OCEANSIDE PUBLIC LIBRARY
330 N. Coast Highway
Oceanside, CA 92054

MW00386792

VOCATIONAL CAREERS SOURCEBOOK

ISSN 1060-5630

A GALE CAREER INFORMATION GUIDE

VOCATIONAL CAREERS SOURCEBOOK

Where to find help planning careers in skilled, trade, and nontechnical vocations

SECOND EDITION

Sara T. Bernstein and Kathleen M. Savage, Editors

Compiled in cooperation with InfoPLACE, the Job, Career, and Education Service of the Cuyahoga County Public Library, Cleveland, Ohio

An ITP Information/Reference Group Company

NEW YORK • LONDON • BONN • BOSTON • DETROIT
MADRID • MELBOURNE • MEXICO CITY • PARIS
SINGAPORE • TOKYO • TORONTO • WASHINGTON
ALBANY NY • BELMONT CA • CINCINNATI OH

Editors: Sara T. Bernstein and Kathleen M. Savage
Associate Editors: Ian Goodhall and Theresa J. MacFarlane
Assistant Editor: Tara Sheets

Research Manager: Victoria B. Cariappa
Research Specialist: Gary J. Oudersluys
Research Associates: Tamara C. Nott and Amy Terese Steel

Production Director: Mary Beth Trimper
Assistant Production Manager: Evi Seoud
Production Assistant: Deborah Milliken
Product Design Manager: Cynthia Baldwin
Graphic Designer: Michelle DiMercurio
Graphic Services Supervisor: Barbara J. Yarrow

Manager, Data Entry Services: Benita L. Spight
Data Entry Supervisor: Gwendolyn S. Tucker
Data Entry Associate: Johnny Carson

Manager, Technical Support Services: Theresa Rocklin
Programmer/Analyst: Charles Beaumont
Programmer: Parveen Parikh

∞™ The paper used in this publication meets the minimum requirements of American National Standard for Information Sciences--Permanence Paper for Printed Library Materials, ANSI Z39.48-1984.

This book is printed on recycled paper that meets Environmental Protection Agency standards.

ISBN 0-8103-8812-X
ISSN 1060-5630

Printed in the United States of America

I(T)P™ Gale Research Inc., an International Thomson Publishing Company.
ITP logo is a trademark under license.

Contents

Highlights . . . vii
Preface . . . ix
Introduction . . . xi
User's Guide . . . xiii
Master List of Profiled Careers . . . xvii

Marketing and Sales Occupations

Cashiers . . . 1
Counter and Rental Clerks . . . 5
Insurance Agents and Brokers . . . 9
Manufacturers' and Wholesale Sales Representatives . . . 18
Real Estate Agents, Brokers, and Appraisers . . . 25
Retail Sales Workers . . . 36
Securities and Financial Services Sales Representatives . . . 43
Services Sales Representatives . . . 50
Travel Agents . . . 56

Administrative Support Occupations, Including Clerical

Adjusters, Investigators and Collectors . . . 65
Bank Tellers . . . 71
Clerical Supervisors and Managers . . . 78
Computer and Peripheral Equipment Operators . . . 82
Credit Clerks and Authorizers . . . 88
General Office Clerks . . . 91
Information Clerks . . . 95
  Hotel and Motel Desk Clerks . . . 98
  Interviewing and New Accounts Clerks . . . 102
  Receptionists . . . 105
  Reservation and Transportation Ticket Agents and Travel Clerks . . . 109
Mail Clerks and Messengers . . . 116
Material Recording, Scheduling, Dispatching, and Distributing Occupations . . . 119
  Dispatchers . . . 121
  Stock Clerks. . . . 125
  Traffic, Shipping, and Receiving Clerks . . . 128
Postal Clerks and Mail Carriers . . . 131
Records Clerks . . . 137
  Billing Clerks . . . 139
  Bookkeeping, Accounting, and Auditing Clerks . . . 141
  Brokerage Clerks and Statement Clerks . . . 147
  File Clerks . . . 149
  Library Assistants and Bookmobile Drivers . . . 153
  Order Clerks . . . 157
  Payroll and Timekeeping Clerks . . . 159
  Personnel Clerks . . . 162
Secretaries . . . 165
Stenographers and Court Reporters . . . 174
Teachers Aides . . . 180
Telephone Operators . . . 184
Typists, Word Processors, and Data Entry Keyers . . . 188

Service Occupations

Protective Service Occupations
Correction Officers . . . 195
Firefighting Occupations . . . 200
Guards . . . 209
Police, Detectives, and Special Agents . . . 213

Food and Beverage Preparation and Service Occupations
Chefs, Cooks, and Other Kitchen Workers . . 226
Food and Beverage Service Occupations . . 236

Health Service Occupations
Dental Assistants . . . 246
Medical Assistants . . . 252
Nursing Aides and Psychiatric Aides . . . 259

Personal Service and Building and Grounds Service Occupations
Animal Caretakers, Except Farm . . . 265
Barbers and Cosmetologists . . . 271
Flight Attendants . . . 279
Gardeners and Groundskeepers . . . 283
Homemaker-Home Health Aides . . . 289
Janitors and Cleaners . . . 293
Preschool Workers . . . 300
Private Household Workers . . . 306

Agriculture, Forestry, Fishing, and Related Occupations

Farm Operators and Managers . . . 309
Fishers, Hunters, and Trappers . . . 320
Forestry and Logging Occupations . . . 328

Mechanics, Installers, and Repairers

Aircraft Mechanics and Engine Specialists . . 334
Automotive Body Repairers . . . 339
Automotive Mechanics . . . 346

Diesel Mechanics 354
Electronic Equipment Repairers 359
Commercial and Industrial Electronic Equipment Repairers 362
Communications Equipment Mechanics . . 367
Computer and Office Machine Repairers . 371
Electronic Home Entertainment Equipment Repairers 377
Telephone Installers and Repairers 382
Elevator Installers and Repairers 385
Farm Equipment Mechanics 388
General Maintenance Mechanics 391
Heating, Air-conditioning, and Refrigeration Mechanics 394
Home Appliance and Power Tool Repairers 401
Industrial Machinery Repairers 405
Line Installers and Cable Splicers 408
Millwrights 412
Mobile Heavy Equipment Mechanics 415
Motorcycle, Boat, and Small Engine Mechanics 418
Musical Instrument Repairers and Tuners . . 422
Vending Machine Servicers and Repairers . 427

Construction Trades and Extractive Occupations

Bricklayers and Stonemasons 430
Carpenters 436
Carpet Installers 443
Concrete Masons and Terrazzo Workers . . . 447
Drywall Workers and Lathers 453
Electricians 458
Glaziers 465
Insulation Workers 469
Painters and Paperhangers 474
Plasterers 479
Plumbers and Pipefitters 483
Roofers 491
Roustabouts 497
Sheet-Metal Workers 501
Structural and Reinforcing Ironworkers 506
Tilesetters 511

Production Occupations

Assemblers
Precision Assemblers 515

Blue-collar Worker Supervisors 518

Food Processing Occupations
Butchers and Meat, Poultry and Fish Cutters 521

Inspectors, Testers, and Graders 525

Metalworking and Plastic-working Occupations
Boilermakers 528
Jewelers 531
Machinists and Tool Programmers 535
Metalworking and Plastic-Working Machine Operators 539
Tool and Die Makers 545
Welders, Cutters, and Welding Machine Operators 549

Plant and Systems Operators
Electric Power Generating Plant Operators and Power Distributors and Dispatchers 555
Stationary Engineers 560
Water and Wastewater Treatment Plant Operators 563

Printing Occupations
Bindery Workers 568
Prepress Workers 572
Printing Press Operators 577

Textile, Apparel, and Furnishings Occupations
Apparel Workers 582
Shoe and Leather Workers and Repairers . . 587
Textile Machinery Operators 591
Upholsterers 595

Woodworking Occupations 599

Miscellaneous Production Occupations
Dental Laboratory Technicians 604
Ophthalmic Laboratory Technicians 609
Painting and Coating Machine Operators . . . 613
Photographic Process Workers 617

Transportation and Material Moving Occupations

Busdrivers 621
Material Moving Equipment Operators 626
Rail Transportation Occupations 631
Taxi Drivers and Chauffeurs 637
Truckdrivers 641
Water Transportation Occupations 650

Handlers, Equipment Cleaners, Helpers, and Laborers 655

Job Opportunities in the Armed Forces . . 661

Appendix I: State Occupational and ProfessionalLicensing Agencies 669
Appendix II: Employment Growth Rankings and Statistics 673
Index to Information Sources 679

Highlights

Students, parents, career changers, and counselors involved with career guidance can turn first to *Vocational Careers Sourcebook* (VCS) to locate essential career planning sources.

VCS identifies and pulls together a broad spectrum of resources used to explore vocational career opportunities. It profiles 131 vocational occupations, ranging from aircraft mechanic and animal caretaker to welder and woodworker. Each profile lists up to 11 categories of career information:

- Job descriptions
- Career guides
- Associations
- Standards/certification agencies
- Test guides and certification examinations
- Educational directories and programs
- Awards, scholarships, grants, and fellowships
- Basic reference guides and handbooks
- Periodicals
- Meetings and conventions
- Other sources of interest to professionals

Each entry includes, as appropriate and available:

- Organization, association, or publication name
- Contact information, including address, phone, toll-free, and facsimile numbers
- Author/editor, dates, and frequency
- Brief description of purpose, services, or content

The second edition is a complete revision, incorporating thousands of organization, title, address, and text changes.

Also included in the second edition:

- A Master List of Profiled Careers referencing covered vocational occupations by job titles, alternate names, popular names, and synonymous and related names
- State Occupational and Professional Licensing Agencies listings
- Employment Growth Rankings and Statistics of profiled careers as projected by the U.S. Department of Labor's Bureau of Labor Statistics
- Index to Information Sources listed in *VCS.*

New Features include:

- Fully updated contact/order information–including addresses and phone, fax, and toll-free numbers
- Over 700 new career guides, test guides, directories, and basic reference guides and handbooks produced by over 25 major publishers of career resources
- Overall entry count has increased by over 15 percent, while the new, three-column format makes a more compact book

Compiled in Cooperation With Career Information Center

Many of the sources listed in *VCS* were identified in the career collection of InfoPlace, the job, career, and education service of the Cuyahoga County Public Library, and are used daily to develop career planning strategies and provide answers to career-related questions.

Career Research Resources— Step by Step

Step 1: Beginning Your Career Search

Occupational Outlook Handbook (OOH)

Describes careers in detail:
- nature of work
- working conditions
- employment statistics
- job outlook
- earnings
- job training, qualifications, and advancement

Provides additional information sources:
- associations, organizations, unions, and governmental agencies
- publications

Step 2: Planning Your Career

Vocational Careers Sourcebook (VCS) and **Professional Careers Sourcebook (PCS)**

Provide concise job descriptions noting:
- employment outlook
- salaries

Offer descriptive listings:
- directories and catalogs of educational programs
- special training programs
- standards/certification agencies

Expand *OOH*'s additional information sources:
- complete information on professional associations and related organizations
- comprehensive entries for professional reference works and trade periodicals

Provide extensive listings for other categories of resources:
- career guides
- test guides
- awards, scholarships, grants, and fellowships
- meetings and conventions

Step 3: Finding the Job You Want

Job Hunter's Sourcebook (JHS)

Features profiles of job-hunting information for specific careers:
- sources of help-wanted ads
- placement and job referral services
- employer directories and networking lists
- handbooks and manuals
- employment agencies and executive search firms
- other leads

Identifies sources of general job-hunting information:
- reference works
- newspapers, magazines, and journals
- audio/visual resources
- online services
- software
- other sources

Includes an essay offering tips on using the public library as a career information center.

Preface

Each of us possesses a unique set of values and abilities, and the ideal job complements these qualities. Someone well suited to a career enjoys not just financial rewards, but personal satisfaction as well. Not everyone is willing or able to go to college or pursue advanced technical training to land a job, but this need not mean a disappointing work life. Many careers do not require advanced education, yet have good growth prospects and offer comfortable living standards. The first step in successfully selecting and developing a career is to become familiar with the opportunities available.

Today's Job Market

As economists continue to search for signs of the long- awaited economic recovery, the job market remains difficult in many areas and uncertain in others. This affects not only those looking for their first full-time job, but workers at all levels displaced by downsizing and company closings. Achieving a management position no longer guarantees security. In retailing, for example, according to the 1991 edition of U.S. Employment Opportunities, "The farther you get away from the customer, the more difficult it will be to justify your salary in a time of declining sales." And increasingly, workers decide to make a career change as they find their goals or needs change.

In addition to economic and personal factors, the evolution of the business community and society as a whole will play an important role in the near-term job market. The Department of Labor reports that seven out of ten workers are now found in service industries. A growing population and increased demand for services of all types are spurring the continued expansion of the service-producing sector, according to the federal government's *Occupational Outlook Handbook*, 1994-95. This will open doors in such vocational occupations as food service, cashiering, and clerical work, along with many more skilled careers. Opportunities for data processors and repair and maintenance workers are also expected to increase, with technical skills often the best hedge in getting and keeping a job.

Making Good Career Choices

Understanding economic trends can doubtless aid someone looking for security and growth in a career, but many important questions are much more specific to the job and the person. Clear knowledge of one's own skills, aptitudes, interests, and goals is crucial to achieving job satisfaction. Coupling that with knowledge of a particular occupation makes it possible to evaluate a career choice on such key factors as:

- Will the work offer personal satisfaction?
- Are special skills or training needed?
- What is the outlook for future growth?
- How are the working conditions?
- What is the typical salary range?

Vocational Careers Sourcebook (VCS) helps jobseekers answer just these types of questions for 131 occupational categories. It provides both a quick summary of specific careers that do not require an advanced degree and a comprehensive list of resources for evaluating and pursuing each one. In today's complex arena of career resources, *VCS* fills a gap in vocational career information in a uniquely accessible way. Those new to the job market, career changers, counselors, and information professionals all will find it a valuable resource.

Introduction

The U.S. Bureau of Labor Statistics predicts that 80% of the occupations traditionally classified as vocational will grow in the next decade, bringing the total employed in these job categories to nearly 72,000,000 workers by the year 2000. A job is usually considered vocational when employment in that occupation does not depend upon a degree from a college or other institution for higher education. Examples of these occupations include construction, clerical, and food service workers; machine operators; mechanics; and salespeople.

Although an advanced degree is not required, many of the better-paying, more stimulating, and more secure vocational careers do require some training. It often begins in high school, where classes in office procedures or automotive mechanics can give graduating students a practical edge in looking for a job. This type of education can also foster an interest in additional training at a technical or trade school. Cosmetology schools and culinary institutes are examples of specialized schools that offer certificate programs denoting a certain level of achievement or training. Still other vocational jobs, such as postal clerks, require applicants to pass a standard examination before they are considered for employment.

Comprehensive Tool for Career Planning

With such diversity in vocational occupations and training requirements, careful research and planning plays an essential role preparing for a career. *Vocational Careers Sourcebook (VCS)* was published to support these activities. *VCS* compiles comprehensive information about 131 specific vocational careers and presents it in a single, easy-to-use volume. Arranged by job type, *VCS* can be used by students, jobseekers, career changers, career librarians, employment and guidance counselors, and others to:

- Research occupations. Brief career descriptions summarize the duties and responsibilities that each profession entails, complete with salary levels and growth potentials for each.
- Explore vocational careers. Specific professions are described in listed career guides, including books, articles, kits, pamphlets, brochures, and other materials that are often difficult to identify or locate quickly.
- Find vocational or certification test guides. Students and jobseekers can locate information on test guides and handbooks designed to assist with preparing for vocational or certification examinations.
- Identify career-enhancing resources. *VCS* identifies newsletters, magazines, newspapers, trade journals, and other serials that offer information to, and are used by people in the profiled careers. Valuable resources such as manuals, textbooks, directories, dictionaries, encyclopedias, films, videocassettes, and other significant reference materials used by professionals are also identified.
- Target associations and organizations for networking. *VCS* lists organizations that will assist individuals seeking advice on career planning, professional development, and networking, including:

  Trade and professional associations and unions
  Standards and certification agencies.
  State vocational and occupational licensing agencies.
  Meetings, conventions, trade shows, and conferences within given fields.
  Award and financial support programs that encourage students and professionals to further pursue a given career.

Easy access to information on specific occupations is facilitated by the Master List of Profiled Careers. This definitive guide to *VCS* contents refers to covered professions by occupation names, job titles, popular names, and by synonymous or related terms. The Index to Information Sources alphabetically lists specific publication titles and organization names.

Please consult the User's Guide for more information about the arrangement, content, and indexing of the information sources cited in *VCS*.

VCS Complements the *Occupational Outlook Handbook*

Owing to the importance of career information to students, parents, counselors, and librarians, *VCS* is designed as a companion to today's foremost career resource–the Department of Labor's *Occupational Outlook Handbook (OOH)*. The *OOH* provides detailed descriptions of some 250 occupations, covering areas such as the nature of the work, working conditions, job outlook, earnings, job training, qualifications, and advancement. It also offers selected sources of additional information for each of the occupations covered, listing the names and addresses of associations, organizations, unions, government agencies, and publications.

VCS has been designed to complement–not replace–*OOH* by augmenting the information about the 131 "vocational" careers included in *OOH*. *VCS* greatly expands the Additional Sources of Information sections in each *OOH* chapter, by providing complete information about professional associations and related organizations and comprehensive entries for professional reference works and trade periodicals. In addition, *VCS* provides extensive listings of career guides, test guides, awards, scholarships, grants, fellowships, professional meetings and conventions, and more. *VCS* career profiles are arranged in the same order as *OOH* chapters on the covered job categories, allowing the books to be used in tandem to create a complete career research program.

VCS Compiled in Cooperation With Career Information Center

Many of the information sources included in this edition of *VCS* were identified in the more than 3,000 books, pamphlets, newspapers, and periodicals that comprise the career collection of InfoPLACE, the highly regarded job, career, and education service of the Cuyahoga County Public Library in Cleveland, Ohio. Kathleen M. Savage, the InfoPLACE information librarian, selected career resources that have been successfully used by patrons and counselors at InfoPLACE. InfoPLACE also conducts individual consultations and sponsors workshops such as "Career Decisions" for career planning and "Career Realities" for job hunters seeking professional positions.

Additional information contained in *VCS* was compiled through direct contact with selected associations, agencies, and organizations; from career collections of other major public libraries; and from selected material from other Gale databases. This second edition represents a complete revision and updating from the first edition of *VCS*.

Comments and Suggestions Are Welcome

Libraries, associations, career counseling firms, agencies, publishers, and other organizations active in career planning and research are encouraged to submit material about their programs, activities, publications, or other resources for use in future editions of *VCS*. Other comments and suggestions from users of this directory also are appreciated. Please contact:

Vocational Careers Sourcebook
Gale Research Inc.
835 Penobscot Bldg.
Detroit, MI 48226-4094
Toll-free: 800-347-GALE
Facsimile: (313)961-6815
Telex: 810 221 7087

User's Guide

Vocational Careers Sourcebook (VCS) consists of:

- Master List of Profiled Careers
- 131 Career Profiles
- State Occupational and Professional Licensing Agencies
- Job Rankings and Statistics
- Employment Growth Rankings and Statistics
- Index to Information Sources

Master List of Profiled Careers

The Master List of Profiled Careers, following this guide, lists in a single alphabetic sequence the job titles used to identify the 131 careers profiled in *VCS*, as well as alternate, popular, synonymous, and related job titles and names, and occupation names contained within job titles. "See" references lead from alternate names to the appropriate career profiles and their beginning page numbers.

Career Profile Content and Arrangement

The order of the 131 career profiles contained in *VCS* reflects the arrangement used in the *Occupational Outlook Handbook*, as listed on the Contents pages. Profiles are organized into ten major sections by general vocation type (which are further subdivided into more specific occupation types in some cases) and are then listed alphabetically.

Each profile contains up to 11 categories of information sources, as described below. Within each category, individual entries are organized alphabetically by name or title. (Entries are numbered and arranged sequentially, beginning with the first entry in the first profile.) The organizations, publications, and other sources listed are fully cited in all relevant chapters and categories, providing the user with a complete selection of information resources for each career in a single, convenient location.

Categories of Information in Career Profiles

- **Job Descriptions.** Each profile contains a summary explaining the duties and responsibilities that a particular occupation or profession entails, including educational and training requirements, if available. The description abstracts the 1994-1995 *Occupational Outlook Handbook's* coverage of the profession. Salaries and growth potential for an occupation also will be noted, with the following phrases used as defined by the *OOH*:

If employment growth reads...	then *OOH* predicts
Faster than the average	20 percent or more increase
Average	11 to 19 percent increase
Slower than the average	4 to 10 percent increase
More slowly than the average	3 percent or less increase

- **Career Guides.** This section lists books, articles, kits, pamphlets, brochures, and other materials that describe a given profession. Often these works will be part of a career/vocational series. Entries in this section will include the source's title; name, address, and phone number of its publisher or distributor; name of the editor or author; publication date or frequency; description of contents; arrangement; indexes; toll-free or additional phone numbers; and facsimile numbers, when applicable. Publication, videocassette, and film titles appear in italics.

- **Associations.** This category of information covers associations that offer career-related information and services. Entries note the association's name, address, and phone number; its membership; purpose and objectives; publications; toll-free or additional phone numbers; and facsimile numbers, when known. Publication titles are rendered in italics. In some cases, the publications mentioned in these entries are described in greater detail as separate entries cited in the Career Guides, Basic Reference Guides and Handbooks, and Professional and Trade Periodicals categories.
- **Standards/Certification Agencies.** This section offers information about accrediting agencies, certification examinations, national or vocational standards programs, or association-sponsored certification and testing programs. Entries in this section provide the certifying agency or program's name, address, and phone number; a description; publication titles; toll-free or additional phone numbers; and facsimile numbers, when available.
- **Test Guides.** This section lists guides and handbooks designed to assist in preparing for vocational or certification examinations; for instance, instruction booklets on how tp prepare for the Civil Service Exam will appear in this section. These entries include the guide's title; its publisher's or distributor's name, address, and phone number; editor's or author's name; publication date or frequency; description of contents; arrangement; indexes; toll-free or additional phone numbers; and facsimile numbers, when available. Publication titles appear in italics.
- **Educational Directories and Programs.** This category notes directories, catalogs, and other publications that list career-related course offerings of schools, associations, and other organizations. Association and special school programs exclusively for the profiled career may be listed here as well. Entries for directories and other publications will offer the title; name, address, and phone number of the publisher or distributor; name of the editor or author; publication date or frequency; description of contents; arrangement; indexes; toll-free or additional phone numbers; and facsimile numbers, when known. Entries for programs will offer the name, address, and phone number of the institution; a description of course offerings; toll-free or additional phone numbers; and facsimile numbers, when available. Publication titles appear in italics.
- **Awards, Scholarships, Grants, and Fellowships.** This section lists awards given in recognition of achievement and financial support programs that aid students and other individuals in fulfilling or continuing their education in a given career. Entries in this section include the name of the award or program; the name, address, and phone number of the sponsoring organization; a description; toll-free or additional phone numbers; and facsimile number, when applicable.
- **Basic Reference Guides and Handbooks.** This category provides information about manuals, textbooks, directories, dictionaries, encyclopedias, films and videocassettes, and other published reference material used by individuals working in the profiled career. Entries offer the resource's title; the name, address, and phone number of its publisher or distributor; the editor's or author's name; publication date or frequency; description of contents; arrangement; indexes; toll-free and additional phone numbers; and facsimile numbers, when applicable. Publication and film title are rendered in italics.
- **Periodicals.**This section lists newsletters, magazines, newspapers, trade journals, and other serials that offer information to individuals in the profiled career. Entries note the resource's title; the name, address, and phone number of the publisher; the editor's name; frequency; description of contents; toll-free and additional phone numbers; and facsimile numbers, when available. Publication titles appear in italics.
- **Meetings and Conventions.** This section includes trade shows, conferences, conventions, and meetings that provide opportunities for networking and development. Entries feature the event's name; the name, address, and phone number of the event's organizer or sponsor; the frequency of the event and forthcoming dates and locations; toll-free and additional phone numbers; and facsimile numbers, when known.
- **Other Sources of Information.** This category lists online databases, compilations of performance standards, statistical sources, sources of supply, special reference works, films and

videocassettes, annual reviews, or other miscellaneous material that might be of interest to individuals working in the given profession. (Material routinely used by individuals in a profiled career will be found in the Basic Reference Guides and Handbooks category.) Entries for sources of information feature the title; the name, address, and phone number of the publisher or distributor; editor's or author's name; publication date or frequency; description of contents; arrangement; indexes; toll-free and additional phone numbers; and facsimile numbers, when known. Publication and film titles appear in italics.

Appendixes Enhance the Usefulness of Career Profiles

Appendix I: State Occupational and Professional Licensing Agencies, following the main section, covers state government agencies responsible for granting professional and occupational licenses. Entries are arranged alphabetically by state and include the state agency's or department's name, address, and phone number.

Appendix II: Employment Growth Rankings and Statistics reprints Bureau of Labor Statistics figures indicating the employment growth for occupations covered in this edition of *VCS*.

Index to Information Sources

VCS includes a comprehensive Index to Information Sources that lists all associations, organizations, agencies, publications, database services, and information sources cited in the career profiles and state agencies section. Entries are arranged alphabetically and are referenced by their entry numbers. Publication and film titles are rendered in italics.

Master List of Profiled Careers

This lists outlines references to covered occupations and professions by job titles, alternate names, occupation names contained within job titles, popular names, and synonymous and related names. Beginning page numbers for each occupation's profile are provided. Title of profiles appear in **boldface**.

Able seamen *See* Water transportation occupations 650
Accident prevention squad police officers *See* Police, detectives, and special agents 213
Accordion repairers *See* Musical instrument repairers and tuners 422
Account analysts *See* Bookkeeping, accounting, and auditing clerks 141
Account information clerks *See* Bookkeeping, accounting, and auditing clerks 141
Acid tank liners *See* Bricklayers and stonemasons . . 430
Adjusters, investigators and collectors 65
Advertising sales representatives *See* Services sales representatives 50
Air and hydronic balancing technicians *See* Heating, air conditioning, and refrigeration mechanics 394
Air-conditioning mechanics *See* Heating, air conditioning, and refrigeration mechanics 394
Air-conditioning window unit installer-repairers *See* Home appliance and power tool repairers 401
Air Force *See* Job opportunities in the Armed Forces 661
Airbrush artists *See* Photographic process workers . . 617
Aircraft accessories mechanics *See* Aircraft mechanics and engine specialists 334
Aircraft body repairers *See* Aircraft mechanics and engine specialists 334
Aircraft mechanics and engine specialists 334
Aircraft rigging and controls *mechanics See* Aircraft mechanics and engine specialists 334
Airline security representatives *See* Guards 209
Airplane charter clerks *See* Counter and rental clerks . . 5
Airplane flight attendants *See* Flight attendants 279
Alarm operators *See* Dispatchers 121
Animal breeders *See* Farm operators and managers . 309
Animal caretakers, except farm 265
Animal keepers *See* Animal caretakers, except farm 265
Animal nursery workers *See* Animal caretakers, except farm 265
Animal trappers *See* Fishers, hunters, and trappers . 320
Apparel workers 582
Appliance repairers *See* Home appliance and power tool repairers 401
Appointment clerks *See* Receptionists 105
Appraisers, real estate *See* Real estate agents, brokers, and appraisers 25
Aquarists *See* Animal caretakers, except farm 265
Arc welders *See* Welders, cutters, and welding machine operators 549
Armed Forces *See* Job opportunities in the Armed Forces 661
Armored car guards and drivers *See* Guards 209
Army *See* Job opportunities in the Armed Forces 661
Artificial-breeding distributors *See* Farm operators and managers 309
Artificial glass-eye makers *See* Ophthalmic laboratory technicians 609
Artificial plastic-eye makers *See* Ophthalmic laboratory technicians 609
Assembler brazers *See* Precision assemblers 515
Welders, cutters, and welding machine operators 549
Assistant chief train dispatchers *See* Dispatchers 121
Audio-video repairers *See* Electronic home entertainment equipment repairers 377
Audiovisual program productions sales representatives *See* Services sales representatives 50
Audit clerks *See* Bookkeeping, accounting, and auditing clerks 141
Auto body repairers *See* Automotive body repairers 339
Automated equipment engineer technicians *See* Millwrights 412
Automatic developers *See* Photographic process workers 617
Automatic equipment technicians *See* Communications equipment mechanics 367
Automatic gluing machine operators *See* Bindery workers 568
Automatic mounters *See* Photographic process workers . . 617
Automatic print developers *See* Photographic process workers 617
Automobile accessories installers *See* Automotive mechanics 346
Automobile body customizers *See* Automotive body repairers 339
Automobile rental clerks *See* Counter and rental clerks 5
Automobile upholsterers *See* Upholsterers 595
Automotive body repairers 339
Automotive generator and starter repairers *See* Automotive mechanics 346
Automotive leasing sales representatives *See* Services sales representatives 50
Automotive mechanics 346
Auxiliary equipment operators *See* Electric power generating plant operators and plant distributors and dispatchers . . 121
Avionics technicians *See* Communications equipment mechanics 367
Bakers *See* Chefs, cooks, and other kitchen workers 226
Bank messengers *See* Mail clerks and messengers 116
Bank tellers 71

Master List of Profiled Careers

Bar attendants *See* Food and beverage service occupations . . . 236
Bar waiters/waitresses *See* Food and beverage service occupations . . . 236
Barbecue cooks *See* Chefs, cooks, and other kitchen workers . . . 226
Barbers and cosmetologists . . . 271
Barge captains *See* Water transportation occupations . . . 650
Bartenders *See* Food and beverage service occupations . . . 236
Battalion chiefs *See* Firefighting occupations . . . 200
Beekeepers *See* Farm operators and managers . . . 309
Billing clerks . . . 139
Billing machine operators *See* Billing clerks . . . 139
Bindery workers . . . 568
Bird trappers *See* Fishers, hunters, and trappers . . . 320
Birth attendants *See* Nursing aides and psychiatric aides . . . 259
Blood donor recruiters *See* Services sales representatives . . . 50
Blood donor recruiters supervisors *See* Services sales representatives . . . 50
Blower insulators *See* Insulation workers . . . 469
Blue-Collar worker supervisors . . . 518
Blueprinting machine operators *See* Prepress operators . . . 572
Boat mechanics *See* Motorcycle, boat, and small engine mechanics . . . 418
Boatswains *See* Water transportation occupations . . 650
Body make-up artists *See* Barbers and cosmetologists . . . 271
Bodyguards *See* Guards . . . 209
Boilerhouse mechanics *See* Boilermakers . . . 528
Boilermakers . . . 528
Bonded structures repairers *See* Aircraft mechanics and engine specialists . . . 334
Automotive body repairers . . . 339
Book binders *See* Bindery workers . . . 568
Book repairers *See* Bindery workers . . . 568
Book sewing machine operators *See* Bindery workers . . . 568
Book trimmers *See* Bindery workers . . . 568
Booking clerks *See* Traffic, shipping and receiving clerks . . . 128
Booking police officers *See* Police, detectives, and special agents . . . 213
Bookkeepers *See* Bookkeeping, accounting, and auditing clerks . . . 141
Bookkeeping, accounting, and auditing clerks . . 141
Bookmobile drivers *See* Library assistants and bookmobile drivers . . . 153
Border guards *See* Police, detectives, and special agents . . . 213
Bouncers *See* Guards . . . 209
Braille and talking books clerks *See* Library assistants and bookmobile drivers . . . 153
Break adjusters *See* Automotive mechanics . . . 346
Break holders *See* Rail transportation occupations . . 631
Bricklayers and stonemasons . . . 430
Bridge carpenters *See* Carpenters . . . 436
Brokerage clerks and statement clerks . . . 148
Broker's floor representatives *See* Securities and financial Sale representatives . . . 43
Brush clearing laborers *See* Forestry and logging occupations . . . 328
Buckers *See* Forestry and logging occupations . . . 328
Buffet waiters/waitresses *See* Food and beverage service occupations . . . 236
Building maintenance repairers *See* General maintenance mechanics . . . 391
Burnishers and bumpers *See* Aircraft mechanics and engine specialists . . . 334
Busdrivers . . . 621
Business services sales agents *See* Services sales representatives . . . 50
Butchers and meat, poultry and fish cutters . . . 521
Cable ferryboat operators *See* Water transportation occupations . . . 650
Cable installer-repairers *See* Line installers and cable splicers . . . 408
Cable splicers *See* Line installers and cable splicers . . . 408
Cafeteria attendants *See* Food and beverage service occupations . . . 236
Cancellation clerks *See* Adjusters, investigators and collectors . . . 65
Canteen operators *See* Food and beverage service occupations . . . 236
Car barn laborers *See* Rail transportation occupations . . . 631
Car checkers *See* Traffic, shipping, and receiving clerks . . 128
Car hops *See* Food and beverage service occupations . . . 236
Car retarder operators *See* Rail transportation occupations . . . 631
Carbide operators *See* Tool and die makers . . . 545
Career guidance technicians *See* General office clerks . . . 91
Carpenters . . . 436
Carpet installers . . . 443
Carvers *See* Chefs, cooks, and other kitchen workers . . . 226
Case making machine operators *See* Bindery workers . . . 568
Casers *See* Bindery workers . . . 568
Cash grain farmers *See* Farm operators and managers . . 309
Cash register servicers *See* Computer and peripheral equipment operators . . . 82
Cashiers . . . 1
Casting-in-line setters *See* Bindery workers . . . 568
Cement masons *See* Concrete masons and terrazzo workers . . . 447
Cemetery workers *See* Gardeners and groundskeepers . . 283
Central office operators *See* Telephone operators . . . 184
Chainsaw operators *See* Forestry and logging occupations . . . 328
Charge account clerks *See* Interviewing and new accounts clerks . . . 102
Chasers *See* Forestry and logging occupations . . . 328
Check cashiers *See* Cashiers . . . 1
Chefs, cooks, and other kitchen workers . . . 226
Chefs de froid *See* Chefs, cooks, and other kitchen workers . . . 226
Chicken and fish butchers *See* Butchers and meat, poultry, and fish cutters . . . 521
Chief deputy sheriffs *See* Police, detectives, and special agents . . . 213
Chief jailers *See* Police, detectives, and special agents . . 213
Childcare workers *See* Preschool workers . . . 300
Children's institution attendants *See* Preschool workers . . 300
Chimney repairers *See* Bricklayers and stonemasons . . . 430
Chimney sweeps *See* Janitors and cleaners . . . 293
Chip tuners *See* Welders, cutters, and welding machine

operators 549
Chiropractic assistants *See* Medical assistants 252
Christmas tree farm managers *See* Farm operators and managers 309
Civil service clerks *See* Personnel clerks 162
Claims adjusters *See* Adjusters, investigators and collectors 65
Claims clerks *See* Adjusters, investigators and collectors 65
Claims examiners *See* Adjusters, investigators and collectors 65
Clarifying plant operators *See* Water and wastewater treatment plant operators 563
Classification clerks *See* File clerks 149
Classification control clerks *See* Bookkeeping, accounting, and auditing clerks 141
Cleaners *See* Janitors and cleaners 293
Clerical supervisors and managers 78
Clerks *See* specific types
Clerk-typists *See* Typists, word processors, and data entry keyers 188
Coating machine operators *See* Painting and coating machine operators 613
Cobblers *See* Shoe and leather workers and repairers 587
Coin machine service repairers *See* Vending machine servicers and repairers 427
Collators *See* Bindery workers 568
Collection and exchange tellers *See* Bank tellers 71
Collectors *See* Adjusters, investigators and collectors 65
Color printer operators *See* Photographic process workers 617
Commercial and industrial electronic equipment repairers 362
Commercial or institutional cleaners *See* Janitors and cleaners 293
Commodity loan clerks *See* Bookkeeping, accounting, and auditing clerks 141
Communication center operators *See* Telephone operators 184
Communications consultants *See* Services sales representatives 50
Communications equipment mechanics 367
Community relations police lieutenants *See* Police, detectives, and special agents 213
Community service officers *See* Police, detectives, and special agents 213
Complaint evaluation officers *See* Police, detectives, and special agents 213
Composition stone applicators *See* Bricklayers and stonemasons 430
Computer and office machine repairers 371
Computer operators *See* Computer and peripheral equipment operators 82
Computer and peripheral equipment operators . . . 82
Concrete masons and terrazzo workers 447
Concrete-mixing truck operators *See* Truckdrivers . . 641
Concrete rubbers *See* Concrete masons and terrazzo workers 447
Concrete stone finishers *See* Concrete masons and terrazzo workers 447
Congressional district aides *See* General office clerks 91
Construction equipment mechanics *See* Mobile heavy equipment mechanics 415
Construction equipment operators *See* Material moving equipment operators 626
Contact lens blockers and cutters *See* Ophthalmic laboratory technicians 609
Contact lens lathe operators *See* Ophthalmic laboratory technicians 609
Contingents supervisors *See* Personnel clerks 162
Cook apprentices *See* Chefs, cooks, and other kitchen workers 226
Cooks *See* Chefs, cooks, and other kitchen workers . . 226
Coppersmiths *See* Plumbers and pipefitters 483
Copy messengers *See* Mail clerks and messengers 116
Corn seed production managers *See* Farm operators and managers 309
Correction officers 195
Cosmetologists *See* Barbers and cosmetologists 271
Counter and rental clerks 5
Court deputies *See* Police, detectives, and special agents 213
Crash, fire, and rescue firefighters *See* Firefighting occupations 200
Crating and moving estimators *See* Services sales representatives 50
Credit authorizers *See* Credit clerks and authorizers 88
Credit clerks and authorizers 88
Credit reference clerks *See* Credit clerks and authorizers . . 88
Crime prevention police officers *See* Police, detectives, and special agents 213
Criminal and patrol division deputy sheriffs *See* Police, detectives, and special agents 213
Cruisers *See* Forestry and logging occupations 328
Cupola patchers *See* Bricklayers and stonemasons 430
Customer complaint clerks *See* Adjusters, investigators and collectors 65
Customs patrol officers *See* Police, detectives, and special agents 213
Cutting and printing machine operators *See* Prepress operators 572
Cutting machine operators *See* Bindery workers 568
Dairy equipment repairers *See* Farm equipment mechanics 388
Dairy farm managers *See* Farm operators and managers 309
Data coder operators *See* Typists, word processors, and data entry keyers 188
Data entry keyers *See* Typists, word processors, and data entry keyers 188
Data processing auxiliary-equipment operators *See* Computer and peripheral equipment operators 82
Data processing services sales representatives *See* Services sales representatives 50
Data typists *See* Typists, word processors, and data entry keyers 188
Day-haul or farm charter busdrivers *See* Busdrivers 621
Deckhands *See* Water transportation occupations 650
Deep submergence vehicle operators *See* Water transportation occupations 650
Deli cutter-slicers *See* Chefs, cooks, and other kitchen workers 226
Dental assistants 246
Dental ceramists *See* Dental laboratory technicians 604
Dental laboratory technicians 604

Master List of Profiled Careers

Denture contour wire specialists *See* Dental laboratory technicians 604
Derrick boat captains *See* Water transportation occupations 650
Desk officers *See* Police, detectives, and special agents 213
Detective chiefs *See* Police, detectives, and special agents 213
Detectives *See* Police, detectives, and special agents 213
Developers *See* Photographic process workers 617
Dictating/transcribing machine servicers *See* Computer and peripheral equipment operators 82
Die makers *See* Tool and die makers 545
Diesel engine erectors *See* Diesel mechanics 354
Diesel engine pipefitters *See* Plumbers and pipefitters 483
Diesel engine testers *See* Diesel mechanics 354
Diesel mechanics 354
Diesel plant operators *See* Electric power generating plant operators and plant distributors and dispatchers . . 121
Digitizer operators *See* Computer and peripheral equipment operators 82
Dining car waiters/waitresses *See* Food and beverage service occupations 236
Dining room attendants *See* Food and beverage service occupations 236
Dinkey operators *See* Rail transportation occupations 631
Direct mail clerks *See* Mail clerks and messengers . . 116
Directory assistance operators *See* Telephone operators 184
Disbursement clerks *See* Credit clerks and authorizers 88
Dispatchers 121
Diving fishers *See* Fishers, hunters, and trappers . . . 320
Dog groomers *See* Animal caretakers, except farm . . 265
Dog licensers *See* Adjusters, investigators and collectors 65
Dredge captains *See* Water transportation occupations 650
Dredge mates *See* Water transportation occupations 650
Drip pumpers *See* Truckdrivers 641
Driver-utility workers *See* Truckdrivers 641
Drivers *See* Truckdrivers 641
Drywall applicators *See* Drywall workers and lathers 453
Drywall workers and lathers 453
Dulsers *See* Fishers, hunters, and trappers 320
Dump truck operators *See* Truckdrivers 641
Electric organ inspectors and repairers *See* Musical instrument repairers and tuners 422
Electric power generating plant operators and power distributors and dispatchers 555
Electric powerline examiners *See* Line installers and cable splicers 408
Electric track and switch maintainers *See* Communications equipment mechanics 367
Electrical appliance servicers and repairers *See* Home appliance and power tool repairers 401
Electrical, plumbing, mechanical installers *See*
  Electricians 458
  Plumbers and pipefitters 483
Electrician apprentices *See* Electricians 458
Electricians 458
Electrologists *See* Barbers and Cosmetologists 271
Electron beam photo mask makers *See* Prepress workers 572
Electron beam welding machine operators *See* Welders, cutters, and welding machine operators 549
Electron beam welding machine setters *See* Welders, cutters, and welding machine operators 549
Electronic Equipment Repairers 359
Electronic home entertainment equipment repairers 377
Electronic organ technicians *See* Musical instrument repairers and tuners 422
Electronic sales and service technicians *See* Commercial and industrial electronic equipment repairers 362
Electronics mechanics *See*
  Commercial and industrial electronic equipment repairers 362
  Computer and peripheral equipment operators 82
Electroslag welding machine operators *See* Welders, cutters, and welding machine operators 549
Elevator constructors *See* Elevator installers and repairers 385
Elevator examiners and adjusters *See* Elevator installers and repairers 385
Elevator installers and repairers 385
Elevator repairers *See* Elevator installers and repairers . . 385
Elevators, escalators, and dumbwaiters service representatives *See* Services sales representatives 50
Employment clerks *See* Personnel clerks 162
Endless track vehicle mechanics *See* Mobile heavy equipment mechanics 415
Environmental control system installer-servicers *See* Heating, air-conditioning, and refrigeration mechanics 394
Equipment cleaners *See* Handlers, equipment cleaners, helpers, and laborers 655
Equipment installers *See* Communications equipment mechanics 367
Escort vehicle drivers *See* Truckdrivers 641
Ethnic specialty cooks *See* Chefs, cooks, and other kitchen workers 226
Evaporative cooler installers *See* Heating, air-conditioning, and refrigeration mechanics 394
Exchange clerks *See* Bank tellers 71
Expedition supervisors *See* Fishers, hunters, and trappers 320
Explosion welders *See* Welders, cutters, and welding machine operators 549
Explosives transporters *See* Truckdrivers 641
Express clerks *See* Mail clerks and messengers 116
Fallers *See* Forestry and logging occupations 328
Farm equipment mechanics 388
Farm machinery set-up mechanics *See* Farm equipment mechanics 388
Farm managers *See* Farm operators and managers 309
Farm operators and managers 309
Fast-foods workers *See* Food and beverage service occupations 236
Feeder switchboard operators *See* Electric power generating plant operators and plant distributors and dispatchers 555
Ferryboat captains *See* Water transportation occupations 650

Field crop farmers *See* Farm operators and managers . . . 309
Field engineers *See* Commercial and industrial electronic equipment repairers . . . 362
Field horticultural specialty growers *See* Farm operators and managers . . . 309
Field service technicians *See* Commercial and industrial electronic equipment repairers . . . 362
Millwrights . . . 412
File clerks . . . 149
Film developers *See* Photographic process workers . 617
Film or tape librarians *See* Stock clerks . . . 125
Film laboratory technicians *See* Photographic process workers . . . 617
Film printers *See* Photographic process workers 617
Film processing utility workers *See* Photographic process workers . . . 617
Financial report service sales agents *See* Services sales representatives . . . 50
Fingerprint clerks *See* File clerks . . . 149
Fire captains *See* Firefighting occupations . . . 200
Fire chief's aides *See* Firefighting occupations . . . 200
Fire extinguisher sprinkler inspectors *See* Firefighting occupations . . . 200
Fire inspectors *See* Firefighting occupations . . . 200
Fire investigation lieutenants *See* Firefighting occupations . . . 200
Fire lookouts *See* Firefighting occupations . . . 200
Fire marshals *See* Firefighting occupations . . . 200
Fire prevention bureau captains *See* Firefighting occupations . . . 200
Fire rangers *See* Firefighting occupations . . . 200
Fire wardens *See* Firefighting occupations . . . 200
Firebrick and refractory tile bricklayers *See* Bricklayers and stonemasons . . . 430
Firefighters *See* Firefighting occupations . . . 200
Firefighting equipment specialists *See* General maintenance mechanics . . . 391
Firefighting occupations . . . 200
First aid attendants *See* Nursing aides and psychiatric aides . . . 259
Fish cleaners *See* Butchers and meat, poultry, and fish cutters . . . 521
Fish farmers *See* Farm operators and managers 309
Fishers, hunters, and trappers . . . 320
Fishing vessel workers *See* Fishers, hunters, and trappers . . . 320
Water transportation occupations . . . 650
Flight attendants . . . 279
Flight test shop mechanics *See* Aircraft mechanics and engine specialists . . . 334
Floor waxers *See* Janitors and cleaners . . . 293
Folding machine workers *See* Bindery workers . . . 568
Food and beverage service occupations . . . 236
Food service drivers *See* Truckdrivers . . . 641
Foreign exchange position clerks *See* Bookkeeping, accounting, and auditing clerks . . . 141
Forestry and logging occupations . . . 328
Form builders *See* Carpenters . . . 436
Formal waiters/waitresses *See* Food and beverage service occupations . . . 236
Forwarders *See* Bindery workers . . . 568
Fountain servers *See* Food and beverage service occupations . . . 236
Frame repairers *See* Automotive body repairers . . . 339
Frame wirers *See* Communications equipment mechanics . . . 367
Franchise sales representatives *See* Services sales representatives . . . 50
Freight rate analysts *See* Billing clerks . . . 139
Fretter instrument repairers *See* Musical instrument repairers and tuners . . . 422
Friction welding machine operators *See* Welders, cutters, and welding machine operators . . . 549
Fuel injection servicers *See* Diesel mechanics . . . 354
Fuel-oil clerks *See* Stock clerks . . . 125
Fund raisers *See* Services sales representatives . . . 50
Fur farmers *See* Farm operators and managers . . . 309
Furnace installers *See* Heating, air conditioning, and refrigeration mechanics . . . 394
Furniture upholsterers *See* Upholsterers . . . 595
Game bird farmers *See* Farm operators and managers . . . 309
Game breeding farm managers *See* Farm operators and managers . . . 309
Game preserve managers *See* Farm operators and managers . . . 309
Garbage truck operators *See* Truckdrivers . . . 641
Gardeners and groundskeepers . . . 283
Gas appliance servicers *See* Home appliance and power tool repairers . . . 401
Gas engine operators *See* Stationary engineers . . . 560
Gas main fitters *See* Plumbers and pipefitters . . . 483
Gas welders *See* Welders, cutters, and welding machine operators . . . 549
Gate agents *See* Reservation and transportation ticket agents and travel clerks . . . 109
Gate tenders *See* Guards . . . 209
Gathering machine feeders *See* Bindery workers . . . 568
General accounting systems operators *See* Bookkeeping, accounting, and auditing clerks . . . 141
General ledger bookkeepers *See* Bookkeeping, accounting, and auditing clerks . . . 141
General maintenance mechanics . . . 391
General office clerks . . . 91
Geriatric nurse assistants *See* Nursing aides and psychiatric aides . . . 259
Glass installers *See* Glaziers . . . 465
Glass tinters *See* Painters and paperhangers . . . 474
Glaziers . . . 465
Golf course rangers *See* Guards . . . 209
Grain elevator clerks *See* Traffic, shipping, and receiving clerks . . . 128
Graphic art sales representatives *See* Services sales representatives . . . 50
Greasers *See* Farm equipment mechanics . . . 388
Greenskeepers *See* Gardeners and groundskeepers . . . 283
Groundskeepers *See* Gardeners and groundskeepers . . . 283
Guards . . . 209
Gun welders *See* Welders, cutters, and welding machine operators . . . 549
Hair stylists *See* Barbers and cosmetologists . . . 271
Hand collators *See* Bindery workers . . . 568
Hand etchers *See* Prepress workers . . . 572
Hand stitchers *See* Bindery workers . . . 568
Hand thermal cutters *See* Welders, cutters, and welding machine operators . . . 549
Handlers, equipment cleaners, helpers, and laborers . . . 655

Master List of Profiled Careers

Harbor police launch commanders *See* Police, detectives, and special agents . . . 213
Harness makers *See* Shoe and leather workers and repairers . . . 587
Harp regulators *See* Musical instrument repairers and tuners . . . 422
Heating, air-conditioning, and refrigeration mechanics . . . 394
Heavy repairers *See* Automobile mechanics . . . 346
Heavy truck operators *See* Truckdrivers . . . 641
Helpers *See* Handlers, equipment cleaners, helpers, and laborers . . . 655
Herbicide service sales representatives *See* Services sales representatives . . . 50
Highway patrol pilots *See* Police, detectives, and special agents . . . 213
Home appliance and power tool repairers . . . 401
Home health technicians *See* Homemaker-home health aides . . . 289
Homemaker-home health aides . . . 289
Homicide squad commanding officers *See* Police, detectives, and special agents . . . 213
Horseshoers *See* Animal caretakers, except farm . . . 265
Horticultural specialty growers *See* Farm operators and managers . . . 309
Horticulture superintendents *See* Farm operators and managers . . . 309
Hospital-admitting clerks *See* Interviewing and new accounts clerks . . . 102
Hospital cleaners *See* Janitors and cleaners . . . 293
Hospital food service workers *See* Food and beverage service occupations . . . 236
Hostlers *See* Rail transportation occupations . . . 631
Truckdrivers . . . 641
Hot top liners *See* Bricklayers and stonemasons . . . 430
Hotel and motel desk clerks . . . 98
Hotel services sales representatives *See* Services sales representatives . . . 50
House repairers *See* Carpenters . . . 436
Housecleaners *See* Janitors and cleaners . . . 293
Household appliance installers *See* Home appliance and power tool repairers . . . 401
Household workers *See* Private household workers . . . 306
Housekeeping cleaners *See* Janitors and cleaners . . . 293
Hunters *See* Fishers, hunters, and trappers . . . 320
Hydroelectric station operators *See* Electric power generating plant operators and power distributors and dispatchers . . . 555
Ice cream chefs *See* Chefs, cooks, and other kitchen workers . . . 226
Identification and communications supervisors *See* Police, detectives, and special agents . . . 213
Identification and records commanders *See* Police, detectives, and special agents . . . 213
Identification clerks *See* Personnel clerks . . . 162
Identification officers *See* Police, detectives, and special agents . . . 213
In-file operators *See* Receptionists . . . 105
Industrial cleaners *See* Janitors and cleaners . . . 293
Industrial-commercial groundskeepers *See* Gardeners and groundskeepers . . . 283
Industrial gas fitters *See* Plumbers and pipefitters . . . 483
Industrial machinery repairers . . . 405
Industrial maintenance repairers *See* General maintenance mechanics . . . 391
Industrial sweeper-cleaners *See* Janitors and cleaners . . . 293
Industrial truck mechanics *See* Diesel mechanics . . . 354
Information clerks . . . 98
Inspectors, testers, and graders . . . 525
Insulation power unit tenders *See* Insulation workers . . . 469
Insulation workers . . . 469
Insurance clerks *See* Adjusters, investigators and collectors . . . 65
Billing clerks . . . 139
Personnel clerks . . . 162
Insurance agents and brokers . . . 9
Internal affairs investigators *See* Police, detectives, and special agents
Interstate bus dispatchers *See* Dispatchers . . . 121
Interviewing and new accounts clerks . . . 102
Inventory clerks *See* Stock clerks . . . 125
Investigation division commanding officers *See* Police, detectives, and special agents . . . 121
Invoicing systems operators *See* Billing clerks . . . 139
Irish moss bleachers/gatherers *See* Fishers, hunters, and trappers . . . 320
Ironworkers *See* Structural and reinforcing ironworkers . . . 506
Jailers *See* Correction officers . . . 195
Janitors and cleaners . . . 293
Jewelers . . . 531
Job opportunities in the Armed Forces . . . 661
Job setters *See* Metalworking and plastic working machine operators . . . 539
Joggers *See* Bindery workers . . . 568
Joiners *See* Carpenters . . . 436
Kelp cutters *See* Fishers, hunters, and trappers . . . 320
Keypunch operators *See* Typists, word processors, and data entry keyers . . . 188
Kitchen food assemblers *See* Chefs, cooks, and other kitchen workers . . . 226
Laborers *See* Handlers, equipment cleaners, helpers, and laborers . . . 655
Landscape laborers *See* Gardeners and groundskeepers . . . 283
Larder cooks *See* Chefs, cooks, and other kitchen workers . . . 226
Laser beam color scanner operators *See* Prepress occupations . . . 572
Laser beam machine operators *See* Welders, cutters, and welding machine operators . . . 549
Lathers *See* Drywall workers and lathers . . . 453
Lawn service workers *See* Gardeners and groundskeepers . . . 283
Layboy tenders *See* Bindery workers . . . 568
Layout technicians *See* Ophthalmic laboratory technicians . . . 609
Lead burners *See* Welders, cutters, and welding machine operators . . . 549
Leather workers *See* Shoe and leather workers and repairers . . . 587
Legal secretaries *See* Secretaries . . . 165
Lens and frames prescription clerks *See* Stock clerks . . . 125
Lens mold setters *See* Ophthalmic laboratory technicians . . . 609
Lens mounters *See* Ophthalmic laboratory technicians . . . 609
Library assistants and bookmobile drivers . . . 153

Light truck operators *See* Truckdrivers 641
Line erectors *See* Line installers and cable splicers . 408
Line fishers *See* Fishers, hunters, and trappers 320
Line installers and cable splicers 408
Line maintainers *See* Line installers and cable splicers 408
Line repairers *See* Line installers and cable splicers . 408
Liquid fertilizer servicers *See* Truckdrivers 641
Prepress workers 572
Livestock ranchers *See* Farm operators and managers 309
Load dispatchers *See* Electric power generating plant operators and plant distributors and dispatchers . . 555
Loan closers *See* Credit clerks and authorizers 88
Lock tenders *See* Rail transportation occupations . . . 631
Locket makers *See* Jewelers 531
Locomotive engineers *See* Rail transportation occupations 631
Locomotive firers *See* Rail transportation occupations 631
Locomotive operator helpers *See* Rail transportation occupations 631
Log markers and sorters *See* Forestry and logging occupations 328
Log truck operators *See* Truckdrivers 641
Loggers *See* Forestry and logging occupations 328
Logging tractor operators *See* Forestry and logging occupations 328
Looseleaf binder coverers *See* Bindery workers 568
Luggage makers and repairers *See* Shoe and leather workers and repairers 587
Machine lead burners *See* Welders, cutters, and welding machine operators 549
Machinery erectors *See* Millwrights 412
Machinists and tool programmers 535
Magazine keepers *See* Stock clerks 125
Magazine repairers *See* Bindery workers 568
Magnetic tape typewriter operators *See* Typists, word processors, and data entry keyers 188
Magneto repairers *See* Motorcycle, boat, and small engine mechanics 418
Maids *See* Janitors and cleaners 293
Private household workers 306
Mail carriers *See* Postal clerks and mail carriers 131
Mail censors *See* Mail clerks and messengers 116
Mail clerks and messengers 116
Mail handlers *See* Postal clerks and mail carriers . . . 131
Mailers *See* Mail clerks and messengers 116
Make-up artists *See* Barbers and cosmetologists . . . 271
Manicurists *See* Barbers and cosmetologists 271
Manufacturers' and wholesale sales representatives 18
Manufacturers' service representative *See* Millwrights 412
Marble setters *See* Bricklayers and stonemasons . . . 430
Margin clerks *See* Brokerage clerks and statement clerks 148
Marine oilers *See* Water transportation occupations . 650
Marines *See* Job opportunities in the Armed Forces . 661
Material moving equipment operators 626
Material recording, scheduling, dispatching, and distributing occupations 119
Meat butchers *See* Butchers and meat, poultry, and fish cutters 521
Meat cutters *See* Butchers and meat, poultry, and fish cutters 521
Mechanics *See* Specific types
Medical assistants 252
Medical secretaries *See* Secretaries 165
Membership secretaries *See* Secretaries 165
Mental retardation aides *See* Nursing aides and psychiatric aides 259
Merchandise distributors *See* Stock clerks 125
Merchant patrollers *See* Guards 209
Mess attendants *See* Food and beverage service occupations 236
Mess cooks *See* Chefs, cooks, and other kitchen workers 223
Messengers *See* Mail clerks and messengers 116
Metal building assemblers *See* Structural and reinforcing ironworkers 506
Metal reed tuners *See* Musical instrument repairers and tuners 422
Metalworking and plastic-working machine operators 539
Milk drivers *See* Truckdrivers 641
Millwrights 412
Mobile heavy equipment mechanics 415
Mobile lounge drivers *See* Busdrivers 621
Mold carpenters *See* Carpenters 436
Molding plasterers *See* Plasterers 479
Money counters *See* Cashiers 1
Morgue librarians *See* File clerks 149
Mortgage accounting clerks *See* Bookkeeping, accounting, and auditing clerks 141
Mortgage processing clerks *See* Credit clerks and authorizers 88
Mortuary beauticians *See* Barbers and cosmetologists . . . 271
Motion picture equipment machinists *See* Machinists and tool programmers 535
Motor boat mechanics *See* Motorcycle, boat, and small engine mechanics 418
Motor room controllers *See* Electric power generating plant operators and power distributors and dispatchers 555
Motor vehicle dispatchers *See* Dispatchers 121
Motorcycle, boat, and small engine mechanics 418
Motorcycle subassembly repairers *See* Motorcycle, boat, and small engine mechanics 418
Motorized squad commanding officers *See* Police, detectives, and special agents 213
Muffler installers *See* Automotive mechanics 346
Musical instrument repairers and tuners 422
Narcotics investigators *See* Police, detectives, and special agents 213
Navy *See* Job opportunities in the Armed Forces 661
Neon sign servicers *See* Electricians 458
Net fishers *See* Fishers, hunters, and trappers 320
Net repairers *See* Fishers, hunters, and trappers 320
New accounts clerks *See* Interviewing and new accounts clerks 102
Notereaders *See* Typists, word processors, and data entry keyers 188
Nursery managers *See* Farm operators and managers . . . 309
Nursery school attendants *See* Preschool workers 300
Nursing aides and psychiatric aides 259
Office clerks *See* General office clerks 91
Office helpers *See* Mail clerks and messengers 116
Office machine repairers and servicers *See* Computer and peripheral equipment operators 82

Master List of Profiled Careers

Oil burner servicers and installers *See* Heating, air conditioning, and refrigeration mechanics 394
Oil dispatchers *See* Dispatchers 121
Ophthalmic laboratory technicians 609
Optical effects layout persons *See* Photographic process workers 617
Optical element coaters *See* Ophthalmic laboratory technicians 609
Optical instrument assemblers *See* Ophthalmic laboratory technicians 609
Opticians *See* Ophthalmic laboratory technicians . . . 609
Optometric assistants *See* Medical assistants 252
Order clerks 157
Order fillers *See* Stock clerks 125
Orderlies *See* Nursing aides and psychiatric aides . . 259
Ordinary seamen *See* Water transportation occupations 650
Organ pipe voicers *See* Welders, cutters, and welding machine operators 549
Orthodontic technicians *See* Dental laboratory technicians 604
Orthopedic boot and shoe designers and makers *See* Shoe and leather workers and repairers 587
Outboard motor mechanics *See* Motorcycle, boat, and small engine mechanics 418
Outdoor advertising leasing agents *See* Services sales representatives 50
Outpatient admitting clerks *See* Interviewing and new accounts clerks 102
Outside deliverers *See* Mail clerks and messengers . 116
Oyster floaters *See* Fishers, hunters, and trappers . . 320
Pad hands *See* Shoe and leather workers and repairers 587
Painters and paperhangers 474
Painting and coating machine operators 613
Pantry goods makers *See* Chefs, cooks, and other kitchen workers 226
Paperhangers *See* Painters and paperhangers 474
Parcel post clerks *See* Mail clerks and messengers . 116
Parts clerks *See* Stock clerks 125
Passenger barge masters *See* Water transportation occupations 650
Passenger car conductors *See* Rail transportation occupations 631
Passenger train brakers *See* Rail transportation occupations 631
Pastry cooks *See* Chefs, cooks, and other kitchen workers 226
Patch workers *See* Janitors and cleaners 293
Patchers *See* Bricklayers and stonemasons 430
Patrol officers *See* Police, detectives, and special agents 213
Patrol police lieutenants *See* Police, detectives, and special agents 213
Paymasters of purses *See* Cashiers 1
Payroll and timekeeping clerks 159
Percussion instrument repairers *See* Musical instrument repairers and tuners 422
Perforating machine operators *See* Bindery workers . 568
Personnel clerks 162
Pest control service sales agents *See* Services sales representatives 50
Photoengravers *See* Prepress workers 572
Photoengraving etchers *See* Prepress workers 572
Photoengraving finishers *See* Prepress workers 572
Photoengraving printers *See* Prepress workers 572
Photoengraving retouchers *See* Prepress workers 572
Photofinishing laboratory workers *See* Photographic process workers 617
Photograph retouchers *See* Photographic process workers 617
Photographic process workers 617
Photographic spotters *See* Photographic process workers 617
Photography colorists *See* Photographic process workers 617
Piano technicians *See* Musical instrument repairers and tuners 422
Pie makers *See* Chefs, cooks, and other kitchen workers 226
Pipe coverers and insulators *See* Insulation workers 469
Pipe cutters *See* Plumbers and pipefitters 483
Pipe organ tuners and repairers *See* Musical instrument repairers and tuners 422
Pipefitters *See* Plumbers and pipefitters 483
Pizza makers *See* Chefs, cooks, and other kitchen workers 226
Plant and maintenance technicians *See* Communications equipment mechanics 367
Plant propagators *See* Farm operators and managers . . . 309
Plasterers 479
Plastic working machine operators *See* Metalworking and plastic working machine operators 539
Plastics heat welders *See* Welders, cutters, and welding machine operators 549
Playroom attendants *See* Preschool workers 300
Pleasure craft sailors *See* Water transportation occupations 650
Plumbers and pipefitters 483
Podiatric assistants *See* Medical assistants 252
Police academy program coordinators *See* Police, detectives, and special agents 213
Police, detectives, and special agents 213
Police district switchboard operators *See* Telephone operators 184
Police officers *See* Correction officers 195
Police, detectives, and special agents 213
Police reserves commanders *See* Police, detectives, and special agents 213
Policy information clerks *See* Receptionists 105
Poser operators *See* Electric power generating plant operators and plant distributors and dispatchers 555
Postal clerks and mail carriers 131
Pot fishers *See* Fishers, hunters, and trappers 320
Poultry breeders *See* Farm operators and managers 309
Poultry cutters *See* Butchers and meat, poultry, and fish cutters 521
Power plant operators *See* Electric power generating plant operators and power distributors and dispatchers 555
Power reactor operators *See* Electric power generating plant operators and plant distributors and dispatchers 555
Power saw mechanics *See* Motorcycle, boat, and small engine mechanics 418
Power tool repairers *See* Home appliance and power tool repairers 401
Power truck operators *See* Truckdrivers 641

Practical nurses *See* Nursing aides and psychiatric aides . . . 259
Precinct police captains *See* Police, detectives, and special agents . . . 213
Precinct police sergeants *See* Police, detectives, and special agents . . . 213
Precision assemblers . . . 515
Precision lens centerers and edgers *See* Ophthalmic laboratory technicians . . . 609
Precision lens grinders and polishers *See* Ophthalmic laboratory technicians . . . 609
Predatory animal hunters *See* Fishers, hunters, and trappers . . . 320
Prepress workers . . . 572
Preschool workers . . . 300
Pressers *See* Bindery workers . . . 568
Pressure sealers and testers *See* Aircraft mechanics and engine specialists . . . 334
Printed circuit board reworkers *See* Commercial and industrial electronic equipment repairers . . . 362
Printing press operators . . . 577
Printing sales representatives *See* Services sales representatives . . . 50
Private branch exchange installers and repairers *See* Communications equipment mechanics . . . 367
Private household workers . . . 306
Probe test card, semiconductor wafers repairers *See* Commercial and industrial electronic equipment repairers . . . 362
Process artists *See* Prepress workers . . . 572
Process strippers *See* Prepress workers . . . 572
Production line welders *See* Welders, cutters, and welding machine operators . . . 549
Production repairers *See* Commercial and industrial electronic equipment repairers . . . 362
Communications equipment mechanics . . . 367
Electronic home entertainment equipment repairers . . . 377
Projection printers *See* Photographic process workers . . . 617
Prop makers *See* Carpenters . . . 436
Protective officers *See* Police, detectives, and special agents . . . 213
Protective signal installers and repairers *See* Electricians . . . 458
Psychiatric aides *See* Nursing aides and psychiatric aides . . . 259
Psychiatric hospital cooks *See* Chefs, cooks, and other kitchen workers . . . 226
Public address servicers *See* Communications equipment mechanics . . . 367
Public safety officers *See* Police, detectives, and special agents . . . 213
Public utilities sales representatives *See* Services sales representatives . . . 50
Pullman conductors *See* Rail transportation occupations . . . 631
Pulp pilers *See* Forestry and logging occupations . . . 328
Quality control clerks *See* Stock clerks . . . 125
Radio and television time sales representatives *See* Services sales representatives . . . 50
Radio dispatchers *See* Dispatchers . . . 121
Radio interference investigators *See* Line installers and cable splicers . . . 408
Radio mechanics *See* Communications equipment mechanics . . . 367
Radio repairers *See* Electronic home entertainment equipment repairers . . . 377
Radioactive waste disposal dispatchers *See* Dispatchers . . . 121
Radioactivity instrument maintenance technicians *See* Commercial and industrial electronic equipment repairers . . . 362
Rafters *See* Forestry and logging occupations . . . 328
Rail Carpenters *See* Carpenters . . . 436
Rail tractor operators *See* Rail transportation occupations . . . 631
Rail transportation occupations . . . 631
Railroad car letterers *See* Painters and paperhangers . . . 474
Railroad cooks *See* Chefs, cooks, and other kitchen workers . . . 226
Raw shellfish preparers *See* Chefs, cooks, and other kitchen workers . . . 226
Real estate agents, brokers, and appraisers . . . 25
Real estate appraisers *See* Real estate agents, brokers, and appraisers . . . 25
Receptionists . . . 105
Reclamation workers *See* Aircraft mechanics and engine specialists . . . 334
Reconcilement clerks *See* Bookkeeping, accounting, and auditing clerks . . . 141
Reconsignment clerks *See* Traffic, shipping, and receiving clerks . . . 128
Records clerks . . . 137
Records custodians *See* Records clerks . . . 137
Rectification printers *See* Photographic process workers . 617
Referral and information aides *See* Receptionists . . . 105
Refrigeration mechanics *See* Heating, air-conditioning, and refrigeration mechanics . . . 394
Refrigeration plant cork insulators *See* Insulation workers . . . 469
Registered mail clerks *See* Mail clerks and messengers . . 116
Registrars *See* Receptionists . . . 105
Registration clerks *See* Hotel and motel desk clerks . . . 98
Reinforcing metal workers *See* Structural and reinforcing ironworkers . . . 506
Relay dispatchers *See* Dispatchers . . . 121
Rental clerks *See* Counter and rental clerks . . . 5
Repeat chiefs *See* Prepress workers . . . 572
Repeat photocomposing machine operators *See* Prepress workers . . . 572
Repossessors *See* Adjusters, investigators and collectors . . . 65
Reproduction technicians *See* Photographic process workers . . . 617
Reptile farmers *See* Farm operators and managers . . . 309
Rescue firefighters *See* Firefighting occupations . . . 200
Reservation and transportation ticket agents and travel clerks . . . 109
Resistance welding machine operators *See* Welders, cutters, and welding machine operators . . . 549
Resistance welding machine setters *See* Welders, cutters, and welding machine operators . . . 549
Restaurant hosts/hostesses *See* Food and beverage service occupations . . . 236
Retail sales workers . . . 36
Reviewers *See* Adjusters, investigators and collectors . . . 65
Riggers *See* Communications equipment mechanics . . . 367

Rigging slingers *See* Forestry and logging occupations 328
Ring makers *See* Jewelers 531
Riverboat masters *See* Water transportation occupations 650
Rivers *See* Forestry and logging occupations 328
Road freight break couplers *See* Rail transportation occupations 631
Road freight conductors *See* Rail transportation occupations 631
Rocket engine mechanics *See* Machinists and tool programmers 535
Roller print tenders *See* Prepress workers 572
Roofer applicators *See* Roofers 491
Roofers 491
Room service waiters/waitresses *See* Food and beverage service occupations 236
Rounding and backing machine operators *See* Bindery workers 568
Roustabouts 497
Saddle and side wire stitchers *See* Bindery workers . 568
Saddle makers *See* Shoe and leather workers and repairers 587
Saddle stitching machine operators *See* Bindery workers 568
Safety instruction police officers *See* Police, detectives, and special agents 213
Salad makers *See* Chefs, cooks, and other kitchen workers 226
Sales representatives *See* Services sales representatives 50
Sales promotion representatives *See* Services sales representatives 50
Sandblaster paint sprayers *See* Automotive body repairers 339
Sandwich makers *See* Chefs, cooks, and other kitchen workers 226
Satellite communications antenna installers *See* Communications equipment mechanics 367
Saw makers *See* Tool and die makers 545
Scalp treatment operators *See* Barbers and cosmetologists 271
Scanner operators *See* Prepress workers 572
Schedulers *See* Receptionists 105
School cafeteria cooks *See* Chefs, cooks, and other kitchen workers 226
School secretaries *See* Secretaries 165
Scullions *See* Chefs, cooks, and other kitchen workers 226
Sealers *See* Fishers, hunters, and trappers 320
Second cooks and bakers *See* Chefs, cooks, and other kitchen workers 226
Secretaries 165
Securities clerks *See* Bookkeeping, accounting, and auditing clerks 141
Brokerage clerks and statement clerks 148
Securities and financial services sales representatives 43
Securities traders *See* Securities and financial services sales representatives 43
Security systems sales representatives *See* Services sales representatives 50
Seed corn production managers *See* Farm operators and managers 309
Service mechanics *See* Automotive body repairers 339
Service representatives *See* Adjusters, investigators and collectors 65
Services sales representatives 50
Sextons *See* Janitors and cleaners 293
Sheetrock applicators *See* Drywall workers and lathers . . 453
Shellfish growers *See* Farm operators and managers 309
Ship masters *See* Water transportation occupations 650
Ship mates *See* Water transportation occupations 650
Ship pilots *See* Water transportation occupations 650
Ship runners *See* Traffic, shipping, and receiving clerks . . 128
Shipping and receiving clerks *See* Traffic, shipping, and receiving clerks 128
Shipping checkers *See* Traffic, shipping, and receiving clerks 128
Shipping services sales representatives *See* Services sales representatives 50
Shipwrights *See* Carpenters 436
Shipyard painters *See* Painters and paperhangers 474
Shoe and leather workers and repairers 587
Shoe repairers *See* Shoe and leather workers and repairers 587
Shoemakers *See* Shoe and leather workers and repairers 587
Shop estimators *See* Automotive body repairers 339
Short order cooks *See* Chefs, cooks, and other kitchen workers 226
Shorthand reporters *See* Stenographers and court reporters 174
Side stitching machine operators *See* Bindery workers . . . 568
Silversmiths *See* Jewelers 531
Singing messengers *See* Mail clerks and messengers . . . 116
Sketch makers *See* Prepress workers 572
Skiff operators *See* Fishers, hunters, and trappers 320
Smoke jumper supervisors *See* Firefighting occupations . . 200
Social secretaries *See* Secretaries 165
Solar energy system installers *See* Heating, air-conditioning and refrigeration mechanics 394
Song pluggers *See* Services sales representatives 50
Sound technicians *See* Communications equipment mechanics 367
Space and storage clerks *See* Stock clerks 125
Special agents *See* Police, detectives, and special agents 209
Specialty cooks *See* Chefs, cooks, and other kitchen workers 226
Spiral binders *See* Bindery workers 568
Sponge clippers and hookers *See* Fishers, hunters, and trappers 320
Sprinkler/irrigation equipment mechanics *See* Farm equipment mechanics 388
Stable attendants *See* Animal caretakers, except farm 265
State police officers *See* Police, detectives, and special agents 213
Stationary engineers 560
Steam service inspectors *See* Plumbers and pipefitters 483
Steel post installers *See* Line installers and cable splicers 408
Stencil machine operators *See* Prepress workers 572
Stenographers and court reporters 174
Stenotype operators *See* Stenographers and court reporters 174

Stitching machine feeder off bearers *See* Bindery workers . . . 568
Stitching machine setters *See* Bindery workers . . . 568
Stock clerks . . . 125
Stone repairers *See* Bricklayers and stonemasons . . 430
Stonemasons *See* Bricklayers and stonemasons . . . 430
Storekeepers *See* Stock clerks . . . 125
Streetcar operators *See* Rail transportation occupations . . . 631
Strippers *See* Prepress workers . . . 572
Stucco masons *See* Plasterers . . . 479
Structural and reinforcing ironworkers . . . 506
Submarine cable equipment technicians *See* Communications equipment mechanics . . . 367
Substation operators *See* Electric power generating plant operators and plant distributors and dispatchers . . 555
Supply clerks *See* Stock clerks . . . 125
Survey workers *See* Interviewing and new accounts clerks . . . 102
Switch inspectors *See* Electricians . . . 458
Tack welders *See* Welders, cutters, and welding machine operators . . . 549
Take-down sorters *See* Photographic process workers . . . 617
Take-out waiters/waitresses *See* Food and beverage service occupations . . . 236
Tanbark laborers *See* Forestry and logging occupations . . . 328
Tank builders and erectors *See* Carpenters . . . 436
Tank setters *See* Structural and reinforcing ironworkers . . . 506
Tank truck operators *See* Truckdrivers . . . 641
Tape recorder repairers *See* Electronic home entertainment and equipment repairers . . . 377
Tapers *See* Drywall workers and lathers . . . 453
Tariff inspectors *See* Adjusters, investigators and collectors . . . 65
Taxi drivers and chauffeurs . . . 637
Taxicab coordinators *See* Dispatchers . . . 121
Teachers aides . . . 180
Telecommunicators *See* Dispatchers . . . 121
Telegraph office telephone clerks *See* Mail clerks and messengers . . . 116
Telephone installers and repairers . . . 382
Telephone maintenance mechanics *See* Telephone installers and repairers . . . 382
Telephone operators . . . 184
Television and radio repairers *See* Electronic home entertainment equipment repairers . . . 377
Television cable service sales representatives *See* Services sales representatives . . . 50
Television installers *See* Electronic home entertainment equipment repairers . . . 377
Tellers *See* Bank tellers . . . 71
Cashiers . . . 1
Temporary-help agency referral clerks *See* Personnel clerks . . . 162
Terrapin fishers *See* Fishers, hunters, and trappers . 320
Terrazzo workers *See* Concrete masons and terrazzo workers . . . 447
Textile machinery operators . . . 591
Thermic welding machine operators *See* Welders, cutters, and welding machine operators . . . 549
Third riggers *See* Forestry and logging occupations . 328
Ticket agents *See* Reservation and transportation ticket agents and travel clerks . . . 109
Ticketing clerks *See* Reservation and transportation ticket agents and travel clerks . . . 109
Tilesetters . . . 511
Timber framers *See* Carpenters . . . 436
Timekeepers *See* Payroll and timekeeping clerks . . . 159
Tippers *See* Bindery workers . . . 568
Toll collectors *See* Cashiers . . . 1
Tool and die makers . . . 545
Tool crib attendants *See* Stock clerks . . . 125
Tooth clerks *See* Stock clerks . . . 125
Torch straighteners and heaters *See* Welders, cutters, and welding machine operators . . . 549
Tow truck operators *See* Truckdrivers . . . 641
Tower erectors *See* Line installers and cable splicers . . . 408
Tower operators *See* Rail transportation occupations . . . 631
Trackmobile operators *See* Rail transportation occupations . . . 631
Tractor trailer truck operators *See* Truckdrivers . . . 641
Traffic lieutenants *See* Police, detectives, and special agents . . . 213
Traffic or system dispatchers *See* Dispatchers . . . 121
Traffic rate clerks *See* Traffic, shipping, and receiving clerks . . . 128
Traffic sergeants *See* Police, detectives, and special agents . . . 213
Traffic, shipping, and receiving clerks . . . 128
Trailer rental clerks *See* Counter and rental clerks . . . 5
Transfer table operators *See* Rail transportation occupations . . . 631
Trappers *See* Fishers, hunters, and trappers . . . 320
Travel agents . . . 56
Travel clerks *See* Reservation and transportation ticket agents and travel clerks . . . 109
Tree cutters *See* Forestry and logging occupations . . . 328
Tree, fruit, and nut crops farmers *See* Farm operators and managers . . . 309
Tree shear operators *See* Forestry and logging occupations . . . 328
Tree trimmers *See* Forestry and logging occupations . . . 328
Truck mechanics *See* Automotive mechanics . . . 346
Diesel mechanics . . . 354
Truckdrivers . . . 641
Tugboat captains *See* Water transportation occupations . . . 650
Tugboat dispatchers *See* Dispatchers . . . 121
Tugboat mates *See* Water transportation occupations . . . 650
Tune-up mechanics *See* Automotive mechanics . . . 346
Turbine operators *See* Electric power generating plant operators and power distributors and dispatchers . . . 555
Typewriter aliners and repairers *See* Computer and peripheral equipment operators . . . 82
Typists, word processors, and data entry keyers . . . 188
Ultrasonic welding machine operators *See* Welders, cutters, and welding machine operators . . . 549
Underwater hunter-trappers *See* Fishers, hunters, and trappers . . . 320
Upholsterers . . . 595
Upholstery and furniture repair sales representatives *See* Services sales representatives . . . 50
Van drivers *See* Truckdrivers . . . 641
Varitype operators *See* Typists, word processors, and data entry keyers . . . 188

Master List of Profiled Careers

Vegetable farmers *See* Farm operators and managers 309
Vehicle fuel systems converters *See* Automotive mechanics 346
Vending machine attendants *See* Vending machine servicers and repairers 427
Vending machine servicers and repairers 427
Vice investigators *See* Police, detectives, and special agents 213
Vine fruit crops farmers *See* Farm operators and managers 309
Violin repairers *See* Musical instrument repairers and tuners 422
Waiters *See* Food and beverage service occupations 236
Waitresses *See* Food and beverage service occupations 236
Wall cleaners *See* Janitors and cleaners 293
Wastewater treatment plant operators *See* Water and wastewater treatment plant operators 563
Water softener servicers and installers *See* Plumbers and pipefitters 483
Water transportation occupations 650
Water and wastewater treatment plant operators 563
Weir fishers *See* Fishers, hunters, and trappers 320
Welders, cutters, and welding machine operators 549
Wheelwrights *See* Automotive mechanics 346
Wholesale sales representatives *See* Manufacturers' and wholesale sales representatives 18
Wig dressers *See* Barbers and cosmetologists 271
Window cleaners *See* Janitors and cleaners 293
Wood boatbuilders *See* Carpenters 436
Woodworking occupations 599
Worm growers *See* Farm operators and managers 309
Yacht masters *See* Water transportation occupations 650
Yard engineers *See* Rail transportation occupations 631

Cashiers

Cashiers are employed by supermarkets, department stores, movie theaters, restaurants, and many other businesses to facilitate the sale of merchandise. Cashiers total bills, receive money, make change, fill out charge forms, and give receipts. Cashiers traditionally have rung up customers' purchases using a cash register, manually entering the price of each product the consumer was buying. An increasing number of establishments are now using more sophisticated equipment such as scanners and computer terminals.

Salaries

Earnings for cashiers range from the minimum wage to several times that amount. Wages tend to be higher in unionized establishments and in areas where there is intense competition for workers.

Lowest 10 percent	$153/week or less
Median	$185-$295/week
Top 10 percent	$414/week and up.

Employment Outlook

Growth rate until the year 2005: Average.

Cashiers

Career Guides

★1★ "Business and Financial Careers" in *The Best Jobs for the 1990s and Into the 21st Century*
Impact Publications
9104-N Manassas Dr.
Manassas Park, VA 22111
Ph: (703)361-7300 Fax: (703)335-9486

Ronald L. Krannich and Caryl Rae Krannich. 1993. Includes information on cashiers, counter and rental clerks, and information clerks.

★2★ *Cashier*
Careers, Inc.
PO Box 135
Largo, FL 34649-0135
Ph: (813)584-7333

1994. Two-page job guide card describing duties, working conditions, personal qualifications, training, earnings and hours, employment outlook, places of employment, related careers and where to write for more information.

★3★ "Cashier" in *Career Information Center* (Vol.10)
Simon and Schuster
200 Old Tappan Rd.
Old Tappan, NJ 07675
Fax: 800-445-6991 Fr: 800-223-2348

Richard Lidz and Dale Anderson, editorial directors. Fifth edition, 1993. For 600 occupations, describes job duties, entry-level requirements, education and training needed, advancement possibilities, employment outlook, earnings and benefits. The set is divided into 12 volumes. Each volume includes jobs related under a broad career field. Volume 13 is the index.

★4★ "Cashier" in *Occu-Facts: Information on 580 Careers in Outline Form*
Careers, Inc.
PO Box 135
Largo, FL 34649-0135
Ph: (813)584-7333

Biennial, 1995-96 edition. Each one-page occupational profile describes duties, working conditions, physical surroundings and demands, aptitudes, temperament, educational requirements, employment outlook, earnings, and places of employment.

★5★ *Cashier/Vault Attendant*
Vocational Biographies, Inc.
PO Box 31
Sauk Centre, MN 56378-0031
Ph: (612)352-6516 Fax: (612)352-5546
Fr: 800-255-0752

1993. Four-page pamphlet containing a personal narrative about a worker's job, work likes and dislikes, career path from high school to the present. Education and training, the rewards and frustrations, and the effects of the job on the rest of the worker's life. The data file portion of this pamphlet gives a concise occupational summary, including work descriptions, working conditions, places of employment, personal characteristics, education and training, job outlook, and salary range.

★6★ "Cashiers" in *Career Discovery Encyclopedia* (Vol.1, pp. 152-153)
J.G. Ferguson Publishing Co.
200 W. Madison St., Ste. 300
Chicago, IL 60606
Ph: (312)580-5480 Fax: (312)580-4948

E. Russell Primm, editor-in-chief. 1993. Contains two-page articles on 504 occupations. Each article describes job duties, earnings, and educational and training requirements.

★7★ *Cashiers and Checkers*
Chronicle Guidance Publications, Inc.
66 Aurora St.
PO Box 1190
Moravia, NY 13118-1190
Ph: (315)497-0330 Fax: (315)497-3359
Fr: 800-622-7284

1991. This career brief describes the nature of the work, working conditions, hours and earnings, education and training, licensure, certification, unions, personal qualifications, social and psychological factors, employment outlook, entry methods, advancement, and related occupations.

★8★ "Cashiers" in *Encyclopedia of Careers and Vocational Guidance* (Vol.2, pp. 259-262)
J.G. Ferguson Publishing Co.
200 W. Madison St., Ste. 300
Chicago, IL 60606
Ph: (312)580-5480 Fax: (312)580-4948

William E. Hopke, editor-in-chief. Ninth edition, 1993. Four-volume set that profiles 500 occupations and describes job trends in 74 industries. Includes career description, educational requirements, history of the job, methods of entry, advancement, employment outlook, earnings, working conditions, social and psychological factors, and sources of additional information.

★9★ "Cashiers" in *Occupational Outlook Handbook*
U.S. Government Printing Office
Superintendent of Documents
Washington, DC 20402
Ph: (202)512-1800 Fax: (202)512-2250

Biennial; latest edition, 1994-95. Encyclopedia of careers describing more than 250 occupations and comprising about 85 percent of all jobs in the economy. Occupations that require lengthy education or training are given the most attention. For each occupation, the handbook describes job duties, working conditions, training, educational preparation, personal qualities, advancement possibilities, job outlook, earnings, and sources of additional information.

★10★ "Cashiers/Retail Clerk" in *American Almanac of Jobs and Salaries* (p. 532)
Avon Books
1350 Avenue of the Americas
New York, NY 10019
Ph: (212)261-6800 Fr: 800-238-0658

John Wright, editor. Revised and updated, 1994-95. A comprehensive guide to the wages of hundreds of occupations in a wide variety of industries and organizations.

★11★ "Cashiers" in *Travel Agent* (pp. 171-172)
Arco Publishing Co.
Macmillan General Reference
15 Columbus Cir.
New York, NY 10023
Fax: 800-835-3202 Fr: 800-858-7674

Wilma Boyd. 1989. Introduction to the travel business. Covers U.S. and foreign travel, time zones, ticketing, world geography, and airline, railroad, and tour bus connections, and accommodations. Outlines entry-level positions in the airline, car rental, and hospitality industries as well as in travel agencies and related travel services. Explains travel agency operations, sales techniques, and the use of computers in travel services. Gives job hunting advice and sales tips.

★12★ *Grocery Checker*
Careers, Inc.
PO Box 135
Largo, FL 34649-0135
Ph: (813)584-7333

1995. Two-page job guide card describing duties, working conditions, personal qualifications, training, earnings and hours, employment outlook, places of employment, related careers and where to write for more information.

★13★ "Grocery Checker" in *Occu-Facts: Information on 580 Careers in Outline Form*
Careers, Inc.
PO Box 135
Largo, FL 34649-0135
Ph: (813)584-7333

Biennial, 1995-96 edition. Each one-page occupational profile describes duties, working conditions, physical surroundings and demands, aptitudes, temperament, educational requirements, employment outlook, earnings, and places of employment.

★14★ "Hospitality Cashier" in *Career Information Center* (Vol.8)
Simon and Schuster
200 Old Tappan Rd.
Old Tappan, NJ 07675
Fax: 800-445-6991 Fr: 800-223-2348

Richard Lidz and Dale Anderson, editorial directors. Fifth edition, 1993. For 600 occupations, describes job duties, entry-level requirements, education and training needed, advancement possibilities, employment outlook, earnings and benefits. The set is divided into 12 volumes. Each volume includes jobs related under a broad career field. Volume 13 is the index.

★15★ *Supermarket Cashier*
Vocational Biographies, Inc.
PO Box 31
Sauk Centre, MN 56378-0031
Ph: (612)352-6516 Fax: (612)352-5546
Fr: 800-255-0752

1990. This pamphlet profiles a person working in the job. Includes information about job duties, working conditions, places of employment, educational preparation, labor market outlook, and salaries.

★16★ *Video Career Library - Clerical & Administrative Support*
Careers, Inc.
PO Box 135
Largo, FL 34649-0135
Ph: (813)584-7333

Videocassette. 1990. 26 mins. Part of the Video Career Library covering 165 occupations. Shows actual workers on the job. Includes secretaries, cashiers, receptionists, bookkeepers and audit clerks, telephone operators, postal clerks/carriers/supervisors, insurance investigators, bank tellers, data entry keyers, and court reporters.

Associations

★17★ United Food and Commercial Workers International Union (UFCW)
1775 K St. NW
Washington, DC 20006
Ph: (202)223-3111

Members: AFL-CIO. **Publications:** *UFCW Action*, bimonthly. • *UFCW Leadership Update*, monthly.

Test Guides

★18★ *Career Examination Series: Assistant Cashier*
National Learning Corp.
212 Michael Dr.
Syosset, NY 11791
Ph: (516)921-8888 Fax: (516)921-8743
Fr: 800-645-6337

Jack Rudman. All examination guides in this series contain questions with answers.

★19★ *Career Examination Series: Associate Cashier*
National Learning Corp.
212 Michael Dr.
Syosset, NY 11791
Ph: (516)921-8888 Fax: (516)921-8743
Fr: 800-645-6337

Jack Rudman. Test guide including questions and answers for students or professionals in the field who seek advancement through examination.

★20★ *Career Examination Series: Cashier*
National Learning Corp.
212 Michael Dr.
Syosset, NY 11791
Ph: (516)921-8888 Fax: (516)921-8743
Fr: 800-645-6337

Jack Rudman. All examination guides in this series contain questions with answers.

★21★ *Career Examination Series: Cashier-Cashier (I-II)*
National Learning Corp.
212 Michael Dr.
Syosset, NY 11791
Ph: (516)921-8888 Fax: (516)921-8743
Fr: 800-645-6337

Jack Rudman. 1989. All examination guides in this series contain questions with answers.

★22★ *Career Examination Series: Principal Cashier*
National Learning Corp.
212 Michael Dr.
Syosset, NY 11791
Ph: (516)921-8888 Fax: (516)921-8743
Fr: 800-645-6337

Jack Rudman. All examination guides in this series contain questions with answers.

★23★ *Career Examination Series: Senior Cashier*
National Learning Corp.
212 Michael Dr.
Syosset, NY 11791
Ph: (516)921-8888 Fax: (516)921-8743
Fr: 800-645-6337

Jack Rudman. All examination guides in this series contain questions with answers.

★24★ *Career Examination Series: Supervising Cashier*
National Learning Corp.
212 Michael Dr.
Syosset, NY 11791
Ph: (516)921-8888 Fax: (516)921-8743
Fr: 800-645-6337

Jack Rudman. 1989. All examination guides in this series contain questions with answers.

Basic Reference Guides and Handbooks

★25★ *Math on the Job: Cashier*
National Center for Research in Vocational Education
Ohio State University
1900 Kenry Rd.
Columbus, OH 43210
Ph: (614)292-4353

1985.

Periodicals

★26★ *UFCW Action*
United Food and Commercial Workers International Union (UFCW)
1775 K St. NW
Washington, DC 20006
Ph: (202)223-3111

Bimonthly. Covers union activities, political and legislative matters, and consumer news.

★27★ *UFCW Leadership Update*
United Food and Commercial Workers International Union (UFCW)
1775 K St. NW
Washington, DC 20006
Ph: (202)223-3111
Monthly.

Counter and Rental Clerks

Counter and rental clerks are responsible for answering questions, taking orders, receiving payments, and accepting returns. Specific duties vary by establishment, and can be very general, or very specialized. Typical employers for counter and rental clerks include dry-cleaning and laundry establishments, video rental and grocery stores, automobile rental firms, leasing services, and equipment rental firms. Regardless of where they work, counter and rental clerks must be knowledgeable about the company's services, policies, and procedures. When taking orders, counter and rental clerks use various types of equipment. In some establishments, they write out tickets and order forms. In others, they use computers and scanners. Other workers with similar duties include food counter clerks, bank tellers, cashiers, retail sales workers, postal service clerks, and toll collectors.

Salaries

Earnings for counter and rental clerks often start at the minimum wage, but in areas with intense competition for workers, wages are often much higher. In addition some receive commissions based on the number of contracts they complete or services they sell.

Lowest 10 percent	$175/week or less
Median	$201-$383/week
Top 10 percent	$514/week and up.

Employment Outlook

Growth rate until the year 2005: Faster than average.

Counter and Rental Clerks

Career Guides

★28★ **"Business and Financial Careers" in *The Best Jobs for the 1990s and Into the 21st Century***
Impact Publications
9104-N Manassas Dr.
Manassas Park, VA 22111
Ph: (703)361-7300 Fax: (703)335-9486

Ronald L. Krannich and Caryl Rae Krannich. 1993. Includes information on cashiers, counter and rental clerks, and information clerks.

★29★ **"Car Rental Agent" in *Career Information Center* (Vol.12)**
Simon and Schuster
200 Old Tappan Rd.
Old Tappan, NJ 07675
Fax: 800-445-6991 Fr: 800-223-2348

Richard Lidz and Dale Anderson, editorial directors. Fifth edition, 1993. For 600 occupations, describes job duties, entry-level requirements, education and training needed, advancement possibilities, employment outlook, earnings and benefits. The set is divided into 12 volumes. Each volume includes jobs related under a broad career field. Volume 13 is the index.

★30★ ***Car Rental Agents***
Chronicle Guidance Publications, Inc.
66 Aurora St.
PO Box 1190
Moravia, NY 13118-1190
Ph: (315)497-0330 Fax: (315)497-3359
Fr: 800-622-7284

1993. This career brief describes the nature of the work, working conditions, hours and earnings, education and training, licensure, certification, unions, personal qualifications, social and psychological factors, employment outlook, entry methods, advancement, and related occupations.

★31★ **"Car Rental Agents" in *Encyclopedia of Careers and Vocational Guidance***
J.G. Ferguson Publishing Co.
200 W. Madison St., Ste. 300
Chicago, IL 60606
Ph: (312)580-5480 Fax: (312)580-4948

William E. Hopke, editor-in-chief. Ninth edition, 1993. Four-volume set that profiles 500 occupations and describes job trends in 74 industries. Includes career description, educational requirements, history of the job, methods of entry, advancement, employment outlook, earnings, working conditions, social and psychological factors, and sources of additional information.

★32★ **"Car or Truck Rental Agent" in *Transportation* (pp. 69-73)**
Franklin Watts, Inc.
387 Park Avenue, S.
New York, NY 10016
Ph: (212)686-7070

Marjorie Rittenberg Schulz. 1990. Surveys the transportation industry including air, water, and rail services. Provides job description, training, salary, and employment outlook. Offers job hunting advice.

★33★ ***Career Insights***
RMI Media Productions, Inc.
1365 N. Winchester
Olathe, KS 66061
Ph: (913)768-1696 Fax: 800-755-6910
Fr: 800-745-5480

Videocassette series. 1987. This videotape series describes 50 occupations, including skill requirements and interviews with people employed in these fields. Occupations include: flight service, air transportation/ground services, data processing, carpentry, clerk in banking/insurance/business, cosmetic personal grooming, firefighting, forestry, insulation/roofing, mechanics, material handling, photographic processing, pipefitting and plumbing, printing, secretarial services, tool and die operations.

★34★ **"The Center of the Travel Industry - Getting Started in Car Rental" in *Travel and Hospitality Career Directory* (pp. 41-46)**
Career Press, Inc.
PO Box 34
62 Beverly Rd.
Hawthorne, NJ 07507
Ph: (201)427-0229

Ronald W. Fry, editor. 1989. Offers advice on career planning and job hunting in hotel, travel, and related industries. Lists companies offering entry level positions in airlines, convention and visitors' bureaus, foreign tourist boards, hotels, travel agencies, car rental firms, and cruise lines. Lists travel and hospitality associations and trade publications.

★35★ **"Clerks" in *Career Discovery Encyclopedia* (Vol.2, pp. 16-17)**
J.G. Ferguson Publishing Co.
200 W. Madison St., Ste. 300
Chicago, IL 60606
Ph: (312)580-5480 Fax: (312)580-4948

E. Russell Primm, editor-in-chief. 1993. Contains two-page articles on 504 occupations. Each article describes job duties, earnings, and educational and training requirements.

★36★ **"Counter and Rental Clerks" in *America's 50 Fastest Growing Jobs* (pp. 93)**
JIST Works, Inc.
720 N. Park Ave.
Indianapolis, IN 46202-3431
Ph: (317)264-3720 Fax: (317)264-3709
Fr: 800-648-5478

Michael J. Farr, compiler. 1994. Describes the 50 fastest growing jobs within major career clusters such as technicians, and marketing and sales. Each job profile explains the nature of the work, skills and abilities required, employment outlook, average earnings, related occupations, education and training requirements, and employment opportunities. Also contains career planning information and job search tips.

★37★ "Counter and Rental Clerks" in *Occupational Outlook Handbook*
U.S. Government Printing Office
Superintendent of Documents
Washington, DC 20402
Ph: (202)512-1800 Fax: (202)512-2250

Biennial; latest edition, 1994-95. Encyclopedia of careers describing more than 250 occupations and comprising about 85 percent of all jobs in the economy. Occupations that require lengthy education or training are given the most attention. For each occupation, the handbook describes job duties, working conditions, training, educational preparation, personal qualities, advancement possibilities, job outlook, earnings, and sources of additional information.

★38★ "Counter and Retail Clerks" in *Encyclopedia of Careers and Vocational Guidance* (Vol.2, pp. 405-407)
J.G. Ferguson Publishing Co.
200 W. Madison St., Ste. 300
Chicago, IL 60606
Ph: (312)580-5480 Fax: (312)580-4948

William E. Hopke, editor-in-chief. Ninth edition, 1993. Four-volume set that profiles 500 occupations and describes job trends in 74 industries. Includes career description, educational requirements, history of the job, methods of entry, advancement, employment outlook, earnings, working conditions, social and psychological factors, and sources of additional information.

★39★ *Counter Worker, Cafeteria*
Careers, Inc.
PO Box 135
Largo, FL 34649-0135
Ph: (813)584-7333

1992. Two-page job guide card describing duties, working conditions, personal qualifications, training, earnings and hours, employment outlook, places of employment, related careers and where to write for more information.

★40★ "Equipment Rental and Leasing Service Agent" in *Career Information Center* (Vol.10)
Simon and Schuster
200 Old Tappan Rd.
Old Tappan, NJ 07675
Fax: 800-445-6991 Fr: 800-223-2348

Richard Lidz and Dale Anderson, editorial directors. Fifth edition, 1993. For 600 occupations, describes job duties, entry-level requirements, education and training needed, advancement possibilities, employment outlook, earnings and benefits. The set is divided into 12 volumes. Each volume includes jobs related under a broad career field. Volume 13 is the index.

★41★ *Internships Volume 4: The Travel and Hospitality Industries*
Career Press, Inc.
PO Box 34
62 Beverly Rd.
Hawthorne, NJ 07507
Ph: (201)427-0229

Ronald W. Fry, editor-in-chief. 1989. Offers advice on obtaining internships with airlines, hotels, cruise ships, convention and visitors centers, car rental companies, and travel agencies. Each company listing includes name, address, phone number, contact person, paid or unpaid internships, duration, qualifications, application procedures, and deadlines.

★42★ *Laundromat Attendant*
Careers, Inc.
PO Box 135
Largo, FL 34649-0135
Ph: (813)584-7333

1992. Two-page job guide card describing duties, working conditions, personal qualifications, training, earnings and hours, employment outlook, places of employment, related careers and where to write for more information.

★43★ "Laundromat Attendant" in *Occu-Facts: Information on 580 Careers in Outline Form*
Careers, Inc.
PO Box 135
Largo, FL 34649-0135
Ph: (813)584-7333

Biennial, 1995-96 edition. Each one-page occupational profile describes duties, working conditions, physical surroundings and demands, aptitudes, temperament, educational requirements, employment outlook, earnings, and places of employment.

★44★ "Rental Clerk" in *Travel Agent* (p. 168)
Arco Publishing Co.
Macmillan General Reference
15 Columbus Cir.
New York, NY 10023
Fax: 800-835-3202 Fr: 800-858-7674

Wilma Boyd. 1989. Introduction to the travel business. Covers U.S. and foreign travel, time zones, ticketing, world geography, and airline, railroad, and tour bus connections, and accommodations. Outlines entry-level positions in the airline, car rental, and hospitality industries as well as in travel agencies and related travel services. Explains travel agency operations, sales techniques, and the use of computers in travel services. Gives job hunting advice and sales tips.

★45★ *Retailing & Merchandising*
Morris Video
2730 Monterey St., No. 105
Monterey Business Park
Torrance, CA 90503
Ph: (213)533-4800 Fr: 800-843-3606

Videocassette. 1987. 15 mins. A look at the variety of career opportunities available in the world of retail.

★46★ *Vehicle Leasing Agent*
Vocational Biographies, Inc.
PO Box 31
Sauk Centre, MN 56378-0031
Ph: (612)352-6516 Fax: (612)352-5546
Fr: 800-255-0752

1988. This pamphlet profiles a person working in the job. Includes information about job duties, working conditions, places of employment, educational preparation, labor market outlook, and salaries.

★47★ *Wings and Wheels*
Walter J. Klein Company, Ltd.
6311 Carmel Rd.
PO Box 472087
Charlotte, NC 28247-2087
Ph: (704)542-1403 Fax: (704)542-0735

Videocassette. 1978. 15 mins. The concept of renting a car has been in existence since the 1920's. The history of automobile rentals is told from its inception to today's "rent it here, leave it there" era.

Associations

★48★ United Food and Commercial Workers International Union (UFCW)
1775 K St. NW
Washington, DC 20006
Ph: (202)223-3111

Members: AFL-CIO. **Publications:** *UFCW Action*, bimonthly. • *UFCW Leadership Update*, monthly.

Test Guides

★49★ *Career Examination Series: Stores Clerk*
National Learning Corp.
212 Michael Dr.
Syosset, NY 11791
Ph: (516)921-8888 Fax: (516)921-8743
Fr: 800-645-6337

Jack Rudman. All examination guides in this series contain questions with answers.

★50★ *Senior Clerical Series*
Prentice Hall Press
Simon & Schuster Inc.
200 Old Tappan Rd.
Old Tappan, NJ 07675
Ph: 800-223-2348

Hy Hammer. Fourth edition, 1983. Complete test preparation for the following senior grade positions: clerk, typist, stenographer, account clerk, file clerk, statistics clerk, stenographer (law), mail and supply clerk, and stores clerk.

Periodicals

★51★ *Counterman*
Babcox Publications
11 S. Forge St.
Akron, OH 44304
Ph: (216)535-7011 Fax: (216)535-0874
Gary A. Molinaro

Monthly. Magazine devoted to improving the effectiveness of professional counter-sales personnel.

★52★ *UFCW Action*
United Food and Commercial Workers International Union (UFCW)
1775 K St. NW
Washington, DC 20006
Ph: (202)223-3111

Bimonthly. Covers union activities, political and legislative matters, and consumer news.

★53★ *UFCW Leadership Update*
United Food and Commercial Workers International Union (UFCW)
1775 K St. NW
Washington, DC 20006
Ph: (202)223-3111

Monthly.

Insurance Agents and Brokers

Insurance sales workers (agents and brokers) sell policies that provide financial protection against loss to individuals and businesses. They plan for the financial security of individuals, families, and businesses; advise about insurance protection for automobiles, homes, businesses, or other properties; prepare reports and maintain records; and help policyholders settle insurance claims. Insurance sales workers sell one or many types of insurance. Life insurance agents offer policies that pay survivors when a policyholder dies. Insurance agents may work for one insurance company or as "independent agents" selling for several companies. Insurance brokers do not sell for a particular company, but place policies for their clients with the company that offers the best rate and coverage. Property/Casualty insurance agents sell policies that protect individuals and businesses from financial loss as a result of automobile accidents, fire, theft, or other losses.

Salaries

Salaries for insurance sales workers vary by level of experience.

Lowest 10 percent	$15,400/year or less
Median	$30,100/year
Top 10 percent	$64,600/year or more

Employment Outlook

Growth rate until the year 2005: Average.

Insurance Agents and Brokers

Career Guides

★54★ *All Pro*
BNA Communications, Inc.
9439 Key West Ave.
Rockville, MD 20850
Ph: (301)948-0540 Fax: (301)948-2085
Fr: 800-233-6067

Videocassette. 1981. 29 mins. Conversations with five top sales professionals. They discuss their careers and the traits that make a top professional.

★55★ *Business and Finance Career Directory*
Career Press, Inc.
PO Box 34
62 Beverly Rd.
Hawthorne, NJ 07507
Ph: (201)427-0229

Ronald W. Fry, editor. 1989. Chapters are written by practitioners in accounting, securities, financial planning and insurance. Describes job duties, educational preparation required, entry into the field, and earnings. Identifies internship opportunities and lists companies actively hiring at entry level.

★56★ *Business Insurance: A Sales Skills Introduction*
Custom Communications
2 E. Hudson
Mazomanie, WI 53560
Ph: (608)795-4222

Videocassette. 19??. 28 mins. This program is designed to develop the vital sales skills an agent needs to make a smooth transition into the lucrative area of business insurance.

★57★ *Career Success Series*
Cambridge Educational
PO Box 2153
Charleston, WV 25328-2153
Ph: (304)744-9323 Fax: (304)744-9351
Fr: 800-468-4227

Videocassette. 1986. 15 mins. A series, available separately, outlining various career choices for students. Occupations include: accounting, flight service, air transportation/ground/flight service, data processing, carpentry, clerk in banking/insurance, commodity sales, cosmetic personal grooming, fire fighting, forestry services, home economics, insulation/roofing, material handling, mechanics, photographic processing, pipefitting and plumbing, police science, printing, carpentry, medical laboratory technicians, secretarial services, and utilities equipment operator.

★58★ *Careers in Insurance: Property and Casualty*
Insurance Information Institute
110 William St.
New York, NY 10038
Ph: (212)669-9200

1987. This 12-page booklet explores careers in property and casualty insurance and covers job duties and training.

★59★ *Consider a Career as an Insurance Agent*
Professional Insurance Agents
National Association
400 N. Washington St.
Alexandria, VA 22314
Ph: (703)836-9340

This six-panel brochure offers career information and advice. Covers qualifications, job duties, future opportunities, and entry into the field.

★60★ *Explore Your Future: A Career in Life Insurance Sales*
National Association of Life Underwriters
1922 F St., N.W.
Washington, DC 20006-4387
Ph: (202)331-6000

This six-panel brochure describes opportunities, qualifications, and training.

★61★ *Hot Tips, Sneaky Tricks, and Last Ditch Tactics: An Insider's Guide to Getting Your First Corporate Job*
John Wiley and Sons, Inc.
605 3rd Ave.
New York, NY 10158-0012
Ph: (212)850-6000 Fax: (212)850-6088
Fr: 800-526-5368

Jeff B. Speck. 1989. Written for college graduates who are looking for jobs in banking, consulting, accounting, insurance, real estate or the Fortune 500. Offers tips on surviving the standardized selection process used by large companies.

★62★ *Insurance Agent*
Vocational Biographies, Inc.
PO Box 31
Sauk Centre, MN 56378-0031
Ph: (612)352-6516 Fax: (612)352-5546
Fr: 800-255-0752

1994. Four-page pamphlet containing a personal narrative about a worker's job, work likes and dislikes, career path from high school to the present. Education and training, the rewards and frustrations, and the effects of the job on the rest of the worker's life. The data file portion of this pamphlet gives a concise occupational summary, including work descriptions, working conditions, places of employment, personal characteristics, education and training, job outlook, and salary range.

★63★ "Insurance Agent and Broker" in *Career Information Center* (Vol.10)
Simon and Schuster
200 Old Tappan Rd.
Old Tappan, NJ 07675
Fax: 800-445-6991 Fr: 800-223-2348

Richard Lidz and Dale Anderson, editorial directors. Fifth edition, 1993. For 600 occupations, describes job duties, entry-level requirements, education and training needed, advancement possibilities, employment outlook, earnings and benefits. The set is divided into 12 volumes. Each volume includes jobs related under a broad career field. Volume 13 is the index.

★64★ *Insurance Agent/Broker, Life*
Careers, Inc.
PO Box 135
Largo, FL 34649-0135
Ph: (813)584-7333

1993. Four-page brief offering the definition, history, duties, working conditions, personal qualifications, educational requirements, earnings, hours, employment outlook, advancement possibilities, and related occupations.

★65★ "Insurance Agent and Broker" in *VGM's Careers Encyclopedia* (pp. 222-225)
National Textbook Co. (NTC)
VGM Career Books
4255 W. Touhy Ave.
Lincolnwood, IL 60646-1975
Ph: (708)679-5500 Fax: (708)679-2494
Fr: 800-323-4900

Third edition, 1991. Contains two- to five-page descriptions of 200 managerial, professional, technical, trade and service occupations. Includes job duties, places of employment, qualifications, educational preparation, training, employment potential, advancement, income, and additional sources of information.

★66★ "Insurance Agent and Broker" in *VGM's Handbook of Business and Management Careers*
National Textbook Co. (NTC)
VGM Career Books
4255 W. Touhy Ave.
Lincolnwood, IL 60646-1975
Ph: (708)679-5500 Fax: (708)679-2494
Fr: 800-323-4900

Annette Selden. Second edition, 1993. Contains 42 two-page occupational profiles describing job duties, places of employment, working conditions, qualifications, education, employment outlook, and income.

★67★ "Insurance Agent" in *Jobs Rated Almanac*
World Almanac
1 International Blvd., Ste. 444
Mahwah, NJ 07495
Ph: (201)529-6900 Fax: (201)529-6901

Les Krantz. Second edition, 1992. Ranks 250 jobs by environment, salary, outlooks, physical demands, stress, security, travel opportunities, and extra perks. Includes jobs the editor feels are the most common, most interesting, and the most rapidly growing.

★68★ *Insurance Agent, Property and Liability*
Careers, Inc.
PO Box 135
Largo, FL 34649-0135
Ph: (813)584-7333

1993. Two-page occupational summary card describing duties, working conditions, personal qualifications, training, earnings and hours, employment outlook, places of employment, related careers and where to write for more information.

★69★ "Insurance Agent/Property & Liability" in *Occu-Facts: Information on 580 Careers in Outline Form*
Careers, Inc.
PO Box 135
Largo, FL 34649-0135
Ph: (813)584-7333

Biennial, 1995-96 edition. Each one-page occupational profile describes duties, working conditions, physical surroundings and demands, aptitudes, temperament, educational requirements, employment outlook, earnings, and places of employment.

★70★ "Insurance Agent" in *Top Professions: The 100 Most Popular, Dynamic, and Profitable Careers in America Today* (pp. 8-9)
Petersons Guides, Inc.
PO Box 2123
Princeton, NJ 08543-2123
Ph: (609)243-9111 Fax: (609)243-9150
Fr: 800-338-3282

Nicholas Basta. 1989. Includes occupations requiring a college or advanced degree. Describes job duties, earnings, some typical job titles, career opportunities at different degree levels, and lists related associations.

★71★ *Insurance Agents and Brokers*
Chronicle Guidance Publications, Inc.
66 Aurora St.
PO Box 1190
Moravia, NY 13118-1190
Ph: (315)497-0330 Fax: (315)497-3359
Fr: 800-622-7284

1993. This career brief describes the nature of the work, working conditions, hours and earnings, education and training, licensure, certification, unions, personal qualifications, social and psychological factors, employment outlook, entry methods, advancement, and related occupations.

★72★ "Insurance Agents and Brokers" in *101 Careers: A Guide to the Fastest-Growing Opportunities* (pp. 17-19)
John Wiley & Sons, Inc.
605 3rd Ave.
New York, NY 10158-0012
Ph: (212)850-6645 Fax: (212)850-6088

Michael Harkavy. 1990. Describes the nature of the job, working conditions, employment growth, qualifications, personal skills, projected salaries, and where to write for more information.

★73★ "Insurance Agents and Brokers" in *Jobs! What They Are—Where They Are—What They Pay* (p. 337)
Simon & Schuster, Inc.
Simon & Schuster Bldg.
1230 Avenue of the Americas
New York, NY 10020
Ph: (212)698-7000

Robert O. Snelling and Anne M. Snelling. Revised edition, 1992. Profiles 241 occupations, describing duties and responsibilities, educational preparation, earnings, employment opportunities, training, and qualifications.

★74★ "Insurance Agents and Brokers, Life" in *Encyclopedia of Careers and Vocational Guidance* (Vol.3, pp. 212-216)
J.G. Ferguson Publishing Co.
200 W. Madison St., Ste. 300
Chicago, IL 60606
Ph: (312)580-5480 Fax: (312)580-4948

William E. Hopke, editor-in-chief. Ninth edition, 1993. Four-volume set that profiles 500 occupations and describes job trends in 74 industries. Includes career description, educational requirements, history of the job, methods of entry, advancement, employment outlook, earnings, working conditions, social and psychological factors, and sources of additional information.

★75★ "Insurance Agents and Brokers: Making it in a Premium Career" in *Careers for Women Without College Degrees* (pp. 239-245)
McGraw-Hill Publishing Co.
11 W. 19th St.
New York, NY 10011
Ph: (212)337-6010

Beatryce Nivens. 1988. Career planning and job hunting guide containing information on decision-making, skills assessment, and resumes for career changers. Profiles careers with the best occupational outlook. Describes the work, educational preparation, employment outlook, salaries, and required skills.

★76★ "Insurance Agents and Brokers" in *Occupational Outlook Handbook*
U.S. Government Printing Office
Superintendent of Documents
Washington, DC 20402
Ph: (202)512-1800 Fax: (202)512-2250

Biennial; latest edition, 1994-95. Encyclopedia of careers describing more than 250 occupations and comprising about 85 percent of all jobs in the economy. Occupations that require lengthy education or training are given the most attention. For each occupation, the handbook describes job duties, working conditions, training, educational preparation, personal qualities, advancement possibilities, job outlook, earnings, and sources of additional information.

★77★ "Insurance Agents and Brokers, Property and Casualty" in *Encyclopedia of Careers and Vocational Guidance* (Vol.3, pp. 217-220)
J.G. Ferguson Publishing Co.
200 W. Madison St., Ste. 300
Chicago, IL 60606
Ph: (312)580-5480 Fax: (312)580-4948

William E. Hopke, editor-in-chief. Ninth edition, 1993. Four-volume set that profiles 900 occupations and describes job trends in 74 industries. Includes career description, educational requirements, history of the job, methods of entry, advancement, employment outlook, earnings, conditions of work, social and psychological factors, and sources of further information.

★78★ "Insurance" in *Black Woman's Career Guide* (pp. 288-294)
Bantam Doubleday Dell
1540 Broadway
New York, NY 10036
Fax: 800-233-3294 Fr: 800-223-5780

Beatryce Nivens. Revised edition, 1987. Offers career planning and job hunting advice. Contains information on 20 different career areas and profiles women working in the field. Each occupational profile describes the work, career paths and earning potential.

★79★ "Insurance" in *Encyclopedia of Careers and Vocational Guidance* (Vol.1, pp. 242-247)
J.G. Ferguson Publishing Co.
200 W. Madison St., Ste. 300
Chicago, IL 60606
Ph: (312)580-5480 Fax: (312)580-4948

William E. Hopke, editor-in-chief. Ninth edition, 1993. Four-volume set that profiles 500 occupations and describes job trends in 74 industries. Includes career description, educational requirements, history of the job, methods of entry, advancement, employment outlook, earnings, working conditions, social and psychological factors, and sources of additional information.

★80★ "Insurance is Fun!" in *Internships Volume 3: Accounting, Banking, Brokerage, Finance & Insurance* (pp. 55-61)
Career Press, Inc.
PO Box 34
62 Beverly Rd.
Hawthorne, NJ 07507
Ph: (201)427-0229

Ronald W. Fry, editor-in-chief. 1989. Offers advice about obtaining internships with accounting, brokerage and investment banking firms, banks, and insurance companies. Lists companies offering internships and includes the contact person, duration, duties, qualifications, and application procedures and deadlines.

★81★ "Insurance" in *Internships 1995*
Petersons Guides, Inc.
PO Box 2123
Princeton, NJ 08543-2123
Ph: (609)243-9111 Fr: 800-338-3282

Fifteenth edition, 1995. Lists internship opportunities under six broad categories: communications, creative, performing, and fine arts, human services, international relations, business and technology, and public affairs. For each internship program, gives the names, phone number, contact person, description, eligibility requirements, and benefits.

★82★ "Insurance" in *Jobs '95* (pp. 373-381)
Prentice Hall Press
1 Gulf & Western Plaza
New York, NY 10023
Ph: (212)373-8500

Kathryn Petras and Ross Petras. Annual, 1995. Discusses employment prospects and trends for 15 professional careers and 29 industries. Lists leading companies, associations, directories, and magazines.

★83★ "Insurance" in *Major Decisions: A Guide to College Majors* (p. 91)
Orchard House, Inc.
112 Balls Hill Rd.
Concord, MA 01742
Ph: (508)369-0467 Fax: (508)369-9472

Richard A. Blumenthal and Joseph A. Despres. 1990. Provides a one-page description of 155 college majors. Included under each major is a description, the plan of study, typical major courses, high school courses and career possibilities.

★84★ "Insurance Sales Agent" in *100 Best Careers for the Year 2000* (pp. 174-176)
Arco Pub.
201 W. 103rd St.
Indianapolis, IN 46290
Ph: 800-428-5331 Fax: 800-835-3202

Shelly Field. 1992. Describes 100 job opportunities expected to grow fast throughout the next decade. Provides information on job duties and responsibilities, training requirements, education, advancement opportunities, experience and qualifications, and typical salaries.

★85★ "Insurance, Sales" in *Career Choices for the 90's for Students of Business* (pp. 163-164)
Walker and Co.
435 Hudson St.
New York, NY 10014
Ph: (212)727-8300 Fax: (212)727-0984
Fr: 800-289-2553

1990. Describes jobs in different industries and includes interviews with people working in related occupations. Presents employment outlook, preferred geographic location, entry-level opportunities, career paths, job responsibilities, advancement, personal and professional qualifications, salaries, working conditions, material for further reading, and associations.

★86★ "Insurance Sales" in *Career Choices for the 90's for Students of Communications and Journalism* (pp. 171-172)
Walker and Co.
435 Hudson St.
New York, NY 10014
Ph: (212)727-8300 Fax: (212)727-0984
Fr: 800-289-2553

1990. Describes jobs in different industries and includes interviews with people working in related occupations. Presents employment outlook, preferred geographic location, entry-level opportunities, career paths, job responsibilities, advancement, personal and professional qualifications, salaries, working conditions, material for further reading, and associations.

★87★ "Insurance, Sales" in *Career Choices for the 90's for Students of Economics* (pp. 72-74)
Walker and Co.
435 Hudson St.
New York, NY 10014
Ph: (212)727-8300 Fax: (212)727-0984
Fr: 800-289-2553

1990. Describes jobs in different industries and includes interviews with people working in related occupations. Presents employment outlook, preferred geographic location, entry-level opportunities, career paths, job responsibilities, advancement, personal and professional qualifications, salaries, working conditions, material for further reading, and associations.

★88★ "Insurance, Sales" in *Career Choices for the 90's for Students of Mathematics* (pp. 97-99)
Walker and Co.
435 Hudson St.
New York, NY 10014
Ph: (212)727-8300 Fax: (212)727-0984
Fr: 800-289-2553

1990. Describes jobs in different industries and includes interviews with people working in related occupations. Presents employment outlook, preferred geographic location, entry-level opportunities, career paths, job responsibilities, advancement, personal and professional qualifications, salaries, working conditions, material for further reading, and associations.

★89★ "Insurance Sales" in *Career Choices for the 90's for Students of Political Science & Government* (pp. 172-173)
Walker and Co.
435 Hudson St.
New York, NY 10014
Ph: (212)727-8300 Fax: (212)727-0984
Fr: 800-289-2553

1990. Describes jobs in different industries and includes interviews with people working in related occupations. Presents employment outlook, preferred geographic location, entry-level opportunities, career paths, job responsibilities, advancement, personal and professional qualifications, salaries, working conditions, material for further reading, and associations.

★90★ "Insurance Sales" in *Career Choices for the 90's for Students of Psychology* (pp. 192-193)
Walker and Co.
435 Hudson St.
New York, NY 10014
Ph: (212)727-8300 Fax: (212)727-0984
Fr: 800-289-2553

1990. Describes jobs in different industries and includes interviews with people working in related occupations. Presents employment outlook, preferred geographic location, entry-level opportunities, career paths, job responsibilities, advancement, personal and professional qualifications, salaries, working conditions, material for further reading, and associations.

★91★ "Insurance Sales" in *Fast-Track Careers: A Guide to the Highest-Paying Jobs* (pp. 152-153)
John Wiley and Sons, Inc.
605 3rd Ave.
New York, NY 10158-0012
Ph: (212)850-6000 Fax: (212)850-6088
Fr: 800-526-5368

William Lewis and Nancy Schuman. 1987. Profiles eight glamorous and high paying careers describing entry-level opportunities, earnings, personal qualities, types of companies, educational preparation and training, and employment outlook. Lists prominent companies in each industry, typical jargon, and professional associations.

★92★ "Insurance Sales" in *Transitions: Military Pathways to Civilian Careers* (pp. 141-142)
Rosen Publishing Group
29 E. 21st St.
New York, NY 10010
Ph: (212)777-3017 Fax: (212)777-0277
Fr: 800-237-9932

Robert W. MacDonald. 1988. Describes how to make the best use of your military service to create a civilian career. Describes skills needed in civilian employment and compares them to skills acquired in the military. Covers career planning, job search, resume writing, and starting a small business. Lists many resources.

★93★ "Insurance Salesperson" in *College Board Guide to Jobs and Career Planning* (pp. 134-136)
College Entrance Examination Board
45 Columbus Ave.
New York, NY 10023-6992
Ph: (212)713-8000

Joyce Slayton Mitchell. 1990. Career planning guide written for high school and college students. Covers 100 careers in 15 occupational groups. Provides job description, educational preparation needed, salaries, related careers, and sources of additional information. Includes information about the 90's labor market.

★94★ "Insurance Salespersons" in *Opportunities in Vocational and Technical Careers* (pp. 59-75)
National Textbook Co. (NTC)
VGM Career Books
4255 W. Touhy Ave.
Lincolnwood, IL 60646-1975
Ph: (708)679-5500 Fax: (708)679-2494
Fr: 800-323-4900

Adrian A. Paradis. 1992. Describes careers which can be prepared for by attending a private vocational or proprietary school—office employee, sales worker, service worker, health services, mechanic, craftworker, and technician. Covers employment outlook, job duties, and salaries. Offers career planning advice.

★95★ "Life Insurance Agent/Broker" in *Occu-Facts: Information on 580 Careers in Outline Form*
Careers, Inc.
PO Box 135
Largo, FL 34649-0135
Ph: (813)584-7333

Biennial, 1995-96 edition. Each one-page occupational profile describes duties, working conditions, physical surroundings and demands, aptitudes, temperament, educational requirements, employment outlook, earnings, and places of employment.

★96★ "Life Insurance Agents and Brokers" in *Career Discovery Encyclopedia* (Vol.4, pp. 12-13)
J.G. Ferguson Publishing Co.
200 W. Madison St., Ste. 300
Chicago, IL 60606
Ph: (312)580-5480 Fax: (312)580-4948

E. Russell Primm, editor-in-chief. 1993. Contains two-page articles on 504 occupations. Each article describes job duties, earnings, and educational and training requirements.

★97★ "Marine Insurance Careers" in *Opportunities in Marine and Maritime Careers* (pp. 111-112)
National Textbook Co. (NTC)
VGM Career Books
4255 W. Touhy Ave.
Lincolnwood, IL 60646-1975
Ph: (708)679-5500 Fax: (708)679-2494
Fr: 800-323-4900

William Ray Heitzmann. 1988. Includes careers related by their proximity to water: cruise ships, oceanography, marine sciences, fishing, commercial diving, maritime transportation, shipbuilding, Navy, Coast Guard. Covers qualifications, job outlook, job duties, educational preparation, and training. Lists associations and schools.

★98★ *Opportunities in Insurance Careers*
National Textbook Co. (NTC)
VGM Career Books
4255 W. Toughy Ave.
Lincolnwood, IL 60646-1975
Ph: (708)679-5500 Fax: (708)679-2494
Fr: 800-323-4900

Robert Schrayer.

★99★ "Property and Casualty Insurance Agents and Brokers" in *Career Discovery Encyclopedia* (Vol.5, pp. 90-91)
J.G. Ferguson Publishing Co.
200 W. Madison St., Ste. 300
Chicago, IL 60606
Ph: (312)580-5480 Fax: (312)580-4948

E. Russell Primm, editor-in-chief. 1993. Contains two-page articles on 504 occupations. Each article describes job duties, earnings, and educational and training requirements.

★100★ "Sales (Insurance)" in *Encyclopedia of Career Choices for the 1990s: A Guide to Entry Level Jobs* (pp. 442-444)
Berkley Pub.
PO Box 506
East Rutherford, NJ 07073
Fax: (201)933-2316 Fr: 800-788-6262

1992. Describes entry-level opportunities in 42 career fields for college graduates. Each chapter covers a single career field, including an overview, employment outlook, major employers, tips on entering the field, international job opportunities, functional job areas with personal and professional qualifications, career paths, job responsibilities, advancement possibilities, salaries, and working conditions. Lists related sources of information.

★101★ *Video Career Library - Marketing and Sales*
Careers, Inc.
PO Box 135
Largo, FL 34649-0135
Ph: (813)584-7333

Videocassette. 1994. Part of the Video Career Library covering 165 occupations. Shows actual workers on the job.

Associations

★102★ American Society of CLU and ChFC (ASCLU & Ch)
270 S. Bryn Mawr Ave.
Bryn Mawr, PA 19010
Ph: (610)526-2500 Fax: (610)527-4010

Members: Professional society of insurance agents and financial services professionals who hold Chartered Life Underwriter (CLU) or Chartered Financial Consultant (ChFC) designations. **Purpose:** Conducts week-long graduate-level educational sessions (CLU Institutes); one-day seminars with experts lecturing on subjects such as law, taxation, estate planning, and business life insurance; symposia and clinics; research. Offers scholarship to society programs. **Publications:** *Assets: A Business, Tax, and Financial Newsletter*, bimonthly. • *Financial Monitor*, bimonthly. • *Journal of the American Society of CLU & ChFC*, bimonthly. • *Keeping Current*, quarterly. • *Query: Questions and Answers About Managing Your Money*, bimonthly. • *Section Subscription Service*, monthly. • *Society Page*, bimonthly.

★103★ Community Associations Institute (CAI)
1630 Duke St.
Alexandria, VA 22314
Ph: (703)548-8600 Fax: (703)684-1581

Members: Builders, developers, lawyers, accountants, condominium associations, homeowners associations, property managers, insurance and real estate agents, and government officials or agencies. **Purpose:** Purpose is to develop and provide the most advanced and effective guidance for the creation, financing, operation, and maintenance of the common facilities and services in condominiums, townhouse projects, planned unit developments, and open-space communities. Seeks to educate new owners about their responsibilities in order to attract more people to leadership positions within housing developments. Compiles statistics. **Publications:** *Board Briefs*, bimonthly. • *Common Ground*, bimonthly. • *Community Association Law Reporter*, monthly. • *Creating a Community Association*. • *Financial Management of Associations*. • *Ledger Quarterly*.

★104★ Health Insurance Association of America (HIAA)
1025 Connecticut Ave. NW, Ste. 1200
Washington, DC 20036
Ph: (202)223-7780

Members: Represents commercial health insurers in the states and in Washington, DC. **Purpose:** Works to create a positive image of the industry. Issues data on benefits and products, tracks legislation and regulations, and offers insurance education. Provides forum for industry leadership. **Publications:** *Research Bulletins*, periodic. • *Sourcebook of Health Insurance Data*, annual.

★105★ Independent Insurance Agents of America (IIAA)
127 S. Peyton
Alexandria, VA 22314
Ph: (703)683-4422 Fax: (703)683-7556

Members: Sales agencies handling property, fire, casualty, and surety insurance. **Purpose:** Organizes technical and sales courses for new and established agents. Sponsors Insurance Youth Golf Classic. **Publications:** *Actiongram*, bimonthly. • *Independent Agent*, monthly. • *Management Service*, bimonthly.

★106★ National Association of Health Underwriters (NAHU)
1000 Connecticut Ave. NW, Ste. 810
Washington, DC 20036
Ph: (202)223-5533 Fax: (202)785-2274

Members: Insurance agencies and individuals engaged in the promotion, sale, and administration of disability income and health insurance. **Purpose:** Sponsors advanced health insurance underwriting and research seminars at universities. Testifies before federal and state committees on pending health insurance legislation. Sponsors leading producers roundtable awards and health insurance quality awards for leading salesmen. Grants RHU certification to qualified Registered Disability Income and Health Insurance Underwriters. Is organizing a speakers' bureau and a political action committee. **Publications:** *Health Insurance Underwriter*, monthly.

★107★ National Association of Life Underwriters (NALU)
1922 F St. NW
Washington, DC 20006-4387
Ph: (202)331-6000 Fax: (202)331-2179

Members: Federation of state (50) and local associations (950) representing 143,000 life insurance agents, general agents, and managers; associate members are home office officials of life companies, life insurance teachers, journalists, and others. **Purpose:** Objectives are to support and maintain the principles of legal reserve life insurance and health insurance; to promote high ethical standards; to inform the public, render community service, and promote public goodwill. Sponsors public service programs. Offers educational programs. **Publications:** *LeaderLine Newsletter*, monthly. • *Life Association News*, monthly.

★108★ National Association of Professional Insurance Agents (NAPIA)
400 N. Washington St.
Alexandria, VA 22314
Ph: (703)836-9340 Fax: (703)836-1279

Members: Independent property and casualty agents. **Purpose:** Activities are educational, representative, and service-oriented. Sponsors over 200 educational programs and seminars each year on all aspects of property and casualty insurance, ranging from the novice to specialist level. Compiles statistics; conducts research programs; develops products/services unique to independent agencies. **Publications:** *PIACTION*, monthly. • *Professional Agent*, monthly.

★109★ National Association for Variable Annuities
2107 Cabots Point Ln.
Reston, VA 22091
Ph: (703)620-0674 Fax: (703)860-8873

Purpose: Seeks to promote knowledge of variable annuities and life insurance products among members. **Publications:** *NAVA Outlook*, bimonthly.

Standards/Certification Agencies

★110★ National Association of Health Underwriters (NAHU)
1000 Connecticut Ave. NW, Ste. 810
Washington, DC 20036
Ph: (202)223-5533 Fax: (202)785-2274

Testifies before federal and state committees on pending health insurance legislation. Grants RHU certification to qualified Registered Disability Income and Health Insurance Underwriters.

Test Guides

★111★ *Career Examination Series: Actuarial Clerk*
National Learning Corp.
212 Michael Dr.
Syosset, NY 11791
Ph: (516)921-8888 Fax: (516)921-8743
Fr: 800-645-6337

Jack Rudman. All examination guides in this series contain questions with answers.

★112★ *Career Examination Series: Insurance Agent (Accident/Health/Fire/Casualty)*
National Learning Corp.
212 Michael Dr.
Syosset, NY 11791
Ph: (516)921-8888 Fax: (516)921-8743
Fr: 800-645-6337

Jack Rudman. Test guide including questions and answers for students or professionals in the field who seek advancement through examination.

★113★ *Career Examination Series: Insurance Salesman*
National Learning Corp.
212 Michael Dr.
Syosset, NY 11791
Ph: (516)921-8888 Fax: (516)921-8743
Fr: 800-645-6337

Jack Rudman. All examination guides in this series contain questions with answers.

Educational Directories and Programs

★114★ *Connecticut/Rhode Island Telephone Tickler*
Underwriter Printing and Publishing Co.
50 E. Palisade Ave.
Englewood, NJ 07631
Ph: (201)569-8808 Fax: (201)569-8817
Fr: 800-526-4700
Joseph G. Crothers, Contact

Annual, December. Covers insurance companies, agents, brokers, and related suppliers in Connecticut and Rhode Island. Entries include: Name, address, phone. Arrangement: Separate alphabetical sections for each state.

★115★ *Finance, Insurance & Real Estate USA: Industry Analyses, Statistics, and Leading Organizations*
Gale Research Inc.
835 Penobscot Bldg.
Detroit, MI 48226-4094
Ph: (313)961-2242 Fax: (313)961-6083
Fr: 800-877-GALE
Kristin Hart, Contact

Latest edition November; new edition expected 1996. Publication includes: Lists of up to 75 leading companies in banking, finance, insurance, real estate, and related sectors, selected on the basis of annual revenue. Entries include: Co. name, address, phone, chief executive, type of company, annual sales, number of employees. Principal content of publication is statistical profiles of the finance, insurance, and real estate industries. Each industry division includes tables, graphs, and maps that provide general statistics on number of firms and employees, compensation, and revenues; changes in these statistics between 1985 and 1991 (1992 where available); inputs and outputs; occupations employed; and industry data by state. Arrangement: Classified by industry, then ranked by annual sales.

★116★ *Legal and Financial Directory*
The Daily Journal
2000 S. Colorado Blvd., Ste. 2000
Denver, CO 80222
Ph: (303)756-9995 Fax: (303)756-4465
Fr: 800-323-2362
Arla Haley, Contact

Annual, summer. Covers over 15,000 firms and individuals serving the law, real estate, insurance, and financial industries in Colorado. Entries include: Name, address, phone, fax, telex, geographical area served, description of product/service. Arrangement: Alphabetical.

★117★ *Register of North American Insurance Companies*
American Preeminent Registry
510 Old Bridge Tpke.
South River, NJ 08882
Ph: (908)651-1650 Fax: (908)651-1126
Fr: 800-229-1650
Jeff Park, Contact

Annual, spring. Covers over 4,500 insurance companies in the U.S. and Canada. Entries include: Co. name, address, phone, types of insurance offered. Arrangement: Alphabetical.

Awards, Scholarships, Grants, and Fellowships

★118★ Health and Disability Insurance Sales Achievement
National Association of Health Underwriters
1000 Connecticut Ave. NW, Ste. 1111
Washington, DC 20036
Ph: (202)223-5533 Fax: (202)785-2274

To recognize health and disability income insurance agents who reach their full potential in professional development, technical competence, and sales performance. Applications must be submitted by March 31. Leading Producers Round Table Annual Sales Achievement certificates are awarded annually. Established in 1942.

★119★ National Quality Award
National Association of Life Underwriters
1922 F St. NW
Washington, DC 20006
Ph: (202)331-6050 Fax: (202)835-9606

To promote and recognize the maintenance of quality business, as reflected by a high persistency standard of insurance sales to benefit the industry and the public. Members of the NALU are eligible. A certificate or a plaque is awarded annually. Established in 1944. Co-sponsored by the Life Insurance Marketing and Research Association.

★120★ National Sales Achievement Award
National Association of Life Underwriters
1922 F St. NW
Washington, DC 20006
Ph: (202)331-6050 Fax: (202)835-9606

To honor successful life underwriters who, during a particular year, excel in placing a substantial amount of life insurance on a large number of lives. Members of local affiliates of NALU are eligible. A certificate or a plaque is awarded annually. Established in 1966.

PERIODICALS

★121★ *AAIS Viewpoint*
American Association of Insurance Services (AAIS)
1035 S. York Rd.
Bensenville, IL 60106
Ph: (708)595-3225 Fax: (708)595-4647
Carol Poynter

Quarterly. Contains news of current insurance issues, AAIS activities, insurance legislation, and other subjects of interest.

★122★ *Actiongram*
Independent Insurance Agents of America (IIAA)
127 S. Peyton
Alexandria, VA 22314
Ph: (703)683-4422 Fax: (703)683-7556

Bimonthly.

★123★ *American Salesman*
National Research Bureau, Inc.
200 N. 4th
PO Box 1
Burlington, IA 52601-0001
Ph: (319)752-5415 Fax: (319)752-3421
Barbara Boeding

Monthly. Salesmanship magazine.

★124★ *Assets: A Business, Tax, and Financial Newsletter*
American Society of CLU and ChFC (ASCLU & Ch)
270 S. Bryn Mawr Ave.
Bryn Mawr, PA 19010
Ph: (610)526-2500 Fax: (610)527-4010

Bimonthly. Covers life insurance, tax, business, and other financial planning topics. Includes question and answer column dealing with financial planning.

★125★ *Best's Review (Life/Health Edition)*
A.M. Best Co.
Ambest Rd.
Oldwick, NJ 08858
Ph: (908)439-2200 Fax: (908)439-3363
Mark L. Schussel, ED

Monthly. Magazine covering issues and trends for the management personnel of life/health insurers, the agents, and brokers who market their products.

★126★ *Best's Review (Property/Casualty Edition)*
A.M. Best Co.
Ambest Rd.
Oldwick, NJ 08858
Ph: (908)439-2200 Fax: (908)439-3363
Mark L. Schussel, ED

Monthly. Magazine covering issues and trends for the management personnel of property/casualty insurers and the agents and brokers who market their products.

★127★ *CLAIMS*
Insurance Week Publications
1001 4th Ave., Ste. 3029
Seattle, WA 98154
Bill Thorness

Monthly. Magazine for the property-casualty insurance claims industry.

★128★ *CPCU Journal*
CPCU Society
PO Box 3009
720 Providence Rd.
Malvern, PA 19355-0709
Ph: (215)251-2728 Fax: (215)251-2761
Lisa A. Fittipaldi

Quarterly. Journal covering property and casualty insurance and related fields.

★129★ *Degree of Honor Review*
Degree of Honor Protective Assn.
445 Minnesota St., No. 1600
St. Paul, MN 55101-1080
Ph: (612)224-7436 Fax: (612)224-7446
Laureen E. Jansky

Quarterly. Fraternal life insurance magazine.

★130★ *E & S Market News*
Merritt Company, Inc.
1661 9th St.
PO Box 955
Santa Monica, CA 90406
Ph: (310)450-7234 Fax: (310)396-4563
Juan Hovey

Biweekly. Covers events and trends related to the excess and surplus insurance industry and specialty insurance. Analyzes coverage, markets, and insurer competition. Offers commentaries on legislative, legal, and judicial developments.

★131★ *Financial Monitor*
American Society of CLU and ChFC (ASCLU & Ch)
270 S. Bryn Mawr Ave.
Bryn Mawr, PA 19010
Ph: (610)526-2500 Fax: (610)527-4010

Bimonthly. Covers investments, estate planning, life insurance, annuities, disability, business planning, and personal business.

★132★ *Independent Agent*
IIAA/MSI, Inc.
127 S. Peyton St.
Alexandria, VA 22310
Ph: (703)683-4422 Fax: (703)683-7556
Howard P. Hoskins

Monthly. Trade magazine featuring information on property/casualty, and life insurance.

★133★ *The Insurance Advocate*
Chase Communications Group Ltd.
PO Box 9001
Mount Vernon, NY 10552-9001
Ph: (914)699-2020 Fax: (914)699-2025
Emanuel Levy

Weekly. Magazine reporting legislative, regulatory, judicial, and industry news for the insurance industry.

★134★ *Insurance Industry Newsletter*
Smith & Associates
PO Box 3006
Savannah, GA 31402-3006
Ph: (912)355-4117 Fax: (912)355-4117
George V.R. Smith

Weekly. Provides news and comment on the insurance industry in the U.S. Contains information on legislation and regulation, trends, promotions, and new products. Recurring features include book reviews, news of research, statistics, obituaries, and meetings in the fields of liability, property, life, and health insurance.

★135★ *Insurance Journal*
Wells Publishing
9191 Town Centre Dr., No. 550
San Diego, CA 92122
Ph: (619)455-7717 Fax: (619)546-1462
Mark WellsPublisher

Biweekly. Property/Casualty magazine of the West.

★136★ *The Insurance Record*
Record Publishing Co.
PO Box 225770
Dallas, TX 75222-5770
Ph: (214)630-0687 Fax: (214)631-2476
Glen E. Hargis

Biweekly. Insurance trade magazine.

★137★ *Insurance Review*
Journal of Commerce, Inc.
2 World Trade Center, 27th Fl.
New York, NY 10048
Ph: (212)837-7000 Fax: (212)837-7035
Olga B. Sciortino

Monthly. Magazine for insurance agents and brokers, insurance company executives, risk managers, and others interested in the property/casualty and health/life insurance businesses.

★138★ *International Insurance Monitor*
Chase Communications Group Ltd.
PO Box 9001
Mount Vernon, NY 10552-9001
Ph: (914)699-2020 Fax: (914)699-2025
Stephen H. Acunto

Monthly. Magazine covering insurance topics worldwide.

★139★ *Journal of the American Society of CLU & ChFC*
American Society of CLU and ChFC (ASCLU & Ch)
270 S. Bryn Mawr Ave.
Bryn Mawr, PA 19010
Ph: (610)526-2500 Fax: (610)527-4010

Bimonthly. Provides information on insurance and financial planning. Includes book reviews.

★140★ *Journal of Insurance Regulation*
National Assn. of Insurance Commissioners
120 W. 12th St., Ste. 1100
Kansas City, MO 64105-1925
Ph: (816)842-3600 Fax: (816)471-7004
Gregory Krohm

Quarterly. Forum for research and public policy analysis of topics dealing with the control of insurance companies/markets by regulatory bodies.

★141★ *Keeping Current*
American Society of CLU and ChFC (ASCLU & Ch)
270 S. Bryn Mawr Ave.
Bryn Mawr, PA 19010
Ph: (610)526-2500 Fax: (610)527-4010

Quarterly. Audio tape and syllabus subscription series. Helps practitioners better understand tax, legislative, and other financial services and developments.

★142★ *LeaderLine Newsletter*
National Association of Life Underwriters (NALU)
1922 F St. NW
Washington, DC 20006-4387
Ph: (202)331-6000 Fax: (202)331-2179

Monthly.

★143★ *Life Association News*
National Association of Life Underwriters (NALU)
1922 F St. NW
Washington, DC 20006-4387
Ph: (202)331-6000 Fax: (202)331-2179

Monthly. Features industry news and instructional articles on sales techniques and business management. Includes book and legislative reviews.

★144★ *LOMA Membership Directory*
Life Office Management Association (LOMA)
5770 Powers Ferry Rd. NW
Atlanta, GA 30327
Ph: (404)951-1770 Fax: (404)984-0441

Annual.

★145★ *Management Service*
Independent Insurance Agents of America (IIAA)
127 S. Peyton
Alexandria, VA 22314
Ph: (703)683-4422 Fax: (703)683-7556

Bimonthly.

★146★ *The National Gleaner Forum*
Gleaner Life Insurance Society
5200 W. U.S. 223
Adrian, MI 49221
Ph: (517)263-2244 Fax: (517)265-7745
Mary Ward-Eaton

Quarterly. Fraternal insurance magazine.

★147★ *National Underwriter Property and Casualty/Risk and Benefits Management*
Thomas Slattery

Weekly. Newsweekly for agents, brokers, executives, and managers in risk and benefit insurance.

★148★ *PIACTION*
National Association of Professional Insurance Agents (NAPIA)
400 N. Washington St.
Alexandria, VA 22314
Ph: (703)836-9340 Fax: (703)836-1279

Monthly.

★149★ *Professional Agent*
National Association of Professional Insurance Agents (NAPIA)
400 N. Washington St.
Alexandria, VA 22314
Ph: (703)836-9340 Fax: (703)836-1279

Monthly. Concerned with educating and informing independent property and casualty insurance agents. Includes tax adviser and insurance policy columns.

★150★ *Professional Insurance Agents*
PIA Management Services Inc.
25 Chamberlain St.
PO Box 997
Glenmont, NY 12077-0997
Ph: (518)434-3111 Fax: (518)434-2342
Mary Morrison Vanniere

Insurance trade magazine.

★151★ *Query: Questions and Answers About Managing Your Money*
American Society of CLU and ChFC (ASCLU & Ch)
270 S. Bryn Mawr Ave.
Bryn Mawr, PA 19010
Ph: (610)526-2500 Fax: (610)527-4010

Bimonthly. Covers insurance, estate, tax, business, and financial planning topics.

★152★ *Research Bulletins*
Health Insurance Association of America (HIAA)
1025 Connecticut Ave. NW, Ste. 1200
Washington, DC 20036
Ph: (202)223-7780

Periodic.

★153★ *Research Reports*
Life Office Management Association (LOMA)
5770 Powers Ferry Rd. NW
Atlanta, GA 30327
Ph: (404)951-1770 Fax: (404)984-0441

★154★ *Resource*
Life Office Management Association (LOMA)
5770 Powers Ferry Rd. NW
Atlanta, GA 30327
Ph: (404)951-1770 Fax: (404)984-0441

Monthly. Covers topics of interest to insurance company management including systems, human resources, corporate planning, and financial management.

★155★ Risk Management
Risk Management Society Publishing, Inc.
205 E. 42nd St.
New York, NY 10017
Ph: (212)286-9364 Fax: (212)922-0716
Alice Oshins, ED

Monthly. Magazine focusing on insurance risk management.

★156★ *Rough Notes*
The Rough Notes Co., Inc.
1200 N. Meridian St.
PO Box 564
Indianapolis, IN 46206
Ph: (317)634-1541 Fax: (317)634-1041
Tom A. McCoy

Monthly. Sales/management magazine for property/casualty insurance agents and brokers.

★157★ *Salesman's Insider*
Marv. Q. Modell Associates
6009 Montgomery Corner
San Jose, CA 95135-1431
Ph: (408)270-4526
Marv. Q. Modell

Monthly. Concerned with selling techniques and methodology in all sales areas. Tracks new sales developments, trends, and profit opportunities. Details negotiating process; offers "tips that work."

★158★ *Salesmanship*
Dartnell Corporation
4660 Ravenswood
Chicago, IL 60640
Ph: (312)561-4000 Fax: (312)561-3801
Fr: 800-621-5463
Terry Breen

Biweekly. Offers sales ideas and inspiration, profiles of top-producing salespeople, and articles on topics related to sales success.

★159★ *Section Subscription Service*
American Society of CLU and ChFC (ASCLU & Ch)
270 S. Bryn Mawr Ave.
Bryn Mawr, PA 19010
Ph: (610)526-2500 Fax: (610)527-4010

Monthly. Available in 3 areas: employee benefits; estate planning; and financial counseling. Includes *Nutshell*, a monthly digest of articles.

★160★ *Society Page*
American Society of CLU and ChFC (ASCLU & Ch)
270 S. Bryn Mawr Ave.
Bryn Mawr, PA 19010
Ph: (610)526-2500 Fax: (610)527-4010

Bimonthly. For insurance and financial planning practitioners.

★161★ *Sourcebook of Health Insurance Data*
Health Insurance Association of America (HIAA)
1025 Connecticut Ave. NW, Ste. 1200
Washington, DC 20036
Ph: (202)223-7780

Annual. Covers the private health insurance business in the U.S. Includes charts, graphs, and tables.

★162★ *Southern Insurance*
Southern Insurance
PO Box 9001
Mount Vernon, NY 10552-9001
Stephen Acunto

Monthly. Insurance industry magazine.

★163★ *The Weekly Insider (IIABC)*
Independent Insurance Agents and Brokers of California (IIABC)
101 Market St., Ste. 702
San Francisco, CA 94105
Ph: (415)957-1212 Fax: (415)541-9184
Fr: 800-772-8998
David Benesh

Weekly. Carries insurance industry news, legislative developments, and insurance technical reviews of workers compensation and commercial and personal lines. Recurring features include interviews, a calendar of events, and legislative and legal reports.

Meetings and Conventions

★164★ American Association of Managing General Agents Trade Mart
Fromm & Associates
9140 Ward Pkwy.
Kansas City, MO 64114
Ph: (816)444-3500 Fax: (816)444-0330

Annual. Always held during May. **Dates and Locations:** 1996 May 19-23; Orlando, FL.

★165★ American Society of Chartered Life Underwriters National Conference
American Society of Chartered Life Underwriters
270 Bryn Mawr Ave.
Bryn Mawr, PA 19010
Ph: (215)526-2500 Fax: (215)527-4010

Annual. **Dates and Locations:** 1996 Oct; Dallas, TX.

★166★ Carolinas Association of Professional Insurance Agents Annual Convention
Carolinas Association of Professional Insurance Agents
3109 Charles B. Root Wynd
Raleigh, NC 27612
Ph: (919)782-5807 Fax: (919)781-6189

Annual. Always held during June. **Dates and Locations:** 1996 Jun; Myrtle Beach, SC.

★167★ National Association of Professional Insurance Agents Convention and Trade Show
Production Group International
2200 Wilson Blvd., Ste. 200
Arlington, VA 22201-3324
Ph: (703)528-8484 Fax: (703)528-1724

Annual.

★168★ Risk and Insurance Management Society Annual Conference
Risk and Insurance Management Society, Inc.
205 E. 42nd St.
New York, NY 10017
Ph: (212)286-9292 Fax: (212)986-9716

Annual.

★169★ Self Insurance Institute of America Annual Conference and Expo
Self Insurance Institute of America
17300 Red Hill Ave., Ste. 100
Irvine, CA 92714-5643
Ph: (714)261-2553 Fax: (714)261-2594

Annual. Always held during the fall.

★170★ Society of Actuaries Convention
Society of Actuaries
475 N. Martingale Rd., Ste. 800
Schaumburg, IL 60173-2226
Ph: (708)706-3500 Fax: (708)706-3599

Annual. **Dates and Locations:** 1995 Oct 15-18; Boston, MA.

★171★ Society of Chartered Property and Casualty Underwriters, Society Expo
Society of Property and Casualty Underwriters
720 Providence Rd.
PO Box 3009
Malvern, PA 19355-0709
Ph: (215)251-2742 Fax: (215)251-2761

Annual. **Dates and Locations:** 1996 Oct 13-15; New York, NY. • 1997 Oct 12-15; Dallas, TX. • 1998 Oct 25-28; San Diego, CA. • 1999 Oct 17-20; Boston, MA. • 2000 Oct 22-25; San Antonio, TX.

Other Sources of Information

★172★ "Insurance Sales Agent" in *Career Selector 2001*
Barron's Educational Series, Inc.
250 Wireless Blvd.
Hauppauge, NY 11788
Ph: (516)434-3311 Fax: (516)434-3723
Fr: 800-645-3476

James C. Gonyea. 1993.

★173★ "Insurance Salesperson" in *100 Best Jobs for the 1990s & Beyond*
Dearborn Financial Publishing, Inc.
520 N. Dearborn St.
Chicago, IL 60610-4354
Ph: (312)836-4400 Fax: (312)836-1021
Fr: 800-621-9621

Carol Kleiman. 1992. Describes 100 jobs ranging from accountants to veterinarians. Each job profile includes such information as education, experience, and certification needed, salaries, and job search suggestions.

★174★ *Vocational Visions Career Series: Insurance Agent*
Cambridge Career Products
PO Box 2153, Dept. CC15
Charleston, WV 25328-2153
Fr: 800-468-4227

Video collection that includes interviews people with various occupations. Describes educational requirements, necessary skills, outlook for the future, and salary range.

Manufacturers' and Wholesale Sales Representatives

Firms employ **manufacturers' and wholesale sales representatives** to market their products to manufacturers, wholesale and retail establishments, government agencies, and other institutions. The primary job of these sales representatives is to interest wholesale and retail buyers and purchasing agents in their merchandise. Manufacturers' and wholesale sales representatives spend much of their time traveling to and visiting with prospective buyers, to inform these potential customers about prices, availability, and how their products can save money and improve productivity. Prospecting for new clients is an important component of this job. Sales representatives whose products are not in wide distribution follow leads generated by other clients, from advertisements in trade journals, and participation in trade shows and conferences. Other duties include analyzing sales statistics, preparing reports, and handling administrative duties, such as filing expense account reports, scheduling appointments, and making travel plans.

Salaries

Compensation methods are usually a combination of salary and commission or salary plus bonus. Median annual salaries are as follows:

Lowest 10 percent	$16,400/year or less
Middle 50 percent	$22,300-$46,500/year
Top 10 percent	$62,000/year or more.

Employment Outlook

Growth rate until the year 2005: More slowly than average.

Manufacturers' and Wholesale Sales Representatives

Career Guides

★175★ *According to Hoyle*
Commonwealth Films, Inc.
223 Commonwealth Ave.
Boston, MA 02116
Ph: (617)262-5634 Fax: (617)262-6948

Videocassette. 1980. 30 mins. An entire business deal is enacted, from the purchasing of goods to the sales.

★176★ *All Pro*
BNA Communications, Inc.
9439 Key West Ave.
Rockville, MD 20850
Ph: (301)948-0540 Fax: (301)948-2085
Fr: 800-233-6067

Videocassette. 1981. 29 mins. Conversations with five top sales professionals. They discuss their careers and the traits that make a top professional.

★177★ *American Professionals Series*
Cambridge Career Products
PO Box 2153
Charleston, WV 25328-2153
Ph: (304)744-9323 Fax: (304)744-9351
Fr: 800-468-4227

Videocassette. 1984. 30 mins. In this series of twenty-one half hour programs, various occupations are examined in depth, including a day in the life of each worker. Included are: fireman, farmer, oil driller, fisherman, horse trainer, auto assembly repairman, nurse, pilot, and paramedic.

★178★ *Career Success Series*
Cambridge Educational
PO Box 2153
Charleston, WV 25328-2153
Ph: (304)744-9323 Fax: (304)744-9351
Fr: 800-468-4227

Videocassette. 1986. 15 mins. A series, available separately, outlining various career choices for students. Occupations include: accounting, flight service, air transportation/ground/flight service, data processing, carpentry, clerk in banking/insurance, commodity sales, cosmetic personal grooming, fire fighting, forestry services, home economics, insulation/roofing, material handling, mechanics, photographic processing, pipefitting and plumbing, police science, printing, carpentry, medical laboratory technicians, secretarial services, and utilities equipment operator.

★179★ "Getting Started in Industrial Sales" in *Marketing and Sales Career Directory* (pp. 18-22)
Career Press, Inc.
PO Box 34
62 Beverly Rd.
Hawthorne, NJ 07507
Ph: (201)427-0229

Ronald W. Fry, editor. Third edition, 1990. Guide to career planning and job hunting in a marketing or sales capacity at a major corporation, market research company, or public relations agency. Lists hundreds of employers seeking entry level employees. Includes job description, work environments, educational preparation, career advancement, earnings, and trends.

★180★ *How Food Brokers Serve You*
National Food Brokers Association
1010 massachusetts Ave., N.W.
Washington, DC 20001
Ph: (202)789-2844

This four-page brochure describes the work of food brokers.

★181★ "Industrial (Business-to-Business) Marketing" in *Opportunities in Marketing Careers* (pp. 36-37)
National Textbook Co. (NTC)
VGM Career Books
4255 W. Touhy Ave.
Lincolnwood, IL 60646-1975
Ph: (708)679-5500 Fax: (708)679-2494
Fr: 800-323-4900

Margery Steinberg. 1988. Defines marketing and surveys marketing fields such as research and retailing. Covers employment outlook, educational and training requirements, and the financial and other rewards of marketing. Offers job hunting advice for this field.

★182★ "Industrial, Wholesale, and Direct Sales" in *Careers in Marketing* (pp. 50-62)
National Textbook Co. (NTC)
VGM Career Books
4255 W. Touhy Ave.
Lincolnwood, IL 60646-1975
Ph: (708)679-5500 Fax: (708)679-2494
Fr: 800-323-4900

Lila B. Stair. 1991. Surveys career opportunities in marketing and related areas such as marketing research, product development, and sales promotion. Includes a description of the work, places of employment, employment outlook, trends, educational preparation, organizational charts, and salaries. Offers job hunting advice.

★183★ "Instrument Sales Representative" in *Career Opportunities in the Music Industry* (pp. 95-96)
Facts on File
460 Park Ave. S.
New York, NY 10016-7382
Ph: (212)683-2244 Fax: 800-678-3633
Fr: 800-322-8755

Shelly Field. Second edition, 1991. Describes more than 70 music related jobs. Each occupational profile covers job duties, employment outlook, career paths, salaries, skills, and educational preparation. Offers tips for entering the field.

★184★ *Making $70,000 Plus a Year as a Self-Employed Manufacturer's Representative*
Ten Speed Press
PO Box 7123
Berkeley, CA 94707
Fax: (510)559-1629 Fr: 800-841-2665

Leigh Silliphant and Sureleigh Silliphant. Revised and updated edition, 1988. Covers deciding what to sell, negotiating with the manufacturer and determining compensation. Offers advice on how to sell, locating outlets and clients, and traveling.

★185★ "Manufactured Products" in *Career Choices for the 90's for Students of Communications and Journalism* (pp. 175-178)
Walker and Co.
435 Hudson St.
New York, NY 10014
Ph: (212)727-8300 Fax: (212)727-0984
Fr: 800-289-2553

1990. Describes jobs in different industries and includes interviews with people working in related occupations. Presents employment outlook, preferred geographic location, entry-level opportunities, career paths, job responsibilities, advancement, personal and professional qualifications, salaries, working conditions, material for further reading, and associations.

★186★ "Manufactured Products" in *Career Choices for the 90's for Students of Political Science & Government* (pp. 178-181)
Walker and Co.
435 Hudson St.
New York, NY 10014
Ph: (212)727-8300 Fax: (212)727-0984
Fr: 800-289-2553

1990. Describes jobs in different industries and includes interviews with people working in related occupations. Presents employment outlook, preferred geographic location, entry-level opportunities, career paths, job responsibilities, advancement, personal and professional qualifications, salaries, working conditions, material for further reading, and associations.

★187★ "Manufactured Products" in *Career Choices for the 90's for Students of Psychology* (pp. 198-201)
Walker and Co.
435 Hudson St.
New York, NY 10014
Ph: (212)727-8300 Fax: (212)727-0984
Fr: 800-289-2553

1990. Describes jobs in different industries and includes interviews with people working in related occupations. Presents employment outlook, preferred geographic location, entry-level opportunities, career paths, job responsibilities, advancement, personal and professional qualifications, salaries, working conditions, material for further reading, and associations.

★188★ "Manufactured Products (Sales)" in *Encyclopedia of Career Choices for the 1990s: A Guide to Entry Level Jobs* (pp. 780-783)
Berkley Pub.
PO Box 506
East Rutherford, NJ 07073
Fax: (201)933-2316 Fr: 800-788-6262

1992. Describes entry-level opportunities in 42 career fields for college graduates. Each chapter covers a single career field, including an overview, employment outlook, major employers, tips on entering the field, international job opportunities, functional job areas with personal and professional qualifications, career paths, job responsibilities, advancement possibilities, salaries, and working conditions. Lists related sources of information.

★189★ "Manufactured Sales" in *Career Choices for the 90's for Students of Business* (pp. 169-172)
Walker and Co.
435 Hudson St.
New York, NY 10014
Ph: (212)727-8300 Fax: (212)727-0984
Fr: 800-289-2553

1990. Describes jobs in different industries and includes interviews with people working in related occupations. Presents employment outlook, preferred geographic location, entry-level opportunities, career paths, job responsibilities, advancement, personal and professional qualifications, salaries, working conditions, material for further reading, and associations.

★190★ *The Manufacturers' Agent*
Manufacturers' Agents National Association
23016 Mill Creek Rd.
PO Box 3467
Laguna Hills, CA 92654
Ph: (714)859-4040

This five-page leaflet covers duties, personal qualifications, working conditions, education, training, earnings, and employment outlook.

★191★ *Manufacturer's Representative*
Careers, Inc.
PO Box 135
Largo, FL 34649-0135
Ph: (813)584-7333

1992. Four-page brief offering the definition, history, duties, working conditions, personal qualifications, educational requirements, earnings, hours, employment outlook, advancement possibilities, and related occupations.

★192★ "Manufacturer's Representative/ Sporting Goods or Equipment Company" in *Career Opportunities in the Sports Industry* (pp. 172-174)
Facts on File
460 Park Ave. S.
New York, NY 10016-7382
Ph: (212)683-2244 Fax: 800-678-3633
Fr: 800-322-8755

Shelly Field. 1991. Describes various jobs in the sports industry. Each occupational profile covers job duties, employment outlook, career paths, salaries, skills, and educational preparation. Offers tips for entering the field.

★193★ *Manufacturers' Representatives*
Chronicle Guidance Publications, Inc.
66 Aurora St.
PO Box 1190
Moravia, NY 13118-1190
Ph: (315)497-0330 Fax: (315)497-3359
Fr: 800-622-7284

1993. This career brief describes the nature of the work, working conditions, hours and earnings, education and training, licensure, certification, unions, personal qualifications, social and psychological factors, employment outlook, entry methods, advancement, and related occupations.

★194★ *Manufacturers Sales Representative*
Vocational Biographies, Inc.
PO Box 31
Sauk Centre, MN 56378-0031
Ph: (612)352-6516 Fax: (612)352-5546
Fr: 800-255-0752

1991. This pamphlet profiles a person working in the job. Includes information about job duties, working conditions, places of employment, educational preparation, labor market outlook, and salaries.

★195★ "Manufacturer's Sales Representative" in *VGM's Careers Encyclopedia* (pp. 257-259)
National Textbook Co. (NTC)
VGM Career Books
4255 W. Touhy Ave.
Lincolnwood, IL 60646-1975
Ph: (708)679-5500 Fax: (708)679-2494
Fr: 800-323-4900

Third edition, 1991. Contains two- to five-page descriptions of 200 managerial, professional, technical, trade, and service occupations. Each profile includes job duties, places of employment, qualifications, educational preparation, training, employment potential, advancement, income, and additional sources of information.

★196★ "Manufacturer's Sales Representative" in *VGM's Handbook of Business and Management Careers* (pp. 57-58)
National Textbook Co. (NTC)
VGM Career Books
4255 W. Touhy Ave.
Lincolnwood, IL 60646-1975
Ph: (708)679-5500 Fax: (708)679-2494
Fr: 800-323-4900

Annette Selden, editor. Second edition , 1993. Contains 42 two-page occupational profiles describing job duties, places of employment, working conditions, qualifications, education, employment outlook, and income.

★197★ "Manufacturers' Sales Representatives" in *Career Discovery Encyclopedia* (Vol.4, pp. 46-47)
J.G. Ferguson Publishing Co.
200 W. Madison St., Ste. 300
Chicago, IL 60606
Ph: (312)580-5480 Fax: (312)580-4948

E. Russell Primm, editor-in-chief. 1993. Contains two-page articles on 504 occupations. Each article describes job duties, earnings, and educational and training requirements.

★198★ "Manufacturers' Sales Representatives" in *Jobs! What They Are—Where They Are—What They Pay* (p. 333)
Simon & Schuster, Inc.
Simon & Schuster Bldg.
1230 Avenue of the Americas
New York, NY 10020
Ph: (212)698-7000

Robert O. Snelling and Anne M. Snelling. Revised edition, 1992. Profiles 241 occupations, describing duties and responsibilities, educational preparation, earnings, employment opportunities, training, and qualifications.

★199★ "Manufacturers' Sales Worker" in *Career Information Center* (Vol.10)
Simon and Schuster
200 Old Tappan Rd.
Old Tappan, NJ 07675
Fax: 800-445-6991 Fr: 800-223-2348

Richard Lidz and Dale Anderson, editorial directors. Fifth edition, 1993. For 600 occupations, describes job duties, entry-level requirements, education and training needed, advancement possibilities, employment outlook, earnings and benefits. The set is divided into 12 volumes. Each volume includes jobs related under a broad career field. Volume 13 is the index.

★200★ "Manufacturers' Sales Workers" in *Encyclopedia of Careers and Vocational Guidance* (Vol.3, pp. 361-365)
J.G. Ferguson Publishing Co.
200 W. Madison St., Ste. 300
Chicago, IL 60606
Ph: (312)580-5480 Fax: (312)580-4948

William E. Hopke, editor-in-chief. Ninth edition, 1993. Four-volume set that profiles 500 occupations and describes job trends in 74 industries. Includes career description, educational requirements, history of the job, methods of entry, advancement, employment outlook, earnings, working conditions, social and psychological factors, and sources of additional information.

★201★ "Manufacturers' Sales Workers" in *Opportunities in Vocational and Technical Careers* (pp. 59-75)
National Textbook Co. (NTC)
VGM Career Books
4255 W. Touhy Ave.
Lincolnwood, IL 60646-1975
Ph: (708)679-5500 Fax: (708)679-2494
Fr: 800-323-4900

Adrian A. Paradis. 1992. Describes careers which can be prepared for by attending a private vocational or proprietary school—office employee, sales worker, service worker, health services, mechanic, craftworker, and technician. Covers employment outlook, job duties, and salaries. Offers career planning advice.

★202★ "Manufacturer's Salespeople: Selling Goods" in *Careers for Women Without College Degrees* (pp. 250-253)
McGraw-Hill Publishing Co.
11 W. 19th St.
New York, NY 10011
Ph: (212)337-6010

Beatryce Nivens. 1988. Career planning and job hunting guide containing information on decision-making, skills assessment, and resumes for career changers. Profiles careers with the best occupational outlook. Describes the work, educational preparation, employment outlook, salaries, and required skills.

★203★ "Manufacturer's Salesperson" in *College Board Guide to Jobs and Career Planning* (pp. 142-143)
The College Board
45 Columbus Ave.
New York, NY 10023-6992
Ph: (212)713-8165 Fax: (212)713-8143
Fr: 800-323-7155

Second edition, 1994. Describes the job, salaries, related careers, education needed, and where to write for more information.

★204★ "Manufacturers' and Wholesale Sales Representatives" in *Occupational Outlook Handbook*
U.S. Government Printing Office
Superintendent of Documents
Washington, DC 20402
Ph: (202)512-1800 Fax: (202)512-2250

Biennial; latest edition, 1994-95. Encyclopedia of careers describing more than 250 occupations and comprising about 85 percent of all jobs in the economy. Occupations that require lengthy education or training are given the most attention. For each occupation, the handbook describes job duties, working conditions, training, educational preparation, personal qualities, advancement possibilities, job outlook, earnings, and sources of additional information.

★205★ "Manufacturing" in *Internships 1995*
Petersons Guides, Inc.
PO Box 2123
Princeton, NJ 08543-2123
Ph: (609)243-9111 Fr: 800-338-3282

Fifteenth edition, 1995. Lists internship opportunities under six broad categories: communications, creative, performing, and fine arts, human services, international relations, business and technology, and public affairs. For each internship program, gives the names, phone number, contact person, description, eligibility requirements, and benefits.

★206★ "Manufacturing Reps" in *New York Times Career Planner* (pp. 237-240)
Times Books
201 E. 50th St.
New York, NY 10022
Ph: (212)751-2600 Fax: (212)572-8700

Elizabeth M. Fowler. 1987. Offers career planning and job hunting advice for the college graduate. Surveys labor market trends. Contains "inside" information on professional careers including educational preparation, employment opportunities, and salaries.

★207★ *Opportunities in Sales Careers*
National Textbook Co. (NTC)
VGM Career Books
4255 W. Touhy Ave.
Lincolnwood, IL 60646-1975
Ph: (708)679-5500 Fax: (708)679-2494
Fr: 800-323-4900

Ralph M. Dahm and James Brescoll. 1988. Surveys jobs in sales and describes the skills needed to succeed. Covers the nature of the work, employment outlook, educational preparation, and training, salary, and rewards of the work.

★208★ "Pharmaceutical Sales Representative" in *Opportunities in Pharmacy Careers* (pp. 106-108)
National Textbook Co. (NTC)
VGM Career Books
4255 W. Touhy Ave.
Lincolnwood, IL 60646-1975
Ph: (708)679-5500 Fax: (708)679-2494
Fr: 800-323-4900

Fred B. Gable. 1990. Surveys the wide variety of career options available to pharmacists including community, industrial, and public pharmacy. Covers job duties, licensure, and salaries. Provides in-depth information about pharmaceutical education including high school preparation, and pharmacy school admissions and curriculum.

★209★ "Sales Representative, Wholesale Distribution" in *Occu-Facts: Information on 580 Careers in Outline Form*
Careers, Inc.
PO Box 135
Largo, FL 34649-0135
Ph: (813)584-7333

Biennial, 1995-96 edition. Each one-page occupational profile describes duties, working conditions, physical surroundings and demands, aptitudes, temperament, educational requirements, employment outlook, earnings, and places of employment.

★210★ *Sales Representatives, Wholesale Distribution*
Careers, Inc.
PO Box 135
Largo, FL 34649-0135
Ph: (813)584-7333

1992. Four-page brief offering the definition, history, duties, working conditions, personal qualifications, educational requirements, earnings, hours, employment outlook, advancement possibilities, and related occupations.

★211★ "Sales" in *Where the Jobs Are: The Hottest Careers for the 90s* (pp. 221-244)
Career Press
180 5th Ave.
Hawthorne, NJ 07507
Ph: (201)427-0229 Fax: (201)427-2037
Fr: 800-CAREER-1

Joyce Hadley. 1995. Offers a job-hunting strategy for the 1990s as well as descriptions of growing careers of the decade. Each profile includes general information, forecasts, growth, education and training, licensing requirements, and salary information.

★212★ *Video Career Library - Marketing and Sales*
Careers, Inc.
PO Box 135
Largo, FL 34649-0135
Ph: (813)584-7333

Videocassette. 1994. Part of the Video Career Library covering 165 occupations. Shows actual workers on the job.

★213★ "Wholesale and Retail Trade" in *Encyclopedia of Career Choices for the 1990s: A Guide to Entry Level Jobs* (pp. 242-243)
Berkley Pub.
PO Box 506
East Rutherford, NJ 07073
Fax: (201)933-2316 Fr: 800-788-6262

1992. Describes entry-level opportunities in 42 career fields for college graduates. Each chapter covers a single career field, including an overview, employment outlook, major employers, tips on entering the field, international job opportunities, functional job areas with personal and professional qualifications, career paths, job responsibilities, advancement possibilities, salaries, and working conditions. Lists related sources of information.

★214★ "Wholesale Sales Worker" in *Career Information Center* (Vol.10)
Simon and Schuster
200 Old Tappan Rd.
Old Tappan, NJ 07675
Fax: 800-445-6991 Fr: 800-223-2348

Richard Lidz and Dale Anderson, editorial directors. Fifth edition, 1993. For 600 occupations, describes job duties, entry-level requirements, education and training needed, advancement possibilities, employment outlook, earnings and benefits. The set is divided into 12 volumes. Each volume includes jobs related under a broad career field. Volume 13 is the index.

★215★ "Wholesale Sales Workers" in *Career Discovery Encyclopedia* (Vol.6, pp. 152-153)
J.G. Ferguson Publishing Co.
200 W. Madison St., Ste. 300
Chicago, IL 60606
Ph: (312)580-5480 Fax: (312)580-4948

E. Russell Primm, editor-in-chief. 1993. Contains two-page articles on 504 occupations. Each article describes job duties, earnings, and educational and training requirements.

★216★ "Wholesale Trade Sales Representative" in *Guide to Careers Without College* (pp. 23-25)
Franklin Watts, Inc.
387 Park Avenue, S.
New York, NY 10016
Ph: (212)686-7070

Kathleen S. Abrams. 1988. Discusses careers that do not require a college degree in fields such as health care, sales and marketing, and the building trades. Describes the work, employment opportunities, and training.

★217★ "Wholesale Trade Sales Representatives" in *Jobs! What They Are—Where They Are—What They Pay* (p. 336)
Simon & Schuster, Inc.
Simon & Schuster Bldg.
1230 Avenue of the Americas
New York, NY 10020
Ph: (212)698-7000

Robert O. Snelling and Anne M. Snelling. Revised edition, 1992. Profiles 241 occupations, describing duties and responsibilities, educational preparation, earnings, employment opportunities, training, and qualifications.

★218★ "Wholesale Trade Sales Workers" in *Encyclopedia of Careers and Vocational Guidance* (Vol.4, pp. 611-614)
J.G. Ferguson Publishing Co.
200 W. Madison St., Ste. 300
Chicago, IL 60606
Ph: (312)580-5480 Fax: (312)580-4948

William E. Hopke, editor-in-chief. Ninth edition, 1993. Four-volume set that profiles 500 occupations and describes job trends in 74 industries. Includes career description, educational requirements, history of the job, methods of entry, advancement, employment outlook, earnings, working conditions, social and psychological factors, and sources of additional information.

★219★ "Wholesale Trade Sales Workers" in *Opportunities in Vocational and Technical Careers* (pp. 59-75)
National Textbook Co. (NTC)
VGM Career Books
4255 W. Touhy Ave.
Lincolnwood, IL 60646-1975
Ph: (708)679-5500 Fax: (708)679-2494
Fr: 800-323-4900

Adrian A. Paradis. 1992. Describes careers which can be prepared for by attending a private vocational or proprietary school—office employee, sales worker, service worker, health services, mechanic, craftworker, and technician. Covers employment outlook, job duties, and salaries. Offers career planning advice.

Associations

★220★ Distributive Education Clubs of America (DECA)
1908 Association Dr.
Reston, VA 22091
Ph: (703)860-5000

Members: High school juniors and seniors; junior college students interested in the field of marketing and distribution (retailing and wholesaling) as a vocation. **Publications:** *DECA Advisor*. • *DECA Guide*, annual. • *New Dimensions*, quarterly.

★221★ Manufacturers' Agents National Association (MANA)
23016 Mill Creek Rd.
PO Box 3467
Laguna Hills, CA 92654
Ph: (714)859-4040 Fax: (714)855-2973

Members: Manufacturers' agents in all fields representing two or more manufacturers on a commission basis; associate members are manufacturers and others interested in improving the agent-principal relationship. **Purpose:** Maintains code of ethics and rules of business and professional conduct; maintains list of attorneys and accountants experienced in agency matters; issues model standard form of agreement. **Publications:** *Agency Sales Magazine*, monthly. • *Annual Directory of Members*. • *Confidential Newsletter*, quarterly. • *MANA Membership Directory of Manufacturers' Sales Agencies*, annual. • *Manufacturers' Agents National Association—Special Report*, periodic.

Standards/Certification Agencies

★222★ Manufacturers' Agents National Association (MANA)
23016 Mill Creek Rd.
PO Box 3467
Laguna Hills, CA 92654
Ph: (714)859-4040 Fax: (714)855-2973

Maintains code of ethics and rules of business and professional conduct; maintains list of attorneys and accountants expericence in agency matter; issues model standard form fo agreement.

Educational Directories and Programs

★223★ *Annual Directory of Members*
Manufacturers' Agents National Association (MANA)
23016 Mill Creek Rd.
PO Box 3467
Laguna Hills, CA 92654
Ph: (714)859-4040 Fax: (714)855-2973

★224★ *MANA Membership Directory of Manufacturers' Sales Agencies*
Manufacturers' Agents National Association (MANA)
23016 Mill Creek Rd.
PO Box 3467
Laguna Hills, CA 92654
Ph: (714)859-4040 Fax: (714)855-2973

Annual. List of manufacturers' sales agencies. Includes survey of sales commissions.

Basic Reference Guides and Handbooks

★225★ *DECA Guide*
Distributive Education Clubs of America (DECA)
1908 Association Dr.
Reston, VA 22091
Ph: (703)860-5000

Annual. Resource guide covering insurance, membership, and competitive events programs; catalog of instructional materials; scholarship information.

PERIODICALS

★226★ *Agency Sales Magazine*
Manufacturers' Agents National Association (MANA)
23016 Mill Creek Rd.
PO Box 3467
Laguna Hills, CA 92654
Ph: (714)859-4040 Fax: (714)855-2973
Monthly. Contains how-to articles for manufacturers' agents and manufacturers. Includes book reviews, industry calendar, and RepLetter.

★227★ *American Salesman*
National Research Bureau, Inc.
200 N. 4th
PO Box 1
Burlington, IA 52601-0001
Ph: (319)752-5415 Fax: (319)752-3421
Barbara Boeding
Monthly. Salesmanship magazine.

★228★ *ARW Counterline*
Air-Conditioning and Refrigeration Wholesalers Association (ARW)
10251 W. Sample Rd., Ste. B
Coral Springs, FL 33065
Ph: (305)755-7000 Fax: (305)491-8100
James S. McMullen
Quarterly. Carries informational and motivational articles to help sales personnel generate customer loyalty, handle customer complaints, and to increase sales.

★229★ *ARW Wholesaler News*
Air-Conditioning and Refrigeration Wholesalers Association (ARW)
10251 W. Sample Rd., Ste. B
Coral Springs, FL 33065
Ph: (305)755-7000 Fax: (305)491-8100
James S. McMullen
Bimonthly. Focuses on Association news and industry information of concern to member wholesalers and suppliers. Recurring features include information on Association programs and services, notices of educational materials available, a calendar of events, and news of members.

★230★ *Bureau of Wholesale Sales Representatives News*
1819 Peachtree St., Ste. 210
Atlanta, GA 30309
Ph: (404)351-7355 Fax: (404)352-5298
Jill Bunch
Monthly. Trade journal for apparel sales reps.

★231★ *Confidential Newsletter*
Manufacturers' Agents National Association (MANA)
23016 Mill Creek Rd.
PO Box 3467
Laguna Hills, CA 92654
Ph: (714)859-4040 Fax: (714)855-2973
Quarterly.

★232★ *DECA Advisor*
Distributive Education Clubs of America (DECA)
1908 Association Dr.
Reston, VA 22091
Ph: (703)860-5000
Covers teaching aids, surveys, corporation support, scholarships, and special events. Includes teaching guide.

★233★ *Health of the Rep Newsletter*
United Association of Manufacturers' Representatives (UAMR)
133 Terrace Trail, W.
Lake Quivira, KS 66106
Ph: (913)268-9466 Fax: (714)859-9131
Karen Kittrell Mazzola
Monthly. Provides manufacturers' representatives "the latest tips on how to stay healthy." Carries information on various diseases and a list of related publications.

★234★ *Manufacturers' Agents National Association—Special Report*
Manufacturers' Agents National Association (MANA)
23016 Mill Creek Rd.
PO Box 3467
Laguna Hills, CA 92654
Ph: (714)859-4040 Fax: (714)855-2973
Periodic. Includes problem-solving reports on issues recurrent in a manufacturer-agency relationship.

★235★ *Manufacturers Representatives of America—Newsline*
Manufacturers Representatives of America
PO Box 150229
Arlington, TX 76015-6229
Ph: (817)465-5511
William R. Bess
Quarterly. Published for member independent manufacturers' representatives handling sanitary supplies and paper and plastic disposable products. Carries articles to help improve agent sales skills, market coverage, and customer service, and to help establish more effective agent/principal communications. Recurring features include news of members, a calendar of events, job listings, notices of publications available, news of educational opportunities, and a column titled President's Report.

★236★ *NAW Report*
National Association of Wholesaler-Distributors (NAW)
1725 K St. NW, 7th Fl.
Washington, DC 20006
Ph: (202)872-0885
Randi Shumaker
Bimonthly. Publishes information on government issues and actions affecting wholesaler-distributors specifically and the business community generally. Recurring features include reports on federal legislative and regulatory developments; legal and insurance trends; industry research and statistics; and business services offered through the association's group purchasing program.

★237★ *New Dimensions*
Distributive Education Clubs of America (DECA)
1908 Association Dr.
Reston, VA 22091
Ph: (703)860-5000
Quarterly. For high school and college students of marketing, merchandising, and management.

★238★ *Personal Selling Power*
Personal Selling Power, Inc.
1127 International Pkwy.
PO Box 5467
Fredericksburg, VA 22403
Ph: (703)752-7000 Fax: (703)752-7001
LB Gschwandtner
Magazine presenting motivational and sales skills and techniques for sales and marketing executives.

★239★ *The Rep Travel Newsletter*
United Association of Manufacturers' Representatives (UAMR)
133 Terrace Trail, W.
Lake Quivira, KS 66106
Ph: (913)268-9466
Karen Mazzola
Monthly. Provides business and vacation travel tips for manufacturers' representatives. Includes information on tours and travel discounts.

★240★ *Rep World*
Albee-Campbell, Inc.
806 Penn Ave.
Sinking Spring, PA 19608
Ph: (215)678-3361
Thomas C. Reinhart
Quarterly. Helps manufacturers' representatives "locate and appoint qualified Rep agencies according to geographic territory and product line compatibility." Shares ideas on direct mail, public relations, telemarketing, imprinted advertising specialites, and company brochures. Also concerned with trade shows, media advertising, line cards, and lead follow-up. Recurring features include book reviews and news of seminars.

★241★ *Retailing News*
Retailing News Co.
14962 Bear Valley Rd., Ste. 288
Victorville, CA 92392-4236
Ph: (619)241-2514 Fax: (619)241-3595
Martin Barsky
Monthly. Trade magazine reaching dealers, retailers, manufacturers, manufacturing reps, and distributors in the consumer electronics and major appliance industries.

★242★ *RWDSU Record*
Retail, Wholesale and Dept. Store Union-AFL-CIO
30 E. 29th St.
New York, NY 10016
Ph: (212)684-5300 Fax: (212)779-2809
Stuart Appelbeum
Bimonthly. Labor union newspaper.

★243★ *Salesman's Insider*
Marv. Q. Modell Associates
6009 Montgomery Corner
San Jose, CA 95135-1431
Ph: (408)270-4526
Marv. Q. Modell

Monthly. Concerned with selling techniques and methodology in all sales areas. Tracks new sales developments, trends, and profit opportunities. Details negotiating process; offers "tips that work."

★244★ *Salesmanship*
Dartnell Corporation
4660 Ravenswood
Chicago, IL 60640
Ph: (312)561-4000 Fax: (312)561-3801
Fr: 800-621-5463
Terry Breen

Biweekly. Offers sales ideas and inspiration, profiles of top-producing salespeople, and articles on topics related to sales success.

★245★ *Supply House Times*
Cahners Publishing Co.
1350 E. Touhy Ave.
PO Box 5080
Des Plaines, IL 60017-5080
Ph: (708)635-8800 Fax: (708)390-2618
Bill EverhamPublisher

Monthly. Trade magazine for wholesalers in plumbing, heating, cooling, piping, and water systems. Areas of major emphasis include: warehousing, materials handling, inventory control, accounting, data processing, merchandising, salesmanship and general management.

★246★ *UAMR Confidential Bulletin*
United Association of Manufacturers' Representatives (UAMR)
PO Box 986
Dana Point, CA 92629
Ph: (714)240-4966 Fax: (714)240-4966
H. Keith Kittrell

Monthly. Covers product lines offered for representation in all fields. Provides details of the company and product, type of accounts to be serviced, and the areas open for representation. Subscription includes three newsletters and bulletin of lines for representatives.

★247★ *UAMR Monthly Bulletin*
United Association of Manufacturers' Representatives (UAMR)
133 Terrace Trail W.
Lake Quivira, KS 66106
Ph: (913)268-9466
H. Keith Kittrell

Monthly. Discusses topics of interest to manufacturers' representatives, "with particular emphasis on selling, tax advantages, world conditions and happenings in Washington." Recurring features include news of members and the Association.

Meetings and Conventions

★248★ International Mass Retail Association Convention and Exhibits
International Mass Retail Association
1901 Pennsylvania Ave., NW, 10t Fl.
Washington, DC 20006-3455
Ph: (202)861-0774 Fax: (202)785-4588

Annual.

★249★ National Agri-Marketing Association Conference
National Agri-Marketing Association
11020 King St., Ste. 205
Overlard Park, KS 66210
Ph: (913)491-6500 Fax: (913)492-6502

Annual. **Dates and Locations:** 1996 Apr 10-12; San Diego, CA.

Real Estate Agents, Brokers, and Appraisers

Real estate agents, brokers, and appraisers assist people in the purchase or sale of a home, or an investment property. They have a thorough knowledge of the housing market in their community, which neighborhoods will best fit their clients' budgets, local zoning and tax laws, and where to obtain financing for the purchase. They also may act as a medium for price negotiations between buyer and seller. Brokers are independent business people who not only sell real estate owned by others, but also rent and manage properties and develop new building projects. Real estate agents are generally independent sales workers who provide their services to a licensed broker on a contract basis. In return, the broker pays agents a portion of the commission earned from property sold through the firm by the agent. Agents' and brokers' jobs involve more than just selling. They must have property to sell to begin with, so spend much time obtaining "listings" (owner agreements to place properties for sale with the firm). Real estate appraisers, objective experts with no vested interest in the property, give unbiased estimates of the quality, value, and best use of a specific property. They do this by compiling information on a property's construction, condition, functional design, and by searching public records of sales, leases, assessments, and other transactions.

Salaries

Commissions on sales are the main source of earnings of real estate brokers and agents. Few receive a salary.

Lowest 10 percent	Less than $223/week
Median	$323-$802/week
Top 10 percent	More than $1,247/week

Employment Outlook

Growth rate until the year 2005: Average.

Real Estate Agents, Brokers, and Appraisers

Career Guides

★250★ **"Appraisal" in *Career Choices for the 90's for Students of Mathematics* (pp. 142-144)**
Walker and Co.
435 Hudson St.
New York, NY 10014
Ph: (212)727-8300 Fax: (212)727-0984
Fr: 800-289-2553
1990. Describes jobs in different industries and includes interviews with people working in related occupations. Presents employment outlook, preferred geographic location, entry-level opportunities, career paths, job responsibilities, advancement, personal and professional qualifications, salaries, working conditions, material for further reading, and associations.

★251★ **"Appraisal" in *Encyclopedia of Career Choices for the 1990s: AGuide to Entry Level Jobs* (pp. 750-752)**
Berkley Pub.
PO Box 506
East Rutherford, NJ 07073
Fax: (201)933-2316 Fr: 800-788-6262
1992. Describes entry-level opportunities in 42 career fields for college graduates. Each chapter covers a single career field, including an overview, employment outlook, major employers, tips on entering the field, international job opportunities, functional job areas with personal and professional qualifications, career paths, job responsibilities, advancement possibilities, salaries, and working conditions. Lists related sources of information.

★252★ **"Appraisal" in *Opportunities in Real Estate Careers* (pp. 81-85)**
National Textbook Co. (NTC)
VGM Career Books
4255 W. Touhy Ave.
Lincolnwood, IL 60646-1975
Ph: (708)679-5500 Fax: (708)679-2494
Fr: 800-323-4900
Mariwyn Evans. 1988. Surveys the real estate industry and its jobs and related careers. Covers the work, academic preparation, future employment outlook, licensing, and financial compensation. Offers information about choosing a firm and job hunting.

★253★ **"Appraiser" in *Career Choices for the 90's for Students of Economics* (pp. 130-132)**
Walker and Co.
435 Hudson St.
New York, NY 10014
Ph: (212)727-8300 Fax: (212)727-0984
Fr: 800-289-2553
1990. Describes jobs in different industries and includes interviews with people working in related occupations. Presents employment outlook, preferred geographic location, entry-level opportunities, career paths, job responsibilities, advancement, personal and professional qualifications, salaries, working conditions, material for further reading, and associations.

★254★ **"Appraiser" in *Career Information Center* (Vol.5)**
Simon and Schuster
200 Old Tappan Rd.
Old Tappan, NJ 07675
Fax: 800-445-6991 Fr: 800-223-2348
Richard Lidz and Dale Anderson, editorial directors. Fifth edition, 1993. For 600 occupations, describes job duties, entry-level requirements, education and training needed, advancement possibilities, employment outlook, earnings and benefits. The set is divided into 12 volumes. Each volume includes jobs related under a broad career field. Volume 13 is the index.

★255★ **"Assessors and Appraisers" in *Career Discovery Encyclopedia* (Vol.1, pp. 68-69)**
J.G. Ferguson Publishing Co.
200 W. Madison St., Ste. 300
Chicago, IL 60606
Ph: (312)580-5480 Fax: (312)580-4948
E. Russell Primm, editor-in-chief. 1993. Contains two-page articles on 504 occupations. Each article describes job duties, earnings, and educational and training requirements.

★256★ **"Assessors and Appraisers" in *Encyclopedia of Careers and Vocational Guidance* (Vol.2, pp. 113-115)**
J.G. Ferguson Publishing Co.
200 W. Madison St., Ste. 300
Chicago, IL 60606
Ph: (312)580-5480 Fax: (312)580-4948
William E. Hopke, editor-in-chief. Ninth edition, 1993. Four-volume set that profiles 500 occupations and describes job trends in 74 industries. Includes career description, educational requirements, history of the job, methods of entry, advancement, employment outlook, earnings, working conditions, social and psychological factors, and sources of additional information.

★257★ **"Business Realtors" in *New York Times Career Planner* (pp. 139-141)**
Times Books
201 E. 50th St.
New York, NY 10022
Ph: (212)751-2600 Fax: (212)572-8700
Elizabeth M. Fowler. 1987. Offers career planning and job hunting advice for the college graduate. Surveys labor market trends. Contains "inside" information on professional careers including educational preparation, employment opportunities, and salaries.

★258★ ***Career Opportunities***
American Inst. of Real Estate Appraisers of the National Assoc. of Realtors
430 N. Michigan Ave.
Chicago, IL 60611-4088
Ph: (312)329-8559
1989. This eight-page booklet describes the work, needed skills, qualifications, educational requirements, income, and working conditions in real estate careers.

★259★ ***Careers in Real Estate***
National Association of Realtors
430 N. MI Ave.
Chicago, IL 60611-4087
Ph: (312)329-8387
1990. This 30-page booklet explores the varied opportunities in real estate sales. Covers educational preparation, licensing requirements, continuing education, preferred skills

and personal characteristics, places of employment, and employment outlook.

★260★ *Hot Tips, Sneaky Tricks, and Last Ditch Tactics: An Insider's Guide to Getting Your First Corporate Job*
John Wiley and Sons, Inc.
605 3rd Ave.
New York, NY 10158-0012
Ph: (212)850-6000 Fax: (212)850-6088
Fr: 800-526-5368

Jeff B. Speck. 1989. Written for college graduates who are looking for jobs in banking, consulting, accounting, insurance, real estate or the Fortune 500. Offers tips on surviving the standardized selection process used by large companies.

★261★ *How About a Career in Real Estate?*
Real Estate Education Co.
520 N. Dearborn St.
Chicago, IL 60610-4354
Ph: (312)836-4400 Fax: (312)836-1021
Fr: 800-621-9621

Carla Cross. 1993. Describes in detail different aspects of real estate. Topics include what it takes to succeed, day-to-day activities, salaries, and licensure.

★262★ "Opportunities in Marketing & Sales" in *Travel and Hospitality Career Directory* (pp. 66-68)
Career Press, Inc.
PO Box 34
62 Beverly Rd.
Hawthorne, NJ 07507
Ph: (201)427-0229

Ronald W. Fry, editor. 1989. Offers advice on career planning and job hunting in hotel, travel, and related industries. Lists companies offering entry level positions in airlines, convention and visitors' bureaus, foreign tourist boards, hotels, travel agencies, car rental firms, and cruise lines. Lists travel and hospitality associations and trade publications.

★263★ *Opportunities in Real Estate Careers*
National Textbook Co. (NTC)
VGM Career Books
4255 W. Touhy Ave.
Lincolnwood, IL 60646-1975
Ph: (708)679-5500 Fax: (708)679-2494
Fr: 800-323-4900

Mariwyn Evans. 1988. Surveys the real estate industry and its jobs and related careers. Covers the work, academic preparation, future employment outlook, licensing, and financial compensation. Offers information about choosing a firm and job hunting.

★264★ "Real Estate Agent" in *100 Best Careers for the Year 2000* (pp. 177-179)
Arco Pub.
201 W. 103rd St.
Indianapolis, IN 46290
Ph: 800-428-5331 Fax: 800-835-3202

Shelly Field. 1992. Describes 100 job opportunities expected to grow fast throughout the next decade. Provides information on job duties and responsibilities, training requirements, education, advancement opportunities, experience and qualifications, and typical salaries.

★265★ "Real Estate Agent/Broker" in *VGM's Careers Encyclopedia* (pp. 395-397)
National Textbook Co. (NTC)
VGM Career Books
4255 W. Touhy Ave.
Lincolnwood, IL 60646-1975
Ph: (708)679-5500 Fax: (708)679-2494
Fr: 800-323-4900

Third edition, 1991. Contains two- to five-page descriptions of 200 managerial, professional, technical, trade, and service occupations. Each profile includes job duties, places of employment, qualifications, educational preparation, training, employment potential, advancement, income, and additional sources of information.

★266★ "Real Estate Agent/Broker" in *VGM's Handbook of Business and Management Careers* (pp. 77-79)
National Textbook Co. (NTC)
VGM Career Books
4255 W. Touhy Ave.
Lincolnwood, IL 60646-1975
Ph: (708)679-5500 Fax: (708)679-2494
Fr: 800-323-4900

Annette Selden, editor. Second edition, 1993. Contains 42 two-page occupational profiles describing job duties, places of employment, working conditions, qualifications, education, employment outlook, and income.

★267★ "Real Estate Agent and Brokers" in *101 Careers: A Guide to the Fastest-Growing Opportunities* (pp. 48-50)
John Wiley & Sons, Inc.
605 3rd Ave.
New York, NY 10158-0012
Ph: (212)850-6645 Fax: (212)850-6088

Michael Harkavy. 1990. Describes the nature of the job, working conditions, employment growth, qualifications, personal skills, projected salaries, and where to write for more information.

★268★ "Real Estate Agent" in *Jobs Rated Almanac*
World Almanac
1 International Blvd., Ste. 444
Mahwah, NJ 07495
Ph: (201)529-6900 Fax: (201)529-6901

Les Krantz. Second edition, 1992. Ranks 250 jobs by environment, salary, outlooks, physical demands, stress, security, travel opportunities, and extra perks. Includes jobs the editor feels are the most common, most interesting, and the most rapidly growing.

★269★ *Real Estate Agents and Brokers*
Chronicle Guidance Publications, Inc.
66 Aurora St.
PO Box 1190
Moravia, NY 13118-1190
Ph: (315)497-0330 Fax: (315)497-3359
Fr: 800-622-7284

1993. This career brief describes the nature of the work, working conditions, hours and earnings, education and training, licensure, certification, unions, personal qualifications, social and psychological factors, employment outlook, entry methods, advancement, and related occupations.

★270★ "Real Estate Agents and Brokers" in *American Almanac of Jobs and Salaries* (pp. 544)
Avon Books
1350 Avenue of the Americas
New York, NY 10019
Ph: (212)261-6800 Fr: 800-238-0658

John Wright, editor. Revised and updated, 1994-95. A comprehensive guide to the wages of hundreds of occupations in a wide variety of industries and organizations.

★271★ "Real Estate Agents, Brokers, and Appraisers" in *Occupational Outlook Handbook*
U.S. Government Printing Office
Superintendent of Documents
Washington, DC 20402
Ph: (202)512-1800 Fax: (202)512-2250

Biennial; latest edition, 1994-95. Encyclopedia of careers describing more than 250 occupations and comprising about 85 percent of all jobs in the economy. Occupations that require lengthy education or training are given the most attention. For each occupation, the handbook describes job duties, working conditions, training, educational preparation, personal qualities, advancement possibilities, job outlook, earnings, and sources of additional information.

★272★ "Real Estate Agents and Brokers" in *Career Discovery Encyclopedia* (Vol.5, pp. 130-131)
J.G. Ferguson Publishing Co.
200 W. Madison St., Ste. 300
Chicago, IL 60606
Ph: (312)580-5480 Fax: (312)580-4948

E. Russell Primm, editor-in-chief. 1993. Contains two-page articles on 504 occupations. Each article describes job duties, earnings, and educational and training requirements.

★273★ "Real Estate Agents and Brokers" in *Encyclopedia of Careers and Vocational Guidance* (Vol.4, pp. 243-247)
J.G. Ferguson Publishing Co.
200 W. Madison St., Ste. 300
Chicago, IL 60606
Ph: (312)580-5480 Fax: (312)580-4948

William E. Hopke, editor-in-chief. Ninth edition, 1993. Four-volume set that profiles 500 occupations and describes job trends in 74 industries. Includes career description, educational requirements, history of the job, methods of entry, advancement, employment outlook, earnings, working conditions, social and psychological factors, and sources of additional information.

★274★ "Real Estate Agents and Brokers" in *Jobs! What They Are—Where They Are—What They Pay* (p. 338)
Simon & Schuster, Inc.
Simon & Schuster Bldg.
1230 Avenue of the Americas
New York, NY 10020
Ph: (212)698-7000

Robert O. Snelling and Anne M. Snelling. Revised edition, 1992. Profiles 241 occupations, describing duties and responsibilities, educational preparation, earnings, employment opportunities, training, and qualifications.

★275★ "Real Estate Agents and Brokers: Sellers of the Land" in *Careers for Women Without College Degrees* (pp. 245-250)
McGraw-Hill Publishing Co.
11 W. 19th St.
New York, NY 10011
Ph: (212)337-6010

Beatryce Nivens. 1988. Career planning and job hunting guide containing information on decision-making, skills assessment, and resumes for career changers. Profiles careers with the best occupational outlook. Describes the work, educational preparation, employment outlook, salaries, and required skills.

★276★ "Real Estate Agents" in *Opportunities in Home Economics Careers* (pp. 95-96)
National Textbook Co. (NTC)
VGM Career Books
4255 W. Touhy Ave.
Lincolnwood, IL 60646-1975
Ph: (708)679-5500 Fax: (708)679-2494
Fr: 800-323-4900

Rhea Shields and Anna K. Williams. 1988. Describes the history of home economics and current trends affecting the field. Explores related careers in interior design, family relations, and home management. Covers the nature of the work, educational preparation, skills, employment outlook, places of employment, and salaries. Lists professional organizations and offers job hunting advice.

★277★ "Real Estate Agents" in *Opportunities in Vocational and Technical Careers* (pp. 59-75)
National Textbook Co. (NTC)
VGM Career Books
4255 W. Touhy Ave.
Lincolnwood, IL 60646-1975
Ph: (708)679-5500 Fax: (708)679-2494
Fr: 800-323-4900

Adrian A. Paradis. 1994. Describes careers which can be prepared for by attending a private vocational or proprietary school—office employee, sales worker, service worker, health services, mechanic, craftworker, and technician. Covers employment outlook, job duties, and salaries. Offers career plannning advice.

★278★ *Real Estate Appraiser*
Careers, Inc.
PO Box 135
Largo, FL 34649-0135
Ph: (813)584-7333

1993. Two-page occupational summary card describing duties, working conditions, personal qualifications, training, earnings and hours, employment outlook, places of employment, related careers and where to write for more information.

★279★ *Real Estate Appraiser*
Vocational Biographies, Inc.
PO Box 31
Sauk Centre, MN 56378-0031
Ph: (612)352-6516 Fax: (612)352-5546
Fr: 800-255-0752

1992. Four-page pamphlet containing a personal narrative about a worker's job, work likes and dislikes, career path from high school to the present. Education and training, the rewards and frustrations, and the effects of the job on the rest of the worker's life. The data file portion of this pamphlet gives a concise occupational summary, including work descriptions, working conditions, places of employment, personal characteristics, education and training, job outlook, and salary range.

★280★ "Real Estate Appraiser" in *Career Choices for the 90's for Students of Business* (pp. 139-141)
Walker and Co.
435 Hudson St.
New York, NY 10014
Ph: (212)727-8300 Fax: (212)727-0984
Fr: 800-289-2553

1990. Describes jobs in different industries and includes interviews with people working in related occupations. Presents employment outlook, preferred geographic location, entry-level opportunities, career paths, job responsibilities, advancement, personal and professional qualifications, salaries, working conditions, material for further reading, and associations.

★281★ "Real Estate Appraiser" in *Career Information Center* (Vol.10)
Simon and Schuster
200 Old Tappan Rd.
Old Tappan, NJ 07675
Fax: 800-445-6991 Fr: 800-223-2348

Richard Lidz and Dale Anderson, editorial directors. Fifth edition, 1993. For 600 occupations, describes job duties, entry-level requirements, education and training needed, advancement possibilities, employment outlook, earnings and benefits. The set is divided into 12 volumes. Each volume includes jobs related under a broad career field. Volume 13 is the index.

★282★ "Real Estate Appraiser" in *Occu-Facts: Information on 580 Careers in Outline Form*
Careers, Inc.
PO Box 135
Largo, FL 34649-0135
Ph: (813)584-7333

Biennial, 1995-96 edition. Each one-page occupational profile describes duties, working conditions, physical surroundings and demands, aptitudes, temperament, educational requirements, employment outlook, earnings, and places of employment.

★283★ "Real Estate Appraiser" in *VGM's Careers Encyclopedia* (pp. 399-400)
National Textbook Co. (NTC)
VGM Career Books
4255 W. Touhy Ave.
Lincolnwood, IL 60646-1975
Ph: (708)679-5500 Fax: (708)679-2494
Fr: 800-323-4900

Third edition, 1991. Contains two- to five-page descriptions of 200 managerial, professional, technical, trade, and service occupations. Each profile includes job duties, places of employment, qualifications, educational preparation, training, employment potential, advancement, income, and additional sources of information.

★284★ "Real Estate Appraiser" in *VGM's Handbook of Business and Management Careers* (pp. 80-81)
National Textbook Co. (NTC)
VGM Career Books
4255 W. Touhy Ave.
Lincolnwood, IL 60646-1975
Ph: (708)679-5500 Fax: (708)679-2494
Fr: 800-323-4900

Annette Selden, editor. Second edition, 1993. Contains 42 two-page occupational profiles describing job duties, places of employment, working conditions, qualifications, education, employment outlook, and income.

★285★ *Real Estate Appraisers*
Chronicle Guidance Publications, Inc.
66 Aurora St.
PO Box 1190
Moravia, NY 13118-1190
Ph: (315)497-0330 Fax: (315)497-3359
Fr: 800-622-7284

1994. This career brief describes the nature of the work, working conditions, hours and earnings, education and training, licensure, certification, unions, personal qualifications, social and psychological factors, employment outlook, entry methods, advancement, and related occupations.

★286★ "Real Estate Appraisers" in *New York Times Career Planner* (pp. 283-285)
Times Books
201 E. 50th St.
New York, NY 10022
Ph: (212)751-2600 Fax: (212)572-8700

Elizabeth M. Fowler. 1987. Offers career planning and job hunting advice for the college graduate. Surveys labor market trends. Contains "inside" information on professional careers including educational preparation, employment opportunities, and salaries.

★287★ "Real Estate" in *Black Woman's Career Guide* (pp. 295-302)
Bantam Doubleday Dell
1540 Broadway
New York, NY 10036
Fax: 800-233-3294 Fr: 800-223-5780

Beatryce Nivens. Revised edition, 1987. Offers career planning and job hunting advice. Contains information on 20 different career areas and profiles women working in the field. Each occupational profile describes the work, career paths and earning potential.

★288★ *Real Estate Broker/Real Estate Sales Agent*
Vocational Biographies, Inc.
PO Box 31
Sauk Centre, MN 56378-0031
Ph: (612)352-6516 Fax: (612)352-5546
Fr: 800-255-0752

1994. Four-page pamphlet containing a personal narrative about a worker's job, work likes and dislikes, career path from high school to the present. Education and training, the rewards and frustrations, and the effects of the job on the rest of the worker's life. The data file portion of this pamphlet gives a concise occupational summary, including work descriptions, working conditions, places of employment, personal characteristics, education and training, job outlook, and salary range.

★289★ "Real Estate Broker" in *Top Professions: The 100 Most Popular, Dynamic, and Profitable Careers in America Today* (pp. 68-69)
Petersons Guides, Inc.
PO Box 2123
Princeton, NJ 08543-2123
Ph: (609)243-9111 Fax: (609)243-9150
Fr: 800-338-3282

Nicholas Basta. 1989. Includes occupations requiring a college or advanced degree. Describes job duties, earnings, some typical job titles, career opportunities at different degree levels, and lists related associations.

★290★ "Real Estate" in *Career Choices for the 90's for Students of Business* (pp. 131-154)
Walker and Co.
435 Hudson St.
New York, NY 10014
Ph: (212)727-8300 Fax: (212)727-0984
Fr: 800-289-2553

1990. Describes jobs in different industries and includes interviews with people working in related occupations. Presents employment outlook, preferred geographic location, entry-level opportunities, career paths, job responsibilities, advancement, personal and professional qualifications, salaries, working conditions, material for further reading, and associations.

★291★ "Real Estate" in *Career Choices for the 90's for Students of Economics* (pp. 122-145)
Walker and Co.
435 Hudson St.
New York, NY 10014
Ph: (212)727-8300 Fax: (212)727-0984
Fr: 800-289-2553

1990. Describes jobs in different industries and includes interviews with people working in related occupations. Presents employment outlook, preferred geographic location, entry-level opportunities, career paths, job responsibilities, advancement, personal and professional qualifications, salaries, working conditions, material for further reading, and associations.

★292★ "Real Estate" in *Career Choices for the 90's for Students of Mathematics* (pp. 134-157)
Walker and Co.
435 Hudson St.
New York, NY 10014
Ph: (212)727-8300 Fax: (212)727-0984
Fr: 800-289-2553

1990. Describes jobs in different industries and includes interviews with people working in related occupations. Presents employment outlook, preferred geographic location, entry-level opportunities, career paths, job responsibilities, advancement, personal and professional qualifications, salaries, working conditions, material for further reading, and associations.

★293★ "Real Estate" in *Career Connection II: A Guide to Technical Majors and Their Related Careers* (pp. 132-133)
Jist Works, Inc.
720 N. Park Ave.
Indianapolis, IN 46202-3431
Ph: (317)264-3720 Fax: (317)264-3709

Fred A. Rowe. 1994. Contains technical majors, such as automotive technology. Describes the major and the job. Lists high school and postsecondary school courses. Includes occupations related to the major, employment outlook, and starting salary.

★294★ *Real Estate Careers: 25 Growing Opportunities*
John Wiley and Sons, Inc.
605 3rd Ave.
New York, NY 10158-0012
Ph: (212)850-6000 Fax: (212)850-6088
Fr: 800-526-5368

Carolyn Janik and Ruth Rejnis. 1994.

★295★ "Real Estate Careers" in *Transitions: Military Pathways to Civilian Careers* (pp. 137-140)
Rosen Publishing Group
29 E. 21st St.
New York, NY 10010
Ph: (212)777-3017 Fax: (212)777-0277
Fr: 800-237-9932

Robert W. MacDonald. 1988. Describes how to make the best use of your military service to create a civilian career. Describes skills needed in civilian employment and compares them to skills acquired in the military. Covers career planning, job search, resume writing, and starting a small business. Lists many resources.

★296★ "Real Estate and Construction" in *Jobs '95* (pp. 417-429)
Prentice Hall Press
1 Gulf & Western Plaza
New York, NY 10023
Ph: (212)373-8500

Kathryn Petras and Ross Petras. Annual, 1995. Discusses employment prospects and trends for 15 professional careers and 29 industries. Lists leading companies, associations, directories, and magazines.

★297★ "Real Estate" in *Encyclopedia of Career Choices for the 1990s: A Guide to Entry Level Jobs* (pp. 742-765)
Berkley Pub.
PO Box 506
East Rutherford, NJ 07073
Fax: (201)933-2316 Fr: 800-788-6262

1992. Describes entry-level opportunities in 42 career fields for college graduates. Each chapter covers a single career field, including an overview, employment outlook, major employers, tips on entering the field, international job opportunities, functional job areas with personal and professional qualifications, career paths, job responsibilities, advancement possibilities, salaries, and working conditions. Lists related sources of information.

★298★ "Real Estate" in *Encyclopedia of Careers and Vocational Guidance* (Vol.1, pp. 405-410)
J.G. Ferguson Publishing Co.
200 W. Madison St., Ste. 300
Chicago, IL 60606
Ph: (312)580-5480 Fax: (312)580-4948

William E. Hopke, editor-in-chief. Ninth edition, 1993. Four-volume set that profiles 500 occupations and describes job trends in 74 industries. Includes career description, educational requirements, history of the job, methods of entry, advancement, employment outlook, earnings, working conditions, social and psychological factors, and sources of additional information.

★299★ "Real Estate" in *Major Decisions: A Guide to College Majors* (p. 142)
Orchard House, Inc.
112 Balls Hill Rd.
Concord, MA 01742
Ph: (508)369-0467 Fax: (508)369-9472

Richard A. Blumenthal and Joseph A. Despres. Second edition, 1992. Provides a one-page description of 155 college majors. Included under each major is a description, the plan of study, typical major courses, high school courses and career possibilities.

★300★ "Real Estate Sales" in *Career Choices for the 90's for Students of Business* (pp. 164-167)
Walker and Co.
435 Hudson St.
New York, NY 10014
Ph: (212)727-8300 Fax: (212)727-0984
Fr: 800-289-2553

1990. Describes jobs in different industries and includes interviews with people working in related occupations. Presents employment outlook, preferred geographic location, entry-level opportunities, career paths, job responsibilities, advancement, personal and professional qualifications, salaries, working conditions, material for further reading, and associations.

★301★ "Real Estate Sales" in *Career Choices for the 90's for Students of Communications and Journalism* (pp. 172-175)
Walker and Co.
435 Hudson St.
New York, NY 10014
Ph: (212)727-8300 Fax: (212)727-0984
Fr: 800-289-2553

1990. Describes jobs in different industries and includes interviews with people working in related occupations. Presents employment outlook, preferred geographic location, entry-level opportunities, career paths, job responsibilities, advancement, personal and professional qualifications, salaries, working conditions, material for further reading, and associations.

★302★ "Real Estate Sales" in *Encyclopedia of Career Choices for the 1990s: A Guide to Entry Level Jobs* (pp. 775-778)
Berkley Pub.
PO Box 506
East Rutherford, NJ 07073
Fax: (201)933-2316 Fr: 800-788-6262

1992. Describes entry-level opportunities in 42 career fields for college graduates. Each chapter covers a single career field, including an overview, employment outlook, major employers, tips on entering the field, international job opportunities, functional job areas with personal and professional qualifications, career paths, job responsibilities, advancement possibilities, salaries, and working conditions. Lists related sources of information.

★303★ "Real Estate Sales" in *Opportunities in Property Management Careers* (pp. 101-105)
National Textbook Co. (NTC)
VGM Career Books
4255 W. Touhy Ave.
Lincolnwood, IL 60646-1975
Ph: (708)679-5500 Fax: (708)679-2494
Fr: 800-323-4900

Mariwyn Evans. 1990. Describes the past, present, and future of property management, job duties, entering the field, licensure, educational preparation, salary, and related careers. Lists books, periodicals, and associations.

★304★ "Real Estate Sales Representative" in *Great Careers for People Who Like Working with People* (pp. 4-9)
Gale Research Inc.
835 Penobscot Bldg.
Detroit, MI 48226
Ph: (313)961-2242 Fr: 800-347-4253

1994.

★305★ "Real Estate Sales Worker and Broker" in *Career Information Center* (Vol.10)
Simon and Schuster
200 Old Tappan Rd.
Old Tappan, NJ 07675
Fax: 800-445-6991 Fr: 800-223-2348

Richard Lidz and Dale Anderson, editorial directors. Fifth edition, 1993. For 600 occupations, describes job duties, entry-level requirements, education and training needed, advancement possibilities, employment outlook, earnings and benefits. The set is divided into 12 volumes. Each volume includes jobs related under a broad career field. Volume 13 is the index.

★306★ *Real Estate Salesperson*
Careers, Inc.
PO Box 135
Largo, FL 34649-0135
Ph: (813)584-7333

1995. Two-page occupational summary card describing duties, working conditions, personal qualifications, training, earnings and hours, employment outlook, places of employment, related careers and where to write for more information.

★307★ "Real Estate Salesperson" in *College Board Guide to Jobs and Career Planning* (pp. 144-145)
The College Board
45 Columbus Ave.
New York, NY 10023-6992
Ph: (212)713-8165 Fax: (212)713-8143
Fr: 800-323-7155

Second edition, 1994. Describes the job, salaries, related careers, education needed, and where to write for more information.

★308★ "Real Estate Salesperson" in *Occu-Facts: Information on 580 Careers in Outline Form*
Careers, Inc.
PO Box 135
Largo, FL 34649-0135
Ph: (813)584-7333

Biennial, 1995-96 edition. Each one-page occupational profile describes duties, working conditions, physical surroundings and demands, aptitudes, temperament, educational requirements, employment outlook, earnings, and places of employment.

★309★ "Real Estate: What's Hot, What's Not" in *Fast-Track Careers: A Guide to the Highest-Paying Jobs* (pp. 99-121)
John Wiley and Sons, Inc.
605 3rd Ave.
New York, NY 10158-0012
Ph: (212)850-6000 Fax: (212)850-6088
Fr: 800-526-5368

William Lewis and Nancy Schuman. 1987. Profiles eight glamorous and high paying careers describing entry-level opportunities, earnings, personal qualities, types of companies, educational preparation and training, and employment outlook. Lists prominent companies in each industry, typical jargon, and professional associations.

★310★ "Sales" in *Where the Jobs Are: The Hottest Careers for the 90s* (pp. 221-244)
Career Press
180 5th Ave.
Hawthorne, NJ 07507
Ph: (201)427-0229 Fax: (201)427-2037
Fr: 800-CAREER-1

Joyce Hadley. 1995. Offers a job-hunting strategy for the 1990s as well as descriptions of growing careers of the decade. Each profile includes general information, forecasts, growth, education and training, licensing requirements, and salary information.

★311★ *Video Career Library - Marketing and Sales*
Careers, Inc.
PO Box 135
Largo, FL 34649-0135
Ph: (813)584-7333

Videocassette. 1994. Part of the Video Career Library covering 165 occupations. Shows actual workers on the job.

★312★ *Your Successful Real Estate Career*
AMACOM
135 W. 50th St.
New York, NY 10020-1201
Ph: (212)903-8089 Fr: 800-262-9699

Kenneth W. Edwards. Describes the work of real estate agents and brokers, skills needed, earnings, and licensure. Offers advice about job hunting and choosing a company. Surveys real estate related careers.

Associations

★313★ American Society of Appraisers (ASA)
PO Box 17265
Washington, DC 20041
Ph: (703)478-2228 Fax: (703)742-8471
Fr: 800-ASA-VALU

Members: Professional appraisal teaching, testing, and accrediting society concerned with all property. **Purpose:** Seeks to "maintain recognition that members are qualified, objective, unbiased appraisers and advisors of property values; establish members' status as expert witnesses before courts, administrative tribunals, agencies, and other governmental and municipal authorities; attain recognition of the profession of value determination in property economics by educational and governmental institutions and bodies." Awards professional designation of A.S.A. to senior members of legal age, with at least five years' valuation experience, who have successfully passed written and oral examinations and other criteria; presents the F.A.S.A. designation to Fellows chosen from among the senior members by the society's board of governors in recognition of outstanding services to the society and the appraisal profession. Sponsors mandatory Recertification Program for all senior members. Offers a consumer information service to the public. **Publications:** *Business Valuation Review*, quarterly. • *Directory of Accredited Business Appraisal Experts*, annual. • *Directory of Accredited Machinery and Technical Specialty Appraisers*, annual. • *Directory of Accredited Personal Property Appraisers*, annual. • *Directory of Accredited Real Property Appraisers*, annual. • *Directory of Professional Appraisal Services*, annual. • *Journal of Appraisal Review*, semiannual. • *Journal of Technical Valuation*, 3/year. • *Machinery and Equipment Appraiser*, quarterly. • *Newsline*, monthly. • *Personal Property Journal*, quarterly. • *Real Property Journal*. • *Valuation Journal*, semiannual.

★314★ Appraisal Institute (AI)
875 N. Michigan Ave., Ste. 2400
Chicago, IL 60611-1980
Ph: (312)335-4100 Fax: (312)335-4400

Members: General appraisers who hold the MAI, SRPA, or SREA designations, and residential members who hold the SRA or RM designations. **Purpose:** Enforces Code of Professional Ethics and Standards of Professional Appraisal Practice. Confers one general designation, the MAI, and one residential designation, the SRA. Provides training in valuation of residential and income properties, market analysis, and standards of professional appraisal practice. Sponsors courses in preparation for state certification and licensing; offers continuing education programs for members. **Publications:** *Appraisal Institute Directory of Members*, annual. • *Appraisal Journal*, quarterly. • *Ap-*

praisal of Real Estate.* • *Appraiser News*, bimonthly. • *Appraiser News in Brief*, 10/year. • *Education Catalog*, annual. • *MarketSource*, quarterly. • *Publications Catalog*, annual. • *Quarterly Byte*, quarterly.

★315★ Community Associations Institute (CAI)
1630 Duke St.
Alexandria, VA 22314
Ph: (703)548-8600 Fax: (703)684-1581

Members: Builders, developers, lawyers, accountants, condominium associations, homeowners associations, property managers, insurance and real estate agents, and government officials or agencies. **Purpose:** Purpose is to develop and provide the most advanced and effective guidance for the creation, financing, operation, and maintenance of the common facilities and services in condominiums, townhouse projects, planned unit developments, and open-space communities. Seeks to educate new owners about their responsibilities in order to attract more people to leadership positions within housing developments. Compiles statistics. **Publications:** *Board Briefs*, bimonthly. • *Common Ground*, bimonthly. • *Community Association Law Reporter*, monthly. • *Creating a Community Association.* • *Financial Management of Associations.* • *Ledger Quarterly.*

★316★ National Association of Counselors (NAC)
303 W. Cypress St.
San Antonio, TX 78212
Ph: (210)225-2897 Fax: (210)225-8450
Fr: 800-486-3676

Members: Real estate counselors. **Purpose:** Promotes the advancement of real estate counseling. Monitors legislation in the field; develops new counseling forms; conducts educational programs. **Publications:** *Advise and Counsel.* • *Registry of Real Estate Counselors*, annual.

★317★ National Association of Realtors (NAR)
430 N. Michigan Ave.
Chicago, IL 60611
Ph: (312)329-8200 Fax: (312)329-8576

Members: Federation of 54 state and territory associations and 1860 local real estate boards whose members are real estate brokers and agents. **Purpose:** Terms are registered by the association in the U.S. Patent and Trademark Office and in the states. Promotes education, high professional standards, and modern techniques in specialized real estate work such as brokerage, appraisal, property management, land development, industrial real estate, farm brokerage, and counseling. Conducts research programs. **Publications:** *Real Estate Outlook*, monthly. • *Real Estate Today.* • *Realtor News*, biweekly. • *Subject Headings for Real Estate.*

Standards/Certification Agencies

★318★ American Society of Appraisers (ASA)
PO Box 17265
Washington, DC 20041
Fr: 800-ASA-VALU

Professional appraisal teaching, testing, and accrediting society concerned with all property. Seeks to "maintain recognition that members are qualified, objective, unbiased appraisers and advisors of property values; establish members' status as expert witnesses before courts, administrative tribunals, agencies, and other governmental and municipal authorities; attain recognition of the profession of value determination in property economics by educational and governmental institutions and bodies."

★319★ Appraisal Institute (AI)
875 N. Michigan Ave., Ste. 2400
Chicago, IL 60611-1980
Ph: (312)335-4100 Fax: (312)335-4400

General appraisers who hold the MAI, SRPA, or SREA designations, and residential members who hold the SRA or RM designations. Enforces Code of Professional Ethics and Standards of Professional Appraisal Practice. Provides training in valuation of residential and income properties, market analysis, and standards of professional appraisal practice. Sponsors courses in preparation for state certification and licensing; offers continuing education programs for members.

Test Guides

★320★ *Career Examination Series: Appraisal Investigator*
National Learning Corp.
212 Michael Dr.
Syosset, NY 11791
Ph: (516)921-8888 Fax: (516)921-8743
Fr: 800-645-6337

Jack Rudman. All examination guides in this series contain questions with answers.

★321★ *Career Examination Series: Appraiser*
National Learning Corp.
212 Michael Dr.
Syosset, NY 11791
Ph: (516)921-8888 Fax: (516)921-8743
Fr: 800-645-6337

Jack Rudman. All examination guides in this series contain questions with answers.

★322★ *Career Examination Series: Assistant Real Estate Agent/Appraiser*
National Learning Corp.
212 Michael Dr.
Syosset, NY 11791
Ph: (516)921-8888 Fax: (516)921-8743
Fr: 800-645-6337

Jack Rudman. All examination guides in this series contain questions with answers.

★323★ *Career Examination Series: Real Estate Agent*
National Learning Corp.
212 Michael Dr.
Syosset, NY 11791
Ph: (516)921-8888 Fax: (516)921-8743
Fr: 800-645-6337

Jack Rudman. All examination guides in this series contain questions with answers.

★324★ *Career Examination Series: Real Estate Aide*
National Learning Corp.
212 Michael Dr.
Syosset, NY 11791
Ph: (516)921-8888 Fax: (516)921-8743
Fr: 800-645-6337

Jack Rudman. All examination guides in this series contain questions with answers.

★325★ *Career Examination Series: Real Estate Appraiser*
National Learning Corp.
212 Michael Dr.
Syosset, NY 11791
Ph: (516)921-8888 Fax: (516)921-8743
Fr: 800-645-6337

Jack Rudman. All examination guides in this series contain questions with answers.

★326★ *Career Examination Series: Real Estate Assistant*
National Learning Corp.
212 Michael Dr.
Syosset, NY 11791
Ph: (516)921-8888 Fax: (516)921-8743
Fr: 800-645-6337

Jack Rudman. All examination guides in this series contain questions with answers.

★327★ *Career Examination Series: Real Estate Broker*
National Learning Corp.
212 Michael Dr.
Syosset, NY 11791
Ph: (516)921-8888 Fax: (516)921-8743
Fr: 800-645-6337

Jack Rudman. All examination guides in this series contain questions with answers.

★328★ *Career Examination Series: Senior Real Estate Agent/Appraiser*
National Learning Corp.
212 Michael Dr.
Syosset, NY 11791
Ph: (516)921-8888 Fax: (516)921-8743
Fr: 800-645-6337

Jack Rudman. All examination guides in this series contain questions with answers.

★329★ *How to Prepare for Real Estate Licensing Examinations—Salesperson and Broker*
Barron's Educational Series, Inc.
250 Wireless Blvd.
Hauppauge, NY 11788
Ph: (516)434-3311 Fax: (516)434-3723
Fr: 800-645-3476

J. Bruce Lindeman and Jack P. Friedman. Fourth edition. 1990. Applicable for all 50 states, this study guide contains over 1,000 questions, five practice tests, and special tests for contracts, closing statements, and the Rectangular survey.

★330★ *Math Review for Real Estate License Examinations*
Prentice Hall Press
Simon & Schuster Inc.
200 Old Tappan Rd.
Old Tappan, NJ 07675
Ph: 800-223-2348

Susan A. Shulman. Third edition, 1990. Includes over 100 practice problems with answers, coverage of the math of real estate financing, and two practice math exams with solutions.

★331★ *Principles of Real Estate*
National Learning Corp.
212 Michael Dr.
Syosset, NY 11791
Ph: (516)921-8888 Fax: (516)921-8743
Fr: 800-645-6337

Jack Rudman. Part of Dantes Subject Standardized Tests.

★332★ *Q & A on the Real Estate License Examinations (RE)*
National Learning Corp.
212 Michael Dr.
Syosset, NY 11791
Ph: (516)921-8888 Fax: (516)921-8743
Fr: 800-645-6337

Jack Rudman. Part of the Admission Test Series. Books in this series provide test practice and drill for actual professional certification and licensure tests.

★333★ *Real Estate Broker (REB)*
National Learning Corp.
212 Michael Dr.
Syosset, NY 11791
Ph: (516)921-8888 Fax: (516)921-8743
Fr: 800-645-6337

Jack Rudman. Part of the Admission Test Series. Books in this series provide test practice and drill for actual professional certification and licensure tests.

★334★ *Real Estate License Examinations*
Arco Pub.
201 W. 103rd St.
Indianapolis, IN 46290
Ph: 800-428-5331 Fax: 800-835-3202

Joseph H. Martin and Eve P. Steinberg, MA. 1993, fourth edition. Offers review of all test subject areas and 5 sample exams with answers.

★335★ *Real Estate Salesman (RES)*
National Learning Corp.
212 Michael Dr.
Syosset, NY 11791
Ph: (516)921-8888 Fax: (516)921-8743
Fr: 800-645-6337

Jack Rudman. Part of the Admission Test Series. Books in this series provide test practice and drill for actual professional certification and licensure tests.

★336★ *SuperCourse for Real Estate Licensing*
Prentice Hall Press
Simon & Schuster Inc.
200 Old Tappan Rd.
Old Tappan, NJ 07675
Ph: 800-223-2348

Julie Garton-Good. First edition, 1990. Features include in-depth review of real estate principles and practices, strategies for both state and multistate exams, hundreds of practice questions, and seven full-length practice tests for salespersons and brokers; answers included.

Educational Directories and Programs

★337★ *Directory of Accredited Business Appraisal Experts*
American Society of Appraisers (ASA)
PO Box 17265
Washington, DC 20041
Ph: (703)478-2228 Fax: (703)742-8471
Fr: 800-ASA-VALU

Annual.

★338★ *Directory of Accredited Machinery and Technical Specialty Appraisers*
American Society of Appraisers (ASA)
PO Box 17265
Washington, DC 20041
Ph: (703)733-2000 Fax: (703)742-8471
Fr: 800-ASA-VALU

Annual.

★339★ *Directory of Accredited Personal Property Appraisers*
American Society of Appraisers (ASA)
PO Box 17265
Washington, DC 20041
Ph: (703)478-2228 Fax: (703)742-8471
Fr: 800-ASA-VALU

Annual.

★340★ *Directory of Accredited Real Property Appraisers*
American Society of Appraisers (ASA)
PO Box 17265
Washington, DC 20041
Ph: (703)478-2228 Fax: (703)742-8471
Fr: 800-ASA-VALU

Annual.

★341★ *Directory of Professional Appraisal Services*
American Society of Appraisers (ASA)
PO Box 17265
Washington, DC 20041
Ph: (703)478-2228 Fax: (703)742-8471
Fr: 800-ASA-VALU

Annual.

★342★ *Finance, Insurance & Real Estate USA: Industry Analyses, Statistics, and Leading Organizations*
Gale Research Inc.
835 Penobscot Bldg.
Detroit, MI 48226-4094
Ph: (313)961-2242 Fax: (313)961-6083
Fr: 800-877-GALE
Kristin Hart, Contact

Latest edition November; new edition expected 1996. Publication includes: Lists of up to 75 leading companies in banking, finance, insurance, real estate, and related sectors, selected on the basis of annual revenue. Entries include: Co. name, address, phone, chief executive, type of company, annual sales, number of employees. Principal content of publication is statistical profiles of the finance, insurance, and real estate industries. Each industry division includes tables, graphs, and maps that provide general statistics on number of firms and employees, compensation, and revenues; changes in these statistics between 1985 and 1991 (1992 where available); inputs and outputs; occupations employed; and industry data by state. Arrangement: Classified by industry, then ranked by annual sales.

★343★ *Legal and Financial Directory*
The Daily Journal
2000 S. Colorado Blvd., Ste. 2000
Denver, CO 80222
Ph: (303)756-9995 Fax: (303)756-4465
Fr: 800-323-2362
Arla Haley, Contact

Annual, summer. Covers over 15,000 firms and individuals serving the law, real estate, insurance, and financial industries in Colorado. Entries include: Name, address, phone, fax, telex, geographical area served, description of product/service. Arrangement: Alphabetical.

★344★ *National Real Estate Directory*
Real Estate Publications, Inc.
322 W. Rio Vista Ct.
Tampa, FL 33604-6941
Ph: (813)237-0484 Fr: 800-356-2317
Barbara Lucier, Contact

Biennial. Covers about 22,500 federal and state agencies, offices, and departments related to the regulation of real estate; real estate associations, publications, and organizations. Entries include: Agency, association, department, or publication name, address, phone. Arrangement: Classified by type of organization, then geographical.

★345★ *Real Estate Schools Directory*
American Business Directories, Inc.
5711 S. 86th Circle
Omaha, NE 68127
Ph: (402)593-4600 Fax: (402)331-1505

Updated continuously; printed on request. Entries include: Name, address, phone, size of advertisement, name of owner or manager, number of employees, year first in "Yellow Pages." Compiled from telephone company "Yellow Pages," nationwide. Arrangement: Geographical.

Awards, Scholarships, Grants, and Fellowships

★346★ Appraisal Institute Scholarships
Appraisal Institute
Education Trust
875 N. Michigan Ave., Ste. 2400
Chicago, IL 60611-1980
Ph: (312)335-4100 Fax: (312)335-4400

Purpose: To support studies in real estate appraisal, land economics, real estate, or allied fields. Qualifications: Applicant must be a U.S. citizen and a full time graduate or undergraduate student majoring in real estate appraisal, land economics, real estate, or an allied field. Funds available: $3,000 Graduate, $2,000 Undergraduate. Application details: Write to the Institute for application form and guidelines. Deadline: 15 March.

★347★ Distinguished Service Award
National Association of Realtors
P.R. Division
430 N. Michigan Ave.
Chicago, IL 60611-4087
Ph: (312)329-8874
To recognize outstanding public service by a realtor over a period of years to the real estate industry and the community at the national, state, and local levels. The person may not have served as president of the Association. An engraved statuette, plaque, and jewelled lapel pin are awarded annually. Established in 1979.

★348★ Harwood Memorial Real Estate Scholarship
Real Estate Educators Association (REEA)
11 S. LaSalle St., Ste. 1400
Chicago, IL 60603-1210
Ph: (312)201-0101
Qualifications: Applicants must be enrolled in an undergraduate or graduate program specializing in real estate, have a GPA or at least 3.2 on a 4.0 scale, have attained an A or B in real estate courses, be at least a sophomore, and plan to pursue a career in some phase of real estate. Funds available: Approximately ten scholarships at $250 each. Application details: Applicants must submit an application, resume, official transcripts, and a letter of recommendation from their real estate instructor. A letter of support from a member of the Real Estate Educators Association will be required if letter of recommendation is not written by an REEA member. Deadline: December.

★349★ Realtor of the Year
National Association of Realtors
P.R. Division
430 N. Michigan Ave.
Chicago, IL 60611-4087
Ph: (312)329-8874
For recognition of the most successful realtor in each of the 50 United States, the District of Columbia, Puerto Rico, the Virgin Islands, and Guam. Awarded annually and honored at the national convention of the Association.

★350★ Percy and Betty Wagner Award
Appraisal Institute
875 N. Michigan Ave., Ste. 2400
Chicago, IL 60611-1980
Ph: (312)335-4100 Fax: (312)335-4400
To foster the training of persons in the science of real estate appraising and related subjects; to encourage improvements of appraisal techniques; to provide for needed research in the field of real estate valuation; to award scholarships to deserving students interested in the study of real estate valuation and related subjects; to give recognition to authors of published articles, writings, papers, or the like that enhance or advance education and knowledge in appraising; and for any other purpose that the Trustees deem worthy to improve the image of the professional appraiser or would further the work of the Institute. A monetary award of $1,000 and a plaque are presented at the January meeting. Established in 1972 in honor of Percy Wagner for his lifelong dedication to real estate and appraisal education, and for the support provided by his wife Betty.

Basic Reference Guides and Handbooks

★351★ *ASA Business Valuation Review*
American Society of Appraisers (ASA)
PO Box 17265
Washington, DC 20041
Ph: (703)478-2228 Fax: (703)742-8471
Fr: 800-ASA-VALU
Quarterly.

★352★ *How to Succeed As a Real Estate Salesperson: A Comprehensive Training Guide*
Betterway Publications, Inc.
Box 219
Crozet, VA 22932
Ph: (804)823-5661
Lowell Hodgkings. 1990.

★353★ *Retirement Housing: Step by Step Guide for Investors, Developers, Accountants, & Other Professionals*
John Wiley and Sons, Inc.
605 3rd Ave.
New York, NY 10158-0012
Ph: (212)850-6000 Fax: (212)850-6088
Fr: 800-526-5368
Laughlin. 1989. Part of Real Estate for Professional Practitioners Series.

Periodicals

★354★ *The Appraisal Journal*
Appraisal Institute
875 N. Michigan Ave., Ste. 2400
Chicago, IL 60611-1980
Ph: (312)335-4100 Fax: (312)335-4400
Jennifer Roberts
Quarterly. Real estate appraisal journal.

★355★ *The Appraisal Review*
National Assn. of Independent Fee Appraisers
7501 Murdoch Ave.
St. Louis, MO 63119
Ph: (314)781-6688 Fax: (314)781-2872
Donna Walter

★356★ *Appraiser Gram*
National Association of Independent Fee Appraisers
7501 Murdoch
St. Louis, MO 63119
Ph: (314)781-6689
Donna J. Walter
Monthly. Publishes information of interest to real estate appraisers, including news of Association activities.

★357★ *Appraiser News*
Appraisal Institute
875 N. Michigan Ave., Ste. 2400
Chicago, IL 60611-1980
Ph: (312)335-4100 Fax: (312)335-4400
Grace Hayek
Monthly. Covers current news and trends in the real estate appraisal field.

★358★ *Business Valuation Review*
American Society of Appraisers (ASA)
PO Box 17265
Washington, DC 20041
Ph: (703)478-2228 Fax: (703)742-8471
Fr: 800-ASA-VALU
Quarterly.

★359★ *Commercial Investment Real Estate Journal*
Commercial Investment Real Estate Institute
430 N. Michigan Ave., Ste. 600, 6th Fl.
Chicago, IL 60611-4092
Ph: (312)321-4470 Fax: (312)321-4530
Lorene Norton Palm
Quarterly. Professional development magazine for commercial and investment realtors and allied professionals.

★360★ *Commercial Real Estate Digest*
Vestal Communications
334 Humphrey Dr.
Evergreen, CO 80439
Ph: (303)674-0501 Fr: 800-776-4515
Robert Vestal, Contact
Quarterly. Furnishes those involved in commercial, industrial or investment real estate to localize and print unlimited quantities for distribution to client base. Provides trends and new ideas for real estate investors, users, and developers.

★361★ *The Commercial Record*
435 Buckland Rd.
South Windsor, CT 06074-0902
Ph: (203)644-3489 Fax: (203)644-7363
Vincent M. Valvo
Weekly. Real estate and financial newspaper.

★362★ *Corporate Real Estate Executive*
NACORE
440 Columbia Dr., Ste. 100
West Palm Beach, FL 33409-6685
Ph: (407)683-8111 Fax: (407)697-4853
Kathleen B. Dempsey
Real estate magazine.

★363★ *The Corridor Real Estate Journal*
The Adler Group, Inc.
8601 Georgia Ave., 4th Fl.
Silver Spring, MD 20910
Ph: (301)588-0681 Fax: (301)588-6314
Heidi Daniel
Weekly. Commercial real estate journal for managers and property owners of offices, retail and industrial space, and multi-family residential units.

★364★ *Journal of Appraisal Review*
American Society of Appraisers (ASA)
PO Box 17265
Washington, DC 20041
Ph: (703)478-2228 Fax: (703)742-8471
Fr: 800-ASA-VALU
Semiannual.

★365★ *Journal of Property Management*
Institute of Real Estate Management
430 N. Michigan Ave.
Chicago, IL 60611
Ph: (312)661-1930 Fax: (312)661-0217
Mariwyn Evans
Bimonthly. Magazine serving real estate managers.

★366★ *Journal of Real Estate Taxation*
Warren, Gorham and Lamont, Inc.
1 Penn Plaza
New York, NY 10119
Ph: (212)971-5000 Fax: (212)971-5025
Eugene Krader
Quarterly. Quarterly journal that updates the reader on the latest real estate tax developments and provides guidance for handling changes due to tax reform. Regular features include: Tax Workshop, The Institutional Investor, Tax Shelters, Condominiums and Cooperatives, The Partnership Corner, Tas Free Real Estate Exchanges, and Recent Casings and Rulings.

★367★ *Journal of Technical Valuation*
American Society of Appraisers (ASA)
PO Box 17265
Washington, DC 20041
Ph: (703)478-2228 Fax: (703)742-8471
Fr: 800-ASA-VALU
3/year.

★368★ *Machinery and Equipment Appraiser*
American Society of Appraisers (ASA)
PO Box 17265
Washington, DC 20041
Ph: (703)478-2228 Fax: (703)742-8471
Fr: 800-ASA-VALU
Quarterly.

★369★ *National Real Estate Investor*
Argus Business
6151 Powers Ferry Rd. NW
Atlanta, GA 30339-2941
Ph: (404)955-2500 Fax: 800-955-0400
Paula Stephens
Monthly. Magazine on real estate investment, development and management.

★370★ *National Relocation & Real Estate*
The Relocation Information Service, Inc.
113 E. Post Rd., No. 2
Westport, CT 06880-3410
Ph: (203)227-3800 Fax: (203)227-7108
Peter S. Featherston
Bimonthly. Trade magazine focusing on the real estate and corporate relocation markets.

★371★ *New Homes Magazine*
MDM Publications
3151 Airway Ave., Ste. D-2
Costa Mesa, CA 92626
Ph: (714)751-5813 Fax: (714)755-5500
Jim Trumbull
Bimonthly. Real estate magazine.

★372★ *Newsline*
American Society of Appraisers (ASA)
PO Box 17265
Washington, DC 20041
Ph: (703)478-2228 Fax: (703)742-8471
Fr: 800-ASA-VALU
Monthly.

★373★ *Personal Property Journal*
American Society of Appraisers (ASA)
PO Box 17265
Washington, DC 20041
Ph: (703)478-2228 Fax: (703)742-8471
Fr: 800-ASA-VALU
Quarterly.

★374★ *Prime Real Estate*
Prime Publishing Co.
123 W. Padre St., No. B
Santa Barbara, CA 93105-3960
Michael Colin
Bimonthly. Magazine featuring displays of luxury residential property ($500,000 and up) for sale; including feature editorials on exclusive towns, neighborhoods, and resort areas where homes are located.

★375★ *Real Estate Business*
PO Box 300
Wheaton, IL 60189
Ph: (708)752-0500 Fax: (708)752-0525
Pierce HollingsworthPublisher
Quarterly. Trade magazine for real estate brokers and residential sales personnel.

★376★ *The Real Estate Entrepreneur*
Real Estate Entrepreneur
PO Box 13246
Reading, PA 19612
Ph: (610)371-9977
Bryan Wittenmyer
Monthly. Focuses on the buying, selling, and renting of smaller investment properties. Provides a how-to format for persons interested in starting their own real estate business. Recurring features include news of educational opportunities and book reviews.

★377★ *Real Estate Finance*
Federal Research Press
210 Lincoln St.
Boston, MA 02111
Ph: (617)423-0978
Barbara Grzincic
Quarterly. Journal covering commercial and industrial real estate finance for lenders, investors, and developers.

★378★ *The Real Estate Finance Journal*
Warren, Gorham and Lamont, Inc.
1 Penn Plaza
New York, NY 10119
Ph: (212)971-5000 Fax: (212)971-5025
William Zucker
Quarterly. Magazine contains articles by industry practitioners on new financing techniques, case studies, issues of interest to the real estate industry, as well as general columns.

★379★ *Real Estate Finance Today*
The Mortgage Bankers Assn. of America
1125 15th St. NW
Washington, DC 20005
Ph: (202)861-6500 Fax: (202)872-0186
Leah R. Young
Biweekly. Tabloid tracing economic trends and government actions that affect mortgage lenders.

★380★ *Real Estate Forum*
Better Buildings New York
12 W. 37th St.
New York, NY 10018
Ph: (212)563-6460 Fax: (212)967-1498
Michael Desiato
Monthly. Magazine providing national coverage of real estate investment and development news.

★381★ *Real Estate News*
2600 W. Peterson Ave.
Chicago, IL 60659
Ph: (312)465-5151 Fax: (312)465-7218
Steven N. Polydoris

★382★ *Real Estate Outlook*
National Association of Realtors (NAR)
430 N. Michigan Ave.
Chicago, IL 60611
Ph: (312)329-8200 Fax: (312)329-8576
Monthly.

★383★ *Real Estate Record and Builders Guide*
TRW Ready
475 5th Ave., Ste. 1901
New York, NY 10017
Ph: (212)532-2705
Venice Kelly
Weekly. Real estate reports magazine.

★384★ *Real Estate Review*
Warren, Gorham and Lamont, Inc.
1 Penn Plaza
New York, NY 10119
Ph: (212)971-5000 Fax: (212)971-5025
Norman Weinberg
Quarterly. Real estate magazine.

★385★ *Real Estate Today*
National Association of Realtors (NAR)
430 N. Michigan Ave.
Chicago, IL 60611
Ph: (312)329-8200 Fax: (312)329-8576
Provides information and ideas for those in residential, brokerage, management, and commercial investment real estate.

★386★ *Real Estate Weekly*
Hagedorn Communications
1 Madison Ave., Ste. 35A
New York, NY 10010
Ph: (212)679-1234 Fax: (212)689-2267
Charles G. Hagedorn
Weekly. Real estate newspaper.

★387★ *Real Estate West*
Grier & Co.
825 E. Speer Blvd., Ste.300
Denver, CO 80218
Ph: (303)744-6692
Marti Kelle
Bimonthly. Magazine (tabloid) for corporate real estate executives, developers, building owners and managers, commercial and industrial retail brokers, investors, appraisers, and financial institutions.

★388★ *Real Property Journal*
American Society of Appraisers (ASA)
PO Box 17265
Washington, DC 20041
Ph: (703)478-2228 Fax: (703)742-8471
Fr: 800-ASA-VALU

★389★ *Realtor News*
National Association of Realtors (NAR)
430 N. Michigan Ave.
Chicago, IL 60611
Ph: (312)329-8200 Fax: (312)329-8576
Biweekly.

★390★ *Realtor News (All Member Issue)*
National Assn. of Realtors
777 14th St. NW
Washington, DC 20005
Ph: (202)383-1193 Fax: (202)383-1231
Marjorie GreenPublisher
Monthly. Real estate newspaper.

★391★ *Realtor News-Broker Issue*
National Assn. of Realtors
777 14th St. NW
Washington, DC 20005-3271
Ph: (202)383-1193 Fax: (202)383-1231
Marjorie Green
Monthly. Real estate newspaper.

★392★ *REALTORS Land Institute*
National Assn. of Realtors
430 N. Michigan Ave.
Chicago, IL 60611
Ph: (312)329-8446
J. Gregory Wiezorek
Newsletter and journal.

★393★ *Realty*
Leader-Observer, Inc.
80-34 Jamaica Ave.
Wood Haven, NY 11421
Ph: (718)296-2200
Lester Sobel
Semiweekly. Real estate trade newspaper.

★394★ *Right of Way*
International Right of Way Assn.
13650 Gramercy Pl.
Gardena, CA 90249
Ph: (310)538-0233 Fax: (310)538-1471
Ken Rose
Bimonthly. Trade magazine offering technical articles on right of way management and acquisition, real estate appraisal, and property management.

★395★ *S/F (Square Foot)*
Mass Tech Times, Inc.
500 W. Cummings Pk., Ste. 3500
Woburn, MA 01801-6514
Ph: (617)935-1100 Fax: (617)935-0308
Douglas GreenPublisher
Bimonthly. Real estate magazine.

★396★ *Southeast Real Estate News*
Communication Channels, Inc.
6255 Barfield Rd.
Atlanta, GA 30328
Ph: (404)256-9800 Fax: (404)256-3116
Coles McKagen
Monthly. Magazine covering commercial and industrial real estate transactions.

★397★ *Southwest Real Estate News*
Communication Channels, Inc.
310 E. Interstate 30, Ste. 240
Garland, TX 75043-4047
Ph: (214)226-1339 Fax: (214)226-5884
James Mitchell
Bimonthly. Commercial real estate tabloid.

★398★ *Subject Headings for Real Estate*
National Association of Realtors (NAR)
430 N. Michigan Ave.
Chicago, IL 60611
Ph: (312)329-8200 Fax: (312)329-8576

★399★ *Tabloid*
Homefinders, inc.
729-122nd Ave. N E
Bellevue, WA 98005
Ph: (206)451-1360 Fax: (206)451-1321
Jack H. HinshawPresident
Monthly. Newspaper focusing on real estate information.

★400★ *Tierra Grande*
Real Estate Center
Texas A&M University
College Station, TX 77843-2115
Ph: (409)845-0369 Fax: (409)845-0460
Fr: 800-244-2144
David S. Jones
Quarterly. Journal covering real estate research.

★401★ *Valuation Journal*
American Society of Appraisers (ASA)
PO Box 17265
Washington, DC 20041
Ph: (703)478-2228 Fax: (703)742-8471
Fr: 800-ASA-VALU
Semiannual.

Meetings and Conventions

★402★ American Real Estate and Investment Show
Miller Marketing Network Ltd.
119 W. 57th St.
New York, NY 10019
Ph: (212)247-6060 Fax: (212)586-5446
Annual. **Dates and Locations:** 1995; Berlin • 1996; New York, NY.

★403★ National Association of Realtors Midyear Trade Exposition
National Association of Realtors
430 N. Michigan Ave.
Chicago, IL 60611
Ph: (312)329-8491 Fax: (312)645-7747
Annual. Always held during April at the Sheraton in Washington, D.C. Annual meeting changes location yearly. **Dates and Locations:** 1996 Apr 26-01; Washington, DC. • 1997 Apr 16-21; Washington, DC. • 1998 Apr 24-29; Washington, DC.

★404★ National Association of Review Appraisers and Mortgage Underwriters Convention
National Association of Review Appraisers and Mortgage Underwriters
8383 E. Evans Rd.
Scottsdale, AZ 85260
Ph: (602)998-3000 Fax: (602)998-8022
Annual.

Other Sources of Information

★405★ "Real Estate Agent/Broker" in *100 Best Jobs for the 1990s & Beyond*
Dearborn Financial Publishing, Inc.
520 N. Dearborn St.
Chicago, IL 60610-4354
Ph: (312)836-4400 Fax: (312)836-1021
Fr: 800-621-9621
Carol Kleiman. 1992. Describes 100 jobs ranging from accountants to veterinarians. Each job profile includes such information as education, experience, and certification needed, salaries, and job search suggestions.

★406★ "Real Estate Sales Agent" in *Career Selector 2001*
Barron's Educational Series, Inc.
250 Wireless Blvd.
Hauppauge, NY 11788
Ph: (516)434-3311 Fax: (516)434-3723
Fr: 800-645-3476
James C. Gonyea. 1993.

Retail Sales Workers

Retail sales workers are employed by virtually every type of retailer to assist customers in the selection and purchase of merchandise. A sales worker's primary job is to interest customers in the product by describing its construction, demonstrating its use, or showing various models or colors. Most retail sales workers also make out sales checks; receive cash, check, and charge payments; and give change and receipts. They may also handle returns and exchanges, perform gift wrapping services, and monitor inventory. A knowledge of the store's policies, procedures, and promotions is essential, in addition to familiarity with the store's security practices. With increased competition and heavy emphasis on pleasing the customer, a store's sales force becomes more important. Sales workers must offer superior service, ensuring customer satisfaction.

Salaries

Compensation systems vary by type of establishment and merchandise being sold. Some sales workers receive salary plus commissions, others are paid only on a salary or commission basis. The starting wage for many part-time positions is the Federal minimum wage, $4.25 per hour.

Employment Outlook

Growth rate until the year 2005: Average.

Retail Sales Workers

Career Guides

★407★ ***According to Hoyle***
Commonwealth Films, Inc.
223 Commonwealth Ave.
Boston, MA 02116
Ph: (617)262-5634 Fax: (617)262-6948

Videocassette. 1980. 30 mins. An entire business deal is enacted, from the purchasing of goods to the sales.

★408★ ***All Pro***
BNA Communications, Inc.
9439 Key West Ave.
Rockville, MD 20850
Ph: (301)948-0540 Fax: (301)948-2085
Fr: 800-233-6067

Videocassette. 1981. 29 mins. Conversations with five top sales professionals. They discuss their careers and the traits that make a top professional.

★409★ **"Art Supply Salesperson" in *Career Opportunities in Art* (p. 155)**
Facts on File
460 Park Ave. S.
New York, NY 10016-7382
Ph: (212)683-2244 Fax: 800-678-3633
Fr: 800-322-8755

Susan H. Haubenstock and David Joselit. 1988. Profiles more than 75 art-related jobs. Each occupational profile covers job duties, employment outlook, career paths, salaries, skills, and educational preparation. Offers tips for entering the field.

★410★ **"Auto and Car-Parts Sales Representatives" in *Jobs! What They Are—Where They Are—What They Pay* (pp. 328)**
Simon & Schuster, Inc.
Simon & Schuster Bldg.
1230 Avenue of the Americas
New York, NY 10020
Ph: (212)698-7000

Robert O. Snelling and Anne M. Snelling. Revised edition, 1992. Profiles 241 occupations, describing duties and responsibilities, educational preparation, earnings, employment opportunities, training, and qualifications.

★411★ **"Auto Parts Counter Worker" in *Career Information Center* (Vol.10)**
Simon and Schuster
200 Old Tappan Rd.
Old Tappan, NJ 07675
Fax: 800-445-6991 Fr: 800-223-2348

Richard Lidz and Dale Anderson, editorial directors. Fifth edition, 1993. For 600 occupations, describes job duties, entry-level requirements, education and training needed, advancement possibilities, employment outlook, earnings and benefits. The set is divided into 12 volumes. Each volume includes jobs related under a broad career field. Volume 13 is the index.

★412★ **"Auto Sales Worker" in *Career Information Center* (Vol.10)**
Simon and Schuster
200 Old Tappan Rd.
Old Tappan, NJ 07675
Fax: 800-445-6991 Fr: 800-223-2348

Richard Lidz and Dale Anderson, editorial directors. Fifth edition, 1993. For 600 occupations, describes job duties, entry-level requirements, education and training needed, advancement possibilities, employment outlook, earnings and benefits. The set is divided into 12 volumes. Each volume includes jobs related under a broad career field. Volume 13 is the index.

★413★ **"Automobile Sales Workers" in *Career Discovery Encyclopedia* (Vol.1, pp. 92-93)**
J.G. Ferguson Publishing Co.
200 W. Madison St., Ste. 300
Chicago, IL 60606
Ph: (312)580-5480 Fax: (312)580-4948

E. Russell Primm, editor-in-chief. 1993. Contains two-page articles on 504 occupations. Each article describes job duties, earnings, and educational and training requirements.

★414★ **"Automobile Sales Workers" in *Encyclopedia of Careers and Vocational Guidance* (Vol.2, pp. 145-147)**
J.G. Ferguson Publishing Co.
200 W. Madison St., Ste. 300
Chicago, IL 60606
Ph: (312)580-5480 Fax: (312)580-4948

William E. Hopke, editor-in-chief. Ninth edition, 1993. Four-volume set that profiles 500 occupations and describes job trends in 74 industries. Includes career description, educational requirements, history of the job, methods of entry, advancement, employment outlook, earnings, working conditions, social and psychological factors, and sources of additional information.

★415★ ***Automobile Salespeople***
Chronicle Guidance Publications, Inc.
66 Aurora St.
PO Box 1190
Moravia, NY 13118-1190
Ph: (315)497-0330 Fax: (315)497-3359
Fr: 800-622-7284

1991. This career brief describes the nature of the work, working conditions, hours and earnings, education and training, licensure, certification, unions, personal qualifications, social and psychological factors, employment outlook, entry methods, advancement, and related occupations.

★416★ **"Automobile Salesperson" in *College Board Guide to Jobs and Career Planning* (pp. 132-134)**
College Entrance Examination Board
45 Columbus Ave.
New York, NY 10023-6992
Ph: (212)713-8000

Joyce Slayton Mitchell. 1990. Career planning guide written for high school and college students. Covers 100 careers in 15 occupational groups. Provides job description, educational preparation needed, salaries, related careers, and sources of additional information. Includes information about the 90's labor market.

★417★ **"Automotive Parts Specialists" in *Opportunities in Automotive Service Careers* (pp. 39-44)**
National Textbook Co. (NTC)
VGM Career Books
4255 W. Touhy Ave.
Lincolnwood, IL 60646-1975
Ph: (708)679-5500 Fax: (708)679-2494
Fr: 800-323-4900

Robert M. Weber. 1989. Describes the work of the automobile mechanic and related occupations such as service station attendant and automobile body repairer. Covers working conditions, places of employment, qualifications, training, apprenticeships, certification, advancement opportunities, employment outlook, tools needed, and earnings.

★418★ *Basic Retail Selling Skills*
United Learning, Inc.
6633 West Howard St.
PO Box 48718
Niles, IL 60714
Ph: (708)647-0600 Fax: (708)647-0918
Fr: 800-424-0362

Videocassette. 1984. 14 mins. This video, originally developed for Walgreens, stresses the basics of selling goods in the retail marketplace.

★419★ *Basic Retail Selling Skills*
American Media, Inc.
4900 University Ave., Ste. 100
West Des Moines, IA 50266-6769
Ph: (515)224-0919 Fax: (515)224-0256
Fr: 800-262-2557

Videocassette. 1988. 26 mins. A step-by-step approach that will improve the performance of a sales team.

★420★ "Career Profile: Interview with a Personal Computer Salesman" in *Exploring Careers in the Computer Field* (pp. 95-101)
Rosen Publishing Group
29 E. 21st St.
New York, NY 10010
Ph: (212)777-3017 Fax: (212)777-0277
Fr: 800-237-9932

Joseph Weintraub. 1990. Surveys the newest growth areas in the computer industry including artificial intelligence, desktop publishing, and personal computers. Discusses entry into the field, salaries, future trends and offers job search advice. Contains interviews with five people who describe their real-life experiences working in computer related jobs. Lists organizations and colleges.

★421★ *Career Success Series*
Cambridge Educational
PO Box 2153
Charleston, WV 25328-2153
Ph: (304)744-9323 Fax: (304)744-9351
Fr: 800-468-4227

Videocassette. 1986. 15 mins. A series, available separately, outlining various career choices for students. Occupations include: accounting, flight service, air transportation/ground/flight service, data processing, carpentry, clerk in banking/insurance, commodity sales, cosmetic personal grooming, fire fighting, forestry services, home economics, insulation/roofing, material handling, mechanics, photographic processing, pipefitting and plumbing, police science, printing, carpentry, medical laboratory technicians, secretarial services, and utilities equipment operator.

★422★ *Careers in a Department Store*
Lerner Publications Co.
241 First Ave., N.
Minneapolis, MN 55401
Fax: (612)332-7615 Fr: 800-328-4920

Jennifer Brooks Dean. 1973. Describes the varied careers possible in a department store including sales clerk, sales manager, and many others.

★423★ *Careers in Fashion Retailing*
Rosen Publishing Group
29 E. 21st St.
New York, NY 10010
Ph: (212)777-3017 Fax: (212)777-0277
Fr: 800-237-9932

Pat Koester. 1990. Describes fashion retailing, industry structure, career paths, and typical jobs such as sales, management, and buying. Profiles persons working in the field and discusses educational preparation. Lists schools that offer programs in fashion retailing.

★424★ "Department Store Retailing" in *Encyclopedia of Career Choices for the 1990s: A Guide to Entry Level Jobs* (pp. 252-272)
Berkley Pub.
PO Box 506
East Rutherford, NJ 07073
Fax: (201)933-2316 Fr: 800-788-6262

1992. Describes entry-level opportunities in 42 career fields for college graduates. Each chapter covers a single career field, including an overview, employment outlook, major employers, tips on entering the field, international job opportunities, functional job areas with personal and professional qualifications, career paths, job responsibilities, advancement possibilities, salaries, and working conditions. Lists related sources of information.

★425★ "Direct Sales Worker" in *Career Information Center* (Vol.10)
Simon and Schuster
200 Old Tappan Rd.
Old Tappan, NJ 07675
Fax: 800-445-6991 Fr: 800-223-2348

Richard Lidz and Dale Anderson, editorial directors. Fifth edition, 1993. For 600 occupations, describes job duties, entry-level requirements, education and training needed, advancement possibilities, employment outlook, earnings and benefits. The set is divided into 12 volumes. Each volume includes jobs related under a broad career field. Volume 13 is the index.

★426★ *Direct Selling: An Income Opportunity for You*
Direct Selling Association
1776 K St. NW, Ste. 600
Washington, DC 20006
Ph: (202)293-5760

1987. This eight-panel brochure describes the nature of direct selling and skills required to succeed.

★427★ "Door to Door Sales Workers" in *Encyclopedia of Careers and Vocational Guidance* (Vol.2, pp. 502-505)
J.G. Ferguson Publishing Co.
200 W. Madison St., Ste. 300
Chicago, IL 60606
Ph: (312)580-5480 Fax: (312)580-4948

William E. Hopke, editor-in-chief. Ninth edition, 1993. Four-volume set that profiles 500 occupations and describes job trends in 74 industries. Includes career description, educational requirements, history of the job, methods of entry, advancement, employment outlook, earnings, working conditions, social and psychological factors, and sources of additional information.

★428★ "Door-to-Door Sales Workers" in *Career Discovery Encyclopedia* (Vol.2, pp. 120-121)
J.G. Ferguson Publishing Co.
200 W. Madison St., Ste. 300
Chicago, IL 60606
Ph: (312)580-5480 Fax: (312)580-4948

E. Russell Primm, editor-in-chief. 1993. Contains two-page articles on 504 occupations. Each article describes job duties, earnings, and educational and training requirements.

★429★ *Exploring Careers in Computer Sales*
Rosen Publishing Group
29 E. 21st St.
New York, NY 10010
Ph: (212)777-3017 Fax: (212)777-0277
Fr: 800-237-9932

Lawrence Epstein. 1990. Part of Career Series.

★430★ *Fact Sheet: Facts About Direct Selling*
Direct Selling Association
1776 K St. NW, Ste. 600
Washington, DC 20006
Ph: (202)293-5760

1987. This two-page leaflet describes the industry, the jobs of salespeople, customers, and products.

★431★ "Health and Fitness Retail Sales" in *Careers in Health and Fitness* (pp. 71-73)
Rosen Publishing Group
29 E. 21st St.
New York, NY 10010
Ph: (212)777-3017 Fax: (212)777-0277
Fr: 800-237-9932

Jackie Heron. 1990. Describes careers related to sports and fitness. Covers job duties, pros and cons, equipment used, employment outlook, educational preparation, certification, licensing, and salaries.

★432★ "Music Shop Salesperson" in *Career Opportunities in the Music Industry* (pp. 89-90)
Facts on File
460 Park Ave. S.
New York, NY 10016-7382
Ph: (212)683-2244 Fax: 800-678-3633
Fr: 800-322-8755

Shelly Field. Second edition, 1991. Describes more than 70 music related jobs. Each occupational profile covers job duties, employment outlook, career paths, salaries, skills, and educational preparation. Offers tips for entering the field.

★433★ *Musical Instrument Salesperson*
Vocational Biographies, Inc.
PO Box 31
Sauk Centre, MN 56378-0031
Ph: (612)352-6516 Fax: (612)352-5546
Fr: 800-255-0752

1990. This pamphlet profiles a person working in the job. Includes information about job duties, working conditions, places of employment, educational preparation, labor market outlook, and salaries.

★434★ "Personal Computer Salesperson" in *Straight Talk on Careers: 80 Pros Take You Into Their Professions* (pp. 8-10)
Garrett Park Press
PO Box 1907
Garrett Park, MD 20896
Ph: (301)946-2553

Mary Barbera-Hogan. 1987. Written for readers in high school and college. Contains candid interviews from professionals who discuss what their days are like and the pros and cons of their occupations.

★435★ "Record Shop Clerk" in *Career Opportunities in the Music Industry* (pp. 93-94)
Facts on File
460 Park Ave. S.
New York, NY 10016-7382
Ph: (212)683-2244 Fax: 800-678-3633
Fr: 800-322-8755

Shelly Field. Second edition, 1991. Describes more than 70 music related jobs. Each occupational profile covers job duties, employment outlook, career paths, salaries, skills, and educational preparation. Offers tips for entering the field.

★436★ "Retail Industry" in *Footsteps in the Ocean: Careers in Diving* (pp. 37-42)
Lodestar Books
2 Park Avenue
New York, NY 10016
Ph: (212)725-1818 Fax: (212)532-6568

Denise V. Lang. 1987. Explores employment opportunities in sport and commercial diving, science and research, in the military, and police work. Describes the work and training. Lists schools.

★437★ "Retail" in *Internships 1995*
Petersons Guides, Inc.
PO Box 2123
Princeton, NJ 08543-2123
Ph: (609)243-9111 Fr: 800-338-3282

Fifteenth edition, 1995. Lists internship opportunities under six broad categories: communications, creative, performing, and fine arts, human services, international relations, business and technology, and public affairs. For each internship program, gives the names, phone number, contact person, description, eligibility requirements, and benefits.

★438★ "Retail Sales" in *Careers in Marketing* (pp. 66-68)
National Textbook Co. (NTC)
VGM Career Books
4255 W. Touhy Ave.
Lincolnwood, IL 60646-1975
Ph: (708)679-5500 Fax: (708)679-2494
Fr: 800-323-4900

Lila B. Stair. 1991. Surveys career opportunities in marketing and related areas such as marketing research, product development, and sales promotion. Includes a description of the work, place of employment, employment outlook, trends, educational preparation, organizational charts, and salaries. Offers job hunting advice.

★439★ *Retail Sales Power*
Professional Development, Inc.
27955 Clemens Rd.
Westlake, OH 44145
Ph: (216)892-0770 Fax: (216)892-0105

Videocassette. 1986. 30 mins. A two-part program for retail clerks, dealing with customer relations, theft and business decisions.

★440★ "Retail Sales Worker" in *Career Discovery Encyclopedia* (Vol.5, pp. 152-153)
J.G. Ferguson Publishing Co.
200 W. Madison St., Ste. 300
Chicago, IL 60606
Ph: (312)580-5480 Fax: (312)580-4948

E. Russell Primm, editor-in-chief. 1993. Contains two-page articles on 504 occupations. Each article describes job duties, earnings, and educational and training requirements.

★441★ "Retail Sales Worker" in *VGM's Careers Encyclopedia* (pp. 409-411)
National Textbook Co. (NTC)
VGM Career Books
4255 W. Touhy Ave.
Lincolnwood, IL 60646-1975
Ph: (708)679-5500 Fax: (708)679-2494
Fr: 800-323-4900

Third edition, 1991. Contains two- to five-page descriptions of 200 managerial, professional, technical, trade, and service occupations. Each profile includes job duties, places of employment, qualifications, educational preparation, training, employment potential, advancement, income, and additional sources of information.

★442★ "Retail Sales Workers" in *Encyclopedia of Careers and Vocational Guidance* (Vol.4, pp. 297-300)
J.G. Ferguson Publishing Co.
200 W. Madison St., Ste. 300
Chicago, IL 60606
Ph: (312)580-5480 Fax: (312)580-4948

William E. Hopke, editor-in-chief. Ninth edition, 1993. Four-volume set that profiles 500 occupations and describes job trends in 74 industries. Includes career description, educational requirements, history of the job, methods of entry, advancement, employment outlook, earnings, working conditions, social and psychological factors, and sources of additional information.

★443★ "Retail Sales Workers" in *Occupational Outlook Handbook*
U.S. Government Printing Office
Superintendent of Documents
Washington, DC 20402
Ph: (202)512-1800 Fax: (202)512-2250

Biennial; latest edition, 1994-95. Encyclopedia of careers describing more than 250 occupations and comprising about 85 percent of all jobs in the economy. Occupations that require lengthy education or training are given the most attention. For each occupation, the handbook describes job duties, working conditions, training, educational preparation, personal qualities, advancement possibilities, job outlook, earnings, and sources of additional information.

★444★ "Retail Sales Workers" in *Opportunities in Vocational and Technical Careers* (pp. 59-75)
National Textbook Co. (NTC)
VGM Career Books
4255 W. Touhy Ave.
Lincolnwood, IL 60646-1975
Ph: (708)679-5500 Fax: (708)679-2494
Fr: 800-323-4900

Adrian A. Paradis. 1992. Describes careers which can be prepared for by attending a private vocational or proprietary school—office employee, sales worker, service worker, health services, mechanic, craftworker, and technician. Covers employment outlook, job duties, and salaries. Offers career planning advice.

★445★ "Retail Salespeople" in *Jobs! What They Are—Where They Are—What They Pay* (pp. 323)
Simon & Schuster, Inc.
Simon & Schuster Bldg.
1230 Avenue of the Americas
New York, NY 10020
Ph: (212)698-7000

Robert O. Snelling and Anne M. Snelling. Revised edition, 1992. Profiles 241 occupations, describing duties and responsibilities, educational preparation, earnings, employment opportunities, training, and qualifications.

★446★ "Retail Store Sales Worker" in *Career Information Center* (Vol.10)
Simon and Schuster
200 Old Tappan Rd.
Old Tappan, NJ 07675
Fax: 800-445-6991 Fr: 800-223-2348

Richard Lidz and Dale Anderson, editorial directors. Fifth edition, 1993. For 600 occupations, describes job duties, entry-level requirements, education and training needed, advancement possibilities, employment outlook, earnings and benefits. The set is divided into 12 volumes. Each volume includes jobs related under a broad career field. Volume 13 is the index.

★447★ *Retailing & Merchandising*
Morris Video
2730 Monterey St., No. 105
Monterey Business Park
Torrance, CA 90503
Ph: (213)533-4800 Fr: 800-843-3606

Videocassette. 1987. 15 mins. A look at the variety of career opportunities available in the world of retail.

★448★ "Sales" in *Where the Jobs Are: The Hottest Careers for the 90s* (pp. 221-244)
Career Press
180 5th Ave.
Hawthorne, NJ 07507
Ph: (201)427-0229 Fax: (201)427-2037
Fr: 800-CAREER-1

Joyce Hadley. 1995. Offers a job-hunting strategy for the 1990s as well as descriptions of growing careers of the decade. Each profile includes general information, forecasts, growth, education and training, licensing requirements, and salary information.

★449★ "Salesclerk" in *Guide to Careers Without College* (pp. 20-21)
Franklin Watts, Inc.
387 Park Avenue, S.
New York, NY 10016
Ph: (212)686-7070

Kathleen S. Abrams. 1988. Discusses careers that do not require a college degree in fields such as health care, sales and marketing, and the building trades. Describes the work, employment opportunities, and training.

★450★ *Salespeople, Household Appliances*
Chronicle Guidance Publications, Inc.
66 Aurora St.
PO Box 1190
Moravia, NY 13118-1190
Ph: (315)497-0330 Fax: (315)497-3359
Fr: 800-622-7284

1993. This career brief describes the nature of the work, working conditions, hours and earnings, education and training, licensure, certification, unions, personal qualifications, social and psychological factors, employment outlook, entry methods, advancement, and related occupations.

★451★ *Salespeople, Retail*
Chronicle Guidance Publications, Inc.
66 Aurora St.
PO Box 1190
Moravia, NY 13118-1190
Ph: (315)497-0330 Fax: (315)497-3359
Fr: 800-622-7284

1993. This career brief describes the nature of the work, working conditions, hours and earnings, education and training, licensure, certification, unions, personal qualifications, social and psychological factors, employment outlook, entry methods, advancement, and related occupations.

★452★ "Salesperson" in *100 Best Careers for the Year 2000* (pp. 185-187)
Arco Pub.
201 W. 103rd St.
Indianapolis, IN 46290
Ph: 800-428-5331 Fax: 800-835-3202

Shelly Field. 1992. Describes 100 job opportunities expected to grow fast throughout the next decade. Provides information on job duties and responsibilities, training requirements, education, advancement opportunities, experience and qualifications, and typical salaries.

★453★ *Salesperson, Automobile*
Careers, Inc.
PO Box 135
Largo, FL 34649-0135
Ph: (813)584-7333

1994. Two-page occupational summary card describing duties, working conditions, personal qualifications, training, earnings and hours, employment outlook, places of employment, related careers and where to write for more information.

★454★ *Salesperson, Automotive Parts*
Careers, Inc.
PO Box 135
Largo, FL 34649-0135
Ph: (813)584-7333

1991. Two-page occupational summary card describing duties, working conditions, personal qualifications, training, earnings and hours, employment outlook, places of employment, related careers and where to write for more information.

★455★ *Salesperson, Camera Store*
Careers, Inc.
PO Box 135
Largo, FL 34649-0135
Ph: (813)584-7333

1993. Two-page occupational summary card describing duties, working conditions, personal qualifications, training, earnings and hours, employment outlook, places of employment, related careers and where to write for more information.

★456★ *Salesperson, Drugstore*
Careers, Inc.
PO Box 135
Largo, FL 34649-0135
Ph: (813)584-7333

1993. Two-page occupational summary card describing duties, working conditions, personal qualifications, training, earnings and hours, employment outlook, places of employment, related careers and where to write for more information.

★457★ "Salesperson, General Merchandise" in *Museum Jobs form A-Z: What They Are, How to Prepare, and Where to Find Them*
Batax Museum Publishing
301 Racquet Club Rd., Ste. 202
Fort Lauderdale, FL 33326

G.W. Bates. 1994.

★458★ *Salesperson, Grocery Products*
Careers, Inc.
PO Box 135
Largo, FL 34649-0135
Ph: (813)584-7333

1993. Two-page occupational summary card describing duties, working conditions, personal qualifications, training, earnings and hours, employment outlook, places of employment, related careers and where to write for more information.

★459★ *Salesperson, Hardware Store*
Careers, Inc.
PO Box 135
Largo, FL 34649-0135
Ph: (813)584-7333

1994. Two-page occupational summary card describing duties, working conditions, personal qualifications, training, earnings and hours, employment outlook, places of employment, related careers and where to write for more information.

★460★ *Salesperson, Music Store*
Careers, Inc.
PO Box 135
Largo, FL 34649-0135
Ph: (813)584-7333

1991. Two-page occupational summary card describing duties, working conditions, personal qualifications, training, earnings and hours, employment outlook, places of employment, related careers and where to write for more information.

★461★ "Salesperson" in *Occu-Facts: Information on 580 Careers in Outline Form*
Careers, Inc.
PO Box 135
Largo, FL 34649-0135
Ph: (813)584-7333

Biennial, 1995-96 edition. Each one-page occupational profile describes duties, working conditions, physical surroundings and demands, aptitudes, temperament, educational requirements, employment outlook, earnings, and places of employment.

★462★ *Salesperson, Retail*
Careers, Inc.
PO Box 135
Largo, FL 34649-0135
Ph: (813)584-7333

1992. Two-page occupational summary card describing duties, working conditions, personal qualifications, training, earnings and hours, employment outlook, places of employment, related careers and where to write for more information.

★463★ *Selling Direct: Choosing the Right Opportunity*
Direct Selling Association
1776 K St. NW, Ste. 600
Washington, DC 20006
Ph: (202)293-5760

1987. Explains direct selling and offers guidelines for choosing a product to sell.

★464★ *Shoe Salesperson*
Vocational Biographies, Inc.
PO Box 31
Sauk Centre, MN 56378-0031
Ph: (612)352-6516 Fax: (612)352-5546
Fr: 800-255-0752

1991. This pamphlet profiles a person working in the job. Includes information about job duties, working conditions, places of employment, educational preparation, labor market outlook, and salaries.

★465★ *So You Want to Be a Success at Selling?*
Video Arts, Inc.
8614 W Catalpa Ave.
Chicago, IL 60656
Ph: (312)693-9966 Fax: (312)693-7030
Fr: 800-553-0091

Videocassette. 1982. 25 mins. A lesson on the fundamental skills of selling, from the initial research to the close.

★466★ "Sporting Goods Salesperson" in *Career Opportunities in the Sports Industry* (pp. 178-180)
Facts on File
460 Park Ave. S.
New York, NY 10016-7382
Ph: (212)683-2244 Fax: 800-678-3633
Fr: 800-322-8755

Shelly Field. 1991. Describes various jobs in the sports industry. Each occupational profile covers job duties, employment outlook, career paths, salaries, skills, and educational preparation. Offers tips for entering the field.

★467★ *Take this Job and Love It!*
Excellence in Training Corp.
11358 Aurora Ave.
Des Moines, IA 50322-7407
Ph: (515)276-6569 Fax: (515)276-9476
Fr: 800-747-6569

Videocassette. 1987. 9 mins. This video orients and motivates new retail employees.

★468★ *Video Career Library - Marketing and Sales*
Careers, Inc.
PO Box 135
Largo, FL 34649-0135
Ph: (813)584-7333

Videocassette. 1994. Part of the Video Career Library covering 165 occupations. Shows actual workers on the job.

★469★ "Video Sales Clerk" in *Career Opportunities in Television, Cable, and Video* (pp. 194-195)
Facts on File
460 Park Ave. S.
New York, NY 10016-7382
Ph: (212)683-2244 Fax: 800-678-3633
Fr: 800-322-8755

Third edition, 1990. Describes 100 media-related jobs. Each occupational profile covers job duties, employment outlook, career paths, salaries, skills, and educational preparation. Offers tips for entering the field.

★470★ *Your Career in Business-to-Business Direct Marketing*
Direct Marketing Educational Foundation, Inc.
3 E 43rd St.
New York, NY 10017
Ph: (212)689-4977

This 12-page booklet explains business-to-business direct marketing, and lists the types of companies engaged in businesses-to-business direct marketing. Lists career opportunities and offers advice on entry into the field.

Associations

★471★ National Retail Federation (NRF)
325 7th St. NW, Ste. 1000
Washington, DC 20004-2802
Ph: (202)783-7971 Fax: (202)737-2849

Members: Purpose: Represents 50 state retail association, several dozen national retail associations as well as large and small corporate members representing the breadth and diversity of the retail industry's establishment and employees. Conducts informational and educational conferences related to all phases of retailing including financial planning and cash management, taxation, economic forecasting, expense planning, shortage control, credit, electronic data processing, telecommunications, merchandise management, buying, traffic, security, supply, materials handling, store planning and construction, personnel administration, recruitment and training, and advertising and display. **Publications:** *STORES Magazine*, monthly. • *Washington Retail Report*, weekly.

Test Guides

★472★ *Career Examination Series: Sales Store Worker*
National Learning Corp.
212 Michael Dr.
Syosset, NY 11791
Ph: (516)921-8888 Fax: (516)921-8743
Fr: 800-645-6337

Jack Rudman. All examination guides in this series contain questions with answers.

Awards, Scholarships, Grants, and Fellowships

★473★ Gold Medal Award
National Retail Merchants Association
100 W. 31st St.
New York, NY 10001
Ph: (212)244-8780 Fax: (212)594-0487

To recognize an individual for distinguished service to the craft of retailing. An engraved gold medal is awarded annually. Established in 1929.

Basic Reference Guides and Handbooks

★474★ *Modern Retailing: Theory and Practice*
BPI
9605 Scranton Rd., Ste. 503
San Diego, CA 92121-1774
Ph: (619)457-7577 Fax: (619)453-1091

J. Barry Mason, Morris L. Mayer, and J.B. Wilkinson. Sixth edition, 1993.

Periodicals

★475★ *American Salesman*
National Research Bureau, Inc.
200 N. 4th
PO Box 1
Burlington, IA 52601-0001
Ph: (319)752-5415 Fax: (319)752-3421
Barbara Boeding

Monthly. Salesmanship magazine.

★476★ *AudioVideo International*
Dempa Publications, Inc.
275 Madison Ave.
New York, NY 10016
Ph: (212)682-3755 Fax: (212)682-2730
Nancy Klosek

Monthly. Magazine for domestic retailers of consumer electronics products. Feature stories include trends and developments in audio, hi-fi, TV, video, car stereo, and home and personal electronics products.

★477★ *Inside Retailing*
Lebhar-Friedman, Inc.
425 Park Ave.
New York, NY 10022
Ph: (212)756-5017 Fax: (516)935-4958
David Mahler

Biweekly. Provides up-to-date information on what is happening in the retail industry and how current economic conditions affect retailing. Summarizes actions, acquisitions, and policies of major retail chains across the U.S. Discusses problems facing retail operations, i.e., shoplifting and retaining customer loyalty.

★478★ *Personal Selling Power*
Personal Selling Power, Inc.
1127 International Pkwy.
PO Box 5467
Fredericksburg, VA 22403
Ph: (703)752-7000 Fax: (703)752-7001
LB Gschwandtner

Magazine presenting motivational and sales skills and techniques for sales and marketing executives.

★479★ *Retail Info Systems News*
Edgell Enterprises, Inc.
PO Box K
Milford, PA 18337
Ph: (717)296-8330 Fax: (717)296-8350

★480★ *Retailing News*
Retailing News Co.
14962 Bear Valley Rd., Ste. 288
Victorville, CA 92392-4236
Ph: (619)241-2514 Fax: (619)241-3595
Martin Barsky

Monthly. Trade magazine reaching dealers, retailers, manufacturers, manufacturing reps, and distributors in the consumer electronics and major appliance industries.

★481★ *RWDSU Record*
Retail, Wholesale and Dept. Store Union-AFL-CIO
30 E. 29th St.
New York, NY 10016
Ph: (212)684-5300 Fax: (212)779-2809
Stuart Appelbeum

Bimonthly. Labor union newspaper.

★482★ *Salesman's Insider*
Marv. Q. Modell Associates
6009 Montgomery Corner
San Jose, CA 95135-1431
Ph: (408)270-4526
Marv. Q. Modell

Monthly. Concerned with selling techniques and methodology in all sales areas. Tracks new sales developments, trends, and profit opportunities. Details negotiating process; offers "tips that work."

★483★ *Salesmanship*
Dartnell Corporation
4660 Ravenswood
Chicago, IL 60640
Ph: (312)561-4000 Fax: (312)561-3801
Fr: 800-621-5463
Terry Breen

Biweekly. Offers sales ideas and inspiration, profiles of top-producing salespeople, and articles on topics related to sales success.

★484★ *STORES Magazine*
National Retail Federation (NRF)
325 7th St. NW, Ste. 1000
Washington, DC 20004-2802
Ph: (202)783-7971 Fax: (202)737-2849

Monthly. Provides retail executives and other retail personnel with information on current trends, concepts, and promotional innovations in retail.

★485★ *Supply House Times*
Cahners Publishing Co.
1350 E. Touhy Ave.
PO Box 5080
Des Plaines, IL 60017-5080
Ph: (708)635-8800 Fax: (708)390-2618
Bill EverhamPublisher

Monthly. Trade magazine for wholesalers in plumbing, heating, cooling, piping, and water systems. Areas of major emphasis include: warehousing, materials handling, inventory control, accounting, data processing, merchandising, salesmanship and general management.

★486★ *Washington Retail Report*
National Retail Federation (NRF)
325 7th St. NW, Ste. 1000
Washington, DC 20004-2802
Ph: (202)783-7971 Fax: (202)737-2849

Weekly. Covers federal legislative and regulatory issues.

Meetings and Conventions

★487★ Southern Apparel Exhibitors Shows
Southern Apparel Exhibitors, Inc.
Miami International Merchandise Mart
777 NW 72nd Ave., Ste. Lobby 18
Miami, FL 33126
Ph: (305)261-2021 Fax: (305)267-0513

Five times per year. Always held at the Miami Mart and Radisson Center in Miami, Florida.

Other Sources of Information

★488★ "Retail Salesperson" in *100 Best Jobs for the 1990s & Beyond*
Dearborn Financial Publishing, Inc.
520 N. Dearborn St.
Chicago, IL 60610-4354
Ph: (312)836-4400 Fax: (312)836-1021
Fr: 800-621-9621

Carol Kleiman. 1992. Describes 100 jobs ranging from accountants to veterinarians. Each job profile includes such information as education, experience, and certification needed, salaries, and job search suggestions.

★489★ *Who's Who in Direct Selling*
Direct Selling Association
1776 K St. NW, Ste. 600
Washington, DC 20006
Ph: (202)293-5760

1988. Lists companies which are members of the Direct Selling Association. Includes address, phone number, contact person, and indicates product sold.

Securities and Financial Services Sales Representatives

Securities sales representatives, sometimes called **registered representatives**, **account executives**, or **brokers**, assist investors in the buying or selling of stocks, bonds, shares in mutual funds, insurance annuities, certificates of deposit, or other financial products. Securities sales representatives may explain the meaning of stock market terms and trading practices, offer financial counseling, devise an individual financial portfolio for the client, and offer advice on the purchase or sale of particular securities. An important part of their job is building a customer base. Beginning securities sales representatives must search for clients, relying heavily on phone solicitation and business contacts. Sometimes they may inherit the clients of representatives who have retired. **Financial services sales representatives** call on various businesses to solicit applications for loans and new deposit accounts for banks or savings and loan associations. They also locate and contact prospective customers to present their bank's financial services and to determine the customer's banking needs.

Salaries

Average earnings for securities sales representatives are listed below.

Beginning securities sales representatives	$28,000/year
Full-time, experienced securities sales representatives who serve individual investors	$78,000/year
Sales representatives who handle institutional accounts	$156,000/year

Employment Outlook

Growth rate until the year 2005: Faster than average.

Securities and Financial Services Sales Representatives

Career Guides

★490★ *All Pro*
BNA Communications, Inc.
9439 Key West Ave.
Rockville, MD 20850
Ph: (301)948-0540 Fax: (301)948-2085
Fr: 800-233-6067

Videocassette. 1981. 29 mins. Conversations with five top sales professionals. They discuss their careers and the traits that make a top professional.

★491★ "Banking and Financial Services" in *Encyclopedia of Careers and Vocational Guidance* (Vol.1, pp. 51-60)
J.G. Ferguson Publishing Co.
200 W. Madison St., Ste. 300
Chicago, IL 60606
Ph: (312)580-5480 Fax: (312)580-4948

William E. Hopke, editor-in-chief. Ninth edition, 1993. Four-volume set that profiles 500 occupations and describes job trends in 74 industries. Includes career description, educational requirements, history of the job, methods of entry, advancement, employment outlook, earnings, working conditions, social and psychological factors, and sources of additional information.

★492★ "Breaking into Sales & Trading on Wall Street" in *Internships Volume 3: Accounting, Banking, Brokerage, Finance & Insurance* (pp. 49-53)
Career Press, Inc.
PO Box 34
62 Beverly Rd.
Hawthorne, NJ 07507
Ph: (201)427-0229

Ronald W. Fry, editor-in-chief. 1989. Offers advice about obtaining internships with accounting, brokerage and investment banking firms, banks, and insurance companies. Lists companies offering internships and includes the contact person, duration, duties, qualifications, and application procedures and deadlines.

★493★ "Broker" in *Careers in Banking and Finance* (pp. 27-33)
Rosen Publishing Group
29 E. 21st St.
New York, NY 10010
Ph: (212)777-3017 Fax: (212)777-0277
Fr: 800-237-9932

Patricia Haddock. 1990. Describes more than 20 jobs at all levels in banking and finance. Contains information about the types of financial organizations where the jobs are found, educational requirements, job duties, and salaries. Offers advice on job hunting.

★494★ "Brokers" in *American Almanac of Jobs and Salaries* (pp. 406)
Avon Books
1350 Avenue of the Americas
New York, NY 10019
Ph: (212)261-6800 Fr: 800-238-0658

John Wright, editor. Revised and updated, 1994-95. A comprehensive guide to the wages of hundreds of occupations in a wide variety of industries and organizations.

★495★ "Brokers: Steady As IT Goes" in *Getting Into Money: A Career Guide* (pp. 58-73)
Ballantine Books
201 E. 50th St.
New York, NY 10022
Ph: (212)751-2600

Cheri Fein. 1988. Describes careers related to finance, what it takes to succeed in the field, and income potential. Contains interviews with people working in the field and offers job hunting tips.

★496★ *Careers in the Investment World*
Chelsea House Publishers
1974 Sproul Rd., Ste. 400
Broomall, PA 19008
Ph: (215)353-5166 Fax: (215)359-1439

Rachel S. Epstein. 1988.

★497★ *Commodities Trader*
Vocational Biographies, Inc.
PO Box 31
Sauk Centre, MN 56378-0031
Ph: (612)352-6516 Fax: (612)352-5546
Fr: 800-255-0752

1991. This pamphlet profiles a person working in the job. Includes information about job duties, working conditions, places of employment, educational preparation, labor market outlook, and salaries.

★498★ "Commodities Traders: Upping the Stakes" in *Getting Into Money: A Career Guide* (pp. 91-107)
Ballantine Books
201 E. 50th St.
New York, NY 10022
Ph: (212)751-2600

Cheri Fein. 1988. Describes careers related to finance, what it takes to succeed in the field, and income potential. Contains interviews with people working in the field and offers job hunting tips.

★499★ "Commodity Trader" in *Careers in Banking and Finance* (pp. 37-39)
Rosen Publishing Group
29 E. 21st St.
New York, NY 10010
Ph: (212)777-3017 Fax: (212)777-0277
Fr: 800-237-9932

Patricia Haddock. 1990. Describes more than 20 jobs at all levels in banking and finance. Contains information about the types of financial organizations where the jobs are found, educational requirements, job duties, and salaries. Offers advice on job hunting.

★500★ "Financial Services" in *Jobs '95* (pp. 331-338)
Prentice Hall Press
1 Gulf & Western Plaza
New York, NY 10023
Ph: (212)373-8500

Kathryn Petras and Ross Petras. Annual, 1995. Discusses employment prospects and trends for 15 professional careers and 29 industries. Lists leading companies, associations, directories, and magazines.

★501★ "Floor Brokers, Traders, and Commodity Traders" in *Jobs! What They Are—Where They Are—What They Pay* (pp. 143)
Simon & Schuster, Inc.
Simon & Schuster Bldg.
1230 Avenue of the Americas
New York, NY 10020
Ph: (212)698-7000

Robert O. Snelling and Anne M. Snelling. Revised edition, 1992. Profiles 241 occupations, describing duties and responsibilities, educational preparation, earnings, employment opportunities, training, and qualifications.

★502★ "Institutional Broker" in *Careers in Banking and Finance* (pp. 54-55)
Rosen Publishing Group
29 E. 21st St.
New York, NY 10010
Ph: (212)777-3017 Fax: (212)777-0277
Fr: 800-237-9932

Patricia Haddock. 1990. Describes more than 20 jobs at all levels in banking and finance. Contains information about the types of financial organizations where the jobs are found, educational requirements, job duties, and salaries. Offers advice on job hunting.

★503★ "Launching a Career on Wall Street" in *Internships Volume 3: Accounting, Banking, Brokerage, Finance & Insurance* (pp. 23-33)
Career Press, Inc.
PO Box 34
62 Beverly Rd.
Hawthorne, NJ 07507
Ph: (201)427-0229

Ronald W. Fry, editor-in-chief. 1989. Offers advice about obtaining internships with accounting, brokerage and investment banking firms, banks, and insurance companies. Lists companies offering internships and includes the contact person, duration, duties, qualifications, and application procedures and deadlines.

★504★ *No Experience Necessary: Make $100,000 a Year as a Stockbroker*
Simon & Schuster, Inc.
Simon & Schuster Bldg.
1230 Avenue of the Americas
New York, NY 10020
Ph: (212)698-7000

Bruce Eaton. 1987. Explains a day in the life of a stockbroker including the work, training, entry into the profession, how to get a job, how to succeed, and earning potential. Offers career planning and job hunting advice.

★505★ "Options Traders" in *New York Times Career Planner* (pp. 261-263)
Times Books
201 E. 50th St.
New York, NY 10022
Ph: (212)751-2600 Fax: (212)572-8700

Elizabeth M. Fowler. 1987. Offers career planning and job hunting advice for the college graduate. Surveys labor market trends. Contains "inside" information on professional careers including educational preparation, employment opportunities, and salaries.

★506★ *Salesperson, Securities*
Careers, Inc.
PO Box 135
Largo, FL 34649-0135
Ph: (813)584-7333

1994. Two-page occupational summary card describing duties, working conditions, personal qualifications, training, earnings and hours, employment outlook, places of employment, related careers and where to write for more information.

★507★ "Securities Broker" in *Career Information Center* (Vol.1)
Simon and Schuster
200 Old Tappan Rd.
Old Tappan, NJ 07675
Fax: 800-445-6991 Fr: 800-223-2348

Richard Lidz and Dale Anderson, editorial directors. Fifth edition, 1993. For 600 occupations, describes job duties, entry-level requirements, education and training needed, advancement possibilities, employment outlook, earnings and benefits. The set is divided into 12 volumes. Each volume includes jobs related under a broad career field. Volume 13 is the index.

★508★ "Securities Brokerage" in *How to Get the Hot Jobs in Business & Finance* (pp. 117-130)
HarperCollins Inc.
10 E. 53rd St.
New York, NY 10022
Ph: (212)207-7000

Mary E. Calhoun. Revised edition, 1988. Job hunting and career guide written for the college graduate. Surveys the highest paying jobs on Wall Street. Each chapter describes the work, certification or licensure, and entry into the field. Lists 500 financial institutions.

★509★ "Securities Brokers" in *Jobs! What They Are—Where They Are—What They Pay* (p. 144)
Simon & Schuster, Inc.
Simon & Schuster Bldg.
1230 Avenue of the Americas
New York, NY 10020
Ph: (212)698-7000

Robert O. Snelling and Anne M. Snelling. Revised edition, 1992. Profiles 241 occupations, describing duties and responsibilities, educational preparation, earnings, employment opportunities, training, and qualifications.

★510★ "Securities" in *Career Choices for the 90's for Students of Business* (pp. 173-193)
Walker and Co.
435 Hudson St.
New York, NY 10014
Ph: (212)727-8300 Fax: (212)727-0984
Fr: 800-289-2553

1990. Describes jobs in different industries and includes interviews with people working in related occupations. Presents employment outlook, preferred geographic location, entry-level opportunities, career paths, job responsibilities, advancement, personal and professional qualifications, salaries, working conditions, material for further reading, and associations.

★511★ "Securities" in *Career Choices for the 90's for Students of Economics* (pp. 146-167)
Walker and Co.
435 Hudson St.
New York, NY 10014
Ph: (212)727-8300 Fax: (212)727-0984
Fr: 800-289-2553

1990. Describes jobs in different industries and includes interviews with people working in related occupations. Presents employment outlook, preferred geographic location, entry-level opportunities, career paths, job responsibilities, advancement, personal and professional qualifications, salaries, working conditions, material for further reading, and associations.

★512★ "Securities" in *Career Choices for the 90's for Students of Mathematics* (pp. 158-179)
Walker and Co.
435 Hudson St.
New York, NY 10014
Ph: (212)727-8300 Fax: (212)727-0984
Fr: 800-289-2553

1990. Describes jobs in different industries and includes interviews with people working in related occupations. Presents employment outlook, preferred geographic location, entry-level opportunities, career paths, job responsibilities, advancement, personal and professional qualifications, salaries, working conditions, material for further reading, and associations.

★513★ "Securities" in *Career Choices for the 90's for Students of M.B.A.* (pp. 176-197)
Walker and Co.
435 Hudson St.
New York, NY 10014
Ph: (212)727-8300 Fax: (212)727-0984
Fr: 800-289-2553

1990. Describes jobs in various industries and contains interviews with people working in related occupations. Presents employment outlook, best geographic location, entry-level opportunities, career paths, job responsibilities, advancement possibilities, personal and professional qualifications, salaries, working conditions, material for further reading, and associations.

★514★ "Securities" in *Encyclopedia of Career Choices for the 1990s: A Guide to Entry Level Jobs* (pp. 784-804)
Berkley Pub.
PO Box 506
East Rutherford, NJ 07073
Fax: (201)933-2316 Fr: 800-788-6262

1992. Describes entry-level opportunities in 42 career fields for college graduates. Each chapter covers a single career field, including an overview, employment outlook, major employers, tips on entering the field, international job opportunities, functional job areas with personal and professional qualifications, career paths, job responsibilities, advancement possibilities, salaries, and working conditions. Lists related sources of information.

★515★ "Securities and Exchange Commission" in *Career Choices for the 90's for Students of Law* (pp. 23-24)
Walker and Co.
435 Hudson St.
New York, NY 10014
Ph: (212)727-8300 Fax: (212)727-0984
Fr: 800-289-2553

1990. Describes jobs in different industries and includes interviews with people working in related occupations. Presents employment outlook, preferred geographic location, entry-level opportunities, career paths, job responsibilities, advancement, personal and professional qualifications, salaries, working conditions, material for further reading, and associations.

★516★ "Securities and Financial Services Sales Representatives" in *America's 50 Fastest Growing Jobs* (pp. 94)
JIST Works, Inc.
720 N. Park Ave.
Indianapolis, IN 46202-3431
Ph: (317)264-3720 Fax: (317)264-3709
Fr: 800-648-5478

Michael J. Farr, compiler. 1994. Describes the 50 fastest growing jobs within major career clusters such as technicians, and marketing and sales. Each job profile explains the nature of the work, skills and abilities required, employment outlook, average earnings, related occupations, education and training requirements, and employment opportunities. Also contains career planning information and job search tips.

★517★ "Securities and Financial Services Sales Representatives" in *Encyclopedia of Careers and Vocational Guidance*
J.G. Ferguson Publishing Co.
200 W. Madison St., Ste. 300
Chicago, IL 60606
Ph: (312)580-5480 Fax: (312)580-4948

William E. Hopke, editor-in-chief. Ninth edition, 1993. Four-volume set that profiles 500 occupations and describes job trends in 74 industries. Includes career description, educational requirements, history of the job, methods of entry, advancement, employment outlook, earnings, working conditions, social and psychological factors, and sources of additional information.

★518★ "Securities and Financial Services Sales Representatives" in *Occupational Outlook Handbook*
U.S. Government Printing Office
Superintendent of Documents
Washington, DC 20402
Ph: (202)512-1800 Fax: (202)512-2250

Biennial; latest edition, 1994-95. Encyclopedia of careers describing more than 250 occupations and comprising about 85 percent of all jobs in the economy. Occupations that require lengthy education or training are given the most attention. For each occupation, the handbook describes job duties, working conditions, training, educational preparation, personal qualities, advancement possibilities, job outlook, earnings, and sources of additional information.

★519★ "Securities Sales Agents" in *Transitions: Military Pathways to Civilian Careers* (pp. 140-141)
Rosen Publishing Group
29 E. 21st St.
New York, NY 10010
Ph: (212)777-3017 Fax: (212)777-0277
Fr: 800-237-9932

Robert W. MacDonald. 1988. Describes how to make the best use of your military service to create a civilian career. Describes skills needed in civilian employment and compares them to skills acquired in the military. Covers career planning, job search, resume writing, and starting a small business. Lists many resources.

★520★ "Securities Sales" in *Career Choices for the 90's for Students of Business* (pp. 160-163, 180-182)
Walker and Co.
435 Hudson St.
New York, NY 10014
Ph: (212)727-8300 Fax: (212)727-0984
Fr: 800-289-2553

1990. Describes jobs in different industries and includes interviews with people working in related occupations. Presents employment outlook, preferred geographic location, entry-level opportunities, career paths, job responsibilities, advancement, personal and professional qualifications, salaries, working conditions, material for further reading, and associations.

★521★ "Securities Sales" in *Career Choices for the 90's for Students of Communications and Journalism* (pp. 169-171)
Walker and Co.
435 Hudson St.
New York, NY 10014
Ph: (212)727-8300 Fax: (212)727-0984
Fr: 800-289-2553

1990. Describes jobs in different industries and includes interviews with people working in related occupations. Presents employment outlook, preferred geographic location, entry-level opportunities, career paths, job responsibilities, advancement, personal and professional qualifications, salaries, working conditions, material for further reading, and associations.

★522★ "Securities Sales" in *Career Choices for the 90's for Students of Political Science & Government* (pp. 169-172)
Walker and Co.
435 Hudson St.
New York, NY 10014
Ph: (212)727-8300 Fax: (212)727-0984
Fr: 800-289-2553

1990. Describes jobs in different industries and includes interviews with people working in related occupations. Presents employment outlook, preferred geographic location, entry-level opportunities, career paths, job responsibilities, advancement, personal and professional qualifications, salaries, working conditions, material for further reading, and associations.

★523★ "Securities Sales" in *Career Choices for the 90's for Students of Psychology* (pp. 189-191)
Walker and Co.
435 Hudson St.
New York, NY 10014
Ph: (212)727-8300 Fax: (212)727-0984
Fr: 800-289-2553

1990. Describes jobs in different industries and includes interviews with people working in related occupations. Presents employment outlook, preferred geographic location, entry-level opportunities, career paths, job responsibilities, advancement, personal and professional qualifications, salaries, working conditions, material for further reading, and associations.

★524★ "Securities Sales" in *Encyclopedia of Career Choices for the 1990s: A Guide to Entry Level Jobs* (pp. 771-774)
Berkley Pub.
PO Box 506
East Rutherford, NJ 07073
Fax: (201)933-2316 Fr: 800-788-6262

1992. Describes entry-level opportunities in 42 career fields for college graduates. Each chapter covers a single career field, including an overview, employment outlook, major employers, tips on entering the field, international job opportunities, functional job areas with personal and professional qualifications, career paths, job responsibilities, advancement possibilities, salaries, and working conditions. Lists related sources of information.

★525★ *Securities Sales Representatives*
Chronicle Guidance Publications, Inc.
66 Aurora St.
PO Box 1190
Moravia, NY 13118-1190
Ph: (315)497-0330 Fax: (315)497-3359
Fr: 800-622-7284

1994. This career brief describes the nature of the work, working conditions, hours and earnings, education and training, licensure, certification, unions, personal qualifications, social and psychological factors, employment outlook, entry methods, advancement, and related occupations.

★526★ "Securities Sales Worker (Stockbroker)" in *VGM's Careers Encyclopedia* (pp. 427-429)
National Textbook Co. (NTC)
VGM Career Books
4255 W. Touhy Ave.
Lincolnwood, IL 60646-1975
Ph: (708)679-5500 Fax: (708)679-2494
Fr: 800-323-4900

Third edition, 1991. Contains two- to five-page descriptions of 200 managerial, professional, technical, trade, and service occupations. Each profile includes job duties, places of employment, qualifications, educational preparation, training, employment potential, advancement, income, and additional sources of information.

★527★ "Securities Sales Worker (Stockbroker)" in *VGM's Handbook of Business and Management Careers* (pp. 86-87)
National Textbook Co. (NTC)
VGM Career Books
4255 W. Touhy Ave.
Lincolnwood, IL 60646-1975
Ph: (708)679-5500 Fax: (708)679-2494
Fr: 800-323-4900

Annette Selden, editor. Second edition, 1993. Contains 42 two-page occupational profiles describing job duties, places of employment, working conditions, qualifications, education, employment outlook, and income.

★528★ "Securities Salesperson" in *Occu-Facts: Information on 580 Careers in Outline Form*
Careers, Inc.
PO Box 135
Largo, FL 34649-0135
Ph: (813)584-7333

Biennial, 1995-96 edition. Each one-page occupational profile describes duties, working conditions, physical surroundings and demands, aptitudes, temperament, educational requirements, employment outlook, earnings, and places of employment.

★529★ "Services Sales Representatives" in *Career Discovery Encyclopedia* (Vol.6, pp. 22-23)
J.G. Ferguson Publishing Co.
200 W. Madison St., Ste. 300
Chicago, IL 60606
Ph: (312)580-5480 Fax: (312)580-4948

E. Russell Primm, editor-in-chief. 1993. Contains two-page articles on 504 occupations. Each article describes job duties, earnings, and educational and training requirements.

★530★ *Stockbroker*
Vocational Biographies, Inc.
PO Box 31
Sauk Centre, MN 56378-0031
Ph: (612)352-6516 Fax: (612)352-5546
Fr: 800-255-0752

1990. This pamphlet profiles a person working in the job. Includes information about job duties, working conditions, places of employment, educational preparation, labor market outlook, and salaries.

★531★ "Stockbroker" in *College Board Guide to Jobs and Career Planning* (pp. 142-144)
College Entrance Examination Board
45 Columbus Ave.
New York, NY 10023-6992
Ph: (212)713-8000

Joyce Slayton Mitchell. 1990. Career planning guide written for high school and college students. Covers 100 careers in 15 occupational groups. Provides job description, educational preparation needed, salaries, related careers, and sources of additional information. Includes information about the 90's labor market.

★532★ "Stockbroker" in *Top Professions: The 100 Most Popular, Dynamic, and Profitable Careers in America Today* (pp. 1-3)
Petersons Guides, Inc.
PO Box 2123
Princeton, NJ 08543-2123
Ph: (609)243-9111 Fax: (609)243-9150
Fr: 800-338-3282

Nicholas Basta. 1989. Includes occupations requiring a college or advanced degree. Describes job duties, earnings, some typical job titles, career opportunities at different degree levels, and lists related associations.

★533★ "Stockbrokers" in *Career Discovery Encyclopedia* (Vol.6, pp. 66-67)
J.G. Ferguson Publishing Co.
200 W. Madison St., Ste. 300
Chicago, IL 60606
Ph: (312)580-5480 Fax: (312)580-4948

E. Russell Primm, editor-in-chief. 1993. Contains two-page articles on 504 occupations. Each article describes job duties, earnings, and educational and training requirements.

★534★ "Stockbrokers" in *New York Times Career Planner* (pp. 308-310)
Times Books
201 E. 50th St.
New York, NY 10022
Ph: (212)751-2600 Fax: (212)572-8700

Elizabeth M. Fowler. 1987. Offers career planning and job hunting advice for the college graduate. Surveys labor market trends. Contains "inside" information on professional careers including educational preparation, employment opportunities, and salaries.

★535★ "Trader" in *Careers in Banking and Finance* (pp. 67-72)
Rosen Publishing Group
29 E. 21st St.
New York, NY 10010
Ph: (212)777-3017 Fax: (212)777-0277
Fr: 800-237-9932

Patricia Haddock. 1990. Describes more than 20 jobs at all levels in banking and finance. Contains information about the types of financial organizations where the jobs are found, educational requirements, job duties, and salaries. Offers advice on job hunting.

★536★ "Traders" in *American Almanac of Jobs and Salaries* (pp. 408)
Avon Books
1350 Avenue of the Americas
New York, NY 10019
Ph: (212)261-6800 Fr: 800-238-0658

John Wright, editor. Revised and updated, 1994-95. A comprehensive guide to the wages of hundreds of occupations in a wide variety of industries and organizations.

★537★ "Traders: Dealing With Uncertainty" in *Getting Into Money: A Career Guide* (pp. 74-90)
Ballantine Books
201 E. 50th St.
New York, NY 10022
Ph: (212)751-2600

Cheri Fein. 1988. Describes careers related to finance, what it takes to succeed in the field, and income potential. Contains interviews with people working in the field and offers job hunting tips.

★538★ *Traders: the Jobs, the Products, the Markets*
New York Institute of Finance
2 Broadway
New York, NY 10004-2207

David M. Weiss. 1990. Provides an overview of the securities industry. Describes the work and procedures of many different types of trades in many different marketplaces.

★539★ "Wall Street Bond Broker" in *Straight Talk on Careers: 80 Pros Take You Into Their Professions* (pp. 21-24)
Garrett Park Press
PO Box 1907
Garrett Park, MD 20896
Ph: (301)946-2553

Mary Barbera-Hogan. 1987. Written for readers in high school and college. Contains candid interviews from professionals who discuss what their days are like and the pros and cons of their occupations.

★540★ "Wall Street: Building a Career in Finance" in *Fast-Track Careers: A Guide to the Highest-Paying Jobs* (pp. 17-39)
John Wiley and Sons, Inc.
605 3rd Ave.
New York, NY 10158-0012
Ph: (212)850-6000 Fax: (212)850-6088
Fr: 800-526-5368

William Lewis and Nancy Schuman. 1987. Profiles eight glamorous and high paying careers describing entry-level opportunities, earnings, personal qualities, types of companies, educational preparation and training, and employment outlook. Lists prominent companies in each industry, typical jargon, and professional associations.

ASSOCIATIONS

★541★ Securities Industry Association (SIA)
120 Broadway
New York, NY 10271
Ph: (212)608-1500 Fax: (212)608-1604

Members: Investment bankers, securities underwriters, and dealers in stocks and bonds. **Purpose:** To represent and serve all segments of the securities industry and provide a unified voice in legislation, regulation, and public information. Conducts studies and compiles statistics on investment, securities markets, and related matters. Sponsors management development programs; conducts roundtables. Maintains offices in New York City, and Washington, DC. **Publications:** *Securities Industry Association—Directory and Guide*, annual. • *Securities Industry Association—Foreign Activity Report*, quarterly. • *Securities Industry Association—Yearbook*. • *Securities Industry Trends*, monthly. • *SIA Washington Report*, bimonthly. • *SOURCES: The Securities Executive's Guide to Products and Services*, annual. • *Tax Briefs from SIA*, periodic.

EDUCATIONAL DIRECTORIES AND PROGRAMS

★542★ *Business and Finance Career Directory*
Career Press, Inc.
PO Box 34
62 Beverly Rd.
Hawthorne, NJ 07507
Ph: (201)427-0229

Ronald W. Fry, editor. 1989. Chapters are written by practitioners in accounting, securities, financial planning and insurance. Describes job duties, educational preparation required, entry into the field, and earnings. Identifies internship opportunities and lists companies actively hiring at entry level.

BASIC REFERENCE GUIDES AND HANDBOOKS

★543★ *Glossary of Financial Services Terminology*
Institute of Financial Education
111 E. Wacker Dr.
Chicago, IL 60601-4389
Ph: (312)644-3100 Fax: (312)856-0497

Fourth edition. 1990.

★544★ *Sales Management in Financial Services: How to Build a Competitive Sales Team*
Bank Administration Institute
60 Gould Center
Rolling Meadows, IL 60008
Fr: 800-323-8552

Jeff Sucec. 1990.

★545★ *Setting Up & Running Financial Systems*
Butterworth Legal Publishers
289 E. 5th St.
St. Paul, MN 55101
Ph: (612)227-4200

Steve Ives. 1989.

★546★ *Smart Selling: Successful Sales Techniques for Bankers*
Bank Administration Institute
60 Gould Center
Rolling Meadows, IL 60008
Fr: 800-323-8552

Judith A. Pennington. 1990.

PERIODICALS

★547★ *American Salesman*
National Research Bureau, Inc.
200 N. 4th
PO Box 1
Burlington, IA 52601-0001
Ph: (319)752-5415 Fax: (319)752-3421
Barbara Boeding

Monthly. Salesmanship magazine.

★548★ *Bank Auditing and Accounting Report*
Warren, Gorham & Lamont, Inc.
31 St. James Ave.
Boston, MA 02116-4112
Ph: (617)423-2020 Fax: (617)695-9699
Stephen Collins

Monthly. Provides information on developments, practices, and techniques in bank accounting, auditing, and financial controls. Covers such topics as procedures for preventing embezzlement, improving management information systems, audit planning and supervision, and electronic data processing developments.

★549★ *Bank Insurance & Protection Bulletin*
American Bankers Association (ABA)
1120 Connecticut Ave. NW
Washington, DC 20036
Ph: (202)663-5071 Fax: (202)828-4540
Fr: 800-338-0626
C. Howie Hodges

Monthly. Monitors the latest trends in risk management, insurance, and security for banks. Reports on current bank crime statistics, methods of deterrence, and other "state of the art information." Recurring features include news of research, notices of publications available, a calendar of events, meeting reports, and news of educational opportunities. Also announces ABA Security & Risk Management Division staff changes.

★550★ *Bank Operations Report*
Warren, Gorham & Lamont, Inc.
31 St. James Ave.
Boston, MA 02116-4112
Ph: (617)423-2020 Fax: (617)695-9699
Fr: 800-922-1201
Nancy Hitchner

Monthly. Focuses on electronic data processing control, check processing, record keeping, cost control, federal regulation, credit and debit cards, electronic funds transfer system, physical security, and office automation, computer, and systems applications.

★551★ *Bank Security Report*
Warren, Gorham & Lamont, Inc.
31 St. James Ave.
Boston, MA 02116-4112
Ph: (617)423-2020 Fax: (617)695-9699
Fr: 800-950-1201
Nancy Hitchner

Monthly. Compiles news, information, case histories, suggestions, and advice on bank security equipment and procedures, forgeries, check alterations, identifications, kiting, counterfeiting, money laundering, internal controls, and new federal announcements on bank security.

★552★ *Banking Policy Report*
Law & Business, Inc.
270 Sylvan Ave.
Englewood Cliffs, NJ 07632
Ph: (201)894-8538 Fax: (201)894-8666
Phillip Meyer

Semimonthly. Discusses new strategies, techniques, and developments in the financial services industry.

★553★ *Financial Marketing*
Charles E. Bartling, Contact
Provides marketing professionals from banks, savings institutions, and credit unions with pertinent information on current trends and developments in the marketing of financial services. Recurring features include letters to the editor, news of research, book reviews, job listing, and a calendar of events.

★554★ *Gold Mining Stock Report*
Robert Bishop
PO Box 1217
Lafayette, CA 94549
Ph: (510)283-4848 Fax: (510)283-8901
Fr: 800-759-7677
Bob Bishop

Monthly. Offers analysis and specific recommendations for investors interested in gold mining stocks, emphasizing junior companies. Carries discussions of market strategy. Recurring features include news of research and interviews.

★555★ *Independent Operations*
American Financial Services Association (AFSA)
919 18th St. NW
Washington, DC 20006
Ph: (202)296-5544 Fax: (202)223-0321
Fr: 800-843-3280
Naomi Romanchor

Quarterly. Furnishes members with news of the financial services industry, small business, and other areas of concern to the members of the Association's Section on Independent Operations. Provides news of current legislation, regulations, and individual/company profiles. Recurring features include letters to the editor, interviews, reports of meetings, news of Association events and conferences, and notices of publications available. Also contains columns titled Chairman's Report, Profile, Marketplace, Want Ads, For Your Information, and Question and Answer.

★556★ *The Journal of Portfolio Management*
Institutional Investor, Inc.
488 Madison Ave.
New York, NY 10022
Ph: (212)303-3300 Fax: (212)303-3527
Frank J. Fabozzi

Quarterly. Journal focusing on portfolio management and investment systems.

★557★ ***Moody's Bond Survey***
Moody's Investors Service
99 Church St.
New York, NY 10007
Ph: (212)553-0403 Fax: (212)553-0010
Martin Hatcher

Weekly. Magazine focusing on the bond market.

★558★ ***OTC Chart Manual***
Standard & Poor's
25 Broadway
New York, NY 10004
Ph: (212)208-8392 Fax: (212)208-0040
Kenneth LutzPublisher

Bimonthly. Price volume charts plotted on a weekly basis, reports on 3 1/2 years of action on over 900 NASDAQ stocks.

★559★ ***Salesman's Insider***
Marv. Q. Modell Associates
6009 Montgomery Corner
San Jose, CA 95135-1431
Ph: (408)270-4526
Marv. Q. Modell

Monthly. Concerned with selling techniques and methodology in all sales areas. Tracks new sales developments, trends, and profit opportunities. Details negotiating process; offers "tips that work."

★560★ ***Salesmanship***
Dartnell Corporation
4660 Ravenswood
Chicago, IL 60640
Ph: (312)561-4000 Fax: (312)561-3801
Fr: 800-621-5463
Terry Breen

Biweekly. Offers sales ideas and inspiration, profiles of top-producing salespeople, and articles on topics related to sales success.

★561★ ***Securities Industry Association—Directory and Guide***
Securities Industry Association (SIA)
120 Broadway
New York, NY 10271
Ph: (212)608-1500 Fax: (212)608-1604

Annual.

★562★ ***Securities Industry Association—Foreign Activity Report***
Securities Industry Association (SIA)
120 Broadway
New York, NY 10271
Ph: (212)608-1500 Fax: (212)608-1604

Quarterly. Covers purchases and sales of U.S. securities by foreign investors; includes statistics and graphs.

★563★ ***Securities Industry Association—Yearbook***
Securities Industry Association (SIA)
120 Broadway
New York, NY 10271
Ph: (212)608-1500 Fax: (212)608-1604

Reference containing detailed information on individual firms, including key personnel and department heads, number of accounts, and capital.

★564★ ***Securities Industry Trends***
Securities Industry Association (SIA)
120 Broadway
New York, NY 10271
Ph: (212)608-1500 Fax: (212)608-1604

Monthly. Covers trends within the securities industry and on economic developments affecting securities firms; includes statistics.

★565★ ***Securities Regulation Law Journal***
Warren, Gorham and Lamont, Inc.
1 Penn Plaza
New York, NY 10019
Ph: (212)971-5000 Fax: (212)971-5025
Fr: 800-950-1205
Brian O'Neil

Quarterly. Securities law journal.

★566★ ***Security Management***
America Society for Industrial Security
1655 N. Fort Myer Dr., Ste. 1200
Arlington, VA 22209
Ph: (703)522-5800 Fax: (703)522-5226
Mary Alice CrawfordPublisher

Monthly. Loss prevention and security magazine.

★567★ ***SIA Washington Report***
Securities Industry Association (SIA)
120 Broadway
New York, NY 10271
Ph: (212)608-1500 Fax: (212)608-1604

Bimonthly. Informs members of legislative and regulatory developments in Washington pertinent to the industry.

★568★ ***SOURCES: The Securities Executive's Guide to Products and Services***
Securities Industry Association (SIA)
120 Broadway
New York, NY 10271
Ph: (212)608-1500 Fax: (212)608-1604

Annual. Includes index of companies.

★569★ ***Standard & Poor's Nasdaq and Regional Exchange Stock Reports***
Standard & Poor's
25 Broadway
New York, NY 10004
Ph: (212)208-8392 Fax: (212)208-0040
Richard J. Albanese

Publication containing two-page reports on the most active and widely traded companies on NASDAQ and U.S. and Canadian regional exchanges.

★570★ ***Tax Briefs from SIA***
Securities Industry Association (SIA)
120 Broadway
New York, NY 10271
Ph: (212)608-1500 Fax: (212)608-1604

Periodic. Informs firms of important tax issues affecting day-to-day operations.

★571★ ***Worth Magazine***
Independent Investor Publications, Inc.
82 Devonshire St.
Boston, MA 02109
Ph: (617)570-7000 Fax: (617)728-6732
Susan Feldman

Bimonthly. Investment and personal finance magazine.

Meetings and Conventions

★572★ **Compliance and Legal Seminar**
Securities Industry Association (SIA)
120 Broadway
New York, NY 10271
Ph: (212)608-1500 Fax: (212)608-1604

Annual.

★573★ **Information Management Conference**
Securities Industry Association (SIA)
120 Broadway
New York, NY 10271
Ph: (212)608-1500 Fax: (212)608-1604

Annual. Always New York City.

★574★ **Local Firms Conference**
Securities Industry Association (SIA)
120 Broadway
New York, NY 10271
Ph: (212)608-1500 Fax: (212)608-1604

Annual.

★575★ **Operations Conference**
Securities Industry Association (SIA)
120 Broadway
New York, NY 10271
Ph: (212)608-1500 Fax: (212)608-1604

Annual.

★576★ **Sales and Marketing Conference**
Securities Industry Association (SIA)
120 Broadway
New York, NY 10271
Ph: (212)608-1500 Fax: (212)608-1604

Annual.

★577★ **Securities Industry Institute**
Securities Industry Association (SIA)
120 Broadway
New York, NY 10271
Ph: (212)608-1500 Fax: (212)608-1604

Annual.

★578★ **Trends Conference**
Securities Industry Association (SIA)
120 Broadway
New York, NY 10271
Ph: (212)608-1500 Fax: (212)608-1604

Annual.

Other Sources of Information

★579★ **"Securities Sales Agent" in *Career Selector 2001***
Barron's Educational Series, Inc.
250 Wireless Blvd.
Hauppauge, NY 11788
Ph: (516)434-3311 Fax: (516)434-3723
Fr: 800-645-3476

James C. Gonyea. 1993.

Services Sales Representatives

Services sales representatives sell a wide variety of services. Sales representatives for data processing services may sell services like inventory control, payroll processing, and financial reporting. Sales representatives for hotels may contact government, business, and social groups in an effort to solicit convention business for the hotel. Other representatives sell automotive leasing, public utilities, and management consulting services. They must establish a client base through use of business directories and personal referrals. Services sales representatives must fully understand and be able to discuss the services their company offers. Often literature or demonstrations are used to describe their company's services. If they fail to make a sale on the first visit, they may follow up with more visits, letters, and phone calls. If a sale is made, representatives call on their customers to ensure that everything is satisfactory. A sales representative's job can vary with the kind of service being sold. In general, highly technical services require more complex and lengthy sales processes. Fundraisers plan programs to raise money for charities or other nonprofit causes. The job may also vary with the size of the company and territory. Those working for large companies usually are more specialized and assigned territorial boundaries.

Salaries

Sales representatives work on different types of compensation plans. Some get a straight salary, others are paid on a commission basis or a combination of both. The median annual earnings of full-time advertising sales representatives are about $26,000. Representatives selling other business services earn $30,000.

Employment Outlook

Growth rate until the year 2005: Faster than average.

Services Sales Representatives

Career Guides

★580★ **"Advertising Sales" in *Careers in Fashion Retailing* (pp. 80-82)**
Rosen Publishing Group
29 E. 21st St.
New York, NY 10010
Ph: (212)777-3017 Fax: (212)777-0277
Fr: 800-237-9932

Pat Koester. 1990. Describes fashion retailing, industry structure, career paths, and typical jobs such as sales, management, and buying. Profiles persons working in the field and discusses educational preparation. Lists schools that offer programs in fashion retailing.

★581★ **"Advertising Sales Person" in *VGM's Handbook of Business and Management Careers* (pp. 11-14)**
National Textbook Co. (NTC)
VGM Career Books
4255 W. Touhy Ave.
Lincolnwood, IL 60646-1975
Ph: (708)679-5500 Fax: (708)679-2494
Fr: 800-323-4900

Annette Selde, editor. Second edition, 1993. Contains 42 two-page occupational profiles describing job duties, places of employment, working conditions, qualifications, education, employment outlook, and income.

★582★ **"Advertising Sales Representatives" in *Jobs! What They Are—Where They Are—What They Pay* (pp. 326)**
Simon & Schuster, Inc.
Simon & Schuster Bldg.
1230 Avenue of the Americas
New York, NY 10020
Ph: (212)698-7000

Robert O. Snelling and Anne M. Snelling. 3rd edition, 1992. Profiles 241 occupations, describing duties and responsibilities, educational preparation, earnings, employment opportunities, training, and qualifications.

★583★ **"Advertising Sales, Television" in *Career Choices for the 90's for Students of Communications and Journalism* (pp. 189-191)**
Walker and Co.
435 Hudson St.
New York, NY 10014
Ph: (212)727-8300 Fax: (212)727-0984
Fr: 800-289-2553

1990. Describes jobs in different industries and includes interviews with people working in related occupations. Presents employment outlook, preferred geographic location, entry-level opportunities, career paths, job responsibilities, advancement, personal and professional qualifications, salaries, working conditions, material for further reading, and associations.

★584★ **"Advertising Sales (Television)" in *Encyclopedia of Career Choices for the 1990s: A Guide to Entry Level Jobs* (pp. 828-830)**
Berkley Pub.
PO Box 506
East Rutherford, NJ 07073
Fax: (201)933-2316 Fr: 800-788-6262

1992. Describes entry-level opportunities in 42 career fields for college graduates. Each chapter covers a single career field, including an overview, employment outlook, major employers, tips on entering the field, international job opportunities, functional job areas with personal and professional qualifications, career paths, job responsibilities, advancement possibilities, salaries, and working conditions. Lists related sources of information.

★585★ **"Advertising Sales Workers" in *Career Discovery Encyclopedia* (Vol.1, pp. 24-25)**
J.G. Ferguson Publishing Co.
200 W. Madison St., Ste. 300
Chicago, IL 60606
Ph: (312)580-5480 Fax: (312)580-4948

E. Russell Primm, editor-in-chief. 1993. Contains two-page articles on 504 occupations. Each article describes job duties, earnings, and educational and training requirements.

★586★ **"Advertising Salesperson" in *Career Opportunities in Television, Cable, and Video* (pp. 110-111)**
Facts on File
460 Park Ave. S.
New York, NY 10016-7382
Ph: (212)683-2244 Fax: 800-678-3633
Fr: 800-322-8755

Third edition, 1990. Describes 100 media-related jobs. Each occupational profile covers job duties, employment outlook, career paths, salaries, skills, and educational preparation. Offers tips for entering the field.

★587★ **"Advertising Space Sales" in *Career Choices for the 90's for Students of Business* (pp. 155-158)**
Walker and Co.
435 Hudson St.
New York, NY 10014
Ph: (212)727-8300 Fax: (212)727-0984
Fr: 800-289-2553

1990. Describes jobs in different industries and includes interviews with people working in related occupations. Presents employment outlook, preferred geographic location, entry-level opportunities, career paths, job responsibilities, advancement, personal and professional qualifications, salaries, working conditions, material for further reading, and associations.

★588★ **"Advertising Space Sales" in *Career Choices for the 90's for Students of Political Science & Government* (pp. 164-167)**
Walker and Co.
435 Hudson St.
New York, NY 10014
Ph: (212)727-8300 Fax: (212)727-0984
Fr: 800-289-2553

1990. Describes jobs in different industries and includes interviews with people working in related occupations. Presents employment outlook, preferred geographic location, entry-level opportunities, career paths, job responsibilities, advancement, personal and professional qualifications, salaries, working conditions, material for further reading, and associations.

★589★ "Advertising Space Sales" in *Encyclopedia of Career Choices for the 1990s: A Guide to Entry Level Jobs* (pp. 610-613, 766-769)
Berkley Pub.
PO Box 506
East Rutherford, NJ 07073
Fax: (201)933-2316 Fr: 800-788-6262

1992. Describes entry-level opportunities in 42 career fields for college graduates. Each chapter covers a single career field, including an overview, employment outlook, major employers, tips on entering the field, international job opportunities, functional job areas with personal and professional qualifications, career paths, job responsibilities, advancement possibilities, salaries, and working conditions. Lists related sources of information.

★590★ "Advertising Space Sales, Newspaper Publishing" in *Career Choices for the 90's for Students of Communications and Journalism*
Walker and Co.
435 Hudson St.
New York, NY 10014
Ph: (212)727-8300 Fax: (212)727-0984
Fr: 800-289-2553

1990. Describes jobs in different industries and includes interviews with people working in related occupations. Presents employment outlook, preferred geographic location, entry-level opportunities, career paths, job responsibilities, advancement, personal and professional qualifications, salaries, working conditions, material for further reading, and associations.

★591★ "Advertising Space Sales, Newspaper Publishing" in *Career Choices for the 90's for Students of Political Science & Government*
Walker and Co.
435 Hudson St.
New York, NY 10014
Ph: (212)727-8300 Fax: (212)727-0984
Fr: 800-289-2553

1990. Describes jobs in different industries and includes interviews with people working in related occupations. Presents employment outlook, preferred geographic location, entry-level opportunities, career paths, job responsibilities, advancement, personal and professional qualifications, salaries, working conditions, material for further reading, and associations.

★592★ "Advertising Space Salesperson" in *Occu-Facts: Information on 580 Careers in Outline Form*
Careers, Inc.
PO Box 135
Largo, FL 34649-0135
Ph: (813)584-7333

Biennial, 1995-96 edition. Each one-page occupational profile describes duties, working conditions, physical surroundings and demands, aptitudes, temperament, educational requirements, employment outlook, earnings, and places of employment.

★593★ *All Pro*
BNA Communications, Inc.
9439 Key West Ave.
Rockville, MD 20850
Ph: (301)948-0540 Fax: (301)948-2085
Fr: 800-233-6067

Videocassette. 1981. 29 mins. Conversations with five top sales professionals. They discuss their careers and the traits that make a top professional.

★594★ "A Bright Future in Classified Ad Sales" in *Newspapers Career Directory* (pp. 17-19)
Career Press, Inc.
PO Box 34
62 Beverly Rd.
Hawthorne, NJ 07507
Ph: (201)427-0229

Ronald W. Fry, editor. Third edition, 1990. Separate chapters written by practitioners describe newspaper careers in classified and retail ad sales, editorial cartooning, circulation, editing, librarianship, production and promotion. Explains job duties, entry into the field, educational preparation, trends, career paths, and skills needed. Lists associations, publications, and companies actively seeking entry level employees.

★595★ "A Career in Outdoor Advertising Sales" in *Advertising Career Directory* (pp. 61-64)
Career Press, Inc.
PO Box 34
62 Beverly Rd.
Hawthorne, NJ 07507
Ph: (201)427-0229

Ronald W. Fry, editor. Fourth edition, 1990. Provides an overview of the advertising industry and describes what agencies do, and four areas of specialization including account management, and the creative, media, and research functions. Lists companies that offer entry-level job opportunities.

★596★ *Classified Sales Representative*
Careers, Inc.
PO Box 135
Largo, FL 34649-0135
Ph: (813)584-7333

1994. Two-page occupational summary card describing duties, working conditions, personal qualifications, training, earnings and hours, employment outlook, places of employment, related careers and where to write for more information.

★597★ "Customer Services Sales" in *Careers in Marketing* (pp. 68-69)
National Textbook Co. (NTC)
VGM Career Books
4255 W. Touhy Ave.
Lincolnwood, IL 60646-1975
Ph: (708)679-5500 Fax: (708)679-2494
Fr: 800-323-4900

Lila B. Stair. 1991. Surveys career opportunities in marketing and related areas such as marketing research, product development, and sales promotion. Includes a description of the work, places of employment, employment outlook, trends, educational preparation, organizational charts, and salaries. Offers job hunting advice.

★598★ *Exploring Careers in Computer Sales*
Rosen Publishing Group
29 E. 21st St.
New York, NY 10010
Ph: (212)777-3017 Fax: (212)777-0277
Fr: 800-237-9932

Lawrence Epstein. 1990. Part of Career Series.

★599★ "Getting Started in Retail Ad Sales" in *Newspapers Career Directory* (pp. 21-24)
Career Press, Inc.
PO Box 34
62 Beverly Rd.
Hawthorne, NJ 07507
Ph: (201)427-0229

Ronald W. Fry, editor. Third edition, 1990. Separate chapters written by practitioners describe newspaper careers in classified and retail ad sales, editorial cartooning, circulation, editing, librarianship, production and promotion. Explains job duties, entry into the field, educational preparation, trends, career paths, and skills needed. Lists associations, publications, and companies actively seeking entry level employees.

★600★ "Magazine Advertising Sales" in *Career Choices for the 90's for Students of Business* (pp. 167-169)
Walker and Co.
435 Hudson St.
New York, NY 10014
Ph: (212)727-8300 Fax: (212)727-0984
Fr: 800-289-2553

1990. Describes jobs in different industries and includes interviews with people working in related occupations. Presents employment outlook, preferred geographic location, entry-level opportunities, career paths, job responsibilities, advancement, personal and professional qualifications, salaries, working conditions, material for further reading, and associations.

★601★ "Magazine Advertising Sales" in *Career Choices for the 90's for Students of Political Science & Government* (pp. 176-178)
Walker and Co.
435 Hudson St.
New York, NY 10014
Ph: (212)727-8300 Fax: (212)727-0984
Fr: 800-289-2553

1990. Describes jobs in different industries and includes interviews with people working in related occupations. Presents employment outlook, preferred geographic location, entry-level opportunities, career paths, job responsibilities, advancement, personal and professional qualifications, salaries, working conditions, material for further reading, and associations.

★602★ "Magazine Advertising Sales" in *Career Choices for the 90's for Students of Psychology* (196-198)
Walker and Co.
435 Hudson St.
New York, NY 10014
Ph: (212)727-8300 Fax: (212)727-0984
Fr: 800-289-2553

1990. Describes jobs in different industries and includes interviews with people working in related occupations. Presents employment outlook, preferred geographic location, entry-level opportunities, career paths, job responsibilities, advancement, personal and professional qualifications, salaries, working conditions, material for further reading, and associations.

★603★ "Magazine Advertising Sales" in *Encyclopedia of Career Choices for the 1990s: A Guide to Entry Level Jobs* (pp. 778-780)
Berkley Pub.
PO Box 506
East Rutherford, NJ 07073
Fax: (201)933-2316 Fr: 800-788-6262
1992. Describes entry-level opportunities in 42 career fields for college graduates. Each chapter covers a single career field, including an overview, employment outlook, major employers, tips on entering the field, international job opportunities, functional job areas with personal and professional qualifications, career paths, job responsibilities, advancement possibilities, salaries, and working conditions. Lists related sources of information.

★604★ "Marketing/Sales" in *Career Choices for the 90's for Students of Business* (pp. 99-101)
Walker and Co.
435 Hudson St.
New York, NY 10014
Ph: (212)727-8300 Fax: (212)727-0984
Fr: 800-289-2553
1990. Describes jobs in different industries and includes interviews with people working in related occupations. Presents employment outlook, preferred geographic location, entry-level opportunities, career paths, job responsibilities, advancement, personal and professional qualifications, salaries, working conditions, material for further reading, and associations.

★605★ "Marketing and Sales" in *Encyclopedia of Career Choices for the 1990s: A Guide to Entry Level Jobs* (pp. 407-409)
Berkley Pub.
PO Box 506
East Rutherford, NJ 07073
Fax: (201)933-2316 Fr: 800-788-6262
1992. Describes entry-level opportunities in 42 career fields for college graduates. Each chapter covers a single career field, including an overview, employment outlook, major employers, tips on entering the field, international job opportunities, functional job areas with personal and professional qualifications, career paths, job responsibilities, advancement possibilities, salaries, and working conditions. Lists related sources of information.

★606★ "Marketing and Sales, Hotel Management" in *Career Choices for the 90's for Students of Psychology* (pp. 101-103)
Walker and Co.
435 Hudson St.
New York, NY 10014
Ph: (212)727-8300 Fax: (212)727-0984
Fr: 800-289-2553
1990. Describes jobs in different industries and includes interviews with people working in related occupations. Presents employment outlook, preferred geographic location, entry-level opportunities, career paths, job responsibilities, advancement, personal and professional qualifications, salaries, working conditions, material for further reading, and associations.

★607★ "Newspaper and Magazine Advertising Sales Representative" in *Career Opportunities in Advertising and Public Relations* (pp. 224-226)
Facts on File
460 Park Ave. S.
New York, NY 10016-7382
Ph: (212)683-2244 Fax: 800-678-3633
Fr: 800-322-8755
Shelly Field, 1990. Contains more than 80 jobs related to advertising and public relations in the private, public, and nonprofit sectors. Each occupational profile describes job duties, salary, employment outlook, career paths, advancement prospects, educational preparation, training, and skills. Offers tips for entering the field.

★608★ "Opportunities in Marketing & Sales" in *Travel and Hospitality Career Directory* (pp. 66-68)
Career Press, Inc.
PO Box 34
62 Beverly Rd.
Hawthorne, NJ 07507
Ph: (201)427-0229
Ronald W. Fry, editor. 1989. Offers advice on career planning and job hunting in hotel, travel, and related industries. Lists companies offering entry level positions in airlines, convention and visitors' bureaus, foreign tourist boards, hotels, travel agencies, car rental firms, and cruise lines. Lists travel and hospitality associations and trade publications.

★609★ "Radio Advertising Salesperson" in *Career Opportunities in Advertising and Public Relations* (pp. 128-130)
Facts on File
460 Park Ave. S.
New York, NY 10016-7382
Ph: (212)683-2244 Fax: 800-678-3633
Fr: 800-322-8755
Shelly Field, 1990. Contains more than 80 jobs related to advertising and public relations in the private, public, and nonprofit sectors. Each occupational profile describes job duties, salary, employment outlook, career paths, advancement prospects, educational preparation, training, and skills. Offers tips for entering the field.

★610★ "Radio, Television, and Print Advertising Sales Workers" in *Encyclopedia of Careers and Vocational Guidance*
J.G. Ferguson Publishing Co.
200 W. Madison St., Ste. 300
Chicago, IL 60606
Ph: (312)580-5480 Fax: (312)580-4948
William E. Hopke, editor-in-chief. Ninth edition, 1993. Four-volume set that profiles 500 occupations and describes job trends in 74 industries. Includes career description, educational requirements, history of the job, methods of entry, advancement, employment outlook, earnings, working conditions, social and psychological factors, and sources of additional information.

★611★ "Resolution, Personal Services and Transportation Careers" in *The Best Jobs for the 1990s and Into the 21st Century*
Impact Publications
9104-N Manassas Dr.
Manassas Park, VA 22111
Ph: (703)361-7300 Fax: (703)335-9486
Ronald L. Krannich and Caryl Rae Krannich. 1993. Includes information on a wide variety of careers including adjusters, investigators, and collectors, animal caretakers, electricians, services sales reps., and truck drivers.

★612★ "Sales Opportunities in Service Industries" in *Opportunities in Sales Careers* (pp. 123-131)
National Textbook Co. (NTC)
VGM Career Books
4255 W. Touhy Ave.
Lincolnwood, IL 60646-1975
Ph: (708)679-5500 Fax: (708)679-2494
Fr: 800-323-4900
James Brescoll and Ralph M. Dahm. 1988. Surveys jobs in sales and describes the skills needed to succeed. Covers the nature of the work, employment outlook, educational preparation, and training, salary, and rewards of the work.

★613★ "Sales" in *Where the Jobs Are: The Hottest Careers for the 90s* (pp. 221-244)
Career Press
180 5th Ave.
Hawthorne, NJ 07507
Ph: (201)427-0229 Fax: (201)427-2037
Fr: 800-CAREER-1
Joyce Hadley. 1995. Offers a job-hunting strategy for the 1990s as well as descriptions of growing careers of the decade. Each profile includes general information, forecasts, growth, education and training, licensing requirements, and salary information.

★614★ *Salesperson, Advertising Space*
Careers, Inc.
PO Box 135
Largo, FL 34649-0135
Ph: (813)584-7333
1993. Two-page occupational summary card describing duties, working conditions, personal qualifications, training, earnings and hours, employment outlook, places of employment, related careers and where to write for more information.

★615★ "Service Sales Representatives" in *America's 50 Fastest Growing Jobs* (pp. 96)
JIST Works, Inc.
720 N. Park Ave.
Indianapolis, IN 46202-3431
Ph: (317)264-3720 Fax: (317)264-3709
Fr: 800-648-5478
Michael J. Farr, compiler. 1994. Describes the 50 fastest growing jobs within major career clusters such as technicians, and marketing and sales. Each job profile explains the nature of the work, skills and abilities required, employment outlook, average earnings, related occupations, education and training requirements, and employment opportunities. Also contains career planning information and job search tips.

★616★ "Service Sales Representatives" in *Encyclopedia of Careers and Vocational Guidance* (Vol.4, pp. 345-348)
J.G. Ferguson Publishing Co.
200 W. Madison St., Ste. 300
Chicago, IL 60606
Ph: (312)580-5480 Fax: (312)580-4948
William E. Hopke, editor-in-chief. Ninth edition, 1993. Four-volume set that profiles 500 occupations and describes job trends in 74 industries. Includes career description, educational requirements, history of the job, methods of entry, advancement, employment outlook, earnings, working conditions, social and psychological factors, and sources of additional information.

★617★ "Services Sales Representatives" in *College Board Guide to Jobs and Career Planning* (pp. 148-149)
The College Board
45 Columbus Ave.
New York, NY 10023-6992
Ph: (212)713-8165 Fax: (212)713-8143
Fr: 800-323-7155
Second edition, 1994. Describes the job, salaries, related careers, education needed, and where to write for more information.

★618★ "Services Sales Representatives" in *Occupational Outlook Handbook*
U.S. Government Printing Office
Superintendent of Documents
Washington, DC 20402
Ph: (202)512-1800 Fax: (202)512-2250
Biennial; latest edition, 1994-95. Encyclopedia of careers describing more than 250 occupations and comprising about 85 percent of all jobs in the economy. Occupations that require lengthy education or training are given the most attention. For each occupation, the handbook describes job duties, working conditions, training, educational preparation, personal qualities, advancement possibilities, job outlook, earnings, and sources of additional information.

★619★ *So You Want to Be a Success at Selling?*
Video Arts, Inc.
8614 W Catalpa Ave.
Chicago, IL 60656
Ph: (312)693-9966 Fax: (312)693-7030
Fr: 800-553-0091
Videocassette. 1982. 25 mins. A lesson on the fundamental skills of selling, from the initial research to the close.

★620★ "Television Advertising Representative" in *Career Opportunities in Advertising and Public Relations* (pp. 137-139)
Facts on File
460 Park Ave. S.
New York, NY 10016-7382
Ph: (212)683-2244 Fax: 800-678-3633
Fr: 800-322-8755
Shelly Field, 1990. Contains more than 80 jobs related to advertising and public relations in the private, public, and nonprofit sectors. Each occupational profile describes job duties, salary, employment outlook, career paths, advancement prospects, educational preparation, training, and skills. Offers tips for entering the field.

★621★ "Television Advertising Sales Assistant" in *Career Opportunities in Advertising and Public Relations* (pp. 140-142)
Facts on File
460 Park Ave. S.
New York, NY 10016-7382
Ph: (212)683-2244 Fax: 800-678-3633
Fr: 800-322-8755
Shelly Field, 1990. Contains more than 80 jobs related to advertising and public relations in the private, public, and nonprofit sectors. Each occupational profile describes job duties, salary, employment outlook, career paths, advancement prospects, educational preparation, training, and skills. Offers tips for entering the field.

★622★ *Video Career Library - Marketing and Sales*
Careers, Inc.
PO Box 135
Largo, FL 34649-0135
Ph: (813)584-7333
Videocassette. 1994. Part of the Video Career Library covering 165 occupations. Shows actual workers on the job.

Basic Reference Guides and Handbooks

★623★ *The AMA Handbook of Marketing for the Service Industries*
AMACOM
135 W. 50th St.
New York, NY 10020-1201
Ph: (212)903-8089 Fr: 800-262-9699
Carole A. Congram, editor. 1990.

★624★ *Managing for Quality in the Service Sector*
Basil Blackwell, Inc.
3 Cambridge Center
Cambridge, MA 02142
Ph: (617)225-0430
Willem Mastenbroek, editor. 1991.

★625★ *Marketing Your Services: A Step-by-Step Guide for Small Businesses & Professionals*
John Wiley and Sons, Inc.
605 3rd Ave.
New York, NY 10158-0012
Ph: (212)850-6000 Fax: (212)850-6088
Fr: 800-526-5368
Anthony O. Putnam. 1990.

★626★ *Multinational Service Firms*
Routledge, Chapman & Hall, Inc.
29 W. 35th St.
New York, NY 10001-2291
Ph: (212)244-3336 Fax: (212)563-2269
Peter Enderwick, editor. 1989.

★627★ *Strategic Trends in Services: An Inquiry into the Global Service Economy*
HarperCollins Inc.
10 E. 53rd St.
New York, NY 10022
Ph: (212)207-7000
Albert Bressand, editor. 1989.

Periodicals

★628★ *AACS News*
American Association of Cosmetology Schools (AACS)
901 N. Washington St., Ste. 206
Alexandria, VA 22314-1535
Ph: (703)845-1333 Fax: (703)845-1336
Bimonthly.

★629★ *American Salesman*
National Research Bureau, Inc.
200 N. 4th
PO Box 1
Burlington, IA 52601-0001
Ph: (319)752-5415 Fax: (319)752-3421
Barbara Boeding
Monthly. Salesmanship magazine.

★630★ *Personal Selling Power*
Personal Selling Power, Inc.
1127 International Pkwy.
PO Box 5467
Fredericksburg, VA 22403
Ph: (703)752-7000 Fax: (703)752-7001
LB Gschwandtner
Magazine presenting motivational and sales skills and techniques for sales and marketing executives.

★631★ *Retailing News*
Retailing News Co.
14962 Bear Valley Rd., Ste. 288
Victorville, CA 92392-4236
Ph: (619)241-2514 Fax: (619)241-3595
Martin Barsky
Monthly. Trade magazine reaching dealers, retailers, manufacturers, manufacturing reps, and distributors in the consumer electronics and major appliance industries.

★632★ *Salesman's Insider*
Marv. Q. Modell Associates
6009 Montgomery Corner
San Jose, CA 95135-1431
Ph: (408)270-4526
Marv. Q. Modell
Monthly. Concerned with selling techniques and methodology in all sales areas. Tracks new sales developments, trends, and profit opportunities. Details negotiating process; offers "tips that work."

★633★ *Salesmanship*
Dartnell Corporation
4660 Ravenswood
Chicago, IL 60640
Ph: (312)561-4000 Fax: (312)561-3801
Fr: 800-621-5463
Terry Breen
Biweekly. Offers sales ideas and inspiration, profiles of top-producing salespeople, and articles on topics related to sales success.

Meetings and Conventions

★634★ National Agri-Marketing Association Conference
National Agri-Marketing Association
11020 King St., Ste. 205
Overlard Park, KS 66210
Ph: (913)491-6500 Fax: (913)492-6502

Annual. **Dates and Locations:** 1996 Apr 10-12; San Diego, CA.

Other Sources of Information

★635★ Seventh Annual Services Marketing Conference Proceedings: Designing a Winning Service Strategy
American Marketing Association
250 S. Wacker Dr.
Chicago, IL 60606
Ph: (312)648-0536 Fax: (312)993-7542

Mary J. Bitner. 1989.

Travel Agents

Travel agents give advice on destinations, make arrangements for transportation, hotel accommodations, car rentals, tours, and recreation. They may also advise on weather conditions, restaurants, and tourist attractions. Travel agents also provide information on customs regulations, required papers like passports and visas, and currency exchange rates. Travel agents use a variety of published and computer-based sources for information on departure and arrival times, fares, and hotel accommodations.

Salaries

Experience, sales ability, and size and location of the agency determine the salary of a travel agent.

Beginning travel agents	$12,428-$15,610/year
Middle travel agents	$17,975-$20,775/year
Experienced travel agents	$25,007/year

Employment Outlook

Growth rate until the year 2005: Much faster than average.

Travel Agents

Career Guides

★636★ *Air Transport-Ground Services*
Morris Video
2730 Monterey St. #105
Monterey Business Park
Torrance, CA 90503
Ph: (213)533-4800

Videocassette. 1986. 10 mins. Discover the different jobs available in ground services from air traffic controller to ramp attendant.

★637★ *Communication Skills*
Travel Text Associates
12605 State Fair
Detroit, MI 48205
Ph: (313)527-6971

Chris Hoosen. 1989. Part of Travel Agent Training Series.

★638★ *Exploring Careers in the Travel Industry*
Rosen Publishing Group
29 E. 21st St.
New York, NY 10010
Ph: (212)777-3017 Fax: (212)777-0277
Fr: 800-237-9932

Edgar Grant. 1989. Provides an overview of the travel and tourism industries. Describes the work of the travel agent, skills, training, pay, and employment outlook. Offers job hunting advice.

★639★ *Flying High in Travel: A Complete Guide to Careers in the Travel Industry*
John Wiley and Sons, Inc.
605 3rd Ave.
New York, NY 10158-0012
Ph: (212)850-6000 Fax: (212)850-6088
Fr: 800-526-5368

Karen Rubin. 1992.

★640★ *Getting Down to Business: Travel Agency*
American Institutes for Research in the Behavioral Sciences
PO Box 11131
Palo Alto, CA 94302
Ph: (415)493-3550 Fax: (415)858-0958

Rachel L. Rassen. 1981.

★641★ *How to Get a Job with A Cruise Line: Adventure-Travel-Romance - How to Sail Around the World on Cruise Ships & Get Paid for It*
Ticket to Adventure, Inc.
PO Box 47622
St. Petersburg, FL 33743
Ph: (813)544-0066

Mary F. Miller. 1990.

★642★ "Professionalism - Certified Travel Counselor" in *Travel Agent: Dealer in Dreams* (pp. 21-22)
Prentice Hall Press
1 Gulf & Western Plaza
New York, NY 10023
Ph: (212)373-8500

Aryear Gregory. Fourth edition, 1993. Comprehensive guide for those interested in the travel industry . Covers the work of the travel agent, agency problems, techniques, and promotion. Describes various jobs within the travel industry including travel consultant, agency manager, and tour operators. Explains the knowledge, skills, training, and educational preparation needed to succeed.

★643★ "Travel Agencies" in *Opportunities in Travel Careers* (pp. 77-90)
National Textbook Co. (NTC)
VGM Career Books
4255 W. Touhy Ave.
Lincolnwood, IL 60646-1975
Ph: (708)679-5500 Fax: (708)679-2494
Fr: 800-323-4900

Robert Scott Milne. 1991. Explores job opportunities in many travel related fields including the airlines, resorts, travel agencies, recreation, and tourism. Covers the work, salaries, educational preparation and training, and advancement possibilities.

★644★ *Travel Agent*
Careers, Inc.
PO Box 135
Largo, FL 34649-0135
Ph: (813)584-7333

1994. Two-page occupational summary card describing duties, working conditions, personal qualifications, training, earnings and hours, employment outlook, places of employment, related careers and where to write for more information.

★645★ *Travel Agent*
Arco Publishing Co.
Macmillan General Reference
15 Columbus Cir.
New York, NY 10023
Fax: 800-835-3202 Fr: 800-858-7674

Wilma Boyd. 1989. Introduction to the travel business. Covers U.S. and foreign travel, time zones, ticketing, world geography, and airline, railroad, and tour bus connections, and accommodations. Outlines entry-level positions in the airline, car rental, and hospitality industries as well as in travel agencies and related travel services. Explains travel agency operations, sales techniques, and the use of computers in travel services. Gives job hunting advice and sales tips.

★646★ "Travel Agent" in *100 Best Careers for the Year 2000* (pp. 236-238)
Arco Pub.
201 W. 103rd St.
Indianapolis, IN 46290
Ph: 800-428-5331 Fax: 800-835-3202

Shelly Field. 1992. Describes 100 job opportunities expected to grow fast throughout the next decade. Provides information on job duties and responsibilities, training requirements, education, advancement opportunities, experience and qualifications, and typical salaries.

★647★ "Travel Agent" in *Career Information Center* (Vol.8)
Simon and Schuster
200 Old Tappan Rd.
Old Tappan, NJ 07675
Fax: 800-445-6991 Fr: 800-223-2348

Richard Lidz and Dale Anderson, editorial directors. Fifth edition, 1993. For 600 occupations, describes job duties, entry-level requirements, education and training needed, advancement possibilities, employment outlook, earnings and benefits. The set is divided into 12 volumes. Each volume includes jobs related under a broad career field. Volume 13 is the index.

★648★ "Travel Agent" in *College Board Guide to Jobs and Career Planning* (pp. 152-154)
The College Board
45 Columbus Ave.
New York, NY 10023-6992
Ph: (212)713-8165 Fax: (212)713-8143
Fr: 800-323-7155

Second edition, 1994. Describes the job, salaries, related careers, education needed, and where to write for more information.

★649★ *The Travel Agent: Dealer in Dreams*
Prentice Hall Press
1 Gulf & Western Plaza
New York, NY 10023
Ph: (212)373-8500

Aryear Gregory. Fourth edition, 1993. Comprehensive guide for those interested in the travel industry. Covers the work of the travel agent, agency problems, techniques, and promotion. Describes various jobs within the travel industry including travel consultant, agency manager, and tour operators. Explains the knowledge, skills, training, and educational preparation needed to succeed.

★650★ "Travel Agent" in *Guide to Careers Without College* (pp. 25-26)
Franklin Watts, Inc.
387 Park Avenue, S.
New York, NY 10016
Ph: (212)686-7070

Kathleen S. Abrams. 1988. Discusses careers that do not require a college degree in fields such as health care, sales and marketing, and the building trades. Describes the work, employment opportunities, and training.

★651★ "Travel Agent" in *Jobs Rated Almanac*
World Almanac
1 International Blvd., Ste. 444
Mahwah, NJ 07495
Ph: (201)529-6900 Fax: (201)529-6901

Les Krantz. Second edition, 1992. Ranks 250 jobs by environment, salary, outlooks, physical demands, stress, security, travel opportunities, and extra perks. Includes jobs the editor feels are the most common, most interesting, and the most rapidly growing.

★652★ "Travel Agent" in *Occu-Facts: Information on 580 Careers in Outline Form*
Careers, Inc.
PO Box 135
Largo, FL 34649-0135
Ph: (813)584-7333

Biennial, 1995-96 edition. Each one-page occupational profile describes duties, working conditions, physical surroundings and demands, aptitudes, temperament, educational requirements, employment outlook, earnings, and places of employment.

★653★ "Travel Agent" in *Opportunities in Vocational and Technical Careers* (pp. 59-61)
National Textbook Co. (NTC)
VGM Career Books
4255 W. Touhy Ave.
Lincolnwood, IL 60646-1975
Ph: (708)679-5500 Fax: (708)679-2494
Fr: 800-323-4900

Describes careers which can be prepared for by attending a private vocational or proprietary school—office employee, sales worker, service worker, health services, mechanic, craftworker, and technician. Covers employment outlook, job duties, and salaries. Offers career planning advice.

★654★ "Travel Agent" in *Top Professions: The 100 Most Popular, Dynamic, and Profitable Careers in America Today* (pp. 57-59)
Petersons Guides, Inc.
PO Box 2123
Princeton, NJ 08543-2123
Ph: (609)243-9111 Fax: (609)243-9150
Fr: 800-338-3282

Nicholas Basta. 1989. Includes occupations requiring a college or advanced degree. Describes job duties, earnings, some typical job titles, career opportunities at different degree levels, and lists related associations.

★655★ "Travel Agent" in *Travel & Tourism* (pp. 27-31)
Franklin Watts, Inc.
387 Park Avenue, S.
New York, NY 10016
Ph: (212)686-7070

Marjorie Rittenberg Schulz. 1990. Surveys employment opportunities in the travel and tourism industry. Provides job description, educational preparation, training, salary, employment outlook, and sources of additional information. Offers job hunting advice.

★656★ "Travel Agent" in *VGM's Careers Encyclopedia* (pp. 468-470)
National Textbook Co. (NTC)
VGM Career Books
4255 W. Touhy Ave.
Lincolnwood, IL 60646-1975
Ph: (708)679-5500 Fax: (708)679-2494
Fr: 800-323-4900

Third edition, 1991. Contains two- to five-page descriptions of 200 managerial, professional, technical, trade, and service occupations. Each profile includes job duties, places of employment, qualifications, educational preparation, training, employment potential, advancement, income, and additional sources of information.

★657★ "Travel Agent" in *VGM's Handbook of Business and Management Careers* (pp. 92-93)
National Textbook Co. (NTC)
VGM Career Books
4255 W. Touhy Ave.
Lincolnwood, IL 60646-1975
Ph: (708)679-5500 Fax: (708)679-2494
Fr: 800-323-4900

Annette Selden, editor. Second edition, 1993. Contains 42 two-page occupational profiles describing job duties, places of employment, working conditions, qualifications, education, employment outlook, and income.

★658★ *Travel Agents*
Chronicle Guidance Publications, Inc.
66 Aurora St.
PO Box 1190
Moravia, NY 13118-1190
Ph: (315)497-0330 Fax: (315)497-3359
Fr: 800-622-7284

1993. This career brief describes the nature of the work, working conditions, hours and earnings, education and training, licensure, certification, unions, personal qualifications, social and psychological factors, employment outlook, entry methods, advancement, and related occupations.

★659★ "Travel Agents" in *101 Careers: A Guide to the Fastest-Growing Opportunities* (pp. 319-322)
John Wiley & Sons, Inc.
605 3rd Ave.
New York, NY 10158-0012
Ph: (212)850-6645 Fax: (212)850-6088

Michael Harkavy. 1990. Describes the nature of the job, working conditions, employment growth, qualifications, personal skills, projected salaries, and where to write for more information.

★660★ "Travel Agents" in *American Almanac of Jobs and Salaries* (pp. 547)
Avon Books
1350 Avenue of the Americas
New York, NY 10019
Ph: (212)261-6800 Fr: 800-238-0658

John Wright, editor. Revised and updated, 1994-95. A comprehensive guide to the wages of hundreds of occupations in a wide variety of industries and organizations.

★661★ "Travel Agents" in *America's 50 Fastest Growing Jobs* (pp. 98)
JIST Works, Inc.
720 N. Park Ave.
Indianapolis, IN 46202-3431
Ph: (317)264-3720 Fax: (317)264-3709
Fr: 800-648-5478

Michael J. Farr, compiler. 1994. Describes the 50 fastest growing jobs within major career clusters such as technicians, and marketing and sales. Each job profile explains the nature of the work, skills and abilities required, employment outlook, average earnings, related occupations, education and training requirements, and employment opportunities. Also contains career planning information and job search tips.

★662★ "Travel Agents" in *Career Discovery Encyclopedia* (Vol.6, pp. 124-125)
J.G. Ferguson Publishing Co.
200 W. Madison St., Ste. 300
Chicago, IL 60606
Ph: (312)580-5480 Fax: (312)580-4948

E. Russell Primm, editor-in-chief. 1993. Contains two-page articles on 504 occupations. Each article describes job duties, earnings, and educational and training requirements.

★663★ "Travel Agents" in *Encyclopedia of Careers and Vocational Guidance* (Vol.4, pp. 565-568)
J.G. Ferguson Publishing Co.
200 W. Madison St., Ste. 300
Chicago, IL 60606
Ph: (312)580-5480 Fax: (312)580-4948

William E. Hopke, editor-in-chief. Ninth edition, 1993. Four-volume set that profiles 500 occupations and describes job trends in 74 industries. Includes career description, educational requirements, history of the job, methods of entry, advancement, employment outlook, earnings, working conditions, social and psychological factors, and sources of additional information.

★664★ "Travel Agents" in *Jobs! What They Are—Where They Are—What They Pay* (pp. 206)
Simon & Schuster, Inc.
Simon & Schuster Bldg.
1230 Avenue of the Americas
New York, NY 10020
Ph: (212)698-7000

Robert O. Snelling and Anne M. Snelling. Revised edition, 1992. Profiles 241 occupations, describing duties and responsibilities, educational preparation, earnings, employment opportunities, training, and qualifications.

★665★ "Travel Agents: Plotters of Unforgettable Trips" in *Careers for Women Without College Degrees* (pp. 234-238)
McGraw-Hill Publishing Co.
11 W. 19th St.
New York, NY 10011
Ph: (212)337-6010

Beatryce Nivens. 1988. Career planning and job hunting guide containing information on decision-making, skills assessment, and resumes for career changers. Profiles careers with the best occupational outlook. Describes the work, educational preparation, employment outlook, salaries, and required skills.

★666★ *Travel Career Development*
Irwin Professional Publishing
1333 Burr Ridge Pkwy.
Burr Ridge, IL 60521
Ph: (708)789-4000 Fax: (708)789-6933

Fifth edition, 1992.

★667★ "Travel Coordinator" in *BLR Encyclopedia of Prewritten Job Descriptions*
Business and Legal Reports, Inc.
39 Academy St.
Madison, CT 06443-1513
Ph: (203)245-7448

Stephen D. Bruce, editor-in-chief. 1994. This book contains hundreds of sample job descriptions arranged by functional job category. The 1-3 page job descriptions cover what the worker normally does in the position, who they report to, and how that position fits in the organizational structure.

★668★ *Travel Free: How to Start and Succeed in Your Own Travel Consultant Business*
Prima Publishing and Communications
4970 Topaz Ave., PO Box 1260
Rocklin, CA 95677
Ph: (916)624-5718

Ben Dominitz. 1984.

★669★ "Travel and Hospitality Careers" in *The Best Jobs for the 1990s and Into the 21st Century*
Impact Publications
9104-N Manassas Dr.
Manassas Park, VA 22111
Ph: (703)361-7300 Fax: (703)335-9486

Ronald L. Krannich and Caryl Rae Krannich. 1993. Includes information on chefs, cooks, flight attendants, food and beverage service workers, hotel and motel desk clerks, reservation and transportation ticket agents and travel clerks, and travel agents.

★670★ "Travel and Hospitality" in *Where the Jobs Are: The Hottest Careers for the 90s* (pp. 279)
Career Press
180 5th Ave.
Hawthorne, NJ 07507
Ph: (201)427-0229 Fax: (201)427-2037
Fr: 800-CAREER-1

Joyce Hadley. 1995. Offers a job-hunting strategy for the 1990s as well as descriptions of growing careers of the decade. Each profile includes general information, forecasts, growth, education and training, licensing requirements, and salary information.

★671★ *Travel Industry Guidelines for Employment*
Travel Text Associates
12605 State Fair
Detroit, MI 48205
Ph: (313)527-6971

Chris Hoosen. 1990. Part of Travel Agent Training Series.

★672★ "Travel and Tourism" in *Career Connection II: A Guide to Technical Majors and Their Related Careers* (pp. 148-149)
Jist Works, Inc.
720 N. Park Ave.
Indianapolis, IN 46202-3431
Ph: (317)264-3720 Fax: (317)264-3709

Fred A. Rowe. 1994. Contains technical majors, such as automotive technology. Describes the major and the job. Lists high school and postsecondary school courses. Includes occupations related to the major, employment outlook, and starting salary.

★673★ *Travel Training Workbook, 1994-95*
Solitaire Publishing
216 S. Bungalow Park Ave.
Tampa, FL 33609
Ph: (813)876-0286 Fr: 800-226-0286

Claudine L. Dervaes. Fifth revised edition, 1994.

★674★ *What is a Travel Agent?*
American Society of Travel Agents
1101 King St., Ste. 200
Alexandria, VA 22314
Ph: (703)739-2782

This six-panel brochure describes industry outlook, education, training, job duties, and working conditions.

ASSOCIATIONS

★675★ American Society of Travel Agents (ASTA)
1101 King St.
Alexandria, VA 22314
Ph: (703)739-2782 Fax: (703)684-8319

Members: Travel agents; allied members are representatives of carriers, hotels, resorts, sightseeing and car rental companies, official tourist organizations, and other travel interests. **Purpose:** Purposes are to: promote and encourage travel among people of all nations; to promote the image and encourage the use of professional travel agents worldwide; serve as an information resource for the travel industry worldwide; promote and represent the views and interests of travel agents to all levels of government and industry; promote professional and ethical conduct in the travel agency industry worldwide; facilitate consumer protection and safety for the traveling public. Maintains biographical archives and travel hall of fame. Conducts research and education programs. **Publications:** *ASTA Educational System Catalog*, annual. • *ASTA Officials Directory*, annual. • *ASTA Travel Agency Management Magazine*, monthly. • *Dateline ASTA*, bimonthly. • *Travel Industry Honors*, periodic.

★676★ Institute of Certified Travel Agents (ICTA)
148 Linden St.
PO Box 812059
Wellesley, MA 02181-0012
Ph: (617)237-0280 Fax: (617)237-3860
Fr: 800-542-4282

Members: Individuals who have been accredited as Certified Travel Counselors (CTC) after meeting the institute's requirements (5 years' travel industry experience, 5 travel management courses, 4 examinations, an original research project, and a presentation). **Purpose:** Seeks to increase the level of competence in the travel industry. Provides continuing education, and examination and certification programs; conducts workshops and professional management seminars. Operates Travel Career Development Program to increase professional skills and Destination Specialist Programs to enhance the geographical knowledge of sales agents. Organizes study groups of instruction with enrolled student bodies in most major cities. **Publications:** *ICTA Update*, bimonthly. • *Sales Skills Development*. • *Travel Counselor Magazine*, bimonthly.

Standards/Certification Agencies

★677★ American Society of Travel Agents (ASTA)
1101 King St.
Alexandria, VA 22314
Ph: (703)739-2782 Fax: (703)684-8319
Promotes and encourage travel among people of all nations; promote professional and ethical conduct in the travel agency industry worldwide; facilitate consumer protection and safety for the traveling public. Conducts research and education programs.

★678★ Institute of Certified Travel Agents (ICTA)
148 Linden St.
PO Box 812059
Wellesley, MA 02181-0012
Ph: (617)237-0280 Fax: (617)237-3860
Fr: 800-542-4282
Provides continuing education, and examination and certification programs; conducts workshops and professional management seminars.

Test Guides

★679★ *Travel Agent*
Arco Pub.
201 W. 103rd St.
Indianapolis, IN 46290
Ph: 800-428-5331 Fax: 800-835-3202
Wilma Boyd. 1989. An entry-level introduction to the travel business.

Educational Directories and Programs

★680★ *ASTA Officials Directory*
American Society of Travel Agents (ASTA)
1101 King St.
Alexandria, VA 22314
Ph: (703)739-2782 Fax: (703)684-8319
Annual. Lists information on committee, council, and task force activities and members. Includes antitrust compliance guidelines, code of ethics, and bylaws.

★681★ *Official Tour Directory*
Thomas Publishing Co.
5 Penn Plaza
New York, NY 10001
Ph: (212)290-7355 Fax: (212)290-7288
David Juman, Contact
Semiannual, spring/summer and fall/winter. Covers Approximately 2,200 tour operators offering tours and vacation packages to over 500 worldwide destinations and 200 special interests and activities; approximately 800 airlines, hotel/motel chains, and car rental companies; more than 850 domestic and international tourist offices. Entries include: Co. name, address, phone. Arrangement: Alphabetical, geographical, and by specialty..

★682★ *Research Supplier Directory*
Travel & Tourism Research Association (TTRA)
10200 W. 44th Ave., No. 304
Wheat Ridge, CO 80033
Ph: (303)940-6557 Fax: (303)422-8894
Francine Butler, Contact
Irregular, previous edition 1986; latest edition 1991. Covers more than 200 organizations engaged in research and consulting on travel and tourism, including government agencies, university departments and private firms. Entries include: Company name, address, phone, fax, date founded, chief officer, name of member, type of organization, number of employees, services available, publications. Arrangement: Alphabetical.

★683★ *Travel Agent—Focus 500 Directory Issue*
Universal Media, Inc.
801 2nd Ave.
New York, NY 10017
Ph: (212)370-5050
Nancy Ness, Contact
Annual, October. Publication includes: Lists of attractions, restaurants, convention and visitor bureaus, hotel chains and management companies, cruise lines, state tourism offices, travel trade associations, tourist railways; coverage includes Canada. Entries include: Company, agency, or center name, address, phone, name and title of contact. Arrangement: Geographical.

★684★ *Travel Industry Career Directory*
Career Press, Inc.
62 Beverly Rd.
Hawthorne, NJ 07507
Ph: (201)427-0229 Fax: (201)427-2037
1989.

Awards, Scholarships, Grants, and Fellowships

★685★ Air Travel Card Grant
American Society of Travel Agents (ASTA) Scholarship Foundation
1101 King St.
Alexandria, VA 22314
Ph: (703)739-2782 Fax: (703)684-8319
Qualifications: Applicants must be United States or Canadian citizens who are undergraduates enrolled in an accredited two- or four-year college (not a proprietary school). A 2.5 grade point average on a 4.0 scale is required. Funds available: One annual award of $3,000. Application details: Students must submit an essay (minimum of 500 words) on the challenges of managing business travel in the 1990's which should contain a brief description of career goals and proof of enrollment in a qualified college. Applicants must also submit transcripts from the last academic year must be attached, unless an applicant has been out of school for at least five year. In that case, a letter explaining the return to school is required. Students must send brochures describing the travel curriculum, tuition, and length of their programs. Statements from at least one professor and/or employer in the travel and tourism field attesting to the applicant's dedication and interest in the travel industry are required. Deadline: June or July.

★686★ American Express Travel Scholarships
ASTA Scholarship Foundation, Inc.
1101 King St.
Alexandria, VA 22314
Ph: (703)739-2782 Fax: (703)684-8319
Purpose: To encourage the pursuit of education in the travel and tourism field and to support the growth and development of tomorrow's travel and tourism work force. Qualifications: Applicants must be enrolled in a travel and tourism program at either a two- or four-year college, university, or proprietary travel school, have a 2.5 grade point average (4.0 scale), and be residents, citizens, or legal aliens of the United States or Canada. Funds available: $1,000. Application details: A 500-word essay detailing the student's plans in travel and tourism, as well as views of the travel industry's future is required. Students must submit proof of enrollment or acceptance to a school, an official school-printed description or listing of the travel curriculum, an official statement of the tuition amount, and a letter of recommendation. Application materials must be mailed in triplicate; faxed entries are not accepted. Deadline: June or July. Winners are notified in September.

★687★ Fernando R. Ayuso Awards
American Society of Travel Agents (ASTA) Scholarship Foundation
1101 King St.
Alexandria, VA 22314
Ph: (703)739-2782 Fax: (703)684-8319
Purpose: To encourage U.S. or Spanish scholars in the field of travel and tourism to visit either Spain or the United States. Qualifications: Candidate must be a citizen of the United States or Spain and be between the ages of 23 to 30 years. Applicant must have at least two years of college education and two years of work experience in a travel-related field. U.S. candidates should have a strong interest and knowledge of Spanish culture and language. U.S. citizens must use the award to visit Spain. Spanish citizens must visit the United States and attend the American Society of Travel Agents World Congress. Funds available: Airfare, accommodations, and meals. Application details: Write for application form and guidelines. Submit form with a 500-word essay describing the benefits of the proposed visit. Deadline: June/July.

★688★ Northern California/Richard Epping Scholarships
American Society of Travel Agents (ASTA) Scholarship Foundation
1101 King St.
Alexandria, VA 22314
Ph: (703)739-2782 Fax: (703)684-8319
Purpose: To promote professionalism in the travel industry. Qualifications: Applicants must be currently enrolled in a travel or tourism curriculum at a college, university, or proprietary travel and tourism school. The estab-

lishment must be located within the geographic boundaries of the Northern California ASTA Chapter. Students must be permanent residents of these same boundaries and must agree to become involved in ASTA's Northern California Chapter, as well as make a presentation to the Chapter at the end of the academic term. In addition, applicants must have a 2.5 grade point average (4.0 scale) and be residents, citizens, or legal aliens of the United States or Canada. Funds available: One $750 award is given annually. Application details: A 500-word essay entitled, "Why I Desire a Profession in the Travel and Tourism Industry," is required. Students must also submit proof of enrollment or acceptance to a school, an official school-printed description or listing of the travel curriculum, an official statement of the tuition amount, and a letter of recommendation. Application materials must be mailed in triplicate; faxed entries are not accepted. Deadline: July 15. Winners are notified by August 31.

★689★ Avis Rent a Car Scholarship; David Halissey Memorial Scholarship; Simmons Scholarship
American Society of Travel Agents (ASTA) Scholarship Foundation
1101 King St.
Alexandria, VA 22314
Ph: (703)739-2782 Fax: (703)684-8319

Purpose: To support further studies related to the travel industry. Qualifications: Candidate for any of the scholarships must be a citizen, resident, or legal alien of the United States or Canada pursuing further studies in the field of travel and tourism at a U.S. or Canadian institution. Applicant for the Avis Scholarship must be an upper-class undergraduate or graduate student who has worked part time in the travel industry. Candidate must submit a 500-word essay on the benefits of automation for travel agents and industry suppliers. Candidate for the Hallissey Scholarship must be a graduate student or travel educator at a recognized college, university or proprietary school. Applicant must submit a 500-word abstract on the proposed topic of research incorporating methodology and objectives. Applicant for a Simmons Scholarship must be pursuing a master's or doctoral degree with emphasis in travel and tourism. An upper-level paper or thesis (15 to 50 pages long) written on some topic of travel and tourism, which has been or will be submitted to a professor, must accompany the candidate's application. Funds available: $1,000-1,200. Application details: Write to the Foundation for application form and guidelines. Deadline: 14 June.

★690★ Healy Scholarship
American Society of Travel Agents (ASTA) Scholarship Foundation
1101 King St.
Alexandria, VA 22314
Ph: (703)739-2782 Fax: (703)684-8319

Qualifications: Applicants must be citizens of the United States or Canada. They must be enrolled in a recognized college, and be a sophomore, junior, or senior. Applicants must be enrolled in travel and tourism courses. A 2.5 grade point average on a 4.0 scale is required. Funds available: The fund offers one award of $1,200 to dedicated undergraduate students. Application details: Students must provide a 500-word essay suggesting improvements for the travel industry. Proof of enrollment in a qualified school or program must be submitted. Transcripts from the last academic year must be attached unless an applicant has been out of school for at least five years. In that case, a letter explaining the return is required. Students must send brochures describing the travel curriculum, tuition, and length of their programs. Statements from at least one professor and/or employer in the travel and tourism field attesting to the applicant's dedication and interest in the travel industry are also required. Deadline: June/July.

★691★ Outstanding International Travel Agent of the Year
Association of Community Travel Clubs
2330 S. Brentwood Blvd.
St. Louis, MO 63144-2096
Ph: (314)961-2300 Fax: (314)961-9828

For recognition of contributions in the field of tourism. Selection is by nomination. A monetary award of $10,000 and a plaque are awarded annually at the convention. Established in 1948.

★692★ Pollard Scholarships
American Society of Travel Agents (ASTA) Scholarship Foundation
1101 King St.
Alexandria, VA 22314
Ph: (703)739-2782 Fax: (703)684-8319

Purpose: To promote professionalism in travel by supporting persons reentering the job market via attendance in recognized proprietary travel schools or two-year junior colleges that specialize in travel or tourism studies. Qualifications: Students must be citizens of the United States or Canada who have been out of high school for at least five years. Funds available: The fund currently awards two $1,000 scholarships. The award may not exceed 50 percent of the annual tuition. A copy of the tuition fee is required. Application details: Students must provide proof of registration in a recognized travel school or two-year college, a 500-word essay on objectives in the travel and tourism industry, and proof that they have been out of high school for at least 5 years. Deadline: June/July.

★693★ Princess Cruises and Princess Tours Scholarship
American Society of Travel Agents (ASTA) Scholarship Foundation
1101 King St.
Alexandria, VA 22314
Ph: (703)739-2782 Fax: (703)684-8319

Qualifications: Candidates must be sophomores, juniors, or seniors studying travel and tourism in a four-year college or university, and they must be a resident, citizen, or legal alien of the United States or Canada. Funds available: One award of $400. Application details: Submit a 500-word essay on the five features that cruise ships will need to offer passengers in the next ten years. Applicants should also submit proof of enrollment; provide and official statement of their tuition; provide an official school-printed description of their travel curriculum; possess at least a 2.5 grade point average on a 4.0 scale or, if the applicant is reentering school after time spent in the work force, submit a cover letter explaining why they are returning to school; and provide a letter of recommendation from a professor, employer, or business colleague that attests to the student's desire to pursue a profession in the travel and tourism industry. Deadline: July 15.

★694★ Simmons Scholarship
ASTA Scholarship Foundation, Inc.
1101 King St.
Alexandria, VA 22314
Ph: (703)739-2782 Fax: (703)684-8319

Purpose: To promote professionalism in the travel industry by providing scholarships for continued education in the field of travel and tourism. Qualifications: Applicants must be graduate students who are pursuing a Masters or Doctorate degree with an emphasis in travel and tourism. They must have a minimum 2.5 grade point average (4.0 scale) and be residents, citizens, or legal aliens of the United States or Canada. Funds available: Two awards of $1,500 each are given. Application details: An upper-level paper or thesis (15 to 20 pages) written on some travel and tourism topic that has been or will be submitted to a professor must be provided. Candidates must also submit proof of enrollment, an official school-printed description or listing of the travel curriculum, an official statement of the tuition amount, and a letter of recommendation. Application materials must be mailed in triplicate; faxed entries are not accepted. Deadline: June or July. Winners are notified in September.

★695★ Southern California Chapter/ Pleasant Hawaiian Holidays Scholarship
American Society of Travel Agents (ASTA) Scholarship Foundation
1101 King St.
Alexandria, VA 22314
Ph: (703)739-2782 Fax: (703)684-8319

Purpose: To promote professionalism in the travel industry by providing scholarships for continued education in the field of travel and tourism. Qualifications: Applicants must be undergraduate students enrolled or accepted to an accredited college, junior college, university, or proprietary travel school in preparation for a profession in the travel and tourism industry. They must also have a 3.0 grade point average (4.0 scale), and submit proof of U.S. citizenship. One parent of the applicant must be employed in the travel industry (i.e., hotel, car rental, airlines, travel agency, etc.) in the Southern California Chapter of ASTA's boundaries. Funds available: $1,000. Application details: A 1,000-word essay entitled, "My Goals in the Travel Industry," is required, as well as a statement as to why applicant should be chosen to receive the award. Students must submit proof of enrollment, an official school-printed description or listing of the travel curriculum, an official statement of the tuition amount, and a letter of recommendation. A statement from the parent's employer must also accompany the student's application. Application materials must be mailed in triplicate; faxed entries are not accepted. Deadline: July 15. Winners are notified by August 31.

★696★ A.J. (Andy) Spielman Scholarships
American Society of Travel Agents (ASTA)
Scholarship Foundation
1101 King St.
Alexandria, VA 22314
Ph: (703)739-2782 Fax: (703)684-8319

Qualifications: Applicants must be citizens of the United States or Canada who are currently enrolled in or scheduled to attend a recognized proprietary travel school for the purpose of re-entering the work force in the field of travel. Funds available: The fund currently awards two $1,000 scholarships. Application details: Applicants must submit a 500-word essay entitled "Why I have chosen the Travel Profession for my Re-entry into the Work Force", and provide proof of registration at a recognized proprietary travel school. Deadline: June/July.

Basic Reference Guides and Handbooks

★697★ Africa's Top Wildlife Countries
Global Travel Publishers, Inc.
PO Box 2567
Pompano Beach, FL 33072
Ph: (305)781-3933 Fax: (305)781-0984
Fr: 800-882-9453
Mark Nolting, Contact

Biennial, February of even years. Publication includes: List of parks, accommodations, banks, and tourist camps and offices in 15 African countries; African embassies; airlines that fly to Africa. Entries include: Name, address, phone, services. Principal content of publication is information and suggestions for tourists on observing wildlife in 15 African countries. Arrangement: Classified by service.

★698★ American Bus Association's Motorcoach Marketer: Complete Directory of the Intercity Bus & Travel/ Tourism Industry
American Bus Association
1100 New York Ave. NW, Ste. 1050
Washington, DC 20005-3934
Ph: (202)842-1645 Fax: (202)842-0850
Fr: 800-283-2877
Lynn Brewer, Contact

Annual, October. Covers over 2,000 hotels and sightseeing services, convention information centers, visitors' centers, and similar businesses and organizations of interest to motorcoach tour organizers; includes about 500 companies which operate intercity scheduled and charter buses; coverage includes Canada and Mexico. Entries include: Co. name, address, phone, name and title of contact. Arrangement: Classified by type of business.

★699★ Business of Travel: Agency Operations & Administration
Macmillian Publishing Co.
866 3rd Ave.
New York, NY 10022
Ph: (212)702-2000

Dennis L. Foster. 1990.

★700★ Travel Agent—Domestic Tour Manual Issue
Universal Media, Inc.
801 2nd Ave.
New York, NY 10017
Ph: (212)370-5050

Annual, February. Publication includes: Lists of leading motorcoach tour companies offering over 500 escort vacation tours with 9,000 departures throughout the U.S. and Canada. Entries include: For tour companies—Name, address, phone. For tours—Dates offered, name of tour, costs, number of days. Arrangement: Alphabetical.

★701★ Travel Industry Association of America-International Travel News Directory
Travel Industry Association of America (TIA)
2 Lafayette Center
1133 21st St., NW
Washington, DC 20036
Ph: (202)293-1433 Fax: (202)293-3155

Thomas Berrigan, editor. Annual. Travel editors of major newspapers, magazines, and broadcast outlets; consumer and travel industry magazines and publications, including guide books, in-flight publications, in-room publications; news and photo services; international coverage for travel trade and consumer travel editors. Entries include: Generally, publication title, address, phone, fax, telex, names of editorial and advertising contacts, target audience, editorial and advertising deadlines. Arrangement: Classified by media, then in separate section for United States and international. Indexes: Media title, geographical.

★702★ Travel Industry Association of America—Travel Media Directory
Travel Industry Association of America (TIA)
2 Lafayette Center
1133 21st St. NW
Washington, DC 20036
Ph: (202)293-1433 Fax: (202)293-3155
Thomas Berrigan, Contact

Annual. Covers travel editors of major newspapers, magazines, and broadcast outlets; consumer and travel industry magazines and publications, including guide books, in-flight publications, in-room publications; news and photo services; international coverage for travel trade and consumer travel editors. Entries include: Generally, publication title, address, phone, fax, telex, names of editorial and advertising contacts, target audience, editorial and advertising deadlines. Arrangement: Classified by media, then in separate section for United States and international.

★703★ Travel & Vacation Discount Guide
Pilot Books
103 Cooper St.
Babylon, NY 11702
Ph: (516)422-2225 Fax: (516)422-2227
Sam Small, Contact

Annual, March. Covers nearly 335 sponsors of discount travel programs, including discount travel clubs, hotels, airlines, and other travel industry firms; also lists tourist information agencies in the United States and abroad. Entries include: Sponsor name, address, phone, description of program. Arrangement: Alphabetical.

★704★ Worldwide Travel Information Contact Book
Gale Research Inc.
835 Penobscot Bldg.
Detroit, MI 48226-4094
Ph: (313)961-2242 Fax: (313)961-6083
Fr: 800-877-GALE
Linda Irvin, Contact

Irregular, latest edition November 1992; no new edition planned. Covers Approximately 45,500 contacts and sources for travel information including: travel agents, associations, tourist authorities, tour operators, lodging associations, and publications. Entries include: Name, address, phone, fax, telex. Arrangement: Geographical, then by subject heading.

Periodicals

★705★ Adventure West
SKI WEST Publications, Inc.
1025 Ridgeview Dr., Ste. 400
Reno, NV 89509
Thomas M. Hill

Quarterly. Magazine featuring exciting places to go and things to do in the American West.

★706★ ARTAFACTS
Association of Retail Travel Agents (ARTA)
1745 Jefferson Davis Pkwy., Ste. 300
Arlington, VA 22202-3402
Ph: (703)553-7777 Fax: (703)413-2225
Fr: 800-969-6069

Monthly. Reviews developments in the travel industry for retail travel agents. Covers topics such as ethics, tour operations, transportation services, educational opportunities, commissions, and political action in pertinent issues. Includes chapter and Association news.

★707★ ASTA Educational System Catalog
American Society of Travel Agents (ASTA)
1101 King St.
Alexandria, VA 22314
Ph: (703)739-2782 Fax: (703)684-8319

Annual. Contains information on ASTA programs including programs in accounting, automation, geography, group travel, law, and management.

★708★ ASTA Travel Agency Management Magazine
American Society of Travel Agents (ASTA)
1101 King St.
Alexandria, VA 22314
Ph: (703)739-2782 Fax: (703)684-8319

Monthly.

★709★ Atterbury Letter
Kirby and Renee Atterbury
PO Box 1197
Bethel Island, CA 94511
Ph: (510)684-3142
Kirby Atterbury

Carries personal opinions from readers and writers on their experience in various locales integrating wine, dining, and travel. Reports on travel fares, accommodations, conditions, tours, restaurants, and vineyards. Recurring features include specific recommendations, off-beat travel ideas, and discussions of seasonal differences in prices and services.

★710★ *Dateline ASTA*
American Society of Travel Agents (ASTA)
1101 King St.
Alexandria, VA 22314
Ph: (703)739-2782 Fax: (703)684-8319
Bimonthly.

★711★ *Developments*
American Resort Development Assn.
1220 L St. NW, No. 510
Washington, DC 20005
Ph: (202)371-6700 Fax: (202)289-8544
Sheila Morris
Monthly. Trade magazine for the American Resort Development Association.

★712★ *Entree*
Entree Travel
1470 E. Valley Rd.
Santa Barbara, CA 93108
Ph: (805)969-5848 Fax: (805)966-7095
William Tomicki
Monthly. Features "an insider's look at hotels, restaurants, and travel around the world." Contains advice and tips on travel, bargains, and services. Recurring features include book reviews and notices of publications available.

★713★ *The Hideaway Report*
Harper Associates, Inc.
PO Box 50
Sun Valley, ID 83353-0050
Ph: (208)622-3183
Andrew Harper
Monthly. Provides informative critiques on small, secluded resorts and executive retreats around the world. Composed of 12-15 hotel descriptions per issue. Recurring features include Hideaway of the Year Awards in December issue and columns titled Reader Requests and Hotel & Travel Watch.

★714★ *Hotel & Travel Index—ABC International Edition*
Reed Travel Group
500 Plaza Drive
Secaucus, NJ 07094-3626
Ph: (201)902-2000
Melinda BushPublisher
Quarterly. International hotel directory.

★715★ *ICTA Update*
Institute of Certified Travel Agents (ICTA)
148 Linden St.
PO Box 812059
Wellesley, MA 02181-0012
Ph: (617)237-0280 Fax: (617)237-3860
Fr: 800-542-4282
Bimonthly. Offers travel management tips and information on ICTA educational programs.

★716★ *OAG Desktop Flight Guide-Worldwide Edition*
Official Airline Guides
2000 Clearwater Drive
Oak Brook, IL 60521
Ph: (708)574-6000 Fax: (708)474-6667
Richard A. NelsonPublisher
Monthly. Guide containing schedules of airlines operating throughout the world (excluding North America and Caribbean), published as a service for business travelers, travel agents, and airlines.

★717★ *Ocean State Traveler*
Ocean State Traveler
172 Bellevue Ave., Ste. 319
Newport, RI 02840
Ph: (401)847-0089 Fax: (401)847-5267
Eleyne Austen
Monthly. Newspaper containing tourist information for the state of Rhode Island.

★718★ *Recommend*
Worth International Communications Corp.
5979 NW, 151 St., Ste. 120
Miami Lakes, FL 33014
Ph: (305)828-0123 Fax: (305)826-6950
Hal Herman
Monthly. Travel industry magazine.

★719★ *Sales Skills Development*
Institute of Certified Travel Agents (ICTA)
148 Linden St.
PO Box 812059
Wellesley, MA 02181-0012
Ph: (617)237-0280 Fax: (617)237-3860
Fr: 800-542-4282
Includes workbook. Used for in-house training at agencies.

★720★ *Schedule of Daily Subsistence Allowance Rates*
United Nations Publications
PO Box 361
Birmingham, AL 35201-0361
Fax: (205)995-1588 Fr: 800-633-4931
Monthly. Journal compiling travel costs throughout the world.

★721★ *Southeast Travel Professional*
Southern Travel Professional
1200 NW 78th Ave., Ste. 201
Miami, FL 33126
Ph: (305)592-6133 Fax: (305)592-9741
Larry Cafiero
Monthly. Travel newspaper (tabloid).

★722★ *Travel Agent*
Universal Media, Inc.
801 2nd Ave., 7th Fl.
New York, NY 10017
Ph: (212)370-5050 Fax: (212)370-4491
Richard P. FriesePublisher
Weekly. Travel industry magazine.

★723★ *Travel Counselor Magazine*
Institute of Certified Travel Agents (ICTA)
148 Linden St.
PO Box 812059
Wellesley, MA 02181-0012
Ph: (617)237-0280 Fax: (617)237-3860
Fr: 800-542-4282
Bimonthly. Provides information to career travel agents.

★724★ *Travel Industry Honors*
American Society of Travel Agents (ASTA)
1101 King St.
Alexandria, VA 22314
Ph: (703)739-2782 Fax: (703)684-8319
Periodic.

MEETINGS AND CONVENTIONS

★725★ American Society of Travel Agents World Travel Congress
American Society of Travel Agents
1101 King St.
Alexandria, VA 22314
Ph: (703)739-2782 Fax: (703)684-8319
Fr: 800-828-2712
Annual. **Dates and Locations:** 1995 Nov 05-10; Philadelphia, PA.

★726★ National Forum
Institute of Certified Travel Agents (ICTA)
148 Linden St.
PO Box 812059
Wellesley, MA 02181-0012
Ph: (617)237-0280 Fax: (617)237-3860
Fr: 800-542-4282
Annual.

★727★ Travel South USA Showcase
Travel South USA Showcase
3400 Peachtree Rd., NE
Atlanta, GA 30326
Ph: (404)231-1790 Fax: (404)231-2364
Annual.

OTHER SOURCES OF INFORMATION

★728★ *Choosing the Right Travel School*
American Society of Travel Agents
1101 King St., Ste. 200
Alexandria, VA 22314
Ph: (703)739-2782
1989. This four-panel brochure offers a list of questions to help prospective students evaluate a travel agent training program.

★729★ *Eurail Guide: How to Travel Europe and All the World by Train*
Houghton Mifflin Co.
222 Berkeley St.
Boston, MA 02116-3764
Ph: (617)523-1670 Fax: (617)523-1021
Barbara F. Saltzman, Contact
Annual, January. Covers rail trips for tourists in 112 countries. Entries include: Departure times, arrival times, on-board services (eating, sleeping, air conditioning facilities), and notable scenery enroute. Arrangement: Geographical.

★730★ *Europe by Train: The Complete Guide to Inter Railing*
HarperCollins
10 E. 53rd St.
New York, NY 10022
Ph: (212)207-7000 Fax: (212)343-3611
Fr: 800-2-HARPER
Helen Moore, Contact

Annual, March. Covers hotels, inns, hostels, and restaurants near European train stations that are recommended by the editors as being reasonably priced; also includes attractions and sites. Arrangement: Geographical.

★731★ *First Class: In Introduction to Travel and Tourism*
Glencoe Publishing Co.
866 3rd Ave.
New York, NY 10022
Ph: (212)702-3276

2nd edition, 1995.

★732★ *Fodor's Guides*
Fodor's Travel Publications, Inc.
201 E. 50th St.
New York, NY 10022
Ph: (212)872-8254 Fr: 800-733-3000

Annual. This series of travel guides now comprises approximately 140 titles; prospective travelers may select coverage at the continental, regional, national, or local scale. The guides offer detailed information about sights and accommodations, as well as general travel advice and commentary.

★733★ *Travel*
Crestwood House
866 3rd Ave.
New York, NY 10022
Ph: (212)702-9632

1994.

★734★ "Travel Agent" in *100 Best Jobs for the 1990s & Beyond*
Dearborn Financial Publishing, Inc.
520 N. Dearborn St.
Chicago, IL 60610-4354
Ph: (312)836-4400 Fax: (312)836-1021
Fr: 800-621-9621

Carol Kleiman. 1992. Describes 100 jobs ranging from accountants to veterinarians. Each job profile includes such information as education, experience, and certification needed, salaries, and job search suggestions.

★735★ "Travel Agent" in *Career Selector 2001*
Barron's Educational Series, Inc.
250 Wireless Blvd.
Hauppauge, NY 11788
Ph: (516)434-3311 Fax: (516)434-3723
Fr: 800-645-3476

James C. Gonyea. 1993.

Adjusters, Investigators and Collectors

Adjusters, investigators and collectors act as intermediaries between an organization and its clients. **Claim representatives** investigate claims, negotiate settlements, and authorize payments to claimants. To expedite the processing, minor claims filed by automobile or homeowner policy holders are usually handled by inside adjusters or telephone adjusters. These workers contact claimants by telephone or by mail to get information on repair costs, medical expenses, or other records needed by the company. More complex cases are referred to a claim adjuster or outside adjuster. **Claim adjusters** plan and schedule the work required to process a claim. Material damage adjusters inspect automobile damage and prepare estimates of the damage. Claim adjusters sometimes testify in court on contested claims. Claim examiners investigate questionable claims or those exceeding a designated amount. Examiners are authorized to investigate and approve payments on all claims up to a certain limit; larger claims are referred to a senior examiner. Policy processing clerks process new policies, modifications to existing policies, and claims. Claim clerks, also called claim interviewers, obtain information from policy-holders regarding claims, prepare reports, and review insurance claim forms. **Adjustment clerks** investigate and resolve customers' complaints about merchandise, service, billing, or credit rating. Sometimes they are called customer service representatives, customer complaint clerks, or adjustment correspondents. **Bill and account collectors**, sometimes called collection correspondents, are responsible for ensuring that customers pay their overdue accounts. This may involve meeting with customers to offer payment advice or review the terms of the original sale, service or credit contract. **Welfare eligibility workers and interviewers**-- sometimes referred to as intake workers, eligibility determination workers, eligibility specialists, or income maintenance specialists-- determine who can receive welfare and other types of social assistance. Adjusters, investigators, and collectors often work for insurance companies, real estate firms, department stores, manufacturing firms, banks and other financial institutions, telephone companies, and credit reporting and collection agencies.

Salaries

Earnings of adjusters, investigators, and collectors vary significantly.

Adjusters and investigators	$310-$510/week
Insurance claims representatives	$340-$580/week
Bill and account collectors	$2900$450/week
Welfare eligibility workers and interviewers	$300-$500/week

Employment Outlook

Growth rate until the year 2005: Average.

Adjusters, Investigators and Collectors

Career Guides

★736★ "Adjusters, Investigators, and Collectors" in *Occupational Outlook Handbook*
U.S. Government Printing Office
Superintendent of Documents
Washington, DC 20402
Ph: (202)512-1800 Fax: (202)512-2250

Biennial; latest edition, 1994-95. Encyclopedia of careers describing more than 250 occupations and comprising about 85 percent of all jobs in the economy. Occupations that require lengthy education or training are given the most attention. For each occupation, the handbook describes job duties, working conditions, training, educational preparation, personal qualities, advancement possibilities, job outlook, earnings, and sources of additional information.

★737★ "Adjusters" in *Opportunities in Insurance Careers* (pp. 42-43)
National Textbook Co. (NTC)
VGM Career Books
4255 W. Touhy Ave.
Lincolnwood, IL 60646-1975
Ph: (708)679-5500 Fax: (708)679-2494
Fr: 800-323-4900

Robert M. Schrayer. 1993. Explores the history of the insurance industry and career opportunities. Describes educational requirements, certification, licensing, salaries, and employment outlook.

★738★ "Benefits Claims Examiner" in *Opportunities in Insurance Careers* (p. 39)
National Textbook Co. (NTC)
VGM Career Books
4255 W. Touhy Ave.
Lincolnwood, IL 60646-1975
Ph: (708)679-5500 Fax: (708)679-2494
Fr: 800-323-4900

Robert M. Schrayer. 1993. Explores the history of the insurance industry and career opportunities. Describes educational requirements, certification, licensing, salaries, and employment outlook.

★739★ *Bill Collector*
Careers, Inc.
PO Box 135
Largo, FL 34649-0135
Ph: (813)584-7333

1992. Two-page occupational summary card describing duties, working conditions, personal qualifications, training, earnings and hours, employment outlook, places of employment, related careers and where to write for more information.

★740★ "Bill Collector" in *Occu-Facts: Information on 580 Careers in Outline Form*
Careers, Inc.
PO Box 135
Largo, FL 34649-0135
Ph: (813)584-7333

Biennial, 1995-96 edition. Each one-page occupational profile describes duties, working conditions, physical surroundings and demands, aptitudes, temperament, educational requirements, employment outlook, earnings, and places of employment.

★741★ *Bill Collectors*
Chronicle Guidance Publications, Inc.
66 Aurora St.
PO Box 1190
Moravia, NY 13118-1190
Ph: (315)497-0330 Fax: (315)497-3359
Fr: 800-622-7284

1994. This career brief describes the nature of the work, working conditions, hours and earnings, education and training, licensure, certification, unions, personal qualifications, social and psychological factors, employment outlook, entry methods, advancement, and related occupations.

★742★ *Careers in Insurance: Property and Casualty*
Insurance Information Institute
110 William St.
New York, NY 10038
Ph: (212)669-9200

1987. This 12-page booklet explores careers in property and casualty insurance and covers job duties and training.

★743★ *Careers in Life and Health Claims*
International Claim Association
Mississippi River at 17th St.
Rock Island, IL 61201
Ph: (309)786-6481

This booklet describes jobs in insurance claims. Covers salaries and future trends.

★744★ "Claim Adjuster" in *Career Information Center* (Vol.1)
Simon and Schuster
200 Old Tappan Rd.
Old Tappan, NJ 07675
Fax: 800-445-6991 Fr: 800-223-2348

Richard Lidz and Dale Anderson, editorial directors. Fifth edition, 1993. For 600 occupations, describes job duties, entry-level requirements, education and training needed, advancement possibilities, employment outlook, earnings and benefits. The set is divided into 12 volumes. Each volume includes jobs related under a broad career field. Volume 13 is the index.

★745★ "Claim Agent" in *Careers in Trucking*
Rosen Publishing Group
29 E. 21st St.
New York, NY 10010
Ph: (212)777-3017 Fax: (212)777-0277
Fr: 800-237-9932

Donald D. Schauer. 1991. Describes employment in the trucking industry including driving, operations, sales, and administration. Covers qualifications, training, future outlook, and salaries. Offers career planning and job hunting advice.

★746★ "Claim Examiner" in *Career Information Center* (Vol.1)
Simon and Schuster
200 Old Tappan Rd.
Old Tappan, NJ 07675
Fax: 800-445-6991 Fr: 800-223-2348

Richard Lidz and Dale Anderson, editorial directors. Fifth edition, 1993. For 600 occupations, describes job duties, entry-level requirements, education and training needed, advancement possibilities, employment outlook, earnings and benefits. The set is divided into 12 volumes. Each volume includes

jobs related under a broad career field. Volume 13 is the index.

★747★ "Claim Representative" in *VGM's Careers Encyclopedia* (pp. 107-111)
National Textbook Co. (NTC)
VGM Career Books
4255 W. Touhy Ave.
Lincolnwood, IL 60646-1975
Ph: (708)679-5500 Fax: (708)679-2494
Fr: 800-323-4900

Third edition, 1991. Contains two- to five-page descriptions of 200 managerial, professional, technical, trade, and service occupations. Each profile includes job duties, places of employment, qualifications, educational preparation, training, employment potential, advancement, income, and additional sources of information.

★748★ "Claim Representative" in *VGM's Handbook of Business and Management Careers* (pp. 30-32)
National Textbook Co. (NTC)
VGM Career Books
4255 W. Touhy Ave.
Lincolnwood, IL 60646-1975
Ph: (708)679-5500 Fax: (708)679-2494
Fr: 800-323-4900

Annette Selden, editor. Second edition, 1993. Contains 42 two-page occupational profiles describing job duties, places of employment, working conditions, qualifications, education, employment outlook, and income.

★749★ "Claim Representatives" in *Jobs! What They Are—Where They Are—What They Pay* (pp. 154)
Simon & Schuster, Inc.
Simon & Schuster Bldg.
1230 Avenue of the Americas
New York, NY 10020
Ph: (212)698-7000

Robert O. Snelling and Anne M. Snelling. Revised edition, 1992. Profiles 241 occupations, describing duties and responsibilities, educational preparation, earnings, employment opportunities, training, and qualifications.

★750★ *Claims Adjusters (Insurance)*
Chronicle Guidance Publications, Inc.
66 Aurora St.
PO Box 1190
Moravia, NY 13118-1190
Ph: (315)497-0330 Fax: (315)497-3359
Fr: 800-622-7284

1993. This career brief describes the nature of the work, working conditions, hours and earnings, education and training, licensure, certification, unions, personal qualifications, social and psychological factors, employment outlook, entry methods, advancement, and related occupations.

★751★ "Claims Representatives" in *Opportunities in Insurance Careers* (p. 37)
National Textbook Co. (NTC)
VGM Career Books
4255 W. Touhy Ave.
Lincolnwood, IL 60646-1975
Ph: (708)679-5500 Fax: (708)679-2494
Fr: 800-323-4900

Robert M. Schrayer. 1993. Explores the history of the insurance industry and career opportunities. Describes educational requirements, certification, licensing, salaries, and employment outlook.

★752★ *Clerks, Insurance*
Careers, Inc.
PO Box 135
Largo, FL 34649-0135
Ph: (813)584-7333

1992. Two-page occupational summary card describing duties, working conditions, personal qualifications, training, earnings and hours, employment outlook, places of employment, related careers and where to write for more information.

★753★ "Collection Workers" in *Career Discovery Encyclopedia* (Vol.2, pp. 26-27)
J.G. Ferguson Publishing Co.
200 W. Madison St., Ste. 300
Chicago, IL 60606
Ph: (312)580-5480 Fax: (312)580-4948

E. Russell Primm, editor-in-chief. 1993. Contains two-page articles on 504 occupations. Each article describes job duties, earnings, and educational and training requirements.

★754★ "Collection Workers" in *Encyclopedia of Careers and Vocational Guidance* (Vol.2, pp. 332-334)
J.G. Ferguson Publishing Co.
200 W. Madison St., Ste. 300
Chicago, IL 60606
Ph: (312)580-5480 Fax: (312)580-4948

William E. Hopke, editor-in-chief. Ninth edition, 1993. Four-volume set that profiles 500 occupations and describes job trends in 74 industries. Includes career description, educational requirements, history of the job, methods of entry, advancement, employment outlook, earnings, working conditions, social and psychological factors, and sources of additional information.

★755★ "Collectors" in *Jobs! What They Are—Where They Are—What They Pay* (pp. 150)
Simon & Schuster, Inc.
Simon & Schuster Bldg.
1230 Avenue of the Americas
New York, NY 10020
Ph: (212)698-7000

Robert O. Snelling and Anne M. Snelling. Revised edition, 1992. Profiles 241 occupations, describing duties and responsibilities, educational preparation, earnings, employment opportunities, training, and qualifications.

★756★ "Credit Collector" in *Career Information Center* (Vol.1)
Simon and Schuster
200 Old Tappan Rd.
Old Tappan, NJ 07675
Fax: 800-445-6991 Fr: 800-223-2348

Richard Lidz and Dale Anderson, editorial directors. Fifth edition, 1993. For 600 occupations, describes job duties, entry-level requirements, education and training needed, advancement possibilities, employment outlook, earnings and benefits. The set is divided into 12 volumes. Each volume includes jobs related under a broad career field. Volume 13 is the index.

★757★ "Customer Service Assistant" in *Career Opportunities in Art* (p. 135)
Facts on File
460 Park Ave. S.
New York, NY 10016-7382
Ph: (212)683-2244 Fax: 800-678-3633
Fr: 800-322-8755

Susan H. Haubenstock and David Joselit. 1988. Profiles more than 75 art-related jobs. Each occupational profile covers job duties, employment outlook, career paths, salaries, skills, and educational preparation. Offers tips for entering the field.

★758★ "Customer Service Representative" in *Career Opportunities in Television, Cable, and Video* (pp. 170-171)
Facts on File
460 Park Ave. S.
New York, NY 10016-7382
Ph: (212)683-2244 Fax: 800-678-3633
Fr: 800-322-8755

Third edition, 1990. Describes 100 media-related jobs. Each occupational profile covers job duties, employment outlook, career paths, salaries, skills, and educational preparation. Offers tips for entering the field.

★759★ "Customer Service Representative" in *Careers in Trucking*
Rosen Publishing Group
29 E. 21st St.
New York, NY 10010
Ph: (212)777-3017 Fax: (212)777-0277
Fr: 800-237-9932

Donald D. Schauer. 1991. Describes employment in the trucking industry including driving, operations, sales, and administration. Covers qualifications, training, future outlook, and salaries. Offers career planning and job hunting advice.

★760★ "Customer Service Representative" in *Jobs! What They Are—Where They Are—What They Pay* (pp. 248)
Simon & Schuster, Inc.
Simon & Schuster Bldg.
1230 Avenue of the Americas
New York, NY 10020
Ph: (212)698-7000

Robert O. Snelling and Anne M. Snelling. Revised edition, 1992. Profiles 241 occupations, describing duties and responsibilities, educational preparation, earnings, employment opportunities, training, and qualifications.

★761★ "Field Representatives" in *Opportunities in Insurance Careers* (pp. 42-43)
National Textbook Co. (NTC)
VGM Career Books
4255 W. Touhy Ave.
Lincolnwood, IL 60646-1975
Ph: (708)679-5500 Fax: (708)679-2494
Fr: 800-323-4900

Robert M. Schrayer. 1993. Explores the history of the insurance industry and career opportunities. Describes educational requirements, certification, licensing, salaries, and employment outlook.

★762★ ***Insurance Adjuster***
Careers, Inc.
PO Box 135
Largo, FL 34649-0135
Ph: (813)584-7333

1991. Two-page occupational summary card describing duties, working conditions, personal qualifications, training, earnings and hours, employment outlook, places of employment, related careers and where to write for more information.

★763★ **"Insurance Adjuster" in *Occu-Facts: Information on 580 Careers in Outline Form***
Careers, Inc.
PO Box 135
Largo, FL 34649-0135
Ph: (813)584-7333

Biennial, 1995-96 edition. Each one-page occupational profile describes duties, working conditions, physical surroundings and demands, aptitudes, temperament, educational requirements, employment outlook, earnings, and places of employment.

★764★ **"Insurance Claims Representatives" in *Career Discovery Encyclopedia* (Vol.3, pp. 136-137)**
J.G. Ferguson Publishing Co.
200 W. Madison St., Ste. 300
Chicago, IL 60606
Ph: (312)580-5480 Fax: (312)580-4948

E. Russell Primm, editor-in-chief. 1993. Contains two-page articles on 504 occupations. Each article describes job duties, earnings, and educational and training requirements.

★765★ **"Insurance Claims Representatives" in *Encyclopedia of Careers and Vocational Guidance* (Vol.3, pp. 221-223)**
J.G. Ferguson Publishing Co.
200 W. Madison St., Ste. 300
Chicago, IL 60606
Ph: (312)580-5480 Fax: (312)580-4948

William E. Hopke, editor-in-chief. Ninth edition, 1993. Four-volume set that profiles 500 occupations and describes job trends in 74 industries. Includes career description, educational requirements, history of the job, methods of entry, advancement, employment outlook, earnings, working conditions, social and psychological factors, and sources of additional information.

★766★ **"Insurance Clerks" in *Occu-Facts: Information on 580 Careers in Outline Form***
Careers, Inc.
PO Box 135
Largo, FL 34649-0135
Ph: (813)584-7333

Biennial, 1995-96 edition. Each one-page occupational profile describes duties, working conditions, physical surroundings and demands, aptitudes, temperament, educational requirements, employment outlook, earnings, and places of employment.

★767★ **"Insurance Policy Processing Occupations" in *Career Discovery Encyclopedia* (Vol.3, pp. 138-139)**
J.G. Ferguson Publishing Co.
200 W. Madison St., Ste. 300
Chicago, IL 60606
Ph: (312)580-5480 Fax: (312)580-4948

E. Russell Primm, editor-in-chief. 1993. Contains two-page articles on 504 occupations. Each article describes job duties, earnings, and educational and training requirements.

★768★ **"Insurance Policy Processing Occupations" in *Encyclopedia of Careers and Vocational Guidance* (Vol.3, pp. 224-226)**
J.G. Ferguson Publishing Co.
200 W. Madison St., Ste. 300
Chicago, IL 60606
Ph: (312)580-5480 Fax: (312)580-4948

William E. Hopke, editor-in-chief. Ninth edition, 1993. Four-volume set that profiles 500 occupations and describes job trends in 74 industries. Includes career description, educational requirements, history of the job, methods of entry, advancement, employment outlook, earnings, working conditions, social and psychological factors, and sources of additional information.

★769★ **"Resolution, Personal Services and Transportation Careers" in *The Best Jobs for the 1990s and Into the 21st Century***
Impact Publications
9104-N Manassas Dr.
Manassas Park, VA 22111
Ph: (703)361-7300 Fax: (703)335-9486

Ronald L. Krannich and Caryl Rae Krannich. 1993. Includes information on a wide variety of careers including adjusters, investigators, and collectors, animal caretakers, electricians, services sales reps., and truck drivers.

★770★ ***Secrets of Locating Past Due Debtors***
Bill Arnold Associates, Inc.
2330 Perkins Rd.
Arlington, TX 76016
Ph: (817)457-6559 Fax: (817)457-2619

Videocassette. 1986. 42 mins. For training debt collectors, how to track down welchers.

★771★ ***Video Career Library - Clerical & Administrative Support***
Careers, Inc.
PO Box 135
Largo, FL 34649-0135
Ph: (813)584-7333

Videocassette. 1990. 26 mins. Part of the Video Career Library covering 165 occupations. Shows actual workers on the job. Includes secretaries, cashiers, receptionists, bookkeepers and audit clerks, telephone operators, postal clerks/carriers/supervisors, insurance investigators, bank tellers, data entry keyers, and court reporters.

ASSOCIATIONS

★772★ **Alliance of American Insurers (ALLIANCE)**
1501 Woodfield Rd., Ste. 400 W
Schaumburg, IL 60173-4980
Ph: (708)330-8500 Fax: (708)330-8602

Members: Property and casualty insurance companies.

★773★ **American Collectors Association (ACA)**
ASAE Bldg.
4040 W. 70th St.
Minneapolis, MN 55435-4199
Ph: (612)926-6547 Fax: (612)926-1624

Members: Collection services handling overdue accounts for retail, professional, and commercial credit grantors. **Purpose:** Maintains Healthcare Client Services Program, which provides services for members who work with the health care industry and providers. Conducts research. Offers specialized education; compiles statistics. **Publications:** *American Collectors Association—Membership Roster*, annual. • *Collector*, monthly. • *Corporate Collector Currents*, biweekly. • *Cred-Alert*, monthly. • *Public Affairs Review*, monthly.

★774★ **Insurance Information Institute (III)**
110 William St.
New York, NY 10038
Ph: (212)669-9200 Fax: (212)732-1916

Members: Property and liability insurance companies. **Purpose:** Provides information and educational services to mass media, educational institutions, trade associations, businesses, government agencies, and the public. Conducts public opinion surveys. Sponsors seminars and briefings on insurance, safety, research, public policy, and economic topics. **Publications:** *Executive Media Alert*, biweekly. • *I.I.I. Insurance Daily*. • *Insurance Facts*, annual. • *Insurance Issues Update*, monthly. • *Insurance Pulse*, quarterly.

★775★ **Life Office Management Association (LOMA)**
5770 Powers Ferry Rd. NW
Atlanta, GA 30327
Ph: (404)951-1770 Fax: (404)984-0441

Members: Life and health insurance companies in the U.S. and Canada; associate members are life insurers in 33 countries; affiliate members are firms that provide professional support to member companies. **Purpose:** Provides research, information, training, and educational activities in areas of operations and systems, human resources, financial planning and employee development. Administers FLMI Insurance Education Program, which awards FLMI (Fellow, Life Management Institute) designation to life and health insurance company employees and others who complete the ten-examination program. **Publications:** *LOMA Membership Directory*, annual. • *Research Reports*. • *Resource*, monthly.

★776★ National Association of Public Insurance Adjusters (NAPIA)
300 Water St., Ste. 400
Baltimore, MD 21202
Ph: (410)539-4141 Fax: (410)659-9491

Members: Professional society of public insurance adjusters. **Purpose:** Sponsors certification and professional education programs. **Publications:** *NAPIA Bulletin*, quarterly.

Standards/Certification Agencies

★777★ Life Office Management Association (LOMA)
5770 Powers Ferry Rd., NW
Atlanta, GA 30327
Ph: (404)951-1770

Administers FLMI Insurance Education Program, which awards FLMI (Fellow, Life Management Institute) designation to life and health insurance company employees and others who complete the ten-examination program.

★778★ National Association of Public Insurance Adjusters (NAPIA)
300 Water St., Ste. 400
Baltimore, MD 21202
Ph: (410)539-4141 Fax: (410)659-9491

Sponsors certification and professional education programs.

Test Guides

★779★ *Career Examination Series: Assessment Assistant*
National Learning Corp.
212 Michael Dr.
Syosset, NY 11791
Ph: (516)921-8888 Fax: (516)921-8743
Fr: 800-645-6337

Jack Rudman. All examination guides in this series contain questions with answers.

★780★ *Career Examination Series: Assessment Clerk*
National Learning Corp.
212 Michael Dr.
Syosset, NY 11791
Ph: (516)921-8888 Fax: (516)921-8743
Fr: 800-645-6337

Jack Rudman. All examination guides in this series contain questions with answers.

★781★ *Career Examination Series: Associate Claim Examiner*
National Learning Corp.
212 Michael Dr.
Syosset, NY 11791
Ph: (516)921-8888 Fax: (516)921-8743
Fr: 800-645-6337

Jack Rudman. All examination guides in this series contain questions with answers.

★782★ *Career Examination Series: Chief Investigator*
National Learning Corp.
212 Michael Dr.
Syosset, NY 11791
Ph: (516)921-8888 Fax: (516)921-8743
Fr: 800-645-6337

Jack Rudman. All examination guides in this series contain questions with answers.

★783★ *Career Examination Series: Claims Clerk*
National Learning Corp.
212 Michael Dr.
Syosset, NY 11791
Ph: (516)921-8888 Fax: (516)921-8743
Fr: 800-645-6337

Jack Rudman. All examination guides in this series contain questions with answers.

★784★ *Career Examination Series: Claims Investigator*
National Learning Corp.
212 Michael Dr.
Syosset, NY 11791
Ph: (516)921-8888 Fax: (516)921-8743
Fr: 800-645-6337

Jack Rudman. All examination guides in this series contain questions with answers.

★785★ *Career Examination Series: Credit and Collection Coordinator*
National Learning Corp.
212 Michael Dr.
Syosset, NY 11791
Ph: (516)921-8888 Fax: (516)921-8743
Fr: 800-645-6337

Jack Rudman. All examination guides in this series contain questions with answers.

★786★ *Investigator/Claim Examiner*
Prentice Hall Press
Simon & Schuster Inc.
200 Old Tappan Rd.
Old Tappan, NJ 07675
Ph: 800-223-2348

John Czukor. First edition, 1990. Complete preparation for the qualifying test for civil service Investigators/Claim Examiners. Includes five practice tests with answers.

Awards, Scholarships, Grants, and Fellowships

★787★ NAFI Man of the Year
National Association of Fire Investigators
PO Box 957257
Hoffman Estates, IL 60195-7257
Ph: (312)427-6320

To recognize significant contributions to the fire investigation profession and NAFI. Firefighters, police officers, attorneys, insurance adjusters, claimsmen, fire experts, fire marshals in the military, or full-time fire investigators may be nominated. An engraved plaque is awarded annually when merited. Established in 1969.

Basic Reference Guides and Handbooks

★788★ *National Association of Public Insurance Adjusters Directory*
National Association of Public Insurance Adjusters (NAPIA)
300 Water St., Ste. 400
Baltimore, MD 21202
Ph: (410)539-4141 Fax: (410)659-9491

Biennial.

Periodicals

★789★ *Adjusters Reference Guide*
Insurance Field Co.
PO Box 24244
Louisville, KY 40224-0244
Ph: (502)491-5857 Fax: (502)491-5905
R.W. Bourne

Quarterly. Reference guide for insurance adjusters. Contains claim information and specimen policies.

★790★ *American Agent & Broker*
Commerce Publishing Co.
330 N. 4th St.
Saint Louis, MO 63102
Ph: (314)421-5445 Fax: (314)421-1070
George Williams

Monthly. Magazine for independent agents in fire, casualty, and surety insurance businesses.

★791★ *American Collectors Association—Membership Roster*
American Collectors Association (ACA)
ASAE Bldg.
4040 W. 70th St.
Minneapolis, MN 55435-4199
Ph: (612)926-6547 Fax: (612)926-1624

Annual.

★792★ *Collector*
American Collectors Association (ACA)
ASAE Bldg.
4040 W. 70th St.
Minneapolis, MN 55435-4199
Ph: (612)926-6547 Fax: (612)926-1624

Monthly. Covers the consumer debt collection industry. Includes regulation, agency management, and collection techniques information.

★793★ *Corporate Collector Currents*
American Collectors Association (ACA)
ASAE Bldg.
4040 W. 70th St.
Minneapolis, MN 55435-4199
Ph: (612)926-6547 Fax: (612)926-1624

Biweekly. Legal and legislative information.

★794★ *Cred-Alert*
American Collectors Association
4040 W. 70th St.
Minneapolis, MN 55435
Ph: (612)926-6547 Fax: (612)926-1624
Sandra Whalen

Monthly. Monitors credit and collection court decisions, legislative decisions, and other general credit matters of interest to credit grantors and collectors.

★795★ *Executive Media Alert*
Insurance Information Institute (III)
110 William St.
New York, NY 10038
Ph: (212)669-9200 Fax: (212)732-1916

Biweekly.

★796★ *I.I.I. Insurance Daily*
Insurance Information Institute (III)
110 William St.
New York, NY 10038
Ph: (212)669-9200 Fax: (212)732-1916

★797★ *Insurance Facts*
Insurance Information Institute (III)
110 William St.
New York, NY 10038
Ph: (212)669-9200 Fax: (212)732-1916

Annual.

★798★ *Insurance Issues Update*
Insurance Information Institute (III)
110 William St.
New York, NY 10038
Ph: (212)669-9200 Fax: (212)732-1916

Monthly.

★799★ *Insurance Pulse*
Insurance Information Institute (III)
110 William St.
New York, NY 10038
Ph: (212)669-9200 Fax: (212)732-1916

Quarterly.

★800★ *NAPIA Bulletin*
National Association of Public Insurance Adjusters (NAPIA)
300 Water St., Ste. 400
Baltimore, MD 21202
Ph: (410)539-4141 Fax: (410)659-9491

Quarterly.

★801★ *Public Affairs Review*
American Collectors Association (ACA)
ASAE Bldg.
4040 W. 70th St.
Minneapolis, MN 55435-4199
Ph: (612)926-6547 Fax: (612)926-1624

Monthly.

★802★ *Southern Insurance*
Southern Insurance
PO Box 9001
Mount Vernon, NY 10552-9001
Stephen Acunto

Monthly. Insurance industry magazine.

Bank Tellers

Bank tellers cash customers' checks and process deposits and withdrawals from checking and savings accounts. Larger banks employ tellers with more specialized duties such as selling savings bonds, handling foreign currency, or computing interest on savings accounts. In most banks, tellers use computer terminals to keep accurate records of all transactions. Although they work independently, bank tellers are closely supervised and work directly with the public.

Salaries

Earnings for bank tellers vary according to responsibility, experience, and size and location of bank.

Lowest 10 percent	$10,500/year
Median	$14,800/year
Top 10 percent	$24,300/year

Employment Outlook

Growth rate until the year 2005: Decline.

Bank Tellers

Career Guides

★803★ "Bank Service Occupations" in *Career Discovery Encyclopedia* (Vol.1, pp. 100-101)
J.G. Ferguson Publishing Co.
200 W. Madison St., Ste. 300
Chicago, IL 60606
Ph: (312)580-5480 Fax: (312)580-4948

E. Russell Primm, editor-in-chief. 1993. Contains two-page articles on 504 occupations. Each article describes job duties, earnings, and educational and training requirements.

★804★ *Bank Teller*
Vocational Biographies, Inc.
PO Box 31
Sauk Centre, MN 56378-0031
Ph: (612)352-6516 Fax: (612)352-5546
Fr: 800-255-0752

1991. This pamphlet profiles a person working in the job. Includes information about job duties, working conditions, places of employment, educational preparation, labor market outlook, and salaries.

★805★ *Bank Teller*
Careers, Inc.
PO Box 135
Largo, FL 34649-0135
Ph: (813)584-7333

1994. Two-page occupational summary card describing duties, working conditions, personal qualifications, training, earnings and hours, employment outlook, places of employment, related careers and where to write for more information.

★806★ "Bank Teller" in *Career Information Center* (Vol.1)
Simon and Schuster
200 Old Tappan Rd.
Old Tappan, NJ 07675
Fax: 800-445-6991 Fr: 800-223-2348

Richard Lidz and Dale Anderson, editorial directors. Fifth edition, 1993. For 600 occupations, describes job duties, entry-level requirements, education and training needed, advancement possibilities, employment outlook, earnings and benefits. The set is divided into 12 volumes. Each volume includes jobs related under a broad career field. Volume 13 is the index.

★807★ "Bank Teller" in *Careers in Banking and Finance* (pp. 21-26)
Rosen Publishing Group
29 E. 21st St.
New York, NY 10010
Ph: (212)777-3017 Fax: (212)777-0277
Fr: 800-237-9932

Patricia Haddock. 1990. Describes more than 20 jobs at all levels in banking and finance. Contains information about the types of financial organizations where the jobs are found, educational requirements, job duties, and salaries. Offers advice on job hunting.

★808★ "Bank Teller" in *Guide to Careers Without College* (pp. 53-56)
Franklin Watts, Inc.
387 Park Avenue, S.
New York, NY 10016
Ph: (212)686-7070

Kathleen S. Abrams. 1988. Discusses careers that do not require a college degree in fields such as health care, sales and marketing, and the building trades. Describes the work, employment opportunities, and training.

★809★ "Bank Teller" in *Jobs Rated Almanac*
World Almanac
1 International Blvd., Ste. 444
Mahwah, NJ 07495
Ph: (201)529-6900 Fax: (201)529-6901

Les Krantz. Second edition, 1992. Ranks 250 jobs by environment, salary, outlooks, physical demands, stress, security, travel opportunities, and extra perks. Includes jobs the editor feels are the most common, most interesting, and the most rapidly growing.

★810★ "Bank Teller" in *Occu-Facts: Information on 580 Careers in Outline Form*
Careers, Inc.
PO Box 135
Largo, FL 34649-0135
Ph: (813)584-7333

Biennial, 1995-96 edition. Each one-page occupational profile describes duties, working conditions, physical surroundings and demands, aptitudes, temperament, educational requirements, employment outlook, earnings, and places of employment.

★811★ "Bank Teller" in *VGM's Careers Encyclopedia* (pp. 60-61)
National Textbook Co. (NTC)
VGM Career Books
4255 W. Touhy Ave.
Lincolnwood, IL 60646-1975
Ph: (708)679-5500 Fax: (708)679-2494
Fr: 800-323-4900

Third edition, 1991. Contains two- to five-page descriptions of 200 managerial, professional, technical, trade, and service occupations. Each profile includes job duties, places of employment, qualifications, educational preparation, training, employment potential, advancement, income, and additional sources of information.

★812★ "Bank Tellers" in *Jobs! What They Are—Where They Are—What They Pay* (pp. 149)
Simon & Schuster, Inc.
Simon & Schuster Bldg.
1230 Avenue of the Americas
New York, NY 10020
Ph: (212)698-7000

Robert O. Snelling and Anne M. Snelling. Revised edition, 1992. Profiles 241 occupations, describing duties and responsibilities, educational preparation, earnings, employment opportunities, training, and qualifications.

★813★ "Bank Tellers" in *Occupational Outlook Handbook*
U.S. Government Printing Office
Superintendent of Documents
Washington, DC 20402
Ph: (202)512-1800 Fax: (202)512-2250

Biennial; latest edition, 1994-95. Encyclopedia of careers describing more than 250 occupations and comprising about 85 percent of all jobs in the economy. Occupations that require lengthy education or training are given the most attention. For each occupation, the handbook describes job duties, working conditions, training, educational preparation, personal qualities, advancement possibilities, job outlook, earnings, and sources of additional information.

★814★ "Bank Worker" in *VGM's Handbook of Business and Management Careers*
National Textbook Co.
4255 W. Touhy Ave.
Lincolnwood, IL 60646-1975
Ph: (708)679-5500 Fax: (708)679-2494
Fr: 800-323-4900

Annette Selden. Second edition, 1993. Contains 42 two-page occupational profiles describing job duties, places of employment, working conditions, qualifications, education, employment outlook, and income.

★815★ "Banking" in *Internships 1995*
Petersons Guides, Inc.
PO Box 2123
Princeton, NJ 08543-2123
Ph: (609)243-9111 Fr: 800-338-3282

Fifteenth edition, 1995. Lists internship opportunities under six broad categories: communications, creative, performing, and fine arts, human services, international relations, business and technology, and public affairs. For each internship program, gives the names, phone number, contact person, description, eligibility requirements, and benefits.

★816★ *Career Success Series*
Cambridge Educational
PO Box 2153
Charleston, WV 25328-2153
Ph: (304)744-9323 Fax: (304)744-9351
Fr: 800-468-4227

Videocassette. 1986. 15 mins. A series, available separately, outlining various career choices for students. Occupations include: accounting, flight service, air transportation/ground/flight service, data processing, carpentry, clerk in banking/insurance, commodity sales, cosmetic personal grooming, fire fighting, forestry services, home economics, insulation/roofing, material handling, mechanics, photographic processing, pipefitting and plumbing, police science, printing, carpentry, medical laboratory technicians, secretarial services, and utilities equipment operator.

★817★ *Careers in the Investment World*
Chelsea House Publishers
1974 Sproul Rd., Ste. 400
Broomall, PA 19008
Ph: (215)353-5166 Fax: (215)359-1439

Rachel S. Epstein. 1988.

★818★ *Clerk: Bank, Insurance and Commerce*
Morris Video
2730 Monterey St., No. 105
Monterey Business Park
Torrance, CA 90503
Ph: (310)533-4800 Fr: 800-843-3606

Videocassette. 1981. 15 mins. The many and varied duties of the clerk are examined.

★819★ "Financial Institution Tellers" in *Encyclopedia of Careers and Vocational Guidance* (Vol.2, pp. 662-664)
J.G. Ferguson Publishing Co.
200 W. Madison St., Ste. 300
Chicago, IL 60606
Ph: (312)580-5480 Fax: (312)580-4948

William E. Hopke, editor-in-chief. Ninth edition, 1993. Four-volume set that profiles 500 occupations and describes job trends in 74 industries. Includes career description, educational requirements, history of the job, methods of entry, advancement, employment outlook, earnings, working conditions, social and psychological factors, and sources of additional information.

★820★ "Tellers and Clerks (Bank)" in *American Almanac of Jobs and Salaries* (pp. 402)
Avon Books
1350 Avenue of the Americas
New York, NY 10019
Ph: (212)261-6800 Fr: 800-238-0658

John Wright, editor. Revised and updated, 1994-95. A comprehensive guide to the wages of hundreds of occupations in a wide variety of industries and organizations.

★821★ *Tellers, Financial Institution*
Chronicle Guidance Publications, Inc.
66 Aurora St.
PO Box 1190
Moravia, NY 13118-1190
Ph: (315)497-0330 Fax: (315)497-3359
Fr: 800-622-7284

1994. This career brief describes the nature of the work, working conditions, hours and earnings, education and training, licensure, certification, unions, personal qualifications, social and psychological factors, employment outlook, entry methods, advancement, and related occupations.

★822★ *Tellers—How Important Are They?*
First Financial Video Network
4811 Emerson St., Ste. 210
Palatine, IL 60067-7417
Ph: (708)397-9000 Fax: (708)397-6721
Fr: 800-442-8662

Videocassette. 1987. 23 mins. The importance of tellers and other platform personnel is the thrust of this program.

★823★ *Video Career Library - Clerical & Administrative Support*
Careers, Inc.
PO Box 135
Largo, FL 34649-0135
Ph: (813)584-7333

Videocassette. 1990. 26 mins. Part of the Video Career Library covering 165 occupations. Shows actual workers on the job. Includes secretaries, cashiers, receptionists, bookkeepers and audit clerks, telephone operators, postal clerks/carriers/supervisors, insurance investigators, bank tellers, data entry keyers, and court reporters.

ASSOCIATIONS

★824★ American Bankers Association (ABA)
1120 Connecticut Ave. NW
Washington, DC 20036
Ph: (202)663-5000 Fax: (202)663-7533

Members: Members are principally commercial banks and trust companies; combined assets of members represent approximately 90% of the U.S. banking industry; approximately 94% of members are community banks with less than $500 million in assets. **Purpose:** Seeks to enhance the role of commercial bankers as preeminent providers of financial services through communications, research, legal action, lobbying of federal legislative and regulatory bodies, and education and training programs. Serves as spokesperson for the banking industry; facilitates exchange of information among members. Maintains the American Institute of Banking, an industry-sponsored adult education program. Conducts educational and training programs for bank employees and officers through a wide range of banking schools and national conferences. Maintains liaison with federal bank regulators; submits draft legislation and lobbies Congress on issues affecting commercial banks; testifies before congressional committees; represents members in U.S. postal rate proceedings. Serves as secretariat of the International Monetary Conference and the Financial Institutions Committee for the American National Standards Institute. Compiles briefs and lawsuits in major court cases affecting the industry. Conducts teleconferences with state banking associations on such issues as regulatory compliance; works to build consensus and coordinate activities of leading bank and financial service trade groups. Provides services to members including: public advocacy; news media contact; insurance program providing directors and officers with liability coverage, financial institution bond, and trust errors and omissions coverage; research service operated through ABA Center for Banking Information; fingerprint set processing in conjunction with the Federal Bureau of Investigation; discounts on operational and income-producing projects through the Corporation for American Banking. Conducts conferences, forums, and workshops covering subjects such as small business, consumer credit, agricultural and community banking, trust management, bank operations, and automation. Sponsors the Personal Economics Program, which educates schoolchildren and the community on banking, economics, and personal finance. **Publications:** *ABA Banking Journal*, monthly. • *ABA Management Update of Personal Trust and Private Banking*, bimonthly. • *AIB Leader Letter*, quarterly. • *Bank Compliance Magazine*, quarterly. • *Bank Insurance and Protection Bulletin*, monthly. • *Bank Operations Bulletin*, monthly. • *Bank Personnel News*, monthly. • *Bank Security News*, monthly. • *Bankers News*, biweekly. • *Commercial Lending Review*, quarterly. • *Consumer Credit Delinquency Bulletin*, quarterly. • *Employee Benefits Quarterly*, quarterly. • *Journal of*

Agricultural Lending, quarterly. • *Network News*, 3/year. • *Retail Banking Digest*, bimonthly. • *Retail Delivery Systems Quarterly*, quarterly. • *Securities Processing Digest*, quarterly. • *Stonier Forum*, semiannual. • *Trends*, bimonthly. • *Trust and Financial Advisor*, quarterly. • *Trust Letter*, monthly.

★825★ *Bank Compliance Magazine*
American Bankers Association (ABA)
1120 Connecticut Ave. NW
Washington, DC 20036
Ph: (202)663-5000 Fax: (202)663-7533

Quarterly.

★826★ Institute of Financial Education (IFE)
111 E. Wacker Dr., 9th Fl.
Chicago, IL 60601-4680
Ph: (312)946-8801 Fax: (312)946-8802

Members: Nationwide educational organization conducting courses for personnel of savings institutions, commercial banks, and credit unions. **Purpose:** Conducts educational programs. **Publications:** *Bringing in Business*. • *Chapter Briefing*, monthly. • *Consumer Lending: From Application to Servicing*. • *Deposit Account Operations*. • *Deposit Accounts and Services*. • *Glossary of Financial Services Terminology*. • *HUD/FHA Quality Control Manual*. • *Insurance of Accounts: A Practical Guide to the FDIC Regulations*. • *IRA Basics*. • *1994 FHA/VA Loan Processing Information Service*. • *1994 FHA/VA Loan Servicing Manual*. • *Person to Person: Helping Customers Make Financial Decisions*. • *Residential Mortgage Lending Documentation*. • *Residential Mortgage Lending: From Application to Servicing*. • *Residential Mortgage Lending Origination*. • *Retail Banking: Serving the Financial Needs of Customers*. • *Sales Skills for Financial Professionals*. • *Service Excellence: New Techniques for Banking Professionals*. • *Supervisory Personnel Management: Building Work Relationships*. • *Supervisory Personnel Management: Maximizing Your Effectiveness*. • *Talking and Listening: Keys to Success with Customers and Co-Workers*. • *Teller Operations*. • *Truth in Savings Handbook for Front-Line Staff*. • *Write with Confidence: Tools for Financial Business Writing*. • *Your New Job: Tips for Career Success*.

Educational Directories and Programs

★827★ *AIB Student Catalog*
American Bankers Association (ABA)
1120 Connecticut Ave. NW
Washington, DC 20036
Ph: (202)663-5000

Annual.

Awards, Scholarships, Grants, and Fellowships

★828★ American Institute of Banking Scholarship
American Institute of Banking
c/o Ken Ambers
1213 Bakers Way
Manhattan, KS 66502
Ph: (913)537-4750

To be applied to tuition at the American Institute of Banking resident courses lasting 10 or 16 weeks. Applicants must be high school graduates or hold a GED. Scholarships are based on merit.

Basic Reference Guides and Handbooks

★829★ *Bank Tellers Do's & Don'ts*
American Bankers Association
1120 Connecticut Ave., NW
Washington, DC 20036
Ph: (202)663-7500 Fax: (202)828-4540

Revised edition, 1963.

★830★ *Bank Tellers Job: A Day to Day Reference Guide*
American Bankers Association
1120 Connecticut Ave., NW
Washington, DC 20036
Ph: (202)663-7500 Fax: (202)828-4540

American Bankers Association Staff. 1980.

★831★ *Glossary of Financial Services Terminology*
Institute of Financial Education
111 E. Wacker Dr.
Chicago, IL 60601-4389
Ph: (312)644-3100 Fax: (312)856-0497

Fourth edition. 1990.

★832★ *Teller Operations Manual*
Bank Administration Institute
60 Gould Center
Rolling Meadows, IL 60008
Fr: 800-323-8552

1990.

★833★ *Teller Performance*
Bank Administration Institute
60 Gould Center
Rolling Meadows, IL 60008
Fr: 800-323-8552

1989.

★834★ *Teller World*
Bank Administration Insitute
60 Gould Center
Rolling Meadows, IL 60008
Fr: 800-323-8552

Third edition, 1989.

Periodicals

★835★ *1994 FHA/VA Loan Processing Information Service*
Institute of Financial Education (IFE)
111 E. Wacker Dr., 9th Fl.
Chicago, IL 60601-4680
Ph: (312)946-8801 Fax: (312)946-8802

Features step-by-step instructions for completing documentation and calculations required by HUD and the VA. Quarterly updates available.

★836★ *1994 FHA/VA Loan Servicing Manual*
Institute of Financial Education (IFE)
111 E. Wacker Dr., 9th Fl.
Chicago, IL 60601-4680
Ph: (312)946-8801 Fax: (312)946-8802

Provides information on servicing government-insured or government-guaranteed loans.

★837★ *ABA Banking Journal*
American Bankers Association (ABA)
1120 Connecticut Ave. NW
Washington, DC 20036
Ph: (202)663-5000 Fax: (202)663-7533

Monthly.

★838★ *ABA Management Update of Personal Trust and Private Banking*
American Bankers Association (ABA)
1120 Connecticut Ave. NW
Washington, DC 20036
Ph: (202)663-5000 Fax: (202)663-7533

Bimonthly.

★839★ *AIB Leader Letter*
American Bankers Association (ABA)
1120 Connecticut Ave. NW
Washington, DC 20036
Ph: (202)663-5000 Fax: (202)663-7533

Quarterly.

★840★ *Bank Auditing and Accounting Report*
Warren, Gorham & Lamont, Inc.
31 St. James Ave.
Boston, MA 02116-4112
Ph: (617)423-2020 Fax: (617)695-9699
Stephen Collins

Monthly. Provides information on developments, practices, and techniques in bank accounting, auditing, and financial controls. Covers such topics as procedures for preventing embezzlement, improving management information systems, audit planning and supervision, and electronic data processing developments.

★841★ *Bank Compliance Magazine*
American Bankers Association (ABA)
1120 Connecticut Ave. NW
Washington, DC 20036
Ph: (202)663-5000 Fax: (202)663-7533

Quarterly.

★842★ *Bank Insurance & Protection Bulletin*
American Bankers Association (ABA)
1120 Connecticut Ave. NW
Washington, DC 20036
Ph: (202)663-5071 Fax: (202)828-4540
Fr: 800-338-0626
C. Howie Hodges

Monthly. Monitors the latest trends in risk management, insurance, and security for banks. Reports on current bank crime statistics, methods of deterrence, and other "state of the art information." Recurring features include news of research, notices of publications available, a calendar of events, meeting reports, and news of educational opportunities. Also announces ABA Security & Risk Management Division staff changes.

★843★ *Bank Operations Bulletin*
American Bankers Association (ABA)
1120 Connecticut Ave. NW
Washington, DC 20036
Ph: (202)663-5000 Fax: (202)663-7533

Monthly.

★844★ *Bank Operations Report*
Warren, Gorham & Lamont, Inc.
31 St. James Ave.
Boston, MA 02116-4112
Ph: (617)423-2020 Fax: (617)695-9699
Fr: 800-922-1201
Nancy Hitchner

Monthly. Focuses on electronic data processing control, check processing, record keeping, cost control, federal regulation, credit and debit cards, electronic funds transfer system, physical security, and office automation, computer, and systems applications.

★845★ *Bank Personnel News*
American Bankers Association (ABA)
1120 Connecticut Ave. NW
Washington, DC 20036
Ph: (202)663-5000 Fax: (202)663-7533

Monthly.

★846★ *Bank Security News*
American Bankers Association (ABA)
1120 Connecticut Ave. NW
Washington, DC 20036
Ph: (202)663-5000 Fax: (202)663-7533

Monthly.

★847★ *Bank Security Report*
Warren, Gorham & Lamont, Inc.
31 St. James Ave.
Boston, MA 02116-4112
Ph: (617)423-2020 Fax: (617)695-9699
Fr: 800-950-1201
Nancy Hitchner

Monthly. Compiles news, information, case histories, suggestions, and advice on bank security equipment and procedures, forgeries, check alterations, identifications, kiting, counterfeiting, money laundering, internal controls, and new federal announcements on bank security.

★848★ *Bank Teller's Report*
Warren, Gorham & Lamont, Inc.
1 Penn Plaza
New York, NY 10119
Ph: (212)971-5000 Fax: (212)971-5024
Fr: 800-950-1205
Joan German

Monthly. Designed to help bank tellers (and also their supervisors) "sharpen their job skills with tips on endorsements, forgeries, kiters, automation, settling, finding errors in computations and various time- and work-savers." Contains articles and briefs that address tellers' concerns and provides them with news, information, and guidance on bank services and customer service. Recurring features include columns titled One of Those Days (where tellers share frustrating or surprising incidents), Tips From Tellers, and Extraordinary Service (in which tellers share instances of service "beyond the call of duty").

★849★ *The Bankers Magazine*
Warren, Gorham and Lamont, Inc.
1 Penn Plaza
New York, NY 10119
Ph: (212)971-5000 Fax: (212)971-5025
Paul Blocklyn

Bimonthly. Magazine on banking.

★850★ *Bankers News*
American Bankers Association (ABA)
1120 Connecticut Ave. NW
Washington, DC 20036
Ph: (202)663-5000 Fax: (202)663-7533

Biweekly.

★851★ *Banking Policy Report*
Law & Business, Inc.
270 Sylvan Ave.
Englewood Cliffs, NJ 07632
Ph: (201)894-8538 Fax: (201)894-8666
Phillip Meyer

Semimonthly. Discusses new strategies, techniques, and developments in the financial services industry.

★852★ *Bringing in Business*
Institute of Financial Education (IFE)
111 E. Wacker Dr., 9th Fl.
Chicago, IL 60601-4680
Ph: (312)946-8801 Fax: (312)946-8802

★853★ *Chapter Briefing*
Institute of Financial Education (IFE)
111 E. Wacker Dr., 9th Fl.
Chicago, IL 60601-4680
Ph: (312)946-8801 Fax: (312)946-8802

Monthly. For chapter officers.

★854★ *Commercial Lending Review*
American Bankers Association (ABA)
1120 Connecticut Ave. NW
Washington, DC 20036
Ph: (202)663-5000 Fax: (202)663-7533

Quarterly. Published by Institutional Investor (endorsed by ABA).

★855★ *Consumer Credit Delinquency Bulletin*
American Bankers Association (ABA)
1120 Connecticut Ave. NW
Washington, DC 20036
Ph: (202)663-5000 Fax: (202)663-7533

Quarterly.

★856★ *Consumer Lending: From Application to Servicing*
Institute of Financial Education (IFE)
111 E. Wacker Dr., 9th Fl.
Chicago, IL 60601-4680
Ph: (312)946-8801 Fax: (312)946-8802

★857★ *Deposit Account Operations*
Institute of Financial Education (IFE)
111 E. Wacker Dr., 9th Fl.
Chicago, IL 60601-4680
Ph: (312)946-8801 Fax: (312)946-8802

Includes regulatory compliance information on reporting interest and currency transactions, federal tax levies, dormant accounts, and loans.

★858★ *Deposit Accounts and Services*
Institute of Financial Education (IFE)
111 E. Wacker Dr., 9th Fl.
Chicago, IL 60601-4680
Ph: (312)946-8801 Fax: (312)946-8802

Features information on account ownership, types of deposit accounts, and regulatory provisions and restrictions related to deposit accounts.

★859★ *Employee Benefits Quarterly*
American Bankers Association (ABA)
1120 Connecticut Ave. NW
Washington, DC 20036
Ph: (202)663-5000 Fax: (202)663-7533

Quarterly.

★860★ *Financial Marketing*
Charles E. Bartling, Contact
Provides marketing professionals from banks, savings institutions, and credit unions with pertinent information on current trends and developments in the marketing of financial services. Recurring features include letters to the editor, news of research, book reviews, job listing, and a calendar of events.

★861★ *HUD/FHA Quality Control Manual*
Institute of Financial Education (IFE)
111 E. Wacker Dr., 9th Fl.
Chicago, IL 60601-4680
Ph: (312)946-8801 Fax: (312)946-8802

Includes step-by-step instructions for implementing a quality control plan.

★862★ *Insurance of Accounts: A Practical Guide to the FDIC Regulations*
Institute of Financial Education (IFE)
111 E. Wacker Dr., 9th Fl.
Chicago, IL 60601-4680
Ph: (312)946-8801 Fax: (312)946-8802

Explains FDIC insurance regulations, ownership categories, and how accounts are insured.

★863★ *IRA Basics*
Institute of Financial Education (IFE)
111 E. Wacker Dr., 9th Fl.
Chicago, IL 60601-4680
Ph: (312)946-8801 Fax: (312)946-8802

Presents an overview of the process of establishing and maintaining IRAs at financial institutions.

★864★ *Journal of Agricultural Lending*
American Bankers Association (ABA)
1120 Connecticut Ave. NW
Washington, DC 20036
Ph: (202)663-5000 Fax: (202)663-7533
Quarterly.

★865★ *Network News*
American Bankers Association (ABA)
1120 Connecticut Ave. NW
Washington, DC 20036
Ph: (202)663-5000 Fax: (202)663-7533
3/year.

★866★ *Person to Person: Helping Customers Make Financial Decisions*
Institute of Financial Education (IFE)
111 E. Wacker Dr., 9th Fl.
Chicago, IL 60601-4680
Ph: (312)946-8801 Fax: (312)946-8802
Provides examples and case studies for identifying the needs of customers of various ages, backgrounds, and personalities.

★867★ *Residential Mortgage Lending Documentation*
Institute of Financial Education (IFE)
111 E. Wacker Dr., 9th Fl.
Chicago, IL 60601-4680
Ph: (312)946-8801 Fax: (312)946-8802
Identifies the documents that must be ordered, prepared, verified and organized before a loan file can be given to an underwriter.

★868★ *Residential Mortgage Lending: From Application to Servicing*
Institute of Financial Education (IFE)
111 E. Wacker Dr., 9th Fl.
Chicago, IL 60601-4680
Ph: (312)946-8801 Fax: (312)946-8802
Outlines the phases of residential mortgage lending, including types of loans, laws and regulations, evaluation procedures, and appraisal basics.

★869★ *Residential Mortgage Lending Origination*
Institute of Financial Education (IFE)
111 E. Wacker Dr., 9th Fl.
Chicago, IL 60601-4680
Ph: (312)946-8801 Fax: (312)946-8802
Provides a step-by-step guide to conducting an interview and completing the application process for conventional fixed and adjustable rate loans.

★870★ *Retail Banking Digest*
American Bankers Association
1120 Connecticut Ave. NW
Washington, DC 20036
Ph: (202)663-5000 Fax: (202)663-7533
Bimonthly.

★871★ *Retail Banking: Serving the Financial Needs of Customers*
Institute of Financial Education (IFE)
111 E. Wacker Dr., 9th Fl.
Chicago, IL 60601-4680
Ph: (312)946-8801 Fax: (312)946-8802
Explains the purpose and function of retail banks. Examines various types of loans and accounts. Includes information on banking regulations.

★872★ *Retail Delivery Systems Quarterly*
American Bankers Association (ABA)
1120 Connecticut Ave. NW
Washington, DC 20036
Ph: (202)663-5000 Fax: (202)663-7533
Quarterly.

★873★ *Sales Skills for Financial Professionals*
Institute of Financial Education (IFE)
111 E. Wacker Dr., 9th Fl.
Chicago, IL 60601-4680
Ph: (312)946-8801 Fax: (312)946-8802
Provides information on a systematic sales approach and methods for improving sales performance, productivity, and professionalism.

★874★ *Securities Processing Digest*
American Bankers Association (ABA)
1120 Connecticut Ave. NW
Washington, DC 20036
Ph: (202)663-5000 Fax: (202)663-7533
Quarterly.

★875★ *Service Excellence: New Techniques for Banking Professionals*
Institute of Financial Education (IFE)
111 E. Wacker Dr., 9th Fl.
Chicago, IL 60601-4680
Ph: (312)946-8801 Fax: (312)946-8802
Explains how to provide excellent service in difficult situations, the basics of customer service, and how to overcome potential problems.

★876★ *Stonier Forum*
American Bankers Association (ABA)
1120 Connecticut Ave. NW
Washington, DC 20036
Ph: (202)663-5000 Fax: (202)663-7533
Semiannual.

★877★ *Supervisory Personnel Management: Building Work Relationships*
Institute of Financial Education (IFE)
111 E. Wacker Dr., 9th Fl.
Chicago, IL 60601-4680
Ph: (312)946-8801 Fax: (312)946-8802
Provides strategies for managing change, increasing productivity, improving relations with staff, developing leadership style, and other skills.

★878★ *Supervisory Personnel Management: Maximizing Your Effectiveness*
Institute of Financial Education (IFE)
111 E. Wacker Dr., 9th Fl.
Chicago, IL 60601-4680
Ph: (312)946-8801 Fax: (312)946-8802
Explores ways to motivate staff, appraise performance, manage time, discipline employees, make decisions, solve conflicts, and manage with authority.

★879★ *Talking and Listening: Keys to Success with Customers and Co-Workers*
Institute of Financial Education (IFE)
111 E. Wacker Dr., 9th Fl.
Chicago, IL 60601-4680
Ph: (312)946-8801 Fax: (312)946-8802
Emphasizes effective communications with peers, subordinates, managers, and customers.

★880★ *Teller Operations*
Institute of Financial Education (IFE)
111 E. Wacker Dr., 9th Fl.
Chicago, IL 60601-4680
Ph: (312)946-8801 Fax: (312)946-8802
Includes strategies for handling cash and checks, reducing errors, managing emergency situations, and determining endorsements.

★881★ *Trends*
American Bankers Association (ABA)
1120 Connecticut Ave. NW
Washington, DC 20036
Ph: (202)663-5000 Fax: (202)663-7533
Bimonthly.

★882★ *Trust and Financial Advisor*
American Bankers Association (ABA)
1120 Connecticut Ave. NW
Washington, DC 20036
Ph: (202)663-5000 Fax: (202)663-7533
Quarterly.

★883★ *Trust Letter*
American Bankers Association (ABA)
1120 Connecticut Ave. NW
Washington, DC 20036
Ph: (202)663-5000 Fax: (202)663-7533
Monthly.

★884★ *Truth in Savings Handbook for Front-Line Staff*
Institute of Financial Education (IFE)
111 E. Wacker Dr., 9th Fl.
Chicago, IL 60601-4680
Ph: (312)946-8801 Fax: (312)946-8802
Explains the Truth in Savings Act and required disclosures.

★885★ *Write with Confidence: Tools for Financial Business Writing*
Institute of Financial Education (IFE)
111 E. Wacker Dr., 9th Fl.
Chicago, IL 60601-4680
Ph: (312)946-8801 Fax: (312)946-8802
Includes information on writing letters, memos, job procedures, and reports.

★886★ *Your New Job: Tips for Career Success*
Institute of Financial Education (IFE)
111 E. Wacker Dr., 9th Fl.
Chicago, IL 60601-4680
Ph: (312)946-8801 Fax: (312)946-8802
Stresses the importance of teamwork, positive attitudes, efficient work habits, first-rate job skills, and clear communications.

Other Sources of Information

★887★ "Bank Teller" in *Career Selector 2001*
Barron's Educational Series, Inc.
250 Wireless Blvd.
Hauppauge, NY 11788
Ph: (516)434-3311 Fax: (516)434-3723
Fr: 800-645-3476
James C. Gonyea. 1993.

Clerical Supervisors and Managers

Clerical supervisors and managers oversee the general operation of an organization's clerical department. They coordinate the work of individual employees to ensure that projects are completed within their allotted time. They also act as liaisons between the clerical staff and other departments. This may involve clarifying instructions, resolving conflicts, monitoring work progress and quality, and keeping management informed. Clerical supervisors and managers generally interview prospective clerical workers and train new employees. Although clerical workers are found in most industries, the largest number of clerical supervisors and managers are found in government agencies, wholesale trade outlets, banks, business service firms, colleges and universities, hospitals, and telephone companies.

Salaries

Salaries for clerical supervisors and managers are listed below.

Lowest 10 percent	Less than $16,200/year
Middle 50 percent	$21,100-$39,400/year
Top 10 percent	More than $51,300/year

Employment Outlook

Growth rate until the year 2005: Average.

Clerical Supervisors and Managers

CAREER GUIDES

★888★ "Clerical Supervisor and Manager" in *Careers in Banking and Finance* (pp. 33-34)
Rosen Publishing Group
29 E. 21st St.
New York, NY 10010
Ph: (212)777-3017 Fax: (212)777-0277
Fr: 800-237-9932

Patricia Haddock. 1990. Describes more than 20 jobs at all levels in banking and finance. Contains information about the types of financial organizations where the jobs are found, educational requirements, job duties, and salaries. Offers advice on job hunting.

★889★ "Clerical Supervisors and Managers" in *Career Discovery Encyclopedia* (Vol.2, pp. 14-15)
J.G. Ferguson Publishing Co.
200 W. Madison St., Ste. 300
Chicago, IL 60606
Ph: (312)580-5480 Fax: (312)580-4948

E. Russell Primm, editor-in-chief. 1993. Contains two-page articles on 504 occupations. Each article describes job duties, earnings, and educational and training requirements.

★890★ "Clerical Supervisors and Managers" in *Encyclopedia of Careers and Vocational Guidance* (Vol.2, pp. 312-313)
J.G. Ferguson Publishing Co.
200 W. Madison St., Ste. 300
Chicago, IL 60606
Ph: (312)580-5480 Fax: (312)580-4948

William E. Hopke, editor-in-chief. Ninth edition, 1993. Four-volume set that profiles 500 occupations and describes job trends in 74 industries. Includes career description, educational requirements, history of the job, methods of entry, advancement, employment outlook, earnings, working conditions, social and psychological factors, and sources of additional information.

★891★ "Clerical Supervisors and Managers" in *Occupational Outlook Handbook*
U.S. Government Printing Office
Superintendent of Documents
Washington, DC 20402
Ph: (202)512-1800 Fax: (202)512-2250

Biennial; latest edition, 1994-95. Encyclopedia of careers describing more than 250 occupations and comprising about 85 percent of all jobs in the economy. Occupations that require lengthy education or training are given the most attention. For each occupation, the handbook describes job duties, working conditions, training, educational preparation, personal qualities, advancement possibilities, job outlook, earnings, and sources of additional information.

★892★ "Office Manager" in *Career Information Center* (Vol.1)
Simon and Schuster
200 Old Tappan Rd.
Old Tappan, NJ 07675
Fax: 800-445-6991 Fr: 800-223-2348

Richard Lidz and Dale Anderson, editorial directors. Fifth edition, 1993. For 600 occupations, describes job duties, entry-level requirements, education and training needed, advancement possibilities, employment outlook, earnings and benefits. The set is divided into 12 volumes. Each volume includes jobs related under a broad career field. Volume 13 is the index.

★893★ "Office Manager" in *Career Opportunities in Art* (pp. 33-34)
Facts on File
460 Park Ave. S.
New York, NY 10016-7382
Ph: (212)683-2244 Fax: 800-678-3633
Fr: 800-322-8755

Susan H. Haubenstock and David Joselit. 1988. Profiles more than 75 art-related jobs. Each occupational profile covers job duties, employment outlook, career paths, salaries, skills, and educational preparation. Offers tips for entering the field.

★894★ "Office Manager" in *Career Opportunities in Television, Cable, and Video* (pp. 168-169)
Facts on File
460 Park Ave. S.
New York, NY 10016-7382
Ph: (212)683-2244 Fax: 800-678-3633
Fr: 800-322-8755

Third edition, 1990. Describes 100 media-related jobs. Each occupational profile covers job duties, employment outlook, career paths, salaries, skills, and educational preparation. Offers tips for entering the field.

★895★ "Office Manager" in *Occu-Facts: Information on 580 Careers in Outline Form*
Careers, Inc.
PO Box 135
Largo, FL 34649-0135
Ph: (813)584-7333

Biennial, 1995-96 edition. Each one-page occupational profile describes duties, working conditions, physical surroundings and demands, aptitudes, temperament, educational requirements, employment outlook, earnings, and places of employment.

★896★ "Office Manager" in *VGM's Careers Encyclopedia* (pp. 312-315)
National Textbook Co. (NTC)
VGM Career Books
4255 W. Touhy Ave.
Lincolnwood, IL 60646-1975
Ph: (708)679-5500 Fax: (708)679-2494
Fr: 800-323-4900

Third edition, 1991. Contains two- to five-page descriptions of 200 managerial, professional, technical, trade, and service occupations. Each profile includes job duties, places of employment, qualifications, educational preparation, training, employment potential, advancement, income, and additional sources of information.

★897★ "Office Manager" in *VGM's Handbook of Business and Management Careers* (pp. 64-65)
National Textbook Co. (NTC)
VGM Career Books
4255 W. Touhy Ave.
Lincolnwood, IL 60646-1975
Ph: (708)679-5500 Fax: (708)679-2494
Fr: 800-323-4900

Annette Selden, editor. Second edition, 1993. Contains 42 two-page occupational profiles describing job duties, places of employment, working conditions, qualifications, education, employment outlook, and income.

★898★ *Vocational Visions*
Center for Humanities, Inc.
Communications Park
Box 1000
Mount Kisco, NY 10549
Ph: (914)666-4100 Fax: (914)666-5319
Fr: 800-431-1242

Videocassette. 1984. 30 mins. This series of programs explains key aspects of actual training and a day in the life of a worker in the specific field mentioned on the videocassette. Occupations include: transportation/mechanics, repair, construction, business/office occupations, health, agriculture, technical/manufacturing, communications, and personal service.

ASSOCIATIONS

★899★ American Management Association (AMA)
135 W. 50th St.
New York, NY 10020-1201
Ph: (212)586-8100 Fax: (212)903-8168

Members: Provides educational forums worldwide to teach members and their colleagues about superior, practical business skills and explore best practices of world-class organizations through interaction with each other and expert faculty practitioners. **Purpose:** Publishing program provides tools individuals use to extend learning beyond the classroom in a process of life-long professional growth and development through education. **Publications:** *Compensation and Benefits Review*, bimonthly. • *CompFlash*, monthly. • *HR Focus*, monthly. • *Management Review*, monthly. • *Organizational Dynamics: A Quarterly Review of Organizational Behavior for Professional Managers*. • *The President*, monthly. • *Supervisory Management*, monthly.

★900★ Association of Management (AoM)
Rte. 17, George Washington Hwy.
PO Box 1301
Grafton, VA 23692-1301
Ph: (804)479-5363 Fax: (804)479-0656

Members: Academics and practitioners of management. **Purpose:** Seeks to align theory and practice in the study of human resource management, information and technology management, computer science, organizational studies, information systems, global health and ecology, transportation, travel and related technology, educational studies and research, management functions and applications, and multidisciplinary related issues. Encourages research in the fields. **Publications:** *AM Proceedings*, annual. • *Global Information Systems*, quarterly. • *Journal of Information Technology Management*, quarterly. • *Journal of Management Systems*, quarterly. • *Leadership & Leaders*, quarterly.

★901★ Data Entry Management Association
101 Merritt 7, 5th Fl.
Norwalk, CT 06851
Ph: (203)846-3777 Fax: (203)846-6883

Members: Data entry managers and others involved with the data entry profession. **Purpose:** Promotes the individual development and education of its members through exchange of ideas and discussion of problems and solutions. Conducts seminars and regional workshops and meetings.

★902★ Data Processing Management Association (DPMA)
505 Busse Hwy.
Park Ridge, IL 60068
Ph: (708)825-8124 Fax: (708)825-1693

Members: Managerial personnel, staff, educators, and individuals interested in the management of information resources. **Purpose:** Founder of the Certificate in Data Processing examination program, now administered by an intersociety organization. Maintains Legislative Communications Network. Professional education programs include EDP-oriented business and management principles self-study courses and a series of videotaped management development seminars. Sponsors student organizations around the country interested in data processing and encourages members to serve as counselors for the Scout computer merit badge. Conducts research projects, including a business information systems curriculum for two- and four-year colleges. **Publications:** *Industry Structure Model, A Framework for Career Develpment for IS Professionals*. • *Information Systems, The DPMA Model Curriculum for a Four-Year Undergraduate Degree for the 1990's*. • *Inside DPMA*, monthly.

STANDARDS/CERTIFICATION AGENCIES

★903★ Data Processing Management Association (DPMA)
505 Busse Hwy.
Park Ridge, IL 60068
Ph: (708)825-8124 Fax: (708)825-1693

Founder of the Certificate in Data Processing examination program, now administered by an intersociety organization.

TEST GUIDES

★904★ *Career Examination Series: Key Punch Supervisor*
National Learning Corp.
212 Michael Dr.
Syosset, NY 11791
Ph: (516)921-8888 Fax: (516)921-8743
Fr: 800-645-6337

Jack Rudman. All examination guides in this series contain questions with answers.

★905★ *Career Examination Series: Word Processing Supervisor*
National Learning Corp.
212 Michael Dr.
Syosset, NY 11791
Ph: (516)921-8888 Fax: (516)921-8743
Fr: 800-645-6337

Jack Rudman. All examination guides in this series contain questions with answers.

EDUCATIONAL DIRECTORIES AND PROGRAMS

★906★ *Industry Directory*
Association of Information Professionals
104 Wilmot Rd., Ste. 201
Deerfield, IL 60015-5195
Ph: (708)940-8800 Fax: (708)940-7218

Manufacturers of office automation equipment; word processing service bureaus; educational institutions offering office automation and associated software courses or curriculums; personnel agencies serving office automation personnel and users; analysts and consultants. Entries include: Name, address. Arrangement: Alphabetical within categories above.

BASIC REFERENCE GUIDES AND HANDBOOKS

★907★ *NOMDA Who's Who*
National Office Machine Dealers Association (NOMDA)
12411 Wornall Rd.
Kansas City, MO 64145
Ph: (816)941-3100 Fax: (816)941-2829
Brent Hoskins, Contact

Annual, August. Publication includes: List of 5,000 retailers and 500 manufacturers of typewriters, calculators, word processors, computers, dictation equipment, copying machines, and other office machines. Entries include: Company name, address, phone, names of executives; dealer listings include codes showing products handled. Arrangement: Dealers and manufacturers are listed both geographically and alphabetically.

Periodicals

★908★ *AM Proceedings*
Association of Management (AoM)
Rte. 17, George Washington Hwy.
PO Box 1301
Grafton, VA 23692-1301
Ph: (804)479-5363 Fax: (804)479-0656
Annual.

★909★ *Compensation and Benefits Review*
American Management Association (AMA)
135 W. 50th St.
New York, NY 10020-1201
Ph: (212)586-8100 Fax: (212)903-8168
Bimonthly. Includes annual index, book reviews, digest service of annotations and selected readings from publications, and information on current trends.

★910★ *CompFlash*
American Management Association (AMA)
135 W. 50th St.
New York, NY 10020-1201
Ph: (212)586-8100 Fax: (212)903-8168
Monthly. Features new developments in the field, salary and wage surveys, government regulations, pension and benefits news, and available publications.

★911★ *From Nine to Five*
Dartnell Corporation
4660 Ravenswood
Chicago, IL 60640
Ph: (312)561-4000 Fax: (312)561-3801
Fr: 800-621-5463
Douglas Leland
Biweekly. Provides "tips, shortcuts, and helpful information for success in the office," particularly secretaries and office workers. Recurring features include columns titled titled Business Skills Clinic, Shortcuts, and The Coffee Break.

★912★ *Global Information Systems*
Association of Management (AoM)
Rte. 17, George Washington Hwy.
PO Box 1301
Grafton, VA 23692-1301
Ph: (804)479-5363 Fax: (804)479-0656
Quarterly. Includes academic and practioner related research and scholarly information systems related articles bridging the academic/practioner experience.

★913★ *HR Focus*
American Management Association (AMA)
135 W. 50th St.
New York, NY 10020-1201
Ph: (212)586-8100 Fax: (212)903-8168
Monthly. Keeps HR managers abreast of the progressive personnel practices and developments in the field.

★914★ *Industry Structure Model, A Framework for Career Develpment for IS Professionals*
Data Processing Management Association (DPMA)
505 Busse Hwy.
Park Ridge, IL 60068
Ph: (708)825-8124 Fax: (708)825-1693

★915★ *Information Systems, The DPMA Model Corriculum for a Four-Year Undergraduate Degree for the 1990's*
Data Processing Management Association (DPMA)
505 Busse Hwy.
Park Ridge, IL 60068
Ph: (708)825-8124 Fax: (708)825-1693

★916★ *Inside DPMA*
Data Processing Management Association (DPMA)
505 Busse Hwy.
Park Ridge, IL 60068
Ph: (708)825-8124 Fax: (708)825-1693
Monthly.

★917★ *Journal of Information Technology Management*
Association of Management (AoM)
Rte. 17, George Washington Hwy.
PO Box 1301
Grafton, VA 23692-1301
Ph: (804)479-5363 Fax: (804)479-0656
Quarterly. Includes cage studies, management applications, info technology, case studies and professional academic and practioner related articles.

★918★ *Journal of Management Systems*
Association of Management (AoM)
Rte. 17, George Washington Hwy.
PO Box 1301
Grafton, VA 23692-1301
Ph: (804)479-5363 Fax: (804)479-0656
Quarterly. Includes academic research and scholarly management systems related articles, case studies, and book reviews.

★919★ *Leadership & Leaders*
Association of Management (AoM)
Rte. 17, George Washington Hwy.
PO Box 1301
Grafton, VA 23692-1301
Ph: (804)479-5363 Fax: (804)479-0656
Quarterly.

★920★ *Management Review*
American Management Association (AMA)
135 W. 50th St.
New York, NY 10020-1201
Ph: (212)586-8100 Fax: (212)903-8168
Monthly. Provides information on management trends and techniques. Includes book reviews and case studies.

★921★ *Organizational Dynamics: A Quarterly Review of Organizational Behavior for Professional Managers*
American Management Association (AMA)
135 W. 50th St.
New York, NY 10020-1201
Ph: (212)586-8100 Fax: (212)903-8168
Includes annual index.

★922★ *The President*
American Management Association (AMA)
135 W. 50th St.
New York, NY 10020-1201
Ph: (212)586-8100 Fax: (212)903-8168
Monthly. Includes calendar of events. Only to members of the Presidents Association, a division of AMA.

★923★ *Supervision*
National Research Bureau, Inc.
200 N. 4th
PO Box 1
Burlington, IA 52601-0001
Ph: (319)752-5415 Fax: (319)752-3421
Barbara Boeding
Monthly. Magazine for first-line foremen, supervisors, and office managers.

★924★ *Supervisory Management*
American Management Association (AMA)
135 W. 50th St.
New York, NY 10020-1201
Ph: (212)586-8100 Fax: (212)903-8168
Monthly. Aimed at first- and second-line managers. Contains how-to articles to help with supervisory problems. Includes annual article index.

Meetings and Conventions

★925★ Human Resources Conference and Exposition
American Management Association (AMA)
135 W. 50th St.
New York, NY 10020-1201
Ph: (212)586-8100 Fax: (212)903-8168
Annual.

Other Sources of Information

★926★ "Clerical Supervisor/Office Manager" in *100 Best Jobs for the 1990s & Beyond*
Dearborn Financial Publishing, Inc.
520 N. Dearborn St.
Chicago, IL 60610-4354
Ph: (312)836-4400 Fax: (312)836-1021
Fr: 800-621-9621
Carol Kleiman. 1992. Describes 100 jobs ranging from accountants to veterinarians. Each job profile includes such information as education, experience, and certification needed, salaries, and job search suggestions.

Computer and Peripheral Equipment Operators

Computer and peripheral equipment operators oversee the operation of computer hardware systems. Their duties vary depending on the size and type of equipment installed. In organizations with smaller systems, computer and peripheral equipment operators run the computer and all the peripheral equipment such as printers, disk drives, and tape readers. In larger organizations, the computer operator may specialize in console operation, while the peripheral equipment operator runs the related devices. The operators run the equipment, or set the controls, to do a particular job as specified by instructions from a programmer or operations manager. Operators also maintain log books of all computer operations, and resolve problems if error messages occur. Computer and peripheral equipment operators are found in many industries including wholesale trade establishments, manufacturing companies, data processing firms, banks, government agencies, and accounting, auditing, and bookkeeping firms.

Salaries

Salaries for computer and peripheral equipment operators are listed below.

Lowest 10 percent	Less than $13,400/year
Middle 50 percent	$16,000-$28,700/year
Top 10 percent	More than $38,700/year

Employment Outlook

Growth rate until the year 2005: Decline sharply.

Computer and Peripheral Equipment Operators

Career Guides

★927★ *Career Choices: Computer Science*
Walker & Company
720 5th Ave.
New York, NY 10019
Ph: (212)265-3632 Fax: (212)307-1764

1990.

★928★ *Careers in Computers & Data Processing*
Petrocelli Books, Inc.
174 Brookstone Dr.
Princeton, NJ 08540-2404
Ph: (609)924-5851

Herman McDaniel. 1978.

★929★ **"Careers in Operations and the Information Center" in *Careers in Computers* (pp. 34-41)**
National Textbook Co. (NTC)
VGM Career Books
4255 W. Touhy Ave.
Lincolnwood, IL 60646-1975
Ph: (708)679-5500 Fax: (708)679-2494
Fr: 800-323-4900

Lila B. Stair. 1991. Describes trends affecting computer careers and explores a wide range of job opportunities from programming to consulting. Provides job qualifications, salary data, job market information, personal and educational requirements, career paths, and the place of the job in the organizational structure. Offers advice on education, certification, and job search.

★930★ *Computer Careers: The Complete Pocket Guide to America's Fastest-Growing Job Market*
Sun Features, Inc.
PO Box 368-P
Cardiff, CA 92007
Ph: (619)753-3489

Joyce L. Kennedy. 1983.

★931★ *Computer Numerical Control Machine Operators*
Chronicle Guidance Publications, Inc.
66 Aurora St.
PO Box 1190
Moravia, NY 13118-1190
Ph: (315)497-0330 Fax: (315)497-3359
Fr: 800-622-7284

1991. This career brief describes the nature of the work, working conditions, hours and earnings, education and training, licensure, certification, unions, personal qualifications, social and psychological factors, employment outlook, entry methods, advancement, and related occupations.

★932★ **"Computer Operating" in *Exploring High Tech Careers***
Rosen Publishing Group
29 E. 21st St.
New York, NY 10010
Ph: (212)777-3017 Fax: (212)777-0277
Fr: 800-237-9932

Scott Southworth. Revised edition, 1993. Provides an orientation to the whole area of high tech and surveys jobs such as computer programming, drafting, and technical illustration. Covers educational preparation, advantages and disadvantages, advancement opportunities, and personal characteristics needed. Offers job hunting advice.

★933★ **"Computer Operating Personnel" in *American Almanac of Jobs and Salaries* (pp. 511)**
Avon Books
1350 Avenue of the Americas
New York, NY 10019
Ph: (212)261-6800 Fr: 800-238-0658

John Wright, editor. Revised and updated, 1994-95. A comprehensive guide to the wages of hundreds of occupations in a wide variety of industries and organizations.

★934★ **"Computer Operations" in *Careers in High Tech* (pp. 34-36)**
Arco Publishing Co.
Macmillan General Reference
15 Columbus Cir.
New York, NY 10023
Fax: 800-835-3202 Fr: 800-858-7674

Connie Winkler. 1987. Surveys career opportunities in data processing, technology, personal computers, telecommunications, manufacturing technology, artificial intelligence, computer graphics, biotechnology, lasers, technical writing, and publishing. Includes information on educational preparation, associations, and periodicals.

★935★ **"Computer Operations" in *Opportunities in Information Systems Careers* (p. 25)**
National Textbook Co. (NTC)
VGM Career Books
4255 W. Touhy Ave.
Lincolnwood, IL 60646-1975
Ph: (708)679-5500 Fax: (708)679-2494
Fr: 800-323-4900

Douglas B. Hoyt. 1991. Provides an overview of information systems with organizational charts and job descriptions. Covers personal characteristics, educational preparation, career paths, places of employment, salaries, and labor market outlook. Offers advice about job hunting and advancement.

★936★ **"Computer Operator" in *100 Best Careers for the Year 2000* (pp. 107-109)**
Arco Pub.
201 W. 103rd St.
Indianapolis, IN 46290
Ph: 800-428-5331 Fax: 800-835-3202

Shelly Field. 1992. Describes 100 job opportunities expected to grow fast throughout the next decade. Provides information on job duties and responsibilities, training requirements, education, advancement opportunities, experience and qualifications, and typical salaries.

★937★ "Computer Operator" in *BLR Encyclopedia of Prewritten Job Descriptions*
Business and Legal Reports, Inc.
39 Academy St.
Madison, CT 06443-1513
Ph: (203)245-7448

Stephen D. Bruce, editor-in-chief. 1994. This book contains hundreds of sample job descriptions arranged by functional job category. The 1-3 page job descriptions cover what the worker normally does in the position, who they report to, and how that position fits in the organizational structure.

★938★ "Computer Operator" in *Career Information Center* (Vol.1)
Simon and Schuster
200 Old Tappan Rd.
Old Tappan, NJ 07675
Fax: 800-445-6991 Fr: 800-223-2348

Richard Lidz and Dale Anderson, editorial directors. Fifth edition, 1993. For 600 occupations, describes job duties, entry-level requirements, education and training needed, advancement possibilities, employment outlook, earnings and benefits. The set is divided into 12 volumes. Each volume includes jobs related under a broad career field. Volume 13 is the index.

★939★ "Computer Operator" in *Careers in Banking and Finance* (pp. 39-41)
Rosen Publishing Group
29 E. 21st St.
New York, NY 10010
Ph: (212)777-3017 Fax: (212)777-0277
Fr: 800-237-9932

Patricia Haddock. 1990. Describes more than 20 jobs at all levels in banking and finance. Contains information about the types of financial organizations where the jobs are found, educational requirements, job duties, and salaries. Offers advice on job hunting.

★940★ "Computer Operator" in *Exploring Careers in the Computer Field*
Rosen Publishing Group
29 E. 21st St.
New York, NY 10010
Ph: (212)777-3017 Fax: (212)777-0277
Fr: 800-237-9932

Joseph Weintraub. 1993. Surveys the newest growth areas in the computer industry including artificial intelligence, desktop publishing, and personal computers. Discusses entry into the field, salaries, future trends and offers job search advice. Contains interviews with five people who describe their real-life experiences working in computer related jobs. Lists organizations and colleges.

★941★ "Computer Operator" in *Guide to Careers Without College* (pp. 51-53)
Franklin Watts, Inc.
387 Park Avenue, S.
New York, NY 10016
Ph: (212)686-7070

Kathleen S. Abrams. 1988. Discusses careers that do not require a college degree in fields such as health care, sales and marketing, and the building trades. Describes the work, employment opportunities, and training.

★942★ "Computer Operator" in *Jobs Rated Almanac*
World Almanac
1 International Blvd., Ste. 444
Mahwah, NJ 07495
Ph: (201)529-6900 Fax: (201)529-6901

Les Krantz. Second edition, 1992. Ranks 250 jobs by environment, salary, outlooks, physical demands, stress, security, travel opportunities, and extra perks. Includes jobs the editor feels are the most common, most interesting, and the most rapidly growing.

★943★ "Computer Operator" in *Opportunities in Data Processing Careers* (pp. 49-51)
National Textbook Co. (NTC)
VGM Career Books
4255 W. Touhy Ave.
Lincolnwood, IL 60646-1975
Ph: (708)679-5500 Fax: (708)679-2494
Fr: 800-323-4900

Norman N. Noerper. 1989. Provides an overview of the history and development of data processing careers. For each job included, describes responsibilities, salary, and job outlook. Contains separate chapters on educational preparation and job hunting. Lists professional organizations, publications, and schools.

★944★ *Computer Operators*
Chronicle Guidance Publications, Inc.
66 Aurora St.
PO Box 1190
Moravia, NY 13118-1190
Ph: (315)497-0330 Fax: (315)497-3359
Fr: 800-622-7284

1993. This career brief describes the nature of the work, working conditions, hours and earnings, education and training, licensure, certification, unions, personal qualifications, social and psychological factors, employment outlook, entry methods, advancement, and related occupations.

★945★ "Computer Operators" in *Career Discovery Encyclopedia* (Vol.2, pp. 42-43)
J.G. Ferguson Publishing Co.
200 W. Madison St., Ste. 300
Chicago, IL 60606
Ph: (312)580-5480 Fax: (312)580-4948

E. Russell Primm, editor-in-chief. 1993. Contains two-page articles on 504 occupations. Each article describes job duties, earnings, and educational and training requirements.

★946★ "Computer Operators" in *Jobs! What They Are—Where They Are—What They Pay* (pp. 75)
Simon & Schuster, Inc.
Simon & Schuster Bldg.
1230 Avenue of the Americas
New York, NY 10020
Ph: (212)698-7000

Robert O. Snelling and Anne M. Snelling. Revised edition, 1992. Profiles 241 occupations, describing duties and responsibilities, educational preparation, earnings, employment opportunities, training, and qualifications.

★947★ "Computer Operators: Keepers of the Machines" in *Careers for Women Without College Degrees* (pp. 189-192)
McGraw-Hill Publishing Co.
11 W. 19th St.
New York, NY 10011
Ph: (212)337-6010

Beatryce Nivens. 1988. Career planning and job hunting guide containing information on decision-making, skills assessment, and resumes for career changers. Profiles careers with the best occupational outlook. Describes the work, educational preparation, employment outlook, salaries, and required skills.

★948★ "Computer Operators" in *Opportunities in Vocational and Technical Careers* (p. 48)
National Textbook Co. (NTC)
VGM Career Books
4255 W. Touhy Ave.
Lincolnwood, IL 60646-1975
Ph: (708)679-5500 Fax: (708)679-2494
Fr: 800-323-4900

Adrian A. Paradis. 1992. Describes careers which can be prepared for by attending a private vocational or proprietary school—office employee, sales worker, service worker, health services, mechanic, craftworker, and technician. Covers employment outlook, job duties, and salaries. Offers career planning advice.

★949★ "Computer and Peripheral Equipment Operators" in *Encyclopedia of Careers and Vocational Guidance*
J.G. Ferguson Publishing Co.
200 W. Madison St., Ste. 300
Chicago, IL 60606
Ph: (312)580-5480 Fax: (312)580-4948

William E. Hopke, editor-in-chief. Ninth edition, 1993. Four-volume set that profiles 500 occupations and describes job trends in 74 industries. Includes career description, educational requirements, history of the job, methods of entry, advancement, employment outlook, earnings, working conditions, social and psychological factors, and sources of additional information.

★950★ "Computer and Peripheral Equipment Operators" in *Occupational Outlook Handbook*
U.S. Government Printing Office
Superintendent of Documents
Washington, DC 20402
Ph: (202)512-1800 Fax: (202)512-2250

Biennial; latest edition, 1994-95. Encyclopedia of careers describing more than 250 occupations and comprising about 85 percent of all jobs in the economy. Occupations that require lengthy education or training are given the most attention. For each occupation, the handbook describes job duties, working conditions, training, educational preparation, personal qualities, advancement possibilities, job outlook, earnings, and sources of additional information.

★951★ *Computers - How to Break into the Field*
T A B Books
Blue Ridge Summit, PA 17294-0850
Ph: (717)794-2191

Peter L. Carron, Jr. Second edition. 1986.

★952★ "Computers" in *Internships 1995*
Petersons Guides, Inc.
PO Box 2123
Princeton, NJ 08543-2123
Ph: (609)243-9111 Fr: 800-338-3282

Fifteenth edition, 1995. Lists internship opportunities under six broad categories: communications, creative, performing, and fine arts, human services, international relations, business and technology, and public affairs. For each internship program, gives the names, phone number, contact person, description, eligibility requirements, and benefits.

★953★ "Computing or Information Center Operations" in *Opportunities in Computer Science Careers*
National Textbook Co. (NTC)
VGM Career Books
4255 W. Touhy Ave.
Lincolnwood, IL 60646-1975
Ph: (708)679-5500 Fax: (708)679-2494
Fr: 800-323-4900

1991. Surveys careers in the computer field including programming, software development, hardware, research, and technical writing. Profiles five people working in the field. Separate chapters discuss educational preparation and employment outlook. An appendix contains salary information.

★954★ *Computing, Operating Personnel, Electronic*
Careers, Inc.
PO Box 135
Largo, FL 34649-0135
Ph: (813)584-7333

1994. Four-page brief offering the definition, history, duties, working conditions, personal qualifications, educational requirements, earnings, hours, employment outlook, advancement possibilities, and related occupations.

★955★ "Electronic Computer Operating Personnel" in *Occu-Facts: Information on 580 Careers in Outline Form*
Careers, Inc.
PO Box 135
Largo, FL 34649-0135
Ph: (813)584-7333

Biennial, 1995-96 edition. Each one-page occupational profile describes duties, working conditions, physical surroundings and demands, aptitudes, temperament, educational requirements, employment outlook, earnings, and places of employment.

★956★ *Exploring Careers in Computer Field*
Rosen Publishing Group
29 E. 21st St.
New York, NY 10010
Ph: (212)777-3017 Fax: (212)777-0277
Fr: 800-237-9932

Joseph Weintraub. 1993.

★957★ *Exploring Computer Careers at Home*
Rosen Publishing Group
29 E. 21st St.
New York, NY 10010
Ph: (212)777-3017 Fax: (212)777-0277
Fr: 800-237-9932

Scott Southworth. 1986. Part of Careers Series.

★958★ *A Guide to Computer Careers*
Camelot Publishing Co.
PO Box 1357
Ormond Beach, FL 32175
Ph: (904)672-5672

Donald D. Spencer. 1984.

★959★ *A Guide to Computer Careers*
Free Press
866 3rd Ave.
New York, NY 10022
Ph: (212)702-3130 Fax: (212)605-9364

Donald D. Spencer. 1984.

★960★ *Opportunities in Computer Science*
National Textbook Co. (NTC)
VGM Career Books
4255 W. Touhy Ave.
Lincolnwood, IL 60646-1975
Ph: (708)679-5500 Fax: (708)679-2494
Fr: 800-323-4900

Julie L. Kling. 1987. Describes job opportunities, how to make a career decision, job hunting techniques, and future trends.

★961★ "Peripheral Equipment Operators" in *Careers in High Tech* (pp. 32-34)
Arco Publishing Co.
Macmillan General Reference
15 Columbus Cir.
New York, NY 10023
Fax: 800-835-3202 Fr: 800-858-7674

Connie Winkler. 1987. Surveys career opportunities in data processing, technology, personal computers, telecommunications, manufacturing technology, artificial intelligence, computer graphics, biotechnology, lasers, technical writing, and publishing. Includes information on educational preparation, associations, and periodicals.

★962★ *Video Career Library - Technical Occupations*
Careers, Inc.
PO Box 135
Largo, FL 34649-0135
Ph: (813)584-7333

Videocassette. 1990. Part of the Video Career Library covering 165 occupations. Shows actual workers on the job.

★963★ *Winning Resumes for Computer Personnel*
Barron's Educational Series, Inc.
250 Wireless Blvd.
Hauppauge, NY 11788
Ph: (516)434-3311 Fax: (516)434-3723
Fr: 800-645-3476

1994.

Associations

★964★ Association for Computer Operations Management (AFCOM)
742 E. Chapman Ave.
Orange, CA 92666
Ph: (714)997-7966 Fax: (714)997-9743

Members: Data center and data processing operations management professionals from medium and large scale main frame, midrange and client/server data centers worldwide. **Purpose:** Dedicated to meeting the professional needs of the data center management community. Provides information and support through educational events, research and assistance hotlines, and surveys. **Publications:** *AFCOM's Fall Program Proceedings*, annual. • *Annual Survey of Data Processing Operations Salaries*, annual. • *The Communique*, bimonthly. • *The Computer Operations Manager*, bimonthly. • *"Focus on Operations" Digest of Conference Sessions*, annual.

Test Guides

★965★ *Advanced Placement Examination in Computer Science*
Prentice Hall
Rte. 9W
Englewood Cliffs, NJ 07632
Ph: (201)592-2000

Elayne Schulman. Second edition, 1988.

★966★ *Career Examination Series: Chief Data Processing Equipment Operator*
National Learning Corp.
212 Michael Dr.
Syosset, NY 11791
Ph: (516)921-8888 Fax: (516)921-8743
Fr: 800-645-6337

Jack Rudman. All examination guides in this series contain questions with answers.

★967★ *Career Examination Series: Computer Operator*
National Learning Corp.
212 Michael Dr.
Syosset, NY 11791
Ph: (516)921-8888 Fax: (516)921-8743
Fr: 800-645-6337

Jack Rudman. Includes a study guide for computer operator trainee. All examination guides in this series contain questions with answers.

★968★ *Career Examination Series: Multi-Keyboard Operator*
National Learning Corp.
212 Michael Dr.
Syosset, NY 11791
Ph: (516)921-8888 Fax: (516)921-8743
Fr: 800-645-6337

Jack Rudman. All examination guides in this series contain questions with answers.

★969★ *Career Examination Series: Principal Data Entry Machine Operator*
National Learning Corp.
212 Michael Dr.
Syosset, NY 11791
Ph: (516)921-8888 Fax: (516)921-8743
Fr: 800-645-6337

Jack Rudman. All examination guides in this series contain questions with answers.

★970★ *Career Examination Series: Senior Business Machine Operator*
National Learning Corp.
212 Michael Dr.
Syosset, NY 11791
Ph: (516)921-8888 Fax: (516)921-8743
Fr: 800-645-6337

Jack Rudman. All examination guides in this series contain questions with answers.

★971★ *Career Examination Series: Senior Data Entry Machine Operator*
National Learning Corp.
212 Michael Dr.
Syosset, NY 11791
Ph: (516)921-8888 Fax: (516)921-8743
Fr: 800-645-6337

Jack Rudman. All examination guides in this series contain questions with answers.

★972★ *Career Examination Series: Senior Data Processing Control Clerk*
National Learning Corp.
212 Michael Dr.
Syosset, NY 11791
Ph: (516)921-8888 Fax: (516)921-8743
Fr: 800-645-6337

Jack Rudman. All examination guides in this series contain questions with answers.

★973★ *Career Examination Series: Senior Data Processing Equipment Operator*
National Learning Corp.
212 Michael Dr.
Syosset, NY 11791
Ph: (516)921-8888 Fax: (516)921-8743
Fr: 800-645-6337

Jack Rudman. All examination guides in this series contain questions with answers.

★974★ *Computer Work & Computer Trainee Exams*
Ken-Books
56 Midcrest Way
San Francisco, CA 94131
Ph: (415)826-6550

Harry W. Koch. Second edition, 1987.

PERIODICALS

★975★ *AFCOM's Fall Program Proceedings*
Association for Computer Operations Management (AFCOM)
742 E. Chapman Ave.
Orange, CA 92666
Ph: (714)997-7966 Fax: (714)997-9743

Annual.

★976★ *Andrew Seybold's Outlook on Professional Computing*
Pinecrest Press, Inc.
PO Box 917
Brookdale, CA 95007-0917
Ph: (408)338-7701 Fax: (408)338-7806

Monthly. Offers news, views, analysis, and informed perspective on issues in the computing industry. Recurring features include new product reviews, interview, a calendar of events, and news of research.

★977★ *Annual Survey of Data Processing Operations Salaries*
Association for Computer Operations Management (AFCOM)
742 E. Chapman Ave.
Orange, CA 92666
Ph: (714)997-7966 Fax: (714)997-9743

Annual.

★978★ *Apple Library Users Group Newsletter*
Apple Computer, Inc.
4 Infinite Loop MS 304-2A
Cupertino, CA 95014
Ph: (408)974-2552 Fax: (408)725-8502
Monica Ertel

Quarterly. Serves as an exchange for information concerning the use of Apple and Macintosh computers in libraries and information centers of all sizes. Recurring features include news of research, book reviews, news from members, answers to readers' questions, a calendar of events, and columns titled News From/About Apple, Software Reviews, and Information From Our Vendors.

★979★ *The Communique*
Association for Computer Operations Management (AFCOM)
742 E. Chapman Ave.
Orange, CA 92666
Ph: (714)997-7966 Fax: (714)997-9743

Bimonthly. Contains news items, product announcements, information requests from members, and classified ads.

★980★ *Computer Business*
TAB/McGraw-Hill, Inc.
PO Box 182607
Columbus, OH 43218-2607
Fax: (614)759-3644 Fr: 800-822-8158
Abe H. Hassan

Monthly. Provides citations and abstracts of articles on computers and communications appearing in business and technical publications. Reports significant market data, including estimates of market share and industry forecasts. Lists abstracts according to subject in such areas as minicomputers, microcomputers, software, peripherals, data communications, legal and regulatory action, consumer electronics, and human factors.

★981★ *Computer Graphics World*
PennWell Publishing Co.
10 Tara Blvd., 5th Fl.
Nashua, NH 03062-2801
Ph: (603)891-0123 Fax: (603)891-0587
Stephen Porter

Monthly. Publication reporting on the use of modeling, animation, and multimedia in the areas of science and engineering, art and entertainment, and presentation and training.

★982★ *Computer Industry Update*
IMR, Inc.
PO Box 681
Los Altos, CA 94022
Ph: (415)941-6679 Fr: 800-875-6610
George Weiser

Monthly. Summarizes vendor announcements and articles from the weekly computer trade press. Organizes summaries into seven categories: mainframes, minicomputers, terminals and workstations, peripherals, personal computers, and networking.

★983★ *The Computer Operations Manager*
Association for Computer Operations Management (AFCOM)
742 E. Chapman Ave.
Orange, CA 92666
Ph: (714)997-7966 Fax: (714)997-9743

Bimonthly. Contains feature articles and columns.

★984★ *Computer Report and PC Street Price Index*
John Murphy
Metro Computing
10 Foster Ave., Ste. E-1
Gibbsboro, NJ 08026
Ph: (609)784-8866
John Murphy

Monthly. Concentrates on the latest developments in computer technology and their effects on the corporate end-user. Covers software, personal computers, computer companies, and industry trends.

★985★ *Computer Wave*
PO Box 19491
Seattle, WA 98109
Ph: (206)284-5476 Fax: (206)283-1020
Robert L. Crowther

Monthly. Newspaper focusing on computers and technology and serving Seattle.

★986★ *Data Entry Awareness Report*
Management Information Corporation
PO Box 5062
Cherry Hill, NJ 08034
Ph: (609)428-1020 Fax: (609)428-1683
Fr: 800-678-4642
Mark Kostic

Monthly. Evaluates a data entry system in each issue, including key to disc, intelligent terminals, optical character readers, portable data recorders, and voice data entry. Describes system hardware, software, and pricing, and analyzes the advantages and disadvantages of the system.

★987★ *DataWorld*
Faulkner Technical Reports, Inc.
114 Cooper Center
7905 Browning Rd.
Pennsauken, NJ 08109-4374
Ph: (609)662-2070 Fax: (609)662-3380
Larry Abbot

Monthly. Information service describing and evaluating mainframe, mini- and microcomputer hardware and software, as well as communications facilities and equipment.

★988★ *Dental Computer Newsletter*
Andent, Inc.
1000 North Ave.
Waukegan, IL 60085
Ph: (708)223-5077 Fax: (708)223-5077
Ellis J. Neiburger

Quarterly. Emphasizes "practical use of all brands of computers for the professional office." Provides news of the computer industry as well as computer-use tips, information on computer gadgets and systems, and system recommendations. Recurring features include editorials, news of research, letters to the editor, news of members, book reviews, and columns titled Education, Hardware, Software, Specials, and Report on Hardware/Software.

★989★ *EDP Weekly*
Computer Age
3918 Prosperity Ave., Ste. 310
Fairfax, VA 22031-3300
Ph: (703)573-8400 Fax: (703)573-8594
Charles Bailey

Weekly. Reports news concerning all aspects of the computer industry. Covers standards, licensing agreements, patents issued, industry growth statistics, new technology, and pertinent legislation. Also includes semimonthly features on robotics, electronic funds transfer, mini and micro computers, data communications, and world trade.

★990★ *"Focus on Operations" Digest of Conference Sessions*
Association for Computer Operations Management (AFCOM)
742 E. Chapman Ave.
Orange, CA 92666
Ph: (714)997-7966 Fax: (714)997-9743

Annual.

★991★ *The Gray Sheet: Computer Industry Report*
International Data Corporation (IDC)
c/o IDG International News Group
41 West St.
Boston, MA 02111
Ph: (617)423-9030 Fax: (617)423-0712
Doug McLeod

Provides news of original research and explains important trends in the worldwide information transmission industry. Analyzes, segments, and sizes worldwide computer markets.

★992★ *Micro Computer Journal*
CQ Communications
76 N. Broadway
Hicksville, NY 11801
Ph: (516)681-2922 Fax: (516)681-2926
Arthur Salsberg

Monthly. Magazine covering electronics and computers.

Meetings and Conventions

★993★ AFCOM's Fall Educational Program
Association for Computer Operations Management (AFCOM)
742 E. Chapman Ave.
Orange, CA 92666
Ph: (714)997-7966 Fax: (714)997-9743

Annual. Usually September. **Dates and Locations:** 1995 Sep 10-13; Anaheim, CA.

★994★ Focus on Operations
Association for Computer Operations Management (AFCOM)
742 E. Chapman Ave.
Orange, CA 92666
Ph: (714)997-7966 Fax: (714)997-9743

Annual. Usually March or April. **Dates and Locations:** 1996 Apr 14-18; Chicago, IL.

Other Sources of Information

★995★ "Computer Operator" in *100 Best Jobs for the 1990s & Beyond*
Dearborn Financial Publishing, Inc.
520 N. Dearborn St.
Chicago, IL 60610-4354
Ph: (312)836-4400 Fax: (312)836-1021
Fr: 800-621-9621

Carol Kleiman. 1992. Describes 100 jobs ranging from accountants to veterinarians. Each job profile includes such information as education, experience, and certification needed, salaries, and job search suggestions.

★996★ "Computer Operator" in *Career Selector 2001*
Barron's Educational Series, Inc.
250 Wireless Blvd.
Hauppauge, NY 11788
Ph: (516)434-3311 Fax: (516)434-3723
Fr: 800-645-3476

James C. Gonyea. 1993.

★997★ *Computer Service and Repair Directory*
American Business Directories, Inc.
5711 S. 86th Circle
Omaha, NE 68127
Ph: (402)593-4600 Fax: (402)331-1505

Annual. Number of listings: 13,755 (U. S. edition); 905 (Canadian edition). Entries include: Name, address, phone (including area code), size of advertisement, year first in "Yellow Pages," name of owner or manager, number of employees. Compiled from telephone company "Yellow Pages," nationwide. Arrangement: Geographical.

★998★ *Computers and Computing Information Resources Directory*
Gale Research Inc.
835 Penobscot Bldg.
Detroit, MI 48226-4094
Ph: (313)961-2242 Fax: (313)961-6083
Fr: 800-877-GALE
Kathy Marcaccio, Contact

Irregular, latest edition October 1986; supplement, 1987. Covers computer-related information sources, including 1,450 consultant and training organizations, 650 trade and professional associations or user groups, 1,000 special libraries and information centers, 900 university computer facilities and research centers; 600 for-profit research services, 240 online services and teleprocessing networks, 1,500 journals, newsletters, and abstracting and indexing services; over 400 trade shows, conventions, and exhibits; 200 publishers, 250 directories; international coverage. Entries include: Name, address, phone, and name of contact; other details (as appropriate), including publications, year founded, target audience, dates and location of exhibit, frequency, price, descriptions Arrangement: By type of organization or service.

★999★ *Microelectronics & Office Jobs: The Impact of the Chip on Women's Employment*
International Labor Office
1828 L St., NW, No. 801
Washington, DC 20036-5104

Diane Werneke. Third edition, 1985.

Credit Clerks and Authorizers

Credit clerks and authorizers review the credit histories of applicants and decide whether or not to approve credit. To obtain the appropriate information, credit clerks contact employers, references, banks, or credit bureaus to verify personal and financial information. Credit authorizers evaluate a customers' computerized credit records and payment histories and make credit decisions. Most charges are automatically approved by computer. The majority of credit clerks and authorizers work in banks or financial institutions, and wholesale and retail trade. Others work for businesses such as credit reporting and collection agencies and computer and data processing services.

Salaries

Salaries for credit clerks and authorizers are listed below.

Loan processors in branch offices	$18,000/year
Loan processors in central offices	$19,200/year
Credit and collection clerks	$20,800/year

Employment Outlook

Growth rate until the year 2005: Average.

Credit Clerks and Authorizers

Career Guides

★1000★ *Career Success Series*
Cambridge Educational
PO Box 2153
Charleston, WV 25328-2153
Ph: (304)744-9323 Fax: (304)744-9351
Fr: 800-468-4227

Videocassette. 1986. 15 mins. A series, available separately, outlining various career choices for students. Occupations include: accounting, flight service, air transportation/ground/flight service, data processing, carpentry, clerk in banking/insurance, commodity sales, cosmetic personal grooming, fire fighting, forestry services, home economics, insulation/roofing, material handling, mechanics, photographic processing, pipefitting and plumbing, police science, printing, carpentry, medical laboratory technicians, secretarial services, and utilities equipment operator.

★1001★ *Credit Analysts (Bankers)*
Chronicle Guidance Publications, Inc.
66 Aurora St.
PO Box 1190
Moravia, NY 13118-1190
Ph: (315)497-0330 Fax: (315)497-3359
Fr: 800-622-7284

1992. Career brief describing the nature of the job, working conditions, hours and earnings, education and training, licensure, certification, unions, personal qualifications, social and psychological factors, location, employment outlook, entry methods, advancement, and related occupations.

★1002★ "Credit Checker" in *Career Information Center* (Vol.1)
Simon and Schuster
200 Old Tappan Rd.
Old Tappan, NJ 07675
Fax: 800-445-6991 Fr: 800-223-2348

Richard Lidz and Dale Anderson, editorial directors. Fifth edition, 1993. For 600 occupations, describes job duties, entry-level requirements, education and training needed, advancement possibilities, employment outlook, earnings and benefits. The set is divided into 12 volumes. Each volume includes jobs related under a broad career field. Volume 13 is the index.

★1003★ "Credit Clerks and Authorizers" in *Jobs! What They Are—Where They Are—What They Pay* (pp. 159)
Fireside
Simon & Schuster Bldg.
1230 Avenue of the Americas
New York, NY 10020
Ph: (212)698-7000 Fr: 800-223-2348

Robert O. Snelling and Anne M. Snelling. Revised and updated, 1992. Describes duties and responsibilities, earnings, employment opportunities, training, and qualifications.

★1004★ "Credit Clerks and Authorizers" in *Occupational Outlook Handbook*
U.S. Government Printing Office
Superintendent of Documents
Washington, DC 20402
Ph: (202)512-1800 Fax: (202)512-2250

Biennial; latest edition, 1994-95. Encyclopedia of careers describing more than 250 occupations and comprising about 85 percent of all jobs in the economy. Occupations that require lengthy education or training are given the most attention. For each occupation, the handbook describes job duties, working conditions, training, educational preparation, personal qualities, advancement possibilities, job outlook, earnings, and sources of additional information.

★1005★ *Credit Workers*
Chronicle Guidance Publications, Inc.
66 Aurora St.
PO Box 1190
Moravia, NY 13118-1190
Ph: (315)497-0330 Fax: (315)497-3359
Fr: 800-622-7284

1993. This career brief describes the nature of the work, working conditions, hours and earnings, education and training, licensure, certification, unions, personal qualifications, social and psychological factors, employment outlook, entry methods, advancement, and related occupations.

★1006★ *Understanding the Lending Process*
First Financial Video Network
4811 Emerson St., Ste. 210
Palatine, IL 60067-7417
Ph: (708)397-9000 Fax: (708)397-6721
Fr: 800-442-8662

Videocassette. 1987. 19 mins. Basic terms and theories of the money lending process are made simple.

Associations

★1007★ International Credit Association (ICA)
243 N. Lindbergh Blvd.
St. Louis, MO 63141
Ph: (314)991-3030 Fax: (314)991-3029

Members: Credit executives and professionals. Conducts educational seminars and conferences; offers group insurance plans. Through its Society of Certified Credit Executives, gives specific designations to members meeting its professional certification program requirements. **Purpose:** Sponsors National Credit Education Week. Maintains speakers' bureau. **Publications:** *Consumer Trends*, monthly. • *Credit World*, bimonthly. • *Who's Who in Credit Management*, annual.

Standards/Certification Agencies

★1008★ International Credit Association (ICA)
243 N. Lindbergh Blvd.
St. Louis, MO 63141
Ph: (314)991-3030 Fax: (314)991-3029

Conducts educational seminars and conferences; offers group insurance plans. Through its Society of Certified Credit Executives, gives specific designations to members meeting its professional certification program requirements.

Awards, Scholarships, Grants, and Fellowships

★1009★ American Institute of Banking Scholarship
American Institute of Banking
c/o Ken Ambers
1213 Bakers Way
Manhattan, KS 66502
Ph: (913)537-4750

To be applied to tuition at the American Institute of Banking resident courses lasting 10 or 16 weeks. Applicants must be high school graduates or hold a GED. Scholarships are based on merit.

★1010★ Quarter-Century Honor Roll
National Association of Federal Credit Unions
PO Box 3769
Washington, DC 20007
Ph: (703)522-4770 Fax: (703)524-1082

To recognize individuals, both paid and volunteer, who have dedicated 25 years of service or more to the credit union community. Individuals who have unselfishly contributed much effort to ensure the success of the credit union movement are eligible. Credit Unions can also submit honorees posthumously. A Quarter-Century Honor Roll certificate signed by the president of NAFCU is forwarded to the Board of Directors at the individual's credit union for appropriate presentation. Those accepted into the Quarter-Century Honor Roll are also acknowledged by NAFCU's bi-monthly magazine, *The Federal Credit Union,* which periodically publishes an Honor Roll list. Established in 1986.

Periodicals

★1011★ *Consumer Credit and Truth-in-Lending Compliance Report*
Warren, Gorham & Lamont, Inc.
1 Penn Plaza
New York, NY 10119
Ph: (212)971-5591 Fax: (212)971-5024
Fr: 800-950-1201
Earl Phillips

Monthly. Reports on recent changes in the consumer credit field. Acts as a compliance guide on the Equal Credit Opportunity Act, Truth-in-Lending, debt collection practices, credit cards, service contracts, insurance, and related areas. Analyzes significant litigation and current and potential changes in consumer credit legislation.

★1012★ *Consumer Finance Newsletter*
Financial Publishing Company
82 Brookline Ave.
Boston, MA 02215
Ph: (617)262-4040
James C. Senay

Provides information on effective and pending credit insurance and installment loan regulations on the state and federal levels. Supplies news of potential state changes in regulations.

★1013★ *Consumer Trends*
International Credit Association (ICA)
243 N. Lindbergh Blvd.
St. Louis, MO 63141
Ph: (314)991-3030 Fax: (314)991-3029

Monthly.

★1014★ *Cred-Alert*
American Collectors Association
4040 W. 70th St.
Minneapolis, MN 55435
Ph: (612)926-6547 Fax: (612)926-1624
Sandra Whalen

Monthly. Monitors credit and collection court decisions, legislative decisions, and other general credit matters of interest to credit grantors and collectors.

★1015★ *Credit Card Management*
Faulkner & Gray, Inc.
11 Penn Plaza, 17th Fl.
New York, NY 10001
Ph: (212)648-0261 Fax: (212)648-0287
John Stewart

Magazine covering credit and card operations and programs in business; providing pertinent information for bankers, retailers, executives, and supervisors.

★1016★ *Credit Memo*
New York Credit & Financial Mgmt. Assn.
49 W. 45th St., 5th Fl.
New York, NY 10036
Ph: (212)944-2400 Fax: (212)944-2663
J. Robert Murray

Bimonthly. Magazine on business and commercial credit and finance.

★1017★ *Credit World*
International Credit Association (ICA)
243 N. Lindbergh Blvd.
St. Louis, MO 63141
Ph: (314)991-3030 Fax: (314)991-3029

Bimonthly.

★1018★ *Financial Marketing*
Charles E. Bartling, Contact

Provides marketing professionals from banks, savings institutions, and credit unions with pertinent information on current trends and developments in the marketing of financial services. Recurring features include letters to the editor, news of research, book reviews, job listing, and a calendar of events.

★1019★ *The Journal of Commercial Lending*
Robert Morris Associates
1 Liberty Place
1650 Market St., Ste. 2300
Philadelphia, PA 19103-7398
Ph: (215)851-9100 Fax: (215)851-9206
Charlotte Weisman

Monthly. Magazine for bank loan and credit officers.

★1020★ *Who's Who in Credit Management*
International Credit Association (ICA)
243 N. Lindbergh Blvd.
St. Louis, MO 63141
Ph: (314)991-3030 Fax: (314)991-3029

Annual. Lists persons certified by the Society of Certified Credit Executives.

Other Sources of Information

★1021★ "Credit Analyst" in *Career Selector 2001*
Barron's Educational Series, Inc.
250 Wireless Blvd.
Hauppauge, NY 11788
Ph: (516)434-3311 Fax: (516)434-3723
Fr: 800-645-3476

James C. Gonyea. 1993.

General Office Clerks

General office clerks do a variety of tasks to support office, business, or administrative operations. Some may specialize in one task such as typing or filing. Others may do many tasks, such as answering phone calls, operating office equipment, or entering data at a computer terminal, depending on the needs of the employer. Experienced employees may handle financial records, inventory, or customer complaints. Inexperienced employees may transcribe data, operator calculators, or record inquiries.

Salaries

Salaries for general office clerks vary by industry.

Lowest 10 percent	$11,400/year or less
Median	$18,500/year
Top 10 percent	$29,500 or more
Beginning office clerks in private firms	$12,700/year
Clerks with more responsibilities	$23,800/year

Employment Outlook

Growth rate until the year 2005: Average.

General Office Clerks

Career Guides

★1022★ ***Career Insights***
RMI Media Productions, Inc.
1365 N. Winchester
Olathe, KS 66061
Ph: (913)768-1696 Fax: 800-755-6910
Fr: 800-745-5480

Videocassette series. 1987. This videotape series describes 50 occupations, including skill requirements and interviews with people employed in these fields. Occupations include: flight service, air transportation/ground services, data processing, carpentry, clerk in banking/insurance/business, cosmetic personal grooming, firefighting, forestry, insulation/roofing, mechanics, material handling, photographic processing, pipefitting and plumbing, printing, secretarial services, tool and die operations.

★1023★ **"Clerk" in *Careers Inside the World of Offices* (pp. 37-41)**
Rosen Publishing Group
29 E. 21st St.
New York, NY 10010
Ph: 800-237-9932 Fax: (212)777-0277

Carolyn Simpson. 1995. Describes job possibilities, attitudes and skills needed, and tips for getting the job. Also includes a self-evaluation test.

★1024★ ***Clerk, General Office***
Careers, Inc.
PO Box 135
Largo, FL 34649-0135
Ph: (813)584-7333

1994. Four-page brief offering the definition, history, duties, working conditions, personal qualifications, educational requirements, earnings, hours, employment outlook, advancement possibilities, and related occupations.

★1025★ **"The Clerk" in *Opportunities in Office Occupations* (pp. 49-83)**
National Textbook Co. (NTC)
VGM Career Books
4255 W. Touhy Ave.
Lincolnwood, IL 60646-1975
Ph: (708)679-5500 Fax: (708)679-2494
Fr: 800-323-4900

Blanche Ettinger. 1989. Describes factors and trends which will affect office occupations including automation, telecommuting, and unionization. Separate chapters cover clerks, records management, information word processing, the secretary, and the bookkeeper-accountant. Describes job duties, skills needed, educational preparation, job hunting, types of equipment, employment outlook, and salaries.

★1026★ **"Clerk-Typist" in *BLR Encyclopedia of Prewritten Job Descriptions***
Business and Legal Reports, Inc.
39 Academy St.
Madison, CT 06443-1513
Ph: (203)245-7448

Stephen D. Bruce, editor-in-chief. 1994. This book contains hundreds of sample job descriptions arranged by functional job category. The 1-3 page job descriptions cover what the worker normally does in the position, who they report to, and how that position fits in the organizational structure.

★1027★ **"Clerks" in *Career Discovery Encyclopedia* (Vol.2, pp. 16-17)**
J.G. Ferguson Publishing Co.
200 W. Madison St., Ste. 300
Chicago, IL 60606
Ph: (312)580-5480 Fax: (312)580-4948

E. Russell Primm, editor-in-chief. 1993. Contains two-page articles on 504 occupations. Each article describes job duties, earnings, and educational and training requirements.

★1028★ **"General Office Clerk" in *Occu-Facts: Information on 580 Careers in Outline Form***
Careers, Inc.
PO Box 135
Largo, FL 34649-0135
Ph: (813)584-7333

Biennial, 1995-96 edition. Each one-page occupational profile describes duties, working conditions, physical surroundings and demands, aptitudes, temperament, educational requirements, employment outlook, earnings, and places of employment.

★1029★ ***General Office Clerks***
Chronicle Guidance Publications, Inc.
66 Aurora St.
PO Box 1190
Moravia, NY 13118-1190
Ph: (315)497-0330 Fax: (315)497-3359
Fr: 800-622-7284

1991. Career brief describing the nature of the job, working conditions, hours and earnings, education and training, licensure, certification, unions, personal qualifications, social and psychological factors, location, employment outlook, entry methods, advancement, and related occupations.

★1030★ **"General Office Clerks" in *Encyclopedia of Careers and Vocational Guidance* (Vol.3, pp. 73-75)**
J.G. Ferguson Publishing Co.
200 W. Madison St., Ste. 300
Chicago, IL 60606
Ph: (312)580-5480 Fax: (312)580-4948

William E. Hopke, editor-in-chief. Ninth edition, 1993. Four-volume set that profiles 500 occupations and describes job trends in 74 industries. Includes career description, educational requirements, history of the job, methods of entry, advancement, employment outlook, earnings, working conditions, social and psychological factors, and sources of additional information.

★1031★ **"General Office Clerks" in *Occupational Outlook Handbook***
U.S. Government Printing Office
Superintendent of Documents
Washington, DC 20402
Ph: (202)512-1800 Fax: (202)512-2250

Biennial; latest edition, 1994-95. Encyclopedia of careers describing more than 250 occupations and comprising about 85 percent of all jobs in the economy. Occupations that require lengthy education or training are given the most attention. For each occupation, the handbook describes job duties, working conditions, training, educational preparation, personal qualities, advancement possibilities, job outlook, earnings, and sources of additional information.

★1032★ "Office Clerk" in *Career Information Center* (Vol.1)
Simon and Schuster
200 Old Tappan Rd.
Old Tappan, NJ 07675
Fax: 800-445-6991 Fr: 800-223-2348

Richard Lidz and Dale Anderson, editorial directors. Fifth edition, 1993. For 600 occupations, describes job duties, entry-level requirements, education and training needed, advancement possibilities, employment outlook, earnings and benefits. The set is divided into 12 volumes. Each volume includes jobs related under a broad career field. Volume 13 is the index.

★1033★ *Office Systems & Careers: A Resource for Administrative Assistants*
Allyn & Bacon, Inc.
160 Gould St.
Needham Heights, MA 02194

Olice D. Church and Anne E. Schatz. 1981.

★1034★ *Vocational Visions*
Center for Humanities, Inc.
Communications Park
Box 1000
Mount Kisco, NY 10549
Ph: (914)666-4100 Fax: (914)666-5319
Fr: 800-431-1242

Videocassette. 1984. 30 mins. This series of programs explains key aspects of actual training and a day in the life of a worker in the specific field mentioned on the videocassette. Occupations include: transportation/mechanics, repair, construction, business/office occupations, health, agriculture, technical/manufacturing, communications, and personal service.

Test Guides

★1035★ *Career Examination Series: Admitting Clerk/Assistant Clerk*
National Learning Corp.
212 Michael Dr.
Syosset, NY 11791
Ph: (516)921-8888 Fax: (516)921-8743
Fr: 800-645-6337

Jack Rudman. Test guide including questions and answers for students or professionals in the field who seek advancement through examination.

★1036★ *Career Examination Series: Beginning Office Worker*
National Learning Corp.
212 Michael Dr.
Syosset, NY 11791
Ph: (516)921-8888 Fax: (516)921-8743
Fr: 800-645-6337

Jack Rudman. All examination guides in this series contain questions with answers.

★1037★ *Career Examination Series: Chief Clerk*
National Learning Corp.
212 Michael Dr.
Syosset, NY 11791
Ph: (516)921-8888 Fax: (516)921-8743
Fr: 800-645-6337

Jack Rudman. All examination guides in this series contain questions with answers.

★1038★ *Career Examination Series: Clerical Careers*
National Learning Corp.
212 Michael Dr.
Syosset, NY 11791
Ph: (516)921-8888 Fax: (516)921-8743
Fr: 800-645-6337

Jack Rudman. All examination guides in this series contain questions with answers.

★1039★ *Career Examination Series: Clerk*
National Learning Corp.
212 Michael Dr.
Syosset, NY 11791
Ph: (516)921-8888 Fax: (516)921-8743
Fr: 800-645-6337

Jack Rudman. Test guide including questions and answers for students or professionals in the field who seek advancement through examination. Also included in the series: Supervising Clerk and Senior Clerk.

★1040★ *Career Examination Series: Principal Clerk*
National Learning Corp.
212 Michael Dr.
Syosset, NY 11791
Ph: (516)921-8888 Fax: (516)921-8743
Fr: 800-645-6337

Jack Rudman. All examination guides in this series contain questions with answers.

★1041★ *Career Examination Series: Principal Office Assistant*
National Learning Corp.
212 Michael Dr.
Syosset, NY 11791
Ph: (516)921-8888 Fax: (516)921-8743
Fr: 800-645-6337

Jack Rudman. All examination guides in this series contain questions with answers.

★1042★ *Career Examination Series: Senior Clerical Series*
National Learning Corp.
212 Michael Dr.
Syosset, NY 11791
Ph: (516)921-8888 Fax: (516)921-8743
Fr: 800-645-6337

Jack Rudman. All examination guides in this series contain questions with answers.

★1043★ *Career Examination Series: Senior Office Assistant/Worker*
National Learning Corp.
212 Michael Dr.
Syosset, NY 11791
Ph: (516)921-8888 Fax: (516)921-8743
Fr: 800-645-6337

Jack Rudman. All examination guides in this series contain questions with answers.

★1044★ *Office Aide*
Prentice Hall Press
Simon & Schuster Inc.
200 Old Tappan Rd.
Old Tappan, NJ 07675
Ph: 800-223-2348

Hy Hammer. Second edition, 1985. Contains seven sample exams for the following entry-level civil service positions: clerk, typist, stenographer, receptionist, office machine operator, telephone operator.

★1045★ *Practice for Clerical, Typing, and Stenographic Tests*
Arco Pub.
201 W. 103rd St.
Indianapolis, IN 46290
Ph: 800-428-5331 Fax: 800-835-3202

1993, eighth edition.

★1046★ *Practice and Drill for the Clerk, Typist, and Stenographer Examinations*
National Learning Corp.
212 Michael Dr.
Syosset, NY 11791
Ph: (516)921-8888 Fax: (516)921-8743
Fr: 800-645-6337

Jack Rudman. Part of the General Aptitude and Abilities Series. Books in this series provide functional, intensive test practice and drill in the basic skills and areas common to many examinations, as well as general aptitude or achievement necessary for entrance into many occupations or positions.

★1047★ *Senior Clerical Series*
Prentice Hall Press
Simon & Schuster Inc.
200 Old Tappan Rd.
Old Tappan, NJ 07675
Ph: 800-223-2348

Hy Hammer. Fourth edition, 1983. Complete test preparation for the following senior grade positions: clerk, typist, stenographer, account clerk, file clerk, statistics clerk, stenographer (law), mail and supply clerk, and stores clerk.

Basic Reference Guides and Handbooks

★1048★ *The A to Z Business Office Handbook*
Prentice Hall
Rte. 9W
Englewood Cliffs, NJ 07632
Ph: (201)592-2000

Robert E. Swindle. 1984.

★1049★ *Career Strategies for Secretaries: How to Get Where You Want to Be*
Contemporary Books, Inc.
180 N. Michigan Ave.
Chicago, IL 60601
Ph: (312)782-9181 Fax: (312)782-2157

Marie Kisiel. 1982.

★1050★ *General Office Procedures for Colleges*
South-Western Publishing Co.
5101 Madison Rd.
Cincinnati, OH 45227
Ph: (513)271-8811

Patsy J. Fulton. Tenth edition, 1988.

★1051★ *Hotel Front Office Management & Operation*
William C. Brown Group
2460 Kerper Blvd.
Dubuque, IA 52001
Ph: (319)588-1451 Fax: (319)589-2955

Peter Dukas. Third edition, 1970.

★1052★ *Math on the Job: Secretary/ Clerk Typist*
National Center for Research in Vocational Education
Ohio State University
1900 Kenry Rd.
Columbus, OH 43210
Ph: (614)292-4353

1985.

★1053★ *Office Procedures*
McGraw-Hill Publishing Co.
1221 Avenue of the Americas
New York, NY 10020
Ph: (212)512-2000

Jeffrey R. Stewart, Jr. 1980.

★1054★ *Procedures for the Office Professional*
South-Western Publishing Co.
5101 Madison Rd.
Cincinnati, OH 45227
Ph: (513)271-8811

Patsy J. Fulton. Second edition, 1990.

★1055★ *Reference Manual: For the Office*
South-Western Publishing Co.
5101 Madison Rd.
Cincinnati, OH 45227
Ph: (513)271-8811

Clifford R. House. Seventh edition, 1988.

★1056★ *Technique of Systems & Procedures*
Office Research Institute
1517 Sparrow St.
Longwood, FL 32750

John H. Ross.

PERIODICALS

★1057★ *Bank Operations Report*
Warren, Gorham & Lamont, Inc.
31 St. James Ave.
Boston, MA 02116-4112
Ph: (617)423-2020 Fax: (617)695-9699
Fr: 800-922-1201
Nancy Hitchner

Monthly. Focuses on electronic data processing control, check processing, record keeping, cost control, federal regulation, credit and debit cards, electronic funds transfer system, physical security, and office automation, computer, and systems applications.

★1058★ *From Nine to Five*
Dartnell Corporation
4660 Ravenswood
Chicago, IL 60640
Ph: (312)561-4000 Fax: (312)561-3801
Fr: 800-621-5463
Douglas Leland

Biweekly. Provides "tips, shortcuts, and helpful information for success in the office," particularly secretaries and office workers. Recurring features include columns titled titled Business Skills Clinic, Shortcuts, and The Coffee Break.

Information Clerks

Information clerks perform a variety of duties related to gathering and providing information in a wide range of employment settings. Many are employed by hotels and motels to deal directly with the public either by taking reservations, greeting guests, or answering questions. Often information clerks use word processors, fax machines, or personal computers to facilitate their work. Many information clerks are also found in the transportation industry, hospitals, and banks.

Salaries

Salaries for information clerks vary by industry.

Lowest 10 percent	Less than $210/week
Median	$320/week
Top 10 percent	More than $580/week

Employment Outlook

Growth rate until the year 2005: Faster than average.

Information Clerks

Career Guides

★1059★ **"Business and Financial Careers" in *The Best Jobs for the 1990s and Into the 21st Century***
Impact Publications
9104-N Manassas Dr.
Manassas Park, VA 22111
Ph: (703)361-7300 Fax: (703)335-9486

Ronald L. Krannich and Caryl Rae Krannich. 1993. Includes information on cashiers, counter and rental clerks, and information clerks.

★1060★ ***Clerk, Information***
Careers, Inc.
PO Box 135
Largo, FL 34649-0135
Ph: (813)584-7333

1994. Two-page job guide card describing duties, working conditions, personal qualifications, training, earnings and hours, employment outlook, places of employment, related careers and where to write for more information.

★1061★ **"Information Clerk" in *Careers Inside the World of Offices* (pp. 7-8)**
Rosen Publishing Group
29 E. 21st St.
New York, NY 10010
Ph: 800-237-9932 Fax: (212)777-0277

Carolyn Simpson. 1995. Describes job possibilities, attitudes and skills needed, and tips for getting the job. Also includes a self-evaluation test.

★1062★ **"Information Clerk" in *Occu-Facts: Information on 580 Careers in Outline Form***
Careers, Inc.
PO Box 135
Largo, FL 34649-0135
Ph: (813)584-7333

Biennial, 1995-96 edition. Each one-page occupational profile describes duties, working conditions, physical surroundings and demands, aptitudes, temperament, educational requirements, employment outlook, earnings, and places of employment.

★1063★ **"Information Clerks" in *America's 50 Fastest Growing Jobs* (pp. 102)**
JIST Works, Inc.
720 N. Park Ave.
Indianapolis, IN 46202-3431
Ph: (317)264-3720 Fax: (317)264-3709
Fr: 800-648-5478

Michael J. Farr, compiler. 1994. Describes the 50 fastest growing jobs within major career clusters such as technicians, and marketing and sales. Each job profile explains the nature of the work, skills and abilities required, employment outlook, average earnings, related occupations, education and training requirements, and employment opportunities. Also contains career planning information and job search tips.

★1064★ **"Information Clerks" in *Occupational Outlook Handbook***
U.S. Government Printing Office
Superintendent of Documents
Washington, DC 20402
Ph: (202)512-1800 Fax: (202)512-2250

Biennial; latest edition, 1994-95. Encyclopedia of careers describing more than 250 occupations and comprising about 85 percent of all jobs in the economy. Occupations that require lengthy education or training are given the most attention. For each occupation, the handbook describes job duties, working conditions, training, educational preparation, personal qualities, advancement possibilities, job outlook, earnings, and sources of additional information.

★1065★ ***The Power of Customer Service***
Nightingale-Conant Corp.
7300 N. Lehigh Ave.
Niles, IL 60714
Ph: (708)647-0300 Fr: 800-323-5552

Videocassette. 1991. 45 mins. Customer oriented service can be the greatest asset for any business. This video discusses the training and building of a service oriented team.

★1066★ **"Reservation and Information Clerks" in *Opportunities in Travel Careers* (p. 53)**
National Textbook Co. (NTC)
VGM Career Books
4255 W. Touhy Ave.
Lincolnwood, IL 60646-1975
Ph: (708)679-5500 Fax: (708)679-2494
Fr: 800-323-4900

Robert Scott Milne. 1991. Explores job opportunities in many travel related fields including the airlines, resorts, travel agencies, recreation, and tourism. Covers the work, salaries, educational preparation and training, and advancement possibilities.

Test Guides

★1067★ ***Career Examination Series: Associate Public Information Specialist***
National Learning Corp.
212 Michael Dr.
Syosset, NY 11791
Ph: (516)921-8888 Fax: (516)921-8743
Fr: 800-645-6337

Jack Rudman. All examination guides in this series contain questions with answers.

★1068★ ***Career Examination Series: Clerical Careers***
National Learning Corp.
212 Michael Dr.
Syosset, NY 11791
Ph: (516)921-8888 Fax: (516)921-8743
Fr: 800-645-6337

Jack Rudman. All examination guides in this series contain questions with answers.

★1069★ ***Career Examination Series: Public Information Assistant***
National Learning Corp.
212 Michael Dr.
Syosset, NY 11791
Ph: (516)921-8888 Fax: (516)921-8743
Fr: 800-645-6337

Jack Rudman. All examination guides in this series contain questions with answers.

★1070★ *Office Aide*
Prentice Hall Press
Simon & Schuster Inc.
200 Old Tappan Rd.
Old Tappan, NJ 07675
Ph: 800-223-2348

Hy Hammer. Second edition, 1985. Contains seven sample exams for the following entry-level civil service positions: clerk, typist, stenographer, receptionist, office machine operator, telephone operator.

★1071★ *Senior Clerical Series*
Prentice Hall Press
Simon & Schuster Inc.
200 Old Tappan Rd.
Old Tappan, NJ 07675
Ph: 800-223-2348

Hy Hammer. Fourth edition, 1983. Complete test preparation for the following senior grade positions: clerk, typist, stenographer, account clerk, file clerk, statistics clerk, stenographer (law), mail and supply clerk, and stores clerk.

Hotel and Motel Desk Clerks

Hotel and motel desk clerks perform a variety of services such as registering guests, assigning rooms, answering questions, and processing payments. In smaller establishments, clerks may also function as bookkeepers, cashiers, or telephone operators. In addition to these duties, clerks keep records of room assignments to maximize profit and coordinate housekeeping and maintenance work. Hotel and motel clerks are in direct contact with the public and, through their attitude, may influence guests positively or negatively about the establishment.

Salaries

The average salary for hotel and motel clerks is $250/week.

Employment Outlook

Growth rate until the year 2005: Faster than average.

Hotel and Motel Desk Clerks

Career Guides

★1072★ *Hospitality Industry*
AIMS Media, Inc.
9710 DeSoto Ave.
Chatsworth, CA 91311
Ph: (818)773-4300 Fax: (818)341-6700
Fr: 800-367-2467

Videocassette. 1988. 40 mins. A section of the "Career Awareness" series which covers the hotel industry.

★1073★ *Hotel Concierge*
Vocational Biographies, Inc.
PO Box 31
Sauk Centre, MN 56378-0031
Ph: (612)352-6516 Fax: (612)352-5546
Fr: 800-255-0752

1991. Four-page pamphlet containing a personal narrative about a worker's job, work likes and dislikes, career path from high school to the present. Education and training, the rewards and frustrations, and the effects of the job on the rest of the worker's life. The data file portion of this pamphlet gives a concise occupational summary, including work descriptions, working conditions, places of employment, personal characteristics, education and training, job outlook, and salary range.

★1074★ "Hotel Desk Clerk" in *Career Information Center* (Vol.8)
Simon and Schuster
200 Old Tappan Rd.
Old Tappan, NJ 07675
Fax: 800-445-6991 Fr: 800-223-2348

Richard Lidz and Dale Anderson, editorial directors. Fifth edition, 1993. For 600 occupations, describes job duties, entry-level requirements, education and training needed, advancement possibilities, employment outlook, earnings and benefits. The set is divided into 12 volumes. Each volume includes jobs related under a broad career field. Volume 13 is the index.

★1075★ *Hotel/Motel Careers: A World of Opportunities*
American Hotel and Motel Association
Educational Institute
1407 S. Harrison Rd.
PO Box 1240
East Lansing, MI 48826

1992. Booklet providing an overview of the lodging industry and its job opportunities.

★1076★ *Hotel/Motel Clerk*
Careers, Inc.
PO Box 135
Largo, FL 34649-0135
Ph: (813)584-7333

1994. Two-page occupational summary card describing duties, working conditions, personal qualifications, training, earnings and hours, employment outlook, places of employment, related careers and where to write for more information.

★1077★ "Hotel/Motel Clerk" in *Occu-Facts: Information on 580 Careers in Outline Form*
Careers, Inc.
PO Box 135
Largo, FL 34649-0135
Ph: (813)584-7333

Biennial, 1995-96 edition. Each one-page occupational profile describes duties, working conditions, physical surroundings and demands, aptitudes, temperament, educational requirements, employment outlook, earnings, and places of employment.

★1078★ "Hotel and Motel Clerks" in *Occupational Outlook Handbook*
U.S. Government Printing Office
Superintendent of Documents
Washington, DC 20402
Ph: (202)512-1800 Fax: (202)512-2250

Biennial; latest edition, 1994-95. Encyclopedia of careers describing more than 250 occupations and comprising about 85 percent of all jobs in the economy. Occupations that require lengthy education or training are given the most attention. For each occupation, the handbook describes job duties, working conditions, training, educational preparation, personal qualities, advancement possibilities, job outlook, earnings, and sources of additional information.

★1079★ "Hotel and Motel Desk Clerk" in *Hospitality & Recreation* (pp. 15-19)
Franklin Watts, Inc.
387 Park Avenue, S.
New York, NY 10016
Ph: (212)686-7070

Marjorie Rittenberg Schulz. 1990. Provides an overview of jobs in the hotel, motel, food service, fitness, and recreation industries. Covers job duties, educational preparation, salary, and employment outlook. Offers job hunting advice.

★1080★ "Hotel and Motel Desk Clerks" in *America's 50 Fastest Growing Jobs* (pp. 101)
JIST Works, Inc.
720 N. Park Ave.
Indianapolis, IN 46202-3431
Ph: (317)264-3720 Fax: (317)264-3709
Fr: 800-648-5478

Michael J. Farr, compiler. 1994. Describes the 50 fastest growing jobs within major career clusters such as technicians, and marketing and sales. Each job profile explains the nature of the work, skills and abilities required, employment outlook, average earnings, related occupations, education and training requirements, and employment opportunities. Also contains career planning information and job search tips.

★1081★ "Hotel and Motel Front Office Clerks" in *Jobs! What They Are—Where They Are—What They Pay* (pp. 201)
Simon & Schuster, Inc.
Simon & Schuster Bldg.
1230 Avenue of the Americas
New York, NY 10020
Ph: (212)698-7000

Robert O. Snelling and Anne M. Snelling. Revised edition, 1992. Profiles 241 occupations, describing duties and responsibilities, educational preparation, earnings, employment opportunities, training, and qualifications.

★1082★ "Hotel and Motel Industry Workers" in *Encyclopedia of Careers and Vocational Guidance* (Vol.3, pp. 143-148)
J.G. Ferguson Publishing Co.
200 W. Madison St., Ste. 300
Chicago, IL 60606
Ph: (312)580-5480 Fax: (312)580-4948

William E. Hopke, editor-in-chief. Ninth edition, 1993. Four-volume set that profiles 500 occupations and describes job trends in 74 industries. Includes career description, educational requirements, history of the job, methods of entry, advancement, employment outlook, earnings, working conditions, social and psychological factors, and sources of additional information.

★1083★ *Introduction to Management in the Hospitality Industry*
John Wiley and Sons, Inc.
605 3rd Ave.
New York, NY 10158-0012
Ph: (212)850-6000 Fax: (212)850-6088
Fr: 800-526-5368

Tom Powers. 1992.

★1084★ "Travel and Hospitality Careers" in *The Best Jobs for the 1990s and Into the 21st Century*
Impact Publications
9104-N Manassas Dr.
Manassas Park, VA 22111
Ph: (703)361-7300 Fax: (703)335-9486

Ronald L. Krannich and Caryl Rae Krannich. 1993. Includes information on chefs, cooks, flight attendants, food and beverage service workers, hotel and motel desk clerks, reservation and transportation ticket agents and travel clerks, and travel agents.

Associations

★1085★ American Hotel & Motel Association (AH&MA)
1201 New York Ave. NW, Ste. 600
Washington, DC 20005-3931
Ph: (202)289-3100 Fax: (202)289-3199

Members: Federation of 50 state and regional hotel associations, representing over 1.4 million hotel and motel rooms. **Purpose:** Promotes business of hotels and motels through publicity and promotion programs. Works to improve operating methods through dissemination of information on industry methods. Conducts educational institute for training at all levels, through home study, adult education, and colleges. Provides guidance on member and labor relations. Reviews proposed legislation affecting hotels. Sponsors study group programs. Maintains speakers' bureau and library; conducts research; compiles statistics; sponsors competitions. Operates the American Hotel Foundation, which absorbed the Hospitality Lodging and Travel Research Foundation in 1993. **Publications:** *AH&MA Reports.* • *Directory of Hotel and Motel Systems*, annual. • *Innside Government.* • *Lodging*, monthly. • *Who's Who Directory*, annual.

Educational Directories and Programs

★1086★ *Directory of Hotel and Motel Systems*
American Hotel & Motel Association (AH&MA)
1201 New York Ave. NW, Ste. 600
Washington, DC 20005
Ph: (202)289-3100 Fax: (202)289-3199

Annual.

★1087★ *Who's Who Directory*
American Hotel & Motel Association (AH&MA)
1201 New York Ave. NW, Ste. 600
Washington, DC 20005-3931
Ph: (202)289-3100 Fax: (202)289-3199

Annual. Listing of names, company affiliations, addresses, and phone numbers for important AH&MA members.

Awards, Scholarships, Grants, and Fellowships

★1088★ Outstanding Lodging Employee of the Year
American Hotel & Motel Association
1201 New York Ave. NW
Washington, DC 20005-3931
Ph: (202)289-3133

To provide hotels and motels an opportunity to recognize exemplary professionalism and exceptional service by an employee in a management or non-management position with the exception of roomkeeper. The nominees are judged on performance that goes above and beyond normal job responsibilities, including outstanding and unusual service to the hotel/motel, to the guests, and/or community. A nominee must have served in the lodging industry for a minimum of three years. Only one nominee may be entered per property. The deadline for nominations is January 24. The award winner is flown to the awards ceremony held during the annual convention in Denver, CO, to receive a special award, $1,000 cash, two roundtrip tickets to a select destination in North America, and 7 days/6 nights accommodations. Awarded annually. Sponsored by Visa U.S.A.

Basic Reference Guides and Handbooks

★1089★ *Hotel Front Office Management & Operation*
William C. Brown Group
2460 Kerper Blvd.
Dubuque, IA 52001
Ph: (319)588-1451 Fax: (319)589-2955

Peter Dukas. Third edition, 1970.

Periodicals

★1090★ *AH&MA Reports*
American Hotel & Motel Association (AH&MA)
1201 New York Ave. NW, Ste. 600
Washington, DC 20005-3931
Ph: (202)289-3100 Fax: (202)289-3199

★1091★ *Hotel & Motel Management*
Advanstar Communications Inc.
7500 Old Oak Blvd.
Cleveland, OH 44130
Ph: (216)896-2839 Fax: (216)891-2726
Robert Nozar

Magazine (tabloid) covering the global lodging industry.

★1092★ *HOTELS*
Cahners Publishing Co.
1350 E. Touhy Ave.
PO Box 5080
Des Plaines, IL 60017-5080
Ph: (708)635-8800 Fax: (708)390-2618
James Carper

Monthly. Magazine covering management and operations as well as foodservice and design in the hospitality industry.

★1093★ *Innside Government*
American Hotel & Motel Association (AH&MA)
1201 New York Ave. NW, Ste. 600
Washington, DC 20005-3931
Ph: (202)289-3100 Fax: (202)289-3199

★1094★ *Lodging*
American Hotel & Motel Association (AH&MA)
1201 New York Ave. NW, Ste. 600
Washington, DC 20005-3931
Ph: (202)289-3100 Fax: (202)289-3199

Monthly.

Meetings and Conventions

★1095★ American Hotel and Motel Association Fall Conference
American Hotel and Motel Association
1201 New York Ave., NW, Ste. 600
Washington, DC 20005-3931
Ph: (202)289-3115 Fax: (202)289-3199

Annual. **Dates and Locations:** 1995 Nov 06-10; New York, NY.

★1096★ IAHA HITEC-Hospitality Industry Technology Exposition and Conference
International Association of Hospitality Accountants
PO Box 203008
Austin, TX 78720-3008
Ph: (512)346-5680 Fax: (512)346-5760

Annual.

OTHER SOURCES OF INFORMATION

★1097★ "Hotel Clerk" in *Career Selector 2001*
Barron's Educational Series, Inc.
250 Wireless Blvd.
Hauppauge, NY 11788
Ph: (516)434-3311 Fax: (516)434-3723
Fr: 800-645-3476

James C. Gonyea. 1993.

★1098★ *Hotel & Motel Equipment & Supplies Directory*
American Business Directories, Inc.
5711 S. 86th Circle
Omaha, NE 68127
Ph: (402)593-4600 Fax: (402)331-1505

Updated continuously; printed on request. Entries include: Name, address, phone, size of advertisement, name of owner or manager, number of employees, year first in "Yellow Pages." Compiled from telephone company "Yellow Pages," nationwide. Arrangement: Geographical.

Interviewing and New Accounts Clerks

Interviewing clerks gather and process various types of information and assist people in filling out forms. In hospitals, an outpatient admitting clerk gathers the preliminary information necessary for admission and provides general information. Survey workers, sometimes called telemarketers, often conduct telephone interviews to gather information and compile statistics. **New accounts clerks** interview applicants and help them fill out applications for credit cards or bank accounts. Interviewing and new accounts clerks are often employed by banks, savings and loan associations, firms providing miscellaneous business services, hospitals, and the Federal Government.

Salaries

The average salary for interviewing and new accounts clerks is $350/week.

Employment Outlook

Growth rate until the year 2005: Average.

Interviewing and New Accounts Clerks

Career Guides

★1099★ "Admitting Clerk" in *Career Information Center* (pp. 39-40)
Simon and Schuster
200 Old Tappan Rd.
Old Tappan, NJ 07675
Fax: 800-445-6991 Fr: 800-223-2348

Richard Lidz and Dale Anderson, editorial directors. Fifth edition, 1993. For 600 occupations, describes job duties, entry-level requirements, education and training needed, advancement possibilities, employment outlook, earnings and benefits. The set is divided into 12 volumes. Each volume includes jobs related under a broad career field. Volume 13 is the index.

★1100★ "Admitting Clerk" in *Health Care* (pp. 39-43)
Franklin Watts, Inc.
387 Park Avenue, S.
New York, NY 10016
Ph: (212)686-7070

Linda Barrett and Galen Guengerich. 1991. Provides an overview of the health care industry. Includes job description, educational preparation, training, salary, and employment outlook. Offers job hunting advice.

★1101★ "Interviewing and New Accounts Clerks" in *Occupational Outlook Handbook*
U.S. Government Printing Office
Superintendent of Documents
Washington, DC 20402
Ph: (202)512-1800 Fax: (202)512-2250

Biennial; latest edition, 1994-95. Encyclopedia of careers describing more than 250 occupations and comprising about 85 percent of all jobs in the economy. Occupations that require lengthy education or training are given the most attention. For each occupation, the handbook describes job duties, working conditions, training, educational preparation, personal qualities, advancement possibilities, job outlook, earnings, and sources of additional information.

★1102★ "Tel-a-marketing" in *Careers in Trucking*
Rosen Publishing Group
29 E. 21st St.
New York, NY 10010
Ph: (212)777-3017 Fax: (212)777-0277
Fr: 800-237-9932

Donald D. Schauer. 1991. Describes employment in the trucking industry including driving, operations, sales, and administration. Covers qualifications, training, future outlook, and salaries. Offers career planning and job hunting advice.

★1103★ *Telemarketer*
Careers, Inc.
PO Box 135
Largo, FL 34649-0135
Ph: (813)584-7333

1992. Two-page occupational summary card describing duties, working conditions, personal qualifications, training, earnings and hours, employment outlook, places of employment, related careers and where to write for more information.

★1104★ "Telemarketer" in *Occu-Facts: Information on 580 Careers in Outline Form*
Careers, Inc.
PO Box 135
Largo, FL 34649-0135
Ph: (813)584-7333

Biennial, 1995-96 edition. Each one-page occupational profile describes duties, working conditions, physical surroundings and demands, aptitudes, temperament, educational requirements, employment outlook, earnings, and places of employment.

★1105★ "Telemarketers" in *Career Discovery Encyclopedia* (Vol.6, pp. 98-99)
J.G. Ferguson Publishing Co.
200 W. Madison St., Ste. 300
Chicago, IL 60606
Ph: (312)580-5480 Fax: (312)580-4948

E. Russell Primm, editor-in-chief. 1993. Contains two-page articles on 504 occupations. Each article describes job duties, earnings, and educational and training requirements.

★1106★ "Telemarketers" in *Encyclopedia of Careers and Vocational Guidance* (Vol.4, pp. 506-509)
J.G. Ferguson Publishing Co.
200 W. Madison St., Ste. 300
Chicago, IL 60606
Ph: (312)580-5480 Fax: (312)580-4948

William E. Hopke, editor-in-chief. Ninth edition, 1993. Four-volume set that profiles 500 occupations and describes job trends in 74 industries. Includes career description, educational requirements, history of the job, methods of entry, advancement, employment outlook, earnings, working conditions, social and psychological factors, and sources of additional information.

★1107★ "Telemarketing" in *Careers in Marketing* (pp. 57-58)
National Textbook Co. (NTC)
VGM Career Books
4255 W. Touhy Ave.
Lincolnwood, IL 60646-1975
Ph: (708)679-5500 Fax: (708)679-2494
Fr: 800-323-4900

Lila B. Stair. 1991. Surveys career opportunities in marketing and related areas such as marketing research, product development, and sales promotion. Includes a description of the work, places of employment, employment outlook, trends, educational preparation, organizational charts, and salaries. Offers job hunting advice.

★1108★ "Telemarketing" in *Opportunities in Telecommunications Careers* (pp. 35-46)
National Textbook Co. (NTC)
VGM Career Books
4255 W. Touhy Ave.
Lincolnwood, IL 60646-1975
Ph: (708)679-5500 Fax: (708)679-2494
Fr: 800-323-4900

Jan Bone. 1990. Discusses the many facets of the telecommunications industry including research and development, manufacturing, sales, telecommunications, services, management, telemarketing, electronic mail, networking, and cellular communication. Explores jobs, educational preparation and training requirements, and provides job hunting tips.

★1109★ "Telemarketing Specialist" in *Career Information Center* (Vol.10)
Simon and Schuster
200 Old Tappan Rd.
Old Tappan, NJ 07675
Fax: 800-445-6991 Fr: 800-223-2348

Richard Lidz and Dale Anderson, editorial directors. Fifth edition, 1993. For 600 occupations, describes job duties, entry-level requirements, education and training needed, advancement possibilities, employment outlook, earnings and benefits. The set is divided into 12 volumes. Each volume includes jobs related under a broad career field. Volume 13 is the index.

★1110★ "Telemarketing: The Fast-Track Medium" in *Marketing and Sales Career Directory* (pp. 68-72)
Career Press, Inc.
PO Box 34
62 Beverly Rd.
Hawthorne, NJ 07507
Ph: (201)427-0229

Ronald W. Fry, editor. Third edition, 1990. Guide to career planning and job hunting in a marketing or sales capacity at a major corporation, market research company, or public relations agency. Lists hundreds of employers seeking entry level employees. Includes job description, work environments, educational preparation, career advancement, earnings, and trends.

★1111★ Telephone Salespeople (Telemarketers)
Chronicle Guidance Publications, Inc.
66 Aurora St.
PO Box 1190
Moravia, NY 13118-1190
Ph: (315)497-0330 Fax: (315)497-3359
Fr: 800-622-7284

1993. This career brief describes the nature of the work, working conditions, hours and earnings, education and training, licensure, certification, unions, personal qualifications, social and psychological factors, employment outlook, entry methods, advancement, and related occupations.

Associations

★1112★ American Bankers Association (ABA)
1120 Connecticut Ave. NW
Washington, DC 20036
Ph: (202)663-5000 Fax: (202)663-7533

Members: Members are principally commercial banks and trust companies; combined assets of members represent approximately 90% of the U.S. banking industry; approximately 94% of members are community banks with less than $500 million in assets. **Purpose:** Seeks to enhance the role of commercial bankers as preeminent providers of financial services through communications, research, legal action, lobbying of federal legislative and regulatory bodies, and education and training programs. Serves as spokesperson for the banking industry; facilitates exchange of information among members. Maintains the American Institute of Banking, an industry-sponsored adult education program. Conducts educational and training programs for bank employees and officers through a wide range of banking schools and national conferences. Maintains liaison with federal bank regulators; submits draft legislation and lobbies Congress on issues affecting commercial banks; testifies before congressional committees; represents members in U.S. postal rate proceedings. Serves as secretariat of the International Monetary Conference and the Financial Institutions Committee for the American National Standards Institute. Compiles briefs and lawsuits in major court cases affecting the industry. Conducts teleconferences with state banking associations on such issues as regulatory compliance; works to build consensus and coordinate activities of leading bank and financial service trade groups. Provides services to members including: public advocacy; news media contact; insurance program providing directors and officers with liability coverage, financial institution bond, and trust errors and omissions coverage; research service operated through ABA Center for Banking Information; fingerprint set processing in conjunction with the Federal Bureau of Investigation; discounts on operational and income-producing projects through the Corporation for American Banking. Conducts conferences, forums, and workshops covering subjects such as small business, consumer credit, agricultural and community banking, trust management, bank operations, and automation. Sponsors the Personal Economics Program, which educates schoolchildren and the community on banking, economics, and personal finance. **Publications:** *ABA Banking Journal*, monthly. • *ABA Management Update of Personal Trust and Private Banking*, bimonthly. • *AIB Leader Letter*, quarterly. • *Bank Compliance Magazine*, quarterly. • *Bank Insurance and Protection Bulletin*, monthly. • *Bank Operations Bulletin*, monthly. • *Bank Personnel News*, monthly. • *Bank Security News*, monthly. • *Bankers News*, biweekly. • *Commercial Lending Review*, quarterly. • *Consumer Credit Delinquency Bulletin*, quarterly. • *Employee Benefits Quarterly*, quarterly. • *Journal of Agricultural Lending*, quarterly. • *Network News*, 3/year. • *Retail Banking Digest*, bimonthly. • *Retail Delivery Systems Quarterly*, quarterly. • *Securities Processing Digest*, quarterly. • *Stonier Forum*, semiannual. • *Trends*, bimonthly. • *Trust and Financial Advisor*, quarterly. • *Trust Letter*, monthly.

Educational Directories and Programs

★1113★ AIB Student Catalog
American Bankers Association (ABA)
1120 Connecticut Ave. NW
Washington, DC 20036
Ph: (202)663-5000

Annual.

Periodicals

★1114★ ABA Banking Journal
American Bankers Association (ABA)
1120 Connecticut Ave. NW
Washington, DC 20036
Ph: (202)663-5000 Fax: (202)663-7533

Monthly.

★1115★ AIB Leader Letter
American Bankers Association (ABA)
1120 Connecticut Ave. NW
Washington, DC 20036
Ph: (202)663-5000 Fax: (202)663-7533

Quarterly.

★1116★ Bank Compliance Magazine
American Bankers Association (ABA)
1120 Connecticut Ave. NW
Washington, DC 20036
Ph: (202)663-5000 Fax: (202)663-7533

Quarterly.

★1117★ Bank Personnel News
American Bankers Association (ABA)
1120 Connecticut Ave. NW
Washington, DC 20036
Ph: (202)663-5000 Fax: (202)663-7533

Monthly.

★1118★ Bankers News
American Bankers Association (ABA)
1120 Connecticut Ave. NW
Washington, DC 20036
Ph: (202)663-5000 Fax: (202)663-7533

Biweekly.

★1119★ Retail Banking Digest
American Bankers Association
1120 Connecticut Ave. NW
Washington, DC 20036
Ph: (202)663-5000 Fax: (202)663-7533

Bimonthly.

Receptionists

Receptionists greet customers and visitors, determine their needs, and refer them to the correct person. This involves daily interaction with people either in person or on the telephone. Depending on where they work, receptionists may schedule appointments, answer questions, open mail, or do bookkeeping. Receptionists often use automated office equipment such as word processors and personal computers to perform their duties. Many receptionists are employed by health care facilities as well as factories, wholesale and retail stores, government agencies, real estate offices, and firms providing business services.

Salaries

The average salary for receptionists is $310/week.

Employment Outlook

Growth rate until the year 2005: Faster than average.

Receptionists

Career Guides

★1120★ *How to Be a Receptionist*
Oddo Publishing, Inc.
PO Box 68
Storybrook Acres
Fayetteville, GA 30214-0068
Ph: (404)461-7627

Johnson.

★1121★ *Receptionist*
Careers, Inc.
PO Box 135
Largo, FL 34649-0135
Ph: (813)584-7333

1994. Two-page occupational summary card describing duties, working conditions, personal qualifications, training, earnings and hours, employment outlook, places of employment, related careers and where to write for more information.

★1122★ *The Receptionist*
McGraw-Hill Publishing Co.
1221 Avenue of the Americas
New York, NY 10020
Ph: (212)512-2000

J. W. Twing. 1983.

★1123★ *Receptionist*
Vocational Biographies, Inc.
PO Box 31
Sauk Centre, MN 56378-0031
Ph: (612)352-6516 Fax: (612)352-5546
Fr: 800-255-0752

1990. This pamphlet profiles a person working in the job. Includes information about job duties, working conditions, places of employment, educational preparation, labor market outlook, and salaries.

★1124★ "Receptionist" in *BLR Encyclopedia of Prewritten Job Descriptions*
Business and Legal Reports, Inc.
39 Academy St.
Madison, CT 06443-1513
Ph: (203)245-7448

Stephen D. Bruce, editor-in-chief. 1994. This book contains hundreds of sample job descriptions arranged by functional job category. The 1-3 page job descriptions cover what the worker normally does in the position, who they report to, and how that position fits in the organizational structure.

★1125★ "Receptionist" in *Career Information Center* (Vol.1)
Simon and Schuster
200 Old Tappan Rd.
Old Tappan, NJ 07675
Fax: 800-445-6991 Fr: 800-223-2348

Richard Lidz and Dale Anderson, editorial directors. Fifth edition, 1993. For 600 occupations, describes job duties, entry-level requirements, education and training needed, advancement possibilities, employment outlook, earnings and benefits. The set is divided into 12 volumes. Each volume includes jobs related under a broad career field. Volume 13 is the index.

★1126★ "Receptionist" in *Careers Inside the World of Offices* (pp. 8-7, 29-34)
Rosen Publishing Group
29 E. 21st St.
New York, NY 10010
Ph: 800-237-9932 Fax: (212)777-0277

Carolyn Simpson. 1995. Describes job possibilities, attitudes and skills needed, and tips for getting the job. Also includes a self-evaluation test.

★1127★ "Receptionist/Clerk-Typist" in *Career Opportunities in Television, Cable, and Video* (pp. 22-23)
Facts on File
460 Park Ave. S.
New York, NY 10016-7382
Ph: (212)683-2244 Fax: 800-678-3633
Fr: 800-322-8755

Third edition, 1990. Describes 100 media-related jobs. Each occupational profile covers job duties, employment outlook, career paths, salaries, skills, and educational preparation. Offers tips for entering the field.

★1128★ "Receptionist" in *Jobs Rated Almanac*
World Almanac
1 International Blvd., Ste. 444
Mahwah, NJ 07495
Ph: (201)529-6900 Fax: (201)529-6901

Les Krantz. Second edition, 1992. Ranks 250 jobs by environment, salary, outlooks, physical demands, stress, security, travel opportunities, and extra perks. Includes jobs the editor feels are the most common, most interesting, and the most rapidly growing.

★1129★ "Receptionist" in *Occu-Facts: Information on 580 Careers in Outline Form*
Careers, Inc.
PO Box 135
Largo, FL 34649-0135
Ph: (813)584-7333

Biennial, 1995-96 edition. Each one-page occupational profile describes duties, working conditions, physical surroundings and demands, aptitudes, temperament, educational requirements, employment outlook, earnings, and places of employment.

★1130★ *Receptionists*
Chronicle Guidance Publications, Inc.
66 Aurora St.
PO Box 1190
Moravia, NY 13118-1190
Ph: (315)497-0330 Fax: (315)497-3359
Fr: 800-622-7284

1992. This career brief describes the nature of the work, working conditions, hours and earnings, education and training, licensure, certification, unions, personal qualifications, social and psychological factors, employment outlook, entry methods, advancement, and related occupations.

★1131★ "Receptionists" in *Career Discovery Encyclopedia* (Vol.5, pp. 132-133)
J.G. Ferguson Publishing Co.
200 W. Madison St., Ste. 300
Chicago, IL 60606
Ph: (312)580-5480 Fax: (312)580-4948

E. Russell Primm, editor-in-chief. 1993. Contains two-page articles on 504 occupations. Each article describes job duties, earnings, and educational and training requirements.

★1132★ "Receptionists" in *Encyclopedia of Careers and Vocational Guidance* (Vol.4, pp. 248-250)
J.G. Ferguson Publishing Co.
200 W. Madison St., Ste. 300
Chicago, IL 60606
Ph: (312)580-5480 Fax: (312)580-4948

William E. Hopke, editor-in-chief. Ninth edition, 1993. Four-volume set that profiles 500

occupations and describes job trends in 74 industries. Includes career description, educational requirements, history of the job, methods of entry, advancement, employment outlook, earnings, working conditions, social and psychological factors, and sources of additional information.

★1133★ "Receptionists" in *Jobs! What They Are—Where They Are—What They Pay* (pp. 251)
Simon & Schuster, Inc.
Simon & Schuster Bldg.
1230 Avenue of the Americas
New York, NY 10020
Ph: (212)698-7000

Robert O. Snelling and Anne M. Snelling. Revised edition, 1992. Profiles 241 occupations, describing duties and responsibilities, educational preparation, earnings, employment opportunities, training, and qualifications.

★1134★ "Receptionists" in *Occupational Outlook Handbook*
U.S. Government Printing Office
Superintendent of Documents
Washington, DC 20402
Ph: (202)512-1800 Fax: (202)512-2250

Biennial; latest edition, 1994-95. Encyclopedia of careers describing more than 250 occupations and comprising about 85 percent of all jobs in the economy. Occupations that require lengthy education or training are given the most attention. For each occupation, the handbook describes job duties, working conditions, training, educational preparation, personal qualities, advancement possibilities, job outlook, earnings, and sources of additional information.

★1135★ "Receptionists" in *Opportunities in Vocational and Technical Careers* (pp. 47-58)
National Textbook Co. (NTC)
VGM Career Books
4255 W. Touhy Ave.
Lincolnwood, IL 60646-1975
Ph: (708)679-5500 Fax: (708)679-2494
Fr: 800-323-4900

Adrian A. Paradis. 1992. Describes careers which can be prepared for by attending a private vocational or proprietary school—office employee, sales worker, service worker, health services, mechanic, craftworker, and technician. Covers employment outlook, job duties, and salaries. Offers career planning advice.

★1136★ "Receptionists and Switchboard Operators" in *American Almanac of Jobs and Salaries* (p. 511)
Avon Books
1350 Avenue of the Americas
New York, NY 10019
Ph: (212)261-6800 Fr: 800-238-0658

John Wright, editor. Revised and updated, 1994-95. A comprehensive guide to the wages of hundreds of occupations in a wide variety of industries and organizations.

★1137★ *Video Career Library - Clerical & Administrative Support*
Careers, Inc.
PO Box 135
Largo, FL 34649-0135
Ph: (813)584-7333

Videocassette. 1990. 26 mins. Part of the Video Career Library covering 165 occupations. Shows actual workers on the job. Includes secretaries, cashiers, receptionists, bookkeepers and audit clerks, telephone operators, postal clerks/carriers/supervisors, insurance investigators, bank tellers, data entry keyers, and court reporters.

★1138★ *Vocational Visions*
Center for Humanities, Inc.
Communications Park
Box 1000
Mount Kisco, NY 10549
Ph: (914)666-4100 Fax: (914)666-5319
Fr: 800-431-1242

Videocassette. 1984. 30 mins. This series of programs explains key aspects of actual training and a day in the life of a worker in the specific field mentioned on the videocassette. Occupations include: transportation/mechanics, repair, construction, business/office occupations, health, agriculture, technical/manufacturing, communications, and personal service.

Test Guides

★1139★ *Career Examination Series: Receptionist*
National Learning Corp.
212 Michael Dr.
Syosset, NY 11791
Ph: (516)921-8888 Fax: (516)921-8743
Fr: 800-645-6337

Jack Rudman. All examination guides in this series contain questions with answers.

★1140★ *Office Aide*
Prentice Hall Press
Simon & Schuster Inc.
200 Old Tappan Rd.
Old Tappan, NJ 07675
Ph: 800-223-2348

Hy Hammer. Second edition, 1985. Contains seven sample exams for the following entry-level civil service positions: clerk, typist, stenographer, receptionist, office machine operator, telephone operator.

Educational Directories and Programs

★1141★ *Industry Directory*
Association of Information Professionals
104 Wilmot Rd., Ste. 201
Deerfield, IL 60015-5195
Ph: (708)940-8800 Fax: (708)940-7218

Manufacturers of office automation equipment; word processing service bureaus; educational institutions offering office automation and associated software courses or curriculums; personnel agencies serving office automation personnel and users; analysts and consultants. Entries include: Name, address. Arrangement: Alphabetical within categories above.

Basic Reference Guides and Handbooks

★1142★ *Career Strategies for Secretaries: How to Get Where You Want to Be*
Contemporary Books, Inc.
180 N. Michigan Ave.
Chicago, IL 60601
Ph: (312)782-9181 Fax: (312)782-2157

Marie Kisiel. 1982.

★1143★ *Math on the Job: Secretary/ Clerk Typist*
National Center for Research in Vocational Education
Ohio State University
1900 Kenry Rd.
Columbus, OH 43210
Ph: (614)292-4353

1985.

★1144★ *Receptionist: A Practical Course in Office Reception Techniques*
McGraw-Hill Publishing Co.
1221 Avenue of the Americas
New York, NY 10020
Ph: (212)512-2000

Merle W. Wood. 1966.

Periodicals

★1145★ *From Nine to Five*
Dartnell Corporation
4660 Ravenswood
Chicago, IL 60640
Ph: (312)561-4000 Fax: (312)561-3801
Fr: 800-621-5463
Douglas Leland

Biweekly. Provides "tips, shortcuts, and helpful information for success in the office," particularly secretaries and office workers. Recurring features include columns titled titled Business Skills Clinic, Shortcuts, and The Coffee Break.

OTHER SOURCES OF INFORMATION

★1146★ *How to Be an Outstanding Receptionist*
Cambridge Career Products
PO Box 2153, Dept. CC15
Charleston, WV 25328-2153
Fr: 800-468-4227

1992. A two volume video series on the techniques needed to be a successful receptionist.

★1147★ "Receptionist" in *Career Selector 2001*
Barron's Educational Series, Inc.
250 Wireless Blvd.
Hauppauge, NY 11788
Ph: (516)434-3311 Fax: (516)434-3723
Fr: 800-645-3476

James C. Gonyea. 1993.

Reservation and Transportation Ticket Agents and Travel Clerks

Reservation and transportation ticket agents and travel clerks help passengers plan trips and assist them during travel. Travel clerks gather information on accommodation and transportation rates, make reservations, and calculate expenses. Reservation agents usually work in central offices answering telephone inquiries and booking reservations. They often use computer terminals to quickly access reservation information. Ticket agents sell tickets, answer inquiries, check baggage, examine visas, and ensure passenger seating. Ticket agents, known as gate agents in airports, assist people when boarding.

Salaries

The average salary for reservation and transportation ticket agents and travel clerks is $400/week.

Employment Outlook

Growth rate until the year 2005: Faster than average.

Reservation and Transportation Ticket Agents and Travel Clerks

Career Guides

★1148★ "Airline Reservations Agent" in *Career Information Center* (Vol.12)
Simon and Schuster
200 Old Tappan Rd.
Old Tappan, NJ 07675
Fax: 800-445-6991 Fr: 800-223-2348

Richard Lidz and Dale Anderson, editorial directors. Fifth edition, 1993. For 600 occupations, describes job duties, entry-level requirements, education and training needed, advancement possibilities, employment outlook, earnings and benefits. The set is divided into 12 volumes. Each volume includes jobs related under a broad career field. Volume 13 is the index.

★1149★ "Airline Reservations Agent" in *Travel & Tourism* (pp. 21-25)
Franklin Watts, Inc.
387 Park Avenue, S.
New York, NY 10016
Ph: (212)686-7070

Marjorie Rittenberg Schulz. 1990. Surveys employment opportunities in the travel and tourism industry. Provides job description, educational preparation, training, salary, employment outlook, and sources of additional information. Offers job hunting advice.

★1150★ *Airline Reservations Sales Agent*
Vocational Biographies, Inc.
PO Box 31
Sauk Centre, MN 56378-0031
Ph: (612)352-6516 Fax: (612)352-5546
Fr: 800-255-0752

1990. This pamphlet profiles a person working in the job. Includes information about job duties, working conditions, places of employment, educational preparation, labor market outlook, and salaries.

★1151★ "Airline Sales and Reservations" in *Travel Agent: Dealer in Dreams* (pp. 113-128)
Prentice Hall Press
1 Gulf & Western Plaza
New York, NY 10023
Ph: (212)373-8500

Aryear Gregory. Fourth edition, 1993. Comprehensive guide for those interested in the travel industry. Covers the work of the travel agent, agency problems, techniques, and promotion. Describes various jobs within the travel industry including travel consultant, agency manager, and tour operators. Explains the knowledge, skills, training, and educational preparation needed to succeed.

★1152★ *Airline Ticket Agent*
Careers, Inc.
PO Box 135
Largo, FL 34649-0135
Ph: (813)584-7333

1992. Two-page occupational summary card describing duties, working conditions, personal qualifications, training, earnings and hours, employment outlook, places of employment, related careers and where to write for more information.

★1153★ "Airline Ticket Agent" in *Career Information Center* (Vol.12)
Simon and Schuster
200 Old Tappan Rd.
Old Tappan, NJ 07675
Fax: 800-445-6991 Fr: 800-223-2348

Richard Lidz and Dale Anderson, editorial directors. Fifth edition, 1993. For 600 occupations, describes job duties, entry-level requirements, education and training needed, advancement possibilities, employment outlook, earnings and benefits. The set is divided into 12 volumes. Each volume includes jobs related under a broad career field. Volume 13 is the index.

★1154★ "Airline Ticket Agent" in *Occu-Facts: Information on 580 Careers in Outline Form*
Careers, Inc.
PO Box 135
Largo, FL 34649-0135
Ph: (813)584-7333

Biennial, 1995-96 edition. Each one-page occupational profile describes duties, working conditions, physical surroundings and demands, aptitudes, temperament, educational requirements, employment outlook, earnings, and places of employment.

★1155★ *Career Insights*
RMI Media Productions, Inc.
1365 N. Winchester
Olathe, KS 66061
Ph: (913)768-1696 Fax: 800-755-6910
Fr: 800-745-5480

Videocassette series. 1987. This videotape series describes 50 occupations, including skill requirements and interviews with people employed in these fields. Occupations include: flight service, air transportation/ground services, data processing, carpentry, clerk in banking/insurance/business, cosmetic personal grooming, firefighting, forestry, insulation/roofing, mechanics, material handling, photographic processing, pipefitting and plumbing, printing, secretarial services, tool and die operations.

★1156★ *Careers in Travel*
Solitaire Publishing
216 S. Bungalow Park Ave.
Tampa, FL 33609
Ph: (813)876-0286 Fr: 800-226-0286

Claudine Dervaes. 1988.

★1157★ *Flying High in Travel: A Complete Guide to Careers in the Travel Industry*
John Wiley and Sons, Inc.
605 3rd Ave.
New York, NY 10158-0012
Ph: (212)850-6000 Fax: (212)850-6088
Fr: 800-526-5368

Karen Rubin. 1992.

★1158★ *Getting Down to Business: Travel Agency*
American Institutes for Research in the Behavioral Sciences
PO Box 11131
Palo Alto, CA 94302
Ph: (415)493-3550 Fax: (415)858-0958
Rachel L. Rassen. 1981.

★1159★ *How to Get a Job with A Cruise Line: Adventure-Travel-Romance - How to Sail Around the World on Cruise Ships & Get Paid for It*
Ticket to Adventure, Inc.
PO Box 47622
St. Petersburg, FL 33743
Ph: (813)544-0066
Mary F. Miller. 1990.

★1160★ "Passenger Agent" in *Opportunities in Airline Careers* (pp. 68-69)
National Textbook Co. (NTC)
VGM Career Books
4255 W. Touhy Ave.
Lincolnwood, IL 60646-1975
Ph: (708)679-5500 Fax: (708)679-2494
Fr: 800-323-4900
Adrian A. Paradis. 1987. Surveys trends in the industry and career opportunities with the airlines including management, sales, customer service, flying, and maintenance. Describes pilots' job duties, working conditions, and basic educational and training requirements.

★1161★ "Reservation Agents" in *Travel Agent* (pp. 167-168)
Arco Publishing Co.
Macmillan General Reference
15 Columbus Cir.
New York, NY 10023
Fax: 800-835-3202 Fr: 800-858-7674
Wilma Boyd. 1989. Introduction to the travel business. Covers U.S. and foreign travel, time zones, ticketing, world geography, and airline, railroad, and tour bus connections, and accommodations. Outlines entry-level positions in the airline, car rental, and hospitality industries as well as in travel agencies and related travel services. Explains travel agency operations, sales techniques, and the use of computers in travel services. Gives job hunting advice and sales tips.

★1162★ "Reservation and Information Clerks" in *Opportunities in Travel Careers* (p. 53)
National Textbook Co. (NTC)
VGM Career Books
4255 W. Touhy Ave.
Lincolnwood, IL 60646-1975
Ph: (708)679-5500 Fax: (708)679-2494
Fr: 800-323-4900
Robert Scott Milne. 1991. Explores job opportunities in many travel related fields including the airlines, resorts, travel agencies, recreation, and tourism. Covers the work, salaries, educational preparation and training, and advancement possibilities.

★1163★ "Reservation and Transportation Ticket Agent" in *Career Discovery Encyclopedia* (Vol.5, pp. 148-149)
J.G. Ferguson Publishing Co.
200 W. Madison St., Ste. 300
Chicago, IL 60606
Ph: (312)580-5480 Fax: (312)580-4948
E. Russell Primm, editor-in-chief. 1993. Contains two-page articles on 504 occupations. Each article describes job duties, earnings, and educational and training requirements.

★1164★ "Reservation and Transportation Ticket Agents" in *Encyclopedia of Careers and Vocational Guidance* (Vol.4, pp. 282-284)
J.G. Ferguson Publishing Co.
200 W. Madison St., Ste. 300
Chicago, IL 60606
Ph: (312)580-5480 Fax: (312)580-4948
William E. Hopke, editor-in-chief. Ninth edition, 1993. Four-volume set that profiles 500 occupations and describes job trends in 74 industries. Includes career description, educational requirements, history of the job, methods of entry, advancement, employment outlook, earnings, working conditions, social and psychological factors, and sources of additional information.

★1165★ "Reservation and Transportation Ticket Agents and Travel Clerks " in *America's 50 Fastest Growing Jobs* (pp. 108)
JIST Works, Inc.
720 N. Park Ave.
Indianapolis, IN 46202-3431
Ph: (317)264-3720 Fax: (317)264-3709
Fr: 800-648-5478
Michael J. Farr, compiler. 1994. Describes the 50 fastest growing jobs within major career clusters such as technicians, and marketing and sales. Each job profile explains the nature of the work, skills and abilities required, employment outlook, average earnings, related occupations, education and training requirements, and employment opportunities. Also contains career planning information and job search tips.

★1166★ "Reservation and Transportation Ticket Agents and Travel Clerks" in *Occupational Outlook Handbook*
U.S. Government Printing Office
Superintendent of Documents
Washington, DC 20402
Ph: (202)512-1800 Fax: (202)512-2250
Biennial; latest edition, 1994-95. Encyclopedia of careers describing more than 250 occupations and comprising about 85 percent of all jobs in the economy. Occupations that require lengthy education or training are given the most attention. For each occupation, the handbook describes job duties, working conditions, training, educational preparation, personal qualities, advancement possibilities, job outlook, earnings, and sources of additional information.

★1167★ "Reservationists and Airline Ticket Agents" in *Jobs! What They Are—Where They Are—What They Pay* (pp. 205)
Simon & Schuster, Inc.
Simon & Schuster Bldg.
1230 Avenue of the Americas
New York, NY 10020
Ph: (212)698-7000
Robert O. Snelling and Anne M. Snelling. Revised edition, 1992. Profiles 241 occupations, describing duties and responsibilities, educational preparation, earnings, employment opportunities, training, and qualifications.

★1168★ "Reservations Agents" in *Opportunities in Airline Careers* (pp. 65-67)
National Textbook Co. (NTC)
VGM Career Books
4255 W. Touhy Ave.
Lincolnwood, IL 60646-1975
Ph: (708)679-5500 Fax: (708)679-2494
Fr: 800-323-4900
Adrian A. Paradis. 1987. Surveys trends in the industry and career opportunities with the airlines including management, sales, customer service, flying, and maintenance. Describes pilots' job duties, working conditions, and basic educational and training requirements.

★1169★ "The Reservations Department" in *Opportunities in Transportation Careers* (pp. 43-44)
National Textbook Co. (NTC)
VGM Career Books
4255 W. Touhy Ave.
Lincolnwood, IL 60646-1975
Ph: (708)679-5500 Fax: (708)679-2494
Fr: 800-323-4900
Adrian A. Paradis. 1988. Describes transportation and related employment in driving occupations, the airlines, merchant marine, and travel services. Covers employment outlook, educational and training requirements, wages, and the work itself, and advantages and disadvantages of transportation careers. Offers job hunting advice.

★1170★ "Reservations Sales Agent" in *Opportunities in Aerospace Careers* (pp. 21-25)
National Textbook Co. (NTC)
VGM Career Books
4255 W. Touhy Ave.
Lincolnwood, IL 60646-1975
Ph: (708)679-5500 Fax: (708)679-2494
Fr: 800-323-4900
Wallace R. Maples. 1991. Surveys jobs with the airlines, airports, the government, the military, in manufacturing, and in research and development. Describes educational requirements, working conditions, salaries, employment outlook and licensure.

★1171★ "Reservations Sales Agent" in *Travel Agent* (pp. 164-165)
Arco Publishing Co.
Macmillan General Reference
15 Columbus Cir.
New York, NY 10023
Fax: 800-835-3202 Fr: 800-858-7674
Wilma Boyd. 1989. Introduction to the travel business. Covers U.S. and foreign travel, time zones, ticketing, world geography, and

airline, railroad, and tour bus connections, and accommodations. Outlines entry-level positions in the airline, car rental, and hospitality industries as well as in travel agencies and related travel services. Explains travel agency operations, sales techniques, and the use of computers in travel services. Gives job hunting advice and sales tips.

★1172★ "Ticket Agent" in *Opportunities in Airline Careers* (pp. 67-68)
National Textbook Co. (NTC)
VGM Career Books
4255 W. Touhy Ave.
Lincolnwood, IL 60646-1975
Ph: (708)679-5500 Fax: (708)679-2494
Fr: 800-323-4900

Adrian A. Paradis. 1987. Surveys trends in the industry and career opportunities with the airlines including management, sales, customer service, flying, and maintenance. Describes pilots' job duties, working conditions, and basic educational and training requirements.

★1173★ *Ticket Agents*
Chronicle Guidance Publications, Inc.
66 Aurora St.
PO Box 1190
Moravia, NY 13118-1190
Ph: (315)497-0330 Fax: (315)497-3359
Fr: 800-622-7284

1991. This career brief describes the nature of the work, working conditions, hours and earnings, education and training, licensure, certification, unions, personal qualifications, social and psychological factors, employment outlook, entry methods, advancement, and related occupations.

★1174★ "Ticket Agents, Reservation Agents, and Clerks" in *Opportunities in Travel Careers* (p. 40-42)
National Textbook Co. (NTC)
VGM Career Books
4255 W. Touhy Ave.
Lincolnwood, IL 60646-1975
Ph: (708)679-5500 Fax: (708)679-2494
Fr: 800-323-4900

Robert Scott Milne. 1991. Explores job opportunities in many travel related fields including the airlines, resorts, travel agencies, recreation, and tourism. Covers the work, salaries, educational preparation and training, and advancement possibilities.

★1175★ *Travel Agent*
Careers, Inc.
PO Box 135
Largo, FL 34649-0135
Ph: (813)584-7333

1994. Two-page occupational summary card describing duties, working conditions, personal qualifications, training, earnings and hours, employment outlook, places of employment, related careers and where to write for more information.

★1176★ *Travel Agent*
Arco Publishing Co.
Macmillan General Reference
15 Columbus Cir.
New York, NY 10023
Fax: 800-835-3202 Fr: 800-858-7674

Wilma Boyd. 1989. Introduction to the travel business. Covers U.S. and foreign travel, time zones, ticketing, world geography, and airline, railroad, and tour bus connections, and accommodations. Outlines entry-level positions in the airline, car rental, and hospitality industries as well as in travel agencies and related travel services. Explains travel agency operations, sales techniques, and the use of computers in travel services. Gives job hunting advice and sales tips.

★1177★ *Travel Career Development*
Irwin Professional Publishing
1333 Burr Ridge Pkwy.
Burr Ridge, IL 60521
Ph: (708)789-4000 Fax: (708)789-6933

Fifth edition, 1992.

★1178★ *Travel Free: How to Start and Succeed in Your Own Travel Consultant Business*
Prima Publishing and Communications
4970 Topaz Ave., PO Box 1260
Rocklin, CA 95677
Ph: (916)624-5718

Ben Dominitz. 1984.

★1179★ "Travel and Hospitality Careers" in *The Best Jobs for the 1990s and Into the 21st Century*
Impact Publications
9104-N Manassas Dr.
Manassas Park, VA 22111
Ph: (703)361-7300 Fax: (703)335-9486

Ronald L. Krannich and Caryl Rae Krannich. 1993. Includes information on chefs, cooks, flight attendants, food and beverage service workers, hotel and motel desk clerks, reservation and transportation ticket agents and travel clerks, and travel agents.

★1180★ *Travel Industry Guidelines for Employment*
Travel Text Associates
12605 State Fair
Detroit, MI 48205
Ph: (313)527-6971

Chris Hoosen. 1990. Part of Travel Agent Training Series.

★1181★ *Travel Training Workbook, 1994-95*
Solitaire Publishing
216 S. Bungalow Park Ave.
Tampa, FL 33609
Ph: (813)876-0286 Fr: 800-226-0286

Claudine L. Dervaes. Fifth revised edition, 1994.

★1182★ *Video Career Library - Marketing and Sales*
Careers, Inc.
PO Box 135
Largo, FL 34649-0135
Ph: (813)584-7333

Videocassette. 1994. Part of the Video Career Library covering 165 occupations. Shows actual workers on the job.

ASSOCIATIONS

★1183★ Air Transport Association of America (ATA)
1301 Pennsylvania Ave., Ste. 1100
Washington, DC 20004-7017
Ph: (202)626-4000 Fax: (202)626-4166

Members: Airlines engaged in transporting persons, goods, and mail by aircraft between fixed terminals on regular schedules. **Publications:** *Air Transport*, annual.

★1184★ American Society of Travel Agents (ASTA)
1101 King St.
Alexandria, VA 22314
Ph: (703)739-2782 Fax: (703)684-8319

Members: Travel agents; allied members are representatives of carriers, hotels, resorts, sightseeing and car rental companies, official tourist organizations, and other travel interests. **Purpose:** Purposes are to: promote and encourage travel among people of all nations; to promote the image and encourage the use of professional travel agents worldwide; serve as an information resource for the travel industry worldwide; promote and represent the views and interests of travel agents to all levels of government and industry; promote professional and ethical conduct in the travel agency industry worldwide; facilitate consumer protection and safety for the traveling public. Maintains biographical archives and travel hall of fame. Conducts research and education programs. **Publications:** *ASTA Educational System Catalog*, annual. • *ASTA Officials Directory*, annual. • *ASTA Travel Agency Management Magazine*, monthly. • *Dateline ASTA*, bimonthly. • *Travel Industry Honors*, periodic.

★1185★ Institute of Certified Travel Agents (ICTA)
148 Linden St.
PO Box 812059
Wellesley, MA 02181-0012
Ph: (617)237-0280 Fax: (617)237-3860
Fr: 800-542-4282

Members: Individuals who have been accredited as Certified Travel Counselors (CTC) after meeting the institute's requirements (5 years' travel industry experience, 5 travel management courses, 4 examinations, an original research project, and a presentation). **Purpose:** Seeks to increase the level of competence in the travel industry. Provides continuing education, and examination and certification programs; conducts workshops and professional management seminars. Operates Travel Career Development Program to increase professional skills and Destination Specialist Programs to enhance the geographical knowledge of sales agents. Organizes study groups of instruction with enrolled student bodies in most major cities. **Publications:** *ICTA Update*, bimonthly. • *Sales Skills Development*. • *Travel Counselor Magazine*, bimonthly.

Standards/Certification Agencies

★1186★ American Society of Travel Agents (ASTA)
1101 King St.
Alexandria, VA 22314
Ph: (703)739-2782 Fax: (703)684-8319
Promotes and encourage travel among people of all nations; promote professional and ethical conduct in the travel agency industry worldwide; facilitate consumer protection and safety for the traveling public. Conducts research and education programs.

★1187★ Institute of Certified Travel Agents (ICTA)
148 Linden St.
PO Box 812059
Wellesley, MA 02181-0012
Ph: (617)237-0280 Fax: (617)237-3860
Fr: 800-542-4282
Provides continuing education, and examination and certification programs; conducts workshops and professional management seminars.

Test Guides

★1188★ *Career Examination Series: Reservation Agent*
National Learning Corp.
212 Michael Dr.
Syosset, NY 11791
Ph: (516)921-8888 Fax: (516)921-8743
Fr: 800-645-6337
Jack Rudman. Test guide including questions and answers for students or professionals in the field who seek advancement through examination.

★1189★ *Career Examination Series: Ticket Agent*
National Learning Corp.
212 Michael Dr.
Syosset, NY 11791
Ph: (516)921-8888 Fax: (516)921-8743
Fr: 800-645-6337
Jack Rudman. All examination guides in this series contain questions with answers.

Educational Directories and Programs

★1190★ *Corporate Travel's Black Book*
Miller Freeman, Inc.
1515 Broadway
New York, NY 10036
Ph: (212)869-1300 Fax: (212)768-3481
Rory Flanagan, Contact
Annual, October. Covers Approximately 2,000 airlines, hotels, car rentals, corporate charge cards, travel agencies, and other businesses offering travel packages to corporations. Entries include: Co. name, address, phone, fax, name and title of contact. Arrangement: Classified by industry.

★1191★ *Eurail Guide: How to Travel Europe and All the World by Train*
Houghton Mifflin Co.
222 Berkeley St.
Boston, MA 02116-3764
Ph: (617)523-1670 Fax: (617)523-1021
Barbara F. Saltzman, Contact
Annual, January. Covers rail trips for tourists in 112 countries. Entries include: Departure times, arrival times, on-board services (eating, sleeping, air conditioning facilities), and notable scenery enroute. Arrangement: Geographical.

★1192★ *Travel Industry Career Directory*
Career Press, Inc.
62 Beverly Rd.
Hawthorne, NJ 07507
Ph: (201)427-0229 Fax: (201)427-2037
1989.

Awards, Scholarships, Grants, and Fellowships

★1193★ American Express Travel Scholarships
ASTA Scholarship Foundation, Inc.
1101 King St.
Alexandria, VA 22314
Ph: (703)739-2782 Fax: (703)684-8319
Purpose: To encourage the pursuit of education in the travel and tourism field and to support the growth and development of tomorrow's travel and tourism work force. Qualifications: Applicants must be enrolled in a travel and tourism program at either a two- or four-year college, university, or proprietary travel school, have a 2.5 grade point average (4.0 scale), and be residents, citizens, or legal aliens of the United States or Canada. Funds available: $1,000. Application details: A 500-word essay detailing the student's plans in travel and tourism, as well as views of the travel industry's future is required. Students must submit proof of enrollment or acceptance to a school, an official school-printed description or listing of the travel curriculum, an official statement of the tuition amount, and a letter of recommendation. Application materials must be mailed in triplicate; faxed entries are not accepted. Deadline: June or July. Winners are notified in September.

★1194★ Northern California/Richard Epping Scholarships
American Society of Travel Agents (ASTA) Scholarship Foundation
1101 King St.
Alexandria, VA 22314
Ph: (703)739-2782 Fax: (703)684-8319
Purpose: To promote professionalism in the travel industry. Qualifications: Applicants must be currently enrolled in a travel or tourism curriculum at a college, university, or proprietary travel and tourism school. The establishment must be located within the geographic boundaries of the Northern California ASTA Chapter. Students must be permanent residents of these same boundaries and must agree to become involved in ASTA's Northern California Chapter, as well as make a presentation to the Chapter at the end of the academic term. In addition, applicants must have a 2.5 grade point average (4.0 scale) and be residents, citizens, or legal aliens of the United States or Canada. Funds available: One $750 award is given annually. Application details: A 500-word essay entitled, "Why I Desire a Profession in the Travel and Tourism Industry," is required. Students must also submit proof of enrollment or acceptance to a school, an official school-printed description or listing of the travel curriculum, an official statement of the tuition amount, and a letter of recommendation. Application materials must be mailed in triplicate; faxed entries are not accepted. Deadline: July 15. Winners are notified by August 31.

★1195★ Avis Rent a Car Scholarship; David Halissey Memorial Scholarship; Simmons Scholarship
American Society of Travel Agents (ASTA) Scholarship Foundation
1101 King St.
Alexandria, VA 22314
Ph: (703)739-2782 Fax: (703)684-8319
Purpose: To support further studies related to the travel industry. Qualifications: Candidate for any of the scholarships must be a citizen, resident, or legal alien of the United States or Canada pursuing further studies in the field of travel and tourism at a U.S. or Canadian institution. Applicant for the Avis Scholarship must be an upper-class undergraduate or graduate student who has worked part time in the travel industry. Candidate must submit a 500-word essay on the benefits of automation for travel agents and industry suppliers. Candidate for the Hallissey Scholarship must be a graduate student or travel educator at a recognized college, university or proprietary school. Applicant must submit a 500-word abstract on the proposed topic of research incorporating methodology and objectives. Applicant for a Simmons Scholarship must be pursuing a master's or doctoral degree with emphasis in travel and tourism. An upper-level paper or thesis (15 to 50 pages long) written on some topic of travel and tourism, which has been or will be submitted to a professor, must accompany the candidate's application. Funds available: $1,000-1,200. Application details: Write to the Foundation for application form and guidelines. Deadline: 14 June.

★1196★ Simmons Scholarship
ASTA Scholarship Foundation, Inc.
1101 King St.
Alexandria, VA 22314
Ph: (703)739-2782 Fax: (703)684-8319
Purpose: To promote professionalism in the travel industry by providing scholarships for continued education in the field of travel and tourism. Qualifications: Applicants must be graduate students who are pursuing a Masters or Doctorate degree with an emphasis in travel and tourism. They must have a minimum 2.5 grade point average (4.0 scale) and

be residents, citizens, or legal aliens of the United States or Canada. Funds available: Two awards of $1,500 each are given. Application details: An upper-level paper or thesis (15 to 20 pages) written on some travel and tourism topic that has been or will be submitted to a professor must be provided. Candidates must also submit proof of enrollment, an official school-printed description or listing of the travel curriculum, an official statement of the tuition amount, and a letter of recommendation. Application materials must be mailed in triplicate; faxed entries are not accepted. Deadline: June or July. Winners are notified in September.

★1197★ Southern California Chapter/ Pleasant Hawaiian Holidays Scholarship
American Society of Travel Agents (ASTA)
Scholarship Foundation
1101 King St.
Alexandria, VA 22314
Ph: (703)739-2782 Fax: (703)684-8319

Purpose: To promote professionalism in the travel industry by providing scholarships for continued education in the field of travel and tourism. Qualifications: Applicants must be undergraduate students enrolled or accepted to an accredited college, junior college, university, or proprietary travel school in preparation for a profession in the travel and tourism industry. They must also have a 3.0 grade point average (4.0 scale), and submit proof of U.S. citizenship. One parent of the applicant must be employed in the travel industry (i.e., hotel, car rental, airlines, travel agency, etc.) in the Southern California Chapter of ASTA's boundaries. Funds available: $1,000. Application details: A 1,000-word essay entitled, "My Goals in the Travel Industry," is required, as well as a statement as to why applicant should be chosen to receive the award. Students must submit proof of enrollment, an official school-printed description or listing of the travel curriculum, an official statement of the tuition amount, and a letter of recommendation. A statement from the parent's employer must also accompany the student's application. Application materials must be mailed in triplicate; faxed entries are not accepted. Deadline: July 15. Winners are notified by August 31.

Basic Reference Guides and Handbooks

★1198★ *Business of Travel: Agency Operations & Administration*
Macmillian Publishing Co.
866 3rd Ave.
New York, NY 10022
Ph: (212)702-2000

Dennis L. Foster. 1990.

★1199★ *Communication Skills*
Travel Text Associates
12605 State Fair
Detroit, MI 48205
Ph: (313)527-6971

Chris Hoosen. 1989. Part of Travel Agent Training Series.

Periodicals

★1200★ *Adventure West*
SKI WEST Publications, Inc.
1025 Ridgeview Dr., Ste. 400
Reno, NV 89509
Thomas M. HillPublisher

Quarterly. Magazine featuring exciting places to go and things to do in the American West.

★1201★ *Air Transport*
Air Transport Association of America (ATA)
1301 Pennsylvania Ave., Ste. 1100
Washington, DC 20004-7017
Ph: (202)626-4000 Fax: (202)626-4166

Annual.

★1202★ *ARTAFACTS*
Association of Retail Travel Agents (ARTA)
1745 Jefferson Davis Pkwy., Ste. 300
Arlington, VA 22202-3402
Ph: (703)553-7777 Fax: (703)413-2225
Fr: 800-969-6069

Monthly. Reviews developments in the travel industry for retail travel agents. Covers topics such as ethics, tour operations, transportation services, educational opportunities, commissions, and political action in pertinent issues. Includes chapter and Association news.

★1203★ *Developments*
American Resort Development Assn.
1220 L St. NW, No. 510
Washington, DC 20005
Ph: (202)371-6700 Fax: (202)289-8544
Sheila Morris

Monthly. Trade magazine for the American Resort Development Association.

★1204★ *Entree*
Entree Travel
1470 E. Valley Rd.
Santa Barbara, CA 93108
Ph: (805)969-5848 Fax: (805)966-7095
William Tomicki

Monthly. Features "an insider's look at hotels, restaurants, and travel around the world." Contains advice and tips on travel, bargains, and services. Recurring features include book reviews and notices of publications available.

★1205★ *Hotel & Travel Index—ABC International Edition*
Reed Travel Group
500 Plaza Drive
Secaucus, NJ 07094-3626
Ph: (201)902-2000
Melinda BushPublisher

Quarterly. International hotel directory.

★1206★ *ICTA Update*
Institute of Certified Travel Agents (ICTA)
148 Linden St.
PO Box 812059
Wellesley, MA 02181-0012
Ph: (617)237-0280 Fax: (617)237-3860
Fr: 800-542-4282

Bimonthly. Offers travel management tips and information on ICTA educational programs.

★1207★ *OAG Desktop Flight Guide-Worldwide Edition*
Official Airline Guides
2000 Clearwater Drive
Oak Brook, IL 60521
Ph: (708)574-6000 Fax: (708)474-6667
Richard A. NelsonPublisher

Monthly. Guide containing schedules of airlines operating throughout the world (excluding North America and Caribbean), published as a service for business travelers, travel agents, and airlines.

★1208★ *OAG Travel Planner, European Edition*
Official Airline Guides
2000 Clearwater Drive
Oak Brook, IL 60521
Ph: (708)574-6000 Fax: (708)474-6667
Martin ShapiroPublisher

Quarterly. Directory containing information on travel to and through Europe, including country basics, city destination data, hotel/ motel listings, airport diagrams, city and country maps, and reservation directories.

★1209★ *Ocean State Traveler*
Ocean State Traveler
172 Bellevue Ave., Ste. 319
Newport, RI 02840
Ph: (401)847-0089 Fax: (401)847-5267
Eleyne Austen

Monthly. Newspaper containing tourist information for the state of Rhode Island.

★1210★ *Recommend*
Worth International Communications Corp.
5979 NW, 151 St., Ste. 120
Miami Lakes, FL 33014
Ph: (305)828-0123 Fax: (305)826-6950
Hal Herman

Monthly. Travel industry magazine.

★1211★ *Schedule of Daily Subsistence Allowance Rates*
United Nations Publications
PO Box 361
Birmingham, AL 35201-0361
Fax: (205)995-1588 Fr: 800-633-4931

Monthly. Journal compiling travel costs throughout the world.

★1212★ *Tour & Travel News*
CMP Publications, Inc.
600 Community Drive
Manhasset, NY 11030
Ph: (516)562-5000 Fax: (516)562-5101
Linda Ball

Weekly. Magazine for the travel industry, covering issues of interest to travel agents.

★1213★ ***Travel Agent***
Universal Media, Inc.
801 2nd Ave., 7th Fl.
New York, NY 10017
Ph: (212)370-5050 Fax: (212)370-4491
Richard P. Friese

Weekly. Travel industry magazine.

★1214★ ***Travel News***
Travel Agents International, Inc.
111 2nd Ave. NE, 15th Fl.
Saint Petersburg, FL 33701
Ph: (813)895-8241 Fax: (813)894-6318
Matthew Wiseman

★1215★ ***Travel People Magazine***
CMP Publications, Inc.
600 Community Drive
Manhasset, NY 11030
Ph: (516)562-5000 Fax: (516)562-5101
Jerry Landress

Monthly. Lifestyle magazine targeted for travel agents.

★1216★ ***Travel Trade***
Travel Trade
15 W. 44th St.
New York, NY 10036
Ph: (212)730-6600 Fax: (212)730-7137
Joel M. Abels

Weekly. Travel industry magazine.

★1217★ ***Travel Weekly***
Reed Travel Group
500 Plaza Drive
Secaucus, NJ 07096
Ph: (201)902-2000 Fax: (201)319-1947
Alan Fredericks

SWM. Travel industry magazine.

Meetings and Conventions

★1218★ **American Society of Travel Agents World Travel Congress**
American Society of Travel Agents
1101 King St.
Alexandria, VA 22314
Ph: (703)739-2782 Fax: (703)684-8319
Fr: 800-828-2712

Annual. **Dates and Locations:** 1995 Nov 05-10; Philadelphia, PA.

★1219★ **Travel South USA Showcase**
Travel South USA Showcase
3400 Peachtree Rd., NE
Atlanta, GA 30326
Ph: (404)231-1790 Fax: (404)231-2364

Annual.

Other Sources of Information

★1220★ ***First Class: In Introduction to Travel and Tourism***
Glencoe Publishing Co.
866 3rd Ave.
New York, NY 10022
Ph: (212)702-3276

2nd edition, 1995.

★1221★ **"Reservations Agent (Airline)" in *Career Selector 2001***
Barron's Educational Series, Inc.
250 Wireless Blvd.
Hauppauge, NY 11788
Ph: (516)434-3311 Fax: (516)434-3723
Fr: 800-645-3476

James C. Gonyea. 1993.

★1222★ **"Ticket Agent" in *Career Selector 2001***
Barron's Educational Series, Inc.
250 Wireless Blvd.
Hauppauge, NY 11788
Ph: (516)434-3311 Fax: (516)434-3723
Fr: 800-645-3476

James C. Gonyea. 1993.

★1223★ ***Travel***
Crestwood House
866 3rd Ave.
New York, NY 10022
Ph: (212)702-9632

1994.

Mail Clerks and Messengers

Mail clerks serve as the link between the U.S. Postal Service and individual offices and workers. They sort and deliver incoming mail, prepare outgoing mail for delivery to the post office, and contact delivery services to handle important letters or parcels. Mail clerks also operate various machines that facilitate the mailing process. **Messengers** pick up and deliver letters, important business documents, or small packages which need to be sent or received in a hurry from one side of town to another.

Salaries

Salaries for mail clerks and messengers are listed below.

Mail clerks	$240-$390/week
Messengers	$250-$560/week

Employment Outlook

Growth rate until the year 2005: More slowly than average.

Mail Clerks and Messengers

Career Guides

★1224★ "Mail Clerk" in *Career Information Center* (Vol.1)
Simon and Schuster
200 Old Tappan Rd.
Old Tappan, NJ 07675
Fax: 800-445-6991 Fr: 800-223-2348

Richard Lidz and Dale Anderson, editorial directors. Fifth edition, 1993. For 600 occupations, describes job duties, entry-level requirements, education and training needed, advancement possibilities, employment outlook, earnings and benefits. The set is divided into 12 volumes. Each volume includes jobs related under a broad career field. Volume 13 is the index.

★1225★ *Mail Clerk, Office*
Careers, Inc.
PO Box 135
Largo, FL 34649-0135
Ph: (813)584-7333

1991. Two-page job guide card describing duties, working conditions, personal qualifications, training, earnings and hours, employment outlook, places of employment, related careers and where to write for more information.

★1226★ *Mail Clerks (Any Industry)*
Chronicle Guidance Publications, Inc.
66 Aurora St.
PO Box 1190
Moravia, NY 13118-1190
Ph: (315)497-0330 Fax: (315)497-3359
Fr: 800-622-7284

1993. This career brief describes the nature of the work, working conditions, hours and earnings, education and training, licensure, certification, unions, personal qualifications, social and psychological factors, employment outlook, entry methods, advancement, and related occupations.

★1227★ "Mail Clerks and Messengers" in *Occupational Outlook Handbook*
U.S. Government Printing Office
Superintendent of Documents
Washington, DC 20402
Ph: (202)512-1800 Fax: (202)512-2250

Biennial; latest edition, 1994-95. Encyclopedia of careers describing more than 250 occupations and comprising about 85 percent of all jobs in the economy. Occupations that require lengthy education or training are given the most attention. For each occupation, the handbook describes job duties, working conditions, training, educational preparation, personal qualities, advancement possibilities, job outlook, earnings, and sources of additional information.

★1228★ "Mailroom Clerk" in *BLR Encyclopedia of Prewritten Job Descriptions*
Business and Legal Reports, Inc.
39 Academy St.
Madison, CT 06443-1513
Ph: (203)245-7448

Stephen D. Bruce, editor-in-chief. 1994. This book contains hundreds of sample job descriptions arranged by functional job category. The 1-3 page job descriptions cover what the worker normally does in the position, who they report to, and how that position fits in the organizational structure.

★1229★ "Messenger Service Worker" in *Career Information Center* (Vol.1)
Simon and Schuster
200 Old Tappan Rd.
Old Tappan, NJ 07675
Fax: 800-445-6991 Fr: 800-223-2348

Richard Lidz and Dale Anderson, editorial directors. Fifth edition, 1993. For 600 occupations, describes job duties, entry-level requirements, education and training needed, advancement possibilities, employment outlook, earnings and benefits. The set is divided into 12 volumes. Each volume includes jobs related under a broad career field. Volume 13 is the index.

★1230★ "Office Mail Clerk" in *Occu-Facts: Information on 580 Careers in Outline Form*
Careers, Inc.
PO Box 135
Largo, FL 34649-0135
Ph: (813)584-7333

Biennial, 1995-96 edition. Each one-page occupational profile describes duties, working conditions, physical surroundings and demands, aptitudes, temperament, educational requirements, employment outlook, earnings, and places of employment.

Test Guides

★1231★ *Career Examination Series: Mail Clerk*
National Learning Corp.
212 Michael Dr.
Syosset, NY 11791
Ph: (516)921-8888 Fax: (516)921-8743
Fr: 800-645-6337

Jack Rudman. All examination guides in this series contain questions with answers.

★1232★ *Career Examination Series: Mail & Supply Clerk*
National Learning Corp.
212 Michael Dr.
Syosset, NY 11791
Ph: (516)921-8888 Fax: (516)921-8743
Fr: 800-645-6337

Jack Rudman. All examination guides in this series contain questions with answers.

★1233★ *Career Examination Series: Messenger*
National Learning Corp.
212 Michael Dr.
Syosset, NY 11791
Ph: (516)921-8888 Fax: (516)921-8743
Fr: 800-645-6337

Jack Rudman. All examination guides in this series contain questions with answers.

★1234★ *Career Examination Series: Principal Mail & Supply Clerk*
National Learning Corp.
212 Michael Dr.
Syosset, NY 11791
Ph: (516)921-8888 Fax: (516)921-8743
Fr: 800-645-6337

Jack Rudman. All examination guides in this series contain questions with answers.

★1235★ *Career Examination Series: Senior Mail Clerk*
National Learning Corp.
212 Michael Dr.
Syosset, NY 11791
Ph: (516)921-8888 Fax: (516)921-8743
Fr: 800-645-6337

Jack Rudman. All examination guides in this series contain questions with answers.

★1236★ *Senior Clerical Series*
Prentice Hall Press
Simon & Schuster Inc.
200 Old Tappan Rd.
Old Tappan, NJ 07675
Ph: 800-223-2348

Hy Hammer. Fourth edition, 1983. Complete test preparation for the following senior grade positions: clerk, typist, stenographer, account clerk, file clerk, statistics clerk, stenographer (law), mail and supply clerk, and stores clerk.

Educational Directories and Programs

★1237★ *Mailing Machines & Equipment Directory*
American Business Directories, Inc.
5711 S. 86th Circle
Omaha, NE 68127
Ph: (402)593-4600 Fax: (402)331-1505

Updated continuously; printed on request. Entries include: Name, address, phone, size of advertisement, name of owner or manager, number of employees, year first in "Yellow Pages." Compiled from telephone company "Yellow Pages," nationwide. Arrangement: Geographical.

Periodicals

★1238★ *The American Postal Worker*
American Postal Workers Union, AFL-CIO
1300 L St. NW
Washington, DC 20005
Ph: (202)842-4200 Fax: (202)842-4297
Moe Biller

Monthly. AFL-CIO postal labor.

Other Sources of Information

★1239★ "Bicycle Messenger" in *Encyclopedia of Danger: Dangerous Professions* (pp. 26-29)
Chelsea House Publishers
1974 Sproul Rd., Ste. 400
Broomall, PA 19008
Ph: (215)353-5166 Fax: (215)359-1439

Missy Allen and Michel Peissel. 1993. Provides descriptions of 24 dangerous occupations, their risky characteristics, and safety precautions.

Material Recording, Scheduling, Dispatching, and Distributing Occupations

Material recording, scheduling, dispatching, and distributing occupations involve coordinating, expediting, and keeping track of materials being sent or received. Some dispatchers also receive requests for service, as in the case of medical emergencies, and they coordinate the movement of the vehicles involved. Shipping and receiving clerks keep track of materials being transferred between businesses and their suppliers and customers. Stock clerks receive and issue merchandise or supplies and maintain an inventory of stock. These occupations are found primarily in wholesale and retail establishments, manufacturing, transportation, communications, utilities, and state and local government.

Salaries

Salaries for workers in material recording, scheduling, dispatching, and distributing occupations vary by occupation and industry setting, with dispatchers earning slightly more than average.

Lowest 10 percent	$226/week or less
Median	$384/week
Top 10 percent	More than $688/week
Dispatchers	$420/week
Traffic, shipping, receiving, and stock clerks	$350-$370/week

Employment Outlook

Growth rate until the year 2005: More slowly than the average.

Material Recording, Scheduling, Dispatching, and Distributing Occupations

Career Guides

★1240★ "Distribution Managers" in *Jobs! What They Are—Where They Are—What They Pay* (pp. 237)
Fireside
Simon & Schuster Bldg.
1230 Avenue of the Americas
New York, NY 10020
Ph: (212)698-7000 Fr: 800-223-2348

Robert O. Snelling and Anne M. Snelling. Revised and updated, 1992. Describes duties and responsibilities, earnings, employment opportunities, training, and qualifications.

★1241★ "Material Recording, Scheduling, Dispatching, and Distributing Occupations" in *Occupational Outlook Handbook*
U.S. Government Printing Office
Superintendent of Documents
Washington, DC 20402
Ph: (202)512-1800 Fax: (202)512-2250

Biennial; latest edition, 1994-95. Encyclopedia of careers describing more than 250 occupations and comprising about 85 percent of all jobs in the economy. Occupations that require lengthy education or training are given the most attention. For each occupation, the handbook describes job duties, working conditions, training, educational preparation, personal qualities, advancement possibilities, job outlook, earnings, and sources of additional information.

Test Guides

★1242★ *Career Examination Series: Assistant Stockman*
National Learning Corp.
212 Michael Dr.
Syosset, NY 11791
Ph: (516)921-8888 Fax: (516)921-8743
Fr: 800-645-6337

Jack Rudman. All examination guides in this series contain questions with answers.

★1243★ *Career Examination Series: Stockroom Worker*
National Learning Corp.
212 Michael Dr.
Syosset, NY 11791
Ph: (516)921-8888 Fax: (516)921-8743
Fr: 800-645-6337

Jack Rudman. All examination guides in this series contain questions with answers.

★1244★ *Career Examination Series: Warehouseman*
National Learning Corp.
212 Michael Dr.
Syosset, NY 11791
Ph: (516)921-8888 Fax: (516)921-8743
Fr: 800-645-6337

Jack Rudman. All examination guides in this series contain questions with answers.

Periodicals

★1245★ *Supply House Times*
Cahners Publishing Co.
1350 E. Touhy Ave.
PO Box 5080
Des Plaines, IL 60017-5080
Ph: (708)635-8800 Fax: (708)390-2618
Bill EverhamPublisher

Monthly. Trade magazine for wholesalers in plumbing, heating, cooling, piping, and water systems. Areas of major emphasis include: warehousing, materials handling, inventory control, accounting, data processing, merchandising, salesmanship and general management.

Dispatchers

Dispatchers respond to requests for service and coordinate the appropriate action depending on where they work. Public safety dispatchers, including police , fire, and ambulance dispatchers, are usually the first people called in an emergency. They quickly decide the type and number of units needed and send them to the scene. Truck dispatchers coordinate the movement of trucks and freight between cities. Other dispatchers working in transportation coordinate the movement of trains, buses, taxicabs, or tow trucks. All dispatchers keep records, logs, and schedules of the calls they receive and the actions they take.

Salaries

The median salary for dispatchers is $420/week but varies by industry setting.

Employment Outlook

Growth rate until the year 2005: Average.

Dispatchers

Career Guides

★1246★ ***Airline Dispatcher***
Careers, Inc.
PO Box 135
Largo, FL 34649-0135
Ph: (813)584-7333

1992. Four-page brief offering the definition, history, duties, working conditions, personal qualifications, educational requirements, earnings, hours, employment outlook, advancement possibilities, and related occupations.

★1247★ **"Airline Dispatcher" in *Career Information Center* (Vol.12)**
Simon and Schuster
200 Old Tappan Rd.
Old Tappan, NJ 07675
Fax: 800-445-6991 Fr: 800-223-2348

Richard Lidz and Dale Anderson, editorial directors. Fifth edition, 1993. For 600 occupations, describes job duties, entry-level requirements, education and training needed, advancement possibilities, employment outlook, earnings and benefits. The set is divided into 12 volumes. Each volume includes jobs related under a broad career field. Volume 13 is the index.

★1248★ **"Airline Dispatcher" in *Occu-Facts: Information on 580 Careers in Outline Form***
Careers, Inc.
PO Box 135
Largo, FL 34649-0135
Ph: (813)584-7333

Biennial, 1995-96 edition. Each one-page occupational profile describes duties, working conditions, physical surroundings and demands, aptitudes, temperament, educational requirements, employment outlook, earnings, and places of employment.

★1249★ ***Airline Dispatchers***
Chronicle Guidance Publications, Inc.
66 Aurora St.
PO Box 1190
Moravia, NY 13118-1190
Ph: (315)497-0330 Fax: (315)497-3359
Fr: 800-622-7284

1991. This career brief describes the nature of the work, working conditions, hours and earnings, education and training, licensure, certification, unions, personal qualifications, social and psychological factors, employment outlook, entry methods, advancement, and related occupations.

★1250★ **"Airplane Dispatchers" in *Encyclopedia of Careers and Vocational Guidance* (Vol.2, pp. 75-78)**
J.G. Ferguson Publishing Co.
200 W. Madison St., Ste. 300
Chicago, IL 60606
Ph: (312)580-5480 Fax: (312)580-4948

William E. Hopke, editor-in-chief. Ninth edition, 1993. Four-volume set that profiles 500 occupations and describes job trends in 74 industries. Includes career description, educational requirements, history of the job, methods of entry, advancement, employment outlook, earnings, working conditions, social and psychological factors, and sources of additional information.

★1251★ **"Dispatcher" in *150 Careers in the Health Care Field***
Reed Reference Publishing
121 Chanlon Rd.
PO Box 31
New Providence, NJ 07974
Fax: (908)665-6688 Fr: 800-521-8110

Stanley Alperin. Third edition, 1993. Each occupational profile covers job functions and responsibilities, work locations, training requirements, certification, and salaries. Lists community colleges, universities, vocational-technical schools, and other educational institutions that provide accredited training programs.

★1252★ **"Dispatcher" in *Careers in Trucking***
Rosen Publishing Group
29 E. 21st St.
New York, NY 10010
Ph: (212)777-3017 Fax: (212)777-0277
Fr: 800-237-9932

Donald D. Schauer. 1991. Describes employment in the trucking industry including driving, operations, sales, and administration. Covers qualifications, training, future outlook, and salaries. Offers career planning and job hunting advice.

★1253★ **"Dispatcher and Communications" in *Opportunities in Fire Protection Services* (pp. 28-29)**
National Textbook Co. (NTC)
VGM Career Books
4255 W. Touhy Ave.
Lincolnwood, IL 60646-1975
Ph: (708)679-5500 Fax: (708)679-2494
Fr: 800-323-4900

Ronny J. Coleman. 1990. Explores fire-fighting and related jobs with not only local fire departments but also with state and federal governments and private fire departments, fire sprinkler and fire equipment manufacturing companies, and insurance companies. Covers personal qualifications, educational preparation and training, advancement possibilities, and salaries. Offers job hunting advice.

★1254★ **"Dispatchers" in *Occupational Outlook Handbook***
U.S. Government Printing Office
Superintendent of Documents
Washington, DC 20402
Ph: (202)512-1800 Fax: (202)512-2250

Biennial; latest edition, 1994-95. Encyclopedia of careers describing more than 250 occupations and comprising about 85 percent of all jobs in the economy. Occupations that require lengthy education or training are given the most attention. For each occupation, the handbook describes job duties, working conditions, training, educational preparation, personal qualities, advancement possibilities, job outlook, earnings, and sources of additional information.

★1255★ "Flight Dispatcher" in *Opportunities in Airline Careers* (pp. 91-93)
National Textbook Co. (NTC)
VGM Career Books
4255 W. Touhy Ave.
Lincolnwood, IL 60646-1975
Ph: (708)679-5500 Fax: (708)679-2494
Fr: 800-323-4900

Adrian A. Paradis. 1987. Surveys trends in the industry and career opportunities with the airlines including management, sales, customer service, flying, and maintenance. Describes pilots' job duties, working conditions, and basic educational and training requirements.

★1256★ "Flight Dispatcher" in *Opportunities in Transportation Careers* (pp. 39-40)
National Textbook Co. (NTC)
VGM Career Books
4255 W. Touhy Ave.
Lincolnwood, IL 60646-1975
Ph: (708)679-5500 Fax: (708)679-2494
Fr: 800-323-4900

Adrian A. Paradis. 1988. Describes transportation and related employment in driving occupations, the airlines, merchant marine, and travel services. Covers employment outlook, educational and training requirements, wages, and the work itself, and advantages and disadvantages of transportation careers. Offers job hunting advice.

★1257★ "Radio Dispatcher" in *BLR Encyclopedia of Prewritten Job Descriptions*
Business and Legal Reports, Inc.
39 Academy St.
Madison, CT 06443-1513
Ph: (203)245-7448

Stephen D. Bruce, editor-in-chief. 1994. This book contains hundreds of sample job descriptions arranged by functional job category. The 1-3 page job descriptions cover what the worker normally does in the position, who they report to, and how that position fits in the organizational structure.

★1258★ *Radio Dispatchers*
Chronicle Guidance Publications, Inc.
66 Aurora St.
PO Box 1190
Moravia, NY 13118-1190
Ph: (315)497-0330 Fax: (315)497-3359
Fr: 800-622-7284

1993. This career brief describes the nature of the work, working conditions, hours and earnings, education and training, licensure, certification, unions, personal qualifications, social and psychological factors, employment outlook, entry methods, advancement, and related occupations.

★1259★ "Railroad Signaler, Telegrapher, Telephoner, and Dispatcher" in *Transportation* (pp. 57-61)
Franklin Watts, Inc.
387 Park Avenue, S.
New York, NY 10016
Ph: (212)686-7070

Marjorie Rittenberg Schulz. 1990. Surveys the transportation industry including air, water, and rail services. Provides job description, training, salary, and employment outlook. Offers job hunting advice.

★1260★ "Taxi Dispatcher" in *Travel & Tourism* (pp. 45-49)
Franklin Watts, Inc.
387 Park Avenue, S.
New York, NY 10016
Ph: (212)686-7070

Marjorie Rittenberg Schulz. 1990. Surveys employment opportunities in the travel and tourism industry. Provides job description, educational preparation, training, salary, employment outlook, and sources of additional information. Offers job hunting advice.

★1261★ "Truck and Bus Dispatcher" in *Career Information Center* (Vol.12)
Simon and Schuster
200 Old Tappan Rd.
Old Tappan, NJ 07675
Fax: 800-445-6991 Fr: 800-223-2348

Richard Lidz and Dale Anderson, editorial directors. Fifth edition, 1993. For 600 occupations, describes job duties, entry-level requirements, education and training needed, advancement possibilities, employment outlook, earnings and benefits. The set is divided into 12 volumes. Each volume includes jobs related under a broad career field. Volume 13 is the index.

Associations

★1262★ American Train Dispatchers Association (ATDA)
1370 Ontario St., Ste. 1040
Cleveland, OH 44113-1701

Members: AFL-CIO. **Publications:** *The Train Dispatcher*, quarterly.

★1263★ Association of Public-Safety Communications Officials - International (APCO)
2040 S. Ridgewood Ave.
Daytona Beach, FL 32119
Ph: (904)322-2500 Fax: (904)322-2501
Fr: 800-949-2726

Members: Employees of municipal, county, state, and federal public safety agencies such as 911 emergency phone line, fire, police, highway maintenance, forestry-conservation, civil defense, special emergency, and local government; individuals who sell public safety communication products. **Purpose:** Objectives are to: foster the development and progress of the art of public safety communications; ensure greater cooperation in the correlation of the work and activities of the several town, county, state, and federal agencies; promote cooperation between these agencies and the Federal Communications Commission. Conducts surveys, management and training seminars, and grant-in-aid projects with federal funding agencies. Offers 40-hour and 80-hour training courses for telecommunications, public safety, and emergency medical dispatchers; provides information service. According to APCO, this is the largest and oldest two-way land mobile radio group in the U.S. and holds the largest annual showing of public safety equipment in the world. Compiles statistics. **Publications:** *APCO Bulletin*, monthly. • *APCO Membership Directory*, annual. • *APCO Reports*, monthly.

★1264★ International Municipal Signal Association (IMSA)
165 E. Union St.
Newark, NY 14513
Ph: (315)331-2182 Fax: (315)331-8205
Fr: 800-723-4672

Members: Professional organization of government officials responsible for municipal signaling, fire alarms, traffic signals, radio communication, street lighting, electric inspection, emergency medical service, signs and marking, and other related services. **Publications:** *Fire Alarm Manual.* • *IMSA*, bimonthly. • *IMSA Journal*, semimonthly. • *Microprocessor Manual for Traffic Signals.* • *Traffic Signal Manual of Installation and Maintenance Procedures.* • *Wire and Cable Specifications.*

★1265★ Service Employees International Union (SEIU)
1313 L St. NW
Washington, DC 20005
Ph: (202)898-3200 Fax: (202)898-3304

Members: AFL-CIO; Canadian Labour Congress. **Publications:** *Union*, bimonthly. • *Update*, quarterly.

Standards/Certification Agencies

★1266★ International Municipal Signal Association (IMSA)
165 E. Union St.
Newark, NY 14513
Ph: (315)331-2182 Fax: (315)331-8205
Fr: 800-723-4672

Maintains more than 20 committees including standardizations.

Test Guides

★1267★ *Career Examination Series: Assistant Train Dispatcher*
National Learning Corp.
212 Michael Dr.
Syosset, NY 11791
Ph: (516)921-8888 Fax: (516)921-8743
Fr: 800-645-6337

Jack Rudman. All examination guides in this series contain questions with answers.

★1268★ *Career Examination Series: Dispatcher*
National Learning Corp.
212 Michael Dr.
Syosset, NY 11791
Ph: (516)921-8888 Fax: (516)921-8743
Fr: 800-645-6337

Jack Rudman. Test guide including questions and answers for students or professionals in the field who seek advancement through examination.

★1269★ *Career Examination Series: Fire Alarm Dispatcher*
National Learning Corp.
212 Michael Dr.
Syosset, NY 11791
Ph: (516)921-8888 Fax: (516)921-8743
Fr: 800-645-6337

Jack Rudman. All examination guides in this series contain questions with answers.

★1270★ *Career Examination Series: Police Dispatcher*
National Learning Corp.
212 Michael Dr.
Syosset, NY 11791
Ph: (516)921-8888 Fax: (516)921-8743
Fr: 800-645-6337

Jack Rudman. All examination guides in this series contain questions with answers.

★1271★ *Career Examination Series: Public Safety Dispatcher*
National Learning Corp.
212 Michael Dr.
Syosset, NY 11791
Ph: (516)921-8888 Fax: (516)921-8743
Fr: 800-645-6337

Jack Rudman. All examination guides in this series contain questions with answers.

★1272★ *Career Examination Series: Train Dispatcher*
National Learning Corp.
212 Michael Dr.
Syosset, NY 11791
Ph: (516)921-8888 Fax: (516)921-8743
Fr: 800-645-6337

Jack Rudman. All examination guides in this series contain questions with answers.

Basic Reference Guides and Handbooks

★1273★ *Fire Alarm Manual*
International Municipal Signal Association (IMSA)
165 E. Union St.
Newark, NY 14513
Ph: (315)331-2182 Fax: (315)331-8205
Fr: 800-723-4672

★1274★ *Microprocessor Manual for Traffic Signals*
International Municipal Signal Association (IMSA)
165 E. Union St.
Newark, NY 14513
Ph: (315)331-2182 Fax: (315)331-8205
Fr: 800-723-4672

★1275★ *Traffic Signal Manual of Installation and Maintenance Procedures*
International Municipal Signal Association (IMSA)
165 E. Union St.
Newark, NY 14513
Ph: (315)331-2182 Fax: (315)331-8205
Fr: 800-723-4672

Periodicals

★1276★ *APCO BULLETIN*
APCO, Inc.
2040 S. Ridgewood Ave.
Daytona Beach, FL 32119-8437
Ph: (904)322-2500 Fax: (904)322-2501
Alan Chase

Monthly. Public safety communications magazine.

★1277★ *APCO Membership Directory*
Association of Public-Safety Communications Officials - International (APCO)
2040 S. Ridgewood Ave.
Daytona Beach, FL 32119
Ph: (904)322-2500 Fax: (904)322-2501
Fr: 800-949-2726

Annual.

★1278★ *APCO Reports*
Association of Public-Safety Communications Officials - International (APCO)
2040 S. Ridgewood Ave.
Daytona Beach, FL 32119
Ph: (904)322-2500 Fax: (904)322-2501
Fr: 800-949-2726

Monthly.

★1279★ *IMSA*
International Municipal Signal Association (IMSA)
165 E. Union St.
Newark, NY 14513
Ph: (315)331-2182 Fax: (315)331-8205
Fr: 800-723-4672

Bimonthly.

★1280★ *IMSA Journal*
International Municipal Signal Association (IMSA)
165 E. Union St.
Newark, NY 14513
Ph: (315)331-2182 Fax: (315)331-8205
Fr: 800-723-4672

Semimonthly.

★1281★ *Union*
Service Employees International Union (SEIU)
1313 L St. NW
Washington, DC 20005
Ph: (202)898-3200 Fax: (202)898-3304

Bimonthly.

★1282★ *Update*
Service Employees International Union (SEIU)
1313 L St. NW
Washington, DC 20005
Ph: (202)898-3200 Fax: (202)898-3304

Quarterly.

★1283★ *Wire and Cable Specifications*
International Municipal Signal Association (IMSA)
165 E. Union St.
Newark, NY 14513
Ph: (315)331-2182 Fax: (315)331-8205
Fr: 800-723-4672

Meetings and Conventions

★1284★ APCO Annual Conference and Exposition
Association of Public-Safety Communications Officials - International (APCO)
2040 S. Ridgewood Ave.
Daytona Beach, FL 32119
Ph: (904)322-2500 Fax: (904)322-2501
Fr: 800-949-2726

Annual. **Dates and Locations:** 1995 Aug 13-17; Detroit, MI • 1996 Aug 11-15; San Antonio, TX • 1997 Aug 10-14; Charlotte, NC • 1998 Aug 09-13; Albuquerque, NM.

Other Sources of Information

★1285★ "Gas Dispatcher" in *Career Selector 2001*
Barron's Educational Series, Inc.
250 Wireless Blvd.
Hauppauge, NY 11788
Ph: (516)434-3311 Fax: (516)434-3723
Fr: 800-645-3476

James C. Gonyea. 1993.

Stock Clerks

Stock clerks receive, record, unpack, and store merchandise or materials. They also organize and label items and report damaged or spoiled goods. Stock clerks sometimes use hand-held scanners connected to computers to keep inventories up to date. In stores, they may be responsible for keeping shelves and racks stocked. In stockrooms and warehouses, they store materials in bins, on the floor, or on shelves. In large establishments they may be responsible for only one specific task. In smaller firms they may be responsible for tasks usually handled by shipping and receiving clerks.

Salaries

The average salary for stock clerks is $350-$370/week.

Employment Outlook

Growth rate until the year 2005: More slowly than the average.

Stock Clerks

Career Guides

★1286★ ***Stock Clerk***
Careers, Inc.
PO Box 135
Largo, FL 34649-0135
Ph: (813)584-7333

1994. Two-page job guide card describing duties, working conditions, personal qualifications, training, earnings and hours, employment outlook, places of employment, related careers and where to write for more information.

★1287★ **"Stock Clerk" in *Career Information Center* (Vol.10)**
Simon and Schuster
200 Old Tappan Rd.
Old Tappan, NJ 07675
Fax: 800-445-6991 Fr: 800-223-2348

Richard Lidz and Dale Anderson, editorial directors. Fifth edition, 1993. For 600 occupations, describes job duties, entry-level requirements, education and training needed, advancement possibilities, employment outlook, earnings and benefits. The set is divided into 12 volumes. Each volume includes jobs related under a broad career field. Volume 13 is the index.

★1288★ **"Stock Clerk" in *Careers Inside the World of Offices* (pp. 10-11)**
Rosen Publishing Group
29 E. 21st St.
New York, NY 10010
Ph: 800-237-9932 Fax: (212)777-0277

Carolyn Simpson. 1995. Describes job possibilities, attitudes and skills needed, and tips for getting the job. Also includes a self-evaluation test.

★1289★ **"Stock Clerk" in *Occu-Facts: Information on 580 Careers in Outline Form***
Careers, Inc.
PO Box 135
Largo, FL 34649-0135
Ph: (813)584-7333

Biennial, 1995-96 edition. Each one-page occupational profile describes duties, working conditions, physical surroundings and demands, aptitudes, temperament, educational requirements, employment outlook, earnings, and places of employment.

★1290★ ***Stock Clerks***
Chronicle Guidance Publications, Inc.
66 Aurora St.
PO Box 1190
Moravia, NY 13118-1190
Ph: (315)497-0330 Fax: (315)497-3359
Fr: 800-622-7284

1993. This career brief describes the nature of the work, working conditions, hours and earnings, education and training, licensure, certification, unions, personal qualifications, social and psychological factors, employment outlook, entry methods, advancement, and related occupations.

★1291★ **"Stock Clerks" in *Encyclopedia of Careers and Vocational Guidance* (Vol.4, pp. 443-445)**
J.G. Ferguson Publishing Co.
200 W. Madison St., Ste. 300
Chicago, IL 60606
Ph: (312)580-5480 Fax: (312)580-4948

William E. Hopke, editor-in-chief. Ninth edition, 1993. Four-volume set that profiles 500 occupations and describes job trends in 74 industries. Includes career description, educational requirements, history of the job, methods of entry, advancement, employment outlook, earnings, working conditions, social and psychological factors, and sources of additional information.

★1292★ **"Stock Clerks" in *Occupational Outlook Handbook***
U.S. Government Printing Office
Superintendent of Documents
Washington, DC 20402
Ph: (202)512-1800 Fax: (202)512-2250

Biennial; latest edition, 1994-95. Encyclopedia of careers describing more than 250 occupations and comprising about 85 percent of all jobs in the economy. Occupations that require lengthy education or training are given the most attention. For each occupation, the handbook describes job duties, working conditions, training, educational preparation, personal qualities, advancement possibilities, job outlook, earnings, and sources of additional information.

★1293★ **"Warehouse Worker" in *Career Information Center* (Vol.10)**
Simon and Schuster
200 Old Tappan Rd.
Old Tappan, NJ 07675
Fax: 800-445-6991 Fr: 800-223-2348

Richard Lidz and Dale Anderson, editorial directors. Fifth edition, 1993. For 600 occupations, describes job duties, entry-level requirements, education and training needed, advancement possibilities, employment outlook, earnings and benefits. The set is divided into 12 volumes. Each volume includes jobs related under a broad career field. Volume 13 is the index.

Associations

★1294★ **Distributive Education Clubs of America (DECA)**
1908 Association Dr.
Reston, VA 22091
Ph: (703)860-5000

Members: High school juniors and seniors; junior college students interested in the field of marketing and distribution (retailing and wholesaling) as a vocation. **Publications:** *DECA Advisor.* • *DECA Guide*, annual. • *New Dimensions*, quarterly.

Test Guides

★1295★ ***Career Examination Series: Shop Clerk***
National Learning Corp.
212 Michael Dr.
Syosset, NY 11791
Ph: (516)921-8888 Fax: (516)921-8743
Fr: 800-645-6337

Jack Rudman. All examination guides in this series contain questions with answers.

★1296★ ***Career Examination Series: Stock Clerk***
National Learning Corp.
212 Michael Dr.
Syosset, NY 11791
Ph: (516)921-8888 Fax: (516)921-8743
Fr: 800-645-6337
Jack Rudman. All examination guides in this series contain questions with answers.

★1297★ ***Senior Clerical Series***
Prentice Hall Press
Simon & Schuster Inc.
200 Old Tappan Rd.
Old Tappan, NJ 07675
Ph: 800-223-2348
Hy Hammer. Fourth edition, 1983. Complete test preparation for the following senior grade positions: clerk, typist, stenographer, account clerk, file clerk, statistics clerk, stenographer (law), mail and supply clerk, and stores clerk.

Meetings and Conventions

★1298★ **Distributive Education Clubs of America Career Development Conference (DECA)**
1908 Association Dr.
Reston, VA 22091
Ph: (703)860-5000
Annual.

Other Sources of Information

★1299★ **"Stock Clerk" in *Career Selector 2001***
Barron's Educational Series, Inc.
250 Wireless Blvd.
Hauppauge, NY 11788
Ph: (516)434-3311 Fax: (516)434-3723
Fr: 800-645-3476
James C. Gonyea. 1993.

Traffic, Shipping, and Receiving Clerks

Traffic, shipping, and receiving clerks keep records of all materials shipped and received. Traffic clerks record the destination, weight, and charges on all incoming and outgoing freight. Shipping clerks are responsible for all outgoing shipments. They make sure each order is filled correctly, label and address packages, and compute postal rates. Receiving clerks see that incoming orders have been filled correctly, record the shipment and its condition. Most traffic, shipping, and receiving clerks are employed by wholesale establishments, retail stores, and manufacturing firms.

Salaries

The average salary for traffic, shipping, and receiving clerks is $350-$370/week.

Employment Outlook

Growth rate until the year 2005: Average.

Traffic, Shipping, and Receiving Clerks

Career Guides

★1300★ **"Department Store Receiving, Delivering, & Related Workers" in *Occu-Facts: Information on 580 Careers in Outline Form***
Careers, Inc.
PO Box 135
Largo, FL 34649-0135
Ph: (813)584-7333

Biennial, 1995-96 edition. Each one-page occupational profile describes duties, working conditions, physical surroundings and demands, aptitudes, temperament, educational requirements, employment outlook, earnings, and places of employment.

★1301★ ***Department Store Receiving and Related Workers***
Careers, Inc.
PO Box 135
Largo, FL 34649-0135
Ph: (813)584-7333

1992. Four-page brief offering the definition, history, duties, working conditions, personal qualifications, educational requirements, earnings, hours, employment outlook, advancement possibilities, and related occupations.

★1302★ ***Shipping Clerk***
Careers, Inc.
PO Box 135
Largo, FL 34649-0135
Ph: (813)584-7333

1991. Two-page job guide card describing duties, working conditions, personal qualifications, training, earnings and hours, employment outlook, places of employment, related careers and where to write for more information.

★1303★ **"Shipping Clerk" in *Occu-Facts: Information on 580 Careers in Outline Form***
Careers, Inc.
PO Box 135
Largo, FL 34649-0135
Ph: (813)584-7333

Biennial, 1995-96 edition. Each one-page occupational profile describes duties, working conditions, physical surroundings and demands, aptitudes, temperament, educational requirements, employment outlook, earnings, and places of employment.

★1304★ **"Shipping and Receiving Clerk" in *Career Information Center* (Vol.10)**
Simon and Schuster
200 Old Tappan Rd.
Old Tappan, NJ 07675
Fax: 800-445-6991 Fr: 800-223-2348

Richard Lidz and Dale Anderson, editorial directors. Fifth edition, 1993. For 600 occupations, describes job duties, entry-level requirements, education and training needed, advancement possibilities, employment outlook, earnings and benefits. The set is divided into 12 volumes. Each volume includes jobs related under a broad career field. Volume 13 is the index.

★1305★ **"Shipping/Receiving Clerk" in *Jobs Rated Almanac***
World Almanac
1 International Blvd., Ste. 444
Mahwah, NJ 07495
Ph: (201)529-6900 Fax: (201)529-6901

Les Krantz. Second edition, 1992. Ranks 250 jobs by environment, salary, outlooks, physical demands, stress, security, travel opportunities, and extra perks. Includes jobs the editor feels are the most common, most interesting, and the most rapidly growing.

★1306★ ***Shipping and Receiving Clerks***
Chronicle Guidance Publications, Inc.
66 Aurora St.
PO Box 1190
Moravia, NY 13118-1190
Ph: (315)497-0330 Fax: (315)497-3359
Fr: 800-622-7284

1987. This career brief describes the nature of the work, working conditions, hours and earnings, education and training, licensure, certification, unions, personal qualifications, social and psychological factors, employment outlook, entry methods, advancement, and related occupations.

★1307★ **"Shipping and Receiving Clerks" in *Encyclopedia of Careers and Vocational Guidance* (Vol.4, pp. 353-356)**
J.G. Ferguson Publishing Co.
200 W. Madison St., Ste. 300
Chicago, IL 60606
Ph: (312)580-5480 Fax: (312)580-4948

William E. Hopke, editor-in-chief. Ninth edition, 1993. Four-volume set that profiles 500 occupations and describes job trends in 74 industries. Includes career description, educational requirements, history of the job, methods of entry, advancement, employment outlook, earnings, working conditions, social and psychological factors, and sources of additional information.

★1308★ **"Traffic Agents and Clerks" in *Encyclopedia of Careers and Vocational Guidance* (Vol.4, pp. 554-556)**
J.G. Ferguson Publishing Co.
200 W. Madison St., Ste. 300
Chicago, IL 60606
Ph: (312)580-5480 Fax: (312)580-4948

William E. Hopke, editor-in-chief. Ninth edition, 1993. Four-volume set that profiles 500 occupations and describes job trends in 74 industries. Includes career description, educational requirements, history of the job, methods of entry, advancement, employment outlook, earnings, working conditions, social and psychological factors, and sources of additional information.

★1309★ **"Traffic Clerk" in *BLR Encyclopedia of Prewritten Job Descriptions***
Business and Legal Reports, Inc.
39 Academy St.
Madison, CT 06443-1513
Ph: (203)245-7448

Stephen D. Bruce, editor-in-chief. 1994. This book contains hundreds of sample job descriptions arranged by functional job category. The 1-3 page job descriptions cover what the worker normally does in the position, who they report to, and how that position fits in the organizational structure.

★1310★ "Traffic, Shipping, and Receiving Clerks" in *Occupational Outlook Handbook*
U.S. Government Printing Office
Superintendent of Documents
Washington, DC 20402
Ph: (202)512-1800 Fax: (202)512-2250

Biennial; latest edition, 1994-95. Encyclopedia of careers describing more than 250 occupations and comprising about 85 percent of all jobs in the economy. Occupations that require lengthy education or training are given the most attention. For each occupation, the handbook describes job duties, working conditions, training, educational preparation, personal qualities, advancement possibilities, job outlook, earnings, and sources of additional information.

Associations

★1311★ International Brotherhood of Teamsters 1991 (IBT)
25 Louisiana Ave. NW
Washington, DC 20001
Ph: (202)624-6800

Publications: *The New Teamster*, 8/year.

Test Guides

★1312★ *Career Examination Series: Shipment Clerk*
National Learning Corp.
212 Michael Dr.
Syosset, NY 11791
Ph: (516)921-8888 Fax: (516)921-8743
Fr: 800-645-6337

Jack Rudman. Test guide including questions and answers for students or professionals in the field who seek advancement through examination.

Awards, Scholarships, Grants, and Fellowships

★1313★ Joseph C. Scheleen Award for Excellence
American Society of Transportation and Logistics
216 E. Church St.
Lock Haven, PA 17745-2010

To recognize distinguished achievement in the field of transportation and business logistics as a part of the Society's continuing program to promote high standards of knowledge, education, and ethics. An inscribed bronze plaque is awarded annually at the Society's conference. Established in 1974 in honor of Joseph C. Scheleen, editor of *Traffic World*.

Periodicals

★1314★ *American Shipper*
33 S.Hogan
PO Box 4728
Jacksonville, FL 32201
Ph: (904)355-2601 Fax: (904)791-8836
Fr: 800-874-6422
David A. Howard

Monthly. Transportation and shipping magazine.

★1315★ *Drop Shipping News*
Consolidated Marketing Services, Inc.
PO Box 1361
New York, NY 10017
Ph: (212)688-8797
Nicholas T. Scheel

Monthly. Supplies data on firms that drop ship their products as a means of distribution. Contains information on sources of consumer and industrial products, formulation of marketing policy, and on the pricing, ordering, packaging, and handling of drop shipments. Includes articles on uses of direct mail and direct-response advertising.

Postal Clerks and Mail Carriers

Postal clerks and **mail carriers** receive, sort, and deliver letters and packages. Postal clerks operate electronic letter-sorting machines and sort odd-sized letters, magazines or newspapers by hand. Clerks at local post offices sort mail for delivery to individual customers, sell stamps, money orders, weigh packages, and provide information. City and rural mail carriers travel established routes by vehicle or on foot delivering and collecting mail.

Salaries

Salaries for postal clerks and carriers are listed below.

Beginning postal carriers and clerks	$23,737/year
Postal carriers and clerks after 10 1/2 years of service	$33,952/year
Experienced city delivery mail carriers	$32,1832/year
Rural delivery mail carriers	$34,951/year

Employment Outlook

Growth rate until the year 2005: Decline.

Postal Clerks and Mail Carriers

Career Guides

★1316★ ***Book of $16,000-$60,000 Post Office Jobs: Where They Are, What They Pay, and How to Get Them***
Bookhaus Publishers
23323 Teppert
East Detroit, MI 48021
Ph: (313)778-7080

Veltisezar B. Bautista. 1989. Describes a variety of jobs with the U.S. Postal Service such as computer programmer, labor relations manager, and building maintenance supervisor. Many of the jobs listed are available only to current postal employees. Describes qualifications, duties, and salaries, and offers advice about filling out the application and taking the examination. Lists postal service testing centers.

★1317★ ***Carrying the Mail: A Career in Public Service***
National Association of Letter Carriers
100 Indiana Ave., N.W.
Washington, DC 20001
Ph: (202)393-4695

1989. This eight-panel brochure describes job duties, working conditions, earnings, qualifications, and how to apply.

★1318★ ***How to Get a Job with the Post Office***
Barnes and Noble Books
105 5th Ave.
New York, NY 10003
Ph: (212)633-3300

Stephen M. Good. Second edition, 1985.

★1319★ ***Mail Carrier***
Careers, Inc.
PO Box 135
Largo, FL 34649-0135
Ph: (813)584-7333

1992. Two-page occupational summary card describing duties, working conditions, personal qualifications, training, earnings and hours, employment outlook, places of employment, related careers and where to write for more information.

★1320★ **"Mail Carrier" in *Jobs Rated Almanac***
World Almanac
1 International Blvd., Ste. 444
Mahwah, NJ 07495
Ph: (201)529-6900 Fax: (201)529-6901

Les Krantz. Second edition, 1992. Ranks 250 jobs by environment, salary, outlooks, physical demands, stress, security, travel opportunities, and extra perks. Includes jobs the editor feels are the most common, most interesting, and the most rapidly growing.

★1321★ **"Mail Carrier" in *Occu-Facts: Information on 580 Careers in Outline Form***
Careers, Inc.
PO Box 135
Largo, FL 34649-0135
Ph: (813)584-7333

Biennial, 1995-96 edition. Each one-page occupational profile describes duties, working conditions, physical surroundings and demands, aptitudes, temperament, educational requirements, employment outlook, earnings, and places of employment.

★1322★ **"Mail Carriers" in *Career Discovery Encyclopedia* (Vol.4, pp. 40-41)**
J.G. Ferguson Publishing Co.
200 W. Madison St., Ste. 300
Chicago, IL 60606
Ph: (312)580-5480 Fax: (312)580-4948

E. Russell Primm, editor-in-chief. 1993. Contains two-page articles on 504 occupations. Each article describes job duties, earnings, and educational and training requirements.

★1323★ **"Mail Carriers" in *Encyclopedia of Careers and Vocational Guidance* (Vol.3, pp. 353-356)**
J.G. Ferguson Publishing Co.
200 W. Madison St., Ste. 300
Chicago, IL 60606
Ph: (312)580-5480 Fax: (312)580-4948

William E. Hopke, editor-in-chief. Ninth edition, 1993. Four-volume set that profiles 500 occupations and describes job trends in 74 industries. Includes career description, educational requirements, history of the job, methods of entry, advancement, employment outlook, earnings, working conditions, social and psychological factors, and sources of additional information.

★1324★ ***Mail Handler: U. S. Postal Service***
Simon & Schuster, Inc.
Simon & Schuster Bldg.
1230 Avenue of the Americas
New York, NY 10020
Ph: (212)698-7000

Hy Hammer, editor. 1985.

★1325★ **"Mail Service Worker" in *Career Information Center* (Vol.1)**
Simon and Schuster
200 Old Tappan Rd.
Old Tappan, NJ 07675
Fax: 800-445-6991 Fr: 800-223-2348

Richard Lidz and Dale Anderson, editorial directors. Fifth edition, 1993. For 600 occupations, describes job duties, entry-level requirements, education and training needed, advancement possibilities, employment outlook, earnings and benefits. The set is divided into 12 volumes. Each volume includes jobs related under a broad career field. Volume 13 is the index.

★1326★ ***Post Office Clerk***
Careers, Inc.
PO Box 135
Largo, FL 34649-0135
Ph: (813)584-7333

1994. Two-page occupational summary card describing duties, working conditions, personal qualifications, training, earnings and hours, employment outlook, places of employment, related careers and where to write for more information.

★1327★ ***Post Office Clerk-Carrier***
Macmillan Publishing Co., Inc.
866 3rd Ave.
New York, NY 10022
Ph: (212)702-2000 Fr: 800-257-5755

Eve P. Steinberg. 19th edition, 1995.

★1328★ **"Post Office Clerk" in *Occu-Facts: Information on 580 Careers in Outline Form***
Careers, Inc.
PO Box 135
Largo, FL 34649-0135
Ph: (813)584-7333

Biennial, 1995-96 edition. Each one-page occupational profile describes duties, working conditions, physical surroundings and demands, aptitudes, temperament, educational requirements, employment outlook, earnings, and places of employment.

★1329★ *Postal Clerk*
Vocational Biographies, Inc.
PO Box 31
Sauk Centre, MN 56378-0031
Ph: (612)352-6516 Fax: (612)352-5546
Fr: 800-255-0752

1992. Four-page pamphlet containing a personal narrative about a worker's job, work likes and dislikes, career path from high school to the present. Education and training, the rewards and frustrations, and the effects of the job on the rest of the worker's life. The data file portion of this pamphlet gives a concise occupational summary, including work descriptions, working conditions, places of employment, personal characteristics, education and training, job outlook, and salary range.

★1330★ "Postal Clerks" in *Encyclopedia of Careers and Vocational Guidance* (Vol.4, pp. 159-162)
J.G. Ferguson Publishing Co.
200 W. Madison St., Ste. 300
Chicago, IL 60606
Ph: (312)580-5480 Fax: (312)580-4948

William E. Hopke, editor-in-chief. Ninth edition, 1993. Four-volume set that profiles 500 occupations and describes job trends in 74 industries. Includes career description, educational requirements, history of the job, methods of entry, advancement, employment outlook, earnings, working conditions, social and psychological factors, and sources of additional information.

★1331★ "Postal Clerks and Mail Carriers" in *Occupational Outlook Handbook*
U.S. Government Printing Office
Superintendent of Documents
Washington, DC 20402
Ph: (202)512-1800 Fax: (202)512-2250

Biennial; latest edition, 1994-95. Encyclopedia of careers describing more than 250 occupations and comprising about 85 percent of all jobs in the economy. Occupations that require lengthy education or training are given the most attention. For each occupation, the handbook describes job duties, working conditions, training, educational preparation, personal qualities, advancement possibilities, job outlook, earnings, and sources of additional information.

★1332★ "Postal Employees" in *Career Discovery Encyclopedia* (Vol.5, pp. 72-73)
J.G. Ferguson Publishing Co.
200 W. Madison St., Ste. 300
Chicago, IL 60606
Ph: (312)580-5480 Fax: (312)580-4948

E. Russell Primm, editor-in-chief. 1993. Contains two-page articles on 504 occupations. Each article describes job duties, earnings, and educational and training requirements.

★1333★ "Postal Service Worker" in *Career Information Center* (Vol.11)
Simon and Schuster
200 Old Tappan Rd.
Old Tappan, NJ 07675
Fax: 800-445-6991 Fr: 800-223-2348

Richard Lidz and Dale Anderson, editorial directors. Fifth edition, 1993. For 600 occupations, describes job duties, entry-level requirements, education and training needed, advancement possibilities, employment outlook, earnings and benefits. The set is divided into 12 volumes. Each volume includes jobs related under a broad career field. Volume 13 is the index.

★1334★ *Postal Service Workers*
Chronicle Guidance Publications, Inc.
66 Aurora St.
PO Box 1190
Moravia, NY 13118-1190
Ph: (315)497-0330 Fax: (315)497-3359
Fr: 800-622-7284

1991. This career brief describes the nature of the work, working conditions, hours and earnings, education and training, licensure, certification, unions, personal qualifications, social and psychological factors, employment outlook, entry methods, advancement, and related occupations.

★1335★ *Rural Mail Carrier*
Vocational Biographies, Inc.
PO Box 31
Sauk Centre, MN 56378-0031
Ph: (612)352-6516 Fax: (612)352-5546
Fr: 800-255-0752

1990. This pamphlet profiles a person working in the job. Includes information about job duties, working conditions, places of employment, educational preparation, labor market outlook, and salaries.

★1336★ *Video Career Library - Clerical & Administrative Support*
Careers, Inc.
PO Box 135
Largo, FL 34649-0135
Ph: (813)584-7333

Videocassette. 1990. 26 mins. Part of the Video Career Library covering 165 occupations. Shows actual workers on the job. Includes secretaries, cashiers, receptionists, bookkeepers and audit clerks, telephone operators, postal clerks/carriers/supervisors, insurance investigators, bank tellers, data entry keyers, and court reporters.

Associations

★1337★ Advertising Mail Marketing Association (AMMA)
1333 F St. NW, Ste. 710
Washington, DC 20004-1108
Ph: (202)347-0055 Fax: (202)347-0789

Members: Represents supporters and users of **Purpose:** third class mail as an advertising, marketing, and fundraising medium. Seeks to protect interests of members with respect to third class postal rates and services before Congress, the U.S. Postal Service, and the Postal Rate Commission. Is conducting a public relations campaign to "enhance public appreciation of the value of advertising mail." **Publications:** *AMMA Bulletin.* • *Postal Issue Summary*, semiannual.

★1338★ National Star Route Mail Contractors Association (NSRMCA)
324 E. Capitol St.
Washington, DC 20003
Ph: (202)543-1661 Fax: (202)543-8863

Members: Highway mail contractors with the U.S. Postal Service transporting mail over the highway on authorized schedules. **Publications:** *Star Carrier*, monthly.

Test Guides

★1339★ *Barron's How to Prepare for the U.S. Postal Service Mail Handler - Mail Processor Examination*
Barron's Educational Series, Inc.
250 Wireless Blvd.
Hauppauge, NY 11788
Ph: (516)434-3311 Fax: (516)434-3723
Fr: 800-645-3476

Philip Barkus. Second edition. 1993.

★1340★ *Career Examination Series: Administrative Clerk (USPS)*
National Learning Corp.
212 Michael Dr.
Syosset, NY 11791
Ph: (516)921-8888 Fax: (516)921-8743
Fr: 800-645-6337

Jack Rudman. All examination guides in this series contain questions with answers.

★1341★ *Career Examination Series: Clerk-Carrier (U. S. P. S.)*
National Learning Corp.
212 Michael Dr.
Syosset, NY 11791
Ph: (516)921-8888 Fax: (516)921-8743
Fr: 800-645-6337

Jack Rudman. 1989. All examination guides in this series contain questions with answers.

★1342★ *Career Examination Series: Clerk-Technician (U. S. P. S.)*
National Learning Corp.
212 Michael Dr.
Syosset, NY 11791
Ph: (516)921-8888 Fax: (516)921-8743
Fr: 800-645-6337

Jack Rudman. 1989. All examination guides in this series contain questions with answers.

★1343★ *Career Examination Series: Mail Clerk*
National Learning Corp.
212 Michael Dr.
Syosset, NY 11791
Ph: (516)921-8888 Fax: (516)921-8743
Fr: 800-645-6337

Jack Rudman. All examination guides in this series contain questions with answers.

★1344★ *Career Examination Series: Mail Handler (USPS)*
National Learning Corp.
212 Michael Dr.
Syosset, NY 11791
Ph: (516)921-8888 Fax: (516)921-8743
Fr: 800-645-6337

Jack Rudman. All examination guides in this series contain questions with answers.

★1345★ *Career Examination Series: Maintenance Mechanic (Automated Mail Processing Equipment) (A.M.P.E.) (U.S.P.S.)*
National Learning Corp.
212 Michael Dr.
Syosset, NY 11791
Ph: (516)921-8888 Fax: (516)921-8743
Fr: 800-645-6337

Jack Rudman. 1989. All examination guides in this series contain questions with answers.

★1346★ *Career Examination Series: Mark-Up Clerk (USPS)*
National Learning Corp.
212 Michael Dr.
Syosset, NY 11791
Ph: (516)921-8888 Fax: (516)921-8743
Fr: 800-645-6337

Jack Rudman. All examination guides in this series contain questions with answers.

★1347★ *Career Examination Series: Motor Vehicle Operator (U.S.P.S.)*
National Learning Corp.
212 Michael Dr.
Syosset, NY 11791
Ph: (516)921-8888 Fax: (516)921-8743
Fr: 800-645-6337

Jack Rudman. 1989. All examination guides in this series contain questions with answers.

★1348★ *Career Examination Series: Postal Inspector (USPS)*
National Learning Corp.
212 Michael Dr.
Syosset, NY 11791
Ph: (516)921-8888 Fax: (516)921-8743
Fr: 800-645-6337

Jack Rudman. All examination guides in this series contain questions with answers.

★1349★ *Career Examination Series: Postal Machines Mechanic (USPS)*
National Learning Corp.
212 Michael Dr.
Syosset, NY 11791
Ph: (516)921-8888 Fax: (516)921-8743
Fr: 800-645-6337

Jack Rudman. All examination guides in this series contain questions with answers.

★1350★ *Career Examination Series: Postal Supervisor (USPS)*
National Learning Corp.
212 Michael Dr.
Syosset, NY 11791
Ph: (516)921-8888 Fax: (516)921-8743
Fr: 800-645-6337

Jack Rudman. All examination guides in this series contain questions with answers.

★1351★ *Career Examination Series: Postal System Examiner (USPS)*
National Learning Corp.
212 Michael Dr.
Syosset, NY 11791
Ph: (516)921-8888 Fax: (516)921-8743
Fr: 800-645-6337

Jack Rudman. All examination guides in this series contain questions with answers.

★1352★ *Career Examination Series: Postal Transportation Clerk (USPS)*
National Learning Corp.
212 Michael Dr.
Syosset, NY 11791
Ph: (516)921-8888 Fax: (516)921-8743
Fr: 800-645-6337

Jack Rudman. All examination guides in this series contain questions with answers.

★1353★ *Career Examination Series: Postmaster (USPS)*
National Learning Corp.
212 Michael Dr.
Syosset, NY 11791
Ph: (516)921-8888 Fax: (516)921-8743
Fr: 800-645-6337

Jack Rudman. Examination guides are available for Postmaster 1st, 2nd, 3rd, and 4th Classes. All examination guides in this series contain questions with answers.

★1354★ *Career Examination Series: Rural Carrier (USPS)*
National Learning Corp.
212 Michael Dr.
Syosset, NY 11791
Ph: (516)921-8888 Fax: (516)921-8743
Fr: 800-645-6337

Jack Rudman. All examination guides in this series contain questions with answers.

★1355★ *Career Examination Series: Window Clerk (USPS)*
National Learning Corp.
212 Michael Dr.
Syosset, NY 11791
Ph: (516)921-8888 Fax: (516)921-8743
Fr: 800-645-6337

Jack Rudman. All examination guides in this series contain questions with answers.

★1356★ *Civil Service Arithmetic and Vocabulary*
Prentice Hall Press
Simon & Schuster Inc.
200 Old Tappan Rd.
Old Tappan, NJ 07675
Ph: 800-223-2348 Fax: (201)767-5852

Barbara Erdsneker, Margaret A. Haller, and Eve P. Steinberg. Tenth edition, 1991. Practical guide reviews the two subjects most frequently tested on civil service exams. Includes sample questions and answers and test-taking tips and strategies.

★1357★ *The Corey Guide to Postal Exams*
Prentice Hall
Rte. 9W
Englewood Cliffs, NJ 07632
Ph: (201)592-2000

Richard J. Corey. Third edition, 1988.

★1358★ *Distribution Clerk, Machine*
Prentice Hall Press
Simon & Schuster Inc.
200 Old Tappan Rd.
Old Tappan, NJ 07675
Ph: 800-223-2348

Eve P. Steinberg. Second edition, 1988. Provides preparation for promotion from Postal Service carrier to distribution clerk. Contains eight sample tests, tips, techniques, and study practice section.

★1359★ *Distribution Clerk, Machine: Letter Sorting Machine Operator-U.S. Postal Service*
Prentice Hall
Rte. 9W
Englewood Cliffs, NJ 07632
Ph: (201)592-2000

Eve P. Steinberg. Second edition, 1988. Part of ARCO Civil Service Test Tutor Series.

★1360★ *Guide to Federal Technical, Trades, and Labor Jobs*
Resource Directories
3361 Executive Pkwy., Ste. 302
Toledo, OH 43606
Ph: 800-274-8515

Provides information on written exams and application procedures for postal workers.

★1361★ *How to Prepare for a Civil Service Examination (Text)*
National Learning Corp.
212 Michael Dr.
Syosset, NY 11791
Ph: (516)921-8888 Fax: (516)921-8743
Fr: 800-645-6337

Jack Rudman. Part of the General Aptitude and Abilities Series. Books in this series provide functional, intensive test practice and drill in the basic skills and areas common to many examinations, as well as general aptitude or achievement necessary for entrance into many occupations or positions.

★1362★ *How to Prepare for the Postal Clerk-Carrier Examination*
Barron's Educational Series, Inc.
250 Wireless Blvd.
Hauppauge, NY 11788
Ph: (516)434-3311 Fax: (516)434-3723
Fr: 800-645-3476

Philip Barkus. Third edition. 1993. This test guide provides study techniques, test-taking strategies, sample questions with answers, and five timed practice tests.

★1363★ *How to Prepare for the U.S. Postal Distribution Machine Clerk Examination*
Barron's Educational Series, Inc.
250 Wireless Blvd.
Hauppauge, NY 11788
Ph: (516)434-3311 Fax: (516)434-3723
Fr: 800-645-3476

Philip Barkus. Second edition. 1992. Manual provides diagnostic test, followed by address-checking and memory drills. Four additional practice tests are also included, with answers provided.

★1364★ *How to Prepare for the U.S. Postal Service Mailhandler/Mail Processor Examination*
Barron's Educational Series, Inc.
250 Wireless Blvd.
Hauppauge, NY 11788
Ph: (516)434-3311 Fax: (516)434-3723
Fr: 800-645-3476

Philip Barkus. Second edition. 1993. Manual contains diagnostic test and five model tests, as well as timed practice drills.

★1365★ *Mail Handler*
Prentice Hall
Rte. 9W
Englewood Cliffs, NJ 07632
Ph: (201)592-2000

Eve P. Steinberg. Ninth edition, 1988. Part of ARCO Civil Service Test Tutor Series.

★1366★ *Mail Handler/Mail Processor*
Arco Pub.
201 W. 103rd St.
Indianapolis, IN 46290
Ph: 800-428-5331 Fax: 800-835-3202

E.P. Steinberg. 1993, 11th edition. Includes six sample exams of the U.S. Postal Service exam.

★1367★ *Mark-up Clerk/Clerk Typist/ Clerk Stenographer - U.S. Postal Service*
Prentice Hall Press
Simon & Schuster Inc.
200 Old Tappan Rd.
Old Tappan, NJ 07675
Ph: 800-223-2348

Eve P. Steinberg. First edition, 1990. Provides practice exams with explanatory answers.

★1368★ *Math and Verbal Review for the Civil Service Exam*
Video Aided Instruction, Inc.
182 Village Rd.
Roslyn Heights, NY 11577
Ph: (516)621-6176 Fax: (516)484-8785
Fr: 800-238-1512

Videocassette. 1986. 120 mins. A college instructor explains and reviews the basic math skills needed for a civil service exam.

★1369★ *Post Office Clerk-Carrier*
Prentice Hall Press
Simon & Schuster Inc.
200 Old Tappan Rd.
Old Tappan, NJ 07675
Ph: 800-223-2348

E.P. Steinberg. 16th edition, 1989. Contains 11 complete model exams with answers.

★1370★ *Post Office Clerk-Carrier*
Arco Pub.
201 W. 103rd St.
Indianapolis, IN 46290
Ph: 800-428-5331 Fax: 800-835-3202

E.P. Steinberg. 1994. Offers 11 complete exams with answers.

★1371★ *Postal Arithmetic*
National Learning Corp.
212 Michael Dr.
Syosset, NY 11791
Ph: (516)921-8888 Fax: (516)921-8743
Fr: 800-645-6337

Jack Rudman. Part of the General Aptitude and Abilities Series. Books in this series provide functional, intensive test practice and drill in the basic skills and areas common to many examinations, as well as general aptitude or achievement necessary for entrance into many occupations or positions.

★1372★ *Postal Clerk-Carrier & Mail Handler Exams*
Ken-Books
56 Midcrest Way
San Francisco, CA 94131
Ph: (415)826-6550

Harry W. Koch. Fourth edition, 1981.

★1373★ *Postal Exam Handbook*
Prentice Hall Press
Simon & Schuster Inc.
200 Old Tappan Rd.
Old Tappan, NJ 07675
Ph: 800-223-2348

E.P. Steinberg. First edition, 1990. Serves as a guide to the tests for the most popular entry-level postal positions, including clerk carrier, mail handler, mark-up clerk, garageman driver, postal police, and more. Contains sample exams and complete information on application procedures.

★1374★ *Precis of Postal Service Manual*
National Learning Corp.
212 Michael Dr.
Syosset, NY 11791
Ph: (516)921-8888 Fax: (516)921-8743
Fr: 800-645-6337

Jack Rudman. Part of the General Aptitude and Abilities Series. Books in this series provide functional, intensive test practice and drill in the basic skills and areas common to many examinations, as well as general aptitude or achievement necessary for entrance into many occupations or positions.

★1375★ *Rural Carrier*
Prentice Hall Press
Simon & Schuster Inc.
200 Old Tappan Rd.
Old Tappan, NJ 07675
Ph: 800-223-2348

E.P. Steinberg. First edition, 1989. Prepares applicants for nationwide postal exam; includes three full-length sample exams with answers.

★1376★ *Test Practice Book for 100 Civil Service Jobs*
National Learning Corp.
212 Michael Dr.
Syosset, NY 11791
Ph: (516)921-8888 Fax: (516)921-8743
Fr: 800-645-6337

Jack Rudman. Part of the General Aptitude and Abilities Series. Books in this series provide functional, intensive test practice and drill in the basic skills and areas common to many examinations, as well as general aptitude or achievement necessary for entrance into many occupations or positions.

Educational Directories and Programs

★1377★ *Mailing Machines & Equipment Directory*
American Business Directories, Inc.
5711 S. 86th Circle
Omaha, NE 68127
Ph: (402)593-4600 Fax: (402)331-1505

Updated continuously; printed on request. Entries include: Name, address, phone, size of advertisement, name of owner or manager, number of employees, year first in "Yellow Pages." Compiled from telephone company "Yellow Pages," nationwide. Arrangement: Geographical.

Periodicals

★1378★ *The American Postal Worker*
American Postal Workers Union, AFL-CIO
1300 L St. NW
Washington, DC 20005
Ph: (202)842-4200 Fax: (202)842-4297
Moe Biller

Monthly. AFL-CIO postal labor.

★1379★ *AMMA Bulletin*
Advertising Mail Marketing Association (AMMA)
1333 F St. NW, Ste. 710
Washington, DC 20004-1108
Ph: (202)347-0055 Fax: (202)347-0789

★1380★ *National Alliance*
National Alliance of Postal and Federal Employees
1628 11th St. NW
Washington, DC 20001
Ph: (202)939-6325 Fax: (202)939-6389
Jacquelyn C. Moore

Monthly. Magazine for postal and federal employees.

★1381★ *The National Rural Letter Carrier*
National Rural Letter Carriers' Assn.
1630 Duke St., 4th Fl.
Alexandria, VA 22314-3465
Ph: (703)684-5545
William R. Brown

Weekly. Magazine covering postal service issues for members.

★1382★ *Postal Bulletin*
U.S. Government Printing Office
Superintendent of Documents
Washington, DC 20402-9322
Ph: (202)783-3238 Fax: (202)512-2250
U.S. Postal ServicePublisher

Biweekly. Bulletin reporting U.S. Postal Service news.

★1383★ *Postal Issue Summary*
Advertising Mail Marketing Association (AMMA)
1333 F St. NW, Ste. 710
Washington, DC 20004-1108
Ph: (202)347-0055 Fax: (202)347-0789

Semiannual.

★1384★ *Postal Record*
National Assn. of Letter Carriers
100 Indiana Ave. NW
Washington, DC 20001-2144
Ph: (202)393-4695 Fax: (202)737-1540
Vincent R. Sombrotto

Monthly. Magazine for active and retired letter carriers.

★1385★ *The Postal Supervisor*
490 L'Enfant Plaza SW, Ste. 3200
Washington, DC 20024-2120
Ph: (202)484-6070
Bob McLean

Quarterly. Postal magazine.

★1386★ *Postmasters Gazette*
National Assn. of Postmasters
8 Herbert St.
Alexandria, VA 22305-2600
Ph: (703)683-9027 Fax: (703)683-6820
Shirlene Fitzner

Monthly. Postal magazine.

Meetings and Conventions

★1387★ National Association of Postmasters of the United States Convention
National Association of Postmasters of the United States
8 Herbert St.
Alexandria, VA 22305-2600
Ph: (703)683-9027 Fax: (703)683-6820

Annual. **Dates and Locations:** 1996 Aug; Salt Lake City, UT. • 1997 Aug; Philadelphia, PA.

★1388★ National Postal Forum
National Postal Forum
PO Box 915
Mc Lean, VA 22101-0915
Ph: (703)442-8198 Fax: (703)442-0435

Semiannual. **Dates and Locations:** 1996 Apr 21-24; Anaheim, CA. • 1996 Aug 25-28; Washington, DC.

Other Sources of Information

★1389★ *Dames Employees: The Feminization of Postal Workers in Nineteenth-Century France*
Haworth Press, Inc.
10 Alice St.
Binghamton, NY 13904
Ph: (607)722-5857 Fax: (607)722-1424

Susan Bachrach. 1984. Part of Women & History Series.

★1390★ "Mail Carrier" in *Career Selector 2001*
Barron's Educational Series, Inc.
250 Wireless Blvd.
Hauppauge, NY 11788
Ph: (516)434-3311 Fax: (516)434-3723
Fr: 800-645-3476

James C. Gonyea. 1993.

★1391★ "Post Office Clerk" in *Career Selector 2001*
Barron's Educational Series, Inc.
250 Wireless Blvd.
Hauppauge, NY 11788
Ph: (516)434-3311 Fax: (516)434-3723
Fr: 800-645-3476

James C. Gonyea. 1993.

★1392★ *The Post Office Worker: A Trade Union & Social History*
Unwin Hyman, Inc.
Cambridge, MA 02139-3107
Fr: 800-933-6402

Alan Clinton. 1984.

★1393★ *Vocational Visions Career Series: Letter Carrier*
Cambridge Career Products
PO Box 2153, Dept. CC15
Charleston, WV 25328-2153
Fr: 800-468-4227

Video collection that includes interviews people with various occupations. Describes educational requirements, necessary skills, outlook for the future, and salary range.

Records Clerks

Records clerks maintain and update either financial or nonfinancial records for a variety of businesses, government agencies, unions, colleges and universities. Some examples of record clerks include brokerage clerks, file clerks, and library assistants. Most record clerks work in an office setting and have skills in typing and word processing. Interaction with the public is often a basic job element.

Salaries

Salaries for record clerks vary by occupation and employment setting.

Order clerks	$22,200/year
Personnel clerks	$20,300/year
Library assistants and bookmobile drivers	$16,400/year
File clerks	$15,700/year

Employment Outlook

Growth rate until the year 2005: More slowly than average.

Records Clerks

Career Guides

★1394★ "Police Records Clerk" in *BLR Encyclopedia of Prewritten Job Descriptions*
Business and Legal Reports, Inc.
39 Academy St.
Madison, CT 06443-1513
Ph: (203)245-7448

Stephen D. Bruce, editor-in-chief. 1994. This book contains hundreds of sample job descriptions arranged by functional job category. The 1-3 page job descriptions cover what the worker normally does in the position, who they report to, and how that position fits in the organizational structure.

★1395★ "Record Clerk" in *Careers Inside the World of Offices* (pp. 38)
Rosen Publishing Group
29 E. 21st St.
New York, NY 10010
Ph: 800-237-9932 Fax: (212)777-0277

Carolyn Simpson. 1995. Describes job possibilities, attitudes and skills needed, and tips for getting the job. Also includes a self-evaluation test.

★1396★ "Record Clerks" in *Occupational Outlook Handbook*
U.S. Government Printing Office
Superintendent of Documents
Washington, DC 20402
Ph: (202)512-1800 Fax: (202)512-2250

Biennial; latest edition, 1994-95. Encyclopedia of careers describing more than 250 occupations and comprising about 85 percent of all jobs in the economy. Occupations that require lengthy education or training are given the most attention. For each occupation, the handbook describes job duties, working conditions, training, educational preparation, personal qualities, advancement possibilities, job outlook, earnings, and sources of additional information.

Test Guides

★1397★ *Career Examination Series: Associate Public Records Officer*
National Learning Corp.
212 Michael Dr.
Syosset, NY 11791
Ph: (516)921-8888 Fax: (516)921-8743
Fr: 800-645-6337

Jack Rudman. All examination guides in this series contain questions with answers.

★1398★ *Career Examination Series: Principal Records Center Assistant*
National Learning Corp.
212 Michael Dr.
Syosset, NY 11791
Ph: (516)921-8888 Fax: (516)921-8743
Fr: 800-645-6337

Jack Rudman. All examination guides in this series contain questions with answers.

★1399★ *Career Examination Series: Recording Clerk*
National Learning Corp.
212 Michael Dr.
Syosset, NY 11791
Ph: (516)921-8888 Fax: (516)921-8743
Fr: 800-645-6337

Jack Rudman. All examination guides in this series contain questions with answers.

★1400★ *Career Examination Series: Records Clerk*
National Learning Corp.
212 Michael Dr.
Syosset, NY 11791
Ph: (516)921-8888 Fax: (516)921-8743
Fr: 800-645-6337

Jack Rudman. Test guide including questions and answers for students or professionals in the field who seek advancement through examination.

★1401★ *Career Examination Series: Senior Records Center Assistant*
National Learning Corp.
212 Michael Dr.
Syosset, NY 11791
Ph: (516)921-8888 Fax: (516)921-8743
Fr: 800-645-6337

Jack Rudman. All examination guides in this series contain questions with answers.

Periodicals

★1402★ *Bank Operations Report*
Warren, Gorham & Lamont, Inc.
31 St. James Ave.
Boston, MA 02116-4112
Ph: (617)423-2020 Fax: (617)695-9699
Fr: 800-922-1201
Nancy Hitchner

Monthly. Focuses on electronic data processing control, check processing, record keeping, cost control, federal regulation, credit and debit cards, electronic funds transfer system, physical security, and office automation, computer, and systems applications.

★1403★ *Records Management Quarterly*
Association of Record Managers and Administrators
4200 Somerset Dr, Ste. 215
Prairie Village, KS 66208
Ph: (913)341-3808 Fax: (913)341-3742
Ira Penn

Quarterly. Professional journal on records technology and information management.

Billing Clerks

Billing clerks compute fees and costs, record data and prepare statements in order to maintain a firm's financial stability. Clerks handling accounts receivable prepare invoices to collect bills from customers. Often they use computers to calculate the amount due from sales tickets, purchase orders, or charge slips. Accounts payable clerks verify billing information and handle payment. Billing clerks are employed in banks, insurance companies, health and business services organizations, wholesale and retail establishments, manufacturing, transportation, communications, and utilities.

Salaries

The average salary for billing clerks and related workers is $18,400/year.

Employment Outlook

Growth rate until the year 2005: Employment is expected to change little.

Billing Clerks

Career Guides

★1404★ "Billing Clerk" in *Careers in Trucking*
Rosen Publishing Group
29 E. 21st St.
New York, NY 10010
Ph: (212)777-3017 Fax: (212)777-0277
Fr: 800-237-9932

Donald D. Schauer. 1991. Describes employment in the trucking industry including driving, operations, sales, and administration. Covers qualifications, training, future outlook, and salaries. Offers career planning and job hunting advice.

★1405★ *Billing Clerks*
Chronicle Guidance Publications, Inc.
66 Aurora St.
PO Box 1190
Moravia, NY 13118-1190
Ph: (315)497-0330 Fax: (315)497-3359
Fr: 800-622-7284

1992. This career brief describes the nature of the work, working conditions, hours and earnings, education and training, licensure, certification, unions, personal qualifications, social and psychological factors, employment outlook, entry methods, advancement, and related occupations.

★1406★ "Billing Clerks" in *Encyclopedia of Careers and Vocational Guidance* (Vol.2, pp. 172-174)
J.G. Ferguson Publishing Co.
200 W. Madison St., Ste. 300
Chicago, IL 60606
Ph: (312)580-5480 Fax: (312)580-4948

William E. Hopke, editor-in-chief. Ninth edition, 1993. Four-volume set that profiles 500 occupations and describes job trends in 74 industries. Includes career description, educational requirements, history of the job, methods of entry, advancement, employment outlook, earnings, working conditions, social and psychological factors, and sources of additional information.

★1407★ "Billing Clerks" in *Occupational Outlook Handbook*
U.S. Government Printing Office
Superintendent of Documents
Washington, DC 20402
Ph: (202)512-1800 Fax: (202)512-2250

Biennial; latest edition, 1994-95. Encyclopedia of careers describing more than 250 occupations and comprising about 85 percent of all jobs in the economy. Occupations that require lengthy education or training are given the most attention. For each occupation, the handbook describes job duties, working conditions, training, educational preparation, personal qualities, advancement possibilities, job outlook, earnings, and sources of additional information.

★1408★ *Clerk: Bank, Insurance and Commerce*
Morris Video
2730 Monterey St., No. 105
Monterey Business Park
Torrance, CA 90503
Ph: (310)533-4800 Fr: 800-843-3606

Videocassette. 1981. 15 mins. The many and varied duties of the clerk are examined.

★1409★ "Clerks" in *Career Discovery Encyclopedia* (Vol.2, pp. 16-17)
J.G. Ferguson Publishing Co.
200 W. Madison St., Ste. 300
Chicago, IL 60606
Ph: (312)580-5480 Fax: (312)580-4948

E. Russell Primm, editor-in-chief. 1993. Contains two-page articles on 504 occupations. Each article describes job duties, earnings, and educational and training requirements.

★1410★ "Rate Clerk" in *Careers in Trucking*
Rosen Publishing Group
29 E. 21st St.
New York, NY 10010
Ph: (212)777-3017 Fax: (212)777-0277
Fr: 800-237-9932

Donald D. Schauer. 1991. Describes employment in the trucking industry including driving, operations, sales, and administration. Covers qualifications, training, future outlook, and salaries. Offers career planning and job hunting advice.

Other Sources of Information

★1411★ "Billing Clerk" in *Career Selector 2001*
Barron's Educational Series, Inc.
250 Wireless Blvd.
Hauppauge, NY 11788
Ph: (516)434-3311 Fax: (516)434-3723
Fr: 800-645-3476

James C. Gonyea. 1993.

Bookkeeping, Accounting, and Auditing Clerks

Bookkeeping, accounting, and auditing clerks compute, classify, and record financial data to develop and maintain financial records. They record debits and credits, compare balance sheets, and monitor accounts payable and receivable. They also verify receipts, prepare bank deposits, and update computer and manual files. Bookkeeping, accounting, and auditing clerks are found in most industries including many in wholesale and retail trade, and organizations providing business, health, educational, and social services.

Salaries

The average salary for bookkeeping, accounting, and auditing clerks is $19,100/year.

Employment Outlook

Growth rate until the year 2005: Employment is expected to remain level.

Bookkeeping, Accounting, and Auditing Clerks

Career Guides

★1412★ *Accounting Clerk*
Careers, Inc.
PO Box 135
Largo, FL 34649-0135
Ph: (813)584-7333

1993. Two-page occupational summary card describing duties, working conditions, personal qualifications, training, earnings and hours, employment outlook, places of employment, related careers and where to write for more information.

★1413★ "Accounting Clerk" in *BLR Encyclopedia of Prewritten Job Descriptions*
Business and Legal Reports, Inc.
39 Academy St.
Madison, CT 06443-1513
Ph: (203)245-7448

Stephen D. Bruce, editor-in-chief. 1994. This book contains hundreds of sample job descriptions arranged by functional job category. The 1-3 page job descriptions cover what the worker normally does in the position, who they report to, and how that position fits in the organizational structure.

★1414★ "Accounting Clerk" in *Careers Inside the World of Offices* (pp. 12, 42-45)
Rosen Publishing Group
29 E. 21st St.
New York, NY 10010
Ph: 800-237-9932 Fax: (212)777-0277

Carolyn Simpson. 1995. Describes job possibilities, attitudes and skills needed, and tips for getting the job. Also includes a self-evaluation test.

★1415★ "Accounting Clerk" in *Occu-Facts: Information on 580 Careers in Outline Form*
Careers, Inc.
PO Box 135
Largo, FL 34649-0135
Ph: (813)584-7333

Biennial, 1995-96 edition. Each one-page occupational profile describes duties, working conditions, physical surroundings and demands, aptitudes, temperament, educational requirements, employment outlook, earnings, and places of employment.

★1416★ "Accounting Clerks" in *American Almanac of Jobs and Salaries* (pp. 509)
Avon Books
1350 Avenue of the Americas
New York, NY 10019
Ph: (212)261-6800 Fr: 800-238-0658

John Wright, editor. Revised and updated, 1994-95. A comprehensive guide to the wages of hundreds of occupations in a wide variety of industries and organizations.

★1417★ "Accounting Clerks and Bookkeepers" in *Opportunities in Vocational and Technical Careers* (pp. 47-58)
National Textbook Co. (NTC)
VGM Career Books
4255 W. Touhy Ave.
Lincolnwood, IL 60646-1975
Ph: (708)679-5500 Fax: (708)679-2494
Fr: 800-323-4900

Adrian A. Paradis. 1992. Describes careers which can be prepared for by attending a private vocational or proprietary school—office employee, sales worker, service worker, health services, mechanic, craftworker, and technician. Covers employment outlook, job duties, and salaries. Offers career planning advice.

★1418★ *Bookkeeper*
Careers, Inc.
PO Box 135
Largo, FL 34649-0135
Ph: (813)584-7333

1992. Four-page brief offering the definition, history, duties, working conditions, personal qualifications, educational requirements, earnings, hours, employment outlook, advancement possibilities, and related occupations.

★1419★ *Bookkeeper*
Vocational Biographies, Inc.
PO Box 31
Sauk Centre, MN 56378-0031
Ph: (612)352-6516 Fax: (612)352-5546
Fr: 800-255-0752

1993. Four-page pamphlet containing a personal narrative about a worker's job, work likes and dislikes, career path from high school to the present. Education and training, the rewards and frustrations, and the effects of the job on the rest of the worker's life. The data file portion of this pamphlet gives a concise occupational summary, including work descriptions, working conditions, places of employment, personal characteristics, education and training, job outlook, and salary range.

★1420★ "The Bookkeeper-Accountant" in *Opportunities in Office Occupations* (pp. 131-140)
National Textbook Co. (NTC)
VGM Career Books
4255 W. Touhy Ave.
Lincolnwood, IL 60646-1975
Ph: (708)679-5500 Fax: (708)679-2494
Fr: 800-323-4900

Blanche Ettinger. 1989. Describes factors and trends which will affect office occupations including automation, telecommuting, and unionization. Separate chapters cover clerks, records management, information word processing, the secretary, and the bookkeeper-accountant. Describes job duties, skills needed, educational preparation, job hunting, types of equipment, employment outlook, and salaries.

★1421★ "Bookkeeper and Accounting Clerk" in *Careers in Banking and Finance* (pp. 26-27)
Rosen Publishing Group
29 E. 21st St.
New York, NY 10010
Ph: (212)777-3017 Fax: (212)777-0277
Fr: 800-237-9932

Patricia Haddock. 1990. Describes more than 20 jobs at all levels in banking and finance. Contains information about the types of financial organizations where the jobs are found, educational requirements, job duties, and salaries. Offers advice on job hunting.

★1422★ "Bookkeeper" in *Career Information Center* (Vol.1)
Simon and Schuster
200 Old Tappan Rd.
Old Tappan, NJ 07675
Fax: 800-445-6991 Fr: 800-223-2348

Richard Lidz and Dale Anderson, editorial directors. Fifth edition, 1993. For 600 occupations, describes job duties, entry-level requirements, education and training needed, advancement possibilities, employment outlook, earnings and benefits. The set is divided into 12 volumes. Each volume includes jobs related under a broad career field. Volume 13 is the index.

★1423★ "Bookkeeper" in *Career Opportunities in Television, Cable, and Video* (pp. 20-21)
Facts on File
460 Park Ave. S.
New York, NY 10016-7382
Ph: (212)683-2244 Fax: 800-678-3633
Fr: 800-322-8755

Third edition, 1990. Describes 100 media-related jobs. Each occupational profile covers job duties, employment outlook, career paths, salaries, skills, and educational preparation. Offers tips for entering the field.

★1424★ "Bookkeeper" in *Jobs Rated Almanac*
World Almanac
1 International Blvd., Ste. 444
Mahwah, NJ 07495
Ph: (201)529-6900 Fax: (201)529-6901

Les Krantz. Second edition, 1992. Ranks 250 jobs by environment, salary, outlooks, physical demands, stress, security, travel opportunities, and extra perks. Includes jobs the editor feels are the most common, most interesting, and the most rapidly growing.

★1425★ "Bookkeeper" in *Occu-Facts: Information on 580 Careers in Outline Form*
Careers, Inc.
PO Box 135
Largo, FL 34649-0135
Ph: (813)584-7333

Biennial, 1995-96 edition. Each one-page occupational profile describes duties, working conditions, physical surroundings and demands, aptitudes, temperament, educational requirements, employment outlook, earnings, and places of employment.

★1426★ "Bookkeeper, Secretary, and Clerk" in *Travel & Tourism* (pp. 69-73)
Franklin Watts, Inc.
387 Park Avenue, S.
New York, NY 10016
Ph: (212)686-7070

Marjorie Rittenberg Schulz. 1990. Surveys employment opportunities in the travel and tourism industry. Provides job description, educational preparation, training, salary, employment outlook, and sources of additional information. Offers job hunting advice.

★1427★ "Bookkeepers and Accounting Clerks" in *Jobs! What They Are—Where They Are—What They Pay* (pp. 158)
Simon & Schuster, Inc.
Simon & Schuster Bldg.
1230 Avenue of the Americas
New York, NY 10020
Ph: (212)698-7000

Robert O. Snelling and Anne M. Snelling. Revised edition, 1992. Profiles 241 occupations, describing duties and responsibilities, educational preparation, earnings, employment opportunities, training, and qualifications.

★1428★ "Bookkeepers" in *Career Discovery Encyclopedia* (Vol.1, pp. 122-123)
J.G. Ferguson Publishing Co.
200 W. Madison St., Ste. 300
Chicago, IL 60606
Ph: (312)580-5480 Fax: (312)580-4948

E. Russell Primm, editor-in-chief. 1993. Contains two-page articles on 504 occupations. Each article describes job duties, earnings, and educational and training requirements.

★1429★ "Bookkeeping, Accounting, and Auditing Clerks" in *Occupational Outlook Handbook*
U.S. Government Printing Office
Superintendent of Documents
Washington, DC 20402
Ph: (202)512-1800 Fax: (202)512-2250

Biennial; latest edition, 1994-95. Encyclopedia of careers describing more than 250 occupations and comprising about 85 percent of all jobs in the economy. Occupations that require lengthy education or training are given the most attention. For each occupation, the handbook describes job duties, working conditions, training, educational preparation, personal qualities, advancement possibilities, job outlook, earnings, and sources of additional information.

★1430★ *Bookkeeping and Accounting Clerks*
Chronicle Guidance Publications, Inc.
66 Aurora St.
PO Box 1190
Moravia, NY 13118-1190
Ph: (315)497-0330 Fax: (315)497-3359
Fr: 800-622-7284

1994. Career brief describing the nature of the job, working conditions, hours and earnings, education and training, licensure, certification, unions, personal qualifications, social and psychological factors, location, employment outlook, entry methods, advancement, and related occupations.

★1431★ "Bookkeeping and Accounting Clerks" in *Encyclopedia of Careers and Vocational Guidance* (Vol.2, pp. 209-212)
J.G. Ferguson Publishing Co.
200 W. Madison St., Ste. 300
Chicago, IL 60606
Ph: (312)580-5480 Fax: (312)580-4948

William E. Hopke, editor-in-chief. Ninth edition, 1993. Four-volume set that profiles 500 occupations and describes job trends in 74 industries. Includes career description, educational requirements, history of the job, methods of entry, advancement, employment outlook, earnings, working conditions, social and psychological factors, and sources of additional information.

★1432★ "Bookkeeping and Accounting" in *Desk Guide to Training and Work Advisement* (pp. 177-178)
Charles C. Thomas, Publisher
2600 S. 1st St.
Springfield, IL 62794-9265
Ph: (217)789-8980 Fax: (217)789-9130
Fr: 800-258-8980

Gail Baugher Kuenstler. 1988. Describes alternative methods of gaining entry into an occupation through different types of educational programs, internships and apprenticeships.

★1433★ "Bookkeeping and Accounting Service" in *100 Best Careers for the Year 2000* (pp. 278)
Arco Pub.
201 W. 103rd St.
Indianapolis, IN 46290
Ph: 800-428-5331 Fax: 800-835-3202

Shelly Field. 1992. Describes 100 job opportunities expected to grow fast throughout the next decade. Provides information on job duties and responsibilities, training requirements, education, advancement opportunities, experience and qualifications, and typical salaries.

★1434★ "Bookkeeping" in *Career Connection II: A Guide to Technical Majors and Their Related Careers* (pp. 28-29)
Jist Works, Inc.
720 N. Park Ave.
Indianapolis, IN 46202-3431
Ph: (317)264-3720 Fax: (317)264-3709

Fred A. Rowe. 1994. Contains technical majors, such as automotive technology. Describes the major and the job. Lists high school and postsecondary school courses. Includes occupations related to the major, employment outlook, and starting salary.

★1435★ "Bookkeeping Systems Operator" in *Occu-Facts: Information on 580 Careers in Outline Form*
Careers, Inc.
PO Box 135
Largo, FL 34649-0135
Ph: (813)584-7333

Biennial, 1995-96 edition. Each one-page occupational profile describes duties, working conditions, physical surroundings and demands, aptitudes, temperament, educational requirements, employment outlook, earnings, and places of employment.

★1436★ *Bookkeeping Systems Operators*
Careers, Inc.
PO Box 135
Largo, FL 34649-0135
Ph: (813)584-7333

1991. Two-page occupational summary card describing duties, working conditions, personal qualifications, training, earnings and hours, employment outlook, places of employment, related careers and where to write for more information.

★1437★ *Career Examination Series: Accounting & Auditing Careers*
National Learning Corporation
212 Michael Dr.
Syosset, NY 11791
Ph: (516)921-8888

1988. All examination guides in this series contain questions with answers.

★1438★ *How to Learn Basic Bookkeeping in Ten Easy Lessons*
Barnes and Noble Books
105 5th Ave.
New York, NY 10003
Ph: (212)633-3300

John Barnes. 1987.

★1439★ *Interviewing for a Career in Public Accounting*
Hampton Press
PO Box 805
Rochester, MI 48063
Ph: (810)852-0980

Richard L. Baird, editor. Second edition, 1989.

★1440★ *Opportunities in Accounting Careers*
National Textbook Co. (NTC)
VGM Career Books
4255 W. Touhy Ave.
Lincolnwood, IL 60646-1975
Ph: (708)679-5500 Fax: (708)679-2494
Fr: 800-323-4900

Martin Rosenberg. Covers the nature of the work, employment outlook, educational preparation and training, salary, and rewards of the work.

★1441★ *Starting & Building Your Own Accounting Business*
John Wiley and Sons, Inc.
605 3rd Ave.
New York, NY 10158-0012
Ph: (212)850-6000 Fax: (212)850-6088
Fr: 800-526-5368

Jack Fox. Second edition, 1991. Part of Ronald National Association of Accounting Series.

★1442★ *Teach Yourself Bookkeeping*
David McKay Co., Inc.
201 E. 50th St.
New York, NY 10022
Ph: (212)751-2600

D. Cousins. 1978. Part of Teach Yourself Series.

★1443★ *Video Career Library - Clerical & Administrative Support*
Careers, Inc.
PO Box 135
Largo, FL 34649-0135
Ph: (813)584-7333

Videocassette. 1990. 26 mins. Part of the Video Career Library covering 165 occupations. Shows actual workers on the job. Includes secretaries, cashiers, receptionists, bookkeepers and audit clerks, telephone operators, postal clerks/carriers/supervisors, insurance investigators, bank tellers, data entry keyers, and court reporters.

ASSOCIATIONS

★1444★ Institute of Internal Auditors (IIA)
249 Maitland Ave.
Altamonte Springs, FL 32701-4201
Ph: (407)830-7600 Fax: (407)831-5171

Members: International professional organization of internal auditors, comptrollers, accountants, educators, and computer specialists in functions of internal auditing in corporations, government agencies, and institutions. **Purpose:** Grants professional certification. Offers benchmarking subscription service and quality reviews. **Publications:** *IIA Educator*, semiannual. • *IIA Today*, bimonthly. • *Institute of Internal Auditors—Membership/Certified Internal Auditor Directory*, biennial. • *Internal Auditor*, bimonthly. • *Pistas de Auditoria*, bimonthly.

★1445★ National Society of Public Accountants (NSPA)
1010 N. Fairfax St.
Alexandria, VA 22314-1574
Ph: (703)549-6400 Fax: (703)549-2984
Fr: 800-966-6679

Members: Professional society of practicing accountants and tax practitioners. **Purpose:** Represents the independent practitioner. Conducts correspondence courses and seminars; operates speakers' bureau. Maintains 21 committees. **Publications:** *Income and Fees of Accountants in Public Practice*, triennial. • *National Public Accountant*, monthly. • *National Society of Public Accountants—Annual Report*. • *National Society of Public Accountants—Yearbook*. • *NSPA Washington Reporter*.

STANDARDS/CERTIFICATION AGENCIES

★1446★ Institute of Internal Auditors (IIA)
249 Maitland Ave.
Altamonte Springs, FL 32701-4201
Ph: (407)830-7600 Fax: (407)831-5171

Grants professional certification. Offers benchmarking subscription service and quality reviews.

★1447★ National Society of Public Accountants (NSPA)
1010 N. Fairfax St.
Alexandria, VA 22314-1574
Ph: (703)549-6400 Fax: (703)549-2984
Fr: 800-966-6679

Conducts correspondence courses and seminars; operates speakers' bureau.

TEST GUIDES

★1448★ *Accounts Payable Practice Set*
McGraw-Hill Publishing Co.
1221 Avenue of the Americas
New York, NY 10020
Ph: (212)512-2000

Fred C. Archer. 1969.

★1449★ *Accounts Receivable Practice Set*
McGraw-Hill Publishing Co.
1221 Avenue of the Americas
New York, NY 10020
Ph: (212)512-2000

Fred C. Archer. 1970.

★1450★ *Assistant Accountant*
Prentice Hall Press
Simon & Schuster Inc.
200 Old Tappan Rd.
Old Tappan, NJ 07675
Ph: 800-223-2348

Michael McDonough. Third edition, 1984. Includes four sample tests for self-instruction course. Topics include opening and closing books, recording transactions, and compiling balance sheets and income statements.

★1451★ *Bookkeeper-Account Clerk*
Arco Pub.
201 W. 103rd St.
Indianapolis, IN 46290
Ph: 800-428-5331 Fax: 800-835-3202

Hy Hammer. 1983. Provides information for the civil service bookkeeper examination.

★1452★ *Career Examination Series: Account Clerk*
National Learning Corp.
212 Michael Dr.
Syosset, NY 11791
Ph: (516)921-8888 Fax: (516)921-8743
Fr: 800-645-6337

Jack Rudman. All examination guides in this series contain questions with answers.

★1453★ *Career Examination Series: Accounting and Auditing Clerk*
National Learning Corp.
212 Michael Dr.
Syosset, NY 11791
Ph: (516)921-8888 Fax: (516)921-8743
Fr: 800-645-6337

Jack Rudman. All examinations guides in this series contain questions with answers.

★1454★ *Career Examination Series: Audit Clerk*
National Learning Corp.
212 Michael Dr.
Syosset, NY 11791
Ph: (516)921-8888 Fax: (516)921-8743
Fr: 800-645-6337

Jack Rudman. Test guide including questions and answers for students or professionals in the field who seek advancement through examination.

★1455★ *Career Examination Series: Bookkeeper*
National Learning Corp.
212 Michael Dr.
Syosset, NY 11791
Ph: (516)921-8888 Fax: (516)921-8743
Fr: 800-645-6337

Jack Rudman. Test guide including questions and answers for students or professionals in the field who seek advancement through examination. Also included in the series: Supervising Bookkeeper, Senior Bookkeeper, and Principal Bookkeeper.

★1456★ *Career Examination Series: Bookkeeping Machine Operator*
National Learning Corp.
212 Michael Dr.
Syosset, NY 11791
Ph: (516)921-8888 Fax: (516)921-8743
Fr: 800-645-6337

Jack Rudman. All examination guides in this series contain questions with answers.

★1457★ *Career Examination Series: Head Account-Audit Clerk*
National Learning Corp.
212 Michael Dr.
Syosset, NY 11791
Ph: (516)921-8888 Fax: (516)921-8743
Fr: 800-645-6337

Jack Rudman. Test guide including questions and answers for students or professionals in the field who seek advancement through examination.

★1458★ *Career Examination Series: Principal Account-Audit Clerk*
National Learning Corp.
212 Michael Dr.
Syosset, NY 11791
Ph: (516)921-8888 Fax: (516)921-8743
Fr: 800-645-6337

Jack Rudman. Test guide including questions and answers for students or professionals in the field who seek advancement through examination.

★1459★ *Senior Clerical Series*
Prentice Hall Press
Simon & Schuster Inc.
200 Old Tappan Rd.
Old Tappan, NJ 07675
Ph: 800-223-2348

Hy Hammer. Fourth edition, 1983. Complete test preparation for the following senior grade positions: clerk, typist, stenographer, account clerk, file clerk, statistics clerk, stenographer (law), mail and supply clerk, and stores clerk.

Basic Reference Guides and Handbooks

★1460★ *Accounting Terms & Bookkeeping Procedures Explained*
Gower Publishing Co.
Old Post Rd.
Brookfield, VT 05036
Ph: (802)276-3162

Diane Houghton. 1980.

★1461★ *The American System of Practical Bookkeeping: Adapted to the Commerce of the United States*
Ayer Company Publishers, Inc.
50 Northwestern Dr., No. 10
PO Box 958
Salem, NH 03079
Ph: (603)898-1200

James A. Bennett. 1976. Part of History of Accounting Series.

★1462★ *Basic Bookkeeping*
Trans-Atlantic Publications, Inc.
311 Bainbridge St.
Philadelphia, PA 19147
Ph: (215)925-5083 Fax: (215)925-1912

J. O. Magee. 1979.

★1463★ *Bookkeeping & Accounts*
Butterworths Legal Publishers
289 E. 5th St.
St. Paul, MN 55101
Ph: (612)227-4200

Paul Gee. 20th edition, 1988.

★1464★ *Bookkeeping for Beginners*
Beekman Publishers, Inc.
Rte. 212
PO Box 888
Woodstock, NY 12498
Ph: (914)679-2300

W. E. Hooper. 1970.

★1465★ *Bookkeeping the Easy Way*
Barron's Eductional Series, Inc.
250 Wireless Blvd.
Hauppauge, NY 11788
Ph: (516)434-3311 Fax: (516)434-3723
Fr: 800-645-3476

Wallace Kravitz. Second edition, 1990. Part of Easy Way Series.

★1466★ *Bookkeeping Made Easy*
HarperCollins Publishers, Inc.
10 E. 53rd St.
New York, NY 10022
Ph: (212)207-7000

Alexander L. Sheff. 1971.

★1467★ *Bookkeeping Made Simple*
Doubleday & Company, Inc.
666 5th Ave.
New York, NY 10103
Ph: (212)765-6500 Fax: (212)492-9700

Louis W. Fields. 1990. Part of Made Simple Series.

★1468★ *Bookkeeping for the Nineteen Nineties*
Regal Books
2300 Knoll Dr.
Ventura, CA 93003
Ph: (805)644-9721

Lynn Grobin. 1990.

★1469★ *Bookkeeping: Outline of Double Entry Bookkeeping for Small Business & Co-Operatives*
State Mutual Book & Periodical Service, Ltd.
521 5th Ave., 17th Fl.
New York, NY 10175
Ph: (212)682-5844

A. S. Walford. 1982.

★1470★ *Bookkeeping for a Small Business*
D B A Books
323 Beacon St.
Boston, MA 02116
Ph: (617)262-0411

Diane Bellavance. Third edition, 1987.

★1471★ *Bookkeeping for Small Organizations: A Handbook for Treasurers & Finance Committees*
Progressive Publisher
401 E. 32nd, No. 1002
Chicago, IL 60616
Ph: (312)225-9181

Kenneth Ives. 1990.

★1472★ *Developing Bookkeeping Skills*
AMSCO School Publications, Inc.
315 Hudson St.
New York, NY 10013
Ph: (212)675-7000

Wallace W. Kravitz. 1978.

★1473★ *Discover Bookkeeping & Accounts*
Trans-Atlantic Publications, Inc.
311 Bainbridge St.
Philadelphia, PA 19147
Ph: (215)925-5083 Fax: (215)925-1912

David Spurling. 1988.

★1474★ *Double Entry by Single: A New Method of Bookkeeping*
Ayer Company Publishers, Inc.
50 Northwestern Dr., No. 10
PO Box 958
Salem, NH 93079
Ph: (603)898-1200

Frederick W. Cronhelm. 1978. Part of Development of Contemporary Accounting Thought Series.

★1475★ *Horsebreeders Bookkeeping System*
Printed Horse
PO Box 1908
Fort Collins, CO 80522
Ph: (303)482-2286

1976.

★1476★ *Jones's English System of Bookkeeping Single or Double Entry*
Ayer Company Publishers, Inc.
50 Northwestern Dr., No. 10
PO Box 958
Salem, NH 03079
Ph: (603)898-1200

Edward T. Jones. 1978. Part of Development of Contemporary Accounting Thought Series.

★1477★ *Munro's Bookkeeping & Accountancy*
Trans-Atlantic Publications, Inc.
311 Bainbridge St.
Philadelphia, PA 19147
Ph: (215)925-5083 Fax: (215)925-1912

Alfred Palmer. 23rd edition, 1975.

★1478★ *A New & Complete System of Bookkeeping by an Improved Method of Double Entry*
Ayer Company Publishers, Inc.
50 Northwestern Dr., No. 10
PO Box 958
Salem, NH 03079
Ph: (603)898-1200

William Mitchell. 1978. Part of Development of Contemporary Accounting Thought Series.

★1479★ *Record Keeping for Small Rural Businesses*
University of Massachusetts, Amherst
Center for International Education
285 Hills House S.
Amherst, MA 01003
Ph: (413)545-0465

Eligia Murcia. Part of Technical Note Series.

★1480★ *Schaum's Outline of Bookkeeping & Accounting*
McGraw-Hill Publishing Co.
1221 Avenue of the Americas
New York, NY 10020
Ph: (212)512-2000

Joel J. Lerner. Second edition, 1988.

★1481★ *Schaum's Outline of Theory & Problems of Bookkeeping*
McGraw-Hill Publishing Company
1221 Avenue of the Americas
New York, NY 10020
Ph: (212)512-2000

Joel J. Lerner. 1994.

★1482★ *Step-by-Step Bookkeeping*
Borgo Press
PO Box 2845
San Bernardino, CA 92406-2845
Ph: (714)884-5813

Robert Ragan. 1989.

★1483★ *Streamlined Bookkeeping for Multi-Level Marketing*
Advantage Press
PO Box 51
Rocklin, CA 95677
Ph: (916)652-0185 Fax: (916)652-0539

Audrey A. Scannell. 1985.

★1484★ *Successfully Managing Your Accounting Career*
John Wiley and Sons, Inc.
605 3rd Ave.
New York, NY 10158-0012
Ph: (212)850-6000 Fax: (212)850-6088
Fr: 800-526-5368

Henry Labus. 1988.

Other Sources of Information

★1485★ *Ancient Double-Entry Bookkeeping*
Scholars Book Company
4431 Mt. Vernon
Houston, TX 77006
Ph: (713)528-4395

John B. Geijsbeek. 1975.

★1486★ *The Auditor's Guide of Eighteen Sixty-Nine*
Garland Publishing, Inc.
136 Madison Ave.
New York, NY 10016
Ph: (212)686-7492 Fax: (212)889-9399
Fr: 800-627-6273

Richard P. Brief, editor. 1988. Part of Foundations of Accounting Series.

★1487★ "Bookkeeper" in *Career Selector 2001*
Barron's Educational Series, Inc.
250 Wireless Blvd.
Hauppauge, NY 11788
Ph: (516)434-3311 Fax: (516)434-3723
Fr: 800-645-3476

James C. Gonyea. 1993.

★1488★ *Four Classics on the Theory of Double Entry Bookkeeping*
Garland Publishing, Inc.
136 Madison Ave.
New York, NY 10016
Ph: (212)686-7492 Fax: (212)889-9399
Fr: 800-627-6273

Richard P. Brief, editor. 1982. Part of Accountancy in Transition Series.

★1489★ *Robert Oliver & Mercantile Bookkeeping in the Early Nineteenth Century*
Ayer Company Publishers, Inc.
50 Northwestern Dr., No. 10
PO Box 958
Salem, NH 03079
Ph: (603)898-1200

Stuart Bruchey. 1976. Part of History of Accounting Series.

Brokerage Clerks and Statement Clerks

Brokerage clerks facilitate the sale and purchase of stocks, bonds, commodities, and other types of investments. Some types of brokerage clerks include purchase-and-sale clerks, dividend clerks, transfer clerks, receive-and-deliver clerks, and margin clerks. **Purchase-and-sale clerks** match orders to buy with orders to sell. **Dividend clerks** handle the payments of stock or cash dividends to clients. **Transfer clerks** check stock certificates to see that they adhere to banking regulations. **Receive-and-deliver clerks** are responsible for receiving and delivering stock certificates. **Margin clerks** monitor customers' accounts. **Statement clerks** are employed by banking institutions to process and mail bank statements with the aid of sophisticated machines. They assemble, verify, and send individual and commercial bank statements every month.

Salaries

The average salary of brokerage clerks is $13,800-26,700/year, with margin clerks, option clerks, and stock loan clerks earning the highest salaries, and transfer clerks, syndicate clerks, registration clerks, and dividend clerks earning the lowest.

Employment Outlook

Growth rate until the year 2005: More slowly than the average.

Brokerage Clerks and Statement Clerks

Career Guides

★1490★ "Brokerage Clerks and Statement Clerks" in *Occupational Outlook Handbook*
U.S. Government Printing Office
Superintendent of Documents
Washington, DC 20402
Ph: (202)512-1800 Fax: (202)512-2250

Biennial; latest edition, 1994-95. Encyclopedia of careers describing more than 250 occupations and comprising about 85 percent of all jobs in the economy. Occupations that require lengthy education or training are given the most attention. For each occupation, the handbook describes job duties, working conditions, training, educational preparation, personal qualities, advancement possibilities, job outlook, earnings, and sources of additional information.

Associations

★1491★ American Stock Exchange (AMEX)
86 Trinity Pl.
New York, NY 10006
Ph: (212)306-1000 Fax: (212)306-1812

Members: A domestic and international equities and derivative securities market organized in the late 18th century, exact year unknown. **Purpose:** Maintains library of books, periodicals, and business records. **Publications:** *American Stock Exchange—Annual Report.* • *AMEX Fact Book,* annual.

Basic Reference Guides and Handbooks

★1492★ *Records Management*
South-Western Publishing Co.
5101 Madison Rd.
Cincinnati, OH 45227
Ph: (513)271-8811

Mina M. Johnson. Fourth edition, 1986.

Periodicals

★1493★ *ABA Banking Journal*
American Bankers Association (ABA)
1120 Connecticut Ave. NW
Washington, DC 20036
Ph: (202)663-5000 Fax: (202)663-7533

Monthly.

★1494★ *American Stock Exchange—Annual Report*
American Stock Exchange (AMEX)
86 Trinity Pl.
New York, NY 10006
Ph: (212)306-1000 Fax: (212)306-1812

Review of previous year's activities on AMEX with financial statement.

★1495★ *AMEX Fact Book*
American Stock Exchange (AMEX)
86 Trinity Pl.
New York, NY 10006
Ph: (212)306-1000 Fax: (212)306-1812

Annual. Statistical reference work covering equities and derivatives; includes directories of company trading statistics and corporate addresses.

★1496★ *Records Management Quarterly*
Association of Record Managers and Administrators
4200 Somerset Dr, Ste. 215
Prairie Village, KS 66208
Ph: (913)341-3808 Fax: (913)341-3742
Ira Penn

Quarterly. Professional journal on records technology and information management.

Other Sources of Information

★1497★ *AMEX Fact Book*
American Stock Exchange (AMEX)
86 Trinity Pl.
New York, NY 10006
Ph: (212)306-1000 Fax: (212)306-1812

Annual. Statistical reference work including equity trading, options, Market Value Index, new stock listings, and a list of issues on AMEX with trading data. Includes subject index.

File Clerks

File clerks also called **records and information clerks** are responsible for maintaining an organized and updated filing system within an organization. They classify, store, update, and retrieve information on request. To keep records updated, file clerks add new material in a timely manner and may have to destroy outdated information or transfer it to a storage system. File clerks may be required to revise the manner of filing to keep pace with the amount of information. Some types of filing systems include file cabinets, microfilm, optical disks, or computerized retrieval systems. In smaller establishments, file clerks sometimes have additional responsibilities such as typing, word processing, or sorting mail.

Salaries

The average salary for file clerks is $15,700/year.

Employment Outlook

Growth rate until the year 2005: Average.

File Clerks

Career Guides

★1498★ "Clerks" in ***Career Discovery Encyclopedia*** **(Vol.2, pp. 16-17)**
J.G. Ferguson Publishing Co.
200 W. Madison St., Ste. 300
Chicago, IL 60606
Ph: (312)580-5480 Fax: (312)580-4948
E. Russell Primm, editor-in-chief. 1993. Contains two-page articles on 504 occupations. Each article describes job duties, earnings, and educational and training requirements.

★1499★ ***File Clerk***
Careers, Inc.
PO Box 135
Largo, FL 34649-0135
Ph: (813)584-7333
1992. Two-page job guide card describing duties, working conditions, personal qualifications, training, earnings and hours, employment outlook, places of employment, related careers and where to write for more information.

★1500★ **"File Clerk" in *Career Information Center* (Vol.1)**
Simon and Schuster
200 Old Tappan Rd.
Old Tappan, NJ 07675
Fax: 800-445-6991 Fr: 800-223-2348
Richard Lidz and Dale Anderson, editorial directors. Fifth edition, 1993. For 600 occupations, describes job duties, entry-level requirements, education and training needed, advancement possibilities, employment outlook, earnings and benefits. The set is divided into 12 volumes. Each volume includes jobs related under a broad career field. Volume 13 is the index.

★1501★ **"File Clerk" in *Careers in Banking and Finance* (pp. 43-45)**
Rosen Publishing Group
29 E. 21st St.
New York, NY 10010
Ph: (212)777-3017 Fax: (212)777-0277
Fr: 800-237-9932
Patricia Haddock. 1990. Describes more than 20 jobs at all levels in banking and finance. Contains information about the types of financial organizations where the jobs are found, educational requirements, job duties, and salaries. Offers advice on job hunting.

★1502★ **"File Clerk" in *Careers Inside the World of Offices* (pp. 11,38)**
Rosen Publishing Group
29 E. 21st St.
New York, NY 10010
Ph: 800-237-9932 Fax: (212)777-0277
Carolyn Simpson.1995. Describes job possibilities, attitudes and skills needed, and tips for getting the job. Also includes a self-evaluation test.

★1503★ ***File Clerk, General Clerk***
Prentice Hall
Rte. 9W
Englewood Cliffs, NJ 07632
Ph: (201)592-2000
Edited by John C. Czukor. Ninth edition, 1993.

★1504★ **"File Clerk" in *Jobs Rated Almanac***
World Almanac
1 International Blvd., Ste. 444
Mahwah, NJ 07495
Ph: (201)529-6900 Fax: (201)529-6901
Les Krantz. Second edition, 1992. Ranks 250 jobs by environment, salary, outlooks, physical demands, stress, security, travel opportunities, and extra perks. Includes jobs the editor feels are the most common, most interesting, and the most rapidly growing.

★1505★ **"File Clerk" in *Occu-Facts: Information on 580 Careers in Outline Form***
Careers, Inc.
PO Box 135
Largo, FL 34649-0135
Ph: (813)584-7333
Biennial, 1995-96 edition. Each one-page occupational profile describes duties, working conditions, physical surroundings and demands, aptitudes, temperament, educational requirements, employment outlook, earnings, and places of employment.

★1506★ **"File Clerks" in *American Almanac of Jobs and Salaries* (pp. 509)**
Avon Books
1350 Avenue of the Americas
New York, NY 10019
Ph: (212)261-6800 Fr: 800-238-0658
John Wright, editor. Revised and updated, 1994-95. A comprehensive guide to the wages of hundreds of occupations in a wide variety of industries and organizations.

★1507★ **"File Clerks" in *Encyclopedia of Careers and Vocational Guidance* (Vol.2, pp. 646-648)**
J.G. Ferguson Publishing Co.
200 W. Madison St., Ste. 300
Chicago, IL 60606
Ph: (312)580-5480 Fax: (312)580-4948
William E. Hopke, editor-in-chief. Ninth edition, 1993. Four-volume set that profiles 500 occupations and describes job trends in 74 industries. Includes career description, educational requirements, history of the job, methods of entry, advancement, employment outlook, earnings, working conditions, social and psychological factors, and sources of additional information.

★1508★ **"File Clerks" in *Jobs! What They Are—Where They Are—What They Pay* (pp. 249)**
Simon & Schuster, Inc.
Simon & Schuster Bldg.
1230 Avenue of the Americas
New York, NY 10020
Ph: (212)698-7000
Robert O. Snelling and Anne M. Snelling. Revised edition, 1992. Profiles 241 occupations, describing duties and responsibilities, educational preparation, earnings, employment opportunities, training, and qualifications.

★1509★ **"File Clerks" in *Occupational Outlook Handbook***
U.S. Government Printing Office
Superintendent of Documents
Washington, DC 20402
Ph: (202)512-1800 Fax: (202)512-2250
Biennial; latest edition, 1994-95. Encyclopedia of careers describing more than 250 occupations and comprising about 85 percent of all jobs in the economy. Occupations that require lengthy education or training are given the most attention. For each occupation, the handbook describes job duties, working con-

ditions, training, educational preparation, personal qualities, advancement possibilities, job outlook, earnings, and sources of additional information.

★1510★ ***Vocational Visions***
Center for Humanities, Inc.
Communications Park
Box 1000
Mount Kisco, NY 10549
Ph: (914)666-4100 Fax: (914)666-5319
Fr: 800-431-1242

Videocassette. 1984. 30 mins. This series of programs explains key aspects of actual training and a day in the life of a worker in the specific field mentioned on the videocassette. Occupations include: transportation/mechanics, repair, construction, business/office occupations, health, agriculture, technical/manufacturing, communications, and personal service.

TEST GUIDES

★1511★ ***Career Examination Series: Chief File Clerk***
National Learning Corp.
212 Michael Dr.
Syosset, NY 11791
Ph: (516)921-8888 Fax: (516)921-8743
Fr: 800-645-6337

Jack Rudman. All examination guides in this series contain questions with answers.

★1512★ ***Career Examination Series: File Clerk***
National Learning Corp.
212 Michael Dr.
Syosset, NY 11791
Ph: (516)921-8888 Fax: (516)921-8743
Fr: 800-645-6337

Jack Rudman. All examination guides in this series contain questions with answers.

★1513★ ***Career Examination Series: Principal File Clerk***
National Learning Corp.
212 Michael Dr.
Syosset, NY 11791
Ph: (516)921-8888 Fax: (516)921-8743
Fr: 800-645-6337

Jack Rudman. All examination guides in this series contain questions with answers.

★1514★ ***Career Examination Series: Senior File Clerk***
National Learning Corp.
212 Michael Dr.
Syosset, NY 11791
Ph: (516)921-8888 Fax: (516)921-8743
Fr: 800-645-6337

Jack Rudman. All examination guides in this series contain questions with answers.

★1515★ ***File Clerk, General Clerk***
Arco Pub.
201 W. 103rd St.
Indianapolis, IN 46290
Ph: 800-428-5331 Fax: 800-835-3202

John Czukor. 1993, ninth edition. Provides preparation for qualifying tests for positions with federal, state, and municipal agencies.

★1516★ ***Senior Clerical Series***
Prentice Hall Press
Simon & Schuster Inc.
200 Old Tappan Rd.
Old Tappan, NJ 07675
Ph: 800-223-2348

Hy Hammer. Fourth edition, 1983. Complete test preparation for the following senior grade positions: clerk, typist, stenographer, account clerk, file clerk, statistics clerk, stenographer (law), mail and supply clerk, and stores clerk.

★1517★ ***Senior Clerical Series***
Prentice Hall Press
Simon & Schuster Inc.
200 Old Tappan Rd.
Old Tappan, NJ 07675
Ph: 800-223-2348

Hy Hammer. Fourth edition, 1983. Complete test preparation for the following senior grade positions: clerk, typist, stenographer, account clerk, file clerk, statistics clerk, stenographer (law), mail and supply clerk, and stores clerk.

★1518★ ***Workbook Exercises in Alphabetic Filing***
McGraw-Hill Publishing Co.
1221 Avenue of the Americas
New York, NY 10020
Ph: (212)512-2000

R. J. Stewart. Third revised edition, 1980.

BASIC REFERENCE GUIDES AND HANDBOOKS

★1519★ ***Alphabetic Filing Rules***
Association of Records Managers & Administrators, Inc.
4200 Somerset, Ste. 215
Prairie Village, KS 66208
Ph: (913)341-3808

1986.

★1520★ ***File Management Techniques***
Krieger Publishing Co.
PO Box 9542
Melbourne, FL 32902
Ph: (407)724-9542 Fax: (407)951-3671

Billy G. Claybrook. 1983.

★1521★ ***File Structure & Design***
Krieger Publishing Co.
PO Box 9542
Melbourne, FL 32902
Ph: (407)724-9542 Fax: (407)951-3671

Margaret Cunningham. 1986.

★1522★ ***Filing Procedures Guideline***
Association of Records Managers & Administrators
4200 Somerset, Ste. 215
Prairie Village, KS 66208
Ph: (913)341-3808

1989.

★1523★ ***Filing & Records Management***
Prentice Hall
Rte. 9W
Englewood Cliffs, NJ 07632
Ph: (201)592-2000

Nathan Krevolin. 1986.

★1524★ ***Filing: Syllabus***
National Book Co.
PO Box 8795
Portland, OR 97207-8795
Ph: (503)228-6345

Joanne Piper. Second edition, 1979.

★1525★ ***Filing Systems & Records Management***
McGraw-Hill Publishing Co.
1221 Avenue of the Americas
New York, NY 10020
Ph: (212)512-2000

Jeffrey R. Stewart, Jr. Third edition, 1981.

★1526★ ***Gregg Quick Filing Practice***
McGraw-Hill Publishing Co.
1221 Avenue of the Americas
New York, NY 10020
Ph: (212)512-2000

Jeffrey R. Stewart, Jr. Second edition, 1979.

★1527★ ***How to Set up an Effective Filing System***
National Association of Credit Management
8815 Centre Park, Dr., Ste. 200
Columbia, MD 21045
Ph: (301)740-5560 Fax: (301)740-5574

Mary S. Taylor. 1981.

★1528★ ***Intensive Files Management***
South-Western Publishing Co.
5101 Madison Rd.
Cincinnati, OH 45227
Ph: (513)271-8811

Andrea R. Henne. Second edition, 1985.

★1529★ ***Numeric Filing Guideline***
Association of Records Managers & Administrators
4200 Somerset, Ste. 215
Prairie Village, KS 66208
Ph: (913)341-3808

1989.

★1530★ ***OJT File Clerk Resource Materials***
McGraw-Hill Publishing Co.
1221 Avenue of the Americas
New York, NY 10020
Ph: (212)512-2000

Joyce A. Sherster. Second edition, 1981. Part of Gregg Office Job Training Program Series.

★1531★ ***OJT File Clerk Training Manual***
McGraw-Hill, Inc.
1221 Avenue of the Americas
New York, NY 10020
Ph: (212)512-2000

Joyce A. Sherster. Second edition, 1981. Part of Gregg Office Job Training Program Series.

★1532★ ***Progressive Filing***
McGraw-Hill Publishing Co.
1221 Avenue of the Americas
New York, NY 10020
Ph: (212)512-2000

Jeffrey R. Stewart. Ninth edition, 1980.

★1533★ ***Records & Database Management***
McGraw-Hill Publishing Co.
1221 Avenue of the Americas
New York, NY 10020
Ph: (212)512-2000

Jeffrey R. Stewart. Fourth edition, 1989.

★1534★ *Records Management*
South-Western Publishing Co.
5101 Madison Rd.
Cincinnati, OH 45227
Ph: (513)271-8811

Mina M. Johnson. Fourth edition, 1986.

★1535★ *Records Management*
South-Western Publishing Co.
5101 Madison Rd.
Cincinnati, OH 45227
Ph: (513)271-8811

Mina M. Johnson. Fourth edition, 1986.

★1536★ *The Vertical File & Its Satellites: A Handbook of Acquisition, Processing, & Organization*
Libraries Unlimited, Inc,
6931 S. Yosemite St.
Englewood, CO 80112
Ph: (303)770-1220

Shirley Miller. Second edition, 1979. Part of Library Science Text Series.

Periodicals

★1537★ *Records Management Quarterly*
Association of Record Managers and Administrators
4200 Somerset Dr, Ste. 215
Prairie Village, KS 66208
Ph: (913)341-3808 Fax: (913)341-3742
Ira Penn

Quarterly. Professional journal on records technology and information management.

Other Sources of Information

★1538★ "Office File Clerk" in *Career Selector 2001*
Barron's Educational Series, Inc.
250 Wireless Blvd.
Hauppauge, NY 11788
Ph: (516)434-3311 Fax: (516)434-3723
Fr: 800-645-3476

James C. Gonyea. 1993.

Library Assistants and Bookmobile Drivers

Library assistants help keep library resources in an orderly condition and make sure they are readily available to users. They are responsible for registering patrons and issuing library cards as well as checking out materials and computing overdue fines. Library assistants also sort returned books and periodicals and return them to the shelves. **Bookmobile drivers** are also employed by many libraries to extend library services by driving a vehicle stocked with books to regular locations.

Salaries

The average salary for library assistants and bookmobile drivers is $16,400/year.

Employment Outlook

Growth rate until the year 2005: Average.

Library Assistants and Bookmobile Drivers

CAREER GUIDES

★1539★ "Library Assistant" in ***Museum Jobs form A-Z: What They Are, How to Prepare, and Where to Find Them***
Batax Museum Publishing
301 Racquet Club Rd., Ste. 202
Fort Lauderdale, FL 33326

G.W. Bates. 1994.

★1540★ **"Library Assistants and Bookmobile Drivers" in *Occupational Outlook Handbook***
U.S. Government Printing Office
Superintendent of Documents
Washington, DC 20402
Ph: (202)512-1800 Fax: (202)512-2250

Biennial; latest edition, 1994-95. Encyclopedia of careers describing more than 250 occupations and comprising about 85 percent of all jobs in the economy. Occupations that require lengthy education or training are given the most attention. For each occupation, the handbook describes job duties, working conditions, training, educational preparation, personal qualities, advancement possibilities, job outlook, earnings, and sources of additional information.

★1541★ **"Library Assistants" in *Career Discovery Encyclopedia* (Vol.4, pp. 8-9)**
J.G. Ferguson Publishing Co.
200 W. Madison St., Ste. 300
Chicago, IL 60606
Ph: (312)580-5480 Fax: (312)580-4948

E. Russell Primm, editor-in-chief. 1993. Contains two-page articles on 504 occupations. Each article describes job duties, earnings, and educational and training requirements.

★1542★ ***Library Clerk***
Careers, Inc.
PO Box 135
Largo, FL 34649-0135
Ph: (813)584-7333

1994. Two-page job guide card describing duties, working conditions, personal qualifications, training, earnings and hours, employment outlook, places of employment, related careers and where to write for more information.

★1543★ ***Library Clerk***
Vocational Biographies, Inc.
PO Box 31
Sauk Centre, MN 56378-0031
Ph: (612)352-6516 Fax: (612)352-5546
Fr: 800-255-0752

1990. This pamphlet profiles a person working in the job. Includes information about job duties, working conditions, places of employment, educational preparation, labor market outlook, and salaries.

★1544★ **"Library Clerk" in *Careers Inside the World of Offices* (pp. 8)**
Rosen Publishing Group
29 E. 21st St.
New York, NY 10010
Ph: 800-237-9932 Fax: (212)777-0277

Carolyn Simpson. 1995. Describes job possibilities, attitudes and skills needed, and tips for getting the job. Also includes a self-evaluation test.

★1545★ **"Library Clerk" in *Occu-Facts: Information on 580 Careers in Outline Form***
Careers, Inc.
PO Box 135
Largo, FL 34649-0135
Ph: (813)584-7333

Biennial, 1995-96 edition. Each one-page occupational profile describes duties, working conditions, physical surroundings and demands, aptitudes, temperament, educational requirements, employment outlook, earnings, and places of employment.

★1546★ ***Library Jobs: How to Fill Them, How to Find Them***
Oryx Press
4041 N. Central at Indian School Rd., Ste. 700
Phoenix, AZ 85012-3397
Ph: (602)265-2651 Fax: (602)253-2741
Fr: 800-279-6799

Barbara I. Dewey. 1987.

★1547★ ***Library Technical Assistant***
Careers, Inc.
PO Box 135
Largo, FL 34649-0135
Ph: (813)584-7333

1994. Two-page occupational summary card describing duties, working conditions, personal qualifications, training, earnings and hours, employment outlook, places of employment, related careers and where to write for more information.

★1548★ **"Library Technical Assistant" in *Occu-Facts: Information on 580 Careers in Outline Form***
Careers, Inc.
PO Box 135
Largo, FL 34649-0135
Ph: (813)584-7333

Biennial, 1995-96 edition. Each one-page occupational profile describes duties, working conditions, physical surroundings and demands, aptitudes, temperament, educational requirements, employment outlook, earnings, and places of employment.

★1549★ ***Library Technicians and Assistants***
Chronicle Guidance Publications, Inc.
66 Aurora St.
PO Box 1190
Moravia, NY 13118-1190
Ph: (315)497-0330 Fax: (315)497-3359
Fr: 800-622-7284

1993. This career brief describes the nature of the work, working conditions, hours and earnings, education and training, licensure, certification, unions, personal qualifications, social and psychological factors, employment outlook, entry methods, advancement, and related occupations.

★1550★ "Library Technicians and Assistants" in *Jobs! What They Are—Where They Are—What They Pay* (p. 113)
Simon & Schuster, Inc.
Simon & Schuster Bldg.
1230 Avenue of the Americas
New York, NY 10020
Ph: (212)698-7000

Robert O. Snelling and Anne M. Snelling. Revised edition, 1992. Profiles 241 occupations, describing duties and responsibilities, educational preparation, earnings, employment opportunities, training, and qualifications.

Associations

★1551★ American Library Association (ALA)
50 E. Huron St.
Chicago, IL 60611
Ph: (312)944-6780 Fax: (312)280-3255
Fr: 800-545-2433

Members: Librarians, libraries, trustees, friends of libraries, and others interested in the responsibilities of libraries in the educational, social, and cultural needs of society. **Purpose:** Promotes and improves library service and librarianship. Establishes standards of service, support, education, and welfare for libraries and library personnel; promotes the adoption of such standards in libraries of all kinds; safeguards the professional status of librarians; encourages the recruiting of competent personnel for professional careers in librarianship; promotes popular understanding and public acceptance of the value of library service and librarianship. Works in liaison with federal agencies to initiate the enactment and administration of legislation that will extend library services. Offers placement services. **Publications:** *ALA Handbook of Organization and Membership Directory*, annual. • *ALA Washington Newsletter*, periodic. • *American Libraries*, 11/year. • *Book Links*, bimonthly. • *Booklist*, biweekly. • *Library Systems Newsletter*, monthly. • *Library Technology Reports*, bimonthly.

★1552★ Council on Library-Media Technical-Assistants (COLT)
c/o Margaret Barron
Cuyahoga Community College
Library/Media Technology Dept., SC 201
2900 Community College Ave.
Cleveland, OH 44115
Ph: (216)987-4296 Fax: (216)987-4404

Members: Persons involved in two-year associate degree programs for the training of library technical assistants (professional-support workers) and graduates of programs employed as library/media technical assistants (B.A. degree holders without M.L.S. degree). Membership includes junior college deans, librarians, curriculum directors, professors, employers, special libraries, university libraries, library schools, publishers, and library technical assistants. Provides a channel of communication among the institutions and personnel that have developed such training programs; attempts to standardize curriculum offerings; develops educational standards; conducts research on graduates of the programs; represents the interests of library technical assistants and support staff . The council's concerns also include development of clear job descriptions and criteria for employment of technicians and dissemination of information to the public and to prospective students. Sponsors workshops for support staff in areas such as management, supervisory skills, interpersonal communication, business writing, and media center management. Maintains speakers' bureau. Is developing a program for certification of library media technicians and a continuing education program for library support staff. **Publications:** *Membership Directory and Data Book*, biennial. • *Mosaic*, monthly.

Standards/Certification Agencies

★1553★ American Library Association (ALA)
50 E. Huron St.
Chicago, IL 60611
Ph: (312)944-6780 Fax: (312)280-3255
Fr: 800-545-2433

Establishes standards of service, support, education, and welfare for libraries and library personnel; promotes the adoption of such standards in libraries of all kinds.

★1554★ Council on Library-Media Technical-Assistants (COLT)
c/o Margaret Barron
Cuyahoga Community College
Library/Media Technology Dept., SC 201
2900 Community College Ave.
Cleveland, OH 44115
Ph: (216)987-4296 Fax: (216)987-4404

Provides a channel of communication among the institutions and personnel that have developed such training programs; attempts to standardize curriculum offerings; develops educational standards; conducts research on graduates of the programs; represents the interests of library technical assistants and support staff. Is developing a program for certification of library media technicians.

Test Guides

★1555★ *Career Examination Series: Department Library Aide*
National Learning Corp.
212 Michael Dr.
Syosset, NY 11791
Ph: (516)921-8888 Fax: (516)921-8743
Fr: 800-645-6337

Jack Rudman. All examination guides in this series contain questions with answers.

★1556★ *Career Examination Series: Library Assistant*
National Learning Corp.
212 Michael Dr.
Syosset, NY 11791
Ph: (516)921-8888 Fax: (516)921-8743
Fr: 800-645-6337

Jack Rudman. Test guide including questions and answers for students or professionals in the field who seek advancement through examination.

★1557★ *Career Examination Series: Principal Library Clerk*
National Learning Corp.
212 Michael Dr.
Syosset, NY 11791
Ph: (516)921-8888 Fax: (516)921-8743
Fr: 800-645-6337

Jack Rudman. All examination guides in this series contain questions with answers.

★1558★ *Career Examination Series: Senior Library Clerk*
National Learning Corp.
212 Michael Dr.
Syosset, NY 11791
Ph: (516)921-8888 Fax: (516)921-8743
Fr: 800-645-6337

Jack Rudman. All examination guides in this series contain questions with answers.

Basic Reference Guides and Handbooks

★1559★ *Records Management*
South-Western Publishing Co.
5101 Madison Rd.
Cincinnati, OH 45227
Ph: (513)271-8811

Mina M. Johnson. Fourth edition, 1986.

Periodicals

★1560★ *The Abbey Newsletter*
Abbey Publications, Inc.
7105 Geneva Dr.
Austin, TX 78723
Ph: (512)929-3992 Fax: (512)929-3995
Ellen R. McCrady

Encourages the development of library and archival conservation, particularly technical advances and cross-disciplinary research in the field. Covers bookbinding and the conservation of books, papers, photographs, and non-paper materials. Recurring features include book reviews, news of research, job listings, convention reports, letters to the editor, a calendar of events, and a column about equipment and supplies.

★1561★ *Apple Library Users Group Newsletter*
Apple Computer, Inc.
4 Infinite Loop MS 304-2A
Cupertino, CA 95014
Ph: (408)974-2552 Fax: (408)725-8502
Monica Ertel

Quarterly. Serves as an exchange for information concerning the use of Apple and Macintosh computers in libraries and information centers of all sizes. Recurring features include news of research, book reviews, news from members, answers to readers' questions, a calendar of events, and columns titled News From/About Apple, Software Reviews, and Information From Our Vendors.

★1562★ *CMC News*
Computers and the Media Center (CMC)
515 Oak St., N.
Cannon Falls, MN 55009
Ph: (507)263-3711
Jim Deacon

Quarterly. Acts as a forum where library/media specialists can share information on computer use. Contains reviews of library utility programs on the microcomputer and articles on the management of microcomputers in library/media centers. Recurring features include columns titled Commercially Speaking (information on new computer products) and User Directory (a list of useful computer products and how they are used).

★1563★ *ERIC/IR Update*
ERIC Clearinghouse on Information and Technology
Syracuse University
4-194 Center for Science and Technology
Syracuse, NY 13244-4100
Ph: (315)443-3640 Fax: (315)443-5448
Jane K. Janis

Semiannual. Concentrates on the areas of education technology and library/information science. Offers informational resources and annotated bibliographies on topics of current interest in the areas of bibliographic instruction, microcomputers, computers and libraries, and television, visual literacy, and videotaping. Covers research reports, conference papers, curriculum guides, and trade books, which are available on microfiche and/or photocopy through ERIC.

★1564★ *FLICC Newsletter*
Federal Library and Information Center Committee (FLICC)
Library of Congress
Washington, DC 20540-5100
Ph: (202)707-4800 Fax: (202)707-4818
Darlene J. Dolan

Quarterly. Provides news and items of interest for federal librarians, information specialists, and administrators. Recurring features include reports on FLICC meetings, descriptions of its programs and projects, working group updates, announcements of educational programs for federal library and information center personnel.

★1565★ *Hot Off the Computer*
Westchester Library System
8 Westchester Plaza
Elmsford, NY 10523
Ph: (914)592-8214
Diane Courtney

Focuses on administrative and public service applications of microcomputers for public libraries. Includes columns titled Practical Uses of Microcomputers, Software Reviews, Database Searches, Book Reviews, and Articles of Interest.

★1566★ *IASL Newsletter*
International Association of School Librarianship (IASL)
PO Box 19586
Kalamazoo, MI 49019-0586
Peter J. Genco

Quarterly. Covers Association activities and developments in school library programs worldwide. Recurring features include book reviews, a schedule of activities, news of research, and reports from IASL Directors.

★1567★ *Library Times International*
Future World Publishing Company
PO Box 15661-0661
Evansville, IN 47716
Ph: (812)473-2420
R.N. Sharma

Quarterly. Monitors international developments and events related to library and information science. Carries items on countries worldwide. Recurring features include interviews, book reviews, a column carrying information science updates, news from library associations and groups, editorials, letters to the editor, listings of new publications, and a calendar of events.

★1568★ *The National Librarian: The NLA Newsletter*
National Librarians Association (NLA)
PO Box 486
Alma, MI 48801
Ph: (517)463-7227 Fax: (517)463-8694
Peter Dollard

Quarterly. Reports on news of concern to professional librarians. Reports on certification, education, relevant legal cases, and news of the Association and related library and educational organizations. Recurring features include book reviews and a section titled Bibliography on Professionalism.

★1569★ *OCLC Newsletter*
Online Computer Library Center (OCLC)
6565 Frantz Rd.
Dublin, OH 43017
Ph: (614)764-6000
Nita Dean

Bimonthly. Published as a service to users and potential users of automated library and information systems. Includes client news and information on Center activities.

★1570★ *Online Libraries and Microcomputers*
Information Intelligence, Inc.
PO Box 31098
Phoenix, AZ 85046
Ph: (602)996-2283 Fr: 800-228-9982
George S. Machovec

Monthly. Covers new library online and automation applications, library-oriented software and hardware for online and CD-ROM use, library networks, new online and CD-ROM databases, and people in the online/CD-ROM fields. Recurring features include editorials and notices of forthcoming meetings and new publications.

★1571★ *Records Management Quarterly*
Association of Record Managers and Administrators
4200 Somerset Dr, Ste. 215
Prairie Village, KS 66208
Ph: (913)341-3808 Fax: (913)341-3742
Ira Penn

Quarterly. Professional journal on records technology and information management.

★1572★ *Sipapu*
Noel Peattie
23311 County Rd. 88
Winters, CA 95694
Ph: (916)752-1032
Noel Peattie

Semiannual. Serves librarians and others concerned with alternative publications. Contains informal listings, annotation, and articles on small and independent presses; Third World, feminist, underground, counter-culture and radical publications; and dissent literature in general.

★1573★ *Technicalities*
Media Periodicals
4050 Pennsylvania Ave., Ste. 310
Kansas City, MO 64111-3051
Ph: (816)756-1490 Fax: (816)756-0159
Fr: 800-347-2665
Brian Alley

Monthly. Presents discussion, opinions, and reviews on library management topics, including computer applications, online public access catalogs, library budgets, collection building, automation, software, library marketplace trends, and the Library of Congress.

Other Sources of Information

★1574★ *A Benefit-Cost Analysis of Alternative Library Delivery Systems*
Greenwood Publishing Group, Inc.
88 Post Rd., W.
PO Box 5007
Westport, CT 06881
Ph: (203)226-3571 Fax: (203)222-1505

Teh-Wei Hu. 1975. Part of the Contributions in Librarianship and Information Science Series.

★1575★ "Library Technical Assistant" in *Career Selector 2001*
Barron's Educational Series, Inc.
250 Wireless Blvd.
Hauppauge, NY 11788
Ph: (516)434-3311 Fax: (516)434-3723
Fr: 800-645-3476

James C. Gonyea. 1993.

Order Clerks

Order clerks receive and process incoming orders for materials, merchandise, or services. They handle orders for a wide variety of items, with some orders coming from within the organization itself. In large companies, such as automobile manufacturers, parts or equipment need to be ordered from the company's warehouses. Employees in this setting are called "inside order clerks." Order clerks who deal primarily with the public are called "outside order clerks." Many order clerks work on video display terminals, which provide easy access to prices and inventory. Orders are received by telephone, mail, and facsimile machines. Order clerks review incoming orders, enter the information on an order form, and compute the customer's cost. The clerk then routes the order to the department that will send or deliver the item. Order clerks are primarily employed by wholesale and retail establishments and manufacturing firms.

Salaries

The average salary for order clerks is $22,200/year.

Employment Outlook

Growth rate until the year 2005: Employment is expected to remain level.

Order Clerks

Career Guides

★1576★ "Catalog Order Clerk" in *Occu-Facts: Information on 580 Careers in Outline Form*
Careers, Inc.
PO Box 135
Largo, FL 34649-0135
Ph: (813)584-7333

Biennial, 1995-96 edition. Each one-page occupational profile describes duties, working conditions, physical surroundings and demands, aptitudes, temperament, educational requirements, employment outlook, earnings, and places of employment.

★1577★ "Order Clerks" in *Occupational Outlook Handbook*
U.S. Government Printing Office
Superintendent of Documents
Washington, DC 20402
Ph: (202)512-1800 Fax: (202)512-2250

Biennial; latest edition, 1994-95. Encyclopedia of careers describing more than 250 occupations and comprising about 85 percent of all jobs in the economy. Occupations that require lengthy education or training are given the most attention. For each occupation, the handbook describes job duties, working conditions, training, educational preparation, personal qualities, advancement possibilities, job outlook, earnings, and sources of additional information.

Basic Reference Guides and Handbooks

★1578★ *Records Management*
South-Western Publishing Co.
5101 Madison Rd.
Cincinnati, OH 45227
Ph: (513)271-8811

Mina M. Johnson. Fourth edition, 1986.

Periodicals

★1579★ *Records Management Quarterly*
Association of Record Managers and Administrators
4200 Somerset Dr, Ste. 215
Prairie Village, KS 66208
Ph: (913)341-3808 Fax: (913)341-3742
Ira Penn

Quarterly. Professional journal on records technology and information management.

Payroll and Timekeeping Clerks

Payroll and timekeeping clerks make sure employees' paychecks are correct and paid on time. Timekeeping clerks distribute and collect time cards each pay period. They review time sheets to verify that the information is correct and properly recorded. Payroll clerks screen the timecards for errors and compute earnings. Payroll clerks also maintain and update employee files when workers resign, retire or transfer. Payroll and timekeeping clerks are found in business, health, education, social services, manufacturing, wholesale and retail trade, and in government.

Salaries

The average salary for payroll and timekeeping clerks is $21,000/year.

Employment Outlook

Growth rate until the year 2005: Decline.

Payroll and Timekeeping Clerks

Career Guides

★1580★ *Payroll Accounting*
South-Western Publishing Co.
5101 Madison Rd.
Cincinnati, OH 45227
Ph: (513)271-8811

Bernard J. Bieg and B. Lewis Keeling. 1994.

★1581★ "Payroll Clerk" in *Career Information Center* (Vol.1)
Simon and Schuster
200 Old Tappan Rd.
Old Tappan, NJ 07675
Fax: 800-445-6991 Fr: 800-223-2348

Richard Lidz and Dale Anderson, editorial directors. Fifth edition, 1993. For 600 occupations, describes job duties, entry-level requirements, education and training needed, advancement possibilities, employment outlook, earnings and benefits. The set is divided into 12 volumes. Each volume includes jobs related under a broad career field. Volume 13 is the index.

★1582★ "Payroll Clerk" in *Careers Inside the World of Offices* (pp. 11)
Rosen Publishing Group
29 E. 21st St.
New York, NY 10010
Ph: 800-237-9932 Fax: (212)777-0277

Carolyn Simpson. 1995. Describes job possibilities, attitudes and skills needed, and tips for getting the job. Also includes a self-evaluation test.

★1583★ "Payroll and Timekeeping Clerks" in *Occupational Outlook Handbook*
U.S. Government Printing Office
Superintendent of Documents
Washington, DC 20402
Ph: (202)512-1800 Fax: (202)512-2250

Biennial; latest edition, 1994-95. Encyclopedia of careers describing more than 250 occupations and comprising about 85 percent of all jobs in the economy. Occupations that require lengthy education or training are given the most attention. For each occupation, the handbook describes job duties, working conditions, training, educational preparation, personal qualities, advancement possibilities, job outlook, earnings, and sources of additional information.

Associations

★1584★ American Payroll Association (APA)
30 E. 33rd St., 5th Fl.
New York, NY 10016
Ph: (212)686-2030 Fax: (212)686-2789

Members: Payroll employees. **Purpose:** Works to increase members' skills and professionalism through education and mutual support. Represents the interest of members before legislative bodies. Conducts training courses. Operates speakers' bureau; conducts educational programs. Administers the certified payroll professional program of recognition. **Publications:** *APA Directory*, annual. • *Basic Guide to Payroll*, annual. • *Guide to Payroll Practice and Management.* • *Payroll Currently*, bimonthly. • *The Payroll Manager's Guide to Successful Direct Deposit.* • *The Payroll Source.* • *Paytech*, bimonthly.

Standards/Certification Agencies

★1585★ American Payroll Association (APA)
30 E. 33rd St., 5th Fl.
New York, NY 10016
Ph: (212)686-2030 Fax: (212)686-2789

Administers the certified payroll professional program of recognition.

Test Guides

★1586★ *Career Examination Series: Assistant Payroll Supervisor*
National Learning Corp.
212 Michael Dr.
Syosset, NY 11791
Ph: (516)921-8888 Fax: (516)921-8743
Fr: 800-645-6337

Jack Rudman. 1989. All examination guides in this series contain questions with answers.

★1587★ *Career Examination Series: Head Clerk (Payroll)*
National Learning Corp.
212 Michael Dr.
Syosset, NY 11791
Ph: (516)921-8888 Fax: (516)921-8743
Fr: 800-645-6337

Jack Rudman. All examination guides in this series contain questions with answers.

★1588★ *Career Examination Series: Payroll Auditor/Clerk*
National Learning Corp.
212 Michael Dr.
Syosset, NY 11791
Ph: (516)921-8888 Fax: (516)921-8743
Fr: 800-645-6337

Jack Rudman. 1988. All examination guides in this series contain questions with answers.

★1589★ *Career Examination Series: Senior Payroll Audit Clerk*
National Learning Corp.
212 Michael Dr.
Syosset, NY 11791
Ph: (516)921-8888 Fax: (516)921-8743
Fr: 800-645-6337

Jack Rudman. All examination guides in this series contain questions with answers.

Educational Directories and Programs

★1590★ *APA Directory*
American Payroll Association (APA)
30 E. 33rd St., 5th Fl.
New York, NY 10016
Ph: (212)686-2030 Fax: (212)686-2789
Annual.

Basic Reference Guides and Handbooks

★1591★ *Buying Payroll Software*
Cambridge University Press
49 W. 20th St.
New York, NY 10011
Ph: (212)924-3900 Fax: (212)691-3239
British Computer Society Staff. 1985. Part of Software Package Buyer's Guides Series.

★1592★ *Payroll Accounting for Microcomputers*
South-Western Publishing Co.
5101 Madison Rd.
Cincinnati, OH 45227
Ph: (513)271-8811
B. Lewis Keeling. 1991.

★1593★ *Payroll Recordkeeping*
McGraw-Hill Publishing Co.
1221 Avenue of the Americas
New York, NY 10020
Ph: (212)512-2000
Hadley Editorial Staff. Seventh edition, 1965.

★1594★ *Payroll Systems & Procedures*
McGraw-Hill Publishing Co.
1221 Avenue of the Americas
New York, NY 10020
Ph: (212)512-2000
B. F. Wigge. 1970.

★1595★ *Principles of Payroll Administration*
Prentice Hall
Rte. 9W
Englewood Cliffs, NJ 07632
Ph: (201)592-2000
Debera J. Salam. 1988.

Periodicals

★1596★ *Basic Guide to Payroll*
American Payroll Association (APA)
30 E. 33rd St., 5th Fl.
New York, NY 10016
Ph: (212)686-2030 Fax: (212)686-2789
Annual.

★1597★ *Guide to Payroll Practice and Management*
American Payroll Association (APA)
30 E. 33rd St., 5th Fl.
New York, NY 10016
Ph: (212)686-2030 Fax: (212)686-2789

★1598★ *Payroll Currently*
American Payroll Association (APA)
30 E. 33rd St., 5th Fl.
New York, NY 10016
Ph: (212)686-2030 Fax: (212)686-2789
Bimonthly. Tracks legislation.

★1599★ *The Payroll Manager's Guide to Successful Direct Deposit*
American Payroll Association (APA)
30 E. 33rd St., 5th Fl.
New York, NY 10016
Ph: (212)686-2030 Fax: (212)686-2789

★1600★ *The Payroll Source*
American Payroll Association (APA)
30 E. 33rd St., 5th Fl.
New York, NY 10016
Ph: (212)686-2030 Fax: (212)686-2789

★1601★ *Paytech*
American Payroll Association (APA)
30 E. 33rd St., 5th Fl.
New York, NY 10016
Ph: (212)686-2030 Fax: (212)686-2789
Bimonthly.

Other Sources of Information

★1602★ *Available Pay Survey Reports for Other Countries: An Annotated Bibliography*
Abbott, Langer & Associates
548 1st St.
Crete, IL 60417
Ph: (708)672-4200
Steven Langer, editor. 1987.

★1603★ *Available Pay Survey for the U.S.: An Annotated Bibliography*
Abbott, Langer & Associates
548 1st St.
Crete, IL 60417
Ph: (708)672-4200
Steven Langer, editor. 1987.

★1604★ "Payroll Clerk" in *Career Selector 2001*
Barron's Educational Series, Inc.
250 Wireless Blvd.
Hauppauge, NY 11788
Ph: (516)434-3311 Fax: (516)434-3723
Fr: 800-645-3476
James C. Gonyea. 1993.

Personnel Clerks

Personnel clerks are responsible for maintaining the personnel records of an organization's employees. These records include name, address, job title, earnings, benefits, absences, and information about job performance. Personnel clerks may also be involved in the hiring process. Once new employees begin work, they are greeted by personnel clerks, who provide information about the organization and help them fill out the necessary forms. In temporary help agencies, personnel clerks are known as referral clerks. They match requests for temporary help with qualified applicants. Other personnel clerks may be known as identification clerks and are responsible for security matters at defense installations. They keep records of all employees and visitors and issue badges, passes and identification cards. Personnel clerks are found in most industries including government, colleges and universities, hospitals, department stores, and banks.

Salaries

The average salary for personnel clerks is $20,300/year.

Employment Outlook

Growth rate until the year 2005: Average.

Personnel Clerks

Career Guides

★1605★ ***Beginning Consultant Training Program***
National Association of Personnel Consultants
3133 Mt. Vernon Ave.
Alexandria, VA 22305
Ph: (703)684-0180

★1606★ ***Career Planning Manual for Human Resource-Management/ Personnel: A Guide to the Practice & Accreditation in the Profession***
Society for Human Resource Management
606 N. Washington
Alexandria, VA 22314
Ph: (703)548-3440 Fax: (703)836-0367

Gladys W. Gruenberg. 1986.

★1607★ **"Personnel Clerk" in *Career Information Center* (Vol.1)**
Simon and Schuster
200 Old Tappan Rd.
Old Tappan, NJ 07675
Fax: 800-445-6991 Fr: 800-223-2348

Richard Lidz and Dale Anderson, editorial directors. Fifth edition, 1993. For 600 occupations, describes job duties, entry-level requirements, education and training needed, advancement possibilities, employment outlook, earnings and benefits. The set is divided into 12 volumes. Each volume includes jobs related under a broad career field. Volume 13 is the index.

★1608★ **"Personnel Clerks" in *Occupational Outlook Handbook***
U.S. Government Printing Office
Superintendent of Documents
Washington, DC 20402
Ph: (202)512-1800 Fax: (202)512-2250

Biennial; latest edition, 1994-95. Encyclopedia of careers describing more than 250 occupations and comprising about 85 percent of all jobs in the economy. Occupations that require lengthy education or training are given the most attention. For each occupation, the handbook describes job duties, working conditions, training, educational preparation, personal qualities, advancement possibilities, job outlook, earnings, and sources of additional information.

Associations

★1609★ **National Association of Personnel Workers (NAPW)**
Norfolk State University
2401 Corprew Ave.
Norfolk, VA 23504
Ph: (804)683-8223 Fax: (804)683-8029

Members: Student affairs personnel at historically black colleges. **Purpose:** Seeks to foster a unified spirit among student affairs personnel at predominantly black universities, colleges, and educational institutions. Works to improve the delivery of student services at black colleges and institutions. Serves as a professional agency for the collection of information and the discussion of scientific studies and problems pertaining to student services administration. Provides professional development for student affairs personnel. Designs projects in accordance with trends in postsecondary education. Monitors legislation that impacts student affairs programs and services. **Publications:** *NAPW Newsletter*, quarterly.

★1610★ **Newspaper Personnel Relations Association (NPRA)**
606 N. Washington St.
Alexandria, VA 22314
Ph: (703)548-3440 Fax: (703)836-0367

Members: Acts as a professional emphasis group within the Society for Human Resource Management. International newspaper human resources and labor relations executives; newspaper executives whose companies do not have human resources departments; associate members suppliers. **Purpose:** Seeks to advance human resources and industrial relations by seeking ways for management to make more effective use of people and by educating members in basic methods and techniques. Conducts research on human resource issues at newspapers. **Publications:** *NPRA News*, bimonthly.

Test Guides

★1611★ ***Career Examination Series: Personnel Clerk***
National Learning Corp.
212 Michael Dr.
Syosset, NY 11791
Ph: (516)921-8888 Fax: (516)921-8743
Fr: 800-645-6337

Jack Rudman. All examination guides in this series contain questions with answers.

★1612★ ***Career Examination Series: Principal Clerk (Personnel)***
National Learning Corp.
212 Michael Dr.
Syosset, NY 11791
Ph: (516)921-8888 Fax: (516)921-8743
Fr: 800-645-6337

Jack Rudman. All examination guides in this series contain questions with answers.

★1613★ ***Career Examination Series: Principal Personnel Clerk***
National Learning Corp.
212 Michael Dr.
Syosset, NY 11791
Ph: (516)921-8888 Fax: (516)921-8743
Fr: 800-645-6337

Jack Rudman. All examination guides in this series contain questions with answers.

★1614★ ***Career Examination Series: Senior Personnel Clerk***
National Learning Corp.
212 Michael Dr.
Syosset, NY 11791
Ph: (516)921-8888 Fax: (516)921-8743
Fr: 800-645-6337

Jack Rudman. All examination guides in this series contain questions with answers.

Educational Directories and Programs

★1615★ *NPRA Directory*
Newspaper Personnel Relations Association (NPRA)
606 N. Washington St.
Alexandria, VA 22314
Ph: (703)548-3440 Fax: (703)836-0367
Annual.

Basic Reference Guides and Handbooks

★1616★ *Records Management*
South-Western Publishing Co.
5101 Madison Rd.
Cincinnati, OH 45227
Ph: (513)271-8811
Mina M. Johnson. Fourth edition, 1986.

Periodicals

★1617★ *Compensation & Benefits Review*
American Management Assn.
135 W. 50th St., 15th Fl.
New York, NY 10020
Ph: (212)903-8160 Fax: (212)903-8168
Linda Bennett
Bimonthly. Journal on employee compensation and benefits.

★1618★ *EAP Digest*
Performance Resource Press
1863 Technology Drive
Troy, MI 48083
Ph: (313)588-7733 Fax: (313)588-6633
Brent Chartier
Bimonthly. Magazine covering planning, development, and administration of employee assistance programs.

★1619★ *Human Resources Abstracts*
Sage Periodicals Press
2455 Teller Rd.
Thousand Oaks, CA 91320
Ph: (805)499-0721 Fax: (805)499-0871
Paul V. McDowell
Quarterly. Journal providing abstracts reffering to employment and labor relations.

★1620★ *NAPW Newsletter*
National Association of Personnel Workers (NAPW)
Norfolk State University
2401 Corprew Ave.
Norfolk, VA 23504
Ph: (804)683-8223 Fax: (804)683-8029
Quarterly.

★1621★ *NPRA News*
Newspaper Personnel Relations Association (NPRA)
606 N. Washington St.
Alexandria, VA 22314
Ph: (703)548-3440 Fax: (703)836-0367
Bimonthly. Covers trends in human resources and labor, management, training, and legal updates.

★1622★ *Personnel Journal*
ACC Communications Inc.
245 Fischer Ave., B-2
Costa Mesa, CA 92626
Ph: (714)751-1883 Fax: (714)751-4106
Allan Halcrow
Monthly.

★1623★ *Personnel Literature*
U.S. Government Printing Office
Superintendent of Documents
Washington, DC 20402-9325
Ph: (202)783-3238
Monthly. Index to publications on personnel issues. Compiled by the Office of Personnel Management Library staff.

★1624★ *Personnel Psychology*
Personnel Psychology, Inc.
745 Haskins Rd., Ste. A
Bowling Green, OH 43402-1600
Ph: (419)352-1562 Fax: (419)352-2645
Michael A. Campion
Quarterly. Journal covering empirical research on personnel, including test validation, selection, labor-management relations, training, compensation, and reward systems. Also publishes related book reviews.

★1625★ *Public Personnel Management*
International Personnel Management Assn.
1617 Duke St.
Alexandria, VA 22314
Ph: (703)549-7100 Fax: (703)684-0948
Sarah Shiffert
Quarterly. Magazine for public personnel administrators responsible for selection, training, and labor relations.

★1626★ *Records Management Quarterly*
Association of Record Managers and Administrators
4200 Somerset Dr, Ste. 215
Prairie Village, KS 66208
Ph: (913)341-3808 Fax: (913)341-3742
Ira Penn
Quarterly. Professional journal on records technology and information management.

Secretaries

Secretaries perform a variety of administrative and clerical duties to help an organization run efficiently. They answer telephone calls, provide information, schedule appointments, maintain files, transcribe dictation, and other related tasks depending on the needs of the employer. There are various types of secretaries who have specified job duties. **Executive secretaries** perform fewer clerical tasks than lower level secretaries. Instead they handle more complex responsibilities like conducting research, training employees, and preparing reports. **Legal secretaries** prepare legal documents for attorneys, such as summonses, complaints, motions, and subpoenas. **Medical secretaries** assist physicians and medical scientists. **Technical secretaries** assist engineers or scientists. In addition to the usual secretarial duties, they prepare much of the correspondence, maintain the technical library, and gather and edit materials for scientific papers.

Salaries

The average salary for secretaries varies, reflecting differences in skill, experience, level of responsibility, and industry. Salaries of secretaries tend to be highest in transportation and public utilities and lowest in retail trade and finance, insurance, and real estate.

Secretaries	$20,000-36,000/year
Inexperienced secretaries in the federal government	$16,400/year
Secretaries in the federal government	$24,000/year

Employment Outlook

Growth rate until the year 2005: More slowly than average.

Secretaries

Career Guides

★1627★ "Administrative Assistants, Clerical Workers, and Secretaries" in *Jobs '95* (pp. 25-29)
Prentice Hall Press
1 Gulf Western Plaza
New York, NY 10023
Ph: (212)373-8500

Kathryn Petras and Ross Petras. Annual, 1995. Discusses employment prospects and trends for 15 professional careers and 29 industries. Lists leading companies, associations, directories, and magazines.

★1628★ *The Administrative Secretary*
McGraw-Hill Publishing Co.
1221 Avenue of the Americas
New York, NY 10020
Ph: (212)512-2000

R. I. Anderson. Second edition, 1976.

★1629★ *Basic Secretarial Skills*
Ambrose Video Publishing
1290 Avenue of the Americas, Ste. 2245
New York, NY 10104
Ph: (212)265-7272 Fax: (212)265-8088
Fr: 800-526-4663

Videocassette. 1989. 61 mins. A video training course for people who want to be secretaries.

★1630★ "Bookkeeper, Secretary, and Clerk" in *Travel & Tourism* (pp. 69-73)
Franklin Watts, Inc.
387 Park Avenue, S.
New York, NY 10016
Ph: (212)686-7070

Marjorie Rittenberg Schulz. 1990. Surveys employment opportunities in the travel and tourism industry. Provides job description, educational preparation, training, salary, employment outlook, and sources of additional information. Offers job hunting advice.

★1631★ *Career Insights*
RMI Media Productions, Inc.
1365 N. Winchester
Olathe, KS 66061
Ph: (913)768-1696 Fax: 800-755-6910
Fr: 800-745-5480

Videocassette series. 1987. This videotape series describes 50 occupations, including skill requirements and interviews with people employed in these fields. Occupations include: flight service, air transportation/ground services, data processing, carpentry, clerk in banking/insurance/business, cosmetic personal grooming, firefighting, forestry, insulation/roofing, mechanics, material handling, photographic processing, pipefitting and plumbing, printing, secretarial services, tool and die operations.

★1632★ *Career Success Series*
Cambridge Educational
PO Box 2153
Charleston, WV 25328-2153
Ph: (304)744-9323 Fax: (304)744-9351
Fr: 800-468-4227

Videocassette. 1986. 15 mins. A series, available separately, outlining various career choices for students. Occupations include: accounting, flight service, air transportation/ground/flight service, data processing, carpentry, clerk in banking/insurance, commodity sales, cosmetic personal grooming, fire fighting, forestry services, home economics, insulation/roofing, material handling, mechanics, photographic processing, pipefitting and plumbing, police science, printing, carpentry, medical laboratory technicians, secretarial services, and utilities equipment operator.

★1633★ "Clerical and Secretarial Work" in *Exploring Careers Using Foreign Languages* (pp. 51-52)
Rosen Publishing Group
29 E. 21st St.
New York, NY 10010
Ph: (212)777-3017 Fax: (212)777-0277
Fr: 800-237-9932

E. W. Edwards. Revised edition, 1990. Explores careers in teaching, translating, interpreting, business and finance, government, communications, and the media. Covers employment ideas, salaries, job duties, and educational preparation. Contains information on accreditation and job hunting.

★1634★ *Complete Secretary's Handbook*
Prentice Hall
Rte. 9W
Englewood Cliffs, NJ 07632
Ph: (201)592-2000

Mary A. DeVries, editor. Seventh edition, revised. 1993.

★1635★ *Considering a Secretarial Service?: Possibilities for Income*
Prosperity & Profits Unlimited
PO Box 570213
Houston, TX 77257
Ph: (713)867-3438

Center for Self-Sufficiency, Research Division Staff. 1983.

★1636★ "Dental and Medical Secretary" in *Career Information Center* (Vol.7)
Simon and Schuster
200 Old Tappan Rd.
Old Tappan, NJ 07675
Fax: 800-445-6991 Fr: 800-223-2348

Richard Lidz and Dale Anderson, editorial directors. Fifth edition, 1993. For 600 occupations, describes job duties, entry-level requirements, education and training needed, advancement possibilities, employment outlook, earnings and benefits. The set is divided into 12 volumes. Each volume includes jobs related under a broad career field. Volume 13 is the index.

★1637★ *The Dynamic Secretary: A Practical Guide to Achieving Success as an Executive Assistant*
Prentice Hall
Rte. 9W
Englewood Cliffs, NJ 07632
Ph: (201)592-2000

Frieda Porat and Mimi Will. 1983.

★1638★ *Executive Secretary*
Vocational Biographies, Inc.
PO Box 31
Sauk Centre, MN 56378-0031
Ph: (612)352-6516 Fax: (612)352-5546
Fr: 800-255-0752

1991. This pamphlet profiles a person working in the job. Includes information about job duties, working conditions, places of employment, educational preparation, labor market outlook, and salaries.

★1639★ *How to Start Your Own Secretarial Services Business at Home*
SK Publictions
7149 Natalie Blvd.
Northfield Center, OH 44067
Ph: (216)467-8059

Stephen G. Kozlow. 1980.

★1640★ "Information/Word Processing: The Secretary" in *Opportunities in Office Occupations* (pp. 93-115)
National Textbook Co. (NTC)
VGM Career Books
4255 W. Touhy Ave.
Lincolnwood, IL 60646-1975
Ph: (708)679-5500 Fax: (708)679-2494
Fr: 800-323-4900

Blanche Ettinger. 1989. Describes factors and trends which will affect office occupations including automation, telecommuting, and unionization. Separate chapters cover clerks, records management, information word processing, the secretary, and the bookkeeper-accountant. Describes job duties, skills needed, educational preparation, job hunting, types of equipment, employment outlook, and salaries.

★1641★ *Instant Secretary's Handbook*
Career Publishing Inc.
905 Allanson Rd.
Mundelein, IL 60060
Ph: (708)949-0011 Fax: (708)566-8552

Martha S. Luck and Donald O. Bolander. 1990.

★1642★ "Legal Secretaries" in *America's 50 Fastest Growing Jobs* (pp. 104)
JIST Works, Inc.
720 N. Park Ave.
Indianapolis, IN 46202-3431
Ph: (317)264-3720 Fax: (317)264-3709
Fr: 800-648-5478

Michael J. Farr, compiler. 1994. Describes the 50 fastest growing jobs within major career clusters such as technicians, and marketing and sales. Each job profile explains the nature of the work, skills and abilities required, employment outlook, average earnings, related occupations, education and training requirements, and employment opportunities. Also contains career planning information and job search tips.

★1643★ "Medical Dental Secretary" in *Career Connection II: A Guide to Technical Majors and Their Related Careers* (pp. 112-113)
Jist Works, Inc.
720 N. Park Ave.
Indianapolis, IN 46202-3431
Ph: (317)264-3720 Fax: (317)264-3709

Fred A. Rowe. 1994. Contains technical majors, such as automotive technology. Describes the major and the job. Lists high school and postsecondary school courses. Includes occupations related to the major, employment outlook, and starting salary.

★1644★ "Medical or Dental Secretary" in *Health Care* (pp. 51-55)
Franklin Watts, Inc.
387 Park Avenue, S.
New York, NY 10016
Ph: (212)686-7070

Linda Barrett and Galen Guengerich. 1991. Provides an overview of the health care industry. Includes job description, educational preparation, training, salary, and employment outlook. Offers job hunting advice.

★1645★ "Medical Secretary" in *Opportunities in Health and Medical Careers* (pp. 106-107)
National Textbook Co. (NTC)
VGM Career Books
4255 W. Touhy Ave.
Lincolnwood, IL 60646-1975
Ph: (708)679-5500 Fax: (708)679-2494
Fr: 800-323-4900

Leo D'Orazio and I. Donald Snook. 1991. Provides an overview of the health care industry with future projections. Describes a wide variety of healthcare jobs covering the nature of the work, educational requirements, employment outlook and salaries. Offers job hunting advice.

★1646★ "Medical Secretary" in *VGM's Careers Encyclopedia* (pp. 279-281)
National Textbook Co. (NTC)
VGM Career Books
4255 W. Touhy Ave.
Lincolnwood, IL 60646-1975
Ph: (708)679-5500 Fax: (708)679-2494
Fr: 800-323-4900

Third edition, 1991. Contains two- to five-page descriptions of 200 managerial, professional, technical, trade, and service occupations. Each profile includes job duties, places of employment, qualifications, educational preparation, training, employment potential, advancement, income, and additional sources of information.

★1647★ "Medical Secretary" in *VGM's Handbook of Health Care Careers*
National Textbook Co.
4255 W. Touhy Ave.
Lincolnwood, IL 60646-1975
Ph: (708)679-5500 Fax: (708)679-2494
Fr: 800-323-4900

Annette Selden. 1993. Contains 42 two-page occupational profiles describing job duties, places of employment, working conditions, qualifications, education, employment outlook, and income.

★1648★ "Membership Secretary" in *Museum Jobs form A-Z: What They Are, How to Prepare, and Where to Find Them*
Batax Museum Publishing
301 Racquet Club Rd., Ste. 202
Fort Lauderdale, FL 33326

G.W. Bates. 1994.

★1649★ *Office Systems & Careers: A Resource for Administrative Assistants*
Allyn & Bacon, Inc.
160 Gould St.
Needham Heights, MA 02194

Olice D. Church and Anne E. Schatz. 1981.

★1650★ *Procedures for the Professional Secretary*
South-Western Publishing Co.
5101 Madison Rd.
Cincinnati, OH 45227
Ph: (513)271-8811

Patsy J. Fulton and Joanna D. Hanks. 1985.

★1651★ *School Secretary*
Vocational Biographies, Inc.
PO Box 31
Sauk Centre, MN 56378-0031
Ph: (612)352-6516 Fax: (612)352-5546
Fr: 800-255-0752

1991. This pamphlet profiles a person working in the job. Includes information about job duties, working conditions, places of employment, educational preparation, labor market outlook, and salaries.

★1652★ "Secretarial Science" in *Career Connection II: A Guide to Technical Majors and Their Related Careers* (pp. 136-137)
Jist Works, Inc.
720 N. Park Ave.
Indianapolis, IN 46202-3431
Ph: (317)264-3720 Fax: (317)264-3709

Fred A. Rowe. 1994. Contains technical majors, such as automotive technology. Describes the major and the job. Lists high school and postsecondary school courses. Includes occupations related to the major, employment outlook, and starting salary.

★1653★ "Secretarial Sciences" in *College Majors and Careers: A Resource Guide for Effective Life Planning* (pp. 119-120)
Garrett Park Press
PO Box 1907
Garrett Park, MD 20896
Ph: (301)946-2553

Paul Phifer. 1993. Lists 61 college majors. Includes a general definition of the field, related occupations requiring either a bachelor or associate degree, related leisure-time activities denoting personal interest in the field, skills needed, values, and personal attributes. Lists organizations.

★1654★ "Secretaries/Administrative Assistants" in *Profitable Careers in Nonprofit* (pp. 149-151)
John Wiley and Sons, Inc.
605 3rd Ave.
New York, NY 10158-0012
Ph: (212)850-6000 Fax: (212)850-6088
Fr: 800-526-5368

William Lewis and Carol Milano. 1987. Examines employment opportunities in various types of nonprofit organizations from entry level to high-level executive. Explains the structure of nonprofit corporations, characteristics of employees, the rewards and drawbacks of the work, and offers tips on how to target positions.

★1655★ "Secretaries" in *American Almanac of Jobs and Salaries* (pp. 506)
Avon Books
1350 Avenue of the Americas
New York, NY 10019
Ph: (212)261-6800 Fr: 800-238-0658

John Wright, editor. Revised and updated, 1994-95. A comprehensive guide to the wages of hundreds of occupations in a wide variety of industries and organizations.

★1656★ "Secretaries" in *Career Discovery Encyclopedia* (Vol.6, pp/ 12-13)
J.G. Ferguson Publishing Co.
200 W. Madison St., Ste. 300
Chicago, IL 60606
Ph: (312)580-5480 Fax: (312)580-4948

E. Russell Primm, editor-in-chief. 1993. Contains two-page articles on 504 occupations. Each article describes job duties, earnings, and educational and training requirements.

★1657★ "Secretaries and Clerical Personnel" in *Opportunities in Real Estate Careers* (pp. 117-118)
National Textbook Co. (NTC)
VGM Career Books
4255 W. Touhy Ave.
Lincolnwood, IL 60646-1975
Ph: (708)679-5500 Fax: (708)679-2494
Fr: 800-323-4900

Mariwyn Evans. 1988. Surveys the real estate industry and related careers. Covers the work, academic preparation, employment outlook, licensing, and financial compensation. Offers job hunting information.

★1658★ "Secretaries" in *Encyclopedia of Careers and Vocational Guidance* (Vol.4, pp. 332-335)
J.G. Ferguson Publishing Co.
200 W. Madison St., Ste. 300
Chicago, IL 60606
Ph: (312)580-5480 Fax: (312)580-4948

William E. Hopke, editor-in-chief. Ninth edition, 1993. Four-volume set that profiles 500 occupations and describes job trends in 74 industries. Includes career description, educational requirements, history of the job, methods of entry, advancement, employment outlook, earnings, working conditions, social and psychological factors, and sources of additional information.

★1659★ *Secretaries, Management & Organizations*
Gower Publishing Co.
Old Post Rd.
Brookfield, VT 05036
Ph: (802)276-3162

S. Vinnicombe. 1980.

★1660★ "Secretaries" in *Occupational Outlook Handbook*
U.S. Government Printing Office
Superintendent of Documents
Washington, DC 20402
Ph: (202)512-1800 Fax: (202)512-2250

Biennial; latest edition, 1994-95. Encyclopedia of careers describing about 250 occupations and comprising about 85 percent of all jobs in the economy. Occupations that require lengthy education or training are given the most attention. Each occupation's profile describes what the worker does on the job, working conditions, education and training requirements, advancement possibilities, job outlook, earnings, and sources of additional information.

★1661★ "Secretaries" in *Opportunities in Vocational and Technical Careers* (pp. 47-58)
National Textbook Co. (NTC)
VGM Career Books
4255 W. Touhy Ave.
Lincolnwood, IL 60646-1975
Ph: (708)679-5500 Fax: (708)679-2494
Fr: 800-323-4900

Adrian A. Paradis. 1992. Describes careers which can be prepared for by attending a private vocational or proprietary school—office employee, sales worker, service worker, health services, mechanic, craftworker, and technician. Covers employment outlook, job duties, and salaries. Offers career planning advice.

★1662★ *Secretaries and Stenographers*
Chronicle Guidance Publications, Inc.
66 Aurora St.
PO Box 1190
Moravia, NY 13118-1190
Ph: (315)497-0330 Fax: (315)497-3359
Fr: 800-622-7284

1991. This career brief describes the nature of the work, working conditions, hours and earnings, education and training, licensure, certification, unions, personal qualifications, social and psychological factors, employment outlook, entry methods, advancement, and related occupations.

★1663★ "Secretaries and Stenographers" in *Jobs! What They Are—Where They Are—What They Pay* (pp. 252)
Simon & Schuster, Inc.
Simon & Schuster Bldg.
1230 Avenue of the Americas
New York, NY 10020
Ph: (212)698-7000

Robert O. Snelling and Anne M. Snelling. Revised edition, 1992. Profiles 241 occupations, describing duties and responsibilities, educational preparation, earnings, employment opportunities, training, and qualifications.

★1664★ *Secretary . . .*
Professional Secretaries International
10502 N.W. Ambassador Dr.
PO Box 20404
Kansas City, MO 64195-0404
Ph: (816)891-6600

1990. This pamphlet describes secretarial work, advancement opportunities, and educational preparation.

★1665★ *Secretary*
Careers, Inc.
PO Box 135
Largo, FL 34649-0135
Ph: (813)584-7333

1992. Four-page brief offering the definition, history, duties, working conditions, personal qualifications, educational requirements, earnings, hours, employment outlook, advancement possibilities, and related occupations.

★1666★ "Secretary" in *100 Best Careers for the Year 2000* (pp. 205-207)
Arco Pub.
201 W. 103rd St.
Indianapolis, IN 46290
Ph: 800-428-5331 Fax: 800-835-3202

Shelly Field. 1992. Describes 100 job opportunities expected to grow fast throughout the next decade. Provides information on job duties and responsibilities, training requirements, education, advancement opportunities, experience and qualifications, and typical salaries.

★1667★ *Secretary: A Career of Distinction*
Professional Secretaries International
10502 N.W. Ambassador Dr.
PO Box 20404
Kansas City, MO 64195-0404
Ph: (816)891-6600

1987. This eight-panel brochure describes educational preparation, travel opportunities, labor market outlook, promotional opportunities, and working conditions.

★1668★ *Secretary, Bilingual*
Careers, Inc.
PO Box 135
Largo, FL 34649-0135
Ph: (813)584-7333

1993. Four-page brief offering the definition, history, duties, working conditions, personal qualifications, educational requirements, earnings, hours, employment outlook, advancement possibilities, and related occupations.

★1669★ "Secretary" in *BLR Encyclopedia of Prewritten Job Descriptions*
Business and Legal Reports, Inc.
39 Academy St.
Madison, CT 06443-1513
Ph: (203)245-7448

Stephen D. Bruce, editor-in-chief. 1994. This book contains hundreds of sample job descriptions arranged by functional job category. The 1-3 page job descriptions cover what the worker normally does in the position, who they report to, and how that position fits in the organizational structure.

★1670★ "Secretary" in *Career Information Center* (Vol.1)
Simon and Schuster
200 Old Tappan Rd.
Old Tappan, NJ 07675
Fax: 800-445-6991 Fr: 800-223-2348

Richard Lidz and Dale Anderson, editorial directors. Fifth edition, 1993. For 600 occupations, describes job duties, entry-level requirements, education and training needed, advancement possibilities, employment outlook, earnings and benefits. The set is divided into 12 volumes. Each volume includes jobs related under a broad career field. Volume 13 is the index.

★1671★ "Secretary" in *Careers in Banking and Finance* (pp. 65-66)
Rosen Publishing Group
29 E. 21st St.
New York, NY 10010
Ph: (212)777-3017 Fax: (212)777-0277
Fr: 800-237-9932

Patricia Haddock. 1990. Describes more than 20 jobs at all levels in banking and finance. Contains information about the types of financial organizations where the jobs are found, educational requirements, job duties, and salaries. Offers advice on job hunting.

★1672★ "Secretary" in *Careers Inside the World of Offices* (pp. 34-37)
Rosen Publishing Group
29 E. 21st St.
New York, NY 10010
Ph: 800-237-9932 Fax: (212)777-0277

Carolyn Simpson. 1995. Describes job possibilities, attitudes and skills needed, and tips for getting the job. Also includes a self-evaluation test.

★1673★ *Secretary, Executive*
Careers, Inc.
PO Box 135
Largo, FL 34649-0135
Ph: (813)584-7333

1991. Four-page brief offering the definition, history, duties, working conditions, personal qualifications, educational requirements, earnings, hours, employment outlook, advancement possibilities, and related occupations.

★1674★ "Secretary" in *Guide to Careers Without College* (pp. 46-49)
Franklin Watts, Inc.
387 Park Avenue, S.
New York, NY 10016
Ph: (212)686-7070

Kathleen S. Abrams. 1988. Discusses careers that do not require a college degree in fields such as health care, sales and marketing, and the building trades. Describes the work, employment opportunities, and training.

★1675★ *Secretary on the Job*
McGraw-Hill Publishing Co.
1221 Avenue of the Americas
New York, NY 10020
Ph: (212)512-2000

Mary Witherow. 1983.

★1676★ "Secretary" in *Jobs Rated Almanac*
World Almanac
1 International Blvd., Ste. 444
Mahwah, NJ 07495
Ph: (201)529-6900 Fax: (201)529-6901

Les Krantz. Second edition, 1992. Ranks 250 jobs by environment, salary, outlooks, physical demands, stress, security, travel opportunities, and extra perks. Includes jobs the editor feels are the most common, most interesting, and the most rapidly growing.

★1677★ *Secretary, Legal*
Careers, Inc.
PO Box 135
Largo, FL 34649-0135
Ph: (813)584-7333

1991. Two-page occupational summary card describing duties, working conditions, personal qualifications, training, earnings and hours, employment outlook, places of employment, related careers and where to write for more information.

★1678★ "Secretary" in *Occu-Facts: Information on 580 Careers in Outline Form*
Careers, Inc.
PO Box 135
Largo, FL 34649-0135
Ph: (813)584-7333

Biennial, 1995-96 edition. Each one-page occupational profile describes duties, working conditions, physical surroundings and demands, aptitudes, temperament, educational requirements, employment outlook, earnings, and places of employment.

★1679★ *Secretary, Technical*
Careers, Inc.
PO Box 135
Largo, FL 34649-0135
Ph: (813)584-7333

1995. Two-page occupational summary card describing duties, working conditions, personal qualifications, training, earnings and hours, employment outlook, places of employment, related careers and where to write for more information.

★1680★ "Secretary" in *VGM's Careers Encyclopedia* (pp. 424-427)
National Textbook Co. (NTC)
VGM Career Books
4255 W. Touhy Ave.
Lincolnwood, IL 60646-1975
Ph: (708)679-5500 Fax: (708)679-2494
Fr: 800-323-4900

Third edition, 1991. Contains two- to five-page descriptions of 200 managerial, professional, technical, trade, and service occupations. Each profile includes job duties, places of employment, qualifications, educational preparation, training, employment potential, advancement, income, and additional sources of information.

★1681★ "Skills Analysis: Secretaries" in *Black Woman's Career Guide* (pp. 52-56)
Bantam Doubleday Dell
1540 Broadway
New York, NY 10036
Fax: 800-233-3294 Fr: 800-223-5780

Beatryce Nivens. Revised edition, 1987. Offers career planning and job hunting advice. Contains information on 20 different career areas and profiles women working in the field. Each occupational profile describes the work, career paths and earning potential.

★1682★ *Starting Your Own Secretarial Business*
Contemporary Books, Inc.
180 N. Michigan Ave.
Chicago, IL 60601
Ph: (312)782-9181 Fax: (312)782-2157

Betty Lonngren. 1982.

★1683★ "Traveling Secretary/ Professional Sports Team" in *Career Opportunities in the Sports Industry* (pp. 43-45)
Facts on File
460 Park Ave. S.
New York, NY 10016-7382
Ph: (212)683-2244 Fax: 800-678-3633
Fr: 800-322-8755

Shelly Field. 1991. Describes various jobs in the sports industry. Each occupational profile covers job duties, employment outlook, career paths, salaries, skills, and educational preparation. Offers tips for entering the field.

★1684★ *Video Career Library - Clerical & Administrative Support*
Careers, Inc.
PO Box 135
Largo, FL 34649-0135
Ph: (813)584-7333

Videocassette. 1990. 26 mins. Part of the Video Career Library covering 165 occupations. Shows actual workers on the job. Includes secretaries, cashiers, receptionists, bookkeepers and audit clerks, telephone operators, postal clerks/carriers/supervisors, insurance investigators, bank tellers, data entry keyers, and court reporters.

★1685★ *Vocational Visions*
Center for Humanities, Inc.
Communications Park
Box 1000
Mount Kisco, NY 10549
Ph: (914)666-4100 Fax: (914)666-5319
Fr: 800-431-1242

Videocassette. 1984. 30 mins. This series of programs explains key aspects of actual training and a day in the life of a worker in the specific field mentioned on the videocassette. Occupations include: transportation/mechanics, repair, construction, business/office occupations, health, agriculture, technical/manufacturing, communications, and personal service.

Associations

★1686★ Association of Independent Colleges and Schools
1 Dupont Circle NW, Ste. 350
Washington, DC 20036
Ph: (202)659-2460 Fax: (202)659-2254

Members: Independent business schools and junior and senior colleges of business. **Purpose:** Sponsors an accrediting commission for postsecondary and collegiate institutions. **Publications:** *AICS Compass*, monthly. • *Capital Comments*, bimonthly. • *Directory of Accredited Institutions*, annual.

★1687★ National Association of Executive Secretaries (NAES)
900 S. Washington St., No. G-13
Falls Church, VA 22046
Ph: (703)237-8616

Members: Professional secretaries united to bring added stature to their profession and to create for members the benefits that are normally limited to members of specialized professional and fraternal groups. **Purpose:**

Sponsors biennial secretarial salary survey. **Publications:** *Exec-U-Tary*, monthly. • *Moving Up: A Career Path Guide for the Executive Secretary.* • *Stress Management in the Workplace—Coping Skills for the Executive Secretary.*

★1688★ National Association of Legal Secretaries (International) (NALS)
2250 E. 73rd St., Ste. 550
Tulsa, OK 74136
Ph: (918)493-3540 Fax: (918)493-5784

Members: Legal secretaries and others employed in work of a legal nature in law offices, banks, and courts. **Purpose:** Sponsors legal secretarial training courses and awards those passing a two-day examination the rating of Certified Professional Legal Secretary. **Publications:** *Career Legal Secretary.* • *Docket*, bimonthly. • *Manual for Lawyer's Assistant.*

★1689★ Professional Secretaries International (PSI)
10502 NW Ambassador Dr.
PO Box 20404
Kansas City, MO 64195-0404
Ph: (816)891-6600 Fax: (816)891-9118

Members: Professional organization of secretaries. **Purpose:** Monitors related legislative and governmental activities; sponsors audiovisual productions; provides group insurance plans. Sponsors Professional Secretaries' Day/Week. Has established the PSI Research and Educational Foundation to develop research and educational projects for secretaries, management, and educators. Has also established Professional Secretaries International Retirement Centers Trust to acquire and maintain a home in Albuquerque, NM for needy and elderly secretaries. Sponsors continuing education programs. **Publications:** *Career Track Monitor*, periodic. • *Office Proficiency Assessment and Certification.* • *The Secretary Magazine*, 9/year. • *Vision*, periodic.

Standards/Certification Agencies

★1690★ Association of Independent Colleges and Schools (AICS)
1 Dupont Circle NW, Ste. 350
Washington, DC 20036
Ph: (202)659-2460

Sponsors an accrediting commission for postsecondary and collegiate institutions.

★1691★ National Association of Legal Secretaries (International) (NALS)
2250 E. 73rd St., Ste. 550
Tulsa, OK 74136
Ph: (918)493-3540 Fax: (918)493-5784

Sponsors legal secretarial training courses and awards those passing a two-day examination the rating of Certified Professional Legal Secretary.

★1692★ Professional Secretaries International (PSI)
10502 NW Ambassador Dr.
PO Box 20404
Kansas City, MO 64195-0404
Ph: (816)891-6600 Fax: (816)891-9118

Has established the PSI Research and Educational Foundation to develop research and educational projects for secretaries, management, and educators. Sponsors continuing education programs.

Test Guides

★1693★ *Career Examination Series: Administrative Secretary*
National Learning Corp.
212 Michael Dr.
Syosset, NY 11791
Ph: (516)921-8888 Fax: (516)921-8743
Fr: 800-645-6337

Jack Rudman. 1989. All examination guides in this series contain questions with answers.

★1694★ *Career Examination Series: College Secretarial Assistant A/B*
National Learning Corp.
212 Michael Dr.
Syosset, NY 11791
Ph: (516)921-8888 Fax: (516)921-8743
Fr: 800-645-6337

Jack Rudman. 1989. All examination guides in this series contain questions with answers.

★1695★ *Career Examination Series: Confidential Secretary*
National Learning Corp.
212 Michael Dr.
Syosset, NY 11791
Ph: (516)921-8888 Fax: (516)921-8743
Fr: 800-645-6337

Jack Rudman. 1989. All examination guides in this series contain questions with answers.

★1696★ *Career Examination Series: Drug Abuse Secretarial Aide*
National Learning Corp.
212 Michael Dr.
Syosset, NY 11791
Ph: (516)921-8888 Fax: (516)921-8743
Fr: 800-645-6337

Jack Rudman. 1989. All examination guides in this series contain questions with answers.

★1697★ *Career Examination Series: Executive Secretary*
National Learning Corp.
212 Michael Dr.
Syosset, NY 11791
Ph: (516)921-8888 Fax: (516)921-8743
Fr: 800-645-6337

Jack Rudman. 1989. All examination guides in this series contain questions with answers.

★1698★ *Career Examination Series: Legal Secretary*
National Learning Corp.
212 Michael Dr.
Syosset, NY 11791
Ph: (516)921-8888 Fax: (516)921-8743
Fr: 800-645-6337

Jack Rudman. Test guide including questions and answers for students or professionals in the field who seek advancement through examination.

★1699★ *Career Examination Series: Secretarial Assistant/Stenographer*
National Learning Corp.
212 Michael Dr.
Syosset, NY 11791
Ph: (516)921-8888 Fax: (516)921-8743
Fr: 800-645-6337

Jack Rudman. All examination guides in this series contain questions with answers.

★1700★ *Career Examination Series: Secretary*
National Learning Corp.
212 Michael Dr.
Syosset, NY 11791
Ph: (516)921-8888 Fax: (516)921-8743
Fr: 800-645-6337

Jack Rudman. All examination guides in this series contain questions with answers.

★1701★ *Career Examination Series: Secretary (Stenography) GS5*
National Learning Corp.
212 Michael Dr.
Syosset, NY 11791
Ph: (516)921-8888 Fax: (516)921-8743
Fr: 800-645-6337

Jack Rudman. All examination guides in this series contain questions with answers.

★1702★ *Career Examination Series: Stenographer-Secretary*
National Learning Corp.
212 Michael Dr.
Syosset, NY 11791
Ph: (516)921-8888 Fax: (516)921-8743
Fr: 800-645-6337

Jack Rudman. All examination guides in this series contain questions with answers.

★1703★ *Certified Professional Secretary (CPS) Examination Review*
Prentice Hall Press
Simon & Schuster Inc.
200 Old Tappan Rd.
Old Tappan, NJ 07675
Ph: 800-223-2348

Sheryl Lindsell and Stanley Alpert. First edition, 1987. Actual CPS questions are used in this prep guide.

Educational Directories and Programs

★1704★ *Directory of Accredited Institutions*
Association of Independent Colleges and Schools (AICS)
1 Dupont Circle NW, Ste. 350
Washington, DC 20036
Ph: (202)659-2460
Annual.

★1705★ *Industry Directory*
Association of Information Professionals
104 Wilmot Rd., Ste. 201
Deerfield, IL 60015-5195
Ph: (708)940-8800 Fax: (708)940-7218
Manufacturers of office automation equipment; word processing service bureaus; educational institutions offering office automation and associated software courses or curriculums; personnel agencies serving office automation personnel and users; analysts and consultants. Entries include: Name, address. Arrangement: Alphabetical within categories above.

Awards, Scholarships, Grants, and Fellowships

★1706★ International Secretary of the Year
Professional Secretaries International
10502 NW Ambassador Dr.
PO Box 20404
Kansas City, MO 64195-0404
Ph: (816)891-6600 Fax: (816)891-9118
To pay tribute to an outstanding member secretary and to encourage other secretaries to strive for professionalism. A bronze plaque is awarded annually. Established in 1949.

Basic Reference Guides and Handbooks

★1707★ *Ansley House Associates: The Executive Secretary - An Office Job Simulation*
South-Western Publishing, Co.
5101 Madison Rd.
Cincinnati, OH 45227
Ph: (513)271-8811
Harriet McIntosh. Second edition, 1985.

★1708★ *Basic Metric Style Manual for Secretaries*
Global Engineering Documents
2805 McGaw Ave.
PO Box 19539
Irvine, CA 92714
Ph: (714)261-1455 Fax: (714)261-7892
Fr: 800-854-7179
John Corbett, editor. 1976.

★1709★ *Canadian Secretary's Handbook: An on-the-job Guide for Office Professionals*
International Self-Counsel Press
1481 Charlotte Rd.
North Vancouver, BC, Canada V7J 1H1
Anne Morton. 1988. Part of Self-Counsel Reference Series.

★1710★ *Career Strategies for Secretaries: How to Get Where You Want to Be*
Contemporary Books, Inc.
180 N. Michigan Ave.
Chicago, IL 60601
Ph: (312)782-9181 Fax: (312)782-2157
Marie Kisiel. 1982.

★1711★ *Common Secretarial Mistakes & How to Avoid Them*
Prentice Hall
Rte. 9W
Englewood Cliffs, NJ 07632
Ph: (201)592-2000
Prentice-Hall Editorial Staff. 1986.

★1712★ *How to Start a Secretarial & Business Service*
Pilot Books
103 Cooper St.
Babylon, NY 11702
Ph: (516)422-2225
Mary Temple. 1989.

★1713★ *Instant Secretary's Handbook*
Career Publishing, Inc.
905 Allanson Dr.
Mundelein, IL 60060
Ph: (708)949-0011 Fax: (708)566-8550
Martha S. Luck. 1972. Part of Instant Series.

★1714★ *Making it Work: The Secretary - Boss Team*
Avatar Press
PO Box 77234
Atlanta, GA 30357
Ph: (404)892-8511
Charles E. Kozoll. 1974.

★1715★ *Manual for the Lawyer's Assistant*
National Association of Legal Secretaries (International) (NALS)
2250 E. 73rd St., Ste. 550
Tulsa, OK 74136
Ph: (918)493-3540 Fax: (918)493-5784

★1716★ *Math on the Job: Secretary/Clerk Typist*
National Center for Research in Vocational Education
Ohio State University
1900 Kenry Rd.
Columbus, OH 43210
Ph: (614)292-4353
1985.

★1717★ *New Secretary: How to Handle People As Well As You Handled Paper*
Facts on File
460 Park Ave. S.
New York, NY 10016-7382
Ph: (212)683-2244 Fax: 800-678-3633
Fr: 800-322-8755
Dianna Booher. 1986.

★1718★ *NOMDA Who's Who*
National Office Machine Dealers Association (NOMDA)
12411 Wornall Rd.
Kansas City, MO 64145
Ph: (816)941-3100 Fax: (816)941-2829
Brent Hoskins, Contact
Annual, August. Publication includes: List of 5,000 retailers and 500 manufacturers of typewriters, calculators, word processors, computers, dictation equipment, copying machines, and other office machines. Entries include: Company name, address, phone, names of executives; dealer listings include codes showing products handled. Arrangement: Dealers and manufacturers are listed both geographically and alphabetically.

★1719★ *Office Organization & Secretarial Procedures*
Trans-Atlantic Publications, Inc.
311 Bainbridge St.
Philadelphia, PA 19147
Ph: (215)925-5083 Fax: (215)925-1912
Helen Harding. 1988.

★1720★ *Personal Shorthand for the Executive Secretary: Syllabus*
National Book Company
PO Box 8795
Portland, OR 97207-8795
Ph: (503)228-6345
Piper. 1977.

★1721★ *Professional Excellence for Secretaries*
Crisp Publications, Inc.
95 1st St.
Los Altos, CA 94022
Ph: (415)949-4888 Fax: (415)949-1610
Marilyn Manning. 1988. Part of Fifty Minute Series.

★1722★ *Professional Secretary's Handbook*
Dartnell Corp.
4660 Ravenswood Ave.
Chicago, IL 60640
Ph: (312)561-4000 Fax: (312)561-3801
Fr: 800-621-5463
Cook. 1988.

★1723★ *Secretarial Administration & Management*
Prentice Hall
Rte. 9W
Englewood Cliffs, NJ 07632
Ph: (201)592-2000
Daniel R. Boyd. 1985.

★1724★ *The Secretarial Handbook on Planning & Organizing Work*
Executive Enterprises Publications Co., Inc.
22 W. 21st St.
New York, NY 10010-6904
Ph: (212)645-7880 Fax: (212)645-8689
Fr: 800-332-1105
1975.

★1725★ *Secretarial Office Procedures*
McGraw-Hill Publishing Co.
1221 Avenue of the Americas
New York, NY 10020
Ph: (212)512-2000
Dorothy E. Lee. Second edition, 1981.

★1726★ *Secretarial Practice*
Advent Books
141 E. 44th St., Ste. 511
New York, NY 10017
Ph: (212)697-0887

M. C. Kuchhal. Tenth edition, 1984.

★1727★ *Secretarial Practice: Syllabus*
National Book Co.
PO Box 8795
Portland, OR 97207-8795
Ph: (503)228-6345

Carl Salser. Second edition, 1977.

★1728★ *Secretarial Procedures for the Automated Office*
Prentice Hall
Rte. 9W
Englewood Cliffs, NJ 07632
Ph: (201)592-2000

Dalton E. McFarland. 1985.

★1729★ *Secretarial Procedures in the Electronic Office*
Trans-Atlantic Pubications, Inc.
311 Bainbridge St
Philadelphia, PA 19147
Ph: (215)925-5083 Fax: (215)925-1912

Desmond Evans. 1989.

★1730★ *The Secretarial Specialist*
P.A.R., Inc.
272 W. Exchange St.
Providence, RI 02903-3416
Ph: (401)331-0130

Alfred C. Pascale. 1968.

★1731★ *Secretary to Paralegal: A Career Manual & Guide*
Prentice Hall
Rte. 9W
Englewood Cliffs, NJ 07632
Ph: (201)592-2000

Lesley J. Prendergast. 1984.

★1732★ *The Secretary's Handbook*
Macmillan Publishing Co., Inc.
866 3rd Ave.
New York, NY 10022
Ph: (212)702-2000

Sarah A. Taintor. Tenth edition, 1988.

★1733★ *The Secretary's Handbook: A Manual for Office Personnel*
Academic Press, Inc.
1250 6th Ave.
San Diego, CA 92101
Ph: (619)699-6412

Fourth edition, 1986.

★1734★ *Secretary's Problem Solver: Word-for-Word Scripts for Coping with Difficult Situations*
Prentice Hall
Rte. 9W
Englewood Cliffs, NJ 07632
Ph: (201)592-2000

Charlotte A. Peterson. 1990.

★1735★ *The Secretary's Quick Reference Handbook*
Arco Pub.
201 W. 103rd St.
Indianapolis, IN 46290
Ph: 800-428-5331 Fax: 800-835-3202

Sheryl L. Lindsell-Roberts. 1992, third edition. Includes business letter styles, records management techniques, postal regulations, electronic mail, and desktop publishing.

★1736★ *Senior Secretarial Duties & Office Organization*
Trans-Atlantic Publications, Inc.
311 Bainbridge St.
Philadelphia, PA 19147
Ph: (215)925-5083 Fax: (215)925-1912

Evelyn Austin. Third edition, 1983.

★1737★ *The Successful Secretary's Handbook*
HarperCollins Publisher, Inc.
10 E. 53rd St.
New York, NY 10022
Ph: (212)207-7000

Esther R. Becker. 1984.

★1738★ *Technical Secretary: Terminology & Transcription*
McGraw-Hill Publishing Co.
1221 Avenue of the Americas
New York, NY 10020
Ph: (212)512-2000

Dorothy Adams. 1967. Part of Diamond Jubilee Series.

★1739★ *Webster's New World Secretarial Handbook*
Prentice Hall
Rte. 9W
Englewood Cliffs, NJ 07632
Ph: (201)592-2000

1989.

Periodicals

★1740★ *Career Legal Secretary*
National Association of Legal Secretaries (International) (NALS)
2250 E. 73rd St., Ste. 550
Tulsa, OK 74136
Ph: (918)493-3540 Fax: (918)493-5784

★1741★ *The Corporate Secretary*
American Society of Corporate Secretaries, Inc.
1270 Ave. of the Americas
New York, NY 10020
Ph: (212)765-2620 Fax: (212)765-8349
Michael E. Goodman

Bimonthly. Provides legal and legislative news involving corporate secretaries and their executive duties. Recurring features include columns titled SEC Update and Society Notes.

★1742★ *Docket*
National Association of Legal Secretaries (International) (NALS)
2250 E. 73rd St., Ste. 550
Tulsa, OK 74136
Ph: (918)493-3540 Fax: (918)493-5784

Bimonthly.

★1743★ *The Exec-U-tary*
National Association of Executive Secretaries
900 S. Washington St., No. G13
Falls Church, VA 22046-4020
Ph: (703)237-8616
Ruth Ludeman

Monthly. Provides information pertaining to the business and personal lives of executive secretaries. Recurring features include Association news.

★1744★ *From Nine to Five*
Dartnell Corporation
4660 Ravenswood
Chicago, IL 60640
Ph: (312)561-4000 Fax: (312)561-3801
Fr: 800-621-5463
Douglas Leland

Biweekly. Provides "tips, shortcuts, and helpful information for success in the office," particularly secretaries and office workers. Recurring features include columns titled titled Business Skills Clinic, Shortcuts, and The Coffee Break.

Meetings and Conventions

★1745★ International Convention
Professional Secretaries International (PSI)
10502 NW Ambassador Dr.
PO Box 20404
Kansas City, MO 64195-0404
Ph: (816)891-6600 Fax: (816)891-9118

Annual. **Dates and Locations:** 1996 Jul 21-24; Des Moines, IA • 1997 Jul 20-23; Buffalo, NY.

Other Sources of Information

★1746★ *Beyond Secretary*
Cambridge Career Products
PO Box 2153, Dept. CC15
Charleston, WV 25328-2153
Fr: 800-468-4227

1993. Describes ways to stay on top of new developments in organizations, getting through a crisis, solving problems, and tips to sharpen the professional image.

★1747★ "Secretary" in *Career Selector 2001*
Barron's Educational Series, Inc.
250 Wireless Blvd.
Hauppauge, NY 11788
Ph: (516)434-3311 Fax: (516)434-3723
Fr: 800-645-3476

James C. Gonyea. 1993.

★1748★ "Secretary/Office Administrator" in *100 Best Jobs for the 1990s & Beyond*
Dearborn Financial Publishing, Inc.
520 N. Dearborn St.
Chicago, IL 60610-4354
Ph: (312)836-4400 Fax: (312)836-1021
Fr: 800-621-9621

Carol Kleiman. 1992. Describes 100 jobs ranging from accountants to veterinarians. Each job profile includes such information as education, experience, and certification needed, salaries, and job search suggestions.

Stenographers and Court Reporters

Stenographers take dictation using shorthand or a stenotype machine and transcribe spoken communications into a written record. General stenographers take routine dictation in addition to performing other office tasks such as typing or filing. More experienced stenographers may sit in on staff meetings and record the proceedings. **Court reporters** record all statements at an official proceeding. Many other shorthand reporters work as freelance reporters who record out-of-court testimony for attorneys, proceedings of meetings and conventions, and other private activities. Still others record the proceedings in the U.S. Congress, in state and local governing bodies, and in government agencies at all levels. Transcribing-machine operators listen to recordings and transcribe what they hear into the proper format. Sometimes they are called dictating-machine transcribers or dictating-machine typists. Print shop stenographers take dictation and transcribe the dictated material to be used by addressing machines.

Salaries

The average salaries for stenographers are listed below. Salaries for stenographers vary by ability and are slightly higher for shorthand reporters than stenographic office workers.

Stenographers in private industry	$21,528/year
Inexperienced clerk-stenographers in the federal government	$12,531/year
Other clerk-stenographers in the federal government	$15,000/year

Employment Outlook

Growth rate until the year 2005: Decline.

Stenographers and Court Reporters

Career Guides

★1749★ ***Court Reporter***
Careers, Inc.
PO Box 135
Largo, FL 34649-0135
Ph: (813)584-7333

1992. Two-page occupational summary card describing duties, working conditions, personal qualifications, training, earnings and hours, employment outlook, places of employment, related careers and where to write for more information.

★1750★ **"Court Reporter" in *Occu-Facts: Information on 580 Careers in Outline Form***
Careers, Inc.
PO Box 135
Largo, FL 34649-0135
Ph: (813)584-7333

Biennial, 1995-96 edition. Each one-page occupational profile describes duties, working conditions, physical surroundings and demands, aptitudes, temperament, educational requirements, employment outlook, earnings, and places of employment.

★1751★ **"Court Reporter (Short Hand Reporter)" in *Career Planning in Criminal Justice* (pp. 62-63)**
Anderson Publishing Co.
PO Box 1576
Cincinnati, OH 45201
Ph: (513)421-4142 Fax: (513)562-8116
Fr: 800-582-7295

Robert C. DeLucia and Thomas J. Doyle. 1994. Surveys a wide range of career and employment opportunities in law enforcement, the courts, corrections, forensic science and private security. Contains career planning and job hunting advice. Profiles 77 criminal justice occupations describing job duties, work environments, and educational requirements.

★1752★ ***Court Reporters***
Chronicle Guidance Publications, Inc.
66 Aurora St.
PO Box 1190
Moravia, NY 13118-1190
Ph: (315)497-0330 Fax: (315)497-3359
Fr: 800-622-7284

1987. This career brief describes the nature of the work, working conditions, hours and earnings, education and training, licensure, certification, unions, personal qualifications, social and psychological factors, employment outlook, entry methods, advancement, and related occupations.

★1753★ **"Court Reporters: $40,000-$50,000 Recorders" in *Careers for Women Without College Degrees* (pp. 231-233)**
McGraw-Hill Publishing Co.
11 W. 19th St.
New York, NY 10011
Ph: (212)337-6010

Beatryce Nivens. 1988. Career planning and job hunting guide containing information on decision-making, skills assessment, and resumes for career changers. Profiles careers with the best occupational outlook. Describes the work, educational preparation, employment outlook, salaries, and required skills.

★1754★ **"Court Reporters" in *Career Discovery Encyclopedia* (Vol.2, pp. 70-71)**
J.G. Ferguson Publishing Co.
200 W. Madison St., Ste. 300
Chicago, IL 60606
Ph: (312)580-5480 Fax: (312)580-4948

E. Russell Primm, editor-in-chief. 1993. Contains two-page articles on 504 occupations. Each article describes job duties, earnings, and educational and training requirements.

★1755★ **"Court Reporters" in *Encyclopedia of Careers and Vocational Guidance* (Vol.2, pp. 408-410)**
J.G. Ferguson Publishing Co.
200 W. Madison St., Ste. 300
Chicago, IL 60606
Ph: (312)580-5480 Fax: (312)580-4948

William E. Hopke, editor-in-chief. Ninth edition, 1993. Four-volume set that profiles 500 occupations and describes job trends in 74 industries. Includes career description, educational requirements, history of the job, methods of entry, advancement, employment outlook, earnings, working conditions, social and psychological factors, and sources of additional information.

★1756★ **"Court Reporting" in *Career Connection II: A Guide to Technical Majors and Their Related Careers* (pp. 46-47)**
Jist Works, Inc.
720 N. Park Ave.
University Station
Indianapolis, IN 46202-3431
Ph: (317)264-3720 Fax: (317)264-3709

Fred A. Rowe. 1994. Contains technical majors, such as automotive technology. Describes the major and the job. Lists high school and postsecondary school courses. Includes occupations related to the major, employment outlook, and starting salary.

★1757★ ***Medical Transcriptionist***
Vocational Biographies, Inc.
PO Box 31
Sauk Centre, MN 56378-0031
Ph: (612)352-6516 Fax: (612)352-5546
Fr: 800-255-0752

1991. This pamphlet profiles a person working in the job. Includes information about job duties, working conditions, places of employment, educational preparation, labor market outlook, and salaries.

★1758★ "Medical Transcriptionist" in *150 Careers in the Health Care Field*
Reed Reference Publishing
121 Chanlon Rd.
PO Box 31
New Providence, NJ 07974
Fax: (908)665-6688 Fr: 800-521-8110

Stanley Alperin. Third edition, 1993. Each occupational profile covers job functions and responsibilities, work locations, training requirements, certification, and salaries. Lists community colleges, universities, vocational-technical schools, and other educational institutions that provide accredited training programs.

★1759★ "Medical Transcriptionist" in *Occu-Facts: Information on 580 Careers in Outline Form*
Careers, Inc.
PO Box 135
Largo, FL 34649-0135
Ph: (813)584-7333

Biennial, 1995-96 edition. Each one-page occupational profile describes duties, working conditions, physical surroundings and demands, aptitudes, temperament, educational requirements, employment outlook, earnings, and places of employment.

★1760★ "Medical Transcriptionist" in *Opportunities in Health and Medical Careers* (p. 122)
National Textbook Co. (NTC)
VGM Career Books
4255 W. Touhy Ave.
Lincolnwood, IL 60646-1975
Ph: (708)679-5500 Fax: (708)679-2494
Fr: 800-323-4900

Leo D'Orazio and I. Donald Snook. 1991. Provides an overview of the health care industry with future projections. Describes a wide variety of healthcare jobs covering the nature of the work, educational requirements, employment outlook and salaries. Offers job hunting advice.

★1761★ *Secretaries and Stenographers*
Chronicle Guidance Publications, Inc.
66 Aurora St.
PO Box 1190
Moravia, NY 13118-1190
Ph: (315)497-0330 Fax: (315)497-3359
Fr: 800-622-7284

1991. This career brief describes the nature of the work, working conditions, hours and earnings, education and training, licensure, certification, unions, personal qualifications, social and psychological factors, employment outlook, entry methods, advancement, and related occupations.

★1762★ "Secretaries and Stenographers" in *Jobs! What They Are—Where They Are—What They Pay* (pp. 252)
Simon & Schuster, Inc.
Simon & Schuster Bldg.
1230 Avenue of the Americas
New York, NY 10020
Ph: (212)698-7000

Robert O. Snelling and Anne M. Snelling. Revised edition, 1992. Profiles 241 occupations, describing duties and responsibilities, educational preparation, earnings, employment opportunities, training, and qualifications.

★1763★ "Shorthand Reporter" in *Career Information Center* (Vol.11)
Simon and Schuster
200 Old Tappan Rd.
Old Tappan, NJ 07675
Fax: 800-445-6991 Fr: 800-223-2348

Richard Lidz and Dale Anderson, editorial directors. Fifth edition, 1993. For 600 occupations, describes job duties, entry-level requirements, education and training needed, advancement possibilities, employment outlook, earnings and benefits. The set is divided into 12 volumes. Each volume includes jobs related under a broad career field. Volume 13 is the index.

★1764★ *Stenographer*
Vocational Biographies, Inc.
PO Box 31
Sauk Centre, MN 56378-0031
Ph: (612)352-6516 Fax: (612)352-5546
Fr: 800-255-0752

1990. This pamphlet profiles a person working in the job. Includes information about job duties, working conditions, places of employment, educational preparation, labor market outlook, and salaries.

★1765★ "Stenographer/Court Reporter" in *Jobs Rated Almanac*
World Almanac
1 International Blvd., Ste. 444
Mahwah, NJ 07495
Ph: (201)529-6900 Fax: (201)529-6901

Les Krantz. Second edition, 1992. Ranks 250 jobs by environment, salary, outlooks, physical demands, stress, security, travel opportunities, and extra perks. Includes jobs the editor feels are the most common, most interesting, and the most rapidly growing.

★1766★ "Stenographer and Transcriber" in *Career Information Center* (Vol.1)
Simon and Schuster
200 Old Tappan Rd.
Old Tappan, NJ 07675
Fax: 800-445-6991 Fr: 800-223-2348

Richard Lidz and Dale Anderson, editorial directors. Fifth edition, 1993. For 600 occupations, describes job duties, entry-level requirements, education and training needed, advancement possibilities, employment outlook, earnings and benefits. The set is divided into 12 volumes. Each volume includes jobs related under a broad career field. Volume 13 is the index.

★1767★ "Stenographers" in *Career Discovery Encyclopedia* (Vol.6, pp. 62-63)
J.G. Ferguson Publishing Co.
200 W. Madison St., Ste. 300
Chicago, IL 60606
Ph: (312)580-5480 Fax: (312)580-4948

E. Russell Primm, editor-in-chief. 1993. Contains two-page articles on 504 occupations. Each article describes job duties, earnings, and educational and training requirements.

★1768★ *"Stenographers and Court Reporters" in Occupational Outlook Handbook*
U.S. Government Printing Office
Superintendent of Documents
Washington, DC 20402
Ph: (202)512-1800 Fax: (202)512-2250

Biennial; latest edition, 1994-95. Encyclopedia of careers describing more than 250 occupations and comprising about 85 percent of all jobs in the economy. Occupations that require lengthy education or training are given the most attention. For each occupation, the handbook describes job duties, working conditions, training, educational preparation, personal qualities, advancement possibilities, job outlook, earnings, and sources of additional information.

★1769★ "Stenographers" in *Encyclopedia of Careers and Vocational Guidance* (Vol.4, pp. 436-438)
J.G. Ferguson Publishing Co.
200 W. Madison St., Ste. 300
Chicago, IL 60606
Ph: (312)580-5480 Fax: (312)580-4948

William E. Hopke, editor-in-chief. Ninth edition, 1993. Four-volume set that profiles 500 occupations and describes job trends in 74 industries. Includes career description, educational requirements, history of the job, methods of entry, advancement, employment outlook, earnings, working conditions, social and psychological factors, and sources of additional information.

★1770★ *A Study of Some Aspects of Satisfaction in the Vocation of Stenography*
AMS Press, Inc.
56 E. 13th St.
New York, NY 10003
Ph: (212)777-4700 Fax: (212)995-5413

Margaret S. Quayle. Part of Columbia University Teachers College. Contributions to Education Series.

★1771★ *Transcriber*
Vocational Biographies, Inc.
PO Box 31
Sauk Centre, MN 56378-0031
Ph: (612)352-6516 Fax: (612)352-5546
Fr: 800-255-0752

1991. This pamphlet profiles a person working in the job. Includes information about job duties, working conditions, places of employment, educational preparation, labor market outlook, and salaries.

★1772★ *Video Career Library - Clerical & Administrative Support*
Careers, Inc.
PO Box 135
Largo, FL 34649-0135
Ph: (813)584-7333

Videocassette. 1990. 26 mins. Part of the Video Career Library covering 165 occupations. Shows actual workers on the job. Includes secretaries, cashiers, receptionists, bookkeepers and audit clerks, telephone operators, postal clerks/carriers/supervisors, insurance investigators, bank tellers, data entry keyers, and court reporters.

★1773★ *What Combines Communications, Law, Technology, Finance, Medicine, Engineering . . .*
National Court Reporters Association
8224 Old Courthouse Rd.
Vienna, VA 22182-3808
Ph: (703)556-6272

This six-panel brochure describes qualifications, work, future outlook, places of employment, and educational preparation of court reporters.

Associations

★1774★ Association of Independent Colleges and Schools
1 Dupont Circle NW, Ste. 350
Washington, DC 20036
Ph: (202)659-2460 Fax: (202)659-2254

Members: Independent business schools and junior and senior colleges of business. **Purpose:** Sponsors an accrediting commission for postsecondary and collegiate institutions. **Publications:** *AICS Compass*, monthly. • *Capital Comments*, bimonthly. • *Directory of Accredited Institutions*, annual.

★1775★ National Court Reporters Association (NCRA)
8224 Old Courthouse Rd.
Vienna, VA 22182
Ph: (703)556-6272 Fax: (703)556-6291

Members: Independent state, regional, and local associations. Verbatim shorthand reporters who work as official reporters for courts and government agencies and as freelance reporters for independent contractors, retired reporters, teachers of shorthand reporting, and school officials; student shorthand reporters. **Purpose:** Conducts research; compiles statistics; offers placement service and Registered Professional Reporter Certification program. **Publications:** *Journal of Court Reporting*, 10/year. • *National Court Reporters Association—Membership Directory and Registry of Professional Reporters*, annual. • *Professional Education Series.*

★1776★ National Shorthand Reporters Association (NSRA)
118 Park St. SE
Vienna, VA 22180
Ph: (703)281-4677

Standards/Certification Agencies

★1777★ Association of Independent Colleges and Schools (AICS)
1 Dupont Circle NW, Ste. 350
Washington, DC 20036
Ph: (202)659-2460

Sponsors an accrediting commission for postsecondary and collegiate institutions.

★1778★ National Court Reporters Association (NCRA)
8224 Old Courthouse Rd.
Vienna, VA 22182
Ph: (703)556-6272 Fax: (703)556-6291

Conducts research; compiles statistics; offers placement service and Registered Professional Reporter Certification program.

★1779★ National Shorthand Reporters Association (NSRA)
118 Park St. SE
Vienna, VA 22180
Ph: (703)281-4677

Offers Registered Professional Reporter Certification program.

Test Guides

★1780★ *Career Examination Series: Certified Shorthand Reporter*
National Learning Corp.
212 Michael Dr.
Syosset, NY 11791
Ph: (516)921-8888 Fax: (516)921-8743
Fr: 800-645-6337

Jack Rudman. All examination guides in this series contain questions with answers.

★1781★ *Career Examination Series: Chief Law Stenographer*
National Learning Corp.
212 Michael Dr.
Syosset, NY 11791
Ph: (516)921-8888 Fax: (516)921-8743
Fr: 800-645-6337

Jack Rudman. All examination guides in this series contain questions with answers.

★1782★ *Career Examination Series: Chief of Stenographic Services*
National Learning Corp.
212 Michael Dr.
Syosset, NY 11791
Ph: (516)921-8888 Fax: (516)921-8743
Fr: 800-645-6337

Jack Rudman. All examination guides in this series contain questions with answers.

★1783★ *Career Examination Series: Clerk-Stenographer*
National Learning Corp.
212 Michael Dr.
Syosset, NY 11791
Ph: (516)921-8888 Fax: (516)921-8743
Fr: 800-645-6337

Jack Rudman. 1989. All examination guides in this series contain questions with answers.

★1784★ *Career Examination Series: Clerk-Stenographer (I-IV)*
National Learning Corp.
212 Michael Dr.
Syosset, NY 11791
Ph: (516)921-8888 Fax: (516)921-8743
Fr: 800-645-6337

Jack Rudman. 1989. All examination guides in this series contain questions with answers.

★1785★ *Career Examination Series: Court Reporter*
National Learning Corp.
212 Michael Dr.
Syosset, NY 11791
Ph: (516)921-8888 Fax: (516)921-8743
Fr: 800-645-6337

Jack Rudman. Test guide including questions and answers for students or professionals in the field who seek advancement through examination.

★1786★ *Career Examination Series: Law Stenographer*
National Learning Corp.
212 Michael Dr.
Syosset, NY 11791
Ph: (516)921-8888 Fax: (516)921-8743
Fr: 800-645-6337

Jack Rudman. 1989. Part of Career Examinations Series.

★1787★ *Career Examination Series: Legal Stenographer*
National Learning Corp.
212 Michael Dr.
Syosset, NY 11791
Ph: (516)921-8888 Fax: (516)921-8743
Fr: 800-645-6337

Jack Rudman. 1989. All examination guides in this series contain questions with answers.

★1788★ *Career Examination Series: Principal Clerk-Stenographer*
National Learning Corp.
212 Michael Dr.
Syosset, NY 11791
Ph: (516)921-8888 Fax: (516)921-8743
Fr: 800-645-6337

Jack Rudman. All examination guides in this series contain questions with answers.

★1789★ *Career Examination Series: Principal Office Stenographer*
National Learning Corp.
212 Michael Dr.
Syosset, NY 11791
Ph: (516)921-8888 Fax: (516)921-8743
Fr: 800-645-6337

Jack Rudman. All examination guides in this series contain questions with answers.

★1790★ *Career Examination Series: Principal Stenographer*
National Learning Corp.
212 Michael Dr.
Syosset, NY 11791
Ph: (516)921-8888 Fax: (516)921-8743
Fr: 800-645-6337

Jack Rudman. All examination guides in this series contain questions with answers.

★1791★ *Career Examination Series: Principal Stenographer (Law)*
National Learning Corp.
212 Michael Dr.
Syosset, NY 11791
Ph: (516)921-8888 Fax: (516)921-8743
Fr: 800-645-6337

Jack Rudman. All examination guides in this series contain questions with answers.

★1792★ *Career Examination Series: Senior Clerk-Stenographer*
National Learning Corp.
212 Michael Dr.
Syosset, NY 11791
Ph: (516)921-8888 Fax: (516)921-8743
Fr: 800-645-6337

Jack Rudman. 1989. All examination guides in this series contain questions with answers.

★1793★ *Career Examination Series: Senior Court Reporter*
National Learning Corp.
212 Michael Dr.
Syosset, NY 11791
Ph: (516)921-8888 Fax: (516)921-8743
Fr: 800-645-6337

Jack Rudman. Test guide including questions and answers for students or professionals in the field who seek advancement through examination.

★1794★ *Career Examination Series: Senior Legal Stenographer*
National Learning Corp.
212 Michael Dr.
Syosset, NY 11791
Ph: (516)921-8888 Fax: (516)921-8743
Fr: 800-645-6337

Jack Rudman. All examination guides in this series contain questions with answers.

★1795★ *Career Examination Series: Senior Office Stenographer*
National Learning Corp.
212 Michael Dr.
Syosset, NY 11791
Ph: (516)921-8888 Fax: (516)921-8743
Fr: 800-645-6337

Jack Rudman. All examination guides in this series contain questions with answers.

★1796★ *Career Examination Series: Senior Stenographer*
National Learning Corp.
212 Michael Dr.
Syosset, NY 11791
Ph: (516)921-8888 Fax: (516)921-8743
Fr: 800-645-6337

Jack Rudman. All examination guides in this series contain questions with answers.

★1797★ *Career Examination Series: Shorthand Reporter*
National Learning Corp.
212 Michael Dr.
Syosset, NY 11791
Ph: (516)921-8888 Fax: (516)921-8743
Fr: 800-645-6337

Jack Rudman. All examination guides in this series contain questions with answers.

★1798★ *Career Examination Series: Stenographer*
National Learning Corp.
212 Michael Dr.
Syosset, NY 11791
Ph: (516)921-8888 Fax: (516)921-8743
Fr: 800-645-6337

Jack Rudman. All examination guides in this series contain questions with answers.

★1799★ *Career Examination Series: Stenographer (Law)*
National Learning Corp.
212 Michael Dr.
Syosset, NY 11791
Ph: (516)921-8888 Fax: (516)921-8743
Fr: 800-645-6337

Jack Rudman. All examination guides in this series contain questions with answers.

★1800★ *Career Examination Series: Stenographer-Secretary*
National Learning Corp.
212 Michael Dr.
Syosset, NY 11791
Ph: (516)921-8888 Fax: (516)921-8743
Fr: 800-645-6337

Jack Rudman. All examination guides in this series contain questions with answers.

★1801★ *Career Examination Series: Stenographer-Typist*
National Learning Corp.
212 Michael Dr.
Syosset, NY 11791
Ph: (516)921-8888 Fax: (516)921-8743
Fr: 800-645-6337

Jack Rudman. All examination guides in this series contain questions with answers.

★1802★ *Career Examination Series: Stenographic/Secretarial Associate*
National Learning Corp.
212 Michael Dr.
Syosset, NY 11791
Ph: (516)921-8888 Fax: (516)921-8743
Fr: 800-645-6337

Jack Rudman. All examination guides in this series contain questions with answers.

★1803★ *Career Examination Series: Stenographic Secretary*
National Learning Corp.
212 Michael Dr.
Syosset, NY 11791
Ph: (516)921-8888 Fax: (516)921-8743
Fr: 800-645-6337

Jack Rudman. All examination guides in this series contain questions with answers.

★1804★ *Career Examination Series: Stenographic Specialist*
National Learning Corp.
212 Michael Dr.
Syosset, NY 11791
Ph: (516)921-8888 Fax: (516)921-8743
Fr: 800-645-6337

Jack Rudman. All examination guides in this series contain questions with answers.

★1805★ *Career Examination Series: Supervising Legal Stenographer*
National Learning Corp.
212 Michael Dr.
Syosset, NY 11791
Ph: (516)921-8888 Fax: (516)921-8743
Fr: 800-645-6337

Jack Rudman. 1989. All examination guides in this series contain questions with answers.

★1806★ *Career Examination Series: Supervising Stenographer*
National Learning Corp.
212 Michael Dr.
Syosset, NY 11791
Ph: (516)921-8888 Fax: (516)921-8743
Fr: 800-645-6337

Jack Rudman. 1989. All examination guides in this series contain questions with answers.

★1807★ *Career Examination Series: Transcribing Typist*
National Learning Corp.
212 Michael Dr.
Syosset, NY 11791
Ph: (516)921-8888 Fax: (516)921-8743
Fr: 800-645-6337

Jack Rudman. 1989. All examination guides in this series contain questions with answers.

★1808★ *Court Officer, Senior Court Officer, Court Clerk*
Arco Pub.
201 W. 103rd St.
Indianapolis, IN 46290
Ph: 800-428-5331 Fax: 800-835-3202

E.P. Steinberg and William Goffen. 1989. Provides four sample exams with explanations.

★1809★ *Federal Clerk - Steno - Typist*
Prentice Hall Press
Simon & Schuster Inc.
200 Old Tappan Rd.
Old Tappan, NJ 07675
Ph: 800-223-2348

Hy Hammer and John Czukor. Sixth edition, 1988. Coverage includes Federal entry-level clerical positions, including clerk, clerk typist, stenographer, transcriber, office machines operator, and office assistant.

★1810★ *Office Aide*
Prentice Hall Press
Simon & Schuster Inc.
200 Old Tappan Rd.
Old Tappan, NJ 07675
Ph: 800-223-2348

Hy Hammer. Second edition, 1985. Contains seven sample exams for the following entry-level civil service positions: clerk, typist, stenographer, receptionist, office machine operator, telephone operator.

★1811★ *Practice for Clerical, Typing and Stenographic Tests*
Prentice Hall Press
Simon & Schuster Inc.
200 Old Tappan Rd.
Old Tappan, NJ 07675
Ph: 800-223-2348

Maryhelen H. Paulick Hoffman. Seventh edition, 1988. Provide preparation for all qualifying tests given by local, state, and federal agencies for all types of clerical positions.

★1812★ *Practice and Drill for the Clerk, Typist, and Stenographer Examinations*
National Learning Corp.
212 Michael Dr.
Syosset, NY 11791
Ph: (516)921-8888 Fax: (516)921-8743
Fr: 800-645-6337

Jack Rudman. Part of the General Aptitude and Abilities Series. Books in this series provide functional, intensive test practice and drill in the basic skills and areas common to many examinations, as well as general aptitude or achievement necessary for entrance into many occupations or positions.

★1813★ *Principal Clerk/Principal Stenographer*
Prentice Hall Press
Simon & Schuster Inc.
200 Old Tappan Rd.
Old Tappan, NJ 07675
Ph: 800-223-2348

Hy Hammer. Third edition, 1983. Contains information to prepare for federal, state, and municipal positions, including five sample exams.

★1814★ *Senior Clerical Series*
Prentice Hall Press
Simon & Schuster Inc.
200 Old Tappan Rd.
Old Tappan, NJ 07675
Ph: 800-223-2348

Hy Hammer. Fourth edition, 1983. Complete test preparation for the following senior grade positions: clerk, typist, stenographer, account clerk, file clerk, statistics clerk, stenographer (law), mail and supply clerk, and stores clerk.

Educational Directories and Programs

★1815★ *Directory of Accredited Institutions*
Association of Independent Colleges and Schools (AICS)
1 Dupont Circle NW, Ste. 350
Washington, DC 20036
Ph: (202)659-2460

Annual.

★1816★ *NSRA List of Approved Court Reporter Education Programs*
National Shorthand Reporters Association
118 Park St., SE
Vienna, VA 22180
Ph: (703)281-4677

1990. State-by-state listing of schools meeting minimum standards established by the National Shorthand Reporters Association. Includes address and phone number.

Awards, Scholarships, Grants, and Fellowships

★1817★ Fellow of the Academy of Professional Reporters
National Court Reporters Association
8224 Old Courthouse Rd.
Vienna, VA 22182-3808
Ph: (703)556-6272 Fax: (703)556-6291

To recognize outstanding and extraordinary qualifications and experience in the field of court reporting. Professional members who have been in the active practice of court reporting for ten years and who have attained distinction as measured by performance are eligible. A certificate and pin are awarded. Established in 1975.

Basic Reference Guides and Handbooks

★1818★ *Professional Education Series*
National Court Reporters Association (NCRA)
8224 Old Courthouse Rd.
Vienna, VA 22180
Ph: (703)556-6272 Fax: (703)556-6291

Periodicals

★1819★ *From Nine to Five*
Dartnell Corporation
4660 Ravenswood
Chicago, IL 60640
Ph: (312)561-4000 Fax: (312)561-3801
Fr: 800-621-5463
Douglas Leland

Biweekly. Provides "tips, shortcuts, and helpful information for success in the office," particularly secretaries and office workers. Recurring features include columns titled titled Business Skills Clinic, Shortcuts, and The Coffee Break.

★1820★ *Journal of Court Reporting*
National Court Reporters Association (NCRA)
8224 Old Courthouse Rd.
Vienna, VA 22182
Ph: (703)556-6272 Fax: (703)556-6291

10/year. For court and freelance shorthand reporters who specialize in hearings, depositions, statements, conferences, and other fields.

★1821★ *National Court Reporters Association—Membership Directory and Registry of Professional Reporters*
National Court Reporters Association (NCRA)
8224 Old Courthouse Rd.
Vienna, VA 22182
Ph: (703)556-6272 Fax: (703)556-6291

Annual. Geographically and alphabetically arranged; lists international shorthand reporters.

Other Sources of Information

★1822★ "Court Reporter" in *100 Best Jobs for the 1990s & Beyond*
Dearborn Financial Publishing, Inc.
520 N. Dearborn St.
Chicago, IL 60610-4354
Ph: (312)836-4400 Fax: (312)836-1021
Fr: 800-621-9621

Carol Kleiman. 1992. Describes 100 jobs ranging from accountants to veterinarians. Each job profile includes such information as education, experience, and certification needed, salaries, and job search suggestions.

Teachers Aides

Teacher aides also called **paraeducators**, assist teachers in a variety of ways to allow them more time for teaching. They help supervise students, record grades, and prepare teaching materials. In some schools, teacher aides perform clerical tasks, while in other districts, they may help instruct students under the guidance of teachers. Many teacher aides work part time during the school year and are concentrated primarily in the lower grades.

Salaries

The average earnings for teacher aides is $8.31/hour.

Employment Outlook

Growth rate until the year 2005: Much faster than average.

Teachers Aides

Career Guides

★1823★ "Early Childhood Center Teacher or Aide" in *Exploring Careers in Child Care Services* (pp. 9-21)
Rosen Publishing Group
29 E. 21st St.
New York, NY 10010
Ph: (212)777-3017 Fax: (212)777-0277
Fr: 800-237-9932

Jean Ispa, Elizabeth Vemer, and Janis Logan. Revised edition, 1990. Covers occupations working with children including those requiring no education and training to those that require advanced training; from babysitting to program director. Describes the work and a typical work day, employment outlook, advantages and disadvantages, and personal characteristics needed for success in the field. Offers job hunting advice.

★1824★ *Teacher Aide*
Careers, Inc.
PO Box 135
Largo, FL 34649-0135
Ph: (813)584-7333

1991. Two-page occupational summary card describing duties, working conditions, personal qualifications, training, earnings and hours, employment outlook, places of employment, related careers and where to write for more information.

★1825★ "Teacher Aide" in *Occu-Facts: Information on 580 Careers in Outline Form*
Careers, Inc.
PO Box 135
Largo, FL 34649-0135
Ph: (813)584-7333

Biennial, 1995-96 edition. Each one-page occupational profile describes duties, working conditions, physical surroundings and demands, aptitudes, temperament, educational requirements, employment outlook, earnings, and places of employment.

★1826★ "Teacher Aides" in *America's 50 Fastest Growing Jobs* (pp. 110)
JIST Works, Inc.
720 N. Park Ave.
Indianapolis, IN 46202-3431
Ph: (317)264-3720 Fax: (317)264-3709
Fr: 800-648-5478

Michael J. Farr, compiler. 1994. Describes the 50 fastest growing jobs within major career clusters such as technicians, and marketing and sales. Each job profile explains the nature of the work, skills and abilities required, employment outlook, average earnings, related occupations, education and training requirements, and employment opportunities. Also contains career planning information and job search tips.

★1827★ "Teacher Aides" in *Career Discovery Encyclopedia* (Vol.6, pp. 92-93)
J.G. Ferguson Publishing Co.
200 W. Madison St., Ste. 300
Chicago, IL 60606
Ph: (312)580-5480 Fax: (312)580-4948

E. Russell Primm, editor-in-chief. 1993. Contains two-page articles on 504 occupations. Each article describes job duties, earnings, and educational and training requirements.

★1828★ "Teacher Aides" in *Encyclopedia of Careers and Vocational Guidance* (Vol.4, pp. 490-492)
J.G. Ferguson Publishing Co.
200 W. Madison St., Ste. 300
Chicago, IL 60606
Ph: (312)580-5480 Fax: (312)580-4948

William E. Hopke, editor-in-chief. Ninth edition, 1993. Four-volume set that profiles 500 occupations and describes job trends in 74 industries. Includes career description, educational requirements, history of the job, methods of entry, advancement, employment outlook, earnings, working conditions, social and psychological factors, and sources of additional information.

★1829★ "Teacher Aides" in *Jobs! What They Are—Where They Are—What They Pay* (pp. 107)
Simon & Schuster, Inc.
Simon & Schuster Bldg.
1230 Avenue of the Americas
New York, NY 10020
Ph: (212)698-7000

Robert O. Snelling and Anne M. Snelling. Revised edition, 1992. Profiles 241 occupations, describing duties and responsibilities, educational preparation, earnings, employment opportunities, training, and qualifications.

★1830★ "Teacher Aides" in *Occupational Outlook Handbook*
U.S. Government Printing Office
Superintendent of Documents
Washington, DC 20402
Ph: (202)512-1800 Fax: (202)512-2250

Biennial; latest edition, 1994-95. Encyclopedia of careers describing more than 250 occupations and comprising about 85 percent of all jobs in the economy. Occupations that require lengthy education or training are given the most attention. For each occupation, the handbook describes job duties, working conditions, training, educational preparation, personal qualities, advancement possibilities, job outlook, earnings, and sources of additional information.

★1831★ "Teacher Aides" in *Opportunities in Child Care Careers* (pp. 58-72)
National Textbook Co. (NTC)
VGM Career Books
4255 W. Touhy Ave.
Lincolnwood, IL 60646-1975
Ph: (708)679-5500 Fax: (708)679-2494
Fr: 800-323-4900

Renee Wittenberg. 1995. Surveys job opportunities related to child care in child development, child life, health services, and psychology. Covers personal qualifications, training programs, job outlook, and salaries. Offers job hunting advice.

★1832★ *Teacher's Aide*
Vocational Biographies, Inc.
PO Box 31
Sauk Centre, MN 56378-0031
Ph: (612)352-6516 Fax: (612)352-5546
Fr: 800-255-0752

1992. Four-page pamphlet containing a personal narrative about a worker's job, work likes and dislikes, career path from high school to the present. Education and training, the rewards and frustrations, and the effects of the job on the rest of the worker's life. The data file portion of this pamphlet gives a concise occupational summary, including work descriptions, working conditions, places of employment, personal characteristics, education and training, job outlook, and salary range.

★1833★ "Teacher's Aide" in *Career Information Center* (Vol.11)
Simon and Schuster
200 Old Tappan Rd.
Old Tappan, NJ 07675
Fax: 800-445-6991 Fr: 800-223-2348

Richard Lidz and Dale Anderson, editorial directors. Fifth edition, 1993. For 600 occupations, describes job duties, entry-level requirements, education and training needed, advancement possibilities, employment outlook, earnings and benefits. The set is divided into 12 volumes. Each volume includes jobs related under a broad career field. Volume 13 is the index.

★1834★ "Teacher's Aide" in *Jobs Rated Almanac*
World Almanac
1 International Blvd., Ste. 444
Mahwah, NJ 07495
Ph: (201)529-6900 Fax: (201)529-6901

Les Krantz. Second edition, 1992. Ranks 250 jobs by environment, salary, outlooks, physical demands, stress, security, travel opportunities, and extra perks. Includes jobs the editor feels are the most common, most interesting, and the most rapidly growing.

★1835★ "Teachers Aides and School Bus Drivers" in *American Almanac of Jobs and Salaries* (pp. 110)
Avon Books
1350 Avenue of the Americas
New York, NY 10019
Ph: (212)261-6800 Fr: 800-238-0658

John Wright, editor. Revised and updated, 1994-95. A comprehensive guide to the wages of hundreds of occupations in a wide variety of industries and organizations.

★1836★ *Teachers Assistants*
Chronicle Guidance Publications, Inc.
66 Aurora St.
PO Box 1190
Moravia, NY 13118-1190
Ph: (315)497-0330 Fax: (315)497-3359
Fr: 800-622-7284

1993. This career brief describes the nature of the work, working conditions, hours and earnings, education and training, licensure, certification, unions, personal qualifications, social and psychological factors, employment outlook, entry methods, advancement, and related occupations.

★1837★ *Video Career Library - Education*
Careers, Inc.
PO Box 135
Largo, FL 34649-0135
Ph: (813)584-7333

Videocassette. 1990. 26 minutes. Part of the Video Career Library series covering 165 occupations. Shows actual workers on the job. Includes teachers' aides.

Associations

★1838★ American Federation of Teachers (AFT)
555 New Jersey Ave. NW
Washington, DC 20001
Ph: (202)879-4400 Fr: 800-238-1133

Members: AFL-CIO. Works with teachers and other educational employees at the state and local level in organizing, collective bargaining, research, educational issues, and public relations. **Purpose:** Conducts research in areas such as educational reform, bilingual education, teacher certification, and evaluation and national assessments and standards. Represents members' concerns through legislative action; offers technical assistance. Seeks to serve professionals with concerns similar to those of teachers, including state employees, healthcare workers, and paraprofessionals. **Publications:** *AFT Action: A Newsletter for AFT Leaders*, weekly. • *American Educator*, quarterly. • *American Teacher*, 8/year. • *Healthwire*, 10/year. • *On Campus*, 9/year. • *Public Sevice Reporter*, 9/year.

Test Guides

★1839★ *Career Examination Series: Assistant Teacher*
National Learning Corp.
212 Michael Dr.
Syosset, NY 11791
Ph: (516)921-8888 Fax: (516)921-8743
Fr: 800-645-6337

Jack Rudman. 1989. All examination guides in this series contain questions with answers.

★1840★ *Career Examination Series: Teaching Assistant*
National Learning Corp.
212 Michael Dr.
Syosset, NY 11791
Ph: (516)921-8888 Fax: (516)921-8743
Fr: 800-645-6337

Jack Rudman. All examination guides in this series contain questions with answers.

Basic Reference Guides and Handbooks

★1841★ *A Handbook of Effective Techniques for Teacher Aides*
Charles C. Thomas, Publisher
2600 S. 1st St.
Springfield, IL 62794-9265
Ph: (217)789-8980 Fax: (217)789-9130

Dick B. Clough. 1978.

★1842★ *Handbook for Teacher Aides*
Pendell Publishing Co.
PO Box 2066
Midland, MI 48640
Ph: (517)496-3337

Howard Brighton. 1972.

★1843★ *The Teacher Aide in the Instructional Team*
McGraw-Hill Publishing Co.
1221 Avenue of the Americas
New York, NY 10020
Ph: (212)512-2000

Don A. Welty. 1976.

Periodicals

★1844★ *AFT Action: A Newsletter for AFT Leaders*
American Federation of Teachers (AFT)
555 New Jersey Ave. NW
Washington, DC 20001
Ph: (202)879-4400 Fr: 800-238-1133

Weekly.

★1845★ *American Educator*
American Federation of Teachers (AFT)
555 New Jersey Ave. NW
Washington, DC 20001
Ph: (202)879-4400 Fr: 800-238-1133

Quarterly.

★1846★ *American Teacher*
American Federation of Teachers (AFT)
555 New Jersey Ave. NW
Washington, DC 20001
Ph: (202)879-4400 Fr: 800-238-1133

8/year. Tabloid covering union news; includes conference report.

★1847★ *ATEA Journal*
American Technical Education Association
North Dakota State College of Science
Wahpeton, ND 58076
Ph: (701)671-2240 Fax: (701)671-2260
Betty Krump

Quarterly. Reports on meetings, conferences, and conventions; equipment and teaching aids; news of members in the field of technical education; and reviews of books, pamphlets, and magazine articles. Recurring features include news from industry, U.S. Government publications, and book reviews.

★1848★ ***Healthwire***
American Federation of Teachers (AFT)
555 New Jersey Ave. NW
Washington, DC 20001
Ph: (202)879-4400 Fr: 800-238-1133

10/year. For AFT members involved in health care.

★1849★ ***On Campus***
American Federation of Teachers (AFT)
555 New Jersey Ave. NW
Washington, DC 20001
Ph: (202)879-4400 Fr: 800-238-1133

9/year.

★1850★ ***Public Sevice Reporter***
American Federation of Teachers (AFT)
555 New Jersey Ave. NW
Washington, DC 20001
Ph: (202)879-4400 Fr: 800-238-1133

9/year.

Telephone Operators

Telephone operators help customers with calls that cannot be dialed directly, such as person-to-person calls or collect calls. They also handle special billing requests, such as charging a call to a third number or to a calling card. Directory assistance operators answer customers' inquiries for telephone numbers by accessing computerized alphabetical and geographical directories. Many businesses, such as hotels, employ their own operators to handle house calls. Operators are also found in such settings as answering services and airport communication centers.

Salaries

The average salary for telephone operators is listed below.

Lowest 10 percent	Less than $232/week
Median	$385/week
Top 10 percent	More than $561/week

Employment Outlook

Growth rate until the year 2005: Sharply decline.

Telephone Operators

Career Guides

★1851★ "Dial O For Operator" in *Telecommunications Careers* (pp. 54-57)
Franklin Watts, Inc.
387 Park Avenue, S.
New York, NY 10016
Ph: (212)686-7070

James L. Schefter. 1988. Describes the telecommunications industry and profiles jobs in manufacturing, the telephone industry, the military, video communications and television broadcasting. Covers job duties, educational requirements, salaries, and promotional possibilities.

★1852★ "Radio and Telegraph Operator" in *Telecommunications* (pp. 51-55)
Franklin Watts, Inc.
387 Park Avenue, S.
New York, NY 10016
Ph: (212)686-7070

Linda Barrett and Galen Guengerich. 1991. Surveys opportunities in telecommunications including telephone, radio, telegraph, and television communications. Includes job description, educational preparation, salary, and employment outlook. Offers job hunting advice.

★1853★ "Radio and Telegraph Operators" in *Career Discovery Encyclopedia* (Vol.5, pp. 120-121)
J.G. Ferguson Publishing Co.
200 W. Madison St., Ste. 300
Chicago, IL 60606
Ph: (312)580-5480 Fax: (312)580-4948

E. Russell Primm, editor-in-chief. 1993. Contains two-page articles on 504 occupations. Each article describes job duties, earnings, and educational and training requirements.

★1854★ "Radio and Telegraph Operators" in *Encyclopedia of Careers and Vocational Guidance* (Vol.4, pp. 220-222)
J.G. Ferguson Publishing Co.
200 W. Madison St., Ste. 300
Chicago, IL 60606
Ph: (312)580-5480 Fax: (312)580-4948

William E. Hopke, editor-in-chief. Ninth edition, 1993. Four-volume set that profiles 500 occupations and describes job trends in 74 industries. Includes career description, educational requirements, history of the job, methods of entry, advancement, employment outlook, earnings, working conditions, social and psychological factors, and sources of additional information.

★1855★ "Receptionists and Switchboard Operators" in *American Almanac of Jobs and Salaries* (p. 511)
Avon Books
1350 Avenue of the Americas
New York, NY 10019
Ph: (212)261-6800 Fr: 800-238-0658

John Wright, editor. Revised and updated, 1994-95. A comprehensive guide to the wages of hundreds of occupations in a wide variety of industries and organizations.

★1856★ *Switchboard Operators*
Chronicle Guidance Publications, Inc.
66 Aurora St.
PO Box 1190
Moravia, NY 13118-1190
Ph: (315)497-0330 Fax: (315)497-3359
Fr: 800-622-7284

1993. This career brief describes the nature of the work, working conditions, hours and earnings, education and training, licensure, certification, unions, personal qualifications, social and psychological factors, employment outlook, entry methods, advancement, and related occupations.

★1857★ "Switchboard Operators" in *Career Discovery Encyclopedia* (Vol.6, pp. 82-83)
J.G. Ferguson Publishing Co.
200 W. Madison St., Ste. 300
Chicago, IL 60606
Ph: (312)580-5480 Fax: (312)580-4948

E. Russell Primm, editor-in-chief. 1993. Contains two-page articles on 504 occupations. Each article describes job duties, earnings, and educational and training requirements.

★1858★ "Switchboard Operators" in *Encyclopedia of Careers and Vocational Guidance* (Vol.4, pp. 474-475)
J.G. Ferguson Publishing Co.
200 W. Madison St., Ste. 300
Chicago, IL 60606
Ph: (312)580-5480 Fax: (312)580-4948

William E. Hopke, editor-in-chief. Ninth edition, 1993. Four-volume set that profiles 500 occupations and describes job trends in 74 industries. Includes career description, educational requirements, history of the job, methods of entry, advancement, employment outlook, earnings, working conditions, social and psychological factors, and sources of additional information.

★1859★ *Telephone Answering Service Operator*
Careers, Inc.
PO Box 135
Largo, FL 34649-0135
Ph: (813)584-7333

1994. Two-page job guide card describing duties, working conditions, personal qualifications, training, earnings and hours, employment outlook, places of employment, related careers and where to write for more information.

★1860★ *Telephone Operator*
Careers, Inc.
PO Box 135
Largo, FL 34649-0135
Ph: (813)584-7333

1994. Two-page occupational summary card describing duties, working conditions, personal qualifications, training, earnings and hours, employment outlook, places of employment, related careers and where to write for more information.

★1861★ "Telephone Operator" in *Career Information Center* (Vol.3)
Simon and Schuster
200 Old Tappan Rd.
Old Tappan, NJ 07675
Fax: 800-445-6991 Fr: 800-223-2348

Richard Lidz and Dale Anderson, editorial directors. Fifth edition, 1993. For 600 occupations, describes job duties, entry-level requirements, education and training needed, advancement possibilities, employment outlook, earnings and benefits. The set is divided into 12 volumes. Each volume includes jobs related under a broad career field. Volume 13 is the index.

★1862★ "Telephone Operators" in *Career Discovery Encyclopedia* (Vol.6, pp. 102-103)
J.G. Ferguson Publishing Co.
200 W. Madison St., Ste. 300
Chicago, IL 60606
Ph: (312)580-5480 Fax: (312)580-4948

E. Russell Primm, editor-in-chief. 1993. Contains two-page articles on 504 occupations. Each article describes job duties, earnings, and educational and training requirements.

★1863★ *Telephone Operators (Central Office)*
Chronicle Guidance Publications, Inc.
66 Aurora St.
PO Box 1190
Moravia, NY 13118-1190
Ph: (315)497-0330 Fax: (315)497-3359
Fr: 800-622-7284

1993. This career brief describes the nature of the work, working conditions, hours and earnings, education and training, licensure, certification, unions, personal qualifications, social and psychological factors, employment outlook, entry methods, advancement, and related occupations.

★1864★ "Telephone Operators" in *Encyclopedia of Careers and Vocational Guidance* (Vol.4, pp. 513-516)
J.G. Ferguson Publishing Co.
200 W. Madison St., Ste. 300
Chicago, IL 60606
Ph: (312)580-5480 Fax: (312)580-4948

William E. Hopke, editor-in-chief. Ninth edition, 1993. Four-volume set that profiles 500 occupations and describes job trends in 74 industries. Includes career description, educational requirements, history of the job, methods of entry, advancement, employment outlook, earnings, working conditions, social and psychological factors, and sources of additional information.

★1865★ "Telephone Operators" in *Jobs! What They Are—Where They Are—What They Pay* (pp. 254)
Simon & Schuster, Inc.
Simon & Schuster Bldg.
1230 Avenue of the Americas
New York, NY 10020
Ph: (212)698-7000

Robert O. Snelling and Anne M. Snelling. Revised edition, 1992. Profiles 241 occupations, describing duties and responsibilities, educational preparation, earnings, employment opportunities, training, and qualifications.

★1866★ "Telephone Operators" in *Occupational Outlook Handbook*
U.S. Government Printing Office
Superintendent of Documents
Washington, DC 20402
Ph: (202)512-1800 Fax: (202)512-2250

Biennial; latest edition, 1994-95. Encyclopedia of careers describing more than 250 occupations and comprising about 85 percent of all jobs in the economy. Occupations that require lengthy education or training are given the most attention. For each occupation, the handbook describes job duties, working conditions, training, educational preparation, personal qualities, advancement possibilities, job outlook, earnings, and sources of additional information.

★1867★ "Telephone and PBX Operator" in *Telecommunications* (pp. 15-19)
Franklin Watts, Inc.
387 Park Avenue, S.
New York, NY 10016
Ph: (212)686-7070

Linda Barrett and Galen Guengerich. 1991. Surveys opportunities in telecommunications including telephone, radio, telegraph, and television communications. Includes job description, educational preparation, salary, and employment outlook. Offers job hunting advice.

★1868★ *Video Career Library - Clerical & Administrative Support*
Careers, Inc.
PO Box 135
Largo, FL 34649-0135
Ph: (813)584-7333

Videocassette. 1990. 26 mins. Part of the Video Career Library covering 165 occupations. Shows actual workers on the job. Includes secretaries, cashiers, receptionists, bookkeepers and audit clerks, telephone operators, postal clerks/carriers/supervisors, insurance investigators, bank tellers, data entry keyers, and court reporters.

★1869★ *What Is Telemarketing and How Do I Get Started?*
First Finanacial Video Network
4811 Emerson St., Ste. 210
Palatine, IL 60067-7417
Ph: (708)397-9000 Fax: (708)397-6721
Fr: 800-442-8662

Videocassette. 1987. 25 mins. Starting a career in telemarketing is explained in this tape.

Associations

★1870★ United States Telephone Association (USTA)
1401 H St., Ste. 600
Washington, DC 20005-2136
Ph: (202)326-7300 Fax: (202)326-7333

Members: Local operating telephone companies or telephone holding companies. Members represent a total of 114 million access lines. **Purpose:** Conducts educational and training programs. Maintains 21 committees. **Publications:** *Holding Company Report*, annual. • *Phonefacts*, annual. • *Statistical Volumes*, annual. • *Teletimes*, quarterly.

Test Guides

★1871★ *Career Examination Series: Principal Telephone Operator*
National Learning Corp.
212 Michael Dr.
Syosset, NY 11791
Ph: (516)921-8888 Fax: (516)921-8743
Fr: 800-645-6337

Jack Rudman. All examination guides in this series contain questions with answers.

★1872★ *Career Examination Series: Radio Telephone Operator*
National Learning Corp.
212 Michael Dr.
Syosset, NY 11791
Ph: (516)921-8888 Fax: (516)921-8743
Fr: 800-645-6337

Jack Rudman. All examination guides in this series contain questions with answers.

★1873★ *Career Examination Series: Senior Telephone Operator*
National Learning Corp.
212 Michael Dr.
Syosset, NY 11791
Ph: (516)921-8888 Fax: (516)921-8743
Fr: 800-645-6337

Jack Rudman. All examination guides in this series contain questions with answers.

★1874★ *Career Examination Series: Telephone Operator*
National Learning Corp.
212 Michael Dr.
Syosset, NY 11791
Ph: (516)921-8888 Fax: (516)921-8743
Fr: 800-645-6337

Jack Rudman. All examination guides in this series contain questions with answers.

★1875★ *Office Aide*
Prentice Hall Press
Simon & Schuster Inc.
200 Old Tappan Rd.
Old Tappan, NJ 07675
Ph: 800-223-2348

Hy Hammer. Second edition, 1985. Contains seven sample exams for the following entry-level civil service positions: clerk, typist, stenographer, receptionist, office machine operator, telephone operator.

★1876★ *The Telephone Company Test*
Arco Pub.
201 W. 103rd St.
Indianapolis, IN 46290
Ph: 800-428-5331 Fax: 800-835-3202

Margaret Ehrlich, Ph.D. 1991. Includes sample exams with explanations.

Periodicals

★1877★ *Dots and Dashes*
Morse Telegraph Club
1101 Maplewood Dr.
Normal, IL 61761
Ph: (309)454-2029
W.K. Dunbar

Quarterly. Perpetuates the tradition of the telegraph profession through articles and anecdotes about the use of Morse and International codes and operators, manufacturers, and users of telegraphs. Recurring features include member and chapter news, letters to the editor, and reports of meetings.

★1878★ *Holding Company Report*
United States Telephone Association (USTA)
1401 H St., Ste. 600
Washington, DC 20005-2136
Ph: (202)326-7300 Fax: (202)326-7333

Annual.

★1879★ *International PBX/Telecommunicators—Newsletter*
International PBX/Telecommunicators
2426 Swan Blvd.
Wauwatosa, WI 53226
Ph: (414)771-5336
Ila Mae Hora

Monthly. Furnishes articles and commentary to assist switchboard operators and communication directors to better communicate with customers and government. Recurring features include letters to the editor, interviews, news of research, a calendar of events, reports of meetings, news of educational opportunities, and columns titled President's Message, New Equipment, and Helpful Hints.

★1880★ *Statistical Volumes*
United States Telephone Association (USTA)
1401 H St., Ste. 600
Washington, DC 20005-2136
Ph: (202)326-7300 Fax: (202)326-7333

Annual.

★1881★ *Telemarketing*
Technology Marketing Corp.
1 Technology Plaza
Norwalk, CT 06854
Ph: (203)852-6800 Fax: (203)853-2845
Fr: 800-243-6002
Linda Driscoll

Monthly. Magazine on telemarketing and business telecommunications technology.

★1882★ *Teletimes*
United States Telephone Association (USTA)
1401 H St., Ste. 600
Washington, DC 20005-2136
Ph: (202)326-7300 Fax: (202)326-7333

Quarterly.

Other Sources of Information

★1883★ *Phonefacts*
United States Telephone Association (USTA)
1401.H. St., Ste. 600
Washington, DC 20006
Ph: (202)326-7300 Fax: (202)326-7333

Annual.

★1884★ *Telegraph & Data Transmission over Shortwave Radio Links: Fundamental Principles & Networks*
John Wiley and Sons, Inc.
605 3rd Ave.
New York, NY 10158-0012
Ph: (212)850-6000 Fax: (212)850-6088
Fr: 800-526-5368

Lother Wiesner. Third edition, 1984.

★1885★ "Telephone Operator" in *Career Selector 2001*
Barron's Educational Series, Inc.
250 Wireless Blvd.
Hauppauge, NY 11788
Ph: (516)434-3311 Fax: (516)434-3723
Fr: 800-645-3476

James C. Gonyea. 1993.

Typists, Word Processors, and Data Entry Keyers

Typists, word processors, and data entry keyers are responsible for the timely processing of information and data. Depending on their experience, typists may prepare simple forms or type technical material from rough drafts. Word processors use word processing equipment to record, edit, store, and revise correspondence, reports, statistical tables, and other materials. Data entry keyers are generally responsible for entering numerical information, such as data from checks or invoices, into computer systems. Typists, word processors, and data entry keyers are employed in a variety of industries, with many found in educational institutions, health care facilities, and firms that provide business services.

Salaries

Average salaries of typists, word processors, and data entry keyers vary by industry.

Typists	$20,000/year
Word processors	$23,000/year
Data entry keyers	$20,000/year

Employment Outlook

Growth rate until the year 2005: Decline.

Typists, Word Processors, and Data Entry Keyers

Career Guides

★1886★ *Business & Data Processing Machine Operators*
Morris Video
2730 Monterey St. #105
Monterey Business Park
Torrance, CA 90503
Ph: (310)533-4800 Fr: 800-843-3606

Videocassette. 1982. 15 mins. Machinery is an integral part of the business world, be it calculator or computer, and women and men are in great demand to operate them.

★1887★ *Career Insights*
RMI Media Productions, Inc.
1365 N. Winchester
Olathe, KS 66061
Ph: (913)768-1696 Fax: 800-755-6910
Fr: 800-745-5480

Videocassette series. 1987. This videotape series describes 50 occupations, including skill requirements and interviews with people employed in these fields. Occupations include: flight service, air transportation/ground services, data processing, carpentry, clerk in banking/insurance/business, cosmetic personal grooming, firefighting, forestry, insulation/roofing, mechanics, material handling, photographic processing, pipefitting and plumbing, printing, secretarial services, tool and die operations.

★1888★ *Career Success Series*
Cambridge Educational
PO Box 2153
Charleston, WV 25328-2153
Ph: (304)744-9323 Fax: (304)744-9351
Fr: 800-468-4227

Videocassette. 1986. 15 mins. A series, available separately, outlining various career choices for students. Occupations include: accounting, flight service, air transportation/ground/flight service, data processing, carpentry, clerk in banking/insurance, commodity sales, cosmetic personal grooming, fire fighting, forestry services, home economics, insulation/roofing, material handling, mechanics, photographic processing, pipefitting and plumbing, police science, printing, carpentry, medical laboratory technicians, secretarial services, and utilities equipment operator.

★1889★ "Clerks" in *Career Discovery Encyclopedia* (Vol.2, pp. 16-17)
J.G. Ferguson Publishing Co.
200 W. Madison St., Ste. 300
Chicago, IL 60606
Ph: (312)580-5480 Fax: (312)580-4948

E. Russell Primm, editor-in-chief. 1993. Contains two-page articles on 504 occupations. Each article describes job duties, earnings, and educational and training requirements.

★1890★ *Computer Program & Systems Analysis*
Morris Video
2730 Monterey St., No. 105
Monterey Business Park
Torrance, CA 90503
Ph: (310)533-4800 Fr: 800-843-3606

Videocassette. 1984. 15 mins. From data processing to program writing, the myriad computer career possibilities are discussed.

★1891★ "Data Entry" in *Careers in High Tech* (pp. 31-32)
Arco Publishing Co.
Macmillan General Reference
15 Columbus Cir.
New York, NY 10023
Fax: 800-835-3202 Fr: 800-858-7674

Connie Winkler. 1987. Surveys career opportunities in data processing, technology, personal computers, telecommunications, manufacturing technology, artificial intelligence, computer graphics, biotechnology, lasers, technical writing, and publishing. Includes information on educational preparation, associations, and periodicals.

★1892★ "Data Entry Clerks" in *Encyclopedia of Careers and Vocational Guidance* (Vol.2, pp. 431-433)
J.G. Ferguson Publishing Co.
200 W. Madison St., Ste. 300
Chicago, IL 60606
Ph: (312)580-5480 Fax: (312)580-4948

William E. Hopke, editor-in-chief. Ninth edition, 1993. Four-volume set that profiles 500 occupations and describes job trends in 74 industries. Includes career description, educational requirements, history of the job, methods of entry, advancement, employment outlook, earnings, working conditions, social and psychological factors, and sources of additional information.

★1893★ "Data Entry Keyer" in *Career Information Center* (Vol.1)
Simon and Schuster
200 Old Tappan Rd.
Old Tappan, NJ 07675
Fax: 800-445-6991 Fr: 800-223-2348

Richard Lidz and Dale Anderson, editorial directors. Fifth edition, 1993. For 600 occupations, describes job duties, entry-level requirements, education and training needed, advancement possibilities, employment outlook, earnings and benefits. The set is divided into 12 volumes. Each volume includes jobs related under a broad career field. Volume 13 is the index.

★1894★ "Data Entry Keyer" in *Careers in Banking and Finance* (pp. 41-42)
Rosen Publishing Group
29 E. 21st St.
New York, NY 10010
Ph: (212)777-3017 Fax: (212)777-0277
Fr: 800-237-9932

Patricia Haddock. 1990. Describes more than 20 jobs at all levels in banking and finance. Contains information about the types of financial organizations where the jobs are found, educational requirements, job duties, and salaries. Offers advice on job hunting.

★1895★ "Data Entry Keyer" in *Careers Inside the World of Offices* (pp. 10,17)
Rosen Publishing Group
29 E. 21st St.
New York, NY 10010
Ph: 800-237-9932 Fax: (212)777-0277

Carolyn Simpson. 1995. Describes job possibilities, attitudes and skills needed, and tips for getting the job. Also includes a self-evaluation test.

★1896★ *Data Entry Operator*
Careers, Inc.
PO Box 135
Largo, FL 34649-0135
Ph: (813)584-7333

1991. Two-page occupational summary card describing duties, working conditions, personal qualifications, training, earnings and hours, employment outlook, places of employment, related careers and where to write for more information.

★1897★ "Data Entry Operator" in *BLR Encyclopedia of Prewritten Job Descriptions*
Business and Legal Reports, Inc.
39 Academy St.
Madison, CT 06443-1513
Ph: (203)245-7448

Stephen D. Bruce, editor-in-chief. 1994. This book contains hundreds of sample job descriptions arranged by functional job category. The 1-3 page job descriptions cover what the worker normally does in the position, who they report to, and how that position fits in the organizational structure.

★1898★ "Data Entry Operator" in *Occu-Facts: Information on 580 Careers in Outline Form*
Careers, Inc.
PO Box 135
Largo, FL 34649-0135
Ph: (813)584-7333

Biennial, 1995-96 edition. Each one-page occupational profile describes duties, working conditions, physical surroundings and demands, aptitudes, temperament, educational requirements, employment outlook, earnings, and places of employment.

★1899★ *Data Entry Operators*
Chronicle Guidance Publications, Inc.
66 Aurora St.
PO Box 1190
Moravia, NY 13118-1190
Ph: (315)497-0330 Fax: (315)497-3359
Fr: 800-622-7284

1993. This career brief describes the nature of the work, working conditions, hours and earnings, education and training, licensure, certification, unions, personal qualifications, social and psychological factors, employment outlook, entry methods, advancement, and related occupations.

★1900★ "Data Entry Specialist" in *Opportunities in Data Processing Careers* (pp. 52-53)
National Textbook Co. (NTC)
VGM Career Books
4255 W. Touhy Ave.
Lincolnwood, IL 60646-1975
Ph: (708)679-5500 Fax: (708)679-2494
Fr: 800-323-4900

Norman N. Noerper. 1989. Provides an overview of the history and development of data processing careers. For each job included, describes responsibilities, salary, and job outlook. Contains separate chapters on educational preparation and job hunting. Lists professional organizations, publications, and schools.

★1901★ *Data Processing: Career Opportunities for Hearing Impaired People*
Journal Films, Inc.
1560 Sherman Ave., Ste. 100
Evanston, IL 60201
Ph: (708)328-6700 Fax: (708)328-6706
Fr: 800-323-9084

Videocassette. 1982. 11 mins. Hearing impaired people are taught how to enter the field of data processing.

★1902★ *Exploring Careers in Word Processing and Desktop Publishing*
Rosen Publishing Group
29 E. 21st St.
New York, NY 10010
Ph: (212)777-3017 Fax: (212)777-0277
Fr: 800-237-9932

Jean W. Spencer. 1990. Describes past, current and future trends in jobs using word processing. Covers the secretarial, information processing, and desktop publishing fields. Explains training needed, skills needed to succeed on the job, and the equipment used. Lists professional organizations and trade publications.

★1903★ "Information Technology, Data Processing" in *Career Connection II: A Guide to Technical Majors and Their Related Careers* (pp. 92-93)
Jist Works, Inc.
720 N. Park Ave.
Indianapolis, IN 46202-3431
Ph: (317)264-3720 Fax: (317)264-3709

Fred A. Rowe. 1994. Contains technical majors, such as automotive technology. Describes the major and the job. Lists high school and postsecondary school courses. Includes occupations related to the major, employment outlook, and starting salary.

★1904★ "Information/Word Processing" in *Opportunities in Office Occupations* (pp. 116-130)
National Textbook Co. (NTC)
VGM Career Books
4255 W. Touhy Ave.
Lincolnwood, IL 60646-1975
Ph: (708)679-5500 Fax: (708)679-2494
Fr: 800-323-4900

Blanche Ettinger. 1989. Describes factors and trends which will affect office occupations including automation, telecommuting, and unionization. Separate chapters cover clerks, records management, information word processing, the secretary, and the bookkeeper-accountant. Describes job duties, skills needed, educational preparation, job hunting, types of equipment, employment outlook, and salaries.

★1905★ *Office Revolution*
Nebraska ETV Council for Higher Education (NETCHE)
1800 N. 33rd St.
Lincoln, NE 68503
Ph: (402)472-3611

Videocassette. 1983. 26 mins. This program is intended as an introduction to word processing.

★1906★ *Opportunities in Data Processing Careers*
National Textbook Co. (NTC)
VGM Career Books
4255 W. Toughy Ave.
Lincolnwood, IL 60646-1975
Ph: (708)679-5500 Fax: (708)679-2494
Fr: 800-323-4900

Norman N. Noerper.

★1907★ *Opportunities in Word Processing Careers*
National Textbook Co. (NTC)
VGM Career Books
4255 W. Touhy Ave.
Lincolnwood, IL 60646-1975
Ph: (708)679-5500 Fax: (708)679-2494
Fr: 800-323-4900

Marianne Forrester Munday. 1991. Describes the role word processing plays in organizations, career opportunities, and effective training programs. Presents employment outlook, qualifications needed, salaries, working conditions, and what word processors like about their jobs. Provides job huntings tips.

★1908★ "Receptionist/Clerk-Typist" in *Career Opportunities in Television, Cable, and Video* (pp. 22-23)
Facts on File
460 Park Ave. S.
New York, NY 10016-7382
Ph: (212)683-2244 Fax: 800-678-3633
Fr: 800-322-8755

Third edition, 1990. Describes 100 media-related jobs. Each occupational profile covers job duties, employment outlook, career paths, salaries, skills, and educational preparation. Offers tips for entering the field.

★1909★ *Typist*
Careers, Inc.
PO Box 135
Largo, FL 34649-0135
Ph: (813)584-7333

1995. Two-page occupational summary card describing duties, working conditions, personal qualifications, training, earnings and hours, employment outlook, places of employment, related careers and where to write for more information.

★1910★ "Typist" in *Occu-Facts: Information on 580 Careers in Outline Form*
Careers, Inc.
PO Box 135
Largo, FL 34649-0135
Ph: (813)584-7333

Biennial, 1995-96 edition. Each one-page occupational profile describes duties, working conditions, physical surroundings and demands, aptitudes, temperament, educational requirements, employment outlook, earnings, and places of employment.

★1911★ "Typist and Word Processors" in *Careers in Banking and Finance* (p. 73)
Rosen Publishing Group
29 E. 21st St.
New York, NY 10010
Ph: (212)777-3017 Fax: (212)777-0277
Fr: 800-237-9932

Patricia Haddock. 1990. Describes more than 20 jobs at all levels in banking and finance. Contains information about the types of financial organizations where the jobs are found, educational requirements, job duties, and salaries. Offers advice on job hunting.

★1912★ "Typists" in *Career Discovery Encyclopedia* (Vol.6, pp. 130-131)
J.G. Ferguson Publishing Co.
200 W. Madison St., Ste. 300
Chicago, IL 60606
Ph: (312)580-5480 Fax: (312)580-4948

E. Russell Primm, editor-in-chief. 1993. Contains two-page articles on 504 occupations. Each article describes job duties, earnings, and educational and training requirements.

★1913★ "Typists" in *Opportunities in Vocational and Technical Careers* (pp. 47-58)
National Textbook Co. (NTC)
VGM Career Books
4255 W. Touhy Ave.
Lincolnwood, IL 60646-1975
Ph: (708)679-5500 Fax: (708)679-2494
Fr: 800-323-4900

Adrian A. Paradis. 1992. Describes careers which can be prepared for by attending a private vocational or proprietary school—office employee, sales worker, service worker, health services, mechanic, craftworker, and technician. Covers employment outlook, job duties, and salaries. Offers career planning advice.

★1914★ "Typists and Word Processor Operators" in *Jobs! What They Are—Where They Are—What They Pay* (pp. 255)
Simon & Schuster, Inc.
Simon & Schuster Bldg.
1230 Avenue of the Americas
New York, NY 10020
Ph: (212)698-7000

Robert O. Snelling and Anne M. Snelling. Revised edition, 1992. Profiles 241 occupations, describing duties and responsibilities, educational preparation, earnings, employment opportunities, training, and qualifications.

★1915★ "Typists, Word Processors, and Data Entry Keyers" in *American Almanac of Jobs and Salaries* (pp. 513)
Avon Books
1350 Avenue of the Americas
New York, NY 10019
Ph: (212)261-6800 Fr: 800-238-0658

John Wright, editor. Revised and updated, 1994-95. A comprehensive guide to the wages of hundreds of occupations in a wide variety of industries and organizations.

★1916★ "Typists, Word Processors, and Data Entry Keyers" in *Occupational Outlook Handbook*
U.S. Government Printing Office
Superintendent of Documents
Washington, DC 20402
Ph: (202)512-1800 Fax: (202)512-2250

Biennial; latest edition, 1994-95. Encyclopedia of careers describing more than 250 occupations and comprising about 85 percent of all jobs in the economy. Occupations that require lengthy education or training are given the most attention. For each occupation, the handbook describes job duties, working conditions, training, educational preparation, personal qualities, advancement possibilities, job outlook, earnings, and sources of additional information.

★1917★ "Typists and Word Processors" in *Encyclopedia of Careers and Vocational Guidance* (Vol.4, pp. 574-577)
J.G. Ferguson Publishing Co.
200 W. Madison St., Ste. 300
Chicago, IL 60606
Ph: (312)580-5480 Fax: (312)580-4948

William E. Hopke, editor-in-chief. Ninth edition, 1993. Four-volume set that profiles 500 occupations and describes job trends in 74 industries. Includes career description, educational requirements, history of the job, methods of entry, advancement, employment outlook, earnings, working conditions, social and psychological factors, and sources of additional information.

★1918★ *Video Career Library - Clerical & Administrative Support*
Careers, Inc.
PO Box 135
Largo, FL 34649-0135
Ph: (813)584-7333

Videocassette. 1990. 26 mins. Part of the Video Career Library covering 165 occupations. Shows actual workers on the job. Includes secretaries, cashiers, receptionists, bookkeepers and audit clerks, telephone operators, postal clerks/carriers/supervisors, insurance investigators, bank tellers, data entry keyers, and court reporters.

★1919★ *Vocational Visions*
Center for Humanities, Inc.
Communications Park
Box 1000
Mount Kisco, NY 10549
Ph: (914)666-4100 Fax: (914)666-5319
Fr: 800-431-1242

Videocassette. 1984. 30 mins. This series of programs explains key aspects of actual training and a day in the life of a worker in the specific field mentioned on the videocassette. Occupations include: transportation/mechanics, repair, construction, business/office occupations, health, agriculture, technical/manufacturing, communications, and personal service.

★1920★ "Word Processing" in *Careers Inside the World of Offices* (pp. 10-11)
Rosen Publishing Group
29 E. 21st St.
New York, NY 10010
Ph: 800-237-9932 Fax: (212)777-0277

Carolyn Simpson. 1995. Describes job possibilities, attitudes and skills needed, and tips for getting the job. Also includes a self-evaluation test.

★1921★ "Word Processing" in *Exploring High Tech Careers*
Rosen Publishing Group
29 E. 21st St.
New York, NY 10010
Ph: (212)777-3017 Fax: (212)777-0277
Fr: 800-237-9932

Scott Southworth. Revised edition, 1993. Provides an orientation to the whole area of high tech and surveys jobs such as computer programming, drafting, and technical illustration. Covers educational preparation, advantages and disadvantages, advancement opportunities, and personal characteristics needed. Offers job hunting advice.

★1922★ *Word Processing Machine Operator*
Careers, Inc.
PO Box 135
Largo, FL 34649-0135
Ph: (813)584-7333

1992. Two-page occupational summary card describing duties, working conditions, personal qualifications, training, earnings and hours, employment outlook, places of employment, related careers and where to write for more information.

★1923★ "Word Processing Specialists: Information Processors" in *Careers for Women Without College Degrees* (pp. 192-196)
McGraw-Hill Publishing Co.
11 W. 19th St.
New York, NY 10011
Ph: (212)337-6010

Beatryce Nivens. 1988. Career planning and job hunting guide containing information on decision-making, skills assessment, and resumes for career changers. Profiles careers with the best occupational outlook. Describes the work, educational preparation, employment outlook, salaries, and required skills.

★1924★ *Word Processing Specialists (Operators)*
Chronicle Guidance Publications, Inc.
66 Aurora St.
PO Box 1190
Moravia, NY 13118-1190
Ph: (315)497-0330 Fax: (315)497-3359
Fr: 800-622-7284

1994. This career brief describes the nature of the work, working conditions, hours and earnings, education and training, licensure, certification, unions, personal qualifications, social and psychological factors, employment outlook, entry methods, advancement, and related occupations.

★1925★ "Word Processor" in *Career Information Center* (Vol.1)
Simon and Schuster
200 Old Tappan Rd.
Old Tappan, NJ 07675
Fax: 800-445-6991 Fr: 800-223-2348

Richard Lidz and Dale Anderson, editorial directors. Fifth edition, 1993. For 600 occupations, describes job duties, entry-level requirements, education and training needed, advancement possibilities, employment outlook, earnings and benefits. The set is divided into 12 volumes. Each volume includes jobs related under a broad career field. Volume 13 is the index.

★1926★ "Word Processor Operator" in *100 Best Careers for the Year 2000* (pp. 104-106)
Arco Pub.
201 W. 103rd St.
Indianapolis, IN 46290
Ph: 800-428-5331 Fax: 800-835-3202

Shelly Field. 1992. Describes 100 job opportunities expected to grow fast throughout the next decade. Provides information on job duties and responsibilities, training requirements, education, advancement opportunities, experience and qualifications, and typical salaries.

★1927★ "Word Processor Operators" in *Career Discovery Encyclopedia* (Vol.6, pp. 158-159)
J.G. Ferguson Publishing Co.
200 W. Madison St., Ste. 300
Chicago, IL 60606
Ph: (312)580-5480 Fax: (312)580-4948

E. Russell Primm, editor-in-chief. 1993. Contains two-page articles on 504 occupations. Each article describes job duties, earnings, and educational and training requirements.

★1928★ "Word Processor" in *VGM's Careers Encyclopedia* (pp. 489-490)
National Textbook Co. (NTC)
VGM Career Books
4255 W. Touhy Ave.
Lincolnwood, IL 60646-1975
Ph: (708)679-5500 Fax: (708)679-2494
Fr: 800-323-4900

Third edition, 1991. Contains two- to five-page descriptions of 200 managerial, professional, technical, trade, and service occupations. Each profile includes job duties, places of employment, qualifications, educational preparation, training, employment potential, advancement, income, and additional sources of information.

★1929★ *Your Future in Word Processing*
Rosen Publishing Group
29 E. 21st St.
New York, NY 10010
Ph: (212)777-3017 Fax: (212)777-0277
Fr: 800-237-9932

Gilbert J. Konkel. First edition, 1981. Discusses a variety of careers in word processing, how to get a job, using word processing as an entry to a specific field, and opportunities of the future.

Associations

★1930★ Data Entry Management Association
101 Merritt 7, 5th Fl.
Norwalk, CT 06851
Ph: (203)846-3777 Fax: (203)846-6883

Members: Data entry managers and others involved with the data entry profession. **Purpose:** Promotes the individual development and education of its members through exchange of ideas and discussion of problems and solutions. Conducts seminars and regional workshops and meetings.

Test Guides

★1931★ *Career Examination Series: Typists*
National Learning Corp.
212 Michael Dr.
Syosset, NY 11791
Ph: (516)921-8888 Fax: (516)921-8743
Fr: 800-645-6337

Jack Rudman. Contains examination guides for careers in data entry and data processing, including typists, key-punch operators, data entry keyers, word processors, typist-clerks, machine operators, and supervisors. The examination guides in this series contain questions with answers.

★1932★ *Data Processing*
National Learning Corp.
212 Michael Dr.
Syosset, NY 11791
Ph: (516)921-8888 Fax: (516)921-8743
Fr: 800-645-6337

Jack Rudman. Part of Occupational Competency Examination Series (OCE).

★1933★ *Data Processing*
National Learning Corp.
212 Michael Dr.
Syosset, NY 11791
Ph: (516)921-8888 Fax: (516)921-8743
Fr: 800-645-6337

Jack Rudman. Part of the Test Your Knowledge Series. Contains multiple choice questions with answers.

★1934★ *Federal Clerk - Steno - Typist*
Prentice Hall Press
Simon & Schuster Inc.
200 Old Tappan Rd.
Old Tappan, NJ 07675
Ph: 800-223-2348

Hy Hammer and John Czukor. Sixth edition, 1988. Coverage includes Federal entry-level clerical positions, including clerk, clerk typist, stenographer, transcriber, office machines operator, and office assistant.

★1935★ *How to Prepare for the Civil Service Examinations for Stenographer, Typist, Clerk, and Office Machine Operator*
Barron's Educational Series, Inc.
250 Wireless Blvd.
Hauppauge, NY 11788
Ph: (516)434-3311 Fax: (516)434-3723
Fr: 800-645-3476

Jerry Bobrow, Ph.D. Third edition. 1994. Test manual includes eleven model tests on verbal and clerical skills, typing, dictation, and office machine operation. All exams have answers explained and each simulates the actual Civil Service Exam.

★1936★ *Office Aide*
Prentice Hall Press
Simon & Schuster Inc.
200 Old Tappan Rd.
Old Tappan, NJ 07675
Ph: 800-223-2348

Hy Hammer. Second edition, 1985. Contains seven sample exams for the following entry-level civil service positions: clerk, typist, stenographer, receptionist, office machine operator, telephone operator.

★1937★ *Practice for Clerical, Typing, and Stenographic Tests*
Arco Pub.
201 W. 103rd St.
Indianapolis, IN 46290
Ph: 800-428-5331 Fax: 800-835-3202

1993, eighth edition.

★1938★ *Practice and Drill for the Clerk, Typist, and Stenographer Examinations*
National Learning Corp.
212 Michael Dr.
Syosset, NY 11791
Ph: (516)921-8888 Fax: (516)921-8743
Fr: 800-645-6337

Jack Rudman. Part of the General Aptitude and Abilities Series. Books in this series provide functional, intensive test practice and drill in the basic skills and areas common to many examinations, as well as general aptitude or achievement necessary for entrance into many occupations or positions.

★1939★ *Senior Clerical Series*
Prentice Hall Press
Simon & Schuster Inc.
200 Old Tappan Rd.
Old Tappan, NJ 07675
Ph: 800-223-2348

Hy Hammer. Fourth edition, 1983. Complete test preparation for the following senior grade positions: clerk, typist, stenographer, account clerk, file clerk, statistics clerk, stenographer (law), mail and supply clerk, and stores clerk.

★1940★ *Senior Clerical Series*
Prentice Hall Press
Simon & Schuster Inc.
200 Old Tappan Rd.
Old Tappan, NJ 07675
Ph: 800-223-2348

Hy Hammer. Fourth edition, 1983. Complete test preparation for the following senior grade positions: clerk, typist, stenographer, account clerk, file clerk, statistics clerk, stenographer (law), mail and supply clerk, and stores clerk.

Educational Directories and Programs

★1941★ *Industry Directory*
Association of Information Professionals
104 Wilmot Rd., Ste. 201
Deerfield, IL 60015-5195
Ph: (708)940-8800 Fax: (708)940-7218

Manufacturers of office automation equipment; word processing service bureaus; educational institutions offering office automation and associated software courses or curriculums; personnel agencies serving office automation personnel and users; analysts and consultants. Entries include: Name, address. Arrangement: Alphabetical within categories above.

★1942★ *YARDSTICK*
Gartner Group
56 Top Gallant Rd.
Stamford, CT 06904
Ph: (203)975-6419 Fax: (203)324-7901
Fr: 800-677-7778
Randall Brophy, Contact

Three times per year, April, June, and August. Covers top 100 U.S. and worldwide data processing equipment manufacturers, selected on the basis of revenue. Entries include: Company name, ticker symbol, line of business, rank, country, address, phone; financial data in calendar format for prior five years. Arrangement: Ranked by revenues.

Awards, Scholarships, Grants, and Fellowships

★1943★ Distinguished Information Sciences Award
DPMA, Association of Information Systems Professionals
505 Busse Hwy.
Park Ridge, IL 60068-3191
Ph: (708)825-8124

To recognize an individual for outstanding contributions to the information processing industry. Nominations must be made by DPMA members but the award is not limited to members. The final selection is made by the DPMA Executive Council. A bronze etched plaque and an honorary lifetime membership in the Association are bestowed annually at the DPMA Conference and Business Exposition. Established in 1969. Additional information is available from Janet L. Milakis, Director Member Services.

Basic Reference Guides and Handbooks

★1944★ *Busy Person's Guide to Selecting the Right Word Processor: A Visual Shortcut to Understanding & Buying, Complete with Checklist & Prod. Guide*
Festival Publications
7944 Capistrano Ave.
West Hills, CA 91304
Ph: (818)340-0175

Alan Gadney. 1984. Part of Busy Person's Computer Buying Guides Series.

★1945★ *Choosing & Using a Word Processor*
Gower Publishing Co.
Old Post Rd.
Brookfield, VT 05036
Ph: (802)276-3162

Kevin Townsend. 1982.

★1946★ *Fullwrite Professional: A User's Guide*
Prentice Hall
Rte. 9W
Englewood Cliffs, NJ 07632
Ph: (201)592-2000

Keith Thompson. 1988.

★1947★ *How to Buy an Office Computer or Word Processor*
Prentice Hall
Rte.9W
Englewood Cliffs, NJ 07632
Ph: (201)592-2000

Brian Donohue. 1983.

★1948★ *How to Typeset from a Wordprocessor: An Interfacing Guide*
R. R. Bowker, Co.
121 Chanlon Rd.
New Providence, NJ 07974
Ph: (908)464-6800 Fax: (908)464-3553

Ronald A. Labuz. 1984.

★1949★ *Low-End Word Processor Market*
Frost & Sullivan, Inc.
106 Fulton St.
New York, NY 10038
Ph: (212)233-1080

1984.

★1950★ *Math on the Job: Secretary/ Clerk Typist*
National Center for Research in Vocational Education
Ohio State University
1900 Kenry Rd.
Columbus, OH 43210
Ph: (614)292-4353

1985.

★1951★ *Mercury Systems Inc.: Practice Set in Word-Information Processing for Conventional & Text-Editing Typewriters*
McGraw-Hill, Inc.
1221 Avenue of the Americas
New York, NY 10020
Ph: (212)512-2000

B. L. Boyce. 1981.

★1952★ *Sprint: A Power User's Guide*
John Wiley and Sons, Inc.
605 3rd Ave.
New York, NY 10158-0012
Ph: (212)850-6000 Fax: (212)850-6088
Fr: 800-526-5368

Charles Ackerman. 1990.

★1953★ *SPRINT Simplified*
T A B Books, Inc.
Blue Ridge Summit, PA 17294-0850
Ph: (717)794-2191

Douglas J. Wolf. 1988.

★1954★ *Word Magic: A Guide to Understanding & Evaluating Word Processing Equipment*
Van Nostrand Reinhold Co., Inc.
115 5th Ave.
New York, NY 10003
Ph: (212)254-3232 Fax: (212)254-9499

Michael Scriven. 1983.

★1955★ *Word Processor & Calculator Development System MVP-Forth*
Mountain View Press, Inc.
PO Box X
Mountain View, CA 94040
Ph: (415)961-4103

Thomas E. Wempe. 1987. Part of MVP-Forth Books Vol. 9.

★1956★ *Word Processor & Calculator Development System Source*
Mountain View Press, Inc.
PO Box X
Mountain View, CA 94040
Ph: (415)961-4103

Thomas E. Wempe. 1987. Part of MVP-Forth Series. Vol. 10.

★1957★ *Word Processors & Information Processing: What They Are & How to Buy*
Para Publishing
PO Box 4232-821
Santa Barbara, CA 93140-4232
Ph: (805)968-7277 Fax: (805)968-1379

Dan Poynter. Second edition, 1982.

★1958★ *Word Processors & Typewriters Worldwide: Opportunities & Pitfalls*
LAAL Companies, Research Group
9 Kaufman Dr.
Westwood, NJ 07675
Ph: (201)664-6222

Villy Diernisse. 1984.

★1959★ *Word Processors & the Writing Process: An Annotated Bibliography*
Greenwood Publishing Group, Inc.
88 Post Rd., W.
PO Box 5007
Westport, CT 06881
Ph: (203)226-3571 Fax: (203)222-1502

Paula R. Nancarrow, editor. 1984.

★1960★ *You Can Type for Doctors at Home!*
Claremont Press
PO Box 177, Cooper Sta.
New York, NY 10003
Ph: (212)260-2812

Ruth de Menezes. 1981.

Periodicals

★1961★ *Bank Operations Report*
Warren, Gorham & Lamont, Inc.
31 St. James Ave.
Boston, MA 02116-4112
Ph: (617)423-2020 Fax: (617)695-9699
Fr: 800-922-1201
Nancy Hitchner

Monthly. Focuses on electronic data processing control, check processing, record keeping, cost control, federal regulation, credit and debit cards, electronic funds transfer system, physical security, and office automation, computer, and systems applications.

★1962★ *Data Entry Awareness Report*
Management Information Corporation
PO Box 5062
Cherry Hill, NJ 08034
Ph: (609)428-1020 Fax: (609)428-1683
Fr: 800-678-4642
Mark Kostic

Monthly. Evaluates a data entry system in each issue, including key to disc, intelligent terminals, optical character readers, portable data recorders, and voice data entry. Describes system hardware, software, and pricing, and analyzes the advantages and disadvantages of the system.

★1963★ *From Nine to Five*
Dartnell Corporation
4660 Ravenswood
Chicago, IL 60640
Ph: (312)561-4000 Fax: (312)561-3801
Fr: 800-621-5463
Douglas Leland

Biweekly. Provides "tips, shortcuts, and helpful information for success in the office," particularly secretaries and office workers. Recurring features include columns titled titled Business Skills Clinic, Shortcuts, and The Coffee Break.

★1964★ *Supply House Times*
Cahners Publishing Co.
1350 E. Touhy Ave.
PO Box 5080
Des Plaines, IL 60017-5080
Ph: (708)635-8800 Fax: (708)390-2618
Bill EverhamPublisher

Monthly. Trade magazine for wholesalers in plumbing, heating, cooling, piping, and water systems. Areas of major emphasis include: warehousing, materials handling, inventory control, accounting, data processing, merchandising, salesmanship and general management.

Other Sources of Information

★1965★ "Clerk-Typist" in *Career Selector 2001*
Barron's Educational Series, Inc.
250 Wireless Blvd.
Hauppauge, NY 11788
Ph: (516)434-3311 Fax: (516)434-3723
Fr: 800-645-3476

James C. Gonyea. 1993.

★1966★ "Typist" in *Career Selector 2001*
Barron's Educational Series, Inc.
250 Wireless Blvd.
Hauppauge, NY 11788
Ph: (516)434-3311 Fax: (516)434-3723
Fr: 800-645-3476

James C. Gonyea. 1993.

★1967★ "Word Processing Machine Operator" in *Career Selector 2001*
Barron's Educational Series, Inc.
250 Wireless Blvd.
Hauppauge, NY 11788
Ph: (516)434-3311 Fax: (516)434-3723
Fr: 800-645-3476

James C. Gonyea. 1993.

Correction Officers

Corrections officers are responsible for the safety and security of persons who have been arrested, are awaiting trial, or who have been tried and convicted of a crime and sentenced to serve time in a correctional institution. They maintain order and enforce rules within the institution by monitoring inmates' activities, such as working, exercising, eating, and bathing. It may sometimes be necessary to search inmates and their living quarters for drugs or weapons, and to settle disputes between inmates. Corrections officers inspect the facilities for unsanitary conditions, fire hazards, and evidence of infractions by inmates such as lock or window tampering. Counseling and helping inmates with problems are increasingly important parts of the correction officer's job. In some institutions, officers receive specialized training and have a more formal counseling role and may lead or participate in group counseling sessions.

Salaries

Earnings for corrections officers are listed below.

Starting salary at the state level	$18,600/year
Starting salary at the federal level	$18,300/year

Employment Outlook

Growth rate until the year 2005: Much faster than average.

Correction Officers

Career Guides

★1968★ *Correction Officer*
Macmillan Publishing Co., Inc.
866 3rd Ave.
New York, NY 10022
Ph: (212)702-2000 Fr: 800-257-5755

Eve P. Steinberg. 10th edition, 1994.

★1969★ "Correction Officer" in *100 Best Careers for the Year 2000* (pp. 194-197)
Arco Pub.
201 W. 103rd St.
Indianapolis, IN 46290
Ph: 800-428-5331 Fax: 800-835-3202

Shelly Field. 1992. Describes 100 job opportunities expected to grow fast throughout the next decade. Provides information on job duties and responsibilities, training requirements, education, advancement opportunities, experience and qualifications, and typical salaries.

★1970★ "Correction Officer" in *Career Information Center* (Vol.11)
Simon and Schuster
200 Old Tappan Rd.
Old Tappan, NJ 07675
Fax: 800-445-6991 Fr: 800-223-2348

Richard Lidz and Dale Anderson, editorial directors. Fifth edition, 1993. For 600 occupations, describes job duties, entry-level requirements, education and training needed, advancement possibilities, employment outlook, earnings and benefits. The set is divided into 12 volumes. Each volume includes jobs related under a broad career field. Volume 13 is the index.

★1971★ "Correction Officer" in *Jobs Rated Almanac*
World Almanac
1 International Blvd., Ste. 444
Mahwah, NJ 07495
Ph: (201)529-6900 Fax: (201)529-6901

Les Krantz. Second edition, 1992. Ranks 250 jobs by environment, salary, outlooks, physical demands, stress, security, travel opportunities, and extra perks. Includes jobs the editor feels are the most common, most interesting, and the most rapidly growing.

★1972★ "Correction Officers" in *America's 50 Fastest Growing Jobs* (pp. 116)
JIST Works, Inc.
720 N. Park Ave.
Indianapolis, IN 46202-3431
Ph: (317)264-3720 Fax: (317)264-3709
Fr: 800-648-5478

Michael J. Farr, compiler. 1994. Describes the 50 fastest growing jobs within major career clusters such as technicians, and marketing and sales. Each job profile explains the nature of the work, skills and abilities required, employment outlook, average earnings, related occupations, education and training requirements, and employment opportunities. Also contains career planning information and job search tips.

★1973★ "Correction Officers" in *Career Discovery Encyclopedia* (Vol.2, pp. 62-63)
J.G. Ferguson Publishing Co.
200 W. Madison St., Ste. 300
Chicago, IL 60606
Ph: (312)580-5480 Fax: (312)580-4948

E. Russell Primm, editor-in-chief. 1993. Contains two-page articles on 504 occupations. Each article describes job duties, earnings, and educational and training requirements.

★1974★ "Correction Officers" in *Encyclopedia of Careers and Vocational Guidance* (Vol.2, pp. 392-395)
J.G. Ferguson Publishing Co.
200 W. Madison St., Ste. 300
Chicago, IL 60606
Ph: (312)580-5480 Fax: (312)580-4948

William E. Hopke, editor-in-chief. Ninth edition, 1993. Four-volume set that profiles 500 occupations and describes job trends in 74 industries. Includes career description, educational requirements, history of the job, methods of entry, advancement, employment outlook, earnings, working conditions, social and psychological factors, and sources of additional information.

★1975★ "Correction Officers" in *Jobs! What They Are—Where They Are—What They Pay* (pp. 227)
Simon & Schuster, Inc.
Simon & Schuster Bldg.
1230 Avenue of the Americas
New York, NY 10020
Ph: (212)698-7000

Robert O. Snelling and Anne M. Snelling. Revised edition, 1992. Profiles 241 occupations, describing duties and responsibilities, educational preparation, earnings, employment opportunities, training, and qualifications.

★1976★ "Correction Officers" in *Occupational Outlook Handbook*
U.S. Government Printing Office
Superintendent of Documents
Washington, DC 20402
Ph: (202)512-1800 Fax: (202)512-2250

Biennial; latest edition, 1994-95. Encyclopedia of careers describing more than 250 occupations and comprising about 85 percent of all jobs in the economy. Occupations that require lengthy education or training are given the most attention. For each occupation, the handbook describes job duties, working conditions, training, educational preparation, personal qualities, advancement possibilities, job outlook, earnings, and sources of additional information.

★1977★ "Correction Officers" in *Opportunities in Vocational and Technical Careers* (pp. 76-90)
National Textbook Co. (NTC)
VGM Career Books
4255 W. Touhy Ave.
Lincolnwood, IL 60646-1975
Ph: (708)679-5500 Fax: (708)679-2494
Fr: 800-323-4900

Adrian A. Paradis. 1992. Describes careers which can be prepared for by attending a private vocational or proprietary school—office employee, sales worker, service worker, health services, mechanic, craftworker, and technician. Covers employment outlook, job duties, and salaries. Offers career planning advice.

★1978★ *Correctional Officer Correspondence Course*
American Correctional Association
8025 Laurel Lakes Ct.
Laurel, MD 20707
Ph: (301)206-5100 Fax: (301)206-5061

American Correctional Association Staff. Revised edition, 1989. In four volumes.

★1979★ "Correctional Officer" in *Great Careers for People Who Like Working with People* (pp. 43)
Gale Research Inc.
835 Penobscot Bldg.
Detroit, MI 48226
Ph: (313)961-2242 Fr: 800-347-4253

1994.

★1980★ *Correctional Officer II Courespondence Course*
American Correctional Association
8025 Laurel Lakes Ct.
Laurel, MD 20707
Ph: (301)206-5100 Fax: (301)206-5061

★1981★ *Correctional Officer Series*
AIMS Media, Inc.
9710 DeSoto Ave.
Chatsworth, CA 91311
Ph: (818)773-4300 Fax: (818)341-6700
Fr: 800-367-2467

Videocassette. 198?. 13 mins. This film combines teaching jobs skills, officer self- evaluation, and human understanding. Draws upon experiences of men and women involved in the operation of correctional facilities.

★1982★ *Correctional Officers*
Chronicle Guidance Publications, Inc.
66 Aurora St.
PO Box 1190
Moravia, NY 13118-1190
Ph: (315)497-0330 Fax: (315)497-3359
Fr: 800-622-7284

1994. This career brief describes the nature of the work, working conditions, hours and earnings, education and training, licensure, certification, unions, personal qualifications, social and psychological factors, employment outlook, entry methods, advancement, and related occupations.

★1983★ "Corrections Officer" in *Career Planning in Criminal Justice* (pp. 70-72)
Anderson Publishing Co.
PO Box 1576
Cincinnati, OH 45201
Ph: (513)421-4142 Fax: (513)562-8116
Fr: 800-582-7295

Robert C. DeLucia and Thomas J. Doyle. 1994. Surveys a wide range of career and employment opportunities in law enforcement, the courts, corrections, forensic science and private security. Contains career planning and job hunting advice. Profiles 77 criminal justice occupations describing job duties, work environments, and educational requirements.

★1984★ "Corrections Officer" in *VGM's Careers Encyclopedia* (pp. 120-122)
National Textbook Co. (NTC)
VGM Career Books
4255 W. Touhy Ave.
Lincolnwood, IL 60646-1975
Ph: (708)679-5500 Fax: (708)679-2494
Fr: 800-323-4900

Third edition, 1991. Contains two- to five-page descriptions of 200 managerial, professional, technical, trade, and service occupations. Each profile includes job duties, places of employment, qualifications, educational preparation, training, employment potential, advancement, income, and additional sources of information.

★1985★ "Corrections Officers" in *American Almanac of Jobs and Salaries* (pp. 96)
Avon Books
1350 Avenue of the Americas
New York, NY 10019
Ph: (212)261-6800 Fr: 800-238-0658

John Wright, editor. Revised and updated, 1994-95. A comprehensive guide to the wages of hundreds of occupations in a wide variety of industries and organizations.

★1986★ "Corrections and Rehabilitation" in *Opportunities in Law Enforcement and Criminal Justice Careers* (pp. 110-124)
National Textbook Co. (NTC)
VGM Career Books
4255 W. Touhy Ave.
Lincolnwood, IL 60646-1975
Ph: (708)679-5500 Fax: (708)679-2494
Fr: 800-323-4900

James D. Stinchcomb. 1990. Describes law enforcement and related positions at the city, county, state, and federal levels and in the military. Covers trends, future outlook, personal qualities, selection requirements, salaries, working conditions, and educational preparation.

★1987★ "Education, Government, and Legal Careers" in *The Best Jobs for the 1990s and Into the 21st Century*
Impact Publications
9104-N Manassas Dr.
Manassas Park, VA 22111
Ph: (703)361-7300 Fax: (703)335-9486

Ronald L. Krannich and Caryl Rae Krannich. 1993. Includes information on correction officers, guards, and police, detectives, and special agents.

★1988★ *Video Career Library - Public and Personal Services*
Careers, Inc.
PO Box 135
Largo, FL 34649-0135
Ph: (813)584-7333

Videocassette. 1990. 35 mins. Part of the Video Career Library covering 165 occupations. Shows actual workers on the job. Includes firefighters, police officers, correctional officers, bartenders, waiters/waitresses, cooks/chefs, child care workers, flight attendants, barbers/cosmetologists, groundskeepers/gardeners, and butchers/meat cutters.

Associations

★1989★ American Correctional Association (ACA)
8025 Laurel Lakes Ct.
Laurel, MD 20707-5075
Ph: (301)206-5100 Fax: (301)206-5061
Fr: 800-222-5646

Members: Correctional administrators, wardens, superintendents, members of prison and parole boards, probation officers, psychologists, educators, sociologists, and other individuals; institutions and associations involved in the correctional field. **Purpose:** Promotes improved correctional standards, including selection of personnel, care, supervision, education, training, employment, treatment, and post-release adjustment of inmates. Develops adequate physical facilities. Studies causes of crime and juvenile delinquency and methods of crime control and prevention through grants and contracts. Compiles statistics. Conducts research programs. **Publications:** *Corrections Today*, bimonthly. • *Directory of Institutions*, annual. • *National Jail and Adult Detention Directory*, semiannual. • *On the Line*. • *Probation and Parole Directory*, semiannual.

Standards/Certification Agencies

★1990★ American Correctional Association (ACA)
8025 Laurel Lakes Ct.
Laurel, MD 20707-5075
Ph: (301)206-5100 Fax: (301)206-5061
Fr: 800-222-5646

Promotes improved correctional standards, including selection of personnel, care, supervision, education, training, employment, treatment, and post-release adjustment of inmates.

Test Guides

★1991★ *Career Examination Series: Correction Counselor*
National Learning Corp.
212 Michael Dr.
Syosset, NY 11791
Ph: (516)921-8888 Fax: (516)921-8743
Fr: 800-645-6337

Jack Rudman. 1989. All examination guides in this series contain questions with answers.

★1992★ *Career Examination Series: Correction Counselor Trainee*
National Learning Corp.
212 Michael Dr.
Syosset, NY 11791
Ph: (516)921-8888 Fax: (516)921-8743
Fr: 800-645-6337

Jack Rudman. 1988. All examination guides in this series contain questions with answers.

★1993★ *Career Examination Series: Correction Officer*
National Learning Corp.
212 Michael Dr.
Syosset, NY 11791
Ph: (516)921-8888 Fax: (516)921-8743
Fr: 800-645-6337

Jack Rudman. 1988. All examination guides in this series contain questions with answers.

★1994★ *Career Examination Series: Correction Officer (I-IV)*
National Learning Corp.
212 Michael Dr.
Syosset, NY 11791
Ph: (516)921-8888 Fax: (516)921-8743
Fr: 800-645-6337

Jack Rudman. 1989. All examination guides in this series contain questions with answers.

★1995★ *Career Examination Series: Warden*
National Learning Corp.
212 Michael Dr.
Syosset, NY 11791
Ph: (516)921-8888 Fax: (516)921-8743
Fr: 800-645-6337

Jack Rudman. Contains many study guides for careers in the corrections field, including Warden, Deputy Warden, Prison Guard, Jail Guard, Correction Captain, Correction Hospital Officer (men and women), Correction Lieutenant, Correction Matron, Correction Officer, Correction Officer trainee, and Correction Youth Camp Officer. All examination guides in this series contain questions with answers.

★1996★ *Correction Officer*
Arco Pub.
201 W. 103rd St.
Indianapolis, IN 46290
Ph: 800-428-5331 Fax: 800-835-3202

Tenth edition.

★1997★ *Correction Officer Promotion Tests*
Prentice Hall Press
Simon & Schuster Inc.
200 Old Tappan Rd.
Old Tappan, NJ 07675
Ph: 800-223-2348

Hugh O'Neill and Hy Hammer. First edition, 1986. Contains seven practice exams with hundreds of actual civil service questions.

★1998★ *Correction Promotion Course (One Volume)*
National Learning Corp.
212 Michael Dr.
Syosset, NY 11791
Ph: (516)921-8888 Fax: (516)921-8743
Fr: 800-645-6337

Jack Rudman. Part of the General Aptitude and Abilities Series. Books in this series provide functional, intensive test practice and drill in the basic skills and areas common to many examinations, as well as general aptitude or achievement necessary for entrance into many occupations or positions.

★1999★ *Probation Officer - Parole Officer*
Prentice Hall Press
Simon & Schuster Inc.
200 Old Tappan Rd.
Old Tappan, NJ 07675
Ph: 800-223-2348

Hy Hammer. Fourth edition, 1984. Contains six sample exams with answers.

Educational Directories and Programs

★2000★ *Directory of Institutions*
American Correctional Association (ACA)
8025 Laurel Lakes Ct.
Laurel, MD 20707-5075
Ph: (301)206-5100 Fax: (301)206-5061
Fr: 800-222-5646

Annual.

★2001★ *National Jail and Adult Detention Directory*
American Correctional Association (ACA)
8025 Laurel Lakes Ct.
Laurel, MD 20707-5075
Ph: (301)206-5100 Fax: (301)206-5061
Fr: 800-222-5646

Semiannual.

★2002★ *Probation and Parole Directory*
American Correctional Association (ACA)
8025 Laurel Lakes Ct.
Laurel, MD 20707-5075
Ph: (301)206-5100 Fax: (301)206-5061
Fr: 800-222-5646

Semiannual.

Awards, Scholarships, Grants, and Fellowships

★2003★ Medal of Valor
American Correctional Association
8025 Laurel Lakes Ct.
Laurel, MD 20707-5075
Ph: (301)206-5100 Fax: (301)206-5061
Fr: 800-ACA-JOIN

To recognize corrections professionals who have gone beyond the call of duty and exhibited extreme bravery and courage either on or off the job. Nominations must be submitted by June 1. Awarded annually at the ACA winter conference. Established in 1989.

Basic Reference Guides and Handbooks

★2004★ *Burnout in Probation & Corrections*
Greenwood Publishing Group, Inc.
88 Post Rd., W.
PO Box 5007
Westport, CT 06881
Ph: (203)226-3571 Fax: (203)222-1502

John T. Whitehead. 1989.

★2005★ *Correctional Officer Resource Guide*
American Correctional Association
8025 Laurel Lakes Ct.
Laurel, MD 20707
Ph: (301)206-5100 Fax: (301)206-5061

Richard L. Phillips, editor. 1989.

★2006★ *Correctional Officers: Power, Pressure & Responsibility*
American Correctional Association
8025 Laurel Lakes Ct.
Laurel, MD 20707
Ph: (301)206-5100 Fax: (301)206-5061

American Correctional Association Staff. 1983.

★2007★ *Potential Liabilities of Probation & Parole Officers*
Anderson Publishing Co.
2035 Reading Rd.
Cincinnati, OH 45202
Ph: (513)421-4142

Rolando V. Del Carmen. Revised edition, 1986.

★2008★ *Practical Law for Jail & Prison Personnel: A Resource Manual & Training Curriculum*
American Correctional Association
8025 Laurel Lakes Ct.
Laurel, MD 20707
Ph: (301)206-5100 Fax: (301)206-5061

1987.

★2009★ *Stress Management for Correctional Officers & Their Families*
American Correctional Association
8025 Laurel Lakes Ct.
Laurel, MD 20707
Ph: (301)206-5100 Fax: (301)206-5061

Frances E. Cheek. 1984.

★2010★ *Survival Thinking: For Police & Corrections Officers*
Charles C. Thomas, Publisher
2600 S. 1st St.
Springfield, IL 62794-9265
Ph: (217)789-8980 Fax: (217)789-9130

James L. Lockard. 1991.

★2011★ *Surviving in Corrections: A Guide for Corrections Professionals*
Charles C. Thomas, Publisher
2600 S. 1st St.
Springfield, IL 62794-9265
Ph: (217)789-8980 Fax: (217)789-9130

David B. Kalinich. 1984.

Periodicals

★2012★ *CEA News and Notes Newsletter*
Correctional Education Association (CEA)
LA County Office of Education
9300 E. Imperial Hwy.
Downey, CA 90242
Ph: (213)803-8204
Jennifer Hartman

Quarterly. Supports Association efforts "to broaden the professional horizons and equip each member with the support to provide relevant educational programs which focus upon life survival skills for the adult and juvenile offender." Promotes the "importance of interaction between the disciplines and services within (correctional) institutions and agencies, in an attempt to improve the delivery of total treatment services." Recurring features include Association news, practioner-oriented articles, and training news.

★2013★ *Corrections Digest*
Washington Crime News Services
3918 Prosperity Ave., Ste. 318
Fairfax, VA 22151-3334
Ph: (703)573-1600 Fax: (703)573-1604
Fr: 800-422-9267
Betty B. Bosarge

Biweekly. Discusses prison-related issues, including reform, overcrowding, current and pending law, legislation and litigation, commutations, juveniles in adult institutions, individual state issues, budgets, and capital punishment. Provides news of recent publications and job openings.

★2014★ *Corrections Forum*
Partisan Publishing
320 Broadway
Bethpage, NY 11714
Ph: (516)942-3601 Fax: (516)942-3606
Thomas S. Kapinos

Journal serving more than 10,000 professional corrections managers and decisionmakers.

★2015★ *Corrections Today*
American Correctional Association (ACA)
8025 Laurel Lakes Ct.
Laurel, MD 20707-5075
Ph: (301)206-5100 Fax: (301)206-5061
Fr: 800-222-5646

Bimonthly. Contains articles about the field of corrections and criminal justice. Contains advertisers and product indexes and book reviews.

★2016★ *Crime Control Digest*
Washington Crime News Services
3918 Prosperity Ave., Ste. 318
Fairfax, VA 22031-3334
Ph: (703)573-1600 Fax: (703)573-1604
Fr: 800-422-9267
Betty B. Bosarge

Weekly. Contains articles on all levels of law enforcement in the U.S., including national, state, county, local, and student concerns, though the focus is on matters of national import. Reports on such items as illegal drug trafficking, terrorism, the accreditation of law enforcement agencies, pending legislation, and the implementation of new laws. Recurring features include information on upcoming seminars and conferences, and announcements of awards.

★2017★ *Criminal Justice Digest*
Washington Crime News Services
3918 Prosperity Ave., Ste. 318
Fairfax, VA 22031-3334
Ph: (703)573-1600 Fax: (703)573-1604
Fr: 800-422-9267
Betty B. Bosarge

Monthly. Discusses prevalent managerial problems and solutions in law enforcement and criminal agencies throughout the country. Covers such topics as cost cutting, efficiency improvement, overcrowded prisons, employee motivation, and employer/employee communication.

★2018★ *On the Line*
American Correctional Association (ACA)
8025 Laurel Lakes Ct.
Laurel, MD 20707-5075
Ph: (301)206-5100 Fax: (301)206-5061
Fr: 800-222-5646

Includes calendar of events, classifieds, and resource information.

Other Sources of Information

★2019★ "Correctional Officer" in *Career Selector 2001*
Barron's Educational Series, Inc.
250 Wireless Blvd.
Hauppauge, NY 11788
Ph: (516)434-3311 Fax: (516)434-3723
Fr: 800-645-3476

James C. Gonyea. 1993.

★2020★ "Correctional Officer" in *Encyclopedia of Danger: Dangerous Professions* (pp. 38-41)
Chelsea House Publishers
1974 Sproul Rd., Ste. 400
Broomall, PA 19008
Ph: (215)353-5166 Fax: (215)359-1439

Missy Allen and Michel Peissel. 1993. Provides descriptions of 24 dangerous occupations, their risky characteristics, and safety precautions.

★2021★ "Corrections Officer/Guard Jailer" in *100 Best Jobs for the 1990s & Beyond*
Dearborn Financial Publishing, Inc.
520 N. Dearborn St.
Chicago, IL 60610-4354
Ph: (312)836-4400 Fax: (312)836-1021
Fr: 800-621-9621

Carol Kleiman. 1992. Describes 100 jobs ranging from accountants to veterinarians. Each job profile includes such information as education, experience, and certification needed, salaries, and job search suggestions.

★2022★ *Treatment Custody Role Conflict in Community Based Correctional Workers: Causes & Effects*
R & E Publishers
PO Box 2008
Saratoga, CA 95070
Ph: (408)866-6303 Fax: (408)866-0825

Ronald J. Scott. 1977.

Firefighting Occupations

Firefighters work to prevent fires and to save lives and property when fires or other emergencies occur. Firefighters perform a variety of tasks in response to a fire emergency. They rescue victims and administer emergency medical aid, ventilate smoke-filled areas, operate equipment, and salvage contents of buildings. Often firefighters assume additional responsibilities, including natural disaster recovery efforts and emergency rescue and cleanup operations. When not responding to an emergency, on-duty firefighters fill out reports, operate training and public awareness programs, maintain and clean equipment, have classroom training, and conduct practice drills.

Salaries

Average earnings vary depending on city size and region of the U.S.; although volunteer firefighters make up the majority of firefighters in the U.S., they are not included when determining the average earnings.

Lowest 10 percent	$362/week or less
Midian for all firefighters	$636/week
Highest 10 percent	$987/week or more

Employment Outlook

Growth rate until the year 2005: Average.

Firefighting Occupations

Career Guides

★2023★ *American Professionals Series*
Cambridge Career Products
PO Box 2153
Charleston, WV 25328-2153
Ph: (304)744-9323 Fax: (304)744-9351
Fr: 800-468-4227

Videocassette. 1984. 30 mins. In this series of twenty-one half hour programs, various occupations are examined in depth, including a day in the life of each worker. Included are: fireman, farmer, oil driller, fisherman, horse trainer, auto assembly repairman, nurse, pilot, and paramedic.

★2024★ *Becoming a Professional Firefighter*
International Association of Fire Fighters
1750 New York Ave. NW
Washington, DC 20006-5395
Ph: (202)737-8484

Leaflet covering basic requirements and working conditions.

★2025★ *Career Insights*
RMI Media Productions, Inc.
1365 N. Winchester
Olathe, KS 66061
Ph: (913)768-1696 Fax: 800-755-6910
Fr: 800-745-5480

Videocassette series. 1987. This videotape series describes 50 occupations, including skill requirements and interviews with people employed in these fields. Occupations include: flight service, air transportation/ground services, data processing, carpentry, clerk in banking/insurance/business, cosmetic personal grooming, firefighting, forestry, insulation/roofing, mechanics, material handling, photographic processing, pipefitting and plumbing, printing, secretarial services, tool and die operations.

★2026★ *Career Success Series*
Cambridge Educational
PO Box 2153
Charleston, WV 25328-2153
Ph: (304)744-9323 Fax: (304)744-9351
Fr: 800-468-4227

Videocassette. 1986. 15 mins. A series, available separately, outlining various career choices for students. Occupations include: accounting, flight service, air transportation/ground/flight service, data processing, carpentry, clerk in banking/insurance, commodity sales, cosmetic personal grooming, fire fighting, forestry services, home economics, insulation/roofing, material handling, mechanics, photographic processing, pipefitting and plumbing, police science, printing, carpentry, medical laboratory technicians, secretarial services, and utilities equipment operator.

★2027★ *Fire Fighter*
Vocational Biographies, Inc.
PO Box 31
Sauk Centre, MN 56378-0031
Ph: (612)352-6516 Fax: (612)352-5546
Fr: 800-255-0752

1992. Four-page pamphlet containing a personal narrative about a worker's job, work likes and dislikes, career path from high school to the present. Education and training, the rewards and frustrations, and the effects of the job on the rest of the worker's life. The data file portion of this pamphlet gives a concise occupational summary, including work descriptions, working conditions, places of employment, personal characteristics, education and training, job outlook, and salary range.

★2028★ *Fire Fighter*
Troll Associates
100 Corporate Dr.
Mahwah, NJ 07430
Ph: (201)529-4000 Fax: (201)529-9347
Fr: 800-526-5289

Michael Pellowski. 1989.

★2029★ *"Fire Fighter" in Action Careers: Employment in the High-Risk Job Market (pp. 59-75)*
Citadel Press/Lyle Stuart Inc.
Carol Publishing Group
120 Enterprise Ave.
Secaucus, NJ 07094
Ph: (201)866-0490

Ragnar Benson. 1988. Describes 24 dangerous careers such as repo man, explosives handler, and river rafting guide. Each profile includes demand for the job, where the jobs can be found, required personal and physical characteristics and training needed.

★2030★ "Fire Fighter" in *Career Information Center* (Vol.11)
Simon and Schuster
200 Old Tappan Rd.
Old Tappan, NJ 07675
Fax: 800-445-6991 Fr: 800-223-2348

Richard Lidz and Dale Anderson, editorial directors. Fifth edition, 1993. For 600 occupations, describes job duties, entry-level requirements, education and training needed, advancement possibilities, employment outlook, earnings and benefits. The set is divided into 12 volumes. Each volume includes jobs related under a broad career field. Volume 13 is the index.

★2031★ "Fire Fighter, Paramedic" in *Straight Talk on Careers: 80 Pros Take You Into Their Professions* (pp. 227-230, 231-232)
Garrett Park Press
PO Box 1907
Garrett Park, MD 20896
Ph: (301)946-2553

Mary Barbera-Hogan. 1987. Written for readers in high school and college. Contains candid interviews from professionals who discuss what their days are like and the pros and cons of their occupations.

★2032★ *Fire Fighters*
Scholastic, Inc.
730 Broadway
New York, NY 10003
Ph: (212)505-3000

Robert Maas. 1989.

★2033★ "Fire Fighters" in *American Almanac of Jobs and Salaries* (pp. 98)
Avon Books
1350 Avenue of the Americas
New York, NY 10019
Ph: (212)261-6800 Fr: 800-238-0658

John Wright, editor. Revised and updated, 1994-95. A comprehensive guide to the wages of hundreds of occupations in a wide variety of industries and organizations.

★2034★ "Fire Fighters" in *Career Discovery Encyclopedia* (Vol.2, pp. 16-17)
J.G. Ferguson Publishing Co.
200 W. Madison St., Ste. 300
Chicago, IL 60606
Ph: (312)580-5480 Fax: (312)580-4948

E. Russell Primm, editor-in-chief. 1993. Contains two-page articles on 504 occupations. Each article describes job duties, earnings, and educational and training requirements.

★2035★ *Fire Fighters and Inspectors*
Chronicle Guidance Publications, Inc.
66 Aurora St.
PO Box 1190
Moravia, NY 13118-1190
Ph: (315)497-0330 Fax: (315)497-3359
Fr: 800-622-7284

1994. This career brief describes the nature of the work, working conditions, hours and earnings, education and training, licensure, certification, unions, personal qualifications, social and psychological factors, employment outlook, entry methods, advancement, and related occupations.

★2036★ "Fire Fighters" in *Jobs! What They Are—Where They Are—What They Pay* (pp. 135)
Simon & Schuster, Inc.
Simon & Schuster Bldg.
1230 Avenue of the Americas
New York, NY 10020
Ph: (212)698-7000

Robert O. Snelling and Anne M. Snelling. Revised edition, 1992. Profiles 241 occupations, describing duties and responsibilities, educational preparation, earnings, employment opportunities, training, and qualifications.

★2037★ *Fire Prevention & Firefighting*
Morris Video
2730 Monterey St., No. 105
Monterey Business Park
Torrance, CA 90503
Ph: (310)533-4800 Fr: 800-843-3606

Videocassette. 1984. 15 mins. Careers dealing with fire prevention, fighting, and emergency rescue are examined.

★2038★ "Fire Protection Engineer" in *Career Information Center* (Vol.6)
Simon and Schuster
200 Old Tappan Rd.
Old Tappan, NJ 07675
Fax: 800-445-6991 Fr: 800-223-2348

Richard Lidz and Linda Perrin, editorial directors. Fifth edition, 1993. This 13-volume set profiles over 600 occupations. Each occupational profile describes job duties, entry-level requirements, educational requirements, advancement possibilities, employment outlook, working conditions, earnings and benefits, and where to write for more information.

★2039★ "Fire Safety Technicians" in *Encyclopedia of Careers and Vocational Guidance* (Vol.2, pp. 673-678)
J.G. Ferguson Publishing Co.
200 W. Madison St., Ste. 300
Chicago, IL 60606
Ph: (312)580-5480 Fax: (312)580-4948

William E. Hopke, editor-in-chief. Ninth edition, 1993. Four-volume set that profiles 900 occupations and describes job trends in 74 industries. Includes career description, educational requirements, history of the job, methods of entry, advancement, employment outlook, earnings, conditions of work, social and psychological factors, and sources of further information.

★2040★ "Fire Science" in *Career Connection II: A Guide to Technical Majors and Their Related Careers* (pp. 80-81)
Jist Works, Inc.
720 N. Park Ave.
Indianapolis, IN 46202-3431
Ph: (317)264-3720 Fax: (317)264-3709

Fred A. Rowe. 1994. Contains technical majors, such as automotive technology. Describes the major and the job. Lists high school and postsecondary school courses. Includes occupations related to the major, employment outlook, and starting salary.

★2041★ *Firefighter*
Careers, Inc.
PO Box 135
Largo, FL 34649-0135
Ph: (813)584-7333

1995. Two-page occupational summary card describing duties, working conditions, personal qualifications, training, earnings and hours, employment outlook, places of employment, related careers and where to write for more information.

★2042★ "Firefighter" in *Hard Hatted Women: Stories of Struggle and Success in the Trades* (pp. 156-170)
Seal Press
3131 Western Ave., Ste. 410
Seattle, WA 98121
Ph: (206)283-7844 Fax: (206)285-9410

Molly Martin, editor. 1988. Twenty-six women recount their experiences working in blue collar occupations. They describe how they got in, the work they do, their relationships in predominantly male occupations, and their training.

★2043★ "Firefighter" in *Jobs Rated Almanac*
World Almanac
1 International Blvd., Ste. 444
Mahwah, NJ 07495
Ph: (201)529-6900 Fax: (201)529-6901

Les Krantz. Second edition, 1992. Ranks 250 jobs by environment, salary, outlooks, physical demands, stress, security, travel opportunities, and extra perks. Includes jobs the editor feels are the most common, most interesting, and the most rapidly growing.

★2044★ "Firefighter" in *Occu-Facts: Information on 580 Careers in Outline Form*
Careers, Inc.
PO Box 135
Largo, FL 34649-0135
Ph: (813)584-7333

Biennial, 1995-96 edition. Each one-page occupational profile describes duties, working conditions, physical surroundings and demands, aptitudes, temperament, educational requirements, employment outlook, earnings, and places of employment.

★2045★ "Firefighter" in *VGM's Careers Encyclopedia* (pp. 176-178)
National Textbook Co. (NTC)
VGM Career Books
4255 W. Touhy Ave.
Lincolnwood, IL 60646-1975
Ph: (708)679-5500 Fax: (708)679-2494
Fr: 800-323-4900

Third edition, 1991. Contains two- to five-page descriptions of 200 managerial, professional, technical, trade, and service occupations. Each profile includes job duties, places of employment, qualifications, educational preparation, training, employment potential, advancement, income, and additional sources of information.

★2046★ *Firefighters: A to Z*
Walker & Co.
720 5th Ave.
New York, NY 10019
Ph: (212)265-3632 Fax: (212)307-1764

Jean Johnson. 1985.

★2047★ "Firefighters" in *Encyclopedia of Careers and Vocational Guidance* (Vol.2, pp. 668-672)
J.G. Ferguson Publishing Co.
200 W. Madison St., Ste. 300
Chicago, IL 60606
Ph: (312)580-5480 Fax: (312)580-4948

William E. Hopke, editor-in-chief. Ninth edition, 1993. Four-volume set that profiles 500 occupations and describes job trends in 74 industries. Includes career description, educational requirements, history of the job, methods of entry, advancement, employment outlook, earnings, working conditions, social and psychological factors, and sources of additional information.

★2048★ "Firefighters" in *Opportunities in Vocational and Technical Careers* (p. 76-90)
National Textbook Co. (NTC)
VGM Career Books
4255 W. Touhy Ave.
Lincolnwood, IL 60646-1975
Ph: (708)679-5500 Fax: (708)679-2494
Fr: 800-323-4900

Adrian A. Paradis. 1992. Describes careers which can be prepared for by attending a private vocational or proprietary school—office employee, sales worker, service worker, health services, mechanic, craftworker, and technician. Covers employment outlook, job duties, and salaries. Offers career planning advice.

★2049★ **"Firefighting Occupations" in *Occupational Outlook Handbook***
U.S. Government Printing Office
Superintendent of Documents
Washington, DC 20402
Ph: (202)512-1800 Fax: (202)512-2250
Biennial; latest edition, 1994-95. Encyclopedia of careers describing more than 250 occupations and comprising about 85 percent of all jobs in the economy. Occupations that require lengthy education or training are given the most attention. For each occupation, the handbook describes job duties, working conditions, training, educational preparation, personal qualities, advancement possibilities, job outlook, earnings, and sources of additional information.

★2050★ ***Making of a Fire Fighter***
Film Communicators
108 Wilmot Rd.
Deerfield, IL 60015-5196
Ph: (708)940-1260 Fr: 800-621-2131
Videocassette. 19??. 16 mins. This film is designed to familiarize prospective recruits and the community with the Fire Service.

★2051★ ***National Professional Qualifications System: Established by the Joint Council of National Fire Service Organizations***
National Fire Protection Association
1 Batterymarch Park
Quincy, MA 02269-9109
Ph: (617)770-3000
American National Standards Institute. 1987.

★2052★ ***NFPA 1001, Fire Fighter Professional Qualifications, 1987 edition***
National Fire Protection Association
1 Batterymarch Park
Quincy, MA 02269-9101
Ph: (617)770-3000
1987.

★2053★ ***Opportunities in Fire Protection Services***
National Textbook Co. (NTC)
VGM Career Books
4255 W. Touhy Ave.
Lincolnwood, IL 60646-1975
Ph: (708)679-5500 Fax: (708)679-2494
Fr: 800-323-4900
Ron J. Coleman. 1990. Explores firefighting and related jobs with not only local fire departments but also with state and federal governments and private fire departments, fire sprinkler and fire equipment manufacturing companies, and insurance companies. Covers personal qualifications, educational preparation and training, advancement possibilities, and salaries. Offers job hunting advice.

★2054★ ***Standard for Professional Qualifications for Fire Inspector, Fire Investigator, & Fire Prevention Education Officer: NFPA 1031***
National Fire Protection Association
1 Batterymarch Park
Quincy, MA 02269-9109
Ph: (617)770-3000
National Fire Protection Association Staff. 1983.

★2055★ ***Standard for Professional Qualifications for Fire Investigator***
National Fire Protection Association
1 Batterymarch Park
Quincy, MA 02269-9109
Ph: (617)770-3000
American National Standards Institute. 1987.

★2056★ ***Standard for Professional Qualifications for Public Fire Educator***
National Fire Protection Association
1 Batterymarch Park
Quincy, MA 02269-9109
Ph: (617)770-3000
American National Standards Institute. 1987.

★2057★ ***Video Career Library - Public and Personal Services***
Careers, Inc.
PO Box 135
Largo, FL 34649-0135
Ph: (813)584-7333
Videocassette. 1990. 35 mins. Part of the Video Career Library covering 165 occupations. Shows actual workers on the job. Includes firefighters, police officers, correctional officers, bartenders, waiters/waitresses, cooks/chefs, child care workers, flight attendants, barbers/cosmetologists, groundskeepers/gardeners, and butchers/meat cutters.

Associations

★2058★ **International Association of Fire Chiefs (IAFC)**
4025 Fair Ridge Dr.
Fairfax, VA 22033-2868
Ph: (703)273-0911 Fax: (703)273-9363
Members: Membership in 26 countries includes: fire chiefs in city and state departments, industry, and military installations; equipment manufacturers; individuals interested in fire prevention, fire protection, and fire fighting. **Purpose:** Conducts research and information gathering projects to promote increased fire department efficiency and better public awareness. **Publications:** *IAFC On Scene*, semimonthly.

★2059★ **International Association of Fire Fighters (IAFF)**
1750 New York Ave. NW
Washington, DC 20006-5395
Ph: (202)737-8484
Members: AFL-CIO, Canadian Labour Congress. **Publications:** *International Fire Fighter*, bimonthly. • *Local Union Officers Directory*, annual.

★2060★ **National Fire Protection Association (NFPA)**
1 Batterymarch Park
PO Box 9101
Quincy, MA 02269-9101
Ph: (617)770-3000 Fax: (617)770-0700
Members: Membership drawn from the fire service, business and industry, health care, educational and other institutions, and individuals in the fields of insurance, government, architecture, and engineering. **Purpose:** Develops, publishes, and disseminates standards, prepared by approximately 250 technical committees, intended to minimize the possibility and effects of fire and explosion; conducts fire safety education programs for the general public. Provides information on fire protection, prevention, and suppression; compiles annual statistics on causes and occupancies of fires, large-loss fires (over $1,000,000), fire deaths, and fire fighter casualties. Provides field service by specialists on electricity, flammable liquids and gases, and marine fire problems. Sponsors National Fire Prevention Week each October and public education campaigns featuring Sparky the Fire Dog. Also sponsors seminars on the Life Safety Code, the National Electrical Code, hotel/motel fire safety, shipyard fire protection, fire safety in detention and correctional facilities, and other timely topics. Conducts research projects that apply statistical methods and operations research to develop computer models and data management systems. Maintains library of 20,000 books, reports, periodicals, audiovisual materials, as well as 13,000 pieces of microform. **Publications:** *Catalogs of Publications and Visual Aids*, annual. • *Fire News*, bimonthly. • *Fire Protection Handbook*. • *Fire Protection Reference Directory and Buyer's Guide*, annual. • *Fire Technology*, quarterly. • *Learn Not to Burn Curriculum*. • *National Fire Codes*, annual. • *National Fire Protection Association—Technical Committee Reports/Technical Committee Documentation*, semiannual. • *NFPA Journal*, bimonthly.

Standards/Certification Agencies

★2061★ **National Fire Protection Association (NFPA)**
1 Batterymarch Park
PO Box 9101
Quincy, MA 02269-9101
Ph: (617)770-3000 Fax: (617)770-0700
Develops, publishes, and disseminates standards, prepared by approximately 250 technical committees, intended to minimize the possibility and effects of fire and explosion; conducts fire safety education programs for the general public.

Test Guides

★2062★ ***Career Examination Series: Administrative Fire Marshal (Uniformed)***
National Learning Corp.
212 Michael Dr.
Syosset, NY 11791
Ph: (516)921-8888 Fax: (516)921-8743
Fr: 800-645-6337
Jack Rudman. Test guide including questions and answers for students or professionals in the field who seek advancement through examination.

★2063★ *Career Examination Series: Assistant Fire Marshal*
National Learning Corp.
212 Michael Dr.
Syosset, NY 11791
Ph: (516)921-8888 Fax: (516)921-8743
Fr: 800-645-6337

Jack Rudman. Test guide including questions and answers for students or professionals in the field who seek advancement through examination.

★2064★ *Career Examination Series: Battalion Chief, Fire Dept.*
National Learning Corp.
212 Michael Dr.
Syosset, NY 11791
Ph: (516)921-8888 Fax: (516)921-8743
Fr: 800-645-6337

Jack Rudman. All examination guides in this series contain questions with answers.

★2065★ *Career Examination Series: Captain, Fire Dept.*
National Learning Corp.
212 Michael Dr.
Syosset, NY 11791
Ph: (516)921-8888 Fax: (516)921-8743
Fr: 800-645-6337

Jack Rudman. All examination guides in this series contain questions with answers.

★2066★ *Career Examination Series: Chief Fire Marshal*
National Learning Corp.
212 Michael Dr.
Syosset, NY 11791
Ph: (516)921-8888 Fax: (516)921-8743
Fr: 800-645-6337

Jack Rudman. All examination guides in this series contain questions with answers.

★2067★ *Career Examination Series: Deputy Chief, Fire Dept.*
National Learning Corp.
212 Michael Dr.
Syosset, NY 11791
Ph: (516)921-8888 Fax: (516)921-8743
Fr: 800-645-6337

Jack Rudman. All examination guides in this series contain questions with answers.

★2068★ *Career Examination Series: Deputy Chief Fire Marshal (Uniformed)*
National Learning Corp.
212 Michael Dr.
Syosset, NY 11791
Ph: (516)921-8888 Fax: (516)921-8743
Fr: 800-645-6337

Jack Rudman. All examination guides in this series contain questions with answers.

★2069★ *Career Examination Series: Director of Fire Safety*
National Learning Corp.
212 Michael Dr.
Syosset, NY 11791
Ph: (516)921-8888 Fax: (516)921-8743
Fr: 800-645-6337

Jack Rudman. Test guide including questions and answers for students or professionals in the field who seek advancement through examination.

★2070★ *Career Examination Series: Fire Engine Driver*
National Learning Corp.
212 Michael Dr.
Syosset, NY 11791
Ph: (516)921-8888 Fax: (516)921-8743
Fr: 800-645-6337

Jack Rudman. All examination guides in this series contain questions with answers.

★2071★ *Career Examination Series: Fire Inspector*
National Learning Corp.
212 Michael Dr.
Syosset, NY 11791
Ph: (516)921-8888 Fax: (516)921-8743
Fr: 800-645-6337

Jack Rudman. All examination guides in this series contain questions with answers.

★2072★ *Career Examination Series: Fire Marshal*
National Learning Corp.
212 Michael Dr.
Syosset, NY 11791
Ph: (516)921-8888 Fax: (516)921-8743
Fr: 800-645-6337

Jack Rudman. All examination guides in this series contain questions with answers.

★2073★ *Career Examination Series: Fire Officer*
National Learning Corp.
212 Michael Dr.
Syosset, NY 11791
Ph: (516)921-8888 Fax: (516)921-8743
Fr: 800-645-6337

Jack Rudman. All examination guides in this series contain questions with answers.

★2074★ *Career Examination Series: Fire Prevention Inspector*
National Learning Corp.
212 Michael Dr.
Syosset, NY 11791
Ph: (516)921-8888 Fax: (516)921-8743
Fr: 800-645-6337

Jack Rudman. All examination guides in this series contain questions with answers.

★2075★ *Career Examination Series: Fire Protection Specialist*
National Learning Corp.
212 Michael Dr.
Syosset, NY 11791
Ph: (516)921-8888 Fax: (516)921-8743
Fr: 800-645-6337

Jack Rudman. All examination guides in this series contain questions with answers.

★2076★ *Career Examination Series: Fire Safety Officer*
National Learning Corp.
212 Michael Dr.
Syosset, NY 11791
Ph: (516)921-8888 Fax: (516)921-8743
Fr: 800-645-6337

Jack Rudman. All examination guides in this series contain questions with answers.

★2077★ *Career Examination Series: Fire & Safety Representative*
National Learning Corp.
212 Michael Dr.
Syosset, NY 11791
Ph: (516)921-8888 Fax: (516)921-8743
Fr: 800-645-6337

Jack Rudman. All examination guides in this series contain questions with answers.

★2078★ *Career Examination Series: Fire Safety Technician*
National Learning Corp.
212 Michael Dr.
Syosset, NY 11791
Ph: (516)921-8888 Fax: (516)921-8743
Fr: 800-645-6337

Jack Rudman. All examination guides in this series contain questions with answers.

★2079★ *Career Examination Series: Firefighter*
National Learning Corp.
212 Michael Dr.
Syosset, NY 11791
Ph: (516)921-8888 Fax: (516)921-8743
Fr: 800-645-6337

Jack Rudman. All examination guides in this series contain questions with answers.

★2080★ *Career Examination Series: Firehouse Attendant*
National Learning Corp.
212 Michael Dr.
Syosset, NY 11791
Ph: (516)921-8888 Fax: (516)921-8743
Fr: 800-645-6337

Jack Rudman. All examination guides in this series contain questions with answers.

★2081★ *Career Examination Series: Fireman Examinations-All States*
National Learning Corp.
212 Michael Dr.
Syosset, NY 11791
Ph: (516)921-8888 Fax: (516)921-8743
Fr: 800-645-6337

Jack Rudman. All examination guides in this series contain questions with answers.

★2082★ *Career Examination Series: Fireman, Fire Dept.*
National Learning Corp.
212 Michael Dr.
Syosset, NY 11791
Ph: (516)921-8888 Fax: (516)921-8743
Fr: 800-645-6337

Jack Rudman. All examination guides in this series contain questions with answers.

★2083★ *Career Examination Series: Fireman-Laborer*
National Learning Corp.
212 Michael Dr.
Syosset, NY 11791
Ph: (516)921-8888 Fax: (516)921-8743
Fr: 800-645-6337

Jack Rudman. All examination guides in this series contain questions with answers.

★2084★ *Career Examination Series: Lieutenant Fire Department*
National Learning Corp.
212 Michael Dr.
Syosset, NY 11791
Ph: (516)921-8888 Fax: (516)921-8743
Fr: 800-645-6337

Jack Rudman. Test guide including questions and answers for students or professionals in the field who seek advancement through examination.

★2085★ *Career Examination Series: Senior Fire Prevention Inspector*
National Learning Corp.
212 Michael Dr.
Syosset, NY 11791
Ph: (516)921-8888 Fax: (516)921-8743
Fr: 800-645-6337

Jack Rudman. Test guide including questions and answers for students or professionals in the field who seek advancement through examination.

★2086★ *Fire Administration & Supervision*
National Learning Corp.
212 Michael Dr.
Syosset, NY 11791
Ph: (516)921-8888 Fax: (516)921-8743
Fr: 800-645-6337

Jack Rudman. Part of the General Aptitude and Abilities Series. Books in this series provide functional, intensive test practice and drill in the basic skills and areas common to many examinations, as well as general aptitude or achievement necessary for entrance into many occupations or positions.

★2087★ *Fire Captain Oral Exam Study Guide*
Information Guides
32 18th St.
Hermosa Beach, CA 90254
Ph: (213)374-1914

Arthur R. Couvillon. 1988.

★2088★ *Fire Department Lieutenant/ Captain/Battalion Chief*
Prentice Hall Press
Simon & Schuster Inc.
200 Old Tappan Rd.
Old Tappan, NJ 07675
Ph: 800-223-2348

Gene Mahony. First edition, 1983. Includes over 600 questions with answers concerning fire department supervision.

★2089★ *Fire Department Lieutenant Captain Battalion Chief: Score High on Firefighter Promotion Exams*
Prentice Hall
Rte. 9W
Englewood Cliffs, NJ 07632
Ph: (201)592-2000

Gene Maloney. 1983.

★2090★ *Fire Engineer Written Exam Study Guide*
Information Guides
32 18th St.
Hermosa Beach, CA 90254
Ph: (213)374-1914

Arthur R. Couvillon. Second revised edition, 1988.

★2091★ *Fire Promotion Course (One Volume)*
National Learning Corp.
212 Michael Dr.
Syosset, NY 11791
Ph: (516)921-8888 Fax: (516)921-8743
Fr: 800-645-6337

Jack Rudman. Part of the General Aptitude and Abilities Series. Books in this series provide functional, intensive test practice and drill in the basic skills and areas common to many examinations, as well as general aptitude or achievement necessary for entrance into many occupations or positions.

★2092★ *Firefighter*
Arco Pub.
201 W. 103rd St.
Indianapolis, IN 46290
Ph: 800-428-5331 Fax: 800-835-3202

Robert Andriuolo. 1993, tenth edition. Provides five full length exams with answers.

★2093★ *Firefighter Entrance Examinations*
Ken-Books
56 Midcrest Way
San Francisco, CA 94131
Ph: (415)826-6550

Harry W. Koch. Second edition, 1989.

★2094★ *How to Prepare for the Fire Fighter Examinations*
Barron's Educational Series, Inc.
250 Wireless Blvd.
Hauppauge, NY 11788
Ph: (516)434-3311 Fax: (516)434-3723
Fr: 800-645-3476

Second edition. 1990. Guide contains four full-length practice firefighter exams plus one diagnostic exam, with answers explained. Practice exams include two recent New York City Fire Dept. exams and two exams modeled after tests used throughout the U.S.

Educational Directories and Programs

★2095★ *Fire Protection Reference Directory and Buyer's Guide*
National Fire Protection Association (NFPA)
1 Batterymarch Park
PO Box 9101
Quincy, MA 02269-9101
Ph: (617)770-3000 Fax: (617)770-0700

Annual. Provides information on products, manufacturers and sales office, and services in the field of fire protection. Includes list of trade names.

★2096★ *Local Union Officers Directory*
International Association of Fire Fighters (IAFF)
1750 New York Ave. NW
Washington, DC 20006-5395
Ph: (202)737-8484

Annual.

★2097★ *National Directory of Fire Chiefs & Emergency Departments*
SPAN Publishing
1308 Main St.
Stevens Point, WI 54481
Ph: (715)345-2772 Fax: (715)345-7288
Fr: 800-647-7579
Laurie Bannach, Contact

Annual, February. Covers Approximately 38,000 fire and emergency departments in the U.S. Entries include: Department name, address, phone, fax, telex, county, name of chief. Arrangement: Geographical.

Awards, Scholarships, Grants, and Fellowships

★2098★ Fire Fighter of the Year
National Burglar and Fire Alarm Association
Public Safety Commitee
7101 Wisconsin Ave. NW, Ste. 901
Bethesda, MD 20814
Ph: (301)907-3202 Fax: (301)907-7897

To honor the fire fighter who has done the most to promote the use of professional fire alarm systems and to advance closer cooperation between the fire prevention community and the alarm industry. Nominations are submitted by Chartered State Associations.

★2099★ *Firehouse* Magazine Heroism and Community Service Award
PTN Publishing Company
445 Broadhollow Rd., Ste. 21
Melville, NY 11747-4722
Ph: (516)845-2700 Fax: (516)496-8013

For recognition of service above and beyond the call of duty. Members of a professional or volunteer fire service organization may be nominated by December 31. Monetary awards and a plaque are awarded annually. Established in 1977.

★2100★ Fireman of the Year
International Fire Buff Associates
7509 Chesapeake Ave.
Baltimore, MD 21219
Ph: (410)477-1544

To acknowledge an outstanding fireman serving in the fire department of the city where the group's annual convention is held. The fireman is chosen by the host city Fire Chief. An inscribed plaque and a $100 United States Savings Bond are awarded annually at the convention banquet. Established in 1971.

★2101★ Everett E. Hudiburg Award
International Fire Service Training Association
Fire Protection Publications
Oklahoma State Univ.
Stillwater, OK 74078-0118
Ph: (405)744-5723 Fax: (405)744-8204

To honor individuals for significant contributions to the training of firefighters. Anyone who works in the fire service field is eligible to submit an application by March 1. Recipients are selected by secret ballot of the Executive Board. A plaque is awarded annually at the Validation Conference in July. Established in

1972 in memory of Everett E. Hudiburg, a past editor.

★2102★ International Benjamin Franklin Fire Service Award
International Association of Fire Chiefs
Publications Dept.
1329 18th St. NW
Washington, DC 20036-6516
Ph: (202)833-3420 Fax: (202)452-0684
To provide worldwide recognition to fire fighters for a life-saving effort involving courage and the demonstration of expert training, professional service and dedication to duty. An active fire fighter of any country may be nominated by his Chief for an incident in which he saved a human life. A plaque and medallion are awarded to the individual, and a plaque and a U.S. Savings Bond are awarded to the department. Awarded when merited. Established in 1948. Co-sponsored by the Motorola Corporation.

★2103★ NAFI Man of the Year
National Association of Fire Investigators
PO Box 957257
Hoffman Estates, IL 60195-7257
Ph: (312)427-6320
To recognize significant contributions to the fire investigation profession and NAFI. Firefighters, police officers, attorneys, insurance adjusters, claimsmen, fire experts, fire marshals in the military, or full-time fire investigators may be nominated. An engraved plaque is awarded annually when merited. Established in 1969.

★2104★ Public Service Award
Scanner Association of North America
PO Box 414
Western Springs, IL 60558
Ph: (312)246-4550
To recognize a police, fire, or other public safety volunteer or official for heroic action. Members of the Association may nominate individuals. A monetary prize and a plaque are awarded six times per year. Established in 1978.

Basic Reference Guides and Handbooks

★2105★ *Engineers, Pump Operators, Drivers Handbook*
Davis Publishing Co.
2015 McFarland Blvd. E.
Tuscaloosa, AL 35405
Ph: (205)759-1508 Fr: 800-538-0762
Robert E. Ford. 1977.

★2106★ *Fire Assessment Centers: The New Concept in Promotional Examinations*
Davis Publishing Co., Inc.
2015 McFarland Blvd. E.
Tuscaloosa, AL 35405
Ph: (205)759-1508 Fr: 800-538-0762
George Tielsch. 1978.

★2107★ *Fire Brigade Training Program: Instructor's Guide*
National Fire Protection Association
1 Batterymarch Park
Quincy, MA 02269-9101
Ph: (617)770-3000

★2108★ *Fire Brigade Training Program: Student Manual*
National Fire Protection Association
1 Batterymarch Park
Quincy, MA 02269-9101

★2109★ *Fire Command Officer's Handbook*
Davis Publishing Co.
2015 McFarland Blvd. E.
Tuscaloosa, AL 35405
Ph: (205)759-1508 Fr: 800-538-0762
Robert E. Ford. 1978.

★2110★ *Fire Department Safety Officer's Reference Guide*
National Fire Protection Association
1 Batterymarch Park
Quincy, MA 02269-9101
Ph: (617)770-3000

★2111★ *Fire Lieutenant's & Captain's Handbook*
Davis Publishing Co.
2015 McFarland Blvd. E.
Tuscaloosa, AL 35405
Ph: (205)759-1508 Fr: 800-538-0762
Robert E. Ford. 1977.

★2112★ *Fire Protection Handbook*
National Fire Protection Association (NFPA)
1 Batterymarch Park
PO Box 9101
Quincy, MA 02269-9101
Ph: (617)770-3000 Fax: (617)770-0700

★2113★ *Firefighter & Paramedic Burnout*
Arco Publishing Co.
Macmillan General Reference
15 Columbus Cir.
New York, NY 10023
Fax: 800-835-3202 Fr: 800-858-7674
Gerald L. Fishkin. 1990.

★2114★ *Firefighter's Entrance Handbook*
Davis Publishing Co.
2015 McFarland Blvd. E.
Tuscaloosa, AL 35405
Ph: (205)759-1508 Fr: 800-538-0762
Robert E. Ford. 1977.

★2115★ *Industrial Fire Brigades Training Manual*
National Fire Protection Association
1 Batterymarch Park
Quincy, MA 02269-9101
Ph: (617)770-3000
Charles A. Tuck, Jr., editor. Fifth edition, 1982.

★2116★ *Learn Not to Burn Curriculum*
National Fire Protection Association (NFPA)
1 Batterymarch Park
PO Box 9101
Quincy, MA 02269-9101
Ph: (617)770-3000 Fax: (617)770-0700

★2117★ *Tentative Standard for Proctective Clothing for Fire Fighters*
National Fire Protection Association
1 Battertmarch Park
Quincy, MA 02269-9101
Ph: (617)770-3000
1986.

★2118★ *Training Reports & Records*
National Fire Protection Association
1 Batterymarch Park
Quincy, MA 02269-9101
Ph: (617)770-3000
1970. Part of Zero Series.

★2119★ *Winning the Fire Service Leadership Game*
Fire Engineering Book & Videos
Park 80 W., Plaza 2, 7th Fl.
Saddle Brook, NJ 07662
H. Caulfield. 1985.

Periodicals

★2120★ *American Fire Journal*
9072 E. Artesia Blvd., Ste. 7
Bellflower, CA 90706-6299
Ph: (310)866-1664 Fax: (310)867-6434
Carol Carlsen Brooks
Monthly. Magazine about fire protection.

★2121★ *Catalogs of Publications and Visual Aids*
National Fire Protection Association (NFPA)
1 Batterymarch Park
PO Box 9101
Quincy, MA 02269-9101
Ph: (617)770-3000 Fax: (617)770-0700
Annual.

★2122★ *Codewatch*
National Fire Sprinkler Association (NFSA)
Robin Hill Corporate Park
Rte. 22, Box 1000
Patterson, NY 12563
Ph: (914)878-4200 Fax: (914)878-4215
Quarterly. Lists changes in model codes and state and local laws and regulations, and amendments to building codes and local ordinances.

★2123★ *Fire Control Digest*
Washington Capital News Reports, Inc.
3918 Prosperity Ave., Ste. 318
Fairfax, VA 22031
Ph: (703)573-1600 Fax: (703)573-1604
Susan Kernus
Monthly. Considers concerns of fire fighting and safety, including arson, construction materials, the toxicity of plastics, fire hazards, emergency medical service (EMS), fire codes, insurance, state concerns, and fire departments that are in the news. Also includes information on seminars and classes.

★2124★ *Fire Engineering*
Pennwell Publishing Co.
Park 80 West Plaza 2
Saddle Brook, NJ 07662-5612
Ph: (201)845-0800 Fax: (201)845-6275
Bill Manning
Monthly. Fire suppression, protection, and prevention magazine.

★2125★ *Fire Management Notes*
U.S. Government Printing Office
Superintendent of Documents
Washington, DC 20402-9322
Ph: (202)783-3238 Fax: (202)512-2250
David W. Dahl
Quarterly. Magazine on forest fire control.

★2126★ *Fire and Materials*
John Wiley and Sons, Inc.
Subscription Dept.
605 3rd Ave.
New York, NY 10158
Ph: (212)850-6000 Fax: (212)850-6799
J.D. Redfern
Bimonthly. Journal which focuses on the fire properties of materials. Topics include heat release, properties of combustion products, and modelling and testing.

★2127★ *Fire News*
National Fire Protection Association (NFPA)
1 Batterymarch Park
PO Box 9101
Quincy, MA 02269-9101
Ph: (617)770-3000 Fax: (617)770-0700
Bimonthly. Features calendar of events and lists job openings.

★2128★ *Fire Technology*
National Fire Protection Association (NFPA)
1 Batterymarch Park
PO Box 9101
Quincy, MA 02269-9101
Ph: (617)770-3000 Fax: (617)770-0700
Quarterly. Professional journal for the fire safety practitioner and the fire safety researcher. Papers describe advances in fire technology.

★2129★ *Firefighter's News*
Lifesaving Communications, Inc.
248 S. Rehoboth Blvd.
PO Box 165
Milford, DE 19963-0165
Ph: (302)422-2772 Fax: (302)422-0552
Steve Stevenson
Bimonthly. Magazine (tabloid) reporting on issues affecting professional and volunteer fire and rescue personnel.

★2130★ *Firehouse Magazine*
PTN Publishing Co.
445 Broad Hollow Rd., Ste. 21
Melville, NY 11747
Ph: (516)845-2700 Fax: (516)845-7109
Bruce BowlingPublisher
Monthly. Magazine focusing on fire protection.

★2131★ *Grass Roots*
National Fire Sprinkler Association (NFSA)
Robin Hill Corporate Park
Rte. 22, Box 1000
Patterson, NY 12563
Ph: (914)878-4200 Fax: (914)878-4215
Monthly.

★2132★ *IAFC On Scene*
International Association of Fire Chiefs (IAFC)
4025 Fair Ridge Dr.
Fairfax, VA 22033-2868
Ph: (703)273-0911 Fax: (703)273-9363
Semimonthly. Covers current news of interest to fire and emergency services managers.

★2133★ *International Fire Fighter*
International Association of Fire Fighters (IAFF)
1750 New York Ave. NW
Washington, DC 20006-5395
Ph: (202)737-8484
Bimonthly. Union tabloid; includes IAFF media awards and death and injury survey.

★2134★ *ISFSI Instruct-O-Gram*
International Society of Fire Service Instructors (ISFSI)
30 Main St.
Ashland, MA 01721
Ph: (508)881-5800 Fax: (508)881-6829
Monthly. Publishes items to be used as a fire training aid.

★2135★ *Labor Line*
National Fire Sprinkler Association (NFSA)
Robin Hill Corporate Park
Rte. 22, Box 1000
Patterson, NY 12563
Ph: (914)878-4200 Fax: (914)878-4215
Bimonthly. Reports to unionized contractors on federal and state labor laws.

★2136★ *Membership List*
National Fire Sprinkler Association (NFSA)
Robin Hill Corporate Park
Rte. 22, Box 1000
Patterson, NY 12563
Ph: (914)878-4200 Fax: (914)878-4215
Periodic.

★2137★ *National Fire Codes*
National Fire Protection Association (NFPA)
1 Batterymarch Park
PO Box 9101
Quincy, MA 02269-9101
Ph: (617)770-3000 Fax: (617)770-0700
Annual. Compilation of over 270 fire codes, standards, recommended practices, manuals, and guides on fire protection.

★2138★ *National Fire Protection Association—Technical Committee Reports/Technical Committee Documentation*
National Fire Protection Association (NFPA)
1 Batterymarch Park
PO Box 9101
Quincy, MA 02269-9101
Ph: (617)770-3000 Fax: (617)770-0700
Semiannual. Committee reports and interim documents on the fire code and standards development process.

★2139★ *NFPA Journal*
National Fire Protection Association (NFPA)
1 Batterymarch Park
PO Box 9101
Quincy, MA 02269-9101
Ph: (617)770-3000 Fax: (617)770-0700
Bimonthly. Features technical, scientific, and industrial applications of fire protection, suppression, investigations, and educations, plus association news.

★2140★ *Regional Report*
National Fire Sprinkler Association (NFSA)
Robin Hill Corporate Park
Rte. 22, Box 1000
Patterson, NY 12563
Ph: (914)878-4200 Fax: (914)878-4215
Monthly.

★2141★ *Sprinkler Quarterly*
National Fire Sprinkler Association (NFSA)
Robin Hill Corporate Park
Rte. 22, Box 1000
Patterson, NY 12563
Ph: (914)878-4200 Fax: (914)878-4215
Quarterly. Provides information on fire sprinkler protection; includes features and technical information for and about the industry. Covers association news.

★2142★ *Sprinkler Technotes*
National Fire Sprinkler Association (NFSA)
Robin Hill Corporate Park
Rte. 22, Box 1000
Patterson, NY 12563
Ph: (914)878-4200 Fax: (914)878-4215
Bimonthly. Lists proposed changes to fire sprinkler codes and standards; also covers developing fire protection technology.

★2143★ *Today's Fireman*
Towerhigh Publications, Inc.
PO Box 875108
Los Angeles, CA 90087
Ph: (213)432-3806
Donald Mack
Quarterly. Fire service magazine.

★2144★ *Turn Out*
International Fire Buff Associates, Inc.
c/o Roman A. Kaminski
7509 Chesapeake Ave.
Baltimore, MD 21219
Ph: (410)477-1544
William M. Mokros
Semiannual. Concerned with the firefighting activities of fire departments across the nation. Includes historical accounts and news of association and member activities.

★2145★ *The Voice*
International Society of Fire Service Instructors (ISFSI)
30 Main St.
Ashland, MA 01721
Ph: (508)881-5800 Fax: (508)881-6829
Ed McCormack
Monthly. Provides professional news for those engaged in fire service instruction in industrial and educational settings. Discusses new products available to fire fighters and safety procedures. Recurring features include book reviews, a calendar of events, and a column titled Across the Country.

MEETINGS AND CONVENTIONS

★2146★ Fire and Rescue Educational Conference and Exposition
International Association of Fire Chiefs
4025 Fair Ridge Dr.
Fairfax, VA 22033-2868
Ph: (703)273-0911

Annual.

★2147★ Industrial Fire Expo
PennWell Conferences and Exhibitions
3050 Post Oak Blvd., Ste. 205
Houston, TX 77056
Ph: (713)621-8833 Fax: (713)963-6284

OTHER SOURCES OF INFORMATION

★2148★ *Careers in Firefighting*
Rosen Publishing Group
29 E. 21st St.
New York, NY 10010
Ph: 800-237-9932 Fax: (212)777-0277

Mary Price Lee and Richard S. Lee. 1993. Presents the requirements need to become a firefighter.

★2149★ *Confined Space Rescue*
Media Resources, Inc.
2614 Fort VanCouver Way
Vancouver, WA 98661-3997
Ph: (206)693-3344 Fax: (206)693-1760
Fr: 800-666-0106

Designed to train fire departments and businesses in OSHA's Permit Required Confined Spaces. Includes information on entering confined spaces. preparing protective clothing and respiratory protection, preparing a pre-incident plan, and more. Instructors guide, discussion questions and a quiz are included.

★2150★ "Fire Fighter" in *Career Selector 2001*
Barron's Educational Series, Inc.
250 Wireless Blvd.
Hauppauge, NY 11788
Ph: (516)434-3311 Fax: (516)434-3723
Fr: 800-645-3476

James C. Gonyea. 1993.

★2151★ *Fire on the Rim: A Firefighter's Season at the Grand Canyon*
Ballantine Books of Canada
1265 Aerowood Dr.
Mississauga, ON, Canada L4W 1B9
Ph: (416)624-0672 Fax: (416)624-6217

Stephen J. Pyne. 1990.

★2152★ "Firefighter" in *100 Best Jobs for the 1990s & Beyond*
Dearborn Financial Publishing, Inc.
520 N. Dearborn St.
Chicago, IL 60610-4354
Ph: (312)836-4400 Fax: (312)836-1021
Fr: 800-621-9621

Carol Kleiman. 1992. Describes 100 jobs ranging from accountants to veterinarians. Each job profile includes such information as education, experience, and certification needed, salaries, and job search suggestions.

★2153★ *Firefighters in Action*
State Mutual Book & Periodical Service, Ltd.
521 5th Ave., 17th Fl.
New York, NY 10175
Ph: (212)682-5844

John Creighton. 1985.

★2154★ *Firefighters: Their Lives in Their Own Words*
Doubleday
666 5th Ave.
New York, NY 10103
Ph: (212)765-6500 Fax: (212)492-9700

Dennis Smith. 1988.

★2155★ *Firehouse Trivia*
Unlimited Publishing Co.
Box 240, Rte. 17K
Bullville, NY 10915
Ph: (914)361-1299

William J. Geis. 1986.

★2156★ *Here Comes the Fireman*
Outlet Book Co.
225 Park Ave. S.
New York, NY 10003
Ph: (212)254-1600

1990.

★2157★ *Industrial Firefighting Series*
Gulf Publishing Co.
PO Box 2680
Houston, TX 77252-2608
Ph: (713)529-4301 Fax: (713)520-4438

Five-part fire training series that provides information on various firefighting topics common to the industrial environment. Also covers common types of firefighting equipment and the techniques used to fight various types of fires.

★2158★ *Last Alarm*
National Fire Protection Association
1 Battertmarch Park
Quincy, MA 02269-9101
Ph: (617)770-3000

Jerry Laughlin. 1986.

★2159★ *National Fire Codes*
National Fire Protection Association (NFPA)
1 Batterymarch Park
PO Box 9101
Quincy, MA 02269-9101
Ph: (617)770-3000 Fax: (617)770-0700

Annual. Compilation of over 250 fire codes, standards, recommended practices, manuals, and guides on fire protection.

★2160★ *National Fire Protection Association—Technical Committee Reports/Technical Committee Documentation*
National Fire Protection Association (NFPA)
1 Batterymarch Park
PO Box 9101
Quincy, MA 02269-9101
Ph: (617)770-3000 Fax: (617)770-0700

Semiannual. Committee reports and interim documents on the fire code and standards development process.

Guards

Guards patrol and inspect property against fire, theft, vandalism, and illegal entry. In office buildings, stores, banks, and hospitals, guards protect records, merchandise, money and equipment. At airports and railroads, guards ensure that nothing is stolen while being loaded or unloaded, and screen passengers and visitors for weapons and other forbidden articles. Guards who work in public buildings such as museums or art galleries protect exhibits and may also answer routine questions from visitors. In those places where valuable property or information is kept, such as laboratories or government buildings, guards check the credentials of persons or vehicles entering or leaving the premises. At public gatherings like sporting events, guards maintain order, give information, and watch for persons who may cause trouble. Armored car guards protect money and valuables during transit. Bodyguards protect individuals from bodily injury, kidnapping, or invasion of privacy. Guards usually patrol on foot, but if the property is large, they may make their rounds by car or scooter. As they make their rounds, guards check all doors and windows, see that no unauthorized persons remain after working hours, and ensure that alarms, and other various electrical and plumbing systems are working properly. Guards usually are uniformed and may carry a gun or nightstick. They may also carry a flashlight, whistle, two-way radio, and a watch clock.

Salaries

Earnings vary according to type or guard duty.

Various service industries, including security and guard agencies	$4.25/hour
Federal guards	$14,600-$16,400/year

Employment Outlook

Growth rate until the year 2005: Much faster than the average.

Guards

Career Guides

★2161★ *"Bodyguard" in Action Careers: Employment in the High-Risk Job Market (pp. 5-14)*
Citadel Press/Lyle Stuart Inc.
Carol Publishing Group
120 Enterprise Ave.
Secaucus, NJ 07094
Ph: (201)866-0490

Ragnar Benson. 1988. Describes 24 dangerous careers such as repo man, explosives handler, and river rafting guide. Each profile includes demand for the job, where the jobs can be found, required personal and physical characteristics and training needed.

★2162★ "Careers in Private Security" in *Career Planning in Criminal Justice* (pp. 95-100)
Anderson Publishing Co.
PO Box 1576
Cincinnati, OH 45201
Ph: (513)421-4142 Fax: (513)562-8116
Fr: 800-582-7295

Robert C. DeLucia and Thomas J. Doyle. 1994. Surveys a wide range of career and employment opportunities in law enforcement, the courts, corrections, forensic science and private security. Contains career planning and job hunting advice. Profiles 77 criminal justice occupations describing job duties, work environments, and educational requirements.

★2163★ *Customs Officers*
Chronicle Guidance Publications, Inc.
66 Aurora St.
PO Box 1190
Moravia, NY 13118-1190
Ph: (315)497-0330 Fax: (315)497-3359
Fr: 800-622-7284

1993. This career brief describes the nature of the work, working conditions, hours and earnings, education and training, licensure, certification, unions, personal qualifications, social and psychological factors, employment outlook, entry methods, advancement, and related occupations.

★2164★ "Education, Government, and Legal Careers" in *The Best Jobs for the 1990s and Into the 21st Century*
Impact Publications
9104-N Manassas Dr.
Manassas Park, VA 22111
Ph: (703)361-7300 Fax: (703)335-9486

Ronald L. Krannich and Caryl Rae Krannich. 1993. Includes information on correction officers, guards, and police, detectives, and special agents.

★2165★ "Guard" in *Career Opportunities in Art* (pp. 25-26)
Facts on File
460 Park Ave. S.
New York, NY 10016-7382
Ph: (212)683-2244 Fax: 800-678-3633
Fr: 800-322-8755

Susan H. Haubenstock and David Joselit. 1988. Profiles more than 75 art-related jobs. Each occupational profile covers job duties, employment outlook, career paths, salaries, skills, and educational preparation. Offers tips for entering the field.

★2166★ "Guard, Museum" in *Museum Jobs form A-Z: What They Are, How to Prepare, and Where to Find Them*
Batax Museum Publishing
301 Racquet Club Rd., Ste. 202
Fort Lauderdale, FL 33326

G.W. Bates. 1994.

★2167★ *Guard, Security*
Careers, Inc.
PO Box 135
Largo, FL 34649-0135
Ph: (813)584-7333

1992. Two-page occupational summary card describing duties, working conditions, personal qualifications, training, earnings and hours, employment outlook, places of employment, related careers and where to write for more information.

★2168★ "Guard Supervisor" in *Career Opportunities in Art* (pp. 27-28)
Facts on File
460 Park Ave. S.
New York, NY 10016-7382
Ph: (212)683-2244 Fax: 800-678-3633
Fr: 800-322-8755

Susan H. Haubenstock and David Joselit. 1988. Profiles more than 75 art-related jobs. Each occupational profile covers job duties, employment outlook, career paths, salaries, skills, and educational preparation. Offers tips for entering the field.

★2169★ "Guard" in *VGM's Careers Encyclopedia* (pp. 84-86)
National Textbook Co. (NTC)
VGM Career Books
4255 W. Touhy Ave.
Lincolnwood, IL 60646-1975
Ph: (708)679-5500 Fax: (708)679-2494
Fr: 800-323-4900

Third edition, 1991. Contains two- to five-page descriptions of 200 managerial, professional, technical, trade, and service occupations. Each profile includes job duties, places of employment, qualifications, educational preparation, training, employment potential, advancement, income, and additional sources of information.

★2170★ "Guards" in *American Almanac of Jobs and Salaries* (pp. 532)
Avon Books
1350 Avenue of the Americas
New York, NY 10019
Ph: (212)261-6800 Fr: 800-238-0658

John Wright, editor. Revised and updated, 1994-95. A comprehensive guide to the wages of hundreds of occupations in a wide variety of industries and organizations.

★2171★ "Guards" in *America's 50 Fastest Growing Jobs* (pp. 122)
JIST Works, Inc.
720 N. Park Ave.
Indianapolis, IN 46202-3431
Ph: (317)264-3720 Fax: (317)264-3709
Fr: 800-648-5478

Michael J. Farr, compiler. 1994. Describes the 50 fastest growing jobs within major career clusters such as technicians, and marketing and sales. Each job profile explains the nature of the work, skills and abilities required, employment outlook, average earnings, related occupations, education and training requirements, and employment opportunities. Also contains career planning information and job search tips.

★2172★ "Guards" in *Occupational Outlook Handbook*
U.S. Government Printing Office
Superintendent of Documents
Washington, DC 20402
Ph: (202)512-1800 Fax: (202)512-2250

Biennial; latest edition, 1994-95. Encyclopedia of careers describing more than 250 occupations and comprising about 85 percent of all jobs in the economy. Occupations that require lengthy education or training are given the most attention. For each occupation, the handbook describes job duties, working conditions, training, educational preparation, personal qualities, advancement possibilities, job outlook, earnings, and sources of additional information.

★2173★ *Health Care Security Training Series*
MTI Teleprograms, Inc.
108 Wilmot Rd.
Deerfield, IL 60015-9990
Ph: (708)940-1260 Fr: 800-621-2131

Videocassette. 198?. 15 mins. This series teaches the basic skills needed for working as a security officer in a health care facility.

★2174★ "Security Guard" in *BLR Encyclopedia of Prewritten Job Descriptions*
Business and Legal Reports, Inc.
39 Academy St.
Madison, CT 06443-1513
Ph: (203)245-7448

Stephen D. Bruce, editor-in-chief. 1994. This book contains hundreds of sample job descriptions arranged by functional job category. The 1-3 page job descriptions cover what the worker normally does in the position, who they report to, and how that position fits in the organizational structure.

★2175★ "Security Guard" in *Career Information Center* (Vol.11)
Simon and Schuster
200 Old Tappan Rd.
Old Tappan, NJ 07675
Fax: 800-445-6991 Fr: 800-223-2348

Richard Lidz and Dale Anderson, editorial directors. Fifth edition, 1993. For 600 occupations, describes job duties, entry-level requirements, education and training needed, advancement possibilities, employment outlook, earnings and benefits. The set is divided into 12 volumes. Each volume includes jobs related under a broad career field. Volume 13 is the index.

★2176★ "Security Guards" in *Career Discovery Encyclopedia* (Vol.6, pp. 16-17)
J.G. Ferguson Publishing Co.
200 W. Madison St., Ste. 300
Chicago, IL 60606
Ph: (312)580-5480 Fax: (312)580-4948

E. Russell Primm, editor-in-chief. 1993. Contains two-page articles on 504 occupations. Each article describes job duties, earnings, and educational and training requirements.

★2177★ "Security Guards" in *Careers in Law Enforcement and Security*
Rosen Publishing Group
29 E. 21st St.
New York, NY 10010
Ph: (212)777-3017 Fax: (212)777-0277
Fr: 800-237-9932

Paul Cohen and Shari Cohen. 1994. Describes jobs such as police, sheriff, detective, FBI, CIA, and Secret Service agents, parole and probation officers, security guards, and private investigators. Covers job duties, qualifications, education, training, income, and advancement possibilities. Offers advice about where and how to apply for jobs.

★2178★ "Security Guards" in *Encyclopedia of Careers and Vocational Guidance* (Vol.4, pp. 340-342)
J.G. Ferguson Publishing Co.
200 W. Madison St., Ste. 300
Chicago, IL 60606
Ph: (312)580-5480 Fax: (312)580-4948

William E. Hopke, editor-in-chief. Ninth edition, 1993. Four-volume set that profiles 500 occupations and describes job trends in 74 industries. Includes career description, educational requirements, history of the job, methods of entry, advancement, employment outlook, earnings, working conditions, social and psychological factors, and sources of additional information.

★2179★ *Security Officers*
Chronicle Guidance Publications, Inc.
66 Aurora St.
PO Box 1190
Moravia, NY 13118-1190
Ph: (315)497-0330 Fax: (315)497-3359
Fr: 800-622-7284

1991. This career brief describes the nature of the work, working conditions, hours and earnings, education and training, licensure, certification, unions, personal qualifications, social and psychological factors, employment outlook, entry methods, advancement, and related occupations.

Associations

★2180★ International Association of Security Service (IASS)
PO Box 8202
Northfield, IL 60093
Ph: (312)973-7712 Fax: (312)973-7677

Members: Companies providing security services, primarily guard services. **Purpose:** Works to establish standardized licensing and training regulations. Operates research programs; maintains speakers' bureau, hall of fame, and museum. Plans to conduct seminars and training workshops.

★2181★ International Security Officer's Police and Guard Union (ISOPGU)
321 86th St.
Brooklyn, NY 11209
Ph: (718)836-3508 Fax: (718)836-6757

Members: Independent.

★2182★ International Union of Security Officers (IUSO)
2404 Merced St.
San Leandro, CA 94577
Ph: (510)895-9905 Fax: (510)895-6974

Members: Independent. Guards and security officers. **Purpose:** Seeks to improve wages, hours, and working conditions for security officers and guards. Conducts charitable program and shop steward training program.

★2183★ Security Industry Association (SIA)
1801 K St. NW, Ste. 1203L
Washington, DC 20006
Ph: (202)466-7420 Fax: (202)466-0010

Members: Security equipment manufacturers and distributors. **Purpose:** Seeks advancement of companies in the security products industry. Promotes the export of American security products. Conducts research programs, educational programs, technical seminars, communications with related industries, and other activities. Maintains speakers' bureau; compiles statistics. **Publications:** *Market Overview*, annual. • *SIA News*, bimonthly.

Standards/Certification Agencies

★2184★ International Association of Security Service (IASS)
PO Box 8202
Northfield, IL 60093
Ph: (312)973-7712 Fax: (312)973-7677

Works to establish standardized licensing and training regulations.

Test Guides

★2185★ *Career Examination Series: Building Guard*
National Learning Corp.
212 Michael Dr.
Syosset, NY 11791
Ph: (516)921-8888 Fax: (516)921-8743
Fr: 800-645-6337

Jack Rudman. All examination guides in this series contain questions with answers.

★2186★ *Career Examination Series: Customs Security Officer (Sky Marshal)*
National Learning Corp.
212 Michael Dr.
Syosset, NY 11791
Ph: (516)921-8888 Fax: (516)921-8743
Fr: 800-645-6337

Jack Rudman. 1989. All examination guides in this series contain questions with answers.

★2187★ *Career Examination Series: Guard Patrolman*
National Learning Corp.
212 Michael Dr.
Syosset, NY 11791
Ph: (516)921-8888 Fax: (516)921-8743
Fr: 800-645-6337

Jack Rudman. All examination guides in this series contain questions with answers.

★2188★ *Career Examination Series: Security Guard*
National Learning Corp.
212 Michael Dr.
Syosset, NY 11791
Ph: (516)921-8888 Fax: (516)921-8743
Fr: 800-645-6337

Jack Rudman. All examination guides in this series contain questions with answers.

★2189★ *Career Examination Series: Security Officer*
National Learning Corp.
212 Michael Dr.
Syosset, NY 11791
Ph: (516)921-8888 Fax: (516)921-8743
Fr: 800-645-6337

Jack Rudman. All examination guides in this series contain questions with answers.

★2190★ *Career Examination Series: Senior Building Guard*
National Learning Corp.
212 Michael Dr.
Syosset, NY 11791
Ph: (516)921-8888 Fax: (516)921-8743
Fr: 800-645-6337

Jack Rudman. All examination guides in this series contain questions with answers.

★2191★ *Career Examination Series: Senior Campus Security Officer*
National Learning Corp.
212 Michael Dr.
Syosset, NY 11791
Ph: (516)921-8888 Fax: (516)921-8743
Fr: 800-645-6337

Jack Rudman. All examination guides in this series contain questions with answers.

Awards, Scholarships, Grants, and Fellowships

★2192★ ISDA Special Commendation
International Security and Detective Alliance
PO Box 6303
Corpus Christi, TX 78466-6303
Ph: (512)888-6164

To honor any individual who significantly promotes the growth and betterment of the private security and investigation professions, or who performs significant acts of heroism, bravery, and/or faithful service. Letters of application with affidavits, statements, etc., as required may be submitted by anyone meeting the above criteria. Certificates are awarded when approved applications are received. Established in 1987.

Periodicals

★2193★ *Campus Safety Newsletter*
National Safety Council
1121 Spring Lake Dr.
Itasca, IL 60143-3201
Ph: (708)775-2282 Fax: (708)775-2285
Diane A. Ghazarian

Bimonthly. Focuses on safety problems and effective precautions for college and university buildings and campuses. Discusses security patrols, facilities for the handicapped, institutional policies, and similar subjects. Promotes safety education as the direct means of accident prevention.

★2194★ *Market Overview*
Security Industry Association (SIA)
1801 K St. NW, Ste. 1203L
Washington, DC 20006
Ph: (202)466-7420 Fax: (202)466-0010

Annual.

★2195★ *Police & Security News*
Days Communications
1690 Quarry Rd.
PO Box 330
Kulpsville, PA 19443
Ph: (215)538-1240 Fax: (215)538-1208
James Devery

Bimonthly. Tabloid for the law enforcement and private security industries. Includes articles on training, new products, and new technology.

★2196★ *SIA News*
Security Industry Association (SIA)
1801 K St. NW, Ste. 1203L
Washington, DC 20006
Ph: (202)466-7420 Fax: (202)466-0010

Bimonthly.

Other Sources of Information

★2197★ "Corrections Officer/Guard Jailer" in *100 Best Jobs for the 1990s & Beyond*
Dearborn Financial Publishing, Inc.
520 N. Dearborn St.
Chicago, IL 60610-4354
Ph: (312)836-4400 Fax: (312)836-1021
Fr: 800-621-9621

Carol Kleiman. 1992. Describes 100 jobs ranging from accountants to veterinarians. Each job profile includes such information as education, experience, and certification needed, salaries, and job search suggestions.

★2198★ "Security Guard" in *Career Selector 2001*
Barron's Educational Series, Inc.
250 Wireless Blvd.
Hauppauge, NY 11788
Ph: (516)434-3311 Fax: (516)434-3723
Fr: 800-645-3476

James C. Gonyea. 1993.

Police, Detectives, and Special Agents

Police, detectives, and special agents work to maintain the safety of the nation's cities, towns, and highways. They do this through a variety of activities ranging from controlling traffic to preventing and investigating crimes. Police and detectives who work in small communities may have a wide variety of duties including traffic enforcement, burglary investigations, or giving first aid to an accident victim. In larger areas, officers are usually assigned to a specific type of duty. Detectives and special agents are plainclothes investigators who gather facts and collect evidence for criminal cases. They conduct interviews, examine records, observe the activities of suspects, and participate in raids or arrests. Federal Bureau of Investigation (FBI) special agents investigate violations of federal laws in connection with bank robberies, theft of government property, organized crime, and terrorism. Special agents employed by the U.S. Department of Treasury may work for the U.S. Customs Service where they enforce laws preventing the illegal smuggling of goods across borders; the Bureau of Alcohol, Tobacco, and Firearms where they might investigate illegal sales of guns or the underpayment of taxes by a liquor or cigarette manufacturer; the U.S. Secret Service who protect high ranking government officials; or the Internal Revenue Service which collects evidence of tax evasion. State police officers (sometimes called State troopers or highway patrol officers) patrol highways and enforce laws and regulations that govern their use. In addition to highway responsibilities, state police in the majority of states also enforce criminal laws.

Salaries

Salaries for police, detectives, and special agents vary greatly depending upon region, size of the department, and experience.

Nonsupervisory police officers	
Lowest 10 percent	$18,400/year or less
Middle	$24,500-$41,200/year
Top 10 percent	$51,200/year or more

Supervisory police officers	
Lowest 10 percent	$23,200/year or less
Middle	$28,300-$49,800/year
Top 10 percent	$58,400/year or more

Employment Outlook

Growth rate until the year 2005: More slowly than the average.

Police, Detectives, and Special Agents

★2199★ "Education, Government, and Legal Careers" in *The Best Jobs for the 1990s and Into the 21st Century*
Impact Publications
9104-N Manassas Dr.
Manassas Park, VA 22111
Ph: (703)361-7300 Fax: (703)335-9486
Ronald L. Krannich and Caryl Rae Krannich. 1993. Includes information on correction officers, guards, and police, detectives, and special agents.

Career Guides

★2200★ *Border Patrol Agent*
Vocational Biographies, Inc.
PO Box 31
Sauk Centre, MN 56378-0031
Ph: (612)352-6516 Fax: (612)352-5546
Fr: 800-255-0752
1994. This pamphlet profiles a person working in the job. Includes information about job duties, working conditions, places of employment, educational preparation, labor market outlook, and salaries.

★2201★ *Border Patrol Agent*
Careers, Inc.
PO Box 135
Largo, FL 34649-0135
Ph: (813)584-7333
1993. Two-page occupational summary card describing duties, working conditions, personal qualifications, training, earnings and hours, employment outlook, places of employment, related careers and where to write for more information.

★2202★ *Career Success Series*
Cambridge Educational
PO Box 2153
Charleston, WV 25328-2153
Ph: (304)744-9323 Fax: (304)744-9351
Fr: 800-468-4227
Videocassette. 1986. 15 mins. A series, available separately, outlining various career choices for students. Occupations include: accounting, flight service, air transportation/ground/flight service, data processing, carpentry, clerk in banking/insurance, commodity sales, cosmetic personal grooming, fire fighting, forestry services, home economics, insulation/roofing, material handling, mechanics, photographic processing, pipefitting and plumbing, police science, printing, carpentry, medical laboratory technicians, secretarial services, and utilities equipment operator.

★2203★ "Careers in Law Enforcement" in *Career Planning in Criminal Justice* (pp. 57)
Anderson Publishing Co.
PO Box 1576
Cincinnati, OH 45201
Ph: (513)421-4142 Fax: (513)562-8116
Fr: 800-582-7295
Robert C. DeLucia and Thomas J. Doyle. 1994. Surveys a wide range of career and employment opportunities in law enforcement, the courts, corrections, forensic science and private security. Contains career planning and job hunting advice. Profiles 77 criminal justice occupations describing job duties, work environments, and educational requirements.

★2204★ *County Sheriff*
Vocational Biographies, Inc.
PO Box 31
Sauk Centre, MN 56378-0031
Ph: (612)352-6516 Fax: (612)352-5546
Fr: 800-255-0752
1991. This pamphlet profiles a person working in the job. Includes information about job duties, working conditions, places of employment, educational preparation, labor market outlook, and salaries.

★2205★ "Customs Worker" in *Career Information Center* (Vol.11)
Simon and Schuster
200 Old Tappan Rd.
Old Tappan, NJ 07675
Fax: 800-445-6991 Fr: 800-223-2348
Richard Lidz and Dale Anderson, editorial directors. Fifth edition, 1993. For 600 occupations, describes job duties, entry-level requirements, education and training needed, advancement possibilities, employment outlook, earnings and benefits. The set is divided into 12 volumes. Each volume includes jobs related under a broad career field. Volume 13 is the index.

★2206★ "Customs Worker" in *Occu-Facts: Information on 580 Careers in Outline Form*
Careers, Inc.
PO Box 135
Largo, FL 34649-0135
Ph: (813)584-7333
Biennial, 1995-96 edition. Each one-page occupational profile describes duties, working conditions, physical surroundings and demands, aptitudes, temperament, educational requirements, employment outlook, earnings, and places of employment.

★2207★ *Customs Workers*
Careers, Inc.
PO Box 135
Largo, FL 34649-0135
Ph: (813)584-7333
1994. Two-page occupational summary card describing duties, working conditions, personal qualifications, training, earnings and hours, employment outlook, places of employment, related careers and where to write for more information.

★2208★ "Detective" in *Career Information Center* (Vol.11)
Simon and Schuster
200 Old Tappan Rd.
Old Tappan, NJ 07675
Fax: 800-445-6991 Fr: 800-223-2348
Richard Lidz and Dale Anderson, editorial directors. Fifth edition, 1993. For 600 occupations, describes job duties, entry-level requirements, education and training needed, advancement possibilities, employment outlook, earnings and benefits. The set is divided into 12 volumes. Each volume includes jobs related under a broad career field. Volume 13 is the index.

★2209★ *Detective, Police*
Careers, Inc.
PO Box 135
Largo, FL 34649-0135
Ph: (813)584-7333

1992. Two-page occupational summary card describing duties, working conditions, personal qualifications, training, earnings and hours, employment outlook, places of employment, related careers and where to write for more information.

★2210★ **"Detectives" in *Encyclopedia of Careers and Vocational Guidance* (Vol.2, pp. 462-465)**
J.G. Ferguson Publishing Co.
200 W. Madison St., Ste. 300
Chicago, IL 60606
Ph: (312)580-5480 Fax: (312)580-4948

William E. Hopke, editor-in-chief. Ninth edition, 1993. Four-volume set that profiles 900 occupations and describes job trends in 74 industries. Includes career description, educational requirements, history of the job, methods of entry, advancement, employment outlook, earnings, conditions of work, social and psychological factors, and sources of further information.

★2211★ *Face Unique Challenges With the FBI: A Career as a Special Agent*
U.S. Department of Justice
Federal Bureau of Investigation
Applicant Recruiting Office
1900 Half St., S.W.
Washington, DC 20535
Ph: (202)324-3000

1989. This eight-page booklet describes the work of an FBI Special Agent. Covers entry requirements, the application process, training, and advancement possibilities. Lists FBI field offices with phone numbers.

★2212★ *"FBI Agent" in Action Careers: Employment in the High-Risk Job Market (pp. 47-58)*
Citadel Press/Lyle Stuart Inc.
Carol Publishing Group
120 Enterprise Ave.
Secaucus, NJ 07094
Ph: (201)866-0490

Ragnar Benson. 1988. Describes 24 dangerous careers such as repo man, explosives handler, and river rafting guide. Each profile includes demand for the job, where the jobs can be found, required personal and physical characteristics and training needed.

★2213★ **"FBI Agents" in *Career Discovery Encyclopedia* (Vol.3, pp. 8-9)**
J.G. Ferguson Publishing Co.
200 W. Madison St., Ste. 300
Chicago, IL 60606
Ph: (312)580-5480 Fax: (312)580-4948

E. Russell Primm, editor-in-chief. 1993. Contains two-page articles on 504 occupations. Each article describes job duties, earnings, and educational and training requirements.

★2214★ **"FBI Agents" in *Encyclopedia of Careers and Vocational Guidance* (Vol.2, pp. 639-642)**
J.G. Ferguson Publishing Co.
200 W. Madison St., Ste. 300
Chicago, IL 60606
Ph: (312)580-5480 Fax: (312)580-4948

William E. Hopke, editor-in-chief. Ninth edition, 1993. Four-volume set that profiles 500 occupations and describes job trends in 74 industries. Includes career description, educational requirements, history of the job, methods of entry, advancement, employment outlook, earnings, working conditions, social and psychological factors, and sources of additional information.

★2215★ **"FBI Special Agent" in *Career Information Center* (Vol.11)**
Simon and Schuster
200 Old Tappan Rd.
Old Tappan, NJ 07675
Fax: 800-445-6991 Fr: 800-223-2348

Richard Lidz and Dale Anderson, editorial directors. Fifth edition, 1993. For 600 occupations, describes job duties, entry-level requirements, education and training needed, advancement possibilities, employment outlook, earnings and benefits. The set is divided into 12 volumes. Each volume includes jobs related under a broad career field. Volume 13 is the index.

★2216★ **"FBI Special Agent" in *VGM's Careers Encyclopedia* (pp. 173-175)**
National Textbook Co. (NTC)
VGM Career Books
4255 W. Touhy Ave.
Lincolnwood, IL 60646-1975
Ph: (708)679-5500 Fax: (708)679-2494
Fr: 800-323-4900

Third edition, 1991. Contains two- to five-page descriptions of 200 managerial, professional, technical, trade, and service occupations. Each profile includes job duties, places of employment, qualifications, educational preparation, training, employment potential, advancement, income, and additional sources of information.

★2217★ *FBI Special Agents*
Careers, Inc.
PO Box 135
Largo, FL 34649-0135
Ph: (813)584-7333

1992. Four-page brief offering the definition, history, duties, working conditions, personal qualifications, educational requirements, earnings, hours, employment outlook, advancement possibilities, and related occupations.

★2218★ *FBI Special Agents*
Chronicle Guidance Publications, Inc.
66 Aurora St.
PO Box 1190
Moravia, NY 13118-1190
Ph: (315)497-0330 Fax: (315)497-3359
Fr: 800-622-7284

1991. This career brief describes the nature of the work, working conditions, hours and earnings, education and training, licensure, certification, unions, personal qualifications, social and psychological factors, employment outlook, entry methods, advancement, and related occupations.

★2219★ **"FBI Special Agents" in *Occu-Facts: Information on 580 Careers in Outline Form***
Careers, Inc.
PO Box 135
Largo, FL 34649-0135
Ph: (813)584-7333

Biennial, 1995-96 edition. Each one-page occupational profile describes duties, working conditions, physical surroundings and demands, aptitudes, temperament, educational requirements, employment outlook, earnings, and places of employment.

★2220★ **"Federal Bureau of Investigation" in *Exploring Careers Using Foreign Languages* (pp. 67-69)**
Rosen Publishing Group
29 E. 21st St.
New York, NY 10010
Ph: (212)777-3017 Fax: (212)777-0277
Fr: 800-237-9932

E. W. Edwards. Revised edition, 1990. Explores careers in teaching, translating, interpreting, business and finance, government, communications, and the media. Covers employment ideas, salaries, job duties, and educational preparation. Contains information on accreditation and job hunting.

★2221★ *"Federal Bureau of Investigation" in Law Enforcement Employment Guide (pp. 130-131)*
Lawman Press
PO Box 1468
Mt. Shasta, CA 96067
Ph: (818)344-6146

Ron Stern. Second edition, 1990. Provides hiring information for 78 federal, state, and local law enforcement agencies across the United States that are currently hiring. Each agency profile contains selection criteria, information about the application and testing process, salaries, benefits, and career ladders. Offers advice on taking tests and interviewing.

★2222★ *How to Get a Job With the Police Department: Police Officer*
Barnes and Noble Books
10 E. 53rd St.
New York, NY 10022

Stephen M. Good. First edition, 1985.

★2223★ *Internal Revenue Agent*
Careers, Inc.
PO Box 135
Largo, FL 34649-0135
Ph: (813)584-7333

1993. Four-page brief offering the definition, history, duties, working conditions, personal qualifications, educational requirements, earnings, hours, employment outlook, advancement possibilities, and related occupations.

★2224★ **"Internal Revenue Agent" in *Occu-Facts: Information on 580 Careers in Outline Form***
Careers, Inc.
PO Box 135
Largo, FL 34649-0135
Ph: (813)584-7333

Biennial, 1995-96 edition. Each one-page occupational profile describes duties, working conditions, physical surroundings and demands, aptitudes, temperament, educational requirements, employment outlook, earnings, and places of employment.

★2225★ "Internal Revenue Agent" in *VGM's Careers Encyclopedia* (pp. 227-229)
National Textbook Co. (NTC)
VGM Career Books
4255 W. Touhy Ave.
Lincolnwood, IL 60646-1975
Ph: (708)679-5500 Fax: (708)679-2494
Fr: 800-323-4900

Third edition, 1991. Contains two- to five-page descriptions of 200 managerial, professional, technical, trade, and service occupations. Each profile includes job duties, places of employment, qualifications, educational preparation, training, employment potential, advancement, income, and additional sources of information.

★2226★ *Internal Revenue Service Agent*
Vocational Biographies, Inc.
PO Box 31
Sauk Centre, MN 56378-0031
Ph: (612)352-6516 Fax: (612)352-5546
Fr: 800-255-0752

1995. This pamphlet profiles a person working in the job. Includes information about job duties, working conditions, places of employment, educational preparation, labor market outlook, and salaries.

★2227★ *Law Enforcement*
AIMS Media, Inc.
9710 DeSoto Ave.
Chatsworth, CA 91311-4409
Ph: (818)773-4300 Fax: (818)341-6700
Fr: 800-367-2467

Videocassette. 1988. 30 mins. This tape from the "Career Awareness" series showcases jobs in law enforcement.

★2228★ "Law Enforcement" in *Career Connection II: A Guide to Technical Majors and Their Related Careers* (pp. 100-101)
Jist Works, Inc.
720 N. Park Ave.
Indianapolis, IN 46202-3431
Ph: (317)264-3720 Fax: (317)264-3709

Fred A. Rowe. 1994. Contains technical majors, such as automotive technology. Describes the major and the job. Lists high school and postsecondary school courses. Includes occupations related to the major, employment outlook, and starting salary.

★2229★ *Law Enforcement Careers: A Complete Guide from Application to Employment*
Lawman Press
PO Box 1468
Mt. Shasta, CA 96067
Ph: (818)344-6146

Ron Stern. 1988. Law enforcement job hunting guide covering the following topics: submitting an application, taking the written examination and oral interview, passing the physical agility test, and going through medical, psychological and polygraph screening. Describes police academy training and life as a police officer. Lists federal and state law enforcement offices.

★2230★ *Law Enforcement Employment Guide*
Lawman Press
PO Box 1468
Mt. Shasta, CA 96067
Ph: (818)344-6146

Ron Stern. Second edition, 1990. Provides hiring information for 78 federal, state, and local law enforcement agencies across the United States that are currently hiring. Each agency profile contains selection criteria, information about the application and testing process, salaries, benefits, and career ladders. Offers advice on taking tests and interviewing.

★2231★ "Law Enforcement Officer" in *100 Best Careers for the Year 2000* (pp. 191-193)
Arco Pub.
201 W. 103rd St.
Indianapolis, IN 46290
Ph: 800-428-5331 Fax: 800-835-3202

Shelly Field. 1992. Describes 100 job opportunities expected to grow fast throughout the next decade. Provides information on job duties and responsibilities, training requirements, education, advancement opportunities, experience and qualifications, and typical salaries.

★2232★ "Municipal Police Officer" in *VGM's Careers Encyclopedia* (pp. 361-364)
National Textbook Co. (NTC)
VGM Career Books
4255 W. Touhy Ave.
Lincolnwood, IL 60646-1975
Ph: (708)679-5500 Fax: (708)679-2494
Fr: 800-323-4900

Third edition, 1991. Contains two- to five-page descriptions of 200 managerial, professional, technical, trade, and service occupations. Each profile includes job duties, places of employment, qualifications, educational preparation, training, employment potential, advancement, income, and additional sources of information.

★2233★ *Obtaining Your Private Investigator's License*
Paladin Press
PO Box 1307
Boulder, CO 80306
Ph: (303)443-7250 Fax: (303)442-8741

Orion Agency, Inc. Staff. 1986.

★2234★ *Opportunities in Law Enforcement and Criminal Justice Careers*
National Textbook Co. (NTC)
VGM Career Books
4255 W. Touhy Ave.
Lincolnwood, IL 60646-1975
Ph: (708)679-5500 Fax: (708)679-2494
Fr: 800-323-4900

James D. Stinchcomb. 1990. Describes law enforcement and related positions at the city, county, state, and federal levels and in the military. Covers trends, future outlook, personal qualities, selection requirements, salaries, working conditions, and educational preparation.

★2235★ *Personal Service Cluster*
Center for Humanities, Inc.
Communications Park
Box 1000
Mount Kisco, NY 10549
Ph: (914)666-4100 Fax: (914)666-5319
Fr: 800-431-1242

Videocassette. 1984. 20 mins. Students get to see the day-by-day lives of people who work in the fields of cosmetology, food service and law enforcement.

★2236★ "Police" in *American Almanac of Jobs and Salaries* (pp. 101)
Avon Books
1350 Avenue of the Americas
New York, NY 10019
Ph: (212)261-6800 Fr: 800-238-0658

John Wright, editor. Revised and updated, 1994-95. A comprehensive guide to the wages of hundreds of occupations in a wide variety of industries and organizations.

★2237★ *The Police Detective Function*
Charles C. Thomas, Publisher
2600 S. 1st St.
Springfield, IL 62794-9265
Ph: (217)789-8980 Fax: (217)789-9130

V. A. Leonard. 1970.

★2238★ "Police Detective" in *Occu-Facts: Information on 580 Careers in Outline Form*
Careers, Inc.
PO Box 135
Largo, FL 34649-0135
Ph: (813)584-7333

Biennial, 1995-96 edition. Each one-page occupational profile describes duties, working conditions, physical surroundings and demands, aptitudes, temperament, educational requirements, employment outlook, earnings, and places of employment.

★2239★ "Police Detective" in *Straight Talk on Careers: 80 Pros Take You Into Their Professions* (pp. 236-238)
Garrett Park Press
PO Box 1907
Garrett Park, MD 20896
Ph: (301)946-2553

Mary Barbera-Hogan. 1987. Written for readers in high school and college. Contains candid interviews from professionals who discuss what their days are like and the pros and cons of their occupations.

★2240★ "Police, Detectives, and Special Agents" in *101 Careers: A Guide to the Fastest-Growing Opportunities* (pp. 140-143)
John Wiley & Sons, Inc.
605 3rd Ave.
New York, NY 10158-0012
Ph: (212)850-6645 Fax: (212)850-6088

Michael Harkavy. 1990. Describes the nature of the job, working conditions, employment growth, qualifications, personal skills, projected salaries, and where to write for more information.

★2241★ "Police, Detectives, and Special Agents" in *Occupational Outlook Handbook*
U.S. Government Printing Office
Superintendent of Documents
Washington, DC 20402
Ph: (202)512-1800 Fax: (202)512-2250
Biennial; latest edition, 1994-95. Encyclopedia of careers describing more than 250 occupations and comprising about 85 percent of all jobs in the economy. Occupations that require lengthy education or training are given the most attention. For each occupation, the handbook describes job duties, working conditions, training, educational preparation, personal qualities, advancement possibilities, job outlook, earnings, and sources of additional information.

★2242★ *Police Officer*
Macmillan Publishing Co., Inc.
866 3rd Ave.
New York, NY 10022
Ph: (212)702-2000 Fr: 800-257-5755
Hugh O'Neill, Hy Hammer, and Eve P. Steinberg. 12th edition, 1994.

★2243★ *Police Officer*
Careers, Inc.
PO Box 135
Largo, FL 34649-0135
Ph: (813)584-7333
1994. Two-page occupational summary card describing duties, working conditions, personal qualifications, training, earnings and hours, employment outlook, places of employment, related careers and where to write for more information.

★2244★ *Police Officer*
Vocational Biographies, Inc.
PO Box 31
Sauk Centre, MN 56378-0031
Ph: (612)352-6516 Fax: (612)352-5546
Fr: 800-255-0752
1990. This pamphlet profiles a person working in the job. Includes information about job duties, working conditions, places of employment, educational preparation, labor market outlook, and salaries.

★2245★ "Police Officer" in *Career Information Center* (Vol.11)
Simon and Schuster
200 Old Tappan Rd.
Old Tappan, NJ 07675
Fax: 800-445-6991 Fr: 800-223-2348
Richard Lidz and Dale Anderson, editorial directors. Fifth edition, 1993. For 600 occupations, describes job duties, entry-level requirements, education and training needed, advancement possibilities, employment outlook, earnings and benefits. The set is divided into 12 volumes. Each volume includes jobs related under a broad career field. Volume 13 is the index.

★2246★ "Police Officer" in *Hard Hatted Women: Stories of Struggle and Success in the Trades* (pp. 71-80)
Seal Press
3131 Western Ave., Ste. 410
Seattle, WA 98121
Ph: (206)283-7844 Fax: (206)285-9410
Molly Martin, editor. 1988. Twenty-six women recount their experiences working in blue collar occupations. They describe how they got in, the work they do, their relationships in predominantly male occupations, and their training.

★2247★ "Police Officer" in *Jobs Rated Almanac*
World Almanac
1 International Blvd., Ste. 444
Mahwah, NJ 07495
Ph: (201)529-6900 Fax: (201)529-6901
Les Krantz. Second edition, 1992. Ranks 250 jobs by environment, salary, outlooks, physical demands, stress, security, travel opportunities, and extra perks. Includes jobs the editor feels are the most common, most interesting, and the most rapidly growing.

★2248★ "Police Officer" in *Occu-Facts: Information on 580 Careers in Outline Form*
Careers, Inc.
PO Box 135
Largo, FL 34649-0135
Ph: (813)584-7333
Biennial, 1995-96 edition. Each one-page occupational profile describes duties, working conditions, physical surroundings and demands, aptitudes, temperament, educational requirements, employment outlook, earnings, and places of employment.

★2249★ "Police Officer" in *Top Professions: The 100 Most Popular, Dynamic, and Profitable Careers in America Today* (pp. 40-41)
Petersons Guides, Inc.
PO Box 2123
Princeton, NJ 08543-2123
Ph: (609)243-9111 Fax: (609)243-9150
Fr: 800-338-3282
Nicholas Basta. 1989. Includes occupations requiring a college or advanced degree. Describes job duties, earnings, some typical job titles, career opportunities at different degree levels, and lists related associations.

★2250★ *Police Officers*
Chronicle Guidance Publications, Inc.
66 Aurora St.
PO Box 1190
Moravia, NY 13118-1190
Ph: (315)497-0330 Fax: (315)497-3359
Fr: 800-622-7284
1991. This career brief describes the nature of the work, working conditions, hours and earnings, education and training, licensure, certification, unions, personal qualifications, social and psychological factors, employment outlook, entry methods, advancement, and related occupations.

★2251★ "Police Officers" in *Career Discovery Encyclopedia* (Vol.5, pp. 64-65)
J.G. Ferguson Publishing Co.
200 W. Madison St., Ste. 300
Chicago, IL 60606
Ph: (312)580-5480 Fax: (312)580-4948
E. Russell Primm, editor-in-chief. 1993. Contains two-page articles on 504 occupations. Each article describes job duties, earnings, and educational and training requirements.

★2252★ "Police Officers" in *Encyclopedia of Careers and Vocational Guidance* (Vol.4, pp. 140-144)
J.G. Ferguson Publishing Co.
200 W. Madison St., Ste. 300
Chicago, IL 60606
Ph: (312)580-5480 Fax: (312)580-4948
William E. Hopke, editor-in-chief. Ninth edition, 1993. Four-volume set that profiles 500 occupations and describes job trends in 74 industries. Includes career description, educational requirements, history of the job, methods of entry, advancement, employment outlook, earnings, working conditions, social and psychological factors, and sources of additional information.

★2253★ "Police Officers" in *Jobs! What They Are—Where They Are—What They Pay* (pp. 229-231)
Simon & Schuster, Inc.
Simon & Schuster Bldg.
1230 Avenue of the Americas
New York, NY 10020
Ph: (212)698-7000
Robert O. Snelling and Anne M. Snelling. Revised edition, 1992. Profiles 241 occupations, describing duties and responsibilities, educational preparation, earnings, employment opportunities, training, and qualifications.

★2254★ "Police Search & Recovery" in *Footsteps in the Ocean: Careers in Diving* (pp. 109-114)
Lodestar Books
2 Park Avenue
New York, NY 10016
Ph: (212)725-1818 Fax: (212)532-6568
Denise V. Lang. 1987. Explores employment opportunities in sport and commercial diving, science and research, in the military, and police work. Describes the work and training. Lists schools.

★2255★ "Police Sergeant" in *Straight Talk on Careers: 80 Pros Take You Into Their Professions* (pp. 233-235)
Garrett Park Press
PO Box 1907
Garrett Park, MD 20896
Ph: (301)946-2553
Mary Barbera-Hogan. 1987. Written for readers in high school and college. Contains candid interviews from professionals who discuss what their days are like and the pros and cons of their occupations.

★2256★ *"Secret Service Agent" in Action Careers: Employment in the High-Risk Job Market (pp. 211-221)*
Citadel Press/Lyle Stuart Inc.
Carol Publishing Group
120 Enterprise Ave.
Secaucus, NJ 07094
Ph: (201)866-0490
Ragnar Benson. 1988. Describes 24 dangerous careers such as repo man, explosives handler, and river rafting guide. Each profile includes demand for the job, where the jobs can be found, required personal and physical characteristics and training needed.

★2257★ "Secret Service Agent" in *VGM's Careers Encyclopedia* (pp. 421-424)
National Textbook Co. (NTC)
VGM Career Books
4255 W. Touhy Ave.
Lincolnwood, IL 60646-1975
Ph: (708)679-5500 Fax: (708)679-2494
Fr: 800-323-4900

Third edition, 1991. Contains two- to five-page descriptions of 200 managerial, professional, technical, trade, and service occupations. Each profile includes job duties, places of employment, qualifications, educational preparation, training, employment potential, advancement, income, and additional sources of information.

★2258★ *So You Want to Be a Cop*
EES Publications
1120 Royal Palm Beach Blvd., No. 216
Royal Palm Beach, FL 33411
Ph: (407)795-7475

Frank Pickens. 1991.

★2259★ *State Police/Highway Patrol Officer*
Careers, Inc.
PO Box 135
Largo, FL 34649-0135
Ph: (813)584-7333

1993. Two-page occupational summary card describing duties, working conditions, personal qualifications, training, earnings and hours, employment outlook, places of employment, related careers and where to write for more information.

★2260★ "State Police/Highway Patrol Officer" in *Occu-Facts: Information on 580 Careers in Outline Form*
Careers, Inc.
PO Box 135
Largo, FL 34649-0135
Ph: (813)584-7333

Biennial, 1995-96 edition. Each one-page occupational profile describes duties, working conditions, physical surroundings and demands, aptitudes, temperament, educational requirements, employment outlook, earnings, and places of employment.

★2261★ "State Police Officer" in *Career Information Center* (Vol.11)
Simon and Schuster
200 Old Tappan Rd.
Old Tappan, NJ 07675
Fax: 800-445-6991 Fr: 800-223-2348

Richard Lidz and Dale Anderson, editorial directors. Fifth edition, 1993. For 600 occupations, describes job duties, entry-level requirements, education and training needed, advancement possibilities, employment outlook, earnings and benefits. The set is divided into 12 volumes. Each volume includes jobs related under a broad career field. Volume 13 is the index.

★2262★ "State Police Officer" in *VGM's Careers Encyclopedia* (pp. 364-366)
National Textbook Co. (NTC)
VGM Career Books
4255 W. Touhy Ave.
Lincolnwood, IL 60646-1975
Ph: (708)679-5500 Fax: (708)679-2494
Fr: 800-323-4900

Third edition, 1991. Contains two- to five-page descriptions of 200 managerial, professional, technical, trade, and service occupations. Each profile includes job duties, places of employment, qualifications, educational preparation, training, employment potential, advancement, income, and additional sources of information.

★2263★ "State Police Officers" in *Career Discovery Encyclopedia* (Vol.6, pp. 60-61)
J.G. Ferguson Publishing Co.
200 W. Madison St., Ste. 300
Chicago, IL 60606
Ph: (312)580-5480 Fax: (312)580-4948

E. Russell Primm, editor-in-chief. 1993. Contains two-page articles on 504 occupations. Each article describes job duties, earnings, and educational and training requirements.

★2264★ *State Trooper*
Vocational Biographies, Inc.
PO Box 31
Sauk Centre, MN 56378-0031
Ph: (612)352-6516 Fax: (612)352-5546
Fr: 800-255-0752

1990. This pamphlet profiles a person working in the job. Includes information about job duties, working conditions, places of employment, educational preparation, labor market outlook, and salaries.

★2265★ "Texas Ranger" in *Offbeat Careers: The Directory of Unusual Work*
Ten Speed Press
PO Box 7123
Berkeley, CA 94707
Fax: (510)559-1629 Fr: 800-841-2665

Al Sacharov. 1991. Profiles eighty-eight unusual careers. Provides job description, history of occupation, salary, and training required. Lists one or more sources of additional information.

★2266★ "United States Customs Service" in *Opportunities in Transportation Careers* (pp. 130-132)
National Textbook Co. (NTC)
VGM Career Books
4255 W. Touhy Ave.
Lincolnwood, IL 60646-1975
Ph: (708)679-5500 Fax: (708)679-2494
Fr: 800-323-4900

Adrian A. Paradis. 1988. Describes transportation and related employment in driving occupations, the airlines, merchant marine, and travel services. Covers employment outlook, educational and training requirements, wages, and the work itself, and advantages and disadvantages of transportation careers. Offers job hunting advice.

★2267★ *U.S. Special Agent*
Vocational Biographies, Inc.
PO Box 31
Sauk Centre, MN 56378-0031
Ph: (612)352-6516 Fax: (612)352-5546
Fr: 800-255-0752

1989. This pamphlet profiles a person working in the job. Includes information about job duties, working conditions, places of employment, educational preparation, labor market outlook, and salaries.

★2268★ *Video Career Library - Public and Personal Services*
Careers, Inc.
PO Box 135
Largo, FL 34649-0135
Ph: (813)584-7333

Videocassette. 1990. 35 mins. Part of the Video Career Library covering 165 occupations. Shows actual workers on the job. Includes firefighters, police officers, correctional officers, bartenders, waiters/waitresses, cooks/chefs, child care workers, flight attendants, barbers/cosmetologists, groundskeepers/gardeners, and butchers/meat cutters.

★2269★ *What's it Like to be a Police Officer?*
Troll Associates
100 Corporate Dr.
Mahwah, NJ 07430
Ph: (201)529-4000 Fax: (201)529-9347
Fr: 800-526-5289

Michael J. Pellowski. 1990.

ASSOCIATIONS

★2270★ American Police Academy (APA)
1000 Conneticut Ave. NW, Ste. 9
Washington, DC 20036
Ph: (202)293-9088 Fax: (202)573-9819

Members: Educational arm of the American Federation of Police and National Association of Chiefs of Police. Law enforcement officers who have completed advanced training offered by the academy for on-duty police officers and security personnel. **Purpose:** Establishes professional certification standards for career officers. Conducts home study programs. Operates speakers' bureau and placement service; compiles statistics. **Publications:** *Police Times Magazine*, bimonthly. • *Who's Who in Law Enforcement*, triennial.

★2271★ Federal Bureau of Investigation (FBI)
Applicant Recruiting Office
1900 Half St. SW
Washington, DC 20535

Provides information concerning qualifications of FBI special agents.

★2272★ Federal Investigators Association (FIA)
PO Box 65864
Washington, DC 20035-5864

Members: Persons currently or formerly engaged in investigations, enforcement, security, and related activities for the federal government. **Purpose:** Goal is to recognize and promote criminal investigation. Has established professional standards of work, education, and conduct. Serves as a vehicle for exchange of ideas and broadening of professional contacts; conducts specialized education programs; offers placement service. Addresses such topics as advanced white collar crime investigations, suitability investigations, terrorism, and adjudication standards. Supports charitable programs. Offers placement service. **Publications:** *Federal Investigator Magazine*, semiannual. • *FIA Newsletter*, bimonthly. • *Investigative and Related Positions in the Federal Government.*

★2273★ National Association of Investigative Specialists (NAIS)
PO Box 33244
Austin, TX 78764
Ph: (512)832-0355

Offers training programs and issues certificates of completion.

★2274★ National Police Officers Association of America (NPOAA)
PO Box 22129
Louisville, KY 40252-0129
Ph: 800-467-6762 Fax: (502)425-9215
Fr: 800-467-6762

Members: Professional and fraternal benefit organization of law enforcement officers of federal, state, county, and local police departments, and civilians supporting law enforcement. **Purpose:** Maintains speakers' bureau; conducts educational programs. **Publications:** *National Police Review*, quarterly.

Standards/Certification Agencies

★2275★ American Police Academy (APA)
1000 Conneticut Ave. NW, Ste. 9
Washington, DC 20036
Ph: (202)293-9088 Fax: (202)573-9819

Law enforcement officers who have completed advanced training offered by the academy for on-duty police officers and security personnel. Establishes professional certification standards for career officers. Conducts home study programs.

★2276★ Association of Federal Investigators (AFI)
3299 K St. NW, 7th Fl.
Washington, DC 20007
Ph: (202)337-5234

Has established professional standards of work, education, and conduct.

★2277★ Federal Bureau of Investigation (FBI)
Applicant Recruiting Office
1900 Half St. SW
Washington, DC 20535

Provides information concerning qualifications of FBI special agents.

★2278★ Federal Investigators Association (FIA)
PO Box 65864
Washington, DC 20035-5864

Has established professional standards of work, education, and conduct.

★2279★ International Security and Detective Alliance (ISDA)
PO Box 6303
Corpus Christi, TX 78466-6303
Ph: (512)888-6164

Sets standards for and awards Professional Trade Designations and certifications.

★2280★ National Association of Investigative Specialists (NAIS)
PO Box 33244
Austin, TX 78764
Ph: (512)832-0355

Offers training programs and issues certificates of completion.

Test Guides

★2281★ *Career Examination Series: Captain, Police Dept.*
National Learning Corp.
212 Michael Dr.
Syosset, NY 11791
Ph: (516)921-8888 Fax: (516)921-8743
Fr: 800-645-6337

Jack Rudman. All examination guides in this series contain questions with answers.

★2282★ *Career Examination Series: Chief Deputy Sheriff*
National Learning Corp.
212 Michael Dr.
Syosset, NY 11791
Ph: (516)921-8888 Fax: (516)921-8743
Fr: 800-645-6337

Jack Rudman. All examination guides in this series contain questions with answers.

★2283★ *Career Examination Series: Chief of Police*
National Learning Corp.
212 Michael Dr.
Syosset, NY 11791
Ph: (516)921-8888 Fax: (516)921-8743
Fr: 800-645-6337

Jack Rudman. All examination guides in this series contain questions with answers.

★2284★ *Career Examination Series: Chief of Staff (Sheriff)*
National Learning Corp.
212 Michael Dr.
Syosset, NY 11791
Ph: (516)921-8888 Fax: (516)921-8743
Fr: 800-645-6337

Jack Rudman. All examination guides in this series contain questions with answers.

★2285★ *Career Examination Series: Deputy Chief Marshal*
National Learning Corp.
212 Michael Dr.
Syosset, NY 11791
Ph: (516)921-8888 Fax: (516)921-8743
Fr: 800-645-6337

Jack Rudman. All examination guides in this series contain questions with answers.

★2286★ *Career Examination Series: Deputy Sheriff*
National Learning Corp.
212 Michael Dr.
Syosset, NY 11791
Ph: (516)921-8888 Fax: (516)921-8743
Fr: 800-645-6337

Jack Rudman. All examination guides in this series contain questions with answers.

★2287★ *Career Examination Series: Detective Investigator*
National Learning Corp.
212 Michael Dr.
Syosset, NY 11791
Ph: (516)921-8888 Fax: (516)921-8743
Fr: 800-645-6337

Jack Rudman. All examination guides in this series contain questions with answers.

★2288★ *Career Examination Series: Police Cadet*
National Learning Corp.
212 Michael Dr.
Syosset, NY 11791
Ph: (516)921-8888 Fax: (516)921-8743
Fr: 800-645-6337

Jack Rudman. All examination guides in this series contain questions with answers.

★2289★ *Career Examination Series: Police Captain*
National Learning Corp.
212 Michael Dr.
Syosset, NY 11791
Ph: (516)921-8888 Fax: (516)921-8743
Fr: 800-645-6337

Jack Rudman. All examination guides in this series contain questions with answers.

★2290★ *Career Examination Series: Police Chief*
National Learning Corp.
212 Michael Dr.
Syosset, NY 11791
Ph: (516)921-8888 Fax: (516)921-8743
Fr: 800-645-6337

Jack Rudman. All examination guides in this series contain questions with answers.

★2291★ *Career Examination Series: Police Inspector*
National Learning Corp.
212 Michael Dr.
Syosset, NY 11791
Ph: (516)921-8888 Fax: (516)921-8743
Fr: 800-645-6337

Jack Rudman. All examination guides in this series contain questions with answers.

★2292★ *Career Examination Series: Police Lieutenant*
National Learning Corp.
212 Michael Dr.
Syosset, NY 11791
Ph: (516)921-8888 Fax: (516)921-8743
Fr: 800-645-6337

Jack Rudman. All examination guides in this series contain questions with answers.

★2293★ *Career Examination Series: Police Officer*
National Learning Corp.
212 Michael Dr.
Syosset, NY 11791
Ph: (516)921-8888 Fax: (516)921-8743
Fr: 800-645-6337

Jack Rudman. Guides are also available for the positions of police patrolman, police trainee, and policewomen. All examination guides in this series contain questions with answers.

★2294★ *Career Examination Series: Policewoman*
National Learning Corp.
212 Michael Dr.
Syosset, NY 11791
Ph: (516)921-8888 Fax: (516)921-8743
Fr: 800-645-6337

Jack Rudman. Test guide including questions and answers for students or professionals in the field who seek advancement through examination.

★2295★ *Career Examination Series: Principal Special Investigator*
National Learning Corp.
212 Michael Dr.
Syosset, NY 11791
Ph: (516)921-8888 Fax: (516)921-8743
Fr: 800-645-6337

Jack Rudman. All examination guides in this series contain questions with answers.

★2296★ *Career Examination Series: Public Safety Officer*
National Learning Corp.
212 Michael Dr.
Syosset, NY 11791
Ph: (516)921-8888 Fax: (516)921-8743
Fr: 800-645-6337

Jack Rudman. All examination guides in this series contain questions with answers.

★2297★ *Career Examination Series: Secret Service Agent (Uniformed)*
National Learning Corp.
212 Michael Dr.
Syosset, NY 11791
Ph: (516)921-8888 Fax: (516)921-8743
Fr: 800-645-6337

Jack Rudman. All examination guides in this series contain questions with answers.

★2298★ *Career Examination Series: Senior Capital Police Officer*
National Learning Corp.
212 Michael Dr.
Syosset, NY 11791
Ph: (516)921-8888 Fax: (516)921-8743
Fr: 800-645-6337

Jack Rudman. All examination guides in this series contain questions with answers.

★2299★ *Career Examination Series: Senior Deputy Sheriff*
National Learning Corp.
212 Michael Dr.
Syosset, NY 11791
Ph: (516)921-8888 Fax: (516)921-8743
Fr: 800-645-6337

Jack Rudman. All examination guides in this series contain questions with answers.

★2300★ *Career Examination Series: Senior Detective Investigator*
National Learning Corp.
212 Michael Dr.
Syosset, NY 11791
Ph: (516)921-8888 Fax: (516)921-8743
Fr: 800-645-6337

Jack Rudman. All examination guides in this series contain questions with answers.

★2301★ *Career Examination Series: Sheriff*
National Learning Corp.
212 Michael Dr.
Syosset, NY 11791
Ph: (516)921-8888 Fax: (516)921-8743
Fr: 800-645-6337

Jack Rudman. All examination guides in this series contain questions with answers.

★2302★ *Career Examination Series: Special Agent, Department of Justice*
National Learning Corp.
212 Michael Dr.
Syosset, NY 11791
Ph: (516)921-8888 Fax: (516)921-8743
Fr: 800-645-6337

Jack Rudman. All examination guides in this series contain questions with answers.

★2303★ *Career Examination Series: Special Agent FBI*
National Learning Corp.
212 Michael Dr.
Syosset, NY 11791
Ph: (516)921-8888 Fax: (516)921-8743
Fr: 800-645-6337

Jack Rudman. All examination guides in this series contain questions with answers.

★2304★ *Career Examination Series: State Policewoman*
National Learning Corp.
212 Michael Dr.
Syosset, NY 11791
Ph: (516)921-8888 Fax: (516)921-8743
Fr: 800-645-6337

Jack Rudman. Test guide including questions and answers for students or professionals in the field who seek advancement through examination.

★2305★ *Career Examination Series: State Trooper*
National Learning Corp.
212 Michael Dr.
Syosset, NY 11791
Ph: (516)921-8888 Fax: (516)921-8743
Fr: 800-645-6337

Jack Rudman. All examination guides in this series contain questions with answers.

★2306★ *Drug Enforcement Agent*
Prentice Hall Press
Simon & Schuster Inc.
200 Old Tappan Rd.
Old Tappan, NJ 07675
Ph: 800-223-2348

Francis Mullen. First edition, 1989. Includes a complete DEA exam battery, information on firearms tests, and review of drugs of abuse.

★2307★ *FBI Entrance Examination*
Prentice Hall Press
Simon & Schuster Inc.
200 Old Tappan Rd.
Old Tappan, NJ 07675
Ph: 800-223-2348

John Quirk. First edition, 1988. Provides sample exam, job application information, breakdown of jobs available with the FBI, interview with FBI personnel, and a history of the FBI.

★2308★ *How to Prepare for the Police Officer Examination Including Transit and Housing Officer*
Barron's Educational Series, Inc.
250 Wireless Blvd.
Hauppauge, NY 11788
Ph: (516)434-3311 Fax: (516)434-3723
Fr: 800-645-3476

Donald J. Schroeder and Frank A. Lombardo. Fourth edition. 1992. Manual offers four full-length practice exams, including the official exams used by the New York City Police Department. Includes answers with explanations and test-taking strategies.

★2309★ *How to Prepare for the Police Sergeant Examination*
Barron's Educational Series, Inc.
250 Wireless Blvd.
Hauppauge, NY 11788
Ph: (516)434-3311 Fax: (516)434-3723
Fr: 800-645-3476

Donald J. Schroeder and Frank A. Lombardo. Second edition. 1992. Manual presents four diagnostic exams with explained answers.

★2310★ *Law Enforcement Exams Handbook*
Arco Pub.
201 W. 103rd St.
Indianapolis, IN 46290
Ph: 800-428-5331 Fax: 800-835-3202

1993, first edition. Includes job descriptions and sample tests.

★2311★ *Police Administration & Supervision*
National Learning Corp.
212 Michael Dr.
Syosset, NY 11791
Ph: (516)921-8888 Fax: (516)921-8743
Fr: 800-645-6337

Jack Rudman. Part of the General Aptitude and Abilities Series. Books in this series provide functional, intensive test practice and drill in the basic skills and areas common to many examinations, as well as general aptitude or achievement necessary for entrance into many occupations or positions.

★2312★ *Police Administrative Aide*
Prentice Hall Press
Simon & Schuster Inc.
200 Old Tappan Rd.
Old Tappan, NJ 07675
Ph: 800-223-2348

Hy Hammer. Second edition, 1983. Complete test preparation for the positions of civilian police aide and 911 operator. Covers all major subject areas and includes two practice exams.

★2313★ *Police Officer*
Arco Pub.
201 W. 103rd St.
Indianapolis, IN 46290
Ph: 800-428-5331 Fax: 800-835-3202

12th edition. Includes five full length sample exams.

★2314★ *Police Officer Exams Review*
Video Aided Instruction, Inc.
182 Village Rd.
Roslyn Heights, NY 11577
Ph: (516)621-6176 Fax: (516)484-8785
Fr: 800-238-1512

Videocassette. 1987. 120 mins. This video summarizes the mental skills and attitudes necessary for work in the city, county, state, and other police agencies. It includes Test Taking Strategies, Reading Police Materials, Sizing up Suspicious Situations, Information Processing, Police Procedures, Police Reports, Maps and Traffic Diagrams, and Memorizing Faces, Scenes, and Facts.

★2315★ *Police Promotion Course (One Volume)*
National Learning Corp.
212 Michael Dr.
Syosset, NY 11791
Ph: (516)921-8888 Fax: (516)921-8743
Fr: 800-645-6337

Jack Rudman. Part of the General Aptitude and Abilities Series. Books in this series provide functional, intensive test practice and drill in the basic skills and areas common to many examinations, as well as general aptitude or achievement necessary for entrance into many occupations or positions.

★2316★ *Police Promotion Examinations*
Prentice Hall Press
Simon & Schuster Inc.
200 Old Tappan Rd.
Old Tappan, NJ 07675
Ph: 800-223-2348

Hugh O'Neill. First edition, 1983. Provides preparation for the examinations that qualify police officers for promotion to sergeant, lieutenant, and other higher-level positions.

★2317★ *Police Reading Comprehension*
National Learning Corp.
212 Michael Dr.
Syosset, NY 11791
Ph: (516)921-8888 Fax: (516)921-8743
Fr: 800-645-6337

Jack Rudman. Part of the General Aptitude and Abilities Series. Books in this series provide functional, intensive test practice and drill in the basic skills and areas common to many examinations, as well as general aptitude or achievement necessary for entrance into many occupations or positions.

★2318★ *Special Agent*
Prentice Hall Press
Simon & Schuster Inc.
200 Old Tappan Rd.
Old Tappan, NJ 07675
Ph: 800-223-2348

E.P. Steinberg. First edition, 1989. Complete guide to the Treasury Enforcement Agent test that all applicants must take for posts within the U.S. Treasury Department, including the branches of Secret Service, Customs Service, Internal Revenue Service, or Bureau of Alcohol, Tobacco, and Firearms. Contains three full-length sample exams with answers.

★2319★ *State Trooper/Highway Patrol Officer/State Traffic Officer*
Prentice Hall Press
Simon & Schuster Inc.
200 Old Tappan Rd.
Old Tappan, NJ 07675
Ph: 800-223-2348

Hy Hammer and Edward Scheinkman. Ninth edition, 1988. Complete guide to all types of state trooper exams given throughout the country. Includes study sections and five sample exams.

Awards, Scholarships, Grants, and Fellowships

★2320★ AFI Honor Roll
Association of Federal Investigators
3299 K St. NW, 7th Fl.
Washington, DC 20007
Ph: (202)337-5234 Fax: (202)333-5365

To recognize individuals who have made the ultimate sacrifice and have given their lives in the line of duty. It is given posthumously each year to those in Federal law enforcement who have made this sacrifice. Their names are added to a special Honor Roll. Established in 1984.

★2321★ Criminal Investigation Award
American Police Hall of Fame
3801 Biscayne Blvd.
Miami, FL 33137
Ph: (305)573-0070 Fax: (305)573-9819

To recognize the men and women who quietly work to solve cases through long hours of detective work and for recognition of their talents that lead to the closing of a difficult case. Nominations of any person, any age, are accepted from another person or him or herself, anytime during the year. A certificate is awarded when merited.

★2322★ Alphonso Deal Scholarship Award
National Black Police Association (NBPA)
3251 Mt. Pleasant St., NW
2nd Fl.
Washington, DC 20010
Ph: (202)986-2070

Purpose: To enhance the higher educational opportunities among qualified high school graduates in the area of law enforcement or other related fields for the betterment of the criminal justice system. Qualifications: Applicants must be U.S. citizens, and high school seniors accepted by a college or university prior to the date of the award, and have maintained at least a 2.5 GPA. Selection criteria: Selection is based upon GPA, recommendations, and extra-curricular activities. Funds available: $500 per recipient. Application details: Candidates should submit information regarding their educational background, biographical information, and transcripts. Deadline: June 1.

★2323★ Distinguished Service Award
American Police Hall of Fame
3801 Biscayne Blvd.
Miami, FL 33137
Ph: (305)573-0070 Fax: (305)573-9819

To recognize police officers and high ranking officials who distinguish themselves with honor in outstanding service to their state and community. Nominations of any person, any age, are accepted from another person or him or herself, anytime during the year. A certificate is awarded.

★2324★ Distinguished Service Award
American Association of Motor Vehicle Administrators
4200 Wilson Blvd., Ste. 1100
Arlington, VA 22203
Ph: (703)522-4200 Fax: (703)522-1553

To recognize the outstanding services, contributions, and accomplishments of individuals in the field of motor vehicle administration and traffic law enforcement. Members of the Association who are employed by a motor vehicle or public safety agency are eligible in either of two categories: Category I - those who are active members of the Association, but have never served on the Board of Directors; and Category II - those who have served on the Board of Directors and have contributed to the advancement of the Association through outstanding services and accomplishments. Nominees in both categories must have worked at a member agency between September of the year prior to the award and June of the year the award is given. A plaque is awarded in each category annually at the international conference held in August. A Lifetime Achievement Award is also presented to an individual who was supportive of and active with the Association and a leader in his or her field, but no longer holds a position at a member agency. A potential candidate need not to have been employed by a member agency during the previous year to be nominated. Established in 1964.

★2325★ General Commendation
American Police Hall of Fame
3801 Biscayne Blvd.
Miami, FL 33137
Ph: (305)573-0070 Fax: (305)573-9819

To recognize officers who have, through an act of service or by professional police work, earned a special commendation on an individual basis. Nominations of any person, any age, are accepted from another person or him or herself, anytime during the year. Awarded when merited.

★2326★ Good Samaritan Award
American Police Hall of Fame
3801 Biscayne Blvd.
Miami, FL 33137
Ph: (305)573-0070 Fax: (305)573-9819

To recognize both law enforcement and civilians for an act of charity that aids those less fortunate, thus carrying on the biblical act of the Good Samaritan. Nominations of any person, any age, are accepted from another person or him or herself, anytime during the year. Awarded when merited.

★2327★ J. Edgar Hoover Foundation Scholarship
Boy Scouts of America
Exploring Division
1325 Walnut Hill Ln.
Irving, TX 75038-3096

Purpose: These scholarships are intended to promote interest in and study of the law enforcement profession. Qualifications: Registered Explorer scouts, active in a post specializing in law enforcement or who have demonstrated meaningful service to or interest in law enforcement agencies, are eligible to apply. Applicants must be at least a high school senior by March 1 of the year for which they are being considered. Applicants must not have reached their 21st birthday by March 31 of the year under consideration. Funds available: Six national winners, one from each of BSA's six regions, are selected. The amount of each scholarship is $1,000. It covers tuition only and does not provide for room and board or incidental expenses. Scholarship funds remain available to winners for a 24-month period, starting with the summer or fall semester, of the year selected. Application details: Applicants must write a statement of at least 250 words giving reasons for seeking a career in law enforcement and must submit a minimum of three letters of recommendation (at least one from a law enforcement official). A high school transcript of grades is required, along with consent and certification by parents, post Advisor and the head of the law enforcement agency chartering the post, and local Boy Scout Council executives. Deadline: Applications must be received in the local Boy Scout Council Exploring office by March 15, and must be received by the National Office Exploring Division by March 31.

★2328★ John Edgar Hoover Police Service Award
American Police Hall of Fame
3801 Biscayne Blvd.
Miami, FL 33137
Ph: (305)573-0070 Fax: (305)573-9819

To honor police and citizens for service and valor nationwide. One award is presented per state. Any person, any age, is and can be nominated either by another person or by him or herself anytime during the year. The Hoover Trophyis awarded during the Police Memorial Day program. Established in 1966 in honor of police officers and friends of police officers.

★2329★ Human Rights Award
International League for Human Rights
432 Park Ave. S., Rm. 1103
New York, NY 10016
Ph: (212)684-1221 Fax: (212)684-1696

To recognize outstanding contributions to the cause of human freedom internationally. Individuals in any country judged to have made such contributions are eligible. Awarded annually. Established in 1968.

★2330★ Individual Award
American Printing History Association
PO Box 4922
Grand Central Sta.
New York, NY 10163
Ph: (212)930-0802 Fax: (212)302-4815

To recognize an individual for distinguished contributions to the study, recording, preservation, and dissemination of printing history. Awarded annually. Established in 1976.

★2331★ Investigator of the Year
Association of Federal Investigators
3299 K St. NW, 7th Fl.
Washington, DC 20007
Ph: (202)337-5234 Fax: (202)333-5365

For recognition of significant contributions to the investigative profession. Investigative professionals, public officials, and citizens of the United States are eligible. Nominations are accepted. Awards are given in the following categories: criminal investigator; financial investigator; general investigator; fraud investigator; and security/counterintelligence investigator. A plaque is awarded annually. Established in 1976.

★2332★ ISDA Special Commendation
International Security and Detective Alliance
PO Box 6303
Corpus Christi, TX 78466-6303
Ph: (512)888-6164

To honor any individual who significantly promotes the growth and betterment of the private security and investigation professions, or who performs significant acts of heroism, bravery, and/or faithful service. Letters of application with affidavits, statements, etc., as required may be submitted by anyone meeting the above criteria. Certificates are awarded when approved applications are received. Established in 1987.

★2333★ Knights of Justice Award
American Police Hall of Fame
3801 Biscayne Blvd.
Miami, FL 33137
Ph: (305)573-0070 Fax: (305)573-9819

To recognize community service and valor by lawmen who are all "Blue Knights of Justice" and are considered to carry out the work of the world's first police officer, Michael the Archangel. Nominations of any person, any age, are accepted from another person or him or herself, anytime during the year. An honorary knighthood is awarded as merited.

★2334★ Law Enforcement Assistance Award
Boy Scouts of America
Exploring Division
1325 Walnut Hill Ln.
Irving, TX 75038-3096

Purpose: These scholarships are intended to promote interest in and study of the law enforcement profession. Qualifications: Registered Explorer scouts, active in a post specializing in law enforcement or who have demonstrated meaningful service to or interest in law enforcement agencies, are eligible to apply. The Law Enforcement Assistance Award, cosponsored by the U.S. Secret Service, is awarded to an Explorer who has acted to assist in the prevention or solution of a serious crime, or who has provided information that assisted law enforcement personnel to apprehend a felony suspect. Funds available: The Law Enforcement Assistance Award provides a certificate, a lapel pin, an engraved medallion, and a $1,000 scholarship to the college of the winner's choice. Application details: Applicants must submit a formal application, noting the act of assistance. Three letters of recommendation (from school officials, post or organization leaders, and church/community leaders) must be submitted, along with a statement of qualification from the post Advisor. Deadline: Applications must be filed in the National Office Exploring Division by March 31.

★2335★ Law Enforcement Leadership Award
Association of Federal Investigators
3299 K St. NW, 7th Fl.
Washington, DC 20007
Ph: (202)337-5234 Fax: (202)333-5365

To recognize individuals in leadership positions in Federal law enforcement who have uniquely provided outstanding leadership contributions towards achieving major law enforcement objectives. A plaque is awarded annually at the awards program. Established in 1966.

★2336★ Man of the Year in Law Enforcement
Society of Professional Investigators
c/o All-Tech Investigations
4812 Ft. Hamilton Pkwy., 3rd Fl.
Brooklyn, NY 11219-5855
Ph: (212)807-5658 Fax: (212)581-3217

For recognition of outstanding service rendered in the crusade against crime, racketeering, and corruption in government. Individuals in the investigative area of law enforcement who are nominated by members of the Society are eligible. An engraved plaque is awarded annually. Established in 1957.

★2337★ McDonnell Douglas Law Enforcement Award
Helicopter Association International
1619 Duke St.
Alexandria, VA 22314-3406
Ph: (703)683-4646 Fax: (703)683-4745

To recognize a worthy contribution to the advancement of the crime-suppression concept of helicopter patrol service. The award is limited to anti-crime patrol service and related activities such as surveillance and pursuit, but not limited to pilots or necessarily restricted to law enforcement personnel. Individuals employed by members in good standing of the Association are eligible. An engraved plaque is awarded annually. Established in 1972 by Hughes Helicopter of Culver City, California.

★2338★ Merit Award for Excellent Arrest
American Police Hall of Fame
3801 Biscayne Blvd.
Miami, FL 33137
Ph: (305)573-0070 Fax: (305)573-9819
For recognition of the apprehension of a felon who was endangering the life and safety of the community. The arrest is considered by the department to be outstanding from the normal day-to-day arrests. Awarded when merited.

★2339★ NAFI Man of the Year
National Association of Fire Investigators
PO Box 957257
Hoffman Estates, IL 60195-7257
Ph: (312)427-6320
To recognize significant contributions to the fire investigation profession and NAFI. Firefighters, police officers, attorneys, insurance adjusters, claimsmen, fire experts, fire marshals in the military, or full-time fire investigators may be nominated. An engraved plaque is awarded annually when merited. Established in 1969.

★2340★ Outstanding Law Enforcement Achievement Award
International Association of Fish and Wildlife Agencies
444 N. Capitol St. NW, Ste. 544
Washington, DC 20001
Ph: (202)624-7890 Fax: (202)624-7891
To recognize outstanding law enforcement efforts in support of wildlife. Individuals and agencies are eligible. Awarded annually. Established in 1982.

★2341★ Patriots Award
American Police Hall of Fame
3801 Biscayne Blvd.
Miami, FL 33137
Ph: (305)573-0070 Fax: (305)573-9819
For recognition of organizations and individuals whose patriotic acts or service promote liberty and justice in the United States. Nominations of any person, any age, are accepted from another person or him or herself, anytime during the year. A certificate is awarded when merited.

★2342★ Police Officer of the Year Award
International Association of Chiefs of Police
515 N. Washington St.
Alexandria, VA 22314-2357
Ph: (703)836-6767 Fax: (703)836-4543
To recognize exemplary performance in police work. Nominations may be made for exceptional achievement in any police endevour, including but not limited to, extraordinary valor, crime prevention, investigative work, community relations, traffic safety, drug control and prevention, juvenile programs, and training efforts. All sworn, full-time local, county, state, or federal officers below the rank of chief are eligible. Recipients are recognized in *PARADE* magazine and at an awards luncheon at the Annual Conference. Sponsored jointly by the IACP and *PARADE*magazine.

★2343★ Public Service Award
Scanner Association of North America
PO Box 414
Western Springs, IL 60558
Ph: (312)246-4550
To recognize a police, fire, or other public safety volunteer or official for heroic action. Members of the Association may nominate individuals. A monetary prize and a plaque are awarded six times per year. Established in 1978.

★2344★ Silver Star for Bravery
American Police Hall of Fame
3801 Biscayne Blvd.
Miami, FL 33137
Ph: (305)573-0070 Fax: (305)573-9819
To recognize an officer for an act of daring and valor in a life-threatening situation that is above and beyond the line of duty. Nominations by any person, any age, are accepted from another person or him or herself, anytime during the year. A silver star is awarded as merited.

★2345★ Sons of the American Revolution Law Enforcement Commendation Medal
National Society
Sons of the American Revolution
1000 S. 4th St.
Louisville, KY 40203
Ph: (502)589-1776
To recognize law enforcement officers for outstanding service in the line of duty. A gold filled enamel medal is awarded irregularly. Established in 1968.

★2346★ Special Achievement Awards
Association of Federal Investigators
3299 K St. NW, 7th Fl.
Washington, DC 20007
Ph: (202)337-5234 Fax: (202)333-5365
To recognize an individual for special achievements in federal investigation law enforcement, or the criminal justice system. Investigative professionals, public officials, and citizens of the United States are eligible. Nominations are accepted. A plaque is awarded annually. Established in 1979.

★2347★ VFW J. Edgar Hoover Award
Veterans of Foreign Wars of the U.S.A.
V.F.W. Bldg.
406 W. 34th St.
Kansas City, MO 64111
Ph: (816)756-3390 Fax: (816)968-1157
To recognize an individual for outstanding service in the field of law enforcement. Awarded on recommendation of the National Committee on Awards and Citations and authorized by the National Council of Administration. An honorarium, medal, and citation are awarded annually at the National Convention. Established in 1966.

★2348★ Woman Officer of the Year
International Association of Women Police
PO Box 371008
Decatur, GA 30037
Ph: (404)244-2856
To recognize outstanding women of the law enforcement profession by a professional network of peer officers. In addition, the award has the following objectives: (1) to provide the members with the benefit of learning about achievements of sister officers; (2) to increase understanding and awareness of women in law enforcement and the International Association of Women Police; (3) to encourage police administrators to support the organization with their own membership as well as that of officers in their agencies; (4) to promote the annual training conference; and (5) to promote membership by all women law enforcement officers in IAWP. Women who are sworn law enforcement officers with the power of arrest, and who are currently employed may be nominated with the approval of the highest ranking official of the agency where the woman is employed. Nominations may be made when a woman officer has demonstrated meritorious police service, i.e., has at imminent risk of life performed deeds of valor or has rendered invaluable police service and is dedicated to her daily tasks. Travel and expenses to attend the annual conference are awarded annually in September or October. Established in 1977.

Basic Reference Guides and Handbooks

★2349★ *Detective Work: A Study of Criminal Investigations*
Free Press
866 3rd Ave.
New York, NY 10022
Ph: (212)702-3130 Fax: (212)605-9364
William B. Sanders. 1977.

★2350★ *Detective's Private Investigation Training Manual*
Paladin Press
PO Box 1307
Boulder, CO 80306
Ph: (303)443-7250 Fax: (303)442-8741
William Patterson. 1979.

★2351★ *Find 'em Fast: A Private Investigator's Workbook*
Paladin Press
PO Box 1307
Boulder, CO 80306
Ph: (303)443-7250 Fax: (303)442-8741
John D. McCann. 1984.

★2352★ *Find Them Fast, Find Them Now: Private Investigators Share Their Secrets for Finding Missing Persons*
Carol Publishing Group
120 Enterprise Ave.
Secaucus, NJ 07094
Ph: (201)866-0490 Fax: (201)866-8159
Frederick C. Hoyer, Jr. 1988.

★2353★ *How to Find Anyone Anywhere*
Thomas Publications
202 S. Stratton St.
PO Box 3031
Gettysburg, PA 17325
Ph: (717)334-1921
Ralph D. Thomas. 1987. Part of Private Investigation Series.

★2354★ *How to Find Cases Anywhere: P.I.'s Guide to Obtaining Cases, Obtaining Free Publicity & Marketing Investigative Services*
Thomas Publications
202 S. Stratton St.
PO Box 3031
Gettysburg, PA 17325
Ph: (717)334-1921

Ralph D. Thomas. 1988.

★2355★ *Law Enforcement Career Planning*
Charles C. Thomas, Publisher
2600 S. 1st St.
Springfield, IL 62794-9265
Ph: (217)789-8980 Fax: (217)789-9130

Thomas Mahoney. 1989.

★2356★ *Police—Buyer's Guide Issue*
Hare Publications
6300 Yarrow Dr.
Carlsbad, CA 92009
Ph: 800-854-6449 Fax: (619)931-5809
Fr: 800-624-6377
Dan Burger, Contact

Annual, August. Publication includes: List of suppliers of police products and services. Entries include: Supplier name, address, phone, products or services supplied. Arrangement: Classified by product or service.

★2357★ *The Police Function & the Investigation of Crime*
Gower Publishing Co.
Old Post Rd.
Brookfield, VT 05036
Ph: (802)276-3162

Brian J. Morgan. 1990.

★2358★ *Police Promotion Manual*
Looseleaf Law Publications, Inc.
41-23 150th St.
Flushing, NY 11355
Fax: (718)539-0941

★2359★ *The Process of Investigation: Concepts & Strategies for the Security Professional*
Butterworth-Heinemann
80 Montvale Ave.
Stoneham, MA 02180
Ph: (617)438-8464 Fax: (617)279-4851

Charles A. Sennewald. 1981.

★2360★ *Professional Thieves & the Detective*
AMS Press, Inc.
56 E. 13th St.
New York, NY 10003
Ph: (212)777-4700 Fax: (212)995-5413

Allan Pinkerton.

★2361★ *Shadowing & Surveillance: A Complete Guide Book*
Loompanics Unlimited
PO Box 1197
Port Townsend, WA 98368
Ph: (206)385-5087

Burt Rapp. 1985.

★2362★ *Top Secret! Codes to Crack*
Albert Whitman & Co.
6340 Oakton St.
Morton Grove, IL 60053-2723
Ph: (708)581-0033 Fax: (708)581-0039
Fr: 800-255-7675

Burton Albert, Jr. 1987.

★2363★ *Undercover Work: A Complete Handbook*
Loompanics Unlimited
PO Box 1197
Port Townsend, WA 98368
Ph: (206)385-5087

Burt Rapp. 1985.

★2364★ *Word Detective Picture Word Book*
EDC Publishing
10302 E. 55th Pl.
Tulsa, OK 74146
Ph: (918)622-4522

King. 1982.

★2365★ *The Young Detective's Handbook*
Little, Brown & Co., Inc.
34 Becon St.
Boston, MA 02108
Ph: (617)227-0730 Fax: (617)723-9422

William V. Butler. 1986.

PERIODICALS

★2366★ *College of Law Enforcement—Newsletter*
College of Law Enforcement
105 Stratton
Richmond, KY 40475
Ph: (606)622-1155 Fax: (606)622-6264
Fr: 800-622-1497
Bruce I. Wolford

Biennial. Reports on the activities in the areas of concentration within the College: law enforcement, fire science, security, and traffic safety. Contains articles on criminal justice, public safety, loss prevention, and related subjects. Recurring features include news of members, a calendar of events, and faculty updates.

★2367★ *Crime Control Digest*
Washington Crime News Services
3918 Prosperity Ave., Ste. 318
Fairfax, VA 22031-3334
Ph: (703)573-1600 Fax: (703)573-1604
Fr: 800-422-9267
Betty B. Bosarge

Weekly. Contains articles on all levels of law enforcement in the U.S., including national, state, county, local, and student concerns, though the focus is on matters of national import. Reports on such items as illegal drug trafficking, terrorism, the accreditation of law enforcement agencies, pending legislation, and the implementation of new laws. Recurring features include information on upcoming seminars and conferences, and announcements of awards.

★2368★ *Federal Investigator Magazine*
Federal Investigators Association (FIA)
PO Box 65864
Washington, DC 20035-5864

Semiannual. Covers current law enforcement issues and studies.

★2369★ *FIA Newsletter*
Federal Investigators Association (FIA)
PO Box 65864
Washington, DC 20035-5864

Bimonthly. Covers legislative issues and other current information affecting federal law enforcement. Includes chapter news, employment opportunities, reports.

★2370★ *First Principles: National Security and Civil Liberties*
Center for National Security Studies
122 Maryland Ave. NE
Washington, DC 20002
Ph: (202)544-1681
Gary Stern

Concerned that intelligence agencies, local police, and other government agencies violate the civil liberties of American citizens. Calls for legislative reforms "to prevent further abuses." Recurring features include reviews of current litigation and legislative activities, and literature in the field.

★2371★ *Investigative and Related Positions in the Federal Government*
Federal Investigators Association (FIA)
PO Box 65864
Washington, DC 20035-5864

★2372★ *Law Enforcement Technology*
PTN Publishing Co.
445 Broad Hollow Rd., Ste. 21
Melville, NY 11747
Ph: (516)845-2700 Fax: (516)845-7109
Donna Rogers

Magazine for police technology and management.

★2373★ *Law Officer's Bulletin*
Bureau of National Affairs, Inc. (BNA)
1231 25th St. NW
Washington, DC 20037
Ph: (202)452-4200 Fax: (202)822-8092
Fr: 800-372-1033
Robert L. Goebes

Biweekly. Provides an update of court decisions, Justice Department proposals, and congressional actions involving law enforcement officers, describing legal reasoning and explaining the impact on the law enforcement community. Recurring features include the features From the Supreme Court, Trends and Developments, You Be the Judge, Perspective, and Training Calendar.

★2374★ *Law and Order*
1000 Skokie Blvd.
Wilmette, IL 60091
Ph: (708)256-8555 Fax: (708)256-8574
Bruce Cameron

Monthly. Law enforcement trade magazine.

★2375★ *National Police Review*
National Police Officers Assn.
PO Box 22129
Louisville, KY 40252-0129
Ph: 800-467-6762 Fax: (502)425-9215
John R. Moore

Magazine serving as a forum for the Police Officers Association of America. Includes articles on new ideas and procedures in law enforcement, reviews of police products and equipment, and association news.

★2376★ *Police*
Hare Publications
6300 Yarrow Dr.
Carlsbad, CA 92009
Ph: (619)438-2511 Fax: (619)931-5809
Dan Burger

Monthly. Law enforcement magazine.

★2377★ *The Police Chief*
International Assn. of Chiefs of Police
515 N. Washington St., #400
Alexandria, VA 22314-2340
Ph: (703)243-6500 Fax: (703)243-0684
Charles E. Higginbotham

Monthly. Law enforcement magazine.

★2378★ *Police & Security News*
Days Communications
1690 Quarry Rd.
PO Box 330
Kulpsville, PA 19443
Ph: (215)538-1240 Fax: (215)538-1208
James Devery

Bimonthly. Tabloid for the law enforcement and private security industries. Includes articles on training, new products, and new technology.

★2379★ *Police Times Magazine*
American Police Academy (APA)
1000 Conneticut Ave. NW, Ste. 9
Washington, DC 20036
Ph: (202)293-9088 Fax: (305)573-9819

Bimonthly. Tabloid reporting on issues in law enforcement.

★2380★ *Sheriff*
National Sheriffs' Assn.
1450 Duke St.
Alexandria, VA 22314-3490
Ph: (703)836-7827 Fax: (703)683-6541
Fr: 800-424-7827
Suzanne D. Bacon

Bimonthly. Professional law enforcement magazine.

★2381★ *Today's Policeman*
Towerhigh Publications, Inc.
PO Box 875108
Los Angeles, CA 90087
Ph: (213)432-3806
Donald Mack

Quarterly. Law enforcement magazine.

★2382★ *Who's Who in Law Enforcement*
American Police Academy (APA)
1000 Conneticut Ave. NW, Ste. 9
Washington, DC 20036
Ph: (202)293-9088 Fax: (202)573-9819

Triennial.

Meetings and Conventions

★2383★ Annual Training Conference and Awards Banquet
Federal Investigators Association (FIA)
PO Box 65864
Washington, DC 20035-5864

Washington, D.C..

★2384★ International Association of Chiefs of Police Annual Conference
International Association of Chiefs of Police
515 N. Washington St.
Alexandria, VA 22314-2357
Ph: (703)836-6767

Annual. Always held during October. **Dates and Locations:** 1995 Oct 14-18; Miami, FL. • 1996 Oct 26-31; Phoenix, AZ. • 1997 Oct; Salt Lake City, UT. • 1998 Oct; Charlotte, NC.

Other Sources of Information

★2385★ *The Breakfast Club*
Suncoast Media, Inc.
122551 Indian Rocks Rd., No. 15
Largo, FL 34644-3009
Ph: (813)596-1112 Fax: (813)587-7942
Fr: 800-899-1008

Provides accurate information and professional guidance to police officers on the subject of how to handle exposure to HIV and AIDS in their daily duties. Includes trainer's manual and handout material.

★2386★ *Career Planning in Criminal Justice*
Anderson Publishing Co.
2035 Reading Rd.
Cincinnati, OH 45202
Ph: (513)421-4142

1990. Includes chapters describing careers in corrections, careers in forensic science, and careers in private security.

★2387★ *A Cowboy Detective: A True Story of Twenty-Two Years with a World-Famous Detective Agency*
University of Nebraska, Lincoln
University of Nebraska Press
901 N. 17th St.
Lincoln, NE 68588
Ph: (402)472-3581 Fax: (402)472-6214

Charles A. Siringo. 1988.

★2388★ "Detective" in *Career Selector 2001*
Barron's Educational Series, Inc.
250 Wireless Blvd.
Hauppauge, NY 11788
Ph: (516)434-3311 Fax: (516)434-3723
Fr: 800-645-3476

James C. Gonyea. 1993.

★2389★ *Front Page Detective: William J. Burns & the Detective Profession, 1880-1930*
Bowling Green State University Popular Press
838 E. Wooster St.
Bowling Green, OH 43403
Ph: (419)372-7866 Fax: (419)372-8095

William R. Hunt. 1990.

★2390★ *The Idea of Police*
Sage Publications, Inc.
2111 W. Hillcrest Dr.
Newbury Park, CA 91320
Ph: (805)499-0721 Fax: (805)499-0871

Carl B. Klockars. 1985. Part of Law & Criminal Justice Series.

★2391★ "Law Enforcement Officer" in *Encyclopedia of Danger: Dangerous Professions* (pp. 58-61)
Chelsea House Publishers
1974 Sproul Rd., Ste. 400
Broomall, PA 19008
Ph: (215)353-5166 Fax: (215)359-1439

Missy Allen and Michel Peissel. 1993. Provides descriptions of 24 dangerous occupations, their risky characteristics, and safety precautions.

★2392★ "Police Officer" in *100 Best Jobs for the 1990s & Beyond*
Dearborn Financial Publishing, Inc.
520 N. Dearborn St.
Chicago, IL 60610-4354
Ph: (312)836-4400 Fax: (312)836-1021
Fr: 800-621-9621

Carol Kleiman. 1992. Describes 100 jobs ranging from accountants to veterinarians. Each job profile includes such information as education, experience, and certification needed, salaries, and job search suggestions.

★2393★ "Police Officer" in *Career Selector 2001*
Barron's Educational Series, Inc.
250 Wireless Blvd.
Hauppauge, NY 11788
Ph: (516)434-3311 Fax: (516)434-3723
Fr: 800-645-3476

James C. Gonyea. 1993.

★2394★ *Successful Private Eyes & Private Spies: Private Spies*
Thomas Publications
202 S. Stratton St.
PO Box 3031
Gettysburg, PA 17325
Ph: (717)334-1921

Barbara L. Thomas. 1986. Part of Private Investigation Series.

Chefs, Cooks, and Other Kitchen Workers

Chefs and cooks are responsible for preparing meals that are tasty and attractively presented. Typical duties include measuring, mixing, and cooking ingredients, using a variety of pots, pans, cutlery, and equipment including ovens, broilers, grills, and blenders. They often direct the work of other kitchen workers. Many chefs have earned fame for themselves and the eateries they work for because of their skill in artfully preparing traditional favorites and exciting new dishes. The terms chef and cook are sometimes used interchangeably, but chefs are generally the most highly skilled and trained, whereas cooks have more limited skills. **Institutional chefs and cooks** work in the kitchens of schools, industrial cafeterias, hospitals, and other institutions. They usually prepare a small selection of entrees in large quantities. **Restaurant chefs and cooks** prepare a wider selection of dishes, cooking individual servings to order. **Bread and pastry bakers** produce baked goods for restaurants, institutions, and retail bakery shops. **Short-order cooks** prepare foods to order in eateries that emphasize fast service. **Specialty fast-food cooks** prepare a limited selection of menu items in fast-food restaurants. Other kitchen workers perform tasks at the direction of chefs and cooks. This may include cleaning and slicing vegetables, and cleaning work areas and equipment.

Salaries

Wages vary depending on region and type of establishment.

Chefs-elegant restaurants, hotels	over $40,000/year
Cooks	$6.57/hour
Assistant cooks and short-order cooks	$6.00/hour
Bread and pastry bakers	$6.25/hour
Salad preparation workers	$5.90/hour
Food preparation workers in fast-food restaurants	$4.68/hour

Employment Outlook

Growth rate until the year 2005: Faster than average.

Chefs, Cooks, and Other Kitchen Workers

Career Guides

★2395★ *Bagel Baker*
Vocational Biographies, Inc.
PO Box 31
Sauk Centre, MN 56378-0031
Ph: (612)352-6516 Fax: (612)352-5546
Fr: 800-255-0752

1990. This pamphlet profiles a person working in the job. Includes information about job duties, working conditions, places of employment, educational preparation, labor market outlook, and salaries.

★2396★ *Baker*
Careers, Inc.
PO Box 135
Largo, FL 34649-0135
Ph: (813)584-7333

1995. Two-page occupational summary card describing duties, working conditions, personal qualifications, training, earnings and hours, employment outlook, places of employment, related careers and where to write for more information.

★2397★ "Baker" in *Occu-Facts: Information on 580 Careers in Outline Form* (p. 17.30)
Careers, Inc.
PO Box 135
Largo, FL 34649-0135
Ph: (813)584-7333

Biennial, 1995-96 edition. Each one-page occupational profile describes duties, working conditions, physical surroundings and demands, aptitudes, temperament, educational requirements, employment outlook, earnings, and places of employment.

★2398★ *Bakers and Bakery Products Workers*
Chronicle Guidance Publications, Inc.
66 Aurora St.
PO Box 1190
Moravia, NY 13118-1190
Ph: (315)497-0330 Fax: (315)497-3359
Fr: 800-622-7284

1993. This career brief describes the nature of the work, working conditions, hours and earnings, education and training, licensure, certification, unions, personal qualifications, social and psychological factors, employment outlook, entry methods, advancement, and related occupations.

★2399★ "Baking and Pastry" in *Opportunities in Culinary Careers* (pp. 99-106)
National Textbook Co. (NTC)
VGM Career Books
4255 W. Touhy Ave.
Lincolnwood, IL 60646-1975
Ph: (708)679-5500 Fax: (708)679-2494
Fr: 800-323-4900

Mary Deirdre Donovan. 1990. Describes the educational preparation and training of chefs and cooks and explores a variety of food service jobs in restaurants, institutions, and research and development. Lists culinary schools and professional organizations.

★2400★ "Becoming a Chef" in *Opportunities in Culinary Careers* (pp. 17-39)
National Textbook Co. (NTC)
VGM Career Books
4255 W. Touhy Ave.
Lincolnwood, IL 60646-1975
Ph: (708)679-5500 Fax: (708)679-2494
Fr: 800-323-4900

Mary Deirdre Donovan. 1990. Describes the educational preparation and training of chefs and cooks and explores a variety of food service jobs in restaurants, institutions, and research and development. Lists culinary schools and professional organizations.

★2401★ *Careers for Gourmets & Others Who Relish Food*
National Textbook Co. (NTC)
VGM Career Books
4255 W. Toughy Ave.
Lincolnwood, IL 60646-1975
Ph: (708)679-5500 Fax: (708)679-2494
Fr: 800-323-4900

Mary Donovan.

★2402★ "Certified Master Chef: the Highest Honor in the Industry" in *Opportunities in Restaurant Careers* (pp. 49-53)
National Textbook Co. (NTC)
VGM Career Books
4255 W. Touhy Ave.
Lincolnwood, IL 60646-1975
Ph: (708)679-5500 Fax: (708)679-2494
Fr: 800-323-4900

Carol Ann Caprione Chmelynski. 1990. Provides an overview of the restaurant industry and surveys entry-level, mid-level, and management jobs. Covers working conditions, educational preparation, training, advancement possibilities, employment outlook, and earnings. Lists schools offering programs in hotel, restaurant, and institutional management.

★2403★ "Chef/Cook" in *Guide to Careers Without College* (pp. 97-100)
Franklin Watts, Inc.
387 Park Avenue, S.
New York, NY 10016
Ph: (212)686-7070

Kathleen S. Abrams. 1988. Discusses careers that do not require a college degree in fields such as health care, sales and marketing, and the building trades. Describes the work, employment opportunities, and training.

★2404★ "Chef" in *VGM's Careers Encyclopedia* (pp. 84-86)
National Textbook Co. (NTC)
VGM Career Books
4255 W. Touhy Ave.
Lincolnwood, IL 60646-1975
Ph: (708)679-5500 Fax: (708)679-2494
Fr: 800-323-4900

Third edition, 1991. Contains two- to five-page descriptions of 200 managerial, professional, technical, trade, and service occupations. Each profile includes job duties, places of employment, qualifications, educational preparation, training, employment potential, advancement, income, and additional sources of information.

★2405★ *Chefs and Cooks*
Careers, Inc.
PO Box 135
Largo, FL 34649-0135
Ph: (813)584-7333

1994. Four-page brief offering the definition, history, duties, working conditions, personal qualifications, educational requirements, earnings, hours, employment outlook, advancement possibilities, and related occupations.

★2406★ *Chefs and Cooks*
Chronicle Guidance Publications, Inc.
66 Aurora St.
PO Box 1190
Moravia, NY 13118-1190
Ph: (315)497-0330 Fax: (315)497-3359
Fr: 800-622-7284

1993. This career brief describes the nature of the work, working conditions, hours and earnings, education and training, licensure, certification, unions, personal qualifications, social and psychological factors, employment outlook, entry methods, advancement, and related occupations.

★2407★ "Chefs and Cooks" in *Jobs! What They Are—Where They Are—What They Pay* (pp. 198)
Simon & Schuster, Inc.
Simon & Schuster Bldg.
1230 Avenue of the Americas
New York, NY 10020
Ph: (212)698-7000

Robert O. Snelling and Anne M. Snelling. Revised edition, 1992. Profiles 241 occupations, describing duties and responsibilities, educational preparation, earnings, employment opportunities, training, and qualifications.

★2408★ "Chefs and Cooks" in *Occu-Facts: Information on 580 Careers in Outline Form*
Careers, Inc.
PO Box 135
Largo, FL 34649-0135
Ph: (813)584-7333

Biennial, 1995-96 edition. Each one-page occupational profile describes duties, working conditions, physical surroundings and demands, aptitudes, temperament, educational requirements, employment outlook, earnings, and places of employment.

★2409★ "Chefs and Cooks" in *Opportunities in Vocational and Technical Careers* (p. 73)
National Textbook Co. (NTC)
VGM Career Books
4255 W. Touhy Ave.
Lincolnwood, IL 60646-1975
Ph: (708)679-5500 Fax: (708)679-2494
Fr: 800-323-4900

Adrian A. Paradis. 1992. Describes careers which can be prepared for by attending a private vocational or proprietary school—office employee, sales worker, service worker, health services, mechanic, craftworker, and technician. Covers employment outlook, job duties, and salaries. Offers career planning advice.

★2410★ "Chefs, Cooks, and Other Kitchen Workers" in *America's 50 Fastest Growing Jobs* (pp. 113)
JIST Works, Inc.
720 N. Park Ave.
Indianapolis, IN 46202-3431
Ph: (317)264-3720 Fax: (317)264-3709
Fr: 800-648-5478

Michael J. Farr, compiler. 1994. Describes the 50 fastest growing jobs within major career clusters such as technicians, and marketing and sales. Each job profile explains the nature of the work, skills and abilities required, employment outlook, average earnings, related occupations, education and training requirements, and employment opportunities. Also contains career planning information and job search tips.

★2411★ "Chefs, Cooks, and Other Kitchen Workers" in *Occupational Outlook Handbook*
U.S. Government Printing Office
Superintendent of Documents
Washington, DC 20402
Ph: (202)512-1800 Fax: (202)512-2250

Biennial; latest edition, 1994-95. Encyclopedia of careers describing more than 250 occupations and comprising about 85 percent of all jobs in the economy. Occupations that require lengthy education or training are given the most attention. For each occupation, the handbook describes job duties, working conditions, training, educational preparation, personal qualities, advancement possibilities, job outlook, earnings, and sources of additional information.

★2412★ "Chefs, Cooks, and Other Kitchen Workers" in *Opportunities in Restaurant Careers* (pp. 22-31)
National Textbook Co. (NTC)
VGM Career Books
4255 W. Touhy Ave.
Lincolnwood, IL 60646-1975
Ph: (708)679-5500 Fax: (708)679-2494
Fr: 800-323-4900

Carol Ann Caprione Chmelynski. 1990. Provides an overview of the restaurant industry and surveys entry-level, mid-level, and management jobs. Covers working conditions, educational preparation, training, advancement possibilities, employment outlook, and earnings. Lists schools offering programs in hotel, restaurant, and institutional management.

★2413★ *The Choice of the Future*
National Restaurant Association
The Educational Foundation
250 S. Wacker Dr., Ste. 1400
Chicago, IL 60606
Ph: (312)715-1010

This 27-page booklet provides an overview of the food service industry and describes jobs, the work, education, training, and advancement possibilities. Contains salary surveys.

★2414★ "Cook" in *BLR Encyclopedia of Prewritten Job Descriptions*
Business and Legal Reports, Inc.
39 Academy St.
Madison, CT 06443-1513
Ph: (203)245-7448

Stephen D. Bruce, editor-in-chief. 1994. This book contains hundreds of sample job descriptions arranged by functional job category. The 1-3 page job descriptions cover what the worker normally does in the position, who they report to, and how that position fits in the organizational structure.

★2415★ "Cook and Chef" in *Career Information Center* (Vol.8)
Simon and Schuster
200 Old Tappan Rd.
Old Tappan, NJ 07675
Fax: 800-445-6991 Fr: 800-223-2348

Richard Lidz and Dale Anderson, editorial directors. Fifth edition, 1993. For 600 occupations, describes job duties, entry-level requirements, education and training needed, advancement possibilities, employment outlook, earnings and benefits. The set is divided into 12 volumes. Each volume includes jobs related under a broad career field. Volume 13 is the index.

★2416★ "Cook and Chef: The Cornerstones of a Good Restaurant" in *Careers in the Restaurant Industry* (pp. 35-45)
Rosen Publishing Group
29 E. 21st St.
New York, NY 10010
Ph: (212)777-3017 Fax: (212)777-0277
Fr: 800-237-9932

Richard S. Lee and Mary Price Lee. Revised edition, 1990. Explores various jobs in the restaurant industry including cooks and chefs, manager, maitre d', bartender, and waiter/waitress. Describes job duties, salaries, educational preparation and job hunting. Contains information about fast food, catering, and small businesses.

★2417★ *Cook, Short Order*
Careers, Inc.
PO Box 135
Largo, FL 34649-0135
Ph: (813)584-7333

1995. Two-page job guide card describing duties, working conditions, personal qualifications, training, earnings and hours, employment outlook, places of employment, related careers and where to write for more information.

★2418★ "Cooks and Chefs" in *American Almanac of Jobs and Salaries* (pp. 528)
Avon Books
1350 Avenue of the Americas
New York, NY 10019
Ph: (212)261-6800 Fr: 800-238-0658

John Wright, editor. Revised and updated, 1994-95. A comprehensive guide to the wages of hundreds of occupations in a wide variety of industries and organizations.

★2419★ "Cooks, Chefs, and Bakers" in *Encyclopedia of Careers and Vocational Guidance* (Vol.2, pp. 384-388)
J.G. Ferguson Publishing Co.
200 W. Madison St., Ste. 300
Chicago, IL 60606
Ph: (312)580-5480 Fax: (312)580-4948

William E. Hopke, editor-in-chief. Ninth edition, 1993. Four-volume set that profiles 500 occupations and describes job trends in 74 industries. Includes career description, educational requirements, history of the job, methods of entry, advancement, employment outlook, earnings, working conditions, social and psychological factors, and sources of additional information.

★2420★ "Cooks and Chefs" in *Career Discovery Encyclopedia* (pp. 58-59)
J.G. Ferguson Publishing Co.
200 W. Madison St., Ste. 300
Chicago, IL 60606
Ph: (312)580-5480 Fax: (312)580-4948

E. Russell Primm, editor-in-chief. 1993. Contains two-page articles on 504 occupations. Each article describes job duties, earnings, and educational and training requirements.

★2421★ *Cosmetologist*
Careers, Inc.
PO Box 135
Largo, FL 34649-0135
Ph: (813)584-7333

1994. Two-page occupational summary card describing duties, working conditions, personal qualifications, training, earnings and hours, employment outlook, places of employment, related careers and where to write for more information.

★2422★ "Culinary Arts" in *College Majors and Careers: A Resource Guide for Effective Life Planning* (pp. 45-46)
Garrett Park Press
PO Box 1907
Garrett Park, MD 20896
Ph: (301)946-2553

Paul Phifer. 1993. Lists 61 college majors. Includes a general definition of the field, related occupations requiring either a bachelor or associate degree, related leisure-time activities denoting personal interest in the field, skills needed, values, and personal attributes. Lists organizations.

★2423★ *Executive Chef*
Vocational Biographies, Inc.
PO Box 31
Sauk Centre, MN 56378-0031
Ph: (612)352-6516 Fax: (612)352-5546
Fr: 800-255-0752

1994. Four-page pamphlet containing a personal narrative about a worker's job, work likes and dislikes, career path from high school to the present. Education and training, the rewards and frustrations, and the effects of the job on the rest of the worker's life. The data file portion of this pamphlet gives a concise occupational summary, including work descriptions, working conditions, places of employment, personal characteristics, education and training, job outlook, and salary range.

★2424★ *Fast Food Workers*
Chronicle Guidance Publications, Inc.
66 Aurora St.
PO Box 1190
Moravia, NY 13118-1190
Ph: (315)497-0330 Fax: (315)497-3359
Fr: 800-622-7284

1993. This career brief describes the nature of the work, working conditions, hours and earnings, education and training, licensure, certification, unions, personal qualifications, social and psychological factors, employment outlook, entry methods, advancement, and related occupations.

★2425★ *Food Careers*
Prentice Hall
Rte. 9W
Englewood Cliffs, NJ 07632
Ph: (201)592-2000

Donna N. Creasy. 1977. Part of Home Economics Careers Series.

★2426★ "Food Service" in *Career Connection II: A Guide to Technical Majors and Their Related Careers* (pp. 82-83)
Jist Works, Inc.
720 N. Park Ave.
Indianapolis, IN 46202-3431
Ph: (317)264-3720 Fax: (317)264-3709

Fred A. Rowe. 1994. Contains technical majors, such as automotive technology. Describes the major and the job. Lists high school and postsecondary school courses. Includes occupations related to the major, employment outlook, and starting salary.

★2427★ "Food Service Workers" in *Encyclopedia of Careers and Vocational Guidance* (Vol.3, pp. 16-20)
J.G. Ferguson Publishing Co.
200 W. Madison St., Ste. 300
Chicago, IL 60606
Ph: (312)580-5480 Fax: (312)580-4948

William E. Hopke, editor-in-chief. Ninth edition, 1993. Four-volume set that profiles 900 occupations and describes job trends in 74 industries. Includes career description, educational requirements, history of the job, methods of entry, advancement, employment outlook, earnings, conditions of work, social and psychological factors, and sources of further information.

★2428★ *Food Services*
Learning Corporation of America
108 Wilmot Rd.
Deerfield, IL 60015
Ph: (708)940-1260 Fax: (708)940-3600
Fr: 800-621-2131

Videocassette. 1982. 21 mins. Four workers in the food industry offer a look at their jobs: chef, restaurant manager, baker and meat wrapper. From the "Working" series.

★2429★ "Hotel Cook or Chef and Baker" in *Hospitality & Recreation* (pp. 27-31)
Franklin Watts, Inc.
387 Park Avenue, S.
New York, NY 10016
Ph: (212)686-7070

Marjorie Rittenberg Schulz. 1990. Provides an overview of jobs in the hotel, motel, food service, fitness, and recreation industries. Covers job duties, educational preparation, salary, and employment outlook. Offers job hunting advice.

★2430★ *Introduction to Management in the Hospitality Industry*
John Wiley and Sons, Inc.
605 3rd Ave.
New York, NY 10158-0012
Ph: (212)850-6000 Fax: (212)850-6088
Fr: 800-526-5368

Tom Powers. 1992.

★2431★ *Kitchen Helper*
Careers, Inc.
PO Box 135
Largo, FL 34649-0135
Ph: (813)584-7333

1994. Two-page job guide card describing duties, working conditions, personal qualifications, training, earnings and hours, employment outlook, places of employment, related careers and where to write for more information.

★2432★ "Kitchen Helper" in *Occu-Facts: Information on 580 Careers in Outline Form*
Careers, Inc.
PO Box 135
Largo, FL 34649-0135
Ph: (813)584-7333

Biennial, 1995-96 edition. Each one-page occupational profile describes duties, working conditions, physical surroundings and demands, aptitudes, temperament, educational requirements, employment outlook, earnings, and places of employment.

★2433★ *Opportunities in Culinary Careers*
National Textbook Co. (NTC)
VGM Career Books
4255 W. Touhy Ave.
Lincolnwood, IL 60646-1975
Ph: (708)679-5500 Fax: (708)679-2494
Fr: 800-323-4900

Mary Donovan. 1990. Describes the educational preparation and training of chefs and cooks and explores a variety of food service jobs in restaurants, institutions, and research and development. Lists culinary schools and professional organizations.

★2434★ *Opportunities in Fast Food Careers*
National Textbook Co. (NTC)
VGM Career Books
4255 W. Toughy Ave.
Lincolnwood, IL 60646-1975
Ph: (708)679-5500 Fax: (708)679-2494
Fr: 800-323-4900

Marjorie Eberts and Margaret Gisler. 1994.

★2435★ *Opportunities in Restaurant Careers*
National Textbook Co. (NTC)
VGM Career Books
4255 W. Touhy Ave.
Lincolnwood, IL 60646-1975
Ph: (708)679-5500 Fax: (708)679-2494
Fr: 800-323-4900

Carol Caprione Chemelynski. Provides an overview of the restaurant industry and surveys entry-level, mid-level, and management jobs. Covers working conditions, educational preparation, training, advancement possibilities, employment outlook, and earnings. Lists schools offering programs in hotel, restaurant, and institutional management.

★2436★ "Pastry Chef and Baker" in *Career Information Center* (Vol.8)
Simon and Schuster
200 Old Tappan Rd.
Old Tappan, NJ 07675
Fax: 800-445-6991 Fr: 800-223-2348

Richard Lidz and Dale Anderson, editorial directors. Fifth edition, 1993. For 600 occupations, describes job duties, entry-level requirements, education and training needed, advancement possibilities, employment outlook, earnings and benefits. The set is divided into 12 volumes. Each volume includes jobs related under a broad career field. Volume 13 is the index.

★2437★ *Personal Service Cluster*
Center for Humanities, Inc.
Communications Park
Box 1000
Mount Kisco, NY 10549
Ph: (914)666-4100 Fax: (914)666-5319
Fr: 800-431-1242

Videocassette. 1984. 20 mins. Students get to see the day-by-day lives of people who work in the fields of cosmetology, food service and law enforcement.

★2438★ "Professional Cooking" in *The Desk Guide to Training and Work Advisement* (pp. 77-79)
Charles C. Thomas, Publisher
2600 S. 1st St.
Springfield, IL 62794-9265
Ph: (217)789-8980 Fax: (217)789-9130
Fr: 800-258-8980

Gail Baugher Kuenstler. 1988. Describes alternative methods of gaining entry into an occupation through different types of educational programs, internships and apprenticeships.

★2439★ "Restaurant Chef" in *Top Professions: The 100 Most Popular, Dynamic, and Profitable Careers in America Today* (pp. 195-197)
Petersons Guides, Inc.
PO Box 2123
Princeton, NJ 08543-2123
Ph: (609)243-9111 Fax: (609)243-9150
Fr: 800-338-3282

Nicholas Basta. 1989. Includes occupations requiring a college or advanced degree. Describes job duties, earnings, some typical job titles, career opportunities at different degree levels, and lists related associations.

★2440★ "Short Order Cook" in *Career Information Center* (pp. 62-64)
Simon and Schuster
200 Old Tappan Rd.
Old Tappan, NJ 07675
Fax: 800-445-6991 Fr: 800-223-2348

Richard Lidz and Dale Anderson, editorial directors. Fifth edition, 1993. For 600 occupations, describes job duties, entry-level requirements, education and training needed, advancement possibilities, employment outlook, earnings and benefits. The set is divided into 12 volumes. Each volume includes jobs related under a broad career field. Volume 13 is the index.

★2441★ "Short Order Cook" in *Occu-Facts: Information on 580 Careers in Outline Form*
Careers, Inc.
PO Box 135
Largo, FL 34649-0135
Ph: (813)584-7333

Biennial, 1995-96 edition. Each one-page occupational profile describes duties, working conditions, physical surroundings and demands, aptitudes, temperament, educational requirements, employment outlook, earnings, and places of employment.

★2442★ "Travel and Hospitality Careers" in *The Best Jobs for the 1990s and Into the 21st Century*
Impact Publications
9104-N Manassas Dr.
Manassas Park, VA 22111
Ph: (703)361-7300 Fax: (703)335-9486

Ronald L. Krannich and Caryl Rae Krannich. 1993. Includes information on chefs, cooks, flight attendants, food and beverage service workers, hotel and motel desk clerks, reservation and transportation ticket agents and travel clerks, and travel agents.

★2443★ *Video Career Library - Public and Personal Services*
Careers, Inc.
PO Box 135
Largo, FL 34649-0135
Ph: (813)584-7333

Videocassette. 1990. 35 mins. Part of the Video Career Library covering 165 occupations. Shows actual workers on the job. Includes firefighters, police officers, correctional officers, bartenders, waiters/waitresses, cooks/chefs, child care workers, flight attendants, barbers/cosmetologists, groundskeepers/gardeners, and butchers/meat cutters.

★2444★ *Waiting Tables*
Filmakers Library, Inc.
124 E. 40th St.
New York, NY 10016
Ph: (212)808-4980 Fax: (212)808-4983

Videocassette. 1986. 20 mins. An enlightening look at the food service industry where the majority of employees are underpaid, non-unionized women.

ASSOCIATIONS

★2445★ American Culinary Federation (ACF)
10 San Bartola Rd.
PO Box 3466
St. Augustine, FL 32085-3466
Ph: (904)824-4468 Fax: (904)825-4758

Members: State and local chapters of professional chefs. **Purpose:** Works to advance the culinary profession by sponsoring a continuing education program to keep members informed on food preparation and new equipment, apprenticeship training, and demonstrations for charitable and professional groups. Has sent a United States team of chefs to the International Culinary Olympic Competition in Frankfurt, Germany since 1960. Sponsors American Academy of Chefs, an honor society that supports the federation's educational program for the benefit of the food service industry. Local chapter activities include gourmet dinners "to perpetuate the fine art of dining among the public," and dinners for underprivileged children and hospital patients. Maintains the Educational Institute of the ACF which operates the National Apprenticeship Program for Cooks. **Publications:** *Art and Science of Food Preparation.* • *Culinary Olympic Cookbook.* • *National Culinary Review*, monthly.

★2446★ Career College Association (CCA)
750 1st St. NE, Ste. 900
Washington, DC 20002
Ph: (202)336-6700 Fax: (202)336-6828

Members: Private postsecondary schools providing career education. **Purpose:** Seeks to inform members of the accreditation process and regulations affecting vocational education. Conducts workshops and institutes for staffs of member schools; provides legislative, administrative, and public relations assistance. Has established Career Training Foundation to support research into private vocational education. Sponsors research programs. Maintains hall of fame; compiles statistics. **Publications:** *Career College Times*, monthly. • *Career Education.* • *Career News Digest.* • *Classroom Companion*, quarterly. • *Directory of Private Accredited Career Colleges and Schools*, annual.

★2447★ Council on Hotel, Restaurant, and Institutional Education (CHRIE)
1200 17th St. NW
Washington, DC 20036-3097
Ph: (202)331-5990 Fax: (202)785-2511

Members: Schools and colleges offering specialized education and training in cooking, baking, tourism and hotel, restaurant, and institutional administration; individuals, executives, and students. **Purpose:** Sponsors competitions. **Publications:** *CHRIE Communique*, biweekly. • *Guide to Hospitality Education*, semiannual. • *Hospitality and Tourism Educator*, quarterly. • *Hospitality Education and Research Journal.* • *Hosteur Magazine*, annual. • *Membership Directory and Research Guide*, annual.

★2448★ National Association of Trade and Technical Schools
2251 Wisconsin Ave. NW
Washington, DC 20007
Ph: (202)333-1021

Members: Private schools providing career education. **Purpose:** Seeks to inform members of the accreditation process and regulations affecting vocational education. Conducts workshops and institutes for staffs of member schools; provides legislative, administrative, and public relations assistance; services as federally recognized accrediting agency. Maintains hall of fame; compiles statistics. **Publications:** *Career News Digest*, 3-4/year. • *Handbook of Trade and Technical Careers and Training.*

★2449★ National Restaurant Association (NRA)
1200 17th St. NW
Washington, DC 20036
Ph: (202)331-5900 Fax: (202)331-2429

Members: Restaurants, cafeterias, clubs, contract foodservice management, drive-ins, caterers, institutional food services, and other members of the foodservice industry; also represents establishments belonging to nonaffiliated state and local restaurant associations in governmental affairs. **Purpose:** Supports foodservice education and research in several educational institutions; conducts traveling management courses and seminars for restaurant personnel. Affiliated with the Educational Foundation of the National Restaurant Association. Provides training and education for operators, food and equipment manufacturers, distributors, and educators. Offers waiter/waitress training programs. Conducts the Great Menu Contest. **Publications:** *Foodservice Information Abstracts*, biweekly. • *National Restaurant Association—Washington Weekly.* • *Restaurant Industry Operations Report*, annual. • *Restaurants USA*, monthly. • *Technical Bulletin*, periodic.

Standards/Certification Agencies

★2450★ National Association of Trade and Technical Schools (NATTS)
2251 Wisconsin Ave. NW
Washington, DC 20007
Ph: (202)333-1021

Informs members of the accreditation process and regulations affecting vocational education. Conducts workshops and institutes for staffs of member schools; provides legislative, administrative, and public relations assistance; serves as a federally recognized accrediting agency.

Test Guides

★2451★ *Career Examination Series: Assistant Cook*
National Learning Corp.
212 Michael Dr.
Syosset, NY 11791
Ph: (516)921-8888 Fax: (516)921-8743
Fr: 800-645-6337

Jack Rudman. All examination guides in this series contain questions with answers.

★2452★ *Career Examination Series: Baker*
National Learning Corp.
212 Michael Dr.
Syosset, NY 11791
Ph: (516)921-8888 Fax: (516)921-8743
Fr: 800-645-6337

Jack Rudman. Test guide including questions and answers for students or professionals in the field who seek advancement through examination.

★2453★ *Career Examination Series: Cook*
National Learning Corp.
212 Michael Dr.
Syosset, NY 11791
Ph: (516)921-8888 Fax: (516)921-8743
Fr: 800-645-6337

Jack Rudman. All examination guides in this series contain questions with answers.

★2454★ *Career Examination Series: Kitchen Supervisor*
National Learning Corp.
212 Michael Dr.
Syosset, NY 11791
Ph: (516)921-8888 Fax: (516)921-8743
Fr: 800-645-6337

Jack Rudman. All examination guides in this series contain questions with answers.

Educational Directories and Programs

★2455★ *Career Guidance Handouts*
National Association of Trade and Technical Schools
NATTS
2251 Wisconsin Ave. NW
Washington, DC 20007
Ph: (202)333-1021

★2456★ *Career Training*
National Association of Trade and Technical Schools (NATTS)
2251 Wisconsin Ave. NW
Washington, DC 20007
Ph: (202)333-1021

Quarterly.

★2457★ *Classroom Companion*
National Association of Trade and Technical Schools (NATTS)
2251 Wisconsin Ave. NW
Washington, DC 20007
Ph: (202)333-1021

Quarterly.

★2458★ *College/University Foodservice Who's Who*
Information Central, Inc.
Box 3900
Prescott, AZ 86302
Ph: (602)778-1513 Fax: (602)445-6407
Julie Woodman, Contact

Triennial, latest edition January 1993; new edition expected 1996. Covers over 2,200 food service programs in colleges and universities. Entries include: Institution name, address, phone, enrollment, total annual food purchases, number of meals served per day; name of management company, principal food service official, services, fast food chains on campus. Arrangement: Geographical.

★2459★ *Directory of French-Fry Potatoes*
Food Information Service Center
21050 SW 93rd Ln. Rd.
Dunnellon, FL 34431
Ph: (904)489-8919 Fax: (904)489-8919
Fr: 800-443-5820
James A. Mixon, Contact

Biennial, even years. Covers French-fry potato suppliers and related service companies. Entries include: Co. name, address, phone, name and title of contact, subsidiary and branch names and locations, products produced. Arrangement: Classified by product or service.

★2460★ *Directory of Private Accredited Career Colleges and Schools*
Career College Association (CCA)
750 1st St. NE, Ste. 900
Washington, DC 20002
Ph: (202)336-6700 Fax: (202)336-6828

Annual.

★2461★ *The Guide to Cooking Schools*
ShawGuides, Inc.
10 W. 66th St. 30H
New York, NY 10023
Ph: (212)799-6464 Fax: (212)724-9287
D. KaplanPresident

Annual, November. Covers Approximately 345 cooking schools including culinary arts colleges, cooking travel programs, institutions offering specialized instruction, and culinary organizations; over 100 cooking programs at vocational/technical schools and junior colleges; international coverage. Entries include: For schools—Name, address, phone, fax, description of program, requirements for admission, faculty credentials, tuition cost. For organizations—Name, address, phone, fax, requirements for admission, services, annual dues. Arrangement: Geographical.

Awards, Scholarships, Grants, and Fellowships

★2462★ Culinary Arts Salon
National Restaurant Association
1200 17th St. NW
Washington, DC 20036
Ph: (202)331-5900 Fr: 800-424-5156

One of the largest culinary competitions of its kind in America, it recognizes chefs, apprentices, students, and culinarians for outstanding food preparation. The event is held at the Association's annual show. Awards are given in Professional and Student categories. Gold, silver, and bronze medals are awarded. Other awards presented are: Best of Show, Best Entry for Junior Culinarian, Most Original Piece of Show, and Grand Prize for Pastry. Established in 1971. Winners often participate in the Culinary Olympics in Frankfort, Germany, with the winners of the other regional competitions: Culinary World Cup (Luxembourg); Salon Culinaire Mondial (Basel, Switzerland); Food & Hotel Asia Competition (Singapore); Hotelympia (London); Culinary Masters (Canada); and Chef Ireland (Ireland). The Culinary Arts Salon is produced by the National Restaurant Association in cooperation with the American Culinary Federation and the ACF, Chicago Chefs of Cuisine.

★2463★ National Restaurant Association Ice Carving Classic
National Restaurant Association
1200 17th St. NW
Washington, DC 20036
Ph: (202)331-5900 Fr: 800-424-5156

To recognize three-person teams for transforming huge blocks of ice into magnificent works of art. The competition pits master ice carvers from around the world against one another in three events: compulsory figures, to be completed in one hour; free-style individual blocks, two hours; and team multiple blocks, three hours. Winners are honored at the Association's annual show. Established in 1988 in cooperation with the National Ice Carving Association. Additional information is available from the National Restaurant Association.

★2464★ National Restaurant Association Undergraduate Scholarships
National Restaurant Association Educational Foundation
250 S. Wacker Dr., Ste. 1400
Chicago, IL 60606-5834
Ph: (312)715-1010 Fax: (312)715-0807
Fr: 800-765-2122

Qualifications: Candidates must be full-time students working toward a foodservice/hospitality degree for the full academic year beginning with the fall term. They must have demonstrated interest in foodservice/hospitality through work experience in the industry and have a cumulative grade point average of at least 3.0 on a 4.0 scale. Eligible majors include: hotel, restaurant, and institutional management, culinary arts, dietetics, food science and technology, and other foodservice related curricula, including manufacturing and distribution. Funds available: More than 100 undergaduate scholarships are awarded, ranging in value from $500 to $10,000. Application details: Candidates must submit a formal applications and transcripts. Applications are available after December 1. Deadline: March 1.

Basic Reference Guides and Handbooks

★2465★ *Baking Buyer—Yearbook Issue*
Sosland Publishing Co.
4800 Main, Ste. 100
Kansas City, MO 64112
Ph: (816)756-1000 Fax: (816)756-0494
Carol D. Kaskie, Contact

Annual, June. Publication includes: List of approximately 1,700 distributors and 1,000 manufacturers of products and equipment for the baking industry. Entries include: For distributors—Co. name, address, phone, fax, name of contact, types of products distributed, geographical area served. For manufacturers—Co. name, address, phone, fax. Arrangement: Distributors are geographical.

★2466★ *Culinary Olympic Cookbook*
American Culinary Federation (ACF)
10 San Bartola Rd.
PO Box 3466
St. Augustine, FL 32085-3466
Ph: (904)824-4468 Fax: (904)825-4758

★2467★ *Food Distribution Magazine—Food Brokers Directory Issue*
National Food Distribution Network
PO Box 87
Barrington, RI 02806-0087
Ph: 800-541-6336 Fax: (401)245-4699
Dara Chadwick

Annual, December. Publication includes: List of brokers in the food business. Entries include: Co. name, address, phone, name and title of contact.

★2468★ *Guide to Hospitality Education*
Council on Hotel, Restaurant, and Institutional Education (CHRIE)
1200 17th St. NW
Washington, DC 20036-3097
Ph: (202)331-5990 Fax: (202)785-2511

Semiannual.

★2469★ *Handbook of Trade and Technical Careers and Training*
National Association of Trade and Technical Schools (NATTS)
2251 Wisconsin Ave. NW
Washington, DC 20007
Ph: (202)333-1021

★2470★ *Whole Foods—Source Book Issue*
Whole Foods Communications, Inc.
3000 Hadley Rd.
South Plainfield, NJ 07080
Ph: (908)769-1160 Fax: (908)769-1171
Daniel McSweeney, Associate Publisher

Annual, May. Publication includes: Lists of 1,400 manufacturers, 175 wholesalers and distributors, and 95 brokers of natural food products; also 90 publishers of information about natural foods and 52 natural food associations. Entries include: For manufacturers—Company name, address, phone, contact person, line of business. For wholesalers and distributors—Company name, address, phone, tollfree phone, contact, description of products and services, territory covered, shipping company, approximate shipping time, size of sales staff. For brokers—Company name, address, phone, contact, geographic territory covered, firms represented, products. For others—Organization name, address, phone, contact, product or Arrangement: Classified by type of business.

Periodicals

★2471★ *Almost Free Cookbooks and Recipes Update*
Update Publicare Company
c/o Prosperity & Profits Unlimited
PO Box 570213
Houston, TX 77257
A.C. Doyle

Annual. Carries information on recipe ingredient substitutions. Recurring features include news of research and lists of "almost free" cookbooks and recipes.

★2472★ *Art and Science of Food Preparation*
American Culinary Federation (ACF)
10 San Bartola Rd.
PO Box 3466
St. Augustine, FL 32085-3466
Ph: (904)824-4468 Fax: (904)825-4758

★2473★ *Bakery Production and Marketing*
Pat Reynolds

Monthly. Bakery industry magazine.

★2474★ *Baking & Snack*
Sosland Publishing Co.
4800 Main St., Ste. 100
Kansas City, MO 64112
Ph: (816)756-1000 Fax: (816)756-0494
Laurie Gorton

Monthly. Equipment, engineering, production and formulating magazine for commercial manufacturers of baked and snack foods.

★2475★ *BC&T News*
Bakery, Confectionery, and Tobacco Workers International Union
10401 Connecticut Ave.
Kensington, MD 20895-3961
Ph: (301)933-8600

★2476★ *Capitol News*
Snack Food Association (SFA)
1711 King St., Ste. 1
Alexandria, VA 22314
Ph: (703)836-4500 Fax: (703)836-8262
Jim McCarthy

Seeks to disseminate information to those involved in the manufacturing of snack foods. Provides chief executive and government relations officers of snack food companies with reports on legislative and regulatory changes of import to the industry.

★2477★ *Career College Times*
Career College Association (CCA)
750 1st St. NE, Ste. 900
Washington, DC 20002
Ph: (202)336-6700 Fax: (202)336-6828
Monthly.

★2478★ *Career Education*
Career College Association (CCA)
750 1st St. NE, Ste. 900
Washington, DC 20002
Ph: (202)336-6700 Fax: (202)336-6828

★2479★ *Career News Digest*
Career College Association (CCA)
750 1st St. NE, Ste. 900
Washington, DC 20002
Ph: (202)336-6700 Fax: (202)336-6828

★2480★ *Catering Industry Employee*
Hotel Employees and Restaurant Employees International Union
1219 28th St. NW
Washington, DC 20007
Ph: (202)393-4373 Fax: (202)333-0468
Herman Leavitt
Bimonthly. Trade journal for culinary and hospitality workers. Official publication of the Hotel Employees and Restaurant Employees International Union.

★2481★ *Chef*
Talcott Communications Corp.
20 N. Wacker Dr., Ste. 3230
Chicago, IL 60606
Ph: (312)849-2220 Fax: (312)549-2184
Danie Von RabenauPublisher
Publication for the food service field.

★2482★ *Chile Pepper*
Out West Publishing
PO Box 80780
Albuquerque, NM 87198
Ph: (505)266-8322 Fax: (505)266-2127
Dave DeWitt
Bimonthly. Magazine on spicy cuisine from around the world.

★2483★ *CHRIE Communique*
Council on Hotel, Restaurant, and Institutional Education (CHRIE)
1200 17th St. NW
Washington, DC 20036-3097
Ph: (202)331-5990 Fax: (202)785-2511
Biweekly.

★2484★ *Classroom Companion*
Career College Association (CCA)
750 1st St. NE, Ste. 900
Washington, DC 20002
Ph: (202)336-6700 Fax: (202)336-6828
Quarterly.

★2485★ *Cookbook Digest*
Grass Roots
950 3rd Ave., 16th Fl.
New York, NY 10022
Ph: (212)888-1855 Fax: (212)838-8420
Robert J. KreftingPublisher
Bimonthly. Magazine featuring recipes from various cookbooks.

★2486★ *Cookies*
P. Wetherill
5426 27th St. NW
Washington, DC 20015
Ph: (202)966-0869
P. Wetherill
Focuses on cookies and cookie shaping. Carries historical items on cookie cutters and other shaping devices, and general cookie-related news items. Recurring features include recipes, sources of new cutters and molds, baking tips, news of research, letters to the editor, news of members, book reviews, and a calendar of events.

★2487★ *Cooking Contest Chronicle*
Karen Martis
PO Box 10792
Merrillville, IN 46411-0792
Ph: (219)887-6983
Karen Martis
Designed to inform readers of cooking contests. Includes entry requirements, closing dates, and news of rapidly changing contest developments. Recurring features include editorials, letters to the editor, news of contestant winners, and cookbook reviews. Also carries tips, news of food trends, and prize-winning recipes.

★2488★ *Country Chronicle*
Metropolitan Newspaper Corp.
PO Box 2467
Green Bay, WI 54306
Ph: (414)432-2941 Fax: (414)432-8581
Cindy Thompson
Weekly. Rural community newspaper.

★2489★ *Dairy-Deli Bake Digest*
International Dairy-Deli-Bakery Association
313 Price P1., Ste. 202
PO Box 5528
Madison, WI 53705-0528
Ph: (608)238-7908 Fax: (608)238-6330
Carol L. Christison
Supports the Association, which seeks to increase dairy-deli-bakery business. Focuses on issues of concern to manufacturers, retailers, brokers, distributors, businesses, and organizations involved with the dairy-deli-bakery industry. Recurring features include research news, reports of meetings, news of educational opportunities and industrial trends, and notices of publications available.

★2490★ *Deli-Bake Advocate*
Gro Com Group
912 Drew St., Ste. 104
Clearwater, FL 34615-4523
Mark A. SadePublisher
Bimonthly. Trade magazine for the deli and bakery industries (food service and retail).

★2491★ *Entree*
Entree Travel
1470 E. Valley Rd.
Santa Barbara, CA 93108
Ph: (805)969-5848 Fax: (805)966-7095
William Tomicki
Monthly. Features "an insider's look at hotels, restaurants, and travel around the world." Contains advice and tips on travel, bargains, and services. Recurring features include book reviews and notices of publications available.

★2492★ *Food Chemical News*
CRC Press, Inc.
1101 Pennsylvania Ave. SE
Washington, DC 20003
Ph: (202)994-0555 Fax: (202)546-3890
Louis Rothschild
Weekly. Provides in-depth, timely coverage of the laws affecting food regulation, including additives, colors, pesticides, and allied products. Recurring features include news of research.

★2493★ *Food Distribution Research Society—Newsletter*
Food Distribution Research Society, Inc.
c/o Richard Bacon
Department of Food and Resource Economics
University of Delaware
Newark, DE 19717-1303
Ph: (302)831-1320 Fax: (302)292-1787
Dale L. Anderson
Reports on the actions of government bodies and other developments affecting the food industry. Reprints articles of interest from other publications, with special attention to results of research, surveys, and studies. Recurring features include announcements of conferences, meetings, and educational programs; notices of resource materials available; news of research; statistics; and book reviews.

★2494★ *Food & Wine*
American Express Publishing Corp.
1120 Avenue of the Americas
New York, NY 10036
Ph: (212)382-5600 Fax: (212)768-1573
Fr: 800-333-6569
Ila Stanger
Monthly. Magazine devoted to food and wine.

★2495★ *Foodletter*
Foodletter
1 TwoPence Rd.
Ridgefield, CT 06877-1220
Doreen Higgins
Analyzes current trends in foods and beverages, forecasts trends, and gives corresponding ideas for new products and packaging. Recurring features include a column titled Consumer Corner.

★2496★ *Foodservice Information Abstracts*
National Restaurant Association (NRA)
1200 17th St. NW
Washington, DC 20036
Ph: (202)331-5900 Fax: (202)331-2429
Biweekly. Abstracts from foodservice trade magazines.

★2497★ *Foodservice Report*
International Foodservice Distributors Association (IFDA)
201 Park Washington Court
Falls Church, VA 22046
Ph: (703)532-9400 Fax: (703)538-4673
John D. Thompson
Monthly. Carries news of the food service industry, including activities of manufacturers, brokers, and distributors, as well as trends in food service operation. Recurring features include profiles of food service distribution companies in the U.S. and Canada, a

calendar of events, and reports of conventions and conferences.

★2498★ *Fresh Baked*
Retail Bakers of America
14239 Bark Center Dr.
Laurel, MD 20707
Ph: (301)725-2149 Fax: (301)725-2187
Margi Berkowitz

Monthly. Examines trends and issues in the bakery industry. Features items on bakery production, marketing, business management, and other topics of interest. Recurring features include news of research, meeting reports, a calendar of events, and columns titled How to, Ingredient Update, and Donut Directions.

★2499★ *Guide to Hospitality Education*
Council on Hotel, Restaurant, and Institutional Education (CHRIE)
1200 17th St. NW
Washington, DC 20036-3097
Ph: (202)331-5990 Fax: (202)785-2511

Semiannual.

★2500★ *Hospitality Education and Research Journal*
Council on Hotel, Restaurant, and Institutional Education (CHRIE)
1200 17th St. NW
Washington, DC 20036-3097
Ph: (202)331-5990 Fax: (202)785-2511

★2501★ *The Hospitality Manager*
Kassis Communications
120 Hayward
Ames, IA 50010
Ph: (515)296-2400 Fax: (515)296-2405
Terry Lowman

Monthly. Trade publication (tabloid) covering restaurant and institutional business in the Midwest. Mailed to restaurants, bars, and institutional food service companies.

★2502★ *Hospitality and Tourism Educator*
Council on Hotel, Restaurant, and Institutional Education (CHRIE)
1200 17th St. NW
Washington, DC 20036-3097
Ph: (202)331-5990 Fax: (202)785-2511

Quarterly.

★2503★ *Hosteur Magazine*
Council on Hotel, Restaurant, and Institutional Education (CHRIE)
1200 17th St. NW
Washington, DC 20036-3097
Ph: (202)331-5990 Fax: (202)785-2511

Annual.

★2504★ *The Independent*
Independent Bakers Association
PO Box 3731
Washington, DC 20007
Ph: (202)333-8190 Fax: (202)337-3809
Robert N. Pyle

Periodic. Carries Association news and brief articles on commodities, taxes, labor, and other matters affecting the baking industry. Recurring features include reports of conferences, meetings, and the annual convention; election slates; membership updates; and presidential reports.

★2505★ *Kitchen Times*
Howard Wilson & Company, Inc.
185 Marlborough St.
Boston, MA 02116
Ph: (617)266-2453 Fax: (617)437-9983
Howard Wilson

Monthly. Contains instructions on buying food and preparing specific dishes. Reviews restaurants, inns, cooks, cookbooks, and wines.

★2506★ *Membership Directory and Research Guide*
Council on Hotel, Restaurant, and Institutional Education (CHRIE)
1200 17th St. NW
Washington, DC 20036-3097
Ph: (202)331-5990 Fax: (202)785-2511

Annual.

★2507★ *Modern Baking*
Donohue-Meehan Publishing Co.
2700 River Rd., Ste. 418
Des Plaines, IL 60018
Ph: (708)299-4430 Fax: (708)296-1968
Ed Lee

Monthly. Magazine on news, products, and trends of the baking industry.

★2508★ *Modern Food Service News*
Grocers Publishing Co., Inc.
15 Emerald St.
Hackensack, NJ 07601
Ph: (201)488-1800
Rob Reis

Monthly. Magazine for restaurateurs, chefs, caterers, purchasing agents in the food service industry.

★2509★ *NACUFS News Wave*
National Association of College and University Food Services (NACUFS)
1405 S. Harrison Rd., Ste. 303-304
Manly Miles Bldg.
East Lansing, MI 48824
Ph: (517)332-2494 Fax: (517)332-8144
C. Dennis Pierce

Covers news of interest to food service industry personnel in academic institutions. Also reports on regional Association activities. Recurring features include columns titled President's Message, Special Features, and Committee Spotlight.

★2510★ *National Culinary Review*
American Culinary Federation (ACF)
10 San Bartola Rd.
PO Box 3466
St. Augustine, FL 32085-3466
Ph: (904)824-4468 Fax: (904)825-4758

Monthly.

★2511★ *National Restaurant Association—Washington Weekly*
National Restaurant Association (NRA)
1200 17th St. NW
Washington, DC 20036
Ph: (202)331-5900 Fax: (202)331-2429

Reports on legislation and regulatory issues affecting the food service industry.

★2512★ *Nation's Restaurant News*
Lebhar-Friedman, Inc.
425 Park Ave.
New York, NY 10022
Ph: (212)756-5000 Fax: (212)756-5125
Rick Van Warner

Weekly.

★2513★ *NNFA Today*
National Nutritional Foods Association (NNFA)
150 Paularino Ave., Ste. 285
Costa Mesa, CA 92626-3302
Ph: (714)966-6632 Fax: (714)641-7005
Burton Kallman

Monthly. Supplies professionals in the health foods industry with analysis of business, legislative, social, technological, scientific, and economic developments affecting the industry. Provides information and suggestions on marketing, merchandising, public relations, and business management. Recurring features include interviews, reports of meetings, book reviews, news of nutrition research, a calendar of events, and columns titled Business Shorts, Science & Technology, and Legal/Legislation.

★2514★ *Quick 'n Easy Country Cookin'*
Parkside Publishing
Box 66
Davis, SD 57021
Ph: (605)238-5704 Fax: (605)238-5399
Pam Schrag

Bimonthly. Cooking magazine emphasizing meats requiring short preparation times. Includes articles on efficient use of microwave oven, crock pot, and food processor; recipes, food information, craft ideas, poems, and human interest stories.

★2515★ *Recipe Ingredient Substitution Update*
Update Publicare Company
c/o Prosperity & Profits Unlimited
PO Box 416
Denver, CO 80201
Ph: (303)575-5676
A.C. Doyle

Annual. Aims to introduce housewives and caterers to new food ideas. Carries recipes and suggestions for ingredient substitutions and recipe variations.

★2516★ *Restaurants & Institutions*
Cahners Publishing Co.
1350 E. Touhy Ave.
PO Box 5080
Des Plaines, IL 60017-5080
Ph: (708)635-8800 Fax: (708)390-2618
Mike Bartlett

Semiweekly. Magazine focusing on foodservice and lodging management.

★2517★ *Restaurants, Resorts & Hotels*
Trade Publishing Co.
41 Shea Terr.
Stratford, CT 06497-2422
Ph: (203)378-1223 Fax: (203)378-7285
James Martone

Monthly. National business magazine serving the food service industry.

★2518★ ***Restaurants USA***
National Restaurant Association (NRA)
1200 17th St. NW
Washington, DC 20036
Ph: (202)331-5900 Fax: (202)331-2429

Monthly. Includes combined June/July issue. Keeps foodservice operators and managers abreast of trends and developments in the industry.

★2519★ ***Seafood Leader***
Waterfront Press Co.
1115 NW 46th St.
Seattle, WA 98107
Ph: (206)789-6506 Fax: (206)789-9193
Peter Redmayne

Bimonthly. Magazine on seafood buying, marketing, and technology. Articles range from seafood processing technology to merchandising to cuisine; featuring seafood from the ocean to the plate.

★2520★ ***Simple Cooking***
Jackdaw Press
PO Box 88
Steuben, ME 04680-0088
John Thorne

Quarterly. Discusses culinary subjects, focusing on traditional recipes "requiring the simple preparation of good ingredients." Contains essays on origins, makings, and relevance of recipes. Recurring features include editorials, recipes, and columns titled Table Talk, Kitchen Diary, and Good Things.

★2521★ ***Technical Bulletin***
National Restaurant Association (NRA)
1200 17th St. NW
Washington, DC 20036
Ph: (202)331-5900 Fax: (202)331-2429

Periodic.

★2522★ ***Total Food Service***
PO Box 2507
Greenwich, CT 06836
Ph: (203)661-9090 Fax: (203)661-9325
Gary Cohen

Monthly. Food service industry magazine.

Meetings and Conventions

★2523★ **American School Food Service Association Conference**
American School Food Service Association
1600 Duke St., 7th Fl.
Alexandria, VA 22314
Ph: (703)739-3900 Fax: (703)739-3915
Fr: 800-877-8822

Annual.

★2524★ **IFT Annual Meeting and Food Expo**
Institute of Food Technologists
221 N. LaSalle St.
Chicago, IL 60601
Ph: (312)782-8424 Fax: (312)782-8348

Annual. Always held during June. 1996 Jun 23-26; New Orleans, LA. • 1997 Jun 14-18; Orlando, FL.

★2525★ **International Baking Industry Exposition**
American Bakers Association
1350 I St. NW, Ste. 1290
Washington, DC 20005
Ph: (202)789-0300 Fax: (202)898-1164

Every four years. **Dates and Locations:** 1997

★2526★ **National Restaurant Association Restaurant, Hotel-Motel Show**
National Restaurant Association
150 N. Michigan Ave., Ste. 2000
Chicago, IL 60601
Ph: (312)853-2525 Fax: (312)853-2548

Annual. Always held during May at the McCormick Place Complex in Chicago, Illinois. **Dates and Locations:** 1996 May 20-18; Chicago, IL.

★2527★ **Retail Confectioners International Annual Convention and Exposition**
Retail Confectioners International
1807 Glenview Rd., Ste. 204
Glenview, IL 60025
Ph: (708)724-6120 Fax: (708)724-2719

Annual. Always held during June.

Other Sources of Information

★2528★ ***Commercial Food Equipment Service Association Directory***
Commercial Food Equipment Service Association (CFESA)
9247 N. Meridian, Ste. 216
Indianapolis, IN 46260
Ph: (317)844-4700
Carla M. Helm, Contact

Annual. Covers independent service companies that repair commercial food equipment.

★2529★ **"Cook" in *Career Selector 2001***
Barron's Educational Series, Inc.
250 Wireless Blvd.
Hauppauge, NY 11788
Ph: (516)434-3311 Fax: (516)434-3723
Fr: 800-645-3476

James C. Gonyea. 1993.

★2530★ ***Frozen Foods—Wholesale Directory***
American Business Directories, Inc.
5711 S. 86th Circle
Omaha, NE 68127
Ph: (402)593-4600 Fax: (402)331-1505

Annual. Number of listings: 1,462. Entries include: Name, address, phone, size of advertisement, name of owner or manager, number of employees, year first in "Yellow Pages." Compiled from telephone company "Yellow Pages," nationwide. Arrangement: Geographical.

★2531★ ***Restaurant Industry Operations Report***
National Restaurant Association (NRA)
1200 17th St. NW
Washington, DC 20036
Ph: (202)331-5900 Fax: (202)331-2429

Annual.

★2532★ ***Vocational Visions Career Series: Chef***
Cambridge Career Products
PO Box 2153, Dept. CC15
Charleston, WV 25328-2153
Fr: 800-468-4227

Video collection that includes interviews people with various occupations. Describes educational requirements, necessary skills, outlook for the future, and salary range.

Food and Beverage Service Occupations

Food and beverage service workers deal with customers in all manner of dining establishments from small, informal diners to large restaurants. **Waiters and waitresses** take customers' orders and serve food and beverages. How this is done varies depending on type of establishment. Coffee shops require fast, efficient service, whereas in finer restaurants the service is more formal and personal. **Bartenders** fill the drink orders given to them by waiters or waitresses. Bartenders must be able to mix drinks accurately and quickly, and may also operate the cash register and clean up. They may also be responsible for ordering and maintaining an inventory of liquor and other bar supplies. **Hosts and hostesses** welcome guests, take coats, and escort patrons to their tables. They also take reservations and arrange parties. **Dining room attendants and bartender helpers** keep the serving area stocked, and perform cleaning and maintenance tasks. **Counter attendants** take orders and serve food at counters. They do food pick-up, prepare short-order items, clean counters and accept payment. **Fast-food workers** take orders and accept payment from customers standing at counters of fast-food restaurants. They may also cook and package foods.

Salaries

Food and beverage workers derive their earnings from a combination of hourly wages and customer tips. Both vary greatly, depending on type of job and establishment. Median full-time hourly earnings (including tips) are listed below.

Waiters and waitresses	$220/week
Bartenders	$250/week
Dining room attendants and bartender helpers	$210/week
Counter attendants and fast-food workers	$220/week

Employment Outlook

Growth rate until the year 2005: Average.

Food and Beverage Service Occupations

Career Guides

★2533★ *Bartender*
Vocational Biographies, Inc.
PO Box 31
Sauk Centre, MN 56378-0031
Ph: (612)352-6516 Fax: (612)352-5546
Fr: 800-255-0752

1992. Four-page pamphlet containing a personal narrative about a worker's job, work likes and dislikes, career path from high school to the present. Education and training, the rewards and frustrations, and the effects of the job on the rest of the worker's life. The data file portion of this pamphlet gives a concise occupational summary, including work descriptions, working conditions, places of employment, personal characteristics, education and training, job outlook, and salary range.

★2534★ "Bartender" in *Career Information Center* (Vol.8)
Simon and Schuster
200 Old Tappan Rd.
Old Tappan, NJ 07675
Fax: 800-445-6991 Fr: 800-223-2348

Richard Lidz and Dale Anderson, editorial directors. Fifth edition, 1993. For 600 occupations, describes job duties, entry-level requirements, education and training needed, advancement possibilities, employment outlook, earnings and benefits. The set is divided into 12 volumes. Each volume includes jobs related under a broad career field. Volume 13 is the index.

★2535★ *Bartenders*
Chronicle Guidance Publications, Inc.
66 Aurora St.
PO Box 1190
Moravia, NY 13118-1190
Ph: (315)497-0330 Fax: (315)497-3359
Fr: 800-622-7284

1991. This career brief describes the nature of the work, working conditions, hours and earnings, education and training, licensure, certification, unions, personal qualifications, social and psychological factors, employment outlook, entry methods, advancement, and related occupations.

★2536★ "Bartenders" in *Career Discovery Encyclopedia* (Vol.1, pp. 102-103)
J.G. Ferguson Publishing Co.
200 W. Madison St., Ste. 300
Chicago, IL 60606
Ph: (312)580-5480 Fax: (312)580-4948

E. Russell Primm, editor-in-chief. 1993. Contains two-page articles on 504 occupations. Each article describes job duties, earnings, and educational and training requirements.

★2537★ "Bartenders" in *Encyclopedia of Careers and Vocational Guidance* (Vol.2, pp. 166-168)
J.G. Ferguson Publishing Co.
200 W. Madison St., Ste. 300
Chicago, IL 60606
Ph: (312)580-5480 Fax: (312)580-4948

William E. Hopke, editor-in-chief. Ninth edition, 1993. Four-volume set that profiles 500 occupations and describes job trends in 74 industries. Includes career description, educational requirements, history of the job, methods of entry, advancement, employment outlook, earnings, working conditions, social and psychological factors, and sources of additional information.

★2538★ "Bartenders" in *Opportunities in Restaurant Careers* (pp. 19-22)
National Textbook Co. (NTC)
VGM Career Books
4255 W. Touhy Ave.
Lincolnwood, IL 60646-1975
Ph: (708)679-5500 Fax: (708)679-2494
Fr: 800-323-4900

Carol Ann Caprione Chmelynski. 1990. Provides an overview of the restaurant industry and surveys entry-level, mid-level, and management jobs. Covers working conditions, educational preparation, training, advancement possibilities, employment outlook, and earnings. Lists schools offering programs in hotel, restaurant, and institutional management.

★2539★ "Bartenders" in *Opportunities in Vocational and Technical Careers* (pp. 72-73)
National Textbook Co. (NTC)
VGM Career Books
4255 W. Touhy Ave.
Lincolnwood, IL 60646-1975
Ph: (708)679-5500 Fax: (708)679-2494
Fr: 800-323-4900

Adrian A. Paradis. 1992. Describes careers which can be prepared for by attending a private vocational or proprietary school—office employee, sales worker, service worker, health services, mechanic, craftworker, and technician. Covers employment outlook, job duties, and salaries. Offers career planning advice.

★2540★ "Bartenders, Waiters, and Bus Persons" in *American Almanac of Jobs and Salaries* (pp. 527)
Avon Books
1350 Avenue of the Americas
New York, NY 10019
Ph: (212)261-6800 Fr: 800-238-0658

John Wright, editor. Revised and updated, 1994-95. A comprehensive guide to the wages of hundreds of occupations in a wide variety of industries and organizations.

★2541★ "Cafeteria Attendant" in *Career Information Center* (Vol.8)
Simon and Schuster
200 Old Tappan Rd.
Old Tappan, NJ 07675
Fax: 800-445-6991 Fr: 800-223-2348

Richard Lidz and Dale Anderson, editorial directors. Fifth edition, 1993. For 600 occupations, describes job duties, entry-level requirements, education and training needed, advancement possibilities, employment outlook, earnings and benefits. The set is divided into 12 volumes. Each volume includes jobs related under a broad career field. Volume 13 is the index.

★2542★ "Cafeteria Counter Worker" in *Occu-Facts: Information on 580 Careers in Outline Form*
Careers, Inc.
PO Box 135
Largo, FL 34649-0135
Ph: (813)584-7333

Biennial, 1995-96 edition. Each one-page occupational profile describes duties, working conditions, physical surroundings and demands, aptitudes, temperament, educational requirements, employment outlook, earnings, and places of employment.

★2543★ *Caterer*
Careers, Inc.
PO Box 135
Largo, FL 34649-0135
Ph: (813)584-7333

1993. Two-page occupational summary card describing duties, working conditions, personal qualifications, training, earnings and hours, employment outlook, places of employment, related careers, and where to write for more information.

★2544★ *Caterers*
Chronicle Guidance Publications, Inc.
66 Aurora St.
PO Box 1190
Moravia, NY 13118-1190
Ph: (315)497-0330 Fax: (315)497-3359
Fr: 800-622-7284

1992. Career brief describing the nature of the job, working conditions, hours and earnings, education and training, licensure, certification, unions, personal qualifications, social and psychological factors, location, employment outlook, entry methods, advancement, and related occupations.

★2545★ *The Choice of the Future*
National Restaurant Association
The Educational Foundation
250 S. Wacker Dr., Ste. 1400
Chicago, IL 60606
Ph: (312)715-1010

This 27-page booklet provides an overview of the food service industry and describes jobs, the work, education, training, and advancement possibilities. Contains salary surveys.

★2546★ *College & University Food Service Manual*
Colman Publishers
1147 Elmwood
Stockton, CA 95204
Ph: (209)464-9503

Paul Fairbrook. 1979.

★2547★ *Dining Room Attendant*
Careers, Inc.
PO Box 135
Largo, FL 34649-0135
Ph: (813)584-7333

1994. Two-page job guide card describing duties, working conditions, personal qualifications, training, earnings and hours, employment outlook, places of employment, related careers and where to write for more information.

★2548★ "Dining Room Attendant" in *Career Information Center* (Vol.8)
Simon and Schuster
200 Old Tappan Rd.
Old Tappan, NJ 07675
Fax: 800-445-6991 Fr: 800-223-2348

Richard Lidz and Dale Anderson, editorial directors. Fifth edition, 1993. For 600 occupations, describes job duties, entry-level requirements, education and training needed, advancement possibilities, employment outlook, earnings and benefits. The set is divided into 12 volumes. Each volume includes jobs related under a broad career field. Volume 13 is the index.

★2549★ "Dining Room Attendant" in *Occu-Facts: Information on 580 Careers in Outline Form*
Careers, Inc.
PO Box 135
Largo, FL 34649-0135
Ph: (813)584-7333

Biennial, 1995-96 edition. Each one-page occupational profile describes duties, working conditions, physical surroundings and demands, aptitudes, temperament, educational requirements, employment outlook, earnings, and places of employment.

★2550★ "Fast Food Franchise Worker" in *Career Information Center* (Vol.8)
Simon and Schuster
200 Old Tappan Rd.
Old Tappan, NJ 07675
Fax: 800-445-6991 Fr: 800-223-2348

Richard Lidz and Dale Anderson, editorial directors. Fifth edition, 1993. For 600 occupations, describes job duties, entry-level requirements, education and training needed, advancement possibilities, employment outlook, earnings and benefits. The set is divided into 12 volumes. Each volume includes jobs related under a broad career field. Volume 13 is the index.

★2551★ *Fast Food Jobs: National Study of Fast Foods Employment*
National Institute for Work and Learning
1255 23rd St., NW, Ste. 400
Washington, DC 20037
Ph: (202)862-8845

Ivan Charner and Bryna Shore Fraser. 1984.

★2552★ "Fast Food Workers" in *Encyclopedia of Careers and Vocational Guidance* (Vol.2, pp. 636-638)
J.G. Ferguson Publishing Co.
200 W. Madison St., Ste. 300
Chicago, IL 60606
Ph: (312)580-5480 Fax: (312)580-4948

William E. Hopke, editor-in-chief. Ninth edition, 1993. Four-volume set that profiles 500 occupations and describes job trends in 74 industries. Includes career description, educational requirements, history of the job, methods of entry, advancement, employment outlook, earnings, working conditions, social and psychological factors, and sources of additional information.

★2553★ "Food and Beverage Industry" in *Jobs '95* (pp. 339-350)
Prentice Hall Press
1 Gulf Western Plaza
New York, NY 10023
Ph: (212)373-8500

Kathryn Petras and Ross Petras. Annual, 1995. Discusses employment prospects and trends for 15 professional careers and 29 industries. Lists leading companies, associations, directories, and magazines.

★2554★ "Food and Beverage Manager" in *Career Information Center* (Vol.8)
Simon and Schuster
200 Old Tappan Rd.
Old Tappan, NJ 07675
Fax: 800-445-6991 Fr: 800-223-2348

Richard Lidz and Linda Perrin, editorial directors. Fifth edition, 1993. This 13-volume set profiles over 600 occupations. Each occupational profile describes job duties, entry-level requirements, educational requirements, advancement possibilities, employment outlook, working conditions, earnings and benefits, and where to write for more information.

★2555★ "Food and Beverage Service Occupations" in *Occupational Outlook Handbook*
U.S. Government Printing Office
Superintendent of Documents
Washington, DC 20402
Ph: (202)512-1800 Fax: (202)512-2250

Biennial; latest edition, 1994-95. Encyclopedia of careers describing more than 250 occupations and comprising about 85 percent of all jobs in the economy. Occupations that require lengthy education or training are given the most attention. For each occupation, the handbook describes job duties, working conditions, training, educational preparation, personal qualities, advancement possibilities, job outlook, earnings, and sources of additional information.

★2556★ *Food Careers*
Prentice Hall
Rte. 9W
Englewood Cliffs, NJ 07632
Ph: (201)592-2000

Donna N. Creasy. 1977. Part of Home Economics Careers Series.

★2557★ *Food Service Careers Guide Book: A Handy Guidebook for Those Seeking a Career in the Hospitality Industry*
Educators' Publications, Inc.
1110 S. Pomona Ave.
Fullerton, CA 92632
Ph: (714)871-2950

Joe Witzman. 1986.

★2558★ *Food Service Officers*
Chronicle Guidance Publications, Inc.
66 Aurora St.
PO Box 1190
Moravia, NY 13118-1190
Ph: (315)497-0330 Fax: (315)497-3359
Fr: 800-622-7284

1992. This career brief describes the nature of the work, working conditions, hours and earnings, education and training, licensure, certification, unions, personal qualifications, social and psychological factors, employment outlook, entry methods, advancement, and related occupations.

★2559★ "Food Service Workers" in *Career Discovery Encyclopedia* (Vol.3, pp. 32-33)
J.G. Ferguson Publishing Co.
200 W. Madison St., Ste. 300
Chicago, IL 60606
Ph: (312)580-5480 Fax: (312)580-4948

Russell E. Primm, editor-in chief. 1993. This six volume set contains two-page articles for 504 occupations. Each article describes job duties, earnings, and educational and training requirements. The whole set is arranged alphabetically by job title. Designed for junior high and older students.

★2560★ *Food Services*
Learning Corporation of America
108 Wilmot Rd.
Deerfield, IL 60015
Ph: (708)940-1260 Fax: (708)940-3600
Fr: 800-621-2131

Videocassette. 1982. 21 mins. Four workers in the food industry offer a look at their jobs: chef, restaurant manager, baker and meat wrapper. From the "Working" series.

★2561★ "Head Waiter and Waitress" in *Career Information Center* (Vol.8)
Simon and Schuster
200 Old Tappan Rd.
Old Tappan, NJ 07675
Fax: 800-445-6991 Fr: 800-223-2348

Richard Lidz and Dale Anderson, editorial directors. Fifth edition, 1993. For 600 occupations, describes job duties, entry-level requirements, education and training needed, advancement possibilities, employment outlook, earnings and benefits. The set is divided into 12 volumes. Each volume includes jobs related under a broad career field. Volume 13 is the index.

★2562★ "Hostessing" in *The Job Hunter's Guide to Japan* (pp. 163-166)
Kodansha International
114 Fifth Ave.
New York, NY 10011
Ph: (212)727-6460

Terra Brockman. 1990. Provides an overview of life in Japan. Describes various types of jobs including hostessing. Outlines necessary qualifications, job hunting strategies, salaries, working hours and conditions, and additional sources of information.

★2563★ *Introduction to Management in the Hospitality Industry*
John Wiley and Sons, Inc.
605 3rd Ave.
New York, NY 10158-0012
Ph: (212)850-6000 Fax: (212)850-6088
Fr: 800-526-5368

Tom Powers. 1992.

★2564★ "Maitre d', Bartender, Waiter/Waitress: The People Who Meet the Public" in *Careers in the Restaurant Industry* (pp. 23-24)
Rosen Publishing Group
29 E. 21st St.
New York, NY 10010
Ph: (212)777-3017 Fax: (212)777-0277
Fr: 800-237-9932

Richard S. Lee and Mary Price Lee. Revised edition, 1990. Explores various jobs in the restaurant industry including cooks and chefs, manager, maitre d', bartender, and waiter/waitress. Describes job duties, salaries, educational preparation and job hunting. Contains information about fast food, catering, and small businesses.

★2565★ *Opportunities in Culinary Careers*
National Textbook Co. (NTC)
VGM Career Books
4255 W. Touhy Ave.
Lincolnwood, IL 60646-1975
Ph: (708)679-5500 Fax: (708)679-2494
Fr: 800-323-4900

Mary Donovan. 1990. Describes the educational preparation and training of chefs and cooks and explores a variety of food service jobs in restaurants, institutions, and research and development. Lists culinary schools and professional organizations.

★2566★ *Opportunities in Fast Food Careers*
National Textbook Co. (NTC)
VGM Career Books
4255 W. Toughy Ave.
Lincolnwood, IL 60646-1975
Ph: (708)679-5500 Fax: (708)679-2494
Fr: 800-323-4900

Marjorie Eberts and Margaret Gisler. 1994.

★2567★ *Opportunities in Food Services*
National Textbook Co. (NTC)
VGM Career Books
4255 W. Touhy Ave.
Lincolnwood, IL 60646-1975
Ph: (708)679-5500 Fax: (708)679-2494
Fr: 800-323-4900

Carol Caprione Chmelynski. 1983.

★2568★ *Opportunities in Restaurant Careers*
National Textbook Co. (NTC)
VGM Career Books
4255 W. Touhy Ave.
Lincolnwood, IL 60646-1975
Ph: (708)679-5500 Fax: (708)679-2494
Fr: 800-323-4900

Carol Caprione Chemelynski. Provides an overview of the restaurant industry and surveys entry-level, mid-level, and management jobs. Covers working conditions, educational preparation, training, advancement possibilities, employment outlook, and earnings. Lists schools offering programs in hotel, restaurant, and institutional management.

★2569★ *Personal Service Cluster*
Center for Humanities, Inc.
Communications Park
Box 1000
Mount Kisco, NY 10549
Ph: (914)666-4100 Fax: (914)666-5319
Fr: 800-431-1242

Videocassette. 1984. 20 mins. Students get to see the day-by-day lives of people who work in the fields of cosmetology, food service and law enforcement.

★2570★ *Restaurant Host/Hostess*
Careers, Inc.
PO Box 135
Largo, FL 34649-0135
Ph: (813)584-7333

1994. Two-page occupational summary card describing duties, working conditions, personal qualifications, training, earnings and hours, employment outlook, places of employment, related careers and where to write for more information.

★2571★ "Restaurant Host and Hostess" in *Career Information Center* (Vol.8)
Simon and Schuster
200 Old Tappan Rd.
Old Tappan, NJ 07675
Fax: 800-445-6991 Fr: 800-223-2348

Richard Lidz and Dale Anderson, editorial directors. Fifth edition, 1993. For 600 occupations, describes job duties, entry-level requirements, education and training needed, advancement possibilities, employment outlook, earnings and benefits. The set is divided into 12 volumes. Each volume includes jobs related under a broad career field. Volume 13 is the index.

★2572★ "Restaurant Host/Hostess" in *Occu-Facts: Information on 580 Careers in Outline Form*
Careers, Inc.
PO Box 135
Largo, FL 34649-0135
Ph: (813)584-7333

Biennial, 1995-96 edition. Each one-page occupational profile describes duties, working conditions, physical surroundings and demands, aptitudes, temperament, educational requirements, employment outlook, earnings, and places of employment.

★2573★ *Table Attendant Training*
Bergwall Productions
540 Baltimore Pike
Chadds Ford, PA 19317
Ph: (215)388-0400 Fax: (215)388-0405
Fr: 800-645-3565

Videocassette. 1983. 75 mins. On 5 tapes, the techniques of becoming a good waiter are explained.

★2574★ "Travel and Hospitality Careers" in *The Best Jobs for the 1990s and Into the 21st Century*
Impact Publications
9104-N Manassas Dr.
Manassas Park, VA 22111
Ph: (703)361-7300 Fax: (703)335-9486

Ronald L. Krannich and Caryl Rae Krannich. 1993. Includes information on chefs, cooks, flight attendants, food and beverage service workers, hotel and motel desk clerks, reservation and transportation ticket agents and travel clerks, and travel agents.

★2575★ *Video Career Library - Public and Personal Services*
Careers, Inc.
PO Box 135
Largo, FL 34649-0135
Ph: (813)584-7333

Videocassette. 1990. 35 mins. Part of the Video Career Library covering 165 occupations. Shows actual workers on the job. Includes firefighters, police officers, correctional officers, bartenders, waiters/waitresses, cooks/chefs, child care workers, flight attendants, barbers/cosmetologists, groundskeepers/gardeners, and butchers/meat cutters.

★2576★ "Waiter" in *VGM's Careers Encyclopedia* (pp. 485-487)
National Textbook Co. (NTC)
VGM Career Books
4255 W. Touhy Ave.
Lincolnwood, IL 60646-1975
Ph: (708)679-5500 Fax: (708)679-2494
Fr: 800-323-4900

Third edition, 1991. Contains two- to five-page descriptions of 200 managerial, professional, technical, trade, and service occupations. Each profile includes job duties, places of employment, qualifications, educational preparation, training, employment potential, advancement, income, and additional sources of information.

★2577★ *Waiter-Waitress*
Careers, Inc.
PO Box 135
Largo, FL 34649-0135
Ph: (813)584-7333

1993. Two-page occupational summary card describing duties, working conditions, personal qualifications, training, earnings and hours, employment outlook, places of employment, related careers and where to write for more information.

★2578★ "Waiter and Waitress" in *Career Information Center* (Vol.8)
Simon and Schuster
200 Old Tappan Rd.
Old Tappan, NJ 07675
Fax: 800-445-6991 Fr: 800-223-2348

Richard Lidz and Dale Anderson, editorial directors. Fifth edition, 1993. For 600 occupations, describes job duties, entry-level requirements, education and training needed, advancement possibilities, employment outlook, earnings and benefits. The set is divided into 12 volumes. Each volume includes jobs related under a broad career field. Volume 13 is the index.

★2579★ "Waiter or Waitress and Host or Hostess" in *Hospitality & Recreation* (pp. 39-43)
Franklin Watts, Inc.
387 Park Avenue, S.
New York, NY 10016
Ph: (212)686-7070

Marjorie Rittenberg Schulz. 1990. Provides an overview of jobs in the hotel, motel, food service, fitness, and recreation industries. Covers job duties, educational preparation, salary, and employment outlook. Offers job hunting advice.

★2580★ "Waiter/Waitress" in *Occu-Facts: Information on 580 Careers in Outline Form*
Careers, Inc.
PO Box 135
Largo, FL 34649-0135
Ph: (813)584-7333

Biennial, 1995-96 edition. Each one-page occupational profile describes duties, working conditions, physical surroundings and demands, aptitudes, temperament, educational requirements, employment outlook, earnings, and places of employment.

★2581★ *Waiters and Waitresses*
Chronicle Guidance Publications, Inc.
66 Aurora St.
PO Box 1190
Moravia, NY 13118-1190
Ph: (315)497-0330 Fax: (315)497-3359
Fr: 800-622-7284

1992. This career brief describes the nature of the work, working conditions, hours and earnings, education and training, licensure, certification, unions, personal qualifications, social and psychological factors, employment outlook, entry methods, advancement, and related occupations.

★2582★ "Waiters and Waitresses" in *Career Discovery Encyclopedia* (Vol.6, p. 144-145)
J.G. Ferguson Publishing Co.
200 W. Madison St., Ste. 300
Chicago, IL 60606
Ph: (312)580-5480 Fax: (312)580-4948

E. Russell Primm, editor-in-chief. 1993. Contains two-page articles on 504 occupations. Each article describes job duties, earnings, and educational and training requirements.

★2583★ "Waiters and Waitresses" in *Opportunities in Restaurant Careers* (p. 10)
National Textbook Co. (NTC)
VGM Career Books
4255 W. Touhy Ave.
Lincolnwood, IL 60646-1975
Ph: (708)679-5500 Fax: (708)679-2494
Fr: 800-323-4900

Carol Ann Caprione Chmelynski. 1990. Provides an overview of the restaurant industry and surveys entry-level, mid-level, and management jobs. Covers working conditions, educational preparation, training, advancement possibilities, employment outlook, and earnings. Lists schools offering programs in hotel, restaurant, and institutional management.

★2584★ *Waiting Tables*
Filmakers Library, Inc.
124 E. 40th St.
New York, NY 10016
Ph: (212)808-4980 Fax: (212)808-4983

Videocassette. 1986. 20 mins. An enlightening look at the food service industry where the majority of employees are underpaid, non-unionized women.

★2585★ *Waitress*
Vocational Biographies, Inc.
PO Box 31
Sauk Centre, MN 56378-0031
Ph: (612)352-6516 Fax: (612)352-5546
Fr: 800-255-0752

1995. Four-page pamphlet containing a personal narrative about a worker's job, work likes and dislikes, career path from high school to the present. Education and training, the rewards and frustrations, and the effects of the job on the rest of the worker's life. The data file portion of this pamphlet gives a concise occupational summary, including work descriptions, working conditions, places of employment, personal characteristics, education and training, job outlook, and salary range.

★2586★ *Who's Hiring in Hospitality*
Educator's Pubications, Inc.
1110 S. Pomona Ave.
Fullerton, CA 92632
Ph: (714)871-2950

Joe Witzman. 1988.

Associations

★2587★ Career College Association (CCA)
750 1st St. NE, Ste. 900
Washington, DC 20002
Ph: (202)336-6700 Fax: (202)336-6828

Members: Private postsecondary schools providing career education. **Purpose:** Seeks to inform members of the accreditation process and regulations affecting vocational education. Conducts workshops and institutes for staffs of member schools; provides legislative, administrative, and public relations assistance. Has established Career Training Foundation to support research into private vocational education. Sponsors research programs. Maintains hall of fame; compiles statistics. **Publications:** *Career College Times*, monthly. • *Career Education.* • *Career News Digest.* • *Classroom Companion*, quarterly. • *Directory of Private Accredited Career Colleges and Schools*, annual.

★2588★ Council on Hotel, Restaurant, and Institutional Education (CHRIE)
1200 17th St. NW
Washington, DC 20036-3097
Ph: (202)331-5990 Fax: (202)785-2511

Members: Schools and colleges offering specialized education and training in cooking, baking, tourism and hotel, restaurant, and institutional administration; individuals, executives, and students. **Purpose:** Sponsors competitions. **Publications:** *CHRIE Communique*, biweekly. • *Guide to Hospitality Education*, semiannual. • *Hospitality and Tourism Educator*, quarterly. • *Hospitality Education and Research Journal.* • *Hosteur Magazine*, annual. • *Membership Directory and Research Guide*, annual.

★2589★ National Association of Church Food Service
76 Ivy Pky. NE
Atlanta, GA 30342-4241
Ph: (404)261-1794

Offers certification to become a certified church food service director. Conducts educational and charitable programs.

★2590★ National Association of Trade and Technical Schools
2251 Wisconsin Ave. NW
Washington, DC 20007
Ph: (202)333-1021

Members: Private schools providing career education. **Purpose:** Seeks to inform members of the accreditation process and regulations affecting vocational education. Conducts workshops and institutes for staffs of member schools; provides legislative, administrative, and public relations assistance; services as federally recognized accrediting agency. Maintains hall of fame; compiles statistics. **Publications:** *Career News Digest*, 3-4/year. • *Handbook of Trade and Technical Careers and Training.*

★2591★ National Restaurant Association (NRA)
1200 17th St. NW
Washington, DC 20036
Ph: (202)331-5900 Fax: (202)331-2429

Members: Restaurants, cafeterias, clubs, contract foodservice management, drive-ins, caterers, institutional food services, and other members of the foodservice industry; also represents establishments belonging to nonaffiliated state and local restaurant associations in governmental affairs. **Purpose:** Supports foodservice education and research in several educational institutions; conducts traveling management courses and seminars for restaurant personnel. Affiliated with the Educational Foundation of the National Restaurant Association. Provides training and education for operators, food and equipment manufacturers, distributors, and educators. Offers waiter/waitress training programs. Conducts the Great Menu Contest. **Publications:** *Foodservice Information Abstracts*, biweekly. • *National Restaurant Association—Washington Weekly.* • *Restaurant Industry Operations Report*, annual. • *Restaurants USA*, monthly. • *Technical Bulletin*, periodic.

Standards/Certification Agencies

★2592★ National Association of Church Food Service
76 Ivy Pky. NE
Atlanta, GA 30342-4241
Ph: (404)261-1794

Offers certification to become a certified church food service director. Conducts educational and charitable programs.

★2593★ National Association of Trade and Technical Schools (NATTS)
2251 Wisconsin Ave. NW
Washington, DC 20007
Ph: (202)333-1021

Informs members of the accreditation process and regulations affecting vocational education. Conducts workshops and institutes for staffs of member schools; provides legislative, administrative, and public relations assistance; serves as a federally recognized accrediting agency.

Test Guides

★2594★ *Career Examination Series: Beverage Control Inspector*
National Learning Corp.
212 Michael Dr.
Syosset, NY 11791
Ph: (516)921-8888 Fax: (516)921-8743
Fr: 800-645-6337

Jack Rudman. All examination guides in this series contain questions with answers.

★2595★ *Career Examination Series: Cafeteria Supervisor*
National Learning Corp.
212 Michael Dr.
Syosset, NY 11791
Ph: (516)921-8888 Fax: (516)921-8743
Fr: 800-645-6337

Jack Rudman. Test guide including questions and answers for students or professionals in the field who seek advancement through examination.

★2596★ *Career Examination Series: Food Service Specialist*
National Learning Corp.
212 Michael Dr.
Syosset, NY 11791
Ph: (516)921-8888 Fax: (516)921-8743
Fr: 800-645-6337

Jack Rudman. 1990. All examination guides in this series contain questions with answers.

★2597★ *Career Examination Series: Senior Beverage Control Investigator*
National Learning Corp.
212 Michael Dr.
Syosset, NY 11791
Ph: (516)921-8888 Fax: (516)921-8743
Fr: 800-645-6337

Jack Rudman. All examination guides in this series contain questions with answers.

Educational Directories and Programs

★2598★ *Baking Buyer—Yearbook Issue*
Sosland Publishing Co.
4800 Main, Ste. 100
Kansas City, MO 64112
Ph: (816)756-1000 Fax: (816)756-0494
Carol D. Kaskie, Contact

Annual, June. Publication includes: List of approximately 1,700 distributors and 1,000 manufacturers of products and equipment for the baking industry. Entries include: For distributors—Co. name, address, phone, fax, name of contact, types of products distributed, geographical area served. For manufacturers—Co. name, address, phone, fax. Arrangement: Distributors are geographical.

★2599★ *Career Guidance Handouts*
National Association of Trade and Technical Schools
NATTS
2251 Wisconsin Ave. NW
Washington, DC 20007
Ph: (202)333-1021

★2600★ *Career Training*
National Association of Trade and Technical Schools (NATTS)
2251 Wisconsin Ave. NW
Washington, DC 20007
Ph: (202)333-1021

Quarterly.

★2601★ *Classroom Companion*
National Association of Trade and Technical Schools (NATTS)
2251 Wisconsin Ave. NW
Washington, DC 20007
Ph: (202)333-1021

Quarterly.

★2602★ *College/University Foodservice Who's Who*
Information Central, Inc.
Box 3900
Prescott, AZ 86302
Ph: (602)778-1513 Fax: (602)445-6407
Julie Woodman, Contact

Triennial, latest edition January 1993; new edition expected 1996. Covers over 2,200 food service programs in colleges and universities. Entries include: Institution name, address, phone, enrollment, total annual food purchases, number of meals served per day; name of management company, principal food service official, services, fast food chains on campus. Arrangement: Geographical.

★2603★ *Commercial Food Equipment Service Association Directory*
Commercial Food Equipment Service Association (CFESA)
9247 N. Meridian, Ste. 216
Indianapolis, IN 46260
Ph: (317)844-4700
Carla M. Helm, Contact

Annual. Covers independent service companies that repair commercial food equipment.

★2604★ *Directory of French-Fry Potatoes*
Food Information Service Center
21050 SW 93rd Ln. Rd.
Dunnellon, FL 34431
Ph: (904)489-8919 Fax: (904)489-8919
Fr: 800-443-5820
James A. Mixon, Contact

Biennial, even years. Covers French-fry potato suppliers and related service companies. Entries include: Co. name, address, phone, name and title of contact, subsidiary and branch names and locations, products produced. Arrangement: Classified by product or service.

★2605★ *Food Distribution Magazine—Food Brokers Directory Issue*
National Food Distribution Network
PO Box 87
Barrington, RI 02806-0087
Ph: 800-541-6336 Fax: (401)245-4699
Dara Chadwick

Annual, December. Publication includes: List of brokers in the food business. Entries include: Co. name, address, phone, name and title of contact.

★2606★ *Whole Foods—Source Book Issue*
Whole Foods Communications, Inc.
3000 Hadley Rd.
South Plainfield, NJ 07080
Ph: (908)769-1160 Fax: (908)769-1171
Daniel McSweeney, Associate Publisher

Annual, May. Publication includes: Lists of 1,400 manufacturers, 175 wholesalers and distributors, and 95 brokers of natural food products; also 90 publishers of information about natural foods and 52 natural food associations. Entries include: For manufacturers—Company name, address, phone, contact person, line of business. For wholesalers and distributors—Company name, address, phone, tollfree phone, contact, description of products and services, territory covered, shipping company, approximate shipping time, size of sales staff. For brokers—Company name, address, phone, contact, geographic territory covered, firms represented, products. For others—Organization name, address, phone, contact, product or Arrangement: Classified by type of business.

Awards, Scholarships, Grants, and Fellowships

★2607★ National Restaurant Association Ice Carving Classic
National Restaurant Association
1200 17th St. NW
Washington, DC 20036
Ph: (202)331-5900 Fr: 800-424-5156

To recognize three-person teams for transforming huge blocks of ice into magnificent works of art. The competition pits master ice carvers from around the world against one another in three events: compulsory figures, to be completed in one hour; free-style individual blocks, two hours; and team multiple blocks, three hours. Winners are honored at the Association's annual show. Established in 1988 in cooperation with the National Ice Carving Association. Additional information is available from the National Restaurant Association.

★2608★ National Restaurant Association Undergraduate Scholarships
National Restaurant Association
Educational Foundation
250 S. Wacker Dr., Ste. 1400
Chicago, IL 60606-5834
Ph: (312)715-1010 Fax: (312)715-0807
Fr: 800-765-2122

Qualifications: Candidates must be full-time students working toward a foodservice/hospitality degree for the full academic year beginning with the fall term. They must have demonstrated interest in foodservice/hospitality through work experience in the industry and have a cumulative grade point average of at least 3.0 on a 4.0 scale. Eligible majors include: hotel, restaurant, and institutional management, culinary arts, dietetics, food science and technology, and other foodservice related curricula, including manufacturing and distribution. Funds available: More than 100 undergaduate scholarships are awarded, ranging in value from $500 to $10,000. Application details: Candidates must submit a formal applications and transcripts. Applications are available after December 1. Deadline: March 1.

Basic Reference Guides and Handbooks

★2609★ *Food Service Management by Checklist: A Handbook of Control Techniques*
John Wiley and Sons, Inc.
605 3rd Ave.
New York, NY 10158-0012
Ph: (212)850-6000 Fax: (212)850-6088
Fr: 800-526-5368

Herman E. Zaccerelli. 1991.

★2610★ *Foodservice Management Study Course*
Iowa State University Press
Iowa State University
2121 S. State Ave.
Ames, IA 50010
Ph: (515)292-0140 Fax: (515)292-3348

Shirley Gilmore. Second edition, 1990.

★2611★ *Guide to Hospitality Education*
Council on Hotel, Restaurant, and Institutional Education (CHRIE)
1200 17th St. NW
Washington, DC 20036-3097
Ph: (202)331-5990 Fax: (202)785-2511

Semiannual.

★2612★ *Guide to Hospitality Education*
Council on Hotel, Restaurant, and Institutional Education (CHRIE)
1200 17th St. NW
Washington, DC 20036-3097
Ph: (202)331-5990 Fax: (202)785-2511

Semiannual.

★2613★ *Handbook of Trade and Technical Careers and Training*
National Association of Trade and Technical Schools (NATTS)
2251 Wisconsin Ave. NW
Washington, DC 20007
Ph: (202)333-1021

★2614★ *Training Programs for Health Care Workers: Food Service Workers*
Hospital Research & Educational Trust
840 N. Lake Shore Dr.
Chicago, IL 60611
Ph: (312)280-6000

1967.

Periodicals

★2615★ *Alcoholic Beverage Control: From the State Capitals*
Wakeman/Walworth, Inc.
300 N. Washington St., Ste. B100
Alexandria, VA 22314
Ph: (703)549-8606 Fax: (703)549-1372
Keyes Walworth

Weekly. Covers state endeavors affecting the production, marketing, sale, consumption, and taxation of alcoholic beverages.

★2616★ *Atlantic Control States Beverage Journal*
Club and Tavern, Inc.
3 Twelfth St.
Wheeling, WV 26003
Ph: (304)232-7620 Fax: (304)232-1236
Arnold Lazarus

Monthly. Magazine for the alcoholic beverage industry.

★2617★ *Bartender Magazine*
Foley Publishing
PO Box 158
Liberty Corner, NJ 07938
Ph: (908)766-6006 Fax: (908)766-6607
Jaclyn W. Foley

Quarterly. Trade magazine.

★2618★ *Beverage Alcohol Market Report*
Peregrine Communications
160 E. 48th St.
New York, NY 10017
Ph: (212)371-5237
Perry Luntz

Covers international beer, wine, and liquor production, importation, marketing, wholesale distribution, and retailing. Recurring features include reports on legislation affecting the industry, news of research, a calendar of events, job changes, and statistics.

★2619★ *Capitol News*
Snack Food Association (SFA)
1711 King St., Ste. 1
Alexandria, VA 22314
Ph: (703)836-4500 Fax: (703)836-8262
Jim McCarthy

Seeks to disseminate information to those involved in the manufacturing of snack foods. Provides chief executive and government relations officers of snack food companies with reports on legislative and regulatory changes of import to the industry.

★2620★ *Career College Times*
Career College Association (CCA)
750 1st St. NE, Ste. 900
Washington, DC 20002
Ph: (202)336-6700 Fax: (202)336-6828

Monthly.

★2621★ *Catering Industry Employee*
Hotel Employees and Restaurant Employees International Union
1219 28th St. NW
Washington, DC 20007
Ph: (202)393-4373 Fax: (202)333-0468
Herman Leavitt

Bimonthly. Trade journal for culinary and hospitality workers. Official publication of the Hotel Employees and Restaurant Employees International Union.

★2622★ *Cheers*
Jobson Publishing Corp.
100 Avenue of the Americas, 9th Fl.
New York, NY 10013
Ph: (212)274-7000 Fax: (212)431-0500
Bob Keane

Bimonthly.

★2623★ *CHRIE Communique*
Council on Hotel, Restaurant, and Institutional Education (CHRIE)
1200 17th St. NW
Washington, DC 20036-3097
Ph: (202)331-5990 Fax: (202)785-2511

Biweekly.

★2624★ *Entree*
Entree Travel
1470 E. Valley Rd.
Santa Barbara, CA 93108
Ph: (805)969-5848 Fax: (805)966-7095
William Tomicki

Monthly. Features "an insider's look at hotels, restaurants, and travel around the world." Contains advice and tips on travel, bargains, and services. Recurring features include book reviews and notices of publications available.

★2625★ *Food Distribution Research Society—Newsletter*
Food Distribution Research Society, Inc.
c/o Richard Bacon
Department of Food and Resource Economics
University of Delaware
Newark, DE 19717-1303
Ph: (302)831-1320 Fax: (302)292-1787
Dale L. Anderson

Reports on the actions of government bodies and other developments affecting the food industry. Reprints articles of interest from other publications, with special attention to results of research, surveys, and studies. Recurring features include announcements of conferences, meetings, and educational programs; notices of resource materials available; news of research; statistics; and book reviews.

★2626★ *Food Reviews International*
Marcel Dekker, Inc.
270 Madison Ave.
New York, NY 10016
Ph: (212)696-9000 Fax: (212)685-4540
Roy Teranishi

Quarterly. Journal covering agricultural production, food processing, nutrition, and health.

★2627★ *Foodletter*
Foodletter
1 TwoPence Rd.
Ridgefield, CT 06877-1220
Doreen Higgins

Analyzes current trends in foods and beverages, forecasts trends, and gives corresponding ideas for new products and packaging. Recurring features include a column titled Consumer Corner.

★2628★ *Foodservice Product News*
Young/Conway Publications, Inc.
1101 Richmond Ave., Ste. 201
Point Pleasant, NJ 08742
Ph: (908)295-5959 Fax: (908)295-5979
Judy Ann Young

Monthly. Magazine serving the restaurant food service market.

★2629★ *Foodservice Report*
International Foodservice Distributors Association (IFDA)
201 Park Washington Court
Falls Church, VA 22046
Ph: (703)532-9400 Fax: (703)538-4673
John D. Thompson

Monthly. Carries news of the food service industry, including activities of manufacturers, brokers, and distributors, as well as trends in food service operation. Recurring features include profiles of food service distribution companies in the U.S. and Canada, a calendar of events, and reports of conventions and conferences.

★2630★ *The Hospitality Manager*
Kassis Communications
120 Hayward
Ames, IA 50010
Ph: (515)296-2400 Fax: (515)296-2405
Terry Lowman

Monthly. Trade publication (tabloid) covering restaurant and institutional business in the Midwest. Mailed to restaurants, bars, and institutional food service companies.

★2631★ *HOTELS*
Cahners Publishing Co.
1350 E. Touhy Ave.
PO Box 5080
Des Plaines, IL 60017-5080
Ph: (708)635-8800 Fax: (708)390-2618
James Carper

Monthly. Magazine covering management and operations as well as foodservice and design in the hospitality industry.

★2632★ *Import Statistics*
National Association of Beverage Importers, Inc.
1025 Vermont Ave. NW, Ste. 1205
Washington, DC 20005
Ph: (202)638-1617 Fax: (202)638-3122

Monthly. Contains Bureau of Census statistics of beverage imports compiled monthly with cumulative comparisons with the same period of the previous year. Presents statistics by the tariff schedules of beer, wines, and spirits categories. Includes statistics of U.S.-produced beer, wines, and spirits.

★2633★ *Jesse Meyers' Beverage Digest*
Tomac & Company, Inc.
PO Box 238
Old Greenwich, CT 06870
Ph: (203)358-8198 Fax: (203)327-9761
Jesse Meyers

Focuses primarily on soft drinks. Reports on industry news in relation to pricing, marketing, and competition.

★2634★ *Kane's Beverage Week*
Whitaker Newsletters, Inc.
313 South Ave.
PO Box 340
Fanwood, NJ 07023-0340
Ph: (908)889-6336 Fax: (908)889-6339
Joel Whitaker

Presents news items pertaining to the marketing, advertising, and distribution of alcoholic and other types of beverages. Also reports on social, health, and legal issues affecting the beverage industry. Recurring features include interviews, news of research, job listings, notices of publications available, and a calendar of events.

★2635★ *Kitchen Times*
Howard Wilson & Company, Inc.
185 Marlborough St.
Boston, MA 02116
Ph: (617)266-2453 Fax: (617)437-9983
Howard Wilson

Monthly. Contains instructions on buying food and preparing specific dishes. Reviews restaurants, inns, cooks, cookbooks, and wines.

★2636★ *Mixin'*
American Bartenders' Association
PO Box 3881
Plant City, FL 33564
Ph: (813)752-6987 Fax: (813)752-2768
Fr: 800-935-3232
Yvonne Fry

Monthly. Supports the Association's dedication to strengthening the position of professional bartenders, bar managers, and bar owners throughout the industry and in the legislature. Includes news of interest to those in the beverage business such as announcements of new products and services, changing prices, alterations in government regulations, and profit-making suggestions. Recurring features include letters to the editor, interviews, news of research, book reviews, notices of publications available, new drink recipes, and a calendar of events.

★2637★ *Modern Food Service News*
Grocers Publishing Co., Inc.
15 Emerald St.
Hackensack, NJ 07601
Ph: (201)488-1800
Rob Reis

Monthly. Magazine for restaurateurs, chefs, caterers, purchasing agents in the food service industry.

★2638★ *NACUFS News Wave*
National Association of College and University Food Services (NACUFS)
1405 S. Harrison Rd., Ste. 303-304
Manly Miles Bldg.
East Lansing, MI 48824
Ph: (517)332-2494 Fax: (517)332-8144
C. Dennis Pierce

Covers news of interest to food service industry personnel in academic institutions. Also reports on regional Association activities. Recurring features include columns titled President's Message, Special Features, and Committee Spotlight.

★2639★ *National Restaurant Association—Washington Weekly*
National Restaurant Association (NRA)
1200 17th St. NW
Washington, DC 20036
Ph: (202)331-5900 Fax: (202)331-2429

Reports on legislation and regulatory issues affecting the food service industry.

★2640★ *Nation's Restaurant News*
Lebhar-Friedman, Inc.
425 Park Ave.
New York, NY 10022
Ph: (212)756-5000 Fax: (212)756-5125
Rick Van Warner

Weekly.

★2641★ *Restaurant Business*
Bill Communications, Inc.
355 Park Ave. S.
New York, NY 10010-1789
Ph: (212)592-6200 Fax: (212)592-6359
Scott Allmendinger

Trade magazine for restaurants and commercial food service.

★2642★ *Restaurants & Institutions*
Cahners Publishing Co.
1350 E. Touhy Ave.
PO Box 5080
Des Plaines, IL 60017-5080
Ph: (708)635-8800 Fax: (708)390-2618
Mike Bartlett

Semiweekly. Magazine focusing on foodservice and lodging management.

★2643★ *Restaurants, Resorts & Hotels*
Trade Publishing Co.
41 Shea Terr.
Stratford, CT 06497-2422
Ph: (203)378-1223 Fax: (203)378-7285
James Martone

Monthly. National business magazine serving the food service industry.

★2644★ *Total Food Service*
PO Box 2507
Greenwich, CT 06836
Ph: (203)661-9090 Fax: (203)661-9325
Gary Cohen

Monthly. Food service industry magazine.

Meetings and Conventions

★2645★ American School Food Service Association Conference
American School Food Service Association
1600 Duke St., 7th Fl.
Alexandria, VA 22314
Ph: (703)739-3900 Fax: (703)739-3915
Fr: 800-877-8822

Annual.

★2646★ Hotel, Motel, and Restaurant Supply Show of the Southeast
Leisure Time Unlimited, Inc.
708 Main St.
PO Box 332
Myrtle Beach, SC 29578
Ph: (803)448-9483 Fax: (803)626-1513

Annual. Always held during January at the Convention Center in Myrtle Beach, South Carolina. **Dates and Locations:** 1996 Jan 30-01; Myrtle Beach, SC. • 1997 Jan 28-30; Myrtle Beach, SC. • 1998 Jan 27-20; Myrtle Beach, SC.

★2647★ IFT Annual Meeting and Food Expo
Institute of Food Technologists
221 N. LaSalle St.
Chicago, IL 60601
Ph: (312)782-8424 Fax: (312)782-8348

Annual. Always held during June. 1996 Jun 23-26; New Orleans, LA. • 1997 Jun 14-18; Orlando, FL.

★2648★ Midwestern Foodservice and Equipment Exposition
Missouri Restaurant Association
PO Box 10277
4049 Pennsylvania
Kansas City, MO 64111
Ph: (816)753-5222 Fax: (816)753-6993

Annual. Always held during October alternating between St. Louis and Kansas City, Missouri.

★2649★ National Association of Food Equipment Manufacturers Convention
National Association of Food Equipment Manufacturers
401 N. Michigan Ave.
Chicago, IL 60611
Ph: (312)644-6610

Biennial. **Dates and Locations:** 1997 Sep; New Orleans, LA.

★2650★ National Restaurant Association Restaurant, Hotel-Motel Show
National Restaurant Association
150 N. Michigan Ave., Ste. 2000
Chicago, IL 60601
Ph: (312)853-2525 Fax: (312)853-2548

Annual. Always held during May at the McCormick Place Complex in Chicago, Illinois. **Dates and Locations:** 1996 May 20-18; Chicago, IL.

★2651★ Northeast Food Service and Lodging Exposition and Conference
Reed Exhibition Companies (World Headquarters)
255 Washington St.
Newton, MA 02158-1630
Ph: (617)630-2200 Fax: (617)630-2222

Annual. Always held during April at the Bayside Exposition Center in Boston, Massachusetts. **Dates and Locations:** 1996 Apr; Boston, MA.

★2652★ Southeastern Restaurant, Hospitality Foodservice Show
Reed Exhibition Companies (World Headquarters)
255 Washington St.
Newton, MA 02158-1630
Ph: (617)630-2200 Fax: (617)630-2222

Annual. Always held during October at the Georgia World Congress Center in Atlanta, Georgia.

★2653★ Tri-State Restaurant Food and Equipment Show
Pennsylvania Restaurant Association
100 State St.
Harrisburg, PA 17101
Ph: (717)232-7726 Fax: (717)263-1202
Fr: 800-346-7767

Annual. Always held during March at the Pittsburgh Expo Mart in Monroeville, Pennsylvania. **Dates and Locations:** 1996 Mar; Monroeville, PA.

★2654★ Upper Midwest Hospitality, Restaurant, and Lodging Show
Upper Midwest Hospitality Inc.
871 Jefferson Ave.
St. Paul, MN 55102
Ph: (612)222-7401 Fax: (612)222-7347

Annual. **Dates and Locations:** 1996 Feb; Minneapolis, MN.

Other Sources of Information

★2655★ *Careers in the Restaurant Industry*
Rosen Publishing Group
29 E. 21st St.
New York, NY 10010
Ph: 800-237-9932 Fax: (212)777-0277

Mary Price Lee and Richard Lee. Revised edition, 1990.

★2656★ "Fast-Foods Worker" in *Career Selector 2001*
Barron's Educational Series, Inc.
250 Wireless Blvd.
Hauppauge, NY 11788
Ph: (516)434-3311 Fax: (516)434-3723
Fr: 800-645-3476

James C. Gonyea. 1993.

★2657★ *Restaurant Industry Operations Report*
National Restaurant Association (NRA)
1200 17th St. NW
Washington, DC 20036
Ph: (202)331-5900 Fax: (202)331-2429

Annual.

★2658★ *To Health! Guidelines for Food Service Sanitation*
West One Video
1995 Bailey Hill Rd.
Eugene, OR 97405
Ph: (503)683-2236 Fax: (503)344-3489
Fr: 800-234-4952

An informative and entertaining explanation of proper food handling, types of food-borne illnesses, and methods of prevention.

Dental Assistants

Dental assistants work alongside dentists as they examine and treat patients. Moreover, dental assistants perform a variety of clinical, office, and laboratory duties. Clinical duties include removing sutures, applying anesthetic and caries-preventive agents to the teeth and oral tissue, removing excess cement used in the filling process, and placing rubber dams on the teeth to isolate them for individual treatment. Office duties include arranging and confirming appointments, receiving patients, keeping treatment records, sending bills, receiving payments, and ordering dental supplies and materials. Laboratory duties include casting teeth and the mouth from impressions taken by the dentist. Most dental assistants work in private dental offices. Others work in dental schools, hospital dental departments, state and public health departments, or private clinics.

Salaries

Average weekly salaries for dental assistants is $332.

Employment Outlook

Growth rate until the year 2005: Faster than average.

Dental Assistants

Career Guides

★2659★ *Careers in the Dental Profession: Dental Assisting*
SELECT
211 E. Chicago Ave., Ste. 1804
Chicago, IL 60611-2678
Ph: (312)440-2500

1991. This eight-page booklet describes what dental assistants do, where they work, educational preparation and certification.

★2660★ *Comprehensive Review of Dental Assisting*
John Wiley and Sons, Inc.
605 3rd Ave.
New York, NY 10158
Ph: (212)850-6000 Fax: (212)850-6088

Jacqueline W. Sapp. 1981.

★2661★ "Dental Assistance" in *Career Connection II: A Guide to Technical Majors and Their Related Careers* (pp. 52-53)
Jist Works, Inc.
720 N. Park Ave.
University Station
Indianapolis, IN 46202-3431
Ph: (317)264-3720 Fax: (317)264-3709

Fred A. Rowe. 1994. Contains technical majors, such as automotive technology. Describes the major and the job. Lists high school and postsecondary school courses. Includes occupations related to the major, employment outlook, and starting salary.

★2662★ *The Dental Assistant*
Lea & Febiger
200 Chester Field Pkwy.
Malvern, PA 19355
Ph: (215)251-2230 Fax: (215)251-2229

Roger E. Barton, editor. Sixth edition, 1988.

★2663★ *Dental Assistant*
Careers, Inc.
PO Box 135
Largo, FL 34649-0135
Ph: (813)584-7333

1994. Two-page occupational summary card describing duties, working conditions, personal qualifications, training, earnings and hours, employment outlook, places of employment, related careers and where to write for more information.

★2664★ "Dental Assistant" in *100 Best Careers for the Year 2000* (pp. 29-31)
Arco Pub.
201 W. 103rd St.
Indianapolis, IN 46290
Ph: 800-428-5331 Fax: 800-835-3202

Shelly Field. 1992. Describes 100 job opportunities expected to grow fast throughout the next decade. Provides information on job duties and responsibilities, training requirements, education, advancement opportunities, experience and qualifications, and typical salaries.

★2665★ "Dental Assistant" in *150 Careers in the Health Care Field*
Reed Reference Publishing
121 Chanlon Rd.
PO Box 31
New Providence, NJ 07974
Fax: (908)665-6688 Fr: 800-521-8110

Stanley Alperin. Third edition, 1993. Each occupational profile covers job functions and responsibilities, work locations, training requirements, certification, and salaries. Lists community colleges, universities, vocational-technical schools, and other educational institutions that provide accredited training programs.

★2666★ "Dental Assistant" in *Career Information Center* (Vol.7)
Simon and Schuster
200 Old Tappan Rd.
Old Tappan, NJ 07675
Fax: 800-445-6991 Fr: 800-223-2348

Richard Lidz and Dale Anderson, editorial directors. Fifth edition, 1993. For 600 occupations, describes job duties, entry-level requirements, education and training needed, advancement possibilities, employment outlook, earnings and benefits. The set is divided into 12 volumes. Each volume includes jobs related under a broad career field. Volume 13 is the index.

★2667★ "Dental Assistant" in *Careers in Health Care* (pp. 50-54)
National Textbook Co. (NTC)
VGM Career Books
4255 W. Touhy Ave.
Lincolnwood, IL 60646-1975
Ph: (708)679-5500 Fax: (708)679-2494
Fr: 800-323-4900

Barbara M. Swanson. 1995. Discusses 58 health careers, providing information about the history of the occupation, job duties, work environments, salaries, educational preparation, licensure, certification, and employment outlook.

★2668★ "Dental Assistant" in *Health Care* (pp. 57-61)
Franklin Watts, Inc.
387 Park Avenue, S.
New York, NY 10016
Ph: (212)686-7070

Linda Barrett and Galen Guengerich. 1991. Provides an overview of the health care industry. Includes job description, educational preparation, training, salary, and employment outlook. Offers job hunting advice.

★2669★ "Dental Assistant" in *Occu-Facts: Information on 580 Careers in Outline Form*
Careers, Inc.
PO Box 135
Largo, FL 34649-0135
Ph: (813)584-7333

Biennial, 1995-96 edition. Each one-page occupational profile describes duties, working conditions, physical surroundings and demands, aptitudes, temperament, educational requirements, employment outlook, earnings, and places of employment.

★2670★ "Dental Assistant" in *Opportunities in Dental Care Careers* (pp. 17-18, 46-47)
National Textbook Co. (NTC)
VGM Career Books
4255 W. Touhy Ave.
Lincolnwood, IL 60646-1975
Ph: (708)679-5500 Fax: (708)679-2494
Fr: 800-323-4900

Bonnie L. Kendall. 1991. Describes the work of dentists and related dental care employees. Covers dental education including admission to dental school, dental specialties, skills, personal qualities, income, and licensure. Lists accredited dental schools, dental hygiene and assisting programs.

★2671★ "Dental Assistant" in *Opportunities in Health and Medical Careers* (p. 15)
National Textbook Co. (NTC)
VGM Career Books
4255 W. Touhy Ave.
Lincolnwood, IL 60646-1975
Ph: (708)679-5500 Fax: (708)679-2494
Fr: 800-323-4900

Leo D'Orazio and I. Donald Snook. 1991. Provides an overview of the health care industry with future projections. Describes a wide variety of healthcare jobs covering the nature of the work, educational requirements, employment outlook and salaries. Offers job hunting advice.

★2672★ "Dental Assistant" in *Opportunities in Paramedical Careers* (pp. 40-49)
National Textbook Co. (NTC)
VGM Career Books
4255 W. Touhy Ave.
Lincolnwood, IL 60646-1975
Ph: (708)679-5500 Fax: (708)679-2494
Fr: 800-323-4900

Alex Kacen. 1994. Describes paraprofessional careers in the health professions such as physician assistant and mental health technician. Covers job functions, educational preparation, certification, earnings, and job outlook. Lists accredited educational programs.

★2673★ "Dental Assistant" in *VGM's Careers Encyclopedia* (pp. 132-134)
National Textbook Co. (NTC)
VGM Career Books
4255 W. Touhy Ave.
Lincolnwood, IL 60646-1975
Ph: (708)679-5500 Fax: (708)679-2494
Fr: 800-323-4900

Third edition, 1991. Contains two- to five-page descriptions of 200 managerial, professional, technical, trade, and service occupations. Each profile includes job duties, places of employment, qualifications, educational preparation, training, employment potential, advancement, income, and additional sources of information.

★2674★ "Dental Assistant" in *VGM's Handbook of Health Care Careers*
National Textbook Co.
4255 W. Touhy Ave.
Lincolnwood, IL 60646-1975
Ph: (708)679-5500 Fax: (708)679-2494
Fr: 800-323-4900

Annette Selden. 1993. Contains 42 two-page occupational profiles describing job duties, places of employment, working conditions, qualifications, education, employment outlook, and income.

★2675★ *Dental Assistants*
Chronicle Guidance Publications, Inc.
66 Aurora St.
PO Box 1190
Moravia, NY 13118-1190
Ph: (315)497-0330 Fax: (315)497-3359
Fr: 800-622-7284

1994. This career brief describes the nature of the work, working conditions, hours and earnings, education and training, licensure, certification, unions, personal qualifications, social and psychological factors, employment outlook, entry methods, advancement, and related occupations.

★2676★ "Dental Assistants" in *America's 50 Fastest Growing Jobs* (pp. 118)
JIST Works, Inc.
720 N. Park Ave.
Indianapolis, IN 46202-3431
Ph: (317)264-3720 Fax: (317)264-3709
Fr: 800-648-5478

Michael J. Farr, compiler. 1994. Describes the 50 fastest growing jobs within major career clusters such as technicians, and marketing and sales. Each job profile explains the nature of the work, skills and abilities required, employment outlook, average earnings, related occupations, education and training requirements, and employment opportunities. Also contains career planning information and job search tips.

★2677★ "Dental Assistants" in *Career Discovery Encyclopedia* (Vol.2, pp. 84-85)
J.G. Ferguson Publishing Co.
200 W. Madison St., Ste. 300
Chicago, IL 60606
Ph: (312)580-5480 Fax: (312)580-4948

E. Russell Primm, editor-in-chief. 1993. Contains two-page articles on 504 occupations. Each article describes job duties, earnings, and educational and training requirements.

★2678★ "Dental Assistants: Chairside Assistants" in *Careers for Women Without College Degrees* (pp. 208-211)
McGraw-Hill Publishing Co.
11 W. 19th St.
New York, NY 10011
Ph: (212)337-6010

Beatryce Nivens. 1988. Career planning and job hunting guide containing information on decision-making, skills assessment, and resumes for career changers. Profiles careers with the best occupational outlook. Describes the work, educational preparation, employment outlook, salaries, and required skills.

★2679★ "Dental Assistants and Dental Hygienists" in *American Almanac of Jobs and Salaries* (pp. 480)
Avon Books
1350 Avenue of the Americas
New York, NY 10019
Ph: (212)261-6800 Fr: 800-238-0658

John Wright, editor. Revised and updated, 1994-95. A comprehensive guide to the wages of hundreds of occupations in a wide variety of industries and organizations.

★2680★ "Dental Assistants" in *Encyclopedia of Careers and Vocational Guidance* (Vol.2, pp. 444-446)
J.G. Ferguson Publishing Co.
200 W. Madison St., Ste. 300
Chicago, IL 60606
Ph: (312)580-5480 Fax: (312)580-4948

William E. Hopke, editor-in-chief. Ninth edition, 1993. Four-volume set that profiles 500 occupations and describes job trends in 74 industries. Includes career description, educational requirements, history of the job, methods of entry, advancement, employment outlook, earnings, working conditions, social and psychological factors, and sources of additional information.

★2681★ "Dental Assistants and Hygienists" in *Jobs! What They Are—Where They Are—What They Pay* (p. 180)
Simon & Schuster, Inc.
Simon & Schuster Bldg.
1230 Avenue of the Americas
New York, NY 10020
Ph: (212)698-7000

Robert O. Snelling and Anne M. Snelling. Revised edition, 1992. Profiles 241 occupations, describing duties and responsibilities, educational preparation, earnings, employment opportunities, training, and qualifications.

★2682★ "Dental Assistants" in *Occupational Outlook Handbook*
U.S. Government Printing Office
Superintendent of Documents
Washington, DC 20402
Ph: (202)512-1800 Fax: (202)512-2250

Biennial; latest edition, 1994-95. Encyclopedia of careers describing more than 250 occupations and comprising about 85 percent of all jobs in the economy. Occupations that require lengthy education or training are given the most attention. For each occupation, the handbook describes job duties, working conditions, training, educational preparation, personal qualities, advancement possibilities, job outlook, earnings, and sources of additional information.

★2683★ *Dental Assisting: Basic & Dental Sciences*
Mosby-Year Book, Inc.
11830 Westline Industrial Dr.
St. Louis, MO 63146
Ph: (314)872-8370 Fax: (314)432-1380
Fr: 800-325-4177

Earl Leimone. 1988.

★2684★ *Dental Assisting Exam Preparation*
W. B. Saunders Co.
Curtis Center
Independence Sq. W.
Philadelphia, PA 19106
Ph: (215)238-7800

Hazel O. Torres and Lois Mazzucchi-Ballard. 1994.

★2685★ *Dental Technicians*
Chronicle Guidance Publications, Inc.
66 Aurora St.
PO Box 1190
Moravia, NY 13118-1190
Ph: (315)497-0330 Fax: (315)497-3359
Fr: 800-622-7284

1994. This career brief describes the nature of the work, working conditions, hours and earnings, education and training, licensure, certification, unions, personal qualifications, social and psychological factors, employment outlook, entry methods, advancement, and related occupations.

★2686★ ***Health Career Planning: A Realistic Guide***
Human Sciences Press
233 Spring St.
New York, NY 10013
Ph: (212)620-8000
Ellen F. Lederman. 1988.

★2687★ ***Health Careers Today***
Mosby-Year Book, Inc.
11830 Westline Industrial Dr.
St. Louis, MO 63146
Ph: (314)872-8370 Fax: (314)432-1380
Fr: 800-325-4177
Judith A. Gerdin. 1991. Surveys health occupations. Includes information on basic health care skills and careers.

★2688★ ***Introduction to the Health Professions***
Jones and Bartlett Publishers, Inc.
1 Exeter Plaza
Boston, MA 02116
Ph: (617)859-3900
Peggy Stanfield. Second edition, 1995.

★2689★ ***Medical and Dental Associations, P.C. Insurance Forms Preparation***
South-Western Publishing Co.
5101 Madison Rd.
Cincinnati, OH 45227
Ph: (513)271-8811
Carol Dehler Gense. Second edition, 1990.

★2690★ ***Student Syllabus for the Dental Assistant: A Correlated, Individualized Instruction Program***
National Book Co.
PO Box 8795
Portland, OR 97207-8795
Ph: (503)228-6345
E.A. Jacobson and Alma Jacobson. 1978.

Associations

★2691★ **American Dental Assistants Association (ADAA)**
203 N. LaSalle St., Ste. 1320
Chicago, IL 60601-1225
Ph: (312)541-1550 Fax: (312)541-1496
Members: Individuals employed as dental assistants in dental offices, clinics, hospitals, or institutions; instructors of dental assistants; dental students. Sponsors workshops and seminars; maintains governmental liaison. **Purpose:** Offers group insurance; maintains scholarship trust fund. Dental Assisting National Board examines members who are candidates for title of Certified Dental Assistant. **Publications:** *The Dental Assistant*, 5/year. • *The Dental Assistant Update*, semiannual.

★2692★ **American Dental Association (ADA)**
211 E. Chicago Ave.
Chicago, IL 60611
Ph: (312)440-2500 Fax: (312)440-7494
Members: Professional society of dentists. Encourages the improvement of the health of the public and promotes the art and science of dentistry in matters of legislation and regulations. **Purpose:** Inspects and accredits dental schools and schools for dental hygienists, assistants, and laboratory technicians. Conducts research programs at ADA Health Foundation Research Institute. Produces most of the dental health education material used in the U.S. Sponsors National Children's Dental Health Month. Compiles statistics on personnel, practice, and dental care needs and attitudes of patients with regard to dental health. Sponsors 12 councils. **Publications:** *American Dental Directory*, annual. • *Dental Teamwork*, bimonthly. • *Index to Dental Literature*, quarterly. • *Journal of the American Dental Association*, monthly. • *News*, biweekly.

★2693★ **American Medical Technologists (AMT)**
710 Higgins Rd.
Park Ridge, IL 60068
Ph: (708)823-5169 Fax: (708)823-0458
Fr: 800-275-1268
Members: National professional registry of medical laboratory technologists, technicians, medical assistants, dental assistants, and phlebotomists. **Purpose:** Maintains job information service. Sponsors AMT Institute for Education, which has developed continuing education programs. **Publications:** *AMT Events and Continuing Education Supplement*, 8/year.

★2694★ **Dental Assisting National Board (DANB)**
216 E. Ontario St.
Chicago, IL 60611
Ph: (312)642-3368
Purpose: Certifying agency that administers examinations to dental assistants.

Standards/Certification Agencies

★2695★ **American Dental Association (ADA)**
211 E. Chicago Ave.
Chicago, IL 60611
Ph: (312)440-2500
Promotes the art and science of dentistry in matters of legislation and regulations. Inspects and accredits dental schools and schools for dental hygienists, assistants, and laboratory technicians. Conducts research programs at ADA Health Foundation Research Institute. Produces most of the dental health education material used in the U.S.

★2696★ ***Dental Assistant Certification***
American Medical Technologists
710 Higgins Rd.
Park Ridge, IL 60068-5765
Ph: (708)823-5169
1991. This six-panel brochure describes the requirements for dental assistant certification.

★2697★ **Dental Assisting National Board (DANB)**
216 E. Ontario St.
Chicago, IL 60611
Ph: (312)642-3368
Certifying agency that administers examinations to dental assistants.

Test Guides

★2698★ ***Career Examination Series: Dental Assistant***
National Learning Corp.
212 Michael Dr.
Syosset, NY 11791
Ph: (516)921-8888 Fax: (516)921-8743
Fr: 800-645-6337
Jack Rudman. All examination guides in this series contain questions with answers.

★2699★ ***Certified Dental Technician (CDT)***
National Learning Corp.
212 Michael Dr.
Syosset, NY 11791
Ph: (516)921-8888 Fax: (516)921-8743
Fr: 800-645-6337
Jack Rudman. Part of the Admission Test series. A sample test for those seeking admission to graduate and professional schools or seeking entrance or advancement in institutional and public career service.

★2700★ ***Dental Assisting***
National Learning Corp.
212 Michael Dr.
Syosset, NY 11791
Ph: (516)921-8888 Fax: (516)921-8743
Fr: 800-645-6337
Jack Rudman. 1989. Part of Occupational Competency Examination Series.

★2701★ ***Essentials of Dental Radiography for Dental Assistants and Dental Hygienists***
Appleton & Lange
25 Van Zant St.
PO Box 5630
East Norwalk, CT 06855
Wolf deLyre and Orlen N. Johnson. Fourth edition, 1989. Contains information needed to pass the licensing, registration, certification, and radiation safety examinations.

★2702★ ***National Dental Assistant Boards (NDAB)***
National Learning Corp.
212 Michael Dr.
Syosset, NY 11791
Ph: (516)921-8888 Fax: (516)921-8743
Fr: 800-645-6337
Jack Rudman. 1989. Part of Admission Test Series.

★2703★ ***Self-Assessment Questions & Answers for Dental Assistants***
Butterworth-Heinemann
80 Montvale Ave.
Stoneham, MA 02180
Ph: (617)438-8464 Fax: (617)279-4851
P. L. Erridge. Second edition, 1988.

Educational Directories and Programs

★2704★ *American Dental Directory*
American Dental Association (ADA)
211 E. Chicago Ave.
Chicago, IL 60611
Ph: (312)440-2500 Fax: (312)440-7494

Annual. Lists dentists in the United States; includes biographical information.

★2705★ *Encyclopedia of Medical Organizations and Agencies*
Gale Research Inc.
835 Penobscot Bldg.
Detroit, MI 48226-4094
Ph: (313)961-2242 Fax: (313)961-6741
Fr: 800-877-GALE
Karen Boyden, Contact

Biennial, November of odd years. Covers over 13,400 state, national, and international medical associations, foundations, research institutes, federal and state agencies, and medical and allied health schools. Entries include: Organization name, address, phone; many listings include names and titles of key personnel, descriptive annotations. Arrangement: Classified by subject, then by type of organization.

★2706★ *Health & Medical Industry Directory*
American Business Directories, Inc.
5711 S. 86th Circle
Omaha, NE 68127
Ph: (402)593-4600 Fax: (402)331-1505

★2707★ *Medical and Health Information Directory*
Gale Research Inc.
835 Penobscot Bldg.
Detroit, MI 48226-4094
Ph: (313)961-2242 Fax: (313)961-6741
Fr: 800-877-GALE
Karen Boyden, Contact

Approximately biennial; latest edition 1994. Covers in Volume 1, almost 18,600 medical and health oriented associations, organizations, institutions, and government agencies, including health maintenance organizations (HMOs), preferred provider organizations (PPOs), insurance companies, pharmaceutical companies, research centers, and medical and allied health schools. In Volume 2, nearly 11,800 medical book publishers; medical periodicals, directories, audiovisual producers and services, medical libraries and information centers, and electronic resources. In Volume 3, nearly 26,000 clinics, treatment centers, care programs, and counseling/diagnostic services for 30 subject areas. Entries include: Institution, service, or firm name, address, phone; many include names of key personnel Arrangement: Classified by organization activity, service, etc..

Awards, Scholarships, Grants, and Fellowships

★2708★ American Medical Technologists Scholarships
American Medical Technologists (AMT)
710 Higgins Rd.
Park Ridge, IL 60068
Ph: (708)823-5169

Qualifications: Applicants must be high schools seniors or graduates in good standing who are planning to attend a college, university, or school accredited by the Accrediting Bureau of Health Education Schools or a regionally accredited university or college in the United States. They must be enrolled in a medical technology, medical assisting, or dental assisting program. Funds available: Five $250 awards annually. Winners must furnish proof of enrollment and good standing. Application details: Applicants must submit completed application with transcript of grades an essay on their career choice, and two letters of personal reference. Applications are available by writing to the above address. Requests should be accompanied by a legal-size, self-addressed, stamped envelope. Deadline: April 1. Winners are determined at the Annual Convention of the American Medical Technologists each summer and notified thereafter.

★2709★ Dental Assisting Scholarship Program
ADA Endowment Fund and Assistance Fund Inc
211 East Chicago Ave., 17th Fl.
Chicago, IL 60611
Ph: (312)440-2567 Fax: (312)440-2822

Purpose: To assist students entering dental assisting that need financial assistance. Qualifications: Applicant must be a U.S. citizen entering an accredited dental assisting program. Selection criteria: 2.8 GPA; 2 letters of reference; financial need; typed summary of personal/professional goals. Funds available: $1,000. Application details: Contact the Fund for guidelines and application forms. Deadline: September 1.

Basic Reference Guides and Handbooks

★2710★ *Dental Assistant Techniques*
Macmillan Publishing Company, Inc.
866 3rd Ave.
New York, NY 10022
Ph: (212)702-2000

Betty Lorenzen. 1976. Part of Allied Health Series.

★2711★ *Dental Assisting Manuals*
University of North Carolina Chapel Hill
University of North Carolina Press
116 S. Boundary St.
PO Box 2288
Chapel Hill, NC 27515-2288
Ph: (919)966-3561 Fax: 800-272-6817
Fr: 800-848-6224

Ethel M. Earl. Third edition.

★2712★ *Effective Dental Assisting*
William C. Brown Group
2460 Kerper Blvd.
Dubuque, IA 52001
Ph: (319)588-1451 Fax: 800-346-2377

Shirley Schwarzrock. 1991.

★2713★ *Essentials of Clinical Dental Assisting*
Mosby-Year Book, Inc.
11830 Westline Industrial Dr.
St. Louis, MO 63146
Ph: (314)872-8370 Fax: (314)432-1380
Fr: 800-325-4177

Joseph Chasteen. 4th edition, 1989.

★2714★ *Handbook of Expanded Dental Auxiliary Practice*
J. B. Lippincott Co.
E. Washington Square
Philadelphia, PA 19105
Ph: (215)238-4200

Francis A. Castano. 1973.

★2715★ *Modern Dental Assisting*
W. B. Saunders, Co.
Curtis Center
Independence Sq. W.
Philadelphia, PA 19106
Ph: (215)238-7800 Fr: 800-545-2522

Hazel O. Torres. Fourth edition, 1990.

★2716★ *Patient Management Skills for Dental Assistants & Hygienist*
Appleton & Lange
25 Van Zant St.
East Norwalk, CT 06855
Ph: (203)838-4400

Barbara D. Ingersoll. 1986.

Periodicals

★2717★ *Corhealth*
American Correctional Health Services Association
11 W. Monument Ave., Ste. 510
PO Box 2307
Dayton, OH 45401
Ph: (513)223-9630 Fax: (513)223-6307
H. A. Rosefield

Quarterly. "Dedicated to improving correctional health services." Covers news of the Association and its chapters and affiliates, who administer and monitor efficiency of health care in correctional institutions. Concerned with the multidisciplinary approach to nursing, dentistry, medicine, surgery, and medical administration. Recurring features include editorials, news of members, statistics, publications available, calls for papers, abstracts, book reviews, and a calendar of events.

★2718★ *Current Opinion in Dentistry*
Current Science
20 N. 3rd St.
Philadelphia, PA 19106-2113
Ph: (215)574-2266 Fax: (215)574-2270
Fr: 800-552-5866
S.T. Sonis

Quarterly. Journal for dental professionals.

★2719★ *Dental Abstracts*
Mosby-Year Book, Inc.
11830 Westline Industrial Dr.
St. Louis, MO 63146
Ph: (314)872-8370 Fax: (314)432-1380
Fr: 800-325-4177
Tracy A. Briggs

Monthly. Dentistry professional magazine.

★2720★ *The Dental Assistant*
American Dental Assistants Assn.
203 N. LaSalle St., Ste. 1320
Chicago, IL 60601-1225
Ph: (312)541-1550 Fax: (312)541-1496
Michael Shaneyfelt

Quarterly.

★2721★ *Dental Clinics of North America*
W.B. Saunders Co.
The Curtis Center
Independence Sq. W.
Philadelphia, PA 19106-3399
Ph: (215)238-7800 Fax: (215)238-6445
Susan C. Short

Quarterly. Journal reviewing current techniques in dentistry.

★2722★ *Dental Office*
Stevens Publishing Corp.
225 N. New Rd.
Waco, TX 76710
Ph: (817)776-9000 Fax: (817)776-9018
Carolyn L. Aydelotte

Bimonthly. Trade magazine for dental assistants.

★2723★ *Dental Products Report*
MEDEC Dental Communications
7400 Skokie Blvd.
Skokie, IL 60077-3339
Ph: (708)674-0110 Fax: (708)674-2991
Teri Reis-Schmidt

Professional tabloid for dentists. Covering new products, new literature, conferences, technical exhibits, aesthetic dentistry techniques, and infection-control procedures.

★2724★ *Dental Teamwork*
American Dental Association (ADA)
211 E. Chicago Ave.
Chicago, IL 60611
Ph: (312)440-2500 Fax: (312)440-7494

Bimonthly.

★2725★ *Dentistry Today*
Dentistry Today
26 Park St.
Montclair, NJ 07042
Ph: (201)783-3935 Fax: (201)783-7112
Paul F. RadcliffePublisher

Dental magazine (tabloid).

★2726★ *The Explorer*
National Association of Dental Assistants
900 S. Washington St., No. G13
Falls Church, VA 22046-4020
Ph: (703)237-8616
Sue Young

Monthly. Reflects the Association's goal of improving the professional and personal lives of dental assistants and other staff. Provides information relating to the field of dentistry.

★2727★ *Healthwire*
Federation of Nurses and Health Professionals
555 New Jersey Ave. NW
Washington, DC 20001
Ph: (202)879-4430
Priscilla M. Nemeth

Explores national news and issues affecting health care workers. Discusses general union developments as well as labor and union concerns specific to the health care field. Recurring features include local member news, book reviews, news of research, and columns titled Clipboard, Pulse Points, Stethescope, Second Opinion, and Making Rounds.

★2728★ *Index to Dental Literature*
American Dental Association (ADA)
211 E. Chicago Ave.
Chicago, IL 60611
Ph: (312)440-2500 Fax: (312)440-7494

Quarterly. Indexes worldwide literature on dentistry.

★2729★ *JADA*
ADA Publishers Inc.
211 E. Chicago Ave.
Chicago, IL 60611
Ph: (312)440-2740 Fax: (312)440-2550
James Berry

Monthly. Dental magazine.

★2730★ *Journal of the American Dental Association*
American Dental Association (ADA)
211 E. Chicago Ave.
Chicago, IL 60611
Ph: (312)440-2500 Fax: (312)440-7494

Monthly.

★2731★ *News*
American Dental Association (ADA)
211 E. Chicago Ave.
Chicago, IL 60611
Ph: (312)440-2500 Fax: (312)440-7494

Biweekly.

★2732★ *Special Care in Dentistry*
Federation of Special Care Organizations in Dentistry
211 E. Chicago Ave.
17th Fl.
Chicago, IL 60611
Ph: (312)440-2660 Fax: (312)440-7494
Roseann Mulligan

Bimonthly. Dental journal.

Other Sources of Information

★2733★ "Dental Assistant" in *Allied Health Professions* (pp. 16-17; 138)
Arco Publishing Co.
Simon & Schuster, Inc.
201 W. 103rd St.
Indianapolis, IN 46290
Ph: 800-428-5331 Fax: 800-835-3202

1993. Contains information on 28 representative careers in health care. Provides a sample of the Allied Health Professions Admission Test, lists professional societies and associations, and offers a directory of schools and programs for the careers listed.

★2734★ "Dental Assistant" in *Career Selector 2001*
Barron's Educational Series, Inc.
250 Wireless Blvd.
Hauppauge, NY 11788
Ph: (516)434-3311 Fax: (516)434-3723
Fr: 800-645-3476

James C. Gonyea. 1993.

Medical Assistants

Medical assistants help physicians examine and treat patients. Most medical assistants generalize, handling both clerical and clinical duties and reporting directly to the office manager or physician. Clinical duties include taking and recording vital signs and medical histories; explaining treatment procedures to patients; preparing patients for examination; assisting during the examination; collecting and preparing laboratory specimens or performing basic laboratory tests on the premises; disposing of contaminated supplies; sterilizing medical instruments. Other clinical duties include instructing patients about medication and special diets, authorizing drug refills as directed, telephoning prescriptions to the pharmacy, drawing blood, preparing patients for X-rays, taking EKG's, and applying dressings. They also arrange instruments and equipment in the examining room; check office and laboratory supplies; and maintain the waiting, consulting, and examination rooms in a neat and orderly condition. Administrative duties include answering the telephone, greeting patients, recording and filing patient medical records, filling out insurance forms, handling correspondences, scheduling appointments, arranging for hospital admission and laboratory services, and handling billing and bookkeeping. Some medical assistants specialize. **Podiatric medical assistants** make castings of the feet, expose and develop X-rays, and assist podiatrists at surgery in addition to handling front office responsibilities. **Ophthalmic medical assistants** help ophthalmologists provide medical eye care. They take medical histories and use precision instruments to administer diagnostic tests, measure and record vision, and test the functioning of eyes and eye muscles. They also instruct patients in the use of eye dressings, protective shields, and safety glasses, as well as in the insertion, removal, and care of contact lenses. At the direction of the physician, they may administer medications. Their responsibilities may include maintaining optical and surgery instruments and assisting the ophthalmologist in surgery.

Salaries

The salary for graduates of the medical assistant programs are as follows:

2 year or less experience	$13,715/year
Over 11 years experience	$20,885/year

Employment Outlook

Growth rate until the year 2005: Much faster than average.

Medical Assistants

CAREER GUIDES

★2735★ *Career in Ophthalmic Medical Assisting*
The Joint Commission on Allied Health Personnel in Ophthalmology
2025 Woodlane Dr.
St. Paul, MN 55125-2995
Ph: (612)731-2944 Fr: 800-284-3937

1991. This six-panel brochure describes the work, qualifications, educational preparation and certification.

★2736★ *Careers in Health Care*
Chelsea House Publishers
1974 Sproul Rd., Ste. 400
Broomall, PA 19008
Ph: (215)353-5166 Fax: (215)359-1439

Rachel S. Epstein. 1989.

★2737★ *Careers in Health Services: Opportunities for You*
Cambridge Career Products
PO Box 2153
Charleston, WV 25328-2153
Ph: (304)744-9323 Fax: (304)744-9351
Fr: 800-468-4227

Videocassette. 1989. 30 mins. This program shows the range of career opportunities in health care fields.

★2738★ "Health Care" in *Where the Jobs Are: The Hottest Careers for the 90s* (pp. 143-166)
Career Press
180 5th Ave.
Hawthorne, NJ 07507
Ph: (201)427-0229 Fax: (201)427-2037
Fr: 800-CAREER-1

Joyce Hadley. 1995. Offers a job-hunting strategy for the 1990s as well as descriptions of growing careers of the decade. Each profile includes general information, forecasts, growth, education and training, licensing requirements, and salary information.

★2739★ *Health Career Planning: A Realistic Guide*
Human Sciences Press
233 Spring St.
New York, NY 10013
Ph: (212)620-8000

Ellen F. Lederman. 1988.

★2740★ *Health Careers Today*
Mosby-Year Book, Inc.
11830 Westline Industrial Dr.
St. Louis, MO 63146
Ph: (314)872-8370 Fax: (314)432-1380
Fr: 800-325-4177

Judith A. Gerdin. 1991. Surveys health occupations. Includes information on basic health care skills and careers.

★2741★ *Introduction to the Health Professions*
Jones and Bartlett Publishers, Inc.
1 Exeter Plaza
Boston, MA 02116
Ph: (617)859-3900

Peggy Stanfield. Second edition, 1995.

★2742★ *Medical Assistant*
Vocational Biographies, Inc.
PO Box 31
Sauk Centre, MN 56378-0031
Ph: (612)352-6516 Fax: (612)352-5546
Fr: 800-255-0752

1990. This pamphlet profiles a person working in the job. Includes information about job duties, working conditions, places of employment, educational preparation, labor market outlook, and salaries.

★2743★ *Medical Assistant*
Careers, Inc.
PO Box 135
Largo, FL 34649-0135
Ph: (813)584-7333

1994. Two-page occupational summary card describing duties, working conditions, personal qualifications, training, earnings and hours, employment outlook, places of employment, related careers and where to write for more information.

★2744★ "Medical Assistant" in *150 Careers in the Health Care Field*
Reed Reference Publishing
121 Chanlon Rd.
PO Box 31
New Providence, NJ 07974
Fax: (908)665-6688 Fr: 800-521-8110

Stanley Alperin. Third edition, 1993. Each occupational profile covers job functions and responsibilities, work locations, training requirements, certification, and salaries. Lists community colleges, universities, vocational-technical schools, and other educational institutions that provide accredited training programs.

★2745★ "Medical Assistant" in *Allied Health Education Directory* (pp. 59-71)
American Medical Association (AMA)
515 N. State St.
Chicago, IL 60610
Ph: (312)464-5000 Fr: 800-621-8335

William R. Burrow, editor. 1994. Describes allied health occupations and lists educational programs accredited by the Committee on Allied Health Education and Accreditation of the American Medical Association.

★2746★ "Medical Assistant" in *Career Connection II: A Guide to Technical Majors and Their Related Careers* (pp. 110-111)
Jist Works, Inc.
720 N. Park Ave.
Indianapolis, IN 46202-3431
Ph: (317)264-3720 Fax: (317)264-3709

Fred A. Rowe. 1994. Contains technical majors, such as automotive technology. Describes the major and the job. Lists high school and postsecondary school courses. Includes occupations related to the major, employment outlook, and starting salary.

★2747★ "Medical Assistant" in *Career Information Center* (Vol.7)
Simon and Schuster
200 Old Tappan Rd.
Old Tappan, NJ 07675
Fax: 800-445-6991 Fr: 800-223-2348

Richard Lidz and Dale Anderson, editorial directors. Fifth edition, 1993. For 600 occupations, describes job duties, entry-level requirements, education and training needed, advancement possibilities, employment outlook, earnings and benefits. The set is di-

vided into 12 volumes. Each volume includes jobs related under a broad career field. Volume 13 is the index.

★2748★ "Medical Assistant" in *Careers in Health Care* (pp. 120-124)
National Textbook Co. (NTC)
VGM Career Books
4255 W. Touhy Ave.
Lincolnwood, IL 60646-1975
Ph: (708)679-5500 Fax: (708)679-2494
Fr: 800-323-4900

Barbara M. Swanson. 1995. Discusses 58 health careers, providing information about the history of the occupation, job duties, work environments, salaries, educational preparation, licensure, certification, and employment outlook.

★2749★ "Medical Assistant" in *Occu-Facts: Information on 580 Careers in Outline Form*
Careers, Inc.
PO Box 135
Largo, FL 34649-0135
Ph: (813)584-7333

Biennial, 1995-96 edition. Each one-page occupational profile describes duties, working conditions, physical surroundings and demands, aptitudes, temperament, educational requirements, employment outlook, earnings, and places of employment.

★2750★ "Medical Assistant" in *Opportunities in Health and Medical Careers* (p. 17)
National Textbook Co. (NTC)
VGM Career Books
4255 W. Touhy Ave.
Lincolnwood, IL 60646-1975
Ph: (708)679-5500 Fax: (708)679-2494
Fr: 800-323-4900

Leo D'Orazio and I. Donald Snook. 1991. Provides an overview of the health care industry with future projections. Describes a wide variety of healthcare jobs covering the nature of the work, educational requirements, employment outlook and salaries. Offers job hunting advice.

★2751★ "Medical Assistant" in *Opportunities in Paramedical Careers* (pp. 30-34)
National Textbook Co. (NTC)
VGM Career Books
4255 W. Touhy Ave.
Lincolnwood, IL 60646-1975
Ph: (708)679-5500 Fax: (708)679-2494
Fr: 800-323-4900

Alex Kacen. 1994. Describes paraprofessional careers in the health professions such as physician assistant and mental health technician. Covers job functions, educational preparation, certification, earnings, and job outlook. Lists accredited educational programs.

★2752★ "Medical Assistant in Pediatrics" in *Opportunities in Health and Medical Careers* (pp. 17-18)
National Textbook Co. (NTC)
VGM Career Books
4255 W. Touhy Ave.
Lincolnwood, IL 60646-1975
Ph: (708)679-5500 Fax: (708)679-2494
Fr: 800-323-4900

Leo D'Orazio and I. Donald Snook. 1991. Provides an overview of the health care industry with future projections. Describes a wide variety of healthcare jobs covering the nature of the work, educational requirements, employment outlook and salaries. Offers job hunting advice.

★2753★ "Medical Assistant" in *VGM's Careers Encyclopedia* (pp. 272-274)
National Textbook Co. (NTC)
VGM Career Books
4255 W. Touhy Ave.
Lincolnwood, IL 60646-1975
Ph: (708)679-5500 Fax: (708)679-2494
Fr: 800-323-4900

Third edition, 1991. Contains two- to five-page descriptions of 200 managerial, professional, technical, trade, and service occupations. Each profile includes job duties, places of employment, qualifications, educational preparation, training, employment potential, advancement, income, and additional sources of information.

★2754★ "Medical Assistant" in *VGM's Handbook of Health Care Careers*
National Textbook Co.
4255 W. Touhy Ave.
Lincolnwood, IL 60646-1975
Ph: (708)679-5500 Fax: (708)679-2494
Fr: 800-323-4900

Annette Selden. 1993. Contains 42 two-page occupational profiles describing job duties, places of employment, working conditions, qualifications, education, employment outlook, and income.

★2755★ *Medical Assistants*
Chronicle Guidance Publications, Inc.
66 Aurora St.
PO Box 1190
Moravia, NY 13118-1190
Ph: (315)497-0330 Fax: (315)497-3359
Fr: 800-622-7284

1993. This career brief describes the nature of the work, working conditions, hours and earnings, education and training, licensure, certification, unions, personal qualifications, social and psychological factors, employment outlook, entry methods, advancement, and related occupations.

★2756★ "Medical Assistants" in *America's 50 Fastest Growing Jobs* (pp. 126)
JIST Works, Inc.
720 N. Park Ave.
Indianapolis, IN 46202-3431
Ph: (317)264-3720 Fax: (317)264-3709
Fr: 800-648-5478

Michael J. Farr, compiler. 1994. Describes the 50 fastest growing jobs within major career clusters such as technicians, and marketing and sales. Each job profile explains the nature of the work, skills and abilities required, employment outlook, average earnings, related occupations, education and training requirements, and employment opportunities. Also contains career planning information and job search tips.

★2757★ "Medical Assistants" in *Career Discovery Encyclopedia* (Vol.4, pp. 74-75)
J.G. Ferguson Publishing Co.
200 W. Madison St., Ste. 300
Chicago, IL 60606
Ph: (312)580-5480 Fax: (312)580-4948

E. Russell Primm, editor-in-chief. 1993. Contains two-page articles on 504 occupations. Each article describes job duties, earnings, and educational and training requirements.

★2758★ "Medical Assistants" in *Encyclopedia of Careers and Vocational Guidance* (Vol.3, pp. 404-406)
J.G. Ferguson Publishing Co.
200 W. Madison St., Ste. 300
Chicago, IL 60606
Ph: (312)580-5480 Fax: (312)580-4948

William E. Hopke, editor-in-chief. Ninth edition, 1993. Four-volume set that profiles 500 occupations and describes job trends in 74 industries. Includes career description, educational requirements, history of the job, methods of entry, advancement, employment outlook, earnings, working conditions, social and psychological factors, and sources of additional information.

★2759★ "Medical Assistants" in *Health Care Job Explosion!* (pp. 271-279)
D-Amp Publications
401 Amherst Ave.
Coraopolis, PA 15108
Ph: (412)262-5578

Dennis V. Damp. 1993. Provides information on the nature of work for the major health care occupational groups. Descriptions include working conditions, training, job outlook, qualifications, and related occupations.

★2760★ "Medical Assistants" in *Occupational Outlook Handbook*
U.S. Government Printing Office
Superintendent of Documents
Washington, DC 20402
Ph: (202)512-1800 Fax: (202)512-2250

Biennial; latest edition, 1994-95. Encyclopedia of careers describing more than 250 occupations and comprising about 85 percent of all jobs in the economy. Occupations that require lengthy education or training are given the most attention. For each occupation, the handbook describes job duties, working conditions, training, educational preparation, personal qualities, advancement possibilities, job outlook, earnings, and sources of additional information.

★2761★ "Medical Assistants" in *The Best Jobs for the 1990s and Into the 21st Century*
Impact Publications
9104-N Manassas Dr.
Manassas Park, VA 22111
Ph: (703)361-7300 Fax: (703)335-9486

Ronald L. Krannich and Caryl Rae Krannich. 1993.

★2762★ *Medical Assisting - A Career for Today and Tomorrow*
Registered Medical Assistants (RMA)
710 Higgins Rd.
Park Ridge, IL 60068-5765
Ph: (708)823-5169

★2763★ *Medical Assisting: Today's Career for Tomorrow's Reward*
American Association of Medical Assistants
20 N. Wacker Dr., Ste. 1575
Chicago, IL 60606-2903
Ph: (312)899-1500 Fr: 800-228-2262

This six-panel brochure describes the work, educational preparation, and working conditions.

★2764★ "Medical Office Assistants" in *Jobs! What They Are—Where They Are—What They Pay* (p. 167)
Simon & Schuster, Inc.
Simon & Schuster Bldg.
1230 Avenue of the Americas
New York, NY 10020
Ph: (212)698-7000

Robert O. Snelling and Anne M. Snelling. Revised edition, 1992. Profiles 241 occupations, describing duties and responsibilities, educational preparation, earnings, employment opportunities, training, and qualifications.

★2765★ "Ophthalmic Medical Assistant" in *150 Careers in the Health Care Field*
Reed Reference Publishing
121 Chanlon Rd.
PO Box 31
New Providence, NJ 07974
Fax: (908)665-6688 Fr: 800-521-8110

Stanley Alperin. Third edition, 1993. Each occupational profile covers job functions and responsibilities, work locations, training requirements, certification, and salaries. Lists community colleges, universities, vocational-technical schools, and other educational institutions that provide accredited training programs.

★2766★ *Whatcha Gonna Do Now?*
Northern Lights Productions
276 Newbury St.
Boston, MA 02116
Ph: (617)267-0391 Fax: (617)267-8957
Fr: 800-284-6521

Videocassette. 1987. 17 mins. This video dramatically examines teenagers attitudes toward their future, including staying in school and different career choices.

Associations

★2767★ American Association of Medical Assistants (AAMA)
20 N. Wacker Dr., Ste. 1575
Chicago, IL 60606-2903
Ph: (312)899-1500 Fax: (312)899-1259

Members: Assistants, receptionists, secretaries, bookkeepers, nurses, and laboratory personnel employed in the offices of physicians and other medical facilities. Activities include a certification program consisting of study and an examination, passage of which entitles the individual to a certificate as a Certified Medical Assistant. Conducts accreditation of one- and two-year programs in medical assisting in conjunction with the Committee on Allied Health Education and Accreditation of the American Medical Association. Provides assistance and information to institutions of higher learning desirous of initiating courses for medical assistants. Offers continuing education to assistants who cannot return to school and home study courses. Awards continuing education units for selected educational programs. **Publications:** *A User's Guide to the Resource Based Relative Value Scale.* • *Accounts Receivable and Collection for the Medical Practice.* • *AIDS Concepts for Medical Assistnts — Part I.* • *Human Relations for the Medical Office.* • *Law for the Medical Office.* • *Managing Managed Care.* • *Medical Office Management — Part I.* • *PMA*, bimonthly. • *Urinalysis Today.*

★2768★ American Medical Technologists (AMT)
710 Higgins Rd.
Park Ridge, IL 60068
Ph: (708)823-5169 Fax: (708)823-0458
Fr: 800-275-1268

Members: National professional registry of medical laboratory technologists, technicians, medical assistants, dental assistants, and phlebotomists. **Purpose:** Maintains job information service. Sponsors AMT Institute for Education, which has developed continuing education programs. **Publications:** *AMT Events and Continuing Education Supplement*, 8/year.

★2769★ American Society of Podiatric Medical Assistants (ASPMA)
2124 S. Austin Blvd.
Cicero, IL 60650
Ph: (708)863-6303 Fax: (708)863-5375

Members: Podiatric assistants. **Purpose:** Purposes are to hold educational seminars and to administer certification examinations.

★2770★ Joint Commission on Allied Health Personnel in Ophthalmology (JCAHPO)
2025 Woodlane Dr.
St. Paul, MN 55125-2995
Ph: (612)731-2944 Fax: (612)731-0410
Fr: 800-284-3937

Members: A certifying agency for allied health personnel. **Purpose:** Objectives are: to encourage the establishment of medically oriented programs for training allied health personnel in ophthalmology; to develop standards of education and training in the field; to examine, certify, and recertify ophthalmic medical personnel, and encourage their continued occupational development. Conducts annual national certifying examinations and continuing education programs. **Publications:** *Directory of Certified Ophthalmic Medical Personnel*, annual. • *JCAHPO Outlook*, bimonthly.

★2771★ Registered Medical Assistants of American Medical Technologists (RMAAMT)
710 Higgins Rd.
Park Ridge, IL 60068-5765
Ph: (708)823-5169 Fax: (708)823-0458
Fr: 800-275-1268

Members: A program of the American Medical Technologists. Certified assistants to physicians in office practice, clinics, hospitals, and private health care facilities. **Purpose:** Works to establish standards of training; provides continuing education and home study programs; promotes quality care in allied health. Works with the Accrediting Bureau of Health Education Schools in regard to certification examinations and student societies. Offers group insurance programs. **Publications:** *AMT Events*, quarterly. • *AMT Events Continuing Education Supplement*, 3/year. • *Medical Assisting - A Career for Today and Tomorrow.*

Standards/Certification Agencies

★2772★ Accrediting Bureau of Health Education Schools (ABHES)
29089 U.S. 20 W.
Elkhart, IN 46514
Ph: (219)293-0124 Fax: (219)295-8564

Independent accrediting agency of the American Medical Technologists. Serves as a nationally recognized accrediting agency of health education institutions and schools conducting medical laboratory technician and medical assistant education programs. Establishes criteria and standards for the administration and operation of health education institutions. Seeks to enhance the profession through the improvement of schools, courses, and the competence of graduates. Schools must apply voluntarily for accreditation; once accredited, they must report to the bureau annually and be reexamined at least every 6 years. Has accredited 29 programs for medical laboratory technicians, 168 medical assistants, and 118 institutions of allied health.

★2773★ American Association of Medical Assistants (AAMA)
20 N. Wacker Dr., Ste. 1575
Chicago, IL 60606-2903
Ph: (312)899-1500 Fax: (312)899-1259

Activities include a certification program consisting of study and an examination, passage of which entitles the individual to a certificate as a Certified Medical Assistant. Conducts accreditation of one- and two-year programs in medical assisting in conjunction with the Committee on Allied Health Education and Accreditation of the American Medical Association.

★2774★ American Society of Podiatric Medical Assistants (ASPMA)
2124 S. Austin Blvd.
Cicero, IL 60650
Ph: (708)863-6303 Fax: (708)863-5375

Purposes are to hold educational seminars and to administer certification examinations.

★2775★ Joint Commission on Allied Health Personnel in Ophthalmology (JCAHPO)
2025 Woodlane Dr.
St. Paul, MN 55125-2995
Ph: (612)731-2944 Fax: (612)731-0410
Fr: 800-284-3937

A certifying agency for allied health personnel. Objectives are: to encourage the establishment of medically oriented programs for training allied health personnel in ophthalmology; to develop standards of education and training in the field; to examine, certify, and recertify ophthalmic medical personnel, and encourage their continued occupational development. Conducts annual national certifying examinations and continuing education programs.

★2776★ Registered Medical Assistants of American Medical Technologists (RMAAMT)
710 Higgins Rd.
Park Ridge, IL 60068-5765
Ph: (708)823-5169 Fax: (708)823-0458
Fr: 800-275-1268

Certified physician assistants in office practice, clinics, hospitals, and private health care facilities. Works to establish standards of training; provides continuing education and home study programs; promotes quality care in allied health. Works with the Accrediting Bureau of Health Education Schools in regard to certification examinations and student societies.

Test Guides

★2777★ Appleton & Lange's Review for the Surgical Technology Examination, ARCO
Appleton & Lange
25 Van Zant St.
PO Box 5630
East Norwalk, CT 06855

Nancy M. Allmers and Joan Ann Verderame. Second edition, 1987. A review for the medical assistant, this title follows the outlines established by the DACUM chart, which defines the entry level skills necessary to function effectively as a medical assistant. The second edition features 1,600 questions with answers and explanations, along with a sample Practice Test simulating the actual exam and test-taking strategies.

★2778★ Career Examination Series: Medical Aide
National Learning Corp.
212 Michael Dr.
Syosset, NY 11791
Ph: (516)921-8888 Fax: (516)921-8743
Fr: 800-645-6337

Jack Rudman. This series of examination guides from National Learning Corp. includes study guides for many medical positions, including medical assistant, medical clerk, medical equipment technician, medical inspector, medical records assistant, medical records clerk, medical stenographer, medical technical assistant, medical technician trainee, medical transcribing machine operator, and medical typist. All examination guides in this series contain questions with answers.

★2779★ Career Examination Series: Medical Assistant
National Learning Corp.
212 Michael Dr.
Syosset, NY 11791
Ph: (516)921-8888 Fax: (516)921-8743
Fr: 800-645-6337

Jack Rudman. Test guide including questions and answers for students or professionals in the field who seek advancement through examination.

★2780★ Certification Examination for Medical Assistants (CMA)
National Learning Corp.
212 Michael Dr.
Syosset, NY 11791
Ph: (516)921-8888 Fax: (516)921-8743
Fr: 800-645-6337

Jack Rudman. Part of the Admission Test Series. Books in this series provide test practice and drill for actual professional certification and licensure tests.

★2781★ Certification— Why and How
The Joint Commission on Allied Health Personnel in Ophthalmology
2025 Woodland Dr.
St. Paul, MN 55125-2995
Ph: (612)731-2944 Fr: 800-284-3937

Briefly describes certification, qualifications needed, and the certifying examinations.

★2782★ Medical Assisting
National Learning Corp.
212 Michael Dr.
Syosset, NY 11791
Ph: (516)921-8888 Fax: (516)921-8743
Fr: 800-645-6337

Jack Rudman. Part of Occupational Competency Examination Series (OCE).

Educational Directories and Programs

★2783★ Encyclopedia of Medical Organizations and Agencies
Gale Research Inc.
835 Penobscot Bldg.
Detroit, MI 48226-4094
Ph: (313)961-2242 Fax: (313)961-6741
Fr: 800-877-GALE
Karen Boyden, Contact

Biennial, November of odd years. Covers over 13,400 state, national, and international medical associations, foundations, research institutes, federal and state agencies, and medical and allied health schools. Entries include: Organization name, address, phone; many listings include names and titles of key personnel, descriptive annotations. Arrangement: Classified by subject, then by type of organization.

★2784★ Health & Medical Industry Directory
American Business Directories, Inc.
5711 S. 86th Circle
Omaha, NE 68127
Ph: (402)593-4600 Fax: (402)331-1505

★2785★ JCAHPO Outlook
Joint Commission on Allied Health Personnel in Ophthalmology (JCAHPO)
2025 Woodlane Dr.
St. Paul, MN 55125-2995
Ph: (612)731-2944

Bimonthly. Tabloid including continuing education course listings.

★2786★ Manual of the Accrediting Bureau of Health Education Schools
American Medical Technologists (AMT)
710 Higgins Rd.
Park Ridge, IL 60068
Ph: (708)823-5169

★2787★ Medical and Health Information Directory
Gale Research Inc.
835 Penobscot Bldg.
Detroit, MI 48226-4094
Ph: (313)961-2242 Fax: (313)961-6741
Fr: 800-877-GALE
Karen Boyden, Contact

Approximately biennial; latest edition 1994. Covers in Volume 1, almost 18,600 medical and health oriented associations, organizations, institutions, and government agencies, including health maintenance organizations (HMOs), preferred provider organizations (PPOs), insurance companies, pharmaceutical companies, research centers, and medical and allied health schools. In Volume 2, nearly 11,800 medical book publishers; medical periodicals, directories, audiovisual producers and services, medical libraries and information centers, and electronic resources. In Volume 3, nearly 26,000 clinics, treatment centers, care programs, and counseling/diagnostic services for 30 subject areas. Entries include: Institution, service, or firm name, address, phone; many include names of key personnel Arrangement: Classified by organization activity, service, etc..

Awards, Scholarships, Grants, and Fellowships

★2788★ American Medical Technologists Scholarships
American Medical Technologists (AMT)
710 Higgins Rd.
Park Ridge, IL 60068
Ph: (708)823-5169

Qualifications: Applicants must be high schools seniors or graduates in good standing who are planning to attend a college, university, or school accredited by the Accrediting Bureau of Health Education Schools or a regionally accredited university or college in the United States. They must be enrolled in a medical technology, medical assisting, or dental assisting program. Funds available: Five $250 awards annually. Winners must furnish proof of enrollment and good standing. Application details: Applicants must submit completed application with transcript of grades an essay on their career choice, and two letters of personal reference. Applications are available by writing to the above address. Requests should be accompanied by a legal-size, self-addressed, stamped envelope. Deadline: April 1. Winners are determined at the Annual Convention of the American Medical Technologists each summer and notified thereafter.

★2789★ Maxine Williams Scholarships
American Association of Medical Assistants' Endowment (AAMA)
20 North Wacker Dr., Ste. 1575
Chicago, IL 60606
Ph: (312)899-1500

Purpose: To support students pursuing careers as medical assistants. Qualifications: Candidate may be of any nationality. Applicant must hold a high school diploma or the equivalent and must be committed to a career as a medical assistant. Candidate must demonstrate financial need. Scholarships are tenable at postsecondary medical assistant training courses. Funds available: $500. Application details: Write to the assistant executive director for application form and guidelines. Submit form with letter of recommendation from the medical assisting program director with most recent transcripts, reasons for wanting to become a medical assistant, and a statement of financial need. Deadline: 1 February, 1 June. Candidates will be notified six weeks after the deadline.

Periodicals

★2790★ *Accounts Receivable and Collection for the Medical Practice*
American Association of Medical Assistants (AAMA)
20 N. Wacker Dr., Ste. 1575
Chicago, IL 60606-2903
Ph: (312)899-1500 Fax: (312)899-1259

★2791★ *AIDS Concepts for Medical Assistnts — Part I*
American Association of Medical Assistants (AAMA)
20 N. Wacker Dr., Ste. 1575
Chicago, IL 60606-2903
Ph: (312)899-1500 Fax: (312)899-1259

★2792★ *AMT Events*
Registered Medical Assistants of American Medical Technologists (RMAAMT)
710 Higgins Rd.
Park Ridge, IL 60068-5765
Ph: (708)823-5169 Fax: (708)823-0458
Fr: 800-275-1268

Quarterly. Includes state chapter news, legislative updates, and book reviews.

★2793★ *AMT Events and Continuing Education Supplement*
American Medical Technologists (AMT)
710 Higgins Rd.
Park Ridge, IL 60068
Ph: (708)823-5169 Fax: (708)823-0458
Fr: 800-275-1268

8/year. Includes book reviews and legislative updates.

★2794★ *Breathline*
American Society of Post Anesthesia Nurses
11512 Allecingie Pkwy.
Richmond, VA 23235
Ph: (804)379-5516 Fax: (804)379-1386
Nancy Burden

Bimonthly. Publishes news of the Society, which is "an organization of licensed nurses engaged in the practice of post anesthesia patient care." Carries legislative updates, scientific articles, and state component society information. Discusses patient care standards, new drugs and treatments, and clinical issues relating to anesthesia and surgery. Recurring features include a calendar of events and columns titled Comment, Keeping Up, Resource Review, President's Message, Ambulatory Surgery, Manager's Minute, and Certification Corner.

★2795★ *Computers & Medicine*
Carol Brierly
PO Box 36
Glencoe, IL 60022
Ph: (708)446-3100
Carol Brierly

Monthly. Covers news and ideas on using computers in the health field for diagnosis, treatment, education, and other purposes. Discusses the social and behavioral implications of computer technology, the utilization of artificial intelligence, and similar considerations. Recurring features include reviews of pertinent articles and books, news of research, and a calendar of events.

★2796★ *Corhealth*
American Correctional Health Services Association
11 W. Monument Ave., Ste. 510
PO Box 2307
Dayton, OH 45401
Ph: (513)223-9630 Fax: (513)223-6307
H. A. Rosefield

Quarterly. "Dedicated to improving correctional health services." Covers news of the Association and its chapters and affiliates, who administer and monitor efficiency of health care in correctional institutions. Concerned with the multidisciplinary approach to nursing, dentistry, medicine, surgery, and medical administration. Recurring features include editorials, news of members, statistics, publications available, calls for papers, abstracts, book reviews, and a calendar of events.

★2797★ *Healthwire*
Federation of Nurses and Health Professionals
555 New Jersey Ave. NW
Washington, DC 20001
Ph: (202)879-4430
Priscilla M. Nemeth

Explores national news and issues affecting health care workers. Discusses general union developments as well as labor and union concerns specific to the health care field. Recurring features include local member news, book reviews, news of research, and columns titled Clipboard, Pulse Points, Stethescope, Second Opinion, and Making Rounds.

★2798★ *Human Relations for the Medical Office*
American Association of Medical Assistants (AAMA)
20 N. Wacker Dr., Ste. 1575
Chicago, IL 60606-2903
Ph: (312)899-1500 Fax: (312)899-1259

★2799★ *Law for the Medical Office*
American Association of Medical Assistants (AAMA)
20 N. Wacker Dr., Ste. 1575
Chicago, IL 60606-2903
Ph: (312)899-1500 Fax: (312)899-1259

★2800★ *Managing Managed Care*
American Association of Medical Assistants (AAMA)
20 N. Wacker Dr., Ste. 1575
Chicago, IL 60606-2903
Ph: (312)899-1500 Fax: (312)899-1259

★2801★ *Medical Office Management — Part I*
American Association of Medical Assistants (AAMA)
20 N. Wacker Dr., Ste. 1575
Chicago, IL 60606-2903
Ph: (312)899-1500 Fax: (312)899-1259

★2802★ *PMA*
American Association of Medical Assistants (AAMA)
20 N. Wacker Dr., Ste. 1575
Chicago, IL 60606-2903
Ph: (312)899-1500 Fax: (312)899-1259

Bimonthly. Includes association news, index of advertisers, continuing education articles, and calendar of events.

★2803★ *Urinalysis Today*
American Association of Medical Assistants (AAMA)
20 N. Wacker Dr., Ste. 1575
Chicago, IL 60606-2903
Ph: (312)899-1500 Fax: (312)899-1259

★2804★ *A User's Guide to the Resource Based Relative Value Scale*
American Association of Medical Assistants (AAMA)
20 N. Wacker Dr., Ste. 1575
Chicago, IL 60606-2903
Ph: (312)899-1500 Fax: (312)899-1259

MEETINGS AND CONVENTIONS

★2805★ American Association of Medical Assistants Regional Conferences
American Association of Medical Assistants
20 N. Wacker Dr., Ste. 1575
Chicago, IL 60606-2903
Ph: (312)899-1500 Fr: 800-228-2262

Annual.

★2806★ AMT Educational Program and National Meeting
Registered Medical Assistants of American Medical Technologists (RMAAMT)
710 Higgins Rd.
Park Ridge, IL 60068-5765
Ph: (708)823-5169 Fax: (708)823-0458
Fr: 800-275-1268

Annual. Always summer.

★2807★ National Medical Assistant Week
Registered Medical Assistants of American Medical Technologists (RMAAMT)
710 Higgins Rd.
Park Ridge, IL 60068-5765
Ph: (708)823-5169 Fax: (708)823-0458
Fr: 800-275-1268

Annual.

★2808★ Physician Assistants Annual Conference
American Academy of Physician Assistants
950 N. Washington St.
Arlington, 22314-1552
Ph: (703)836-2272 Fax: (703)684-1924

Annual. **Dates and Locations:** 1996 May 25-30; New York, NY.

Nursing Aides and Psychiatric Aides

Nursing aides and psychiatric aides help care for physically or mentally ill, injured, disabled, or infirm individuals confined to hospitals, long term care facilities such as nursing homes, and mental health settings. Nursing aides are sometimes known as nursing assistants or hospital attendants, and work under the supervision of registered and licensed practical nurses. Nursing aides employed in nursing homes are sometimes called geriatric aides and, like nursing aides, work under the supervision of registered and licensed practical nurses. Psychiatric aides, also known as **mental health assistants, psychiatric nursing assistants**, or **ward attendants**, care for mentally impaired or emotionally disturbed individuals. They work under a team that may include psychiatrists, psychologists, psychiatric nurses, social workers, and therapists. Almost half of all nursing aides work in nursing homes, and about 25 percent work in hospitals and state and county mental institutions. Almost all psychiatric aides work in psychiatric hospitals, state and county mental institutions, or private psychiatric facilities.

Salaries

Annual earnings of nursing and psychiatric aides are as follows:

Lowest 10 percent	$9,500/year or less
Middle 50 percent	$11,000--$$17,900/year
Top 10 percent	$23,900/year or more

Employment Outlook

Growth rate until the year 2005: Much faster than average.

Nursing Aides and Psychiatric Aides

CAREER GUIDES

★2809★ ***Being a Long-Term Care Nursing Assistant***
Prentice Hall
Rte. 9W
Englewood Cliffs, NJ 07632
Ph: (201)592-2000

Connie A. Will-Black and Judith B. Eighmy. Fourth edition, 1996.

★2810★ ***Careers in Health Care***
Chelsea House Publishers
1974 Sproul Rd., Ste. 400
Broomall, PA 19008
Ph: (215)353-5166 Fax: (215)359-1439

Rachel S. Epstein. 1989.

★2811★ **"Geriatric Aide" in *Career Information Center* (Vol.11)**
Simon and Schuster
200 Old Tappan Rd.
Old Tappan, NJ 07675
Fax: 800-445-6991 Fr: 800-223-2348

Richard Lidz and Dale Anderson, editorial directors. Fifth edition, 1993. For 600 occupations, describes job duties, entry-level requirements, education and training needed, advancement possibilities, employment outlook, earnings and benefits. The set is divided into 12 volumes. Each volume includes jobs related under a broad career field. Volume 13 is the index.

★2812★ ***Health Career Planning: A Realistic Guide***
Human Sciences Press
233 Spring St.
New York, NY 10013
Ph: (212)620-8000

Ellen F. Lederman. 1988.

★2813★ ***Health Careers Today***
Mosby-Year Book, Inc.
11830 Westline Industrial Dr.
St. Louis, MO 63146
Ph: (314)872-8370 Fax: (314)432-1380
Fr: 800-325-4177

Judith A. Gerdin. 1991. Surveys health occupations. Includes information on basic health care skills and careers.

★2814★ ***Hospital Attendant***
Careers, Inc.
PO Box 135
Largo, FL 34649-0135
Ph: (813)584-7333

1995. Two-page job guide card describing duties, working conditions, personal qualifications, training, earnings and hours, employment outlook, places of employment, related careers and where to write for more information.

★2815★ **"Hospital Attendant" in *Occu-Facts: Information on 580 Careers in Outline Form***
Careers, Inc.
PO Box 135
Largo, FL 34649-0135
Ph: (813)584-7333

Biennial, 1995-96 edition. Each one-page occupational profile describes duties, working conditions, physical surroundings and demands, aptitudes, temperament, educational requirements, employment outlook, earnings, and places of employment.

★2816★ **"Hospital Attendants" in *Career Discovery Encyclopedia* (Vol.3, pp. 102-103)**
J.G. Ferguson Publishing Co.
200 W. Madison St., Ste. 300
Chicago, IL 60606
Ph: (312)580-5480 Fax: (312)580-4948

E. Russell Primm, editor-in-chief. 1993. Contains two-page articles on 504 occupations. Each article describes job duties, earnings, and educational and training requirements.

★2817★ ***Introduction to the Health Professions***
Jones and Bartlett Publishers, Inc.
1 Exeter Plaza
Boston, MA 02116
Ph: (617)859-3900

Peggy Stanfield. Second edition, 1995.

★2818★ **"Mental Health Technician/ Human Services Technician/Psychiatric Aide" in *150 Careers in the Health Care Field***
Reed Reference Publishing
121 Chanlon Rd.
PO Box 31
New Providence, NJ 07974
Fax: (908)665-6688 Fr: 800-521-8110

Stanley Alperin. Third edition, 1993. Each occupational profile covers job functions and responsibilities, work locations, training requirements, certification, and salaries. Lists community colleges, universities, vocational-technical schools, and other educational institutions that provide accredited training programs.

★2819★ ***Nursery and Landscape Workers***
Careers, Inc.
PO Box 135
Largo, FL 34649-0135
Ph: (813)584-7333

1994. Two-page occupational summary card describing duties, working conditions, personal qualifications, training, earnings and hours, employment outlook, places of employment, related careers and where to write for more information.

★2820★ **"Nurse's Aide" in *100 Best Careers for the Year 2000* (pp. 17-19)**
Arco Pub.
201 W. 103rd St.
Indianapolis, IN 46290
Ph: 800-428-5331 Fax: 800-835-3202

Shelly Field. 1992. Describes 100 job opportunities expected to grow fast throughout the next decade. Provides information on job duties and responsibilities, training requirements, education, advancement opportunities, experience and qualifications, and typical salaries.

★2850★ *Career Examination Series: Nurse's Aide*
National Learning Corp.
212 Michael Dr.
Syosset, NY 11791
Ph: (516)921-8888 Fax: (516)921-8743
Fr: 800-645-6337

Jack Rudman. 1989. All examination guides in this series contain questions with answers.

★2851★ *Career Examination Series: Nursing Assistant*
National Learning Corp.
212 Michael Dr.
Syosset, NY 11791
Ph: (516)921-8888 Fax: (516)921-8743
Fr: 800-645-6337

Jack Rudman. 1989. All examination guides in this series contain questions with answers.

★2852★ *Career Examination Series: Psychiatric Therapy Aide*
National Learning Corp.
212 Michael Dr.
Syosset, NY 11791
Ph: (516)921-8888 Fax: (516)921-8743
Fr: 800-645-6337

Jack Rudman. Includes study guides for many health-related careers. All examination guides in this series contain questions with answers.

★2853★ *Civil Service Tests for Basic Skills Jobs*
Prentice Hall Press
Simon & Schuster Inc.
200 Old Tappan Rd.
Old Tappan, NJ 07675
Ph: 800-223-2348

Hy Hammer. First edition, 1985. Contains nine sample examinations to prepare candidates for entry-level positions that include hospital attendant, building groundskeeper, and custodial assistant, among others.

Educational Directories and Programs

★2854★ *Encyclopedia of Medical Organizations and Agencies*
Gale Research Inc.
835 Penobscot Bldg.
Detroit, MI 48226-4094
Ph: (313)961-2242 Fax: (313)961-6741
Fr: 800-877-GALE
Karen Boyden, Contact

Biennial, November of odd years. Covers over 13,400 state, national, and international medical associations, foundations, research institutes, federal and state agencies, and medical and allied health schools. Entries include: Organization name, address, phone; many listings include names and titles of key personnel, descriptive annotations. Arrangement: Classified by subject, then by type of organization.

★2855★ *Health & Medical Industry Directory*
American Business Directories, Inc.
5711 S. 86th Circle
Omaha, NE 68127
Ph: (402)593-4600 Fax: (402)331-1505

★2856★ *Medical and Health Information Directory*
Gale Research Inc.
835 Penobscot Bldg.
Detroit, MI 48226-4094
Ph: (313)961-2242 Fax: (313)961-6741
Fr: 800-877-GALE
Karen Boyden, Contact

Approximately biennial; latest edition 1994. Covers in Volume 1, almost 18,600 medical and health oriented associations, organizations, institutions, and government agencies, including health maintenance organizations (HMOs), preferred provider organizations (PPOs), insurance companies, pharmaceutical companies, research centers, and medical and allied health schools. In Volume 2, nearly 11,800 medical book publishers; medical periodicals, directories, audiovisual producers and services, medical libraries and information centers, and electronic resources. In Volume 3, nearly 26,000 clinics, treatment centers, care programs, and counseling/diagnostic services for 30 subject areas. Entries include: Institution, service, or firm name, address, phone; many include names of key personnel Arrangement: Classified by organization activity, service, etc..

★2857★ *Nursing Aides and Psychiatric Aides*
Accrediting Bureau of Health Education
Oak Manor Office
29089 U.S. 20 W.
Elkhart, IN 46514
Ph: (219)293-0124

1991. State-by-state listing of schools offering nurse aide training programs. Lists address, phone number, and contact person.

Awards, Scholarships, Grants, and Fellowships

★2858★ Nurse Education Scholarships
American Association of Homes for the Aging
901 E. St. NW, Ste. 500
Washington, DC 20004-2037
Ph: (202)783-2242 Fax: (202)783-2255

Purpose: To provide financial support to nursing assistants pursuing careers in the field of long-term care nursing. Qualifications: Applicants must have been accepted for future or current enrollment in an accredited LPN or RN program and must be presently employed as nursing assistants in an American Association of Homes for the Aging (AAHA) member organization. They also must pledge to practice nursing skills at an AAHA member facility for at least one year upon successful completion of the courses. Selection criteria: Selections based on applicant's merit as a future asset to the long-term care industry, the letters of acceptance from the LPN or RN schools, and letters of recommendation. Selections are not based on financial need. Funds available: One $1,000 scholarship; five $750 scholarships; ten $500 scholarships. None of the scholarships are renewable. Application details: Applicants must submit an official application available from AAHA's Office of Educational Services. They must also submit letters of recommendation from the Director of Nursing of the facility in which the applicant is currently employed and the direct supervisor at the same facility, and a character reference from a teacher, counselor, pastor, rabbi, or facility administrator. References from family members are not accepted. The three references must be filled out and returned by the persons completing them.

Basic Reference Guides and Handbooks

★2859★ *A Clinical Manual for Nursing Assistants*
Jones & Bartlett Publishers, Inc.
1 Exeter Plaza
Boston, MA 02116
Ph: (617)859-3900

Sharon McClelland. 1985.

★2860★ *Geriatric Nursing Assistants: An Annotated Bibliography with Models to Enhance Practice*
Greenwood Publishing Group, Inc.
88 Post Rd., W.
PO Box 5007
Westport, CT 06881
Ph: (203)226-3571 Fax: (203)222-1502

George H. Weber. 1991. Part of Bibliographies & Indexes in Gerontology Series.

★2861★ *Mosby's Textbook for Nursing Assistants*
Mosby-Year Book, Inc.
11830 Westline Industrial Dr.
St. Louis, MO 63146
Ph: (314)872-8370 Fax: (314)432-1380
Fr: 800-325-4177

Sorrentino. Third edition, 1991.

★2862★ *Successful Nurse Aide Management in Nursing Homes*
Oryx Press
4041 N. Central at Indian School Rd., Ste. 700
Phoenix, AZ 85012-3397
Ph: (602)265-2651 Fax: 800-279-4663
Fr: 800-279-6799

Joann M. Day, editor. 1989.

★2863★ *Textbook for Nursing Assistants*
Mosby-Year Book, Inc.
11830 Westline Industrial Dr.
St. Louis, MO 63146
Ph: (314)872-8370 Fax: (314)432-1380
Fr: 800-325-4177

Sorretino. Second edition, 1988.

PERIODICALS

★2864★ *AHANews*
American Hospital Association (AHA)
1 N. Franklin, Ste. 27
Chicago, IL 60606
Ph: (312)422-3000 Fax: (312)422-4796
Weekly.

★2865★ *AHCA Notes*
American Health Care Association (AHCA)
1201 L St. NW
Washington, DC 20005
Ph: (202)842-4444 Fax: (202)842-3860
Monthly. Covers legislation and regulations.

★2866★ *Breathline*
American Society of Post Anesthesia Nurses
11512 Allecingie Pkwy.
Richmond, VA 23235
Ph: (804)379-5516 Fax: (804)379-1386
Nancy Burden
Bimonthly. Publishes news of the Society, which is "an organization of licensed nurses engaged in the practice of post anesthesia patient care." Carries legislative updates, scientific articles, and state component society information. Discusses patient care standards, new drugs and treatments, and clinical issues relating to anesthesia and surgery. Recurring features include a calendar of events and columns titled Comment, Keeping Up, Resource Review, President's Message, Ambulatory Surgery, Manager's Minute, and Certification Corner.

★2867★ *Computers & Medicine*
Carol Brierly
PO Box 36
Glencoe, IL 60022
Ph: (708)446-3100
Carol Brierly
Monthly. Covers news and ideas on using computers in the health field for diagnosis, treatment, education, and other purposes. Discusses the social and behavioral implications of computer technology, the utilization of artificial intelligence, and similar considerations. Recurring features include reviews of pertinent articles and books, news of research, and a calendar of events.

★2868★ *Corhealth*
American Correctional Health Services Association
11 W. Monument Ave., Ste. 510
PO Box 2307
Dayton, OH 45401
Ph: (513)223-9630 Fax: (513)223-6307
H. A. Rosefield
Quarterly. "Dedicated to improving correctional health services." Covers news of the Association and its chapters and affiliates, who administer and monitor efficiency of health care in correctional institutions. Concerned with the multidisciplinary approach to nursing, dentistry, medicine, surgery, and medical administration. Recurring features include editorials, news of members, statistics, publications available, calls for papers, abstracts, book reviews, and a calendar of events.

★2869★ *Guide to the Health Care Field*
American Hospital Association (AHA)
1 N. Franklin, Ste. 27
Chicago, IL 60606
Ph: (312)422-3000 Fax: (312)422-4796
Annual.

★2870★ *Healthwire*
Federation of Nurses and Health Professionals
555 New Jersey Ave. NW
Washington, DC 20001
Ph: (202)879-4430
Priscilla M. Nemeth
Explores national news and issues affecting health care workers. Discusses general union developments as well as labor and union concerns specific to the health care field. Recurring features include local member news, book reviews, news of research, and columns titled Clipboard, Pulse Points, Stethescope, Second Opinion, and Making Rounds.

★2871★ *Hospital Statistics*
American Hospital Association (AHA)
1 N. Franklin, Ste. 27
Chicago, IL 60606
Ph: (312)422-3000 Fax: (312)422-4796
Annual.

★2872★ *Hospitals and Health Networks*
American Hospital Association (AHA)
1 N. Franklin, Ste. 27
Chicago, IL 60606
Ph: (312)422-3000 Fax: (312)422-4796
Biweekly.

★2873★ *The Nightingale*
National Association of Physician Nurses
900 S. Washington St., No. G13
Falls Church, VA 22046-4020
Ph: (703)237-8616
Sue Young
Monthly. Presents items on "medical and personal subjects pertaining to office nurses and other staff."

★2874★ *Provider: For Long Term Care Professionals*
American Health Care Association (AHCA)
1201 L St. NW
Washington, DC 20005
Ph: (202)842-4444 Fax: (202)842-3860
Monthly. Includes buyers' guide, news reports, advertisers' index, a listing of new products and services, and calendar of events.

★2875★ *Quickening*
American College of Nurse-Midwives
818 Connecticut Ave., No. 900
Washington, DC 20006
Ph: (202)289-0171
Charles Honaker
Bimonthly. Promotes the training and certification of nurse-midwives. Recurring features include membership, board and convention news, announcements of relevant meetings and workshops, help-wanted items, and lists of significant publications.

★2876★ *Thinking About a Nursing Home?*
American Health Care Association (AHCA)
1201 L St. NW
Washington, DC 20005
Ph: (202)842-4444 Fax: (202)842-3860

★2877★ *Welcome to Our Nursing Home*
American Health Care Association (AHCA)
1201 L St. NW
Washington, DC 20005
Ph: (202)842-4444 Fax: (202)842-3860

OTHER SOURCES OF INFORMATION

★2878★ *Caring for the Alzheimer's Resident: A Day in the Life of Nancy Moore*
Terra Nova Films
9848 S. Winchester Ave.
Chicago, IL 60643
Ph: (312)881-8491 Fax: (312)881-3368
Fr: 800-779-8491
1992. See how a real nurse's aide gets through a day on the job. Motivating and informative, both students and family members can learn valuable lessons.

★2879★ "Nurse's Aide" in *Career Selector 2001*
Barron's Educational Series, Inc.
250 Wireless Blvd.
Hauppauge, NY 11788
Ph: (516)434-3311 Fax: (516)434-3723
Fr: 800-645-3476
James C. Gonyea. 1993.

Animal Caretakers, except Farm

Animal caretakers, sometimes called **animal attendants**, feed, water, groom, bathe, and exercise animals and clean and repair their cages. They also provide social interaction for the animals with play and companionship. Job titles and duties of caretakers vary by employment setting. People who specialize in maintaining dogs' appearance are called **dog groomers**. Some groomers work in kennels and others operate their own grooming business. **Veterinary technicians**, also known as **animal health technicians**, keep records, take specimens, perform laboratory tests, prepare animals and instruments for surgery, take and develop radiographs, dress wounds, and assist the veterinarian with examinations and surgery. **Veterinary assistants** feed and bathe the animals, administer medication as prescribed by the veterinarian, and assist the veterinarian and veterinary technician in the treatment of the animal. Animal attendants clean cages, exercise the animals, and monitor the animals for symptoms of illnesses. **Laboratory animal technologists** supervise the daily care and maintenance of animals by a technician and assistant; they may also assist in surgical care and other laboratory procedures. The animal laboratory technician provides the daily care of animals--giving prescribed dosages and medications, taking specimens, performing laboratory tests, and assisting with minor surgery. Technicians also keep daily records of the animals' diets, behavior, and health. The assistant laboratory animal technician sanitizes cages and feeds the animals. **Zookeepers** prepare the diets, clean the enclosures, and monitor the behavior of exotic animals. Keepers sometimes assist in research studies, train animals, and put on special shows and give lectures to the public. Caretakers are employed at kennels, animal shelters, pet stores, stables, veterinary facilities, laboratories, and zoological parks.

Salaries

Weekly salaries of caretakers is $250.

Employment Outlook

Growth rate until the year 2005: Faster than average.

Animal Caretakers except Farm

Career Guides

★2880★ *Animal Care Attendant*
Careers, Inc.
PO Box 135
Largo, FL 34649-0135
Ph: (813)584-7333

1992. Two-page job guide card describing duties, working conditions, personal qualifications, training, earnings and hours, employment outlook, places of employment, related careers and where to write for more information.

★2881★ "Animal Care Attendant" in *Careers for Animal Lovers and Other Zoological Types* (pp. 17-19)
National Textbook Co. (NTC)
VGM Career Books
4255 W. Touhy Ave.
Lincolnwood, IL 60646-1975
Ph: (708)679-5500 Fax: (708)679-2494
Fr: 800-323-4900

Louise Miller. 1991. Surveys a wide range of career opportunities working with animals in both the public and profit sectors. Lists job titles and describes qualifications, salaries, benefits, educational requirements, employment outlook, and places of employment. Includes animal trainers and handlers, animal-related businesses, and animal writers, photographers, and illustrators.

★2882★ "Animal Care Attendant" in *Occu-Facts: Information on 580 Careers in Outline Form*
Careers, Inc.
PO Box 135
Largo, FL 34649-0135
Ph: (813)584-7333

Biennial, 1995-96 edition. Each one-page occupational profile describes duties, working conditions, physical surroundings and demands, aptitudes, temperament, educational requirements, employment outlook, earnings, and places of employment.

★2883★ "Animal Caretaker" in *150 Careers in the Health Care Field*
Reed Reference Publishing
121 Chanlon Rd.
PO Box 31
New Providence, NJ 07974
Fax: (908)665-6688 Fr: 800-521-8110

Stanley Alperin. Third edition, 1993. Profiles health care occupations requiring a bachelor's degree or less. Describes the nature of the work, educational preparation, licensing requirements, and salary. Lists accredited educational programs.

★2884★ "Animal Caretaker" in *Career Information Center* (Vol.8)
Simon and Schuster
200 Old Tappan Rd.
Old Tappan, NJ 07675
Fax: 800-445-6991 Fr: 800-223-2348

Richard Lidz and Dale Anderson, editorial directors. Fifth edition, 1993. For 600 occupations, describes job duties, entry-level requirements, education and training needed, advancement possibilities, employment outlook, earnings and benefits. The set is divided into 12 volumes. Each volume includes jobs related under a broad career field. Volume 13 is the index.

★2885★ *Animal Caretakers*
Chronicle Guidance Publications, Inc.
66 Aurora St.
PO Box 1190
Moravia, NY 13118-1190
Ph: (315)497-0330 Fax: (315)497-3359
Fr: 800-622-7284

1994. This career brief describes the nature of the work, working conditions, hours and earnings, education and training, licensure, certification, unions, personal qualifications, social and psychological factors, employment outlook, entry methods, advancement, and related occupations.

★2886★ "Animal Caretakers, except Farm" in *America's 50 Fastest Growing Jobs* (pp. 112)
JIST Works, Inc.
720 N. Park Ave.
Indianapolis, IN 46202-3431
Ph: (317)264-3720 Fax: (317)264-3709
Fr: 800-648-5478

Michael J. Farr, compiler. 1994. Describes the 50 fastest growing jobs within major career clusters such as technicians, and marketing and sales. Each job profile explains the nature of the work, skills and abilities required, employment outlook, average earnings, related occupations, education and training requirements, and employment opportunities. Also contains career planning information and job search tips.

★2887★ "Animal Caretakers, except Farm" in *Occupational Outlook Handbook*
U.S. Government Printing Office
Superintendent of Documents
Washington, DC 20402
Ph: (202)512-1800 Fax: (202)512-2250

Biennial; latest edition, 1994-95. Encyclopedia of careers describing more than 250 occupations and comprising about 85 percent of all jobs in the economy. Occupations that require lengthy education or training are given the most attention. For each occupation, the handbook describes job duties, working conditions, training, educational preparation, personal qualities, advancement possibilities, job outlook, earnings, and sources of additional information.

★2888★ "Animal Health Technicians" in *Career Discovery Encyclopedia* (Vol.1, pp. 46-47)
J.G. Ferguson Publishing Co.
200 W. Madison St., Ste. 300
Chicago, IL 60606
Ph: (312)580-5480 Fax: (312)580-4948

E. Russell Primm, editor-in-chief. 1993. Contains two-page articles on 504 occupations. Each article describes job duties, earnings, and educational and training requirements.

★2889★ "Animal Health Technicians" in *Encyclopedia of Careers and Vocational Guidance* (Vol.2, pp. 79-83)
J.G. Ferguson Publishing Co.
200 W. Madison St., Ste. 300
Chicago, IL 60606
Ph: (312)580-5480 Fax: (312)580-4948

William E. Hopke, editor-in-chief. Ninth edition, 1993. Four-volume set that profiles 500 occupations and describes job trends in 74 industries. Includes career description, educational requirements, history of the job, methods of entry, advancement, employment outlook, earnings, working conditions, social

and psychological factors, and sources of additional information.

★2890★ *Animal Technicians*
Chronicle Guidance Publications, Inc.
66 Aurora St.
PO Box 1190
Moravia, NY 13118-1190
Ph: (315)497-0330 Fax: (315)497-3359
Fr: 800-622-7284

1987. This career brief describes the nature of the work, working conditions, hours and earnings, education and training, licensure, certification, unions, personal qualifications, social and psychological factors, employment outlook, entry methods, advancement, and related occupations.

★2891★ "Animal Technicians and Other Paramedical Personnel" in *Opportunities in Veterinary Medicine* (pp. 115-116)
National Textbook Co. (NTC)
VGM Career Books
4255 W. Touhy Ave.
Lincolnwood, IL 60646-1975
Ph: (708)679-5500 Fax: (708)679-2494
Fr: 800-323-4900

Robert E. Swope. 1987. Discusses history, educational requirements, and employment opportunities for veterinarians in industry, government, academia, and the military.

★2892★ "Animal Technology" in *150 Careers in the Health Care Field*
Reed Reference Publishing
121 Chanlon Rd.
PO Box 31
New Providence, NJ 07974
Fax: (908)665-6688 Fr: 800-521-8110

Stanley Alperin. Third edition, 1993. Each occupational profile covers job functions and responsibilities, work locations, training requirements, certification, and salaries. Lists community colleges, universities, vocational-technical schools, and other educational institutions that provide accredited training programs.

★2893★ "Animal Trainers/Handlers" in *Jobs! What They Are—Where They Are—What They Pay* (pp. 48)
Fireside
Simon & Schuster Bldg.
1230 Avenue of the Americas
New York, NY 10020
Ph: (212)698-7000 Fr: 800-223-2348

Robert O. Snelling and Anne M. Snelling. Revised and updated, 1992. Describes duties and responsibilities, earnings, employment opportunities, training, and qualifications.

★2894★ *Careers Working With Animals: An Introduction to Occupational Opportunities in Animal Welfare . . .*
Acropolis Books
11741 Bowman Greene Dr.
Reston, VA 22090
Ph: (703)709-0006 Fax: (703)709-0942

Guy R. Hodge. 1979.

★2895★ *Careers at a Zoo*
Lerner Publications Co.
241 First Ave., N.
Minneapolis, MN 55401
Fax: (612)332-7615 Fr: 800-328-4920

Mark Lerner. 1980. Describes 15 careers at a zoo, including zoo keeper and animal commissary keeper.

★2896★ *The Challenge of a Lifetime: Careers in Animal Science*
American Association for Laboratory Animal Science
17 Timber Creek Dr., Ste. 5
Cordova, TN 38018
Ph: (901)754-8620

This 10-page booklet surveys careers in animal laboratory science. Covers entry-level positions and places of employment.

★2897★ *Dog Groomer*
Careers, Inc.
PO Box 135
Largo, FL 34649-0135
Ph: (813)584-7333

1991. Two-page occupational summary card describing duties, working conditions, personal qualifications, training, earnings and hours, employment outlook, places of employment, related careers and where to write for more information.

★2898★ "Dog Groomer" in *Occu-Facts: Information on 580 Careers in Outline Form*
Careers, Inc.
PO Box 135
Largo, FL 34649-0135
Ph: (813)584-7333

Biennial, 1995-96 edition. Each one-page occupational profile describes duties, working conditions, physical surroundings and demands, aptitudes, temperament, educational requirements, employment outlook, earnings, and places of employment.

★2899★ *Dog Groomers*
Chronicle Guidance Publications, Inc.
66 Aurora St.
PO Box 1190
Moravia, NY 13118-1190
Ph: (315)497-0330 Fax: (315)497-3359
Fr: 800-622-7284

1993. This career brief describes the nature of the work, working conditions, hours and earnings, education and training, licensure, certification, unions, personal qualifications, social and psychological factors, employment outlook, entry methods, advancement, and related occupations.

★2900★ "Dog Groomers" in *Career Discovery Encyclopedia* (Vol.2, pp. 118-119)
J.G. Ferguson Publishing Co.
200 W. Madison St., Ste. 300
Chicago, IL 60606
Ph: (312)580-5480 Fax: (312)580-4948

E. Russell Primm, editor-in-chief. 1993. Contains two-page articles on 504 occupations. Each article describes job duties, earnings, and educational and training requirements.

★2901★ "Dog Groomers" in *Encyclopedia of Careers and Vocational Guidance* (Vol.2, pp. 498-501)
J.G. Ferguson Publishing Co.
200 W. Madison St., Ste. 300
Chicago, IL 60606
Ph: (312)580-5480 Fax: (312)580-4948

William E. Hopke, editor-in-chief. Ninth edition, 1993. Four-volume set that profiles 500 occupations and describes job trends in 74 industries. Includes career description, educational requirements, history of the job, methods of entry, advancement, employment outlook, earnings, working conditions, social and psychological factors, and sources of additional information.

★2902★ "Laboratory Animal Care Worker" in *Career Information Center* (Vol.7)
Simon and Schuster
200 Old Tappan Rd.
Old Tappan, NJ 07675
Fax: 800-445-6991 Fr: 800-223-2348

Richard Lidz and Dale Anderson, editorial directors. Fifth edition, 1993. For 600 occupations, describes job duties, entry-level requirements, education and training needed, advancement possibilities, employment outlook, earnings and benefits. The set is divided into 12 volumes. Each volume includes jobs related under a broad career field. Volume 13 is the index.

★2903★ "Pet Care Worker" in *Career Information Center* (Vol.5)
Simon and Schuster
200 Old Tappan Rd.
Old Tappan, NJ 07675
Fax: 800-445-6991 Fr: 800-223-2348

Richard Lidz and Dale Anderson, editorial directors. Fifth edition, 1993. For 600 occupations, describes job duties, entry-level requirements, education and training needed, advancement possibilities, employment outlook, earnings and benefits. The set is divided into 12 volumes. Each volume includes jobs related under a broad career field. Volume 13 is the index.

★2904★ "Pet Care Worker" in *Personal Services* (pp. 45-49)
Franklin Watts, Inc.
387 Park Avenue, S.
New York, NY 10016
Ph: (212)686-7070

Linda Barrett and Galen Guengerich. 1991. Surveys personal services jobs. Describes job duties, educational preparation, salaries, and employment outlook. Offers job hunting advice.

★2905★ "Pet Grooming" in *Careers for Animal Lovers and Other Zoological Types* (pp. 59-61)
National Textbook Co. (NTC)
VGM Career Books
4255 W. Touhy Ave.
Lincolnwood, IL 60646-1975
Ph: (708)679-5500 Fax: (708)679-2494
Fr: 800-323-4900

Louise Miller. 1991. Surveys a wide range of career opportunities working with animals in both the public and profit sectors. Lists job titles and describes qualifications, salaries, benefits, educational requirements, employment outlook, and places of employment. Includes animal trainers and handlers, animal-related businesses, and animal writers, photographers, and illustrators.

★2906★ "Resolution, Personal Services and Transportation Careers" in *The Best Jobs for the 1990s and Into the 21st Century*
Impact Publications
9104-N Manassas Dr.
Manassas Park, VA 22111
Ph: (703)361-7300 Fax: (703)335-9486

Ronald L. Krannich and Caryl Rae Krannich. 1993. Includes information on a wide variety of careers including adjusters, investigators, and collectors, animal caretakers, electricians, services sales reps., and truck drivers.

★2907★ "Veterinary Technician" in *Careers for Animal Lovers and Other Zoological Types* (pp. 15-17)
National Textbook Co. (NTC)
VGM Career Books
4255 W. Touhy Ave.
Lincolnwood, IL 60646-1975
Ph: (708)679-5500 Fax: (708)679-2494
Fr: 800-323-4900

Louise Miller. 1991. Surveys a wide range of career opportunities working with animals in both the public and profit sectors. Lists job titles and describes qualifications, salaries, benefits, educational requirements, employment outlook, and places of employment. Includes animal trainers and handlers, animal-related businesses, and animal writers, photographers, and illustrators.

★2908★ "Veterinary Technician" in *Careers in Veterinary Medicine*
Rosen Publishing Group
29 E. 21st St.
New York, NY 10010
Ph: (212)777-3017 Fax: (212)777-0277
Fr: 800-237-9932

Jane Caryl Duncan. 1994. Surveys job opportunities for veterinarians in teaching, private practice, private industry, and zoos. Covers educational preparation, the nature of the work, salaries, licensure, and continuing education.

★2909★ "Veterinary Technicians and Assistants" in *Jobs! What They Are—Where They Are—What They Pay* (p. 54)
Simon & Schuster, Inc.
Simon & Schuster Bldg.
1230 Avenue of the Americas
New York, NY 10020
Ph: (212)698-7000

Robert O. Snelling and Anne M. Snelling. Revised edition, 1992. Profiles 241 occupations, describing duties and responsibilities, educational preparation, earnings, employment opportunities, training, and qualifications.

★2910★ *Your Career in Veterinary Technology*
American Veterinary Medical Association
930 N. Mecham Rd.
Schaumburg, IL 60196-1074
Ph: (708)605-8070

1989. This eight-panel brochure describes the work, places of employment, educational preparation, personal attributes, and earnings of veterinary medical technologists.

★2911★ "Zookeeper" in *Careers for Animal Lovers and Other Zoological Types* (pp. 90-93)
National Textbook Co. (NTC)
VGM Career Books
4255 W. Touhy Ave.
Lincolnwood, IL 60646-1975
Ph: (708)679-5500 Fax: (708)679-2494
Fr: 800-323-4900

Louise Miller. 1991. Surveys a wide range of career opportunities working with animals in both the public and profit sectors. Lists job titles and describes qualifications, salaries, benefits, educational requirements, employment outlook, and places of employment. Includes animal trainers and handlers, animal-related businesses, and animal writers, photographers, and illustrators.

Associations

★2912★ American Association for Laboratory Animal Science (AALAS)
70 Timber Creek, Ste. 5
Cordova, TN 38018
Ph: (901)754-8620 Fax: (901)753-0046

Members: Persons and institutions professionally concerned with the production, use, care, and study of laboratory animals. **Purpose:** Serves as clearinghouse for collection and exchange of information on all phases of laboratory animal care and management and on the care, use, and procurement of laboratory animals used in biomedical research. Conducts examinations and certification through its Animal Technician Certification Program. **Publications:** *American Association for Laboratory Animal Science—Membership Directory*, annual. • *Contemporary Topics in Laboratory Animal Science*, bimonthly. • *Laboratory Animal Science*, bimonthly.

★2913★ American Boarding Kennels Association (ABKA)
4575 Galley Rd., No. 400A
Colorado Springs, CO 80915
Ph: (719)591-1113 Fax: (719)597-0006

Members: Persons or firms that board pets; kennel suppliers; others interested in the boarding kennel industry. **Purpose:** Seeks to upgrade the industry through educational programs, seminars and conventions. Provides insurance plans for members and supplies pet care information to the public. Promotes code of ethics and accreditation program for recognition and training of superior kennel operators. Compiles statistics. **Publications:** *Boarderline Newsletter*, bimonthly. • *Pet Services Journal*, bimonthly.

★2914★ Humane Society of the United States (HSUS)
2100 L St. NW
Washington, DC 20037
Ph: (202)452-1100 Fax: (202)778-6132

Members: Purpose: Promotes public education to foster respect, understanding, and compassion for all creatures. Programs include: reducing the overbreeding of cats and dogs and promoting responsible pet ownership; eliminating cruelty in hunting and trapping; exposing and eliminating painful uses of animals in research and testing; eliminating the abuse of animals in movies, television productions, circuses, and competitive events such as dogfights, racing, pulling contests, and shows; correcting inhumane conditions for animals in zoos, menageries, pet shops, puppy mills, and kennels; stopping cruelty in the raising, handling, and transporting of animals used for food; addressing critical environmental issues in terms of their impact on animals and humans; protecting endangered wildlife and marine mammals; making national wildlife refuges and parks into true sanctuaries for wildlife; halting the cruelty and destruction of the international trade in wildlife, especially exotic birds and elephant ivory; campaigns to create public awareness and rejection of harvested or farm-raised fur-bearing animals. Campaigns for or against legislation affecting animal protection and monitors enforcement of existing animal protection statutes; works with animal control agencies and local humane societies to establish effective and humane programs. Assists local humane societies in improving their administrative, organizational, and sheltering techniques. Sponsors HSUS Animal Control Academy and the National Association for Humane and Environmental Education. **Publications:** *Animal Activist Alert*, quarterly. • *HSUS Close-Up Reports*, quarterly. • *HSUS News*, quarterly. • *Kind News*. • *Kind Teacher*, annual. • *Shelter Sense*, 10/year.

★2915★ National Dog Groomers Association of America (NDGAA)
Box 101
Clark, PA 16113
Ph: (412)962-2711 Fax: (412)962-1919

Members: Dog groomers and supply distributors organized to upgrade the profession. **Purpose:** Conducts state and local workshops; sponsors competitions and certification testing. Makes groomer referrals. **Publications:** *Convention Manual*, annual. • *Groomers Voice*, quarterly.

Standards/Certification Agencies

★2916★ American Association for Laboratory Animal Science (AALAS)
70 Timber Creek, Ste. 5
Cordova, TN 38018
Ph: (901)754-8620 Fax: (901)753-0046

Conducts examinations and certification through its Animal Technician Certification Program.

★2917★ **American Boarding Kennels Association (ABKA)**
4575 Galley Rd., No. 400A
Colorado Springs, CO 80915
Ph: (719)591-1113 Fax: (719)597-0006
Promotes code of ethics and accreditation program for recognition and training of superior kennel operators. Compiles statistics.

★2918★ **National Dog Groomers Association of America (NDGAA)**
Box 101
Clark, PA 16113
Ph: (412)962-2711 Fax: (412)962-1919
Conducts state and local workshops; sponsors competitions and certification testing.

Test Guides

★2919★ ***Career Examination Series: Animal Caretaker***
National Learning Corp.
212 Michael Dr.
Syosset, NY 11791
Ph: (516)921-8888 Fax: (516)921-8743
Fr: 800-645-6337
Jack Rudman. Includes study guides for animal caretaker, animal health aide, and animal warden. All examination guides in this series contain questions with answers.

★2920★ ***Career Examination Series: Animal Health Aide***
National Learning Corp.
212 Michael Dr.
Syosset, NY 11791
Ph: (516)921-8888 Fax: (516)921-8743
Fr: 800-645-6337
Jack Rudman. All examination guides in this series contain questions with answers.

★2921★ ***Career Examination Series: Animal Warden***
National Learning Corp.
212 Michael Dr.
Syosset, NY 11791
Ph: (516)921-8888 Fax: (516)921-8743
Fr: 800-645-6337
Jack Rudman. All examination guides in this series contain questions with answers.

★2922★ ***Career Examination Series: Dog Warden***
National Learning Corp.
212 Michael Dr.
Syosset, NY 11791
Ph: (516)921-8888 Fax: (516)921-8743
Fr: 800-645-6337
Jack Rudman. All examination guides in this series contain questions with answers.

★2923★ ***Career Examination Series: Senior Dog Warden***
National Learning Corp.
212 Michael Dr.
Syosset, NY 11791
Ph: (516)921-8888 Fax: (516)921-8743
Fr: 800-645-6337
Jack Rudman. All examination guides in this series contain questions with answers.

Awards, Scholarships, Grants, and Fellowships

★2924★ **Excellence in Zookeeping Award**
American Association of Zoo Keepers
Topeka Zoological Park
635 Gage Blvd.
Topeka, KS 66606
Ph: (913)272-5821
To recognize an individual for achievement and determination in the zookeeping field, and to foster professionalism. Full-time zookeepers employed for at least two years in any North American zoo or aquarium may be nominated by June 1. A certificate, a letter to the institution's director, and national recognition by professional journals are awarded annually at the AAZK Conference. Established in 1974 to honor zoologist R. Marlin Perkins.

Basic Reference Guides and Handbooks

★2925★ ***NDGAA Convention Manual***
National Dog Groomers Association of America (NDGAA)
Box 101
Clark, PA 16113
Ph: (412)962-2711 Fax: (412)962-1919
Annual.

Periodicals

★2926★ ***American Association for Laboratory Animal Science—Membership Directory***
American Association for Laboratory Animal Science (AALAS)
70 Timber Creek, Ste. 5
Cordova, TN 38018
Ph: (901)754-8620 Fax: (901)753-0046
Annual. Arranged alphabetically by name and geographically.

★2927★ ***Animal Activist Alert***
Humane Society of the United States (HSUS)
2100 L St. NW
Washington, DC 20037
Ph: (202)452-1100 Fax: (202)778-6132
Quarterly. Covers animal legislation.

★2928★ ***Boarderline Newsletter***
American Boarding Kennels Association (ABKA)
4575 Galley Rd., No. 400A
Colorado Springs, CO 80915
Ph: (719)591-1113 Fax: (719)597-0006
Bimonthly.

★2929★ ***Contemporary Topics in Laboratory Animal Science***
American Association for Laboratory Animal Science (AALAS)
70 Timber Creek, Ste. 5
Cordova, TN 38018
Ph: (901)754-8620 Fax: (901)753-0046
Bimonthly. Contains refereed papers covering topics in laboratory animal science; covers association activities.

★2930★ ***Convention Manual***
National Dog Groomers Association of America (NDGAA)
Box 101
Clark, PA 16113
Ph: (412)962-2711 Fax: (412)962-1919
Annual.

★2931★ ***Groomers Voice***
National Dog Groomers Association of America (NDGAA)
Box 101
Clark, PA 16113
Ph: (412)962-2711 Fax: (412)962-1919
Quarterly. Includes information on shows, new grooming techniques, and new products. Contains workshop and certification test sites and dates.

★2932★ ***HSUS Close-Up Reports***
Humane Society of the United States (HSUS)
2100 L St. NW
Washington, DC 20037
Ph: (202)452-1100 Fax: (202)778-6132
Quarterly. Covers critical problems affecting animals.

★2933★ ***HSUS News***
Humane Society of the United States (HSUS)
2100 L St. NW
Washington, DC 20037
Ph: (202)452-1100 Fax: (202)778-6132
Quarterly. Covers society activities.

★2934★ ***International Society for Animal Rights—Report***
International Society for Animal Rights, Inc.
421 S. State St.
Clarks Summit, PA 18411
Ph: (717)586-2200 Fax: (717)586-9580
Lynn Manheim
Reports on programs undertaken by the Society, on legislative issues affecting animals, and on news of the national and international field of animal rights.

★2935★ ***Kind News***
Humane Society of the United States (HSUS)
2100 L St. NW
Washington, DC 20037
Ph: (202)452-1100 Fax: (202)778-6132

★2936★ ***Kind Teacher***
Humane Society of the United States (HSUS)
2100 L St. NW
Washington, DC 20037
Ph: (202)452-1100 Fax: (202)778-6132
Annual. Contains educational program information and activities for teachers and students.

★2937★ *Laboratory Animal Science*
American Association for Laboratory Animal Science (AALAS)
70 Timber Creek, Ste. 5
Cordova, TN 38018
Ph: (901)754-8620 Fax: (901)753-0046

Bimonthly. Covers comparative and experimental medicine related to laboratory animal science.

★2938★ *Pet Services Journal*
American Boarding Kennels Association (ABKA)
4575 Galley Rd., No. 400A
Colorado Springs, CO 80915
Ph: (719)591-1113 Fax: (719)597-0006

Bimonthly. Covers animal care and business management, with statistics and association news. Includes kennel profiles.

★2939★ *Shelter Sense*
Humane Society of the United States (HSUS)
2100 L St. NW
Washington, DC 20037
Ph: (202)452-1100 Fax: (202)778-6132

10/year. For individuals employed in or concerned with community animal control.

★2940★ *Veterinary Technician*
Veterinary Learning Systems
8717 W. 110th St., Ste. 160
Shawnee Mission, KS 66210
Ph: (913)451-3475 Fax: (913)451-3929
Richard B. Ford

Official journal of the North American Veterinary Technician Association. Published for veterinary technicians, nurses, and assistants.

Meetings and Conventions

★2941★ American Animal Hospital Association Annual Meeting
American Animal Hospital Association
PO Box 150899
Denver, CO 80215-0899
Ph: (303)986-2800 Fax: (303)986-1700
Fr: 800-252-2242

Annual. Always held during March or April.

★2942★ American Humane Association Annual Meeting and Training Conference/Animal Protection
American Humane Association
63 Inverness Dr., E.
Englewood, CO 80112-5117
Ph: (303)792-9900 Fax: (303)792-5333

Annual. Usually held during October.

★2943★ Pet Services Annual Connecticut and Trade Show
American Boarding Kennels Association (ABKA)
4575 Galley Rd., No. 400A
Colorado Springs, CO 80915
Ph: (719)591-1113 Fax: (719)597-0006

Annual. Always fall.

Other Sources of Information

★2944★ "Animal Caretaker" in *Career Selector 2001*
Barron's Educational Series, Inc.
250 Wireless Blvd.
Hauppauge, NY 11788
Ph: (516)434-3311 Fax: (516)434-3723
Fr: 800-645-3476

James C. Gonyea. 1993.

Barbers and Cosmetologists

The basic job of barbers and cosmetologists is to help people look their best. **Barbers** cut, trim, shampoo, and style hair; they also offer hair and scalp treatments, shaves, and facial massages. They may also provide additional services, such as hairstyling and permanents. They cut and style hair to suit each customer and may color or straighten hair and fit hairpieces. **Cosmetologists** primarily shampoo, cut, and style hair. They also may lighten or darken hair color, give manicures, supply scalp and facial treatments, provides makeup analysis, and clean and style wigs and hairpieces.

Salaries

Barbers and cosmetologists generally earn between $20,000 and $30,000/year, including tips.

Employment Outlook

Growth rate until the year 2005: Faster than average.

Barbers and Cosmetologists

Career Guides

★2945★ *Barber*
Vocational Biographies, Inc.
PO Box 31
Sauk Centre, MN 56378-0031
Ph: (612)352-6516 Fax: (612)352-5546
Fr: 800-255-0752

1994. This pamphlet profiles a person working in the job. Includes information about job duties, working conditions, places of employment, educational preparation, labor market outlook, and salaries.

★2946★ *Barber*
Careers, Inc.
PO Box 135
Largo, FL 34649-0135
Ph: (813)584-7333

1994. Two-page occupational summary card describing duties, working conditions, personal qualifications, training, earnings and hours, employment outlook, places of employment, related careers and where to write for more information.

★2947★ "Barber and Hairstylist" in *Career Information Center* (Vol.5)
Simon and Schuster
200 Old Tappan Rd.
Old Tappan, NJ 07675
Fax: 800-445-6991 Fr: 800-223-2348

Richard Lidz and Dale Anderson, editorial directors. Fifth edition, 1993. For 600 occupations, describes job duties, entry-level requirements, education and training needed, advancement possibilities, employment outlook, earnings and benefits. The set is divided into 12 volumes. Each volume includes jobs related under a broad career field. Volume 13 is the index.

★2948★ "Barber" in *Occu-Facts: Information on 580 Careers in Outline Form*
Careers, Inc.
PO Box 135
Largo, FL 34649-0135
Ph: (813)584-7333

Biennial, 1995-96 edition. Each one-page occupational profile describes duties, working conditions, physical surroundings and demands, aptitudes, temperament, educational requirements, employment outlook, earnings, and places of employment.

★2949★ *Barber-Stylists*
Chronicle Guidance Publications, Inc.
66 Aurora St.
PO Box 1190
Moravia, NY 13118-1190
Ph: (315)497-0330 Fax: (315)497-3359
Fr: 800-622-7284

1993. This career brief describes the nature of the work, working conditions, hours and earnings, education and training, licensure, certification, unions, personal qualifications, social and psychological factors, employment outlook, entry methods, advancement, and related occupations.

★2950★ "Barbers and Cosmetologists" in *American Almanac of Jobs and Salaries* (pp. 530)
Avon Books
1350 Avenue of the Americas
New York, NY 10019
Ph: (212)261-6800 Fr: 800-238-0658

John Wright, editor. Revised and updated, 1994-95. A comprehensive guide to the wages of hundreds of occupations in a wide variety of industries and organizations.

★2951★ "Barbers and Cosmetologists" in *Occupational Outlook Handbook*
U.S. Government Printing Office
Superintendent of Documents
Washington, DC 20402
Ph: (202)512-1800 Fax: (202)512-2250

Biennial; latest edition, 1994-95. Encyclopedia of careers describing more than 250 occupations and comprising about 85 percent of all jobs in the economy. Occupations that require lengthy education or training are given the most attention. For each occupation, the handbook describes job duties, working conditions, training, educational preparation, personal qualities, advancement possibilities, job outlook, earnings, and sources of additional information.

★2952★ "Barbers" in *Encyclopedia of Careers and Vocational Guidance* (Vol.2, pp. 163-165)
J.G. Ferguson Publishing Co.
200 W. Madison St., Ste. 300
Chicago, IL 60606
Ph: (312)580-5480 Fax: (312)580-4948

William E. Hopke, editor-in-chief. Ninth edition, 1993. Four-volume set that profiles 500 occupations and describes job trends in 74 industries. Includes career description, educational requirements, history of the job, methods of entry, advancement, employment outlook, earnings, working conditions, social and psychological factors, and sources of additional information.

★2953★ "Barbers" in *Opportunities in Vocational and Technical Careers* (pp. 76-77)
National Textbook Co. (NTC)
VGM Career Books
4255 W. Touhy Ave.
Lincolnwood, IL 60646-1975
Ph: (708)679-5500 Fax: (708)679-2494
Fr: 800-323-4900

Adrian A. Paradis. 1992. Describes careers which can be prepared for by attending a private vocational or proprietary school—office employee, sales worker, service worker, health services, mechanic, craftworker, and technician. Covers employment outlook, job duties, and salaries. Offers career planning advice.

★2954★ "Beautician" in *How to Get a Job With a Cruise Line* (p. 4)
Ticket to Adventure, Inc.
8800 49th St., N., Ste. 410, Rm. 3
Pinellas Park, FL 34666
Ph: (813)544-0066

Mary Fallon Miller. 1991. Explores jobs with cruise ships, describing duties, responsibilities, benefits, and training. Lists cruise ship lines and schools offering cruise line training. Offers job hunting advice.

★2955★ *Career Insights*
RMI Media Productions, Inc.
1365 N. Winchester
Olathe, KS 66061
Ph: (913)768-1696 Fax: 800-755-6910
Fr: 800-745-5480

Videocassette series. 1987. This videotape series describes 50 occupations, including skill requirements and interviews with people employed in these fields. Occupations include: flight service, air transportation/ground services, data processing, carpentry, clerk in banking/insurance/business, cosmetic personal grooming, firefighting, forestry, insulation/roofing, mechanics, material handling, photographic processing, pipefitting and plumbing, printing, secretarial services, tool and die operations.

★2956★ *A Career for Looking Good, Feeling Great*
National Association of Accredited Cosmetology Schools
5201 Leesburg Pike, Ste. 205
Falls Church, VA 22041
Ph: (703)845-1333

This six-panel brochure surveys cosmetology related jobs and offers tips on judging the quality of a cosmetology school.

★2957★ *Career Success Series*
Cambridge Educational
PO Box 2153
Charleston, WV 25328-2153
Ph: (304)744-9323 Fax: (304)744-9351
Fr: 800-468-4227

Videocassette. 1986. 15 mins. A series, available separately, outlining various career choices for students. Occupations include: accounting, flight service, air transportation/ground/flight service, data processing, carpentry, clerk in banking/insurance, commodity sales, cosmetic personal grooming, fire fighting, forestry services, home economics, insulation/roofing, material handling, mechanics, photographic processing, pipefitting and plumbing, police science, printing, carpentry, medical laboratory technicians, secretarial services, and utilities equipment operator.

★2958★ *Careers in Beauty Culture*
Rosen Publishing Group
29 E. 21st St.
New York, NY 10010
Ph: (212)777-3017 Fax: (212)777-0277
Fr: 800-237-9932

Barbara L. Johnson. 1989. Discusses job opportunities for cosmetologists. Describes personal characteristics, training, licensing requirements, working conditions, advancement opportunities, employment outlook, and advantages and disadvantages of the job. Offers advice on job hunting and succeeding on the job. Contains information on owning a salon.

★2959★ *Cosmetic and Personal Services*
Morris Video
2730 Monterey St., No. 105
Monterey Business Park
Torrance, CA 90503
Ph: (310)533-4800 Fr: 800-843-3606

Videocassette. 1985. 15 mins. Occupations involving cosmetology, hair styling and manicures are covered.

★2960★ "Cosmetologist" in *Career Information Center* (Vol.5)
Simon and Schuster
200 Old Tappan Rd.
Old Tappan, NJ 07675
Fax: 800-445-6991 Fr: 800-223-2348

Richard Lidz and Dale Anderson, editorial directors. Fifth edition, 1993. For 600 occupations, describes job duties, entry-level requirements, education and training needed, advancement possibilities, employment outlook, earnings and benefits. The set is divided into 12 volumes. Each volume includes jobs related under a broad career field. Volume 13 is the index.

★2961★ "Cosmetologist" in *Occu-Facts: Information on 580 Careers in Outline Form*
Careers, Inc.
PO Box 135
Largo, FL 34649-0135
Ph: (813)584-7333

Biennial, 1995-96 edition. Each one-page occupational profile describes duties, working conditions, physical surroundings and demands, aptitudes, temperament, educational requirements, employment outlook, earnings, and places of employment.

★2962★ "Cosmetologist" in *VGM's Careers Encyclopedia* (pp. 122-124)
National Textbook Co. (NTC)
VGM Career Books
4255 W. Touhy Ave.
Lincolnwood, IL 60646-1975
Ph: (708)679-5500 Fax: (708)679-2494
Fr: 800-323-4900

Third edition, 1991. Contains two- to five-page descriptions of 200 managerial, professional, technical, trade, and service occupations. Each profile includes job duties, places of employment, qualifications, educational preparation, training, employment potential, advancement, income, and additional sources of information.

★2963★ *Cosmetologists*
Chronicle Guidance Publications, Inc.
66 Aurora St.
PO Box 1190
Moravia, NY 13118-1190
Ph: (315)497-0330 Fax: (315)497-3359
Fr: 800-622-7284

1987. This career brief describes the nature of the work, working conditions, hours and earnings, education and training, licensure, certification, unions, personal qualifications, social and psychological factors, employment outlook, entry methods, advancement, and related occupations.

★2964★ "Cosmetologists: Beauty Preservers" in *Careers for Women Without College Degrees* (pp. 254-257)
McGraw-Hill Publishing Co.
11 W. 19th St.
New York, NY 10011
Ph: (212)337-6010

Beatryce Nivens. 1988. Career planning and job hunting guide containing information on decision-making, skills assessment, and resumes for career changers. Profiles careers with the best occupational outlook. Describes the work, educational preparation, employment outlook, salaries, and required skills.

★2965★ "Cosmetologists" in *Career Discovery Encyclopedia* (Vol.2, pp. 64-65)
J.G. Ferguson Publishing Co.
200 W. Madison St., Ste. 300
Chicago, IL 60606
Ph: (312)580-5480 Fax: (312)580-4948

E. Russell Primm, editor-in-chief. 1993. Contains two-page articles on 504 occupations. Each article describes job duties, earnings, and educational and training requirements.

★2966★ "Cosmetologists" in *Encyclopedia of Careers and Vocational Guidance* (Vol.2, pp. 396-398)
J.G. Ferguson Publishing Co.
200 W. Madison St., Ste. 300
Chicago, IL 60606
Ph: (312)580-5480 Fax: (312)580-4948

William E. Hopke, editor-in-chief. Ninth edition, 1993. Four-volume set that profiles 500 occupations and describes job trends in 74 industries. Includes career description, educational requirements, history of the job, methods of entry, advancement, employment outlook, earnings, working conditions, social and psychological factors, and sources of additional information.

★2967★ "Cosmetologists" in *Opportunities in Vocational and Technical Careers* (pp. 76-90)
National Textbook Co. (NTC)
VGM Career Books
4255 W. Touhy Ave.
Lincolnwood, IL 60646-1975
Ph: (708)679-5500 Fax: (708)679-2494
Fr: 800-323-4900

Adrian A. Paradis. 1987. Describes careers which can be prepared for by attending a private vocational or proprietary school—office employee, sales worker, service worker, health services, mechanic, craftworker, and technician. Covers employment outlook, job duties, and salaries. Offers career planning advice.

★2968★ "Cosmetology and Barbering" in *Career Connection II: A Guide to Technical Majors and Their Related Careers* (pp. 44-45)
Jist Works, Inc.
720 N. Park Ave.
Indianapolis, IN 46202-3431
Ph: (317)264-3720 Fax: (317)264-3709

Fred A. Rowe. 1994. Contains technical majors, such as automotive technology. Describes the major and the job. Lists high school and postsecondary school courses. Includes occupations related to the major, employment outlook, and starting salary.

★2969★ *Cosmetology . . . Excellent Opportunities . . .*
National Cosmetology Association, Inc.
3510 Olive St.
St. Louis, MO 63103
Ph: (314)534-7980

This two-page leaflet surveys job opportunities for cosmetologists as salon managers, owners and teachers. Outlines preferred personal characteristics and licensure requirements. Offers advice on selecting a cosmetology school.

★2970★ "Electrologist" in *Career Information Center* (Vol.5)
Simon and Schuster
200 Old Tappan Rd.
Old Tappan, NJ 07675
Fax: 800-445-6991 Fr: 800-223-2348
Richard Lidz and Dale Anderson, editorial directors. Fifth edition, 1993. For 600 occupations, describes job duties, entry-level requirements, education and training needed, advancement possibilities, employment outlook, earnings and benefits. The set is divided into 12 volumes. Each volume includes jobs related under a broad career field. Volume 13 is the index.

★2971★ *Electrologists*
Chronicle Guidance Publications, Inc.
66 Aurora St.
PO Box 1190
Moravia, NY 13118-1190
Ph: (315)497-0330 Fax: (315)497-3359
Fr: 800-622-7284
1991. This career brief describes the nature of the work, working conditions, hours and earnings, education and training, licensure, certification, unions, personal qualifications, social and psychological factors, employment outlook, entry methods, advancement, and related occupations.

★2972★ "Electrologists" in *Encyclopedia of Careers and Vocational Guidance* (Vol.2, pp. 559-561)
J.G. Ferguson Publishing Co.
200 W. Madison St., Ste. 300
Chicago, IL 60606
Ph: (312)580-5480 Fax: (312)580-4948
William E. Hopke, editor-in-chief. Ninth edition, 1993. Four-volume set that profiles 500 occupations and describes job trends in 74 industries. Includes career description, educational requirements, history of the job, methods of entry, advancement, employment outlook, earnings, working conditions, social and psychological factors, and sources of additional information.

★2973★ *Face Painter*
Vocational Biographies, Inc.
PO Box 31
Sauk Centre, MN 56378-0031
Ph: (612)352-6516 Fax: (612)352-5546
Fr: 800-255-0752
1992. Four-page pamphlet containing a personal narrative about a worker's job, work likes and dislikes, career path from high school to the present. Education and training, the rewards and frustrations, and the effects of the job on the rest of the worker's life. The data file portion of this pamphlet gives a concise occupational summary, including work descriptions, working conditions, places of employment, personal characteristics, education and training, job outlook, and salary range.

★2974★ *Getting Down to Business: Hair Styling Shop*
American Institutes for Research in the Behavioral Sciences
PO Box 1113
Palo Alto, CA 94302
Ph: (415)493-3550 Fax: (415)858-0958
Joyce P. Gall. 1981.

★2975★ "Hair Stylist" in *Career Opportunities in Television, Cable, and Video* (pp. 140-141)
Facts on File
460 Park Ave. S.
New York, NY 10016-7382
Ph: (212)683-2244 Fax: 800-678-3633
Fr: 800-322-8755
Third edition, 1990. Describes 100 media-related jobs. Each occupational profile covers job duties, employment outlook, career paths, salaries, skills, and educational preparation. Offers tips for entering the field.

★2976★ "Hairdresser" in *Great Careers for People Who Like to Work with Their Hands* (pp. 43)
Gale Research Inc.
835 Penobscot Bldg.
Detroit, MI 48226
Ph: (313)961-2242 Fr: 800-347-4253
1994.

★2977★ "Hairdressers" in *Jobs! What They Are—Where They Are—What They Pay* (p. 350)
Simon & Schuster, Inc.
Simon & Schuster Bldg.
1230 Avenue of the Americas
New York, NY 10020
Ph: (212)698-7000
Robert O. Snelling and Anne M. Snelling. Revised edition, 1992. Profiles 241 occupations, describing duties and responsibilities, educational preparation, earnings, employment opportunities, training, and qualifications.

★2978★ "Hairstylist" in *100 Best Careers for the Year 2000* (pp. 200-204)
Arco Pub.
201 W. 103rd St.
Indianapolis, IN 46290
Ph: 800-428-5331 Fax: 800-835-3202
Shelly Field. 1992. Describes 100 job opportunities expected to grow fast throughout the next decade. Provides information on job duties and responsibilities, training requirements, education, advancement opportunities, experience and qualifications, and typical salaries.

★2979★ "Hairstylist" in *Guide to Careers Without College* (pp. 100-102)
Franklin Watts, Inc.
387 Park Avenue, S.
New York, NY 10016
Ph: (212)686-7070
Kathleen S. Abrams. 1988. Discusses careers that do not require a college degree in fields such as health care, sales and marketing, and the building trades. Describes the work, employment opportunities, and training.

★2980★ *Hairstylist/Salon Owner*
Vocational Biographies, Inc.
PO Box 31
Sauk Centre, MN 56378-0031
Ph: (612)352-6516 Fax: (612)352-5546
Fr: 800-255-0752
1993. Four-page pamphlet containing a personal narrative about a worker's job, work likes and dislikes, career path from high school to the present. Education and training, the rewards and frustrations, and the effects of the job on the rest of the worker's life. The data file portion of this pamphlet gives a concise occupational summary, including work descriptions, working conditions, places of employment, personal characteristics, education and training, job outlook, and salary range.

★2981★ *Makeup Artist/Modeling Coach*
Vocational Biographies, Inc.
PO Box 31
Sauk Centre, MN 56378-0031
Ph: (612)352-6516 Fax: (612)352-5546
Fr: 800-255-0752
1994. This pamphlet profiles a person working in the job. Includes information about job duties, working conditions, places of employment, educational preparation, labor market outlook, and salaries.

★2982★ *Manicurist*
Careers, Inc.
PO Box 135
Largo, FL 34649-0135
Ph: (813)584-7333
1995. Two-page job guide card describing duties, working conditions, personal qualifications, training, earnings and hours, employment outlook, places of employment, related careers and where to write for more information.

★2983★ "Manicurist" in *Occu-Facts: Information on 580 Careers in Outline Form*
Careers, Inc.
PO Box 135
Largo, FL 34649-0135
Ph: (813)584-7333
Biennial, 1995-96 edition. Each one-page occupational profile describes duties, working conditions, physical surroundings and demands, aptitudes, temperament, educational requirements, employment outlook, earnings, and places of employment.

★2984★ *Manicurists and Nail Technicians*
Chronicle Guidance Publications, Inc.
66 Aurora St.
PO Box 1190
Moravia, NY 13118-1190
Ph: (315)497-0330 Fax: (315)497-3359
Fr: 800-622-7284
1993. This career brief describes the nature of the work, working conditions, hours and earnings, education and training, licensure, certification, unions, personal qualifications, social and psychological factors, employment outlook, entry methods, advancement, and related occupations.

★2985★ *Personal Service Cluster*
Center for Humanities, Inc.
Communications Park
Box 1000
Mount Kisco, NY 10549
Ph: (914)666-4100 Fax: (914)666-5319
Fr: 800-431-1242
Videocassette. 1984. 20 mins. Students get to see the day-by-day lives of people who work in the fields of cosmetology, food service and law enforcement.

★2986★ *Video Career Library - Public and Personal Services*
Careers, Inc.
PO Box 135
Largo, FL 34649-0135
Ph: (813)584-7333

Videocassette. 1990. 35 mins. Part of the Video Career Library covering 165 occupations. Shows actual workers on the job. Includes firefighters, police officers, correctional officers, bartenders, waiters/waitresses, cooks/chefs, child care workers, flight attendants, barbers/cosmetologists, groundskeepers/gardeners, and butchers/meat cutters.

★2987★ *Video Tapes for Cosmetology*
Golden West College
15744 Golden West St.
Huntington Beach, CA 92647
Ph: (714)892-7711 Fax: (714)895-8243

Videocassette. 1984. 25 mins. This series of six programs is a course in cosmetology from haircutting to manicuring.

★2988★ *Your Career in Professional Barber Styling*
National Association of Barber Styling Schools
304 S. 11th St.
Lincoln, NE 68508
Ph: (402)474-4244

This six-panel brochure describes the advantages of working as a barber.

Associations

★2989★ **American Association of Cosmetology Schools (AACS)**
901 N. Washington St., Ste. 206
Alexandria, VA 22314-1535
Ph: (703)845-1333 Fax: (703)845-1336

Members: Owners and instructors of schools of cosmetology; associate members are manufacturers and jobbers of beauty products and others interested in beauty culture and training. **Purpose:** Sponsors competitions and seminars. **Publications:** *AACS News*, bimonthly. • *OSHA Hazard Communication Standard: A Compliance Manual for Cosmetology Schools.* • *Washington Update*, monthly.

★2990★ **Hair International/Associated Master Barbers and Beauticians of America (HI/AMBBA)**
124-B E. Main St.
PO Box 273
Palmyra, PA 17078
Ph: (717)838-0795 Fax: (717)838-0796

Members: Barber styling and cosmetology school and business owners and employees; manufacturers. **Purpose:** Operates speakers' bureau; conducts hairstyling show, classes, and seminars. Sponsors hair cutting and styling competitions. **Publications:** *Hair International News*, bimonthly. • *National Bulletin*, quarterly. • *Standardized Textbook of Barbering and Styling.*

★2991★ **National Cosmetology Association (NCA)**
3510 Olive St.
St. Louis, MO 63103
Ph: (314)534-7980 Fax: (314)534-8618
Fr: 800-527-1683

Members: Owners of cosmetology salons; cosmetologists. **Purpose:** Sponsors: advanced cosmetology courses at universities throughout the U.S.; National Cosmetology Month; National Beauty Show. Provides special sections for estheticians, school owners, salon owners, and nail technicians. Maintains hall of fame and museum. Conducts educational and charitable programs. **Publications:** *American Looks*, semiannual. • *American Salon Magazine*, monthly. • *Association Bulletin*, periodic.

Standards/Certification Agencies

★2992★ **American Association of Cosmetology Schools (AACS)**
901 N. Washington St., Ste. 206
Alexandria, VA 22314-1535
Ph: (703)845-1333 Fax: (703)845-1336

Owners and instructors of schools of cosmetology; associate members are manufacturers and jobbers of beauty products and others interested in beauty culture and training.

★2993★ **National Accrediting Commission of Cosmetology Arts and Sciences (NACCAS)**
901 N. Stuart St., No. 900
Arlington, VA 22203
Ph: (703)527-7600 Fax: (703)527-8811

Accrediting body for schools of cosmetology; presently there are 1565 accredited schools. Objectives are to: raise standards of cosmetology schools throughout the country; encourage use of modern educational methods and techniques; stimulate self-improvement by the schools. Sponsors standards and professional team training workshops.

★2994★ **National Association of Accredited Cosmetology Schools (NAACS)**
5201 Leesburg Pike, Ste. 205
Falls Church, VA 22041
Ph: (703)845-1333 Fax: (703)845-1336

Owners and instructors of schools of cosmetology; associate members are manufacturers and jobbers of beauty products and others interested in beauty culture and training. Presents annual awards; sponsors competitions and seminars.

★2995★ **National Association of Barber Styling Schools (NABS)**
304 S. 11th St.
Lincoln, NE 68508
Ph: (402)474-4244

Seeks to improve barber school training and instructor qualifications in an effort to increase professional standards in barbering.

Test Guides

★2996★ *Career Examination Series: Barber*
National Learning Corp.
212 Michael Dr.
Syosset, NY 11791
Ph: (516)921-8888 Fax: (516)921-8743
Fr: 800-645-6337

Jack Rudman. All examination guides in this series contain questions with answers.

★2997★ *Career Examination Series: Cosmetologist*
National Learning Corp.
212 Michael Dr.
Syosset, NY 11791
Ph: (516)921-8888 Fax: (516)921-8743
Fr: 800-645-6337

Jack Rudman. All examination guides in this series contain questions with answers.

★2998★ *Cosmetologist's State Board Exam Review in English*
Milady Publishing Co
220 White Plains Rd.
Tarrytown, NY 10591
Ph: (914)332-4800 Fax: (212)881-5624

Milady Editors. 1985.

★2999★ *Cosmetology*
National Learning Corp.
212 Michael Dr.
Syosset, NY 11791
Ph: (516)921-8888 Fax: (516)921-8743
Fr: 800-645-6337

Jack Rudman. Part of Occupational Competency Examination Series.

★3000★ *Cosmetology*
National Learning Corp.
212 Michael Dr.
Syosset, NY 11791
Ph: (516)921-8888 Fax: (516)921-8743
Fr: 800-645-6337

Jack Rudman. Part of the Test Your Knowledge Series. Contains multiple choice questions with answers.

★3001★ *Professional Barber Styling State Board Exam Review*
Milady Publishing
220 Whie Plains Rd.
Tarrytown, NY 10591
Ph: (914)332-4800 Fax: (212)881-5624

1983.

★3002★ *State Board Review Examinations In Cosmetology*
Keystone Publications, Inc.
1657 Broadway
New York, NY 10019
Ph: (212)582-2254

Anthony B. Colletti. 1976.

Educational Directories and Programs

★3003★ *Beauty Supplies Dealers Directory*
American Business Directories, Inc.
5711 S. 86th Circle
Omaha, NE 68127
Ph: (402)593-4600 Fax: (402)331-1505

Annual. Number of listings: 15,247 (U.S. edition); 2,195 (Canadian edition). Entries include: Name, address, phone (including area code), size of advertisement, year first in "Yellow Pages," name of owner or manager, number of employees. Compiled from telephone company "Yellow Pages," nationwide. Arrangement: Geographical.

★3004★ *Directory of Accredited Cosmetology Schools*
National Accrediting Commission of Cosmetology Arts & Sciences
901 N. Stuart St., Ste. 900
Arlington, VA 22203-1816
Ph: (703)527-7600 Fax: (703)527-8811
Mark Gross, Contact

Annual, August. Covers over 1,569 accredited cosmetology schools in the United States, Puerto Rico, and Guam. Entries include: School name, address, phone, date accredited, curriculum offered. Arrangement: Geographical.

★3005★ *Members of the National Association of Barber Styling Schools*
National Association of Barber Styling Schools
304 S. 11th St.
Lincoln, NE 68508
Ph: (402)474-4244

!990. Lists schools accredited by the association. Provides address, phone number and contact person.

Awards, Scholarships, Grants, and Fellowships

★3006★ Academy of Legends
Aestheticians International Association
4447 McKinney Ave.
Dallas, TX 75205
Ph: (214)526-0752 Fax: (214)526-2925
Fr: 800-285-5277

For recognition of outstanding achievements in the field of skin care, make-up, and appearance. A trophy is awarded bimonthly and the winner is featured on the cover of *DermaScope Magazine.* Established in 1986 in memory of Ida Mae Mixon Green.

★3007★ Barbering Hall of Fame
National Association of Barber Styling Schools
304 S. 11th St.
Lincoln, NE 68508
Ph: (402)474-4244

To honor those who have made an outstanding contribution in the barber industry. Individuals with 20 years of service to the barber industry are eligible. A plaque, and a picture and accomplishments displayed in the Hall of Fame are awarded annually at the Convention. Established in 1966.

★3008★ Make-Up Competition
Aestheticians International Association
4447 McKinney Ave.
Dallas, TX 75205
Ph: (214)526-0752 Fax: (214)526-2925
Fr: 800-285-5277

For recognition of outstanding make-up artistry, and to encourage personal growth and creativity in make-up. Both professional and student make-up artists may enter. The deadline is usually 30 days prior to show dates. A monetary award and plaque are bestowed for the first, second, and third prizes. Presented annually at the convention.

★3009★ North American Hairstyling Awards
Beauty and Barber Supply Institute (BBSI)
271 Rte. 46 W., Ste. F-209
Fairfield, NJ 07004-2415
Ph: (201)808-7444 Fax: (201)808-9099

To recognize the best hairstylists in North America. Awards are given in the following eleven categories: Men's Makeover - "Before" and "After" photographs of a single model; Women's Makeover - "Before" and "After" photographs of a single model; Avant Garde - an individual interpretation of fashion-forward hair; Classic - Photographs of commercial styles designed to flatter and enhance the "total look;" Permanent Waving; Enhanced Nails; Natural Nails; Multicultural; North American Student Hairstylist of the Year; and North American Stylist of the Year. All entries are judged on originality, creativity, style and fashion appeal, overall suitability to model, and technical execution. The deadline is January 15. Nominees must be licensed cosmetologists or licensed men's hairstylists. One trophy is awarded for each category at the annual BBSI Winter Conference. The awards ceremony includes the introduction of all winners, the announcement of the North American Stylist of the Year, and the presentation of a Lifetime Achievement Award to a well known contemporary hair designer. All winning entries are published in an upcoming issue of *Modern Salon.* Established in 1982. Previously administered by *Modern Salon* of the Vance Publishing Corporation.

★3010★ WINBA Championship Title
World International Nail and Beauty Association
1221 N. Lakeview
Anaheim, CA 92807
Ph: (714)779-9883

For recognition of achievement and field activity in cosmetology. World Championship Titles are given in the following categories: Student, Nails, Nail Arts, Professional Sculptured Acrylic Nails, U.S. Championship Nails, and Nail Wrapping. Monetary awards, medallions, jewelry, and travel are awarded annually in each category. Awards are also given in the following categories: Professional Haircutting Two Phase, Student Haircutting Two Phase, Student Mannequin Two Phase Comb Out, Student Styling Contest, Professional Hairstyling; Fantasy Make-up, and Evening Corrective Make-up. First, second, and third prizes include trophies, cash, and gift packages. Established in 1980 by James George.

Basic Reference Guides and Handbooks

★3011★ *OSHA Hazard Communication Standard: A Compliance Manual for Cosmetology Schools*
American Association of Cosmetology Schools (AACS)
901 N. Washington St., Ste. 206
Alexandria, VA 22314
Ph: (703)845-1333 Fax: (703)845-1336

★3012★ *Standardized Textbook of Barbering and Styling*
Hair International/Associated Master Barbers and Beauticians of America (HI/AMBBA)
124-B E. Main St.
PO Box 273
Palmyra, PA 17078
Ph: (717)838-0795 Fax: (717)838-0796

★3013★ *Workbook for Professional Barber Styling*
Milady Publishing Co.
220 White Plains Rd.
Tarrytown, NY 10591
Ph: (914)332-4800 Fax: (212)881-5624

Milady Editors. 1984.

Periodicals

★3014★ *AACS News*
American Association of Cosmetology Schools (AACS)
901 N. Washington St., Ste. 206
Alexandria, VA 22314-1535
Ph: (703)845-1333 Fax: (703)845-1336

Bimonthly.

★3015★ *American Looks*
National Cosmetology Association (NCA)
3510 Olive St.
St. Louis, MO 63103
Ph: (314)534-7980 Fax: (314)534-8618
Fr: 800-527-1683

Semiannual.

★3016★ *American Salon Magazine*
National Cosmetology Association (NCA)
3510 Olive St.
St. Louis, MO 63103
Ph: (314)534-7980 Fax: (314)534-8618
Fr: 800-527-1683

Monthly.

★3017★ *Association Bulletin*
National Cosmetology Association (NCA)
3510 Olive St.
St. Louis, MO 63103
Ph: (314)534-7980 Fax: (314)534-8618
Fr: 800-527-1683

Periodic.

★3018★ *Cosmetic Insiders' Report*
Cosmetic Insider's Report
270 Madison Ave.
New York, NY 10016
Ph: (212)951-6600 Fax: (212)481-6563
Don Davis

Semimonthly. Carries news and current insider views of the cosmetic, toiletries, and fragrance industries. Includes items on marketing, advertising, regulation, technology, consumer buying patterns, new products, company developments, and people in the industry.

★3019★ *Hair International News*
Hair International/Associated Master Barbers and Beauticians of America (HI/AMBBA)
124-B E. Main St.
PO Box 273
Palmyra, PA 17078
Ph: (717)838-0795 Fax: (717)838-0796

Bimonthly.

★3020★ *NACCAS Handbook*
National Accrediting Commission of Cosmetology Arts and Sciences (NACCAS)
901 N. Stuart St., No. 900
Arlington, VA 22203
Ph: (703)527-7600 Fax: (703)527-8811

Annual.

★3021★ *NACCAS Review*
National Accrediting Commission of Cosmetology Arts and Sciences (NACCAS)
901 N. Stuart St., No. 900
Arlington, VA 22203
Ph: (703)527-7600 Fax: (703)527-8811

★3022★ *National Bulletin*
Hair International/Associated Master Barbers and Beauticians of America (HI/AMBBA)
124-B E. Main St.
PO Box 273
Palmyra, PA 17078
Ph: (717)838-0795 Fax: (717)838-0796

Quarterly.

★3023★ *Skin Inc.*
Allured Publishing Corp.
362 S. Schmale Rd.
Carol Stream, IL 60188-2787
Ph: (708)653-2155 Fax: (708)653-2192
Jean E. AlluredPublisher

Bimonthly. The business magazine for skin care facilities.

★3024★ *Soap/Cosmetics/Chemical Specialties*
PTN Publishing Co.
445 Broad Hollow Rd., Ste. 21
Melville, NY 11747-3601
Ph: (516)845-2700 Fax: (516)845-2797
Anita Hipius Shaw

Monthly. Soap, cosmetics, and chemical specialties trade magazine.

★3025★ *Toiletries, Fragrances and Skin Care—The Rose Sheet*
F-D-C Reports, Inc.
5550 Friendship Blvd., Ste. 1
Chevy Chase, MD 20815
Ph: (301)657-9830 Fax: (301)656-3094
Christine Harrington

Weekly. Covers the cosmetics industry, including regulatory and legal issues, scientific developments, testing methodologies, mergers and acquisitions, Europe 1992 factors, marketing strategies, new product launches, and advertising and retail promotions. Recurring features include columns titled In Brief, Marketing in Briefs, and Trademark Review.

★3026★ *Washington Update*
American Association of Cosmetology Schools (AACS)
901 N. Washington St., Ste. 206
Alexandria, VA 22314-1535
Ph: (703)845-1333 Fax: (703)845-1336

Monthly.

★3027★ *Where They Stand: A Digest of Organizational Policies on Child Care and Education*
Child Care Action Campaign (CCAC)
330 7th Ave., 17th Fl.
New York, NY 10001
Ph: (212)239-0138 Fax: (212)268-6515

Provides a guide to 45 national organizations' policy positions on quality child care, early childhood education, and education reform.

Meetings and Conventions

★3028★ AACS - Association of Accredited Cosmetology Schools Annual Convention & Exhibition
Association of Accredited Cosmetology Schools (AACS)
5201 Leesburg Pike, Ste. 205
Falls Church, VA 22041
Ph: (703)845-1333 Fax: (703)845-1336

Annual.

★3029★ Big Show Expo Beauty and Hair Care Show
Big Show Expo, Inc.
1841 Broadway
New York, NY 10023
Ph: (212)757-7589 Fax: (212)757-3611

Annual.

★3030★ Cosmetics, Hair & Beauty/Shanghai
Glahe International, INc.
1700 K St., NW, Ste. 403
Washington, DC 20006-4557
Ph: (202)659-4557 Fax: (202)457-0776

Biennial. **Dates and Locations:** 1996; Shanghai

★3031★ Cosmetics Hair & Beauty/Shenzhen
Glahe International, Inc.
1700 K St., NW, Ste. 403
Washington, DC 20006-4557
Ph: (202)659-4557 Fax: (202)457-0776

Biennial. **Dates and Locations:** 1996; Shenzhen

★3032★ EID Spring Shopping Fair - International Trade Fair for Household Goods, Cosmetics, Fashionware, Gifts, Jewelry & Furniture
Glahe International, Inc.
1700 K St., NW, Ste. 403
Washington, DC 20006-4557
Ph: (202)659-4557 Fax: (202)457-0776

Biennial. **Dates and Locations:** 1996; Dhahran

★3033★ IBS - New York
Advanstar Expositions
7500 Old Oak Blvd.
Cleveland, OH 44130
Ph: (216)826-2810 Fax: (216)826-2801
Fr: 800-225-4569

Annual.

★3034★ National Beauty Show
National Cosmetology Association
3510 Olive St.
St. Louis, MO 63103
Ph: (314)534-7980 Fax: (314)534-8618
Fr: 800-527-1683

Annual. Always held during January. **Dates and Locations:** 1996 Jan.

★3035★ National Cosmetology Association Convention
National Cosmetology Association
3510 Olive St.
St. Louis, MO 63103
Ph: (314)534-7980 Fax: (314)534-8618
Fr: 800-527-1683

Annual. **Dates and Locations:** 1996 Aug 07-09; Washington, DC. • 1997 Aug 10-13; Washington, DC.

Other Sources of Information

★3036★ "Barber" in *Career Selector 2001*
Barron's Educational Series, Inc.
250 Wireless Blvd.
Hauppauge, NY 11788
Ph: (516)434-3311 Fax: (516)434-3723
Fr: 800-645-3476

James C. Gonyea. 1993.

★3037★ *Barbers' Equipment & Supplies—Wholesale Directory*
American Business Directories, Inc.
5711 S. 86th Circle
Omaha, NE 68127
Ph: (402)593-4600 Fax: (402)331-1505

Updated continuously; printed on request. Entries include: Name, address, phone, size of advertisement, name of owner or manager, number of employees, year first in "Yellow Pages." Compiled from telephone company

"Yellow Pages," nationwide. Arrangement: Geographical.

★3038★ *Basic Make Up Film 2*
Allan Keith Productions
425 E. 79th St., Ste. 1-D
New York, NY 10021
Ph: (212)535-6301 Fr: 800-962-9966

Features a complete make-up application demonstration by a specialist.

★3039★ "Beautician" in *Encyclopedia of Danger: Dangerous Professions* (pp. 22-25)
Chelsea House Publishers
1974 Sproul Rd., Ste. 400
Broomall, PA 19008
Ph: (215)353-5166 Fax: (215)359-1439

Missy Allen and Michel Peissel. 1993. Provides descriptions of 24 dangerous occupations, their risky characteristics, and safety precautions.

★3040★ *Braiding*
Allan Keith Productions
425 E 79th St., Ste. 1-D
New York, NY 10021
Ph: (212)535-6301 Fr: 800-962-9966

This tape demonstrates a method of braiding hair.

★3041★ "Cosmetologist" in *100 Best Jobs for the 1990s & Beyond*
Dearborn Financial Publishing, Inc.
520 N. Dearborn St.
Chicago, IL 60610-4354
Ph: (312)836-4400 Fax: (312)836-1021
Fr: 800-621-9621

Carol Kleiman. 1992. Describes 100 jobs ranging from accountants to veterinarians. Each job profile includes such information as education, experience, and certification needed, salaries, and job search suggestions.

★3042★ "Cosmetologist" in *Career Selector 2001*
Barron's Educational Series, Inc.
250 Wireless Blvd.
Hauppauge, NY 11788
Ph: (516)434-3311 Fax: (516)434-3723
Fr: 800-645-3476

James C. Gonyea. 1993.

★3043★ *Hair Shaping Lessons Series*
Allan Keith Productions
425 E. 79th St., Ste. 1-D
New York, NY 10021
Ph: (212)535-6301 Fr: 800-962-9966

Demonstrates modern hair cutting, styling and curling techniques for hairdressers and students. Programs include: Low Layered Cut; High Layered Cut; The Wedge Haircut; The Unisex Haircut; High Graduated Haircut.

★3044★ *The Journeymen Barbers' International Union of America*
AMS Press, Inc.
56 E. 13th St.
New York, NY 10003
Ph: (212)777-4700 Fax: (212)995-5413

William S. Hall. Part of Johns Hopkins University. Studies in the Social Sciences. Fifty-Fourth Series.

★3045★ *NABS Research Reports*
National Association of Barber Styling Schools (NABS)
304 S. 11th St.
Lincoln, NE 68508
Ph: (402)474-4244

Annual.

Flight Attendants

Flight attendants are aboard all passenger planes to look after the passengers' flight safety and comfort. At least one hour before each flight, the attendants see that the passenger cabin is in order. As the passengers board the plane, attendants assist them. Before the plane takes off, attendants instruct passengers in the use of emergency equipment and check to see that all passengers have their seat belts fastened and seat backs forward. In the air, attendants serve refreshments and, on many flights, heat and distribute precooked meals. After the plane has landed, the flight attendants assist passengers as they leave the plane. Assisting passengers in the rare event of an emergency is the most important function of attendants. Lead or first flight attendants aboard planes oversee the work of the other attendants while performing most of the same duties. Commercial airlines employ the vast majority of all flight attendants. A small number of flight attendants work for large companies that operate their own aircraft for business purposes.

Salaries

Median annual salaries for flight attendants are as follows:

Beginning flight attendants	$13,000/year
Flight attendants with six years of flying experience	$20,000/year
Senior flight attendants	$40,000/year

Employment Outlook

Growth rate until the year 2005: Much faster than average.

Flight Attendants

Career Guides

★3046★ "Airline Flight Attendant" in *Career Information Center* (Vol.12)
Simon and Schuster
200 Old Tappan Rd.
Old Tappan, NJ 07675
Fax: 800-445-6991 Fr: 800-223-2348

Richard Lidz and Dale Anderson, editorial directors. Fifth edition, 1993. For 600 occupations, describes job duties, entry-level requirements, education and training needed, advancement possibilities, employment outlook, earnings and benefits. The set is divided into 12 volumes. Each volume includes jobs related under a broad career field. Volume 13 is the index.

★3047★ *Airline Flight Attendants*
Chronicle Guidance Publications, Inc.
66 Aurora St.
PO Box 1190
Moravia, NY 13118-1190
Ph: (315)497-0330 Fax: (315)497-3359
Fr: 800-622-7284

1994. This career brief describes the nature of the work, working conditions, hours and earnings, education and training, licensure, certification, unions, personal qualifications, social and psychological factors, employment outlook, entry methods, advancement, and related occupations.

★3048★ *Career Insights*
RMI Media Productions, Inc.
1365 N. Winchester
Olathe, KS 66061
Ph: (913)768-1696 Fax: 800-755-6910
Fr: 800-745-5480

Videocassette series. 1987. This videotape series describes 50 occupations, including skill requirements and interviews with people employed in these fields. Occupations include: flight service, air transportation/ground services, data processing, carpentry, clerk in banking/insurance/business, cosmetic personal grooming, firefighting, forestry, insulation/roofing, mechanics, material handling, photographic processing, pipefitting and plumbing, printing, secretarial services, tool and die operations.

★3049★ *Career Success Series*
Cambridge Educational
PO Box 2153
Charleston, WV 25328-2153
Ph: (304)744-9323 Fax: (304)744-9351
Fr: 800-468-4227

Videocassette. 1986. 15 mins. A series, available separately, outlining various career choices for students. Occupations include: accounting, flight service, air transportation/ground/flight service, data processing, carpentry, clerk in banking/insurance, commodity sales, cosmetic personal grooming, fire fighting, forestry services, home economics, insulation/roofing, material handling, mechanics, photographic processing, pipefitting and plumbing, police science, printing, carpentry, medical laboratory technicians, secretarial services, and utilities equipment operator.

★3050★ *Careers as a Flight Attendant*
Rosen Publishing Group
29 E. 21st St.
New York, NY 10010
Ph: (212)777-3017 Fax: (212)777-0277
Fr: 800-237-9932

Catherine Okray Lobus. 1991. Discusses the work, personal characteristics of successful flight attendants, physical and educational qualifications, the application process, and airline training programs. Lists major airlines and outlines their application processes, policies and benefits, and training programs.

★3051★ *Flight Attendant*
Careers, Inc.
PO Box 135
Largo, FL 34649-0135
Ph: (813)584-7333

1992. Four-page brief offering the definition, history, duties, working conditions, personal qualifications, educational requirements, earnings, hours, employment outlook, advancement possibilities, and related occupations.

★3052★ *Flight Attendant*
Vocational Biographies, Inc.
PO Box 31
Sauk Centre, MN 56378-0031
Ph: (612)352-6516 Fax: (612)352-5546
Fr: 800-255-0752

1993. Four-page pamphlet containing a personal narrative about a worker's job, work likes and dislikes, career path from high school to the present. Education and training, the rewards and frustrations, and the effects of the job on the rest of the worker's life. The data file portion of this pamphlet gives a concise occupational summary, including work descriptions, working conditions, places of employment, personal characteristics, education and training, job outlook, and salary range.

★3053★ "Flight Attendant" in *100 Best Careers for the Year 2000* (pp. 242-245)
Arco Pub.
201 W. 103rd St.
Indianapolis, IN 46290
Ph: 800-428-5331 Fax: 800-835-3202

Shelly Field. 1992. Describes 100 job opportunities expected to grow fast throughout the next decade. Provides information on job duties and responsibilities, training requirements, education, advancement opportunities, experience and qualifications, and typical salaries.

★3054★ "Flight Attendant" in *American Almanac of Jobs and Salaries* (pp. 392)
Avon Books
1350 Avenue of the Americas
New York, NY 10019
Ph: (212)261-6800 Fr: 800-238-0658

John Wright, editor. Revised and updated, 1994-95. A comprehensive guide to the wages of hundreds of occupations in a wide variety of industries and organizations.

★3055★ "Flight Attendant" in *Careers in Aviation* (pp. 15-18)
Rosen Publishing Group
29 E. 21st St.
New York, NY 10010
Ph: (212)777-3017 Fax: (212)777-0277
Fr: 800-237-9932

Sharon Carter. 1990. Explores a wide variety of piloting jobs including aerial patrolling, corporate flying, flying for the media, law enforcement, and the airlines, helicopter ambulance flying, and stunt flying. Discusses being licensed, and opportunities for women. Most of the book is based on interviews with people who describe what they do on the job.

★3056★ "Flight Attendant" in *College Board Guide to Jobs and Career Planning* (pp. 83-84)
The College Board
45 Columbus Ave.
New York, NY 10023-6992
Ph: (212)713-8165 Fax: (212)713-8143
Fr: 800-323-7155

Second edition, 1994. Describes the job, salaries, related careers, education needed, and where to write for more information.

★3057★ *Flight Attendant Interview Handbook*
Plane Sense
1516 Roslyn St.
Denver, CO 80220-1935
Ph: (303)388-8488

Ken Jabalais. Second edition, 1992.

★3058★ "Flight Attendant" in *Jobs Rated Almanac*
World Almanac
1 International Blvd., Ste. 444
Mahwah, NJ 07495
Ph: (201)529-6900 Fax: (201)529-6901

Les Krantz. Second edition, 1992. Ranks 250 jobs by environment, salary, outlooks, physical demands, stress, security, travel opportunities, and extra perks. Includes jobs the editor feels are the most common, most interesting, and the most rapidly growing.

★3059★ "Flight Attendant" in *Occu-Facts: Information on 580 Careers in Outline Form*
Careers, Inc.
PO Box 135
Largo, FL 34649-0135
Ph: (813)584-7333

Biennial, 1995-96 edition. Each one-page occupational profile describes duties, working conditions, physical surroundings and demands, aptitudes, temperament, educational requirements, employment outlook, earnings, and places of employment.

★3060★ "Flight Attendant" in *Opportunities in Airline Careers* (pp. 63-76)
National Textbook Co. (NTC)
VGM Career Books
4255 W. Touhy Ave.
Lincolnwood, IL 60646-1975
Ph: (708)679-5500 Fax: (708)679-2494
Fr: 800-323-4900

Adrian A. Paradis. 1987. Surveys trends in the industry and career opportunities with the airlines including management, sales, customer service, flying, and maintenance. Describes pilots' job duties, working conditions, and basic educational and training requirements.

★3061★ "Flight Attendant" in *The Complete Aviation/Aerospace Career Guide* (pp. 159-164)
Aero Publishers, Inc.
13311 Monterey Ave.
Blue Ridge Summit, PA 17294
Ph: (717)794-2191 Fax: (717)794-2080

Robert Calderone. 1989. This is a comprehensive guide to hundreds of aviation related jobs. Provides job description, training requirements, advancement opportunities and employment outlook.

★3062★ "Flight Attendant" in *Transportation* (pp. 51-55)
Franklin Watts, Inc.
387 Park Avenue, S.
New York, NY 10016
Ph: (212)686-7070

Marjorie Rittenberg Schulz. 1990. Surveys the transportation industry including air, water, and rail services. Provides job description, training, salary, and employment outlook. Offers job hunting advice.

★3063★ "Flight Attendant" in *VGM's Careers Encyclopedia* (pp. 178-181)
National Textbook Co. (NTC)
VGM Career Books
4255 W. Touhy Ave.
Lincolnwood, IL 60646-1975
Ph: (708)679-5500 Fax: (708)679-2494
Fr: 800-323-4900

Third edition, 1991. Contains two- to five-page descriptions of 200 managerial, professional, technical, trade, and service occupations. Each profile includes job duties, places of employment, qualifications, educational preparation, training, employment potential, advancement, income, and additional sources of information.

★3064★ "Flight Attendants" in *101 Careers: A Guide to the Fastest-Growing Opportunities* (pp. 316-318)
John Wiley & Sons, Inc.
605 3rd Ave.
New York, NY 10158-0012
Ph: (212)850-6645 Fax: (212)850-6088

Michael Harkavy. 1990. Describes the nature of the job, working conditions, employment growth, qualifications, personal skills, projected salaries, and where to write for more information.

★3065★ "Flight Attendants" in *America's 50 Fastest Growing Jobs* (pp. 119)
JIST Works, Inc.
720 N. Park Ave.
Indianapolis, IN 46202-3431
Ph: (317)264-3720 Fax: (317)264-3709
Fr: 800-648-5478

Michael J. Farr, compiler. 1994. Describes the 50 fastest growing jobs within major career clusters such as technicians, and marketing and sales. Each job profile explains the nature of the work, skills and abilities required, employment outlook, average earnings, related occupations, education and training requirements, and employment opportunities. Also contains career planning information and job search tips.

★3066★ "Flight Attendants" in *Career Discovery Encyclopedia* (Vol.3, pp. 22-23)
J.G. Ferguson Publishing Co.
200 W. Madison St., Ste. 300
Chicago, IL 60606
Ph: (312)580-5480 Fax: (312)580-4948

E. Russell Primm, editor-in-chief. 1993. Contains two-page articles on 504 occupations. Each article describes job duties, earnings, and educational and training requirements.

★3067★ "Flight Attendants" in *Encyclopedia of Careers and Vocational Guidance* (Vol.3, pp. 5-8)
J.G. Ferguson Publishing Co.
200 W. Madison St., Ste. 300
Chicago, IL 60606
Ph: (312)580-5480 Fax: (312)580-4948

William E. Hopke, editor-in-chief. Ninth edition, 1993. Four-volume set that profiles 500 occupations and describes job trends in 74 industries. Includes career description, educational requirements, history of the job, methods of entry, advancement, employment outlook, earnings, working conditions, social and psychological factors, and sources of additional information.

★3068★ "Flight Attendants" in *Jobs! What They Are—Where They Are—What They Pay* (pp. 199)
Simon & Schuster, Inc.
Simon & Schuster Bldg.
1230 Avenue of the Americas
New York, NY 10020
Ph: (212)698-7000

Robert O. Snelling and Anne M. Snelling. Revised edition, 1992. Profiles 241 occupations, describing duties and responsibilities, educational preparation, earnings, employment opportunities, training, and qualifications.

★3069★ "Flight Attendants" in *Occupational Outlook Handbook*
U.S. Government Printing Office
Superintendent of Documents
Washington, DC 20402
Ph: (202)512-1800 Fax: (202)512-2250

Biennial; latest edition, 1994-95. Encyclopedia of careers describing more than 250 occupations and comprising about 85 percent of all jobs in the economy. Occupations that require lengthy education or training are given the most attention. For each occupation, the handbook describes job duties, working conditions, training, educational preparation, personal qualities, advancement possibilities, job outlook, earnings, and sources of additional information.

★3070★ "Flight Attendants" in *Opportunities in Travel Careers* (pp. 37-39)
National Textbook Co. (NTC)
VGM Career Books
4255 W. Touhy Ave.
Lincolnwood, IL 60646-1975
Ph: (708)679-5500 Fax: (708)679-2494
Fr: 800-323-4900

Robert Scott Milne. 1991. Explores job opportunities in many travel related fields including the airlines, resorts, travel agencies, recreation, and tourism. Covers the work, salaries, educational preparation and training, and advancement possibilities.

★3071★ "Flight Attendants" in *Travel Agent* (pp. 165-166)
Arco Publishing Co.
Macmillan General Reference
15 Columbus Cir.
New York, NY 10023
Fax: 800-835-3202 Fr: 800-858-7674

Wilma Boyd. 1989. Introduction to the travel business. Covers U.S. and foreign travel, time zones, ticketing, world geography, and airline, railroad, and tour bus connections, and accommodations. Outlines entry-level positions in the airline, car rental, and hospitality industries as well as in travel agencies and related travel services. Explains travel agency operations, sales techniques, and the use of computers in travel services. Gives job hunting advice and sales tips.

★3072★ *A Guide to Becoming a Flight Attendant*
Bob Adams, Inc.
260 Center St.
Holbrook, MA 02343
Ph: (617)268-9570

Douglas K. Kinan. 1987. Job hunting guide for flight attendants. Describes qualifications. Offers advice on getting an interview, writing resumes and cover letters, filling out the application, and interviewing. Contains 45 sample interview questions with sample "preferred" answers.

★3073★ *How You Too Can Become a Flight Attendant!: A Step by Step Guide*
Ross Publishing Co.
Rte. 3, 188 Forester Rd.
Slippery Rock, PA 16057
Ph: (412)794-2837

Debby Shearer. 1987.

★3074★ "Travel and Hospitality Careers" in *The Best Jobs for the 1990s and Into the 21st Century*
Impact Publications
9104-N Manassas Dr.
Manassas Park, VA 22111
Ph: (703)361-7300 Fax: (703)335-9486

Ronald L. Krannich and Caryl Rae Krannich. 1993. Includes information on chefs, cooks, flight attendants, food and beverage service workers, hotel and motel desk clerks, reservation and transportation ticket agents and travel clerks, and travel agents.

★3075★ *Video Career Library - Public and Personal Services*
Careers, Inc.
PO Box 135
Largo, FL 34649-0135
Ph: (813)584-7333

Videocassette. 1990. 35 mins. Part of the Video Career Library covering 165 occupations. Shows actual workers on the job. Includes firefighters, police officers, correctional officers, bartenders, waiters/waitresses, cooks/chefs, child care workers, flight attendants, barbers/cosmetologists, groundskeepers/gardeners, and butchers/meat cutters.

★3076★ *Walking on Air*
Aviation Book Co.
25133 Anza Dr., No. E.
Santa Clarita, CA 91355-3412
Ph: (805)294-0101 Fax: (805)294-0035

Helen E. McLaughlin. 1986.

Associations

★3077★ Future Aviation Professional of America
4959 Massachusetts Blvd.
Atlanta, GA 30337
Ph: (404)997-8097 Fax: (404)997-8111

Members: Commercial pilots, flight attendants, aviation maintenance personnel, and persons aspiring to careers in those areas. **Purpose:** To channel career information to aviation personnel and those seeking careers in aviation. Conducts bimonthly seminar and job fair.

Test Guides

★3078★ *Career Examination Series: Flight Attendant Skills Test (FAST)*
National Learning Corp.
212 Michael Dr.
Syosset, NY 11791
Ph: (516)921-8888 Fax: (516)921-8743
Fr: 800-645-6337

Jack Rudman. All examination guides in this series contain questions with answers.

Basic Reference Guides and Handbooks

★3079★ *The Official Airline Career Handbook*
Market Plus Inc.
PO Box 2255
Silverthorne, CO 80498

Ron Hooson. 25th edition, 1995. Offers job descriptions and requirements, salaries information, and application and interview procedures. Also provides a list of national, regional, and charter airlines.

Periodicals

★3080★ *Air Line Pilot*
Air Line Pilots Assn.
535 Herndon Pkwy.
PO Box 1169
Herndon, VA 22070
Ph: (703)689-4176 Fax: (703)689-4370
Esperison Martinez

Monthly. Magazine covering industry trends and developments, flight technology, and air safety.

★3081★ *Airport Journal*
PO Box 273
Clarendon Hills, IL 60514
Ph: (708)318-6872 Fax: (708)986-5010
John Andrews

Monthly. Magazine serving the air transport industry in the Chicago area.

★3082★ *Flightlog*
Association of Flight Attendants, AFL-CIO
1625 Massachusetts Ave. NW
Washington, DC 20036
Ph: (202)328-5400 Fax: (202)328-5424
Molly Charboneau

Bimonthly. Covers aviation industry news, aviation safety, legislative and government issues affecting flight attendants, union activities, and related topics.

Other Sources of Information

★3083★ "Airplane Flight Attendant" in *Career Selector 2001*
Barron's Educational Series, Inc.
250 Wireless Blvd.
Hauppauge, NY 11788
Ph: (516)434-3311 Fax: (516)434-3723
Fr: 800-645-3476

James C. Gonyea. 1993.

★3084★ *Choosing an Airline Career: In-Depth Descriptions of Entry-Level Positions, Travel Benefits, How to Apply and Interview*
Capri Publishing Co.
PO Box 625 FDR Station
New York, NY 10150-0625
Ph: (212)421-3709 Fax: (212)223-2878
Fr: 800-247-6553

1992.

★3085★ "Flight Attendant" in *100 Best Jobs for the 1990s & Beyond*
Dearborn Financial Publishing, Inc.
520 N. Dearborn St.
Chicago, IL 60610-4354
Ph: (312)836-4400 Fax: (312)836-1021
Fr: 800-621-9621

Carol Kleiman. 1992. Describes 100 jobs ranging from accountants to veterinarians. Each job profile includes such information as education, experience, and certification needed, salaries, and job search suggestions.

Gardeners and Groundskeepers

Gardeners are responsible for the overall care of the property, ranging from feeding, watering, and pruning the flowering plants and trees to mowing and watering the lawn. Some landscape gardeners, called lawn service workers, specialize in maintaining lawns and shrubs for a fee. **Groundskeepers** who care for athletic fields keep both natural and artificial turf fields in top condition and mark boundaries and paint team logos and names on the playing fields before each athletic event. **Greenskeepers** maintain golf courses. In order to keep the putting greens in good condition, greenskeepers periodically relocate the hole. The greenskeepers also must keep golf course equipment in good working order. Cemetery workers prepare graves and maintain cemetery grounds. They dig graves to specified depth. Basic duties of groundskeepers in parks and recreation facilities include caring for lawns, trees, and shrubs, maintaining athletic fields and playgrounds, and keeping parking lots, picnic areas, and other public spaces free of litter.

Salaries

Weekly earnings for gardeners and groundskeepers are as follows:

Lowest 10 percent	$175/week or less
Middle 50 percent	$210-$365/week
Top 10 percent	$475/week or more

Employment Outlook

Growth rate until the year 2005: Faster than average.

Gardeners and Groundskeepers

Career Guides

★3086★ *Career Profiles: Environmental Series*
Cambridge Educational
PO Box 2153
Charleston, WV 25328-2153
Ph: (304)744-9323 Fax: (304)744-9351
Fr: 800-468-4227

Videocassette. 1989. 15 mins. Environmental careers of all sorts are examined, including grounds and turf management, landscaping, and wastewater treatment plant operator.

★3087★ "Garden Worker" and "Groundskeeper" in *Museum Jobs form A-Z: What They Are, How to Prepare, and Where to Find Them*
Batax Museum Publishing
301 Racquet Club Rd., Ste. 202
Fort Lauderdale, FL 33326

G.W. Bates. 1994.

★3088★ "Gardener and Grounds Keeper" in *Career Inormation Center* (Vol.5)
Simon and Schuster
200 Old Tappan Rd.
Old Tappan, NJ 07675
Fax: 800-445-6991 Fr: 800-223-2348

Richard Lidz and Dale Anderson, editorial directors. Fifth edition, 1993. For 600 occupations, describes job duties, entry-level requirements, education and training needed, advancement possibilities, employment outlook, earnings and benefits. The set is divided into 12 volumes. Each volume includes jobs related under a broad career field. Volume 13 is the index.

★3089★ "Gardeners and Groundskeepers" in *America's 50 Fastest Growing Jobs* (pp. 121)
JIST Works, Inc.
720 N. Park Ave.
Indianapolis, IN 46202-3431
Ph: (317)264-3720 Fax: (317)264-3709
Fr: 800-648-5478

Michael J. Farr, compiler. 1994. Describes the 50 fastest growing jobs within major career clusters such as technicians, and marketing and sales. Each job profile explains the nature of the work, skills and abilities required, employment outlook, average earnings, related occupations, education and training requirements, and employment opportunities. Also contains career planning information and job search tips.

★3090★ "Gardeners and Groundskeepers" in *Occupational Outlook Handbook*
U.S. Government Printing Office
Superintendent of Documents
Washington, DC 20402
Ph: (202)512-1800 Fax: (202)512-2250

Biennial; latest edition, 1994-95. Encyclopedia of careers describing more than 250 occupations and comprising about 85 percent of all jobs in the economy. Occupations that require lengthy education or training are given the most attention. For each occupation, the handbook describes job duties, working conditions, training, educational preparation, personal qualities, advancement possibilities, job outlook, earnings, and sources of additional information.

★3091★ *Grounds Keeper*
Careers, Inc.
PO Box 135
Largo, FL 34649-0135
Ph: (813)584-7333

1995. Two-page job guide card describing duties, working conditions, personal qualifications, training, earnings and hours, employment outlook, places of employment, related careers and where to write for more information.

★3092★ *Grounds Maintenance Estimating Guidelines*
Professional Grounds Management Society (PGMS)
120 Cockeysville Rd., Ste. 104
Hunt Valley, MD 21031
Ph: (410)584-9754 Fax: (410)584-9756

Sixth edition, 1990.

★3093★ *Grounds Management Forms and Job Descriptions Guide*
Professional Gounds Management Society (PGMS)
120 Cockeysville Rd., Ste. 104
Hunt Valley, MD 21031
Ph: (410)584-9754 Fax: (410)584-9756

Fourth edition, 1993.

★3094★ *Grounds Manager Certification Proram*
Professional Grounds Management Society (PGMS)
120 Cockeysville Rd., Ste. 104
Hunt Valley, MD 21031
Ph: (410)584-9754 Fax: (410)584-9756

An 8 panel pamphlet.

★3095★ "Groundskeeper" in *Occu-Facts: Information on 580 Careers in Outline Form*
Careers, Inc.
PO Box 135
Largo, FL 34649-0135
Ph: (813)584-7333

Biennial, 1995-96 edition. Each one-page occupational profile describes duties, working conditions, physical surroundings and demands, aptitudes, temperament, educational requirements, employment outlook, earnings, and places of employment.

★3096★ "Groundskeeper and Stadium Worker" in *Hospitality & Recreation* (pp. 57-61)
Franklin Watts, Inc.
387 Park Avenue, S.
New York, NY 10016
Ph: (212)686-7070

Marjorie Rittenberg Schulz. 1990. Provides an overview of jobs in the hotel, motel, food service, fitness, and recreation industries. Covers job duties, educational preparation, salary, and employment outlook. Offers job hunting advice.

★3097★ "Landscapers and Grounds Managers" in *Career Discovery Encyclopedia* (Vol.4, pp. 160-161)
J.G. Ferguson Publishing Co.
200 W. Madison St., Ste. 300
Chicago, IL 60606
Ph: (312)580-5480 Fax: (312)580-4948

E. Russell Primm, editor-in-chief. 1993. Contains two-page articles on 504 occupations. Each article describes job duties, earnings, and educational and training requirements.

★3098★ "Landscapers and Grounds Managers" in *Encyclopedia of Careers and Vocational Guidance* (Vol.3, pp. 267-269)
J.G. Ferguson Publishing Co.
200 W. Madison St., Ste. 300
Chicago, IL 60606
Ph: (312)580-5480 Fax: (312)580-4948

William E. Hopke, editor-in-chief. Ninth edition, 1993. Four-volume set that profiles 500 occupations and describes job trends in 74 industries. Includes career description, educational requirements, history of the job, methods of entry, advancement, employment outlook, earnings, working conditions, social and psychological factors, and sources of additional information.

★3099★ "Nursery and Landscape Workers" in *Occu-Facts: Information on 580 Careers in Outline Form*
Careers, Inc.
PO Box 135
Largo, FL 34649-0135
Ph: (813)584-7333

Biennial, 1995-96 edition. Each one-page occupational profile describes duties, working conditions, physical surroundings and demands, aptitudes, temperament, educational requirements, employment outlook, earnings, and places of employment.

★3100★ *Video Career Library - Public and Personal Services*
Careers, Inc.
PO Box 135
Largo, FL 34649-0135
Ph: (813)584-7333

Videocassette. 1990. 35 mins. Part of the Video Career Library covering 165 occupations. Shows actual workers on the job. Includes firefighters, police officers, correctional officers, bartenders, waiters/waitresses, cooks/chefs, child care workers, flight attendants, barbers/cosmetologists, groundskeepers/gardeners, and butchers/meat cutters.

Associations

★3101★ Associated Landscape Contractors of America (ALCA)
12200 Sunrise Valley, Ste. 150
Reston, VA 22091
Ph: (703)620-6363 Fax: (703)620-6365

Members: Landscape contractors. **Purpose:** Works to represent, lead, and unify the interior and exterior landscape industry by working together on a national basis; addressing environmental and legislative issues; and creating increased opportunities in business. Provides forum to encourage members' profitability, personal growth, and professional advancement. **Publications:** *Landscape Contractor News*, monthly. • *Who's Who In Landscape Contracting*, annual.

★3102★ Building Service Contractors Association International (BSCAI)
10201 Lee Hwy., Ste. 225
Fairfax, VA 22030
Ph: (703)359-7090 Fax: (703)352-0493
Fr: 800-368-3414

Members: Firms and corporations in 40 countries engaged in contracting building maintenance services including the provision of labor, purchasing materials, and janitorial cleaning and maintenance of a building or its surroundings; associate members are manufacturers of cleaning supplies and equipment. **Purpose:** Seeks to provide a unified voice for building service contractors and to promote increased recognition by government, property owners, and the general business and professional public. Conducts continuing study and action, through committees and special task groups on areas such as public affairs, costs and ratios, uniform accounting, industrial relations and personnel, marketing and sales, contract improvement, research and planning, materials and supplies sources, group insurance, management training, statistics collection, safety, and insurance costs. Has developed a certification program for building service executives, and a registration program for building service managers. **Publications:** *Building Service Contractors Association International—Services*, monthly. • *Information Central Guide*, annual. • *Who's Who in Building Service Contracting*, annual.

★3103★ National Landscape Association (NLA)
1250 Eye St. NW, Ste. 500
Washington, DC 20005
Ph: (202)789-2900 Fax: (202)789-1893

Members: Landscape firms. **Purpose:** Works to: enhance the professionalism of its member firms in designing, building, and maintaining quality landscapes in a profitable and environmentally responsible manner; represent the landscape perspective within the industry. Sponsors annual landscape tour in conjunction with American Association of Nurserymen. **Publications:** *NLA Landscape News*, bimonthly.

★3104★ Professional Grounds Management Society (PGMS)
120 Cockeysville Rd., Ste. 104
Hunt Valley, MD 21031
Ph: (410)584-9754 Fax: (410)584-9756
Fr: 800-609-7467

Members: Professional society of grounds managers of large institutions of all sorts and independent landscape contractors. **Purpose:** Establishes grounds management as a profession; secures opportunities for professional advancement of well-qualified grounds managers; acquaints the public with "the distinction between competent ground managers, equipped through practical experience and systematic study, and self-styled maintenance' personnel, lacking these essentials." Original sponsor of International Peace Garden, located in North Dakota on the U.S.-Canadian border. Provides employment referral service to members. Sponsors contests. Conducts research and surveys; sponsors certification program for professional grounds managers. Takes action with the legislative and executive branches of government on issues affecting grounds managers; keeps members informed on matters affecting the profession. **Publications:** *Grounds Maintenance Estimating Guidelines*, periodic. • *Grounds Maintenance Management Guidelines.* • *Grounds Management Forms and Job Descriptions Guide.* • *Grounds Management Forum*, monthly. • *Grounds Management Guide.* • *Grounds Manager Certification Program.* • *Guide to Grounds Maintenance Estimating.* • *Landscape Management Supervisory Training Manual.* • *Professional Grounds Management Society—Membership Directory*, annual. • *The Professional Grounds Manager.*

Standards/Certification Agencies

★3105★ Professional Grounds Management Society (PGMS)
120 Cockeysville Rd., Ste. 104
Hunt Valley, MD 21031
Ph: (410)584-9754 Fax: (410)584-9756
Fr: 800-609-7467

Conducts research and surveys; sponsors certification program for professional grounds managers.

Test Guides

★3106★ *Career Examination Series: Assistant Gardener*
National Learning Corp.
212 Michael Dr.
Syosset, NY 11791
Ph: (516)921-8888 Fax: (516)921-8743
Fr: 800-645-6337

Jack Rudman. All examination guides in this series contain questions with answers.

★3107★ *Career Examination Series: Chief Groundskeeper*
National Learning Corp.
212 Michael Dr.
Syosset, NY 11791
Ph: (516)921-8888 Fax: (516)921-8743
Fr: 800-645-6337

Jack Rudman. All examination guides in this series contain questions with answers.

★3108★ *Career Examination Series: Foreman of Gardeners*
National Learning Corp.
212 Michael Dr.
Syosset, NY 11791
Ph: (516)921-8888 Fax: (516)921-8743
Fr: 800-645-6337

Jack Rudman. All examination guides in this series contain questions with answers.

★3109★ *Career Examination Series: Gardener*
National Learning Corp.
212 Michael Dr.
Syosset, NY 11791
Ph: (516)921-8888 Fax: (516)921-8743
Fr: 800-645-6337

Jack Rudman. All examination guides in this series contain questions with answers.

★3110★ *Career Examination Series: Greenskeeper*
National Learning Corp.
212 Michael Dr.
Syosset, NY 11791
Ph: (516)921-8888 Fax: (516)921-8743
Fr: 800-645-6337

Jack Rudman. All examination guides in this series contain questions with answers.

★3111★ *Career Examination Series: Groundskeeper*
National Learning Corp.
212 Michael Dr.
Syosset, NY 11791
Ph: (516)921-8888 Fax: (516)921-8743
Fr: 800-645-6337

Jack Rudman. All examination guides in this series contain questions with answers.

★3112★ *Career Examination Series: Principal Groundskeeper*
National Learning Corp.
212 Michael Dr.
Syosset, NY 11791
Ph: (516)921-8888 Fax: (516)921-8743
Fr: 800-645-6337

Jack Rudman. All examination guides in this series contain questions with answers.

★3113★ *Career Examination Series: Senior Groundskeeper*
National Learning Corp.
212 Michael Dr.
Syosset, NY 11791
Ph: (516)921-8888 Fax: (516)921-8743
Fr: 800-645-6337

Jack Rudman. All examination guides in this series contain questions with answers.

★3114★ *Civil Service Tests for Basic Skills Jobs*
Prentice Hall Press
Simon & Schuster Inc.
200 Old Tappan Rd.
Old Tappan, NJ 07675
Ph: 800-223-2348

Hy Hammer. First edition, 1985. Contains nine sample examinations to prepare candidates for entry-level positions that include hospital attendant, building groundskeeper, and custodial assistant, among others.

★3115★ *Gardener - Grounds Maintenance Worker*
Prentice Hall Press
Simon & Schuster Inc.
200 Old Tappan Rd.
Old Tappan, NJ 07675
Ph: 800-223-2348

Hy Hammer. Fourth edition, 1986. Contains eight sample exams with answers for applicants for civil service landscaping and grounds maintenance positions.

★3116★ *Gardening*
National Learning Corp.
212 Michael Dr.
Syosset, NY 11791
Ph: (516)921-8888 Fax: (516)921-8743
Fr: 800-645-6337

Jack Rudman. Part of the Test Your Knowledge Series. Contains multiple choice questions with answers.

Awards, Scholarships, Grants, and Fellowships

★3117★ AAN American Beautification Award
American Association of Nurserymen
1250 I St. NW, Ste. 500
Washington, DC 20005
Ph: (202)789-2900 Fax: (202)789-1893

To recognize outstanding contributions to environmental improvement through the use of living plants. Recipients may be individuals (however, not residential homes), companies, branches of government, churches, clubs, communities, etc. Each AAN Governor is authorized to present one award each year to an outstanding publicly accessible interior or exterior planting. A walnut plaque is presented at a ceremony at the locale of the planting. Established in 1980.

★3118★ W. Allison and Elizabeth Stubbs Davis Award
Municipal Art Society of New York
457 Madison Ave.
New York, NY 10022
Ph: (212)935-3960 Fax: (212)753-1816

To recognize an employee of the Parks Department for exceptional dedication in the service of the city's parks. The recipient is honored with a Certificate of Merit and $500. Established to honor the parents of former Parks Commissioner Gordon J. Davis.

★3119★ *Grounds Maintenance* Awards
Professional Grounds Management Society
120 Cockeysville Rd., Ste.. 104
Hunt Valley, MD 21031
Ph: (410)584-9754 Fax: (410)584-9756

To recognize outstanding achievement in the grounds maintenance field. Awards are given for the best maintained area in the following categories: industrial or office park; condominium, apartment complex, or planned community; hotel, motel, or resort grounds; golf course; cemetery or memorial park; park, recreation area, or athletic field; school or university grounds; government building or complex; shopping area; hospital or institution; small business or residential landscape; and interior landscape. All entries must include photos and slides with captions, and a brief explanation of the year-round maintenance procedures. Plaques are presented to the grand winners and certificates are presented to honor winners in each category. Awarded annually at the awards banquet at the PGMS Annual Conference in the fall.

★3120★ G. B. Gunlogson Medal
American Horticultural Society
7931 E. Boulevard Dr.
Alexandria, VA 22308
Ph: (703)768-5700 Fax: (703)765-6032
Fr: 800-777-7931

To recognize the creative use of new technology to make home gardening more productive and enjoyable. Selection is based on creativeness and inventiveness in the design, construction, and maintenance of home gardens, flower and/or vegetable. A sterling silver medal is awarded each year when merited at the annual meetings. Established in 1974 by G. B. Gunlogson of Racine, Wisconsin.

★3121★ Frances Jones Poetker Award
American Horticultural Society
7931 E. Boulevard Dr.
Alexandria, VA 22308
Ph: (703)768-5700 Fax: (703)765-6032
Fr: 800-777-7931

To recognize a floral artist, either amateur or professional, of national reputation who has, over an extended period of time, generously given inspirational talent that encompasses designing, teaching, and/or writing, and has enhanced the American aesthetic by the use of plant material. Established in 1987.

Basic Reference Guides and Handbooks

★3122★ *Grounds Maintenance Management Guidelines*
Professional Grounds Management Society (PGMS)
120 Cockeysville Rd., Ste. 104
Hunt Valley, MD 21031
Ph: (410)584-9754 Fax: (410)584-9756
Fr: 800-609-7467

Periodic.

★3123★ *Grounds Management Guide,*
Professional Grounds Management Society (PGMS)
120 Cockeysville Rd., Ste. 104
Hunt Valley, MD 21031
Ph: (410)584-9754 Fax: (410)584-9756
Fr: 800-609-7467

★3124★ *Guide to Grounds Maintenance Estimating*
Professional Grounds Management Society
120 Cockeysville Rd., Ste. 104
Hunt Valley, MD 21031
Ph: (410)584-9754 Fax: (410)584-9756
Fr: 800-609-7467

★3125★ *Park and Grounds Management—Athletic Area and Facilities Buyer's Guide Issue*
Madisen Publishing Co.
PO Box 1936
Appleton, WI 54913-1936
Ph: (414)733-2301
Erik Madisen, Contact

Annual, April. Publication includes: Lists of companies and products of interest to managers of parks, campuses, golf courses, or other large grounds areas. Principal content is articles on park or grounds management, operation, and maintenance. Arrangement: Alphabetical.

★3126★ *The Professional Grounds Manager*
Professional Grounds Management Society (PGMS)
120 Cockeysville Rd., Ste. 104
Hunt Valley, MD 21031
Ph: (410)584-9754 Fax: (410)584-9756
Fr: 800-609-7467

PERIODICALS

★3127★ *American Horticulturist*
American Horticultural Society
7931 E. Boulevard Dr.
Alexandria, VA 22308
Ph: (703)768-5700 Fax: (703)765-6032
Fr: 800-777-7931
Kathleen Fisher

Bimonthly. Publishes news of the Society and its interest in gardening and horticulture. Reports on scientific developments, new plants, ecology and environment, and cultivation methods. Recurring features include regional news, a calendar of events, book reviews, and a column titled Plants Wanted.

★3128★ *American Nurseryman*
American Nurseryman Publishing Co.
77 W. Washington St., Ste. 2100
Chicago, IL 60602-2801
Ph: (312)782-5505 Fax: (312)782-3232
Fr: 800-621-5727
Julie S. Higginbotham

Semiweekly. Magazine containing information on horticulture and nursery, landscape and garden center management.

★3129★ *The American Rose*
American Rose Society
PO Box 30,000
Shreveport, LA 71130
Ph: (318)938-5402 Fax: (318)938-5405
William Johnson

Monthly. Magazine concerning rose growing.

★3130★ *Amerigold Bulletin*
Marigold Society of America
PO Box 5112
New Britain, PA 18901
Jeannette Lowe

Quarterly. Highlights events of the Society and discusses topics of interest to horticulturists and marigold lovers. Examines varieties, plant culture, and history of marigold cultivation. Recurring features include convention reports, news of members, commentary, news of upcoming events, a seed exchange, and the column President's Message.

★3131★ *The Avant Gardener*
Horticultural Data Processors
PO Box 489
New York, NY 10028
Thomas Powell

Monthly. Contains information on such subjects as indoor and outdoor plants, edible plants, new products, methods of cultivation, breeding and growing techniques, pest control, fertilizers, and landscaping. Recurring features include several special issues per year on specific topics.

★3132★ *The Cultivator*
Red Butte Gardens and Arboretum
390 Wakara Way
Salt Lake City, UT 84108
Ph: (801)581-5322
Edward R. Mitchell

Covers gardening, general arboreta news, and related items of interest, with particular attention to seasonal information concerning plants and their cultivation. Recurring features include practical gardening tips, book reviews, news of volunteers, reports of field trips and lectures, news of research, a calendar of events, list of current contributors, and columns titled From the Director, From the Garden, Special Events and Happenings, Home Gardening, Fun for Sprouts, and Garden Queries.

★3133★ *The Gardener*
The Gardeners of America, Inc.
5560 Merle Hay Rd.
PO Box 241
Johnston, IA 50131
Ph: (515)278-0295 Fax: (515)278-6245
Carol Donovan

Bimonthly. Gardening and horticulture magazine.

★3134★ *Green World News*
Bonsai & Orchid Association
26 Pine St.
Dover, DE 19901
Ph: (302)736-6781 Fax: (302)736-6763

Monthly. Updates members of the bonsai and orchid industry on the latest technical information in the field. Reviews new products, growing methods, pertinent regulations, and industry trends. Recurring features include news of research, editorials, news of members, and a calendar of events.

★3135★ *Grounds Management Forum*
Professional Grounds Management Society
120 Cockeysville Rd., Ste. 104
Hunt Valley, MD 21031
Ph: (410)584-9754
John Gillan

Monthly. Reports news of the Society and its members. Provides information on upcoming conferences, recent government action, and on current topics of interest to members. Recurring features include book reviews.

★3136★ *Harvests*
Lawn Institute
1509 Johnson Ferry Rd. NE, Ste. 190
Marietta, GA 30062-8122
Eliot C. Roberts

Quarterly. Summarizes results of current research on lawns and sports turf. Recurring features include editorials, news of members, book reviews, letters to the editor, reports on turfgrass conferences and field days, and columns titled Lawn Institute Pitch and Director's Dialogue.

★3137★ *Horticulture*
98 N. Washington St.
Boston, MA 02114
Ph: (617)742-5600 Fax: (617)367-6364
Thomas C. Cooper

Magazine for the amateur gardener.

★3138★ *Hortldeas*
Greg and Pat Williams
Box 302, Rte. 1
Gravel Switch, KY 40328
Ph: (606)332-7606
Greg Williams

Monthly. Reviews the latest research on vegetable, fruit, and flower gardening. Provides practical information and tips on growing techniques, tools, plant varieties, and resources in abstract form with full references to original sources. Recurring features include book reviews.

★3139★ *Landscape Contractor News*
Associated Landscape Contractors of America (ALCA)
12200 Sunrise Valley, Ste. 150
Reston, VA 22091
Ph: (703)620-6363 Fax: (703)620-6365

Monthly. Covers association and industry news.

★3140★ *Magnolia: Journal of the Magnolia Society*
Magnolia Society, Inc.
907 S. Chestnut St.
Hammond, LA 70403-5102
Ph: (504)542-9477 Fax: (504)345-4294
Larry W. Langford

Semiannual. Discusses aspects of magnolia culture. Covers hybridization, seed collection, storing, mailing, genetics, the search for new species abroad, and similar subjects. Recurring features include reports of the seed counter program, news of research, book reviews, and Society news.

★3141★ *National Gardening*
National Gardening Assn.
180 Flynn Ave.
Burlington, VT 05401
Ph: (802)863-1308 Fax: (802)863-5962
Michael MacCaskey

Bimonthly. Magazine covering fruit, vegetable, and ornamental gardening for home and community gardeners.

★3142★ *New Horizons*
Horticultural Research Institute
1250 I St. NW, Ste. 500
Washington, DC 20005
Ph: (202)789-2900 Fax: (202)789-1893
Ashby P. Ruden

Explores research of the science and art of nursery, retail garden center, and landscape plant production, marketing, and care.

★3143★ *NLA Landscape News*
National Landscape Association (NLA)
1250 Eye St. NW, Ste. 500
Washington, DC 20005
Ph: (202)789-2900 Fax: (202)789-1893

Bimonthly.

★3144★ *Organic Gardening*
Rodale Press, Inc.
33 E. Minor St.
Emmaus, PA 18098
Ph: (610)967-8650 Fax: (610)967-8181
Mike McGrath

Horticulture and gardening magazine.

★3145★ *Plants & Gardens*
Brooklyn Botanic Garden
1000 Washington Ave.
Brooklyn, NY 11225
Ph: (718)622-4433 Fax: (718)857-2430
Barbara Pesch

Quarterly. Horticultural and botanical magazine.

★3146★ *Rocky Mountain Construction*
Golden Bell Press
2403 Champa St.
Denver, CO 80205
Ph: (303)295-0630 Fax: (303)295-2159
F. Hol Wagner

Semiweekly. Magazine serving the construction industry of America's mountain regions. Covering heavy engineering, building, landscaping, soil conservation, mining and logging, and federal, state, county, and city projects. Includes weekly construction reports.

★3147★ *Who's Who In Landscape Contracting*
Associated Landscape Contractors of America (ALCA)
12200 Sunrise Valley, Ste. 150
Reston, VA 22091
Ph: (703)620-6363 Fax: (703)620-6365

Annual.

Meetings and Conventions

★3148★ Annual Conference and Green Industry Expo
Professional Grounds Management Society (PGMS)
120 Cockeysville Rd., Ste. 104
Hunt Valley, MD 21031
Ph: (410)584-9754 Fax: (410)584-9756
Fr: 800-609-7467

Annual. Always November. **Dates and Locations:** 1995 Nov; Ft. Worth, TX • 1996 Nov; Cincinnati, OH • 1997 Nov; Charlotte, NC.

★3149★ Eastern Regional Nurserymen Show
Eastern Regional Nurserymen Association
24 West Rd., Ste. 53
Vernon, CT 06066
Ph: (203)872-2095

Annual. Always held at the Concord Resort Hotel in Kiamesha Lake, New York. **Dates and Locations:** 1995; Kiamesha Lake, NY.

★3150★ Executive Forum
Associated Landscape Contractors of America (ALCA)
12200 Sunrise Valley, Ste. 150
Reston, VA 22091
Ph: (703)620-6363 Fax: (703)620-6365

Annual. Always January or February.

★3151★ Interior Plantscape Conference and Trade Show
Associated Landscape Contractors of America (ALCA)
12200 Sunrise Valley, Ste. 150
Reston, VA 22091
Ph: (703)620-6363 Fax: (703)620-6365

Annual. Always September.

★3152★ International Lawn, Garden, and Power Equipment Expo
Andry Montgomery California Inc.
8930 Keith Ave.
Los Angeles, CA 90069
Ph: (213)271-3200 Fax: (213)271-8409

Annual. Always held during July at the Kentucky Fair and Exposition Center in Louisville, Kentucky. **Dates and Locations:** 1996 Jul; Louisville, KY.

★3153★ Landscape and Grounds Maintenance Conference
Associated Landscape Contractors of America (ALCA)
12200 Sunrise Valley, Ste. 150
Reston, VA 22091
Ph: (703)620-6363 Fax: (703)620-6365

Annual. Always November.

★3154★ Mid-Atlantic Nurserymen's Winter Trade Show
Mid-Atlantic Nurserymen's Trade Show, Inc.
PO Box 314
Perry Hall, MD 21128
Ph: (410)256-6474 Fax: (410)256-2268

Semiannual. Always held at the Convention Center in Baltimore, Maryland.

★3155★ National Institute on Park and Grounds Management Convention
National Institute on Park and Grounds Management
PO Box 1936
Appleton, WI 54913
Ph: (414)733-2301

Annual.

★3156★ New England Nurserymen's Annual Trade Show
Connecticut/Eastern Regional Nurserymen's Association
Management Specialties Inc.
1148 Centre St., Ste. 163
Newton, MA 02159-1539
Ph: (617)964-8209

Annual. Always held during January in Boston, Massachusetts.

★3157★ Professional Lawn Care Association of America Annual Conference and Show
Professional Lawn Care Association of America
1000 Johnson Ferry Rd., Ste. C-135
Marietta, GA 30068
Ph: (404)977-5222 Fax: (404)578-6071
Fr: 800-458-3466

Annual. **Dates and Locations:** 1995 Nov 13-16; Fort Worth, TX.

★3158★ Southern Nurserymen Association Horticultural Trade Show
Southern Nurserymen Association
1000 Johnson Ferry Rd., Ste. 130 E.
Marietta, GA 30068-2100
Ph: (404)973-9026 Fax: (404)973-9097

Annual. Always held during the first weekend in August at the Georgia World Congress Center in Atlanta, Georgia. **Dates and Locations:** 1996 Aug 09-11; Atlanta, GA. • 1997 Aug 01-03; Atlanta, GA. • 1998 Jul 31-02; Atlanta, GA.

Other Sources of Information

★3159★ *Government Product News—Buyers Guide for Grounds Maintenance Issue*
Penton Publishing Co.
1100 Superior Ave.
Cleveland, OH 44114-2543
Ph: (216)696-7000 Fax: (216)696-0177
P. K. Gibson, Contact

Annual, November. Publication includes: List of over 1,000 manufacturers of grounds maintenance equipment. Entries include: Company name, address, phone, name and title of contact. Arrangement: Alphabetical.

★3160★ *Pruning Bare Root Trees for the Garden Center and Shearing Pine, Sprouce and Fir*
American Nurseryman Publishing Co.
77 W. Washington St., Ste. 2100
Chicago, IL 60602
Ph: (312)782-5505 Fax: (312)782-3232
Fr: 800-621-5727

Two-part program offers employees a look at proper pruning and shearing techniques.

Homemaker-Home Health Aides

Homemaker-home health aides provide home management services, personal care, and emotional support for elderly, disabled, and ill persons. Aides perform management services such as light housekeeping chores. Among the personal care services that aides perform are assisting with bathing or giving a bed bath, shampooing hair, and helping the client move from bed to a chair or another room. Providing emotional support and understanding is a particularly important aspect of the work since a client's progress in regaining strength and independence may be greatly influenced by his or her mental attitude. In agency settings, homemaker-home health aides are assigned specific duties by a supervisor--usually a registered nurse, physical therapist, or social worker.

Salaries

Earnings for homemaker-home health aides vary considerably. Some aides start at $6.31/hour. Aides in agencies in large cities that have high living costs generally pay higher wages, up to $8.28/hour to start. Agencies that have union contracts usually pay higher wages and offer more benefits. While some agencies pay the same rate to all aides, most agencies give slight pay increases as aides gain experience and are given more responsibility.

Employment Outlook

Growth rate until the year 2005: Much faster than the average.

Homemaker-Home Health Aides

Career Guides

★3161★ *Becoming a Helper*
Brooks/Cole Publishing Co.
511 Forest Lodge Rd.
Pacific Grove, CA 93950-5098
Ph: (408)373-0728 Fax: (408)375-6414

Marianne Schneider Corey and Gerald Corey. Second edition, 1993.

★3162★ *Geriatric Aides*
Chronicle Guidance Publications, Inc.
66 Aurora St.
PO Box 1190
Moravia, NY 13118-1190
Ph: (315)497-0330 Fax: (315)497-3359
Fr: 800-622-7284

1993. This career brief describes the nature of the work, working conditions, hours and earnings, education and training, licensure, certification, unions, personal qualifications, social and psychological factors, employment outlook, entry methods, advancement, and related occupations.

★3163★ "Health Care" in *Where the Jobs Are: The Hottest Careers for the 90s* (pp. 143-166)
Career Press
180 5th Ave.
Hawthorne, NJ 07507
Ph: (201)427-0229 Fax: (201)427-2037
Fr: 800-CAREER-1

Joyce Hadley. 1995. Offers a job-hunting strategy for the 1990s as well as descriptions of growing careers of the decade. Each profile includes general information, forecasts, growth, education and training, licensing requirements, and salary information.

★3164★ "Home Care Aide" in *Careers in Health Care* (pp. 112-115)
National Textbook Co. (NTC)
VGM Career Books
4255 W. Touhy Ave.
Lincolnwood, IL 60646-1975
Ph: (708)679-5500 Fax: (708)679-2494
Fr: 800-323-4900

Barbara M. Swanson. 1995. Discusses 58 health careers, providing information about the history of the occupation, job duties, work environments, salaries, educational preparation, licensure, certification, and employment outlook.

★3165★ *Home Health Aide*
Careers, Inc.
PO Box 135
Largo, FL 34649-0135
Ph: (813)584-7333

1991. Two-page job guide card describing duties, working conditions, personal qualifications, training, earnings and hours, employment outlook, places of employment, related careers and where to write for more information.

★3166★ "Home Health Aide" in *100 Best Careers for the Year 2000* (pp. 20-22)
Arco Pub.
201 W. 103rd St.
Indianapolis, IN 46290
Ph: 800-428-5331 Fax: 800-835-3202

Shelly Field. 1992. Describes 100 job opportunities expected to grow fast throughout the next decade. Provides information on job duties and responsibilities, training requirements, education, advancement opportunities, experience and qualifications, and typical salaries.

★3167★ "Home Health Aide" in *Career Information Center* (Vol.7)
Simon and Schuster
200 Old Tappan Rd.
Old Tappan, NJ 07675
Fax: 800-445-6991 Fr: 800-223-2348

Richard Lidz and Dale Anderson, editorial directors. Fifth edition, 1993. For 600 occupations, describes job duties, entry-level requirements, education and training needed, advancement possibilities, employment outlook, earnings and benefits. The set is divided into 12 volumes. Each volume includes jobs related under a broad career field. Volume 13 is the index.

★3168★ "Home Health Aide" in *Health Care* (pp. 45-49)
Franklin Watts, Inc.
387 Park Avenue, S.
New York, NY 10016
Ph: (212)686-7070

Linda Barrett and Galen Guengerich. 1991. Provides an overview of the health care industry. Includes job description, educational preparation, training, salary, and employment outlook. Offers job hunting advice.

★3169★ "Home Health Aide" in *Occu-Facts: Information on 580 Careers in Outline Form*
Careers, Inc.
PO Box 135
Largo, FL 34649-0135
Ph: (813)584-7333

Biennial, 1995-96 edition. Each one-page occupational profile describes duties, working conditions, physical surroundings and demands, aptitudes, temperament, educational requirements, employment outlook, earnings, and places of employment.

★3170★ *Home Health Care Nurse*
Vocational Biographies, Inc.
PO Box 31
Sauk Centre, MN 56378-0031
Ph: (612)352-6516 Fax: (612)352-5546
Fr: 800-255-0752

1993. Four-page pamphlet containing a personal narrative about a worker's job, work likes and dislikes, career path from high school to the present. Education and training, the rewards and frustrations, and the effects of the job on the rest of the worker's life. The data file portion of this pamphlet gives a concise occupational summary, including work descriptions, working conditions, places of employment, personal characteristics, education and training, job outlook, and salary range.

★3171★ "Homemaker" in *Career Information Center* (Vol.5)
Simon and Schuster
200 Old Tappan Rd.
Old Tappan, NJ 07675
Fax: 800-445-6991 Fr: 800-223-2348

Richard Lidz and Dale Anderson, editorial directors. Fifth edition, 1993. For 600 occupations, describes job duties, entry-level requirements, education and training needed, advancement possibilities, employment outlook, earnings and benefits. The set is divided into 12 volumes. Each volume includes jobs related under a broad career field. Volume 13 is the index.

★3172★ "Homemaker-Home Health Aide" in *150 Careers in the Health Care Field*
Reed Reference Publishing
121 Chanlon Rd.
PO Box 31
New Providence, NJ 07974
Fax: (908)665-6688 Fr: 800-521-8110

Stanley Alperin. Third edition, 1993. Each occupational profile covers job functions and responsibilities, work locations, training requirements, certification, and salaries. Lists community colleges, universities, vocational-technical schools, and other educational institutions that provide accredited training programs.

★3173★ "Homemaker Home Health Aide" in *Opportunities in Health and Medical Careers* (pp. 32-33)
National Textbook Co. (NTC)
VGM Career Books
4255 W. Touhy Ave.
Lincolnwood, IL 60646-1975
Ph: (708)679-5500 Fax: (708)679-2494
Fr: 800-323-4900

Leo D'Orazio and I. Donald Snook. 1991. Provides an overview of the health care industry with future projections. Describes a wide variety of healthcare jobs covering the nature of the work, educational requirements, employment outlook and salaries. Offers job hunting advice.

★3174★ *Homemaker Home Health Aides*
Chronicle Guidance Publications, Inc.
66 Aurora St.
PO Box 1190
Moravia, NY 13118-1190
Ph: (315)497-0330 Fax: (315)497-3359
Fr: 800-622-7284

1993. This career brief describes the nature of the work, working conditions, hours and earnings, education and training, licensure, certification, unions, personal qualifications, social and psychological factors, employment outlook, entry methods, advancement, and related occupations.

★3175★ "Homemaker-Home Health Aides" in *America's 50 Fastest Growing Jobs* (pp. 124)
JIST Works, Inc.
720 N. Park Ave.
Indianapolis, IN 46202-3431
Ph: (317)264-3720 Fax: (317)264-3709
Fr: 800-648-5478

Michael J. Farr, compiler. 1994. Describes the 50 fastest growing jobs within major career clusters such as technicians, and marketing and sales. Each job profile explains the nature of the work, skills and abilities required, employment outlook, average earnings, related occupations, education and training requirements, and employment opportunities. Also contains career planning information and job search tips.

★3176★ "Homemaker Home Health Aides" in *Career Discovery Encyclopedia* (Vol.3, pp. 98-99)
J.G. Ferguson Publishing Co.
200 W. Madison St., Ste. 300
Chicago, IL 60606
Ph: (312)580-5480 Fax: (312)580-4948

E. Russell Primm, editor-in-chief. 1993. Contains two-page articles on 504 occupations. Each article describes job duties, earnings, and educational and training requirements.

★3177★ "Homemaker Home Health Aides" in *Encyclopedia of Careers and Vocational Guidance* (Vol.3, pp. 139-142)
J.G. Ferguson Publishing Co.
200 W. Madison St., Ste. 300
Chicago, IL 60606
Ph: (312)580-5480 Fax: (312)580-4948

William E. Hopke, editor-in-chief. Ninth edition, 1993. Four-volume set that profiles 500 occupations and describes job trends in 74 industries. Includes career description, educational requirements, history of the job, methods of entry, advancement, employment outlook, earnings, working conditions, social and psychological factors, and sources of additional information.

★3178★ "Homemaker-Home Health Aides" in *Health Care Job Explosion!* (pp. 253-260)
D-Amp Publications
401 Amherst Ave.
Coraopolis, PA 15108
Ph: (412)262-5578

Dennis V. Damp. 1993. Provides information on the nature of work for the major health care occupational groups. Descriptions include working conditions, training, job outlook, qualifications, and related occupations.

★3179★ "Homemaker-Home Health Aides" in *Occupational Outlook Handbook*
U.S. Government Printing Office
Superintendent of Documents
Washington, DC 20402
Ph: (202)512-1800 Fax: (202)512-2250

Biennial; latest edition, 1994-95. Encyclopedia of careers describing more than 250 occupations and comprising about 85 percent of all jobs in the economy. Occupations that require lengthy education or training are given the most attention. For each occupation, the handbook describes job duties, working conditions, training, educational preparation, personal qualities, advancement possibilities, job outlook, earnings, and sources of additional information.

★3180★ "Homemaker—Home Health Aides" in *The Best Jobs for the 1990s and Into the 21st Century*
Impact Publications
9104-N Manassas Dr.
Manassas Park, VA 22111
Ph: (703)361-7300 Fax: (703)335-9486

Ronald L. Krannich and Caryl Rae Krannich. 1993.

★3181★ "Homemaker" in *Opportunities in Home Economics Careers* (pp. 51-52)
National Textbook Co. (NTC)
VGM Career Books
4255 W. Touhy Ave.
Lincolnwood, IL 60646-1975
Ph: (708)679-5500 Fax: (708)679-2494
Fr: 800-323-4900

Rhea Shields and Anna K. Williams. 1988. Describes the history of home economics and current trends affecting the field. Explores related careers in interior design, family relations, and home management. Covers the nature of the work, educational preparation, skills, employment outlook, places of employment, and salaries. Lists professional organizations and offers job hunting advice.

★3182★ "Household Workers" in *Encyclopedia of Careers and Vocational Guidance* (Vol.3, pp. 152-154)
J.G. Ferguson Publishing Co.
200 W. Madison St., Ste. 300
Chicago, IL 60606
Ph: (312)580-5480 Fax: (312)580-4948

William E. Hopke, editor-in-chief. Ninth edition, 1993. Four-volume set that profiles 900 occupations and describes job trends in 74 industries. Includes career description, educational requirements, history of the job, methods of entry, advancement, employment outlook, earnings, conditions of work, social and psychological factors, and sources of further information.

★3183★ *Opportunities in Homecare Services Careers*
National Textbook Co. (NTC)
VGM Career Books
4255 W. Toughy Ave.
Lincolnwood, IL 60646-1975
Ph: (708)679-5500 Fax: (708)679-2494
Fr: 800-323-4900

Anne Cardoza.

Associations

★3184★ National Association for Home Care (NAHC)
519 C St. NE
Stanton Park
Washington, DC 20002
Ph: (202)547-7424 Fax: (202)547-3540

Members: Providers of home health care, hospice, and homemaker-home health aide services; interested individuals and organizations. **Purpose:** Develops and promotes high standards of patient care in home care services. Seeks to affect legislative and regulatory processes concerning home care services; gathers and disseminates home care industry data; develops public relations strategies; works to increase political visibility of home care services. Interprets home care services to governmental and private sector bodies affecting the delivery and financing of such services. Provides legal and accounting consulting services; conducts market research and compiles statistics. Offers members insurance discounts. Sponsors educational programs for organizations and individuals concerned with home care services. **Publications:** *Caring*, monthly. • *Homecare News*, monthly. • *Hospice Forum*, biweekly. • *NAHC Report*, weekly. • *National Home Care and Hospice Directory*, annual.

Standards/Certification Agencies

★3185★ National Association for Home Care (NAHC)
519 C St. NE
Stanton Park
Washington, DC 20002
Ph: (202)547-7424 Fax: (202)547-3540

Develops and promotes high standards of patient care in home care services. Seeks to affect legislative and regulatory processes concerning home care services; gathers and disseminates home care industry data; develops public relations strategies; works to increase political visibility of home care services.

Test Guides

★3186★ *Career Examination Series: Home Health Aide/Homemaker*
National Learning Corp.
212 Michael Dr.
Syosset, NY 11791
Ph: (516)921-8888 Fax: (516)921-8743
Fr: 800-645-6337

Jack Rudman. Test guide including questions and answers for students or professionals in the field who seek advancement through examination.

Educational Directories and Programs

★3187★ *National Home Care and Hospice Directory*
National Association for Home Care (NAHC)
519 C St. NE
Stanton Park
Washington, DC 20002
Ph: (202)547-7424 Fax: (202)547-3540

Annual.

Periodicals

★3188★ *AAHA Provider News*
American Association of Homes for the Aging (AAHA)
901 E St. NW, Ste. 500
Washington, DC 20004
Ph: (202)783-2242 Fax: (202)783-2255
Jean E. Van Ryzin

Discusses topics concerning nonprofit homes and services for the aging, including legislative, regulatory, and judicial developments in long-term care and housing; issues in the field of gerontology; and new developments in alternative services for the aging. Publicizes Association events, services and growth, membership accomplishments, and professional opportunities. Recurring features include columns titled Job Mart, Health Issues, Employer Tips, Trends, and Housing Issues.

★3189★ *AHEA ACTION*
American Home Economics Assn.
1555 King St.
Alexandria, VA 22314
Ph: (703)706-4600 Fax: (703)706-HOME
Marjorie Harter

Home economics publication.

★3190★ *Caring*
National Association for Home Care (NAHC)
519 C St. NE
Stanton Park
Washington, DC 20002
Ph: (202)547-7424 Fax: (202)547-3540

Monthly.

★3191★ *Home Health Line*
Karen Rak
PO Box 250
Port Republic, MD 20676
Ph: (410)535-4103 Fax: (410)535-0632
Richard Falknor

Weekly. Reports on Medicare, Medicaid, and other federal and commercial coverage and payment for home health care, including hospice care, home medical equipment, home infusion therapy, and the home care industry as a business.

★3192★ *Homecare News*
National Association for Home Care (NAHC)
519 C St. NE
Stanton Park
Washington, DC 20002
Ph: (202)547-7424 Fax: (202)547-3540

Monthly. Tabloid covering association news; serves as an information exchange between state associations and providers/suppliers to the industry.

★3193★ *Hospice Forum*
National Association for Home Care (NAHC)
519 C St. NE
Stanton Park
Washington, DC 20002
Ph: (202)547-7424 Fax: (202)547-3540

Biweekly. Covers legislative and research news.

★3194★ *NAHC Report*
National Association for Home Care (NAHC)
519 C St. NE
Stanton Park
Washington, DC 20002
Ph: (202)547-7424 Fax: (202)547-3540

Weekly. Covers legislative and regulatory issues related to the home health care industry. Contains employment opportunity listings.

Meetings and Conventions

★3195★ American Association for Continuity of Care Annual Conference
American Association for Continuity of Care
1730 N. Lynn St., Ste. 502
Arlington, VA 22209-2004
Ph: (305)386-3855 Fax: (703)276-8196

Annual. Always held during September. **Dates and Locations:** 1996; New York, NY.

★3196★ National Association for Home Care Annual Meeting and Home Care Exhibition
National Association for Home Care
519 C St., NE
Washington, DC 20002
Ph: (202)547-7424 Fax: (202)547-3540

Annual.

Other Sources of Information

★3197★ "Home Health Aide" in *100 Best Jobs for the 1990s & Beyond*
Dearborn Financial Publishing, Inc.
520 N. Dearborn St.
Chicago, IL 60610-4354
Ph: (312)836-4400 Fax: (312)836-1021
Fr: 800-621-9621

Carol Kleiman. 1992. Describes 100 jobs ranging from accountants to veterinarians. Each job profile includes such information as education, experience, and certification needed, salaries, and job search suggestions.

Janitors and Cleaners

Janitors or **cleaners**--also called **building custodians**--keep office buildings, hospitals, stores, apartment houses, hotels, and other types of buildings clean and in good condition. Some janitors can only do cleaning; others have a wide range of duties. Custodians work in every type of establishment. About 20 percent work in a school, including colleges and universities. Twenty percent work for a firm supplying building maintenance services on a contract basis. Ten percent work in a hotel and another ten percent in a hospital. Others were employed by restaurants, operators of apartment buildings, office buildings, and other types of real estate, churches and other religious organizations, manufacturing firms, and government agencies.

Salaries

Average weekly earnings of janitors and cleaners are as follows:

Janitors and cleaners lowest 10 percent	$176/week or less
Janitors and cleaners middle 10 percent	$212-$374/week
Janitors and cleaners top 10 percent	$477/week or more
Cleaning supervisors lowest 10 percent	$228/week or less
Cleaning supervisors middle 10 percent	$285-$497/week
Cleaning supervisors top 10 percent	$690/week or more

Employment Outlook

Growth rate until the year 2005: Average.

Janitors and Cleaners

Career Guides

★3198★ "Building Custodian" in *Career Information Center* (Vol.11)
Simon and Schuster
200 Old Tappan Rd.
Old Tappan, NJ 07675
Fax: 800-445-6991 Fr: 800-223-2348

Richard Lidz and Dale Anderson, editorial directors. Fifth edition, 1993. For 600 occupations, describes job duties, entry-level requirements, education and training needed, advancement possibilities, employment outlook, earnings and benefits. The set is divided into 12 volumes. Each volume includes jobs related under a broad career field. Volume 13 is the index.

★3199★ "Building Custodian" in *Exploring Nontraditional Jobs for Women* (pp. 99-105)
Rosen Publishing Group
29 E. 21st St.
New York, NY 10010
Ph: (212)777-3017 Fax: (212)777-0277
Fr: 800-237-9932

Rose Neufeld. 1989. Describes blue-collar, male dominated occupations. Discusses what is done on the job, training, where to apply for jobs, tools used, salaries, and advantages and disadvantages. Relates the experiences of women who are working in the field.

★3200★ "Building Custodian" in *Personal Services* (pp. 21-25)
Franklin Watts, Inc.
387 Park Avenue, S.
New York, NY 10016
Ph: (212)686-7070

Linda Barrett and Galen Guengerich. 1991. Surveys personal services jobs. Describes job duties, educational preparation, salaries, and employment outlook. Offers job hunting advice.

★3201★ *Career Examination Series: Assistant Building Inspector*
National Learning Corp.
212 Michael Dr.
Syosset, NY 11791
Ph: (516)921-8888

1989. All examination guides in this series contain questions with answers.

★3202★ *Career Examination Series: Building Maintenance Custodian (U.S.P.S.)*
National Learning Corp.
212 Michael Dr.
Syosset, NY 11791
Ph: (516)921-8888

1988. All examination guides in this series contain questions with answers.

★3203★ "Cleaning Service" in *100 Best Careers for the Year 2000* (pp. 274)
Arco Pub.
201 W. 103rd St.
Indianapolis, IN 46290
Ph: 800-428-5331 Fax: 800-835-3202

Shelly Field. 1992. Describes 100 job opportunities expected to grow fast throughout the next decade. Provides information on job duties and responsibilities, training requirements, education, advancement opportunities, experience and qualifications, and typical salaries.

★3204★ "Custodial Services Manager" in *BLR Encyclopedia of Prewritten Job Descriptions*
Business and Legal Reports, Inc.
39 Academy St.
Madison, CT 06443-1513
Ph: (203)245-7448

Stephen D. Bruce, editor-in-chief. 1994. This book contains hundreds of sample job descriptions arranged by functional job category. The 1-3 page job descriptions cover what the worker normally does in the position, who they report to, and how that position fits in the organizational structure.

★3205★ "Custodial Workers" in *American Almanac of Jobs and Salaries* (p. 531)
Avon Books
1350 Avenue of the Americas
New York, NY 10019
Ph: (212)261-6800 Fr: 800-238-0658

John Wright, editor. Revised and updated, 1994-95. A comprehensive guide to the wages of hundreds of occupations in a wide variety of industries and organizations.

★3206★ *Custodian*
Vocational Biographies, Inc.
PO Box 31
Sauk Centre, MN 56378-0031
Ph: (612)352-6516 Fax: (612)352-5546
Fr: 800-255-0752

1994. Four-page pamphlet containing a personal narrative about a worker's job, work likes and dislikes, career path from high school to the present. Education and training, the rewards and frustrations, and the effects of the job on the rest of the worker's life. The data file portion of this pamphlet gives a concise occupational summary, including work descriptions, working conditions, places of employment, personal characteristics, education and training, job outlook, and salary range.

★3207★ *Custodian, Building*
Careers, Inc.
PO Box 135
Largo, FL 34649-0135
Ph: (813)584-7333

1994. Two-page job guide card describing duties, working conditions, personal qualifications, training, earnings and hours, employment outlook, places of employment, related careers and where to write for more information.

★3208★ "Custodian, Building" in *Occu-Facts: Information on 580 Careers inOutline Form*
Careers, Inc.
PO Box 135
Largo, FL 34649-0135
Ph: (813)584-7333

Biennial, 1995-96 edition. Each one-page occupational profile describes duties, working conditions, physical surroundings and demands, aptitudes, temperament, educational requirements, employment outlook, earnings, and places of employment.

★3209★ *Custodians*
Chronicle Guidance Publications, Inc.
66 Aurora St.
PO Box 1190
Moravia, NY 13118-1190
Ph: (315)497-0330 Fax: (315)497-3359
Fr: 800-622-7284

1993. This career brief describes the nature of the work, working conditions, hours and earnings, education and training, licensure, certification, unions, personal qualifications, social and psychological factors, employment outlook, entry methods, advancement, and related occupations.

★3210★ "Hotel, Motel Cleaner" in *Occu-Facts: Information on 580 Careers in Outline Form*
Careers, Inc.
PO Box 135
Largo, FL 34649-0135
Ph: (813)584-7333

Biennial, 1995-96 edition. Each one-page occupational profile describes duties, working conditions, physical surroundings and demands, aptitudes, temperament, educational requirements, employment outlook, earnings, and places of employment.

★3211★ *Inside the Janitorial Business: How to Start from Scratch & Succeed in Professional Cleaning*
MBM Books
PO Box 1087
Valley Center, CA 92082
Ph: (619)749-2380

Frederick R. Massey. Second edition, 1989.

★3212★ "Janitor" in *VGM's Careers Encyclopedia* (pp. 235-236)
National Textbook Co. (NTC)
VGM Career Books
4255 W. Touhy Ave.
Lincolnwood, IL 60646-1975
Ph: (708)679-5500 Fax: (708)679-2494
Fr: 800-323-4900

Third edition, 1991. Contains two- to five-page descriptions of 200 managerial, professional, technical, trade, and service occupations. Each profile includes job duties, places of employment, qualifications, educational preparation, training, employment potential, advancement, income, and additional sources of information.

★3213★ *Janitors*
Chronicle Guidance Publications, Inc.
66 Aurora St.
PO Box 1190
Moravia, NY 13118-1190
Ph: (315)497-0330 Fax: (315)497-3359
Fr: 800-622-7284

1993. Career brief describing the nature of the job, working conditions, hours and earnings, education and training, licensure, certification, unions, personal qualifications, social and psychological factors, location, employment outlook, entry methods, advancement, and related occupations.

★3214★ "Janitors and Cleaners" in *Career Discovery Encyclopedia* (Vol.3, pp. 148-149)
J.G. Ferguson Publishing Co.
200 W. Madison St., Ste. 300
Chicago, IL 60606
Ph: (312)580-5480 Fax: (312)580-4948

E. Russell Primm, editor-in-chief. 1993. Contains two-page articles on 504 occupations. Each article describes job duties, earnings, and educational and training requirements.

★3215★ "Janitors and Cleaners" in *Encyclopedia of Careers and Vocational Guidance* (Vol.3, pp. 244-245)
J.G. Ferguson Publishing Co.
200 W. Madison St., Ste. 300
Chicago, IL 60606
Ph: (312)580-5480 Fax: (312)580-4948

William E. Hopke, editor-in-chief. Ninth edition, 1993. Four-volume set that profiles 500 occupations and describes job trends in 74 industries. Includes career description, educational requirements, history of the job, methods of entry, advancement, employment outlook, earnings, working conditions, social and psychological factors, and sources of additional information.

★3216★ "Janitors and Cleaners" in *Occupational Outlook Handbook*
U.S. Government Printing Office
Superintendent of Documents
Washington, DC 20402
Ph: (202)512-1800 Fax: (202)512-2250

Biennial; latest edition, 1994-95. Encyclopedia of careers describing more than 250 occupations and comprising about 85 percent of all jobs in the economy. Occupations that require lengthy education or training are given the most attention. For each occupation, the handbook describes job duties, working conditions, training, educational preparation, personal qualities, advancement possibilities, job outlook, earnings, and sources of additional information.

★3217★ *Motel Maid*
Vocational Biographies, Inc.
PO Box 31
Sauk Centre, MN 56378-0031
Ph: (612)352-6516 Fax: (612)352-5546
Fr: 800-255-0752

1993. Four-page pamphlet containing a personal narrative about a worker's job, work likes and dislikes, career path from high school to the present. Education and training, the rewards and frustrations, and the effects of the job on the rest of the worker's life. The data file portion of this pamphlet gives a concise occupational summary, including work descriptions, working conditions, places of employment, personal characteristics, education and training, job outlook, and salary range.

Associations

★3218★ Building Service Contractors Association International (BSCAI)
10201 Lee Hwy., Ste. 225
Fairfax, VA 22030
Ph: (703)359-7090 Fax: (703)352-0493
Fr: 800-368-3414

Members: Firms and corporations in 40 countries engaged in contracting building maintenance services including the provision of labor, purchasing materials, and janitorial cleaning and maintenance of a building or its surroundings; associate members are manufacturers of cleaning supplies and equipment. **Purpose:** Seeks to provide a unified voice for building service contractors and to promote increased recognition by government, property owners, and the general business and professional public. Conducts continuing study and action, through committees and special task groups on areas such as public affairs, costs and ratios, uniform accounting, industrial relations and personnel, marketing and sales, contract improvement, research and planning, materials and supplies sources, group insurance, management training, statistics collection, safety, and insurance costs. Has developed a certification program for building service executives, and a registration program for building service managers. **Publications:** *Building Service Contractors Association International—Services*, monthly. • *Information Central Guide*, annual. • *Who's Who in Building Service Contracting*, annual.

★3219★ National Executive Housekeepers Association (N.E.H.A.)
1001 Eastwind Dr., Ste. 301
Westerville, OH 43081-3361
Ph: (614)895-7166 Fax: (614)895-1248
Fr: 800-200-NEHA

Members: Persons engaged in institutional housekeeping management in hospitals, hotels and motels, schools, and industrial establishments. Has established educational standards. Sponsors certificate and collegiate degree programs. Holds annual National Housekeepers Week celebration during the second week in September. Created the N.E.H.A. Educational Foundation to allocate financial awards to recognized schools to assist students in institutional housekeeping. Maintains referral service. **Publications:** *Executive Housekeeping Today*, monthly. • *Shop Talk*, quarterly.

Standards/Certification Agencies

★3220★ Building Service Contractors Association International (BSCAI)
10201 Lee Hwy., Ste. 225
Fairfax, VA 22030
Ph: (703)359-7090 Fax: (703)352-0493
Fr: 800-368-3414

Has developed a certification program for building service executives, and a registration program for building service managers.

★3221★ National Executive Housekeepers Association (N.E.H.A.)
1001 Eastwind Dr., Ste. 301
Westerville, OH 43081
Ph: (614)895-7166

Has established educational standards. Sponsors certificate and collegiate degree programs.

Test Guides

★3222★ *Building Custodian, Building Superintendent, Custodian Engineer*
Arco Pub.
201 W. 103rd St.
Indianapolis, IN 46290
Ph: 800-428-5331 Fax: 800-835-3202

Robert Padula and Hy Hammer. 1990, eighth edition. Contains questions on plumbing, electrical and structural repairs, and the maintenance of the heating system.

★3223★ *Career Examination Series: Assistant Building Custodian*
National Learning Corp.
212 Michael Dr.
Syosset, NY 11791
Ph: (516)921-8888 Fax: (516)921-8743
Fr: 800-645-6337

★3224★ *Career Examination Series: Assistant Buildings Superintendent*
National Learning Corp.
212 Michael Dr.
Syosset, NY 11791
Ph: (516)921-8888 Fax: (516)921-8743
Fr: 800-645-6337

Jack Rudman. 1989. All examination guides in this series contain questions with answers.

★3225★ *Career Examination Series: Assistant Custodial Work Supervisor*
National Learning Corp.
212 Michael Dr.
Syosset, NY 11791
Ph: (516)921-8888 Fax: (516)921-8743
Fr: 800-645-6337

Jack Rudman. 1989. All examination guides in this series contain questions with answers.

★3226★ *Career Examination Series: Assistant Custodian*
National Learning Corp.
212 Michael Dr.
Syosset, NY 11791
Ph: (516)921-8888 Fax: (516)921-8743
Fr: 800-645-6337

Jack Rudman. 1989. All examination guides in this series contain questions with answers.

★3227★ *Career Examination Series: Assistant Custodian-Engineer*
National Learning Corp.
212 Michael Dr.
Syosset, NY 11791
Ph: (516)921-8888 Fax: (516)921-8743
Fr: 800-645-6337

Jack Rudman. 1989. All examination guides in this series contain questions with answers.

★3228★ *Career Examination Series: Assistant Head Custodian*
National Learning Corp.
212 Michael Dr.
Syosset, NY 11791
Ph: (516)921-8888 Fax: (516)921-8743
Fr: 800-645-6337

Jack Rudman. Test guide including questions and answers for students or professionals in the field who seek advancement through examination.

★3229★ *Career Examination Series: Assistant School Custodian-Engineer*
National Learning Corp.
212 Michael Dr.
Syosset, NY 11791
Ph: (516)921-8888 Fax: (516)921-8743
Fr: 800-645-6337

Jack Rudman. 1989. All examination guides in this series contain questions with answers.

★3230★ *Career Examination Series: Assistant Superintendent of Buildings & Grounds*
National Learning Corp.
212 Michael Dr.
Syosset, NY 11791
Ph: (516)921-8888 Fax: (516)921-8743
Fr: 800-645-6337

Jack Rudman. 1989. All examination guides in this series contain questions with answers.

★3231★ *Career Examination Series: Borough Supervisor of School Custodians*
National Learning Corp.
212 Michael Dr.
Syosset, NY 11791
Ph: (516)921-8888 Fax: (516)921-8743
Fr: 800-645-6337

Jack Rudman. 1988. All examination guides in this series contain questions with answers.

★3232★ *Career Examination Series: Building Custodian*
National Learning Corp.
212 Michael Dr.
Syosset, NY 11791
Ph: (516)921-8888 Fax: (516)921-8743
Fr: 800-645-6337

Jack Rudman. All examination guides in this series contain questions with answers.

★3233★ *Career Examination Series: Chief Custodian*
National Learning Corp.
212 Michael Dr.
Syosset, NY 11791
Ph: (516)921-8888 Fax: (516)921-8743
Fr: 800-645-6337

Jack Rudman. 1989. All examination guides in this series contain questions with answers.

★3234★ *Career Examination Series: Chief Housekeeper*
National Learning Corp.
212 Michael Dr.
Syosset, NY 11791
Ph: (516)921-8888 Fax: (516)921-8743
Fr: 800-645-6337

★3235★ *Career Examination Series: Cleaner, Custodian USPS*
National Learning Corp.
212 Michael Dr.
Syosset, NY 11791
Ph: (516)921-8888 Fax: (516)921-8743
Fr: 800-645-6337

Jack Rudman. 1988. All examination guides in this series contain questions with answers.

★3236★ *Career Examination Series: Cleaner (T. A.)*
National Learning Corp.
212 Michael Dr.
Syosset, NY 11791
Ph: (516)921-8888 Fax: (516)921-8743
Fr: 800-645-6337

Jack Rudman. 1990. All examination guides in this series contain questions with answers.

★3237★ *Career Examination Series: Custodial Assistants, Laborers, Workers, and Supervisors*
National Learning Corp.
212 Michael Dr.
Syosset, NY 11791
Ph: (516)921-8888 Fax: (516)921-8743
Fr: 800-645-6337

★3238★ *Career Examination Series: Custodial Foreman*
National Learning Corp.
212 Michael Dr.
Syosset, NY 11791
Ph: (516)921-8888 Fax: (516)921-8743
Fr: 800-645-6337

Jack Rudman. 1989. All examination guides in this series contain questions with answers.

★3239★ *Career Examination Series: Custodial Laborer (USPS)*
National Learning Corp.
212 Michael Dr.
Syosset, NY 11791
Ph: (516)921-8888 Fax: (516)921-8743
Fr: 800-645-6337

Jack Rudman. 1988. All examination guides in this series contain questions with answers.

★3240★ *Career Examination Series: Custodial Work Supervisor*
National Learning Corp.
212 Michael Dr.
Syosset, NY 11791
Ph: (516)921-8888 Fax: (516)921-8743
Fr: 800-645-6337

Jack Rudman. 1989. All examination guides in this series contain questions with answers.

★3241★ *Career Examination Series: Custodial Worker*
National Learning Corp.
212 Michael Dr.
Syosset, NY 11791
Ph: (516)921-8888 Fax: (516)921-8743
Fr: 800-645-6337

Jack Rudman. 1989. All examination guides in this series contain questions with answers.

★3242★ *Career Examination Series: Custodian*
National Learning Corp.
212 Michael Dr.
Syosset, NY 11791
Ph: (516)921-8888 Fax: (516)921-8743
Fr: 800-645-6337

Jack Rudman. 1989. All examination guides in this series contain questions with answers.

★3243★ *Career Examination Series: Custodian-Engineer*
National Learning Corp.
212 Michael Dr.
Syosset, NY 11791
Ph: (516)921-8888 Fax: (516)921-8743
Fr: 800-645-6337

Jack Rudman. 1989. All examination guides in this series contain questions with answers.

★3244★ *Career Examination Series: District Supervisor of School Custodians*
National Learning Corp.
212 Michael Dr.
Syosset, NY 11791
Ph: (516)921-8888 Fax: (516)921-8743
Fr: 800-645-6337

Jack Rudman. 1989. All examination guides in this series contain questions with answers.

★3245★ *Career Examination Series: Grounds Superintendent*
National Learning Corp.
212 Michael Dr.
Syosset, NY 11791
Ph: (516)921-8888 Fax: (516)921-8743
Fr: 800-645-6337

Jack Rudman. 1988. All examination guides in this series contain questions with answers.

★3246★ *Career Examination Series: Head Custodian*
National Learning Corp.
212 Michael Dr.
Syosset, NY 11791
Ph: (516)921-8888 Fax: (516)921-8743
Fr: 800-645-6337

Jack Rudman. 1989. All examination guides in this series contain questions with answers.

★3247★ *Career Examination Series: Head Janitor*
National Learning Corp.
212 Michael Dr.
Syosset, NY 11791
Ph: (516)921-8888 Fax: (516)921-8743
Fr: 800-645-6337

Jack Rudman. 1988. All examination guides in this series contain questions with answers.

★3248★ *Career Examination Series: Housing Caretaker*
National Learning Corp.
212 Michael Dr.
Syosset, NY 11791
Ph: (516)921-8888 Fax: (516)921-8743
Fr: 800-645-6337

Jack Rudman. 1989. All examination guides in this series contain questions with answers.

★3249★ *Career Examination Series: Institution Steward*
National Learning Corp.
212 Michael Dr.
Syosset, NY 11791
Ph: (516)921-8888 Fax: (516)921-8743
Fr: 800-645-6337

Jack Rudman. 1989. All examination guides in this series contain questions with answers.

★3250★ *Career Examination Series: Junior Building Custodian*
National Learning Corp.
212 Michael Dr.
Syosset, NY 11791
Ph: (516)921-8888 Fax: (516)921-8743
Fr: 800-645-6337

Jack Rudman. 1989. All examination guides in this series contain questions with answers.

★3251★ *Career Examination Series: Maintenance Crew Chief*
National Learning Corp.
212 Michael Dr.
Syosset, NY 11791
Ph: (516)921-8888 Fax: (516)921-8743
Fr: 800-645-6337

Jack Rudman. 1988. All examination guides in this series contain questions with answers.

★3252★ *Career Examination Series: Maintenance (Custodial) Branch Initial-Level Supervisor Examination (U.S.P.S.)*
National Learning Corp.
212 Michael Dr.
Syosset, NY 11791
Ph: (516)921-8888 Fax: (516)921-8743
Fr: 800-645-6337

Jack Rudman. 1989. All examination guides in this series contain questions with answers.

★3253★ *Career Examination Series: Principal Custodial Foreman*
National Learning Corp.
212 Michael Dr.
Syosset, NY 11791
Ph: (516)921-8888 Fax: (516)921-8743
Fr: 800-645-6337

Jack Rudman. 1989. All examination guides in this series contain questions with answers.

★3254★ *Career Examination Series: Resident Buildings Superintendent*
National Learning Corp.
212 Michael Dr.
Syosset, NY 11791
Ph: (516)921-8888 Fax: (516)921-8743
Fr: 800-645-6337

Jack Rudman. 1989. All examination guides in this series contain questions with answers.

★3255★ *Career Examination Series: School Custodial Supervisor*
National Learning Corp.
212 Michael Dr.
Syosset, NY 11791
Ph: (516)921-8888 Fax: (516)921-8743
Fr: 800-645-6337

Jack Rudman. 1989. All examination guides in this series contain questions with answers.

★3256★ *Career Examination Series: School Custodian*
National Learning Corp.
212 Michael Dr.
Syosset, NY 11791
Ph: (516)921-8888 Fax: (516)921-8743
Fr: 800-645-6337

Jack Rudman. 1989. All examination guides in this series contain questions with answers.

★3257★ *Career Examination Series: School Custodian-Engineer*
National Learning Corp.
212 Michael Dr.
Syosset, NY 11791
Ph: (516)921-8888 Fax: (516)921-8743
Fr: 800-645-6337

Jack Rudman. 1989. All examination guides in this series contain questions with answers.

★3258★ *Career Examination Series: Senior Building Custodian*
National Learning Corp.
212 Michael Dr.
Syosset, NY 11791
Ph: (516)921-8888 Fax: (516)921-8743
Fr: 800-645-6337

Jack Rudman. 1989. All examination guides in this series contain questions with answers.

★3259★ *Career Examination Series: Senior Custodial Assistant (Men)*
National Learning Corp.
212 Michael Dr.
Syosset, NY 11791
Ph: (516)921-8888 Fax: (516)921-8743
Fr: 800-645-6337

Jack Rudman. 1989. All examination guides in this series contain questions with answers.

★3260★ *Career Examination Series: Senior Custodial Foreman*
National Learning Corp.
212 Michael Dr.
Syosset, NY 11791
Ph: (516)921-8888 Fax: (516)921-8743
Fr: 800-645-6337

Jack Rudman. 1988. All examination guides in this series contain questions with answers.

★3261★ *Career Examination Series: Superintendent Building Service (U.S.P.S.)*
National Learning Corp.
212 Michael Dr.
Syosset, NY 11791
Ph: (516)921-8888 Fax: (516)921-8743
Fr: 800-645-6337

Jack Rudman. 1989. All examination guides in this series contain questions with answers.

★3262★ *Career Examination Series: Supervising Custodial Foreman*
National Learning Corp.
212 Michael Dr.
Syosset, NY 11791
Ph: (516)921-8888 Fax: (516)921-8743
Fr: 800-645-6337

Jack Rudman. 1989. All examination guides in this series contain questions with answers.

★3263★ *Career Examination Series: Supervising Janitor*
National Learning Corp.
212 Michael Dr.
Syosset, NY 11791
Ph: (516)921-8888 Fax: (516)921-8743
Fr: 800-645-6337

Jack Rudman. 1988. All examination guides in this series contain questions with answers.

★3264★ *Career Examination Series: Supervisor of Building Custodians*
National Learning Corp.
212 Michael Dr.
Syosset, NY 11791
Ph: (516)921-8888 Fax: (516)921-8743
Fr: 800-645-6337

Jack Rudman. 1989. All examination guides in this series contain questions with answers.

★3265★ *Career Examination Series: Window Cleaner*
National Learning Corp.
212 Michael Dr.
Syosset, NY 11791
Ph: (516)921-8888 Fax: (516)921-8743
Fr: 800-645-6337

Jack Rudman. 1989. All examination guides in this series contain questions with answers.

★3266★ *Civil Service Tests for Basic Skills Jobs*
Prentice Hall Press
Simon & Schuster Inc.
200 Old Tappan Rd.
Old Tappan, NJ 07675
Ph: 800-223-2348

Hy Hammer. First edition, 1985. Contains nine sample examinations to prepare candidates for entry-level positions that include hospital attendant, building groundskeeper, and custodial assistant, among others.

★3267★ *Janitorial & Maintenance Examinations*
Ken Books
56 Midcrest Way
San Francisco, CA 94131
Ph: (415)826-6550

Harry W. Koch. Second edition, 1975.

Educational Directories and Programs

★3268★ *Vacuum Cleaning Systems Directory*
American Business Directories, Inc.
5711 S. 86th Circle
Omaha, NE 68127
Ph: (402)593-4600 Fax: (402)331-1505

Updated continuously; printed on request. Entries include: Name, address, phone, size of advertisement, name of owner or manager, number of employees, year first in "Yellow Pages." Compiled from telephone company "Yellow Pages," nationwide. Arrangement: Geographical.

Awards, Scholarships, Grants, and Fellowships

★3269★ Roomkeeper of the Year
American Hotel & Motel Association
1201 New York Ave. NW
Washington, DC 20005-3931
Ph: (202)289-3133

To provide managers, owners, and executive housekeepers with the opportunity to reward a staff person for exceptional service that they have rendered to a guest, the management, or the community. The award is limited to non-supervisory (housekeeping) employees of association member properties. The nominee must be in the lodging industry for a minimum of three years. The entry deadline is January 24. Prizes include a commemorative plaque, two roundtrip tickets anywhere in the United States for seven days/six nights, and travel expenses to the association's convention. Awarded annually. Sponsored by Visa U.S.A.

Basic Reference Guides and Handbooks

★3270★ *BSCAI Information Central Guide*
Building Service Contractors Association International (BSCAI)
10201 Lee Hwy., Ste. 225
Fairfax, VA 22030
Ph: (703)359-7090 Fax: (703)352-0493
Fr: 800-368-3414

Annual.

★3271★ *The Complete Custodial Handbook*
Prentice Hall
Rte. 9W
Englewood Cliffs, NJ 07632
Ph: (201)592-2000

William R. Griffin. 1989.

★3272★ *The Comprehensive Custodial Training Manual*
Cleaning Consultant Services, Inc.
1512 Western Ave.
Seattle, WA 98101
Ph: (206)284-9954

Cleaning Consultant Services, Inc. Staff. 1980.

★3273★ *Custodial Methods and Procedures Manual*
Association of School Business Officials International
11401 N. Shore Dr.
Reston, VA 22090
Ph: (703)478-0405

1986.

★3274★ *Supervisors' Guide to Successful Training*
Cleaning Consultant Services, Inc.
1512 Western Ave.
Seattle, WA 98101
Ph: (206)284-9954

William R. Griffin. 1977.

★3275★ *Vacuum Cleaners Supplies & Parts Directory*
American Business Directories, Inc.
5711 S. 86th Circle
Omaha, NE 68127
Ph: (402)593-4600 Fax: (402)331-1505

Updated continuously; printed on request. Entries include: Name, address, phone, size of advertisement, name of owner or manager, number of employees, year first in "Yellow Pages." Compiled from telephone company "Yellow Pages," nationwide. Arrangement: Geographical.

Periodicals

★3276★ *Building Service Contractors Association International—Services*
Building Service Contractors Association International (BSCAI)
10201 Lee Hwy., Ste. 225
Fairfax, VA 22030
Ph: (703)359-7090 Fax: (703)352-0493
Fr: 800-368-3414

Monthly. Includes calendar of events, classified ads, new product information, new members, industry promotions and appointments, and new literature.

★3277★ *Executive Housekeeping Today*
National Executive Housekeepers Association (N.E.H.A.)
1001 Eastwind Dr., Ste. 301
Westerville, OH 43081-3361
Ph: (614)895-7166 Fax: (614)895-1248
Fr: 800-200-NEHA

Monthly. Primarily for management executives of the health care and hospitality industries; also includes association news.

★3278★ *Information Central Guide*
Building Service Contractors Association International (BSCAI)
10201 Lee Hwy., Ste. 225
Fairfax, VA 22030
Ph: (703)359-7090 Fax: (703)352-0493
Fr: 800-368-3414

Annual.

★3279★ *Installation & Cleaning Specialist*
Specialist Publications, Inc.
17835 Ventura Blvd., Ste. 312
Encino, CA 91316
Ph: (818)345-3550 Fax: (818)344-9647
Howard Olansky

Monthly. Trade magazine for floor covering installers, workrooms, contractors, installing retailers, cleaning and maintenance firms, and distributors.

★3280★ *Sanitary Maintenance*
Trade Press Publishing Corp.
2100 W. Florist Ave.
Milwaukee, WI 53209
Ph: (414)228-7701 Fax: (414)228-1134
Austin Weber

Monthly. Magazine for sanitary supply and paper distributors.

★3281★ *Shop Talk*
National Executive Housekeepers Association (N.E.H.A.)
1001 Eastwind Dr., Ste. 301
Westerville, OH 43081-3361
Ph: (614)895-7166 Fax: (614)895-1248
Fr: 800-200-NEHA

Quarterly. Contains compliance information and news on book sales.

★3282★ *Who's Who in Building Service Contracting*
Building Service Contractors Association International (BSCAI)
10201 Lee Hwy., Ste. 225
Fairfax, VA 22030
Ph: (703)359-7090 Fax: (703)352-0493
Fr: 800-368-3414

Annual. Lists companies and contains buyer's guide. Includes photo gallery of company representatives.

Other Sources of Information

★3283★ *An Analysis of Janitor Service in Elementary Schools*
AMS Press, Inc.
56 E. 13th St.
New York, NY 10003
Ph: (212)777-4700 Fax: (212)995-5413

Charles E. Reeves. Part of Columbia University. Teachers College. Contributions to Education Series.

★3284★ *Basic Terms of Maintenance*
Tel-A-Train, Inc.
309 N. Market St.
PO Box 4752
Chattanooga, TN 37405
Ph: (615)266-0113 Fax: (615)267-2555
Fr: 800-251-6018

Serves as a fundamental illustrated glossary of 87 common maintenance and engineering terms.

★3285★ *Guide to Industrial Housekeeping*
Gulf Publishing Co.
PO Box 2680
Houston, TX 77252
Ph: (713)529-4301 Fax: (713)520-4438

Offers vocational training information on the importance of a clean work area to a more efficient and safer work environment.

★3286★ "Janitor" in *Career Selector 2001*
Barron's Educational Series, Inc.
250 Wireless Blvd.
Hauppauge, NY 11788
Ph: (516)434-3311 Fax: (516)434-3723
Fr: 800-645-3476

James C. Gonyea. 1993.

★3287★ "Sanitation Worker" in *Encyclopedia of Danger: Dangerous Professions* (pp. 86-89)
Chelsea House Publishers
1974 Sproul Rd., Ste. 400
Broomall, PA 19008
Ph: (215)353-5166 Fax: (215)359-1439

Missy Allen and Michel Peissel. 1993. Provides descriptions of 24 dangerous occupations, their risky characteristics, and safety precautions.

Preschool Workers

Preschool workers nurture and train preschool children who are 5 years old or younger. They attend to basic needs and, in addition, organize activities that stimulate the children's physical, emotional, intellectual, and social growth. They work in daycare centers or in their own homes. In large daycare centers, each worker is in charge of a group of children under the supervision of a director, who lays out specific objectives and activities. Preschool workers, also known as childcare workers or family daycare providers, care for a few children in their own homes. These workers are subject to state licensing requirements that regulate the number of children one worker may care for and the environment in which care is provided. In addition to their childcare duties, they are responsible for all aspects of running a small business. About half of all preschool workers are self-employed. Most of these are family daycare providers who take care of children in their own homes. The rest work in daycare centers sponsored by a variety of organizations. Many centers are for-profit operations, affiliated in some instances with a local or national chain. Others are run by churches, synagogues, community agencies, school systems, and state and local governments. A small number are operated by business firms for the children of their employees.

Salaries

Weekly salaries for preschool workers are as follows:

Lowest 10 percent	\$140/week
Middle 50 percent	\$210-\$320/week
Top 10 percent	\$460/week

Employment Outlook

Growth rate until the year 2005: Much faster than average.

Preschool Workers

CAREER GUIDES

★3288★ ***Becoming a Helper***
Brooks/Cole Publishing Co.
511 Forest Lodge Rd.
Pacific Grove, CA 93950-5098
Ph: (408)373-0728 Fax: (408)375-6414
Marianne Schneider Corey and Gerald Corey. Second edition, 1993.

★3289★ ***Careers in Child Care***
National Textbook Co. (NTC)
VGM Career Books
4255 W. Toughy Ave.
Lincolnwood, IL 60646-1975
Ph: (708)679-5500 Fax: (708)679-2494
Fr: 800-323-4900
Marjorie Eberts and Margaret Gidler. Provides information on establishing a career in professional child care.

★3290★ ***Careers in Early Childhood Education***
National Association for the Education of Young Children
1834 Connecticut Ave., N.W.
Washington, DC 20009
Ph: (202)232-8777 Fr: 800-424-2460
1990. This six-panel pamphlet covers the work, educational preparation, qualifications, and employment opportunities.

★3291★ **"Child Care Assistant" in *Guide to Careers Without College* (pp. 95-97)**
Franklin Watts, Inc.
387 Park Avenue, S.
New York, NY 10016
Ph: (212)686-7070
Kathleen S. Abrams. 1988. Discusses careers that do not require a college degree in fields such as health care, sales and marketing, and the building trades. Describes the work, employment opportunities, and training.

★3292★ ***Child-Care Attendant***
Careers, Inc.
PO Box 135
Largo, FL 34649-0135
Ph: (813)584-7333
1994. Two-page occupational summary card describing duties, working conditions, personal qualifications, training, earnings and hours, employment outlook, places of employment, related careers, and where to write for more information.

★3293★ **"Child Care Attendant" in *Occu-Facts: Information on 580 Careers in Outline Form***
Careers, Inc.
PO Box 135
Largo, FL 34649-0135
Ph: (813)584-7333
Biennial, 1995-96 edition. Each one-page occupational profile describes duties, working conditions, physical surroundings and demands, aptitudes, temperament, educational requirements, employment outlook, earnings, and places of employment.

★3294★ **"Child Care Center Workers" in *Career Discovery Encyclopedia* (Vol.1, pp. 166-167)**
J.G. Ferguson Publishing Co.
200 W. Madison St., Ste. 300
Chicago, IL 60606
Ph: (312)580-5480 Fax: (312)580-4948
E. Russell Primm, editor-in-chief. 1993. Contains two-page articles on 504 occupations. Each article describes job duties, earnings, and educational and training requirements.

★3295★ **"Child Care Service" in *100 Best Careers for the Year 2000* (pp. 268)**
Arco Pub.
201 W. 103rd St.
Indianapolis, IN 46290
Ph: 800-428-5331 Fax: 800-835-3202
Shelly Field. 1992. Describes 100 job opportunities expected to grow fast throughout the next decade. Provides information on job duties and responsibilities, training requirements, education, advancement opportunities, experience and qualifications, and typical salaries.

★3296★ ***Child Care Workers***
Chronicle Guidance Publications, Inc.
66 Aurora St.
PO Box 1190
Moravia, NY 13118-1190
Ph: (315)497-0330 Fax: (315)497-3359
Fr: 800-622-7284
1994. Career brief describing the nature of the job, working conditions, hours and earnings, education and training, licensure, certification, unions, personal qualifications, social and psychological factors, location, employment outlook, entry methods, advancement, and related occupations.

★3297★ **"Child Care Workers" in *Encyclopedia of Careers and Vocational Guidance* (Vol.2, pp. 288-290)**
J.G. Ferguson Publishing Co.
200 W. Madison St., Ste. 300
Chicago, IL 60606
Ph: (312)580-5480 Fax: (312)580-4948
William E. Hopke, editor-in-chief. Ninth edition, 1993. Four-volume set that profiles 500 occupations and describes job trends in 74 industries. Includes career description, educational requirements, history of the job, methods of entry, advancement, employment outlook, earnings, working conditions, social and psychological factors, and sources of additional information.

★3298★ ***Child Care Workers (Institutions)***
Chronicle Guidance Publications, Inc.
66 Aurora St.
PO Box 1190
Moravia, NY 13118-1190
Ph: (315)497-0330 Fax: (315)497-3359
Fr: 800-622-7284
1993. This career brief describes the nature of the work, working conditions, hours and earnings, education and training, licensure, certification, unions, personal qualifications, social and psychological factors, employment outlook, entry methods, advancement, and related occupations.

★3299★ **"Child-Care Workers" in *Jobs! What They Are—Where They Are—What They Pay* (pp. 347)**
Fireside
Simon & Schuster Bldg.
1230 Avenue of the Americas
New York, NY 10020
Ph: (212)698-7000 Fr: 800-223-2348
Robert O. Snelling and Anne M. Snelling. Revised and updated, 1992. Describes duties and responsibilities, earnings, employment opportunities, training, and qualifications.

★3300★ "Child Development Associate" in *Exploring Careers in Child Care Services* (pp. 17-18)
Rosen Publishing Group
29 E. 21st St.
New York, NY 10010
Ph: (212)777-3017 Fax: (212)777-0277
Fr: 800-237-9932

Jean Ispa, Elizabeth Vemer, and Janis Logan. Revised edition, 1990. Covers occupations working with children including those requiring no education and training to those that require advanced training; from babysitting to program director. Describes the work and a typical work day, employment outlook, advantages and disadvantages, and personal characteristics needed for success in the field. Offers job hunting advice.

★3301★ "Child Development Associate" in *Opportunities in Child Care Careers* (pp. 37-57)
National Textbook Co. (NTC)
VGM Career Books
4255 W. Touhy Ave.
Lincolnwood, IL 60646-1975
Ph: (708)679-5500 Fax: (708)679-2494
Fr: 800-323-4900

Renee Wittenberg. 1995. Surveys job opportunities related to child care in child development, child life, health services, and psychology. Covers personal qualifications, training programs, job outlook, and salaries. Offers job hunting advice.

★3302★ "Childcare" in *How to Get a Job With a Cruise Line* (pp. 7-13)
Ticket to Adventure, Inc.
8800 49th St., N., Ste. 410, Rm. 3
Pinellas Park, FL 34666
Ph: (813)544-0066

Mary Fallon Miller. 1991. Explores jobs with cruise ships, describing duties, responsibilities, benefits, and training. Lists cruise ship lines and schools offering cruise line training. Offers job hunting advice.

★3303★ "Childcare Worker" in *100 Best Careers for the Year 2000* (pp. 202-204)
Arco Pub.
201 W. 103rd St.
Indianapolis, IN 46290
Ph: 800-428-5331 Fax: 800-835-3202

Shelly Field. 1992. Describes 100 job opportunities expected to grow fast throughout the next decade. Provides information on job duties and responsibilities, training requirements, education, advancement opportunities, experience and qualifications, and typical salaries.

★3304★ "Childcare Worker" in *VGM's Careers Encyclopedia* (pp. 91-93)
National Textbook Co. (NTC)
VGM Career Books
4255 W. Touhy Ave.
Lincolnwood, IL 60646-1975
Ph: (708)679-5500 Fax: (708)679-2494
Fr: 800-323-4900

Third edition, 1991. Contains two- to five-page descriptions of 200 managerial, professional, technical, trade, and service occupations. Each profile includes job duties, places of employment, qualifications, educational preparation, training, employment potential, advancement, income, and additional sources of information.

★3305★ "Childcare Workers" in *Opportunities in Vocational and Technical Careers* (pp. 77-78)
National Textbook Co. (NTC)
VGM Career Books
4255 W. Touhy Ave.
Lincolnwood, IL 60646-1975
Ph: (708)679-5500 Fax: (708)679-2494
Fr: 800-323-4900

Adrian A. Paradis. 1992. Describes careers which can be prepared for by attending a private vocational or proprietary school—office employee, sales worker, service worker, health services, mechanic, craftworker, and technician. Covers employment outlook, job duties, and salaries. Offers career planning advice.

★3306★ *Children's Day-Care Nurse*
Vocational Biographies, Inc.
PO Box 31
Sauk Centre, MN 56378-0031
Ph: (612)352-6516 Fax: (612)352-5546
Fr: 800-255-0752

1993. Four-page pamphlet containing a personal narrative about a worker's job, work likes and dislikes, career path from high school to the present. Education and training, the rewards and frustrations, and the effects of the job on the rest of the worker's life. The data file portion of this pamphlet gives a concise occupational summary, including work descriptions, working conditions, places of employment, personal characteristics, education and training, job outlook, and salary range.

★3307★ *Day Care Provider*
Vocational Biographies, Inc.
PO Box 31
Sauk Centre, MN 56378-0031
Ph: (612)352-6516 Fax: (612)352-5546
Fr: 800-255-0752

1990. This pamphlet profiles a person working in the job. Includes information about job duties, working conditions, places of employment, educational preparation, labor market outlook, and salaries.

★3308★ "Day Care Providers" in *Opportunities in Child Care Careers* (pp. 42-43)
National Textbook Co. (NTC)
VGM Career Books
4255 W. Touhy Ave.
Lincolnwood, IL 60646-1975
Ph: (708)679-5500 Fax: (708)679-2494
Fr: 800-323-4900

Renee Wittenberg. 1987. Surveys job opportunities related to child care in child development, child life, health services, and psychology. Covers personal qualifications, training programs, job outlook, and salaries. Offers job hunting advice.

★3309★ "Day Care Worker" in *Career Information Center* (Vol.11)
Simon and Schuster
200 Old Tappan Rd.
Old Tappan, NJ 07675
Fax: 800-445-6991 Fr: 800-223-2348

Richard Lidz and Dale Anderson, editorial directors. Fifth edition, 1993. For 600 occupations, describes job duties, entry-level requirements, education and training needed, advancement possibilities, employment outlook, earnings and benefits. The set is divided into 12 volumes. Each volume includes jobs related under a broad career field. Volume 13 is the index.

★3310★ *Day Care Workers*
Chronicle Guidance Publications, Inc.
66 Aurora St.
PO Box 1190
Moravia, NY 13118-1190
Ph: (315)497-0330 Fax: (315)497-3359
Fr: 800-622-7284

1993. This career brief describes the nature of the work, working conditions, hours and earnings, education and training, licensure, certification, unions, personal qualifications, social and psychological factors, employment outlook, entry methods, advancement, and related occupations.

★3311★ "Education and Training" in *Where the Jobs Are: The Hottest Careers for the 90s* (pp. 97-110)
Career Press
180 5th Ave.
Hawthorne, NJ 07507
Ph: (201)427-0229 Fax: (201)427-2037
Fr: 800-CAREER-1

Joyce Hadley. 1995. Offers a job-hunting strategy for the 1990s as well as descriptions of growing careers of the decade. Each profile includes general information, forecasts, growth, education and training, licensing requirements, and salary information.

★3312★ *Educational Career Directory*
Gale Research Inc.
835 Penobscot Bldg.
Detroit, MI 48226
Ph: (313)961-2242 Fr: 800-877-GALE

1994.

★3313★ "Family Day-Care Providers" in *Exploring Careers in Child Care Services* (pp. 22-31)
Rosen Publishing Group
29 E. 21st St.
New York, NY 10010
Ph: (212)777-3017 Fax: (212)777-0277
Fr: 800-237-9932

Jean Ispa, Elizabeth Vemer, and Janis Logan. Revised edition, 1990. Covers occupations working with children including those requiring no education and training to those that require advanced training; from babysitting to program director. Describes the work and a typical work day, employment outlook, advantages and disadvantages, and personal characteristics needed for success in the field. Offers job hunting advice.

★3314★ "Institutional Child Care Worker" in *Career Information Center* (Vol.11)
Simon and Schuster
200 Old Tappan Rd.
Old Tappan, NJ 07675
Fax: 800-445-6991 Fr: 800-223-2348

Richard Lidz and Dale Anderson, editorial directors. Fifth edition, 1993. For 600 occupations, describes job duties, entry-level requirements, education and training needed, advancement possibilities, employment outlook, earnings and benefits. The set is divided into 12 volumes. Each volume includes

jobs related under a broad career field. Volume 13 is the index.

★3315★ *Opportunities in Child Carer Careers*
National Textbook Co. (NTC)
VGM Career Books
4255 W. Toughy Ave.
Lincolnwood, IL 60646-1975
Ph: (708)679-5500 Fax: (708)679-2494
Fr: 800-323-4900

Renee Wittenberg. 1994.

★3316★ "Preschool and Childcare Workers" in *101 Careers: A Guide to the Fastest-Growing Opportunities* (pp. 178-180)
John Wiley & Sons, Inc.
605 3rd Ave.
New York, NY 10158-0012
Ph: (212)850-6645 Fax: (212)850-6088

Michael Harkavy. 1990. Describes the nature of the job, working conditions, employment growth, qualifications, personal skills, projected salaries, and where to write for more information.

★3317★ "Preschool Teachers" in *Career Discovery Encyclopedia* (Vol.5, pp. 78-79)
J.G. Ferguson Publishing Co.
200 W. Madison St., Ste. 300
Chicago, IL 60606
Ph: (312)580-5480 Fax: (312)580-4948

Russell E. Primm, editor-in chief. 1993. This six volume set contains two-page articles for 504 occupations. Each article describes job duties, earnings, and educational and training requirements. The whole set is arranged alphabetically by job title. Designed for junior high and older students.

★3318★ "Preschool Workers" in *America's 50 Fastest Growing Jobs* (pp. 129)
JIST Works, Inc.
720 N. Park Ave.
Indianapolis, IN 46202-3431
Ph: (317)264-3720 Fax: (317)264-3709
Fr: 800-648-5478

Michael J. Farr, compiler. 1994. Describes the 50 fastest growing jobs within major career clusters such as technicians, and marketing and sales. Each job profile explains the nature of the work, skills and abilities required, employment outlook, average earnings, related occupations, education and training requirements, and employment opportunities. Also contains career planning information and job search tips.

★3319★ "Preschool Workers" in *Occupational Outlook Handbook*
U.S. Government Printing Office
Superintendent of Documents
Washington, DC 20402
Ph: (202)512-1800 Fax: (202)512-2250

Biennial; latest edition, 1994-95. Encyclopedia of careers describing more than 250 occupations and comprising about 85 percent of all jobs in the economy. Occupations that require lengthy education or training are given the most attention. For each occupation, the handbook describes job duties, working conditions, training, educational preparation, personal qualities, advancement possibilities, job outlook, earnings, and sources of additional information.

★3320★ *Questions and Answers About Entering the Child Care Profession*
Child Care Employee Project
6536 Telegraph Ave., Ste. A-201
Oakland, CA 94609-1114
Ph: (415)653-9889

This one-page leaflet answers questions about training, earnings, employment outlook, and advancement opportunities.

★3321★ "Teachers, Preschool" in *Encyclopedia of Careers and Vocational Guidance* (Vol.4, pp. 498-500)
J.G. Ferguson Publishing Co.
200 W. Madison St., Ste. 300
Chicago, IL 60606
Ph: (312)580-5480 Fax: (312)580-4948

William E. Hopke, editor-in-chief. Ninth edition, 1993. Four-volume set that profiles 900 occupations and describes job trends in 74 industries. Includes career description, educational requirements, history of the job, methods of entry, advancement, employment outlook, earnings, conditions of work, social and psychological factors, and sources of further information.

★3322★ *Video Career Library - Public and Personal Services*
Careers, Inc.
PO Box 135
Largo, FL 34649-0135
Ph: (813)584-7333

Videocassette. 1990. 35 mins. Part of the Video Career Library covering 165 occupations. Shows actual workers on the job. Includes firefighters, police officers, correctional officers, bartenders, waiters/waitresses, cooks/chefs, child care workers, flight attendants, barbers/cosmetologists, groundskeepers/gardeners, and butchers/meat cutters.

★3323★ *Wages and Benefits in Child Care*
Child Care Action Campaign
330 Seventh Ave., 18th Fl.
New York, NY 10001
Ph: (212)239-0138

CCAC Information Guide #16. A two-page pamphlet realistically describes the low salaries and few benefits awarded childcare workers.

Associations

★3324★ Child Care Action Campaign (CCAC)
330 7th Ave., 17th Fl.
New York, NY 10001
Ph: (212)239-0138 Fax: (212)268-6515

Members: Individuals and organizations interested and active in child care; corporations and financial institutions; labor organizations; editors of leading women's magazines; leaders in government and representatives of civic organizations. **Purpose:** Purposes are to alert the country to the problems of and need for child care services; prepare and disseminate information responsive to inquiries resulting from publicity; analyze existing services and identify gaps; work directly with communities to stimulate the development of local task forces and long-range plans for improved and coordinated services. Brings pressing legislative action or inaction to public attention. Has worked to help make liability insurance available for child care providers. Compiles statistics. **Publications:** *An Employer's Guide to Child Care Consultants.* • *Building Links: Developer Initiatives for Financing Child Care.* • *Child Care ActioNews*, bimonthly. • *Investing in the Future: Child Care Financing Options for the Public and Private Sectors.* • *Not Too Small to Care: Small Businesses and Child Care.* • *Where They Stand: A Digest of Organizational Policies on Child Care and Education.*

★3325★ Council for Early Childhood Professional Recognition (CECPR)
1341 G St. NW, Ste. 400
Washington, DC 20005
Ph: (202)265-9090 Fax: (202)265-9161
Fr: 800-424-4310

Members: Purpose: Promotes availability of quality child care through the Child Development Associate National Credentialing Program. Credentials are awarded to family day care, center-based, home visitor, and infant/toddler caregivers. Plans to develop the CDA Professional Preparation Program to provide uniform and accessible training for individuals who would like to become certified. **Publications:** *Competence.* • *Essentials.* • *Improving Child Care Through the Child Development Associate Program.*

★3326★ National Association for the Education of Young Children (NAEYC)
1509 16th St. NW
Washington, DC 20036
Ph: (202)232-8777 Fax: (202)328-1846
Fr: 800-424-2460

Members: Teachers and directors of preschool and primary schools, kindergartens, child care centers, cooperatives, church schools, and groups having similar programs for young children; early childhood education and child development professors, trainers, and researchers. Open to all individuals interested in serving and acting on behalf of the needs and rights of young children, with primary focus on the provision of educational services and resources. **Purpose:** Sponsors a public education campaign entitled "Week of the Young Child." Offers voluntary accreditation for early childhood schools and centers through the National Academy of Early Childhood Programs. **Publications:** *Young Children*, bimonthly.

★3327★ National Center for the Early Childhood Work Force
733 15th St. NW, Ste. 800
Washington, DC 20005-2112
Fr: 800-879-6784

Members: Purpose: Purposes are: to improve salaries, working conditions, and status of child care workers; to increase public awareness about the importance of child care work and the training and skill it demands; to develop resources and create an information sharing network for child care workers nationwide. Gathers current information on salaries and benefits; offers consultation services. Sponsors research projects; compiles statistics; operates speakers' bureau. Maintains extensive file of materials on working conditions and research on child care workers. Launched the Worthy Wage Campaign: 1991. **Publications:** *Child Care Employee News*, quarterly. • *National Child Care Staffing Study.*

Standards/Certification Agencies

★3328★ *CDA in State Child Care Licensing*
Council for Early Childhood Professional Recognition
1718 Connecticut Ave., NW, Ste. 500
Washington, DC 20009-1148
Ph: (202)265-9090 Fr: 800-424-4310
1991. This four-page pamphlet lists 49 states which recognize CDA credentialing as a qualification for child care center teachers and/or directors.

★3329★ National Association for the Education of Young Children (NAEYC)
1509 16th St. NW
Washington, DC 20036
Ph: (202)232-8777 Fax: (202)328-1846
Fr: 800-424-2460
Offers voluntary accreditation for early childhood schools and centers through the National Academy of Early Childhood Programs.

Test Guides

★3330★ *Career Examination Series: Day Care Center Aide*
National Learning Corp.
212 Michael Dr.
Syosset, NY 11791
Ph: (516)921-8888 Fax: (516)921-8743
Fr: 800-645-6337
Jack Rudman. All examination guides in this series contain questions with answers.

Educational Directories and Programs

★3331★ *Child Care Database (CCARE)*
Care Connectors, Inc.
PO Box 14452
Research Triangle Park, NC 27709
Ph: (919)544-7300 Fax: (919)544-3558
Monthly, Current. Database covers over 100,000 licensed, registered, or certified child care establishments in 45 states. Database includes: Facility name, address, phone, county, business type, days and hours of operation, caregiver training in first aid and CPR, training frequency, professional program managers on staff, type of care available (full-day, half-day, before and after school, hourly, or part-week), maximum child care capacity, youngest and oldest ages accepted, handicapped children admission policy, mildly ill children admission policy, supply of toys and equipment, developmental program activities, field trips conducted, program activity schedule provided, size of playground or backyard, whether transportation to school is provided or

★3332★ *Directory of Family Day Care Associations & Support Groups*
Children's Foundation
725 15th St. NW, Ste. 505
Washington, DC 20005-2109
Ph: (202)347-3300 Fax: (202)347-3382
Kay Hollestelle, Executive Director
Annual, February. Covers over 1,400 organizations and support groups for child care providers in the U.S. Entries include: Organization name, address, phone, subsidiary and branch names and locations. Arrangement: Geographical.

★3333★ *Kin Care and the American Corporation: Solving the Work/Family Dilemma*
Irwin Professional Publishing
1333 Burr Ridge Pkwy.
Burr Ridge, IL 60521
Ph: (708)789-4000 Fax: (708)798-6388
Fr: 800-448-3343
Kathleen McGowan, Contact
Latest edition 1991. Publication includes: List of eldercare and childcare organizations in the U.S. Entries include: Organization name, address.

Basic Reference Guides and Handbooks

★3334★ *Improving Child Care Through the Child Development Associate Program*
Council for Early Childhood Professional Recognition (CECPR)
1341 G St. NW, Ste. 400
Washington, DC 20005
Ph: (202)265-9090 Fax: (202)265-9161
Fr: 800-424-4310

Periodicals

★3335★ *Building Links: Developer Initiatives for Financing Child Care*
Child Care Action Campaign (CCAC)
330 7th Ave., 17th Fl.
New York, NY 10001
Ph: (212)239-0138 Fax: (212)268-6515
Covers financing alternatives for child care and examines the ways in which communities have begun to involve real estate developers in child care.

★3336★ *Child Care ActioNews*
Child Care Action Campaign (CCAC)
330 7th Ave., 17th Fl.
New York, NY 10001
Ph: (212)239-0138 Fax: (212)268-6515
Bimonthly. Covers innovations in the field of child care for working parents. Includes calendar of events, legislative update, and resource information.

★3337★ *An Employer's Guide to Child Care Consultants*
Child Care Action Campaign (CCAC)
330 7th Ave., 17th Fl.
New York, NY 10001
Ph: (212)239-0138 Fax: (212)268-6515
Focuses on the reasons for using a child care consultant, services that consultants can offer, and how to choose the child care consultant for you.

★3338★ *Family Day Care Bulletin*
Children's Foundation
725 15th St. NW, Ste. 505
Washington, DC 20005-2109
Ph: (202)347-3300
Kay Hollestelle
Bimonthly. Serves as a national information resource on family day care systems and supports. Covers topics such as government program and legislative developments, day care insurance, day care licensing, and current research concerning child development and behavior. Recurring features include listings of Foundation publications and a calendar of events.

★3339★ *Investing in the Future: Child Care Financing Options for the Public and Private Sectors*
Child Care Action Campaign (CCAC)
330 7th Ave., 17th Fl.
New York, NY 10001
Ph: (212)239-0138 Fax: (212)268-6515
Highlights successful financing models, including grants and loans, bank reinvestment strategies, community initiatives, bonds and pension funds.

★3340★ *Not Too Small to Care: Small Businesses and Child Care*
Child Care Action Campaign (CCAC)
330 7th Ave., 17th Fl.
New York, NY 10001
Ph: (212)239-0138 Fax: (212)268-6515
Profiles 29 small businesses that have implemented child care benefits: on-or-near-site child care centers, employee subsidies, and parental leave.

★3341★ *School Age Notes*
Richard T. Scofield
PO Box 40205
Nashville, TN 37204
Ph: (615)242-8464
Richard T. Scofield
Monthly. Carries ideas for activities and games that are developmentally oriented. Offers curricula, advice, news, and think-pieces for improving child care. Recurring features include book reviews, a list of resources, notices of events, and columns titled Director's Corner, Developmental Notes, Activities, Curriculum Corner, and Administrative Notes.

★3342★ *Young Children*
National Association for the Education of Young Children (NAEYC)
1509 16th St. NW
Washington, DC 20036
Ph: (202)232-8777 Fax: (202)328-1846
Fr: 800-424-2460

Bimonthly. Covers developments in the practice, research, and theory of early childhood education. Includes book reviews and calendary of events.

Meetings and Conventions

★3343★ **Mother & Infant Expo**
Glahe International, Inc.
1700 K St., NW, Ste. 403
Washington, DC 20006-4557
Ph: (202)659-4557 Fax: (202)457-0776

Biennial.

★3344★ **National Association for the Education of Young Children Annual Conference**
National Association for the Education of Young Children
1509 16th St., NW
Washington, DC 20036
Ph: (202)232-8777 Fax: (202)328-1846

Annual. Usually held during November.

★3345★ **Southern Early Childhood Association Annual Meeting**
Southern Early Childhood Association
7107 W. 12th., No. 102
Box 56130
Little Rock, AR 72215-6130
Ph: (501)663-0353

Annual. **Dates and Locations:** 1996 Mar 12-16; Little Rock, AR.

Other Sources of Information

★3346★ **"Nursery School Attendant" in *Career Selector 2001***
Barron's Educational Series, Inc.
250 Wireless Blvd.
Hauppauge, NY 11788
Ph: (516)434-3311 Fax: (516)434-3723
Fr: 800-645-3476

James C. Gonyea. 1993.

★3347★ **"Teacher (Preschool)" in *Career Selector 2001***
Barron's Educational Series, Inc.
250 Wireless Blvd.
Hauppauge, NY 11788
Ph: (516)434-3311 Fax: (516)434-3723
Fr: 800-645-3476

James C. Gonyea. 1993.

Private Household Workers

Private household workers clean homes, care for children, plan and cook meals, do laundry, administer the household, and perform numerous other duties. Private household workers are employed by many types of households of various income levels. Although wealthy families may employ a large staff, it is much more common for one worker to be employed in a household where both parents work. Most household workers are general houseworkers and usually the only worker employed in the home. They dust and polish furniture; sweep, mop, and wax floors; vacuum; and clean ovens, refrigerators, and bathrooms. Other duties include looking after a child or an elderly person, cooking, feeding pets, answering the telephone and doorbell, and calling and waiting for repair workers. Household workers whose primary responsibility is taking care of children are called **childcare workers**. Those employed on an hourly basis are usually called **babysitters**. Those who are in charge of infants are sometimes called **infant nurses** or **nannies**. Tutors or **governesses** look after older children. Those who assist elderly, handicapped, or convalescent people are called companions or **personal attendants**. Households with a large staff may include a housekeeper or a butler, a cook, a caretaker, and a launderer. Housekeepers and butlers hire, supervise, and coordinate the work of the household staff and keep the household running smoothly. Cooks plan and prepare meals, clean the kitchen, order groceries and supplies, and may also serve meals. Caretakers do heavy housework and general home maintenance.

Salaries

Some full-time live-in housekeepers or butlers, nannies, and governesses earn much higher wages than full-time private household workers and cleaners. Median weekly earnings for full-time household workers are as follows:

Private household workers	$179/week
Cleaners	$191/week
Childcare workers	$154/week

Employment Outlook

Growth rate until the year 2005: Decline.

Private Household Workers

Career Guides

★3348★ *American Nanny*
TAN Press
PO Box 3721
Georgetown Station
Washington, DC 20007

Robin D. Rice. 1985. Written for the person interested in hiring a nanny. Covers qualifications, job description, employment outlook, and advantages and disadvantages. Lists nanny schools.

★3349★ "Baby-sitting: Caring for Children in Their Home" in *Exploring Careers in Child Care Services* (pp. 1-8)
Rosen Publishing Group
29 E. 21st St.
New York, NY 10010
Ph: (212)777-3017 Fax: (212)777-0277
Fr: 800-237-9932

Jean Ispa, Elizabeth Vemer, and Janis Logan. Revised edition, 1990. Covers occupations working with children including those requiring no education and training to those that require advanced training; from babysitting to program director. Describes the work and a typical work day, employment outlook, advantages and disadvantages, and personal characteristics needed for success in the field. Offers job hunting advice.

★3350★ *Becoming a Helper*
Brooks/Cole Publishing Co.
511 Forest Lodge Rd.
Pacific Grove, CA 93950-5098
Ph: (408)373-0728 Fax: (408)375-6414

Marianne Schneider Corey and Gerald Corey. Second edition, 1993.

★3351★ "Companion" in *Career Information Center* (Vol.5)
Simon and Schuster
200 Old Tappan Rd.
Old Tappan, NJ 07675
Fax: 800-445-6991 Fr: 800-223-2348

Richard Lidz and Dale Anderson, editorial directors. Fifth edition, 1993. For 600 occupations, describes job duties, entry-level requirements, education and training needed, advancement possibilities, employment outlook, earnings and benefits. The set is divided into 12 volumes. Each volume includes jobs related under a broad career field. Volume 13 is the index.

★3352★ *Cook, Domestic Service*
Careers, Inc.
PO Box 135
Largo, FL 34649-0135
Ph: (813)584-7333

1994. Two-page job guide card describing duties, working conditions, personal qualifications, training, earnings and hours, employment outlook, places of employment, related careers and where to write for more information.

★3353★ "Domestic Housekeeper" in *Career Information Center* (Vol.5)
Simon and Schuster
200 Old Tappan Rd.
Old Tappan, NJ 07675
Fax: 800-445-6991 Fr: 800-223-2348

Richard Lidz and Dale Anderson, editorial directors. Fifth edition, 1993. For 600 occupations, describes job duties, entry-level requirements, education and training needed, advancement possibilities, employment outlook, earnings and benefits. The set is divided into 12 volumes. Each volume includes jobs related under a broad career field. Volume 13 is the index.

★3354★ "Domestic Service Cook" in *Occu-Facts: Information on 580 Careers in Outline Form*
Careers, Inc.
PO Box 135
Largo, FL 34649-0135
Ph: (813)584-7333

Biennial, 1995-96 edition. Each one-page occupational profile describes duties, working conditions, physical surroundings and demands, aptitudes, temperament, educational requirements, employment outlook, earnings, and places of employment.

★3355★ *Household Service Workers*
Chronicle Guidance Publications, Inc.
66 Aurora St.
PO Box 1190
Moravia, NY 13118-1190
Ph: (315)497-0330 Fax: (315)497-3359
Fr: 800-622-7284

1992. This career brief describes the nature of the work, working conditions, hours and earnings, education and training, licensure, certification, unions, personal qualifications, social and psychological factors, employment outlook, entry methods, advancement, and related occupations.

★3356★ *Nannies*
Chronicle Guidance Publications, Inc.
66 Aurora St.
PO Box 1190
Moravia, NY 13118-1190
Ph: (315)497-0330 Fax: (315)497-3359
Fr: 800-622-7284

1993. This career brief describes the nature of the work, working conditions, hours and earnings, education and training, licensure, certification, unions, personal qualifications, social and psychological factors, employment outlook, entry methods, advancement, and related occupations.

★3357★ "Nannies" in *Career Discovery Encyclopedia* (Vol.4, pp. 118-119)
J.G. Ferguson Publishing Co.
200 W. Madison St., Ste. 300
Chicago, IL 60606
Ph: (312)580-5480 Fax: (312)580-4948

E. Russell Primm, editor-in-chief. 1993. Contains two-page articles on 504 occupations. Each article describes job duties, earnings, and educational and training requirements.

★3358★ "Nannies" in *Encyclopedia of Careers and Vocational Guidance* (Vol.3, pp. 540-542)
J.G. Ferguson Publishing Co.
200 W. Madison St., Ste. 300
Chicago, IL 60606
Ph: (312)580-5480 Fax: (312)580-4948

William E. Hopke, editor-in-chief. Ninth edition, 1993. Four-volume set that profiles 500 occupations and describes job trends in 74 industries. Includes career description, educational requirements, history of the job, methods of entry, advancement, employment outlook, earnings, working conditions, social

and psychological factors, and sources of additional information.

★3359★ "Nanny" in *Career Information Center* (Vol.5)
Simon and Schuster
200 Old Tappan Rd.
Old Tappan, NJ 07675
Fax: 800-445-6991 Fr: 800-223-2348

Richard Lidz and Dale Anderson, editorial directors. Fifth edition, 1993. For 600 occupations, describes job duties, entry-level requirements, education and training needed, advancement possibilities, employment outlook, earnings and benefits. The set is divided into 12 volumes. Each volume includes jobs related under a broad career field. Volume 13 is the index.

★3360★ "Nanny" in *Offbeat Careers: The Directory of Unusual Work*
Ten Speed Press
PO Box 7123
Berkeley, CA 94707
Fax: (510)559-1629 Fr: 800-841-2665

Al Sacharov. 1991. Profiles eighty-eight unusual careers. Provides job description, history of occupation, salary, and training required. Lists one or more sources of additional information.

★3361★ "Private Child Care Worker" in *Career Information Center* (Vol.5)
Simon and Schuster
200 Old Tappan Rd.
Old Tappan, NJ 07675
Fax: 800-445-6991 Fr: 800-223-2348

Richard Lidz and Dale Anderson, editorial directors. Fifth edition, 1993. For 600 occupations, describes job duties, entry-level requirements, education and training needed, advancement possibilities, employment outlook, earnings and benefits. The set is divided into 12 volumes. Each volume includes jobs related under a broad career field. Volume 13 is the index.

★3362★ "Private Household Worker" in *Personal Services* (pp. 15-19)
Franklin Watts, Inc.
387 Park Avenue, S.
New York, NY 10016
Ph: (212)686-7070

Linda Barrett and Galen Guengerich. 1991. Surveys personal services jobs. Describes job duties, educational preparation, salaries, and employment outlook. Offers job hunting advice.

★3363★ "Private Household Workers" in *Career Discovery Encyclopedia* (Vol.5, pp. 84-85)
J.G. Ferguson Publishing Co.
200 W. Madison St., Ste. 300
Chicago, IL 60606
Ph: (312)580-5480 Fax: (312)580-4948

E. Russell Primm, editor-in-chief. 1993. Contains two-page articles on 504 occupations. Each article describes job duties, earnings, and educational and training requirements.

★3364★ "Private Household Workers" in *Encyclopedia of Careers and Vocational Guidance*
J.G. Ferguson Publishing Co.
200 W. Madison St., Ste. 300
Chicago, IL 60606
Ph: (312)580-5480 Fax: (312)580-4948

William E. Hopke, editor-in-chief. Ninth edition, 1993. Four-volume set that profiles 500 occupations and describes job trends in 74 industries. Includes career description, educational requirements, history of the job, methods of entry, advancement, employment outlook, earnings, working conditions, social and psychological factors, and sources of additional information.

★3365★ "Private Household Workers" in *Occupational Outlook Handbook*
U.S. Government Printing Office
Superintendent of Documents
Washington, DC 20402
Ph: (202)512-1800 Fax: (202)512-2250

Biennial; latest edition, 1994-95. Encyclopedia of careers describing more than 250 occupations and comprising about 85 percent of all jobs in the economy. Occupations that require lengthy education or training are given the most attention. For each occupation, the handbook describes job duties, working conditions, training, educational preparation, personal qualities, advancement possibilities, job outlook, earnings, and sources of additional information.

Associations

★3366★ American Council of Nanny Schools (ACNS)
Delta Coll.
University Center, MI 48710
Ph: (517)686-9417 Fax: (517)686-8736

Members: Schools involved in training programs for nannies. **Purpose:** Purposes include: promoting professionalism of nannies and others in the field of child care; compiling information on nanny training programs and placement agencies available; establishing and maintaining a national competency test for nannies; creating standards for schools initiating nanny programs and providing a means for exchanging experiences in the curriculum. Maintains speakers' bureau and placement service; compiles statistics. **Publications:** *ACNewS*.

Standards/Certification Agencies

★3367★ American Council of Nanny Schools (ACNS)
Delta Coll.
University Center, MI 48710
Ph: (517)686-9417 Fax: (517)686-8736

Purposes include: establishing and maintaining a national competency test for nannies; creating standards for schools initiating nanny programs and providing a means for exchanging experiences in the curriculum.

Test Guides

★3368★ *Career Examination Series: Domestic Worker*
National Learning Corp.
212 Michael Dr.
Syosset, NY 11791
Ph: (516)921-8888 Fax: (516)921-8743
Fr: 800-645-6337

Jack Rudman. All examination guides in this series contain questions with answers.

Periodicals

★3369★ *ACNewS*
American Council of Nanny Schools (ACNS)
Delta Coll.
University Center, MI 48710
Ph: (517)686-9417 Fax: (517)686-8736

Provides information on child development, nutrition, health care, and other topics.

Meetings and Conventions

★3370★ National Executive Housekeepers Association Exposition
National Executive Housekeepers Association
1001 Eastwind Dr., Ste. 301
Westerville, OH 43081
Ph: (614)895-7166 Fax: (614)895-1248

Biennial. **Dates and Locations:** 1996 Jul; Dallas, TX.

Farm Operators and Managers

Farm operators and managers in the United States direct the activities of one of the world's largest and most productive agricultural sectors. Farm operators may be farmer owners or tenant farmers (renters). On crop farms, farm operators are responsible for planning, tilling, planting, fertilizing, cultivating, spraying, and harvesting. After the harvest, they make sure that the crops are packaged, loaded, and promptly marketed or stored for resale. On livestock, dairy, and poultry farms, farm operators must plan, feed, and care for the animals and keep barns, pens, coops, and other farm buildings clean and in repair. They also oversee breeding, some slaughtering, and marketing activities. On horticultural specialty farms, farm operators oversee the production of ornamental plants, nursery products, and fruits and vegetables grown in greenhouses. In addition, farm operators must make many managerial decisions and perform tasks ranging from setting up and operating machinery to erecting fences and sheds. Farm managers handle some or all farm operations or oversee tenant operators. Most farm operators and managers handle crop production activities while others manage livestock production activities. A relatively small number are involved in agricultural services such as contract harvesting and farm labor contracting.

Salaries

Incomes vary greatly from year to year, since prices of farm products fluctuate depending upon weather conditions. Farm income also varies greatly depending upon the type and size of farm. Vegetable and melon, cotton, horticultural, specialty, and rice farms generate an average income of over $100,000. Cattle, general crop, corn, tobacco, and other livestock farms generate less than $15,000 in income.

Top 10 percent	$696/week
Middle	$382-$545/week
Lowest 10 percents	$!85/week

Employment Outlook

Growth rate until the year 2005: Decline.

Farm Operators and Managers

Career Guides

★3371★ *Agricultural Cluster*
Center for Humanities, Inc.
Communications Park
Box 1000
Mount Kisco, NY 10549
Ph: (914)666-4100 Fax: (914)666-5319
Fr: 800-431-1242

Videocassette. 1984. 20 mins. People who work in agriculture describe their daily work routines for students interested in entering this occupation.

★3372★ *American Professionals Series*
Cambridge Career Products
PO Box 2153
Charleston, WV 25328-2153
Ph: (304)744-9323 Fax: (304)744-9351
Fr: 800-468-4227

Videocassette. 1984. 30 mins. In this series of twenty-one half hour programs, various occupations are examined in depth, including a day in the life of each worker. Included are: fireman, farmer, oil driller, fisherman, horse trainer, auto assembly repairman, nurse, pilot, and paramedic.

★3373★ *Career Summary: Farm Manager*
American Society of Farm Managers and Rural Appriasers
950 S. Cherry St., Ste. 106
Denver, CO 80222
Ph: (303)758-3513

1984. This two-page leaflet describes the work of a farm manager, as well as working conditions, personal qualifications, training, and outlook.

★3374★ *Crop Farming Workers*
Chronicle Guidance Publications, Inc.
66 Aurora St.
PO Box 1190
Moravia, NY 13118-1190
Ph: (315)497-0330 Fax: (315)497-3359
Fr: 800-622-7284

1993. This career brief describes the nature of the work, working conditions, hours and earnings, education and training, licensure, certification, unions, personal qualifications, social and psychological factors, employment outlook, entry methods, advancement, and related occupations.

★3375★ *Dairy Farmers*
Chronicle Guidance Publications, Inc.
66 Aurora St.
PO Box 1190
Moravia, NY 13118-1190
Ph: (315)497-0330 Fax: (315)497-3359
Fr: 800-622-7284

1993. This career brief describes the nature of the work, working conditions, hours and earnings, education and training, licensure, certification, unions, personal qualifications, social and psychological factors, employment outlook, entry methods, advancement, and related occupations.

★3376★ "Dairy Farmers" in *Career Discovery Encyclopedia* (Vol.2, pp. 74-75)
J.G. Ferguson Publishing Co.
200 W. Madison St., Ste. 300
Chicago, IL 60606
Ph: (312)580-5480 Fax: (312)580-4948

E. Russell Primm, editor-in-chief. 1993. Contains two-page articles on 504 occupations. Each article describes job duties, earnings, and educational and training requirements.

★3377★ *Employment Opportunities for College Graduates in Food & Agricultural Sciences: Agriculture, Natural Resources, & Veterinary Medicine: 1990-1995*
U.S. Department of Agriculture
Cooperative State Research Service
Higher Education Programs
Washington, DC 20250
Ph: (202)447-7854

1990. This 26-page booklet describes the labor market outlook for agriculture related careers, including farm operators and managers, from 1990 to 1995.

★3378★ "Farm Management" in *Career Connection II: A Guide to Technical Majors and Their Related Careers* (pp. 74-75)
Jist Works, Inc.
720 N. Park Ave.
Indianapolis, IN 46202-3431
Ph: (317)264-3720 Fax: (317)264-3709

Fred A. Rowe. 1994. Contains technical majors, such as automotive technology. Describes the major and the job. Lists high school and postsecondary school courses. Includes occupations related to the major, employment outlook, and starting salary.

★3379★ *Farm Manager*
Vocational Biographies, Inc.
PO Box 31
Sauk Centre, MN 56378-0031
Ph: (612)352-6516 Fax: (612)352-5546
Fr: 800-255-0752

1990. This pamphlet profiles a person working in the job. Includes information about job duties, working conditions, places of employment, educational preparation, labor market outlook, and salaries.

★3380★ *Farm Manager*
Careers, Inc.
PO Box 135
Largo, FL 34649-0135
Ph: (813)584-7333

1993. Two-page occupational summary card describing duties, working conditions, personal qualifications, training, earnings and hours, employment outlook, places of employment, related careers and where to write for more information.

★3381★ "Farm Manager" in *Career Information Center* (Vol.2)
Simon and Schuster
200 Old Tappan Rd.
Old Tappan, NJ 07675
Fax: 800-445-6991 Fr: 800-223-2348

Richard Lidz and Dale Anderson, editorial directors. Fifth edition, 1993. For 600 occupations, describes job duties, entry-level requirements, education and training needed, advancement possibilities, employment outlook, earnings and benefits. The set is divided into 12 volumes. Each volume includes jobs related under a broad career field. Volume 13 is the index.

★3382★ "Farm Manager" in *Top Professions: The 100 Most Popular, Dynamic, and Profitable Careers in America Today* (pp. 77-78)
Petersons Guides, Inc.
PO Box 2123
Princeton, NJ 08543-2123
Ph: (609)243-9111 Fax: (609)243-9150
Fr: 800-338-3282

Nicholas Basta. 1989. Includes occupations requiring a college or advanced degree. Describes job duties, earnings, some typical job titles, career opportunities at different degree levels, and lists related associations.

★3383★ "Farm Operatives and Managers" in *Encyclopedia of Careers and Vocational Guidance*
J.G. Ferguson Publishing Co.
200 W. Madison St., Ste. 300
Chicago, IL 60606
Ph: (312)580-5480 Fax: (312)580-4948

William E. Hopke, editor-in-chief. Ninth edition, 1993. Four-volume set that profiles 500 occupations and describes job trends in 74 industries. Includes career description, educational requirements, history of the job, methods of entry, advancement, employment outlook, earnings, working conditions, social and psychological factors, and sources of additional information.

★3384★ "Farm Operators and Managers" in *Jobs! What They Are—Where They Are—What They Pay* (pp. 49-50)
Fireside
Simon & Schuster Bldg.
1230 Avenue of the Americas
New York, NY 10020
Ph: (212)698-7000 Fr: 800-223-2348

Robert O. Snelling and Anne M. Snelling. Revised and updated, 1992. Describes duties and responsibilities, earnings, employment opportunities, training, and qualifications.

★3385★ "Farm Operators and Managers" in *Occupational Outlook Handbook*
U.S. Government Printing Office
Superintendent of Documents
Washington, DC 20402
Ph: (202)512-1800 Fax: (202)512-2250

Biennial; latest edition, 1994-95. Encyclopedia of careers describing more than 250 occupations and comprising about 85 percent of all jobs in the economy. Occupations that require lengthy education or training are given the most attention. For each occupation, the handbook describes job duties, working conditions, training, educational preparation, personal qualities, advancement possibilities, job outlook, earnings, and sources of additional information.

★3386★ "Farmer" in *Career Information Center* (Vol.2)
Simon and Schuster
200 Old Tappan Rd.
Old Tappan, NJ 07675
Fax: 800-445-6991 Fr: 800-223-2348

Richard Lidz and Dale Anderson, editorial directors. Fifth edition, 1993. For 600 occupations, describes job duties, entry-level requirements, education and training needed, advancement possibilities, employment outlook, earnings and benefits. The set is divided into 12 volumes. Each volume includes jobs related under a broad career field. Volume 13 is the index.

★3387★ *Farmer, Cattle*
Careers, Inc.
PO Box 135
Largo, FL 34649-0135
Ph: (813)584-7333

1992. Two-page occupational summary card describing duties, working conditions, personal qualifications, training, earnings and hours, employment outlook, places of employment, related careers and where to write for more information.

★3388★ *Farmer, Dairy*
Careers, Inc.
PO Box 135
Largo, FL 34649-0135
Ph: (813)584-7333

1995. Two-page occupational summary card describing duties, working conditions, personal qualifications, training, earnings and hours, employment outlook, places of employment, related careers and where to write for more information.

★3389★ *Farmer, Fruit*
Careers, Inc.
PO Box 135
Largo, FL 34649-0135
Ph: (813)584-7333

1994. Two-page occupational summary card describing duties, working conditions, personal qualifications, training, earnings and hours, employment outlook, places of employment, related careers and where to write for more information.

★3390★ *Farmer, Poultry*
Careers, Inc.
PO Box 135
Largo, FL 34649-0135
Ph: (813)584-7333

1991. Two-page occupational summary card describing duties, working conditions, personal qualifications, training, earnings and hours, employment outlook, places of employment, related careers and where to write for more information.

★3391★ *Farmer, Vegetable Crops*
Careers, Inc.
PO Box 135
Largo, FL 34649-0135
Ph: (813)584-7333

1992. Two-page occupational summary card describing duties, working conditions, personal qualifications, training, earnings and hours, employment outlook, places of employment, related careers and where to write for more information.

★3392★ "Farmer" in *VGM's Careers Encyclopedia* (pp. 169-171)
National Textbook Co. (NTC)
VGM Career Books
4255 W. Touhy Ave.
Lincolnwood, IL 60646-1975
Ph: (708)679-5500 Fax: (708)679-2494
Fr: 800-323-4900

Third edition, 1991. Contains two- to five-page descriptions of 200 managerial, professional, technical, trade, and service occupations. Each profile includes job duties, places of employment, qualifications, educational preparation, training, employment potential, advancement, income, and additional sources of information.

★3393★ *Farmers*
Careers, Inc.
PO Box 135
Largo, FL 34649-0135
Ph: (813)584-7333

1991. Four-page brief offering the definition, history, duties, working conditions, personal qualifications, educational requirements, earnings, hours, employment outlook, advancement possibilities, and related occupations.

★3394★ "Farmers" in *Career Discovery Encyclopedia* (Vol.2, pp. 174-175)
J.G. Ferguson Publishing Co.
200 W. Madison St., Ste. 300
Chicago, IL 60606
Ph: (312)580-5480 Fax: (312)580-4948

E. Russell Primm, editor-in-chief. 1993. Contains two-page articles on 504 occupations. Each article describes job duties, earnings, and educational and training requirements.

★3395★ "Farmers" in *Encyclopedia of Careers and Vocational Guidance* (Vol.2, pp. 628-632)
J.G. Ferguson Publishing Co.
200 W. Madison St., Ste. 300
Chicago, IL 60606
Ph: (312)580-5480 Fax: (312)580-4948

William E. Hopke, editor-in-chief. Ninth edition, 1993. Four-volume set that profiles 500 occupations and describes job trends in 74 industries. Includes career description, educational requirements, history of the job, methods of entry, advancement, employment outlook, earnings, working conditions, social and psychological factors, and sources of additional information.

★3396★ *Farmers, General*
Chronicle Guidance Publications, Inc.
66 Aurora St.
PO Box 1190
Moravia, NY 13118-1190
Ph: (315)497-0330 Fax: (315)497-3359
Fr: 800-622-7284

1992. This career brief describes the nature of the work, working conditions, hours and earnings, education and training, licensure, certification, unions, personal qualifications, social and psychological factors, employment outlook, entry methods, advancement, and related occupations.

★3397★ "Farmers" in *Occu-Facts: Information on 580 Careers in Outline Form*
Careers, Inc.
PO Box 135
Largo, FL 34649-0135
Ph: (813)584-7333

Biennial, 1995-96 edition. Each one-page occupational profile describes duties, working conditions, physical surroundings and demands, aptitudes, temperament, educational requirements, employment outlook, earnings, and places of employment.

★3398★ *Grain Farmer*
Vocational Biographies, Inc.
PO Box 31
Sauk Centre, MN 56378-0031
Ph: (612)352-6516 Fax: (612)352-5546
Fr: 800-255-0752

1990. This pamphlet profiles a person working in the job. Includes information about job duties, working conditions, places of employment, educational preparation, labor market outlook, and salaries.

★3399★ *Stew Leonard's Creating the Customer's Dream*
United Training Media
6633 West Howard St.
PO Box 47818
Niles, IL 60714-0718
Ph: (708)647-0600 Fax: (708)647-0918
Fr: 800-424-0364

Videocassette. 1990. 59 mins. Stew Leonard runs a huge dairy in Norwalk, Connecticut, and on this video he attributes his success primarily to the high level of customer service he delivers.

★3400★ *There's a New "Challenge in Agriculture"*
American Farm Bureau Federation
225 Touhy Ave.
Park Ridge, IL 60068
Ph: (312)399-5700

1991. This booklet surveys opportunities in farming and agriculture. Lists land grant colleges offering degree programs in agriculture. Includes a bibliography of sources for more information about careers in agriculture.

★3401★ *Vocational Visions*
Center for Humanities, Inc.
Communications Park
Box 1000
Mount Kisco, NY 10549
Ph: (914)666-4100 Fax: (914)666-5319
Fr: 800-431-1242

Videocassette. 1984. 30 mins. This series of programs explains key aspects of actual training and a day in the life of a worker in the specific field mentioned on the videocassette. Occupations include: transportation/mechanics, repair, construction, business/office occupations, health, agriculture, technical/manufacturing, communications, and personal service.

★3402★ *Vocations U.S.A.*
Info-Disc Corporation
4 Professional Dr., Ste. 134
Gaithersburg, MD 20879
Ph: (301)948-2300 Fr: 800-648-6422

Videocassette. 1987. 60 mins. A disc collection outlining the requirements and methods of various career areas. Occupations include: transportation, mechanical/repair, health, agriculture, technical/manufacturing, and construction.

★3403★ *When Do You Need a Professional, Accredited Farm Manager?*
American Society of Farm Managers and Rural Appriasers
950 S. Cherry St., Ste. 106
Denver, CO 80222
Ph: (303)758-3513

Six-panel brochure describing the job duties and responsibilities of an accredited farm manager.

Associations

★3404★ American Farm Bureau Federation (AFBF)
225 Touhy Ave.
Park Ridge, IL 60068
Ph: (312)399-5700 Fax: (312)399-5896

Members: Federation of 50 state farm bureaus and Puerto Rico, with membership on a family basis. **Purpose:** Analyzes problems of members and formulates action to achieve educational improvement, economic opportunity, and social advancement. Maintains speakers' bureau; sponsors specialized education program. **Publications:** *Farm Bureau News*, weekly.

★3405★ American Society of Farm Managers and Rural Appraisers (ASFMRA)
950 S. Cherry St., Ste. 508
Denver, CO 80222
Ph: (303)758-3513 Fax: (303)758-0190

Members: Professional farm managers, appraisers, lenders, and researchers in farm and ranch management and/or rural appraisal. **Purpose:** Bestows registered ARA (Accredited Rural Appraiser) and AFM (Accredited Farm Manager) designations. Operates managing and appraisal schools, seminars, and conferences. Maintains placement service. **Publications:** *American Society of Farm Managers and Rural Appraisers-General Membership Directory*, annual. • *Farm Management Manual.* • *FMRA News.* • *Journal of the American Society of Farm Managers and Rural Appraisers*, annual. • *Rural Appraisal Manual.*

★3406★ Demeter Association
Britt Rd.
Aurora, NY 13026
Ph: (315)364-5617 Fax: (315)364-5224

Certifies biodynamic farms. (Biodynamic farming predates organic farming and is based on lectures by Austrian philosopher Rudolf Steiner.)

★3407★ National FFA Organization (NFFAO)
5632 Mount Vernon Memorial Hwy.
Box 15160
Alexandria, VA 22309-0160
Ph: (703)360-3600 Fax: (703)360-5524

Members: Students of agriculture/agribusiness in public schools. Organized under the National Vocational Education Act to foster character development, agricultural leadership, and responsible citizenship and to supplement training opportunities for students preparing for careers in farming and agribusiness. **Purpose:** Works with youth specialists in approximately 38 countries. Maintains Hall of Achievement. National FFA Alumni Association is supportive group. Sponsored by Agriculture/Agribusiness and Natural Resources Staff of the Division of Vocational and Technical Education, U.S. Department of Education. **Publications:** *FFA Advisors Making a Difference*, bimonthly. • *FFA New Horizons Magazine*, bimonthly. • *National FFA Convention Proceedings*, annual. • *National FFA Organization—Update*, monthly.

Standards/Certification Agencies

★3408★ American Society of Farm Managers and Rural Appraisers (ASFMRA)
950 S. Cherry St., Ste. 508
Denver, CO 80222
Ph: (303)758-3513 Fax: (303)758-0190

Bestows registered ARA (Accredited Rural Appraiser) and AFM (Accredited Farm Manager) designations. Operates managing and appraisal schools, seminars, and conferences.

★3409★ Demeter Association
Britt Rd.
Aurora, NY 13026
Ph: (315)364-5617 Fax: (315)364-5224

Certifies biodynamic farms. (Biodynamic farming predates organic farming and is based on lectures by Austrian philosopher Rudolf Steiner.)

★3410★ National Postsecondary Agricultural Student Organization (PAS)
PO Box 15440
Alexandria, VA 22309
Ph: (703)780-4922 Fax: (703)780-4378

Promotes leadership experiences and assists students in job placement. Sponsors Speakers for Agriculture and Employment Interview. Conducts Planning for Progress Project to recognize achievement by students.

Educational Directories and Programs

★3411★ *International Green Front Report*
Friends of the Trees
PO Box 1064
Tonasket, WA 98855
Ph: (509)485-2705 Fax: (509)485-2705
Michael Pilarski, Office Manager

Irregular, latest edition 1988. Covers Organizations and periodicals concerned with sustainable forestry and agriculture and related fields. Entries include: Organization or publisher name, address, phone, description of projects and activities, or description of periodical coverage. Arrangement: Classified by subject.

★3412★ *New England Farm Bulletin & Garden Gazette—Farmer-Consumer Connection*
Jacob's Meadow, Inc.
PO Box 67
Taunton, MA 02780-0067
Ph: (508)998-5424
Pam Comstock

Annual, June. Covers about 1,000 suppliers of farm products, farmers' markets, agricultural fairs, and farm museums in New England. Entries include: Name, address, phone, services provided, descriptions of services. Arrangement: Classified by line of service.

★3413★ *New England Farm Bulletin & Garden Gazette—NEFB Almanack Issue*
Jacob's Meadow, Inc.
PO Box 67
Taunton, MA 02780-0067
Ph: (508)998-5424
Pam Comstock

Annual, January. Publication includes: List of farming and gardening organizations in New England. Entries include: Organization name, address, phone, name and title of contact. Principal content of publication is information on issues affecting farming and gardening. Arrangement: Classified by type of organization.

★3414★ *Tractor Equipment & Parts Directory*
American Business Directories, Inc.
5711 S. 86th Circle
Omaha, NE 68127
Ph: (402)593-4600 Fax: (402)331-1505

Updated continuously; printed on request. Entries include: Name, address, phone, size of advertisement, name of owner or manager, number of employees, year first in "Yellow Pages." Compiled from telephone company "Yellow Pages," nationwide. Arrangement: Geographical.

AWARDS, SCHOLARSHIPS, GRANTS, AND FELLOWSHIPS

★3415★ Agricultural Hall of Fame
National Agricultural Center and Hall of Fame
630 N. 126 St.
Bonner Springs, KS 66012
Ph: (913)721-1075 Fax: (913)721-1202

To honor individuals who have helped make this nation great by their outstanding contributions to the establishment, development, advancement, or improvement of agriculture in the United States. Farmers, farm women, farm leaders, teachers, scientists, inventors, governmental leaders, and other individuals are eligible. Usually, candidates must have been deceased at least ten years. A unanimous vote by the board of governors may declare a living person (or person deceased less than 10 years) as an eligible candidate. Portraits of recipients are hung in the Hall of Honorees. Awarded only when merited. Established in 1960.

★3416★ Distinguished Dairy Cattle Breeder Award
Dairy Shrine
100 MBC Dr.
Shawano, WI 54166
Ph: (608)846-3721 Fax: (608)846-6444

To recognize an outstanding dairy cattle breeder. Awarded annually. Established in 1973.

★3417★ Distinguished Service to Agriculture
American Society of Farm Managers and Rural Appraisers
950 S. Cherry St., Ste. 508
Denver, CO 80222
Ph: (303)758-3513 Fax: (303)758-0190

To recognize individuals who have made contributions to agriculture. A plaque is awarded annually if merited. Established in 1974.

★3418★ D. Howard Doane Award
American Society of Farm Managers and Rural Appraisers
950 S. Cherry St., Ste. 508
Denver, CO 80222
Ph: (303)758-3513 Fax: (303)758-0190

To recognize an individual who has made an outstanding contribution in the field of agriculture, with emphasis on farm management and rural appraising. Preference is given to members of the society. A wood and metal plaque are awarded annually if merited. Established in 1951 in honor of D. Howard Doane, first president of the society.

★3419★ Guest of Honor Award
Dairy Shrine
100 MBC Dr.
Shawano, WI 54166
Ph: (608)846-3721 Fax: (608)846-6444

To recognize contemporary dairy leaders for outstanding accomplishments and contributions to the dairy industry. One individual is selected annually. Established in 1949.

★3420★ Outstanding Grassland Farmer or Rancher Award
American Forage and Grassland Council
PO Box 891
Georgetown, TX 78627
Ph: (512)863-2444

To recognize farmers, farm managers or ranchers who have done an exceptional job of forage crop production or grassland or range management and utilization. The state or Provincial Forage Council is responsible for nominations and selecting the winners. As many as ten farmers or ranchers in each state or province having a Forage Council affiliated with AFGC are eligible. Awarded annually at suitable functions as established by the state or provincial council, where feasible.

★3421★ Outstanding Young Farmer Awards
United States Junior Chamber of Commerce
PO Box 7
Tulsa, OK 74102-0007
Ph: (918)584-2481 Fax: (918)584-4422
Fr: 800-JAY-CEES

To foster better urban-rural relations by creating an understanding and interest in today's farmers, their professional abilities, and problems as a world food supplier. Individuals between the ages of 21 and 39 who are actual farm operators, deriving a minimum of two-thirds of their income from farming are eligible. Selection is based on progress in agricultural career, extent of soil and water conservation practices, and contributions to well-being of the community, state, and nation. Each state participating in the awards program selects one state winner; the national organization then selects four national winners. Awarded annually. Established in 1954. Sponsored by Deere and Company.

★3422★ Pioneer of the Year Award
Northwest Farm Managers Association
PO Box 3437
Fargo, ND 58105
Ph: (701)237-7378 Fax: (701)237-8520

For recognition of outstanding achievement and lifelong service to agriculture. Nominations are accepted from former winners, and present and former officers of the organization. A plaque is presented annually at the Convention in Febuary. Established in 1959.

★3423★ Lillian B. Wood Rowe & John O. Rowe Citizen of the Year Award
American Milking Shorthorn Society
PO Box 449
Beloit, WI 53512-0449
Ph: (608)365-3332

To recognize outstanding service and contributions made by an individual for the Milking Shorthorn breed. Those involved in some way with the dairy industry are eligible. A plaque is awarded at the convention in April. Established in 1983 by Stuart and Lillian Rowe in memory of John O. Rowe, a California Milking Shorthorn breeder who possessed strong dairy skills. Additional information is available from J. Stuart Rowe, Rt. 1, Box 2800 Davis, CA 95616

★3424★ Wall of Honors
National Agricultural Center and Hall of Fame
630 N. 126 St.
Bonner Springs, KS 66012
Ph: (913)721-1075 Fax: (913)721-1202

To honor individuals, clubs, associations and/or businesses that have contributed to the (financial and otherwise) success and development of the Agricultural Hall of Fame. Nominees may or may not have an agricultural background and may or may not be deceased. A certificate or plaque is awarded. A framed portrait and a brief description of the honoree's achievements and contributions are noted on the Wall of Honors, the official name of the place of induction.

Basic Reference Guides and Handbooks

★3425★ *American Farmer*
ESP, Inc.
1201 E. Johnson
Jonesboro, AR 72401
Ph: (501)935-3533
Ethel Cole. 1976.

★3426★ *Conservation Gains in the Tax Reform Act*
Natural Resources Defense Council
40 W. 20th St.
New York, NY 10011
Ph: (212)727-4412
Kaid Benfield. 1987.

★3427★ *Farm Management Manual.*
American Society of Farm Managers and Rural Appraisers (ASFMRA)
950 S. Cherry St., Ste. 508
Denver, CO 80222
Ph: (303)758-3513 Fax: (303)758-0190

★3428★ *Farmers as Hunters: The Implications of Sedentism*
Cambridge University Press
40 W. 20th St.
New York, NY 10011
Ph: (212)924-3900 Fax: (212)691-3239
Susan Kent, editor. 1989. Part of New Directions in Archaeology Series.

★3429★ *Rural Appraisal Manual*
American Society of Farm Managers and Rural Appraisers (ASFMRA)
950 S. Cherry St., Ste. 508
Denver, CO 80222
Ph: (303)758-3513 Fax: (303)758-0190

Periodicals

★3430★ *Ag Alert*
California Farm Bureau Federation
1601 Exposition Blvd., No. FB9
Sacramento, CA 95815
Ph: (916)924-4140 Fax: (916)923-5318
Steve Adler
Weekly. Agricultural magazine (tabloid).

★3431★ *AG Consultant*
Meister Publishing Co.
37733 Euclid Ave.
Willoughby, OH 44094-5992
Ph: (216)942-2000 Fax: (216)942-0662
Judy Ferguson
Crop advisory magazine.

★3432★ *AG-PILOT International*
Graphics Plus
PO Box 1607
Mount Vernon, WA 98273
Ph: (206)336-9737 Fax: (206)336-2506
Tom J. Wood
Monthly. Magazine covering agricultural aviation.

★3433★ *Agri-Equipment & Chemical*
Clintron Publishers, Inc.
PO Box 6
Spokane, WA 99210
Ph: (509)575-6774 Fax: (509)457-3885
Ron Riggan
Monthly. Agriculture magazine.

★3434★ *Agri Finance*
Century Communications Inc.
6201 Howard St.
Niles, IL 60714
Ph: (708)647-1200 Fax: (708)647-7055
Fr: 800-322-5510
David Pelzer
Trade magazine on agriculture banking, professional farm management, and crop consultant news and features.

★3435★ *Agri-News*
Box 30755
Billings, MT 59107-0755
Ph: (406)259-5406 Fax: (406)259-6888
Rebecca K. Tescher
Weekly. Newspaper covering agriculture in Montana, northern Wyoming, and western North Dakota.

★3436★ *Agri News*
Post Bulletin Co.
PO Box 6118
Rochester, MN 55903-6118
Ph: (507)285-7657 Fax: (507)281-7436
Kelly J. Boldan
Weekly. Farm newspaper distributed in southern Minnesota, central Minnesota, and northeastern Iowa.

★3437★ *Agri-View*
Krause Publications, Inc.
700 E. State St.
Iola, WI 54990
Rick GrothPublisher
SWY. Agricultural newspaper for farmers with 100 acres or more.

★3438★ *Agribusiness*
John Wiley and Sons, Inc.
605 3rd Ave.
New York, NY 10158
Ph: (212)850-6000 Fax: (212)850-6799
Michael W. Woolverton
Bimonthly. Publication focusing on applied research in agribusiness, including agricultural inputs, agricultural production, commodity processing, food manufacturing, and food distribution.

★3439★ *Agricultural Aviation*
National Agricultural Aviation Assn.
1005 E St. SE
Washington, DC 20003
Ph: (202)546-5722 Fax: (202)546-5726
Jim Boillot
Magazine covering trends in the agricultural aviation industry.

★3440★ *The Agricultural Education Magazine*
2441 Suzanne Drive
Mechanicsville, VA 23111-4028
Philip Zurbrick
Monthly. Vocational agriculture education magazine.

★3441★ *Agricultural Engineering*
American Society of Agricultural Engineers
2950 Niles Rd.
Saint Joseph, MI 49085-9659
Ph: (616)429-0300 Fax: (616)429-3852
Denise Sicking
Bimonthly. Magazine covering technology for food and agriculture.

★3442★ *Agricultural & Food: An Abstract Newsletter*
National Technical Information Service (NTIS)
5285 Port Royal Rd.
Springfield, VA 22161
Ph: (703)487-4630
Biweekly. Publishes abstracts of reports on agricultural chemistry, agricultural equipment, facilities, and operations. Also covers agronomy, horticulture, and plant pathology; fisheries and aquaculture; animal husbandry and veterinary medicine; and food technology.

★3443★ *Agronomy Journal*
American Society of Agronomy
677 S. Segoe Rd.
Madison, WI 53711
Ph: (608)273-8080 Fax: (608)273-2021
J.L. Hatfield
Bimonthly. Agriculture science trade journal.

★3444★ *AgVenture*
Wisconsin Farm Bureau Federation
PO Box 5550
Madison, WI 53705
Ph: (608)833-8070
Joyce Munz Hach
Bimonthly. Agriculture magazine.

★3445★ *Agway Cooperator*
Agway, Inc.
PO Box 4933
Syracuse, NY 13221
Ph: (315)449-6117 Fax: (315)449-6253
S. Zarins
Bimonthly. Magazine for farm cooperative members.

★3446★ *AGWEEK*
Grand Forks Herald, Inc.
120 N. 4th St.
PO Box 6008
Grand Forks, ND 58206-6008
Ph: (701)780-1230 Fax: (701)780-1188
Fr: 800-477-6572
Juan Pedraza
Weekly. Newsmagazine covering markets, prices, and global news affecting American farmers.

★3447★ *American Agriculturist*
Farm Progress Companies
191 S. Gary Ave.
Carol Stream, IL 60188
Ph: (708)690-5600 Fax: (708)462-2924
Allan JohnsonPresident
Monthly. Magazine on agriculture and homemaking.

★3448★ *American Beef Cattleman*
Box 357
Allen, KS 66833
Ph: (316)528-3556 Fax: (316)528-3226
Hayes Walker
Monthly. Newspaper (tabloid) for beef-cow/calf producers including test stations research reports.

★3449★ *American Journal of Agricultural Economics*
American Agricultural Economics Assn.
1110 Buckeye Ave.
Ames, IA 50010-8063
Ph: (515)233-3234 Fax: (515)233-3101
Rich Adams
Journal on agriculture and resource economics.

★3450★ *American Society of Farm Managers and Rural Appraisers-General Membership Directory*
American Society of Farm Managers and Rural Appraisers (ASFMRA)
950 S. Cherry St., Ste. 508
Denver, CO 80222
Ph: (303)758-3513 Fax: (303)758-0190
Annual.

★3451★ *The Back Forty*
Prairie West Publications
601 Dakota Ave.
PO Box 1018
Wahpeton, ND 58075
Ph: (701)642-1501
Patricia Estes
Monthly. Farm newspaper.

★3452★ *BEEF*
Webb Division, Intertec Publishing Corp.
7900 International Dr., Ste. 300
Minneapolis, MN 55425
Ph: (612)851-9329 Fax: (612)851-4601
Paul D. Andre
Monthly.

★3453★ *Beef Today*
Farm Journal, Inc.
230 W. Washington Sq.
Philadelphia, PA 19106
Ph: (215)829-4700 Fax: (215)829-4757
Fr: 800-523-1538
Dale E. SmithPresident
Magazine for farmers and ranchers raising beef cows, feeders, and backgrounder cattle.

★3454★ *Biodynamics*
Biodynamic Farming & Gardening Association
PO Box 550
Kimberton, PA 19442-0550
Ph: (215)935-7797 Fax: (215)983-3196
Fr: 800-516-7797
Jean W. Yeager
Bimonthly. Magazine on biodynamic agriculture, nutrition, soil health and goethean science.

★3455★ *The Brahman Journal*
Sagebrush Publishing Co., Inc.
PO Box 220
Eddy, TX 76524
Ph: (817)859-5507 Fax: (817)859-5451
Joe Brockett
Monthly. Livestock and breed journal.

★3456★ *Brangus Journal*
5750 Epsilon
San Antonio, TX 78249
Ph: (210)696-4343 Fax: (210)696-3713
Ellen H. Godwin
Monthly. Cattle breeding industry magazine.

★3457★ *BUFFALO!*
National Buffalo Assn.
4 E. Main St.
PO Box 580
Fort Pierre, SD 57532
Ph: (605)223-2829 Fax: (605)223-2669
Kim Dowling
Quarterly. Magazine serving ranchers, farmers, and others interested in the American buffalo.

★3458★ *Business Farmer-Stockman*
Business Farmer Printing Inc.
1617 Avenue A
Box 770
Scottsbluff, NE 69361
Ph: (308)635-2045 Fax: (308)635-2348
Penny YekelPublisher
Weekly. Agricultural newspaper.

★3459★ *Calavo Newsletter*
Calavo Growers of California
PO Box 26081
Santa Ana, CA 92799-6081
Ph: (714)259-1166 Fax: (714)259-1973
Bob Duke
Quarterly. Contains news of avocado production, marketing, and the Calavo Growers of California.

★3460★ *CALF News Magazine*
CALF News Magazine Ltd.
PO Box 88312
Colorado Springs, CO 80908-8312
Ph: (719)495-0303 Fax: (719)495-9204
Steve Dittmer
Monthly. Magazine for commercial feedlot operators (1,000 head or more).

★3461★ *Cattle Business*
Mississippi Cattlemen's Assn.
1202 Mississippi St.
Jackson, MS 39202-3535
Ph: (601)354-8951 Fax: (601)355-7128
Shari Holloway
Livestock magazine.

★3462★ *Cattle Guard*
Colorado Cattlemen's Assn.
8833 Ralston Rd.
Arvada, CO 80002-2839
Ph: (303)431-6422 Fax: (303)431-6446
Todd Inglee
Monthly. Magazine covering cattle breeding and feeders.

★3463★ *Citrus and Vegetable Magazine*
4902 Eisenhower Blvd., Ste. 291
Tampa, FL 33634
Ph: (813)886-8988 Fax: (813)888-5290
Gordon Smith
Monthly. Magazine serving citrus and vegetable growers, packers, and processors.

★3464★ *Cooperative Farmer*
Southern States Cooperative, Inc.
PO Box 26234
Richmond, VA 23260
Ph: (804)281-1317 Fax: (804)281-1141
Don R. Tindall
Agricultural magazine.

★3465★ *Corn Farmer*
Meredith Corp.
1716 Locust St.
Des Moines, IA 50336
Ph: (515)284-3000 Fax: (515)284-2700
James CornickPublisher
Quarterly. Magazine reporting current information on corn production.

★3466★ *Cotton Farming*
Little Publications, Inc.
6263 Poplar Ave., Ste. 540
Memphis, TN 38119
Ph: (901)767-4020 Fax: (901)767-4026
Carroll Headley
Agriculture trade magazine.

★3467★ *Cotton Grower*
Meister Publishing Co.
37733 Euclid Ave.
Willoughby, OH 44094-5992
Ph: (216)942-2000 Fax: (216)942-0662
Bill Spencer
Monthly. Magazine for commercial cotton growers throughout the U.S.

★3468★ *Cotton Trade Report*
New York Cotton Exchange
4 World Trade Center
New York, NY 10048
Ph: (212)938-7909 Fax: (212)839-8061
Tom Bertolini
Weekly. Contains analyses of conditions, trends, and prospects in the cotton trade; domestic cotton crop progress during the growing season; U.S. Government activities in the cotton trade; and economic conditions affecting the cotton trade and market. Recurring features include charts showing daily and weekly fluctuations of spot and futures cotton prices and a weekly market review.

★3469★ *Country Folks*
Lee Publications, Inc.
W. Grand St.
PO Box 121
Palatine Bridge, NY 13428
Ph: (518)673-3237 Fax: (518)673-3237
Janice Handy
Weekly. Farm newspaper.

★3470★ *Crop Science*
Crop Science Society of America
677 S. Segoe Rd.
Madison, WI 53711
Ph: (608)273-8080 Fax: (608)273-2021
E.L. Klepper
Bimonthly. Agricultural science journal.

★3471★ *Dairy and Field Crops Digest*
Regional Cooperative Extension Dairy Program
56 Main St.
Owego, NY 13827
Ph: (607)687-4020 Fax: (607)687-6162
William Menzi
Bimonthly. Agricultural and dairy magazine.

★3472★ *Delta Farm Press*
Farm Press Publications, Inc.
14920 U.S. Hwy. 61
PO Box 1420
Clarksdale, MS 38614
Ph: (601)624-8503 Fax: (601)627-1977
Ben Pryor

Weekly. Agriculture tabloid.

★3473★ *Doane's Agricultural Report*
Doane Information Service
11701 Borman Dr.
St. Louis, MO 63146
Ph: (314)569-2700
Paul Justis

Covers the marketing of commodities (such as cattle, hogs, corn, wheat, and soybeans), as well as providing agricultural, economic, management, and production information. Discusses such topics as profit management, prices, outlook, machinery, buildings, equipment, taxes, social security, law, and government.

★3474★ *Experimental Agriculture*
Cambridge University Press
40 W. 20th St.
New York, NY 10011
Ph: (212)924-3900 Fax: (212)691-3239
F.G.H. Lupton

Quarterly. Journal publishing research into the agronomy of crops. Also prints related book reviews.

★3475★ *Farm/Ranch Exchange*
Star-Herald
1405 Broadway
PO Box 1709
Scottsbluff, NE 69363-1709
Ph: (308)632-0670
Ken Campbell

Monthly. Farm newspaper.

★3476★ *Farm & Ranch Living*
Reiman Publications, L.P.
5400 S. 60th St.
Greendale, WI 53129
Ph: (414)423-0100
Bob Ottum

Bimonthly. Lifestyle magazine for farmers and ranchers.

★3477★ *The Farmers' Advance*
Camden Publications, Inc.
331 E. Bell St.
Camden, MI 49232
Ph: (517)368-0365 Fax: (517)368-5131
Fr: 800-222-6336
Kurt GreenhoePublisher

Weekly. Agricultural newspaper.

★3478★ *Farmer's Exchange*
Exchange Publishing Corp.
PO Box 45
New Paris, IN 46553
Ph: (219)831-2138 Fax: (219)831-2131
Paul Hershberger

Weekly. Agricultural newspaper.

★3479★ *Farmer's Report*
211 Hwy. 38E
Rochelle, IL 61068
Ph: (815)562-4171 Fax: (815)562-7048
Laurie Parli

Monthly. Agricultural publication.

★3480★ *Farmland News*
104 Depot St.
PO Box 240
Archbold, OH 43502-0240
Ph: (419)445-9456 Fax: (419)445-4444
Jeremy J. Rohrs

Weekly. Agriculture newspaper (tabloid).

★3481★ *FFA Advisors Making a Difference*
National FFA Organization (NFFAO)
5632 Mount Vernon Memorial Hwy.
Box 15160
Alexandria, VA 22309-0160
Ph: (703)360-3600 Fax: (703)360-5524

Bimonthly.

★3482★ *FFA New Horizons Magazine*
National FFA Organization (NFFAO)
5632 Mount Vernon Memorial Hwy.
Box 15160
Alexandria, VA 22309-0160
Ph: (703)360-3600 Fax: (703)360-5524

Bimonthly. Profiles members who have made outstanding contributions to the farming industry. Covers new developments and trends in agriculture and agribusiness.

★3483★ *The Flue Cured Tobacco Farmer*
Specialized Agricultural Publications, Inc.
3000 Highwoods Blvd., Ste. 300
Raleigh, NC 27604-1029
Ph: (919)872-5040 Fax: (919)876-6531
Dayton Matlick

Business magazine for tobacco farmers.

★3484★ *FMRA News*
American Society of Farm Managers and Rural Appraisers (ASFMRA)
950 S. Cherry St., Ste. 508
Denver, CO 80222
Ph: (303)758-3513 Fax: (303)758-0190

★3485★ *Focus on Farming*
Focus on Farming
6 Central St.
Moravia, NY 13118
Ph: (315)497-1551 Fax: (315)497-1551
Bernard F. McGuertyPublisher

Biweekly. Farm oriented newspaper.

★3486★ *Grain & Feed Market News*
Livestock and Seed Division
South Bldg., Rm. 2623
PO Box 96456
Washington, DC 20090-6456
Ph: (202)720-6231 Fax: (202)690-3732
Mike O'Connor

Weekly. Publishes weekly grain and feed marketing statistics. Includes narrative summaries of the grain and feed marketing situation in the U.S. and abroad.

★3487★ *Grass & Grain*
Ag Press, Inc.
1531 Yuma
Box 1009
Manhattan, KS 66502
Ph: (913)539-7558 Fax: (913)539-2679
Steve Suther

Weekly. Agricultural tabloid.

★3488★ *Hay There!*
National Hay Association, Inc.
102 Treasure Island Causeway, Ste. 201
St. Petersburg, FL 33706
Ph: (813)367-9702 Fax: (813)367-9608
Donald F. Kieffer

Monthly. Reports current developments in the hay industry, including marketing and shipping information.

★3489★ *High Plains Journal*
1500 E. Wyatt Earp
PO Box 760
Dodge City, KS 67801
Ph: (316)227-7171 Fax: (316)227-7173
Galen Hubbs

Weekly. Agricultural newspaper.

★3490★ *Hjort Associates, Inc.—Viewpoint*
Hjort Associates, Inc.
1400 50th St., Ste. 140
West Des Moines, IA 50266
Ph: (515)223-5541 Fax: (515)223-2222
Douglas C. Hjort

Weekly. Addresses marketing problems faced by U.S. agricultural producers. Provides marketing recommendations and analysis projecting cash and futures prices activity for agricultural commodities, including corn, soybeans, wheat, feeder cattle, live cattle, hogs, cotton, and sunflowers. Recurring features include statistics and a column titled As It Is.

★3491★ *Journal of the American Society of Farm Managers and Rural Appraisers*
American Society of Farm Managers and Rural Appraisers (ASFMRA)
950 S. Cherry St., Ste. 508
Denver, CO 80222
Ph: (303)758-3513 Fax: (303)758-0190

Annual.

★3492★ *Limousin World*
PO Box 850870
1050 Andrew Dr.
Yukon, OK 73085
Ph: (405)350-0040 Fax: (405)350-0054
Jim Eischen

Monthly. Magazine for cattle breeders.

★3493★ *Livestock Market Digest*
Livestock Market Digest, Inc.
PO Box 7458
Albuquerque, NM 87194
Ph: (505)243-9515 Fax: (505)243-4598
Emil Reutzel

Weekly. Livestock and agriculture business (tabloid).

★3494★ *Livestock, Meat, and Wool Market News*
Livestock and Seed Division
South Bldg., Rm. 2623
PO Box 96456
Washington, DC 20090-6456
Ph: (202)720-6231 Fax: (202)690-3732
Mike O'Connor

Weekly. Publishes weekly livestock, meat, and wool marketing statistics. Includes narrative summaries of the week's livestock, meat, and wool marketing situation in the United States.

★3495★ *Livestock Weekly*
Southwest Publishers, Inc.
PO Box 3306
San Angelo, TX 76902
Ph: (915)949-4611
Stanley R. Frank
Weekly. Newspaper (tabloid) for the livestock industry.

★3496★ *Living Among Nature Daringly*
4466 Ike Mooney Rd.
Silverton, OR 97381
Ph: (503)873-8829
Bill Anderson
Magazine for trappers, farmers, and nature lovers.

★3497★ *National Farmers Union—Washington Newsletter*
National Farmers Union
PO Box 372790
Denver, CO 80237-7914
Ph: (303)337-5500 Fax: (303)368-1390
Fr: 800-347-1961
Milt Hakel
Carries legislative and economic news pertaining to family farm agriculture. Gives explanations for actions taken by the House of Representatives and the Senate, congressional committees, and various agencies of the administration.

★3498★ *National FFA Convention Proceedings*
National FFA Organization (NFFAO)
5632 Mount Vernon Memorial Hwy.
Box 15160
Alexandria, VA 22309-0160
Ph: (703)360-3600 Fax: (703)360-5524
Annual.

★3499★ *National FFA Organization—Update*
National FFA Organization (NFFAO)
5632 Mount Vernon Memorial Hwy.
Box 15160
Alexandria, VA 22309-0160
Ph: (703)360-3600 Fax: (703)360-5524
Monthly. Includes calendar of events.

★3500★ *National Hog Farmer*
Webb Division, Intertec Publishing Corp.
7900 International Dr., Ste. 300
Minneapolis, MN 55425
Ph: (612)851-9329 Fax: (612)851-4601
William Fleming
Monthly. Trade magazine for hog producers.

★3501★ *The New Farm*
Rodale Institute
222 Main St.
Emmaus, PA 18098
Ph: (610)967-8563 Fax: (610)967-8963
Mike BruskoPublisher
Specialized farming magazine devoted to helping commercial farmers cut production costs and boost profits.

★3502★ *Nut Grower*
Western Agricultural Publishing Co., Inc.
4974 E. Clinton Way, Ste. 214
Fresno, CA 93727
Ph: (209)252-7000 Fax: (209)252-7387
Harry Cline
Magazine on nut growing.

★3503★ *Onion World*
Columbia Publishing & Design
2809-A Fruitvale Blvd.
PO Box 1467
Yakima, WA 98902
Ph: (509)248-2452 Fax: (509)248-4056
D. Brent Clement
Agricultural magazine.

★3504★ *The Peanut Farmer*
Specialized Agricultural Publications, Inc.
3000 Highwoods Blvd., Ste. 300
Raleigh, NC 27604-1029
Ph: (919)872-5040 Fax: (919)876-6531
Dayton Matlick
Business magazine for peanut farmers.

★3505★ *The Peanut Grower*
Vance Publishing
PO Box 83, 128 1st St., Ste. 223
Tifton, GA 31793
Ph: (912)386-8591 Fax: (912)386-9772
Catherine Andrews
Magazine on peanut farming. Includes information on production, research, and marketing.

★3506★ *Pest Alerts*
Cooperative Extension Service
c/o Mark Schriber
Department of Entomology
243 Natural Science Bldg.
East Lansing, MI 48824-1115
Ph: (517)353-3890 Fax: (517)353-4354
Weekly. Provides pest predictions and control recommendations in areas including vegetables, fruits, grains, ornamentals, and forestry. Supplies detailed maps and statistics.

★3507★ *Premium Grower*
Napa Valley Grape Growers Association
4075 Solano Ave.
Napa, CA 94558
Ph: (707)944-8311 Fax: (707)224-7836
Teresa Geremia-Chart
Bimonthly. Supplies grape commodity and vineyard news. Carries technical information on grape and wine production, legislative updates, news of research, and Association and valley news.

★3508★ *The Rice World*
PO Box 3083
Lake Charles, LA 70602
John Hart
Monthly. Tabloid reporting information of interest to rice and soybean farmers and processors.

★3509★ *Rocky Mountain Union Farmer*
Rocky Mountain Farmers Union
10800 E. Bethany Dr., 4th Fl.
Aurora, CO 80014-2632
Ph: (303)752-5800 Fax: (303)752-5810
Melissa Elliott
Agricultural magazine (tabloid) featuring articles on issues affecting family operated farms and ranches.

★3510★ *Rural Living*
Michigan Farm Bureau
7373 W. Saginaw Hwy.
PO Box 30690
Lansing, MI 48909-8460
Ph: (517)323-7000 Fax: (517)323-6793
Dennis Rudat
Quarterly. Regional agriculture lifestyle magazine.

★3511★ *San Joaquin Farm Bureau News*
San Joaquin Farm Bureau Federation
PO Box 8444
Stockton, CA 95208-0444
Ph: (209)931-4931 Fax: (209)931-1433
Robert J. CabralPublisher
Monthly. Agricultural newspaper.

★3512★ *Southwest Farm Press*
Farm Press Publications, Inc.
14920 U.S. Hwy. 61
PO Box 1420
Clarksdale, MS 38614
Ph: (601)624-8503 Fax: (601)627-1977
James Calvin Pigg
Semiweekly. Agriculture tabloid.

★3513★ *Spokesman*
Iowa Farm Bureau Federation
606 8th St.
Grundy Center, IA 50638
Ph: (319)824-5454
Darryl Jahn
Weekly. Agricultural newspaper.

★3514★ *The Stockman Grass Farmer*
Mississippi Valley Publishing Corp.
5135 Galaxie Dr., Ste. 300-C
PO Box 9607
Jackson, MS 39206
Ph: (601)981-4805
H. Allan Nation
Monthly. Magazine reporting on livestock and grass farming.

★3515★ *The Sugar Producer*
Harris Publishing, Inc.
520 Park Ave.
Idaho Falls, ID 83402
Ph: (208)524-7000 Fax: (208)522-5241
Steve Janes
Bimonthly. Magazine for sugar beet growers.

★3516★ *The Sunflower*
National Sunflower Assn.
4023 State St.
Bismarck, ND 58501
Ph: (701)221-5105 Fax: (701)221-5101
Larry Kleingartner
Bimonthly. Magazine for sunflower producers in the U.S.

★3517★ *Times-Plain Dealer*
Times-Plain Dealer Publishing, Inc.
214 N. Elm
PO Box 350
Cresco, IA 52136
Ph: (319)547-3601 Fax: (319)547-4602
H. Denis Moore
Weekly. Agricultural newspaper.

★3518★ *Tree Farmer*
1250 Connecticut Ave. NW
Washington, DC 20036
Ph: (202)463-2455 Fax: (202)463-2461
Luke Popovich

Quarterly. Forestry journal.

★3519★ *Turf News*
American Sod Producers Assn.
1855 A Hicks Rd.
Rolling Meadows, IL 60008-1215
Ph: (708)705-9898 Fax: (708)705-8347
Wendell Mathews

Bimonthly. Trade magazine.

★3520★ *United Caprine News*
PO Drawer A
Rotan, TX 79546
Ph: (915)735-2562 Fax: (915)735-2230
Jeff Klein

Monthly. Newspaper (tabloid) serving dairy goat producers.

★3521★ *Vegetables and Specialties Situation and Outlook Report*
Economic Research Service
1301 New York Ave. NW
Washington, DC 20005-4788
Ph: (202)219-0886 Fax: (202)219-0042
Gary Lucien

Discusses fresh and processed vegetable crops and products. Provides data on supply, demand, prices, imports and exports for vegetables, including potatoes, sweet potatoes, mushrooms, dried beans, peas, lentils, and specialty vegetables. Carries the official USDA estimate of per capita vegetable utilization in the August issue.

★3522★ *The Wheat Grower*
National Association of Wheat Growers
415 2nd St. NE, Ste. 300
Washington, DC 20002-4993
Ph: (202)547-7800 Fax: (202)546-2638
Barry Jenkins

Magazine on growing, harvesting, storing, transporting, and marketing wheat. Covers economic conditions, weather, policies, and politics affecting U.S. and world grain trade.

★3523★ *The Wool Sack*
North Central Wool Marketing Corp.
315 5th St
PO Box 328
Brookings, SD 57006
Ph: (605)692-2324 Fax: (605)692-8182
Dick Boniface

BIE. Newspaper about wool marketing and sheep raising.

★3524★ *Yorkshire Journal*
American Yorkshire Club Inc.
1769 U.S. 52 N.
PO Box 2417
West Lafayette, IN 47906
Ph: (317)463-3593 Fax: (317)497-2959
Darrell Anderson

Monthly. Magazine serving breeders of Yorkshire swine.

Meetings and Conventions

★3525★ Ag Expo
South Dakota Fertilizer and Chemical Association
121 N. Grand
Pierre, SD 57501
Ph: (605)224-2445 Fax: (605)224-9913

Annual. Always held during January at the Ramkota Exhibition Hall in Sioux Falls, South Dakota. **Dates and Locations:** 1996 Jan 10-11; Sioux Falls, SD. • 1997 Jan 08-09; Sioux Falls, SD. • 1998 Jan 14-15; Sioux Falls, SD.

★3526★ Agri News Farm Show
Agri News Farm Show
PO Box 6118
Rochester, MN 55903-6118
Ph: (507)285-7600 Fax: (507)281-7436
Fr: 800-533-1727

Annual. Always held at the Olmsted County Fairgrounds in the Graham Arena in Rochester, Minnesota.

★3527★ American Feed Industry Association Feed Industries Show
American Feed Industry Association
1501 Wilson Blvd., Ste. 1100
Arlington, VA 22209
Ph: (703)524-0810 Fax: (703)524-1921

Biennial. Always held during May. **Dates and Locations:** 1997.

★3528★ American Soybean Association Annual Conference
American Soybean Association
PO Box 419200
St. Louis, MO 63141
Ph: (314)576-1770 Fax: (314)576-2786

Annual. Always held during late July or early August.

★3529★ Electric Power and Farm Equipment Show
Midwest Equipment Dealers Association
PO Box 44364
Madison, WI 53744-4364
Ph: (608)276-6700 Fax: (608)276-6719

Annual. Always held during March at the Dane County Exposition Center in Madison, Wisconsin. **Dates and Locations:** 1996 Mar 13-15; Madison, WI. • 1997 Mar 09-21; Madison, WI. • 1998 Mar 08-20; Madison, WI.

★3530★ Empire Farm Days
Empire Farm Days
PO Box 566
Stanley, NY 14561
Ph: (716)526-5356

Annual. Always held during August at the Rodman Lott & Sons Farm in Sensca Falls, New York. **Dates and Locations:** 1996 Aug 06-08; Sensca Falls, NY. • 1997 Aug 05-07; Sensca Falls, NY. • 1998 Aug 11-13; Sensca Falls, NY.

★3531★ Farm Progress Show
Farm Progress Companies, Inc.
191 S. Gary Ave.
Carol Stream, IL 60188
Ph: (708)462-2892 Fax: (708)462-2869

Annual. Always held during September. **Dates and Locations:** 1996 Sep.

★3532★ Mid-America Farm Exposition
Salina Area Chamber of Commerce
PO Box 586
Salina, KS 67402-0586
Ph: (913)827-9301 Fax: (913)827-9758

Annual. Always held during March at Kenwood and Oakdale Parks in Salina, Kansas. **Dates and Locations:** 1996 Mar; Salina, KS.

★3533★ Mid-South Farm and Gin Supply Exhibit
Southern Cotton Ginners Association
874 Cotton Gin Pl.
Memphis, TN 38106
Ph: (901)947-3104 Fax: (901)947-3103

Annual. Always held in Memphis, Tennessee. **Dates and Locations:** 1996 Mar 01-02; Memphis, TN. • 1997 Feb 28-01; Memphis, TN.

★3534★ Midwest Farm Show
American Farm Shows
PO Box 1
Chippewa Falls, WI 54729-0001
Ph: (715)723-5061 Fax: (715)723-5061

Annual. **Dates and Locations:** 1996 Jan 17-18; LaCrosse, WI.

★3535★ Midwest Poultry Federation Convention
Midwest Poultry Federation
2380 Wycliff St.
St. Paul, MN 55114
Ph: (612)646-4553 Fax: (612)646-4554

Annual. Always held during February at the Convention Center in Minneapolis, Minnesota. **Dates and Locations:** 1996 Feb.

★3536★ National Association of Wheat Growers Convention
National Association of Wheat Growers
415 2nd St., NE, Ste. 300
Washington, DC 20002
Ph: (202)547-7800 Fax: (202)546-2638

Annual.

★3537★ National Cattlemen's Association Annual Convention and Trade Show
National Cattlemen's Association
5420 S. Quebec St.
PO Box 3469
Englewood, CO 80155
Ph: (303)694-0305 Fax: (303)694-2851

Annual. **Dates and Locations:** 1996 Jan 31-03; San Antonio, TX. • 1997 Feb 05-08; Orlando, FL.

★3538★ National Farm Machinery Show and Championship Tractor Pull
Kentucky Fair & Exposition Center
PO Box 37130
Louisville, KY 40233
Ph: (502)367-5000 Fax: (502)367-5299

Annual. Always held during February at the Kentucky Fair and Exposition Center in Louisville, Kentucky. **Dates and Locations:** 1996 Feb 14-17; Louisville, KY.

★3539★ North American Farm and Power Show
Farm Equipment Association of Minnesota and South Dakota
121 E. Park Sq.
Owatonna, MN 55060
Ph: (507)451-1136 Fax: (507)455-5909
Fr: 800-949-3976

Semiannual. Always held during December at the Convention Center in Minneapolis and August at Nobles Fairgrounds in Worthington, Minnesota. **Dates and Locations:** 1995 Nov 30-02; Minneapolis, MN.

★3540★ Northwest Agricultural Show
Northwest Agricultural Congress
4672 Drift Creek Rd., SE
Sublimity, OR 97385
Ph: (503)769-7120 Fax: (503)769-3549

Annual. Always held during January at the Expo Center in Portland, Oregon.

★3541★ Society for Range Management Annual Conference
Society for Range Management
1839 York St.
Denver, CO 80206
Ph: (303)355-7070 Fax: (303)355-5059

Annual. **Dates and Locations:** 1996 Feb 10-15; Wichita, KS. • 1997 Feb 16-21; Rapid City, SD.

★3542★ Triumph of Agriculture Exposition Farm and Ranch Machinery Show
Mid-America Expositions, Inc.
1613 Farnam St., Ste. 666
Omaha, NE 68102-2142
Ph: (402)346-8003 Fax: (402)346-5412

Annual. Always held during March at the Civic Auditorium in Omaha, Nebraska. **Dates and Locations:** 1996 Mar; Omaha, NE.

★3543★ United Fresh Fruit and Vegetable Association Annual Convention and Exposition
TAB/McGraw-Hill, Inc.
PO Box 182607
Columbus, OH 43218-2607
Fax: (614)759-3644 Fr: 800-822-8158

Annual. Always held during February **Dates and Locations:** 1996 Feb 11-13; New Orleans, LA. • 1997 Feb 23-25; Orlando, FL. • 1998 Feb 21-24; Dallas, TX.

★3544★ Western Farm Show
Western Retail Implement and Hardware Association
PO Box 419264
Kansas City, MO 64141
Ph: (816)561-5323 Fax: (816)561-1249

Annual. Always held during February at the American Royal Buildings in Kansas City, Missouri. **Dates and Locations:** 1996 Feb 25-27; Kansas City, MO.

★3545★ World Pork Expo
National Pork Producers Council
PO Box 10383
Des Moines, IA 50306
Ph: (515)223-2600 Fax: (515)223-2646

Annual. Always held during June. **Dates and Locations:** 1996 Jun 07-09; Des Moines, IA. • 1997 Jun 06-08 • 1998 Jun 05-07 • 1999 Jun 11-13 • 2000 Jun 09-11.

Other Sources of Information

★3546★ *The Family Farm: Can It Be Saved?*
Brethren Press
1451 Dundee Ave.
Elgin, IL 60120
Ph: (708)742-5100 Fax: (708)742-6103

Shantilal P. Bhagat. 1985.

★3547★ *Farm: A Year in the Life of an American Farmer*
Simon & Schuster Inc.
Simon & Schuster Bldg.
1230 Avenue of the Americas
New York, NY 10020
Ph: (212)698-7000

Richard Rhodes. 1990.

★3548★ "Farm Manager" in *100 Best Jobs for the 1990s & Beyond*
Dearborn Financial Publishing, Inc.
520 N. Dearborn St.
Chicago, IL 60610-4354
Ph: (312)836-4400 Fax: (312)836-1021
Fr: 800-621-9621

Carol Kleiman. 1992. Describes 100 jobs ranging from accountants to veterinarians. Each job profile includes such information as education, experience, and certification needed, salaries, and job search suggestions.

★3549★ "Farmer" in *Career Selector 2001*
Barron's Educational Series, Inc.
250 Wireless Blvd.
Hauppauge, NY 11788
Ph: (516)434-3311 Fax: (516)434-3723
Fr: 800-645-3476

James C. Gonyea. 1993.

★3550★ "Farmer" in *Encyclopedia of Danger: Dangerous Professions* (pp. 42-45)
Chelsea House Publishers
1974 Sproul Rd., Ste. 400
Broomall, PA 19008
Ph: (215)353-5166 Fax: (215)359-1439

Missy Allen and Michel Peissel. 1993. Provides descriptions of 24 dangerous occupations, their risky characteristics, and safety precautions.

★3551★ *Farming Is in Our Blood: Farm Families in Economic Crisis*
Iowa State University Press
Iowa State University
2121 S. State Ave.
Ames, IA 50010
Ph: (515)292-0140 Fax: (515)292-3348

Paul C. Rosenblatt. 1990.

★3552★ *The Last Farmer*
Thorndike Press
PO Box 159
Thorndike, ME 04986
Ph: (207)948-2962 Fax: (207)948-2863
Fr: 800-257-5755

Howard Kohn. 1989.

★3553★ *Men of Earth*
Ayer Company Publishers, Inc.
50 Northwestern Dr., No. 10
PO Box 958
Salem, NH 03079
Ph: (603)898-1200

Russell Lord. Facsimile edition, 1975. Part of American Farmers & the Rise of Agribusiness Series.

Fishers, Hunters, and Trappers

Fishers, hunters, and trappers gather marine and animal life for human consumption and for animal feed, bait, and other industrial uses, and manage animal life for research and control purposes. Gathering sea life hundreds of miles from shore with vessels requires a crew of up to 30 fishers-- captain, or skipper, a first mate and sometimes a second mate, and boatswains and other deckhands. Engineers operate, repair, and maintain the vessel's engines and equipment. Most full-time and virtually all part-time fishers work on motorboats in relatively shallow waters and often in sight of land. Crews are small and collaborate on all aspects of the fishing operation. This includes placing gill nets across the mouths of rivers or inlets, entrapment nets in bays and lakes, and pots and traps for shellfish such as lobsters and crabs. Dredges and scrapes are also used to gather shellfish such as oysters and scallops. In very shallow waters, fish are caught from small boats with an outboard motor, rowboats, or by wading. While most fishers are involved with commercial fishing, some captains and deckhands are primarily involved with recreational fishing. Hunters track, stalk, and kill their quarry. They usually operate alone or as members of a very small hunting party and may use dogs to locate and corner the quarry. They use guns and bows and arrows to hunt predatory animals such as bears, eradicate animal pests such as coyotes, and control the population of large game animals such as deer. Divers hunt fish with spear guns or nets, and alligator hunters shoot their quarry after snaring it with baited hooks. Trappers catch animals or birds using baited, scented, or camouflaged traps, snares, cages, or nets. Many trappers prepare and sell pelts and skins. Many trappers are also involved with animal damage control, wildlife management, disease control, and research activities.

Salaries

Annual income of fishers, hunters, and trappers are generally highest in the summer and fall-when demand for their services peaks and environmental conditions are favorable-and lowest during the winter.

Employment Outlook

Growth rate until the year 2005: Slower than average.

Fishers, Hunters, and Trappers

Career Guides

★3554★ *American Professionals Series*
Cambridge Career Products
PO Box 2153
Charleston, WV 25328-2153
Ph: (304)744-9323 Fax: (304)744-9351
Fr: 800-468-4227

Videocassette. 1984. 30 mins. In this series of twenty-one half hour programs, various occupations are examined in depth, including a day in the life of each worker. Included are: fireman, farmer, oil driller, fisherman, horse trainer, auto assembly repairman, nurse, pilot, and paramedic.

★3555★ "Baitfish Catcher" in *Opportunities in Marine and Maritime Careers* (pp. 110-111)
National Textbook Co. (NTC)
VGM Career Books
4255 W. Touhy Ave.
Lincolnwood, IL 60646-1975
Ph: (708)679-5500 Fax: (708)679-2494
Fr: 800-323-4900

William Ray Heitzmann. 1988. Includes careers related by their proximity to water; cruise ships, oceanography, marine sciences, fishing, commercial diving, maritime transportation, shipbuilding, Navy, and Coast Guard. Covers qualifications, job outlook, job duties, educational preparation, and training. Lists associations and schools.

★3556★ "Commercial Diver" in *Occu-Facts: Information on 580 Careers in Outline Form*
Careers, Inc.
PO Box 135
Largo, FL 34649-0135
Ph: (813)584-7333

Biennial, 1995-96 edition. Each one-page occupational profile describes duties, working conditions, physical surroundings and demands, aptitudes, temperament, educational requirements, employment outlook, earnings, and places of employment.

★3557★ *Commercial Fisher*
Vocational Biographies, Inc.
PO Box 31
Sauk Centre, MN 56378-0031
Ph: (612)352-6516 Fax: (612)352-5546
Fr: 800-255-0752

1993. This pamphlet profiles a person working in the job. Includes information about job duties, working conditions, places of employment, educational preparation, labor market outlook, and salaries.

★3558★ "Commercial Fisher" in *Occu-Facts: Information on 580 Careers in Outline Form*
Careers, Inc.
PO Box 135
Largo, FL 34649-0135
Ph: (813)584-7333

Biennial, 1995-96 edition. Each one-page occupational profile describes duties, working conditions, physical surroundings and demands, aptitudes, temperament, educational requirements, employment outlook, earnings, and places of employment.

★3559★ "Diver" in *Career Information Center* (Vol.2)
Simon and Schuster
200 Old Tappan Rd.
Old Tappan, NJ 07675
Fax: 800-445-6991 Fr: 800-223-2348

Richard Lidz and Dale Anderson, editorial directors. Fifth edition, 1993. For 600 occupations, describes job duties, entry-level requirements, education and training needed, advancement possibilities, employment outlook, earnings and benefits. The set is divided into 12 volumes. Each volume includes jobs related under a broad career field. Volume 13 is the index.

★3560★ *Divers, Commercial*
Careers, Inc.
PO Box 135
Largo, FL 34649-0135
Ph: (813)584-7333

1994. Two-page occupational summary card describing duties, working conditions, personal qualifications, training, earnings and hours, employment outlook, places of employment, related careers and where to write for more information.

★3561★ "Diving Technicians" in *Career Discovery Encyclopedia* (Vol.2, pp. 116-117)
J.G. Ferguson Publishing Co.
200 W. Madison St., Ste. 300
Chicago, IL 60606
Ph: (312)580-5480 Fax: (312)580-4948

E. Russell Primm, editor-in-chief. 1993. Contains two-page articles on 504 occupations. Each article describes job duties, earnings, and educational and training requirements.

★3562★ "Diving Technicians" in *Encyclopedia of Careers and Vocational Guidance* (Vol.2, pp. 491-497)
J.G. Ferguson Publishing Co.
200 W. Madison St., Ste. 300
Chicago, IL 60606
Ph: (312)580-5480 Fax: (312)580-4948

William E. Hopke, editor-in-chief. Ninth edition, 1993. Four-volume set that profiles 500 occupations and describes job trends in 74 industries. Includes career description, educational requirements, history of the job, methods of entry, advancement, employment outlook, earnings, working conditions, social and psychological factors, and sources of additional information.

★3563★ *Fish Farmer*
Vocational Biographies, Inc.
PO Box 31
Sauk Centre, MN 56378-0031
Ph: (612)352-6516 Fax: (612)352-5546
Fr: 800-255-0752

1993. Four-page pamphlet containing a personal narrative about a worker's job, work likes and dislikes, career path from high school to the present. Education and training, the rewards and frustrations, and the effects of the job on the rest of the worker's life. The data file portion of this pamphlet gives a concise occupational summary, including work descriptions, working conditions, places of employment, personal characteristics, education and training, job outlook, and salary range.

★3564★ *Fish Farming Workers*
Chronicle Guidance Publications, Inc.
66 Aurora St.
PO Box 1190
Moravia, NY 13118-1190
Ph: (315)497-0330 Fax: (315)497-3359
Fr: 800-622-7284

1991. Career brief describing the nature of the job, working conditions, hours and earnings, education and training, licensure, certification, unions, personal qualifications, social and psychological factors, location, employment outlook, entry methods, advancement, and related occupations.

★3565★ "Fisher" in *Career Information Center* (Vol.2)
Simon and Schuster
200 Old Tappan Rd.
Old Tappan, NJ 07675
Fax: 800-445-6991 Fr: 800-223-2348

Richard Lidz and Dale Anderson, editorial directors. Fifth edition, 1993. For 600 occupations, describes job duties, entry-level requirements, education and training needed, advancement possibilities, employment outlook, earnings and benefits. The set is divided into 12 volumes. Each volume includes jobs related under a broad career field. Volume 13 is the index.

★3566★ *Fisher, Commercial*
Careers, Inc.
PO Box 135
Largo, FL 34649-0135
Ph: (813)584-7333

1992. Two-page job guide card describing duties, working conditions, personal qualifications, training, earnings and hours, employment outlook, places of employment, related careers and where to write for more information.

★3567★ "Fisher" in *Hard Hatted Women: Stories of Struggle and Success in the Trades* (pp. 81-87)
Seal Press
3131 Western Ave., Ste. 410
Seattle, WA 98121
Ph: (206)283-7844 Fax: (206)285-9410

Molly Martin, editor. 1988. Twenty-six women recount their experiences working in blue collar occupations. They describe how they got in, the work they do, their relationships in predominantly male occupations, and their training.

★3568★ *Fisherman*
Morris Video
2730 Monterey St., No. 105
Monterey Business Park
Torrance, CA 90503
Ph: (310)533-4800 Fr: 800-843-3606

Videocassette. 1982. 30 mins. A North Carolina fisherman discusses the pros and cons of a career in fishing.

★3569★ *Fishers, Commercial*
Chronicle Guidance Publications, Inc.
66 Aurora St.
PO Box 1190
Moravia, NY 13118-1190
Ph: (315)497-0330 Fax: (315)497-3359
Fr: 800-622-7284

1993. This career brief describes the nature of the work, working conditions, hours and earnings, education and training, licensure, certification, unions, personal qualifications, social and psychological factors, employment outlook, entry methods, advancement, and related occupations.

★3570★ "Fishers, Commercial" in *Career Discovery Encyclopedia* (Vol.3, pp. 20-21)
J.G. Ferguson Publishing Co.
200 W. Madison St., Ste. 300
Chicago, IL 60606
Ph: (312)580-5480 Fax: (312)580-4948

E. Russell Primm, editor-in-chief. 1993. Contains two-page articles on 504 occupations. Each article describes job duties, earnings, and educational and training requirements.

★3571★ "Fishers, Commercial" in *Encyclopedia of Careers and Vocational Guidance* (Vol.3, pp. 2-4)
J.G. Ferguson Publishing Co.
200 W. Madison St., Ste. 300
Chicago, IL 60606
Ph: (312)580-5480 Fax: (312)580-4948

William E. Hopke, editor-in-chief. Ninth edition, 1993. Four-volume set that profiles 500 occupations and describes job trends in 74 industries. Includes career description, educational requirements, history of the job, methods of entry, advancement, employment outlook, earnings, working conditions, social and psychological factors, and sources of additional information.

★3572★ "Fishers, Hunters, and Trappers" in *Occupational Outlook Handbook*
U.S. Government Printing Office
Superintendent of Documents
Washington, DC 20402
Ph: (202)512-1800 Fax: (202)512-2250

Biennial; latest edition, 1994-95. Encyclopedia of careers describing more than 250 occupations and comprising about 85 percent of all jobs in the economy. Occupations that require lengthy education or training are given the most attention. For each occupation, the handbook describes job duties, working conditions, training, educational preparation, personal qualities, advancement possibilities, job outlook, earnings, and sources of additional information.

★3573★ *Footsteps in the Ocean: Careers in Diving*
Lodestar Books
2 Park Avenue
New York, NY 10016
Ph: (212)725-1818 Fax: (212)532-6568

Denise V. Lang. 1987. Explores employment opportunities in sport and commercial diving, science and research, in the military, and police work. Describes the work and training. Lists schools.

★3574★ *Fur Trapping*
New Win Publishing, Inc.
PO Box 5159
Clinton, NJ 08809
Ph: (201)735-9701 Fax: (201)735-9703

Bill Musgrove and Gerry Blair. 1979.

★3575★ *Fur Trapping in North America*
New Win Publishing, Inc.
PO Box 5159
Clinton, NJ 08809
Ph: (201)735-9701 Fax: (201)735-9703

Steven M. Geary. Revised and expanded edition, 1984.

★3576★ *Hunting and Fishing Guides*
Chronicle Guidance Publications, Inc.
66 Aurora St.
PO Box 1190
Moravia, NY 13118-1190
Ph: (315)497-0330 Fax: (315)497-3359
Fr: 800-622-7284

1990. Career brief describing the nature of the job, working conditions, hours and earnings, education and training, licensure, certification, unions, personal qualifications, social and psychological factors, location, employment outlook, entry methods, advancement, and related occupations.

★3577★ "Professional Diver" in *Offbeat Careers: The Directory of Unusual Work*
Ten Speed Press
PO Box 7123
Berkeley, CA 94707
Fax: (510)559-1629 Fr: 800-841-2665

Al Sacharov. 1991. Profiles eighty-eight unusual careers. Provides job description, history of occupation, salary, and training required. Lists one or more sources of additional information.

★3578★ *Transportation*
Learning Corporation of America
108 Wilmot Rd.
Deerfield, IL 60015
Ph: (708)940-1260 Fax: (708)940-3600
Fr: 800-621-2131

Videocassette. 1982. 21 mins. In this program from the "Working" series, we meet five employees in transportation-related jobs: fishing boat captain, auto body repair shop owner, construction equipment operator, air traffic controller and truck driver.

★3579★ "Wildlife Management Trapper" in *Action Careers: Employment in the High-Risk Job Market* (pp. 291-299)
Citadel Press/Lyle Stuart Inc.
Carol Publishing Group
120 Enterprise Ave.
Secaucus, NJ 07094
Ph: (201)866-0490

Ragnar Benson. 1988. Describes 24 dangerous careers such as repo man, explosives handler, and river rafting guide. Each profile includes demand for the job, where the jobs can be found, required personal and physical characteristics and training needed.

Associations

★3580★ Marine Technology Society (MTS)
1828 L St. NW, No. 906
Washington, DC 20036
Ph: (202)775-5966 Fax: (202)429-9417
Members: Scientists, engineers, educators, and others with professional interests in the marine sciences or related fields; includes institutional and corporate members. **Purpose:** Disseminates marine scientific and technical information, including institutional, environmental, physical, and biological aspects; fosters a deeper understanding of the world's seas and attendant technologies. Maintains 14 sections and 28 professional committees. Conducts tutorials. **Publications:** *Marine Technology Society Journal*, quarterly.

★3581★ National Association of Underwater Instructors (NAUI)
PO Box 14650
Montclair, CA 91763
Ph: (714)621-5801 Fax: (714)621-6405
Fr: 800-553-6284
Members: Certified instructors of basic, advanced, and specialized courses in underwater diving. Offers instructor certification programs and training programs. Conducts seminars, workshops, and symposia. Sells diving education books. Sponsors competitions; maintains speakers' bureau and placement service; conducts charitable programs. **Publications:** *Sources: The Journal of Underwater Education*, bimonthly.

★3582★ National Rifle Association of America (NRA)
11250 Waples Mill Rd.
Fairfax, VA 22030
Ph: (703)267-1000 Fr: 800-368-5714
Members: Target shooters, hunters, gun collectors, gunsmiths, police officers, and others interested in firearms. **Purpose:** Promotes rifle, pistol, and shotgun shooting, hunting, gun collecting, home firearm safety, and wildlife conservation. Encourages civilian marksmanship. Educates police firearms instructors. Maintains national and international records of shooting competitions; sponsors teams to compete in world championships. Also maintains comprehensive collection of antique and modern firearms. Administers the NRA Political Victory Fund. Compiles statistics; sponsors research and education programs; maintains speakers' bureau and museum. Lobbies on firearms issues. **Publications:** *American Hunter*, monthly. • *American Rifleman*, monthly. • *InSights*, monthly. • *NRAction*, monthly.

★3583★ National Trappers Association (NTA)
PO Box 3667
Bloomington, IL 61702
Ph: (309)829-2422 Fax: (309)829-7615
Members: Harvesters of furbearers (muskrat, fox, coyote, mink, beaver, raccoon, bobcat, and others) for the purpose of wildlife management, animal damage control, and outdoor recreation. **Purpose:** Promotes sound environmental education programs and conservation of natural resources. Compiles statistics. **Publications:** *American Trapper*, bimonthly. • *Facts About Fur.* • *Furbearer Management.* • *Traps Today.*

Standards/Certification Agencies

★3584★ National Association of Underwater Instructors (NAUI)
PO Box 14650
Montclair, CA 91763
Ph: (714)621-5801 Fax: (714)621-6405
Fr: 800-553-6284
Certified instructors of basic, advanced, and specialized courses in underwater diving. Offers instructor certification programs and training programs.

★3585★ U.S. Coast Guard
Merchant Vessel Personnel Division
2100 Second St., SW
Washington, DC 20593
Provides information on the licensing of captains and mates and requirements for merchant mariner documentation.

Awards, Scholarships, Grants, and Fellowships

★3586★ Don Harger Memorial Award
Federation of Fly Fishers
PO Box 1595
Bozeman, MT 59771
Ph: (406)585-7592 Fax: (406)585-7596
Fr: 800-618-0808
To recognize an individual (or, in his or her memory, to a family member) who is or has been actively engaged or closely related to some aspect of fly fishing as a vocation or avocation, and has made some noteworthy contribution as an educator, writer, environmental conservationist, photographer, flytier, or proponent of fishing rights. A life membership in the Federation is awarded annually. Established in 1978 to honor Don Harger, a noted author, photographer, and flytier from Salem, Oregon.

Basic Reference Guides and Handbooks

★3587★ *Furbearer Management*
National Trappers Association (NTA)
PO Box 3667
Bloomington, IL 61702
Ph: (309)829-2422 Fax: (309)829-7615

★3588★ *Get Set to Trap*
Outdoor Empire Publishing, Inc.
PO Box 19000
Seattle, WA 98109
Ph: (206)624-3845
1982.

★3589★ *Handy Medical Guide for Seafarers, Fisherman, Trawlermen & Yachtsmen*
State Mutual Book & Periodical Service, Ltd.
521 5th Ave., 17th Fl.
New York, NY 10175
Ph: (212)682-5844
R. W. Scott. 1978.

★3590★ *Muskrats & Marsh Management*
University of Nebraska, Lincoln
University of Nebraska Press
901 N. 17th St.
Lincoln, NE 68588
Ph: (402)472-3581 Fax: (402)472-6214
Paul L. Errington. 1978.

★3591★ *NTA Trapping Handbook: A Guide for Better Trapping*
National Trappers Association
PO Box 3667
Bloomington, IL 61702
Ph: (309)829-2422
Tom Krause. 1984.

★3592★ *Part Time Cash for the Sportsman: Twenty-Five Ways for the Fisherman & Hunter to Earn Extra Money*
Northeast Sportsman's Press
PO Box 188
Tarrytown, NY 10591
Ph: (914)762-7193
Jim Capossela. 1984.

★3593★ *Ragnar's Ten Best Traps & a Few Others That Are Damn Good, Too*
Paladin Press
PO Box 1307
Boulder, CO 80306
Ph: (303)443-7250 Fax: (303)442-8741
Ragnar Benson. 1985.

★3594★ *The Trapper's Bible: Traps, Snares, & Pathguards*
Paladin Press
PO Box 1307
Boulder, CO 80306
Ph: (303)443-7250 Fax: (303)442-8741
Dale Martin. 1987.

★3595★ *Trapper's Handbook*
DBI Books, Inc.
4092 Commercial Ave.
Northbrook, IL 60062
Ph: (708)272-6310 Fax: (708)272-2051
Rick Jamison. 1983.

★3596★ *Traps Today*
National Trappers Association (NTA)
PO Box 3667
Bloomington, IL 61702
Ph: (309)829-2422 Fax: (309)829-7615

PERIODICALS

★3597★ *American Hunter*
National Rifle Assn. of America
11250 Waples Mill Rd.
Fairfax, VA 22030
Ph: (703)267-1584 Fax: (703)267-3994
Thomas Fulgham
Monthly. Hunting magazine emphasizing technique, sportsmanship, and safety.

★3598★ *American Rifleman*
National Rifle Association of America (NRA)
11250 Waples Mill Rd.
Fairfax, VA 22030
Ph: (703)267-1000 Fr: 800-368-5714
Monthly. Contains reports on equipment, tournaments, Olympics, collector items, and NRA news. Also includes book reviews and calendar of events.

★3599★ *American Trapper*
National Trappers Assn.
PO Box 3667
Bloomington, IL 61702
Ph: (309)829-2422 Fax: (309)827-7615
Tom Krause
Bimonthly. Fur trade magazine.

★3600★ *Atlantic Offshore Fisherman's Association—Newsletter*
Atlantic Offshore Fisherman's Association
221 3rd St.
PO Box 3001
Newport, RI 02840
Ph: (401)849-3232 Fax: (401)847-9966
Susan Cortis
Quarterly. Discusses news and concerns of the organization, fishing policies, and trade news affecting the fishing industry. Recurring features include news of members.

★3601★ *The Badger Sportsman*
19 E. Main St.
Chilton, WI 53014
Ph: (414)849-7036 Fax: (414)849-4651
Tom Woodrow
Monthly. Hunting, fishing, and camping magazine.

★3602★ *Bassin'*
NatCom Inc.
5300 CityPlex Tower
PO Box 5300
Jenks, OK 74037-5300
Ph: (918)366-4441 Fax: (918)366-4439
Fr: 800-554-1999
Gerald W. PopePublisher
Bass fishing magazine featuring articles on equipment, techniques, and locations; as well as profiles of successful bass fishermen.

★3603★ *Bassmaster Magazine*
B.A.S.S. Inc.
5845 Carmichael Pkwy.
PO Box 17151
Montgomery, AL 36141
Ph: (205)272-9530 Fax: (205)279-7148
Dave Precht
Magazine covering boating and freshwater bass fishing.

★3604★ *Bowhunter Magazine*
Cowles Magazines
6405 Flank Drive
PO Box 8200
Harrisburg, PA 17105-8200
Ph: (717)657-9555 Fax: (717)657-9526
M.R. James
The magazine is dedicated to the sport of Bowhunting.

★3605★ *The Chase*
1150 Industry Rd.
Lexington, KY 40505
Ph: (606)254-4262
Jo Ann Stone
Monthly. Magazine on fox hunting.

★3606★ *Commercial Fisheries News*
Compass Publications, Inc., Fisheries Division
PO Box 37
Stonington, ME 04681
Ph: (207)367-2396 Fax: (207)367-2490
Robin Alden
Monthly. Magazine for commercial fishermen.

★3607★ *Delta Pride News*
Delta Catfish Processors, Inc.
Industrial Park
PO Box 850
Indianola, MS 38751
Ph: (601)887-5401
Walter Harrison
Quarterly. Informs customers and stockholders of new developments and techniques within Delta Catfish Processors and within the fresh fish processing industry. Recurring features include news of research, staff news, items on the annual Brokers' Conference and on awards won by Delta Catfish, new product introductions, information on training materials available, and columns titled A Message From the President and Outlook on Supply and Demand.

★3608★ *Field & Stream*
Times Mirror Magazines, Inc.
2 Park Ave.
New York, NY 10016
Ph: (212)779-5000 Fax: (212)779-5465
Duncan Barnes
Monthly. Magazine focusing on hunting, fishing, camping, and boating.

★3609★ *Fins & Feathers*
Fins Publications
318 Franklin W.
Minneapolis, MN 55404
Ph: (612)490-9408
Dave Greer
Monthly. Magazine featuring fishing, hunting, and conservation.

★3610★ *Fish and Game Finder Magazine*
Fish Finder Industries, Inc.
1233 W. Jackson St.
Orlando, FL 32805
Ph: (407)425-0045 Fax: (407)425-1529
Harold F. "Skip" HallPublisher
Monthly. Magazines covering fishing and hunting markets in 32 states. Published in 22 regional editions.

★3611★ *The Fisherman*
L.I. Fisherman Publishing Corp.
14 Ramsey Rd.
Shirley, NY 11967
Ph: (516)345-5200 Fax: (516)345-5304
Peter Barrett
Weekly. Magazine covering local fresh and salt water sportfishing.

★3612★ *Fishing Facts Magazine*
Fishing Facts Magazine
312 E. Buffalo
Milwaukee, WI 53202
Ph: (414)273-0021 Fax: (414)273-0016
Spence Petros
Magazine on freshwater sport fishing.

★3613★ *Fishing and Hunting News*
PO Box 19000
Seattle, WA 98109
Ph: (206)624-3845 Fax: (206)340-9816
Vince Malernee
Semiweekly. Hunting, fishing and outdoor sports magazine.

★3614★ *Flashes*
National Fisheries Institute
1525 Wilson Blvd., Ste. 500
Arlington, VA 22209
Ph: (703)524-8880 Fax: (703)524-4619
Emily Holt-Chambers
Monthly. Publishes information on the activities of the Institute and other fishery organizations and on seafood consumption. Covers government actions which affect fishing, such as the National Marine Fisheries Service budget, EPA water quality standards, endangered fishes, fishing rules and regulations, and commercial shipping and trade laws. Recurring features include news of members, news of research, book reviews, and a calendar of events.

★3615★ *Fly Fisherman*
Cowles Magazines
6405 Flank Drive
PO Box 8200
Harrisburg, PA 17105-8200
Ph: (717)657-9555 Fax: (717)657-9526
John Randolph
Bimonthly. Magazine of interest to fly fishermen.

★3616★ *Fly Rod & Reel*
Down East Enterprise, Inc.
Rte. 1 Roxmont
Rockport, ME 04856
Ph: (207)594-9544 Fax: (207)594-7215
Jim Butler
Bimonthly. Publication focuses on all aspects of fly-fishing; travel, equipment, technique.

★3617★ *Flyfishing*
Frank Amato Publications
PO Box 82112
Portland, OR 97282
Ph: (503)653-8151 Fax: (503)653-2766
Marty Sherman
Flyfishing magazine.

★3618★ *FUR-FISH-GAME*
A.R. Harding Publishing Co.
2878 E. Main St.
Columbus, OH 43209
Ph: (614)231-9585
Mitch Cox

Monthly. Magazine featuring hunting, trapping, fishing, dogs, and conservation.

★3619★ *Game & Fish Magazine*
Game & Fish Publications, Inc.
2250 Newmarket Pkwy., Ste. 110
PO Box 741
Marietta, GA 30061
Ph: (404)953-9222 Fax: (404)933-9510
David Morris

Monthly. Magazine with specific state editions providing in-depth information on the wheres, whens, and hows of hunting and fishing in these states.

★3620★ *Gray's Sporting Journal*
North American Publications, Inc.
PO Box 1207
Augusta, GA 30903-1207
Ph: (706)722-6060 Fax: (706)724-3873
David Foster

Bimonthly. Hunting and fishing magazine.

★3621★ *Grit and Steel*
De Camp Publishing Co.
Drawer 280
Gaffney, SC 29342
Ph: (803)489-2324
Mary M. Hodge

Monthly. Game fowl magazine.

★3622★ *Hook, Line & Sinker*
Rte. 3, Box 337-C
Harrisburg, AR 72432
Ph: (501)578-9501 Fax: (501)578-5480
William J. Beasley

Quarterly. Fishing magazine.

★3623★ *Hooks and Lines*
International Women's Fishing Association
P.O. Drawer 3125
Palm Beach, FL 33480
Joan S. Willmott

Bimonthly. Covers the fishing activities of the members, with news items and stories. Recurring features include a calendar of events.

★3624★ *The Hospitality Manager*
Kassis Communications
120 Hayward
Ames, IA 50010
Ph: (515)296-2400 Fax: (515)296-2405
Terry Lowman

Monthly. Trade publication (tabloid) covering restaurant and institutional business in the Midwest. Mailed to restaurants, bars, and institutional food service companies.

★3625★ *The Hunting Report for Big Game Hunters*
Oxpecker Enterprises, Inc.
9300 S. Dadeland Blvd., Ste. 605
Miami, FL 33156
Ph: (305)598-0158 Fax: (305)670-1376
Fr: (305)598-0735
Don Causey

Quarterly. Comments on big game hunting conditions, cost, and likelihood of success. Reports recent big game hunting trips by subscribers.

★3626★ *IIFET Newsletter*
International Institute of Fisheries Economics and Trade (IIFET)
Oregon State University
232 Ballard Hall
Corvallis, OR 97331-1641
Ph: (503)737-1420 Fax: (503)737-2563
Ann L. Shriver

Semiannual. Keeps members abreast of events in the fisheries sectors around the world and facilitates cooperative research in the field. Also covers association workshops, conferences, and training programs. Recurring features include notices of publications available, news of research, and information on new companies and business opportunities.

★3627★ *InSights*
National Rifle Association of America (NRA)
11250 Waples Mill Rd.
Fairfax, VA 22030
Ph: (703)267-1000 Fr: 800-368-5714

Monthly. Includes articles on firearm education and safety and hunting tips.

★3628★ *The International Angler*
International Game Fish Association
3000 E. Las Olas Blvd.
Ft. Lauderdale, FL 33316
Ph: (305)467-0161
Ray Crawford

Bimonthly. Provides information on recreational angling throughout the world. Covers subjects including game fish legislation and conservation efforts, scientific tag and release and other data collection programs, and world record fish catches. Recurring features include information on new fishing areas, new publications, and activities of the Association.

★3629★ *International Light Tackle Tournament Association—Bulletin*
International Light Tackle Tournament Association
2044 Federal Ave.
Costa Mesa, CA 92627
Ph: (714)548-4273 Fax: (714)631-7642
Helen R. Smith

Provides members with detailed formal and informal accounts of light tackle fishing tournaments.

★3630★ *Living Among Nature Daringly*
4466 Ike Mooney Rd.
Silverton, OR 97381
Ph: (503)873-8829
Bill Anderson

Magazine for trappers, farmers, and nature lovers.

★3631★ *Marine Fish Management*
Nautilus Press, Inc.
1054 National Press Bldg.
Washington, DC 20045
Ph: (202)347-6643
John R. Botzum

Monthly. Discusses the organizational, legislative, and ideological issues confronting fisheries management, particularly of the living resources in the U.S. 200-mile fisheries zone. Provides information on aquaculture world fish management news. Recurring features include a calendar of events and news of research.

★3632★ *Marine Technology Society Journal*
Marine Technology Society (MTS)
1828 L St. NW, No. 906
Washington, DC 20036
Ph: (202)775-5966 Fax: (202)429-9417

Quarterly. Includes book reviews and peer-reviewed articles.

★3633★ *Musky Hunter*
ESOX Publishing, Inc.
PO Box 11796
Green Bay, WI 54307-1796
Ph: (414)496-0334 Fax: (414)496-0332
Joe Bucher

Bimonthly. Magazine about musky fishing.

★3634★ *National Fisherman*
120 Tillson Ave.
PO Box 908
Rockland, ME 04841
Ph: (207)594-6222 Fax: (207)594-8978
James W. Fullilove

Monthly. Magazine covering commercial fishing and boat building.

★3635★ *North American Fisherman*
North American Outdoor Group, Inc.
12301 Whitewater Dr., Ste. 260
Minnetonka, MN 55343
Ph: (612)936-9333 Fax: (612)936-9755
Steve Pennaz

Bimonthly. Fishing magazine.

★3636★ *North American Hunter*
North American Outdoor Group, Inc.
12301 Whitewater Dr., Ste. 260
Minnetonka, MN 55343
Ph: (612)936-9333 Fax: (612)936-9755
Bill Miller

Hunting magazine.

★3637★ *North American Journal of Fisheries Management*
American Fisheries Society
5410 Grosvenor Ln., Ste. 110
Bethesda, MD 20814-2199
Ph: (301)897-8616 Fax: (301)897-8096
Phyllis Cahn

Quarterly. Fisheries management journal.

★3638★ *NRAction*
National Rifle Association of America (NRA)
11250 Waples Mill Rd.
Fairfax, VA 22030
Ph: (703)267-1000 Fr: 800-368-5714

Monthly.

★3639★ *Pacific States Marine Fisheries Commission—Newsletter*
Pacific States Marine Fisheries Commission
45 82nd Dr. No. 100
Gladstone, OR 97027-2522
Ph: (503)650-5400 Fax: (503)650-5426
Al Didier

Carries Commission news and articles concerned with Pacific coast fisheries. Reviews Commission activities with U.S. Congress. Recurring features include contract reports, statistics, news of research, and management activities.

★3640★ *PRODUCT NEWS*
Compass Publications, Inc., Fisheries Division
PO Box 37
Stonington, ME 04681
Ph: (207)367-2396 Fax: (207)367-2490
Robin AldenPublisher

Bimonthly. New product publication for commercial fishermen, seafood processors, and aquaculturists.

★3641★ *Salmon Trout Steelheader*
PO Box 82112
Portland, OR 97282
Ph: (503)653-8108
Nick Amato

Bimonthly. Magazine featuring salmon, trout, and steelhead sport fishing.

★3642★ *Salt Water Sportsman*
Times Mirror Magazines, Inc.
2 Park Ave.
New York, NY 10016
Ph: (212)779-5000 Fax: (212)779-5465
Colin M. Cunningham

Monthly. Magazine on salt water fishing and boating

★3643★ *Sea Grant Extension Program Newsletter*
Department of Wildlife & Fisheries Biology
Davis, CA 95616-8751
Ph: (916)752-1497
Christopher M. Dewees

Discusses commercial fishing, seafood processing, vessel and gear operation and maintenance, recreational fishing, and oceanography. Also examines maritime law, marine education, marine recreation, and government regulations and guidelines affecting marine activity.

★3644★ *SFI Bulletin*
Sport Fishing Institute (SFI)
1010 Massachusetts Ave. NW, Ste. 320
Washington, DC 20001
Ph: (202)898-0770 Fax: (202)371-2085
Gilbert C. Radonski

Serves as an educational tool regarding the Institute's efforts in fish conservation. Covers fisheries science and management, habitat protection, aquatic ecology and ecosystems management, water pollution control and abatement, and recreational fisheries development. Recurring features include book reviews, editorials, staff commentaries on developments in the field, and coverage of relevant government actions.

★3645★ *Shooting Times*
PJS Publications, Inc.
News Plaza
PO Box 1790
Peoria, IL 61656
Ph: (309)682-6626 Fax: (309)682-7394
Jim Bequette

Monthly. Magazine focusing on guns and shooting sports.

★3646★ *Southern Outdoors*
B.A.S.S., Inc.
PO Box 17915
Montgomery, AL 36141
Ph: (205)277-3940
Larry Teague

Outdoor magazine covering fishing, hunting, camping, boating, and outdoor recreation.

★3647★ *Sport Fishing*
World Publications, Inc.
PO Box 2456
Winter Park, FL 32790
Ph: (407)628-4802 Fax: (407)628-7061
Terry SnowPublisher

Magazine about offshore saltwater fishing.

★3648★ *SPORTING CLASSICS*
Live Oak Press, Inc.
PO Box 1017
Camden, SC 29020
Ph: (803)425-1003 Fax: (803)432-8056
Charles A. Wechsler

Bimonthly. Hunting and fishing magazine.

★3649★ *The Trapper and Predator Caller*
Krause Publications, Inc.
700 E. State St.
Iola, WI 54990-0001
Ph: (715)445-2214 Fax: (715)445-4087
Gordy Krahn

Monthly. Magazine on hunting, trapping, and predator calling.

★3650★ *The Trout & Salmon Leader*
The Trout & Salmon Leader
2401 Bristol Ct. SW
Olympia, WA 98502
Bill Lindstrom

Official publication of the Northwest Region of Trout Unlimited.

★3651★ *The Turkey Hunter*
Krause Publications, Inc.
700 E. State St.
Iola, WI 54990-0001
Ph: (715)445-2214 Fax: (715)445-4087
Gerry Blair

Sportsmen magazine featuring turkey hunting.

★3652★ *Wildfowl*
Stover Publishing Co., Inc.
1901 Bell Ave., Ste. 4
PO Box 35098
Des Moines, IA 50315
Ph: (515)243-2472 Fax: (515)243-0233
Bob Wilbanks

Bimonthly.

★3653★ *Wildlife Harvest*
Wildlife Harvest Publications
PO Box 96
Goose Lake, IA 52750
Ph: (319)242-3046
John M. Mullin

Monthly. Magazine for hunting resorts, sportsmen's clubs, gun clubs, dog kennels, and commercial gamebird producers.

★3654★ *Wing & Shot*
Stover Publishing Co., Inc.
1901 Bell Ave., Ste. 4
PO Box 35098
Des Moines, IA 50315
Ph: (515)243-2472 Fax: (515)243-0233
Robert Wilbanks

Bimonthly.

Meetings and Conventions

★3655★ American Convention of Meat Processors
American Association of Meat Processors
PO Box 269
Elizabethtown, PA 17022
Ph: (717)367-1168 Fax: (717)367-9096

Annual. Always held during July. **Dates and Locations:** 1996 Jul.

★3656★ American Fisheries Society Convention
American Fisheries Society
5410 Grosvenor Ln.
Bethesda, MD 20814
Ph: (301)897-8616 Fax: (301)897-8096

Annual.

★3657★ Fish Expo
Diversified Expositions
5 Milk St.
PO Box 7437
Portland, ME 04112-7437
Ph: (207)772-3005 Fax: (207)772-5059

Annual. Always held in Seattle, Washington, in odd-numbered years and in Boston, Massachusetts, in even-numbered years.

Other Sources of Information

★3658★ *Book of the Free Trapper*
Pioneer Press
DGW Bldg.
PO Box 684
Union City, TN 38261
Ph: (901)885-0374

Keith Walters. 1981.

★3659★ *Distant Water: The Fate of the North Atlantic Fisherman*
Viking Penguin
375 Hudson St.
New York, NY 10014
Ph: (212)366-2000

William W. Warner. 1984.

★3660★ *Facts About Fur*
National Trappers Association (NTA)
PO Box 3667
Bloomington, IL 61702
Ph: (309)829-2422 Fax: (309)829-7615

★3661★ "Fish Farmer" in *Career Selector 2001*
Barron's Educational Series, Inc.
250 Wireless Blvd.
Hauppauge, NY 11788
Ph: (516)434-3311 Fax: (516)434-3723
Fr: 800-645-3476

James C. Gonyea. 1993.

★3662★ *Lake Erie Fisherman: Work, Identity & Tradition*
University of Illinois
University of Illinois Press
54 E. Gregory Dr.
Champaign, IL 61820
Ph: (217)333-0950 Fax: (217)244-8082

Timothy C. Lloyd. 1990.

Forestry and Logging Occupations

Forestry and conservation workers help develop, maintain, and protect these forests by growing and planting new tree seedlings, fighting insects and diseases that attack trees, and helping to control soil erosion. Timber cutting and logging workers harvest thousands of acres of forests each year for the timber that provides the raw material for countless consumer and industrial products. Fallers cut down trees with chain saws or mechanical felling equipment. Buckers trim off the tops and branches and buck (cut) the resulting logs into specified lengths. These workers usually use gas-powered chain saws. Choker setters fasten chokers (steel cables or chains) around logs to be skidded (dragged) by tractors or forwarded by the cable yarding system to the landing. Included are riggers, who set up and dismantle the cables and guy wires of the cable yarding system. Logging tractor operators drive crawler or wheeled tractors to skid logs from the felling site to the landing. Some operate harvesters-- tractors outfitted with specialized equipment that can cut and delimb trees. Others operate forwarders that haul the logs to the landing and load them onto trucks. Log handling equipment operators operate tracked and wheeled equipment to load or unload logs and pulpwood onto or off trucks or gondola railroad cars. Log graders and scalers inspect logs for defects, measure logs to determine their volume, and estimate the marketable content or value of logs or pulpwood. Cruisers hike through forests to assess logging conditions and estimate the volume of marketable timber. Brush clearing laborers clear areas of brush and other growth to prepare for logging activities and to promote growth of desirable species of trees. Tree trimmers prune tree tops and branches, using saws or pruning shears. Pickers select and place logs onto skidders and log blocks onto conveyors to be sent to other machines for further processing. Log markers determine the bucking points at which logs will be sawn into sections. Rivers use sledge hammers, mallets, wedges, and froes (cleaving tools) to split logs to form posts, pickets, shakes, and other objects. Rigging slingers determine the sequence of logs to be yarded by the cable yarding system. Chasers direct the placement of logs at landings and disengage their chokers. Pulp pilers stack pulpwood logs at landings near logging roads.

Salaries

Median weekly earning for full-time logging workers is $296.

Lowest 10 percent	$159/week or less
Middle	$210-$408/week
Top 10 percent	$556/week or more

Employment Outlook

Growth rate until the year 2005: Little change.

Forestry and Logging Occupations

Career Guides

★3663★ ***Career Success Series***
Cambridge Educational
PO Box 2153
Charleston, WV 25328-2153
Ph: (304)744-9323 Fax: (304)744-9351
Fr: 800-468-4227
Videocassette. 1986. 15 mins. A series, available separately, outlining various career choices for students. Occupations include: accounting, flight service, air transportation/ground/flight service, data processing, carpentry, clerk in banking/insurance, commodity sales, cosmetic personal grooming, fire fighting, forestry services, home economics, insulation/roofing, material handling, mechanics, photographic processing, pipefitting and plumbing, police science, printing, carpentry, medical laboratory technicians, secretarial services, and utilities equipment operator.

★3664★ ***Forest Technician***
Careers, Inc.
PO Box 135
Largo, FL 34649-0135
Ph: (813)584-7333
1994. Two-page occupational summary card describing duties, working conditions, personal qualifications, training, earnings and hours, employment outlook, places of employment, related careers, and where to write for more information.

★3665★ **"Foresters" in *Career Discovery Encyclopedia* (Vol.3, pp. 40-41)**
J.G. Ferguson Publishing Co.
200 W. Madison St., Ste. 300
Chicago, IL 60606
Ph: (312)580-5480 Fax: (312)580-4948
Russell E. Primm, editor-in chief. 1993. This six volume set contains two-page articles for 504 occupations. Each article describes job duties, earnings, and educational and training requirements. The whole set is arranged alphabetically by job title. Designed for junior high and older students.

★3666★ **"Forestry and Logging Occupations" in *Occupational Outlook Handbook***
U.S. Government Printing Office
Superintendent of Documents
Washington, DC 20402
Ph: (202)512-1800 Fax: (202)512-2250
Biennial; latest edition, 1994-95. Encyclopedia of careers describing more than 250 occupations and comprising about 85 percent of all jobs in the economy. Occupations that require lengthy education or training are given the most attention. For each occupation, the handbook describes job duties, working conditions, training, educational preparation, personal qualities, advancement possibilities, job outlook, earnings, and sources of additional information.

★3667★ ***Logger***
Careers, Inc.
PO Box 135
Largo, FL 34649-0135
Ph: (813)584-7333
1992. Two-page occupational summary card describing duties, working conditions, personal qualifications, training, earnings and hours, employment outlook, places of employment, related careers and where to write for more information.

★3668★ **"Logger" in *Career Information Center* (Vol.2)**
Simon and Schuster
200 Old Tappan Rd.
Old Tappan, NJ 07675
Fax: 800-445-6991 Fr: 800-223-2348
Richard Lidz and Dale Anderson, editorial directors. Fifth edition, 1993. For 600 occupations, describes job duties, entry-level requirements, education and training needed, advancement possibilities, employment outlook, earnings and benefits. The set is divided into 12 volumes. Each volume includes jobs related under a broad career field. Volume 13 is the index.

★3669★ **"Logger" in *Occu-Facts: Information on 580 Careers in Outline Form***
Careers, Inc.
PO Box 135
Largo, FL 34649-0135
Ph: (813)584-7333
Biennial, 1995-96 edition. Each one-page occupational profile describes duties, working conditions, physical surroundings and demands, aptitudes, temperament, educational requirements, employment outlook, earnings, and places of employment.

★3670★ ***Logging Industry Workers***
Chronicle Guidance Publications, Inc.
66 Aurora St.
PO Box 1190
Moravia, NY 13118-1190
Ph: (315)497-0330 Fax: (315)497-3359
Fr: 800-622-7284
1994. This career brief describes the nature of the work, working conditions, hours and earnings, education and training, licensure, certification, unions, personal qualifications, social and psychological factors, employment outlook, entry methods, advancement, and related occupations.

★3671★ **"Logging Industry Workers" in *Career Discovery Encyclopedia* (Vol.4, pp. 30-31)**
J.G. Ferguson Publishing Co.
200 W. Madison St., Ste. 300
Chicago, IL 60606
Ph: (312)580-5480 Fax: (312)580-4948
E. Russell Primm, editor-in-chief. 1993. Contains two-page articles on 504 occupations. Each article describes job duties, earnings, and educational and training requirements.

★3672★ **"Logging Industry Workers" in *Encyclopedia of Careers and Vocational Guidance* (Vol.3, pp. 328-331)**
J.G. Ferguson Publishing Co.
200 W. Madison St., Ste. 300
Chicago, IL 60606
Ph: (312)580-5480 Fax: (312)580-4948
William E. Hopke, editor-in-chief. Ninth edition, 1993. Four-volume set that profiles 500 occupations and describes job trends in 74

industries. Includes career description, educational requirements, history of the job, methods of entry, advancement, employment outlook, earnings, working conditions, social and psychological factors, and sources of additional information.

★3673★ *Timber & the Forest Service*
University of Kansas, Lawrence
University Press of Kansas
Lawrence, KS 66049
Ph: (913)864-4154 Fax: (913)864-4586

David A. Clary. 1986. Part of Development of Western Resources Series.

Associations

★3674★ Northeastern Loggers Association (NELA)
PO Box 69
Old Forge, NY 13420
Ph: (315)369-3078 Fax: (315)369-3736

Members: Timberland owners, independent loggers, professional foresters, and primary wood products industries. **Purpose:** Works to improve the industry in the Northeast and educate the public about the policies, practices, and products of the industry. Maintains Forest Industries Exhibit Hall. Cooperates in research by public and private agencies. Operates museum; conducts educational program. **Publications:** *Northern Logger and Timber Processor*, monthly.

★3675★ Pacific Logging Congress (PLC)
2300 SW 6th Ave., Ste. 200
Portland, OR 97201
Ph: (503)224-8406 Fax: (503)224-7211

Members: Logging firms, manufacturers of wood products and logging equipment, and distributors in Canada, New Zealand, and the United States.

★3676★ Society of American Foresters (SAF)
5400 Grosvenor Ln.
Bethesda, MD 20814
Ph: (301)897-8720 Fax: (301)897-3690

Members: Professional society of foresters and scientists working in related fields. **Purpose:** Serves as accrediting agency for professional forestry education. Provides professional training. Supports 28 subject-oriented working groups. **Publications:** *Forest Science*, quarterly. • *Journal of Forestry*, monthly. • *Northern Journal of Applied Forestry*, quarterly. • *Southern Journal of Applied Forestry*, quarterly. • *Western Journal of Applied Forestry*, quarterly.

Standards/Certification Agencies

★3677★ Society of American Foresters (SAF)
5400 Grosvenor Ln.
Bethesda, MD 20814
Ph: (301)897-8720 Fax: (301)897-3690

Serves as accrediting agency for professional forestry education.

Test Guides

★3678★ *Career Examination Series: Forester*
National Learning Corp.
212 Michael Dr.
Syosset, NY 11791
Ph: (516)921-8888 Fax: (516)921-8743
Fr: 800-645-6337

Jack Rudman. Test guide including questions and answers for students or professionals in the field who seek advancement through examination.

★3679★ *Career Examination Series: Forestry Technician*
National Learning Corp.
212 Michael Dr.
Syosset, NY 11791
Ph: (516)921-8888 Fax: (516)921-8743
Fr: 800-645-6337

Jack Rudman. Test guide including questions and answers for students or professionals in the field who seek advancement through examination. Also included in the series: Senior Forestry Technician and Principal Forestry Technician.

Educational Directories and Programs

★3680★ *International Green Front Report*
Friends of the Trees
PO Box 1064
Tonasket, WA 98855
Ph: (509)485-2705 Fax: (509)485-2705
Michael Pilarski, Office Manager

Irregular, latest edition 1988. Covers Organizations and periodicals concerned with sustainable forestry and agriculture and related fields. Entries include: Organization or publisher name, address, phone, description of projects and activities, or description of periodical coverage. Arrangement: Classified by subject.

★3681★ *Society of American Foresters Accredited Professional and Recognized Technical Forestry Degree Programs*
Society of American Foresters
5400 Grosvenor Ln.
Bethesda, MD 20814
Ph: (301)897-8720 Fax: (301)897-3690
P. Gregory Smith, Contact

Annual, January. Covers nearly 50 forestry schools and institutions offering programs in professional forestry; about 20 institutions offering forestry technician programs are also listed. Entries include: Institution name, address; date of first accreditation, date of last on-site accreditation, date accreditation expires. Arrangement: Geographical.

Awards, Scholarships, Grants, and Fellowships

★3682★ Northeastern Loggers' Association Annual Scholarships
Northeastern Loggers' Association
PO Box 69
Old Forge, NY 13420

Purpose: To promote good writing skills among forestry and wood science students. Qualifications: Candidates must be second-year students in two-year forestry and wood science programs or juniors in four-year programs. Entrants must also be attending school in one of the northeastern states in the area roughly bounded by Maine and Maryland on the east and Minnesota and Missouri on the west. Funds available: Two awards of $2,000 each and two awards of $1,000 each are given. Application details: Students must submit a paper on a specific topic along with a resume and academic transcripts. Deadline: January 31.

★3683★ Northeastern Loggers' Association Awards Program
Northeastern Loggers' Association
PO Box 69
Old Forge, NY 13420
Ph: (315)369-3078 Fax: (315)369-3736

To recognize significant achievement in forestry and wood utilization during the year in nine major categories: outstanding logging operator, outstanding sawmill operator, outstanding service to the forest industry, outstanding management of resources, outstanding leadership in industry, outstanding contributions to forest industry education, outstanding use of wood, outstanding contribution to safety, and outstanding industry activist. Persons or organizations need not be members of the Northeastern Loggers' Association. The nominee must reside in or conduct business in the Northeastern or Lake States Region of the United States as delineated by the USFA. The deadline for nominations is January 31. A maximum of one award is given in each category when merited. A plaque and $300 is awarded in each of the categories with the exception of the Safety Award. Presented at the annual Northeastern Loggers' Congress. Established in 1955. The

Safety Award is sponsored by Forest Products Agency of Norwich, CT.

Basic Reference Guides and Handbooks

★3684★ *International Tropical Timber Agreement*
United Nations Publishing Service
Rm. DC2-0853
New York, NY 10017
Fax: (212)963-3489
1985.

★3685★ *Logging Companies Directory*
American Business Directories, Inc.
5711 S. 86th Circle
Omaha, NE 68127
Ph: (402)593-4600 Fax: (402)331-1505
Updated continuously; printed on request. Entries include: Name, address, phone, size of advertisement, name of owner or manager, number of employees, year first in "Yellow Pages." Compiled from telephone company "Yellow Pages," nationwide. Arrangement: Geographical.

★3686★ *The Practical Design of Structural Elements of Timber*
Gower Publishing Co.
Old Post Rd.
Brookfield, VT 05036
Ph: (802)276-3162
John W. Bull. 1994.

★3687★ *Promoting Timber Cropping*
Gower Publishing Comapany
Old Post Rd.
Brookfield, VT 05036
Ph: (802)276-3162
Paul A. Huber.

★3688★ *Timber Cutting Practices*
Miller Freeman Publications, Inc.
600 Harrison St.
San Francisco, CA 94105
Ph: (415)397-1881
Steve Conway. Third edition, 1978.

★3689★ *Timber Designer's Manual*
Beekman Publishers, Inc.
Rte. 212
PO Box 888
Woodstock, NY 12498
Ph: (914)679-2300
J. A. Baird. Second edition, 1988.

★3690★ *Timber: Its Nature & Behavior*
Van Nostrand Reinhold Co., Inc.
115 5th Ave.
New York, NY 10003
Ph: (212)254-3232 Fax: (212)254-9499
Dinwoodie. 1981.

★3691★ *Timber: Its Structure, Properties & Utilization*
Timber Press
9999 SW Wilshire
Portland, OR 97225
Ph: (503)292-0745 Fax: (503)292-6607
H. E. Desch. Sixth edition, 1980.

★3692★ *Timber Management: A Quantitative Approach*
John Wiley and Sons, Inc.
605 3rd Ave.
New York, NY 10158-0012
Ph: (212)850-6000 Fax: (212)850-6088
Fr: 800-526-5368
Jerome L. Clutter. 1983.

★3693★ *Timber!: Problems, Prospects, Policies*
Iowa State University Press
Iowa State University
2121 S. State Ave.
Ames, IA 50010
Ph: (515)292-0140 Fax: (515)292-3348
William A. Duerr, editor. 1973.

★3694★ *Timber Resources for America's Future: Forest Resource Report No. 14*
Ayer Company Publishers, Inc.
50 Northwestern Dr., No. 10
PO Box 958
Salem, NH 03079
Ph: (603)898-1200
U.S. Department of Agriculture, Forest Service Staff. 1972. Part of Use & Abuse of America's Natural Resources Series.

★3695★ *Timber Specifier's Guide: Understanding & Specifying Softwoods in Buildings*
Blackwell Scientific Publications, Inc.
3 Cambridge Center, Ste. 208
Cambridge, MA 02142
Ph: (617)225-0401 Fax: (617)225-0412
J. A. Baird. 1990.

★3696★ *Timber Supply: Issues & Options*
Forest Products Research Society
2801 Marshall Ct.
Madison, WI 53705
Ph: (608)231-1361 Fax: (608)231-2152
1979.

★3697★ *Vanishing Forest Reserves*
Ayer Company Publishers, Inc.
50 Northwestern Dr., No. 10
PO Box 958
Salem, NH 03079
Ph: (603)898-1200
Willard G. Van Name. 1979. Part of Management of Public Lands in the U.S. Series.

Periodicals

★3698★ *American Forests*
PO Box 2000
Washington, DC 20013-2000
Ph: (202)667-3300 Fax: (202)667-7751
Bill Rooney
Bimonthly. Forest conservation magazine.

★3699★ *Case 'n Base News*
Wood Moulding and Millwork Producers Association
PO Box 25278
Portland, OR 97225
Ph: (503)292-9288 Fax: (503)292-3490
James E. Mongrain
Monthly. Represents the Association, providing members with information concerning the promotion, standardization, and marketing of millwork products. Also provides general news of the industry. Recurring features include news of educational opportunities, job listings, notices of publications available, and a calendar of events.

★3700★ *Christmas Trees*
Tree Publishers, Inc.
Box 107
Lecompton, KS 66050
Ph: (913)887-6324 Fax: (913)887-6734
Charles (Chuck) W. Wright
Quarterly. Magazine covering the Christmas tree industry.

★3701★ *Crow's Weekly Letter*
C.C. Crow Publications, Inc.
PO Box 25749
Portland, OR 97225
Ph: (503)646-8075
Sam Sherrill
Weekly. Serves as a market report on lumber, plywood, and panel wood products, supplying news, analysis, and price information as a guide to sales. Carries market data on the transportation industry as it pertains to the shipment of forest products. Recurring features include housing market updates and news of industry events and personnel.

★3702★ *Environmental Report*
American Forest & Paper Association
1111 19th St. NW, Ste. 800
Washington, DC 20036
Ph: (202)463-2785 Fax: (202)463-2785
Marilyn Haugen
Monthly. Supplies the paper and forest products industry with information on environmental issues developments. Includes a 2-page status report on recent regulations, legislation, and litigation.

★3703★ *Forest & Conservation History*
Forest History Society
701 Vickers Ave.
Durham, NC 27701
Ph: (919)682-9319 Fax: (919)682-2349
Kevin C. Foy
Quarterly. Journal on the history of forest use and conservation.

★3704★ *Log Trucker*
Loggers World Publications
4206 Jackson Hwy.
Chehalis, WA 98532
Ph: (206)262-3376 Fax: (206)262-3337
Fr: 800-462-8283
Bill Palmroth
Monthly. Magazine focusing on the transportation of logs from the woods to the mills and sorting yards.

★3705★ *Logger and Lumberman*
Dixie Publications
210 N. Main St.
PO Box 489
Wadley, GA 30477
Ph: (912)252-5237 Fax: (912)252-1140
Jack D. Smith

Monthly. Magazine for the forest products industry.

★3706★ *Loggers World*
Loggers World Publications
4206 Jackson Hwy.
Chehalis, WA 98532
Ph: (206)262-3376 Fax: (206)262-3337
Fr: 800-462-8283
Finley Hays

Monthly. Trade magazine reporting on the logging industry.

★3707★ *Modern Woodworking*
Target Marketing Magazine Group
167 Hwy. 72 E.
PO Box 640
Collierville, TN 38017
Ph: (901)853-7470 Fax: (901)853-6437
Joyce Powell

Monthly. Magazine for management in the primary and secondary wood products industry.

★3708★ *Monthly F.O.B. Price Summary, Past Sales (Coast Mills)*
Western Wood Products Assn.
522 SW 5th Ave.
Portland, OR 97204-2122
Ph: (503)224-3930 Fax: (503)224-3934
Jim Yuhas

Monthly. Statistical report covering lumber species produced by Coast Mills.

★3709★ *Monthly F.O.B. Price Summary, Past Sales (Inland Mills)*
Western Wood Products Assn.
522 SW 5th Ave.
Portland, OR 97204-2122
Ph: (503)224-3930 Fax: (503)224-3934
Jim Yuhas

Monthly. Statistical reports on lumber species produced in the Inland area.

★3710★ *National Catholic Forester*
National Catholic Society of Foresters
446 E. Ontario
Chicago, IL 60611
Ph: (312)266-6250 Fax: (312)266-6256
Robert Nasenbeny

Quarterly. Magazine informing membership of new products and activities.

★3711★ *Northeastern Lumber Manufacturers Association—Information Log*
Northeastern Lumber Manufacturers Association
272 Tuttle Rd.
PO Box 87A
Cumberland Center, ME 04021
Ph: (207)829-6901 Fax: (207)829-4293
Donna J. Reynolds

Monthly. Discusses the growth, harvesting, production, and marketing of Northeastern lumber. Includes news of federal and state activities and of business of the Association.

★3712★ *Northern Journal of Applied Forestry*
Society of American Foresters
5400 Grosvenor Ln.
Bethesda, MD 20814-2198
Ph: (301)897-8720 Fax: (301)897-3690
Harry V. Wiant

Quarterly. Forestry industry magazine covering an area eastern Kansas and the areas northward and eastward (including all or part of 25 states and 6 provinces of Canada).

★3713★ *Northern Logger and Timber Processor*
N.L. Publishing, Inc.
PO Box 69
Old Forge, NY 13420
Ph: (315)369-3078 Fax: (315)369-3736
Eric A. Johnson

Monthly. Magazine for the logging and lumber industries.

★3714★ *Out of the Woods*
Western Forest Industries Association
1500 SW Taylor
Portland, OR 97205
Ph: (503)224-5455 Fax: (503)224-0592
David Ford

Weekly. Covers news of the forest products industry, including significant government and legislative actions and business statistics and trends. Recurring features include reprints of relevant articles from newspapers around the country.

★3715★ *Random Lengths*
Random Lengths Publications, Inc.
PO Box 867
Eugene, OR 97440-0867
Ph: (503)686-9925 Fax: (503)686-9629
Burrle Elmore

Weekly. Publishes market reports on North American forest products (lumber, softwood panels, shingles, shakes, and particle board) plus an insert listing prices. Contains articles on topics affecting the economy of the industry and analyses of the major North American softwood species. Recurring features include editorials, industry personnel news, and statistics.

★3716★ *Rocky Mountain Construction*
Golden Bell Press
2403 Champa St.
Denver, CO 80205
Ph: (303)295-0630 Fax: (303)295-2159
F. Hol Wagner

Semiweekly. Magazine serving the construction industry of America's mountain regions. Covering heavy engineering, building, landscaping, soil conservation, mining and logging, and federal, state, county, and city projects. Includes weekly construction reports.

★3717★ *SF Newsletter*
Southern Forest Products Association
PO Box 641700
Kenner, LA 70064-1700
Ph: (504)443-4464 Fax: (504)443-6612
David Kellogg

Weekly. Concerned with forest products, timber resources, home building, transportation, lumber manufacturing, and business and Association news.

★3718★ *Southern Journal of Applied Forestry*
Society of American Foresters
5400 Grosvenor Ln.
Bethesda, MD 20814-2198
Ph: (301)897-8720 Fax: (301)897-3690
William T. Gladstone

Quarterly. Forestry industry magazine covering an area south of Maryland and westward into Texas and Oklahoma and other areas with similar conditions.

★3719★ *Southern Loggin' Times*
Hatton-Brown Publishers, Inc.
225 Hanrick St.
Montgomery, AL 36104
Ph: (205)834-1170 Fax: (205)834-4525
D.K. KnightPublisher

Monthly. Magazine serving the Southern U.S. logging industry.

★3720★ *Southern Lumberman*
Greysmith Publishing
128 Holiday Ct., Ste. 116
PO Box 681629
Franklin, TN 37068-1629
Ph: (615)794-4338 Fax: (615)790-6188
Nanci P. Gregg

Monthly. Industry publication for sawmill operators.

★3721★ *Timber Bulletin*
United Nations Publications
PO Box 361
Birmingham, AL 35201-0361
Fax: (205)995-1588 Fr: 800-633-4931

Journal providing information on forest products, including a survey of monthly prices, a market review and trade flow data.

★3722★ *Timber Equipment Trader*
Dixie Publications
210 N. Main St.
PO Box 489
Wadley, GA 30477
Ph: (912)252-5237 Fax: (912)252-1140
David Lumpkin

Monthly. Magazine for buyers and sellers of timber equipment.

★3723★ *Timber Harvesting*
Hatton-Brown Publishers, Inc.
225 Hanrick St.
Montgomery, AL 36104
Ph: (205)834-1170 Fax: (205)834-4525
D.K. KnightPublisher

Monthly. National magazine for the U.S. logging industry.

★3724★ *Timber Mart-South*
Timber Marts, Inc.
PO Box 1278
Highlands, NC 28741
Ph: (704)526-3653 Fax: (704)526-3683
Frank Norris

Quarterly. Reports market prices for raw forest products, and provides a finished lumber price index for 13 Southeastern states. Data includes current prices (stumpage) plus current F.O.B. Mill delivered prices actually paid for sawtimber, pulpwood, veneer, chip-n-saw, poles, cross ties, and chips, both pine and hardwood.

★3725★ *The Timber Producer*
PO Box 39
Tomahawk, WI 54487
Ph: (715)453-5159 Fax: (715)453-4177
Carl F. Theiler

Monthly. Magazine for timber producers covering production and markets.

★3726★ *Timber West*
Timber West Publications
PO Box 610
Edmonds, WA 98020
Ph: (206)778-3388 Fax: (206)771-3623
John L. Nederlee

Logging and sawmill news.

Meetings and Conventions

★3727★ American Forestry Association Convention and Exposition
Offinger Management Co.
1100-H Brandywine Blvd.
PO Box 2188
Zanesville, OH 43702-2188
Ph: (614)452-4541 Fax: (614)452-2552

Every two to four years.

★3728★ Forest Industries Clinic and Show
Miller Freeman Expositions
600 Harrison St.
San Francisco, CA 94107
Ph: (415)905-2626

Annual. Always held during March at the Oregon State Convention Center in Portland, Oregon. **Dates and Locations:** 1996 Mar 13-15; Portland, OR. • 1997 Mar 12-14; Portland, OR.

★3729★ Forest Products Machinery and Equipment Exposition
Southern Forest Products Association
PO Box 641700
Kenner, LA 70064
Ph: (504)443-4464 Fax: (504)443-6612

Biennial.

★3730★ Northeastern Loggers Congress and Equipment Exposition
Northeastern Loggers Association
PO Box 69
Old Forge, NY 13420
Ph: (315)369-3078 Fax: (315)369-3736

Annual. Rotates between Bangor, Maine; Springfield, Massachusetts; and Syracuse, New York. **Dates and Locations:** 1996 Apr 26-27; Springfield, MA.

★3731★ Pacific Logging Congress, Equipment Exhibit
Pacific Logging Congress
2300 SW 6th Ave. Ste. 200
Portland, OR 97201
Ph: (503)224-8406 Fax: (503)224-7211

Annual.

★3732★ Redwood Region Logging Conference
Redwood Region Logging Conference
1725 H St.
Eureka, CA 95501-2339
Ph: (707)443-4091 Fax: (707)443-4187

Annual.

★3733★ Society of American Foresters National Convention
Society of American Foresters
5400 Grosvenor Ln.
Bethesda, MD 20814
Ph: (301)897-8720 Fax: (301)897-3690

Annual. **Dates and Locations:** 1995 Oct 28-01; Portland, ME. • 1996 Oct 17-20; Atlanta, GA.

Other Sources of Information

★3734★ "Forester Aide" in *Career Selector 2001*
Barron's Educational Series, Inc.
250 Wireless Blvd.
Hauppauge, NY 11788
Ph: (516)434-3311 Fax: (516)434-3723
Fr: 800-645-3476

James C. Gonyea. 1993.

★3735★ *Timbers of the New World*
Ayer Company Publishers, Inc.
50 Northwestern Dr., No. 10
PO Box 958
Salem, NH 03079
Ph: (603)898-1200

Samuel J. Record. 1972. Part of Use & Abuse of America's Natural Resources Series.

Aircraft Mechanics and Engine Specialists

Aircraft mechanics and engine specialists inspect the engine, landing gear, instruments, pressurized sections, accessories, brakes, valves, pumps, and other aircraft equipment and perform the necessary maintenance. Such maintenance usually follows a schedule based on hours flown, calendar days, and cycles of operation. Mechanics specializing in repair work rely on the pilot's description of a problem to find and fix faulty equipment. They may also work on many different types of aircraft, or specialize on one type or one section of aircraft. Technological advancements require aircraft mechanics and engine specialists to spend an increasing amount of time repairing electronic systems and computerized controls.

Salaries

The median annual salary of aircraft mechanics is about $26,000.

Top 10 percent	$47,500/year
Middle	$25,000-$39,000/year
Lowest 10 percent	$17,700/year

Employment Outlook

Growth rate until the year 2005: Slower than the average.

Aircraft Mechanics and Engine Specialists

Career Guides

★3736★ "Aircraft Mechanic" in *Career Information Center* (Vol.12)
Simon and Schuster
200 Old Tappan Rd.
Old Tappan, NJ 07675
Fax: 800-445-6991 Fr: 800-223-2348
Richard Lidz and Dale Anderson, editorial directors. Fifth edition, 1993. For 600 occupations, describes job duties, entry-level requirements, education and training needed, advancement possibilities, employment outlook, earnings and benefits. The set is divided into 12 volumes. Each volume includes jobs related under a broad career field. Volume 13 is the index.

★3737★ "Aircraft Mechanic" in *Careers in Aviation* (pp. 19-22)
Rosen Publishing Group
29 E. 21st St.
New York, NY 10010
Ph: (212)777-3017 Fax: (212)777-0277
Fr: 800-237-9932
Sharon Carter. 1990. Explores a wide variety of piloting jobs including aerial patrolling, corporate flying, flying for the media, law enforcement, and the airlines, helicopter ambulance flying, and stunt flying. Discusses being licensed, and opportunities for women. Most of the book is based on interviews with people who describe what they do on the job.

★3738★ "Aircraft Mechanic" in *Exploring Nontraditional Jobs for Women* (pp. 83-89)
Rosen Publishing Group
29 E. 21st St.
New York, NY 10010
Ph: (212)777-3017 Fax: (212)777-0277
Fr: 800-237-9932
Rose Neufeld. 1989. Describes blue-collar, male dominated occupations. Discusses what is done on the job, training, where to apply for jobs, tools used, salaries, and advantages and disadvantages. Relates the experiences of women who are working in the field.

★3739★ "Aircraft Mechanic" in *Jobs Rated Almanac*
World Almanac
1 International Blvd., Ste. 444
Mahwah, NJ 07495
Ph: (201)529-6900 Fax: (201)529-6901
Les Krantz. Second edition, 1992. Ranks 250 jobs by environment, salary, outlooks, physical demands, stress, security, travel opportunities, and extra perks. Includes jobs the editor feels are the most common, most interesting, and the most rapidly growing.

★3740★ "Aircraft Mechanics" in *101 Careers: A Guide to the Fastest-Growing Opportunities* (pp. 307-309)
John Wiley & Sons, Inc.
605 3rd Ave.
New York, NY 10158-0012
Ph: (212)850-6645 Fax: (212)850-6088
Michael Harkavy. 1990. Describes the nature of the job, working conditions, employment growth, qualifications, personal skills, projected salaries, and where to write for more information.

★3741★ "Aircraft Mechanics" in *Career Discovery Encyclopedia* (Vol.1, pp. 44-45)
J.G. Ferguson Publishing Co.
200 W. Madison St., Ste. 300
Chicago, IL 60606
Ph: (312)580-5480 Fax: (312)580-4948
E. Russell Primm, editor-in-chief. 1993. Contains two-page articles on 504 occupations. Each article describes job duties, earnings, and educational and training requirements.

★3742★ "Aircraft Mechanics and Engine Specialists" in *Encyclopedia of Careers and Vocational Guidance* (Vol.2, pp. 71-74)
J.G. Ferguson Publishing Co.
200 W. Madison St., Ste. 300
Chicago, IL 60606
Ph: (312)580-5480 Fax: (312)580-4948
William E. Hopke, editor-in-chief. Ninth edition, 1993. Four-volume set that profiles 500 occupations and describes job trends in 74 industries. Includes career description, educational requirements, history of the job, methods of entry, advancement, employment outlook, earnings, working conditions, social and psychological factors, and sources of additional information.

★3743★ "Aircraft Mechanics and Engine Specialists" in *Occupational Outlook Handbook*
U.S. Government Printing Office
Superintendent of Documents
Washington, DC 20402
Ph: (202)512-1800 Fax: (202)512-2250
Biennial; latest edition, 1994-95. Encyclopedia of careers describing more than 250 occupations and comprising about 85 percent of all jobs in the economy. Occupations that require lengthy education or training are given the most attention. For each occupation, the handbook describes job duties, working conditions, training, educational preparation, personal qualities, advancement possibilities, job outlook, earnings, and sources of additional information.

★3744★ "Aircraft Mechanics" in *Jobs! What They Are—Where They Are—What They Pay* (pp. 210)
Simon & Schuster, Inc.
Simon & Schuster Bldg.
1230 Avenue of the Americas
New York, NY 10020
Ph: (212)698-7000
Robert O. Snelling and Anne M. Snelling. 3rd edition, 1992. Profiles 241 occupations, describing duties and responsibilities, educational preparation, earnings, employment opportunities, training, and qualifications.

★3745★ "Aircraft Mechanics" in *Opportunities in Travel Careers* (pp. 37-39)
National Textbook Co. (NTC)
VGM Career Books
4255 W. Touhy Ave.
Lincolnwood, IL 60646-1975
Ph: (708)679-5500 Fax: (708)679-2494
Fr: 800-323-4900
Robert Scott Milne. 1991. Explores job opportunities in many travel related fields including the airlines, resorts, travel agencies, recreation, and tourism. Covers the work, salaries, educational preparation and training, and advancement possibilities.

★3746★ *Aircraft Technician*
Careers, Inc.
PO Box 135
Largo, FL 34649-0135
Ph: (813)584-7333

1994. Four-page brief offering the definition, history, duties, working conditions, personal qualifications, educational requirements, earnings, hours, employment outlook, advancement, and careers related to this position.

★3747★ "Aircraft Technician" in *Occu-Facts: Information on 580 Careers in Outline Form*
Careers, Inc.
PO Box 135
Largo, FL 34649-0135
Ph: (813)584-7333

Biennial, 1995-96 edition. Each one-page occupational profile describes duties, working conditions, physical surroundings and demands, aptitudes, temperament, educational requirements, employment outlook, earnings, and places of employment.

★3748★ *Aircraft Technicians*
Chronicle Guidance Publications, Inc.
66 Aurora St.
PO Box 1190
Moravia, NY 13118-1190
Ph: (315)497-0330 Fax: (315)497-3359
Fr: 800-622-7284

1993. This career brief describes the nature of the work, working conditions, hours and earnings, education and training, licensure, certification, unions, personal qualifications, social and psychological factors, employment outlook, entry methods, advancement, and related occupations.

★3749★ "The Airline Mechanic" in *Opportunities in Airline Careers* (pp. 101-105)
National Textbook Co. (NTC)
VGM Career Books
4255 W. Touhy Ave.
Lincolnwood, IL 60646-1975
Ph: (708)679-5500 Fax: (708)679-2494
Fr: 800-323-4900

Adrian A. Paradis. 1987. Surveys trends in the industry and career opportunities with the airlines including management, sales, customer service, flying, and maintenance. Describes pilots' job duties, working conditions, and basic educational and training requirements.

★3750★ "Airplane Mechanic" in *VGM's Careers Encyclopedia* (pp. 32-34)
National Textbook Co. (NTC)
VGM Career Books
4255 W. Touhy Ave.
Lincolnwood, IL 60646-1975
Ph: (708)679-5500 Fax: (708)679-2494
Fr: 800-323-4900

Third edition, 1991. Contains two- to five-page descriptions of 200 managerial, professional, technical, trade, and service occupations. Each profile includes job duties, places of employment, qualifications, educational preparation, training, employment potential, advancement, income, and additional sources of information.

★3751★ "Airplane Mechanics" in *American Almanac of Jobs and Salaries* (pp. 394)
Avon Books
1350 Avenue of the Americas
New York, NY 10019
Ph: (212)261-6800 Fr: 800-238-0658

John Wright, editor. Revised and updated, 1994-95. A comprehensive guide to the wages of hundreds of occupations in a wide variety of industries and organizations.

★3752★ "Aviation Maintenance" in *Complete Aviation/Aerospace Career Guide* (pp. 165-169)
Aero Publishers, Inc.
13311 Monterey Ave.
Blue Ridge Summit, PA 17294
Ph: (717)794-2191 Fax: (717)794-2080

Robert Calderone. 1989. This is a comprehensive guide to hundreds of aviation related jobs. Provides job description, training requirements, advancement opportunities and employment outlook.

★3753★ "Aviation Maintenance Technology" in *Career Connection II: A Guide to Technical Majors and Their Related Careers* (pp. 26-27)
Jist Works, Inc.
720 N. Park Ave.
Indianapolis, IN 46202-3431
Ph: (317)264-3720 Fax: (317)264-3709

Fred A. Rowe. 1994. Contains technical majors, such as automotive technology. Describes the major and the job. Lists high school and postsecondary school courses. Includes occupations related to the major, employment outlook, and starting salary.

★3754★ *Career Success Series*
Cambridge Educational
PO Box 2153
Charleston, WV 25328-2153
Ph: (304)744-9323 Fax: (304)744-9351
Fr: 800-468-4227

Videocassette. 1986. 15 mins. A series, available separately, outlining various career choices for students. Occupations include: accounting, flight service, air transportation/ground/flight service, data processing, carpentry, clerk in banking/insurance, commodity sales, cosmetic personal grooming, fire fighting, forestry services, home economics, insulation/roofing, material handling, mechanics, photographic processing, pipefitting and plumbing, police science, printing, carpentry, medical laboratory technicians, secretarial services, and utilities equipment operator.

★3755★ *Do Your Own Thing . . . in the Mechanical Field*
AIMS Media, Inc.
9710 DeSoto Ave.
Chatsworth, CA 91311
Ph: (818)773-4300 Fax: (818)341-6700
Fr: 800-367-2467

Videocassette. 1979. 16 mins. Various job levels in the mechanical field are outlined for students.

★3756★ "Maintenance Technician" in *Opportunities in Aerospace Careers* (pp. 16-21)
National Textbook Co. (NTC)
VGM Career Books
4255 W. Touhy Ave.
Lincolnwood, IL 60646-1975
Ph: (708)679-5500 Fax: (708)679-2494
Fr: 800-323-4900

Wallace R. Maples. 1991. Surveys jobs with the airlines, airports, the government, the military, in manufacturing, and in research and development. Describes educational requirements, working conditions, salaries, employment outlook and licensure.

★3757★ *Mechanics*
Morris Video
2730 Monterey St., No. 105
Monterey Business Park
Torrance, CA 90503
Ph: (213)533-4800 Fr: 800-843-3606

Videocassette. 1984. 15 mins. Various careers in repair are examined including aircraft, motorcycle, diesel, refrigeration and heavy equipment.

★3758★ "Mechanics" in *Opportunities in Transportation Careers* (pp. 38-39)
National Textbook Co. (NTC)
VGM Career Books
4255 W. Touhy Ave.
Lincolnwood, IL 60646-1975
Ph: (708)679-5500 Fax: (708)679-2494
Fr: 800-323-4900

Adrian A. Paradis. 1988. Describes transportation and related employment in driving occupations, the airlines, merchant marine, and travel services. Covers employment outlook, educational and training requirements, wages, and the work itself, and advantages and disadvantages of transportation careers. Offers job hunting advice.

★3759★ *Video Career Library - Mechanical Fields*
Careers, Inc.
PO Box 135
Largo, FL 34649-0135
Ph: (813)584-7333

Videocassette. 1990. 22 mins. Part of the Video Career Library covering 165 occupations. Shows actual workers on the job. Includes automobile mechanics, diesel engine mechanics, aircraft engine mechanics, automobile body repairers, heavy equipment mechanics, and heating/air-conditioning/refrigeration mechanics.

★3760★ *Vocational Visions*
Center for Humanities, Inc.
Communications Park
Box 1000
Mount Kisco, NY 10549
Ph: (914)666-4100 Fax: (914)666-5319
Fr: 800-431-1242

Videocassette. 1984. 30 mins. This series of programs explains key aspects of actual training and a day in the life of a worker in the specific field mentioned on the videocassette. Occupations include: transportation/mechanics, repair, construction, business/office occupations, health, agriculture, technical/manufacturing, communications, and personal service.

★3761★ *Vocations U.S.A.*
Info-Disc Corporation
4 Professional Dr., Ste. 134
Gaithersburg, MD 20879
Ph: (301)948-2300 Fr: 800-648-6422

Videocassette. 1987. 60 mins. A disc collection outlining the requirements and methods of various career areas. Occupations include: transportation, mechanical/repair, health, agriculture, technical/manufacturing, and construction.

★3762★ *Your Career in Aviation Maintenance*
Professional Aviation Maintenance Association
500 N.W. Plaza, Ste. 809
St. Ann, MO 63074
Ph: (314)739-2580

1991. This 48-page booklet describes the work of airframe and powerplant technicians. Covers eligibility, experience, and knowledge requirements and offers advice for selecting a school. Lists schools nationwide and includes accreditation, programs offered, length of the course of study, and admissions requirements.

Associations

★3763★ **Aviation Maintenance Foundation International (AMFI)**
PO Box 2826
Redmond, WA 98073
Ph: (206)827-2295 Fax: (206)827-2320

Members: Trade association consisting of licensed aircraft mechanics, students, and schools as well as companies involved in the aviation maintenance industry. **Purpose:** To promote and improve the industry through education and research. Conducts surveys and market studies. Appoints professional aviation maintenance delegates to foreign countries. Sponsors competitions. Conducts seminars; maintains speakers' bureau and placement service; compiles statistics. Operates charitable program; compiles statistics. **Publications:** *AMFI Industry News*, bimonthly. • *Industry Report*, annual. • *Job Opportunities Listing*, monthly. • *Samolyot*, quarterly.

★3764★ **Future Aviation Professional of America**
4959 Massachusetts Blvd.
Atlanta, GA 30337
Ph: (404)997-8097 Fax: (404)997-8111

Members: Commercial pilots, flight attendants, aviation maintenance personnel, and persons aspiring to careers in those areas. **Purpose:** To channel career information to aviation personnel and those seeking careers in aviation. Conducts bimonthly seminar and job fair.

★3765★ **Professional Aviation Maintenance Association (PAMA)**
500 Northwest Plz., Ste. 1016
St. Ann, MO 63074-2209
Ph: (314)739-2580 Fax: (314)739-2039

Members: General aviation airframe and powerplant (A & P) technicians and aviation industry-related companies. **Purpose:** Strives to increase the professionalism of the individual aviation technician through greater technical knowledge and better understanding of safety requirements. Establishes communication among technicians throughout the country. Fosters and improves methods, skills, learning, and achievement in the aviation maintenance field. Maintains job referral assistance program. **Publications:** *Membership Directory and Information Guide*, annual. • *PAMA News Magazine*, 10/year. • *Your Career in Aviation Maintenance.*

Awards, Scholarships, Grants, and Fellowships

★3766★ **Helicopter Maintenance Award**
Helicopter Association International
1619 Duke St.
Alexandria, VA 22314-3406
Ph: (703)683-4646 Fax: (703)683-4745

To recognize a distinguished contribution to aviation safety through good practice in the field of helicopter maintenance or through significant innovation. Individuals employed by a regular or associate class C member in good standing of the Association are eligible. An engraved plaque commemorating the individual's achievement is awarded annually. Established in 1973.

Basic Reference Guides and Handbooks

★3767★ *Aircraft Cabin Cleaning & Refurbishing Operations*
National Fire Protection Association
1 Batterymarch Park
Quincy, MA 02269-9101
Ph: (617)770-3000

1994. Part of Four Hundred Series.

★3768★ *Aircraft Cleaning, Painting & Paint Removal*
National Fire Protection Association
1 Batterymarch Park
Quincy, MA 02269-9101
Ph: (617)770-3000

1989. Part of Four Hundred Series.

★3769★ *Aircraft Fuel System Maintenance*
National Fire Protection Association
1 Batterymarch Park
Quincy, MA 02269-9101
Ph: (617)770-3000

★3770★ *Aircraft Maintenance & Repair*
McGraw-Hill Publishing Co.
1221 Avenue of the Americas
New York, NY 10020
Ph: (212)512-2000

F. Delp. Fifth edition, 1987.

★3771★ *Aircraft Mechanics Digest*
Palomar Books
PO Box 915
Marquette, MI 49855
Ph: (906)346-6781

Larry Reithmaier, editor. 1982.

★3772★ *Aircraft Mechanic's Shop Manual*
Palomar Books
PO Box 915
Marquette, MI 49855
Ph: (906)346-6781

Larry Reithmaier. New edition, 1979.

★3773★ *Aircraft Repair Manual*
Palomar Books
PO Box 915
Marquette, MI 49855
Ph: (906)346-6781

Larry Reithmaier, editor. 1981.

★3774★ *Aviation Maintenance Management*
Southern Illinois University, Carbondale
Southern Illinois University Press
PO Box 3697
Carbondale, IL 62902-3697
Ph: (618)453-2281 Fax: (618)453-1221

Frank King. 1968. Part of Aviation Management Series.

★3775★ *Lightplane Refurbishing Techniques*
TAB/McGraw-Hill, Inc.
PO Box 182607
Columbus, OH 43218-2607
Fax: (614)759-3644 Fr: 800-822-8158

Joe Christy. 1986.

★3776★ *Make Your Airplane Last Forever*
TAB/McGraw-Hill, Inc.
PO Box 182607
Columbus, OH 43218-2607
Fax: (614)759-3644 Fr: 800-822-8158

Nicholas E. Silitch. 1982.

★3777★ *The Official Airline Career Handbook*
Market Plus Inc.
PO Box 2255
Silverthorne, CO 80498

Ron Hooson. 25th edition, 1995. Offers job descriptions and requirements, salaries information, and application and interview procedures. Also provides a list of national, regional, and charter airlines.

Periodicals

★3778★ *Air Line Pilot*
Air Line Pilots Assn.
535 Herndon Pkwy.
PO Box 1169
Herndon, VA 22070
Ph: (703)689-4176 Fax: (703)689-4370
Esperison Martinez

Monthly. Magazine covering industry trends and developments, flight technology, and air safety.

★3779★ *Aircraft Technician*
Johnson Hill Press, Inc.
1233 Janesville Ave.
PO Box 803
Fort Atkinson, WI 53538-0803
Ph: (414)563-6388 Fax: (414)563-1699
Greg Napert

Bimonthly. Magazine addressing the professional and technical needs of the aviation maintenance professional.

★3780★ *Airport Journal*
PO Box 273
Clarendon Hills, IL 60514
Ph: (708)318-6872 Fax: (708)986-5010
John Andrews

Monthly. Magazine serving the air transport industry in the Chicago area.

★3781★ *Airport Press*
P.A.T.I., Inc.
PO Box 879
JFK Station
Jamaica, NY 11430-0879
Ph: (718)244-6788 Fax: (718)995-3432
Fr: 800-982-5832
Albert Chioda

Monthly. Newspaper for the air transport industry.

★3782★ *Aviation Equipment Maintenance*
Phillips Business Information, Inc.
1201 Seven Locks Rd.
Potomac, MD 20854
Ph: (301)340-1520 Fax: (301)340-0542
Clifton C. Stroud

Monthly. Magazine covering aviation maintenance.

★3783★ *Aviation Mechanics Bulletin*
Flight Safety Foundation, Inc.
2200 Wilson Blvd., Ste. 500
Arlington, VA 22201-3324
Ph: (703)522-8300 Fax: (703)525-6047
Roger Rozelle

Bimonthly. Aviation magazine.

★3784★ *Business & Commercial Aviation*
4 International Dr., Ste. 260
Rye Brook, NY 10573-1065
Ph: (914)939-0300 Fax: (914)939-1184
John Olcott

Monthly. Magazine focusing on operation and maintenance of business and commercial aircraft.

★3785★ *FAA Aviation News*
DOT/FAA
AFS-810
Washington, DC 20591
Ph: (202)267-8017 Fax: (202)267-5219
Phyllis Duncan

Bimonthly. Magazine containing aviation news.

★3786★ *Membership Directory and Information Guide*
Professional Aviation Maintenance Association (PAMA)
500 Northwest Plz., Ste. 1016
St. Ann, MO 63074-2209
Ph: (314)739-2580 Fax: (314)739-2039

Annual.

★3787★ *PAMA News Magazine*
Professional Aviation Maintenance Association (PAMA)
500 Northwest Plz., Ste. 1016
St. Ann, MO 63074-2209
Ph: (314)739-2580 Fax: (314)739-2039

10/year. Covers aviation parts and maintenance and association activities. Includes list of new members and company profiles.

★3788★ *ROTOR*
Helicopter Assoc. International
1635 Prince St.
Alexandria, VA 22314
Ph: (703)683-4646 Fax: (703)683-4745
Fr: 800-435-4976
Daniel P. Warsley

Quarterly. Civil helicopter industry magazine.

★3789★ *Rotor & Wing International*
Phillips Business Information, Inc.
7811 Montrose Rd.
Potomac, MD 20854
Ph: (301)340-2100 Fax: (301)340-0542
David Jensen

Monthly. Magazine covering helicopters.

Meetings and Conventions

★3790★ AMFI Aviation Maintenance Symposium
Aviation Maintenance Foundation International (AMFI)
PO Box 2826
Redmond, WA 98073
Ph: (206)827-2295 Fax: (206)827-2320

Annual. **Dates and Locations:** 1996 Oct; Atlanta, GA.

★3791★ Annual Aviation Maintenance Symposium and Trade Show
Professional Aviation Maintenance Association (PAMA)
500 Northwest Plz., Ste. 1016
St. Ann, MO 63074-2209
Ph: (314)739-2580 Fax: (314)739-2039

Annual. **Dates and Locations:** 1996; Dallas, TX.

Other Sources of Information

★3792★ "Aircraft Technician" in *100 Best Jobs for the 1990s & Beyond*
Dearborn Financial Publishing, Inc.
520 N. Dearborn St.
Chicago, IL 60610-4354
Ph: (312)836-4400 Fax: (312)836-1021
Fr: 800-621-9621

Carol Kleiman. 1992. Describes 100 jobs ranging from accountants to veterinarians. Each job profile includes such information as education, experience, and certification needed, salaries, and job search suggestions.

★3793★ *AMFI Industry Report*
Aviation Maintenance Foundation International (AMFI)
PO Box 2826
Redmond, WA 98073
Ph: (206)827-2295 Fax: (206)827-2320

Annual.

★3794★ *AMFI Job Opportunities Listing*
Aviation Maintenance Foundation International (AMFI)
PO Box 2826
Redmond, WA 98073
Ph: (206)827-2295 Fax: (206)827-2320

Monthly. Directory of job listings for aircraft mechanics.

Automotive Body Repairers

Automotive body repairers fix motor vehicle bodies that have been damaged in accidents. Often with instructions from supervisors, automotive body repairers restore damaged metal frames and body sections to their original shape and location, and remove badly damaged sections and replace them with new ones. Body repairers also repair or replace the plastic body parts increasingly used on newer model vehicles. They routinely use special tools and machines like alignment machines and hydraulic jacks. In large shops, body repairers may specialize in one type of repair, such as frame straightening or glass installing. Most automotive body repairers work for shops that specialize in body repairs and painting. Others work for trucking companies and automobile rental companies. A few work for motor vehicle manufacturers.

Salaries

Weekly earnings for automotive body repairers are as follows:

Lowest 10 percent	$227/week
Middle 50 percent	$289-$525/week
Highest 10 percent	$757/week

Employment Outlook

Growth rate until the year 2005: Faster than average.

Automotive Body Repairers

Career Guides

★3795★ *Auto Assembly Line General Repairman*
Morris Video
2730 Monterey St., No. 105
Monterey Business Park
Torrance, CA 90503
Ph: (213)533-4800 Fax: 800-843-3606

Videocassette. 1982. 30 mins. A fifteen year employee of auto manufacturing offers his insights on the industry for those wishing to pursue such a career.

★3796★ *Auto Body Repairer*
Vocational Biographies, Inc.
PO Box 31
Sauk Centre, MN 56378-0031
Ph: (612)352-6516 Fax: (612)352-5546
Fr: 800-255-0752

1990. This pamphlet profiles a person working in the job. Includes information about job duties, working conditions, places of employment, educational preparation, labor market outlook, and salaries.

★3797★ "Auto Body Repairer" in *Career Information Center* (Vol.12)
Simon and Schuster
200 Old Tappan Rd.
Old Tappan, NJ 07675
Fax: 800-445-6991 Fr: 800-223-2348

Richard Lidz and Dale Anderson, editorial directors. Fifth edition, 1993. For 600 occupations, describes job duties, entry-level requirements, education and training needed, advancement possibilities, employment outlook, earnings and benefits. The set is divided into 12 volumes. Each volume includes jobs related under a broad career field. Volume 13 is the index.

★3798★ *Auto Shop Safety*
Bergwall Productions
540 Baltimore Pike
Chadds Ford, PA 19317
Ph: (215)388-0400 Fax: (215)388-0405
Fr: 800-645-3565

Videocassette. 1987. 10 mins. The basics of working safely in an auto shop are given. The entire series is also available as a single tape for the same cost.

★3799★ "Automobile Body Repairer" in *Jobs Rated Almanac*
World Almanac
1 International Blvd., Ste. 444
Mahwah, NJ 07495
Ph: (201)529-6900 Fax: (201)529-6901

Les Krantz. Second edition, 1992. Ranks 250 jobs by environment, salary, outlooks, physical demands, stress, security, travel opportunities, and extra perks. Includes jobs the editor feels are the most common, most interesting, and the most rapidly growing.

★3800★ "Automobile Body Repairers" in *Career Discovery Encyclopedia* (Vol.1, pp. 88-89)
J.G. Ferguson Publishing Co.
200 W. Madison St., Ste. 300
Chicago, IL 60606
Ph: (312)580-5480 Fax: (312)580-4948

E. Russell Primm, editor-in-chief. 1993. Contains two-page articles on 504 occupations. Each article describes job duties, earnings, and educational and training requirements.

★3801★ "Automobile Body Repairers" in *Opportunities in Automotive Service Careers* (pp. 25-30)
National Textbook Co. (NTC)
VGM Career Books
4255 W. Touhy Ave.
Lincolnwood, IL 60646-1975
Ph: (708)679-5500 Fax: (708)679-2494
Fr: 800-323-4900

Robert M. Weber. 1989. Describes the work of the automobile mechanic and related occupations such as service station attendant and automobile body repairer. Covers working conditions, places of employment, qualifications, training, apprenticeships, certification, advancement opportunities, employment outlook, tools needed, and earnings.

★3802★ "Automobile Repairers" in *Encyclopedia of Careers and Vocational Guidance* (Vol.2, pp. 140-144)
J.G. Ferguson Publishing Co.
200 W. Madison St., Ste. 300
Chicago, IL 60606
Ph: (312)580-5480 Fax: (312)580-4948

William E. Hopke, editor-in-chief. Ninth edition, 1993. Four-volume set that profiles 500 occupations and describes job trends in 74 industries. Includes career description, educational requirements, history of the job, methods of entry, advancement, employment outlook, earnings, working conditions, social and psychological factors, and sources of additional information.

★3803★ *Automotive Body Repairer*
Careers, Inc.
PO Box 135
Largo, FL 34649-0135
Ph: (813)584-7333

1995. Two-page occupational summary card describing duties, working conditions, personal qualifications, training, earnings and hours, employment outlook, places of employment, related careers and where to write for more information.

★3804★ "Automotive Body Repairer" in *Career Connection II: A Guide to Technical Majors and Their Related Careers* (pp. 22-23)
Jist Works, Inc.
720 N. Park Ave.
Indianapolis, IN 46202-3431
Ph: (317)264-3720 Fax: (317)264-3709

Fred A. Rowe. 1994. Contains technical majors, such as automotive technology. Describes the major and the job. Lists high school and postsecondary school courses. Includes occupations related to the major, employment outlook, and starting salary.

★3805★ "Automotive Body Repairer" in *Occu-Facts: Information on 580 Careers in Outline Form*
Careers, Inc.
PO Box 135
Largo, FL 34649-0135
Ph: (813)584-7333

Biennial, 1995-96 edition. Each one-page occupational profile describes duties, working conditions, physical surroundings and demands, aptitudes, temperament, educational requirements, employment outlook, earnings, and places of employment.

★3806★ *Automotive Body Repairers*
Chronicle Guidance Publications, Inc.
66 Aurora St.
PO Box 1190
Moravia, NY 13118-1190
Ph: (315)497-0330 Fax: (315)497-3359
Fr: 800-622-7284

1987. This career brief describes the nature of the work, working conditions, hours and earnings, education and training, licensure, certification, unions, personal qualifications, social and psychological factors, employment outlook, entry methods, advancement, and related occupations.

★3807★ "Automotive Body Repairers" in *Occupational Outlook Handbook*
U.S. Government Printing Office
Superintendent of Documents
Washington, DC 20402
Ph: (202)512-1800 Fax: (202)512-2250

Biennial; latest edition, 1994-95. Encyclopedia of careers describing more than 250 occupations and comprising about 85 percent of all jobs in the economy. Occupations that require lengthy education or training are given the most attention. For each occupation, the handbook describes job duties, working conditions, training, educational preparation, personal qualities, advancement possibilities, job outlook, earnings, and sources of additional information.

★3808★ *Automotive Painters*
Chronicle Guidance Publications, Inc.
66 Aurora St.
PO Box 1190
Moravia, NY 13118-1190
Ph: (315)497-0330 Fax: (315)497-3359
Fr: 800-622-7284

1992. Career brief describing the nature of the job, working conditions, hours and earnings, education and training, licensure, certification, unions, personal qualifications, social and psychological factors, location, employment outlook, entry methods, advancement, and related occupations.

★3809★ *Career Opportunities . . . in the Automotive Collision Repair and Refinishing Industry*
Automotive Service Association
PO Box 929
Bedford, TX 76095-0929
Ph: (817)283-6205

Booklet describing the work, training, areas of specialization, places of employment, hours, and outlook for automotive repair and refinishing specialists.

★3810★ *Opportunities in Automotive Services*
National Textbook Co. (NTC)
VGM Career Books
4255 W. Toughy Ave.
Lincolnwood, IL 60646-1975
Ph: (708)679-5500 Fax: (708)679-2494
Fr: 800-323-4900

Robert Weber.

★3811★ *Transportation*
Learning Corporation of America
108 Wilmot Rd.
Deerfield, IL 60015
Ph: (708)940-1260 Fax: (708)940-3600
Fr: 800-621-2131

Videocassette. 1982. 21 mins. In this program from the "Working" series, we meet five employees in transportation-related jobs: fishing boat captain, auto body repair shop owner, construction equipment operator, air traffic controller and truck driver.

★3812★ *Transportation/Mechanical Cluster*
Center for Humanities, Inc.
Communications Park
Box 1000
Mount Kisco, NY 10549
Ph: (914)666-4100 Fax: (914)666-5319
Fr: 800-431-1242

Videocassette. 1984. 20 mins. The key aspects of working in the fields of Auto Body Repair, Truck Driving, and Auto Mechanics are explained.

★3813★ *Video Career Library - Mechanical Fields*
Careers, Inc.
PO Box 135
Largo, FL 34649-0135
Ph: (813)584-7333

Videocassette. 1990. 22 mins. Part of the Video Career Library covering 165 occupations. Shows actual workers on the job. Includes automobile mechanics, diesel engine mechanics, aircraft engine mechanics, automobile body repairers, heavy equipment mechanics, and heating/air-conditioning/refrigeration mechanics.

★3814★ *Vocational Visions*
Center for Humanities, Inc.
Communications Park
Box 1000
Mount Kisco, NY 10549
Ph: (914)666-4100 Fax: (914)666-5319
Fr: 800-431-1242

Videocassette. 1984. 30 mins. This series of programs explains key aspects of actual training and a day in the life of a worker in the specific field mentioned on the videocassette. Occupations include: transportation/mechanics, repair, construction, business/office occupations, health, agriculture, technical/manufacturing, communications, and personal service.

★3815★ *Vocations U.S.A.*
Info-Disc Corporation
4 Professional Dr., Ste. 134
Gaithersburg, MD 20879
Ph: (301)948-2300 Fr: 800-648-6422

Videocassette. 1987. 60 mins. A disc collection outlining the requirements and methods of various career areas. Occupations include: transportation, mechanical/repair, health, agriculture, technical/manufacturing, and construction.

Associations

★3816★ Automotive Service Association (ASA)
1901 Airport Fwy., Ste. 100
PO Box 929
Bedford, TX 76095-0929
Ph: (817)283-6205 Fax: (817)685-0225
Fr: 800-272-7467

Members: Automotive service businesses including body, paint, and trim shops, engine rebuilders, radiator shops, brake and wheel alignment services, transmission shops, tune-up services, and air conditioning services; associate members are manufacturers and wholesalers of automotive parts, and the trade press. **Purpose:** Represents independent business owners and managers before private agencies and national and state legislative bodies. Promotes confidence between consumer and automotive technician, safety inspection of motor vehicles, and better highways. **Publications:** *AutoInc*, monthly. • *Collision Repair Report*, monthly. • *Mechanical News*, bimonthly. • *TransTechnical News*, monthly.

★3817★ Automotive Service Industry Association (ASIA)
25 Northwest Point
Elk Grove Village, IL 60007-1035
Ph: (708)228-1310 Fax: (708)228-1510

Members: Executives representing independent automotive wholesalers, warehouse distributors, heavy-duty vehicle and equipment parts distributors, automotive electrical service and supply wholesalers and distributors, manufacturers' representatives, and manufacturers and remanufacturers of replacement parts, tools, equipment, chemicals, refinishing materials, supplies, and accessories. Holds educational and research programs and seminars; compiles statistics. **Publications:** *Aftermarket Today*, quarterly. • *Automotive Service Industry Association—Membership Directory*, periodic. • *Automotive Service Industry Association—Product Directory*, annual. • *Automotive Service Industry Association—Survey of Profitability*, annual. • *Hotline Divisional Newsletter*, monthly. • *Washington Insights Public Affairs Newsletter*, monthly.

★3818★ Career College Association (CCA)
750 1st St. NE, Ste. 900
Washington, DC 20002
Ph: (202)336-6700 Fax: (202)336-6828

Members: Private postsecondary schools providing career education. **Purpose:** Seeks to inform members of the accreditation process and regulations affecting vocational education. Conducts workshops and institutes for staffs of member schools; provides legislative, administrative, and public relations assistance. Has established Career Training Foundation to support research into private vocational education. Sponsors research programs. Maintains hall of fame; compiles statistics. **Publications:** *Career College Times*, monthly. • *Career Education*. • *Career News Digest*. • *Classroom Companion*, quarterly. • *Directory of Private Accredited Career Colleges and Schools*, annual.

★3819★ National Association of Trade and Technical Schools
2251 Wisconsin Ave. NW
Washington, DC 20007
Ph: (202)333-1021

Members: Private schools providing career education. **Purpose:** Seeks to inform members of the accreditation process and regulations affecting vocational education. Conducts workshops and institutes for staffs of member schools; provides legislative, administrative, and public relations assistance; services as federally recognized accrediting agency. Maintains hall of fame; compiles statistics. **Publications:** *Career News Digest*, 3-4/year. • *Handbook of Trade and Technical Careers and Training.*

★3820★ National Institute for Automotive Service Excellence (ASE)
13505 Dulles Technology Dr.
Herndon, VA 22071-3415
Ph: (703)713-3800 Fax: (703)713-0727

Members: Governed by a 40-member board of directors selected from all sectors of the automotive service industry and from education, government, and consumer groups. Encourages and promotes the highest standards of automotive service in the public interest. **Purpose:** Conducts continuing research to determine the best methods for training automotive technicians; encourages the development of effective training programs. Tests and certifies the competence of automobile, medium/heavy truck, collision repair, and engine machinist technicians as well as parts specialists. **Publications:** *ASE Preparation Guide*, annual. • *ASE Test Registration Booklet*, semiannual. • *The Blue Seal*, semiannual.

Standards/Certification Agencies

★3821★ Auto Body Repairmen! Painters/Refinishers! Become a Proven Pro: Get ASE Certified
National Institute for Automotive Service Excellence
13505 Dulles Technology Dr.
Herndon, VA 22071-3415
Ph: (703)742-3800

This four-panel brochure describes the examinations for certification for automotive body repairers and painters.

★3822★ National Association of Trade and Technical Schools (NATTS)
2251 Wisconsin Ave. NW
Washington, DC 20007
Ph: (202)333-1021

Informs members of the accreditation process and regulations affecting vocational education. Conducts workshops and institutes for staffs of member schools; provides legislative, administrative, and public relations assistance; serves as a federally recognized accrediting agency.

★3823★ National Institute for Automotive Service Excellence (ASE)
13505 Dulles Technology Dr.
Herndon, VA 22071-3415
Ph: (703)713-3800 Fax: (703)713-0727

Encourages and promotes the highest standards of automotive service in the public interest. Tests and certifies the competence of automobile, medium/heavy truck, collision repair, and engine machinist technicians as well as parts specialists.

Test Guides

★3824★ ASE Test Registration Booklet
National Institute for Automotive Service Excellence (ASE)
13505 Dulles Technology Dr.
Herndon, VA 22071-3415
Ph: (703)742-3800

Semiannual. Registration for technicians who wish to become ASE certified. Provides registration information and sample questions.

★3825★ ASE Training Guide
National Institute for Automotive Service Excellence (ASE)
13505 Dulles Technology Dr.
Herndon, VA 22071-3415
Ph: (703)742-3800

Annual. Bibliographic listing of training materials available for upgrading technicians' skills in automotive repair, including sample ASE test questions and test specifications.

★3826★ Auto Body Repair
National Learning Corp.
212 Michael Dr.
Syosset, NY 11791
Ph: (516)921-8888 Fax: (516)921-8743
Fr: 800-645-6337

Jack Rudman. Part of Occupational Competency Examination Series.

★3827★ Career Examination Series: Auto Body Repairmen
National Learning Corp.
212 Michael Dr.
Syosset, NY 11791
Ph: (516)921-8888 Fax: (516)921-8743
Fr: 800-645-6337

Jack Rudman. All examination guides in this series contain questions with answers.

★3828★ Career Examination Series: Body Repair Inspector
National Learning Corp.
212 Michael Dr.
Syosset, NY 11791
Ph: (516)921-8888 Fax: (516)921-8743
Fr: 800-645-6337

Jack Rudman. All examination guides in this series contain questions with answers.

★3829★ Career Examination Series: Senior Automotive Serviceman
National Learning Corp.
212 Michael Dr.
Syosset, NY 11791
Ph: (516)921-8888 Fax: (516)921-8743
Fr: 800-645-6337

Jack Rudman. All examination guides in this series contain questions with answers.

★3830★ The Official ASE Preparation Guide to ASE Automobile and Body/Paint Tests
National Institute for Automotive Service Excellence
13505 Dulles Technology Dr.
Herndon, VA 22071-3415
Ph: (703)742-3800

Describes the certification process for automobile mechanics and auto body repairers. Offers tips on preparing for the test. Contains sample test questions.

Educational Directories and Programs

★3831★ Automotive Service Industry Association—Product Directory
Automotive Service Industry Association (ASIA)
25 Northwest Point
Elk Grove Village, IL 60007-1035
Ph: (708)228-1310 Fax: (708)228-1510

Annual.

★3832★ Career Guidance Handouts
National Association of Trade and Technical Schools
NATTS
2251 Wisconsin Ave. NW
Washington, DC 20007
Ph: (202)333-1021

★3833★ Career Training
National Association of Trade and Technical Schools (NATTS)
2251 Wisconsin Ave. NW
Washington, DC 20007
Ph: (202)333-1021

Quarterly.

★3834★ Classroom Companion
National Association of Trade and Technical Schools (NATTS)
2251 Wisconsin Ave. NW
Washington, DC 20007
Ph: (202)333-1021

Quarterly.

★3835★ Directory of Certified Aftermarket Body Parts
Certified Automotive Parts Association (CAPA)
1518 K St. NW, Ste. 302
Washington, DC 20005
Ph: (202)737-2212 Fax: (202)737-2214
Jack Gillis, Contact

Three times a year. Covers a listing of approximately 1,100 aftermarket automotive body parts which meet CAPA certification standards and the distributors which sell the parts. Entries include: Part name, manufacturer name, address, phone, fax, description. Arrangement: Parts classified by vehicle make and model.

Basic Reference Guides and Handbooks

★3836★ *Advances in Exterior Body Panels*
Society of Automotive Engineers
400 Commonwealth Dr.
Warrendale, PA 15096-0001
Ph: (412)776-4841
1987.

★3837★ *Advances & Trends in Automotive Sheet Steel Stamping*
Society of Automotive Engineers, Inc.
400 Commonwealth Dr.
Warrendale, PA 15096-0001
Ph: (412)776-4841
1988.

★3838★ *Auto Body Repairing & Repainting*
Goodheart-Willcox Company
123 Taft Dr.
South Holland, IL 60473
Ph: (708)333-7200 Fax: (708)331-9130
Bill Toboldt. Revised edition, 1982.

★3839★ *Autobody Refinishing Handbook*
Prentice Hall
Rte 9W
Englewood Cliffs, NJ 07632
Ph: (201)592-2000
Andre G. Deroche. 1988.

★3840★ *Autobody Repair & Refinishing*
Prentice Hall
Rte 9W
Englewood Cliffs, NJ 07632
Ph: (201)592-2000
Robert P. Schmidt. 1981.

★3841★ *Automotive Chassis & Body*
McGraw-Hill Publishing Company
1221 Avenue of the Americas
New York, NY 10020
Ph: (212)512-2000
William H. Crouse. Fifth edition, 1975. Part of Automotive Technology Series.

★3842★ *Automotive Exterior Body Panels*
Society of Automotive Engineers, Inc.
400 Commonwealth Dr.
Warrendale, PA 15096-0001
Ph: (412)776-4841
1988.

★3843★ *Collision Repair Guide*
McGraw-Hill Publishing Company
1221 Avenue of the Americas
New York, NY 10020
Ph: (212)512-2000
Robert C. MacPherson. 1971.

★3844★ *The Complete Guide to Automotive Refinishing*
Prentice Hall
Rte 9W
Englewood Cliffs, NJ 07632
Ph: (201)592-2000
Harry T. Chudy. Second edition, 1988.

★3845★ *Exterior Body Panel Developments*
Society of Automotive Engineers, Inc.
400 Commonwealth Dr.
Warrendale, PA 15096-0001
Ph: (412)776-4841
1985.

★3846★ *Fixing Cars*
Rose Pubishing Co.
1148 Holly St.
Alameda, CA 94501
Ph: (415)523-5913
Rick Greenspan. 1974.

★3847★ *Handbook of Trade and Technical Careers and Training*
National Association of Trade and Technical Schools (NATTS)
2251 Wisconsin Ave. NW
Washington, DC 20007
Ph: (202)333-1021

★3848★ *How to Restore Wooden Body Framing*
Motorbooks International Publishers & Wholesalers, Inc.
729 Prospect Ave., Box 2
Osceola, WI 54020
Ph: (715)294-3345
A. Alderwyck. 1984. Part of Osprey Restoration Guide Series.

★3849★ *New Polymer Technology for Auto Body Exteriors*
American Institute of Chemical Engineers
345 E. 47th St.
New York, NY 10017
Ph: (212)705-7338 Fax: (212)752-3294
W. R. Schmeal, editor. 1988. Part of AIChE Symposium Series.

★3850★ *Structural Design & Crashworthiness of Automobiles*
Springer-Verlag New York, Inc.
175 5th Ave., 19th Fl.
New York, NY 10010
Ph: (212)460-1500
T. K. Murthy, editor. 1987.

★3851★ *Total Auto Body Repair*
Macmillan Publishing Company, Inc.
866 3rd Ave.
New York, NY 10022
Ph: (212)702-2000
L. C. Rhone. 1985.

★3852★ *Vehicle Body Building One*
State Mutual Book & Periodical Service, Ltd.
521 5th Ave., 17th Fl.
New York, NY 10175
Ph: (212)682-5844
1989.

★3853★ *Vehicle Body Building Two*
State Mutual Book & Periodical Service, Ltd.
521 5th Ave., 17th Fl.
New York, NY 10175
Ph: (212)682-5844
1989.

Periodicals

★3854★ *Aftermarket Today*
Automotive Service Industry Association (ASIA)
25 Northwest Point
Elk Grove Village, IL 60007-1035
Ph: (708)228-1310 Fax: (708)228-1510
Quarterly.

★3855★ *ASE Preparation Guide*
National Institute for Automotive Service Excellence (ASE)
13505 Dulles Technology Dr.
Herndon, VA 22071-3415
Ph: (703)713-3800 Fax: (703)713-0727
Annual. Bibliographic listing of training materials for upgrading technicians' skills in automotive repair; sample test questions; and task lists.

★3856★ *Auto and Flat Glass Journal*
Grawine Publications
PO Box 12099
Seattle, WA 98102-0099
Ph: (206)322-5120
Burton Winters
Monthly.

★3857★ *Auto Inc.*
Automotive Service Association
PO Box 929
Bedford, TX 76021-0929
Ph: (817)283-6205 Fax: (817)685-0225
Monica Buchholz
Monthly. Carries automotive technical and management material, news of the automotive industry, information on relevant legislation, and news of the Automotive Service Association.

★3858★ *The Auto Index*
7 Clinton Pl.
Suffern, NY 10901
Ph: (914)357-3695
Bimonthly. Magazine providing a general purpose index to 14 automotive periodicals.

★3859★ *Auto and Truck International*
Johnston International Publishing Corp.
25 Northwest Point Blvd., Ste. 800
Elk Grove Village, IL 60007
Ph: (708)427-2089 Fax: (708)427-2013
Gary L. Hynes
Bimonthly. International magazine of auto service and repairs. Printed in English and Spanish; published quarterly in Arabic.

★3860★ *AutoGlass*
National Glass Association
8200 Greensboro Dr., No. 302
Mc Lean, VA 22102
Ph: (703)442-4890 Fax: (703)442-0630
Nicole HarrisPublisher

Bimonthly. Trade publication for auto glass manufacturers, distributors, and installers.

★3861★ *AutoInc*
Automotive Service Association (ASA)
1901 Airport Fwy., Ste. 100
PO Box 929
Bedford, TX 76095-0929
Ph: (817)283-6205 Fax: (817)685-0225
Fr: 800-272-7467

Monthly. Covers technical and management information of interest to members; contains shop profiles, legislative news, and industry events.

★3862★ *Automotive Body Repair News*
Capital Cities/ABC/Chilton Co.
Chilton Way
Radnor, PA 19087
Ph: (215)964-4000 Fax: (215)964-4647
Tony Molla

Monthly. Magazine reporting automotive repair industry news.

★3863★ *The Automotive Messenger*
Hansen Publishing, Inc.
427 Chez Paree
Hazelwood, MO 63042
Ph: (314)831-4000 Fax: (314)831-3610
B. Hank HansenPublisher

Monthly. Automotive magazine (tabloid).

★3864★ *Automotive Service Industry Association—Membership Directory*
Automotive Service Industry Association (ASIA)
25 Northwest Point
Elk Grove Village, IL 60007-1035
Ph: (708)228-1310 Fax: (708)228-1510

Periodic.

★3865★ *Automotive Service Industry Association—Survey of Profitability*
Automotive Service Industry Association (ASIA)
25 Northwest Point
Elk Grove Village, IL 60007-1035
Ph: (708)228-1310 Fax: (708)228-1510

Annual.

★3866★ *The Blue Seal*
National Institute for Automotive Service Excellence
13505 Dulles Technology Dr.
Herndon, VA 22071
Ph: (703)713-3800 Fax: (703)713-0727
Martin Lawson

Semiannual. Covers news of the Institute's efforts to certify auto, medium/heavy truck, engine machinists, collision repair technicians, and parts specialists. Discusses industry trends, vehicle repair tips, and training information, and highlights activities of ASE-certified technicians.

★3867★ *Career College Times*
Career College Association (CCA)
750 1st St. NE, Ste. 900
Washington, DC 20002
Ph: (202)336-6700 Fax: (202)336-6828

Monthly.

★3868★ *Collision Repair Report*
Automotive Service Association (ASA)
1901 Airport Fwy., Ste. 100
PO Box 929
Bedford, TX 76095-0929
Ph: (817)283-6205 Fax: (817)685-0225
Fr: 800-272-7467

Monthly. Speciality publication for members of the ASA Collision Division.

★3869★ *Convenient Automotive Services Retailer*
Graphics Concepts
1801 Rockville Pike, Ste. 330
Rockville, MD 20852
Ph: (301)984-4000 Fax: (301)984-7340
Louise Classon

Bimonthly. Trade magazine for professionals in the automotive services industry.

★3870★ *Gasoline and Automotive Service Dealers Association—Bulletin*
Gasoline and Automotive Service Dealers Association (GASDA)
9520 Seaview Ave.
Brooklyn, NY 11236
Ph: (718)241-1111 Fax: (718)241-1111
Stanley M. Schuer

Monthly. Reports on industry news, laws, and regulations affecting service station operators in New York. Updates Association news and provides general tips on operation. Recurring features include news of research, news of educational opportunities and Association programs, reports of meetings, and a calendar of events.

★3871★ *Hotline Divisional Newsletter*
Automotive Service Industry Association (ASIA)
25 Northwest Point
Elk Grove Village, IL 60007-1035
Ph: (708)228-1310 Fax: (708)228-1510

Monthly.

★3872★ *Import Service*
Gemini Communications
306 N. Cleveland Massillon Rd.
Akron, OH 44333
Ph: (216)666-9553 Fax: (216)666-8912
Karl Seyfert

Monthly. Magazine covering the service and repair of imported cars.

★3873★ *Mechanical News*
Automotive Service Association (ASA)
1901 Airport Fwy., Ste. 100
PO Box 929
Bedford, TX 76095-0929
Ph: (817)283-6205 Fax: (817)685-0225
Fr: 800-272-7467

Bimonthly. Speciality publication for members of the ASA Mechanical Division.

★3874★ *Motor/Age*
Capital Cities/ABC/Chilton Co.
Chilton Way
Radnor, PA 19087
Ph: (215)964-4000 Fax: (215)964-4647
Tony Molla

Monthly. Trade magazine for the automotive service industry.

★3875★ *Motor Service*
Hunter Publishing Ltd. Partnership
25 Northwest Point Blvd.
Suite 800
Elk Grove Village, IL 60007
Ph: (708)427-9512 Fax: (708)427-2079
Jim Halloran

Monthly. Magazine for auto repair shops.

★3876★ *Tech Center News*
Monday Morning Newspapers, Inc.
31201 Chicago Rd. S.
PO Box 300
Warren, MI 48093
Ph: (313)939-6800 Fax: (313)939-5850
Peter Salinas

Weekly. Newspaper (tabloid) containing automotive and business news for the business community, including General Motors Technical Center, Warren, Michigan.

★3877★ *TransTechnical News*
Automotive Service Association (ASA)
1901 Airport Fwy., Ste. 100
PO Box 929
Bedford, TX 76095-0929
Ph: (817)283-6205 Fax: (817)685-0225
Fr: 800-272-7467

Monthly. Speciality publication for members of the ASA Transmission Division.

★3878★ *Washington Insights Public Affairs Newsletter*
Automotive Service Industry Association (ASIA)
25 Northwest Point
Elk Grove Village, IL 60007-1035
Ph: (708)228-1310 Fax: (708)228-1510

Monthly.

MEETINGS AND CONVENTIONS

★3879★ Aftermarket Symposium
Automotive Service Industry Association (ASIA)
25 Northwest Point
Elk Grove Village, IL 60007-1035
Ph: (708)228-1310 Fax: (708)228-1510

Annual. Always Las Vegas, NV. **Dates and Locations:** 1995 Oct 24-27.

★3880★ Automotive Aftermarket Industry Week
Automotive Service Industry Association (ASIA)
25 Northwest Point
Elk Grove Village, IL 60007-1035
Ph: (708)228-1310 Fax: (708)228-1510

★3881★ Congress of Automotive Repair and Service Cars
Automotive Service Association (ASA)
1901 Airport Fwy., Ste. 100
PO Box 929
Bedford, TX 76095-0929
Ph: (817)283-6205 Fax: (817)685-0225
Fr: 800-272-7467

Annual.

★3882★ National Auto Body Congress and Exposition
Automotive Service Association (ASA)
1901 Airport Fwy., Ste. 100
PO Box 929
Bedford, TX 76095-0929
Ph: (817)283-6205 Fax: (817)685-0225
Fr: 800-272-7467

Annual.

Other Sources of Information

★3883★ "Automobile Body Repairer" in *Career Selector 2001*
Barron's Educational Series, Inc.
250 Wireless Blvd.
Hauppauge, NY 11788
Ph: (516)434-3311 Fax: (516)434-3723
Fr: 800-645-3476

James C. Gonyea. 1993.

★3884★ *Automotive Aerodynamics: An Update*
Society of Automotive Engineers
400 Commonwealth Dr.
Warrendale, PA 15096-0001
Ph: (412)776-4841

1987.

★3885★ *Automotive Instrument Panels: Design, Materials & Manufacturing*
Society of Automotive Engineers, Inc.
400 Commonwealth Dr.
Warrendale, PA 15096-0001
Ph: (412)776-4841

1987.

★3886★ *Computers in Design Construction & Operation of Automobiles*
Springer-Verlag New York, Inc.
175 5th Ave., 19th Fl.
New York, NY 10010
Ph: (212)460-1500

T. K. Murthy, editor. 1987.

★3887★ National Automotive Technicians Education Foundation (NATEF)
13505 Dulles Technology Dr.
Herndon, VA 22071-3415
Ph: (703)713-0100 Fax: (703)713-0727

Makes recommendations that lead to program certification by the National Institute of Automotive Service Excellence.

★3888★ *Racing & Sports Car Chassis Design*
Robert Bentley, Inc, Publishers
1000 Massachusetts Ave.
Cambridge, MA 02138
Ph: (617)547-4170 Fax: (617)876-9235

Michael Costin. 1965.

Automotive Mechanics

Automotive mechanics, often called **automotive service technicians**, repair and service automobiles and occasionally light trucks, with gasoline engines. Based on a description of the symptoms, the mechanic may test drive, or use diagnostic equipment to find the problem. Many mechanics consider the diagnostic process the most challenging and satisfying part of the job. Once the cause of the problem is found, mechanics make adjustments or repairs. If a part is worn or damaged beyond repair, or cannot be fixed at a reasonable cost, they replace it, usually after consultation with the vehicle owner. During routine service, mechanics inspect, lubricate, and adjust various components to prevent breakdowns. A variety of tools are used such as pneumatic wrenches, grinding machines, and a growing variety of electronic and computerized service equipment. In larger shops, specialization is common, including automatic transmission mechanics that work on gear trains and other transmission parts, tune-up mechanics that adjust timing mechanisms and ensure efficient engine performance, brake repairers, and many other specialists. The majority of automotive mechanics work for automotive dealers, independent repair shops, and gasoline service stations. Others are employed at automotive service facilities at department and other stores. Some maintain auto fleets for taxicab and leasing companies, government facilities, and other organizations. Motor vehicle manufacturers may also employ mechanics to make final adjustments and repairs at the end of assembly.

Salaries

Earnings for automotive mechanics:

Lowest 10 percent	$230/week
Middle 50 percent	$320-$523/week
Highest 10 percent	$746/week

Employment Outlook

Growth rate until the year 2005: Average.

Automotive Mechanics

CAREER GUIDES

★3889★ *Auto Assembly Line General Repairman*
Morris Video
2730 Monterey St., No. 105
Monterey Business Park
Torrance, CA 90503
Ph: (213)533-4800 Fax: 800-843-3606
Videocassette. 1982. 30 mins. A fifteen year employee of auto manufacturing offers his insights on the industry for those wishing to pursue such a career.

★3890★ "Auto Mechanic" in *Exploring Nontraditional Jobs for Women* (pp. 89-95)
Rosen Publishing Group
29 E. 21st St.
New York, NY 10010
Ph: (212)777-3017 Fax: (212)777-0277
Fr: 800-237-9932
Rose Neufeld. 1989. Describes blue-collar, male dominated occupations. Discusses what is done on the job, training, where to apply for jobs, tools used, salaries, and advantages and disadvantages. Relates the experiences of women who are working in the field.

★3891★ "Auto Mechanic" in *The Desk Guide to Training and Work Advisement* (p. 85)
Charles C. Thomas, Publisher
2600 S. 1st St.
Springfield, IL 62794-9265
Ph: (217)789-8980 Fax: (217)789-9130
Fr: 800-258-8980
Gail Baugher Kuenstler. 1988. Describes alternative methods of gaining entry into an occupation through different types of educational programs, internships and apprenticeships.

★3892★ *Auto Shop Safety*
Bergwall Productions
540 Baltimore Pike
Chadds Ford, PA 19317
Ph: (215)388-0400 Fax: (215)388-0405
Fr: 800-645-3565
Videocassette. 1987. 10 mins. The basics of working safely in an auto shop are given. The entire series is also available as a single tape for the same cost.

★3893★ "Automobile Mechanic" in *Jobs Rated Almanac*
World Almanac
1 International Blvd., Ste. 444
Mahwah, NJ 07495
Ph: (201)529-6900 Fax: (201)529-6901
Les Krantz. Second edition, 1992. Ranks 250 jobs by environment, salary, outlooks, physical demands, stress, security, travel opportunities, and extra perks. Includes jobs the editor feels are the most common, most interesting, and the most rapidly growing.

★3894★ "Automobile Mechanics" in *American Almanac of Jobs and Salaries* (pp. 524)
Avon Books
1350 Avenue of the Americas
New York, NY 10019
Ph: (212)261-6800 Fr: 800-238-0658
John Wright, editor. Revised and updated, 1994-95. A comprehensive guide to the wages of hundreds of occupations in a wide variety of industries and organizations.

★3895★ "Automobile Mechanics" in *Career Discovery Encyclopedia* (Vol.1, pp. 90-91)
J.G. Ferguson Publishing Co.
200 W. Madison St., Ste. 300
Chicago, IL 60606
Ph: (312)580-5480 Fax: (312)580-4948
E. Russell Primm, editor-in-chief. 1993. Contains two-page articles on 504 occupations. Each article describes job duties, earnings, and educational and training requirements.

★3896★ "Automobile Mechanics" in *Encyclopedia of Careers and Vocational Guidance* (Vol.2, pp. 135-139)
J.G. Ferguson Publishing Co.
200 W. Madison St., Ste. 300
Chicago, IL 60606
Ph: (312)580-5480 Fax: (312)580-4948
William E. Hopke, editor-in-chief. Ninth edition, 1993. Four-volume set that profiles 500 occupations and describes job trends in 74 industries. Includes career description, educational requirements, history of the job, methods of entry, advancement, employment outlook, earnings, working conditions, social and psychological factors, and sources of additional information.

★3897★ *Automobile Technicians (Mechanics)*
Chronicle Guidance Publications, Inc.
66 Aurora St.
PO Box 1190
Moravia, NY 13118-1190
Ph: (315)497-0330 Fax: (315)497-3359
Fr: 800-622-7284
1993. This career brief describes the nature of the work, working conditions, hours and earnings, education and training, licensure, certification, unions, personal qualifications, social and psychological factors, employment outlook, entry methods, advancement, and related occupations.

★3898★ *Automotive Brake Specialist*
Careers, Inc.
PO Box 135
Largo, FL 34649-0135
Ph: (813)584-7333
1992. Two-page occupational summary card describing duties, working conditions, personal qualifications, training, earnings and hours, employment outlook, places of employment, related careers and where to write for more information.

★3899★ "Automotive Brake Specialist" in *Occu-Facts: Information on 580 Careers in Outline Form*
Careers, Inc.
PO Box 135
Largo, FL 34649-0135
Ph: (813)584-7333
Biennial, 1995-96 edition. Each one-page occupational profile describes duties, working conditions, physical surroundings and demands, aptitudes, temperament, educational requirements, employment outlook, earnings, and places of employment.

★3900★ "Automotive Cooling System Technicians" in *Encyclopedia of Careers and Vocational Guidance* (Vol.2, pp. 148-152)
J.G. Ferguson Publishing Co.
200 W. Madison St., Ste. 300
Chicago, IL 60606
Ph: (312)580-5480 Fax: (312)580-4948
William E. Hopke, editor-in-chief. Ninth edition, 1993. Four-volume set that profiles 500

occupations and describes job trends in 74 industries. Includes career description, educational requirements, history of the job, methods of entry, advancement, employment outlook, earnings, working conditions, social and psychological factors, and sources of additional information.

★3901★ "Automotive Engine Technicians" in *Career Discovery Encyclopedia* (Vol.1, pp. 94-95)
J.G. Ferguson Publishing Co.
200 W. Madison St., Ste. 300
Chicago, IL 60606
Ph: (312)580-5480 Fax: (312)580-4948
E. Russell Primm, editor-in-chief. 1993. Contains two-page articles on 504 occupations. Each article describes job duties, earnings, and educational and training requirements.

★3902★ *Automotive Mechanic*
Careers, Inc.
PO Box 135
Largo, FL 34649-0135
Ph: (813)584-7333
1993. Four-page brief offering the definition, history, duties, working conditions, personal qualifications, educational requirements, earnings, hours, employment outlook, advancement possibilities, and related occupations.

★3903★ "Automotive Mechanic" in *Career Information Center* (Vol.12)
Simon and Schuster
200 Old Tappan Rd.
Old Tappan, NJ 07675
Fax: 800-445-6991 Fr: 800-223-2348
Richard Lidz and Dale Anderson, editorial directors. Fifth edition, 1993. For 600 occupations, describes job duties, entry-level requirements, education and training needed, advancement possibilities, employment outlook, earnings and benefits. The set is divided into 12 volumes. Each volume includes jobs related under a broad career field. Volume 13 is the index.

★3904★ "Automotive Mechanic" in *Occu-Facts: Information on 580 Careers in Outline Form*
Careers, Inc.
PO Box 135
Largo, FL 34649-0135
Ph: (813)584-7333
Biennial, 1995-96 edition. Each one-page occupational profile describes duties, working conditions, physical surroundings and demands, aptitudes, temperament, educational requirements, employment outlook, earnings, and places of employment.

★3905★ "Automotive Mechanic" in *VGM's Careers Encyclopedia* (pp. 54-56)
National Textbook Co. (NTC)
VGM Career Books
4255 W. Touhy Ave.
Lincolnwood, IL 60646-1975
Ph: (708)679-5500 Fax: (708)679-2494
Fr: 800-323-4900
Third edition, 1991. Contains two- to five-page descriptions of 200 managerial, professional, technical, trade, and service occupations. Each profile includes job duties, places of employment, qualifications, educational preparation, training, employment potential, advancement, income, and additional sources of information.

★3906★ "Automotive Mechanics" in *Jobs! What They Are—Where They Are—What They Pay* (pp. 211-212)
Simon & Schuster, Inc.
Simon & Schuster Bldg.
1230 Avenue of the Americas
New York, NY 10020
Ph: (212)698-7000
Robert O. Snelling and Anne M. Snelling. Revised edition, 1992. Profiles 241 occupations, describing duties and responsibilities, educational preparation, earnings, employment opportunities, training, and qualifications.

★3907★ "Automotive Mechanics" in *Occupational Outlook Handbook*
U.S. Government Printing Office
Superintendent of Documents
Washington, DC 20402
Ph: (202)512-1800 Fax: (202)512-2250
Biennial; latest edition, 1994-95. Encyclopedia of careers describing more than 250 occupations and comprising about 85 percent of all jobs in the economy. Occupations that require lengthy education or training are given the most attention. For each occupation, the handbook describes job duties, working conditions, training, educational preparation, personal qualities, advancement possibilities, job outlook, earnings, and sources of additional information.

★3908★ *Automotive Technician: A Challenging and Changing Career*
Automotive Service Association
PO Box 929
Bedford, TX 76095-0929
Ph: (817)283-6205
1994. This eight-page booklet describes the work, job duties, places of employment, labor market outlook, advancement prospects, training, certification, and earnings of the automotive technician.

★3909★ "Automotive Technology" in *Career Connection II: A Guide to Technical Majors and Their Related Careers* (pp. 24-25)
Jist Works, Inc.
720 N. Park Ave.
Indianapolis, IN 46202-3431
Ph: (317)264-3720 Fax: (317)264-3709
Fred A. Rowe. 1994. Contains technical majors, such as automotive technology. Describes the major and the job. Lists high school and postsecondary school courses. Includes occupations related to the major, employment outlook, and starting salary.

★3910★ "Brake Specialist" in *Opportunities in Automotive Service Careers* (p. 54)
National Textbook Co. (NTC)
VGM Career Books
4255 W. Touhy Ave.
Lincolnwood, IL 60646-1975
Ph: (708)679-5500 Fax: (708)679-2494
Fr: 800-323-4900
Robert M. Weber. 1989. Describes the work of the automobile mechanic and related occupations such as service station attendant and automobile body repairer. Covers working conditions, places of employment, qualifications, training, apprenticeships, certification, advancement opportunities, employment outlook, tools needed, and earnings.

★3911★ *Career Success Series*
Cambridge Educational
PO Box 2153
Charleston, WV 25328-2153
Ph: (304)744-9323 Fax: (304)744-9351
Fr: 800-468-4227
Videocassette. 1986. 15 mins. A series, available separately, outlining various career choices for students. Occupations include: accounting, flight service, air transportation/ground/flight service, data processing, carpentry, clerk in banking/insurance, commodity sales, cosmetic personal grooming, fire fighting, forestry services, home economics, insulation/roofing, material handling, mechanics, photographic processing, pipefitting and plumbing, police science, printing, carpentry, medical laboratory technicians, secretarial services, and utilities equipment operator.

★3912★ *Certified Automotive Technician*
Vocational Biographies, Inc.
PO Box 31
Sauk Centre, MN 56378-0031
Ph: (612)352-6516 Fax: (612)352-5546
Fr: 800-255-0752
1990. This pamphlet profiles a person working in the job. Includes information about job duties, working conditions, places of employment, educational preparation, labor market outlook, and salaries.

★3913★ *Do Your Own Thing . . . in the Mechanical Field*
AIMS Media, Inc.
9710 DeSoto Ave.
Chatsworth, CA 91311
Ph: (818)773-4300 Fax: (818)341-6700
Fr: 800-367-2467
Videocassette. 1979. 16 mins. Various job levels in the mechanical field are outlined for students.

★3914★ "Mechanic" in *Guide to Careers Without College* (pp. 92-95)
Franklin Watts, Inc.
387 Park Avenue, S.
New York, NY 10016
Ph: (212)686-7070
Kathleen S. Abrams. 1988. Discusses careers that do not require a college degree in fields such as health care, sales and marketing, and the building trades. Describes the work, employment opportunities, and training.

★3915★ "Motor Vehicle Mechanic" in *BLR Encyclopedia of Prewritten Job Descriptions*
Business and Legal Reports, Inc.
39 Academy St.
Madison, CT 06443-1513
Ph: (203)245-7448
Stephen D. Bruce, editor-in-chief. 1994. This book contains hundreds of sample job descriptions arranged by functional job category. The 1-3 page job descriptions cover what the worker normally does in the position, who they report to, and how that position fits in the organizational structure.

★3916★ *Opportunities in Automotive Services*
National Textbook Co. (NTC)
VGM Career Books
4255 W. Toughy Ave.
Lincolnwood, IL 60646-1975
Ph: (708)679-5500 Fax: (708)679-2494
Fr: 800-323-4900

Robert Weber.

★3917★ *Rewarding Careers in the Automotive Service Industry*
Motor Vehicle Manufacturers Association of the United States, Inc.
7430 Second Ave., Ste. 300
Detroit, MI 48202
Ph: (313)872-4311

1990. This 12-page booklet describes the demand for, work, earnings, and training of automotive mechanics.

★3918★ *Transportation/Mechanical Cluster*
Center for Humanities, Inc.
Communications Park
Box 1000
Mount Kisco, NY 10549
Ph: (914)666-4100 Fax: (914)666-5319
Fr: 800-431-1242

Videocassette. 1984. 20 mins. The key aspects of working in the fields of Auto Body Repair, Truck Driving, and Auto Mechanics are explained.

★3919★ *Video Career Library - Mechanical Fields*
Careers, Inc.
PO Box 135
Largo, FL 34649-0135
Ph: (813)584-7333

Videocassette. 1990. 22 mins. Part of the Video Career Library covering 165 occupations. Shows actual workers on the job. Includes automobile mechanics, diesel engine mechanics, aircraft engine mechanics, automobile body repairers, heavy equipment mechanics, and heating/air-conditioning/refrigeration mechanics.

★3920★ *Vocational Visions*
Center for Humanities, Inc.
Communications Park
Box 1000
Mount Kisco, NY 10549
Ph: (914)666-4100 Fax: (914)666-5319
Fr: 800-431-1242

Videocassette. 1984. 30 mins. This series of programs explains key aspects of actual training and a day in the life of a worker in the specific field mentioned on the videocassette. Occupations include: transportation/mechanics, repair, construction, business/office occupations, health, agriculture, technical/manufacturing, communications, and personal service.

★3921★ *Vocations U.S.A.*
Info-Disc Corporation
4 Professional Dr., Ste. 134
Gaithersburg, MD 20879
Ph: (301)948-2300 Fr: 800-648-6422

Videocassette. 1987. 60 mins. A disc collection outlining the requirements and methods of various career areas. Occupations include: transportation, mechanical/repair, health, agriculture, technical/manufacturing, and construction.

ASSOCIATIONS

★3922★ Automotive Service Association (ASA)
1901 Airport Fwy., Ste. 100
PO Box 929
Bedford, TX 76095-0929
Ph: (817)283-6205 Fax: (817)685-0225
Fr: 800-272-7467

Members: Automotive service businesses including body, paint, and trim shops, engine rebuilders, radiator shops, brake and wheel alignment services, transmission shops, tune-up services, and air conditioning services; associate members are manufacturers and wholesalers of automotive parts, and the trade press. **Purpose:** Represents independent business owners and managers before private agencies and national and state legislative bodies. Promotes confidence between consumer and automotive technician, safety inspection of motor vehicles, and better highways. **Publications:** *AutoInc*, monthly. • *Collision Repair Report*, monthly. • *Mechanical News*, bimonthly. • *TransTechnical News*, monthly.

★3923★ Automotive Service Industry Association (ASIA)
25 Northwest Point
Elk Grove Village, IL 60007-1035
Ph: (708)228-1310 Fax: (708)228-1510

Members: Executives representing independent automotive wholesalers, warehouse distributors, heavy-duty vehicle and equipment parts distributors, automotive electrical service and supply wholesalers and distributors, manufacturers' representatives, and manufacturers and remanufacturers of replacement parts, tools, equipment, chemicals, refinishing materials, supplies, and accessories. Holds educational and research programs and seminars; compiles statistics. **Publications:** *Aftermarket Today*, quarterly. • *Automotive Service Industry Association—Membership Directory*, periodic. • *Automotive Service Industry Association—Product Directory*, annual. • *Automotive Service Industry Association—Survey of Profitability*, annual. • *Hotline Divisional Newsletter*, monthly. • *Washington Insights Public Affairs Newsletter*, monthly.

★3924★ Motor and Equipment Manufacturers Association (MEMA)
10 Laboratory Dr.
PO Box 13966
Research Triangle Park, NC 27709-3966
Ph: (919)549-4800 Fax: (919)549-4824

Members: Manufacturers of automotive and heavy-duty original equipment and aftermarket components, maintenance equipment, chemicals, accessories, refinishing supplies, tools, and service equipment united for research into all aspects of the automotive and heavy-duty markets. **Purpose:** Provides manufacturer-oriented services and programs including marketing consultation for the automotive industry; federal and state legal, safety, and legislative representation and consultation; personnel services; manpower development workshops; international information. Cosponsors Automotive Aftermarket Industry Week, and automotive aftermarket trade show. Maintains credit reporting service covering wholesalers, retailers, chain stores, and warehouse distributors; offers electronic order-entry, price-update, and electronic document exchange services through MEMA/Transnet and MEMA/Ansinet systems. Maintains international liaison. Administers U.S. Automotive Parts Industry Japan Office, Tokyo in conjunction with the U.S. Department of Commerce and the United States Automotive Parts Industry European Office, Brussels. Compiles statistics on automotive and heavy duty OE market and aftermarkets for use by members and as a public service. **Publications:** *Autobody Supply and Equipment Market*, biennial. • *Automotive Distributor Trends and Financial Analysis*, periodic. • *Automotive Jobbers in the U.S.A.*, biennial. • *Car Maintenance in the U.S.A.*. • *Credit and Sales Reference Directory*. • *Distributors Financial Analysis*. • *Europe Automotive Insight*, monthly. • *Foreign Vehicle Maintenance in the U.S.A.*. • *Heavy Duty Truck Maintenance in the U.S.A.*. • *International Buyer's Guide of U.S. Automotive and Heavy Duty Products*, biennial. • *Japan Automotive Insight*, monthly. • *Legislative Insight*, weekly. • *Market Analysts*, bimonthly. • *Marketing Insight*, weekly. • *Toxic Labeling Compliance Newsletter*, quarterly. • *Washington Digest*, biweekly.

★3925★ National Automotive Technicians Education Foundation (NATEF)
13505 Dulles Technology Dr.
Herndon, VA 22071-3415
Ph: (703)713-0100 Fax: (703)713-0727

Members: Encourages the development of automotive technical education and the maintenance of national standards set by the automotive industry for secondary and postsecondary educational facilities. **Purpose:** Evaluates and reviews the structure and resources of automobile, autobody and truck training programs in areas such as learning resources, student services, instruction, and facilities. Makes recommendations that lead to program certification by the National Institute of Automotive Service Excellence.

★3926★ National Institute for Automotive Service Excellence (ASE)
13505 Dulles Technology Dr.
Herndon, VA 22071-3415
Ph: (703)713-3800 Fax: (703)713-0727

Members: Governed by a 40-member board of directors selected from all sectors of the automotive service industry and from education, government, and consumer groups. Encourages and promotes the highest standards of automotive service in the public interest. **Purpose:** Conducts continuing research to determine the best methods for training automotive technicians; encourages the development of effective training programs. Tests and certifies the competence of automobile, medium/heavy truck, collision repair, and engine machinist technicians as well as parts specialists. **Publications:** *ASE Preparation Guide*, annual. • *ASE Test Reg-*

istration Booklet, semiannual. • *The Blue Seal*, semiannual.

Standards/Certification Agencies

★3927★ National Automotive Technicians Education Foundation (NATEF)
13505 Dulles Technology Dr.
Herndon, VA 22071-3415
Ph: (703)713-0100 Fax: (703)713-0727

Makes recommendations that lead to program certification by the National Institute of Automotive Service Excellence.

★3928★ National Institute for Automotive Service Excellence (ASE)
13505 Dulles Technology Dr.
Herndon, VA 22071-3415
Ph: (703)713-3800 Fax: (703)713-0727

Encourages and promotes the highest standards of automotive service in the public interest. Tests and certifies the competence of automobile, medium/heavy truck, collision repair, and engine machinist technicians as well as parts specialists.

Test Guides

★3929★ *ASE Test Registration Booklet*
National Institute for Automotive Service Excellence (ASE)
13505 Dulles Technology Dr.
Herndon, VA 22071-3415
Ph: (703)742-3800

Semiannual. Registration for technicians who wish to become ASE certified. Provides registration information and sample questions.

★3930★ *ASE Training Guide*
National Institute for Automotive Service Excellence (ASE)
13505 Dulles Technology Dr.
Herndon, VA 22071-3415
Ph: (703)742-3800

Annual. Bibliographic listing of training materials available for upgrading technicians' skills in automotive repair, including sample ASE test questions and test specifications.

★3931★ *Auto Mechanic/Automotive Serviceman*
Prentice Hall Press
Simon & Schuster Inc.
200 Old Tappan Rd.
Old Tappan, NJ 07675
Ph: 800-223-2348

Hy Hammer. Sixth edition, 1982. Preparation for the complete civil service exam for journeymen, automobile mechanics, and automotive servicemen. Contains actual past exams given for these positions.

★3932★ *Auto Mechanics*
National Learning Corp.
212 Michael Dr.
Syosset, NY 11791
Ph: (516)921-8888 Fax: (516)921-8743
Fr: 800-645-6337

Jack Rudman. 1988. Part of Dantes Series.

★3933★ *Auto Mechanics*
National Learning Corp.
212 Michael Dr.
Syosset, NY 11791
Ph: (516)921-8888 Fax: (516)921-8743
Fr: 800-645-6337

Jack Rudman. 1989. Part of Occupational Competency Examination Series.

★3934★ *Auto Mechanics*
National Learning Corp.
212 Michael Dr.
Syosset, NY 11791
Ph: (516)921-8888 Fax: (516)921-8743
Fr: 800-645-6337

Jack Rudman. Part of the Test Your Knowledge Series. Contains multiple choice questions with answers.

★3935★ *Automobile Mechanic Certification Tests*
Prentice Hall Press
Simon & Schuster Inc.
200 Old Tappan Rd.
Old Tappan, NJ 07675
Ph: 800-223-2348

David Sharp. Second edition, 1985. Provides sample tests, basic technical review, glossary of terms, and information on the certification exams and programs of the National Institute for Automotive Service Excellence (NIASE).

★3936★ *Automobile Technician Certification Tests*
Arco Pub.
201 W. 103rd St.
Indianapolis, IN 46290
Ph: 800-428-5331 Fax: 800-835-3202

1994, third edition. Provides practice tests in all certification areas.

★3937★ *Career Examination Series: Auto Engineman*
National Learning Corp.
212 Michael Dr.
Syosset, NY 11791
Ph: (516)921-8888 Fax: (516)921-8743
Fr: 800-645-6337

Jack Rudman. All examination guides in this series contain test questions with answers.

★3938★ *Career Examination Series: Auto Maintenance Coordinator*
National Learning Corp.
212 Michael Dr.
Syosset, NY 11791
Ph: (516)921-8888 Fax: (516)921-8743
Fr: 800-645-6337

Jack Rudman. All examination guides in this series contain test questions with answers.

★3939★ *Career Examination Series: Auto Mechanic*
National Learning Corp.
212 Michael Dr.
Syosset, NY 11791
Ph: (516)921-8888 Fax: (516)921-8743
Fr: 800-645-6337

Jack Rudman. All examination guides in this series contain test questions with answers.

★3940★ *Career Examination Series: Automotive Mechanic*
National Learning Corp.
212 Michael Dr.
Syosset, NY 11791
Ph: (516)921-8888 Fax: (516)921-8743
Fr: 800-645-6337

Jack Rudman. 1989. All examination guides in this series contain questions with answers.

★3941★ *Career Examination Series: Automotive Serviceman*
National Learning Corp.
212 Michael Dr.
Syosset, NY 11791
Ph: (516)921-8888 Fax: (516)921-8743
Fr: 800-645-6337

Jack Rudman. All examination guides in this series contain test questions with answers.

★3942★ *Career Examination Series: Certified General Automobile Mechanic (CGAM)*
National Learning Corp.
212 Michael Dr.
Syosset, NY 11791
Ph: (516)921-8888 Fax: (516)921-8743
Fr: 800-645-6337

Jack Rudman. All examination guides in this series contain questions with answers.

★3943★ *Career Examination Series: Foreman Auto Mechanic*
National Learning Corp.
212 Michael Dr.
Syosset, NY 11791
Ph: (516)921-8888 Fax: (516)921-8743
Fr: 800-645-6337

Jack Rudman. All examination guides in this series contain questions with answers.

★3944★ *Career Examination Series: Garageman*
National Learning Corp.
212 Michael Dr.
Syosset, NY 11791
Ph: (516)921-8888 Fax: (516)921-8743
Fr: 800-645-6337

Jack Rudman. 1989. All examination guides in this series contain questions with answers.

★3945★ *Career Examination Series: Garageman (USPS)*
National Learning Corp.
212 Michael Dr.
Syosset, NY 11791
Ph: (516)921-8888 Fax: (516)921-8743
Fr: 800-645-6337

Jack Rudman. 1989. All examination guides in this series contain questions with answers.

★3946★ *Career Examination Series: Head Automotive Mechanic*
National Learning Corp.
212 Michael Dr.
Syosset, NY 11791
Ph: (516)921-8888 Fax: (516)921-8743
Fr: 800-645-6337

Jack Rudman. All examination guides in this series contain questions with answers.

★3947★ *Career Examination Series: Senior Automotive Mechanic*
National Learning Corp.
212 Michael Dr.
Syosset, NY 11791
Ph: (516)921-8888 Fax: (516)921-8743
Fr: 800-645-6337

Jack Rudman. All examination guides in this series contain questions with answers.

★3948★ *GMC Apprentice Program Battery Tests (GMC)*
National Learning Corp.
212 Michael Dr.
Syosset, NY 11791
Ph: (516)921-8888 Fax: (516)921-8743
Fr: 800-645-6337

Jack Rudman. Part of the Admission Test Series. Books in this series provide test practice and drill for actual professional certification and licensure tests.

★3949★ *The Official ASE Preparation Guide to ASE Automobile and Body/ Paint Tests*
National Institute for Automotive Service Excellence
13505 Dulles Technology Dr.
Herndon, VA 22071-3415
Ph: (703)742-3800

1990. Describes the certification process for automobile mechanics and auto body repairers. Offers tips on preparing for the test. Contains sample test questions.

Educational Directories and Programs

★3950★ *Automotive Service Industry Association—Product Directory*
Automotive Service Industry Association (ASIA)
25 Northwest Point
Elk Grove Village, IL 60007-1035
Ph: (708)228-1310 Fax: (708)228-1510

Annual.

Basic Reference Guides and Handbooks

★3951★ *Auto Mechanics for the Complete Dummy*
Motormatics Publications
PO Box 91051
Long Beach, CA 90809
Ph: (213)434-6701

Philip R. Martin. Second edition, 1983.

★3952★ *Auto Mechanics Refresher Course*
H. M. Gousha Co.
2001 The Alameda
San Jose, CA 95126
Ph: (408)296-1060

Chek-Chart Staff.

★3953★ *Automechanics*
Prentice Hall
Rte. 9W
Englewood Cliffs, NJ 07632
Ph: (201)592-2000

Herbert E. Ellinger. Fourth edition, 1988.

★3954★ *Automechanic's Guide to Electronic Instrumentation & Microprocessor*
Prentice Hall
Rte. 9W
Englewood Cliffs, NJ 07632
Ph: (201)592-2000

Lynn S. Mosher. 1987.

★3955★ *Automechanics: Understanding the New Technology*
Prentice Hall
Rte. 9W
Englewood Cliffs, NJ 07632
Ph: (201)592-2000

Don Knowles. 1987.

★3956★ *Automotive Mechanics*
McGraw-Hill Publishing Company
1221 Avenue of the Americas
New York, NY 10020
Ph: (212)512-2000

William H. Crouse. Ninth edition, 1985.

★3957★ *Car Maintenance in the U.S.A.*
Motor and Equipment Manufacturers Association (MEMA)
10 Laboratory Dr.
PO Box 13966
Research Triangle Pk., NC 27709
Ph: (919)549-4800 Fax: (919)549-4824

★3958★ *Heavy Duty Truck Maintenance in the U.S.A.*
Motor and Equipment Manufacturers Association (MEMA)
10 Laboratory Dr.
PO Box 13966
Research Triangle Pk., NC 27709
Ph: (919)549-4800 Fax: (919)549-4824

★3959★ *Mathematics for Auto Mechanics*
Delmar Publishers, Inc.
PO Box 15015
2 Computer Dr., W.
Albany, NY 12212
Ph: (518)459-1150 Fax: (518)453-6472

T. G. Hendrix. 1978.

★3960★ *Mercruiser Stern Drive Shop Manual 1964-1987*
Clymer Publications
PO Box 120901
Overland Park, KS 66212
Ph: (913)541-6752 Fax: (913)541-6769
Fr: 800-633-6219

Kalton Lahue.

★3961★ *Motor Service—Tool & Equipment Buyers Guide Issue*
Hunter Publishing Limited Partnership
25 NW Point Blvd., Ste. 800
Elk Grove Village, IL 60007
Ph: (708)427-2018 Fax: (708)427-2018
James J. Halloran, Contact

Annual, December. Publication includes: List of companies that manufacture tools and equipment for the automotive service industry.

Periodicals

★3962★ *Aftermarket Today*
Automotive Service Industry Association (ASIA)
25 Northwest Point
Elk Grove Village, IL 60007-1035
Ph: (708)228-1310 Fax: (708)228-1510

Quarterly.

★3963★ *ASE Preparation Guide*
National Institute for Automotive Service Excellence (ASE)
13505 Dulles Technology Dr.
Herndon, VA 22071-3415
Ph: (703)713-3800 Fax: (703)713-0727

Annual. Bibliographic listing of training materials for upgrading technicians' skills in automotive repair; sample test questions; and task lists.

★3964★ *Auto Inc.*
Automotive Service Association
PO Box 929
Bedford, TX 76021-0929
Ph: (817)283-6205 Fax: (817)685-0225
Monica Buchholz

Monthly. Carries automotive technical and management material, news of the automotive industry, information on relevant legislation, and news of the Automotive Service Association.

★3965★ *The Auto Index*
7 Clinton Pl.
Suffern, NY 10901
Ph: (914)357-3695

Bimonthly. Magazine providing a general purpose index to 14 automotive periodicals.

★3966★ *Auto and Truck International*
Johnston International Publishing Corp.
25 Northwest Point Blvd., Ste. 800
Elk Grove Village, IL 60007
Ph: (708)427-2089 Fax: (708)427-2013
Gary L. Hynes

Bimonthly. International magazine of auto service and repairs. Printed in English and Spanish; published quarterly in Arabic.

★3967★ *Autobody Supply and Equipment Market*
Motor and Equipment Manufacturers Association (MEMA)
10 Laboratory Dr.
PO Box 13966
Research Triangle Park, NC 27709-3966
Ph: (919)549-4800 Fax: (919)549-4824

Biennial.

★3968★ *AutoGlass*
National Glass Association
8200 Greensboro Dr., No. 302
Mc Lean, VA 22102
Ph: (703)442-4890 Fax: (703)442-0630
Nicole HarrisPublisher

Bimonthly. Trade publication for auto glass manufacturers, distributors, and installers.

★3969★ *AutoInc*
Automotive Service Association (ASA)
1901 Airport Fwy., Ste. 100
PO Box 929
Bedford, TX 76095-0929
Ph: (817)283-6205 Fax: (817)685-0225
Fr: 800-272-7467

Monthly. Covers technical and management information of interest to members; contains shop profiles, legislative news, and industry events.

★3970★ *Automotive Distributor Trends and Financial Analysis*
Motor and Equipment Manufacturers Association (MEMA)
10 Laboratory Dr.
PO Box 13966
Research Triangle Park, NC 27709-3966
Ph: (919)549-4800 Fax: (919)549-4824

Periodic.

★3971★ *Automotive Jobbers in the U.S.A.*
Motor and Equipment Manufacturers Association (MEMA)
10 Laboratory Dr.
PO Box 13966
Research Triangle Park, NC 27709-3966
Ph: (919)549-4800 Fax: (919)549-4824

Biennial.

★3972★ *The Automotive Messenger*
Hansen Publishing, Inc.
427 Chez Paree
Hazelwood, MO 63042
Ph: (314)831-4000 Fax: (314)831-3610
B. Hank HansenPublisher

Monthly. Automotive magazine (tabloid).

★3973★ *Automotive News*
Crain Communications, Inc.
1400 Woodbridge Ave.
Detroit, MI 48207
Ph: (313)446-1600 Fax: (313)446-0383
Peter Brown, ED

Weekly. Tabloid reporting on all facets of the automotive and truck industry, as well as related businesses.

★3974★ *Automotive Service Industry Association—Membership Directory*
Automotive Service Industry Association (ASIA)
25 Northwest Point
Elk Grove Village, IL 60007-1035
Ph: (708)228-1310 Fax: (708)228-1510

Periodic.

★3975★ *Convenient Automotive Services Retailer*
Graphics Concepts
1801 Rockville Pike, Ste. 330
Rockville, MD 20852
Ph: (301)984-4000 Fax: (301)984-7340
Louise Classon

Bimonthly. Trade magazine for professionals in the automotive services industry.

★3976★ *Credit and Sales Reference Directory*
Motor and Equipment Manufacturers Association (MEMA)
10 Laboratory Dr.
PO Box 13966
Research Triangle Park, NC 27709-3966
Ph: (919)549-4800 Fax: (919)549-4824

★3977★ *Distributors Financial Analysis*
Motor and Equipment Manufacturers Association (MEMA)
10 Laboratory Dr.
PO Box 13966
Research Triangle Park, NC 27709-3966
Ph: (919)549-4800 Fax: (919)549-4824

★3978★ *Europe Automotive Insight*
Motor and Equipment Manufacturers Association (MEMA)
10 Laboratory Dr.
PO Box 13966
Research Triangle Park, NC 27709-3966
Ph: (919)549-4800 Fax: (919)549-4824

Monthly.

★3979★ *Exhaust News*
PO Box 120937
Arlington, TX 76012
Ph: (817)860-2375 Fax: (817)548-0004
Lee Cruse

Monthly. Automotive magazine.

★3980★ *Foreign Vehicle Maintenance in the U.S.A.*
Motor and Equipment Manufacturers Association (MEMA)
10 Laboratory Dr.
PO Box 13966
Research Triangle Park, NC 27709-3966
Ph: (919)549-4800 Fax: (919)549-4824

★3981★ *Gasoline and Automotive Service Dealers Association—Bulletin*
Gasoline and Automotive Service Dealers Association (GASDA)
9520 Seaview Ave.
Brooklyn, NY 11236
Ph: (718)241-1111 Fax: (718)241-1111
Stanley M. Schuer

Monthly. Reports on industry news, laws, and regulations affecting service station operators in New York. Updates Association news and provides general tips on operation. Recurring features include news of research, news of educational opportunities and Association programs, reports of meetings, and a calendar of events.

★3982★ *Import Service*
Gemini Communications
306 N. Cleveland Massillon Rd.
Akron, OH 44333
Ph: (216)666-9553 Fax: (216)666-8912
Karl Seyfert

Monthly. Magazine covering the service and repair of imported cars.

★3983★ *International Buyer's Guide of U.S. Automotive and Heavy Duty Products*
Motor and Equipment Manufacturers Association (MEMA)
10 Laboratory Dr.
PO Box 13966
Research Triangle Park, NC 27709-3966
Ph: (919)549-4800 Fax: (919)549-4824

Biennial.

★3984★ *Japan Automotive Insight*
Motor and Equipment Manufacturers Association (MEMA)
10 Laboratory Dr.
PO Box 13966
Research Triangle Park, NC 27709-3966
Ph: (919)549-4800 Fax: (919)549-4824

Monthly.

★3985★ *Legislative Insight*
Motor and Equipment Manufacturers Association (MEMA)
10 Laboratory Dr.
PO Box 13966
Research Triangle Park, NC 27709-3966
Ph: (919)549-4800 Fax: (919)549-4824

Weekly.

★3986★ *Market Analysts*
Motor and Equipment Manufacturers Association (MEMA)
10 Laboratory Dr.
PO Box 13966
Research Triangle Park, NC 27709-3966
Ph: (919)549-4800 Fax: (919)549-4824

Bimonthly.

★3987★ *Marketing Insight*
Motor and Equipment Manufacturers Association (MEMA)
10 Laboratory Dr.
PO Box 13966
Research Triangle Park, NC 27709-3966
Ph: (919)549-4800 Fax: (919)549-4824

Weekly.

★3988★ *Motor/Age*
Capital Cities/ABC/Chilton Co.
Chilton Way
Radnor, PA 19087
Ph: (215)964-4000 Fax: (215)964-4647
Tony Molla

Monthly. Trade magazine for the automotive service industry.

★3989★ *Motor Service*
Hunter Publishing Ltd. Partnership
25 Northwest Point Blvd.
Suite 800
Elk Grove Village, IL 60007
Ph: (708)427-9512 Fax: (708)427-2079
Jim Halloran

Monthly. Magazine for auto repair shops.

★3990★ *SuperAutomotive Service*
Irving-Cloud Publications Co.
417 N. Hough St.
Barrington, IL 60010-3028
Ph: (708)382-3405 Fax: (708)382-3426
Bob Weber

Monthly. Trade magazine covering the technical aspects of normal service station/tire dealership/garage repair and service operations.

★3991★ *Toxic Labeling Compliance Newsletter*
Motor and Equipment Manufacturers Association (MEMA)
10 Laboratory Dr.
PO Box 13966
Research Triangle Park, NC 27709-3966
Ph: (919)549-4800 Fax: (919)549-4824

Quarterly.

★3992★ *Undercar Digest*
M D Publications, Inc.
PO Box 2210
Springfield, MO 65801-2210
Ph: (417)866-3917 Fax: (417)866-2781
James R. Wilder

Monthly. Magazine for the undercar service and supply industry.

★3993★ *Washington Digest*
Motor and Equipment Manufacturers Association (MEMA)
10 Laboratory Dr.
PO Box 13966
Research Triangle Park, NC 27709-3966
Ph: (919)549-4800 Fax: (919)549-4824

Biweekly.

Meetings and Conventions

★3994★ **Aftermarket Symposium**
Automotive Service Industry Association (ASIA)
25 Northwest Point
Elk Grove Village, IL 60007-1035
Ph: (708)228-1310 Fax: (708)228-1510

Annual. Always Las Vegas, NV. **Dates and Locations:** 1995 Oct 24-27.

★3995★ **Automotive Engine Rebuilders Tech Show**
Automotive Engine Rebuilders Association
330 Lexington Dr.
Buffalo Grove, IL 60089
Ph: (708)541-6550 Fax: (708)541-5808

Annual.

★3996★ **Congress of Automotive Repair and Service Cars**
Automotive Service Association (ASA)
1901 Airport Fwy., Ste. 100
PO Box 929
Bedford, TX 76095-0929
Ph: (817)283-6205 Fax: (817)685-0225
Fr: 800-272-7467

Annual.

★3997★ **National Automotive Radiator Service Association Annual Trade Show and Convention**
National Automotive Radiator Service Association
PO Box 97
East Greenville, PA 18041
Ph: (215)541-4500 Fax: (215)679-4977

Annual.

Other Sources of Information

★3998★ *ASSET: Q: Where Can You . . . ?*
Ford Motor Company
Ford Parts and Service Division
Training Department
Dearborn, MI 48121
Ph: 800-392-3673

This eight-page booklet describes the ASSET work-study program to train entry-level automotive service technicians for Ford and Lincoln Mercury dealerships.

★3999★ **"Automotive Mechanic" in *100 Best Jobs for the 1990s & Beyond***
Dearborn Financial Publishing, Inc.
520 N. Dearborn St.
Chicago, IL 60610-4354
Ph: (312)836-4400 Fax: (312)836-1021
Fr: 800-621-9621

Carol Kleiman. 1992. Describes 100 jobs ranging from accountants to veterinarians. Each job profile includes such information as education, experience, and certification needed, salaries, and job search suggestions.

★4000★ *Automotive Technology Development Contractor's Coordination Meeting, 24th: Proceedings*
Society of Automotive Engineers, Inc.
400 Commonwealth Dr.
Warrendale, PA 15096-0001
Ph: (412)776-4841

1987.

★4001★ *Brakes and Clutches*
Tel-A-Train, Inc.
309 N. Market St.
PO Box 4752
Chattanooga, TN 37405
Ph: (615)266-0113 Fax: (615)267-2555
Fr: 800-251-6018

This program takes a look at the most common types of brakes and clutches, and how they are used and maintained.

★4002★ *CAP Orientation Guide*
Chryser Corporation
National C.A.P. Development Dept.
Attn.: Rich Hund
26001 Lawrence Ave.
Center Line, MI 48015-1718
Ph: (313)445-7290

1991. This eight-page guide describes the Chrysler Dealer Apprenticeship work-study program designed to train automotive technicians for Chrysler dealerships.

★4003★ *Distributors Financial Analysis*
Motor and Equipment Manufacturers Association (MEMA)
10 Laboratory Dr.
PO Box 13966
Research Triangle Pk., NC 27709
Ph: (919)549-4800 Fax: (919)549-4824

★4004★ *Do-It-Yourself Car Repairs with Norm Wynne*
Educational Video Network
1401 19th St.
Huntsville, TX 77340
Ph: (409)295-5767 Fax: (409)294-0233

Provides step-by-step methods for basic automotive repair, covering brake service, oil changes, preventative maintenance, and tune-ups.

★4005★ *Vocational Visions Career Series: Automotive Mechanic*
Cambridge Career Products
PO Box 2153, Dept. CC15
Charleston, WV 25328-2153
Fr: 800-468-4227

Video collection that includes interviews people with various occupations. Describes educational requirements, necessary skills, outlook for the future, and salary range.

Diesel Mechanics

Diesel mechanics repair and maintain diesel engines that power transportation equipment, such as heavy trucks, buses, and locomotives; construction equipment such as bulldozers, cranes, and road graders; and farm equipment such as tractors and combines. A small number work on diesel-powered automobiles. Diesel mechanics spend much time doing preventive maintenance like brake and steering system inspections. In some shops, mechanics do all kinds of repairs, while in other shops, the mechanics may specialize in one or two types of work, like transmissions or electrical systems. Diesel mechanics use a variety of tools like pneumatic wrenches, lathes and grinding machines, and a wide range of testing equipment like ohmmeters and tachometers. Over 30% of diesel mechanics work for vehicle and equipment dealers, leasing companies, and independent automotive repair shops. More than 20% are employed by local and long-distance trucking companies, and nearly 25% for buslines, public transit companies, school systems, and federal, state, and local government. The remainder maintain the fleets of trucks and other equipment of manufacturing, construction, and other companies. A relatively small number are self-employed.

Salaries

Diesel mechanics employed by trucking companies, buslines, and other firms that maintain their own vehicles have average hourly earnings of $14.10.

Employment Outlook

Growth rate until the year 2005: Average.

Diesel Mechanics

Career Guides

★4006★ *Diesel Mechanic*
Careers, Inc.
PO Box 135
Largo, FL 34649-0135
Ph: (813)584-7333

1995. Two-page occupational summary card describing duties, working conditions, personal qualifications, training, earnings and hours, employment outlook, places of employment, related careers and where to write for more information.

★4007★ **"Diesel Mechanic" in *Career Information Center* (Vol.12)**
Simon and Schuster
200 Old Tappan Rd.
Old Tappan, NJ 07675
Fax: 800-445-6991 Fr: 800-223-2348

Richard Lidz and Dale Anderson, editorial directors. Fifth edition, 1993. For 600 occupations, describes job duties, entry-level requirements, education and training needed, advancement possibilities, employment outlook, earnings and benefits. The set is divided into 12 volumes. Each volume includes jobs related under a broad career field. Volume 13 is the index.

★4008★ **"Diesel Mechanic" in *Careers in Trucking***
Rosen Publishing Group
29 E. 21st St.
New York, NY 10010
Ph: (212)777-3017 Fax: (212)777-0277
Fr: 800-237-9932

Donald D. Schauer. 1991. Describes employment in the trucking industry including driving, operations, sales, and administration. Covers qualifications, training, future outlook, and salaries. Offers career planning and job hunting advice.

★4009★ **"Diesel Mechanic" in *Jobs Rated Almanac***
World Almanac
1 International Blvd., Ste. 444
Mahwah, NJ 07495
Ph: (201)529-6900 Fax: (201)529-6901

Les Krantz. Second edition, 1992. Ranks 250 jobs by environment, salary, outlooks, physical demands, stress, security, travel opportunities, and extra perks. Includes jobs the editor feels are the most common, most interesting, and the most rapidly growing.

★4010★ **"Diesel Mechanic" in *Occu-Facts: Information on 580 Careers in Outline Form***
Careers, Inc.
PO Box 135
Largo, FL 34649-0135
Ph: (813)584-7333

Biennial, 1995-96 edition. Each one-page occupational profile describes duties, working conditions, physical surroundings and demands, aptitudes, temperament, educational requirements, employment outlook, earnings, and places of employment.

★4011★ *Diesel Mechanics*
Chronicle Guidance Publications, Inc.
66 Aurora St.
PO Box 1190
Moravia, NY 13118-1190
Ph: (315)497-0330 Fax: (315)497-3359
Fr: 800-622-7284

1990. Career brief describing the nature of the job, working conditions, hours and earnings, education and training, licensure, certification, unions, personal qualifications, social and psychological factors, location, employment outlook, entry methods, advancement, and related occupations.

★4012★ **"Diesel Mechanics" in *Career Discovery Encyclopedia* (Vol.2, pp. 100-101)**
J.G. Ferguson Publishing Co.
200 W. Madison St., Ste. 300
Chicago, IL 60606
Ph: (312)580-5480 Fax: (312)580-4948

E. Russell Primm, editor-in-chief. 1993. Contains two-page articles on 504 occupations. Each article describes job duties, earnings, and educational and training requirements.

★4013★ **"Diesel Mechanics" in *Encyclopedia of Careers and Vocational Guidance* (Vol.2, pp. 472-475)**
J.G. Ferguson Publishing Co.
200 W. Madison St., Ste. 300
Chicago, IL 60606
Ph: (312)580-5480 Fax: (312)580-4948

William E. Hopke, editor-in-chief. Ninth edition, 1993. Four-volume set that profiles 500 occupations and describes job trends in 74 industries. Includes career description, educational requirements, history of the job, methods of entry, advancement, employment outlook, earnings, working conditions, social and psychological factors, and sources of additional information.

★4014★ **"Diesel Mechanics" in *Occupational Outlook Handbook***
U.S. Government Printing Office
Superintendent of Documents
Washington, DC 20402
Ph: (202)512-1800 Fax: (202)512-2250

Biennial; latest edition, 1994-95. Encyclopedia of careers describing more than 250 occupations and comprising about 85 percent of all jobs in the economy. Occupations that require lengthy education or training are given the most attention. For each occupation, the handbook describes job duties, working conditions, training, educational preparation, personal qualities, advancement possibilities, job outlook, earnings, and sources of additional information.

★4015★ **"Diesel Technology" in *Career Connection II: A Guide to Technical Majors and Their Related Careers* (pp. 56-57)**
Jist Works, Inc.
720 N. Park Ave.
Indianapolis, IN 46202-3431
Ph: (317)264-3720 Fax: (317)264-3709

Fred A. Rowe. 1994. Contains technical majors, such as automotive technology. Describes the major and the job. Lists high school and postsecondary school courses. Includes occupations related to the major, employment outlook, and starting salary.

★4016★ *Do Your Own Thing . . . in the Mechanical Field*
AIMS Media, Inc.
9710 DeSoto Ave.
Chatsworth, CA 91311
Ph: (818)773-4300 Fax: (818)341-6700
Fr: 800-367-2467

Videocassette. 1979. 16 mins. Various job levels in the mechanical field are outlined for students.

★4017★ *Mechanics*
Morris Video
2730 Monterey St., No. 105
Monterey Business Park
Torrance, CA 90503
Ph: (213)533-4800 Fr: 800-843-3606

Videocassette. 1984. 15 mins. Various careers in repair are examined including aircraft, motorcycle, diesel, refrigeration and heavy equipment.

★4018★ *Video Career Library - Mechanical Fields*
Careers, Inc.
PO Box 135
Largo, FL 34649-0135
Ph: (813)584-7333

Videocassette. 1990. 22 mins. Part of the Video Career Library covering 165 occupations. Shows actual workers on the job. Includes automobile mechanics, diesel engine mechanics, aircraft engine mechanics, automobile body repairers, heavy equipment mechanics, and heating/air-conditioning/refrigeration mechanics.

★4019★ *Vocational Visions*
Center for Humanities, Inc.
Communications Park
Box 1000
Mount Kisco, NY 10549
Ph: (914)666-4100 Fax: (914)666-5319
Fr: 800-431-1242

Videocassette. 1984. 30 mins. This series of programs explains key aspects of actual training and a day in the life of a worker in the specific field mentioned on the videocassette. Occupations include: transportation/mechanics, repair, construction, business/office occupations, health, agriculture, technical/manufacturing, communications, and personal service.

★4020★ *Vocations U.S.A.*
Info-Disc Corporation
4 Professional Dr., Ste. 134
Gaithersburg, MD 20879
Ph: (301)948-2300 Fr: 800-648-6422

Videocassette. 1987. 60 mins. A disc collection outlining the requirements and methods of various career areas. Occupations include: transportation, mechanical/repair, health, agriculture, technical/manufacturing, and construction.

ASSOCIATIONS

★4021★ Automotive Service Association (ASA)
1901 Airport Fwy., Ste. 100
PO Box 929
Bedford, TX 76095-0929
Ph: (817)283-6205 Fax: (817)685-0225
Fr: 800-272-7467

Members: Automotive service businesses including body, paint, and trim shops, engine rebuilders, radiator shops, brake and wheel alignment services, transmission shops, tune-up services, and air conditioning services; associate members are manufacturers and wholesalers of automotive parts, and the trade press. **Purpose:** Represents independent business owners and managers before private agencies and national and state legislative bodies. Promotes confidence between consumer and automotive technician, safety inspection of motor vehicles, and better highways. **Publications:** *AutoInc*, monthly. • *Collision Repair Report*, monthly. • *Mechanical News*, bimonthly. • *TransTechnical News*, monthly.

★4022★ Automotive Service Industry Association (ASIA)
25 Northwest Point
Elk Grove Village, IL 60007-1035
Ph: (708)228-1310 Fax: (708)228-1510

Members: Executives representing independent automotive wholesalers, warehouse distributors, heavy-duty vehicle and equipment parts distributors, automotive electrical service and supply wholesalers and distributors, manufacturers' representatives, and manufacturers and remanufacturers of replacement parts, tools, equipment, chemicals, refinishing materials, supplies, and accessories. Holds educational and research programs and seminars; compiles statistics. **Publications:** *Aftermarket Today*, quarterly. • *Automotive Service Industry Association—Membership Directory*, periodic. • *Automotive Service Industry Association—Product Directory*, annual. • *Automotive Service Industry Association—Survey of Profitability*, annual. • *Hotline Divisional Newsletter*, monthly. • *Washington Insights Public Affairs Newsletter*, monthly.

★4023★ Career College Association (CCA)
750 1st St. NE, Ste. 900
Washington, DC 20002
Ph: (202)336-6700 Fax: (202)336-6828

Members: Private postsecondary schools providing career education. **Purpose:** Seeks to inform members of the accreditation process and regulations affecting vocational education. Conducts workshops and institutes for staffs of member schools; provides legislative, administrative, and public relations assistance. Has established Career Training Foundation to support research into private vocational education. Sponsors research programs. Maintains hall of fame; compiles statistics. **Publications:** *Career College Times*, monthly. • *Career Education*. • *Career News Digest*. • *Classroom Companion*, quarterly. • *Directory of Private Accredited Career Colleges and Schools*, annual.

★4024★ International Association of Machinists and Aerospace Workers (IAM)
9000 Machinists PL
Upper Marlboro, MD 20772
Ph: (301)967-4500 Fax: (301)967-4588

Members: AFL-CIO. **Publications:** *The Machinist*, monthly.

★4025★ Motor and Equipment Manufacturers Association (MEMA)
10 Laboratory Dr.
PO Box 13966
Research Triangle Park, NC 27709-3966
Ph: (919)549-4800 Fax: (919)549-4824

Members: Manufacturers of automotive and heavy-duty original equipment and aftermarket components, maintenance equipment, chemicals, accessories, refinishing supplies, tools, and service equipment united for research into all aspects of the automotive and heavy-duty markets. **Purpose:** Provides manufacturer-oriented services and programs including marketing consultation for the automotive industry; federal and state legal, safety, and legislative representation and consultation; personnel services; manpower development workshops; international information. Cosponsors Automotive Aftermarket Industry Week, and automotive aftermarket trade show. Maintains credit reporting service covering wholesalers, retailers, chain stores, and warehouse distributors; offers electronic order-entry, price-update, and electronic document exchange services through MEMA/Transnet and MEMA/Ansinet systems. Maintains international liaison. Administers U.S. Automotive Parts Industry Japan Office, Tokyo in conjunction with the U.S. Department of Commerce and the United States Automotive Parts Industry European Office, Brussels. Compiles statistics on automotive and heavy duty OE market and aftermarkets for use by members and as a public service. **Publications:** *Autobody Supply and Equipment Market*, biennial. • *Automotive Distributor Trends and Financial Analysis*, periodic. • *Automotive Jobbers in the U.S.A.*, biennial. • *Car Maintenance in the U.S.A.*. • *Credit and Sales Reference Directory*. • *Distributors Financial Analysis*. • *Europe Automotive Insight*, monthly. • *Foreign Vehicle Maintenance in the U.S.A.*. • *Heavy Duty Truck Maintenance in the U.S.A.*. • *International Buyer's Guide of U.S. Automotive and Heavy Duty Products*, biennial. • *Japan Automotive Insight*, monthly. • *Legislative Insight*, weekly. • *Market Analysts*, bimonthly. • *Marketing Insight*, weekly. • *Toxic Labeling Compliance Newsletter*, quarterly. • *Washington Digest*, biweekly.

★4026★ National Association of Trade and Technical Schools
2251 Wisconsin Ave. NW
Washington, DC 20007
Ph: (202)333-1021

Members: Private schools providing career education. **Purpose:** Seeks to inform members of the accreditation process and regulations affecting vocational education. Conducts workshops and institutes for staffs of member schools; provides legislative, administrative, and public relations assistance; services as federally recognized accrediting agency. Maintains hall of fame; compiles statistics. **Publications:** *Career News Digest*, 3-4/year. • *Handbook of Trade and Technical Careers and Training*.

★4027★ National Institute for Automotive Service Excellence (ASE)
13505 Dulles Technology Dr.
Herndon, VA 22071-3415
Ph: (703)713-3800 Fax: (703)713-0727

Members: Governed by a 40-member board of directors selected from all sectors of the automotive service industry and from education, government, and consumer groups. Encourages and promotes the highest standards of automotive service in the public interest. **Purpose:** Conducts continuing research to determine the best methods for training automotive technicians; encourages the development of effective training programs. Tests and certifies the competence of automobile, medium/heavy truck, collision repair, and engine machinist technicians as well as parts specialists. **Publications:** *ASE Preparation Guide*, annual. • *ASE Test Registration Booklet*, semiannual. • *The Blue Seal*, semiannual.

Standards/Certification Agencies

★4028★ National Association of Trade and Technical Schools (NATTS)
2251 Wisconsin Ave. NW
Washington, DC 20007
Ph: (202)333-1021

Informs members of the accreditation process and regulations affecting vocational education. Conducts workshops and institutes for staffs of member schools; provides legislative, administrative, and public relations assistance; serves as a federally recognized accrediting agency.

★4029★ National Institute for Automotive Service Excellence (ASE)
13505 Dulles Technology Dr.
Herndon, VA 22071-3415
Ph: (703)713-3800 Fax: (703)713-0727

Encourages and promotes the highest standards of automotive service in the public interest. Tests and certifies the competence of automobile, medium/heavy truck, collision repair, and engine machinist technicians as well as parts specialists.

Test Guides

★4030★ *ASE Test Registration Booklet*
National Institute for Automotive Service Excellence (ASE)
13505 Dulles Technology Dr.
Herndon, VA 22071-3415
Ph: (703)742-3800

Semiannual. Registration for technicians who wish to become ASE certified. Provides registration information and sample questions.

★4031★ *ASE Training Guide*
National Institute for Automotive Service Excellence (ASE)
13505 Dulles Technology Dr.
Herndon, VA 22071-3415
Ph: (703)742-3800

Annual. Bibliographic listing of training materials available for upgrading technicians' skills in automotive repair, including sample ASE test questions and test specifications.

★4032★ *Career Examination Series: Auto Mechanic (Diesel)*
National Learning Corp.
212 Michael Dr.
Syosset, NY 11791
Ph: (516)921-8888 Fax: (516)921-8743
Fr: 800-645-6337

Jack Rudman. All examination guides in this series contain questions with answers.

★4033★ *Diesel Engine Repair*
National Learning Corp.
212 Michael Dr.
Syosset, NY 11791
Ph: (516)921-8888 Fax: (516)921-8743
Fr: 800-645-6337

Jack Rudman. Part of Occupational Competency Examination Series (OCE).

★4034★ *Diesel Engine Repair*
National Learning Corp.
212 Michael Dr.
Syosset, NY 11791
Ph: (516)921-8888 Fax: (516)921-8743
Fr: 800-645-6337

Jack Rudman. Part of the Test Your Knowledge Series. Contains multiple choice questions with answers.

Educational Directories and Programs

★4035★ *Automotive Service Industry Association—Product Directory*
Automotive Service Industry Association (ASIA)
25 Northwest Point
Elk Grove Village, IL 60007-1035
Ph: (708)228-1310 Fax: (708)228-1510

Annual.

★4036★ *Career Guidance Handouts*
National Association of Trade and Technical Schools
NATTS
2251 Wisconsin Ave. NW
Washington, DC 20007
Ph: (202)333-1021

★4037★ *Career Training*
National Association of Trade and Technical Schools (NATTS)
2251 Wisconsin Ave. NW
Washington, DC 20007
Ph: (202)333-1021

Quarterly.

★4038★ *Classroom Companion*
National Association of Trade and Technical Schools (NATTS)
2251 Wisconsin Ave. NW
Washington, DC 20007
Ph: (202)333-1021

Quarterly.

Awards, Scholarships, Grants, and Fellowships

★4039★ Dodge Trucks Scholarships
National FFA Foundation
5632 Mt. Vernon Memorial Hwy.
PO Box 15160
Alexandria, VA 22309-0160
Ph: (703)360-3600

Qualifications: Applicants must be FFA members pursuing a degree in agricultural mechanics/diesel engines. Selection criteria: Preference will be given to those members with established financial need. Funds available: One $1,250 scholarship and nine $1,000 scholarships. Application details: Application material is available from FFA. Applicants must complete the parental analysis section. Deadline: The 1993 deadline was February 15.

Basic Reference Guides and Handbooks

★4040★ *Car Maintenance in the U.S.A.*
Motor and Equipment Manufacturers Association (MEMA)
10 Laboratory Dr.
PO Box 13966
Research Triangle Pk., NC 27709
Ph: (919)549-4800 Fax: (919)549-4824

★4041★ *Handbook of Trade and Technical Careers and Training*
National Association of Trade and Technical Schools (NATTS)
2251 Wisconsin Ave. NW
Washington, DC 20007
Ph: (202)333-1021

★4042★ *Heavy Duty Truck Maintenance in the U.S.A.*
Motor and Equipment Manufacturers Association (MEMA)
10 Laboratory Dr.
PO Box 13966
Research Triangle Pk., NC 27709
Ph: (919)549-4800 Fax: (919)549-4824

★4043★ *Troubleshooting & Repairing Diesel Engines*
TAB/McGraw-Hill, Inc.
PO Box 182607
Columbus, OH 43218-2607
Fax: (614)759-3644 Fr: 800-822-8158

Paul Dempsey. Third edition.

Periodicals

★4044★ *Aftermarket Today*
Automotive Service Industry Association (ASIA)
25 Northwest Point
Elk Grove Village, IL 60007-1035
Ph: (708)228-1310 Fax: (708)228-1510

Quarterly.

★4045★ *ASE Preparation Guide*
National Institute for Automotive Service Excellence (ASE)
13505 Dulles Technology Dr.
Herndon, VA 22071-3415
Ph: (703)713-3800 Fax: (703)713-0727

Annual. Bibliographic listing of training materials for upgrading technicians' skills in automotive repair; sample test questions; and task lists.

★4046★ *Autobody Supply and Equipment Market*
Motor and Equipment Manufacturers Association (MEMA)
10 Laboratory Dr.
PO Box 13966
Research Triangle Park, NC 27709-3966
Ph: (919)549-4800 Fax: (919)549-4824

Biennial.

★4047★ *Automotive Service Industry Association—Membership Directory*
Automotive Service Industry Association (ASIA)
25 Northwest Point
Elk Grove Village, IL 60007-1035
Ph: (708)228-1310 Fax: (708)228-1510

Periodic.

★4048★ *Career College Times*
Career College Association (CCA)
750 1st St. NE, Ste. 900
Washington, DC 20002
Ph: (202)336-6700 Fax: (202)336-6828

Monthly.

★4049★ *Diesel & Gas Turbine Worldwide*
Diesel & Gas Turbine Publications
13555 Bishop's Ct.
Brookfield, WI 53005-6286
Ph: (414)784-9177 Fax: (414)784-8133
Paul L. Johnson

Monthly. International magazine covering the design, application, and operation of diesel, natural gas, and gas turbine engine systems.

★4050★ *Diesel Progress Engines & Drives*
Diesel & Gas Turbine Publications
13555 Bishop's Ct.
Brookfield, WI 53005-6286
Ph: (414)784-9177 Fax: (414)784-8133
Michael J. Osenga

Monthly. Technical magazine covering engine-powered drive systems in mobile, stationary, and marine equipment.

Meetings and Conventions

★4051★ Association of Diesel Specialists International Convention and Exhibit
Association of Diesel Specialists
9140 Ward Pkwy.
Kansas City, MO 64114
Ph: (816)444-3500 Fax: (816)444-0330

Annual. **Dates and Locations:** 1995; Las Vegas, NV.

Other Sources of Information

★4052★ *Distributors Financial Analysis*
Motor and Equipment Manufacturers Association (MEMA)
10 Laboratory Dr.
PO Box 13966
Research Triangle Pk., NC 27709
Ph: (919)549-4800 Fax: (919)549-4824

Electronic Equipment Repairers

Electronic equipment repairers install, maintain, and repair electronic equipment used in offices, factories, homes, hospitals, aircraft, and other places. Equipment includes televisions, radar, industrial equipment controls, computerrs, telephone systems, and medical diagnosing equipment.

Salaries

The median weekly earnings of full-time electronic equipment repariers are $521.

Lowest 10 percent	$312/week or less
Middle 50 percent	$400-$629/week
Highest 10 percent	$729/week or more

Employment Outlook

Growth rate until the year 2005: Decline.

Electronic Equipment Repairers

Career Guides

★4053★ *Electronic Equipment Repair Technician*
Vocational Biographies, Inc.
PO Box 31
Sauk Centre, MN 56378-0031
Ph: (612)352-6516 Fax: (612)352-5546
Fr: 800-255-0752

1994. Four-page pamphlet containing a personal narrative about a worker's job, work likes and dislikes, career path from high school to the present. Education and training, the rewards and frustrations, and the effects of the job on the rest of the worker's life. The data file portion of this pamphlet gives a concise occupational summary, including work descriptions, working conditions, places of employment, personal characteristics, education and training, job outlook, and salary range.

★4054★ "Electronic Equipment Repairers" in *Occupational Outlook Handbook*
U.S. Government Printing Office
Superintendent of Documents
Washington, DC 20402
Ph: (202)512-1800 Fax: (202)512-2250

Biennial; latest edition, 1994-95. Encyclopedia of careers describing about 250 occupations and comprising about 85 percent of all jobs in the economy. Occupations that require lengthy education or training are given the most attention. Each occupation's profile describes what the worker does on the job, working conditions, education and training requirements, advancement possibilities, job outlook, earnings, and sources of additional information.

★4055★ "Electronics Repair" in *Career Connection for Technical Education* (pp. 64-65)
JIST Works, Inc.
720 N. Park Ave.
Indianapolis, IN 46202-3431
Ph: (317)264-3720 Fax: (317)264-3709

Fred A. Rowe. 1994, second edition. Describes in detail technical occupations. Includes information on recommended high school courses, course requirements, related careers, and a self-assessment guide.

Basic Reference Guides and Handbooks

★4056★ *Home VCR Repair Illustrated*
TAB/McGraw-Hill, Inc.
PO Box 182607
Columbus, OH 43218-2607
Fax: (614)759-3644 Fr: 800-822-8158

Richard C. Wilkins and Cheryl A. Hubbard. Guide to basic VCR maintenance and repair.

★4057★ *Maintaining and Repairing VCRs*
TAB/McGraw-Hill, Inc.
PO Box 182607
Columbus, OH 43218-2607
Fax: (614)759-3644 Fr: 800-822-8158

Robert L. Goodman. Third edition.

★4058★ *Troubleshooting & Repairing Audio & Video Cassette Players and Recorders*
TAB/McGraw-Hill, Inc.
PO Box 182607
Columbus, OH 43218-2607
Fax: (614)759-3644 Fr: 800-822-8158

Homer L. Davidson. Covers repair procedures for digital audio tapes, compact discs, stereos, and camcorders.

★4059★ *Troubleshooting and Repairing Camcorders*
TAB/McGraw-Hill, Inc.
PO Box 182607
Columbus, OH 43218-2607
Fax: (614)759-3644 Fr: 800-822-8158

Homer L. Davidson.

★4060★ *Troubleshooting and Repairing Solid-State TVs*
TAB/McGraw-Hill, Inc.
PO Box 182607
Columbus, OH 43218-2607
Fax: (614)759-3644 Fr: 800-822-8158

Homer L. Davidson. Second edition.

★4061★ *TV Repair for Beginners*
TAB/McGraw-Hill, Inc.
PO Box 182607
Columbus, OH 43218-2607
Fax: (614)759-3644 Fr: 800-822-8158

George Zwick and Homer Davidson. Describes how to repair such problems as horizontal streaking, interference, and color smears.

Periodicals

★4062★ *Electronic Servicing & Technology*
CQ Communications
76 N. Broadway
Hicksville, NY 11801
Ph: (516)681-2922 Fax: (516)681-2926
Conrad Persson

Monthly. Consumer electronics servicing magazine.

Meetings and Conventions

★4063★ ELECTRO - Electronics Show and Convention
Miller Freeman Expositions
13760 Noel Rd., Ste. 500
Dallas, TX 75240
Fax: (214)419-7938 Fr: 800-527-0207

Annual. Alternates between New York, New York and Boston, Massachusetts. **Dates and Locations:** 1996 May 07-09; Boston, MA.

★4064★ Electronic & Components Expo -International Tradeshow for the Electronics Equipment and Components Industry
Glahe International, Inc.
1700 K St., NW, Ste. 403
Washington, DC 20006-4557
Ph: (202)659-4557 Fax: (202)457-0776

Biennial.

★4065★ Electronic Distribution Show and Conference
Electronic Industry Show Corp.
222 S. Riverside Plaza, Ste. 2710
Chicago, IL 60606
Ph: (312)648-1140 Fax: (312)648-4282

Annual. Always held during April/May in Las Vegas, Nevada.

Commercial and Industrial Electronic Equipment Repairers

Commercial and industrial electronic equipment repairers, also called **industrial electronics technicians,** install and repair electronic equipment used in industrial automated equipment controls, missile control systems, radar systems, medical diagnostic equipment, transmitters, and antennas. Those who install radar, missile control and communication systems on aircrafts, ships, building, and other structures work for the Department of Defense.

Salaries

The average earnings for commercial and industrial electronic equipment repairers is $454/week.

Employment Outlook

Growth rate until the year 2005: More slowly than average.

Commercial and Industrial Electronic Equipment Repairers

Career Guides

★4066★ *Careers in the Electronics Industry*
International Society of Certified Electronics Technicians
2708 W. Berry St.
Fort Worth, TX 76109
Ph: (817)921-9101

This 16-page booklet provides an overview of the electronics industry and describes training and qualifications, employment outlook, earnings, and working conditions. Includes a state-by-state listing of electronic technician training schools.

★4067★ "Commercial and Industrial Electronic Equipment Repairers" in *Occupational Outlook Handbook*
U.S. Government Printing Office
Superintendent of Documents
Washington, DC 20402
Ph: (202)512-1800 Fax: (202)512-2250

Biennial; latest edition, 1994-95. Encyclopedia of careers describing more than 250 occupations and comprising about 85 percent of all jobs in the economy. Occupations that require lengthy education or training are given the most attention. For each occupation, the handbook describes job duties, working conditions, training, educational preparation, personal qualities, advancement possibilities, job outlook, earnings, and sources of additional information.

★4068★ *The Complete Electronics Career Guide*
TAB/McGraw-Hill, Inc.
PO Box 182607
Columbus, OH 43218-2607
Fax: (614)759-3644 Fr: 800-822-8158

Joseph A. Risse. First edition, 1989.

★4069★ *Electrical Maintenance Training Program*
NUS Training Corporation
910 Clopper Rd.
Gaithersburg, MD 20878-1399
Ph: (301)258-2500 Fax: (301)258-1295
Fr: 800-848-1717

Videocassette. 1982. 60 mins. This program is designed to improve the skills of electrical maintenance personnel currently in the field and to train new entrees into the field. Programs available as an entire series or individually.

★4070★ *The Professional Electronics Technician*
Electronics Technicians Association
602 N Jackson St.
Greencastle, IN 46135
Ph: (317)653-8262

This six-page brochure describes job duties, training, skills and aptitudes, salaries, employment outlook, and certification.

★4071★ *Tools for the Electrical Trades*
Bergwall Productions
540 Baltimore Pike
Chadds Ford, PA 19317
Ph: (215)388-0400 Fax: (215)388-0405
Fr: 800-645-3565

Videocassette. 1986. 58 mins. A look at various electronic tools; on four tapes.

★4072★ *Video Career Library - Repair Fields*
Careers, Inc.
PO Box 135
Largo, FL 34649-0135
Ph: (813)584-7333

Videocassette. 1990. 23 mins. Part of the Video Career Library covering 165 occupations. Shows actual workers on the job. Includes industrial machinery repairers, communications equipment repairers, data processing equipment repairers, home entertainment equipment repairers, office machine repairers, electrical power installers and repairers, and electrical and electronic repairers.

Associations

★4073★ Electronics Technicians Association, International (ETA-I)
602 N. Jackson
Greencastle, IN 46135
Ph: (317)653-8262 Fax: (317)653-8262

Members: Skilled electronics technicians. **Purpose:** Provides placement service; offers certification examinations for electronics technicians and satellite installers. Compiles wage and manpower statistics. **Publications:** *Directory of Professional Electronics Technicians*, annual. • *EEA Training Program*, monthly. • *Management Update*, monthly. • *Technician Association News*, monthly.

★4074★ International Society of Certified Electronics Technicians (ISCET)
2708 W. Berry, Ste. 3
Fort Worth, TX 76109
Ph: (817)921-9101 Fax: (817)921-3741

Members: Technicians in 37 countries who have been certified by the society. **Purpose:** Seeks to provide a fraternal bond among certified electronics technicians, raise their public image, and improve the effectiveness of industry education programs for technicians. Offers training programs in new electronics information. Maintains library of service literature for consumer electronic equipment, including manuals and schematics for out-of-date equipment. Offers general radiotelephone license. Sponsors testing program for certification of electronics technicians in the fields of audio, communications, computer, consumer, industrial, medical electronics, radar, radio-television, and video. Operates Hall of Fame. **Publications:** *ISCET Update*, quarterly. • *Professional Electronics Magazine*, bimonthly. • *Technical Log*, quarterly.

STANDARDS/CERTIFICATION AGENCIES

★4075★ Electronics Technicians Association, International (ETA-I)
602 N. Jackson
Greencastle, IN 46135
Ph: (317)653-8262

Offers certification examinations for electronics technicians. Maintains VCR tapes for certification practice exams.

★4076★ Federal Communications Commission
1919 M St., NW
Washington, DC 20554

Provides information on the general radiotelephone operator license, upon request.

★4077★ International Society of Certified Electronics Technicians (ISCET)
2708 W. Berry, Ste. 3
Fort Worth, TX 76109
Ph: (817)921-9101

Sponsors testing program for certification of electronics technicians in the fields of audio, communications, computer, consumer, industrial, medical electronics, radar, radio-television, and video.

★4078★ *Professionals . . . Are Certified by the Electronics Technicians Association, International*
Electronics Technicians Association
602 N Jackson St.
Greencastle, IN 46135
Ph: (317)653-8262

This six-panel brochure describes the certification process for electronics technicians. Covers eligibility requirements, examination contents, and specialties.

TEST GUIDES

★4079★ *Career Examination Series: Assistant Electronic Technician*
National Learning Corp.
212 Michael Dr.
Syosset, NY 11791
Ph: (516)921-8888 Fax: (516)921-8743
Fr: 800-645-6337

Jack Rudman. All examination guides in this series contain questions with answers.

★4080★ *Career Examination Series: Electronic Equipment Repairer*
National Learning Corp.
212 Michael Dr.
Syosset, NY 11791
Ph: (516)921-8888 Fax: (516)921-8743
Fr: 800-645-6337

Jack Rudman. All examination guides in this series contain questions with answers.

★4081★ *Career Examination Series: Electronic Mechanic*
National Learning Corp.
212 Michael Dr.
Syosset, NY 11791
Ph: (516)921-8888 Fax: (516)921-8743
Fr: 800-645-6337

Jack Rudman. 1989. All examination guides in this series contain questions with answers.

★4082★ *Certified Electronic Technician (CET)*
National Learning Corp.
212 Michael Dr.
Syosset, NY 11791
Ph: (516)921-8888 Fax: (516)921-8743
Fr: 800-645-6337

Jack Rudman. Part of the Admission Test Series. Books in this series provide test practice and drill for actual professional certification and licensure tests.

★4083★ *The CET Exam: ISCET: Certified Electronics Technician*
International Society of Certified Electronics Technicians
2708 W. Berry St.
Fort Worth, TX 76109
Ph: (817)921-9101

This six-panel brochure describes certification for electronic technicians. Outlines examination contents.

★4084★ *EEA Training Program*
Electronics Technicians Association, International (ETA-I)
602 N. Jackson
Greencastle, IN 46135
Ph: (317)653-8262

Monthly.

★4085★ *Industrial Electronics*
National Learning Corp.
212 Michael Dr.
Syosset, NY 11791
Ph: (516)921-8888 Fax: (516)921-8743
Fr: 800-645-6337

Jack Rudman. 1989. Part of Occupational Competency Examination Series.

EDUCATIONAL DIRECTORIES AND PROGRAMS

★4086★ *Directory of Professional Electronics Technicians*
Electronics Technicians Association, International (ETA-I)
602 N. Jackson
Greencastle, IN 46135
Ph: (317)653-8262 Fax: (317)653-8262

Annual.

AWARDS, SCHOLARSHIPS, GRANTS, AND FELLOWSHIPS

★4087★ Electronics Technicians Association, International Technician of the Year
Electronics Technicians Association, International
604 N. Jackson
Greencastle, IN 46135
Ph: (317)653-8262

To honor a practicing electronics technician as an incentive for all other technicans to achieve higher goals. A plaque is awarded annually at the convention. Established in 1979 in memory of Norris R. Browne, CET, Houston, Tx.

★4088★ ISCET Tech-of-the-Year Award
International Society of Certified Electronics Technicians
c/o Alice Johnson
2708 W. Berry St.
Fort Worth, TX 76109
Ph: (817)921-9101

To recognize a technician for outstanding work in the field of electronics. Established in 1976.

BASIC REFERENCE GUIDES AND HANDBOOKS

★4089★ *Electronic Maintenance*
State Mutual Book & Periodical Service, Ltd.
521 5th Ave., 17th Fl.
New York, NY 10175
Ph: (212)682-5844

1982.

★4090★ *Electronic Maintenance Two*
State Mutual Book & Periodical Service Ltd.
521 5th Ave., 17th Fl.
New York, NY 10175
Ph: (212)682-5844

1982.

★4091★ *Electronics for Industrial Electricians*
Delmar Publishers, Inc.
PO Box 15015
2 Computer Dr., W.
Albany, NY 12212
Ph: (518)459-1150 Fax: (518)453-6472

Stephen L. Herman. Second edition, 1985.

★4092★ *Electronics in Industry*
McGraw-Hill Publishing Company
1221 Avenue of the Americas
New York, NY 10020
Ph: (212)512-2000

George M. Chute. Fifth edition, 1979.

★4093★ *The Electronics Manual to Industrial Automation*
TAB/McGraw-Hill, Inc.
PO Box 182607
Columbus, OH 43218-2607
Fax: (614)759-3644 Fr: 800-822-8158
G. R. Slone. 1987.

★4094★ *Guide to Electronic Components*
Van Nostrand Reinhold
115 5th Ave.
New York, NY 10003
Ph: (212)254-3232 Fax: (212)254-9499
Segalis.

★4095★ *Handbook of Basic Electronic Troubleshooting*
Prentice Hall
Rte. 9W
Englewood Cliffs, NJ 07632
Ph: (201)592-2000
John D. Lenk. 1979.

★4096★ *Home Electronics*
Time Life Books, Inc.
777 Duke St.
Alexandria, VA 22314
Ph: (703)838-7000
1988. Part of Fix-It-Yourself Series.

★4097★ *How to Locate Needed Servicing Information*
ARS Enterprises
PO Box 997
Mercer Island, WA 98040
Ph: (206)236-7071

★4098★ *The Illustrated Home Electronics Fix-it Book*
TAB/McGraw-Hill, Inc.
PO Box 182607
Columbus, OH 43218-2607
Fax: (614)759-3644 Fr: 800-822-8158
Homer L. Davidson. Second edition, 1988.

★4099★ *Industrial Circuits & Automated Manufacturing*
Holt, Rinehart & Winston, Inc.
6277 Sea Harbor Dr.
Orlando, FL 32887
Ph: (407)345-2500
Clyde Kale. 1989.

★4100★ *Industrial Control Electronics*
Prentice Hall
Rte. 9W
Englewood Cliffs, NJ 07632
Ph: (201)592-2000
David P. Beach. 1990.

★4101★ *Industrial Electronics: A Text-Lab Manual*
McGraw-Hill Publishing Company
1221 Avenue of the Americas
New York, NY 10020
Ph: (212)512-2000
Paul B Zbar. Third edition, 1981.

★4102★ *Industrial Electronics and Controls*
Prentice Hall
Rte. 9W
Englewood Cliffs, NJ 07632
Ph: (201)592-2000
Martin Newman. 1986. Part of Electronic Technology Series.

★4103★ *Industrial Electronics: Devices & Systems*
Prentice Hall
Rte. 9W
Englewood Cliffs, NJ 07632
Ph: (201)592-2000
Dale R. Patrick. 1986.

★4104★ *Manual of Electronic Servicing Test & Measurements*
Prentice Hall
Rte. 9W
Englewood Cliffs, NJ 07632
Ph: (201)592-2000
Robert C. Genn, Jr. Second edition, 1990.

★4105★ *New Manufacturing Technologies*
State Mutual Book & Periodical Service, Ltd.
521 5th Ave., 17th Fl.
New York, NY 10175
Ph: (212)682-5844
Network Staff. 1984.

★4106★ *New Ways to Use Test Meters: A Modern Guide to Electronic Servicing*
Prentice Hall
Rte. 9W
Englewood Cliffs, NJ 07632
Ph: (201)592-2000
Robert G. Middleton. 1986.

★4107★ *Repairing Appliances*
Time Life Books, Inc.
777 Duke St.
Alexandria, VA 22314
Ph: (703)838-7000
1981. Part of Home Repair & Improvement Series.

★4108★ *Troubleshooting Electronics Equipment Without Service Data*
Prentice Hall
Rte. 9W
Englewood Cliffs, NJ 07632
Ph: (201)592-2000
Robert G. Middleton. 1989.

Periodicals

★4109★ *American Electronics Association—Update*
American Electronics Association
5201 Great America Pkwy.
Santa Clara, CA 95054
Ph: (408)987-4234 Fax: (408)970-8565
April Nellson
Carries electronics industry news and statistics. Discusses international trade; federal tax laws; and public affairs, finance, sales and marketing, and management issues facing the electronics industry. Lists Association activities and events. Recurring features include a calendar of events.

★4110★ *Carolina Retailer*
Halco Communications
841 Post Road Circle
PO Box 830034
Stone Mountain, GA 30083-0001
Ph: (404)879-9682 Fax: (404)879-6791
David Hollingsworth
Monthly. Regional trade tabloid for the electronics, appliances, consumer outdoor power equipment, and TVRO satellite industries.

★4111★ *EASA Currents*
Electrical Apparatus Service Association, Inc. (EASA)
1331 Baur Blvd.
St. Louis, MO 63132
Ph: (314)993-2220 Fax: (314)993-1269
Carl Fields
Monthly. Provides news of the electric motor sales and repair industry and related topics, including safety, financial management, and market trends. Recurring features include articles by the staff engineers and committees, chapter news, and news of members.

★4112★ *Electronic Business Forecast*
Cahners Economics
275 Washington St.
Newton, MA 02158
Ph: (617)630-2119 Fax: (617)558-4700
Madeline Franchi
Bimonthly. Provides news, analysis, and forecasts of developments in the electronics industry. Recurring features include one-page columns on electronic end markets, supply conditions, and international developments.

★4113★ *Electronic Industries Association—Executive Report*
Electronic Industries Association
2001 Pennsylvania Ave. NW
Washington, DC 20006
Ph: (202)457-4980 Fax: (202)457-4985
Mack V. Rosenker
Bimonthly. Provides news of electronics and the electronics industry. Focuses on legislative proposals and hearings, engineering standards, sales trends in the industry and general Association news. Recurring features include news of Association business and meetings, seminars, and notices of publications available.

★4114★ *Electronic Servicing & Technology*
CQ Communications
76 N. Broadway
Hicksville, NY 11801
Ph: (516)681-2922 Fax: (516)681-2926
Conrad Persson
Monthly. Consumer electronics servicing magazine.

★4115★ *ETA Technician Association News*
Electronic Technicians Association (ETA)
602 N. Jackson St.
Greencastle, IN 46135
Ph: (317)653-5541 Fax: (317)653-8262
Fr: 800-359-6706
Dick Glass
Monthly. Serves member technicians with news of the Association and the electronics industry, including items on service, education, employment, management, and events. Contains information on membership, man-

agement, telecommunications, and business and technical training programs. Recurring features include editorials, news of research, letters to the editor, book reviews, and a calendar of events.

★4116★ *International Society of Certified Electronics Technicians—Update*
International Society of Certified Electronics Technicians
2708 W. Berry St.
Ft. Worth, TX 76109
Ph: (817)921-9101 Fax: (817)921-3741
Barbara Rubin

Quarterly. Reflects the aims of the Society, which are to raise the public image of certified electronics technicians and to improve the effectiveness of industry education programs for technicians. Recurring features include news of research, a calendar of events, reports of meetings, news of educational opportunities, and job listings.

★4117★ *ISCET Update*
International Society of Certified Electronics Technicians (ISCET)
2708 W. Berry, Ste. 3
Fort Worth, TX 76109
Ph: (817)921-9101 Fax: (817)921-3741

Quarterly. Includes job listings.

★4118★ *Link Review of Interactive Services*
Link Resources Corporation
79 5th Ave., 12th Fl.
New York, NY 10003
Ph: (212)627-1500 Fax: (212)620-3099
Steven K. Sieck

Monthly. Concerned with the interactive communications industry. Covers integrated networks, electronic entertainment and information, videotex, and electronic home offices. Recurring features include a column titled Statistical Spotlight and a calendar of events.

★4119★ *Management Update*
Electronics Technicians Association, International (ETA-I)
602 N. Jackson
Greencastle, IN 46135
Ph: (317)653-8262 Fax: (317)653-8262

Monthly.

★4120★ *NESDA—Update*
National Electronics Service Dealers Association (NESDA)
2708 W. Berry St., Ste. 3
Fort Worth, TX 76109
Ph: (817)921-9061 Fax: (817)921-3741

Bimonthly. Provides information on legislation, regulations, legal, and industry news.

★4121★ *Professional Electronics Magazine*
International Society of Certified Electronics Technicians (ISCET)
2708 W. Berry, Ste. 3
Fort Worth, TX 76109
Ph: (817)921-9101 Fax: (817)921-3741

Bimonthly.

★4122★ *Technical Log*
International Society of Certified Electronics Technicians (ISCET)
2708 W. Berry, Ste. 3
Fort Worth, TX 76109
Ph: (817)921-9101 Fax: (817)921-3741

Quarterly.

★4123★ *Technician Association News*
Electronics Technicians Association, International (ETA-I)
602 N. Jackson
Greencastle, IN 46135
Ph: (317)653-8262 Fax: (317)653-8262

Monthly. *EEA Program* and *Management Update* are now monographs of this publication. Includes book reviews, obituaries and information on new products.

MEETINGS AND CONVENTIONS

★4124★ Consumers Electronics Instructors Conference
International Society of Certified Electronics Technicians (ISCET)
2708 W. Berry, Ste. 3
Fort Worth, TX 76109
Ph: (817)921-9101 Fax: (817)921-3741

Annual.

★4125★ Electronic Technicians Association Annual Convention
Electronic Technicians Association, International (ETA)
602 N. Jackson St.
Greencastle, IN 46135
Ph: (317)653-5541

Annual.

Communications Equipment Mechanics

Communications equipment mechanics install, repair, and maintain an array of complex and sophisticated communications equipment. Most communications equipment mechanics, sometimes referred to as **telecommunications technicians**, work either in telephone company central offices, or on customers' premises installing and repairing telephone switching and transmission systems. Central office equipment installers set up, rearrange and remove switching and dialing equipment used in central offices. Frame wirers, sometimes referred to as frame workers or frame attendants, connect, disconnect, inspect, and repair wires that run from telephone lines and cables to the central office. **Central office repairers**, often referred to as central office technicians or switching equipment technicians, test, repair, and maintain all types of local and toll switching equipment that automatically connects lines when customers dial numbers. Trouble locators work at special switchboards to find the source of the problem. **PBX installers**, often called systems technicians, specialize in complex telephone system installation. They create switchboard systems for businesses with unique communications requirements. PBX repairers, with the assistance of trouble locators, locate the malfunction in customers' PBX, CENTREX, KEY, or other telephone systems and make the necessary repairs. Most communications equipment mechanics work for telephone and telegraph companies. A small number work for cable television and related companies, as well as for railroad companies and electrical repair shops.

Salaries

Wage rates for communications equipment mechanics vary by employer and locality; specific information may be obtained from local telephone companies. Central office installers, central office technicians, and PBX installers employed by AT & T and the Bell Operating Companies and represented by the Communications Workers of America earn an average weekly salary of $752-$824.

Employment Outlook

Growth rate until the year 2005: Decline sharply.

Communications Equipment Mechanics

Career Guides

★4126★ "Avionic Technicians" in *Career Discovery Encyclopedia* (Vol.1, pp. 98-99)
J.G. Ferguson Publishing Co.
200 W. Madison St., Ste. 300
Chicago, IL 60606
Ph: (312)580-5480 Fax: (312)580-4948

E. Russell Primm, editor-in-chief. 1993. Contains two-page articles on 504 occupations. Each article describes job duties, earnings, and educational and training requirements.

★4127★ "Avionics and Marine Electronics" in *Electronic Service Careers* (pp. 71-76)
Franklin Watts, Inc.
387 Park Avenue, S.
New York, NY 10016
Ph: (212)686-7070

Robert Laurance. 1987. Discusses the work of an electronic service technician, employment outlook, places of employment, and educational preparation and training. Describes jobs with computers, consumer electronics, industrial electronics and the military.

★4128★ "Avionics Technician" in *Career Information Center* (pp. 96-98)
Simon and Schuster
200 Old Tappan Rd.
Old Tappan, NJ 07675
Fax: 800-445-6991 Fr: 800-223-2348

Richard Lidz and Dale Anderson, editorial directors. Fifth edition, 1993. For 600 occupations, describes job duties, entry-level requirements, education and training needed, advancement possibilities, employment outlook, earnings and benefits. The set is divided into 12 volumes. Each volume includes jobs related under a broad career field. Volume 13 is the index.

★4129★ "Avionics Technician" in *Opportunities in Aerospace Careers* (pp. 34-37)
National Textbook Co. (NTC)
VGM Career Books
4255 W. Touhy Ave.
Lincolnwood, IL 60646-1975
Ph: (708)679-5500 Fax: (708)679-2494
Fr: 800-323-4900

Wallace R. Maples. 1991. Surveys jobs with the airlines, airports, the government, the military, in manufacturing, and in research and development. Describes educational requirements, working conditions, salaries, employment outlook and licensure.

★4130★ "Avionics Technicians" in *Encyclopedia of Careers and Vocational Guidance* (Vol.2, pp. 156-158)
J.G. Ferguson Publishing Co.
200 W. Madison St., Ste. 300
Chicago, IL 60606
Ph: (312)580-5480 Fax: (312)580-4948

William E. Hopke, editor-in-chief. Ninth edition, 1993. Four-volume set that profiles 500 occupations and describes job trends in 74 industries. Includes career description, educational requirements, history of the job, methods of entry, advancement, employment outlook, earnings, working conditions, social and psychological factors, and sources of additional information.

★4131★ "Central Office Technician" in *Exploring Nontraditional Jobs for Women* (pp. 32-37)
Rosen Publishing Group
29 E. 21st St.
New York, NY 10010
Ph: (212)777-3017 Fax: (212)777-0277
Fr: 800-237-9932

Rose Neufeld. 1989. Describes blue-collar, male dominated occupations. Discusses what is done on the job, training, where to apply for jobs, tools used, salaries, and advantages and disadvantages. Relates the experiences of women who are working in the field.

★4132★ "Communications Equipment Mechanic" in *Jobs Rated Almanac*
World Almanac
1 International Blvd., Ste. 444
Mahwah, NJ 07495
Ph: (201)529-6900 Fax: (201)529-6901

Les Krantz. Second edition, 1992. Ranks 250 jobs by environment, salary, outlooks, physical demands, stress, security, travel opportunities, and extra perks. Includes jobs the editor feels are the most common, most interesting, and the most rapidly growing.

★4133★ "Communications Equipment Mechanic" in *VGM's Careers Encyclopedia* (pp. 111-114)
National Textbook Co. (NTC)
VGM Career Books
4255 W. Touhy Ave.
Lincolnwood, IL 60646-1975
Ph: (708)679-5500 Fax: (708)679-2494
Fr: 800-323-4900

Third edition, 1991. Contains two- to five-page descriptions of 200 managerial, professional, technical, trade, and service occupations. Each profile includes job duties, places of employment, qualifications, educational preparation, training, employment potential, advancement, income, and additional sources of information.

★4134★ "Communications Equipment Mechanics" in *Career Discovery Encyclopedia* (Vol.2, pp. 38-39)
J.G. Ferguson Publishing Co.
200 W. Madison St., Ste. 300
Chicago, IL 60606
Ph: (312)580-5480 Fax: (312)580-4948

E. Russell Primm, editor-in-chief. 1993. Contains two-page articles on 504 occupations. Each article describes job duties, earnings, and educational and training requirements.

★4135★ "Communications Equipment Mechanics" in *Encyclopedia of Careers and Vocational Guidance* (Vol.2, pp. 352-355)
J.G. Ferguson Publishing Co.
200 W. Madison St., Ste. 300
Chicago, IL 60606
Ph: (312)580-5480 Fax: (312)580-4948

William E. Hopke, editor-in-chief. Ninth edition, 1993. Four-volume set that profiles 500 occupations and describes job trends in 74 industries. Includes career description, educational requirements, history of the job, methods of entry, advancement, employment outlook, earnings, working conditions, social and psychological factors, and sources of additional information.

★4136★ "Communications Equipment Mechanics" in *Occupational Outlook Handbook*
U.S. Government Printing Office
Superintendent of Documents
Washington, DC 20402
Ph: (202)512-1800 Fax: (202)512-2250

Biennial; latest edition, 1994-95. Encyclopedia of careers describing more than 250 occupations and comprising about 85 percent of all jobs in the economy. Occupations that require lengthy education or training are given the most attention. For each occupation, the handbook describes job duties, working conditions, training, educational preparation, personal qualities, advancement possibilities, job outlook, earnings, and sources of additional information.

★4137★ "Communications Mechanic" in *Opportunities in Electrical Trades* (pp. 83-84)
National Textbook Co. (NTC)
VGM Career Books
4255 W. Touhy Ave.
Lincolnwood, IL 60646-1975
Ph: (708)679-5500 Fax: (708)679-2494
Fr: 800-323-4900

Robert Wood. 1990. Provides an overview of the electrical industry describing current trends and future projections. Surveys electrician jobs and covers the nature of the work, working conditions, job outlook, advancement possibilities, education and training, earnings, and specialization. Offers career planning advice.

★4138★ "Communications Technician" in *VGM's Handbook of Scientific and Technical Careers* (pp. 28-30)
National Textbook Co. (NTC)
VGM Career Books
4255 W. Touhy Ave.
Lincolnwood, IL 60646-1975
Ph: (708)679-5500 Fax: (708)679-2494
Fr: 800-323-4900

Craig T. Norback, editor. 1990. Includes 50 occupations in science and technology and describes job duties, qualifications, education, training, potential advancement, income. Lists sources of additional information.

★4139★ "Communications or Telecommunications" in *Careers in High Tech* (p. 104)
Arco Publishing Co.
Macmillan General Reference
15 Columbus Cir.
New York, NY 10023
Fax: 800-835-3202 Fr: 800-858-7674

Connie Winkler. 1987. Surveys career opportunities in data processing, technology, personal computers, telecommunications, manufacturing technology, artificial intelligence, computer graphics, biotechnology, lasers, technical writing, and publishing. Includes information on educational preparation, associations, and periodicals.

★4140★ *Do Your Own Thing . . . in the Mechanical Field*
AIMS Media, Inc.
9710 DeSoto Ave.
Chatsworth, CA 91311
Ph: (818)773-4300 Fax: (818)341-6700
Fr: 800-367-2467

Videocassette. 1979. 16 mins. Various job levels in the mechanical field are outlined for students.

★4141★ *The Professional Electronics Technician*
Electronics Technicians Association
602 N Jackson St.
Greencastle, IN 46135
Ph: (317)653-8262

This six-page brochure describes job duties, training, skills and aptitudes, salaries, employment outlook, and certification.

★4142★ "Railroad Signaler and Signal Maintainer" in *Career Information Center* (Vol.12)
Simon and Schuster
200 Old Tappan Rd.
Old Tappan, NJ 07675
Fax: 800-445-6991 Fr: 800-223-2348

Richard Lidz and Dale Anderson, editorial directors. Fifth edition, 1993. For 600 occupations, describes job duties, entry-level requirements, education and training needed, advancement possibilities, employment outlook, earnings and benefits. The set is divided into 12 volumes. Each volume includes jobs related under a broad career field. Volume 13 is the index.

★4143★ "Signal Mechanics" in *Encyclopedia of Careers and Vocational Guidance* (Vol.4, pp. 362-364)
J.G. Ferguson Publishing Co.
200 W. Madison St., Ste. 300
Chicago, IL 60606
Ph: (312)580-5480 Fax: (312)580-4948

William E. Hopke, editor-in-chief. Ninth edition, 1993. Four-volume set that profiles 500 occupations and describes job trends in 74 industries. Includes career description, educational requirements, history of the job, methods of entry, advancement, employment outlook, earnings, working conditions, social and psychological factors, and sources of additional information.

★4144★ "Telecommunications Technicians" in *Career Discovery Encyclopedia* (Vol.6, pp. 96-97)
J.G. Ferguson Publishing Co.
200 W. Madison St., Ste. 300
Chicago, IL 60606
Ph: (312)580-5480 Fax: (312)580-4948

E. Russell Primm, editor-in-chief. 1993. Contains two-page articles on 504 occupations. Each article describes job duties, earnings, and educational and training requirements.

★4145★ "Telecommunications Technicians" in *Encyclopedia of Careers and Vocational Guidance* (Vol.4, p. 505)
J.G. Ferguson Publishing Co.
200 W. Madison St., Ste. 300
Chicago, IL 60606
Ph: (312)580-5480 Fax: (312)580-4948

William E. Hopke, editor-in-chief. Ninth edition, 1993. Four-volume set that profiles 500 occupations and describes job trends in 74 industries. Includes career description, educational requirements, history of the job, methods of entry, advancement, employment outlook, earnings, working conditions, social and psychological factors, and sources of additional information.

★4146★ "Telecommunications Technology" in *Career Connection II: A Guide to Technical Majors and Their Related Careers* (pp. 142-143)
Jist Works, Inc.
720 N. Park Ave.
Indianapolis, IN 46202-3431
Ph: (317)264-3720 Fax: (317)264-3709

Fred A. Rowe. 1994. Contains technical majors, such as automotive technology. Describes the major and the job. Lists high school and postsecondary school courses. Includes occupations related to the major, employment outlook, and starting salary.

★4147★ "Telephone Central Office Technician" in *Career Information Center* (Vol.3)
Simon and Schuster
200 Old Tappan Rd.
Old Tappan, NJ 07675
Fax: 800-445-6991 Fr: 800-223-2348

Richard Lidz and Dale Anderson, editorial directors. Fifth edition, 1993. For 600 occupations, describes job duties, entry-level requirements, education and training needed, advancement possibilities, employment outlook, earnings and benefits. The set is divided into 12 volumes. Each volume includes jobs related under a broad career field. Volume 13 is the index.

★4148★ "Telephone Central Office Technician" in *Telecommunications* (pp. 39-43)
Franklin Watts, Inc.
387 Park Avenue, S.
New York, NY 10016
Ph: (212)686-7070

Linda Barrett and Galen Guengerich. 1991. Surveys opportunities in telecommunications including telephone, radio, telegraph, and television communications. Includes job description, educational preparation, salary, and employment outlook. Offers job hunting advice.

★4149★ "Telephone and PBX Installers and Repairers" in *Encyclopedia of Careers and Vocational Guidance* (Vol.4, pp. 510-512)
J.G. Ferguson Publishing Co.
200 W. Madison St., Ste. 300
Chicago, IL 60606
Ph: (312)580-5480 Fax: (312)580-4948

William E. Hopke, editor-in-chief. Ninth edition, 1993. Four-volume set that profiles 500 occupations and describes job trends in 74 industries. Includes career description, educational requirements, history of the job, methods of entry, advancement, employment outlook, earnings, working conditions, social and psychological factors, and sources of additional information.

★4150★ *Video Career Library - Repair Fields*
Careers, Inc.
PO Box 135
Largo, FL 34649-0135
Ph: (813)584-7333

Videocassette. 1990. 23 mins. Part of the Video Career Library covering 165 occupations. Shows actual workers on the job. Includes industrial machinery repairers, communications equipment repairers, data processing equipment repairers, home entertainment equipment repairers, office machine repairers, electrical power installers and repairers, and electrical and electronic repairers.

ASSOCIATIONS

★4151★ National Association of Radio and Telecommunications Engineers (NARTE)
PO Box 678
Medway, MA 02053
Ph: (508)533-8333 Fax: (508)533-3815
Fr: 800-89-NARTE

Members: Purpose: Provides certification of Radio, telecommunications, and Electromagnetic Compatibility (EMC) engineers and technicians. Designated and accredited by the Federal Communications Commission as a Commercial Operators License Examination Manager. Objectives are to: foster professionalism; develop and implement guidelines for certification; promote radio, telecommunications, and EMC education in colleges and universities. **Publications:** *NARTE News*, quarterly.

★4152★ United States Telephone Association (USTA)
1401 H St., Ste. 600
Washington, DC 20005-2136
Ph: (202)326-7300 Fax: (202)326-7333

Members: Local operating telephone companies or telephone holding companies. Members represent a total of 114 million access lines. **Purpose:** Conducts educational and training programs. Maintains 21 committees. **Publications:** *Holding Company Report*, annual. • *Phonefacts*, annual. • *Statistical Volumes*, annual. • *Teletimes*, quarterly.

STANDARDS/CERTIFICATION AGENCIES

★4153★ National Association of Radio and Telecommunications Engineers (NARTE)
PO Box 678
Medway, MA 02053
Ph: (508)533-8333 Fax: (508)533-3815
Fr: 800-89-NARTE

Provides certification of Radio, telecommunications, and Electromagnetic Compatibility (EMC) engineers and technicians. Designated and accredited by the Federal Communications Commission as a Commercial Operators License Examination Manager. Objectives are to: foster professionalism; develop and implement guidelines for certification; promote radio, telecommunications, and EMC education in colleges and universities.

TEST GUIDES

★4154★ *Career Examination Series: Police Communications Technician*
National Learning Corp.
212 Michael Dr.
Syosset, NY 11791
Ph: (516)921-8888 Fax: (516)921-8743
Fr: 800-645-6337

Jack Rudman. All examination guides in this series contain questions with answers.

PERIODICALS

★4155★ *Sound & Communications Magazine*
Testa Communications
25 Willowdale Ave.
Port Washington, NY 11050
Ph: (516)767-2500 Fax: (516)767-9335
Judith Morrison

Monthly. Magazine focusing on sound and communications systems equipment, installations, and technology.

OTHER SOURCES OF INFORMATION

★4156★ *Phonefacts*
United States Telephone Association (USTA)
1401 H. St., Ste. 600
Washington, DC 20006
Ph: (202)326-7300 Fax: (202)326-7333

Annual.

Computer and Office Machine Repairers

Computer and office machine repairers (often called field engineers, customer service engineers, or service technicians) install, do preventive maintenance, or correct emergency problems on computers and other office equipment. Field technicians visit the offices and stores of customers in their assigned area to perform routine maintenance such as cleaning, oiling, and adjusting parts. In the case of machine breakdown, technicians run special diagnostic programs that pinpoint the malfunction. Once the problem has been located, fixing the equipment may take only a few minutes because most repairs merely involve the replacement of malfunctioning parts. About 75% of repairers are employed by wholesalers of computers and other office equipment and by firms that provide maintenance services for a fee. The remainder work for equipment manufacturers, retail establishments, and organizations with enough equipment and funding to warrant a full-time service staff.

Salaries

Median weekly earnings of full-time computer and office machine repairers is about $476.

Employment Outlook

Growth rate until the year 2005: Faster than average.

Computer and Office Machine Repairers

Career Guides

★4157★ "Business Computers and Office Equipment Service" in *Electronic Service Careers* (pp. 46-56)
Franklin Watts, Inc.
387 Park Avenue, S.
New York, NY 10016
Ph: (212)686-7070

Robert Laurance. 1987. Discusses the work of an electronic service technician, employment outlook, places of employment, and educational preparation and training. Describes jobs with computers, consumer electronics, industrial electronics and the military.

★4158★ "Business Machine Operator" in *Career Information Center* (Vol.1)
Simon and Schuster
200 Old Tappan Rd.
Old Tappan, NJ 07675
Fax: 800-445-6991 Fr: 800-223-2348

Richard Lidz and Dale Anderson, editorial directors. Fifth edition, 1993. For 600 occupations, describes job duties, entry-level requirements, education and training needed, advancement possibilities, employment outlook, earnings and benefits. The set is divided into 12 volumes. Each volume includes jobs related under a broad career field. Volume 13 is the index.

★4159★ "Business Machine Repairers" in *Jobs! What They Are—Where They Are—What They Pay* (pp. 247)
Simon & Schuster, Inc.
Simon & Schuster Bldg.
1230 Avenue of the Americas
New York, NY 10020
Ph: (212)698-7000

Robert O. Snelling and Anne M. Snelling. Revised edition, 1992. Profiles 241 occupations, describing duties and responsibilities, educational preparation, earnings, employment opportunities, training, and qualifications.

★4160★ "Business Machine Service Technician" in *VGM's Careers Encyclopedia* (pp. 72-73)
National Textbook Co. (NTC)
VGM Career Books
4255 W. Touhy Ave.
Lincolnwood, IL 60646-1975
Ph: (708)679-5500 Fax: (708)679-2494
Fr: 800-323-4900

Third edition, 1991. Contains two- to five-page descriptions of 200 managerial, professional, technical, trade, and service occupations. Each profile includes job duties, places of employment, qualifications, educational preparation, training, employment potential, advancement, income, and additional sources of information.

★4161★ "Business Machine Service Technician" in *VGM's Handbook of Scientific and Technical Careers* (pp. 18-19)
National Textbook Co. (NTC)
VGM Career Books
4255 W. Touhy Ave.
Lincolnwood, IL 60646-1975
Ph: (708)679-5500 Fax: (708)679-2494
Fr: 800-323-4900

Craig T. Norback, editor. 1990. Includes 50 occupations in science and technology and describes job duties, qualifications, education, training, potential advancement, income. Lists sources of additional information.

★4162★ "Computer Maintenance" in *Career Connection II: A Guide to Technical Majors and Their Related Careers* (pp. 40-41)
Jist Works, Inc.
720 N. Park Ave.
University Station
Indianapolis, IN 46202-3431
Ph: (317)264-3720 Fax: (317)264-3709

Fred A. Rowe. 1994. Contains technical majors, such as automotive technology. Describes the major and the job. Lists high school and postsecondary school courses. Includes occupations related to the major, employment outlook, and starting salary.

★4163★ "Computer and Office Machine Repairers" in *America's 50 Fastest Growing Jobs* (pp. 131)
JIST Works, Inc.
720 N. Park Ave.
Indianapolis, IN 46202-3431
Ph: (317)264-3720 Fax: (317)264-3709
Fr: 800-648-5478

Michael J. Farr, compiler. 1994. Describes the 50 fastest growing jobs within major career clusters such as technicians, and marketing and sales. Each job profile explains the nature of the work, skills and abilities required, employment outlook, average earnings, related occupations, education and training requirements, and employment opportunities. Also contains career planning information and job search tips.

★4164★ "Computer and Office Machine Repairers" in *Occupational Outlook Handbook*
U.S. Government Printing Office
Superintendent of Documents
Washington, DC 20402
Ph: (202)512-1800 Fax: (202)512-2250

Biennial; latest edition, 1994-95. Encyclopedia of careers describing more than 250 occupations and comprising about 85 percent of all jobs in the economy. Occupations that require lengthy education or training are given the most attention. For each occupation, the handbook describes job duties, working conditions, training, educational preparation, personal qualities, advancement possibilities, job outlook, earnings, and sources of additional information.

★4165★ "Computer and Office Machine Repairers" in *The Best Jobs for the 1990s and Into the 21st Century*
Impact Publications
9104-N Manassas Dr.
Manassas Park, VA 22111
Ph: (703)361-7300 Fax: (703)335-9486

Ronald L. Krannich and Caryl Rae Krannich. 1993.

★4166★ *Computer Repair Technician*
Vocational Biographies, Inc.
PO Box 31
Sauk Centre, MN 56378-0031
Ph: (612)352-6516 Fax: (612)352-5546
Fr: 800-255-0752

1992. Four-page pamphlet containing a personal narrative about a worker's job, work likes and dislikes, career path from high school to the present. Education and training, the rewards and frustrations, and the effects of the job on the rest of the worker's life. The data file portion of this pamphlet gives a concise occupational summary, including work descriptions, working conditions, places of employment, personal characteristics, education and training, job outlook, and salary range.

★4167★ **"Computer Service" in *Opportunities in Vocational and Technical Careers* (pp. 108-109)**
National Textbook Co. (NTC)
VGM Career Books
4255 W. Touhy Ave.
Lincolnwood, IL 60646-1975
Ph: (708)679-5500 Fax: (708)679-2494
Fr: 800-323-4900

Adrian A. Paradis. 1992. Describes careers requiring instruction at a private vocational or proprietary school including office employee, sales worker, service worker, health services, mechanic, craftworker, and technician. Covers employment outlook, job duties and salaries. Offers career planning advice.

★4168★ *Computer Service Technician*
Careers, Inc.
PO Box 135
Largo, FL 34649-0135
Ph: (813)584-7333

1993. Two-page occupational summary card describing duties, working conditions, personal qualifications, training, earnings and hours, employment outlook, places of employment, related careers and where to write for more information.

★4169★ **"Computer Service Technician" in *100 Best Careers for the Year 2000* (pp. 123-125)**
Arco Pub.
201 W. 103rd St.
Indianapolis, IN 46290
Ph: 800-428-5331 Fax: 800-835-3202

Shelly Field. 1992. Describes 100 job opportunities expected to grow fast throughout the next decade. Provides information on job duties and responsibilities, training requirements, education, advancement opportunities, experience and qualifications, and typical salaries.

★4170★ **"Computer Service Technician" in *Occu-Facts: Information on 580 Careers in Outline Form***
Careers, Inc.
PO Box 135
Largo, FL 34649-0135
Ph: (813)584-7333

Biennial, 1995-96 edition. Each one-page occupational profile describes duties, working conditions, physical surroundings and demands, aptitudes, temperament, educational requirements, employment outlook, earnings, and places of employment.

★4171★ **"Computer Service Technician" in *Opportunities in Data Processing Careers* (pp. 66-67)**
National Textbook Co. (NTC)
VGM Career Books
4255 W. Touhy Ave.
Lincolnwood, IL 60646-1975
Ph: (708)679-5500 Fax: (708)679-2494
Fr: 800-323-4900

Norman N. Noerper. 1989. Provides an overview of the history and development of data processing careers. For each job included, describes responsibilities, salary, and job outlook. Contains separate chapters on educational preparation and job hunting. Lists professional organizations, publications, and schools.

★4172★ **"Computer Service Technician" in *VGM's Careers Encyclopedia* (pp. 116-118)**
National Textbook Co. (NTC)
VGM Career Books
4255 W. Touhy Ave.
Lincolnwood, IL 60646-1975
Ph: (708)679-5500 Fax: (708)679-2494
Fr: 800-323-4900

Third edition, 1991. Contains two- to five-page descriptions of 200 managerial, professional, technical, trade and service occupations. Each profile includes job duties, places of employment, qualifications, educational preparation and job hunting. Lists professional organizations, publications, and schools.

★4173★ **"Computer Service Technician" in *VGM's Handbook of Scientific and Technical Careers***
National Textbook Co. (NTC)
VGM Career Books
4255 W. Touhy Ave.
Lincolnwood, IL 60646-1975
Ph: (708)679-5500 Fax: (708)679-2494
Fr: 800-323-4900

Craig T. Norback, editor. 1990. Includes 50 occupations in science and technology and describes job duties, qualifications, education, training, potential advancement, and income. Lists sources of additional information.

★4174★ *Computer Service Technicians*
Chronicle Guidance Publications, Inc.
66 Aurora St.
PO Box 1190
Moravia, NY 13118-1190
Ph: (315)497-0330 Fax: (315)497-3359
Fr: 800-622-7284

1994. This career brief describes the nature of the work, working conditions, hours and earnings, education and training, licensure, certification, unions, personal qualifications, social and psychological factors, employment outlook, entry methods, advancement, and related occupations.

★4175★ **"Computer Service Technicians" in *Career Discovery Encyclopedia* (Vol.2, pp. 46-47)**
J.G. Ferguson Publishing Co.
200 W. Madison St., Ste. 300
Chicago, IL 60606
Ph: (312)580-5480 Fax: (312)580-4948

E. Russell Primm, editor-in-chief. 1993. Contains two-page articles on 504 occupations. Each article describes job duties, earnings, and educational and training requirements.

★4176★ **"Computer Service Technicians" in *Encyclopedia of Careers and Vocational Guidance* (Vol.2, pp. 363-367)**
J.G. Ferguson Publishing Co.
200 W. Madison St., Ste. 300
Chicago, IL 60606
Ph: (312)580-5480 Fax: (312)580-4948

William E. Hopke, editor-in-chief. Ninth edition, 1993. Four-volume set that profiles 500 occupations and describes job trends in 74 industries. Includes career description, educational requirements, history of the job, methods of entry, advancement, employment outlook, earnings, working conditions, social and psychological factors, and sources of additional information.

★4177★ **"Computer Service Technicians" in *Jobs! What They Are—Where They Are—What They Pay* (pp. 76)**
Simon & Schuster, Inc.
Simon & Schuster Bldg.
1230 Avenue of the Americas
New York, NY 10020
Ph: (212)698-7000

Robert O. Snelling and Anne M. Snelling. Revised edition, 1992. Profiles 241 occupations, describing duties and responsibilities, educational preparation, earnings, employment opportunities, training, and qualifications.

★4178★ **"Computer Service Technicians: Troubleshooting in High Tech" in *Careers for Women Without College Degrees* (pp. 185-189)**
McGraw-Hill Publishing Co.
11 W. 19th St.
New York, NY 10011
Ph: (212)337-6010

Beatryce Nivens. 1988. Career planning and job hunting guide containing information on decision-making, skills assessment, and resumes for career changers. Profiles careers with the best occupational outlook. Describes the work, educational preparation, employment outlook, salaries, and required skills.

★4179★ **"Computer Servicer" in *Career Information Center* (Vol.1)**
Simon and Schuster
200 Old Tappan Rd.
Old Tappan, NJ 07675
Fax: 800-445-6991 Fr: 800-223-2348

Richard Lidz and Dale Anderson, editorial directors. Fifth edition, 1993. For 600 occupations, describes job duties, entry-level requirements, education and training needed, advancement possibilities, employment outlook, earnings and benefits. The set is divided into 12 volumes. Each volume includes jobs related under a broad career field. Volume 13 is the index.

★4180★ **"Computer Servicing and Troubleshooting" in *The Complete Electronics Career Guide* (pp. 81-86)**
TAB/McGraw-Hill, Inc.
PO Box 182607
Columbus, OH 43218-2607
Fax: (614)759-3644 Fr: 800-822-8158

Joe Risse. 1989. Explores opportunities for electronic technicians in industry, broadcasting, appliance repair, telecommunications, computer servicing, and technical writing. Offers advice on educational preparation, training, finding or changing jobs, and career advancement. Lists trade publications and professional associations.

★4181★ "Computers and Information Systems" in *Where the Jobs Are: The Hottest Careers for the 90s* (pp. 77-96)
Career Press
180 5th Ave.
Hawthorne, NJ 07507
Ph: (201)427-0229 Fax: (201)427-2037
Fr: 800-CAREER-1

Joyce Hadley. 1995. Offers a job-hunting strategy for the 1990s as well as descriptions of growing careers of the decade. Each profile includes general information, forecasts, growth, education and training, licensing requirements, and salary information.

★4182★ "Computers" in *Internships 1995*
Petersons Guides, Inc.
PO Box 2123
Princeton, NJ 08543-2123
Ph: (609)243-9111 Fr: 800-338-3282

Fifteenth edition, 1995. Lists internship opportunities under six broad categories: communications, creative, performing, and fine arts, human services, international relations, business and technology, and public affairs. For each internship program, gives the names, phone number, contact person, description, eligibility requirements, and benefits.

★4183★ *Copier Repair Technician*
Vocational Biographies, Inc.
PO Box 31
Sauk Centre, MN 56378-0031
Ph: (612)352-6516 Fax: (612)352-5546
Fr: 800-255-0752

1991. This pamphlet profiles a person working in the job. Includes information about job duties, working conditions, places of employment, educational preparation, labor market outlook, and salaries.

★4184★ *Exploring Careers as a Computer Technician*
Rosen Publishing Group
29 E. 21st St.
New York, NY 10010
Ph: (212)777-3017 Fax: (212)777-0277
Fr: 800-237-9932

Jean W. Spencer. Revised edition, 1989. Covers job prospects and duties, educational preparation, equipment, tools, work environment, advancement possibilities, job satisfaction, and salaries. Lists schools, journals and professional associations.

★4185★ *Office Machine Service Technician*
Careers, Inc.
PO Box 135
Largo, FL 34649-0135
Ph: (813)584-7333

1994. Four-page brief offering the definition, history, duties, working conditions, personal qualifications, educational requirements, earnings, hours, employment outlook, advancement possibilities, and related occupations.

★4186★ "Office Machine Service Technician" in *Occu-Facts: Information on 580 Careers in Outline Form*
Careers, Inc.
PO Box 135
Largo, FL 34649-0135
Ph: (813)584-7333

Biennial, 1995-96 edition. Each one-page occupational profile describes duties, working conditions, physical surroundings and demands, aptitudes, temperament, educational requirements, employment outlook, earnings, and places of employment.

★4187★ "Office Machine Servicer" in *Career Information Center* (Vol.1)
Simon and Schuster
200 Old Tappan Rd.
Old Tappan, NJ 07675
Fax: 800-445-6991 Fr: 800-223-2348

Richard Lidz and Dale Anderson, editorial directors. Fifth edition, 1993. For 600 occupations, describes job duties, entry-level requirements, education and training needed, advancement possibilities, employment outlook, earnings and benefits. The set is divided into 12 volumes. Each volume includes jobs related under a broad career field. Volume 13 is the index.

★4188★ "Office Machine Servicers" in *Career Discovery Encyclopedia* (Vol.4, pp. 140-141)
J.G. Ferguson Publishing Co.
200 W. Madison St., Ste. 300
Chicago, IL 60606
Ph: (312)580-5480 Fax: (312)580-4948

E. Russell Primm, editor-in-chief. 1993. Contains two-page articles on 504 occupations. Each article describes job duties, earnings, and educational and training requirements.

★4189★ "Office Machine Servicers" in *Encyclopedia of Careers and Vocational Guidance* (Vol.3, pp. 611-614)
J.G. Ferguson Publishing Co.
200 W. Madison St., Ste. 300
Chicago, IL 60606
Ph: (312)580-5480 Fax: (312)580-4948

William E. Hopke, editor-in-chief. Ninth edition, 1993. Four-volume set that profiles 500 occupations and describes job trends in 74 industries. Includes career description, educational requirements, history of the job, methods of entry, advancement, employment outlook, earnings, working conditions, social and psychological factors, and sources of additional information.

★4190★ *Office Machine Technicians*
Chronicle Guidance Publications, Inc.
66 Aurora St.
PO Box 1190
Moravia, NY 13118-1190
Ph: (315)497-0330 Fax: (315)497-3359
Fr: 800-622-7284

1993. This career brief describes the nature of the work, working conditions, hours and earnings, education and training, licensure, certification, unions, personal qualifications, social and psychological factors, employment outlook, entry methods, advancement, and related occupations.

★4191★ *Opportunities in Computer Maintenance Careers*
National Textbook Co. (NTC)
VGM Career Books
4255 W. Touhy Ave.
Lincolnwood, IL 60646-1975
Ph: (708)679-5500 Fax: (708)679-2494
Fr: 800-323-4900

Elliott S. Kanter. 1988. Provides an overview of the work of a computer service technician, places of employment, educational preparation, employment outlook, and salaries. Offers job hunting advice. Profiles people working in the field.

★4192★ "PC Technicians" in *Careers in High Tech* (pp. 81-82)
Arco Publishing Co.
Macmillan General Reference
15 Columbus Cir.
New York, NY 10023
Fax: 800-835-3202 Fr: 800-858-7674

Connie Winkler. 1987. Surveys career opportunities in data processing, technology, personal computers, telecommunications, manufacturing technology, artificial intelligence, computer graphics, biotechnology, lasers, technical writing, and publishing. Includes information on educational preparation, associations, and periodicals.

★4193★ *The Professional Electronics Technician*
Electronics Technicians Association
602 N Jackson St.
Greencastle, IN 46135
Ph: (317)653-8262

This six-page brochure describes job duties, training, skills and aptitudes, salaries, employment outlook, and certification.

★4194★ "Service Technician/Customer Service" in *Careers in High Tech* (pp. 65-70)
Arco Publishing Co.
Macmillan General Reference
15 Columbus Cir.
New York, NY 10023
Fax: 800-835-3202 Fr: 800-858-7674

Connie Winkler. 1987. Surveys career opportunities in data processing, technology, personal computers, telecommunications, manufacturing technology, artificial intelligence, computer graphics, biotechnology, lasers, technical writing, and publishing. Includes information on educational preparation, associations, and periodicals.

★4195★ *Troubleshooting and Repairing Computer Printers*
TAB/McGraw-Hill, Inc.
PO Box 182607
Columbus, OH 43218-2607
Fax: (614)759-3644 Fr: 800-822-8158

★4196★ *Video Career Library - Repair Fields*
Careers, Inc.
PO Box 135
Largo, FL 34649-0135
Ph: (813)584-7333

Videocassette. 1990. 23 mins. Part of the Video Career Library covering 165 occupations. Shows actual workers on the job. Includes industrial machinery repairers, communications equipment repairers, data processing equipment repairers, home entertainment equipment repairers, office machine repairers, electrical power installers and repairers, and electrical and electronic repairers.

Associations

★4197★ Business Technology Association
12411 Wornall
Kansas City, MO 64145
Ph: (816)941-3100 Fax: (816)941-2829
Members: Resellers of office equipment and networking products and services. **Purpose:** Offers 60 seminars on management, service, technology, and business systems. Conducts research; provides buiness-supporting services and benefits, including insurance, and legal counsel. **Publications:** *BTA Membership Directory*, annual. • *Business Technology Solutions*, monthly. • *Hotline*, semimonthly.

Test Guides

★4198★ *Career Examination Series: Business Machine Maintainer & Repairer*
National Learning Corp.
212 Michael Dr.
Syosset, NY 11791
Ph: (516)921-8888 Fax: (516)921-8743
Fr: 800-645-6337
Jack Rudman. 1989. All examination guides in this series contain questions with answers.

Basic Reference Guides and Handbooks

★4199★ *Advances in Cooling Techniques for Computers*
Hemisphere Publishing Corp.
1900 Frost Rd., Ste. 101
Bristol, PA 19007
Ph: (215)785-5800 Fax: (215)785-5515
Win Aung, editor. 1991.

★4200★ *Computer Parts and Supplies Directory*
American Business Directories, Inc.
5711 S. 86th Circle
Omaha, NE 68127
Ph: (402)593-4600 Fax: (402)331-1505
Annual. Number of listings: 15,468 (U. S. edition); 2,402 (Canadian edition). Entries include: Name, address, phone (including area code), size of advertisement, year first in "Yellow Pages," name of owner or manager, number of employees. Compiled from telephone company "Yellow Pages," nationwide. Arrangement: Geographical.

★4201★ *Computer Technician's Handbook*
TAB/McGraw-Hill, Inc.
PO Box 182607
Columbus, OH 43218-2607
Fax: (614)759-3644 Fr: 800-822-8158
Art Margolis.

★4202★ *Computer Troubleshooting & Maintenance*
Arco Publishing Co.
Macmillan General Reference
15 Columbus Cir.
New York, NY 10023
Fax: 800-835-3202 Fr: 800-858-7674
Walter J. McBride. 1988.

★4203★ *Computerized Maintenance Management Systems*
Industrial Press, Inc.
200 Madison Ave.
New York, NY 10016
Ph: (212)889-6330 Fax: (212)545-8327
Terry Wireman. 1994.

★4204★ *Handbook of Software Maintenance*
John Wiley and Sons, Inc.
605 3rd Ave.
New York, NY 10158-0012
Ph: (212)850-6000 Fax: (212)850-6088
Fr: 800-526-5368
Girish Parikh. 1986.

★4205★ *IBM PC Advanced Troubleshooting & Repair*
Howard W. Sams & Co., Publishers
2647 Waterfront Pkwy., E. Dr.
Indianapolis, IN 46214-2012
Fax: (317)298-5604 Fr: 800-257-5755
Robert Brenner. 1988.

★4206★ *Installing Personal Computer*
QED Information Sciences, Inc.
Box 82-181
Wellesley, MA 02181
Ph: (617)237-5656 Fax: (617)235-0826
William E. Perry. 1984. Part of QED Personal Computing Series.

★4207★ *The Plain English Maintenance & Repair Guide for the IBM PC & PCjr*
Simon & Schuster, Inc.
Simon & Schuster Bldg.
1230 Avenue of the Americas
New York, NY 10020
Ph: (212)698-7000
Henry F. Beechhold. 1985.

★4208★ *Professional Photocopier Troubleshooting & Repair*
TAB/McGraw-Hill, Inc.
PO Box 182607
Columbus, OH 43218-2607
Fax: (614)759-3644 Fr: 800-822-8158
Eric Kuaimoku. Maps out the tools and techniques for servicing business and personal photocopiers.

★4209★ *Service Management: Principles & Practices*
Instrument Society of America
67 Alexander Dr.
PO Box 12277
Research Triangle Park, NC 27709
Ph: (919)549-8411
W. H. Bleuel. Second edition, 1986.

★4210★ *Start Your Own Computer Repair Business*
TAB/McGraw-Hill, Inc.
PO Box 182607
Columbus, OH 43218-2607
Fax: (614)759-3644 Fr: 800-822-8158
Linda Rohrbough and Michael F. Hordeski.

★4211★ *Troubleshooting and Repairing Computer Monitors*
TAB/McGraw-Hill, Inc.
PO Box 182607
Columbus, OH 43218-2607
Fax: (614)759-3644 Fr: 800-822-8158
Stephen J. Bigelow. A Guide devoted exclusively to monitor maintenance and repair.

★4212★ *Troubleshooting & Repairing TVRO Systems*
TAB/McGraw-Hill, Inc.
PO Box 182607
Columbus, OH 43218-2607
Fax: (614)759-3644 Fr: 800-822-8158
Stan Prentiss. 1988.

Periodicals

★4213★ *BTA Membership Directory*
Business Technology Association
12411 Wornall
Kansas City, MO 64145
Ph: (816)941-3100 Fax: (816)941-2829
Annual.

★4214★ *Business Technology Solutions*
Business Technology Association
12411 Wornall
Kansas City, MO 64145
Ph: (816)941-3100 Fax: (816)941-2829
Monthly. Includes reports on new technologies, industry trends, association news, and columns.

★4215★ *Computer Wave*
PO Box 19491
Seattle, WA 98109
Ph: (206)284-5476 Fax: (206)283-1020
Robert L. Crowther
Monthly. Newspaper focusing on computers and technology and serving Seattle.

★4216★ *EDP Weekly*
Computer Age
3918 Prosperity Ave., Ste. 310
Fairfax, VA 22031-3300
Ph: (703)573-8400 Fax: (703)573-8594
Charles Bailey
Weekly. Reports news concerning all aspects of the computer industry. Covers standards, licensing agreements, patents issued, industry growth statistics, new technology, and pertinent legislation. Also includes semimonthly features on robotics, electronic funds

transfer, mini and micro computers, data communications, and world trade.

★4217★ *Hotline*
Business Technology Association
12411 Wornall
Kansas City, MO 64145
Ph: (816)941-3100 Fax: (816)941-2829

Semimonthly. Includes industry and association news.

Other Sources of Information

★4218★ "Computer Service Technician" in *100 Best Jobs for the 1990s & Beyond*
Dearborn Financial Publishing, Inc.
520 N. Dearborn St.
Chicago, IL 60610-4354
Ph: (312)836-4400 Fax: (312)836-1021
Fr: 800-621-9621

Carol Kleiman. 1992. Describes 100 jobs ranging from accountants to veterinarians. Each job profile includes such information as education, experience, and certification needed, salaries, and job search suggestions.

★4219★ "Office/Business Machine Repairer" in *100 Best Jobs for the 1990s & Beyond*
Dearborn Financial Publishing, Inc.
520 N. Dearborn St.
Chicago, IL 60610-4354
Ph: (312)836-4400 Fax: (312)836-1021
Fr: 800-621-9621

Carol Kleiman. 1992. Describes 100 jobs ranging from accountants to veterinarians. Each job profile includes such information as education, experience, and certification needed, salaries, and job search suggestions.

Electronic Home Entertainment Equipment Repairers

Electronic home entertainment equipment repairers, also called service technicians, repair radios, televisions, stereo systems, home security systems, and video systems. Some may specialize in only one kind of equipment. Repairers conduct routine checks to locate the trouble. When these checks fail to find the problem, the repairers refer to wiring diagrams and service manuals. Repairs usually consist of part replacements or adjustments using tools such as soldering guns, wire cutters, and other hand tools. Self-employed electronic home entertainment equipment repairers also have managerial responsibilities, including ordering supplies and keeping records.

Salaries

Repairers earnings vary depending upon skill level, type of employer, and geographic location.

Lowest 10 percent	Less than $312/week
Median	$521/week
Top 10 percent	More than $729/week

Employment Outlook

Growth rate until the year 2005: Decline.

Electronic Home Entertainment Equipment Repairers

Career Guides

★4220★ *Aim For A Job As An Electronic Technician*
Rosen Publishing Group
29 E. 21st St.
New York, NY 10010
Ph: (212)777-3017 Fax: (212)777-0277
Fr: 800-237-9932

John E. Keefe. Revised edition, 1978. Describes the training requirements and the advantages and disadvantages of various jobs available in electronics.

★4221★ *Careers in Electronics*
RMI Media Productions, Inc.
2807 West 47th St.
Shawnee Mission, KS 66205
Ph: (913)262-3974 Fax: (913)362-6910
Fr: 800-745-5480

Videocassette. 1984. 19 mins. This program shows the wide variety of occupations in the electronics field.

★4222★ *Careers in the Electronics Industry*
International Society of Certified Electronics Technicians
2708 W. Berry St.
Fort Worth, TX 76109
Ph: (817)921-9101

This 16-page booklet provides an overview of the electronics industry and describes training and qualifications, employment outlook, earnings, and working conditions. Includes a state-by-state listing of electronic technician training schools.

★4223★ "Consumer Electronic Services" in *Electronic Service Careers* (pp. 57-62)
Franklin Watts, Inc.
387 Park Avenue, S.
New York, NY 10016
Ph: (212)686-7070

Robert Laurance. 1987. Discusses the work of an electronic service technician, employment outlook, places of employment, and educational preparation and training. Describes jobs with computers, consumer electronics, industrial electronics and the military.

★4224★ *Consumer Electronics Service Technician*
Careers, Inc.
PO Box 135
Largo, FL 34649-0135
Ph: (813)584-7333

1994. Two-page occupational summary card describing duties, working conditions, personal qualifications, training, earnings and hours, employment outlook, places of employment, related careers and where to write for more information.

★4225★ *Consumer Electronics Technicians*
Chronicle Guidance Publications, Inc.
66 Aurora St.
PO Box 1190
Moravia, NY 13118-1190
Ph: (315)497-0330 Fax: (315)497-3359
Fr: 800-622-7284

1991. This career brief describes the nature of the work, working conditions, hours and earnings, education and training, licensure, certification, unions, personal qualifications, social and psychological factors, employment outlook, entry methods, advancement, and related occupations.

★4226★ "Consumer Electronics" in *The Complete Electronics Career Guides* (pp. 30-32)
TAB/McGraw-Hill, Inc.
PO Box 182607
Columbus, OH 43218-2607
Fax: (614)759-3644 Fr: 800-822-8158

Joe Risse. 1989. Explores opportunities for electronic technicians in industry, broadcasting, appliance repair, telecommunications, computer servicing, and technical writing. Offers advice on educational preparation, training, finding or changing jobs, and career advancement. Lists trade publications and professional associations.

★4227★ "Consumer Servicing" in *The Complete Electronics Career Guide* (pp. 65-69)
TAB/McGraw-Hill, Inc.
PO Box 182607
Columbus, OH 43218-2607
Fax: (614)759-3644 Fr: 800-822-8158

Joe Risse. 1989. Explores opportunities for electronic technicians in industry, broadcasting, appliance repair, telecommunications, computer servicing, and technical writing. Offers advice on educational preparation, training, finding or changing jobs, and career advancement. Lists trade publications and professional associations.

★4228★ "Electronic Home Entertainment Equipment Repairers" in *Occupational Outlook Handbook*
U.S. Government Printing Office
Superintendent of Documents
Washington, DC 20402
Ph: (202)512-1800 Fax: (202)512-2250

Biennial; latest edition, 1994-95. Encyclopedia of careers describing more than 250 occupations and comprising about 85 percent of all jobs in the economy. Occupations that require lengthy education or training are given the most attention. For each occupation, the handbook describes job duties, working conditions, training, educational preparation, personal qualities, advancement possibilities, job outlook, earnings, and sources of additional information.

★4229★ "Electronic Organ Technicians" in *Encyclopedia of Careers and Vocational Guidance*
J.G. Ferguson Publishing Co.
200 W. Madison St., Ste. 300
Chicago, IL 60606
Ph: (312)580-5480 Fax: (312)580-4948

William E. Hopke, editor-in-chief. Ninth edition, 1993. Four-volume set that profiles 500 occupations and describes job trends in 74 industries. Includes career description, educational requirements, history of the job, methods of entry, advancement, employment outlook, earnings, working conditions, social and psychological factors, and sources of additional information.

★4230★ *Electronic Service Careers*
Franklin Watts, Inc.
387 Park Ave., S.
New York, NY 10016
Ph: (212)686-7070 Fax: (212)213-6435

Robert Laurance. 1987. Describes the career opportunities in electronics and the education and training requirements.

★4231★ "Electronics Repairers" in *Career Discovery Encyclopedia* (Vol.2, pp. 148-149)
J.G. Ferguson Publishing Co.
200 W. Madison St., Ste. 300
Chicago, IL 60606
Ph: (312)580-5480 Fax: (312)580-4948

E. Russell Primm, editor-in-chief. 1993. Contains two-page articles on 504 occupations. Each article describes job duties, earnings, and educational and training requirements.

★4232★ *Electronics Technician: A Career for Tomorrow*
Electronic Industries Association
Consumer Electronics Group
2001 Eye St. NW
PO Box 19100
Washington, DC 20006
Ph: (202)457-4919

1987. This eight-panel brochure describes the work, employment outlook, training, earnings, and opportunities for advancement.

★4233★ *The Professional Electronics Technician*
Electronics Technicians Association
602 N Jackson St.
Greencastle, IN 46135
Ph: (317)653-8262

This six-page brochure describes job duties, training, skills and aptitudes, salaries, employment outlook, and certification.

★4234★ "Radio and Television Technician" in *Telecommunications* (pp. 63-67)
Franklin Watts, Inc.
387 Park Avenue, S.
New York, NY 10016
Ph: (212)686-7070

Linda Barrett and Galen Guengerich. 1991. Surveys opportunities in telecommunications including telephone, radio, telegraph, and television communications. Includes job description, educational preparation, salary, and employment outlook. Offers job hunting advice.

★4235★ *Repair Cluster*
Center for Humanities, Inc.
Communications Park
Box 1000
Mount Kisco, NY 10549
Ph: (914)666-4100 Fax: (914)666-5319
Fr: 800-431-1242

Videocassette. 1984. 15 mins. People who work in the fields of Heating/Air Conditioning Repair, and Radio/TV Repair describe what it's like to work at their jobs.

★4236★ "Television and Radio Service Technician" in *Career Information Center* (Vol.3)
Simon and Schuster
200 Old Tappan Rd.
Old Tappan, NJ 07675
Fax: 800-445-6991 Fr: 800-223-2348

Richard Lidz and Dale Anderson, editorial directors. Fifth edition, 1993. For 600 occupations, describes job duties, entry-level requirements, education and training needed, advancement possibilities, employment outlook, earnings and benefits. The set is divided into 12 volumes. Each volume includes jobs related under a broad career field. Volume 13 is the index.

★4237★ "Television and Radio Service Technician" in *VGM's Careers Encyclopedia* (pp. 460-462)
National Textbook Co. (NTC)
VGM Career Books
4255 W. Touhy Ave.
Lincolnwood, IL 60646-1975
Ph: (708)679-5500 Fax: (708)679-2494
Fr: 800-323-4900

Third edition, 1991. Contains two- to five-page descriptions of 200 managerial, professional, technical, trade, and service occupations. Each profile includes job duties, places of employment, qualifications, educational preparation, training, employment potential, advancement, income, and additional sources of information.

★4238★ *Television Repairer*
Vocational Biographies, Inc.
PO Box 31
Sauk Centre, MN 56378-0031
Ph: (612)352-6516 Fax: (612)352-5546
Fr: 800-255-0752

1990. This pamphlet profiles a person working in the job. Includes information about job duties, working conditions, places of employment, educational preparation, labor market outlook, and salaries.

★4239★ *Tools for the Electrical Trades*
Bergwall Productions
540 Baltimore Pike
Chadds Ford, PA 19317
Ph: (215)388-0400 Fax: (215)388-0405
Fr: 800-645-3565

Videocassette. 1986. 58 mins. A look at various electronic tools; on four tapes.

★4240★ *Video Career Library - Repair Fields*
Careers, Inc.
PO Box 135
Largo, FL 34649-0135
Ph: (813)584-7333

Videocassette. 1990. 23 mins. Part of the Video Career Library covering 165 occupations. Shows actual workers on the job. Includes industrial machinery repairers, communications equipment repairers, data processing equipment repairers, home entertainment equipment repairers, office machine repairers, electrical power installers and repairers, and electrical and electronic repairers.

★4241★ "Video Service Technician" in *Career Opportunities in Television, Cable, and Video* (pp. 196-197)
Facts on File
460 Park Ave. S.
New York, NY 10016-7382
Ph: (212)683-2244 Fax: 800-678-3633
Fr: 800-322-8755

Third edition, 1990. Describes 100 media-related jobs. Each occupational profile covers job duties, employment outlook, career paths, salaries, skills, and educational preparation. Offers tips for entering the field.

Associations

★4242★ Electronic Industries Association (EIA)
2500 Wilson Blvd.
Arlington, VA 22201
Ph: (703)907-7500 Fax: (703)457-4985

Members: Purpose: Trade organization representing manufacturers of electronic components, parts, systems and equipment for communications, industrial, government, and consumer use. **Publications:** *EIA Publications Index*, semiannual.

★4243★ Electronics Technicians Association, International (ETA-I)
602 N. Jackson
Greencastle, IN 46135
Ph: (317)653-8262 Fax: (317)653-8262

Members: Skilled electronics technicians. **Purpose:** Provides placement service; offers certification examinations for electronics technicians and satellite installers. Compiles wage and manpower statistics. **Publications:** *Directory of Professional Electronics Technicians*, annual. • *EEA Training Program*, monthly. • *Management Update*, monthly. • *Technician Association News*, monthly.

★4244★ International Society of Certified Electronics Technicians (ISCET)
2708 W. Berry, Ste. 3
Fort Worth, TX 76109
Ph: (817)921-9101 Fax: (817)921-3741

Members: Technicians in 37 countries who have been certified by the society. **Purpose:** Seeks to provide a fraternal bond among certified electronics technicians, raise their public image, and improve the effectiveness of industry education programs for technicians. Offers training programs in new electronics information. Maintains library of service literature for consumer electronic equipment, including manuals and schematics for out-of-date equipment. Offers general radiotelephone license. Sponsors testing program for certification of electronics technicians in the fields of audio, communications, computer, consumer, industrial, medical electronics, radar, radio-television, and video. Operates Hall of Fame. **Publications:** *ISCET Update*, quarterly. • *Professional Electronics Magazine*, bimonthly. • *Technical Log*, quarterly.

★4245★ National Electronics Service Dealers Association (NESDA)
2708 W. Berry St., Ste. 3
Fort Worth, TX 76109
Ph: (817)921-9061 Fax: (817)921-3741

Members: Local and state electronic service associations and companies representing 4200 individuals. **Purpose:** Provides educational assistance in electronic training to public schools; supplies technical service information on business management training to electronic service dealers. Offers certification, apprenticeship, and training programs through International Society of Certified Electronics Technicians. Compiles statistics on electronics service business; conducts technical service and business management seminars. **Publications:** *Industry Alert*, periodic. • *Legislative Alert*, periodic. • *National Electronics Service Dealers Association—Inside NESDA*, bimonthly. • *NESDA—Update*, bimonthly. • *Professional Electronics*, bimonthly. • *Professional Electronics Directory*.

Standards/Certification Agencies

★4246★ Electronics Technicians Association, International (ETA-I)
602 N. Jackson
Greencastle, IN 46135
Ph: (317)653-8262

Offers certification examinations for electronics technicians. Maintains VCR tapes for certification practice exams.

★4247★ International Society of Certified Electronics Technicians (ISCET)
2708 W. Berry, Ste. 3
Fort Worth, TX 76109
Ph: (817)921-9101

Sponsors testing program for certification of electronics technicians in the fields of audio, communications, computer, consumer, industrial, medical electronics, radar, radio-television, and video.

★4248★ National Electronics Service Dealers Association (NESDA)
2708 W. Berry St., Ste. 3
Fort Worth, TX 76109
Ph: (817)921-9061 Fax: (817)921-3741

Provides educational assistance in electronic training to public schools; supplies technical service information on business management training to electronic service dealers. Offers certification, apprenticeship, and training programs through International Society of Certified Electronics Technicians. Compiles statistics on electronics service business; conducts technical service and business management seminars.

★4249★ *Professionals . . . Are Certified by the Electronics Technicians Association, International*
Electronics Technicians Association
602 N Jackson St.
Greencastle, IN 46135
Ph: (317)653-8262

This six-panel brochure describes the certification process for electronics technicians. Covers eligibility requirements, examination contents, and specialties.

Test Guides

★4250★ *Certified Electronic Technician (CET)*
National Learning Corp.
212 Michael Dr.
Syosset, NY 11791
Ph: (516)921-8888 Fax: (516)921-8743
Fr: 800-645-6337

Jack Rudman. Part of the Admission Test Series. Books in this series provide test practice and drill for actual professional certification and licensure tests.

★4251★ *The CET Exam: ISCET: Certified Electronics Technician*
International Society of Certified Electronics Technicians
2708 W. Berry St.
Fort Worth, TX 76109
Ph: (817)921-9101

This six-panel brochure describes certification for electronic technicians. Outlines examination contents.

★4252★ *EEA Training Program*
Electronics Technicians Association, International (ETA-I)
602 N. Jackson
Greencastle, IN 46135
Ph: (317)653-8262

Monthly.

Educational Directories and Programs

★4253★ *Directory of Professional Electronics Technicians*
Electronics Technicians Association, International (ETA-I)
602 N. Jackson
Greencastle, IN 46135
Ph: (317)653-8262 Fax: (317)653-8262

Annual.

★4254★ *Professional Electronics Directory*
National Electronic Sales and Service Dealers Association (NESDA)
2708 W. Berry St., Ste. 3
Ft. Worth, TX 76109
Ph: (817)921-9061 Fax: (817)921-3741

Lists parts distributers, service contract vendors/administrators, software/systems vendors, trade associations, trade publications, and other services.

Awards, Scholarships, Grants, and Fellowships

★4255★ Electronics Technicians Association, International Technician of the Year
Electronics Technicians Association, International
604 N. Jackson
Greencastle, IN 46135
Ph: (317)653-8262

To honor a practicing electronics technician as an incentive for all other technicans to achieve higher goals. A plaque is awarded annually at the convention. Established in 1979 in memory of Norris R. Browne, CET, Houston, Tx.

★4256★ ISCET Tech-of-the-Year Award
International Society of Certified Electronics Technicians
c/o Alice Johnson
2708 W. Berry St.
Fort Worth, TX 76109
Ph: (817)921-9101

To recognize a technician for outstanding work in the field of electronics. Established in 1976.

★4257★ Technician of the Year
Electronics Technicians Association, International
602 N. Jackson
Greencastle, IN 46135
Ph: (317)653-8262

To honor a practicing electronics technician as an incentive for all other technicians to achieve higher goals. A plaque is awarded annually at the convention. Established in 1979 in memory of Norris R. Browne, CET, Houston, Texas.

★4258★ Technician of the Year Award
International Society of Certified Electronics Technicians
2708 W. Berry St.
Fort Worth, TX 76109
Ph: (817)921-9101 Fax: (817)921-3741

To recognize a technician for outstanding work in the field of electronics. Established in 1976.

Basic Reference Guides and Handbooks

★4259★ *Home VCR Repair Illustrated*
TAB/McGraw-Hill, Inc.
PO Box 182607
Columbus, OH 43218-2607
Fax: (614)759-3644 Fr: 800-822-8158

Richard C. Wilkins and Cheryl A. Hubbard. Guide to basic VCR maintenance and repair.

★4260★ *Maintaining and Repairing VCRs*
TAB/McGraw-Hill, Inc.
PO Box 182607
Columbus, OH 43218-2607
Fax: (614)759-3644 Fr: 800-822-8158
Robert L. Goodman. Third edition.

★4261★ *Troubleshooting & Repairing Audio & Video Cassette Players and Recorders*
TAB/McGraw-Hill, Inc.
PO Box 182607
Columbus, OH 43218-2607
Fax: (614)759-3644 Fr: 800-822-8158
Homer L. Davidson. Covers repair procedures for digital audio tapes, compact discs, stereos, and camcorders.

★4262★ *Troubleshooting and Repairing Camcorders*
TAB/McGraw-Hill, Inc.
PO Box 182607
Columbus, OH 43218-2607
Fax: (614)759-3644 Fr: 800-822-8158
Homer L. Davidson.

★4263★ *Troubleshooting and Repairing Solid-State TVs*
TAB/McGraw-Hill, Inc.
PO Box 182607
Columbus, OH 43218-2607
Fax: (614)759-3644 Fr: 800-822-8158
Homer L. Davidson. Second edition.

★4264★ *TV Repair for Beginners*
TAB/McGraw-Hill, Inc.
PO Box 182607
Columbus, OH 43218-2607
Fax: (614)759-3644 Fr: 800-822-8158
George Zwick and Homer Davidson. Describes how to repair such problems as horizontal streaking, interference, and color smears.

Periodicals

★4265★ *Carolina Retailer*
Halco Communications
841 Post Road Circle
PO Box 830034
Stone Mountain, GA 30083-0001
Ph: (404)879-9682 Fax: (404)879-6791
David Hollingsworth
Monthly. Regional trade tabloid for the electronics, appliances, consumer outdoor power equipment, and TVRO satellite industries.

★4266★ *Industry Alert*
National Electronics Service Dealers Association (NESDA)
2708 W. Berry St., Ste. 3
Fort Worth, TX 76109
Ph: (817)921-9061 Fax: (817)921-3741
Periodic.

★4267★ *International Society of Certified Electronics Technicians—Update*
International Society of Certified Electronics Technicians
2708 W. Berry St.
Ft. Worth, TX 76109
Ph: (817)921-9101 Fax: (817)921-3741
Barbara Rubin
Quarterly. Reflects the aims of the Society, which are to raise the public image of certified electronics technicians and to improve the effectiveness of industry education programs for technicians. Recurring features include news of research, a calendar of events, reports of meetings, news of educational opportunities, and job listings.

★4268★ *ISCET Update*
International Society of Certified Electronics Technicians (ISCET)
2708 W. Berry, Ste. 3
Fort Worth, TX 76109
Ph: (817)921-9101 Fax: (817)921-3741
Quarterly. Includes job listings.

★4269★ *Legislative Alert*
National Electronics Service Dealers Association (NESDA)
2708 W. Berry St., Ste. 3
Fort Worth, TX 76109
Ph: (817)921-9061 Fax: (817)921-3741
Periodic.

★4270★ *National Electronics Service Dealers Association—Inside NESDA*
National Electronics Service Dealers Association (NESDA)
2708 W. Berry St., Ste. 3
Fort Worth, TX 76109
Ph: (817)921-9061 Fax: (817)921-3741
Bimonthly.

★4271★ *NESDA—Update*
National Electronics Service Dealers Association (NESDA)
2708 W. Berry St., Ste. 3
Fort Worth, TX 76109
Ph: (817)921-9061 Fax: (817)921-3741
Bimonthly. Provides information on legislation, regulations, legal, and industry news.

★4272★ *Professional Electronics*
National Electronics Service Dealers Association (NESDA)
2708 W. Berry St., Ste. 3
Fort Worth, TX 76109
Ph: (817)921-9061 Fax: (817)921-3741
Bimonthly. For owners, operators, and employees of retail electronics sales/service firms. Includes technical articles as well as general interest articles.

Meetings and Conventions

★4273★ Consumers Electronics Instructors Conference
International Society of Certified Electronics Technicians (ISCET)
2708 W. Berry, Ste. 3
Fort Worth, TX 76109
Ph: (817)921-9101 Fax: (817)921-3741
Annual.

★4274★ ELECTRO - Electronics Show and Convention
Miller Freeman Expositions
13760 Noel Rd., Ste. 500
Dallas, TX 75240
Fax: (214)419-7938 Fr: 800-527-0207
Annual. Alternates between New York, New York and Boston, Massachusetts. **Dates and Locations:** 1996 May 07-09; Boston, MA.

★4275★ Electronic & Components Expo -International Tradeshow for the Electronics Equipment and Components Industry
Glahe International, Inc.
1700 K St., NW, Ste. 403
Washington, DC 20006-4557
Ph: (202)659-4557 Fax: (202)457-0776
Biennial.

★4276★ Electronic Distribution Show and Conference
Electronic Industry Show Corp.
222 S. Riverside Plaza, Ste. 2710
Chicago, IL 60606
Ph: (312)648-1140 Fax: (312)648-4282
Annual. Always held during April/May in Las Vegas, Nevada.

Telephone Installers and Repairers

Telephone installers and repairers install, service, and repair telephones and other communications equipment on customers' property. Telephone installers and repairers, sometimes called station installers or service technicians, relocate telephones or make changes on existing equipment, such as adding extensions or replacing an old phone with a newer model. In homes under construction they may install all necessary wiring and telephone jacks in the desired locations. Installers and technicians connect telephones to outside service wires, sometimes climbing poles or ladders to do so. In diagnosing problems, they work closely with trouble locators in the central office. Repairers find the source of the problem by connecting a test set to the customer's telephone line and then testing in conjunction with the trouble locator. Some experienced service technicians have learned additional skills in line installation and cable splicing. Those with multiple skills and the ability to handle emergencies quickly are considered especially valuable by many small companies.

Salaries

Pay scales vary greatly across the country. Specific information may be obtained from local telephone companies. However, telephone installers and repairers employed by AT & T and the Bell Operating Companies, and represented by the Communications Workers of America, earn an average weekly salary of $752-$824.

Employment Outlook

Growth rate until the year 2005: Decline sharply.

Telephone Installers and Repairers

Career Guides

★4277★ "Phone Repair Technician" in *Hard Hatted Women: Stories of Struggle and Success in the Trades* (pp. 235-253)
Seal Press
3131 Western Ave., Ste. 410
Seattle, WA 98121
Ph: (206)283-7844 Fax: (206)285-9410

Molly Martin, editor. 1988. Twenty-six women recount their experiences working in blue collar occupations. They describe how they got in, the work they do, their relationships in predominantly male occupations, and their training.

★4278★ "Telephone Installer" in *Exploring Nontraditional Jobs for Women* (pp. 43-48)
Rosen Publishing Group
29 E. 21st St.
New York, NY 10010
Ph: (212)777-3017 Fax: (212)777-0277
Fr: 800-237-9932

Rose Neufeld. 1989. Describes blue-collar, male dominated occupations. Discusses what is done on the job, training, where to apply for jobs, tools used, salaries, and advantages and disadvantages. Relates the experiences of women who are working in the field.

★4279★ *Telephone Installer/Repair Technician*
Careers, Inc.
PO Box 135
Largo, FL 34649-0135
Ph: (813)584-7333

1993. Two-page occupational summary card describing duties, working conditions, personal qualifications, training, earnings and hours, employment outlook, places of employment, related careers and where to write for more information.

★4280★ "Telephone Installer/Repair Technician" in *Occu-Facts: Information on 580 Careers in Outline Form*
Careers, Inc.
PO Box 135
Largo, FL 34649-0135
Ph: (813)584-7333

Biennial, 1995-96 edition. Each one-page occupational profile describes duties, working conditions, physical surroundings and demands, aptitudes, temperament, educational requirements, employment outlook, earnings, and places of employment.

★4281★ "Telephone Installer/Repairer" in *Jobs Rated Almanac*
World Almanac
1 International Blvd., Ste. 444
Mahwah, NJ 07495
Ph: (201)529-6900 Fax: (201)529-6901

Les Krantz. Second edition, 1992. Ranks 250 jobs by environment, salary, outlooks, physical demands, stress, security, travel opportunities, and extra perks. Includes jobs the editor feels are the most common, most interesting, and the most rapidly growing.

★4282★ "Telephone Installers and Repairers" in *Career Discovery Encyclopedia* (Vol.6, pp. 100-101)
J.G. Ferguson Publishing Co.
200 W. Madison St., Ste. 300
Chicago, IL 60606
Ph: (312)580-5480 Fax: (312)580-4948

E. Russell Primm, editor-in-chief. 1993. Contains two-page articles on 504 occupations. Each article describes job duties, earnings, and educational and training requirements.

★4283★ "Telephone Installers and Repairers" in *Occupational Outlook Handbook*
U.S. Government Printing Office
Superintendent of Documents
Washington, DC 20402
Ph: (202)512-1800 Fax: (202)512-2250

Biennial; latest edition, 1994-95. Encyclopedia of careers describing more than 250 occupations and comprising about 85 percent of all jobs in the economy. Occupations that require lengthy education or training are given the most attention. For each occupation, the handbook describes job duties, working conditions, training, educational preparation, personal qualities, advancement possibilities, job outlook, earnings, and sources of additional information.

★4284★ "Telephone Service Technician" in *Career Information Center* (Vol.3)
Simon and Schuster
200 Old Tappan Rd.
Old Tappan, NJ 07675
Fax: 800-445-6991 Fr: 800-223-2348

Richard Lidz and Dale Anderson, editorial directors. Fifth edition, 1993. For 600 occupations, describes job duties, entry-level requirements, education and training needed, advancement possibilities, employment outlook, earnings and benefits. The set is divided into 12 volumes. Each volume includes jobs related under a broad career field. Volume 13 is the index.

★4285★ "Telephone Service Technician" in *Telecommunications* (pp. 27-31)
Franklin Watts, Inc.
387 Park Avenue, S.
New York, NY 10016
Ph: (212)686-7070

Linda Barrett and Galen Guengerich. 1991. Surveys opportunities in telecommunications including telephone, radio, telegraph, and television communications. Includes job description, educational preparation, salary, and employment outlook. Offers job hunting advice.

Associations

★4286★ North American Telecommunications Association (NATA)
2000 M St. NW, Ste. 550
Washington, DC 20036
Ph: (202)296-9800 Fax: (202)296-4993

Members: Manufacturers and distributors of communications, computer, and office equipment; suppliers, consultants, and users of voice and data technology; related service and information providers. **Purpose:** Provides legal, legislative, public relations, research, and membership services. Conducts specialized education and research programs. Presents annual exhibition showcase. Compiles statistics. **Publications:** *Directory of Telecommunications and Education Programs*, periodic. • *Export Guide.* • *Industry Basics.* • *NATA Communicator*, monthly. • *NATA Sourcebook*, annual. • *Sales Agency: A Comparative Analysis.* • *Telecom Export Guide*, biennial. • *Telecom Market Review and Forecast*, annual. • *Voice Messaging Industry Review.* • *Voice Processing Industry Review.* • *Washington Update*, biweekly.

★4287★ United States Telephone Association (USTA)
1401 H St., Ste. 600
Washington, DC 20005-2136
Ph: (202)326-7300 Fax: (202)326-7333
Members: Local operating telephone companies or telephone holding companies. Members represent a total of 114 million access lines. **Purpose:** Conducts educational and training programs. Maintains 21 committees. **Publications:** *Holding Company Report*, annual. • *Phonefacts*, annual. • *Statistical Volumes*, annual. • *Teletimes*, quarterly.

Educational Directories and Programs

★4288★ Directory of Telecommunications and Education Programs
North American Telecommunications Association (NATA)
2000 M St. NW, Ste. 550
Washington, DC 20036
Ph: (202)296-9800 Fax: (202)296-4993
Periodic.

Basic Reference Guides and Handbooks

★4289★ NATA Industry Basics
North American Telecommunications Association (NATA)
2000 M St. NW, Ste. 550
Washington, DC 20036
Ph: (202)296-9800 Fax: (202)296-4993

★4290★ NATA Sourcebook
North American Telecommunications Association (NATA)
2000 M St. NW, Ste. 550
Washington, DC 20036
Ph: (202)296-9800 Fax: (202)296-4993
Annual. Directory.

★4291★ Ready-To-Build Telephone Enhancements
TAB/McGraw-Hill, Inc.
PO Box 182607
Columbus, OH 43218-2607
Fax: (614)759-3644 Fr: 800-822-8158
Delton T. Horn. Describes ways to turn an average telephone into a fully functionals, multi-purpose home communication system. Includes step-by-step instructions, parts list, and parts layout diagram.

★4292★ Telephone Repair Illustrated
TAB/McGraw-Hill, Inc.
PO Box 182607
Columbus, OH 43218-2607
Fax: (614)759-3644 Fr: 800-822-8158
Stephen J. Bigelow. Shows how to install, maintain, and repair telephones and answering machines. Includes coverage of rotary, electronic, cordless, cellular, and classic telephones.

Periodicals

★4293★ Export Guide
North American Telecommunications Association (NATA)
2000 M St. NW, Ste. 550
Washington, DC 20036
Ph: (202)296-9800 Fax: (202)296-4993

★4294★ Industry Basics
North American Telecommunications Association (NATA)
2000 M St. NW, Ste. 550
Washington, DC 20036
Ph: (202)296-9800 Fax: (202)296-4993

★4295★ NATA Communicator
North American Telecommunications Association (NATA)
2000 M St. NW, Ste. 550
Washington, DC 20036
Ph: (202)296-9800 Fax: (202)296-4993
Monthly.

★4296★ Rural Telecommunications
National Telephone Cooperative Assn.
2626 Pennsylvania Ave. NW
Washington, DC 20037
Ph: (202)298-2300 Fax: (202)298-2320
Lisa Westbrook
Bimonthly.

★4297★ Sales Agency: A Comparative Analysis
North American Telecommunications Association (NATA)
2000 M St. NW, Ste. 550
Washington, DC 20036
Ph: (202)296-9800 Fax: (202)296-4993

★4298★ Telecom Export Guide
North American Telecommunications Association (NATA)
2000 M St. NW, Ste. 550
Washington, DC 20036
Ph: (202)296-9800 Fax: (202)296-4993
Biennial.

★4299★ Telecom Market Review and Forecast
North American Telecommunications Association (NATA)
2000 M St. NW, Ste. 550
Washington, DC 20036
Ph: (202)296-9800 Fax: (202)296-4993
Annual. Statistical review of the telecommunications industry.

★4300★ Voice Messaging Industry Review
North American Telecommunications Association (NATA)
2000 M St. NW, Ste. 550
Washington, DC 20036
Ph: (202)296-9800 Fax: (202)296-4993

★4301★ Voice Processing Industry Review
North American Telecommunications Association (NATA)
2000 M St. NW, Ste. 550
Washington, DC 20036
Ph: (202)296-9800 Fax: (202)296-4993

★4302★ Washington Update
North American Telecommunications Association (NATA)
2000 M St. NW, Ste. 550
Washington, DC 20036
Ph: (202)296-9800 Fax: (202)296-4993
Biweekly.

Other Sources of Information

★4303★ Phonefacts
United States Telephone Association (USTA)
1401 H. St., Ste. 600
Washington, DC 20006
Ph: (202)326-7300 Fax: (202)326-7333
Annual.

Elevator Installers and Repairers

Elevator installers and repairers, also called **elevator constructors** or mechanics, assemble, install, and replace elevators, escalators, and similar equipment in new and old buildings. Once the equipment is in service, they maintain and repair it. These duties require thorough knowledge of electronics, electricity, and hydraulics. Elevator constructors usually specialize in installation, maintenance, or repair work. Maintenance and repair workers generally need more knowledge of electricity and electronics than installers because a large part of maintenance and repair work is troubleshooting. Similarly, construction "adjustors," who fine-tune the newly installed equipment, need a thorough knowledge of electricity, electronics, and computers. Most elevator installers and repairers are employed by field offices of elevator manufacturers; small, local elevator maintenance and repair contractors; or by government agencies or businesses that do their own elevator maintenance and repair.

Salaries

Weekly earnings for elevator installers and repairers are listed below.

Elevator installers and repairers	$740/week
Probationary helpers	$370/week
Non-probationary helpers	$518/week
Mechanics-in-charge	$830/week

Employment Outlook

Growth rate until the year 2005: Average.

Elevator Installers and Repairers

Career Guides

★4304★ "Elevator Constructor and Repair Worker" in *Career Information Center* (Vol.4)
Simon and Schuster
200 Old Tappan Rd.
Old Tappan, NJ 07675
Fax: 800-445-6991 Fr: 800-223-2348

Richard Lidz and Dale Anderson, editorial directors. Fifth edition, 1993. For 600 occupations, describes job duties, entry-level requirements, education and training needed, advancement possibilities, employment outlook, earnings and benefits. The set is divided into 12 volumes. Each volume includes jobs related under a broad career field. Volume 13 is the index.

★4305★ *Elevator Constructors (Mechanics)*
Chronicle Guidance Publications, Inc.
66 Aurora St.
PO Box 1190
Moravia, NY 13118-1190
Ph: (315)497-0330 Fax: (315)497-3359
Fr: 800-622-7284

1992. This career brief describes the nature of the work, working conditions, hours and earnings, education and training, licensure, certification, unions, personal qualifications, social and psychological factors, employment outlook, entry methods, advancement, and related occupations.

★4306★ "Elevator Constructors" in *Opportunities in Building Construction Trades* (p. 52)
National Textbook Co. (NTC)
VGM Career Books
4255 W. Touhy Ave.
Lincolnwood, IL 60646-1975
Ph: (708)679-5500 Fax: (708)679-2494
Fr: 800-323-4900

Michael Sumichrast. 1989. Gives an overview of the construction industry and describes the jobs of various craftworkers. Covers different kinds of builders: home, custom; and describes management skills needed and industry trends affecting opportunities.

★4307★ "Elevator Installers and Repairers" in *Career Discovery Encyclopedia* (Vol.2, pp. 156-157)
J.G. Ferguson Publishing Co.
200 W. Madison St., Ste. 300
Chicago, IL 60606
Ph: (312)580-5480 Fax: (312)580-4948

E. Russell Primm, editor-in-chief. 1993. Contains two-page articles on 504 occupations. Each article describes job duties, earnings, and educational and training requirements.

★4308★ "Elevator Installers and Repairers" in *Encyclopedia of Careers and Vocational Guidance* (Vol.2, pp. 581-584)
J.G. Ferguson Publishing Co.
200 W. Madison St., Ste. 300
Chicago, IL 60606
Ph: (312)580-5480 Fax: (312)580-4948

William E. Hopke, editor-in-chief. Ninth edition, 1993. Four-volume set that profiles 500 occupations and describes job trends in 74 industries. Includes career description, educational requirements, history of the job, methods of entry, advancement, employment outlook, earnings, working conditions, social and psychological factors, and sources of additional information.

★4309★ "Elevator Installers and Repairers" in *Occupational Outlook Handbook*
U.S. Government Printing Office
Superintendent of Documents
Washington, DC 20402
Ph: (202)512-1800 Fax: (202)512-2250

Biennial; latest edition, 1994-95. Encyclopedia of careers describing more than 250 occupations and comprising about 85 percent of all jobs in the economy. Occupations that require lengthy education or training are given the most attention. For each occupation, the handbook describes job duties, working conditions, training, educational preparation, personal qualities, advancement possibilities, job outlook, earnings, and sources of additional information.

Associations

★4310★ International Union of Elevator Constructors (IUEC)
Clark Bldg., Ste. 530
5565 Sterrett Pl., Ste. 310
Columbia, MD 21044
Ph: (410)997-9000

Members: Elevator constructor unions in the U.S. and Canada. **Purpose:** Supplies companies with referrals to elevator installers. **Publications:** *The Constructor*, monthly.

Test Guides

★4311★ *Career Examination Series: Chief Elevator Starter*
National Learning Corp.
212 Michael Dr.
Syosset, NY 11791
Ph: (516)921-8888 Fax: (516)921-8743
Fr: 800-645-6337

Jack Rudman. All examination guides in this series contain questions with answers.

★4312★ *Career Examination Series: Elevator Inspector*
National Learning Corp.
212 Michael Dr.
Syosset, NY 11791
Ph: (516)921-8888 Fax: (516)921-8743
Fr: 800-645-6337

Jack Rudman. 1989. All examination guides in this series contain questions with answers.

★4313★ *Career Examination Series: Elevator Mechanic*
National Learning Corp.
212 Michael Dr.
Syosset, NY 11791
Ph: (516)921-8888 Fax: (516)921-8743
Fr: 800-645-6337

Jack Rudman. Other guides are available for elevator mechanic's helper, elevator inspector, and elevator starter. All examination guides in this series contain questions with answers.

★4314★ *Career Examination Series: Foreman Elevator Mechanic*
National Learning Corp.
212 Michael Dr.
Syosset, NY 11791
Ph: (516)921-8888 Fax: (516)921-8743
Fr: 800-645-6337

Jack Rudman. All examination guides in this series contain questions with answers.

★4315★ *Career Examination Series: Foreman (Elevators & Escalators)*
National Learning Corp.
212 Michael Dr.
Syosset, NY 11791
Ph: (516)921-8888 Fax: (516)921-8743
Fr: 800-645-6337

Jack Rudman. 1989. All examination guides in this series contain questions with answers.

★4316★ *Maintenance Mechanic*
Prentice Hall Press
Simon & Schuster Inc.
200 Old Tappan Rd.
Old Tappan, NJ 07675
Ph: 800-223-2348

Hy Hammer. First edition, 1988. Provides information for applicants interested in the following entry-level civil service positions: mason's helper, elevator mechanic's helper, mechanical maintainer's helper, among others.

Basic Reference Guides and Handbooks

★4317★ *Elevators & Engineering: An Architectural Guide*
Vance Bibliographies
112 N. Charter St.
Monticello, IL 61856
Ph: (217)762-3831

Coppa & Avery Consultants Staff. 1987.

★4318★ *Lift Practice*
State Mutual Book & Periodical Service, Ltd.
521 5th Ave., 17th Fl.
New York, NY 10175
Ph: (212)682-5844

1982.

★4319★ *Lift Servicing & Maintenance*
State Mutual Book & Periodical Service, Ltd.
521 5th Ave. 17th Fl.
New York, NY 10175
Ph: (212)682-5844

1982.

★4320★ *Safety Code for Elevators & Escalators*
American Society of Mechanical Engineers
345 E. 47th St.
New York, NY 10017
Ph: (212)705-7722

1987.

★4321★ *Safety Code for Elevators & Escalators: Handbook on A17.1*
American Society of Mechanical Engineers
345 E. 47th St.
New York, NY 10017
Ph: (212)705-7722

E. A. Donoghue, editor. 1987.

Periodicals

★4322★ *Elevator World, Inc.*
Elevator World, Inc.
354 Morgan Ave.
PO Box 6507
Mobile, AL 36606
Ph: (205)479-4514 Fax: (205)479-7043
W.C. Sturgeon

Monthly. Magazine for the elevator industry.

Other Sources of Information

★4323★ *The Elevator*
Walker & Company
720 5th Ave.
New York, NY 10019
Ph: (212)265-3632 Fax: (212)307-1764

Barbara Ford. 1982. Part of Inventions that Changed Our Lives Series.

★4324★ "Elevator Operator" in *Career Selector 2001*
Barron's Educational Series, Inc.
250 Wireless Blvd.
Hauppauge, NY 11788
Ph: (516)434-3311 Fax: (516)434-3723
Fr: 800-645-3476

James C. Gonyea. 1993.

★4325★ *Lift Erection*
State Mutual Book & Periodical Services, Ltd.
521 5th Ave., 17th Fl.
New York, NY 10175
Ph: (212)682-5844

1982.

★4326★ *Vertical Transportation: Elevators & Escalators*
John Wiley and Sons, Inc.
605 3rd Ave.
New York, NY 10158-0012
Ph: (212)850-6000 Fax: (212)850-6088
Fr: 800-526-5368

George R. Strakosch. Second edition, 1983.

Farm Equipment Mechanics

Farm equipment mechanics perform preventive maintenance and repair all manners of farm equipment like tractors, combines, planters, and tillage equipment. As farm machinery has grown larger with more electronic and hydraulic controls, farmers have increasingly turned to farm equipment dealers for service and repair of the machines they sell. Therefore, almost every dealer employs farm equipment mechanics, often called service technicians, to do this work. Some mechanics specialize in certain types of work such as hydraulics or transmission repair. A variety of basic hand tools are used in addition to sophisticated precision equipment. While most farm equipment mechanics work in service departments of farm equipment dealers, others work in independent repair shops and in shops on large farms.

Salaries

Farm equipment mechanics have median weekly earnings of about $355. The top 10 percent earn over $608/week.

Employment Outlook

Growth rate until the year 2005: More slowly than average.

Farm Equipment Mechanics

CAREER GUIDES

★4327★ *Careers in Farm Equipment Mechanics*
North American Equipment Dealers Association/NAED Foundation
10877 Watson Rd.
St. Louis, MO 63127-1081
Ph: (314)821-7220

This six-panel brochure describes the nature of the work, working conditions, places of employment, training, and advancement opportunities, employment outlook, and earnings.

★4328★ *Do Your Own Thing . . . in the Mechanical Field*
AIMS Media, Inc.
9710 DeSoto Ave.
Chatsworth, CA 91311
Ph: (818)773-4300 Fax: (818)341-6700
Fr: 800-367-2467

Videocassette. 1979. 16 mins. Various job levels in the mechanical field are outlined for students.

★4329★ *Farm Equipment Mechanic*
Careers, Inc.
PO Box 135
Largo, FL 34649-0135
Ph: (813)584-7333

1994. Two-page occupational summary card describing duties, working conditions, personal qualifications, training, earnings and hours, employment outlook, places of employment, related careers and where to write for more information.

★4330★ "Farm Equipment Mechanic" in *Occu-Facts: Information on 580 Careers in Outline Form*
Careers, Inc.
PO Box 135
Largo, FL 34649-0135
Ph: (813)584-7333

Biennial, 1995-96 edition. Each one-page occupational profile describes duties, working conditions, physical surroundings and demands, aptitudes, temperament, educational requirements, employment outlook, earnings, and places of employment.

★4331★ *Farm Equipment Mechanics*
Chronicle Guidance Publications, Inc.
66 Aurora St.
PO Box 1190
Moravia, NY 13118-1190
Ph: (315)497-0330 Fax: (315)497-3359
Fr: 800-622-7284

1993. This career brief describes the nature of the work, working conditions, hours and earnings, education and training, licensure, certification, unions, personal qualifications, social and psychological factors, employment outlook, entry methods, advancement, and related occupations.

★4332★ "Farm Equipment Mechanics" in *Career Discovery Encyclopedia* (Vol.3, pp. 172-173)
J.G. Ferguson Publishing Co.
200 W. Madison St., Ste. 300
Chicago, IL 60606
Ph: (312)580-5480 Fax: (312)580-4948

E. Russell Primm, editor-in-chief. 1993. Contains two-page articles on 504 occupations. Each article describes job duties, earnings, and educational and training requirements.

★4333★ "Farm Equipment Mechanics" in *Encyclopedia of Careers and Vocational Guidance* (Vol.2, pp. 623-627)
J.G. Ferguson Publishing Co.
200 W. Madison St., Ste. 300
Chicago, IL 60606
Ph: (312)580-5480 Fax: (312)580-4948

William E. Hopke, editor-in-chief. Ninth edition, 1993. Four-volume set that profiles 500 occupations and describes job trends in 74 industries. Includes career description, educational requirements, history of the job, methods of entry, advancement, employment outlook, earnings, working conditions, social and psychological factors, and sources of additional information.

★4334★ "Farm Equipment Mechanics" in *Occupational Outlook Handbook*
U.S. Government Printing Office
Superintendent of Documents
Washington, DC 20402
Ph: (202)512-1800 Fax: (202)512-2250

Biennial; latest edition, 1994-95. Encyclopedia of careers describing more than 250 occupations and comprising about 85 percent of all jobs in the economy. Occupations that require lengthy education or training are given the most attention. For each occupation, the handbook describes job duties, working conditions, training, educational preparation, personal qualities, advancement possibilities, job outlook, earnings, and sources of additional information.

ASSOCIATIONS

★4335★ Motor and Equipment Manufacturers Association (MEMA)
10 Laboratory Dr.
PO Box 13966
Research Triangle Park, NC 27709-3966
Ph: (919)549-4800 Fax: (919)549-4824

Members: Manufacturers of automotive and heavy-duty original equipment and aftermarket components, maintenance equipment, chemicals, accessories, refinishing supplies, tools, and service equipment united for research into all aspects of the automotive and heavy-duty markets. **Purpose:** Provides manufacturer-oriented services and programs including marketing consultation for the automotive industry; federal and state legal, safety, and legislative representation and consultation; personnel services; manpower development workshops; international information. Cosponsors Automotive Aftermarket Industry Week, and automotive aftermarket trade show. Maintains credit reporting service covering wholesalers, retailers, chain stores, and warehouse distributors; offers electronic order-entry, price-update, and electronic document exchange services through MEMA/Transnet and MEMA/Ansinet systems. Maintains international liaison. Administers U.S. Automotive Parts Industry Japan Office, Tokyo in conjunction with the U.S. Department of Commerce and the United States Automotive Parts Industry European Office, Brussels. Compiles statistics on automotive and heavy duty OE market and aftermarkets for use by members and as a public service. **Publications:** *Autobody Supply and Equipment Market*, biennial. • *Automotive Distributor Trends and Financial Analysis*, periodic. • *Automotive Jobbers in the U.S.A.*, biennial. • *Car Maintenance in the U.S.A.*. • *Credit and*

Sales Reference Directory. • *Distributors Financial Analysis*. • *Europe Automotive Insight*, monthly. • *Foreign Vehicle Maintenance in the U.S.A.*. • *Heavy Duty Truck Maintenance in the U.S.A.*. • *International Buyer's Guide of U.S. Automotive and Heavy Duty Products*, biennial. • *Japan Automotive Insight*, monthly. • *Legislative Insight*, weekly. • *Market Analysts*, bimonthly. • *Marketing Insight*, weekly. • *Toxic Labeling Compliance Newsletter*, quarterly. • *Washington Digest*, biweekly.

★4336★ North American Equipment Dealers Association (NAEDA)
10877 Watson Rd.
St. Louis, MO 63127
Ph: (314)821-7220 Fax: (314)821-0674

Members: Retailers of farm machinery, implements, light industrial machinery, tools, vehicles, outdoor power equipment, and related supplies. **Purpose:** Conducts programs on management training, and governmental and trade relations. Sponsors group health and accident insurance program for members and their employees. Compiles statistics. **Publications:** *Cost of Doing Business Study*, annual. • *Farm and Power Equipment Dealer*, monthly. • *Official Guide—Tractors and Farm Equipment*, semiannual. • *Official Industrial Equipment Guide*, semiannual. • *Outdoor Power Equipment Official Guide*, annual.

Basic Reference Guides and Handbooks

★4337★ Heavy Duty Truck Maintenance in the U.S.A.
Motor and Equipment Manufacturers Association (MEMA)
10 Laboratory Dr.
PO Box 13966
Research Triangle Pk., NC 27709
Ph: (919)549-4800 Fax: (919)549-4824

★4338★ Official Guide—Tractors and Farm Equipment
North American Equipment Dealers Association (NAEDA)
10877 Watson Rd.
St. Louis, MO 63127
Ph: (314)821-7220 Fax: (314)821-0674

Semiannual. Guide for evaluating used tractors and other farm equipment.

★4339★ Official Industrial Equipment Guide
North American Equipment Dealers Association (NAEDA)
10877 Watson Rd.
St. Louis, MO 63127
Ph: (314)821-7220 Fax: (314)821-0674

Semiannual. Guide for evaluating used industrial equipment. Includes rental information.

★4340★ Outdoor Power Equipment Official Guide
North American Equipment Dealers Association (NAEDA)
10877 Watson Rd.
St. Louis, MO 63127
Ph: (314)821-7220 Fax: (314)821-0674

Annual. Guide for evaluating used outdoor power equipment. Includes rental information.

★4341★ Tractor Equipment & Parts Directory
American Business Directories, Inc.
5711 S. 86th Circle
Omaha, NE 68127
Ph: (402)593-4600 Fax: (402)331-1505

Updated continuously; printed on request. Entries include: Name, address, phone, size of advertisement, name of owner or manager, number of employees, year first in "Yellow Pages." Compiled from telephone company "Yellow Pages," nationwide. Arrangement: Geographical.

Periodicals

★4342★ Agri-Equipment & Chemical
Clintron Publishers, Inc.
PO Box 6
Spokane, WA 99210
Ph: (509)575-6774 Fax: (509)457-3885
Ron Riggan

Monthly. Agriculture magazine.

★4343★ Autobody Supply and Equipment Market
Motor and Equipment Manufacturers Association (MEMA)
10 Laboratory Dr.
PO Box 13966
Research Triangle Park, NC 27709-3966
Ph: (919)549-4800 Fax: (919)549-4824

Biennial.

★4344★ Cost of Doing Business Study
North American Equipment Dealers Association (NAEDA)
10877 Watson Rd.
St. Louis, MO 63127
Ph: (314)821-7220 Fax: (314)821-0674

Annual.

★4345★ Farm and Power Equipment Dealer
North American Equipment Dealers Association (NAEDA)
10877 Watson Rd.
St. Louis, MO 63127
Ph: (314)821-7220 Fax: (314)821-0674

Monthly. Provides management and marketing information for farm, lawn and garden, and industrial equipment dealers. Includes tax and legislative information.

Other Sources of Information

★4346★ Distributors Financial Analysis
Motor and Equipment Manufacturers Association (MEMA)
10 Laboratory Dr.
PO Box 13966
Research Triangle Pk., NC 27709
Ph: (919)549-4800 Fax: (919)549-4824

General Maintenance Mechanics

General maintenance mechanics repair and maintain all manner of mechanical equipment, machines, and buildings, as opposed to most craft workers who specialize in one kind of work. They may work on plumbing, electrical, and heating and cooling systems. Other projects may include drywall repairs, and roof, floor, and window maintenance and repairs. They also have knowledge of specialized equipment and machinery often found in cafeterias, laundries, hospitals, and factories. General maintenance mechanics inspect and diagnose problems and plan how the work will be done. They use a variety of common hand and power tools such as drills and wrenches. Nearly 30% of general maintenance mechanics work in service industries; most work for elementary and secondary schools, colleges, and universities, hospitals and nursing homes, and hotels. About 25% are employed by the manufacturing industry. Others work for real estate firms that operate office and apartment buildings and for wholesale and retail firms, government agencies, and gas and electric companies.

Salaries

Earnings vary widely by industry, geographic area, and skill level but generally are between $7.85 and $11.05 an hour.

Employment Outlook

Growth rate until the year 2005: Faster than average.

General Maintenance Mechanics

Career Guides

★4347★ *Building Maintenance Management*
Sheridan House, Inc.
145 Palisade St.
Dobbs Ferry, NY 10522
Ph: (914)693-2410

Reginald Lee. Third edition, 1987.

★4348★ *Career Success Series*
Cambridge Educational
PO Box 2153
Charleston, WV 25328-2153
Ph: (304)744-9323 Fax: (304)744-9351
Fr: 800-468-4227

Videocassette. 1986. 15 mins. A series, available separately, outlining various career choices for students. Occupations include: accounting, flight service, air transportation/ground/flight service, data processing, carpentry, clerk in banking/insurance, commodity sales, cosmetic personal grooming, fire fighting, forestry services, home economics, insulation/roofing, material handling, mechanics, photographic processing, pipefitting and plumbing, police science, printing, carpentry, medical laboratory technicians, secretarial services, and utilities equipment operator.

★4349★ "General Maintenance Mechanics" in *Career Discovery Encyclopedia* (Vol.3, pp. 56-57)
J.G. Ferguson Publishing Co.
200 W. Madison St., Ste. 300
Chicago, IL 60606
Ph: (312)580-5480 Fax: (312)580-4948

E. Russell Primm, editor-in-chief. 1993. Contains two-page articles on 504 occupations. Each article describes job duties, earnings, and educational and training requirements.

★4350★ "General Maintenance Mechanics" in *Encyclopedia of Careers and Vocational Guidance* (Vol.3, pp. 70-72)
J.G. Ferguson Publishing Co.
200 W. Madison St., Ste. 300
Chicago, IL 60606
Ph: (312)580-5480 Fax: (312)580-4948

William E. Hopke, editor-in-chief. Ninth edition, 1993. Four-volume set that profiles 500 occupations and describes job trends in 74 industries. Includes career description, educational requirements, history of the job, methods of entry, advancement, employment outlook, earnings, working conditions, social and psychological factors, and sources of additional information.

★4351★ "General Maintenance Mechanics" in *Occupational Outlook Handbook*
U.S. Government Printing Office
Superintendent of Documents
Washington, DC 20402
Ph: (202)512-1800 Fax: (202)512-2250

Biennial; latest edition, 1994-95. Encyclopedia of careers describing more than 250 occupations and comprising about 85 percent of all jobs in the economy. Occupations that require lengthy education or training are given the most attention. For each occupation, the handbook describes job duties, working conditions, training, educational preparation, personal qualities, advancement possibilities, job outlook, earnings, and sources of additional information.

★4352★ *General and Mechanical Maintenance Training Program*
NUS Training Corporation
910 Clopper Rd.
Gaithersburg, MD 20878-1399
Ph: (301)258-2500 Fax: (301)258-1205
Fr: 800-848-1717

Videocassette. 1980. 60 mins. This series is designed to improve the skills of personnel currently assigned to maintenance work or to provide newly assigned personnel with the skills required to become accomplished maintenance personnel. Programs available as a series or individually.

★4353★ *Lawn and Garden Equipment Technicians*
Chronicle Guidance Publications, Inc.
66 Aurora St.
PO Box 1190
Moravia, NY 13118-1190
Ph: (315)497-0330 Fax: (315)497-3359
Fr: 800-622-7284

1992. This career brief describes the nature of the work, working conditions, hours and earnings, education and training, licensure, certification, unions, personal qualifications, social and psychological factors, employment outlook, entry methods, advancement, and related occupations.

★4354★ "Maintenance Mechanics" in *American Almanac of Jobs and Salaries* (pp. 504)
Avon Books
1350 Avenue of the Americas
New York, NY 10019
Ph: (212)261-6800 Fr: 800-238-0658

John Wright, editor. Revised and updated, 1994-95. A comprehensive guide to the wages of hundreds of occupations in a wide variety of industries and organizations.

★4355★ *Maintenance Mechanics Qualification Program*
Technical Association of the Pulp & Paper Industry
Technology Park/Atlanta
PO Box 105113
Atlanta, GA 30348
Ph: (404)446-1400

Clint C. Bell. Second edition, 1989.

★4356★ *Mechanics*
Morris Video
2730 Monterey St., No. 105
Monterey Business Park
Torrance, CA 90503
Ph: (213)533-4800 Fr: 800-843-3606

Videocassette. 1984. 15 mins. Various careers in repair are examined including aircraft, motorcycle, diesel, refrigeration and heavy equipment.

★4357★ *Vocations U.S.A.*
Info-Disc Corporation
4 Professional Dr., Ste. 134
Gaithersburg, MD 20879
Ph: (301)948-2300 Fr: 800-648-6422

Videocassette. 1987. 60 mins. A disc collection outlining the requirements and methods of various career areas. Occupations include: transportation, mechanical/repair, health, agriculture, technical/manufacturing, and construction.

Test Guides

★4358★ *Career Examination Series: Director of Maintenance*
National Learning Corp.
212 Michael Dr.
Syosset, NY 11791
Ph: (516)921-8888 Fax: (516)921-8743
Fr: 800-645-6337

Jack Rudman. 1988. All examination guides in this series contain questions with answers.

★4359★ *Career Examination Series: Electronic Equipment Maintainer*
National Learning Corp.
212 Michael Dr.
Syosset, NY 11791
Ph: (516)921-8888 Fax: (516)921-8743
Fr: 800-645-6337

Jack Rudman. All examination guides in this series contain questions with answers.

★4360★ *Career Examination Series: Foreman of Mechanics*
National Learning Corp.
212 Michael Dr.
Syosset, NY 11791
Ph: (516)921-8888 Fax: (516)921-8743
Fr: 800-645-6337

Jack Rudman. All examination guides in this series contain questions with answers.

★4361★ *Career Examination Series: Mechanical Maintainer*
National Learning Corp.
212 Michael Dr.
Syosset, NY 11791
Ph: (516)921-8888 Fax: (516)921-8743
Fr: 800-645-6337

Jack Rudman. All examination guides in this series contain questions with answers.

★4362★ *Career Examination Series: Toll Equipment Maintenance Supervisor*
National Learning Corp.
212 Michael Dr.
Syosset, NY 11791
Ph: (516)921-8888 Fax: (516)921-8743
Fr: 800-645-6337

Jack Rudman. 1989. All examination guides in this series contain questions with answers.

★4363★ *Maintenance Mechanic*
Prentice Hall Press
Simon & Schuster Inc.
200 Old Tappan Rd.
Old Tappan, NJ 07675
Ph: 800-223-2348

Hy Hammer. First edition, 1988. Provides information for applicants interested in the following entry-level civil service positions: mason's helper, elevator mechanic's helper, mechanical maintainer's helper, among others.

Basic Reference Guides and Handbooks

★4364★ *Maintenance Management Handbook*
Fairmont Press, Inc.
700 Indian Trail
Lilburn, GA 30247
Ph: (404)925-9388

S. T. Cordero.

★4365★ *The Maintenance Mechanic's-Machinist's Toolbox Manual*
Prentice Hall
Rte. 9W
Englewood Cliffs, NJ 07632
Ph: (201)592-2000

John D. Bies. 1989.

★4366★ *Maintenance Supplies—Buyers' Guide Issue*
PTN Publishing Co.
445 Broad Hollow Rd., Ste. 21
Melville, NY 11747
Ph: (516)845-2700 Fax: (516)845-2726
Linda Bruder

Annual, December. Covers Approximately 1,000 manufacturers and associations for commercial, industrial, and institutional janitorial supplies; international coverage. Entries include: Co. name, address, phone, fax, product/service. Arrangement: Classified by product/service.

★4367★ *Planned Maintenance*
Didactic Systems, Inc.
PO Box 457
Cranford, NJ 07016
Ph: (201)789-2194

Didactic Systems Staff. 1969. Part of Simulation Game Series.

★4368★ *Practical Guide Maintenance Engineering*
Butterworth-Heinemann
80 Montvale Ave.
Stoneham, MA 02180
Ph: (617)438-8464 Fax: (617)279-4851

C. Dunlop. 1990.

Periodicals

★4369★ *Installation & Cleaning Specialist*
Specialist Publications, Inc.
17835 Ventura Blvd., Ste. 312
Encino, CA 91316
Ph: (818)345-3550 Fax: (818)344-9647
Howard Olansky

Monthly. Trade magazine for floor covering installers, workrooms, contractors, installing retailers, cleaning and maintenance firms, and distributors.

Meetings and Conventions

★4370★ International Maintenance Institute Show and Technical Conference
International Maintenance Institute
PO Box 266695
Houston, TX 77207
Ph: (713)481-0869 Fax: (713)481-8337

Annual.

Heating, Air-Conditioning, and Refrigeration Technicians

Heating, air-conditioning, and refrigeration technicians, install, maintain, and repair heating, air-conditioning and refrigeration systems in residential, commercial, industrial, and other buildings. Mechanics must be able to maintain, diagnose, and correct problems within the entire system. They adjust system controls to recommended settings and test the performance of the entire system using special tools and test equipment. Mechanics may specialize in installation or maintenance and repair. They may also specialize in a particular type of equipment. However, more and more technicians do both installation and servicing, and work with a variety of equipment. Heating equipment technicians, also called furnace installers, follow blueprints or other specifications to install oil, gas, electric, solid-fuel, and multifuel heating systems. After installation, they perform routine maintenance to keep the system operating efficiently. Air-conditioning and refrigeration mechanics install and service central air-conditioning systems and a variety of refrigeration equipment following blueprints, design specifications, and manufacturers' instructions. Once installed, they also perform necessary maintenance. Technicians use a wide range of tools including drills and torches. They also use a variety of testing devices such as voltmeters and pressure gauges.

Salaries

Median weekly earnings of air-conditioning, heating, and refrigeration mechanics who are wage and salary workers is $474.

Lowest 10 percent	$280/week or less
Middle 50 percent	$356-$596/week
Top 10 percent	$743/week or more

Employment Outlook

Growth rate until the year 2005: Faster than the average.

Heating, Air-Conditioning, and Refrigeration Technicians

Career Guides

★4371★ "Air Conditioning, Heating, and Refrigeration Mechanic" in *Career Information Center* (Vol.4)
Simon and Schuster
200 Old Tappan Rd.
Old Tappan, NJ 07675
Fax: 800-445-6991 Fr: 800-223-2348

Richard Lidz and Dale Anderson, editorial directors. Fifth edition, 1993. For 600 occupations, describes job duties, entry-level requirements, education and training needed, advancement possibilities, employment outlook, earnings and benefits. The set is divided into 12 volumes. Each volume includes jobs related under a broad career field. Volume 13 is the index.

★4372★ "Air Conditioning, Heating, and Refrigeration Mechanics" in *American Almanac of Jobs and Salaries* (p. 522)
Avon Books
1350 Avenue of the Americas
New York, NY 10019
Ph: (212)261-6800 Fr: 800-238-0658

John Wright, editor. Revised and updated, 1994-95. A comprehensive guide to the wages of hundreds of occupations in a wide variety of industries and organizations.

★4373★ *Air Conditioning/Heating/Solar Technician*
Careers, Inc.
PO Box 135
Largo, FL 34649-0135
Ph: (813)584-7333

1992. Two-page occupational summary card describing duties, working conditions, personal qualifications, training, earnings and hours, employment outlook, places of employment, related careers and where to write for more information.

★4374★ "Air-Conditioning/Heating/Solar Technician" in *Occu-Facts: Information on 580 Careers in Outline Form*
Careers, Inc.
PO Box 135
Largo, FL 34649-0135
Ph: (813)584-7333

Biennial, 1995-96 edition. Each one-page occupational profile describes duties, working conditions, physical surroundings and demands, aptitudes, temperament, educational requirements, employment outlook, earnings, and places of employment.

★4375★ "Air Conditioning and Heating Technician" in *Career Information Center* (Vol.4)
Simon and Schuster
200 Old Tappan Rd.
Old Tappan, NJ 07675
Fax: 800-445-6991 Fr: 800-223-2348

Richard Lidz and Dale Anderson, editorial directors. Fifth edition, 1993. For 600 occupations, describes job duties, entry-level requirements, education and training needed, advancement possibilities, employment outlook, earnings and benefits. The set is divided into 12 volumes. Each volume includes jobs related under a broad career field. Volume 13 is the index.

★4376★ "Air Conditioning, Refrigeration, and Heating Mechanic" in *Exploring Nontraditional Jobs for Women* (pp. 76-82)
Rosen Publishing Group
29 E. 21st St.
New York, NY 10010
Ph: (212)777-3017 Fax: (212)777-0277
Fr: 800-237-9932

Rose Neufeld. 1989. Describes blue-collar, male dominated occupations. Discusses what is done on the job, training, where to apply for jobs, tools used, salaries, and advantages and disadvantages. Relates the experiences of women who are working in the field.

★4377★ "Air-Conditioning, Refrigeration, and Heating Mechanic" in *VGM's Careers Encyclopedia* (pp. 29-32)
National Textbook Co. (NTC)
VGM Career Books
4255 W. Touhy Ave.
Lincolnwood, IL 60646-1975
Ph: (708)679-5500 Fax: (708)679-2494
Fr: 800-323-4900

Third edition, 1991. Contains two- to five-page descriptions of 200 managerial, professional, technical, trade, and service occupations. Each profile includes job duties, places of employment, qualifications, educational preparation, training, employment potential, advancement, income, and additional sources of information.

★4378★ "Air-Conditioning, Refrigeration, and Heating Mechanics" in *Encyclopedia of Careers and Vocational Guidance* (Vol.2, pp. 60-64)
J.G. Ferguson Publishing Co.
200 W. Madison St., Ste. 300
Chicago, IL 60606
Ph: (312)580-5480 Fax: (312)580-4948

William E. Hopke, editor-in-chief. Ninth edition, 1993. Four-volume set that profiles 500 occupations and describes job trends in 74 industries. Includes career description, educational requirements, history of the job, methods of entry, advancement, employment outlook, earnings, working conditions, social and psychological factors, and sources of additional information.

★4379★ "Air-Conditioning and Refrigeration Mechanic" in *Occu-Facts: Information on 580 Careers in Outline Form*
Careers, Inc.
PO Box 135
Largo, FL 34649-0135
Ph: (813)584-7333

Biennial, 1995-96 edition. Each one-page occupational profile describes duties, working conditions, physical surroundings and demands, aptitudes, temperament, educational requirements, employment outlook, earnings, and places of employment.

★4380★ *Air-Conditioning and Refrigeration Service Technicians*
Chronicle Guidance Publications, Inc.
66 Aurora St.
PO Box 1190
Moravia, NY 13118-1190
Ph: (315)497-0330 Fax: (315)497-3359
Fr: 800-622-7284

1994. This career brief describes the nature of the work, working conditions, hours and earnings, education and training, licensure, certification, unions, personal qualifications, social and psychological factors, employment outlook, entry methods, advancement, and related occupations.

★4381★ *Air Conditioning and Refrigeration Technician*
Careers, Inc.
PO Box 135
Largo, FL 34649-0135
Ph: (813)584-7333

1991. Two-page occupational summary card describing duties, working conditions, personal qualifications, training, earnings and hours, employment outlook, places of employment, related careers and where to write for more information.

★4382★ *Construction: Basic Principles*
RMI Media Productions, Inc.
2807 West 47th St.
Shawnee Mission, KS 66205
Ph: (913)262-3974 Fax: (913)362-6910
Fr: 800-745-5480

Videocassette. 1984. 20 mins. This series of five programs of varying lengths covers different aspects of career opportunities in the construction trades. Included are: concrete masonry, carpentry, electrical work, plumbing, and heating and air conditioning.

★4383★ *Do Your Own Thing . . . in the Mechanical Field*
AIMS Media, Inc.
9710 DeSoto Ave.
Chatsworth, CA 91311
Ph: (818)773-4300 Fax: (818)341-6700
Fr: 800-367-2467

Videocassette. 1979. 16 mins. Various job levels in the mechanical field are outlined for students.

★4384★ "Heating and Air Conditioning Installers" in *Opportunities in Building Construction Trades* (pp. 57-58)
National Textbook Co. (NTC)
VGM Career Books
4255 W. Touhy Ave.
Lincolnwood, IL 60646-1975
Ph: (708)679-5500 Fax: (708)679-2494
Fr: 800-323-4900

Michael Sumichrast. 1989. Gives an overview of the construction industry and describes the jobs of various craftworkers. Covers different kinds of builders: home, custom; and describes management skills needed and industry trends affecting opportunities.

★4385★ "Heating, Air-Conditioning, and Refrigeration Mechanics" in *Jobs! What They Are—Where They Are—What They Pay* (pp. 213)
Simon & Schuster, Inc.
Simon & Schuster Bldg.
1230 Avenue of the Americas
New York, NY 10020
Ph: (212)698-7000

Robert O. Snelling and Anne M. Snelling. Revised edition, 1992. Profiles 241 occupations, describing duties and responsibilities, educational preparation, earnings, employment opportunities, training, and qualifications.

★4386★ "Heating, Air-Conditioning, and Refrigeration Technicians" in *Occupational Outlook Handbook*
U.S. Government Printing Office
Superintendent of Documents
Washington, DC 20402
Ph: (202)512-1800 Fax: (202)512-2250

Biennial; latest edition, 1994-95. Encyclopedia of careers describing more than 250 occupations and comprising about 85 percent of all jobs in the economy. Occupations that require lengthy education or training are given the most attention. For each occupation, the handbook describes job duties, working conditions, training, educational preparation, personal qualities, advancement possibilities, job outlook, earnings, and sources of additional information.

★4387★ "Heating and Cooling Mechanics" in *Career Discovery Encyclopedia* (Vol.3, pp. 90-91)
J.G. Ferguson Publishing Co.
200 W. Madison St., Ste. 300
Chicago, IL 60606
Ph: (312)580-5480 Fax: (312)580-4948

E. Russell Primm, editor-in-chief. 1993. Contains two-page articles on 504 occupations. Each article describes job duties, earnings, and educational and training requirements.

★4388★ "Heating, Cooling, and Refrigeration" in *Opportunities in Plumbing and Pipefitting Careers* (pp. 83-85)
National Textbook Co. (NTC)
VGM Career Books
4255 W. Touhy Ave.
Lincolnwood, IL 60646-1975
Ph: (708)679-5500 Fax: (708)679-2494
Fr: 800-323-4900

Patrick J. Galvin. 1989. Describes the work, jobs, educational preparation, training, apprenticeships, a typical working day, salaries, future trends, and related fields.

★4389★ "Heating and Cooling Technicians" in *Career Discovery Encyclopedia* (Vol.3, pp. 92-93)
J.G. Ferguson Publishing Co.
200 W. Madison St., Ste. 300
Chicago, IL 60606
Ph: (312)580-5480 Fax: (312)580-4948

E. Russell Primm, editor-in-chief. 1993. Contains two-page articles on 504 occupations. Each article describes job duties, earnings, and educational and training requirements.

★4390★ "Heating/Refrigeration Mechanic" in *Jobs Rated Almanac*
World Almanac
1 International Blvd., Ste. 444
Mahwah, NJ 07495
Ph: (201)529-6900 Fax: (201)529-6901

Les Krantz. Second edition, 1992. Ranks 250 jobs by environment, salary, outlooks, physical demands, stress, security, travel opportunities, and extra perks. Includes jobs the editor feels are the most common, most interesting, and the most rapidly growing.

★4391★ "Heating, Ventilation and Air Conditioning" in *Career Connection II: A Guide to Technical Majors and Their Related Careers* (pp. 86-87)
Jist Works, Inc.
720 N. Park Ave.
Indianapolis, IN 46202-3431
Ph: (317)264-3720 Fax: (317)264-3709

Fred A. Rowe. 1994. Contains technical majors, such as automotive technology. Describes the major and the job. Lists high school and postsecondary school courses. Includes occupations related to the major, employment outlook, and starting salary.

★4392★ *Mechanics*
Morris Video
2730 Monterey St., No. 105
Monterey Business Park
Torrance, CA 90503
Ph: (213)533-4800 Fr: 800-843-3606

Videocassette. 1984. 15 mins. Various careers in repair are examined including aircraft, motorcycle, diesel, refrigeration and heavy equipment.

★4393★ *Repair Cluster*
Center for Humanities, Inc.
Communications Park
Box 1000
Mount Kisco, NY 10549
Ph: (914)666-4100 Fax: (914)666-5319
Fr: 800-431-1242

Videocassette. 1984. 15 mins. People who work in the fields of Heating/Air Conditioning Repair, and Radio/TV Repair describe what it's like to work at their jobs.

★4394★ *Video Career Library - Mechanical Fields*
Careers, Inc.
PO Box 135
Largo, FL 34649-0135
Ph: (813)584-7333

Videocassette. 1990. 22 mins. Part of the Video Career Library covering 165 occupations. Shows actual workers on the job. Includes automobile mechanics, diesel engine mechanics, aircraft engine mechanics, automobile body repairers, heavy equipment mechanics, and heating/air-conditioning/refrigeration mechanics.

★4395★ *Would You Like a Career That Pays Well, Helps People, and Provides Exceptional Opportunities?*
Air Conditioning and Refrigeration Institute
1501 Wilson Blvd., 6th Fl.
Arlington, VA 22209
Ph: (703)534-8800

An eight-panel brochure describes job opportunities in the air conditioning and refrigeration industry.

★4396★ *Your Future in the Plumbing Heating Cooling Industry*
National Association of Plumbing, Heating, and Cooling Contractors
P.O. Box 6808
180 S. Washington St.
Washington, DC 20046
Ph: (202)331-7675

1988. This eight-panel brochure describes the work, opportunities, working conditions, and entry into the field.

Associations

★4397★ American Society of Heating, Refrigerating and Air-Conditioning Engineers (ASHRAE)
1791 Tullie Cir. NE
Atlanta, GA 30329
Ph: (404)636-8400 Fax: (404)321-5478
Fr: 800-5-ASHRAE

Technical society of heating, ventilating, refrigeration, and air-conditioning engineers. Sponsors numerous research programs in cooperation with universities, research laboratories, and government agencies on subjects such as human and animal environmental studies, effects of air-conditioning, quality of inside air, heat transfer, flow, and cooling processes. Research and general technical programs are conducted through 90 technical committees organized in 11 sections. Conducts professional development seminars. **Publications:** *American Society of Heating, Refrigerating, and Air-Conditioning Engineers—Insights*, monthly. • *ASHRAE Journal*, monthly. • *ASHRAE Transactions*, semiannual.

★4398★ Associated Builders and Contractors (ABC)
1300 N. 17th St.
Rossyln, VA 22209
Ph: (703)812-2000

Members: Construction contractors, subcontractors, suppliers, and associates. **Purpose:** Aim is to foster and perpetuate the principles of rewarding construction workers and management on the basis of merit. Sponsors management education programs and craft training; also sponsors apprenticeship and skill training programs. Disseminates technological and labor relations information. Maintains placement service. Compiles statistics. **Publications:** *ABC Today*, semimonthly. • *National Membership Directory and Users Guide*, annual.

★4399★ National Association of Home Builders of the U.S. (NAHB)
1201 15th St. NW
Washington, DC 20005
Ph: (202)822-0200 Fax: (202)822-0559

Members: Single and multifamily home builders, commercial builders, and others associated with the building industry. **Purpose:** Lobbies on behalf of the housing industry and conducts public affairs activities to increase public understanding of housing and the economy. Collects and disseminates data on current developments in home building and home builders' plans through its Economics Department and nationwide Metropolitan Housing Forecast. Maintains NAHB Research Center, which functions as the research arm of the home building industry. Sponsors seminars and workshops on construction, mortgage credit, labor relations, cost reduction, land use, remodeling, and business management. Compiles statistics; offers charitable program, spokesman training, and placement service; maintains speakers' bureau, and hall of fame. Subsidiaries include Home Builders Institute and National Council of the Housing Industry. Maintains over 50 committees in many areas of construction; operates National Commercial Builders Council, National Council of the Multifamily Housing Industry, National Remodelers Council and National Sales and Marketing Council. **Publications:** *Builder Magazine*, monthly. • *Forecast of Housing Activity*, monthly. • *Housing Economics*, monthly. • *Housing Market Statistics*, monthly. • *Nation's Building News*, semimonthly. • *Reference Guide to Homebuilding Articles*, quarterly.

★4400★ National Association of Plumbing-Heating-Cooling Contractors (NAPHCC)
180 S. Washington St.
PO Box 6808
Falls Church, VA 22040
Ph: (703)237-8100 Fax: (703)237-7442
Fr: 800-533-7694

Members: Federation of state and local associations of plumbing, heating, and cooling contractors. **Purpose:** Seeks to advance sanitation, encourage sanitary laws, and generally improve the plumbing, heating, ventilating, and air conditioning industries. Conducts apprenticeship training programs, workshops, and seminars; cooperates with Plumbing-Heating-Cooling Information Bureau. Maintains speakers' bureau and political action committee. Conducts educational and research programs. **Publications:** *Connection*, monthly. • *Leadership Directory*, annual. • *News*, monthly.

★4401★ Refrigeration Service Engineers Society (RSES)
1666 Rand Rd.
Des Plaines, IL 60016-3552
Ph: (708)297-6464 Fax: (708)297-5038
Fr: 800-4-CERTIFY

Members: Persons engaged in refrigeration, air-conditioning and heating installation, service, sales, and maintenance. **Purpose:** Conducts training courses and certification testing. Maintains a hall of fame and a speakers' bureau. Has 3 boards and 23 committees. **Publications:** *Refrigeration Service and Contracting*, monthly. • *Service Application Manual.*

★4402★ Sheet Metal and Air Conditioning Contractors' National Association (SMACNA)
4201 Lafayette Center Dr.
Chantilly, VA 22021
Ph: (703)803-2980 Fax: (703)803-3732

Members: Ventilating, air handling, warm air heating, architectural and industrial sheet metal, kitchen equipment, testing and balancing, siding, and decking and specialty fabrication contractors. **Purpose:** Prepares standards and codes; sponsors research and educational programs on sheet metal duct construction and fire damper (single and multi-blade) construction. Engages in legislative and labor activities; conducts business management and contractor education programs. **Publications:** *Chaptergram.* • *SMACNEWS*, monthly.

Standards/Certification Agencies

★4403★ Refrigeration Service Engineers Society (RSES)
1666 Rand Rd.
Des Plaines, IL 60016-3552
Ph: (708)297-6464 Fax: (708)297-5038
Fr: 800-4-CERTIFY

Conducts training courses and certification testing. Maintains a hall of fame and a speakers' bureau.

★4404★ Sheet Metal and Air Conditioning Contractors' National Association (SMACNA)
4201 Lafayette Center Dr.
Chantilly, VA 22021
Ph: (703)803-2980 Fax: (703)803-3732

Prepares standards and codes; sponsors research and educational programs on sheet metal duct construction and fire damper (single and multi-blade) construction.

Test Guides

★4405★ *Air Conditioning and Refrigeration*
National Learning Corp.
212 Michael Dr.
Syosset, NY 11791
Ph: (516)921-8888 Fax: (516)921-8743
Fr: 800-645-6337

Jack Rudman. Part of Occupational Competency Examination Series (OCE).

★4406★ *Automatic Heating*
National Learning Corp.
212 Michael Dr.
Syosset, NY 11791
Ph: (516)921-8888 Fax: (516)921-8743
Fr: 800-645-6337

Jack Rudman. 1989. Part of Occupational Competency Examination Series.

★4407★ *Career Examination Series: Air Conditioning, Heating & Refrigeration Mechanic*
National Learning Corp.
212 Michael Dr.
Syosset, NY 11791
Ph: (516)921-8888 Fax: (516)921-8743
Fr: 800-645-6337

Jack Rudman. All examination guides in this series contain questions with answers.

★4408★ *Career Examination Series: Refrigerating Machine Mechanic*
National Learning Corp.
212 Michael Dr.
Syosset, NY 11791
Ph: (516)921-8888 Fax: (516)921-8743
Fr: 800-645-6337

Jack Rudman. All examination guides in this series contain questions with answers.

★4409★ *Introduction to Air Conditioning, Refrigeration & Heating*
National Learning Corp.
212 Michael Dr.
Syosset, NY 11791
Ph: (516)921-8888 Fax: (516)921-8743
Fr: 800-645-6337

Jack Rudman. 1989. Part of Dantes Series.

★4410★ *Principles of Refrigeration*
National Learning Corp.
212 Michael Dr.
Syosset, NY 11791
Ph: (516)921-8888 Fax: (516)921-8743
Fr: 800-645-6337

Jack Rudman. Part of Dantes Subject Standardized Tests.

★4411★ *Refrigeration License Examinations*
Arco Pub.
201 W. 103rd St.
Indianapolis, IN 46290
Ph: 800-428-5331 Fax: 800-835-3202

Antonio I. Mejas. 1993. Provides review, illustrations, and test taking practice.

★4412★ *What Do You Know about Air Conditioning, Refrigeration & Heating*
National Learning Corp.
212 Michael Dr.
Syosset, NY 11791
Ph: (516)921-8888 Fax: (516)921-8743
Fr: 800-645-6337

Jack Rudman. 1990. Part of Test Your Knowledge Series.

Educational Directories and Programs

★4413★ *Directory of Certified Room Air Conditioners*
Association of Home Appliance Manufacturers (AHAM)
20 N. Wacker Dr., Ste. 1500
Chicago, IL 60606
Ph: (312)984-5800 Fax: (312)984-5823

Semiannual. Describes AHAM Certification Program for room air conditioners and gives data in tabular form for cooling capacity and energy requirements.

★4414★ *Leadership Directory*
National Association of Plumbing-Heating-Cooling Contractors (NAPHCC)
180 S. Washington St.
PO Box 6808
Falls Church, VA 22040
Ph: (703)237-8100 Fax: (703)237-7442
Fr: 800-533-7694

Annual.

★4415★ *National Membership Directory and Users Guide*
Associated Builders and Contractors (ABC)
1300 N. 17th St.
Rosslyn, VA 22209
Ph: (703)812-2000

Annual.

★4416★ *PM Directory & Reference Issue*
Business News Publishing Co.
755 W. Big Beaver Rd., 10th Fl.
Troy, MI 48084
Ph: (810)362-3700 Fax: (313)362-0317
Fr: 800-837-7370
Tim Fausch, Contact

Annual, December. Covers manufacturers, wholesalers, exporters, associations, products, consultants, and manufacturers' representatives in the industries of plumbing, piping, and hydronic heating. Entries include: Contact name, company, address, phone, fax, and product descriptions. Arrangement: Alphabetical.

Basic Reference Guides and Handbooks

★4417★ *The Air Conditioning/ Refrigeration Toolbox Manual*
Arco Pub.
201 W. 103rd St.
Indianapolis, IN 46290
Ph: 800-428-5331 Fax: 800-835-3202

David Tenenbaum. 1990.

★4418★ *ASHRAE Pocket Guide for Air-Conditioning, Heating, Ventilation & Refrigeration*
American Society of Heating, Refrigerating & Air Conditioning Engineers
1791 Tullie Circle NE
Atlanta, GA 30329
Ph: (404)636-8400 Fax: (404)321-5478

Carl McPhee, editor. Revised edition, 1994.

★4419★ *Combustion Hot Spot Analysis for Fired Process Heaters: Prediction, Control, Troubleshooting*
Gulf Publishing Company
PO Box 2608
Houston, TX 77252
Ph: (713)529-4301 Fax: (713)520-4438

E. Talmor. 1982.

★4420★ *Faber & Kell's Heating & Air Conditioning of Buildings*
Butterworth-Heinemann
80 Montvale Ave.
Stoneham, MA 02180
Ph: (617)438-8464 Fax: (617)279-4851

P. L. Martin. Seventh edition, 1989.

★4421★ *Heating, Cooling & Lighting*
John Wiley and Sons, Inc.
605 3rd Ave.
New York, NY 10158-0012
Ph: (212)850-6000 Fax: (212)850-6088
Fr: 800-526-5368

Herbert M. Lechner. 1991.

★4422★ *Heating System Troubleshooting Handbook*
Prentice Hall
Rte. 9W
Englewood Cliffs, NJ 07632
Ph: (201)592-2000

Billy C. Langley. 1988.

★4423★ *Heating, Ventilating & Air Conditioning*
Prentice Hall
Rte. 9W
Englewood Cliffs, NJ 07632
Ph: (201)592-2000

George Clifford. 1984.

★4424★ *Home Heating & Air Conditioning Systems*
TAB/McGraw-Hill, Inc.
PO Box 182607
Columbus, OH 43218-2607
Fax: (614)759-3644 Fr: 800-822-8158

James L. Kittle. 1989.

★4425★ *IBPAT Directory*
International Brotherhood of Painters and Allied Trades (IBPAT)
United Unions Bldg.
1750 New York Ave., NW
Washington, DC 20006
Ph: (202)637-0720 Fax: (202)637-0771

Annual.

★4426★ *Mathematics for the Heating, Ventilating & Cooling Trades*
Prentice Hall
Rte. 9W
Englewood Cliffs, NJ 07632
Ph: (201)592-2000

David L. Goetsch. 1988.

★4427★ *Modern Heating, Ventilating & Air Conditioning*
Prentice Hall
Rte. 9W
Englewood Cliffs, NJ 07632
Ph: (201)592-2000

George Clifford. 1990.

★4428★ *Oil Heat Technician's Manual*
Kendall/Hunt Publishing Company
2460 Kerper Blvd.
Dubuque, IA 52001
Ph: (319)588-1451

P.M.E.F. Staff. 1990.

★4429★ *Residential Heating Operations & Troubleshooting*
Prentice Hall
Rte 9W
Englewood Cliffs, NJ 07632
Ph: (201)592-2000

John E. Traister. 1985.

★4430★ *Troubleshooting & Repairing Heat Pumps*
TAB/McGraw-Hill, Inc.
PO Box 182607
Columbus, OH 43218-2607
Fax: (614)759-3644 Fr: 800-822-8158

R. Dodge Woodson.

★4431★ *Wholesaler—"Wholesaling 100" Issue*
TMB Publishing Inc.
1838 Techny Ct.
Northbrook, IL 60062
Ph: (708)564-1127 Fax: (708)564-1264
John A. Schweizer

Annual, July. Publication includes: List of 100 leading wholesalers of plumbing, heating, air conditioning, refrigeration equipment, and supplies such as industrial pipe, valves and fittings. Entries include: Co. name, address, phone, fax, names and titles of key personnel, number of employees, business breakdown (percentage). Arrangement: Ranked by sales.

Periodicals

★4432★ *ABC Today*
Associated Builders and Contractors (ABC)
1300 N. 17th St.
Rosslyn, VA 22209
Ph: (703)812-2000

Semimonthly. News magazine for merit shop contractors.

★4433★ *ACCA News*
Air Conditioning Contractors of America (ACCA)
1513 16th St. NW
Washington, DC 20036
Ph: (202)483-9370 Fax: (202)234-4721
Elaine W. Smith

Reports on ACCA members, activities, and issues. Covers trends in the heating, ventilating, and air conditioning industries that affect contractors. Discusses management, legal issues, and new technology. Recurring features include editorials and a calendar of events.

★4434★ *Air Conditioning, Heating and Refrigeration News*
Business News Publishing Co.
PO Box 2600
Troy, MI 48007
Ph: (313)362-3700 Fax: (313)362-0317
Wayne Johnson

Weekly. Tabloid for HVAC and commercial refrigeration contractors, wholesalers, manufacturers, engineers, and owners/managers.

★4435★ *Appliance Service News*
Gamit Enterprises, Inc.
110 W. St. Charles Rd.
PO Box 789
Lombard, IL 60148
Ph: (708)932-9550 Fax: (708)932-9552
William Wingstedt

Monthly. Magazine for appliance repairmen.

★4436★ *ASHRAE Journal*
American Society of Heating, Refrigerating and Air-Conditioning Engineers
1791 Tullie Circle NE
Atlanta, GA 30329
Ph: (404)636-8400 Fax: (404)321-4578
William R. Coker

Monthly. Magazine for the heating, refrigeration, and air conditioning trade.

★4437★ *Builder Magazine*
National Association of Home Builders of the U.S. (NAHB)
1201 15th St. NW
Washington, DC 20005
Ph: (202)822-0200 Fax: (202)822-0559

Monthly.

★4438★ *Connection*
National Association of Plumbing-Heating-Cooling Contractors (NAPHCC)
180 S. Washington St.
PO Box 6808
Falls Church, VA 22040
Ph: (703)237-8100 Fax: (703)237-7442
Fr: 800-533-7694

Monthly.

★4439★ *Distributor*
Technical Reporting Co./Palmer Publishing Co.
651 W. Washington St., Ste. 300
Chicago, IL 60606
Ph: (312)993-0929 Fax: (312)993-0960
Phil PalmerPublisher

Bimonthly. Magazine focusing on air conditioning, heating, ventilation, refrigeration and appliance parts.

★4440★ *District Heating and Cooling*
International District Heating and Cooling Assn.
1200 19th St. NW, Ste. 300
Washington, DC 20036
Ph: (202)429-5111 Fax: (202)429-5113
John L. FiegelPublisher

Quarterly. Heating and cooling magazine.

★4441★ *Forecast of Housing Activity*
National Association of Home Builders of the U.S. (NAHB)
1201 15th St. NW
Washington, DC 20005
Ph: (202)822-0200 Fax: (202)822-0559

Monthly.

★4442★ *Housing Economics*
National Association of Home Builders of the U.S. (NAHB)
1201 15th St. NW
Washington, DC 20005
Ph: (202)822-0200 Fax: (202)822-0559

Monthly.

★4443★ *Housing Market Statistics*
National Association of Home Builders of the U.S. (NAHB)
1201 15th St. NW
Washington, DC 20005
Ph: (202)822-0200 Fax: (202)822-0559

Monthly.

★4444★ *HVAC*
Roland Winkler

Monthly. Heating, ventilating, and air conditioning magazine (tabloid).

★4445★ *Nation's Building News*
National Association of Home Builders of the U.S. (NAHB)
1201 15th St. NW
Washington, DC 20005
Ph: (202)822-0200 Fax: (202)822-0559

Semimonthly. Provides the latest information concerning the housing industry, including finance, legislation, new technologies, and membership news.

★4446★ *News*
National Association of Plumbing-Heating-Cooling Contractors (NAPHCC)
180 S. Washington St.
PO Box 6808
Falls Church, VA 22040
Ph: (703)237-8100 Fax: (703)237-7442
Fr: 800-533-7694

Monthly.

★4447★ *Palmetto Piper*
Mechanical Contractor's Assn. of South Carolina
1504 Morninghill Drive
PO Box 384
Columbia, SC 29202
Ph: (803)772-7834 Fax: (803)731-0390

Monthly. Plumbing, heating, air conditioning, and electrical journal.

★4448★ *Reeves Journal: Plumbing Heating Cooling*
Business News Publishing Co.
23187 La Cadena Dr., Ste. 101
PO Box 30700
Laguna Hills, CA 92654
Ph: (714)830-0881 Fax: (714)859-7845
Dick Peck

Monthly. Regional plumbing, heating, and cooling magazine.

★4449★ *Reference Guide to Homebuilding Articles*
National Association of Home Builders of the U.S. (NAHB)
1201 15th St. NW
Washington, DC 20005
Ph: (202)822-0200 Fax: (202)822-0559

Quarterly.

★4450★ *Refrigeration Service and Contracting*
Refrigeration Service Engineers Society (RSES)
1666 Rand Rd.
Des Plaines, IL 60016-3552
Ph: (708)297-6464 Fax: (708)297-5038
Fr: 800-4-CERTIFY

Monthly.

★4451★ *RSC (Refrigeration Service and Contracting)*
Business News Publishing Co.
PO Box 2600
Troy, MI 48007
Ph: (313)362-3700 Fax: (313)362-0317
Peter Powell

Monthly. Official magazine of the Refrigeration Service Engineer's Society; reporting on service, repair, installation, and replacement articles.

★4452★ *Service Application Manual*
Refrigeration Service Engineers Society (RSES)
1666 Rand Rd.
Des Plaines, IL 60016-3552
Ph: (708)297-6464 Fax: (708)297-5038
Fr: 800-4-CERTIFY

★4453★ *Service Reporter*
Technical Reporting Co./Palmer Publishing Co.
651 W. Washington St., Ste. 300
Chicago, IL 60606
Ph: (312)993-0929 Fax: (312)993-0960
Ed Schwenn
Monthly. Magazine (tabloid) focusing on air conditioning and ventilation, heating, and refrigeration.

★4454★ *Snips Magazine*
1949 Cornell Ave.
Melrose Park, IL 60160-9953
Ph: (708)544-3870 Fax: (708)544-3884
Nick Carter
Monthly. Magazine for the sheet metal, warm-air heating, ventilating, and air conditioning industry.

★4455★ *Southern Plumbing, Heating, Cooling Magazine*
Southern Trade Publications, Inc.
Box 18343
Greensboro, NC 27419
Ph: (919)454-3516
Emmet Atkins
Monthly. Trade magazine covering plumbing, heating, and air conditioning.

★4456★ *Supply House Times*
Cahners Publishing Co.
1350 E. Touhy Ave.
PO Box 5080
Des Plaines, IL 60017-5080
Ph: (708)635-8800 Fax: (708)390-2618
Bill EverhamPublisher
Monthly. Trade magazine for wholesalers in plumbing, heating, cooling, piping, and water systems. Areas of major emphasis include: warehousing, materials handling, inventory control, accounting, data processing, merchandising, salesmanship and general management.

MEETINGS AND CONVENTIONS

★4457★ International Air-Conditioning, Heating, Refrigerating Exposition
International Exposition Co.
15 Franklin St.
Westport, CT 06880-5903
Ph: (203)221-9262 Fax: (203)221-9260
Annual. **Dates and Locations:** 1996 Feb 19-21; Atlanta, GA. • 1997 Jan; Philadelphia, PA. • 1998 Jan; San Francisco, CA.

★4458★ Mobile Air Conditioning Society Trade Show and Technical Conference
Mobile Air Conditioning Society
PO Box 97
East Greenville, PA 18041
Ph: (215)541-4500 Fax: (215)679-4977
Annual. Always held during mid-January. **Dates and Locations:** 1996 Jan.

★4459★ Sheet Metal and Air-Conditioning Contractors National Association Convention
Sheet Metal and Air-Conditioning Contractors National Association
PO Box 221230
Chantilly, VA 22022-1230
Ph: (703)803-2980 Fax: (703)803-3732
Annual.

OTHER SOURCES OF INFORMATION

★4460★ "Air-Conditioning Installer" in *Career Selector 2001*
Barron's Educational Series, Inc.
250 Wireless Blvd.
Hauppauge, NY 11788
Ph: (516)434-3311 Fax: (516)434-3723
Fr: 800-645-3476
James C. Gonyea. 1993.

★4461★ *Careers in Plumbing, Heating, and Cooling*
Rosen Publishing Group
29 E. 21st St.
New York, NY 10010
Ph: 800-237-9932 Fax: (212)777-0277
Elizabeth Stewart Lytle. 1995. Describes some of the skills needed to be qualified to work in the fields of plumbing, heating, cooling, and ventilation.

Home Appliance and Power Tool Repairers

Home appliance and power tool repairers, sometimes called service technicians, install and service a variety of household appliances such as ovens, washers and dryers, vacuum cleaners, lawnmowers, and power tools. Repairers in large shops generally specialize. Some may handle small appliances, others may service power tools. To determine why a piece of equipment fails, repairers look for frequent sources of trouble such as faulty wiring, and also consult service manuals. After diagnosing the problem, they make the necessary repairs or replacements. This often involves removing old parts and installing new ones. Repairers also answer customers' questions and complaints about appliances, and provide estimates of the cost of repairs. About 70% of repairers in this field work in retail trade establishments such as department stores, household appliance stores, and dealers that sell or service appliances and power tools. Others work for gas and electric utility companies, wholesalers, and electrical repair shops. About 10% of repairers in this field are self-employed.

Salaries

Earnings of home appliance and power tool repairers vary widely according to skill level, geographic location, and the type of equipment serviced.

Lowest 10 percent	Less than $257/week
Median	$300-$656/week
Top 10 percent	More than $780/week

Employment Outlook

Growth rate until the year 2005: Decline slightly.

Home Appliance and Power Tool Repairers

CAREER GUIDES

★4462★ *Appliance Repairer*
Vocational Biographies, Inc.
PO Box 31
Sauk Centre, MN 56378-0031
Ph: (612)352-6516 Fax: (612)352-5546
Fr: 800-255-0752

1990. This pamphlet profiles a person working in the job. Includes information about job duties, working conditions, places of employment, educational preparation, labor market outlook, and salaries.

★4463★ "Appliance Repairer" in *VGM's Careers Encyclopedia* (pp. 44-46)
National Textbook Co. (NTC)
VGM Career Books
4255 W. Touhy Ave.
Lincolnwood, IL 60646-1975
Ph: (708)679-5500 Fax: (708)679-2494
Fr: 800-323-4900

Third edition, 1991. Contains two- to five-page descriptions of 200 managerial, professional, technical, trade, and service occupations. Each profile includes job duties, places of employment, qualifications, educational preparation, training, employment potential, advancement, income, and additional sources of information.

★4464★ "Appliance Repairers" in *American Almanac of Jobs and Salaries* (pp. 523)
Avon Books
1350 Avenue of the Americas
New York, NY 10019
Ph: (212)261-6800 Fr: 800-238-0658

John Wright, editor. Revised and updated, 1994-95. A comprehensive guide to the wages of hundreds of occupations in a wide variety of industries and organizations.

★4465★ "Appliance Repairers" in *Career Discovery Encyclopedia* (Vol.1, pp. 52-53)
J.G. Ferguson Publishing Co.
200 W. Madison St., Ste. 300
Chicago, IL 60606
Ph: (312)580-5480 Fax: (312)580-4948

E. Russell Primm, editor-in-chief. 1993. Contains two-page articles on 504 occupations. Each article describes job duties, earnings, and educational and training requirements.

★4466★ "Appliance Repairers" in *Encyclopedia of Careers and Vocational Guidance* (Vol.2, pp. 91-93)
J.G. Ferguson Publishing Co.
200 W. Madison St., Ste. 300
Chicago, IL 60606
Ph: (312)580-5480 Fax: (312)580-4948

William E. Hopke, editor-in-chief. Ninth edition, 1993. Four-volume set that profiles 500 occupations and describes job trends in 74 industries. Includes career description, educational requirements, history of the job, methods of entry, advancement, employment outlook, earnings, working conditions, social and psychological factors, and sources of additional information.

★4467★ *Appliance Service Technician, Electrical*
Careers, Inc.
PO Box 135
Largo, FL 34649-0135
Ph: (813)584-7333

1993. Four-page brief offering the definition, history, duties, working conditions, personal qualifications, educational requirements, earnings, hours, employment outlook, advancement possibilities, and related occupations.

★4468★ "Appliance Service Worker" in *Career Information Center* (Vol.5)
Simon and Schuster
200 Old Tappan Rd.
Old Tappan, NJ 07675
Fax: 800-445-6991 Fr: 800-223-2348

Richard Lidz and Dale Anderson, editorial directors. Fifth edition, 1993. For 600 occupations, describes job duties, entry-level requirements, education and training needed, advancement possibilities, employment outlook, earnings and benefits. The set is divided into 12 volumes. Each volume includes jobs related under a broad career field. Volume 13 is the index.

★4469★ "Electrical Appliance Service Technician" in *Occu-Facts: Information on 580 Careers in Outline Form*
Careers, Inc.
PO Box 135
Largo, FL 34649-0135
Ph: (813)584-7333

Biennial, 1995-96 edition. Each one-page occupational profile describes duties, working conditions, physical surroundings and demands, aptitudes, temperament, educational requirements, employment outlook, earnings, and places of employment.

★4470★ *Gas Appliance Service Technicians*
Chronicle Guidance Publications, Inc.
66 Aurora St.
PO Box 1190
Moravia, NY 13118-1190
Ph: (315)497-0330 Fax: (315)497-3359
Fr: 800-622-7284

1994. This career brief describes the nature of the work, working conditions, hours and earnings, education and training, licensure, certification, unions, personal qualifications, social and psychological factors, employment outlook, entry methods, advancement, and related occupations.

★4471★ "Home Appliance and Power Tool Repairers" in *Occupational Outlook Handbook*
U.S. Government Printing Office
Superintendent of Documents
Washington, DC 20402
Ph: (202)512-1800 Fax: (202)512-2250

Biennial; latest edition, 1994-95. Encyclopedia of careers describing more than 250 occupations and comprising about 85 percent of all jobs in the economy. Occupations that require lengthy education or training are given the most attention. For each occupation, the handbook describes job duties, working conditions, training, educational preparation, personal qualities, advancement possibilities, job outlook, earnings, and sources of additional information.

★4472★ "Home Appliance Repairer" in *Personal Services* (pp. 51-55)
Franklin Watts, Inc.
387 Park Avenue, S.
New York, NY 10016
Ph: (212)686-7070

Linda Barrett and Galen Guengerich. 1991. Surveys personal services jobs. Describes job duties, educational preparation, salaries, and employment outlook. Offers job hunting advice.

★4473★ "Power Tool Repairer" in *Career Information Center* (Vol.4)
Simon and Schuster
200 Old Tappan Rd.
Old Tappan, NJ 07675
Fax: 800-445-6991 Fr: 800-223-2348

Richard Lidz and Dale Anderson, editorial directors. Fifth edition, 1993. For 600 occupations, describes job duties, entry-level requirements, education and training needed, advancement possibilities, employment outlook, earnings and benefits. The set is divided into 12 volumes. Each volume includes jobs related under a broad career field. Volume 13 is the index.

★4474★ *Vocations U.S.A.*
Info-Disc Corporation
4 Professional Dr., Ste. 134
Gaithersburg, MD 20879
Ph: (301)948-2300 Fr: 800-648-6422

Videocassette. 1987. 60 mins. A disc collection outlining the requirements and methods of various career areas. Occupations include: transportation, mechanical/repair, health, agriculture, technical/manufacturing, and construction.

Associations

★4475★ Association of Home Appliance Manufacturers (AHAM)
20 N. Wacker Dr., Ste. 1500
Chicago, IL 60606
Ph: (312)984-5800 Fax: (312)984-5823

Members: Companies manufacturing major and portable appliances; supplier members provide products and services to the appliance industry. **Purpose:** Major areas of activity include: market research and reporting of industry statistics; development of standard methods for measuring appliance performance and certification of certain characteristics of room air conditioners, refrigerators, freezers, humidifiers, dehumidifiers, and room air cleaners; public relations and press relations. Represents the appliance industry before government at the federal, state, and local levels. Sponsors the Major Appliance Consumer Action Panel. Maintains committees and boards in communications, engineering, consumer relations, market research, economics, and other service areas. **Publications:** *AHAM Factory Shipment Release*, monthly. • *AHAM Major Appliance Industry Factbook*, annual. • *AHAM Membership Directory*, annual. • *Directory of Certified Dehumidifiers*, semiannual. • *Directory of Certified Humidifiers*, semiannual. • *Directory of Certified Refrigerators and Freezers*, semiannual. • *Directory of Certified Room Air Conditioners*, semiannual. • *MACAP Statistical Report*, annual. • *Trends and Forecasts*, quarterly.

★4476★ Power Tool Institute (PTI)
1300 Sumner Ave.
Cleveland, OH 44115-2851
Ph: (216)241-7333 Fax: (216)241-0105

Members: Manufacturers of portable, lawn and garden, and stationary tools, both electric and battery operated. **Purpose:** Distributes brochures, slides, and cassettes on power tool safety. Offers educational programs.

Standards/Certification Agencies

★4477★ Association of Home Appliance Manufacturers (AHAM)
20 N. Wacker Dr., Ste. 1500
Chicago, IL 60606
Ph: (312)984-5800 Fax: (312)984-5823

Major areas of activity include: market research and reporting of industry statistics; development of standard methods for measuring appliance performance and certification of certain characteristics of room air conditioners, refrigerators, freezers, humidifiers, dehumidifiers, and room air cleaners; public relations and press relations. Represents the appliance industry before government at the federal, state, and local levels.

Educational Directories and Programs

★4478★ *AHAM Membership Directory*
Association of Home Appliance Manufacturers (AHAM)
20 N. Wacker Dr., Ste. 1500
Chicago, IL 60606
Ph: (312)984-5800 Fax: (312)984-5823

Annual.

★4479★ *Directory of Certified Dehumidifiers*
Association of Home Appliance Manufacturers (AHAM)
20 N. Wacker Dr., Ste. 1500
Chicago, IL 60606
Ph: (312)984-5800 Fax: (312)984-5823

Semiannual. Lists certified brands and models of dehumidifiers, providing water-removal capacity. Includes dehumidification selection guide for consumers.

★4480★ *Directory of Certified Humidifiers*
Association of Home Appliance Manufacturers (AHAM)
20 N. Wacker Dr., Ste. 1500
Chicago, IL 60606
Ph: (312)984-5800 Fax: (312)984-5823

Semiannual. Listing of AHAM-certified brands and models of humidifiers, providing water-output capacity. Includes humidification selection guide for consumers.

★4481★ *Directory of Certified Refrigerators and Freezers*
Association of Home Appliance Manufacturers (AHAM)
20 N. Wacker Dr., Ste. 1500
Chicago, IL 60606
Ph: (312)984-5800 Fax: (312)984-5823

Semiannual. Describes AHAM Certification Program for refrigerators and freezers; provides energy, mechanical, and storage capacity data in tabular arrangement.

★4482★ *Directory of Certified Room Air Conditioners*
Association of Home Appliance Manufacturers (AHAM)
20 N. Wacker Dr., Ste. 1500
Chicago, IL 60606
Ph: (312)984-5800 Fax: (312)984-5823

Semiannual. Describes AHAM Certification Program for room air conditioners and gives data in tabular form for cooling capacity and energy requirements.

Basic Reference Guides and Handbooks

★4483★ *Home VCR Repair Illustrated*
TAB/McGraw-Hill, Inc.
PO Box 182607
Columbus, OH 43218-2607
Fax: (614)759-3644 Fr: 800-822-8158

Richard C. Wilkins and Cheryl A. Hubbard. Guide to basic VCR maintenance and repair.

★4484★ *Maintaining and Repairing VCRs*
TAB/McGraw-Hill, Inc.
PO Box 182607
Columbus, OH 43218-2607
Fax: (614)759-3644 Fr: 800-822-8158

Robert L. Goodman. Third edition.

★4485★ *Power Tool Maintenance*
McGraw-Hill Publishing
1221 Avenue of the Americas
New York, NY 10020
Ph: (212)512-2000

D. Irvin. 1971.

★4486★ *Shop Savvy*
Borgo Press
PO Box 2845
San Bernardino, CA 92406-2845
Ph: (714)884-5813

Roy Moungovan. 1990.

★4487★ *Troubleshooting & Repairing Audio & Video Cassette Players and Recorders*
TAB/McGraw-Hill, Inc.
PO Box 182607
Columbus, OH 43218-2607
Fax: (614)759-3644 Fr: 800-822-8158

Homer L. Davidson. Covers repair procedures for digital audio tapes, compact discs, stereos, and camcorders.

★4488★ *Troubleshooting and Repairing Camcorders*
TAB/McGraw-Hill, Inc.
PO Box 182607
Columbus, OH 43218-2607
Fax: (614)759-3644 Fr: 800-822-8158

Homer L. Davidson.

★4489★ *Troubleshooting & Repairing Power Tools*
TAB/McGraw-Hill, Inc.
PO Box 182607
Columbus, OH 43218-2607
Fax: (614)759-3644 Fr: 800-822-8158

Homer L. Davidson. 1990.

★4490★ *Troubleshooting and Repairing Solid-State TVs*
TAB/McGraw-Hill, Inc.
PO Box 182607
Columbus, OH 43218-2607
Fax: (614)759-3644 Fr: 800-822-8158

Homer L. Davidson. Second edition.

★4491★ *Troubleshooting & Repairing VCRs*
TAB/McGraw-Hill, Inc.
PO Box 182607
Columbus, OH 43218-2607
Fax: (614)759-3644 Fr: 800-822-8158

Gordon McComb. Third edition. Describes every aspect of VCR maintenance and repair. Includes information on self-cleaning heads, digital tracking, and beltless drives.

★4492★ *TV Repair for Beginners*
TAB/McGraw-Hill, Inc.
PO Box 182607
Columbus, OH 43218-2607
Fax: (614)759-3644 Fr: 800-822-8158

George Zwick and Homer Davidson. Describes how to repair such problems as horizontal streaking, interference, and color smears.

Periodicals

★4493★ *AHAM Factory Shipment Release*
Association of Home Appliance Manufacturers (AHAM)
20 N. Wacker Dr., Ste. 1500
Chicago, IL 60606
Ph: (312)984-5800 Fax: (312)984-5823

Monthly. Press release and statistics on major appliance factory shipments.

★4494★ *AHAM Major Appliance Industry Factbook*
Association of Home Appliance Manufacturers (AHAM)
20 N. Wacker Dr., Ste. 1500
Chicago, IL 60606
Ph: (312)984-5800 Fax: (312)984-5823

Annual.

★4495★ *Appliance*
Dana Chase Publications, Inc.
1110 Jorie Blvd., CS 9019, Ste. 203
Hinsdale, IL 60521
Ph: (708)990-3484 Fax: (708)990-0078
Scot M. Stevens

Monthly. Trade magazine focusing on appliances: commercial, consumer, and business.

★4496★ *Appliance Service News*
Gamit Enterprises, Inc.
110 W. St. Charles Rd.
PO Box 789
Lombard, IL 60148
Ph: (708)932-9550 Fax: (708)932-9552
William Wingstedt

Monthly. Magazine for appliance repairmen.

★4497★ *Carolina Retailer*
Halco Communications
841 Post Road Circle
PO Box 830034
Stone Mountain, GA 30083-0001
Ph: (404)879-9682 Fax: (404)879-6791
David Hollingsworth

Monthly. Regional trade tabloid for the electronics, appliances, consumer outdoor power equipment, and TVRO satellite industries.

★4498★ *MACAP Statistical Report*
Association of Home Appliance Manufacturers (AHAM)
20 N. Wacker Dr., Ste. 1500
Chicago, IL 60606
Ph: (312)984-5800 Fax: (312)984-5823

Annual. Detailed tabular statistical report presented after the end of a calendar year about complaints received by the MACAP concerning appliances.

★4499★ *Trends and Forecasts*
Association of Home Appliance Manufacturers (AHAM)
20 N. Wacker Dr., Ste. 1500
Chicago, IL 60606
Ph: (312)984-5800 Fax: (312)984-5823

Quarterly. A one-page tabular statistical report giving trends and forecasts of domestic and export shipments of major appliances.

Other Sources of Information

★4500★ "Appliance/Power Tool Repairer" in *100 Best Jobs for the 1990s & Beyond*
Dearborn Financial Publishing, Inc.
520 N. Dearborn St.
Chicago, IL 60610-4354
Ph: (312)836-4400 Fax: (312)836-1021
Fr: 800-621-9621

Carol Kleiman. 1992. Describes 100 jobs ranging from accountants to veterinarians. Each job profile includes such information as education, experience, and certification needed, salaries, and job search suggestions.

Industrial Machinery Repairers

Industrial machinery repairers, often called maintenance mechanics, do preventive maintenance and repairs for machinery used in factories and plants. This includes inspecting machinery and spotting and correcting minor problems. Mechanics diagnose major problems, and disassemble the equipment and repair or replace necessary parts. The final step is to test the machine to ensure that it is running smoothly. When repairing electronically controlled machinery, these mechanics may work closely with electronic repairers or electricians who maintain the machine's electric parts. A wide range of tools may be used in doing maintenance and repair work, from a screwdriver to adjust engine parts, to a hoist to lift heavy equipment.

Salaries

Earnings for Industrial machinery repairers are below:

Lowest 10 percent	$296/week or less
Middle 50 percent	$384-$626/week
Top 10 percent	$773/week or more.

Employment Outlook

Growth rate until the year 2005: Decline.

Industrial Machinery Repairers

CAREER GUIDES

★4501★ ***American Professionals Series***
Cambridge Career Products
PO Box 2153
Charleston, WV 25328-2153
Ph: (304)744-9323 Fax: (304)744-9351
Fr: 800-468-4227

Videocassette. 1984. 30 mins. In this series of twenty-one half hour programs, various occupations are examined in depth, including a day in the life of each worker. Included are: fireman, farmer, oil driller, fisherman, horse trainer, auto assembly repairman, nurse, pilot, and paramedic.

★4502★ ***Chemical Plant Operations Training Program***
NUS Training Corporation
910 Clopper Rd.
Gaithersburg, MD 20878-1399
Ph: (301)258-8763

Videocassette. 1984. 60 mins. A comprehensive view for vocational purposes of industrial chemical plant maintenance, functions, processes and repair.

★4503★ **"Industrial Machine Repairer" in *Jobs Rated Almanac***
World Almanac
1 International Blvd., Ste. 444
Mahwah, NJ 07495
Ph: (201)529-6900 Fax: (201)529-6901

Les Krantz. Second edition, 1992. Ranks 250 jobs by environment, salary, outlooks, physical demands, stress, security, travel opportunities, and extra perks. Includes jobs the editor feels are the most common, most interesting, and the most rapidly growing.

★4504★ ***Industrial Machinery Mechanics***
Chronicle Guidance Publications, Inc.
66 Aurora St.
PO Box 1190
Moravia, NY 13118-1190
Ph: (315)497-0330 Fax: (315)497-3359
Fr: 800-622-7284

1991. This career brief describes the nature of the work, working conditions, hours and earnings, education and training, licensure, certification, unions, personal qualifications, social and psychological factors, employment outlook, entry methods, advancement, and related occupations.

★4505★ **"Industrial Machinery Mechanics" in *Career Discovery Encyclopedia* (Vol.3, pp. 116-117)**
J.G. Ferguson Publishing Co.
200 W. Madison St., Ste. 300
Chicago, IL 60606
Ph: (312)580-5480 Fax: (312)580-4948

E. Russell Primm, editor-in-chief. 1993. Contains two-page articles on 504 occupations. Each article describes job duties, earnings, and educational and training requirements.

★4506★ **"Industrial Machinery Mechanics" in *Encyclopedia of Careers and Vocational Guidance* (Vol.3, pp. 182-184)**
J.G. Ferguson Publishing Co.
200 W. Madison St., Ste. 300
Chicago, IL 60606
Ph: (312)580-5480 Fax: (312)580-4948

William E. Hopke, editor-in-chief. Ninth edition, 1993. Four-volume set that profiles 500 occupations and describes job trends in 74 industries. Includes career description, educational requirements, history of the job, methods of entry, advancement, employment outlook, earnings, working conditions, social and psychological factors, and sources of additional information.

★4507★ **"Industrial Machinery Repairer" in *Career Information Center* (Vol.9)**
Simon and Schuster
200 Old Tappan Rd.
Old Tappan, NJ 07675
Fax: 800-445-6991 Fr: 800-223-2348

Richard Lidz and Dale Anderson, editorial directors. Fifth edition, 1993. For 600 occupations, describes job duties, entry-level requirements, education and training needed, advancement possibilities, employment outlook, earnings and benefits. The set is divided into 12 volumes. Each volume includes jobs related under a broad career field. Volume 13 is the index.

★4508★ **"Industrial Machinery Repairer" in *Occu-Facts: Information on 580 Careers in Outline Form***
Careers, Inc.
PO Box 135
Largo, FL 34649-0135
Ph: (813)584-7333

Biennial, 1995-96 edition. Each one-page occupational profile describes duties, working conditions, physical surroundings and demands, aptitudes, temperament, educational requirements, employment outlook, earnings, and places of employment.

★4509★ **"Industrial Machinery Repairers" in *American Almanac of Jobs and Salaries* (pp. 525)**
Avon Books
1350 Avenue of the Americas
New York, NY 10019
Ph: (212)261-6800 Fr: 800-238-0658

John Wright, editor. Revised and updated, 1994-95. A comprehensive guide to the wages of hundreds of occupations in a wide variety of industries and organizations.

★4510★ **"Industrial Machinery Repairers" in *Occupational Outlook Handbook***
U.S. Government Printing Office
Superintendent of Documents
Washington, DC 20402
Ph: (202)512-1800 Fax: (202)512-2250

Biennial; latest edition, 1994-95. Encyclopedia of careers describing more than 250 occupations and comprising about 85 percent of all jobs in the economy. Occupations that require lengthy education or training are given the most attention. For each occupation, the handbook describes job duties, working conditions, training, educational preparation, personal qualities, advancement possibilities, job outlook, earnings, and sources of additional information.

★4511★ ***Machinery Repairer, Industrial***
Careers, Inc.
PO Box 135
Largo, FL 34649-0135
Ph: (813)584-7333

1993. Four-page brief offering the definition, history, duties, working conditions, personal qualifications, educational requirements, earnings, hours, employment outlook, advancement possibilities, and related occupations.

★4512★ *Video Career Library - Repair Fields*
Careers, Inc.
PO Box 135
Largo, FL 34649-0135
Ph: (813)584-7333

Videocassette. 1990. 23 mins. Part of the Video Career Library covering 165 occupations. Shows actual workers on the job. Includes industrial machinery repairers, communications equipment repairers, data processing equipment repairers, home entertainment equipment repairers, office machine repairers, electrical power installers and repairers, and electrical and electronic repairers.

Associations

★4513★ International Union of Electronic, Electrical, Salaried, Machine, and Furniture Workers (IUE)
1126 16th St. NW
Washington, DC 20036
Ph: (202)296-1200 Fax: (202)785-4563

Members: AFL-CIO.**Purpose:** Negotiates collective bargaining agreements; maintains apprenticeship programs. Conducts district education directors meeting and training programs. Compiles statistics. **Publications:** *Health and Safety*. • *International Union of Electronic, Electrical, Salaried, Machine, and Furniture Workers—Convention Proceedings*, biennial. • *IUE News*, bimonthly. • *Research Information*, monthly.

Test Guides

★4514★ *Machinist - Machinist's Helper*
Prentice Hall Press
Simon & Schuster Inc.
200 Old Tappan Rd.
Old Tappan, NJ 07675
Ph: 800-223-2348

Hy Hammer. Fourth edition, 1984. For applicants for civil service entry level and advanced level positions. Includes nine sample exams with answers.

★4515★ *Maintenance Worker/ Mechanical Maintainer*
Prentice Hall Press
Simon & Schuster Inc.
200 Old Tappan Rd.
Old Tappan, NJ 07675
Ph: 800-223-2348

Hy Hammer. Fourth edition, 1984. Provides information for applicants interested in the following civil service positions: carpenter, mason, plumber, electrician, painter, machinist. Includes eight sample tests.

Periodicals

★4516★ *Health and Safety*
International Union of Electronic, Electrical, Salaried, Machine, and Furniture Workers (IUE)
1126 16th St. NW
Washington, DC 20036
Ph: (202)296-1200 Fax: (202)785-4563

★4517★ *International Union of Electronic, Electrical, Salaried, Machine, and Furniture Workers—Convention Proceedings*
International Union of Electronic, Electrical, Salaried, Machine, and Furniture Workers (IUE)
1126 16th St. NW
Washington, DC 20036
Ph: (202)296-1200 Fax: (202)785-4563
Biennial.

★4518★ *IUE News*
International Union of Electronic, Electrical, Salaried, Machine, and Furniture Workers (IUE)
1126 16th St., NW
Washington, DC 20036
Ph: (202)296-1200 Fax: (202)785-4563
Bimonthly.

★4519★ *Research Information*
International Union of Electronic, Electrical, Salaried, Machine, and Furniture Workers (IUE)
1126 16th St. NW
Washington, DC 20036
Ph: (202)296-1200 Fax: (202)785-4563
Monthly.

★4520★ *Research Information Monthly*
International Union of Electronic, Electrical, Salaried, Machine, and Furniture Workers (IUE)
1126 16th St., NW
Washington, DC 20036
Ph: (202)296-1200 Fax: (202)785-4563
Monthly.

Meetings and Conventions

★4521★ International Union of Electronic, Electrical, Salaried, Machine and Furnityre Workers (IUE)
1126 16th St., NW
Washington, DC 20036
Ph: (202)296-1200 Fax: (202)785-4563
Biennial.

Line Installers and Cable Splicers

Line installers and cable splicers construct and maintain the network of wires and cables that link the electric power produced in generating plants to individual customers, connects telephone central offices to customers' telephones and switchboards, and extends cable TV to residential and commercial customers. In installing new electric power or telephone lines, line installers, often referred to as outside plant technicians or construction line workers, install poles and terminals and place wires and cables that lead from the source of the transmission to the customers' premises. They also lay cable television lines underground or hang them on poles with the telephone and utility wires. Cable splicers, or cable splicing technicians, complete the line connections after the line installers have done their job. Cable splicers connect individual wires or fibers within the cable and rearrange wires when lines have to be changed. After determining the proper splicing specifications, splices are made by twisting, soldering, or joining wires and cables with small hand tools and epoxy. Line installers and cable splicers also maintain and repair telephone, power, and cable TV lines. Preventive maintenance is extremely important, because a single defect may interrupt service for many customers. Nearly all line installers and cable splicers work for telephone companies, cable television companies, power companies, and construction companies.

Salaries

Line installers and repairers earn a median weekly wage of $648.

Lowest 10 percent	$350/week or less
Middle 50 percent	$503-$770/week
Top 10 percent	$874/week or more

Employment Outlook

Growth rate until the year 2005: Decline.

Line Installers and Cable Splicers

Career Guides

★4522★ *Cable Job Guide*
Cable Television Information Center
1700 Shaker Church Rd., NW
Olympia, WA 98502-9514

Janet Quigley. Second edition, 1985.

★4523★ "Cable Splicer" in *Exploring Nontraditional Jobs for Women* (pp. 26-31)
Rosen Publishing Group
29 E. 21st St.
New York, NY 10010
Ph: (212)777-3017 Fax: (212)777-0277
Fr: 800-237-9932

Rose Neufeld. 1989. Describes blue-collar, male dominated occupations. Discusses what is done on the job, training, where to apply for jobs, tools used, salaries, and advantages and disadvantages. Relates the experiences of women who are working in the field.

★4524★ "Cable Splicer" in *Opportunities in Electrical Trades* (pp. 58-60)
National Textbook Co. (NTC)
VGM Career Books
4255 W. Touhy Ave.
Lincolnwood, IL 60646-1975
Ph: (708)679-5500 Fax: (708)679-2494
Fr: 800-323-4900

Robert Wood. 1990. Provides an overview of the electrical industry describing current trends and future projections. Surveys electrician jobs and covers the nature of the work, working conditions, job outlook, advancement possibilities, education and training, earnings, and specialization. Offers career planning advice.

★4525★ *Cable Television Systems Technicians and Installers*
Chronicle Guidance Publications, Inc.
66 Aurora St.
PO Box 1190
Moravia, NY 13118-1190
Ph: (315)497-0330 Fax: (315)497-3359
Fr: 800-622-7284

1993. Career brief describing the nature of the job, working conditions, hours and earnings, education and training, licensure, certification, unions, personal qualifications, social and psychological factors, location, employment outlook, entry methods, advancement, and related occupations.

★4526★ *Careers with an Electric Company*
Lerner Publications Co.
241 First Ave., N.
Minneapolis, MN 55401
Fax: (612)332-7615 Fr: 800-328-4920

Pam Fricke. 1984. Describes fifteen career possibilities with an electric company including such jobs as lineman and system operator.

★4527★ *The IBEW Leads to Electrifying Careers*
International Brotherhood of Electrical Workers
1125 15th St. NW
Washington, DC 20005
Ph: (202)833-7000

1988. This 15-page booklet describes the electrician apprenticeship program and the jobs of electricians, communications, and utility workers and licensure.

★4528★ "Line Installer" in *Exploring Nontraditional Jobs for Women* (pp. 37-43)
Rosen Publishing Group
29 E. 21st St.
New York, NY 10010
Ph: (212)777-3017 Fax: (212)777-0277
Fr: 800-237-9932

Rose Neufeld. 1989. Describes blue-collar, male dominated occupations. Discusses what is done on the job, training, where to apply for jobs, tools used, salaries, and advantages and disadvantages. Relates the experiences of women who are working in the field.

★4529★ "Line Installer" in *Jobs Rated Almanac*
World Almanac
1 International Blvd., Ste. 444
Mahwah, NJ 07495
Ph: (201)529-6900 Fax: (201)529-6901

Les Krantz. Second edition, 1992. Ranks 250 jobs by environment, salary, outlooks, physical demands, stress, security, travel opportunities, and extra perks. Includes jobs the editor feels are the most common, most interesting, and the most rapidly growing.

★4530★ "Line Installers and Cable Splicers" in *Career Discovery Encyclopedia* (Vol.4, pp. 16-17)
J.G. Ferguson Publishing Co.
200 W. Madison St., Ste. 300
Chicago, IL 60606
Ph: (312)580-5480 Fax: (312)580-4948

E. Russell Primm, editor-in-chief. 1993. Contains two-page articles on 504 occupations. Each article describes job duties, earnings, and educational and training requirements.

★4531★ "Line Installers and Cable Splicers" in *Encyclopedia of Careers and Vocational Guidance* (Vol.3, pp. 301-304)
J.G. Ferguson Publishing Co.
200 W. Madison St., Ste. 300
Chicago, IL 60606
Ph: (312)580-5480 Fax: (312)580-4948

William E. Hopke, editor-in-chief. Ninth edition, 1993. Four-volume set that profiles 500 occupations and describes job trends in 74 industries. Includes career description, educational requirements, history of the job, methods of entry, advancement, employment outlook, earnings, working conditions, social and psychological factors, and sources of additional information.

★4532★ "Line Installers and Cable Splicers" in *Occupational Outlook Handbook*
U.S. Government Printing Office
Superintendent of Documents
Washington, DC 20402
Ph: (202)512-1800 Fax: (202)512-2250

Biennial; latest edition, 1994-95. Encyclopedia of careers describing more than 250 occupations and comprising about 85 percent of all jobs in the economy. Occupations that require lengthy education or training are given the most attention. For each occupation, the handbook describes job duties, working conditions, training, educational preparation, personal qualities, advancement possibilities, job outlook, earnings, and sources of additional information.

★4533★ *Line Workers (Electric Power)*
Chronicle Guidance Publications, Inc.
66 Aurora St.
PO Box 1190
Moravia, NY 13118-1190
Ph: (315)497-0330 Fax: (315)497-3359
Fr: 800-622-7284

1994. This career brief describes the nature of the work, working conditions, hours and earnings, education and training, licensure, certification, unions, personal qualifications, social and psychological factors, employment outlook, entry methods, advancement, and related occupations.

★4534★ *Linemen*
Film Library
3450 Wilshire Blvd., No. 700
Los Angeles, CA 90010
Ph: 800-421-9585

Videocassette. 198?. 14 mins. This film shows a group of linemen discussing why they became involved in their profession.

★4535★ "Lineperson" in *Opportunities in Electrical Trades* (p. 56)
National Textbook Co. (NTC)
VGM Career Books
4255 W. Touhy Ave.
Lincolnwood, IL 60646-1975
Ph: (708)679-5500 Fax: (708)679-2494
Fr: 800-323-4900

Robert Wood. 1990. Provides an overview of the electrical industry describing current trends and future projections. Surveys electrician jobs and covers the nature of the work, working conditions, job outlook, advancement possibilities, education and training, earnings, and specialization. Offers career planning advice.

★4536★ *Live Line Maintenance*
L & K International Video Training
295 Evans Ave.
PO Box 940, Sta. U
Toronto, ON, Canada M8Z 5P9
Ph: (416)252-6407 Fax: (416)252-8331
Fr: 800-668-6064

Videocassette. 1984. 60 mins. This program explains the training techniques for Electrical Utility Linemen.

★4537★ "On the Line" in *Telecommunications Careers* (pp. 50-54)
Franklin Watts, Inc.
387 Park Avenue, S.
New York, NY 10016
Ph: (212)686-7070

James L. Schefter. 1988. Describes the telecommunications industry and profiles jobs in manufacturing, the telephone industry, the military, video communications and television broadcasting. Covers job duties, educational requirements, salaries, and promotional possibilities.

★4538★ *Opportunities in Cable Television*
National Textbook Co. (NTC)
VGM Career Books
4255 W. Toughy Ave.
Lincolnwood, IL 60646-1975
Ph: (708)679-5500 Fax: (708)679-2494
Fr: 800-323-4900

Jan Bone.

★4539★ *Our Wiremen*
International Brotherhood of Electrical Workers
1125 15th St. NW
Washington, DC 20005
Ph: (202)833-7000

Brochure describing the work, skills needed, and training.

★4540★ *Telephone Line Installers and Cable Splicers*
Careers, Inc.
PO Box 135
Largo, FL 34649-0135
Ph: (813)584-7333

1994. Four-page brief offering the definition, history, duties, working conditions, personal qualifications, educational requirements, earnings, hours, employment outlook, advancement possibilities, and related occupations.

★4541★ "Telephone Line Installers and Cable Splicers" in *Occu-Facts: Information on 580 Careers in Outline Form*
Careers, Inc.
PO Box 135
Largo, FL 34649-0135
Ph: (813)584-7333

Biennial, 1995-96 edition. Each one-page occupational profile describes duties, working conditions, physical surroundings and demands, aptitudes, temperament, educational requirements, employment outlook, earnings, and places of employment.

★4542★ "Telephone Line Worker and Cable Splicer" in *Career Information Center* (Vol.3)
Simon and Schuster
200 Old Tappan Rd.
Old Tappan, NJ 07675
Fax: 800-445-6991 Fr: 800-223-2348

Richard Lidz and Dale Anderson, editorial directors. Fifth edition, 1993. For 600 occupations, describes job duties, entry-level requirements, education and training needed, advancement possibilities, employment outlook, earnings and benefits. The set is divided into 12 volumes. Each volume includes jobs related under a broad career field. Volume 13 is the index.

★4543★ "Telephone Line Worker and Cable Splicer" in *Telecommunications* (pp. 33-37)
Franklin Watts, Inc.
387 Park Avenue, S.
New York, NY 10016
Ph: (212)686-7070

Linda Barrett and Galen Guengerich. 1991. Surveys opportunities in telecommunications including telephone, radio, telegraph, and television communications. Includes job description, educational preparation, salary, and employment outlook. Offers job hunting advice.

★4544★ *Video Career Library - Repair Fields*
Careers, Inc.
PO Box 135
Largo, FL 34649-0135
Ph: (813)584-7333

Videocassette. 1990. 23 mins. Part of the Video Career Library covering 165 occupations. Shows actual workers on the job. Includes industrial machinery repairers, communications equipment repairers, data processing equipment repairers, home entertainment equipment repairers, office machine repairers, electrical power installers and repairers, and electrical and electronic repairers.

★4545★ *Your Guardian Angel*
Film Library
3450 Wilshire Blvd., No. 700
Los Angeles, CA 90010-2215
Ph: (213)384-8114 Fr: 800-421-9585

Videocassette. 198?. 15 mins. Harry Sparks, the guardian angel of electrical workers looks at the hazards and characteristics of 600-volt lines and equipment.

ASSOCIATIONS

★4546★ International Brotherhood of Electrical Workers (IBEW)
1125 15th St. NW
Washington, DC 20005
Ph: (202)833-7000 Fax: (202)467-6316

Members: AFL-CIO. **Publications:** *IBEW Journal*, monthly.

★4547★ United States Telephone Association (USTA)
1401 H St., Ste. 600
Washington, DC 20005-2136
Ph: (202)326-7300 Fax: (202)326-7333

Members: Local operating telephone companies or telephone holding companies. Members represent a total of 114 million access lines. **Purpose:** Conducts educational and training programs. Maintains 21 committees. **Publications:** *Holding Company Report*, annual. • *Phonefacts*, annual. • *Statistical Volumes*, annual. • *Teletimes*, quarterly.

Test Guides

★4548★ *Career Examination Series: Cable Splicer*
National Learning Corp.
212 Michael Dr.
Syosset, NY 11791
Ph: (516)921-8888 Fax: (516)921-8743
Fr: 800-645-6337

Jack Rudman. Test guide including questions and answers for students or professionals in the field who seek advancement through examination.

★4549★ *Career Examination Series: Foreman Cable Splicer*
National Learning Corp.
212 Michael Dr.
Syosset, NY 11791
Ph: (516)921-8888 Fax: (516)921-8743
Fr: 800-645-6337

Jack Rudman. All examination guides in this series contain questions with answers.

★4550★ *Career Examination Series: Foreman (Power Cables)*
National Learning Corp.
212 Michael Dr.
Syosset, NY 11791
Ph: (516)921-8888 Fax: (516)921-8743
Fr: 800-645-6337

Jack Rudman. All examination guides in this series contain questions with answers.

★4551★ *Career Examination Series: Lineman (Electrical Power)*
National Learning Corp.
212 Michael Dr.
Syosset, NY 11791
Ph: (516)921-8888 Fax: (516)921-8743
Fr: 800-645-6337

Jack Rudman. All examination guides in this series contain questions with answers.

Basic Reference Guides and Handbooks

★4552★ *Cable Hardware & Technology*
Frost & Sullivan, Inc.
106 Fulton St.
New York, NY 10038
Ph: (212)233-1080

1987.

★4553★ *Cable Television Technology Handbook*
Artech House, Inc.
685 Canton St.
Norwood, MA 02062
Ph: (617)769-9750 Fax: (617)769-6334

Bobby Harrell. 1985.

Periodicals

★4554★ *The Electricity Journal*
1932 1st Ave., No. 809
Seattle, WA 98101-1040
Ph: (206)448-4078 Fax: (206)441-7443
Robert O. Marritz

Magazine serving the electric utility industry.

★4555★ *Rural Telecommunications*
National Telephone Cooperative Assn.
2626 Pennsylvania Ave. NW
Washington, DC 20037
Ph: (202)298-2300 Fax: (202)298-2320
Lisa Westbrook

Bimonthly.

Meetings and Conventions

★4556★ Eastern Cable Television Trade Show and Convention
Convention and Show Management Co.
6175 Barfield Rd., Ste. 220
Atlanta, GA 30328
Ph: (404)252-2454 Fax: (404)252-0215

Annual.

★4557★ Great Lakes Cable Expo
Great Lakes Cable Expo
6910 N. Shadeland Ave., Ste. 206
Indianapolis, IN 46220
Ph: (317)845-8100 Fax: (317)578-0621

Annual. Always held during August or September in Indianapolis, Indiana.

★4558★ Western Cable Television Convention and Exposition
Trade Associates, Inc.
6001 Montrose Rd., Ste. 900
Rockville, MD 20852-1608
Ph: (301)468-3210 Fax: (301)468-3662

Annual. Always held at the Convention Center in Anaheim, California. **Dates and Locations:** 1995 Nov 28-01; Anaheim, CA.

Other Sources of Information

★4559★ *Phonefacts*
United States Telephone Association (USTA)
1401 H. St., Ste. 600
Washington, DC 20006
Ph: (202)326-7300 Fax: (202)326-7333

Annual.

Millwrights

Millwrights install, repair, replace, and dismantle the machinery and heavy equipment used in almost every industry. The machinery must be lifted and moved, therefore millwrights use a variety of rigging and hoisting devices. A knowledge of load-bearing properties of ropes, cables, and hoists is essential. New machinery sometimes requires a new foundation and millwrights prepare or supervise the construction. This requires a background on blueprint reading and building materials. When assembling machinery, millwrights fit bearings, align gears and wheels, and connect belts according to the manufacturer's blueprints and drawings. Millwrights are also involved in the installation of industrial robots and other automated equipment. In addition to installing and dismantling machinery, millwrights also repair and maintain equipment. Millwrights employed in factories tend to specialize in the particular types of machinery used by their employers. Those employed by contract installation and construction companies must know how to do a variety of installation work.

Salaries

Full-time millwrights have median weekly earnings of $596.

Lowest 10 percent	$335/week or less
Middle 50 percent	$479-$724/week
Top 10 percent	$849/week or more.

Employment Outlook

Growth rate until the year 2005: More slowly than the average.

Millwrights

Career Guides

★4560★ *Millwright*
Careers, Inc.
PO Box 135
Largo, FL 34649-0135
Ph: (813)584-7333

1995. Four-page brief offering the definition, history, duties, working conditions, personal qualifications, educational requirements, earnings, hours, employment outlook, advancement possibilities, and related occupations.

★4561★ *Millwright*
Vocational Biographies, Inc.
PO Box 31
Sauk Centre, MN 56378-0031
Ph: (612)352-6516 Fax: (612)352-5546
Fr: 800-255-0752

1993. Four-page pamphlet containing a personal narrative about a worker's job, work likes and dislikes, career path from high school to the present. Education and training, the rewards and frustrations, and the effects of the job on the rest of the worker's life. The data file portion of this pamphlet gives a concise occupational summary, including work descriptions, working conditions, places of employment, personal characteristics, education and training, job outlook, and salary range.

★4562★ "Millwright" in *BLR Encyclopedia of Prewritten Job Descriptions*
Business and Legal Reports, Inc.
39 Academy St.
Madison, CT 06443-1513
Ph: (203)245-7448

Stephen D. Bruce, editor-in-chief. 1994. This book contains hundreds of sample job descriptions arranged by functional job category. The 1-3 page job descriptions cover what the worker normally does in the position, who they report to, and how that position fits in the organizational structure.

★4563★ "Millwright" in *Jobs Rated Almanac*
World Almanac
1 International Blvd., Ste. 444
Mahwah, NJ 07495
Ph: (201)529-6900 Fax: (201)529-6901

Les Krantz. Second edition, 1992. Ranks 250 jobs by environment, salary, outlooks, physical demands, stress, security, travel opportunities, and extra perks. Includes jobs the editor feels are the most common, most interesting, and the most rapidly growing.

★4564★ "Millwright" in *Occu-Facts: Information on 580 Careers in Outline Form*
Careers, Inc.
PO Box 135
Largo, FL 34649-0135
Ph: (813)584-7333

Biennial, 1995-96 edition. Each one-page occupational profile describes duties, working conditions, physical surroundings and demands, aptitudes, temperament, educational requirements, employment outlook, earnings, and places of employment.

★4565★ "Millwright" in *Opportunities in Carpentry Careers* (p. 52)
National Textbook Co. (NTC)
VGM Career Books
4255 W. Touhy Ave.
Lincolnwood, IL 60646-1975
Ph: (708)679-5500 Fax: (708)679-2494
Fr: 800-323-4900

Roger Sheldon. 1987. Covers the history of the crafts, a typical carpenter's workday, future opportunities for carpenters, qualifications, training, apprenticeships, and special advice for women and minorities. Surveys various training opportunities.

★4566★ *Millwrights*
Chronicle Guidance Publications, Inc.
66 Aurora St.
PO Box 1190
Moravia, NY 13118-1190
Ph: (315)497-0330 Fax: (315)497-3359
Fr: 800-622-7284

1987. This career brief describes the nature of the work, working conditions, hours and earnings, education and training, licensure, certification, unions, personal qualifications, social and psychological factors, employment outlook, entry methods, advancement, and related occupations.

★4567★ "Millwrights" in *Career Discovery Encyclopedia* (Vol.4, pp. 92-93)
J.G. Ferguson Publishing Co.
200 W. Madison St., Ste. 300
Chicago, IL 60606
Ph: (312)580-5480 Fax: (312)580-4948

E. Russell Primm, editor-in-chief. 1993. Contains two-page articles on 504 occupations. Each article describes job duties, earnings, and educational and training requirements.

★4568★ "Millwrights" in *Encyclopedia of Careers and Vocational Guidance* (Vol.3, pp. 447-449)
J.G. Ferguson Publishing Co.
200 W. Madison St., Ste. 300
Chicago, IL 60606
Ph: (312)580-5480 Fax: (312)580-4948

William E. Hopke, editor-in-chief. Ninth edition, 1993. Four-volume set that profiles 500 occupations and describes job trends in 74 industries. Includes career description, educational requirements, history of the job, methods of entry, advancement, employment outlook, earnings, working conditions, social and psychological factors, and sources of additional information.

★4569★ "Millwrights" in *Occupational Outlook Handbook*
U.S. Government Printing Office
Superintendent of Documents
Washington, DC 20402
Ph: (202)512-1800 Fax: (202)512-2250

Biennial; latest edition, 1994-95. Encyclopedia of careers describing more than 250 occupations and comprising about 85 percent of all jobs in the economy. Occupations that require lengthy education or training are given the most attention. For each occupation, the handbook describes job duties, working conditions, training, educational preparation, personal qualities, advancement possibilities, job outlook, earnings, and sources of additional information.

★4570★ *Video Career Library - Construction*
Careers, Inc.
PO Box 135
Largo, FL 34649-0135
Ph: (813)584-7333

Videocassette. 1990. 36 mins. Part of the Video Career Library covering 165 occupations. Shows actual workers on the job. Includes millwrights, brickmasons, carpenters, drywall installers, electricians, painters, plumbers and pipefitters, carpenter and soft tile installers, insulation workers, paving equipment operators, and structural metal workers.

Associations

★4571★ Associated General Contractors of America (AGC)
1957 E St. NW
Washington, DC 20006
Ph: (202)393-2040 Fax: (202)347-4004

Members: General construction contractors; subcontractors; industry suppliers; service firms. **Purpose:** Provides market services through its divisions. Conducts special conferences and seminars designed specifically for construction firms. Compiles statistics on job accidents reported by member firms. ors. Maintains 65 committees, including joint cooperative committees with other associations and liaison committees with federal agencies. **Publications:** *AGC Membership Directory and Buyers' Guide*, annual. • *AGC Mobile Directory.* • *Associated General Contractors of America—National Newsletter*, biweekly. • *Constructor*, monthly.

Educational Directories and Programs

★4572★ *AGC Membership Directory and Buyers' Guide*
Associated General Contractors of America (AGC)
1957 E St. NW
Washington, DC 20006
Ph: (202)393-2040 Fax: (202)347-4004

Annual.

★4573★ *AGC Mobile Directory*
Associated General Contractors of America (AGC)
1957 E St. NW
Washington, DC 20006
Ph: (202)393-2040 Fax: (202)347-4004

Periodicals

★4574★ *Associated General Contractors of America—National Newsletter*
Associated General Contractors of America (AGC)
1957 E St. NW
Washington, DC 20006
Ph: (202)393-2040 Fax: (202)347-4004

Biweekly.

★4575★ *Constructor*
Associated General Contractors of America (AGC)
1957 E St. NW
Washington, DC 20006
Ph: (202)393-2040 Fax: (202)347-4004

Monthly. For general contractors engaged in construction.

Meetings and Conventions

★4576★ Association of Operative Millers Technical Conference and Trade Show
Association of Operative Millers
5001 College Blvd., Ste. 104
Leawood, KS 66211
Ph: (913)338-3377 Fax: (913)338-3553

Annual.

Mobile Heavy Equipment Mechanics

Mobile heavy equipment mechanics service and repair the engines, transmissions, and other components of equipment such as motor graders, trenches and backhoes, crawler-loaders, and stripping and loading shovels that are used at construction sites. Mobile heavy equipment mechanics perform routine maintenance and repairs on the engines of heavy equipment. After diagnosis, they repair, replace, clean, and lubricate parts as necessary. Repairing malfunctioning hydraulic components is one of a mechanic's major responsibilities. Diagnosing and correcting electrical problems is another important task. They use a variety of tools from common hand tools to more technical equipment such as dynamometers and voltmeters. Most mechanics work in small repair shops of construction contractors, logging and mining companies, and local government road maintenance departments.

Salaries

Mobile heavy equipment mechanics have median weekly earnings of about $516.

Lowest 10 percent	$318/week or less
Middle 50 percent	$412-$644/week
Top 10 percent	$845/week or more.

Employment Outlook

Growth rate until the year 2005: More slowly than the average.

Mobile Heavy Equipment Mechanics

Career Guides

★4577★ "Construction Equipment Mechanic" in *Career Information Center* (Vol.4)
Simon and Schuster
200 Old Tappan Rd.
Old Tappan, NJ 07675
Fax: 800-445-6991 Fr: 800-223-2348

Richard Lidz and Dale Anderson, editorial directors. Fifth edition, 1993. For 600 occupations, describes job duties, entry-level requirements, education and training needed, advancement possibilities, employment outlook, earnings and benefits. The set is divided into 12 volumes. Each volume includes jobs related under a broad career field. Volume 13 is the index.

★4578★ *Do Your Own Thing . . . in the Mechanical Field*
AIMS Media, Inc.
9710 DeSoto Ave.
Chatsworth, CA 91311
Ph: (818)773-4300 Fax: (818)341-6700
Fr: 800-367-2467

Videocassette. 1979. 16 mins. Various job levels in the mechanical field are outlined for students.

★4579★ *Mechanics*
Morris Video
2730 Monterey St., No. 105
Monterey Business Park
Torrance, CA 90503
Ph: (213)533-4800 Fr: 800-843-3606

Videocassette. 1984. 15 mins. Various careers in repair are examined including aircraft, motorcycle, diesel, refrigeration and heavy equipment.

★4580★ "Mobile Heavy Equipment Mechanics" in *Career Discovery Encyclopedia* (Vol.4, pp. 96-97)
J.G. Ferguson Publishing Co.
200 W. Madison St., Ste. 300
Chicago, IL 60606
Ph: (312)580-5480 Fax: (312)580-4948

E. Russell Primm, editor-in-chief. 1993. Contains two-page articles on 504 occupations. Each article describes job duties, earnings, and educational and training requirements.

★4581★ "Mobile Heavy Equipment Mechanics" in *Occupational Outlook Handbook*
U.S. Government Printing Office
Superintendent of Documents
Washington, DC 20402
Ph: (202)512-1800 Fax: (202)512-2250

Biennial; latest edition, 1994-95. Encyclopedia of careers describing more than 250 occupations and comprising about 85 percent of all jobs in the economy. Occupations that require lengthy education or training are given the most attention. For each occupation, the handbook describes job duties, working conditions, training, educational preparation, personal qualities, advancement possibilities, job outlook, earnings, and sources of additional information.

★4582★ *Video Career Library - Mechanical Fields*
Careers, Inc.
PO Box 135
Largo, FL 34649-0135
Ph: (813)584-7333

Videocassette. 1990. 22 mins. Part of the Video Career Library covering 165 occupations. Shows actual workers on the job. Includes automobile mechanics, diesel engine mechanics, aircraft engine mechanics, automobile body repairers, heavy equipment mechanics, and heating/air-conditioning/refrigeration mechanics.

★4583★ *Vocations U.S.A.*
Info-Disc Corporation
4 Professional Dr., Ste. 134
Gaithersburg, MD 20879
Ph: (301)948-2300 Fr: 800-648-6422

Videocassette. 1987. 60 mins. A disc collection outlining the requirements and methods of various career areas. Occupations include: transportation, mechanical/repair, health, agriculture, technical/manufacturing, and construction.

Associations

★4584★ Motor and Equipment Manufacturers Association (MEMA)
10 Laboratory Dr.
PO Box 13966
Research Triangle Park, NC 27709-3966
Ph: (919)549-4800 Fax: (919)549-4824

Members: Manufacturers of automotive and heavy-duty original equipment and aftermarket components, maintenance equipment, chemicals, accessories, refinishing supplies, tools, and service equipment united for research into all aspects of the automotive and heavy-duty markets. **Purpose:** Provides manufacturer-oriented services and programs including marketing consultation for the automotive industry; federal and state legal, safety, and legislative representation and consultation; personnel services; manpower development workshops; international information. Cosponsors Automotive Aftermarket Industry Week, and automotive aftermarket trade show. Maintains credit reporting service covering wholesalers, retailers, chain stores, and warehouse distributors; offers electronic order-entry, price-update, and electronic document exchange services through MEMA/Transnet and MEMA/Ansinet systems. Maintains international liaison. Administers U.S. Automotive Parts Industry Japan Office, Tokyo in conjunction with the U.S. Department of Commerce and the United States Automotive Parts Industry European Office, Brussels. Compiles statistics on automotive and heavy duty OE market and aftermarkets for use by members and as a public service. **Publications:** *Autobody Supply and Equipment Market*, biennial. • *Automotive Distributor Trends and Financial Analysis*, periodic. • *Automotive Jobbers in the U.S.A.*, biennial. • *Car Maintenance in the U.S.A.*. • *Credit and Sales Reference Directory*. • *Distributors Financial Analysis*. • *Europe Automotive Insight*, monthly. • *Foreign Vehicle Maintenance in the U.S.A.*. • *Heavy Duty Truck Maintenance in the U.S.A.*. • *International Buyer's Guide of U.S. Automotive and Heavy Duty Products*, biennial. • *Japan Automotive Insight*, monthly. • *Legislative Insight*, weekly. • *Market Analysts*, bimonthly. • *Marketing Insight*, weekly. • *Toxic Labeling Compliance Newsletter*, quarterly. • *Washington Digest*, biweekly.

Test Guides

★4585★ *Career Examination Series: Heavy Equipment Mechanic*
National Learning Corp.
212 Michael Dr.
Syosset, NY 11791
Ph: (516)921-8888 Fax: (516)921-8743
Fr: 800-645-6337

Jack Rudman. All examination guides in this series contain questions with answers.

Basic Reference Guides and Handbooks

★4586★ *Car Maintenance in the U.S.A.*
Motor and Equipment Manufacturers Association (MEMA)
10 Laboratory Dr.
PO Box 13966
Research Triangle Pk., NC 27709
Ph: (919)549-4800 Fax: (919)549-4824

★4587★ *Heavy Duty Truck Maintenance in the U.S.A.*
Motor and Equipment Manufacturers Association (MEMA)
10 Laboratory Dr.
PO Box 13966
Research Triangle Pk., NC 27709
Ph: (919)549-4800 Fax: (919)549-4824

Periodicals

★4588★ *Autobody Supply and Equipment Market*
Motor and Equipment Manufacturers Association (MEMA)
10 Laboratory Dr.
PO Box 13966
Research Triangle Park, NC 27709-3966
Ph: (919)549-4800 Fax: (919)549-4824

Biennial.

Meetings and Conventions

★4589★ Heating, Ventilation, and Air Conditioning Product and Equipment Show
Institute of Heating and Air Conditioning Industries
606 N. Larchmont Blvd., Ste. 4A
Los Angeles, CA 90004
Ph: (213)467-1158 Fax: (213)461-2588

Annual. Always held during November at the Convention Center in Pasadena, California.

★4590★ Midwest Specialty Exposition
Kansas Plumbing, Heating, and Cooling Contractors Association
320 Laura St.
Wichita, KS 67211
Ph: (316)262-8860 Fax: (316)262-2782

Annual.

Other Sources of Information

★4591★ *Distributors Financial Analysis*
Motor and Equipment Manufacturers Association (MEMA)
10 Laboratory Dr.
PO Box 13966
Research Triangle Pk., NC 27709
Ph: (919)549-4800 Fax: (919)549-4824

Motorcycle, Boat, and Small Engine Mechanics

Motorcycle, boat, and small engine mechanics repair and service power equipment that includes boats, motorcycles, lawn and garden equipment, and occasionally outdoor power equipment. Routine maintenance like adjusting, cleaning, and lubricating parts is a major part of the mechanic's work. When breakdowns do occur, mechanics diagnose the cause and repair or replace the faulty parts. This is accomplished by using common hand tools such as pliers and screwdrivers, and a variety of testing devices such as engine analyzers and voltmeters. Mechanics usually specialize in the service and repair of one type of equipment. **Motorboat mechanics** repair and adjust the engines and electrical and mechanical equipment of inboard and outboard marine engines. **Small engine mechanics** service and repair outdoor power equipment such as lawnmowers, garden tractors, and chain saws.

Salaries

Full-time motorcycle, boat, and small engine mechanics have median weekly earnings of about $435.

Lowest 10 percent	$263/week or less
Middle 50 percent	$330-$499/week
Highest 10 percent	$749/week or more

Employment Outlook

Growth rate until the year 2005: Average.

Motorcycle, Boat, and Small Engine Mechanics

Career Guides

★4592★ "Boat Motor Mechanic" in *Career Information Center* (Vol.12)
Simon and Schuster
200 Old Tappan Rd.
Old Tappan, NJ 07675
Fax: 800-445-6991 Fr: 800-223-2348

Richard Lidz and Dale Anderson, editorial directors. Fifth edition, 1993. For 600 occupations, describes job duties, entry-level requirements, education and training needed, advancement possibilities, employment outlook, earnings and benefits. The set is divided into 12 volumes. Each volume includes jobs related under a broad career field. Volume 13 is the index.

★4593★ *Do Your Own Thing . . . in the Mechanical Field*
AIMS Media, Inc.
9710 DeSoto Ave.
Chatsworth, CA 91311
Ph: (818)773-4300 Fax: (818)341-6700
Fr: 800-367-2467

Videocassette. 1979. 16 mins. Various job levels in the mechanical field are outlined for students.

★4594★ "Marine Engine Mechanic" in *Opportunities in Marine and Maritime Careers* (pp. 105-107)
National Textbook Co. (NTC)
VGM Career Books
4255 W. Touhy Ave.
Lincolnwood, IL 60646-1975
Ph: (708)679-5500 Fax: (708)679-2494
Fr: 800-323-4900

William Ray Heitzmann. 1988. Includes careers related by their proximity to water; cruise ships, oceanography, marine sciences, fishing, commercial diving, maritime transportation, shipbuilding, Navy, and Coast Guard. Covers qualifications, job outlook, job duties, educational preparation, and training. Lists associations and schools.

★4595★ "Marine Services Technician" in *Career Information Center* (Vol.12)
Simon and Schuster
200 Old Tappan Rd.
Old Tappan, NJ 07675
Fax: 800-445-6991 Fr: 800-223-2348

Richard Lidz and Dale Anderson, editorial directors. Fifth edition, 1993. For 600 occupations, describes job duties, entry-level requirements, education and training needed, advancement possibilities, employment outlook, earnings and benefits. The set is divided into 12 volumes. Each volume includes jobs related under a broad career field. Volume 13 is the index.

★4596★ *Mechanics*
Morris Video
2730 Monterey St., No. 105
Monterey Business Park
Torrance, CA 90503
Ph: (213)533-4800 Fr: 800-843-3606

Videocassette. 1984. 15 mins. Various careers in repair are examined including aircraft, motorcycle, diesel, refrigeration and heavy equipment.

★4597★ *Motorboat Mechanics*
Chronicle Guidance Publications, Inc.
66 Aurora St.
PO Box 1190
Moravia, NY 13118-1190
Ph: (315)497-0330 Fax: (315)497-3359
Fr: 800-622-7284

1993. This career brief describes the nature of the work, working conditions, hours and earnings, education and training, licensure, certification, unions, personal qualifications, social and psychological factors, employment outlook, entry methods, advancement, and related occupations.

★4598★ "Motorcycle, Boat, and Small-Engine Mechanics" in *Occupatiional Outlook Handbook*
U.S. Government Printing Office
Superintendent of Documents
Washington, DC 20402
Ph: (202)512-1800 Fax: (202)512-2250

Biennial; latest edition, 1994-95. Encyclopedia of careers describing more than 250 occupations and comprising about 85 percent of all jobs in the economy. Occupations that require lengthy education or training are given the most attention. For each occupation, the handbook describes job duties, working conditions, training, educational preparation, personal qualities, advancement possibilities, job outlook, earnings, and sources of additional information.

★4599★ *Motorcycle Mechanic*
Careers, Inc.
PO Box 135
Largo, FL 34649-0135
Ph: (813)584-7333

1995. Two-page occupational summary card describing duties, working conditions, personal qualifications, training, earnings and hours, employment outlook, places of employment, related careers and where to write for more information.

★4600★ *Motorcycle Mechanic*
Vocational Biographies, Inc.
PO Box 31
Sauk Centre, MN 56378-0031
Ph: (612)352-6516 Fax: (612)352-5546
Fr: 800-255-0752

1994. Four-page pamphlet containing a personal narrative about a worker's job, work likes and dislikes, career path from high school to the present. Education and training, the rewards and frustrations, and the effects of the job on the rest of the worker's life. The data file portion of this pamphlet gives a concise occupational summary, including work descriptions, working conditions, places of employment, personal characteristics, education and training, job outlook, and salary range.

★4601★ "Motorcycle Mechanic" in *Career Information Center* (Vol.12)
Simon and Schuster
200 Old Tappan Rd.
Old Tappan, NJ 07675
Fax: 800-445-6991 Fr: 800-223-2348

Richard Lidz and Dale Anderson, editorial directors. Fifth edition, 1993. For 600 occupations, describes job duties, entry-level requirements, education and training needed, advancement possibilities, employment outlook, earnings and benefits. The set is di-

vided into 12 volumes. Each volume includes jobs related under a broad career field. Volume 13 is the index.

★4602★ "Motorcycle Mechanic" in *Occu-Facts: Information on 580 Careers in Outline Form*
Careers, Inc.
PO Box 135
Largo, FL 34649-0135
Ph: (813)584-7333

Biennial, 1995-96 edition. Each one-page occupational profile describes duties, working conditions, physical surroundings and demands, aptitudes, temperament, educational requirements, employment outlook, earnings, and places of employment.

★4603★ "Motorcycle Mechanics" in *Career Discovery Encyclopedia* (Vol.4, pp. 102-103)
J.G. Ferguson Publishing Co.
200 W. Madison St., Ste. 300
Chicago, IL 60606
Ph: (312)580-5480 Fax: (312)580-4948

E. Russell Primm, editor-in-chief. 1993. Contains two-page articles on 504 occupations. Each article describes job duties, earnings, and educational and training requirements.

★4604★ "Motorcycle Mechanics" in *Opportunities in Automotive Service Careers* (p. 59)
National Textbook Co. (NTC)
VGM Career Books
4255 W. Touhy Ave.
Lincolnwood, IL 60646-1975
Ph: (708)679-5500 Fax: (708)679-2494
Fr: 800-323-4900

Robert M. Weber. 1989. Describes the work of the automobile mechanic and related occupations such as service station attendant and automobile body repairer. Covers working conditions, places of employment, qualifications, training, apprenticeships, certification, advancement opportunities, employment outlook, tools needed, and earnings.

★4605★ *Motorcycle Technicians*
Chronicle Guidance Publications, Inc.
66 Aurora St.
PO Box 1190
Moravia, NY 13118-1190
Ph: (315)497-0330 Fax: (315)497-3359
Fr: 800-622-7284

1993. This career brief describes the nature of the work, working conditions, hours and earnings, education and training, licensure, certification, unions, personal qualifications, social and psychological factors, employment outlook, entry methods, advancement, and related occupations.

ASSOCIATIONS

★4606★ Motor and Equipment Manufacturers Association (MEMA)
10 Laboratory Dr.
PO Box 13966
Research Triangle Park, NC 27709-3966
Ph: (919)549-4800 Fax: (919)549-4824

Members: Manufacturers of automotive and heavy-duty original equipment and aftermarket components, maintenance equipment, chemicals, accessories, refinishing supplies, tools, and service equipment united for research into all aspects of the automotive and heavy-duty markets. **Purpose:** Provides manufacturer-oriented services and programs including marketing consultation for the automotive industry; federal and state legal, safety, and legislative representation and consultation; personnel services; manpower development workshops; international information. Cosponsors Automotive Aftermarket Industry Week, and automotive aftermarket trade show. Maintains credit reporting service covering wholesalers, retailers, chain stores, and warehouse distributors; offers electronic order-entry, price-update, and electronic document exchange services through MEMA/Transnet and MEMA/Ansinet systems. Maintains international liaison. Administers U.S. Automotive Parts Industry Japan Office, Tokyo in conjunction with the U.S. Department of Commerce and the United States Automotive Parts Industry European Office, Brussels. Compiles statistics on automotive and heavy duty OE market and aftermarkets for use by members and as a public service. **Publications:** *Autobody Supply and Equipment Market*, biennial. • *Automotive Distributor Trends and Financial Analysis*, periodic. • *Automotive Jobbers in the U.S.A.*, biennial. • *Car Maintenance in the U.S.A.*. • *Credit and Sales Reference Directory*. • *Distributors Financial Analysis*. • *Europe Automotive Insight*, monthly. • *Foreign Vehicle Maintenance in the U.S.A.*. • *Heavy Duty Truck Maintenance in the U.S.A.*. • *International Buyer's Guide of U.S. Automotive and Heavy Duty Products*, biennial. • *Japan Automotive Insight*, monthly. • *Legislative Insight*, weekly. • *Market Analysts*, bimonthly. • *Marketing Insight*, weekly. • *Toxic Labeling Compliance Newsletter*, quarterly. • *Washington Digest*, biweekly.

TEST GUIDES

★4607★ *Career Examination Series: Motor Equipment Mechanic*
National Learning Corp.
212 Michael Dr.
Syosset, NY 11791
Ph: (516)921-8888 Fax: (516)921-8743
Fr: 800-645-6337

Jack Rudman. All examination guides in this series contain questions with answers.

★4608★ *Small Engine Repair*
National Learning Corp.
212 Michael Dr.
Syosset, NY 11791
Ph: (516)921-8888 Fax: (516)921-8743
Fr: 800-645-6337

Jack Rudman. Part of Occupational Competency Examination Series (OCE).

★4609★ *Small Engine Repair*
National Learning Corp.
212 Michael Dr.
Syosset, NY 11791
Ph: (516)921-8888 Fax: (516)921-8743
Fr: 800-645-6337

Jack Rudman. Part of the Test Your Knowledge Series. Contains multiple choice questions with answers.

BASIC REFERENCE GUIDES AND HANDBOOKS

★4610★ *Care & Repair of Small Marine Diesels*
International Marine Publishing Company
PO Box 220
Camden, ME 04843
Ph: (207)236-4837 Fax: (207)236-6314

Chris Thompson. 1987.

★4611★ *The Complete Guide to Motorcycle Mechanics*
Prentice Hall
Rte. 9W
Englewood Cliffs, NJ 07632
Ph: (201)592-2000

Motorcycle Mechanics Institute Staff. 1984.

★4612★ *Metal Corrosion in Boats*
International Marine Publishing Company
PO Box 220
Camden, ME 04843
Ph: (207)236-4837 Fax: (207)236-6314

Nigel Warren. 1987.

★4613★ *Motorcycle Electrics Without Pain*
M. Arman Publishing, Inc.
PO Box 785
Ormond Beach, FL 32175
Ph: (904)673-5576

Mike Arman. 1980.

★4614★ *Motorcycle Mechanics*
McGraw-Hill Publishing Company
1221 Avenue of the Americas
New York, NY 10020
Ph: (212)512-2000

William H. Crouse. 1982.

★4615★ *Small Steel Craft: Design, Construction & Maintenance*
Sheridan House, Inc.
145 Palisade St.
Dobbs Ferry, NY 10522
Ph: (914)693-2410

Ian Nicolson. Second edition, 1986.

PERIODICALS

★4616★ *ABYC News*
American Boat and Yacht Council, Inc. (ABYC)
3069 Solomons Island Rd.
Edgewater, MD 21037-1416
Ph: (410)956-1050 Fax: (410)956-2737
Louise Lincoln

Quarterly. Reports on the activities of the Council. Updates members on current events, seminars, and meetings. Discusses technical boating topics and current boating standards and related issues. Recurring features include a calendar of events, reports of meetings, job listings, and notices of publications available.

★4617★ *American Boat Builders & Repairers Association—Bulletin*
American Boat Builders & Repairers Association
PO Box 1236
Stamford, CT 06904
Ph: (203)967-4745 Fax: (203)967-4618
Adair Garis

Bimonthly. Covers matters of interest and concern to boatbuilders, boatyards, and marinas.

★4618★ *Autobody Supply and Equipment Market*
Motor and Equipment Manufacturers Association (MEMA)
10 Laboratory Dr.
PO Box 13966
Research Triangle Park, NC 27709-3966
Ph: (919)549-4800 Fax: (919)549-4824

Biennial.

OTHER SOURCES OF INFORMATION

★4619★ *Distributors Financial Analysis*
Motor and Equipment Manufacturers Association (MEMA)
10 Laboratory Dr.
PO Box 13966
Research Triangle Pk., NC 27709
Ph: (919)549-4800 Fax: (919)549-4824

Musical Instrument Repairers and Tuners

Musical instrument repairers and tuners maintain piano, pipe-organ, brass, wind, and string instruments so they perform properly. **Piano tuners** adjust piano strings to the proper pitch by setting them in relation to a properly adjusted "A" string. They also diagnose and correct any problems that may affect proper operation. **Pipe-organ repairers** tune, repair, and install organs that make music by forcing air through flue pipes or reed pipes. Like piano tuners, pipe-organ repairers tune the various pipes in relation to the "A" pipe. Repairers also do maintenance work cleaning the pipes, and may assemble organs onsite in churches and auditoriums. **Violin repairers** adjust and repair bowed instruments like violins and cellos. **Brass and wind instrument repairers** clean, adjust, and repair instruments such as flutes, saxophones and trumpets. **Guitar repairers** inspect and play the instrument to determine defects. They reassemble and string guitars. **Percussion instrument repairers** work on drums, cymbals, and xylophones.

Salaries

Earnings for musical instrument repairers and tuners average between $20,000-$40,000/year.

Employment Outlook

Growth rate until the year 2005: Slower than average.

Musical Instrument Repairers and Tuners

Career Guides

★4620★ **"Bow Repairer and Restorer" in *Career Opportunities in the Music Industry* (pp. 131-132)**
Facts on File
460 Park Ave. S.
New York, NY 10016-7382
Ph: (212)683-2244 Fax: 800-678-3633
Fr: 800-322-8755

Shelly Field. Second edition, 1991. Describes more than 70 music related jobs. Each occupational profile covers job duties, employment outlook, career paths, salaries, skills, and educational preparation. Offers tips for entering the field.

★4621★ **"Instrument Repair & Restoration Specialist" in *Career Opportunities in the Music Industry* (pp. 127-128)**
Facts on File
460 Park Ave. S.
New York, NY 10016-7382
Ph: (212)683-2244 Fax: 800-678-3633
Fr: 800-322-8755

Shelly Field. Second edition, 1991. Describes more than 70 music related jobs. Each occupational profile covers job duties, employment outlook, career paths, salaries, skills, and educational preparation. Offers tips for entering the field.

★4622★ ***Instrument Repairers***
Chronicle Guidance Publications, Inc.
66 Aurora St.
PO Box 1190
Moravia, NY 13118-1190
Ph: (315)497-0330 Fax: (315)497-3359
Fr: 800-622-7284

1993. This career brief describes the nature of the work, working conditions, hours and earnings, education and training, licensure, certification, unions, personal qualifications, social and psychological factors, employment outlook, entry methods, advancement, and related occupations.

★4623★ ***Musical Instrument Repairer***
Vocational Biographies, Inc.
PO Box 31
Sauk Centre, MN 56378-0031
Ph: (612)352-6516 Fax: (612)352-5546
Fr: 800-255-0752

1991. Four-page pamphlet containing a personal narrative about a worker's job, work likes and dislikes, career path from high school to the present. Education and training, the rewards and frustrations, and the effects of the job on the rest of the worker's life. The data file portion of this pamphlet gives a concise occupational summary, including work descriptions, working conditions, places of employment, personal characteristics, education and training, job outlook, and salary range.

★4624★ **"Musical Instrument Repairer" in *Jobs Rated Almanac***
World Almanac
1 International Blvd., Ste. 444
Mahwah, NJ 07495
Ph: (201)529-6900 Fax: (201)529-6901

Les Krantz. Second edition, 1992. Ranks 250 jobs by environment, salary, outlooks, physical demands, stress, security, travel opportunities, and extra perks. Includes jobs the editor feels are the most common, most interesting, and the most rapidly growing.

★4625★ **"Musical Instrument Repairers" in *Career Discovery Encyclopedia* (Vol.4, pp. 114-115)**
J.G. Ferguson Publishing Co.
200 W. Madison St., Ste. 300
Chicago, IL 60606
Ph: (312)580-5480 Fax: (312)580-4948

E. Russell Primm, editor-in-chief. 1993. Contains two-page articles on 504 occupations. Each article describes job duties, earnings, and educational and training requirements.

★4626★ **"Musical Instrument Repairers and Tuners" in *Encyclopedia of Careers and Vocational Guidance* (Vol.3, pp. 529-532)**
J.G. Ferguson Publishing Co.
200 W. Madison St., Ste. 300
Chicago, IL 60606
Ph: (312)580-5480 Fax: (312)580-4948

William E. Hopke, editor-in-chief. Ninth edition, 1993. Four-volume set that profiles 500 occupations and describes job trends in 74 industries. Includes career description, educational requirements, history of the job, methods of entry, advancement, employment outlook, earnings, working conditions, social and psychological factors, and sources of additional information.

★4627★ **"Musical Instrument Repairers and Tuners" in *Occupational Outlook Handbook***
U.S. Government Printing Office
Superintendent of Documents
Washington, DC 20402
Ph: (202)512-1800 Fax: (202)512-2250

Biennial; latest edition, 1994-95. Encyclopedia of careers describing more than 250 occupations and comprising about 85 percent of all jobs in the economy. Occupations that require lengthy education or training are given the most attention. For each occupation, the handbook describes job duties, working conditions, training, educational preparation, personal qualities, advancement possibilities, job outlook, earnings, and sources of additional information.

★4628★ **"Piano and Organ Technicians" in *Encyclopedia of Careers and Vocational Guidance* (Vol.4, pp. 103-108)**
J.G. Ferguson Publishing Co.
200 W. Madison St., Ste. 300
Chicago, IL 60606
Ph: (312)580-5480 Fax: (312)580-4948

William E. Hopke, editor-in-chief. Ninth edition, 1993. Four-volume set that profiles 500 occupations and describes job trends in 74 industries. Includes career description, educational requirements, history of the job, methods of entry, advancement, employment outlook, earnings, working conditions, social

and psychological factors, and sources of additional information.

★4629★ "Piano and Organ Tuner, Technician" in *Career Information Center* (Vol.5)
Simon and Schuster
200 Old Tappan Rd.
Old Tappan, NJ 07675
Fax: 800-445-6991 Fr: 800-223-2348

Richard Lidz and Dale Anderson, editorial directors. Fifth edition, 1993. For 600 occupations, describes job duties, entry-level requirements, education and training needed, advancement possibilities, employment outlook, earnings and benefits. The set is divided into 12 volumes. Each volume includes jobs related under a broad career field. Volume 13 is the index.

★4630★ "Piano Tuner" in *Offbeat Careers: The Directory of Unusual Work*
Ten Speed Press
PO Box 7123
Berkeley, CA 94707
Fax: (510)559-1629 Fr: 800-841-2665

Al Sacharov. 1991. Profiles eighty-eight unusual careers. Provides job description, history of occupation, salary, and training required. Lists one or more sources of additional information.

★4631★ *The Piano Tuner-Technician*
Piano Technicians Guild
4510 Belleview, Ste. 100
Kansas City, MO 64111
Ph: (816)753-7747

1984. This pamphlet describes the work, the skills needed, places of employment, and earnings.

★4632★ *Piano Tuner-Technician*
Careers, Inc.
PO Box 135
Largo, FL 34649-0135
Ph: (813)584-7333

1994. Two-page occupational summary card describing duties, working conditions, personal qualifications, training, earnings and hours, employment outlook, places of employment, related careers and where to write for more information.

★4633★ "Piano Tuner Technician" in *Career Opportunities in the Music Industry* (pp. 129-130)
Facts on File
460 Park Ave. S.
New York, NY 10016-7382
Ph: (212)683-2244 Fax: 800-678-3633
Fr: 800-322-8755

Shelly Field. Second edition, 1991. Describes more than 70 music related jobs. Each occupational profile covers job duties, employment outlook, career paths, salaries, skills, and educational preparation. Offers tips for entering the field.

★4634★ "Piano Tuner-Technician" in *Occu-Facts: Information on 580 Careers in Outline Form*
Careers, Inc.
PO Box 135
Largo, FL 34649-0135
Ph: (813)584-7333

Biennial, 1995-96 edition. Each one-page occupational profile describes duties, working conditions, physical surroundings and demands, aptitudes, temperament, educational requirements, employment outlook, earnings, and places of employment.

★4635★ *Piano Tuners and Technicians*
Chronicle Guidance Publications, Inc.
66 Aurora St.
PO Box 1190
Moravia, NY 13118-1190
Ph: (315)497-0330 Fax: (315)497-3359
Fr: 800-622-7284

1991. This career brief describes the nature of the work, working conditions, hours and earnings, education and training, licensure, certification, unions, personal qualifications, social and psychological factors, employment outlook, entry methods, advancement, and related occupations.

★4636★ "Tuner/Technician" in *Opportunities in Music Careers* (pp. 134-135)
National Textbook Co. (NTC)
VGM Career Books
4255 W. Touhy Ave.
Lincolnwood, IL 60646-1975
Ph: (708)679-5500 Fax: (708)679-2494
Fr: 800-323-4900

Robert Gerardi. 1991. Covers many aspects of the music business including careers in music performance and publishing, the recording industry, and teaching. Lists resources, associations, and unions.

★4637★ *Violin Bow Maker*
Vocational Biographies, Inc.
PO Box 31
Sauk Centre, MN 56378-0031
Ph: (612)352-6516 Fax: (612)352-5546
Fr: 800-255-0752

1995. Four-page pamphlet containing a personal narrative about a worker's job, work likes and dislikes, career path from high school to the present. Education and training, the rewards and frustrations, and the effects of the job on the rest of the worker's life. The data file portion of this pamphlet gives a concise occupational summary, including work descriptions, working conditions, places of employment, personal characteristics, education and training, job outlook, and salary range.

ASSOCIATIONS

★4638★ American Federation of Violin and Bow Makers (AFVBM)
288 Richmond Terrace
Staten Island, NY 10301
Ph: (718)816-7818

Elevates professional standards of craftsmanship and ethical conduct among members. Grants journeyman and master status in the field.

★4639★ American Institute of Organbuilders (AIO)
PO Box 130982
Houston, TX 77219
Ph: (713)529-2212

Conducts examinations and bestows certification at the journeyman and master levels.

★4640★ National Association of Professional Band Instrument Repair Technicians (NAPBIRT)
PO Box 51
Normal, IL 61761
Ph: (309)452-4257

Members: Professional technicians who repair or restore band instruments. **Purpose:** Purpose is to promote technical integrity in the craft. Conducts self-evaluation programs, local parts and services exchange programs, and problem solution services. Surveys tools and procedures to improve work quality. Serves as liaison between manufacturers/suppliers and technicians by providing a technical audience for the introduction and evaluation of new products and policies. Makes available emergency maintenance and repair of band instruments to college and university instructors, thus allowing musicians to continue in concert. Has established a code of ethics; is developing library on the construction, repair, and restoration of band instruments. Provides placement service. **Publications:** *Administrative Newsletter*, quarterly. • *Regional Newsletter*, quarterly. • *TechniCom*, bimonthly.

★4641★ Piano Technicians Guild (PTG)
3930 Washington
Kansas City, MO 64111
Ph: (816)753-7747 Fax: (816)531-0070

Members: Piano tuners and technicians. **Purpose:** Conducts technical institutes at conventions, seminars, and local chapter meetings. Promotes public education in piano care; maintains liaison with piano manufacturers and teachers. Maintains hall of fame. **Publications:** *Piano Action Handbook.* • *Piano Parts and Their Functions, Illustrated.* • *Piano Technicians Journal*, annual.

STANDARDS/CERTIFICATION AGENCIES

★4642★ American Federation of Violin and Bow Makers (AFVBM)
288 Richmond Terrace
Staten Island, NY 10301
Ph: (718)816-7818

Elevates professional standards of craftsmanship and ethical conduct among members. Grants journeyman and master status in the field.

★4643★ American Institute of Organbuilders (AIO)
PO Box 130982
Houston, TX 77219
Ph: (713)529-2212

Conducts examinations and bestows certification at the journeyman and master levels.

Test Guides

★4644★ *Career Examination Series: Instrumentman*
National Learning Corp.
212 Michael Dr.
Syosset, NY 11791
Ph: (516)921-8888 Fax: (516)921-8743
Fr: 800-645-6337

Jack Rudman. All examination guides in this series contain questions with answers.

Educational Directories and Programs

★4645★ *NAPBIRT Directory*
National Association of Professional Band Instrument Repair Technicians (NAPBIRT)
8 Ardith Dr.
PO Box 51
Normal, IL 61761
Ph: (309)452-4257

Periodic.

Awards, Scholarships, Grants, and Fellowships

★4646★ Golden Hammer Award
Piano Technicians Guild
3930 Washington
Kansas City, MO 64111
Ph: (816)753-7747 Fax: (816)561-0070

To recognize an individual for exceptional personal service in and to the piano technological profession over many years. Members of PTG are eligible. A gold-plated tuning hammer displayed in a hand-made case in the shape of a grand piano is awarded annually. Established in 1969.

★4647★ Hall of Fame
Piano Technicians Guild
3930 Washington
Kansas City, MO 64111
Ph: (816)753-7747 Fax: (816)561-0070

To perpetuate the memory of piano industry greats and to recognize a lifetime of very special services to the music industry. A framed certificate and pin are presented to the honoree, whose picture and resume are in the Hall of Fame book at the home office. Awarded annually. Established in 1976.

Basic Reference Guides and Handbooks

★4648★ *Complete Course in Professional Piano Tuning, Repair & Rebuilding*
Nelson-Hall, Inc.
111 N. Canal St.
Chicago, IL 60606
Ph: (312)930-9446

Floyd A. Stevens. 1972.

★4649★ *Guitar Repair*
Bold Strummer, Ltd
20 Turkey Hill Circle
PO Box 2037
Westport, CT 06880
Ph: (203)259-3021 Fax: (203)259-7369

Irving Sloane. Revised edition, 1989.

★4650★ *How to Tune, Repair & Regulate Pianos: A Practical Guide*
Hill Springs Publications
5023 Kentucky St.
South Charleston, WV 23509

Jack Bradley. 1986.

★4651★ *Piano Servicing, Tuning & Rebuilding*
Vestal Press, Ltd.
320 N. Jensen Rd.
PO Box 97
Vestal, NY 13851-0097
Ph: (607)797-4872 Fax: (607)797-4898

Arthur A. Reblitz. 1993.

★4652★ *Player Piano Servicing & Rebuilding*
Vestal Press, Ltd.
320 N. Jensen Rd.
PO Box 97
Vestal, NY 13851-0097
Ph: (607)797-4872

Arthur A. Reblitz. 1985. (607)797-4898.

Periodicals

★4653★ *Administrative Newsletter*
National Association of Professional Band Instrument Repair Technicians (NAPBIRT)
PO Box 51
Normal, IL 61761
Ph: (309)452-4257

Quarterly.

★4654★ *Catgut Acoustical Society—Journal*
Catgut Acoustical Society
112 Essex Ave.
Montclair, NJ 07042
Ph: (201)744-4029 Fax: (201)744-9197
Daniel W. Haines

Semiannual. Deals with the practical, technical, and acoustical aspects of musical instrument making. Discusses the history and performance of musical instruments and musical composition. Covers new developments in the field. Recurring features include book reviews and bibliographies.

★4655★ *Experimental Musical Instruments*
Bart Hopkin
PO Box 784
Nicasio, CA 94946
Ph: (415)662-2182
Bart Hopkin

Quarterly. Explores new and unconventional musical instruments and sound sculpture. Covers all types of instruments and musical forms, discussing acoustics, tools and techniques, recording, and composition. Recurring features include news of research, letters to the editor, and reviews of books and recordings.

★4656★ *FIGA Newsletter*
Fretted Instrument Guild of America (FIGA)
c/o Ann Pertoney
2344 S. Oakley Ave.
Chicago, IL 60608
Ph: (312)376-1143
Glen Lemmer

Bimonthly. Publishes news of the Guild and musical pieces for fretted instruments, including the banjo, guitar, violin, fiddle, mandolin, lute, and bass.

★4657★ *Piano Action Handbook*
Piano Technicians Guild (PTG)
3930 Washington
Kansas City, MO 64111
Ph: (816)753-7747 Fax: (816)531-0070

★4658★ *Piano Parts and Their Functions, Illustrated*
Piano Technicians Guild (PTG)
3930 Washington
Kansas City, MO 64111
Ph: (816)753-7747 Fax: (816)531-0070

★4659★ *Piano Technicians Journal*
Piano Technicians Guild, Inc.
3930 Washington
Kansas City, MO 64111
Ph: (816)753-7747 Fax: (816)531-0070
Larry Goldsmith

Monthly. Magazine for piano technicians.

★4660★ *Regional Newsletter*
National Association of Professional Band Instrument Repair Technicians (NAPBIRT)
PO Box 51
Normal, IL 61761
Ph: (309)452-4257

Quarterly.

★4661★ *STRINGS*
The String Letter Press
412 Red Hill Ave., Ste. 16
PO Box 767
San Anselmo, CA 94960-0767
Ph: (415)485-6946 Fax: (415)485-0831
Fr: 800-827-6837
Mary Van Clay

Bimonthly.

★4662★ *TECHNICOM*
National Association of Professional Band Instrument Repair Technicians
PO Box 51
Normal, IL 61761
Ph: (309)452-4257 Fax: (309)452-4825
Chuck Hagler

Serves as an exchange of information among band instrument repair technicians, providing news of developments in the field and articles by Association members. Carries updates on Association activities and profiles of industry professionals.

Vending Machine Servicers and Repairers

Vending machine servicers and repairers install, service, and stock vending machines and keep them in good working order. Servicers make sure machines operate correctly by checking that refrigeration and heating units work properly, handles, springs, and merchandise chutes operate, and that coin and change making mechanisms are functional. When installing the machines, they make the necessary water and electrical connections and recheck the machines for proper operation. Another major duty of these workers is preventive maintenance. This involves cleaning and lubrication of various parts and making necessary adjustments. In case of machine breakdown, repairers inspect it for obvious problems, consult troubleshooting manuals and use testing devices to locate the defect. Once the problem is found, they use a variety of tools in repair such as pipe cutters, soldering guns and other power tools. Because many vending machines dispense food, these workers must comply with state and local public health and sanitation standards. They also must comply with local plumbing and electrical codes. Most repairers work for vending companies that sell food and other items through machines. Others work for soft drink bottling companies that have their own coin-operated machines. Some work for companies that own video games, pin-ball machines, jukeboxes, and similar types of amusement equipment.

Salaries

Wage rates for experienced vending machine servicers and repairers range from $5.00-14.00/hour depending on the size of the firm and the region of the country.

Employment Outlook

Growth rate until the year 2005: Decline slightly.

Vending Machine Servicers and Repairers

Career Guides

★4663★ *Vending Machine Mechanic*
Careers, Inc.
PO Box 135
Largo, FL 34649-0135
Ph: (813)584-7333

1991. Two-page occupational summary card describing duties, working conditions, personal qualifications, training, earnings and hours, employment outlook, places of employment, related careers and where to write for more information.

★4664★ "Vending Machine Mechanic" in *Occu-Facts: Information on 580 Careers in Outline Form*
Careers, Inc.
PO Box 135
Largo, FL 34649-0135
Ph: (813)584-7333

Biennial, 1995-96 edition. Each one-page occupational profile describes duties, working conditions, physical surroundings and demands, aptitudes, temperament, educational requirements, employment outlook, earnings, and places of employment.

★4665★ "Vending Machine Mechanics" in *Career Discovery Encyclopedia* (Vol.6, pp. 136-137)
J.G. Ferguson Publishing Co.
200 W. Madison St., Ste. 300
Chicago, IL 60606
Ph: (312)580-5480 Fax: (312)580-4948

E. Russell Primm, editor-in-chief. 1993. Contains two-page articles on 504 occupations. Each article describes job duties, earnings, and educational and training requirements.

★4666★ "Vending Machine Repairer" in *Jobs Rated Almanac*
World Almanac
1 International Blvd., Ste. 444
Mahwah, NJ 07495
Ph: (201)529-6900 Fax: (201)529-6901

Les Krantz. Second edition, 1992. Ranks 250 jobs by environment, salary, outlooks, physical demands, stress, security, travel opportunities, and extra perks. Includes jobs the editor feels are the most common, most interesting, and the most rapidly growing.

★4667★ *Vending Machine Repairers*
Chronicle Guidance Publications, Inc.
66 Aurora St.
PO Box 1190
Moravia, NY 13118-1190
Ph: (315)497-0330 Fax: (315)497-3359
Fr: 800-622-7284

1991. This career brief describes the nature of the work, working conditions, hours and earnings, education and training, licensure, certification, unions, personal qualifications, social and psychological factors, employment outlook, entry methods, advancement, and related occupations.

★4668★ *Vending Machine Route Driver*
Vocational Biographies, Inc.
PO Box 31
Sauk Centre, MN 56378-0031
Ph: (612)352-6516 Fax: (612)352-5546
Fr: 800-255-0752

1991. This pamphlet profiles a person working in the job. Includes information about job duties, working conditions, places of employment, educational preparation, labor market outlook, and salaries.

★4669★ "Vending Machine Route Worker" in *Career Information Center* (Vol.10)
Simon and Schuster
200 Old Tappan Rd.
Old Tappan, NJ 07675
Fax: 800-445-6991 Fr: 800-223-2348

Richard Lidz and Dale Anderson, editorial directors. Fifth edition, 1993. For 600 occupations, describes job duties, entry-level requirements, education and training needed, advancement possibilities, employment outlook, earnings and benefits. The set is divided into 12 volumes. Each volume includes jobs related under a broad career field. Volume 13 is the index.

★4670★ *Vending Machine Route Workers*
Careers, Inc.
PO Box 135
Largo, FL 34649-0135
Ph: (813)584-7333

1993. Two-page job guide card describing duties, working conditions, personal qualifications, training, earnings and hours, employment outlook, places of employment, related careers and where to write for more information.

★4671★ "Vending Machine Route Workers" in *Occu-Facts: Information on 580 Careers in Outline Form*
Careers, Inc.
PO Box 135
Largo, FL 34649-0135
Ph: (813)584-7333

Biennial, 1995-96 edition. Each one-page occupational profile describes duties, working conditions, physical surroundings and demands, aptitudes, temperament, educational requirements, employment outlook, earnings, and places of employment.

★4672★ "Vending Machine Servicers and Repairers" in *Occupational Outlook Handbook*
U.S. Government Printing Office
Superintendent of Documents
Washington, DC 20402
Ph: (202)512-1800 Fax: (202)512-2250

Biennial; latest edition, 1994-95. Encyclopedia of careers describing more than 250 occupations and comprising about 85 percent of all jobs in the economy. Occupations that require lengthy education or training are given the most attention. For each occupation, the handbook describes job duties, working conditions, training, educational preparation, personal qualities, advancement possibilities, job outlook, earnings, and sources of additional information.

Associations

★4673★ National Automatic Merchandising Association (NAMA)
20 N. Wacker Dr.
Chicago, IL 60606
Ph: (312)346-0370 Fax: (312)704-4140

Members: Manufacturing and operating companies in the automatic vending machine industry; food service management firms; office coffee machine operators; suppliers of products and services such as food, candy, beverages, cigarettes, and packaging. **Purpose:** Compiles industry profit ratios; conducts manufacturing census. **Publications:** *National Automatic Merchandising Association—Directory of Members*, annual. • *National Automatic Merchandising Association-Newsletter*, bimonthly. • *National Automatic Merchandising Association—State Legislative Review*, periodic. • *Quarterly Labor Relations Comprehensive Bulletin*, quarterly.

Periodicals

★4674★ National Automatic Merchandising Association—Directory of Members
National Automatic Merchandising Association (NAMA)
20 N. Wacker Dr.
Chicago, IL 60606
Ph: (312)346-0370 Fax: (312)704-4140

Annual. Includes service firms, alphabetically by state; machine manufacturers, alphabetically by company name; suppliers, alphabetically by name.

★4675★ National Automatic Merchandising Association-Newsletter
National Automatic Merchandising Association (NAMA)
20 N. Wacker Dr.
Chicago, IL 60606
Ph: (312)346-0370 Fax: (312)704-4140

Bimonthly.

★4676★ National Automatic Merchandising Association—State Legislative Review
National Automatic Merchandising Association (NAMA)
20 N. Wacker Dr.
Chicago, IL 60606
Ph: (312)346-0370 Fax: (312)704-4140

Periodic. Contains state legislation affecting the vending/foodservice management industry.

★4677★ Quarterly Labor Relations Comprehensive Bulletin
National Automatic Merchandising Association (NAMA)
20 N. Wacker Dr.
Chicago, IL 60606
Ph: (312)346-0370 Fax: (312)704-4140

Quarterly. Concerned with technical-legal aspects of employee relations policies in the vending/foodservice management industry.

Bricklayers and Stonemasons

Bricklayers build walls, floors, partitions, fireplaces, and other structures with brick, cinder or concrete block, and other masonry materials. They also install firebrick linings in industrial furnaces. **Stonemasons** build stone walls as well as set stone exteriors and floors. Because stone is expensive, stonemasons work mostly on high-cost buildings, such as churches, hotels, and office buildings. Bricklayers and stonemasons also repair imperfections and cracks or replace broken or missing masonry units in walls and floors. Refractory repairers or masons are bricklayers who install firebrick and refractory tile in high-temperature boilers, furnaces, cupolas, ladles and soaking pits in industrial establishments. Most work in steel mills, where molten materials flow on refractory beds from furnaces to rolling machines.

Salaries

Apprentices or helpers in each trade start at about 50 percent of the wage rate paid to experienced workers. The rate increases as they gain experience. Weekly earnings for bricklayers and stonemasons are as follows:

Lowest 10 percent	$260/week or less
Median	$335-$640/week
Top 10 percent	$785/week or more

Employment Outlook

Growth rate until the year 2005: Average.

Bricklayers and Stonemasons

Career Guides

★4678★ *Bricklayer*
Careers, Inc.
PO Box 135
Largo, FL 34649-0135
Ph: (813)584-7333

1994. Two-page occupational summary card describing duties, working conditions, personal qualifications, training, earnings and hours, employment outlook, places of employment, related careers and where to write for more information.

★4679★ "Bricklayer" in *Career Information Center* (Vol.4)
Simon and Schuster
200 Old Tappan Rd.
Old Tappan, NJ 07675
Fax: 800-445-6991 Fr: 800-223-2348

Richard Lidz and Dale Anderson, editorial directors. Fifth edition, 1993. For 600 occupations, describes job duties, entry-level requirements, education and training needed, advancement possibilities, employment outlook, earnings and benefits. The set is divided into 12 volumes. Each volume includes jobs related under a broad career field. Volume 13 is the index.

★4680★ "Bricklayer" in *Jobs Rated Almanac*
World Almanac
1 International Blvd., Ste. 444
Mahwah, NJ 07495
Ph: (201)529-6900 Fax: (201)529-6901

Les Krantz. Second edition, 1992. Ranks 250 jobs by environment, salary, outlooks, physical demands, stress, security, travel opportunities, and extra perks. Includes jobs the editor feels are the most common, most interesting, and the most rapidly growing.

★4681★ "Bricklayer" in *Occu-Facts: Information on 580 Careers in Outline Form*
Careers, Inc.
PO Box 135
Largo, FL 34649-0135
Ph: (813)584-7333

Biennial, 1995-96 edition. Each one-page occupational profile describes duties, working conditions, physical surroundings and demands, aptitudes, temperament, educational requirements, employment outlook, earnings, and places of employment.

★4682★ "Bricklayers" in *American Almanac of Jobs and Salaries* (pp. 501)
Avon Books
1350 Avenue of the Americas
New York, NY 10019
Ph: (212)261-6800 Fr: 800-238-0658

John Wright, editor. Revised and updated, 1994-95. A comprehensive guide to the wages of hundreds of occupations in a wide variety of industries and organizations.

★4683★ "Bricklayers" in *Opportunities in Building Construction Trades* (pp. 49-52)
National Textbook Co. (NTC)
VGM Career Books
4255 W. Touhy Ave.
Lincolnwood, IL 60646-1975
Ph: (708)679-5500 Fax: (708)679-2494
Fr: 800-323-4900

Michael Sumichrast. 1989. Gives an overview of the construction industry and describes the jobs of various craftworkers. Covers different kinds of builders: home, custom; and describes management skills needed and industry trends affecting opportunities.

★4684★ *Bricklayers and Stonemasons*
Chronicle Guidance Publications, Inc.
66 Aurora St.
PO Box 1190
Moravia, NY 13118-1190
Ph: (315)497-0330 Fax: (315)497-3359
Fr: 800-622-7284

1993. This career brief describes the nature of the work, working conditions, hours and earnings, education and training, licensure, certification, unions, personal qualifications, social and psychological factors, employment outlook, entry methods, advancement, and related occupations.

★4685★ "Bricklayers and Stonemasons" in *Career Discovery Encyclopedia* (Vol.1, pp. 128-129)
J.G. Ferguson Publishing Co.
200 W. Madison St., Ste. 300
Chicago, IL 60606
Ph: (312)580-5480 Fax: (312)580-4948

E. Russell Primm, editor-in-chief. 1993. Contains two-page articles on 504 occupations. Each article describes job duties, earnings, and educational and training requirements.

★4686★ "Bricklayers and Stonemasons" in *Encyclopedia of Careers and Vocational Guidance* (Vol.2, pp. 219-221)
J.G. Ferguson Publishing Co.
200 W. Madison St., Ste. 300
Chicago, IL 60606
Ph: (312)580-5480 Fax: (312)580-4948

William E. Hopke, editor-in-chief. Ninth edition, 1993. Four-volume set that profiles 500 occupations and describes job trends in 74 industries. Includes career description, educational requirements, history of the job, methods of entry, advancement, employment outlook, earnings, working conditions, social and psychological factors, and sources of additional information.

★4687★ "Bricklayers and Stonemasons" in *Occupational Outlook Handbook*
U.S. Government Printing Office
Superintendent of Documents
Washington, DC 20402
Ph: (202)512-1800 Fax: (202)512-2250

Biennial; latest edition, 1994-95. Encyclopedia of careers describing more than 250 occupations and comprising about 85 percent of all jobs in the economy. Occupations that require lengthy education or training are given the most attention. For each occupation, the handbook describes job duties, working conditions, training, educational preparation, personal qualities, advancement possibilities, job outlook, earnings, and sources of additional information.

★4688★ *Bricklaying*
Brick Institute of America
1750 Old Meadow Rd.
Mc Lean, VA 22102
Ph: (703)893-4010

This four-page pamphlet describes skills, benefits, and how to get started as a bricklayer.

★4689★ *Construction Cluster*
Center for Humanities, Inc.
Communications Park
Box 1000
Mount Kisco, NY 10549
Ph: (914)666-4100 Fax: (914)666-5319
Fr: 800-431-1242

Videocassette. 1984. 15 mins. Construction workers describe what it's like to work at their jobs, and show the special equipment they use in their field.

★4690★ "Marble Setters" in *Career Discovery Encyclopedia* (Vol.4, pp. 50-51)
J.G. Ferguson Publishing Co.
200 W. Madison St., Ste. 300
Chicago, IL 60606
Ph: (312)580-5480 Fax: (312)580-4948

E. Russell Primm, editor-in-chief. 1993. Contains two-page articles on 504 occupations. Each article describes job duties, earnings, and educational and training requirements.

★4691★ "Marble Setters, Tile Setters, and Terrazzo Workers" in *Encyclopedia of Careers and Vocational Guidance* (Vol.3, pp. 366-368)
J.G. Ferguson Publishing Co.
200 W. Madison St., Ste. 300
Chicago, IL 60606
Ph: (312)580-5480 Fax: (312)580-4948

William E. Hopke, editor-in-chief. Ninth edition, 1993. Four-volume set that profiles 500 occupations and describes job trends in 74 industries. Includes career description, educational requirements, history of the job, methods of entry, advancement, employment outlook, earnings, working conditions, social and psychological factors, and sources of additional information.

★4692★ *Marble, Tile Setters, Terrazzo, and Stone Workers*
Careers, Inc.
PO Box 135
Largo, FL 34649-0135
Ph: (813)584-7333

1993. Four-page brief offering the definition, history, duties, working conditions, personal qualifications, educational requirements, earnings, hours, employment outlook, advancement possibilities, and related occupations.

★4693★ "Marble, Tile, Terrazzo, and Stone Workers" in *Occu-Facts: Information on 580 Careers in Outline Form*
Careers, Inc.
PO Box 135
Largo, FL 34649-0135
Ph: (813)584-7333

Biennial, 1995-96 edition. Each one-page occupational profile describes duties, working conditions, physical surroundings and demands, aptitudes, temperament, educational requirements, employment outlook, earnings, and places of employment.

★4694★ "Marble, Tile, and Terrazzo Worker" in *Career Information Center* (Vol.4)
Simon and Schuster
200 Old Tappan Rd.
Old Tappan, NJ 07675
Fax: 800-445-6991 Fr: 800-223-2348

Richard Lidz and Dale Anderson, editorial directors. Fifth edition, 1993. For 600 occupations, describes job duties, entry-level requirements, education and training needed, advancement possibilities, employment outlook, earnings and benefits. The set is divided into 12 volumes. Each volume includes jobs related under a broad career field. Volume 13 is the index.

★4695★ *Masons*
Chronicle Guidance Publications, Inc.
66 Aurora St.
PO Box 1190
Moravia, NY 13118-1190
Ph: (315)497-0330 Fax: (315)497-3359
Fr: 800-622-7284

1992. Career brief describing the nature of the job, working conditions, hours and earnings, education and training, licensure, certification, unions, personal qualifications, social and psychological factors, location, employment outlook, entry methods, advancement, and related occupations.

★4696★ *Opportunities in Masonry Careers*
National Textbook Co. (NTC)
VGM Career Books
4255 W. Toughy Ave.
Lincolnwood, IL 60646-1975
Ph: (708)679-5500 Fax: (708)679-2494
Fr: 800-323-4900

Chris Santilli.

★4697★ *Stonemason*
Careers, Inc.
PO Box 135
Largo, FL 34649-0135
Ph: (813)584-7333

1995. Two-page occupational summary card describing duties, working conditions, personal qualifications, training, earnings and hours, employment outlook, places of employment, related careers and where to write for more information.

★4698★ "Stonemason" in *Career Information Center* (Vol.4)
Simon and Schuster
200 Old Tappan Rd.
Old Tappan, NJ 07675
Fax: 800-445-6991 Fr: 800-223-2348

Richard Lidz and Dale Anderson, editorial directors. Fifth edition, 1993. For 600 occupations, describes job duties, entry-level requirements, education and training needed, advancement possibilities, employment outlook, earnings and benefits. The set is divided into 12 volumes. Each volume includes jobs related under a broad career field. Volume 13 is the index.

★4699★ "Stonemason" in *Exploring Nontraditional Jobs for Women* (pp. 11-16)
Rosen Publishing Group
29 E. 21st St.
New York, NY 10010
Ph: (212)777-3017 Fax: (212)777-0277
Fr: 800-237-9932

Rose Neufeld. 1989. Describes blue-collar, male dominated occupations. Discusses what is done on the job, training, where to apply for jobs, tools used, salaries, and advantages and disadvantages. Relates the experiences of women who are working in the field.

★4700★ "Stonemason" in *Occu-Facts: Information on 580 Careers in Outline Form*
Careers, Inc.
PO Box 135
Largo, FL 34649-0135
Ph: (813)584-7333

Biennial, 1995-96 edition. Each one-page occupational profile describes duties, working conditions, physical surroundings and demands, aptitudes, temperament, educational requirements, employment outlook, earnings, and places of employment.

★4701★ "Stonemasons" in *Opportunities in Building Construction Trades* (pp. 70-72)
National Textbook Co. (NTC)
VGM Career Books
4255 W. Touhy Ave.
Lincolnwood, IL 60646-1975
Ph: (708)679-5500 Fax: (708)679-2494
Fr: 800-323-4900

Michael Sumichrast. 1989. Gives an overview of the construction industry and describes the jobs of various craftworkers. Covers different kinds of builders: home, custom; and describes management skills needed and industry trends affecting opportunities.

★4702★ *The Trowel Trades*
International Masonry Institute
823 15th St. NW, Ste. 1001
Washington, DC 20005
Ph: (202)783-3908

This six-panel brochure describes skills, advancement opportunities, and apprentice training.

★4703★ *Video Career Library - Construction*
Careers, Inc.
PO Box 135
Largo, FL 34649-0135
Ph: (813)584-7333

Videocassette. 1990. 36 mins. Part of the Video Career Library covering 165 occupations. Shows actual workers on the job. Includes millwrights, brickmasons, carpenters, drywall installers, electricians, painters, plumbers and pipefitters, carpenter and soft tile installers, insulation workers, paving equipment operators, and structural metal workers.

★4704★ *Vocational Visions*
Center for Humanities, Inc.
Communications Park
Box 1000
Mount Kisco, NY 10549
Ph: (914)666-4100 Fax: (914)666-5319
Fr: 800-431-1242

Videocassette. 1984. 30 mins. This series of programs explains key aspects of actual training and a day in the life of a worker in the specific field mentioned on the videocassette. Occupations include: transportation/mechanics, repair, construction, business/office occupations, health, agriculture, technical/manufacturing, communications, and personal service.

★4705★ *Vocations U.S.A.*
Info-Disc Corporation
4 Professional Dr., Ste. 134
Gaithersburg, MD 20879
Ph: (301)948-2300 Fr: 800-648-6422

Videocassette. 1987. 60 mins. A disc collection outlining the requirements and methods of various career areas. Occupations include: transportation, mechanical/repair, health, agriculture, technical/manufacturing, and construction.

★4706★ *You Can Become a Tile, Marble, Terrazzo and Dimensional Stone Installer*
United Brotherhood of Carpenters and Joiners of America
101 Constitution Ave., N.W.
Washington, DC 20001
Ph: (202)546-6206

This six-panel brochure describes apprenticeship training, hours, and working conditions.

Associations

★4707★ Associated General Contractors of America (AGC)
1957 E St. NW
Washington, DC 20006
Ph: (202)393-2040 Fax: (202)347-4004

Members: General construction contractors; subcontractors; industry suppliers; service firms. **Purpose:** Provides market services through its divisions. Conducts special conferences and seminars designed specifically for construction firms. Compiles statistics on job accidents reported by member firms. ors. Maintains 65 committees, including joint cooperative committees with other associations and liaison committees with federal agencies. **Publications:** *AGC Membership Directory and Buyers' Guide*, annual. • *AGC Mobile Directory*. • *Associated General Contractors of America—National Newsletter*, biweekly. • *Constructor*, monthly.

★4708★ Brick Institute of America (BIA)
11490 Commerce Park Dr.
Reston, VA 22091
Ph: (703)620-0010 Fax: (703)620-3928

Members: Manufacturers of clay brick. **Publications:** *BIA News*, monthly. • *Brick in Architecture*, quarterly. • *Builder Notes*, bimonthly. • *Technical Notes*, bimonthly.

★4709★ International Union of Bricklayers and Allied Craftsmen (BAC)
815 15th St. NW
Washington, DC 20005
Ph: (202)783-3788 Fax: (202)393-0219

Members: AFL-CIO. **Publications:** *Chalkline*, periodic.

Test Guides

★4710★ *Career Examination Series: Bricklayer*
National Learning Corp.
212 Michael Dr.
Syosset, NY 11791
Ph: (516)921-8888 Fax: (516)921-8743
Fr: 800-645-6337

Jack Rudman. All examination guides in this series contain questions with answers.

★4711★ *Career Examination Series: Foreman Bricklayer*
National Learning Corp.
212 Michael Dr.
Syosset, NY 11791
Ph: (516)921-8888 Fax: (516)921-8743
Fr: 800-645-6337

Jack Rudman. All examination guides in this series contain questions with answers.

★4712★ *Career Examination Series: Maintenance Mason*
National Learning Corp.
212 Michael Dr.
Syosset, NY 11791
Ph: (516)921-8888 Fax: (516)921-8743
Fr: 800-645-6337

Jack Rudman. 1989. All examination guides in this series contain questions with answers.

★4713★ *Career Examination Series: Maintenance Mason Foreman*
National Learning Corp.
212 Michael Dr.
Syosset, NY 11791
Ph: (516)921-8888 Fax: (516)921-8743
Fr: 800-645-6337

Jack Rudman. 1989. All examination guides in this series contain questions with answers.

★4714★ *Masonry*
National Learning Corp.
212 Michael Dr.
Syosset, NY 11791
Ph: (516)921-8888 Fax: (516)921-8743
Fr: 800-645-6337

Jack Rudman. Part of Occupational Competency Examination Series (OCE).

★4715★ *Masonry and Bricklaying*
National Learning Corp.
212 Michael Dr.
Syosset, NY 11791
Ph: (516)921-8888 Fax: (516)921-8743
Fr: 800-645-6337

Jack Rudman. Part of the Test Your Knowledge Series. Contains multiple choice questions with answers.

Educational Directories and Programs

★4716★ *AGC Membership Directory and Buyers' Guide*
Associated General Contractors of America (AGC)
1957 E St. NW
Washington, DC 20006
Ph: (202)393-2040 Fax: (202)347-4004

Annual.

★4717★ *AGC Mobile Directory*
Associated General Contractors of America (AGC)
1957 E St. NW
Washington, DC 20006
Ph: (202)393-2040 Fax: (202)347-4004

★4718★ *BIA Directory*
Brick Institute of America (BIA)
11490 Commerce Park Dr.
Reston, VA 22091
Ph: (703)620-0010 Fax: (703)620-3928

Annual.

★4719★ *International Directory of Building Research, Information and Development Organizations*
29 W. 35th St.
New York, NY 10001
Ph: (212)244-3336

Over 600 universities, institutions, government agencies, and other construction-related research institutions. Entries include: Institution name, address, phone, telex, name and title of contact, number of staff, source of finance, area of interest, publications.

Basic Reference Guides and Handbooks

★4720★ *Gauged Brickwork: A Technical Handbook*
Gower Publishing Company
Old Post Rd.
Brookfield, VT 05036
Ph: (802)276-3162

Gerard Lynch. 1990.

★4721★ *Intelligent Buildings Institute—Directory of Products and Services*
Intelligent Buildings Institute (IBI)
2101 L St., NW, Ste. 300
Washington, DC 20037
Ph: (202)457-1988 Fax: (202)457-8468

S. Hunt, Associate Executive Director, editor. Annual, September. Member consultants, associations, research organizations, and other suppliers of products and services to the construction and building industry. Entries include: Company name, address, phone. Arrangement: Alphabetical. Indexes: Product/service.

★4722★ *The Mason's Toolbox Manual*
Arco Pub.
201 W. 103rd St.
Indianapolis, IN 46290
Ph: 800-428-5331 Fax: 800-835-3202
David Tenenbaum. 1990.

PERIODICALS

★4723★ *ABC Today*
Associated Builders and Contractors, Inc. (ABC)
N. 17th St.
Rosslyn, VA 22209
Ph: (703)637-8800 Fax: (703)812-8203
Pamela E. Hunter
Semimonthly. Designed to keep readers alerted to important changes within ABC and the construction industry. Reports on legislative issues, construction trends, conferences and meetings, and ABC services. Recurring features include news of members and columns titled Industry Briefs, Safety Notebook, Computer Corner, Bottom Line, and Chapter News.

★4724★ *ABC Today*
Associated Builders and Contractors, Inc. (ABC)
1300 N. 17th St., 8th Floor
Arlington, VA 22209-3803
Ph: (703)812-2000 Fax: (703)812-8203
Pamela E. Hunter
Semiweekly. Magazine for open shop contractors and subcontractors. Includes articles on national and regional construction news, construction management, project case histories, new products, building design, and legislative and regulatory updates.

★4725★ *American Architectural Manufacturers Association—Quarterly Review*
American Architectural Manufacturers Association
1540 E. Dundee Rd., Ste. 310
Palatine, IL 60067-8321
Ph: (708)202-1350 Fax: (708)202-1480
Tony Coorlim
Annual. Contains industry news on architectural products. Covers prime and combination storm windows, sliding glass and combination storm doors, window and curtainwalls, store fronts and entrances, siding, soffits, fascia, gutters, downspouts, skylights, space enclosures, and mobile home components. Recurring features include news of research, notices of publications available, and announcements by the Association.

★4726★ *American Institute of Constructors—Newsletter*
American Institute of Constructors
9887 Gandy Blvd. N., Ste. 104
St. Petersburg, FL 33702
Ph: (813)578-1962 Fax: (813)578-9982
Cheryl P. Harris
Bimonthly. Concerned with construction practice, design, administration, and teaching. Carries news of members, listings of job opportunities, local chapter reports, notices of new publications, and conferences on construction topics.

★4727★ *Associated General Contractors of America—National Newsletter*
Associated General Contractors of America (AGC)
1957 E St. NW
Washington, DC 20006
Ph: (202)393-2040 Fax: (202)347-4004
Biweekly.

★4728★ *BIA News*
Brick Institute of America (BIA)
11490 Commerce Park Dr.
Reston, VA 22091
Ph: (703)620-0010 Fax: (703)620-3928
Monthly.

★4729★ *Blue Reports, Inc.*
Construction News Service
7325 Steel Mill Dr.
Springfield, VA 22050
Ph: (703)644-5884 Fax: (703)644-1929
Calvin S. Oren
Daily. Reports on public and private construction projects in the Washington, DC, Virginia, and Maryland areas. Provides owner's and architect's names, plan status, date bids due, prospective bidders, low bids received, and specification details.

★4730★ *Brick in Architecture*
Brick Institute of America (BIA)
11490 Commerce Park Dr.
Reston, VA 22091
Ph: (703)620-0010 Fax: (703)620-3928
Quarterly.

★4731★ *Builder*
Hanley-Wood, Inc.
1 Thomas Circle, Ste. 600
Washington, DC 20005
Ph: (202)452-0800
Mitchell Rouda
Monthly. Magazine covering housing, commercial, and industrial building.

★4732★ *Builder Architect*
Sunshine Media, Inc.
PO Box 37707
Phoenix, AZ 85069-7707
Ph: (602)433-7393 Fax: (602)433-2963
Marie Vere
Monthly. Home builders magazine.

★4733★ *Builder/Dealer*
Peterson Bros. Inc., Publishing
14 W. South St.
Corry, PA 16407-1894
Ph: (814)664-8624 Fax: (814)664-8506
Charles P. MancinoPublisher
Monthly. Trade magazine.

★4734★ *Builder Insider*
Divibest, Inc.
PO Box 191125
Dallas, TX 75219
Ph: (214)871-2913
Michael J. Anderson
Monthly. Magazine (tabloid) for builders, architects, and remodelers.

★4735★ *Builder Notes*
Brick Institute of America (BIA)
11490 Commerce Park Dr.
Reston, VA 22091
Ph: (703)620-0010 Fax: (703)620-3928
Bimonthly.

★4736★ *Building Business & Apartment Management*
Builders Association of Southeastern Michigan
30375 Northwestern Hwy.
Farmington Hills, MI 48334
Ph: (810)737-4477 Fax: (810)737-5741
Susan Adler
Monthly. Construction and apartment industry magazine.

★4737★ *Building Concerns*
National Association of Minority Contractors (NAMC)
1333 F St. NW, Ste. 500
Washington, DC 20004
Ph: (202)347-8259 Fax: (202)628-1876
Agreta Hester
Quarterly. Concentrates on national and regional news regarding minority construction contractors. Contains articles on issues generally affecting the industry—especially issues affecting minorities—including topics such as legislative and regulatory activity and reports on major corporation developments. Recurring features include reports of meetings, news of educational opportunities, a calendar of events, and news of NAMC chapters, affiliates, and members.

★4738★ *Building Industry*
Trade Publishing Co.
287 Mokauea St.
Honolulu, HI 96819
Ph: (808)848-0711 Fax: (808)841-3053
Jay McWilliams
Monthly. Construction and design magazine.

★4739★ *Building Industry Technology: An Abstract Newsletter*
National Technical Information Service (NTIS)
5285 Port Royal Rd.
Springfield, VA 22161
Ph: (703)487-4630
Biweekly. Consists of abstracts of reports on architectural and environmental design, building standards, construction materials and equipment, and structural analyses. Recurring features include a form for ordering reports from NTIS.

★4740★ *Buildings*
Stamats Communications, Inc.
427 6th Ave. SE
PO Box 1888
Cedar Rapids, IA 52406
Ph: (319)364-6167 Fax: (319)364-4278
Linda Monroe
Monthly. Publication featuring management techniques, development, and ownership of facilities.

★4741★ *Capital Comments*
National Lumber & Building Material Dealers Association
40 Ivy St. SE
Washington, DC 20003
Ph: (202)547-2230 Fax: (202)547-7640
Matt Geitner

Semimonthly. Reports on news of legislation pertaining to lumber, other building materials, and housing. Discusses such issues as lumber subsidies, interest rates on homes, health and safety, and jobs.

★4742★ *Chalkline*
International Union of Bricklayers and Allied Craftsmen (BAC)
815 15th St. NW
Washington, DC 20005
Ph: (202)783-3788 Fax: (202)393-0219

Periodic.

★4743★ *ConnStruction*
McHugh Design, Advertising & Publishing
62 Lasalle Rd., Ste. 211
West Hartford, CT 06107
Ph: (203)523-7518 Fax: (203)231-8808
Tracy E. McHughPublisher

Quarterly. Magazine for construction industry.

★4744★ *CONSTRUCTION*
HES, Inc.
26 Long Hill Rd.
PO Box 362
Guilford, CT 06437-0362
Ph: (203)453-3717 Fax: (203)453-4390
Jack C. Lewis

Semiweekly. Journal for the construction industry.

★4745★ *Construction News*
10835 Financial Centre Pkwy., Ste. 133
Little Rock, AR 72211-3555
Ph: (501)376-1931 Fax: (501)375-5831
Robert Alvey

Weekly. Construction industry magazine.

★4746★ *Construction Newsletter*
National Safety Council
1121 Spring Lake Dr.
Itasca, IL 60143-3201
Ph: (708)775-2282 Fax: (708)775-2285
Diane A. Ghazarian

Bimonthly. Focuses on industrial and occupational safety in the construction industry. Carries items on such topics as safe work practices and products; accident prevention; and successful industrial safety programs and policies.

★4747★ *Daily Construction Reporter*
7670 Opprtunity Rd.
San Diego, CA 92111-1112
Ph: (619)492-1402 Fax: (619)565-4182
Bernado RomanowskyPublisher

Daily. Construction newspaper covering jobs that are out for bid, bid results, building permits, and other information.

★4748★ *Dimensional Stone*
Dimensional Stone Institute, Inc.
6300 Variel Ave., Suite I
Woodland Hills, CA 91367
Ph: (818)704-5555 Fax: (818)704-6500
Jerry FisherdPublisher

Monthly. International trade publication covering the natural stone industry (marble, granite and other dimensional stone).

★4749★ *Fine Homebuilding*
The Taunton Press, Inc.
63 S. Main St.
PO Box 5506
Newtown, CT 06470
Ph: (203)426-8171 Fax: (203)426-3434
Fr: 800-283-7252
Mark Feirer

Magazine for builders, architects, designers, and owner-builders.

★4750★ *International Construction*
Maclean Hunter Publishing Co.
29 N. Wacker Drive
Chicago, IL 60606
Ph: (312)726-2802 Fax: (312)726-2574
Alan Peterson

Monthly. Trade magazine.

★4751★ *Journal of the International Union of Bricklayers & Allied Craftsmen*
815 15th St. NW
Washington, DC 20005
Ph: (202)783-3788 Fax: (202)393-0219
Paul Ruffins

Monthly. Tabloid for trade union members.

★4752★ *The Journal of Light Construction*
RR 2, Box 146
Richmond, VT 05477-9607
Ph: (802)434-4747 Fax: (802)434-4467
Steve Bliss

Monthly. Magazine (tabloid) for residential and light professionals involved in new and rehabilitative construction. Each issue covers a single aspect of construction.

★4753★ *Masonry*
Mason Contractors Association of America
1550 Spring Rd., Ste. 320
Oak Brook, IL 60521-1363
Ph: (708)782-6767 Fax: (708)782-6786
Gene Adams

Bimonthly. Trade magazine on construction, architecture, and engineering.

★4754★ *Nation's Building News*
1201 15th St. NW
Washington, DC 20005-2800
Ph: (202)822-0525 Fax: (202)861-2131
Tim Ahern

Semiweekly. Trade magazine (tabloid) covering home building and all related industries.

★4755★ *Nation's Building News*
National Association of Home Builders of the U.S. (NAHB)
1201 15th St. NW
Washington, DC 20005
Ph: (202)822-0200 Fax: (202)822-0559

Semimonthly. Provides the latest information concerning the housing industry, including finance, legislation, new technologies, and membership news.

★4756★ *Professional Builder & Remodeler*
Cahners Publishing Co.
1350 E. Touhy Ave.
PO Box 5080
Des Plaines, IL 60018-5080
Ph: (708)635-8800 Fax: (708)635-9950
Ed Fitch

Monthly.

★4757★ *The SPEC-DATA Program*
Construction Specifications Institute
601 Madison St.
Alexandria, VA 22314
Ph: (703)684-0300 Fax: (703)684-0465
Carol E. Duke

Quarterly. Magazine (loose-leaf) for the construction industry covering technical product and specification information.

★4758★ *Stone Review*
National Stone Assn.
1415 Elliot Pl. NW
Washington, DC 20007
Ph: (202)342-1100 Fax: (202)342-0702
Kash H. McClure

Bimonthly. Trade magazine for stone producers and suppliers of equipment to the aggregates industry.

★4759★ *Stone World*
Business News Publishing
1 Kalisa Way, Suite 205
Paramus, NJ 07652
Ph: (201)599-0136 Fax: (201)599-2378
Michael Reis

Monthly. Trade magazine on natural stone products.

★4760★ *Technical Notes*
Brick Institute of America (BIA)
11490 Commerce Park Dr.
Reston, VA 22091
Ph: (703)620-0010 Fax: (703)620-3928

Bimonthly.

Meetings and Conventions

★4761★ National Association of Brick Distributors Trade Exhibit
National Association of Brick Distributors
1600 Spring Hill Rd., Ste. 305
Vienna, VA 22182
Ph: (703)749-6223 Fax: (703)549-6227

Annual.

Other Sources of Information

★4762★ "Bricklayer" in *Career Selector 2001*
Barron's Educational Series, Inc.
250 Wireless Blvd.
Hauppauge, NY 11788
Ph: (516)434-3311 Fax: (516)434-3723
Fr: 800-645-3476

James C. Gonyea. 1993.

Carpenters

Carpenters working on construction projects constitute the largest group of building trade workers. A carpenter employed by a special trade contractor may specialize in setting forms for concrete construction, while one who is employed by a general building contractor may perform many tasks, such as framing walls and partitions, putting in doors and windows, and installing paneling and tile ceilings. Carpenters employed outside the construction industry are involved in a variety of installation and maintenance work. In manufacturing firms, carpenters may assist in moving or installing machinery. Local building codes often dictate where certain materials can and cannot be used, and carpenters have to know these requirements. All carpenters work in teams or are assisted by a helper.

Salaries

Maintenance carpenters, who generally have more steady employment, average $425/week.

Lowest 10 percent	$255/week or less
Median	$320-$585/week
Top 10 percent	$750/week or more

Employment Outlook

Growth rate until the year 2005: Average.

Carpenters

Career Guides

★4763★ *Career Insights*
RMI Media Productions, Inc.
1365 N. Winchester
Olathe, KS 66061
Ph: (913)768-1696 Fax: 800-755-6910
Fr: 800-745-5480

Videocassette series. 1987. This videotape series describes 50 occupations, including skill requirements and interviews with people employed in these fields. Occupations include: flight service, air transportation/ground services, data processing, carpentry, clerk in banking/insurance/business, cosmetic personal grooming, firefighting, forestry, insulation/roofing, mechanics, material handling, photographic processing, pipefitting and plumbing, printing, secretarial services, tool and die operations.

★4764★ *Career Success Series*
Cambridge Educational
PO Box 2153
Charleston, WV 25328-2153
Ph: (304)744-9323 Fax: (304)744-9351
Fr: 800-468-4227

Videocassette. 1986. 15 mins. A series, available separately, outlining various career choices for students. Occupations include: accounting, flight service, air transportation/ground/flight service, data processing, carpentry, clerk in banking/insurance, commodity sales, cosmetic personal grooming, fire fighting, forestry services, home economics, insulation/roofing, material handling, mechanics, photographic processing, pipefitting and plumbing, police science, printing, carpentry, medical laboratory technicians, secretarial services, and utilities equipment operator.

★4765★ "Carpenter" in *BLR Encyclopedia of Prewritten Job Descriptions*
Business and Legal Reports, Inc.
39 Academy St.
Madison, CT 06443-1513
Ph: (203)245-7448

Stephen D. Bruce, editor-in-chief. 1994. This book contains hundreds of sample job descriptions arranged by functional job category. The 1-3 page job descriptions cover what the worker normally does in the position, who they report to, and how that position fits in the organizational structure.

★4766★ "Carpenter" in *Career Information Center* (Vol.4)
Simon and Schuster
200 Old Tappan Rd.
Old Tappan, NJ 07675
Fax: 800-445-6991 Fr: 800-223-2348

Richard Lidz and Dale Anderson, editorial directors. Fifth edition, 1993. For 600 occupations, describes job duties, entry-level requirements, education and training needed, advancement possibilities, employment outlook, earnings and benefits. The set is divided into 12 volumes. Each volume includes jobs related under a broad career field. Volume 13 is the index.

★4767★ *Carpenter, Construction*
Careers, Inc.
PO Box 135
Largo, FL 34649-0135
Ph: (813)584-7333

1993. Four-page brief offering the definition, history, duties, working conditions, personal qualifications, educational requirements, earnings, hours, employment outlook, advancement possibilities, and related occupations.

★4768★ "Carpenter" in *Exploring Nontraditional Jobs for Women* (pp. 6-11)
Rosen Publishing Group
29 E. 21st St.
New York, NY 10010
Ph: (212)777-3017 Fax: (212)777-0277
Fr: 800-237-9932

Rose Neufeld. 1989. Describes blue-collar, male dominated occupations. Discusses what is done on the job, training, where to apply for jobs, tools used, salaries, and advantages and disadvantages. Relates the experiences of women who are working in the field.

★4769★ "Carpenter" in *Great Careers for People Who Like to Work with Their Hands* (pp. 28-33)
Gale Research Inc.
835 Penobscot Bldg.
Detroit, MI 48226
Ph: (313)961-2242 Fr: 800-347-4253

1994.

★4770★ "Carpenter" in *Hard Hatted Women: Stories of Struggle and Success in the Trades* (pp. 45-54)
Seal Press
3131 Western Ave., Ste. 410
Seattle, WA 98121
Ph: (206)283-7844 Fax: (206)285-9410

Molly Martin, editor. 1988. Twenty-six women recount their experiences working in blue collar occupations. They describe how they got in, the work they do, their relationships in predominantly male occupations, and their training.

★4771★ "Carpenter" in *Jobs Rated Almanac*
World Almanac
1 International Blvd., Ste. 444
Mahwah, NJ 07495
Ph: (201)529-6900 Fax: (201)529-6901

Les Krantz. Second edition, 1992. Ranks 250 jobs by environment, salary, outlooks, physical demands, stress, security, travel opportunities, and extra perks. Includes jobs the editor feels are the most common, most interesting, and the most rapidly growing.

★4772★ "Carpenter" in *Opportunities in Crafts Careers* (pp. 29-30)
National Textbook Co. (NTC)
VGM Career Books
4255 W. Touhy Ave.
Lincolnwood, IL 60646-1975
Ph: (708)679-5500 Fax: (708)679-2494
Fr: 800-323-4900

Marianne F. Munday. 1994. Covers crafts such as woodworking, ceramics, and leatherworking, and crafts-related careers such as writing and teaching. Offers advice on planning a career in crafts, starting a crafts business, and selling crafts.

★4773★ "Carpenter" in *VGM's Careers Encyclopedia* (pp. 75-78)
National Textbook Co. (NTC)
VGM Career Books
4255 W. Touhy Ave.
Lincolnwood, IL 60646-1975
Ph: (708)679-5500 Fax: (708)679-2494
Fr: 800-323-4900

Third edition, 1991. Contains two- to five-page descriptions of 200 managerial, professional, technical, trade, and service occupations. Each profile includes job duties, places of employment, qualifications, educational preparation, training, employment potential, advancement, income, and additional sources of information.

★4774★ *Carpenters*
Chronicle Guidance Publications, Inc.
66 Aurora St.
PO Box 1190
Moravia, NY 13118-1190
Ph: (315)497-0330 Fax: (315)497-3359
Fr: 800-622-7284

1993. This career brief describes the nature of the work, working conditions, hours and earnings, education and training, licensure, certification, unions, personal qualifications, social and psychological factors, employment outlook, entry methods, advancement, and related occupations.

★4775★ "Carpenters" in *American Almanac of Jobs and Salaries* (pp. 501)
Avon Books
1350 Avenue of the Americas
New York, NY 10019
Ph: (212)261-6800 Fr: 800-238-0658

John Wright, editor. Revised and updated, 1994-95. A comprehensive guide to the wages of hundreds of occupations in a wide variety of industries and organizations.

★4776★ "Carpenters" in *Career Discovery Encyclopedia* (Vol.1, pp. 146-147)
J.G. Ferguson Publishing Co.
200 W. Madison St., Ste. 300
Chicago, IL 60606
Ph: (312)580-5480 Fax: (312)580-4948

E. Russell Primm, editor-in-chief. 1993. Contains two-page articles on 504 occupations. Each article describes job duties, earnings, and educational and training requirements.

★4777★ "Carpenters" in *Encyclopedia of Careers and Vocational Guidance* (Vol.2, pp. 250-253)
J.G. Ferguson Publishing Co.
200 W. Madison St., Ste. 300
Chicago, IL 60606
Ph: (312)580-5480 Fax: (312)580-4948

William E. Hopke, editor-in-chief. Ninth edition, 1993. Four-volume set that profiles 500 occupations and describes job trends in 74 industries. Includes career description, educational requirements, history of the job, methods of entry, advancement, employment outlook, earnings, working conditions, social and psychological factors, and sources of additional information.

★4778★ "Carpenters" in *Occupational Outlook Handbook*
U.S. Government Printing Office
Superintendent of Documents
Washington, DC 20402
Ph: (202)512-1800 Fax: (202)512-2250

Biennial; latest edition, 1994-95. Encyclopedia of careers describing more than 250 occupations and comprising about 85 percent of all jobs in the economy. Occupations that require lengthy education or training are given the most attention. For each occupation, the handbook describes job duties, working conditions, training, educational preparation, personal qualities, advancement possibilities, job outlook, earnings, and sources of additional information.

★4779★ "Carpenters" in *Opportunities in Building Construction Trades* (pp. 23-29)
National Textbook Co. (NTC)
VGM Career Books
4255 W. Touhy Ave.
Lincolnwood, IL 60646-1975
Ph: (708)679-5500 Fax: (708)679-2494
Fr: 800-323-4900

Michael Sumichrast. 1989. Gives an overview of the construction industry and describes the jobs of various craftworkers. Covers different kinds of builders: home, custom; and describes management skills needed and industry trends affecting opportunities.

★4780★ *Carpentry*
Morris Video
2730 Monterey St., No. 105
Monterey Business Park
Torrance, CA 90503
Ph: (310)533-4800 Fr: 800-843-3606

Videocassette. 1984. 15 mins. The various levels of carpentry, plus the tools of the trade, are discussed.

★4781★ "Carpentry and Cabinetmaking" in *The Desk Guide to Training and Work Advisement* (pp. 71-73)
Charles C. Thomas, Publisher
2600 S. 1st St.
Springfield, IL 62794-9265
Ph: (217)789-8980 Fax: (217)789-9130
Fr: 800-258-8980

Gail Baugher Kuenstler. 1988. Describes alternative methods of gaining entry into an occupation through different types of educational programs, internships and apprenticeships.

★4782★ "Carpentry" in *Career Connection II: A Guide to Technical Magors and Their Related Careers* (pp. 38-39)
Jist Works, Inc.
720 N. Park Ave.
Indianapolis, IN 46202-3431
Ph: (317)264-3720 Fax: (317)264-3709

Fred A. Rowe. 1994. Contains technical majors, such as automotive technology. Describes the major and the job. Lists high school and postsecondary school courses. Includes occupations related to the major, employment outlook, and starting salary.

★4783★ *Carpentry & Construction*
TAB/McGraw-Hill, Inc.
PO Box 182607
Columbus, OH 43218-2607
Fax: (614)759-3644 Fr: 800-822-8158

Rex Miller and Glenn E. Baker. Second edition, 1991.

★4784★ *Construction: Basic Principles*
RMI Media Productions, Inc.
2807 West 47th St.
Shawnee Mission, KS 66205
Ph: (913)262-3974 Fax: (913)362-6910
Fr: 800-745-5480

Videocassette. 1984. 20 mins. This series of five programs of varying lengths covers different aspects of career opportunities in the construction trades. Included are: concrete masonry, carpentry, electrical work, plumbing, and heating and air conditioning.

★4785★ "Construction Carpenter" in *Occu-Facts: Information on 580 Careers in Outline Form*
Careers, Inc.
PO Box 135
Largo, FL 34649-0135
Ph: (813)584-7333

Biennial, 1995-96 edition. Each one-page occupational profile describes duties, working conditions, physical surroundings and demands, aptitudes, temperament, educational requirements, employment outlook, earnings, and places of employment.

★4786★ *Construction Cluster*
Center for Humanities, Inc.
Communications Park
Box 1000
Mount Kisco, NY 10549
Ph: (914)666-4100 Fax: (914)666-5319
Fr: 800-431-1242

Videocassette. 1984. 15 mins. Construction workers describe what it's like to work at their jobs, and show the special equipment they use in their field.

★4787★ *Getting Down to Business: Carpentry Business*
American Institutes for Research
PO Box 11131
Palo Alto, CA 94302
Ph: (415)493-3550 Fax: (415)858-0958

Joyce P. Gall. 1981.

★4788★ *Getting Down to Business: Construction Electrician Business*
American Institutes for Research in the Behavioral Sciences
PO Box 11131
Palo Alto, CA 94302
Ph: (415)493-3550 Fax: (415)858-0958

Joyce P. Gall. 1981.

★4789★ *Opportunities in Carpentry Careers*
National Textbook Co. (NTC)
VGM Career Books
4255 W. Touhy Ave.
Lincolnwood, IL 60646-1975
Ph: (708)679-5500 Fax: (708)679-2494
Fr: 800-323-4900

Roger Sheldon. 1987. Covers the history of the crafts, a typical carpenter's workday, future opportunities for carpenters, qualifications, training, apprenticeships, and special advice for women and minorities. Surveys various training opportunities.

★4790★ *Video Career Library - Construction*
Careers, Inc.
PO Box 135
Largo, FL 34649-0135
Ph: (813)584-7333

Videocassette. 1990. 36 mins. Part of the Video Career Library covering 165 occupations. Shows actual workers on the job. Includes millwrights, brickmasons, carpenters, drywall installers, electricians, painters, plumbers and pipefitters, carpenter and soft tile installers, insulation workers, paving equipment operators, and structural metal workers.

★4791★ *Vocational Visions*
Center for Humanities, Inc.
Communications Park
Box 1000
Mount Kisco, NY 10549
Ph: (914)666-4100 Fax: (914)666-5319
Fr: 800-431-1242

Videocassette. 1984. 30 mins. This series of programs explains key aspects of actual training and a day in the life of a worker in the specific field mentioned on the videocassette. Occupations include: transportation/mechanics, repair, construction, business/office occupations, health, agriculture, technical/manufacturing, communications, and personal service.

★4792★ *Vocations U.S.A.*
Info-Disc Corporation
4 Professional Dr., Ste. 134
Gaithersburg, MD 20879
Ph: (301)948-2300 Fr: 800-648-6422

Videocassette. 1987. 60 mins. A disc collection outlining the requirements and methods of various career areas. Occupations include: transportation, mechanical/repair, health, agriculture, technical/manufacturing, and construction.

Associations

★4793★ Associated Builders and Contractors (ABC)
1300 N. 17th St.
Rossyln, VA 22209
Ph: (703)812-2000

Members: Construction contractors, subcontractors, suppliers, and associates. **Purpose:** Aim is to foster and perpetuate the principles of rewarding construction workers and management on the basis of merit. Sponsors management education programs and craft training; also sponsors apprenticeship and skill training programs. Disseminates technological and labor relations information. Maintains placement service. Compiles statistics. **Publications:** *ABC Today*, semimonthly. • *National Membership Directory and Users Guide*, annual.

★4794★ Associated General Contractors of America (AGC)
1957 E St. NW
Washington, DC 20006
Ph: (202)393-2040 Fax: (202)347-4004

Members: General construction contractors; subcontractors; industry suppliers; service firms. **Purpose:** Provides market services through its divisions. Conducts special conferences and seminars designed specifically for construction firms. Compiles statistics on job accidents reported by member firms. ors. Maintains 65 committees, including joint cooperative committees with other associations and liaison committees with federal agencies. **Publications:** *AGC Membership Directory and Buyers' Guide*, annual. • *AGC Mobile Directory*. • *Associated General Contractors of America—National Newsletter*, biweekly. • *Constructor*, monthly.

★4795★ National Association of Home Builders of the U.S. (NAHB)
1201 15th St. NW
Washington, DC 20005
Ph: (202)822-0200 Fax: (202)822-0559

Members: Single and multifamily home builders, commercial builders, and others associated with the building industry. **Purpose:** Lobbies on behalf of the housing industry and conducts public affairs activities to increase public understanding of housing and the economy. Collects and disseminates data on current developments in home building and home builders' plans through its Economics Department and nationwide Metropolitan Housing Forecast. Maintains NAHB Research Center, which functions as the research arm of the home building industry. Sponsors seminars and workshops on construction, mortgage credit, labor relations, cost reduction, land use, remodeling, and business management. Compiles statistics; offers charitable program, spokesman training, and placement service; maintains speakers' bureau, and hall of fame. Subsidiaries include Home Builders Institute and National Council of the Housing Industry. Maintains over 50 committees in many areas of construction; operates National Commercial Builders Council, National Council of the Multifamily Housing Industry, National Remodelers Council and National Sales and Marketing Council. **Publications:** *Builder Magazine*, monthly. • *Forecast of Housing Activity*, monthly. • *Housing Economics*, monthly. • *Housing Market Statistics*, monthly. • *Nation's Building News*, semimonthly. • *Reference Guide to Homebuilding Articles*, quarterly.

★4796★ United Brotherhood of Carpenters and Joiners of America (UBC)
101 Constitution Ave. NW
Washington, DC 20001
Ph: (202)546-6206

Members: AFL-CIO. **Publications:** *Carpenter*, bimonthly.

Test Guides

★4797★ *Career Examination Series: Carpenter*
National Learning Corp.
212 Michael Dr.
Syosset, NY 11791
Ph: (516)921-8888 Fax: (516)921-8743
Fr: 800-645-6337

Jack Rudman. All examination guides in this series contain questions with answers.

★4798★ *Career Examination Series: Foreman Carpenter*
National Learning Corp.
212 Michael Dr.
Syosset, NY 11791
Ph: (516)921-8888 Fax: (516)921-8743
Fr: 800-645-6337

Jack Rudman. All examination guides in this series contain questions with answers.

★4799★ *Career Examination Series: Maintenance Carpenter*
National Learning Corp.
212 Michael Dr.
Syosset, NY 11791
Ph: (516)921-8888 Fax: (516)921-8743
Fr: 800-645-6337

Jack Rudman. 1989. All examination guides in this series contain questions with answers.

★4800★ *Career Examination Series: Maintenance Carpenter Foreman*
National Learning Corp.
212 Michael Dr.
Syosset, NY 11791
Ph: (516)921-8888 Fax: (516)921-8743
Fr: 800-645-6337

Jack Rudman. 1989. All examination guides in this series contain questions with answers.

★4801★ *Career Examination Series: Shop Carpenter*
National Learning Corp.
212 Michael Dr.
Syosset, NY 11791
Ph: (516)921-8888 Fax: (516)921-8743
Fr: 800-645-6337

Jack Rudman. 1989. All examination guides in this series contain questions with answers.

★4802★ *Carpenter*
Prentice Hall Press
Simon & Schuster Inc.
200 Old Tappan Rd.
Old Tappan, NJ 07675
Ph: 800-223-2348

Hy Hammer. Fifth edition, 1982. Helps prepare for the civil service exam or to gain employment in the private sector. Includes past exams and answer keys, and glossary of construction terms.

★4803★ *Carpentry*
National Learning Corp.
212 Michael Dr.
Syosset, NY 11791
Ph: (516)921-8888 Fax: (516)921-8743
Fr: 800-645-6337

Jack Rudman. 1989. Part of Occupational Competency Examination Series.

★4804★ *Introduction to Carpentry*
National Learning Corp.
212 Michael Dr.
Syosset, NY 11791
Ph: (516)921-8888 Fax: (516)921-8743
Fr: 800-645-6337

Jack Rudman. Part of Dantes Subject Standardized Tests.

★4805★ *Maintenance Worker/ Mechanical Maintainer*
Prentice Hall Press
Simon & Schuster Inc.
200 Old Tappan Rd.
Old Tappan, NJ 07675
Ph: 800-223-2348

Hy Hammer. Fourth edition, 1984. Provides information for applicants interested in the following civil service positions: carpenter, mason, plumber, electrician, painter, machinist. Includes eight sample tests.

★4806★ *What Do You Know about Carpentry*
National Learning Corp.
212 Michael Dr.
Syosset, NY 11791
Ph: (516)921-8888 Fax: (516)921-8743
Fr: 800-645-6337

Jack Rudman. 1990. Part of Test Your Knowledge Series.

Educational Directories and Programs

★4807★ *AGC Membership Directory and Buyers' Guide*
Associated General Contractors of America (AGC)
1957 E St. NW
Washington, DC 20006
Ph: (202)393-2040 Fax: (202)347-4004

Annual.

★4808★ *AGC Mobile Directory*
Associated General Contractors of America (AGC)
1957 E St. NW
Washington, DC 20006
Ph: (202)393-2040 Fax: (202)347-4004

★4809★ *International Directory of Building Research, Information and Development Organizations*
29 W. 35th St.
New York, NY 10001
Ph: (212)244-3336

Over 600 universities, institutions, government agencies, and other construction-related research institutions. Entries include: Institution name, address, phone, telex, name and title of contact, number of staff, source of finance, area of interest, publications.

Basic Reference Guides and Handbooks

★4810★ *Carpenter's Manifesto*
Henry Holt & Company
115 W. 18th St.
New York, NY 10011
Ph: (212)886-9200

Jefferey Ehrlich. 1990.

★4811★ *Carpenter's Toolbox Manual*
Prentice Hall
Rte. 9W
Englewood Cliffs, NJ 07632
Ph: (201)592-2000

Gary D. Meyers. 1989. Part of On-The-Job Reference Series.

★4812★ *The Carpenter's Toolbox Manual*
Arco Pub.
201 W. 103rd St.
Indianapolis, IN 46290
Ph: 800-428-5331 Fax: 800-835-3202

Gary D. Meers. 1989.

★4813★ *Carpentry: Framing & Finishing*
Prentice Hall
Rte. 9W
Englewood Cliffs, NJ 07632
Ph: (201)592-2000

Byron W. Maguire. 1989.

★4814★ *Finish Carpentry Illustrated*
TAB/McGraw-Hill, Inc.
PO Box 182607
Columbus, OH 43218-2607
Fax: (614)759-3644 Fr: 800-822-8158

R. Williams. 1991.

★4815★ *Intelligent Buildings Institute—Directory of Products and Services*
Intelligent Buildings Institute (IBI)
2101 L St., NW, Ste. 300
Washington, DC 20037
Ph: (202)457-1988 Fax: (202)457-8468

S. Hunt, Associate Executive Director, editor. Annual, September. Member consultants, associations, research organizations, and other suppliers of products and services to the construction and building industry. Entries include: Company name, address, phone. Arrangement: Alphabetical. Indexes: Product/ service.

★4816★ *Outdoor Structures*
Rodale Press, Inc.
33 E. Minor St.
Emmaus, PA 18098
Ph: (215)967-5171 Fax: (215)967-8963
Fr: 800-441-7761

Nick Engler . 1990. Part of Built-It-Better-Yourself Series.

★4817★ *Roof Framing*
Craftsman Book Company
PO Box 6500
6058 Corte del Cedro
Carlsbad, CA 92009
Ph: (619)438-7828 Fax: (619)438-0398

Marshal Gross. 1989.

★4818★ *Roof Framing*
American Association for Vocational Instructional Materials
745 Goines School Rd.
Athens, GA 30605
Ph: (404)543-7557 Fax: (404)613-6779

Charley G. Chadwick. 1991. Part of Basic Carpentry Skills Series.

★4819★ *Shelving & Storage*
Rodale Press, Inc.
33 E. Minor St.
Emmaus, PA 18098
Ph: (215)967-5171 Fax: (215)967-8963
Fr: 800-441-7761

Nick Engler. 1989. Part of Build-It-Better-Yourself Series.

★4820★ *Trim Carpentry Techniques: Installing Doors, Windows, Base & Crown*
Peter Smith Publisher, Inc.
6 Lexington Ave.
Magnolia, MA 01930
Ph: (617)525-3562

Craig Savage. 1991.

Periodicals

★4821★ *ABC Today*
Associated Builders and Contractors, Inc. (ABC)
N. 17th St.
Rosslyn, VA 22209
Ph: (703)637-8800 Fax: (703)812-8203
Pamela E. Hunter

Semimonthly. Designed to keep readers alerted to important changes within ABC and the construction industry. Reports on legislative issues, construction trends, conferences and meetings, and ABC services. Recurring features include news of members and columns titled Industry Briefs, Safety Notebook, Computer Corner, Bottom Line, and Chapter News.

★4822★ *ABC Today*
Associated Builders and Contractors, Inc. (ABC)
1300 N. 17th St., 8th Floor
Arlington, VA 22209-3803
Ph: (703)812-2000 Fax: (703)812-8203
Pamela E. Hunter

Semiweekly. Magazine for open shop contractors and subcontractors. Includes articles on national and regional construction news, construction management, project case histories, new products, building design, and legislative and regulatory updates.

★4823★ *ABC Today*
Associated Builders and Contractors (ABC)
1300 N. 17th St.
Rosslyn, VA 22209
Ph: (703)812-2000

Semimonthly. News magazine for merit shop contractors.

★4824★ *American Architectural Manufacturers Association—Quarterly Review*
American Architectural Manufacturers Association
1540 E. Dundee Rd., Ste. 310
Palatine, IL 60067-8321
Ph: (708)202-1350 Fax: (708)202-1480
Tony Coorlim

Annual. Contains industry news on architectural products. Covers prime and combination storm windows, sliding glass and combination storm doors, window and curtainwalls, store fronts and entrances, siding, soffits, fascia, gutters, downspouts, skylights, space enclosures, and mobile home components. Recurring features include news of research, notices of publications available, and announcements by the Association.

★4825★ *American Institute of Constructors—Newsletter*
American Institute of Constructors
9887 Gandy Blvd. N., Ste. 104
St. Petersburg, FL 33702
Ph: (813)578-1962 Fax: (813)578-9982
Cheryl P. Harris

Bimonthly. Concerned with construction practice, design, administration, and teaching. Carries news of members, listings of job opportunities, local chapter reports, notices of new publications, and conferences on construction topics.

★4826★ *Associated General Contractors of America—National Newsletter*
Associated General Contractors of America (AGC)
1957 E St. NW
Washington, DC 20006
Ph: (202)393-2040 Fax: (202)347-4004

Biweekly.

★4827★ *Blue Reports, Inc.*
Construction News Service
7325 Steel Mill Dr.
Springfield, VA 22050
Ph: (703)644-5884 Fax: (703)644-1929
Calvin S. Oren

Daily. Reports on public and private construction projects in the Washington, DC, Virginia, and Maryland areas. Provides owner's and architect's names, plan status, date bids due, prospective bidders, low bids received, and specification details.

★4828★ *Builder*
Hanley-Wood, Inc.
1 Thomas Circle, Ste. 600
Washington, DC 20005
Ph: (202)452-0800
Mitchell Rouda

Monthly. Magazine covering housing, commercial, and industrial building.

★4829★ *Builder Architect*
Sunshine Media, Inc.
PO Box 37707
Phoenix, AZ 85069-7707
Ph: (602)433-7393 Fax: (602)433-2963
Marie Vere

Monthly. Home builders magazine.

★4830★ *Builder/Dealer*
Peterson Bros. Inc., Publishing
14 W. South St.
Corry, PA 16407-1894
Ph: (814)664-8624 Fax: (814)664-8506
Charles P. MancinoPublisher

Monthly. Trade magazine.

★4831★ *Builder Insider*
Divibest, Inc.
PO Box 191125
Dallas, TX 75219
Ph: (214)871-2913
Michael J. Anderson

Monthly. Magazine (tabloid) for builders, architects, and remodelers.

★4832★ *Builder Notes*
Brick Institute of America (BIA)
11490 Commerce Park Dr.
Reston, VA 22091
Ph: (703)620-0010 Fax: (703)620-3928

Bimonthly.

★4833★ *Building Business & Apartment Management*
Builders Association of Southeastern Michigan
30375 Northwestern Hwy.
Farmington Hills, MI 48334
Ph: (810)737-4477 Fax: (810)737-5741
Susan Adler

Monthly. Construction and apartment industry magazine.

★4834★ *Building Concerns*
National Association of Minority Contractors (NAMC)
1333 F St. NW, Ste. 500
Washington, DC 20004
Ph: (202)347-8259 Fax: (202)628-1876
Agreta Hester

Quarterly. Concentrates on national and regional news regarding minority construction contractors. Contains articles on issues generally affecting the industry—especially issues affecting minorities—including topics such as legislative and regulatory activity and reports on major corporation developments. Recurring features include reports of meetings, news of educational opportunities, a calendar of events, and news of NAMC chapters, affiliates, and members.

★4835★ *Building Design & Construction*
Cahners Publishing Co.
1350 E. Touhy Ave.
PO Box 5080
Des Plaines, IL 60017-5080
Ph: (708)635-8800 Fax: (708)390-2618
Jack HollfelderPublisher

Monthly. Magazine on business and technology for commercial, institutional, and industrial buildings.

★4836★ *Building Industry*
Trade Publishing Co.
287 Mokauea St.
Honolulu, HI 96819
Ph: (808)848-0711 Fax: (808)841-3053
Jay McWilliams

Monthly. Construction and design magazine.

★4837★ *Building Industry Technology: An Abstract Newsletter*
National Technical Information Service (NTIS)
5285 Port Royal Rd.
Springfield, VA 22161
Ph: (703)487-4630

Biweekly. Consists of abstracts of reports on architectural and environmental design, building standards, construction materials and equipment, and structural analyses. Recurring features include a form for ordering reports from NTIS.

★4838★ *Buildings*
Stamats Communications, Inc.
427 6th Ave. SE
PO Box 1888
Cedar Rapids, IA 52406
Ph: (319)364-6167 Fax: (319)364-4278
Linda Monroe

Monthly. Publication featuring management techniques, development, and ownership of facilities.

★4839★ *Capital Comments*
National Lumber & Building Material Dealers Association
40 Ivy St. SE
Washington, DC 20003
Ph: (202)547-2230 Fax: (202)547-7640
Matt Geitner

Semimonthly. Reports on news of legislation pertaining to lumber, other building materials, and housing. Discusses such issues as lumber subsidies, interest rates on homes, health and safety, and jobs.

★4840★ *The Carpenter*
United Brotherhood of Carpenters and Joiners of America, AFL-CIO
101 Constitution Ave. NW
Washington, DC 20001
Ph: (202)546-6206 Fax: (202)543-5724
Sigurd. Lucassen

Bimonthly. Official magazine of the Carpenters' Union.

★4841★ *ConnStruction*
McHugh Design, Advertising & Publishing
62 Lasalle Rd., Ste. 211
West Hartford, CT 06107
Ph: (203)523-7518 Fax: (203)231-8808
Tracy E. McHughPublisher

Quarterly. Magazine for construction industry.

★4842★ *CONSTRUCTION*
HES, Inc.
26 Long Hill Rd.
PO Box 362
Guilford, CT 06437-0362
Ph: (203)453-3717 Fax: (203)453-4390
Jack C. Lewis

Semiweekly. Journal for the construction industry.

★4843★ *Construction News*
10835 Financial Centre Pkwy., Ste. 133
Little Rock, AR 72211-3555
Ph: (501)376-1931 Fax: (501)375-5831
Robert Alvey

Weekly. Construction industry magazine.

★4844★ *Construction Newsletter*
National Safety Council
1121 Spring Lake Dr.
Itasca, IL 60143-3201
Ph: (708)775-2282 Fax: (708)775-2285
Diane A. Ghazarian

Bimonthly. Focuses on industrial and occupational safety in the construction industry. Carries items on such topics as safe work practices and products; accident prevention; and successful industrial safety programs and policies.

★4845★ *Daily Construction Reporter*
7670 Opprtunity Rd.
San Diego, CA 92111-1112
Ph: (619)492-1402 Fax: (619)565-4182
Bernado Romanowsky

Daily. Construction newspaper covering jobs that are out for bid, bid results, building permits, and other information.

★4846★ *Fine Homebuilding*
The Taunton Press, Inc.
63 S. Main St.
PO Box 5506
Newtown, CT 06470
Ph: (203)426-8171 Fax: (203)426-3434
Fr: 800-283-7252
Mark Feirer

Magazine for builders, architects, designers, and owner-builders.

★4847★ *International Construction*
Maclean Hunter Publishing Co.
29 N. Wacker Drive
Chicago, IL 60606
Ph: (312)726-2802 Fax: (312)726-2574
Alan Peterson

Monthly. Trade magazine.

★4848★ *The Journal of Light Construction*
RR 2, Box 146
Richmond, VT 05477-9607
Ph: (802)434-4747 Fax: (802)434-4467
Steve Bliss

Monthly. Magazine (tabloid) for residential and light professionals involved in new and rehabilitative construction. Each issue covers a single aspect of construction.

★4849★ *Professional Builder & Remodeler*
Cahners Publishing Co.
1350 E. Touhy Ave.
PO Box 5080
Des Plaines, IL 60018-5080
Ph: (708)635-8800 Fax: (708)635-9950
Ed Fitch

Monthly.

★4850★ *Southwest Contractor*
McGraw-Hill, Inc.
2050 E. University Dr., Ste. 1
Phoenix, AZ 85034-6731
Ph: (602)258-1641 Fax: (602)495-9407
Bill Davis

Monthly. Regional trade magazine for the contracting industries including highway, municipal, utility, heavy construction, and mining.

★4851★ *The SPEC-DATA Program*
Construction Specifications Institute
601 Madison St.
Alexandria, VA 22314
Ph: (703)684-0300 Fax: (703)684-0465
Carol E. Duke

Quarterly. Magazine (loose-leaf) for the construction industry covering technical product and specification information.

Meetings and Conventions

★4852★ Associated General Contractors National Convention and Constructor Exposition
Associated General Contractors
1957 E St., NW
Washington, DC 20006
Ph: (202)393-2040 Fax: (202)347-4004

Annual. **Dates and Locations:** 1996 Feb 29-05; San Diego, CA.

Other Sources of Information

★4853★ "Carpenter" in *100 Best Jobs for the 1990s & Beyond*
Dearborn Financial Publishing, Inc.
520 N. Dearborn St.
Chicago, IL 60610-4354
Ph: (312)836-4400 Fax: (312)836-1021
Fr: 800-621-9621

Carol Kleiman. 1992. Describes 100 jobs ranging from accountants to veterinarians. Each job profile includes such information as education, experience, and certification needed, salaries, and job search suggestions.

★4854★ "Carpenter" in *Career Selector 2001*
Barron's Educational Series, Inc.
250 Wireless Blvd.
Hauppauge, NY 11788
Ph: (516)434-3311 Fax: (516)434-3723
Fr: 800-645-3476

James C. Gonyea. 1993.

Carpet Installers

Carpet installers measure, cut, and fit carpet materials in homes, offices, stores, restaurants, and other buildings. Many work for flooring contractors or floor covering retailers. Many other carpet installers are self-employed.

Salaries

Weekly earnings for carpet installers are as follows:

Lowest 10 percent	$185/week or less
Middle 50 percent	$275-$500/week
Top 10 percent	$700/week or more

Employment Outlook

Growth rate until the year 2005: Average.

Carpet Installers

Career Guides

★4855★ *Carpet Installer*
Careers, Inc.
PO Box 135
Largo, FL 34649-0135
Ph: (813)584-7333

1993. Two-page job guide card describing duties, working conditions, personal qualifications, training, earnings and hours, employment outlook, places of employment, related careers and where to write for more information.

★4856★ **"Carpet Installer" in *Occu-Facts: Information on 580 Careers in Outline Form***
Careers, Inc.
PO Box 135
Largo, FL 34649-0135
Ph: (813)584-7333

Biennial, 1995-96 edition. Each one-page occupational profile describes duties, working conditions, physical surroundings and demands, aptitudes, temperament, educational requirements, employment outlook, earnings, and places of employment.

★4857★ **"Carpet Installers" in *Occupational Outlook Handbook***
U.S. Government Printing Office
Superintendent of Documents
Washington, DC 20402
Ph: (202)512-1800 Fax: (202)512-2250

Biennial; latest edition, 1994-95. Encyclopedia of careers describing more than 250 occupations and comprising about 85 percent of all jobs in the economy. Occupations that require lengthy education or training are given the most attention. For each occupation, the handbook describes job duties, working conditions, training, educational preparation, personal qualities, advancement possibilities, job outlook, earnings, and sources of additional information.

★4858★ **"Carpet/Tile Installer" in *Jobs Rated Almanac***
World Almanac
1 International Blvd., Ste. 444
Mahwah, NJ 07495
Ph: (201)529-6900 Fax: (201)529-6901

Les Krantz. Second edition, 1992. Ranks 250 jobs by environment, salary, outlooks, physical demands, stress, security, travel opportunities, and extra perks. Includes jobs the editor feels are the most common, most interesting, and the most rapidly growing.

★4859★ **"Floor Covering Installer" in *Career Information Center* (Vol.4)**
Simon and Schuster
200 Old Tappan Rd.
Old Tappan, NJ 07675
Fax: 800-445-6991 Fr: 800-223-2348

Richard Lidz and Dale Anderson, editorial directors. Fifth edition, 1993. For 600 occupations, describes job duties, entry-level requirements, education and training needed, advancement possibilities, employment outlook, earnings and benefits. The set is divided into 12 volumes. Each volume includes jobs related under a broad career field. Volume 13 is the index.

★4860★ *Floor Covering Installer (Resilient)*
Careers, Inc.
PO Box 135
Largo, FL 34649-0135
Ph: (813)584-7333

1993. Two-page occupational summary card describing duties, working conditions, personal qualifications, training, earnings and hours, employment outlook, places of employment, related careers, and where to write for more information.

★4861★ **"Floor Covering Installer (Resilient)" in *Occu-Facts: Information on 580 Careers in Outline Form***
Careers, Inc.
PO Box 135
Largo, FL 34649-0135
Ph: (813)584-7333

Biennial, 1995-96 edition. Each one-page occupational profile describes duties, working conditions, physical surroundings and demands, aptitudes, temperament, educational requirements, employment outlook, earnings, and places of employment.

★4862★ *Floor Covering Installers*
Chronicle Guidance Publications, Inc.
66 Aurora St.
PO Box 1190
Moravia, NY 13118-1190
Ph: (315)497-0330 Fax: (315)497-3359
Fr: 800-622-7284

1990. Career brief describing the nature of the job, working conditions, hours and earnings, education and training, licensure, certification, unions, personal qualifications, social and psychological factors, location, employment outlook, entry methods, advancement, and related occupations.

★4863★ *Floor Covering Installers*
Vocational Biographies, Inc.
PO Box 31
Sauk Centre, MN 56378-0031
Ph: (612)352-6516 Fax: (612)352-5546
Fr: 800-255-0752

1990. Four-page pamphlet containing a personal narrative about a worker's job, work likes and dislikes, career path from high school to the present. Education and training, the rewards and frustrations, and the effects of the job on the rest of the worker's life. The data file portion of this pamphlet gives a concise occupational summary, including work descriptions, working conditions, places of employment, personal characteristics, education and training, job outlook, and salary range.

★4864★ **"Floor Covering Installers" in *Career Discovery Encyclopedia* (Vol.3, pp. 26-27)**
J.G. Ferguson Publishing Co.
200 W. Madison St., Ste. 300
Chicago, IL 60606
Ph: (312)580-5480 Fax: (312)580-4948

E. Russell Primm, editor-in-chief. 1993. Contains two-page articles on 504 occupations. Each article describes job duties, earnings, and educational and training requirements.

★4865★ **"Floor Covering Installers" in *Encyclopedia of Careers and Vocational Guidance* (Vol.3, pp. 11-14)**
J.G. Ferguson Publishing Co.
200 W. Madison St., Ste. 300
Chicago, IL 60606
Ph: (312)580-5480 Fax: (312)580-4948

William E. Hopke, editor-in-chief. Ninth edition, 1993. Four-volume set that profiles 500

occupations and describes job trends in 74 industries. Includes career description, educational requirements, history of the job, methods of entry, advancement, employment outlook, earnings, working conditions, social and psychological factors, and sources of additional information.

★4866★ "Floor Covering Installers" in *Opportunities in Building Construction Trades* (pp. 53-55)
National Textbook Co. (NTC)
VGM Career Books
4255 W. Touhy Ave.
Lincolnwood, IL 60646-1975
Ph: (708)679-5500 Fax: (708)679-2494
Fr: 800-323-4900

Michael Sumichrast. 1989. Gives an overview of the construction industry and describes the jobs of various craftworkers. Covers different kinds of builders: home, custom; and describes management skills needed and industry trends affecting opportunities.

★4867★ "Resilient Floor Layer" in *Opportunities in Carpentry Careers* (pp. 52-53)
National Textbook Co. (NTC)
VGM Career Books
4255 W. Touhy Ave.
Lincolnwood, IL 60646-1975
Ph: (708)679-5500 Fax: (708)679-2494
Fr: 800-323-4900

Roger Sheldon. 1987. Covers the history of the crafts, a typical carpenter's workday, future opportunities for carpenters, qualifications, training, apprenticeships, and special advice for women and minorities. Surveys various training opportunities.

Associations

★4868★ Floor Covering Installation Contractors Association (FCICA)
PO Box 948
Dalton, GA 30722-0948
Ph: (706)226-5488 Fax: (706)226-1775

Members: Installation contractors, carpet manufacturers, and suppliers to the installation trade. **Purpose:** Goals are to establish acceptable levels of performance for the carpet installation industry; promote standards of business ethics; encourage quality installations. Represents the interests of the floor covering installation industry by addressing issues such as minimum standards, clear and equitable specifications, uniform training, and quality craftsmanship. Acts as liaison with retailers, manufacturers, and suppliers; represents the industry before government agencies regarding proposed or enacted regulation and legislation. Fosters the sale and use of the industry's products and services. Serves as clearinghouse for resolving problems of mutual interest inside and outside the industry; exchanges information on problems, trends, techniques, and other matters concerning management. Assists local installation workrooms/contractors groups. Sponsors training programs and refresher courses. Compiles statistics. **Publications:** *Floor Covering Installation Contractors Association—Newsletter*, monthly.

Periodicals

★4869★ *ABC Today*
Associated Builders and Contractors, Inc. (ABC)
N. 17th St.
Rosslyn, VA 22209
Ph: (703)637-8800 Fax: (703)812-8203
Pamela E. Hunter

Semimonthly. Designed to keep readers alerted to important changes within ABC and the construction industry. Reports on legislative issues, construction trends, conferences and meetings, and ABC services. Recurring features include news of members and columns titled Industry Briefs, Safety Notebook, Computer Corner, Bottom Line, and Chapter News.

★4870★ *ABC Today*
Associated Builders and Contractors, Inc. (ABC)
1300 N. 17th St., 8th Floor
Arlington, VA 22209-3803
Ph: (703)812-2000 Fax: (703)812-8203
Pamela E. Hunter

Semiweekly. Magazine for open shop contractors and subcontractors. Includes articles on national and regional construction news, construction management, project case histories, new products, building design, and legislative and regulatory updates.

★4871★ *American Architectural Manufacturers Association—Quarterly Review*
American Architectural Manufacturers Association
1540 E. Dundee Rd., Ste. 310
Palatine, IL 60067-8321
Ph: (708)202-1350 Fax: (708)202-1480
Tony Coorlim

Annual. Contains industry news on architectural products. Covers prime and combination storm windows, sliding glass and combination storm doors, window and curtainwalls, store fronts and entrances, siding, soffits, fascia, gutters, downspouts, skylights, space enclosures, and mobile home components. Recurring features include news of research, notices of publications available, and announcements by the Association.

★4872★ *American Institute of Constructors—Newsletter*
American Institute of Constructors
9887 Gandy Blvd. N., Ste. 104
St. Petersburg, FL 33702
Ph: (813)578-1962 Fax: (813)578-9982
Cheryl P. Harris

Bimonthly. Concerned with construction practice, design, administration, and teaching. Carries news of members, listings of job opportunities, local chapter reports, notices of new publications, and conferences on construction topics.

★4873★ *Blue Reports, Inc.*
Construction News Service
7325 Steel Mill Dr.
Springfield, VA 22050
Ph: (703)644-5884 Fax: (703)644-1929
Calvin S. Oren

Daily. Reports on public and private construction projects in the Washington, DC, Virginia, and Maryland areas. Provides owner's and architect's names, plan status, date bids due, prospective bidders, low bids received, and specification details.

★4874★ *Building Concerns*
National Association of Minority Contractors (NAMC)
1333 F St. NW, Ste. 500
Washington, DC 20004
Ph: (202)347-8259 Fax: (202)628-1876
Agreta Hester

Quarterly. Concentrates on national and regional news regarding minority construction contractors. Contains articles on issues generally affecting the industry—especially issues affecting minorities—including topics such as legislative and regulatory activity and reports on major corporation developments. Recurring features include reports of meetings, news of educational opportunities, a calendar of events, and news of NAMC chapters, affiliates, and members.

★4875★ *Building Industry Technology: An Abstract Newsletter*
National Technical Information Service (NTIS)
5285 Port Royal Rd.
Springfield, VA 22161
Ph: (703)487-4630

Biweekly. Consists of abstracts of reports on architectural and environmental design, building standards, construction materials and equipment, and structural analyses. Recurring features include a form for ordering reports from NTIS.

★4876★ *Capital Comments*
National Lumber & Building Material Dealers Association
40 Ivy St. SE
Washington, DC 20003
Ph: (202)547-2230 Fax: (202)547-7640
Matt Geitner

Semimonthly. Reports on news of legislation pertaining to lumber, other building materials, and housing. Discusses such issues as lumber subsidies, interest rates on homes, health and safety, and jobs.

★4877★ *ConnStruction*
McHugh Design, Advertising & Publishing
62 Lasalle Rd., Ste. 211
West Hartford, CT 06107
Ph: (203)523-7518 Fax: (203)231-8808
Tracy E. McHughPublisher

Quarterly. Magazine for construction industry.

★4878★ *CONSTRUCTION*
HES, Inc.
26 Long Hill Rd.
PO Box 362
Guilford, CT 06437-0362
Ph: (203)453-3717 Fax: (203)453-4390
Jack C. Lewis

Semiweekly. Journal for the construction industry.

★4879★ *Construction News*
10835 Financial Centre Pkwy., Ste. 133
Little Rock, AR 72211-3555
Ph: (501)376-1931 Fax: (501)375-5831
Robert Alvey

Weekly. Construction industry magazine.

★4880★ *Construction Newsletter*
National Safety Council
1121 Spring Lake Dr.
Itasca, IL 60143-3201
Ph: (708)775-2282 Fax: (708)775-2285
Diane A. Ghazarian

Bimonthly. Focuses on industrial and occupational safety in the construction industry. Carries items on such topics as safe work practices and products; accident prevention; and successful industrial safety programs and policies.

★4881★ *Daily Construction Reporter*
7670 Opprtunity Rd.
San Diego, CA 92111-1112
Ph: (619)492-1402 Fax: (619)565-4182
Bernado Romanowsky

Daily. Construction newspaper covering jobs that are out for bid, bid results, building permits, and other information.

★4882★ *Floor Covering Installation Contractors Association—Newsletter*
Floor Covering Installation Contractors Association (FCICA)
PO Box 948
Dalton, GA 30722-0948
Ph: (706)226-5488 Fax: (706)226-1775

Monthly.

★4883★ *Floor Covering Weekly*
Hearst Business Communications, Inc.
645 Stewart Ave.
Garden City, NY 11530-4709
Ph: (212)541-4080 Fax: (212)541-4699
Janet Morgan Daly

Weekly. Business newspaper of the floor covering industry.

★4884★ *International Construction*
Maclean Hunter Publishing Co.
29 N. Wacker Drive
Chicago, IL 60606
Ph: (312)726-2802 Fax: (312)726-2574
Alan Peterson

Monthly. Trade magazine.

★4885★ *The Journal of Light Construction*
RR 2, Box 146
Richmond, VT 05477-9607
Ph: (802)434-4747 Fax: (802)434-4467
Steve Bliss

Monthly. Magazine (tabloid) for residential and light professionals involved in new and rehabilitative construction. Each issue covers a single aspect of construction.

★4886★ *Nation's Building News*
1201 15th St. NW
Washington, DC 20005-2800
Ph: (202)822-0525 Fax: (202)861-2131
Tim Ahern

Semiweekly. Trade magazine (tabloid) covering home building and all related industries.

★4887★ *Nation's Building News*
National Association of Home Builders of the U.S. (NAHB)
1201 15th St. NW
Washington, DC 20005
Ph: (202)822-0200 Fax: (202)822-0559

Semimonthly. Provides the latest information concerning the housing industry, including finance, legislation, new technologies, and membership news.

★4888★ *Professional Builder & Remodeler*
Cahners Publishing Co.
1350 E. Touhy Ave.
PO Box 5080
Des Plaines, IL 60018-5080
Ph: (708)635-8800 Fax: (708)635-9950
Ed Fitch

Monthly.

MEETINGS AND CONVENTIONS

★4889★ Installation Supplies and Ideas Expo
National Association of Floor Covering Distributors
401 N. Michigan Ave.
Chicago, IL 60611-4207
Ph: (312)644-6610 Fax: (312)245-1084

Annual.

Concrete Masons and Terrazzo Workers

Concrete masons place and finish concrete for such projects as highways, bridges, shopping malls, or large buildings such as factories, schools, and hospitals. They also color concrete surfaces, expose aggregate in walls and sidewalks, or fabricate concrete beams, columns, and panels. Most concrete masons work for concrete contractors or for general contractors; a small number are employed by firms that manufacture concrete products. **Terrazzo workers** create attractive walkways, floors, patios, and panels by exposing marble chips and other fine aggregates on the surface of finished concrete. They work for special trade contractors who install decorative floors and wall panels. The few concrete masons and terrazzo workers that are self-employed specialize in small jobs, such as driveways, sidewalks, and patios.

Salaries

Nonunion workers generally have lower wage rates than union workers. Apprentices usually start at 50 to 60 percent of the rate paid to experienced workers. Median hourly salaries for concrete masons and terrazzo workers are between $15 and $37.

Employment Outlook

Growth rate until the year 2005: More slowly than the average.

Concrete Masons and Terrazzo Workers

Career Guides

★4890★ ***Cement Mason***
Careers, Inc.
PO Box 135
Largo, FL 34649-0135
Ph: (813)584-7333

1991. Two-page occupational summary card describing duties, working conditions, personal qualifications, training, earnings and hours, employment outlook, places of employment, related careers and where to write for more information.

★4891★ "Cement Mason" in *Career Information Center* (pp. 43-45)
Simon and Schuster
200 Old Tappan Rd.
Old Tappan, NJ 07675
Fax: 800-445-6991 Fr: 800-223-2348

Richard Lidz and Dale Anderson, editorial directors. Fifth edition, 1993. For 600 occupations, describes job duties, entry-level requirements, education and training needed, advancement possibilities, employment outlook, earnings and benefits. The set is divided into 12 volumes. Each volume includes jobs related under a broad career field. Volume 13 is the index.

★4892★ "Cement Mason" in *Occu-Facts: Information on 580 Careers in Outline Form*
Careers, Inc.
PO Box 135
Largo, FL 34649-0135
Ph: (813)584-7333

Biennial, 1995-96 edition. Each one-page occupational profile describes duties, working conditions, physical surroundings and demands, aptitudes, temperament, educational requirements, employment outlook, earnings, and places of employment.

★4893★ ***Cement Masons***
Chronicle Guidance Publications, Inc.
66 Aurora St.
PO Box 1190
Moravia, NY 13118-1190
Ph: (315)497-0330 Fax: (315)497-3359
Fr: 800-622-7284

1993. This career brief describes the nature of the work, working conditions, hours and earnings, education and training, licensure, certification, unions, personal qualifications, social and psychological factors, employment outlook, entry methods, advancement, and related occupations.

★4894★ "Cement Masons" in *Career Discovery Encyclopedia* (Vol.1, pp. 156-157)
J.G. Ferguson Publishing Co.
200 W. Madison St., Ste. 300
Chicago, IL 60606
Ph: (312)580-5480 Fax: (312)580-4948

E. Russell Primm, editor-in-chief. 1993. Contains two-page articles on 504 occupations. Each article describes job duties, earnings, and educational and training requirements.

★4895★ "Cement Masons" in *Encyclopedia of Careers and Vocational Guidance* (Vol.2, pp. 267-270)
J.G. Ferguson Publishing Co.
200 W. Madison St., Ste. 300
Chicago, IL 60606
Ph: (312)580-5480 Fax: (312)580-4948

William E. Hopke, editor-in-chief. Ninth edition, 1993. Four-volume set that profiles 500 occupations and describes job trends in 74 industries. Includes career description, educational requirements, history of the job, methods of entry, advancement, employment outlook, earnings, working conditions, social and psychological factors, and sources of additional information.

★4896★ "Cement Masons" in *Opportunities in Building Construction Trades* (pp. 29-30)
National Textbook Co. (NTC)
VGM Career Books
4255 W. Touhy Ave.
Lincolnwood, IL 60646-1975
Ph: (708)679-5500 Fax: (708)679-2494
Fr: 800-323-4900

Michael Sumichrast. 1989. Gives an overview of the construction industry and describes the jobs of various craftworkers. Covers different kinds of builders: home, custom; and describes management skills needed and industry trends affecting opportunities.

★4897★ "Concrete Masons and Terrazzo Workers" in *Occupational Outlook Handbook*
U.S. Government Printing Office
Superintendent of Documents
Washington, DC 20402
Ph: (202)512-1800 Fax: (202)512-2250

Biennial; latest edition, 1994-95. Encyclopedia of careers describing more than 250 occupations and comprising about 85 percent of all jobs in the economy. Occupations that require lengthy education or training are given the most attention. For each occupation, the handbook describes job duties, working conditions, training, educational preparation, personal qualities, advancement possibilities, job outlook, earnings, and sources of additional information.

★4898★ ***Construction: Basic Principles***
RMI Media Productions, Inc.
2807 West 47th St.
Shawnee Mission, KS 66205
Ph: (913)262-3974 Fax: (913)362-6910
Fr: 800-745-5480

Videocassette. 1984. 20 mins. This series of five programs of varying lengths covers different aspects of career opportunities in the construction trades. Included are: concrete masonry, carpentry, electrical work, plumbing, and heating and air conditioning.

★4899★ ***Construction Cluster***
Center for Humanities, Inc.
Communications Park
Box 1000
Mount Kisco, NY 10549
Ph: (914)666-4100 Fax: (914)666-5319
Fr: 800-431-1242

Videocassette. 1984. 15 mins. Construction workers describe what it's like to work at their jobs, and show the special equipment they use in their field.

★4900★ **"Marble Setter, Tilesetters, and Terrazzo Workers" in *Opportunities in Building Construction Trades* (pp. 63-65)**
National Textbook Co. (NTC)
VGM Career Books
4255 W. Touhy Ave.
Lincolnwood, IL 60646-1975
Ph: (708)679-5500 Fax: (708)679-2494
Fr: 800-323-4900

Michael Sumichrast. 1989. Gives an overview of the construction industry and describes the jobs of various craftworkers. Covers different kinds of builders: home, custom; and describes management skills needed and industry trends affecting opportunities.

★4901★ ***Marble Setters, Tile Layers and Terrazzo Workers***
Chronicle Guidance Publications, Inc.
66 Aurora St.
PO Box 1190
Moravia, NY 13118-1190
Ph: (315)497-0330 Fax: (315)497-3359
Fr: 800-622-7284

1993. This career brief describes the nature of the work, working conditions, hours and earnings, education and training, licensure, certification, unions, personal qualifications, social and psychological factors, employment outlook, entry methods, advancement, and related occupations.

★4902★ **"Marble Setters, Tile Setters, and Terrazzo Workers" in *Encyclopedia of Careers and Vocational Guidance* (Vol.3, pp. 366-368)**
J.G. Ferguson Publishing Co.
200 W. Madison St., Ste. 300
Chicago, IL 60606
Ph: (312)580-5480 Fax: (312)580-4948

William E. Hopke, editor-in-chief. Ninth edition, 1993. Four-volume set that profiles 500 occupations and describes job trends in 74 industries. Includes career description, educational requirements, history of the job, methods of entry, advancement, employment outlook, earnings, working conditions, social and psychological factors, and sources of additional information.

★4903★ ***Marble, Tile Setters, Terrazzo, and Stone Workers***
Careers, Inc.
PO Box 135
Largo, FL 34649-0135
Ph: (813)584-7333

1993. Four-page brief offering the definition, history, duties, working conditions, personal qualifications, educational requirements, earnings, hours, employment outlook, advancement possibilities, and related occupations.

★4904★ **"Marble, Tile, Terrazzo, and Stone Workers" in *Occu-Facts: Information on 580 Careers in Outline Form***
Careers, Inc.
PO Box 135
Largo, FL 34649-0135
Ph: (813)584-7333

Biennial, 1995-96 edition. Each one-page occupational profile describes duties, working conditions, physical surroundings and demands, aptitudes, temperament, educational requirements, employment outlook, earnings, and places of employment.

★4905★ **"Marble, Tile, and Terrazzo Worker" in *Career Information Center* (Vol.4)**
Simon and Schuster
200 Old Tappan Rd.
Old Tappan, NJ 07675
Fax: 800-445-6991 Fr: 800-223-2348

Richard Lidz and Dale Anderson, editorial directors. Fifth edition, 1993. For 600 occupations, describes job duties, entry-level requirements, education and training needed, advancement possibilities, employment outlook, earnings and benefits. The set is divided into 12 volumes. Each volume includes jobs related under a broad career field. Volume 13 is the index.

★4906★ ***The Trowel Trades***
International Masonry Institute
823 15th St. NW, Ste. 1001
Washington, DC 20005
Ph: (202)783-3908

This six-panel brochure describes skills, advancement opportunities, and apprentice training.

★4907★ ***Vocational Visions***
Center for Humanities, Inc.
Communications Park
Box 1000
Mount Kisco, NY 10549
Ph: (914)666-4100 Fax: (914)666-5319
Fr: 800-431-1242

Videocassette. 1984. 30 mins. This series of programs explains key aspects of actual training and a day in the life of a worker in the specific field mentioned on the videocassette. Occupations include: transportation/mechanics, repair, construction, business/office occupations, health, agriculture, technical/manufacturing, communications, and personal service.

★4908★ ***Vocations U.S.A.***
Info-Disc Corporation
4 Professional Dr., Ste. 134
Gaithersburg, MD 20879
Ph: (301)948-2300 Fr: 800-648-6422

Videocassette. 1987. 60 mins. A disc collection outlining the requirements and methods of various career areas. Occupations include: transportation, mechanical/repair, health, agriculture, technical/manufacturing, and construction.

★4909★ ***You Can Become a Tile, Marble, Terrazzo and Dimensional Stone Installer***
United Brotherhood of Carpenters and Joiners of America
101 Constitution Ave., N.W.
Washington, DC 20001
Ph: (202)546-6206

This six-panel brochure describes apprenticeship training, hours, and working conditions.

Associations

★4910★ **Associated General Contractors of America (AGC)**
1957 E St. NW
Washington, DC 20006
Ph: (202)393-2040 Fax: (202)347-4004

Members: General construction contractors; subcontractors; industry suppliers; service firms. **Purpose:** Provides market services through its divisions. Conducts special conferences and seminars designed specifically for construction firms. Compiles statistics on job accidents reported by member firms. ors. Maintains 65 committees, including joint cooperative committees with other associations and liaison committees with federal agencies. **Publications:** *AGC Membership Directory and Buyers' Guide*, annual. • *AGC Mobile Directory.* • *Associated General Contractors of America—National Newsletter*, biweekly. • *Constructor*, monthly.

★4911★ **Concrete Sawing and Drilling Association**
6077 Roswell Rd., NE, Ste. 205
Atlanta, GA 30328
Ph: (404)257-1177

Develops standards for products and procedures related to concrete sawing and drilling.

★4912★ **International Union of Bricklayers and Allied Craftsmen (BAC)**
815 15th St. NW
Washington, DC 20005
Ph: (202)783-3788 Fax: (202)393-0219

Members: AFL-CIO. **Publications:** *Chalkline*, periodic.

★4913★ **National Terrazzo and Mosaic Association (NTMA)**
3166 Des Plaines Ave., Ste. 121
Des Plaines, IL 60018
Ph: (708)635-7744 Fax: (708)635-9127
Fr: 800-323-9736

Members: Contractors who install terrazzo and mosaic work; firms that produce or manufacture materials. **Purpose:** Provides information to building owners, architects, builders, and terrazzo contractors. Conducts research on installation methods. **Publications:** *Design Book.* • *Terrazzo and Mosiac Catalog.*

★4914★ Operative Plasterers and Cement Masons International Association of U.S. and Canada (OPCMIA)
1125 17th St. NW
Washington, DC 20036
Ph: (202)393-6569 Fax: (202)393-2514

Members: AFL-CIO. **Publications:** *Plasterer and Cement Mason*, monthly.

★4915★ Portland Cement Association (PCA)
5420 Old Orchard Rd.
Skokie, IL 60077
Ph: (708)966-6200 Fax: (708)966-8389

Members: Manufacturers and marketers of portland cement in the U.S. and Canada. **Purpose:** Seeks to improve and extend the uses of portland cement and concrete through market promotion, research and development, educational programs, and representation with governmental entities. Conducts research on concrete technology and durability; concrete pavement design; load-bearing capacities, field performance, and fire resistance of concrete; transportation, building, and structural uses of concrete. Operates Construction Technology Laboratories, which conducts research and technical services in construction materials, products, and applications. Sponsors a public affairs program in Washington, DC. **Publications:** *Includes technical, promotional publications..*
• *List of Member Companies*, periodic.

Standards/Certification Agencies

★4916★ Concrete Sawing and Drilling Association
6077 Roswell Rd., NE, Ste. 205
Atlanta, GA 30328
Ph: (404)257-1177

Develops standards for products and procedures related to concrete sawing and drilling.

★4917★ Interlocking Concrete Pavement Institute (ICPI)
1323 Shepard Dr., Ste. D
Sterling, VA 20164
Ph: (703)450-4998 Fax: (703)450-0482
Fr: 800-241-3652

Develops product and installation specifications for concrete pavers, contractor certifications programs, and curriculum for training installers and university students.

★4918★ National Terrazzo and Mosaic Association (NTMA)
3166 Des Plaines Ave., Ste. 121
Des Plaines, IL 60018
Ph: (708)635-7744 Fax: (708)635-9127
Fr: 800-323-9736

Provides information to building owners, architects, builders, and terrazzo contractors. Conducts research on installation methods.

Test Guides

★4919★ *Career Examination Series: Cement Mason*
National Learning Corp.
212 Michael Dr.
Syosset, NY 11791
Ph: (516)921-8888 Fax: (516)921-8743
Fr: 800-645-6337

Jack Rudman. All examination guides in this series contain questions with answers.

★4920★ *Career Examination Series: Mason*
National Learning Corp.
212 Michael Dr.
Syosset, NY 11791
Ph: (516)921-8888 Fax: (516)921-8743
Fr: 800-645-6337

Jack Rudman. All examination guides in this series contain questions with answers.

★4921★ *Career Examination Series: Mason's Helper*
National Learning Corp.
212 Michael Dr.
Syosset, NY 11791
Ph: (516)921-8888 Fax: (516)921-8743
Fr: 800-645-6337

Jack Rudman. All examination guides in this series contain questions with answers.

★4922★ *Maintenance Mechanic*
Prentice Hall Press
Simon & Schuster Inc.
200 Old Tappan Rd.
Old Tappan, NJ 07675
Ph: 800-223-2348

Hy Hammer. First edition, 1988. Provides information for applicants interested in the following entry-level civil service positions: mason's helper, elevator mechanic's helper, mechanical maintainer's helper, among others.

★4923★ *Maintenance Worker/ Mechanical Maintainer*
Prentice Hall Press
Simon & Schuster Inc.
200 Old Tappan Rd.
Old Tappan, NJ 07675
Ph: 800-223-2348

Hy Hammer. Fourth edition, 1984. Provides information for applicants interested in the following civil service positions: carpenter, mason, plumber, electrician, painter, machinist. Includes eight sample tests.

★4924★ *Masonry*
National Learning Corp.
212 Michael Dr.
Syosset, NY 11791
Ph: (516)921-8888 Fax: (516)921-8743
Fr: 800-645-6337

Jack Rudman. Part of Occupational Competency Examination Series (OCE).

Educational Directories and Programs

★4925★ *AGC Membership Directory and Buyers' Guide*
Associated General Contractors of America (AGC)
1957 E St. NW
Washington, DC 20006
Ph: (202)393-2040 Fax: (202)347-4004

Annual.

★4926★ *AGC Mobile Directory*
Associated General Contractors of America (AGC)
1957 E St. NW
Washington, DC 20006
Ph: (202)393-2040 Fax: (202)347-4004

★4927★ *International Directory of Building Research, Information and Development Organizations*
29 W. 35th St.
New York, NY 10001
Ph: (212)244-3336

Over 600 universities, institutions, government agencies, and other construction-related research institutions. Entries include: Institution name, address, phone, telex, name and title of contact, number of staff, source of finance, area of interest, publications.

★4928★ *NTMA Directory*
National Terrazzo and Mosaic Association (NTMA)
3166 Des Plaines Ave., Ste. 121
Des Plaines, IL 60018
Ph: (708)635-7744 Fax: (708)635-9127
Fr: 800-323-9736

Annual.

Basic Reference Guides and Handbooks

★4929★ *Intelligent Buildings Institute—Directory of Products and Services*
Intelligent Buildings Institute (IBI)
2101 L St., NW, Ste. 300
Washington, DC 20037
Ph: (202)457-1988 Fax: (202)457-8468

S. Hunt, Associate Executive Director, editor. Annual, September. Member consultants, associations, research organizations, and other suppliers of products and services to the construction and building industry. Entries include: Company name, address, phone. Arrangement: Alphabetical. Indexes: Product/ service.

★4930★ *Mason Contractors' Equipment & Supplies Directory*
American Business Directories, Inc.
5711 S. 86th Circle
Omaha, NE 68127
Ph: (402)593-4600 Fax: (402)331-1505

Updated continuously; printed on request. Entries include: Name, address, phone, size of advertisement, name of owner or manager, number of employees, year first in "Yellow Pages." Compiled from telephone company "Yellow Pages," nationwide. Arrangement: Geographical.

★4931★ *NTMA Design Book*
National Terrazzo and Mosaic Association (NTMA)
3166 Des Plaines Ave., Ste. 121
Des Plaines, IL 60018
Ph: (708)635-7744 Fax: (708)635-9127
Fr: 800-323-9736

PERIODICALS

★4932★ *ABC Today*
Associated Builders and Contractors, Inc. (ABC)
N. 17th St.
Rosslyn, VA 22209
Ph: (703)637-8800 Fax: (703)812-8203
Pamela E. Hunter

Semimonthly. Designed to keep readers alerted to important changes within ABC and the construction industry. Reports on legislative issues, construction trends, conferences and meetings, and ABC services. Recurring features include news of members and columns titled Industry Briefs, Safety Notebook, Computer Corner, Bottom Line, and Chapter News.

★4933★ *ABC Today*
Associated Builders and Contractors, Inc. (ABC)
1300 N. 17th St., 8th Floor
Arlington, VA 22209-3803
Ph: (703)812-2000 Fax: (703)812-8203
Pamela E. Hunter

Semiweekly. Magazine for open shop contractors and subcontractors. Includes articles on national and regional construction news, construction management, project case histories, new products, building design, and legislative and regulatory updates.

★4934★ *Aberdeen's Magazine of Masonry Construction*
The Aberdeen Group
426 S. Westgate
Addison, IL 60101-9929
Ph: (708)543-0870 Fax: (708)543-3112
Kenneth A. Hooker

Monthly. Trade magazine.

★4935★ *ACI Structural Journal*
American Concrete Institute
PO Box 19150
Detroit, MI 48219-0150
Ph: (313)532-2600 Fax: (313)538-0655
Helayne Beavers

Bimonthly. Journal containing information on structural design and analysis of concrete elements and structures; includes design and analysis theory, and related ACI standards and committee reports.

★4936★ *American Architectural Manufacturers Association—Quarterly Review*
American Architectural Manufacturers Association
1540 E. Dundee Rd., Ste. 310
Palatine, IL 60067-8321
Ph: (708)202-1350 Fax: (708)202-1480
Tony Coorlim

Annual. Contains industry news on architectural products. Covers prime and combination storm windows, sliding glass and combination storm doors, window and curtainwalls, store fronts and entrances, siding, soffits, fascia, gutters, downspouts, skylights, space enclosures, and mobile home components. Recurring features include news of research, notices of publications available, and announcements by the Association.

★4937★ *American Institute of Constructors—Newsletter*
American Institute of Constructors
9887 Gandy Blvd. N., Ste. 104
St. Petersburg, FL 33702
Ph: (813)578-1962 Fax: (813)578-9982
Cheryl P. Harris

Bimonthly. Concerned with construction practice, design, administration, and teaching. Carries news of members, listings of job opportunities, local chapter reports, notices of new publications, and conferences on construction topics.

★4938★ *Anti-Corrosion Times*
Concrete Reinforcing Steel Institute (CRSI)
933 N. Plum Grove Rd.
Schaumburg, IL 60173-4758
Ph: (708)517-1200 Fax: (708)517-1206
Theodore L. Neff

Biennial. Focuses on developments in the reinforced concrete construction industry. Reports on advances and applications of the fusion-bonded coating system for corrosion prevention. Recurring features include profiles of successful construction projects, news of the Institute and its members, and a calendar of events.

★4939★ *Associated General Contractors of America—National Newsletter*
Associated General Contractors of America (AGC)
1957 E St. NW
Washington, DC 20006
Ph: (202)393-2040 Fax: (202)347-4004

Biweekly.

★4940★ *Blue Reports, Inc.*
Construction News Service
7325 Steel Mill Dr.
Springfield, VA 22050
Ph: (703)644-5884 Fax: (703)644-1929
Calvin S. Oren

Daily. Reports on public and private construction projects in the Washington, DC, Virginia, and Maryland areas. Provides owner's and architect's names, plan status, date bids due, prospective bidders, low bids received, and specification details.

★4941★ *Building Concerns*
National Association of Minority Contractors (NAMC)
1333 F St. NW, Ste. 500
Washington, DC 20004
Ph: (202)347-8259 Fax: (202)628-1876
Agreta Hester

Quarterly. Concentrates on national and regional news regarding minority construction contractors. Contains articles on issues generally affecting the industry—especially issues affecting minorities—including topics such as legislative and regulatory activity and reports on major corporation developments. Recurring features include reports of meetings, news of educational opportunities, a calendar of events, and news of NAMC chapters, affiliates, and members.

★4942★ *Building Industry Technology: An Abstract Newsletter*
National Technical Information Service (NTIS)
5285 Port Royal Rd.
Springfield, VA 22161
Ph: (703)487-4630

Biweekly. Consists of abstracts of reports on architectural and environmental design, building standards, construction materials and equipment, and structural analyses. Recurring features include a form for ordering reports from NTIS.

★4943★ *Capital Comments*
National Lumber & Building Material Dealers Association
40 Ivy St. SE
Washington, DC 20003
Ph: (202)547-2230 Fax: (202)547-7640
Matt Geitner

Semimonthly. Reports on news of legislation pertaining to lumber, other building materials, and housing. Discusses such issues as lumber subsidies, interest rates on homes, health and safety, and jobs.

★4944★ *Chalkline*
International Union of Bricklayers and Allied Craftsmen (BAC)
815 15th St. NW
Washington, DC 20005
Ph: (202)783-3788 Fax: (202)393-0219

Periodic.

★4945★ *Concrete Abstracts*
American Concrete Institute
PO Box 19150
Detroit, MI 48219-0150
Ph: (313)532-2600 Fax: (313)538-0655
Helayne H. Beavers

Bimonthly. Magazine summarizing and indexing U.S. and international publications that report developments in concrete and concrete technology.

★4946★ *Concrete Construction Magazine*
The Aberdeen Group
426 S. Westgate
Addison, IL 60101-9929
Ph: (708)543-0870 Fax: (708)543-3112
Ward R. Malisch

Monthly. Trade magazine for contractors, subcontractors, and others involved in concrete construction.

★4947★ *Concrete International*
American Concrete Institute
PO Box 19150
Detroit, MI 48219
Ph: (313)532-2600 Fax: (313)538-0655
Roger Wood

Monthly. Trade magazine covering engineering, construction, structural design, and the technology of concrete.

★4948★ *Concrete Masonry News*
National Concrete Masonry Association
2302 Horse Pen Rd.
Herndon, VA 22071
Ph: (703)713-1900 Fax: (703)713-1910
Scott Ramminger

Monthly. Focuses on the manufacturing and marketing of concrete masonry products and the management of production plants. Covers fire safety, energy efficiency, pertinent legislative and regulatory developments, production and marketing developments, and new products and services of interest to the industry. Also reports the news and activities of the Association. Recurring features include editorials, news of research, news of members, letters to the editor, and a calendar of events.

★4949★ *Concrete Products*
Maclean Hunter Publishing Co.
29 N. Wacker Drive
Chicago, IL 60606
Ph: (312)726-2802 Fax: (312)726-2574
Don Marsh

Monthly. Magazine on concrete products and ready-mixed concrete.

★4950★ *ConnStruction*
McHugh Design, Advertising & Publishing
62 Lasalle Rd., Ste. 211
West Hartford, CT 06107
Ph: (203)523-7518 Fax: (203)231-8808
Tracy E. McHugh

Quarterly. Magazine for construction industry.

★4951★ *CONSTRUCTION*
HES, Inc.
26 Long Hill Rd.
PO Box 362
Guilford, CT 06437-0362
Ph: (203)453-3717 Fax: (203)453-4390
Jack C. Lewis

Semiweekly. Journal for the construction industry.

★4952★ *Construction News*
10835 Financial Centre Pkwy., Ste. 133
Little Rock, AR 72211-3555
Ph: (501)376-1931 Fax: (501)375-5831
Robert Alvey

Weekly. Construction industry magazine.

★4953★ *Construction Newsletter*
National Safety Council
1121 Spring Lake Dr.
Itasca, IL 60143-3201
Ph: (708)775-2282 Fax: (708)775-2285
Diane A. Ghazarian

Bimonthly. Focuses on industrial and occupational safety in the construction industry. Carries items on such topics as safe work practices and products; accident prevention; and successful industrial safety programs and policies.

★4954★ *Daily Construction Reporter*
7670 Opprtunity Rd.
San Diego, CA 92111-1112
Ph: (619)492-1402 Fax: (619)565-4182
Bernado Romanowsky

Daily. Construction newspaper covering jobs that are out for bid, bid results, building permits, and other information.

★4955★ *International Construction*
Maclean Hunter Publishing Co.
29 N. Wacker Drive
Chicago, IL 60606
Ph: (312)726-2802 Fax: (312)726-2574
Alan Peterson

Monthly. Trade magazine.

★4956★ *Journal of the International Union of Bricklayers & Allied Craftsmen*
815 15th St. NW
Washington, DC 20005
Ph: (202)783-3788 Fax: (202)393-0219
Paul Ruffins

Monthly. Tabloid for trade union members.

★4957★ *The Journal of Light Construction*
RR 2, Box 146
Richmond, VT 05477-9607
Ph: (802)434-4747 Fax: (802)434-4467
Steve Bliss

Monthly. Magazine (tabloid) for residential and light professionals involved in new and rehabilitative construction. Each issue covers a single aspect of construction.

★4958★ *Masonry*
Mason Contractors Association of America
1550 Spring Rd., Ste. 320
Oak Brook, IL 60521-1363
Ph: (708)782-6767 Fax: (708)782-6786
Gene Adams

Bimonthly. Trade magazine on construction, architecture, and engineering.

★4959★ *Nation's Building News*
1201 15th St. NW
Washington, DC 20005-2800
Ph: (202)822-0525 Fax: (202)861-2131
Tim Ahern

Semiweekly. Trade magazine (tabloid) covering home building and all related industries.

★4960★ *Nation's Building News*
National Association of Home Builders of the U.S. (NAHB)
1201 15th St. NW
Washington, DC 20005
Ph: (202)822-0200 Fax: (202)822-0559

Semimonthly. Provides the latest information concerning the housing industry, including finance, legislation, new technologies, and membership news.

★4961★ *PCI Journal*
Precast/Prestressed Concrete Institute
175 W. Jackson Blvd., Ste. 1859
Chicago, IL 60604
Ph: (312)786-0300 Fax: (312)786-0353
George D. Nasser

Bimonthly. Concrete engineering journal.

★4962★ *Professional Builder & Remodeler*
Cahners Publishing Co.
1350 E. Touhy Ave.
PO Box 5080
Des Plaines, IL 60018-5080
Ph: (708)635-8800 Fax: (708)635-9950
Ed Fitch

Monthly.

MEETINGS AND CONVENTIONS

★4963★ International Concrete and Aggregates Show
National Aggregates Association/National Ready Mixed Concrete Association
900 Spring St.
Silver Spring, MD 20910
Ph: (301)587-1400 Fax: (301)587-4260
Fr: 800-233-0823

Biennial. **Dates and Locations:** 1996 Jan 28-01; Atlanta, GA.

★4964★ World of Concrete USA Exposition
The Aberdeen Group
426 S. Westgate
Addison, IL 60101
Ph: (708)543-0870 Fax: (708)543-3112
Fr: 800-837-0870

Annual. Always held during January or February. **Dates and Locations:** 1996 Jan 18-21; Las Vegas, NV. • 1999 Jan 26-29; Las Vegas, NV.

Drywall Workers and Lathers

Drywall installers, also called applicators, and drywall finishers, or tapers, work with drywall, a substitute for wet plaster used for walls and ceilings in most buildings. **Lathers** apply metal or gypsum lath to walls, ceilings, or ornamental frameworks to form the support base for plaster coatings. Most drywall workers and lathers work for contractors who specialize in drywall or lathing installation; others work for contractors who do many kinds of construction.

Salaries

Median weekly earnings for drywall workers and lathers are about $420/week. Trainees start at about half the rate paid to experienced workers.

Lowest 10 percent	$235/week or less
Middle 50 percent	$305-$645/week
Highest 10 percent	$870/week or more

Employment Outlook

Growth rate until the year 2005: Faster than the average.

Drywall Workers and Lathers

Career Guides

★4965★ *Automatic Lathe Operator*
Careers, Inc.
PO Box 135
Largo, FL 34649-0135
Ph: (813)584-7333

1993. Two-page occupational summary card describing duties, working conditions, personal qualifications, training, earnings and hours, employment outlook, places of employment, related careers, and where to write for more information.

★4966★ *Big Questions?*
National Joint Painting, Decorating and Drywall
Apprenticeship and Training Committee
1750 New York Ave., N.W., Lower Level
Washington, DC 20006
Ph: (202)783-7770

This four-page brochure describes requirements, the work, employment opportunities, working conditions, and earnings.

★4967★ "Drywall Applicator/Finisher" in *Jobs Rated Almanac*
World Almanac
1 International Blvd., Ste. 444
Mahwah, NJ 07495
Ph: (201)529-6900 Fax: (201)529-6901

Les Krantz. Second edition, 1992. Ranks 250 jobs by environment, salary, outlooks, physical demands, stress, security, travel opportunities, and extra perks. Includes jobs the editor feels are the most common, most interesting, and the most rapidly growing.

★4968★ *Drywall Installer*
Vocational Biographies, Inc.
PO Box 31
Sauk Centre, MN 56378-0031
Ph: (612)352-6516 Fax: (612)352-5546
Fr: 800-255-0752

1993. Four-page pamphlet containing a personal narrative about a worker's job, work likes and dislikes, career path from high school to the present. Education and training, the rewards and frustrations, and the effects of the job on the rest of the worker's life. The data file portion of this pamphlet gives a concise occupational summary, including work descriptions, working conditions, places of employment, personal characteristics, education and training, job outlook, and salary range.

★4969★ "Drywall Installer and Finisher" in *Career Information Center* (Vol.4)
Simon and Schuster
200 Old Tappan Rd.
Old Tappan, NJ 07675
Fax: 800-445-6991 Fr: 800-223-2348

Richard Lidz and Dale Anderson, editorial directors. Fifth edition, 1993. For 600 occupations, describes job duties, entry-level requirements, education and training needed, advancement possibilities, employment outlook, earnings and benefits. The set is divided into 12 volumes. Each volume includes jobs related under a broad career field. Volume 13 is the index.

★4970★ *Drywall Installers and Finishers*
Chronicle Guidance Publications, Inc.
66 Aurora St.
PO Box 1190
Moravia, NY 13118-1190
Ph: (315)497-0330 Fax: (315)497-3359
Fr: 800-622-7284

1987. This career brief describes the nature of the work, working conditions, hours and earnings, education and training, licensure, certification, unions, personal qualifications, social and psychological factors, employment outlook, entry methods, advancement, and related occupations.

★4971★ "Drywall Installers and Finishers" in *Career Discovery Encyclopedia* (Vol.2, pp. 128-129)
J.G. Ferguson Publishing Co.
200 W. Madison St., Ste. 300
Chicago, IL 60606
Ph: (312)580-5480 Fax: (312)580-4948

E. Russell Primm, editor-in-chief. 1993. Contains two-page articles on 504 occupations. Each article describes job duties, earnings, and educational and training requirements.

★4972★ "Drywall Installers and Finishers" in *Encyclopedia of Careers and Vocational Guidance* (Vol.2, pp. 518-521)
J.G. Ferguson Publishing Co.
200 W. Madison St., Ste. 300
Chicago, IL 60606
Ph: (312)580-5480 Fax: (312)580-4948

William E. Hopke, editor-in-chief. Ninth edition, 1993. Four-volume set that profiles 500 occupations and describes job trends in 74 industries. Includes career description, educational requirements, history of the job, methods of entry, advancement, employment outlook, earnings, working conditions, social and psychological factors, and sources of additional information.

★4973★ "Drywall Rocker and Taper" in *Hard Hatted Women: Stories of Struggle and Success in the Trades* (pp. 63-70)
Seal Press
3131 Western Ave., Ste. 410
Seattle, WA 98121
Ph: (206)283-7844 Fax: (206)285-9410

Molly Martin, editor. 1988. Twenty-six women recount their experiences working in blue collar occupations. They describe how they got in, the work they do, their relationships in predominantly male occupations, and their training.

★4974★ "Drywall Workers and Lathers" in *Occupational Outlook Handbook*
U.S. Government Printing Office
Superintendent of Documents
Washington, DC 20402
Ph: (202)512-1800 Fax: (202)512-2250

Biennial; latest edition, 1994-95. Encyclopedia of careers describing more than 250 occupations and comprising about 85 percent of all jobs in the economy. Occupations that require lengthy education or training are given the most attention. For each occupation, the handbook describes job duties, working conditions, training, educational preparation, personal qualities, advancement possibilities, job outlook, earnings, and sources of additional information.

★4975★ *Lather*
Careers, Inc.
PO Box 135
Largo, FL 34649-0135
Ph: (813)584-7333

1993. Two-page occupational summary card describing duties, working conditions, personal qualifications, training, earnings and hours, employment outlook, places of employment, related careers and where to write for more information.

★4976★ "Lather" in *Career Information Center* (Vol.4)
Simon and Schuster
200 Old Tappan Rd.
Old Tappan, NJ 07675
Fax: 800-445-6991 Fr: 800-223-2348

Richard Lidz and Dale Anderson, editorial directors. Fifth edition, 1993. For 600 occupations, describes job duties, entry-level requirements, education and training needed, advancement possibilities, employment outlook, earnings and benefits. The set is divided into 12 volumes. Each volume includes jobs related under a broad career field. Volume 13 is the index.

★4977★ "Lather" in *Occu-Facts: Information on 580 Careers in Outline Form*
Careers, Inc.
PO Box 135
Largo, FL 34649-0135
Ph: (813)584-7333

Biennial, 1995-96 edition. Each one-page occupational profile describes duties, working conditions, physical surroundings and demands, aptitudes, temperament, educational requirements, employment outlook, earnings, and places of employment.

★4978★ *Lathers*
Chronicle Guidance Publications, Inc.
66 Aurora St.
PO Box 1190
Moravia, NY 13118-1190
Ph: (315)497-0330 Fax: (315)497-3359
Fr: 800-622-7284

1994. This career brief describes the nature of the work, working conditions, hours and earnings, education and training, licensure, certification, unions, personal qualifications, social and psychological factors, employment outlook, entry methods, advancement, and related occupations.

★4979★ "Lathers" in *Career Discovery Encyclopedia* (Vol.3, pp. 164-165)
J.G. Ferguson Publishing Co.
200 W. Madison St., Ste. 300
Chicago, IL 60606
Ph: (312)580-5480 Fax: (312)580-4948

Russell E. Primm, editor-in chief. 1993. This six volume set contains two-page articles for 504 occupations. Each article describes job duties, earnings, and educational and training requirements. The whole set is arranged alphabetically by job title. Designed for junior high and older students.

★4980★ "Lathers" in *Encyclopedia of Careers and Vocational Guidance* (Vol.3, pp. 277-280)
J.G. Ferguson Publishing Co.
200 W. Madison St., Ste. 300
Chicago, IL 60606
Ph: (312)580-5480 Fax: (312)580-4948

William E. Hopke, editor-in-chief. Ninth edition, 1993. Four-volume set that profiles 500 occupations and describes job trends in 74 industries. Includes career description, educational requirements, history of the job, methods of entry, advancement, employment outlook, earnings, working conditions, social and psychological factors, and sources of additional information.

★4981★ "Lathers" in *Opportunities in Building Construction Trades* (pp. 59-61)
National Textbook Co. (NTC)
VGM Career Books
4255 W. Touhy Ave.
Lincolnwood, IL 60646-1975
Ph: (708)679-5500 Fax: (708)679-2494
Fr: 800-323-4900

Michael Sumichrast. 1989. Gives an overview of the construction industry and describes the jobs of various craftworkers. Covers different kinds of builders: home, custom; and describes management skills needed and industry trends affecting opportunities.

★4982★ *Video Career Library - Construction*
Careers, Inc.
PO Box 135
Largo, FL 34649-0135
Ph: (813)584-7333

Videocassette. 1990. 36 mins. Part of the Video Career Library covering 165 occupations. Shows actual workers on the job. Includes millwrights, brickmasons, carpenters, drywall installers, electricians, painters, plumbers and pipefitters, carpenter and soft tile installers, insulation workers, paving equipment operators, and structural metal workers.

ASSOCIATIONS

★4983★ Associated Builders and Contractors (ABC)
1300 N. 17th St.
Rossyln, VA 22209
Ph: (703)812-2000

Members: Construction contractors, subcontractors, suppliers, and associates. **Purpose:** Aim is to foster and perpetuate the principles of rewarding construction workers and management on the basis of merit. Sponsors management education programs and craft training; also sponsors apprenticeship and skill training programs. Disseminates technological and labor relations information. Maintains placement service. Compiles statistics. **Publications:** *ABC Today*, semimonthly. • *National Membership Directory and Users Guide*, annual.

★4984★ International Brotherhood of Painters and Allied Trades (IBPAT)
United Unions Bldg.
1750 New York Ave. NW
Washington, DC 20006
Ph: (202)637-0720 Fax: (202)637-0771

Members: AFL-CIO. **Publications:** *Painters and Allied Trades Journal*, monthly.

★4985★ International Joint Painting, Decorating and Drywall Apprenticeship and Manpower Training Fund
1750 New York Ave. NW, 8th Fl.
Washington, DC 20006
Ph: (202)783-7770 Fax: (202)628-4897

Members: Representatives of labor and management. Labor is represented by the International Brotherhood of Painters and Allied Trades Management by Painting and Decorating Contractors of America and the Association of Wall and Ceiling Industries - International. Seeks to increase apprenticeship and training activities so that prospective apprentices can obtain the training necessary to equip themselves and to assume a high level of skill and responsibility. Develops and supplies materials necessary for training tradespersons and journeypersons with emphasis on changing techniques, materials, and tools of the trade; maintains library. Qualifications, selection, instruction, and terms of apprenticeship are suggested for use as the national standards for painting, decorating, and drywall trades nationally. Also supplies instructional materials for advanced journeyperson programs. Holds workshops and seminars for instructors and coordinators; sponsors international Apprenticeship Panel contests.

★4986★ National Association of Home Builders of the U.S. (NAHB)
1201 15th St. NW
Washington, DC 20005
Ph: (202)822-0200 Fax: (202)822-0559

Members: Single and multifamily home builders, commercial builders, and others associated with the building industry. **Purpose:** Lobbies on behalf of the housing industry and conducts public affairs activities to increase public understanding of housing and the economy. Collects and disseminates data on current developments in home building and home builders' plans through its Economics Department and nationwide Metropolitan Housing Forecast. Maintains NAHB Research Center, which functions as the research arm of the home building industry. Sponsors seminars and workshops on construction, mortgage credit, labor relations, cost reduction, land use, remodeling, and business management. Compiles statistics; offers charitable program, spokesman training, and placement service; maintains speakers' bureau, and hall of fame. Subsidiaries include Home Builders Institute and National Council of the Housing Industry. Maintains over 50 committees in many areas of construction; operates National Commercial Builders Council, National Council of the Multifamily Housing Industry, National Remodelers Council and National Sales and Marketing Council. **Publications:** *Builder Magazine*, monthly. • *Forecast of Housing Activity*, monthly. • *Housing Economics*, monthly. • *Housing Market Statistics*, monthly. • *Nation's Building News*, semi-monthly. • *Reference Guide to Homebuilding Articles*, quarterly.

★4987★ United Brotherhood of Carpenters and Joiners of America (UBC)
101 Constitution Ave. NW
Washington, DC 20001
Ph: (202)546-6206

Members: AFL-CIO. **Publications:** *Carpenter*, bimonthly.

Basic Reference Guides and Handbooks

★4988★ *IBPAT Directory*
International Brotherhood of Painters and Allied Trades (IBPAT)
United Unions Bldg.
1750 New York Ave., NW
Washington, DC 20006
Ph: (202)637-0720 Fax: (202)637-0771

Annual.

Periodicals

★4989★ *ABC Today*
Associated Builders and Contractors, Inc. (ABC)
N. 17th St.
Rosslyn, VA 22209
Ph: (703)637-8800 Fax: (703)812-8203
Pamela E. Hunter

Semimonthly. Designed to keep readers alerted to important changes within ABC and the construction industry. Reports on legislative issues, construction trends, conferences and meetings, and ABC services. Recurring features include news of members and columns titled Industry Briefs, Safety Notebook, Computer Corner, Bottom Line, and Chapter News.

★4990★ *ABC Today*
Associated Builders and Contractors, Inc. (ABC)
1300 N. 17th St., 8th Floor
Arlington, VA 22209-3803
Ph: (703)812-2000 Fax: (703)812-8203
Pamela E. Hunter

Semiweekly. Magazine for open shop contractors and subcontractors. Includes articles on national and regional construction news, construction management, project case histories, new products, building design, and legislative and regulatory updates.

★4991★ *ABC Today*
Associated Builders and Contractors (ABC)
1300 N. 17th St.
Rosslyn, VA 22209
Ph: (703)812-2000

Semimonthly. News magazine for merit shop contractors.

★4992★ *American Architectural Manufacturers Association—Quarterly Review*
American Architectural Manufacturers Association
1540 E. Dundee Rd., Ste. 310
Palatine, IL 60067-8321
Ph: (708)202-1350 Fax: (708)202-1480
Tony Coorlim

Annual. Contains industry news on architectural products. Covers prime and combination storm windows, sliding glass and combination storm doors, window and curtainwalls, store fronts and entrances, siding, soffits, fascia, gutters, downspouts, skylights, space enclosures, and mobile home components. Recurring features include news of research, notices of publications available, and announcements by the Association.

★4993★ *American Institute of Constructors—Newsletter*
American Institute of Constructors
9887 Gandy Blvd. N., Ste. 104
St. Petersburg, FL 33702
Ph: (813)578-1962 Fax: (813)578-9982
Cheryl P. Harris

Bimonthly. Concerned with construction practice, design, administration, and teaching. Carries news of members, listings of job opportunities, local chapter reports, notices of new publications, and conferences on construction topics.

★4994★ *Blue Reports, Inc.*
Construction News Service
7325 Steel Mill Dr.
Springfield, VA 22050
Ph: (703)644-5884 Fax: (703)644-1929
Calvin S. Oren

Daily. Reports on public and private construction projects in the Washington, DC, Virginia, and Maryland areas. Provides owner's and architect's names, plan status, date bids due, prospective bidders, low bids received, and specification details.

★4995★ *Builder*
Hanley-Wood, Inc.
1 Thomas Circle, Ste. 600
Washington, DC 20005
Ph: (202)452-0800
Mitchell Rouda

Monthly. Magazine covering housing, commercial, and industrial building.

★4996★ *Builder Architect*
Sunshine Media, Inc.
PO Box 37707
Phoenix, AZ 85069-7707
Ph: (602)433-7393 Fax: (602)433-2963
Marie Vere

Monthly. Home builders magazine.

★4997★ *Builder/Dealer*
Peterson Bros. Inc., Publishing
14 W. South St.
Corry, PA 16407-1894
Ph: (814)664-8624 Fax: (814)664-8506
Charles P. Mancino

Monthly. Trade magazine.

★4998★ *Builder Insider*
Divibest, Inc.
PO Box 191125
Dallas, TX 75219
Ph: (214)871-2913
Michael J. Anderson

Monthly. Magazine (tabloid) for builders, architects, and remodelers.

★4999★ *Builder Notes*
Brick Institute of America (BIA)
11490 Commerce Park Dr.
Reston, VA 22091
Ph: (703)620-0010 Fax: (703)620-3928

Bimonthly.

★5000★ *Building Business & Apartment Management*
Builders Association of Southeastern Michigan
30375 Northwestern Hwy.
Farmington Hills, MI 48334
Ph: (810)737-4477 Fax: (810)737-5741
Susan Adler

Monthly. Construction and apartment industry magazine.

★5001★ *Building Concerns*
National Association of Minority Contractors (NAMC)
1333 F St. NW, Ste. 500
Washington, DC 20004
Ph: (202)347-8259 Fax: (202)628-1876
Agreta Hester

Quarterly. Concentrates on national and regional news regarding minority construction contractors. Contains articles on issues generally affecting the industry—especially issues affecting minorities—including topics such as legislative and regulatory activity and reports on major corporation developments. Recurring features include reports of meetings, news of educational opportunities, a calendar of events, and news of NAMC chapters, affiliates, and members.

★5002★ *Building Design & Construction*
Cahners Publishing Co.
1350 E. Touhy Ave.
PO Box 5080
Des Plaines, IL 60017-5080
Ph: (708)635-8800 Fax: (708)390-2618
Jack Hollfelderl

Monthly. Magazine on business and technology for commercial, institutional, and industrial buildings.

★5003★ *Building Industry*
Trade Publishing Co.
287 Mokauea St.
Honolulu, HI 96819
Ph: (808)848-0711 Fax: (808)841-3053
Jay McWilliams

Monthly. Construction and design magazine.

★5004★ *Building Industry Technology: An Abstract Newsletter*
National Technical Information Service (NTIS)
5285 Port Royal Rd.
Springfield, VA 22161
Ph: (703)487-4630

Biweekly. Consists of abstracts of reports on architectural and environmental design, building standards, construction materials and equipment, and structural analyses. Recurring features include a form for ordering reports from NTIS.

★5005★ *Buildings*
Stamats Communications, Inc.
427 6th Ave. SE
PO Box 1888
Cedar Rapids, IA 52406
Ph: (319)364-6167 Fax: (319)364-4278
Linda Monroe

Monthly. Publication featuring management techniques, development, and ownership of facilities.

★5006★ *Capital Comments*
National Lumber & Building Material Dealers Association
40 Ivy St. SE
Washington, DC 20003
Ph: (202)547-2230 Fax: (202)547-7640
Matt Geitner

Semimonthly. Reports on news of legislation pertaining to lumber, other building materials, and housing. Discusses such issues as lumber subsidies, interest rates on homes, health and safety, and jobs.

★5007★ *ConnStruction*
McHugh Design, Advertising & Publishing
62 Lasalle Rd., Ste. 211
West Hartford, CT 06107
Ph: (203)523-7518 Fax: (203)231-8808
Tracy E. McHugh

Quarterly. Magazine for construction industry.

★5008★ *CONSTRUCTION*
HES, Inc.
26 Long Hill Rd.
PO Box 362
Guilford, CT 06437-0362
Ph: (203)453-3717 Fax: (203)453-4390
Jack C. Lewis

Semiweekly. Journal for the construction industry.

★5009★ *Construction News*
10835 Financial Centre Pkwy., Ste. 133
Little Rock, AR 72211-3555
Ph: (501)376-1931 Fax: (501)375-5831
Robert Alvey

Weekly. Construction industry magazine.

★5010★ *Construction Newsletter*
National Safety Council
1121 Spring Lake Dr.
Itasca, IL 60143-3201
Ph: (708)775-2282 Fax: (708)775-2285
Diane A. Ghazarian

Bimonthly. Focuses on industrial and occupational safety in the construction industry. Carries items on such topics as safe work practices and products; accident prevention; and successful industrial safety programs and policies.

★5011★ *Daily Construction Reporter*
7670 Opprtunity Rd.
San Diego, CA 92111-1112
Ph: (619)492-1402 Fax: (619)565-4182
Bernado Romanowsky

Daily. Construction newspaper covering jobs that are out for bid, bid results, building permits, and other information.

★5012★ *Fine Homebuilding*
The Taunton Press, Inc.
63 S. Main St.
PO Box 5506
Newtown, CT 06470
Ph: (203)426-8171 Fax: (203)426-3434
Fr: 800-283-7252
Mark Feirer

Magazine for builders, architects, designers, and owner-builders.

★5013★ *International Construction*
Maclean Hunter Publishing Co.
29 N. Wacker Drive
Chicago, IL 60606
Ph: (312)726-2802 Fax: (312)726-2574
Alan Peterson

Monthly. Trade magazine.

★5014★ *The Journal of Light Construction*
RR 2, Box 146
Richmond, VT 05477-9607
Ph: (802)434-4747 Fax: (802)434-4467
Steve Bliss

Monthly. Magazine (tabloid) for residential and light professionals involved in new and rehabilitative construction. Each issue covers a single aspect of construction.

★5015★ *Painters and Allied Trades Journal*
International Brotherhood of Painters and Allied Trades (IBPAT)
United Unions Bldg.
1750 New York Ave. NW
Washington, DC 20006
Ph: (202)637-0720 Fax: (202)637-0771

Monthly.

★5016★ *Professional Builder & Remodeler*
Cahners Publishing Co.
1350 E. Touhy Ave.
PO Box 5080
Des Plaines, IL 60018-5080
Ph: (708)635-8800 Fax: (708)635-9950
Ed Fitch

Monthly.

★5017★ *The SPEC-DATA Program*
Construction Specifications Institute
601 Madison St.
Alexandria, VA 22314
Ph: (703)684-0300 Fax: (703)684-0465
Carol E. Duke

Quarterly. Magazine (loose-leaf) for the construction industry covering technical product and specification information.

★5018★ *Walls & Ceilings*
LMRector Corp.
8602 N. 40th St.
Tampa, FL 33604
Ph: (813)989-9300 Fax: (813)980-3982
Robert F. Welch

Monthly. Trade magazine for contractors, suppliers, and distributors of drywall, plaster, stucco, exterior insulation, acoustics, metal framing, and ceilings.

Meetings and Conventions

★5019★ Western Lath/Plaster/Drywall Industries Association Annual Convention
Western Lath/Plaster/Drywall Industries Association
8635 Navajo Rd.
San Diego, CA 92119
Ph: (619)466-9070 Fax: (619)466-9149

Annual. Always held in Reno or Las Vegas, Nevada.

Electricians

Electricians install and maintain electrical systems for climate control, security, and communications purposes. They may also install and maintain the electronic controls for machines in business and industry. Electricians must follow the National Electric Code and comply with state and local building codes when they install these systems. Slightly more than half are employed in the construction industry. Others worked as maintenance electricians and are employed in virtually every industry. In addition, a small percentage of electricians are self-employed.

Salaries

Median weekly salaries for electricians are as follows:

Lowest 10 percent	$321/week or less
Median	$412-$717/week
Top 10 percent	$887/week or more

Employment Outlook

Growth rate until the year 2005: Average.

Electricians

Career Guides

★5020★ *Aim For A Job As An Electronic Technician*
Rosen Publishing Group
29 E. 21st St.
New York, NY 10010
Ph: (212)777-3017 Fax: (212)777-0277
Fr: 800-237-9932

John E. Keefe. Revised edition, 1978. Describes the training requirements and the advantages and disadvantages of various jobs available in electronics.

★5021★ *Careers with an Electric Company*
Lerner Publications Co.
241 First Ave., N.
Minneapolis, MN 55401
Fax: (612)332-7615 Fr: 800-328-4920

Pam Fricke. 1984. Describes fifteen career possibilities with an electric company including such jobs as lineman and system operator.

★5022★ *Construction: Basic Principles*
RMI Media Productions, Inc.
2807 West 47th St.
Shawnee Mission, KS 66205
Ph: (913)262-3974 Fax: (913)362-6910
Fr: 800-745-5480

Videocassette. 1984. 20 mins. This series of five programs of varying lengths covers different aspects of career opportunities in the construction trades. Included are: concrete masonry, carpentry, electrical work, plumbing, and heating and air conditioning.

★5023★ *Construction Cluster*
Center for Humanities, Inc.
Communications Park
Box 1000
Mount Kisco, NY 10549
Ph: (914)666-4100 Fax: (914)666-5319
Fr: 800-431-1242

Videocassette. 1984. 15 mins. Construction workers describe what it's like to work at their jobs, and show the special equipment they use in their field.

★5024★ "Construction Electrician" in *Career Information Center* (Vol.4)
Simon and Schuster
200 Old Tappan Rd.
Old Tappan, NJ 07675
Fax: 800-445-6991 Fr: 800-223-2348

Richard Lidz and Dale Anderson, editorial directors. Fifth edition, 1993. For 600 occupations, describes job duties, entry-level requirements, education and training needed, advancement possibilities, employment outlook, earnings and benefits. The set is divided into 12 volumes. Each volume includes jobs related under a broad career field. Volume 13 is the index.

★5025★ "Construction Electrician" in *Occu-Facts: Information on 580 Careers in Outline Form*
Careers, Inc.
PO Box 135
Largo, FL 34649-0135
Ph: (813)584-7333

Biennial, 1995-96 edition. Each one-page occupational profile describes duties, working conditions, physical surroundings and demands, aptitudes, temperament, educational requirements, employment outlook, earnings, and places of employment.

★5026★ "Construction Electrician" in *Opportunities in Electrical Trades* (pp. 44-46)
National Textbook Co. (NTC)
VGM Career Books
4255 W. Touhy Ave.
Lincolnwood, IL 60646-1975
Ph: (708)679-5500 Fax: (708)679-2494
Fr: 800-323-4900

Robert Wood. 1990. Provides an overview of the electrical industry describing current trends and future projections. Surveys electricians jobs and covers the nature of the work, working conditions, job outlook, advancement possibilities, education and training, earnings, and specialization. Offers career planning advice.

★5027★ *Electrician*
Vocational Biographies, Inc.
PO Box 31
Sauk Centre, MN 56378-0031
Ph: (612)352-6516 Fax: (612)352-5546
Fr: 800-255-0752

1993. Four-page pamphlet containing a personal narrative about a worker's job, work likes and dislikes, career path from high school to the present. Education and training, the rewards and frustrations, and the effects of the job on the rest of the worker's life. The data file portion of this pamphlet gives a concise occupational summary, including work descriptions, working conditions, places of employment, personal characteristics, education and training, job outlook, and salary range.

★5028★ "Electrician" in *BLR Encyclopedia of Prewritten Job Descriptions*
Business and Legal Reports, Inc.
39 Academy St.
Madison, CT 06443-1513
Ph: (203)245-7448

Stephen D. Bruce, editor-in-chief. 1994. This book contains hundreds of sample job descriptions arranged by functional job category. The 1-3 page job descriptions cover what the worker normally does in the position, who they report to, and how that position fits in the organizational structure.

★5029★ "Electrician" in *Career Connection II: A Guide to Technical Majors and Their Related Careers* (pp. 62-63)
Jist Works, Inc.
720 N. Park Ave.
Indianapolis, IN 46202-3431
Ph: (317)264-3720 Fax: (317)264-3709

Fred A. Rowe. 1994. Contains technical majors, such as automotive technology. Describes the major and the job. Lists high school and postsecondary school courses. Includes occupations related to the major, employment outlook, and starting salary.

★5030★ *Electrician, Construction*
Careers, Inc.
PO Box 135
Largo, FL 34649-0135
Ph: (813)584-7333

1994. Two-page occupational summary card describing duties, working conditions, personal qualifications, training, earnings and hours, employment outlook, places of employment, related careers and where to write for more information.

★5031★ "Electrician" in *Guide to Careers Without College* (pp. 85-86)
Franklin Watts, Inc.
387 Park Avenue, S.
New York, NY 10016
Ph: (212)686-7070

Kathleen S. Abrams. 1988. Discusses careers that do not require a college degree in fields such as health care, sales and marketing, and the building trades. Describes the work, employment opportunities, and training.

★5032★ "Electrician" in *Hard Hatted Women: Stories of Struggle and Success in the Trades* (pp. 216-224)
Seal Press
3131 Western Ave., Ste. 410
Seattle, WA 98121
Ph: (206)283-7844 Fax: (206)285-9410

Molly Martin, editor. 1988. Twenty-six women recount their experiences working in blue collar occupations. They describe how they got in, the work they do, their relationships in predominantly male occupations, and their training.

★5033★ "Electrician" in *Jobs Rated Almanac*
World Almanac
1 International Blvd., Ste. 444
Mahwah, NJ 07495
Ph: (201)529-6900 Fax: (201)529-6901

Les Krantz. Second edition, 1992. Ranks 250 jobs by environment, salary, outlooks, physical demands, stress, security, travel opportunities, and extra perks. Includes jobs the editor feels are the most common, most interesting, and the most rapidly growing.

★5034★ *Electrician, Maintenance*
Careers, Inc.
PO Box 135
Largo, FL 34649-0135
Ph: (813)584-7333

1995. Four-page brief offering the definition, history, duties, working conditions, personal qualifications, educational requirements, earnings, hours, employment outlook, advancement possibilities, and related occupations.

★5035★ "Electrician" in *VGM's Careers Encyclopedia* (pp. 155-158)
National Textbook Co. (NTC)
VGM Career Books
4255 W. Touhy Ave.
Lincolnwood, IL 60646-1975
Ph: (708)679-5500 Fax: (708)679-2494
Fr: 800-323-4900

Third edition, 1991. Contains two- to five-page descriptions of 200 managerial, professional, technical, trade, and service occupations. Each profile includes job duties, places of employment, qualifications, educational preparation, training, employment potential, advancement, income, and additional sources of information.

★5036★ "Electricians" in *American Almanac of Jobs and Salaries* (pp. 502)
Avon Books
1350 Avenue of the Americas
New York, NY 10019
Ph: (212)261-6800 Fr: 800-238-0658

John Wright, editor. Revised and updated, 1994-95. A comprehensive guide to the wages of hundreds of occupations in a wide variety of industries and organizations.

★5037★ "Electricians" in *Career Discovery Encyclopedia* (Vol.2, pp. 144-145)
J.G. Ferguson Publishing Co.
200 W. Madison St., Ste. 300
Chicago, IL 60606
Ph: (312)580-5480 Fax: (312)580-4948

E. Russell Primm, editor-in-chief. 1993. Contains two-page articles on 504 occupations. Each article describes job duties, earnings, and educational and training requirements.

★5038★ *Electricians, Construction*
Chronicle Guidance Publications, Inc.
66 Aurora St.
PO Box 1190
Moravia, NY 13118-1190
Ph: (315)497-0330 Fax: (315)497-3359
Fr: 800-622-7284

1987. This career brief describes the nature of the work, working conditions, hours and earnings, education and training, licensure, certification, unions, personal qualifications, social and psychological factors, employment outlook, entry methods, advancement, and related occupations.

★5039★ "Electricians" in *Encyclopedia of Careers and Vocational Guidance* (Vol.2, pp. 546-549)
J.G. Ferguson Publishing Co.
200 W. Madison St., Ste. 300
Chicago, IL 60606
Ph: (312)580-5480 Fax: (312)580-4948

William E. Hopke, editor-in-chief. Ninth edition, 1993. Four-volume set that profiles 500 occupations and describes job trends in 74 industries. Includes career description, educational requirements, history of the job, methods of entry, advancement, employment outlook, earnings, working conditions, social and psychological factors, and sources of additional information.

★5040★ *Electricians, Maintenance*
Chronicle Guidance Publications, Inc.
66 Aurora St.
PO Box 1190
Moravia, NY 13118-1190
Ph: (315)497-0330 Fax: (315)497-3359
Fr: 800-622-7284

1994. This career brief describes the nature of the work, working conditions, hours and earnings, education and training, licensure, certification, unions, personal qualifications, social and psychological factors, employment outlook, entry methods, advancement, and related occupations.

★5041★ "Electricians" in *Occupational Outlook Handbook*
U.S. Government Printing Office
Superintendent of Documents
Washington, DC 20402
Ph: (202)512-1800 Fax: (202)512-2250

Biennial; latest edition, 1994-95. Encyclopedia of careers describing more than 250 occupations and comprising about 85 percent of all jobs in the economy. Occupations that require lengthy education or training are given the most attention. For each occupation, the handbook describes job duties, working conditions, training, educational preparation, personal qualities, advancement possibilities, job outlook, earnings, and sources of additional information.

★5042★ "Electricians" in *Opportunities in Building Construction Trades* (pp. 31-34)
National Textbook Co. (NTC)
VGM Career Books
4255 W. Touhy Ave.
Lincolnwood, IL 60646-1975
Ph: (708)679-5500 Fax: (708)679-2494
Fr: 800-323-4900

Michael Sumichrast. 1989. Gives an overview of the construction industry and describes the jobs of various craftworkers. Covers different kinds of builders: home, custom; and describes management skills needed and industry trends affecting opportunities.

★5043★ *Electronic Service Careers*
Franklin Watts, Inc.
387 Park Ave., S.
New York, NY 10016
Ph: (212)686-7070 Fax: (212)213-6435

Robert Laurance. 1987. Describes the career opportunities in electronics and the education and training requirements.

★5044★ *Exploring Careers as an Electrician*
Rosen Publishing Group
29 E. 21st St.
New York, NY 10010
Ph: (212)777-3017 Fax: (212)777-0277
Fr: 800-237-9932

Elizabeth Stewart Lytle. 1993. Electricians in the field describe their work, training, and owning a business. Covers employment outlook.

★5045★ *Get Wired for Life as a Construction Electrician*
Independent Electrical Contractors, Inc.
PO Box 10379
Alexandria, VA 22310-0379
Ph: (703)549-7351

This six-panel brochure describes high school preparation and minimum qualifications for an electrician's apprenticeship.

★5046★ *Getting Down to Business: Construction Electrician Business*
American Institutes for Research in the Behavioral Sciences
PO Box 11131
Palo Alto, CA 94302
Ph: (415)493-3550 Fax: (415)858-0958

Joyce P. Gall. 1981.

★5047★ ***The IBEW Leads to Electrifying Careers***
International Brotherhood of Electrical Workers
1125 15th St. NW
Washington, DC 20005
Ph: (202)833-7000

1988. This 15-page booklet describes the electrician apprenticeship program and the jobs of electricians, communications, and utility workers and licensure.

★5048★ **"Maintenance Electrician" in *Career Information Center* (Vol.4)**
Simon and Schuster
200 Old Tappan Rd.
Old Tappan, NJ 07675
Fax: 800-445-6991 Fr: 800-223-2348

Richard Lidz and Dale Anderson, editorial directors. Fifth edition, 1993. For 600 occupations, describes job duties, entry-level requirements, education and training needed, advancement possibilities, employment outlook, earnings and benefits. The set is divided into 12 volumes. Each volume includes jobs related under a broad career field. Volume 13 is the index.

★5049★ **"Maintenance Electrician" in *Exploring Nontraditional Jobs for Women* (pp. 118-124)**
Rosen Publishing Group
29 E. 21st St.
New York, NY 10010
Ph: (212)777-3017 Fax: (212)777-0277
Fr: 800-237-9932

Rose Neufeld. 1989. Describes blue-collar, male dominated occupations. Discusses what is done on the job, training, where to apply for jobs, tools used, salaries, and advantages and disadvantages. Relates the experiences of women who are working in the field.

★5050★ **"Maintenance Electrician" in *Occu-Facts: Information on 580 Careers in Outline Form***
Careers, Inc.
PO Box 135
Largo, FL 34649-0135
Ph: (813)584-7333

Biennial, 1995-96 edition. Each one-page occupational profile describes duties, working conditions, physical surroundings and demands, aptitudes, temperament, educational requirements, employment outlook, earnings, and places of employment.

★5051★ **"Maintenance Electrician" in *Opportunities in Electrical Trades* (pp. 46-49)**
National Textbook Co. (NTC)
VGM Career Books
4255 W. Touhy Ave.
Lincolnwood, IL 60646-1975
Ph: (708)679-5500 Fax: (708)679-2494
Fr: 800-323-4900

Robert Wood. 1990. Provides an overview of the electrical industry describing current trends and future projections. Surveys electricians jobs and covers the nature of the work, working conditions, job outlook, advancement possibilities, education and training, earnings, and specialization. Offers career planning advice.

★5052★ **"Marine Electrician" in *Opportunities in Electrical Trades* (pp. 51-53)**
National Textbook Co. (NTC)
VGM Career Books
4255 W. Touhy Ave.
Lincolnwood, IL 60646-1975
Ph: (708)679-5500 Fax: (708)679-2494
Fr: 800-323-4900

Robert Wood. 1990. Provides an overview of the electrical industry describing current trends and future projections. Surveys electricians jobs and covers the nature of the work, working conditions, job outlook, advancement possibilities, education and training, earnings, and specialization. Offers career planning advice.

★5053★ **"Resolution, Personal Services and Transportation Careers" in *The Best Jobs for the 1990s and Into the 21st Century***
Impact Publications
9104-N Manassas Dr.
Manassas Park, VA 22111
Ph: (703)361-7300 Fax: (703)335-9486

Ronald L. Krannich and Caryl Rae Krannich. 1993. Includes information on a wide variety of careers including adjusters, investigators, and collectors, animal caretakers, electricians, services sales reps., and truck drivers.

★5054★ **"Utility and Power Plant Occupations" in *Opportunities in Electrical Trades* (pp. 43-64)**
National Textbook Co. (NTC)
VGM Career Books
4255 W. Touhy Ave.
Lincolnwood, IL 60646-1975
Ph: (708)679-5500 Fax: (708)679-2494
Fr: 800-323-4900

Robert Wood. 1990. Provides an overview of the electrical industry describing current trends and future projections. Surveys electricians jobs and covers the nature of the work, working conditions, job outlook, advancement possibilities, education and training, earnings, and specialization. Offers career planning advice.

★5055★ ***Video Career Library - Construction***
Careers, Inc.
PO Box 135
Largo, FL 34649-0135
Ph: (813)584-7333

Videocassette. 1990. 36 mins. Part of the Video Career Library covering 165 occupations. Shows actual workers on the job. Includes millwrights, brickmasons, carpenters, drywall installers, electricians, painters, plumbers and pipefitters, carpenter and soft tile installers, insulation workers, paving equipment operators, and structural metal workers.

ASSOCIATIONS

★5056★ **Associated Builders and Contractors (ABC)**
1300 N. 17th St.
Rossyln, VA 22209
Ph: (703)812-2000

Members: Construction contractors, subcontractors, suppliers, and associates. **Purpose:** Aim is to foster and perpetuate the principles of rewarding construction workers and management on the basis of merit. Sponsors management education programs and craft training; also sponsors apprenticeship and skill training programs. Disseminates technological and labor relations information. Maintains placement service. Compiles statistics. **Publications:** *ABC Today*, semimonthly. • *National Membership Directory and Users Guide*, annual.

★5057★ **Independent Electrical Contractors (IEC)**
507 Wythe St.
Alexandria, VA 22314
Ph: (703)549-7351 Fax: (703)549-7448

Members: Independent electrical contractors, small and large, primarily open shop. **Purpose:** Promotes the interests of members; works to eliminate "unwise and unfair business practices" and to protect its members against "unfair or unjust taxes and legislative enactments." Sponsors electrical apprenticeship programs; conducts educational programs on cost control and personnel motivation. Represents independent electrical contractors to the National Electrical Code panel. Conducts surveys on volume of sales and purchases and on type of products used. Has formulated National Pattern Standards for Apprentice Training for Electricians. **Publications:** *IEC Quarterly*, quarterly.

★5058★ **International Brotherhood of Electrical Workers (IBEW)**
1125 15th St. NW
Washington, DC 20005
Ph: (202)833-7000 Fax: (202)467-6316

Members: AFL-CIO. **Publications:** *IBEW Journal*, monthly.

★5059★ **National Electrical Contractors Association (NECA)**
3 Bethesda Metro Ctr., Ste. 1100
Bethesda, MD 20814
Ph: (301)657-3110 Fax: (301)215-4500

Members: Contractors erecting, installing, repairing, servicing, and maintaining electric wiring, equipment, and appliances. **Purpose:** Provides management services and labor relations programs for electrical contractors; conducts seminars for contractor sales and training. Conducts research and educational programs; compiles statistics. Sponsors honorary society, the Academy of Electrical Contracting. **Publications:** *Electrical Contractor Magazine*, monthly. • *Electrical Design Library*. • *Electro Fact File*, bimonthly. • *NECA News*, weekly. • *NECA Standard of Installation*.

Standards/Certification Agencies

★5060★ Independent Electrical Contractors (IEC)
507 Wythe St.
Alexandria, VA 22314
Ph: (703)549-7351 Fax: (703)549-7448

Sponsors electrical apprenticeship programs; conducts educational programs on cost control and personnel motivation. Represents independent electrical contractors to the National Electrical Code panel. Has formulated National Pattern Standards for Apprentice Training for Electricians.

Test Guides

★5061★ *Career Examination Series: Electrician*
National Learning Corp.
212 Michael Dr.
Syosset, NY 11791
Ph: (516)921-8888 Fax: (516)921-8743
Fr: 800-645-6337

Jack Rudman. All examination guides in this series contain questions with answers.

★5062★ *Career Examination Series: Electrician's Helper*
National Learning Corp.
212 Michael Dr.
Syosset, NY 11791
Ph: (516)921-8888 Fax: (516)921-8743
Fr: 800-645-6337

Jack Rudman. All examination guides in this series contain questions with answers.

★5063★ *Career Examination Series: Foreman (Electrical Power)*
National Learning Corp.
212 Michael Dr.
Syosset, NY 11791
Ph: (516)921-8888 Fax: (516)921-8743
Fr: 800-645-6337

Jack Rudman. 1989. All examination guides in this series contain questions with answers.

★5064★ *Career Examination Series: Foreman Electrician*
National Learning Corp.
212 Michael Dr.
Syosset, NY 11791
Ph: (516)921-8888 Fax: (516)921-8743
Fr: 800-645-6337

Jack Rudman. All examination guides in this series contain questions with answers.

★5065★ *Career Examination Series: Master Electrician*
National Learning Corp.
212 Michael Dr.
Syosset, NY 11791
Ph: (516)921-8888 Fax: (516)921-8743
Fr: 800-645-6337

Jack Rudman. All examination guides in this series contain questions with answers.

★5066★ *Career Examination Series: Special Electrical License*
National Learning Corp.
212 Michael Dr.
Syosset, NY 11791
Ph: (516)921-8888 Fax: (516)921-8743
Fr: 800-645-6337

Jack Rudman. All examination guides in this series contain questions with answers.

★5067★ *Career Examination Series: Transit Electrical Helper Series*
National Learning Corp.
212 Michael Dr.
Syosset, NY 11791
Ph: (516)921-8888 Fax: (516)921-8743
Fr: 800-645-6337

Jack Rudman. 1989. All examination guides in this series contain questions with answers.

★5068★ *Electrician, Electrician's Helper*
Arco Pub.
201 W. 103rd St.
Indianapolis, IN 46290
Ph: 800-428-5331 Fax: 800-835-3202

Dr. Rex Miller. 1991, sixth edition. Includes five exams with answers.

★5069★ *Maintenance Worker/Mechanical Maintainer*
Prentice Hall Press
Simon & Schuster Inc.
200 Old Tappan Rd.
Old Tappan, NJ 07675
Ph: 800-223-2348

Hy Hammer. Fourth edition, 1984. Provides information for applicants interested in the following civil service positions: carpenter, mason, plumber, electrician, painter, machinist. Includes eight sample tests.

Educational Directories and Programs

★5070★ *International Directory of Building Research, Information and Development Organizations*
29 W. 35th St.
New York, NY 10001
Ph: (212)244-3336

Over 600 universities, institutions, government agencies, and other construction-related research institutions. Entries include: Institution name, address, phone, telex, name and title of contact, number of staff, source of finance, area of interest, publications.

Basic Reference Guides and Handbooks

★5071★ *Electrical Design Library*
National Electrical Contractors Association (NECA)
7315 Wisconsin Ave.
Bethesda, MD 20814
Ph: (301)657-3110

★5072★ *The Electrician's Toolbox Manual*
Prentice Hall
Rte. 9W
Englewood Cliffs, NJ 07632
Ph: (201)592-2000

Rex Miller. 1989.

★5073★ *The Electrician's Toolbox Manual*
Arco Pub.
201 W. 103rd St.
Indianapolis, IN 46290
Ph: 800-428-5331 Fax: 800-835-3202

Rex Miller. 1989.

★5074★ *Intelligent Buildings Institute—Directory of Products and Services*
Intelligent Buildings Institute (IBI)
2101 L St., NW, Ste. 300
Washington, DC 20037
Ph: (202)457-1988 Fax: (202)457-8468

S. Hunt, Associate Executive Director, editor. Annual, September. Member consultants, associations, research organizations, and other suppliers of products and services to the construction and building industry. Entries include: Company name, address, phone. Arrangement: Alphabetical. Indexes: Product/service.

★5075★ *Math on the Job: Electrician*
National Center for Research in Vocational Education
Ohio State University
1900 Kenry Rd.
Columbus, OH 43210
Ph: (614)292-4353

1985.

Periodicals

★5076★ *ABC Today*
Associated Builders and Contractors, Inc. (ABC)
N. 17th St.
Rosslyn, VA 22209
Ph: (703)637-8800 Fax: (703)812-8203
Pamela E. Hunter

Semimonthly. Designed to keep readers alerted to important changes within ABC and the construction industry. Reports on legislative issues, construction trends, conferences and meetings, and ABC services. Recurring features include news of members and columns titled Industry Briefs, Safety Notebook, Computer Corner, Bottom Line, and Chapter News.

★5077★ *ABC Today*
Associated Builders and Contractors, Inc. (ABC)
1300 N. 17th St., 8th Floor
Arlington, VA 22209-3803
Ph: (703)812-2000 Fax: (703)812-8203
Pamela E. Hunter

Semiweekly. Magazine for open shop contractors and subcontractors. Includes articles on national and regional construction news, construction management, project case histories, new products, building design, and legislative and regulatory updates.

★5078★ *ABC Today*
Associated Builders and Contractors (ABC)
1300 N. 17th St.
Rosslyn, VA 22209
Ph: (703)812-2000

Semimonthly. News magazine for merit shop contractors.

★5079★ *American Architectural Manufacturers Association—Quarterly Review*
American Architectural Manufacturers Association
1540 E. Dundee Rd., Ste. 310
Palatine, IL 60067-8321
Ph: (708)202-1350 Fax: (708)202-1480
Tony Coorlim

Annual. Contains industry news on architectural products. Covers prime and combination storm windows, sliding glass and combination storm doors, window and curtainwalls, store fronts and entrances, siding, soffits, fascia, gutters, downspouts, skylights, space enclosures, and mobile home components. Recurring features include news of research, notices of publications available, and announcements by the Association.

★5080★ *American Institute of Constructors—Newsletter*
American Institute of Constructors
9887 Gandy Blvd. N., Ste. 104
St. Petersburg, FL 33702
Ph: (813)578-1962 Fax: (813)578-9982
Cheryl P. Harris

Bimonthly. Concerned with construction practice, design, administration, and teaching. Carries news of members, listings of job opportunities, local chapter reports, notices of new publications, and conferences on construction topics.

★5081★ *Blue Reports, Inc.*
Construction News Service
7325 Steel Mill Dr.
Springfield, VA 22050
Ph: (703)644-5884 Fax: (703)644-1929
Calvin S. Oren

Daily. Reports on public and private construction projects in the Washington, DC, Virginia, and Maryland areas. Provides owner's and architect's names, plan status, date bids due, prospective bidders, low bids received, and specification details.

★5082★ *Building Concerns*
National Association of Minority Contractors (NAMC)
1333 F St. NW, Ste. 500
Washington, DC 20004
Ph: (202)347-8259 Fax: (202)628-1876
Agreta Hester

Quarterly. Concentrates on national and regional news regarding minority construction contractors. Contains articles on issues generally affecting the industry—especially issues affecting minorities—including topics such as legislative and regulatory activity and reports on major corporation developments. Recurring features include reports of meetings, news of educational opportunities, a calendar of events, and news of NAMC chapters, affiliates, and members.

★5083★ *Building Industry Technology: An Abstract Newsletter*
National Technical Information Service (NTIS)
5285 Port Royal Rd.
Springfield, VA 22161
Ph: (703)487-4630

Biweekly. Consists of abstracts of reports on architectural and environmental design, building standards, construction materials and equipment, and structural analyses. Recurring features include a form for ordering reports from NTIS.

★5084★ *Capital Comments*
National Lumber & Building Material Dealers Association
40 Ivy St. SE
Washington, DC 20003
Ph: (202)547-2230 Fax: (202)547-7640
Matt Geitner

Semimonthly. Reports on news of legislation pertaining to lumber, other building materials, and housing. Discusses such issues as lumber subsidies, interest rates on homes, health and safety, and jobs.

★5085★ *CEE News*
Intertec Publishing Corp.
9800 Metcalf
Overland Park, KS 66212-2215
Ph: (913)341-1300 Fax: (913)967-1898
Stuart M. Lewis

Monthly. Electrical construction industry magazine.

★5086★ *ConnStruction*
McHugh Design, Advertising & Publishing
62 Lasalle Rd., Ste. 211
West Hartford, CT 06107
Ph: (203)523-7518 Fax: (203)231-8808
Tracy E. McHughPublisher

Quarterly. Magazine for construction industry.

★5087★ *CONSTRUCTION*
HES, Inc.
26 Long Hill Rd.
PO Box 362
Guilford, CT 06437-0362
Ph: (203)453-3717 Fax: (203)453-4390
Jack C. Lewis

Semiweekly. Journal for the construction industry.

★5088★ *Construction News*
10835 Financial Centre Pkwy., Ste. 133
Little Rock, AR 72211-3555
Ph: (501)376-1931 Fax: (501)375-5831
Robert Alvey

Weekly. Construction industry magazine.

★5089★ *Construction Newsletter*
National Safety Council
1121 Spring Lake Dr.
Itasca, IL 60143-3201
Ph: (708)775-2282 Fax: (708)775-2285
Diane A. Ghazarian

Bimonthly. Focuses on industrial and occupational safety in the construction industry. Carries items on such topics as safe work practices and products; accident prevention; and successful industrial safety programs and policies.

★5090★ *Daily Construction Reporter*
7670 Opprtunity Rd.
San Diego, CA 92111-1112
Ph: (619)492-1402 Fax: (619)565-4182
Bernado RomanowskyPublisher

Daily. Construction newspaper covering jobs that are out for bid, bid results, building permits, and other information.

★5091★ *Electrical Contractor Magazine*
National Electrical Contractors Association (NECA)
3 Bethesda Metro Ctr., Ste. 1100
Bethesda, MD 20814
Ph: (301)657-3110 Fax: (301)215-4500

Monthly.

★5092★ *The Electricity Journal*
1932 1st Ave., No. 809
Seattle, WA 98101-1040
Ph: (206)448-4078 Fax: (206)441-7443
Robert O. Marritz

Magazine serving the electric utility industry.

★5093★ *Electro Fact File*
National Electrical Contractors Association (NECA)
3 Bethesda Metro Ctr., Ste. 1100
Bethesda, MD 20814
Ph: (301)657-3110 Fax: (301)215-4500

Bimonthly.

★5094★ *IEC Quarterly*
Independent Electrical Contractors (IEC)
507 Wythe St.
Alexandria, VA 22314
Ph: (703)549-7351 Fax: (703)549-7448

Quarterly.

★5095★ *Interior Construction*
Ceilings and Interior Systems Construction Assn.
579 W. North Ave. Ste. 301
Elmhurst, IL 60126
Ph: (708)833-1919 Fax: (708)833-1940
Jan FoxenPublisher

Bimonthly. Magazine covering interior system construction.

★5096★ *International Construction*
Maclean Hunter Publishing Co.
29 N. Wacker Drive
Chicago, IL 60606
Ph: (312)726-2802 Fax: (312)726-2574
Alan Peterson

Monthly. Trade magazine.

★5097★ *The Journal of Light Construction*
RR 2, Box 146
Richmond, VT 05477-9607
Ph: (802)434-4747 Fax: (802)434-4467
Steve Bliss

Monthly. Magazine (tabloid) for residential and light professionals involved in new and rehabilitative construction. Each issue covers a single aspect of construction.

★5098★ *Nation's Building News*
1201 15th St. NW
Washington, DC 20005-2800
Ph: (202)822-0525 Fax: (202)861-2131
Tim Ahern

Semiweekly. Trade magazine (tabloid) covering home building and all related industries.

★5099★ *Nation's Building News*
National Association of Home Builders of the U.S. (NAHB)
1201 15th St. NW
Washington, DC 20005
Ph: (202)822-0200 Fax: (202)822-0559
Semimonthly. Provides the latest information concerning the housing industry, including finance, legislation, new technologies, and membership news.

★5100★ *NECA News*
National Electrical Contractors Association (NECA)
3 Bethesda Metro Ctr., Ste. 1100
Bethesda, MD 20814
Ph: (301)657-3110 Fax: (301)215-4500
Weekly.

★5101★ *NECA Standard of Installation*
National Electrical Contractors Association (NECA)
3 Bethesda Metro Ctr., Ste. 1100
Bethesda, MD 20814
Ph: (301)657-3110 Fax: (301)215-4500

★5102★ *Palmetto Piper*
Mechanical Contractor's Assn. of South Carolina
1504 Morninghill Drive
PO Box 384
Columbia, SC 29202
Ph: (803)772-7834 Fax: (803)731-0390
Monthly. Plumbing, heating, air conditioning, and electrical journal.

★5103★ *Professional Builder & Remodeler*
Cahners Publishing Co.
1350 E. Touhy Ave.
PO Box 5080
Des Plaines, IL 60018-5080
Ph: (708)635-8800 Fax: (708)635-9950
Ed Fitch
Monthly.

Meetings and Conventions

★5104★ Electric Expo
The Electrical Association of Philadelphia
40 Monument Rd., Ste. 107
Bala Cynwyd, PA 19004
Ph: (215)668-1700 Fax: (215)668-1703
Biennial. Always held during October odd-numbered years at the Valley Forge Convention Center in King of Prussia, Pennsylvania. **Dates and Locations:** 1995 Oct 17-18; King of Prussia, PA.

★5105★ Electrical Industry Exposition
National Electrical Contractors Association
3 Bethesda Metro Center, Ste. 1100
Bethesda, MD 20814
Ph: (301)657-3110 Fax: (301)215-4500
Annual. **Dates and Locations:** 1995 Oct 08-10; Anaheim, CA.

★5106★ Midwest Specialty Exposition
Kansas Plumbing, Heating, and Cooling Contractors Association
320 Laura St.
Wichita, KS 67211
Ph: (316)262-8860 Fax: (316)262-2782
Annual.

★5107★ Upper Midwest Electrical Expo
North Central Electrical League
4930 77th St., W., Ste. 150
Minneapolis, MN 55435
Ph: (612)835-4808 Fax: (612)835-4809
Biennial. Always held at the Convention Center in Minneapolis, Minnesota. **Dates and Locations:** 1996 Apr 10-11; Minneapolis, MN.

Other Sources of Information

★5108★ *Basic Principles of Electricity*
BNA Communications, Inc.
9439 Key West Ave.
Rockville, MD 20850
Ph: (301)948-0540 Fax: (301)948-2085
Fr: 800-233-6067
A dramatic reenactment of an actual electrocution shows employees how electricity affects the body and what can be done to prevent electrical accidents and injuries.

★5109★ *Career Connections Video Series: Electrician*
Cambridge Career Products
PO Box 2153, Dept. CC15
Charleston, WV 25328-2153
Fr: 800-468-4227
1993. Contains interviews with workers in specific fields and includes on-the-job footage.

★5110★ *Electrical Safety Related Work Practices*
Gulf Publishing Co.
PO Box 2680
Houston, TX 77252-2608
Ph: (713)529-4301 Fax: (713)520-4438
1992. Six-part training program that offers educational material on electrical safety. Centers on the new OSHA requirements for work performed on or near exposed energized and de-energized parts of electrical equipment, the use of electrical protective equipment, and the safe use of electrical equipment.

★5111★ *Electrical Symbols and Abbreviations*
Vis-Tech Services, Inc.
815 Arndd Ave.
PO Box 2131
Rockford, IL 61130
Ph: (815)282-2100 Fax: (815)229-1528
Describes various electrical symbols and abbreviations that are used in blue prints. Includes training test with answer key.

★5112★ "Electrician" in *Career Selector 2001*
Barron's Educational Series, Inc.
250 Wireless Blvd.
Hauppauge, NY 11788
Ph: (516)434-3311 Fax: (516)434-3723
Fr: 800-645-3476
James C. Gonyea. 1993.

★5113★ *Switching Circuits*
Vis-Tech Services, Inc.
815 Arndd Ave.
PO Box 2131
Rockford, IL 61130
Ph: (815)282-2100 Fax: (815)229-1528
Provides information on the operation of general use snap switches and the associated circuitry.

★5114★ *Working Safely with Electricity*
Bergwall Productions, Inc.
540 Baltimore Pk.
Chadds Ford, PA 19317
Ph: (610)388-0400 Fax: (610)388-0405
Fr: 800-645-4565
1992. Workers who treat hazardous materials carelessly may benefit from the concepts of electricity presented in this program. Details what happens when electrical currents flow through the body. Introduces the concepts of grounding and outlines proper emergency response.

Glaziers

Glaziers select, cut, install, and remove all types of glass as well as plastics and similar materials. They also install mirrors, shower doors and bathtub enclosures, and glass for table tops and display cases. They may mount steel and aluminum sashes or frames and attach locks and hinges to glass doors. The majority of glaziers work for glazing contractors engaged in new construction, alteration, and repair. Others work for retail glass shops that install or replace glass and wholesale distributors of products containing glass.

Salaries

Median weekly earnings for glaziers is $446.

Lowest 10 percent	$279/week or less
Middle 50 percent	$334-$608/week
Top 10 percent	$790/week or more

Employment Outlook

Growth rate until the year 2005: Much faster than the average.

Glaziers

Career Guides

★5115★ *Construction Cluster*
Center for Humanities, Inc.
Communications Park
Box 1000
Mount Kisco, NY 10549
Ph: (914)666-4100 Fax: (914)666-5319
Fr: 800-431-1242

Videocassette. 1984. 15 mins. Construction workers describe what it's like to work at their jobs, and show the special equipment they use in their field.

★5116★ *Glazier*
Careers, Inc.
PO Box 135
Largo, FL 34649-0135
Ph: (813)584-7333

1993. Two-page occupational summary card describing duties, working conditions, personal qualifications, training, earnings and hours, employment outlook, places of employment, related careers and where to write for more information.

★5117★ "Glazier" in *Career Information Center* (Vol.4)
Simon and Schuster
200 Old Tappan Rd.
Old Tappan, NJ 07675
Fax: 800-445-6991 Fr: 800-223-2348

Richard Lidz and Dale Anderson, editorial directors. Fifth edition, 1993. For 600 occupations, describes job duties, entry-level requirements, education and training needed, advancement possibilities, employment outlook, earnings and benefits. The set is divided into 12 volumes. Each volume includes jobs related under a broad career field. Volume 13 is the index.

★5118★ "Glazier" in *Exploring Nontraditional Jobs for Women* (pp. 16-20)
Rosen Publishing Group
29 E. 21st St.
New York, NY 10010
Ph: (212)777-3017 Fax: (212)777-0277
Fr: 800-237-9932

Rose Neufeld. 1989. Describes blue-collar, male dominated occupations. Discusses what is done on the job, training, where to apply for jobs, tools used, salaries, and advantages and disadvantages. Relates the experiences of women who are working in the field.

★5119★ "Glazier" in *Jobs Rated Almanac*
World Almanac
1 International Blvd., Ste. 444
Mahwah, NJ 07495
Ph: (201)529-6900 Fax: (201)529-6901

Les Krantz. Second edition, 1992. Ranks 250 jobs by environment, salary, outlooks, physical demands, stress, security, travel opportunities, and extra perks. Includes jobs the editor feels are the most common, most interesting, and the most rapidly growing.

★5120★ "Glazier" in *Occu-Facts: Information on 580 Careers in Outline Form*
Careers, Inc.
PO Box 135
Largo, FL 34649-0135
Ph: (813)584-7333

Biennial, 1995-96 edition. Each one-page occupational profile describes duties, working conditions, physical surroundings and demands, aptitudes, temperament, educational requirements, employment outlook, earnings, and places of employment.

★5121★ *Glaziers*
Chronicle Guidance Publications, Inc.
66 Aurora St.
PO Box 1190
Moravia, NY 13118-1190
Ph: (315)497-0330 Fax: (315)497-3359
Fr: 800-622-7284

1993. This career brief describes the nature of the work, working conditions, hours and earnings, education and training, licensure, certification, unions, personal qualifications, social and psychological factors, employment outlook, entry methods, advancement, and related occupations.

★5122★ "Glaziers" in *Career Discovery Encyclopedia* (Vol.3, pp. 66-67)
J.G. Ferguson Publishing Co.
200 W. Madison St., Ste. 300
Chicago, IL 60606
Ph: (312)580-5480 Fax: (312)580-4948

E. Russell Primm, editor-in-chief. 1993. Contains two-page articles on 504 occupations. Each article describes job duties, earnings, and educational and training requirements.

★5123★ "Glaziers" in *Encyclopedia of Careers and Vocational Guidance* (Vol.3, pp. 94-96)
J.G. Ferguson Publishing Co.
200 W. Madison St., Ste. 300
Chicago, IL 60606
Ph: (312)580-5480 Fax: (312)580-4948

William E. Hopke, editor-in-chief. Ninth edition, 1993. Four-volume set that profiles 500 occupations and describes job trends in 74 industries. Includes career description, educational requirements, history of the job, methods of entry, advancement, employment outlook, earnings, working conditions, social and psychological factors, and sources of additional information.

★5124★ "Glaziers" in *Occupational Outlook Handbook*
U.S. Government Printing Office
Superintendent of Documents
Washington, DC 20402
Ph: (202)512-1800 Fax: (202)512-2250

Biennial; latest edition, 1994-95. Encyclopedia of careers describing more than 250 occupations and comprising about 85 percent of all jobs in the economy. Occupations that require lengthy education or training are given the most attention. For each occupation, the handbook describes job duties, working conditions, training, educational preparation, personal qualities, advancement possibilities, job outlook, earnings, and sources of additional information.

★5125★ "Glaziers" in *Opportunities in Building Construction Trades* (pp. 55-57)
National Textbook Co. (NTC)
VGM Career Books
4255 W. Touhy Ave.
Lincolnwood, IL 60646-1975
Ph: (708)679-5500 Fax: (708)679-2494
Fr: 800-323-4900

Michael Sumichrast. 1989. Gives an overview of the construction industry and describes the jobs of various craftworkers. Covers different kinds of builders: home, custom; and describes management skills needed and industry trends affecting opportunities.

Associations

★5126★ International Brotherhood of Painters and Allied Trades (IBPAT)
United Unions Bldg.
1750 New York Ave. NW
Washington, DC 20006
Ph: (202)637-0720 Fax: (202)637-0771

Members: AFL-CIO. **Publications:** *Painters and Allied Trades Journal*, monthly.

★5127★ National Glass Association (NGA)
8200 Greensboro Dr., 3rd Fl.
Mc Lean, VA 22102-3881
Ph: (703)442-4890 Fax: (703)442-0630

Members: Manufacturers, installers, retailers, distributors, and fabricators of flat, architectural, automotive, and specialty glass and metal products, mirrors, shower and patio doors, windows, and table tops. **Purpose:** Provides informational, educational and technical services. **Publications:** *AutoGlass Magazine*, bimonthly. • *Catalog of Products and Services*, annual. • *Glass Magazine*, monthly. • *Index of Publications and Resource Catalogue*, periodic.

Test Guides

★5128★ *Career Examination Series: Glazier*
National Learning Corp.
212 Michael Dr.
Syosset, NY 11791
Ph: (516)921-8888 Fax: (516)921-8743
Fr: 800-645-6337

Jack Rudman. All examination guides in this series contain questions with answers.

★5129★ *Career Examination Series: Supervising Glazier*
National Learning Corp.
212 Michael Dr.
Syosset, NY 11791
Ph: (516)921-8888 Fax: (516)921-8743
Fr: 800-645-6337

Jack Rudman. Test guide including questions and answers for students or professionals in the field who seek advancement through examination.

Educational Directories and Programs

★5130★ *International Directory of Building Research, Information and Development Organizations*
29 W. 35th St.
New York, NY 10001
Ph: (212)244-3336

Over 600 universities, institutions, government agencies, and other construction-related research institutions. Entries include: Institution name, address, phone, telex, name and title of contact, number of staff, source of finance, area of interest, publications.

★5131★ *National Glaziers' Architectural Metal and Glassworkers' Industries Apprenticeship Training and Journeymen Education Fund*
9030 Red Branch Rd.
Columbia, MD 21045

Provides information on training for glaziers.

Basic Reference Guides and Handbooks

★5132★ *Intelligent Buildings Institute—Directory of Products and Services*
Intelligent Buildings Institute (IBI)
2101 L St., NW, Ste. 300
Washington, DC 20037
Ph: (202)457-1988 Fax: (202)457-8468

S. Hunt, Associate Executive Director, editor. Annual, September. Member consultants, associations, research organizations, and other suppliers of products and services to the construction and building industry. Entries include: Company name, address, phone. Arrangement: Alphabetical. Indexes: Product/service.

★5133★ *U.S. Glass, Metal and Glazing—Directory of Suppliers of Machinery & Equipment Issue*
Key Communications, Inc.
PO Box 569
Garrisonville, VA 22463
Ph: (703)720-5584 Fax: (703)295-2903
Debra Levy, Publisher

Annual, May. Publication includes: List of suppliers of machinery and equipment for the glass, metal, and glazing industry. Entries include: Co. name, address, phone, telex, names and titles of key personnel, subsidiary and branch names and locations. Arrangement: Alphabetical.

★5134★ *U.S. Glass, Metal and Glazing—Directory of Suppliers of Sealants & Glazing Systems Issue*
Key Communications, Inc.
PO Box 569
Garrisonville, VA 22463
Ph: (703)720-5584 Fax: (703)295-2903
Debra A. Levy, Publisher

Annual, July. Publication includes: List of about 90 suppliers of sealants and glazing systems for the glass, metal, and glazing industry. Entries include: Co. name, address, phone, fax. Arrangement: Classified by product of service.

Periodicals

★5135★ *ABC Today*
Associated Builders and Contractors, Inc. (ABC)
N. 17th St.
Rosslyn, VA 22209
Ph: (703)637-8800 Fax: (703)812-8203
Pamela E. Hunter

Semimonthly. Designed to keep readers alerted to important changes within ABC and the construction industry. Reports on legislative issues, construction trends, conferences and meetings, and ABC services. Recurring features include news of members and columns titled Industry Briefs, Safety Notebook, Computer Corner, Bottom Line, and Chapter News.

★5136★ *ABC Today*
Associated Builders and Contractors, Inc. (ABC)
1300 N. 17th St., 8th Floor
Arlington, VA 22209-3803
Ph: (703)812-2000 Fax: (703)812-8203
Pamela E. Hunter

Semiweekly. Magazine for open shop contractors and subcontractors. Includes articles on national and regional construction news, construction management, project case histories, new products, building design, and legislative and regulatory updates.

★5137★ *American Architectural Manufacturers Association—Quarterly Review*
American Architectural Manufacturers Association
1540 E. Dundee Rd., Ste. 310
Palatine, IL 60067-8321
Ph: (708)202-1350 Fax: (708)202-1480
Tony Coorlim

Annual. Contains industry news on architectural products. Covers prime and combination storm windows, sliding glass and combination storm doors, window and curtainwalls, store fronts and entrances, siding, soffits, fascia, gutters, downspouts, skylights, space enclosures, and mobile home components. Recurring features include news of research, notices of publications available, and announcements by the Association.

★5138★ *American Institute of Constructors—Newsletter*
American Institute of Constructors
9887 Gandy Blvd. N., Ste. 104
St. Petersburg, FL 33702
Ph: (813)578-1962 Fax: (813)578-9982
Cheryl P. Harris

Bimonthly. Concerned with construction practice, design, administration, and teaching. Carries news of members, listings of job opportunities, local chapter reports, notices of new publications, and conferences on construction topics.

★5139★ *AutoGlass*
National Glass Association
8200 Greensboro Dr., No. 302
Mc Lean, VA 22102
Ph: (703)442-4890 Fax: (703)442-0630
Nicole Harris

Bimonthly. Trade publication for auto glass manufacturers, distributors, and installers.

★5140★ *Blue Reports, Inc.*
Construction News Service
7325 Steel Mill Dr.
Springfield, VA 22050
Ph: (703)644-5884 Fax: (703)644-1929
Calvin S. Oren

Daily. Reports on public and private construction projects in the Washington, DC, Virginia, and Maryland areas. Provides owner's and architect's names, plan status, date bids due, prospective bidders, low bids received, and specification details.

★5141★ *Building Concerns*
National Association of Minority Contractors (NAMC)
1333 F St. NW, Ste. 500
Washington, DC 20004
Ph: (202)347-8259 Fax: (202)628-1876
Agreta Hester

Quarterly. Concentrates on national and regional news regarding minority construction contractors. Contains articles on issues generally affecting the industry—especially issues affecting minorities—including topics such as legislative and regulatory activity and reports on major corporation developments. Recurring features include reports of meetings, news of educational opportunities, a calendar of events, and news of NAMC chapters, affiliates, and members.

★5142★ *Building Industry Technology: An Abstract Newsletter*
National Technical Information Service (NTIS)
5285 Port Royal Rd.
Springfield, VA 22161
Ph: (703)487-4630

Biweekly. Consists of abstracts of reports on architectural and environmental design, building standards, construction materials and equipment, and structural analyses. Recurring features include a form for ordering reports from NTIS.

★5143★ *Capital Comments*
National Lumber & Building Material Dealers Association
40 Ivy St. SE
Washington, DC 20003
Ph: (202)547-2230 Fax: (202)547-7640
Matt Geitner

Semimonthly. Reports on news of legislation pertaining to lumber, other building materials, and housing. Discusses such issues as lumber subsidies, interest rates on homes, health and safety, and jobs.

★5144★ *Catalog of Products and Services*
National Glass Association (NGA)
8200 Greensboro Dr., 3rd Fl.
Mc Lean, VA 22102-3881
Ph: (703)442-4890 Fax: (703)442-0630

Annual.

★5145★ *ConnStruction*
McHugh Design, Advertising & Publishing
62 Lasalle Rd., Ste. 211
West Hartford, CT 06107
Ph: (203)523-7518 Fax: (203)231-8808
Tracy E. McHugh

Quarterly. Magazine for construction industry.

★5146★ *CONSTRUCTION*
HES, Inc.
26 Long Hill Rd.
PO Box 362
Guilford, CT 06437-0362
Ph: (203)453-3717 Fax: (203)453-4390
Jack C. Lewis

Semiweekly. Journal for the construction industry.

★5147★ *Construction News*
10835 Financial Centre Pkwy., Ste. 133
Little Rock, AR 72211-3555
Ph: (501)376-1931 Fax: (501)375-5831
Robert Alvey

Weekly. Construction industry magazine.

★5148★ *Construction Newsletter*
National Safety Council
1121 Spring Lake Dr.
Itasca, IL 60143-3201
Ph: (708)775-2282 Fax: (708)775-2285
Diane A. Ghazarian

Bimonthly. Focuses on industrial and occupational safety in the construction industry. Carries items on such topics as safe work practices and products; accident prevention; and successful industrial safety programs and policies.

★5149★ *Daily Construction Reporter*
7670 Opprtunity Rd.
San Diego, CA 92111-1112
Ph: (619)492-1402 Fax: (619)565-4182
Bernado RomanowskyPublisher

Daily. Construction newspaper covering jobs that are out for bid, bid results, building permits, and other information.

★5150★ *Glass Magazine*
National Glass Association (NGA)
8200 Greensboro Dr., 3rd Fl.
Mc Lean, VA 22102-3881
Ph: (703)442-4890 Fax: (703)442-0630

Monthly. Contains news and information on glass industry management. Topics include architectural glass, storefronts, curtainwall, skylights, and greenhouses.

★5151★ *Index of Publications and Resource Catalogue*
National Glass Association (NGA)
8200 Greensboro Dr., 3rd Fl.
Mc Lean, VA 22102-3881
Ph: (703)442-4890 Fax: (703)442-0630

Periodic.

★5152★ *International Construction*
Maclean Hunter Publishing Co.
29 N. Wacker Drive
Chicago, IL 60606
Ph: (312)726-2802 Fax: (312)726-2574
Alan Peterson

Monthly. Trade magazine.

★5153★ *The Journal of Light Construction*
RR 2, Box 146
Richmond, VT 05477-9607
Ph: (802)434-4747 Fax: (802)434-4467
Steve Bliss

Monthly. Magazine (tabloid) for residential and light professionals involved in new and rehabilitative construction. Each issue covers a single aspect of construction.

★5154★ *Nation's Building News*
1201 15th St. NW
Washington, DC 20005-2800
Ph: (202)822-0525 Fax: (202)861-2131
Tim Ahern

Semiweekly. Trade magazine (tabloid) covering home building and all related industries.

★5155★ *Nation's Building News*
National Association of Home Builders of the U.S. (NAHB)
1201 15th St. NW
Washington, DC 20005
Ph: (202)822-0200 Fax: (202)822-0559

Semimonthly. Provides the latest information concerning the housing industry, including finance, legislation, new technologies, and membership news.

★5156★ *Professional Builder & Remodeler*
Cahners Publishing Co.
1350 E. Touhy Ave.
PO Box 5080
Des Plaines, IL 60018-5080
Ph: (708)635-8800 Fax: (708)635-9950
Ed Fitch

Monthly.

MEETINGS AND CONVENTIONS

★5157★ National Glass Association Annual Convention and National Glass and Machinery Show
National Glass Association
8200 Greensboro Dr., 3rd Fl.
Mc Lean, VA 22102
Ph: (703)442-4890 Fax: (703)442-0630

Annual. **Dates and Locations:** 1996 May 09-11; Phoenix, AZ. • 1997 May 15-18; Atlanta, GA.

Insulation Workers

Insulation workers cement, staple, wire, tape, or spray insulation. Most work for insulation or other construction contractors. Others work for the federal government, in shipbuilding, and in other manufacturing industries, such as chemicals and petroleum refining.

Salaries

Median weekly salaries for insulation workers are as follows:

Lowest 10 percent	$279/week or less
Median	$334-$608/week
Top 10 percent	$796/week or more

Employment Outlook

Growth rate until the year 2005: Much faster than the average.

Insulation Workers

Career Guides

★5158★ "Asbestos and Insulating Worker" in *Opportunities in Building Construction Trades* (pp. 47-49)
National Textbook Co. (NTC)
VGM Career Books
4255 W. Touhy Ave.
Lincolnwood, IL 60646-1975
Ph: (708)679-5500 Fax: (708)679-2494
Fr: 800-323-4900

Michael Sumichrast. 1989. Gives an overview of the construction industry and describes the jobs of various craftworkers. Covers different kinds of builders: home, custom; and describes management skills needed and industry trends affecting opportunities.

★5159★ *Career Insights*
RMI Media Productions, Inc.
1365 N. Winchester
Olathe, KS 66061
Ph: (913)768-1696 Fax: 800-755-6910
Fr: 800-745-5480

Videocassette series. 1987. This videotape series describes 50 occupations, including skill requirements and interviews with people employed in these fields. Occupations include: flight service, air transportation/ground services, data processing, carpentry, clerk in banking/insurance/business, cosmetic personal grooming, firefighting, forestry, insulation/roofing, mechanics, material handling, photographic processing, pipefitting and plumbing, printing, secretarial services, tool and die operations.

★5160★ *Career Success Series*
Cambridge Educational
PO Box 2153
Charleston, WV 25328-2153
Ph: (304)744-9323 Fax: (304)744-9351
Fr: 800-468-4227

Videocassette. 1986. 15 mins. A series, available separately, outlining various career choices for students. Occupations include: accounting, flight service, air transportation/ground/flight service, data processing, carpentry, clerk in banking/insurance, commodity sales, cosmetic personal grooming, fire fighting, forestry services, home economics, insulation/roofing, material handling, mechanics, photographic processing, pipefitting and plumbing, police science, printing, carpentry, medical laboratory technicians, secretarial services, and utilities equipment operator.

★5161★ *Construction Cluster*
Center for Humanities, Inc.
Communications Park
Box 1000
Mount Kisco, NY 10549
Ph: (914)666-4100 Fax: (914)666-5319
Fr: 800-431-1242

Videocassette. 1984. 15 mins. Construction workers describe what it's like to work at their jobs, and show the special equipment they use in their field.

★5162★ *Insulating & Roofing Occupations*
Morris Video
2730 Monterey St., No. 105
Monterey Business Park
Torrance, CA 90503
Ph: (310)533-4800 Fr: 800-843-3606

Videocassette. 1987. 15 mins. A look at the various careers that involve the reduction of the flow of cold, heat or sound.

★5163★ "Insulation Worker" in *Career Information Center* (Vol.4)
Simon and Schuster
200 Old Tappan Rd.
Old Tappan, NJ 07675
Fax: 800-445-6991 Fr: 800-223-2348

Richard Lidz and Dale Anderson, editorial directors. Fifth edition, 1993. For 600 occupations, describes job duties, entry-level requirements, education and training needed, advancement possibilities, employment outlook, earnings and benefits. The set is divided into 12 volumes. Each volume includes jobs related under a broad career field. Volume 13 is the index.

★5164★ *Insulation Workers*
Careers, Inc.
PO Box 135
Largo, FL 34649-0135
Ph: (813)584-7333

1992. Two-page occupational summary card describing duties, working conditions, personal qualifications, training, earnings and hours, employment outlook, places of employment, related careers and where to write for more information.

★5165★ "Insulation Workers" in *Career Discovery Encyclopedia* (Vol.3, pp. 134-135)
J.G. Ferguson Publishing Co.
200 W. Madison St., Ste. 300
Chicago, IL 60606
Ph: (312)580-5480 Fax: (312)580-4948

E. Russell Primm, editor-in-chief. 1993. Contains two-page articles on 504 occupations. Each article describes job duties, earnings, and educational and training requirements.

★5166★ *Insulation Workers, Industrial*
Chronicle Guidance Publications, Inc.
66 Aurora St.
PO Box 1190
Moravia, NY 13118-1190
Ph: (315)497-0330 Fax: (315)497-3359
Fr: 800-622-7284

1991. Career brief describing the nature of the job, working conditions, hours and earnings, education and training, licensure, certification, unions, personal qualifications, social and psychological factors, location, employment outlook, entry methods, advancement, and related occupations.

★5167★ "Insulation Workers" in *Occu-Facts: Information on 580 Careers in Outline Form*
Careers, Inc.
PO Box 135
Largo, FL 34649-0135
Ph: (813)584-7333

Biennial, 1995-96 edition. Each one-page occupational profile describes duties, working conditions, physical surroundings and demands, aptitudes, temperament, educational requirements, employment outlook, earnings, and places of employment.

★5168★ "Insulation Workers" in *Occupational Outlook Handbook*
U.S. Government Printing Office
Superintendent of Documents
Washington, DC 20402
Ph: (202)512-1800 Fax: (202)512-2250

Biennial; latest edition, 1994-95. Encyclopedia of careers describing more than 250 occupations and comprising about 85 percent of all jobs in the economy. Occupations that require lengthy education or training are given the most attention. For each occupation, the handbook describes job duties, working conditions, training, educational preparation, personal qualities, advancement possibilities, job outlook, earnings, and sources of additional information.

★5169★ *Video Career Library - Construction*
Careers, Inc.
PO Box 135
Largo, FL 34649-0135
Ph: (813)584-7333

Videocassette. 1990. 36 mins. Part of the Video Career Library covering 165 occupations. Shows actual workers on the job. Includes millwrights, brickmasons, carpenters, drywall installers, electricians, painters, plumbers and pipefitters, carpenter and soft tile installers, insulation workers, paving equipment operators, and structural metal workers.

Associations

★5170★ National Insulation and Abatement Contractors Association (NIAC)
99 Canal Center Plz., Ste. 222
Alexandria, VA 22314
Ph: (703)683-6422 Fax: (703)549-4838

Members: Insulation and asbestos abatement contractors, distributors, and manufacturers. **Publications:** *Estimator's Handbook.* • *Financial and Compensation Survey.* • *Hazard Classification Guide.* • *Insulation Industry File.* • *Insulation Outlook*, monthly. • *NIAC News*, monthly. • *Owner/Contractor Asbestos Abatement Agreement Guide.* • *Safety Handbook.*

Educational Directories and Programs

★5171★ *International Directory of Building Research, Information and Development Organizations*
29 W. 35th St.
New York, NY 10001
Ph: (212)244-3336

Over 600 universities, institutions, government agencies, and other construction-related research institutions. Entries include: Institution name, address, phone, telex, name and title of contact, number of staff, source of finance, area of interest, publications.

Basic Reference Guides and Handbooks

★5172★ *Intelligent Buildings Institute—Directory of Products and Services*
Intelligent Buildings Institute (IBI)
2101 L St., NW, Ste. 300
Washington, DC 20037
Ph: (202)457-1988 Fax: (202)457-8468

S. Hunt, Associate Executive Director, editor. Annual, September. Member consultants, associations, research organizations, and other suppliers of products and services to the construction and building industry. Entries include: Company name, address, phone. Arrangement: Alphabetical. Indexes: Product/service.

★5173★ *NIAC Commercial and Industrial Standards Manual*
National Insulation and Abatement Contractors Association (NIAC)
99 Canal Center Plaza, Ste. 222
Alexandria, VA 22314
Ph: (703)683-6422 Fax: (703)549-4838

Periodicals

★5174★ *ABC Today*
Associated Builders and Contractors, Inc. (ABC)
N. 17th St.
Rosslyn, VA 22209
Ph: (703)637-8800 Fax: (703)812-8203
Pamela E. Hunter

Semimonthly. Designed to keep readers alerted to important changes within ABC and the construction industry. Reports on legislative issues, construction trends, conferences and meetings, and ABC services. Recurring features include news of members and columns titled Industry Briefs, Safety Notebook, Computer Corner, Bottom Line, and Chapter News.

★5175★ *ABC Today*
Associated Builders and Contractors, Inc. (ABC)
1300 N. 17th St., 8th Floor
Arlington, VA 22209-3803
Ph: (703)812-2000 Fax: (703)812-8203
Pamela E. Hunter

Semiweekly. Magazine for open shop contractors and subcontractors. Includes articles on national and regional construction news, construction management, project case histories, new products, building design, and legislative and regulatory updates.

★5176★ *American Architectural Manufacturers Association—Quarterly Review*
American Architectural Manufacturers Association
1540 E. Dundee Rd., Ste. 310
Palatine, IL 60067-8321
Ph: (708)202-1350 Fax: (708)202-1480
Tony Coorlim

Annual. Contains industry news on architectural products. Covers prime and combination storm windows, sliding glass and combination storm doors, window and curtainwalls, store fronts and entrances, siding, soffits, fascia, gutters, downspouts, skylights, space enclosures, and mobile home components. Recurring features include news of research, notices of publications available, and announcements by the Association.

★5177★ *American Institute of Constructors—Newsletter*
American Institute of Constructors
9887 Gandy Blvd. N., Ste. 104
St. Petersburg, FL 33702
Ph: (813)578-1962 Fax: (813)578-9982
Cheryl P. Harris

Bimonthly. Concerned with construction practice, design, administration, and teaching. Carries news of members, listings of job opportunities, local chapter reports, notices of new publications, and conferences on construction topics.

★5178★ *Blue Reports, Inc.*
Construction News Service
7325 Steel Mill Dr.
Springfield, VA 22050
Ph: (703)644-5884 Fax: (703)644-1929
Calvin S. Oren

Daily. Reports on public and private construction projects in the Washington, DC, Virginia, and Maryland areas. Provides owner's and architect's names, plan status, date bids due, prospective bidders, low bids received, and specification details.

★5179★ *Building Concerns*
National Association of Minority Contractors (NAMC)
1333 F St. NW, Ste. 500
Washington, DC 20004
Ph: (202)347-8259 Fax: (202)628-1876
Agreta Hester

Quarterly. Concentrates on national and regional news regarding minority construction contractors. Contains articles on issues generally affecting the industry—especially issues affecting minorities—including topics such as legislative and regulatory activity and reports on major corporation developments. Recurring features include reports of meetings, news of educational opportunities, a calendar of events, and news of NAMC chapters, affiliates, and members.

★5180★ *Building Industry Technology: An Abstract Newsletter*
National Technical Information Service (NTIS)
5285 Port Royal Rd.
Springfield, VA 22161
Ph: (703)487-4630

Biweekly. Consists of abstracts of reports on architectural and environmental design, building standards, construction materials and equipment, and structural analyses. Recurring features include a form for ordering reports from NTIS.

★5181★ *Capital Comments*
National Lumber & Building Material Dealers Association
40 Ivy St. SE
Washington, DC 20003
Ph: (202)547-2230 Fax: (202)547-7640
Matt Geitner

Semimonthly. Reports on news of legislation pertaining to lumber, other building materials, and housing. Discusses such issues as lumber subsidies, interest rates on homes, health and safety, and jobs.

★5182★ *ConnStruction*
McHugh Design, Advertising & Publishing
62 Lasalle Rd., Ste. 211
West Hartford, CT 06107
Ph: (203)523-7518 Fax: (203)231-8808
Tracy E. McHugh

Quarterly. Magazine for construction industry.

★5183★ *CONSTRUCTION*
HES, Inc.
26 Long Hill Rd.
PO Box 362
Guilford, CT 06437-0362
Ph: (203)453-3717 Fax: (203)453-4390
Jack C. Lewis

Semiweekly. Journal for the construction industry.

★5184★ *Construction News*
10835 Financial Centre Pkwy., Ste. 133
Little Rock, AR 72211-3555
Ph: (501)376-1931 Fax: (501)375-5831
Robert Alvey

Weekly. Construction industry magazine.

★5185★ *Construction Newsletter*
National Safety Council
1121 Spring Lake Dr.
Itasca, IL 60143-3201
Ph: (708)775-2282 Fax: (708)775-2285
Diane A. Ghazarian

Bimonthly. Focuses on industrial and occupational safety in the construction industry. Carries items on such topics as safe work practices and products; accident prevention; and successful industrial safety programs and policies.

★5186★ *Contractors Guide*
Century Publishing Co.
990 Grove St.
Evanston, IL 60201-4370
Ph: (708)491-6440 Fax: (708)491-0867
Greg Ettling

Monthly. Trade magazine on roofing and insulation.

★5187★ *Daily Construction Reporter*
7670 Opprtunity Rd.
San Diego, CA 92111-1112
Ph: (619)492-1402 Fax: (619)565-4182
Bernado Romanowsky

Daily. Construction newspaper covering jobs that are out for bid, bid results, building permits, and other information.

★5188★ *Estimator's Handbook*
National Insulation and Abatement Contractors Association (NIAC)
99 Canal Center Plz., Ste. 222
Alexandria, VA 22314
Ph: (703)683-6422 Fax: (703)549-4838

★5189★ *Financial and Compensation Survey*
National Insulation and Abatement Contractors Association (NIAC)
99 Canal Center Plz., Ste. 222
Alexandria, VA 22314
Ph: (703)683-6422 Fax: (703)549-4838

★5190★ *Hazard Classification Guide*
National Insulation and Abatement Contractors Association (NIAC)
99 Canal Center Plz., Ste. 222
Alexandria, VA 22314
Ph: (703)683-6422 Fax: (703)549-4838

★5191★ *ICAA News*
Insulation Contractors Association of America (ICAA)
PO Box 26237
Alexandria, VA 22313-6337
Ph: (703)739-0356 Fax: (703)739-0412
R. Hartley Edes

Monthly. Focuses on the insulation industry, including contracting materials, codes and standards, marketing, legislation, and regulation. Promotes professionalism among insulation contractors and quality industry standards.

★5192★ *Insulation Industry File*
National Insulation and Abatement Contractors Association (NIAC)
99 Canal Center Plz., Ste. 222
Alexandria, VA 22314
Ph: (703)683-6422 Fax: (703)549-4838

★5193★ *Insulation Outlook*
National Insulation and Abatement Contractors Assn.
99 Canal Center Plaza, Ste. 222
Alexandria, VA 22314
Ph: (703)683-6480 Fax: (703)549-4838
Stuart C. Hales

Monthly. Official magazine of the National Insulation and Abatement Contractors Association.

★5194★ *International Construction*
Maclean Hunter Publishing Co.
29 N. Wacker Drive
Chicago, IL 60606
Ph: (312)726-2802 Fax: (312)726-2574
Alan Peterson

Monthly. Trade magazine.

★5195★ *The Journal of Light Construction*
RR 2, Box 146
Richmond, VT 05477-9607
Ph: (802)434-4747 Fax: (802)434-4467
Steve Bliss

Monthly. Magazine (tabloid) for residential and light professionals involved in new and rehabilitative construction. Each issue covers a single aspect of construction.

★5196★ *Nation's Building News*
1201 15th St. NW
Washington, DC 20005-2800
Ph: (202)822-0525 Fax: (202)861-2131
Tim Ahern

Semiweekly. Trade magazine (tabloid) covering home building and all related industries.

★5197★ *Nation's Building News*
National Association of Home Builders of the U.S. (NAHB)
1201 15th St. NW
Washington, DC 20005
Ph: (202)822-0200 Fax: (202)822-0559

Semimonthly. Provides the latest information concerning the housing industry, including finance, legislation, new technologies, and membership news.

★5198★ *NIAC News*
National Insulation and Abatement Contractors Association (NIAC)
99 Canal Center Plz., Ste. 222
Alexandria, VA 22314
Ph: (703)683-6422 Fax: (703)549-4838

Monthly.

★5199★ *Owner/Contractor Asbestos Abatement Agreement Guide*
National Insulation and Abatement Contractors Association (NIAC)
99 Canal Center Plz., Ste. 222
Alexandria, VA 22314
Ph: (703)683-6422 Fax: (703)549-4838

★5200★ *Professional Builder & Remodeler*
Cahners Publishing Co.
1350 E. Touhy Ave.
PO Box 5080
Des Plaines, IL 60018-5080
Ph: (708)635-8800 Fax: (708)635-9950
Ed Fitch

Monthly.

★5201★ *Safety Handbook*
National Insulation and Abatement Contractors Association (NIAC)
99 Canal Center Plz., Ste. 222
Alexandria, VA 22314
Ph: (703)683-6422 Fax: (703)549-4838

★5202★ *Walls & Ceilings*
LMRector Corp.
8602 N. 40th St.
Tampa, FL 33604
Ph: (813)989-9300 Fax: (813)980-3982
Robert F. Welch

Monthly. Trade magazine for contractors, suppliers, and distributors of drywall, plaster, stucco, exterior insulation, acoustics, metal framing, and ceilings.

Meetings and Conventions

★5203★ Insulation Contractors Association of America Convention
Insulation Contractors Association of America
15819 Crabbs Branch Way
Rockville, MD 20855
Ph: (301)590-0030 Fax: (301)590-0713

Annual. Always held during September. **Dates and Locations:** 1996 Sep.

Other Sources of Information

★5204★ *First Biannual Commercial and Industrial Insulation Industry Financial Survey*
National Insulation and Abatement Contractors Association (NIAC)
99 Canal Center Plaza, Ste. 222
Alexandria, VA 22314
Ph: (703)683-6422

Industry statistics.

★5205★ "Insulation Worker" in *Encyclopedia of Danger: Dangerous Professions* (pp. 50-53)
Chelsea House Publishers
1974 Sproul Rd., Ste. 400
Broomall, PA 19008
Ph: (215)353-5166 Fax: (215)359-1439

Missy Allen and Michel Peissel. 1993. Provides descriptions of 24 dangerous occupations, their risky characteristics, and safety precautions.

Painters and Paperhangers

Painters apply paint, stain, varnish, and other finishes to buildings and other structures. **Paperhangers** cover walls and ceilings with decorative wall coverings made of paper, vinyl, or fabric. Many painters and paperhangers work for contractors engaged in new construction, repair, restoration, or remodeling work. In addition, organizations that own or manage large buildings, such as hotels, offices, and apartment complexes, employ maintenance painters, as do some schools, hospitals, and factories. Nearly half of painters and paperhangers are self-employed.

Salaries

Median weekly earnings for painters who are not self-employed are as follows:

Lowest 10 percent	$202/week or less
Median	$283-$534/week
Top 10 percent	$703/week or more

Employment Outlook

Growth rate until the year 2005: Faster than the average.

Painters and Paperhangers

Career Guides

★5206★ *Big Questions?*
National Joint Painting, Decorating and Drywall
Apprenticeship and Training Committee
1750 New York Ave., N.W., Lower Level
Washington, DC 20006
Ph: (202)783-7770

This four-page brochure describes requirements, the work, employment opportunities, working conditions, and earnings.

★5207★ "Construction Painter" in *Occu-Facts: Information on 580 Careers in Outline Form*
Careers, Inc.
PO Box 135
Largo, FL 34649-0135
Ph: (813)584-7333

Biennial, 1995-96 edition. Each one-page occupational profile describes duties, working conditions, physical surroundings and demands, aptitudes, temperament, educational requirements, employment outlook, earnings, and places of employment.

★5208★ *Paint and Coatings Industry Workers*
Chronicle Guidance Publications, Inc.
66 Aurora St.
PO Box 1190
Moravia, NY 13118-1190
Ph: (315)497-0330 Fax: (315)497-3359
Fr: 800-622-7284

1991. This career brief describes the nature of the work, working conditions, hours and earnings, education and training, licensure, certification, unions, personal qualifications, social and psychological factors, employment outlook, entry methods, advancement, and related occupations.

★5209★ *Painter*
Vocational Biographies, Inc.
PO Box 31
Sauk Centre, MN 56378-0031
Ph: (612)352-6516 Fax: (612)352-5546
Fr: 800-255-0752

1994. Four-page pamphlet containing a personal narrative about a worker's job, work likes and dislikes, career path from high school to the present. Education and training, the rewards and frustrations, and the effects of the job on the rest of the worker's life. The data file portion of this pamphlet gives a concise occupational summary, including work descriptions, working conditions, places of employment, personal characteristics, education and training, job outlook, and salary range.

★5210★ "Painter" in *BLR Encyclopedia of Prewritten Job Descriptions*
Business and Legal Reports, Inc.
39 Academy St.
Madison, CT 06443-1513
Ph: (203)245-7448

Stephen D. Bruce, editor-in-chief. 1994. This book contains hundreds of sample job descriptions arranged by functional job category. The 1-3 page job descriptions cover what the worker normally does in the position, who they report to, and how that position fits in the organizational structure.

★5211★ *Painter, Construction*
Careers, Inc.
PO Box 135
Largo, FL 34649-0135
Ph: (813)584-7333

1994. Four-page brief offering the definition, history, duties, working conditions, personal qualifications, educational requirements, earnings, hours, employment outlook, advancement possibilities, and related occupations.

★5212★ "Painter" in *Exploring Nontraditional Jobs for Women* (pp. 20-25)
Rosen Publishing Group
29 E. 21st St.
New York, NY 10010
Ph: (212)777-3017 Fax: (212)777-0277
Fr: 800-237-9932

Rose Neufeld. 1989. Describes blue-collar, male dominated occupations. Discusses what is done on the job, training, where to apply for jobs, tools used, salaries, and advantages and disadvantages. Relates the experiences of women who are working in the field.

★5213★ "Painter" in *Great Careers for People Who Like to Work with Their Hands* (pp. 42)
Gale Research Inc.
835 Penobscot Bldg.
Detroit, MI 48226
Ph: (313)961-2242 Fr: 800-347-4253

1994.

★5214★ "Painter and Paperhanger" in *Career Information Center* (Vol.4)
Simon and Schuster
200 Old Tappan Rd.
Old Tappan, NJ 07675
Fax: 800-445-6991 Fr: 800-223-2348

Richard Lidz and Dale Anderson, editorial directors. Fifth edition, 1993. For 600 occupations, describes job duties, entry-level requirements, education and training needed, advancement possibilities, employment outlook, earnings and benefits. The set is divided into 12 volumes. Each volume includes jobs related under a broad career field. Volume 13 is the index.

★5215★ "Painters" in *American Almanac of Jobs and Salaries* (pp. 502)
Avon Books
1350 Avenue of the Americas
New York, NY 10019
Ph: (212)261-6800 Fr: 800-238-0658

John Wright, editor. Revised and updated, 1994-95. A comprehensive guide to the wages of hundreds of occupations in a wide variety of industries and organizations.

★5216★ *Painters (Construction)*
Chronicle Guidance Publications, Inc.
66 Aurora St.
PO Box 1190
Moravia, NY 13118-1190
Ph: (315)497-0330 Fax: (315)497-3359
Fr: 800-622-7284

1993. This career brief describes the nature of the work, working conditions, hours and earnings, education and training, licensure, certification, unions, personal qualifications, social and psychological factors, employment outlook, entry methods, advancement, and related occupations.

★5217★ "Painters" in *Opportunities in Building Construction Trades* (pp. 35-37)
National Textbook Co. (NTC)
VGM Career Books
4255 W. Touhy Ave.
Lincolnwood, IL 60646-1975
Ph: (708)679-5500 Fax: (708)679-2494
Fr: 800-323-4900

Michael Sumichrast. 1989. Gives an overview of the construction industry and describes the jobs of various craftworkers. Covers different kinds of builders: home, custom; and describes management skills needed and industry trends affecting opportunities.

★5218★ "Painters and Paperhangers" in *Career Discovery Encyclopedia* (Vol.4, pp. 162-163)
J.G. Ferguson Publishing Co.
200 W. Madison St., Ste. 300
Chicago, IL 60606
Ph: (312)580-5480 Fax: (312)580-4948

E. Russell Primm, editor-in-chief. 1993. Contains two-page articles on 504 occupations. Each article describes job duties, earnings, and educational and training requirements.

★5219★ "Painters and Paperhangers" in *Encyclopedia of Careers and Vocational Guidance* (Vol.3, pp. 659-662)
J.G. Ferguson Publishing Co.
200 W. Madison St., Ste. 300
Chicago, IL 60606
Ph: (312)580-5480 Fax: (312)580-4948

William E. Hopke, editor-in-chief. Ninth edition, 1993. Four-volume set that profiles 500 occupations and describes job trends in 74 industries. Includes career description, educational requirements, history of the job, methods of entry, advancement, employment outlook, earnings, working conditions, social and psychological factors, and sources of additional information.

★5220★ "Painters and Paperhangers" in *Occupational Outlook Handbook*
U.S. Government Printing Office
Superintendent of Documents
Washington, DC 20402
Ph: (202)512-1800 Fax: (202)512-2250

Biennial; latest edition, 1994-95. Encyclopedia of careers describing more than 250 occupations and comprising about 85 percent of all jobs in the economy. Occupations that require lengthy education or training are given the most attention. For each occupation, the handbook describes job duties, working conditions, training, educational preparation, personal qualities, advancement possibilities, job outlook, earnings, and sources of additional information.

★5221★ *Paperhanger*
Careers, Inc.
PO Box 135
Largo, FL 34649-0135
Ph: (813)584-7333

1994. Two-page occupational summary card describing duties, working conditions, personal qualifications, training, earnings and hours, employment outlook, places of employment, related careers and where to write for more information.

★5222★ "Paperhanger" in *Occu-Facts: Information on 580 Careers in Outline Form*
Careers, Inc.
PO Box 135
Largo, FL 34649-0135
Ph: (813)584-7333

Biennial, 1995-96 edition. Each one-page occupational profile describes duties, working conditions, physical surroundings and demands, aptitudes, temperament, educational requirements, employment outlook, earnings, and places of employment.

★5223★ "Paperhanger" and "Painter" in *Jobs Rated Almanac*
World Almanac
1 International Blvd., Ste. 444
Mahwah, NJ 07495
Ph: (201)529-6900 Fax: (201)529-6901

Les Krantz. Second edition, 1992. Ranks 250 jobs by environment, salary, outlooks, physical demands, stress, security, travel opportunities, and extra perks. Includes jobs the editor feels are the most common, most interesting, and the most rapidly growing.

★5224★ *Paperhangers*
Chronicle Guidance Publications, Inc.
66 Aurora St.
PO Box 1190
Moravia, NY 13118-1190
Ph: (315)497-0330 Fax: (315)497-3359
Fr: 800-622-7284

1991. This career brief describes the nature of the work, working conditions, hours and earnings, education and training, licensure, certification, unions, personal qualifications, social and psychological factors, employment outlook, entry methods, advancement, and related occupations.

★5225★ "Paperhangers" in *Opportunities in Building Construction Trades* (pp. 37-39)
National Textbook Co. (NTC)
VGM Career Books
4255 W. Touhy Ave.
Lincolnwood, IL 60646-1975
Ph: (708)679-5500 Fax: (708)679-2494
Fr: 800-323-4900

Michael Sumichrast. 1989. Gives an overview of the construction industry and describes the jobs of various craftworkers. Covers different kinds of builders: home, custom; and describes management skills needed and industry trends affecting opportunities.

★5226★ *Video Career Library - Construction*
Careers, Inc.
PO Box 135
Largo, FL 34649-0135
Ph: (813)584-7333

Videocassette. 1990. 36 mins. Part of the Video Career Library covering 165 occupations. Shows actual workers on the job. Includes millwrights, brickmasons, carpenters, drywall installers, electricians, painters, plumbers and pipefitters, carpenter and soft tile installers, insulation workers, paving equipment operators, and structural metal workers.

★5227★ *Wallpaper Hanger*
Vocational Biographies, Inc.
PO Box 31
Sauk Centre, MN 56378-0031
Ph: (612)352-6516 Fax: (612)352-5546
Fr: 800-255-0752

1990. This pamphlet profiles a person working in the job. Includes information about job duties, working conditions, places of employment, educational preparation, labor market outlook, and salaries.

ASSOCIATIONS

★5228★ Associated Builders and Contractors (ABC)
1300 N. 17th St.
Rossyln, VA 22209
Ph: (703)812-2000

Members: Construction contractors, subcontractors, suppliers, and associates. **Purpose:** Aim is to foster and perpetuate the principles of rewarding construction workers and management on the basis of merit. Sponsors management education programs and craft training; also sponsors apprenticeship and skill training programs. Disseminates technological and labor relations information. Maintains placement service. Compiles statistics. **Publications:** *ABC Today*, semimonthly. • *National Membership Directory and Users Guide*, annual.

★5229★ International Brotherhood of Painters and Allied Trades (IBPAT)
United Unions Bldg.
1750 New York Ave. NW
Washington, DC 20006
Ph: (202)637-0720 Fax: (202)637-0771

Members: AFL-CIO. **Publications:** *Painters and Allied Trades Journal*, monthly.

TEST GUIDES

★5230★ *Career Examination Series: Foreman Painter*
National Learning Corp.
212 Michael Dr.
Syosset, NY 11791
Ph: (516)921-8888 Fax: (516)921-8743
Fr: 800-645-6337

Jack Rudman. All examination guides in this series contain questions with answers.

★5231★ *Career Examination Series: House Painter*
National Learning Corp.
212 Michael Dr.
Syosset, NY 11791
Ph: (516)921-8888 Fax: (516)921-8743
Fr: 800-645-6337

Jack Rudman. All examination guides in this series contain questions with answers.

★5232★ *Career Examination Series: Painter*
National Learning Corp.
212 Michael Dr.
Syosset, NY 11791
Ph: (516)921-8888 Fax: (516)921-8743
Fr: 800-645-6337

Jack Rudman. All examination guides in this series contain questions with answers.

★5233★ *Career Examination Series: Supervising Painter*
National Learning Corp.
212 Michael Dr.
Syosset, NY 11791
Ph: (516)921-8888 Fax: (516)921-8743
Fr: 800-645-6337

Jack Rudman. Test guide including questions and answers for students or professionals in the field who seek advancement through examination.

★5234★ *Maintenance Worker/ Mechanical Maintainer*
Prentice Hall Press
Simon & Schuster Inc.
200 Old Tappan Rd.
Old Tappan, NJ 07675
Ph: 800-223-2348

Hy Hammer. Fourth edition, 1984. Provides information for applicants interested in the following civil service positions: carpenter, mason, plumber, electrician, painter, machinist. Includes eight sample tests.

Educational Directories and Programs

★5235★ *IBPAT Directory*
International Brotherhood of Painters and Allied Trades (IBPAT)
United Unions Bldg.
1750 New York Ave., NW
Washington, DC 20006
Ph: (202)637-0720 Fax: (202)637-0771

Annual.

★5236★ *Painters' Equipment & Supplies Directory*
American Business Directories, Inc.
5711 S. 86th Circle
Omaha, NE 68127
Ph: (402)593-4600 Fax: (402)331-1505

Updated continuously; printed on request. Entries include: Name, address, phone, size of advertisement, name of owner or manager, number of employees, year first in "Yellow Pages." Compiled from telephone company "Yellow Pages," nationwide. Arrangement: Geographical.

Basic Reference Guides and Handbooks

★5237★ *The Painting, Patching, and Wallcovering Toolbox Manual*
Arco Pub.
201 W. 103rd St.
Indianapolis, IN 46290
Ph: 800-428-5331 Fax: 800-835-3202

David Tenenbaum. 1991.

Periodicals

★5238★ *ABC Today*
Associated Builders and Contractors (ABC)
1300 N. 17th St.
Rosslyn, VA 22209
Ph: (703)812-2000

Semimonthly. News magazine for merit shop contractors.

★5239★ *ABC Today*
Associated Builders and Contractors, Inc. (ABC)
N. 17th St.
Rosslyn, VA 22209
Ph: (703)637-8800 Fax: (703)812-8203
Pamela E. Hunter

Semimonthly. Designed to keep readers alerted to important changes within ABC and the construction industry. Reports on legislative issues, construction trends, conferences and meetings, and ABC services. Recurring features include news of members and columns titled Industry Briefs, Safety Notebook, Computer Corner, Bottom Line, and Chapter News.

★5240★ *ABC Today*
Associated Builders and Contractors, Inc. (ABC)
1300 N. 17th St., 8th Floor
Arlington, VA 22209-3803
Ph: (703)812-2000 Fax: (703)812-8203
Pamela E. Hunter

Semiweekly. Magazine for open shop contractors and subcontractors. Includes articles on national and regional construction news, construction management, project case histories, new products, building design, and legislative and regulatory updates.

★5241★ *American Architectural Manufacturers Association—Quarterly Review*
American Architectural Manufacturers Association
1540 E. Dundee Rd., Ste. 310
Palatine, IL 60067-8321
Ph: (708)202-1350 Fax: (708)202-1480
Tony Coorlim

Annual. Contains industry news on architectural products. Covers prime and combination storm windows, sliding glass and combination storm doors, window and curtainwalls, store fronts and entrances, siding, soffits, fascia, gutters, downspouts, skylights, space enclosures, and mobile home components. Recurring features include news of research, notices of publications available, and announcements by the Association.

★5242★ *American Institute of Constructors—Newsletter*
American Institute of Constructors
9887 Gandy Blvd. N., Ste. 104
St. Petersburg, FL 33702
Ph: (813)578-1962 Fax: (813)578-9982
Cheryl P. Harris

Bimonthly. Concerned with construction practice, design, administration, and teaching. Carries news of members, listings of job opportunities, local chapter reports, notices of new publications, and conferences on construction topics.

★5243★ *American Painting Contractor*
American Paint Journal Co.
2911 Washington Ave.
Saint Louis, MO 63103
Ph: (314)534-0301 Fax: (314)534-4458
Paul Stoecklein

Monthly. Magazine serving paint and wallcovering contractors and in-house maintenance crews.

★5244★ *Blue Reports, Inc.*
Construction News Service
7325 Steel Mill Dr.
Springfield, VA 22050
Ph: (703)644-5884 Fax: (703)644-1929
Calvin S. Oren

Daily. Reports on public and private construction projects in the Washington, DC, Virginia, and Maryland areas. Provides owner's and architect's names, plan status, date bids due, prospective bidders, low bids received, and specification details.

★5245★ *Building Concerns*
National Association of Minority Contractors (NAMC)
1333 F St. NW, Ste. 500
Washington, DC 20004
Ph: (202)347-8259 Fax: (202)628-1876
Agreta Hester

Quarterly. Concentrates on national and regional news regarding minority construction contractors. Contains articles on issues generally affecting the industry—especially issues affecting minorities—including topics such as legislative and regulatory activity and reports on major corporation developments. Recurring features include reports of meetings, news of educational opportunities, a calendar of events, and news of NAMC chapters, affiliates, and members.

★5246★ *Building Industry Technology: An Abstract Newsletter*
National Technical Information Service (NTIS)
5285 Port Royal Rd.
Springfield, VA 22161
Ph: (703)487-4630

Biweekly. Consists of abstracts of reports on architectural and environmental design, building standards, construction materials and equipment, and structural analyses. Recurring features include a form for ordering reports from NTIS.

★5247★ *Capital Comments*
National Lumber & Building Material Dealers Association
40 Ivy St. SE
Washington, DC 20003
Ph: (202)547-2230 Fax: (202)547-7640
Matt Geitner

Semimonthly. Reports on news of legislation pertaining to lumber, other building materials, and housing. Discusses such issues as lumber subsidies, interest rates on homes, health and safety, and jobs.

★5248★ *ConnStruction*
McHugh Design, Advertising & Publishing
62 Lasalle Rd., Ste. 211
West Hartford, CT 06107
Ph: (203)523-7518 Fax: (203)231-8808
Tracy E. McHugh

Quarterly. Magazine for construction industry.

★5249★ *CONSTRUCTION*
HES, Inc.
26 Long Hill Rd.
PO Box 362
Guilford, CT 06437-0362
Ph: (203)453-3717 Fax: (203)453-4390
Jack C. Lewis

Semiweekly. Journal for the construction industry.

★5250★ *Construction News*
10835 Financial Centre Pkwy., Ste. 133
Little Rock, AR 72211-3555
Ph: (501)376-1931 Fax: (501)375-5831
Robert Alvey

Weekly. Construction industry magazine.

★5251★ *Construction Newsletter*
National Safety Council
1121 Spring Lake Dr.
Itasca, IL 60143-3201
Ph: (708)775-2282 Fax: (708)775-2285
Diane A. Ghazarian

Bimonthly. Focuses on industrial and occupational safety in the construction industry. Carries items on such topics as safe work practices and products; accident prevention; and successful industrial safety programs and policies.

★5252★ *Daily Construction Reporter*
7670 Opprtunity Rd.
San Diego, CA 92111-1112
Ph: (619)492-1402 Fax: (619)565-4182
Bernado Romanowsky

Daily. Construction newspaper covering jobs that are out for bid, bid results, building permits, and other information.

★5253★ *Interior Construction*
Ceilings and Interior Systems Construction Assn.
579 W. North Ave. Ste. 301
Elmhurst, IL 60126
Ph: (708)833-1919 Fax: (708)833-1940
Jan Foxen

Bimonthly. Magazine covering interior system construction.

★5254★ *International Construction*
Maclean Hunter Publishing Co.
29 N. Wacker Drive
Chicago, IL 60606
Ph: (312)726-2802 Fax: (312)726-2574
Alan Peterson

Monthly. Trade magazine.

★5255★ *Nation's Building News*
1201 15th St. NW
Washington, DC 20005-2800
Ph: (202)822-0525 Fax: (202)861-2131
Tim Ahern

Semiweekly. Trade magazine (tabloid) covering home building and all related industries.

★5256★ *Nation's Building News*
National Association of Home Builders of the U.S. (NAHB)
1201 15th St. NW
Washington, DC 20005
Ph: (202)822-0200 Fax: (202)822-0559

Semimonthly. Provides the latest information concerning the housing industry, including finance, legislation, new technologies, and membership news.

★5257★ *Painting & Wallcovering Contractor*
Finan Publishing Co., Inc.
8730 Big Bend Blvd.
Saint Louis, MO 63119
Ph: (314)961-6644 Fax: (314)961-4809
Jeffery Beckner

Bimonthly. Magazine covering painting and decorating industry-current research; new trends in techniques and products; and commercial, industrial, institutional, and residential application.

★5258★ *Professional Builder & Remodeler*
Cahners Publishing Co.
1350 E. Touhy Ave.
PO Box 5080
Des Plaines, IL 60018-5080
Ph: (708)635-8800 Fax: (708)635-9950
Ed Fitch

Monthly.

Meetings and Conventions

★5259★ Paint and Paper Pro Show
Painting and Decorating Contractors of America
3913 Old Lee Hwy., Ste. 33B
Fairfax, VA 22030
Ph: (703)359-0826 Fax: (703)359-2576

Annual.

Other Sources of Information

★5260★ "Painter" and "Paperhanger" in *Career Selector 2001*
Barron's Educational Series, Inc.
250 Wireless Blvd.
Hauppauge, NY 11788
Ph: (516)434-3311 Fax: (516)434-3723
Fr: 800-645-3476

James C. Gonyea. 1993.

Plasterers

Plasterers finish interior walls and ceilings with plaster materials that form fire-resistant and relatively soundproof surfaces. They also apply durable cement plasters, polymer-based acrylic finishes, and stucco to exterior surfaces, and may cast ornamental designs in plaster. Increasingly today, plasterers apply insulation to the exteriors of new and old buildings. Most plasterers work on new construction, particularly where special architectural and lighting effects are part of the work. Some repair and renovate older buildings. Most plasterers work for independent contractors; a small percentage are self-employed.

Salaries

Median hourly earnings for plasterers who belong to a union are $15-$33/hour. Apprentice wage rates start at about half the rate paid to experienced plasterers.

Employment Outlook

Growth rate until the year 2005: Average.

Plasterers

Career Guides

★5261★ *Construction Cluster*
Center for Humanities, Inc.
Communications Park
Box 1000
Mount Kisco, NY 10549
Ph: (914)666-4100 Fax: (914)666-5319
Fr: 800-431-1242

Videocassette. 1984. 15 mins. Construction workers describe what it's like to work at their jobs, and show the special equipment they use in their field.

★5262★ *Plasterer*
Careers, Inc.
PO Box 135
Largo, FL 34649-0135
Ph: (813)584-7333

1995. Two-page occupational summary card describing duties, working conditions, personal qualifications, training, earnings and hours, employment outlook, places of employment, related careers and where to write for more information.

★5263★ "Plasterer" in *Career Information Center* (Vol.4)
Simon and Schuster
200 Old Tappan Rd.
Old Tappan, NJ 07675
Fax: 800-445-6991 Fr: 800-223-2348

Richard Lidz and Dale Anderson, editorial directors. Fifth edition, 1993. For 600 occupations, describes job duties, entry-level requirements, education and training needed, advancement possibilities, employment outlook, earnings and benefits. The set is divided into 12 volumes. Each volume includes jobs related under a broad career field. Volume 13 is the index.

★5264★ "Plasterer" in *Jobs Rated Almanac*
World Almanac
1 International Blvd., Ste. 444
Mahwah, NJ 07495
Ph: (201)529-6900 Fax: (201)529-6901

Les Krantz. Second edition, 1992. Ranks 250 jobs by environment, salary, outlooks, physical demands, stress, security, travel opportunities, and extra perks. Includes jobs the editor feels are the most common, most interesting, and the most rapidly growing.

★5265★ "Plasterer" in *Occu-Facts: Information on 580 Careers in Outline Form*
Careers, Inc.
PO Box 135
Largo, FL 34649-0135
Ph: (813)584-7333

Biennial, 1995-96 edition. Each one-page occupational profile describes duties, working conditions, physical surroundings and demands, aptitudes, temperament, educational requirements, employment outlook, earnings, and places of employment.

★5266★ *Plasterers*
Chronicle Guidance Publications, Inc.
66 Aurora St.
PO Box 1190
Moravia, NY 13118-1190
Ph: (315)497-0330 Fax: (315)497-3359
Fr: 800-622-7284

1992. This career brief describes the nature of the work, working conditions, hours and earnings, education and training, licensure, certification, unions, personal qualifications, social and psychological factors, employment outlook, entry methods, advancement, and related occupations.

★5267★ "Plasterers" in *American Almanac of Jobs and Salaries* (pp. 503)
Avon Books
1350 Avenue of the Americas
New York, NY 10019
Ph: (212)261-6800 Fr: 800-238-0658

John Wright, editor. Revised and updated, 1994-95. A comprehensive guide to the wages of hundreds of occupations in a wide variety of industries and organizations.

★5268★ "Plasterers" in *Career Discovery Encyclopedia* (Vol.5, pp. 54-55)
J.G. Ferguson Publishing Co.
200 W. Madison St., Ste. 300
Chicago, IL 60606
Ph: (312)580-5480 Fax: (312)580-4948

E. Russell Primm, editor-in-chief. 1993. Contains two-page articles on 504 occupations. Each article describes job duties, earnings, and educational and training requirements.

★5269★ "Plasterers" in *Encyclopedia of Careers and Vocational Guidance* (Vol.4, pp. 123-125)
J.G. Ferguson Publishing Co.
200 W. Madison St., Ste. 300
Chicago, IL 60606
Ph: (312)580-5480 Fax: (312)580-4948

William E. Hopke, editor-in-chief. Ninth edition, 1993. Four-volume set that profiles 500 occupations and describes job trends in 74 industries. Includes career description, educational requirements, history of the job, methods of entry, advancement, employment outlook, earnings, working conditions, social and psychological factors, and sources of additional information.

★5270★ "Plasterers" in *Occupational Outlook Handbook*
U.S. Government Printing Office
Superintendent of Documents
Washington, DC 20402
Ph: (202)512-1800 Fax: (202)512-2250

Biennial; latest edition, 1994-95. Encyclopedia of careers describing more than 250 occupations and comprising about 85 percent of all jobs in the economy. Occupations that require lengthy education or training are given the most attention. For each occupation, the handbook describes job duties, working conditions, training, educational preparation, personal qualities, advancement possibilities, job outlook, earnings, and sources of additional information.

★5271★ "Plasterers" in *Opportunities in Building Construction Trades* (pp. 39-41)
National Textbook Co. (NTC)
VGM Career Books
4255 W. Touhy Ave.
Lincolnwood, IL 60646-1975
Ph: (708)679-5500 Fax: (708)679-2494
Fr: 800-323-4900

Michael Sumichrast. 1989. Gives an overview of the construction industry and describes the jobs of various craftworkers. Covers different kinds of builders: home, custom; and describes management skills needed and industry trends affecting opportunities.

★5272★ *The Trowel Trades*
International Masonry Institute
823 15th St. NW, Ste. 1001
Washington, DC 20005
Ph: (202)783-3908

This six-panel brochure describes skills, advancement opportunities, and apprentice training.

Associations

★5273★ **International Union of Bricklayers and Allied Craftsmen (BAC)**
815 15th St. NW
Washington, DC 20005
Ph: (202)783-3788 Fax: (202)393-0219

Members: AFL-CIO. **Publications:** *Chalkline*, periodic.

★5274★ **Operative Plasterers and Cement Masons International Association of U.S. and Canada (OPCMIA)**
1125 17th St. NW
Washington, DC 20036
Ph: (202)393-6569 Fax: (202)393-2514

Members: AFL-CIO. **Publications:** *Plasterer and Cement Mason*, monthly.

Test Guides

★5275★ *Career Examination Series: Foreman Plasterer*
National Learning Corp.
212 Michael Dr.
Syosset, NY 11791
Ph: (516)921-8888 Fax: (516)921-8743
Fr: 800-645-6337

Jack Rudman. All examination guides in this series contain questions with answers.

★5276★ *Career Examination Series: Plasterer*
National Learning Corp.
212 Michael Dr.
Syosset, NY 11791
Ph: (516)921-8888 Fax: (516)921-8743
Fr: 800-645-6337

Jack Rudman. All examination guides in this series contain questions with answers.

Basic Reference Guides and Handbooks

★5277★ *Plastering: A Craftman's Encyclopedia*
Blackwell Scientific Publications
3 Cambridge Center, Ste. 208
Cambridge, MA 02142
Ph: (617)225-0401 Fax: (617)225-0412

Don W. Stagg. Second edition, 1989.

Periodicals

★5278★ *ABC Today*
Associated Builders and Contractors, Inc. (ABC)
N. 17th St.
Rosslyn, VA 22209
Ph: (703)637-8800 Fax: (703)812-8203
Pamela E. Hunter

Semimonthly. Designed to keep readers alerted to important changes within ABC and the construction industry. Reports on legislative issues, construction trends, conferences and meetings, and ABC services. Recurring features include news of members and columns titled Industry Briefs, Safety Notebook, Computer Corner, Bottom Line, and Chapter News.

★5279★ *ABC Today*
Associated Builders and Contractors, Inc. (ABC)
1300 N. 17th St., 8th Floor
Arlington, VA 22209-3803
Ph: (703)812-2000 Fax: (703)812-8203
Pamela E. Hunter

Semiweekly. Magazine for open shop contractors and subcontractors. Includes articles on national and regional construction news, construction management, project case histories, new products, building design, and legislative and regulatory updates.

★5280★ *American Architectural Manufacturers Association—Quarterly Review*
American Architectural Manufacturers Association
1540 E. Dundee Rd., Ste. 310
Palatine, IL 60067-8321
Ph: (708)202-1350 Fax: (708)202-1480
Tony Coorlim

Annual. Contains industry news on architectural products. Covers prime and combination storm windows, sliding glass and combination storm doors, window and curtainwalls, store fronts and entrances, siding, soffits, fascia, gutters, downspouts, skylights, space enclosures, and mobile home components. Recurring features include news of research, notices of publications available, and announcements by the Association.

★5281★ *American Institute of Constructors—Newsletter*
American Institute of Constructors
9887 Gandy Blvd. N., Ste. 104
St. Petersburg, FL 33702
Ph: (813)578-1962 Fax: (813)578-9982
Cheryl P. Harris

Bimonthly. Concerned with construction practice, design, administration, and teaching. Carries news of members, listings of job opportunities, local chapter reports, notices of new publications, and conferences on construction topics.

★5282★ *Blue Reports, Inc.*
Construction News Service
7325 Steel Mill Dr.
Springfield, VA 22050
Ph: (703)644-5884 Fax: (703)644-1929
Calvin S. Oren

Daily. Reports on public and private construction projects in the Washington, DC, Virginia, and Maryland areas. Provides owner's and architect's names, plan status, date bids due, prospective bidders, low bids received, and specification details.

★5283★ *Builder*
Hanley-Wood, Inc.
1 Thomas Circle, Ste. 600
Washington, DC 20005
Ph: (202)452-0800
Mitchell Rouda

Monthly. Magazine covering housing, commercial, and industrial building.

★5284★ *Builder Architect*
Sunshine Media, Inc.
PO Box 37707
Phoenix, AZ 85069-7707
Ph: (602)433-7393 Fax: (602)433-2963
Marie Vere

Monthly. Home builders magazine.

★5285★ *Builder/Dealer*
Peterson Bros. Inc., Publishing
14 W. South St.
Corry, PA 16407-1894
Ph: (814)664-8624 Fax: (814)664-8506
Charles P. Mancino

Monthly. Trade magazine.

★5286★ *Builder Insider*
Divibest, Inc.
PO Box 191125
Dallas, TX 75219
Ph: (214)871-2913
Michael J. Anderson

Monthly. Magazine (tabloid) for builders, architects, and remodelers.

★5287★ *Builder Notes*
Brick Institute of America (BIA)
11490 Commerce Park Dr.
Reston, VA 22091
Ph: (703)620-0010 Fax: (703)620-3928

Bimonthly.

★5288★ *Building Business & Apartment Management*
Builders Association of Southeastern Michigan
30375 Northwestern Hwy.
Farmington Hills, MI 48334
Ph: (810)737-4477 Fax: (810)737-5741
Susan Adler

Monthly. Construction and apartment industry magazine.

★5289★ *Building Concerns*
National Association of Minority Contractors (NAMC)
1333 F St. NW, Ste. 500
Washington, DC 20004
Ph: (202)347-8259 Fax: (202)628-1876
Agreta Hester

Quarterly. Concentrates on national and regional news regarding minority construction contractors. Contains articles on issues generally affecting the industry—especially issues affecting minorities—including topics such as legislative and regulatory activity and reports on major corporation developments. Recurring features include reports of meetings, news of educational opportunities, a calendar of events, and news of NAMC chapters, affiliates, and members.

★5290★ *Building Design & Construction*
Cahners Publishing Co.
1350 E. Touhy Ave.
PO Box 5080
Des Plaines, IL 60017-5080
Ph: (708)635-8800 Fax: (708)390-2618
Jack Hollfelder

Monthly. Magazine on business and technology for commercial, institutional, and industrial buildings.

★5291★ *Building Industry*
Trade Publishing Co.
287 Mokauea St.
Honolulu, HI 96819
Ph: (808)848-0711 Fax: (808)841-3053
Jay McWilliams

Monthly. Construction and design magazine.

★5292★ *Building Industry Technology: An Abstract Newsletter*
National Technical Information Service (NTIS)
5285 Port Royal Rd.
Springfield, VA 22161
Ph: (703)487-4630

Biweekly. Consists of abstracts of reports on architectural and environmental design, building standards, construction materials and equipment, and structural analyses. Recurring features include a form for ordering reports from NTIS.

★5293★ *Buildings*
Stamats Communications, Inc.
427 6th Ave. SE
PO Box 1888
Cedar Rapids, IA 52406
Ph: (319)364-6167 Fax: (319)364-4278
Linda Monroe

Monthly. Publication featuring management techniques, development, and ownership of facilities.

★5294★ *Capital Comments*
National Lumber & Building Material Dealers Association
40 Ivy St. SE
Washington, DC 20003
Ph: (202)547-2230 Fax: (202)547-7640
Matt Geitner

Semimonthly. Reports on news of legislation pertaining to lumber, other building materials, and housing. Discusses such issues as lumber subsidies, interest rates on homes, health and safety, and jobs.

★5295★ *Chalkline*
International Union of Bricklayers and Allied Craftsmen (BAC)
815 15th St. NW
Washington, DC 20005
Ph: (202)783-3788 Fax: (202)393-0219

Periodic.

★5296★ *ConnStruction*
McHugh Design, Advertising & Publishing
62 Lasalle Rd., Ste. 211
West Hartford, CT 06107
Ph: (203)523-7518 Fax: (203)231-8808
Tracy E. McHugh

Quarterly. Magazine for construction industry.

★5297★ *CONSTRUCTION*
HES, Inc.
26 Long Hill Rd.
PO Box 362
Guilford, CT 06437-0362
Ph: (203)453-3717 Fax: (203)453-4390
Jack C. Lewis

Semiweekly. Journal for the construction industry.

★5298★ *Construction News*
10835 Financial Centre Pkwy., Ste. 133
Little Rock, AR 72211-3555
Ph: (501)376-1931 Fax: (501)375-5831
Robert Alvey

Weekly. Construction industry magazine.

★5299★ *Construction Newsletter*
National Safety Council
1121 Spring Lake Dr.
Itasca, IL 60143-3201
Ph: (708)775-2282 Fax: (708)775-2285
Diane A. Ghazarian

Bimonthly. Focuses on industrial and occupational safety in the construction industry. Carries items on such topics as safe work practices and products; accident prevention; and successful industrial safety programs and policies.

★5300★ *Daily Construction Reporter*
7670 Opprtunity Rd.
San Diego, CA 92111-1112
Ph: (619)492-1402 Fax: (619)565-4182
Bernado Romanowsky

Daily. Construction newspaper covering jobs that are out for bid, bid results, building permits, and other information.

★5301★ *Fine Homebuilding*
The Taunton Press, Inc.
63 S. Main St.
PO Box 5506
Newtown, CT 06470
Ph: (203)426-8171 Fax: (203)426-3434
Fr: 800-283-7252
Mark Feirer

Magazine for builders, architects, designers, and owner-builders.

★5302★ *International Construction*
Maclean Hunter Publishing Co.
29 N. Wacker Drive
Chicago, IL 60606
Ph: (312)726-2802 Fax: (312)726-2574
Alan Peterson

Monthly. Trade magazine.

★5303★ *Nation's Building News*
1201 15th St. NW
Washington, DC 20005-2800
Ph: (202)822-0525 Fax: (202)861-2131
Tim Ahern

Semiweekly. Trade magazine (tabloid) covering home building and all related industries.

★5304★ *Nation's Building News*
National Association of Home Builders of the U.S. (NAHB)
1201 15th St. NW
Washington, DC 20005
Ph: (202)822-0200 Fax: (202)822-0559

Semimonthly. Provides the latest information concerning the housing industry, including finance, legislation, new technologies, and membership news.

★5305★ *Professional Builder & Remodeler*
Cahners Publishing Co.
1350 E. Touhy Ave.
PO Box 5080
Des Plaines, IL 60018-5080
Ph: (708)635-8800 Fax: (708)635-9950
Ed Fitch

Monthly.

★5306★ *The SPEC-DATA Program*
Construction Specifications Institute
601 Madison St.
Alexandria, VA 22314
Ph: (703)684-0300 Fax: (703)684-0465
Carol E. Duke

Quarterly. Magazine (loose-leaf) for the construction industry covering technical product and specification information.

★5307★ *Walls & Ceilings*
LMRector Corp.
8602 N. 40th St.
Tampa, FL 33604
Ph: (813)989-9300 Fax: (813)980-3982
Robert F. Welch

Monthly. Trade magazine for contractors, suppliers, and distributors of drywall, plaster, stucco, exterior insulation, acoustics, metal framing, and ceilings.

Meetings and Conventions

★5308★ Western Lath/Plaster/Drywall Industries Association Annual Convention
Western Lath/Plaster/Drywall Industries Association
8635 Navajo Rd.
San Diego, CA 92119
Ph: (619)466-9070 Fax: (619)466-9149

Annual. Always held in Reno or Las Vegas, Nevada.

Plumbers and Pipefitters

Plumbers install and repair the water, waste disposal, drainage, and gas systems in homes and commercial and industrial buildings. They also install plumbing fixtures, such as bathtubs, sinks, and toilets, and appliances such as dishwashers and water heaters. **Pipefitters** install and repair both high- and low-pressure pipe systems that are used in manufacturing, in the generation of electricity, and in heating and cooling buildings. Some pipefitters specialize in only one type of system. Steamfitters, for example, install pipe systems that move liquids or gases under high pressure. Sprinklerfitters install automatic fire sprinkler systems in buildings. Most plumbers and pipefitters work for mechanical and plumbing contractors engaged in new construction, repair, modernization, or maintenance work. Others do maintenance work for a variety of industrial, commercial, and government employers, such as the petroleum and chemical industries. Only 20 percent of all plumbers and pipefitters are self-employed.

Salaries

Median hourly earnings for plumbers and pipefitters are $16.15-$19.66.

Employment Outlook

Growth rate until the year 2005: More slowly than the average.

Plumbers and Pipefitters

Career Guides

★5309★ *Career Insights*
RMI Media Productions, Inc.
1365 N. Winchester
Olathe, KS 66061
Ph: (913)768-1696 Fax: 800-755-6910
Fr: 800-745-5480

Videocassette series. 1987. This videotape series describes 50 occupations, including skill requirements and interviews with people employed in these fields. Occupations include: flight service, air transportation/ground services, data processing, carpentry, clerk in banking/insurance/business, cosmetic personal grooming, firefighting, forestry, insulation/roofing, mechanics, material handling, photographic processing, pipefitting and plumbing, printing, secretarial services, tool and die operations.

★5310★ *Career Opportunities in the Fire Sprinkler Industry*
National Fire Sprinkler Association, Inc.
Robin Hill Corporate Park
Route 22
PO Box 1000
Patterson, NY 12563
Ph: (914)878-4200

1991. This eight-page booklet describes the industry, training, earnings, and certification.

★5311★ *Career Success Series*
Cambridge Educational
PO Box 2153
Charleston, WV 25328-2153
Ph: (304)744-9323 Fax: (304)744-9351
Fr: 800-468-4227

Videocassette. 1986. 15 mins. A series, available separately, outlining various career choices for students. Occupations include: accounting, flight service, air transportation/ground/flight service, data processing, carpentry, clerk in banking/insurance, commodity sales, cosmetic personal grooming, fire fighting, forestry services, home economics, insulation/roofing, material handling, mechanics, photographic processing, pipefitting and plumbing, police science, printing, carpentry, medical laboratory technicians, secretarial services, and utilities equipment operator.

★5312★ *Construction: Basic Principles*
RMI Media Productions, Inc.
2807 West 47th St.
Shawnee Mission, KS 66205
Ph: (913)262-3974 Fax: (913)362-6910
Fr: 800-745-5480

Videocassette. 1984. 20 mins. This series of five programs of varying lengths covers different aspects of career opportunities in the construction trades. Included are: concrete masonry, carpentry, electrical work, plumbing, and heating and air conditioning.

★5313★ *Construction Cluster*
Center for Humanities, Inc.
Communications Park
Box 1000
Mount Kisco, NY 10549
Ph: (914)666-4100 Fax: (914)666-5319
Fr: 800-431-1242

Videocassette. 1984. 15 mins. Construction workers describe what it's like to work at their jobs, and show the special equipment they use in their field.

★5314★ *Getting Down to Business: Plumbing Business*
American Institutes for Research in the Behavioral Sciences
PO Box 11131
Palo Alto, CA 94302
Ph: (415)493-3550 Fax: (415)858-0958

Barbara Sanderson. 1981.

★5315★ *Opportunities in Plumbing and Pipefitting Careers*
National Textbook Co. (NTC)
VGM Career Books
4255 W. Toughy Ave.
Lincolnwood, IL 60646-1975
Ph: (708)679-5500 Fax: (708)679-2494
Fr: 800-323-4900

Patrick J. Galvin. 1994.

★5316★ *Pipe Fitters and Steam Fitters*
Chronicle Guidance Publications, Inc.
66 Aurora St.
PO Box 1190
Moravia, NY 13118-1190
Ph: (315)497-0330 Fax: (315)497-3359
Fr: 800-622-7284

1993. This career brief describes the nature of the work, working conditions, hours and earnings, education and training, licensure, certification, unions, personal qualifications, social and psychological factors, employment outlook, entry methods, advancement, and related occupations.

★5317★ "Pipe Fitters and Steam Fitters" in *Encyclopedia of Careers and Vocational Guidance* (Vol.4, pp. 117-120)
J.G. Ferguson Publishing Co.
200 W. Madison St., Ste. 300
Chicago, IL 60606
Ph: (312)580-5480 Fax: (312)580-4948

William E. Hopke, editor-in-chief. Ninth edition, 1993. Four-volume set that profiles 500 occupations and describes job trends in 74 industries. Includes career description, educational requirements, history of the job, methods of entry, advancement, employment outlook, earnings, working conditions, social and psychological factors, and sources of additional information.

★5318★ "Pipefitter" in *BLR Encyclopedia of Prewritten Job Descriptions*
Business and Legal Reports, Inc.
39 Academy St.
Madison, CT 06443-1513
Ph: (203)245-7448

Stephen D. Bruce, editor-in-chief. 1994. This book contains hundreds of sample job descriptions arranged by functional job category. The 1-3 page job descriptions cover what the worker normally does in the position, who they report to, and how that position fits in the organizational structure.

★5319★ "Pipefitters and Steamfitters" in *Career Discovery Encyclopedia* (Vol.5, pp. 52-53)
J.G. Ferguson Publishing Co.
200 W. Madison St., Ste. 300
Chicago, IL 60606
Ph: (312)580-5480 Fax: (312)580-4948

E. Russell Primm, editor-in-chief. 1993. Contains two-page articles on 504 occupations. Each article describes job duties, earnings, and educational and training requirements.

★5320★ *Pipefitting and Plumbing*
Morris Video
2730 Monterey St., No. 105
Monterey Business Park
Torrance, CA 90503
Ph: (213)533-4800 Fr: 800-843-3606

Videocassette. 1983. 15 mins. A look at the many fields to which plumbing may be applied.

★5321★ *Plumber*
Vocational Biographies, Inc.
PO Box 31
Sauk Centre, MN 56378-0031
Ph: (612)352-6516 Fax: (612)352-5546
Fr: 800-255-0752

1990. This pamphlet profiles a person working in the job. Includes information about job duties, working conditions, places of employment, educational preparation, labor market outlook, and salaries.

★5322★ *Plumber*
Vocational Biographies, Inc.
PO Box 31
Sauk Centre, MN 56378-0031
Ph: (612)352-6516 Fax: (612)352-5546
Fr: 800-255-0752

1990. Four-page pamphlet containing a personal narrative about a worker's job, work likes and dislikes, career path from high school to the present. Education and training, the rewards and frustrations, and the effects of the job on the rest of the worker's life. The data file portion of this pamphlet gives a concise occupational summary, including work descriptions, working conditions, places of employment, personal characteristics, education and training, job outlook, and salary range.

★5323★ "Plumber" in *Guide to Careers Without College* (pp. 82-85)
Franklin Watts, Inc.
387 Park Avenue, S.
New York, NY 10016
Ph: (212)686-7070

Kathleen S. Abrams. 1988. Discusses careers that do not require a college degree in fields such as health care, sales and marketing, and the building trades. Describes the work, employment opportunities, and training.

★5324★ "Plumber" in *Jobs Rated Almanac*
World Almanac
1 International Blvd., Ste. 444
Mahwah, NJ 07495
Ph: (201)529-6900 Fax: (201)529-6901

Les Krantz. Second edition, 1992. Ranks 250 jobs by environment, salary, outlooks, physical demands, stress, security, travel opportunities, and extra perks. Includes jobs the editor feels are the most common, most interesting, and the most rapidly growing.

★5325★ "Plumber and Pipe Fitter" in *Career Information Center* (Vol.4)
Simon and Schuster
200 Old Tappan Rd.
Old Tappan, NJ 07675
Fax: 800-445-6991 Fr: 800-223-2348

Richard Lidz and Dale Anderson, editorial directors. Fifth edition, 1993. For 600 occupations, describes job duties, entry-level requirements, education and training needed, advancement possibilities, employment outlook, earnings and benefits. The set is divided into 12 volumes. Each volume includes jobs related under a broad career field. Volume 13 is the index.

★5326★ "Plumber and Pipefitter" in *VGM's Careers Encyclopedia* (pp. 357-359)
National Textbook Co. (NTC)
VGM Career Books
4255 W. Touhy Ave.
Lincolnwood, IL 60646-1975
Ph: (708)679-5500 Fax: (708)679-2494
Fr: 800-323-4900

Third edition, 1991. Contains two- to five-page descriptions of 200 managerial, professional, technical, trade, and service occupations. Each profile includes job duties, places of employment, qualifications, educational preparation, training, employment potential, advancement, income, and additional sources of information.

★5327★ "Plumber" in *The Desk Guide to Training and Work Advisement* (p. 83)
Charles C. Thomas, Publisher
2600 S. 1st St.
Springfield, IL 62794-9265
Ph: (217)789-8980 Fax: (217)789-9130
Fr: 800-258-8980

Gail Baugher Kuenstler. 1988. Describes alternative methods of gaining entry into an occupation through different types of educational programs, internships and apprenticeships.

★5328★ *Plumbers*
Chronicle Guidance Publications, Inc.
66 Aurora St.
PO Box 1190
Moravia, NY 13118-1190
Ph: (315)497-0330 Fax: (315)497-3359
Fr: 800-622-7284

1994. This career brief describes the nature of the work, working conditions, hours and earnings, education and training, licensure, certification, unions, personal qualifications, social and psychological factors, employment outlook, entry methods, advancement, and related occupations.

★5329★ "Plumbers" in *Career Discovery Encyclopedia* (Vol.5, pp. 60-61)
J.G. Ferguson Publishing Co.
200 W. Madison St., Ste. 300
Chicago, IL 60606
Ph: (312)580-5480 Fax: (312)580-4948

E. Russell Primm, editor-in-chief. 1993. Contains two-page articles on 504 occupations. Each article describes job duties, earnings, and educational and training requirements.

★5330★ "Plumbers" in *Encyclopedia of Careers and Vocational Guidance* (Vol.4, pp. 134-146)
J.G. Ferguson Publishing Co.
200 W. Madison St., Ste. 300
Chicago, IL 60606
Ph: (312)580-5480 Fax: (312)580-4948

William E. Hopke, editor-in-chief. Ninth edition, 1993. Four-volume set that profiles 500 occupations and describes job trends in 74 industries. Includes career description, educational requirements, history of the job, methods of entry, advancement, employment outlook, earnings, working conditions, social and psychological factors, and sources of additional information.

★5331★ *Plumbers and Pipefitters*
Careers, Inc.
PO Box 135
Largo, FL 34649-0135
Ph: (813)584-7333

1994. Four-page brief offering the definition, history, duties, working conditions, personal qualifications, educational requirements, earnings, hours, employment outlook, advancement possibilities, and related occupations.

★5332★ "Plumbers and Pipefitters" in *American Almanac of Jobs and Salaries* (pp. 503)
Avon Books
1350 Avenue of the Americas
New York, NY 10019
Ph: (212)261-6800 Fr: 800-238-0658

John Wright, editor. Revised and updated, 1994-95. A comprehensive guide to the wages of hundreds of occupations in a wide variety of industries and organizations.

★5333★ "Plumbers and Pipefitters" in *Occu-Facts: Information on 580 Careers in Outline Form*
Careers, Inc.
PO Box 135
Largo, FL 34649-0135
Ph: (813)584-7333

Biennial, 1995-96 edition. Each one-page occupational profile describes duties, working conditions, physical surroundings and demands, aptitudes, temperament, educational requirements, employment outlook, earnings, and places of employment.

★5334★ "Plumbers and Pipefitters" in *Occupational Outlook Handbook*
U.S. Government Printing Office
Superintendent of Documents
Washington, DC 20402
Ph: (202)512-1800 Fax: (202)512-2250

Biennial; latest edition, 1994-95. Encyclopedia of careers describing more than 250 occupations and comprising about 85 percent of all jobs in the economy. Occupations that require lengthy education or training are given the most attention. For each occupation, the handbook describes job duties, working conditions, training, educational preparation, personal qualities, advancement possibilities, job outlook, earnings, and sources of additional information.

★5335★ "Plumbers and Pipefitters" in *Opportunities in Building Construction Trades* (pp. 41-45)
National Textbook Co. (NTC)
VGM Career Books
4255 W. Touhy Ave.
Lincolnwood, IL 60646-1975
Ph: (708)679-5500 Fax: (708)679-2494
Fr: 800-323-4900

Michael Sumichrast. 1989. Gives an overview of the construction industry and describes the jobs of various craftworkers. Covers different kinds of builders: home, custom; and describes management skills needed and industry trends affecting opportunities.

★5336★ "Plumbing" in *Career Connection II: A Guide to Technical Majors and Their Related Careers* (pp. 126-127)
Jist Works, Inc.
720 N. Park Ave.
Indianapolis, IN 46202-3431
Ph: (317)264-3720 Fax: (317)264-3709

Fred A. Rowe. 1994. Contains technical majors, such as automotive technology. Describes the major and the job. Lists high school and postsecondary school courses. Includes occupations related to the major, employment outlook, and starting salary.

★5337★ "Sprinkler Fitter" in *Hard Hatted Women: Stories of Struggle and Success in the Trades* (pp. 143-149)
Seal Press
3131 Western Ave., Ste. 410
Seattle, WA 98121
Ph: (206)283-7844 Fax: (206)285-9410

Molly Martin, editor. 1988. Twenty-six women recount their experiences working in blue collar occupations. They describe how they got in, the work they do, their relationships in predominantly male occupations, and their training.

★5338★ "Sprinkler Fitting" in *Opportunities in Plumbing and Pipefitting Careers* (pp. 85-88)
National Textbook Co. (NTC)
VGM Career Books
4255 W. Touhy Ave.
Lincolnwood, IL 60646-1975
Ph: (708)679-5500 Fax: (708)679-2494
Fr: 800-323-4900

Patrick J. Galvin. 1989. Describes the work, jobs, educational preparation, training, apprenticeships, a typical working day, salaries, future trends, and related fields.

★5339★ *Video Career Library - Construction*
Careers, Inc.
PO Box 135
Largo, FL 34649-0135
Ph: (813)584-7333

Videocassette. 1990. 36 mins. Part of the Video Career Library covering 165 occupations. Shows actual workers on the job. Includes millwrights, brickmasons, carpenters, drywall installers, electricians, painters, plumbers and pipefitters, carpenter and soft tile installers, insulation workers, paving equipment operators, and structural metal workers.

★5340★ *Your Future in the Plumbing Heating Cooling Industry*
National Association of Plumbing, Heating, and Cooling Contractors
P.O. Box 6808
180 S. Washington St.
Washington, DC 20046
Ph: (202)331-7675

1988. This eight-panel brochure describes the work, opportunities, working conditions, and entry into the field.

Associations

★5341★ Associated Builders and Contractors (ABC)
1300 N. 17th St.
Rossyln, VA 22209
Ph: (703)812-2000

Members: Construction contractors, subcontractors, suppliers, and associates. **Purpose:** Aim is to foster and perpetuate the principles of rewarding construction workers and management on the basis of merit. Sponsors management education programs and craft training; also sponsors apprenticeship and skill training programs. Disseminates technological and labor relations information. Maintains placement service. Compiles statistics. **Publications:** *ABC Today*, semimonthly. • *National Membership Directory and Users Guide*, annual.

★5342★ Mechanical Contractors Association of America (MCAA)
1385 Piccard Dr.
Rockville, MD 20850-4329
Ph: (301)869-5800 Fax: (301)990-9690

Members: Contractors who furnish, install, and service piping systems and related equipment for heating, cooling, refrigeration, ventilating, and air conditioning systems. **Purpose:** Works to standardize materials and methods used in the industry. Conducts business overhead, labor wage, and statistical surveys. Maintains dialogue with key officials in building trade unions. Promotes apprenticeship training programs. Conducts seminars on contracts, labor estimating, job cost control, project management, marketing, collective bargaining, contractor insurance, and other management topics. Promotes methods to conserve energy in new and existing buildings. Sponsors Industrial Relations Council for the Plumbing and Pipe Fitting Industry. **Publications:** *Reporter*, monthly.

★5343★ National Association of Plumbing-Heating-Cooling Contractors (NAPHCC)
180 S. Washington St.
PO Box 6808
Falls Church, VA 22040
Ph: (703)237-8100 Fax: (703)237-7442
Fr: 800-533-7694

Members: Federation of state and local associations of plumbing, heating, and cooling contractors. **Purpose:** Seeks to advance sanitation, encourage sanitary laws, and generally improve the plumbing, heating, ventilating, and air conditioning industries. Conducts apprenticeship training programs, workshops, and seminars; cooperates with Plumbing-Heating-Cooling Information Bureau. Maintains speakers' bureau and political action committee. Conducts educational and research programs. **Publications:** *Connection*, monthly. • *Leadership Directory*, annual. • *News*, monthly.

★5344★ National Fire Sprinkler Association (NFSA)
Robin Hill Corporate Park
Rte. 22, Box 1000
Patterson, NY 12563
Ph: (914)878-4200 Fax: (914)878-4215

Members: Manufacturers, suppliers, contractors, and installers of fire sprinklers and related products and services. **Purpose:** Conducts Labor negotiations for the industry with 19 Local unions. Conducts education program to promote the concept of automatic fire sprinkler protection. Acts as Liaison for the industry and participates in fire test research with insurance organizations and fire services. Acts as consultant for building codes; has developed model fire protection coders. Conducts research; compiles statistics. Maintains speakers' bureau and hall of fame. **Publications:** *Codewatch*, quarterly. • *Grass Roots*, monthly. • *Labor Line*, bimonthly. • *Membership List*, periodic. • *Regional Report*, monthly. • *Sprinkler Quarterly*, quarterly. • *Sprinkler Technotes*, bimonthly.

Standards/Certification Agencies

★5345★ Mechanical Contractors Association of America (MCAA)
1385 Piccard Dr.
Rockville, MD 20832
Ph: (301)869-5800 Fax: (301)990-9690

Works to standardize materials and methods used in the industry.

★5346★ National Fire Sprinkler Association (NFSA)
Robin Hill Corporate Park
Rte. 22, Box 1000
Patterson, NY 12563
Ph: (914)878-4200 Fax: (914)878-4215

Acts as consultant for building codes; has developed model fire protection coders.

Test Guides

★5347★ *Career Examination Series: Foreman Plumber*
National Learning Corp.
212 Michael Dr.
Syosset, NY 11791
Ph: (516)921-8888 Fax: (516)921-8743
Fr: 800-645-6337

Jack Rudman. All examination guides in this series contain questions with answers.

★5348★ *Career Examination Series: Foreman Steamfitter*
National Learning Corp.
212 Michael Dr.
Syosset, NY 11791
Ph: (516)921-8888 Fax: (516)921-8743
Fr: 800-645-6337

Jack Rudman. 1989. All examination guides in this series contain questions with answers.

★5349★ ***Career Examination Series: Gang Foreman (Structures-Group E) (Plumbing)***
National Learning Corp.
212 Michael Dr.
Syosset, NY 11791
Ph: (516)921-8888 Fax: (516)921-8743
Fr: 800-645-6337

Jack Rudman. 1989. All examination guides in this series contain questions with answers.

★5350★ ***Career Examination Series: Maintenance Plumber***
National Learning Corp.
212 Michael Dr.
Syosset, NY 11791
Ph: (516)921-8888 Fax: (516)921-8743
Fr: 800-645-6337

Jack Rudman. 1989. All examination guides in this series contain questions with answers.

★5351★ ***Career Examination Series: Maintenance Plumber Foreman***
National Learning Corp.
212 Michael Dr.
Syosset, NY 11791
Ph: (516)921-8888 Fax: (516)921-8743
Fr: 800-645-6337

Jack Rudman. 1989. All examination guides in this series contain questions with answers.

★5352★ ***Career Examination Series: Master Plumber***
National Learning Corp.
212 Michael Dr.
Syosset, NY 11791
Ph: (516)921-8888 Fax: (516)921-8743
Fr: 800-645-6337

Jack Rudman. All examination guides in this series contain questions with answers.

★5353★ ***Career Examination Series: Pipefitter***
National Learning Corp.
212 Michael Dr.
Syosset, NY 11791
Ph: (516)921-8888 Fax: (516)921-8743
Fr: 800-645-6337

Jack Rudman. All examination guides in this series contain questions with answers.

★5354★ ***Career Examination Series: Plumber***
National Learning Corp.
212 Michael Dr.
Syosset, NY 11791
Ph: (516)921-8888 Fax: (516)921-8743
Fr: 800-645-6337

Jack Rudman. Guides are also available for the plumber's helper, plumbing engineer, plumbing inspector, and plumbing supervisor. All examination guides in this series contain questions with answers.

★5355★ ***Maintenance Worker/ Mechanical Maintainer***
Prentice Hall Press
Simon & Schuster Inc.
200 Old Tappan Rd.
Old Tappan, NJ 07675
Ph: 800-223-2348

Hy Hammer. Fourth edition, 1984. Provides information for applicants interested in the following civil service positions: carpenter, mason, plumber, electrician, painter, machinist. Includes eight sample tests.

★5356★ ***Plumber—Steam Fitter***
Prentice Hall Press
Simon & Schuster Inc.
200 Old Tappan Rd.
Old Tappan, NJ 07675
Ph: 800-223-2348

Frank Sparandero. Fourth edition, 1987. Includes 11 practice exams, plus information on plumbing terms, regulations, and mathematical formulas.

★5357★ ***Plumbing***
National Learning Corp.
212 Michael Dr.
Syosset, NY 11791
Ph: (516)921-8888 Fax: (516)921-8743
Fr: 800-645-6337

Jack Rudman. Part of Occupational Competency Examination Series (OCE).

★5358★ ***Plumbing***
National Learning Corp.
212 Michael Dr.
Syosset, NY 11791
Ph: (516)921-8888 Fax: (516)921-8743
Fr: 800-645-6337

Jack Rudman. Part of the Test Your Knowledge Series. Contains multiple choice questions with answers.

Educational Directories and Programs

★5359★ ***Plumbing Engineer—Product Directory Issue***
TMB Publishing Inc.
1884 Techny Ct.
Northbrook, IL 60062
Ph: (708)564-1127 Fax: (708)564-1264
Arthur Klein, Contact

Annual, January. Covers over 400 plumbing products from approximately 250 manufacturers. Entries include: Company name, phone, fax; name of engineering contact with the firm.

★5360★ ***PM Directory & Reference Issue***
Business News Publishing Co.
755 W. Big Beaver Rd., 10th Fl.
Troy, MI 48084
Ph: (810)362-3700 Fax: (313)362-0317
Fr: 800-837-7370
Tim Fausch, Contact

Annual, December. Covers manufacturers, wholesalers, exporters, associations, products, consultants, and manufacturers' representatives in the industries of plumbing, piping, and hydronic heating. Entries include: Contact name, company, address, phone, fax, and product descriptions. Arrangement: Alphabetical.

Awards, Scholarships, Grants, and Fellowships

★5361★ **Industry Award**
Institute of Nuclear Materials Management
60 Revere Dr., Ste. 500
Northbrook, IL 60062
Ph: (708)480-9080 Fax: (708)480-9282

No further information was provided for this edition.

Basic Reference Guides and Handbooks

★5362★ ***Basic Plumbing Skills***
American Association for Vocational Instructional Materials
745 Goines School Rd.
Athens, GA 30605
Ph: (404)543-7557 Fax: (404)613-6779

William H. Annis. 1990.

★5363★ ***Blueprint Reading for Plumbers: Residential & Commercial***
Delmar Publishers, Inc.
PO Box 15015
2 Computer Dr., W.
Albany, NY 12212
Ph: (518)459-1150 Fax: (518)453-6472

Bartholomew D'Arcangelo. Fifth revised edition, 1989. Part of Blueprint Reading Series.

★5364★ ***Do-It-Yourself Plumbing***
Borgo Press
PO Box 2845
San Bernardino, CA 92406-2845
Ph: (714)884-5813

Max Alth. 1989.

★5365★ ***Math on the Job: Plumber***
National Center for Research in Vocational Education
Ohio State University
1900 Kenry Rd.
Columbus, OH 43210
Ph: (614)292-4353

1985.

★5366★ ***Plumbers Handbook***
Macmillan Publishing Co., Inc.
866 3rd Ave.
New York, NY 10022
Ph: (212)702-2000

Joseph Almond. Eighth edition, 1991.

★5367★ ***Plumbers & Pipefitters Library***
Macmillan Publishing Company, Inc.
866 3rd Ave.
New York, NY 10022
Ph: (212)702-2000

Charles N. McConnell. 1990.

★5368★ *The Plumber's Toolbox Manual*
Prentice Hall
Rte. 9W
Englewood Cliffs, NJ 07632
Ph: (201)592-2000

Louis J. Mahiau. 1989. Part of On-the-Job Reference Series.

★5369★ *The Plumber's Toolbox Manual*
Arco Pub.
201 W. 103rd St.
Indianapolis, IN 46290
Ph: 800-428-5331 Fax: 800-835-3202

Louis J. Mahieu. 1989.

★5370★ *Plumbing*
Time-Life Books, Inc.
777 Duke St.
Alexandria, VA 22314
Ph: (703)838-7000

Time-Life Books Editors. Revised edition, 1989. Part of Home Repair & Improvement Series.

★5371★ *The Plumbing Apprentice Handbook*
McGraw-Hill
1221 Avenue of the Americas
New York, NY 10020
Ph: (212)512-3493 Fax: (212)512-3050

1994.

★5372★ *Residential Plumbing*
Taunton Press, Inc.
63 S. Main St.
Box 5506
Newtown, CT 06470-9989
Ph: (203)426-8171 Fax: (203)426-3434
Fr: 800-888-8286

Peter Hemp. 1992.

★5373★ *Wholesaler—"Wholesaling 100" Issue*
TMB Publishing Inc.
1838 Techny Ct.
Northbrook, IL 60062
Ph: (708)564-1127 Fax: (708)564-1264
John A. Schweizer

Annual, July. Publication includes: List of 100 leading wholesalers of plumbing, heating, air conditioning, refrigeration equipment, and supplies such as industrial pipe, valves and fittings. Entries include: Co. name, address, phone, fax, names and titles of key personnel, number of employees, business breakdown (percentage). Arrangement: Ranked by sales.

PERIODICALS

★5374★ *ABC Today*
Associated Builders and Contractors, Inc. (ABC)
N. 17th St.
Rosslyn, VA 22209
Ph: (703)637-8800 Fax: (703)812-8203
Pamela E. Hunter

Semimonthly. Designed to keep readers alerted to important changes within ABC and the construction industry. Reports on legislative issues, construction trends, conferences and meetings, and ABC services. Recurring features include news of members and columns titled Industry Briefs, Safety Notebook, Computer Corner, Bottom Line, and Chapter News.

★5375★ *ABC Today*
Associated Builders and Contractors, Inc. (ABC)
1300 N. 17th St., 8th Floor
Arlington, VA 22209-3803
Ph: (703)812-2000 Fax: (703)812-8203
Pamela E. Hunter

Semiweekly. Magazine for open shop contractors and subcontractors. Includes articles on national and regional construction news, construction management, project case histories, new products, building design, and legislative and regulatory updates.

★5376★ *ABC Today*
Associated Builders and Contractors (ABC)
1300 N. 17th St.
Rosslyn, VA 22209
Ph: (703)812-2000

Semimonthly. News magazine for merit shop contractors.

★5377★ *American Architectural Manufacturers Association—Quarterly Review*
American Architectural Manufacturers Association
1540 E. Dundee Rd., Ste. 310
Palatine, IL 60067-8321
Ph: (708)202-1350 Fax: (708)202-1480
Tony Coorlim

Annual. Contains industry news on architectural products. Covers prime and combination storm windows, sliding glass and combination storm doors, window and curtainwalls, store fronts and entrances, siding, soffits, fascia, gutters, downspouts, skylights, space enclosures, and mobile home components. Recurring features include news of research, notices of publications available, and announcements by the Association.

★5378★ *American Institute of Constructors—Newsletter*
American Institute of Constructors
9887 Gandy Blvd. N., Ste. 104
St. Petersburg, FL 33702
Ph: (813)578-1962 Fax: (813)578-9982
Cheryl P. Harris

Bimonthly. Concerned with construction practice, design, administration, and teaching. Carries news of members, listings of job opportunities, local chapter reports, notices of new publications, and conferences on construction topics.

★5379★ *ASA News*
American Supply Association (ASA)
222 Merchandise Mart Plaza, Ste. 1360
Chicago, IL 60654
Ph: (312)464-0090 Fax: (312)464-0091
Inge Calderon

Bimonthly. Covers Association events and news from member companies in the plumbing industry, regional and national industry events, and items of interest.

★5380★ *Blue Reports, Inc.*
Construction News Service
7325 Steel Mill Dr.
Springfield, VA 22050
Ph: (703)644-5884 Fax: (703)644-1929
Calvin S. Oren

Daily. Reports on public and private construction projects in the Washington, DC, Virginia, and Maryland areas. Provides owner's and architect's names, plan status, date bids due, prospective bidders, low bids received, and specification details.

★5381★ *Building Concerns*
National Association of Minority Contractors (NAMC)
1333 F St. NW, Ste. 500
Washington, DC 20004
Ph: (202)347-8259 Fax: (202)628-1876
Agreta Hester

Quarterly. Concentrates on national and regional news regarding minority construction contractors. Contains articles on issues generally affecting the industry—especially issues affecting minorities—including topics such as legislative and regulatory activity and reports on major corporation developments. Recurring features include reports of meetings, news of educational opportunities, a calendar of events, and news of NAMC chapters, affiliates, and members.

★5382★ *Building Industry Technology: An Abstract Newsletter*
National Technical Information Service (NTIS)
5285 Port Royal Rd.
Springfield, VA 22161
Ph: (703)487-4630

Biweekly. Consists of abstracts of reports on architectural and environmental design, building standards, construction materials and equipment, and structural analyses. Recurring features include a form for ordering reports from NTIS.

★5383★ *Capital Comments*
National Lumber & Building Material Dealers Association
40 Ivy St. SE
Washington, DC 20003
Ph: (202)547-2230 Fax: (202)547-7640
Matt Geitner

Semimonthly. Reports on news of legislation pertaining to lumber, other building materials, and housing. Discusses such issues as lumber subsidies, interest rates on homes, health and safety, and jobs.

★5384★ *Codewatch*
National Fire Sprinkler Association (NFSA)
Robin Hill Corporate Park
Rte. 22, Box 1000
Patterson, NY 12563
Ph: (914)878-4200 Fax: (914)878-4215

Quarterly. Lists changes in model codes and state and local laws and regulations, and amendments to building codes and local ordinances.

★5385★ *Connection*
National Association of Plumbing-Heating-Cooling Contractors (NAPHCC)
180 S. Washington St.
PO Box 6808
Falls Church, VA 22040
Ph: (703)237-8100 Fax: (703)237-7442
Fr: 800-533-7694
Monthly.

★5386★ *ConnStruction*
McHugh Design, Advertising & Publishing
62 Lasalle Rd., Ste. 211
West Hartford, CT 06107
Ph: (203)523-7518 Fax: (203)231-8808
Tracy E. McHugh
Quarterly. Magazine for construction industry.

★5387★ *CONSTRUCTION*
HES, Inc.
26 Long Hill Rd.
PO Box 362
Guilford, CT 06437-0362
Ph: (203)453-3717 Fax: (203)453-4390
Jack C. Lewis
Semiweekly. Journal for the construction industry.

★5388★ *Construction News*
10835 Financial Centre Pkwy., Ste. 133
Little Rock, AR 72211-3555
Ph: (501)376-1931 Fax: (501)375-5831
Robert Alvey
Weekly. Construction industry magazine.

★5389★ *Construction Newsletter*
National Safety Council
1121 Spring Lake Dr.
Itasca, IL 60143-3201
Ph: (708)775-2282 Fax: (708)775-2285
Diane A. Ghazarian
Bimonthly. Focuses on industrial and occupational safety in the construction industry. Carries items on such topics as safe work practices and products; accident prevention; and successful industrial safety programs and policies.

★5390★ *Daily Construction Reporter*
7670 Opprtunity Rd.
San Diego, CA 92111-1112
Ph: (619)492-1402 Fax: (619)565-4182
Bernado Romanowsky
Daily. Construction newspaper covering jobs that are out for bid, bid results, building permits, and other information.

★5391★ *Distributor*
Technical Reporting Co./Palmer Publishing Co.
651 W. Washington St., Ste. 300
Chicago, IL 60606
Ph: (312)993-0929 Fax: (312)993-0960
Phil Palmer
Bimonthly. Magazine focusing on air conditioning, heating, ventilation, refrigeration and appliance parts.

★5392★ *International Construction*
Maclean Hunter Publishing Co.
29 N. Wacker Drive
Chicago, IL 60606
Ph: (312)726-2802 Fax: (312)726-2574
Alan Peterson
Monthly. Trade magazine.

★5393★ *Mechanical Contractors Association of America—Reporter*
Mechanical Contractors Association of America, Inc.
1385 Piccard Dr.
Rockville, MD 20850
Ph: (301)869-5800 Fax: (301)990-9690
Victoria L. Tanner
Monthly. Covers labor issues and government affairs as they affect mechanical contractors in the plumbing and pipefitting industry. Recurring features include reports on the activities of the Association and notices of pertinent seminars and meetings.

★5394★ *Nation's Building News*
National Association of Home Builders of the U.S. (NAHB)
1201 15th St. NW
Washington, DC 20005
Ph: (202)822-0200 Fax: (202)822-0559
Semimonthly. Provides the latest information concerning the housing industry, including finance, legislation, new technologies, and membership news.

★5395★ *Nation's Building News*
1201 15th St. NW
Washington, DC 20005-2800
Ph: (202)822-0525 Fax: (202)861-2131
Tim Ahern
Semiweekly. Trade magazine (tabloid) covering home building and all related industries.

★5396★ *Official Magazine*
International Assn. of Plumbing & Mechanical Officials
20001 Walnut Dr. S.
Walnut, CA 91789-2825
Ph: (909)595-8449 Fax: (909)594-3690
Arthur J. Lettenmaier
Bimonthly. Trade publication containing articles of interest to anyone involved in the plumbing industry.

★5397★ *Palmetto Piper*
Mechanical Contractor's Assn. of South Carolina
1504 Morninghill Drive
PO Box 384
Columbia, SC 29202
Ph: (803)772-7834 Fax: (803)731-0390
Monthly. Plumbing, heating, air conditioning, and electrical journal.

★5398★ *Plumb*
Georgia Association of Plumbing, Heating and Cooling Contractors
3338 Gwinnett Plantation Way
Duluth, GA 30136-4647
Dianne Olson
Plumbing industry magazine.

★5399★ *Plumbing Heating Piping*
Delta Communications Inc.
455 N. Cityfront Plaza
Chicago, IL 60611
Ph: (312)222-2000 Fax: (312)222-2026
Cari T. Laird
Monthly. Magazine on the plumbing, piping, and hydronics industries.

★5400★ *Professional Builder & Remodeler*
Cahners Publishing Co.
1350 E. Touhy Ave.
PO Box 5080
Des Plaines, IL 60018-5080
Ph: (708)635-8800 Fax: (708)635-9950
Ed Fitch
Monthly.

★5401★ *Reeves Journal: Plumbing Heating Cooling*
Business News Publishing Co.
23187 La Cadena Dr., Ste. 101
PO Box 30700
Laguna Hills, CA 92654
Ph: (714)830-0881 Fax: (714)859-7845
Dick Peck
Monthly. Regional plumbing, heating, and cooling magazine.

★5402★ *Reporter*
Mechanical Contractors Association of America (MCAA)
1385 Piccard Dr.
Rockville, MD 20850-4329
Ph: (301)869-5800 Fax: (301)990-9690
Monthly.

★5403★ *Supply House Times*
Cahners Publishing Co.
1350 E. Touhy Ave.
PO Box 5080
Des Plaines, IL 60017-5080
Ph: (708)635-8800 Fax: (708)390-2618
Bill Everham
Monthly. Trade magazine for wholesalers in plumbing, heating, cooling, piping, and water systems. Areas of major emphasis include: warehousing, materials handling, inventory control, accounting, data processing, merchandising, salesmanship and general management.

★5404★ *U.A. Journal*
United Assn. of Journeymen & Apprentices of the Plumbing & Pipefitting Industry of the U.S. & Canada
901 Massachusetts Ave. NW
Washington, DC 20001
Ph: (202)628-5823
Marion A. Lee
Monthly. Labor magazine.

MEETINGS AND CONVENTIONS

★5405★ Midwest Specialty Exposition
Kansas Plumbing, Heating, and Cooling Contractors Association
320 Laura St.
Wichita, KS 67211
Ph: (316)262-8860 Fax: (316)262-2782
Annual.

Other Sources of Information

★5406★ *Career Connections Video Series: Plumber and Pipefitter*
Cambridge Career Products
PO Box 2153, Dept. CC15
Charleston, WV 25328-2153
Fr: 800-468-4227

1993. Contains interviews with workers in specific fields and includes on-the-job footage.

★5407★ *Careers in Plumbing, Heating, and Cooling*
Rosen Publishing Group
29 E. 21st St.
New York, NY 10010
Ph: 800-237-9932 Fax: (212)777-0277

Elizabeth Stewart Lytle. 1995. Describes some of the skills needed to be qualified to work in the fields of plumbing, heating, cooling, and ventilation.

★5408★ "Plumber" in *Career Selector 2001*
Barron's Educational Series, Inc.
250 Wireless Blvd.
Hauppauge, NY 11788
Ph: (516)434-3311 Fax: (516)434-3723
Fr: 800-645-3476

James C. Gonyea. 1993.

Roofers

Roofers repair and install roofs of tar or asphalt and gravel, rubber, thermoplastic, and metal; and shingles made of slate, asphalt, fiberglass, wood, or tile. Repair and reroofing provide many work opportunities for these workers. Roofers also may waterproof and dampproof masonry and concrete walls and floors. Most roofers work for roofing contractors. About 30 percent of all roofers are self-employed and specialize in residential work.

Salaries

Median weekly earnings for roofers are as follows:

Lowest 10 percent	$230/week or less
Median	$295-$595/week
Top 10 percent	$830/week or more

Employment Outlook

Growth rate until the year 2005: Average.

Roofers

Career Guides

★5409★ *Career Insights*
RMI Media Productions, Inc.
1365 N. Winchester
Olathe, KS 66061
Ph: (913)768-1696 Fax: 800-755-6910
Fr: 800-745-5480

Videocassette series. 1987. This videotape series describes 50 occupations, including skill requirements and interviews with people employed in these fields. Occupations include: flight service, air transportation/ground services, data processing, carpentry, clerk in banking/insurance/business, cosmetic personal grooming, firefighting, forestry, insulation/roofing, mechanics, material handling, photographic processing, pipefitting and plumbing, printing, secretarial services, tool and die operations.

★5410★ *Career Success Series*
Cambridge Educational
PO Box 2153
Charleston, WV 25328-2153
Ph: (304)744-9323 Fax: (304)744-9351
Fr: 800-468-4227

Videocassette. 1986. 15 mins. A series, available separately, outlining various career choices for students. Occupations include: accounting, flight service, air transportation/ground/flight service, data processing, carpentry, clerk in banking/insurance, commodity sales, cosmetic personal grooming, fire fighting, forestry services, home economics, insulation/roofing, material handling, mechanics, photographic processing, pipefitting and plumbing, police science, printing, carpentry, medical laboratory technicians, secretarial services, and utilities equipment operator.

★5411★ *Construction Cluster*
Center for Humanities, Inc.
Communications Park
Box 1000
Mount Kisco, NY 10549
Ph: (914)666-4100 Fax: (914)666-5319
Fr: 800-431-1242

Videocassette. 1984. 15 mins. Construction workers describe what it's like to work at their jobs, and show the special equipment they use in their field.

★5412★ *Insulating & Roofing Occupations*
Morris Video
2730 Monterey St., No. 105
Monterey Business Park
Torrance, CA 90503
Ph: (310)533-4800 Fr: 800-843-3606

Videocassette. 1987. 15 mins. A look at the various careers that involve the reduction of the flow of cold, heat or sound.

★5413★ *Roofer*
Careers, Inc.
PO Box 135
Largo, FL 34649-0135
Ph: (813)584-7333

1992. Two-page occupational summary card describing duties, working conditions, personal qualifications, training, earnings and hours, employment outlook, places of employment, related careers and where to write for more information.

★5414★ "Roofer" in *Career Information Center* (Vol.4)
Simon and Schuster
200 Old Tappan Rd.
Old Tappan, NJ 07675
Fax: 800-445-6991 Fr: 800-223-2348

Richard Lidz and Dale Anderson, editorial directors. Fifth edition, 1993. For 600 occupations, describes job duties, entry-level requirements, education and training needed, advancement possibilities, employment outlook, earnings and benefits. The set is divided into 12 volumes. Each volume includes jobs related under a broad career field. Volume 13 is the index.

★5415★ "Roofer" in *Jobs Rated Almanac*
World Almanac
1 International Blvd., Ste. 444
Mahwah, NJ 07495
Ph: (201)529-6900 Fax: (201)529-6901

Les Krantz. Second edition, 1992. Ranks 250 jobs by environment, salary, outlooks, physical demands, stress, security, travel opportunities, and extra perks. Includes jobs the editor feels are the most common, most interesting, and the most rapidly growing.

★5416★ "Roofer" in *Occu-Facts: Information on 580 Careers in Outline Form*
Careers, Inc.
PO Box 135
Largo, FL 34649-0135
Ph: (813)584-7333

Biennial, 1995-96 edition. Each one-page occupational profile describes duties, working conditions, physical surroundings and demands, aptitudes, temperament, educational requirements, employment outlook, earnings, and places of employment.

★5417★ *Roofers*
Chronicle Guidance Publications, Inc.
66 Aurora St.
PO Box 1190
Moravia, NY 13118-1190
Ph: (315)497-0330 Fax: (315)497-3359
Fr: 800-622-7284

1994. This career brief describes the nature of the work, working conditions, hours and earnings, education and training, licensure, certification, unions, personal qualifications, social and psychological factors, employment outlook, entry methods, advancement, and related occupations.

★5418★ "Roofers" in *Career Discovery Encyclopedia* (Vol.5, pp. 162-163)
J.G. Ferguson Publishing Co.
200 W. Madison St., Ste. 300
Chicago, IL 60606
Ph: (312)580-5480 Fax: (312)580-4948

E. Russell Primm, editor-in-chief. 1993. Contains two-page articles on 504 occupations. Each article describes job duties, earnings, and educational and training requirements.

★5419★ "Roofers" in *Encyclopedia of Careers and Vocational Guidance* (Vol.4, pp. 312-314)
J.G. Ferguson Publishing Co.
200 W. Madison St., Ste. 300
Chicago, IL 60606
Ph: (312)580-5480 Fax: (312)580-4948

William E. Hopke, editor-in-chief. Ninth edition, 1993. Four-volume set that profiles 500 occupations and describes job trends in 74 industries. Includes career description, educational requirements, history of the job, methods of entry, advancement, employment outlook, earnings, working conditions, social

and psychological factors, and sources of additional information.

★5420★ "Roofers" in *Occupational Outlook Handbook*
U.S. Government Printing Office
Superintendent of Documents
Washington, DC 20402
Ph: (202)512-1800 Fax: (202)512-2250

Biennial; latest edition, 1994-95. Encyclopedia of careers describing more than 250 occupations and comprising about 85 percent of all jobs in the economy. Occupations that require lengthy education or training are given the most attention. For each occupation, the handbook describes job duties, working conditions, training, educational preparation, personal qualities, advancement possibilities, job outlook, earnings, and sources of additional information.

★5421★ "Roofers" in *Opportunities in Building Construction Trades* (pp. 45-47)
National Textbook Co. (NTC)
VGM Career Books
4255 W. Touhy Ave.
Lincolnwood, IL 60646-1975
Ph: (708)679-5500 Fax: (708)679-2494
Fr: 800-323-4900

Michael Sumichrast. 1989. Gives an overview of the construction industry and describes the jobs of various craftworkers. Covers different kinds of builders: home, custom; and describes management skills needed and industry trends affecting opportunities.

★5422★ *Roofer's Pitch*
International Film Bureau, Inc. (IFB)
332 S. Michigan Ave.
Chicago, IL 60604-4382
Ph: (312)427-4545

Videocassette. 198?. 21 mins. This program shows what happens to a roofer when he is not careful on the job and how the crew corrects the problem.

★5423★ *Roofing and Waterproofing: A Trade Worth Learning Through Apprenticeship*
United Union of Roofers, Waterproofers and Allied Workers
1125 17th St., N.W.
Washington, DC 20036
Ph: (202)638-3228

This eight-panel brochure describes the apprentice roofer program including earnings, the work, and qualifications needed.

Associations

★5424★ National Roofing Contractors Association (NRCA)
10255 W. Higgins Rd., Ste. 600
Rosemont, IL 60018-5607
Ph: (708)299-9070 Fax: (708)299-1183

Members: Roofing, roof deck, and waterproofing contractors and industry-related associate members. **Purpose:** Assists members to successfully satisfy their customers through technical support, testing and research, education, marketing, government relations, and consultation. **Publications:** *Professional Roofing*, monthly. • *Roofing Manual.* • *Roofing Materials Guide.*

★5425★ United Union of Roofers, Waterproofers and Allied Workers (UURWAW)
1125 17th St. NW
Washington, DC 20036
Ph: (202)638-3228 Fax: (202)737-3621

Members: AFL-CIO.

Test Guides

★5426★ *Career Examination Series: Foreman Roofer*
National Learning Corp.
212 Michael Dr.
Syosset, NY 11791
Ph: (516)921-8888 Fax: (516)921-8743
Fr: 800-645-6337

Jack Rudman. All examination guides in this series contain questions with answers.

★5427★ *Career Examination Series: Roofer*
National Learning Corp.
212 Michael Dr.
Syosset, NY 11791
Ph: (516)921-8888 Fax: (516)921-8743
Fr: 800-645-6337

Jack Rudman. All examination guides in this series contain questions with answers.

Educational Directories and Programs

★5428★ *International Directory of Building Research, Information and Development Organizations*
29 W. 35th St.
New York, NY 10001
Ph: (212)244-3336

Over 600 universities, institutions, government agencies, and other construction-related research institutions. Entries include: Institution name, address, phone, telex, name and title of contact, number of staff, source of finance, area of interest, publications.

★5429★ *NRCA Directory*
National Roofing Contractors Association (NRCA)
O'Hare International Center
10255 W. Higgins Rd., Ste. 600
Rosemont, IL 60018-5607
Ph: (708)299-9070 Fax: (708)299-1183

Annual.

Awards, Scholarships, Grants, and Fellowships

★5430★ National Roofing Foundation Scholarship Award
National Roofing Foundation
O'Hare International Center
10255 W. Higgins, Ste. 600
Rosemont, IL 60018
Ph: (708)299-9070 Fax: (708)299-1183

Purpose: To develop qualified professional roofing contractors or related professionals for the benefit of the roofing industry. Qualifications: Applicants must be United States citizens and full-time students (high school senior, undergraduate, or graduate) undertaking architecture, engineering, or another curriculum related to the roofing industry. Selection criteria: Academic performance, faculty recommendation, extracurricular activities, employment experience, and a demonstrated interest in the construction industry. Funds available: $2,000. Application details: Candidates must submit an official application, which may be obtained by sending a self-addressed, stamped envelope. Deadline: January 15.

Basic Reference Guides and Handbooks

★5431★ *Intelligent Buildings Institute—Directory of Products and Services*
Intelligent Buildings Institute (IBI)
2101 L St., NW, Ste. 300
Washington, DC 20037
Ph: (202)457-1988 Fax: (202)457-8468

S. Hunt, Associate Executive Director, editor. Annual, September. Member consultants, associations, research organizations, and other suppliers of products and services to the construction and building industry. Entries include: Company name, address, phone. Arrangement: Alphabetical. Indexes: Product/service.

★5432★ *The NCRA Roofing & Waterproofing Manual*
National Roofing Contractors Association
O'Hare Intl. Center
10255 W. Higgins Rd., Ste. 600
Rosemont, IL 60018-5607
Ph: (708)299-9070

Third edition, 1989.

★5433★ *Roof Framing*
Craftsman Book Company
PO Box 6500
6058 Corte del Cedro
Carlsbad, CA 92009
Ph: (619)438-7828 Fax: (619)438-0398

Marshal Gross. 1989.

★5434★ *Roof Framing*
American Association for Vocational Instructional Materials
745 Goines School Rd.
Athens, GA 30605
Ph: (404)543-7557 Fax: (404)613-6779

Charley G. Chadwick. 1991. Part of Basic Carpentry Skills Series.

★5435★ *Roofing: Design Criteria, Options, Selection*
R. S. Means Company, Inc.
100 Construction Plaza
Kingston, MA 02364
Ph: (617)585-7880 Fax: (617)585-7466

Robert D. Herbert, III. 1989.

★5436★ *Roofing Manual*
National Roofing Contractors Association (NRCA)
O'Hare Intl. Center
10255 W. Higgins Rd., Ste. 600
Rosemont, IL 60018-5607
Ph: (708)299-9070 Fax: (708)299-1183

★5437★ *Roofing the Right Way*
TAB/McGraw-Hill, Inc.
PO Box 182607
Columbus, OH 43218-2607
Fax: (614)759-3644 Fr: 800-822-8158

Steven Bolt. Second edition, 1990.

Periodicals

★5438★ *ABC Today*
Associated Builders and Contractors, Inc. (ABC)
N. 17th St.
Rosslyn, VA 22209
Ph: (703)637-8800 Fax: (703)812-8203
Pamela E. Hunter

Semimonthly. Designed to keep readers alerted to important changes within ABC and the construction industry. Reports on legislative issues, construction trends, conferences and meetings, and ABC services. Recurring features include news of members and columns titled Industry Briefs, Safety Notebook, Computer Corner, Bottom Line, and Chapter News.

★5439★ *ABC Today*
Associated Builders and Contractors, Inc. (ABC)
1300 N. 17th St., 8th Floor
Arlington, VA 22209-3803
Ph: (703)812-2000 Fax: (703)812-8203
Pamela E. Hunter

Semiweekly. Magazine for open shop contractors and subcontractors. Includes articles on national and regional construction news, construction management, project case histories, new products, building design, and legislative and regulatory updates.

★5440★ *American Architectural Manufacturers Association—Quarterly Review*
American Architectural Manufacturers Association
1540 E. Dundee Rd., Ste. 310
Palatine, IL 60067-8321
Ph: (708)202-1350 Fax: (708)202-1480
Tony Coorlim

Annual. Contains industry news on architectural products. Covers prime and combination storm windows, sliding glass and combination storm doors, window and curtainwalls, store fronts and entrances, siding, soffits, fascia, gutters, downspouts, skylights, space enclosures, and mobile home components. Recurring features include news of research, notices of publications available, and announcements by the Association.

★5441★ *American Institute of Constructors—Newsletter*
American Institute of Constructors
9887 Gandy Blvd. N., Ste. 104
St. Petersburg, FL 33702
Ph: (813)578-1962 Fax: (813)578-9982
Cheryl P. Harris

Bimonthly. Concerned with construction practice, design, administration, and teaching. Carries news of members, listings of job opportunities, local chapter reports, notices of new publications, and conferences on construction topics.

★5442★ *Asphalt Roofing Manufacturers Association—Newsletter*
Asphalt Roofing Manufacturers Association (ARMA)
6000 Executive Blvd., Ste. 201
Rockville, MD 20852-3803
Ph: (301)231-9050
Russell K. Snyder

Bimonthly. Reports news and information of interest to professionals in the asphalt roofing industry. Highlights Association activities and discusses developments in the industry, including occupational safety and health measures, changes in industry codes and standards, environmental issues, and legislative and regulatory actions.

★5443★ *Blue Reports, Inc.*
Construction News Service
7325 Steel Mill Dr.
Springfield, VA 22050
Ph: (703)644-5884 Fax: (703)644-1929
Calvin S. Oren

Daily. Reports on public and private construction projects in the Washington, DC, Virginia, and Maryland areas. Provides owner's and architect's names, plan status, date bids due, prospective bidders, low bids received, and specification details.

★5444★ *Builder*
Hanley-Wood, Inc.
1 Thomas Circle, Ste. 600
Washington, DC 20005
Ph: (202)452-0800
Mitchell Rouda

Monthly. Magazine covering housing, commercial, and industrial building.

★5445★ *Builder Architect*
Sunshine Media, Inc.
PO Box 37707
Phoenix, AZ 85069-7707
Ph: (602)433-7393 Fax: (602)433-2963
Marie Vere

Monthly. Home builders magazine.

★5446★ *Builder/Dealer*
Peterson Bros. Inc., Publishing
14 W. South St.
Corry, PA 16407-1894
Ph: (814)664-8624 Fax: (814)664-8506
Charles P. Mancino

Monthly. Trade magazine.

★5447★ *Builder Insider*
Divibest, Inc.
PO Box 191125
Dallas, TX 75219
Ph: (214)871-2913
Michael J. Anderson

Monthly. Magazine (tabloid) for builders, architects, and remodelers.

★5448★ *Builder Notes*
Brick Institute of America (BIA)
11490 Commerce Park Dr.
Reston, VA 22091
Ph: (703)620-0010 Fax: (703)620-3928

Bimonthly.

★5449★ *Building Business & Apartment Management*
Builders Association of Southeastern Michigan
30375 Northwestern Hwy.
Farmington Hills, MI 48334
Ph: (810)737-4477 Fax: (810)737-5741
Susan Adler

Monthly. Construction and apartment industry magazine.

★5450★ *Building Concerns*
National Association of Minority Contractors (NAMC)
1333 F St. NW, Ste. 500
Washington, DC 20004
Ph: (202)347-8259 Fax: (202)628-1876
Agreta Hester

Quarterly. Concentrates on national and regional news regarding minority construction contractors. Contains articles on issues generally affecting the industry—especially issues affecting minorities—including topics such as legislative and regulatory activity and reports on major corporation developments. Recurring features include reports of meetings, news of educational opportunities, a calendar of events, and news of NAMC chapters, affiliates, and members.

★5451★ *Building Design & Construction*
Cahners Publishing Co.
1350 E. Touhy Ave.
PO Box 5080
Des Plaines, IL 60017-5080
Ph: (708)635-8800 Fax: (708)390-2618
Jack Hollfelder

Monthly. Magazine on business and technology for commercial, institutional, and industrial buildings.

★5452★ ***Building Industry***
Trade Publishing Co.
287 Mokauea St.
Honolulu, HI 96819
Ph: (808)848-0711 Fax: (808)841-3053
Jay McWilliams

Monthly. Construction and design magazine.

★5453★ ***Building Industry Technology: An Abstract Newsletter***
National Technical Information Service (NTIS)
5285 Port Royal Rd.
Springfield, VA 22161
Ph: (703)487-4630

Biweekly. Consists of abstracts of reports on architectural and environmental design, building standards, construction materials and equipment, and structural analyses. Recurring features include a form for ordering reports from NTIS.

★5454★ ***Buildings***
Stamats Communications, Inc.
427 6th Ave. SE
PO Box 1888
Cedar Rapids, IA 52406
Ph: (319)364-6167 Fax: (319)364-4278
Linda Monroe

Monthly. Publication featuring management techniques, development, and ownership of facilities.

★5455★ ***Capital Comments***
National Lumber & Building Material Dealers Association
40 Ivy St. SE
Washington, DC 20003
Ph: (202)547-2230 Fax: (202)547-7640
Matt Geitner

Semimonthly. Reports on news of legislation pertaining to lumber, other building materials, and housing. Discusses such issues as lumber subsidies, interest rates on homes, health and safety, and jobs.

★5456★ ***ConnStruction***
McHugh Design, Advertising & Publishing
62 Lasalle Rd., Ste. 211
West Hartford, CT 06107
Ph: (203)523-7518 Fax: (203)231-8808
Tracy E. McHugh

Quarterly. Magazine for construction industry.

★5457★ ***CONSTRUCTION***
HES, Inc.
26 Long Hill Rd.
PO Box 362
Guilford, CT 06437-0362
Ph: (203)453-3717 Fax: (203)453-4390
Jack C. Lewis

Semiweekly. Journal for the construction industry.

★5458★ ***Construction News***
10835 Financial Centre Pkwy., Ste. 133
Little Rock, AR 72211-3555
Ph: (501)376-1931 Fax: (501)375-5831
Robert Alvey

Weekly. Construction industry magazine.

★5459★ ***Construction Newsletter***
National Safety Council
1121 Spring Lake Dr.
Itasca, IL 60143-3201
Ph: (708)775-2282 Fax: (708)775-2285
Diane A. Ghazarian

Bimonthly. Focuses on industrial and occupational safety in the construction industry. Carries items on such topics as safe work practices and products; accident prevention; and successful industrial safety programs and policies.

★5460★ ***Contractors Guide***
Century Publishing Co.
990 Grove St.
Evanston, IL 60201-4370
Ph: (708)491-6440 Fax: (708)491-0867
Greg Ettling

Monthly. Trade magazine on roofing and insulation.

★5461★ ***Daily Construction Reporter***
7670 Opprtunity Rd.
San Diego, CA 92111-1112
Ph: (619)492-1402 Fax: (619)565-4182
Bernado Romanowsky

Daily. Construction newspaper covering jobs that are out for bid, bid results, building permits, and other information.

★5462★ ***Fine Homebuilding***
The Taunton Press, Inc.
63 S. Main St.
PO Box 5506
Newtown, CT 06470
Ph: (203)426-8171 Fax: (203)426-3434
Fr: 800-283-7252
Mark Feirer

Magazine for builders, architects, designers, and owner-builders.

★5463★ ***International Construction***
Maclean Hunter Publishing Co.
29 N. Wacker Drive
Chicago, IL 60606
Ph: (312)726-2802 Fax: (312)726-2574
Alan Peterson

Monthly. Trade magazine.

★5464★ ***Journeyman Roofer***
Union of Roofers, Waterproofers & Allied Workers
1125 17th St. NW
Washington, DC 20036
Ph: (202)638-3228 Fax: (202)737-3621
John A. McConaty

Monthly. Trade journal.

★5465★ ***Metal Construction News***
Modern Trade Communications, Inc.
7450 N. Skokie Blvd.
Skokie, IL 60077
Ph: (708)674-2200 Fax: (708)674-3676
Shawn Zuver

Monthly. Magazine focusing on metal building, metal roof, and sidewall news.

★5466★ ***Nation's Building News***
1201 15th St. NW
Washington, DC 20005-2800
Ph: (202)822-0525 Fax: (202)861-2131
Tim Ahern

Semiweekly. Trade magazine (tabloid) covering home building and all related industries.

★5467★ ***Nation's Building News***
National Association of Home Builders of the U.S. (NAHB)
1201 15th St. NW
Washington, DC 20005
Ph: (202)822-0200 Fax: (202)822-0559

Semimonthly. Provides the latest information concerning the housing industry, including finance, legislation, new technologies, and membership news.

★5468★ ***Professional Builder & Remodeler***
Cahners Publishing Co.
1350 E. Touhy Ave.
PO Box 5080
Des Plaines, IL 60018-5080
Ph: (708)635-8800 Fax: (708)635-9950
Ed Fitch

Monthly.

★5469★ ***Professional Roofing***
National Roofing Contractors Assn.
10255 W. Higgins Rd., Ste. 600
Rosemont, IL 60018
Ph: (708)299-9070 Fax: (708)299-1183
Mari Ujka

Monthly. Roofing industry magazine.

★5470★ ***RIEI Information Letter***
The Roofing Industry Educational Institute (RIEI)
14 Inverness Dr. E., No. H-110
Englewood, CO 80112-5608
Ph: (303)790-7200 Fax: (303)790-9006
Susan E. Kaminski

Quarterly. Features technical articles on aspects of the roofing industry. Covers the educational activities of the Institute. Recurring features include a calendar of events.

★5471★ ***ROOFER Magazine***
Construction Publications, Inc.
6719 Winkler Rd. St. 214
Fort Myers, FL 33919
Ph: (813)489-2929 Fax: (813)489-1747
Greg P. Abrell

Independent national trade magazine for the roofing industry.

★5472★ ***The SPEC-DATA Program***
Construction Specifications Institute
601 Madison St.
Alexandria, VA 22314
Ph: (703)684-0300 Fax: (703)684-0465
Carol E. Duke

Quarterly. Magazine (loose-leaf) for the construction industry covering technical product and specification information.

MEETINGS AND CONVENTIONS

★5473★ **Conference on Roofing Technology**
National Roofing Contractors Association (NRCA)
10255 W. Higgins Rd., Ste. 600
Rosemont, IL 60018-5607
Ph: (708)299-9070 Fax: (708)299-1183
Biennial.

★5474★ National Roofing Contractors Association Annual Convention and Trade Show
National Roofing Contractors Association
O'Hare Intl. Center
10255 W. Higgins Rd., Ste. 600
Rosemont, IL 60018-5607
Ph: (708)299-9070 Fax: (708)299-1183

Annual. **Dates and Locations:** 1996 Feb 27-01; San Diego, CA. • 1997 Feb 04-07; Orlando, FL. • 1998 Feb 08-11; Las Vegas, NV. • 1999 Feb 07-10; Phoenix, AZ. • 2000 Feb 27-01; Miami, FL.

Other Sources of Information

★5475★ *Roofinig Technology Conference, 9th: Proceedings*
National Roofing Contractors Association
O'Hare Intl. Center
10255 W. Higgins Rd., Ste. 600
Rosemont, IL 60018-5607
Ph: (708)299-9070

Walter J. Rossiter, Jr., editor. 1989.

★5476★ *Standard for Safety for Roof Trusses for Manufactured Homes*
Underwriters Laboratories, Inc.
1285 Walt Whitman Rd.
Melville, NY 11747
Ph: (516)271-6200

Third edition, 1990.

Roustabouts

Roustabouts perform much of the routine physical labor and maintenance in and around oil fields and pipelines, such as digging ditches for foundations or for drainage, loading and unloading trucks and boats, and mixing concrete. Roustabouts are employed in the oil and gas field services industry and the contract drilling industry in primarily eight states--Texas, Louisiana, Oklahoma, California, Colorado, Wyoming, Alaska, and New Mexico.

Salaries

Hourly salaries for roustabouts are listed below.

Onshore roustabouts in the oil and gas industry	$12.50/hour
Offshore roustabouts in the oil and gas industry	$14.40/hour
Onshore roustabouts in the contract drilling industry	$9.70/hour
Offshore roustabouts in the contract drilling industry	$10.60/hour

Employment Outlook

Growth rate until the year 2005: Decline.

Roustabouts

Career Guides

★5477★ *American Professionals Series*
Cambridge Career Products
PO Box 2153
Charleston, WV 25328-2153
Ph: (304)744-9323 Fax: (304)744-9351
Fr: 800-468-4227

Videocassette. 1984. 30 mins. In this series of twenty-one half hour programs, various occupations are examined in depth, including a day in the life of each worker. Included are: fireman, farmer, oil driller, fisherman, horse trainer, auto assembly repairman, nurse, pilot, and paramedic.

★5478★ *The Green Man*
Film Library
3450 Wilshire Blvd., No. 700
Los Angeles, CA 90010
Ph: 800-421-9585

Videocassette. 198?. 20 mins. This film shows how a new employee on a drilling rig is orientated, trained, counselled and begins to gain confidence in himself during his first days on the job.

★5479★ *Profile: The Petroleum Industry*
University of Texas at Austin
Petroleum Extension Service
Austin, TX 78712
Ph: (512)471-5940 Fax: (512)471-9410

Videocassette. 1981. 30 mins. An overview of the petroleum industry from exploration to refining is provided.

★5480★ *Roustabout*
Chronicle Guidance Publications, Inc.
66 Aurora St.
PO Box 1190
Moravia, NY 13118-1190
Ph: (315)497-0330 Fax: (315)497-3359
Fr: 800-622-7284

1992. This career brief describes the nature of the work, working conditions, hours and earnings, education and training, licensure, certification, unions, personal qualifications, social and psychological factors, employment outlook, entry methods, advancement, and related occupations.

★5481★ "Roustabout" in *Jobs Rated Almanac*
World Almanac
1 International Blvd., Ste. 444
Mahwah, NJ 07495
Ph: (201)529-6900 Fax: (201)529-6901

Les Krantz. Second edition, 1992. Ranks 250 jobs by environment, salary, outlooks, physical demands, stress, security, travel opportunities, and extra perks. Includes jobs the editor feels are the most common, most interesting, and the most rapidly growing.

★5482★ "Roustabouts" in *Career Discovery Encyclopedia* (Vol.5, pp. 164-165)
J.G. Ferguson Publishing Co.
200 W. Madison St., Ste. 300
Chicago, IL 60606
Ph: (312)580-5480 Fax: (312)580-4948

E. Russell Primm, editor-in-chief. 1993. Contains two-page articles on 504 occupations. Each article describes job duties, earnings, and educational and training requirements.

★5483★ "Roustabouts" in *Encyclopedia of Careers and Vocational Guidance* (Vol.4, pp. 315-317)
J.G. Ferguson Publishing Co.
200 W. Madison St., Ste. 300
Chicago, IL 60606
Ph: (312)580-5480 Fax: (312)580-4948

William E. Hopke, editor-in-chief. Ninth edition, 1993. Four-volume set that profiles 500 occupations and describes job trends in 74 industries. Includes career description, educational requirements, history of the job, methods of entry, advancement, employment outlook, earnings, working conditions, social and psychological factors, and sources of additional information.

★5484★ "Roustabouts" in *Occupational Outlook Handbook*
U.S. Government Printing Office
Superintendent of Documents
Washington, DC 20402
Ph: (202)512-1800 Fax: (202)512-2250

Biennial; latest edition, 1994-95. Encyclopedia of careers describing more than 250 occupations and comprising about 85 percent of all jobs in the economy. Occupations that require lengthy education or training are given the most attention. For each occupation, the handbook describes job duties, working conditions, training, educational preparation, personal qualities, advancement possibilities, job outlook, earnings, and sources of additional information.

★5485★ *Wellhead Operations*
University of Texas at Austin
Petroleum Extension Service
Balcones Research Ctr., Bldg. 2
Austin, TX 78712
Ph: (512)471-5940 Fax: (512)471-9410

Videocassette. 1981. 23 mins. This program introduces gas field operators to routine wellhead operations.

★5486★ *Work Procedures for a Derrickman*
Gulf Publishing Co.
PO Box 2608
Houston, TX 77252-2608
Ph: (713)529-4301 Fax: (713)520-4438

Videocassette. 1984. 50 mins. This program discusses job responsibilities of the derrickman, both in the derrick and in the pump room. This program is part of the "Working Offshore" series.

★5487★ *Work Procedures for a Roustabout*
Gulf Publishing Co.
PO Box 2608
Houston, TX 77252-2608
Ph: (713)529-4438 Fax: (713)520-4438

Videocassette. 1984. 50 mins. This program takes a look at the life of a roustabout. This program is part of the "Working Offshore" series.

Associations

★5488★ American Petroleum Institute (API)
1220 L St. NW
Washington, DC 20005
Ph: (202)682-8000 Fax: (202)682-8232

Members: Corporations in the petroleum and allied industries, including producers, refiners, marketers, and transporters of crude oil, lubricating oil, gasoline, and natural gas. **Purpose:** Provides public policy development, advocacy, research, and technical services to enhance the ability of the petroleum industry to fulfill its mission: meeting the nation's energy needs; enhancing the environmental, health, and safety performance of the industry; conducting research to advance petroleum technology, equipment, and standards. Seeks to maintain cooperation between government and industry on all matters of national concern; fosters foreign and domestic trade in American petroleum products; promotes the interests of the petroleum industry; encourages the study of the arts and sciences connected with the petroleum industry. Provides information services; conducts fundamental research on petroleum. Operates functional departments to support the work of the institute including a Central Abstracting and Information Service in New York City. **Publications:** *American Petroleum Institute—Publications and Materials*, annual. • *API Report to the Membership*, annual. • *API Reports*, quarterly. • *Basic Petroleum Data Book.* • *Imported Crude Oil and Petroleum Products*, monthly. • *Inventories of Natural Gas Liquids and Liquefied Refinery Gases*, monthly. • *Joint Association Survey*, annual. • *Monthly Completion Report.* • *Monthly Statistical Report.* • *Quarterly Completion Report.* • *Weekly Statistical Bulletin.*

Basic Reference Guides and Handbooks

★5489★ *Basic Petroleum Data Book*
American Petroleum Institute (API)
1220 L St. NW
Washington, DC 20005
Ph: (202)682-8000 Fax: (202)682-8232

3 updates/year. Domestic and world statistical background data (since 1947) on energy, reserves, exploration and drilling, production, finance, prices, demand, and refining.

Periodicals

★5490★ *ABC Today*
Associated Builders and Contractors, Inc. (ABC)
N. 17th St.
Rosslyn, VA 22209
Ph: (703)637-8800 Fax: (703)812-8203
Pamela E. Hunter

Semimonthly. Designed to keep readers alerted to important changes within ABC and the construction industry. Reports on legislative issues, construction trends, conferences and meetings, and ABC services. Recurring features include news of members and columns titled Industry Briefs, Safety Notebook, Computer Corner, Bottom Line, and Chapter News.

★5491★ *ABC Today*
Associated Builders and Contractors, Inc. (ABC)
1300 N. 17th St., 8th Floor
Arlington, VA 22209-3803
Ph: (703)812-2000 Fax: (703)812-8203
Pamela E. Hunter

Semiweekly. Magazine for open shop contractors and subcontractors. Includes articles on national and regional construction news, construction management, project case histories, new products, building design, and legislative and regulatory updates.

★5492★ *American Petroleum Institute—Publications and Materials*
American Petroleum Institute (API)
1220 L St. NW
Washington, DC 20005
Ph: (202)682-8000 Fax: (202)682-8232

Annual. Lists publications and audiovisual materials available through API.

★5493★ *API Report to the Membership*
American Petroleum Institute (API)
1220 L St. NW
Washington, DC 20005
Ph: (202)682-8000 Fax: (202)682-8232

Annual. Review of API activities.

★5494★ *API Reports*
American Petroleum Institute (API)
1220 L St. NW
Washington, DC 20005
Ph: (202)682-8000 Fax: (202)682-8232

Quarterly. Covers current issues and activities.

★5495★ *Drilling Contractor*
Drilling Contractor Publications, Inc.
15810 Park 10 Pl., Ste. 222
Houston, TX 77084
Ph: (713)578-7171 Fax: (713)578-0589
Alvaro Franco

Bimonthly. Magazine covering technical, economic, and political developments affecting the drilling and production segments of the international petroleum industry.

★5496★ *Imported Crude Oil and Petroleum Products*
American Petroleum Institute (API)
1220 L St. NW
Washington, DC 20005
Ph: (202)682-8000 Fax: (202)682-8232

Monthly. Data on crude oil imports and major products detailing the importer, port of entry, country of origin, recipient, and destination.

★5497★ *Inventories of Natural Gas Liquids and Liquefied Refinery Gases*
American Petroleum Institute (API)
1220 L St. NW
Washington, DC 20005
Ph: (202)682-8000 Fax: (202)682-8232

Monthly. Geographical listing of inventories of liquefied petroleum and liquefied refinery gases at plants and refineries, and in underground storage.

★5498★ *IUPIW Views*
International Union of Petroleum & Industrial Workers, SIUNA (IUPIW)
8131 E. Rosecranes
Paramount, CA 90723
Ph: (310)630-6232 Fax: (310)408-1073
Fr: 800-624-5842
Robert Davidson

Bimonthly. Presents labor, safety, and consumer news for petroleum and industrial workers. Recurring features include obituaries, a schedule of activities, editorials, news of research, letters to the editor, news of members, and a calendar of events.

★5499★ *Joint Association Survey*
American Petroleum Institute (API)
1220 L St. NW
Washington, DC 20005
Ph: (202)682-8000 Fax: (202)682-8232

Annual. Report of the estimated cost of drilling oil wells, gas wells, and dry holes by depth range for regions in the U.S.

★5500★ *Monthly Completion Report*
American Petroleum Institute (API)
1220 L St. NW
Washington, DC 20005
Ph: (202)682-8000 Fax: (202)682-8232

Report of the cumulative number of wells and footage, by type of well and by month of completion, for the current year and two prior years.

★5501★ *Monthly Statistical Report*
American Petroleum Institute (API)
1220 L St. NW
Washington, DC 20005
Ph: (202)682-8000 Fax: (202)682-8232

Summary of the estimated U.S. petroleum balance with analyses of the trends reflected in the Weekly Statistical Bulletin.

★5502★ *Ocean Industry*
Gulf Publishing Co.
3301 Allen Pkwy.
PO Box 2608
Houston, TX 77252-2608
Ph: (713)529-4301 Fax: (713)520-4433
Robert Snyder

Magazine covering offshore drilling production and pipeline construction projects.

★5503★ *Ocean Oil Weekly Report*
PennWell Publishing Company
3050 Post Oak, Ste. 200
PO Box 1941
Houston, TX 77251
Ph: (713)621-9720 Fax: (713)963-6285
Fr: 800-874-1510
Michael Crowder

Weekly. Provides weekly news of the offshore oil industry and analysis of significant events. Includes information on offshore concessions, mobile rigs, exploration and productions, pipeline and construction, contractors stock market report, and personnel notes.

★5504★ *Offshore Field Development International*
Offshore Data Services, Inc.
PO Box 19909
Houston, TX 77224-9909
Ph: (713)781-2713 Fax: (713)781-9594
Paul Hillegeist

Monthly. Reports on petroleum-related offshore construction projects worldwide, from the planning stage through final installation. Covers platforms, pipelines, subsea completions, and mooring terminals. Recurring features include sections on construction barge locations and possible areas for future development.

★5505★ *Offshore Rig Locator*
Offshore Data Services, Inc.
PO Box 19909
Houston, TX 77224
Ph: (713)781-2713 Fax: (713)781-9594
John Chadderdon

Monthly. Provides information on the location of offshore drilling rigs. Tracks each of the more than 800 mobile rigs and 400 platform rigs currently operating and under construction, both in the U.S. and in international waters. Categorizes by geographical areas and rig type and includes contract status and major sub-contractors.

★5506★ *Offshore Rig Newsletter*
Offshore Data Services, Inc.
PO Box 19909
Houston, TX 77224
Ph: (713)781-2713 Fax: (713)781-9594
Richard Maddox

Monthly. Contains information on drilling rigs. Covers performance, design, and new construction of rigs. Discusses insurance, labor problems, costs, accidents, and industry trends. Recurring features include a market outlook each month.

★5507★ *Quarterly Completion Report*
American Petroleum Institute (API)
1220 L St. NW
Washington, DC 20005
Ph: (202)682-8000 Fax: (202)682-8232

Regional report by quarter of completion for total wells drilled and by depth intervals; also provides annual summary table on total wells.

★5508★ *Weekly Statistical Bulletin*
American Petroleum Institute (API)
1220 L St. NW
Washington, DC 20005
Ph: (202)682-8000 Fax: (202)682-8232

Data on U.S. refinery activity and principal inventories, crude oil and product imports, and crude oil production.

Other Sources of Information

★5509★ *API Monthly Statistical Report*
American Petroleum Institute (API)
1220 L St. NW
Washington, DC 20005
Ph: (202)682-8000 Fax: (202)682-8232

Summary of the estimated U.S. petroleum balance with analyses of the trends reflected in the *Weekly Statistical Bulletin*.

Sheet-metal Workers

Sheet-metal workers fabricate, install, and maintain air-conditioning, heating, ventilation, and pollution control duct systems; roofs; siding; rain gutters and downspouts; skylights; restaurant equipment; outdoor signs; and many other building parts and products made from metal sheets. They may also work with fiberglass and plastic materials. Although some workers specialize in fabrication, installation, or maintenance, most do all three jobs. Approximately 75% of sheet-metal workers are employed by plumbing, heating, and air-conditioning contractors; about 20% work for roofing and sheet-metal contractors; and the rest work for general contractors engaged in residential and commercial building. Unlike many other construction trades, very few sheet-metal workers are self-employed.

Salaries

Union sheet-metal workers' average earnings are $27.62/hour. Apprentices generally start at about 40 percent of the rate paid to experienced workers. Throughout the course of the apprenticeship program, they receive periodic increases as they acquire the skills of the trade.

Employment Outlook

Growth rate until the year 2005: Faster than the average.

Sheet-Metal Workers

Career Guides

★5510★ ***Careers in Sheet Metal***
National Training Fund/Sheet Metal and Air Conditioning Industry
601 N. Fairfax St.
Alexandria, VA 22314

Fifth edition, 1994. This 24-page booklet describes needed qualities, basic requirements, working conditions, and training. Explains the sheet metal industry's apprenticeship program.

★5511★ ***Construction Cluster***
Center for Humanities, Inc.
Communications Park
Box 1000
Mount Kisco, NY 10549
Ph: (914)666-4100 Fax: (914)666-5319
Fr: 800-431-1242

Videocassette. 1984. 15 mins. Construction workers describe what it's like to work at their jobs, and show the special equipment they use in their field.

★5512★ **"Sheet Metal Duct Systems for Heating and Air Conditioning . . . " in *Opportunities in Refrigeration and Air Conditioning Trades***
National Textbook Co. (NTC)
VGM Career Books
4255 W. Touhy Ave.
Lincolnwood, IL 60646-1975
Ph: (708)679-5500 Fax: (708)679-2494
Fr: 800-323-4900

Richard Budzik. 1989. Surveys the air conditioning and refrigeration industry. Describes jobs, educational and training requirements, small business opportunities, places of employment, and job outlook. Offers job hunting advice.

★5513★ **"Sheet Metal Work" in *Opportunities in Plumbing and Pipefitting Careers* (pp. 79-82)**
National Textbook Co. (NTC)
VGM Career Books
4255 W. Touhy Ave.
Lincolnwood, IL 60646-1975
Ph: (708)679-5500 Fax: (708)679-2494
Fr: 800-323-4900

Patrick J. Galvin. 1989. Describes the work, jobs, educational preparation, training, apprenticeships, a typical working day, salaries, future trends, and related fields.

★5514★ ***Sheet Metal Worker***
Careers, Inc.
PO Box 135
Largo, FL 34649-0135
Ph: (813)584-7333

1994. Two-page occupational summary card describing duties, working conditions, personal qualifications, training, earnings and hours, employment outlook, places of employment, related careers and where to write for more information.

★5515★ **"Sheet Metal Worker" in *BLR Encyclopedia of Prewritten Job Descriptions***
Business and Legal Reports, Inc.
39 Academy St.
Madison, CT 06443-1513
Ph: (203)245-7448

Stephen D. Bruce, editor-in-chief. 1994. This book contains hundreds of sample job descriptions arranged by functional job category. The 1-3 page job descriptions cover what the worker normally does in the position, who they report to, and how that position fits in the organizational structure.

★5516★ **"Sheet Metal Worker" in *Career Information Center* (Vol.4)**
Simon and Schuster
200 Old Tappan Rd.
Old Tappan, NJ 07675
Fax: 800-445-6991 Fr: 800-223-2348

Richard Lidz and Dale Anderson, editorial directors. Fifth edition, 1993. For 600 occupations, describes job duties, entry-level requirements, education and training needed, advancement possibilities, employment outlook, earnings and benefits. The set is divided into 12 volumes. Each volume includes jobs related under a broad career field. Volume 13 is the index.

★5517★ **"Sheet Metal Worker" in *Hard Hatted Women: Stories of Struggle and Success in the Trades* (pp. 17-32)**
Seal Press
3131 Western Ave., Ste. 410
Seattle, WA 98121
Ph: (206)283-7844 Fax: (206)285-9410

Molly Martin, editor. 1988. Twenty-six women recount their experiences working in blue collar occupations. They describe how they got in, the work they do, their relationships in predominantly male occupations, and their training.

★5518★ **"Sheet Metal Worker" in *Jobs Rated Almanac***
World Almanac
1 International Blvd., Ste. 444
Mahwah, NJ 07495
Ph: (201)529-6900 Fax: (201)529-6901

Les Krantz. Second edition, 1992. Ranks 250 jobs by environment, salary, outlooks, physical demands, stress, security, travel opportunities, and extra perks. Includes jobs the editor feels are the most common, most interesting, and the most rapidly growing.

★5519★ **"Sheet Metal Worker" in *Occu-Facts: Information on 580 Careers in Outline Form***
Careers, Inc.
PO Box 135
Largo, FL 34649-0135
Ph: (813)584-7333

Biennial, 1995-96 edition. Each one-page occupational profile describes duties, working conditions, physical surroundings and demands, aptitudes, temperament, educational requirements, employment outlook, earnings, and places of employment.

★5520★ ***Sheet Metal Workers***
Chronicle Guidance Publications, Inc.
66 Aurora St.
PO Box 1190
Moravia, NY 13118-1190
Ph: (315)497-0330 Fax: (315)497-3359
Fr: 800-622-7284

1994. This career brief describes the nature of the work, working conditions, hours and earnings, education and training, licensure, certification, unions, personal qualifications, social and psychological factors, employment outlook, entry methods, advancement, and related occupations.

★5521★ "Sheet Metal Workers" in *Career Discovery Encyclopedia* (Vol.6, pp. 24-25)
J.G. Ferguson Publishing Co.
200 W. Madison St., Ste. 300
Chicago, IL 60606
Ph: (312)580-5480 Fax: (312)580-4948

E. Russell Primm, editor-in-chief. 1993. Contains two-page articles on 504 occupations. Each article describes job duties, earnings, and educational and training requirements.

★5522★ "Sheet Metal Workers" in *Encyclopedia of Careers and Vocational Guidance* (Vol.4, pp. 349-352)
J.G. Ferguson Publishing Co.
200 W. Madison St., Ste. 300
Chicago, IL 60606
Ph: (312)580-5480 Fax: (312)580-4948

William E. Hopke, editor-in-chief. Ninth edition, 1993. Four-volume set that profiles 500 occupations and describes job trends in 74 industries. Includes career description, educational requirements, history of the job, methods of entry, advancement, employment outlook, earnings, working conditions, social and psychological factors, and sources of additional information.

★5523★ "Sheet-Metal Workers" in *Occupational Outlook Handbook*
U.S. Government Printing Office
Superintendent of Documents
Washington, DC 20402
Ph: (202)512-1800 Fax: (202)512-2250

Biennial; latest edition, 1994-95. Encyclopedia of careers describing more than 250 occupations and comprising about 85 percent of all jobs in the economy. Occupations that require lengthy education or training are given the most attention. For each occupation, the handbook describes job duties, working conditions, training, educational preparation, personal qualities, advancement possibilities, job outlook, earnings, and sources of additional information.

★5524★ "Sheet Metal Working" in *Opportunities in Metalworking Careers* (pp. 17-26)
National Textbook Co. (NTC)
VGM Career Books
4255 W. Touhy Ave.
Lincolnwood, IL 60646-1975
Ph: (708)679-5500 Fax: (708)679-2494
Fr: 800-323-4900

Mark Rowh. 1991. Covers sheet metal work, machining, structural and reinforcing metalworking, and jewelry making. Describes the work performed, skills needed, training and working conditions. Lists unions that sponsor apprenticeship and technical schools which offer training.

★5525★ *Technical/Manufacturing Cluster One*
Center for Humanities, Inc.
Communications Park
Box 1000
Mount Kisco, NY 10549
Ph: (914)666-4100 Fax: (914)666-5319
Fr: 800-431-1242

Videocassette. 1984. 20 mins. An upclose look at people who work in the fields of welding, drafting, and sheet metal.

★5526★ *Video Career Library - Production II*
Careers, Inc.
PO Box 135
Largo, FL 34649-0135
Ph: (813)584-7333

Videocassette. 1990. 32 mins. Part of the Video Career Library covering 165 occupations. Shows actual workers on the job. Includes tool and die makers, machinists, sheet metal workers, cabinet and bench carpenters, opticians, precision electronic equipment assemblers, industrial machine operators, welders and cutters, and assemblers.

Associations

★5527★ Associated Builders and Contractors (ABC)
1300 N. 17th St.
Rossyln, VA 22209
Ph: (703)812-2000

Members: Construction contractors, subcontractors, suppliers, and associates. **Purpose:** Aim is to foster and perpetuate the principles of rewarding construction workers and management on the basis of merit. Sponsors management education programs and craft training; also sponsors apprenticeship and skill training programs. Disseminates technological and labor relations information. Maintains placement service. Compiles statistics. **Publications:** *ABC Today*, semimonthly. • *National Membership Directory and Users Guide*, annual.

★5528★ Sheet Metal and Air Conditioning Contractors' National Association (SMACNA)
4201 Lafayette Center Dr.
Chantilly, VA 22021
Ph: (703)803-2980 Fax: (703)803-3732

Members: Ventilating, air handling, warm air heating, architectural and industrial sheet metal, kitchen equipment, testing and balancing, siding, and decking and specialty fabrication contractors. **Purpose:** Prepares standards and codes; sponsors research and educational programs on sheet metal duct construction and fire damper (single and multi-blade) construction. Engages in legislative and labor activities; conducts business management and contractor education programs. **Publications:** *Chaptergram*. • *SMACNEWS*, monthly.

Standards/Certification Agencies

★5529★ Sheet Metal and Air Conditioning Contractors' National Association (SMACNA)
4201 Lafayette Center Dr.
Chantilly, VA 22021
Ph: (703)803-2980 Fax: (703)803-3732

Prepares standards and codes; sponsors research and educational programs on sheet metal duct construction and fire damper (single and multi-blade) construction.

Test Guides

★5530★ *Career Examination Series: Foreman Sheet Metal Worker*
National Learning Corp.
212 Michael Dr.
Syosset, NY 11791
Ph: (516)921-8888 Fax: (516)921-8743
Fr: 800-645-6337

Jack Rudman. All examination guides in this series contain questions with answers.

★5531★ *Career Examination Series: Gang Foreman (Structures-Group D) (Sheet Metal)*
National Learning Corp.
212 Michael Dr.
Syosset, NY 11791
Ph: (516)921-8888 Fax: (516)921-8743
Fr: 800-645-6337

Jack Rudman. 1989. All examination guides in this series contain questions with answers.

★5532★ *Career Examination Series: Sheet Metal Worker*
National Learning Corp.
212 Michael Dr.
Syosset, NY 11791
Ph: (516)921-8888 Fax: (516)921-8743
Fr: 800-645-6337

Jack Rudman. All examination guides in this series contain questions with answers.

★5533★ *Sheet Metal Fabrication*
National Learning Corp.
212 Michael Dr.
Syosset, NY 11791
Ph: (516)921-8888 Fax: (516)921-8743
Fr: 800-645-6337

Jack Rudman. 1989. Part of Occupational Competency Examination Series.

★5534★ *Sheet Metal Work*
National Learning Corp.
212 Michael Dr.
Syosset, NY 11791
Ph: (516)921-8888 Fax: (516)921-8743
Fr: 800-645-6337

Jack Rudman. Part of the Test Your Knowledge Series. Contains multiple choice questions with answers.

Educational Directories and Programs

★5535★ *Intelligent Buildings Institute—Directory of Products and Services*
Intelligent Buildings Institute (IBI)
2101 L St., NW, Ste. 300
Washington, DC 20037
Ph: (202)457-1988 Fax: (202)457-8468

S. Hunt, Associate Executive Director, editor. Annual, September. Member consultants, associations, research organizations, and other suppliers of products and services to the construction and building industry. Entries include: Company name, address, phone. Arrangement: Alphabetical. Indexes: Product/service.

★5536★ *International Directory of Building Research, Information and Development Organizations*
29 W. 35th St.
New York, NY 10001
Ph: (212)244-3336

Over 600 universities, institutions, government agencies, and other construction-related research institutions. Entries include: Institution name, address, phone, telex, name and title of contact, number of staff, source of finance, area of interest, publications.

Basic Reference Guides and Handbooks

★5537★ *The Sheet Metal Toolbox Manual*
Arco Pub.
201 W. 103rd St.
Indianapolis, IN 46290
Ph: 800-428-5331 Fax: 800-835-3202

David Tenenbaum. 1991.

Periodicals

★5538★ *ABC Today*
Associated Builders and Contractors (ABC)
1300 N. 17th St.
Rosslyn, VA 22209
Ph: (703)812-2000

Semimonthly. News magazine for merit shop contractors.

★5539★ *ABC Today*
Associated Builders and Contractors, Inc. (ABC)
N. 17th St.
Rosslyn, VA 22209
Ph: (703)637-8800 Fax: (703)812-8203
Pamela E. Hunter

Semimonthly. Designed to keep readers alerted to important changes within ABC and the construction industry. Reports on legislative issues, construction trends, conferences and meetings, and ABC services. Recurring features include news of members and columns titled Industry Briefs, Safety Notebook, Computer Corner, Bottom Line, and Chapter News.

★5540★ *ABC Today*
Associated Builders and Contractors, Inc. (ABC)
1300 N. 17th St., 8th Floor
Arlington, VA 22209-3803
Ph: (703)812-2000 Fax: (703)812-8203
Pamela E. Hunter

Semiweekly. Magazine for open shop contractors and subcontractors. Includes articles on national and regional construction news, construction management, project case histories, new products, building design, and legislative and regulatory updates.

★5541★ *American Architectural Manufacturers Association—Quarterly Review*
American Architectural Manufacturers Association
1540 E. Dundee Rd., Ste. 310
Palatine, IL 60067-8321
Ph: (708)202-1350 Fax: (708)202-1480
Tony Coorlim

Annual. Contains industry news on architectural products. Covers prime and combination storm windows, sliding glass and combination storm doors, window and curtainwalls, store fronts and entrances, siding, soffits, fascia, gutters, downspouts, skylights, space enclosures, and mobile home components. Recurring features include news of research, notices of publications available, and announcements by the Association.

★5542★ *American Institute of Constructors—Newsletter*
American Institute of Constructors
9887 Gandy Blvd. N., Ste. 104
St. Petersburg, FL 33702
Ph: (813)578-1962 Fax: (813)578-9982
Cheryl P. Harris

Bimonthly. Concerned with construction practice, design, administration, and teaching. Carries news of members, listings of job opportunities, local chapter reports, notices of new publications, and conferences on construction topics.

★5543★ *Blue Reports, Inc.*
Construction News Service
7325 Steel Mill Dr.
Springfield, VA 22050
Ph: (703)644-5884 Fax: (703)644-1929
Calvin S. Oren

Daily. Reports on public and private construction projects in the Washington, DC, Virginia, and Maryland areas. Provides owner's and architect's names, plan status, date bids due, prospective bidders, low bids received, and specification details.

★5544★ *Building Concerns*
National Association of Minority Contractors (NAMC)
1333 F St. NW, Ste. 500
Washington, DC 20004
Ph: (202)347-8259 Fax: (202)628-1876
Agreta Hester

Quarterly. Concentrates on national and regional news regarding minority construction contractors. Contains articles on issues generally affecting the industry—especially issues affecting minorities—including topics such as legislative and regulatory activity and reports on major corporation developments. Recurring features include reports of meetings, news of educational opportunities, a calendar of events, and news of NAMC chapters, affiliates, and members.

★5545★ *Building Industry Technology: An Abstract Newsletter*
National Technical Information Service (NTIS)
5285 Port Royal Rd.
Springfield, VA 22161
Ph: (703)487-4630

Biweekly. Consists of abstracts of reports on architectural and environmental design, building standards, construction materials and equipment, and structural analyses. Recurring features include a form for ordering reports from NTIS.

★5546★ *Capital Comments*
National Lumber & Building Material Dealers Association
40 Ivy St. SE
Washington, DC 20003
Ph: (202)547-2230 Fax: (202)547-7640
Matt Geitner

Semimonthly. Reports on news of legislation pertaining to lumber, other building materials, and housing. Discusses such issues as lumber subsidies, interest rates on homes, health and safety, and jobs.

★5547★ *Chaptergram*
Sheet Metal and Air Conditioning Contractors' National Association (SMACNA)
4201 Lafayette Center Dr.
Chantilly, VA 22021
Ph: (703)803-2980 Fax: (703)803-3732

★5548★ *ConnStruction*
McHugh Design, Advertising & Publishing
62 Lasalle Rd., Ste. 211
West Hartford, CT 06107
Ph: (203)523-7518 Fax: (203)231-8808
Tracy E. McHugh

Quarterly. Magazine for construction industry.

★5549★ *CONSTRUCTION*
HES, Inc.
26 Long Hill Rd.
PO Box 362
Guilford, CT 06437-0362
Ph: (203)453-3717 Fax: (203)453-4390
Jack C. Lewis

Semiweekly. Journal for the construction industry.

★5550★ *Construction News*
10835 Financial Centre Pkwy., Ste. 133
Little Rock, AR 72211-3555
Ph: (501)376-1931 Fax: (501)375-5831
Robert Alvey

Weekly. Construction industry magazine.

★5551★ *Construction Newsletter*
National Safety Council
1121 Spring Lake Dr.
Itasca, IL 60143-3201
Ph: (708)775-2282 Fax: (708)775-2285
Diane A. Ghazarian

Bimonthly. Focuses on industrial and occupational safety in the construction industry. Carries items on such topics as safe work practices and products; accident prevention; and successful industrial safety programs and policies.

★5552★ *Daily Construction Reporter*
7670 Opprtunity Rd.
San Diego, CA 92111-1112
Ph: (619)492-1402 Fax: (619)565-4182
Bernado Romanowsky

Daily. Construction newspaper covering jobs that are out for bid, bid results, building permits, and other information.

★5553★ *International Construction*
Maclean Hunter Publishing Co.
29 N. Wacker Drive
Chicago, IL 60606
Ph: (312)726-2802 Fax: (312)726-2574
Alan Peterson

Monthly. Trade magazine.

★5554★ *Nation's Building News*
1201 15th St. NW
Washington, DC 20005-2800
Ph: (202)822-0525 Fax: (202)861-2131
Tim Ahern

Semiweekly. Trade magazine (tabloid) covering home building and all related industries.

★5555★ *Nation's Building News*
National Association of Home Builders of the U.S. (NAHB)
1201 15th St. NW
Washington, DC 20005
Ph: (202)822-0200 Fax: (202)822-0559

Semimonthly. Provides the latest information concerning the housing industry, including finance, legislation, new technologies, and membership news.

★5556★ *Professional Builder & Remodeler*
Cahners Publishing Co.
1350 E. Touhy Ave.
PO Box 5080
Des Plaines, IL 60018-5080
Ph: (708)635-8800 Fax: (708)635-9950
Ed Fitch

Monthly.

★5557★ *SMACNA Newsletter*
Sheet Metal and Air Conditioning Contractors' National Association (SMACNA)
4201 Lafayette Center Dr.
Chantilly, VA 22021-1209
Ph: (703)803-2980 Fax: (703)803-3732
Rosalind P. Raymond

Monthly. Provides information on the sheet metal industry. Covers labor, legislative, and governmental actions affecting the industry. Recurring features include Association news, contractors in the News, and a President's column.

★5558★ *SMACNEWS*
Sheet Metal and Air Conditioning Contractors' National Association (SMACNA)
4201 Lafayette Center Dr.
Chantilly, VA 22021
Ph: (703)803-2980 Fax: (703)803-3732

Monthly.

★5559★ *Snips Magazine*
1949 Cornell Ave.
Melrose Park, IL 60160-9953
Ph: (708)544-3870 Fax: (708)544-3884
Nick Carter

Monthly. Magazine for the sheet metal, warm-air heating, ventilating, and air conditioning industry.

Meetings and Conventions

★5560★ Heating, Ventilation, and Air Conditioning Product and Equipment Show
Institute of Heating and Air Conditioning Industries
606 N. Larchmont Blvd., Ste. 4A
Los Angeles, CA 90004
Ph: (213)467-1158 Fax: (213)461-2588

Annual. Always held during November at the Convention Center in Pasadena, California.

★5561★ Sheet Metal and Air-Conditioning Contractors National Association Convention
Sheet Metal and Air-Conditioning Contractors National Association
PO Box 221230
Chantilly, VA 22022-1230
Ph: (703)803-2980 Fax: (703)803-3732

Annual.

Structural and Reinforcing Ironworkers

Structural and reinforcing ironworkers fabricate, assemble, and install such products as structural steel, reinforced concrete, and ornamental iron. These workers also repair, renovate, and maintain older buildings and structures such as steel mills, utility plants, automobile factories, highways, and bridges. Almost all structural and reinforcing ironworkers are employed in the construction industry. About 50% work for structural steel erection contractors; most of the remainder worked for a variety of contractors specializing in the construction of homes, factories, commercial buildings, churches, schools, bridges and tunnels, and water, sewer, communications, and power lines. A few work for government agencies, utilities, and manufacturing firms that do some of their own construction work. Very few are self-employed.

Salaries

Median earnings for ironworkers is about $27/hour. Apprentices usually start at 40 to 60 percent of the wages paid to experienced workers.

Employment Outlook

Growth rate until the year 2005: Average.

Structural and Reinforcing Ironworkers

Career Guides

★5562★ ***Construction Cluster***
Center for Humanities, Inc.
Communications Park
Box 1000
Mount Kisco, NY 10549
Ph: (914)666-4100 Fax: (914)666-5319
Fr: 800-431-1242

Videocassette. 1984. 15 mins. Construction workers describe what it's like to work at their jobs, and show the special equipment they use in their field.

★5563★ ***Construction Ironworkers***
Chronicle Guidance Publications, Inc.
66 Aurora St.
PO Box 1190
Moravia, NY 13118-1190
Ph: (315)497-0330 Fax: (315)497-3359
Fr: 800-622-7284

1993. This career brief describes the nature of the work, working conditions, hours and earnings, education and training, licensure, certification, unions, personal qualifications, social and psychological factors, employment outlook, entry methods, advancement, and related occupations.

★5564★ **"Iron and Steel Industry" in *Career Information Center* (Vol.9)**
Simon and Schuster
200 Old Tappan Rd.
Old Tappan, NJ 07675
Fax: 800-445-6991 Fr: 800-223-2348

Richard Lidz and Dale Anderson, editorial directors. Fifth edition, 1993. For 600 occupations, describes job duties, entry-level requirements, education and training needed, advancement possibilities, employment outlook, earnings and benefits. The set is divided into 12 volumes. Each volume includes jobs related under a broad career field. Volume 13 is the index.

★5565★ ***Iron and Steel Industry Workers***
Chronicle Guidance Publications, Inc.
66 Aurora St.
PO Box 1190
Moravia, NY 13118-1190
Ph: (315)497-0330 Fax: (315)497-3359
Fr: 800-622-7284

1993. This career brief describes the nature of the work, working conditions, hours and earnings, education and training, licensure, certification, unions, personal qualifications, social and psychological factors, employment outlook, entry methods, advancement, and related occupations.

★5566★ **"Iron and Steel Industry Workers" in *Career Discovery Encyclopedia* (Vol.3, pp. 146-147)**
J.G. Ferguson Publishing Co.
200 W. Madison St., Ste. 300
Chicago, IL 60606
Ph: (312)580-5480 Fax: (312)580-4948

E. Russell Primm, editor-in-chief. 1993. Contains two-page articles on 504 occupations. Each article describes job duties, earnings, and educational and training requirements.

★5567★ **"Iron and Steel Industry Workers" in *Encyclopedia of Careers and Vocational Guidance* (Vol.3, pp. 241-243)**
J.G. Ferguson Publishing Co.
200 W. Madison St., Ste. 300
Chicago, IL 60606
Ph: (312)580-5480 Fax: (312)580-4948

William E. Hopke, editor-in-chief. Ninth edition, 1993. Four-volume set that profiles 500 occupations and describes job trends in 74 industries. Includes career description, educational requirements, history of the job, methods of entry, advancement, employment outlook, earnings, working conditions, social and psychological factors, and sources of additional information.

★5568★ **"Iron and Steel Worker" in *Career Information Center* (Vol.4)**
Simon and Schuster
200 Old Tappan Rd.
Old Tappan, NJ 07675
Fax: 800-445-6991 Fr: 800-223-2348

Richard Lidz and Linda Perrin, editorial directors. Fifth edition, 1993. This 13-volume set profiles over 600 occupations. Each occupational profile describes job duties, entry-level requirements, educational requirements, advancement possibilities, employment outlook, working conditions, earnings and benefits, and where to write for more information.

★5569★ ***Iron Workers and Riggers***
Careers, Inc.
PO Box 135
Largo, FL 34649-0135
Ph: (813)584-7333

1992. Four-page brief offering the definition, history, duties, working conditions, personal qualifications, educational requirements, earnings, hours, employment outlook, advancement possibilities, and related occupations.

★5570★ **"Iron Workers and Riggers" in *Occu-Facts: Information on 580 Careers in Outline Form***
Careers, Inc.
PO Box 135
Largo, FL 34649-0135
Ph: (813)584-7333

Biennial, 1995-96 edition. Each one-page occupational profile describes duties, working conditions, physical surroundings and demands, aptitudes, temperament, educational requirements, employment outlook, earnings, and places of employment.

★5571★ **"Ironworker" in *Hard Hatted Women: Stories of Struggle and Success in the Trades* (pp. 102-108)**
Seal Press
3131 Western Ave., Ste. 410
Seattle, WA 98121
Ph: (206)283-7844 Fax: (206)285-9410

Molly Martin, editor. 1988. Twenty-six women recount their experiences working in blue collar occupations. They describe how they got in, the work they do, their relationships in predominantly male occupations, and their training.

★5572★ "Ironworker" in *Jobs Rated Almanac*
World Almanac
1 International Blvd., Ste. 444
Mahwah, NJ 07495
Ph: (201)529-6900 Fax: (201)529-6901

Les Krantz. Second edition, 1992. Ranks 250 jobs by environment, salary, outlooks, physical demands, stress, security, travel opportunities, and extra perks. Includes jobs the editor feels are the most common, most interesting, and the most rapidly growing.

★5573★ "Ironworkers and Steelworkers" in *Opportunities in Building Construction Trades* (pp. 68-70)
National Textbook Co. (NTC)
VGM Career Books
4255 W. Touhy Ave.
Lincolnwood, IL 60646-1975
Ph: (708)679-5500 Fax: (708)679-2494
Fr: 800-323-4900

Michael Sumichrast. 1989. Gives an overview of the construction industry and describes the jobs of various craftworkers. Covers different kinds of builders: home, custom; and describes management skills needed and industry trends affecting opportunities.

★5574★ *Men of Iron*
International Film Bureau, Inc. (IFB)
332 S. Michigan Ave.
Chicago, IL 60604-4382
Ph: (312)427-4545

Videocassette. 198?. 20 mins. This program follows an apprentice ironworker as he learns the trade and how to do it safely.

★5575★ "Structural and Reinforcing Ironworkers" in *Occupational Outlook Handbook*
U.S. Government Printing Office
Superintendent of Documents
Washington, DC 20402
Ph: (202)512-1800 Fax: (202)512-2250

Biennial; latest edition, 1994-95. Encyclopedia of careers describing more than 250 occupations and comprising about 85 percent of all jobs in the economy. Occupations that require lengthy education or training are given the most attention. For each occupation, the handbook describes job duties, working conditions, training, educational preparation, personal qualities, advancement possibilities, job outlook, earnings, and sources of additional information.

★5576★ "Structural Steel Workers" in *Encyclopedia of Careers and Vocational Guidance* (Vol.4, pp. 446-449)
J.G. Ferguson Publishing Co.
200 W. Madison St., Ste. 300
Chicago, IL 60606
Ph: (312)580-5480 Fax: (312)580-4948

William E. Hopke, editor-in-chief. Ninth edition, 1993. Four-volume set that profiles 500 occupations and describes job trends in 74 industries. Includes career description, educational requirements, history of the job, methods of entry, advancement, employment outlook, earnings, working conditions, social and psychological factors, and sources of additional information.

★5577★ *Video Career Library - Construction*
Careers, Inc.
PO Box 135
Largo, FL 34649-0135
Ph: (813)584-7333

Videocassette. 1990. 36 mins. Part of the Video Career Library covering 165 occupations. Shows actual workers on the job. Includes millwrights, brickmasons, carpenters, drywall installers, electricians, painters, plumbers and pipefitters, carpenter and soft tile installers, insulation workers, paving equipment operators, and structural metal workers.

Associations

★5578★ American Foundrymen's Society
505 State St.
Des Plaines, IL 60016-8399
Ph: (708)824-0181

Members: Foundrymen, patternmakers, technologists, and educators. **Purpose:** Sponsors training courses through the Cast Metal Institute; conducts educational and instructional exhibits of foundry industry; sponsors regional conferences, technical meetings, and seminars.

★5579★ Associated General Contractors of America (AGC)
1957 E St. NW
Washington, DC 20006
Ph: (202)393-2040 Fax: (202)347-4004

Members: General construction contractors; subcontractors; industry suppliers; service firms. **Purpose:** Provides market services through its divisions. Conducts special conferences and seminars designed specifically for construction firms. Compiles statistics on job accidents reported by member firms. ors. Maintains 65 committees, including joint cooperative committees with other associations and liaison committees with federal agencies. **Publications:** *AGC Membership Directory and Buyers' Guide*, annual. • *AGC Mobile Directory*. • *Associated General Contractors of America—National Newsletter*, biweekly. • *Constructor*, monthly.

★5580★ International Association of Bridge, Structural and Ornamental Iron Workers (IABSOIW)
1750 New York Ave. NW
Washington, DC 20006
Ph: (202)383-4810 Fax: (202)638-4856

Members: AFL-CIO. **Publications:** *Ironworker*, monthly.

★5581★ National Association of Reinforcing Steel Contractors (NARSC)
10382 Main St., Ste. 300
PO Box 280
Fairfax, VA 22030
Ph: (703)591-1870 Fax: (703)591-1895

Members: Companies engaged primarily in the placing of reinforcing steel and post-tensioning systems; associate members are suppliers of services and materials. **Purpose:** Serves as a unified voice for reinforcing steel contractors. Disseminates information on topics such as trade practices, construction techniques, efficient operation, safety standards, and welfare. Advises members on congressional legislation, wage settlements throughout the country, and other matters. Conducts studies on apprenticeship and training, equal employment, and labor relations.

★5582★ National Erectors Association (NEA)
1501 Lee Hwy., No. 202
Arlington, VA 22209
Ph: (703)524-3336 Fax: (703)524-3364

Members: Active members are erector, ironworking, industrial, and maintenance contracting firms engaged in the erection of steel or allied materials. Associate members are engaged in the manufacture of products and equipment or providing services generally used in the fabrication, erection, or transportation of structural steel. **Purpose:** Objectives include developing industry standards, communicating governmental regulations to members, promoting safe work practices, and expanding opportunities for job training and increasing job skills. Represents the industry engaged in the erection of structural steel, allied work, and industrial maintenance before all divisions of government. Conducts activities with labor organizations to prevent strikes and promote cooperation with labor groups in areas of mutual interest. Conducts research. **Publications:** *NEA Notes Newsletter*, monthly.

Standards/Certification Agencies

★5583★ National Association of Reinforcing Steel Contractors (NARSC)
10382 Main St., Ste. 300
PO Box 280
Fairfax, VA 22030
Ph: (703)591-1870 Fax: (703)591-1895

Serves as a unified voice for reinforcing steel contractors. Disseminates information on topics such as trade practices, construction techniques, efficient operation, safety standards, and welfare. Advises members on congressional legislation, wage settlements throughout the country, and other matters. Conducts studies on apprenticeship and training, equal employment, and labor relations.

★5584★ National Erectors Association (NEA)
1501 Lee Hwy., No. 202
Arlington, VA 22209
Ph: (703)524-3336 Fax: (703)524-3364

Objectives include developing industry standards, communicating governmental regulations to members, promoting safe work practices, and expanding opportunities for job training and increasing job skills. Represents the industry engaged in the erection of structural steel, allied work, and industrial maintenance before all divisions of government.

Educational Directories and Programs

★5585★ *AGC Membership Directory and Buyers' Guide*
Associated General Contractors of America (AGC)
1957 E St. NW
Washington, DC 20006
Ph: (202)393-2040 Fax: (202)347-4004

Annual.

★5586★ *AGC Mobile Directory*
Associated General Contractors of America (AGC)
1957 E St. NW
Washington, DC 20006
Ph: (202)393-2040 Fax: (202)347-4004

★5587★ *International Directory of Building Research, Information and Development Organizations*
29 W. 35th St.
New York, NY 10001
Ph: (212)244-3336

Over 600 universities, institutions, government agencies, and other construction-related research institutions. Entries include: Institution name, address, phone, telex, name and title of contact, number of staff, source of finance, area of interest, publications.

Basic Reference Guides and Handbooks

★5588★ *Intelligent Buildings Institute—Directory of Products and Services*
Intelligent Buildings Institute (IBI)
2101 L St., NW, Ste. 300
Washington, DC 20037
Ph: (202)457-1988 Fax: (202)457-8468

S. Hunt, Associate Executive Director, editor. Annual, September. Member consultants, associations, research organizations, and other suppliers of products and services to the construction and building industry. Entries include: Company name, address, phone. Arrangement: Alphabetical. Indexes: Product/service.

Periodicals

★5589★ *ABC Today*
Associated Builders and Contractors, Inc. (ABC)
N. 17th St.
Rosslyn, VA 22209
Ph: (703)637-8800 Fax: (703)812-8203
Pamela E. Hunter

Semimonthly. Designed to keep readers alerted to important changes within ABC and the construction industry. Reports on legislative issues, construction trends, conferences and meetings, and ABC services. Recurring features include news of members and columns titled Industry Briefs, Safety Notebook, Computer Corner, Bottom Line, and Chapter News.

★5590★ *ABC Today*
Associated Builders and Contractors, Inc. (ABC)
1300 N. 17th St., 8th Floor
Arlington, VA 22209-3803
Ph: (703)812-2000 Fax: (703)812-8203
Pamela E. Hunter

Semiweekly. Magazine for open shop contractors and subcontractors. Includes articles on national and regional construction news, construction management, project case histories, new products, building design, and legislative and regulatory updates.

★5591★ *American Architectural Manufacturers Association—Quarterly Review*
American Architectural Manufacturers Association
1540 E. Dundee Rd., Ste. 310
Palatine, IL 60067-8321
Ph: (708)202-1350 Fax: (708)202-1480
Tony Coorlim

Annual. Contains industry news on architectural products. Covers prime and combination storm windows, sliding glass and combination storm doors, window and curtainwalls, store fronts and entrances, siding, soffits, fascia, gutters, downspouts, skylights, space enclosures, and mobile home components. Recurring features include news of research, notices of publications available, and announcements by the Association.

★5592★ *American Institute of Constructors—Newsletter*
American Institute of Constructors
9887 Gandy Blvd. N., Ste. 104
St. Petersburg, FL 33702
Ph: (813)578-1962 Fax: (813)578-9982
Cheryl P. Harris

Bimonthly. Concerned with construction practice, design, administration, and teaching. Carries news of members, listings of job opportunities, local chapter reports, notices of new publications, and conferences on construction topics.

★5593★ *Associated General Contractors of America—National Newsletter*
Associated General Contractors of America (AGC)
1957 E St. NW
Washington, DC 20006
Ph: (202)393-2040 Fax: (202)347-4004

Biweekly.

★5594★ *Blue Reports, Inc.*
Construction News Service
7325 Steel Mill Dr.
Springfield, VA 22050
Ph: (703)644-5884 Fax: (703)644-1929
Calvin S. Oren

Daily. Reports on public and private construction projects in the Washington, DC, Virginia, and Maryland areas. Provides owner's and architect's names, plan status, date bids due, prospective bidders, low bids received, and specification details.

★5595★ *Boilermaker Reporter*
International Brotherhood of Boilermakers, Iron Shipbuilders
753 State Ave., No. 570
Kansas City, KS 66101-2511
Ph: (913)371-2640
Donald Caswell, Contact

Bimonthly. Discusses news of interest to members of the union. Recurring features include letters to the editor and columns titled Safety & Health and Retiree News.

★5596★ *Building Concerns*
National Association of Minority Contractors (NAMC)
1333 F St. NW, Ste. 500
Washington, DC 20004
Ph: (202)347-8259 Fax: (202)628-1876
Agreta Hester

Quarterly. Concentrates on national and regional news regarding minority construction contractors. Contains articles on issues generally affecting the industry—especially issues affecting minorities—including topics such as legislative and regulatory activity and reports on major corporation developments. Recurring features include reports of meetings, news of educational opportunities, a calendar of events, and news of NAMC chapters, affiliates, and members.

★5597★ *Building Industry Technology: An Abstract Newsletter*
National Technical Information Service (NTIS)
5285 Port Royal Rd.
Springfield, VA 22161
Ph: (703)487-4630

Biweekly. Consists of abstracts of reports on architectural and environmental design, building standards, construction materials and equipment, and structural analyses. Recurring features include a form for ordering reports from NTIS.

★5598★ *Capital Comments*
National Lumber & Building Material Dealers Association
40 Ivy St. SE
Washington, DC 20003
Ph: (202)547-2230 Fax: (202)547-7640
Matt Geitner

Semimonthly. Reports on news of legislation pertaining to lumber, other building materials, and housing. Discusses such issues as lumber subsidies, interest rates on homes, health and safety, and jobs.

★5599★ *ConnStruction*
McHugh Design, Advertising & Publishing
62 Lasalle Rd., Ste. 211
West Hartford, CT 06107
Ph: (203)523-7518 Fax: (203)231-8808
Tracy E. McHugh

Quarterly. Magazine for construction industry.

★5600★ *CONSTRUCTION*
HES, Inc.
26 Long Hill Rd.
PO Box 362
Guilford, CT 06437-0362
Ph: (203)453-3717 Fax: (203)453-4390
Jack C. Lewis

Semiweekly. Journal for the construction industry.

★5601★ *Construction News*
10835 Financial Centre Pkwy., Ste. 133
Little Rock, AR 72211-3555
Ph: (501)376-1931 Fax: (501)375-5831
Robert Alvey

Weekly. Construction industry magazine.

★5602★ *Construction Newsletter*
National Safety Council
1121 Spring Lake Dr.
Itasca, IL 60143-3201
Ph: (708)775-2282 Fax: (708)775-2285
Diane A. Ghazarian

Bimonthly. Focuses on industrial and occupational safety in the construction industry. Carries items on such topics as safe work practices and products; accident prevention; and successful industrial safety programs and policies.

★5603★ *Daily Construction Reporter*
7670 Opprtunity Rd.
San Diego, CA 92111-1112
Ph: (619)492-1402 Fax: (619)565-4182
Bernado Romanowsky

Daily. Construction newspaper covering jobs that are out for bid, bid results, building permits, and other information.

★5604★ *Industrial Machinery News*
Hartland Communications
1003 Central Ave.
Ft. Dodge, IA 50501
Ph: (515)955-1600 Fax: (515)955-3753
Lucky D. Slate

Monthly. Magazine reporting on machinery, equipment, and supplies for manufacturing operations in the metal-working industry.

★5605★ *International Construction*
Maclean Hunter Publishing Co.
29 N. Wacker Drive
Chicago, IL 60606
Ph: (312)726-2802 Fax: (312)726-2574
Alan Peterson

Monthly. Trade magazine.

★5606★ *Metal Construction News*
Modern Trade Communications, Inc.
7450 N. Skokie Blvd.
Skokie, IL 60077
Ph: (708)674-2200 Fax: (708)674-3676
Shawn Zuver

Monthly. Magazine focusing on metal building, metal roof, and sidewall news.

★5607★ *Nation's Building News*
1201 15th St. NW
Washington, DC 20005-2800
Ph: (202)822-0525 Fax: (202)861-2131
Tim Ahern

Semiweekly. Trade magazine (tabloid) covering home building and all related industries.

★5608★ *Nation's Building News*
National Association of Home Builders of the U.S. (NAHB)
1201 15th St. NW
Washington, DC 20005
Ph: (202)822-0200 Fax: (202)822-0559

Semimonthly. Provides the latest information concerning the housing industry, including finance, legislation, new technologies, and membership news.

★5609★ *NEA Notes Newsletter*
National Erectors Association (NEA)
1501 Lee Hwy., No. 202
Arlington, VA 22209
Ph: (703)524-3336 Fax: (703)524-3364

Monthly.

★5610★ *Professional Builder & Remodeler*
Cahners Publishing Co.
1350 E. Touhy Ave.
PO Box 5080
Des Plaines, IL 60018-5080
Ph: (708)635-8800 Fax: (708)635-9950
Ed Fitch

Monthly.

★5611★ *Roads & Bridges Magazine*
Scranton Gillette Communications, Inc.
380 E. Northwest Hwy.
Des Plaines, IL 60016-2282
Ph: (708)298-6622 Fax: (708)390-0408
Tom Kuennen

Monthly. Magazine containing information on highway, road, and bridge design, construction, and maintenance for government agencies, contractors, and consulting engineers.

★5612★ *Steel Digest*
Intersteel Technology, Inc.
PO Box 560786
Charlotte, NC 28256-0786
Ph: (704)549-4177 Fax: (704)549-4178
John A. Vallomy

Bimonthly. Highlights new technologies, new equipment, and innovative concepts in the iron and steel industry. Discusses technology pertinent to blast furnaces, oxygen converters, electric arc furnaces, ladle metallurgy, continuous casting, and general steelmaking. Recurring features include editorials and news of research.

Meetings and Conventions

★5613★ American Foundrymen's Society Casting Congress and Cast Expo
American Foundrymen's Society, Inc.
505 State St.
Des Plaines, IL 60016-8399
Ph: (708)824-0181 Fax: (708)824-7848
Fr: 800-537-4237

Congress is annual; exposition is held every three years. **Dates and Locations:** 1996 Apr 20-23; Philadelphia, PA. • 1997 Apr 12-17; Seattle, WA.

Other Sources of Information

★5614★ "Ironworker Machine Operator" in *Career Selector 2001*
Barron's Educational Series, Inc.
250 Wireless Blvd.
Hauppauge, NY 11788
Ph: (516)434-3311 Fax: (516)434-3723
Fr: 800-645-3476

James C. Gonyea. 1993.

Tilesetters

Tilesetters apply tile to floors, walls, and ceilings. One of every 2 tilesetters is self-employed, compared to 1 of every 4 construction workers. Most self-employed tilesetters work on residential projects. Tilesetters are employed throughout the country but are found largely in urban areas.

Salaries

Salaries for experienced tilesetters range from $10.00/hour to $28.00/hour. Apprentices usually start earning 50% of journeymen's wages.

Employment Outlook

Growth rate until the year 2005: Average.

Tilesetters

Career Guides

★5615★ **"Marble Setter, Tilesetters, and Terrazzo Workers" in *Opportunities in Building Construction Trades* (pp. 63-65)**
National Textbook Co. (NTC)
VGM Career Books
4255 W. Touhy Ave.
Lincolnwood, IL 60646-1975
Ph: (708)679-5500 Fax: (708)679-2494
Fr: 800-323-4900

Michael Sumichrast. 1989. Gives an overview of the construction industry and describes the jobs of various craftworkers. Covers different kinds of builders: home, custom; and describes management skills needed and industry trends affecting opportunities.

★5616★ ***Marble Setters, Tile Layers and Terrazzo Workers***
Chronicle Guidance Publications, Inc.
66 Aurora St.
PO Box 1190
Moravia, NY 13118-1190
Ph: (315)497-0330 Fax: (315)497-3359
Fr: 800-622-7284

1993. This career brief describes the nature of the work, working conditions, hours and earnings, education and training, licensure, certification, unions, personal qualifications, social and psychological factors, employment outlook, entry methods, advancement, and related occupations.

★5617★ **"Marble Setters, Tile Setters, and Terrazzo Workers" in *Encyclopedia of Careers and Vocational Guidance* (Vol.3, pp. 366-368)**
J.G. Ferguson Publishing Co.
200 W. Madison St., Ste. 300
Chicago, IL 60606
Ph: (312)580-5480 Fax: (312)580-4948

William E. Hopke, editor-in-chief. Ninth edition, 1993. Four-volume set that profiles 500 occupations and describes job trends in 74 industries. Includes career description, educational requirements, history of the job, methods of entry, advancement, employment outlook, earnings, working conditions, social and psychological factors, and sources of additional information.

★5618★ ***Marble, Tile Setters, Terrazzo, and Stone Workers***
Careers, Inc.
PO Box 135
Largo, FL 34649-0135
Ph: (813)584-7333

1993. Four-page brief offering the definition, history, duties, working conditions, personal qualifications, educational requirements, earnings, hours, employment outlook, advancement possibilities, and related occupations.

★5619★ **"Marble, Tile, Terrazzo, and Stone Workers" in *Occu-Facts: Information on 580 Careers in Outline Form***
Careers, Inc.
PO Box 135
Largo, FL 34649-0135
Ph: (813)584-7333

Biennial, 1995-96 edition. Each one-page occupational profile describes duties, working conditions, physical surroundings and demands, aptitudes, temperament, educational requirements, employment outlook, earnings, and places of employment.

★5620★ **"Marble, Tile, and Terrazzo Worker" in *Career Information Center* (Vol.4)**
Simon and Schuster
200 Old Tappan Rd.
Old Tappan, NJ 07675
Fax: 800-445-6991 Fr: 800-223-2348

Richard Lidz and Dale Anderson, editorial directors. Fifth edition, 1993. For 600 occupations, describes job duties, entry-level requirements, education and training needed, advancement possibilities, employment outlook, earnings and benefits. The set is divided into 12 volumes. Each volume includes jobs related under a broad career field. Volume 13 is the index.

★5621★ ***Tile Setter***
Vocational Biographies, Inc.
PO Box 31
Sauk Centre, MN 56378-0031
Ph: (612)352-6516 Fax: (612)352-5546
Fr: 800-255-0752

1991. This pamphlet profiles a person working in the job. Includes information about job duties, working conditions, places of employment, educational preparation, labor market outlook, and salaries.

★5622★ **"Tilesetters" in *Occupational Outlook Handbook***
U.S. Government Printing Office
Superintendent of Documents
Washington, DC 20402
Ph: (202)512-1800 Fax: (202)512-2250

Biennial; latest edition, 1994-95. Encyclopedia of careers describing more than 250 occupations and comprising about 85 percent of all jobs in the economy. Occupations that require lengthy education or training are given the most attention. For each occupation, the handbook describes job duties, working conditions, training, educational preparation, personal qualities, advancement possibilities, job outlook, earnings, and sources of additional information.

★5623★ ***The Trowel Trades***
International Masonry Institute
823 15th St. NW, Ste. 1001
Washington, DC 20005
Ph: (202)783-3908

This six-panel brochure describes skills, advancement opportunities, and apprentice training.

★5624★ ***Video Career Library - Construction***
Careers, Inc.
PO Box 135
Largo, FL 34649-0135
Ph: (813)584-7333

Videocassette. 1990. 36 mins. Part of the Video Career Library covering 165 occupations. Shows actual workers on the job. Includes millwrights, brickmasons, carpenters, drywall installers, electricians, painters, plumbers and pipefitters, carpenter and soft tile installers, insulation workers, paving equipment operators, and structural metal workers.

★5625★ *You Can Become a Tile, Marble, Terrazzo and Dimensional Stone Installer*
United Brotherhood of Carpenters and Joiners of America
101 Constitution Ave., N.W.
Washington, DC 20001
Ph: (202)546-6206
This six-panel brochure describes apprenticeship training, hours, and working conditions.

Associations

★5626★ International Union of Bricklayers and Allied Craftsmen (BAC)
815 15th St. NW
Washington, DC 20005
Ph: (202)783-3788 Fax: (202)393-0219
Members: AFL-CIO. **Publications:** *Chalkline*, periodic.

★5627★ United Brotherhood of Carpenters and Joiners of America (UBC)
101 Constitution Ave. NW
Washington, DC 20001
Ph: (202)546-6206
Members: AFL-CIO. **Publications:** *Carpenter*, bimonthly.

Educational Directories and Programs

★5628★ *Ceramic Source*
American Ceramic Society
735 Ceramic Pl.
Westerville, OH 43081-8720
Ph: (614)890-4700 Fax: (614)899-6109
Doris L. Isaac, Contact
Annual, November. Publication includes: List of about 3,000 manufacturers, educational institutions, associations, publications, etc., in the ceramic industry; international coverage. Entries include: Name, address, phone, telex, and cable address; year established; description of products, services, or activities; names and titles of executives; number of employees. Arrangement: Alphabetical.

Periodicals

★5629★ *ABC Today*
Associated Builders and Contractors, Inc. (ABC)
N. 17th St.
Rosslyn, VA 22209
Ph: (703)637-8800 Fax: (703)812-8203
Pamela E. Hunter
Semimonthly. Designed to keep readers alerted to important changes within ABC and the construction industry. Reports on legislative issues, construction trends, conferences and meetings, and ABC services. Recurring features include news of members and columns titled Industry Briefs, Safety Notebook, Computer Corner, Bottom Line, and Chapter News.

★5630★ *ABC Today*
Associated Builders and Contractors, Inc. (ABC)
1300 N. 17th St., 8th Floor
Arlington, VA 22209-3803
Ph: (703)812-2000 Fax: (703)812-8203
Pamela E. Hunter
Semiweekly. Magazine for open shop contractors and subcontractors. Includes articles on national and regional construction news, construction management, project case histories, new products, building design, and legislative and regulatory updates.

★5631★ *American Architectural Manufacturers Association—Quarterly Review*
American Architectural Manufacturers Association
1540 E. Dundee Rd., Ste. 310
Palatine, IL 60067-8321
Ph: (708)202-1350 Fax: (708)202-1480
Tony Coorlim
Annual. Contains industry news on architectural products. Covers prime and combination storm windows, sliding glass and combination storm doors, window and curtainwalls, store fronts and entrances, siding, soffits, fascia, gutters, downspouts, skylights, space enclosures, and mobile home components. Recurring features include news of research, notices of publications available, and announcements by the Association.

★5632★ *American Institute of Constructors—Newsletter*
American Institute of Constructors
9887 Gandy Blvd. N., Ste. 104
St. Petersburg, FL 33702
Ph: (813)578-1962 Fax: (813)578-9982
Cheryl P. Harris
Bimonthly. Concerned with construction practice, design, administration, and teaching. Carries news of members, listings of job opportunities, local chapter reports, notices of new publications, and conferences on construction topics.

★5633★ *Blue Reports, Inc.*
Construction News Service
7325 Steel Mill Dr.
Springfield, VA 22050
Ph: (703)644-5884 Fax: (703)644-1929
Calvin S. Oren
Daily. Reports on public and private construction projects in the Washington, DC, Virginia, and Maryland areas. Provides owner's and architect's names, plan status, date bids due, prospective bidders, low bids received, and specification details.

★5634★ *Building Concerns*
National Association of Minority Contractors (NAMC)
1333 F St. NW, Ste. 500
Washington, DC 20004
Ph: (202)347-8259 Fax: (202)628-1876
Agreta Hester
Quarterly. Concentrates on national and regional news regarding minority construction contractors. Contains articles on issues generally affecting the industry—especially issues affecting minorities—including topics such as legislative and regulatory activity and reports on major corporation developments. Recurring features include reports of meetings, news of educational opportunities, a calendar of events, and news of NAMC chapters, affiliates, and members.

★5635★ *Building Industry Technology: An Abstract Newsletter*
National Technical Information Service (NTIS)
5285 Port Royal Rd.
Springfield, VA 22161
Ph: (703)487-4630
Biweekly. Consists of abstracts of reports on architectural and environmental design, building standards, construction materials and equipment, and structural analyses. Recurring features include a form for ordering reports from NTIS.

★5636★ *Capital Comments*
National Lumber & Building Material Dealers Association
40 Ivy St. SE
Washington, DC 20003
Ph: (202)547-2230 Fax: (202)547-7640
Matt Geitner
Semimonthly. Reports on news of legislation pertaining to lumber, other building materials, and housing. Discusses such issues as lumber subsidies, interest rates on homes, health and safety, and jobs.

★5637★ *Chalkline*
International Union of Bricklayers and Allied Craftsmen (BAC)
815 15th St. NW
Washington, DC 20005
Ph: (202)783-3788 Fax: (202)393-0219
Periodic.

★5638★ *ConnStruction*
McHugh Design, Advertising & Publishing
62 Lasalle Rd., Ste. 211
West Hartford, CT 06107
Ph: (203)523-7518 Fax: (203)231-8808
Tracy E. McHughPublisher
Quarterly. Magazine for construction industry.

★5639★ *CONSTRUCTION*
HES, Inc.
26 Long Hill Rd.
PO Box 362
Guilford, CT 06437-0362
Ph: (203)453-3717 Fax: (203)453-4390
Jack C. Lewis
Semiweekly. Journal for the construction industry.

★5640★ *Construction News*
10835 Financial Centre Pkwy., Ste. 133
Little Rock, AR 72211-3555
Ph: (501)376-1931 Fax: (501)375-5831
Robert Alvey
Weekly. Construction industry magazine.

★5641★ *Construction Newsletter*
National Safety Council
1121 Spring Lake Dr.
Itasca, IL 60143-3201
Ph: (708)775-2282 Fax: (708)775-2285
Diane A. Ghazarian

Bimonthly. Focuses on industrial and occupational safety in the construction industry. Carries items on such topics as safe work practices and products; accident prevention; and successful industrial safety programs and policies.

★5642★ *Daily Construction Reporter*
7670 Opprtunity Rd.
San Diego, CA 92111-1112
Ph: (619)492-1402 Fax: (619)565-4182
Bernado Romanowsky

Daily. Construction newspaper covering jobs that are out for bid, bid results, building permits, and other information.

★5643★ *International Construction*
Maclean Hunter Publishing Co.
29 N. Wacker Drive
Chicago, IL 60606
Ph: (312)726-2802 Fax: (312)726-2574
Alan Peterson

Monthly. Trade magazine.

★5644★ *Nation's Building News*
1201 15th St. NW
Washington, DC 20005-2800
Ph: (202)822-0525 Fax: (202)861-2131
Tim Ahern

Semiweekly. Trade magazine (tabloid) covering home building and all related industries.

★5645★ *Nation's Building News*
National Association of Home Builders of the U.S. (NAHB)
1201 15th St. NW
Washington, DC 20005
Ph: (202)822-0200 Fax: (202)822-0559

Semimonthly. Provides the latest information concerning the housing industry, including finance, legislation, new technologies, and membership news.

★5646★ *Professional Builder & Remodeler*
Cahners Publishing Co.
1350 E. Touhy Ave.
PO Box 5080
Des Plaines, IL 60018-5080
Ph: (708)635-8800 Fax: (708)635-9950
Ed Fitch

Monthly.

★5647★ *Tile & Decorative Surfaces*
20335 Ventura Blvd., No. 400
Woodland Hills, CA 91364
Ph: (818)704-5555 Fax: (818)704-6500
Jerry Fisher

Monthly. International trade publication available to the hand surfaces industries: ceramic tile, natural stone tiles, terrazzo, cement tiles, glass tiles and agglomerated marble and granite tiles.

Meetings and Conventions

★5648★ Installation Supplies and Ideas Expo
National Association of Floor Covering Distributors
401 N. Michigan Ave.
Chicago, IL 60611-4207
Ph: (312)644-6610 Fax: (312)245-1084

Annual.

Precision Assemblers

Assemblers are workers who put together the parts of manufactured articles. In some instances, hundreds of assemblers work on a single product; in others, a single assembler is responsible for each product. Assembly work varies from simple, repetitive jobs that are relatively easy to learn to those requiring great precision and many months of experience and training. The following industries provide wage and salary jobs for precision assemblers: Electrical and electronic machinery and equipment; machinery, except electrical ; transportation equipment; professional and scientific instruments; and fabricated metal products.

Salaries

Average earnings of assemblers in various industries are as follows:

Full-time workers who assemble electrical and electronic equipment	$248-$418/week
Union aircraft assemblers	$400-$600/week

Employment Outlook

Growth rate until the year 2005: Decline.

Precision Assemblers

Career Guides

★5649★ ***Aerospace Assembly Worker***
Vocational Biographies, Inc.
PO Box 31
Sauk Centre, MN 56378-0031
Ph: (612)352-6516 Fax: (612)352-5546
Fr: 800-255-0752

1990. This pamphlet profiles a person working in the job. Includes information about job duties, working conditions, places of employment, educational preparation, labor market outlook, and salaries.

★5650★ **"Aircraft Assembler" in *Occu-Facts: Information on 580 Careers in Outline Form***
Careers, Inc.
PO Box 135
Largo, FL 34649-0135
Ph: (813)584-7333

Biennial, 1995-96 edition. Each one-page occupational profile describes duties, working conditions, physical surroundings and demands, aptitudes, temperament, educational requirements, employment outlook, earnings, and places of employment.

★5651★ ***Alternatives to Assembly Lines: Modern Times—Revisited***
Britannica Films
310 S. Michigan Ave.
Chicago, IL 60604
Ph: (312)347-7900 Fax: (312)347-7966
Fr: 800-554-9862

Videocassette. 1988. 29 mins. In this program we visit assembly plants in Sweden and Italy to see how Volvo and Olivetti use self-pacing work teams, replacing the classic assembly line.

★5652★ ***Assembler, Aircraft***
Careers, Inc.
PO Box 135
Largo, FL 34649-0135
Ph: (813)584-7333

1993. Two-page occupational summary card describing duties, working conditions, personal qualifications, training, earnings and hours, employment outlook, places of employment, related careers and where to write for more information.

★5653★ **"Assembler" in *Career Information Center* (Vol.9)**
Simon and Schuster
200 Old Tappan Rd.
Old Tappan, NJ 07675
Fax: 800-445-6991 Fr: 800-223-2348

Richard Lidz and Dale Anderson, editorial directors. Fifth edition, 1993. For 600 occupations, describes job duties, entry-level requirements, education and training needed, advancement possibilities, employment outlook, earnings and benefits. The set is divided into 12 volumes. Each volume includes jobs related under a broad career field. Volume 13 is the index.

★5654★ **"Assemblers" in *Career Discovery Encyclopedia* (Vol.1, pp. 66-67)**
J.G. Ferguson Publishing Co.
200 W. Madison St., Ste. 300
Chicago, IL 60606
Ph: (312)580-5480 Fax: (312)580-4948

E. Russell Primm, editor-in-chief. 1993. Contains two-page articles on 504 occupations. Each article describes job duties, earnings, and educational and training requirements.

★5655★ ***Assemblers, Electronics Manufacturing***
Careers, Inc.
PO Box 135
Largo, FL 34649-0135
Ph: (813)584-7333

1993. Two-page occupational summary card describing duties, working conditions, personal qualifications, training, earnings and hours, employment outlook, places of employment, related careers and where to write for more information.

★5656★ **"Assemblers" in *Encyclopedia of Careers and Vocational Guidance* (Vol.2, pp. 109-112)**
J.G. Ferguson Publishing Co.
200 W. Madison St., Ste. 300
Chicago, IL 60606
Ph: (312)580-5480 Fax: (312)580-4948

William E. Hopke, editor-in-chief. Ninth edition, 1993. Four-volume set that profiles 500 occupations and describes job trends in 74 industries. Includes career description, educational requirements, history of the job, methods of entry, advancement, employment outlook, earnings, working conditions, social and psychological factors, and sources of additional information.

★5657★ **"Electronics Assemblers" in *The Complete Electronics Career Guide* (pp. 40-43)**
TAB/McGraw-Hill, Inc.
PO Box 182607
Columbus, OH 43218-2607
Fax: (614)759-3644 Fr: 800-822-8158

Joe Risse. 1989. Explores opportunities for electronic technicians in industry, broadcasting, appliance repair, telecommunications, computer servicing, and technical writing. Offers advice on educational preparation, training, finding or changing jobs, and career advancement. Lists trade publications and professional associations.

★5658★ **"Electronics Manufacturing Assemblers" in *Occu-Facts: Information on 580 Careers in Outline Form***
Careers, Inc.
PO Box 135
Largo, FL 34649-0135
Ph: (813)584-7333

Biennial, 1995-96 edition. Each one-page occupational profile describes duties, working conditions, physical surroundings and demands, aptitudes, temperament, educational requirements, employment outlook, earnings, and places of employment.

★5659★ **"Precision Assembler" in *Jobs Rated Almanac***
World Almanac
1 International Blvd., Ste. 444
Mahwah, NJ 07495
Ph: (201)529-6900 Fax: (201)529-6901

Les Krantz. Second edition, 1992. Ranks 250 jobs by environment, salary, outlooks, physical demands, stress, security, travel opportunities, and extra perks. Includes jobs the editor feels are the most common, most interesting, and the most rapidly growing.

★5660★ "Precision Assemblers" in *American Almanac of Jobs and Salaries* (pp. 529)
Avon Books
1350 Avenue of the Americas
New York, NY 10019
Ph: (212)261-6800 Fr: 800-238-0658
John Wright, editor. Revised and updated, 1994-95. A comprehensive guide to the wages of hundreds of occupations in a wide variety of industries and organizations.

★5661★ "Precision Assemblers" in *Occupational Outlook Handbook*
U.S. Government Printing Office
Superintendent of Documents
Washington, DC 20402
Ph: (202)512-1800 Fax: (202)512-2250
Biennial; latest edition, 1994-95. Encyclopedia of careers describing more than 250 occupations and comprising about 85 percent of all jobs in the economy. Occupations that require lengthy education or training are given the most attention. For each occupation, the handbook describes job duties, working conditions, training, educational preparation, personal qualities, advancement possibilities, job outlook, earnings, and sources of additional information.

★5662★ "Semi-Skilled Assemblers" in *Occu-Facts: Information on 580 Careers in Outline Form*
Careers, Inc.
PO Box 135
Largo, FL 34649-0135
Ph: (813)584-7333
Biennial, 1995-96 edition. Each one-page occupational profile describes duties, working conditions, physical surroundings and demands, aptitudes, temperament, educational requirements, employment outlook, earnings, and places of employment.

★5663★ *Video Career Library - Production II*
Careers, Inc.
PO Box 135
Largo, FL 34649-0135
Ph: (813)584-7333
Videocassette. 1990. 32 mins. Part of the Video Career Library covering 165 occupations. Shows actual workers on the job. Includes tool and die makers, machinists, sheet metal workers, cabinet and bench carpenters, opticians, precision electronic equipment assemblers, industrial machine operators, welders and cutters, and assemblers.

Associations

★5664★ International Association of Machinists and Aerospace Workers (IAM)
9000 Machinists PL
Upper Marlboro, MD 20772
Ph: (301)967-4500 Fax: (301)967-4588
Members: AFL-CIO. **Publications:** *The Machinist*, monthly.

★5665★ International Brotherhood of Electrical Workers (IBEW)
1125 15th St. NW
Washington, DC 20005
Ph: (202)833-7000 Fax: (202)467-6316
Members: AFL-CIO. **Publications:** *IBEW Journal*, monthly.

★5666★ International Union of Electronic, Electrical, Salaried, Machine, and Furniture Workers (IUE)
1126 16th St. NW
Washington, DC 20036
Ph: (202)296-1200 Fax: (202)785-4563
Members: AFL-CIO.**Purpose:** Negotiates collective bargaining agreements; maintains apprenticeship programs. Conducts district education directors meeting and training programs. Compiles statistics. **Publications:** *Health and Safety*. • *International Union of Electronic, Electrical, Salaried, Machine, and Furniture Workers—Convention Proceedings*, biennial. • *IUE News*, bimonthly. • *Research Information*, monthly.

Periodicals

★5667★ *Health and Safety*
International Union of Electronic, Electrical, Salaried, Machine, and Furniture Workers (IUE)
1126 16th St. NW
Washington, DC 20036
Ph: (202)296-1200 Fax: (202)785-4563

★5668★ *International Union of Electronic, Electrical, Salaried, Machine, and Furniture Workers—Convention Proceedings*
International Union of Electronic, Electrical, Salaried, Machine, and Furniture Workers (IUE)
1126 16th St. NW
Washington, DC 20036
Ph: (202)296-1200 Fax: (202)785-4563
Biennial.

★5669★ *IUE News*
International Union of Electronic, Electrical, Salaried, Machine, and Furniture Workers (IUE)
1126 16th St., NW
Washington, DC 20036
Ph: (202)296-1200 Fax: (202)785-4563
Bimonthly.

★5670★ *Research Information Monthly*
International Union of Electronic, Electrical, Salaried, Machine, and Furniture Workers (IUE)
1126 16th St., NW
Washington, DC 20036
Ph: (202)296-1200 Fax: (202)785-4563
Monthly.

Meetings and Conventions

★5671★ International Union of Electronic, Electrical, Salaried, Machine and Furnityre Workers (IUE)
1126 16th St., NW
Washington, DC 20036
Ph: (202)296-1200 Fax: (202)785-4563
Biennial.

Blue-Collar Worker Supervisors

Supervisors ensure that workers, equipment, and materials are used properly and efficiently. They make sure machinery is set up correctly and schedule or perform repairs and maintenance work. Supervisors tell other workers what to do and make sure it is done safely, correctly, and on time. **Blue-collar worker supervisors** may have other titles, such as first-line supervisors, foreman, or forewomen. In the textile industry, they may be referred to as second hands; on ships, boatswains; in the construction industry, they may be called superintendents or crew chiefs; and in oil drilling, toolpushers or gang pushers. Although blue-collar worker supervisors are found in almost all industries, more than 40 percent work in manufacturing; about 15 percent work in the construction industry and 10 percent in wholesale and retail trade. Others were in public utilities, repair shops, transportation, and government agencies.

Salaries

Weekly earnings for blue-collar worker supervisors are as follows:

Lowest 10 percent	$323/week or less
Middle 50 percent	$347-$790/week
Top 10 percent	$1,010/week or more

Employment Outlook

Growth rate until the year 2005: More slowly than average.

Blue-Collar Worker Supervisors

Career Guides

★5672★ "Blue Collar Worker Supervisors" in *Encyclopedia of Careers and Vocational Guidance*
J.G. Ferguson Publishing Co.
200 W. Madison St., Ste. 300
Chicago, IL 60606
Ph: (312)580-5480 Fax: (312)580-4948

William E. Hopke, editor-in-chief. Ninth edition, 1993. Four-volume set that profiles 500 occupations and describes job trends in 74 industries. Includes career description, educational requirements, history of the job, methods of entry, advancement, employment outlook, earnings, working conditions, social and psychological factors, and sources of additional information.

★5673★ "Blue-Collar Worker Supervisors" in *Occupational Outlook Handbook*
U.S. Government Printing Office
Superintendent of Documents
Washington, DC 20402
Ph: (202)512-1800 Fax: (202)512-2250

Biennial; latest edition, 1994-95. Encyclopedia of careers describing more than 250 occupations and comprising about 85 percent of all jobs in the economy. Occupations that require lengthy education or training are given the most attention. For each occupation, the handbook describes job duties, working conditions, training, educational preparation, personal qualities, advancement possibilities, job outlook, earnings, and sources of additional information.

★5674★ "Carpenter Foreman" in *Hard Hatted Women: Stories of Struggle and Success in the Trades* (pp. 122-134)
Seal Press
3131 Western Ave., Ste. 410
Seattle, WA 98121
Ph: (206)283-7844 Fax: (206)285-9410

Molly Martin, editor. 1988. Twenty-six women recount their experiences working in blue collar occupations. They describe how they got in, the work they do, their relationships in predominantly male occupations, and their training.

★5675★ "Dock Foreman/Supervisor" in *Careers in Trucking*
Rosen Publishing Group
29 E. 21st St.
New York, NY 10010
Ph: (212)777-3017 Fax: (212)777-0277
Fr: 800-237-9932

Donald D. Schauer. 1991. Describes employment in the trucking industry including driving, operations, sales, and administration. Covers qualifications, training, future outlook, and salaries. Offers career planning and job hunting advice.

★5676★ "Production Supervisor" in *Career Information Center* (Vol.9)
Simon and Schuster
200 Old Tappan Rd.
Old Tappan, NJ 07675
Fax: 800-445-6991 Fr: 800-223-2348

Richard Lidz and Dale Anderson, editorial directors. Fifth edition, 1993. For 600 occupations, describes job duties, entry-level requirements, education and training needed, advancement possibilities, employment outlook, earnings and benefits. The set is divided into 12 volumes. Each volume includes jobs related under a broad career field. Volume 13 is the index.

★5677★ *Successful Strategies for Manufacturing Management*
Deltak, Inc.
East-West Technological Center
1751 Diehl Rd.
Naperville, IL 60563
Ph: (708)369-3000

Videocassette. 1984. 40 mins. This series of programs examines how to plan and design strategies to use the new systems of manufacturing technology.

★5678★ *Supervisory Planning and Control*
Bureau of Business Practice
24 Rope Ferry Rd.
Waterford, CT 06386-0001
Ph: (203)442-4365 Fax: (203)434-3341
Fr: 800-243-0876

Videocassette. 1986. 21 mins. For businesses, this tape shows how to manage and run a smooth production line.

Associations

★5679★ American Management Association (AMA)
135 W. 50th St.
New York, NY 10020-1201
Ph: (212)586-8100 Fax: (212)903-8168

Members: Provides educational forums worldwide to teach members and their colleagues about superior, practical business skills and explore best practices of world-class organizations through interaction with each other and expert faculty practitioners. **Purpose:** Publishing program provides tools individuals use to extend learning beyond the classroom in a process of life-long professional growth and development through education. **Publications:** *Compensation and Benefits Review*, bimonthly. • *CompFlash*, monthly. • *HR Focus*, monthly. • *Management Review*, monthly. • *Organizational Dynamics: A Quarterly Review of Organizational Behavior for Professional Managers.* • *The President*, monthly. • *Supervisory Management*, monthly.

Test Guides

★5680★ *Career Examination Series: Assistant Foreman*
National Learning Corp.
212 Michael Dr.
Syosset, NY 11791
Ph: (516)921-8888 Fax: (516)921-8743
Fr: 800-645-6337

Jack Rudman. All examination guides in this series contain questions with answers.

★5681★ *Career Examination Series: Foreman*
National Learning Corp.
212 Michael Dr.
Syosset, NY 11791
Ph: (516)921-8888 Fax: (516)921-8743
Fr: 800-645-6337

Jack Rudman. All examination guides in this series contain questions with answers.

★5682★ *Career Examination Series: Foreman of Laborers*
National Learning Corp.
212 Michael Dr.
Syosset, NY 11791
Ph: (516)921-8888 Fax: (516)921-8743
Fr: 800-645-6337

Jack Rudman. All examination guides in this series contain questions with answers.

PERIODICALS

★5683★ *Construction Supervision & Safety Letter*
Bureau of Business Practice
24 Rope Ferry Rd.
Waterford, CT 06386
Ph: (203)442-4365 Fax: (203)592-3179
Fr: 800-243-0876
Barry Richardson

Semimonthly. Serves supervisors of blue-collar workers with discussion and advice on organizing, planning, and operating. Covers construction safety, the use of communication and motivation as productive management tools, ways to simplify discipline, and building teamwork. Recurring features include interviews with safety professionals, case histories, and cartoons.

★5684★ *Supervision*
National Research Bureau, Inc.
200 N. 4th
PO Box 1
Burlington, IA 52601-0001
Ph: (319)752-5415 Fax: (319)752-3421
Barbara Boeding

Monthly. Magazine for first-line foremen, supervisors, and office managers.

Butchers and Meat, Poultry and Fish Cutters

Butchers and meat, poultry, and fish cutters reduce animal carcasses into small pieces of meat suitable for sale to consumers. In meatpacking plants, butchers slaughter cattle, hogs, goats, and sheep and cut the carcasses into large wholesale cuts to facilitate handling, distribution, and marketing. Meatcutters separate the wholesale cuts into retail cuts or individual size servings. Poultry cuts slaughter and cut up chickens, turkeys, and other types of poultry. Fish cleaners cut, scale, and dress fish in fish processing plants and wholesale and retail fish markets. Over 80 percent of all butchers and meat, poultry, and fish cutters work in meatpacking and poultry and fish processing plants and retail grocery stores, while others are employed by meat and fish markets, restaurants, hotels, and wholesale establishments.

Salaries

Weekly earnings of butchers and meatcutters are as follows:

Middle 50 percent	$230-$490/week
Top 10 percent	$630/week or more

Employment Outlook

Growth rate until the year 2005: More slowly than average.

Butchers and Meat, Poultry and Fish Cutters

Career Guides

★5685★ "Butcher or Boucher" in *Opportunities in Culinary Careers* (pp. 61-62)
National Textbook Co. (NTC)
VGM Career Books
4255 W. Touhy Ave.
Lincolnwood, IL 60646-1975
Ph: (708)679-5500 Fax: (708)679-2494
Fr: 800-323-4900

Mary Deirdre Donovan. 1990. Describes the educational preparation and training of chefs and cooks and explores a variety of food service jobs in restaurants, institutions, and research and development. Lists culinary schools and professional organizations.

★5686★ "Butchers and Meat, Poultry, and Fish Cutters" in *Occupational Outlook Handbook*
U.S. Government Printing Office
Superintendent of Documents
Washington, DC 20402
Ph: (202)512-1800 Fax: (202)512-2250

Biennial; latest edition, 1994-95. Encyclopedia of careers describing more than 250 occupations and comprising about 85 percent of all jobs in the economy. Occupations that require lengthy education or training are given the most attention. For each occupation, the handbook describes job duties, working conditions, training, educational preparation, personal qualities, advancement possibilities, job outlook, earnings, and sources of additional information.

★5687★ "Fish Production Technicians" in *Career Discovery Encyclopedia* (Vol.3, pp. 18-19)
J.G. Ferguson Publishing Co.
200 W. Madison St., Ste. 300
Chicago, IL 60606
Ph: (312)580-5480 Fax: (312)580-4948

E. Russell Primm, editor-in-chief. 1993. Contains two-page articles on 504 occupations. Each article describes job duties, earnings, and educational and training requirements.

★5688★ "Fish Production Technicians" in *Encyclopedia of Careers and Vocational Guidance* (Vol.3, p.1)
J.G. Ferguson Publishing Co.
200 W. Madison St., Ste. 300
Chicago, IL 60606
Ph: (312)580-5480 Fax: (312)580-4948

William E. Hopke, editor-in-chief. Ninth edition, 1993. Four-volume set that profiles 500 occupations and describes job trends in 74 industries. Includes career description, educational requirements, history of the job, methods of entry, advancement, employment outlook, earnings, working conditions, social and psychological factors, and sources of additional information.

★5689★ *Food Services*
Learning Corporation of America
108 Wilmot Rd.
Deerfield, IL 60015
Ph: (708)940-1260 Fax: (708)940-3600
Fr: 800-621-2131

Videocassette. 1982. 21 mins. Four workers in the food industry offer a look at their jobs: chef, restaurant manager, baker and meat wrapper. From the "Working" series.

★5690★ *Meat Cutter*
Careers, Inc.
PO Box 135
Largo, FL 34649-0135
Ph: (813)584-7333

1995. Two-page occupational summary card describing duties, working conditions, personal qualifications, training, earnings and hours, employment outlook, places of employment, related careers and where to write for more information.

★5691★ *Meat Cutter/Market Manager*
Vocational Biographies, Inc.
PO Box 31
Sauk Centre, MN 56378-0031
Ph: (612)352-6516 Fax: (612)352-5546
Fr: 800-255-0752

1991. Four-page pamphlet containing a personal narrative about a worker's job, work likes and dislikes, career path from high school to the present. Education and training, the rewards and frustrations, and the effects of the job on the rest of the worker's life. The data file portion of this pamphlet gives a concise occupational summary, including work descriptions, working conditions, places of employment, personal characteristics, education and training, job outlook, and salary range.

★5692★ "Meat Cutter" in *Occu-Facts: Information on 580 Careers in Outline Form*
Careers, Inc.
PO Box 135
Largo, FL 34649-0135
Ph: (813)584-7333

Biennial, 1995-96 edition. Each one-page occupational profile describes duties, working conditions, physical surroundings and demands, aptitudes, temperament, educational requirements, employment outlook, earnings, and places of employment.

★5693★ "Meat Packing Production Workers" in *Career Discovery Encyclopedia* (Vol.4, pp. 62-63)
J.G. Ferguson Publishing Co.
200 W. Madison St., Ste. 300
Chicago, IL 60606
Ph: (312)580-5480 Fax: (312)580-4948

E. Russell Primm, editor-in-chief. 1993. Contains two-page articles on 504 occupations. Each article describes job duties, earnings, and educational and training requirements.

★5694★ "Meat Packing Production Workers" in *Encyclopedia of Careers and Vocational Guidance* (Vol.3, pp. 381-384)
J.G. Ferguson Publishing Co.
200 W. Madison St., Ste. 300
Chicago, IL 60606
Ph: (312)580-5480 Fax: (312)580-4948

William E. Hopke, editor-in-chief. Ninth edition, 1993. Four-volume set that profiles 500 occupations and describes job trends in 74 industries. Includes career description, educational requirements, history of the job, methods of entry, advancement, employment outlook, earnings, working conditions, social and psychological factors, and sources of additional information.

★5695★ "Meat Packing Worker" in *Career Information Center* (Vol.2)
Simon and Schuster
200 Old Tappan Rd.
Old Tappan, NJ 07675
Fax: 800-445-6991 Fr: 800-223-2348

Richard Lidz and Dale Anderson, editorial directors. Fifth edition, 1993. For 600 occupations, describes job duties, entry-level requirements, education and training needed, advancement possibilities, employment outlook, earnings and benefits. The set is divided into 12 volumes. Each volume includes jobs related under a broad career field. Volume 13 is the index.

★5696★ "Meat Wrapper (Supermarket)" in *Occu-Facts: Information on 580 Careers in Outline Form*
Careers, Inc.
PO Box 135
Largo, FL 34649-0135
Ph: (813)584-7333

Biennial, 1995-96 edition. Each one-page occupational profile describes duties, working conditions, physical surroundings and demands, aptitudes, temperament, educational requirements, employment outlook, earnings, and places of employment.

★5697★ *Meatcutters*
Chronicle Guidance Publications, Inc.
66 Aurora St.
PO Box 1190
Moravia, NY 13118-1190
Ph: (315)497-0330 Fax: (315)497-3359
Fr: 800-622-7284

1993. This career brief describes the nature of the work, working conditions, hours and earnings, education and training, licensure, certification, unions, personal qualifications, social and psychological factors, employment outlook, entry methods, advancement, and related occupations.

★5698★ "Meatcutters" in *American Almanac of Jobs and Salaries* (pp. 533)
Avon Books
1350 Avenue of the Americas
New York, NY 10019
Ph: (212)261-6800 Fr: 800-238-0658

John Wright, editor. Revised and updated, 1994-95. A comprehensive guide to the wages of hundreds of occupations in a wide variety of industries and organizations.

★5699★ "Meatcutters" in *Career Discovery Encyclopedia* (Vol.4, pp. 64-65)
J.G. Ferguson Publishing Co.
200 W. Madison St., Ste. 300
Chicago, IL 60606
Ph: (312)580-5480 Fax: (312)580-4948

E. Russell Primm, editor-in-chief. 1993. Contains two-page articles on 504 occupations. Each article describes job duties, earnings, and educational and training requirements.

★5700★ "Meatcutters" in *Encyclopedia of Careers and Vocational Guidance* (Vol.3, pp. 385-387)
J.G. Ferguson Publishing Co.
200 W. Madison St., Ste. 300
Chicago, IL 60606
Ph: (312)580-5480 Fax: (312)580-4948

William E. Hopke, editor-in-chief. Ninth edition, 1993. Four-volume set that profiles 500 occupations and describes job trends in 74 industries. Includes career description, educational requirements, history of the job, methods of entry, advancement, employment outlook, earnings, working conditions, social and psychological factors, and sources of additional information.

★5701★ "Retail Butcher" in *Career Information Center* (Vol.10)
Simon and Schuster
200 Old Tappan Rd.
Old Tappan, NJ 07675
Fax: 800-445-6991 Fr: 800-223-2348

Richard Lidz and Dale Anderson, editorial directors. Fifth edition, 1993. For 600 occupations, describes job duties, entry-level requirements, education and training needed, advancement possibilities, employment outlook, earnings and benefits. The set is divided into 12 volumes. Each volume includes jobs related under a broad career field. Volume 13 is the index.

★5702★ "Seafood Processing and Marketing" in *Opportunities in Marine and Maritime Careers* (pp. 112-113)
National Textbook Co. (NTC)
VGM Career Books
4255 W. Touhy Ave.
Lincolnwood, IL 60646-1975
Ph: (708)679-5500 Fax: (708)679-2494
Fr: 800-323-4900

William Ray Heitzmann. 1988. Includes careers related by their proximity to water; cruise ships, oceanography, marine sciences, fishing, commercial diving, maritime transportation, shipbuilding, Navy, and Coast Guard. Covers qualifications, job outlook, job duties, educational preparation, and training. Lists associations and schools.

★5703★ *Video Career Library - Public and Personal Services*
Careers, Inc.
PO Box 135
Largo, FL 34649-0135
Ph: (813)584-7333

Videocassette. 1990. 35 mins. Part of the Video Career Library covering 165 occupations. Shows actual workers on the job. Includes firefighters, police officers, correctional officers, bartenders, waiters/waitresses, cooks/chefs, child care workers, flight attendants, barbers/cosmetologists, groundskeepers/gardeners, and butchers/meat cutters.

Associations

★5704★ American Association of Meat Processors (AAMP)
PO Box 269
Elizabethtown, PA 17022
Ph: (717)367-1168

Members: Retail and wholesale operators of meat processing plants, locker plants, frozen food centers, freezer food suppliers and food plants. **Purpose:** Sponsors American Cured Meat Championship and American Meat Platter Competition.

★5705★ United Food and Commercial Workers International Union (UFCW)
1775 K St. NW
Washington, DC 20006
Ph: (202)223-3111

Members: AFL-CIO. **Publications:** *UFCW Action*, bimonthly. • *UFCW Leadership Update*, monthly.

Test Guides

★5706★ *Career Examination Series: Butcher*
National Learning Corp.
212 Michael Dr.
Syosset, NY 11791
Ph: (516)921-8888 Fax: (516)921-8743
Fr: 800-645-6337

Jack Rudman. All examination guides in this series contain questions with answers.

★5707★ *Career Examination Series: Chief Meat Inspector*
National Learning Corp.
212 Michael Dr.
Syosset, NY 11791
Ph: (516)921-8888 Fax: (516)921-8743
Fr: 800-645-6337

Jack Rudman. All examination guides in this series contain questions with answers.

★5708★ *Career Examination Series: Meat Cutter*
National Learning Corp.
212 Michael Dr.
Syosset, NY 11791
Ph: (516)921-8888 Fax: (516)921-8743
Fr: 800-645-6337

Jack Rudman. All examination guides in this series contain questions with answers.

★5709★ *Career Examination Series: Senior Meat Cutter*
National Learning Corp.
212 Michael Dr.
Syosset, NY 11791
Ph: (516)921-8888 Fax: (516)921-8743
Fr: 800-645-6337

Jack Rudman. All examination guides in this series contain questions with answers.

Periodicals

★5710★ *American Meat Institute—Newsletter*
American Meat Institute
PO Box 3556
Washington, DC 20007
Janet M. Riley

Weekly. Contains news of legislative and government regulations and actions relevant to the meat industry. Recurring features include Institute news and livestock and slaughter reports.

★5711★ *National Broiler Council—Washington Report*
National Broiler Council
1155 15th St. NW, Ste. 614
Washington, DC 20005
Ph: (202)296-2622 Fax: (202)293-4005
Margaret Ernst

Weekly. Centers on issues affecting the marketing of poultry for the broiler processing industry. Covers government actions, export markets, and grain supplies.

★5712★ *Seafood Leader*
Waterfront Press Co.
1115 NW 46th St.
Seattle, WA 98107
Ph: (206)789-6506 Fax: (206)789-9193
Peter Redmayne

Bimonthly. Magazine on seafood buying, marketing, and technology. Articles range from seafood processing technology to merchandising to cuisine; featuring seafood from the ocean to the plate.

★5713★ *UFCW Action*
United Food and Commercial Workers International Union (UFCW)
1775 K St. NW
Washington, DC 20006
Ph: (202)223-3111

Bimonthly. Covers union activities, political and legislative matters, and consumer news.

Meetings and Conventions

★5714★ American Convention of Meat Processors
American Association of Meat Processors
PO Box 269
Elizabethtown, PA 17022
Ph: (717)367-1168 Fax: (717)367-9096

Annual. Always held during July. **Dates and Locations:** 1996 Jul.

★5715★ Food & Dairy Expo
Dairy and Food Industries Supply Association
6245 Executive Blvd.
Rockville, MD 20852
Ph: (301)984-1444 Fax: (301)881-7832

Biennial. Always held during October or November at the McCormick Place Complex in Chicago, Illinois. **Dates and Locations:** 1995 Nov 04-07; Chicago, IL. • 1997 Oct 18-21; Chicago, IL.

★5716★ Midwest Poultry Federation Convention
Midwest Poultry Federation
2380 Wycliff St.
St. Paul, MN 55114
Ph: (612)646-4553 Fax: (612)646-4554

Annual. Always held during February at the Convention Center in Minneapolis, Minnesota. **Dates and Locations:** 1996 Feb.

★5717★ Western States Meat Association Bi-Annual Exposition
Western States Meat Association
PO Box 12944
Oakland, CA 94604
Ph: (510)763-1533 Fax: (415)763-6186

Biennial.

Inspectors, Testers, and Graders

Inspectors, testers, and graders compare products to samples or to specifications in blueprints or graphs to ensure that the products meet quality standards. If the product checks out, inspectors certify it in some manner. They may reject defective items outright, send them for rework, or, in the case of minor problems, fix them themselves. Inspectors, testers, and graders record the results of their inspections, compute the percentage of defects and other statistical parameters, prepare inspection and test reports, notify supervisors of problems, and may help analyze and correct problems. Senior inspectors may also set up tests and test equipment. Over 80 percent of all inspectors, testers, and graders work in manufacturing industries. Some work in wholesale trade, transportation, testing and photofinishing labs, engineering services, and government agencies.

Salaries

Weekly earnings for inspectors, testers, and graders are as follows:

Lowest 10 percent	$209/week or less
Middle 50 percent	$282-$534/week
Top 10 percent	$691/week or more

Employment Outlook

Growth rate until the year 2005: Decline.

Inspectors, Testers, and Graders

Career Guides

★5718★ **"Electronics Inspector" in *Hard Hatted Women: Stories of Struggle and Success in the Trades* (pp. 212-215)**
Seal Press
3131 Western Ave., Ste. 410
Seattle, WA 98121
Ph: (206)283-7844 Fax: (206)285-9410

Molly Martin, editor. 1988. Twenty-six women recount their experiences working in blue collar occupations. They describe how they got in, the work they do, their relationships in predominantly male occupations, and their training.

★5719★ **"Inspectors, Testers, and Graders" in *Occupational Outlook Handbook***
U.S. Government Printing Office
Superintendent of Documents
Washington, DC 20402
Ph: (202)512-1800 Fax: (202)512-2250

Biennial; latest edition, 1994-95. Encyclopedia of careers describing more than 250 occupations and comprising about 85 percent of all jobs in the economy. Occupations that require lengthy education or training are given the most attention. For each occupation, the handbook describes job duties, working conditions, training, educational preparation, personal qualities, advancement possibilities, job outlook, earnings, and sources of additional information.

★5720★ **"Quality Control Inspector" in *Career Information Center* (Vol.9)**
Simon and Schuster
200 Old Tappan Rd.
Old Tappan, NJ 07675
Fax: 800-445-6991 Fr: 800-223-2348

Richard Lidz and Dale Anderson, editorial directors. Fifth edition, 1993. For 600 occupations, describes job duties, entry-level requirements, education and training needed, advancement possibilities, employment outlook, earnings and benefits. The set is divided into 12 volumes. Each volume includes jobs related under a broad career field. Volume 13 is the index.

Associations

★5721★ **American Society for Quality Control (ASQC)**
611 E. Wisconsin Ave.
PO Box 3005
Milwaukee, WI 53201-3005
Ph: (414)272-8575 Fax: (414)272-1734
Fr: 800-248-1946

Members: Individuals and organizations dedicated to the on-going development, advancement, and promotion of quality concepts, principles, and technologies. Through its Professional Development Department, offers courses in quality engineering, reliability engineering, managing for quality, management of quality costs, quality audit-development and administration, management of the inspection function, probability and statistics for engineers and scientists, and product liability and prevention. Offers personnel listing service. **Publications:** *Journal of Quality Technology*, quarterly. • *Quality Engineering*, quarterly. • *Quality Management Journal*, quarterly. • *Quality Progress*, monthly. • *Technical Congress Transactions*, annual. • *Technometrics*, quarterly.

★5722★ **National Tooling and Machining Association (NTMA)**
9300 Livingston Rd.
Fort Washington, MD 20744
Ph: (301)248-6200 Fax: (301)248-7104
Fr: 800-248-NTMA

Members: Manufacturers of tools, dies, jigs, fixtures, molds, gages, or special machinery; companies that do precision machining on a contract basis; past service and associate members. **Purpose:** Provides management services; represents members in legislative matters. Promotes apprenticeship programs. Compiles management surveys; conducts management training workshops; maintains speakers' bureau. Has produced motion pictures and videocassettes on tool, die, and precision machining for educational showings. **Publications:** *Business Management Advisories*, periodic. • *Buyers Guide of Special Tooling and Precision Machining Services*, annual. • *Catalog of Publications and Training Materials*, periodic. • *Precision*, bimonthly. • *Record*, monthly.

Test Guides

★5723★ ***Career Examination Series: Associate Quality Assurance Specialist***
National Learning Corp.
212 Michael Dr.
Syosset, NY 11791
Ph: (516)921-8888 Fax: (516)921-8743
Fr: 800-645-6337

Jack Rudman. All examination guides in this series contain questions with answers.

★5724★ ***Career Examination Series: Beverage Control Inspector***
National Learning Corp.
212 Michael Dr.
Syosset, NY 11791
Ph: (516)921-8888 Fax: (516)921-8743
Fr: 800-645-6337

Jack Rudman. All examination guides in this series contain questions with answers.

★5725★ ***Career Examination Series: Chief Meat Inspector***
National Learning Corp.
212 Michael Dr.
Syosset, NY 11791
Ph: (516)921-8888 Fax: (516)921-8743
Fr: 800-645-6337

Jack Rudman. All examination guides in this series contain questions with answers.

★5726★ *Career Examination Series: Food Inspector*
National Learning Corp.
212 Michael Dr.
Syosset, NY 11791
Ph: (516)921-8888 Fax: (516)921-8743
Fr: 800-645-6337

Jack Rudman. Study guide is also available for food inspector trainee positions. All examination guides in this series contain questions with answers.

★5727★ *Career Examination Series: Meat Inspector*
National Learning Corp.
212 Michael Dr.
Syosset, NY 11791
Ph: (516)921-8888 Fax: (516)921-8743
Fr: 800-645-6337

Jack Rudman. Study guide for meat inspector trainee also available. All examination guides in this series contain questions with answers.

★5728★ *Career Examination Series: Meat Inspector-Poultry Inspector*
National Learning Corp.
212 Michael Dr.
Syosset, NY 11791
Ph: (516)921-8888 Fax: (516)921-8743
Fr: 800-645-6337

Jack Rudman. All examination guides in this series contain questions with answers.

★5729★ *Career Examination Series: Quality Control Inspector (USPS)*
National Learning Corp.
212 Michael Dr.
Syosset, NY 11791
Ph: (516)921-8888 Fax: (516)921-8743
Fr: 800-645-6337

Jack Rudman. All examination guides in this series contain questions with answers.

★5730★ *Career Examination Series: Senior Boiler Inspector*
National Learning Corp.
212 Michael Dr.
Syosset, NY 11791
Ph: (516)921-8888 Fax: (516)921-8743
Fr: 800-645-6337

Jack Rudman. All examination guides in this series contain questions with answers.

★5731★ *Career Examination Series: Senior Food Inspector*
National Learning Corp.
212 Michael Dr.
Syosset, NY 11791
Ph: (516)921-8888 Fax: (516)921-8743
Fr: 800-645-6337

Jack Rudman. All examination guides in this series contain questions with answers.

★5732★ *Career Examination Series: Senior Inspector, Meat & Poultry*
National Learning Corp.
212 Michael Dr.
Syosset, NY 11791
Ph: (516)921-8888 Fax: (516)921-8743
Fr: 800-645-6337

Jack Rudman. All examination guides in this series contain questions with answers.

★5733★ *Career Examination Series: Senior Meat Inspector*
National Learning Corp.
212 Michael Dr.
Syosset, NY 11791
Ph: (516)921-8888 Fax: (516)921-8743
Fr: 800-645-6337

Jack Rudman. All examination guides in this series contain questions with answers.

Periodicals

★5734★ *Business Management Advisories*
National Tooling and Machining Association (NTMA)
9300 Livingston Rd.
Fort Washington, MD 20744
Ph: (301)248-6200 Fax: (301)248-7104
Fr: 800-248-NTMA

Periodic.

★5735★ *Buyers Guide of Special Tooling and Precision Machining Services*
National Tooling and Machining Association (NTMA)
9300 Livingston Rd.
Fort Washington, MD 20744
Ph: (301)248-6200 Fax: (301)248-7104
Fr: 800-248-NTMA

Annual.

★5736★ *Journal of Quality Technology*
American Society for Quality Control (ASQC)
611 E. Wisconsin Ave.
PO Box 3005
Milwaukee, WI 53201-3005
Ph: (414)272-8575 Fax: (414)272-1734
Fr: 800-248-1946

Quarterly.

★5737★ *Precision*
National Tooling and Machining Association (NTMA)
9300 Livingston Rd.
Fort Washington, MD 20744
Ph: (301)248-6200 Fax: (301)248-7104
Fr: 800-248-NTMA

Bimonthly.

★5738★ *Quality Engineering*
American Society for Quality Control (ASQC)
611 E. Wisconsin Ave.
PO Box 3005
Milwaukee, WI 53201-3005
Ph: (414)272-8575 Fax: (414)272-1734
Fr: 800-248-1946

Quarterly.

★5739★ *Quality Management Journal*
American Society for Quality Control (ASQC)
611 E. Wisconsin Ave.
PO Box 3005
Milwaukee, WI 53201-3005
Ph: (414)272-8575 Fax: (414)272-1734
Fr: 800-248-1946

Quarterly.

★5740★ *Quality Progress*
American Society for Quality Control (ASQC)
611 E. Wisconsin Ave.
PO Box 3005
Milwaukee, WI 53201-3005
Ph: (414)272-8575 Fax: (414)272-1734
Fr: 800-248-1946

Monthly.

★5741★ *Record*
National Tooling and Machining Association (NTMA)
9300 Livingston Rd.
Fort Washington, MD 20744
Ph: (301)248-6200 Fax: (301)248-7104
Fr: 800-248-NTMA

Monthly.

★5742★ *Technical Congress Transactions*
American Society for Quality Control (ASQC)
611 E. Wisconsin Ave.
PO Box 3005
Milwaukee, WI 53201-3005
Ph: (414)272-8575 Fax: (414)272-1734
Fr: 800-248-1946

Annual.

★5743★ *Technometrics*
American Society for Quality Control (ASQC)
611 E. Wisconsin Ave.
PO Box 3005
Milwaukee, WI 53201-3005
Ph: (414)272-8575 Fax: (414)272-1734
Fr: 800-248-1946

Quarterly. Published with American Statistical Association.

Other Sources of Information

★5744★ *Catalog of Publications and Training Materials*
National Tooling and Machining Association (NTMA)
9300 Livingston Rd.
Ft. Washington, MD 20744
Ph: (301)248-6200 Fax: (301)248-7104
Fr: 800-248-NTMA

Periodic.

Boilermakers

Boilermakers and boilermaker mechanics construct, assemble, and repair boilers, vats, and other large vessels that hold liquids and gases. In construction and assembly, boilermakers locate reference points for installation, attach rigging, align sections, and attach water tubes, stacks, and other parts. They then test for leaks or other defects. Usually, they assemble large vessels temporarily in a fabrication shop to ensure a proper fit and again on their permanent site. Boilermaker mechanics maintain and repair boilers and similar vessels. They clean and repair various components and replace defective parts. Over 50 percent of all boilermakers work in the construction industry. About 25 percent work in manufacturing, primarily in boiler manufacturing shops, iron and steel plants, petroleum refineries, chemical plants, and shipyards. Some also work for boiler repair firms, railroads, and in Navy shipyards, and federal power facilities.

Salaries

Full-time boilermakers average about $553/week.

Employment Outlook

Growth rate until the year 2005: Decline.

Boilermakers

CAREER GUIDES

★5745★ *Boilermaker*
Careers, Inc.
PO Box 135
Largo, FL 34649-0135
Ph: (813)584-7333

1994. Two-page occupational summary card describing duties, working conditions, personal qualifications, training, earnings and hours, employment outlook, places of employment, related careers and where to write for more information.

★5746★ "Boilermaker" in *Jobs Rated Almanac*
World Almanac
1 International Blvd., Ste. 444
Mahwah, NJ 07495
Ph: (201)529-6900 Fax: (201)529-6901

Les Krantz. Second edition, 1992. Ranks 250 jobs by environment, salary, outlooks, physical demands, stress, security, travel opportunities, and extra perks. Includes jobs the editor feels are the most common, most interesting, and the most rapidly growing.

★5747★ "Boilermaker" in *Occu-Facts: Information on 580 Careers in Outline Form*
Careers, Inc.
PO Box 135
Largo, FL 34649-0135
Ph: (813)584-7333

Biennial, 1995-96 edition. Each one-page occupational profile describes duties, working conditions, physical surroundings and demands, aptitudes, temperament, educational requirements, employment outlook, earnings, and places of employment.

★5748★ *Boilermakers*
Chronicle Guidance Publications, Inc.
66 Aurora St.
PO Box 1190
Moravia, NY 13118-1190
Ph: (315)497-0330 Fax: (315)497-3359
Fr: 800-622-7284

1992. This career brief describes the nature of the work, working conditions, hours and earnings, education and training, licensure, certification, unions, personal qualifications, social and psychological factors, employment outlook, entry methods, advancement, and related occupations.

★5749★ "Boilermakers" in *Occupational Outlook Handbook*
U.S. Government Printing Office
Superintendent of Documents
Washington, DC 20402
Ph: (202)512-1800 Fax: (202)512-2250

Biennial; latest edition, 1994-95. Encyclopedia of careers describing more than 250 occupations and comprising about 85 percent of all jobs in the economy. Occupations that require lengthy education or training are given the most attention. For each occupation, the handbook describes job duties, working conditions, training, educational preparation, personal qualities, advancement possibilities, job outlook, earnings, and sources of additional information.

★5750★ "Boilermaking Occupations" in *Encyclopedia of Careers and Vocational Guidance* (Vol.2, pp. 200-203)
J.G. Ferguson Publishing Co.
200 W. Madison St., Ste. 300
Chicago, IL 60606
Ph: (312)580-5480 Fax: (312)580-4948

William E. Hopke, editor-in-chief. Ninth edition, 1993. Four-volume set that profiles 500 occupations and describes job trends in 74 industries. Includes career description, educational requirements, history of the job, methods of entry, advancement, employment outlook, earnings, working conditions, social and psychological factors, and sources of additional information.

★5751★ "Boilermaking Worker" in *Career Information Center* (Vol.9)
Simon and Schuster
200 Old Tappan Rd.
Old Tappan, NJ 07675
Fax: 800-445-6991 Fr: 800-223-2348

Richard Lidz and Dale Anderson, editorial directors. Fifth edition, 1993. For 600 occupations, describes job duties, entry-level requirements, education and training needed, advancement possibilities, employment outlook, earnings and benefits. The set is divided into 12 volumes. Each volume includes jobs related under a broad career field. Volume 13 is the index.

★5752★ "Boilermaking Workers" in *Career Discovery Encyclopedia* (Vol.1, pp. 118-119)
J.G. Ferguson Publishing Co.
200 W. Madison St., Ste. 300
Chicago, IL 60606
Ph: (312)580-5480 Fax: (312)580-4948

E. Russell Primm, editor-in-chief. 1993. Contains two-page articles on 504 occupations. Each article describes job duties, earnings, and educational and training requirements.

ASSOCIATIONS

★5753★ International Association of Machinists and Aerospace Workers (IAM)
9000 Machinists PL
Upper Marlboro, MD 20772
Ph: (301)967-4500 Fax: (301)967-4588

Members: AFL-CIO. **Publications:** *The Machinist*, monthly.

★5754★ International Brotherhood of Boilermakers, Iron Ship Builders, Blacksmiths, Forgers and Helpers (BSF)
753 State Ave., Ste. 570
New Brotherhood
Kansas City, KS 66101
Ph: (913)371-2640 Fax: (913)281-8101

Members: AFL-CIO, CFL. **Publications:** *Boilermakers-Blacksmiths Reporter*, bimonthly. • *Membership Roster*, triennial. • *NTL News*, quarterly.

★5755★ International Union, United Automobile, Aerospace and Agricultural Implement Workers of America (UAW)
8000 E. Jefferson
Detroit, MI 48214
Ph: (313)926-5000 Fax: (313)823-6016

Members: AFL-CIO. **Publications:** *Ammo*, monthly. • *Skill*, quarterly. • *Solidarity*, 10/year.

★5756★ United Steelworkers of America (USWA)
5 Gateway Center
Pittsburgh, PA 15222
Ph: (412)562-2400 Fax: (412)562-2445

Members: AFL-CIO. **Publications:** *Steellabor*, bimonthly. • *Steelworker Old Time*, quarterly.

TEST GUIDES

★5757★ Career Examination Series: Boiler Inspector
National Learning Corp.
212 Michael Dr.
Syosset, NY 11791
Ph: (516)921-8888 Fax: (516)921-8743
Fr: 800-645-6337

Jack Rudman. All examination guides in this series contain questions with answers.

★5758★ Career Examination Series: Boiler Room Helper
National Learning Corp.
212 Michael Dr.
Syosset, NY 11791
Ph: (516)921-8888 Fax: (516)921-8743
Fr: 800-645-6337

Jack Rudman. All examination guides in this series contain questions with answers.

★5759★ Career Examination Series: Boilermaker
National Learning Corp.
212 Michael Dr.
Syosset, NY 11791
Ph: (516)921-8888 Fax: (516)921-8743
Fr: 800-645-6337

Jack Rudman. All examination guides in this series contain questions with answers.

AWARDS, SCHOLARSHIPS, GRANTS, AND FELLOWSHIPS

★5760★ AIRCO Welding Award
American Welding Society
550 NW LeJeune Rd.
PO Box 351040
Miami, FL 33135
Ph: (305)443-9353 Fax: (305)443-7559
Fr: 800-443-9353

For recognition of distinguished accomplishments in the joining of or severing of metals that have improved and benefited mankind and furthered the welding industry. An honorarium of $1,000 and a certificate are awarded annually. Established in 1967 and sponsored by Airco Distributor Gases, Division of BOC.

PERIODICALS

★5761★ Ammo
International Union, United Automobile, Aerospace and Agricultural Implement Workers of America (UAW)
8000 E. Jefferson
Detroit, MI 48214
Ph: (313)926-5000 Fax: (313)823-6016

Monthly.

★5762★ Boilermaker Reporter
International Brotherhood of Boilermakers, Iron Shipbuilders
753 State Ave., No. 570
Kansas City, KS 66101-2511
Ph: (913)371-2640
Donald Caswell, Contact

Bimonthly. Discusses news of interest to members of the union. Recurring features include letters to the editor and columns titled Safety & Health and Retiree News.

★5763★ Boilermakers-Blacksmiths Reporter
International Brotherhood of Boilermakers, Iron Ship Builders, Blacksmiths, Forgers and Helpers (BSF)
753 State Ave., Ste. 570
New Brotherhood
Kansas City, KS 66101
Ph: (913)371-2640 Fax: (913)281-8101

Bimonthly. Includes annual index.

★5764★ Membership Roster
International Brotherhood of Boilermakers, Iron Ship Builders, Blacksmiths, Forgers and Helpers (BSF)
753 State Ave., Ste. 570
New Brotherhood
Kansas City, KS 66101
Ph: (913)371-2640 Fax: (913)281-8101

Triennial.

★5765★ NTL News
International Brotherhood of Boilermakers, Iron Ship Builders, Blacksmiths, Forgers and Helpers (BSF)
753 State Ave., Ste. 570
New Brotherhood
Kansas City, KS 66101
Ph: (913)371-2640 Fax: (913)281-8101

Quarterly.

★5766★ Skill
International Union, United Automobile, Aerospace and Agricultural Implement Workers of America (UAW)
8000 E. Jefferson
Detroit, MI 48214
Ph: (313)926-5000 Fax: (313)823-6016

Quarterly.

★5767★ Solidarity
International Union, United Automobile, Aerospace and Agricultural Implement Workers of America (UAW)
8000 E. Jefferson
Detroit, MI 48214
Ph: (313)926-5000 Fax: (313)823-6016

10/year. Covers labor, economic, social, and political affairs affecting union members. Includes book and film reviews.

★5768★ Steelabor
United Steelworkers of America (USWA)
5 Gateway Center
Pittsburgh, PA 15222
Ph: (412)562-2400 Fax: (412)562-2445

Bimonthly. Reports on legislation and regulation affecting the union, union activities at the national and chapter levels, economic developments, pension news.

★5769★ Steelworker Old Time
United Steelworkers of America (USWA)
5 Gateway Center
Pittsburgh, PA 15222
Ph: (412)562-2400 Fax: (412)562-2445

Quarterly.

Jewelers

Jewelers make, repair, and adjust all types of jewelry such as rings, necklaces, and earrings. Using drills, jeweler's soldering torches, and a variety of other handtools, they mold and shape metal, and set precious and semiprecious stones. Jewelers' work varies by the type of establishment in which they work. Those in retail stores and repair shops primarily do adjustments and repairs like resetting stones and replacing broken clasps. Jewelers in manufacturing specialize in a single operation such as engraving. Nearly 50 percent of all salaried jewelers work in retail establishments, while approximately 33 percent are employed in manufacturing plants. About 40 percent of all jewelers are self-employed.

Salaries

Earnings for jewelers vary by type of establishment. Some median salaries are listed below.

Jewelers in retail stores	$28,000/year
Jewelry repair workers	$22,000/year

Employment Outlook

Growth rate until the year 2005: Average.

Jewelers

Career Guides

★5770★ *Bench Jewelers*
Chronicle Guidance Publications, Inc.
66 Aurora St.
PO Box 1190
Moravia, NY 13118-1190
Ph: (315)497-0330 Fax: (315)497-3359
Fr: 800-622-7284

1992. Career brief describing the nature of the job, working conditions, hours and earnings, education and training, licensure, certification, unions, personal qualifications, social and psychological factors, location, employment outlook, entry methods, advancement, and related occupations.

★5771★ *Careers for Crafty People & Other Dextrous Types*
National Textbook Co. (NTC)
VGM Career Books
4255 W. Toughy Ave.
Lincolnwood, IL 60646-1975
Ph: (708)679-5500 Fax: (708)679-2494
Fr: 800-323-4900

Mark Rowh. Provides information for careers for crafts people.

★5772★ *Jeweler*
Vocational Biographies, Inc.
PO Box 31
Sauk Centre, MN 56378-0031
Ph: (612)352-6516 Fax: (612)352-5546
Fr: 800-255-0752

1990. This pamphlet profiles a person working in the job. Includes information about job duties, working conditions, places of employment, educational preparation, labor market outlook, and salaries.

★5773★ *Jeweler*
Careers, Inc.
PO Box 135
Largo, FL 34649-0135
Ph: (813)584-7333

1993. Four-page brief offering the definition, history, duties, working conditions, personal qualifications, educational requirements, earnings, hours, employment outlook, advancement possibilities, and related occupations.

★5774★ "Jeweler" in *Career Information Center* (Vol.5)
Simon and Schuster
200 Old Tappan Rd.
Old Tappan, NJ 07675
Fax: 800-445-6991 Fr: 800-223-2348

Richard Lidz and Dale Anderson, editorial directors. Fifth edition, 1993. For 600 occupations, describes job duties, entry-level requirements, education and training needed, advancement possibilities, employment outlook, earnings and benefits. The set is divided into 12 volumes. Each volume includes jobs related under a broad career field. Volume 13 is the index.

★5775★ "Jeweler" in *Occu-Facts: Information on 580 Careers in Outline Form*
Careers, Inc.
PO Box 135
Largo, FL 34649-0135
Ph: (813)584-7333

Biennial, 1995-96 edition. Each one-page occupational profile describes duties, working conditions, physical surroundings and demands, aptitudes, temperament, educational requirements, employment outlook, earnings, and places of employment.

★5776★ "Jewelers" in *Career Discovery Encyclopedia* (Vol.3, pp. 150-151)
J.G. Ferguson Publishing Co.
200 W. Madison St., Ste. 300
Chicago, IL 60606
Ph: (312)580-5480 Fax: (312)580-4948

E. Russell Primm, editor-in-chief. 1993. Contains two-page articles on 504 occupations. Each article describes job duties, earnings, and educational and training requirements.

★5777★ "Jewelers and Jewelry Repairers" in *Encyclopedia of Careers and Vocational Guidance* (Vol.3, pp. 246-249)
J.G. Ferguson Publishing Co.
200 W. Madison St., Ste. 300
Chicago, IL 60606
Ph: (312)580-5480 Fax: (312)580-4948

William E. Hopke, editor-in-chief. Ninth edition, 1993. Four-volume set that profiles 500 occupations and describes job trends in 74 industries. Includes career description, educational requirements, history of the job, methods of entry, advancement, employment outlook, earnings, working conditions, social and psychological factors, and sources of additional information.

★5778★ "Jewelers" in *Jobs! What They Are—Where They Are—What They Pay* (p. 351)
Simon & Schuster, Inc.
Simon & Schuster Bldg.
1230 Avenue of the Americas
New York, NY 10020
Ph: (212)698-7000

Robert O. Snelling and Anne M. Snelling. Revised edition, 1992. Profiles 241 occupations, describing duties and responsibilities, educational preparation, earnings, employment opportunities, training, and qualifications.

★5779★ "Jewelers" in *Occupational Outlook Handbook*
U.S. Government Printing Office
Superintendent of Documents
Washington, DC 20402
Ph: (202)512-1800 Fax: (202)512-2250

Biennial; latest edition, 1994-95. Encyclopedia of careers describing more than 250 occupations and comprising about 85 percent of all jobs in the economy. Occupations that require lengthy education or training are given the most attention. For each occupation, the handbook describes job duties, working conditions, training, educational preparation, personal qualities, advancement possibilities, job outlook, earnings, and sources of additional information.

★5780★ *Jewelers, Retail*
Chronicle Guidance Publications, Inc.
66 Aurora St.
PO Box 1190
Moravia, NY 13118-1190
Ph: (315)497-0330 Fax: (315)497-3359
Fr: 800-622-7284

1991. Career brief describing the nature of the job, working conditions, hours and earnings, education and training, licensure, certification, unions, personal qualifications, social and psychological factors, location, employment outlook, entry methods, advancement, and related occupations.

★5781★ "Jewelry Design and Metal Smithing" in *Career Connection II: A Guide to Technical Majors and Their Related Careers* (pp. 96-97)
Jist Works, Inc.
720 N. Park Ave.
Indianapolis, IN 46202-3431
Ph: (317)264-3720 Fax: (317)264-3709

Fred A. Rowe. 1994. Contains technical majors, such as automotive technology. Describes the major and the job. Lists high school and postsecondary school courses. Includes occupations related to the major, employment outlook, and starting salary.

★5782★ *Jewelry Maker*
Vocational Biographies, Inc.
PO Box 31
Sauk Centre, MN 56378-0031
Ph: (612)352-6516 Fax: (612)352-5546
Fr: 800-255-0752

1992. Four-page pamphlet containing a personal narrative about a worker's job, work likes and dislikes, career path from high school to the present. Education and training, the rewards and frustrations, and the effects of the job on the rest of the worker's life. The data file portion of this pamphlet gives a concise occupational summary, including work descriptions, working conditions, places of employment, personal characteristics, education and training, job outlook, and salary range.

★5783★ "Jewelry Making" in *Opportunities in Metalworking Careers* (pp. 59-66)
National Textbook Co. (NTC)
VGM Career Books
4255 W. Touhy Ave.
Lincolnwood, IL 60646-1975
Ph: (708)679-5500 Fax: (708)679-2494
Fr: 800-323-4900

Mark Rowh. 1991. Covers sheet metal work, machining, structural and reinforcing metalworking, and jewelry making. Describes the work performed, skills needed, training and working conditions. Lists unions that sponsor apprenticeship and technical schools which offer training.

★5784★ "Jewelry Worker" in *Offbeat Careers: The Directory of Unusual Work*
Ten Speed Press
PO Box 7123
Berkeley, CA 94707
Fax: (510)559-1629 Fr: 800-841-2665

Al Sacharov. 1991. Profiles eighty-eight unusual careers. Provides job description, history of occupation, salary, and training required. Lists one or more sources of additional information.

Associations

★5785★ Jewelers of America (JA)
1185 6th Ave., 30th Fl.
New York, NY 10036
Ph: (212)768-8777 Fax: (212)768-8087
Fr: 800-223-0673

Members: Retailers of jewelry, watches, silver, and allied merchandise. Conducts surveys and compiles statistics. **Publications:** *'J' Report*, monthly.

Awards, Scholarships, Grants, and Fellowships

★5786★ International Art Competition - New York
Artitudes
PO Box 380
Larchmont, NY 10538

To recognize artists working in all media and styles. Awards are presented in various categories including jewelry. 35mm slides may be submitted by June 23. Awarded annually. Established in 1983.

★5787★ Washington Craft Schow
Smithsonian Associates Women's Committee
Art and Industries Bldg., Rm. 1278
Smithsonian Institute
Washington, DC 20560
Ph: (202)357-4000

To enable craftsmen to exhibit and sell crafts as fine art. Artisans working in several categories including wood are eligible. One hundred exhibitors are selected on the basis of originality, artistic conception, and quality of workmanship.

Basic Reference Guides and Handbooks

★5788★ *Jewelers' Circular/Keystone—Almanac Issue*
Chilton Co.
1 Chilton Way
Radnor, PA 19089
Ph: (610)964-4487 Fax: (610)964-4481
Karnila Moravec, Contact

Annual, July. Publication includes: List of jewelery associations. Entries include: Association name, address, phone. Principal content of publication is jewelry industry statistics as well as a complete listing of industry associations.

★5789★ *Professional Goldsmithing: A Contemporary Guide to Traditional Jewelry Techniques*
Van Nostrand Reinhold
115 5th Ave.
New York, NY 10003
Ph: (212)254-3232 Fax: (212)254-9499

Alan Revere. 1991.

Periodicals

★5790★ *Accent Magazine*
Larkin Publications
485 7th Ave., Ste. 1400
New York, NY 10018
Ph: (212)594-0880 Fax: (212)594-8556
Lauren Parker

Monthly. Fashion jewelry trade magazine.

★5791★ *American Jewelry Manufacturer*
Capital Cities/ABC/Chilton Co.
Chilton Way
Radnor, PA 19087
Ph: (215)964-4000 Fax: (215)964-4647
Ellen Berkovitch

Monthly. Trade magazine. Official publication of Manufacturing Jewelers and Silversmiths of America, Inc.

★5792★ *The Diamond Registry Bulletin*
Joseph Schlussel
580 5th Ave., Ste. 806
New York, NY 10036
Ph: (212)575-0444 Fax: (212)575-0722
Fr: 800-223-7955
Joseph Schlussel

Monthly. Supplies current data on the present and future outlook of the diamond market. Provides information concerning trends in jewelry and investment companies and actual wholesale prices by size, quality, and shape for certified and commercial diamonds. Recurring features include reviews of fashion trends, diamond sales boosters, quotes, and anecdotes.

★5793★ *Gem and Jewelry Fact Sheets Quarterly Supplement*
American Gem Society
1050 E. Flamingo Rd., No. 130
Las Vegas, NV 89119
Ph: (702)255-6500 Fax: (702)255-7420
Patty Fry

Quarterly. Highlights jewelry industry developments. Discusses market projections, new sources of gemstones, and major marketing ideas.

★5794★ *Gems & Gemology*
Gemological Institute of America
1660 Stewart St.
Santa Monica, CA 90404
Ph: (310)829-2991 Fax: (310)453-4478
Fr: 800-421-7250
Alice S. Keller

Quarterly. Gemology and mineralogy magazine featuring articles on gemstone identification, localities, synthetics, simulants, treatments, and antique jewelry.

★5795★ *'J' Report*
Jewelers of America (JA)
1185 6th Ave., 30th Fl.
New York, NY 10036
Ph: (212)768-8777 Fax: (212)768-8087
Fr: 800-223-0673
Monthly.

★5796★ *Jewelry Newsletter International*
Newsletters International, Inc.
2600 S. Gessner Rd.
Houston, TX 77063
Ph: (713)783-0100
Len Fox
Monthly. Reports news and developments in the jewelry industry, with brief items on people, companies, products, the changing scene and tastes, retailers, jobbers, and manufacturers. Recurring features include cost-cutting tips, listings of recommended books, professional opportunity notices, and items on economic trends.

★5797★ *Lapidary Journal*
Lapidary Journal, Inc.
60 Chestnut Ave., Ste. 201
Devon, PA 19333-1312
Ph: (610)293-1112 Fax: (610)293-1717
Merle Berk
Monthly. Magazine for gem cutters, collectors, and jewelry craftsmen.

★5798★ *MJSA Benchmark*
Manufacturing Jewelers and Silversmiths of America Inc. (MJSA)
100 India St.
Providence, RI 02903
Ph: (401)274-3840 Fax: (401)274-3840
Fr: 800-444-6572
David Lafleur
Bimonthly. Informs jewelry manufacturers of legislative news concerning their industry, expositions around the country, export news, tax news, and advances in technology. Presents information in the form of brief updates. Recurring features include member profiles and industry news.

★5799★ *Modern Jeweler*
Vance Publishing Corp.
7950 College Blvd.
PO Box 2939
Overland Park, KS 66202
Ph: (913)451-2200 Fax: (913)451-5821
Fr: 800-255-5113
Joseph Thompson
Monthly. Trade magazine for retail jewelers.

★5800★ *National Jeweler*
Miller Freeman, Inc.
1515 Broadway
New York, NY 10036
Ph: (212)869-1300 Fax: (212)768-0002
S. Lynn DiamondPublisher
Semiweekly. Jewelry industry magazine.

★5801★ *Ornament Magazine*
PO Box 2349
San Marcos, CA 92079
Ph: (619)599-0222 Fax: (619)599-0228
Quarterly. Jewelry and wearables magazine.

★5802★ *Rock & Gem*
Miller Magazines, Inc.
4880 Market St.
Ventura, CA 93003-7783
Ph: (805)644-3824 Fax: (805)644-3875
W.R.C. Shedenhelm
Monthly. Magazine about rocks, gold prospecting, lapidary, and jewelry making.

★5803★ *Spectra*
American Gem Society
1050 E. Flamingo Rd., No. 130
Las Vegas, NV 89119
Ph: (702)255-6500 Fax: (702)255-7420
Patty Fry
Informs members of Society activities promoting ethical business standards and professional excellence in the retail jewelry industry. Features articles about technical advances in the field and profiles of members.

Meetings and Conventions

★5804★ Jewelers International Showcase
Jewelers International Showcase, Inc.
6405 Congress Ave., Ste. 125
Boca Raton, FL 33487
Ph: (407)998-0205
Held up to 6 times yearly.

★5805★ Manufacturing Jewelers and Silversmiths of America Exposition/ Providence
Manufacturing Jewelers and Silversmiths of America
100 India St.
Providence, RI 02903
Ph: (401)274-3840 Fax: (401)274-0265
Annual.

★5806★ Mid-America Jewelry Show
Ohio Jewelers Association
50 W. Broad St., Ste. 1616
Columbus, OH 43215
Ph: (614)221-7833 Fax: (614)221-7020
Annual. Always held during August at the Ohio Center in Columbus, Ohio.

Other Sources of Information

★5807★ "Jeweler" in *Career Selector 2001*
Barron's Educational Series, Inc.
250 Wireless Blvd.
Hauppauge, NY 11788
Ph: (516)434-3311 Fax: (516)434-3723
Fr: 800-645-3476
James C. Gonyea. 1993.

Machinists and Tool Programmers

Machinists produce precision metal parts, usually using machine tools such as lathes, drill presses, and milling machines. Although machinists can and sometimes do produce large quantities of one part, they often produce small batches of one-of-a-kind items. They set up and operate a wide variety of machine tools and know the working properties of metals such as steel, cast iron, aluminum, and brass. Using their skill with machine tools and their knowledge of metals, machinists plan and carry out the operations needed to make machined products that meet precise specifications. metal goods that are made in numbers too small to produce with automated machinery. **Tool programmers** begin as machinists do-by analyzing blueprints, computing the size and position of the cuts, determining the sequence of machine operations, selecting tools, and calculating the machine speed and feed rates. They then write the program in the language of the machine's controller and store it.

Salaries

The median weekly earnings for machinists is about $435.

Lowest 10 percent	$275/week or less
Middle 50 percent	$376-$623/week
Top 10 percent	$750/week or more

Employment Outlook

Growth rate until the year 2005: Decline slightly.

Machinists and Tool Programmers

Career Guides

★5808★ "All Round Machinist" in *Career Information Center* (Vol.9)
Simon and Schuster
200 Old Tappan Rd.
Old Tappan, NJ 07675
Fax: 800-445-6991 Fr: 800-223-2348

Richard Lidz and Dale Anderson, editorial directors. Fifth edition, 1993. For 600 occupations, describes job duties, entry-level requirements, education and training needed, advancement possibilities, employment outlook, earnings and benefits. The set is divided into 12 volumes. Each volume includes jobs related under a broad career field. Volume 13 is the index.

★5809★ "All-Round Machinist" in *Occu-Facts: Information on 580 Careers in Outline Form*
Careers, Inc.
PO Box 135
Largo, FL 34649-0135
Ph: (813)584-7333

Biennial, 1995-96 edition. Each one-page occupational profile describes duties, working conditions, physical surroundings and demands, aptitudes, temperament, educational requirements, employment outlook, earnings, and places of employment.

★5810★ *Career Information for Precision Machining Technology*
National Tooling and Machining Association
9300 Livingston Rd.
Ft. Washington, MD 20744
Ph: (301)248-6200

This six-panel brochure lists the advantages of working in the machine tool industry, study course contents, and how to get started.

★5811★ *How Valuable is Your Future?*
Tooling and Manufacturing Association
1177 S. Dee Rd.
Park Ridge, IL 60068-9809
Ph: (708)825-1120

1989. This ten-panel brochure describes the work of precision metalworkers, the skills, entry into the field, internships, and earnings.

★5812★ *Machinist, All-Round*
Careers, Inc.
PO Box 135
Largo, FL 34649-0135
Ph: (813)584-7333

1994. Four-page brief offering the definition, history, duties, working conditions, personal qualifications, educational requirements, earnings, hours, employment outlook, advancement possibilities, and related occupations.

★5813★ "Machinist" in *BLR Encyclopedia of Prewritten Job Descriptions*
Business and Legal Reports, Inc.
39 Academy St.
Madison, CT 06443-1513
Ph: (203)245-7448

Stephen D. Bruce, editor-in-chief. 1994. This book contains hundreds of sample job descriptions arranged by functional job category. The 1-3 page job descriptions cover what the worker normally does in the position, who they report to, and how that position fits in the organizational structure.

★5814★ "Machinist" in *Hard Hatted Women: Stories of Struggle and Success in the Trades* (pp. 187-191, 254-262)
Seal Press
3131 Western Ave., Ste. 410
Seattle, WA 98121
Ph: (206)283-7844 Fax: (206)285-9410

Molly Martin, editor. 1988. Twenty-six women recount their experiences working in blue collar occupations. They describe how they got in, the work they do, their relationships in predominantly male occupations, and their training.

★5815★ "Machinist" in *Jobs Rated Almanac*
World Almanac
1 International Blvd., Ste. 444
Mahwah, NJ 07495
Ph: (201)529-6900 Fax: (201)529-6901

Les Krantz. Second edition, 1992. Ranks 250 jobs by environment, salary, outlooks, physical demands, stress, security, travel opportunities, and extra perks. Includes jobs the editor feels are the most common, most interesting, and the most rapidly growing.

★5816★ "Machinist" in *VGM's Careers Encyclopedia* (pp. 253-255)
National Textbook Co. (NTC)
VGM Career Books
4255 W. Touhy Ave.
Lincolnwood, IL 60646-1975
Ph: (708)679-5500 Fax: (708)679-2494
Fr: 800-323-4900

Third edition, 1991. Contains two- to five-page descriptions of 200 managerial, professional, technical, trade, and service occupations. Each profile includes job duties, places of employment, qualifications, educational preparation, training, employment potential, advancement, income, and additional sources of information.

★5817★ *Machinists*
Chronicle Guidance Publications, Inc.
66 Aurora St.
PO Box 1190
Moravia, NY 13118-1190
Ph: (315)497-0330 Fax: (315)497-3359
Fr: 800-622-7284

1993. This career brief describes the nature of the work, working conditions, hours and earnings, education and training, licensure, certification, unions, personal qualifications, social and psychological factors, employment outlook, entry methods, advancement, and related occupations.

★5818★ "Machinists" in *Career Discovery Encyclopedia* (Vol.4, pp. 34-35)
J.G. Ferguson Publishing Co.
200 W. Madison St., Ste. 300
Chicago, IL 60606
Ph: (312)580-5480 Fax: (312)580-4948

E. Russell Primm, editor-in-chief. 1993. Contains two-page articles on 504 occupations. Each article describes job duties, earnings, and educational and training requirements.

★5819★ "Machinists" in *Encyclopedia of Careers and Vocational Guidance* (Vol.3, pp. 342-345)
J.G. Ferguson Publishing Co.
200 W. Madison St., Ste. 300
Chicago, IL 60606
Ph: (312)580-5480 Fax: (312)580-4948

William E. Hopke, editor-in-chief. Ninth edition, 1993. Four-volume set that profiles 500 occupations and describes job trends in 74 industries. Includes career description, educational requirements, history of the job, methods of entry, advancement, employment outlook, earnings, working conditions, social and psychological factors, and sources of additional information.

★5820★ "Machinists" in *Jobs! What They Are—Where They Are—What They Pay* (pp. 215)
Simon & Schuster, Inc.
Simon & Schuster Bldg.
1230 Avenue of the Americas
New York, NY 10020
Ph: (212)698-7000

Robert O. Snelling and Anne M. Snelling. Revised edition, 1992. Profiles 241 occupations, describing duties and responsibilities, educational preparation, earnings, employment opportunities, training, and qualifications.

★5821★ "Machinists" in *Opportunities in Metalworking Careers* (pp. 28-29)
National Textbook Co. (NTC)
VGM Career Books
4255 W. Touhy Ave.
Lincolnwood, IL 60646-1975
Ph: (708)679-5500 Fax: (708)679-2494
Fr: 800-323-4900

Mark Rowh. 1991. Separate chapters cover sheet metal work, machining, structural and reinforcing metalworking and jewelry making. Describes the work performed, skills needed, training, and working conditions. Lists unions that sponsor apprenticeship, and technical schools and colleges that offer training.

★5822★ "Machinists and Tool Programmers" in *Occupational Outlook Handbook*
U.S. Government Printing Office
Superintendent of Documents
Washington, DC 20402
Ph: (202)512-1800 Fax: (202)512-2250

Biennial; latest edition, 1994-95. Encyclopedia of careers describing more than 250 occupations and comprising about 85 percent of all jobs in the economy. Occupations that require lengthy education or training are given the most attention. For each occupation, the handbook describes job duties, working conditions, training, educational preparation, personal qualities, advancement possibilities, job outlook, earnings, and sources of additional information.

★5823★ *Opportunities in Machine Trades Careers*
National Textbook Co. (NTC)
VGM Career Books
4255 W. Toughy Ave.
Lincolnwood, IL 60646-1975
Ph: (708)679-5500 Fax: (708)679-2494
Fr: 800-323-4900

Lonny D. Garvey.

★5824★ *Video Career Library - Production II*
Careers, Inc.
PO Box 135
Largo, FL 34649-0135
Ph: (813)584-7333

Videocassette. 1990. 32 mins. Part of the Video Career Library covering 165 occupations. Shows actual workers on the job. Includes tool and die makers, machinists, sheet metal workers, cabinet and bench carpenters, opticians, precision electronic equipment assemblers, industrial machine operators, welders and cutters, and assemblers.

Associations

★5825★ AMT - Association for Manufacturing Technology
7901 Westpark Dr.
Mc Lean, VA 22102
Ph: (703)893-2900 Fax: (703)893-1151
Fr: 800-544-3597

Members: Makers of power driven machines used in the process of transforming man-made materials into durable goods, including machine tools, assembly machines, inspection and testing machinery, robots, parts loaders, and plastics molding machines; associate members are producers of tools and tooling parts and components, attachments and accessories, controls and software, and engineering and systems design services. **Purpose:** Seeks to improve methods of producing and marketing machine tools; promotes research and development in the industry. Sponsors: seminars for training production supervisors, accident prevention and safety, and advertising management; industry standards and technical aspects of the industry. Serves as a clearinghouse for technical aspects of the industry. Promotes orderly disposal of government-owned surplus machine tools. **Publications:** *Directories of Machine Tools*, annual. • *Economic Handbook of the Machine Tool Industry*, annual.

★5826★ National Screw Machine Products Association (NSMPA)
6700 W. Snowville Rd.
Brecksville, OH 44141
Ph: (216)526-0300 Fax: (216)526-5803

Members: Manufacturers of component parts to customer's order, machined from rod, bar, or tube stock, of metal, fiber, plastic, or other material, using automatic or hand screw machines, automatic bar machines, and CNC machines.

★5827★ National Tooling and Machining Association (NTMA)
9300 Livingston Rd.
Fort Washington, MD 20744
Ph: (301)248-6200 Fax: (301)248-7104
Fr: 800-248-NTMA

Members: Manufacturers of tools, dies, jigs, fixtures, molds, gages, or special machinery; companies that do precision machining on a contract basis; past service and associate members. **Purpose:** Provides management services; represents members in legislative matters. Promotes apprenticeship programs. Compiles management surveys; conducts management training workshops; maintains speakers' bureau. Has produced motion pictures and videocassettes on tool, die, and precision machining for educational showings. **Publications:** *Business Management Advisories*, periodic. • *Buyers Guide of Special Tooling and Precision Machining Services*, annual. • *Catalog of Publications and Training Materials*, periodic. • *Precision*, bimonthly. • *Record*, monthly.

★5828★ Tool and Manufacturing Association
1177 S. Dee Rd.
Park Ridge, IL 60068

PUR Provides information on opportunities in high production precision machining.

Standards/Certification Agencies

★5829★ AMT - Association for Manufacturing Technology
7901 Westpark Dr.
Mc Lean, VA 22102
Ph: (703)893-2900 Fax: (703)893-1151
Fr: 800-544-3597

Sponsors: seminars for training production supervisors, accident prevention and safety, and advertising management; industry standards and technical aspects of the industry. Serves as a clearinghouse for technical aspects of the industry.

★5830★ NMTBA - Association for Manufacturing Technology
7901 Westpark Dr.
Mc Lean, VA 22102
Ph: (703)893-2900

Develops and supervises standards for training apprentices. Participates in programs of standardization of design and performance of machine tools and components.

Test Guides

★5831★ *Career Examination Series: Foreman Machinist*
National Learning Corp.
212 Michael Dr.
Syosset, NY 11791
Ph: (516)921-8888 Fax: (516)921-8743
Fr: 800-645-6337

Jack Rudman. All examination guides in this series contain questions with answers.

★5832★ *Career Examination Series: Machinist*
National Learning Corp.
212 Michael Dr.
Syosset, NY 11791
Ph: (516)921-8888 Fax: (516)921-8743
Fr: 800-645-6337

Jack Rudman. All examination guides in this series contain questions with answers.

★5833★ *Career Examination Series: Machinist's Helper*
National Learning Corp.
212 Michael Dr.
Syosset, NY 11791
Ph: (516)921-8888 Fax: (516)921-8743
Fr: 800-645-6337

Jack Rudman. All examination guides in this series contain questions with answers.

Educational Directories and Programs

★5834★ *Directories of Machine Tools*
AMT - Association for Manufacturing Technology
7901 Westpark Dr.
Mc Lean, VA 22102
Ph: (703)893-2900 Fax: (703)893-1151
Fr: 800-544-3597

Annual.

Basic Reference Guides and Handbooks

★5835★ *Economic Handbook of the Machine Tool Industry*
AMT - Association for Manufacturing Technology
7901 Westpark Dr.
Mc Lean, VA 22102
Ph: (703)893-2900 Fax: (703)893-1151
Fr: 800-544-3597

Annual.

Periodicals

★5836★ *Locator*
Machinery Information Systems, Inc.
1110 Spring St.
Silver Spring, MD 20910
Ph: (301)585-9498 Fax: (301)585-9460
Rick ShontzPublisher

Monthly. Magazine on metalworking, plastic and electrical machinery, and power equipment.

★5837★ *NTMA Record*
National Tooling and Machining Association (NTMA)
9300 Livingston Rd.
Fort Washington, MD 20744
Ph: (301)248-6200 Fax: (301)248-7104
Fr: 800-248-6862
Sandra S. Bailey

Monthly. Focuses on business management techniques and government relations for the contract tool, die, and precision machining industry. Supplies information on Association activities. Recurring features include editorials, tax information, and technical notes.

Meetings and Conventions

★5838★ MAQUINAMEX - Metalworking Machine Tool Expo
Marketing International Corp.
200 N. Glebe Rd., Ste. 900
Arlington, VA 22203
Ph: (703)527-8000 Fax: (703)527-8006

Annual. Always held during June at the Exhibition Center in Mexico City.

★5839★ METALFORM
Precision Metalforming Association
27027 Chardon Rd.
Richmond Heights, OH 44143
Ph: (216)585-8800 Fax: (216)585-3126

Annual. Held during odd-numbered years in Rosemont, Illinois. Held during even-numbered years in the Southeast. **Dates and Locations:** 1996 Mar 17-20; Nashville, TN.

★5840★ Pacific Coast Industrial and Machine Tool Show
Industrial Shows of America
20 W. Aylesbury Rd.
Timonium, MD 21093
Ph: (410)252-1167 Fax: (410)560-0477
Fr: 800-638-6396

Annual. Always held during November at the Convention Center in Santa Clara, California. **Dates and Locations:** 1995 Nov; Santa Clara, CA.

Other Sources of Information

★5841★ *American Machinist—Buyers' Guide Issue*
Penton Publishing Co.
1100 Superior Ave.
Cleveland, OH 44114-2543
Ph: (216)696-7000 Fax: (216)696-0177
P. K. Gibson, Contact

Annual, April. Publication includes: Guide to over 2,600 manufacturers of products and services used by metalworking industries. Entries include: Co. name, address, phone, fax. Arrangement: Separate alphabetical sections for manufacturers and products.

★5842★ *Catalog of Publications and Training Materials*
National Tooling and Machining Association (NTMA)
9300 Livingston Rd.
Ft. Washington, MD 20744
Ph: (301)248-6200 Fax: (301)248-7104
Fr: 800-248-NTMA

Periodic.

★5843★ *Heinz Bloch: Machinery Component Maintenance and Repair*
Gulf Publishing Co.
PO Box 2680
Houston, TX 77252-2680
Ph: (713)529-4301 Fax: (713)520-4438

12 part training series that outlines maintenance and repair techniques on various types of machinery. Provides lectures, graphic presentations, and drawings.

★5844★ "Machinist" in *Career Selector 2001*
Barron's Educational Series, Inc.
250 Wireless Blvd.
Hauppauge, NY 11788
Ph: (516)434-3311 Fax: (516)434-3723
Fr: 800-645-3476

James C. Gonyea. 1993.

Metalworking and Plastics-Working Machine Operators

Metalworking machine setters and operators set up, and tend the machines that cut and form all types of metal parts. Traditionally, setup workers plan and set up the sequence of operations according to blueprints, layouts, or other instructions. They adjust speed, feed, and other controls, choose the proper coolants and lubricants, and select the tools for each operation. Using micrometers, gauges, and other precision measuring instruments, they may compare the completed work with the tolerance limits stated in the specifications. **Plastics working machine operators** set up and tend machines that transform plastics compounds-chemical based products that can be produced in powder, pellet, or syrup form-into a wide variety of consumer goods such as toys, tubing, and auto parts.

Salaries

Metal and plastics-working machine operators weekly earnings are as follows:

Lowest 10 percent	$236/week or less
Middle 50 percent	$300-$536/week
Top 10 percent	$697/week or more

Employment Outlook

Growth rate until the year 2005: Decline.

Metalworking and Plastics-Working Machine Operators

Career Guides

★5845★ *A Good Part of Your Life*
National Screw Machine Products
6700 W. Snowville Rd.
Brecksville, OH 44141
Ph: (216)526-0300

This six-panel brochure describes the screw machine products industry, workers' skills and earnings.

★5846★ "Heavy Equipment Operator" in *Great Careers for People Who Like to Work with Their Hands* (pp. 22-27)
Gale Research Inc.
835 Penobscot Bldg.
Detroit, MI 48226
Ph: (313)961-2242 Fr: 800-347-4253

1994.

★5847★ *An Important Message To All Mechanical Minded People*
National Screw Machine Products
6700 W. Snowville Rd.
Brecksville, OH 44141
Ph: (216)526-0300

This six-panel brochure describes needed skills, the work, and employment opportunities in the screw machine products industry.

★5848★ "Machine Operator—Casemaking" in *BLR Encyclopedia of Prewritten Job Descriptions*
Business and Legal Reports, Inc.
39 Academy St.
Madison, CT 06443-1513
Ph: (203)245-7448

Stephen D. Bruce, editor-in-chief. 1994. This book contains hundreds of sample job descriptions arranged by functional job category. The 1-3 page job descriptions cover what the worker normally does in the position, who they report to, and how that position fits in the organizational structure.

★5849★ "Machine Tool Operator" in *Career Information Center* (Vol.9)
Simon and Schuster
200 Old Tappan Rd.
Old Tappan, NJ 07675
Fax: 800-445-6991 Fr: 800-223-2348

Richard Lidz and Dale Anderson, editorial directors. Fifth edition, 1993. For 600 occupations, describes job duties, entry-level requirements, education and training needed, advancement possibilities, employment outlook, earnings and benefits. The set is divided into 12 volumes. Each volume includes jobs related under a broad career field. Volume 13 is the index.

★5850★ "Machine Tool Operator" in *Jobs Rated Almanac*
World Almanac
1 International Blvd., Ste. 444
Mahwah, NJ 07495
Ph: (201)529-6900 Fax: (201)529-6901

Les Krantz. Second edition, 1992. Ranks 250 jobs by environment, salary, outlooks, physical demands, stress, security, travel opportunities, and extra perks. Includes jobs the editor feels are the most common, most interesting, and the most rapidly growing.

★5851★ *Machine Tool Operators*
Chronicle Guidance Publications, Inc.
66 Aurora St.
PO Box 1190
Moravia, NY 13118-1190
Ph: (315)497-0330 Fax: (315)497-3359
Fr: 800-622-7284

1991. This career brief describes the nature of the work, working conditions, hours and earnings, education and training, licensure, certification, unions, personal qualifications, social and psychological factors, employment outlook, entry methods, advancement, and related occupations.

★5852★ *Machine Tool Operators*
Careers, Inc.
PO Box 135
Largo, FL 34649-0135
Ph: (813)584-7333

1992. Two-page occupational summary card describing duties, working conditions, personal qualifications, training, earnings and hours, employment outlook, places of employment, related careers and where to write for more information.

★5853★ "Machine Tool Operators" in *Encyclopedia of Careers and Vocational Guidance* (Vol.3, pp. 338-341)
J.G. Ferguson Publishing Co.
200 W. Madison St., Ste. 300
Chicago, IL 60606
Ph: (312)580-5480 Fax: (312)580-4948

William E. Hopke, editor-in-chief. Ninth edition, 1993. Four-volume set that profiles 500 occupations and describes job trends in 74 industries. Includes career description, educational requirements, history of the job, methods of entry, advancement, employment outlook, earnings, working conditions, social and psychological factors, and sources of additional information.

★5854★ "Machine Tool Operators" in *Occu-Facts: Information on 580 Careers in Outline Form*
Careers, Inc.
PO Box 135
Largo, FL 34649-0135
Ph: (813)584-7333

Biennial, 1995-96 edition. Each one-page occupational profile describes duties, working conditions, physical surroundings and demands, aptitudes, temperament, educational requirements, employment outlook, earnings, and places of employment.

★5855★ "Machining and Machine Operation" in *Opportunities in Metalworking Careers* (pp. 27-38)
National Textbook Co. (NTC)
VGM Career Books
4255 W. Touhy Ave.
Lincolnwood, IL 60646-1975
Ph: (708)679-5500 Fax: (708)679-2494
Fr: 800-323-4900

Mark Rowh. 1991. Covers sheet metal work, machining, structural and reinforcing metalworking, and jewelry making. Describes the work performed, skills needed, training and working conditions. Lists unions that sponsor apprenticeship and technical schools which offer training.

★5856★ "Metalworking and Plastics-Working Machine Operators" in *Occupational Outlook Handbook*
U.S. Government Printing Office
Superintendent of Documents
Washington, DC 20402
Ph: (202)512-1800 Fax: (202)512-2250
Biennial; latest edition, 1994-95. Encyclopedia of careers describing more than 250 occupations and comprising about 85 percent of all jobs in the economy. Occupations that require lengthy education or training are given the most attention. For each occupation, the handbook describes job duties, working conditions, training, educational preparation, personal qualities, advancement possibilities, job outlook, earnings, and sources of additional information.

★5857★ "Milling Machine Tender" in *Occu-Facts: Information on 580 Careers in Outline Form*
Careers, Inc.
PO Box 135
Largo, FL 34649-0135
Ph: (813)584-7333
Biennial, 1995-96 edition. Each one-page occupational profile describes duties, working conditions, physical surroundings and demands, aptitudes, temperament, educational requirements, employment outlook, earnings, and places of employment.

★5858★ "Numerical Control Machine Operator" in *Career Information Center* (Vol.9)
Simon and Schuster
200 Old Tappan Rd.
Old Tappan, NJ 07675
Fax: 800-445-6991 Fr: 800-223-2348
Richard Lidz and Dale Anderson, editorial directors. Fifth edition, 1993. For 600 occupations, describes job duties, entry-level requirements, education and training needed, advancement possibilities, employment outlook, earnings and benefits. The set is divided into 12 volumes. Each volume includes jobs related under a broad career field. Volume 13 is the index.

★5859★ "Numerical Control Machine Operator" in *Careers in High Tech* (pp. 138-139)
Arco Publishing Co.
Macmillan General Reference
15 Columbus Cir.
New York, NY 10023
Fax: 800-835-3202 Fr: 800-858-7674
Connie Winkler. 1987. Surveys career opportunities in data processing, technology, personal computers, telecommunications, manufacturing technology, artificial intelligence, computer graphics, biotechnology, lasers, technical writing, and publishing. Includes information on educational preparation, associations, and periodicals.

★5860★ "Numerical Control Machine Tool Operator" in *Guide To Careers Without College* (pp. 61-63)
Franklin Watts, Inc.
387 Park Avenue, S.
New York, NY 10016
Ph: (212)686-7070
Kathleen S. Abrams. 1988. Discusses careers that do not require a college degree in fields such as health care, sales and marketing, and the building trades. Describes the work, employment opportunities, and training.

★5861★ *Numerical-Control Setup Technician*
Vocational Biographies, Inc.
PO Box 31
Sauk Centre, MN 56378-0031
Ph: (612)352-6516 Fax: (612)352-5546
Fr: 800-255-0752
1994. Four-page pamphlet containing a personal narrative about a worker's job, work likes and dislikes, career path from high school to the present. Education and training, the rewards and frustrations, and the effects of the job on the rest of the worker's life. The data file portion of this pamphlet gives a concise occupational summary, including work descriptions, working conditions, places of employment, personal characteristics, education and training, job outlook, and salary range.

★5862★ *Numerical Control Tool Programmers*
Chronicle Guidance Publications, Inc.
66 Aurora St.
PO Box 1190
Moravia, NY 13118-1190
Ph: (315)497-0330 Fax: (315)497-3359
Fr: 800-622-7284
1994. Career brief describing the nature of the job, working conditions, hours and earnings, education and training, licensure, certification, unions, personal qualifications, social and psychological factors, location, employment outlook, entry methods, advancement, and related occupations.

★5863★ *Opportunities in Machine Trades Careers*
National Textbook Co. (NTC)
VGM Career Books
4255 W. Toughy Ave.
Lincolnwood, IL 60646-1975
Ph: (708)679-5500 Fax: (708)679-2494
Fr: 800-323-4900
Lonny D. Garvey.

★5864★ *Opportunities in Metalworking Careers*
National Textbook Co. (NTC)
VGM Career Books
4255 W. Toughy Ave.
Lincolnwood, IL 60646-1975
Ph: (708)679-5500 Fax: (708)679-2494
Fr: 800-323-4900
Mark Rowh.

★5865★ *Opportunities in Plastics Careers*
National Textbook Co. (NTC)
VGM Career Books
4255 W. Touhy Ave.
Lincolnwood, IL 60646-1975
Ph: (708)679-5500 Fax: (708)679-2494
Fr: 800-323-4900
Jan Bone. 1991. Explores career opportunities for chemists, engineers, machinists, moldmakers, technicians, salespeople, and business executives in plastics manufacturing, research and development, and recycling. Describes educational preparation, preferred personal qualities, job hunting strategies, and continuing education.

★5866★ "Plastics" in *Encyclopedia of Careers and Vocational Guidance* (Vol.1, pp. 368-373)
J.G. Ferguson Publishing Co.
200 W. Madison St., Ste. 300
Chicago, IL 60606
Ph: (312)580-5480 Fax: (312)580-4948
William E. Hopke, editor-in-chief. Ninth edition, 1993. Four-volume set that profiles 500 occupations and describes job trends in 74 industries. Includes career description, educational requirements, history of the job, methods of entry, advancement, employment outlook, earnings, working conditions, social and psychological factors, and sources of additional information.

★5867★ "Plastics Industry" in *Career Information Center* (Vol.9)
Simon and Schuster
200 Old Tappan Rd.
Old Tappan, NJ 07675
Fax: 800-445-6991 Fr: 800-223-2348
Richard Lidz and Dale Anderson, editorial directors. Fifth edition, 1993. For 600 occupations, describes job duties, entry-level requirements, education and training needed, advancement possibilities, employment outlook, earnings and benefits. The set is divided into 12 volumes. Each volume includes jobs related under a broad career field. Volume 13 is the index.

★5868★ *Plastics Products Manufacturing Workers*
Chronicle Guidance Publications, Inc.
66 Aurora St.
PO Box 1190
Moravia, NY 13118-1190
Ph: (315)497-0330 Fax: (315)497-3359
Fr: 800-622-7284
1994. Career brief describing the nature of the job, working conditions, hours and earnings, education and training, licensure, certification, unions, personal qualifications, social and psychological factors, location, employment outlook, entry methods, advancement, and related occupations.

★5869★ "Plastics Products Manufacturing Workers" in *Career Discovery Encyclopedia* (Vol.5, pp. 56-57)
J.G. Ferguson Publishing Co.
200 W. Madison St., Ste. 300
Chicago, IL 60606
Ph: (312)580-5480 Fax: (312)580-4948
E. Russell Primm, editor-in-chief. 1993. Contains two-page articles on 504 occupations. Each article describes job duties, earnings, and educational and training requirements.

★5870★ "Plastics Products Manufacturing Workers" in *Encyclopedia of Careers and Vocational Guidance* (Vol.4, pp. 126-128)
J.G. Ferguson Publishing Co.
200 W. Madison St., Ste. 300
Chicago, IL 60606
Ph: (312)580-5480 Fax: (312)580-4948
William E. Hopke, editor-in-chief. Ninth edition, 1993. Four-volume set that profiles 500 occupations and describes job trends in 74 industries. Includes career description, educational requirements, history of the job,

methods of entry, advancement, employment outlook, earnings, working conditions, social and psychological factors, and sources of additional information.

★5871★ *Setup Operators (Machine Shop)*
Chronicle Guidance Publications, Inc.
66 Aurora St.
PO Box 1190
Moravia, NY 13118-1190
Ph: (315)497-0330 Fax: (315)497-3359
Fr: 800-622-7284

1993. This career brief describes the nature of the work, working conditions, hours and earnings, education and training, licensure, certification, unions, personal qualifications, social and psychological factors, employment outlook, entry methods, advancement, and related occupations.

★5872★ *Stamp of Approval*
Film Video Library
University of Michigan
919 S University Ave., Rm. 207
Ann Arbor, MI 48109-1185
Ph: (313)764-5360

Videocassette. 198?. 21 mins. This program documents the process of metal stamping from the time steel is delivered to a modern plant, through cutting, blanking, and forming operations.

★5873★ *Vertical Milling Machine Explained*
Bergwall Productions
540 Baltimore Pike
Chadds Ford, PA 19317
Ph: (215)388-0400 Fax: (215)388-0405
Fr: 800-645-3565

Videocassette. 1980. 75 mins. On 6 tapes, here is a look at how milling machines work.

★5874★ *Video Career Library - Production II*
Careers, Inc.
PO Box 135
Largo, FL 34649-0135
Ph: (813)584-7333

Videocassette. 1990. 32 mins. Part of the Video Career Library covering 165 occupations. Shows actual workers on the job. Includes tool and die makers, machinists, sheet metal workers, cabinet and bench carpenters, opticians, precision electronic equipment assemblers, industrial machine operators, welders and cutters, and assemblers.

ASSOCIATIONS

★5875★ American Foundrymen's Society
505 State St.
Des Plaines, IL 60016-8399
Ph: (708)824-0181

Members: Foundrymen, patternmakers, technologists, and educators. **Purpose:** Sponsors training courses through the Cast Metal Institute; conducts educational and instructional exhibits of foundry industry; sponsors regional conferences, technical meetings, and seminars.

★5876★ AMT - Association for Manufacturing Technology
7901 Westpark Dr.
Mc Lean, VA 22102
Ph: (703)893-2900 Fax: (703)893-1151
Fr: 800-544-3597

Members: Makers of power driven machines used in the process of transforming man-made materials into durable goods, including machine tools, assembly machines, inspection and testing machinery, robots, parts loaders, and plastics molding machines; associate members are producers of tools and tooling parts and components, attachments and accessories, controls and software, and engineering and systems design services. **Purpose:** Seeks to improve methods of producing and marketing machine tools; promotes research and development in the industry. Sponsors: seminars for training production supervisors, accident prevention and safety, and advertising management; industry standards and technical aspects of the industry. Serves as a clearinghouse for technical aspects of the industry. Promotes orderly disposal of government-owned surplus machine tools. **Publications:** *Directories of Machine Tools*, annual. • *Economic Handbook of the Machine Tool Industry*, annual.

★5877★ National Tooling and Machining Association (NTMA)
9300 Livingston Rd.
Fort Washington, MD 20744
Ph: (301)248-6200 Fax: (301)248-7104
Fr: 800-248-NTMA

Members: Manufacturers of tools, dies, jigs, fixtures, molds, gages, or special machinery; companies that do precision machining on a contract basis; past service and associate members. **Purpose:** Provides management services; represents members in legislative matters. Promotes apprenticeship programs. Compiles management surveys; conducts management training workshops; maintains speakers' bureau. Has produced motion pictures and videocassettes on tool, die, and precision machining for educational showings. **Publications:** *Business Management Advisories*, periodic. • *Buyers Guide of Special Tooling and Precision Machining Services*, annual. • *Catalog of Publications and Training Materials*, periodic. • *Precision*, bimonthly. • *Record*, monthly.

★5878★ Society of Plastics Engineers (SPE)
14 Fairfield Dr.
Brookfield, CT 06804-0403
Ph: (203)775-0471 Fax: (203)775-8490

Members: Professional society of plastics scientists, engineers, sales professionals, educators, students, and others interested in the design, development, production, and utilization of plastics materials, products, and equipment. **Purpose:** Conducts seminars. Maintains 92 sections. **Publications:** *Journal of Vinyl Additive Technology*, quarterly. • *Plastics Engineering*, monthly. • *Plastics Engineering Series.* • *Polymer Composites*, bimonthly. • *Polymer Engineering and Science*, semimonthly. • *Preprint Volumes.*

★5879★ Tool and Manufacturing Association
1177 S. Dee Rd.
Park Ridge, IL 60068

PUR Provides information on opportunities in high production precision machining.

STANDARDS/CERTIFICATION AGENCIES

★5880★ AMT - Association for Manufacturing Technology
7901 Westpark Dr.
Mc Lean, VA 22102
Ph: (703)893-2900 Fax: (703)893-1151
Fr: 800-544-3597

Sponsors: seminars for training production supervisors, accident prevention and safety, and advertising management; industry standards and technical aspects of the industry. Serves as a clearinghouse for technical aspects of the industry.

★5881★ NMTBA - Association for Manufacturing Technology
7901 Westpark Dr.
Mc Lean, VA 22102
Ph: (703)893-2900

Develops and supervises standards for training apprentices. Participates in programs of standardization of design and performance of machine tools and components.

TEST GUIDES

★5882★ *Career Examination Series: Machinist*
National Learning Corp.
212 Michael Dr.
Syosset, NY 11791
Ph: (516)921-8888 Fax: (516)921-8743
Fr: 800-645-6337

Jack Rudman. All examination guides in this series contain questions with answers.

★5883★ *Career Examination Series: Maintenance Machinist*
National Learning Corp.
212 Michael Dr.
Syosset, NY 11791
Ph: (516)921-8888 Fax: (516)921-8743
Fr: 800-645-6337

Jack Rudman. 1989. All examination guides in this series contain questions with answers.

Educational Directories and Programs

★5884★ *American Machinist—Buyers' Guide Issue*
Penton Publishing Co.
1100 Superior Ave.
Cleveland, OH 44114-2543
Ph: (216)696-7000 Fax: (216)696-0177
P. K. Gibson, Contact

Annual, April. Publication includes: Guide to over 2,600 manufacturers of products and services used by metalworking industries. Entries include: Co. name, address, phone, fax. Arrangement: Separate alphabetical sections for manufacturers and products.

★5885★ *Directories of Machine Tools*
AMT - Association for Manufacturing Technology
7901 Westpark Dr.
Mc Lean, VA 22102
Ph: (703)893-2900 Fax: (703)893-1151
Fr: 800-544-3597

Annual.

Awards, Scholarships, Grants, and Fellowships

★5886★ AMT's Two-Year Scholarships
The Association for Manufacturing Technology (AMT)
7901 Westpark Dr.
Mc Lean, VA 22102-4269
Ph: (703)827-2900 Fax: (703)893-1151

Purpose: To encourage students to pursue careers in the machine tool industry and to foster a closer working relationship between AMT member companies and the educational institutions in their communities. Qualifications: Applicants must be recent or upcoming high school graduates who are planning to enroll full-time in a two-year public community, junior, or technical college and are interested in seeking a career in a manufacturing technology related discipline. They must also be employable in the machine tool industry. Selection criteria: The AMT member companies that wish to participate will work with a regionally accredited colleges or high schools in its geographic area to select a deserving student and will act as the student's sponsor by providing work-training employment during the two summers of the scholarship, working with the school and student to assure appropriateness of the student's course of study, maintaining contact with the school in monitoring student's academic progress, and to monitor student's work-training performance to assure that work assignments contribute to the student's educational development. Selection is based on academic performance, demonstrated interest in a manufacturing technology related discipline, and ability to meet entrance requirements of the participating college and employment standards of the participating member company. Each participating member company can only select one recipient. Funds available: Up to $2,000 per year for two years for tuition, academic fees, and books. Application details: Students should apply through the participating colleges. Each candidate should have an endorsement and recommendation from the secondary school. Deadline: None.

Basic Reference Guides and Handbooks

★5887★ *Economic Handbook of the Machine Tool Industry*
AMT - Association for Manufacturing Technology
7901 Westpark Dr.
Mc Lean, VA 22102
Ph: (703)893-2900 Fax: (703)893-1151
Fr: 800-544-3597

Annual.

★5888★ *Preprint Volumes*
Society of Plastics Engineers (SPE)
14 Fairfield Dr.
Brookfield, CT 06804-0403
Ph: (203)775-0471 Fax: (203)775-8490

★5889★ *U.S. Glass, Metal and Glazing—Directory of Suppliers of Machinery & Equipment Issue*
Key Communications, Inc.
PO Box 569
Garrisonville, VA 22463
Ph: (703)720-5584 Fax: (703)295-2903
Debra Levy, Publisher

Annual, May. Publication includes: List of suppliers of machinery and equipment for the glass, metal, and glazing industry. Entries include: Co. name, address, phone, telex, names and titles of key personnel, subsidiary and branch names and locations. Arrangement: Alphabetical.

★5890★ *U.S. Glass, Metal and Glazing—Directory of Suppliers of Sealants & Glazing Systems Issue*
Key Communications, Inc.
PO Box 569
Garrisonville, VA 22463
Ph: (703)720-5584 Fax: (703)295-2903
Debra A. Levy, Publisher

Annual, July. Publication includes: List of about 90 suppliers of sealants and glazing systems for the glass, metal, and glazing industry. Entries include: Co. name, address, phone, fax. Arrangement: Classified by product of service.

Periodicals

★5891★ *International Journal for Numerical Methods in Fluids*
John Wiley and Sons, Inc.
Subscription Dept.
605 3rd Ave.
New York, NY 10158
Ph: (212)850-6000 Fax: (212)850-6799
C. Taylor

Bimonthly. Journal focussing on computer-based problem-solving techniques for fluids. Topics include potential flow and viscous flow.

★5892★ *Journal of Vinyl Additive Technology*
Society of Plastics Engineers (SPE)
14 Fairfield Dr.
Brookfield, CT 06804-0403
Ph: (203)775-0471 Fax: (203)775-8490

Quarterly. Covers problem solving and use of vinyl polymers in plastics; includes graphs, tables, charts.

★5893★ *Locator*
Machinery Information Systems, Inc.
1110 Spring St.
Silver Spring, MD 20910
Ph: (301)585-9498 Fax: (301)585-9460
Rick ShontzPublisher

Monthly. Magazine on metalworking, plastic and electrical machinery, and power equipment.

★5894★ *Metals Newsletter*
National Safety Council
1121 Spring Lake Dr.
Itasca, IL 60143-3201
Ph: (708)775-2282 Fax: (708)775-2285
Diane A. Ghazarian

Monthly. Promotes safe work practices and products in the metals industry. Carries accident case histories, items on successful accident prevention programs, and articles on safety at home and elsewhere.

★5895★ *Modern Plastics*
McGraw-Hill, Inc.
1221 Avenue of the Americas
New York, NY 10020
Ph: (212)512-4686 Fax: (212)512-4256
Keith Kreisher

Monthly. Magazine for the plastics industry.

★5896★ *Plastics Compounding*
Advanstar Communications, Inc.
859 Williamette St.
Eugene, OR 97401-6806
Ph: (503)343-1200 Fax: (503)344-3514
Mary C. McMurrer

Bimonthly. Magazine on formulation, production, and compounding of plastics, resins, alloys, and blends.

★5897★ *Plastics Engineering*
Society of Plastics Engineers (SPE)
14 Fairfield Dr.
Brookfield, CT 06804-0403
Ph: (203)775-0471 Fax: (203)775-8490

Monthly.

★5898★ *Plastics Engineering Series*
Society of Plastics Engineers (SPE)
14 Fairfield Dr.
Brookfield, CT 06804-0403
Ph: (203)775-0471 Fax: (203)775-8490

★5899★ *Plastics Machinery & Equipment*
Advanstar Communications, Inc.
859 Williamette St.
Eugene, OR 97401-6806
Ph: (503)343-1200 Fax: (503)344-3514
M. Jane Ganter

Monthly. Magazine on plastics processing machinery and equipment.

★5900★ *Plastics News*
Crain Communications Inc
1725 Merriman Rd., Ste. 300
Akron, OH 44313-5251
Ph: (216)836-9180 Fax: (216)836-2831
Robert Grace

Weekly. Magazine (tabloid) for the plastics industry.

★5901★ *Plastics World*
PTN Publishing Co.
445 Broad Hollow Rd., Ste. 21
Melville, NY 11747
Ph: (516)845-2700 Fax: (516)845-7109
Doug Smock

Monthly. Plastics magazine.

★5902★ *Polymer Composites*
Society of Plastics Engineers (SPE)
14 Fairfield Dr.
Brookfield, CT 06804-0403
Ph: (203)775-0471 Fax: (203)775-8490

Bimonthly. Covers developments in reinforced plastics and polymer composites; includes graphs, tables, charts.

★5903★ *Polymer Engineering and Science*
Society of Plastics Engineers (SPE)
14 Fairfield Dr.
Brookfield, CT 06804-0403
Ph: (203)775-0471 Fax: (203)775-8490

Semimonthly. Contains symposium papers and translations of foreign technical papers dealing with polymers.

★5904★ *Production*
Gardner Publications, Inc.
6600 Clough Pike
Cincinnati, OH 45244
Ph: (513)231-8020 Fax: (513)231-2818
Robert F. Huber

Monthly. Magazine helping managers and executives in the metalworking manufacturing industry interpret, evaluate, and implement new technologies, methods, and equipment.

★5905★ *Rubber and Plastics Newsletter*
National Safety Council
1121 Spring Lake Dr.
Itasca, IL 60143-3201
Ph: (708)775-2282 Fax: (708)775-2285
Diane A. Ghazarian

Bimonthly. Carries accident prevention information and promotes safety awareness in the rubber and plastics industries. Emphasizes safe work practices, conditions, and products and reports on successful industrial safety programs.

Meetings and Conventions

★5906★ American Foundrymen's Society Casting Congress and Cast Expo
American Foundrymen's Society, Inc.
505 State St.
Des Plaines, IL 60016-8399
Ph: (708)824-0181 Fax: (708)824-7848
Fr: 800-537-4237

Congress is annual; exposition is held every three years. **Dates and Locations:** 1996 Apr 20-23; Philadelphia, PA. • 1997 Apr 12-17; Seattle, WA.

★5907★ MAQUINAMEX - Metalworking Machine Tool Expo
Marketing International Corp.
200 N. Glebe Rd., Ste. 900
Arlington, VA 22203
Ph: (703)527-8000 Fax: (703)527-8006

Annual. Always held during June at the Exhibition Center in Mexico City.

★5908★ METALFORM
Precision Metalforming Association
27027 Chardon Rd.
Richmond Heights, OH 44143
Ph: (216)585-8800 Fax: (216)585-3126

Annual. Held during odd-numbered years in Rosemont, Illinois. Held during even-numbered years in the Southeast. **Dates and Locations:** 1996 Mar 17-20; Nashville, TN.

Other Sources of Information

★5909★ *American Machinist—Buyers' Guide Issue*
Penton Publishing Co.
1100 Superior Ave.
Cleveland, OH 44114-2543
Ph: (216)696-7000 Fax: (216)696-0177
P. K. Gibson, Contact

Annual, April. Publication includes: Guide to over 2,600 manufacturers of products and services used by metalworking industries. Entries include: Co. name, address, phone, fax. Arrangement: Separate alphabetical sections for manufacturers and products.

★5910★ *Catalog of Publications and Training Materials*
National Tooling and Machining Association (NTMA)
9300 Livingston Rd.
Ft. Washington, MD 20744
Ph: (301)248-6200 Fax: (301)248-7104
Fr: 800-248-NTMA

Periodic.

★5911★ "Machine Operator" in *Career Selector 2001*
Barron's Educational Series, Inc.
250 Wireless Blvd.
Hauppauge, NY 11788
Ph: (516)434-3311 Fax: (516)434-3723
Fr: 800-645-3476

James C. Gonyea. 1993.

★5912★ "Numerical-Control Lathe Operator" in *Career Selector 2001*
Barron's Educational Series, Inc.
250 Wireless Blvd.
Hauppauge, NY 11788
Ph: (516)434-3311 Fax: (516)434-3723
Fr: 800-645-3476

James C. Gonyea. 1993.

Tool and Die Makers

Tool and die makers are highly skilled workers produce tools, dies, and special guiding and holding devices that are used in machines that produce a variety of products. Working from blueprints and instructions, tool and die makers plan the sequence of operations necessary to manufacture the tool or die. They measure and mark the pieces of metal that will be cut or form parts of the final product. They then do the cutting, boring, or drilling that is required. They check the accuracy of what they have done to ensure that the final product will meet specifications. Then they assemble the parts and perform finishing jobs such as filing, grinding, and smoothing surfaces. Most tool and die makers work in industries that manufacture metalworking machinery and equipment, motor vehicles, aircraft, and plastics products.

Salaries

Weekly earnings for tool and die makers are as follows:

Lowest 10 percent	$409/week or less
Middle 50 percent	$499-$803/week
Top 10 percent	$911/week or more

Employment Outlook

Growth rate until the year 2005: Decline.

Tool and Die Makers

Career Guides

★5913★ ***Career Information for Precision Machining Technology***
National Tooling and Machining Association
9300 Livingston Rd.
Ft. Washington, MD 20744
Ph: (301)248-6200
This six-panel brochure lists the advantages of working in the machine tool industry, study course contents, and how to get started.

★5914★ ***Career Insights***
RMI Media Productions, Inc.
1365 N. Winchester
Olathe, KS 66061
Ph: (913)768-1696 Fax: 800-755-6910
Fr: 800-745-5480
Videocassette series. 1987. This videotape series describes 50 occupations, including skill requirements and interviews with people employed in these fields. Occupations include: flight service, air transportation/ground services, data processing, carpentry, clerk in banking/insurance/business, cosmetic personal grooming, firefighting, forestry, insulation/roofing, mechanics, material handling, photographic processing, pipefitting and plumbing, printing, secretarial services, tool and die operations.

★5915★ ***How Valuable is Your Future?***
Tooling and Manufacturing Association
1177 S. Dee Rd.
Park Ridge, IL 60068-9809
Ph: (708)825-1120
1989. This ten-panel brochure describes the work of precision metalworkers, the skills, entry into the field, internships, and earnings.

★5916★ **"Job and Die Setters" in *Encyclopedia of Careers and Vocational Guidance* (Vol.3, pp. 250-251)**
J.G. Ferguson Publishing Co.
200 W. Madison St., Ste. 300
Chicago, IL 60606
Ph: (312)580-5480 Fax: (312)580-4948
William E. Hopke, editor-in-chief. Ninth edition, 1993. Four-volume set that profiles 500 occupations and describes job trends in 74 industries. Includes career description, educational requirements, history of the job, methods of entry, advancement, employment outlook, earnings, working conditions, social and psychological factors, and sources of additional information.

★5917★ ***Opportunities in Tool and Die Careers***
National Textbook Co. (NTC)
VGM Career Books
4255 W. Toughy Ave.
Lincolnwood, IL 60646-1975
Ph: (708)679-5500 Fax: (708)679-2494
Fr: 800-323-4900
George Dudzinski.

★5918★ **"Tap and Die Maker Technicians" in *Encyclopedia of Careers and Vocational Guidance* (Vol.4, pp. 481)**
J.G. Ferguson Publishing Co.
200 W. Madison St., Ste. 300
Chicago, IL 60606
Ph: (312)580-5480 Fax: (312)580-4948
William E. Hopke, editor-in-chief. Ninth edition, 1993. Four-volume set that profiles 500 occupations and describes job trends in 74 industries. Includes career description, educational requirements, history of the job, methods of entry, advancement, employment outlook, earnings, working conditions, social and psychological factors, and sources of additional information.

★5919★ **"Tool-and-Die Maker" in *Jobs Rated Almanac***
World Almanac
1 International Blvd., Ste. 444
Mahwah, NJ 07495
Ph: (201)529-6900 Fax: (201)529-6901
Les Krantz. Second edition, 1992. Ranks 250 jobs by environment, salary, outlooks, physical demands, stress, security, travel opportunities, and extra perks. Includes jobs the editor feels are the most common, most interesting, and the most rapidly growing.

★5920★ **"Tool Design Technician" in *Occu-Facts: Information on 580 Careers in Outline Form***
Careers, Inc.
PO Box 135
Largo, FL 34649-0135
Ph: (813)584-7333
Biennial, 1995-96 edition. Each one-page occupational profile describes duties, working conditions, physical surroundings and demands, aptitudes, temperament, educational requirements, employment outlook, earnings, and places of employment.

★5921★ **"Tool and Die Design" in *Career Connection II: A Guide to Technical Majors and Their Related Careers* (pp. 144-145)**
Jist Works, Inc.
720 N. Park Ave.
Indianapolis, IN 46202-3431
Ph: (317)264-3720 Fax: (317)264-3709
Fred A. Rowe. 1994. Contains technical majors, such as automotive technology. Describes the major and the job. Lists high school and postsecondary school courses. Includes occupations related to the major, employment outlook, and starting salary.

★5922★ ***Tool and Die Maker***
Careers, Inc.
PO Box 135
Largo, FL 34649-0135
Ph: (813)584-7333
1993. Two-page occupational summary card describing duties, working conditions, personal qualifications, training, earnings and hours, employment outlook, places of employment, related careers and where to write for more information.

★5923★ **"Tool and Die Maker" in *BLR Encyclopedia of Prewritten Job Descriptions***
Business and Legal Reports, Inc.
39 Academy St.
Madison, CT 06443-1513
Ph: (203)245-7448
Stephen D. Bruce, editor-in-chief. 1994. This book contains hundreds of sample job descriptions arranged by functional job category. The 1-3 page job descriptions cover what the worker normally does in the position, who they report to, and how that position fits in the organizational structure.

★5924★ "Tool and Die Maker" in *Career Information Center* (Vol.9)
Simon and Schuster
200 Old Tappan Rd.
Old Tappan, NJ 07675
Fax: 800-445-6991 Fr: 800-223-2348

Richard Lidz and Dale Anderson, editorial directors. Fifth edition, 1993. For 600 occupations, describes job duties, entry-level requirements, education and training needed, advancement possibilities, employment outlook, earnings and benefits. The set is divided into 12 volumes. Each volume includes jobs related under a broad career field. Volume 13 is the index.

★5925★ "Tool and Die Maker" in *Occu-Facts: Information on 580 Careers in Outline Form*
Careers, Inc.
PO Box 135
Largo, FL 34649-0135
Ph: (813)584-7333

Biennial, 1995-96 edition. Each one-page occupational profile describes duties, working conditions, physical surroundings and demands, aptitudes, temperament, educational requirements, employment outlook, earnings, and places of employment.

★5926★ "Tool and Die Maker" in *VGM's Careers Encyclopedia* (pp. 462-464)
National Textbook Co. (NTC)
VGM Career Books
4255 W. Touhy Ave.
Lincolnwood, IL 60646-1975
Ph: (708)679-5500 Fax: (708)679-2494
Fr: 800-323-4900

Third edition, 1991. Contains two- to five-page descriptions of 200 managerial, professional, technical, trade, and service occupations. Each profile includes job duties, places of employment, qualifications, educational preparation, training, employment potential, advancement, income, and additional sources of information.

★5927★ "Tool and Die Makers" in *Career Discovery Encyclopedia* (Vol.6, pp. 116-117)
J.G. Ferguson Publishing Co.
200 W. Madison St., Ste. 300
Chicago, IL 60606
Ph: (312)580-5480 Fax: (312)580-4948

E. Russell Primm, editor-in-chief. 1993. Contains two-page articles on 504 occupations. Each article describes job duties, earnings, and educational and training requirements.

★5928★ "Tool and Die Makers" in *Jobs! What They Are—Where They Are—What They Pay* (pp. 217)
Simon & Schuster, Inc.
Simon & Schuster Bldg.
1230 Avenue of the Americas
New York, NY 10020
Ph: (212)698-7000

Robert O. Snelling and Anne M. Snelling. Revised edition, 1992. Profiles 241 occupations, describing duties and responsibilities, educational preparation, earnings, employment opportunities, training, and qualifications.

★5929★ "Tool and Die Makers" in *Occupational Outlook Handbook*
U.S. Government Printing Office
Superintendent of Documents
Washington, DC 20402
Ph: (202)512-1800 Fax: (202)512-2250

Biennial; latest edition, 1994-95. Encyclopedia of careers describing more than 250 occupations and comprising about 85 percent of all jobs in the economy. Occupations that require lengthy education or training are given the most attention. For each occupation, the handbook describes job duties, working conditions, training, educational preparation, personal qualities, advancement possibilities, job outlook, earnings, and sources of additional information.

★5930★ *Tool and Die Sharpener*
Vocational Biographies, Inc.
PO Box 31
Sauk Centre, MN 56378-0031
Ph: (612)352-6516 Fax: (612)352-5546
Fr: 800-255-0752

1990. Four-page pamphlet containing a personal narrative about a worker's job, work likes and dislikes, career path from high school to the present. Education and training, the rewards and frustrations, and the effects of the job on the rest of the worker's life. The data file portion of this pamphlet gives a concise occupational summary, including work descriptions, working conditions, places of employment, personal characteristics, education and training, job outlook, and salary range.

★5931★ "Tool Makers and Die Setters" in *Encyclopedia of Careers and Vocational Guidance* (Vol.4, pp. 540-543)
J.G. Ferguson Publishing Co.
200 W. Madison St., Ste. 300
Chicago, IL 60606
Ph: (312)580-5480 Fax: (312)580-4948

William E. Hopke, editor-in-chief. Ninth edition, 1993. Four-volume set that profiles 500 occupations and describes job trends in 74 industries. Includes career description, educational requirements, history of the job, methods of entry, advancement, employment outlook, earnings, working conditions, social and psychological factors, and sources of additional information.

★5932★ *Toolmakers and Diemakers*
Chronicle Guidance Publications, Inc.
66 Aurora St.
PO Box 1190
Moravia, NY 13118-1190
Ph: (315)497-0330 Fax: (315)497-3359
Fr: 800-622-7284

1993. This career brief describes the nature of the work, working conditions, hours and earnings, education and training, licensure, certification, unions, personal qualifications, social and psychological factors, employment outlook, entry methods, advancement, and related occupations.

★5933★ *Video Career Library - Production II*
Careers, Inc.
PO Box 135
Largo, FL 34649-0135
Ph: (813)584-7333

Videocassette. 1990. 32 mins. Part of the Video Career Library covering 165 occupations. Shows actual workers on the job. Includes tool and die makers, machinists, sheet metal workers, cabinet and bench carpenters, opticians, precision electronic equipment assemblers, industrial machine operators, welders and cutters, and assemblers.

Associations

★5934★ AMT - Association for Manufacturing Technology
7901 Westpark Dr.
Mc Lean, VA 22102
Ph: (703)893-2900 Fax: (703)893-1151
Fr: 800-544-3597

Members: Makers of power driven machines used in the process of transforming man-made materials into durable goods, including machine tools, assembly machines, inspection and testing machinery, robots, parts loaders, and plastics molding machines; associate members are producers of tools and tooling parts and components, attachments and accessories, controls and software, and engineering and systems design services. **Purpose:** Seeks to improve methods of producing and marketing machine tools; promotes research and development in the industry. Sponsors: seminars for training production supervisors, accident prevention and safety, and advertising management; industry standards and technical aspects of the industry. Serves as a clearinghouse for technical aspects of the industry. Promotes orderly disposal of government-owned surplus machine tools. **Publications:** *Directories of Machine Tools*, annual. • *Economic Handbook of the Machine Tool Industry*, annual.

★5935★ National Tooling and Machining Association (NTMA)
9300 Livingston Rd.
Fort Washington, MD 20744
Ph: (301)248-6200 Fax: (301)248-7104
Fr: 800-248-NTMA

Members: Manufacturers of tools, dies, jigs, fixtures, molds, gages, or special machinery; companies that do precision machining on a contract basis; past service and associate members. **Purpose:** Provides management services; represents members in legislative matters. Promotes apprenticeship programs. Compiles management surveys; conducts management training workshops; maintains speakers' bureau. Has produced motion pictures and videocassettes on tool, die, and precision machining for educational showings. **Publications:** *Business Management Advisories*, periodic. • *Buyers Guide of Special Tooling and Precision Machining Services*, annual. • *Catalog of Publications and Training Materials*, periodic. • *Precision*, bimonthly. • *Record*, monthly.

★5936★ Tool and Manufacturing Association
1177 S. Dee Rd.
Park Ridge, IL 60068
PUR Provides information on opportunities in high production precision machining.

Standards/Certification Agencies

★5937★ AMT - Association for Manufacturing Technology
7901 Westpark Dr.
Mc Lean, VA 22102
Ph: (703)893-2900 Fax: (703)893-1151
Fr: 800-544-3597
Sponsors: seminars for training production supervisors, accident prevention and safety, and advertising management; industry standards and technical aspects of the industry. Serves as a clearinghouse for technical aspects of the industry.

★5938★ NMTBA - Association for Manufacturing Technology
7901 Westpark Dr.
Mc Lean, VA 22102
Ph: (703)893-2900
Develops and supervises standards for training apprentices. Participates in programs of standardization of design and performance of machine tools and components.

Test Guides

★5939★ *Career Examination Series: Toolmaker*
National Learning Corp.
212 Michael Dr.
Syosset, NY 11791
Ph: (516)921-8888 Fax: (516)921-8743
Fr: 800-645-6337
Jack Rudman. Test guide including questions and answers for students or professionals in the field who seek advancement through examination.

Educational Directories and Programs

★5940★ *Directories of Machine Tools*
AMT - Association for Manufacturing Technology
7901 Westpark Dr.
Mc Lean, VA 22102
Ph: (703)893-2900 Fax: (703)893-1151
Fr: 800-544-3597
Annual.

★5941★ *MAN—Modern Applications News—Cutting Tools Buyers' Guide*
Nelson Publishing
504 N. Tamiami Trail
Nokomis, FL 34275
Ph: (813)966-9521 Fax: (813)966-2590
Margaret P. Bouse, Contact
Annual, August. Publication includes: List of manufacturers and distributors of cutting tools. Entries include: Co. name, address, phone, name and title of contact, products. Arrangement: Alphabetical.

Basic Reference Guides and Handbooks

★5942★ *Economic Handbook of the Machine Tool Industry*
AMT - Association for Manufacturing Technology
7901 Westpark Dr.
Mc Lean, VA 22102
Ph: (703)893-2900 Fax: (703)893-1151
Fr: 800-544-3597
Annual.

Periodicals

★5943★ *Die Casting*
Engineering Research Center for Net Shape Manufacturing, Ohio State University
339 Baker Systems/1971 Neil Avenue
Columbus, OH 43210
Ph: (614)292-5063 Fax: (614)292-7219
Darline Wine, Contact
Covers net shape manufacturing of die casting project descriptions and plans. Also contains die casting reports. Recurring features include news of research and notices of publications available.

★5944★ *NTMA Record*
National Tooling and Machining Association (NTMA)
9300 Livingston Rd.
Fort Washington, MD 20744
Ph: (301)248-6200 Fax: (301)248-7104
Fr: 800-248-6862
Sandra S. Bailey
Monthly. Focuses on business management techniques and government relations for the contract tool, die, and precision machining industry. Supplies information on Association activities. Recurring features include editorials, tax information, and technical notes.

Other Sources of Information

★5945★ *Catalog of Publications and Training Materials*
National Tooling and Machining Association (NTMA)
9300 Livingston Rd.
Ft. Washington, MD 20744
Ph: (301)248-6200 Fax: (301)248-7104
Fr: 800-248-NTMA
Periodic.

Welders, Cutters, and Welding Machine Operators

Welding is the most common way of permanently joining metal parts. Welding is used to join beams and steel reinforcing rods when constructing buildings, bridges, and other structures, and also in utilities such as nuclear power plants and refineries. **Welders** use all types of welding equipment in a variety of positions, such as flat, vertical, horizontal, and overhead. They select and set up welding equipment and may also examine welds to insure they meet standards or specifications. In many production processes automated welding is used. In this process, a **welding machine operator** monitors the machine, which performs the welding tasks. Welding machine operators set up and operate welding machines as specified by layouts, work orders, or blueprints. **Cutters** use the heat from burning gases or an electric arc to cut and trim metal objects to specific dimensions. Cutters also dismantle large objects, such as ships, railroad cars, automobiles or aircrafts.

Salaries

Weekly earnings for welders and welding machine operators are as follows:

Lowest 10 percent	\$278/week or less
Middle 50 percent	\$342-\$562/week
Top 10 percent	\$715.00/week or more

Employment Outlook

Growth rate until the year 2005: Slower than average.

Welders, Cutters, and Welding Machine Operators

Career Guides

★5946★ *Getting Down to Business: Welding Business*
American Institutes for Research
PO Box 11131
Palo Alto, CA 94302
Ph: (415)493-3550 Fax: (415)858-0958

Joyce P. Gall. 1981.

★5947★ *Opportunities in Welding Careers*
National Textbook Co. (NTC)
VGM Career Books
4255 W. Touhy Ave.
Lincolnwood, IL 60646-1975
Ph: (708)679-5500 Fax: (708)679-2494
Fr: 800-323-4900

Mark Rowh. 1990. Covers employment outlook, educational and training requirements, wages, and the work itself, and advantages and disadvantages of welding careers. Offers job hunting advice.

★5948★ *The Science & Practice of Welding*
Cambridge University Press
40 W. 20th St.
New York, NY 10011
Ph: (212)924-3900 Fax: (212)691-3239

A. C. Davies. Tenth edition, 1993.

★5949★ *Soldering: Instruction and Vocabulary*
RMI Media Productions, Inc.
2807 West 47th St.
Shawnee Mission, KS 66205
Ph: (913)262-3974 Fax: (913)362-6910
Fr: 800-745-5480

Videocassette. 1984. 19 mins. This program provides an introduction to soldering, explaining the terms, materials and tools that relate to the process.

★5950★ *Technical/Manufacturing Cluster One*
Center for Humanities, Inc.
Communications Park
Box 1000
Mount Kisco, NY 10549
Ph: (914)666-4100 Fax: (914)666-5319
Fr: 800-431-1242

Videocassette. 1984. 20 mins. An upclose look at people who work in the fields of welding, drafting, and sheet metal.

★5951★ *Video Career Library - Production II*
Careers, Inc.
PO Box 135
Largo, FL 34649-0135
Ph: (813)584-7333

Videocassette. 1990. 32 mins. Part of the Video Career Library covering 165 occupations. Shows actual workers on the job. Includes tool and die makers, machinists, sheet metal workers, cabinet and bench carpenters, opticians, precision electronic equipment assemblers, industrial machine operators, welders and cutters, and assemblers.

★5952★ "Welder" in *BLR Encyclopedia of Prewritten Job Descriptions*
Business and Legal Reports, Inc.
39 Academy St.
Madison, CT 06443-1513
Ph: (203)245-7448

Stephen D. Bruce, editor-in-chief. 1994. This book contains hundreds of sample job descriptions arranged by functional job category. The 1-3 page job descriptions cover what the worker normally does in the position, who they report to, and how that position fits in the organizational structure.

★5953★ "Welder" in *Career Information Center* (Vol.4)
Simon and Schuster
200 Old Tappan Rd.
Old Tappan, NJ 07675
Fax: 800-445-6991 Fr: 800-223-2348

Richard Lidz and Dale Anderson, editorial directors. Fifth edition, 1993. For 600 occupations, describes job duties, entry-level requirements, education and training needed, advancement possibilities, employment outlook, earnings and benefits. The set is divided into 12 volumes. Each volume includes jobs related under a broad career field. Volume 13 is the index.

★5954★ "Welder" in *Guide to Careers Without College* (pp. 67-70)
Franklin Watts, Inc.
387 Park Avenue, S.
New York, NY 10016
Ph: (212)686-7070

Kathleen S. Abrams. 1988. Discusses careers that do not require a college degree in fields such as health care, sales and marketing, and the building trades. Describes the work, employment opportunities, and training.

★5955★ "Welder" in *Hard Hatted Women: Stories of Struggle and Success in the Trades* (pp. 33-36)
Seal Press
3131 Western Ave., Ste. 410
Seattle, WA 98121
Ph: (206)283-7844 Fax: (206)285-9410

Molly Martin, editor. 1988. Twenty-six women recount their experiences working in blue collar occupations. They describe how they got in, the work they do, their relationships in predominantly male occupations, and their training.

★5956★ "Welder" in *Jobs Rated Almanac*
World Almanac
1 International Blvd., Ste. 444
Mahwah, NJ 07495
Ph: (201)529-6900 Fax: (201)529-6901

Les Krantz. Second edition, 1992. Ranks 250 jobs by environment, salary, outlooks, physical demands, stress, security, travel opportunities, and extra perks. Includes jobs the editor feels are the most common, most interesting, and the most rapidly growing.

★5957★ *Welders*
Chronicle Guidance Publications, Inc.
66 Aurora St.
PO Box 1190
Moravia, NY 13118-1190
Ph: (315)497-0330 Fax: (315)497-3359
Fr: 800-622-7284

1991. This career brief describes the nature of the work, working conditions, hours and earnings, education and training, licensure, certification, unions, personal qualifications, social and psychological factors, employment outlook, entry methods, advancement, and related occupations.

★5958★ "Welders" in *Career Discovery Encyclopedia* (Vol.6, pp. 150-151)
J.G. Ferguson Publishing Co.
200 W. Madison St., Ste. 300
Chicago, IL 60606
Ph: (312)580-5480 Fax: (312)580-4948

E. Russell Primm, editor-in-chief. 1993. Contains two-page articles on 504 occupations. Each article describes job duties, earnings, and educational and training requirements.

★5959★ "Welders, Cutters, and Welding Machine Operators" in *Occupational Outlook Handbook*
U.S. Government Printing Office
Superintendent of Documents
Washington, DC 20402
Ph: (202)512-1800 Fax: (202)512-2250

Biennial; latest edition, 1994-95. Encyclopedia of careers describing more than 250 occupations and comprising about 85 percent of all jobs in the economy. Occupations that require lengthy education or training are given the most attention. For each occupation, the handbook describes job duties, working conditions, training, educational preparation, personal qualities, advancement possibilities, job outlook, earnings, and sources of additional information.

★5960★ "Welders" in *Encyclopedia of Careers and Vocational Guidance* (Vol.4, pp. 604-606)
J.G. Ferguson Publishing Co.
200 W. Madison St., Ste. 300
Chicago, IL 60606
Ph: (312)580-5480 Fax: (312)580-4948

William E. Hopke, editor-in-chief. Ninth edition, 1993. Four-volume set that profiles 500 occupations and describes job trends in 74 industries. Includes career description, educational requirements, history of the job, methods of entry, advancement, employment outlook, earnings, working conditions, social and psychological factors, and sources of additional information.

★5961★ *Welders and Oxygen Cutters*
Careers, Inc.
PO Box 135
Largo, FL 34649-0135
Ph: (813)584-7333

1995. Four-page brief offering the definition, history, duties, working conditions, personal qualifications, educational requirements, earnings, hours, employment outlook, advancement possibilities, and related occupations.

★5962★ "Welders and Oxygen Cutters" in *Occu-Facts: Information on 580 Careers in Outline Form*
Careers, Inc.
PO Box 135
Largo, FL 34649-0135
Ph: (813)584-7333

Biennial, 1995-96 edition. Each one-page occupational profile describes duties, working conditions, physical surroundings and demands, aptitudes, temperament, educational requirements, employment outlook, earnings, and places of employment.

★5963★ *Welding and Joining . . . Build a Career to Build a Country*
American Welding Society
550 NW LeJeune Rd.
PO Box 351040
Miami, FL 33135
Ph: (305)443-9353

This eight-panel brochure describes required skills and employment opportunities.

★5964★ *Welding Machine Operator*
Careers, Inc.
PO Box 135
Largo, FL 34649-0135
Ph: (813)584-7333

1994. Two-page job guide card describing duties, working conditions, personal qualifications, training, earnings and hours, employment outlook, places of employment, related careers and where to write for more information.

★5965★ "Welding Machine Operator" in *Occu-Facts: Information on 580 Careers in Outline Form*
Careers, Inc.
PO Box 135
Largo, FL 34649-0135
Ph: (813)584-7333

Biennial, 1995-96 edition. Each one-page occupational profile describes duties, working conditions, physical surroundings and demands, aptitudes, temperament, educational requirements, employment outlook, earnings, and places of employment.

★5966★ "Welding" in *Opportunities in Metalworking Careers* (pp. 47-58)
National Textbook Co. (NTC)
VGM Career Books
4255 W. Touhy Ave.
Lincolnwood, IL 60646-1975
Ph: (708)679-5500 Fax: (708)679-2494
Fr: 800-323-4900

Mark Rowh. 1991. Covers sheet metal work, machining, structural and reinforcing metalworking, and jewelry making. Describes the work performed, skills needed, training and working conditions. Lists unions that sponsor apprenticeship and technical schools which offer training.

★5967★ "Welding Technicians" in *Encyclopedia of Careers and Vocational Guidance* (Vol.4, pp. 607-610)
J.G. Ferguson Publishing Co.
200 W. Madison St., Ste. 300
Chicago, IL 60606
Ph: (312)580-5480 Fax: (312)580-4948

William E. Hopke, editor-in-chief. Ninth edition, 1993. Four-volume set that profiles 500 occupations and describes job trends in 74 industries. Includes career description, educational requirements, history of the job, methods of entry, advancement, employment outlook, earnings, working conditions, social and psychological factors, and sources of additional information.

★5968★ "Welding Technology" in *Career Connection II: A Guide to Technical Majors and Their Related Careers* (pp. 152-153)
Jist Works, Inc.
720 N. Park Ave.
Indianapolis, IN 46202-3431
Ph: (317)264-3720 Fax: (317)264-3709

Fred A. Rowe. 1994. Contains technical majors, such as automotive technology. Describes the major and the job. Lists high school and postsecondary school courses. Includes occupations related to the major, employment outlook, and starting salary.

Associations

★5969★ American Welding Society (AWS)
550 LeJeune Rd. NW
Miami, FL 33126
Ph: (305)443-9353 Fax: (305)443-7559
Fr: 800-443-9353

Members: One of several sponsors of the Welding Research Council and the Materials Properties Council. Professional engineering society in the field of welding. **Purpose:** Sponsors seminars. Maintains over 130 technical committees and handbook committees and 144 sections, educational committees, and task forces. **Publications:** *Directory of Technical Council Committees*, annual. • *Welding Handbook*, biennial. • *Welding Journal*, monthly.

★5970★ Career College Association (CCA)
750 1st St. NE, Ste. 900
Washington, DC 20002
Ph: (202)336-6700 Fax: (202)336-6828

Members: Private postsecondary schools providing career education. **Purpose:** Seeks to inform members of the accreditation process and regulations affecting vocational education. Conducts workshops and institutes for staffs of member schools; provides legislative, administrative, and public relations assistance. Has established Career Training Foundation to support research into private vocational education. Sponsors research programs. Maintains hall of fame; compiles statistics. **Publications:** *Career College Times*, monthly. • *Career Education.* • *Career News Digest.* • *Classroom Companion*, quarterly. • *Directory of Private Accredited Career Colleges and Schools*, annual.

★5971★ National Association of Trade and Technical Schools
2251 Wisconsin Ave. NW
Washington, DC 20007
Ph: (202)333-1021

Members: Private schools providing career education. **Purpose:** Seeks to inform members of the accreditation process and regulations affecting vocational education. Conducts workshops and institutes for staffs of member schools; provides legislative, administrative, and public relations assistance; services as federally recognized accrediting agency. Maintains hall of fame; compiles statistics. **Publications:** *Career News Digest*, 3-4/year. • *Handbook of Trade and Technical Careers and Training.*

Standards/Certification Agencies

★5972★ American Welding Society (AWS)
550 LeJeune Rd. NW
Miami, FL 33126
Ph: (305)443-9353 Fax: (305)443-7559
Fr: 800-443-9353

Maintains over 130 technical committees and handbook committees and 144 sections, educational committees, and task forces. Publishes codes, standards, specifications, and books on welding.

★5973★ National Association of Trade and Technical Schools (NATTS)
2251 Wisconsin Ave. NW
Washington, DC 20007
Ph: (202)333-1021

Informs members of the accreditation process and regulations affecting vocational education. Conducts workshops and institutes for staffs of member schools; provides legislative, administrative, and public relations assistance; serves as a federally recognized accrediting agency.

Test Guides

★5974★ *Career Examination Series: Gas & Electric Welder*
National Learning Corp.
212 Michael Dr.
Syosset, NY 11791
Ph: (516)921-8888 Fax: (516)921-8743
Fr: 800-645-6337

Jack Rudman. All examination guides in this series contain questions with answers.

★5975★ *Career Examination Series: Maintenance Welder*
National Learning Corp.
212 Michael Dr.
Syosset, NY 11791
Ph: (516)921-8888 Fax: (516)921-8743
Fr: 800-645-6337

Jack Rudman. 1989. All examination guides in this series contain questions with answers.

★5976★ *Career Examination Series: Structural Welder*
National Learning Corp.
212 Michael Dr.
Syosset, NY 11791
Ph: (516)921-8888 Fax: (516)921-8743
Fr: 800-645-6337

Jack Rudman. All examination guides in this series contain questions with answers.

★5977★ *Career Examination Series: Welder*
National Learning Corp.
212 Michael Dr.
Syosset, NY 11791
Ph: (516)921-8888 Fax: (516)921-8743
Fr: 800-645-6337

Jack Rudman. All examination guides in this series contain questions with answers.

★5978★ *Career Examination Series: Welding Engineer*
National Learning Corp.
212 Michael Dr.
Syosset, NY 11791
Ph: (516)921-8888 Fax: (516)921-8743
Fr: 800-645-6337

Jack Rudman. 1989. All examination guides in this series contain questions with answers.

★5979★ *Welding*
National Learning Corp.
212 Michael Dr.
Syosset, NY 11791
Ph: (516)921-8888 Fax: (516)921-8743
Fr: 800-645-6337

Jack Rudman. Part of Occupational Competency Examination Series (OCE).

★5980★ *Welding*
National Learning Corp.
212 Michael Dr.
Syosset, NY 11791
Ph: (516)921-8888 Fax: (516)921-8743
Fr: 800-645-6337

Jack Rudman. Part of the Test Your Knowledge Series. Contains multiple choice questions with answers.

Educational Directories and Programs

★5981★ *Career Guidance Handouts*
National Association of Trade and Technical Schools
NATTS
2251 Wisconsin Ave. NW
Washington, DC 20007
Ph: (202)333-1021

★5982★ *Career Training*
National Association of Trade and Technical Schools (NATTS)
2251 Wisconsin Ave. NW
Washington, DC 20007
Ph: (202)333-1021

Quarterly.

★5983★ *Classroom Companion*
National Association of Trade and Technical Schools (NATTS)
2251 Wisconsin Ave. NW
Washington, DC 20007
Ph: (202)333-1021

Quarterly.

★5984★ *Directory of Technical Council Committees*
American Welding Society (AWS)
550 LeJeune Rd. NW
Miami, FL 33126
Ph: (305)443-9353 Fax: (305)443-7559
Fr: 800-443-9353

Annual.

Awards, Scholarships, Grants, and Fellowships

★5985★ AIRCO Welding Award
American Welding Society
550 NW LeJeune Rd.
PO Box 351040
Miami, FL 33135
Ph: (305)443-9353 Fax: (305)443-7559
Fr: 800-443-9353

For recognition of distinguished accomplishments in the joining of or severing of metals that have improved and benefited mankind and furthered the welding industry. An honorarium of $1,000 and a certificate are awarded annually. Established in 1967 and sponsored by Airco Distributor Gases, Division of BOC.

★5986★ Division II Arc Welding Awards
James F. Lincoln Arc Welding Foundation
PO Box 17305
Cleveland, OH 44117-0035
Ph: (216)481-4300

Purpose: To recognize outstanding student talent in arc welding. Qualifications: Applicant must be a U.S. resident who is at least 18 years old and who is engaged in arc-welding training at a vocational level. Individuals enrolled in bachelor's or master's degree courses are not eligible to apply. There are two categories of competition: in Division II-A, candidates are invited to submit designs and photos from completed arc-welded projects. In Division II-B, applicants submit a solution to a problem concerned with the use and knowledge of arc welding. For either category, project must have been completed during the year prior to the application deadline. Funds available: Best of the Program Prize: $1,000; Gold Award: $500; Silver Award: $250; Bronze Award: $125. Application details: Write to the secretary for application guidelines; there is no application form. Submit project. Deadline: June 1.

★5987★ Excellence in Arc Welding Awards; Graduate and Professional Awards for Achievement in Arc-Welded Design, Engineering and Fabrication
James F. Lincoln Arc Welding Foundation
PO Box 17305
Cleveland, OH 44117-0035
Ph: (216)481-4300

Purpose: To recognize professionals with innovative ideas in arc welding and related technologies. Qualifications: Applicant must be a U.S. resident. Applicant to the Graduate Award division must be enrolled in a master's or doctoral degree program. For the Professional Awards, candidate must be employed in a design, engineering, research, fabricating, production, or maintenance group that has reduced costs or achieved some other noteworthy objective relevant to arc welding. Individuals who do not qualify for the Graduate or Professional Awards but who use arc welding in their occupations are eligible for the Excellence Awards. Awards are given to recognize specific projects that successfully used arc welding. Submissions are judged on practicality, innovation, and presentation. Funds available: Best of Program Award: $2,000 (Excellence and Graduate categories), $10,000 (Professional category); Gold Award: $1,000 (Excellence and Graduate), $5,000 (Professional). Application details: Write to the secretary for application form and guidelines. Submit two copies of the following: completed form, a written description of the project, appropriate photos and illustrations, and a one-page abstract. Actual projects may not be submitted. Deadline: May 1. Awards are made in the fall.

Basic Reference Guides and Handbooks

★5988★ *AWS Directory of Technical Council Committees*
American Welding Society (AWS)
550 LeJeune Rd. NW
Miami, FL 33126
Ph: (305)443-9353 Fax: (305)443-7559
Fr: 800-443-9353

Annual.

★5989★ *Consumable Electrode Processes in Welding Automation*
Springer-Verlag New York, Inc.
175 5th Ave., 19th Fl.
New York, NY 10010
Ph: (212)460-1500

J. Cornu. 1989. Part of Advanced Welding Systems Series.

★5990★ *Fire Prevention in Use of Cutting & Welding Processes*
National Fire Protection Association
1 Batterymarch Park
Quincy, MA 02269-9101
Ph: (617)770-3000

1994. Part of Fifty Series.

★5991★ *Guide to Welding*
Kendall/Hunt Publishing Co.
2460 Kerper Blvd.
Dubuque, IA 52001
Ph: (319)588-1451

Kenneth Brown. 1990.

★5992★ *Handbook of Trade and Technical Careers and Training*
National Association of Trade and Technical Schools (NATTS)
2251 Wisconsin Ave. NW
Washington, DC 20007
Ph: (202)333-1021

★5993★ *International Welding Thesaurus*
Air Science Company
PO Box 143
Corning, NY 14830
Ph: (607)962-5591 Fax: (607)962-3101

International Institute of Welding Staff. Third edition, 1989.

★5994★ *MAN—Modern Applications News—Cutting Tools Buyers' Guide*
Nelson Publishing
504 N. Tamiami Trail
Nokomis, FL 34275
Ph: (813)966-9521 Fax: (813)966-2590
Margaret P. Bouse, Contact

Annual, August. Publication includes: List of manufacturers and distributors of cutting tools. Entries include: Co. name, address, phone, name and title of contact, products. Arrangement: Alphabetical.

★5995★ *Math for Welders*
Goodheart-Willcox Company
123 Taft Dr.
South Holland, IL 60473
Ph: (708)333-7200

Nino Marion. 1995.

★5996★ *Practical Problems in Mathematics for Welders*
Delmar Publishers, Inc.
PO Box 15015
2 Computer Dr., W.
Albany, NY 12212
Ph: (518)459-1150 Fax: (518)453-6472

Frank R. Schell. Third edition, 1989. Part of Practical Problems in Mathematics Series.

★5997★ *Quality Assurance of Welded Construction*
Elsevier Science Publishing Company, Inc.
655 Avenue of the Americas
New York, NY 10010
Ph: (212)989-5800

N. T. Burgess. Second edition, 1989.

★5998★ *Rational Fabrication Specifications for Steel Structures*
Air Science Company
PO Box 143
Corning, NY 14830
Ph: (607)962-5591 Fax: (607)962-3101

Welding Institute Staff. 1989.

★5999★ *TIG & Related Processes in Welding Automation*
Springer-Verlag New York, Inc.
175 5th Ave., 19th Fl.
New York, NY 10010
Ph: (212)460-1500

J. Cornu. 1989. Part of Advanced Welding Systems Series.

★6000★ *Tools—Cutting Directory*
American Business Directories, Inc.
5711 S. 86th Circle
Omaha, NE 68127
Ph: (402)593-4600 Fax: (402)331-1505

Annual. Number of listings: 1,676. Entries include: Name, address, phone, size of advertisement, name of owner or manager, number of employees, year first in "Yellow Pages." Compiled from telephone company "Yellow Pages," nationwide. Arrangement: Geographical.

★6001★ *Welding & Cutting: A Guide to Fusion Welding & Associated Cutting Processes*
Industrial Press, Inc.
200 Madison Ave.
New York, NY 10016
Ph: (212)889-6330 Fax: (212)545-8327

Peter Houldcroft. 1989.

★6002★ *Welding: Principles & Applications*
Delmar Publishers, Inc.
PO Box 15015
2 Computer Dr., W.
Albany, NY 12212
Ph: (518)459-1150 Fax: (518)453-6472

Larry Jeffus. Second edition, 1989.

★6003★ *Welding Technology Fundamentals*
Goodheart-Willcox Co.
123 Taft Dr.
South Holland, IL 60473
Ph: (708)333-7200 Fax: (708)331-9130

William A. Bowditch. 1991.

★6004★ *Welding Technology Today: Principles & Practices*
Prentice Hall
Rte. 9W
Englewood Cliffs, NJ 07632
Ph: (201)592-2000

Craig Stinchcomb. 1989.

Periodicals

★6005★ *Career College Times*
Career College Association (CCA)
750 1st St. NE, Ste. 900
Washington, DC 20002
Ph: (202)336-6700 Fax: (202)336-6828

Monthly.

★6006★ *Welding Design & Fabrication*
Penton Publishing
1100 Superior Ave.
Cleveland, OH 44114
Ph: (216)696-7000 Fax: (216)696-7932
Rosalie Brosilow

Monthly. Magazine for the fabricated metal-products industry.

★6007★ *The Welding Distributor*
Penton Publishing
1100 Superior Ave.
Cleveland, OH 44114
Ph: (216)696-7000 Fax: (216)696-7932
Mike Vasilakes

Bimonthly. Distributors magazine featuring welding, welding safety equipment, industrial gases, and distribution issues.

★6008★ *Welding Handbook*
American Welding Society (AWS)
550 LeJeune Rd. NW
Miami, FL 33126
Ph: (305)443-9353 Fax: (305)443-7559
Fr: 800-443-9353

Biennial.

★6009★ *Welding Innovation Quarterly*
James F. Lincoln Arc Welding Foundation
PO Box 17035
Cleveland, OH 44117
Ph: (216)481-4300 Fax: (216)486-1751
John M. Gerken

Quarterly. Magazine covering arc welding design, engineering, and fabrication.

★6010★ *Welding Journal*
American Welding Society (AWS)
550 LeJeune Rd. NW
Miami, FL 33126
Ph: (305)443-9353 Fax: (305)443-7559
Fr: 800-443-9353

Monthly. Covers developments in welding technology, the industry, and the society. Includes book reviews, calendar of events, and employment listings.

Other Sources of Information

★6011★ *Career Connections Video Series: Welding*
Cambridge Career Products
PO Box 2153, Dept. CC15
Charleston, WV 25328-2153
Fr: 800-468-4227

1993. Contains interviews with workers in specific fields and includes on-the-job footage.

★6012★ *Recent Trends in Welding Science & Technology*
ASM International
96389 Kinsman Rd.
Materials Park, OH 44073
Ph: (216)338-5151 Fax: (216)338-4634

1990.

Electric Power Generating Plant Operators and Power Distributors and Dispatchers

Electric power generating plant operators who work in plants fueled by coal, oil, or natural gas regulate and monitor boilers, turbines, generators, auxiliary equipment, such as coal crushers, and switching gears. They operate switches to distribute power demands among generators, combine the current from several generators, and regulate the flow of electricity into powerlines. Operators who work in newer plants work mainly in a central control room and usually are called control room operators and control room operator trainees and assistants. Auxiliary equipment operators work throughout the plant, while switchboard operators control the flow of electricity from a central point. NRC-licensed reactor operators are authorized to operate all equipment in a nuclear powerplant. In addition, an NRC-licensed senior reactor operator acts as the supervisor of the plant for each shift. **Power distributors and dispatchers**, also called load dispatchers or systems operators, oversee the flow of electricity through substations and over a network of transmission and distribution lines to users. Most electric power generating plant operators and power distributors and dispatchers work for electric utility companies and government agencies that produce electricity. Some work for manufacturing establishments that produce electricity for their own use.

Salaries

Median weekly earnings in the electric utility industry are as follows:

Conventional power plant operators	$750/week
Senior power plant operators	$565-$910/week
Power plant operators	$510-$802/week
Nuclear power plant operators	$960/week

Employment Outlook

Growth rate until the year 2005: More slowly than the average.

Electric Power Generating Plant Operators and Power Distributors and Dispatchers

CAREER GUIDES

★6013★ *Career Success Series*
Cambridge Educational
PO Box 2153
Charleston, WV 25328-2153
Ph: (304)744-9323 Fax: (304)744-9351
Fr: 800-468-4227

Videocassette. 1986. 15 mins. A series, available separately, outlining various career choices for students. Occupations include: accounting, flight service, air transportation/ground/flight service, data processing, carpentry, clerk in banking/insurance, commodity sales, cosmetic personal grooming, fire fighting, forestry services, home economics, insulation/roofing, material handling, mechanics, photographic processing, pipefitting and plumbing, police science, printing, carpentry, medical laboratory technicians, secretarial services, and utilities equipment operator.

★6014★ *Careers with an Electric Company*
Lerner Publications Co.
241 First Ave., N.
Minneapolis, MN 55401
Fax: (612)332-7615 Fr: 800-328-4920

Pam Fricke. 1984. Describes fifteen career possibilities with an electric company including such jobs as lineman and system operator.

★6015★ *Careers in Electricity*
RMI Media Productions, Inc.
2807 West 47th St.
Shawnee Mission, KS 66205
Ph: (913)262-3974 Fax: (913)362-6910
Fr: 800-745-5480

Videocassette. 1984. 16 mins. This program examines career opportunities in the power field branch of electricity.

★6016★ "Electric Power Generating Plant Operators and Power Distributors and Dispatchers" in *Occupational Outlook Handbook*
U.S. Government Printing Office
Superintendent of Documents
Washington, DC 20402
Ph: (202)512-1800 Fax: (202)512-2250

Biennial; latest edition, 1994-95. Encyclopedia of careers describing more than 250 occupations and comprising about 85 percent of all jobs in the economy. Occupations that require lengthy education or training are given the most attention. For each occupation, the handbook describes job duties, working conditions, training, educational preparation, personal qualities, advancement possibilities, job outlook, earnings, and sources of additional information.

★6017★ *Electric Power Plant Occupations*
Careers, Inc.
PO Box 135
Largo, FL 34649-0135
Ph: (813)584-7333

1993. Four-page brief offering the definition, history, duties, working conditions, personal qualifications, educational requirements, earnings, hours, employment outlook, advancement possibilities, and related occupations.

★6018★ "Electric Power Plant Occupations" in *Occu-Facts: Information on 580 Careers in Outline Form*
Careers, Inc.
PO Box 135
Largo, FL 34649-0135
Ph: (813)584-7333

Biennial, 1995-96 edition. Each one-page occupational profile describes duties, working conditions, physical surroundings and demands, aptitudes, temperament, educational requirements, employment outlook, earnings, and places of employment.

★6019★ "Electric Power Service Worker" in *Career Information Center* (Vol.11)
Simon and Schuster
200 Old Tappan Rd.
Old Tappan, NJ 07675
Fax: 800-445-6991 Fr: 800-223-2348

Richard Lidz and Dale Anderson, editorial directors. Fifth edition, 1993. For 600 occupations, describes job duties, entry-level requirements, education and training needed, advancement possibilities, employment outlook, earnings and benefits. The set is divided into 12 volumes. Each volume includes jobs related under a broad career field. Volume 13 is the index.

★6020★ "Electric Power Transmission, Distribution Worker" in *Career Information Center* (Vol.11)
Simon and Schuster
200 Old Tappan Rd.
Old Tappan, NJ 07675
Fax: 800-445-6991 Fr: 800-223-2348

Richard Lidz and Dale Anderson, editorial directors. Fifth edition, 1993. For 600 occupations, describes job duties, entry-level requirements, education and training needed, advancement possibilities, employment outlook, earnings and benefits. The set is divided into 12 volumes. Each volume includes jobs related under a broad career field. Volume 13 is the index.

★6021★ "Electrical Operator" in *Great Careers for People Who Like to Work with Their Hands* (pp. 40)
Gale Research Inc.
835 Penobscot Bldg.
Detroit, MI 48226
Ph: (313)961-2242 Fr: 800-347-4253

1994.

★6022★ "Electrical Power Worker" in *Career Discovery Encyclopedia* (Vol.2, pp. 136-137)
J.G. Ferguson Publishing Co.
200 W. Madison St., Ste. 300
Chicago, IL 60606
Ph: (312)580-5480 Fax: (312)580-4948
E. Russell Primm, editor-in-chief. 1993. Contains two-page articles on 504 occupations. Each article describes job duties, earnings, and educational and training requirements.

★6023★ *Electrical Transmission and Distribution Occupations*
Careers, Inc.
PO Box 135
Largo, FL 34649-0135
Ph: (813)584-7333
1993. Four-page brief offering the definition, history, duties, working conditions, personal qualifications, educational requirements, earnings, hours, employment outlook, advancement possibilities, and related occupations.

★6024★ "Electrical Transmission and Distribution Occupations" in *Occu-Facts: Information on 580 Careers in Outline Form*
Careers, Inc.
PO Box 135
Largo, FL 34649-0135
Ph: (813)584-7333
Biennial, 1995-96 edition. Each one-page occupational profile describes duties, working conditions, physical surroundings and demands, aptitudes, temperament, educational requirements, employment outlook, earnings, and places of employment.

★6025★ "Nuclear Reactor Operator Technicians" in *Career Discovery Encyclopedia* (Vol.4, pp. 128-129)
J.G. Ferguson Publishing Co.
200 W. Madison St., Ste. 300
Chicago, IL 60606
Ph: (312)580-5480 Fax: (312)580-4948
E. Russell Primm, editor-in-chief. 1993. Contains two-page articles on 504 occupations. Each article describes job duties, earnings, and educational and training requirements.

★6026★ "Nuclear Reactor Operator Technicians" in *Encyclopedia of Careers and Vocational Guidance* (Vol.3, pp. 583-588)
J.G. Ferguson Publishing Co.
200 W. Madison St., Ste. 300
Chicago, IL 60606
Ph: (312)580-5480 Fax: (312)580-4948
William E. Hopke, editor-in-chief. Ninth edition, 1993. Four-volume set that profiles 500 occupations and describes job trends in 74 industries. Includes career description, educational requirements, history of the job, methods of entry, advancement, employment outlook, earnings, working conditions, social and psychological factors, and sources of additional information.

★6027★ "Power Plant Occupations" in *Encyclopedia of Careers and Vocational Guidance* (Vol.4, pp. 163-165)
J.G. Ferguson Publishing Co.
200 W. Madison St., Ste. 300
Chicago, IL 60606
Ph: (312)580-5480 Fax: (312)580-4948
William E. Hopke, editor-in-chief. Ninth edition, 1993. Four-volume set that profiles 500 occupations and describes job trends in 74 industries. Includes career description, educational requirements, history of the job, methods of entry, advancement, employment outlook, earnings, working conditions, social and psychological factors, and sources of additional information.

★6028★ "Power Plant Worker" in *Career Information Center* (Vol.11)
Simon and Schuster
200 Old Tappan Rd.
Old Tappan, NJ 07675
Fax: 800-445-6991 Fr: 800-223-2348
Richard Lidz and Dale Anderson, editorial directors. Fifth edition, 1993. For 600 occupations, describes job duties, entry-level requirements, education and training needed, advancement possibilities, employment outlook, earnings and benefits. The set is divided into 12 volumes. Each volume includes jobs related under a broad career field. Volume 13 is the index.

★6029★ "Power Plant Workers" in *Career Discovery Encyclopedia* (Vol.5, pp. 76-77)
J.G. Ferguson Publishing Co.
200 W. Madison St., Ste. 300
Chicago, IL 60606
Ph: (312)580-5480 Fax: (312)580-4948
E. Russell Primm, editor-in-chief. 1993. Contains two-page articles on 504 occupations. Each article describes job duties, earnings, and educational and training requirements.

★6030★ "Transmission and Distribution Occupations" in *Encyclopedia of Careers and Vocational Guidance* (Vol.4, pp. 558-561)
J.G. Ferguson Publishing Co.
200 W. Madison St., Ste. 300
Chicago, IL 60606
Ph: (312)580-5480 Fax: (312)580-4948
William E. Hopke, editor-in-chief. Ninth edition, 1993. Four-volume set that profiles 500 occupations and describes job trends in 74 industries. Includes career description, educational requirements, history of the job, methods of entry, advancement, employment outlook, earnings, working conditions, social and psychological factors, and sources of additional information.

★6031★ "Utility Switch Operator" in *Hard Hatted Women: Stories of Struggle and Success in the Trades* (pp. 150-155)
Seal Press
3131 Western Ave., Ste. 410
Seattle, WA 98121
Ph: (206)283-7844 Fax: (206)285-9410
Molly Martin, editor. 1988. Twenty-six women recount their experiences working in blue collar occupations. They describe how they got in, the work they do, their relationships in predominantly male occupations, and their training.

★6032★ *Video Career Library - Production I*
Careers, Inc.
PO Box 135
Largo, FL 34649-0135
Ph: (813)584-7333
Videocassette. 1990. 28 mins. Part of the Video Career Library covering 165 occupations. Shows actual workers on the job. Includes layout workers, precision typesetters, lithographers/photoengravers, bookbinders, hand tailors/dressmakers, upholsterers, water/sewage plant operators, chemical plant operators, and power plant operators.

★6033★ *Your Guardian Angel*
Film Library
3450 Wilshire Blvd., No. 700
Los Angeles, CA 90010-2215
Ph: (213)384-8114 Fr: 800-421-9585
Videocassette. 198?. 15 mins. Harry Sparks, the guardian angel of electrical workers looks at the hazards and characteristics of 600-volt lines and equipment.

Associations

★6034★ Edison Electric Institute (EEI)
701 Pennsylvania Ave. NW
Washington, DC 20004-2696
Ph: (202)508-5000 Fax: (202)508-5786
Members: Investor-owned electric utility companies operating in the U.S. Has affiliate members in North, Central, and South America. **Purpose:** Maintains library; sponsors educational programs; compiles statistics. Maintains speakers' bureau. **Publications:** *Electric Perspectives*, bimonthly. • *Electric Power Surveys*. • *Electrical Reports*, weekly. • *Rate Book*, annual. • *Statistical Reports*, weekly. • *Statistical YearBook*.

★6035★ Electrical Women's Round Table (EWRT)
PO Box 292793
Nashville, TN 37229-2793
Ph: (615)890-1272
Members: Women and men holding positions connected with the electrical industry or allied fields in roles such as communicator, educator, information specialist, and researcher. **Purpose:** Seeks to provide opportunities for professional growth and development; increase knowledge and understanding among members of issues affecting the electric and allied fields; educate the public. Acts as a forum, promotes research, conducts workshops, and reviews new audiovisual and printed materials. **Publications:** *Electrical Women's Round Table—Membership Directory*, annual. • *Electrical Women's Round Table—National Newsletter*, quarterly.

★6036★ International Brotherhood of Electrical Workers (IBEW)
1125 15th St. NW
Washington, DC 20005
Ph: (202)833-7000 Fax: (202)467-6316
Members: AFL-CIO. **Publications:** *IBEW Journal*, monthly.

★6037★ Utility Workers Union of America (UWUA)
815 16th St. NW, Ste. 605
Washington, DC 20006
Ph: (202)347-8105 Fax: (202)347-4872
Members: AFL-CIO. Sponsors ten educational conferences each year for local officers. **Publications:** *Light*, monthly.

Test Guides

★6038★ *Career Examination Series: Assistant Power Plant Operator*
National Learning Corp.
212 Michael Dr.
Syosset, NY 11791
Ph: (516)921-8888 Fax: (516)921-8743
Fr: 800-645-6337
Jack Rudman. All examination guides in this series contain questions with answers.

★6039★ *Career Examination Series: Foreman (Power Distribution)*
National Learning Corp.
212 Michael Dr.
Syosset, NY 11791
Ph: (516)921-8888 Fax: (516)921-8743
Fr: 800-645-6337
Jack Rudman. All examination guides in this series contain questions with answers.

★6040★ *Career Examination Series: High Pressure Plant Tender*
National Learning Corp.
212 Michael Dr.
Syosset, NY 11791
Ph: (516)921-8888 Fax: (516)921-8743
Fr: 800-645-6337
Jack Rudman. All examination guides in this series contain questions with answers.

★6041★ *Career Examination Series: Power Plant Operator*
National Learning Corp.
212 Michael Dr.
Syosset, NY 11791
Ph: (516)921-8888 Fax: (516)921-8743
Fr: 800-645-6337
Jack Rudman. All examination guides in this series contain questions with answers.

★6042★ *Stationary Engineer, High Pressure Boiler Operating Engineer, High Pressure Plant Tender*
Prentice Hall Press
Simon & Schuster Inc.
200 Old Tappan Rd.
Old Tappan, NJ 07675
Ph: 800-223-2348
Harry Mahler. Sixth edition, 1986. Complete preparation for civil service and certification exams. Includes 12 sample exams and tips to help readers raise their test scores. Includes a special section on boiler operation.

Educational Directories and Programs

★6043★ *Electrical Women's Round Table—Membership Directory*
TAB/McGraw-Hill, Inc. (EWRT)
PO Box 182607
Columbus, OH 43218-2607
Fax: (614)759-3644 Fr: 800-822-8158
Annual.

Basic Reference Guides and Handbooks

★6044★ *Electric Power Surveys*
Edison Electric Institute (EEI)
701 Pennsylvania Ave. NW
Washington, DC 20004-2696
Ph: (202)508-5000 Fax: (202)508-5786

★6045★ *Industrial Load Management: Theory, Practice, & Simulations*
Elsevier Science Publishing Company, Inc.
655 Avenue of the Americas
New York, NY 10010
Ph: (212)989-5800
C. O. Bjork. 1989. Part of Energy Research Series.

Periodicals

★6046★ *EGSA Powerline*
Electrical Generating Systems Association (EGSA)
10251 W. Sample Rd., Ste. SU-B
Coral Springs, FL 33065-3939
Ph: (305)755-2677 Fax: (305)755-2679
Gordon Johnson
Bimonthly. Contains news of the Association and articles on technological and legislative developments, new standards, and unusual applications for generator sets. Recurring features include news of members, news of research, convention and committee reports, and columns titled Industry News and People On the Move.

★6047★ *Electric Light & Power*
PennWell Publishing Co.
1250 S. Grove Ave., Ste. 302
Barrington, IL 60010
Ph: (708)382-2450 Fax: (708)382-2977
Robert W. SmockDirector
Monthly. Tabloid providing news of electric utility industry developments and activities and coverage of new products and technology.

★6048★ *Electric Perspectives*
Edison Electric Institute (EEI)
701 Pennsylvania Ave. NW
Washington, DC 20004-2696
Ph: (202)508-5000 Fax: (202)508-5786
Bimonthly.

★6049★ *Electrical Reports*
Edison Electric Institute (EEI)
701 Pennsylvania Ave. NW
Washington, DC 20004-2696
Ph: (202)508-5000 Fax: (202)508-5786
Weekly.

★6050★ *Electrical Women's Round Table—National Newsletter*
TAB/McGraw-Hill, Inc. (EWRT)
PO Box 182607
Columbus, OH 43218-2607
Fax: (614)759-3644 Fr: 800-822-8158
Quarterly. Addresses the efficient use of electrical energy from an administrative standpoint.

★6051★ *Electrical World*
McGraw-Hill, Inc.
11 W. 19th St., 2nd Fl.
New York, NY 10011
Ph: (212)337-4062 Fax: (212)627-3811
Robert SchwiegerDirector
Monthly. Trade magazine on the business of generating, transmitting, and distributing electric power.

★6052★ *Nuclear Plant Journal*
799 Roosevelt Rd., Bldg. 6, Ste. 208
Glen Ellyn, IL 60137
Ph: (708)858-6161 Fax: (708)858-8787
Newal K. Agnihotri
Magazine focusing on nuclear power plants.

★6053★ *Rate Book*
Edison Electric Institute (EEI)
701 Pennsylvania Ave. NW
Washington, DC 20004-2696
Ph: (202)508-5000 Fax: (202)508-5786
Annual.

★6054★ *Rural Electrification Magazine*
National Rural Electric Cooperative Assn.
1800 Massachusetts Ave. NW
Washington, DC 20036
Ph: (202)857-9500 Fax: (202)857-9791
Frank K. Gallant
Monthly. Magazine for directors and employees of rural electric cooperatives.

★6055★ *Ruralite*
Ruralite Services, Inc.
PO Box 558
Forest Grove, OR 97116
Ph: (503)357-2105 Fax: (503)357-8615
Curtis Condon
Monthly. Consumer magazine for customers of specific consumer-owned utilities throughout Alaska, Washington, Wyoming, California, Idaho, Nevada, and Utah.

★6056★ *Southwest Contractor*
McGraw-Hill, Inc.
2050 E. University Dr., Ste. 1
Phoenix, AZ 85034-6731
Ph: (602)258-1641 Fax: (602)495-9407
Bill Davis
Monthly. Regional trade magazine for the contracting industries including highway, mu-

nicipal, utility, heavy construction, and mining.

★6057★ *Statistical Reports*
Edison Electric Institute (EEI)
701 Pennsylvania Ave. NW
Washington, DC 20004-2696
Ph: (202)508-5000 Fax: (202)508-5786
Weekly.

★6058★ *Statistical YearBook*
Edison Electric Institute (EEI)
701 Pennsylvania Ave. NW
Washington, DC 20004-2696
Ph: (202)508-5000 Fax: (202)508-5786

Stationary Engineers

Stationary engineers operate and maintain equipment to provide heating, air-conditioning, and ventilation. This can include boilers, air-conditioning and refrigeration equipment, diesel engines, turbines, generators, pumps, condensers, and compressors. Engineers might also direct the work of assistant stationary engineers, turbine operators, boiler tenders, and air-conditioning and refrigeration operators and mechanics. These workers are called stationary engineers because much of the equipment they operate is similar to the equipment operated by locomotive or marine engineers except that it is not a moving vehicle. They work in a variety of places, including office and apartment buildings, hospitals, schools, factories, shopping malls, and hotels.

Salaries

Weekly earnings for stationary engineers are as follows:

Lowest 10 percent	$302/week or less
Middle 50 percent	$414-$775/week
Top 10 percent	$920/week or more

Employment Outlook

Growth rate until the year 2005: More slowly than average.

Stationary Engineers

Career Guides

★6059★ ***Stationary Engineer***
Careers, Inc.
PO Box 135
Largo, FL 34649-0135
Ph: (813)584-7333

1992. Four-page brief offering the definition, history, duties, working conditions, personal qualifications, educational requirements, earnings, hours, employment outlook, advancement possibilities, and related occupations.

★6060★ "Stationary Engineer" in *Career Information Center* (Vol.9)
Simon and Schuster
200 Old Tappan Rd.
Old Tappan, NJ 07675
Fax: 800-445-6991 Fr: 800-223-2348

Richard Lidz and Dale Anderson, editorial directors. Fifth edition, 1993. For 600 occupations, describes job duties, entry-level requirements, education and training needed, advancement possibilities, employment outlook, earnings and benefits. The set is divided into 12 volumes. Each volume includes jobs related under a broad career field. Volume 13 is the index.

★6061★ "Stationary Engineer" in *Hard Hatted Women: Stories of Struggle and Success in the Trades* (pp. 37-44)
Seal Press
3131 Western Ave., Ste. 410
Seattle, WA 98121
Ph: (206)283-7844 Fax: (206)285-9410

Molly Martin, editor. 1988. Twenty-six women recount their experiences working in blue collar occupations. They describe how they got in, the work they do, their relationships in predominantly male occupations, and their training.

★6062★ "Stationary Engineer" in *Occu-Facts: Information on 580 Careers in Outline Form*
Careers, Inc.
PO Box 135
Largo, FL 34649-0135
Ph: (813)584-7333

Biennial, 1995-96 edition. Each one-page occupational profile describes duties, working conditions, physical surroundings and demands, aptitudes, temperament, educational requirements, employment outlook, earnings, and places of employment.

★6063★ ***Stationary Engineers***
Chronicle Guidance Publications, Inc.
66 Aurora St.
PO Box 1190
Moravia, NY 13118-1190
Ph: (315)497-0330 Fax: (315)497-3359
Fr: 800-622-7284

1991. Career brief describing the nature of the job, working conditions, hours and earnings, education and training, licensure, certification, unions, personal qualifications, social and psychological factors, location, employment outlook, entry methods, advancement, and related occupations.

★6064★ "Stationary Engineers" in *Encyclopedia of Careers and Vocational Guidance* (Vol.4, pp. 424-426)
J.G. Ferguson Publishing Co.
200 W. Madison St., Ste. 300
Chicago, IL 60606
Ph: (312)580-5480 Fax: (312)580-4948

William E. Hopke, editor-in-chief. Ninth edition, 1993. Four-volume set that profiles 500 occupations and describes job trends in 74 industries. Includes career description, educational requirements, history of the job, methods of entry, advancement, employment outlook, earnings, working conditions, social and psychological factors, and sources of additional information.

★6065★ "Stationary Engineers" in *Occupational Outlook Handbook*
U.S. Government Printing Office
Superintendent of Documents
Washington, DC 20402
Ph: (202)512-1800 Fax: (202)512-2250

Biennial; latest edition, 1994-95. Encyclopedia of careers describing more than 250 occupations and comprising about 85 percent of all jobs in the economy. Occupations that require lengthy education or training are given the most attention. For each occupation, the handbook describes job duties, working conditions, training, educational preparation, personal qualities, advancement possibilities, job outlook, earnings, and sources of additional information.

★6066★ ***Video Career Library - Production I***
Careers, Inc.
PO Box 135
Largo, FL 34649-0135
Ph: (813)584-7333

Videocassette. 1990. 28 mins. Part of the Video Career Library covering 165 occupations. Shows actual workers on the job. Includes layout workers, precision typesetters, lithographers/photoengravers, bookbinders, hand tailors/dressmakers, upholsterers, water/sewage plant operators, chemical plant operators, and power plant operators.

Associations

★6067★ International Union of Operating Engineers (IUOE)
1125 17th St. NW
Washington, DC 20036
Ph: (202)429-9100 Fax: (202)429-0316

Members: AFL-CIO. **Publications:** *International Operating Engineer*, bimonthly.

★6068★ National Association of Power Engineers (NAPE)
1 Springfield St.
Chicopee, MA 01013
Ph: (413)592-6273 Fax: (413)592-1998

Members: Professional society of power and stationary engineers; associate members are sales engineers and teachers of any phase of engineering. **Purpose:** Areas of interest include air conditioning, compressed air, electric power, refrigeration, steam, and water. Promotes education in the power engineering areas. Secures and enforces engineers' license laws to prevent the destruction of life and property in the generation and transmission of power and for the conservation of fuel resources of the nation. **Publications:** *NAPE Directory*, annual. • *National Engineer*, monthly.

TEST GUIDES

★6069★ *Career Examination Series: Chief Stationary Engineer*
National Learning Corp.
212 Michael Dr.
Syosset, NY 11791
Ph: (516)921-8888 Fax: (516)921-8743
Fr: 800-645-6337

Jack Rudman. All examination guides in this series contain questions with answers.

★6070★ *Career Examination Series: Head Stationary Engineer*
National Learning Corp.
212 Michael Dr.
Syosset, NY 11791
Ph: (516)921-8888 Fax: (516)921-8743
Fr: 800-645-6337

Jack Rudman. Test guide including questions and answers for students or professionals in the field who seek advancement through examination.

★6071★ *Career Examination Series: Incinerator Stationary Engineer*
National Learning Corp.
212 Michael Dr.
Syosset, NY 11791
Ph: (516)921-8888 Fax: (516)921-8743
Fr: 800-645-6337

Jack Rudman. All examination guides in this series contain questions with answers.

★6072★ *Career Examination Series: Principal Stationary Engineer*
National Learning Corp.
212 Michael Dr.
Syosset, NY 11791
Ph: (516)921-8888 Fax: (516)921-8743
Fr: 800-645-6337

Jack Rudman. All examination guides in this series contain questions with answers.

★6073★ *Career Examination Series: Senior Incinerator Stationary Engineer*
National Learning Corp.
212 Michael Dr.
Syosset, NY 11791
Ph: (516)921-8888 Fax: (516)921-8743
Fr: 800-645-6337

Jack Rudman. All examination guides in this series contain questions with answers.

★6074★ *Career Examination Series: Senior Stationary Engineer*
National Learning Corp.
212 Michael Dr.
Syosset, NY 11791
Ph: (516)921-8888 Fax: (516)921-8743
Fr: 800-645-6337

Jack Rudman. All examination guides in this series contain questions with answers.

★6075★ *Career Examination Series: Senior Stationary Engineer (Electric)*
National Learning Corp.
212 Michael Dr.
Syosset, NY 11791
Ph: (516)921-8888 Fax: (516)921-8743
Fr: 800-645-6337

Jack Rudman. All examination guides in this series contain questions with answers.

★6076★ *Career Examination Series: Stationary Engineer*
National Learning Corp.
212 Michael Dr.
Syosset, NY 11791
Ph: (516)921-8888 Fax: (516)921-8743
Fr: 800-645-6337

Jack Rudman. All examination guides in this series contain questions with answers.

★6077★ *Career Examination Series: Stationary Engineer (Electric)*
National Learning Corp.
212 Michael Dr.
Syosset, NY 11791
Ph: (516)921-8888 Fax: (516)921-8743
Fr: 800-645-6337

Jack Rudman. All examination guides in this series contain questions with answers.

★6078★ *Stationary Engineer, High Pressure Boiler Operating Engineer, High Pressure Plant Tender*
Prentice Hall Press
Simon & Schuster Inc.
200 Old Tappan Rd.
Old Tappan, NJ 07675
Ph: 800-223-2348

Harry Mahler. Sixth edition, 1986. Complete preparation for civil service and certification exams. Includes 12 sample exams and tips to help readers raise their test scores. Includes a special section on boiler operation.

PERIODICALS

★6079★ *NAPE Directory*
National Association of Power Engineers (NAPE)
1 Springfield St.
Chicopee, MA 01013
Ph: (413)592-6273 Fax: (413)592-1998

Annual.

★6080★ *National Engineer*
National Association of Power Engineers (NAPE)
1 Springfield St.
Chicopee, MA 01013
Ph: (413)592-6273 Fax: (413)592-1998

Monthly.

MEETINGS AND CONVENTIONS

★6081★ Heating, Ventilation, and Air Conditioning Product and Equipment Show
Institute of Heating and Air Conditioning Industries
606 N. Larchmont Blvd., Ste. 4A
Los Angeles, CA 90004
Ph: (213)467-1158 Fax: (213)461-2588

Annual. Always held during November at the Convention Center in Pasadena, California.

★6082★ International Air-Conditioning, Heating, Refrigerating Exposition
International Exposition Co.
15 Franklin St.
Westport, CT 06880-5903
Ph: (203)221-9262 Fax: (203)221-9260

Annual. **Dates and Locations:** 1996 Feb 19-21; Atlanta, GA. • 1997 Jan; Philadelphia, PA. • 1998 Jan; San Francisco, CA.

OTHER SOURCES OF INFORMATION

★6083★ "Stationary Engineer" in *Career Selector 2001*
Barron's Educational Series, Inc.
250 Wireless Blvd.
Hauppauge, NY 11788
Ph: (516)434-3311 Fax: (516)434-3723
Fr: 800-645-3476

James C. Gonyea. 1993.

Water and Wastewater Treatment Plant Operators

Water treatment plant operators treat water so that it is safe to drink. **Wastewater treatment plant operators** remove harmful domestic and industrial pollution from wastewater. Operators in both types of plants control processes and equipment to remove solid materials, chemicals, and micro-organisms from the water or to render them harmless. By operating and maintaining the pumps, valves, and processing equipment of the treatment facility, operators move the water or wastewater through the various treatment processes. Water and wastewater treatment plant operators work for local governments; some work for private water supply and sanitary services companies, many of which provide operation and management services to local governments on a contract basis.

Salaries

Annual salaries for wastewater treatment plant operators are as follows:

Lowest 10 percent	$15,700/year or less
Middle	$19,600-$33,100/year
Top 10 percent	$39,200/year or more

Employment Outlook

Growth rate until the year 2005: Average.

Water and Wastewater Treatment Plant Operators

Career Guides

★6084★ *Career Profiles: Environmental Series*
Cambridge Educational
PO Box 2153
Charleston, WV 25328-2153
Ph: (304)744-9323 Fax: (304)744-9351
Fr: 800-468-4227

Videocassette. 1989. 15 mins. Environmental careers of all sorts are examined, including grounds and turf management, landscaping, and wastewater treatment plant operator.

★6085★ "Environmental Technician (Water and Wastewater)" in *100 Best Careers for the Year 2000* (pp. 135-136)
Arco Pub.
201 W. 103rd St.
Indianapolis, IN 46290
Ph: 800-428-5331 Fax: 800-835-3202

Shelly Field. 1992. Describes 100 job opportunities expected to grow fast throughout the next decade. Provides information on job duties and responsibilities, training requirements, education, advancement opportunities, experience and qualifications, and typical salaries.

★6086★ *Opportunities in Waste Management Careers*
National Textbook Co. (NTC)
VGM Career Books
4255 W. Toughy Ave.
Lincolnwood, IL 60646-1975
Ph: (708)679-5500 Fax: (708)679-2494
Fr: 800-323-4900

Mark Rowh.

★6087★ *Video Career Library - Production I*
Careers, Inc.
PO Box 135
Largo, FL 34649-0135
Ph: (813)584-7333

Videocassette. 1990. 28 mins. Part of the Video Career Library covering 165 occupations. Shows actual workers on the job. Includes layout workers, precision typesetters, lithographers/photoengravers, bookbinders, hand tailors/dressmakers, upholsterers, water/sewage plant operators, chemical plant operators, and power plant operators.

★6088★ *Wastewater Plant Operator*
Vocational Biographies, Inc.
PO Box 31
Sauk Centre, MN 56378-0031
Ph: (612)352-6516 Fax: (612)352-5546
Fr: 800-255-0752

1992. Four-page pamphlet containing a personal narrative about a worker's job, work likes and dislikes, career path from high school to the present. Education and training, the rewards and frustrations, and the effects of the job on the rest of the worker's life. The data file portion of this pamphlet gives a concise occupational summary, including work descriptions, working conditions, places of employment, personal characteristics, education and training, job outlook, and salary range.

★6089★ *Wastewater Treatment Plant Operators*
Chronicle Guidance Publications, Inc.
66 Aurora St.
PO Box 1190
Moravia, NY 13118-1190
Ph: (315)497-0330 Fax: (315)497-3359
Fr: 800-622-7284

1994. This career brief describes the nature of the work, working conditions, hours and earnings, education and training, licensure, certification, unions, personal qualifications, social and psychological factors, employment outlook, entry methods, advancement, and related occupations.

★6090★ "Wastewater Treatment Plant Operators" in *Encyclopedia of Careers and Vocational Guidance* (Vol.4, pp. 595-597)
J.G. Ferguson Publishing Co.
200 W. Madison St., Ste. 300
Chicago, IL 60606
Ph: (312)580-5480 Fax: (312)580-4948

William E. Hopke, editor-in-chief. Ninth edition, 1993. Four-volume set that profiles 500 occupations and describes job trends in 74 industries. Includes career description, educational requirements, history of the job, methods of entry, advancement, employment outlook, earnings, working conditions, social and psychological factors, and sources of additional information.

★6091★ *Water/Wastewater Operator*
Vocational Biographies, Inc.
PO Box 31
Sauk Centre, MN 56378-0031
Ph: (612)352-6516 Fax: (612)352-5546
Fr: 800-255-0752

1989. This pamphlet profiles a person working in the job. Includes information about job duties, working conditions, places of employment, educational preparation, labor market outlook, and salaries.

★6092★ "Water and Wastewater Treatment Plant Operators" in *Career Discovery Encyclopedia* (Vol.6, pp. 148-149)
J.G. Ferguson Publishing Co.
200 W. Madison St., Ste. 300
Chicago, IL 60606
Ph: (312)580-5480 Fax: (312)580-4948

E. Russell Primm, editor-in-chief. 1993. Contains two-page articles on 504 occupations. Each article describes job duties, earnings, and educational and training requirements.

★6093★ "Water and Wastewater Treatment Plant Operators" in *Occupational Outlook Handbook*
U.S. Government Printing Office
Superintendent of Documents
Washington, DC 20402
Ph: (202)512-1800 Fax: (202)512-2250

Biennial; latest edition, 1994-95. Encyclopedia of careers describing more than 250 occupations and comprising about 85 percent of all jobs in the economy. Occupations that require lengthy education or training are given the most attention. For each occupation, the handbook describes job duties, working conditions, training, educational preparation, personal qualities, advancement possibilities, job outlook, earnings, and sources of additional information.

Associations

★6094★ Association of Boards of Certification (ABC)
208 5th St., Ste. 1A
Ames, IA 50010-6259
Ph: (515)232-3623 Fax: (515)232-3778

Members: Governmental certification authorities for environmental control operating personnel and laboratories, including those that deal with hazardous wastes. **Purpose:** Seeks to strengthen state certification laws, their administration and effectiveness, and to establish uniform certification requirements among members. Promotes certification as a means to more efficient operation of public utilities; assists newly created boards in implementing certification programs. Conducts Uniform Program for Reciprocity, wherein certified operators are recognized as such by member boards after passing a standardized test produced by the ABC. **Publications:** *Certifier*, monthly.

★6095★ Water Environment Federation (WEF)
601 Wythe St.
Alexandria, VA 22314-1994
Ph: (703)684-2400 Fax: (703)684-2492
Fr: 800-666-0206

Members: Technical societies representing chemists, biologists, ecologists, geologists, operators, educational and research personnel, industrial wastewater engineers, consultant engineers, municipal officials, equipment manufacturers, and university professors and students dedicated to the enhancement and preservation of water quality and resources. **Purpose:** Seeks to advance fundamental and practical knowledge concerning the nature, collection, treatment, and disposal of domestic and industrial wastewaters, and the design, construction, operation, and management of facilities for these purposes. Disseminates technical information; promotes good public relations and regulations that improve water quality and the status of individuals working in this field. Conducts educational and research programs. **Publications:** *Highlights*, monthly. • *Industrial Wastewater*, bimonthly. • *Literature Review*, annual. • *Manuals of Practice*. • *Operations Forum*, monthly. • *Water, Environment, and Technology*, monthly. • *Water Environment Laboratory Solutions*, 9/year. • *Water Environment Regulation Watch*, monthly. • *Water Environment Research*, bimonthly.

Standards/Certification Agencies

★6096★ Association of Boards of Certification (ABC)
208 5th St., Ste. 1A
Ames, IA 50010-6259
Ph: (515)232-3623 Fax: (515)232-3778

Governmental certification authorities for environmental control operating personnel and laboratories, including those that deal with hazardous wastes. Seeks to strengthen state certification laws, their administration and effectiveness, and to establish uniform certification requirements among members. Promotes certification as a means to more efficient operation of public utilities; assists newly created boards in implementing certification programs. Conducts Uniform Program for Reciprocity, wherein certified operators are recognized as such by member boards after passing a standardized test produced by the ABC.

Test Guides

★6097★ *Career Examination Series: Assistant Water Maintenance Foreman*
National Learning Corp.
212 Michael Dr.
Syosset, NY 11791
Ph: (516)921-8888 Fax: (516)921-8743
Fr: 800-645-6337

Jack Rudman. All examination guides in this series contain questions with answers.

★6098★ *Career Examination Series: Chief Sewage Treatment Plant Operator*
National Learning Corp.
212 Michael Dr.
Syosset, NY 11791
Ph: (516)921-8888 Fax: (516)921-8743
Fr: 800-645-6337

Jack Rudman. All examination guides in this series contain questions with answers.

★6099★ *Career Examination Series: Chief Water Treatment Plant Operator*
National Learning Corp.
212 Michael Dr.
Syosset, NY 11791
Ph: (516)921-8888 Fax: (516)921-8743
Fr: 800-645-6337

Jack Rudman. All examination guides in this series contain questions with answers.

★6100★ *Career Examination Series: Principal Water Plant Supervisor*
National Learning Corp.
212 Michael Dr.
Syosset, NY 11791
Ph: (516)921-8888 Fax: (516)921-8743
Fr: 800-645-6337

Jack Rudman. All examination guides in this series contain questions with answers.

★6101★ *Career Examination Series: Senior Sewage Treatment Plant Operator*
National Learning Corp.
212 Michael Dr.
Syosset, NY 11791
Ph: (516)921-8888 Fax: (516)921-8743
Fr: 800-645-6337

Jack Rudman. All examination guides in this series contain questions with answers.

★6102★ *Career Examination Series: Senior Sewage Treatment Worker*
National Learning Corp.
212 Michael Dr.
Syosset, NY 11791
Ph: (516)921-8888 Fax: (516)921-8743
Fr: 800-645-6337

Jack Rudman. All examination guides in this series contain questions with answers.

★6103★ *Career Examination Series: Senior Water Plant Operator*
National Learning Corp.
212 Michael Dr.
Syosset, NY 11791
Ph: (516)921-8888 Fax: (516)921-8743
Fr: 800-645-6337

Jack Rudman. All examination guides in this series contain questions with answers.

★6104★ *Career Examination Series: Senior Water Plant Supervisor*
National Learning Corp.
212 Michael Dr.
Syosset, NY 11791
Ph: (516)921-8888 Fax: (516)921-8743
Fr: 800-645-6337

Jack Rudman. All examination guides in this series contain questions with answers.

★6105★ *Career Examination Series: Sewage Plant Operations Supervisor*
National Learning Corp.
212 Michael Dr.
Syosset, NY 11791
Ph: (516)921-8888 Fax: (516)921-8743
Fr: 800-645-6337

Jack Rudman. All examination guides in this series contain questions with answers.

★6106★ *Career Examination Series: Sewage Plant Operator*
National Learning Corp.
212 Michael Dr.
Syosset, NY 11791
Ph: (516)921-8888 Fax: (516)921-8743
Fr: 800-645-6337

Jack Rudman. All examination guides in this series contain questions with answers.

★6107★ *Career Examination Series: Sewage Pump Operator*
National Learning Corp.
212 Michael Dr.
Syosset, NY 11791
Ph: (516)921-8888 Fax: (516)921-8743
Fr: 800-645-6337

Jack Rudman. All examination guides in this series contain questions with answers.

★6108★ *Career Examination Series: Sewage Treatment Operator*
National Learning Corp.
212 Michael Dr.
Syosset, NY 11791
Ph: (516)921-8888 Fax: (516)921-8743
Fr: 800-645-6337

Jack Rudman. All examination guides in this series contain questions with answers.

★6109★ *Career Examination Series: Sewage Treatment Operator Trainee*
National Learning Corp.
212 Michael Dr.
Syosset, NY 11791
Ph: (516)921-8888 Fax: (516)921-8743
Fr: 800-645-6337

Jack Rudman. All examination guides in this series contain questions with answers.

★6110★ *Career Examination Series: Sewage Treatment Plant Supervisor*
National Learning Corp.
212 Michael Dr.
Syosset, NY 11791
Ph: (516)921-8888 Fax: (516)921-8743
Fr: 800-645-6337

Jack Rudman. All examination guides in this series contain questions with answers.

★6111★ *Career Examination Series: Sewage Treatment Worker*
National Learning Corp.
212 Michael Dr.
Syosset, NY 11791
Ph: (516)921-8888 Fax: (516)921-8743
Fr: 800-645-6337

Jack Rudman. All examination guides in this series contain questions with answers.

★6112★ *Career Examination Series: Sewage Treatment Worker Trainee*
National Learning Corp.
212 Michael Dr.
Syosset, NY 11791
Ph: (516)921-8888 Fax: (516)921-8743
Fr: 800-645-6337

Jack Rudman. All examination guides in this series contain questions with answers.

★6113★ *Career Examination Series: Wastewater Treatment Plant Maintenance Supervisor*
National Learning Corp.
212 Michael Dr.
Syosset, NY 11791
Ph: (516)921-8888 Fax: (516)921-8743
Fr: 800-645-6337

Jack Rudman. All examination guides in this series contain questions with answers.

★6114★ *Recommended Standards for Waste Water Facilities*
Professional Publications, Inc.
1250 5th Ave.
Belmont, CA 94002-3863
Ph: 800-426-1178

1990.

★6115★ *Sanitation Worker*
Prentice Hall Press
Simon & Schuster Inc.
200 Old Tappan Rd.
Old Tappan, NJ 07675
Ph: 800-223-2348

Hy Hammer. Sixth edition, 1983. Contains ten previous tests for practice; includes section on training for physical tests.

★6116★ *WPCF Manuals of Practice*
Water Pollution Control Federation (WPCF)
601 Wythe St.
Alexandria, VA 22314-1994
Ph: (703)684-2400

Educational Directories and Programs

★6117★ *Directory of Certification and Training Contacts*
Association of Boards of Certification (ABC)
426 1/2 5th St.
PO Box 786
Ames, IA 50010-0786
Ph: (515)232-3623

Periodic. Lists state and provincial certification and training contacts in the fields of distribution and collection of water and waste water and industrial waste treatment.

Awards, Scholarships, Grants, and Fellowships

★6118★ William D. Hatfield Award
Water Environment Federation
601 Wythe St.
Alexandria, VA 22314-1994
Ph: (703)684-2400 Fax: (703)684-2492

To recognize outstanding operation of a wastewater treatment plant. Members of the Federation are eligible. Established in 1946 to correspond with the Bedell Award, in honor of Dr. William D. Hatfield, who served as President of the Federation in 1958-59.

Periodicals

★6119★ *CEES Report*
Arlene Horowitz, Contact
Quarterly. Furnishes environmental research activities at the Institute and its related consortia on the areas of hazardous waste management, pollution prevention, and risk communication. Recurring features include interviews and news of research.

★6120★ *Certifier*
Association of Boards of Certification (ABC)
208 5th St., Ste. 1A
Ames, IA 50010-6259
Ph: (515)232-3623 Fax: (515)232-3778

Monthly.

★6121★ *Clean Water Report*
Business Publishers, Inc.
951 Pershing Dr.
Silver Spring, MD 20910
Ph: (301)587-6300 Fax: (301)587-1081
Fr: 800-274-0122
Elaine Eiserer

Biweekly. Provides information on water pollution control, drinking water supply and safety, and water resources issues. Covers national policy, legislation, regulations, enforcement and litigation, and state and local news.

★6122★ *EI Digest*
Environmental Information Ltd.
4801 W. 81st St., Ste. 119
Minneapolis, MN 55437
Ph: (612)831-2473 Fax: (612)831-6550
Cary L. Perket

Monthly. Journal covering issues on industrial and hazardous waste management.

★6123★ *Highlights*
Water Environment Federation (WEF)
601 Wythe St.
Alexandria, VA 22314-1994
Ph: (703)684-2400 Fax: (703)684-2492
Fr: 800-666-0206

Monthly.

★6124★ *Industrial Wastewater*
Water Environment Federation (WEF)
601 Wythe St.
Alexandria, VA 22314-1994
Ph: (703)684-2400 Fax: (703)684-2492
Fr: 800-666-0206

Bimonthly.

★6125★ *Journal of the American Water Works Association*
American Water Works Assn.
6666 W. Quincy Ave.
Denver, CO 80235
Ph: (303)794-7711 Fax: (303)794-7310

Monthly. Magazine dealing with water supply, treatment, quality, and distribution.

★6126★ *Literature Review*
Water Environment Federation (WEF)
601 Wythe St.
Alexandria, VA 22314-1994
Ph: (703)684-2400 Fax: (703)684-2492
Fr: 800-666-0206

Annual.

★6127★ *Manuals of Practice*
Water Environment Federation (WEF)
601 Wythe St.
Alexandria, VA 22314-1994
Ph: (703)684-2400 Fax: (703)684-2492
Fr: 800-666-0206

★6128★ *Operations Forum*
Water Environment Federation
601 Wythe St.
Alexandria, VA 22314-1994
Ph: (703)684-2400
Lisa Preston

Monthly. Magazine covering water/wastewater technology for industry professionals.

★6129★ *Pollution Engineering*
Cahners Publishing Co.
1350 E. Touhy Ave.
PO Box 5080
Des Plaines, IL 60017-5080
Ph: (708)635-8800 Fax: (708)390-2618
Diane Pirocanac

Semiweekly. Magazine focusing on pollution control, air, water, solid waste, and toxic/hazardous waste.

★6130★ *Water Conditioning & Purification*
Publicom Inc.
2800 E. Fort Lowell Rd.
Tucson, AZ 85716-1518
Ph: (602)293-5446 Fax: (602)887-2383
Darlene J. Scheel

Monthly. Magazine on Domestic and commercial water conditioning and purification.

★6131★ *Water Environment Laboratory Solutions*
Water Environment Federation (WEF)
601 Wythe St.
Alexandria, VA 22314-1994
Ph: (703)684-2400 Fax: (703)684-2492
Fr: 800-666-0206

9/year.

★6132★ *Water Environment Regulation Watch*
Water Environment Federation (WEF)
601 Wythe St.
Alexandria, VA 22314-1994
Ph: (703)684-2400 Fax: (703)684-2492
Fr: 800-666-0206

Monthly.

★6133★ *Water Environment Research*
Water Environment Federation (WEF)
601 Wythe St.
Alexandria, VA 22314-1994
Ph: (703)684-2400 Fax: (703)684-2492
Fr: 800-666-0206

Bimonthly.

★6134★ *Water, Environment, and Technology*
Water Environment Federation (WEF)
601 Wythe St.
Alexandria, VA 22314-1994
Ph: (703)684-2400 Fax: (703)684-2492
Fr: 800-666-0206

Monthly.

★6135★ *Water Research*
Pergamon Press, Inc.
660 White Plains Rd.
Tarrytown, NY 10591-5153
Ph: (914)524-9200 Fax: (914)333-2444
K.J. Ives

Monthly. Journal covering research in water pollution.

★6136★ *Water Technology*
National Trade Publications, Inc.
13 Century Hill Drive
Latham, NY 12110
Ph: (518)783-1281 Fax: (518)783-1386
Alice Savino

Monthly. Magazine focusing on point of use water treatment.

★6137★ *Water & Wastes Digest*
Scranton Gillette Communications, Inc.
380 E. Northwest Hwy.
Des Plaines, IL 60016-2282
Ph: (708)298-6622 Fax: (708)390-0408
Gail Hanczar

Bimonthly. Magazine (tabloid) featuring product news for decision makers in the municipal and industrial water and water pollution control industries.

★6138★ *WSTB Newsletter*
National Academy Press
Water Science and Technology Board (WSTB)
National Research Council
2101 Constitution Ave. NW
Washington, DC 20418
Jackie MacDonald, Contact

Quarterly. Reports on studies being carried out by the Water Science and Technology Board. Study topics include a wide range of water-related environmental issues from ground water cleanup to watershed management. Recurring features include news of research, a calendar of events, and notices of publications available.

Meetings and Conventions

★6139★ Annual Meeting and Exhibition of the Air and Waste Management Association
Air and Waste Management Association
PO Box 2861
Pittsburgh, PA 15230
Ph: (412)232-3444 Fax: (412)232-3450

Annual. Always held during June. **Dates and Locations:** 1996 Jun 23-28; Nashville, TN.

Other Sources of Information

★6140★ "Water-Treatment Plant Operator" in *Career Selector 2001*
Barron's Educational Series, Inc.
250 Wireless Blvd.
Hauppauge, NY 11788
Ph: (516)434-3311 Fax: (516)434-3723
Fr: 800-645-3476

James C. Gonyea. 1993.

★6141★ *WPCF Literature Review*
Water Environment Federation (WEF)
601 Wythe St.
Alexandria, VA 22314-1994
Ph: (703)684-2400 Fax: (703)684-2492
Fr: 800-666-0206

Annual.

Bindery Workers

Bindery workers operate and maintain the machines that perform the various tasks of cutting, folding, gathering, gluing, stitching, trimming, sewing, wrapping, and other finishing operations. In firms that do edition binding, workers bind books produced in large numbers or runs, while job binding workers bind books produced in smaller quantities. In firms that specialize in library binding, workers repair books and provide other specialized binding services to libraries. Pamphlet binding workers produce leaflets and folders, while manifold binding workers bind business forms such as ledgers and books of sales receipts. Blankbook binding workers bind blank pages to produce notebooks, checkbooks, address books, diaries, calendars, and note pads. Although some bindery workers are employed by large libraries and others work for book publishers, most jobs are in commercial printing plants. Bindery trade shops, which specialize in binding, are the second largest employer of bindery workers.

Salaries

Weekly earnings for bindery workers are as follows:

Lesser skilled

Lowest 10 percent	$200/week or less
Middle 50 percent	$240-$480/week
Highest 10 percent	$570/week or more

Highly skilled

Lowest 10 percent	$220/week or less
Middle 50 percent	$270-$70/week
Highest 10 percent	$650/week or more

Employment Outlook

Growth rate until the year 2005: Average.

Bindery Workers

Career Guides

★6142★ "Bindery Workers" in *Career Discovery Encyclopedia* (Vol.1, pp. 106-107)
J.G. Ferguson Publishing Co.
200 W. Madison St., Ste. 300
Chicago, IL 60606
Ph: (312)580-5480 Fax: (312)580-4948

E. Russell Primm, editor-in-chief. 1993. Contains two-page articles on 504 occupations. Each article describes job duties, earnings, and educational and training requirements.

★6143★ "Bindery Workers" in *Encyclopedia of Careers and Vocational Guidance* (Vol.2, pp. 175-178)
J.G. Ferguson Publishing Co.
200 W. Madison St., Ste. 300
Chicago, IL 60606
Ph: (312)580-5480 Fax: (312)580-4948

William E. Hopke, editor-in-chief. Ninth edition, 1993. Four-volume set that profiles 500 occupations and describes job trends in 74 industries. Includes career description, educational requirements, history of the job, methods of entry, advancement, employment outlook, earnings, working conditions, social and psychological factors, and sources of additional information.

★6144★ "Bindery Workers" in *Occupational Outlook Handbook*
U.S. Government Printing Office
Superintendent of Documents
Washington, DC 20402
Ph: (202)512-1800 Fax: (202)512-2250

Biennial; latest edition, 1994-95. Encyclopedia of careers describing more than 250 occupations and comprising about 85 percent of all jobs in the economy. Occupations that require lengthy education or training are given the most attention. For each occupation, the handbook describes job duties, working conditions, training, educational preparation, personal qualities, advancement possibilities, job outlook, earnings, and sources of additional information.

★6145★ *Book Bindery Worker*
Vocational Biographies, Inc.
PO Box 31
Sauk Centre, MN 56378-0031
Ph: (612)352-6516 Fax: (612)352-5546
Fr: 800-255-0752

1990. This pamphlet profiles a person working in the job. Includes information about job duties, working conditions, places of employment, educational preparation, labor market outlook, and salaries.

★6146★ *Bookbinder and Bindery Workers*
Careers, Inc.
PO Box 135
Largo, FL 34649-0135
Ph: (813)584-7333

1994. Two-page occupational summary card describing duties, working conditions, personal qualifications, training, earnings and hours, employment outlook, places of employment, related careers and where to write for more information.

★6147★ "Bookbinder and Bindery Workers" in *Occu-Facts: Information on 580 Careers in Outline Form*
Careers, Inc.
PO Box 135
Largo, FL 34649-0135
Ph: (813)584-7333

Biennial, 1995-96 edition. Each one-page occupational profile describes duties, working conditions, physical surroundings and demands, aptitudes, temperament, educational requirements, employment outlook, earnings, and places of employment.

★6148★ "Bookbinder" in *Career Information Center* (Vol.3)
Simon and Schuster
200 Old Tappan Rd.
Old Tappan, NJ 07675
Fax: 800-445-6991 Fr: 800-223-2348

Richard Lidz and Dale Anderson, editorial directors. Fifth edition, 1993. For 600 occupations, describes job duties, entry-level requirements, education and training needed, advancement possibilities, employment outlook, earnings and benefits. The set is divided into 12 volumes. Each volume includes jobs related under a broad career field. Volume 13 is the index.

★6149★ *Career Success Series*
Cambridge Educational
PO Box 2153
Charleston, WV 25328-2153
Ph: (304)744-9323 Fax: (304)744-9351
Fr: 800-468-4227

Videocassette. 1986. 15 mins. A series, available separately, outlining various career choices for students. Occupations include: accounting, flight service, air transportation/ground/flight service, data processing, carpentry, clerk in banking/insurance, commodity sales, cosmetic personal grooming, fire fighting, forestry services, home economics, insulation/roofing, material handling, mechanics, photographic processing, pipefitting and plumbing, police science, printing, carpentry, medical laboratory technicians, secretarial services, and utilities equipment operator.

★6150★ *Video Career Library - Production I*
Careers, Inc.
PO Box 135
Largo, FL 34649-0135
Ph: (813)584-7333

Videocassette. 1990. 28 mins. Part of the Video Career Library covering 165 occupations. Shows actual workers on the job. Includes layout workers, precision typesetters, lithographers/photoengravers, bookbinders, hand tailors/dressmakers, upholsterers, water/sewage plant operators, chemical plant operators, and power plant operators.

Associations

★6151★ Graphic Arts Technical Foundation (GATF)
4615 Forbes Ave.
Pittsburgh, PA 15213
Ph: (412)621-6941 Fax: (412)621-3049

Members: Scientific, research, technical, and educational organization serving the international graphic communications industries. **Purpose:** Conducts research in all graphic processes and their commercial applications. Conducts seminars, workshops, and forums on graphic arts and environmental subjects. Conducts educational programs, including the publishing of graphic arts textbooks and learning modules, audiovisuals, videotapes, aptitude testing, in-plant and school counseling, and national career and manpower recruitment program. Conducts the GATF training and certification program in sheet-fed offset press operating, Web Offset press operating, Image Assembly, and desktop publishing. Produces test images and quality control devices for the industry. Performs technical services for the graphic arts industry, including problem-solving, material evaluation, and plant audits. Compiles statistics. **Publications:** *GATFWORLD*, bimonthly. • *Product Catalog*, annual. • *Quality Control Device Catalog*, semiannual. • *Second Sight Technical Reports.* • *Technology Forecast.* • *Training Materials Catalog*, semiannual. • *Training Programs Catalog*, semiannual. • *Workshop Catalog*, periodic.

★6152★ Graphic Communications International Union (GCIU)
1900 L St. NW
Washington, DC 20036
Ph: (202)462-1400 Fax: (202)331-9516

Members: AFL-CIO; Canadian Labour Congress. **Publications:** *GraphiCommunicator: The Newspaper of the Graphic Communications Union.*

Standards/Certification Agencies

★6153★ Graphic Arts Technical Foundation (GATF)
4615 Forbes Ave.
Pittsburgh, PA 15213
Ph: (412)621-6941 Fax: (412)621-3049

Conducts the GATF training and certification program in sheet-fed offset press operating, Web Offset press operating, Image Assembly, and desktop publishing. Produces test images and quality control devices for the industry. Performs technical services for the graphic arts industry, including problem-solving, material evaluation, and plant audits.

Test Guides

★6154★ Career Examination Series: Bindery Worker
National Learning Corp.
212 Michael Dr.
Syosset, NY 11791
Ph: (516)921-8888 Fax: (516)921-8743
Fr: 800-645-6337

Jack Rudman. Test guide including questions and answers for students or professionals in the field who seek advancement through examination.

★6155★ Career Examination Series: Journeyman in the Printing Crafts
National Learning Corp.
212 Michael Dr.
Syosset, NY 11791
Ph: (516)921-8888 Fax: (516)921-8743
Fr: 800-645-6337

Jack Rudman. All examination guides in this series contain questions with answers.

Periodicals

★6156★ American Printer
Maclean Hunter Publishing Co.
29 N. Wacker Drive
Chicago, IL 60606
Ph: (312)726-2802 Fax: (312)726-2574
Jill Roth

Monthly. Magazine covering the printing and publishing market.

★6157★ Around the Bargaining Loop
Graphic Arts Employers of America
100 Daingerfield Rd.
Alexandria, VA 22314
Ph: (703)519-8150 Fax: (703)548-3227
Holly T. Kachman

Monthly. Provides "detailed summaries of recent settlements within the printing and other related industries. Wage and fringe benefit provisions are given for both the old and new agreements for quick comparisons."

★6158★ Binders Bulletin
Binding Industries of America
70 E. Lake St.
Chicago, IL 60601
Ph: (312)372-7606 Fax: (312)704-5025
James R. Niesen

Contains management tips and industry news for this association of trade binders and loose leaf manufacturers. Recurring features include a calendar of events, news of members, and listings of equipment wanted or for sale.

★6159★ Binders' Guild—Newsletter
Binders' Guild
9229 Dukes Lake Rd.
Zebulon, NC 27597
Ph: (919)269-6381
Jim Dorsey

Focuses on hand bookbinding. Conveys news of the craft and of persons prominent in the field; describes techniques; and reprints relevant pieces from other publications. Recurring features include announcements of workshops and special courses, book reviews, and occasional inserts of related material.

★6160★ GATFWORLD
Graphic Arts Technical Foundation (GATF)
4615 Forbes Ave.
Pittsburgh, PA 15213
Ph: (412)621-6941 Fax: (412)621-3049

Bimonthly. Includes technical and research reports.

★6161★ In-Plant Printer & Electronic Publisher
Innes Publishing Co.
PO Box 368
Northbrook, IL 60065
Ph: (708)564-5940 Fax: (708)564-8361
Andrea Cody

Bimonthly. Magazine serving printing, graphics, typesetting facilities, educational, government, and non-profit organizations.

★6162★ Instant and Small Commercial Printer
Innes Publishing Co.
PO Box 368
Northbrook, IL 60065
Ph: (708)564-5940 Fax: (708)564-8361
Jeanette Clinkunbroomer

Magazine serving the field of instant/quick printers, copy shops, small commercial printers, combination printers, industry suppliers and others allied to the field, including typesetters and thermographers.

★6163★ Koob Stra
Center for Book Arts
626 Broadway
New York, NY 10012
Ph: (212)460-9768
Brian Hannon

Promotes the arts of the book: printing, bookbinding, papermaking, calligraphy, and preservation. Composed of interviews with people active in book arts; reviews of exhibitions, lectures, conferences, and books; and international calendar of readings, workshops, and seminars; news of educational programs sponsored by the Center; news of small presses; and book arts suppliers information.

★6164★ MCBA Newsletter
Minnesota Center for Book Arts (MCBA)
24 N. 3rd St.
Minneapolis, MN 55401
Ph: (612)338-3634 Fax: (612)338-1562
Loring Johnson

Quarterly. Focuses on the field of book arts, including letterpress printing, bookbinding, and papermaking. Reviews current and future Center exhibitions and announces classes available at the Center.

★6165★ Package Printing and Converting
North American Publishing Co.
401 N. Broad St.
Philadelphia, PA 19108
Ph: (215)238-5300 Fax: (215)238-5457
David H. Luttenberger

Monthly. Magazine.

★6166★ Product Catalog
Graphic Arts Technical Foundation (GATF)
4615 Forbes Ave.
Pittsburgh, PA 15213
Ph: (412)621-6941 Fax: (412)621-3049

Annual.

★6167★ Quality Control Device Catalog
Graphic Arts Technical Foundation (GATF)
4615 Forbes Ave.
Pittsburgh, PA 15213
Ph: (412)621-6941 Fax: (412)621-3049

Semiannual.

★6168★ *Quick Printing*
Coast Publishing, Inc.
Zedcoast Center
1680 SW Bayshore Blvd.
Port Saint Lucie, FL 34984
Ph: (407)879-6666 Fax: (407)879-7388
Bob Hall

Monthly.

★6169★ *Second Sight Technical Reports*
Graphic Arts Technical Foundation (GATF)
4615 Forbes Ave.
Pittsburgh, PA 15213
Ph: (412)621-6941 Fax: (412)621-3049

★6170★ *Southern Graphics*
Coast Publishing, Inc.
Zedcoast Center
1680 SW Bayshore Blvd.
Port Saint Lucie, FL 34984
Ph: (407)879-6666 Fax: (407)879-7388
Cathy Donohue

Monthly. Graphic arts magazine serving the printing and graphic arts industry in 14 southern states.

★6171★ *Technology Forecast*
Graphic Arts Technical Foundation (GATF)
4615 Forbes Ave.
Pittsburgh, PA 15213
Ph: (412)621-6941 Fax: (412)621-3049

★6172★ *Training Programs Catalog*
Graphic Arts Technical Foundation (GATF)
4615 Forbes Ave.
Pittsburgh, PA 15213
Ph: (412)621-6941 Fax: (412)621-3049

Semiannual.

★6173★ *Workshop Catalog*
Graphic Arts Technical Foundation (GATF)
4615 Forbes Ave.
Pittsburgh, PA 15213
Ph: (412)621-6941 Fax: (412)621-3049

Periodic.

Other Sources of Information

★6174★ *Training Materials Catalog*
Graphic Arts Technical Foundation (GATF)
4615 Forbes Ave.
Pittsburgh, PA 15213
Ph: (412)621-6941 Fax: (412)621-3049

Annual.

Prepress Workers

Prepress workers prepare material for printing presses. They perform a variety of tasks such as typesetting, designing page layout, photographing text and pictures, and making printing plates. Prepress workers increasingly share typesetting and page layout tasks with their customers. Most prepress jobs are found in firms that handle commercial or business printing and in newspaper plants. Additional jobs are found in printing trade service firms and "in-plant" operations. Job prospects may be best in large printing centers such as New York, Chicago, Los Angeles, Philadelphia, Washington DC, and Dallas.

Salaries

Wage rates for prepress workers vary according to occupation, level or experience and training, location and size of the firm, and whether they are union members.

Lithographers and photoengravers	$518/week
Typesetters and compositors	$402/week
Scanner operators	$21.86/hour
Strippers	$17.57/hour

Employment Outlook

Growth rate until the year 2005: More slowly than the average.

Prepress Workers

CAREER GUIDES

★6175★ *A Career in Computer Typesetting*
Graphic Arts Technical Foundation
4615 Forbes Ave.
Pittsburgh, PA 15213-3796
Ph: (412)621-6941

This 12-page booklet describes the work of a computer typesetter and covers the skills required.

★6176★ *Career Success Series*
Cambridge Educational
PO Box 2153
Charleston, WV 25328-2153
Ph: (304)744-9323 Fax: (304)744-9351
Fr: 800-468-4227

Videocassette. 1986. 15 mins. A series, available separately, outlining various career choices for students. Occupations include: accounting, flight service, air transportation/ground/flight service, data processing, carpentry, clerk in banking/insurance, commodity sales, cosmetic personal grooming, fire fighting, forestry services, home economics, insulation/roofing, material handling, mechanics, photographic processing, pipefitting and plumbing, police science, printing, carpentry, medical laboratory technicians, secretarial services, and utilities equipment operator.

★6177★ "Compositor/Typesetter" in *Jobs Rated Almanac*
World Almanac
1 International Blvd., Ste. 444
Mahwah, NJ 07495
Ph: (201)529-6900 Fax: (201)529-6901

Les Krantz. Second edition, 1992. Ranks 250 jobs by environment, salary, outlooks, physical demands, stress, security, travel opportunities, and extra perks. Includes jobs the editor feels are the most common, most interesting, and the most rapidly growing.

★6178★ "Compositors and Typesetters" in *Encyclopedia of Careers and Vocational Guidance* (Vol.2, pp. 356-359)
J.G. Ferguson Publishing Co.
200 W. Madison St., Ste. 300
Chicago, IL 60606
Ph: (312)580-5480 Fax: (312)580-4948

William E. Hopke, editor-in-chief. Ninth edition, 1993. Four-volume set that profiles 500 occupations and describes job trends in 74 industries. Includes career description, educational requirements, history of the job, methods of entry, advancement, employment outlook, earnings, working conditions, social and psychological factors, and sources of additional information.

★6179★ "Lithographer/Photoengraver" in *Jobs Rated Almanac*
World Almanac
1 International Blvd., Ste. 444
Mahwah, NJ 07495
Ph: (201)529-6900 Fax: (201)529-6901

Les Krantz. Second edition, 1992. Ranks 250 jobs by environment, salary, outlooks, physical demands, stress, security, travel opportunities, and extra perks. Includes jobs the editor feels are the most common, most interesting, and the most rapidly growing.

★6180★ "Lithographic Occupations" in *Encyclopedia of Careers and Vocational Guidance* (Vol.3, pp. 312-315)
J.G. Ferguson Publishing Co.
200 W. Madison St., Ste. 300
Chicago, IL 60606
Ph: (312)580-5480 Fax: (312)580-4948

William E. Hopke, editor-in-chief. Ninth edition, 1993. Four-volume set that profiles 500 occupations and describes job trends in 74 industries. Includes career description, educational requirements, history of the job, methods of entry, advancement, employment outlook, earnings, working conditions, social and psychological factors, and sources of additional information.

★6181★ "Lithographic Platemaker" in *Occu-Facts: Information on 580 Careers in Outline Form*
Careers, Inc.
PO Box 135
Largo, FL 34649-0135
Ph: (813)584-7333

Biennial, 1995-96 edition. Each one-page occupational profile describes duties, working conditions, physical surroundings and demands, aptitudes, temperament, educational requirements, employment outlook, earnings, and places of employment.

★6182★ "Lithographic Worker" in *Career Information Center* (Vol.3)
Simon and Schuster
200 Old Tappan Rd.
Old Tappan, NJ 07675
Fax: 800-445-6991 Fr: 800-223-2348

Richard Lidz and Dale Anderson, editorial directors. Fifth edition, 1993. For 600 occupations, describes job duties, entry-level requirements, education and training needed, advancement possibilities, employment outlook, earnings and benefits. The set is divided into 12 volumes. Each volume includes jobs related under a broad career field. Volume 13 is the index.

★6183★ "Lithographic Workers" in *Career Discovery Encyclopedia* (Vol.4, pp. 20-21)
J.G. Ferguson Publishing Co.
200 W. Madison St., Ste. 300
Chicago, IL 60606
Ph: (312)580-5480 Fax: (312)580-4948

E. Russell Primm, editor-in-chief. 1993. Contains two-page articles on 504 occupations. Each article describes job duties, earnings, and educational and training requirements.

★6184★ "Photoengraver" in *Career Information Center* (Vol.3)
Simon and Schuster
200 Old Tappan Rd.
Old Tappan, NJ 07675
Fax: 800-445-6991 Fr: 800-223-2348

Richard Lidz and Dale Anderson, editorial directors. Fifth edition, 1993. For 600 occupations, describes job duties, entry-level requirements, education and training needed, advancement possibilities, employment outlook, earnings and benefits. The set is divided into 12 volumes. Each volume includes

jobs related under a broad career field. Volume 13 is the index.

★6185★ "Photoengravers" in *Career Discovery Encyclopedia* (Vol.5, pp. 34-35)
J.G. Ferguson Publishing Co.
200 W. Madison St., Ste. 300
Chicago, IL 60606
Ph: (312)580-5480 Fax: (312)580-4948

E. Russell Primm, editor-in-chief. 1993. Contains two-page articles on 504 occupations. Each article describes job duties, earnings, and educational and training requirements.

★6186★ "Photoengravers" in *Encyclopedia of Careers and Vocational Guidance* (Vol.4, pp. 67-69)
J.G. Ferguson Publishing Co.
200 W. Madison St., Ste. 300
Chicago, IL 60606
Ph: (312)580-5480 Fax: (312)580-4948

William E. Hopke, editor-in-chief. Ninth edition, 1993. Four-volume set that profiles 500 occupations and describes job trends in 74 industries. Includes career description, educational requirements, history of the job, methods of entry, advancement, employment outlook, earnings, working conditions, social and psychological factors, and sources of additional information.

★6187★ "Platemaker" in *Career Information Center* (Vol.3)
Simon and Schuster
200 Old Tappan Rd.
Old Tappan, NJ 07675
Fax: 800-445-6991 Fr: 800-223-2348

Richard Lidz and Dale Anderson, editorial directors. Fifth edition, 1993. For 600 occupations, describes job duties, entry-level requirements, education and training needed, advancement possibilities, employment outlook, earnings and benefits. The set is divided into 12 volumes. Each volume includes jobs related under a broad career field. Volume 13 is the index.

★6188★ *Platemaker, Lithographic*
Careers, Inc.
PO Box 135
Largo, FL 34649-0135
Ph: (813)584-7333

1993. Two-page occupational summary card describing duties, working conditions, personal qualifications, training, earnings and hours, employment outlook, places of employment, related careers and where to write for more information.

★6189★ "Prepress Workers" in *Occupational Outlook Handbook*
U.S. Government Printing Office
Superintendent of Documents
Washington, DC 20402
Ph: (202)512-1800 Fax: (202)512-2250

Biennial; latest edition, 1994-95. Encyclopedia of careers describing more than 250 occupations and comprising about 85 percent of all jobs in the economy. Occupations that require lengthy education or training are given the most attention. For each occupation, the handbook describes job duties, working conditions, training, educational preparation, personal qualities, advancement possibilities, job outlook, earnings, and sources of additional information.

★6190★ *Typesetter*
Vocational Biographies, Inc.
PO Box 31
Sauk Centre, MN 56378-0031
Ph: (612)352-6516 Fax: (612)352-5546
Fr: 800-255-0752

1992. Four-page pamphlet containing a personal narrative about a worker's job, work likes and dislikes, career path from high school to the present. Education and training, the rewards and frustrations, and the effects of the job on the rest of the worker's life. The data file portion of this pamphlet gives a concise occupational summary, including work descriptions, working conditions, places of employment, personal characteristics, education and training, job outlook, and salary range.

★6191★ *Typesetters*
Chronicle Guidance Publications, Inc.
66 Aurora St.
PO Box 1190
Moravia, NY 13118-1190
Ph: (315)497-0330 Fax: (315)497-3359
Fr: 800-622-7284

1993. This career brief describes the nature of the work, working conditions, hours and earnings, education and training, licensure, certification, unions, personal qualifications, social and psychological factors, employment outlook, entry methods, advancement, and related occupations.

★6192★ "Typesetters" in *Career Discovery Encyclopedia* (Vol.6, pp. 128-129)
J.G. Ferguson Publishing Co.
200 W. Madison St., Ste. 300
Chicago, IL 60606
Ph: (312)580-5480 Fax: (312)580-4948

E. Russell Primm, editor-in-chief. 1993. Contains two-page articles on 504 occupations. Each article describes job duties, earnings, and educational and training requirements.

★6193★ *Video Career Library - Production I*
Careers, Inc.
PO Box 135
Largo, FL 34649-0135
Ph: (813)584-7333

Videocassette. 1990. 28 mins. Part of the Video Career Library covering 165 occupations. Shows actual workers on the job. Includes layout workers, precision typesetters, lithographers/photoengravers, bookbinders, hand tailors/dressmakers, upholsterers, water/sewage plant operators, chemical plant operators, and power plant operators.

Associations

★6194★ Graphic Arts Technical Foundation (GATF)
4615 Forbes Ave.
Pittsburgh, PA 15213
Ph: (412)621-6941 Fax: (412)621-3049

Members: Scientific, research, technical, and educational organization serving the international graphic communications industries. **Purpose:** Conducts research in all graphic processes and their commercial applications. Conducts seminars, workshops, and forums on graphic arts and environmental subjects. Conducts educational programs, including the publishing of graphic arts textbooks and learning modules, audiovisuals, videotapes, aptitude testing, in-plant and school counseling, and national career and manpower recruitment program. Conducts the GATF training and certification program in sheet-fed offset press operating, Web Offset press operating, Image Assembly, and desktop publishing. Produces test images and quality control devices for the industry. Performs technical services for the graphic arts industry, including problem-solving, material evaluation, and plant audits. Compiles statistics. **Publications:** *GATFWORLD*, bimonthly. • *Product Catalog*, annual. • *Quality Control Device Catalog*, semiannual. • *Second Sight Technical Reports*. • *Technology Forecast*. • *Training Materials Catalog*, semiannual. • *Training Programs Catalog*, semiannual. • *Workshop Catalog*, periodic.

★6195★ Graphic Communications International Union (GCIU)
1900 L St. NW
Washington, DC 20036
Ph: (202)462-1400 Fax: (202)331-9516

Members: AFL-CIO; Canadian Labour Congress. **Publications:** *GraphiCommunicator: The Newspaper of the Graphic Communications Union.*

Standards/Certification Agencies

★6196★ Graphic Arts Technical Foundation (GATF)
4615 Forbes Ave.
Pittsburgh, PA 15213
Ph: (412)621-6941 Fax: (412)621-3049

Conducts the GATF training and certification program in sheet-fed offset press operating, Web Offset press operating, Image Assembly, and desktop publishing. Produces test images and quality control devices for the industry. Performs technical services for the graphic arts industry, including problem-solving, material evaluation, and plant audits.

Test Guides

★6197★ *Career Examination Series: Composing Machine Operator*
National Learning Corp.
212 Michael Dr.
Syosset, NY 11791
Ph: (516)921-8888 Fax: (516)921-8743
Fr: 800-645-6337

Jack Rudman. All examination guides in this series contain questions with answers.

★6198★ *Career Examination Series: Journeyman in the Printing Crafts*
National Learning Corp.
212 Michael Dr.
Syosset, NY 11791
Ph: (516)921-8888 Fax: (516)921-8743
Fr: 800-645-6337

Jack Rudman. All examination guides in this series contain questions with answers.

★6199★ *Career Examination Series: Lithographic Pressman*
National Learning Corp.
212 Michael Dr.
Syosset, NY 11791
Ph: (516)921-8888 Fax: (516)921-8743
Fr: 800-645-6337

Jack Rudman. 1989. All examination guides in this series contain questions with answers.

★6200★ *Offset Lithography*
National Learning Corp.
212 Michael Dr.
Syosset, NY 11791
Ph: (516)921-8888 Fax: (516)921-8743
Fr: 800-645-6337

Jack Rudman. 1989. Part of Occupational Competency Examination Series.

Basic Reference Guides and Handbooks

★6201★ *Graphics Master 5*
Dean Lem Associates, Inc.
PO Box 959
Kihei, HI 96753-0959
Ph: (808)874-5461 Fax: (808)875-1404
Fr: 800-562-2562

A technical manual and reference guide for new and experienced professionals. Sections include color separation, photography, scanners, typography, printing papers, and binding and finishing.

Periodicals

★6202★ *American Printer*
Maclean Hunter Publishing Co.
29 N. Wacker Drive
Chicago, IL 60606
Ph: (312)726-2802 Fax: (312)726-2574
Jill Roth

Monthly. Magazine covering the printing and publishing market.

★6203★ *American Typecasting Fellowship—Newsletter*
American Typecasting Fellowship
PO Box 263
Terra Alta, WV 26764
Ph: (304)789-2455
Richard L. Hopkins

Periodic. Devoted to conveying information on the preservation of equipment and technology related to metal typecasting. Covers type founding, type design, matrix making, and letterpress printing. Recurring features include letters to the editor and news of members.

★6204★ *Around the Bargaining Loop*
Graphic Arts Employers of America
100 Daingerfield Rd.
Alexandria, VA 22314
Ph: (703)519-8150 Fax: (703)548-3227
Holly T. Kachman

Monthly. Provides "detailed summaries of recent settlements within the printing and other related industries. Wage and fringe benefit provisions are given for both the old and new agreements for quick comparisons."

★6205★ *Flexo*
Flexographic Technical Assn.
900 Marconi Ave.
Ronkonkoma, NY 11779
Ph: (516)737-6023 Fax: (516)737-6813
Linda Casatelli

Monthly. Magazine covering the flexographic printing method.

★6206★ *Graphic Arts Monthly*
Cahners Publishing Co.
249 W. 17th St.
New York, NY 10011
Ph: (212)463-6759 Fax: (212)463-6734
Roger Ynostroza

Monthly. Magazine featuring commercial printing and graphic arts.

★6207★ *In-Plant Printer & Electronic Publisher*
Innes Publishing Co.
PO Box 368
Northbrook, IL 60065
Ph: (708)564-5940 Fax: (708)564-8361
Andrea Cody

Bimonthly. Magazine serving printing, graphics, typesetting facilities, educational, government, and non-profit organizations.

★6208★ *Instant and Small Commercial Printer*
Innes Publishing Co.
PO Box 368
Northbrook, IL 60065
Ph: (708)564-5940 Fax: (708)564-8361
Jeanette Clinkunbroomer

Magazine serving the field of instant/quick printers, copy shops, small commercial printers, combination printers, industry suppliers and others allied to the field, including typesetters and thermographers.

★6209★ *Koob Stra*
Center for Book Arts
626 Broadway
New York, NY 10012
Ph: (212)460-9768
Brian Hannon

Promotes the arts of the book: printing, bookbinding, papermaking, calligraphy, and preservation. Composed of interviews with people active in book arts; reviews of exhibitions, lectures, conferences, and books; and international calendar of readings, workshops, and seminars; news of educational programs sponsored by the Center; news of small presses; and book arts suppliers information.

★6210★ *MCBA Newsletter*
Minnesota Center for Book Arts (MCBA)
24 N. 3rd St.
Minneapolis, MN 55401
Ph: (612)338-3634 Fax: (612)338-1562
Loring Johnson

Quarterly. Focuses on the field of book arts, including letterpress printing, bookbinding, and papermaking. Reviews current and future Center exhibitions and announces classes available at the Center.

★6211★ *Package Printing and Converting*
North American Publishing Co.
401 N. Broad St.
Philadelphia, PA 19108
Ph: (215)238-5300 Fax: (215)238-5457
David H. Luttenberger

Monthly. Magazine.

★6212★ *Quick Printing*
Coast Publishing, Inc.
Zedcoast Center
1680 SW Bayshore Blvd.
Port Saint Lucie, FL 34984
Ph: (407)879-6666 Fax: (407)879-7388
Bob Hall

Monthly.

★6213★ *Southern Graphics*
Coast Publishing, Inc.
Zedcoast Center
1680 SW Bayshore Blvd.
Port Saint Lucie, FL 34984
Ph: (407)879-6666 Fax: (407)879-7388
Cathy Donohue

Monthly. Graphic arts magazine serving the printing and graphic arts industry in 14 southern states.

★6214★ *Type and Press*
24667 Heather Ct.
Hayward, CA 94545
Ph: (415)782-3674
Fred C. Williams

Quarterly. Trade magazine covering letterpress printing.

Meetings and Conventions

★6215★ Color Electronic Prepress Conference
Graphic Arts Technical Foundation (GATF)
4615 Forbes Ave.
Pittsburgh, PA 15213
Ph: (412)621-6941 Fax: (412)621-3049

Annual. Always August.

★6216★ GATF/NSTF Annual Conference
Graphic Arts Technical Foundation (GATF)
4615 Forbes Ave.
Pittsburgh, PA 15213
Ph: (412)621-6941 Fax: (412)621-3049

Annual.

★6217★ National Association of Professional Engravers Annual Trade Show and Exhibit
National Association of Professional Engravers
21010 Center Ridge Rd.
Rocky River, OH 44116
Ph: (216)333-7417 Fax: (216)333-1868

Annual.

Other Sources of Information

★6218★ *Training Materials Catalog*
Graphic Arts Technical Foundation (GATF)
4615 Forbes Ave.
Pittsburgh, PA 15213
Ph: (412)621-6941 Fax: (412)621-3049
Annual.

Printing Press Operators

Printing press operators are responsible for the preparation, operation, and maintenance of the press. Preparation involves installing and adjusting the printing plate, mixing fountain solution, adjusting pressure, inking presses, loading paper, and adjusting the press to paper size. Operation involves running the press and maintaining the feeders. Preventive maintenance involves oiling and cleaning the presses and making minor repairs to keep presses running smoothly. Press operators are generally classified according to the type of press they operate--offset, gravure, flexography, screen printing, or letterpress--and duties vary accordingly. Most press operator jobs are in newspaper plants or in firms that handle commercial or business printing. Commercial printing firms print newspaper. Additional jobs are in the *in-plant* section of organizations and businesses that do their own printing--among them, banks, insurance companies, and government agencies.

Salaries

Weekly earnings for printing press operators are as follows:

Lowest 10 percent	$215/week or less
Middle 50 percent	$300-$570/week
Top 10 percent	$710/week or more

Employment Outlook

Growth rate until the year 2005: Average.

Printing Press Operators

Career Guides

★6219★ *Career Insights*
RMI Media Productions, Inc.
1365 N. Winchester
Olathe, KS 66061
Ph: (913)768-1696 Fax: 800-755-6910
Fr: 800-745-5480

Videocassette series. 1987. This videotape series describes 50 occupations, including skill requirements and interviews with people employed in these fields. Occupations include: flight service, air transportation/ground services, data processing, carpentry, clerk in banking/insurance/business, cosmetic personal grooming, firefighting, forestry, insulation/roofing, mechanics, material handling, photographic processing, pipefitting and plumbing, printing, secretarial services, tool and die operations.

★6220★ *Career Success Series*
Cambridge Educational
PO Box 2153
Charleston, WV 25328-2153
Ph: (304)744-9323 Fax: (304)744-9351
Fr: 800-468-4227

Videocassette. 1986. 15 mins. A series, available separately, outlining various career choices for students. Occupations include: accounting, flight service, air transportation/ground/flight service, data processing, carpentry, clerk in banking/insurance, commodity sales, cosmetic personal grooming, fire fighting, forestry services, home economics, insulation/roofing, material handling, mechanics, photographic processing, pipefitting and plumbing, police science, printing, carpentry, medical laboratory technicians, secretarial services, and utilities equipment operator.

★6221★ *Offset Press Operator*
Careers, Inc.
PO Box 135
Largo, FL 34649-0135
Ph: (813)584-7333

1993. Four-page brief offering the definition, history, duties, working conditions, personal qualifications, educational requirements, earnings, hours, employment outlook, advancement possibilities, and related occupations.

★6222★ "Offset Press Operator" in *Occu-Facts: Information on 580 Careers in Outline Form*
Careers, Inc.
PO Box 135
Largo, FL 34649-0135
Ph: (813)584-7333

Biennial, 1995-96 edition. Each one-page occupational profile describes duties, working conditions, physical surroundings and demands, aptitudes, temperament, educational requirements, employment outlook, earnings, and places of employment.

★6223★ "Printing" in *Encyclopedia of Careers and Vocational Guidance* (Vol.1, pp. 380-386)
J.G. Ferguson Publishing Co.
200 W. Madison St., Ste. 300
Chicago, IL 60606
Ph: (312)580-5480 Fax: (312)580-4948

William E. Hopke, editor-in-chief. Ninth edition, 1993. Four-volume set that profiles 500 occupations and describes job trends in 74 industries. Includes career description, educational requirements, history of the job, methods of entry, advancement, employment outlook, earnings, working conditions, social and psychological factors, and sources of additional information.

★6224★ *Printing Platemakers*
Chronicle Guidance Publications, Inc.
66 Aurora St.
PO Box 1190
Moravia, NY 13118-1190
Ph: (315)497-0330 Fax: (315)497-3359
Fr: 800-622-7284

1991. This career brief describes the nature of the work, working conditions, hours and earnings, education and training, licensure, certification, unions, personal qualifications, social and psychological factors, employment outlook, entry methods, advancement, and related occupations.

★6225★ *Printing Press Operator*
Vocational Biographies, Inc.
PO Box 31
Sauk Centre, MN 56378-0031
Ph: (612)352-6516 Fax: (612)352-5546
Fr: 800-255-0752

1994. Four-page pamphlet containing a personal narrative about a worker's job, work likes and dislikes, career path from high school to the present. Education and training, the rewards and frustrations, and the effects of the job on the rest of the worker's life. The data file portion of this pamphlet gives a concise occupational summary, including work descriptions, working conditions, places of employment, personal characteristics, education and training, job outlook, and salary range.

★6226★ "Printing Press Operator" in *BLR Encyclopedia of Prewritten Job Descriptions*
Business and Legal Reports, Inc.
39 Academy St.
Madison, CT 06443-1513
Ph: (203)245-7448

Stephen D. Bruce, editor-in-chief. 1994. This book contains hundreds of sample job descriptions arranged by functional job category. The 1-3 page job descriptions cover what the worker normally does in the position, who they report to, and how that position fits in the organizational structure.

★6227★ "Printing Press Operator" in *Career Information Center* (Vol.3)
Simon and Schuster
200 Old Tappan Rd.
Old Tappan, NJ 07675
Fax: 800-445-6991 Fr: 800-223-2348

Richard Lidz and Dale Anderson, editorial directors. Fifth edition, 1993. For 600 occupations, describes job duties, entry-level requirements, education and training needed, advancement possibilities, employment outlook, earnings and benefits. The set is divided into 12 volumes. Each volume includes jobs related under a broad career field. Volume 13 is the index.

★6228★ "Printing Press Operator" in *VGM's Careers Encyclopedia* (pp. 368-370)
National Textbook Co. (NTC)
VGM Career Books
4255 W. Touhy Ave.
Lincolnwood, IL 60646-1975
Ph: (708)679-5500 Fax: (708)679-2494
Fr: 800-323-4900

Third edition, 1991. Contains two- to five-page descriptions of 200 managerial, professional, technical, trade, and service occupations. Each profile includes job duties, places of employment, qualifications, educational preparation, training, employment potential, advancement, income, and additional sources of information.

★6229★ *Printing Press Operators*
Chronicle Guidance Publications, Inc.
66 Aurora St.
PO Box 1190
Moravia, NY 13118-1190
Ph: (315)497-0330 Fax: (315)497-3359
Fr: 800-622-7284

1994. This career brief describes the nature of the work, working conditions, hours and earnings, education and training, licensure, certification, unions, personal qualifications, social and psychological factors, employment outlook, entry methods, advancement, and related occupations.

★6230★ "Printing Press Operators and Assistants" in *Encyclopedia of Careers and Vocational Guidance* (Vol.4, pp. 166-169)
J.G. Ferguson Publishing Co.
200 W. Madison St., Ste. 300
Chicago, IL 60606
Ph: (312)580-5480 Fax: (312)580-4948

William E. Hopke, editor-in-chief. Ninth edition, 1993. Four-volume set that profiles 500 occupations and describes job trends in 74 industries. Includes career description, educational requirements, history of the job, methods of entry, advancement, employment outlook, earnings, working conditions, social and psychological factors, and sources of additional information.

★6231★ "Printing Press Operators" in *Career Discovery Encyclopedia* (Vol.5, pp. 82-83)
J.G. Ferguson Publishing Co.
200 W. Madison St., Ste. 300
Chicago, IL 60606
Ph: (312)580-5480 Fax: (312)580-4948

E. Russell Primm, editor-in-chief. 1993. Contains two-page articles on 504 occupations. Each article describes job duties, earnings, and educational and training requirements.

★6232★ "Printing Press Operators" in *Jobs! What They Are—Where They Are—What They Pay* (pp. 216)
Simon & Schuster, Inc.
Simon & Schuster Bldg.
1230 Avenue of the Americas
New York, NY 10020
Ph: (212)698-7000

Robert O. Snelling and Anne M. Snelling. Revised edition, 1992. Profiles 241 occupations, describing duties and responsibilities, educational preparation, earnings, employment opportunities, training, and qualifications.

★6233★ "Printing Press Operators" in *Occupational Outlook Handbook*
U.S. Government Printing Office
Superintendent of Documents
Washington, DC 20402
Ph: (202)512-1800 Fax: (202)512-2250

Biennial; latest edition, 1994-95. Encyclopedia of careers describing more than 250 occupations and comprising about 85 percent of all jobs in the economy. Occupations that require lengthy education or training are given the most attention. For each occupation, the handbook describes job duties, working conditions, training, educational preparation, personal qualities, advancement possibilities, job outlook, earnings, and sources of additional information.

★6234★ "Printing Technology" in *Career Connection II: A Guide to Technical Majors and Their Related Careers* (pp. 128-129)
Jist Works, Inc.
720 N. Park Ave.
Indianapolis, IN 46202-3431
Ph: (317)264-3720 Fax: (317)264-3709

Fred A. Rowe. 1994. Contains technical majors, such as automotive technology. Describes the major and the job. Lists high school and postsecondary school courses. Includes occupations related to the major, employment outlook, and starting salary.

★6235★ *Video Career Library - Production I*
Careers, Inc.
PO Box 135
Largo, FL 34649-0135
Ph: (813)584-7333

Videocassette. 1990. 28 mins. Part of the Video Career Library covering 165 occupations. Shows actual workers on the job. Includes layout workers, precision typesetters, lithographers/photoengravers, bookbinders, hand tailors/dressmakers, upholsterers, water/sewage plant operators, chemical plant operators, and power plant operators.

Associations

★6236★ Graphic Arts Technical Foundation (GATF)
4615 Forbes Ave.
Pittsburgh, PA 15213
Ph: (412)621-6941 Fax: (412)621-3049

Members: Scientific, research, technical, and educational organization serving the international graphic communications industries. **Purpose:** Conducts research in all graphic processes and their commercial applications. Conducts seminars, workshops, and forums on graphic arts and environmental subjects. Conducts educational programs, including the publishing of graphic arts textbooks and learning modules, audiovisuals, videotapes, aptitude testing, in-plant and school counseling, and national career and manpower recruitment program. Conducts the GATF training and certification program in sheet-fed offset press operating, Web Offset press operating, Image Assembly, and desktop publishing. Produces test images and quality control devices for the industry. Performs technical services for the graphic arts industry, including problem-solving, material evaluation, and plant audits. Compiles statistics. **Publications:** *GATFWORLD*, bimonthly. • *Product Catalog*, annual. • *Quality Control Device Catalog*, semiannual. • *Second Sight Technical Reports.* • *Technology Forecast.* • *Training Materials Catalog*, semiannual. • *Training Programs Catalog*, semiannual. • *Workshop Catalog*, periodic.

★6237★ Graphic Communications International Union (GCIU)
1900 L St. NW
Washington, DC 20036
Ph: (202)462-1400 Fax: (202)331-9516

Members: AFL-CIO; Canadian Labour Congress. **Publications:** *GraphiCommunicator: The Newspaper of the Graphic Communications Union.*

Standards/Certification Agencies

★6238★ Graphic Arts Technical Foundation (GATF)
4615 Forbes Ave.
Pittsburgh, PA 15213
Ph: (412)621-6941 Fax: (412)621-3049

Conducts the GATF training and certification program in sheet-fed offset press operating, Web Offset press operating, Image Assembly, and desktop publishing. Produces test images and quality control devices for the industry. Performs technical services for the graphic arts industry, including problem-solving, material evaluation, and plant audits.

Test Guides

★6239★ *Career Examination Series: Journeyman in the Printing Crafts*
National Learning Corp.
212 Michael Dr.
Syosset, NY 11791
Ph: (516)921-8888 Fax: (516)921-8743
Fr: 800-645-6337

Jack Rudman. All examination guides in this series contain questions with answers.

★6240★ *Career Examination Series: Offset Printing Machine Operator*
National Learning Corp.
212 Michael Dr.
Syosset, NY 11791
Ph: (516)921-8888 Fax: (516)921-8743
Fr: 800-645-6337

Jack Rudman. All examination guides in this series contain questions with answers.

★6241★ *Career Examination Series: Press Operator*
National Learning Corp.
212 Michael Dr.
Syosset, NY 11791
Ph: (516)921-8888 Fax: (516)921-8743
Fr: 800-645-6337

Jack Rudman. All examination guides in this series contain questions with answers.

★6242★ *Career Examination Series: Senior Offset Printing Machine Operator*
National Learning Corp.
212 Michael Dr.
Syosset, NY 11791
Ph: (516)921-8888 Fax: (516)921-8743
Fr: 800-645-6337

Jack Rudman. All examination guides in this series contain questions with answers.

Basic Reference Guides and Handbooks

★6243★ *Aligning & Adjusting Cylinders—Instructor Guide*
Graphic Arts Technical Foundation
4615 Forbes Ave.
Pittsburgh, PA 15213-3796
Ph: (412)621-6941 Fax: (412)621-3049

Robert J. Schneider, Jr. 1990.

★6244★ *Aligning & Adjusting Cylinders on the Sheetfed Offset Press*
Graphic Arts Technical Foundation
4615 Forbes Ave.
Pittsburgh, PA 15213-3796
Ph: (412)621-6941 Fax: (412)621-3049

Robert J. Schneider, Jr. 1990.

★6245★ *Operating the Dampening System, Instructor Guide*
Graphic Arts Technical Foundation
4615 Forbes Ave.
Pittsburgh, PA 15213-3796
Ph: (412)621-6941 Fax: (412)621-3049

Robert J. Schneider, Jr. 1990.

★6246★ *Operating the Dampening System on a Sheetfed Offset Press*
Graphic Arts Technical Foundation
4615 Forbes Ave.
Pittsburgh, PA 15213-3796
Ph: (412)621-6941 Fax: (412)621-3049

Robert J. Schneider, Jr. 1990.

★6247★ *Operating the Inking System—Instructor's Guide*
Graphic Arts Technical Foundation
4615 Forbes Ave.
Pittsburgh, PA 15213-3796
Ph: (412)621-6941 Fax: (412)621-3049

Robert J. Schneider, Jr. 1990.

Periodicals

★6248★ *American Ink Maker*
PTN Publishing Co.
445 Broad Hollow Rd., Ste. 21
Melville, NY 11747
Ph: (516)845-2700 Fax: (516)845-7109
Hope Gaines

Monthly. Trade magazine on printing inks and pigments.

★6249★ *American Printer*
Maclean Hunter Publishing Co.
29 N. Wacker Drive
Chicago, IL 60606
Ph: (312)726-2802 Fax: (312)726-2574
Jill Roth

Monthly. Magazine covering the printing and publishing market.

★6250★ *Around the Bargaining Loop*
Graphic Arts Employers of America
100 Daingerfield Rd.
Alexandria, VA 22314
Ph: (703)519-8150 Fax: (703)548-3227
Holly T. Kachman

Monthly. Provides "detailed summaries of recent settlements within the printing and other related industries. Wage and fringe benefit provisions are given for both the old and new agreements for quick comparisons."

★6251★ *Flexo*
Flexographic Technical Assn.
900 Marconi Ave.
Ronkonkoma, NY 11779
Ph: (516)737-6023 Fax: (516)737-6813
Linda Casatelli

Monthly. Magazine covering the flexographic printing method.

★6252★ *Graphic Arts Monthly*
Cahners Publishing Co.
249 W. 17th St.
New York, NY 10011
Ph: (212)463-6759 Fax: (212)463-6734
Roger Ynostroza

Monthly. Magazine featuring commercial printing and graphic arts.

★6253★ *In-Plant Printer & Electronic Publisher*
Innes Publishing Co.
PO Box 368
Northbrook, IL 60065
Ph: (708)564-5940 Fax: (708)564-8361
Andrea Cody

Bimonthly. Magazine serving printing, graphics, typesetting facilities, educational, government, and non-profit organizations.

★6254★ *Instant and Small Commercial Printer*
Innes Publishing Co.
PO Box 368
Northbrook, IL 60065
Ph: (708)564-5940 Fax: (708)564-8361
Jeanette Clinkunbroomer

Magazine serving the field of instant/quick printers, copy shops, small commercial printers, combination printers, industry suppliers and others allied to the field, including typesetters and thermographers.

★6255★ *Koob Stra*
Center for Book Arts
626 Broadway
New York, NY 10012
Ph: (212)460-9768
Brian Hannon

Promotes the arts of the book: printing, bookbinding, papermaking, calligraphy, and preservation. Composed of interviews with people active in book arts; reviews of exhibitions, lectures, conferences, and books; and international calendar of readings, workshops, and seminars; news of educational programs sponsored by the Center; news of small presses; and book arts suppliers information.

★6256★ *MCBA Newsletter*
Minnesota Center for Book Arts (MCBA)
24 N. 3rd St.
Minneapolis, MN 55401
Ph: (612)338-3634 Fax: (612)338-1562
Loring Johnson

Quarterly. Focuses on the field of book arts, including letterpress printing, bookbinding, and papermaking. Reviews current and future Center exhibitions and announces classes available at the Center.

★6257★ *Package Printing and Converting*
North American Publishing Co.
401 N. Broad St.
Philadelphia, PA 19108
Ph: (215)238-5300 Fax: (215)238-5457
David H. Luttenberger

Monthly. Magazine.

★6258★ *Quick Printing*
Coast Publishing, Inc.
Zedcoast Center
1680 SW Bayshore Blvd.
Port Saint Lucie, FL 34984
Ph: (407)879-6666 Fax: (407)879-7388
Bob Hall

Monthly.

★6259★ *Southern Graphics*
Coast Publishing, Inc.
Zedcoast Center
1680 SW Bayshore Blvd.
Port Saint Lucie, FL 34984
Ph: (407)879-6666 Fax: (407)879-7388
Cathy Donohue

Monthly. Graphic arts magazine serving the printing and graphic arts industry in 14 southern states.

★6260★ *Type and Press*
24667 Heather Ct.
Hayward, CA 94545
Ph: (415)782-3674
Fred C. Williams

Quarterly. Trade magazine covering letterpress printing.

Other Sources of Information

★6261★ *Training Materials Catalog*
Graphic Arts Technical Foundation (GATF)
4615 Forbes Ave.
Pittsburgh, PA 15213
Ph: (412)621-6941 Fax: (412)621-3049

Annual.

★6262★ *Troubleshooting Ink Problems, Part 1*
Graphic Arts Technical Foundation
4615 Forbes Ave.
Pittsburgh, PA 15213-3796
Ph: (412)621-6941 Fax: (412)621-3049

1992. Solution to inking problems are presented with tips from experts.

★6263★ *Troubleshooting Inking Problems, Part 2*
Graphic Arts Technical Foundation
4615 Forbes Ave.
Pittsburgh, PA 15213-3796
Ph: (412)621-6941 Fax: (412)621-3049

1992. Includes several tips on identifying and solving paper and ink-related problems such as kickeys, erratic dot gain, mottling, and paper curl.

Apparel Workers

Apparel workers transform cloth, as well as leather and fur, into clothing and other consumer products. Apparel production begins with a design, created by a designer, that has been made into a sample product. Once the pattern has been created, the fabric must be spread and cut. Using an electric knife or other cutting tools, other workers cut out the various pieces of material following the outline of the pattern. Once the material has been cut, it is ready to be sewn together. This is done by sewing machine operators. Sometime sewing is done by hand rather than on a machine. When sewing operations have been completed, there is a final inspection of the product. More than 50 percent of all pressers are employed in the laundry and dry-cleaning industry. In addition, more than 60 percent of all custom tailors and sewers work in retail clothing establishments; many others are self-employed.

Salaries

Earnings of apparel workers vary by industry and by occupation. Median weekly earnings of apparel workers are as follows:

Production workers in the apparel industry	$258/week
Sewing machine operators	$217/week

Employment Outlook

Growth rate until the year 2005: Decline.

Apparel Workers

CAREER GUIDES

★6264★ "Apparel" in *Encyclopedia of Careers and Vocational Guidance*
J.G. Ferguson Publishing Co.
200 W. Madison St., Ste. 300
Chicago, IL 60606
Ph: (312)580-5480 Fax: (312)580-4948

William E. Hopke, editor-in-chief. Ninth edition, 1993. Four-volume set that profiles 500 occupations and describes job trends in 74 industries. Includes career description, educational requirements, history of the job, methods of entry, advancement, employment outlook, earnings, working conditions, social and psychological factors, and sources of additional information.

★6265★ "Apparel Industry" in *Career Information Center* (Vol.9)
Simon and Schuster
200 Old Tappan Rd.
Old Tappan, NJ 07675
Fax: 800-445-6991 Fr: 800-223-2348

Richard Lidz and Dale Anderson, editorial directors. Fifth edition, 1993. For 600 occupations, describes job duties, entry-level requirements, education and training needed, advancement possibilities, employment outlook, earnings and benefits. The set is divided into 12 volumes. Each volume includes jobs related under a broad career field. Volume 13 is the index.

★6266★ *Apparel Industry Workers*
Chronicle Guidance Publications, Inc.
66 Aurora St.
PO Box 1190
Moravia, NY 13118-1190
Ph: (315)497-0330 Fax: (315)497-3359
Fr: 800-622-7284

1987. This career brief describes the nature of the work, working conditions, hours and earnings, education and training, licensure, certification, unions, personal qualifications, social and psychological factors, employment outlook, entry methods, advancement, and related occupations.

★6267★ "Apparel Workers" in *Occupational Outlook Handbook*
U.S. Government Printing Office
Superintendent of Documents
Washington, DC 20402
Ph: (202)512-1800 Fax: (202)512-2250

Biennial; latest edition, 1994-95. Encyclopedia of careers describing more than 250 occupations and comprising about 85 percent of all jobs in the economy. Occupations that require lengthy education or training are given the most attention. For each occupation, the handbook describes job duties, working conditions, training, educational preparation, personal qualities, advancement possibilities, job outlook, earnings, and sources of additional information.

★6268★ "Custom Tailor and Dressmaker" in *Career Information Center* (Vol.5)
Simon and Schuster
200 Old Tappan Rd.
Old Tappan, NJ 07675
Fax: 800-445-6991 Fr: 800-223-2348

Richard Lidz and Dale Anderson, editorial directors. Fifth edition, 1993. For 600 occupations, describes job duties, entry-level requirements, education and training needed, advancement possibilities, employment outlook, earnings and benefits. The set is divided into 12 volumes. Each volume includes jobs related under a broad career field. Volume 13 is the index.

★6269★ "Drapery Sewer" in *Occu-Facts: Information on 580 Careers in Outline Form*
Careers, Inc.
PO Box 135
Largo, FL 34649-0135
Ph: (813)584-7333

Biennial, 1995-96 edition. Each one-page occupational profile describes duties, working conditions, physical surroundings and demands, aptitudes, temperament, educational requirements, employment outlook, earnings, and places of employment.

★6270★ *Dressmaker*
Careers, Inc.
PO Box 135
Largo, FL 34649-0135
Ph: (813)584-7333

1993. Two-page occupational summary card describing duties, working conditions, personal qualifications, training, earnings and hours, employment outlook, places of employment, related careers and where to write for more information.

★6271★ *Dressmakers (Sewing Professionals)*
Chronicle Guidance Publications, Inc.
66 Aurora St.
PO Box 1190
Moravia, NY 13118-1190
Ph: (315)497-0330 Fax: (315)497-3359
Fr: 800-622-7284

1993. This career brief describes the nature of the work, working conditions, hours and earnings, education and training, licensure, certification, unions, personal qualifications, social and psychological factors, employment outlook, entry methods, advancement, and related occupations.

★6272★ "Furniture Upholsterer and Tailor or Dressmaker" in *Personal Services* (pp. 39-43)
Franklin Watts, Inc.
387 Park Avenue, S.
New York, NY 10016
Ph: (212)686-7070

Linda Barrett and Galen Guengerich. 1991. Surveys personal services jobs. Describes job duties, educational preparation, salaries, and employment outlook. Offers job hunting advice.

★6273★ *Garment Cutter*
Careers, Inc.
PO Box 135
Largo, FL 34649-0135
Ph: (813)584-7333

1993. Two-page occupational summary card describing duties, working conditions, personal qualifications, training, earnings and hours, employment outlook, places of employment, related careers and where to write for more information.

★6274★ "Garment Cutter" in *Occu-Facts: Information on 580 Careers in Outline Form*
Careers, Inc.
PO Box 135
Largo, FL 34649-0135
Ph: (813)584-7333

Biennial, 1995-96 edition. Each one-page occupational profile describes duties, working conditions, physical surroundings and demands, aptitudes, temperament, educational requirements, employment outlook, earnings, and places of employment.

★6275★ "Garment Presser" in *Occu-Facts: Information on 580 Careers in Outline Form*
Careers, Inc.
PO Box 135
Largo, FL 34649-0135
Ph: (813)584-7333

Biennial, 1995-96 edition. Each one-page occupational profile describes duties, working conditions, physical surroundings and demands, aptitudes, temperament, educational requirements, employment outlook, earnings, and places of employment.

★6276★ "Hand Sewer" in *Occu-Facts: Information on 580 Careers in Outline Form*
Careers, Inc.
PO Box 135
Largo, FL 34649-0135
Ph: (813)584-7333

Biennial, 1995-96 edition. Each one-page occupational profile describes duties, working conditions, physical surroundings and demands, aptitudes, temperament, educational requirements, employment outlook, earnings, and places of employment.

★6277★ *Presser, Garment*
Careers, Inc.
PO Box 135
Largo, FL 34649-0135
Ph: (813)584-7333

1993. Two-page job guide card describing duties, working conditions, personal qualifications, training, earnings and hours, employment outlook, places of employment, related careers and where to write for more information.

★6278★ *Seamstress*
Vocational Biographies, Inc.
PO Box 31
Sauk Centre, MN 56378-0031
Ph: (612)352-6516 Fax: (612)352-5546
Fr: 800-255-0752

1991. This pamphlet profiles a person working in the job. Includes information about job duties, working conditions, places of employment, educational preparation, labor market outlook, and salaries.

★6279★ *Sewer, Drapery*
Careers, Inc.
PO Box 135
Largo, FL 34649-0135
Ph: (813)584-7333

1994. Two-page job guide card describing duties, working conditions, personal qualifications, training, earnings and hours, employment outlook, places of employment, related careers and where to write for more information.

★6280★ *Sewer, Hand*
Careers, Inc.
PO Box 135
Largo, FL 34649-0135
Ph: (813)584-7333

1992. Two-page job guide card describing duties, working conditions, personal qualifications, training, earnings and hours, employment outlook, places of employment, related careers and where to write for more information.

★6281★ *Sewing Machine Operator*
Careers, Inc.
PO Box 135
Largo, FL 34649-0135
Ph: (813)584-7333

1992. Two-page occupational summary card describing duties, working conditions, personal qualifications, training, earnings and hours, employment outlook, places of employment, related careers and where to write for more information.

★6282★ "Sewing Machine Operator" in *Occu-Facts: Information on 580 Careers in Outline Form*
Careers, Inc.
PO Box 135
Largo, FL 34649-0135
Ph: (813)584-7333

Biennial, 1995-96 edition. Each one-page occupational profile describes duties, working conditions, physical surroundings and demands, aptitudes, temperament, educational requirements, employment outlook, earnings, and places of employment.

★6283★ *Sewing Machine Operators (Apparel)*
Chronicle Guidance Publications, Inc.
66 Aurora St.
PO Box 1190
Moravia, NY 13118-1190
Ph: (315)497-0330 Fax: (315)497-3359
Fr: 800-622-7284

1993. This career brief describes the nature of the work, working conditions, hours and earnings, education and training, licensure, certification, unions, personal qualifications, social and psychological factors, employment outlook, entry methods, advancement, and related occupations.

★6284★ *Tailors*
Chronicle Guidance Publications, Inc.
66 Aurora St.
PO Box 1190
Moravia, NY 13118-1190
Ph: (315)497-0330 Fax: (315)497-3359
Fr: 800-622-7284

1994. This career brief describes the nature of the work, working conditions, hours and earnings, education and training, licensure, certification, unions, personal qualifications, social and psychological factors, employment outlook, entry methods, advancement, and related occupations.

★6285★ *Tailors*
Careers, Inc.
PO Box 135
Largo, FL 34649-0135
Ph: (813)584-7333

1991. Four-page brief offering the definition, history, duties, working conditions, personal qualifications, educational requirements, earnings, hours, employment outlook, advancement possibilities, and related occupations.

★6286★ "Tailors" in *Occu-Facts: Information on 580 Careers in Outline Form*
Careers, Inc.
PO Box 135
Largo, FL 34649-0135
Ph: (813)584-7333

Biennial, 1995-96 edition. Each one-page occupational profile describes duties, working conditions, physical surroundings and demands, aptitudes, temperament, educational requirements, employment outlook, earnings, and places of employment.

★6287★ *Video Career Library - Production I*
Careers, Inc.
PO Box 135
Largo, FL 34649-0135
Ph: (813)584-7333

Videocassette. 1990. 28 mins. Part of the Video Career Library covering 165 occupations. Shows actual workers on the job. Includes layout workers, precision typesetters, lithographers/photoengravers, bookbinders, hand tailors/dressmakers, upholsterers, water/sewage plant operators, chemical plant operators, and power plant operators.

Associations

★6288★ American Apparel Manufacturers Association (AAMA)
2500 Wilson Blvd., Ste. 301
Arlington, VA 22201
Ph: (703)524-1864 Fax: (703)522-6741

Members: Manufacturers (434) of infants', children's, boys', girls', juniors', men's, and women's wearing apparel; associate members (381) are suppliers of fabrics, equipment, accessories, and services to the apparel industry. **Purpose:** Operates the Apparel Foundation; offers placement service through newsletter. Compiles statistics. **Publications:** *AAMA Directory of Members and Associate Members*, annual. • *AAMA Newsletter*, monthly. • *Apparel College Directory*, biennial. • *Apparel Import Digest*, annual. • *Apparel Plant Wages Survey*, annual. • *Apparel Research Notes*, periodic. • *Apparel Sales/Marketing Compensation Survey*, annual. • *Committee Manual*, annual. • *Economic Profile*, annual. • *Personnel Policy Survey*, biennial. • *Technical Advisory Committee Bulletin*, periodic. • *Technical Advisory Committee Research Paper*, annual. • *Washington Letter.*

★6289★ National Association of Hosiery Manufacturers (NAHM)
200 N. Sharon Amity Rd.
Charlotte, NC 28211
Ph: (704)365-0913 Fax: (704)362-2056

Members: Hosiery manufacturers and suppliers. **Purpose:** Develops standards for hosiery measurement. Sponsors annual National Hosiery Week to educate consumers on hosiery varieties. Conducts field visitations for assistance in technical areas. Compiles statistics; conducts research programs. Operates Group Purchasing Program. **Publications:** *Annual Hosiery Statistics.* • *Hosiery News*, monthly. • *NAHM Directory of Hosiery Manufacturers*, periodic. • *NAHM Directory of Hosiery Mill Suppliers*, periodic.

Standards/Certification Agencies

★6290★ National Association of Hosiery Manufacturers (NAHM)
200 N. Sharon Amity Rd.
Charlotte, NC 28211
Ph: (704)365-0913 Fax: (704)362-2056

Develops standards for hosiery measurement.

Basic Reference Guides and Handbooks

★6291★ *Apparel Import Digest*
American Apparel Manufacturers Association (AAMA)
2500 Wilson Blvd., Ste. 301
Arlington, VA 22201
Ph: (703)524-1864 Fax: (703)522-6741

Annual.

Periodicals

★6292★ *AAMA Directory of Members and Associate Members*
American Apparel Manufacturers Association (AAMA)
2500 Wilson Blvd., Ste. 301
Arlington, VA 22201
Ph: (703)524-1864 Fax: (703)522-6741

Annual.

★6293★ *AAMA Newsletter*
American Apparel Manufacturers Association (AAMA)
2500 Wilson Blvd., Ste. 301
Arlington, VA 22201
Ph: (703)524-1864 Fax: (703)522-6741

Monthly.

★6294★ *Apparel College Directory*
American Apparel Manufacturers Association (AAMA)
2500 Wilson Blvd., Ste. 301
Arlington, VA 22201
Ph: (703)524-1864 Fax: (703)522-6741

Biennial.

★6295★ *Apparel Industry Magazine*
Shore Communications, Inc.
180 Allen Rd. NE, Bldg. N, Ste. 300
Atlanta, GA 30328
Ph: (404)252-8831 Fax: (404)252-4436
Karen SchaffrerPublisher

Monthly. Magazine covering technology, management, and marketing for American apparel manufacturers.

★6296★ *Apparel Plant Wages Survey*
American Apparel Manufacturers Association (AAMA)
2500 Wilson Blvd., Ste. 301
Arlington, VA 22201
Ph: (703)524-1864 Fax: (703)522-6741

Annual.

★6297★ *Apparel Research Notes*
American Apparel Manufacturers Association (AAMA)
2500 Wilson Blvd., Ste. 301
Arlington, VA 22201
Ph: (703)524-1864 Fax: (703)522-6741

Periodic.

★6298★ *Apparel Sales/Marketing Compensation Survey*
American Apparel Manufacturers Association (AAMA)
2500 Wilson Blvd., Ste. 301
Arlington, VA 22201
Ph: (703)524-1864 Fax: (703)522-6741

Annual.

★6299★ *Clothing Manufacturers Association—News Bulletin*
Clothing Manufacturers Association of the United States of America
1290 Avenue of the Americas
New York, NY 10104
Ph: (212)757-6664
Robert A. Kaplan

Disseminates information for the Association relating to developments in or affecting the manufacturing of men's and boy's tailored clothing in the U.S. Contains statistics on sales, production, earnings, size, and industry earnings. Recurring features include notices of publications available, labor advisories, import advisories, and news of business opportunities.

★6300★ *Committee Manual*
American Apparel Manufacturers Association (AAMA)
2500 Wilson Blvd., Ste. 301
Arlington, VA 22201
Ph: (703)524-1864 Fax: (703)522-6741

Annual.

★6301★ *Economic Profile*
American Apparel Manufacturers Association (AAMA)
2500 Wilson Blvd., Ste. 301
Arlington, VA 22201
Ph: (703)524-1864 Fax: (703)522-6741

Annual.

★6302★ *Hosiery News*
National Association of Hosiery Manufacturers (NAHM)
200 N. Sharon Amity Rd.
Charlotte, NC 28211
Ph: (704)365-0913 Fax: (704)362-2056

Monthly. Covers legislative and regulatory issues; technology and equipment; new hosiery products at retail; hosiery production, shipments, and foreign trade.

★6303★ *Justice*
International Ladies' Garment Workers' Union
1710 Broadway, 3rd Fl.
New York, NY 10019
Ph: (212)265-7000 Fax: (212)307-6904
Dwight Burton

Monthly. Labor magazine.

★6304★ *Labor Unity*
Amalgamated Clothing & Textile Workers Union
15 Union Sq.
New York, NY 10003
Ph: (212)242-0700 Fax: (212)255-7230
Anne Rivera

Bimonthly. Tabloid magazine for union members. Contains news of union activities and reports on organizing, collective bargaining, union policy, and legislative positions.

★6305★ *NAHM Directory of Hosiery Manufacturers*
National Association of Hosiery Manufacturers (NAHM)
200 N. Sharon Amity Rd.
Charlotte, NC 28211
Ph: (704)365-0913 Fax: (704)362-2056

Periodic.

★6306★ *NAHM Directory of Hosiery Mill Suppliers*
National Association of Hosiery Manufacturers (NAHM)
200 N. Sharon Amity Rd.
Charlotte, NC 28211
Ph: (704)365-0913 Fax: (704)362-2056

Periodic.

★6307★ *The Needle's Eye*
Union Special Corp.
1 Union Special Plaza
Huntley, IL 60142
Ph: (708)669-4334 Fax: (708)669-3534
Sharon McNelis

Bimonthly. Sewing industry magazine.

★6308★ *Personnel Policy Survey*
American Apparel Manufacturers Association (AAMA)
2500 Wilson Blvd., Ste. 301
Arlington, VA 22201
Ph: (703)524-1864 Fax: (703)522-6741

Biennial.

★6309★ *Technical Advisory Committee Bulletin*
American Apparel Manufacturers Association (AAMA)
2500 Wilson Blvd., Ste. 301
Arlington, VA 22201
Ph: (703)524-1864 Fax: (703)522-6741

Periodic.

★6310★ *Technical Advisory Committee Research Paper*
American Apparel Manufacturers Association (AAMA)
2500 Wilson Blvd., Ste. 301
Arlington, VA 22201
Ph: (703)524-1864 Fax: (703)522-6741

Annual.

★6311★ *Washington Letter*
American Apparel Manufacturers Association (AAMA)
2500 Wilson Blvd., Ste. 301
Arlington, VA 22201
Ph: (703)524-1864 Fax: (703)522-6741

Other Sources of Information

★6312★ *AAMA Technical Advisory Committee Research Paper*
American Apparel Manufacturers Association (AAMA)
2500 Wilson Blvd., Ste. 301
Arlington, VA 22201
Ph: (703)524-1864 Fax: (703)522-6741

Annual.

★6313★ *Annual Hosiery Statistics*
National Association of Hosiery Manufacturers (NAHM)
200 N. Sharon Amity Rd.
Charlotte, NC 28211
Ph: (704)365-0913 Fax: (704)362-2056

Annual. Includes information on inventories, per capita consumption, imports/exports, and number of hosiery companies, plants, and employees in the industry.

★6314★ *Apparel Plant Wages Survey*
American Apparel Manufacturers Association (AAMA)
2500 Wilson Blvd., Ste. 301
Arlington, VA 22201
Ph: (703)524-1864 Fax: (703)522-6741

Annual.

Shoe and Leather Workers and Repairers

Shoe and leather workers create stylish and durable leather products; **shoe and leather repairers** keep them in good condition. Among the workers who do leather work and repair are custom luggage makers and orthopedic shoemakers, saddlemakers, and harnessmakers. Self-employed shoe repairers and owners of custom-made shoe and leather shops have managerial responsibilities in addition to their regular duties. They hold over 30 percent of all shoe and leather work and repair jobs. The rest are employed in the manufacture of leather goods. Other areas of employment include large shops operated by shoe stores, department stores, and dry-cleaning establishments.

Salaries

Beginning workers often start near minimum wage.

Employment Outlook

Growth rate until the year 2005: Decline.

Shoe and Leather Workers and Repairers

Career Guides

★6315★ *Career Information in Shoe Repair*
Shoe Service Industry Council
154 W. Hubbard St.
Chicago, IL 60610
Ph: (312)670-3732

This eight-panel brochure describes skills required, job duties, working conditions, places of employment, and earnings. Illustrates the costs of owning a shoe repair business. Includes a state-by-state list of shoe repair schools.

★6316★ "Leather and Shoe Industries" in *Career Information Center* (Vol.9)
Simon and Schuster
200 Old Tappan Rd.
Old Tappan, NJ 07675
Fax: 800-445-6991 Fr: 800-223-2348

Richard Lidz and Dale Anderson, editorial directors. Fifth edition, 1993. For 600 occupations, describes job duties, entry-level requirements, education and training needed, advancement possibilities, employment outlook, earnings and benefits. The set is divided into 12 volumes. Each volume includes jobs related under a broad career field. Volume 13 is the index.

★6317★ "Leatherworking" in *Opportunities in Crafts Careers* (p. 65-78)
National Textbook Co. (NTC)
VGM Career Books
4255 W. Touhy Ave.
Lincolnwood, IL 60646-1975
Ph: (708)679-5500 Fax: (708)679-2494
Fr: 800-323-4900

Marianne F. Munday. 1994. Covers crafts such as woodworking, ceramics, and leatherworking, and crafts-related careers such as writing and teaching. Offers advice on planning a career in crafts, starting a crafts business, and selling crafts.

★6318★ *Pedorthics: Providing Footwear and Related Services to Aid in the Care of the Foot*
Prescription Footwear Association
The Board for Certification in Pedorthics
9861 Broken Land Parkway, Ste. 255
Columbia, MD 21046-1151
Ph: (410)381-7278

1991. This 12-page booklet describes the work of a pedorthist. Covers areas of specialization and certification.

★6319★ "Saddlemaker" in *Offbeat Careers: The Directory of Unusual Work*
Ten Speed Press
PO Box 7123
Berkeley, CA 94707
Fax: (510)559-1629 Fr: 800-841-2665

Al Sacharov. 1991. Profiles eighty-eight unusual careers. Provides job description, history of occupation, salary, and training required. Lists one or more sources of additional information.

★6320★ *Shoe Industry Workers*
Chronicle Guidance Publications, Inc.
66 Aurora St.
PO Box 1190
Moravia, NY 13118-1190
Ph: (315)497-0330 Fax: (315)497-3359
Fr: 800-622-7284

1991. This career brief describes the nature of the work, working conditions, hours and earnings, education and training, licensure, certification, unions, personal qualifications, social and psychological factors, employment outlook, entry methods, advancement, and related occupations.

★6321★ "Shoe Industry Workers" in *Career Discovery Encyclopedia* (Vol.6, pp. 26-27)
J.G. Ferguson Publishing Co.
200 W. Madison St., Ste. 300
Chicago, IL 60606
Ph: (312)580-5480 Fax: (312)580-4948

E. Russell Primm, editor-in-chief. 1993. Contains two-page articles on 504 occupations. Each article describes job duties, earnings, and educational and training requirements.

★6322★ "Shoe Industry Workers" in *Encyclopedia of Careers and Vocational Guidance* (Vol.4, pp. 359-361)
J.G. Ferguson Publishing Co.
200 W. Madison St., Ste. 300
Chicago, IL 60606
Ph: (312)580-5480 Fax: (312)580-4948

William E. Hopke, editor-in-chief. Ninth edition, 1993. Four-volume set that profiles 500 occupations and describes job trends in 74 industries. Includes career description, educational requirements, history of the job, methods of entry, advancement, employment outlook, earnings, working conditions, social and psychological factors, and sources of additional information.

★6323★ "Shoe and Leather Workers and Repairers" in *Encyclopedia of Careers and Vocational Guidance* (Vol.4, pp. 357-358)
J.G. Ferguson Publishing Co.
200 W. Madison St., Ste. 300
Chicago, IL 60606
Ph: (312)580-5480 Fax: (312)580-4948

William E. Hopke, editor-in-chief. Ninth edition, 1993. Four-volume set that profiles 500 occupations and describes job trends in 74 industries. Includes career description, educational requirements, history of the job, methods of entry, advancement, employment outlook, earnings, working conditions, social and psychological factors, and sources of additional information.

★6324★ "Shoe and Leather Workers and Repairers" in *Occupational Outlook Handbook*
U.S. Government Printing Office
Superintendent of Documents
Washington, DC 20402
Ph: (202)512-1800 Fax: (202)512-2250

Biennial; latest edition, 1994-95. Encyclopedia of careers describing more than 250 occupations and comprising about 85 percent of all jobs in the economy. Occupations that require lengthy education or training are given the most attention. For each occupation, the handbook describes job duties, working conditions, training, educational preparation, personal qualities, advancement possibilities, job outlook, earnings, and sources of additional information.

★6325★ "Shoe Maker/Repairer" in *Jobs Rated Almanac*
World Almanac
1 International Blvd., Ste. 444
Mahwah, NJ 07495
Ph: (201)529-6900 Fax: (201)529-6901

Les Krantz. Second edition, 1992. Ranks 250 jobs by environment, salary, outlooks, physical demands, stress, security, travel opportunities, and extra perks. Includes jobs the editor feels are the most common, most interesting, and the most rapidly growing.

★6326★ *Shoe Repairer*
Vocational Biographies, Inc.
PO Box 31
Sauk Centre, MN 56378-0031
Ph: (612)352-6516 Fax: (612)352-5546
Fr: 800-255-0752

1990. Four-page pamphlet containing a personal narrative about a worker's job, work likes and dislikes, career path from high school to the present. Education and training, the rewards and frustrations, and the effects of the job on the rest of the worker's life. The data file portion of this pamphlet gives a concise occupational summary, including work descriptions, working conditions, places of employment, personal characteristics, education and training, job outlook, and salary range.

★6327★ *Shoe Repairer*
Careers, Inc.
PO Box 135
Largo, FL 34649-0135
Ph: (813)584-7333

1993. Two-page occupational summary card describing duties, working conditions, personal qualifications, training, earnings and hours, employment outlook, places of employment, related careers and where to write for more information.

★6328★ "Shoe Repairer" in *Career Information Center* (Vol.5)
Simon and Schuster
200 Old Tappan Rd.
Old Tappan, NJ 07675
Fax: 800-445-6991 Fr: 800-223-2348

Richard Lidz and Dale Anderson, editorial directors. Fifth edition, 1993. For 600 occupations, describes job duties, entry-level requirements, education and training needed, advancement possibilities, employment outlook, earnings and benefits. The set is divided into 12 volumes. Each volume includes jobs related under a broad career field. Volume 13 is the index.

★6329★ "Shoe Repairer" in *Occu-Facts: Information on 580 Careers in Outline Form*
Careers, Inc.
PO Box 135
Largo, FL 34649-0135
Ph: (813)584-7333

Biennial, 1995-96 edition. Each one-page occupational profile describes duties, working conditions, physical surroundings and demands, aptitudes, temperament, educational requirements, employment outlook, earnings, and places of employment.

★6330★ "Shoe Repairer" in *Personal Services* (pp. 63-67)
Franklin Watts, Inc.
387 Park Avenue, S.
New York, NY 10016
Ph: (212)686-7070

Linda Barrett and Galen Guengerich. 1991. Surveys personal services jobs. Describes job duties, educational preparation, salaries, and employment outlook. Offers job hunting advice.

★6331★ *Shoe Repairers*
Chronicle Guidance Publications, Inc.
66 Aurora St.
PO Box 1190
Moravia, NY 13118-1190
Ph: (315)497-0330 Fax: (315)497-3359
Fr: 800-622-7284

1992. This career brief describes the nature of the work, working conditions, hours and earnings, education and training, licensure, certification, unions, personal qualifications, social and psychological factors, employment outlook, entry methods, advancement, and related occupations.

★6332★ "Shoe Repairers" in *American Almanac of Jobs and Salaries* (pp. 526)
Avon Books
1350 Avenue of the Americas
New York, NY 10019
Ph: (212)261-6800 Fr: 800-238-0658

John Wright, editor. Revised and updated, 1994-95. A comprehensive guide to the wages of hundreds of occupations in a wide variety of industries and organizations.

★6333★ "Shoe Repairers" in *Career Discovery Encyclopedia* (Vol.6, pp. 28-29)
J.G. Ferguson Publishing Co.
200 W. Madison St., Ste. 300
Chicago, IL 60606
Ph: (312)580-5480 Fax: (312)580-4948

E. Russell Primm, editor-in-chief. 1993. Contains two-page articles on 504 occupations. Each article describes job duties, earnings, and educational and training requirements.

Associations

★6334★ Pedorthic Footwear Association (PFA)
9861 Broken Land Pky., Ste. 255
Columbia, MD 21046-1151
Ph: (410)381-7278 Fax: (410)381-1167
Fr: 800-673-8447

Members: Manufacturers and retailers of orthopedic footware; associate members are affiliated branch stores. **Purpose:** Works to enhance and educate retailers in the comfort shoe business to provide for improved customer service. Conducts seminars on orthopedic footwear for adults and children. Provides donations to the Prescription Footwear Research Fund. Operates placement service; conducts research and educational programs; compiles statistics. **Publications:** *Dealing With Diabetes*, annual. • *Pedoscope*, bimonthly. • *PFA Directory*, annual.

Educational Directories and Programs

★6335★ *PFA Directory*
Pedorthic Footwear Association (PFA)
9861 Broken Land Pkwy., Ste. 255
Columbia, MD 21046
Ph: (410)381-7278 Fax: (410)381-1167
Fr: 800-673-8447

Annual.

★6336★ *PFA Directory*
Pedorthic Footwear Association (PFA)
9861 Broken Land Pky., Ste. 255
Columbia, MD 21046-1151
Ph: (410)381-7278 Fax: (410)381-1167
Fr: 800-673-8447

Annual.

Basic Reference Guides and Handbooks

★6337★ *The Complete Handbook of Leathercrafting*
Krieger Publishing Company
PO Box 9542
Melbourne, FL 32902
Ph: (407)724-9542 Fax: (407)951-3671

Jane E. Garnes. 1986.

★6338★ *Easy-to-Do Leathercraft Projects with Full-Size Templates*
Dover Publications, Inc.
31 E. Second St.
Mineola, NY 11501
Ph: (516)294-7000

David Dorne. 1976.

★6339★ *Leather Braiding*
Cornell Maritime Press, Inc.
PO Box 456
Centreville, MD 21617
Ph: (301)758-1075

Bruce Grant. 1950.

★6340★ *Leather Makin': A Manual of Primitive and Modern Leather Skills*
Horizon Publishers & Distributors
PO Box 490
Bountiful, UT 84011-0490
Ph: (801)295-9451

Larry J. Wells. 1985.

★6341★ *Leather Tooling & Carving*
Dover Publications, Inc.
31 E. Second St.
Mineola, NY 11501
Ph: (516)294-7000

Chris H. Groneman. 1974.

★6342★ *Projects in Leather*
International Specialized Book Services
5602 NE Hassalo St.
Portland, OR 97213
Ph: (503)287-3093 Fax: (503)284-8859

Thor Kristinsson. 1985.

Periodicals

★6343★ *American Shoemaking*
PO Box 198
Cambridge, MA 02140
Ph: (617)648-8160 Fax: (617)492-0126
James D. Sutton

Monthly. Magazine reporting on shoe manufacturing.

★6344★ *Dealing With Diabetes*
Pedorthic Footwear Association (PFA)
9861 Broken Land Pky., Ste. 255
Columbia, MD 21046-1151
Ph: (410)381-7278 Fax: (410)381-1167
Fr: 800-673-8447

Annual.

★6345★ *FIA Executive Digest*
Footwear Industries of America, Inc. (FIA)
1420 K St. NW, Ste. 600
Washington, DC 20005
Ph: (202)789-1420
Sarah Olson

Monthly. Publishes Association activities in the areas of footwear technology, finance and management, national affairs, and marketing. Provides current industry statistics.

★6346★ *FN (Footwear News)*
Fairchild Publications
7 W. 34th St.
New York, NY 10001
Ph: (212)630-4880 Fax: (212)630-4879
Mark Sullivan

Weekly. Newspaper covering retailing and merchandising of footwear, accessories, and leather industries.

★6347★ *The Leather Manufacturer*
PO Box 198
Cambridge, MA 02140
Ph: (617)648-8160 Fax: (617)492-0126
James Sutton

Monthly. Magazine on tanning and finishing leather.

★6348★ *Pedoscope*
Pedorthic Footwear Association (PFA)
9861 Broken Land Pky., Ste. 255
Columbia, MD 21046-1151
Ph: (410)381-7278 Fax: (410)381-1167
Fr: 800-673-8447

Bimonthly.

★6349★ *Shoe Service*
SSIA Service Corp.
5024 R. Campbell Blvd.
Baltimore, MD 21236
Ph: (410)931-8100 Fax: (410)931-8111
Mitchell Lebovic

Monthly. Magazine for the shoe repair industry.

★6350★ *Show Reporter*
335 Boylston St.
Newton Center, MA 02159
Ph: (617)965-4577 Fax: (617)965-0558
Irving B. Roberts

Footwear and related industries publication.

Textile Machinery Operators

Textile machinery operators tend machines that manufacture textile goods used in all types of consumer and industrial products. There are many phases in the textile production process, and operators' duties and responsibilities depend on the product and the type of machinery in use. Extruding and forming machine operators and tenders maintain the machinery that produces manufactured fiber. Because this fiber is created by a chemical process, the majority of these workers are employed by chemical companies. Textile machine operators and tenders operate the machinery that prepares manufactured or natural fibers for spinning. Textile machine setters and setup operators prepare the machinery prior to a production run and maintain the equipment. Textile bleaching and dyeing machine operators and tenders oversee machines that dye and finish the product either at the textile mill or at a plant specializing in textile finishing. The majority of textile machinery operators are employed in weaving, finishing, yarn, and thread mills. Other significant employers are knitting mills and manufactured fiber producers.

Salaries

The average weekly earnings of production workers in the textile and manufactured fiber industries $353. The average weekly earnings for production workers in the chemical industry is $623.

Employment Outlook

Growth rate until the year 2005: Decline.

Textile Machinery Operators

Career Guides

★6351★ *Fashion & Textile Careers*
Prentice Hall
Rte. 9W
Englewood Cliffs, NJ 07632
Ph: (201)592-2000

Martha S. Servian. 1977. Part of Home Economics Careers Series.

★6352★ *Staple Yarn Production*
North Carolina State University
College of Textiles
Campus Box 8301
2401 Research Dr.
Raleigh, NC 27695-8301
Ph: (919)515-6524 Fax: (919)515-3057

Videocassette. 1987. 18 mins. A detailed look at the art and machinery of staple yarn production.

★6353★ "Textile Industry" in *Career Information Center* (Vol.9)
Simon and Schuster
200 Old Tappan Rd.
Old Tappan, NJ 07675
Fax: 800-445-6991 Fr: 800-223-2348

Richard Lidz and Dale Anderson, editorial directors. Fifth edition, 1993. For 600 occupations, describes job duties, entry-level requirements, education and training needed, advancement possibilities, employment outlook, earnings and benefits. The set is divided into 12 volumes. Each volume includes jobs related under a broad career field. Volume 13 is the index.

★6354★ "Textile Machinery Operators" in *Occupational Outlook Handbook*
U.S. Government Printing Office
Superintendent of Documents
Washington, DC 20402
Ph: (202)512-1800 Fax: (202)512-2250

Biennial; latest edition, 1994-95. Encyclopedia of careers describing more than 250 occupations and comprising about 85 percent of all jobs in the economy. Occupations that require lengthy education or training are given the most attention. For each occupation, the handbook describes job duties, working conditions, training, educational preparation, personal qualities, advancement possibilities, job outlook, earnings, and sources of additional information.

★6355★ "Textile Manufacturing Occupations" in *Encyclopedia of Careers and Vocational Guidance* (Vol.4, pp. 518-520)
J.G. Ferguson Publishing Co.
200 W. Madison St., Ste. 300
Chicago, IL 60606
Ph: (312)580-5480 Fax: (312)580-4948

William E. Hopke, editor-in-chief. Ninth edition, 1993. Four-volume set that profiles 500 occupations and describes job trends in 74 industries. Includes career description, educational requirements, history of the job, methods of entry, advancement, employment outlook, earnings, working conditions, social and psychological factors, and sources of additional information.

★6356★ *Textile Mill Worker*
Vocational Biographies, Inc.
PO Box 31
Sauk Centre, MN 56378-0031
Ph: (612)352-6516 Fax: (612)352-5546
Fr: 800-255-0752

1990. This pamphlet profiles a person working in the job. Includes information about job duties, working conditions, places of employment, educational preparation, labor market outlook, and salaries.

★6357★ *Textile Production Workers*
Chronicle Guidance Publications, Inc.
66 Aurora St.
PO Box 1190
Moravia, NY 13118-1190
Ph: (315)497-0330 Fax: (315)497-3359
Fr: 800-622-7284

1993. This career brief describes the nature of the work, working conditions, hours and earnings, education and training, licensure, certification, unions, personal qualifications, social and psychological factors, employment outlook, entry methods, advancement, and related occupations.

★6358★ "Textile Workers" in *Career Discovery Encyclopedia* (Vol.6, pp. 106-107)
J.G. Ferguson Publishing Co.
200 W. Madison St., Ste. 300
Chicago, IL 60606
Ph: (312)580-5480 Fax: (312)580-4948

E. Russell Primm, editor-in-chief. 1993. Contains two-page articles on 504 occupations. Each article describes job duties, earnings, and educational and training requirements.

★6359★ "Textiles" in *Encyclopedia of Careers and Vocational Guidance* (Vol.1, pp. 456-462)
J.G. Ferguson Publishing Co.
200 W. Madison St., Ste. 300
Chicago, IL 60606
Ph: (312)580-5480 Fax: (312)580-4948

William E. Hopke, editor-in-chief. Ninth edition, 1993. Four-volume set that profiles 500 occupations and describes job trends in 74 industries. Includes career description, educational requirements, history of the job, methods of entry, advancement, employment outlook, earnings, working conditions, social and psychological factors, and sources of additional information.

Associations

★6360★ American Fiber Manufacturers Association (AFMA)
1150 17th St. NW, Ste. 310
Washington, DC 20036
Ph: (202)296-6508 Fax: (202)296-3052

Members: Producers of manufactured fibers used in apparel, household goods, industrial materials, and other types of products. **Purpose:** Represents the industry in educational, governmental, and foreign trade matters. Distributes a video depicting production and end uses of manufactured fibers. **Publications:** *Manufactured Fiber Fact Book.* • *Manufactured Fiber Guide*, periodic.

★6361★ American Textile Manufacturers Institute (ATMI)
1801 K St. NW, Ste. 900
Washington, DC 20006
Ph: (202)862-0500 Fax: (202)862-0570

Members: Textile mill firms operating machinery for manufacturing and processing cotton, man-made, wool, and silk textile products; includes spinning, weaving, bleaching, finishing, knitting, and allied plants; does not include manufacturers of hosiery or firms that produce man-made fibers and yarn by a chemical process. **Purpose:** Operates public relations program for the industry, government relations program, textile market program, and statistical and economic information service. Holds seminars and meetings. Maintains 1200 volume library. Sponsors safety contest among textile mills. **Publications:** *ATMI Member Product Directory*, periodic. • *Official Directory*, annual. • *Textile Hi-Lights*, quarterly. • *Textile Trends*, weekly.

★6362★ National Association of Hosiery Manufacturers (NAHM)
200 N. Sharon Amity Rd.
Charlotte, NC 28211
Ph: (704)365-0913 Fax: (704)362-2056

Members: Hosiery manufacturers and suppliers. **Purpose:** Develops standards for hosiery measurement. Sponsors annual National Hosiery Week to educate consumers on hosiery varieties. Conducts field visitations for assistance in technical areas. Compiles statistics; conducts research programs. Operates Group Purchasing Program. **Publications:** *Annual Hosiery Statistics.* • *Hosiery News*, monthly. • *NAHM Directory of Hosiery Manufacturers*, periodic. • *NAHM Directory of Hosiery Mill Suppliers*, periodic.

Standards/Certification Agencies

★6363★ National Association of Hosiery Manufacturers (NAHM)
200 N. Sharon Amity Rd.
Charlotte, NC 28211
Ph: (704)365-0913 Fax: (704)362-2056

Develops standards for hosiery measurement.

Basic Reference Guides and Handbooks

★6364★ *America's Textiles International—Buyer's Guide Issue*
Billian Publishing Co.
2100 Powers Ferry Rd., Ste. 300
Atlanta, GA 30339
Ph: (404)955-5656 Fax: (404)952-0669
Monte G. Plott, Contact

Annual, July. Publication includes: List of 2,800 suppliers for the textile industry. Entries include: Supplier name, address, phone, telex, fax; separate section lists products for each supplier. Arrangement: Alphabetical.

★6365★ *Manufactured Fiber Guide*
American Fiber Manufacturers Association (AFMA)
1150 17th St. NW, Ste. 310
Washington, DC 20036
Ph: (202)296-6508 Fax: (202)296-3052

Periodic.

Periodicals

★6366★ *American Dyestuff Reporter*
SAF International Publications, Inc.
Harmon Cove Towers
Promenade A, Ste. 2
Secaucus, NJ 07094
Ph: (201)867-9230 Fax: (201)867-0545
Edward Fox

Monthly. Magazine covering textile wet-processing.

★6367★ *ATI America's Textiles International*
Billian Publishing
2100 Powers Ferry Rd. NW, Ste. 300
Atlanta, GA 30339
Ph: (404)955-5656 Fax: (404)952-0669
Monte G. Plott

Monthly. Magazine for the textile industry; including fiber producers, carpet mills, dyeing and finishing plants, and spinning, weaving, and knitting operations.

★6368★ *ATMI Member Product Directory*
American Textile Manufacturers Institute (ATMI)
1801 K St. NW, Ste. 900
Washington, DC 20006
Ph: (202)862-0500 Fax: (202)862-0570

Periodic. Contains information about textile products made in the U.S. by ATMI member companies.

★6369★ *Journal of Coated Fabrics*
TECHNOMIC Publishing Co., Inc.
851 New Holland Ave.
PO Box 3535
Lancaster, PA 17604
Ph: (717)291-5609 Fax: (717)295-4538
Fr: 800-233-9936
William C. Smith

Quarterly. Journal for the coated fabrics and textiles industry.

★6370★ *Knitting Times*
National Knitwear & Sportswear Assn.
386 Park Ave. S.
New York, NY 10016
Ph: (212)683-7520 Fax: (212)532-0766
David Gross

Monthly.

★6371★ *Labor Unity*
Amalgamated Clothing & Textile Workers Union
15 Union Sq.
New York, NY 10003
Ph: (212)242-0700 Fax: (212)255-7230
Anne Rivera

Bimonthly. Tabloid magazine for union members. Contains news of union activities and reports on organizing, collective bargaining, union policy, and legislative positions.

★6372★ *Official Directory*
American Textile Manufacturers Institute (ATMI)
1801 K St. NW, Ste. 900
Washington, DC 20006
Ph: (202)862-0500 Fax: (202)862-0570

Annual.

★6373★ *Textile Chemist and Colorist*
American Assn. of Textile Chemists and Colorists
PO Box 12215
Research Triangle Park, NC 27709
Ph: (919)549-8141 Fax: (919)549-8933
Jack Kissiah

Monthly. Magazine focusing on dyeing, finishing of fibers and fabrics.

★6374★ *Textile Hi-Lights*
American Textile Manufacturers Institute (ATMI)
1801 K St. NW, Ste. 900
Washington, DC 20006
Ph: (202)862-0500 Fax: (202)862-0570

Quarterly. Includes monthly supplements.

★6375★ *Textile Research Journal*
Textile Research Institute
PO Box 625
Princeton, NJ 08542
Ph: (609)924-3150 Fax: (609)683-7836
Richard J. Toner

Monthly. Scientific journal on the textile and allied industries.

★6376★ *Textile Technology Digest*
Institute of Textile Technology
PO Box 391
Charlottesville, VA 22902
Ph: (804)296-5511 Fax: (804)977-5400
Dennis Loy

Monthly. Textile journal.

★6377★ *Textile Trends*
American Textile Manufacturers Institute (ATMI)
1801 K St. NW, Ste. 900
Washington, DC 20006
Ph: (202)862-0500 Fax: (202)862-0570

Weekly.

★6378★ *Textile World*
Maclean Hunter Publishing Co.
4170 Ashford Dunwoody Rd., Ste. 420
Atlanta, GA 30319
Ph: (404)847-2770 Fax: (404)252-6150
McAllister Isaacs

Monthly. Magazine on textiles and man-made fiber products.

Meetings and Conventions

★6379★ American Textile Machinery Exhibition International
Textile Hall Corp.
PO Box 5823
Greenville, SC 29606
Ph: (803)233-2562 Fax: (803)233-0619

Annual. Always held at the Palmetto International Exposition Center in Greenville, South Carolina. **Dates and Locations:** 1996 Oct 07-11; Greenville, SC. • 1997 Apr 07-11; Greenville, SC.

Other Sources of Information

★6380★ *Annual Hosiery Statistics*
National Association of Hosiery Manufacturers (NAHM)
200 N. Sharon Amity Rd.
Charlotte, NC 28211
Ph: (704)365-0913 Fax: (704)362-2056

Annual. Includes information on inventories, per capita consumption, imports/exports, and number of hosiery companies, plants, and employees in the industry.

★6381★ *Manufactured Fiber Fact Book*
American Fiber Manufacturers Association (AFMA)
1150 17th St. NW, Ste. 310
Washington, DC 20036
Ph: (202)296-6508 Fax: (202)295-3052

★6382★ "Textile Worker" in *Encyclopedia of Danger: Dangerous Professions* (pp. 98-101)
Chelsea House Publishers
1974 Sproul Rd., Ste. 400
Broomall, PA 19008
Ph: (215)353-5166 Fax: (215)359-1439

Missy Allen and Michel Peissel. 1993. Provides descriptions of 24 dangerous occupations, their risky characteristics, and safety precautions.

Upholsterers

Upholsterers are skilled craft workers who make new furniture and recondition old furniture. Some repair and replace automobile upholstery and convertible and vinyl tops. Most work in upholstery shops. About 1 out of 3 are self-employed. Companies that manufacture household and office furniture employ about 61% and shops that reupholster and repair furniture employ another 17%. Another 10% specialize in reupholstering the seats of automobiles and other motor vehicles.

Salaries

Average weekly earnings for upholsterers are as follows:

Lowest 10 percent	$200/week or less
Middle 50 percent	$260-$470/week
Top 10 percent	$670/week or more

Employment Outlook

Growth rate until the year 2005: More slowly than average.

Upholsterers

Career Guides

★6383★ "Custom Upholsterer" in *Career Information Center* (Vol.5)
Simon and Schuster
200 Old Tappan Rd.
Old Tappan, NJ 07675
Fax: 800-445-6991 Fr: 800-223-2348

Richard Lidz and Dale Anderson, editorial directors. Fifth edition, 1993. For 600 occupations, describes job duties, entry-level requirements, education and training needed, advancement possibilities, employment outlook, earnings and benefits. The set is divided into 12 volumes. Each volume includes jobs related under a broad career field. Volume 13 is the index.

★6384★ *Furniture: An Opportunity Career*
American Furniture Manufacturers
PO Box HP-7
High Point, NC 27261

This eight-page booklet briefly describes career opportunities in the furniture manufacturing industry.

★6385★ *Furniture Upholsterer*
Vocational Biographies, Inc.
PO Box 31
Sauk Centre, MN 56378-0031
Ph: (612)352-6516 Fax: (612)352-5546
Fr: 800-255-0752

1988. This pamphlet profiles a person working in the job. Includes information about job duties, working conditions, places of employment, educational preparation, labor market outlook, and salaries.

★6386★ "Furniture Upholsterer" in *Jobs Rated Almanac*
World Almanac
1 International Blvd., Ste. 444
Mahwah, NJ 07495
Ph: (201)529-6900 Fax: (201)529-6901

Les Krantz. Second edition, 1992. Ranks 250 jobs by environment, salary, outlooks, physical demands, stress, security, travel opportunities, and extra perks. Includes jobs the editor feels are the most common, most interesting, and the most rapidly growing.

★6387★ "Furniture Upholsterer" in *Occu-Facts: Information on 580 Careers in Outline Form*
Careers, Inc.
PO Box 135
Largo, FL 34649-0135
Ph: (813)584-7333

Biennial, 1995-96 edition. Each one-page occupational profile describes duties, working conditions, physical surroundings and demands, aptitudes, temperament, educational requirements, employment outlook, earnings, and places of employment.

★6388★ "Furniture Upholsterer and Tailor or Dressmaker" in *Personal Services* (pp. 39-43)
Franklin Watts, Inc.
387 Park Avenue, S.
New York, NY 10016
Ph: (212)686-7070

Linda Barrett and Galen Guengerich. 1991. Surveys personal services jobs. Describes job duties, educational preparation, salaries, and employment outlook. Offers job hunting advice.

★6389★ "Furniture Upholsterers" in *Encyclopedia of Careers and Vocational Guidance*
J.G. Ferguson Publishing Co.
200 W. Madison St., Ste. 300
Chicago, IL 60606
Ph: (312)580-5480 Fax: (312)580-4948

William E. Hopke, editor-in-chief. Ninth edition, 1993. Four-volume set that profiles 500 occupations and describes job trends in 74 industries. Includes career description, educational requirements, history of the job, methods of entry, advancement, employment outlook, earnings, working conditions, social and psychological factors, and sources of additional information.

★6390★ "Industrial Upholsterer" in *Career Information Center* (Vol.9)
Simon and Schuster
200 Old Tappan Rd.
Old Tappan, NJ 07675
Fax: 800-445-6991 Fr: 800-223-2348

Richard Lidz and Dale Anderson, editorial directors. Fifth edition, 1993. For 600 occupations, describes job duties, entry-level requirements, education and training needed, advancement possibilities, employment outlook, earnings and benefits. The set is divided into 12 volumes. Each volume includes jobs related under a broad career field. Volume 13 is the index.

★6391★ *Upholsterer, Furniture*
Careers, Inc.
PO Box 135
Largo, FL 34649-0135
Ph: (813)584-7333

1995. Two-page occupational summary card describing duties, working conditions, personal qualifications, training, earnings and hours, employment outlook, places of employment, related careers and where to write for more information.

★6392★ *Upholsterers (Furniture)*
Chronicle Guidance Publications, Inc.
66 Aurora St.
PO Box 1190
Moravia, NY 13118-1190
Ph: (315)497-0330 Fax: (315)497-3359
Fr: 800-622-7284

1993. This career brief describes the nature of the work, working conditions, hours and earnings, education and training, licensure, certification, unions, personal qualifications, social and psychological factors, employment outlook, entry methods, advancement, and related occupations.

★6393★ "Upholsterers" in *Occupational Outlook Handbook*
U.S. Government Printing Office
Superintendent of Documents
Washington, DC 20402
Ph: (202)512-1800 Fax: (202)512-2250

Biennial; latest edition, 1994-95. Encyclopedia of careers describing more than 250 occupations and comprising about 85 percent of all jobs in the economy. Occupations that require lengthy education or training are given the most attention. For each occupation, the handbook describes job duties, working conditions, training, educational preparation, personal qualities, advancement possibilities, job outlook, earnings, and sources of additional information.

★6394★ *Video Career Library - Production I*
Careers, Inc.
PO Box 135
Largo, FL 34649-0135
Ph: (813)584-7333

Videocassette. 1990. 28 mins. Part of the Video Career Library covering 165 occupations. Shows actual workers on the job. Includes layout workers, precision typesetters, lithographers/photoengravers, bookbinders, hand tailors/dressmakers, upholsterers, water/sewage plant operators, chemical plant operators, and power plant operators.

Associations

★6395★ Autoleather Guild (AG)
776 Waddington Rd.
Birmingham, MI 48009
Ph: (810)646-5250 Fax: (810)646-6721

Members: Promotes the use of genuine leather seating in the automotive industry. Conducts dealer seminars.

★6396★ International Institute of Carpet and Upholstery Certification (IICUC)
2715 E. Mill Plain Blvd.
Vancouver, WA 98661
Ph: (206)693-5675 Fax: (206)693-4858

Members: Fabric restoration firms and technicians. **Purpose:** Sets standards of skill and ethics in the fabric restoration industry; works with regulatory bodies to establish proficiency standards. Certifies technicians, firms, and inspectors. **Publications:** *International Directory of Certified Professionals*, annual.

★6397★ National Association of Furniture Repair and Refinishing Specialists
321 S. Houghton
Milford, MI 48381
Ph: (810)684-0319 Fax: (810)684-0224
Fr: 800-274-9918

Promotes the productivity, profitability, and professionalism of its members. Provides discounts on professional courses, supplies, and fees for trade shows and seminars. Developing professional certification program.

★6398★ Upholstered Furniture Action Council (UFAC)
PO Box 2436
High Point, NC 27261
Ph: (919)885-5065 Fax: (919)884-5303

Members: National furniture manufacturers' and retailers' associations. **Purpose:** Conducts research and disseminates information regarding the development and adoption of voluntary guidelines for production of more cigarette-resistant upholstered furniture; educates the public in the safe use of smoking materials. Maintains speakers' bureau; compiles statistics. **Publications:** *UFAC: Action Guide*, annual. • *Upholstered Furniture Action Council—Directory of Materials Suppliers*, biennial.

Standards/Certification Agencies

★6399★ International Institute of Carpet and Upholstery Certification (IICUC)
2715 E. Mill Plain Blvd.
Vancouver, WA 98661
Ph: (206)693-5675 Fax: (206)693-4858

Sets standards of skill and ethics in the fabric restoration industry; works with regulatory bodies to establish proficiency standards. Certifies technicians, firms, and inspectors.

★6400★ National Association of Furniture Repair and Refinishing Specialists
321 S. Houghton
Milford, MI 48381
Ph: (810)684-0319 Fax: (810)684-0224
Fr: 800-274-9918

Promotes the productivity, profitability, and professionalism of its members. Provides discounts on professional courses, supplies, and fees for trade shows and seminars. Developing professional certification program.

Basic Reference Guides and Handbooks

★6401★ *A Concise Guide to Upholstery Fabrics*
State Mutual Book & Periodical Service, Ltd.
521 5th Ave. 17th Fl.
New York, NY 10175
Ph: (212)682-5844

1985.

★6402★ *Flammability Regulations & Standards in the United States for Upholstered Furniture*
Technomic Publishing Company
851 Holland Ave.
PO Box 3535
Lancaster, PA 17604-3535
Ph: (717)291-5609 Fax: (717)295-4538

Sharon Sue Williams. 1985.

★6403★ *Industrial Fabrics in Upholstery*
Industrial Fabrics Association International
345 Cedar St.
St. Paul, MN 55101
Ph: (612)222-2508

1981.

★6404★ *Machine Developments in Upholstery Sewing*
State Mutual Book & Periodical Service, Ltd.
521 5th Ave., 17th Fl.
New York, NY 10175
Ph: (212)682-5844

1985.

★6405★ *Professional Upholster Cleaning Techniques: The Basics*
Cleaning Consultant Services, Inc.
1512 Western Ave.
Seattle, WA 98101
Ph: (206)284-9954

Roy Moore. Revised edition, 1987.

★6406★ *Re-Upholstery Techniques*
Little, Brown & Co., Inc.
34 Beacon St.
Boston, MA 02108
Ph: (617)227-0730 Fax: (617)723-9422

Derek Balfour. 1986.

★6407★ *Upholsterers' Supplies Directory*
American Business Directories, Inc.
5711 S. 86th Circle
Omaha, NE 68127
Ph: (402)593-4600 Fax: (402)331-1505

Updated continuously; printed on request. Entries include: Name, address, phone, size of advertisement, name of owner or manager, number of employees, year first in "Yellow Pages." Compiled from telephone company "Yellow Pages," nationwide. Arrangement: Geographical.

★6408★ *Upholstering*
Macmillan Publishing Company, Inc.
866 3rd Ave.
New York, NY 10022
Ph: (212)702-2000

James E. Brumbaugh. Second edition, 1984.

★6409★ *Upholstering Methods*
Goodheart-Willcox Company
123 Taft Dr.
South Holland, IL 60473
Ph: (708)333-7200 Fax: (708)331-9130

Fred W. Zimmerman. 1992.

★6410★ *Upholstery*
Sterling Publishing Company, Inc.
387 Park Ave. S.
New York, NY 10016-8810
Ph: (212)532-7160 Fax: (212)213-2495
Fr: 800-367-9692

Dorothy Gates. 1990. Part of Living Style Series.

★6411★ *Upholstery Styles: A Design Sourcebook*
Van Nostrand Reinhold
115 5th Ave.
New York, NY 10003
Ph: (212)254-3232 Fax: (212)254-9499

Gillian Walking. 1989.

★6412★ *Upholstery Techniques Illustrated*
TAB/McGraw-Hill, Inc.
PO Box 182607
Columbus, OH 43218-2607
Fax: (614)759-3644 Fr: 800-822-8158

Lloyd W. Gheen. 1986.

Periodicals

★6413★ *UFAC: Action Guide*
Upholstered Furniture Action Council (UFAC)
PO Box 2436
High Point, NC 27261
Ph: (919)885-5065 Fax: (919)884-5303

Annual. Guide to UFAC's voluntary program to promote cigarette-resistant upholstered furniture. Includes construction criteria, compliance, and history.

★6414★ *Upholstered Furniture Action Council—Directory of Materials Suppliers*
Upholstered Furniture Action Council (UFAC)
PO Box 2436
High Point, NC 27261
Ph: (919)885-5065 Fax: (919)884-5303

Biennial. Suppliers who certify that certain of their materials conform to UFAC test criteria for cigarette resistance.

★6415★ *Upholstery Manufacturing Management*
Stormy Fitzgerald

Monthly. Upholstery trade magazine.

Other Sources of Information

★6416★ *The Upholstery Fact Book 1986*
State Mutal Book & Periodical Service, Ltd.
521 5th Ave., 17th Fl.
New York, NY 10175
Ph: (212)682-5844

1986.

Woodworking Occupations

Woodworkers take raw wood and cut and assemble it to make wooden items. Production woodworkers are found in primary industries such as sawmills and plywood mills, as well as in secondary manufactures such as furniture, kitchen cabinets, musical instruments, and other fabricated wood products. Precision woodworkers, such as cabinetmakers, wood pattern and model makers, wood machinists, and furniture and wood finishers, are found in small shops making architectural woodwork, furniture, and many other specialty firms. They often work on a customized basis, often building one-of-a-kind items. Less skilled workers set up, operate, or tend production equipment or machinery. Wood machine operators in sawmills cut logs into planks, timbers, or boards. In planing mills, they cut veneer sheets from logs for making plywood. And in furniture plants, they make furniture components such as table legs, drawers, rails, and spindles.

Salaries

Median weekly earnings for precision woodworkers and woodworking machine operators are as follows:

Precision woodworkers	$385.00/week
Woodworking machine operators	$306.00/week

Employment Outlook

Growth rate until the year 2005: More slowly than average.

Woodworking Occupations

Career Guides

★6417★ *Cabinetmaker*
Careers, Inc.
PO Box 135
Largo, FL 34649-0135
Ph: (813)584-7333

1993. Two-page occupational summary card describing duties, working conditions, personal qualifications, training, earnings and hours, employment outlook, places of employment, related careers and where to write for more information.

★6418★ "Cabinetmaker" in *Occu-Facts: Information on 580 Careers in Outline Form*
Careers, Inc.
PO Box 135
Largo, FL 34649-0135
Ph: (813)584-7333

Biennial, 1995-96 edition. Each one-page occupational profile describes duties, working conditions, physical surroundings and demands, aptitudes, temperament, educational requirements, employment outlook, earnings, and places of employment.

★6419★ "Cabinetmaker" in *Opportunities in Carpentry Careers* (p. 51)
National Textbook Co. (NTC)
VGM Career Books
4255 W. Touhy Ave.
Lincolnwood, IL 60646-1975
Ph: (708)679-5500 Fax: (708)679-2494
Fr: 800-323-4900

Roger Sheldon. 1987. Covers the history of the crafts, a typical carpenter's workday, future opportunities for carpenters, qualifications, training, apprenticeships, and special advice for women and minorities. Surveys various training opportunities.

★6420★ "Cabinetmaker" in *Opportunities in Crafts Careers* (pp. 30-31)
National Textbook Co. (NTC)
VGM Career Books
4255 W. Touhy Ave.
Lincolnwood, IL 60646-1975
Ph: (708)679-5500 Fax: (708)679-2494
Fr: 800-323-4900

Marianne F. Munday. 1988. Covers crafts such as woodworking, ceramics, and leatherworking, and crafts-related careers such as writing and teaching. Offers advice on planning a career in crafts, starting a crafts business, and selling crafts.

★6421★ "Cabinetmaking" in *Career Connection II: A Guide to Technical Majors and Their Related Careers* (pp. 36-37)
Jist Works, Inc.
720 N. Park Ave.
Indianapolis, IN 46202-3431
Ph: (317)264-3720 Fax: (317)264-3709

Fred A. Rowe. 1994. Contains technical majors, such as automotive technology. Describes the major and the job. Lists high school and postsecondary school courses. Includes occupations related to the major, employment outlook, and starting salary.

★6422★ *Careers for Crafty People & Other Dextrous Types*
National Textbook Co. (NTC)
VGM Career Books
4255 W. Toughy Ave.
Lincolnwood, IL 60646-1975
Ph: (708)679-5500 Fax: (708)679-2494
Fr: 800-323-4900

Mark Rowh. Provides information for careers for crafts people.

★6423★ "Carver" in *Great Careers for People Who Like to Work with Their Hands* (pp. 10-15)
Gale Research Inc.
835 Penobscot Bldg.
Detroit, MI 48226
Ph: (313)961-2242 Fr: 800-347-4253

1994.

★6424★ *Furniture: An Opportunity Career*
American Furniture Manufacturers
PO Box HP-7
High Point, NC 27261

This eight-page booklet briefly describes career opportunities in the furniture manufacturing industry.

★6425★ *Furniture Finisher*
Careers, Inc.
PO Box 135
Largo, FL 34649-0135
Ph: (813)584-7333

1994. Two-page occupational summary card describing duties, working conditions, personal qualifications, training, earnings and hours, employment outlook, places of employment, related careers and where to write for more information.

★6426★ "Furniture Finisher" in *Occu-Facts: Information on 580 Careers in Outline Form*
Careers, Inc.
PO Box 135
Largo, FL 34649-0135
Ph: (813)584-7333

Biennial, 1995-96 edition. Each one-page occupational profile describes duties, working conditions, physical surroundings and demands, aptitudes, temperament, educational requirements, employment outlook, earnings, and places of employment.

★6427★ "Furniture Industry" in *Career Information Center* (Vol.9)
Simon and Schuster
200 Old Tappan Rd.
Old Tappan, NJ 07675
Fax: 800-445-6991 Fr: 800-223-2348

Richard Lidz and Dale Anderson, editorial directors. Fifth edition, 1993. For 600 occupations, describes job duties, entry-level requirements, education and training needed, advancement possibilities, employment outlook, earnings and benefits. The set is divided into 12 volumes. Each volume includes jobs related under a broad career field. Volume 13 is the index.

★6428★ *Furniture Manufacturing*
L & K International Video Training
295 Evans Ave.
PO Box 940, Sta. U
Toronto, ON, Canada M8Z 5P9
Ph: (416)252-6407 Fax: (416)252-8331
Fr: 800-668-6064

Videocassette. 1984. 45 mins. This program is designed for wood-working machine operators in the furniture manufacturing industry.

★6429★ "Furniture Manufacturing Occupations" in *Encyclopedia of Careers and Vocational Guidance* (Vol.3, pp. 53-56)
J.G. Ferguson Publishing Co.
200 W. Madison St., Ste. 300
Chicago, IL 60606
Ph: (312)580-5480 Fax: (312)580-4948

William E. Hopke, editor-in-chief. Ninth edition, 1993. Four-volume set that profiles 500 occupations and describes job trends in 74 industries. Includes career description, educational requirements, history of the job, methods of entry, advancement, employment outlook, earnings, working conditions, social and psychological factors, and sources of additional information.

★6430★ "Furniture Manufacturing Workers" in *Career Discovery Encyclopedia* (Vol.3, pp. 50-51)
J.G. Ferguson Publishing Co.
200 W. Madison St., Ste. 300
Chicago, IL 60606
Ph: (312)580-5480 Fax: (312)580-4948

E. Russell Primm, editor-in-chief. 1993. Contains two-page articles on 504 occupations. Each article describes job duties, earnings, and educational and training requirements.

★6431★ "Sawmill Workers" in *Career Discovery Encyclopedia* (Vol.5, pp. 168-169)
J.G. Ferguson Publishing Co.
200 W. Madison St., Ste. 300
Chicago, IL 60606
Ph: (312)580-5480 Fax: (312)580-4948

E. Russell Primm, editor-in-chief. 1993. Contains two-page articles on 504 occupations. Each article describes job duties, earnings, and educational and training requirements.

★6432★ *Video Career Library - Production II*
Careers, Inc.
PO Box 135
Largo, FL 34649-0135
Ph: (813)584-7333

Videocassette. 1990. 32 mins. Part of the Video Career Library covering 165 occupations. Shows actual workers on the job. Includes tool and die makers, machinists, sheet metal workers, cabinet and bench carpenters, opticians, precision electronic equipment assemblers, industrial machine operators, welders and cutters, and assemblers.

★6433★ "Wood Patternmaker" in *Occu-Facts: Information on 580 Careers in Outline Form*
Careers, Inc.
PO Box 135
Largo, FL 34649-0135
Ph: (813)584-7333

Biennial, 1995-96 edition. Each one-page occupational profile describes duties, working conditions, physical surroundings and demands, aptitudes, temperament, educational requirements, employment outlook, earnings, and places of employment.

★6434★ *Woodcarver*
Vocational Biographies, Inc.
PO Box 31
Sauk Centre, MN 56378-0031
Ph: (612)352-6516 Fax: (612)352-5546
Fr: 800-255-0752

1992. Four-page pamphlet containing a personal narrative about a worker's job, work likes and dislikes, career path from high school to the present. Education and training, the rewards and frustrations, and the effects of the job on the rest of the worker's life. The data file portion of this pamphlet gives a concise occupational summary, including work descriptions, working conditions, places of employment, personal characteristics, education and training, job outlook, and salary range.

★6435★ *Woodworking Machine Operator*
Careers, Inc.
PO Box 135
Largo, FL 34649-0135
Ph: (813)584-7333

1993. Two-page occupational summary card describing duties, working conditions, personal qualifications, training, earnings and hours, employment outlook, places of employment, related careers and where to write for more information.

★6436★ "Woodworking Machine Operator" in *Occu-Facts: Information on 580 Careers in Outline Form*
Careers, Inc.
PO Box 135
Largo, FL 34649-0135
Ph: (813)584-7333

Biennial, 1995-96 edition. Each one-page occupational profile describes duties, working conditions, physical surroundings and demands, aptitudes, temperament, educational requirements, employment outlook, earnings, and places of employment.

★6437★ "Woodworking Occupations" in *Occupational Outlook Handbook*
U.S. Government Printing Office
Superintendent of Documents
Washington, DC 20402
Ph: (202)512-1800 Fax: (202)512-2250

Biennial; latest edition, 1994-95. Encyclopedia of careers describing more than 250 occupations and comprising about 85 percent of all jobs in the economy. Occupations that require lengthy education or training are given the most attention. For each occupation, the handbook describes job duties, working conditions, training, educational preparation, personal qualities, advancement possibilities, job outlook, earnings, and sources of additional information.

Associations

★6438★ American Furniture Manufacturers Association (AFMA)
PO Box HP-7
High Point, NC 27261
Ph: (919)884-5000 Fax: (910)884-5303

Members: Furniture manufacturers seeking to provide a unified voice for the furniture industry and to aid in the development of industry personnel. **Purpose:** Provides: market research data; industrial relations services; costs and operating statistics; transportation information; general management and information services. Compiles statistics; develops quarterly Econometric Forecast.

★6439★ Northeastern Loggers Association (NELA)
PO Box 69
Old Forge, NY 13420
Ph: (315)369-3078 Fax: (315)369-3736

Members: Timberland owners, independent loggers, professional foresters, and primary wood products industries. **Purpose:** Works to improve the industry in the Northeast and educate the public about the policies, practices, and products of the industry. Maintains Forest Industries Exhibit Hall. Cooperates in research by public and private agencies. Operates museum; conducts educational program. **Publications:** *Northern Logger and Timber Processor*, monthly.

Awards, Scholarships, Grants, and Fellowships

★6440★ International Art Competition - New York
Artitudes
PO Box 380
Larchmont, NY 10538

To recognize artists working in all media and styles. Awards are presented in various categories including jewelry. 35mm slides may be submitted by June 23. Awarded annually. Established in 1983.

★6441★ Northeastern Loggers' Association Annual Scholarships
Northeastern Loggers' Association
PO Box 69
Old Forge, NY 13420

Purpose: To promote good writing skills among forestry and wood science students. Qualifications: Candidates must be second-year students in two-year forestry and wood science programs or juniors in four-year programs. Entrants must also be attending school in one of the northeastern states in the area roughly bounded by Maine and Maryland on the east and Minnesota and Missouri on the west. Funds available: Two awards of $2,000 each and two awards of $1,000 each are given. Application details: Students must submit a paper on a specific topic along with a resume and academic transcripts. Deadline: January 31.

★6442★ Northeastern Loggers' Association Awards Program
Northeastern Loggers' Association
PO Box 69
Old Forge, NY 13420
Ph: (315)369-3078 Fax: (315)369-3736

To recognize significant achievement in forestry and wood utilization during the year in nine major categories: outstanding logging operator, outstanding sawmill operator, outstanding service to the forest industry, outstanding management of resources, outstanding leadership in industry, outstanding contributions to forest industry education, outstanding use of wood, outstanding contribution to safety, and outstanding industry activist. Persons or organizations need not be members of the Northeastern Loggers' Association. The nominee must reside in or conduct business in the Northeastern or Lake States Region of the United States as delineated by the USFA. The deadline for nominations is January 31. A maximum of one award is given in each category when merited. A plaque and $300 is awarded in each of the categories with the exception of the Safety Award. Presented at the annual Northeastern Loggers' Congress. Established in 1955. The Safety Award is sponsored by Forest Products Agency of Norwich, CT.

★6443★ Washington Craft Schow
Smithsonian Associates Women's Committee
Art and Industries Bldg., Rm. 1278
Smithsonian Institute
Washington, DC 20560
Ph: (202)357-4000

To enable craftsmen to exhibit and sell crafts as fine art. Artisans working in several categories including wood are eligible. One hundred exhibitors are selected on the basis of originality, artistic conception, and quality of workmanship.

Basic Reference Guides and Handbooks

★6444★ *Artistic Woodturning*
Brigham Young University Press
PO Box 7113
University Sta.
Provo, UT 84602
Ph: (801)378-3295

Dale L. Nish. 1980.

★6445★ *The Complete Book of Birdhouse Contruction for Woodworkers*
Dover Publications, Inc.
31 E. Second St.
Mineola, NY 11501
Ph: (516)294-7000

Scott D. Campbell. 1984. Part of Crafts Series.

★6446★ *The Conversion & Seasoning of Wood*
Linden Publishing Co., Inc.
3845 N. Blackstone
Fresno, CA 93726
Ph: (209)227-2901 Fax: (209)227-3520
Fr: 800-345-4447

William Brown. 1989.

★6447★ *Custom Tools for Woodworkers*
Stackpole Books
Cameron and Kelker Sts.
Box 1831
Harrisburg, PA 17105
Ph: (717)234-5041 Fax: (717)234-1359

J. Petrovich. 1990.

★6448★ *General Woodworking*
McGraw-Hill Publishing Company
1221 Avenue of the Americas
New York, NY 10020
Ph: (212)512-2000

Chris H. Groneman. Sixth edition, 1982. Part of Publications in Industrial Education Series.

★6449★ *Technical Woodworking*
McGraw-Hill Publishing Company
1221 Avenue of the Americas
New York, NY 10020
Ph: (212)512-2000

Chris H. Groneman. Second edition, 1975.

★6450★ *Woodworking*
Goodheart-Willcox Company
123 Taft Dr.
South Holland, IL 60473
Ph: (708)333-7200 Fax: (708)331-9130

Willis H. Wagner. Revised edition, 1989. Part of Build-a-Course Series.

Periodicals

★6451★ *American Woodworker*
Rodale Press, Inc.
33 E. Minor St.
Emmaus, PA 18098
Ph: (610)967-8650 Fax: (610)967-8181
David Sloan

Bimonthly. Magazine devoted to helping woodworkers improve their skills.

★6452★ *Bits 'n Chips*
Woodworking Machinery Distributors' Association
Adams Bldg., No. 109
251 W. DeKalb Pike
King of Prussia, PA 19406
Ph: (215)265-6658 Fax: (215)265-3419
R. Franklin Brown

Monthly. Provides news of the woodworking machinery distribution industry. Contains items on pertinent governmental and legislative actions, Association activities, and business trends. Recurring features include news of members.

★6453★ *Chip Chats*
National Wood Carvers Assn.
7424 Miami Ave.
PO Box 43218
Cincinnati, OH 45243
Ph: (513)561-0627
Edward F. Gallenstein

Bimonthly. Journal for amateur and professional wood carvers.

★6454★ *Crow's Weekly Letter*
C.C. Crow Publications, Inc.
PO Box 25749
Portland, OR 97225
Ph: (503)646-8075
Sam Sherrill

Weekly. Serves as a market report on lumber, plywood, and panel wood products, supplying news, analysis, and price information as a guide to sales. Carries market data on the transportation industry as it pertains to the shipment of forest products. Recurring features include housing market updates and news of industry events and personnel.

★6455★ *CWB: Custom Woodworking Business*
Vance Publishing Corp.
400 Knightsbridge Pkwy.
Lincolnshire, IL 60069
Ph: (708)634-2600 Fax: (708)634-4379
Helen Kuhl

Bimonthly. Magazine for custom woodworkers.

★6456★ *Decorative Wood Crafts*
Meredith Publishing
100 Park Ave.
New York, NY 10017
Ph: (212)953-7070 Fax: (212)351-3650

Magazine for women who enjoy making wood crafts.

★6457★ *Modern Woodworking*
Target Marketing Magazine Group
167 Hwy. 72 E.
PO Box 640
Collierville, TN 38017
Ph: (901)853-7470 Fax: (901)853-6437
Joyce Powell

Monthly. Magazine for management in the primary and secondary wood products industry.

★6458★ *Super Scrollsaw Patterns*
Meredith Publishing
100 Park Ave.
New York, NY 10017
Ph: (212)953-7070 Fax: (212)351-3650

Magazine for woodworkers who use a scroll saw.

★6459★ *Wood*
Meredith Publishing
100 Park Ave.
New York, NY 10017
Ph: (212)953-7070 Fax: (212)351-3650

Magazine for people who enjoy woodworking.

★6460★ *Wood Machining News*
Wood Machining Institute
PO Box 476
Berkeley, CA 94701
Ph: (510)943-5240 Fax: (510)945-0947
Ryszard Szymani

Bimonthly. Provides news and technical information on the latest worldwide developments in the field of wood machining. Covers equipment and technology of saws and sawing, planing and sanding operations, and the production of veneer and chips. Recurring features include items on workers' safety and on patents, book reviews, notices of short courses and seminars, editorials, and a calendar of events.

★6461★ *Wood & Wood Products*
Vance Publishing Corp.
400 Knightsbridge Pkwy.
Lincolnshire, IL 60069
Ph: (708)634-2600 Fax: (708)634-4379
Rich Christianson

Monthly. Magazine for furniture, cabinet, and woodworking industry.

★6462★ *Woodshop News*
Soundings Publications, Inc.
35 Pratt St.
Essex, CT 06426-1185
Ph: (203)767-3200 Fax: (203)767-1048
Ian Bowen

Monthly. Newspaper (tabloid) focusing on people and businesses involved in woodworking.

★6463★ *Woodwork*
Ross Periodicals
42 Digital Dr., No. 5
Novato, CA 94949
Ph: (415)382-0580 Fax: (415)382-0587
John McDonald

Bimonthly. High quality covering all aspects of woodworking

★6464★ *The Woodworker's Journal*
517 Litchfield Rd.
PO Box 1629
New Milford, CT 06776
Ph: (203)355-2694 Fax: (203)350-2165
Thomas G. Begnal

Bimonthly. Magazine providing project plans for hobbyist woodworkers; including the basics, special techniques, and shop and finishing tips.

Meetings and Conventions

★6465★ Architectural Woodwork Institute Annual Trade Show and Convention
Architectural Woodwork Institute
13924 Braddock Rd.
Centreville, VA 22020
Ph: (703)222-1100 Fax: (703)222-2499

Annual.

★6466★ International Woodworking Machinery and Furniture Supply Fair - USA
Reed Exhibition Companies (World Headquarters)
255 Washington St.
Newton, MA 02158-1630
Ph: (617)630-2200 Fax: (617)630-2222

Biennial. Always held during August at the World Congress Center in Atlanta, Georgia. **Dates and Locations:** 1996 Aug 23-26; Atlanta, GA. • 1998 Aug; Atlanta, GA.

★6467★ Northeastern Loggers Congress and Equipment Exposition
Northeastern Loggers Association
PO Box 69
Old Forge, NY 13420
Ph: (315)369-3078 Fax: (315)369-3736

Annual. Rotates between Bangor, Maine; Springfield, Massachusetts; and Syracuse, New York. **Dates and Locations:** 1996 Apr 26-27; Springfield, MA.

★6468★ WOODWORKING - Machinery and Equipment for the Forestry, Timber and Woodworking Industries
Glahe International, Inc.
1700 K St., NW, Ste. 403
Washington, DC 20006-3824
Ph: (202)659-4557 Fax: (202)457-0776

Annual.

Other Sources of Information

★6469★ *Dimension Purchasing Guide*
National Dimension Manufacturers Association (NDMA)
1000 Johnson Ferry Rd., Ste. A-130
Marietta, GA 30068
Ph: (404)565-6660
Steven V. Lawser, Contact

Annual, Summer. Covers over 100 member manufacturers of wood components. Entries include: Co. name, address, phone, fax, name and title of contact, description of products and services. Arrangement: Alphabetical.

★6470★ *Easy Woodworking Projects*
Educational Video Network
1401 19th St.
Huntsville, TX 77340
Ph: (409)295-5767 Fax: (409)294-0233

Offers step-by-step instruction on woodworking projects, including bandsaw boxes, towel racks, and turning bowls.

★6471★ *A Reverence for Wood*
Henry Holt & Company
115 W. 18th St.
New York, NY 10011
Ph: (212)886-9200

Eric Sloane. 1990.

Dental Laboratory Technicians

Dental laboratory technicians are skilled craftworkers that make dentures, bridges, crowns, and other dental prosthetics. Most dental laboratory technicians do not specialize, though some do. Orthodontic technicians make appliances for straightening teeth and treating speech impediments. Removable partial denture technicians make and repair contoured metal frames and retainers for teeth used in removable partial dentures. Most dental laboratory technicians work in commercial dental laboratories. About 12 percent of all technicians work in dentists' offices. Others work for hospitals that provide dental services, including Veterans Administration hospitals and clinics. More than 20 percent of all technicians are self-employed, a higher proportion than in most other occupations.

Salaries

Dental laboratory technicians who work full time in commercial laboratories earn about $13.30/hour to start.

Employment Outlook

Growth rate until the year 2005: No change.

Dental Laboratory Technician

Career Guides

★6472★ ***Careers in the Dental Profession: Dental Laboratory Technology***
SELECT
211 E. Chicago Ave., Ste. 1804
Chicago, IL 60611-2678
Ph: (312)440-2500

1992. This ten-page booklet describes what dental laboratory technicians do, where they work, educational preparation and certification.

★6473★ ***Dental Laboratory Technician***
Careers, Inc.
PO Box 135
Largo, FL 34649-0135
Ph: (813)584-7333

1992. Two-page occupational summary card describing duties, working conditions, personal qualifications, training, earnings and hours, employment outlook, places of employment, related careers and where to write for more information.

★6474★ **"Dental Laboratory Technician" in *150 Careers in the Health Care Field***
Reed Reference Publishing
121 Chanlon Rd.
PO Box 31
New Providence, NJ 07974
Fax: (908)665-6688 Fr: 800-521-8110

Stanley Alperin. Third edition, 1993. Each occupational profile covers job functions and responsibilities, work locations, training requirements, certification, and salaries. Lists community colleges, universities, vocational-technical schools, and other educational institutions that provide accredited training programs.

★6475★ **"Dental Laboratory Technician" in *Career Information Center* (Vol.7)**
Simon and Schuster
200 Old Tappan Rd.
Old Tappan, NJ 07675
Fax: 800-445-6991 Fr: 800-223-2348

Richard Lidz and Dale Anderson, editorial directors. Fifth edition, 1993. For 600 occupations, describes job duties, entry-level requirements, education and training needed, advancement possibilities, employment outlook, earnings and benefits. The set is divided into 12 volumes. Each volume includes jobs related under a broad career field. Volume 13 is the index.

★6476★ **"Dental Laboratory Technician" in *Careers in Health Care* (pp. 59-61)**
National Textbook Co. (NTC)
VGM Career Books
4255 W. Touhy Ave.
Lincolnwood, IL 60646-1975
Ph: (708)679-5500 Fax: (708)679-2494
Fr: 800-323-4900

Barbara M. Swanson. 1995. Discusses 58 health careers, providing information about the history of the occupation, job duties, work environments, salaries, educational preparation, licensure, certification, and employment outlook.

★6477★ **"Dental Laboratory Technician" in *Health Care* (pp. 63-67)**
Franklin Watts, Inc.
387 Park Avenue, S.
New York, NY 10016
Ph: (212)686-7070

Linda Barrett and Galen Guengerich. 1991. Provides an overview of the health care industry. Includes job description, educational preparation, training, salary, and employment outlook. Offers job hunting advice.

★6478★ **"Dental Laboratory Technician" in *Jobs Rated Almanac***
World Almanac
1 International Blvd., Ste. 444
Mahwah, NJ 07495
Ph: (201)529-6900 Fax: (201)529-6901

Les Krantz. Second edition, 1992. Ranks 250 jobs by environment, salary, outlooks, physical demands, stress, security, travel opportunities, and extra perks. Includes jobs the editor feels are the most common, most interesting, and the most rapidly growing.

★6479★ **"Dental Laboratory Technician" in *Occu-Facts: Information on 580 Careers in Outline Form***
Careers, Inc.
PO Box 135
Largo, FL 34649-0135
Ph: (813)584-7333

Biennial, 1995-96 edition. Each one-page occupational profile describes duties, working conditions, physical surroundings and demands, aptitudes, temperament, educational requirements, employment outlook, earnings, and places of employment.

★6480★ **"Dental Laboratory Technician" in *Opportunities in Health and Medical Careers* (p. 75)**
National Textbook Co. (NTC)
VGM Career Books
4255 W. Touhy Ave.
Lincolnwood, IL 60646-1975
Ph: (708)679-5500 Fax: (708)679-2494
Fr: 800-323-4900

Leo D'Orazio and I. Donald Snook. 1991. Provides an overview of the health care industry with future projections. Describes a wide variety of healthcare jobs covering the nature of the work, educational requirements, employment outlook and salaries. Offers job hunting advice.

★6481★ **"Dental Laboratory Technician" in *VGM's Handbook of Health Care Careers***
National Textbook Co.
4255 W. Touhy Ave.
Lincolnwood, IL 60646-1975
Ph: (708)679-5500 Fax: (708)679-2494
Fr: 800-323-4900

Annette Selden. 1993. Contains 42 two-page occupational profiles describing job duties, places of employment, working conditions, qualifications, education, employment outlook, and income.

★6482★ **"Dental Laboratory Technicians" in *Career Discovery Encyclopedia* (Vol.2, pp. 88-89)**
J.G. Ferguson Publishing Co.
200 W. Madison St., Ste. 300
Chicago, IL 60606
Ph: (312)580-5480 Fax: (312)580-4948

E. Russell Primm, editor-in-chief. 1993. Contains two-page articles on 504 occupations. Each article describes job duties, earnings, and educational and training requirements.

★6483★ "Dental Laboratory Technicians" in *Encyclopedia of Careers and Vocational Guidance* (Vol.2, pp. 450-454)
J.G. Ferguson Publishing Co.
200 W. Madison St., Ste. 300
Chicago, IL 60606
Ph: (312)580-5480 Fax: (312)580-4948

William E. Hopke, editor-in-chief. Ninth edition, 1993. Four-volume set that profiles 500 occupations and describes job trends in 74 industries. Includes career description, educational requirements, history of the job, methods of entry, advancement, employment outlook, earnings, working conditions, social and psychological factors, and sources of additional information.

★6484★ "Dental Laboratory Technicians" in *Health Care Job Explosion!* (pp. 113-119)
D-Amp Publications
401 Amherst Ave.
Coraopolis, PA 15108
Ph: (412)262-5578

Dennis V. Damp. 1993. Provides information on the nature of work for the major health care occupational groups. Descriptions include working conditions, training, job outlook, qualifications, and related occupations.

★6485★ "Dental Laboratory Technicians" in *Jobs! What They Are—Where They Are—What They Pay* (pp. 181)
Simon & Schuster, Inc.
Simon & Schuster Bldg.
1230 Avenue of the Americas
New York, NY 10020
Ph: (212)698-7000

Robert O. Snelling and Anne M. Snelling. Revised edition, 1992. Profiles 241 occupations, describing duties and responsibilities, educational preparation, earnings, employment opportunities, training, and qualifications.

★6486★ "Dental Laboratory Technicians" in *Occupational Outlook Handbook*
U.S. Government Printing Office
Superintendent of Documents
Washington, DC 20402
Ph: (202)512-1800 Fax: (202)512-2250

Biennial; latest edition, 1994-95. Encyclopedia of careers describing more than 250 occupations and comprising about 85 percent of all jobs in the economy. Occupations that require lengthy education or training are given the most attention. For each occupation, the handbook describes job duties, working conditions, training, educational preparation, personal qualities, advancement possibilities, job outlook, earnings, and sources of additional information.

★6487★ "Dental Laboratory Technicians" in *Opportunities in Dental Care Careers* (pp. 47-49)
National Textbook Co. (NTC)
VGM Career Books
4255 W. Touhy Ave.
Lincolnwood, IL 60646-1975
Ph: (708)679-5500 Fax: (708)679-2494
Fr: 800-323-4900

Bonnie L. Kendall. 1991. Describes the work of dentists and related dental care employees. Covers dental education including admission to dental school, dental specialists, skills, personal qualities, income, and licensure. Lists accredited dental schools, dental hygiene, and assisting programs.

★6488★ "Dental Technology" in *Career Connection for Technical Education* (pp. 54-55)
JIST Works, Inc.
720 N. Park Ave.
Indianapolis, IN 46202-3431
Ph: (317)264-3720 Fax: (317)264-3709

Fred A. Rowe. 1994, second edition. Describes in detail technical occupations. Includes information on recommended high school courses, course requirements, related careers, and a self-assessment guide.

★6489★ *Hands That Think: A Word About Careers in Modern Dental Laboratory Technology*
National Association of Dental Laboratories
3801 Mt. Vernon Ave.
Alexandria, VA 22305
Ph: (703)683-5263

This six-panel brochure describes the work, employment opportunities, earnings, training, and qualifications for dental laboratory technicians.

★6490★ *Video Career Library - Careers in Allied Health Fields*
Careers, Inc.
PO Box 135
Largo, FL 34649-0135
Ph: (813)584-7333

Videocassette. 1990. 60 mins. Part of the Video Career Library covering 16 5 occupations. Shows actual workers on the job. Includes dental laboratory technicians.

ASSOCIATIONS

★6491★ American Dental Association (ADA)
211 E. Chicago Ave.
Chicago, IL 60611
Ph: (312)440-2500 Fax: (312)440-7494

Members: Professional society of dentists. Encourages the improvement of the health of the public and promotes the art and science of dentistry in matters of legislation and regulations. **Purpose:** Inspects and accredits dental schools and schools for dental hygienists, assistants, and laboratory technicians. Conducts research programs at ADA Health Foundation Research Institute. Produces most of the dental health education material used in the U.S. Sponsors National Children's Dental Health Month. Compiles statistics on personnel, practice, and dental care needs and attitudes of patients with regard to dental health. Sponsors 12 councils. **Publications:** *American Dental Directory*, annual. • *Dental Teamwork*, bimonthly. • *Index to Dental Literature*, quarterly. • *Journal of the American Dental Association*, monthly. • *News*, biweekly.

★6492★ National Association of Dental Laboratories (NADL)
555 E. Braddock Rd.
Alexandria, VA 22314-2106
Ph: (703)683-5263 Fax: (703)549-4788
Fr: 800-950-1150

Members: Federation of state associations representing 2900 commercial dental laboratories serving the dental profession. **Purpose:** Develops criteria for ethical dental laboratories. Offers business and personal insurance programs, Hazardous Materials Training Program, and an infectious disease prevention training program. Compiles statistics; maintains speakers' bureau and museum; conducts educational and charitable programs. **Publications:** *Directory of Speakers and Lecturers*, periodic. • *Executive Information Series*, periodic. • *Fabrication Procedures*, periodic. • *Hazard Communication Manual*, periodic. • *Leadership Newsletter*, periodic. • *Managing for Profit.* • *Trends and Techniques in the Contemporary Dental Laboratory*, 10/year. • *Who's Who in the Dental Laboratory Industry*, annual.

STANDARDS/CERTIFICATION AGENCIES

★6493★ American Dental Association (ADA)
211 E. Chicago Ave.
Chicago, IL 60611
Ph: (312)440-2500

Promotes the art and science of dentistry in matters of legislation and regulations. Inspects and accredits dental schools and schools for dental hygienists, assistants, and laboratory technicians. Conducts research programs at ADA Health Foundation Research Institute. Produces most of the dental health education material used in the U.S.

★6494★ National Association of Dental Laboratories (NADL)
555 E. Braddock Rd.
Alexandria, VA 22314-2106
Ph: (703)683-5263 Fax: (703)549-4788
Fr: 800-950-1150

Compiles statistics; maintains speakers' bureau and museum; conducts educational and charitable programs.

Educational Directories and Programs

★6495★ *Accredited Dental Assisting, Dental Hygiene and Dental Laboratory Technology Educational Programs*
American Dental Association
Commission on Dental Accreditation
211 E. Chicago Ave.
Chicago, IL 60611
Ph: (312)440-2500

1991. State-by-state listing of accredited educational programs.

★6496★ *American Dental Directory*
American Dental Association (ADA)
211 E. Chicago Ave.
Chicago, IL 60611
Ph: (312)440-2500 Fax: (312)440-7494

Annual. Lists dentists in the United States; includes biographical information.

★6497★ *Encyclopedia of Medical Organizations and Agencies*
Gale Research Inc.
835 Penobscot Bldg.
Detroit, MI 48226-4094
Ph: (313)961-2242 Fax: (313)961-6741
Fr: 800-877-GALE
Karen Boyden, Contact

Biennial, November of odd years. Covers over 13,400 state, national, and international medical associations, foundations, research institutes, federal and state agencies, and medical and allied health schools. Entries include: Organization name, address, phone; many listings include names and titles of key personnel, descriptive annotations. Arrangement: Classified by subject, then by type of organization.

★6498★ *Medical and Health Information Directory*
Gale Research Inc.
835 Penobscot Bldg.
Detroit, MI 48226-4094
Ph: (313)961-2242 Fax: (313)961-6741
Fr: 800-877-GALE
Karen Boyden, Contact

Approximately biennial; latest edition 1994. Covers in Volume 1, almost 18,600 medical and health oriented associations, organizations, institutions, and government agencies, including health maintenance organizations (HMOs), preferred provider organizations (PPOs), insurance companies, pharmaceutical companies, research centers, and medical and allied health schools. In Volume 2, nearly 11,800 medical book publishers; medical periodicals, directories, audiovisual producers and services, medical libraries and information centers, and electronic resources. In Volume 3, nearly 26,000 clinics, treatment centers, care programs, and counseling/diagnostic services for 30 subject areas. Entries include: Institution, service, or firm name, address, phone; many include names of key personnel Arrangement: Classified by organization activity, service, etc..

Awards, Scholarships, Grants, and Fellowships

★6499★ Dental Lab Tech Scholarship Program
ADA Endowment Fund and Assistance Fund Inc
211 East Chicago Ave., 17th Fl.
Chicago, IL 60611
Ph: (312)440-2567 Fax: (312)440-2822

Purpose: To assist students who are in need of financial assistance. Qualifications: Applicant must be a U.S. citizen enrolled as an entering or first year student at an accredited laboratory technology school. Selection criteria: 2.8 GPA; demonstrate financial need; 21 letters of reference; typed summary of personal/professional goals. Funds available: $1,000. Application details: Contact the Fund for guidelines and application forms. Deadline: August 15.

Basic Reference Guides and Handbooks

★6500★ *Complete Handbook for Dental Auxiliaries*
Quintessence Publishing Company, Inc.
551 N. Kimberly Dr.
Carol Stream, IL 60188-1881
Ph: (708)682-3223 Fax: (708)682-3288
Fr: 800-621-0387

Charles A. Reap, Jr. 1981.

★6501★ *Dental Laboratory Technology*
Prentice Hall
Rte. 9W
Englewood Cliffs, NJ 07632
Ph: (201)592-2000

Chester A. Halterman. 1985.

★6502★ *Directory of Speakers and Lecturers*
National Association of Dental Laboratories (NADL)
555 E. Braddock Rd.
Alexandria, VA 22314
Ph: (703)683-5263 Fax: (703)549-4788
Fr: 800-950-1150

Periodic.

★6503★ *Managing for Profit*
National Association of Dental Laboratories
555 E. Braddock Rd.
Alexandria, VA 22314
Ph: (703)683-5263 Fax: (703)549-4788
Fr: 800-950-1150

★6504★ *NADL Hazard Communication Manual*
National Association of Dental Laboratories (NADL)
555 E. Braddock Rd.
Alexandria, VA 22314
Ph: (703)683-5263 Fax: (703)549-4788
Fr: 800-950-1150

Periodic.

Periodicals

★6505★ *ADA News*
American Dental Association
211 E. Chicago Ave.
Chicago, IL 60611
Ph: (312)440-2791 Fax: (312)440-3538
Judy Jakush

Biweekly. Dental newspaper (tabloid).

★6506★ *Directory of Speakers and Lecturers*
National Association of Dental Laboratories (NADL)
555 E. Braddock Rd.
Alexandria, VA 22314-2106
Ph: (703)683-5263 Fax: (703)549-4788
Fr: 800-950-1150

Periodic.

★6507★ *Executive Information Series*
National Association of Dental Laboratories (NADL)
555 E. Braddock Rd.
Alexandria, VA 22314-2106
Ph: (703)683-5263 Fax: (703)549-4788
Fr: 800-950-1150

Periodic.

★6508★ *Fabrication Procedures*
National Association of Dental Laboratories (NADL)
555 E. Braddock Rd.
Alexandria, VA 22314-2106
Ph: (703)683-5263 Fax: (703)549-4788
Fr: 800-950-1150

Periodic.

★6509★ *Hazard Communication Manual*
National Association of Dental Laboratories (NADL)
555 E. Braddock Rd.
Alexandria, VA 22314-2106
Ph: (703)683-5263 Fax: (703)549-4788
Fr: 800-950-1150

Periodic.

★6510★ *Leadership Newsletter*
National Association of Dental Laboratories (NADL)
555 E. Braddock Rd.
Alexandria, VA 22314-2106
Ph: (703)683-5263 Fax: (703)549-4788
Fr: 800-950-1150

Periodic.

★6511★ *Quintessence International*
Quintessence Publishing Co., Inc.
551 Kimberly Drive N.
Carol Stream, IL 60188-1881
Ph: (708)682-3223 Fax: (708)682-3288
Fr: 800-621-0387
Richard J. Simonsen

Monthly. Dental journal.

★6512★ *Trends and Techniques in the Contemporary Dental Laboratory*
National Association of Dental Laboratories (NADL)
555 E. Braddock Rd.
Alexandria, VA 22314-2106
Ph: (703)683-5263 Fax: (703)549-4788
Fr: 800-950-1150

10/year.

★6513★ *Who's Who in the Dental Laboratory Industry*
National Association of Dental Laboratories (NADL)
555 E. Braddock Rd.
Alexandria, VA 22314-2106
Ph: (703)683-5263 Fax: (703)549-4788
Fr: 800-950-1150

Annual.

OTHER SOURCES OF INFORMATION

★6514★ *Ethics, Jurisprudence & History for the Dental Hygienist*
Lea & Febiger
200 Chester Field Pkwy.
Malvern, PA 19355
Ph: (215)251-2230 Fax: (215)251-2229
Wilma E. Motley. Third edition, 1983.

Ophthalmic Laboratory Technicians

Ophthalmic laboratory technicians--also known as manufacturing opticians, optical mechanics, or optical goods workers--make prescription eyeglass lenses. Ophthalmic laboratory technicians cut, grind, edge, and finish lenses according to specifications provided by dispensing opticians, optometrists, or ophthalmologists, and then assemble the lenses with frames to produce finished glasses. About 50 percent of all ophthalmic laboratory technicians work in retail stores that manufacture prescription glasses, mostly optical goods store chains or independent retailers. Most of the rest work in optical laboratories. A few work for optometrists or ophthalmologists who dispense glasses directly to patients.

Salaries

Most beginning ophthalmic laboratory technicians earn between $15,040-$16,700/year. Trainees are generally paid the minimum wage.

Employment Outlook

Growth rate until the year 2005: Average.

Ophthalmic Laboratory Technicians

Career Guides

★6515★ "Manufacturing Opticians" in *Opportunities in Eye Care Careers* (pp. 79-83)
National Textbook Co. (NTC)
VGM Career Books
4255 W. Touhy Ave.
Lincolnwood, IL 60646-1975
Ph: (708)679-5500 Fax: (708)679-2494
Fr: 800-323-4900

Kathleen M. Ahrens. 1991. Explores careers in ophthalmology, optometry, and support positions. Describes the work, working conditions, educational preparation, salary, and employment outlook. Lists accredited educational programs.

★6516★ "Ophthalmic Laboratory Technician" in *150 Careers in the Health Care Field*
Reed Reference Publishing
121 Chanlon Rd.
PO Box 31
New Providence, NJ 07974
Fax: (908)665-6688 Fr: 800-521-8110

Stanley Alperin. Third edition, 1993. Each occupational profile covers job functions and responsibilities, work locations, training requirements, certification, and salaries. Lists community colleges, universities, vocational-technical schools, and other educational institutions that provide accredited training programs.

★6517★ "Ophthalmic Laboratory Technician" in *Careers in Health Care* (pp. 182-184)
National Textbook Co. (NTC)
VGM Career Books
4255 W. Touhy Ave.
Lincolnwood, IL 60646-1975
Ph: (708)679-5500 Fax: (708)679-2494
Fr: 800-323-4900

Barbara M. Swanson 1995. Discusses 58 health careers, providing information about the history of the occupation, job duties, work environments, salaries, educational preparation, licensure, certification, and employment outlook.

★6518★ "Ophthalmic Laboratory Technician" in *Health Care* (pp. 69-73)
Franklin Watts, Inc.
387 Park Avenue, S.
New York, NY 10016
Ph: (212)686-7070

Linda Barrett and Galen Guengerich. 1991. Provides an overview of the health care industry. Includes job description, educational preparation, training, salary, and employment outlook. Offers job hunting advice.

★6519★ "Ophthalmic Laboratory Technician" in *VGM's Handbook of Health Care Careers*
National Textbook Co.
4255 W. Touhy Ave.
Lincolnwood, IL 60646-1975
Ph: (708)679-5500 Fax: (708)679-2494
Fr: 800-323-4900

Annette Selden. 1993. Contains 42 two-page occupational profiles describing job duties, places of employment, working conditions, qualifications, education, employment outlook, and income.

★6520★ "Ophthalmic Laboratory Technicians" in *Encyclopedia of Careers and Vocational Guidance* (Vol.3, pp. 621-624)
J.G. Ferguson Publishing Co.
200 W. Madison St., Ste. 300
Chicago, IL 60606
Ph: (312)580-5480 Fax: (312)580-4948

William E. Hopke, editor-in-chief. Ninth edition, 1993. Four-volume set that profiles 500 occupations and describes job trends in 74 industries. Includes career description, educational requirements, history of the job, methods of entry, advancement, employment outlook, earnings, working conditions, social and psychological factors, and sources of additional information.

★6521★ "Ophthalmic Laboratory Technicians" in *Health Care Job Explosion!* (pp. 142-148)
D-Amp Publications
401 Amherst Ave.
Coraopolis, PA 15108
Ph: (412)262-5578

Dennis V. Damp. 1993. Provides information on the nature of work for the major health care occupational groups. Descriptions include working conditions, training, job outlook, qualifications, and related occupations.

★6522★ "Ophthalmic Laboratory Technicians" in *Jobs! What They Are—Where They Are—What They Pay* (p. 189)
Simon & Schuster, Inc.
Simon & Schuster Bldg.
1230 Avenue of the Americas
New York, NY 10020
Ph: (212)698-7000

Robert O. Snelling and Anne M. Snelling. Revised edition, 1992. Profiles 241 occupations, describing duties and responsibilities, educational preparation, earnings, employment opportunities, training, and qualifications.

★6523★ "Ophthalmic Laboratory Technicians" in *Occupational Outlook Handbook*
U.S. Government Printing Office
Superintendent of Documents
Washington, DC 20402
Ph: (202)512-1800 Fax: (202)512-2250

Biennial; latest edition, 1994-95. Encyclopedia of careers describing more than 250 occupations and comprising about 85 percent of all jobs in the economy. Occupations that require lengthy education or training are given the most attention. For each occupation, the handbook describes job duties, working conditions, training, educational preparation, personal qualities, advancement possibilities, job outlook, earnings, and sources of additional information.

★6524★ "Ophthalmic Medical Technician/Technologist" in *Allied Health Education Directory* (pp. 166-167)
American Medical Association (AMA)
515 N. State St.
Chicago, IL 60610
Ph: (312)464-5000 Fr: 800-621-8335

William R. Burrow, editor. 1994. Describes allied health occupations and lists educational programs accredited by the Committee on Allied Health Education and Accreditation of the American Medical Association.

★6525★ "Opticians and Optical Mechanics" in *Encyclopedia of Careers and Vocational Guidance* (Vol.3, pp. 625-627)
J.G. Ferguson Publishing Co.
200 W. Madison St., Ste. 300
Chicago, IL 60606
Ph: (312)580-5480 Fax: (312)580-4948

William E. Hopke, editor-in-chief. Ninth edition, 1993. Four-volume set that profiles 500 occupations and describes job trends in 74 industries. Includes career description, educational requirements, history of the job, methods of entry, advancement, employment outlook, earnings, working conditions, social and psychological factors, and sources of additional information.

★6526★ *Video Career Library - Technical Occupations*
Careers, Inc.
PO Box 135
Largo, FL 34649-0135
Ph: (813)584-7333

Videocassette. 1990. Part of the Video Career Library covering 165 occupations. Shows actual workers on the job.

Associations

★6527★ American Academy of Ophthalmology (AAO)
655 Beach St.
San Francisco, CA 94109
Ph: (415)561-8500 Fax: (415)561-8533

Members: Purpose: Ophthalmologists concerned with high-quality eye care and the continuing education of members. Sponsors Basic and Clinical Science Course for practitioners and residents to maintain current status (includes annual self-assessment); offers information on new techniques. Operates museum of ophthalmological instruments and artifacts. Operates American Academy of Ophthalmology Government Affairs Office which serves as a liaison between the AAO and the federal government, monitors pending legislation affecting ophthalmology, and prepares statements and testimonies to be presented to congressional committees and regulatory agencies. Also operates Foundation of the American Academy of Ophthalmology, which functions as the charitable arm of the academy. Current activities of the foundation include National Eye Care Project; Centennial Program. **Publications:** *Argus*, monthly. • *Basic and Clinical Science Course*. • *Ophthalmology*, monthly.

★6528★ Prevent Blindness America
500 E. Remington Rd.
Schaumburg, IL 60173
Ph: (708)843-2020 Fax: (708)843-8458
Fr: 800-331-2020

Members: Professional and laypersons interested in preventing blindness and conserving sight through nationwide comprehensive programs of public and professional education, research, industrial, and community services. **Purpose:** Services include promotion and support of local glaucoma screening programs, preschool vision testing, industrial eye safety, and collection of statistical and other data on nature and extent of causes of blindness and defective vision. Operates NSPB Center for Sight, an information line dealing with eye health and safety topics. Through the NSPB Fight for Sight Research Division, the organization awards student fellowships, postdoctoral awards and grants in aid for medical research. Sponsors Wise Owl Program to promote widespread use of safety eyewear for various activities and occupations. Compiles statistics. **Publications:** *Member New/Wise Owl News*. • *Member News*, quarterly. • *National Society to Prevent Blindness—Annual Report*.

Standards/Certification Agencies

★6529★ Commission on Opticianry Accreditation (COA)
10111 Martin Luther King, Jr. Hwy., No. 100
Bowie, MD 20720
Ph: (301)459-8075

Accrediting agency for ophthalmic dispensing and ophthalmic laboratory technology training programs in postsecondary institutions.

Educational Directories and Programs

★6530★ *Encyclopedia of Medical Organizations and Agencies*
Gale Research Inc.
835 Penobscot Bldg.
Detroit, MI 48226-4094
Ph: (313)961-2242 Fax: (313)961-6741
Fr: 800-877-GALE
Karen Boyden, Contact

Biennial, November of odd years. Covers over 13,400 state, national, and international medical associations, foundations, research institutes, federal and state agencies, and medical and allied health schools. Entries include: Organization name, address, phone; many listings include names and titles of key personnel, descriptive annotations. Arrangement: Classified by subject, then by type of organization.

★6531★ *Medical and Health Information Directory*
Gale Research Inc.
835 Penobscot Bldg.
Detroit, MI 48226-4094
Ph: (313)961-2242 Fax: (313)961-6741
Fr: 800-877-GALE
Karen Boyden, Contact

Approximately biennial; latest edition 1994. Covers in Volume 1, almost 18,600 medical and health oriented associations, organizations, institutions, and government agencies, including health maintenance organizations (HMOs), preferred provider organizations (PPOs), insurance companies, pharmaceutical companies, research centers, and medical and allied health schools. In Volume 2, nearly 11,800 medical book publishers; medical periodicals, directories, audiovisual producers and services, medical libraries and information centers, and electronic resources. In Volume 3, nearly 26,000 clinics, treatment centers, care programs, and counseling/diagnostic services for 30 subject areas. Entries include: Institution, service, or firm name, address, phone; many include names of key personnel Arrangement: Classified by organization activity, service, etc..

Periodicals

★6532★ *Contact Lens Spectrum*
Viscom Publications, Inc.
50 Washington St., 11th Fl.
Norwalk, CT 06854
Ph: (203)838-9100 Fax: (203)838-2550
Joseph T. Barr

Monthly. Magazine for eyecare professionals providing contact lens care and contact lens products.

★6533★ *Member New/Wise Owl News*
Prevent Blindness America (NSPB)
500 E. Remington Rd.
Schaumburg, IL 60173
Ph: (708)843-2020 Fax: (708)843-8458
Fr: 800-331-2020

★6534★ *Member News*
Prevent Blindness America (NSPB)
500 E. Remington Rd.
Schaumburg, IL 60173
Ph: (708)843-2020 Fax: (708)843-8458
Fr: 800-331-2020

Quarterly. Newsletter on eye health and safety.

★6535★ *National Society to Prevent Blindness—Annual Report*
Prevent Blindness America (NSPB)
500 E. Remington Rd.
Schaumburg, IL 60173
Ph: (708)843-2020 Fax: (708)843-8458
Fr: 800-331-2020

Covers highlights and accomplishments of the previous fiscal year. Includes financial statements.

★6536★ *Ocular Surgery News*
Slack, Inc.
6900 Grove Rd.
Thorofare, NJ 08086-9447
Ph: (609)848-1000 Fax: (609)853-5991
Keith Croes

Semiweekly. Medical newspaper for ophthalmologists. Covering scientific meetings and events, with emphasis on cataract/IOL, glaucoma treatment, laser therapy, clinical anterior segment issues, and legislative and regulatory developments.

★6537★ *Ophthalmic Research*
S. Karger Publishers, Inc.
26 W. Avon Rd.
PO Box 529
Farmington, CT 06085
Ph: (203)675-7834 Fax: (203)675-7302
O. Hockwin

Bimonthly. Research journal.

★6538★ *Ophthalmic Surgery*
Slack, Inc.
6900 Grove Rd.
Thorofare, NJ 08086-9447
Ph: (609)848-1000 Fax: (609)853-5991
George Spaeth

Monthly. Journal publishing articles on ophthalmic surgery, research, and clinical approaches.

★6539★ *Ophthalmologica*
S. Karger Publishers, Inc.
26 W. Avon Rd.
PO Box 529
Farmington, CT 06085
Ph: (203)675-7834 Fax: (203)675-7302
W. Straub

Medical research journal (English, French, and German).

★6540★ *Ophthalmology Times*
Advanstar Communications, Inc.
270 Madison Ave.
New York, NY 10016-0601
Ph: (212)951-6600 Fax: (212)481-6561
Dean Celia

Semiweekly.

★6541★ *Optometric Management*
Viscom Publications, Inc.
50 Washington St., 11th Fl.
Norwalk, CT 06854
Ph: (203)838-9100 Fax: (203)838-2550
Herve Byron

Medical professional journal.

★6542★ *Review of Optometry*
Capital Cities/ABC/Chilton Co.
Chilton Way
Radnor, PA 19087
Ph: (215)964-4000 Fax: (215)964-4647
Richard BayPublisher

Monthly. Journal for the optometric profession and optical industry.

Other Sources of Information

★6543★ "Ophthalmic Laboratory Technician" in *100 Best Jobs for the 1990s & Beyond*
Dearborn Financial Publishing, Inc.
520 N. Dearborn St.
Chicago, IL 60610-4354
Ph: (312)836-4400 Fax: (312)836-1021
Fr: 800-621-9621

Carol Kleiman. 1992. Describes 100 jobs ranging from accountants to veterinarians. Each job profile includes such information as education, experience, and certification needed, salaries, and job search suggestions.

Painting and Coating Machine Operators

Painting and coating machine operators control the machinery and equipment that applies the many types of paints and coatings to a wide range of manufactured products. Dippers and impregnators immerse racks and baskets of articles in vats of paint, liquid plastic, or other solutions using a power hoist. Tumbling barrel painters deposit articles of porous materials in a barrel of paint, varnish, or other coating, which is then rotated to ensure thorough coverage. Spray-machine operators use equipment with spray guns to coat metal, wood, ceramic, fabric, paper, and even food products with paint and other coating solutions. Paper coating machine operators spray *size,* a coating mixture, on the surface of paper to give it its gloss or finish. Silvering applicators spray silver, tin, and copper solutions on glass in the manufacture of mirrors. Enrobing machine operators coat, or *enrobe,* confectionery, bakery, and other food products with melted chocolate, cheese, oils, sugar, and other substances. Although the majority of painting and coating machine operators are employed in manufacturing, the largest group works in automotive body repair and paint shops. Fewer than 10 percent of all painting and coating machine operators are self-employed; most are automotive painters.

Salaries

Weekly earnings of painting and coating machine operators are as follows:

Middle 50 percent	$252-$503/week
Top 10 percent	$637/week or more

Employment Outlook

Growth rate until the year 2005: Little change.

Painting and Coating Machine Operators

Career Guides

★6544★ *Auto Painter*
Vocational Biographies, Inc.
PO Box 31
Sauk Centre, MN 56378-0031
Ph: (612)352-6516 Fax: (612)352-5546
Fr: 800-255-0752

1990. This pamphlet profiles a person working in the job. Includes information about job duties, working conditions, places of employment, educational preparation, labor market outlook, and salaries.

★6545★ "Automobile Painters" in *Opportunities in Automotive Service Careers* (pp. 51-52)
National Textbook Co. (NTC)
VGM Career Books
4255 W. Touhy Ave.
Lincolnwood, IL 60646-1975
Ph: (708)679-5500 Fax: (708)679-2494
Fr: 800-323-4900

Robert M. Weber. 1989. Describes the work of the automobile mechanic and related occupations such as service station attendant and automobile body repairer. Covers working conditions, places of employment, qualifications, training, apprenticeships, certification, advancement opportunities, employment outlook, tools needed, and earnings.

★6546★ "Automotive Painters" in *Career Discovery Encyclopedia* (Vol.1, pp. 96-97)
J.G. Ferguson Publishing Co.
200 W. Madison St., Ste. 300
Chicago, IL 60606
Ph: (312)580-5480 Fax: (312)580-4948

E. Russell Primm, editor-in-chief. 1993. Contains two-page articles on 504 occupations. Each article describes job duties, earnings, and educational and training requirements.

★6547★ "Automotive Painters" in *Encyclopedia of Careers and Vocational Guidance*
J.G. Ferguson Publishing Co.
200 W. Madison St., Ste. 300
Chicago, IL 60606
Ph: (312)580-5480 Fax: (312)580-4948

William E. Hopke, editor-in-chief. Ninth edition, 1993. Four-volume set that profiles 500 occupations and describes job trends in 74 industries. Includes career description, educational requirements, history of the job, methods of entry, advancement, employment outlook, earnings, working conditions, social and psychological factors, and sources of additional information.

★6548★ *Career Opportunities . . . in the Automotive Collision Repair and Refinishing Industry*
Automotive Service Association
PO Box 929
Bedford, TX 76095-0929
Ph: (817)283-6205

Booklet describing the work, training, areas of specialization, places of employment, hours, and outlook for automotive repair and refinishing specialists.

★6549★ "Paint and Coatings Industry" in *Encyclopedia of Careers and Vocational Guidance* (Vol.3, pp. 656-658)
J.G. Ferguson Publishing Co.
200 W. Madison St., Ste. 300
Chicago, IL 60606
Ph: (312)580-5480 Fax: (312)580-4948

William E. Hopke, editor-in-chief. Ninth edition, 1993. Four-volume set that profiles 500 occupations and describes job trends in 74 industries. Includes career description, educational requirements, history of the job, methods of entry, advancement, employment outlook, earnings, working conditions, social and psychological factors, and sources of additional information.

★6550★ *Painter, Spray*
Careers, Inc.
PO Box 135
Largo, FL 34649-0135
Ph: (813)584-7333

1992. Two-page occupational summary card describing duties, working conditions, personal qualifications, training, earnings and hours, employment outlook, places of employment, related careers and where to write for more information.

★6551★ "Painting and Coating Machine Operators" in *Occupational Outlook Handbook*
U.S. Government Printing Office
Superintendent of Documents
Washington, DC 20402
Ph: (202)512-1800 Fax: (202)512-2250

Biennial; latest edition, 1994-95. Encyclopedia of careers describing more than 250 occupations and comprising about 85 percent of all jobs in the economy. Occupations that require lengthy education or training are given the most attention. For each occupation, the handbook describes job duties, working conditions, training, educational preparation, personal qualities, advancement possibilities, job outlook, earnings, and sources of additional information.

★6552★ "Production Painter" in *Career Information Center* (Vol.9)
Simon and Schuster
200 Old Tappan Rd.
Old Tappan, NJ 07675
Fax: 800-445-6991 Fr: 800-223-2348

Richard Lidz and Dale Anderson, editorial directors. Fifth edition, 1993. For 600 occupations, describes job duties, entry-level requirements, education and training needed, advancement possibilities, employment outlook, earnings and benefits. The set is divided into 12 volumes. Each volume includes jobs related under a broad career field. Volume 13 is the index.

★6553★ "Spray Painter (Production)" in *Occu-Facts: Information on 580 Careers in Outline Form*
Careers, Inc.
PO Box 135
Largo, FL 34649-0135
Ph: (813)584-7333

Biennial, 1995-96 edition. Each one-page occupational profile describes duties, working conditions, physical surroundings and demands, aptitudes, temperament, educational requirements, employment outlook, earnings, and places of employment.

Associations

★6554★ Automotive Service Association (ASA)
1901 Airport Fwy., Ste. 100
PO Box 929
Bedford, TX 76095-0929
Ph: (817)283-6205 Fax: (817)685-0225
Fr: 800-272-7467

Members: Automotive service businesses including body, paint, and trim shops, engine rebuilders, radiator shops, brake and wheel alignment services, transmission shops, tune-up services, and air conditioning services; associate members are manufacturers and wholesalers of automotive parts, and the trade press. **Purpose:** Represents independent business owners and managers before private agencies and national and state legislative bodies. Promotes confidence between consumer and automotive technician, safety inspection of motor vehicles, and better highways. **Publications:** *AutoInc*, monthly. • *Collision Repair Report*, monthly. • *Mechanical News*, bimonthly. • *TransTechnical News*, monthly.

★6555★ Automotive Service Industry Association (ASIA)
25 Northwest Point
Elk Grove Village, IL 60007-1035
Ph: (708)228-1310 Fax: (708)228-1510

Members: Executives representing independent automotive wholesalers, warehouse distributors, heavy-duty vehicle and equipment parts distributors, automotive electrical service and supply wholesalers and distributors, manufacturers' representatives, and manufacturers and remanufacturers of replacement parts, tools, equipment, chemicals, refinishing materials, supplies, and accessories. Holds educational and research programs and seminars; compiles statistics. **Publications:** *Aftermarket Today*, quarterly. • *Automotive Service Industry Association—Membership Directory*, periodic. • *Automotive Service Industry Association—Product Directory*, annual. • *Automotive Service Industry Association—Survey of Profitability*, annual. • *Hotline Divisional Newsletter*, monthly. • *Washington Insights Public Affairs Newsletter*, monthly.

★6556★ International Association of Machinists and Aerospace Workers (IAM)
9000 Machinists PL
Upper Marlboro, MD 20772
Ph: (301)967-4500 Fax: (301)967-4588

Members: AFL-CIO. **Publications:** *The Machinist*, monthly.

★6557★ International Brotherhood of Teamsters 1991 (IBT)
25 Louisiana Ave. NW
Washington, DC 20001
Ph: (202)624-6800

Publications: *The New Teamster*, 8/year.

★6558★ International Union, United Automobile, Aerospace and Agricultural Implement Workers of America (UAW)
8000 E. Jefferson
Detroit, MI 48214
Ph: (313)926-5000 Fax: (313)823-6016

Members: AFL-CIO. **Publications:** *Ammo*, monthly. • *Skill*, quarterly. • *Solidarity*, 10/year.

★6559★ National Institute for Automotive Service Excellence (ASE)
13505 Dulles Technology Dr.
Herndon, VA 22071-3415
Ph: (703)713-3800 Fax: (703)713-0727

Members: Governed by a 40-member board of directors selected from all sectors of the automotive service industry and from education, government, and consumer groups. Encourages and promotes the highest standards of automotive service in the public interest. **Purpose:** Conducts continuing research to determine the best methods for training automotive technicians; encourages the development of effective training programs. Tests and certifies the competence of automobile, medium/heavy truck, collision repair, and engine machinist technicians as well as parts specialists. **Publications:** *ASE Preparation Guide*, annual. • *ASE Test Registration Booklet*, semiannual. • *The Blue Seal*, semiannual.

Standards/Certification Agencies

★6560★ *Auto Body Repairmen! Painters/Refinishers! Become a Proven Pro: Get ASE Certified*
National Institute for Automotive Service Excellence
13505 Dulles Technology Dr.
Herndon, VA 22071-3415
Ph: (703)742-3800

This four-panel brochure describes the examinations for certification for automotive body repairers and painters.

★6561★ National Institute for Automotive Service Excellence (ASE)
13505 Dulles Technology Dr.
Herndon, VA 22071-3415
Ph: (703)713-3800 Fax: (703)713-0727

Encourages and promotes the highest standards of automotive service in the public interest. Tests and certifies the competence of automobile, medium/heavy truck, collision repair, and engine machinist technicians as well as parts specialists.

Test Guides

★6562★ *ASE Test Registration Booklet*
National Institute for Automotive Service Excellence (ASE)
13505 Dulles Technology Dr.
Herndon, VA 22071-3415
Ph: (703)742-3800

Semiannual. Registration for technicians who wish to become ASE certified. Provides registration information and sample questions.

★6563★ *ASE Training Guide*
National Institute for Automotive Service Excellence (ASE)
13505 Dulles Technology Dr.
Herndon, VA 22071-3415
Ph: (703)742-3800

Annual. Bibliographic listing of training materials available for upgrading technicians' skills in automotive repair, including sample ASE test questions and test specifications.

★6564★ *The Official ASE Preparation Guide to ASE Automobile and Body/Paint Tests*
National Institute for Automotive Service Excellence
13505 Dulles Technology Dr.
Herndon, VA 22071-3415
Ph: (703)742-3800

Describes the certification process for automobile mechanics and auto body repairers. Offers tips on preparing for the test. Contains sample test questions.

Educational Directories and Programs

★6565★ *Automotive Service Industry Association—Product Directory*
Automotive Service Industry Association (ASIA)
25 Northwest Point
Elk Grove Village, IL 60007-1035
Ph: (708)228-1310 Fax: (708)228-1510

Annual.

PERIODICALS

★6566★ *Aftermarket Today*
Automotive Service Industry Association (ASIA)
25 Northwest Point
Elk Grove Village, IL 60007-1035
Ph: (708)228-1310 Fax: (708)228-1510

Quarterly.

★6567★ *Ammo*
International Union, United Automobile, Aerospace and Agricultural Implement Workers of America (UAW)
8000 E. Jefferson
Detroit, MI 48214
Ph: (313)926-5000 Fax: (313)823-6016

Monthly.

★6568★ *ASE Preparation Guide*
National Institute for Automotive Service Excellence (ASE)
13505 Dulles Technology Dr.
Herndon, VA 22071-3415
Ph: (703)713-3800 Fax: (703)713-0727

Annual. Bibliographic listing of training materials for upgrading technicians' skills in automotive repair; sample test questions; and task lists.

★6569★ *AutoInc*
Automotive Service Association (ASA)
1901 Airport Fwy., Ste. 100
PO Box 929
Bedford, TX 76095-0929
Ph: (817)283-6205 Fax: (817)685-0225
Fr: 800-272-7467

Monthly. Covers technical and management information of interest to members; contains shop profiles, legislative news, and industry events.

★6570★ *Automotive Service Industry Association—Membership Directory*
Automotive Service Industry Association (ASIA)
25 Northwest Point
Elk Grove Village, IL 60007-1035
Ph: (708)228-1310 Fax: (708)228-1510

Periodic.

Photographic Process Workers

Photographic process workers in photofinishing or custom photo laboratories develop film, make prints and slides, and do related tasks. All-around darkroom technicians perform delicate tasks by hand. Occupations in this field vary by film development and printing processes. Color film operators use specialized machines to process color film in professional photo processing labs. Developers produce negatives by following a sequence of steps. Printer operators focus light through a negative onto light-sensitive paper in order to make prints. Airbrush artists restore damaged and faded photographs and color drawings to simulate photographs. Photographic retouchers alter photographic negatives and prints to accentuate the desired features of a subject or remove undesirable ones. Colorists apply oil colors to portrait photographs to create a natural, lifelike appearance. Photographic spotters cover or spot out imperfections on photographic prints. Color laboratory technicians produce color prints, negatives, and slides by hand, or operate automated machines. Film developers operate equipment that develops still or motion picture film automatically. Color-printer operators control the equipment used to produce color prints from negatives. Automatic print developers operate machines that develop strips of exposed photographic paper. Takedown sorters sort processed film. Automatic mounters tend the automatic mounting presses that cut slide film into individual transparencies and seal them in mounting frames.

Salaries

Weekly earnings of photo process workers are as follows:

Lowest 10 percent	$210/week or less
Middle 50 percent	$250-$460/week
Top 10 percent	$520/week or more

Employment Outlook

Growth rate until the year 2005: Average.

Photographic Process Workers

Career Guides

★6571★ *Career Insights*
RMI Media Productions, Inc.
1365 N. Winchester
Olathe, KS 66061
Ph: (913)768-1696 Fax: 800-755-6910
Fr: 800-745-5480

Videocassette series. 1987. This videotape series describes 50 occupations, including skill requirements and interviews with people employed in these fields. Occupations include: flight service, air transportation/ground services, data processing, carpentry, clerk in banking/insurance/business, cosmetic personal grooming, firefighting, forestry, insulation/roofing, mechanics, material handling, photographic processing, pipefitting and plumbing, printing, secretarial services, tool and die operations.

★6572★ *Career Success Series*
Cambridge Educational
PO Box 2153
Charleston, WV 25328-2153
Ph: (304)744-9323 Fax: (304)744-9351
Fr: 800-468-4227

Videocassette. 1986. 15 mins. A series, available separately, outlining various career choices for students. Occupations include: accounting, flight service, air transportation/ground/flight service, data processing, carpentry, clerk in banking/insurance, commodity sales, cosmetic personal grooming, fire fighting, forestry services, home economics, insulation/roofing, material handling, mechanics, photographic processing, pipefitting and plumbing, police science, printing, carpentry, medical laboratory technicians, secretarial services, and utilities equipment operator.

★6573★ "Darkroom Technician" in *Career Information Center* (Vol.3)
Simon and Schuster
200 Old Tappan Rd.
Old Tappan, NJ 07675
Fax: 800-445-6991 Fr: 800-223-2348

Richard Lidz and Dale Anderson, editorial directors. Fifth edition, 1993. For 600 occupations, describes job duties, entry-level requirements, education and training needed, advancement possibilities, employment outlook, earnings and benefits. The set is divided into 12 volumes. Each volume includes jobs related under a broad career field. Volume 13 is the index.

★6574★ "Darkroom Technicians" in *Career Discovery Encyclopedia* (Vol.2, pp. 78-79)
J.G. Ferguson Publishing Co.
200 W. Madison St., Ste. 300
Chicago, IL 60606
Ph: (312)580-5480 Fax: (312)580-4948

E. Russell Primm, editor-in-chief. 1993. Contains two-page articles on 504 occupations. Each article describes job duties, earnings, and educational and training requirements.

★6575★ "Darkroom Technicians" in *Encyclopedia of Careers and Vocational Guidance*
J.G. Ferguson Publishing Co.
200 W. Madison St., Ste. 300
Chicago, IL 60606
Ph: (312)580-5480 Fax: (312)580-4948

William E. Hopke, editor-in-chief. Ninth edition, 1993. Four-volume set that profiles 500 occupations and describes job trends in 74 industries. Includes career description, educational requirements, history of the job, methods of entry, advancement, employment outlook, earnings, working conditions, social and psychological factors, and sources of additional information.

★6576★ "Film Laboratory Technicians" in *Encyclopedia of Careers and Vocational Guidance*
J.G. Ferguson Publishing Co.
200 W. Madison St., Ste. 300
Chicago, IL 60606
Ph: (312)580-5480 Fax: (312)580-4948

William E. Hopke, editor-in-chief. Ninth edition, 1993. Four-volume set that profiles 500 occupations and describes job trends in 74 industries. Includes career description, educational requirements, history of the job, methods of entry, advancement, employment outlook, earnings, working conditions, social and psychological factors, and sources of additional information.

★6577★ *Film Processing Specialist*
Careers, Inc.
PO Box 135
Largo, FL 34649-0135
Ph: (813)584-7333

1994. Two-page occupational summary card describing duties, working conditions, personal qualifications, training, earnings and hours, employment outlook, places of employment, related careers and where to write for more information.

★6578★ *Photofinishing Laboratory Technicians*
Chronicle Guidance Publications, Inc.
66 Aurora St.
PO Box 1190
Moravia, NY 13118-1190
Ph: (315)497-0330 Fax: (315)497-3359
Fr: 800-622-7284

1993. This career brief describes the nature of the work, working conditions, hours and earnings, education and training, licensure, certification, unions, personal qualifications, social and psychological factors, employment outlook, entry methods, advancement, and related occupations.

★6579★ *Photographic Equipment Technicians*
Chronicle Guidance Publications, Inc.
66 Aurora St.
PO Box 1190
Moravia, NY 13118-1190
Ph: (315)497-0330 Fax: (315)497-3359
Fr: 800-622-7284

1994. Career brief describing the nature of the job, working conditions, hours and earnings, education and training, licensure, certification, unions, personal qualifications, social and psychological factors, location, employment outlook, entry methods, advancement, and related occupations.

★6580★ "Photographic Process Worker" in *Jobs Rated Almanac*
World Almanac
1 International Blvd., Ste. 444
Mahwah, NJ 07495
Ph: (201)529-6900 Fax: (201)529-6901

Les Krantz. Second edition, 1992. Ranks 250 jobs by environment, salary, outlooks, physical demands, stress, security, travel opportunities, and extra perks. Includes jobs the editor feels are the most common, most interesting, and the most rapidly growing.

★6581★ "Photographic Process Workers" in *Occupational Outlook Handbook*
U.S. Government Printing Office
Superintendent of Documents
Washington, DC 20402
Ph: (202)512-1800 Fax: (202)512-2250
Biennial; latest edition, 1994-95. Encyclopedia of careers describing more than 250 occupations and comprising about 85 percent of all jobs in the economy. Occupations that require lengthy education or training are given the most attention. For each occupation, the handbook describes job duties, working conditions, training, educational preparation, personal qualities, advancement possibilities, job outlook, earnings, and sources of additional information.

★6582★ *Photographic Processing*
Morris Video
2730 Monterey St., No. 105
Monterey Business Park
Torrance, CA 90503
Ph: (213)533-4800 Fr: 800-843-3606
Videocassette. 1987. 15 mins. A guide to photographic and motion picture processing, covering careers such as color timing, printer operating, film mounting, developing and much more.

★6583★ *PhotoIndustry Careers: A Lifelong Commitment to Excellence and Creativity*
Photo Marketing Association International
3000 Picture Place
Jackson, MI 49201-8898
Ph: (517)783-2809
This four-page pamphlet describes the work and lists photofinishing schools.

Associations

★6584★ National Association of Photo Equipment Technicians (NAPET)
3000 Picture Pl.
Jackson, MI 49201
Ph: (517)788-8100
Members: A division of Photo Marketing Association International. **Purpose:** Providers of photo/video repair services. **Publications:** *NAPET News*, quarterly. • *Who's Who in Photographic Management*, semiannual.

★6585★ Photo Marketing Association International (PMA)
3000 Picture Pl.
Jackson, MI 49201
Ph: (517)788-8100 Fax: (517)788-8371
Members: Retailers of photo and video equipment, film, and supplies; firms developing and printing film. Maintains hall of fame. Compiles statistics; conducts research and educational programs. **Publications:** *Mini Lab Focus*, monthly. • *NAPET News*, bimonthly. • *Photo Marketing Association International—Newsline*, semimonthly. • *Photo Marketing Magazine*, monthly. • *Sales Counter*, monthly. • *Specialty Lab Update*, monthly. • *SPFE Newsletter*, bimonthly. • *Who's Who in Photographic Management*, annual.

Test Guides

★6586★ *Career Examination Series: Senior Photographic Machine Operator*
National Learning Corp.
212 Michael Dr.
Syosset, NY 11791
Ph: (516)921-8888 Fax: (516)921-8743
Fr: 800-645-6337
Jack Rudman. All examination guides in this series contain questions with answers.

Awards, Scholarships, Grants, and Fellowships

★6587★ NAPET La Croix Award
National Association of Photo Equipment Technicians
Photo Marketing Association International
3000 Picture Pl.
Jackson, MI 49201
Ph: (517)788-8100 Fax: (517)788-8271
For recognition of achievement or contribution to the photo equipment repair industry. Officers of the Association make nominations and the members vote. A trophy is awarded biennially. Established in 1976 in honor of George La Croix.

Basic Reference Guides and Handbooks

★6588★ *Basic Guide to Black & White Darkroom Techniques*
Price Stern Sloan, Inc.
11150 Olympic Blvd.
Los Angeles, CA 90064
Ph: (213)657-6100 Fax: (213)855-8993
H P Books Staff, editor. 1982.

★6589★ *Better Black & White Darkroom Techniques*
Prentice Hall
Rte. 9W
Englewood Cliffs, NJ 07632
Ph: (201)592-2000
Robert Casagrande. 1984. Part of Master Class Photography Series.

★6590★ *Black & White Darkroom Techniques*
Simon & Schuster, Inc.
Simon & Schuster Bldg.
1230 Avenue of the Americas
New York, NY 10020
Ph: (212)698-7000
Eastman Kodak Company Editors. 1986.

★6591★ *Carbon & Carbro Tissue: You Can Make It!*
Tracy Diers
58-14 84th St.
Elmhurst, NY 11373
Ph: (718)651-2798
Tracy Diers, 1986.

★6592★ *Creative Projects & Processes*
Embee Press
82 Pine Grove Ave.
Kingston, NY 12401
Ph: (914)338-0427
Mark Baczynsky. 1982.

★6593★ *Darkroom*
Lustrum Press
PO Box 450
Canal St. Sta.
New York, NY 10013
Ph: (212)254-9692
Eleanor Lewis, editor. 1979.

★6594★ *The Darkroom Book*
Watson-Guptill Publications, Inc.
1515 Broadway
New York, NY 10036
Ph: (212)764-7300 Fax: (212)536-5359
Jack Schofield, editor. 1985.

★6595★ *The Darkroom Handbook*
Alfred A. Knopf, Inc.
201 E. 50th St.
New York, NY 10022
Michael Langford. 1984.

★6596★ *Darkroom Two*
Lustrum Press
PO Box 450
Canal St. Sta.
New York, NY 10013
Ph: (212)254-9692
Jain Kelley. 1979.

★6597★ *The Double Exposure Book*
Wayne Floyd
1407 Darlene
Arlington, TX 76010
Ph: (817)861-1683
Wayne Floyd. 1985.

★6598★ *Elementary Darkroom Practices: A Basic Photography Manual*
Kendall/Hunt Publishing Company
2460 Kerper Blvd.
Dubuque, IA 52001
Ph: (319)588-1451
Eugene Groppetti. 1987.

★6599★ *The Essential Darkroom Book*
Watson-Guptill Publications, Inc.
1515 Broadway
New York, NY 10036
Ph: (212)764-7300 Fax: (212)536-5359
Tom Grill. 1983.

★6600★ *Essential Darkroom Techniques*
Sterling Publishing Company, Inc.
387 Park Ave. S.
New York, NY 10016-8810
Ph: (212)532-7160 Fax: (212)213-2495
Fr: 800-367-9692
Jonathan Eastland. 1987.

★6601★ *Graphics Master 5*
Dean Lem Associates, Inc.
PO Box 959
Kihei, HI 96753-0959
Ph: (808)874-5461 Fax: (808)875-1404
Fr: 800-562-2562

A technical manual and reference guide for new and experienced professionals. Sections include color separation, photography, scanners, typography, printing papers, and binding and finishing.

★6602★ *Into Your Darkroom Step-by-Step*
Amherst Media
PO Box 645
Calistoga, CA 94515

Dennis Curtin. Revised edition, 1991.

★6603★ *John Hedgecoe's Darkroom Techniques*
Simon & Schuster
Simon & Schuster Bldg.
1230 Avenue of the Americas
New York, NY 10020
Ph: (212)698-7000

John Hedgecoe. 1988.

★6604★ *Society of Photo-technologists—Journal & Service Notes—Parts and Services Directory Issue*
Society of Photo-Technologists (SPT)
367 Windsor Hwy., Ste. 404
New Windsor, NY 12553
Ph: (914)782-4248 Fax: (914)782-2691
June Holecek, Executive Director

Annual. Publication includes: About 300 suppliers of parts and services for camera repair; international coverage. Entries include: Co. name, address, phone, trade and brand names handled, product or service. Arrangement: Classified by product/brand name.

PERIODICALS

★6605★ *American Photo*
Hachette Publications, Inc.
1633 Broadway
New York, NY 10019
Ph: (212)767-5800 Fax: (212)486-4216
David Schonauer

Bimonthly. Photography magazine.

★6606★ *Camera & Darkroom Magazine*
L.F.P., Inc.
9171 Wilshire Blvd., Ste. 300
Beverly Hills, CA 90210
Ph: (310)858-7100 Fax: (310)275-3857
Ana Jones

Monthly. Photographic techniques magazine including product reviews, fine art photography, and portfolios.

★6607★ *Mini Lab Focus*
Photo Marketing Association International (PMA)
3000 Picture Pl.
Jackson, MI 49201
Ph: (517)788-8100 Fax: (517)788-8371

Monthly. Provides association mini lab members with information on industry trends and activities, and advertising and marketing techniques.

★6608★ *NAPET News*
Photo Marketing Association International (PMA)
3000 Picture Pl.
Jackson, MI 49201
Ph: (517)788-8100 Fax: (517)788-8371

Bimonthly. Provides information on association activities, trends in photo/video field, manufacturers' training programs for repair people, and new products.

★6609★ *PHOTO Electronic Imaging*
PPA Publications & Events, Inc.
57 Forsyth Street, NW
Atlanta, GA 30303
Ph: (404)522-8600 Fax: (404)614-6405
Kim Brady

Monthly. Technical business magazine.

★6610★ *Photo Lab Management*
PLM Publishing Inc.
1312 Lincoln Blvd.
PO Box 1700
Santa Monica, CA 90406
Ph: (310)451-1344 Fax: (310)395-9058
Carolyn Ryan

Monthly. Magazine covering photo lab process chemistries, digital imaging, equipment, personnel, and technicians for photo lab owners and managers.

★6611★ *Photo Marketing*
Photo Marketing Assn. Intl.
3000 Picture Pl.
Jackson, MI 49201
Ph: (517)788-8100 Fax: (517)788-8371
Margaret Hooks

Monthly. Trade magazine for photo/video dealers and photo finishers.

★6612★ *Photo Marketing Association International—Newsline*
Photo Marketing Association International (PMA)
3000 Picture Pl.
Jackson, MI 49201
Ph: (517)788-8100 Fax: (517)788-8371

Semimonthly. Provides a digest of pertinent information about the photo industry. Includes surveys of industry leaders on current topics and people profiles.

★6613★ *Photo Marketing Magazine*
Photo Marketing Association International (PMA)
3000 Picture Pl.
Jackson, MI 49201
Ph: (517)788-8100 Fax: (517)788-8371

Monthly. Features articles examining industry issues, product innovations, business management, and interviews with leading industry experts.

★6614★ *PTN (Photographic Trade News)*
PTN Publishing Co.
445 Broad Hollow Rd., Ste. 21
Melville, NY 11747
Ph: (516)845-2700 Fax: (516)845-7109
Bill Schiffner

Semiweekly. Magazine reporting photo industry products news.

★6615★ *Sales Counter*
Photo Marketing Association International (PMA)
3000 Picture Pl.
Jackson, MI 49201
Ph: (517)788-8100 Fax: (517)788-8371

Monthly. Contains articles on techniques of selling photographic products, market trends and innovations, and other consumer information.

★6616★ *Specialty Lab Update*
Photo Marketing Association International (PMA)
3000 Picture Pl.
Jackson, MI 49201
Ph: (517)788-8100 Fax: (517)788-8371

Monthly. Provides information on marketing techniques, business financing and management, government regulations, technical developments in the industry.

★6617★ *SPFE Newsletter*
Photo Marketing Association International (PMA)
3000 Picture Pl.
Jackson, MI 49201
Ph: (517)788-8100 Fax: (517)788-8371

Bimonthly. Covers society activities, technical developments, and EPA guidelines. Contains information on APFT titles awarded and new products.

★6618★ *Who's Who in Photographic Management*
Photo Marketing Association International (PMA)
3000 Picture Pl.
Jackson, MI 49201
Ph: (517)788-8100 Fax: (517)788-8371

Annual.

★6619★ *Who's Who in Photographic Management*
National Association of Photo Equipment Technicians (NAPET)
3000 Picture Pl.
Jackson, MI 49201
Ph: (517)788-8100

Semiannual.

OTHER SOURCES OF INFORMATION

★6620★ *The Keepers of Light: A History & Working Guide to Early Photographic Processes*
Morgan & Morgan, Inc.
145 Palisade St.
Dobbs Ferry, NY 10522
Ph: (914)693-0023

William Crawford. 1979.

★6621★ *The Photographer's Assistant*
Allworth Press
10 E. 23rd St., Ste. 400
New York, NY 10010
Ph: (212)777-8395 Fax: (212)777-8261
Fr: 800-247-6553

1992.

Busdrivers

Intercity **busdrivers** transport people between regions of a state or of the country; local transit busdrivers, within a metropolitan area or county; and school busdrivers, to and from schools and related events. Busdrivers provide transportation for millions of Americans every day. They follow time schedules and routes over highways and city and suburban streets to provide passengers with an alternative the automobile.

Salaries

Weekly earnings for busdrivers are as follows:

Lowest 10 percent	$206.00/week or less
Middle 50 percent	$288-$580/week
Top 10 percent	$721/week or more

Employment Outlook

Growth rate until the year 2005: Average.

Busdrivers

Career Guides

★6622★ "Bus Driver" in *Exploring Nontraditional Jobs for Women* (pp. 63-69)
Rosen Publishing Group
29 E. 21st St.
New York, NY 10010
Ph: (212)777-3017 Fax: (212)777-0277
Fr: 800-237-9932

Rose Neufeld. 1989. Describes blue-collar, male dominated occupations. Discusses what is done on the job, training, where to apply for jobs, tools used, salaries, and advantages and disadvantages. Relates the experiences of women who are working in the field.

★6623★ "Bus Driver" in *Jobs Rated Almanac*
World Almanac
1 International Blvd., Ste. 444
Mahwah, NJ 07495
Ph: (201)529-6900 Fax: (201)529-6901

Les Krantz. Second edition, 1992. Ranks 250 jobs by environment, salary, outlooks, physical demands, stress, security, travel opportunities, and extra perks. Includes jobs the editor feels are the most common, most interesting, and the most rapidly growing.

★6624★ "Bus Driver" in *Transportation* (pp. 27-31)
Franklin Watts, Inc.
387 Park Avenue, S.
New York, NY 10016
Ph: (212)686-7070

Marjorie Rittenberg Schulz. 1990. Surveys the transportation industry including air, water, and rail services. Provides job description, training, salary, and employment outlook. Offers job hunting advice.

★6625★ *Bus Drivers*
Chronicle Guidance Publications, Inc.
66 Aurora St.
PO Box 1190
Moravia, NY 13118-1190
Ph: (315)497-0330 Fax: (315)497-3359
Fr: 800-622-7284

1993. This career brief describes the nature of the work, working conditions, hours and earnings, education and training, licensure, certification, unions, personal qualifications, social and psychological factors, employment outlook, entry methods, advancement, and related occupations.

★6626★ "Bus Lines" in *Opportunities in Travel Careers* (p. 59-63)
National Textbook Co. (NTC)
VGM Career Books
4255 W. Touhy Ave.
Lincolnwood, IL 60646-1975
Ph: (708)679-5500 Fax: (708)679-2494
Fr: 800-323-4900

Robert Scott Milne. 1991. Explores job opportunities in many travel related fields including the airlines, resorts, travel agencies, recreation, and tourism. Covers the work, salaries, educational preparation and training, and advancement possibilities.

★6627★ *Busdrivers*
Careers, Inc.
PO Box 135
Largo, FL 34649-0135
Ph: (813)584-7333

1993. Two-page occupational summary card describing duties, working conditions, personal qualifications, training, earnings and hours, employment outlook, places of employment, related careers and where to write for more information.

★6628★ "Busdrivers" in *Occu-Facts: Information on 580 Careers in Outline Form*
Careers, Inc.
PO Box 135
Largo, FL 34649-0135
Ph: (813)584-7333

Biennial, 1995-96 edition. Each one-page occupational profile describes duties, working conditions, physical surroundings and demands, aptitudes, temperament, educational requirements, employment outlook, earnings, and places of employment.

★6629★ "Busdrivers" in *Occupational Outlook Handbook*
U.S. Government Printing Office
Superintendent of Documents
Washington, DC 20402
Ph: (202)512-1800 Fax: (202)512-2250

Biennial; latest edition, 1994-95. Encyclopedia of careers describing more than 250 occupations and comprising about 85 percent of all jobs in the economy. Occupations that require lengthy education or training are given the most attention. For each occupation, the handbook describes job duties, working conditions, training, educational preparation, personal qualities, advancement possibilities, job outlook, earnings, and sources of additional information.

★6630★ *City Bus Driver*
Vocational Biographies, Inc.
PO Box 31
Sauk Centre, MN 56378-0031
Ph: (612)352-6516 Fax: (612)352-5546
Fr: 800-255-0752

1995. Four-page pamphlet containing a personal narrative about a worker's job, work likes and dislikes, career path from high school to the present. Education and training, the rewards and frustrations, and the effects of the job on the rest of the worker's life. The data file portion of this pamphlet gives a concise occupational summary, including work descriptions, working conditions, places of employment, personal characteristics, education and training, job outlook, and salary range.

★6631★ "Intercity Bus Driver" in *Career Information Center* (Vol.12)
Simon and Schuster
200 Old Tappan Rd.
Old Tappan, NJ 07675
Fax: 800-445-6991 Fr: 800-223-2348

Richard Lidz and Dale Anderson, editorial directors. Fifth edition, 1993. For 600 occupations, describes job duties, entry-level requirements, education and training needed, advancement possibilities, employment outlook, earnings and benefits. The set is divided into 12 volumes. Each volume includes jobs related under a broad career field. Volume 13 is the index.

★6632★ "The Intercity People Movers" in *Opportunities in Transportation Careers* (pp. 19-29)
National Textbook Co. (NTC)
VGM Career Books
4255 W. Touhy Ave.
Lincolnwood, IL 60646-1975
Ph: (708)679-5500 Fax: (708)679-2494
Fr: 800-323-4900

Adrian A. Paradis. 1988. Describes transportation and related employment in driving occupations, the airlines, merchant marine, and travel services. Covers employment outlook, educational and training requirements, wages, and the work itself, and advantages and disadvantages of transportation careers. Offers job hunting advice.

★6633★ *School Bus Driver*
Vocational Biographies, Inc.
PO Box 31
Sauk Centre, MN 56378-0031
Ph: (612)352-6516 Fax: (612)352-5546
Fr: 800-255-0752

1990. This pamphlet profiles a person working in the job. Includes information about job duties, working conditions, places of employment, educational preparation, labor market outlook, and salaries.

★6634★ "Special Service Bus Driver" in *Career Information Center* (Vol.12)
Simon and Schuster
200 Old Tappan Rd.
Old Tappan, NJ 07675
Fax: 800-445-6991 Fr: 800-223-2348

Richard Lidz and Dale Anderson, editorial directors. Fifth edition, 1993. For 600 occupations, describes job duties, entry-level requirements, education and training needed, advancement possibilities, employment outlook, earnings and benefits. The set is divided into 12 volumes. Each volume includes jobs related under a broad career field. Volume 13 is the index.

★6635★ "Teachers Aides and School Bus Drivers" in *American Almanac of Jobs and Salaries* (pp. 110)
Avon Books
1350 Avenue of the Americas
New York, NY 10019
Ph: (212)261-6800 Fr: 800-238-0658

John Wright, editor. Revised and updated, 1994-95. A comprehensive guide to the wages of hundreds of occupations in a wide variety of industries and organizations.

★6636★ "Tour Bus Driver" in *Travel & Tourism* (pp. 35-37)
Franklin Watts, Inc.
387 Park Avenue, S.
New York, NY 10016
Ph: (212)686-7070

Marjorie Rittenberg Schulz. 1990. Surveys employment opportunities in the travel and tourism industry. Provides job description, educational preparation, training, salary, employment outlook, and sources of additional information. Offers job hunting advice.

★6637★ *Video Career Library - Transportation & Materials Moving*
Careers, Inc.
PO Box 135
Largo, FL 34649-0135
Ph: (813)584-7333

Videocassette. 1990. 20 mins. Part of the Video Career Library covering 165 occupations. Shows actual workers on the job. Includes tractor/trailer truck drivers, heavy truck drivers, bus drivers, airplane pilots and navigators, grader/dozer/scraper operators, and forklift operators.

★6638★ *Vocational Visions*
Center for Humanities, Inc.
Communications Park
Box 1000
Mount Kisco, NY 10549
Ph: (914)666-4100 Fax: (914)666-5319
Fr: 800-431-1242

Videocassette. 1984. 30 mins. This series of programs explains key aspects of actual training and a day in the life of a worker in the specific field mentioned on the videocassette. Occupations include: transportation/mechanics, repair, construction, business/office occupations, health, agriculture, technical/manufacturing, communications, and personal service.

★6639★ *Vocations U.S.A.*
Info-Disc Corporation
4 Professional Dr., Ste. 134
Gaithersburg, MD 20879
Ph: (301)948-2300 Fr: 800-648-6422

Videocassette. 1987. 60 mins. A disc collection outlining the requirements and methods of various career areas. Occupations include: transportation, mechanical/repair, health, agriculture, technical/manufacturing, and construction.

Associations

★6640★ American Public Transit Association (APTA)
1201 New York Ave. NW, Ste. 400
Washington, DC 20005
Ph: (202)898-4000 Fax: (202)898-4070

Members: Rapid rail and motor bus transit systems in the U.S., Canada, and Mexico; manufacturers and suppliers of materials and services. Maintains hall of fame; compiles statistics; operates placement service and speakers' bureau; conducts seminars. Sponsors research, eduational, and charitable programs. **Publications:** *APTA Directory*, annual. • *Passenger Transport: The Weekly Newspaper of the Transit Industry*, semiannual. • *Transit Fact Book*, annual.

★6641★ Association of Professional Drivers
PO Box 491
Paoli, PA 19301
Ph: (215)647-0818

For-profit organization that encourages professionalism among truck, school bus, and passenger car drivers.

Standards/Certification Agencies

★6642★ *CDL Commercial Driver License: 104 Helpful CDL Facts*
Professional Truck Driver Institute of America
8788 Elk Grove Blvd., Ste. 20
Elk Grove, CA 95624
Ph: (916)686-5146

1990. This 32-page booklet explains the Commercial Driver License, a set of minimum standards for licensing and testing commercial drivers established by the federal government. Covers the law, classes of licenses, and test content.

Test Guides

★6643★ *Bus Driver's Guide to Commercial Driver Licensing*
Prentice Hall Press
Simon & Schuster Inc.
200 Old Tappan Rd.
Old Tappan, NJ 07675
Ph: 800-223-2348

Highway Users Federation for Safety and Mobility. First edition, 1990. Contains information and practice material on new state licensing tests for certification and recertification of all bus drivers.

★6644★ *Bus Operator-Conductor*
Arco Pub.
201 W. 103rd St.
Indianapolis, IN 46290
Ph: 800-428-5331 Fax: 800-835-3202

Hy Hammer. 1993, seventh edition. Includes 5 sample exams.

★6645★ *Career Examination Series: Bus Driver*
National Learning Corp.
212 Michael Dr.
Syosset, NY 11791
Ph: (516)921-8888 Fax: (516)921-8743
Fr: 800-645-6337

Jack Rudman. All examination guides in this series contain questions with answers.

★6646★ *Career Examination Series: Head Bus Driver*
National Learning Corp.
212 Michael Dr.
Syosset, NY 11791
Ph: (516)921-8888 Fax: (516)921-8743
Fr: 800-645-6337

Jack Rudman. All examination guides in this series contain questions with answers.

★6647★ *Career Examination Series: Transportation Specialist*
National Learning Corp.
212 Michael Dr.
Syosset, NY 11791
Ph: (516)921-8888 Fax: (516)921-8743
Fr: 800-645-6337

Jack Rudman. All examinations in this series contain questions with answers.

Educational Directories and Programs

★6648★ *American Bus Association's Motorcoach Marketer: Complete Directory of the Intercity Bus & Travel/ Tourism Industry*
American Bus Association
1100 New York Ave. NW, Ste. 1050
Washington, DC 20005-3934
Ph: (202)842-1645 Fax: (202)842-0850
Fr: 800-283-2877
Lynn Brewer, Contact

Annual, October. Covers over 2,000 hotels and sightseeing services, convention information centers, visitors' centers, and similar businesses and organizations of interest to motorcoach tour organizers; includes about 500 companies which operate intercity scheduled and charter buses; coverage includes Canada and Mexico. Entries include: Co. name, address, phone, name and title of contact. Arrangement: Classified by type of business.

Awards, Scholarships, Grants, and Fellowships

★6649★ Transportation Man of the Year
Delta Nu Alpha Transportation Fraternity
621 Plainfield, Ste. 308
Willowbrook, IL 60521

To recognize contributions to the field of transportation. A plaque is awarded annually. Established in 1952.

Periodicals

★6650★ *APTA Directory*
American Public Transit Association (APTA)
1201 New York Ave. NW, Ste. 400
Washington, DC 20005
Ph: (202)898-4000 Fax: (202)898-4070

Annual.

★6651★ *Bus World*
Stauss Publications
PO Box 39
Woodland Hills, CA 91367
Ph: (818)710-0208 Fax: (818)710-0208
Ed Stauss

Quarterly. Magazine covering transit and intercity bus systems; provides information on new bus design and technology.

★6652★ *Mass Transit*
PTN Publishing Co.
445 Broad Hollow Rd., Ste. 21
Melville, NY 11747
Ph: (516)845-2700 Fax: (516)845-7109
Tom Kapinos

Urban mass transportation publication.

★6653★ *Metro Magazine*
Bobit Publishing
2512 Artesia Blvd.
Redondo Beach, CA 90278
Ph: (310)376-8788 Fax: (310)376-9043
Frank Di GiacomoPublisher

Magazine on public transportation.

★6654★ *Passenger Transport*
American Public Transit Assn.
1201 New York Ave. NW, Ste. 400
Washington, DC 20005
Ph: (202)898-4119 Fax: (202)898-4095
Dennis Kouba

Weekly. Magazine covering the public transit industry in the U.S. and Canada.

★6655★ *Passenger Transport: The Weekly Newspaper of the Transit Industry*
American Public Transit Association (APTA)
1201 New York Ave. NW, Ste. 400
Washington, DC 20005
Ph: (202)898-4000 Fax: (202)898-4070

Semiannual. Covers the mass transit industry including annual index, obituaries, and industry personnel promotions.

★6656★ *Russell's Official National Motor Coach Guide*
Russell's Guides, Inc.
834 3rd Ave. SE
PO Box 278
Cedar Rapids, IA 52406-0278
Ph: (319)364-6138 Fax: (319)364-4853
Gary Widel

Monthly. Magazine containing national bus schedules.

★6657★ *School Bus Fleet*
Bobit Publishing
2512 Artesia Blvd.
Redondo Beach, CA 90278
Ph: (310)376-8788 Fax: (310)376-9043
Frank Di GiacomoPublisher

Magazine on pupil transportation.

★6658★ *SCTA Hi-Lights*
South Carolina Trucking Assn.
2425 Devine St.
PO Box 50166
Columbia, SC 29250-0166
Ph: (803)799-4306 Fax: (803)254-7148
J. Richards Todd

Monthly. Newspaper (tabloid) serving South Carolina Trucking Association members, truck operators, bus operators, and fleet owners in South Carolina and adjoining states.

★6659★ *TMTA Newsletter*
Texas Motor Transportation Assn.
700 E. 11th St.
PO Box 1669
Austin, TX 78767
Ph: (512)478-2541 Fax: (512)474-6494
Debra Buss

TRW. Magazine covering the Texas truck and bus industry.

★6660★ *Transit Fact Book*
American Public Transit Association (APTA)
1201 New York Ave. NW, Ste. 400
Washington, DC 20005
Ph: (202)898-4000 Fax: (202)898-4070

Annual. Statistical data book breaking down the trends of transit finances and operations by modes of travel. Contains glossary of transit terms.

★6661★ *Transportation: An Abstract Newsletter*
National Technical Information Service (NTIS)
5285 Port Royal Rd.
Springfield, VA 22161
Ph: (703)487-4630

Biweekly. Provides abstracts of publications in the areas of air, rail, water, pipeline, and road transportation; global navigation systems; and transportation safety.

★6662★ *Transportation Quarterly*
Eno Transportation Foundation
44211 Slatestone Ct.
Lansdowne, VA 22075
Ph: (703)883-8243 Fax: (703)227-3928
Tracy Dunleavy

Quarterly. Trade magazine on transportation.

★6663★ *UTU News*
United Transportation Union
14600 Detroit Ave.
Cleveland, OH 44107-4250
Ph: (216)228-9400 Fax: (216)228-5755
G.T. DuBose

Railroad and bus labor newspaper (tabloid).

Other Sources of Information

★6664★ "Bus Driver" in *Career Selector 2001*
Barron's Educational Series, Inc.
250 Wireless Blvd.
Hauppauge, NY 11788
Ph: (516)434-3311 Fax: (516)434-3723
Fr: 800-645-3476

James C. Gonyea. 1993.

★6665★ *General Driving Safety*
Gulf Publishing Co.
PO Box 2680
Houston, TX 77252
Ph: (713)529-4301 Fax: (713)520-4438

11 part series that provides instruction on driving safety, including information on road conditions and speed, drunk driving, accidents, sleepiness and driving, mountain driving, and safety devices.

★6666★ "Transportation" in *Second Careers: New Ways to Work After 50* (pp. 260-268)
Little, Brown and Co.
34 Beacon St.
Boston, MA 02108
Ph: (617)227-0730 Fax: (617)723-9422

Caroline Bird. 1992. Offers suggestions for people over 50 on careers in transportation. Jobs discussed include taxi drivers, bus drivers, truck drivers, and railway conductors.

Material Moving Equipment Operators

Material moving equipment operators use machinery to move construction materials and other manufactured goods, earth, logs, petroleum products, grain, coal, and other heavy materials over short distances. Crane and tower operators operate mechanical boom and cable or tower and cable equipment to lift and move materials, machinery, or other heavy objects. Excavation and loading machine operators operate and tend machinery equipped with scoops, shovels, or buckets to excavate earth at construction sites and to load and move loose materials. Grader, dozer, and scraper operators operate vehicles equipped with blades to remove, distribute, level, and grade earth. In addition to the bulldozers, they operate trench excavators, road graders, and similar equipment. Hoist and winch operators operate or tend machines which lift and pull loads using power-operated cable equipment. Most work in loading operations in manufacturing, mining, or logging. Operating engineers are qualified to operate more than one type of the construction equipment. Industrial truck and tractor operators drive and control industrial trucks or tractors, such as a forklift.

Salaries

Weekly median earnings for material moving equipment operators are as follows:

Crane and tower operators	$570.00/week
Excavation and loading machine operators	$441.00/week
Grader, dozer, and scraper operators	$444.00/week
Industrial truck and tractor operators	$375.00/week
Operating engineers	$514.00/week
Other material moving equipment operators	$379.00/week

Employment Outlook

Growth rate until the year 2005: More slowly than average.

Material Moving Equipment Operators

Career Guides

★6667★ "Asphalt Paving Machine Operators" in *Encyclopedia of Careers and Vocational Guidance*
J.G. Ferguson Publishing Co.
200 W. Madison St., Ste. 300
Chicago, IL 60606
Ph: (312)580-5480 Fax: (312)580-4948

William E. Hopke, editor-in-chief. Ninth edition, 1993. Four-volume set that profiles 500 occupations and describes job trends in 74 industries. Includes career description, educational requirements, history of the job, methods of entry, advancement, employment outlook, earnings, working conditions, social and psychological factors, and sources of additional information.

★6668★ *Bulldozer Operator*
Careers, Inc.
PO Box 135
Largo, FL 34649-0135
Ph: (813)584-7333

1994. Two-page occupational summary card describing duties, working conditions, personal qualifications, training, earnings and hours, employment outlook, places of employment, related careers and where to write for more information.

★6669★ "Bulldozer Operator" in *Occu-Facts: Information on 580 Careers in Outline Form*
Careers, Inc.
PO Box 135
Largo, FL 34649-0135
Ph: (813)584-7333

Biennial, 1995-96 edition. Each one-page occupational profile describes duties, working conditions, physical surroundings and demands, aptitudes, temperament, educational requirements, employment outlook, earnings, and places of employment.

★6670★ *Career Insights*
RMI Media Productions, Inc.
1365 N. Winchester
Olathe, KS 66061
Ph: (913)768-1696 Fax: 800-755-6910
Fr: 800-745-5480

Videocassette series. 1987. This videotape series describes 50 occupations, including skill requirements and interviews with people employed in these fields. Occupations include: flight service, air transportation/ground services, data processing, carpentry, clerk in banking/insurance/business, cosmetic personal grooming, firefighting, forestry, insulation/roofing, mechanics, material handling, photographic processing, pipefitting and plumbing, printing, secretarial services, tool and die operations.

★6671★ "Construction Machinery Operator" in *Guide to Careers Without College* (pp. 77-79)
Franklin Watts, Inc.
387 Park Avenue, S.
New York, NY 10016
Ph: (212)686-7070

Kathleen S. Abrams. 1988. Discusses careers that do not require a college degree in fields such as health care, sales and marketing, and the building trades. Describes the work, employment opportunities, and training.

★6672★ *Crane Operator*
Vocational Biographies, Inc.
PO Box 31
Sauk Centre, MN 56378-0031
Ph: (612)352-6516 Fax: (612)352-5546
Fr: 800-255-0752

1990. This pamphlet profiles a person working in the job. Includes information about job duties, working conditions, places of employment, educational preparation, labor market outlook, and salaries.

★6673★ *Craneman*
Film Library
3450 Wilshire Blvd., No. 700
Los Angeles, CA 90010
Ph: 800-421-9585

Videocassette. 198?. 20 mins. The basic functions and safe operation of the over head travelling crane are demonstrated in this tape.

★6674★ *Forklift Operator Training*
Film Library
3450 Wilshire Blvd., No. 700
Los Angeles, CA 90010
Ph: 800-421-9585

Videocassette. 198?. 14 mins. This course will train forklift operators in OSHA requirements.

★6675★ *Front-End Loader Operator*
Vocational Biographies, Inc.
PO Box 31
Sauk Centre, MN 56378-0031
Ph: (612)352-6516 Fax: (612)352-5546
Fr: 800-255-0752

1990. This pamphlet profiles a person working in the job. Includes information about job duties, working conditions, places of employment, educational preparation, labor market outlook, and salaries.

★6676★ "Heavy Equipment Operations" in *Career Connection II: A Guide to Technical Majors and Their Related Careers* (pp. 69-70)
Jist Works, Inc.
720 N. Park Ave.
University Station
Indianapolis, IN 46202-3431
Ph: (317)264-3720 Fax: (317)264-3709

Fred A. Rowe. 1994. Contains technical majors, such as automotive technology. Describes the major and the job. Lists high school and postsecondary school courses. Includes occupations related to the major, employment outlook, and starting salary.

★6677★ "Heavy Equipment Operator" in *Career Information Center* (Vol.4)
Simon and Schuster
200 Old Tappan Rd.
Old Tappan, NJ 07675
Fax: 800-445-6991 Fr: 800-223-2348

Richard Lidz and Dale Anderson, editorial directors. Fifth edition, 1993. For 600 occupations, describes job duties, entry-level requirements, education and training needed, advancement possibilities, employment outlook, earnings and benefits. The set is di-

vided into 12 volumes. Each volume includes jobs related under a broad career field. Volume 13 is the index.

★6678★ "Industrial Truck Operator" in *Occu-Facts: Information on 580 Careers in Outline Form*
Careers, Inc.
PO Box 135
Largo, FL 34649-0135
Ph: (813)584-7333

Biennial, 1995-96 edition. Each one-page occupational profile describes duties, working conditions, physical surroundings and demands, aptitudes, temperament, educational requirements, employment outlook, earnings, and places of employment.

★6679★ "Industrial Truck Operators" in *Career Discovery Encyclopedia* (Vol.3, pp. 122-123)
J.G. Ferguson Publishing Co.
200 W. Madison St., Ste. 300
Chicago, IL 60606
Ph: (312)580-5480 Fax: (312)580-4948

E. Russell Primm, editor-in-chief. 1993. Contains two-page articles on 504 occupations. Each article describes job duties, earnings, and educational and training requirements.

★6680★ "Industrial Truck Operators" in *Encyclopedia of Careers and Vocational Guidance* (Vol.3, pp. 198-199)
J.G. Ferguson Publishing Co.
200 W. Madison St., Ste. 300
Chicago, IL 60606
Ph: (312)580-5480 Fax: (312)580-4948

William E. Hopke, editor-in-chief. Ninth edition, 1993. Four-volume set that profiles 500 occupations and describes job trends in 74 industries. Includes career description, educational requirements, history of the job, methods of entry, advancement, employment outlook, earnings, working conditions, social and psychological factors, and sources of additional information.

★6681★ "Material Moving Equipment Operators" in *Occupational Outlook Handbook*
U.S. Government Printing Office
Superintendent of Documents
Washington, DC 20402
Ph: (202)512-1800 Fax: (202)512-2250

Biennial; latest edition, 1994-95. Encyclopedia of careers describing more than 250 occupations and comprising about 85 percent of all jobs in the economy. Occupations that require lengthy education or training are given the most attention. For each occupation, the handbook describes job duties, working conditions, training, educational preparation, personal qualities, advancement possibilities, job outlook, earnings, and sources of additional information.

★6682★ *Operating Engineer*
Careers, Inc.
PO Box 135
Largo, FL 34649-0135
Ph: (813)584-7333

1991. Four-page brief offering the definition, history, duties, working conditions, personal qualifications, educational requirements, earnings, hours, employment outlook, advancement possibilities, and related occupations.

★6683★ "Operating Engineer" in *Hard Hatted Women: Stories of Struggle and Success in the Trades* (pp. 88-101)
Seal Press
3131 Western Ave., Ste. 410
Seattle, WA 98121
Ph: (206)283-7844 Fax: (206)285-9410

Molly Martin, editor. 1988. Twenty-six women recount their experiences working in blue collar occupations. They describe how they got in, the work they do, their relationships in predominantly male occupations, and their training.

★6684★ "Operating Engineer" in *VGM's Careers Encyclopedia* (pp. 315-317)
National Textbook Co. (NTC)
VGM Career Books
4255 W. Touhy Ave.
Lincolnwood, IL 60646-1975
Ph: (708)679-5500 Fax: (708)679-2494
Fr: 800-323-4900

Third edition, 1991. Contains two- to five-page descriptions of 200 managerial, professional, technical, trade, and service occupations. Each profile includes job duties, places of employment, qualifications, educational preparation, training, employment potential, advancement, income, and additional sources of information.

★6685★ "Operating Engineer" in *VGM's Handbook of Scientific and Technical Careers* (pp. 79-82)
National Textbook Co. (NTC)
VGM Career Books
4255 W. Touhy Ave.
Lincolnwood, IL 60646-1975
Ph: (708)679-5500 Fax: (708)679-2494
Fr: 800-323-4900

Craig T. Norback, editor. 1990. Includes 50 occupations in science and technology and describes job duties, qualifications, education, training, potential advancement, and income. Lists sources of additional information.

★6686★ "Operating Engineers" in *Career Discovery Encyclopedia* (Vol.4, pp. 142-143)
J.G. Ferguson Publishing Co.
200 W. Madison St., Ste. 300
Chicago, IL 60606
Ph: (312)580-5480 Fax: (312)580-4948

E. Russell Primm, editor-in-chief. 1993. Contains two-page articles on 504 occupations. Each article describes job duties, earnings, and educational and training requirements.

★6687★ "Operating Engineers" in *Encyclopedia of Careers and Vocational Guidance* (Vol.3, pp. 615-617)
J.G. Ferguson Publishing Co.
200 W. Madison St., Ste. 300
Chicago, IL 60606
Ph: (312)580-5480 Fax: (312)580-4948

William E. Hopke, editor-in-chief. Ninth edition, 1993. Four-volume set that profiles 500 occupations and describes job trends in 74 industries. Includes career description, educational requirements, history of the job, methods of entry, advancement, employment outlook, earnings, working conditions, social and psychological factors, and sources of additional information.

★6688★ "Operating Engineers" in *Occu-Facts: Information on 580 Careers in Outline Form*
Careers, Inc.
PO Box 135
Largo, FL 34649-0135
Ph: (813)584-7333

Biennial, 1995-96 edition. Each one-page occupational profile describes duties, working conditions, physical surroundings and demands, aptitudes, temperament, educational requirements, employment outlook, earnings, and places of employment.

★6689★ "Operating Engineers" in *Opportunities in Building Construction Trades* (pp. 66-68)
National Textbook Co. (NTC)
VGM Career Books
4255 W. Touhy Ave.
Lincolnwood, IL 60646-1975
Ph: (708)679-5500 Fax: (708)679-2494
Fr: 800-323-4900

Michael Sumichrast. 1989. Gives an overview of the construction industry and describes the jobs of various craftworkers. Covers different kinds of builders: home, custom; and describes management skills needed and industry trends affecting opportunities.

★6690★ "Power Shovel Crane Operator" in *Occu-Facts: Information on 580 Careers in Outline Form* (p. 19.16)
Careers, Inc.
PO Box 135
Largo, FL 34649-0135
Ph: (813)584-7333

Biennial, 1995-96 edition. Each one-page occupational profile describes duties, working conditions, physical surroundings and demands, aptitudes, temperament, educational requirements, employment outlook, earnings, and places of employment.

★6691★ "Power Truck Operator" in *Career Information Center* (Vol.12)
Simon and Schuster
200 Old Tappan Rd.
Old Tappan, NJ 07675
Fax: 800-445-6991 Fr: 800-223-2348

Richard Lidz and Dale Anderson, editorial directors. Fifth edition, 1993. For 600 occupations, describes job duties, entry-level requirements, education and training needed, advancement possibilities, employment outlook, earnings and benefits. The set is divided into 12 volumes. Each volume includes jobs related under a broad career field. Volume 13 is the index.

★6692★ *Shovel-Crave Operator, Power*
Careers, Inc.
PO Box 135
Largo, FL 34649-0135
Ph: (813)584-7333

1993. Two-page occupational summary card describing duties, working conditions, personal qualifications, training, earnings and hours, employment outlook, places of employment, related careers and where to write for more information.

★6693★ *Transportation*
Learning Corporation of America
108 Wilmot Rd.
Deerfield, IL 60015
Ph: (708)940-1260 Fax: (708)940-3600
Fr: 800-621-2131

Videocassette. 1982. 21 mins. In this program from the "Working" series, we meet five employees in transportation-related jobs: fishing boat captain, auto body repair shop owner, construction equipment operator, air traffic controller and truck driver.

★6694★ *Truck Operator, Industrial*
Careers, Inc.
PO Box 135
Largo, FL 34649-0135
Ph: (813)584-7333

1992. Two-page occupational summary card describing duties, working conditions, personal qualifications, training, earnings and hours, employment outlook, places of employment, related careers and where to write for more information.

★6695★ *Video Career Library - Transportation & Materials Moving*
Careers, Inc.
PO Box 135
Largo, FL 34649-0135
Ph: (813)584-7333

Videocassette. 1990. 20 mins. Part of the Video Career Library covering 165 occupations. Shows actual workers on the job. Includes tractor/trailer truck drivers, heavy truck drivers, bus drivers, airplane pilots and navigators, grader/dozer/scraper operators, and forklift operators.

ASSOCIATIONS

★6696★ Associated Builders and Contractors (ABC)
1300 N. 17th St.
Rossyln, VA 22209
Ph: (703)812-2000

Members: Construction contractors, subcontractors, suppliers, and associates. **Purpose:** Aim is to foster and perpetuate the principles of rewarding construction workers and management on the basis of merit. Sponsors management education programs and craft training; also sponsors apprenticeship and skill training programs. Disseminates technological and labor relations information. Maintains placement service. Compiles statistics. **Publications:** *ABC Today*, semimonthly. • *National Membership Directory and Users Guide*, annual.

★6697★ Associated General Contractors of America (AGC)
1957 E St. NW
Washington, DC 20006
Ph: (202)393-2040 Fax: (202)347-4004

Members: General construction contractors; subcontractors; industry suppliers; service firms. **Purpose:** Provides market services through its divisions. Conducts special conferences and seminars designed specifically for construction firms. Compiles statistics on job accidents reported by member firms. ors. Maintains 65 committees, including joint cooperative committees with other associations and liaison committees with federal agencies. **Publications:** *AGC Membership Directory and Buyers' Guide*, annual. • *AGC Mobile Directory*. • *Associated General Contractors of America—National Newsletter*, biweekly. • *Constructor*, monthly.

★6698★ Industrial Truck Association (ITA)
1750 K St. NW, Ste. 460
Washington, DC 20006
Ph: (202)296-9880

Members: Purpose: Manufacturers of powered industrial lift trucks, electric storage batteries, tires, engines, attachments, and hydraulic systems for powered industrial lift trucks.

★6699★ International Union of Operating Engineers (IUOE)
1125 17th St. NW
Washington, DC 20036
Ph: (202)429-9100 Fax: (202)429-0316

Members: AFL-CIO. **Publications:** *International Operating Engineer*, bimonthly.

EDUCATIONAL DIRECTORIES AND PROGRAMS

★6700★ *AGC Membership Directory and Buyers' Guide*
Associated General Contractors of America (AGC)
1957 E St. NW
Washington, DC 20006
Ph: (202)393-2040 Fax: (202)347-4004

Annual.

★6701★ *AGC Mobile Directory*
Associated General Contractors of America (AGC)
1957 E St. NW
Washington, DC 20006
Ph: (202)393-2040 Fax: (202)347-4004

PERIODICALS

★6702★ *ABC Today*
Associated Builders and Contractors (ABC)
1300 N. 17th St.
Rosslyn, VA 22209
Ph: (703)812-2000

Semimonthly. News magazine for merit shop contractors.

★6703★ *American Mover*
American Movers Conference
1611 Duke St.
Alexandria, VA 22314-4654
Ph: (703)683-7410 Fax: (703)683-7527
Michael Hayes

Monthly. Magazine for the moving industry.

★6704★ *Associated General Contractors of America—National Newsletter*
Associated General Contractors of America (AGC)
1957 E St. NW
Washington, DC 20006
Ph: (202)393-2040 Fax: (202)347-4004

Biweekly.

★6705★ *Network for Material Handling*
PO Box 2338
East Peoria, IL 61611
Fax: (309)698-0801 Fr: 800-447-6901
Mike HawkinsGen Mgr

Monthly. Trade magazine for the materials handling industry.

★6706★ *Rock and Dirt*
TAP Publishing Co.
410 W. 4th St.
PO Box 489
Crossville, TN 38557
Ph: (615)484-5139 Fax: (615)484-2532
Michael D. StonePublisher

Buy and sell trade newspaper (tabloid) for heavy construction earth moving machinery.

★6707★ *Southwest Contractor*
McGraw-Hill, Inc.
2050 E. University Dr., Ste. 1
Phoenix, AZ 85034-6731
Ph: (602)258-1641 Fax: (602)495-9407
Bill Davis

Monthly. Regional trade magazine for the contracting industries including highway, municipal, utility, heavy construction, and mining.

MEETINGS AND CONVENTIONS

★6708★ American Movers Association Trade Show
American Movers Association
1611 Duke St.
Alexandria, VA 22314
Ph: (703)683-7410 Fax: (703)683-7527

Annual.

★6709★ NASSTRAC
NASSTRAC
1750 Pennsylvania Ave., Ste. 1105
Washington, DC 20006
Ph: (202)393-5505 Fax: (202)347-8978

Semiannual.

OTHER SOURCES OF INFORMATION

★6710★ *Forklift Truck: Operator Training*
Du Pont
Brandywine Bldg., No. 11266
Wilmington, DE 19898
Ph: (302)774-2168 Fax: (302)774-2134
Fr: 800-532-7233

Accompanied by self-study courses for either experienced or novice drivers, this tape outlines the training for forklift handlers.

Rail Transportation Occupations

Rail transportation workers facilitate the movement of passengers and cargo by trains, subways, and streetcars. **Locomotive engineers and rail yard engineers** operate locomotives in yards, stations, and on the road between stations. Locomotive engineers transport cargo and passengers between stations, while yard engineers move cars within yards to assemble or disassemble trains. Some engineers called dickey operators work at industrial sites or mines operating engines that help transport coal, rock, or supplies. **Road conductors and yard conductors** are in charge of train and yard crews. Conductors assigned to freight trains keep records of each car's contents and destination and make sure that cars are added and removed at the proper points along the route. Conductors assigned to passenger trains collect tickets and fares and assist passengers. Yard conductors supervise the crews that assemble and disassemble trains. **Brake operators** send information to conductors and dispatchers regarding needed repairs while underway or the removal of defective cars at the nearest station or stop. **Subway operators** guide subway trains, observing the signal system. **Streetcar operators** drive electric-powered streetcars to transport passengers, collect fares from passengers, and issues change and transfers.

Salaries

Average annual earnings for rail transportation workers are as follows:

Yard engineers	$43,300/year
Through engineers in passenger service	$57,900/year
Through engineers in freight service	$54,100/year
Conductors in passenger service	$40,400/year
Conductors in freight service	$35,200/year
Brake operators in freight service	$33,600/year
Brake operators in yard service	$25,600/year

Employment Outlook

Growth rate until the year 2005: Average.

Rail Transportation Occupations

Career Guides

★6711★ "Brake Operators, Brakers" in *Encyclopedia of Careers and Vocational Guidance* (Vol.2, pp. 216-218)
J.G. Ferguson Publishing Co.
200 W. Madison St., Ste. 300
Chicago, IL 60606
Ph: (312)580-5480 Fax: (312)580-4948

William E. Hopke, editor-in-chief. Ninth edition, 1993. Four-volume set that profiles 500 occupations and describes job trends in 74 industries. Includes career description, educational requirements, history of the job, methods of entry, advancement, employment outlook, earnings, working conditions, social and psychological factors, and sources of additional information.

★6712★ "Brakers" in *Career Discovery Encyclopedia* (Vol.1, pp. 126-127)
J.G. Ferguson Publishing Co.
200 W. Madison St., Ste. 300
Chicago, IL 60606
Ph: (312)580-5480 Fax: (312)580-4948

E. Russell Primm, editor-in-chief. 1993. Contains two-page articles on 504 occupations. Each article describes job duties, earnings, and educational and training requirements.

★6713★ "Conductors" in *American Almanac of Jobs and Salaries* (pp. 446)
Avon Books
1350 Avenue of the Americas
New York, NY 10019
Ph: (212)261-6800 Fr: 800-238-0658

John Wright, editor. Revised and updated, 1994-95. A comprehensive guide to the wages of hundreds of occupations in a wide variety of industries and organizations.

★6714★ "Conductors" in *Career Discovery Encyclopedia* (Vol.2, pp. 48-49)
J.G. Ferguson Publishing Co.
200 W. Madison St., Ste. 300
Chicago, IL 60606
Ph: (312)580-5480 Fax: (312)580-4948

E. Russell Primm, editor-in-chief. 1993. Contains two-page articles on 504 occupations. Each article describes job duties, earnings, and educational and training requirements.

★6715★ "Conductors" in *Opportunities in Travel Careers* (p. 54)
National Textbook Co. (NTC)
VGM Career Books
4255 W. Touhy Ave.
Lincolnwood, IL 60646-1975
Ph: (708)679-5500 Fax: (708)679-2494
Fr: 800-323-4900

Robert Scott Milne. 1991. Explores job opportunities in many travel related fields including the airlines, resorts, travel agencies, recreation, and tourism. Covers the work, salaries, educational preparation and training, and advancement possibilities.

★6716★ "Engineers and Engineer Helpers" in *Opportunities in Travel Careers* (pp. 54-55)
National Textbook Co. (NTC)
VGM Career Books
4255 W. Touhy Ave.
Lincolnwood, IL 60646-1975
Ph: (708)679-5500 Fax: (708)679-2494
Fr: 800-323-4900

Robert Scott Milne. 1991. Explores job opportunities in many travel related fields including the airlines, resorts, travel agencies, recreation, and tourism. Covers the work, salaries, educational preparation and training, and advancement possibilities.

★6717★ *The Human Side of Railroading*
Association of American Railroads
Information and Public Affairs Department
50 F St., NW
Washington, DC 20001
Ph: (202)639-2100

1987. Booklet describing the jobs of train and engine service workers and track and equipment maintenance workers. Lists headquarters of major railroads.

★6718★ "Locomotive Engineer" in *Occu-Facts: Information on 580 Careers in Outline Form*
Careers, Inc.
PO Box 135
Largo, FL 34649-0135
Ph: (813)584-7333

Biennial, 1995-96 edition. Each one-page occupational profile describes duties, working conditions, physical surroundings and demands, aptitudes, temperament, educational requirements, employment outlook, earnings, and places of employment.

★6719★ "Locomotive Engineers" in *Career Discovery Encyclopedia* (Vol.4, pp. 28-29)
J.G. Ferguson Publishing Co.
200 W. Madison St., Ste. 300
Chicago, IL 60606
Ph: (312)580-5480 Fax: (312)580-4948

E. Russell Primm, editor-in-chief. 1993. Contains two-page articles on 504 occupations. Each article describes job duties, earnings, and educational and training requirements.

★6720★ "Locomotive Engineers" in *Encyclopedia of Careers and Vocational Guidance* (Vol.3, pp. 325-327)
J.G. Ferguson Publishing Co.
200 W. Madison St., Ste. 300
Chicago, IL 60606
Ph: (312)580-5480 Fax: (312)580-4948

William E. Hopke, editor-in-chief. Ninth edition, 1993. Four-volume set that profiles 500 occupations and describes job trends in 74 industries. Includes career description, educational requirements, history of the job, methods of entry, advancement, employment outlook, earnings, working conditions, social and psychological factors, and sources of additional information.

★6721★ "New Horizons for Rail Careers" in *Opportunities in Transportation Careers* (pp. 81-93)
National Textbook Co. (NTC)
VGM Career Books
4255 W. Touhy Ave.
Lincolnwood, IL 60646-1975
Ph: (708)679-5500 Fax: (708)679-2494
Fr: 800-323-4900

Adrian A. Paradis. 1988. Describes transportation and related employment in driving occupations, the airlines, merchant marine, and travel services. Covers employment outlook, educational and training requirements, wages, and the work itself, and advantages and disadvantages of transportation careers. Offers job hunting advice.

★6722★ *"Rail Transportation Occupation" in Occupational Outlook Handbook*
U.S. Government Printing Office
Superintendent of Documents
Washington, DC 20402
Ph: (202)512-1800 Fax: (202)512-2250

Biennial; latest edition, 1994-95. Encyclopedia of careers describing more than 250 occupations and comprising about 85 percent of all jobs in the economy. Occupations that require lengthy education or training are given the most attention. For each occupation, the handbook describes job duties, working conditions, training, educational preparation, personal qualities, advancement possibilities, job outlook, earnings, and sources of additional information.

★6723★ *Railroad Brake Operator*
Careers, Inc.
PO Box 135
Largo, FL 34649-0135
Ph: (813)584-7333

1992. Two-page occupational summary card describing duties, working conditions, personal qualifications, training, earnings and hours, employment outlook, places of employment, related careers and where to write for more information.

★6724★ "Railroad Brake Operator" in *Occu-Facts: Information on 580 Careers in Outline Form*
Careers, Inc.
PO Box 135
Largo, FL 34649-0135
Ph: (813)584-7333

Biennial, 1995-96 edition. Each one-page occupational profile describes duties, working conditions, physical surroundings and demands, aptitudes, temperament, educational requirements, employment outlook, earnings, and places of employment.

★6725★ "Railroad Braker" in *Career Information Center* (Vol.12)
Simon and Schuster
200 Old Tappan Rd.
Old Tappan, NJ 07675
Fax: 800-445-6991 Fr: 800-223-2348

Richard Lidz and Dale Anderson, editorial directors. Fifth edition, 1993. For 600 occupations, describes job duties, entry-level requirements, education and training needed, advancement possibilities, employment outlook, earnings and benefits. The set is divided into 12 volumes. Each volume includes jobs related under a broad career field. Volume 13 is the index.

★6726★ "Railroad Braker and Conductor" in *Transportation* (pp. 39-43)
Franklin Watts, Inc.
387 Park Avenue, S.
New York, NY 10016
Ph: (212)686-7070

Marjorie Rittenberg Schulz. 1990. Surveys the transportation industry including air, water, and rail services. Provides job description, training, salary, and employment outlook. Offers job hunting advice.

★6727★ "Railroad Clerks" in *Encyclopedia of Careers and Vocational Guidance* (Vol.4, pp. 236-238)
J.G. Ferguson Publishing Co.
200 W. Madison St., Ste. 300
Chicago, IL 60606
Ph: (312)580-5480 Fax: (312)580-4948

William E. Hopke, editor-in-chief. Ninth edition, 1993. Four-volume set that profiles 500 occupations and describes job trends in 74 industries. Includes career description, educational requirements, history of the job, methods of entry, advancement, employment outlook, earnings, working conditions, social and psychological factors, and sources of additional information.

★6728★ *Railroad Conductor*
Vocational Biographies, Inc.
PO Box 31
Sauk Centre, MN 56378-0031
Ph: (612)352-6516 Fax: (612)352-5546
Fr: 800-255-0752

1989. This pamphlet profiles a person working in the job. Includes information about job duties, working conditions, places of employment, educational preparation, labor market outlook, and salaries.

★6729★ *Railroad Conductor*
Careers, Inc.
PO Box 135
Largo, FL 34649-0135
Ph: (813)584-7333

1992. Two-page occupational summary card describing duties, working conditions, personal qualifications, training, earnings and hours, employment outlook, places of employment, related careers and where to write for more information.

★6730★ "Railroad Conductor" in *Career Information Center* (Vol.12)
Simon and Schuster
200 Old Tappan Rd.
Old Tappan, NJ 07675
Fax: 800-445-6991 Fr: 800-223-2348

Richard Lidz and Dale Anderson, editorial directors. Fifth edition, 1993. For 600 occupations, describes job duties, entry-level requirements, education and training needed, advancement possibilities, employment outlook, earnings and benefits. The set is divided into 12 volumes. Each volume includes jobs related under a broad career field. Volume 13 is the index.

★6731★ "Railroad Conductor" in *Jobs Rated Almanac*
World Almanac
1 International Blvd., Ste. 444
Mahwah, NJ 07495
Ph: (201)529-6900 Fax: (201)529-6901

Les Krantz. Second edition, 1992. Ranks 250 jobs by environment, salary, outlooks, physical demands, stress, security, travel opportunities, and extra perks. Includes jobs the editor feels are the most common, most interesting, and the most rapidly growing.

★6732★ "Railroad Conductor" in *Occu-Facts: Information on 580 Careers in Outline Form*
Careers, Inc.
PO Box 135
Largo, FL 34649-0135
Ph: (813)584-7333

Biennial, 1995-96 edition. Each one-page occupational profile describes duties, working conditions, physical surroundings and demands, aptitudes, temperament, educational requirements, employment outlook, earnings, and places of employment.

★6733★ "Railroad Engineer" in *Career Information Center* (Vol.12)
Simon and Schuster
200 Old Tappan Rd.
Old Tappan, NJ 07675
Fax: 800-445-6991 Fr: 800-223-2348

Richard Lidz and Dale Anderson, editorial directors. Fifth edition, 1993. For 600 occupations, describes job duties, entry-level requirements, education and training needed, advancement possibilities, employment outlook, earnings and benefits. The set is divided into 12 volumes. Each volume includes jobs related under a broad career field. Volume 13 is the index.

★6734★ *Railroad Industry Workers*
Chronicle Guidance Publications, Inc.
66 Aurora St.
PO Box 1190
Moravia, NY 13118-1190
Ph: (315)497-0330 Fax: (315)497-3359
Fr: 800-622-7284

1991. This career brief describes the nature of the work, working conditions, hours and earnings, education and training, licensure, certification, unions, personal qualifications, social and psychological factors, employment outlook, entry methods, advancement, and related occupations.

★6735★ *She's a Railroader*
Phoenix/BFA Films
PO Box 1850
New York, NY 10156-1850
Ph: (212)684-5910 Fr: 800-221-1274

Videocassette. 1980. 10 mins. This program tells the story of a woman who works on the railroad and how she manages in a traditionally male field.

★6736★ "Subway Conductor" in *Hard Hatted Women: Stories of Struggle and Success in the Trades* (pp. 193-201)
Seal Press
3131 Western Ave., Ste. 410
Seattle, WA 98121
Ph: (206)283-7844 Fax: (206)285-9410
Molly Martin, editor. 1988. Twenty-six women recount their experiences working in blue collar occupations. They describe how they got in, the work they do, their relationships in predominantly male occupations, and their training.

Associations

★6737★ Association of American Railroads (AAR)
50 F St. NW
Washington, DC 20001
Ph: (202)639-2100 Fax: (202)639-2986
Members: Coordinating and research agency of the American freight railway industry. **Purpose:** Fields of interest include railroad operation and maintenance, statistics, research, public relations, communications, signals, car exchange rules, safety, police and security matters, and testing and standards of railroad equipment. **Publications:** *Analysis of Class I Railroads*, annual. • *Rail News Update*, biweekly. • *Railroad Facts*, annual.

Test Guides

★6738★ *Career Examination Series: Assistant Superintendent (Track)*
National Learning Corp.
212 Michael Dr.
Syosset, NY 11791
Ph: (516)921-8888 Fax: (516)921-8743
Fr: 800-645-6337
Jack Rudman. 1989. All examination guides in this series contain questions with answers.

★6739★ *Career Examination Series: Assistant Train Dispatcher*
National Learning Corp.
212 Michael Dr.
Syosset, NY 11791
Ph: (516)921-8888 Fax: (516)921-8743
Fr: 800-645-6337
Jack Rudman. All examination guides in this series contain questions with answers.

★6740★ *Career Examination Series: Foreman (Railroad Watchman)*
National Learning Corp.
212 Michael Dr.
Syosset, NY 11791
Ph: (516)921-8888 Fax: (516)921-8743
Fr: 800-645-6337
Jack Rudman. All examination guides in this series contain questions with answers.

★6741★ *Career Examination Series: Foreman (Signals)*
National Learning Corp.
212 Michael Dr.
Syosset, NY 11791
Ph: (516)921-8888 Fax: (516)921-8743
Fr: 800-645-6337
Jack Rudman. 1989. All examination guides in this series contain questions with answers.

★6742★ *Career Examination Series: Foreman (Track)*
National Learning Corp.
212 Michael Dr.
Syosset, NY 11791
Ph: (516)921-8888 Fax: (516)921-8743
Fr: 800-645-6337
Jack Rudman. 1989. All examination guides in this series contain questions with answers.

★6743★ *Career Examination Series: Gang Foreman (Track)*
National Learning Corp.
212 Michael Dr.
Syosset, NY 11791
Ph: (516)921-8888 Fax: (516)921-8743
Fr: 800-645-6337
Jack Rudman. 1989. All examination guides in this series contain questions with answers.

★6744★ *Career Examination Series: Railroad Caretaker*
National Learning Corp.
212 Michael Dr.
Syosset, NY 11791
Ph: (516)921-8888 Fax: (516)921-8743
Fr: 800-645-6337
Jack Rudman. All examination guides in this series contain questions with answers.

★6745★ *Career Examination Series: Railroad Clerk*
National Learning Corp.
212 Michael Dr.
Syosset, NY 11791
Ph: (516)921-8888 Fax: (516)921-8743
Fr: 800-645-6337
Jack Rudman. All examination guides in this series contain questions with answers.

★6746★ *Career Examination Series: Railroad Equipment Inspector*
National Learning Corp.
212 Michael Dr.
Syosset, NY 11791
Ph: (516)921-8888 Fax: (516)921-8743
Fr: 800-645-6337
Jack Rudman. All examination guides in this series contain questions with answers.

★6747★ *Career Examination Series: Railroad Inspector*
National Learning Corp.
212 Michael Dr.
Syosset, NY 11791
Ph: (516)921-8888 Fax: (516)921-8743
Fr: 800-645-6337
Jack Rudman. All examination guides in this series contain questions with answers.

★6748★ *Career Examination Series: Railroad Porter*
National Learning Corp.
212 Michael Dr.
Syosset, NY 11791
Ph: (516)921-8888 Fax: (516)921-8743
Fr: 800-645-6337
Jack Rudman. All examination guides in this series contain questions with answers.

★6749★ *Career Examination Series: Railroad Signal Specialist*
National Learning Corp.
212 Michael Dr.
Syosset, NY 11791
Ph: (516)921-8888 Fax: (516)921-8743
Fr: 800-645-6337
Jack Rudman. All examination guides in this series contain questions with answers.

★6750★ *Career Examination Series: Railroad Stock Assistant*
National Learning Corp.
212 Michael Dr.
Syosset, NY 11791
Ph: (516)921-8888 Fax: (516)921-8743
Fr: 800-645-6337
Jack Rudman. All examination guides in this series contain questions with answers.

★6751★ *Career Examination Series: Railroad Stockman*
National Learning Corp.
212 Michael Dr.
Syosset, NY 11791
Ph: (516)921-8888 Fax: (516)921-8743
Fr: 800-645-6337
Jack Rudman. All examination guides in this series contain questions with answers.

★6752★ *Career Examination Series: Railroad Track and Structure Inspector*
National Learning Corp.
212 Michael Dr.
Syosset, NY 11791
Ph: (516)921-8888 Fax: (516)921-8743
Fr: 800-645-6337
Jack Rudman. All examination guides in this series contain questions with answers.

★6753★ *Career Examination Series: Supervisor (Track)*
National Learning Corp.
212 Michael Dr.
Syosset, NY 11791
Ph: (516)921-8888 Fax: (516)921-8743
Fr: 800-645-6337
Jack Rudman. 1988. All examination guides in this series contain questions with answers.

★6754★ *Career Examination Series: Track Equipment Maintainer*
National Learning Corp.
212 Michael Dr.
Syosset, NY 11791
Ph: (516)921-8888 Fax: (516)921-8743
Fr: 800-645-6337
Jack Rudman. All examination guides in this series contain questions with answers.

★6755★ *Career Examination Series: Trackman*
National Learning Corp.
212 Michael Dr.
Syosset, NY 11791
Ph: (516)921-8888 Fax: (516)921-8743
Fr: 800-645-6337

Jack Rudman. All examination guides in this series contain questions with answers.

★6756★ *Career Examination Series: Train Dispatcher*
National Learning Corp.
212 Michael Dr.
Syosset, NY 11791
Ph: (516)921-8888 Fax: (516)921-8743
Fr: 800-645-6337

Jack Rudman. All examination guides in this series contain questions with answers.

★6757★ *Career Examination Series: Train Operator*
National Learning Corp.
212 Michael Dr.
Syosset, NY 11791
Ph: (516)921-8888 Fax: (516)921-8743
Fr: 800-645-6337

Jack Rudman. All examination guides in this series contain questions with answers.

★6758★ *Career Examination Series: Trainmaster*
National Learning Corp.
212 Michael Dr.
Syosset, NY 11791
Ph: (516)921-8888 Fax: (516)921-8743
Fr: 800-645-6337

Jack Rudman. All examination guides in this series contain questions with answers.

★6759★ *Railroad Clerk*
Prentice Hall Press
Simon & Schuster Inc.
200 Old Tappan Rd.
Old Tappan, NJ 07675
Ph: 800-223-2348

Hy Hammer. Third edition, 1984. Provides seven sample examinations with answers for applicants of the New York City rapid transit system.

★6760★ *Railroad Clerk*
Arco Pub.
201 W. 103rd St.
Indianapolis, IN 46290
Ph: 800-428-5331 Fax: 800-835-3202

Hy Hammer. 1994, third edition. Contains seven practice examinations.

Educational Directories and Programs

★6761★ *Railway Age—Railroad Financial Desk Book Issue*
Simmons-Boardman Publishing Corp.
345 Hudson St.
New York, NY 10014
Ph: (212)620-7200 Fax: (212)633-1165
Tony Kruglinski

Annual. Publication includes: Directory of institutions and individuals involved in railroad finance, including banks, arrangers, operating lessors, consultants, accountants, and attorneys. Entries include: Co. name, address, phone, fax, names and titles of key personnel, description. Arrangement: Classified by line of business, then alphabetical.

Awards, Scholarships, Grants, and Fellowships

★6762★ Branding Hammer Award
Railway Tie Association
PO Box 1039
Gulf Shores, AL 36547-1039
Ph: (205)968-5927 Fax: (205)968-5929

To recognize an associate member of the Railway Tie Association who is an employee of a railroad and participated over a period of years in the activities and programs of the Association. A crosstie branding hammer mounted on an inscribed plaque is awarded annually. Established in 1975.

★6763★ *Modern Railroad* Man of the Year
Modern Railroads
K-III Press, Inc.
424 W. 33rd St.
New York, NY 10001

To honor the individual making the greatest contribution to successful railroading. Selection is made by the editors of the magazine. A bronze plaque is awarded annually. Established in 1963.

★6764★ Transportation Man of the Year
Delta Nu Alpha Transportation Fraternity
621 Plainfield, Ste. 308
Willowbrook, IL 60521

To recognize contributions to the field of transportation. A plaque is awarded annually. Established in 1952.

Periodicals

★6765★ *American Railway Engineering Association Bulletin*
American Railway Engineering Assn.
50 F St. NW, No. 7702
Washington, DC 20001
Ph: (202)639-2190 Fax: (202)639-2183
Louis T. Cerny

Magazine of the American Railway Engineering Association. Contains technical committee reports; proposed changes to the Manual for Railway Engineering and Portfolio of Trackwork Plans; reports on railway engineering, construction, and maintenance; results of research investigations and service tests; and proceedings of the Annual Technical Conference.

★6766★ *Analysis of Class I Railroads*
Association of American Railroads (AAR)
50 F St. NW
Washington, DC 20001
Ph: (202)639-2100 Fax: (202)639-2986

Annual.

★6767★ *BMWE Journal*
Brotherhood of Maintenance of Way Employes
26555 Evergreen Rd., Ste. 200
Southfield, MI 48076-4225
Ph: (810)948-1010 Fax: (810)948-7150
Mac A. Fleming

Monthly. Railroad labor tabloid.

★6768★ *Government Tender Report*
American Trucking Associations, Inc.
2200 Mill Rd.
Alexandria, VA 22314
Ph: (703)838-1794
Emry Williams

Semiweekly. Summarizes tenders (except those pertaining to household goods) which have been submitted to the Interstate Commerce Commission by motor, water, and rail carriers and bureaus, and freight forwarders in compliance with Section 10721 of the Interstate Commerce Act. Also identifies carriers, tender numbers, effective and expiration dates, commodities, origins, destinations, and rates. Lists and cross-references entries according to regions of origin.

★6769★ *Government Traffic Bulletin Trucking Information*
American Trucking Information Services, Inc.
2200 Mill Rd.
Alexandria, VA 22314
Ph: (703)838-1793
Susan Stowell

Weekly. Summarizes current traffic requirements of major U.S. Government agencies and reports changes in federal transportation policies, procedures, and personnel. Provides names and phone numbers of individuals who may be contacted for additional information.

★6770★ *International Railway Journal*
Simmons-Boardman Publishing
345 Hudson St.
New York, NY 10014
Ph: (212)620-7200 Fax: (212)633-1165
Mike KnuttonPublisher

Monthly. Magazine focusing on international railways and rail transit. Summaries in French, German and Spanish.

★6771★ *Locomotive Engineers Journal*
Brotherhood of Locomotive Engineers
1370 Ontario St.
Cleveland, OH 44113-1702
Ph: (216)241-2630 Fax: (216)861-0932
Stephen W. FitzGerald

Quarterly. Railroad industry magazine.

★6772★ *NITL Notice*
National Industrial Transportation League (NITL)
1700 N. Moore St., Ste. 1900
Arlington, VA 22209
Ph: (703)524-5011 Fax: (703)524-5017
Patricia A. Mascari

Weekly. Carries transportation news—railroad, motor carrier, airline, and maritime—in the interest of industrial and commercial shippers. Covers rate-hike proposals, transportation legislation, regulatory agency actions, postal service developments, union actions, and court cases. Recurring features include coverage of the Interstate Commerce Commission, U.S. Postal Service, Department of Transportation, and other regulatory agencies.

★6773★ *The Official Railway Equipment Register*
K-III Directory Co.
424 W. 33rd St.
New York, NY 10001
Ph: (212)714-3100
Bob DeMarcoPublisher

Quarterly. Railroad freight car directory.

★6774★ *Passenger Transport*
American Public Transit Assn.
1201 New York Ave. NW, Ste. 400
Washington, DC 20005
Ph: (202)898-4119 Fax: (202)898-4095
Dennis Kouba

Weekly. Magazine covering the public transit industry in the U.S. and Canada.

★6775★ *Pocket List of Railroad Officials*
K-III Directory Co.
424 W. 33rd St.
New York, NY 10001
Ph: (212)714-3100
Robert DeMarcoPublisher

Quarterly. Comprehensive guide to officials in the freight railroad, rail transit, and rail supply industries.

★6776★ *Progressive Railroading*
Murphy-Richter Publishing Co.
230 W. Monroe St., Ste. 2210
Chicago, IL 60606
Ph: (312)629-1200 Fax: (312)629-1304
Tom Judge

Monthly. Railroad magazine.

★6777★ *Rail News Update*
Association of American Railroads (AAR)
50 F St. NW
Washington, DC 20001
Ph: (202)639-2100 Fax: (202)639-2986

Biweekly.

★6778★ *Railroad Facts*
Association of American Railroads (AAR)
50 F St. NW
Washington, DC 20001
Ph: (202)639-2100 Fax: (202)639-2986

Annual.

★6779★ *Railroad Newsletter*
National Safety Council
1121 Spring Lake Dr.
Itasca, IL 60143-3201
Ph: (708)775-2282 Fax: (708)775-2285
Diane M. Ghazarian

Bimonthly. Devoted to accident prevention for railroad personnel. Considers related safety factors, such as noise levels, health hazards, attitudes, and environmental conditions. Provides safety pointers for leisure as well as work activities.

★6780★ *Railway Age*
Simmons-Boardman Publishing
345 Hudson St.
New York, NY 10014
Ph: (212)620-7200 Fax: (212)633-1165
Luther Miller

Monthly. Magazine focusing on railroad and rail transit.

★6781★ *Railway Track & Structures*
Simmons-Boardman Publishing
345 Hudson St.
New York, NY 10014
Ph: (212)620-7200 Fax: (212)633-1165
Robert E. Tuzik

Monthly. Magazine focusing on railroad engineering and maintenance.

★6782★ *Signalman's Journal*
Brotherhood of Railroad Signalmen
601 W. Golf Rd.
PO Box U
Mount Prospect, IL 60056
Ph: (708)439-3732 Fax: (708)439-3743
J.C. Sinclair

Bimonthly.

★6783★ *Southern and Southwestern Railway Club Proceedings*
Southern and Southwestern Railway Assn.
717 Pinecliffe Drive
Chesapeake, VA 23320
Ph: (804)547-5891

Quarterly. Railroad magazine.

★6784★ *Tiempo Latino*
3288 21st Street
PO Box 9
San Francisco, CA 94110
Ph: (415)821-4452
Gail E. NeiraPublisher

Weekly. Publication focusing on Hispanic/Latin issues in Northern California.

★6785★ *Trains*
Kalmbach Publishing Co.
PO Box 1612
Waukesha, WI 53187
Ph: (414)796-8776 Fax: (414)796-0126
J.D. Ingles

Monthly. Magazine featuring railroads past and present.

★6786★ *Transportation: An Abstract Newsletter*
National Technical Information Service (NTIS)
5285 Port Royal Rd.
Springfield, VA 22161
Ph: (703)487-4630

Biweekly. Provides abstracts of publications in the areas of air, rail, water, pipeline, and road transportation; global navigation systems; and transportation safety.

★6787★ *Transportation & Distribution*
Penton Publishing
1100 Superior Ave.
Cleveland, OH 44114
Ph: (216)696-7000 Fax: (216)696-7932
Perry Trunick

Monthly. Magazine covering traffic and physical distribution.

★6788★ *Transportation Quarterly*
Eno Transportation Foundation
44211 Slatestone Ct.
Lansdowne, VA 22075
Ph: (703)883-8243 Fax: (703)227-3928
Tracy Dunleavy

Quarterly. Trade magazine on transportation.

★6789★ *TWU Express*
Transport Workers Union of America
80 West End Ave.
New York, NY 10023
Ph: (212)873-6000 Fax: (212)721-1431
James Gannon

Monthly. Labor magazine.

★6790★ *UTU News*
United Transportation Union
14600 Detroit Ave.
Cleveland, OH 44107-4250
Ph: (216)228-9400 Fax: (216)228-5755
G.T. DuBose

Railroad and bus labor newspaper (tabloid).

OTHER SOURCES OF INFORMATION

★6791★ "Transportation" in *Second Careers: New Ways to Work After 50* (pp. 260-268)
Little, Brown and Co.
34 Beacon St.
Boston, MA 02108
Ph: (617)227-0730 Fax: (617)723-9422

Caroline Bird. 1992. Offers suggestions for people over 50 on careers in transportation. Jobs discussed include taxi drivers, bus drivers, truck drivers, and railway conductors.

Taxi Drivers and Chauffeurs

Taxi drivers and chauffeurs pick up and drive people to their destination in cars, limousines, or vans. Taxi drivers, also known as cab drivers, drive taxicabs, which are custom automobiles modified for transporting passengers. Taxi drivers take customers to such places as airports, convention centers and hotels, or places of entertainment. Chauffeurs drive passengers in private automobiles, limousines, or vans owned by limousine companies. Some drive people between hotels and airports, others drive luxury automobiles to popular entertainment and social events.

Salaries

Earnings vary greatly, depending on the number of hours worked, customers' tips, and other factors.

Lowest 10 percent	$187/week or less
Middle 50 percent	$228-$481/week
Highest 10 percent	$604/week or more

Employment Outlook

Growth rate until the year 2005: Average.

Taxi Drivers and Chauffeurs

Career Guides

★6792★ "Chauffeur" in *BLR Encyclopedia of Prewritten Job Descriptions*
Business and Legal Reports, Inc.
39 Academy St.
Madison, CT 06443-1513
Ph: (203)245-7448

Stephen D. Bruce, editor-in-chief. 1994. This book contains hundreds of sample job descriptions arranged by functional job category. The 1-3 page job descriptions cover what the worker normally does in the position, who they report to, and how that position fits in the organizational structure.

★6793★ "Chauffeur" in *Career Information Center* (Vol.5)
Simon and Schuster
200 Old Tappan Rd.
Old Tappan, NJ 07675
Fax: 800-445-6991 Fr: 800-223-2348

Richard Lidz and Linda Perrin, editorial directors. Fifth edition, 1993. This 13-volume set profiles over 600 occupations. Each occupational profile describes job duties, entry-level requirements, educational requirements, advancement possibilities, employment outlook, working conditions, earnings and benefits, and where to write for more information.

★6794★ "Chauffeur" in *Jobs Rated Almanac*
World Almanac
1 International Blvd., Ste. 444
Mahwah, NJ 07495
Ph: (201)529-6900 Fax: (201)529-6901

Les Krantz. Second edition, 1992. Ranks 250 jobs by environment, salary, outlooks, physical demands, stress, security, travel opportunities, and extra perks. Includes jobs the editor feels are the most common, most interesting, and the most rapidly growing.

★6795★ "Taxi Dispatcher" in *Travel & Tourism* (pp. 45-49)
Franklin Watts, Inc.
387 Park Avenue, S.
New York, NY 10016
Ph: (212)686-7070

Marjorie Rittenberg Schulz. 1990. Surveys employment opportunities in the travel and tourism industry. Provides job description, educational preparation, training, salary, employment outlook, and sources of additional information. Offers job hunting advice.

★6796★ *Taxi Driver*
Careers, Inc.
PO Box 135
Largo, FL 34649-0135
Ph: (813)584-7333

1992. Two-page occupational summary card describing duties, working conditions, personal qualifications, training, earnings and hours, employment outlook, places of employment, related careers, and where to write for more information.

★6797★ "Taxi Driver" in *Career Information Center* (Vol.12)
Simon and Schuster
200 Old Tappan Rd.
Old Tappan, NJ 07675
Fax: 800-445-6991 Fr: 800-223-2348

Richard Lidz and Linda Perrin, editorial directors. Fifth edition, 1993. This 13-volume set profiles over 600 occupations. Each occupational profile describes job duties, entry-level requirements, educational requirements, advancement possibilities, employment outlook, working conditions, earnings and benefits, and where to write for more information.

★6798★ "Taxi Driver" in *Jobs Rated Almanac*
World Almanac
1 International Blvd., Ste. 444
Mahwah, NJ 07495
Ph: (201)529-6900 Fax: (201)529-6901

Les Krantz. Second edition, 1992. Ranks 250 jobs by environment, salary, outlooks, physical demands, stress, security, travel opportunities, and extra perks. Includes jobs the editor feels are the most common, most interesting, and the most rapidly growing.

★6799★ *Taxi Drivers*
Chronicle Guidance Publications, Inc.
66 Aurora St.
PO Box 1190
Moravia, NY 13118-1190
Ph: (315)497-0330 Fax: (315)497-3359
Fr: 800-622-7284

1994. Career brief describing the nature of the job, working conditions, hours and earnings, education and training, licensure, certification, unions, personal qualifications, social and psychological factors, location, employment outlook, entry methods, advancement, and related occupations.

★6800★ "Taxi Drivers and Chauffeurs" in *Occupational Outlook Handbook*
U.S. Government Printing Office
Superintendent of Documents
Washington, DC 20402
Ph: (202)512-1800 Fax: (202)512-2250

Biennial; latest edition, 1994-95. Encyclopedia of careers describing about 250 occupations and comprising about 85 percent of all jobs in the economy. Occupations that require lengthy education or training are given the most attention. Each occupation's profile describes what the worker does on the job, working conditions, education and training requirements, advancement possibilities, job outlook, earnings, and sources of additional information.

★6801★ "Taxi Drivers" in *Encyclopedia of Careers and Vocational Guidance* (Vol.4, pp. 485-487)
J.G. Ferguson Publishing Co.
200 W. Madison St., Ste. 300
Chicago, IL 60606
Ph: (312)580-5480 Fax: (312)580-4948

William E. Hopke, editor-in-chief. Ninth edition, 1993. Four-volume set that profiles 900 occupations and describes job trends in 74 industries. Includes career description, educational requirements, history of the job, methods of entry, advancement, employment outlook, earnings, conditions of work, social and psychological factors, and sources of further information.

Associations

★6802★ Airport Ground Transportation Association
901 Scenic Dr.
Knoxville, TN 37919
Ph: (615)525-1108

Members: Include airport ground transportation operators, suppliers, and related government agencies.

★6803★ Association of Professional Drivers
PO Box 491
Paoli, PA 19301
Ph: (215)647-0818

For-profit organization that encourages professionalism among truck, school bus, and passenger car drivers.

★6804★ International Taxicab and Livery Association
3849 Farragut Ave.
Kensington, MD 20895
Ph: (301)946-5601

Association of ground transportation fleet owners operating 70,000 passenger vehicles including taxicabs, liveries, vans, and minibuses. Formed by a merger of the National Association of Taxicab Owners, Cab Research Bureau, and American Taxicab Association. Formerly known as the International Taxicab Association.

★6805★ Taxicab Industry Group
c/o Capital Cab
1033 3rd St., NE
Washington, DC 20002
Ph: (202)722-2485

Taxicab lobbying group.

Test Guides

★6806★ *Career Examination Series: Chauffeur*
National Learning Corp.
212 Michael Dr.
Syosset, NY 11791
Ph: (516)921-8888 Fax: (516)921-8743
Fr: 800-645-6337

Jack Rudman. Test guide including questions and answers for students or professionals in the field who seek advancement through examination.

Educational Directories and Programs

★6807★ *Taxi & Livery Management—Buyer's Guide Issue*
International Taxicab & Livery Association
3849 Farragut Ave.
Kensington, MD 20895
Ph: (301)946-5701 Fax: (301)946-4641
Irene Kiebuzinski

Publication includes: List of manufacturers of taxicabs, minibuses, vans, limousines, parts, service equipment, wheelchair lifts, communications systems; also includes consultants, insurance agencies, advertising services, propane or natural gas systems; dealers in used vehicles, two-way radios, and meters; and other companies servicing the for-hire vehicle fleet industry (taxicabs, limousines, vans, and minibuses). Entries include: Company name, address, phone, contact person, and brief description of product or service.

★6808★ *Taxicab Companies Directory*
American Business Directories, Inc.
5711 S. 86th Circle
Omaha, NE 68127
Ph: (402)593-4600 Fax: (402)331-1505

Number of listings: 7,163 (U.S. edition); 1,843 (Canadian edition). Entries include: Name, address, phone (including area code), size of advertisement, year first in "Yellow Pages," name of owner or manager, number of employees. Compiled from telephone company "Yellow Pages," nationwide.

★6809★ *Transit Atlas: Bus and Taxi Service in Iowa*
Office of Public Transportation
Park Fair Mall, Ste. 7
Des Moines, IA 50313
Ph: (515)237-3302 Fax: (515)237-3323
Peter H. HallockDirector

Covers: 35 public transportation agencies, 15 regional planning agencies, over 65 taxi companies, 49 intercity and charter bus companies, and commuter service firms in Iowa. Entries include: For transportation agencies—Name, address, phone, contact, type of service, system profile, number of vehicles, number of employees, days and hours of operation, number of users, total system miles, fare. For planning agencies—Name, address, phone. For intercity bus companies—Name, address, phone, service offered. For commuter service firms—Name, address, phone, cities or industrial plants serviced.

Awards, Scholarships, Grants, and Fellowships

★6810★ Transportation Man of the Year
Delta Nu Alpha Transportation Fraternity
621 Plainfield, Ste. 308
Willowbrook, IL 60521

To recognize contributions to the field of transportation. A plaque is awarded annually. Established in 1952.

Basic Reference Guides and Handbooks

★6811★ *Taxi Driving Made Simple: How to Do It Profitably, Pleasurably, and Professionally*
Round Robin Press
PO Box 11245
Oakland, CA 94611
Ph: (510)652-1354

Michael Santee. 1989. Describes the ins and outs of taxi driving including, how to choose a company to work for, equipment, supplies, and clothing needed, techniques and strategies, and how to deal with trouble.

Periodicals

★6812★ *Dispatch: The Business Report of the Taxicab/Paratransit Industry*
International Taxicab and Livery Association
3849 Farragut Ave.
Kensington, MD 20895
Ph: (301)946-5701

Association and industry newsletter for members.

★6813★ *Insurance Journal*
Wells Publishing
9191 Town Centre Dr., No. 550
San Diego, CA 92122
Ph: (619)455-7717 Fax: (619)546-1462
Mark WellsPublisher

Biweekly. Property/Casualty magazine of the West.

★6814★ *Limousine and Chauffeur*
Bobit Publishing
2512 Artesia Blvd.
Redondo Beach, CA 90278-3296
Ph: (310)376-8788

Magazine for the limousine service industry. Published 7 times a year.

★6815★ *Metro Magazine*
Bobit Publishing
2512 Artesia Blvd.
Redondo Beach, CA 90278
Ph: (310)376-8788 Fax: (310)376-9043
Frank Di GiacomoPublisher

Magazine on public transportation.

★6816★ *Taxi and Livery Management*
International Taxicab and Livery Association (ITLA)
3849 Farragut Ave.
Kensington, MD 20895
Ph: (301)946-5701 Fax: (301)946-4641
Lisa Cherubini, ED

Quarterly. Magazine for owners and operators of taxicab, limousine, livery, van, and minibus fleets. Includes advertisers' index, legal column, buyer's guide, convention previews, and a marketing column.

★6817★ *Transportation: An Abstract Newsletter*
National Technical Information Service (NTIS)
5285 Port Royal Rd.
Springfield, VA 22161
Ph: (703)487-4630

Biweekly. Provides abstracts of publications in the areas of air, rail, water, pipeline, and road transportation; global navigation systems; and transportation safety.

★6818★ *Transportation & Distribution*
Penton Publishing
1100 Superior Ave.
Cleveland, OH 44114
Ph: (216)696-7000 Fax: (216)696-7932
Perry Trunick

Monthly. Magazine covering traffic and physical distribution.

Meetings and Conventions

★6819★ ITLA Annual Trade Show and Convention
International Taxicab and Livery Association
3849 Farragut Ave.
Kensington, MD 20895
Ph: (301)946-5701

Annual convention with exhibits. Held in October or November.

Other Sources of Information

★6820★ "Chauffeur" in *Career Selector 2001*
Barron's Educational Series, Inc.
250 Wireless Blvd.
Hauppauge, NY 11788
Ph: (516)434-3311 Fax: (516)434-3723
Fr: 800-645-3476

James C. Gonyea. 1993.

★6821★ *General Driving Safety*
Gulf Publishing Co.
PO Box 2680
Houston, TX 77252
Ph: (713)529-4301 Fax: (713)520-4438

11 part series that provides instruction on driving safety, including information on road conditions and speed, drunk driving, accidents, sleepiness and driving, mountain driving, and safety devices.

★6822★ "Taxi Driver" in *Career Selector 2001*
Barron's Educational Series, Inc.
250 Wireless Blvd.
Hauppauge, NY 11788
Ph: (516)434-3311 Fax: (516)434-3723
Fr: 800-645-3476

James C. Gonyea. 1993.

★6823★ "Taxicab Driver" in *Encyclopedia of Danger: Dangerous Professions* (pp. 94-97)
Chelsea House Publishers
1974 Sproul Rd., Ste. 400
Broomall, PA 19008
Ph: (215)353-5166 Fax: (215)359-1439

Missy Allen and Michel Peissel. 1993. Provides descriptions of 24 dangerous occupations, their risky characteristics, and safety precautions.

★6824★ "Transportation" in *Second Careers: New Ways to Work After 50* (pp. 260-268)
Little, Brown and Co.
34 Beacon St.
Boston, MA 02108
Ph: (617)227-0730 Fax: (617)723-9422

Caroline Bird. 1992. Offers suggestions for people over 50 on careers in transportation. Jobs discussed include taxi drivers, bus drivers, truck drivers, and railway conductors.

Truckdrivers

Long-distance **Truckdrivers** make the initial pickup from factories, consolidate cargo at terminals for intercity shipment, and deliver goods from terminals to stores and homes. Local Truckdrivers--called driver-sales workers or route drivers--primarily have sales and customer relations responsibilities. Driver-sales workers, such as wholesale bakery driver-sales workers and vending machine driver-sales workers, mostly have wholesale routes--that is, they deliver to businesses and stores. A few pick up and deliver items to homes, but retail routes are now rare. Trucking companies employ nearly 33 percent of all Truck drivers, and another 33 percent work for companies engaged in wholesale or retail trade. The rest are scattered throughout the economy, including government agencies. Fewer than 10 percent of all Truck drivers are self-employed; of these, a significant number are owner-operators, who either operate independently or lease their services and their trucks to a trucking company.

Salaries

Hourly earnings for Truck drivers, depending on the size of the truck, are as follows:

Medium trucks	$13.50/hour
Tractor-trailers	$12.94/hour
Heavy straight trucks	$11.91/hour
Light trucks	$8.51/hour

Employment Outlook

Growth rate until the year 2005: Average.

Truckdrivers

Career Guides

★6825★ *Careers in Truck Driving*
American Trucking Association
Office of Public Affairs
2200 Mill Rd.
Alexandria, VA 22314-4677
Ph: (703)838-1873

1992. Eight-panel brochure describing types of truck drivers, required qualifications, training, working conditions, employment outlook, earnings, and advancement opportunities.

★6826★ *Careers in Trucking*
Rosen Publishing Group
29 E. 21st St.
New York, NY 10010
Ph: (212)777-3017 Fax: (212)777-0277
Fr: 800-237-9932

Donald D. Schauer. 1991. Describes employment in the trucking industry including driving, operations, sales, and administration. Covers qualifications, training, future outlook, and salaries. Offers career planning and job hunting advice.

★6827★ *Driver, Heavy-Truck*
Careers, Inc.
PO Box 135
Largo, FL 34649-0135
Ph: (813)584-7333

1991. Two-page occupational summary card describing duties, working conditions, personal qualifications, training, earnings and hours, employment outlook, places of employment, related careers and where to write for more information.

★6828★ "Heavy Truck Driver" in *Occu-Facts: Information on 580 Careers in Outline Form*
Careers, Inc.
PO Box 135
Largo, FL 34649-0135
Ph: (813)584-7333

Biennial, 1995-96 edition. Each one-page occupational profile describes duties, working conditions, physical surroundings and demands, aptitudes, temperament, educational requirements, employment outlook, earnings, and places of employment.

★6829★ "Local Truck Driver" in *Career Information Center* (Vol.12)
Simon and Schuster
200 Old Tappan Rd.
Old Tappan, NJ 07675
Fax: 800-445-6991 Fr: 800-223-2348

Richard Lidz and Dale Anderson, editorial directors. Fifth edition, 1993. For 600 occupations, describes job duties, entry-level requirements, education and training needed, advancement possibilities, employment outlook, earnings and benefits. The set is divided into 12 volumes. Each volume includes jobs related under a broad career field. Volume 13 is the index.

★6830★ "Local Truck Driver" in *Exploring Nontraditional Jobs for Women* (pp. 69-75)
Rosen Publishing Group
29 E. 21st St.
New York, NY 10010
Ph: (212)777-3017 Fax: (212)777-0277
Fr: 800-237-9932

Rose Neufeld. 1989. Describes blue-collar, male dominated occupations. Discusses what is done on the job, training, where to apply for jobs, tools used, salaries, and advantages and disadvantages. Relates the experiences of women who are working in the field.

★6831★ "Long Distance Truck Drivers" in *Opportunities in Transportation Careers* (pp. 69-72)
National Textbook Co. (NTC)
VGM Career Books
4255 W. Touhy Ave.
Lincolnwood, IL 60646-1975
Ph: (708)679-5500 Fax: (708)679-2494
Fr: 800-323-4900

Adrian A. Paradis. 1988. Describes transportation and related employment in driving occupations, the airlines, merchant marine, and travel services. Covers employment outlook, educational and training requirements, wages, and the work itself, and advantages and disadvantages of transportation careers. Offers job hunting advice.

★6832★ "Long Haul Truck Driver" in *Career Information Center* (Vol.12)
Simon and Schuster
200 Old Tappan Rd.
Old Tappan, NJ 07675
Fax: 800-445-6991 Fr: 800-223-2348

Richard Lidz and Dale Anderson, editorial directors. Fifth edition, 1993. For 600 occupations, describes job duties, entry-level requirements, education and training needed, advancement possibilities, employment outlook, earnings and benefits. The set is divided into 12 volumes. Each volume includes jobs related under a broad career field. Volume 13 is the index.

★6833★ *Opportunities in Trucking Careers*
National Textbook Co. (NTC)
VGM Career Books
4255 W. Toughy Ave.
Lincolnwood, IL 60646-1975
Ph: (708)679-5500 Fax: (708)679-2494
Fr: 800-323-4900

Ken Schamberg.

★6834★ "Resolution, Personal Services and Transportation Careers" in *The Best Jobs for the 1990s and Into the 21st Century*
Impact Publications
9104-N Manassas Dr.
Manassas Park, VA 22111
Ph: (703)361-7300 Fax: (703)335-9486

Ronald L. Krannich and Caryl Rae Krannich. 1993. Includes information on a wide variety of careers including adjusters, investigators, and collectors, animal caretakers, electricians, services sales reps., and truck drivers.

★6835★ *Standards for Selection of Truck Fleet Personnel: A Guide for Hiring Professional Drivers & Other Employees in the Trucking Industry*
American Trucking Associations, Inc.
2200 Mill Rd.
Alexandria, VA 22314-4677
Ph: (703)838-1700 Fr: 800-225-8382

American Trucking Associations Department of Safety. Revised edition, 1986.

★6836★ *Tank Truck Driver*
Vocational Biographies, Inc.
PO Box 31
Sauk Centre, MN 56378-0031
Ph: (612)352-6516 Fax: (612)352-5546
Fr: 800-255-0752

1995. Four-page pamphlet containing a personal narrative about a worker's job, work likes and dislikes, career path from high school to the present. Education and training, the rewards and frustrations, and the effects of the job on the rest of the worker's life. The data file portion of this pamphlet gives a concise occupational summary, including work descriptions, working conditions, places of employment, personal characteristics, education and training, job outlook, and salary range.

★6837★ "Tow Truck Operator" in *Career Information Center* (Vol.12)
Simon and Schuster
200 Old Tappan Rd.
Old Tappan, NJ 07675
Fax: 800-445-6991 Fr: 800-223-2348

Richard Lidz and Dale Anderson, editorial directors. Fifth edition, 1993. For 600 occupations, describes job duties, entry-level requirements, education and training needed, advancement possibilities, employment outlook, earnings and benefits. The set is divided into 12 volumes. Each volume includes jobs related under a broad career field. Volume 13 is the index.

★6838★ "Tow Truck Operator" in *Occu-Facts: Information on 580 Careers in Outline Form*
Careers, Inc.
PO Box 135
Largo, FL 34649-0135
Ph: (813)584-7333

Biennial, 1995-96 edition. Each one-page occupational profile describes duties, working conditions, physical surroundings and demands, aptitudes, temperament, educational requirements, employment outlook, earnings, and places of employment.

★6839★ *Transportation*
Learning Corporation of America
108 Wilmot Rd.
Deerfield, IL 60015
Ph: (708)940-1260 Fax: (708)940-3600
Fr: 800-621-2131

Videocassette. 1982. 21 mins. In this program from the "Working" series, we meet five employees in transportation-related jobs: fishing boat captain, auto body repair shop owner, construction equipment operator, air traffic controller and truck driver.

★6840★ *Transportation/Mechanical Cluster*
Center for Humanities, Inc.
Communications Park
Box 1000
Mount Kisco, NY 10549
Ph: (914)666-4100 Fax: (914)666-5319
Fr: 800-431-1242

Videocassette. 1984. 20 mins. The key aspects of working in the fields of Auto Body Repair, Truck Driving, and Auto Mechanics are explained.

★6841★ "Transportation Services" in *Opportunities in Vocational and Technical Careers* (pp. 76-90)
National Textbook Co. (NTC)
VGM Career Books
4255 W. Touhy Ave.
Lincolnwood, IL 60646-1975
Ph: (708)679-5500 Fax: (708)679-2494
Fr: 800-323-4900

Adrian A. Paradis. 1992. Describes careers which can be prepared for by attending a private vocational or proprietary school—office employee, sales worker, service worker, health services, mechanic, craftworker, and technician. Covers employment outlook, job duties, and salaries. Offers career planning advice.

★6842★ "Truck and Delivery Drivers" in *Career Discovery Encyclopedia* (Vol.6, pp. 126-127)
J.G. Ferguson Publishing Co.
200 W. Madison St., Ste. 300
Chicago, IL 60606
Ph: (312)580-5480 Fax: (312)580-4948

E. Russell Primm, editor-in-chief. 1993. Contains two-page articles on 504 occupations. Each article describes job duties, earnings, and educational and training requirements.

★6843★ *Truck Driver*
Vocational Biographies, Inc.
PO Box 31
Sauk Centre, MN 56378-0031
Ph: (612)352-6516 Fax: (612)352-5546
Fr: 800-255-0752

1990. This pamphlet profiles a person working in the job. Includes information about job duties, working conditions, places of employment, educational preparation, labor market outlook, and salaries.

★6844★ "Truck Driver" in *Jobs Rated Almanac*
World Almanac
1 International Blvd., Ste. 444
Mahwah, NJ 07495
Ph: (201)529-6900 Fax: (201)529-6901

Les Krantz. Second edition, 1992. Ranks 250 jobs by environment, salary, outlooks, physical demands, stress, security, travel opportunities, and extra perks. Includes jobs the editor feels are the most common, most interesting, and the most rapidly growing.

★6845★ "Truck Driver" in *Transportation* (pp. 21-25)
Franklin Watts, Inc.
387 Park Avenue, S.
New York, NY 10016
Ph: (212)686-7070

Marjorie Rittenberg Schulz. 1990. Surveys the transportation industry including air, water, and rail services. Provides job description, training, salary, and employment outlook. Offers job hunting advice.

★6846★ "Truck Driver" in *VGM's Careers Encyclopedia* (pp. 471-474)
National Textbook Co. (NTC)
VGM Career Books
4255 W. Touhy Ave.
Lincolnwood, IL 60646-1975
Ph: (708)679-5500 Fax: (708)679-2494
Fr: 800-323-4900

Third edition, 1991. Contains two- to five-page descriptions of 200 managerial, professional, technical, trade, and service occupations. Each profile includes job duties, places of employment, qualifications, educational preparation, training, employment potential, advancement, income, and additional sources of information.

★6847★ *Truck Drivers*
Chronicle Guidance Publications, Inc.
66 Aurora St.
PO Box 1190
Moravia, NY 13118-1190
Ph: (315)497-0330 Fax: (315)497-3359
Fr: 800-622-7284

1993. This career brief describes the nature of the work, working conditions, hours and earnings, education and training, licensure, certification, unions, personal qualifications, social and psychological factors, employment outlook, entry methods, advancement, and related occupations.

★6848★ "Truck Drivers" in *Encyclopedia of Careers and Vocational Guidance* (Vol.4, pp. 569-573)
J.G. Ferguson Publishing Co.
200 W. Madison St., Ste. 300
Chicago, IL 60606
Ph: (312)580-5480 Fax: (312)580-4948

William E. Hopke, editor-in-chief. Ninth edition, 1993. Four-volume set that profiles 900 occupations and describes job trends in 74 industries. Includes career description, educational requirements, history of the job, methods of entry, advancement, employment outlook, earnings, conditions of work, social and psychological factors, and sources of further information.

★6849★ "Truck Drivers" in *Jobs! What They Are—Where They Are—What They Pay* (pp. 218)
Simon & Schuster, Inc.
Simon & Schuster Bldg.
1230 Avenue of the Americas
New York, NY 10020
Ph: (212)698-7000

Robert O. Snelling and Anne M. Snelling. Revised edition, 1992. Profiles 241 occupations, describing duties and responsibilities, educational preparation, earnings, employment opportunities, training, and qualifications.

★6850★ "Truck Driving" in *Career Connection II: A Guide to Technical Majors and Their Related Careers* (pp. 150-151)
Jist Works, Inc.
720 N. Park Ave.
Indianapolis, IN 46202-3431
Ph: (317)264-3720 Fax: (317)264-3709

Fred A. Rowe. 1994. Contains technical majors, such as automotive technology. Describes the major and the job. Lists high school and postsecondary school courses.

Includes occupations related to the major, employment outlook, and starting salary.

★6851★ "Truckdrivers" in *Occupational Outlook Handbook*
U.S. Government Printing Office
Superintendent of Documents
Washington, DC 20402
Ph: (202)512-1800 Fax: (202)512-2250

Biennial; latest edition, 1994-95. Encyclopedia of careers describing more than 250 occupations and comprising about 85 percent of all jobs in the economy. Occupations that require lengthy education or training are given the most attention. For each occupation, the handbook describes job duties, working conditions, training, educational preparation, personal qualities, advancement possibilities, job outlook, earnings, and sources of additional information.

★6852★ *Trucker*
Macmillan Publishing Company, Inc.
866 3rd Ave.
New York, NY 10022
Ph: (212)702-2000

Hope H. Wurmfeld. 1990.

★6853★ "Trucker" in *Hard Hatted Women: Stories of Struggle and Success in the Trades* (pp. 225-234)
Seal Press
3131 Western Ave., Ste. 410
Seattle, WA 98121
Ph: (206)283-7844 Fax: (206)285-9410

Molly Martin, editor. 1988. Twenty-six women recount their experiences working in blue collar occupations. They describe how they got in, the work they do, their relationships in predominantly male occupations, and their training.

★6854★ *Trucksource: Sources of Trucking Industry Information: The Trucking Information Buyer's Guide*
American Trucking Associations, Inc.
2200 Mill Rd.
Alexandria, VA 22314-4677
Ph: (703)838-1700 Fr: 800-225-8382

Catherine M. Mahe and Linda S. Rothbart. 1994.

★6855★ *Video Career Library - Transportation & Materials Moving*
Careers, Inc.
PO Box 135
Largo, FL 34649-0135
Ph: (813)584-7333

Videocassette. 1990. 20 mins. Part of the Video Career Library covering 165 occupations. Shows actual workers on the job. Includes tractor/trailer truck drivers, heavy truck drivers, bus drivers, airplane pilots and navigators, grader/dozer/scraper operators, and forklift operators.

★6856★ *Vocational Visions*
Center for Humanities, Inc.
Communications Park
Box 1000
Mount Kisco, NY 10549
Ph: (914)666-4100 Fax: (914)666-5319
Fr: 800-431-1242

Videocassette. 1984. 30 mins. This series of programs explains key aspects of actual training and a day in the life of a worker in the specific field mentioned on the videocassette. Occupations include: transportation/mechanics, repair, construction, business/office occupations, health, agriculture, technical/manufacturing, communications, and personal service.

★6857★ *Vocations U.S.A.*
Info-Disc Corporation
4 Professional Dr., Ste. 134
Gaithersburg, MD 20879
Ph: (301)948-2300 Fr: 800-648-6422

Videocassette. 1987. 60 mins. A disc collection outlining the requirements and methods of various career areas. Occupations include: transportation, mechanical/repair, health, agriculture, technical/manufacturing, and construction.

Associations

★6858★ American Trucking Associations (ATA)
2200 Mill Rd.
Alexandria, VA 22314
Ph: (703)838-1700 Fax: (703)684-5720
Fr: 800-ATA-LINE

Members: Motor carriers, suppliers, state trucking associations, and national conferences of trucking companies. **Purpose:** Works to influence the decisions of federal, state, and local government bodies; promotes increased efficiency, productivity, and competitiveness in the trucking industries; sponsors American Trucking Associations Foundation. Operates Motor Carrier Advisory Service, a guide to federal and state regulations; provides quarterly financial and operating statistics service. Offers comprehensive accounting service for all sizes of carriers. Promotes highway and driver safety; supports highway research projects; and studies technical and regulatory problems of the trucking industry. Sponsors competitions; compiles statistics. Maintains numerous programs and services including: Portrait of a Professional Truck Driver; Management Information Systems Directory; Compensation Survey; Electronic Data Interchange Standards. **Publications:** *American Trucking Trends*, annual. • *ATA Catalog*, quarterly. • *Motor Carrier Professional Services Directory*, annual. • *Transport Topics*, weekly. • *TruckSource*, annual.

★6859★ Association of Professional Drivers
PO Box 491
Paoli, PA 19301
Ph: (215)647-0818

For-profit organization that encourages professionalism among truck, school bus, and passenger car drivers.

★6860★ Professional Truck Driver Institute of America (PTDIA)
8788 Elk Grove Blvd., Ste. 20
Elk Grove, CA 95624
Ph: (916)686-5146 Fax: (916)686-4878

Members: Trade associations, manufacturers, and suppliers to the trucking industry. Develops professional standards for the certification of truck driver training courses; certifies commercial truck driving training courses.

Standards/Certification Agencies

★6861★ American Trucking Associations (ATA)
2200 Mill Rd.
Alexandria, VA 22314
Ph: (703)838-1700 Fax: (703)684-5720
Fr: 800-ATA-LINE

Operates Motor Carrier Advisory Service, a guide to federal and state regulations. Supports highway research projects; and studies technical and regulatory problems of the trucking industry. Maintains numerous programs and services including: Portrait of a Professional Truck Driver; Management Information Systems Directory; Compensation Survey; Electronic Data Interchange Standards.

★6862★ *CDL Commercial Driver License: 104 Helpful CDL Facts*
Professional Truck Driver Institute of America
8788 Elk Grove Blvd., Ste. 20
Elk Grove, CA 95624
Ph: (916)686-5146

1990. This 32-page booklet explains the Commercial Driver License, a set of minimum standards for licensing and testing commercial drivers established by the federal government. Covers the law, classes of licenses, and test content.

★6863★ Professional Truck Driver Institute of America (PTDIA)
8788 Elk Grove Blvd., Ste. 20
Elk Grove, CA 95624
Ph: (916)686-5146 Fax: (916)686-4878

Develops professional standards for the certification of truck driver training courses; certifies commercial truck driving training courses.

Test Guides

★6864★ *Career Examination Series: Tractor Operator*
National Learning Corp.
212 Michael Dr.
Syosset, NY 11791
Ph: (516)921-8888 Fax: (516)921-8743
Fr: 800-645-6337

Jack Rudman. All examination guides in this series contain questions with answers.

★6865★ *Career Examination Series: Tractor-Trailer Operator*
National Learning Corp.
212 Michael Dr.
Syosset, NY 11791
Ph: (516)921-8888 Fax: (516)921-8743
Fr: 800-645-6337

Jack Rudman. All examination guides in this series contain questions with answers.

★6866★ *Career Examination Series: Truck Driver*
National Learning Corp.
212 Michael Dr.
Syosset, NY 11791
Ph: (516)921-8888 Fax: (516)921-8743
Fr: 800-645-6337

Jack Rudman. All examination guides in this series contain questions with answers.

★6867★ *How to Prepare for the Commercial Driver's License Truck Driver's Test (CDL)*
Barron's Educational Series, Inc.
250 Wireless Blvd.
Hauppauge, NY 11788
Ph: (516)434-3311 Fax: (516)434-3723
Fr: 800-645-3476

Mike Byrnes, et al. 1991. This manual provides information on the Commercial Driver's License tests administered in all 50 states under the same U.S. Department of Transportation standards. Included are model tests with answers, explanations, and diagrams, along with charts and line drawings.

★6868★ *National Highway Traffic Safety Administration's Truck Operator Qualification Examination (NTSATOQ)*
National Learning Corp.
212 Michael Dr.
Syosset, NY 11791
Ph: (516)921-8888 Fax: (516)921-8743
Fr: 800-645-6337

Jack Rudman. Part of the Admission Test Series. Books in this series provide test practice and drill for actual professional certification and licensure tests.

★6869★ *Truck Driver's Guide to Commercial Driver Licensing*
Prentice Hall Press
Simon & Schuster Inc.
200 Old Tappan Rd.
Old Tappan, NJ 07675
Ph: 800-223-2348

Highway Users Federation for Safety and Mobility. First edition, 1990. Contains information and practice material on new state licensing tests for certification and recertification of all truck drivers.

Educational Directories and Programs

★6870★ *Schools with PTDIA Certified Coures Listed by State*
Professional Truck Driver Institute of America (PTDIA)
8788 Elk Grove Blvd., Ste. 20
Elk Grove, CA 95624
Ph: (916)686-5146

1991. State-by-state listing of schools offering entry-level training. Indicates day or evening courses, part-time or full-time study, and the length of the program.

Awards, Scholarships, Grants, and Fellowships

★6871★ AMC Van Operator Lifetime Achievement Award
American Movers Conference
1600 Duke St.
Alexandria, VA 22314
Ph: (703)683-7410 Fax: (703)683-7527

To recognize veteran drivers for their outstanding careers over many years in the moving industry. The award honors the van operator who consistently achieved excellence during a lifetime of commercial driving.

★6872★ ATA National Truck Driving Championships
American Trucking Association
Safety Management Council
220 Mill Rd.
Alexandria, VA 22314
Ph: (703)838-1919 Fax: (703)836-6070

To recognize National Champion Truck Drivers of eight basic types of trucks and combination units. Eligibility is based on one year of accident-free driving, plus one year of continuous employment with the entering driver. The following special awards are presented: Vehicle Condition Award, Sontheime Award, Team Trophy Award, Grand Champion, and Rookie of the Year. Monetary awards, trophies, and plaques are awarded annually. Established in 1937.

★6873★ Distinguished Service Award
Towing and Recovery Association of America
2200 Mill Rd.
Alexandria, VA 22314-4677
Ph: (703)838-1897 Fax: (703)684-6720
Fr: 800-728-0136

For recognition of an individual's outstanding contribution, untiring devotion, and dedicated sacrifice to the towing-recovery-storage industry. Individuals who are actively engaged in the towing industry and members of TRAA are eligible. A plaque is awarded annually at the national convention. Established in 1982.

★6874★ Driver of the Year
Truck Renting and Leasing Association
2011 Pennsylvania Ave. NW, Ste. 500
Washington, DC 20006
Ph: (202)775-4859 Fax: (202)457-9121

To encourage professional development of all drivers and to promote safe, professional truck driving. Selection is by nomination and application. A plaque and a trip to the annual convention are awarded annually. Established in 1987.

★6875★ Driver of the Year Award
American Trucking Association
Safety Management Council
220 Mill Rd.
Alexandria, VA 22314
Ph: (703)838-1919 Fax: (703)836-6070

To recognize the best safety record among truck drivers of the United States and to encourage improved driving performance and a greater appreciation for highway safety. A Driver of the Year pin, trophy, and certificate are awarded annually. Established in 1947.

★6876★ Safe Worker Award
American Trucking Association
Safety Management Council
220 Mill Rd.
Alexandria, VA 22314
Ph: (703)838-1919 Fax: (703)836-6070

To recognize those employees who successfully meet the challenge of working without injury, and to provide incentive to all employees to work in a safe manner. Local drivers, intercity drivers, dockmen, shop employees, working foremen in the above classifications, miscellaneous-custodial employees, watchmen, and spotters are eligible. The award consists of a distinctive pin showing the number of years worked without injury, and a wallet-size card attesting to this record, signed by the ATA Director of Safety.

★6877★ Super Van Operator of the Year
American Movers Conference
1600 Duke St.
Alexandria, VA 22314
Ph: (703)683-7410 Fax: (703)683-7527

To recognize drivers in the moving industry who have had outstanding driving and service records for the past five years. Both younger and older drivers are considered for the award on an equal basis. Five drivers are chosen as Super Van Operators, and one of the five is named Super Van Operator of the Year.

★6878★ Transportation Man of the Year
Delta Nu Alpha Transportation Fraternity
621 Plainfield, Ste. 308
Willowbrook, IL 60521

To recognize contributions to the field of transportation. A plaque is awarded annually. Established in 1952.

Basic Reference Guides and Handbooks

★6879★ *The Art of Giving Quality Service in the Motor Carrier Industry*
American Trucking Associations, Inc.
2200 Mill Rd.
Alexandria, VA 22314-4677
Ph: (703)838-1700 Fr: 800-225-8382
Charles W. Clowdis, Jr. 1984.

★6880★ *Emergency & Trip Permit Handbook: Important Permit Information for Interstate Trucking Operatiobns in the United States & Canada*
J.J. Keller & Associates, Inc.
3003 W. Breezewood
PO Box 368
Neenah, WI 54957-0368
Ph: (414)722-2848 Fax: (414)727-7516
Fr: 800-327-6868
J.J. Keller & Associates, Inc. Fifteenth edition.

★6881★ *Federal Motor Carrier Safety Regulations*
American Trucking Associations, Inc.
2200 Mill Rd.
Alexandria, VA 22314-4677
Ph: (703)838-1700 Fr: 800-225-8382
American Trucking Associations Safety Department. 1994.

★6882★ *Federal Motor Carrier Safety Regulations Pocketbook*
J. J. Keller & Associates, Inc.
3003 W. Breezewood
PO Box 368
Neenah, WI 54957-0368
Ph: (414)722-2848 Fax: (414)727-7516
Fr: 800-327-6868
J. J. Keller & Associates, Inc. Staff. Revised edition, 1991.

★6883★ *The Hazardous Materials Handbook for Motor Carriers*
J.J. Keller & Associates, Inc.
3003 W. Breezewood
PO Box 368
Neenah, WI 54957-0368
Ph: (414)722-2848 Fax: (414)727-7516
Fr: 800-327-6868
1977.

★6884★ *Heavy Vehicle Use Tax: Regulations & Instructions*
American Trucking Associations, Inc.
2200 Mill Rd.
Alexandria, VA 22314-4677
Ph: (703)838-1700 Fr: 800-225-8382
American Trucking Associations State Laws Department. 1985.

★6885★ *How to Achieve a Satisfactory DOT Safety Rating*
American Trucking Associations, Inc.
2200 Mill Rd.
Alexandria, VA 22314-4677
Ph: (703)838-1700 Fr: 800-225-8382
1990.

★6886★ *Interstate Motor Carrier Forms Manual, 2G: Private, Contract, Exempt*
J.J. Keller & Associates, Inc.
3003 W. Breezewood
PO Box 368
Neenah, WI 54957-0368
Ph: (414)722-2848 Fax: (414)727-7516
Fr: 800-327-6868
J.J. Keller & Associates, Inc. Staff. Revised edition, 1991.

★6887★ *Managing Your Independent Contractor Fleet Survey: A Nationwide Survey of Trucking Companies Utilizing Owner-Operators*
American Trucking Associations, Inc.
2200 Mill Rd.
Alexandria, VA 22314-4677
Ph: (703)838-1700 Fr: 800-225-8382
American Trucking Associations Staff. 1993.

★6888★ *Math on the Job: Local Truck Driver*
National Center for Research in Vocational Education
Ohio State University
1900 Kenry Rd.
Columbus, OH 43210
Ph: (614)292-4353
1985.

★6889★ *Modern Bulk Transporter—Truck Specifications Directory Issue*
Tunnell Publications, Inc.
PO Box 66010
Houston, TX 77266
Ph: (713)523-8124 Fax: (713)523-8384
Jay Norem, Circulation Manager
Annual, November. Publication includes: Listing of approximately 150 truck models. Entries include: Company name, address, phone, model names and specifications. Arrangement: Classified by product/service.

★6890★ *Motor Carrier Employees Handbook for the Prevention of Freight Loss & Damages*
American Trucking Associations, Inc.
2200 Mill Rd.
Alexandria, VA 22313-4677
Ph: (703)838-1700 Fr: 800-225-8382
American Trucking Association, National Freight Claim & Security Council. Revised edition, 1987.

★6891★ *Motor Carrier Insurance*
American Trucking Associations, Inc.
2200 Mill Rd.
Alexandria, VA 22314-4677
Ph: (703)838-1700 Fr: 800-255-8382
American Trucking Associations, National Accounting & Finance Council. 1986.

★6892★ *Motor Carrier Management Systems*
American Trucking Associations, Inc.
2200 Mill Rd.
Alexandria, VA 22314-4677
Ph: (703)838-1700 Fr: 800-225-8382
Clifford R. Buys. Revised edition, 1987.

★6893★ *Out of Service Tire Analysis Guide*
American Trucking Associations, Inc.
2200 Mill Rd.
Alexandria, VA 22314-4677
Ph: (703)838-1700 Fr: 800-225-8382
American Trucking Association Maintenance Council. 1984.

★6894★ *Radial Tire Wear Condition & Causes: A Guide to Wear Pattern Analysis*
American Trucking Associations, Inc.
2200 Mill Rd.
Alexandria, VA 22314-4677
Ph: (703)838-1700 Fr: 800-225-8382
American Trucking Association Maintenance Council. 1984.

★6895★ *Risk Management Manual for Motor Carriers*
American Trucking Associations, Inc.
2200 Mill Rd.
Alexandria, VA 22314-4677
Ph: (703)838-1700 Fr: 800-225-8382
American Trucking Associations National Accounting & Finance Council. 1986.

★6896★ *Small Carrier Safety Program*
American Trucking Associations, Inc.
2200 Mill Rd.
Alexandria, VA 22314-4677
Ph: (703)838-1700 Fr: 800-225-8382
1992.

★6897★ *Summary of Size & Weight Limits*
American Trucking Associations, Inc.
2200 Mill Rd.
Alexandria, VA 22314-4677
Ph: (703)838-1700 Fr: 800-225-8382
American Trucking Associations, Inc., Department of State Laws. 1994.

★6898★ *Truckers Atlas*
American Trucking Associations, Inc.
2200 Mill Rd.
Alexandria, VA 22314-4677
Ph: (703)838-1700 Fr: 800-225-8382
American Trucking Associations & Creative Sales Corporation. 1994.

★6899★ *Trucking Permit Guide, 1G: Private, Contract, Common, Exempt*
J. J. Keller & Associates, Inc.
3003 W. Breezewood
PO Box 368
Neenah, WI 54957-0368
Ph: (414)722-2848 Fax: (414)727-7516
Fr: 800-327-6868
J.J. Keller & Associates, Inc. Staff, editor. Revised edition, 1987.

★6900★ *Wheel & Rim out of Service Guide*
American Trucking Associations, Inc.
2200 Mill Rd.
Alexandria, VA 22314-4677
Ph: (703)838-1700 Fr: 800-225-8382
American Trucking Associations, Inc. Maintenance Council. 1987.

PERIODICALS

★6901★ *Automotive News*
Crain Communications, Inc.
1400 Woodbridge Ave.
Detroit, MI 48207
Ph: (313)446-1600 Fax: (313)446-0383
Peter Brown, ED

Weekly. Tabloid reporting on all facets of the automotive and truck industry, as well as related businesses.

★6902★ *CALTRUX*
California Trucking Association
1251 Beacon Blvd.
PO Box 923
West Sacramento, CA 95691
Ph: (916)373-3531
Jay Van Rein

Weekly. Provides news, commentary, announcements, and advertising of interest to California truck fleet owners and managers. Carries congressional updates, news of developments in the state Public Utilities Commission, a calendar of events.

★6903★ *Commercial Carrier Journal*
Capital Cities/ABC/Chilton Co.
Chilton Way
Radnor, PA 19087
Ph: (215)964-4000 Fax: (215)964-4647
Gerald F. Standley

Monthly. Magazine containing management, maintenance, and operations information for truck and bus fleets.

★6904★ *Fruit and Vegetable Truck Rate Report*
Federal-State Market News
630 Sansome St., Rm. 727
San Francisco, CA 94111
Ph: (415)705-1300 Fax: (415)705-1301
Fred Teensma

Weekly. Lists truck rates per load to selected markets throughout the U.S. Also reports on trucks available in relation to shippers' needs. Recurring features include statistics on the total reported domestic and import truck shipments of fresh fruit and vegetables.

★6905★ *Government Tender Report*
American Trucking Associations, Inc.
2200 Mill Rd.
Alexandria, VA 22314
Ph: (703)838-1794
Emry Williams

Semiweekly. Summarizes tenders (except those pertaining to household goods) which have been submitted to the Interstate Commerce Commission by motor, water, and rail carriers and bureaus, and freight forwarders in compliance with Section 10721 of the Interstate Commerce Act. Also identifies carriers, tender numbers, effective and expiration dates, commodities, origins, destinations, and rates. Lists and cross-references entries according to regions of origin.

★6906★ *Government Traffic Bulletin Trucking Information*
American Trucking Information Services, Inc.
2200 Mill Rd.
Alexandria, VA 22314
Ph: (703)838-1793
Susan Stowell

Weekly. Summarizes current traffic requirements of major U.S. Government agencies and reports changes in federal transportation policies, procedures, and personnel. Provides names and phone numbers of individuals who may be contacted for additional information.

★6907★ *Heavy Duty Trucking*
Newport Communications
PO Box W
Newport Beach, CA 92658-8910
Ph: (714)261-1636 Fax: (714)261-2904
Doug Condra

Monthly. Magazine covering long and short haul operations for heavy truck owners and managers.

★6908★ *Highway Common Carrier Newsletter*
Regular Common Carrier Conference
2200 Mill Rd., Ste. 350
Alexandria, VA 22314-4677
Ph: (703)838-1970 Fax: (703)684-4328
Shawn Fields

Biweekly. Focuses on the trucking industry. Covers regulatory, legislative, and judicial matters which affect transportation on the national and state levels. Monitors the activities of the Interstate Commerce Commission and the Department of Transportation. Recurring features include news of the programs of the Conference.

★6909★ *Land Line*
Owner-Operator Independent Drivers Assn. Inc.
311 R.D. Mize Rd.
Grain Valley, MO 64029
Ph: (816)229-5791 Fax: (816)229-0518
Todd Spencer

Bimonthly.

★6910★ *Movin' Out*
Pollock Enterprises, Ltd.
Box 777
118 1/2 Franklin St.
Slippery Rock, PA 16057
Ph: (412)794-6857 Fax: (412)794-1314
Pamela Pollock

Monthly. Trade magazine.

★6911★ *NATSO Truckers News*
Newport Communications
PO Box W
Newport Beach, CA 92658-8910
Ph: (714)261-1636 Fax: (714)261-2904
Jack Thiessen

Monthly. Magazine (tabloid) for professional truck drivers and owner-operators. Official publication of National Association of Truck Stop Operators.

★6912★ *NITL Notice*
National Industrial Transportation League (NITL)
1700 N. Moore St., Ste. 1900
Arlington, VA 22209
Ph: (703)524-5011 Fax: (703)524-5017
Patricia A. Mascari

Weekly. Carries transportation news—railroad, motor carrier, airline, and maritime—in the interest of industrial and commercial shippers. Covers rate-hike proposals, transportation legislation, regulatory agency actions, postal service developments, union actions, and court cases. Recurring features include coverage of the Interstate Commerce Commission, U.S. Postal Service, Department of Transportation, and other regulatory agencies.

★6913★ *Owner Operator*
Capital Cities/ABC/Chilton Co.
Chilton Way
Radnor, PA 19087
Ph: (215)964-4000 Fax: (215)964-4647
Leon E. Witconis

Magazine.

★6914★ *Pro Trucker*
Ramp Publishing Group
610 Colonial Park Drive
Roswell, GA 30075
Ph: (404)587-0311 Fax: (404)642-8874
Carol Prins

Monthly. Trucking industry magazine.

★6915★ *Refrigerated Transporter*
Tunnell Publications, Inc.
PO Box 66010
Houston, TX 77266
Ph: (713)523-8124 Fax: (713)523-8384
Gary Macklin

Monthly. Trade magazine on refrigerated hauling and delivery.

★6916★ *Rolling Along*
North Dakota Motor Carriers Assoc., Inc.
PO Box 874
Bismarck, ND 58502
Ph: (701)223-2700
Leroy H. Ernst

Quarterly. Motor trucking magazine.

★6917★ *SCTA Hi-Lights*
South Carolina Trucking Assn.
2425 Devine St.
PO Box 50166
Columbia, SC 29250-0166
Ph: (803)799-4306 Fax: (803)254-7148
J. Richards Todd

Monthly. Newspaper (tabloid) serving South Carolina Trucking Association members, truck operators, bus operators, and fleet owners in South Carolina and adjoining states.

★6918★ *Southern Motor Cargo*
Wallace Witmer Co.
1509 Madison Ave.
Memphis, TN 38104
Ph: (901)276-5424 Fax: (901)276-5400
Randy Duke

Monthly. Magazine for and about the trucking industry.

★6919★ *Tarheel Wheels' Magazine*
North Carolina Trucking Assn., Inc.
219 W. Martin St.
PO Box 2977
Raleigh, NC 27602
Ph: (919)834-0387 Fax: (919)832-0390
Elbert L. Peters

Quarterly. Magazine on the trucking industry.

★6920★ *Tiempo Latino*
3288 21st Street
PO Box 9
San Francisco, CA 94110
Ph: (415)821-4452
Gail E. NeiraPublisher

Weekly. Publication focusing on Hispanic/ Latin issues in Northern California.

★6921★ *TMTA Newsletter*
Texas Motor Transportation Assn.
700 E. 11th St.
PO Box 1669
Austin, TX 78767
Ph: (512)478-2541 Fax: (512)474-6494
Debra Buss

TRW. Magazine covering the Texas truck and bus industry.

★6922★ *Transport Fleet News*
Transport Publishing Co.
1962 N. Bissell St., Fl. 3
Chicago, IL 60614-5015
Ph: (312)523-6669 Fax: (312)523-9062
Phillip Scopelite

Monthly. Trucking magazine.

★6923★ *Transportation: An Abstract Newsletter*
National Technical Information Service (NTIS)
5285 Port Royal Rd.
Springfield, VA 22161
Ph: (703)487-4630

Biweekly. Provides abstracts of publications in the areas of air, rail, water, pipeline, and road transportation; global navigation systems; and transportation safety.

★6924★ *Transportation & Distribution*
Penton Publishing
1100 Superior Ave.
Cleveland, OH 44114
Ph: (216)696-7000 Fax: (216)696-7932
Perry Trunick

Monthly. Magazine covering traffic and physical distribution.

★6925★ *Transportation Quarterly*
Eno Transportation Foundation
44211 Slatestone Ct.
Lansdowne, VA 22075
Ph: (703)883-8243 Fax: (703)227-3928
Tracy Dunleavy

Quarterly. Trade magazine on transportation.

★6926★ *Truck Paper*
Peed Corp.
120 W. Harvest Drive
PO Box 85518
Lincoln, NE 68521-5380
Ph: (402)477-8900 Fax: (402)477-9252
Lee Chapin

Weekly. Tabloid featuring trucks and trailers for sale.

★6927★ *Truck Parts & Service*
Kona Communications, Inc.
707 Lake Cook Rd., Ste. 300
Deerfield, IL 60015
Ph: (708)498-3180 Fax: (708)498-3197
Fr: 800-767-5662
David Zaritz

Monthly. Trade magazine for truck parts and service market.

★6928★ *TRUCKS Magazine*
765 Churchville Rd.
Southampton, PA 18966
John Stevens

Bimonthly. Magazine covering health, safety, image, and profitability for drivers of heavy duty trucks.

★6929★ *TWU Express*
Transport Workers Union of America
80 West End Ave.
New York, NY 10023
Ph: (212)873-6000 Fax: (212)721-1431
James Gannon

Monthly. Labor magazine.

Meetings and Conventions

★6930★ American Trucking Associations Management Conference & Exhibition
American Trucking Associations
2200 Mill Rd.
Alexandria, VA 22314
Ph: (703)838-1755 Fax: (703)684-3935

Annual. Usually held in autumn. **Dates and Locations:** 1995 Oct 29-01; Chicago, IL. • 1996 Oct 20-23; Washington, DC. • 1997 Oct 26-29; Las Vegas, NV.

★6931★ ATA Management Conference and Exhibition
American Trucking Associations (ATA)
2200 Mill Rd.
Alexandria, VA 22314
Ph: (703)838-1700 Fax: (703)684-5720
Fr: 800-ATA-LINE

Annual. **Dates and Locations:** 1996 Oct 20-23; Washington, DC

★6932★ International Trucking Show
Independent Trade Show Management
1155 Chess Dr., Ste. 102
Foster City, CA 94404
Ph: (415)349-4876 Fax: (415)349-5169
Fr: 800-227-5992

Annual. Always held during the summer at the Convention Center in Anaheim, California. **Dates and Locations:** 1996 May 02-04; Anaheim, CA.

★6933★ Mid-America Trucking Show
Exhibit Management Associates, Inc.
3701 Taylorville Rd., Ste. 4
Louisville, KY 40220
Ph: (502)458-4487 Fr: 800-626-2370

Annual. Always held during March at the Kentucky Fair and Exposition Center in Louisville. **Dates and Locations:** 1996 Mar 21-23; Louisville, KY. • 1997 Mar 20-22; Louisville, KY. • 1998 Mar 19-21; Louisville, KY. • 1999 Mar 25-27; Louisville, KY. • 2000 Mar 23-25; Louisville, KY.

★6934★ Mid-West Truck Show
Mid-West Truckers Association
2727 N. Dirksen Pkwy.
Springfield, IL 62702
Ph: (217)525-0310 Fax: (217)525-0342

Annual. Always held during February at the Prairie Capital Convention Center in Springfield, Illinois. **Dates and Locations:** 1996 Feb 15-17; Springfield, IL. • 1997 Feb 20-22; Springfield, IL.

★6935★ NASSTRAC
NASSTRAC
1750 Pennsylvania Ave., Ste. 1105
Washington, DC 20006
Ph: (202)393-5505 Fax: (202)347-8978

Semiannual.

★6936★ National Truck Equipment Association (SUPERSHOW)
National Truck Equipment Association
37400 Hills Tech Dr.
Farmington Hills, MI 48331-3414
Ph: (810)489-7090 Fax: (810)489-8590
Fr: 800-441-6832

Annual. **Dates and Locations:** 1996 Feb 06-09; Orlando, FL. • 1997; Charlotte, NC.

★6937★ New Jersey Motor Truck Association Annual Convention
New Jersey Motor Truck Association
160 Tices Ln.
East Brunswick, NJ 08816
Ph: (908)254-5000 Fax: (908)613-1745

Biennial.

★6938★ Southwest Trucking Show
Texas Motor Transportation Association
700 E. 11th St.
PO Box 1669
Austin, TX 78701
Ph: (512)478-2541 Fax: (512)474-6494
Fr: 800-876-2161

Annual. **Dates and Locations:** 1996 Jun 13-15; San Antonio, TX.

★6939★ Wisconsin Truck Expo
Wisconsin Motor Carriers Association
PO Box 44849
Madison, WI 53744-4849
Ph: (608)833-8200 Fax: (608)833-2875

Annual. Always held during April at the Milwaukee Exposition-Conference Center and Arena (MECCA) in Wisconsin. **Dates and Locations:** 1996 Jan 17-18; Madison, WI.

Other Sources of Information

★6940★ *American Trucking Trends, 1991-92*
American Trucking Associations, Inc.
2200 Mill Rd.
Alexandria, VA 22314-4677
Ph: (703)838-1700 Fr: 800-225-8382

American Trucking Associations Statistical Analysis Department. 1991.

★6941★ *Encouraging Cooperation among Competitors: The Case of Motor Carrier Deregulation & Collective Ratemaking*
Greenwood Publishing Group, Inc.
88 Post Rd., W
PO Box 5007
Westport, CT 06881
Ph: (203)226-3571 Fax: (203)222-1502
William B. Tye. 1987.

★6942★ *Facts for Consumers From the Federal Trade Commission: Truck-Driving Schools*
Federal Trade Commission
Office of Consumer/Business Education
6th & Pennsylvania Ave. NW
Washington, DC 20580
Ph: (202)326-2222
1990. This four-page leaflet offers consumers guidelines for selecting and evaluating a truck-driver training school.

★6943★ *Forklift Truck: Operator Training*
Du Pont
Brandywine Bldg., No. 11266
Wilmington, DE 19898
Ph: (302)774-2168 Fax: (302)774-2134
Fr: 800-532-7233
Accompanied by self-study courses for either experienced or novice drivers, this tape outlines the training for forklift handlers.

★6944★ *General Driving Safety*
Gulf Publishing Co.
PO Box 2680
Houston, TX 77252
Ph: (713)529-4301 Fax: (713)520-4438
11 part series that provides instruction on driving safety, including information on road conditions and speed, drunk driving, accidents, sleepiness and driving, mountain driving, and safety devices.

★6945★ *Motor Carrier Annual Report*
American Trucking Associations, Inc.
2200 Mill Rd.
Alexandria, VA 22314-4677
Ph: (703)838-1700 Fr: 800-225-8382
American Trucking Association, Statistical Analysis Department. 1992. Part of Financial and Operating Statistics Series.

★6946★ *Motor Carrier Professional Services Directory*
American Trucking Associations, Inc.
2200 Mill Rd.
Alexandria, VA 22314-4677
Ph: (703)838-1700 Fr: 800-225-8382
American Trucking Associations, Inc. 1994.

★6947★ *Roadtester Video*
Increase/SilverMine Video
6860 Canby Ave., Ste. 188
Reseda, CA 91335
Ph: (818)342-2880 Fax: (818)342-4029
Fr: 800-233-2880
Commercial and truck drivers can learn to pass the CDL pre-trip inspection test by watching this easy-to-understand comprehensive video. Contains information on passing the test and detailed mechanical information. Aimed at both new and experienced drivers. Although this video tells how to pass the test in California, it can be used anywhere.

★6948★ "Transportation" in *Second Careers: New Ways to Work After 50* (pp. 260-268)
Little, Brown and Co.
34 Beacon St.
Boston, MA 02108
Ph: (617)227-0730 Fax: (617)723-9422
Caroline Bird. 1992. Offers suggestions for people over 50 on careers in transportation. Jobs discussed include taxi drivers, bus drivers, truck drivers, and railway conductors.

★6949★ "Truck Driver" in *100 Best Jobs for the 1990s & Beyond*
Dearborn Financial Publishing, Inc.
520 N. Dearborn St.
Chicago, IL 60610-4354
Ph: (312)836-4400 Fax: (312)836-1021
Fr: 800-621-9621
Carol Kleiman. 1992. Describes 100 jobs ranging from accountants to veterinarians. Each job profile includes such information as education, experience, and certification needed, salaries, and job search suggestions.

★6950★ "Truck Driver" in *Career Selector 2001*
Barron's Educational Series, Inc.
250 Wireless Blvd.
Hauppauge, NY 11788
Ph: (516)434-3311 Fax: (516)434-3723
Fr: 800-645-3476
James C. Gonyea. 1993.

★6951★ "Truck Driver" in *Encyclopedia of Danger: Dangerous Professions* (pp. 102-105)
Chelsea House Publishers
1974 Sproul Rd., Ste. 400
Broomall, PA 19008
Ph: (215)353-5166 Fax: (215)359-1439
Missy Allen and Michel Peissel. 1993. Provides descriptions of 24 dangerous occupations, their risky characteristics, and safety precautions.

★6952★ *UFAC: Action Guide*
Upholstered Furniture Action Council (UFAC)
PO Box 2436
High Point, NC 27261
Ph: (919)885-5065 Fax: (919)884-5303
Annual. Guide to UFAC's voluntary program to promote cigarette-resistant upholstered furniture. Includes construction criteria, compliance, and history, plus list of directors, member associations, and supporting organizations.

★6953★ *What to Look for in a Truck Driver*
American Trucking Association
Office of Public Affairs
2200 Mill Rd.
Alexandria, VA 22314-4677
Ph: (703)838-1873
1990. This six-panel brochure describes truck driver qualifications and offers advice on truck driver training school facilities, curriculum, and instructors. Lists the criteria required for a school to be certified by the Professional Truck Driver Institute of America.

Water Transportation Occupations

Workers in **water transportation occupations** operate and maintain deep sea merchant ships, tugboats, towboats, ferries, dredges, research vessels, and other waterborne craft on the oceans and the Great Lakes, in harbors, on rivers and canals, and on other waterways. Captains or masters supervise the operation of a vessel and the work of the other officers and the crew. On large vessels, captains are assisted by deck officers or mates; on some inland vessels, they are called pilots. Mates stand watch for specified periods, usually four hours on and eight hours off, overseeing the operation of the vessel. Engineers or marine engineers operate, maintain, and repair propulsion engines, boilers, generators, pumps, and other machinery. Seamen, also called deckhands, particularly on inland waters, help navigate the vessel, operate deck equipment, and keep the nonengineering areas in good condition. Larger vessels have a boatswain or head seaman. Marine oilers lubricate gears, shafts, bearings, and other moving parts of engines and motors, read pressure and temperature gauges and record data, and may repair and adjust machinery. About 33 percent of all water transportation workers are employed on board merchant marine ships or U.S. Navy Military Sealift ships operating on the oceans or Great Lakes. Almost half work on tugs, towboats, ferries, dredges, and other watercraft in harbors, on rivers and canals, and other waterways. Others work in water transportation services such as boatyards and marinas; boat chartering; piloting services; and marine construction, salvaging, and surveying.

Salaries

Weekly earnings for water transportation workers are as follows:

Lowest 10 percent	$350/week or less
Middle 50 percent	$463-$900/week
Top 10 percent	$1,050/week or more

Employment Outlook

Growth rate until the year 2005: Decline.

Water Transportation Occupations

Career Guides

★6954★ "Able Seaman" in *Occu-Facts: Information on 580 Careers in Outline Form*
Careers, Inc.
PO Box 135
Largo, FL 34649-0135
Ph: (813)584-7333

Biennial, 1995-96 edition. Each one-page occupational profile describes duties, working conditions, physical surroundings and demands, aptitudes, temperament, educational requirements, employment outlook, earnings, and places of employment.

★6955★ *Hanging On*
Pennsylvania State University AV Services
University Division of Media & Learning Resources
Special Services Building
1127 Fox Hill Rd.
State College, PA 16803-1824
Ph: (814)865-6314 Fax: (814)863-2574
Fr: 800-826-0132

Videocassette. 1980. 29 mins. Tugboat workers in New York harbor talk about their jobs and their concerns about inflation in this part of the "U.S. Chronicle" series.

★6956★ *Longshore Workers*
Chronicle Guidance Publications, Inc.
66 Aurora St.
PO Box 1190
Moravia, NY 13118-1190
Ph: (315)497-0330 Fax: (315)497-3359
Fr: 800-622-7284

1993. This career brief describes the nature of the work, working conditions, hours and earnings, education and training, licensure, certification, unions, personal qualifications, social and psychological factors, employment outlook, entry methods, advancement, and related occupations.

★6957★ "Marine Engineer" in *Career Information Center* (Vol.2)
Simon and Schuster
200 Old Tappan Rd.
Old Tappan, NJ 07675
Fax: 800-445-6991 Fr: 800-223-2348

Richard Lidz and Dale Anderson, editorial directors. Fifth edition, 1993. For 600 occupations, describes job duties, entry-level requirements, education and training needed, advancement possibilities, employment outlook, earnings and benefits. The set is divided into 12 volumes. Each volume includes jobs related under a broad career field. Volume 13 is the index.

★6958★ "Marine Engineer (Shipboard)" in *Occu-Facts: Information on 580 Careers in Outline Form*
Careers, Inc.
PO Box 135
Largo, FL 34649-0135
Ph: (813)584-7333

Biennial, 1995-96 edition. Each one-page occupational profile describes duties, working conditions, physical surroundings and demands, aptitudes, temperament, educational requirements, employment outlook, earnings, and places of employment.

★6959★ "Marine Engineers" in *Career Discovery Encyclopedia* (Vol.4, pp. 54-55)
J.G. Ferguson Publishing Co.
200 W. Madison St., Ste. 300
Chicago, IL 60606
Ph: (312)580-5480 Fax: (312)580-4948

E. Russell Primm, editor-in-chief. 1993. Contains two-page articles on 504 occupations. Each article describes job duties, earnings, and educational and training requirements.

★6960★ "Marine Engineers" in *Encyclopedia of Careers and Vocational Guidance* (Vol.4, pp. 54-55)
J.G. Ferguson Publishing Co.
200 W. Madison St., Ste. 300
Chicago, IL 60606
Ph: (312)580-5480 Fax: (312)580-4948

William E. Hopke, editor-in-chief. Ninth edition, 1993. Six-volume set that profiles 500 occupations and describes job trends in 74 industries. Includes career description, educational requirements, history of the job, methods of entry, advancement, employment outlook, earnings, working conditions, social and psychological factors, and sources of additional information.

★6961★ "Marine/Ocean Engineering and Naval Architecture" in *Opportunities in Engineering Careers* (pp. 114-116)
National Textbook Co. (NTC)
VGM Career Books
4255 W. Touhy Ave.
Lincolnwood, IL 60646-1975
Ph: (708)679-5500 Fax: (708)679-2494
Fr: 800-323-4900

Nicholas Basta. 1990. Covers the advantages and disadvantages of working as an engineer, employment trends, work environments, and educational preparation.

★6962★ "Maritime Jobs" in *Opportunities in Transportation Careers* (pp. 53-54)
National Textbook Co. (NTC)
VGM Career Books
4255 W. Touhy Ave.
Lincolnwood, IL 60646-1975
Ph: (708)679-5500 Fax: (708)679-2494
Fr: 800-323-4900

Adrian A. Paradis. 1988. Describes transportation and related employment in driving occupations, the airlines, merchant marine, and travel services. Covers employment outlook, educational and training requirements, wages, and the work itself, and advantages and disadvantages of transportation careers. Offers job hunting advice.

★6963★ "Merchant Marine Captain" in *Career Information Center* (Vol.12)
Simon and Schuster
200 Old Tappan Rd.
Old Tappan, NJ 07675
Fax: 800-445-6991 Fr: 800-223-2348

Richard Lidz and Dale Anderson, editorial directors. Fifth edition, 1993. For 600 occupations, describes job duties, entry-level requirements, education and training needed, advancement possibilities, employment outlook, earnings and benefits. The set is divided into 12 volumes. Each volume includes

jobs related under a broad career field. Volume 13 is the index.

★6964★ "Merchant Marine Engineer and Chief Engineer" in *Career Information Center* (Vol.12)
Simon and Schuster
200 Old Tappan Rd.
Old Tappan, NJ 07675
Fax: 800-445-6991 Fr: 800-223-2348

Richard Lidz and Dale Anderson, editorial directors. Fifth edition, 1993. For 600 occupations, describes job duties, entry-level requirements, education and training needed, advancement possibilities, employment outlook, earnings and benefits. The set is divided into 12 volumes. Each volume includes jobs related under a broad career field. Volume 13 is the index.

★6965★ "Merchant Marine Engineer" in *Transportation* (pp. 63-67)
Franklin Watts, Inc.
387 Park Avenue, S.
New York, NY 10016
Ph: (212)686-7070

Marjorie Rittenberg Schulz. 1990. Surveys the transportation industry including air, water, and rail services. Provides job description, training, salary, and employment outlook. Offers job hunting advice.

★6966★ *Merchant Marine Occupations*
Chronicle Guidance Publications, Inc.
66 Aurora St.
PO Box 1190
Moravia, NY 13118-1190
Ph: (315)497-0330 Fax: (315)497-3359
Fr: 800-622-7284

1993. This career brief describes the nature of the work, working conditions, hours and earnings, education and training, licensure, certification, unions, personal qualifications, social and psychological factors, employment outlook, entry methods, advancement, and related occupations.

★6967★ "Merchant Marine Occupations" in *Encyclopedia of Careers and Vocational Guidance* (Vol.3, pp. 425-428)
J.G. Ferguson Publishing Co.
200 W. Madison St., Ste. 300
Chicago, IL 60606
Ph: (312)580-5480 Fax: (312)580-4948

William E. Hopke, editor-in-chief. Ninth edition, 1993. Four-volume set that profiles 500 occupations and describes job trends in 74 industries. Includes career description, educational requirements, history of the job, methods of entry, advancement, employment outlook, earnings, working conditions, social and psychological factors, and sources of additional information.

★6968★ "Merchant Marine Officers" in *Jobs! What They Are—Where They Are—What They Pay* (pp. 297)
Simon & Schuster, Inc.
Simon & Schuster Bldg.
1230 Avenue of the Americas
New York, NY 10020
Ph: (212)698-7000

Robert O. Snelling and Anne M. Snelling. Revised edition, 1992. Profiles 241 occupations, describing duties and responsibilities, educational preparation, earnings, employment opportunities, training, and qualifications.

★6969★ "Merchant Marine Officers" in *Opportunities in Transportation Careers* (pp. 59-60)
National Textbook Co. (NTC)
VGM Career Books
4255 W. Touhy Ave.
Lincolnwood, IL 60646-1975
Ph: (708)679-5500 Fax: (708)679-2494
Fr: 800-323-4900

Adrian A. Paradis. 1988. Describes transportation and related employment in driving occupations, the airlines, merchant marine, and travel services. Covers employment outlook, educational and training requirements, wages, and the work itself, and advantages and disadvantages of transportation careers. Offers job hunting advice.

★6970★ "Merchant Marine Unlicensed Sailors" in *Opportunities in Transportation Careers* (pp. 54-58)
National Textbook Co. (NTC)
VGM Career Books
4255 W. Touhy Ave.
Lincolnwood, IL 60646-1975
Ph: (708)679-5500 Fax: (708)679-2494
Fr: 800-323-4900

Adrian A. Paradis. 1988. Describes transportation and related employment in driving occupations, the airlines, merchant marine, and travel services. Covers employment outlook, educational and training requirements, wages, and the work itself, and advantages and disadvantages of transportation careers. Offers job hunting advice.

★6971★ "Merchant Sailor" in *Hard Hatted Women: Stories of Struggle and Success in the Trades* (pp. 176-186)
Seal Press
3131 Western Ave., Ste. 410
Seattle, WA 98121
Ph: (206)283-7844 Fax: (206)285-9410

Molly Martin, editor. 1988. Twenty-six women recount their experiences working in blue collar occupations. They describe how they got in, the work they do, their relationships in predominantly male occupations, and their training.

★6972★ *Opportunities in Marine and Maritime Careers*
National Textbook Co. (NTC)
VGM Career Books
4255 W. Touhy Ave.
Lincolnwood, IL 60646-1975
Ph: (708)679-5500 Fax: (708)679-2494
Fr: 800-323-4900

William Ray Heitzmann. 1988. Includes careers related by their proximity to water; cruise ships, oceanography, marine sciences, fishing, commercial diving, maritime transportation, shipbuilding, Navy, and Coast Guard. Covers qualifications, job outlook, job duties, educational preparation, and training. Lists associations and schools.

★6973★ "Ordinary and Able Seaman" in *Career Information Center* (Vol.12)
Simon and Schuster
200 Old Tappan Rd.
Old Tappan, NJ 07675
Fax: 800-445-6991 Fr: 800-223-2348

Richard Lidz and Dale Anderson, editorial directors. Fifth edition, 1993. For 600 occupations, describes job duties, entry-level requirements, education and training needed, advancement possibilities, employment outlook, earnings and benefits. The set is divided into 12 volumes. Each volume includes jobs related under a broad career field. Volume 13 is the index.

★6974★ *Seaman, Able*
Careers, Inc.
PO Box 135
Largo, FL 34649-0135
Ph: (813)584-7333

1992. Two-page occupational summary card describing duties, working conditions, personal qualifications, training, earnings and hours, employment outlook, places of employment, related careers and where to write for more information.

★6975★ "Seaman, Steward, Cook" in *Transportation* (pp. 33-37)
Franklin Watts, Inc.
387 Park Avenue, S.
New York, NY 10016
Ph: (212)686-7070

Marjorie Rittenberg Schulz. 1990. Surveys the transportation industry including air, water, and rail services. Provides job description, training, salary, and employment outlook. Offers job hunting advice.

★6976★ "Tall Ship Crew Member" in *Offbeat Careers: The Directory of Unusual Work*
Ten Speed Press
PO Box 7123
Berkeley, CA 94707
Fax: (510)559-1629 Fr: 800-841-2665

Al Sacharov. 1991. Profiles eighty-eight unusual careers. Provides job description, history of occupation, salary, and training required. Lists one or more sources of additional information.

★6977★ "Water Transportation Occupations" in *Occupational Outlook Handbook*
U.S. Government Printing Office
Superintendent of Documents
Washington, DC 20402
Ph: (202)512-1800 Fax: (202)512-2250

Biennial; latest edition, 1994-95. Encyclopedia of careers describing more than 250 occupations and comprising about 85 percent of all jobs in the economy. Occupations that require lengthy education or training are given the most attention. For each occupation, the handbook describes job duties, working conditions, training, educational preparation, personal qualities, advancement possibilities, job outlook, earnings, and sources of additional information.

★6978★ "Yacht Crew Member" in ***Offbeat Careers: The Directory of Unusual Work***
Ten Speed Press
PO Box 7123
Berkeley, CA 94707
Fax: (510)559-1629 Fr: 800-841-2665

Al Sacharov. 1991. Profiles eighty-eight unusual careers. Provides job description, history of occupation, salary, and training required. Lists one or more sources of additional information.

Test Guides

★6979★ ***Assistant Bridge Operator***
National Learning Corp.
212 Michael Dr.
Syosset, NY 11791
Ph: (516)921-8888 Fax: (516)921-8743
Fr: 800-645-6337

Jack Rudman. All examination guides in this series contain questions with answers. Test guide for assistant bridge operator trainee is also available.

★6980★ ***Career Examination Series: Able Seaman***
National Learning Corp.
212 Michael Dr.
Syosset, NY 11791
Ph: (516)921-8888 Fax: (516)921-8743
Fr: 800-645-6337

Jack Rudman. All examination guides in this series contain questions with answers.

★6981★ ***Career Examination Series: Assistant Captain***
National Learning Corp.
212 Michael Dr.
Syosset, NY 11791
Ph: (516)921-8888 Fax: (516)921-8743
Fr: 800-645-6337

Jack Rudman. All examination guides in this series contain questions with answers.

★6982★ ***Career Examination Series: Deckhand***
National Learning Corp.
212 Michael Dr.
Syosset, NY 11791
Ph: (516)921-8888 Fax: (516)921-8743
Fr: 800-645-6337

Jack Rudman. All examination guides in this series contain questions with answers.

★6983★ ***Career Examination Series: Harbormaster***
National Learning Corp.
212 Michael Dr.
Syosset, NY 11791
Ph: (516)921-8888 Fax: (516)921-8743
Fr: 800-645-6337

Jack Rudman. All examination guides in this series contain questions with answers.

★6984★ ***Career Examination Series: Marine Stoker***
National Learning Corp.
212 Michael Dr.
Syosset, NY 11791
Ph: (516)921-8888 Fax: (516)921-8743
Fr: 800-645-6337

Jack Rudman. All examination guides in this series contain questions with answers.

★6985★ ***Career Examination Series: Mate***
National Learning Corp.
212 Michael Dr.
Syosset, NY 11791
Ph: (516)921-8888 Fax: (516)921-8743
Fr: 800-645-6337

Jack Rudman. All examination guides in this series contain questions with answers.

★6986★ ***Career Examination Series: Senior Harbormaster***
National Learning Corp.
212 Michael Dr.
Syosset, NY 11791
Ph: (516)921-8888 Fax: (516)921-8743
Fr: 800-645-6337

Jack Rudman. All examination guides in this series contain questions with answers.

★6987★ ***Merchant Marine Examination Questions—Volume 12: Electricity***
Superintendent of Documents
U.S. Government Printing Office
Washington, DC 20402
Ph: (202)783-3238

1988. Part of a series of volumes produced by the U.S. government; contains questions used in examinations for merchant marine licenses and documents. Also provides sources and answers.

★6988★ ***Merchant Marine Examination Questions—Volume 13: Steam Plants***
Superintendent of Documents
U.S. Government Printing Office
Washington, DC 20402
Ph: (202)783-3238

1988. Part of a series of volumes produced by the U.S. government; contains questions used in examinations for merchant marine licenses and documents. Also provides sources and answers.

★6989★ ***Merchant Marine Examination Questions—Volume 2: Navigation Problems***
Superintendent of Documents
U.S. Government Printing Office
Washington, DC 20402
Ph: (202)783-3238

1989. Part of a series of volumes produced by the U.S. government; contains questions used in examinations for merchant marine licenses and documents. Also provides sources and answers.

Awards, Scholarships, Grants, and Fellowships

★6990★ **Transportation Man of the Year**
Delta Nu Alpha Transportation Fraternity
621 Plainfield, Ste. 308
Willowbrook, IL 60521

To recognize contributions to the field of transportation. A plaque is awarded annually. Established in 1952.

Periodicals

★6991★ ***ABYC News***
American Boat and Yacht Council, Inc. (ABYC)
3069 Solomons Island Rd.
Edgewater, MD 21037-1416
Ph: (410)956-1050 Fax: (410)956-2737
Louise Lincoln

Quarterly. Reports on the activities of the Council. Updates members on current events, seminars, and meetings. Discusses technical boating topics and current boating standards and related issues. Recurring features include a calendar of events, reports of meetings, job listings, and notices of publications available.

★6992★ ***Government Tender Report***
American Trucking Associations, Inc.
2200 Mill Rd.
Alexandria, VA 22314
Ph: (703)838-1794
Emry Williams

Semiweekly. Summarizes tenders (except those pertaining to household goods) which have been submitted to the Interstate Commerce Commission by motor, water, and rail carriers and bureaus, and freight forwarders in compliance with Section 10721 of the Interstate Commerce Act. Also identifies carriers, tender numbers, effective and expiration dates, commodities, origins, destinations, and rates. Lists and cross-references entries according to regions of origin.

★6993★ ***Government Traffic Bulletin Trucking Information***
American Trucking Information Services, Inc.
2200 Mill Rd.
Alexandria, VA 22314
Ph: (703)838-1793
Susan Stowell

Weekly. Summarizes current traffic requirements of major U.S. Government agencies and reports changes in federal transportation policies, procedures, and personnel. Provides names and phone numbers of individuals who may be contacted for additional information.

★6994★ *MARINE DIGEST*
Marine Publishing, Inc.
1201 1st Ave. S, No. 200
PO Box 3905
Seattle, WA 98124
Ph: (206)682-3607 Fax: (206)682-4023
Alec FiskenPublisher

Monthly. Magazine for shipbuilding, transport, international trade, and allied industries.

★6995★ *Marine Log*
Simmons-Boardman Publishing
345 Hudson St.
New York, NY 10014
Ph: (212)620-7200 Fax: (212)633-1165
Nicholas Blenkey

Monthly. Magazine serving ship, boat, and barge owners, builders, and operators; port authorities, and the Navy.

★6996★ *NITL Notice*
National Industrial Transportation League (NITL)
1700 N. Moore St., Ste. 1900
Arlington, VA 22209
Ph: (703)524-5011 Fax: (703)524-5017
Patricia A. Mascari

Weekly. Carries transportation news—railroad, motor carrier, airline, and maritime—in the interest of industrial and commercial shippers. Covers rate-hike proposals, transportation legislation, regulatory agency actions, postal service developments, union actions, and court cases. Recurring features include coverage of the Interstate Commerce Commission, U.S. Postal Service, Department of Transportation, and other regulatory agencies.

★6997★ *Ocean Navigator*
Navigator Publishing Corp.
18 Danforth St.
Portland, ME 04101
Ph: (207)772-2466
Tim Queeney

Magazine on Marine navigation and voyaging equipment and techniques.

★6998★ *Passenger Transport*
American Public Transit Assn.
1201 New York Ave. NW, Ste. 400
Washington, DC 20005
Ph: (202)898-4119 Fax: (202)898-4095
Dennis Kouba

Weekly. Magazine covering the public transit industry in the U.S. and Canada.

★6999★ *Seafarers LOG*
Seafarers Intl. Union
5201 Auth Way
Camp Springs, MD 20746
Ph: (301)899-0675 Fax: (301)899-7355
Jessica Smith

Monthly. Monthly tabloid on maritime labor.

★7000★ *Seatrade Review*
Seatrade North America, Inc.
125 Village Blvd., No. 220
Princeton, NJ 08540-6703
Ph: (609)452-9414 Fax: (609)452-9374
Ian Middleton

Monthly. Trade magazine presenting analyses of the business of sea transport.

★7001★ *Seaway Review*
Harbor House Publishers, Inc.
221 Water St.
Boyne City, MI 49712
Ph: (616)582-2814 Fax: (616)582-3392
Michelle Cortright

Quarterly. Magazine on maritime transportation, business, and international and economic news and analyses.

★7002★ *Tiempo Latino*
3288 21st Street
PO Box 9
San Francisco, CA 94110
Ph: (415)821-4452
Gail E. NeiraPublisher

Weekly. Publication focusing on Hispanic/ Latin issues in Northern California.

★7003★ *Transportation: An Abstract Newsletter*
National Technical Information Service (NTIS)
5285 Port Royal Rd.
Springfield, VA 22161
Ph: (703)487-4630

Biweekly. Provides abstracts of publications in the areas of air, rail, water, pipeline, and road transportation; global navigation systems; and transportation safety.

★7004★ *Transportation & Distribution*
Penton Publishing
1100 Superior Ave.
Cleveland, OH 44114
Ph: (216)696-7000 Fax: (216)696-7932
Perry Trunick

Monthly. Magazine covering traffic and physical distribution.

★7005★ *Transportation Quarterly*
Eno Transportation Foundation
44211 Slatestone Ct.
Lansdowne, VA 22075
Ph: (703)883-8243 Fax: (703)227-3928
Tracy Dunleavy

Quarterly. Trade magazine on transportation.

★7006★ *TWU Express*
Transport Workers Union of America
80 West End Ave.
New York, NY 10023
Ph: (212)873-6000 Fax: (212)721-1431
James Gannon

Monthly. Labor magazine.

★7007★ *Water Law*
John Wiley and Sons, Inc.
605 3rd Ave.
New York, NY 10158-0012
Ph: (212)850-6000 Fax: (212)850-6088
Fr: 800-526-5368
Simon Ball

Bimonthly. Journal publishing a legal analysis of environmental, business, and regulatory changes that impact the water industry.

★7008★ *WWS/World Wide Shipping*
World Wide Shipping Guide, Inc.
77 Moehring Drive
Blauvelt, NY 10913-2093
Ph: (914)359-1934 Fax: (914)359-1938
Ann H. Hagen

Magazine reporting trends, developments, and government regulations effecting the shipping business. Serves ports, carriers, shippers, customs brokers, distributors, agents, stevedores, and terminal operators.

Meetings and Conventions

★7009★ International WorkBoat Show
Diversified Expositions
5 Milk St.
PO Box 7437 DTS
Portland, ME 04112-7437
Ph: (207)772-3005 Fax: (207)772-5059

Annual. Show held annually in New Orleans.

Handlers, Equipment Cleaners, Helpers, and Laborers

Freight, stock, and material movers include stock handlers and baggers, machine feeders and offbearers, stevedores, and related occupations. They move materials to and from storage areas, loading docks, delivery vehicles, ships' holds, machines, and containers either manually or with forklifts, dollies, handtrucks, or carts. **Helpers** assist construction trades workers, mechanics and repairers, and workers in production and extractive occupations. They aid machine operators and tenders by moving materials, supplies, and tools to and from work areas. **Construction laborers** provide much of the routine physical labor at building sites. They supply tools, materials, and equipment to carpenters, electricians, masons, plumbers, and other construction workers. Tenders for bricklayers and plasterers mix and supply materials, set up and move scaffolding, and provide other services. Laborers dig trenches, set braces to support the sides of excavations, and clean up rubble and debris. Hand packers and packagers manually package or wrap materials. Refuse collectors collect trash and garbage and drive garbage trucks. Service station attendants conduct various services on automobiles, buses, trucks, and other vehicles. Parking lot attendants assist customers in parking their cars in lots or storage areas and collect fees from customers. Vehicle washers and equipment cleaners clean machinery, vehicles, storage tanks, pipelines, and similar equipment.

Salaries

Weekly earnings for handlers, equipment cleaners, helpers, and laborers are as follows:

Lowest 10 percent	$180.00/week
Middle 50 percent	$220.00-$420.00/week
Top 10 percent	$550.00/week

Employment Outlook

Growth rate until the year 2005: Average.

Handlers, Equipment Cleaners, Helpers, and Laborers

Career Guides

★7010★ "Airline Baggage and Freight Handler" in *Career Information Center* (Vol.12)
Simon and Schuster
200 Old Tappan Rd.
Old Tappan, NJ 07675
Fax: 800-445-6991 Fr: 800-223-2348

Richard Lidz and Dale Anderson, editorial directors. Fifth edition, 1993. For 600 occupations, describes job duties, entry-level requirements, education and training needed, advancement possibilities, employment outlook, earnings and benefits. The set is divided into 12 volumes. Each volume includes jobs related under a broad career field. Volume 13 is the index.

★7011★ "Airline Freight Handler" in *Transportation* (pp. 15-17)
Franklin Watts, Inc.
387 Park Avenue, S.
New York, NY 10016
Ph: (212)686-7070

Marjorie Rittenberg Schulz. 1990. Surveys the transportation industry including air, water, and rail services. Provides job description, training, salary, and employment outlook. Offers job hunting advice.

★7012★ *Airplane Cleaner*
Careers, Inc.
PO Box 135
Largo, FL 34649-0135
Ph: (813)584-7333

1993. Two-page job guide card describing duties, working conditions, personal qualifications, training, earnings and hours, employment outlook, places of employment, related careers and where to write for more information.

★7013★ "Airplane Cleaner" in *Occu-Facts: Information on 580 Careers in Outline Form*
Careers, Inc.
PO Box 135
Largo, FL 34649-0135
Ph: (813)584-7333

Biennial, 1995-96 edition. Each one-page occupational profile describes duties, working conditions, physical surroundings and demands, aptitudes, temperament, educational requirements, employment outlook, earnings, and places of employment.

★7014★ *Asphalt Paving Machine Operators*
Chronicle Guidance Publications, Inc.
66 Aurora St.
PO Box 1190
Moravia, NY 13118-1190
Ph: (315)497-0330 Fax: (315)497-3359
Fr: 800-622-7284

1987. This career brief describes the nature of the work, working conditions, hours and earnings, education and training, licensure, certification, unions, personal qualifications, social and psychological factors, employment outlook, entry methods, advancement, and related occupations.

★7015★ *Auto Body Repair Helper*
Careers, Inc.
PO Box 135
Largo, FL 34649-0135
Ph: (813)584-7333

1994. Two-page job guide card describing duties, working conditions, personal qualifications, training, earnings and hours, employment outlook, places of employment, related careers and where to write for more information.

★7016★ "Auto Body Repair Helper" in *Occu-Facts: Information on 580 Careers in Outline Form*
Careers, Inc.
PO Box 135
Largo, FL 34649-0135
Ph: (813)584-7333

Biennial, 1995-96 edition. Each one-page occupational profile describes duties, working conditions, physical surroundings and demands, aptitudes, temperament, educational requirements, employment outlook, earnings, and places of employment.

★7017★ *Automobile Parking Attendant*
Careers, Inc.
PO Box 135
Largo, FL 34649-0135
Ph: (813)584-7333

1995. Two-page job guide card describing duties, working conditions, personal qualifications, training, earnings and hours, employment outlook, places of employment, related careers and where to write for more information.

★7018★ *Automobile Washer*
Careers, Inc.
PO Box 135
Largo, FL 34649-0135
Ph: (813)584-7333

1995. Two-page job guide card describing duties, working conditions, personal qualifications, training, earnings and hours, employment outlook, places of employment, related careers and where to write for more information.

★7019★ "Automobile Washer" in *Occu-Facts: Information on 580 Careers in Outline Form*
Careers, Inc.
PO Box 135
Largo, FL 34649-0135
Ph: (813)584-7333

Biennial, 1995-96 edition. Each one-page occupational profile describes duties, working conditions, physical surroundings and demands, aptitudes, temperament, educational requirements, employment outlook, earnings, and places of employment.

★7020★ *Automotive Mechanic Helper*
Careers, Inc.
PO Box 135
Largo, FL 34649-0135
Ph: (813)584-7333

1991. Two-page job guide card describing duties, working conditions, personal qualifications, training, earnings and hours, employment outlook, places of employment, related careers and where to write for more information.

★7021★ "Automotive Mechanic Helper" in *Occu-Facts: Information on 580 Careers in Outline Form*
Careers, Inc.
PO Box 135
Largo, FL 34649-0135
Ph: (813)584-7333

Biennial, 1995-96 edition. Each one-page occupational profile describes duties, working conditions, physical surroundings and demands, aptitudes, temperament, educational requirements, employment outlook, earnings, and places of employment.

★7022★ *Automotive Service Station Attendant*
Careers, Inc.
PO Box 135
Largo, FL 34649-0135
Ph: (813)584-7333

1994. Two-page occupational summary card describing duties, working conditions, personal qualifications, training, earnings and hours, employment outlook, places of employment, related careers and where to write for more information.

★7023★ "Automotive Service Station Attendant" in *Occu-Facts: Information on 580 Careers in Outline Form*
Careers, Inc.
PO Box 135
Largo, FL 34649-0135
Ph: (813)584-7333

Biennial, 1995-96 edition. Each one-page occupational profile describes duties, working conditions, physical surroundings and demands, aptitudes, temperament, educational requirements, employment outlook, earnings, and places of employment.

★7024★ *Bricklayer Helper*
Careers, Inc.
PO Box 135
Largo, FL 34649-0135
Ph: (813)584-7333

1993. Two-page job guide card describing duties, working conditions, personal qualifications, training, earnings and hours, employment outlook, places of employment, related careers and where to write for more information.

★7025★ "Bricklayer Helper" in *Occu-Facts: Information on 580 Careers in Outline Form*
Careers, Inc.
PO Box 135
Largo, FL 34649-0135
Ph: (813)584-7333

Biennial, 1995-96 edition. Each one-page occupational profile describes duties, working conditions, physical surroundings and demands, aptitudes, temperament, educational requirements, employment outlook, earnings, and places of employment.

★7026★ *Car Wash Attendants*
Chronicle Guidance Publications, Inc.
66 Aurora St.
PO Box 1190
Moravia, NY 13118-1190
Ph: (315)497-0330 Fax: (315)497-3359
Fr: 800-622-7284

1993. This career brief describes the nature of the work, working conditions, hours and earnings, education and training, licensure, certification, unions, personal qualifications, social and psychological factors, employment outlook, entry methods, advancement, and related occupations.

★7027★ *Car Wash Operator*
Vocational Biographies, Inc.
PO Box 31
Sauk Centre, MN 56378-0031
Ph: (612)352-6516 Fax: (612)352-5546
Fr: 800-255-0752

1990. This pamphlet profiles a person working in the job. Includes information about job duties, working conditions, places of employment, educational preparation, labor market outlook, and salaries.

★7028★ *Career Insights*
RMI Media Productions, Inc.
1365 N. Winchester
Olathe, KS 66061
Ph: (913)768-1696 Fax: 800-755-6910
Fr: 800-745-5480

Videocassette series. 1987. This videotape series describes 50 occupations, including skill requirements and interviews with people employed in these fields. Occupations include: flight service, air transportation/ground services, data processing, carpentry, clerk in banking/insurance/business, cosmetic personal grooming, firefighting, forestry, insulation/roofing, mechanics, material handling, photographic processing, pipefitting and plumbing, printing, secretarial services, tool and die operations.

★7029★ *Carpenter Helper*
Careers, Inc.
PO Box 135
Largo, FL 34649-0135
Ph: (813)584-7333

1992. Two-page job guide card describing duties, working conditions, personal qualifications, training, earnings and hours, employment outlook, places of employment, related careers and where to write for more information.

★7030★ "Carpenter Helper" in *Occu-Facts: Information on 580 Careers in Outline Form*
Careers, Inc.
PO Box 135
Largo, FL 34649-0135
Ph: (813)584-7333

Biennial, 1995-96 edition. Each one-page occupational profile describes duties, working conditions, physical surroundings and demands, aptitudes, temperament, educational requirements, employment outlook, earnings, and places of employment.

★7031★ "Construction Electrician Helper" in *Occu-Facts: Information on 580 Careers in Outline Form*
Careers, Inc.
PO Box 135
Largo, FL 34649-0135
Ph: (813)584-7333

Biennial, 1995-96 edition. Each one-page occupational profile describes duties, working conditions, physical surroundings and demands, aptitudes, temperament, educational requirements, employment outlook, earnings, and places of employment.

★7032★ *Construction Helpers*
Careers, Inc.
PO Box 135
Largo, FL 34649-0135
Ph: (813)584-7333

1992. Four-page brief offering the definition, history, duties, working conditions, personal qualifications, educational requirements, earnings, hours, employment outlook, advancement possibilities, and related occupations.

★7033★ "Construction Helpers" in *Occu-Facts: Information on 580 Careers in Outline Form*
Careers, Inc.
PO Box 135
Largo, FL 34649-0135
Ph: (813)584-7333

Biennial, 1995-96 edition. Each one-page occupational profile describes duties, working conditions, physical surroundings and demands, aptitudes, temperament, educational requirements, employment outlook, earnings, and places of employment.

★7034★ "Construction Laborer" in *Career Information Center* (Vol.4)
Simon and Schuster
200 Old Tappan Rd.
Old Tappan, NJ 07675
Fax: 800-445-6991 Fr: 800-223-2348

Richard Lidz and Dale Anderson, editorial directors. Fifth edition, 1993. For 600 occupations, describes job duties, entry-level requirements, education and training needed, advancement possibilities, employment outlook, earnings and benefits. The set is divided into 12 volumes. Each volume includes jobs related under a broad career field. Volume 13 is the index.

★7035★ *Construction Laborers*
Chronicle Guidance Publications, Inc.
66 Aurora St.
PO Box 1190
Moravia, NY 13118-1190
Ph: (315)497-0330 Fax: (315)497-3359
Fr: 800-622-7284

1993. This career brief describes the nature of the work, working conditions, hours and earnings, education and training, licensure, certification, unions, personal qualifications, social and psychological factors, employment outlook, entry methods, advancement, and related occupations.

★7036★ *Construction Machine Operators*
Chronicle Guidance Publications, Inc.
66 Aurora St.
PO Box 1190
Moravia, NY 13118-1190
Ph: (315)497-0330 Fax: (315)497-3359
Fr: 800-622-7284

1993. This career brief describes the nature of the work, working conditions, hours and earnings, education and training, licensure, certification, unions, personal qualifications, social and psychological factors, employment outlook, entry methods, advancement, and related occupations.

★7037★ "Display Worker Helper" in *Occu-Facts: Information on 580 Careers in Outline Form*
Careers, Inc.
PO Box 135
Largo, FL 34649-0135
Ph: (813)584-7333

Biennial, 1995-96 edition. Each one-page occupational profile describes duties, working conditions, physical surroundings and demands, aptitudes, temperament, educational requirements, employment outlook, earnings, and places of employment.

★7038★ *Divers*
Chronicle Guidance Publications, Inc.
66 Aurora St.
PO Box 1190
Moravia, NY 13118-1190
Ph: (315)497-0330 Fax: (315)497-3359
Fr: 800-622-7284

1994. This career brief describes the nature of the work, working conditions, hours and earnings, education and training, licensure, certification, unions, personal qualifications, social and psychological factors, employment outlook, entry methods, advancement, and related occupations.

★7039★ "Dock Worker" in *Career Information Center* (Vol.12)
Simon and Schuster
200 Old Tappan Rd.
Old Tappan, NJ 07675
Fax: 800-445-6991 Fr: 800-223-2348

Richard Lidz and Dale Anderson, editorial directors. Fifth edition, 1993. For 600 occupations, describes job duties, entry-level requirements, education and training needed, advancement possibilities, employment outlook, earnings and benefits. The set is divided into 12 volumes. Each volume includes jobs related under a broad career field. Volume 13 is the index.

★7040★ "Dockworker" in *Transportation* (pp. 18-19)
Franklin Watts, Inc.
387 Park Avenue, S.
New York, NY 10016
Ph: (212)686-7070

Marjorie Rittenberg Schulz. 1990. Surveys the transportation industry including air, water, and rail services. Provides job description, training, salary, and employment outlook. Offers job hunting advice.

★7041★ *Electricain Helper, Construction*
Careers, Inc.
PO Box 135
Largo, FL 34649-0135
Ph: (813)584-7333

1993. Two-page job guide card describing duties, working conditions, personal qualifications, training, earnings and hours, employment outlook, places of employment, related careers and where to write for more information.

★7042★ *Electrical Equipment Manufacturing Workers*
Chronicle Guidance Publications, Inc.
66 Aurora St.
PO Box 1190
Moravia, NY 13118-1190
Ph: (315)497-0330 Fax: (315)497-3359
Fr: 800-622-7284

1994. This career brief describes the nature of the work, working conditions, hours and earnings, education and training, licensure, certification, unions, personal qualifications, social and psychological factors, employment outlook, entry methods, advancement, and related occupations.

★7043★ "Furnace Cleaner" in *Occu-Facts: Information on 580 Careers in Outline Form*
Careers, Inc.
PO Box 135
Largo, FL 34649-0135
Ph: (813)584-7333

Biennial, 1995-96 edition. Each one-page occupational profile describes duties, working conditions, physical surroundings and demands, aptitudes, temperament, educational requirements, employment outlook, earnings, and places of employment.

★7044★ *Garbage Collector*
Careers, Inc.
PO Box 135
Largo, FL 34649-0135
Ph: (813)584-7333

1993. Two-page job guide card describing duties, working conditions, personal qualifications, training, earnings and hours, employment outlook, places of employment, related careers and where to write for more information.

★7045★ "Gasoline Service Station Attendants" in *Encyclopedia of Careers and Vocational Guidance* (Vol.3, pp. 63-65)
J.G. Ferguson Publishing Co.
200 W. Madison St., Ste. 300
Chicago, IL 60606
Ph: (312)580-5480 Fax: (312)580-4948

William E. Hopke, editor-in-chief. Ninth edition, 1993. Four-volume set that profiles 500 occupations and describes job trends in 74 industries. Includes career description, educational requirements, history of the job, methods of entry, advancement, employment outlook, earnings, working conditions, social and psychological factors, and sources of additional information.

★7046★ "Hand Packager" in *Occu-Facts: Information on 580 Careers in Outline Form*
Careers, Inc.
PO Box 135
Largo, FL 34649-0135
Ph: (813)584-7333

Biennial, 1995-96 edition. Each one-page occupational profile describes duties, working conditions, physical surroundings and demands, aptitudes, temperament, educational requirements, employment outlook, earnings, and places of employment.

★7047★ *Material Handler*
Careers, Inc.
PO Box 135
Largo, FL 34649-0135
Ph: (813)584-7333

1992. Two-page job guide card describing duties, working conditions, personal qualifications, training, earnings and hours, employment outlook, places of employment, related careers and where to write for more information.

★7048★ "Material Handler" in *Occu-Facts: Information on 580 Careers in Outline Form*
Careers, Inc.
PO Box 135
Largo, FL 34649-0135
Ph: (813)584-7333

Biennial, 1995-96 edition. Each one-page occupational profile describes duties, working conditions, physical surroundings and demands, aptitudes, temperament, educational requirements, employment outlook, earnings, and places of employment.

★7049★ *Material Handlers*
Chronicle Guidance Publications, Inc.
66 Aurora St.
PO Box 1190
Moravia, NY 13118-1190
Ph: (315)497-0330 Fax: (315)497-3359
Fr: 800-622-7284

1993. This career brief describes the nature of the work, working conditions, hours and earnings, education and training, licensure, certification, unions, personal qualifications, social and psychological factors, employment outlook, entry methods, advancement, and related occupations.

★7050★ *Packager, Hand*
Careers, Inc.
PO Box 135
Largo, FL 34649-0135
Ph: (813)584-7333

1991. Two-page job guide card describing duties, working conditions, personal qualifications, training, earnings and hours, employment outlook, places of employment, related careers and where to write for more information.

★7051★ *Parking Attendants*
Chronicle Guidance Publications, Inc.
66 Aurora St.
PO Box 1190
Moravia, NY 13118-1190
Ph: (315)497-0330 Fax: (315)497-3359
Fr: 800-622-7284

1994. This career brief describes the nature of the work, working conditions, hours and earnings, education and training, licensure, certification, unions, personal qualifications, social and psychological factors, employment outlook, entry methods, advancement, and related occupations.

★7052★ *Plasterer Helper*
Careers, Inc.
PO Box 135
Largo, FL 34649-0135
Ph: (813)584-7333

1994. Two-page job guide card describing duties, working conditions, personal qualifications, training, earnings and hours, employment outlook, places of employment, related careers and where to write for more information.

★7053★ "Plasterer Helper" in *Occu-Facts: Information on 580 Careers in Outline Form*
Careers, Inc.
PO Box 135
Largo, FL 34649-0135
Ph: (813)584-7333

Biennial, 1995-96 edition. Each one-page occupational profile describes duties, working conditions, physical surroundings and demands, aptitudes, temperament, educational requirements, employment outlook, earnings, and places of employment.

★7054★ *Plumber Helper*
Careers, Inc.
PO Box 135
Largo, FL 34649-0135
Ph: (813)584-7333

1993. Two-page job guide card describing duties, working conditions, personal qualifications, training, earnings and hours, employment outlook, places of employment, related careers and where to write for more information.

★7055★ "Plumber Helper" in *Occu-Facts: Information on 580 Careers in Outline Form*
Careers, Inc.
PO Box 135
Largo, FL 34649-0135
Ph: (813)584-7333

Biennial, 1995-96 edition. Each one-page occupational profile describes duties, working conditions, physical surroundings and demands, aptitudes, temperament, educational requirements, employment outlook, earnings, and places of employment.

★7056★ *Refuse Collectors*
Chronicle Guidance Publications, Inc.
66 Aurora St.
PO Box 1190
Moravia, NY 13118-1190
Ph: (315)497-0330 Fax: (315)497-3359
Fr: 800-622-7284

1987. This career brief describes the nature of the work, working conditions, hours and earnings, education and training, licensure, certification, unions, personal qualifications, social and psychological factors, employment outlook, entry methods, advancement, and related occupations.

★7057★ "Refuse Collectors" in *Career Discovery Encyclopedia* (Vol.5, pp. 138-139)
J.G. Ferguson Publishing Co.
200 W. Madison St., Ste. 300
Chicago, IL 60606
Ph: (312)580-5480 Fax: (312)580-4948

E. Russell Primm, editor-in-chief. 1993. Contains two-page articles on 504 occupations. Each article describes job duties, earnings, and educational and training requirements.

★7058★ "Refuse Collectors" in *Encyclopedia of Careers and Vocational Guidance* (Vol.4, pp. 262-264)
J.G. Ferguson Publishing Co.
200 W. Madison St., Ste. 300
Chicago, IL 60606
Ph: (312)580-5480 Fax: (312)580-4948

William E. Hopke, editor-in-chief. Ninth edition, 1993. Four-volume set that profiles 500 occupations and describes job trends in 74 industries. Includes career description, educational requirements, history of the job, methods of entry, advancement, employment outlook, earnings, working conditions, social and psychological factors, and sources of additional information.

★7059★ "Refuse Worker" in *Career Information Center* (Vol.11)
Simon and Schuster
200 Old Tappan Rd.
Old Tappan, NJ 07675
Fax: 800-445-6991 Fr: 800-223-2348

Richard Lidz and Dale Anderson, editorial directors. Fifth edition, 1993. For 600 occupations, describes job duties, entry-level requirements, education and training needed, advancement possibilities, employment outlook, earnings and benefits. The set is divided into 12 volumes. Each volume includes jobs related under a broad career field. Volume 13 is the index.

★7060★ *Roofer Helper*
Careers, Inc.
PO Box 135
Largo, FL 34649-0135
Ph: (813)584-7333

1993. Two-page job guide card describing duties, working conditions, personal qualifications, training, earnings and hours, employment outlook, places of employment, related careers and where to write for more information.

★7061★ "Roofer Helper" in *Occu-Facts: Information on 580 Careers in Outline Form*
Careers, Inc.
PO Box 135
Largo, FL 34649-0135
Ph: (813)584-7333

Biennial, 1995-96 edition. Each one-page occupational profile describes duties, working conditions, physical surroundings and demands, aptitudes, temperament, educational requirements, employment outlook, earnings, and places of employment.

★7062★ "Sanitation Workers" in *American Almanac of Jobs and Salaries* (pp. 104)
Avon Books
1350 Avenue of the Americas
New York, NY 10019
Ph: (212)261-6800 Fr: 800-238-0658

John Wright, editor. Revised and updated, 1994-95. A comprehensive guide to the wages of hundreds of occupations in a wide variety of industries and organizations.

★7063★ *Service Station Attendants*
Chronicle Guidance Publications, Inc.
66 Aurora St.
PO Box 1190
Moravia, NY 13118-1190
Ph: (315)497-0330 Fax: (315)497-3359
Fr: 800-622-7284

1993. This career brief describes the nature of the work, working conditions, hours and earnings, education and training, licensure, certification, unions, personal qualifications, social and psychological factors, employment outlook, entry methods, advancement, and related occupations.

★7064★ "Service Station Attendants" in *Career Discovery Encyclopedia* (Vol.6, pp. 20-21)
J.G. Ferguson Publishing Co.
200 W. Madison St., Ste. 300
Chicago, IL 60606
Ph: (312)580-5480 Fax: (312)580-4948

E. Russell Primm, editor-in-chief. 1993. Contains two-page articles on 504 occupations. Each article describes job duties, earnings, and educational and training requirements.

★7065★ "Service Station Attendants" in *Opportunities in Automotive Service Careers* (pp. 25-30)
National Textbook Co. (NTC)
VGM Career Books
4255 W. Touhy Ave.
Lincolnwood, IL 60646-1975
Ph: (708)679-5500 Fax: (708)679-2494
Fr: 800-323-4900

Robert M. Weber. 1989. Describes the work of the automobile mechanic and related occupations such as service station attendant and automobile body repairer. Covers working conditions, places of employment, qualifications, training, apprenticeships, certification, advancement opportunities, employment outlook, tools needed, and earnings.

★7066★ *Sheet Metal Worker Helper*
Careers, Inc.
PO Box 135
Largo, FL 34649-0135
Ph: (813)584-7333

1994. Two-page job guide card describing duties, working conditions, personal qualifications, training, earnings and hours, employment outlook, places of employment, related careers and where to write for more information.

★7067★ "Sheet Metal Worker Helper" in *Occu-Facts: Information on 580 Careers in Outline Form*
Careers, Inc.
PO Box 135
Largo, FL 34649-0135
Ph: (813)584-7333

Biennial, 1995-96 edition. Each one-page occupational profile describes duties, working conditions, physical surroundings and demands, aptitudes, temperament, educational requirements, employment outlook, earnings, and places of employment.

★7068★ "Stevedores" in *Career Discovery Encyclopedia* (Vol.6, pp. 64-65)
J.G. Ferguson Publishing Co.
200 W. Madison St., Ste. 300
Chicago, IL 60606
Ph: (312)580-5480 Fax: (312)580-4948

E. Russell Primm, editor-in-chief. 1993. Contains two-page articles on 504 occupations. Each article describes job duties, earnings, and educational and training requirements.

★7069★ "Stevedoring Occupations" in *Encyclopedia of Careers and Vocational Guidance* (Vol.4, pp. 439-442)
J.G. Ferguson Publishing Co.
200 W. Madison St., Ste. 300
Chicago, IL 60606
Ph: (312)580-5480 Fax: (312)580-4948

William E. Hopke, editor-in-chief. Ninth edition, 1993. Four-volume set that profiles 500 occupations and describes job trends in 74 industries. Includes career description, educational requirements, history of the job, methods of entry, advancement, employment outlook, earnings, working conditions, social and psychological factors, and sources of additional information.

★7070★ "Surveyor Helpers" in *Occu-Facts: Information on 580 Careers in Outline Form*
Careers, Inc.
PO Box 135
Largo, FL 34649-0135
Ph: (813)584-7333

Biennial, 1995-96 edition. Each one-page occupational profile describes duties, working conditions, physical surroundings and demands, aptitudes, temperament, educational requirements, employment outlook, earnings, and places of employment.

★7071★ "Surveyor's Helper" in *Career Information Center* (Vol.4)
Simon and Schuster
200 Old Tappan Rd.
Old Tappan, NJ 07675
Fax: 800-445-6991 Fr: 800-223-2348

Richard Lidz and Dale Anderson, editorial directors. Fifth edition, 1993. For 600 occupations, describes job duties, entry-level requirements, education and training needed, advancement possibilities, employment outlook, earnings and benefits. The set is divided into 12 volumes. Each volume includes jobs related under a broad career field. Volume 13 is the index.

Associations

★7072★ Laborers' International Union of North America (LIUNA)
905 16th St. NW
Washington, DC 20006
Ph: (202)737-8320 Fax: (202)737-2754

Members: AFL-CIO. **Publications:** *The Laborer*, bimonthly. • *LIUNA - Leadership News.*

Test Guides

★7073★ *Career Examination Series: Cleaner-Helper*
National Learning Corp.
212 Michael Dr.
Syosset, NY 11791
Ph: (516)921-8888 Fax: (516)921-8743
Fr: 800-645-6337

Jack Rudman. All examination guides in this series contain questions with answers.

★7074★ *Career Examination Series: Foreman of Laborers*
National Learning Corp.
212 Michael Dr.
Syosset, NY 11791
Ph: (516)921-8888 Fax: (516)921-8743
Fr: 800-645-6337

Jack Rudman. All examination guides in this series contain questions with answers.

★7075★ *Career Examination Series: Stockman*
National Learning Corp.
212 Michael Dr.
Syosset, NY 11791
Ph: (516)921-8888 Fax: (516)921-8743
Fr: 800-645-6337

Jack Rudman. All examination guides in this series contain questions with answers.

★7076★ *Career Examination Series: Warehouseman*
National Learning Corp.
212 Michael Dr.
Syosset, NY 11791
Ph: (516)921-8888 Fax: (516)921-8743
Fr: 800-645-6337

Jack Rudman. All examination guides in this series contain questions with answers.

Awards, Scholarships, Grants, and Fellowships

★7077★ Driver of the Year Award
American Trucking Association
Safety Management Council
220 Mill Rd.
Alexandria, VA 22314
Ph: (703)838-1919 Fax: (703)836-6070

To recognize the best safety record among truck drivers of the United States and to encourage improved driving performance and a greater appreciation for highway safety. A Driver of the Year pin, trophy, and certificate are awarded annually. Established in 1947.

Periodicals

★7078★ *The Laborer*
Laborers' International Union of North America (LIUNA)
905 16th St. NW
Washington, DC 20006
Ph: (202)737-8320 Fax: (202)737-2754

Bimonthly.

★7079★ *LIUNA - Leadership News*
Laborers' International Union of North America (LIUNA)
905 16th St. NW
Washington, DC 20006
Ph: (202)737-8320 Fax: (202)737-2754

Job Opportunities in the Armed Forces

Military service provides educational opportunities and work experience in literally thousands of occupations. There are more than 2,000 basic and advanced military occupational specialties for enlisted personnel and 1,600 for officers. Over 75 percent of these occupational specialties have civilian counterparts. Those in electrical and mechanical equipment repair occupations maintain aircraft, motor vehicles, and ships. Officers manage the maintenance of aircraft, missiles, conventional and nuclear-powered ships, trucks, earth-moving equipment, and other vehicles. Enlisted personnel serve as mechanics, engine men, and boiler technicians. Infantry, gun crews, and seamanship specialists includes both officers and enlisted personnel. Officers plan and direct military operations, oversee security activities, and serve as combat troop leaders. Enlisted personnel serve as infantrymen, gunners' mates, weapons specialists, armored vehicle operators, demolition experts, artillery crew, rocket specialists, special operations forces, and combat engineers. Functional support and administrative jobs in military service also require the support of officers and enlistees. Officers in this category work as directors, executives, adjutants, administrative officers, personnel managers, training administrators, budget officers, finance officers, accountants, hospital administrators, inspectors, computer systems managers, and lawyers. Enlisted personnel in this category work as accounting clerks, payroll clerks, personnel clerks, computer programmers, computer operators, electric accounting machine operators, chaplain assistants, counseling aides, typists, stenographers, storekeepers, and other clerks. Enlisted personnel work as mapping technicians, computer programmers, air traffic controllers, interpreters and translators, and radio and radar operators. Military personnel in service and supply occupations handle food service, security, and personal services and supply. Officers work as logistics officers, supply managers, transportation and traffic managers, and procurement officers. Enlisted personnel include military police, correction specialists, detectives, firefighters, and food preparation and other service workers. Military medical and dental occupations all have civilian counterparts. Holding the rank of medical officer are physicians, dentists, optometrists, nurses, therapists, veterinarians, pharmacists, and others in health diagnosing and treating occupations. Enlisted personnel are trained to work as medical laboratory technologists and technicians, radiologic technologists, emergency medical technicians, dental assistants, pharmaceutical assistants, sanitation specialists, and veterinary assistants. Military personnel assigned to craft occupations are skilled craft workers.

Salaries

Military basic pay by grade for active duty personnel with less than two years of service are as follows:

Enlisted personnel E-1	$814.80/month
Enlisted personnel E-2	$913.20/month
Enlisted personnel E-3	$948.90/month
Enlisted personnel E-4	$1007.10/month
Warrant officers W-1	$1392.60/month
Warrant officers W-2	$1671.60/month

Employment Outlook

Growth rate until the year 2005: Faster than average. However, if the Armed Forces are reduced, fewer job opportunities will be available.

Job Opportunities in the Armed Forces

Career Guides

★7080★ *Air Force Academy: Commitment to Excellence*
Finley-Holiday Film Corporation
PO Box 619
Whittier, CA 90601
Ph: (213)945-3325 Fax: (310)693-4756
Fr: 800-345-6707

Videocassette. 19??. 30 mins. Prospective officer candidates for the U.S. Air Force Academy in Colorado Springs will be interested in this informative video, which explores the military college and chronicles the entire academic careers of the airmen and airwomen.

★7081★ *Air Force Career Opportunities*
Careers, Inc.
PO Box 135
Largo, FL 34649-0135
Ph: (813)584-7333

1993. Four-page brief offering the definition, history, duties, working conditions, personal qualifications, educational requirements, earnings, hours, employment outlook, advancement possibilities, and related occupations.

★7082★ "Air Force Nurse" in *150 Careers in the Health Care Field*
Reed Reference Publishing
121 Chanlon Rd.
PO Box 31
New Providence, NJ 07974
Fax: (908)665-6688 Fr: 800-521-8110

Stanley Alperin. Third edition, 1993. Each occupational profile covers job functions and responsibilities, work locations, training requirements, certification, and salaries. Lists community colleges, universities, vocational-technical schools, and other educational institutions that provide accredited training programs.

★7083★ "Air Force Nurse Corps" in *Opportunities in Nursing Careers* (pp. 112-113)
National Textbook Co. (NTC)
VGM Career Books
4255 W. Touhy Ave.
Lincolnwood, IL 60646-1975
Ph: (708)679-5500 Fax: (708)679-2494
Fr: 800-323-4900

Keville Frederickson. 1989. Covers the history and scope of nursing, educational preparation, job hunting, types and places of employment, and nursing organizations. The appendices list state nurses' associations and state boards of nursing.

★7084★ *America at Its Best: Opportunities in the National Guard*
Rosen Publishing Group
29 E. 21st St.
New York, NY 10010
Ph: (212)777-3017 Fax: (212)777-0277
Fr: 800-237-9932

Robert F. Collins. 1989. Describes the purpose of the national guard, enlistment qualifications and procedures, basic training, pay, and daily routines. The appendices list career fields and federal and state military installations.

★7085★ *Armed Forces Careers*
Chronicle Guidance Publications, Inc.
66 Aurora St.
PO Box 1190
Moravia, NY 13118-1190
Ph: (315)497-0330 Fax: (315)497-3359
Fr: 800-622-7284

1993. This career brief describes the nature of the work, working conditions, hours and earnings, education and training, licensure, certification, unions, personal qualifications, social and psychological factors, employment outlook, entry methods, advancement, and related occupations.

★7086★ "Armed Forces" in *Opportunities in Business Communication Careers* (pp. 38-39)
National Textbook Co. (NTC)
VGM Career Books
4255 W. Touhy Ave.
Lincolnwood, IL 60646-1975
Ph: (708)679-5500 Fax: (708)679-2494
Fr: 800-323-4900

Robert L. Deen. 1987. Describes what business communicators do, the skills they need, and where they work. Covers educational preparation, salaries, entry into the profession, and career paths. Offers job hunting advice and information about freelancing.

★7087★ "Armed Forces" in *Opportunities in Pharmacy Careers* (pp. 115-117)
National Textbook Co. (NTC)
VGM Career Books
4255 W. Touhy Ave.
Lincolnwood, IL 60646-1975
Ph: (708)679-5500 Fax: (708)679-2494
Fr: 800-323-4900

Fred B. Gable. 1990. Surveys the wide variety of career options available to pharmacists including community, industrial, and public pharmacy. Covers job duties, licensure, and salaries. Provides in-depth information about pharmaceutical education including high school and college preparation, and pharmacy school admissions and curriculum.

★7088★ "Armed Forces" in *Opportunities in Transportation Careers* (pp. 127-129)
National Textbook Co. (NTC)
VGM Career Books
4255 W. Touhy Ave.
Lincolnwood, IL 60646-1975
Ph: (708)679-5500 Fax: (708)679-2494
Fr: 800-323-4900

Adrian A. Paradis. 1988. Describes transportation and related employment in driving occupations, the airlines, merchant marine, and travel services. Covers employment outlook, educational and training requirements, wages, and the work itself, and advantages and disadvantages of transportation careers. Offers job hunting advice.

★7089★ "Armed Forces" in *Opportunities in Vocational and Technical Careers* (pp. 37-41)
National Textbook Co. (NTC)
VGM Career Books
4255 W. Touhy Ave.
Lincolnwood, IL 60646-1975
Ph: (708)679-5500 Fax: (708)679-2494
Fr: 800-323-4900

Adrian A. Paradis. 1992. Describes careers which can be prepared for by attending a private vocational or proprietary school—office employee, sales worker, service worker, health services, mechanic, craftworker, and technician. Covers employment outlook, job duties, and salaries. Offers career planning advice.

★7090★ "Armed Forces Training" in *Careers With Robots* (pp. 111-115)
Facts on File
460 Park Ave. S.
New York, NY 10016-7382
Ph: (212)683-2244 Fax: 800-678-3633
Fr: 800-322-8755

Texe W. Marrs. 1988. Describes jobs developing from a boom in robotics. Offers career planning advice and covers educational and training requirements, transferable skills, and industries using robots. Includes a state-by-state listing of major robotics employers, and additional sources of information.

★7091★ "Armed Services Careers" in *Career Information Center* (Vol.11)
Simon and Schuster
200 Old Tappan Rd.
Old Tappan, NJ 07675
Fax: 800-445-6991 Fr: 800-223-2348

Richard Lidz and Dale Anderson, editorial directors. Fifth edition, 1993. For 600 occupations, describes job duties, entry-level requirements, education and training needed, advancement possibilities, employment outlook, earnings and benefits. The set is divided into 12 volumes. Each volume includes jobs related under a broad career field. Volume 13 is the index.

★7092★ *Army Career Opportunities*
Careers, Inc.
PO Box 135
Largo, FL 34649-0135
Ph: (813)584-7333

1993. Four-page brief offering the definition, history, duties, working conditions, personal qualifications, educational requirements, earnings, hours, employment outlook, advancement possibilities, and related occupations.

★7093★ "Army Nurse" in *150 Careers in the Health Care Field*
Reed Reference Publishing
121 Chanlon Rd.
PO Box 31
New Providence, NJ 07974
Fax: (908)665-6688 Fr: 800-521-8110

Stanley Alperin. Third edition, 1993. Each occupational profile covers job functions and responsibilities, work locations, training requirements, certification, and salaries. Lists community colleges, universities, vocational-technical schools, and other educational institutions that provide accredited training programs.

★7094★ "Army Nurse Corps" in *Opportunities in Nursing Careers* (pp. 110-111)
National Textbook Co. (NTC)
VGM Career Books
4255 W. Touhy Ave.
Lincolnwood, IL 60646-1975
Ph: (708)679-5500 Fax: (708)679-2494
Fr: 800-323-4900

Keville Frederickson. 1989. Covers the history and scope of nursing, educational preparation, job hunting, types and places of employment, and nursing organizations. The appendices list state nurses' associations and state boards of nursing.

★7095★ *Basic Training: What to Expect and How to Prepare*
Rosen Publishing Group
29 E. 21st St.
New York, NY 10010
Ph: (212)777-3017 Fax: (212)777-0277
Fr: 800-237-9932

Robert F. Collins. 1988. Describes basic training in the Army, Navy, Air Force, Marines and Coast Guard. Includes information on enlistment and initial training, processing, and terminology used in each service.

★7096★ *Citizen Soldier: Opportunities in the Reserves*
Rosen Publishing Group
29 E. 21st St.
New York, NY 10010
Ph: (212)777-3017 Fax: (212)777-0277
Fr: 800-237-9932

Carl White. 1990. Describes the function of the armed forces reserve units, pay, retirement income, basic and specialty training, and ROTC programs.

★7097★ *Coast Guard Career Opportunities*
Careers, Inc.
PO Box 135
Largo, FL 34649-0135
Ph: (813)584-7333

1995. Four-page brief offering the definition, history, duties, working conditions, personal qualifications, educational requirements, earnings, hours, employment outlook, advancement possibilities, and related occupations.

★7098★ "Coast Guard" in *Opportunities in Marine and Maritime Careers* (pp. 97-100)
National Textbook Co. (NTC)
VGM Career Books
4255 W. Touhy Ave.
Lincolnwood, IL 60646-1975
Ph: (708)679-5500 Fax: (708)679-2494
Fr: 800-323-4900

William Ray Heitzmann. 1988. Includes careers related by their proximity to water including cruise ships, oceanography, marine sciences, fishing, commercial diving, maritime transportation, shipbuilding, Navy, and Coast Guard. Covers qualifications, job outlook, job duties, educational preparation, and training. Lists associations and schools.

★7099★ *Coping With Sexism in the Military*
Rosen Publishing Group
29 E. 21st St.
New York, NY 10010
Ph: (212)777-3017 Fax: (212)777-0277
Fr: 800-237-9932

Mary V. Stremlow. 1990. Covers the history of women's participation in the armed forces. Describes and defines sexism and sexual harassment and offers advice on how to cope. Discusses the pros and cons of dress, living quarters, physical fitness standards, marriage, pregnancy, and promotional opportunities for women in the armed forces.

★7100★ *Exploring Careers in the Military Services*
Rosen Publishing Group
29 E. 21st St.
New York, NY 10010
Ph: (212)777-3017 Fax: (212)777-0277
Fr: 800-237-9932

Robert W. Macdonald. 1991. Describes the role of the military services, how to begin a military career, and taking the armed services vocational aptitude battery. Lists military occupations and equivalent civilian jobs. Gives information about the military service academies. A separate chapter covers each branch of the military, what they do, organization, enlistment, training, advancement and career development, and becoming an officer.

★7101★ "Job Opportunities in the Armed Forces" in *Occupational Outlook Handbook*
U.S. Government Printing Office
Superintendent of Documents
Washington, DC 20402
Ph: (202)512-1800 Fax: (202)512-2250

Biennial; latest edition, 1994-95. Encyclopedia of careers describing more than 250 occupations and comprising about 85 percent of all jobs in the economy. Occupations that require lengthy education or training are given the most attention. For each occupation, the handbook describes job duties, working conditions, training, educational preparation, personal qualities, advancement possibilities, job outlook, earnings, and sources of additional information.

★7102★ *The Men of Company 208*
Centre Productions, Inc.
1800 30th St., Ste. 207
Boulder, CO 80301
Ph: (303)444-1166 Fax: (303)444-1168
Fr: 800-886-1166

Videocassette. 1986. 28 mins. This video is an informative presentation for young men and women interested or curious about enlisting in the Armed Forces.

★7103★ "Military Careers" in *Career Discovery Encyclopedia* (Vol.4, pp. 90-91)
J.G. Ferguson Publishing Co.
200 W. Madison St., Ste. 300
Chicago, IL 60606
Ph: (312)580-5480 Fax: (312)580-4948

E. Russell Primm, editor-in-chief. 1993. Contains two-page articles on 504 occupations. Each article describes job duties, earnings, and educational and training requirements.

★7104★ "Military Careers" in *Encyclopedia of Careers and Vocational Guidance* (Vol.4, pp. 90-91)
J.G. Ferguson Publishing Co.
200 W. Madison St., Ste. 300
Chicago, IL 60606
Ph: (312)580-5480 Fax: (312)580-4948

William E. Hopke, editor-in-chief. Ninth edition, 1993. Six-volume set that profiles 500 occupations and describes job trends in 74 industries. Includes career description, educational requirements, history of the job, methods of entry, advancement, employment outlook, earnings, working conditions, social and psychological factors, and sources of additional information.

★7105★ "Military Chaplain" in *Opportunities in Religious Service Careers* (pp. 85-87)
National Textbook Co. (NTC)
VGM Career Books
4255 W. Touhy Ave.
Lincolnwood, IL 60646-1975
Ph: (708)679-5500 Fax: (708)679-2494
Fr: 800-323-4900

John Oliver Nelson. 1988. Explores the concept of religious "calling" and offers advice about choosing a career with the clergy in the Protestant, Catholic, or Jewish religions. Surveys many religious related careers including missionary work and education. Covers educational preparation and employment outlook. Lists accredited theological schools in the United States.

★7106★ "Military" in *College Board Guide to Jobs and Career Planning* (pp. 208-210)
College Entrance Examination Board
45 Columbus Ave.
New York, NY 10023-6992
Ph: (212)713-8000

Joyce Slayton Mitchell. 1990. Career planning guide written for high school and college students. Covers 100 careers in 15 occupational groups. Provides job description, educational preparation needed, salaries, related careers, and sources of additional information. Includes information about the 90's labor market.

★7107★ "Military Counselor" in *Careers in Counseling and Human Development* (pp. 102-104)
American Association for Counseling and Development
5999 Stevenson Ave.
Alexandria, VA 22304
Ph: (703)823-9800

Brooke B. Collison and Nancy J. Garfield, authors and managing editors. 1990. Surveys jobs in the human services, human development, and counseling fields. Provides an overview of ten different work settings such as private practice, schools, and public agencies. Includes information about certification, credentialing and licensure.

★7108★ "The Military" in *Electronic Service Careers* (pp. 88-99)
Franklin Watts, Inc.
387 Park Avenue, S.
New York, NY 10016
Ph: (212)686-7070

Robert Laurance. 1987. Discusses the work of an electronic service technician, employment outlook, places of employment, and educational preparation and training. Describes jobs with computers, consumer electronics, industrial electronics and the military.

★7109★ "Military Fire Protection" in *Opportunities in Fire Protection Services* (pp. 32-33)
National Textbook Co. (NTC)
VGM Career Books
4255 W. Touhy Ave.
Lincolnwood, IL 60646-1975
Ph: (708)679-5500 Fax: (708)679-2494
Fr: 800-323-4900

Ronny J. Coleman. 1990. Explores firefighting and related jobs with not only local fire departments but also with state and federal governments and private fire departments, fire sprinkler and fire equipment manufacturing companies, and insurance companies. Covers personal qualifications, educational preparation and training, advancement possibilities, and salaries. Offers job hunting advice.

★7110★ "Military" in *Footsteps in the Ocean: Careers in Diving* (pp. 115-122)
Lodestar Books
2 Park Avenue
New York, NY 10016
Ph: (212)725-1818 Fax: (212)532-6568

Denise V. Lang. 1987. Explores employment opportunities in sport and commercial diving, science and research, in the military, and police work. Describes the work and training. Lists schools.

★7111★ "Military" in *International Careers: An Insider's Guide, Where to Find Them, How to Build Them* (pp. 174-176)
Williamson Publishing Co.
185 Church Hill Rd.
Charlotte, VT 05445
Ph: (802)425-2102

David Win. 1987. Gives an overview of the international business field and its structure. Surveys employment opportunities in government, business, and nonprofit organizations. Offers job hunting advice.

★7112★ *"Military Nursing" in Your Career in Nursing (pp. 156-160)*
National League for Nursing
350 Hudson St.
New York, NY 10014
Ph: (212)989-9393

Lila Anastas. Second edition, 1988. Career planning and information guide. Provides job description, educational preparation, interests, aptitudes and abilities needed, and nursing specialties. Includes an overview of the trends affecting the nursing profession. Explores the differences in diploma, associate degree, and bachelor degree nursing programs.

★7113★ "Military Science" in *College Majors and Careers: A Resource Guide for Effective Life Planning* (pp. 99-100)
Garrett Park Press
PO Box 1907
Garrett Park, MD 20896
Ph: (301)946-2553

Paul Phifer. 1993. Lists 61 college majors. Includes a general definition of the field, related occupations requiring either a bachelor or associate degree, related leisure-time activities denoting personal interest in the field, skills needed, values, and personal attributes. Lists organizations.

★7114★ "Military Service" in *Exploring Careers Using Foreign Languages* (pp. 73-74)
Rosen Publishing Group
29 E. 21st St.
New York, NY 10010
Ph: (212)777-3017 Fax: (212)777-0277
Fr: 800-237-9932

E. W. Edwards. Revised edition, 1990. Explores careers in teaching, translating, interpreting, business and finance, government, communications, and the media. Covers employment ideas, salaries, job duties, and educational preparation. Contains information on accreditation and job hunting.

★7115★ *Military Service Occupations*
Careers, Inc.
PO Box 135
Largo, FL 34649-0135
Ph: (813)584-7333

1993. Four-page brief offering the definition, history, duties, working conditions, personal qualifications, educational requirements, earnings, hours, employment outlook, advancement, and careers related to this position.

★7116★ "Military Services" in *Jobs! What They Are—Where They Are—What They Pay* (pp. 294-296)
Simon & Schuster, Inc.
Simon & Schuster Bldg.
1230 Avenue of the Americas
New York, NY 10020
Ph: (212)698-7000

Robert O. Snelling and Anne M. Snelling. Revised edition, 1992. Profiles 241 occupations, describing duties and responsibilities, educational preparation, earnings, employment opportunities, training, and qualifications.

★7117★ "Military" in *Straight Talk on Careers: 80 Pros Take You Into Their Professions* (pp. 203-224)
Garrett Park Press
PO Box 1907
Garrett Park, MD 20896
Ph: (301)946-2553

Mary Barbera-Hogan. 1987. Written for readers in high school and college. Contains candid interviews from professionals who discuss what their days are like and the pros and cons of their occupations.

★7118★ "The Military Veterinarian" in *Opportunities in Veterinary Medicine* (pp. 105-105)
National Textbook Co. (NTC)
VGM Career Books
4255 W. Touhy Ave.
Lincolnwood, IL 60646-1975
Ph: (708)679-5500 Fax: (708)679-2494
Fr: 800-323-4900

Robert E. Swope. 1993. Discusses history, educational requirements, and employment opportunities for veterinarians in industry, government, academia, and the military.

★7119★ *Navy Career Opportunities*
Careers, Inc.
PO Box 135
Largo, FL 34649-0135
Ph: (813)584-7333

1993. Four-page brief offering the definition, history, duties, working conditions, personal qualifications, educational requirements, earnings, hours, employment outlook, advancement possibilities, and related occupations.

★7120★ "Navy Military Sealift Command" in *Opportunities in Transportation Careers* (pp. 129-130)
National Textbook Co. (NTC)
VGM Career Books
4255 W. Touhy Ave.
Lincolnwood, IL 60646-1975
Ph: (708)679-5500 Fax: (708)679-2494
Fr: 800-323-4900

Adrian A. Paradis. 1988. Describes transportation and related employment in driving occupations, the airlines, merchant marine, and travel services. Covers employment outlook, educational and training requirements, wages, and the work itself, and advantages and disadvantages of transportation careers. Offers job hunting advice.

★7121★ "Navy Nurse" in *150 Careers in the Health Care Field*
Reed Reference Publishing
121 Chanlon Rd.
PO Box 31
New Providence, NJ 07974
Fax: (908)665-6688 Fr: 800-521-8110

Stanley Alperin. Third edition, 1993. Each occupational profile covers job functions and responsibilities, work locations, training requirements, certification, and salaries. Lists community colleges, universities, vocational-technical schools, and other educational institutions that provide accredited training programs.

★7122★ "Officer, U.S. Armed Forces" in *VGM's Careers Encyclopedia* (pp. 315-317)
National Textbook Co. (NTC)
VGM Career Books
4255 W. Touhy Ave.
Lincolnwood, IL 60646-1975
Ph: (708)679-5500 Fax: (708)679-2494
Fr: 800-323-4900

Third edition, 1991. Contains two- to five-page descriptions of 200 managerial, professional, technical, trade, and service occupations. Each profile includes job duties, places of employment, qualifications, educational preparation, training, employment potential, advancement, income, and additional sources of information.

★7123★ "Opportunities in the Armed Services" in *Opportunities in Medical Technology Careers* (pp. 71-83)
National Textbook Co. (NTC)
VGM Career Books
4255 W. Touhy Ave.
Lincolnwood, IL 60646-1975
Ph: (708)679-5500 Fax: (708)679-2494
Fr: 800-323-4900

Karen R. Karni and Jane Sidney Oliver. 1990. Defines the field of medical technology and describes trends, employment outlook, salaries, job satisfaction, educational preparation, and opportunities for advancement. Lists associations and accredited educational programs.

★7124★ *Opportunities in Military Careers*
National Textbook Co. (NTC)
VGM Career Books
4255 W. Touhy Ave.
Lincolnwood, IL 60646-1975
Ph: (708)679-5500 Fax: (708)679-2494
Fr: 800-323-4900

Adrian A. Paradis. 1989. Discusses enlistment in the Armed Services as a career choice. Covers the Army, Navy, Marine Corps, Air Force, and Coast Guard. Describes training opportunities for enlisted men and officers, and related civilian careers. Lists colleges and universities offering ROTC.

★7125★ "Opportunities in the U.S. Armed Forces" in *Opportunities in Refrigeration and Air Conditioning Trades* (pp. 117-122)
National Textbook Co. (NTC)
VGM Career Books
4255 W. Touhy Ave.
Lincolnwood, IL 60646-1975
Ph: (708)679-5500 Fax: (708)679-2494
Fr: 800-323-4900

Richard Budzik. 1989. Surveys the air conditioning and refrigeration industry. Describes jobs, educational and training requirements, small business opportunities, places of employment, and job outlook. Offers job hunting advice.

★7126★ *The Profession of Arms*
National Film Board of Canada
1251 Avenue of the Americas, 16th Fl.
New York, NY 10020-1173
Ph: (212)596-1770 Fr: 800-542-2164

Videocassette. 1987. 57 mins. Career officers in the military are profiled in this film.

★7127★ *Qualifying for Admission to the Service Academies: A Student's Guide*
Rosen Publishing Group
29 E. 21st St.
New York, NY 10010
Ph: (212)777-3017 Fax: (212)777-0277
Fr: 800-237-9932

Robert F. Collins. 1990. Describes application procedures, academic standards, physical qualifications, and academy life for the five military service academies. Explains the characteristics needed by today's military officers.

★7128★ *Soldier Girls*
Churchill Films
12210 Nebraska Ave.
Los Angeles, CA 90025
Ph: (310)207-6600 Fax: (310)207-1330
Fr: 800-334-7830

Videocassette. 1981. 87 mins. An account of the experiences of a group of young women newly inducted into the US Army.

★7129★ *Sound Off!: American Military Women Speak Out*
E.P. Dutton
2 Park Avenue
New York, NY 10016
Ph: (212)725-1818

Dorothy Schneider and Carl J. Schneider. 1988. Includes interviews with 300 women in the five branches of the Armed Services. The women talk about their work, their lives, and their concerns and ideas. Also discusses career opportunities.

★7130★ *Transitions: Military Pathways to Civilian Careers*
Rosen Publishing Group
29 E. 21st St.
New York, NY 10010
Ph: (212)777-3017 Fax: (212)777-0277
Fr: 800-237-9932

Robert W. MacDonald. 1988. Describes how to make the best use of your military service to create a civilian career. Describes skills needed in civilian employment and compares them to skills acquired in the military. Covers career planning, job search, resume writing, and starting a small business. Lists many resources.

★7131★ *"U.S. Navy Officer" in Careers for Number Lovers (pp. 55-57)*
The Milbrook Press
2 Old Milford Rd.
Brookfield, CT 06804

Andrew Kaplan. 1991. Contains interviews with 14 people in math related careers. Provides job description, methods of entry into the field, pros and cons, educational preparation, and earnings.

★7132★ "United States Navy" in *Opportunities in Marine and Maritime Careers* (pp. 85-97)
National Textbook Co. (NTC)
VGM Career Books
4255 W. Touhy Ave.
Lincolnwood, IL 60646-1975
Ph: (708)679-5500 Fax: (708)679-2494
Fr: 800-323-4900

William Ray Heitzmann. 1988. Includes careers related by their proximity to water including cruise ships, oceanography, marine sciences, fishing, commercial diving, maritime transportation, shipbuilding, Navy, and Coast Guard. Covers qualifications, job outlook, job duties, educational preparation, and training. Lists associations and schools.

Associations

★7133★ Air Force Association (AFA)
1501 Lee Hwy.
Arlington, VA 22209
Ph: (703)247-5800

Members: U.S. citizens, both civilian and military. **Purpose:** Addresses the responsibilities imposed by the impact of aerospace technology on modern society; supports armed strength adequate to maintain the security and peace of the United States and the Free World.

Test Guides

★7134★ *Armed Forces Test (AFT/ASVAB)*
National Learning Corp.
212 Michael Dr.
Syosset, NY 11791
Ph: (516)921-8888 Fax: (516)921-8743
Fr: 800-645-6337

Jack Rudman. Part of the Admission Test Series. Books in this series provide test practice and drill for actual professional certification and licensure tests.

★7135★ *ASVAB Basics*
Prentice Hall Press
Simon & Schuster Inc.
200 Old Tappan Rd.
Old Tappan, NJ 07675
Ph: 800-223-2348

Ronald Kappraff and Ronald Bronk. First edition, 1990. Provides intensive preparation for the four ASVAB subtests needed to qualify. Includes sample subtests with explanatory answers, basic skills drills, and test-taking tips.

★7136★ *ASVAB Review*
Careers, Inc.
PO Box 135
Largo, FL 34649-0135
Ph: (813)584-7333

Fourth edition. 1992. Study guide for the Armed Services Vocational Aptitude Battery test that must be taken when joining the Armed Forces. Areas reviewed include English, technical knowledge, and math skills.

★7137★ *Barron's How to Prepare for the Armed Forces Test - ASVAB*
Barron's Educational Series, Inc.
250 Wireless Blvd.
Hauppauge, NY 11788
Ph: (516)434-3311 Fax: (516)434-3723
Fr: 800-645-3476

Fourth edition. 1992. Manual presents nine complete review courses and features four full-length practice exams with answers and explanations. Applicable for all branches of military service.

★7138★ *Practice for Air Force Placement Tests*
Prentice Hall Press
Simon & Schuster Inc.
200 Old Tappan Rd.
Old Tappan, NJ 07675
Ph: 800-223-2348

Solomon Wiener and E.P. Steinberg. Seventh edition, 1989. Complete preparation for the enlistment and placement tests required for Air Force entry. Four practice exams are included.

★7139★ *Practice for the Armed Forces Test - ASVAB*
Prentice Hall Press
Simon & Schuster Inc.
200 Old Tappan Rd.
Old Tappan, NJ 07675
Ph: 800-223-2348

Solomon Wiener. 13th edition, 1988. Contains four practice exams with explanations. Reviews all ten subject areas covered on the exam.

★7140★ *Practice for Army Placement Tests*
Prentice Hall Press
Simon & Schuster Inc.
200 Old Tappan Rd.
Old Tappan, NJ 07675
Ph: 800-223-2348

Solomon Wiener and E.P. Steinberg. Fourth edition, 1989. Complete preparation for the enlistment and placement tests required for Army entry. Four practice exams are included.

★7141★ *Practice for Navy Placement Tests*
Prentice Hall Press
Simon & Schuster Inc.
200 Old Tappan Rd.
Old Tappan, NJ 07675
Ph: 800-223-2348

E.P. Steinberg. Third edition, 1986. Complete practice for the Navy and Marine Corps entrance and placement exams. Four practice tests are included.

Awards, Scholarships, Grants, and Fellowships

★7142★ AFCEA ROTC Scholarship Program
Armed Forces Communications & Electronics Association (AFCEA)
Educational Foundation
4400 Fair Lakes Ct.
Fairfax, VA 22033-3899
Ph: (703)631-6149 Fax: (703)631-4693

Purpose: To encourage and reward outstanding and deserving students in the ROTC program. Qualifications: Applicants must be United States citizens enrolled in an ROTC program and working toward a degree in electronics, electrical or communications engineering, mathematics, physics, computer science or technology, or information management. Candidates must also be of "good moral character," have proven academic excellence, and demonstrate motivation and potential for completing a college education and serving as an officer of the Armed Forces of the United States. The student's need for financial assistance is also considered. Selection criteria: Selection is made by a board of active duty officers representing the four services. Scholarship recipients are chosen based on merit and financial need and distributed equally among the Army, Navy/Marine Corps, and Air Force ROTC programs. Funds available: Sixty awards are given annually. Thirty scholarships of $1,000 each are presented to ten Army, ten Navy/Marine Corps, and ten Air Force ROTC students from the junior class for the year they matriculate as seniors. Thirty $1,000 scholarships are given to ten Army, ten Navy/Marine Corps, and ten Air Force ROTC students from the sophomore class for the year they matriculate as juniors. Each scholarship is paid in full to the recipients in August. Application details: Application forms are available from school ROTC units. Professors of Military Science, Naval Science, and Aerospace studies review applications and submit nominations to the AFCEA. Deadline: May 1 for nominations. All individuals nominated are notified. Scholarship recipients are notified in June.

★7143★ Air Force ROTC Scholarships
Air Force Reserve Officers Training Corps (AFROTC)
HQ AFROTC/RRO (Recruiting Division)
551 East Maxwell Blvd.
Maxwell AFB, AL 36112-6106
Ph: (205)953-2091 Fax: (205)953-5271
Fr: 800-522-0033

Purpose: To educate and prepare college students to be AirForce officers. Qualifications: Applicants must be high school seniors, high school graduates not enrolled full-time in college who want to work toward certain (mostly technical) degrees, and college students. They must enroll in AirForce ROTC to receive scholarships. Selection criteria: High school students and high school graduates are selected on the basis of grade point average, interview evaluation, SAT and ACT scores, recommendations from high school officials, extracurricular activities, medical examination, and acceptance and attendance at a college or university offering Air Force ROTC. College students competing for scholarships will also be selected on the basis of scores on the Air Force Officer Qualifying Test, college GPA, extracurricular activities, and medical examination. Funds available: One- to four-year college scholarship. In selected majors scholarships may be extended to meet a five-year degree program requirement. The one-year scholarship is offered to students majoring in career fields in which the Air Force has a shortage, such as nursing. Two- to four-year scholarships are for students pursuing degrees in certain technical fields such as engineering, science, math, and nursing, as well as students enrolled in certain non-technical degree programs, such as business administration, accounting, economics, and management. Application details: Application packages are available from high school officials, admissions liaison officers, Air Force recruiters, Air Force ROTC admissions counselors, professors of aerospace studies at colleges and universities, and the Air Force ROTC Recruiting Division at the above address. Deadline: December 1 of the high school senior year for high school seniors and graduates, and during the freshman, sophomore, or junior years for college students.

PERIODICALS

★7144★ *Air Force Times*
Army Times Publishing Co.
6883 Commercial Drive
Springfield, VA 22159
Ph: (703)750-8646 Fax: (703)750-8622
Fr: 800-424-9335
Lee Ewing

Weekly. Independent newspaper serving Air Force personnel worldwide.

★7145★ *Air University Library Index to Military Periodicals*
Government Printing Office
AUL/LSP, Maxwell AFB
Montgomery, AL 36112-5564
Ph: (205)953-2504 Fax: (205)953-2329
Martha M. Stewart

Quarterly. Subject index to 78 English language journals in the fields of military science, defense, foreign affairs, and aerospace.

★7146★ *Airpower Journal*
Airpower Journal
Maxwell Air Force Base
401 Chennault Cir.
Montgomery, AL 36112-6428
Ph: (205)953-5322 Fax: (205)953-6739
Richard B. Clark

Quarterly. Professional military journal covering the development, fielding, and application of combat power.

★7147★ *All Hands*
U.S. Government Printing Office
Superintendent of Documents
Washington, DC 20402-9322
Ph: (202)783-3238 Fax: (202)512-2250
Bureau of Navy PersonnelPublisher

Monthly. General interest magazine covering the United States Navy.

★7148★ *Armed Forces Journal International*
2000 L St. NW, Ste. 520
Washington, DC 20036
Ph: (202)296-0450 Fax: (202)296-5727
Benjamin F. Schemmer

Monthly. Magazine concerning the armed services, national security, and defense.

★7149★ *Armor*
U.S. Army Armor Center
ATSB-MAG
Fort Knox, KY 40121
Ph: (502)624-2249
Major James D. Brewer

Bimonthly. Military news magazine.

★7150★ *Army Aviation Magazine*
Army Aviation Publications, Inc.
49 Richmondville Ave.
Westport, CT 06880
Ph: (203)226-8184 Fax: (203)222-9863
William R. Harris

★7151★ *Army Communicator*
U.S. Army Signal Corps
Signal Towers, 706
Fort Gordon, GA 30905
Ph: (706)791-7204 Fax: (706)791-3917
Richard Davis

Quarterly. Magazine providing information about the Signal Corps.

★7152★ *Army Families*
Army Family Liaison Office, Department of the Army
HQDA DAPE-ZXF
Washington, DC 20310-0300
Joe Wasserman, Contact

Quarterly. Directed toward army families and provides tips and policy on jobs, benefits, education, finances, and government programs. Recurring features include news of educational opportunities, book reviews, and columns titled Guard/Reserve, Money Savers, Health, and News Roundup.

★7153★ *ARMY Magazine*
Assn. of the U.S. Army (AUSA)
2425 Wilson Blvd.
Arlington, VA 22201-3385
Ph: (703)841-4300 Fax: (703)525-9039
Fr: 800-336-4570
Mary French

Monthly. Magazine for Regular Army officers, noncommissioned officers, warrant officers, and senior enlisted personnel; industrialists; civilians with an interest in national defense; and members of the Army National Guard and Reserve.

★7154★ *Army Reserve Magazine*
1815 N. Fort Myer Dr., Suite 203
Arlington, VA 22209-1805
Ph: (703)696-6212 Fax: (703)696-3745
James M. Nielsen

Quarterly. Military magazine.

★7155★ *Army Times*
Army Times Publishing Co.
6883 Commercial Drive
Springfield, VA 22159
Ph: (703)750-8646 Fax: (703)750-8622
Fr: 800-424-9335
Tom Donnelly

Weekly. U.S. Army periodical.

★7156★ *Marine Corps Gazette*
Marine Corps Assn.
Box 1775
Quantico, VA 22134
Ph: (703)640-6161 Fax: (703)640-0823
Fr: 800-336-0291
J.E. Greenwood

Monthly. Written by and for U.S. Marines covering all aspects of the U.S. Marine Corps.

★7157★ *Marine Log*
Simmons-Boardman Publishing
345 Hudson St.
New York, NY 10014
Ph: (212)620-7200 Fax: (212)633-1165
Nicholas Blenkey

Monthly. Magazine serving ship, boat, and barge owners, builders, and operators; port authorities, and the Navy.

★7158★ *Military Intelligence Professional Bulletin*
U.S. Army Intelligence Center
ATZS-TDL-B
Fort Huachuca, AZ 85613-6000
Ph: (602)538-0797 Fax: (602)533-6308
Annette Castro

Quarterly. Military journal.

★7159★ *Military Lifestyle*
Downey Communications, Inc.
4800 Montgomery Ln., Ste. 710
Bethesda, MD 20814-5341
Ph: (301)718-7600 Fax: (301)718-7652
Hope M. Daniels

Magazine for military families.

★7160★ *Naval Aviation News*
U.S. Government Printing Office
Superintendent of Documents
Washington, DC 20402-9322
Ph: (202)783-3238 Fax: (202)512-2250
Chief of Naval OperationsPublisher

Bimonthly. Magazine presenting articles on all phases of Navy and Marine air activity.

★7161★ *Navy News*
2429 Bowland Parkland, Ste. 118
PO Box 8918
Virginia Beach, VA 23450
Ph: (804)486-8000 Fax: (804)486-8017
Nancy Hoeflaak

Weekly. Navy newspaper (tabloid).

★7162★ *Navy Times*
Army Times Publishing Co.
6883 Commercial Drive
Springfield, VA 22159
Ph: (703)750-8646 Fax: (703)750-8622
Fr: 800-424-9335
Tobias Naegele

Weekly. Independent newspaper serving Navy, Marine, and Coast Guard personnel.

★7163★ *NCOCall*
Chief of Public Affairs
Command Information Unit
1500 Army Pentagon 2D622
Washington, DC 20310-1500
Willard. K. Morris

Aims to contribute to the professional development of Army squad leaders, platoon sergeants, first sergeants, and sergeants major. Recurring features include a column titled A Sergeant's Viewpoint.

★7164★ *Officers' Call*
Chief of Public Affairs
Command Information Unit
1500 Army Pentagon 2D622
Washington, DC 20310-1500
Willard K. Morris

Discusses items of interest to Army officers. Carries articles on various aspects of Army life, including professional development and personal affairs.

★7165★ *On Target*
On Target
Public Affairs Office
Newark Air Force Base
831 Irving-Wick Drive West
Newark, OH 43057-0031
Ph: (614)522-7779 Fax: (614)522-7449
Sandy Layman

Biweekly. Newspaper for Air Force base personnel.

★7166★ *Recorder-Times*
Times Publications, Inc.
8603 Botts Ln.
PO Box 17947
San Antonio, TX 78217
Ph: (210)828-3321 Fax: (210)828-3787
Ed Leal

Daily. Military community newspaper.

★7167★ *Robins Rev-Up*
Office of Public Affairs, Robins Air Force Base
1553 Watson Blvd.
PO Box 6129
Warner Robins, GA 31095-6129
Ph: (912)926-2137 Fax: (912)328-7682
H. Thomas ReedPublisher

Weekly. Military newspaper (tabloid).

★7168★ *Seabee Coverall*
Holden Advertising
1767 Goodyear Ave., Ste. 101
Ventura, CA 93001
Kim Taft

Bimonthly. Military and family-interest magazine (tabloid) distributed worldwide to Navy bases and government offices.

★7169★ *Sergeants*
Air Force Sergeants Assn.
PO Box 50
Temple Hills, MD 20748
Ph: (301)899-3500 Fax: (301)899-8136
David W. Givans

Monthly. Military magazine.

★7170★ *Shipmate*
U.S. Naval Academy Alumni Assn.
Alumni House
247 King George St.
Annapolis, MD 21402
Ph: (410)263-4469
Col. James W. Hammond.

Magazine on naval and naval alumni interests.

★7171★ *SIGNAL*
Armed Forces Communications & Electronics Assn. (AFCEA)
4400 Fair Lakes Court
Fairfax, VA 22033
Ph: (703)631-6178 Fax: (703)631-4693
Fr: 800-336-4583
James B. Busey IV,

Monthly. Magazine on military and industrial command, control, computers, and electronics.

★7172★ *SOLDIERS*
Dept. of the Army
Cameron Sta., Bldg. 2, Door 11
Alexandria, VA 22304-5050
Ph: (703)274-6671 Fax: (703)274-1896
Lt. Col. Eileen M. Bratz

Monthly.

★7173★ *Soldiers' Scene*
Chief of Public Affairs
Command Information Unit
1500 Army Pentagon 2D622
Washington, DC 20310-1500
Willard K. Morris

Informs junior enlisted soldiers of the Army's professional development opportunities and encourages soldiers to take advantage of them. "Provides information on careers, pay and benefits, quality of life, and Army modernization."

★7174★ *Soundoff!*
Patuxent Publishing Co.
10750 Little Patuxent Pkwy.
Columbia, MD 21044
Ph: (410)730-3620 Fax: (410)730-7053
K.L. Vantran

Weekly. Fort Meade military newspaper (tabloid).

★7175★ *Strategic Review*
U.S. Strategic Institute
PO Box 618, Kenmore Sta.
Boston, MA 02215
Ph: (617)353-8700 Fax: (617)353-7330
Mackubin T. Owens

Quarterly. Military and political magazine.

★7176★ *Surface Warfare Magazine*
U.S. Government Printing Office
Superintendent of Documents
Washington, DC 20402
Ph: (202)783-3238 Fax: (202)275-0019
U.S. Department of the NavyPublisher

Bimonthly. Military magazine.

Meetings and Conventions

★7177★ AFCEA INFOTECH - Armed Forces Communications and Electronics Association Midwest Conference and Exposition
Armed Forces Communications and Electronics Association
4400 Fair Lakes Ct.
Fairfax, VA 22033
Ph: (703)631-6200 Fax: (703)631-4693
Fr: 800-336-4583

Annual. Always held during October at the Convention Center in Dayton, Ohio. **Dates and Locations:** 1995 Oct 10-12; Dayton, OH.

★7178★ Armed Forces Communications and Electronics Association Western Conference and Exposition
Armed Forces Communications and Electronics Association
4400 Fair Lakes Ct.
Fairfax, VA 22033
Ph: (703)631-6200 Fax: (703)818-9177

Annual.

★7179★ Army Aviation Association of America Convention
Army Aviation Association of America
49 Richmondville Ave.
Westport, CT 06880-2000
Ph: (203)226-8184 Fax: (203)222-9863

Annual.

★7180★ Association of the United States Army Annual Meeting
Association of the United States Army
2425 Wilson Blvd.
Arlington, VA 22201
Ph: (703)841-4300 Fax: (703)243-2589
Fr: 800-336-4570

Annual. Always held in Washington, D.C.

Other Sources of Information

★7181★ *The Air force and You*
Crestwood House
866 3rd Ave.
New York, NY 10022
Ph: (212)702-9632

1993.

★7182★ *The Army and You*
Crestwood House
866 3rd Ave.
New York, NY 10022
Ph: (212)702-9632

1993.

★7183★ *Guide to Military Careers*
Franklin Watts, Inc.
387 Park Ave., S.
New York, NY 10016
Ph: (212)686-7070 Fax: (212)213-6435

1992.

★7184★ *The Marines and You*
Crestwood House
866 3rd Ave.
New York, NY 10022
Ph: (212)702-9632

1993.

★7185★ *The Navy and You*
Crestwood House
866 3rd Ave.
New York, NY 10022
Ph: (212)702-9632

1993.

★7186★ *Up or Out: How to Get Promoted as the Army Draws Down*
Impact Inc.
Box H
Syracuse, NE 68446
Ph: (402)269-3327

1993.

Appendix I: State Occupational and Professional Licensing Agencies

This appendix covers state government agencies responsible for granting professional and occupational licenses. Entries are arranged alphabetically by state and include the state agency's or department's name, address, and phone number.

State Occupational and Professional Licensing Agencies

★7187★ Alaska State Division of Occupational Licensing
PO Box 110806
Juneau, AK 99811-0806
Ph: (907)465-2534 Fax: (907)465-2974

★7188★ Arizona State Department of Administration
State Boards Office
1400 W. Jefferson St., St. 230
Phoenix, AZ 85007
Ph: (602)542-3095

★7189★ California Department of Consumer Affairs
400 R St., Ste. 3000
Sacramento, CA 95814-6200
Ph: (916)445-1591

★7190★ Colorado State Department of Regulatory Agencies
1560 Broadway, Ste. 1300
Denver, CO 80202
Ph: (303)894-7711 Fax: (303)894-7692

★7191★ Connecticut State Department of Consumer Protection
Bureau of Licensing and Administration
165 Capitol Ave.
Hartford, CT 06106
Ph: (203)566-4999

★7192★ Delaware State Department of Administrative Services
Division of Professional Regulations
PO Box 1401
Dover, DE 19903
Ph: (302)739-4522

★7193★ District of Columbia Department of Consumer and Regulatory Affairs
Occupational and Professional Licensing Administration
614 H St. NW
Washington, DC 20001
Ph: (202)727-7480

★7194★ Florida State Department of Business and Professional Regulation
1940 N. Monroe St.
Tallahassee, FL 32399-0797
Ph: (904)488-7176 Fax: (904)922-3040

★7195★ Georgia Secretary of State
Professional Examining Boards
166 Pryor St. SW
Atlanta, GA 30303
Ph: (404)656-3900 Fax: (404)651-9532

★7196★ Hawaii State Department of Commerce and Consumer Affairs
PO Box 3469
Honolulu, HI 96801
Ph: (808)586-2850 Fax: (808)586-2856

★7197★ Idaho State Board of Occupational Licenses
1109 Main St.
Owyhee Plaza, Ste. 220
Boise, ID 83702-5642
Ph: (208)334-3233 Fax: (208)334-3945

★7198★ Illinois Department of Professional Regulation
320 W. Washington, 3rd Fl.
Springfield, IL 62786
Ph: (217)785-0820

★7199★ Illinois State Department of Professional Regulation
320 W. Washington St., 3rd Fl.
Springfield, IL 62786
Ph: (217)785-2145 Fax: (217)524-2470

★7200★ Indiana Professional Licensing Agency
1021 Government Center N.
100 N. Senate Ave.
Indianapolis, IN 46204
Ph: (317)232-2980 Fax: (317)232-2312

★7201★ Iowa State Department of Commerce
Professional Licensing and Regulation Division
1918 SE Hulsizer Ave.
Ankeny, IA 50021
Ph: (515)281-5602 Fax: (515)281-7372

★7202★ Kentucky Division of Occupations and Professions
PO Box 456
Frankfort, KY 40602-0456
Ph: (502)564-3296 Fax: (502)564-4818

★7203★ Louisiana State Department of Health and Human Resources
Office of Licensing Regulation
PO Box 3767
Baton Rouge, LA 70821-3767
Ph: (504)342-0138

★7204★ Maine State Division of Licensing and Enforcement
State House Station 35
Augusta, ME 04333
Ph: (207)582-8723

★7205★ Maryland State Department of Licensing and Regulation
Division of Occupational and Professional Licensing
501 St. Paul Pl., 15th Fl.
Baltimore, MD 21202-2272
Ph: (410)333-6209 Fax: (410)333-1229

★7206★ Massachusetts State Executive Office of Consumer Affairs
100 Cambridge St., Rm. 1520
Boston, MA 02202
Ph: (617)727-3074 Fax: (617)727-7378

★7207★ Michigan State Department of Commerce
Bureau of Occupational and Professional Regulation
PO Box 30018
Lansing, MI 48909
Ph: (517)373-1870 Fax: (517)335-6696

★7208★ Minnesota State Department of Commerce
133 E. 7th St.
St. Paul, MN 55101
Ph: (612)296-3528

★7209★ Mississippi Secretary of State
401 Mississippi St.
Jackson, MS 39215
Ph: (601)359-1350

★7210★ Missouri State Department of Professional Registration
PO Box 135
Jefferson City, MO 65102-0293
Ph: (314)751-1081 Fax: (314)751-4176

★7211★ Montana State Department of Commerce
Bureau of Professional and Occupational Licensing
111 N. Jackson
PO Box 200513
Helena, MT 59620-0513
Ph: (406)444-1488

★7212★ Nebraska State Bureau of Examining Boards
Department of Health
301 Centennial Mall S.
Box 95007
Lincoln, NE 68509
Ph: (402)471-2115

★7213★ New Jersey State Department of Law and Public Safety
Division of Consumer Affairs
124 Halsey St.
PO Box 45027
Newark, NJ 07102
Fax: (201)648-3538

★7214★ New Mexico State Department of Regulation and Licensing
725 St. Michaels Dr.
PO Box 25101
Santa Fe, NM 87504
Ph: (505)827-7000 Fax: (505)827-7095

★7215★ New York Education Department
Division of Professional Licensing Services
Cultural Education Center, Rm. 3029
Albany, NY 12230
Ph: (518)486-1765

★7216★ North Dakota Secretary of State
600 E. Blvd. Ave.
State Capitol, 1st Fl.
Bismarck, ND 58505-0500
Ph: (701)224-2905 Fax: (701)224-2992

★7217★ Ohio State Department of Commerce
Division of Licensing
77 S. High St., 23rd Fl.
Columbus, OH 43266-0546
Ph: (614)466-4130

★7218★ Oregon State Department of Insurance and Finance
350 Winter St., NW
Salem, OR 97310
Ph: (503)378-4100

★7219★ Pennsylvania State Department
Bureau of Professional and Occupational Affairs
618 Transportation and Safety Bldg.
Harrisburg, PA 17120
Ph: (717)787-8503 Fax: (717)787-7769

★7220★ Rhode Island State Department of Health
Division of Professional Regulation
3 Capitol Hill, Cannon Bldg.
Providence, RI 02908-5097
Ph: (401)277-2827 Fax: (401)277-1272

★7221★ South Carolina Department of Labor
Division of Licensing and Regulations
PO Box 11329
Columbia, SC 29211
Ph: (803)734-9600

★7222★ South Dakota State Department of Commerce
Professional and Occupational Licensing Department
910 E. Sioux Ave.
Pierre, SD 57501
Ph: (605)773-3178 Fax: (605)773-5369

★7223★ Tennessee State Department of Commerce and Insurance
Division of Regulatory Boards
500 James Roberston Pkwy., 2nd Fl.
Nashville, TN 37243-0572
Ph: (615)741-3449 Fax: (615)741-6470

★7224★ Texas State Department of Licensing and Regulation
PO Box 12157
Austin, TX 78711
Ph: (512)463-5520

★7225★ Utah State Division of Occupational and Professional Licensing
PO Box 45805
Salt Lake City, UT 84145-0805
Ph: (801)530-6628 Fax: (801)530-6511

★7226★ Vermont Secretary of State
Office od Professional Regulation
109 State St.
Montpelier, VT 05609-1106
Ph: (802)828-2458

★7227★ Virginia Department of Health Professions
6606 W. Broad St., 4th Fl.
Richmond, VA 23230-1717
Ph: (804)662-9904

★7228★ Virginia State Department of Professional and Occupational Regulation
3600 W. Broad St.
Richmond, VA 23230
Ph: (804)367-8519

★7229★ Washington State Department of Licensing
Highway-Licenses Bldg.
PO Box 01
Olympia, WA 98504-8001
Ph: (206)753-6918

★7230★ Wisconsin State Department of Regulation and Licensing
PO Box 8935
Madison, WI 53708
Ph: (608)266-2811

Appendix I: Employment Growth Rankings and Statistics

This section provides U.S. Bureau of Labor Statistics figures indicating expected employment growth for the occupations covered in this edition of *VCS*.

Bureau of Labor Statistics Occupational Data

Below is an extract of the Bureau of Labor Statistics' Industry-Occupation Matrix (1994). Occupations listed in *Vocational Careers Sourcebook* are ranked alphabetically and in order of growth. Annual figures are presented in thousands.

Occupational Growth from 1992 to 2005 (Occupations in Alphabetical Order)

	1992	2005	% Change
Adjusters, investigators, and collectors	1152	1510	31.1
Aircraft mechanics and engine specialists	131	148	12.7
Animal caretakers, except farm	103	143	39.8
Apparel workers	266	260	-2.3
Automotive body repairers	202	263	30.2
Automotive mechanics	739	907	22.7
Bank tellers	525	502	-4.5
Barbers and cosmetologists	71	69	-1.7
Billing clerks	315	355	12.4
Bindery workers	375	444	18.3
Blue collar worker supervisors	1757	1974	12.4
Boilermakers	26	25	-4.2
Bookkeeping, accounting, and auditing clerks	2112	2186	3.5
Bricklayers and stonemasons	139	174	25.7
Brokerage clerks and statement clerks	57	69	20.9
Busdrivers	562	681	21.2
Butchers and meat, poultry, and fish cutters	222	191	-13.9
Carpenters	978	1176	20.2
Carpet installers	62	75	21.6
Cashiers	2747	3417	24.4
Chefs, cooks, and other kitchen workers	3092	4282	38.5
Clerical supervisors and managers clerks	1267	1568	23.8
Compositors and typesetters	11	8	-26.5
Computer and peripheral equipment operators	296	173	-41.4
Concrete masons and terrazzo workers	100	113	13.4
Correction officers	282	479	69.9
Counter and rental clerks	242	331	36.3
Credit clerks and authorizers	218	272	24.4
Dental assistants	183	254	39.3
Dental laboratory technicians	48	50	3.1
Dispatchers	222	268	20.9
Drywall workers and lathers	121	165	36.9
Electric power generating plant operators and power	43	47	9.9
Electricians	518	618	19.3
Electronic home entertainment equipment repairers	39	37	-5.4
Elevator installers and repairers	22	25	18.1
Farm equipment mechanics	47	53	12.8
Farm operators and managers	1218	1014	-16.7
File clerks	257	305	18.9
Financial records processors	2686	2770	3.1
Firefighting occupations	305	354	16.3
Fishers, hunters, and trappers	52	55	4.7
Flight attendants	93	140	51.0
Food and beverage service occupations	4365	5489	25.8
Forestry and logging occupations	131	134	2.5
Gardeners and groundskeepers	884	1195	35.2
General office clerks	2688	3342	24.3
Glaziers	39	51	30.2
Guards	803	1211	50.8
Heating, air-conditioning, and refrigeration mechanics	212	274	29.4
Home appliance and power Tool repairers	74	74	-.1
Homemaker-home health aides	475	1120	135.9
Hotel and motel desk clerks	122	172	41.3
Industrial machinery repairers	477	462	-3.2

Employment Growth Rankings and Statistics

	1992	2005	% Change
Information clerks	1333	1762	32.2
Inspectors, testers, and graders	625	559	-10.5
Insulation workers	57	79	39.8
Insurance agents and brokers	415	477	15.0
Interviewing and new accounts clerks	71	95	34.4
Janitors and cleaners	2862	3410	19.1
Jewelers	30	35	19.1
Library assistants and bookmobile drivers	114	135	17.8
Machinists and tool programmers	352	34.8	-1.1
Mail clerks and messengers	271	298	9.6
Material moving equipment operators	·983	1111	13.1
Material recording, scheduling, dispatching, and ...	3588	4043	12.7
Medical assistants	181	308	70.5
Metalworking machine operators	96	1111	13.1
Millwrights	73	79	8.7
Mobile heavy equipment mechanics	46	53	14.9
Motorcycle, boat, and small engine mechanics	46	53	14.9
Musical instrument repairers and tuners	12	13	9.0
Numerical-control machine-tool operators	73	87	19.9
Nursing aides and psychiatric aides	1389	2006	44.4
Order clerks	300	313	4.4
Painters and paperhangers	440	569	29.2
Painting and coating machine operators	151	152	1.2
Payroll and timekeeping clerks	165	164	-.4
Photographic process workers	14	18	26.1
Plasterers	32	37	16.3
Plumbers, pipefitters and steamfitters	351	378	7.8
Police, detectives, and special agents	700	792	13.1
Postal clerks and mail carriers	361	362	.4
Precision assemblers	334	316	-5.5
Prepress operators	130	143	9.8
Preschool workers	684	1135	65.8

	1992	2005	% Change
Printing press occupations	217	255	17.6
Private household workers	869	583	-32.9
Rail transportation occupations	116	141	21.4
Real estate agents, brokers, and appraisers	397	461	15.9
Receptionists	904	1210	33.8
Reservation and transportation ticket agents and travel	131	171	30.1
Roofers	127	155	21.7
Roustabouts	33	22	-33.2
Secretaries	3324	3710	11.6
Securities and financial services sales representatives	200	265	32.8
Sheet-metal workers	208	244	17.5
Shoe and leather workers and repairers	22	17	-19.6
Stationary engineers	31	33	5.1
Stenographers	115	113	-1.5
Stock clerks	1782	1940	8.8
Structural and reinforcing ironworkers	66	81	22.4
Taxi drivers and chauffeurs	120	142	18.3
Teacher aides	885	1266	43.1
Telephone installers and repairers	165	125	-24.4
Telephone operators	314	225	-28.3
Textile machinery operators	39	32	-17.2
Timber cutting and logging workers	96	91	-4.8
Tool and die makers	138	128	-6.8
Traffic, shipping, and receiving clerks	824	971	17.8
Travel agents	115	191	65.7
Truckdrivers	2720	3428	26.0
Typists, word processors, and data entry keyers	789	664	-15.8
Upholsterers	60	67	11.2
Vending machine servicers and repairers	20	20	-.2
Water transportation occupations	134	144	7.7
Water and wastewater occupations	86	102	18.4
Welders, etc.	97	80	-17.0
Woodworking occupations	220	272	23.6

Occupational Growth from 1992 to 2005 (Occupations by Percentage of Change)

	1990	2005	% Change
Homemaker-home health aides	475	1120	135.9
Medical assistants	181	308	70.5
Correction officers	282	479	69.9

	1992	2005	% Change
Preschool workers	684	1135	65.8
Travel agents	115	191	65.7
Flight attendants	93	140	51.0

	1990	2005	% Change
Guards	803	1211	50.8
Nursing aides and psychiatric aides	1389	2006	44.4
Teacher aides	885	1266	43.1
Hotel and motel desk clerks	122	172	41.3
Animal caretakers, except farm	103	143	39.8
Insulation workers	57	79	39.8
Dental assistants	183	254	39.3
Chefs, cooks, and other kitchen workers	3092	4282	38.5
Drywall workers and lathers	121	165	36.9
Counter and rental clerks	242	331	36.3
Gardeners and groundskeepers	884	1195	35.2
Interviewing and new accounts clerks	71	95	34.4
Receptionists	904	1210	33.8
Securities and financial services sales representatives	200	265	32.8
Information clerks	1333	1762	32.2
Adjusters, investigators, and collectors	1152	1510	31.1
Automotive body repairers	202	263	30.2
Glaziers	39	51	30.2
Reservation and transportation ticket agents and travel	131	171	30.1
Heating, air-conditioning, and refrigeration mechanics	212	274	29.4
Painters and paperhangers	440	569	29.2
Photographic process workers	14	18	26.1
Truckdrivers	2720	3428	26.0
Food and beverage service occupations	4365	5489	25.8
Bricklayers and stonemasons	139	174	25.7
Cashiers	2747	3417	24.4
Credit clerks and authorizers	218	272	24.4
General office clerks	2688	3342	24.3
Clerical supervisors and managers clerks	1267	1568	23.8
Woodworking occupations	220	272	23.6
Automotive mechanics	739	907	22.7
Structural and reinforcing ironworkers	66	81	22.4
Roofers	127	155	21.7
Carpet installers	62	75	21.6
Rail transportation occupations	116	141	21.4
Busdrivers	562	681	21.2
Brokerage clerks and statement clerks	57	69	20.9
Dispatchers	222	268	20.9
Carpenters	978	1176	20.2
Electricians	518	618	19.3
Janitors and cleaners	2862	3410	19.1
Jewelers	30	35	19.1
File clerks	257	305	18.9
Water and wastewater occupations	86	102	18.4
Bindery workers	375	444	18.3
Taxi drivers and chauffeurs	120	142	18.3
Elevator installers and repairers	22	25	18.1

	1992	2005	% Change
Library assistants and bookmobile drivers	114	135	17.8
Traffic, shipping, and receiving clerks	824	971	17.8
Printing press occupations	217	255	17.6
Sheet-metal workers	208	244	17.5
Firefighting occupations	305	354	16.3
Plasterers	32	37	16.3
Real estate agents, brokers, and appraisers	397	461	15.9
Insurance agents and brokers	415	477	15.0
Mobile heavy equipment mechanics	46	53	14.9
Motorcycle, boat, and small engine mechanics	46	53	14.9
Concrete masons and terrazzo workers	100	113	13.4
Material moving equipment operators	983	1111	13.1
Metalworking machine operators	96	1111	13.1
Police, detectives, and special agents	700	792	13.1
Farm equipment mechanics	47	53	12.8
Aircraft mechanics and engine specialists	131	148	12.7
Material recording, scheduling, dispatching, and ...	3588	4043	12.7
Billing clerks	315	355	12.4
Blue collar worker supervisors	1757	1974	12.4
Secretaries	3324	3710	11.6
Upholsterers	60	67	11.2
Electric power generating plant operators and power	43	47	9.9
Prepress operators	130	143	9.8
Mail clerks and messengers	271	298	9.6
Musical instrument repairers and tuners	12	13	9.0
Stock clerks	1782	1940	8.8
Millwrights	73	79	8.7
Plumbers, pipefitters and steamfitters	351	378	7.8
Water transportation occupations	134	144	7.7
Stationary engineers	31	33	5.1
Fishers, hunters, and trappers	52	55	4.7
Order clerks	300	313	4.4
Bookkeeping, accounting, and auditing clerks	2112	2186	3.5
Dental laboratory technicians	48	50	3.1
Financial records processors	2686	2770	3.1
Forestry and logging occupations	131	134	2.5
Painting and coating machine operators	151	152	1.2
Postal clerks and mail carriers	361	362	.4
Home appliance and power Tool repairers	74	74	-.1
Vending machine servicers and repairers	20	20	-.2

	1990	2005	% Change
Payroll and timekeeping clerks	165	164	-.4
Machinists and tool programmers	352	34.8	-1.1
Stenographers	115	113	-1.5
Barbers and cosmetologists	71	69	-1.7
Apparel workers	266	260	-2.3
Industrial machinery repairers	477	462	-3.2
Boilermakers	26	25	-4.2
Bank tellers	525	502	-4.5
Timber cutting and logging workers	96	91	-4.8
Electronic home entertainment equipment repairers	39	37	-5.4
Precision assemblers	334	316	-5.5
Tool and die makers	138	128	-6.8
Inspectors, testers, and graders	625	559	-10.5

	1992	2005	% Change
Butchers and meat, poultry, and fish cutters	222	191	-13.9
Typists, word processors, and data entry keyers	789	664	-15.8
Farm operators and managers	1218	1014	-16.7
Welders, etc.	97	80	-17.0
Textile machinery operators	39	32	-17.2
Shoe and leather workers and repairers	22	17	-19.6
Telephone installers and repairers	165	125	-24.4
Compositors and typesetters	11	8	-26.5
Telephone operators	314	225	-28.3
Roustabouts	33	22	-33.2
Private household workers	869	583	-32.9
Computer and peripheral equipment operators	296	173	-41.4

Index to Information Sources

This Index is an alphabetical listing of all organizations, agencies, and publications included in *VCS*. Index references are to **entry numbers** rather than to page numbers. Publication and film titles are rendered in italics. Consult the "User's Guide" for more detailed information about the index.

A

The A to Z Business Office Handbook **1048**
AACS - Association of Accredited Cosmetology Schools Annual Convention & Exhibition **3028**
AACS News **628**, **3014**
AAHA Provider News **3188**
AAIS Viewpoint **121**
AAMA Directory of Members and Associate Members **6292**
AAMA Newsletter **6293**
AAMA Technical Advisory Committee Research Paper **6312**
AAN American Beautification Award **3117**
ABA Banking Journal **837**, **1114**, **1493**
ABA Management Update of Personal Trust and Private Banking **838**
The Abbey Newsletter **1560**
ABC Today **4432**, **4723**, **4724**, **4821-4823**, **4869**, **4870**, **4932**, **4933**, **4989-4991**, **5076-5078**, **5135**, **5136**, **5174**, **5175**, **5238-5240**, **5278**, **5279**, **5374-5376**, **5438**, **5439**, **5490**, **5491**, **5538-5540**, **5589**, **5590**, **5629**, **5630**, **6702**
Aberdeen's Magazine of Masonry Construction **4934**
"Able Seaman" in *Occu-Facts: Information on 580 Careers in Outline Form* **6954**
ABYC News **4616**, **6991**
Academy of Legends **3006**
ACCA News **4433**
Accent Magazine **5790**
According to Hoyle **175**, **407**
Accounting Clerk **1412**
"Accounting Clerk" in *BLR Encyclopedia of Prewritten Job Descriptions* **1413**
"Accounting Clerk" in *Careers Inside the World of Offices* (pp. 12, 42-45) **1414**
"Accounting Clerk" in *Occu-Facts: Information on 580 Careers in Outline Form* **1415**
"Accounting Clerks" in *American Almanac of Jobs and Salaries* (pp. 509) **1416**
"Accounting Clerks and Bookkeepers" in *Opportunities in Vocational and Technical Careers* (pp. 47-58) **1417**
Accounting Terms & Bookkeeping Procedures Explained **1460**
Accounts Payable Practice Set **1448**
Accounts Receivable and Collection for the Medical Practice **2790**
Accounts Receivable Practice Set **1449**
Accredited Dental Assisting, Dental Hygiene and Dental Laboratory Technology Educational Programs **6495**
Accrediting Bureau of Health Education Schools **2772**
ACI Structural Journal **4935**
ACNewS **3369**
Actiongram **122**
ADA News **6505**
"Adjusters, Investigators, and Collectors" in *Occupational Outlook Handbook* **736**
"Adjusters" in *Opportunities in Insurance Careers* (pp. 42-43) **737**
Adjusters Reference Guide **789**
"Administrative Assistants, Clerical Workers, and Secretaries" in *Jobs '95* (pp. 25-29) **1627**
Administrative Newsletter **4653**
The Administrative Secretary **1628**
"Admitting Clerk" in *Career Information Center* (pp. 39-40) **1099**
"Admitting Clerk" in *Health Care* (pp. 39-43) **1100**
Advanced Placement Examination in Computer Science **965**
Advances in Cooling Techniques for Computers **4199**
Advances in Exterior Body Panels **3836**
Advances & Trends in Automotive Sheet Steel Stamping **3837**
Adventure West **705**, **1200**
Advertising Mail Marketing Association **1337**
"Advertising Sales" in *Careers in Fashion Retailing* (pp. 80-82) **580**
"Advertising Sales Person" in *VGM's Handbook of Business and Management Careers* (pp. 11-14) **581**
"Advertising Sales Representatives" in *Jobs! What They Are—Where They Are—What They Pay* (pp. 326) **582**
"Advertising Sales, Television" in *Career Choices for the 90's for Students of Communications and Journalism* (pp. 189-191) **583**
"Advertising Sales (Television)" in *Encyclopedia of Career Choices for the 1990s: A Guide to Entry Level Jobs* (pp. 828-830) **584**
"Advertising Sales Workers" in *Career Discovery Encyclopedia* (Vol.1, pp. 24-25) **585**
"Advertising Salesperson" in *Career Opportunities in Television, Cable, and Video* (pp. 110-111) **586**
"Advertising Space Sales" in *Career Choices for the 90's for Students of Business* (pp. 155-158) **587**
"Advertising Space Sales" in *Career Choices for the 90's for Students of Political Science & Government* (pp. 164-167) **588**
"Advertising Space Sales" in *Encyclopedia of Career Choices for the 1990s: A Guide to Entry Level Jobs* (pp. 610-613, 766-769) **589**
"Advertising Space Sales, Newspaper Publishing" in *Career Choices for the 90's for Students of Communications and Journalism* **590**
"Advertising Space Sales, Newspaper Publishing" in *Career Choices for the 90's for Students of Political Science & Government* **591**
"Advertising Space Salesperson" in *Occu-Facts: Information on 580 Careers in Outline Form* **592**
Aerospace Assembly Worker **5649**
AFCEA INFOTECH - Armed Forces Communications and Electronics Association Midwest Conference and Exposition **7177**
AFCEA ROTC Scholarship Program **7142**
AFCOM's Fall Educational Program **993**
AFCOM's Fall Program Proceedings **975**
AFI Honor Roll **2320**
Africa's Top Wildlife Countries **697**
AFT Action: A Newsletter for AFT Leaders **1844**
Aftermarket Symposium **3879**, **3994**
Aftermarket Today **3854**, **3962**, **4044**, **6566**
Ag Alert **3430**
AG Consultant **3431**
Ag Expo **3525**
AG-PILOT International **3432**
AGC Membership Directory and Buyers' Guide **4572**, **4716**, **4807**, **4925**, **5585**, **6700**
AGC Mobile Directory **4573**, **4717**, **4808**, **4926**, **5586**, **6701**
Agency Sales Magazine **226**
Agri-Equipment & Chemical **3433**, **4342**
Agri Finance **3434**
Agri-News **3435**, **3436**
Agri News Farm Show **3526**
Agri-View **3437**
Agribusiness **3438**
Agricultural Aviation **3439**
Agricultural Cluster **3371**
The Agricultural Education Magazine **3440**
Agricultural Engineering **3441**
Agricultural & Food: An Abstract Newsletter **3442**
Agricultural Hall of Fame **3415**
Agronomy Journal **3443**
AgVenture **3444**
Agway Cooperator **3445**
AGWEEK **3446**
AHAM Factory Shipment Release **4493**
AHAM Major Appliance Industry Factbook **4494**
AHAM Membership Directory **4478**
AH&MA Reports **1090**
AHANews **2864**
AHCA Notes **2865**
AHEA ACTION **3189**
AIB Leader Letter **839**, **1115**
AIB Student Catalog **827**, **1113**
AIDS Concepts for Medical Assistnts — Part I **2791**
Aim For A Job As An Electronic Technician **4220**, **5020**
"Air Conditioning, Heating, and Refrigeration Mechanic" in *Career Information Center* (Vol.4) **4371**
"Air Conditioning, Heating, and Refrigeration Mechanics" in *American Almanac of Jobs and Salaries* (p. 522) **4372**

Air Conditioning, Heating and Refrigeration News **4434**
Air Conditioning/Heating/Solar Technician **4373**
"Air-Conditioning/Heating/Solar Technician" in *Occu-Facts: Information on 580 Careers in Outline Form* **4374**
"Air Conditioning and Heating Technician" in *Career Information Center* (Vol.4) **4375**
"Air-Conditioning Installer" in *Career Selector 2001* **4460**
Air Conditioning and Refrigeration **4405**
"Air Conditioning, Refrigeration, and Heating Mechanic" in *Exploring Nontraditional Jobs for Women* (pp. 76-82) **4376**
"Air-Conditioning, Refrigeration, and Heating Mechanic" in *VGM's Careers Encyclopedia* (pp. 29-32) **4377**
"Air-Conditioning, Refrigeration, and Heating Mechanics" in *Encyclopedia of Careers and Vocational Guidance* (Vol.2, pp. 60-64) **4378**
"Air-Conditioning and Refrigeration Mechanic" in *Occu-Facts: Information on 580 Careers in Outline Form* **4379**
Air-Conditioning and Refrigeration Service Technicians **4380**
Air Conditioning and Refrigeration Technician **4381**
The Air Conditioning/Refrigeration Toolbox Manual **4417**
Air Force Academy: Commitment to Excellence **7080**
Air Force Association **7133**
Air Force Career Opportunities **7081**
"Air Force Nurse" in *150 Careers in the Health Care Field* **7082**
"Air Force Nurse Corps" in *Opportunities in Nursing Careers* (pp. 112-113) **7083**
Air Force ROTC Scholarships **7143**
Air Force Times **7144**
Air Line Pilot **3080**, **3778**
Air Transport **1201**
Air Transport Association of America **1183**
Air Transport-Ground Services **636**
Air Travel Card Grant **685**
Air University Library Index to Military Periodicals **7145**
The Air force and You **7181**
AIRCO Welding Award **5760**, **5985**
"Aircraft Assembler" in *Occu-Facts: Information on 580 Careers in Outline Form* **5650**
Aircraft Cabin Cleaning & Refurbishing Operations **3767**
Aircraft Cleaning, Painting & Paint Removal **3768**
Aircraft Fuel System Maintenance **3769**
Aircraft Maintenance & Repair **3770**
"Aircraft Mechanic" in *Career Information Center* (Vol.12) **3736**
"Aircraft Mechanic" in *Careers in Aviation* (pp. 19-22) **3737**
"Aircraft Mechanic" in *Exploring Nontraditional Jobs for Women* (pp. 83-89) **3738**
"Aircraft Mechanic" in *Jobs Rated Almanac* **3739**
"Aircraft Mechanics" in *101 Careers: A Guide to the Fastest-Growing Opportunities* (pp. 307-309) **3740**
"Aircraft Mechanics" in *Career Discovery Encyclopedia* (Vol.1, pp. 44-45) **3741**
Aircraft Mechanics Digest **3771**
"Aircraft Mechanics and Engine Specialists" in *Encyclopedia of Careers and Vocational Guidance* (Vol.2, pp. 71-74) **3742**
"Aircraft Mechanics and Engine Specialists" in *Occupational Outlook Handbook* **3743**
"Aircraft Mechanics" in *Jobs! What They Are—Where They Are—What They Pay* (pp. 210) **3744**
"Aircraft Mechanics" in *Opportunities in Travel Careers* (pp. 37-39) **3745**
Aircraft Mechanic's Shop Manual **3772**
Aircraft Repair Manual **3773**
Aircraft Technician **3746**, **3779**
"Aircraft Technician" in *100 Best Jobs for the 1990s & Beyond* **3792**
"Aircraft Technician" in *Occu-Facts: Information on 580 Careers in Outline Form* **3747**
Aircraft Technicians **3748**
"Airline Baggage and Freight Handler" in *Career Information Center* (Vol.12) **7010**
Airline Dispatcher **1246**
"Airline Dispatcher" in *Career Information Center* (Vol.12) **1247**
"Airline Dispatcher" in *Occu-Facts: Information on 580 Careers in Outline Form* **1248**
Airline Dispatchers **1249**
"Airline Flight Attendant" in *Career Information Center* (Vol.12) **3046**
Airline Flight Attendants **3047**
"Airline Freight Handler" in *Transportation* (pp. 15-17) **7011**
"The Airline Mechanic" in *Opportunities in Airline Careers* (pp. 101-105) **3749**
"Airline Reservations Agent" in *Career Information Center* (Vol.12) **1148**
"Airline Reservations Agent" in *Travel & Tourism* (pp. 21-25) **1149**
Airline Reservations Sales Agent **1150**
"Airline Sales and Reservations" in *Travel Agent: Dealer in Dreams* (pp. 113-128) **1151**
Airline Ticket Agent **1152**
"Airline Ticket Agent" in *Career Information Center* (Vol.12) **1153**
"Airline Ticket Agent" in *Occu-Facts: Information on 580 Careers in Outline Form* **1154**
Airplane Cleaner **7012**
"Airplane Cleaner" in *Occu-Facts: Information on 580 Careers in Outline Form* **7013**
"Airplane Dispatchers" in *Encyclopedia of Careers and Vocational Guidance* (Vol.2, pp. 75-78) **1250**
"Airplane Flight Attendant" in *Career Selector 2001* **3083**
"Airplane Mechanic" in *VGM's Careers Encyclopedia* (pp. 32-34) **3750**
"Airplane Mechanics" in *American Almanac of Jobs and Salaries* (pp. 394) **3751**
Airport Ground Transportation Association **6802**
Airport Journal **3081**, **3780**
Airport Press **3781**
Airpower Journal **7146**
A.J. (Andy) Spielman Scholarships **696**
Alaska State Division of Occupational Licensing **7187**
Alcoholic Beverage Control: From the State Capitals **2615**
Aligning & Adjusting Cylinders—Instructor Guide **6243**
Aligning & Adjusting Cylinders on the Sheetfed Offset Press **6244**
All Hands **7147**
All Pro **54**, **176**, **408**, **490**, **593**
"All Round Machinist" in *Career Information Center* (Vol.9) **5808**
"All-Round Machinist" in *Occu-Facts: Information on 580 Careers in Outline Form* **5809**
Alliance of American Insurers **772**
Almost Free Cookbooks and Recipes Update **2471**
Alphabetic Filing Rules **1519**
Alphonso Deal Scholarship Award **2322**
Alternatives to Assembly Lines: Modern Times—Revisited **5651**
AM Proceedings **908**
The AMA Handbook of Marketing for the Service Industries **623**
AMC Van Operator Lifetime Achievement Award **6871**
America at Its Best: Opportunities in the National Guard **7084**
American Academy of Ophthalmology **6527**
American Agent & Broker **790**
American Agriculturist **3447**
American Animal Hospital Association Annual Meeting **2941**
American Apparel Manufacturers Association **6288**
American Architectural Manufacturers Association—Quarterly Review **4725**, **4824**, **4871**, **4936**, **4992**, **5079**, **5137**, **5176**, **5241**, **5280**, **5377**, **5440**, **5541**, **5591**, **5631**
American Association for Continuity of Care Annual Conference **3195**
American Association of Cosmetology Schools **2989**, **2992**
American Association for Laboratory Animal Science **2912**, **2916**
American Association for Laboratory Animal Science—Membership Directory **2926**
American Association of Managing General Agents Trade Mart **164**
American Association of Meat Processors **5704**
American Association of Medical Assistants **2767**, **2773**
American Association of Medical Assistants Regional Conferences **2805**
American Bankers Association **824**, **1112**
American Beef Cattleman **3448**
American Boarding Kennels Association **2913**, **2917**
American Boat Builders & Repairers Association—Bulletin **4617**
American Bus Association's Motorcoach Marketer: Complete Directory of the Intercity Bus & Travel/Tourism Industry **698**, **6648**
American Collectors Association **773**
American Collectors Association—Membership Roster **791**
American Convention of Meat Processors **3655**, **5714**
American Correctional Association **1989**, **1990**
American Council of Nanny Schools **3366**, **3367**
American Culinary Federation **2445**
American Dental Assistants Association **2691**
American Dental Association **2692**, **2695**, **6491**, **6493**
American Dental Directory **2704**, **6496**
American Dyestuff Reporter **6366**
American Educator **1845**
American Electronics Association—Update **4109**
American Express Travel Scholarships **686**, **1193**
American Farm Bureau Federation **3404**
American Farmer **3425**
American Federation of Teachers **1838**
American Federation of Violin and Bow Makers **4638**, **4642**
American Feed Industry Association Feed Industries Show **3527**
American Fiber Manufacturers Association **6360**
American Fire Journal **2120**
American Fisheries Society Convention **3656**
American Forestry Association Convention and Exposition **3727**
American Forests **3698**
American Foundrymen's Society **5578**, **5875**
American Foundrymen's Society Casting Congress and Cast Expo **5613**, **5906**
American Furniture Manufacturers Association **6438**
American Health Care Association **2846**, **2848**
American Horticulturist **3127**
American Hospital Association **2847**
American Hotel & Motel Association **1085**
American Hotel and Motel Association Fall Conference **1095**
American Humane Association Annual Meeting and Training Conference/Animal Protection **2942**
American Hunter **3597**
American Ink Maker **6248**
American Institute of Banking Scholarship **828**, **1009**
American Institute of Constructors—Newsletter **4726**, **4825**, **4872**, **4937**, **4993**, **5080**, **5138**, **5177**, **5242**, **5281**, **5378**, **5441**, **5542**, **5592**, **5632**

American Institute of Organbuilders **4639**, **4643**
American Jewelry Manufacturer **5791**
American Journal of Agricultural Economics **3449**
American Library Association **1551**, **1553**
American Looks **3015**
American Machinist—Buyers' Guide Issue **5841**, **5884**, **5909**
American Management Association **899**, **5679**
American Meat Institute—Newsletter **5710**
American Medical Technologists **2693**, **2768**
American Medical Technologists Scholarships **2708**, **2788**
American Mover **6703**
American Movers Association Trade Show **6708**
American Nanny **3348**
American Nurseryman **3128**
American Painting Contractor **5243**
American Payroll Association **1584**, **1585**
American Petroleum Institute **5488**
American Petroleum Institute—Publications and Materials **5492**
American Photo **6605**
American Police Academy **2270**, **2275**
The American Postal Worker **1238**, **1378**
American Printer **6156**, **6202**, **6249**, **6283**
American Professionals Series **177**, **2023**, **3372**, **3554**, **4501**, **5477**
American Public Transit Association **6640**
American Railway Engineering Association Bulletin **6765**
American Real Estate and Investment Show **402**
American Rifleman **3598**
The American Rose **3129**
American Salesman **123**, **227**, **475**, **547**, **629**
American Salon Magazine **3016**
American School Food Service Association Conference **2523**, **2645**
American Shipper **1314**
American Shoemaking **6343**
American Society of Appraisers **313**, **318**
American Society of Chartered Life Underwriters National Conference **165**
American Society of CLU and ChFC **102**
American Society of Farm Managers and Rural Appraisers **3405**, **3408**
American Society of Farm Managers and Rural Appraisers-General Membership Directory **3450**
American Society of Heating, Refrigerating and Air-Conditioning Engineers **4397**
American Society of Podiatric Medical Assistants **2769**, **2774**
American Society for Quality Control **5721**
American Society of Travel Agents **675**, **677**, **1184**, **1186**
American Society of Travel Agents World Travel Congress **725**, **1218**
American Soybean Association Annual Conference **3528**
American Stock Exchange **1491**
American Stock Exchange—Annual Report **1494**
The American System of Practical Bookkeeping: Adapted to the Commerce of the United States **1461**
American Teacher **1846**
American Textile Machinery Exhibition International **6379**
American Textile Manufacturers Institute **6361**
American Train Dispatchers Association **1262**
American Trapper **3599**
American Trucking Associations **6858**, **6861**
American Trucking Associations Management Conference & Exhibition **6930**
American Trucking Trends, 1991-92 **6940**
American Typecasting Fellowship—Newsletter **6203**
American Welding Society **5969**, **5972**
American Woodworker **6451**
America's Textiles International—Buyer's Guide Issue **6364**
Amerigold Bulletin **3130**
AMEX Fact Book **1495**, **1497**
AMFI Aviation Maintenance Symposium **3790**
AMFI Industry Report **3793**
AMFI Job Opportunities Listing **3794**
AMMA Bulletin **1379**
Ammo **5761**, **6567**
AMT - Association for Manufacturing Technology **5825**, **5829**, **5876**, **5880**, **5917**, **5921**, **5934**, **5937**
AMT Educational Program and National Meeting **2806**
AMT Events **2792**
AMT Events and Continuing Education Supplement **2793**
AMT's Two-Year Scholarships **5886**
Analysis of Class I Railroads **6766**
An Analysis of Janitor Service in Elementary Schools **3283**
Ancient Double-Entry Bookkeeping **1485**
Andrew Seybold's Outlook on Professional Computing **976**
Animal Activist Alert **2927**
Animal Care Attendant **2880**
"Animal Care Attendant" in *Careers for Animal Lovers and Other Zoological Types* (pp. 17-19) **2881**
"Animal Care Attendant" in *Occu-Facts: Information on 580 Careers in Outline Form* **2882**
"Animal Caretaker" in *150 Careers in the Health Care Field* **2883**
"Animal Caretaker" in *Career Information Center* (Vol.8) **2884**
"Animal Caretaker" in *Career Selector 2001* **2944**
Animal Caretakers **2885**
"Animal Caretakers, except Farm" in *America's 50 Fastest Growing Jobs* (pp. 112) **2886**
"Animal Caretakers, except Farm" in *Occupational Outlook Handbook* **2887**
"Animal Health Technicians" in *Career Discovery Encyclopedia* (Vol.1, pp. 46-47) **2888**
"Animal Health Technicians" in *Encyclopedia of Careers and Vocational Guidance* (Vol.2, pp. 79-83) **2889**
Animal Technicians **2890**
"Animal Technicians and Other Paramedical Personnel" in *Opportunities in Veterinary Medicine* (pp. 115-116) **2891**
"Animal Technology" in *150 Careers in the Health Care Field* **2892**
"Animal Trainers/Handlers" in *Jobs! What They Are—Where They Are—What They Pay* (pp. 48) **2893**
Annual Aviation Maintenance Symposium and Trade Show **3791**
Annual Conference and Green Industry Expo **3148**
Annual Directory of Members **223**
Annual Hosiery Statistics **6313**, **6380**
Annual Meeting and Exhibition of the Air and Waste Management Association **6139**
Annual Survey of Data Processing Operations Salaries **977**
Annual Training Conference and Awards Banquet **2383**
Ansley House Associates: The Executive Secretary - An Office Job Simulation **1707**
Anti-Corrosion Times **4938**
APA Directory **1590**
APCO Annual Conference and Exposition **1284**
APCO BULLETIN **1276**
APCO Membership Directory **1277**
APCO Reports **1278**
API Monthly Statistical Report **5509**
API Report to the Membership **5493**
API Reports **5494**
Apparel College Directory **6294**
"Apparel" in *Encyclopedia of Careers and Vocational Guidance* **6264**
Apparel Import Digest **6291**
"Apparel Industry" in *Career Information Center* (Vol.9) **6265**
Apparel Industry Magazine **6295**
Apparel Industry Workers **6266**
Apparel Plant Wages Survey **6296**, **6314**
Apparel Research Notes **6297**
Apparel Sales/Marketing Compensation Survey **6298**
"Apparel Workers" in *Occupational Outlook Handbook* **6267**
Apple Library Users Group Newsletter **978**, **1561**
Appleton & Lange's Review for the Surgical Technology Examination, ARCO **2777**
Appliance **4495**
"Appliance/Power Tool Repairer" in *100 Best Jobs for the 1990s & Beyond* **4500**
Appliance Repairer **4462**
"Appliance Repairer" in *VGM's Careers Encyclopedia* (pp. 44-46) **4463**
"Appliance Repairers" in *American Almanac of Jobs and Salaries* (pp. 523) **4464**
"Appliance Repairers" in *Career Discovery Encyclopedia* (Vol.1, pp. 52-53) **4465**
"Appliance Repairers" in *Encyclopedia of Careers and Vocational Guidance* (Vol.2, pp. 91-93) **4466**
Appliance Service News **4435**, **4496**
Appliance Service Technician, Electrical **4467**
"Appliance Service Worker" in *Career Information Center* (Vol.5) **4468**
"Appraisal" in *Career Choices for the 90's for Students of Mathematics* (pp. 142-144) **250**
"Appraisal" in *Encyclopedia of Career Choices for the 1990s: AGuide to Entry Level Jobs* (pp. 750-752) **251**
Appraisal Institute **314**, **319**
Appraisal Institute Scholarships **346**
The Appraisal Journal **354**
"Appraisal" in *Opportunities in Real Estate Careers* (pp. 81-85) **252**
The Appraisal Review **355**
"Appraiser" in *Career Choices for the 90's for Students of Economics* (pp. 130-132) **253**
"Appraiser" in *Career Information Center* (Vol.5) **254**
Appraiser Gram **356**
Appraiser News **357**
APTA Directory **6650**
Architectural Woodwork Institute Annual Trade Show and Convention **6465**
Arizona State Department of Administration - State Boards Office **7188**
Armed Forces Careers **7085**
Armed Forces Communications and Electronics Association Western Conference and Exposition **7178**
Armed Forces Journal International **7148**
"Armed Forces" in *Opportunities in Business Communication Careers* (pp. 38-39) **7086**
"Armed Forces" in *Opportunities in Pharmacy Careers* (pp. 115-117) **7087**
"Armed Forces" in *Opportunities in Transportation Careers* (pp. 127-129) **7088**
"Armed Forces" in *Opportunities in Vocational and Technical Careers* (pp. 37-41) **7089**
Armed Forces Test (AFT/ASVAB) **7134**
"Armed Forces Training" in *Careers With Robots* (pp. 111-115) **7090**
"Armed Services Careers" in *Career Information Center* (Vol.11) **7091**
Armor **7149**
Army Aviation Association of America Convention **7179**
Army Aviation Magazine **7150**
Army Career Opportunities **7092**
Army Communicator **7151**
Army Families **7152**
ARMY Magazine **7153**
"Army Nurse" in *150 Careers in the Health Care Field* **7093**
"Army Nurse Corps" in *Opportunities in Nursing Careers* (pp. 110-111) **7094**
Army Reserve Magazine **7154**
Army Times **7155**
The Army and You **7182**
Around the Bargaining Loop **6157**, **6204**, **6250**, **6284**

The Art of Giving Quality Service in the Motor Carrier Industry **6879**
Art and Science of Food Preparation **2472**
"Art Supply Salesperson" in *Career Opportunities in Art* (p. 155) **409**
ARTAFACTS **706**, **1202**
Artistic Woodturning **6444**
ARW Counterline **228**
ARW Wholesaler News **229**
ASA Business Valuation Review **351**
ASA News **5379**
"Asbestos and Insulating Worker" in *Opportunities in Building Construction Trades* (pp. 47-49) **5158**
ASE Preparation Guide **3855**, **3963**, **4045**, **6568**
ASE Test Registration Booklet **3824**, **3929**, **4030**, **6562**
ASE Training Guide **3825**, **3930**, **4031**, **6563**
ASHRAE Journal **4436**
ASHRAE Pocket Guide for Air-Conditioning, Heating, Ventilation & Refrigeration **4418**
Asphalt Paving Machine Operators **7014**
"Asphalt Paving Machine Operators" in *Encyclopedia of Careers and Vocational Guidance* **6667**
Asphalt Roofing Manufacturers Association—Newsletter **5442**
Assembler, Aircraft **5652**
"Assembler" in *Career Information Center* (Vol.9) **5653**
"Assemblers" in *Career Discovery Encyclopedia* (Vol.1, pp. 66-67) **5654**
Assemblers, Electronics Manufacturing **5655**
"Assemblers" in *Encyclopedia of Careers and Vocational Guidance* (Vol.2, pp. 109-112) **5656**
"Assessors and Appraisers" in *Career Discovery Encyclopedia* (Vol.1, pp. 68-69) **255**
"Assessors and Appraisers" in *Encyclopedia of Careers and Vocational Guidance* (Vol.2, pp. 113-115) **256**
ASSET: Q: Where Can You . . . ? **3998**
Assets: A Business, Tax, and Financial Newsletter **124**
Assistant Accountant **1450**
Assistant Bridge Operator **6979**
Associated Builders and Contractors **4398**, **4793**, **4983**, **5056**, **5228**, **5341**, **5527**, **6696**
Associated General Contractors of America **4571**, **4707**, **4794**, **4910**, **5579**, **6697**
Associated General Contractors of America—National Newsletter **4574**, **4727**, **4826**, **4939**, **5593**, **6704**
Associated General Contractors National Convention and Constructor Exposition **4852**
Associated Landscape Contractors of America **3101**
Association of American Railroads **6737**
Association of Boards of Certification **6094**, **6096**
Association Bulletin **3017**
Association for Computer Operations Management **964**
Association of Diesel Specialists International Convention and Exhibit **4051**
Association of Federal Investigators **2276**
Association of Home Appliance Manufacturers **4475**, **4477**
Association of Independent Colleges and Schools **1018**, **1686**, **1690**, **1696**, **1774**, **1777**
Association of Management **900**
Association of Operative Millers Technical Conference and Trade Show **4576**
Association of Professional Drivers **6641**, **6803**, **6859**
Association of Public-Safety Communications Officials - International **1263**
Association of the United States Army Annual Meeting **7180**
ASTA Educational System Catalog **707**
ASTA Officials Directory **680**
ASTA Travel Agency Management Magazine **708**
ASVAB Basics **7135**
ASVAB Review **7136**
ATA Management Conference and Exhibition **6931**
ATA National Truck Driving Championships **6872**
ATEA Journal **1847**
ATI America's Textiles International **6367**
Atlantic Control States Beverage Journal **2616**
Atlantic Offshore Fisherman's Association—Newsletter **3600**
ATMI Member Product Directory **6368**
Atterbury Letter **709**
AudioVideo International **476**
The Auditor's Guide of Eighteen Sixty-Nine **1486**
Auto Assembly Line General Repairman **3795**, **3889**
Auto Body Repair **3826**
Auto Body Repair Helper **7015**
"Auto Body Repair Helper" in *Occu-Facts: Information on 580 Careers in Outline Form* **7016**
Auto Body Repairer **3796**
"Auto Body Repairer" in *Career Information Center* (Vol.12) **3797**
Auto Body Repairing & Repainting **3838**
Auto Body Repairmen! Painters/Refinishers! Become a Proven Pro: Get ASE Certified **3821**, **6560**
"Auto and Car-Parts Sales Representatives" in *Jobs! What They Are—Where They Are—What They Pay* (pp. 328) **410**
Auto and Flat Glass Journal **3856**
Auto Inc. **3857**, **3964**
The Auto Index **3858**, **3965**
Auto Mechanic/Automotive Serviceman **3931**
"Auto Mechanic" in *Exploring Nontraditional Jobs for Women* (pp. 89-95) **3890**
"Auto Mechanic" in *The Desk Guide to Training and Work Advisement* (p. 85) **3891**
Auto Mechanics **3932-3934**
Auto Mechanics for the Complete Dummy **3951**
Auto Mechanics Refresher Course **3952**
Auto Painter **6544**
"Auto Parts Counter Worker" in *Career Information Center* (Vol.10) **411**
"Auto Sales Worker" in *Career Information Center* (Vol.10) **412**
Auto Shop Safety **3798**, **3892**
Auto and Truck International **3859**, **3966**
Autobody Refinishing Handbook **3839**
Autobody Repair & Refinishing **3840**
Autobody Supply and Equipment Market **3967**, **4046**, **4343**, **4588**, **4618**
AutoGlass **3860**, **3968**, **5139**
AutoInc **3861**, **3969**, **6569**
Autoleather Guild **6395**
Automatic Heating **4406**
Automatic Lathe Operator **4965**
Automechanics **3953**
Automechanic's Guide to Electronic Instrumentation & Microprocessor **3954**
Automechanics: Understanding the New Technology **3955**
"Automobile Body Repairer" in *Career Selector 2001* **3883**
"Automobile Body Repairer" in *Jobs Rated Almanac* **3799**
"Automobile Body Repairers" in *Career Discovery Encyclopedia* (Vol.1, pp. 88-89) **3800**
"Automobile Body Repairers" in *Opportunities in Automotive Service Careers* (pp. 25-30) **3801**
Automobile Mechanic Certification Tests **3935**
"Automobile Mechanic" in *Jobs Rated Almanac* **3893**
"Automobile Mechanics" in *American Almanac of Jobs and Salaries* (pp. 524) **3894**
"Automobile Mechanics" in *Career Discovery Encyclopedia* (Vol.1, pp. 90-91) **3895**
"Automobile Mechanics" in *Encyclopedia of Careers and Vocational Guidance* (Vol.2, pp. 135-139) **3896**
"Automobile Painters" in *Opportunities in Automotive Service Careers* (pp. 51-52) **6545**
Automobile Parking Attendant **7017**
"Automobile Repairers" in *Encyclopedia of Careers and Vocational Guidance* (Vol.2, pp. 140-144) **3802**
"Automobile Sales Workers" in *Career Discovery Encyclopedia* (Vol.1, pp. 92-93) **413**
"Automobile Sales Workers" in *Encyclopedia of Careers and Vocational Guidance* (Vol.2, pp. 145-147) **414**
Automobile Salespeople **415**
"Automobile Salesperson" in *College Board Guide to Jobs and Career Planning* (pp. 132-134) **416**
Automobile Technician Certification Tests **3936**
Automobile Technicians (Mechanics) **3897**
Automobile Washer **7018**
"Automobile Washer" in *Occu-Facts: Information on 580 Careers in Outline Form* **7019**
Automotive Aerodynamics: An Update **3884**
Automotive Aftermarket Industry Week **3880**
Automotive Body Repair News **3862**
Automotive Body Repairer **3803**
"Automotive Body Repairer" in *Career Connection II: A Guide to Technical Majors and Their Related Careers* (pp. 22-23) **3804**
"Automotive Body Repairer" in *Occu-Facts: Information on 580 Careers in Outline Form* **3805**
Automotive Body Repairers **3806**
"Automotive Body Repairers" in *Occupational Outlook Handbook* **3807**
Automotive Brake Specialist **3898**
"Automotive Brake Specialist" in *Occu-Facts: Information on 580 Careers in Outline Form* **3899**
Automotive Chassis & Body **3841**
"Automotive Cooling System Technicians" in *Encyclopedia of Careers and Vocational Guidance* (Vol.2, pp. 148-152) **3900**
Automotive Distributor Trends and Financial Analysis **3970**
Automotive Engine Rebuilders Tech Show **3995**
"Automotive Engine Technicians" in *Career Discovery Encyclopedia* (Vol.1, pp. 94-95) **3901**
Automotive Exterior Body Panels **3842**
Automotive Instrument Panels: Design, Materials & Manufacturing **3885**
Automotive Jobbers in the U.S.A. **3971**
Automotive Mechanic **3902**
"Automotive Mechanic" in *100 Best Jobs for the 1990s & Beyond* **3999**
"Automotive Mechanic" in *Career Information Center* (Vol.12) **3903**
Automotive Mechanic Helper **7020**
"Automotive Mechanic Helper" in *Occu-Facts: Information on 580 Careers in Outline Form* **7021**
"Automotive Mechanic" in *Occu-Facts: Information on 580 Careers in Outline Form* **3904**
"Automotive Mechanic" in *VGM's Careers Encyclopedia* (pp. 54-56) **3905**
Automotive Mechanics **3956**
"Automotive Mechanics" in *Jobs! What They Are—Where They Are—What They Pay* (pp. 211-212) **3906**
"Automotive Mechanics" in *Occupational Outlook Handbook* **3907**
The Automotive Messenger **3863**, **3972**
Automotive News **3973**, **6901**
Automotive Painters **3808**
"Automotive Painters" in *Career Discovery Encyclopedia* (Vol.1, pp. 96-97) **6546**
"Automotive Painters" in *Encyclopedia of Careers and Vocational Guidance* **6547**

"Automotive Parts Specialists" in *Opportunities in Automotive Service Careers* (pp. 39-44) **417**
Automotive Service Association **3816**, **3922**, **4021**, **6554**
Automotive Service Industry Association **3817**, **3923**, **4022**, **6555**
Automotive Service Industry Association—Membership Directory **3864**, **3974**, **4047**, **6570**
Automotive Service Industry Association—Product Directory **3831**, **3950**, **4035**, **6565**
Automotive Service Industry Association—Survey of Profitability **3865**
Automotive Service Station Attendant **7022**
"Automotive Service Station Attendant" in *Occu-Facts: Information on 580 Careers in Outline Form* **7023**
Automotive Technician: A Challenging and Changing Career **3908**
"Automotive Technology" in *Career Connection II: A Guide to Technical Majors and Their Related Careers* (pp. 24-25) **3909**
Automotive Technology Development Contractor's Coordination Meeting, 24th: Proceedings **4000**
Available Pay Survey Reports for Other Countries: An Annotated Bibliography **1602**
Available Pay Survey for the U.S.: An Annotated Bibliography **1603**
The Avant Gardener **3131**
Aviation Equipment Maintenance **3782**
"Aviation Maintenance" in *Complete Aviation/Aerospace Career Guide* (pp. 165-169) **3752**
Aviation Maintenance Foundation International **3763**
Aviation Maintenance Management **3774**
"Aviation Maintenance Technology" in *Career Connection II: A Guide to Technical Majors and Their Related Careers* (pp. 26-27) **3753**
Aviation Mechanics Bulletin **3783**
"Avionic Technicians" in *Career Discovery Encyclopedia* (Vol.1, pp. 98-99) **4126**
"Avionics and Marine Electronics" in *Electronic Service Careers* (pp. 71-76) **4127**
"Avionics Technician" in *Career Information Center* (pp. 96-98) **4128**
"Avionics Technician" in *Opportunities in Aerospace Careers* (pp. 34-37) **4129**
"Avionics Technicians" in *Encyclopedia of Careers and Vocational Guidance* (Vol.2, pp. 156-158) **4130**
Avis Rent a Car Scholarship; David Halissey Memorial Scholarship; Simmons Scholarship **689**, **1195**
AWS Directory of Technical Council Committees **5988**
Ayuso Awards; Fernando R. **687**

B

"Baby-sitting: Caring for Children in Their Home" in *Exploring Careers in Child Care Services* (pp. 1-8) **3349**
The Back Forty **3451**
The Badger Sportsman **3601**
Bagel Baker **2395**
"Baitfish Catcher" in *Opportunities in Marine and Maritime Careers* (pp. 110-111) **3555**
Baker **2396**
"Baker" in *Occu-Facts: Information on 580 Careers in Outline Form* (p. 17.30) **2397**
Bakers and Bakery Products Workers **2398**
Bakery Production and Marketing **2473**
Baking Buyer—Yearbook Issue **2465**, **2598**
"Baking and Pastry" in *Opportunities in Culinary Careers* (pp. 99-106) **2399**
Baking & Snack **2474**
Bank Auditing and Accounting Report **548**, **840**
Bank Compliance Magazine **825**, **841**, **1116**
Bank Insurance & Protection Bulletin **549**, **842**
Bank Operations Bulletin **843**
Bank Operations Report **550**, **844**, **1057**, **1402**, **1961**
Bank Personnel News **845**, **1117**
Bank Security News **846**
Bank Security Report **551**, **847**
"Bank Service Occupations" in *Career Discovery Encyclopedia* (Vol.1, pp. 100-101) **803**
Bank Teller **804**, **805**
"Bank Teller" in *Career Information Center* (Vol.1) **806**
"Bank Teller" in *Career Selector 2001* **887**
"Bank Teller" in *Careers in Banking and Finance* (pp. 21-26) **807**
"Bank Teller" in *Guide to Careers Without College* (pp. 53-56) **808**
"Bank Teller" in *Jobs Rated Almanac* **809**
"Bank Teller" in *Occu-Facts: Information on 580 Careers in Outline Form* **810**
"Bank Teller" in *VGM's Careers Encyclopedia* (pp. 60-61) **811**
Bank Tellers Do's & Don'ts **829**
Bank Tellers Job: A Day to Day Reference Guide **830**
"Bank Tellers" in *Jobs! What They Are—Where They Are—What They Pay* (pp. 149) **812**
"Bank Tellers" in *Occupational Outlook Handbook* **813**
Bank Teller's Report **848**
"Bank Worker" in *VGM's Handbook of Business and Management Careers* **814**
The Bankers Magazine **849**
Bankers News **850**, **1118**
"Banking and Financial Services" in *Encyclopedia of Careers and Vocational Guidance* (Vol.1, pp. 51-60) **491**
"Banking" in *Internships 1995* **815**
Banking Policy Report **552**, **851**
Barber **2945**, **2946**
"Barber" in *Career Selector 2001* **3036**
"Barber and Hairstylist" in *Career Information Center* (Vol.5) **2947**
"Barber" in *Occu-Facts: Information on 580 Careers in Outline Form* **2948**
Barber-Stylists **2949**
Barbering Hall of Fame **3007**
"Barbers and Cosmetologists" in *American Almanac of Jobs and Salaries* (pp. 530) **2950**
"Barbers and Cosmetologists" in *Occupational Outlook Handbook* **2951**
"Barbers" in *Encyclopedia of Careers and Vocational Guidance* (Vol.2, pp. 163-165) **2952**
Barbers' Equipment & Supplies—Wholesale Directory **3037**
"Barbers" in *Opportunities in Vocational and Technical Careers* (pp. 76-77) **2953**
Barron's How to Prepare for the Armed Forces Test - ASVAB **7137**
Barron's How to Prepare for the U.S. Postal Service Mail Handler - Mail Processor Examination **1339**
Bartender **2533**
"Bartender" in *Career Information Center* (Vol.8) **2534**
Bartender Magazine **2617**
Bartenders **2535**
"Bartenders" in *Career Discovery Encyclopedia* (Vol.1, pp. 102-103) **2536**
"Bartenders" in *Encyclopedia of Careers and Vocational Guidance* (Vol.2, pp. 166-168) **2537**
"Bartenders" in *Opportunities in Restaurant Careers* (pp. 19-22) **2538**
"Bartenders" in *Opportunities in Vocational and Technical Careers* (pp. 72-73) **2539**
"Bartenders, Waiters, and Bus Persons" in *American Almanac of Jobs and Salaries* (pp. 527) **2540**
Basic Bookkeeping **1462**
Basic Guide to Black & White Darkroom Techniques **6588**
Basic Guide to Payroll **1596**
Basic Make Up Film 2 **3038**
Basic Metric Style Manual for Secretaries **1708**
Basic Petroleum Data Book **5489**
Basic Plumbing Skills **5362**
Basic Principles of Electricity **5108**
Basic Retail Selling Skills **418**, **419**
Basic Secretarial Skills **1629**
Basic Terms of Maintenance **3284**
Basic Training: What to Expect and How to Prepare **7095**
Bassin' **3602**
Bassmaster Magazine **3603**
BC&T News **2475**
"Beautician" in *Encyclopedia of Danger: Dangerous Professions* (pp. 22-25) **3039**
"Beautician" in *How to Get a Job With a Cruise Line* (p. 4) **2954**
Beauty Supplies Dealers Directory **3003**
"Becoming a Chef" in *Opportunities in Culinary Careers* (pp. 17-39) **2400**
Becoming a Helper **3161**, **3288**, **3350**
Becoming a Professional Firefighter **2024**
BEEF **3452**
Beef Today **3453**
Beginning Consultant Training Program **1605**
Being a Long-Term Care Nursing Assistant **2809**
Bench Jewelers **5770**
A Benefit-Cost Analysis of Alternative Library Delivery Systems **1574**
"Benefits Claims Examiner" in *Opportunities in Insurance Careers* (p. 39) **738**
Best's Review (Life/Health Edition) **125**
Best's Review (Property/Casualty Edition) **126**
Better Black & White Darkroom Techniques **6589**
Beverage Alcohol Market Report **2618**
Beyond Secretary **1746**
BIA Directory **4718**
BIA News **4728**
"Bicycle Messenger" in *Encyclopedia of Danger: Dangerous Professions* (pp. 26-29) **1239**
Big Questions? **4966**, **5206**
Big Show Expo Beauty and Hair Care Show **3029**
Bill Collector **739**
"Bill Collector" in *Occu-Facts: Information on 580 Careers in Outline Form* **740**
Bill Collectors **741**
"Billing Clerk" in *Career Selector 2001* **1411**
"Billing Clerk" in *Careers in Trucking* **1404**
Billing Clerks **1405**
"Billing Clerks" in *Encyclopedia of Careers and Vocational Guidance* (Vol.2, pp. 172-174) **1406**
"Billing Clerks" in *Occupational Outlook Handbook* **1407**
Binders Bulletin **6158**
Binders' Guild—Newsletter **6159**
"Bindery Workers" in *Career Discovery Encyclopedia* (Vol.1, pp. 106-107) **6142**
"Bindery Workers" in *Encyclopedia of Careers and Vocational Guidance* (Vol.2, pp. 175-178) **6143**
"Bindery Workers" in *Occupational Outlook Handbook* **6144**
Biodynamics **3454**
Bits 'n Chips **6452**
Black & White Darkroom Techniques **6590**
"Blue Collar Worker Supervisors" in *Encyclopedia of Careers and Vocational Guidance* **5672**
"Blue-Collar Worker Supervisors" in *Occupational Outlook Handbook* **5673**
Blue Reports, Inc. **4729**, **4827**, **4873**, **4940**, **4994**, **5081**, **5140**, **5178**, **5244**, **5282**, **5380**, **5443**, **5543**, **5594**, **5633**
The Blue Seal **3866**
Blueprint Reading for Plumbers: Residential & Commercial **5363**
BMWE Journal **6767**
Boarderline Newsletter **2928**
"Boat Motor Mechanic" in *Career Information Center* (Vol.12) **4592**

"Bodyguard" in Action Careers: Employment in the High-Risk Job Market (pp. 5-14) **2161**
Boilermaker **5745**
"Boilermaker" in *Jobs Rated Almanac* **5746**
"Boilermaker" in *Occu-Facts: Information on 580 Careers in Outline Form* **5747**
Boilermaker Reporter **5595, 5762**
Boilermakers **5748**
Boilermakers-Blacksmiths Reporter **5763**
"Boilermakers" in *Occupational Outlook Handbook* **5749**
"Boilermaking Occupations" in *Encyclopedia of Careers and Vocational Guidance* (Vol.2, pp. 200-203) **5750**
"Boilermaking Worker" in *Career Information Center* (Vol.9) **5751**
"Boilermaking Workers" in *Career Discovery Encyclopedia* (Vol.1, pp. 118-119) **5752**
Book of $16,000-$60,000 Post Office Jobs: Where They Are, What They Pay, and How to Get Them **1316**
Book Bindery Worker **6145**
Book of the Free Trapper **3658**
Bookbinder and Bindery Workers **6146**
"Bookbinder and Bindery Workers" in *Occu-Facts: Information on 580 Careers in Outline Form* **6147**
"Bookbinder" in *Career Information Center* (Vol.3) **6148**
Bookkeeper **1418, 1419**
Bookkeeper-Account Clerk **1451**
"The Bookkeeper-Accountant" in *Opportunities in Office Occupations* (pp. 131-140) **1420**
"Bookkeeper and Accounting Clerk" in *Careers in Banking and Finance* (pp. 26-27) **1421**
"Bookkeeper" in *Career Information Center* (Vol.1) **1422**
"Bookkeeper" in *Career Opportunities in Television, Cable, and Video* (pp. 20-21) **1423**
"Bookkeeper" in *Career Selector 2001* **1487**
"Bookkeeper" in *Jobs Rated Almanac* **1424**
"Bookkeeper" in *Occu-Facts: Information on 580 Careers in Outline Form* **1425**
"Bookkeeper, Secretary, and Clerk" in *Travel & Tourism* (pp. 69-73) **1426, 1630**
"Bookkeepers and Accounting Clerks" in *Jobs! What They Are—Where They Are—What They Pay* (pp. 158) **1427**
"Bookkeepers" in *Career Discovery Encyclopedia* (Vol.1, pp. 122-123) **1428**
"Bookkeeping, Accounting, and Auditing Clerks" in *Occupational Outlook Handbook* **1429**
Bookkeeping and Accounting Clerks **1430**
"Bookkeeping and Accounting Clerks" in *Encyclopedia of Careers and Vocational Guidance* (Vol.2, pp. 209-212) **1431**
"Bookkeeping and Accounting" in *Desk Guide to Training and Work Advisement* (pp. 177-178) **1432**
"Bookkeeping and Accounting Service" in *100 Best Careers for the Year 2000* (pp. 278) **1433**
Bookkeeping & Accounts **1463**
Bookkeeping for Beginners **1464**
"Bookkeeping" in *Career Connection II: A Guide to Technical Majors and Their Related Careers* (pp. 28-29) **1434**
Bookkeeping the Easy Way **1465**
Bookkeeping Made Easy **1466**
Bookkeeping Made Simple **1467**
Bookkeeping for the Nineteen Nineties **1468**
Bookkeeping: Outline of Double Entry Bookkeeping for Small Business & Co-Operatives **1469**
Bookkeeping for a Small Business **1470**
Bookkeeping for Small Organizations: A Handbook for Treasurers & Finance Committees **1471**
"Bookkeeping Systems Operator" in *Occu-Facts: Information on 580 Careers in Outline Form* **1435**
Bookkeeping Systems Operators **1436**
Border Patrol Agent **2200, 2201**
"Bow Repairer and Restorer" in *Career Opportunities in the Music Industry* (pp. 131-132) **4620**
Bowhunter Magazine **3604**
The Brahman Journal **3455**
Braiding **3040**
"Brake Operators, Brakers" in *Encyclopedia of Careers and Vocational Guidance* (Vol.2, pp. 216-218) **6711**
"Brake Specialist" in *Opportunities in Automotive Service Careers* (p. 54) **3910**
"Brakers" in *Career Discovery Encyclopedia* (Vol.1, pp. 126-127) **6712**
Brakes and Clutches **4001**
Branding Hammer Award **6762**
Brangus Journal **3456**
The Breakfast Club **2385**
"Breaking into Sales & Trading on Wall Street" in *Internships Volume 3: Accounting, Banking, Brokerage, Finance & Insurance* (pp. 49-53) **492**
Breathline **2794, 2866**
Brick in Architecture **4730**
Brick Institute of America **4708**
Bricklayer **4678**
"Bricklayer" in *Career Information Center* (Vol.4) **4679**
"Bricklayer" in *Career Selector 2001* **4762**
Bricklayer Helper **7024**
"Bricklayer Helper" in *Occu-Facts: Information on 580 Careers in Outline Form* **7025**
"Bricklayer" in *Jobs Rated Almanac* **4680**
"Bricklayer" in *Occu-Facts: Information on 580 Careers in Outline Form* **4681**
"Bricklayers" in *American Almanac of Jobs and Salaries* (pp. 501) **4682**
"Bricklayers" in *Opportunities in Building Construction Trades* (pp. 49-52) **4683**
Bricklayers and Stonemasons **4684**
"Bricklayers and Stonemasons" in *Career Discovery Encyclopedia* (Vol.1, pp. 128-129) **4685**
"Bricklayers and Stonemasons" in *Encyclopedia of Careers and Vocational Guidance* (Vol.2, pp. 219-221) **4686**
"Bricklayers and Stonemasons" in *Occupational Outlook Handbook* **4687**
Bricklaying **4688**
"A Bright Future in Classified Ad Sales" in *Newspapers Career Directory* (pp. 17-19) **594**
Bringing in Business **852**
"Broker" in *Careers in Banking and Finance* (pp. 27-33) **493**
"Brokerage Clerks and Statement Clerks" in *Occupational Outlook Handbook* **1490**
"Brokers" in *American Almanac of Jobs and Salaries* (pp. 406) **494**
"Brokers: Steady As IT Goes" in *Getting Into Money: A Career Guide* (pp. 58-73) **495**
BSCAI Information Central Guide **3270**
BTA Membership Directory **4213**
BUFFALO! **3457**
Builder **4731, 4828, 4995, 5283, 5444**
Builder Architect **4732, 4829, 4996, 5284, 5445**
Builder/Dealer **4733, 4830, 4997, 5285, 5446**
Builder Insider **4734, 4831, 4998, 5286, 5447**
Builder Magazine **4437**
Builder Notes **4735, 4832, 4999, 5287, 5448**
Building Business & Apartment Management **4736, 4833, 5000, 5288, 5449**
Building Concerns **4737, 4834, 4874, 4941, 5001, 5082, 5141, 5179, 5245, 5289, 5381, 5450, 5544, 5596, 5634**
Building Custodian, Building Superintendent, Custodian Engineer **3222**
"Building Custodian" in *Career Information Center* (Vol.11) **3198**
"Building Custodian" in *Exploring Nontraditional Jobs for Women* (pp. 99-105) **3199**
"Building Custodian" in *Personal Services* (pp. 21-25) **3200**
Building Design & Construction **4835, 5002, 5290, 5451**
Building Industry **4738, 4836, 5003, 5291, 5452**
Building Industry Technology: An Abstract Newsletter **4739, 4837, 4875, 4942, 5004, 5083, 5142, 5180, 5246, 5292, 5382, 5453, 5545, 5597, 5635**
Building Links: Developer Initiatives for Financing Child Care **3335**
Building Maintenance Management **4347**
Building Service Contractors Association International **3102, 3218, 3220**
Building Service Contractors Association International—Services **3276**
Buildings **4740, 4838, 5005, 5293, 5454**
Bulldozer Operator **6668**
"Bulldozer Operator" in *Occu-Facts: Information on 580 Careers in Outline Form* **6669**
Bureau of Wholesale Sales Representatives News **230**
Burnout in Probation & Corrections **2004**
"Bus Driver" in *Career Selector 2001* **6664**
"Bus Driver" in *Exploring Nontraditional Jobs for Women* (pp. 63-69) **6622**
"Bus Driver" in *Jobs Rated Almanac* **6623**
"Bus Driver" in *Transportation* (pp. 27-31) **6624**
Bus Drivers **6625**
Bus Driver's Guide to Commercial Driver Licensing **6643**
"Bus Lines" in *Opportunities in Travel Careers* (p. 59-63) **6626**
Bus Operator-Conductor **6644**
Bus World **6651**
Busdrivers **6627**
"Busdrivers" in *Occu-Facts: Information on 580 Careers in Outline Form* **6628**
"Busdrivers" in *Occupational Outlook Handbook* **6629**
Business & Commercial Aviation **3784**
"Business Computers and Office Equipment Service" in *Electronic Service Careers* (pp. 46-56) **4157**
Business & Data Processing Machine Operators **1886**
Business Farmer-Stockman **3458**
Business and Finance Career Directory **55, 542**
"Business and Financial Careers" in *The Best Jobs for the 1990s and Into the 21st Century* **1, 28, 1059**
Business Insurance: A Sales Skills Introduction **56**
"Business Machine Operator" in *Career Information Center* (Vol.1) **4158**
"Business Machine Repairers" in *Jobs! What They Are—Where They Are—What They Pay* (pp. 247) **4159**
"Business Machine Service Technician" in *VGM's Careers Encyclopedia* (pp. 72-73) **4160**
"Business Machine Service Technician" in *VGM's Handbook of Scientific and Technical Careers* (pp. 18-19) **4161**
Business Management Advisories **5734**
"Business Realtors" in *New York Times Career Planner* (pp. 139-141) **257**
Business Technology Association **4197**
Business Technology Solutions **4214**
Business of Travel: Agency Operations & Administration **699, 1198**
Business Valuation Review **358**
Busy Person's Guide to Selecting the Right Word Processor: A Visual Shortcut to Understanding & Buying, Complete with Checklist & Prod. Guide **1944**
"Butcher or Boucher" in *Opportunities in Culinary Careers* (pp. 61-62) **5685**
"Butchers and Meat, Poultry, and Fish Cutters" in *Occupational Outlook Handbook* **5686**
Buyers Guide of Special Tooling and Precision Machining Services **5735**
Buying Payroll Software **1591**

C

Cabinetmaker **6417**
"Cabinetmaker" in *Occu-Facts: Information on 580 Careers in Outline Form* **6418**
"Cabinetmaker" in *Opportunities in Carpentry Careers* (p. 51) **6419**
"Cabinetmaker" in *Opportunities in Crafts Careers* (pp. 30-31) **6420**
"Cabinetmaking" in *Career Connection II: A Guide to Technical Majors and Their Related Careers* (pp. 36-37) **6421**
Cable Hardware & Technology **4552**
Cable Job Guide **4522**
"Cable Splicer" in *Exploring Nontraditional Jobs for Women* (pp. 26-31) **4523**
"Cable Splicer" in *Opportunities in Electrical Trades* (pp. 58-60) **4524**
Cable Television Systems Technicians and Installers **4525**
Cable Television Technology Handbook **4553**
"Cafeteria Attendant" in *Career Information Center* (Vol.8) **2541**
"Cafeteria Counter Worker" in *Occu-Facts: Information on 580 Careers in Outline Form* **2542**
Calavo Newsletter **3459**
CALF News Magazine **3460**
California Department of Consumer Affairs **7189**
CALTRUX **6902**
Camera & Darkroom Magazine **6606**
Campus Safety Newsletter **2193**
Canadian Secretary's Handbook: An on-the-job Guide for Office Professionals **1709**
CAP Orientation Guide **4002**
Capital Comments **4741**, **4839**, **4876**, **4943**, **5006**, **5084**, **5143**, **5181**, **5247**, **5294**, **5383**, **5455**, **5546**, **5598**, **5636**
Capitol News **2476**, **2619**
Car Maintenance in the U.S.A. **3957**, **4040**, **4388**, **4586**
"Car Rental Agent" in *Career Information Center* (Vol.12) **29**
Car Rental Agents **30**
"Car Rental Agents" in *Encyclopedia of Careers and Vocational Guidance* **31**
"Car or Truck Rental Agent" in *Transportation* (pp. 69-73) **32**
Car Wash Attendants **7026**
Car Wash Operator **7027**
Carbon & Carbro Tissue: You Can Make It! **6591**
Care & Repair of Small Marine Diesels **4610**
Career Choices: Computer Science **927**
Career College Association **2446**, **2587**, **3818**, **4023**, **5970**
Career College Times **2477**, **2620**, **3867**, **4048**, **6005**
A Career in Computer Typesetting **6175**
Career Connections Video Series: Electrician **5109**
Career Connections Video Series: Plumber and Pipefitter **5406**
Career Connections Video Series: Welding **6011**
Career Education **2478**
Career Examination Series: Able Seaman **6980**
Career Examination Series: Account Clerk **1452**
Career Examination Series: Accounting & Auditing Careers **1437**
Career Examination Series: Accounting and Auditing Clerk **1453**
Career Examination Series: Actuarial Clerk **111**
Career Examination Series: Administrative Clerk (USPS) **1340**
Career Examination Series: Administrative Fire Marshal (Uniformed) **2062**
Career Examination Series: Administrative Secretary **1693**
Career Examination Series: Admitting Clerk/Assistant Clerk **1035**
Career Examination Series: Air Conditioning, Heating & Refrigeration Mechanic **4407**
Career Examination Series: Animal Caretaker **2919**
Career Examination Series: Animal Health Aide **2920**
Career Examination Series: Animal Warden **2921**
Career Examination Series: Appraisal Investigator **320**
Career Examination Series: Appraiser **321**
Career Examination Series: Assessment Assistant **779**
Career Examination Series: Assessment Clerk **780**
Career Examination Series: Assistant Building Custodian **3223**
Career Examination Series: Assistant Building Inspector **3201**
Career Examination Series: Assistant Buildings Superintendent **3224**
Career Examination Series: Assistant Captain **6981**
Career Examination Series: Assistant Cashier **18**
Career Examination Series: Assistant Cook **2451**
Career Examination Series: Assistant Custodial Work Supervisor **3225**
Career Examination Series: Assistant Custodian **3226**
Career Examination Series: Assistant Custodian-Engineer **3227**
Career Examination Series: Assistant Electronic Technician **4079**
Career Examination Series: Assistant Fire Marshal **2063**
Career Examination Series: Assistant Foreman **5680**
Career Examination Series: Assistant Gardener **3106**
Career Examination Series: Assistant Head Custodian **3228**
Career Examination Series: Assistant Payroll Supervisor **1586**
Career Examination Series: Assistant Power Plant Operator **6038**
Career Examination Series: Assistant Real Estate Agent/Appraiser **322**
Career Examination Series: Assistant School Custodian-Engineer **3229**
Career Examination Series: Assistant Stockman **1242**
Career Examination Series: Assistant Superintendent of Buildings & Grounds **3230**
Career Examination Series: Assistant Superintendent (Track) **6738**
Career Examination Series: Assistant Teacher **1839**
Career Examination Series: Assistant Train Dispatcher **1267**, **6739**
Career Examination Series: Assistant Water Maintenance Foreman **6097**
Career Examination Series: Associate Cashier **19**
Career Examination Series: Associate Claim Examiner **781**
Career Examination Series: Associate Public Information Specialist **1067**
Career Examination Series: Associate Public Records Officer **1397**
Career Examination Series: Associate Quality Assurance Specialist **5723**
Career Examination Series: Audit Clerk **1454**
Career Examination Series: Auto Body Repairmen **3827**
Career Examination Series: Auto Engineman **3937**
Career Examination Series: Auto Maintenance Coordinator **3938**
Career Examination Series: Auto Mechanic **3939**
Career Examination Series: Auto Mechanic (Diesel) **4032**
Career Examination Series: Automotive Mechanic **3940**
Career Examination Series: Automotive Serviceman **3941**
Career Examination Series: Baker **2452**
Career Examination Series: Barber **2996**
Career Examination Series: Battalion Chief, Fire Dept. **2064**
Career Examination Series: Beginning Office Worker **1036**
Career Examination Series: Beverage Control Inspector **2594**, **5724**
Career Examination Series: Bindery Worker **6154**
Career Examination Series: Body Repair Inspector **3828**
Career Examination Series: Boiler Inspector **5757**
Career Examination Series: Boiler Room Helper **5758**
Career Examination Series: Boilermaker **5759**
Career Examination Series: Bookkeeper **1455**
Career Examination Series: Bookkeeping Machine Operator **1456**
Career Examination Series: Borough Supervisor of School Custodians **3231**
Career Examination Series: Bricklayer **4710**
Career Examination Series: Building Custodian **3232**
Career Examination Series: Building Guard **2185**
Career Examination Series: Building Maintenance Custodian (U.S.P.S.) **3202**
Career Examination Series: Bus Driver **6645**
Career Examination Series: Business Machine Maintainer & Repairer **4198**
Career Examination Series: Butcher **5706**
Career Examination Series: Cable Splicer **4548**
Career Examination Series: Cafeteria Supervisor **2595**
Career Examination Series: Captain, Fire Dept. **2065**
Career Examination Series: Captain, Police Dept. **2281**
Career Examination Series: Carpenter **4797**
Career Examination Series: Cashier **20**
Career Examination Series: Cashier-Cashier (I-II) **21**
Career Examination Series: Cement Mason **4919**
Career Examination Series: Certified General Automobile Mechanic (CGAM) **3942**
Career Examination Series: Certified Shorthand Reporter **1780**
Career Examination Series: Chauffeur **6806**
Career Examination Series: Chief Clerk **1037**
Career Examination Series: Chief Custodian **3233**
Career Examination Series: Chief Data Processing Equipment Operator **966**
Career Examination Series: Chief Deputy Sheriff **2282**
Career Examination Series: Chief Elevator Starter **4311**
Career Examination Series: Chief File Clerk **1511**
Career Examination Series: Chief Fire Marshal **2066**
Career Examination Series: Chief Groundskeeper **3107**
Career Examination Series: Chief Housekeeper **3234**
Career Examination Series: Chief Investigator **782**
Career Examination Series: Chief Law Stenographer **1781**
Career Examination Series: Chief Meat Inspector **5707**, **5725**
Career Examination Series: Chief of Police **2283**
Career Examination Series: Chief Sewage Treatment Plant Operator **6098**
Career Examination Series: Chief of Staff (Sheriff) **2284**
Career Examination Series: Chief Stationary Engineer **6069**

Career Examination Series: Chief of Stenographic Services **1782**
Career Examination Series: Chief Water Treatment Plant Operator **6099**
Career Examination Series: Claims Clerk **783**
Career Examination Series: Claims Investigator **784**
Career Examination Series: Cleaner, Custodian USPS **3235**
Career Examination Series: Cleaner-Helper **7073**
Career Examination Series: Cleaner (T. A.) **3236**
Career Examination Series: Clerical Careers **1038**, **1068**
Career Examination Series: Clerk **1039**
Career Examination Series: Clerk-Carrier (U. S. P. S.) **1341**
Career Examination Series: Clerk-Stenographer **1783**
Career Examination Series: Clerk-Stenographer (I-IV) **1784**
Career Examination Series: Clerk-Technician (U. S. P. S.) **1342**
Career Examination Series: College Secretarial Assistant A/B **1694**
Career Examination Series: Composing Machine Operator **6197**
Career Examination Series: Computer Operator **967**
Career Examination Series: Confidential Secretary **1695**
Career Examination Series: Cook **2453**
Career Examination Series: Correction Counselor **1991**
Career Examination Series: Correction Counselor Trainee **1992**
Career Examination Series: Correction Officer **1993**
Career Examination Series: Correction Officer (I-IV) **1994**
Career Examination Series: Cosmetologist **2997**
Career Examination Series: Court Reporter **1785**
Career Examination Series: Credit and Collection Coordinator **785**
Career Examination Series: Custodial Assistants, Laborers, Workers, and Supervisors **3237**
Career Examination Series: Custodial Foreman **3238**
Career Examination Series: Custodial Laborer (USPS) **3239**
Career Examination Series: Custodial Work Supervisor **3240**
Career Examination Series: Custodial Worker **3241**
Career Examination Series: Custodian **3242**
Career Examination Series: Custodian-Engineer **3243**
Career Examination Series: Customs Security Officer (Sky Marshal) **2186**
Career Examination Series: Day Care Center Aide **3330**
Career Examination Series: Deckhand **6982**
Career Examination Series: Dental Assistant **2698**
Career Examination Series: Department Library Aide **1555**
Career Examination Series: Deputy Chief, Fire Dept. **2067**
Career Examination Series: Deputy Chief Fire Marshal (Uniformed) **2068**
Career Examination Series: Deputy Chief Marshal **2285**
Career Examination Series: Deputy Sheriff **2286**
Career Examination Series: Detective Investigator **2287**
Career Examination Series: Director of Fire Safety **2069**
Career Examination Series: Director of Maintenance **4358**
Career Examination Series: Dispatcher **1268**
Career Examination Series: District Supervisor of School Custodians **3244**
Career Examination Series: Dog Warden **2922**
Career Examination Series: Domestic Worker **3368**
Career Examination Series: Drug Abuse Secretarial Aide **1696**
Career Examination Series: Electrician **5061**
Career Examination Series: Electrician's Helper **5062**
Career Examination Series: Electronic Equipment Maintainer **4359**
Career Examination Series: Electronic Equipment Repairer **4080**
Career Examination Series: Electronic Mechanic **4081**
Career Examination Series: Elevator Inspector **4312**
Career Examination Series: Elevator Mechanic **4313**
Career Examination Series: Executive Secretary **1697**
Career Examination Series: File Clerk **1512**
Career Examination Series: Fire Alarm Dispatcher **1269**
Career Examination Series: Fire Engine Driver **2070**
Career Examination Series: Fire Inspector **2071**
Career Examination Series: Fire Marshal **2072**
Career Examination Series: Fire Officer **2073**
Career Examination Series: Fire Prevention Inspector **2074**
Career Examination Series: Fire Protection Specialist **2075**
Career Examination Series: Fire Safety Officer **2076**
Career Examination Series: Fire & Safety Representative **2077**
Career Examination Series: Fire Safety Technician **2078**
Career Examination Series: Firefighter **2079**
Career Examination Series: Firehouse Attendant **2080**
Career Examination Series: Fireman Examinations-All States **2081**
Career Examination Series: Fireman, Fire Dept. **2082**
Career Examination Series: Fireman-Laborer **2083**
Career Examination Series: Flight Attendant Skills Test **3078**
Career Examination Series: Food Inspector **5726**
Career Examination Series: Food Service Specialist **2596**
Career Examination Series: Foreman **5681**
Career Examination Series: Foreman Auto Mechanic **3943**
Career Examination Series: Foreman Bricklayer **4711**
Career Examination Series: Foreman Cable Splicer **4549**
Career Examination Series: Foreman Carpenter **4798**
Career Examination Series: Foreman (Electrical Power) **5063**
Career Examination Series: Foreman Electrician **5064**
Career Examination Series: Foreman Elevator Mechanic **4314**
Career Examination Series: Foreman (Elevators & Escalators) **4315**
Career Examination Series: Foreman of Gardeners **3108**
Career Examination Series: Foreman of Laborers **5682**, **7074**
Career Examination Series: Foreman Machinist **5831**
Career Examination Series: Foreman of Mechanics **4360**
Career Examination Series: Foreman Painter **5230**
Career Examination Series: Foreman Plasterer **5275**
Career Examination Series: Foreman Plumber **5347**
Career Examination Series: Foreman (Power Cables) **4550**
Career Examination Series: Foreman (Power Distribution) **6039**
Career Examination Series: Foreman (Railroad Watchman) **6740**
Career Examination Series: Foreman Roofer **5426**
Career Examination Series: Foreman Sheet Metal Worker **5530**
Career Examination Series: Foreman (Signals) **6741**
Career Examination Series: Foreman Steamfitter **5348**
Career Examination Series: Foreman (Track) **6742**
Career Examination Series: Forester **3678**
Career Examination Series: Forestry Technician **3679**
Career Examination Series: Gang Foreman (Structures-Group D) (Sheet Metal) **5531**
Career Examination Series: Gang Foreman (Structures-Group E) (Plumbing) **5349**
Career Examination Series: Gang Foreman (Track) **6743**
Career Examination Series: Garageman **3944**
Career Examination Series: Garageman (USPS) **3945**
Career Examination Series: Gardener **3109**
Career Examination Series: Gas & Electric Welder **5974**
Career Examination Series: Glazier **5128**
Career Examination Series: Greenskeeper **3110**
Career Examination Series: Grounds Superintendent **3245**
Career Examination Series: Groundskeeper **3111**
Career Examination Series: Guard Patrolman **2187**
Career Examination Series: Harbormaster **6983**
Career Examination Series: Head Account-Audit Clerk **1457**
Career Examination Series: Head Automotive Mechanic **3946**
Career Examination Series: Head Bus Driver **6646**
Career Examination Series: Head Clerk (Payroll) **1587**
Career Examination Series: Head Custodian **3246**
Career Examination Series: Head Janitor **3247**
Career Examination Series: Head Stationary Engineer **6070**
Career Examination Series: Heavy Equipment Mechanic **4585**
Career Examination Series: High Pressure Plant Tender **6040**
Career Examination Series: Home Health Aide/Homemaker **3186**
Career Examination Series: House Painter **5231**
Career Examination Series: Housing Caretaker **3248**
Career Examination Series: Incinerator Stationary Engineer **6071**
Career Examination Series: Institution Steward **3249**
Career Examination Series: Instrumentman **4644**
Career Examination Series: Insurance Agent (Accident/Health/Fire/Casualty) **112**
Career Examination Series: Insurance Salesman **113**
Career Examination Series: Journeyman in the Printing Crafts **6155**, **6198**, **6239**, **6279**
Career Examination Series: Junior Building Custodian **3250**
Career Examination Series: Key Punch Supervisor **904**
Career Examination Series: Kitchen Supervisor **2454**

Career Examination Series: Law Stenographer **1786**
Career Examination Series: Legal Secretary **1698**
Career Examination Series: Legal Stenographer **1787**
Career Examination Series: Library Assistant **1556**
Career Examination Series: Lieutenant Fire Department **2084**
Career Examination Series: Lineman (Electrical Power) **4551**
Career Examination Series: Lithographic Pressman **6199**
Career Examination Series: Machinist **5832**, **5882**
Career Examination Series: Machinist's Helper **5833**
Career Examination Series: Mail Clerk **1231**, **1343**
Career Examination Series: Mail Handler (USPS) **1344**
Career Examination Series: Mail & Supply Clerk **1232**
Career Examination Series: Maintenance Carpenter **4799**
Career Examination Series: Maintenance Carpenter Foreman **4800**
Career Examination Series: Maintenance Crew Chief **3251**
Career Examination Series: Maintenance (Custodial) Branch Initial-Level Supervisor Examination (U.S.P.S.) **3252**
Career Examination Series: Maintenance Machinist **5883**
Career Examination Series: Maintenance Mason **4712**
Career Examination Series: Maintenance Mason Foreman **4713**
Career Examination Series: Maintenance Mechanic (Automated Mail Processing Equipment) (A.M.P.E.) (U.S.P.S.) **1345**
Career Examination Series: Maintenance Plumber **5350**
Career Examination Series: Maintenance Plumber Foreman **5351**
Career Examination Series: Maintenance Welder **5975**
Career Examination Series: Marine Stoker **6984**
Career Examination Series: Mark-Up Clerk (USPS) **1346**
Career Examination Series: Mason **4920**
Career Examination Series: Mason's Helper **4921**
Career Examination Series: Master Electrician **5065**
Career Examination Series: Master Plumber **5352**
Career Examination Series: Mate **6985**
Career Examination Series: Meat Cutter **5708**
Career Examination Series: Meat Inspector **5727**
Career Examination Series: Meat Inspector-Poultry Inspector **5728**
Career Examination Series: Mechanical Maintainer **4361**
Career Examination Series: Medical Aide **2778**
Career Examination Series: Medical Assistant **2779**
Career Examination Series: Mental Health Assistant **2849**
Career Examination Series: Messenger **1233**
Career Examination Series: Motor Equipment Mechanic **4607**
Career Examination Series: Motor Vehicle Operator (U.S.P.S.) **1347**
Career Examination Series: Multi-Keyboard Operator **968**
Career Examination Series: Nurse's Aide **2850**
Career Examination Series: Nursing Assistant **2851**
Career Examination Series: Offset Printing Machine Operator **6240**
Career Examination Series: Painter **5232**
Career Examination Series: Payroll Auditor/Clerk **1588**
Career Examination Series: Personnel Clerk **1611**
Career Examination Series: Pipefitter **5353**
Career Examination Series: Plasterer **5276**
Career Examination Series: Plumber **5354**
Career Examination Series: Police Cadet **2288**
Career Examination Series: Police Captain **2289**
Career Examination Series: Police Chief **2290**
Career Examination Series: Police Communications Technician **4154**
Career Examination Series: Police Dispatcher **1270**
Career Examination Series: Police Inspector **2291**
Career Examination Series: Police Lieutenant **2292**
Career Examination Series: Police Officer **2293**
Career Examination Series: Policewoman **2294**
Career Examination Series: Postal Inspector (USPS) **1348**
Career Examination Series: Postal Machines Mechanic (USPS) **1349**
Career Examination Series: Postal Supervisor (USPS) **1350**
Career Examination Series: Postal System Examiner (USPS) **1351**
Career Examination Series: Postal Transportation Clerk (USPS) **1352**
Career Examination Series: Postmaster (USPS) **1353**
Career Examination Series: Power Plant Operator **6041**
Career Examination Series: Press Operator **6241**
Career Examination Series: Principal Account-Audit Clerk **1458**
Career Examination Series: Principal Cashier **22**
Career Examination Series: Principal Clerk **1040**
Career Examination Series: Principal Clerk (Personnel) **1612**
Career Examination Series: Principal Clerk-Stenographer **1788**
Career Examination Series: Principal Custodial Foreman **3253**
Career Examination Series: Principal Data Entry Machine Operator **969**
Career Examination Series: Principal File Clerk **1513**
Career Examination Series: Principal Groundskeeper **3112**
Career Examination Series: Principal Library Clerk **1557**
Career Examination Series: Principal Mail & Supply Clerk **1234**
Career Examination Series: Principal Office Assistant **1041**
Career Examination Series: Principal Office Stenographer **1789**
Career Examination Series: Principal Personnel Clerk **1613**
Career Examination Series: Principal Records Center Assistant **1398**
Career Examination Series: Principal Special Investigator **2295**
Career Examination Series: Principal Stationary Engineer **6072**
Career Examination Series: Principal Stenographer **1790**
Career Examination Series: Principal Stenographer (Law) **1791**
Career Examination Series: Principal Telephone Operator **1871**
Career Examination Series: Principal Water Plant Supervisor **6100**
Career Examination Series: Psychiatric Therapy Aide **2852**
Career Examination Series: Public Information Assistant **1069**
Career Examination Series: Public Safety Dispatcher **1271**
Career Examination Series: Public Safety Officer **2296**
Career Examination Series: Quality Control Inspector (USPS) **5729**
Career Examination Series: Radio Telephone Operator **1872**
Career Examination Series: Railroad Caretaker **6744**
Career Examination Series: Railroad Clerk **6745**
Career Examination Series: Railroad Equipment Inspector **6746**
Career Examination Series: Railroad Inspector **6747**
Career Examination Series: Railroad Porter **6748**
Career Examination Series: Railroad Signal Specialist **6749**
Career Examination Series: Railroad Stock Assistant **6750**
Career Examination Series: Railroad Stockman **6751**
Career Examination Series: Railroad Track and Structure Inspector **6752**
Career Examination Series: Real Estate Agent **323**
Career Examination Series: Real Estate Aide **324**
Career Examination Series: Real Estate Appraiser **325**
Career Examination Series: Real Estate Assistant **326**
Career Examination Series: Real Estate Broker **327**
Career Examination Series: Receptionist **1139**
Career Examination Series: Recording Clerk **1399**
Career Examination Series: Records Clerk **1400**
Career Examination Series: Refrigerating Machine Mechanic **4408**
Career Examination Series: Reservation Agent **1188**
Career Examination Series: Resident Buildings Superintendent **3254**
Career Examination Series: Roofer **5427**
Career Examination Series: Rural Carrier (USPS) **1354**
Career Examination Series: Sales Store Worker **472**
Career Examination Series: School Custodial Supervisor **3255**
Career Examination Series: School Custodian **3256**
Career Examination Series: School Custodian-Engineer **3257**
Career Examination Series: Secret Service Agent (Uniformed) **2297**
Career Examination Series: Secretarial Assistant/Stenographer **1699**
Career Examination Series: Secretary **1700**
Career Examination Series: Secretary (Stenography) GS5 **1701**
Career Examination Series: Security Guard **2188**
Career Examination Series: Security Officer **2189**
Career Examination Series: Senior Automotive Mechanic **3947**
Career Examination Series: Senior Automotive Serviceman **3829**
Career Examination Series: Senior Beverage Control Investigator **2597**
Career Examination Series: Senior Boiler Inspector **5730**
Career Examination Series: Senior Building Custodian **3258**
Career Examination Series: Senior Building Guard **2190**
Career Examination Series: Senior Business Machine Operator **970**

Career Examination Series: Senior Campus Security Officer **2191**
Career Examination Series: Senior Capital Police Officer **2298**
Career Examination Series: Senior Cashier **23**
Career Examination Series: Senior Clerical Series **1042**
Career Examination Series: Senior Clerk-Stenographer **1792**
Career Examination Series: Senior Court Reporter **1793**
Career Examination Series: Senior Custodial Assistant (Men) **3259**
Career Examination Series: Senior Custodial Foreman **3260**
Career Examination Series: Senior Data Entry Machine Operator **971**
Career Examination Series: Senior Data Processing Control Clerk **972**
Career Examination Series: Senior Data Processing Equipment Operator **973**
Career Examination Series: Senior Deputy Sheriff **2299**
Career Examination Series: Senior Detective Investigator **2300**
Career Examination Series: Senior Dog Warden **2923**
Career Examination Series: Senior File Clerk **1514**
Career Examination Series: Senior Fire Prevention Inspector **2085**
Career Examination Series: Senior Food Inspector **5731**
Career Examination Series: Senior Groundskeeper **3113**
Career Examination Series: Senior Harbormaster **6986**
Career Examination Series: Senior Incinerator Stationary Engineer **6073**
Career Examination Series: Senior Inspector, Meat & Poultry **5732**
Career Examination Series: Senior Legal Stenographer **1794**
Career Examination Series: Senior Library Clerk **1558**
Career Examination Series: Senior Mail Clerk **1235**
Career Examination Series: Senior Meat Cutter **5709**
Career Examination Series: Senior Meat Inspector **5733**
Career Examination Series: Senior Office Assistant/Worker **1043**
Career Examination Series: Senior Office Stenographer **1795**
Career Examination Series: Senior Offset Printing Machine Operator **6242**
Career Examination Series: Senior Payroll Audit Clerk **1589**
Career Examination Series: Senior Personnel Clerk **1614**
Career Examination Series: Senior Photographic Machine Operator **6586**
Career Examination Series: Senior Real Estate Agent/Appraiser **328**
Career Examination Series: Senior Records Center Assistant **1401**
Career Examination Series: Senior Sewage Treatment Plant Operator **6101**
Career Examination Series: Senior Sewage Treatment Worker **6102**
Career Examination Series: Senior Stationary Engineer **6074**
Career Examination Series: Senior Stationary Engineer (Electric) **6075**
Career Examination Series: Senior Stenographer **1796**
Career Examination Series: Senior Telephone Operator **1873**
Career Examination Series: Senior Water Plant Operator **6103**
Career Examination Series: Senior Water Plant Supervisor **6104**
Career Examination Series: Sewage Plant Operations Supervisor **6105**
Career Examination Series: Sewage Plant Operator **6106**
Career Examination Series: Sewage Pump Operator **6107**
Career Examination Series: Sewage Treatment Operator **6108**
Career Examination Series: Sewage Treatment Operator Trainee **6109**
Career Examination Series: Sewage Treatment Plant Supervisor **6110**
Career Examination Series: Sewage Treatment Worker **6111**
Career Examination Series: Sewage Treatment Worker Trainee **6112**
Career Examination Series: Sheet Metal Worker **5532**
Career Examination Series: Sheriff **2301**
Career Examination Series: Shipment Clerk **1312**
Career Examination Series: Shop Carpenter **4801**
Career Examination Series: Shop Clerk **1295**
Career Examination Series: Shorthand Reporter **1797**
Career Examination Series: Special Agent, Department of Justice **2302**
Career Examination Series: Special Agent FBI **2303**
Career Examination Series: Special Electrical License **5066**
Career Examination Series: State Policewoman **2304**
Career Examination Series: State Trooper **2305**
Career Examination Series: Stationary Engineer **6076**
Career Examination Series: Stationary Engineer (Electric) **6077**
Career Examination Series: Stenographer **1798**
Career Examination Series: Stenographer (Law) **1799**
Career Examination Series: Stenographer-Secretary **1702**, **1800**
Career Examination Series: Stenographer-Typist **1801**
Career Examination Series: Stenographic/Secretarial Associate **1802**
Career Examination Series: Stenographic Secretary **1803**
Career Examination Series: Stenographic Specialist **1804**
Career Examination Series: Stock Clerk **1296**
Career Examination Series: Stockman **7075**
Career Examination Series: Stockroom Worker **1243**
Career Examination Series: Stores Clerk **49**
Career Examination Series: Structural Welder **5976**
Career Examination Series: Superintendent Building Service (U.S.P.S.) **3261**
Career Examination Series: Supervising Cashier **24**
Career Examination Series: Supervising Custodial Foreman **3262**
Career Examination Series: Supervising Glazier **5129**
Career Examination Series: Supervising Janitor **3263**
Career Examination Series: Supervising Legal Stenographer **1805**
Career Examination Series: Supervising Painter **5233**
Career Examination Series: Supervising Stenographer **1806**
Career Examination Series: Supervisor of Building Custodians **3264**
Career Examination Series: Supervisor (Track) **6753**
Career Examination Series: Teaching Assistant **1840**
Career Examination Series: Telephone Operator **1874**
Career Examination Series: Ticket Agent **1189**
Career Examination Series: Toll Equipment Maintenance Supervisor **4362**
Career Examination Series: Toolmaker **5939**
Career Examination Series: Track Equipment Maintainer **6754**
Career Examination Series: Trackman **6755**
Career Examination Series: Tractor Operator **6864**
Career Examination Series: Tractor-Trailer Operator **6865**
Career Examination Series: Train Dispatcher **1272**, **6756**
Career Examination Series: Train Operator **6757**
Career Examination Series: Trainmaster **6758**
Career Examination Series: Transcribing Typist **1807**
Career Examination Series: Transit Electrical Helper Series **5067**
Career Examination Series: Transportation Specialist **6647**
Career Examination Series: Truck Driver **6866**
Career Examination Series: Typists **1931**
Career Examination Series: Warden **1995**
Career Examination Series: Warehouseman **1244**, **7076**
Career Examination Series: Wastewater Treatment Plant Maintenance Supervisor **6113**
Career Examination Series: Welder **5977**
Career Examination Series: Welding Engineer **5978**
Career Examination Series: Window Cleaner **3265**
Career Examination Series: Window Clerk (USPS) **1355**
Career Examination Series: Word Processing Supervisor **905**
Career Guidance Handouts **2455**, **2599**, **3832**, **4036**, **5981**
Career Information for Precision Machining Technology **5810**, **5913**
Career Information in Shoe Repair **6315**
Career Insights **33**, **1022**, **1155**, **1631**, **1887**, **2025**, **2955**, **3048**, **4763**, **5159**, **5309**, **5409**, **5914**, **6219**, **6571**, **6670**, **7028**
Career Legal Secretary **1740**
A Career for Looking Good, Feeling Great **2956**
Career News Digest **2479**
Career in Ophthalmic Medical Assisting **2735**
Career Opportunities **258**
Career Opportunities in the Fire Sprinkler Industry **5310**
Career Opportunities . . . in the Automotive Collision Repair and Refinishing Industry **3809**, **6548**
"A Career in Outdoor Advertising Sales" in *Advertising Career Directory* (pp. 61-64) **595**
Career Planning in Criminal Justice **2386**
Career Planning Manual for Human Resource-Management/Personnel: A Guide to the Practice & Accreditation in the Profession **1606**
"Career Profile: Interview with a Personal Computer Salesman" in *Exploring Careers in the Computer Field* (pp. 95-101) **420**
Career Profiles: Environmental Series **3086**, **6084**
Career Strategies for Secretaries: How to Get Where You Want to Be **1049**, **1142**, **1710**
Career Success Series **57**, **178**, **421**, **816**, **1000**, **1014**, **1632**, **1888**, **2026**, **2202**, **2957**, **3049**, **3663**, **3754**, **3911**, **4348**, **4764**, **5160**, **5311**, **5410**, **6013**, **6149**, **6176**, **6220**, **6263**, **6572**
Career Summary: Farm Manager **3373**
Career Training **2456**, **2600**, **3833**, **4037**, **5982**
Careers in Beauty Culture **2958**
Careers in Child Care **3289**
Careers in Computers & Data Processing **928**
Careers for Crafty People & Other Dextrous Types **5771**, **6422**
Careers in the Dental Profession: Dental Assisting **2659**
Careers in the Dental Profession: Dental Laboratory Technology **6472**
Careers in a Department Store **422**

Careers in Early Childhood Education **3290**
Careers with an Electric Company **4526**, **5021**, **6014**
Careers in Electricity **6015**
Careers in Electronics **4221**
Careers in the Electronics Industry **4066**, **4222**
Careers in Farm Equipment Mechanics **4327**
Careers in Fashion Retailing **423**
Careers in Firefighting **2148**
Careers as a Flight Attendant **3050**
Careers for Gourmets & Others Who Relish Food **2401**
Careers in Health Care **2736**, **2810**
Careers in Health Services: Opportunities for You **2737**
Careers in Insurance: Property and Casualty **58**, **742**
Careers in the Investment World **496**, **817**
"Careers in Law Enforcement" in *Career Planning in Criminal Justice* (pp. 57) **2203**
Careers in Life and Health Claims **743**
"Careers in Operations and the Information Center" in *Careers in Computers* (pp. 34-41) **929**
Careers in Plumbing, Heating, and Cooling **4461**, **5407**
"Careers in Private Security" in *Career Planning in Criminal Justice* (pp. 95-100) **2162**
Careers in Real Estate **259**
Careers in the Restaurant Industry **2655**
Careers in Sheet Metal **5510**
Careers in Travel **1156**
Careers in Truck Driving **6825**
Careers in Trucking **6826**
Careers Working With Animals: An Introduction to Occupational Opportunities in Animal Welfare . . . **2894**
Careers at a Zoo **2895**
Caring **3190**
Caring for the Alzheimer's Resident: A Day in the Life of Nancy Moore **2878**
Carolina Retailer **4110**, **4265**, **4497**
Carolinas Association of Professional Insurance Agents Annual Convention **166**
Carpenter **4802**, **4840**
"Carpenter" in *100 Best Jobs for the 1990s & Beyond* **4853**
"Carpenter" in *BLR Encyclopedia of Prewritten Job Descriptions* **4765**
"Carpenter" in *Career Information Center* (Vol.4) **4766**
"Carpenter" in *Career Selector 2001* **4854**
Carpenter, Construction **4767**
"Carpenter" in *Exploring Nontraditional Jobs for Women* (pp. 6-11) **4768**
"Carpenter Foreman" in *Hard Hatted Women: Stories of Struggle and Success in the Trades* (pp. 122-134) **5674**
"Carpenter" in *Great Careers for People Who Like to Work with Their Hands* (pp. 28-33) **4769**
"Carpenter" in *Hard Hatted Women: Stories of Struggle and Success in the Trades* (pp. 45-54) **4770**
Carpenter Helper **7029**
"Carpenter Helper" in *Occu-Facts: Information on 580 Careers in Outline Form* **7030**
"Carpenter" in *Jobs Rated Almanac* **4771**
"Carpenter" in *Opportunities in Crafts Careers* (pp. 29-30) **4772**
"Carpenter" in *VGM's Careers Encyclopedia* (pp. 75-78) **4773**
Carpenters **4774**
"Carpenters" in *American Almanac of Jobs and Salaries* (pp. 501) **4775**
"Carpenters" in *Career Discovery Encyclopedia* (Vol.1, pp. 146-147) **4776**
"Carpenters" in *Encyclopedia of Careers and Vocational Guidance* (Vol.2, pp. 250-253) **4777**
Carpenter's Manifesto **4810**
"Carpenters" in *Occupational Outlook Handbook* **4778**
"Carpenters" in *Opportunities in Building Construction Trades* (pp. 23-29) **4779**
Carpenter's Toolbox Manual **4811**, **4812**
Carpentry **4780**, **4803**
"Carpentry and Cabinetmaking" in *The Desk Guide to Training and Work Advisement* (pp. 71-73) **4781**
"Carpentry" in *Career Connection II: A Guide to Technical Magors and Their Related Careers* (pp. 38-39) **4782**
Carpentry & Construction **4783**
Carpentry: Framing & Finishing **4813**
Carpet Installer **4855**
"Carpet Installer" in *Occu-Facts: Information on 580 Careers in Outline Form* **4856**
"Carpet Installers" in *Occupational Outlook Handbook* **4857**
"Carpet/Tile Installer" in *Jobs Rated Almanac* **4858**
Carrying the Mail: A Career in Public Service **1317**
"Carver" in *Great Careers for People Who Like to Work with Their Hands* (pp. 10-15) **6423**
Case 'n Base News **3699**
Cashier **2**
"Cashier" in *Career Information Center* (Vol.10) **3**
"Cashier" in *Occu-Facts: Information on 580 Careers in Outline Form* **4**
Cashier/Vault Attendant **5**
"Cashiers" in *Career Discovery Encyclopedia* (Vol.1, pp. 152-153) **6**
Cashiers and Checkers **7**
"Cashiers" in *Encyclopedia of Careers and Vocational Guidance* (Vol.2, pp. 259-262) **8**
"Cashiers" in *Occupational Outlook Handbook* **9**
"Cashiers/Retail Clerk" in *American Almanac of Jobs and Salaries* (p. 532) **10**
"Cashiers" in *Travel Agent* (pp. 171-172) **11**
"Catalog Order Clerk" in *Occu-Facts: Information on 580 Careers in Outline Form* **1576**
Catalog of Products and Services **5144**
Catalog of Publications and Training Materials **5744**, **5842**, **5910**, **5945**, **5959**
Catalogs of Publications and Visual Aids **2121**
Caterer **2543**
Caterers **2544**
Catering Industry Employee **2480**, **2621**
Catgut Acoustical Society—Journal **4654**
Cattle Business **3461**
Cattle Guard **3462**
CDA in State Child Care Licensing **3328**
CDL Commercial Driver License: 104 Helpful CDL Facts **6642**, **6862**
CEA News and Notes Newsletter **2012**
CEE News **5085**
CEES Report **6119**
Cement Mason **4890**
"Cement Mason" in *Career Information Center* (pp. 43-45) **4891**
"Cement Mason" in *Occu-Facts: Information on 580 Careers in Outline Form* **4892**
Cement Masons **4893**
"Cement Masons" in *Career Discovery Encyclopedia* (Vol.1, pp. 156-157) **4894**
"Cement Masons" in *Encyclopedia of Careers and Vocational Guidance* (Vol.2, pp. 267-270) **4895**
"Cement Masons" in *Opportunities in Building Construction Trades* (pp. 29-30) **4896**
"The Center of the Travel Industry - Getting Started in Car Rental" in *Travel and Hospitality Career Directory* (pp. 41-46) **34**
"Central Office Technician" in *Exploring Nontraditional Jobs for Women* (pp. 32-37) **4131**
Ceramic Source **5628**
Certification Examination for Medical Assistants (CMA) **2780**
Certification— Why and How **2781**
Certified Automotive Technician **3912**
Certified Dental Technician **2699**
Certified Electronic Technician (CET) **4082**, **4250**
"Certified Master Chef: the Highest Honor in the Industry" in *Opportunities in Restaurant Careers* (pp. 49-53) **2402**
Certified Professional Secretary (CPS) Examination Review **1703**
Certifier **6120**
The CET Exam: ISCET: Certified Electronics Technician **4083**, **4251**
Chalkline **4742**, **4944**, **5295**, **5637**
The Challenge of a Lifetime: Careers in Animal Science **2896**
Chapter Briefing **853**
Chaptergram **5547**
The Chase **3605**
"Chauffeur" in *BLR Encyclopedia of Prewritten Job Descriptions* **6792**
"Chauffeur" in *Career Information Center* (Vol.5) **6793**
"Chauffeur" in *Career Selector 2001* **6820**
"Chauffeur" in *Jobs Rated Almanac* **6794**
Cheers **2622**
Chef **2481**
"Chef/Cook" in *Guide to Careers Without College* (pp. 97-100) **2403**
"Chef" in *VGM's Careers Encyclopedia* (pp. 84-86) **2404**
Chefs and Cooks **2405**, **2406**
"Chefs and Cooks" in *Jobs! What They Are—Where They Are—What They Pay* (pp. 198) **2407**
"Chefs and Cooks" in *Occu-Facts: Information on 580 Careers in Outline Form* **2408**
"Chefs and Cooks" in *Opportunities in Vocational and Technical Careers* (p. 73) **2409**
"Chefs, Cooks, and Other Kitchen Workers" in *America's 50 Fastest Growing Jobs* (pp. 113) **2410**
"Chefs, Cooks, and Other Kitchen Workers" in *Occupational Outlook Handbook* **2411**
"Chefs, Cooks, and Other Kitchen Workers" in *Opportunities in Restaurant Careers* (pp. 22-31) **2412**
Chemical Plant Operations Training Program **4502**
Child Care Action Campaign **3324**
Child Care ActioNews **3336**
"Child Care Assistant" in *Guide to Careers Without College* (pp. 95-97) **3291**
Child-Care Attendant **3292**
"Child Care Attendant" in *Occu-Facts: Information on 580 Careers in Outline Form* **3293**
"Child Care Center Workers" in *Career Discovery Encyclopedia* (Vol.1, pp. 166-167) **3294**
Child Care Database (CCARE) **3331**
"Child Care Service" in *100 Best Careers for the Year 2000* (pp. 268) **3295**
Child Care Workers **3296**
"Child Care Workers" in *Encyclopedia of Careers and Vocational Guidance* (Vol.2, pp. 288-290) **3297**
Child Care Workers (Institutions) **3298**
"Child-Care Workers" in *Jobs! What They Are—Where They Are—What They Pay* (pp. 347) **3299**
"Child Development Associate" in *Exploring Careers in Child Care Services* (pp. 17-18) **3300**
"Child Development Associate" in *Opportunities in Child Care Careers* (pp. 37-57) **3301**
"Childcare" in *How to Get a Job With a Cruise Line* (pp. 7-13) **3302**
"Childcare Worker" in *100 Best Careers for the Year 2000* (pp. 202-204) **3303**
"Childcare Worker" in *VGM's Careers Encyclopedia* (pp. 91-93) **3304**
"Childcare Workers" in *Opportunities in Vocational and Technical Careers* (pp. 77-78) **3305**
Children's Day-Care Nurse **3306**
Chile Pepper **2482**
Chip Chats **6453**
The Choice of the Future **2413**, **2545**

Choosing an Airline Career: In-Depth Descriptions of Entry-Level Positions, Travel Benefits, How to Apply and Interview **3084**
Choosing the Right Travel School **728**
Choosing & Using a Word Processor **1945**
CHRIE Communique **2483, 2623**
Christmas Trees **3700**
Citizen Soldier: Opportunities in the Reserves **7096**
Citrus and Vegetable Magazine **3463**
City Bus Driver **6630**
Civil Service Arithmetic and Vocabulary **1356**
Civil Service Tests for Basic Skills Jobs **2853, 3114, 3266**
"Claim Adjuster" in *Career Information Center* (Vol.1) **744**
"Claim Agent" in *Careers in Trucking* **745**
"Claim Examiner" in *Career Information Center* (Vol.1) **746**
"Claim Representative" in *VGM's Careers Encyclopedia* (pp. 107-111) **747**
"Claim Representative" in *VGM's Handbook of Business and Management Careers* (pp. 30-32) **748**
"Claim Representatives" in *Jobs! What They Are—Where They Are—What They Pay* (pp. 154) **749**
CLAIMS **127**
Claims Adjusters (Insurance) **750**
"Claims Representatives" in *Opportunities in Insurance Careers* (p. 37) **751**
Classified Sales Representative **596**
Classroom Companion **2457, 2484, 2601, 3834, 4038, 5983**
Clean Water Report **6121**
"Cleaning Service" in *100 Best Careers for the Year 2000* (pp. 274) **3203**
"Clerical and Secretarial Work" in *Exploring Careers Using Foreign Languages* (pp. 51-52) **1633**
"Clerical Supervisor and Manager" in *Careers in Banking and Finance* (pp. 33-34) **888**
"Clerical Supervisor/Office Manager" in *100 Best Jobs for the 1990s & Beyond* **926**
"Clerical Supervisors and Managers" in *Career Discovery Encyclopedia* (Vol.2, pp. 14-15) **889**
"Clerical Supervisors and Managers" in *Encyclopedia of Careers and Vocational Guidance* (Vol.2, pp. 312-313) **890**
"Clerical Supervisors and Managers" in *Occupational Outlook Handbook* **891**
Clerk: Bank, Insurance and Commerce **818, 1408**
"Clerk" in *Careers Inside the World of Offices* (pp. 37-41) **1023**
Clerk, General Office **1024**
Clerk, Information **1060**
"The Clerk" in *Opportunities in Office Occupations* (pp. 49-83) **1025**
"Clerk-Typist" in *BLR Encyclopedia of Prewritten Job Descriptions* **1026**
"Clerk-Typist" in *Career Selector 2001* **1965**
"Clerks" in *Career Discovery Encyclopedia* (Vol.2, pp. 16-17) **35, 1027, 1409, 1498, 1889**
Clerks, Insurance **752**
A Clinical Manual for Nursing Assistants **2859**
Clothing Manufacturers Association—News Bulletin **6299**
CMC News **1562**
Coast Guard Career Opportunities **7097**
"Coast Guard" in *Opportunities in Marine and Maritime Careers* (pp. 97-100) **7098**
Codewatch **2122, 5384**
"Collection Workers" in *Career Discovery Encyclopedia* (Vol.2, pp. 26-27) **753**
"Collection Workers" in *Encyclopedia of Careers and Vocational Guidance* (Vol.2, pp. 332-334) **754**
Collector **792**
"Collectors" in *Jobs! What They Are—Where They Are—What They Pay* (pp. 150) **755**
College of Law Enforcement—Newsletter **2366**
College & University Food Service Manual **2546**
College/University Foodservice Who's Who **2458, 2602**
Collision Repair Guide **3843**
Collision Repair Report **3868**
Color Electronic Prepress Conference **6215**
Colorado State Department of Regulatory Agencies **7190**
Combustion Hot Spot Analysis for Fired Process Heaters: Prediction, Control, Troubleshooting **4419**
Commercial Carrier Journal **6903**
"Commercial Diver" in *Occu-Facts: Information on 580 Careers in Outline Form* **3556**
Commercial Fisher **3557**
"Commercial Fisher" in *Occu-Facts: Information on 580 Careers in Outline Form* **3558**
Commercial Fisheries News **3606**
Commercial Food Equipment Service Association Directory **2528, 2603**
"Commercial and Industrial Electronic Equipment Repairers" in *Occupational Outlook Handbook* **4067**
Commercial Investment Real Estate Journal **359**
Commercial Lending Review **854**
Commercial Real Estate Digest **360**
The Commercial Record **361**
Commission on Opticianry Accreditation **6529**
Committee Manual **6300**
Commodities Trader **497**
"Commodities Traders: Upping the Stakes" in *Getting Into Money: A Career Guide* (pp. 91-107) **498**
"Commodity Trader" in *Careers in Banking and Finance* (pp. 37-39) **499**
Common Secretarial Mistakes & How to Avoid Them **1711**
Communication Skills **637, 1199**
"Communications Equipment Mechanic" in *Jobs Rated Almanac* **4132**
"Communications Equipment Mechanic" in *VGM's Careers Encyclopedia* (pp. 111-114) **4133**
"Communications Equipment Mechanics" in *Career Discovery Encyclopedia* (Vol.2, pp. 38-39) **4134**
"Communications Equipment Mechanics" in *Encyclopedia of Careers and Vocational Guidance* (Vol.2, pp. 352-355) **4135**
"Communications Equipment Mechanics" in *Occupational Outlook Handbook* **4136**
"Communications Mechanic" in *Opportunities in Electrical Trades* (pp. 83-84) **4137**
"Communications Technician" in *VGM's Handbook of Scientific and Technical Careers* (pp. 28-30) **4138**
"Communications or Telecommunications" in *Careers in High Tech* (p. 104) **4139**
The Communique **979**
Community Associations Institute **103, 315**
"Companion" in *Career Information Center* (Vol.5) **3351**
Compensation and Benefits Review **909, 1617**
CompFlash **910**
The Complete Book of Birdhouse Contruction for Woodworkers **6445**
Complete Course in Professional Piano Tuning, Repair & Rebuilding **4648**
The Complete Custodial Handbook **3271**
The Complete Electronics Career Guide **4068**
The Complete Guide to Automotive Refinishing **3844**
The Complete Guide to Motorcycle Mechanics **4611**
Complete Handbook for Dental Auxiliaries **6500**
The Complete Handbook of Leathercrafting **6337**
Complete Secretary's Handbook **1634**
Compliance and Legal Seminar **572**
"Compositor/Typesetter" in *Jobs Rated Almanac* **6177**
"Compositors and Typesetters" in *Encyclopedia of Careers and Vocational Guidance* (Vol.2, pp. 356-359) **6178**
The Comprehensive Custodial Training Manual **3272**
Comprehensive Review of Dental Assisting **2660**
Computer Business **980**
Computer Careers: The Complete Pocket Guide to America's Fastest-Growing Job Market **930**
Computer Graphics World **981**
Computer Industry Update **982**
"Computer Maintenance" in *Career Connection II: A Guide to Technical Majors and Their Related Careers* (pp. 40-41) **4162**
Computer Numerical Control Machine Operators **931**
"Computer and Office Machine Repairers" in *America's 50 Fastest Growing Jobs* (pp. 131) **4163**
"Computer and Office Machine Repairers" in *Occupational Outlook Handbook* **4164**
"Computer and Office Machine Repairers" in *The Best Jobs for the 1990s and Into the 21st Century* **4165**
"Computer Operating" in *Exploring High Tech Careers* **932**
"Computer Operating Personnel" in *American Almanac of Jobs and Salaries* (pp. 511) **933**
"Computer Operations" in *Careers in High Tech* (pp. 34-36) **934**
The Computer Operations Manager **983**
"Computer Operations" in *Opportunities in Information Systems Careers* (p. 25) **935**
"Computer Operator" in *100 Best Careers for the Year 2000* (pp. 107-109) **936**
"Computer Operator" in *100 Best Jobs for the 1990s & Beyond* **995**
"Computer Operator" in *BLR Encyclopedia of Prewritten Job Descriptions* **937**
"Computer Operator" in *Career Information Center* (Vol.1) **938**
"Computer Operator" in *Career Selector 2001* **996**
"Computer Operator" in *Careers in Banking and Finance* (pp. 39-41) **939**
"Computer Operator" in *Exploring Careers in the Computer Field* **940**
"Computer Operator" in *Guide to Careers Without College* (pp. 51-53) **941**
"Computer Operator" in *Jobs Rated Almanac* **942**
"Computer Operator" in *Opportunities in Data Processing Careers* (pp. 49-51) **943**
Computer Operators **944**
"Computer Operators" in *Career Discovery Encyclopedia* (Vol.2, pp. 42-43) **945**
"Computer Operators" in *Jobs! What They Are—Where They Are—What They Pay* (pp. 75) **946**
"Computer Operators: Keepers of the Machines" in *Careers for Women Without College Degrees* (pp. 189-192) **947**
"Computer Operators" in *Opportunities in Vocational and Technical Careers* (p. 48) **948**
Computer Parts and Supplies Directory **4200**
"Computer and Peripheral Equipment Operators" in *Encyclopedia of Careers and Vocational Guidance* **949**
"Computer and Peripheral Equipment Operators" in *Occupational Outlook Handbook* **950**
Computer Program & Systems Analysis **1890**
Computer Repair Technician **4166**
Computer Report and PC Street Price Index **984**
"Computer Service" in *Opportunities in Vocational and Technical Careers* (pp. 108-109) **4167**
Computer Service and Repair Directory **997**
Computer Service Technician **4168**
"Computer Service Technician" in *100 Best Careers for the Year 2000* (pp. 123-125) **4169**

"Computer Service Technician" in *100 Best Jobs for the 1990s & Beyond* **4218**
"Computer Service Technician" in *Occu-Facts: Information on 580 Careers in Outline Form* **4170**
"Computer Service Technician" in *Opportunities in Data Processing Careers* (pp. 66-67) **4171**
"Computer Service Technician" in *VGM's Careers Encyclopedia* (pp. 116-118) **4172**
"Computer Service Technician" in *VGM's Handbook of Scientific and Technical Careers* **4173**
Computer Service Technicians **4174**
"Computer Service Technicians" in *Career Discovery Encyclopedia* (Vol.2, pp. 46-47) **4175**
"Computer Service Technicians" in *Encyclopedia of Careers and Vocational Guidance* (Vol.2, pp. 363-367) **4176**
"Computer Service Technicians" in *Jobs! What They Are—Where They Are—What They Pay* (pp. 76) **4177**
"Computer Service Technicians: Troubleshooting in High Tech" in *Careers for Women Without College Degrees* (pp. 185-189) **4178**
"Computer Servicer" in *Career Information Center* (Vol.1) **4179**
"Computer Servicing and Troubleshooting" in *The Complete Electronics Career Guide* (pp. 81-86) **4180**
Computer Technician's Handbook **4201**
Computer Troubleshooting & Maintenance **4202**
Computer Wave **985**, **4215**
Computer Work & Computer Trainee Exams **974**
Computerized Maintenance Management Systems **4203**
Computers and Computing Information Resources Directory **998**
Computers in Design Construction & Operation of Automobiles **3886**
Computers - How to Break into the Field **951**
"Computers and Information Systems" in *Where the Jobs Are: The Hottest Careers for the 90s* (pp. 77-96) **4181**
"Computers" in *Internships 1995* **952**, **4182**
Computers & Medicine **2795**, **2867**
"Computing or Information Center Operations" in *Opportunities in Computer Science Careers* **953**
Computing, Operating Personnel, Electronic **954**
A Concise Guide to Upholstery Fabrics **6401**
Concrete Abstracts **4945**
Concrete Construction Magazine **4946**
Concrete International **4947**
Concrete Masonry News **4948**
"Concrete Masons and Terrazzo Workers" in *Occupational Outlook Handbook* **4897**
Concrete Products **4949**
Concrete Sawing and Drilling Association **4911**, **4916**
"Conductors" in *American Almanac of Jobs and Salaries* (pp. 446) **6713**
"Conductors" in *Career Discovery Encyclopedia* (Vol.2, pp. 48-49) **6714**
"Conductors" in *Opportunities in Travel Careers* (p. 54) **6715**
Conference on Roofing Technology **5473**
Confidential Newsletter **231**
Confined Space Rescue **2149**
Congress of Automotive Repair and Service Cars **3881**, **3996**
Connecticut/Rhode Island Telephone Tickler **114**
Connecticut State Department of Consumer Protection - Bureau of Licensing and Administration **7191**
Connection **4438**, **5385**
ConnStruction **4743**, **4841**, **4877**, **4950**, **5007**, **5086**, **5145**, **5182**, **5248**, **5296**, **5386**, **5456**, **5548**, **5599**, **5638**
Conservation Gains in the Tax Reform Act **3426**
Consider a Career as an Insurance Agent **59**
Considering a Secretarial Service?: Possibilities for Income **1635**
CONSTRUCTION **4744**, **4842**, **4878**, **4951**, **5008**, **5087**, **5146**, **5183**, **5249**, **5297**, **5387**, **5457**, **5549**, **5600**, **5639**
Construction: Basic Principles **4382**, **4784**, **4898**, **5022**, **5312**
"Construction Carpenter" in *Occu-Facts: Information on 580 Careers in Outline Form* **4785**
Construction Cluster **4689**, **4786**, **4899**, **5023**, **5115**, **5161**, **5261**, **5313**, **5411**, **5511**, **5562**
"Construction Electrician" in *Career Information Center* (Vol.4) **5024**
"Construction Electrician Helper" in *Occu-Facts: Information on 580 Careers in Outline Form* **7031**
"Construction Electrician" in *Occu-Facts: Information on 580 Careers in Outline Form* **5025**
"Construction Electrician" in *Opportunities in Electrical Trades* (pp. 44-46) **5026**
"Construction Equipment Mechanic" in *Career Information Center* (Vol.4) **4577**
Construction Helpers **7032**
"Construction Helpers" in *Occu-Facts: Information on 580 Careers in Outline Form* **7033**
Construction Ironworkers **5563**
"Construction Laborer" in *Career Information Center* (Vol.4) **7034**
Construction Laborers **7035**
Construction Machine Operators **7036**
"Construction Machinery Operator" in *Guide to Careers Without College* (pp. 77-79) **6671**
Construction News **4745**, **4843**, **4879**, **4952**, **5009**, **5088**, **5147**, **5184**, **5250**, **5298**, **5388**, **5458**, **5550**, **5601**, **5640**
Construction Newsletter **4746**, **4844**, **4880**, **4953**, **5010**, **5089**, **5148**, **5185**, **5251**, **5299**, **5389**, **5459**, **5551**, **5602**, **5641**
"Construction Painter" in *Occu-Facts: Information on 580 Careers in Outline Form* **5207**
Construction Supervision & Safety Letter **5683**
Constructor **4575**
Consumable Electrode Processes in Welding Automation **5989**
Consumer Credit Delinquency Bulletin **855**
Consumer Credit and Truth-in-Lending Compliance Report **1011**
"Consumer Electronic Services" in *Electronic Service Careers* (pp. 57-62) **4223**
Consumer Electronics Service Technician **4224**
Consumer Electronics Technicians **4225**
"Consumer Electronics" in *The Complete Electronics Career Guides* (pp. 30-32) **4226**
Consumer Finance Newsletter **1012**
Consumer Lending: From Application to Servicing **856**
"Consumer Servicing" in *The Complete Electronics Career Guide* (pp. 65-69) **4227**
Consumer Trends **1013**
Consumers Electronics Instructors Conference **4124**, **4273**
Contact Lens Spectrum **6532**
Contemporary Topics in Laboratory Animal Science **2929**
Contractors Guide **5186**, **5460**
Convenient Automotive Services Retailer **3869**, **3975**
Convention Manual **2930**
The Conversion & Seasoning of Wood **6446**
"Cook" in *BLR Encyclopedia of Prewritten Job Descriptions* **2414**
"Cook" in *Career Selector 2001* **2529**
"Cook and Chef" in *Career Information Center* (Vol.8) **2415**
"Cook and Chef: The Cornerstones of a Good Restaurant" in *Careers in the Restaurant Industry* (pp. 35-45) **2416**
Cook, Domestic Service **3352**
Cook, Short Order **2417**
Cookbook Digest **2485**
Cookies **2486**
Cooking Contest Chronicle **2487**
"Cooks and Chefs" in *American Almanac of Jobs and Salaries* (pp. 528) **2418**
"Cooks, Chefs, and Bakers" in *Encyclopedia of Careers and Vocational Guidance* (Vol.2, pp. 384-388) **2419**
"Cooks and Chefs" in *Career Discovery Encyclopedia* (pp. 58-59) **2420**
Cooperative Farmer **3464**
Copier Repair Technician **4183**
Coping With Sexism in the Military **7099**
The Corey Guide to Postal Exams **1357**
Corhealth **2717**, **2796**, **2868**
Corn Farmer **3465**
Corporate Collector Currents **793**
Corporate Real Estate Executive **362**
The Corporate Secretary **1741**
Corporate Travel's Black Book **1190**
Correction Officer **1968**, **1996**
"Correction Officer" in *100 Best Careers for the Year 2000* (pp. 194-197) **1969**
"Correction Officer" in *Career Information Center* (Vol.11) **1970**
"Correction Officer" in *Jobs Rated Almanac* **1971**
Correction Officer Promotion Tests **1997**
"Correction Officers" in *America's 50 Fastest Growing Jobs* (pp. 116) **1972**
"Correction Officers" in *Career Discovery Encyclopedia* (Vol.2, pp. 62-63) **1973**
"Correction Officers" in *Encyclopedia of Careers and Vocational Guidance* (Vol.2, pp. 392-395) **1974**
"Correction Officers" in *Jobs! What They Are—Where They Are—What They Pay* (pp. 227) **1975**
"Correction Officers" in *Occupational Outlook Handbook* **1976**
"Correction Officers" in *Opportunities in Vocational and Technical Careers* (pp. 76-90) **1977**
Correction Promotion Course (One Volume) **1998**
"Correctional Officer" in *Career Selector 2001* **2019**
Correctional Officer Correspondence Course **1978**
"Correctional Officer" in *Encyclopedia of Danger: Dangerous Professions* (pp. 38-41) **2020**
"Correctional Officer" in *Great Careers for People Who Like Working with People* (pp. 43) **1979**
Correctional Officer II Courespondence Course **1980**
Correctional Officer Resource Guide **2005**
Correctional Officer Series **1981**
Correctional Officers **1982**
Correctional Officers: Power, Pressure & Responsibility **2006**
Corrections Digest **2013**
Corrections Forum **2014**
"Corrections Officer" in *Career Planning in Criminal Justice* (pp. 70-72) **1983**
"Corrections Officer/Guard Jailer" in *100 Best Jobs for the 1990s & Beyond* **2021**, **2197**
"Corrections Officer" in *VGM's Careers Encyclopedia* (pp. 120-122) **1984**
"Corrections Officers" in *American Almanac of Jobs and Salaries* (pp. 96) **1985**
"Corrections and Rehabilitation" in *Opportunities in Law Enforcement and Criminal Justice Careers* (pp. 110-124) **1986**
Corrections Today **2015**
The Corridor Real Estate Journal **363**
Cosmetic Insiders' Report **3018**
Cosmetic and Personal Services **2959**
Cosmetics, Hair & Beauty/Shanghai **3030**
Cosmetics Hair & Beauty/Shenzhen **3031**
Cosmetologist **2421**
"Cosmetologist" in *100 Best Jobs for the 1990s & Beyond* **3041**

"Cosmetologist" in *Career Information Center* (Vol.5) **2960**
"Cosmetologist" in *Career Selector 2001* **3042**
"Cosmetologist" in *Occu-Facts: Information on 580 Careers in Outline Form* **2961**
"Cosmetologist" in *VGM's Careers Encyclopedia* (pp. 122-124) **2962**
Cosmetologists **2963**
"Cosmetologists: Beauty Preservers" in *Careers for Women Without College Degrees* (pp. 254-257) **2964**
"Cosmetologists" in *Career Discovery Encyclopedia* (Vol.2, pp. 64-65) **2965**
"Cosmetologists" in *Encyclopedia of Careers and Vocational Guidance* (Vol.2, pp. 396-398) **2966**
"Cosmetologists" in *Opportunities in Vocational and Technical Careers* (pp. 76-90) **2967**
Cosmetologist's State Board Exam Review in English **2998**
Cosmetology **2999**, **3000**
"Cosmetology and Barbering" in *Career Connection II: A Guide to Technical Majors and Their Related Careers* (pp. 44-45) **2968**
Cosmetology . . . Excellent Opportunities . . . **2969**
Cost of Doing Business Study **4344**
Cotton Farming **3466**
Cotton Grower **3467**
Cotton Trade Report **3468**
Council for Early Childhood Professional Recognition **3325**
Council on Hotel, Restaurant, and Institutional Education **2447**, **2588**
Council on Library-Media Technical-Assistants **1552**, **1554**
"Counter and Rental Clerks" in *America's 50 Fastest Growing Jobs* (pp. 93) **36**
"Counter and Rental Clerks" in *Occupational Outlook Handbook* **37**
"Counter and Retail Clerks" in *Encyclopedia of Careers and Vocational Guidance* (Vol.2, pp. 405-407) **38**
Counter Worker, Cafeteria **39**
Counterman **51**
Country Chronicle **2488**
Country Folks **3469**
County Sheriff **2204**
Court Officer, Senior Court Officer, Court Clerk **1808**
Court Reporter **1749**
"Court Reporter" in *100 Best Jobs for the 1990s & Beyond* **1822**
"Court Reporter" in *Occu-Facts: Information on 580 Careers in Outline Form* **1750**
"Court Reporter (Short Hand Reporter)" in *Career Planning in Criminal Justice* (pp. 62-63) **1751**
Court Reporters **1752**
"Court Reporters: $40,000-$50,000 Recorders" in *Careers for Women Without College Degrees* (pp. 231-233) **1753**
"Court Reporters" in *Career Discovery Encyclopedia* (Vol.2, pp. 70-71) **1754**
"Court Reporters" in *Encyclopedia of Careers and Vocational Guidance* (Vol.2, pp. 408-410) **1755**
"Court Reporting" in *Career Connection II: A Guide to Technical Majors and Their Related Careers* (pp. 46-47) **1756**
A Cowboy Detective: A True Story of Twenty-Two Years with a World-Famous Detective Agency **2387**
CPCU Journal **128**
Crane Operator **6672**
Craneman **6673**
Creative Projects & Processes **6592**
Cred-Alert **794**, **1014**
"Credit Analyst" in *Career Selector 2001* **1021**
Credit Analysts (Bankers) **1001**
Credit Card Management **1015**
"Credit Checker" in *Career Information Center* (Vol.1) **1002**
"Credit Clerks and Authorizers" in *Jobs! What They Are—Where They Are—What They Pay* (pp. 159) **1003**
"Credit Clerks and Authorizers" in *Occupational Outlook Handbook* **1004**
"Credit Collector" in *Career Information Center* (Vol.1) **756**
Credit Memo **1016**
Credit and Sales Reference Directory **3976**
Credit Workers **1005**
Credit World **1017**
Crime Control Digest **2016**, **2367**
Criminal Investigation Award **2321**
Criminal Justice Digest **2017**
Crop Farming Workers **3374**
Crop Science **3470**
Crow's Weekly Letter **3701**, **6454**
"Culinary Arts" in *College Majors and Careers: A Resource Guide for Effective Life Planning* (pp. 45-46) **2422**
Culinary Arts Salon **2462**
Culinary Olympic Cookbook **2466**
The Cultivator **3132**
Current Opinion in Dentistry **2718**
Custodial Methods and Procedures Manual **3273**
"Custodial Services Manager" in *BLR Encyclopedia of Prewritten Job Descriptions* **3204**
"Custodial Workers" in *American Almanac of Jobs and Salaries* (p. 531) **3205**
Custodian **3206**
Custodian, Building **3207**
"Custodian, Building" in *Occu-Facts: Information on 580 Careers inOutline Form* **3208**
Custodians **3209**
"Custom Tailor and Dressmaker" in *Career Information Center* (Vol.5) **6268**
Custom Tools for Woodworkers **6447**
"Custom Upholsterer" in *Career Information Center* (Vol.5) **6383**
"Customer Service Assistant" in *Career Opportunities in Art* (p. 135) **757**
"Customer Service Representative" in *Career Opportunities in Television, Cable, and Video* (pp. 170-171) **758**
"Customer Service Representative" in *Careers in Trucking* **759**
"Customer Service Representative" in *Jobs! What They Are—Where They Are—What They Pay* (pp. 248) **760**
"Customer Services Sales" in *Careers in Marketing* (pp. 68-69) **597**
Customs Officers **2163**
"Customs Worker" in *Career Information Center* (Vol.11) **2205**
"Customs Worker" in *Occu-Facts: Information on 580 Careers in Outline Form* **2206**
Customs Workers **2207**
CWB: Custom Woodworking Business **6455**

D

D. Howard Doane Award **3418**
Daily Construction Reporter **4747**, **4845**, **4881**, **4954**, **5011**, **5090**, **5149**, **5187**, **5252**, **5300**, **5390**, **5461**, **5552**, **5603**, **5642**
Dairy-Deli Bake Digest **2489**
Dairy Farmers **3375**
"Dairy Farmers" in *Career Discovery Encyclopedia* (Vol.2, pp. 74-75) **3376**
Dairy and Field Crops Digest **3471**
Dames Employees: The Feminization of Postal Workers in Nineteenth-Century France **1389**
Darkroom **6593**
The Darkroom Book **6594**
The Darkroom Handbook **6595**
"Darkroom Technician" in *Career Information Center* (Vol.3) **6573**
"Darkroom Technicians" in *Career Discovery Encyclopedia* (Vol.2, pp. 78-79) **6574**
"Darkroom Technicians" in *Encyclopedia of Careers and Vocational Guidance* **6575**
Darkroom Two **6596**
Data Entry Awareness Report **986**, **1962**
"Data Entry" in *Careers in High Tech* (pp. 31-32) **1891**
"Data Entry Clerks" in *Encyclopedia of Careers and Vocational Guidance* (Vol.2, pp. 431-433) **1892**
"Data Entry Keyer" in *Career Information Center* (Vol.1) **1893**
"Data Entry Keyer" in *Careers in Banking and Finance* (pp. 41-42) **1894**
"Data Entry Keyer" in *Careers Inside the World of Offices* (pp. 10,17) **1895**
Data Entry Management Association **901**, **1930**
Data Entry Operator **1896**
"Data Entry Operator" in *BLR Encyclopedia of Prewritten Job Descriptions* **1897**
"Data Entry Operator" in *Occu-Facts: Information on 580 Careers in Outline Form* **1898**
Data Entry Operators **1899**
"Data Entry Specialist" in *Opportunities in Data Processing Careers* (pp. 52-53) **1900**
Data Processing **1932**, **1933**
Data Processing: Career Opportunities for Hearing Impaired People **1901**
Data Processing Management Association **902**, **903**
DataWorld **987**
Dateline ASTA **710**
Davis Award; W. Allison and Elizabeth Stubbs **3118**
Day Care Provider **3307**
"Day Care Providers" in *Opportunities in Child Care Careers* (pp. 42-43) **3308**
"Day Care Worker" in *Career Information Center* (Vol.11) **3309**
Day Care Workers **3310**
Deal Scholarship Award; Alphonso **2322**
Dealing With Diabetes **6344**
DECA Advisor **232**
DECA Guide **225**
Decorative Wood Crafts **6456**
Degree of Honor Review **129**
Delaware State Department of Administrative Services - Division of Professional Regulations **7192**
Deli-Bake Advocate **2490**
Delta Farm Press **3472**
Delta Pride News **3607**
Demeter Association **3406**, **3409**
Dental Abstracts **2719**
"Dental Assistance" in *Career Connection II: A Guide to Technical Majors and Their Related Careers* (pp. 52-53) **2661**
The Dental Assistant **2662**, **2663**, **2720**
"Dental Assistant" in *100 Best Careers for the Year 2000* (pp. 29-31) **2664**
"Dental Assistant" in *150 Careers in the Health Care Field* **2665**
"Dental Assistant" in *Allied Health Professions* (pp. 16-17; 138) **2733**
"Dental Assistant" in *Career Information Center* (Vol.7) **2666**
"Dental Assistant" in *Career Selector 2001* **2734**
"Dental Assistant" in *Careers in Health Care* (pp. 50-54) **2667**
Dental Assistant Certification **2696**
"Dental Assistant" in *Health Care* (pp. 57-61) **2668**
"Dental Assistant" in *Occu-Facts: Information on 580 Careers in Outline Form* **2669**
"Dental Assistant" in *Opportunities in Dental Care Careers* (pp. 17-18, 46-47) **2670**
"Dental Assistant" in *Opportunities in Health and Medical Careers* (p. 15) **2671**
"Dental Assistant" in *Opportunities in Paramedical Careers* (pp. 40-49) **2672**
Dental Assistant Techniques **2710**
"Dental Assistant" in *VGM's Careers Encyclopedia* (pp. 132-134) **2673**

"Dental Assistant" in *VGM's Handbook of Health Care Careers* **2674**
Dental Assistants **2675**
"Dental Assistants" in *America's 50 Fastest Growing Jobs* (pp. 118) **2676**
"Dental Assistants" in *Career Discovery Encyclopedia* (Vol.2, pp. 84-85) **2677**
"Dental Assistants: Chairside Assistants" in *Careers for Women Without College Degrees* (pp. 208-211) **2678**
"Dental Assistants and Dental Hygienists" in *American Almanac of Jobs and Salaries* (pp. 480) **2679**
"Dental Assistants" in *Encyclopedia of Careers and Vocational Guidance* (Vol.2, pp. 444-446) **2680**
"Dental Assistants and Hygienists" in *Jobs! What They Are—Where They Are—What They Pay* (p. 180) **2681**
"Dental Assistants" in *Occupational Outlook Handbook* **2682**
Dental Assisting **2700**
Dental Assisting: Basic & Dental Sciences **2683**
Dental Assisting Exam Preparation **2684**
Dental Assisting Manuals **2711**
Dental Assisting National Board **2694, 2697**
Dental Assisting Scholarship Program **2709**
Dental Clinics of North America **2721**
Dental Computer Newsletter **988**
Dental Lab Tech Scholarship Program **6499**
Dental Laboratory Technician **6473**
"Dental Laboratory Technician" in *150 Careers in the Health Care Field* **6474**
"Dental Laboratory Technician" in *Career Information Center* (Vol.7) **6475**
"Dental Laboratory Technician" in *Careers in Health Care* (pp. 59-61) **6476**
"Dental Laboratory Technician" in *Health Care* (pp. 63-67) **6477**
"Dental Laboratory Technician" in *Jobs Rated Almanac* **6478**
"Dental Laboratory Technician" in *Occu-Facts: Information on 580 Careers in Outline Form* **6479**
"Dental Laboratory Technician" in *Opportunities in Health and Medical Careers* (p. 75) **6480**
"Dental Laboratory Technician" in *VGM's Handbook of Health Care Careers* **6481**
"Dental Laboratory Technicians" in *Career Discovery Encyclopedia* (Vol.2, pp. 88-89) **6482**
"Dental Laboratory Technicians" in *Encyclopedia of Careers and Vocational Guidance* (Vol.2, pp. 450-454) **6483**
"Dental Laboratory Technicians" in *Health Care Job Explosion!* (pp. 113-119) **6484**
"Dental Laboratory Technicians" in *Jobs! What They Are—Where They Are—What They Pay* (pp. 181) **6485**
"Dental Laboratory Technicians" in *Occupational Outlook Handbook* **6486**
"Dental Laboratory Technicians" in *Opportunities in Dental Care Careers* (pp. 47-49) **6487**
Dental Laboratory Technology **6501**
"Dental and Medical Secretary" in *Career Information Center* (Vol.7) **1636**
Dental Office **2722**
Dental Products Report **2723**
Dental Teamwork **2724**
Dental Technicians **2685**
"Dental Technology" in *Career Connection for Technical Education* (pp. 54-55) **6488**
Dentistry Today **2725**
"Department Store Receiving, Delivering, & Related Workers" in *Occu-Facts: Information on 580 Careers in Outline Form* **1300**
Department Store Receiving and Related Workers **1301**
"Department Store Retailing" in *Encyclopedia of Career Choices for the 1990s: A Guide to Entry Level Jobs* (pp. 252-272) **424**
Deposit Account Operations **857**
Deposit Accounts and Services **858**
"Detective" in *Career Information Center* (Vol.11) **2208**
"Detective" in *Career Selector 2001* **2388**
Detective, Police **2209**
Detective Work: A Study of Criminal Investigations **2349**
"Detectives" in *Encyclopedia of Careers and Vocational Guidance* (Vol.2, pp. 462-465) **2210**
Detective's Private Investigation Training Manual **2350**
Developing Bookkeeping Skills **1472**
Developments **711, 1203**
"Dial O For Operator" in *Telecommunications Careers* (pp. 54-57) **1851**
The Diamond Registry Bulletin **5792**
Die Casting **5943**
Diesel Engine Repair **4033, 4034**
Diesel & Gas Turbine Worldwide **4049**
Diesel Mechanic **4006**
"Diesel Mechanic" in *Career Information Center* (Vol.12) **4007**
"Diesel Mechanic" in *Careers in Trucking* **4008**
"Diesel Mechanic" in *Jobs Rated Almanac* **4009**
"Diesel Mechanic" in *Occu-Facts: Information on 580 Careers in Outline Form* **4010**
Diesel Mechanics **4011**
"Diesel Mechanics" in *Career Discovery Encyclopedia* (Vol.2, pp. 100-101) **4012**
"Diesel Mechanics" in *Encyclopedia of Careers and Vocational Guidance* (Vol.2, pp. 472-475) **4013**
"Diesel Mechanics" in *Occupational Outlook Handbook* **4014**
Diesel Progress Engines & Drives **4050**
"Diesel Technology" in *Career Connection II: A Guide to Technical Majors and Their Related Careers* (pp. 56-57) **4015**
Dimension Purchasing Guide **6469**
Dimensional Stone **4748**
Dining Room Attendant **2547**
"Dining Room Attendant" in *Career Information Center* (Vol.8) **2548**
"Dining Room Attendant" in *Occu-Facts: Information on 580 Careers in Outline Form* **2549**
"Direct Sales Worker" in *Career Information Center* (Vol.10) **425**
Direct Selling: An Income Opportunity for You **426**
Directories of Machine Tools **5834, 5885, 5926, 5940, 5960**
Directory of Accredited Business Appraisal Experts **337**
Directory of Accredited Cosmetology Schools **3004**
Directory of Accredited Institutions **1019, 1704, 1815**
Directory of Accredited Machinery and Technical Specialty Appraisers **338**
Directory of Accredited Personal Property Appraisers **339**
Directory of Accredited Real Property Appraisers **340**
Directory of Certification and Training Contacts **6117**
Directory of Certified Aftermarket Body Parts **3835**
Directory of Certified Dehumidifiers **4479**
Directory of Certified Humidifiers **4480**
Directory of Certified Refrigerators and Freezers **4481**
Directory of Certified Room Air Conditioners **4413, 4482**
Directory of Family Day Care Associations & Support Groups **3332**
Directory of French-Fry Potatoes **2459, 2604**
Directory of Hotel and Motel Systems **1086**
Directory of Institutions **2000**
Directory of Private Accredited Career Colleges and Schools **2460**
Directory of Professional Appraisal Services **341**
Directory of Professional Electronics Technicians **4086, 4253**
Directory of Speakers and Lecturers **6502, 6506**
Directory of Technical Council Committees **5984**
Directory of Telecommunications and Education Programs **4288**
Discover Bookkeeping & Accounts **1473**
Dispatch: The Business Report of the Taxicab/Paratransit Industry **6812**
"Dispatcher" in *150 Careers in the Health Care Field* **1251**
"Dispatcher" in *Careers in Trucking* **1252**
"Dispatcher and Communications" in *Opportunities in Fire Protection Services* (pp. 28-29) **1253**
"Dispatchers" in *Occupational Outlook Handbook* **1254**
"Display Worker Helper" in *Occu-Facts: Information on 580 Careers in Outline Form* **7037**
Distant Water: The Fate of the North Atlantic Fisherman **3659**
Distinguished Dairy Cattle Breeder Award **3416**
Distinguished Information Sciences Award **1943**
Distinguished Service to Agriculture **3417**
Distinguished Service Award **347, 2323, 2324, 6873**
Distribution Clerk, Machine **1358**
Distribution Clerk, Machine: Letter Sorting Machine Operator-U.S. Postal Service **1359**
"Distribution Managers" in *Jobs! What They Are—Where They Are—What They Pay* (pp. 237) **1240**
Distributive Education Clubs of America **220, 1294**
Distributive Education Clubs of America Career Development Conference **1298**
Distributor **4439, 5391**
Distributors Financial Analysis **3977, 4003, 4052, 4346, 4591, 4619**
District of Columbia Department of Consumer and Regulatory Affairs - Occupational and Professional Licensing Administration **7193**
District Heating and Cooling **4440**
"Diver" in *Career Information Center* (Vol.2) **3559**
Divers **7038**
Divers, Commercial **3560**
"Diving Technicians" in *Career Discovery Encyclopedia* (Vol.2, pp. 116-117) **3561**
"Diving Technicians" in *Encyclopedia of Careers and Vocational Guidance* (Vol.2, pp. 491-497) **3562**
Division II Arc Welding Awards **5986**
Do-It-Yourself Car Repairs with Norm Wynne **4004**
Do-It-Yourself Plumbing **5364**
Do Your Own Thing . . . in the Mechanical Field **3755, 3913, 4016, 4140, 4328, 4383, 4578, 4593**
Doane Award; D. Howard **3418**
Doane's Agricultural Report **3473**
"Dock Foreman/Supervisor" in *Careers in Trucking* **5675**
"Dock Worker" in *Career Information Center* (Vol.12) **7039**
Docket **1742**
"Dockworker" in *Transportation* (pp. 18-19) **7040**
Dodge Trucks Scholarships **4039**
Dog Groomer **2897**
"Dog Groomer" in *Occu-Facts: Information on 580 Careers in Outline Form* **2898**
Dog Groomers **2899**
"Dog Groomers" in *Career Discovery Encyclopedia* (Vol.2, pp. 118-119) **2900**
"Dog Groomers" in *Encyclopedia of Careers and Vocational Guidance* (Vol.2, pp. 498-501) **2901**
"Domestic Housekeeper" in *Career Information Center* (Vol.5) **3353**

"Domestic Service Cook" in *Occu-Facts: Information on 580 Careers in Outline Form* **3354**
Don Harger Memorial Award **3586**
"Door to Door Sales Workers" in *Encyclopedia of Careers and Vocational Guidance* (Vol.2, pp. 502-505) **427**
"Door-to-Door Sales Workers" in *Career Discovery Encyclopedia* (Vol.2, pp. 120-121) **428**
Dots and Dashes **1877**
Double Entry by Single: A New Method of Bookkeeping **1474**
The Double Exposure Book **6597**
"Drapery Sewer" in *Occu-Facts: Information on 580 Careers in Outline Form* **6269**
Dressmaker **6270**
Dressmakers (Sewing Professionals) **6271**
Drilling Contractor **5495**
Driver, Heavy-Truck **6827**
Driver of the Year **6874**
Driver of the Year Award **6875**, **7077**
Drop Shipping News **1315**
Drug Enforcement Agent **2306**
"Drywall Applicator/Finisher" in *Jobs Rated Almanac* **4967**
Drywall Installer **4968**
"Drywall Installer and Finisher" in *Career Information Center* (Vol.4) **4969**
Drywall Installers and Finishers **4970**
"Drywall Installers and Finishers" in *Career Discovery Encyclopedia* (Vol.2, pp. 128-129) **4971**
"Drywall Installers and Finishers" in *Encyclopedia of Careers and Vocational Guidance* (Vol.2, pp. 518-521) **4972**
"Drywall Rocker and Taper" in *Hard Hatted Women: Stories of Struggle and Success in the Trades* (pp. 63-70) **4973**
"Drywall Workers and Lathers" in *Occupational Outlook Handbook* **4974**
The Dynamic Secretary: A Practical Guide to Achieving Success as an Executive Assistant **1637**

E

E & S Market News **130**
EAP Digest **1618**
"Early Childhood Center Teacher or Aide" in *Exploring Careers in Child Care Services* (pp. 9-21) **1823**
EASA Currents **4111**
Eastern Cable Television Trade Show and Convention **4556**
Eastern Regional Nurserymen Show **3149**
Easy-to-Do Leathercraft Projects with Full-Size Templates **6338**
Easy Woodworking Projects **6470**
Economic Handbook of the Machine Tool Industry **5835**, **5887**, **5923**, **5942**, **5943**
Economic Profile **6301**
Edison Electric Institute **6034**
EDP Weekly **989**, **4216**
"Education, Government, and Legal Careers" in *The Best Jobs for the 1990s and Into the 21st Century* **1987**, **2164**, **2199**
"Education and Training" in *Where the Jobs Are: The Hottest Careers for the 90s* (pp. 97-110) **3311**
Educational Career Directory **3312**
EEA Training Program **4084**, **4252**
Effective Dental Assisting **2712**
EGSA Powerline **6046**
EI Digest **6122**
EID Spring Shopping Fair - International Trade Fair for Household Goods, Cosmetics, Fashionware, Gifts, Jewelry & Furniture **3032**
Electric Expo **5104**
Electric Light & Power **6047**
Electric Perspectives **6048**
Electric Power and Farm Equipment Show **3529**
"Electric Power Generating Plant Operators and Power Distributors and Dispatchers" in *Occupational Outlook Handbook* **6016**
Electric Power Plant Occupations **6017**
"Electric Power Plant Occupations" in *Occu-Facts: Information on 580 Careers in Outline Form* **6018**
"Electric Power Service Worker" in *Career Information Center* (Vol.11) **6019**
Electric Power Surveys **6044**
"Electric Power Transmission, Distribution Worker" in *Career Information Center* (Vol.11) **6020**
Electricain Helper, Construction **7041**
"Electrical Appliance Service Technician" in *Occu-Facts: Information on 580 Careers in Outline Form* **4469**
Electrical Contractor Magazine **5091**
Electrical Design Library **5071**
Electrical Equipment Manufacturing Workers **7042**
Electrical Industry Exposition **5105**
Electrical Maintenance Training Program **4069**
"Electrical Operator" in *Great Careers for People Who Like to Work with Their Hands* (pp. 40) **6021**
"Electrical Power Worker" in *Career Discovery Encyclopedia* (Vol.2, pp. 136-137) **6022**
Electrical Reports **6049**
Electrical Safety Related Work Practices **5110**
Electrical Symbols and Abbreviations **5111**
Electrical Transmission and Distribution Occupations **6023**
"Electrical Transmission and Distribution Occupations" in *Occu-Facts: Information on 580 Careers in Outline Form* **6024**
Electrical Women's Round Table **6035**
Electrical Women's Round Table—Membership Directory **6043**
Electrical Women's Round Table—National Newsletter **6050**
Electrical World **6051**
Electrician **5027**
"Electrician" in *BLR Encyclopedia of Prewritten Job Descriptions* **5028**
"Electrician" in *Career Connection II: A Guide to Technical Majors and Their Related Careers* (pp. 62-63) **5029**
"Electrician" in *Career Selector 2001* **5112**
Electrician, Construction **5030**
Electrician, Electrician's Helper **5068**
"Electrician" in *Guide to Careers Without College* (pp. 85-86) **5031**
"Electrician" in *Hard Hatted Women: Stories of Struggle and Success in the Trades* (pp. 216-224) **5032**
"Electrician" in *Jobs Rated Almanac* **5033**
Electrician, Maintenance **5034**
"Electrician" in *VGM's Careers Encyclopedia* (pp. 155-158) **5035**
"Electricians" in *American Almanac of Jobs and Salaries* (pp. 502) **5036**
"Electricians" in *Career Discovery Encyclopedia* (Vol.2, pp. 144-145) **5037**
Electricians, Construction **5038**
"Electricians" in *Encyclopedia of Careers and Vocational Guidance* (Vol.2, pp. 546-549) **5039**
Electricians, Maintenance **5040**
"Electricians" in *Occupational Outlook Handbook* **5041**
"Electricians" in *Opportunities in Building Construction Trades* (pp. 31-34) **5042**
The Electrician's Toolbox Manual **5072**, **5073**
The Electricity Journal **4554**, **5092**
ELECTRO - Electronics Show and Convention **4063**, **4274**
Electro Fact File **5093**
"Electrologist" in *Career Information Center* (Vol.5) **2970**
Electrologists **2971**
"Electrologists" in *Encyclopedia of Careers and Vocational Guidance* (Vol.2, pp. 559-561) **2972**
Electronic Business Forecast **4112**
Electronic & Components Expo -International Tradeshow for the Electronics Equipment and Components Industry **4064**, **4275**
"Electronic Computer Operating Personnel" in *Occu-Facts: Information on 580 Careers in Outline Form* **955**
Electronic Distribution Show and Conference **4065**, **4276**
Electronic Equipment Repair Technician **4053**
"Electronic Equipment Repairers" in *Occupational Outlook Handbook* **4054**
"Electronic Home Entertainment Equipment Repairers" in *Occupational Outlook Handbook* **4228**
Electronic Industries Association **4242**
Electronic Industries Association—Executive Report **4113**
Electronic Maintenance **4089**
Electronic Maintenance Two **4090**
"Electronic Organ Technicians" in *Encyclopedia of Careers and Vocational Guidance* **4229**
Electronic Service Careers **4230**, **5043**
Electronic Servicing & Technology **4062**, **4114**
Electronic Technicians Association Annual Convention **4125**
"Electronics Assemblers" in *The Complete Electronics Career Guide* (pp. 40-43) **5657**
Electronics for Industrial Electricians **4091**
Electronics in Industry **4092**
"Electronics Inspector" in *Hard Hatted Women: Stories of Struggle and Success in the Trades* (pp. 212-215) **5718**
The Electronics Manual to Industrial Automation **4093**
"Electronics Manufacturing Assemblers" in *Occu-Facts: Information on 580 Careers in Outline Form* **5658**
"Electronics Repair" in *Career Connection for Technical Education* (pp. 64-65) **4055**
"Electronics Repairers" in *Career Discovery Encyclopedia* (Vol.2, pp. 148-149) **4231**
Electronics Technician: A Career for Tomorrow **4232**
Electronics Technicians Association, International **4073**, **4075**, **4243**, **4246**
Electronics Technicians Association, International Technician of the Year **4087**, **4255**
Elementary Darkroom Practices: A Basic Photography Manual **6598**
The Elevator **4323**
"Elevator Constructor and Repair Worker" in *Career Information Center* (Vol.4) **4304**
Elevator Constructors (Mechanics) **4305**
"Elevator Constructors" in *Opportunities in Building Construction Trades* (p. 52) **4306**
"Elevator Installers and Repairers" in *Career Discovery Encyclopedia* (Vol.2, pp. 156-157) **4307**
"Elevator Installers and Repairers" in *Encyclopedia of Careers and Vocational Guidance* (Vol.2, pp. 581-584) **4308**
"Elevator Installers and Repairers" in *Occupational Outlook Handbook* **4309**
"Elevator Operator" in *Career Selector 2001* **4324**
Elevator World, Inc. **4322**
Elevators & Engineering: An Architectural Guide **4317**
Emergency & Trip Permit Handbook: Important Permit Information for Interstate Trucking Operatiobns in the United States & Canada **6880**
Empire Farm Days **3530**
Employee Benefits Quarterly **859**
An Employer's Guide to Child Care Consultants **3337**
Employment Opportunities for College Graduates in Food & Agricultural Sciences: Agriculture, Natural Resources, & Veterinary Medicine: 1990-1995 **3377**
Encouraging Cooperation among Competitors: The Case of Motor Carrier Deregulation & Collective Ratemaking **6941**

Encyclopedia of Medical Organizations and Agencies **2705**, **2783**, **2854**, **6497**, **6530**
"Engineers and Engineer Helpers" in *Opportunities in Travel Careers* (pp. 54-55) **6716**
Engineers, Pump Operators, Drivers Handbook **2105**
Entree **712**, **1204**, **2491**, **2624**
Environmental Report **3702**
"Environmental Technician (Water and Wastewater)" in *100 Best Careers for the Year 2000* (pp. 135-136) **6085**
Epping Scholarships; Northern California/Richard **688**, **1194**
"Equipment Rental and Leasing Service Agent" in *Career Information Center* (Vol.10) **40**
ERIC/IR Update **1563**
The Essential Darkroom Book **6599**
Essential Darkroom Techniques **6600**
Essentials of Clinical Dental Assisting **2713**
Essentials of Dental Radiography for Dental Assistants and Dental Hygienists **2701**
Estimator's Handbook **5188**
ETA Technician Association News **4115**
Ethics, Jurisprudence & History for the Dental Hygienist **6514**
Eurail Guide: How to Travel Europe and All the World by Train **729**, **1191**
Europe Automotive Insight **3978**
Europe by Train: The Complete Guide to Inter Railing **730**
Everett E. Hudiburg Award **2101**
Excellence in Arc Welding Awards; Graduate and Professional Awards for Achievement in Arc-Welded Design, Engineering and Fabrication **5987**
Excellence in Zookeeping Award **2924**
The Exec-U-tary **1743**
Executive Chef **2423**
Executive Forum **3150**
Executive Housekeeping Today **3277**
Executive Information Series **6507**
Executive Media Alert **795**
Executive Secretary **1638**
Exhaust News **3979**
Experimental Agriculture **3474**
Experimental Musical Instruments **4655**
Explore Your Future: A Career in Life Insurance Sales **60**
The Explorer **2726**
Exploring Careers in Computer Field **956**
Exploring Careers in Computer Sales **429**, **598**
Exploring Careers as a Computer Technician **4184**
Exploring Careers as an Electrician **5044**
Exploring Careers in the Military Services **7100**
Exploring Careers in the Travel Industry **638**
Exploring Careers in Word Processing and Desktop Publishing **1902**
Exploring Computer Careers at Home **957**
Export Guide **4293**
Exterior Body Panel Developments **3845**

F

FAA Aviation News **3785**
Faber & Kell's Heating & Air Conditioning of Buildings **4420**
Fabrication Procedures **6508**
Face Painter **2973**
Face Unique Challenges With the FBI: A Career as a Special Agent **2211**
Fact Sheet: Facts About Direct Selling **430**
Facts About Fur **3660**
Facts for Consumers From the Federal Trade Commission: Truck-Driving Schools **6942**
Family Day Care Bulletin **3338**
"Family Day-Care Providers" in *Exploring Careers in Child Care Services* (pp. 22-31) **3313**
The Family Farm: Can It Be Saved? **3546**
Farm: A Year in the Life of an American Farmer **3547**
Farm Equipment Mechanic **4329**
"Farm Equipment Mechanic" in *Occu-Facts: Information on 580 Careers in Outline Form* **4330**
Farm Equipment Mechanics **4331**
"Farm Equipment Mechanics" in *Career Discovery Encyclopedia* (Vol.3, pp. 172-173) **4332**
"Farm Equipment Mechanics" in *Encyclopedia of Careers and Vocational Guidance* (Vol.2, pp. 623-627) **4333**
"Farm Equipment Mechanics" in *Occupational Outlook Handbook* **4334**
"Farm Management" in *Career Connection II: A Guide to Technical Majors and Their Related Careers* (pp. 74-75) **3378**
Farm Management Manual. **3427**
Farm Manager **3379**, **3380**
"Farm Manager" in *100 Best Jobs for the 1990s & Beyond* **3548**
"Farm Manager" in *Career Information Center* (Vol.2) **3381**
"Farm Manager" in *Top Professions: The 100 Most Popular, Dynamic, and Profitable Careers in America Today* (pp. 77-78) **3382**
"Farm Operatives and Managers" in *Encyclopedia of Careers and Vocational Guidance* **3383**
"Farm Operators and Managers" in *Jobs! What They Are—Where They Are—What They Pay* (pp. 49-50) **3384**
"Farm Operators and Managers" in *Occupational Outlook Handbook* **3385**
Farm and Power Equipment Dealer **4345**
Farm Progress Show **3531**
Farm/Ranch Exchange **3475**
Farm & Ranch Living **3476**
"Farmer" in *Career Information Center* (Vol.2) **3386**
"Farmer" in *Career Selector 2001* **3549**
Farmer, Cattle **3387**
Farmer, Dairy **3388**
"Farmer" in *Encyclopedia of Danger: Dangerous Professions* (pp. 42-45) **3550**
Farmer, Fruit **3389**
Farmer, Poultry **3390**
Farmer, Vegetable Crops **3391**
"Farmer" in *VGM's Careers Encyclopedia* (pp. 169-171) **3392**
Farmers **3393**
The Farmers' Advance **3477**
"Farmers" in *Career Discovery Encyclopedia* (Vol.2, pp. 174-175) **3394**
"Farmers" in *Encyclopedia of Careers and Vocational Guidance* (Vol.2, pp. 628-632) **3395**
Farmer's Exchange **3478**
Farmers, General **3396**
Farmers as Hunters: The Implications of Sedentism **3428**
"Farmers" in *Occu-Facts: Information on 580 Careers in Outline Form* **3397**
Farmer's Report **3479**
Farming Is in Our Blood: Farm Families in Economic Crisis **3551**
Farmland News **3480**
Fashion & Textile Careers **6351**
"Fast Food Franchise Worker" in *Career Information Center* (Vol.8) **2550**
Fast Food Jobs: National Study of Fast Foods Employment **2551**
Fast Food Workers **2424**
"Fast Food Workers" in *Encyclopedia of Careers and Vocational Guidance* (Vol.2, pp. 636-638) **2552**
"Fast-Foods Worker" in *Career Selector 2001* **2656**
"FBI Agent" in Action Careers: Employment in the High-Risk Job Market (pp. 47-58) **2212**
"FBI Agents" in *Career Discovery Encyclopedia* (Vol.3, pp. 8-9) **2213**
"FBI Agents" in *Encyclopedia of Careers and Vocational Guidance* (Vol.2, pp. 639-642) **2214**
FBI Entrance Examination **2307**
"FBI Special Agent" in *Career Information Center* (Vol.11) **2215**
"FBI Special Agent" in *VGM's Careers Encyclopedia* (pp. 173-175) **2216**
FBI Special Agents **2217**, **2218**
"FBI Special Agents" in *Occu-Facts: Information on 580 Careers in Outline Form* **2219**
Federal Bureau of Investigation **2271**, **2277**
"Federal Bureau of Investigation" in *Exploring Careers Using Foreign Languages* (pp. 67-69) **2220**
"Federal Bureau of Investigation" in Law Enforcement Employment Guide (pp. 130-131) **2221**
Federal Clerk - Steno - Typist **1809**, **1934**
Federal Communications Commission **4076**
Federal Investigator Magazine **2368**
Federal Investigators Association **2272**, **2278**
Federal Motor Carrier Safety Regulations **6881**
Federal Motor Carrier Safety Regulations Pocketbook **6882**
Fellow of the Academy of Professional Reporters **1817**
Fernando R. Ayuso Awards **687**
FFA Advisors Making a Difference **3481**
FFA New Horizons Magazine **3482**
FIA Executive Digest **6345**
FIA Newsletter **2369**
"Field Representatives" in *Opportunities in Insurance Careers* (pp. 42-43) **761**
Field & Stream **3608**
FIGA Newsletter **4656**
File Clerk **1499**
"File Clerk" in *Career Information Center* (Vol.1) **1500**
"File Clerk" in *Careers in Banking and Finance* (pp. 43-45) **1501**
"File Clerk" in *Careers Inside the World of Offices* (pp. 11,38) **1502**
File Clerk, General Clerk **1503**, **1515**
"File Clerk" in *Jobs Rated Almanac* **1504**
"File Clerk" in *Occu-Facts: Information on 580 Careers in Outline Form* **1505**
"File Clerks" in *American Almanac of Jobs and Salaries* (pp. 509) **1506**
"File Clerks" in *Encyclopedia of Careers and Vocational Guidance* (Vol.2, pp. 646-648) **1507**
"File Clerks" in *Jobs! What They Are—Where They Are—What They Pay* (pp. 249) **1508**
"File Clerks" in *Occupational Outlook Handbook* **1509**
File Management Techniques **1520**
File Structure & Design **1521**
Filing Procedures Guideline **1522**
Filing & Records Management **1523**
Filing: Syllabus **1524**
Filing Systems & Records Management **1525**
"Film Laboratory Technicians" in *Encyclopedia of Careers and Vocational Guidance* **6576**
Film Processing Specialist **6577**
Finance, Insurance & Real Estate USA: Industry Analyses, Statistics, and Leading Organizations **115**, **342**
Financial and Compensation Survey **5189**
"Financial Institution Tellers" in *Encyclopedia of Careers and Vocational Guidance* (Vol.2, pp. 662-664) **819**
Financial Marketing **553**, **860**, **1018**
Financial Monitor **131**
"Financial Services" in *Jobs '95* (pp. 331-338) **500**
Find 'em Fast: A Private Investigator's Workbook **2351**
Find Them Fast, Find Them Now: Private Investigators Share Their Secrets for Finding Missing Persons **2352**
Fine Homebuilding **4749**, **4846**, **5012**, **5301**, **5462**
Finish Carpentry Illustrated **4814**
Fins & Feathers **3609**
Fire Administration & Supervision **2086**
Fire Alarm Manual **1273**

Fire Assessment Centers: The New Concept in Promotional Examinations **2106**
Fire Brigade Training Program: Instructor's Guide **2107**
Fire Brigade Training Program: Student Manual **2108**
Fire Captain Oral Exam Study Guide **2087**
Fire Command Officer's Handbook **2109**
Fire Control Digest **2123**
Fire Department Lieutenant/Captain/Battalion Chief **2088**
Fire Department Lieutenant Captain Battalion Chief: Score High on Firefighter Promotion Exams **2089**
Fire Department Safety Officer's Reference Guide **2110**
Fire Engineer Written Exam Study Guide **2090**
Fire Engineering **2124**
Fire Fighter **2027, 2028**
"Fire Fighter" in Action Careers: Employment in the High-Risk Job Market (pp. 59-75) **2029**
"Fire Fighter" in *Career Information Center* (Vol.11) **2030**
"Fire Fighter" in *Career Selector 2001* **2150**
"Fire Fighter, Paramedic" in *Straight Talk on Careers: 80 Pros Take You Into Their Professions* (pp. 227-230, 231-232) **2031**
Fire Fighter of the Year **2098**
Fire Fighters **2032**
"Fire Fighters" in *American Almanac of Jobs and Salaries* (pp. 98) **2033**
"Fire Fighters" in *Career Discovery Encyclopedia* (Vol.2, pp. 16-17) **2034**
Fire Fighters and Inspectors **2035**
"Fire Fighters" in *Jobs! What They Are—Where They Are—What They Pay* (pp. 135) **2036**
Fire Lieutenant's & Captain's Handbook **2111**
Fire Management Notes **2125**
Fire and Materials **2126**
Fire News **2127**
Fire Prevention & Firefighting **2037**
Fire Prevention in Use of Cutting & Welding Processes **5990**
Fire Promotion Course (One Volume) **2091**
"Fire Protection Engineer" in *Career Information Center* (Vol.6) **2038**
Fire Protection Handbook **2112**
Fire Protection Reference Directory and Buyer's Guide **2095**
Fire and Rescue Educational Conference and Exposition **2146**
Fire on the Rim: A Firefighter's Season at the Grand Canyon **2151**
"Fire Safety Technicians" in *Encyclopedia of Careers and Vocational Guidance* (Vol.2, pp. 673-678) **2039**
"Fire Science" in *Career Connection II: A Guide to Technical Majors and Their Related Careers* (pp. 80-81) **2040**
Fire Technology **2128**
Firefighter **2041, 2092**
"Firefighter" in *100 Best Jobs for the 1990s & Beyond* **2152**
Firefighter Entrance Examinations **2093**
"Firefighter" in *Hard Hatted Women: Stories of Struggle and Success in the Trades* (pp. 156-170) **2042**
"Firefighter" in *Jobs Rated Almanac* **2043**
"Firefighter" in *Occu-Facts: Information on 580 Careers in Outline Form* **2044**
Firefighter & Paramedic Burnout **2113**
"Firefighter" in *VGM's Careers Encyclopedia* (pp. 176-178) **2045**
Firefighters: A to Z **2046**
Firefighters in Action **2153**
"Firefighters" in *Encyclopedia of Careers and Vocational Guidance* (Vol.2, pp. 668-672) **2047**
Firefighter's Entrance Handbook **2114**
Firefighter's News **2129**
"Firefighters" in *Opportunities in Vocational and Technical Careers* (p. 76-90) **2048**
Firefighters: Their Lives in Their Own Words **2154**
"Firefighting Occupations" in *Occupational Outlook Handbook* **2049**
Firehouse Magazine **2130**
Firehouse Magazine Heroism and Community Service Award **2099**
Firehouse Trivia **2155**
Fireman of the Year **2100**
First Biannual Commercial and Industrial Insulation Industry Financial Survey **5204**
First Class: In Introduction to Travel and Tourism **731, 1220**
First Principles: National Security and Civil Liberties **2370**
Fish Expo **3657**
Fish Farmer **3563**
"Fish Farmer" in *Career Selector 2001* **3661**
Fish Farming Workers **3564**
Fish and Game Finder Magazine **3610**
"Fish Production Technicians" in *Career Discovery Encyclopedia* (Vol.3, pp. 18-19) **5687**
"Fish Production Technicians" in *Encyclopedia of Careers and Vocational Guidance* (Vol.3, p.1) **5688**
"Fisher" in *Career Information Center* (Vol.2) **3565**
Fisher, Commercial **3566**
"Fisher" in *Hard Hatted Women: Stories of Struggle and Success in the Trades* (pp. 81-87) **3567**
Fisherman **3568, 3611**
Fishers, Commercial **3569**
"Fishers, Commercial" in *Career Discovery Encyclopedia* (Vol.3, pp. 20-21) **3570**
"Fishers, Commercial" in *Encyclopedia of Careers and Vocational Guidance* (Vol.3, pp. 2-4) **3571**
"Fishers, Hunters, and Trappers" in *Occupational Outlook Handbook* **3572**
Fishing Facts Magazine **3612**
Fishing and Hunting News **3613**
Fixing Cars **3846**
Flammability Regulations & Standards in the United States for Upholstered Furniture **6402**
Flashes **3614**
Flexo **6205, 6251**
FLICC Newsletter **1564**
Flight Attendant **3051, 3052**
"Flight Attendant" in *100 Best Careers for the Year 2000* (pp. 242-245) **3053**
"Flight Attendant" in *100 Best Jobs for the 1990s & Beyond* **3085**
"Flight Attendant" in *American Almanac of Jobs and Salaries* (pp. 392) **3054**
"Flight Attendant" in *Careers in Aviation* (pp. 15-18) **3055**
"Flight Attendant" in *College Board Guide to Jobs and Career Planning* (pp. 83-84) **3056**
Flight Attendant Interview Handbook **3057**
"Flight Attendant" in *Jobs Rated Almanac* **3058**
"Flight Attendant" in *Occu-Facts: Information on 580 Careers in Outline Form* **3059**
"Flight Attendant" in *Opportunities in Airline Careers* (pp. 63-76) **3060**
"Flight Attendant" in *The Complete Aviation/Aerospace Career Guide* (pp. 159-164) **3061**
"Flight Attendant" in *Transportation* (pp. 51-55) **3062**
"Flight Attendant" in *VGM's Careers Encyclopedia* (pp. 178-181) **3063**
"Flight Attendants" in *101 Careers: A Guide to the Fastest-Growing Opportunities* (pp. 316-318) **3064**
"Flight Attendants" in *America's 50 Fastest Growing Jobs* (pp. 119) **3065**
"Flight Attendants" in *Career Discovery Encyclopedia* (Vol.3, pp. 22-23) **3066**
"Flight Attendants" in *Encyclopedia of Careers and Vocational Guidance* (Vol.3, pp. 5-8) **3067**
"Flight Attendants" in *Jobs! What They Are—Where They Are—What They Pay* (pp. 199) **3068**
"Flight Attendants" in *Occupational Outlook Handbook* **3069**
"Flight Attendants" in *Opportunities in Travel Careers* (pp. 37-39) **3070**
"Flight Attendants" in *Travel Agent* (pp. 165-166) **3071**
"Flight Dispatcher" in *Opportunities in Airline Careers* (pp. 91-93) **1255**
"Flight Dispatcher" in *Opportunities in Transportation Careers* (pp. 39-40) **1256**
Flightlog **3082**
"Floor Brokers, Traders, and Commodity Traders" in *Jobs! What They Are—Where They Are—What They Pay* (pp. 143) **501**
Floor Covering Installation Contractors Association **4868**
Floor Covering Installation Contractors Association—Newsletter **4882**
"Floor Covering Installer" in *Career Information Center* (Vol.4) **4859**
Floor Covering Installer (Resilient) **4860**
"Floor Covering Installer (Resilient)" in *Occu-Facts: Information on 580 Careers in Outline Form* **4861**
Floor Covering Installers **4862, 4863**
"Floor Covering Installers" in *Career Discovery Encyclopedia* (Vol.3, pp. 26-27) **4864**
"Floor Covering Installers" in *Encyclopedia of Careers and Vocational Guidance* (Vol.3, pp. 11-14) **4865**
"Floor Covering Installers" in *Opportunities in Building Construction Trades* (pp. 53-55) **4866**
Floor Covering Weekly **4883**
Florida State Department of Business and Professional Regulation **7194**
The Flue Cured Tobacco Farmer **3483**
Fly Fisherman **3615**
Fly Rod & Reel **3616**
Flyfishing **3617**
Flying High in Travel: A Complete Guide to Careers in the Travel Industry **639, 1157**
FMRA News **3484**
FN (Footwear News) **6346**
Focus on Farming **3485**
Focus on Operations **994**
"Focus on Operations" Digest of Conference Sessions **990**
Fodor's Guides **732**
"Food and Beverage Industry" in *Jobs '95* (pp. 339-350) **2553**
"Food and Beverage Manager" in *Career Information Center* (Vol.8) **2554**
"Food and Beverage Service Occupations" in *Occupational Outlook Handbook* **2555**
Food Careers **2425, 2556**
Food Chemical News **2492**
Food & Dairy Expo **5715**
Food Distribution Magazine—Food Brokers Directory Issue **2467, 2605**
Food Distribution Research Society—Newsletter **2493, 2625**
Food Reviews International **2626**
"Food Service" in *Career Connection II: A Guide to Technical Majors and Their Related Careers* (pp. 82-83) **2426**
Food Service Careers Guide Book: A Handy Guidebook for Those Seeking a Career in the Hospitality Industry **2557**
Food Service Management by Checklist: A Handbook of Control Techniques **2609**
Food Service Officers **2558**
"Food Service Workers" in *Career Discovery Encyclopedia* (Vol.3, pp. 32-33) **2559**
"Food Service Workers" in *Encyclopedia of Careers and Vocational Guidance* (Vol.3, pp. 16-20) **2427**
Food Services **2428, 2560, 5689**
Food & Wine **2494**
Foodletter **2495, 2627**
Foodservice Information Abstracts **2496**
Foodservice Management Study Course **2610**
Foodservice Product News **2628**
Foodservice Report **2497, 2629**
Footsteps in the Ocean: Careers in Diving **3573**
Forecast of Housing Activity **4441**

Foreign Vehicle Maintenance in the U.S.A. **3980**
Forest & Conservation History **3703**
Forest Industries Clinic and Show **3728**
Forest Products Machinery and Equipment Exposition **3729**
Forest Technician **3664**
"Forester Aide" in *Career Selector 2001* **3734**
"Foresters" in *Career Discovery Encyclopedia* (Vol.3, pp. 40-41) **3665**
"Forestry and Logging Occupations" in *Occupational Outlook Handbook* **3666**
Forklift Operator Training **6674**
Forklift Truck: Operator Training **6710**, **6943**
Four Classics on the Theory of Double Entry Bookkeeping **1488**
Frances Jones Poetker Award **3121**
Fresh Baked **2498**
From Nine to Five **911**, **1058**, **1145**, **1744**, **1819**, **1963**
Front-End Loader Operator **6675**
Front Page Detective: William J. Burns & the Detective Profession, 1880-1930 **2389**
Frozen Foods—Wholesale Directory **2530**
Fruit and Vegetable Truck Rate Report **6904**
Fullwrite Professional: A User's Guide **1946**
FUR-FISH-GAME **3618**
Fur Trapping **3574**
Fur Trapping in North America **3575**
Furbearer Management **3587**
"Furnace Cleaner" in *Occu-Facts: Information on 580 Careers in Outline Form* **7043**
Furniture: An Opportunity Career **6384**, **6424**
Furniture Finisher **6425**
"Furniture Finisher" in *Occu-Facts: Information on 580 Careers in Outline Form* **6426**
"Furniture Industry" in *Career Information Center* (Vol.9) **6427**
Furniture Manufacturing **6428**
"Furniture Manufacturing Occupations" in *Encyclopedia of Careers and Vocational Guidance* (Vol.3, pp. 53-56) **6429**
"Furniture Manufacturing Workers" in *Career Discovery Encyclopedia* (Vol.3, pp. 50-51) **6430**
Furniture Upholsterer **6385**
"Furniture Upholsterer" in *Jobs Rated Almanac* **6386**
"Furniture Upholsterer" in *Occu-Facts: Information on 580 Careers in Outline Form* **6387**
"Furniture Upholsterer and Tailor or Dressmaker" in *Personal Services* (pp. 39-43) **6272**, **6388**
"Furniture Upholsterers" in *Encyclopedia of Careers and Vocational Guidance* **6389**
Future Aviation Professional of America **3077**, **3764**

G

G. B. Gunlogson Medal **3120**
Game & Fish Magazine **3619**
Garbage Collector **7044**
"Garden Worker" and "Groundskeeper" in *Museum Jobs form A-Z: What They Are, How to Prepare, and Where to Find Them* **3087**
The Gardener **3133**
"Gardener and Grounds Keeper" in *Career Inormation Center* (Vol.5) **3088**
Gardener - Grounds Maintenance Worker **3115**
"Gardeners and Groundskeepers" in *America's 50 Fastest Growing Jobs* (pp. 121) **3089**
"Gardeners and Groundskeepers" in *Occupational Outlook Handbook* **3090**
Gardening **3116**
Garment Cutter **6273**
"Garment Cutter" in *Occu-Facts: Information on 580 Careers in Outline Form* **6274**
"Garment Presser" in *Occu-Facts: Information on 580 Careers in Outline Form* **6275**
Gas Appliance Service Technicians **4470**
"Gas Dispatcher" in *Career Selector 2001* **1285**
Gasoline and Automotive Service Dealers Association—Bulletin **3870**, **3981**
"Gasoline Service Station Attendants" in *Encyclopedia of Careers and Vocational Guidance* (Vol.3, pp. 63-65) **7045**
GATF/NSTF Annual Conference **6216**
GATFWORLD **6160**
Gauged Brickwork: A Technical Handbook **4720**
Gem and Jewelry Fact Sheets Quarterly Supplement **5793**
Gems & Gemology **5794**
General Commendation **2325**
General Driving Safety **6665**, **6821**, **6944**
"General Maintenance Mechanics" in *Career Discovery Encyclopedia* (Vol.3, pp. 56-57) **4349**
"General Maintenance Mechanics" in *Encyclopedia of Careers and Vocational Guidance* (Vol.3, pp. 70-72) **4350**
"General Maintenance Mechanics" in *Occupational Outlook Handbook* **4351**
General and Mechanical Maintenance Training Program **4352**
"General Office Clerk" in *Occu-Facts: Information on 580 Careers in Outline Form* **1028**
General Office Clerks **1029**
"General Office Clerks" in *Encyclopedia of Careers and Vocational Guidance* (Vol.3, pp. 73-75) **1030**
"General Office Clerks" in *Occupational Outlook Handbook* **1031**
General Office Procedures for Colleges **1050**
General Woodworking **6448**
Georgia Secretary of State - Professional Examining Boards **7195**
"Geriatric Aide" in *Career Information Center* (Vol.11) **2811**
Geriatric Aides **3162**
Geriatric Nursing Assistants: An Annotated Bibliography with Models to Enhance Practice **2860**
Get Set to Trap **3588**
Get Wired for Life as a Construction Electrician **5045**
Getting Down to Business: Carpentry Business **4787**
Getting Down to Business: Construction Electrician Business **4788**, **5046**
Getting Down to Business: Hair Styling Shop **2974**
Getting Down to Business: Plumbing Business **5314**
Getting Down to Business: Travel Agency **640**, **1158**
Getting Down to Business: Welding Business **5946**
"Getting Started in Industrial Sales" in *Marketing and Sales Career Directory* (pp. 18-22) **179**
"Getting Started in Retail Ad Sales" in *Newspapers Career Directory* (pp. 21-24) **599**
Glass Magazine **5150**
Glazier **5116**
"Glazier" in *Career Information Center* (Vol.4) **5117**
"Glazier" in *Exploring Nontraditional Jobs for Women* (pp. 16-20) **5118**
"Glazier" in *Jobs Rated Almanac* **5119**
"Glazier" in *Occu-Facts: Information on 580 Careers in Outline Form* **5120**
Glaziers **5121**
"Glaziers" in *Career Discovery Encyclopedia* (Vol.3, pp. 66-67) **5122**
"Glaziers" in *Encyclopedia of Careers and Vocational Guidance* (Vol.3, pp. 94-96) **5123**
"Glaziers" in *Occupational Outlook Handbook* **5124**
"Glaziers" in *Opportunities in Building Construction Trades* (pp. 55-57) **5125**
Global Information Systems **912**
Glossary of Financial Services Terminology **543**, **831**
GMC Apprentice Program Battery Tests (GMC) **3948**
Gold Medal Award **473**
Gold Mining Stock Report **554**
Golden Hammer Award **4646**
A Good Part of Your Life **5845**
Good Samaritan Award **2326**
Government Product News—Buyers Guide for Grounds Maintenance Issue **3159**
Government Tender Report **6768**, **6905**, **6992**
Government Traffic Bulletin Trucking Information **6769**, **6906**, **6993**
Grain Farmer **3398**
Grain & Feed Market News **3486**
Graphic Arts Monthly **6206**, **6252**
Graphic Arts Technical Foundation **6151**, **6153**, **6194**, **6196**, **6236**, **6238**
Graphic Communications International Union **6152**, **6195**, **6237**, **6277**
Graphics Master 5 **6201**, **6282**, **6601**
Grass & Grain **3487**
Grass Roots **2131**
The Gray Sheet: Computer Industry Report **991**
Gray's Sporting Journal **3620**
Great Lakes Cable Expo **4557**
The Green Man **5478**
Green World News **3134**
Gregg Quick Filing Practice **1526**
Grit and Steel **3621**
Grocery Checker **12**
"Grocery Checker" in *Occu-Facts: Information on 580 Careers in Outline Form* **13**
Groomers Voice **2931**
Grounds Keeper **3091**
Grounds Maintenance Awards **3119**
Grounds Maintenance Estimating Guidelines **3092**
Grounds Maintenance Management Guidelines **3122**
Grounds Management Forms and Job Descriptions Guide **3093**
Grounds Management Forum **3135**
Grounds Management Guide, **3123**
Grounds Manager Certification Proram **3094**
"Groundskeeper" in *Occu-Facts: Information on 580 Careers in Outline Form* **3095**
"Groundskeeper and Stadium Worker" in *Hospitality & Recreation* (pp. 57-61) **3096**
"Guard" in *Career Opportunities in Art* (pp. 25-26) **2165**
"Guard, Museum" in *Museum Jobs form A-Z: What They Are, How to Prepare, and Where to Find Them* **2166**
Guard, Security **2167**
"Guard Supervisor" in *Career Opportunities in Art* (pp. 27-28) **2168**
"Guard" in *VGM's Careers Encyclopedia* (pp. 84-86) **2169**
"Guards" in *American Almanac of Jobs and Salaries* (pp. 532) **2170**
"Guards" in *America's 50 Fastest Growing Jobs* (pp. 122) **2171**
"Guards" in *Occupational Outlook Handbook* **2172**
Guest of Honor Award **3419**
A Guide to Becoming a Flight Attendant **3072**
A Guide to Computer Careers **958**, **959**
The Guide to Cooking Schools **2461**
Guide to Electronic Components **4094**
Guide to Federal Technical, Trades, and Labor Jobs **1360**
Guide to Grounds Maintenance Estimating **3124**
Guide to the Health Care Field **2869**
Guide to Hospitality Education **2468**, **2499**, **2611**, **2612**
Guide to Industrial Housekeeping **3285**
Guide to Military Careers **7183**
Guide to Payroll Practice and Management **1597**
Guide to Welding **5991**
Guitar Repair **4649**
Gunlogson Medal; G. B. **3120**

H

Hair International/Associated Master Barbers and Beauticians of America **2990**
Hair International News **3019**
Hair Shaping Lessons Series **3043**
"Hair Stylist" in *Career Opportunities in Television, Cable, and Video* (pp. 140-141) **2975**
"Hairdresser" in *Great Careers for People Who Like to Work with Their Hands* (pp. 43) **2976**
"Hairdressers" in *Jobs! What They Are—Where They Are—What They Pay* (p. 350) **2977**
"Hairstylist" in *100 Best Careers for the Year 2000* (pp. 200-204) **2978**
"Hairstylist" in *Guide to Careers Without College* (pp. 100-102) **2979**
Hairstylist/Salon Owner **2980**
Halissey Memorial Scholarship; Simmons Scholarship Avis Rent a Car Scholarship; David **689**, **1195**
Hall of Fame **4647**
"Hand Packager" in *Occu-Facts: Information on 580 Careers in Outline Form* **7046**
"Hand Sewer" in *Occu-Facts: Information on 580 Careers in Outline Form* **6276**
Handbook of Basic Electronic Troubleshooting **4095**
A Handbook of Effective Techniques for Teacher Aides **1841**
Handbook of Expanded Dental Auxiliary Practice **2714**
Handbook of Software Maintenance **4204**
Handbook for Teacher Aides **1842**
Handbook of Trade and Technical Careers and Training **2469**, **2613**, **3847**, **4041**, **5992**
Hands That Think: A Word About Careers in Modern Dental Laboratory Technology **6489**
Handy Medical Guide for Seafarers, Fisherman, Trawlermen & Yachtsmen **3589**
Hanging On **6955**
Harger Memorial Award; Don **3586**
Harvests **3136**
Harwood Memorial Real Estate Scholarship **348**
Hatfield Award; William D. **6118**
Hawaii State Department of Commerce and Consumer Affairs **7196**
Hay There! **3488**
Hazard Classification Guide **5190**
Hazard Communication Manual **6509**
The Hazardous Materials Handbook for Motor Carriers **6883**
"Head Waiter and Waitress" in *Career Information Center* (Vol.8) **2561**
Health Care Security Training Series **2173**
"Health Care" in *Where the Jobs Are: The Hottest Careers for the 90s* (pp. 143-166) **2738**, **3163**
Health Career Planning: A Realistic Guide **2686**, **2739**, **2812**
Health Careers Today **2687**, **2740**, **2813**
Health and Disability Insurance Sales Achievement **118**
"Health and Fitness Retail Sales" in *Careers in Health and Fitness* (pp. 71-73) **431**
Health Insurance Association of America **104**
Health & Medical Industry Directory **2706**, **2784**, **2855**
Health of the Rep Newsletter **233**
Health and Safety **4516**, **5667**
Healthwire **1848**, **2727**, **2797**, **2870**
Healy Scholarship **690**
"Heating and Air Conditioning Installers" in *Opportunities in Building Construction Trades* (pp. 57-58) **4384**
"Heating, Air-Conditioning, and Refrigeration Mechanics" in *Jobs! What They Are—Where They Are—What They Pay* (pp. 213) **4385**
"Heating, Air-Conditioning, and Refrigeration Technicians" in *Occupational Outlook Handbook* **4386**
Heating, Cooling & Lighting **4421**
"Heating and Cooling Mechanics" in *Career Discovery Encyclopedia* (Vol.3, pp. 90-91) **4387**
"Heating, Cooling, and Refrigeration" in *Opportunities in Plumbing and Pipefitting Careers* (pp. 83-85) **4388**
"Heating and Cooling Technicians" in *Career Discovery Encyclopedia* (Vol.3, pp. 92-93) **4389**
"Heating/Refrigeration Mechanic" in *Jobs Rated Almanac* **4390**
Heating System Troubleshooting Handbook **4422**
Heating, Ventilating & Air Conditioning **4423**
"Heating, Ventilation and Air Conditioning" in *Career Connection II: A Guide to Technical Majors and Their Related Careers* (pp. 86-87) **4391**
Heating, Ventilation, and Air Conditioning Product and Equipment Show **4589**, **5560**, **6081**
Heavy Duty Truck Maintenance in the U.S.A. **3958**, **4042**, **4337**, **4587**
Heavy Duty Trucking **6907**
"Heavy Equipment Operations" in *Career Connection II: A Guide to Technical Majors and Their Related Careers* (pp. 69-70) **6676**
"Heavy Equipment Operator" in *Career Information Center* (Vol.4) **6677**
"Heavy Equipment Operator" in *Great Careers for People Who Like to Work with Their Hands* (pp. 22-27) **5846**
"Heavy Truck Driver" in *Occu-Facts: Information on 580 Careers in Outline Form* **6828**
Heavy Vehicle Use Tax: Regulations & Instructions **6884**
Heinz Bloch: Machinery Component Maintenance and Repair **5843**
Helicopter Maintenance Award **3766**
Here Comes the Fireman **2156**
The Hideaway Report **713**
High Plains Journal **3489**
Highlights **6123**
Highway Common Carrier Newsletter **6908**
Hjort Associates, Inc.—Viewpoint **3490**
Holding Company Report **1878**
"Home Appliance and Power Tool Repairers" in *Occupational Outlook Handbook* **4471**
"Home Appliance Repairer" in *Personal Services* (pp. 51-55) **4472**
"Home Care Aide" in *Careers in Health Care* (pp. 112-115) **3164**
Home Electronics **4096**
Home Health Aide **3165**
"Home Health Aide" in *100 Best Careers for the Year 2000* (pp. 20-22) **3166**
"Home Health Aide" in *100 Best Jobs for the 1990s & Beyond* **3197**
"Home Health Aide" in *Career Information Center* (Vol.7) **3167**
"Home Health Aide" in *Health Care* (pp. 45-49) **3168**
"Home Health Aide" in *Occu-Facts: Information on 580 Careers in Outline Form* **3169**
Home Health Care Nurse **3170**
Home Health Line **3191**
Home Heating & Air Conditioning Systems **4424**
Home VCR Repair Illustrated **4056**, **4259**, **4483**
Homecare News **3192**
"Homemaker" in *Career Information Center* (Vol.5) **3171**
"Homemaker-Home Health Aide" in *150 Careers in the Health Care Field* **3172**
"Homemaker Home Health Aide" in *Opportunities in Health and Medical Careers* (pp. 32-33) **3173**
Homemaker Home Health Aides **3174**
"Homemaker-Home Health Aides" in *America's 50 Fastest Growing Jobs* (pp. 124) **3175**
"Homemaker Home Health Aides" in *Career Discovery Encyclopedia* (Vol.3, pp. 98-99) **3176**
"Homemaker Home Health Aides" in *Encyclopedia of Careers and Vocational Guidance* (Vol.3, pp. 139-142) **3177**
"Homemaker-Home Health Aides" in *Health Care Job Explosion!* (pp. 253-260) **3178**
"Homemaker-Home Health Aides" in *Occupational Outlook Handbook* **3179**
"Homemaker—Home Health Aides" in *The Best Jobs for the 1990s and Into the 21st Century* **3180**
"Homemaker" in *Opportunities in Home Economics Careers* (pp. 51-52) **3181**
Hook, Line & Sinker **3622**
Hooks and Lines **3623**
Hoover Award; VFW J. Edgar **2347**
Hoover Foundation Scholarship; J. Edgar **2327**
Hoover Police Service Award; John Edgar **2328**
Horsebreeders Bookkeeping System **1475**
Horticulture **3137**
HortIdeas **3138**
Hosiery News **6302**
Hospice Forum **3193**
Hospital Attendant **2814**
"Hospital Attendant" in *Occu-Facts: Information on 580 Careers in Outline Form* **2815**
"Hospital Attendants" in *Career Discovery Encyclopedia* (Vol.3, pp. 102-103) **2816**
Hospital Statistics **2871**
"Hospitality Cashier" in *Career Information Center* (Vol.8) **14**
Hospitality Education and Research Journal **2500**
Hospitality Industry **1072**
The Hospitality Manager **2501**, **2630**, **3624**
Hospitality and Tourism Educator **2502**
Hospitals and Health Networks **2872**
"Hostessing" in *The Job Hunter's Guide to Japan* (pp. 163-166) **2562**
Hosteur Magazine **2503**
Hot Off the Computer **1565**
Hot Tips, Sneaky Tricks, and Last Ditch Tactics: An Insider's Guide to Getting Your First Corporate Job **61**, **260**
"Hotel Clerk" in *Career Selector 2001* **1097**
Hotel Concierge **1073**
"Hotel Cook or Chef and Baker" in *Hospitality & Recreation* (pp. 27-31) **2429**
"Hotel Desk Clerk" in *Career Information Center* (Vol.8) **1074**
Hotel Front Office Management & Operation **1051**, **1089**
Hotel/Motel Careers: A World of Opportunities **1075**
"Hotel, Motel Cleaner" in *Occu-Facts: Information on 580 Careers in Outline Form* **3210**
Hotel/Motel Clerk **1076**
"Hotel/Motel Clerk" in *Occu-Facts: Information on 580 Careers in Outline Form* **1077**
"Hotel and Motel Clerks" in *Occupational Outlook Handbook* **1078**
"Hotel and Motel Desk Clerk" in *Hospitality & Recreation* (pp. 15-19) **1079**
"Hotel and Motel Desk Clerks" in *America's 50 Fastest Growing Jobs* (pp. 101) **1080**
Hotel & Motel Equipment & Supplies Directory **1098**
"Hotel and Motel Front Office Clerks" in *Jobs! What They Are—Where They Are—What They Pay* (pp. 201) **1081**
"Hotel and Motel Industry Workers" in *Encyclopedia of Careers and Vocational Guidance* (Vol.3, pp. 143-148) **1082**
Hotel & Motel Management **1091**
Hotel, Motel, and Restaurant Supply Show of the Southeast **2646**
Hotel & Travel Index—ABC International Edition **714**, **1205**
HOTELS **1092**, **2631**
Hotline **4217**

Hotline Divisional Newsletter **3871**
Household Service Workers **3355**
"Household Workers" in *Encyclopedia of Careers and Vocational Guidance* (Vol.3, pp. 152-154) **3182**
Housing Economics **4442**
Housing Market Statistics **4443**
How About a Career in Real Estate? **261**
How to Achieve a Satisfactory DOT Safety Rating **6885**
How to Be an Outstanding Receptionist **1146**
How to Be a Receptionist **1120**
How to Buy an Office Computer or Word Processor **1947**
How to Find Anyone Anywhere **2353**
How to Find Cases Anywhere: P.I.'s Guide to Obtaining Cases, Obtaining Free Publicity & Marketing Investigative Services **2354**
How Food Brokers Serve You **180**
How to Get a Job with A Cruise Line: Adventure-Travel-Romance - How to Sail Around the World on Cruise Ships & Get Paid for It **641**, **1159**
How to Get a Job with the Post Office **1318**
How to Get a Job With the Police Department: Police Officer **2222**
How to Learn Basic Bookkeeping in Ten Easy Lessons **1438**
How to Locate Needed Servicing Information **4097**
How to Prepare for a Civil Service Examination (Text) **1361**
How to Prepare for the Civil Service Examinations for Stenographer, Typist, Clerk, and Office Machine Operator **1935**
How to Prepare for the Commercial Driver's License Truck Driver's Test (CDL) **6867**
How to Prepare for the Fire Fighter Examinations **2094**
How to Prepare for the Police Officer Examination Including Transit and Housing Officer **2308**
How to Prepare for the Police Sergeant Examination **2309**
How to Prepare for the Postal Clerk-Carrier Examination **1362**
How to Prepare for Real Estate Licensing Examinations—Salesperson and Broker **329**
How to Prepare for the U.S. Postal Distribution Machine Clerk Examination **1363**
How to Prepare for the U.S. Postal Service Mailhandler/Mail Processor Examination **1364**
How to Restore Wooden Body Framing **3848**
How to Set up an Effective Filing System **1527**
How to Start a Secretarial & Business Service **1712**
How to Start Your Own Secretarial Services Business at Home **1639**
How to Succeed As a Real Estate Salesperson: A Comprehensive Training Guide **352**
How to Tune, Repair & Regulate Pianos: A Practical Guide **4650**
How to Typeset from a Wordprocessor: An Interfacing Guide **1948**
How Valuable is Your Future? **5811**, **5915**
How You Too Can Become a Flight Attendant!: A Step by Step Guide **3073**
HR Focus **913**
HSUS Close-Up Reports **2932**
HSUS News **2933**
HUD/FHA Quality Control Manual **861**
Hudiburg Award; Everett E. **2101**
Human Relations for the Medical Office **2798**
Human Resources Abstracts **1619**
Human Resources Conference and Exposition **925**
Human Rights Award **2329**
The Human Side of Railroading **6717**
Humane Society of the United States **2914**
Hunting and Fishing Guides **3576**
The Hunting Report for Big Game Hunters **3625**
HVAC **4444**

I

IAFC On Scene **2132**
IAHA HITEC-Hospitality Industry Technology Exposition and Conference **1096**
IASL Newsletter **1566**
The IBEW Leads to Electrifying Careers **4527**, **5047**
IBM PC Advanced Troubleshooting & Repair **4205**
IBPAT Directory **4425**, **4988**, **5235**
IBS - New York **3033**
ICAA News **5191**
ICTA Update **715**, **1206**
Idaho State Board of Occupational Licenses **7197**
The Idea of Police **2390**
IEC Quarterly **5094**
IFT Annual Meeting and Food Expo **2524**, **2647**
IIFET Newsletter **3626**
I.I.I. Insurance Daily **796**
Illinois Department of Professional Regulation **7198**
Illinois State Department of Professional Regulation **7199**
The Illustrated Home Electronics Fix-it Book **4098**
Import Service **3872**, **3982**
Import Statistics **2632**
An Important Message To All Mechanical Minded People **5847**
Imported Crude Oil and Petroleum Products **5496**
Improving Child Care Through the Child Development Associate Program **3334**
IMSA **1279**
IMSA Journal **1280**
In-Plant Printer & Electronic Publisher **6161**, **6207**, **6253**, **6287**
The Independent **2504**
Independent Agent **132**
Independent Electrical Contractors **5057**, **5060**
Independent Insurance Agents of America **105**
Independent Operations **555**
Index to Dental Literature **2728**
Index of Publications and Resource Catalogue **5151**
Indiana Professional Licensing Agency **7200**
Individual Award **2330**
"Industrial (Business-to-Business) Marketing" in *Opportunities in Marketing Careers* (pp. 36-37) **181**
Industrial Circuits & Automated Manufacturing **4099**
Industrial Control Electronics **4100**
Industrial Electronics **4085**
Industrial Electronics: A Text-Lab Manual **4101**
Industrial Electronics and Controls **4102**
Industrial Electronics: Devices & Systems **4103**
Industrial Fabrics in Upholstery **6403**
Industrial Fire Brigades Training Manual **2115**
Industrial Fire Expo **2147**
Industrial Firefighting Series **2157**
Industrial Load Management: Theory, Practice, & Simulations **6045**
"Industrial Machine Repairer" in *Jobs Rated Almanac* **4503**
Industrial Machinery Mechanics **4504**
"Industrial Machinery Mechanics" in *Career Discovery Encyclopedia* (Vol.3, pp. 116-117) **4505**
"Industrial Machinery Mechanics" in *Encyclopedia of Careers and Vocational Guidance* (Vol.3, pp. 182-184) **4506**
Industrial Machinery News **5604**
"Industrial Machinery Repairer" in *Career Information Center* (Vol.9) **4507**
"Industrial Machinery Repairer" in *Occu-Facts: Information on 580 Careers in Outline Form* **4508**
"Industrial Machinery Repairers" in *American Almanac of Jobs and Salaries* (pp. 525) **4509**
"Industrial Machinery Repairers" in *Occupational Outlook Handbook* **4510**
Industrial Truck Association **6698**
"Industrial Truck Operator" in *Occu-Facts: Information on 580 Careers in Outline Form* **6678**
"Industrial Truck Operators" in *Career Discovery Encyclopedia* (Vol.3, pp. 122-123) **6679**
"Industrial Truck Operators" in *Encyclopedia of Careers and Vocational Guidance* (Vol.3, pp. 198-199) **6680**
"Industrial Upholsterer" in *Career Information Center* (Vol.9) **6390**
Industrial Wastewater **6124**
"Industrial, Wholesale, and Direct Sales" in *Careers in Marketing* (pp. 50-62) **182**
Industry Alert **4266**
Industry Award **5361**
Industry Basics **4294**
Industry Directory **906**, **1141**, **1705**, **1941**
Industry Structure Model, A Framework for Career Develpment for IS Professionals **914**
Information Central Guide **3278**
"Information Clerk" in *Careers Inside the World of Offices* (pp. 7-8) **1061**
"Information Clerk" in *Occu-Facts: Information on 580 Careers in Outline Form* **1062**
"Information Clerks" in *America's 50 Fastest Growing Jobs* (pp. 102) **1063**
"Information Clerks" in *Occupational Outlook Handbook* **1064**
Information Management Conference **573**
Information Systems, The DPMA Model Corriculum for a Four-Year Undergraduate Degree for the 1990's **915**
"Information Technology, Data Processing" in *Career Connection II: A Guide to Technical Majors and Their Related Careers* (pp. 92-93) **1903**
"Information/Word Processing" in *Opportunities in Office Occupations* (pp. 116-130) **1904**
"Information/Word Processing: The Secretary" in *Opportunities in Office Occupations* (pp. 93-115) **1640**
Innside Government **1093**
Inside DPMA **916**
Inside the Janitorial Business: How to Start from Scratch & Succeed in Professional Cleaning **3211**
Inside Retailing **477**
InSights **3627**
"Inspectors, Testers, and Graders" in *Occupational Outlook Handbook* **5719**
Installation & Cleaning Specialist **3279**, **4369**
Installation Supplies and Ideas Expo **4889**, **5648**
Installing Personal Computer **4206**
Instant Secretary's Handbook **1641**, **1713**
Instant and Small Commercial Printer **6162**, **6208**, **6254**, **6288**
Institute of Certified Travel Agents **676**, **678**, **1185**, **1187**
Institute of Financial Education **826**
Institute of Internal Auditors **1444**, **1446**
"Institutional Broker" in *Careers in Banking and Finance* (pp. 54-55) **502**
"Institutional Child Care Worker" in *Career Information Center* (Vol.11) **3314**
"Instrument Repair & Restoration Specialist" in *Career Opportunities in the Music Industry* (pp. 127-128) **4621**
Instrument Repairers **4622**
"Instrument Sales Representative" in *Career Opportunities in the Music Industry* (pp. 95-96) **183**
Insulating & Roofing Occupations **5162**, **5412**
Insulation Contractors Association of America Convention **5203**
Insulation Industry File **5192**
Insulation Outlook **5193**
"Insulation Worker" in *Career Information Center* (Vol.4) **5163**

"Insulation Worker" in *Encyclopedia of Danger: Dangerous Professions* (pp. 50-53) **5205**
Insulation Workers **5164**
"Insulation Workers" in *Career Discovery Encyclopedia* (Vol.3, pp. 134-135) **5165**
Insulation Workers, Industrial **5166**
"Insulation Workers" in *Occu-Facts: Information on 580 Careers in Outline Form* **5167**
"Insulation Workers" in *Occupational Outlook Handbook* **5168**
Insurance of Accounts: A Practical Guide to the FDIC Regulations **862**
Insurance Adjuster **762**
"Insurance Adjuster" in *Occu-Facts: Information on 580 Careers in Outline Form* **763**
The Insurance Advocate **133**
Insurance Agent **62**
"Insurance Agent and Broker" in *Career Information Center* (Vol.10) **63**
Insurance Agent/Broker, Life **64**
"Insurance Agent and Broker" in *VGM's Careers Encyclopedia* (pp. 222-225) **65**
"Insurance Agent and Broker" in *VGM's Handbook of Business and Management Careers* **66**
"Insurance Agent" in *Jobs Rated Almanac* **67**
Insurance Agent, Property and Liability **68**
"Insurance Agent/Property & Liability" in *Occu-Facts: Information on 580 Careers in Outline Form* **69**
"Insurance Agent" in *Top Professions: The 100 Most Popular, Dynamic, and Profitable Careers in America Today* (pp. 8-9) **70**
Insurance Agents and Brokers **71**
"Insurance Agents and Brokers" in *101 Careers: A Guide to the Fastest-Growing Opportunities* (pp. 17-19) **72**
"Insurance Agents and Brokers" in *Jobs! What They Are—Where They Are—What They Pay* (p. 337) **73**
"Insurance Agents and Brokers, Life" in *Encyclopedia of Careers and Vocational Guidance* (Vol.3, pp. 212-216) **74**
"Insurance Agents and Brokers: Making it in a Premium Career" in *Careers for Women Without College Degrees* (pp. 239-245) **75**
"Insurance Agents and Brokers" in *Occupational Outlook Handbook* **76**
"Insurance Agents and Brokers, Property and Casualty" in *Encyclopedia of Careers and Vocational Guidance* (Vol.3, pp. 217-220) **77**
"Insurance" in *Black Woman's Career Guide* (pp. 288-294) **78**
"Insurance Claims Representatives" in *Career Discovery Encyclopedia* (Vol.3, pp. 136-137) **764**
"Insurance Claims Representatives" in *Encyclopedia of Careers and Vocational Guidance* (Vol.3, pp. 221-223) **765**
"Insurance Clerks" in *Occu-Facts: Information on 580 Careers in Outline Form* **766**
"Insurance" in *Encyclopedia of Careers and Vocational Guidance* (Vol.1, pp. 242-247) **79**
Insurance Facts **797**
"Insurance is Fun!" in *Internships Volume 3: Accounting, Banking, Brokerage, Finance & Insurance* (pp. 55-61) **80**
Insurance Industry Newsletter **134**
Insurance Information Institute **774**
"Insurance" in *Internships 1995* **81**
Insurance Issues Update **798**
"Insurance" in *Jobs '95* (pp. 373-381) **82**
Insurance Journal **135, 6813**
"Insurance" in *Major Decisions: A Guide to College Majors* (p. 91) **83**
"Insurance Policy Processing Occupations" in *Career Discovery Encyclopedia* (Vol.3, pp. 138-139) **767**
"Insurance Policy Processing Occupations" in *Encyclopedia of Careers and Vocational Guidance* (Vol.3, pp. 224-226) **768**
Insurance Pulse **799**
The Insurance Record **136**
Insurance Review **137**
"Insurance Sales Agent" in *100 Best Careers for the Year 2000* (pp. 174-176) **84**
"Insurance Sales Agent" in *Career Selector 2001* **172**
"Insurance, Sales" in *Career Choices for the 90's for Students of Business* (pp. 163-164) **85**
"Insurance Sales" in *Career Choices for the 90's for Students of Communications and Journalism* (pp. 171-172) **86**
"Insurance, Sales" in *Career Choices for the 90's for Students of Economics* (pp. 72-74) **87**
"Insurance, Sales" in *Career Choices for the 90's for Students of Mathematics* (pp. 97-99) **88**
"Insurance Sales" in *Career Choices for the 90's for Students of Political Science & Government* (pp. 172-173) **89**
"Insurance Sales" in *Career Choices for the 90's for Students of Psychology* (pp. 192-193) **90**
"Insurance Sales" in *Fast-Track Careers: A Guide to the Highest-Paying Jobs* (pp. 152-153) **91**
"Insurance Sales" in *Transitions: Military Pathways to Civilian Careers* (pp. 141-142) **92**
"Insurance Salesperson" in *100 Best Jobs for the 1990s & Beyond* **173**
"Insurance Salesperson" in *College Board Guide to Jobs and Career Planning* (pp. 134-136) **93**
"Insurance Salespersons" in *Opportunities in Vocational and Technical Careers* (pp. 59-75) **94**
Intelligent Buildings Institute—Directory of Products and Services **4721, 4815, 4929, 5074, 5132, 5172, 5431, 5535, 5588**
Intensive Files Management **1528**
"Intercity Bus Driver" in *Career Information Center* (Vol.12) **6631**
"The Intercity People Movers" in *Opportunities in Transportation Careers* (pp. 19-29) **6632**
Interior Construction **5095, 5253**
Interior Plantscape Conference and Trade Show **3151**
Interlocking Concrete Pavement Institute **4917**
Internal Revenue Agent **2223**
"Internal Revenue Agent" in *Occu-Facts: Information on 580 Careers in Outline Form* **2224**
"Internal Revenue Agent" in *VGM's Careers Encyclopedia* (pp. 227-229) **2225**
Internal Revenue Service Agent **2226**
International Air-Conditioning, Heating, Refrigerating Exposition **4457, 6082**
The International Angler **3628**
International Art Competition - New York **5786, 6440**
International Association of Bridge, Structural and Ornamental Iron Workers **5580**
International Association of Chiefs of Police Annual Conference **2384**
International Association of Fire Chiefs **2058**
International Association of Fire Fighters **2059**
International Association of Machinists and Aerospace Workers **4024, 5664, 5753, 6556**
International Association of Security Service **2180, 2184**
International Baking Industry Exposition **2525**
International Benjamin Franklin Fire Service Award **2102**
International Brotherhood of Boilermakers, Iron Ship Builders, Blacksmiths, Forgers and Helpers **5754**
International Brotherhood of Electrical Workers **4546, 5058, 5665, 6036**
International Brotherhood of Painters and Allied Trades **4984, 5126, 5229**
International Brotherhood of Teamsters 1991 **1311, 6557**
International Buyer's Guide of U.S. Automotive and Heavy Duty Products **3983**
International Concrete and Aggregates Show **4963**
International Construction **4750, 4847, 4884, 4955, 5013, 5096, 5152, 5194, 5254, 5302, 5392, 5463, 5553, 5605, 5643**
International Convention **1745**
International Credit Association **1007, 1008**
International Directory of Building Research, Information and Development Organizations **4719, 4809, 4927, 5070, 5130, 5171, 5428, 5536, 5587**
International Fire Fighter **2133**
International Green Front Report **3411, 3680**
International Institute of Carpet and Upholstery Certification **6396, 6399**
International Insurance Monitor **138**
International Joint Painting, Decorating and Drywall Apprenticeship and Manpower Training Fund **4985**
International Journal for Numerical Methods in Fluids **5891**
International Lawn, Garden, and Power Equipment Expo **3152**
International Light Tackle Tournament Association—Bulletin **3629**
International Maintenance Institute Show and Technical Conference **4370**
International Mass Retail Association Convention and Exhibits **248**
International Municipal Signal Association **1264, 1266**
International PBX/Telecommunicators—Newsletter **1879**
International Railway Journal **6770**
International Secretary of the Year **1706**
International Security and Detective Alliance **2279**
International Security Officer's Police and Guard Union **2181**
International Society for Animal Rights—Report **2934**
International Society of Certified Electronics Technicians **4074, 4077, 4244, 4247**
International Society of Certified Electronics Technicians—Update **4116, 4267**
International Taxicab and Livery Association **6804**
International Tropical Timber Agreement **3684**
International Trucking Show **6932**
International Union of Bricklayers and Allied Craftsmen **4709, 4912, 5273, 5626**
International Union of Electronic, Electrical, Salaried, Machine, and Furniture Workers **4513, 5666**
International Union of Electronic, Electrical, Salaried, Machine, and Furniture Workers—Convention Proceedings **4517, 5668**
International Union of Electronic, Electrical, Salaried, Machine and Furnityre Workers **4521, 5671**
International Union of Elevator Constructors **4310**
International Union of Operating Engineers **6067, 6699**
International Union of Security Officers **2182**
International Union, United Automobile, Aerospace and Agricultural Implement Workers of America **5755, 6558**
International Welding Thesaurus **5993**
International Woodworking Machinery and Furniture Supply Fair - USA **6466**
International WorkBoat Show **7009**
Internships Volume 4: The Travel and Hospitality Industries **41**
Interstate Motor Carrier Forms Manual, 2G: Private, Contract, Exempt **6886**
Interviewing for a Career in Public Accounting **1439**
"Interviewing and New Accounts Clerks" in *Occupational Outlook Handbook* **1101**
Into Your Darkroom Step-by-Step **6602**
Introduction to Air Conditioning, Refrigeration & Heating **4409**
Introduction to Carpentry **4804**
Introduction to the Health Professions **2688, 2741, 2817**

Introduction to Management in the Hospitality Industry **1083**, **2430**, **2563**
Inventories of Natural Gas Liquids and Liquefied Refinery Gases **5497**
Investigative and Related Positions in the Federal Government **2371**
Investigator/Claim Examiner **786**
Investigator of the Year **2331**
Investing in the Future: Child Care Financing Options for the Public and Private Sectors **3339**
Iowa State Department of Commerce - Professional Licensing and Regulation Division **7201**
IRA Basics **863**
"Iron and Steel Industry" in *Career Information Center* (Vol.9) **5564**
Iron and Steel Industry Workers **5565**
"Iron and Steel Industry Workers" in *Career Discovery Encyclopedia* (Vol.3, pp. 146-147) **5566**
"Iron and Steel Industry Workers" in *Encyclopedia of Careers and Vocational Guidance* (Vol.3, pp. 241-243) **5567**
"Iron and Steel Worker" in *Career Information Center* (Vol.4) **5568**
Iron Workers and Riggers **5569**
"Iron Workers and Riggers" in *Occu-Facts: Information on 580 Careers in Outline Form* **5570**
"Ironworker" in *Hard Hatted Women: Stories of Struggle and Success in the Trades* (pp. 102-108) **5571**
"Ironworker" in *Jobs Rated Almanac* **5572**
"Ironworker Machine Operator" in *Career Selector 2001* **5614**
"Ironworkers and Steelworkers" in *Opportunities in Building Construction Trades* (pp. 68-70) **5573**
ISCET Tech-of-the-Year Award **4088**, **4256**
ISCET Update **4117**, **4268**
ISDA Special Commendation **2192**, **2332**
ISFSI Instruct-O-Gram **2134**
ITLA Annual Trade Show and Convention **6819**
IUE News **4518**, **5669**
IUPIW Views **5498**

J

J. Edgar Hoover Foundation Scholarship **2327**
'J' Report **5795**
JADA **2729**
"Janitor" in *Career Selector 2001* **3286**
"Janitor" in *VGM's Careers Encyclopedia* (pp. 235-236) **3212**
Janitorial & Maintenance Examinations **3267**
Janitors **3213**
"Janitors and Cleaners" in *Career Discovery Encyclopedia* (Vol.3, pp. 148-149) **3214**
"Janitors and Cleaners" in *Encyclopedia of Careers and Vocational Guidance* (Vol.3, pp. 244-245) **3215**
"Janitors and Cleaners" in *Occupational Outlook Handbook* **3216**
Japan Automotive Insight **3984**
JCAHPO Outlook **2785**
Jesse Meyers' Beverage Digest **2633**
Jeweler **5772**, **5773**
"Jeweler" in *Career Information Center* (Vol.5) **5774**
"Jeweler" in *Career Selector 2001* **5807**
"Jeweler" in *Occu-Facts: Information on 580 Careers in Outline Form* **5775**
Jewelers of America **5785**
"Jewelers" in *Career Discovery Encyclopedia* (Vol.3, pp. 150-151) **5776**
Jewelers' Circular/Keystone—Almanac Issue **5788**
Jewelers International Showcase **5804**
"Jewelers and Jewelry Repairers" in *Encyclopedia of Careers and Vocational Guidance* (Vol.3, pp. 246-249) **5777**
"Jewelers" in *Jobs! What They Are—Where They Are—What They Pay* (p. 351) **5778**
"Jewelers" in *Occupational Outlook Handbook* **5779**
Jewelers, Retail **5780**
"Jewelry Design and Metal Smithing" in *Career Connection II: A Guide to Technical Majors and Their Related Careers* (pp. 96-97) **5781**
Jewelry Maker **5782**
"Jewelry Making" in *Opportunities in Metalworking Careers* (pp. 59-66) **5783**
Jewelry Newsletter International **5796**
"Jewelry Worker" in *Offbeat Careers: The Directory of Unusual Work* **5784**
"Job and Die Setters" in *Encyclopedia of Careers and Vocational Guidance* (Vol.3, pp. 250-251) **5916**
"Job Opportunities in the Armed Forces" in *Occupational Outlook Handbook* **7101**
John Edgar Hoover Police Service Award **2328**
John Hedgecoe's Darkroom Techniques **6603**
Joint Association Survey **5499**
Joint Commission on Allied Health Personnel in Ophthalmology **2770**, **2775**
Jones's English System of Bookkeeping Single or Double Entry **1476**
Joseph C. Scheleen Award for Excellence **1313**
Journal of Agricultural Lending **864**
Journal of the American Dental Association **2730**
Journal of the American Society of CLU & ChFC **139**
Journal of the American Society of Farm Managers and Rural Appraisers **3491**
Journal of the American Water Works Association **6125**
Journal of Appraisal Review **364**
Journal of Coated Fabrics **6369**
The Journal of Commercial Lending **1019**
Journal of Court Reporting **1820**
Journal of Information Technology Management **917**
Journal of Insurance Regulation **140**
Journal of the International Union of Bricklayers & Allied Craftsmen **4751**, **4956**
The Journal of Light Construction **4752**, **4848**, **4885**, **4957**, **5014**, **5097**, **5153**, **5195**
Journal of Management Systems **918**
The Journal of Portfolio Management **556**
Journal of Property Management **365**
Journal of Quality Technology **5736**
Journal of Real Estate Taxation **366**
Journal of Technical Valuation **367**
Journal of Vinyl Additive Technology **5892**
Journeyman Roofer **5464**
The Journeymen Barbers' International Union of America **3044**
Justice **6303**

K

Kane's Beverage Week **2634**
The Keepers of Light: A History & Working Guide to Early Photographic Processes **6620**
Keeping Current **141**
Kentucky Division of Occupations and Professions **7202**
Kin Care and the American Corporation: Solving the Work/Family Dilemma **3333**
Kind News **2935**
Kind Teacher **2936**
Kitchen Helper **2431**
"Kitchen Helper" in *Occu-Facts: Information on 580 Careers in Outline Form* **2432**
Kitchen Times **2505**, **2635**
Knights of Justice Award **2333**
Knitting Times **6370**
Koob Stra **6163**, **6209**, **6255**, **6289**

L

Labor Line **2135**
Labor Unity **6304**, **6371**
"Laboratory Animal Care Worker" in *Career Information Center* (Vol.7) **2902**
Laboratory Animal Science **2937**
The Laborer **7078**
Laborers' International Union of North America **7072**
Lake Erie Fisherman: Work, Identity & Tradition **3662**
Land Line **6909**
Landscape Contractor News **3139**
Landscape and Grounds Maintenance Conference **3153**
"Landscapers and Grounds Managers" in *Career Discovery Encyclopedia* (Vol.4, pp. 160-161) **3097**
"Landscapers and Grounds Managers" in *Encyclopedia of Careers and Vocational Guidance* (Vol.3, pp. 267-269) **3098**
Lapidary Journal **5797**
Last Alarm **2158**
The Last Farmer **3552**
Lather **4975**
"Lather" in *Career Information Center* (Vol.4) **4976**
"Lather" in *Occu-Facts: Information on 580 Careers in Outline Form* **4977**
Lathers **4978**
"Lathers" in *Career Discovery Encyclopedia* (Vol.3, pp. 164-165) **4979**
"Lathers" in *Encyclopedia of Careers and Vocational Guidance* (Vol.3, pp. 277-280) **4980**
"Lathers" in *Opportunities in Building Construction Trades* (pp. 59-61) **4981**
"Launching a Career on Wall Street" in *Internships Volume 3: Accounting, Banking, Brokerage, Finance & Insurance* (pp. 23-33) **503**
Laundromat Attendant **42**
"Laundromat Attendant" in *Occu-Facts: Information on 580 Careers in Outline Form* **43**
Law Enforcement **2227**
Law Enforcement Assistance Award **2334**
"Law Enforcement" in *Career Connection II: A Guide to Technical Majors and Their Related Careers* (pp. 100-101) **2228**
Law Enforcement Career Planning **2355**
Law Enforcement Careers: A Complete Guide from Application to Employment **2229**
Law Enforcement Employment Guide **2230**
Law Enforcement Exams Handbook **2310**
Law Enforcement Leadership Award **2335**
"Law Enforcement Officer" in *100 Best Careers for the Year 2000* (pp. 191-193) **2231**
"Law Enforcement Officer" in *Encyclopedia of Danger: Dangerous Professions* (pp. 58-61) **2391**
Law Enforcement Technology **2372**
Law for the Medical Office **2799**
Law Officer's Bulletin **2373**
Law and Order **2374**
Lawn and Garden Equipment Technicians **4353**
LeaderLine Newsletter **142**
Leadership Directory **4414**
Leadership & Leaders **919**
Leadership Newsletter **6510**
Learn Not to Burn Curriculum **2116**
Leather Braiding **6339**
Leather Makin': A Manual of Primitive and Modern Leather Skills **6340**
The Leather Manufacturer **6347**
"Leather and Shoe Industries" in *Career Information Center* (Vol.9) **6316**
Leather Tooling & Carving **6341**
"Leatherworking" in *Opportunities in Crafts Careers* (p. 65-78) **6317**
Legal and Financial Directory **116**, **343**
"Legal Secretaries" in *America's 50 Fastest Growing Jobs* (pp. 104) **1642**

Legislative Alert **4269**
Legislative Insight **3985**
"Library Assistant" in *Museum Jobs form A-Z: What They Are, How to Prepare, and Where to Find Them* **1539**
"Library Assistants and Bookmobile Drivers" in *Occupational Outlook Handbook* **1540**
"Library Assistants" in *Career Discovery Encyclopedia* (Vol.4, pp. 8-9) **1541**
Library Clerk **1542, 1543**
"Library Clerk" in *Careers Inside the World of Offices* (pp. 8) **1544**
"Library Clerk" in *Occu-Facts: Information on 580 Careers in Outline Form* **1545**
Library Jobs: How to Fill Them, How to Find Them **1546**
Library Technical Assistant **1547**
"Library Technical Assistant" in *Career Selector 2001* **1575**
"Library Technical Assistant" in *Occu-Facts: Information on 580 Careers in Outline Form* **1548**
Library Technicians and Assistants **1549**
"Library Technicians and Assistants" in *Jobs! What They Are—Where They Are—What They Pay* (p. 113) **1550**
Library Times International **1567**
Life Association News **143**
"Life Insurance Agent/Broker" in *Occu-Facts: Information on 580 Careers in Outline Form* **95**
"Life Insurance Agents and Brokers" in *Career Discovery Encyclopedia* (Vol.4, pp. 12-13) **96**
Life Office Management Association **775, 777**
Lift Erection **4325**
Lift Practice **4318**
Lift Servicing & Maintenance **4319**
Lightplane Refurbishing Techniques **3775**
Lillian B. Wood Rowe & John O. Rowe Citizen of the Year Award **3423**
Limousin World **3492**
Limousine and Chauffeur **6814**
"Line Installer" in *Exploring Nontraditional Jobs for Women* (pp. 37-43) **4528**
"Line Installer" in *Jobs Rated Almanac* **4529**
"Line Installers and Cable Splicers" in *Career Discovery Encyclopedia* (Vol.4, pp. 16-17) **4530**
"Line Installers and Cable Splicers" in *Encyclopedia of Careers and Vocational Guidance* (Vol.3, pp. 301-304) **4531**
"Line Installers and Cable Splicers" in *Occupational Outlook Handbook* **4532**
Line Workers (Electric Power) **4533**
Linemen **4534**
"Lineperson" in *Opportunities in Electrical Trades* (p. 56) **4535**
Link Review of Interactive Services **4118**
Literature Review **6126**
"Lithographer/Photoengraver" in *Jobs Rated Almanac* **6179**
"Lithographic Occupations" in *Encyclopedia of Careers and Vocational Guidance* (Vol.3, pp. 312-315) **6180**
"Lithographic Platemaker" in *Occu-Facts: Information on 580 Careers in Outline Form* **6181**
"Lithographic Worker" in *Career Information Center* (Vol.3) **6182**
"Lithographic Workers" in *Career Discovery Encyclopedia* (Vol.4, pp. 20-21) **6183**
LIUNA - Leadership News **7079**
Live Line Maintenance **4536**
Livestock Market Digest **3493**
Livestock, Meat, and Wool Market News **3494**
Livestock Weekly **3495**
Living Among Nature Daringly **3496, 3630**
Local Firms Conference **574**
"Local Truck Driver" in *Career Information Center* (Vol.12) **6829**
"Local Truck Driver" in *Exploring Nontraditional Jobs for Women* (pp. 69-75) **6830**
Local Union Officers Directory **2096**
Locator **5836, 5893, 5947**
"Locomotive Engineer" in *Occu-Facts: Information on 580 Careers in Outline Form* **6718**
"Locomotive Engineers" in *Career Discovery Encyclopedia* (Vol.4, pp. 28-29) **6719**
"Locomotive Engineers" in *Encyclopedia of Careers and Vocational Guidance* (Vol.3, pp. 325-327) **6720**
Locomotive Engineers Journal **6771**
Lodging **1094**
Lodging Exposition and Conference; Northeast Food Service and **2651**
Log Trucker **3704**
Logger **3667**
"Logger" in *Career Information Center* (Vol.2) **3668**
Logger and Lumberman **3705**
"Logger" in *Occu-Facts: Information on 580 Careers in Outline Form* **3669**
Loggers World **3706**
Logging Companies Directory **3685**
Logging Industry Workers **3670**
"Logging Industry Workers" in *Career Discovery Encyclopedia* (Vol.4, pp. 30-31) **3671**
"Logging Industry Workers" in *Encyclopedia of Careers and Vocational Guidance* (Vol.3, pp. 328-331) **3672**
LOMA Membership Directory **144**
"Long Distance Truck Drivers" in *Opportunities in Transportation Careers* (pp. 69-72) **6831**
"Long Haul Truck Driver" in *Career Information Center* (Vol.12) **6832**
Longshore Workers **6956**
Louisiana State Department of Health and Human Resources - Office of Licensing Regulation **7203**
Low-End Word Processor Market **1949**

M

MACAP Statistical Report **4498**
Machine Developments in Upholstery Sewing **6404**
"Machine Operator" in *Career Selector 2001* **5911**
"Machine Operator—Casemaking" in *BLR Encyclopedia of Prewritten Job Descriptions* **5848**
"Machine Tool Operator" in *Career Information Center* (Vol.9) **5849**
"Machine Tool Operator" in *Jobs Rated Almanac* **5850**
Machine Tool Operators **5851, 5852**
"Machine Tool Operators" in *Encyclopedia of Careers and Vocational Guidance* (Vol.3, pp. 338-341) **5853**
"Machine Tool Operators" in *Occu-Facts: Information on 580 Careers in Outline Form* **5854**
Machinery and Equipment Appraiser **368**
Machinery Repairer, Industrial **4511**
"Machining and Machine Operation" in *Opportunities in Metalworking Careers* (pp. 27-38) **5855**
Machinist, All-Round **5812**
"Machinist" in *BLR Encyclopedia of Prewritten Job Descriptions* **5813**
"Machinist" in *Career Selector 2001* **5844**
"Machinist" in *Hard Hatted Women: Stories of Struggle and Success in the Trades* (pp. 187-191, 254-262) **5814**
"Machinist" in *Jobs Rated Almanac* **5815**
Machinist - Machinist's Helper **4514**
"Machinist" in *VGM's Careers Encyclopedia* (pp. 253-255) **5816**
Machinists **5817**
"Machinists" in *Career Discovery Encyclopedia* (Vol.4, pp. 34-35) **5818**
"Machinists" in *Encyclopedia of Careers and Vocational Guidance* (Vol.3, pp. 342-345) **5819**
"Machinists" in *Jobs! What They Are—Where They Are—What They Pay* (pp. 215) **5820**
"Machinists" in *Opportunities in Metalworking Careers* (pp. 28-29) **5821**
"Machinists and Tool Programmers" in *Occupational Outlook Handbook* **5822**
"Magazine Advertising Sales" in *Career Choices for the 90's for Students of Business* (pp. 167-169) **600**
"Magazine Advertising Sales" in *Career Choices for the 90's for Students of Political Science & Government* (pp. 176-178) **601**
"Magazine Advertising Sales" in *Career Choices for the 90's for Students of Psychology* (196-198) **602**
"Magazine Advertising Sales" in *Encyclopedia of Career Choices for the 1990s: A Guide to Entry Level Jobs* (pp. 778-780) **603**
Magnolia: Journal of the Magnolia Society **3140**
Mail Carrier **1319**
"Mail Carrier" in *Career Selector 2001* **1390**
"Mail Carrier" in *Jobs Rated Almanac* **1320**
"Mail Carrier" in *Occu-Facts: Information on 580 Careers in Outline Form* **1321**
"Mail Carriers" in *Career Discovery Encyclopedia* (Vol.4, pp. 40-41) **1322**
"Mail Carriers" in *Encyclopedia of Careers and Vocational Guidance* (Vol.3, pp. 353-356) **1323**
"Mail Clerk" in *Career Information Center* (Vol.1) **1224**
Mail Clerk, Office **1225**
Mail Clerks (Any Industry) **1226**
"Mail Clerks and Messengers" in *Occupational Outlook Handbook* **1227**
Mail Handler **1365**
Mail Handler/Mail Processor **1366**
Mail Handler: U. S. Postal Service **1324**
"Mail Service Worker" in *Career Information Center* (Vol.1) **1325**
Mailing Machines & Equipment Directory **1237, 1377**
"Mailroom Clerk" in *BLR Encyclopedia of Prewritten Job Descriptions* **1228**
Maine State Division of Licensing and Enforcement **7204**
Maintaining and Repairing VCRs **4057, 4260, 4484**
"Maintenance Electrician" in *Career Information Center* (Vol.4) **5048**
"Maintenance Electrician" in *Exploring Nontraditional Jobs for Women* (pp. 118-124) **5049**
"Maintenance Electrician" in *Occu-Facts: Information on 580 Careers in Outline Form* **5050**
"Maintenance Electrician" in *Opportunities in Electrical Trades* (pp. 46-49) **5051**
Maintenance Management Handbook **4364**
Maintenance Mechanic **4316, 4363, 4922**
"Maintenance Mechanics" in *American Almanac of Jobs and Salaries* (pp. 504) **4354**
The Maintenance Mechanic's-Machinist's Toolbox Manual **4365**
Maintenance Mechanics Qualification Program **4355**
Maintenance Supplies—Buyers' Guide Issue **4366**
"Maintenance Technician" in *Opportunities in Aerospace Careers* (pp. 16-21) **3756**
Maintenance Worker/Mechanical Maintainer **4515, 4805, 4923, 5069, 5234, 5355**
"Maitre d', Bartender, Waiter/Waitress: The People Who Meet the Public" in *Careers in the Restaurant Industry* (pp. 23-24) **2564**
Make-Up Competition **3008**
Make Your Airplane Last Forever **3776**
Makeup Artist/Modeling Coach **2981**
Making $70,000 Plus a Year as a Self-Employed Manufacturer's Representative **184**
Making of a Fire Fighter **2050**

Making it Work: The Secretary - Boss Team **1714**
MAN—Modern Applications News—Cutting Tools Buyers' Guide **5941, 5994**
Man of the Year in Law Enforcement **2336**
MANA Membership Directory of Manufacturers' Sales Agencies **224**
Management Review **920**
Management Service **145**
Management Update **4119**
Managing Managed Care **2800**
Managing for Profit **6503**
Managing for Quality in the Service Sector **624**
Managing Your Independent Contractor Fleet Survey: A Nationwide Survey of Trucking Companies Utilizing Owner-Operators **6887**
Manicurist **2982**
"Manicurist" in *Occu-Facts: Information on 580 Careers in Outline Form* **2983**
Manicurists and Nail Technicians **2984**
Manual of the Accrediting Bureau of Health Education Schools **2786**
Manual of Electronic Servicing Test & Measurements **4104**
Manual for the Lawyer's Assistant **1715**
Manuals of Practice **6127**
Manufactured Fiber Fact Book **6381**
Manufactured Fiber Guide **6365**
"Manufactured Products" in *Career Choices for the 90's for Students of Communications and Journalism* (pp. 175-178) **185**
"Manufactured Products" in *Career Choices for the 90's for Students of Political Science & Government* (pp. 178-181) **186**
"Manufactured Products" in *Career Choices for the 90's for Students of Psychology* (pp. 198-201) **187**
"Manufactured Products (Sales)" in *Encyclopedia of Career Choices for the 1990s: A Guide to Entry Level Jobs* (pp. 780-783) **188**
"Manufactured Sales" in *Career Choices for the 90's for Students of Business* (pp. 169-172) **189**
The Manufacturers' Agent **190**
Manufacturers' Agents National Association **221, 222**
Manufacturers' Agents National Association—Special Report **234**
Manufacturer's Representative **191**
"Manufacturer's Representative/Sporting Goods or Equipment Company" in *Career Opportunities in the Sports Industry* (pp. 172-174) **192**
Manufacturers' Representatives **193**
Manufacturers Representatives of America—Newsline **235**
Manufacturers Sales Representative **194**
"Manufacturer's Sales Representative" in *VGM's Careers Encyclopedia* (pp. 257-259) **195**
"Manufacturer's Sales Representative" in *VGM's Handbook of Business and Management Careers* (pp. 57-58) **196**
"Manufacturers' Sales Representatives" in *Career Discovery Encyclopedia* (Vol.4, pp. 46-47) **197**
"Manufacturers' Sales Representatives" in *Jobs! What They Are—Where They Are—What They Pay* (p. 333) **198**
"Manufacturers' Sales Worker" in *Career Information Center* (Vol.10) **199**
"Manufacturers' Sales Workers" in *Encyclopedia of Careers and Vocational Guidance* (Vol.3, pp. 361-365) **200**
"Manufacturers' Sales Workers" in *Opportunities in Vocational and Technical Careers* (pp. 59-75) **201**
"Manufacturer's Salespeople: Selling Goods" in *Careers for Women Without College Degrees* (pp. 250-253) **202**
"Manufacturer's Salesperson" in *College Board Guide to Jobs and Career Planning* (pp. 142-143) **203**
"Manufacturers' and Wholesale Sales Representatives" in *Occupational Outlook Handbook* **204**
"Manufacturing" in *Internships 1995* **205**
Manufacturing Jewelers and Silversmiths of America Exposition/Providence **5805**
"Manufacturing Opticians" in *Opportunities in Eye Care Careers* (pp. 79-83) **6515**
"Manufacturing Reps" in *New York Times Career Planner* (pp. 237-240) **206**
MAQUINAMEX - Metalworking Machine Tool Expo **5838, 5907**
"Marble Setter, Tilesetters, and Terrazzo Workers" in *Opportunities in Building Construction Trades* (pp. 63-65) **4900, 5615**
"Marble Setters" in *Career Discovery Encyclopedia* (Vol.4, pp. 50-51) **4690**
Marble Setters, Tile Layers and Terrazzo Workers **4901, 5616**
"Marble Setters, Tile Setters, and Terrazzo Workers" in *Encyclopedia of Careers and Vocational Guidance* (Vol.3, pp. 366-368) **4691, 4902, 5617**
Marble, Tile Setters, Terrazzo, and Stone Workers **4692, 4903, 5618**
"Marble, Tile, Terrazzo, and Stone Workers" in *Occu-Facts: Information on 580 Careers in Outline Form* **4693, 4904, 5619**
"Marble, Tile, and Terrazzo Worker" in *Career Information Center* (Vol.4) **4694, 4905, 5620**
Marine Corps Gazette **7156**
MARINE DIGEST **6994**
"Marine Electrician" in *Opportunities in Electrical Trades* (pp. 51-53) **5052**
"Marine Engine Mechanic" in *Opportunities in Marine and Maritime Careers* (pp. 105-107) **4594**
"Marine Engineer" in *Career Information Center* (Vol.2) **6957**
"Marine Engineer (Shipboard)" in *Occu-Facts: Information on 580 Careers in Outline Form* **6958**
"Marine Engineers" in *Career Discovery Encyclopedia* (Vol.4, pp. 54-55) **6959**
"Marine Engineers" in *Encyclopedia of Careers and Vocational Guidance* (Vol.4, pp. 54-55) **6960**
Marine Fish Management **3631**
"Marine Insurance Careers" in *Opportunities in Marine and Maritime Careers* (pp. 111-112) **97**
Marine Log **6995, 7157**
"Marine/Ocean Engineering and Naval Architecture" in *Opportunities in Engineering Careers* (pp. 114-116) **6961**
"Marine Services Technician" in *Career Information Center* (Vol.12) **4595**
Marine Technology Society **3580**
Marine Technology Society Journal **3632**
The Marines and You **7184**
"Maritime Jobs" in *Opportunities in Transportation Careers* (pp. 53-54) **6962**
Mark-up Clerk/Clerk Typist/Clerk Stenographer - U.S. Postal Service **1367**
Market Analysts **3986**
Market Overview **2194**
Marketing Insight **3987**
"Marketing/Sales" in *Career Choices for the 90's for Students of Business* (pp. 99-101) **604**
"Marketing and Sales" in *Encyclopedia of Career Choices for the 1990s: A Guide to Entry Level Jobs* (pp. 407-409) **605**
"Marketing and Sales, Hotel Management" in *Career Choices for the 90's for Students of Psychology* (pp. 101-103) **606**
Marketing Your Services: A Step-by-Step Guide for Small Businesses & Professionals **625**
Maryland State Department of Licensing and Regulation - Division of Occupational and Professional Licensing **7205**
Mason Contractors' Equipment & Supplies Directory **4930**
Masonry **4714, 4753, 4924, 4958**
Masonry and Bricklaying **4715**
Masons **4695**
The Mason's Toolbox Manual **4722**
Mass Transit **6652**
Massachusetts State Executive Office of Consumer Affairs **7206**
Material Handler **7047**
"Material Handler" in *Occu-Facts: Information on 580 Careers in Outline Form* **7048**
Material Handlers **7049**
"Material Moving Equipment Operators" in *Occupational Outlook Handbook* **6681**
"Material Recording, Scheduling, Dispatching, and Distributing Occupations" in *Occupational Outlook Handbook* **1241**
Math on the Job: Cashier **25**
Math on the Job: Electrician **5075**
Math on the Job: Local Truck Driver **6888**
Math on the Job: Plumber **5365**
Math on the Job: Secretary/Clerk Typist **1052, 1143, 1716, 1950**
Math Review for Real Estate License Examinations **330**
Math and Verbal Review for the Civil Service Exam **1368**
Math for Welders **5995**
Mathematics for Auto Mechanics **3959**
Mathematics for the Heating, Ventilating & Cooling Trades **4426**
Maxine Williams Scholarships **2789**
MCBA Newsletter **6164, 6210, 6256, 6290**
McDonnell Douglas Law Enforcement Award **2337**
Meat Cutter **5690**
Meat Cutter/Market Manager **5691**
"Meat Cutter" in *Occu-Facts: Information on 580 Careers in Outline Form* **5692**
"Meat Packing Production Workers" in *Career Discovery Encyclopedia* (Vol.4, pp. 62-63) **5693**
"Meat Packing Production Workers" in *Encyclopedia of Careers and Vocational Guidance* (Vol.3, pp. 381-384) **5694**
"Meat Packing Worker" in *Career Information Center* (Vol.2) **5695**
"Meat Wrapper (Supermarket)" in *Occu-Facts: Information on 580 Careers in Outline Form* **5696**
Meatcutters **5697**
"Meatcutters" in *American Almanac of Jobs and Salaries* (pp. 533) **5698**
"Meatcutters" in *Career Discovery Encyclopedia* (Vol.4, pp. 64-65) **5699**
"Meatcutters" in *Encyclopedia of Careers and Vocational Guidance* (Vol.3, pp. 385-387) **5700**
"Mechanic" in *Guide to Careers Without College* (pp. 92-95) **3914**
Mechanical Contractors Association of America **5342, 5345**
Mechanical Contractors Association of America—Reporter **5393**
Mechanical News **3873**
Mechanics **3757, 4017, 4356, 4392, 4579, 4596**
"Mechanics" in *Opportunities in Transportation Careers* (pp. 38-39) **3758**
Medal of Valor **2003**
Medical Assistant **2742, 2743**
"Medical Assistant" in *150 Careers in the Health Care Field* **2744**
"Medical Assistant" in *Allied Health Education Directory* (pp. 59-71) **2745**
"Medical Assistant" in *Career Connection II: A Guide to Technical Majors and Their Related Careers* (pp. 110-111) **2746**
"Medical Assistant" in *Career Information Center* (Vol.7) **2747**
"Medical Assistant" in *Careers in Health Care* (pp. 120-124) **2748**
"Medical Assistant" in *Occu-Facts: Information on 580 Careers in Outline Form* **2749**
"Medical Assistant" in *Opportunities in Health and Medical Careers* (p. 17) **2750**
"Medical Assistant" in *Opportunities in Paramedical Careers* (pp. 30-34) **2751**

"Medical Assistant in Pediatrics" in *Opportunities in Health and Medical Careers* (pp. 17-18) **2752**
"Medical Assistant" in *VGM's Careers Encyclopedia* (pp. 272-274) **2753**
"Medical Assistant" in *VGM's Handbook of Health Care Careers* **2754**
Medical Assistants **2755**
"Medical Assistants" in *America's 50 Fastest Growing Jobs* (pp. 126) **2756**
"Medical Assistants" in *Career Discovery Encyclopedia* (Vol.4, pp. 74-75) **2757**
"Medical Assistants" in *Encyclopedia of Careers and Vocational Guidance* (Vol.3, pp. 404-406) **2758**
"Medical Assistants" in *Health Care Job Explosion!* (pp. 271-279) **2759**
"Medical Assistants" in *Occupational Outlook Handbook* **2760**
"Medical Assistants" in *The Best Jobs for the 1990s and Into the 21st Century* **2761**
Medical Assisting **2782**
Medical Assisting - A Career for Today and Tomorrow **2762**
Medical Assisting: Today's Career for Tomorrow's Reward **2763**
Medical and Dental Associations, P.C. Insurance Forms Preparation **2689**
"Medical Dental Secretary" in *Career Connection II: A Guide to Technical Majors and Their Related Careers* (pp. 112-113) **1643**
"Medical or Dental Secretary" in *Health Care* (pp. 51-55) **1644**
Medical and Health Information Directory **2707**, **2787**, **2856**, **6498**, **6531**
"Medical Office Assistants" in *Jobs! What They Are—Where They Are—What They Pay* (p. 167) **2764**
Medical Office Management — Part I **2801**
"Medical Secretary" in *Opportunities in Health and Medical Careers* (pp. 106-107) **1645**
"Medical Secretary" in *VGM's Careers Encyclopedia* (pp. 279-281) **1646**
"Medical Secretary" in *VGM's Handbook of Health Care Careers* **1647**
Medical Transcriptionist **1757**
"Medical Transcriptionist" in *150 Careers in the Health Care Field* **1758**
"Medical Transcriptionist" in *Occu-Facts: Information on 580 Careers in Outline Form* **1759**
"Medical Transcriptionist" in *Opportunities in Health and Medical Careers* (p. 122) **1760**
Member New/Wise Owl News **6533**
Member News **6534**
Members of the National Association of Barber Styling Schools **3005**
Membership Directory and Information Guide **3786**
Membership Directory and Research Guide **2506**
Membership List **2136**
Membership Roster **5764**
"Membership Secretary" in *Museum Jobs form A-Z: What They Are, How to Prepare, and Where to Find Them* **1648**
The Men of Company 208 **7102**
Men of Earth **3553**
Men of Iron **5574**
"Mental Health Technician/Human Services Technician/Psychiatric Aide" in *150 Careers in the Health Care Field* **2818**
"Merchant Marine Captain" in *Career Information Center* (Vol.12) **6963**
"Merchant Marine Engineer and Chief Engineer" in *Career Information Center* (Vol.12) **6964**
"Merchant Marine Engineer" in *Transportation* (pp. 63-67) **6965**
Merchant Marine Examination Questions—Volume 12: Electricity **6987**
Merchant Marine Examination Questions—Volume 13: Steam Plants **6988**
Merchant Marine Examination Questions—Volume 2: Navigation Problems **6989**
Merchant Marine Occupations **6966**
"Merchant Marine Occupations" in *Encyclopedia of Careers and Vocational Guidance* (Vol.3, pp. 425-428) **6967**
"Merchant Marine Officers" in *Jobs! What They Are—Where They Are—What They Pay* (pp. 297) **6968**
"Merchant Marine Officers" in *Opportunities in Transportation Careers* (pp. 59-60) **6969**
"Merchant Marine Unlicensed Sailors" in *Opportunities in Transportation Careers* (pp. 54-58) **6970**
"Merchant Sailor" in *Hard Hatted Women: Stories of Struggle and Success in the Trades* (pp. 176-186) **6971**
Mercruiser Stern Drive Shop Manual 1964-1987 **3960**
Mercury Systems Inc.: Practice Set in Word-Information Processing for Conventional & Text-Editing Typewriters **1951**
Merit Award for Excellent Arrest **2338**
"Messenger Service Worker" in *Career Information Center* (Vol.1) **1229**
Metal Construction News **5465**, **5606**
Metal Corrosion in Boats **4612**
METALFORM **5839**, **5908**
Metals Newsletter **5894**
"Metalworking and Plastics-Working Machine Operators" in *Occupational Outlook Handbook* **5856**
Metro Magazine **6653**, **6815**
Michigan State Department of Commerce - Bureau of Occupational and Professional Regulation **7207**
Micro Computer Journal **992**
Microelectronics & Office Jobs: The Impact of the Chip on Women's Employment **999**
Microprocessor Manual for Traffic Signals **1274**
Mid-America Farm Exposition **3532**
Mid-America Jewelry Show **5806**
Mid-America Trucking Show **6933**
Mid-Atlantic Nurserymen's Winter Trade Show **3154**
Mid-South Farm and Gin Supply Exhibit **3533**
Mid-West Truck Show **6934**
Midwest Farm Show **3534**
Midwest Poultry Federation Convention **3535**, **5716**
Midwest Specialty Exposition **4590**, **5106**, **5405**
Midwestern Foodservice and Equipment Exposition **2648**
"Military Careers" in *Career Discovery Encyclopedia* (Vol.4, pp. 90-91) **7103**
"Military Careers" in *Encyclopedia of Careers and Vocational Guidance* (Vol.4, pp. 90-91) **7104**
"Military Chaplain" in *Opportunities in Religious Service Careers* (pp. 85-87) **7105**
"Military" in *College Board Guide to Jobs and Career Planning* (pp. 208-210) **7106**
"Military Counselor" in *Careers in Counseling and Human Development* (pp. 102-104) **7107**
"The Military" in *Electronic Service Careers* (pp. 88-99) **7108**
"Military Fire Protection" in *Opportunities in Fire Protection Services* (pp. 32-33) **7109**
"Military" in *Footsteps in the Ocean: Careers in Diving* (pp. 115-122) **7110**
Military Intelligence Professional Bulletin **7158**
"Military" in *International Careers: An Insider's Guide, Where to Find Them, How to Build Them* (pp. 174-176) **7111**
Military Lifestyle **7159**
"Military Nursing" in Your Career in Nursing (pp. 156-160) **7112**
"Military Science" in *College Majors and Careers: A Resource Guide for Effective Life Planning* (pp. 99-100) **7113**
"Military Service" in *Exploring Careers Using Foreign Languages* (pp. 73-74) **7114**
Military Service Occupations **7115**
"Military Services" in *Jobs! What They Are—Where They Are—What They Pay* (pp. 294-296) **7116**
"Military" in *Straight Talk on Careers: 80 Pros Take You Into Their Professions* (pp. 203-224) **7117**
"The Military Veterinarian" in *Opportunities in Veterinary Medicine* (pp. 105-105) **7118**
"Milling Machine Tender" in *Occu-Facts: Information on 580 Careers in Outline Form* **5857**
Millwright **4560**, **4561**
"Millwright" in *BLR Encyclopedia of Prewritten Job Descriptions* **4562**
"Millwright" in *Jobs Rated Almanac* **4563**
"Millwright" in *Occu-Facts: Information on 580 Careers in Outline Form* **4564**
"Millwright" in *Opportunities in Carpentry Careers* (p. 52) **4565**
Millwrights **4566**
"Millwrights" in *Career Discovery Encyclopedia* (Vol.4, pp. 92-93) **4567**
"Millwrights" in *Encyclopedia of Careers and Vocational Guidance* (Vol.3, pp. 447-449) **4568**
"Millwrights" in *Occupational Outlook Handbook* **4569**
Mini Lab Focus **6607**
Minnesota State Department of Commerce **7208**
Mississippi Secretary of State **7209**
Missouri State Department of Professional Registration **7210**
Mixin' **2636**
MJSA Benchmark **5798**
Mobile Air Conditioning Society Trade Show and Technical Conference **4458**
"Mobile Heavy Equipment Mechanics" in *Career Discovery Encyclopedia* (Vol.4, pp. 96-97) **4580**
"Mobile Heavy Equipment Mechanics" in *Occupational Outlook Handbook* **4581**
Modern Baking **2507**
Modern Bulk Transporter—Truck Specifications Directory Issue **6889**
Modern Dental Assisting **2715**
Modern Food Service News **2508**, **2637**
Modern Heating, Ventilating & Air Conditioning **4427**
Modern Jeweler **5799**
Modern Plastics **5895**
Modern Railroad Man of the Year **6763**
Modern Retailing: Theory and Practice **474**
Modern Woodworking **3707**, **6457**
Montana State Department of Commerce - Bureau of Professional and Occupational Licensing **7211**
Monthly Completion Report **5500**
Monthly F.O.B. Price Summary, Past Sales (Coast Mills) **3708**
Monthly F.O.B. Price Summary, Past Sales (Inland Mills) **3709**
Monthly Statistical Report **5501**
Moody's Bond Survey **557**
Mosby's Textbook for Nursing Assistants **2861**
Motel Maid **3217**
Mother & Infant Expo **3343**
Motor/Age **3874**, **3988**
Motor Carrier Annual Report **6945**
Motor Carrier Employees Handbook for the Prevention of Freight Loss & Damages **6890**
Motor Carrier Insurance **6891**
Motor Carrier Management Systems **6892**
Motor Carrier Professional Services Directory **6946**
Motor and Equipment Manufacturers Association **3924**, **4025**, **4335**, **4584**, **4606**
Motor Service **3875**, **3989**
Motor Service—Tool & Equipment Buyers Guide Issue **3961**
"Motor Vehicle Mechanic" in *BLR Encyclopedia of Prewritten Job Descriptions* **3915**
Motorboat Mechanics **4597**

"Motorcycle, Boat, and Small-Engine Mechanics" in *Occupatiional Outlook Handbook* **4598**
Motorcycle Electrics Without Pain **4613**
Motorcycle Mechanic **4599**, **4600**
"Motorcycle Mechanic" in *Career Information Center* (Vol.12) **4601**
"Motorcycle Mechanic" in *Occu-Facts: Information on 580 Careers in Outline Form* **4602**
Motorcycle Mechanics **4614**
"Motorcycle Mechanics" in *Career Discovery Encyclopedia* (Vol.4, pp. 102-103) **4603**
"Motorcycle Mechanics" in *Opportunities in Automotive Service Careers* (p. 59) **4604**
Motorcycle Technicians **4605**
Movin' Out **6910**
Multinational Service Firms **626**
"Municipal Police Officer" in *VGM's Careers Encyclopedia* (pp. 361-364) **2232**
Munro's Bookkeeping & Accountancy **1477**
"Music Shop Salesperson" in *Career Opportunities in the Music Industry* (pp. 89-90) **432**
Musical Instrument Repairer **4623**
"Musical Instrument Repairer" in *Jobs Rated Almanac* **4624**
"Musical Instrument Repairers" in *Career Discovery Encyclopedia* (Vol.4, pp. 114-115) **4625**
"Musical Instrument Repairers and Tuners" in *Encyclopedia of Careers and Vocational Guidance* (Vol.3, pp. 529-532) **4626**
"Musical Instrument Repairers and Tuners" in *Occupational Outlook Handbook* **4627**
Musical Instrument Salesperson **433**
Muskrats & Marsh Management **3590**
Musky Hunter **3633**

N

NABS Research Reports **3045**
NACCAS Handbook **3020**
NACCAS Review **3021**
NACUFS News Wave **2509**, **2638**
NADL Hazard Communication Manual **6504**
NAFI Man of the Year **787**, **2103**, **2339**
NAHC Report **3194**
NAHM Directory of Hosiery Manufacturers **6305**
NAHM Directory of Hosiery Mill Suppliers **6306**
Nannies **3356**
"Nannies" in *Career Discovery Encyclopedia* (Vol.4, pp. 118-119) **3357**
"Nannies" in *Encyclopedia of Careers and Vocational Guidance* (Vol.3, pp. 540-542) **3358**
"Nanny" in *Career Information Center* (Vol.5) **3359**
"Nanny" in *Offbeat Careers: The Directory of Unusual Work* **3360**
NAPBIRT Directory **4645**
NAPE Directory **6079**
NAPET La Croix Award **6587**
NAPET News **6608**
NAPIA Bulletin **800**
NAPW Newsletter **1620**
NASSTRAC **6709**, **6935**
NATA Communicator **4295**
NATA Industry Basics **4289**
NATA Sourcebook **4290**
National Accrediting Commission of Cosmetology Arts and Sciences **2993**
National Agri-Marketing Association Conference **249**, **634**
National Alliance **1380**
National Association of Accredited Cosmetology Schools **2994**
National Association of Barber Styling Schools **2995**
National Association of Brick Distributors Trade Exhibit **4761**
National Association of Church Food Service **2589**, **2592**
National Association of Counselors **316**
National Association of Dental Laboratories **6492**, **6494**
National Association for the Education of Young Children **3326**, **3329**
National Association for the Education of Young Children Annual Conference **3344**
National Association of Executive Secretaries **1687**
National Association of Food Equipment Manufacturers Convention **2649**
National Association of Furniture Repair and Refinishing Specialists **6397**, **6400**
National Association of Health Underwriters **106**, **110**
National Association of Home Builders of the U.S. **4399**, **4795**, **4986**
National Association for Home Care **3184**, **3185**
National Association for Home Care Annual Meeting and Home Care Exhibition **3196**
National Association of Hosiery Manufacturers **6289**, **6290**, **6362**, **6363**
National Association of Investigative Specialists **2273**, **2280**
National Association of Legal Secretaries (International) **1688**, **1691**
National Association of Life Underwriters **107**
National Association of Personnel Workers **1609**
National Association of Photo Equipment Technicians **6584**
National Association of Plumbing-Heating-Cooling Contractors **4400**, **5343**
National Association of Postmasters of the United States Convention **1387**
National Association of Power Engineers **6068**
National Association of Professional Band Instrument Repair Technicians **4640**
National Association of Professional Engravers Annual Trade Show and Exhibit **6217**
National Association of Professional Insurance Agents **108**
National Association of Professional Insurance Agents Convention and Trade Show **167**
National Association of Public Insurance Adjusters **776**, **778**
National Association of Public Insurance Adjusters Directory **788**
National Association of Radio and Telecommunications Engineers **4151**, **4153**
National Association of Realtors **317**
National Association of Realtors Midyear Trade Exposition **403**
National Association of Reinforcing Steel Contractors **5581**, **5583**
National Association of Review Appraisers and Mortgage Underwriters Convention **404**
National Association of Trade and Technical Schools **2448**, **2450**, **2590**, **2593**, **3819**, **3822**, **4026**, **4028**, **5971**, **5973**
National Association of Underwater Instructors **3581**, **3584**
National Association for Variable Annuities **109**
National Association of Wheat Growers Convention **3536**
National Auto Body Congress and Exposition **3882**
National Automatic Merchandising Association **4673**
National Automatic Merchandising Association—Directory of Members **4674**
National Automatic Merchandising Association-Newsletter **4675**
National Automatic Merchandising Association—State Legislative Review **4676**
National Automotive Radiator Service Association Annual Trade Show and Convention **3997**
National Automotive Technicians Education Foundation **3887**, **3925**, **3927**
National Beauty Show **3034**
National Broiler Council—Washington Report **5711**
National Bulletin **3022**
National Catholic Forester **3710**
National Cattlemen's Association Annual Convention and Trade Show **3537**
National Center for the Early Childhood Work Force **3327**
National Cosmetology Association **2991**
National Cosmetology Association Convention **3035**
National Court Reporters Association **1775**, **1778**
National Court Reporters Association—Membership Directory and Registry of Professional Reporters **1821**
National Culinary Review **2510**
National Dental Assistant Boards **2702**
National Directory of Fire Chiefs & Emergency Departments **2097**
National Dog Groomers Association of America **2915**, **2918**
National Electrical Contractors Association **5059**
National Electronics Service Dealers Association **4245**, **4248**
National Electronics Service Dealers Association—Inside NESDA **4270**
National Engineer **6080**
National Erectors Association **5582**, **5584**
National Executive Housekeepers Association **3219**, **3221**
National Executive Housekeepers Association Exposition **3370**
National Farm Machinery Show and Championship Tractor Pull **3538**
National Farmers Union—Washington Newsletter **3497**
National FFA Convention Proceedings **3498**
National FFA Organization **3407**
National FFA Organization—Update **3499**
National Fire Codes **2137**, **2159**
National Fire Protection Association **2060**, **2061**
National Fire Protection Association—Technical Committee Reports/Technical Committee Documentation **2138**, **2160**
National Fire Sprinkler Association **5344**, **5346**
National Fisherman **3634**
National Forum **726**
National Gardening **3141**
National Glass Association **5127**
National Glass Association Annual Convention and National Glass and Machinery Show **5157**
National Glaziers' Architectural Metal and Glassworkers' Industries Apprenticeship Training and Journeymen Education Fund **5131**
The National Gleaner Forum **146**
National Highway Traffic Safety Administration's Truck Operator Qualification Examination **6868**
National Hog Farmer **3500**
National Home Care and Hospice Directory **3187**
National Institute for Automotive Service Excellence **3820**, **3823**, **3926**, **3928**, **4027**, **4029**, **6559**, **6561**
National Institute on Park and Grounds Management Convention **3155**
National Insulation and Abatement Contractors Association **5170**
National Jail and Adult Detention Directory **2001**
National Jeweler **5800**
National Landscape Association **3103**
The National Librarian: The NLA Newsletter **1568**
National Medical Assistant Week **2807**
National Membership Directory and Users Guide **4415**
National Police Officers Association of America **2274**
National Police Review **2375**
National Postal Forum **1388**

National Postsecondary Agricultural Student Organization **3410**
National Professional Qualifications System: Established by the Joint Council of National Fire Service Organizations **2051**
National Quality Award **119**
National Real Estate Directory **344**
National Real Estate Investor **369**
National Relocation & Real Estate **370**
National Restaurant Association **2449, 2591**
National Restaurant Association Ice Carving Classic **2463, 2607**
National Restaurant Association Restaurant, Hotel-Motel Show **2526, 2650**
National Restaurant Association Undergraduate Scholarships **2464, 2608**
National Restaurant Association—Washington Weekly **2511, 2639**
National Retail Federation **471**
National Rifle Association of America **3582**
National Roofing Contractors Association **5424**
National Roofing Contractors Association Annual Convention and Trade Show **5474**
National Roofing Foundation Scholarship Award **5430**
The National Rural Letter Carrier **1381**
National Sales Achievement Award **120**
National Screw Machine Products Association **5826**
National Shorthand Reporters Association **1776, 1779**
National Society to Prevent Blindness—Annual Report **6535**
National Society of Public Accountants **1445, 1447**
National Star Route Mail Contractors Association **1338**
National Terrazzo and Mosaic Association **4913, 4918**
National Tooling and Machining Association **5722, 5827, 5877, 5919, 5935, 5938**
National Trappers Association **3583**
National Truck Equipment Association (SUPERSHOW) **6936**
National Underwriter Property and Casualty/Risk and Benefits Management **147**
Nation's Building News **4445, 4754, 4755, 4886, 4887, 4959, 4960, 5098, 5099, 5154, 5155, 5196, 5197, 5255, 5256, 5303, 5304, 5394, 5395, 5466, 5467, 5554, 5555, 5607, 5608, 5644, 5645**
Nation's Restaurant News **2512, 2640**
NATSO Truckers News **6911**
Naval Aviation News **7160**
Navy Career Opportunities **7119**
"Navy Military Sealift Command" in *Opportunities in Transportation Careers* (pp. 129-130) **7120**
Navy News **7161**
"Navy Nurse" in *150 Careers in the Health Care Field* **7121**
Navy Times **7162**
The Navy and You **7185**
NAW Report **236**
NCOCall **7163**
The NCRA Roofing & Waterproofing Manual **5432**
NDGAA Convention Manual **2925**
NEA Notes Newsletter **5609**
Nebraska State Bureau of Examining Boards - Department of Health **7212**
NECA News **5100**
NECA Standard of Installation **5101**
The Needle's Eye **6307**
NESDA—Update **4120, 4271**
Network for Material Handling **6705**
Network News **865**
A New & Complete System of Bookkeeping by an Improved Method of Double Entry **1478**
New Dimensions **237**
New England Farm Bulletin & Garden Gazette—Farmer-Consumer Connection **3412**
New England Farm Bulletin & Garden Gazette—NEFB Almanack Issue **3413**
New England Nurserymen's Annual Trade Show **3156**
The New Farm **3501**
New Homes Magazine **371**
New Horizons **3142**
"New Horizons for Rail Careers" in *Opportunities in Transportation Careers* (pp. 81-93) **6721**
New Jersey Motor Truck Association Annual Convention **6937**
New Jersey State Department of Law and Public Safety - Division of Consumer Affairs **7213**
New Manufacturing Technologies **4105**
New Mexico State Department of Regulation and Licensing **7214**
New Polymer Technology for Auto Body Exteriors **3849**
New Secretary: How to Handle People As Well As You Handled Paper **1717**
New Ways to Use Test Meters: A Modern Guide to Electronic Servicing **4106**
New York Education Department - Division of Professional Licensing Services **7215**
News **2731, 4446**
Newsline **372**
"Newspaper and Magazine Advertising Sales Representative" in *Career Opportunities in Advertising and Public Relations* (pp. 224-226) **607**
Newspaper Personnel Relations Association **1610**
NFPA 1001, Fire Fighter Professional Qualifications, 1987 edition **2052**
NFPA Journal **2139**
NIAC Commercial and Industrial Standards Manual **5173**
NIAC News **5198**
The Nightingale **2873**
1994 FHA/VA Loan Processing Information Service **835**
1994 FHA/VA Loan Servicing Manual **836**
NITL Notice **6772, 6912, 6996**
NLA Landscape News **3143**
NMTBA - Association for Manufacturing Technology **5830, 5881, 5938, 5942**
NNFA Today **2513**
No Experience Necessary: Make $100,000 a Year as a Stockbroker **504**
NOMDA Who's Who **907, 1718**
North American Equipment Dealers Association **4336**
North American Farm and Power Show **3539**
North American Fisherman **3635**
North American Hairstyling Awards **3009**
North American Hunter **3636**
North American Journal of Fisheries Management **3637**
North American Telecommunications Association **4286**
North Dakota Secretary of State **7216**
Northeast Food Service and Lodging Exposition and Conference **2651**
Northeastern Loggers Association **3674, 6439**
Northeastern Loggers' Association Annual Scholarships **3682, 6441**
Northeastern Loggers' Association Awards Program **3683, 6442**
Northeastern Loggers Congress and Equipment Exposition **3730, 6467**
Northeastern Lumber Manufacturers Association—Information Log **3711**
Northern California/Richard Epping Scholarships **688, 1194**
Northern Journal of Applied Forestry **3712**
Northern Logger and Timber Processor **3713**
Northwest Agricultural Show **3540**
Not Too Small to Care: Small Businesses and Child Care **3340**
NPRA Directory **1615**
NPRA News **1621**
NRAction **3638**
NRCA Directory **5429**
NSRA List of Approved Court Reporter Education Programs **1816**
NTA Trapping Handbook: A Guide for Better Trapping **3591**
NTL News **5765**
NTMA Design Book **4931**
NTMA Directory **4928**
NTMA Record **5837, 5944**
Nuclear Plant Journal **6052**
"Nuclear Reactor Operator Technicians" in *Career Discovery Encyclopedia* (Vol.4, pp. 128-129) **6025**
"Nuclear Reactor Operator Technicians" in *Encyclopedia of Careers and Vocational Guidance* (Vol.3, pp. 583-588) **6026**
Numeric Filing Guideline **1529**
"Numerical-Control Lathe Operator" in *Career Selector 2001* **5912**
"Numerical Control Machine Operator" in *Career Information Center* (Vol.9) **5858**
"Numerical Control Machine Operator" in *Careers in High Tech* (pp. 138-139) **5859**
"Numerical Control Machine Tool Operator" in *Guide To Careers Without College* (pp. 61-63) **5860**
Numerical-Control Setup Technician **5861**
Numerical Control Tool Programmers **5862**
Nurse Education Scholarships **2858**
Nursery and Landscape Workers **2819**
"Nursery and Landscape Workers" in *Occu-Facts: Information on 580 Careers in Outline Form* **3099**
"Nursery School Attendant" in *Career Selector 2001* **3346**
"Nurse's Aide" in *100 Best Careers for the Year 2000* (pp. 17-19) **2820**
"Nurse's Aide" in *Career Connection II: A Guide to Technical Majors and Their Related Careers* (pp. 116-117) **2821**
"Nurse's Aide" in *Career Selector 2001* **2879**
"Nurse's Aide" in *Jobs Rated Almanac* **2822**
"Nurse's Aide and Orderly" in *Career Information Center* (Vol.7) **2823**
"Nurse's Aide/Psychiatric Aide" in *Careers in Counseling and Human Development* (pp. 115-116) **2824**
"Nurses' Aides and Orderlies" in *American Almanac of Jobs and Salaries* (pp. 464) **2825**
"Nursing Aide/Orderly" in *150 Careers in the Health Care Field* **2826**
"Nursing Aide and Psychiatric Aide" in *Careers in Health Care* (pp. 173-175) **2827**
"Nursing Aide" in *VGM's Handbook of Health Care Careers* **2828**
"Nursing Aides/Assistants" in *Opportunities in Health and Medical Careers* (pp. 38-39) **2829**
Nursing Aides and Psychiatric Aides **2857**
"Nursing Aides and Psychiatric Aides" in *America's 50 Fastest Growing Jobs* (pp. 127) **2830**
"Nursing Aides and Psychiatric Aides" in *Health Care Job Explosion!* (pp. 226-234) **2831**
"Nursing Aides and Psychiatric Aides" in *Jobs! What They Are—Where They Are—What They Pay* (pp. 172) **2832**
"Nursing Aides and Psychiatric Aides" in *Occupational Outlook Handbook* **2833**
"Nursing Aides and Psychiatric Aides" in *The Best Jobs for the 1990s and Into the 21st Century* **2834**
"Nursing Assistant" in *BLR Encyclopedia of Prewritten Job Descriptions* **2835**
Nursing Assistants **2836**
Nursing Assistants & the Long-Term Health Care Facility **2837**
"Nursing or Psychiatric Aide" in *Health Care* (pp. 21-25) **2838**
"Nursing and Psychiatric Aides" in *Career Discovery Encyclopedia* (Vol.4, pp. 134-135) **2839**
"Nursing and Psychiatric Aides" in *Encyclopedia of Careers and Vocational Guidance* (Vol.3, pp. 597-599) **2840**

Nut Grower **3502**

O

OAG Desktop Flight Guide-Worldwide Edition **716**, **1207**
OAG Travel Planner, European Edition **1208**
Obtaining Your Private Investigator's License **2233**
Ocean Industry **5502**
Ocean Navigator **6997**
Ocean Oil Weekly Report **5503**
Ocean State Traveler **717**, **1209**
OCLC Newsletter **1569**
Ocular Surgery News **6536**
Office Aide **1044**, **1070**, **1140**, **1810**, **1875**, **1936**
"Office/Business Machine Repairer" in *100 Best Jobs for the 1990s & Beyond* **4219**
"Office Clerk" in *Career Information Center* (Vol.1) **1032**
"Office File Clerk" in *Career Selector 2001* **1538**
Office Machine Service Technician **4185**
"Office Machine Service Technician" in *Occu-Facts: Information on 580 Careers in Outline Form* **4186**
"Office Machine Servicer" in *Career Information Center* (Vol.1) **4187**
"Office Machine Servicers" in *Career Discovery Encyclopedia* (Vol.4, pp. 140-141) **4188**
"Office Machine Servicers" in *Encyclopedia of Careers and Vocational Guidance* (Vol.3, pp. 611-614) **4189**
Office Machine Technicians **4190**
"Office Mail Clerk" in *Occu-Facts: Information on 580 Careers in Outline Form* **1230**
"Office Manager" in *Career Information Center* (Vol.1) **892**
"Office Manager" in *Career Opportunities in Art* (pp. 33-34) **893**
"Office Manager" in *Career Opportunities in Television, Cable, and Video* (pp. 168-169) **894**
"Office Manager" in *Occu-Facts: Information on 580 Careers in Outline Form* **895**
"Office Manager" in *VGM's Careers Encyclopedia* (pp. 312-315) **896**
"Office Manager" in *VGM's Handbook of Business and Management Careers* (pp. 64-65) **897**
Office Organization & Secretarial Procedures **1719**
Office Procedures **1053**
Office Revolution **1905**
Office Systems & Careers: A Resource for Administrative Assistants **1033**, **1649**
"Officer, U.S. Armed Forces" in *VGM's Careers Encyclopedia* (pp. 315-317) **7122**
Officers' Call **7164**
The Official Airline Career Handbook **3079**, **3777**
The Official ASE Preparation Guide to ASE Automobile and Body/Paint Tests **3830**, **3949**, **6564**
Official Directory **6372**
Official Guide—Tractors and Farm Equipment **4338**
Official Industrial Equipment Guide **4339**
Official Magazine **5396**
The Official Railway Equipment Register **6773**
Official Tour Directory **681**
Offset Lithography **6200**
Offset Press Operator **6221**
"Offset Press Operator" in *Occu-Facts: Information on 580 Careers in Outline Form* **6222**
Offshore Field Development International **5504**
Offshore Rig Locator **5505**
Offshore Rig Newsletter **5506**
Ohio State Department of Commerce - Division of Licensing **7217**
Oil Heat Technician's Manual **4428**
OJT File Clerk Resource Materials **1530**
OJT File Clerk Training Manual **1531**
On Campus **1849**
On the Line **2018**
"On the Line" in *Telecommunications Careers* (pp. 50-54) **4537**
On Target **7165**
Onion World **3503**
Online Libraries and Microcomputers **1570**
Operating the Dampening System, Instructor Guide **6245**
Operating the Dampening System on a Sheetfed Offset Press **6246**
Operating Engineer **6682**
"Operating Engineer" in *Hard Hatted Women: Stories of Struggle and Success in the Trades* (pp. 88-101) **6683**
"Operating Engineer" in *VGM's Careers Encyclopedia* (pp. 315-317) **6684**
"Operating Engineer" in *VGM's Handbook of Scientific and Technical Careers* (pp. 79-82) **6685**
"Operating Engineers" in *Career Discovery Encyclopedia* (Vol.4, pp. 142-143) **6686**
"Operating Engineers" in *Encyclopedia of Careers and Vocational Guidance* (Vol.3, pp. 615-617) **6687**
"Operating Engineers" in *Occu-Facts: Information on 580 Careers in Outline Form* **6688**
"Operating Engineers" in *Opportunities in Building Construction Trades* (pp. 66-68) **6689**
Operating the Inking System—Instructor's Guide **6247**
Operations Conference **575**
Operations Forum **6128**
Operative Plasterers and Cement Masons International Association of U.S. and Canada **4914**, **5274**
"Ophthalmic Laboratory Technician" in *100 Best Jobs for the 1990s & Beyond* **6543**
"Ophthalmic Laboratory Technician" in *150 Careers in the Health Care Field* **6516**
"Ophthalmic Laboratory Technician" in *Careers in Health Care* (pp. 182-184) **6517**
"Ophthalmic Laboratory Technician" in *Health Care* (pp. 69-73) **6518**
"Ophthalmic Laboratory Technician" in *VGM's Handbook of Health Care Careers* **6519**
"Ophthalmic Laboratory Technicians" in *Encyclopedia of Careers and Vocational Guidance* (Vol.3, pp. 621-624) **6520**
"Ophthalmic Laboratory Technicians" in *Health Care Job Explosion!* (pp. 142-148) **6521**
"Ophthalmic Laboratory Technicians" in *Jobs! What They Are—Where They Are—What They Pay* (p. 189) **6522**
"Ophthalmic Laboratory Technicians" in *Occupational Outlook Handbook* **6523**
"Ophthalmic Medical Assistant" in *150 Careers in the Health Care Field* **2765**
"Ophthalmic Medical Technician/Technologist" in *Allied Health Education Directory* (pp. 166-167) **6524**
Ophthalmic Research **6537**
Ophthalmic Surgery **6538**
Ophthalmologica **6539**
Ophthalmology Times **6540**
Opportunities in Accounting Careers **1440**
"Opportunities in the Armed Services" in *Opportunities in Medical Technology Careers* (pp. 71-83) **7123**
Opportunities in Automotive Services **3810**, **3916**
Opportunities in Cable Television **4538**
Opportunities in Carpentry Careers **4789**
Opportunities in Child Carer Careers **3315**
Opportunities in Computer Maintenance Careers **4191**
Opportunities in Computer Science **960**
Opportunities in Culinary Careers **2433**, **2565**
Opportunities in Data Processing Careers **1906**
Opportunities in Fast Food Careers **2434**, **2566**
Opportunities in Fire Protection Services **2053**
Opportunities in Food Services **2567**
Opportunities in Homecare Services Careers **3183**
Opportunities in Insurance Careers **98**
Opportunities in Law Enforcement and Criminal Justice Careers **2234**
Opportunities in Machine Trades Careers **5823**, **5863**
Opportunities in Marine and Maritime Careers **6972**
"Opportunities in Marketing & Sales" in *Travel and Hospitality Career Directory* (pp. 66-68) **262**, **608**
Opportunities in Masonry Careers **4696**
Opportunities in Metalworking Careers **5864**
Opportunities in Military Careers **7124**
Opportunities in Plastics Careers **5865**
Opportunities in Plumbing and Pipefitting Careers **5315**
Opportunities in Real Estate Careers **263**
Opportunities in Restaurant Careers **2435**, **2568**
Opportunities in Sales Careers **207**
Opportunities in Tool and Die Careers **5917**
Opportunities in Trucking Careers **6833**
"Opportunities in the U.S. Armed Forces" in *Opportunities in Refrigeration and Air Conditioning Trades* (pp. 117-122) **7125**
Opportunities in Waste Management Careers **6086**
Opportunities in Welding Careers **5947**
Opportunities in Word Processing Careers **1907**
"Opticians and Optical Mechanics" in *Encyclopedia of Careers and Vocational Guidance* (Vol.3, pp. 625-627) **6525**
"Options Traders" in *New York Times Career Planner* (pp. 261-263) **505**
Optometric Management **6541**
"Order Clerks" in *Occupational Outlook Handbook* **1577**
"Orderly" in *Opportunities in Health and Medical Careers* (p. 39) **2841**
"Ordinary and Able Seaman" in *Career Information Center* (Vol.12) **6973**
Oregon State Department of Insurance and Finance **7218**
Organic Gardening **3144**
Organizational Dynamics: A Quarterly Review of Organizational Behavior for Professional Managers **921**
Ornament Magazine **5801**
OSHA Hazard Communication Standard: A Compliance Manual for Cosmetology Schools **3011**
OTC Chart Manual **558**
Our Wiremen **4539**
Out of Service Tire Analysis Guide **6893**
Out of the Woods **3714**
Outdoor Power Equipment Official Guide **4340**
Outdoor Structures **4816**
Outstanding Grassland Farmer or Rancher Award **3420**
Outstanding International Travel Agent of the Year **691**
Outstanding Law Enforcement Achievement Award **2340**
Outstanding Lodging Employee of the Year **1088**
Outstanding Young Farmer Awards **3421**
Owner/Contractor Asbestos Abatement Agreement Guide **5199**
Owner Operator **6913**

P

Pacific Coast Industrial and Machine Tool Show **5840**
Pacific Logging Congress **3675**
Pacific Logging Congress, Equipment Exhibit **3731**

Pacific States Marine Fisheries Commission—Newsletter **3639**
Package Printing and Converting **6165, 6211, 6257, 6291**
Packager, Hand **7050**
"Paint and Coatings Industry" in *Encyclopedia of Careers and Vocational Guidance* (Vol.3, pp. 656-658) **6549**
Paint and Coatings Industry Workers **5208**
Paint and Paper Pro Show **5259**
Painter **5209**
"Painter" in *BLR Encyclopedia of Prewritten Job Descriptions* **5210**
Painter, Construction **5211**
"Painter" in *Exploring Nontraditional Jobs for Women* (pp. 20-25) **5212**
"Painter" in *Great Careers for People Who Like to Work with Their Hands* (pp. 42) **5213**
"Painter and Paperhanger" in *Career Information Center* (Vol.4) **5214**
"Painter" and "Paperhanger" in *Career Selector 2001* **5260**
Painter, Spray **6550**
Painters and Allied Trades Journal **5015**
"Painters" in *American Almanac of Jobs and Salaries* (pp. 502) **5215**
Painters (Construction) **5216**
Painters' Equipment & Supplies Directory **5236**
"Painters" in *Opportunities in Building Construction Trades* (pp. 35-37) **5217**
"Painters and Paperhangers" in *Career Discovery Encyclopedia* (Vol.4, pp. 162-163) **5218**
"Painters and Paperhangers" in *Encyclopedia of Careers and Vocational Guidance* (Vol.3, pp. 659-662) **5219**
"Painters and Paperhangers" in *Occupational Outlook Handbook* **5220**
"Painting and Coating Machine Operators" in *Occupational Outlook Handbook* **6551**
The Painting, Patching, and Wallcovering Toolbox Manual **5237**
Painting & Wallcovering Contractor **5257**
Palmetto Piper **4447, 5102, 5397**
PAMA News Magazine **3787**
Paperhanger **5221**
"Paperhanger" in *Occu-Facts: Information on 580 Careers in Outline Form* **5222**
"Paperhanger" and "Painter" in *Jobs Rated Almanac* **5223**
Paperhangers **5224**
"Paperhangers" in *Opportunities in Building Construction Trades* (pp. 37-39) **5225**
Park and Grounds Management—Athletic Area and Facilities Buyer's Guide Issue **3125**
Parking Attendants **7051**
Part Time Cash for the Sportsman: Twenty-Five Ways for the Fisherman & Hunter to Earn Extra Money **3592**
"Passenger Agent" in *Opportunities in Airline Careers* (pp. 68-69) **1160**
Passenger Transport **6654, 6774, 6998**
Passenger Transport: The Weekly Newspaper of the Transit Industry **6655**
"Pastry Chef and Baker" in *Career Information Center* (Vol.8) **2436**
Patient Management Skills for Dental Assistants & Hygienist **2716**
Patriots Award **2341**
Payroll Accounting **1580**
Payroll Accounting for Microcomputers **1592**
"Payroll Clerk" in *Career Information Center* (Vol.1) **1581**
"Payroll Clerk" in *Career Selector 2001* **1604**
"Payroll Clerk" in *Careers Inside the World of Offices* (pp. 11) **1582**
Payroll Currently **1598**
The Payroll Manager's Guide to Successful Direct Deposit **1599**
Payroll Recordkeeping **1593**
The Payroll Source **1600**
Payroll Systems & Procedures **1594**
"Payroll and Timekeeping Clerks" in *Occupational Outlook Handbook* **1583**
Paytech **1601**
"PC Technicians" in *Careers in High Tech* (pp. 81-82) **4192**
PCI Journal **4961**
The Peanut Farmer **3504**
The Peanut Grower **3505**
Pedorthic Footwear Association **6334**
Pedorthics: Providing Footwear and Related Services to Aid in the Care of the Foot **6318**
Pedoscope **6348**
Pennsylvania State Department - Bureau of Professional and Occupational Affairs **7219**
Percy and Betty Wagner Award **350**
"Peripheral Equipment Operators" in *Careers in High Tech* (pp. 32-34) **961**
Person to Person: Helping Customers Make Financial Decisions **866**
"Personal Computer Salesperson" in *Straight Talk on Careers: 80 Pros Take You Into Their Professions* (pp. 8-10) **434**
Personal Property Journal **373**
Personal Selling Power **238, 478, 630**
Personal Service Cluster **2235, 2437, 2569, 2985**
Personal Shorthand for the Executive Secretary: Syllabus **1720**
"Personnel Clerk" in *Career Information Center* (Vol.1) **1607**
"Personnel Clerks" in *Occupational Outlook Handbook* **1608**
Personnel Journal **1622**
Personnel Literature **1623**
Personnel Policy Survey **6308**
Personnel Psychology **1624**
Pest Alerts **3506**
"Pet Care Worker" in *Career Information Center* (Vol.5) **2903**
"Pet Care Worker" in *Personal Services* (pp. 45-49) **2904**
"Pet Grooming" in *Careers for Animal Lovers and Other Zoological Types* (pp. 59-61) **2905**
Pet Services Annual Connecticut and Trade Show **2943**
Pet Services Journal **2938**
PFA Directory **6335, 6336**
"Pharmaceutical Sales Representative" in *Opportunities in Pharmacy Careers* (pp. 106-108) **208**
"Phone Repair Technician" in *Hard Hatted Women: Stories of Struggle and Success in the Trades* (pp. 235-253) **4277**
Phonefacts **1883, 4156, 4303, 4559**
PHOTO Electronic Imaging **6609**
Photo Lab Management **6610**
Photo Marketing **6611**
Photo Marketing Association International **6585**
Photo Marketing Association International—Newsline **6612**
Photo Marketing Magazine **6613**
"Photoengraver" in *Career Information Center* (Vol.3) **6184**
"Photoengravers" in *Career Discovery Encyclopedia* (Vol.5, pp. 34-35) **6185**
"Photoengravers" in *Encyclopedia of Careers and Vocational Guidance* (Vol.4, pp. 67-69) **6186**
Photofinishing Laboratory Technicians **6578**
The Photographer's Assistant **6621**
Photographic Equipment Technicians **6579**
"Photographic Process Worker" in *Jobs Rated Almanac* **6580**
"Photographic Process Workers" in *Occupational Outlook Handbook* **6581**
Photographic Processing **6582**
PhotoIndustry Careers: A Lifelong Commitment to Excellence and Creativity **6583**
Physician Assistants Annual Conference **2808**
PIACTION **148**
Piano Action Handbook **4657**
"Piano and Organ Technicians" in *Encyclopedia of Careers and Vocational Guidance* (Vol.4, pp. 103-108) **4628**
"Piano and Organ Tuner, Technician" in *Career Information Center* (Vol.5) **4629**
Piano Parts and Their Functions, Illustrated **4658**
Piano Servicing, Tuning & Rebuilding **4651**
Piano Technicians Guild **4641**
Piano Technicians Journal **4659**
"Piano Tuner" in *Offbeat Careers: The Directory of Unusual Work* **4630**
The Piano Tuner-Technician **4631, 4632**
"Piano Tuner Technician" in *Career Opportunities in the Music Industry* (pp. 129-130) **4633**
"Piano Tuner-Technician" in *Occu-Facts: Information on 580 Careers in Outline Form* **4634**
Piano Tuners and Technicians **4635**
Pioneer of the Year Award **3422**
Pipe Fitters and Steam Fitters **5316**
"Pipe Fitters and Steam Fitters" in *Encyclopedia of Careers and Vocational Guidance* (Vol.4, pp. 117-120) **5317**
"Pipefitter" in *BLR Encyclopedia of Prewritten Job Descriptions* **5318**
"Pipefitters and Steamfitters" in *Career Discovery Encyclopedia* (Vol.5, pp. 52-53) **5319**
Pipefitting and Plumbing **5320**
The Plain English Maintenance & Repair Guide for the IBM PC & PCjr **4207**
Planned Maintenance **4367**
Plants & Gardens **3145**
Plasterer **5262**
"Plasterer" in *Career Information Center* (Vol.4) **5263**
Plasterer Helper **7052**
"Plasterer Helper" in *Occu-Facts: Information on 580 Careers in Outline Form* **7053**
"Plasterer" in *Jobs Rated Almanac* **5264**
"Plasterer" in *Occu-Facts: Information on 580 Careers in Outline Form* **5265**
Plasterers **5266**
"Plasterers" in *American Almanac of Jobs and Salaries* (pp. 503) **5267**
"Plasterers" in *Career Discovery Encyclopedia* (Vol.5, pp. 54-55) **5268**
"Plasterers" in *Encyclopedia of Careers and Vocational Guidance* (Vol.4, pp. 123-125) **5269**
"Plasterers" in *Occupational Outlook Handbook* **5270**
"Plasterers" in *Opportunities in Building Construction Trades* (pp. 39-41) **5271**
Plastering: A Craftman's Encyclopedia **5277**
Plastics Compounding **5896**
"Plastics" in *Encyclopedia of Careers and Vocational Guidance* (Vol.1, pp. 368-373) **5866**
Plastics Engineering **5897**
Plastics Engineering Series **5898**
"Plastics Industry" in *Career Information Center* (Vol.9) **5867**
Plastics Machinery & Equipment **5899**
Plastics News **5900**
Plastics Products Manufacturing Workers **5868**
"Plastics Products Manufacturing Workers" in *Career Discovery Encyclopedia* (Vol.5, pp. 56-57) **5869**
"Plastics Products Manufacturing Workers" in *Encyclopedia of Careers and Vocational Guidance* (Vol.4, pp. 126-128) **5870**
Plastics World **5901**
"Platemaker" in *Career Information Center* (Vol.3) **6187**
Platemaker, Lithographic **6188**
Player Piano Servicing & Rebuilding **4652**
Plumb **5398**
Plumber **5321, 5322**
"Plumber" in *Career Selector 2001* **5408**
"Plumber" in *Guide to Careers Without College* (pp. 82-85) **5323**
Plumber Helper **7054**
"Plumber Helper" in *Occu-Facts: Information on 580 Careers in Outline Form* **7055**
"Plumber" in *Jobs Rated Almanac* **5324**

"Plumber and Pipe Fitter" in *Career Information Center* (Vol.4) **5325**
"Plumber and Pipefitter" in *VGM's Careers Encyclopedia* (pp. 357-359) **5326**
Plumber—Steam Fitter **5356**
"Plumber" in *The Desk Guide to Training and Work Advisement* (p. 83) **5327**
Plumbers **5328**
"Plumbers" in *Career Discovery Encyclopedia* (Vol.5, pp. 60-61) **5329**
"Plumbers" in *Encyclopedia of Careers and Vocational Guidance* (Vol.4, pp. 134-146) **5330**
Plumbers Handbook **5366**
Plumbers and Pipefitters **5331**
"Plumbers and Pipefitters" in *American Almanac of Jobs and Salaries* (pp. 503) **5332**
Plumbers & Pipefitters Library **5367**
"Plumbers and Pipefitters" in *Occu-Facts: Information on 580 Careers in Outline Form* **5333**
"Plumbers and Pipefitters" in *Occupational Outlook Handbook* **5334**
"Plumbers and Pipefitters" in *Opportunities in Building Construction Trades* (pp. 41-45) **5335**
The Plumber's Toolbox Manual **5368, 5369**
Plumbing **5357, 5358, 5370**
The Plumbing Apprentice Handbook **5371**
"Plumbing" in *Career Connection II: A Guide to Technical Majors and Their Related Careers* (pp. 126-127) **5336**
Plumbing Engineer—Product Directory Issue **5359**
Plumbing Heating Piping **5399**
PM Directory & Reference Issue **4416, 5360**
PMA **2802**
Pocket List of Railroad Officials **6775**
Poetker Award; Frances Jones **3121**
Police **2376**
Police Administration & Supervision **2311**
Police Administrative Aide **2312**
"Police" in *American Almanac of Jobs and Salaries* (pp. 101) **2236**
Police—Buyer's Guide Issue **2356**
The Police Chief **2377**
The Police Detective Function **2237**
"Police Detective" in *Occu-Facts: Information on 580 Careers in Outline Form* **2238**
"Police Detective" in *Straight Talk on Careers: 80 Pros Take You Into Their Professions* (pp. 236-238) **2239**
"Police, Detectives, and Special Agents" in *101 Careers: A Guide to the Fastest-Growing Opportunities* (pp. 140-143) **2240**
"Police, Detectives, and Special Agents" in *Occupational Outlook Handbook* **2241**
The Police Function & the Investigation of Crime **2357**
Police Officer **2242-2244, 2313**
"Police Officer" in *100 Best Jobs for the 1990s & Beyond* **2392**
"Police Officer" in *Career Information Center* (Vol.11) **2245**
"Police Officer" in *Career Selector 2001* **2393**
Police Officer Exams Review **2314**
"Police Officer" in *Hard Hatted Women: Stories of Struggle and Success in the Trades* (pp. 71-80) **2246**
"Police Officer" in *Jobs Rated Almanac* **2247**
"Police Officer" in *Occu-Facts: Information on 580 Careers in Outline Form* **2248**
"Police Officer" in *Top Professions: The 100 Most Popular, Dynamic, and Profitable Careers in America Today* (pp. 40-41) **2249**
Police Officer of the Year Award **2342**
Police Officers **2250**
"Police Officers" in *Career Discovery Encyclopedia* (Vol.5, pp. 64-65) **2251**
"Police Officers" in *Encyclopedia of Careers and Vocational Guidance* (Vol.4, pp. 140-144) **2252**
"Police Officers" in *Jobs! What They Are—Where They Are—What They Pay* (pp. 229-231) **2253**
Police Promotion Course (One Volume) **2315**
Police Promotion Examinations **2316**
Police Promotion Manual **2358**
Police Reading Comprehension **2317**
"Police Records Clerk" in *BLR Encyclopedia of Prewritten Job Descriptions* **1394**
"Police Search & Recovery" in *Footsteps in the Ocean: Careers in Diving* (pp. 109-114) **2254**
Police & Security News **2195, 2378**
"Police Sergeant" in *Straight Talk on Careers: 80 Pros Take You Into Their Professions* (pp. 233-235) **2255**
Police Times Magazine **2379**
Pollard Scholarships **692**
Pollution Engineering **6129**
Polymer Composites **5902**
Polymer Engineering and Science **5903**
Portland Cement Association **4915**
Post Office Clerk **1326**
"Post Office Clerk" in *Career Selector 2001* **1391**
Post Office Clerk-Carrier **1327, 1369, 1370**
"Post Office Clerk" in *Occu-Facts: Information on 580 Careers in Outline Form* **1328**
The Post Office Worker: A Trade Union & Social History **1392**
Postal Arithmetic **1371**
Postal Bulletin **1382**
Postal Clerk **1329**
Postal Clerk-Carrier & Mail Handler Exams **1372**
"Postal Clerks" in *Encyclopedia of Careers and Vocational Guidance* (Vol.4, pp. 159-162) **1330**
"Postal Clerks and Mail Carriers" in *Occupational Outlook Handbook* **1331**
"Postal Employees" in *Career Discovery Encyclopedia* (Vol.5, pp. 72-73) **1332**
Postal Exam Handbook **1373**
Postal Issue Summary **1383**
Postal Record **1384**
"Postal Service Worker" in *Career Information Center* (Vol.11) **1333**
Postal Service Workers **1334**
The Postal Supervisor **1385**
Postmasters Gazette **1386**
Potential Liabilities of Probation & Parole Officers **2007**
The Power of Customer Service **1065**
"Power Plant Occupations" in *Encyclopedia of Careers and Vocational Guidance* (Vol.4, pp. 163-165) **6027**
"Power Plant Worker" in *Career Information Center* (Vol.11) **6028**
"Power Plant Workers" in *Career Discovery Encyclopedia* (Vol.5, pp. 76-77) **6029**
"Power Shovel Crane Operator" in *Occu-Facts: Information on 580 Careers in Outline Form* (p. 19.16) **6690**
Power Tool Institute **4476**
Power Tool Maintenance **4485**
"Power Tool Repairer" in *Career Information Center* (Vol.4) **4473**
"Power Truck Operator" in *Career Information Center* (Vol.12) **6691**
The Practical Design of Structural Elements of Timber **3686**
Practical Guide Maintenance Engineering **4368**
Practical Law for Jail & Prison Personnel: A Resource Manual & Training Curriculum **2008**
Practical Problems in Mathematics for Welders **5996**
Practice for Air Force Placement Tests **7138**
Practice for the Armed Forces Test - ASVAB **7139**
Practice for Army Placement Tests **7140**
Practice for Clerical, Typing, and Stenographic Tests **1045, 1811, 1937**
Practice and Drill for the Clerk, Typist, and Stenographer Examinations **1046, 1812, 1938**
Practice for Navy Placement Tests **7141**
Precis of Postal Service Manual **1374**
Precision **5737**
"Precision Assembler" in *Jobs Rated Almanac* **5659**
"Precision Assemblers" in *American Almanac of Jobs and Salaries* (pp. 529) **5660**
"Precision Assemblers" in *Occupational Outlook Handbook* **5661**
Premium Grower **3507**
"Prepress Workers" in *Occupational Outlook Handbook* **6189**
Preprint Volumes **5888**
"Preschool and Childcare Workers" in *101 Careers: A Guide to the Fastest-Growing Opportunities* (pp. 178-180) **3316**
"Preschool Teachers" in *Career Discovery Encyclopedia* (Vol.5, pp. 78-79) **3317**
"Preschool Workers" in *America's 50 Fastest Growing Jobs* (pp. 129) **3318**
"Preschool Workers" in *Occupational Outlook Handbook* **3319**
The President **922**
Presser, Garment **6277**
Prevent Blindness America **6528**
Prime Real Estate **374**
Princess Cruises and Princess Tours Scholarship **693**
Principal Clerk/Principal Stenographer **1813**
Principles of Payroll Administration **1595**
Principles of Real Estate **331**
Principles of Refrigeration **4410**
"Printing" in *Encyclopedia of Careers and Vocational Guidance* (Vol.1, pp. 380-386) **6223**
Printing Platemakers **6224**
Printing Press Operator **6225**
"Printing Press Operator" in *BLR Encyclopedia of Prewritten Job Descriptions* **6226**
"Printing Press Operator" in *Career Information Center* (Vol.3) **6227**
"Printing Press Operator" in *VGM's Careers Encyclopedia* (pp. 368-370) **6228**
Printing Press Operators **6229**
"Printing Press Operators and Assistants" in *Encyclopedia of Careers and Vocational Guidance* (Vol.4, pp. 166-169) **6230**
"Printing Press Operators" in *Career Discovery Encyclopedia* (Vol.5, pp. 82-83) **6231**
"Printing Press Operators" in *Jobs! What They Are—Where They Are—What They Pay* (pp. 216) **6232**
"Printing Press Operators" in *Occupational Outlook Handbook* **6233**
"Printing Technology" in *Career Connection II: A Guide to Technical Majors and Their Related Careers* (pp. 128-129) **6234**
"Private Child Care Worker" in *Career Information Center* (Vol.5) **3361**
"Private Household Worker" in *Personal Services* (pp. 15-19) **3362**
"Private Household Workers" in *Career Discovery Encyclopedia* (Vol.5, pp. 84-85) **3363**
"Private Household Workers" in *Encyclopedia of Careers and Vocational Guidance* **3364**
"Private Household Workers" in *Occupational Outlook Handbook* **3365**
Pro Trucker **6914**
Probation Officer - Parole Officer **1999**
Probation and Parole Directory **2002**
Procedures for the Office Professional **1054**
Procedures for the Professional Secretary **1650**
The Process of Investigation: Concepts & Strategies for the Security Professional **2359**
Product Catalog **6166**
PRODUCT NEWS **3640**
Production **5904**
"Production Painter" in *Career Information Center* (Vol.9) **6552**
"Production Supervisor" in *Career Informa Center* (Vol.9) **5676**
The Profession of Arms **7126**
Professional Agent **149**

Professional Aviation Maintenance Association **3765**
Professional Barber Styling State Board Exam Review **3001**
Professional Builder & Remodeler **4756, 4849, 4888, 4962, 5016, 5103, 5156, 5200, 5258, 5305, 5400, 5468, 5556, 5610, 5646**
"Professional Cooking" in *The Desk Guide to Training and Work Advisement* (pp. 77-79) **2438**
"Professional Diver" in *Offbeat Careers: The Directory of Unusual Work* **3577**
Professional Education Series **1818**
Professional Electronics **4272**
Professional Electronics Directory **4254**
Professional Electronics Magazine **4121**
The Professional Electronics Technician **4070, 4141, 4193, 4233**
Professional Excellence for Secretaries **1721**
Professional Goldsmithing: A Contemporary Guide to Traditional Jewelry Techniques **5789**
Professional Grounds Management Society **3104, 3105**
The Professional Grounds Manager **3126**
Professional Insurance Agents **150**
Professional Lawn Care Association of America Annual Conference and Show **3157**
Professional Photocopier Troubleshooting & Repair **4208**
Professional Roofing **5469**
Professional Secretaries International **1689, 1692**
Professional Secretary's Handbook **1722**
Professional Thieves & the Detective **2360**
Professional Truck Driver Institute of America **6860, 6863**
Professional Upholster Cleaning Techniques: The Basics **6405**
"Professionalism - Certified Travel Counselor" in *Travel Agent: Dealer in Dreams* (pp. 21-22) **642**
Professionals . . . Are Certified by the Electronics Technicians Association, International **4078, 4249**
Profile: The Petroleum Industry **5479**
Progressive Filing **1532**
Progressive Railroading **6776**
Projects in Leather **6342**
Promoting Timber Cropping **3687**
"Property and Casualty Insurance Agents and Brokers" in *Career Discovery Encyclopedia* (Vol.5, pp. 90-91) **99**
Provider: For Long Term Care Professionals **2874**
Pruning Bare Root Trees for the Garden Center and Shearing Pine, Sprouce and Fir **3160**
Psychiatric Aide **2842**
"Psychiatric Aide" in *Occu-Facts: Information on 580 Careers in Outline Form* **2843**
Psychiatric Aides and Technicians **2844**
PTN (Photographic Trade News) **6614**
Public Affairs Review **801**
Public Personnel Management **1625**
Public Service Award **2104, 2343**
Public Sevice Reporter **1850**

Q

Q & A on the Real Estate License Examinations (RE) **332**
Qualifying for Admission to the Service Academies: A Student's Guide **7127**
Quality Assurance of Welded Construction **5997**
Quality Control Device Catalog **6167**
"Quality Control Inspector" in *Career Information Center* (Vol.9) **5720**
Quality Engineering **5738**
Quality Management Journal **5739**
Quality Progress **5740**
Quarter-Century Honor Roll **1010**
Quarterly Completion Report **5507**
Quarterly Labor Relations Comprehensive Bulletin **4677**
Query: Questions and Answers About Managing Your Money **151**
Questions and Answers About Entering the Child Care Profession **3320**
Quick 'n Easy Country Cookin' **2514**
Quick Printing **6168, 6212, 6258, 6292**
Quickening **2875**
Quintessence International **6511**

R

Racing & Sports Car Chassis Design **3888**
Radial Tire Wear Condition & Causes: A Guide to Wear Pattern Analysis **6894**
"Radio Advertising Salesperson" in *Career Opportunities in Advertising and Public Relations* (pp. 128-130) **609**
"Radio Dispatcher" in *BLR Encyclopedia of Prewritten Job Descriptions* **1257**
Radio Dispatchers **1258**
"Radio and Telegraph Operator" in *Telecommunications* (pp. 51-55) **1852**
"Radio and Telegraph Operators" in *Career Discovery Encyclopedia* (Vol.5, pp. 120-121) **1853**
"Radio and Telegraph Operators" in *Encyclopedia of Careers and Vocational Guidance* (Vol.4, pp. 220-222) **1854**
"Radio, Television, and Print Advertising Sales Workers" in *Encyclopedia of Careers and Vocational Guidance* **610**
"Radio and Television Technician" in *Telecommunications* (pp. 63-67) **4234**
Ragnar's Ten Best Traps & a Few Others That Are Damn Good, Too **3593**
Rail News Update **6777**
"Rail Transportation Occupation" in Occupational Outlook Handbook **6722**
Railroad Brake Operator **6723**
"Railroad Brake Operator" in *Occu-Facts: Information on 580 Careers in Outline Form* **6724**
"Railroad Braker" in *Career Information Center* (Vol.12) **6725**
"Railroad Braker and Conductor" in *Transportation* (pp. 39-43) **6726**
Railroad Clerk **6759, 6760**
"Railroad Clerks" in *Encyclopedia of Careers and Vocational Guidance* (Vol.4, pp. 236-238) **6727**
Railroad Conductor **6728, 6729**
"Railroad Conductor" in *Career Information Center* (Vol.12) **6730**
"Railroad Conductor" in *Jobs Rated Almanac* **6731**
"Railroad Conductor" in *Occu-Facts: Information on 580 Careers in Outline Form* **6732**
"Railroad Engineer" in *Career Information Center* (Vol.12) **6733**
Railroad Facts **6778**
Railroad Industry Workers **6734**
Railroad Newsletter **6779**
"Railroad Signaler and Signal Maintainer" in *Career Information Center* (Vol.12) **4142**
"Railroad Signaler, Telegrapher, Telephoner, and Dispatcher" in *Transportation* (pp. 57-61) **1259**
Railway Age **6780**
Railway Age—Railroad Financial Desk Book Issue **6761**
Railway Track & Structures **6781**
Random Lengths **3715**
Rate Book **6053**
"Rate Clerk" in *Careers in Trucking* **1410**
Rational Fabrication Specifications for Steel Structures **5998**
Re-Upholstery Techniques **6406**
Ready-To-Build Telephone Enhancements **4291**
"Real Estate Agent" in *100 Best Careers for the Year 2000* (pp. 177-179) **264**
"Real Estate Agent/Broker" in *100 Best Jobs for the 1990s & Beyond* **405**
"Real Estate Agent/Broker" in *VGM's Careers Encyclopedia* (pp. 395-397) **265**
"Real Estate Agent/Broker" in *VGM's Handbook of Business and Management Careers* (pp. 77-79) **266**
"Real Estate Agent and Brokers" in *101 Careers: A Guide to the Fastest-Growing Opportunities* (pp. 48-50) **267**
"Real Estate Agent" in *Jobs Rated Almanac* **268**
Real Estate Agents and Brokers **269**
"Real Estate Agents and Brokers" in *American Almanac of Jobs and Salaries* (pp. 544) **270**
"Real Estate Agents, Brokers, and Appraisers" in *Occupational Outlook Handbook* **271**
"Real Estate Agents and Brokers" in *Career Discovery Encyclopedia* (Vol.5, pp. 130-131) **272**
"Real Estate Agents and Brokers" in *Encyclopedia of Careers and Vocational Guidance* (Vol.4, pp. 243-247) **273**
"Real Estate Agents and Brokers" in *Jobs! What They Are—Where They Are—What They Pay* (p. 338) **274**
"Real Estate Agents and Brokers: Sellers of the Land" in *Careers for Women Without College Degrees* (pp. 245-250) **275**
"Real Estate Agents" in *Opportunities in Home Economics Careers* (pp. 95-96) **276**
"Real Estate Agents" in *Opportunities in Vocational and Technical Careers* (pp. 59-75) **277**
Real Estate Appraiser **278, 279**
"Real Estate Appraiser" in *Career Choices for the 90's for Students of Business* (pp. 139-141) **280**
"Real Estate Appraiser" in *Career Information Center* (Vol.10) **281**
"Real Estate Appraiser" in *Occu-Facts: Information on 580 Careers in Outline Form* **282**
"Real Estate Appraiser" in *VGM's Careers Encyclopedia* (pp. 399-400) **283**
"Real Estate Appraiser" in *VGM's Handbook of Business and Management Careers* (pp. 80-81) **284**
Real Estate Appraisers **285**
"Real Estate Appraisers" in *New York Times Career Planner* (pp. 283-285) **286**
"Real Estate" in *Black Woman's Career Guide* (pp. 295-302) **287**
Real Estate Broker **333**
Real Estate Broker/Real Estate Sales Agent **288**
"Real Estate Broker" in *Top Professions: The 100 Most Popular, Dynamic, and Profitable Careers in America Today* (pp. 68-69) **289**
Real Estate Business **375**
"Real Estate" in *Career Choices for the 90's for Students of Business* (pp. 131-154) **290**
"Real Estate" in *Career Choices for the 90's for Students of Economics* (pp. 122-145) **291**
"Real Estate" in *Career Choices for the 90's for Students of Mathematics* (pp. 134-157) **292**
"Real Estate" in *Career Connection II: A Guide to Technical Majors and Their Related Careers* (pp. 132-133) **293**
Real Estate Careers: 25 Growing Opportunities **294**
"Real Estate Careers" in *Transitions: Military Pathways to Civilian Careers* (pp. 137-140) **295**
"Real Estate and Construction" in *Jobs '95* (pp. 417-429) **296**
"Real Estate" in *Encyclopedia of Career Choices for the 1990s: A Guide to Entry Level Jobs* (pp. 742-765) **297**
"Real Estate" in *Encyclopedia of Careers and Vocational Guidance* (Vol.1, pp. 405-410) **298**

The Real Estate Entrepreneur **376**
Real Estate Finance **377**
The Real Estate Finance Journal **378**
Real Estate Finance Today **379**
Real Estate Forum **380**
Real Estate License Examinations **334**
"Real Estate" in *Major Decisions: A Guide to College Majors* (p. 142) **299**
Real Estate News **381**
Real Estate Outlook **382**
Real Estate Record and Builders Guide **383**
Real Estate Review **384**
"Real Estate Sales Agent" in *Career Selector 2001* **406**
"Real Estate Sales" in *Career Choices for the 90's for Students of Business* (pp. 164-167) **300**
"Real Estate Sales" in *Career Choices for the 90's for Students of Communications and Journalism* (pp. 172-175) **301**
"Real Estate Sales" in *Encyclopedia of Career Choices for the 1990s: A Guide to Entry Level Jobs* (pp. 775-778) **302**
"Real Estate Sales" in *Opportunities in Property Management Careers* (pp. 101-105) **303**
"Real Estate Sales Representative" in *Great Careers for People Who Like Working with People* (pp. 4-9) **304**
"Real Estate Sales Worker and Broker" in *Career Information Center* (Vol.10) **305**
Real Estate Salesman **335**
Real Estate Salesperson **306**
"Real Estate Salesperson" in *College Board Guide to Jobs and Career Planning* (pp. 144-145) **307**
"Real Estate Salesperson" in *Occu-Facts: Information on 580 Careers in Outline Form* **308**
Real Estate Schools Directory **345**
Real Estate Today **385**
Real Estate Weekly **386**
Real Estate West **387**
"Real Estate: What's Hot, What's Not" in *Fast-Track Careers: A Guide to the Highest-Paying Jobs* (pp. 99-121) **309**
Real Property Journal **388**
Realtor News **389**
Realtor News (All Member Issue) **390**
Realtor News-Broker Issue **391**
Realtor of the Year **349**
REALTORS Land Institute **392**
Realty **393**
Recent Trends in Welding Science & Technology **6012**
Receptionist **1121-1123**
Receptionist: A Practical Course in Office Reception Techniques **1144**
"Receptionist" in *BLR Encyclopedia of Prewritten Job Descriptions* **1124**
"Receptionist" in *Career Information Center* (Vol.1) **1125**
"Receptionist" in *Career Selector 2001* **1147**
"Receptionist" in *Careers Inside the World of Offices* (pp. 8-7, 29-34) **1126**
"Receptionist/Clerk-Typist" in *Career Opportunities in Television, Cable, and Video* (pp. 22-23) **1127, 1908**
"Receptionist" in *Jobs Rated Almanac* **1128**
"Receptionist" in *Occu-Facts: Information on 580 Careers in Outline Form* **1129**
Receptionists **1130**
"Receptionists" in *Career Discovery Encyclopedia* (Vol.5, pp. 132-133) **1131**
"Receptionists" in *Encyclopedia of Careers and Vocational Guidance* (Vol.4, pp. 248-250) **1132**
"Receptionists" in *Jobs! What They Are—Where They Are—What They Pay* (pp. 251) **1133**
"Receptionists" in *Occupational Outlook Handbook* **1134**
"Receptionists" in *Opportunities in Vocational and Technical Careers* (pp. 47-58) **1135**
"Receptionists and Switchboard Operators" in *American Almanac of Jobs and Salaries* (p. 511) **1136, 1855**
Recipe Ingredient Substitution Update **2515**
Recommend **718, 1210**
Recommended Standards for Waste Water Facilities **6114**
Record **5741**
"Record Clerk" in *Careers Inside the World of Offices* (pp. 38) **1395**
"Record Clerks" in *Occupational Outlook Handbook* **1396**
Record Keeping for Small Rural Businesses **1479**
"Record Shop Clerk" in *Career Opportunities in the Music Industry* (pp. 93-94) **435**
Recorder-Times **7166**
Records & Database Management **1533**
Records Management **1492, 1535, 1559, 1578, 1616**
Records Management Quarterly **1403, 1496, 1537, 1571, 1579, 1626**
Redwood Region Logging Conference **3732**
Reeves Journal: Plumbing Heating Cooling **4448, 5401**
Reference Guide to Homebuilding Articles **4449**
Reference Manual: For the Office **1055**
Refrigerated Transporter **6915**
Refrigeration License Examinations **4411**
Refrigeration Service and Contracting **4450**
Refrigeration Service Engineers Society **4401, 4403**
Refuse Collectors **7056**
"Refuse Collectors" in *Career Discovery Encyclopedia* (Vol.5, pp. 138-139) **7057**
"Refuse Collectors" in *Encyclopedia of Careers and Vocational Guidance* (Vol.4, pp. 262-264) **7058**
"Refuse Worker" in *Career Information Center* (Vol.11) **7059**
Regional Newsletter **4660**
Regional Report **2140**
Register of North American Insurance Companies **117**
Registered Medical Assistants of American Medical Technologists **2771, 2776**
"Rental Clerk" in *Travel Agent* (p. 168) **44**
The Rep Travel Newsletter **239**
Rep World **240**
Repair Cluster **4235, 4393**
Repairing Appliances **4107**
Reporter **5402**
Research Bulletins **152**
Research Information **4519**
Research Information Monthly **4520, 5670**
Research Reports **153**
Research Supplier Directory **682**
"Reservation Agents" in *Travel Agent* (pp. 167-168) **1161**
"Reservation and Information Clerks" in *Opportunities in Travel Careers* (p. 53) **1066, 1162**
"Reservation and Transportation Ticket Agent" in *Career Discovery Encyclopedia* (Vol.5, pp. 148-149) **1163**
"Reservation and Transportation Ticket Agents" in *Encyclopedia of Careers and Vocational Guidance* (Vol.4, pp. 282-284) **1164**
"Reservation and Transportation Ticket Agents and Travel Clerks " in *America's 50 Fastest Growing Jobs* (pp. 108) **1165**
"Reservation and Transportation Ticket Agents and Travel Clerks" in *Occupational Outlook Handbook* **1166**
"Reservationists and Airline Ticket Agents" in *Jobs! What They Are—Where They Are—What They Pay* (pp. 205) **1167**
"Reservations Agent (Airline)" in *Career Selector 2001* **1221**
"Reservations Agents" in *Opportunities in Airline Careers* (pp. 65-67) **1168**
"The Reservations Department" in *Opportunities in Transportation Careers* (pp. 43-44) **1169**
"Reservations Sales Agent" in *Opportunities in Aerospace Careers* (pp. 21-25) **1170**
"Reservations Sales Agent" in *Travel Agent* (pp. 164-165) **1171**
Residential Heating Operations & Troubleshooting **4429**
Residential Mortgage Lending Documentation **867**
Residential Mortgage Lending: From Application to Servicing **868**
Residential Mortgage Lending Origination **869**
Residential Plumbing **5372**
"Resilient Floor Layer" in *Opportunities in Carpentry Careers* (pp. 52-53) **4867**
"Resolution, Personal Services and Transportation Careers" in *The Best Jobs for the 1990s and Into the 21st Century* **611, 769, 2906, 5053, 6834**
Resource **154**
Restaurant Business **2641**
"Restaurant Chef" in *Top Professions: The 100 Most Popular, Dynamic, and Profitable Careers in America Today* (pp. 195-197) **2439**
Restaurant Host/Hostess **2570**
"Restaurant Host and Hostess" in *Career Information Center* (Vol.8) **2571**
"Restaurant Host/Hostess" in *Occu-Facts: Information on 580 Careers in Outline Form* **2572**
Restaurant Industry Operations Report **2531, 2657**
Restaurants & Institutions **2516, 2642**
Restaurants, Resorts & Hotels **2517, 2643**
Restaurants USA **2518**
Retail Banking Digest **870, 1119**
Retail Banking: Serving the Financial Needs of Customers **871**
"Retail Butcher" in *Career Information Center* (Vol.10) **5701**
Retail Confectioners International Annual Convention and Exposition **2527**
Retail Delivery Systems Quarterly **872**
"Retail Industry" in *Footsteps in the Ocean: Careers in Diving* (pp. 37-42) **436**
Retail Info Systems News **479**
"Retail" in *Internships 1995* **437**
"Retail Sales" in *Careers in Marketing* (pp. 66-68) **438**
Retail Sales Power **439**
"Retail Sales Worker" in *Career Discovery Encyclopedia* (Vol.5, pp. 152-153) **440**
"Retail Sales Worker" in *VGM's Careers Encyclopedia* (pp. 409-411) **441**
"Retail Sales Workers" in *Encyclopedia of Careers and Vocational Guidance* (Vol.4, pp. 297-300) **442**
"Retail Sales Workers" in *Occupational Outlook Handbook* **443**
"Retail Sales Workers" in *Opportunities in Vocational and Technical Careers* (pp. 59-75) **444**
"Retail Salespeople" in *Jobs! What They Are—Where They Are—What They Pay* (pp. 323) **445**
"Retail Salesperson" in *100 Best Jobs for the 1990s & Beyond* **488**
"Retail Store Sales Worker" in *Career Information Center* (Vol.10) **446**
Retailing & Merchandising **45, 447**
Retailing News **241, 480, 631**
Retirement Housing: Step by Step Guide for Investors, Developers, Accountants, & Other Professionals **353**
A Reverence for Wood **6471**
Review of Optometry **6542**
Rewarding Careers in the Automotive Service Industry **3917**
Rhode Island State Department of Health - Division of Professional Regulation **7220**
The Rice World **3508**
RIEI Information Letter **5470**
Right of Way **394**
Risk and Insurance Management Society Annual Conference **168**
Risk Management **155**

Risk Management Manual for Motor Carriers **6895**
Roads & Bridges Magazine **5611**
Roadtester Video **6947**
Robert Oliver & Mercantile Bookkeeping in the Early Nineteenth Century **1489**
Robins Rev-Up **7167**
Rock and Dirt **6706**
Rock & Gem **5802**
Rocky Mountain Construction **3146, 3716**
Rocky Mountain Union Farmer **3509**
Rolling Along **6916**
Roof Framing **4817, 4818, 5433, 5434**
Roofer **5413**
"Roofer" in *Career Information Center* (Vol.4) **5414**
Roofer Helper **7060**
"Roofer Helper" in *Occu-Facts: Information on 580 Careers in Outline Form* **7061**
"Roofer" in *Jobs Rated Almanac* **5415**
ROOFER Magazine **5471**
"Roofer" in *Occu-Facts: Information on 580 Careers in Outline Form* **5416**
Roofers **5417**
"Roofers" in *Career Discovery Encyclopedia* (Vol.5, pp. 162-163) **5418**
"Roofers" in *Encyclopedia of Careers and Vocational Guidance* (Vol.4, pp. 312-314) **5419**
"Roofers" in *Occupational Outlook Handbook* **5420**
"Roofers" in *Opportunities in Building Construction Trades* (pp. 45-47) **5421**
Roofer's Pitch **5422**
Roofing: Design Criteria, Options, Selection **5435**
Roofing Manual **5436**
Roofing the Right Way **5437**
Roofing and Waterproofing: A Trade Worth Learning Through Apprenticeship **5423**
Roofinig Technology Conference, 9th: Proceedings **5475**
Roomkeeper of the Year **3269**
ROTOR **3788**
Rotor & Wing International **3789**
Rough Notes **156**
Roustabout **5480**
"Roustabout" in *Jobs Rated Almanac* **5481**
"Roustabouts" in *Career Discovery Encyclopedia* (Vol.5, pp. 164-165) **5482**
"Roustabouts" in *Encyclopedia of Careers and Vocational Guidance* (Vol.4, pp. 315-317) **5483**
"Roustabouts" in *Occupational Outlook Handbook* **5484**
Rowe & John O. Rowe Citizen of the Year Award; Lillian B. Wood **3423**
RSC (Refrigeration Service and Contracting) **4451**
Rubber and Plastics Newsletter **5905**
Rural Appraisal Manual **3429**
Rural Carrier **1375**
Rural Electrification Magazine **6054**
Rural Living **3510**
Rural Mail Carrier **1335**
Rural Telecommunications **4296, 4555**
Ruralite **6055**
Russell's Official National Motor Coach Guide **6656**
RWDSU Record **242, 481**

S

S/F (Square Foot) **395**
"Saddlemaker" in *Offbeat Careers: The Directory of Unusual Work* **6319**
Safe Worker Award **6876**
Safety Code for Elevators & Escalators **4320**
Safety Code for Elevators & Escalators: Handbook on A17.1 **4321**
Safety Handbook **5201**
Sales Agency: A Comparative Analysis **4297**
Sales Counter **6615**
"Sales (Insurance)" in *Encyclopedia of Career Choices for the 1990s: A Guide to Entry Level Jobs* (pp. 442-444) **100**
Sales Management in Financial Services: How to Build a Competitive Sales Team **544**
Sales and Marketing Conference **576**
"Sales Opportunities in Service Industries" in *Opportunities in Sales Careers* (pp. 123-131) **612**
"Sales Representative, Wholesale Distribution" in *Occu-Facts: Information on 580 Careers in Outline Form* **209**
Sales Representatives, Wholesale Distribution **210**
Sales Skills Development **719**
Sales Skills for Financial Professionals **873**
"Sales" in *Where the Jobs Are: The Hottest Careers for the 90s* (pp. 221-244) **211, 310, 448, 613**
"Salesclerk" in *Guide to Careers Without College* (pp. 20-21) **449**
Salesman's Insider **157, 243, 482, 559, 632**
Salesmanship **158, 244, 483, 560, 633**
Salespeople, Household Appliances **450**
Salespeople, Retail **451**
"Salesperson" in *100 Best Careers for the Year 2000* (pp. 185-187) **452**
Salesperson, Advertising Space **614**
Salesperson, Automobile **453**
Salesperson, Automotive Parts **454**
Salesperson, Camera Store **455**
Salesperson, Drugstore **456**
"Salesperson, General Merchandise" in *Museum Jobs form A-Z: What They Are, How to Prepare, and Where to Find Them* **457**
Salesperson, Grocery Products **458**
Salesperson, Hardware Store **459**
Salesperson, Music Store **460**
"Salesperson" in *Occu-Facts: Information on 580 Careers in Outline Form* **461**
Salesperson, Retail **462**
Salesperson, Securities **506**
Salmon Trout Steelheader **3641**
Salt Water Sportsman **3642**
San Joaquin Farm Bureau News **3511**
Sanitary Maintenance **3280**
Sanitation Worker **6115**
"Sanitation Worker" in *Encyclopedia of Danger: Dangerous Professions* (pp. 86-89) **3287**
"Sanitation Workers" in *American Almanac of Jobs and Salaries* (pp. 104) **7062**
"Sawmill Workers" in *Career Discovery Encyclopedia* (Vol.5, pp. 168-169) **6431**
Schaum's Outline of Bookkeeping & Accounting **1480**
Schaum's Outline of Theory & Problems of Bookkeeping **1481**
Schedule of Daily Subsistence Allowance Rates **720, 1211**
Scheleen Award for Excellence; Joseph C. **1313**
School Age Notes **3341**
School Bus Driver **6633**
School Bus Fleet **6657**
School Secretary **1651**
Schools with PTDIA Certified Coures Listed by State **6870**
The Science & Practice of Welding **5948**
SCTA Hi-Lights **6658, 6917**
Sea Grant Extension Program Newsletter **3643**
Seabee Coverall **7168**
Seafarers LOG **6999**
Seafood Leader **2519, 5712**
"Seafood Processing and Marketing" in *Opportunities in Marine and Maritime Careers* (pp. 112-113) **5702**
Seaman, Able **6974**
"Seaman, Steward, Cook" in *Transportation* (pp. 33-37) **6975**
Seamstress **6278**
Seatrade Review **7000**
Seaway Review **7001**
Second Sight Technical Reports **6169**
"Secret Service Agent" in Action Careers: Employment in the High-Risk Job Market (pp. 211-221) **2256**
"Secret Service Agent" in *VGM's Careers Encyclopedia* (pp. 421-424) **2257**
Secretarial Administration & Management **1723**
The Secretarial Handbook on Planning & Organizing Work **1724**
Secretarial Office Procedures **1725**
Secretarial Practice **1726**
Secretarial Practice: Syllabus **1727**
Secretarial Procedures for the Automated Office **1728**
Secretarial Procedures in the Electronic Office **1729**
"Secretarial Science" in *Career Connection II: A Guide to Technical Majors and Their Related Careers* (pp. 136-137) **1652**
"Secretarial Sciences" in *College Majors and Careers: A Resource Guide for Effective Life Planning* (pp. 119-120) **1653**
The Secretarial Specialist **1730**
"Secretaries/Administrative Assistants" in *Profitable Careers in Nonprofit* (pp. 149-151) **1654**
"Secretaries" in *American Almanac of Jobs and Salaries* (pp. 506) **1655**
"Secretaries" in *Career Discovery Encyclopedia* (Vol.6, pp/ 12-13) **1656**
"Secretaries and Clerical Personnel" in *Opportunities in Real Estate Careers* (pp. 117-118) **1657**
"Secretaries" in *Encyclopedia of Careers and Vocational Guidance* (Vol.4, pp. 332-335) **1658**
Secretaries, Management & Organizations **1659**
"Secretaries" in *Occupational Outlook Handbook* **1660**
"Secretaries" in *Opportunities in Vocational and Technical Careers* (pp. 47-58) **1661**
Secretaries and Stenographers **1662, 1761**
"Secretaries and Stenographers" in *Jobs! What They Are—Where They Are—What They Pay* (pp. 252) **1663, 1762**
Secretary . . . **1664, 1665**
"Secretary" in *100 Best Careers for the Year 2000* (pp. 205-207) **1666**
Secretary: A Career of Distinction **1667**
Secretary, Bilingual **1668**
"Secretary" in *BLR Encyclopedia of Prewritten Job Descriptions* **1669**
"Secretary" in *Career Information Center* (Vol.1) **1670**
"Secretary" in *Career Selector 2001* **1747**
"Secretary" in *Careers in Banking and Finance* (pp. 65-66) **1671**
"Secretary" in *Careers Inside the World of Offices* (pp. 34-37) **1672**
Secretary, Executive **1673**
"Secretary" in *Guide to Careers Without College* (pp. 46-49) **1674**
Secretary on the Job **1675**
"Secretary" in *Jobs Rated Almanac* **1676**
Secretary, Legal **1677**
"Secretary" in *Occu-Facts: Information on 580 Careers in Outline Form* **1678**
"Secretary/Office Administrator" in *100 Best Jobs for the 1990s & Beyond* **1748**
Secretary to Paralegal: A Career Manual & Guide **1731**
Secretary, Technical **1679**
"Secretary" in *VGM's Careers Encyclopedia* (pp. 424-427) **1680**
The Secretary's Handbook **1732**
The Secretary's Handbook: A Manual for Office Personnel **1733**
Secretary's Problem Solver: Word-for-Word Scripts for Coping with Difficult Situations **1734**
The Secretary's Quick Reference Handbook **1735**
Secrets of Locating Past Due Debtors **770**
Section Subscription Service **159**

"Securities Broker" in *Career Information Center* (Vol.1) **507**
"Securities Brokerage" in *How to Get the Hot Jobs in Business & Finance* (pp. 117-130) **508**
"Securities Brokers" in *Jobs! What They Are—Where They Are—What They Pay* (p. 144) **509**
"Securities" in *Career Choices for the 90's for Students of Business* (pp. 173-193) **510**
"Securities" in *Career Choices for the 90's for Students of Economics* (pp. 146-167) **511**
"Securities" in *Career Choices for the 90's for Students of Mathematics* (pp. 158-179) **512**
"Securities" in *Career Choices for the 90's for Students of M.B.A.* (pp. 176-197) **513**
"Securities" in *Encyclopedia of Career Choices for the 1990s: A Guide to Entry Level Jobs* (pp. 784-804) **514**
"Securities and Exchange Commission" in *Career Choices for the 90's for Students of Law* (pp. 23-24) **515**
"Securities and Financial Services Sales Representatives" in *America's 50 Fastest Growing Jobs* (pp. 94) **516**
"Securities and Financial Services Sales Representatives" in *Encyclopedia of Careers and Vocational Guidance* **517**
"Securities and Financial Services Sales Representatives" in *Occupational Outlook Handbook* **518**
Securities Industry Association **541**
Securities Industry Association—Directory and Guide **561**
Securities Industry Association—Foreign Activity Report **562**
Securities Industry Association—Yearbook **563**
Securities Industry Institute **577**
Securities Industry Trends **564**
Securities Processing Digest **874**
Securities Regulation Law Journal **565**
"Securities Sales Agent" in *Career Selector 2001* **579**
"Securities Sales Agents" in *Transitions: Military Pathways to Civilian Careers* (pp. 140-141) **519**
"Securities Sales" in *Career Choices for the 90's for Students of Business* (pp. 160-163, 180-182) **520**
"Securities Sales" in *Career Choices for the 90's for Students of Communications and Journalism* (pp. 169-171) **521**
"Securities Sales" in *Career Choices for the 90's for Students of Political Science & Government* (pp. 169-172) **522**
"Securities Sales" in *Career Choices for the 90's for Students of Psychology* (pp. 189-191) **523**
"Securities Sales" in *Encyclopedia of Career Choices for the 1990s: A Guide to Entry Level Jobs* (pp. 771-774) **524**
Securities Sales Representatives **525**
"Securities Sales Worker (Stockbroker)" in *VGM's Careers Encyclopedia* (pp. 427-429) **526**
"Securities Sales Worker (Stockbroker)" in *VGM's Handbook of Business and Management Careers* (pp. 86-87) **527**
"Securities Salesperson" in *Occu-Facts: Information on 580 Careers in Outline Form* **528**
"Security Guard" in *BLR Encyclopedia of Prewritten Job Descriptions* **2174**
"Security Guard" in *Career Information Center* (Vol.11) **2175**
"Security Guard" in *Career Selector 2001* **2198**
"Security Guards" in *Career Discovery Encyclopedia* (Vol.6, pp. 16-17) **2176**
"Security Guards" in *Careers in Law Enforcement and Security* **2177**
"Security Guards" in *Encyclopedia of Careers and Vocational Guidance* (Vol.4, pp. 340-342) **2178**
Security Industry Association **2183**
Security Management **566**
Security Officers **2179**
Self-Assessment Questions & Answers for Dental Assistants **2703**
Self Insurance Institute of America Annual Conference and Expo **169**
Selling Direct: Choosing the Right Opportunity **463**
"Semi-Skilled Assemblers" in *Occu-Facts: Information on 580 Careers in Outline Form* **5662**
Senior Clerical Series **50, 1047, 1071, 1236, 1297, 1459, 1516, 1517, 1814, 1939, 1940**
Senior Secretarial Duties & Office Organization **1736**
Sergeants **7169**
Service Application Manual **4452**
Service Employees International Union **1265**
Service Excellence: New Techniques for Banking Professionals **875**
Service Management: Principles & Practices **4209**
Service Reporter **4453**
"Service Sales Representatives" in *America's 50 Fastest Growing Jobs* (pp. 96) **615**
"Service Sales Representatives" in *Encyclopedia of Careers and Vocational Guidance* (Vol.4, pp. 345-348) **616**
Service Station Attendants **7063**
"Service Station Attendants" in *Career Discovery Encyclopedia* (Vol.6, pp. 20-21) **7064**
"Service Station Attendants" in *Opportunities in Automotive Service Careers* (pp. 25-30) **7065**
"Service Technician/Customer Service" in *Careers in High Tech* (pp. 65-70) **4194**
"Services Sales Representatives" in *Career Discovery Encyclopedia* (Vol.6, pp. 22-23) **529**
"Services Sales Representatives" in *College Board Guide to Jobs and Career Planning* (pp. 148-149) **617**
"Services Sales Representatives" in *Occupational Outlook Handbook* **618**
Setting Up & Running Financial Systems **545**
Setup Operators (Machine Shop) **5871**
Seventh Annual Services Marketing Conference Proceedings: Designing a Winning Service Strategy **635**
Sewer, Drapery **6279**
Sewer, Hand **6280**
Sewing Machine Operator **6281**
"Sewing Machine Operator" in *Occu-Facts: Information on 580 Careers in Outline Form* **6282**
Sewing Machine Operators (Apparel) **6283**
SF Newsletter **3717**
SFI Bulletin **3644**
Shadowing & Surveillance: A Complete Guide Book **2361**
Sheet Metal and Air Conditioning Contractors' National Association **4402, 4404, 5528, 5529**
Sheet Metal and Air-Conditioning Contractors National Association Convention **4459, 5561**
"Sheet Metal Duct Systems for Heating and Air Conditioning . . . " in *Opportunities in Refrigeration and Air Conditioning Trades* **5512**
Sheet Metal Fabrication **5533**
The Sheet Metal Toolbox Manual **5537**
Sheet Metal Work **5534**
"Sheet Metal Work" in *Opportunities in Plumbing and Pipefitting Careers* (pp. 79-82) **5513**
Sheet Metal Worker **5514**
"Sheet Metal Worker" in *BLR Encyclopedia of Prewritten Job Descriptions* **5515**
"Sheet Metal Worker" in *Career Information Center* (Vol.4) **5516**
"Sheet Metal Worker" in *Hard Hatted Women: Stories of Struggle and Success in the Trades* (pp. 17-32) **5517**
Sheet Metal Worker Helper **7066**
"Sheet Metal Worker Helper" in *Occu-Facts: Information on 580 Careers in Outline Form* **7067**
"Sheet Metal Worker" in *Jobs Rated Almanac* **5518**
"Sheet Metal Worker" in *Occu-Facts: Information on 580 Careers in Outline Form* **5519**
Sheet Metal Workers **5520**
"Sheet Metal Workers" in *Career Discovery Encyclopedia* (Vol.6, pp. 24-25) **5521**
"Sheet Metal Workers" in *Encyclopedia of Careers and Vocational Guidance* (Vol.4, pp. 349-352) **5522**
"Sheet-Metal Workers" in *Occupational Outlook Handbook* **5523**
"Sheet Metal Working" in *Opportunities in Metalworking Careers* (pp. 17-26) **5524**
Shelter Sense **2939**
Shelving & Storage **4819**
Sheriff **2380**
She's a Railroader **6735**
Shipmate **7170**
Shipping Clerk **1302**
"Shipping Clerk" in *Occu-Facts: Information on 580 Careers in Outline Form* **1303**
"Shipping and Receiving Clerk" in *Career Information Center* (Vol.10) **1304**
"Shipping/Receiving Clerk" in *Jobs Rated Almanac* **1305**
Shipping and Receiving Clerks **1306**
"Shipping and Receiving Clerks" in *Encyclopedia of Careers and Vocational Guidance* (Vol.4, pp. 353-356) **1307**
Shoe Industry Workers **6320**
"Shoe Industry Workers" in *Career Discovery Encyclopedia* (Vol.6, pp. 26-27) **6321**
"Shoe Industry Workers" in *Encyclopedia of Careers and Vocational Guidance* (Vol.4, pp. 359-361) **6322**
"Shoe and Leather Workers and Repairers" in *Encyclopedia of Careers and Vocational Guidance* (Vol.4, pp. 357-358) **6323**
"Shoe and Leather Workers and Repairers" in *Occupational Outlook Handbook* **6324**
"Shoe Maker/Repairer" in *Jobs Rated Almanac* **6325**
Shoe Repairer **6326, 6327**
"Shoe Repairer" in *Career Information Center* (Vol.5) **6328**
"Shoe Repairer" in *Occu-Facts: Information on 580 Careers in Outline Form* **6329**
"Shoe Repairer" in *Personal Services* (pp. 63-67) **6330**
Shoe Repairers **6331**
"Shoe Repairers" in *American Almanac of Jobs and Salaries* (pp. 526) **6332**
"Shoe Repairers" in *Career Discovery Encyclopedia* (Vol.6, pp. 28-29) **6333**
Shoe Salesperson **464**
Shoe Service **6349**
Shooting Times **3645**
Shop Savvy **4486**
Shop Talk **3281**
"Short Order Cook" in *Career Information Center* (pp. 62-64) **2440**
"Short Order Cook" in *Occu-Facts: Information on 580 Careers in Outline Form* **2441**
"Shorthand Reporter" in *Career Information Center* (Vol.11) **1763**
Shovel-Crave Operator, Power **6692**
Show Reporter **6350**
SIA News **2196**
SIA Washington Report **567**
SIGNAL **7171**
"Signal Mechanics" in *Encyclopedia of Careers and Vocational Guidance* (Vol.4, pp. 362-364) **4143**
Signalman's Journal **6782**
Silver Star for Bravery **2344**
Simmons Scholarship **694, 1196**
Simple Cooking **2520**
Sipapu **1572**
Skill **5766**

"Skills Analysis: Secretaries" in *Black Woman's Career Guide* (pp. 52-56) **1681**
Skin Inc. **3023**
SMACNA Newsletter **5557**
SMACNEWS **5558**
Small Carrier Safety Program **6896**
Small Engine Repair **4608**, **4609**
Small Steel Craft: Design, Construction & Maintenance **4615**
Smart Selling: Successful Sales Techniques for Bankers **546**
Snips Magazine **4454**, **5559**
So You Want to Be a Cop **2258**
So You Want to Be a Success at Selling? **465**, **619**
Soap/Cosmetics/Chemical Specialties **3024**
Society of Actuaries Convention **170**
Society of American Foresters **3676**, **3677**
Society of American Foresters Accredited Professional and Recognized Technical Forestry Degree Programs **3681**
Society of American Foresters National Convention **3733**
Society of Chartered Property and Casualty Underwriters, Society Expo **171**
Society Page **160**
Society of Photo-technologists—Journal & Service Notes—Parts and Services Directory Issue **6604**
Society of Plastics Engineers **5878**
Society for Range Management Annual Conference **3541**
Soldering: Instruction and Vocabulary **5949**
Soldier Girls **7128**
SOLDIERS **7172**
Soldiers' Scene **7173**
Solidarity **5767**
Sons of the American Revolution Law Enforcement Commendation Medal **2345**
Sound & Communications Magazine **4155**
Sound Off!: American Military Women Speak Out **7129**
Soundoff! **7174**
Sourcebook of Health Insurance Data **161**
SOURCES: The Securities Executive's Guide to Products and Services **568**
South Carolina Department of Labor - Division of Licensing and Regulations **7221**
South Dakota State Department of Commerce - Professional and Occupational Licensing Department **7222**
Southeast Real Estate News **396**
Southeast Travel Professional **721**
Southeastern Restaurant, Hospitality Foodservice Show **2652**
Southern Apparel Exhibitors Shows **487**
Southern California Chapter/Pleasant Hawaiian Holidays Scholarship **695**, **1197**
Southern Early Childhood Association Annual Meeting **3345**
Southern Graphics **6170**, **6213**, **6259**, **6293**
Southern Insurance **162**, **802**
Southern Journal of Applied Forestry **3718**
Southern Loggin' Times **3719**
Southern Lumberman **3720**
Southern Motor Cargo **6918**
Southern Nurserymen Association Horticultural Trade Show **3158**
Southern Outdoors **3646**
Southern Plumbing, Heating, Cooling Magazine **4455**
Southern and Southwestern Railway Club Proceedings **6783**
Southwest Contractor **4850**, **6056**, **6707**
Southwest Farm Press **3512**
Southwest Real Estate News **397**
Southwest Trucking Show **6938**
The SPEC-DATA Program **4757**, **4851**, **5017**, **5306**, **5472**
Special Achievement Awards **2346**
Special Agent **2318**
Special Care in Dentistry **2732**
"Special Service Bus Driver" in *Career Information Center* (Vol.12) **6634**
Specialty Lab Update **6616**
Spectra **5803**
SPFE Newsletter **6617**
Spielman Scholarships; A.J. (Andy) **696**
Spokesman **3513**
Sport Fishing **3647**
SPORTING CLASSICS **3648**
"Sporting Goods Salesperson" in *Career Opportunities in the Sports Industry* (pp. 178-180) **466**
"Spray Painter (Production)" in *Occu-Facts: Information on 580 Careers in Outline Form* **6553**
"Sprinkler Fitter" in *Hard Hatted Women: Stories of Struggle and Success in the Trades* (pp. 143-149) **5337**
"Sprinkler Fitting" in *Opportunities in Plumbing and Pipefitting Careers* (pp. 85-88) **5338**
Sprinkler Quarterly **2141**
Sprinkler Technotes **2142**
Sprint: A Power User's Guide **1952**
SPRINT Simplified **1953**
Stamp of Approval **5872**
Standard & Poor's Nasdaq and Regional Exchange Stock Reports **569**
Standard for Professional Qualifications for Fire Inspector, Fire Investigator, & Fire Prevention Education Officer: NFPA 1031 **2054**
Standard for Professional Qualifications for Fire Investigator **2055**
Standard for Professional Qualifications for Public Fire Educator **2056**
Standard for Safety for Roof Trusses for Manufactured Homes **5476**
Standardized Textbook of Barbering and Styling **3012**
Standards for Selection of Truck Fleet Personnel: A Guide for Hiring Professional Drivers & Other Employees in the Trucking Industry **6835**
Staple Yarn Production **6352**
Start Your Own Computer Repair Business **4210**
Starting & Building Your Own Accounting Business **1441**
Starting Your Own Secretarial Business **1682**
State Board Review Examinations In Cosmetology **3002**
State Police/Highway Patrol Officer **2259**
"State Police/Highway Patrol Officer" in *Occu-Facts: Information on 580 Careers in Outline Form* **2260**
"State Police Officer" in *Career Information Center* (Vol.11) **2261**
"State Police Officer" in *VGM's Careers Encyclopedia* (pp. 364-366) **2262**
"State Police Officers" in *Career Discovery Encyclopedia* (Vol.6, pp. 60-61) **2263**
State Trooper **2264**
State Trooper/Highway Patrol Officer/State Traffic Officer **2319**
Stationary Engineer **6059**
"Stationary Engineer" in *Career Information Center* (Vol.9) **6060**
"Stationary Engineer" in *Career Selector 2001* **6083**
"Stationary Engineer" in *Hard Hatted Women: Stories of Struggle and Success in the Trades* (pp. 37-44) **6061**
Stationary Engineer, High Pressure Boiler Operating Engineer, High Pressure Plant Tender **6042**, **6078**
"Stationary Engineer" in *Occu-Facts: Information on 580 Careers in Outline Form* **6062**
Stationary Engineers **6063**
"Stationary Engineers" in *Encyclopedia of Careers and Vocational Guidance* (Vol.4, pp. 424-426) **6064**
"Stationary Engineers" in *Occupational Outlook Handbook* **6065**
Statistical Reports **6057**
Statistical Volumes **1880**
Statistical YearBook **6058**
Steel Digest **5612**
Steelabor **5768**
Steelworker Old Time **5769**
Stenographer **1764**
"Stenographer/Court Reporter" in *Jobs Rated Almanac* **1765**
"Stenographer and Transcriber" in *Career Information Center* (Vol.1) **1766**
"Stenographers" in *Career Discovery Encyclopedia* (Vol.6, pp. 62-63) **1767**
"Stenographers and Court Reporters" in Occupational Outlook Handbook **1768**
"Stenographers" in *Encyclopedia of Careers and Vocational Guidance* (Vol.4, pp. 436-438) **1769**
Step-by-Step Bookkeeping **1482**
"Stevedores" in *Career Discovery Encyclopedia* (Vol.6, pp. 64-65) **7068**
"Stevedoring Occupations" in *Encyclopedia of Careers and Vocational Guidance* (Vol.4, pp. 439-442) **7069**
Stew Leonard's Creating the Customer's Dream **3399**
Stock Clerk **1286**
"Stock Clerk" in *Career Information Center* (Vol.10) **1287**
"Stock Clerk" in *Career Selector 2001* **1299**
"Stock Clerk" in *Careers Inside the World of Offices* (pp. 10-11) **1288**
"Stock Clerk" in *Occu-Facts: Information on 580 Careers in Outline Form* **1289**
Stock Clerks **1290**
"Stock Clerks" in *Encyclopedia of Careers and Vocational Guidance* (Vol.4, pp. 443-445) **1291**
"Stock Clerks" in *Occupational Outlook Handbook* **1292**
Stockbroker **530**
"Stockbroker" in *College Board Guide to Jobs and Career Planning* (pp. 142-144) **531**
"Stockbroker" in *Top Professions: The 100 Most Popular, Dynamic, and Profitable Careers in America Today* (pp. 1-3) **532**
"Stockbrokers" in *Career Discovery Encyclopedia* (Vol.6, pp. 66-67) **533**
"Stockbrokers" in *New York Times Career Planner* (pp. 308-310) **534**
The Stockman Grass Farmer **3514**
Stone Review **4758**
Stone World **4759**
Stonemason **4697**
"Stonemason" in *Career Information Center* (Vol.4) **4698**
"Stonemason" in *Exploring Nontraditional Jobs for Women* (pp. 11-16) **4699**
"Stonemason" in *Occu-Facts: Information on 580 Careers in Outline Form* **4700**
"Stonemasons" in *Opportunities in Building Construction Trades* (pp. 70-72) **4701**
Stonier Forum **876**
STORES Magazine **484**
Strategic Review **7175**
Strategic Trends in Services: An Inquiry into the Global Service Economy **627**
Streamlined Bookkeeping for Multi-Level Marketing **1483**
Stress Management for Correctional Officers & Their Families **2009**
STRINGS **4661**
Structural Design & Crashworthiness of Automobiles **3850**
"Structural and Reinforcing Ironworkers" in *Occupational Outlook Handbook* **5575**
"Structural Steel Workers" in *Encyclopedia of Careers and Vocational Guidance* (Vol.4, pp. 446-449) **5576**
Student Syllabus for the Dental Assistant: A Correlated, Individualized Instruction Program **2690**
A Study of Some Aspects of Satisfaction in the Vocation of Stenography **1770**
Subject Headings for Real Estate **398**
"Subway Conductor" in *Hard Hatted Women: Stories of Struggle and Success in the Trades* (pp. 193-201) **6736**
Successful Nurse Aide Management in Nursing Homes **2862**
Successful Private Eyes & Private Spies: Private Spies **2394**

The Successful Secretary's Handbook **1737**
Successful Strategies for Manufacturing Management **5677**
Successfully Managing Your Accounting Career **1484**
The Sugar Producer **3515**
Summary of Size & Weight Limits **6897**
The Sunflower **3516**
Super Scrollsaw Patterns **6458**
Super Van Operator of the Year **6877**
SuperAutomotive Service **3990**
SuperCourse for Real Estate Licensing **336**
Supermarket Cashier **15**
Supervision **923**, **5684**
Supervisors' Guide to Successful Training **3274**
Supervisory Management **924**
Supervisory Personnel Management: Building Work Relationships **877**
Supervisory Personnel Management: Maximizing Your Effectiveness **878**
Supervisory Planning and Control **5678**
Supply House Times **245**, **485**, **1245**, **1964**, **4456**, **5403**
Surface Warfare Magazine **7176**
"Surveyor Helpers" in *Occu-Facts: Information on 580 Careers in Outline Form* **7070**
"Surveyor's Helper" in *Career Information Center* (Vol.4) **7071**
Survival Thinking: For Police & Corrections Officers **2010**
Surviving in Corrections: A Guide for Corrections Professionals **2011**
Switchboard Operators **1856**
"Switchboard Operators" in *Career Discovery Encyclopedia* (Vol.6, pp. 82-83) **1857**
"Switchboard Operators" in *Encyclopedia of Careers and Vocational Guidance* (Vol.4, pp. 474-475) **1858**
Switching Circuits **5113**

T

Table Attendant Training **2573**
Tabloid **399**
Tailors **6284**, **6285**
"Tailors" in *Occu-Facts: Information on 580 Careers in Outline Form* **6286**
Take this Job and Love It! **467**
Talking and Listening: Keys to Success with Customers and Co-Workers **879**
"Tall Ship Crew Member" in *Offbeat Careers: The Directory of Unusual Work* **6976**
Tank Truck Driver **6836**
"Tap and Die Maker Technicians" in *Encyclopedia of Careers and Vocational Guidance* (Vol.4, pp. 481) **5918**
Tarheel Wheels' Magazine **6919**
Tax Briefs from SIA **570**
"Taxi Dispatcher" in *Travel & Tourism* (pp. 45-49) **1260**, **6795**
Taxi Driver **6796**
"Taxi Driver" in *Career Information Center* (Vol.12) **6797**
"Taxi Driver" in *Career Selector 2001* **6822**
"Taxi Driver" in *Jobs Rated Almanac* **6798**
Taxi Drivers **6799**
"Taxi Drivers and Chauffeurs" in *Occupational Outlook Handbook* **6800**
"Taxi Drivers" in *Encyclopedia of Careers and Vocational Guidance* (Vol.4, pp. 485-487) **6801**
Taxi Driving Made Simple: How to Do It Profitably, Pleasurably, and Professionally **6811**
Taxi and Livery Management **6816**
Taxi & Livery Management—Buyer's Guide Issue **6807**
Taxicab Companies Directory **6808**
"Taxicab Driver" in *Encyclopedia of Danger: Dangerous Professions* (pp. 94-97) **6823**
Taxicab Industry Group **6805**
Teach Yourself Bookkeeping **1442**
Teacher Aide **1824**
The Teacher Aide in the Instructional Team **1843**
"Teacher Aide" in *Occu-Facts: Information on 580 Careers in Outline Form* **1825**
"Teacher Aides" in *America's 50 Fastest Growing Jobs* (pp. 110) **1826**
"Teacher Aides" in *Career Discovery Encyclopedia* (Vol.6, pp. 92-93) **1827**
"Teacher Aides" in *Encyclopedia of Careers and Vocational Guidance* (Vol.4, pp. 490-492) **1828**
"Teacher Aides" in *Jobs! What They Are—Where They Are—What They Pay* (pp. 107) **1829**
"Teacher Aides" in *Occupational Outlook Handbook* **1830**
"Teacher Aides" in *Opportunities in Child Care Careers* (pp. 58-72) **1831**
"Teacher (Preschool)" in *Career Selector 2001* **3347**
Teacher's Aide **1832**
"Teacher's Aide" in *Career Information Center* (Vol.11) **1833**
"Teacher's Aide" in *Jobs Rated Almanac* **1834**
"Teachers Aides and School Bus Drivers" in *American Almanac of Jobs and Salaries* (pp. 110) **1835**, **6635**
Teachers Assistants **1836**
"Teachers, Preschool" in *Encyclopedia of Careers and Vocational Guidance* (Vol.4, pp. 498-500) **3321**
Tech Center News **3876**
Technical Advisory Committee Bulletin **6309**
Technical Advisory Committee Research Paper **6310**
Technical Bulletin **2521**
Technical Congress Transactions **5742**
Technical Log **4122**
Technical/Manufacturing Cluster One **5525**, **5950**
Technical Notes **4760**
Technical Secretary: Terminology & Transcription **1738**
Technical Woodworking **6449**
Technicalities **1573**
Technician Association News **4123**
Technician of the Year **4257**
Technician of the Year Award **4258**
TECHNICOM **4662**
Technique of Systems & Procedures **1056**
Technology Forecast **6171**
Technometrics **5743**
"Tel-a-marketing" in *Careers in Trucking* **1102**
Telecom Export Guide **4298**
Telecom Market Review and Forecast **4299**
"Telecommunications Technicians" in *Career Discovery Encyclopedia* (Vol.6, pp. 96-97) **4144**
"Telecommunications Technicians" in *Encyclopedia of Careers and Vocational Guidance* (Vol.4, p. 505) **4145**
"Telecommunications Technology" in *Career Connection II: A Guide to Technical Majors and Their Related Careers* (pp. 142-143) **4146**
Telegraph & Data Transmission over Shortwave Radio Links: Fundamental Principles & Networks **1884**
Telemarketer **1103**
"Telemarketer" in *Occu-Facts: Information on 580 Careers in Outline Form* **1104**
"Telemarketers" in *Career Discovery Encyclopedia* (Vol.6, pp. 98-99) **1105**
"Telemarketers" in *Encyclopedia of Careers and Vocational Guidance* (Vol.4, pp. 506-509) **1106**
Telemarketing **1881**
"Telemarketing" in *Careers in Marketing* (pp. 57-58) **1107**
"Telemarketing" in *Opportunities in Telecommunications Careers* (pp. 35-46) **1108**
"Telemarketing Specialist" in *Career Information Center* (Vol.10) **1109**
"Telemarketing: The Fast-Track Medium" in *Marketing and Sales Career Directory* (pp. 68-72) **1110**
Telephone Answering Service Operator **1859**
"Telephone Central Office Technician" in *Career Information Center* (Vol.3) **4147**
"Telephone Central Office Technician" in *Telecommunications* (pp. 39-43) **4148**
The Telephone Company Test **1876**
"Telephone Installer" in *Exploring Nontraditional Jobs for Women* (pp. 43-48) **4278**
Telephone Installer/Repair Technician **4279**
"Telephone Installer/Repair Technician" in *Occu-Facts: Information on 580 Careers in Outline Form* **4280**
"Telephone Installer/Repairer" in *Jobs Rated Almanac* **4281**
"Telephone Installers and Repairers" in *Career Discovery Encyclopedia* (Vol.6, pp. 100-101) **4282**
"Telephone Installers and Repairers" in *Occupational Outlook Handbook* **4283**
Telephone Line Installers and Cable Splicers **4540**
"Telephone Line Installers and Cable Splicers" in *Occu-Facts: Information on 580 Careers in Outline Form* **4541**
"Telephone Line Worker and Cable Splicer" in *Career Information Center* (Vol.3) **4542**
"Telephone Line Worker and Cable Splicer" in *Telecommunications* (pp. 33-37) **4543**
Telephone Operator **1860**
"Telephone Operator" in *Career Information Center* (Vol.3) **1861**
"Telephone Operator" in *Career Selector 2001* **1885**
"Telephone Operators" in *Career Discovery Encyclopedia* (Vol.6, pp. 102-103) **1862**
Telephone Operators (Central Office) **1863**
"Telephone Operators" in *Encyclopedia of Careers and Vocational Guidance* (Vol.4, pp. 513-516) **1864**
"Telephone Operators" in *Jobs! What They Are—Where They Are—What They Pay* (pp. 254) **1865**
"Telephone Operators" in *Occupational Outlook Handbook* **1866**
"Telephone and PBX Installers and Repairers" in *Encyclopedia of Careers and Vocational Guidance* (Vol.4, pp. 510-512) **4149**
"Telephone and PBX Operator" in *Telecommunications* (pp. 15-19) **1867**
Telephone Repair Illustrated **4292**
Telephone Salespeople (Telemarketers) **1111**
"Telephone Service Technician" in *Career Information Center* (Vol.3) **4284**
"Telephone Service Technician" in *Telecommunications* (pp. 27-31) **4285**
Teletimes **1882**
"Television Advertising Representative" in *Career Opportunities in Advertising and Public Relations* (pp. 137-139) **620**
"Television Advertising Sales Assistant" in *Career Opportunities in Advertising and Public Relations* (pp. 140-142) **621**
"Television and Radio Service Technician" in *Career Information Center* (Vol.3) **4236**
"Television and Radio Service Technician" in *VGM's Careers Encyclopedia* (pp. 460-462) **4237**
Television Repairer **4238**
Teller Operations **880**
Teller Operations Manual **832**
Teller Performance **833**
Teller World **834**
"Tellers and Clerks (Bank)" in *American Almanac of Jobs and Salaries* (pp. 402) **820**
Tellers, Financial Institution **821**
Tellers—How Important Are They? **822**
Tennessee State Department of Commerce and Insurance - Division of Regulatory Boards **7223**
Tentative Standard for Proctective Clothing for Fire Fighters **2117**

Test Practice Book for 100 Civil Service Jobs **1376**
"Texas Ranger" in *Offbeat Careers: The Directory of Unusual Work* **2265**
Texas State Department of Licensing and Regulation **7224**
Textbook for Nursing Assistants **2863**
Textile Chemist and Colorist **6373**
Textile Hi-Lights **6374**
"Textile Industry" in *Career Information Center* (Vol.9) **6353**
"Textile Machinery Operators" in *Occupational Outlook Handbook* **6354**
"Textile Manufacturing Occupations" in *Encyclopedia of Careers and Vocational Guidance* (Vol.4, pp. 518-520) **6355**
Textile Mill Worker **6356**
Textile Production Workers **6357**
Textile Research Journal **6375**
Textile Technology Digest **6376**
Textile Trends **6377**
"Textile Worker" in *Encyclopedia of Danger: Dangerous Professions* (pp. 98-101) **6382**
"Textile Workers" in *Career Discovery Encyclopedia* (Vol.6, pp. 106-107) **6358**
Textile World **6378**
"Textiles" in *Encyclopedia of Careers and Vocational Guidance* (Vol.1, pp. 456-462) **6359**
There's a New "Challenge in Agriculture" **3400**
Thinking About a Nursing Home? **2876**
"Ticket Agent" in *Career Selector 2001* **1222**
"Ticket Agent" in *Opportunities in Airline Careers* (pp. 67-68) **1172**
Ticket Agents **1173**
"Ticket Agents, Reservation Agents, and Clerks" in *Opportunities in Travel Careers* (p. 40-42) **1174**
Tiempo Latino **6784**, **6920**, **7002**
Tierra Grande **400**
TIG & Related Processes in Welding Automation **5999**
Tile & Decorative Surfaces **5647**
Tile Setter **5621**
"Tilesetters" in *Occupational Outlook Handbook* **5622**
Timber Bulletin **3721**
Timber Cutting Practices **3688**
Timber Designer's Manual **3689**
Timber Equipment Trader **3722**
Timber & the Forest Service **3673**
Timber Harvesting **3723**
Timber: Its Nature & Behavior **3690**
Timber: Its Structure, Properties & Utilization **3691**
Timber Management: A Quantitative Approach **3692**
Timber Mart-South **3724**
Timber!: Problems, Prospects, Policies **3693**
The Timber Producer **3725**
Timber Resources for America's Future: Forest Resource Report No. 14 **3694**
Timber Specifier's Guide: Understanding & Specifying Softwoods in Buildings **3695**
Timber Supply: Issues & Options **3696**
Timber West **3726**
Timbers of the New World **3735**
Times-Plain Dealer **3517**
TMTA Newsletter **6659**, **6921**
To Health! Guidelines for Food Service Sanitation **2658**
Today's Fireman **2143**
Today's Policeman **2381**
Toiletries, Fragrances and Skin Care—The Rose Sheet **3025**
"Tool-and-Die Maker" in *Jobs Rated Almanac* **5919**
"Tool Design Technician" in *Occu-Facts: Information on 580 Careers in Outline Form* **5920**
"Tool and Die Design" in *Career Connection II: A Guide to Technical Majors and Their Related Careers* (pp. 144-145) **5921**
Tool and Die Maker **5922**
"Tool and Die Maker" in *BLR Encyclopedia of Prewritten Job Descriptions* **5923**
"Tool and Die Maker" in *Career Information Center* (Vol.9) **5924**
"Tool and Die Maker" in *Occu-Facts: Information on 580 Careers in Outline Form* **5925**
"Tool and Die Maker" in *VGM's Careers Encyclopedia* (pp. 462-464) **5926**
"Tool and Die Makers" in *Career Discovery Encyclopedia* (Vol.6, pp. 116-117) **5927**
"Tool and Die Makers" in *Jobs! What They Are—Where They Are—What They Pay* (pp. 217) **5928**
"Tool and Die Makers" in *Occupational Outlook Handbook* **5929**
Tool and Die Sharpener **5930**
"Tool Makers and Die Setters" in *Encyclopedia of Careers and Vocational Guidance* (Vol.4, pp. 540-543) **5931**
Tool and Manufacturing Association **5828**, **5879**, **5920**, **5936**, **5940**, **5967**
Toolmakers and Diemakers **5932**
Tools—Cutting Directory **6000**
Tools for the Electrical Trades **4071**, **4239**
Top Secret! Codes to Crack **2362**
Total Auto Body Repair **3851**
Total Food Service **2522**, **2644**
"Tour Bus Driver" in *Travel & Tourism* (pp. 35-37) **6636**
Tour & Travel News **1212**
"Tow Truck Operator" in *Career Information Center* (Vol.12) **6837**
"Tow Truck Operator" in *Occu-Facts: Information on 580 Careers in Outline Form* **6838**
Toxic Labeling Compliance Newsletter **3991**
Tractor Equipment & Parts Directory **3414**, **4341**
"Trader" in *Careers in Banking and Finance* (pp. 67-72) **535**
"Traders" in *American Almanac of Jobs and Salaries* (pp. 408) **536**
"Traders: Dealing With Uncertainty" in *Getting Into Money: A Career Guide* (pp. 74-90) **537**
Traders: the Jobs, the Products, the Markets **538**
"Traffic Agents and Clerks" in *Encyclopedia of Careers and Vocational Guidance* (Vol.4, pp. 554-556) **1308**
"Traffic Clerk" in *BLR Encyclopedia of Prewritten Job Descriptions* **1309**
"Traffic, Shipping, and Receiving Clerks" in *Occupational Outlook Handbook* **1310**
Traffic Signal Manual of Installation and Maintenance Procedures **1275**
Training Materials Catalog **6174**, **6218**, **6261**, **6262**
Training Programs Catalog **6172**
Training Programs for Health Care Workers: Food Service Workers **2614**
Training Reports & Records **2118**
Trains **6785**
Transcriber **1771**
Transit Atlas: Bus and Taxi Service in Iowa **6809**
Transit Fact Book **6660**
Transitions: Military Pathways to Civilian Careers **7130**
"Transmission and Distribution Occupations" in *Encyclopedia of Careers and Vocational Guidance* (Vol.4, pp. 558-561) **6030**
Transport Fleet News **6922**
Transportation **3578**, **3811**, **6693**, **6839**
Transportation: An Abstract Newsletter **6661**, **6786**, **6817**, **6923**, **7003**
Transportation & Distribution **6787**, **6818**, **6924**, **7004**
Transportation Man of the Year **6649**, **6764**, **6810**, **6878**, **6990**
Transportation/Mechanical Cluster **3812**, **3918**, **6840**
Transportation Quarterly **6662**, **6788**, **6925**, **7005**
"Transportation" in *Second Careers: New Ways to Work After 50* (pp. 260-268) **6666**, **6791**, **6824**, **6948**
"Transportation Services" in *Opportunities in Vocational and Technical Careers* (pp. 76-90) **6841**
TransTechnical News **3877**
The Trapper and Predator Caller **3649**
The Trapper's Bible: Traps, Snares, & Pathguards **3594**
Trapper's Handbook **3595**
Traps Today **3596**
Travel **733**, **1223**
"Travel Agencies" in *Opportunities in Travel Careers* (pp. 77-90) **643**
Travel Agent **644**, **645**, **679**, **722**, **1175**, **1176**, **1213**
"Travel Agent" in *100 Best Careers for the Year 2000* (pp. 236-238) **646**
"Travel Agent" in *100 Best Jobs for the 1990s & Beyond* **734**
"Travel Agent" in *Career Information Center* (Vol.8) **647**
"Travel Agent" in *Career Selector 2001* **735**
"Travel Agent" in *College Board Guide to Jobs and Career Planning* (pp. 152-154) **648**
The Travel Agent: Dealer in Dreams **649**
Travel Agent—Domestic Tour Manual Issue **700**
Travel Agent—Focus 500 Directory Issue **683**
"Travel Agent" in *Guide to Careers Without College* (pp. 25-26) **650**
"Travel Agent" in *Jobs Rated Almanac* **651**
"Travel Agent" in *Occu-Facts: Information on 580 Careers in Outline Form* **652**
"Travel Agent" in *Opportunities in Vocational and Technical Careers* (pp. 59-61) **653**
"Travel Agent" in *Top Professions: The 100 Most Popular, Dynamic, and Profitable Careers in America Today* (pp. 57-59) **654**
"Travel Agent" in *Travel & Tourism* (pp. 27-31) **655**
"Travel Agent" in *VGM's Careers Encyclopedia* (pp. 468-470) **656**
"Travel Agent" in *VGM's Handbook of Business and Management Careers* (pp. 92-93) **657**
Travel Agents **658**
"Travel Agents" in *101 Careers: A Guide to the Fastest-Growing Opportunities* (pp. 319-322) **659**
"Travel Agents" in *American Almanac of Jobs and Salaries* (pp. 547) **660**
"Travel Agents" in *America's 50 Fastest Growing Jobs* (pp. 98) **661**
"Travel Agents" in *Career Discovery Encyclopedia* (Vol.6, pp. 124-125) **662**
"Travel Agents" in *Encyclopedia of Careers and Vocational Guidance* (Vol.4, pp. 565-568) **663**
"Travel Agents" in *Jobs! What They Are—Where They Are—What They Pay* (pp. 206) **664**
"Travel Agents: Plotters of Unforgettable Trips" in *Careers for Women Without College Degrees* (pp. 234-238) **665**
Travel Career Development **666**, **1177**
"Travel Coordinator" in *BLR Encyclopedia of Prewritten Job Descriptions* **667**
Travel Counselor Magazine **723**
Travel Free: How to Start and Succeed in Your Own Travel Consultant Business **668**, **1178**
"Travel and Hospitality Careers" in *The Best Jobs for the 1990s and Into the 21st Century* **669**, **1084**, **1179**, **2442**, **2574**, **3074**
"Travel and Hospitality" in *Where the Jobs Are: The Hottest Careers for the 90s* (pp. 279) **670**
Travel Industry Association of America—International Travel News Directory **701**
Travel Industry Association of America—Travel Media Directory **702**
Travel Industry Career Directory **684**, **1192**
Travel Industry Guidelines for Employment **671**, **1180**

Travel Industry Honors **724**
Travel News **1214**
Travel People Magazine **1215**
Travel South USA Showcase **727**, **1219**
"Travel and Tourism" in *Career Connection II: A Guide to Technical Majors and Their Related Careers* (pp. 148-149) **672**
Travel Trade **1216**
Travel Training Workbook, 1994-95 **673**, **1181**
Travel & Vacation Discount Guide **703**
Travel Weekly **1217**
"Traveling Secretary/Professional Sports Team" in *Career Opportunities in the Sports Industry* (pp. 43-45) **1683**
Treatment Custody Role Conflict in Community Based Correctional Workers: Causes & Effects **2022**
Tree Farmer **3518**
Trends **881**
Trends Conference **578**
Trends and Forecasts **4499**
Trends and Techniques in the Contemporary Dental Laboratory **6512**
Tri-State Restaurant Food and Equipment Show **2653**
Trim Carpentry Techniques: Installing Doors, Windows, Base & Crown **4820**
Triumph of Agriculture Exposition Farm and Ranch Machinery Show **3542**
Troubleshooting Electronics Equipment Without Service Data **4108**
Troubleshooting Ink Problems, Part 1 **6262**
Troubleshooting Inking Problems, Part 2 **6263**
Troubleshooting & Repairing Audio & Video Cassette Players and Recorders **4058**, **4261**, **4487**
Troubleshooting and Repairing Camcorders **4059**, **4262**, **4488**
Troubleshooting and Repairing Computer Monitors **4211**
Troubleshooting and Repairing Computer Printers **4195**
Troubleshooting & Repairing Diesel Engines **4043**
Troubleshooting & Repairing Heat Pumps **4430**
Troubleshooting & Repairing Power Tools **4489**
Troubleshooting and Repairing Solid-State TVs **4060**, **4263**, **4490**
Troubleshooting & Repairing TVRO Systems **4212**
Troubleshooting & Repairing VCRs **4491**
The Trout & Salmon Leader **3650**
The Trowel Trades **4702**, **4906**, **5272**, **5623**
"Truck and Bus Dispatcher" in *Career Information Center* (Vol.12) **1261**
"Truck and Delivery Drivers" in *Career Discovery Encyclopedia* (Vol.6, pp. 126-127) **6842**
Truck Driver **6843**
"Truck Driver" in *100 Best Jobs for the 1990s & Beyond* **6949**
"Truck Driver" in *Career Selector 2001* **6950**
"Truck Driver" in *Encyclopedia of Danger: Dangerous Professions* (pp. 102-105) **6951**
"Truck Driver" in *Jobs Rated Almanac* **6844**
"Truck Driver" in *Transportation* (pp. 21-25) **6845**
"Truck Driver" in *VGM's Careers Encyclopedia* (pp. 471-474) **6846**
Truck Drivers **6847**
"Truck Drivers" in *Encyclopedia of Careers and Vocational Guidance* (Vol.4, pp. 569-573) **6848**
Truck Driver's Guide to Commercial Driver Licensing **6869**
"Truck Drivers" in *Jobs! What They Are—Where They Are—What They Pay* (pp. 218) **6849**
"Truck Driving" in *Career Connection II: A Guide to Technical Majors and Their Related Careers* (pp. 150-151) **6850**
Truck Operator, Industrial **6694**
Truck Paper **6926**
Truck Parts & Service **6927**
"Truckdrivers" in *Occupational Outlook Handbook* **6851**
Trucker **6852**
"Trucker" in *Hard Hatted Women: Stories of Struggle and Success in the Trades* (pp. 225-234) **6853**
Truckers Atlas **6898**
Trucking Permit Guide, 1G: Private, Contract, Common, Exempt **6899**
TRUCKS Magazine **6928**
Trucksource: Sources of Trucking Industry Information: The Trucking Information Buyer's Guide **6854**
Trust and Financial Advisor **882**
Trust Letter **883**
Truth in Savings Handbook for Front-Line Staff **884**
"Tuner/Technician" in *Opportunities in Music Careers* (pp. 134-135) **4636**
Turf News **3519**
The Turkey Hunter **3651**
Turn Out **2144**
TV Repair for Beginners **4061**, **4264**, **4492**
TWU Express **6789**, **6929**, **7006**
Type and Press **6214**, **6260**
Typesetter **6190**
Typesetters **6191**
"Typesetters" in *Career Discovery Encyclopedia* (Vol.6, pp. 128-129) **6192**
Typist **1909**
"Typist" in *Career Selector 2001* **1966**
"Typist" in *Occu-Facts: Information on 580 Careers in Outline Form* **1910**
"Typist and Word Processors" in *Careers in Banking and Finance* (p. 73) **1911**
"Typists" in *Career Discovery Encyclopedia* (Vol.6, pp. 130-131) **1912**
"Typists" in *Opportunities in Vocational and Technical Careers* (pp. 47-58) **1913**
"Typists and Word Processor Operators" in *Jobs! What They Are—Where They Are—What They Pay* (pp. 255) **1914**
"Typists, Word Processors, and Data Entry Keyers" in *American Almanac of Jobs and Salaries* (pp. 513) **1915**
"Typists, Word Processors, and Data Entry Keyers" in *Occupational Outlook Handbook* **1916**
"Typists and Word Processors" in *Encyclopedia of Careers and Vocational Guidance* (Vol.4, pp. 574-577) **1917**

U

U.A. Journal **5404**
UAMR Confidential Bulletin **246**
UAMR Monthly Bulletin **247**
UFAC: Action Guide **6413**, **6952**
UFCW Action **26**, **52**, **5713**
UFCW Leadership Update **27**, **53**
Undercar Digest **3992**
Undercover Work: A Complete Handbook **2363**
Understanding the Lending Process **1006**
Union **1281**
United Brotherhood of Carpenters and Joiners of America **4796**, **4987**, **5627**
United Caprine News **3520**
United Food and Commercial Workers International Union **17**, **48**, **5705**
United Fresh Fruit and Vegetable Association Annual Convention and Exposition **3543**
U.S. Coast Guard - Merchant Vessel Personnel Division **3585**
"United States Customs Service" in *Opportunities in Transportation Careers* (pp. 130-132) **2266**
U.S. Glass, Metal and Glazing—Directory of Suppliers of Machinery & Equipment Issue **5133**, **5889**
U.S. Glass, Metal and Glazing—Directory of Suppliers of Sealants & Glazing Systems Issue **5134**, **5890**
"U.S. Navy Officer" in Careers for Number Lovers (pp. 55-57) **7131**
"United States Navy" in *Opportunities in Marine and Maritime Careers* (pp. 85-97) **7132**
U.S. Special Agent **2267**
United States Telephone Association **1870**, **4152**, **4287**, **4547**
United Steelworkers of America **5756**
United Union of Roofers, Waterproofers and Allied Workers **5425**
Up or Out: How to Get Promoted as the Army Draws Down **7186**
Update **1282**
Upholstered Furniture Action Council **6398**
Upholstered Furniture Action Council—Directory of Materials Suppliers **6414**
Upholsterer, Furniture **6391**
Upholsterers (Furniture) **6392**
"Upholsterers" in *Occupational Outlook Handbook* **6393**
Upholsterers' Supplies Directory **6407**
Upholstering **6408**
Upholstering Methods **6409**
Upholstery **6410**
The Upholstery Fact Book 1986 **6416**
Upholstery Manufacturing Management **6415**
Upholstery Styles: A Design Sourcebook **6411**
Upholstery Techniques Illustrated **6412**
Upper Midwest Electrical Expo **5107**
Upper Midwest Hospitality, Restaurant, and Lodging Show **2654**
Urinalysis Today **2803**
A User's Guide to the Resource Based Relative Value Scale **2804**
Utah State Division of Occupational and Professional Licensing **7225**
"Utility and Power Plant Occupations" in *Opportunities in Electrical Trades* (pp. 43-64) **5054**
"Utility Switch Operator" in *Hard Hatted Women: Stories of Struggle and Success in the Trades* (pp. 150-155) **6031**
Utility Workers Union of America **6037**
UTU News **6663**, **6790**

V

Vacuum Cleaners Supplies & Parts Directory **3275**
Vacuum Cleaning Systems Directory **3268**
Valuation Journal **401**
Vanishing Forest Reserves **3697**
Vegetables and Specialties Situation and Outlook Report **3521**
Vehicle Body Building One **3852**
Vehicle Body Building Two **3853**
Vehicle Leasing Agent **46**
Vending Machine Mechanic **4663**
"Vending Machine Mechanic" in *Occu-Facts: Information on 580 Careers in Outline Form* **4664**
"Vending Machine Mechanics" in *Career Discovery Encyclopedia* (Vol.6, pp. 136-137) **4665**
"Vending Machine Repairer" in *Jobs Rated Almanac* **4666**
Vending Machine Repairers **4667**
Vending Machine Route Driver **4668**
"Vending Machine Route Worker" in *Career Information Center* (Vol.10) **4669**
Vending Machine Route Workers **4670**
"Vending Machine Route Workers" in *Occu-Facts: Information on 580 Careers in Outline Form* **4671**
"Vending Machine Servicers and Repairers" in *Occupational Outlook Handbook* **4672**
Vermont Secretary of State - Office od Professional Regulation **7226**
The Vertical File & Its Satellites: A Handbook of Acquisition, Processing, & Organization **1536**
Vertical Milling Machine Explained **5873**

Vertical Transportation: Elevators & Escalators **4326**
Veterinary Technician **2940**
"Veterinary Technician" in *Careers for Animal Lovers and Other Zoological Types* (pp. 15-17) **2907**
"Veterinary Technician" in *Careers in Veterinary Medicine* **2908**
"Veterinary Technicians and Assistants" in *Jobs! What They Are—Where They Are—What They Pay* (p. 54) **2909**
VFW J. Edgar Hoover Award **2347**
Video Career Library - Careers in Allied Health Fields **6490**
Video Career Library - Clerical & Administrative Support **16, 771, 823, 1137, 1336, 1443, 1684, 1772, 1868, 1918**
Video Career Library - Construction **4570, 4703, 4790, 4982, 5055, 5169, 5226, 5339, 5577, 5624**
Video Career Library - Education **1837**
Video Career Library - Marketing and Sales **101, 212, 311, 468, 622, 1182**
Video Career Library - Mechanical Fields **3759, 3813, 3919, 4018, 4394, 4582**
Video Career Library - Production I **6032, 6066, 6087, 6150, 6193, 6235, 6275, 6287, 6394**
Video Career Library - Production II **5526, 5663, 5824, 5874, 5933, 5936, 5951, 6432**
Video Career Library - Public and Personal Services **1988, 2057, 2268, 2443, 2575, 2986, 3075, 3100, 3322, 5703**
Video Career Library - Repair Fields **4072, 4150, 4196, 4240, 4512, 4544**
Video Career Library - Technical Occupations **962, 6526**
Video Career Library - Transportation & Materials Moving **6637, 6695, 6855**
"Video Sales Clerk" in *Career Opportunities in Television, Cable, and Video* (pp. 194-195) **469**
"Video Service Technician" in *Career Opportunities in Television, Cable, and Video* (pp. 196-197) **4241**
Video Tapes for Cosmetology **2987**
Violin Bow Maker **4637**
Virginia Department of Health Professions **7227**
Virginia State Department of Professional and Occupational Regulation **7228**
Vocational Visions **898, 1034, 1138, 1510, 1685, 1919, 3401, 3760, 3814, 3920, 4019, 4704, 4791, 4907, 6638, 6856**
Vocational Visions Career Series: Automotive Mechanic **4005**
Vocational Visions Career Series: Chef **2532**
Vocational Visions Career Series: Insurance Agent **174**
Vocational Visions Career Series: Letter Carrier **1393**
Vocations U.S.A. **3402, 3761, 3815, 3921, 4020, 4357, 4474, 4583, 4705, 4792, 4908, 6639, 6857**
The Voice **2145**
Voice Messaging Industry Review **4300**
Voice Processing Industry Review **4301**

W

W. Allison and Elizabeth Stubbs Davis Award **3118**
Wages and Benefits in Child Care **3323**
Wagner Award; Percy and Betty **350**
"Waiter" in *VGM's Careers Encyclopedia* (pp. 485-487) **2576**
Waiter-Waitress **2577**
"Waiter and Waitress" in *Career Information Center* (Vol.8) **2578**
"Waiter or Waitress and Host or Hostess" in *Hospitality & Recreation* (pp. 39-43) **2579**
"Waiter/Waitress" in *Occu-Facts: Information on 580 Careers in Outline Form* **2580**
Waiters and Waitresses **2581**
"Waiters and Waitresses" in *Career Discovery Encyclopedia* (Vol.6, p. 144-145) **2582**
"Waiters and Waitresses" in *Opportunities in Restaurant Careers* (p. 10) **2583**
Waiting Tables **2444, 2584**
Waitress **2585**
Walking on Air **3076**
Wall of Honors **3424**
"Wall Street Bond Broker" in *Straight Talk on Careers: 80 Pros Take You Into Their Professions* (pp. 21-24) **539**
"Wall Street: Building a Career in Finance" in *Fast-Track Careers: A Guide to the Highest-Paying Jobs* (pp. 17-39) **540**
Wallpaper Hanger **5227**
Walls & Ceilings **5018, 5202, 5307**
"Warehouse Worker" in *Career Information Center* (Vol.10) **1293**
Washington Craft Schow **5787, 6443**
Washington Digest **3993**
Washington Insights Public Affairs Newsletter **3878**
Washington Letter **6311**
Washington Retail Report **486**
Washington State Department of Licensing **7229**
Washington Update **3026, 4302**
Wastewater Plant Operator **6088**
Wastewater Treatment Plant Operators **6089**
"Wastewater Treatment Plant Operators" in *Encyclopedia of Careers and Vocational Guidance* (Vol.4, pp. 595-597) **6090**
Water Conditioning & Purification **6130**
Water Environment Federation **6095**
Water Environment Laboratory Solutions **6131**
Water Environment Regulation Watch **6132**
Water Environment Research **6133**
Water, Environment, and Technology **6134**
Water Law **7007**
Water Research **6135**
Water Technology **6136**
"Water Transportation Occupations" in *Occupational Outlook Handbook* **6977**
"Water-Treatment Plant Operator" in *Career Selector 2001* **6140**
Water & Wastes Digest **6137**
Water/Wastewater Operator **6091**
"Water and Wastewater Treatment Plant Operators" in *Career Discovery Encyclopedia* (Vol.6, pp. 148-149) **6092**
"Water and Wastewater Treatment Plant Operators" in *Occupational Outlook Handbook* **6093**
Webster's New World Secretarial Handbook **1739**
The Weekly Insider (IIABC) **163**
Weekly Statistical Bulletin **5508**
Welcome to Our Nursing Home **2877**
"Welder" in *BLR Encyclopedia of Prewritten Job Descriptions* **5952**
"Welder" in *Career Information Center* (Vol.4) **5953**
"Welder" in *Guide to Careers Without College* (pp. 67-70) **5954**
"Welder" in *Hard Hatted Women: Stories of Struggle and Success in the Trades* (pp. 33-36) **5955**
"Welder" in *Jobs Rated Almanac* **5956**
Welders **5957**
"Welders" in *Career Discovery Encyclopedia* (Vol.6, pp. 150-151) **5958**
"Welders, Cutters, and Welding Machine Operators" in *Occupational Outlook Handbook* **5959**
"Welders" in *Encyclopedia of Careers and Vocational Guidance* (Vol.4, pp. 604-606) **5960**
Welders and Oxygen Cutters **5961**
"Welders and Oxygen Cutters" in *Occu-Facts: Information on 580 Careers in Outline Form* **5962**
Welding **5979, 5980**
Welding & Cutting: A Guide to Fusion Welding & Associated Cutting Processes **6001**
Welding Design & Fabrication **6006**
The Welding Distributor **6007**
Welding Handbook **6008**
Welding Innovation Quarterly **6009**
Welding and Joining . . . Build a Career to Build a Country **5963**
Welding Journal **6010**
Welding Machine Operator **5964**
"Welding Machine Operator" in *Occu-Facts: Information on 580 Careers in Outline Form* **5965**
"Welding" in *Opportunities in Metalworking Careers* (pp. 47-58) **5966**
Welding: Principles & Applications **6002**
"Welding Technicians" in *Encyclopedia of Careers and Vocational Guidance* (Vol.4, pp. 607-610) **5967**
"Welding Technology" in *Career Connection II: A Guide to Technical Majors and Their Related Careers* (pp. 152-153) **5968**
Welding Technology Fundamentals **6003**
Welding Technology Today: Principles & Practices **6004**
Wellhead Operations **5485**
Western Cable Television Convention and Exposition **4558**
Western Farm Show **3544**
Western Lath/Plaster/Drywall Industries Association Annual Convention **5019, 5308**
Western States Meat Association Bi-Annual Exposition **5717**
What Combines Communications, Law, Technology, Finance, Medicine, Engineering . . . **1773**
What Do You Know about Air Conditioning, Refrigeration & Heating **4412**
What Do You Know about Carpentry **4806**
What Is Telemarketing and How Do I Get Started? **1869**
What to Look for in a Truck Driver **6953**
What is a Travel Agent? **674**
Whatcha Gonna Do Now? **2766, 2845**
What's it Like to be a Police Officer? **2269**
The Wheat Grower **3522**
Wheel & Rim out of Service Guide **6900**
When Do You Need a Professional, Accredited Farm Manager? **3403**
Where They Stand: A Digest of Organizational Policies on Child Care and Education **3027**
Whole Foods—Source Book Issue **2470, 2606**
"Wholesale and Retail Trade" in *Encyclopedia of Career Choices for the 1990s: A Guide to Entry Level Jobs* (pp. 242-243) **213**
"Wholesale Sales Worker" in *Career Information Center* (Vol.10) **214**
"Wholesale Sales Workers" in *Career Discovery Encyclopedia* (Vol.6, pp. 152-153) **215**
"Wholesale Trade Sales Representative" in *Guide to Careers Without College* (pp. 23-25) **216**
"Wholesale Trade Sales Representatives" in *Jobs! What They Are—Where They Are—What They Pay* (p. 336) **217**
"Wholesale Trade Sales Workers" in *Encyclopedia of Careers and Vocational Guidance* (Vol.4, pp. 611-614) **218**
"Wholesale Trade Sales Workers" in *Opportunities in Vocational and Technical Careers* (pp. 59-75) **219**
Wholesaler—"Wholesaling 100" Issue **4431, 5373**
Who's Hiring in Hospitality **2586**
Who's Who in Building Service Contracting **3282**
Who's Who in Credit Management **1020**
Who's Who in the Dental Laboratory Industry **6513**
Who's Who in Direct Selling **489**
Who's Who Directory **1087**
Who's Who In Landscape Contracting **3147**
Who's Who in Law Enforcement **2382**
Who's Who in Photographic Management **6618, 6619**
Wildfowl **3652**
Wildlife Harvest **3653**

"Wildlife Management Trapper" in *Action Careers: Employment in the High-Risk Job Market* (pp. 291-299) **3579**
William D. Hatfield Award **6118**
Williams Scholarships; Maxine **2789**
WINBA Championship Title **3010**
Wing & Shot **3654**
Wings and Wheels **47**
Winning the Fire Service Leadership Game **2119**
Winning Resumes for Computer Personnel **963**
Wire and Cable Specifications **1283**
Wisconsin State Department of Regulation and Licensing **7230**
Wisconsin Truck Expo **6939**
Woman Officer of the Year **2348**
Wood **6459**
Wood Machining News **6460**
"Wood Patternmaker" in *Occu-Facts: Information on 580 Careers in Outline Form* **6433**
Wood & Wood Products **6461**
Woodcarver **6434**
Woodshop News **6462**
Woodwork **6463**
The Woodworker's Journal **6464**
Woodworking **6450**
Woodworking Machine Operator **6435**
"Woodworking Machine Operator" in *Occu-Facts: Information on 580 Careers in Outline Form* **6436**
WOODWORKING - Machinery and Equipment for the Forestry, Timber and Woodworking Industries **6468**
"Woodworking Occupations" in *Occupational Outlook Handbook* **6437**
The Wool Sack **3523**
Word Detective Picture Word Book **2364**
Word Magic: A Guide to Understanding & Evaluating Word Processing Equipment **1954**
"Word Processing" in *Careers Inside the World of Offices* (pp. 10-11) **1920**
"Word Processing" in *Exploring High Tech Careers* **1921**
Word Processing Machine Operator **1922**
"Word Processing Machine Operator" in *Career Selector 2001* **1967**
"Word Processing Specialists: Information Processors" in *Careers for Women Without College Degrees* (pp. 192-196) **1923**
Word Processing Specialists (Operators) **1924**
Word Processor & Calculator Development System MVP-Forth **1955**
Word Processor & Calculator Development System Source **1956**
"Word Processor" in *Career Information Center* (Vol.1) **1925**
"Word Processor Operator" in *100 Best Careers for the Year 2000* (pp. 104-106) **1926**
"Word Processor Operators" in *Career Discovery Encyclopedia* (Vol.6, pp. 158-159) **1927**
"Word Processor" in *VGM's Careers Encyclopedia* (pp. 489-490) **1928**
Word Processors & Information Processing: What They Are & How to Buy **1957**
Word Processors & Typewriters Worldwide: Opportunities & Pitfalls **1958**
Word Processors & the Writing Process: An Annotated Bibliography **1959**
Work Procedures for a Derrickman **5486**
Work Procedures for a Roustabout **5487**
Workbook Exercises in Alphabetic Filing **1518**
Workbook for Professional Barber Styling **3013**
Working Safely with Electricity **5114**
Workshop Catalog **6173**
World of Concrete USA Exposition **4964**
World Pork Expo **3545**
Worldwide Travel Information Contact Book **704**
Worth Magazine **571**
Would You Like a Career That Pays Well, Helps People, and Provides Exceptional Opportunities? **4395**
WPCF Literature Review **6141**
WPCF Manuals of Practice **6116**
Write with Confidence: Tools for Financial Business Writing **885**
WSTB Newsletter **6138**
WWS/World Wide Shipping **7008**

Y

"Yacht Crew Member" in *Offbeat Careers: The Directory of Unusual Work* **6978**
YARDSTICK **1942**
Yorkshire Journal **3524**
You Can Become a Tile, Marble, Terrazzo and Dimensional Stone Installer **4706**, **4909**, **5625**
You Can Type for Doctors at Home! **1960**
Young Children **3342**
The Young Detective's Handbook **2365**
Your Career in Aviation Maintenance **3762**
Your Career in Business-to-Business Direct Marketing **470**
Your Career in Professional Barber Styling **2988**
Your Career in Veterinary Technology **2910**
Your Future in the Plumbing Heating Cooling Industry **4396**, **5340**
Your Future in Word Processing **1929**
Your Guardian Angel **4545**, **6033**
Your New Job: Tips for Career Success **886**
Your Successful Real Estate Career **312**

Z

"Zookeeper" in *Careers for Animal Lovers and Other Zoological Types* (pp. 90-93) **2911**